HEATH READINGS IN THE LITERATURE OF ENGLAND

SELECTED AND EDITED BY

TOM PEETE CROSS, Ph.D.

PROFESSOR OF ENGLISH AND COMPARATIVE LITERATURE, AND
CHAIRMAN OF THE DEPARTMENT OF GENERAL LITERATURE
UNIVERSITY OF CHICAGO

AND

CLEMENT TYSON GOODE, Ph.D.

BOSTWICK PROFESSOR OF ENGLISH
UNIVERSITY OF RICHMOND

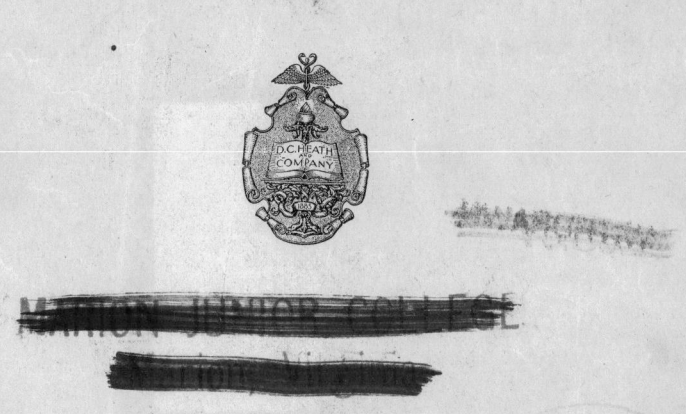

D. C. HEATH AND COMPANY

BOSTON NEW YORK CHICAGO
ATLANTA SAN FRANCISCO DALLAS
LONDON

2 F 9

PRINTED IN U.S.A.

PREFACE

Heath's Readings is designed (1) to meet the needs of the student, or general reader, who desires an acquaintance with the greater masterpieces of British literature, and (2) to afford an adequate background for the undergraduate who wishes to specialize or "major" in the subject of English. The works included therefore comprise not only poems and prose pieces that illustrate the historical development of the literature of England but those writings as well whose claims upon the student's attention are justified not so much by their purely historical value as by their long-continued popularity or intrinsic merit. Particularly in the earlier periods, works of unusual literary excellence or human appeal have occasionally been substituted for documents which, though sometimes included in anthologies because of their historical value, seldom if ever arouse the enthusiasm of the undergraduate or of the general reader. In making the selections, the editors have been constantly guided by accepted critical opinion, seconded by their own judgment, and by a sympathetic respect for the taste of the student who is to use the book. Although specimens of the drama and the novel have been omitted because of the limitations of space, lists of suggested readings in these types are given at the beginnings of the several larger divisions.

The book aims to represent adequately, as far as is practicable, all the major types and authors, along with a sufficient number of minor writers to illustrate the continuity of literary history and the great diversity in subject matter and method of treatment. To this end the compilers have departed somewhat from the common practice in anthologies of excluding all literary works of the earlier period that were not actually written in Anglo-Saxon or in Middle English. Too often the fact is overlooked that before the Renaissance some of the finest flowerings of literary genius in Britain found expression in languages other than English. During the centuries when English was regarded as a medium not sufficiently dignified for universal literary usage, Latin was the language of scholarship and religion as Anglo-Norman French was of chivalry and courtly society; hence it is in works composed in Latin or French that we must seek for the reflection of the most advanced culture of England during a considerable part of the Middle Ages. Moreover, before the close of the twelfth century there had appeared in Irish and in Cymric (Welsh), the ancient language of Britain, writings of unexpected literary excellence that give us fascinating glimpses of the native foundations of British literary tradition and are indispensable to an adequate understanding of the history of British fiction, particularly Arthurian romance. In all selections mere fragments have been avoided, as usually being misleading and, in accordance with present methods of instruction, pedagogically unsound. In the few cases where it has been judged inadvisable to give a work entire, an effort has been made to choose a passage that is at once representative of the whole work and within itself possessed of artistic unity.

The work recognizes the conventional arrangement of material by periods, but it goes a step farther. It groups the special ages that are united by common interests into larger wholes that are themselves distinguished by more marked differences one from another. Within each age the works are classified according to types or forms. Within each type the examples are arranged as far as possible in order of time. Each selection is followed by a date. When placed at the left, as is done in all cases before the art of printing was introduced into England, the date indicates the time of composition; when placed at the right, it indicates the time of first publication. The abbreviation c. signifies "century"; *ca.* stands for *circa,* "about."

The book is supplied with notes and other helps that should enable the student to obtain an adequate notion of English literary history without the aid of a manual. Similarly the mythological references are given fully enough to serve the general purposes of interpretation without a supplementary text on the subject. Each general period is preceded by an introduction giving the main contemporary currents of society and literature. Biographical sketches of the various authors represented, and brief critical notes indicating the historical and æsthetic value of their works, are included. Because of their frequency, the merely glossarial notes in the Old and Middle periods are placed at the foot of the pages. Cross-references make possible the comparison of important themes and ideas as treated by various authors or in various periods. Prefixed to the readings is a Chronological Outline, which is intended to assist the student in placing the chief authors and works in relation to English political history and to some of the great landmarks of continental and American history and literature. A literary map of England, especially prepared for the volume, has been included in the hope that its use may encourage a better acquaintance with the geographical conditions which have entered so largely into the making of our literature.

The compilers are indebted to numerous predecessors for assistance in establishing or elucidating the texts employed. The following list, arranged chronologically, gives the special editions or texts used in the instances of all the major writers:

Malory, Temple Classics; Chaucer, Oxford; Spenser, Cambridge; Shakespeare, Oxford; Bacon, Works, 10 vols., London, 1824; Milton, Cambridge (Poetry) and Bohn's Standard Library (Prose); Dryden, Cambridge; Pope, Cambridge; Johnson, Works, new Edition, 6 vols., Philadelphia, 1825; Burns, Cambridge; Wordsworth, Oxford; Coleridge, Oxford; Byron, Oxford; Shelley, Oxford; Keats, Oxford; Carlyle, Essays, 7 vols., Chapman & Hall, London; Tennyson, Globe; Browning, Oxford ("Epilogue to Asolando," Globe); Arnold, Oxford (Poetry), and Essays, Macmillan (Prose); Ruskin, Works, 30 vols., Crowell.

In all other cases the best available texts have been followed. In every instance the attempt has been to produce not merely a readable text but one of commendable accuracy.

It is a pleasure to acknowledge obligations for many words of interest and encouragement and for a generous spirit of helpfulness: to Professor W. H. Vann of Baylor College; to Dr. Grace Landrum and Messrs. Dunning, Jones, and Hart of the department of English in the University of Richmond; to Dr. H. R. McIlwaine and staff of the Virginia State Library; and to Mr. Edwin E. Willoughby of the Newberry Library, Chicago.

Publishers and Authors who have kindly extended copyright privileges, elsewhere acknowledged specifically, are as follows:

Ginn & Company; Oxford University Press; Open Court Publishing Company; Irish Texts Society; David Nutt; Jessie L. Weston; J. M. Dent & Sons; Chatto & Windus; The Macmillan Company; E. P. Dutton & Company; Charles Scribner's Sons; Harper and Brothers; The Modern Library, Inc.; Dodd, Mead & Company; John Murray; Doubleday, Page & Company; Frederick A. Stokes Company; Brentano's; Sir William Watson; Rudyard Kipling; Sir Edmund Gosse; G. K. Chesterton; H. G. Wells; John Galsworthy.

T. P. C.
C. T. G.

CONTENTS

BALLADS

LYRICS

16th century - 1660

ELIZABETHAN AND PURITAN PERIODS

RENAISSANCE

POETRY

LYRICS

PROSE

ELIZABETHAN AGE

POETRY

NON-DRAMATIC

LYRICS

SONNET CYCLES

PROSE

CHRONICLE HISTORY AND BIOGRAPHY

CRITICISM

LITERATURE OF TRAVEL AND THE SEA

PAMPHLETS

ESSAYS

CHARACTERS

BIBLE

PURITAN AGE

POETRY

LYRICS

PROSE

RESTORATION AND EIGHTEENTH CENTURY

RESTORATION

POETRY

SATIRE

ODES

LYRICS

PROSE

ESSAYS

CRITICISM

JOURNALS

AGE OF POPE

POETRY

PROSE

SATIRE

ESSAYS

ROMANTIC BEGINNINGS

AGE OF JOHNSON

POETRY

ROMANTIC PROGRESS

HYMNS

PROSE

ESSAYS

CRITICISM

BIOGRAPHY

PRIVATE LETTERS

NINETEENTH CENTURY

AGE OF ROMANTICISM

POETRY

PROSE

CRITICISM

ESSAYS

BIOGRAPHY

VICTORIAN AGE

POETRY

PROSE

ESSAYS

CRITICISM

MODERN PERIOD

POETRY

PROSE

CHRONOLOGICAL OUTLINE

OF

ENGLISH LITERATURE AND HISTORY

Names of English sovereigns are printed in small capitals under the dates of their accession; events in foreign literature and history are in italics.

OLD ENGLISH PERIOD

A.D.	
428	First landing of Anglo-Saxon tribes in Britain
563	Columba comes as missionary to Scotland
597	Augustine comes as missionary to England
600–700	Cædmon died *ca.* 680 Adamnan (*ca.* 625–709)
664	Council of Whitby
673	Venerable Bede born. Died 735
700–800	"Beowulf" (late 7th or early 8th c.) Cædmon's Hymn in Northumbrian form
787	First landing of Danes in England
800–900	"Judith" Alfred the Great: Translations Feast of Bricriu and other older Irish sagas ALFRED, King 871–901 *Charlemagne, Emperor of the Roman Empire, 800–814*
900–1000	Ælfric (955?–1020)
1033	Anselm born. Died 1109
1042	EDWARD THE CONFESSOR
1066	Battle of Hastings. Norman Conquest of England WILLIAM I ("THE CONQUEROR")
1086	Domesday Book completed
1087	WILLIAM II ("THE RED")
1095	First Crusade HENRY I

MIDDLE ENGLISH PERIOD

A.D.	
1100–1200	Welsh Mabinogion, 11th or 12th c. *Chanson de Roland (Old French epic), early 12th c.* Geoffrey of Monmouth: "History of the Kings of Britain," *ca.* 1136 Walter Map: Material contained in "Courtiers' Trifles" collected *ca.* 1150–*ca.* 1190 Marie de France: Breton Lays, *ca.* 1165 *Chrétien de Troyes: First Arthurian romances in verse, ca. 1150–ca. 1200*
1153	STEPHEN
1154	HENRY II Anglo-Saxon Chronicle ends
1172	English conquest of Ireland
1189	RICHARD I ("THE LION HEARTED")
1190	Richard's Crusade. Ends 1192
1199	JOHN
1200–1300	Layamon: "Brut," *ca.* 1205 *"Nibelungenlied" (German epic) composed in present form* Roger Bacon (1214?–1294) Lyrics — "Summer is icumen in," etc., 1250–1300
1215	The Great Charter (Magna Carta)
1216	HENRY III
1265	*Dante (Italian poet) born. Died 1321*
1272	EDWARD I
1274	Robert Bruce born. Died 1329
1277	English conquest of Wales
1297	Revolt of William Wallace

A.D.

1300–1400
- Richard de Bury: "Philobiblon," 1345(?)
- Various romances, mostly translated from French, 1300–1350
- Hundred Years' War (1337–1453)
- Chaucer (1340?–1400)
- "Gawain and the Green Knight," *ca.* 1375
- Wycliffe: Translation of the Bible, *ca.* 1382
- Miracle and Mystery Plays

1304 *Petrarch (Italian poet) born. Died 1374*
1307 EDWARD II
1313 *Boccaccio (Italian poet and prose writer) born. Died 1375*
1314 Battle of Bannockburn
1327 EDWARD III
1337 *Froissart (French chronicler) born. Died 1410*
1346 *Battle of Crecy*
1348 First appearance of the Black Death in England
1356 *Battle of Poitiers*
1362 "Piers the Plowman." Revised, 1377, *ca.* 1397
1377 RICHARD II
1381 Wat Tyler's rebellion
1388 Battle of Otterburn
1390 Gower: "Confessio Amantis"
1399 HENRY IV

1400–1500
- Henryson (1425?–1506?)
- Wars of the Roses, 1455–1485
- Dunbar (1465?–1530?)
- First English printed book, printed by Caxton, *ca.* 1474
- *Rabelais (French humorist, satirist) (1490?–1553)*
- Morality Plays
- "Nutbrowne Maide," *ca.* 1500

1403 Revolt of the Percies
1413 HENRY V
1415 *Battle of Agincourt*
1422 HENRY VI
1431 *Death of Joan of Arc*
François Villon (French poet) born. Died after 1463
1461 EDWARD IV
Warwick "the King-Maker." Died 1471
1474 *Ariosto (Italian poet) born. Died 1533*
1483 EDWARD V
RICHARD III
1485 HENRY VII
Sir Thomas Malory: "Morte Darthur"
1492 *Discovery of America by Columbus*

ELIZABETHAN AND PURITAN PERIODS

A.D.

1503 Wyatt born (?). Died 1542
1509 HENRY VIII
1515 Sir Thomas More: "Utopia" (begun)
1516 Surrey born (?). Died 1547
1529 Fall of Cardinal Wolsey
Suppression of the greater monasteries
1533 *Montaigne (French essayist) born. Died 1592*
1544 *Tasso (Italian poet) born. Died 1595*
1547 EDWARD VI
Cervantes (Spanish novelist) born. Died 1616
1552 Edmund Spenser born (?). Died 1599
Sir Walter Ralegh born (?). Died 1618
1553 MARY ("THE BLOODY")
1557 Wyatt, Surrey, Vaux, and others: Poems in Tottel's "Miscellany"
1558 Loss of Calais and death of Mary
ELIZABETH
1561 Francis Bacon born. Died 1626
1563 Foxe: "Acts and Monuments" (Book of Martyrs)
1564 Marlowe born. Died 1593
Shakespeare born. Died 1616
Galileo (Italian astronomer) born. Died 1642
1572 *Massacre of St. Bartholomew*
1573 Ben Jonson born (?). Died 1637
1576 First London theatre
1577 Holinshed: "Chronicles"
1579 Spenser: "Shepheard's Calendar"
North: Translation of "Plutarch's Lives"
Lyly: "Euphues"
1580 *Montaigne: Essais (Books I and II)*
1585 Ralegh's unsuccessful effort to colonize Virginia
1587 Mary Queen of Scots executed
Marlowe's dramatic work begun. Ended 1593
1588 Spanish Armada defeated
1589 *Henry IV (of Navarre), King of France*
Hakluyt: "Voyages," 1589–1600
1590 Spenser: "Faerie Queene" (Books I and II)
Sidney (died 1586): "Arcadia"
Battle of Ivry
Shakespeare's dramatic work probably begun. Ended about 1612–13
1591 Sidney: "Astrophel and Stella"
1592 Greene: "Groatsworth of Wit." First

A.D.

1592 reference to Shakespeare as play-wright. Greene died same year

1595 Sidney: "Defense of Poesy"

Spenser: "Amoretti"

1597 Bacon: Essays (10 essays in this edition). Other essays added 1612, 1625

Ben Jonson's dramatic work begun. Ended 1637

1599 Globe theatre built (many of Shakespeare's plays performed here)

1600 East India Company incorporated

1603 JAMES I

John Florio: Translation of Montaigne's Essays

1605 *Cervantes (Spanish novelist): Don Quixote (Part I). Part II, 1615*

Gunpowder Plot

1606 *Corneille (French dramatist) born. Died 1684*

1607 *Foundation of Virginia, first permanent English settlement in America*

1608 Milton born. Died 1674

1609 Shakespeare: Sonnets

1611 Authorized ("King James") Version of the Bible

1620 Bacon: "Novum Organum"

Pilgrim Fathers emigrate to New England

1622 *Molière (French dramatist) born. Died 1673*

1623 First Folio edition of Shakespeare's plays

1625 CHARLES I

1631 Dryden born. Died 1700

1632 John Locke born. Died 1704

1634 Milton: "Comus" (acted). Published, 1637

1636 *Corneille: "Le Cid"*

1638 Milton: "Lycidas"

1639 *Racine (French dramatist) born. Died 1699*

1642 Outbreak of Civil War in England

Theatres closed

Sir Isaac Newton born. Died 1727

1643 *Louis XIV, King of France. Died 1715*

1644 Milton: "Areopagitica"

1645 Milton: Poems

1648 Royal Society founded

1649 Charles I executed. Abolition of Monarchy and establishment of Commonwealth in England

1652 Beginning of Quakers

1653 OLIVER CROMWELL, LORD PROTECTOR. Died 1658

RESTORATION AND EIGHTEENTH CENTURY

A.D.

1660 CHARLES II

The Restoration

Defoe born (?). Died 1731

1663 Samuel Butler: "Hudibras" (Parts I and II). Part III, 1678

1665 Great plague in London

1666 Great fire in London

1667 Milton: "Paradise Lost"

Swift born. Died 1745

1672 Dryden: "Conquest of Granada" (printed, with preface Of Heroic Plays)

Addison born. Died 1719

1674 *Boileau: L'Art Poétique*

1678 Bunyan: "Pilgrim's Progress" (Part I). Part II, 1684

Popish Plot

1681 Dryden: "Absalom and Achitophel"

1682 Dryden: "Mac Flecknoe"

1685 JAMES II

Revocation of the Edict of Nantes

Monmouth's Rebellion

Sir Isaac Newton: "Principia"

1688 Alexander Pope born. Died 1744

Arrival of William of Orange and flight of James II

1689 WILLIAM AND MARY

Richardson born. Died 1761

Toleration Act

1694 Bank of England established

Voltaire (French philosopher, poet) born. Died 1778

1697 Dryden: "Alexander's Feast"

1701 Defoe: "True-Born Englishman"

1702 ANNE

1703 John Wesley born. Died 1791

1704 *Battle of Blenheim*

Addison: "The Campaign"

Swift: "Battle of the Books" (probably written by 1698)

1707 Fielding born. Died 1754

1709 Samuel Johnson born. Died 1784

1709–1710 Steele, Addison, and others: "The Tatler"*

1711–1712 Steele, Addison, and others: "The Spectator"*

1711 Pope: "Essay on Criticism"

1712 *Rousseau (French philosopher, novelist) born. Died 1778*

1712 Pope: "Rape of the Lock." Revised 1714

* Containing Sir Roger de Coverley Papers. "The Spectator" was revived for a few months in 1714.

A.D.	
1713	Sterne born. Died 1768
1714	GEORGE I
1715	Pope: Translation of Homer's "Iliad" (Books I–IV). Completed 1720
	Le Sage: Gil Blas
1719	Defoe: "Robinson Crusoe" (Part I). Parts II and III, 1720
1720	South Sea Bubble
1724	*Immanuel Kant* (*German philosopher*) *born. Died 1804*
1726	Swift: "Gulliver's Travels"
	Thomson: "Winter" (the first of the "Seasons" published)
1727	GEORGE II
1728	Goldsmith born. Died 1774
1729	Burke born. Died 1797
1730	Beginning of Methodists (at Oxford)
1732	Pope: "Essay on Man" (Epistles I and II). Epistle III, 1733
	Epistle IV, 1734
1742	Young: "Night Thoughts" (Books I–III)
1743	Blair: "The Grave"
1746	Battle of Culloden. Defeat of Charles Edward, the Pretender
1748	Richardson: "Clarissa Harlowe"
	Thomson: "Castle of Indolence"
1749	Fielding: "Tom Jones"
	Goethe (*German novelist, dramatist, poet*) *born. Died 1832*
1751	Gray: "Elegy Written in a Country Churchyard"
	Richard Brinsley Sheridan born. Died 1816
1755	Johnson: "Dictionary of the English Language"
1756	Beginning of Seven Years' War
1757	William Blake born. Died 1827
1759	Sterne: "Tristram Shandy" (begun). Publication continued until 1767
	Robert Burns born. Died 1796
1760	GEORGE III
	Macpherson: "Fragments of Ancient Poetry" (first of spurious poems attributed to Ossian)
1761	*Rousseau: "La Nouvelle Héloïse"* (*The New Eloise*)
1764	Horace Walpole: "Castle of Otranto"
	Foundation of the Literary Club, consisting of Johnson, Goldsmith, Burke, Garrick, Reynolds, and others

A.D.	
1764	Chatterton begins his imitations of mediæval poetry
	Spinning jenny invented
1765	Percy: "Reliques of Ancient English Poetry"
	Steam engine invented
1766	Goldsmith: "Vicar of Wakefield"
1768	Spinning machine invented
1770	Goldsmith: "Deserted Village"
	Wordsworth born. Died 1850
1771	"Encyclopedia Britannica," first edition
	Walter Scott born. Died 1832
1772	Coleridge born. Died 1834
1773	Goldsmith: "She Stoops to Conquer"
	Boston Tea Party
1775	Burke: "Speech on Conciliation with America"
	Sheridan: "The Rivals"
	Jane Austen born. Died 1817
	Charles Lamb born. Died 1834
	War of American Independence begun
1776	Adam Smith: "Wealth of Nations"
	Declaration of American Independence
1777	Sheridan: "School for Scandal"
1783	Crabbe: "The Village"
	Washington Irving born. Died 1859
1786	Burns: Poems (the famous Kilmarnock edition)
1788	Byron born. Died 1824
1789	Blake: "Songs of Innocence"
	James Fenimore Cooper born. Died 1851
	Outbreak of the French Revolution. Storming of the Bastille
1790	*Goethe: "Faust: ein Fragment." "Faust" completed, 1831*
1791	Thomas Paine: "Rights of Man" (Part I). Part II, 1792
1792	Shelley born. Died 1822
1793	*Execution of Louis XVI of France*
1794	Ann Radcliffe: "Mysteries of Udolpho"

NINETEENTH CENTURY

1795	Keats born. Died 1821
	Carlyle born. Died 1881
1796–1816	Jane Austen's novels written
1796–1817	Scott: Poems
1798	Wordsworth and Coleridge: "Lyrical Ballads," containing "Expostulation

A.D.

1798 and Reply," "The Ancient Mariner," and other important poems. Second edition 1800

1799 *Balzac (French novelist) born. Died 1850*

Heinrich Heine (German poet, satirist) born (?). Died 1856

1800 Macaulay born. Died 1859

1802 *Victor Hugo (French poet, novelist) born. Died 1885*

1802–1803 Scott: "Minstrelsy of the Scottish Border" (Vols. I and II)

1803 *Ralph Waldo Emerson born. Died 1882*

1804 *Nathaniel Hawthorne born. Died 1864*

"George Sand" (Madame Dudevant, French novelist) born. Died 1876

1805 Battle of Trafalgar. Death of Nelson

1807–1824 Byron: Works

1807 Moore: "Irish Melodies" (Part I). Other parts later; last published, 1834

Henry Wadsworth Longfellow born. Died 1882

First successful steamboat launched in America

1808 *Peninsular War begun. Ended 1814*

1809 *Battle of Corunna*

Tennyson born. Died 1892

Edgar Allan Poe born. Died 1849

1810 *Alfred de Musset (French poet, dramatist) born. Died 1857*

1810–1822 Shelley: Works composed

1811 Thackeray born. Died 1863

1812 Byron: "Childe Harold" (Cantos I and II). Canto III, 1816. Canto IV, 1818

Dickens born. Died 1870

Browning born. Died 1889

The Brothers Grimm: "Kinder- und Hausmärchen" (Household Tales)

War between England and the United States

1814 Wordsworth: "The Excursion"

1814–1831 Scott: Novels

1815 *Battle of Waterloo*

1816 Byron: "The Prisoner of Chillon"

Coleridge: "Christabel"

1817 Coleridge: "Biographia Literaria"

1817–1820 Keats: Poems

1819 Byron: "Don Juan" (Cantos I and II). Cantos III–IV, 1821. Cantos VI–XVI, 1823

A.D.

1819 Washington Irving: "Sketch Book"

John Ruskin born. Died 1900

Walt Whitman born. Died 1892

1820 George IV

"George Eliot" (Mary Ann Evans) born. Died 1880

1820–1833 Charles Lamb: "Essays of Elia"

1822 Matthew Arnold born. Died 1888

1824–1853 Walter Savage Landor: "Imaginary Conversations"

1826 *James Fenimore Cooper: "The Last of the Mohicans"*

1828 Dante Gabriel Rossetti born. Died 1882

Henrik Ibsen (Norwegian poet, dramatist) born. Died 1906

George Meredith born. Died 1909

1830 William IV

Alfred Tennyson: "Poems Chiefly Lyrical"

Opening of first railway, between Liverpool and Manchester

1831 *Edgar Allan Poe: "The Raven"*

Victor Hugo: "Notre Dame de Paris"

1832 Reform Bill passed

1833 Carlyle: "Sartor Resartus." Publication completed, 1834

1834 William Morris born. Died 1896

Balzac (French novelist): "Père Goriot" (Old Goriot)

1835 *"Mark Twain" (Samuel L. Clemens) born. Died 1910*

The telegraph invented

1836–1870 Dickens: Novels

Whittier: "Voices of Freedom"

1837 Victoria

Carlyle: "French Revolution"

Swinburne born. Died 1909

Thomas Hardy born

1840 *Émile Zola (French novelist) born. Died 1902*

1841 Browning: "Pippa Passes"

1842 Tennyson: Poems

Longfellow: "Poems on Slavery"

1843 Macaulay: Essays (collected edition)

Ruskin: "Modern Painters" (Vol I). Publication completed, 1860

Establishment of the Free Church of Scotland

1844 Robert Bridges (Poet Laureate) born

A.D.

1844 *"Anatole France" (Jacques Anatole Thibault) born. Died 1924*

1845 Browning: "Dramatic Romances and Lyrics"

1847 Tennyson: "The Princess"

Longfellow: "Evangeline"

1847–1859 Thackeray: most important novels

1848 John S. Mill: "Principles of Political Economy"

Matthew Arnold: "The Strayed Reveller and Other Poems"

Suppression of Chartism, a movement for the extension of political power to the working classes

Revolution in France. Abdication of Louis Philippe

1848–1861 Macaulay: "History of England from the Accession of James II." (unfinished)

1849 Browning: Poems

Ruskin: "Seven Lamps of Architecture"

Sainte-Beuve (French literary critic): "Causeries de Lundi" (Monday Chats) begun

1849–1850 Dickens: "David Copperfield"

1850 Elizabeth Barrett Browning: "Sonnets from the Portuguese"

Robert Louis Stevenson born. Died 1894

1851 *Hawthorne: "House of Seven Gables"*

Longfellow: "Golden Legend"

1852 Tennyson: "Ode on the Death of the Duke of Wellington"

1853 *Thomas Nelson Page born. Died 1922*

1853–1861 De Quincey: Collected Works (including Essays)

1854 *Crimean War*

Tennyson: "Charge of the Light Brigade"

1855 Tennyson: "Maud and Other Poems"

Longfellow: "Hiawatha"

1856 *Emerson: "English Traits"*

George Bernard Shaw born

Peace of Paris

1856–1895 George Meredith: Novels published

1857 *Flaubert: "Madame Bovary"*

Joseph Conrad (Teodor Josef Konrad Korzeniowski) born. Died 1926

Indian Mutiny

A.D.

1858 William Morris: "Defence of Guinevere and Other Poems"

1859 Tennyson: "Idylls of the King" (containing Enid, Vivien, Elaine, and Guinevere). Continued 1869–1888

Darwin: "Origin of Species"

Edward Fitzgerald: translation of the "Rubaiyat of Omar Khayyam"

Washington Irving: "Life of Washington"

1859–1879 George Eliot: novels

1861 *William I, King of Prussia. Bismarck his chief adviser*

Beginning of Civil War in America

1864 Newman: "Apologia pro vita sua"

1865 Rudyard Kipling born

William Butler Yeats born

Assassination of President Lincoln

1866 Swinburne: "Poems and Ballads"

H. G. Wells born

1867 Matthew Arnold: "On the Study of Celtic Literature"

Arnold Bennett born

John Galsworthy born

George W. Russell ("A.E.") born

1868 Browning: "The Ring and the Book"

1868–1870 William Morris: "The Earthly Paradise"

1869 Matthew Arnold: "Culture and Anarchy"

William Vaughn Moody born. Died 1910

Suez Canal opened

1870 Dante Gabriel Rossetti: Poems

Bret Harte: "The Luck of Roaring Camp"

War between France and Prussia

1871 Swinburne: "Songs before Sunrise"

Darwin: "Descent of Man"

John M. Synge born. Died 1909

1871–1919 Thomas Hardy: Novels and poems

1873–1896 Walter Pater: Works on Criticism, Art, etc.

1874 James Thomson: "City of Dreadful Night"

G. K. Chesterton born

1875 *Telephone invented by Bell*

John Masefield born

1876 Robert Bridges: first published work

William Morris: "Sigurd the Volsung and the Fall of the Niblungs"

A.D.

1877 *Ibsen: "Pillars of Society" (first of his problem plays)*
Tolstoi: "Anna Karénina"
Zola: "L'Assammoir" (The Slaughter-house)
1878 Tennyson: "Sir Richard Grenville"
1879 *Ibsen: "A Doll's House"*
1880 Alfred Noyes born
1881 Stevenson: "Virginibus Puerisque"
1883 Stevenson: "Treasure Island"
Gladstone adopts Home Rule
1886 Tennyson: "Locksley Hall, Sixty Years After and Other Poems"
Kipling: "Departmental Ditties" (first published collection)
1887 Rupert Brooke born. Died 1915
Queen's Jubilee
1889 Browning died
1892 Tennyson died
George Bernard Shaw: first drama

A.D.

1894 G. W. Russell ("A.E."): "Homeward, Songs by the Way"
1895 Joseph Conrad (Teodor Josef Konrad Korzeniowski): first novel published
H. G. Wells: first published collection
1898 *War between the United States and Spain. Annexation of Cuba*
Arnold Bennett: first published novel
1899 *Boer War begun*
1900 G. K. Chesterton: first published work
1901 EDWARD VII
1902 Alfred Noyes: earliest published work
1903 Samuel Butler: "The Way of All Flesh." Butler died in 1902
1904 John Galsworthy: first published novel
1910 GEORGE V
1911–1915 Rupert Brooke: Poems
1912 John Masefield: "The Everlasting Mercy"
1914 World War begun

OLD ENGLISH PERIOD

EPIC AND CHRONICLE

About the end of the first quarter of the fifth century after Christ (ca. 428) there arrived in Britain a group of pagan Germanic tribes known as Anglo-Saxons. These invaders brought with them numerous literary and historical traditions preserved by their poets — scops or gleemen. In 597 Augustine introduced into the south of England the Roman form of Christianity; a few years earlier (563) the great Irish missionary, Columba (Columcille), had brought the doctrines of Celtic Christianity into Scotland, whence they spread southward as far as Yarrow and Whitby (the monasteries of Bede and of Cædmon) before they were met and displaced (in 664) by the doctrines of Rome.

It is to the Christian scholars and poets of England that we owe the preservation of the small body of native Anglo-Saxon literature which has come down to us. To them also are due several Old-English versions of Biblical stories, numerous homilies and saints' lives in the language of the people, and certain Latin works on themes introduced in part from the Continent. Several translations from Latin into Anglo-Saxon are attributed to Alfred the Great (849–901).

The monks who composed or recorded Anglo-Saxon poetry on secular subjects were influenced by conflicting motives. Though they were Christians, they were close kin to warlike men whose ideals were far from those of the meek and lowly Jesus, and they retell the old tales with a scarcely suppressed gusto. Yet being Christians, they naturally purify and ennoble their themes and idealize their characters by the omission of much that is barbaric and by the infusion of a spirit which is in part chivalric and is altogether Christian. Their attitude toward their material may be compared with that of Tennyson, who long afterward attempted to reconcile the dubious moral standards of mediæval Arthurian story with the ideals of Victorian society — to explain the unfaithfulness of Guinevere on the basis of nineteenth-century ethics. Even when retelling Biblical stories, the Anglo-Saxon poets interpret their stories in terms of pagan society. Their lack of historical sense, which seems to us childish, is thus responsible for what most clearly reflects contemporary life in the Old English Christian epic (e.g., *Judith*). Hence we cannot regard Anglo-Saxon epic literature as reflecting perfectly the life of our barbaric ancestors. Even *Beowulf* is not properly Anglo-Saxon either in subject or in treatment. In subject it is continental — probably Scandinavian — ; in form and treatment it is sophisticated and Christian. Anglo-Saxon prose reveals a love of learning and an acquaintance with Greek and Roman literary culture and philosophy which proves that England during the Dark Ages was by no means isolated from what was best in the great stream of Classical and Early Christian culture which survived the barbarian invasions of southern Europe. Both in religious prose and in poetry, whether written in Latin or in the vernacular, the literature of early England reveals a mysticism, an exalted faith, and a divine enthusiasm hardly to be found elsewhere except in the early Christian literature of Ireland.

But the Old English writings discussed above by no means constitute the whole foundation of the literary culture which has since flourished so abundantly in Britain. In this connection, several significant facts, seldom brought out in histories of literature, should be constantly borne in mind if we are to read intelligently the later pages of this volume. Before the Germanic invaders ever set foot on British soil, the land was inhabited by a group of tribes known as Celts, who had a literature of their own, which, though not written down till late in the Christian era, is known to have been varied in content and rich in imaginative power. Here for example are to be sought the beginnings of the legends about King Arthur. Moreover, by 428 these same Celts had for several centuries been under the rulership of Rome, from whom they had received Christianity as well as much pagan culture. From the fifth century till the Norman conquest (1066) frequent contact between British and Irish monasteries was the means of introducing the literary culture which the Irish people, Christian since the early fifth century, had imported from the Continent or had developed independently. Finally, it was during the Anglo-Saxon period that England was invaded by the Scandinavians, who in their turn made contributions to the literature and culture of the island. In short, we should never forget that although the foundation of our language is Anglo-Saxon, the background of our literature extends far beyond the limits of strictly Anglo-Saxon writings.

POETRY

BEOWULF [1]

BEOWULF AND GRENDEL

I

Scyld and his descendants. Hrothgar and the building of Heorot. The coming of Grendel, and his evil deeds. Hrothgar's great sorrow.

Lo! we of the Spear-Danes', in days of yore,
Warrior-kings' glory have heard,
How the princes heroic deeds wrought.
Oft Scyld, son of Scef, from hosts of foes,
From many tribes, their mead-seats took;
The earl caused terror since first he was
Found thus forlorn: gained he comfort for that,
Grew under the clouds, in honors throve,
Until each one of those dwelling around
Over the whale-road, him should obey,
Should tribute pay: that was a good king!
To him was a son afterwards born,
Young in his palace, one whom God sent
To the people for comfort: their distress He perceived
That they ere suffered life-eating care
So long a while. Him therefor life's Lord,
King of glory, world-honor gave:
Beowulf was noted (wide spread his fame),
The son of Scyld in Scedelands.
So shall a young man with presents cause,
With rich money-gifts in his father's house,
That him in old age may after attend
Willing comrades; when war shall come,
May stand by their chief; by deeds of praise shall
In every tribe a hero thrive!
Then Scyld departed at the hour of fate,
The warlike to go into his Lord's keeping:
They him then bore to the ocean's wave,
His trusty comrades, as he himself bade,
Whilst with words ruled the friend of the Scyldings,
Belovèd land-prince; long wielded he power.
There stood at haven with curvèd prow,
Shining and ready, the prince's ship:
The people laid their dear war-lord,
Giver of rings, on the deck of the ship,
The mighty by th' mast. Many treasures were there,
From distant lands, ornaments brought;
Ne'er heard I of keel more comelily filled
With warlike weapons and weeds of battle,
With bills and burnies! On his bosom lay
A heap of jewels, which with him should
Into the flood's keeping afar depart:
Not at all with less gifts did they him provide,
With princely treasures, than those had done,
Who him at his birth had erst sent forth
Alone o'er the sea when but a child.
Then placed they yet a golden standard
High over his head, let the waves bear
Their gift to the sea; sad was their soul,
Mourning their mood. Men indeed cannot
Say now in sooth, hall-possessors,
Heroes 'neath heavens, who that heap took.
Then was in the cities Beowulf, the Scyldings'
Belovèd folk-king, for a long time
Renowned 'mid the nation (elsewhere went his father
The prince from his home), till from him after sprang
The great Healfdene: he ruled while he lived,
Agèd and warlike, kindly the Scyldings.
To him were four children, reckoned in order,
Born into the world, to the prince of the people,
Heorogar and Hrothgar and Halga the good.
I heard that Elan wife of Ongentheow was,
The warlike Scylfing's bed-companion.
Then was to Hrothgar war-speed given,
Honor in battle, that him his dear kinsmen
Gladly obeyed, until the youth grew,
A great band of men. It came into his mind
That he a great hall would then command,
A greater mead-hall his men to build
Than children of men ever had heard of,
And there within would he all deal out
To young and to old, as God him gave,
Except the folk-land and lives of men.
Then far and wide heard I the work was ordered
To many a tribe throughout this mid-earth
The folk-hall to deck. Him in time it befell
Quickly with men, that it was all ready,
The greatest of halls: Heorot as name gave he it,
He who with his word power far and wide had.
He belied not his promise, bracelets he dealt,
Treasure at banquet. The hall arose

[1] Translation by James M. Garnett, 1882. By permission of Ginn & Co., Publishers.

Lofty and pinnacled; hostile waves it awaited
Of hateful fire. Nor was it yet long
Before fierce hatred to the frightened men,
For deadly enmity, was to arise,
Since the fell spirit most spitefully
For a time endured, who in darkness abode,
That he on each day the sound of joy heard
Loud in the hall: there was harp's sound,
Clear song of the minstrel. He said, he who could
The creation of men from of old relate,
Quoth that the Almighty the earth had wrought,
The beautiful plain which water surrounds,
Victorious had set the sun and the moon
As lights for light to the land-dwellers,
And had adorned the regions of earth
With limbs and leaves, life also created
For every kind of living beings.
Thus were the warriors living in joys
Happily then, until one began
Great woes to work, a fiend of hell:
The wrathful spirit was Grendel named,
The mighty mark-stepper who the moors held,
Fen and fastness: the sea-fiend's abode
The joyless being a while in-dwelt,
Since the Creator him had proscribed.
(Upon Cain's kin that crime avenged
The Lord eternal, for that he slew Abel:
Joyed he not in that feud, but him afar banished
For that crime the Creator away from mankind:
Thence evil demons all were produced,
Eotens and elves and monsters of sea,
Such were the giants who strove against God
For a long time: He repaid them for that.)
Then went he to seek out, after night came,
The high-built house, how the Ring-Danes,
After their beer-feast, it had arranged.
He found then therein a band of nobles
Asleep after feasting: sorrows they knew not,
Misfortunes of men. The demon of death,
Grim and greedy, soon was ready,
Fierce and furious, and on their beds took
Thirty of thanes; thence back he departed,
Exulting in booty, homeward to go,
With this fill of slaughter to seek out his dwelling.
Then at early morn was with dawn of day
Grendel's war-craft made known to men:
Then after his meal was wailing upraised,
A great morning-cry: the mighty prince,
The honored chief, sorrowful sat,
The strong man suffered, thane-sorrow endured,
After the foeman's footsteps they beheld,
The cursed demon's: too severe was that sorrow,
Loathsome and lasting. No longer time was it,
But after one night he again wrought
More deeds of murder, and did not shrink from
Hatred and evil: too firm he was in them.
Then was easy to find one who elsewhere,
Farther removed, rest for himself sought,
A bed next the chambers, since to him was shown,
Truly was said by a manifest sign
The hall-thane's hatred: he held himself after
Further and firmer, who 'scaped from the fiend.
So then he reigned and strove against right
Alone against all, until empty stood
The finest of houses. Long was the time:
Twelve winters' time suffering endured
The friend of the Scyldings, each one of woes,
Of sorrows extreme: therefore was this misery
Openly known to the children of men,
Sadly in songs, that Grendel contended
A while against Hrothgar, hateful war waged,
Evil and enmity many half-years,
Contests continual; peacefully would not
From any one man of the might of the Danes
Life-bale remove, nor with money compound;
No one of the wise men need there expect
A ransom more splendid at the murderer's hands.
The terrible demon harassing was,
Dark death-shadow, the old and the young,
Caught and entrapped them; in constant night held
The misty moors: men know not indeed
Whither hell's demons wander in crowds.
So many foul deeds the foe of mankind,
The terrible lone one, often enacted,
Direful afflictions; Heorot he dwelt in,
The costly-decked hall, on the dark nights;
Yet must he not the rich gift-stool approach
For the Creator, nor wish for it know.
That was great sorrow of the friend of the Scyldings,
Misery of mind! Many oft sat
Mighty in council; plans they devised,
What with bold mind then would be best
'Gainst the sudden attacks for them to do.
Sometimes they vowed at their temples of idols
To their gods worship, with words they prayed

The destroyer of spirits would render them help
Against their folk-sorrows. Such was their custom,
Hope of the heathen: hell they remembered
In their minds' thoughts; the Creator they knew not,
Judge of their deeds: the good Lord they knew not,
Heaven's protector could they not praise,
The King of glory. Woe be to him who shall,
Through deadly hate, thrust down his soul
Into the fire-abyss; for comfort he'll hope not,
By no means return! Well be to him who may,
After his death-day, seek for the Lord,
In the Father's bosom mercy beseech!

II

The arrival of Beowulf. His talk with the warden. His reception by Hrothgar. He makes known his errand.

So then great sorrow Healfdene's son
Continually suffered: might not the wise chieftain
His woes remove: too great was that pain,
Loathsome and lasting, that came on the people,
Dreadful distress, greatest of night-bales.
That from home learnt Higelac's thane,
Good 'mong the Geats, the deeds of Grendel:
He was of mankind strongest in might
In the day then of this mortal life,
Noble and great. For him a ship bade he
A good one prepare, quoth, he the war-king
Over the swan-road wished to seek out,
The mighty prince, since he need had of men.
That journey to him the cunning churls
Not at all blamed, though he dear to them was.
They whetted the brave one, good omens they saw
The good one had of the Geats' people
Warriors chosen, of those whom he bravest
Was able to find: one of fifteen
The vessel he sought: a warrior made known,
A sea-crafty man, the neighboring landmarks.
Thus time went on: on the waves was the ship,
Boat under the mountain. The heroes ready
On the prow stied: the billows rolled
The sea 'gainst the sand. The warriors bore
On the deck of the ship ornaments bright,
Equipments ornate: the men shoved out,
Men on willing journey, the well-fitted wood.
Went then o'er the waves, by the wind hastened,
The foamy-necked float to a fowl most like,
Till at the same hour of the following day
The curvèd prow had traversed the water,
So that the sailors then saw the land,
The sea-cliffs shine, the mountains steep,
The broad sea-nesses. Then was the sea-goer
At the end of its voyage. Thence quickly up
The Weders' people on the plain stied,
The sea-wood tied, their battle-sarks rattled,
Their weeds of war: thanked they then God
That for them the sea-paths easy were found.
Then saw from the wall the guard of the Scyldings,
He who the sea-cliffs was set to hold,
Bear o'er the bulwarks bright-looking shields,
Weapons ready for war: wonder aroused him
In his mind's thoughts as to what these men were.
Went he then to the sea on his steed riding,
The thane of Hrothgar; with might he shook
The strong wood in his hands, with formal words spoke:
'What now are ye of arms-bearing men
With burnies protected, who thus a high keel
Over the sea-path bringing have come
O'er the waves hither, clad in helmets?
I was the coast-guard, sea-watch I kept
That no one of foes on the Danes' land
With a ship-army injury might do.
Not here more openly ever have come
Bearers of shields! Ye the permission
Of warlike men did not well know,
Consent of kinsmen! Ne'er saw I a greater
Earl upon earth than is one of you,
A hero in armor: that is no home-stayer
With weapons adorned, unless looks belie him,
His peerless appearance. Now I of you shall
The origin learn, ere ye far hence,
Like to false spies, in the land of the Danes
Further advance. Now ye far-dwelling,
Sea-faring men, give willing ear
To my simple thought: haste now is best
To make plainly known whence is your coming.'
To him then the princely one quickly replied,
The war-band's leader his word-hoard unlocked:
'We are of the race of the Geats' people,
And are of Hygelac hearth-companions.
My own father was well-known to the folk,
A princely ruler, Ecgtheow called:
Many winters he lived ere he away went
Aged from his dwelling: him well remembers

Each one of the wise men wide through the earth.
With friendly mind we thine own lord,
Healfdene's son, seeking are come,
The people's protector. Be thou our informant.
We have to the mighty a mickle errand,
To the lord of the Danes: nor shall aught be hidden
Of this, as I think. Thou knowest, if it is,
As we indeed truly have heard it said,
That 'mong the Scyldings I know not what foe,
A secret enemy, on the dark nights,
Shows by his terror hatred unknown,
Oppression and slaughter. I for that Hrothgar
With kindly mind counsel may give,
How he, old and good, shall the foe overcome,
If yet for him ever should cease
The misery of woes, release again come,
And the care-waves cooler become;
Or ever hereafter a time of trouble,
Oppression he'll suffer, while there remains
In its high place the noblest of houses.'
The warden spoke, where on his horse sat
The fearless warrior: 'Of each of these shall
A wise shield-warrior the difference know,
Of words and works, he who well judgeth.
I that do hear, that this band is friendly
To the lord of the Scyldings; go then forth bearing
Your weapons and war-weeds; I shall direct you:
Likewise my war-thanes I shall command
Against any foe this vessel of yours,
The newly-tarred boat, on the sea-sand
With honor to hold, till back shall bear
O'er the sea-waves the friendly man
The curved-prowed craft to Wedermark.
To such a good-doer will it be granted,
That this battle-storm he safe shall escape.'
Then journeyed they on: the boat remained still,
In the bay rested the broad-bosomed ship,
At anchor fast. The boar's likeness shone:
Over the visor, with gold adorned,
Bright and fire-hardened, the boar kept guard.
The fierce-minded hurried, the heroes hastened,
Together they went, till the well-built hall,
Shining and gold-adorned, they might perceive:
That was the foremost to dwellers on earth
Of halls under heavens, in which the king dwelt;
The light from it shone o'er many of lands.
To them then the warrior the court of the proud
Glittering showed, that they to it might
Straightway proceed, one of war-heroes:
Turned he his horse, his word then spoke:
'My time 't is to go. May the Father Almighty
With His gracious favor you now preserve
Safe on your journey! I will at the sea
'Gainst hostile band keep guard of the coast.'
The road was stone-laid, the path directed
The men together. The war-burnie shone,
Hard and hand-locked, the bright ringèd-iron
Sang in the armor, when they to the hall
In their war-weeds at first approached.
Sea-wearied they set their broad-shapen shields,
Their stout-made bucklers, against the hall's wall,
Went then to the benches; their burnies rang,
War-armor of men; their long spears stood,
The sea-men's weapons, all together,
Grey ash-shaft above; the armored band was
With weapons adorned. There then a bold warrior
Inquired of the heroes concerning their kinship:
'Whence do ye bear your gilded shields,
Gray-colored sarks and grim-looking helmets,
Heap of war-shafts? I am of Hrothgar
Attendant and servant. Ne'er saw I strangers,
So many men, with prouder looks.
I think ye for valor, and not in exile,
But for high-mindedness Hrothgar have sought.'
Him then the hero famed-for-strength answered,
The brave Weders' prince, his word then spoke,
Bold under his helmet: 'We are of Hygelac
Table-companions, Beowulf's my name.
I wish to tell to the son of Healfdene,
The illustrious prince, my errand to him,
Thy lord, and to know if he will us grant
That we him so good friendly may greet.'
Wulfgar then spoke (he was Vandals' chief,
His strength of mind was to many well-known,
His prowess and wisdom): 'I the Danes' friend,
The lord of the Scyldings, therefore will ask,
The giver of rings, as thou art a suppliant,
The illustrious prince, concerning thy errand,
And to thee the answer at once will announce,

Which to me the good one thinketh to give.'
Went he then quickly to where Hrothgar sat,
Old and gray-headed, with his band of earls;
The warlike went, till he stood in the presence
Of the lord of the Danes; he knew the court's custom.
Wulfgar then spoke to his own dear lord:
'Here are arrived, come from afar
Over the sea-waves, men of the Geats;
The one most distinguished the warriors brave
Beowulf name. They are thy suppliants
That they, my prince, may with thee now
Greetings exchange: do not thou refuse them
Thy converse in turn, friendly Hrothgar!
They in their war-weeds seem very worthy
Contenders with earls: the chief is renowned
Who these war-heroes hither has led.'
Hrothgar then spoke, defence of the Scyldings:
'I knew him of old when he was a child:
His agèd father was Ecgtheow named;
To him at home gave Hrethel the Geat
His only daughter: his son has now
Boldly come here, a trusty friend sought.
Then this was said by the sea-farers,
Those who did tribute for the Geats carry
Thither for favor, that he thirty men's
Great strength of might in his hand-grip,
Brave in war, has. Him holy God
For gracious help to us has sent,
To the West-Danes, as I have hope,
Against Grendel's terror: I shall to the good one
For his boldness of mind costly gifts offer.
Be thou in haste, bid them come in,
A friendly band see all together!
Tell them too in words that they are welcome
To the Danes' people.'—[To the hall-door
Wulfgar then went], words within spoke:
'To you bade me say my victor-lord,
Prince of the East-Danes, that your kinship he knows,
And ye are to him over the sea-waves,
Bold-minded men, welcome hither.
Now ye may go in your war-armor,
Under your helmets, Hrothgar to see:
Let ye your battle-shields here then await,
Your spears, deadly shafts, the converse of words.'
Then rose the mighty, many warriors around him,
A brave band of thanes: some there abode,
The battle-weeds kept, as them the chief bade.
They hastened together, as the guide them directed,
Under Heorot's roof: the valiant one went
Bold under his helmet, till he in the hall stood.
Beowulf spoke (on him shone the burnie,
The linkèd net-work forged by the smith's craft):
'Be thou, Hrothgar, hail! I am of Hygelac
Kinsman and war-thane: many exploits have I
Undertaken in youth. To me Grendel's deed
In my native land clearly was known:
The sea-farers say that this mead-hall stands,
Noblest of halls, for each one of heroes
Empty and useless, when even-light
In the brightness of heaven has been concealed.
Then did my people give me advice,
The noblest of men, craftiest of churls,
Princely Hrothgar, that I thee should seek;
For that they knew my own strength of might:
They themselves saw when I came from the battle,
Blood-stained from my foes, where sea-monsters I bound,
The eoten-race killed, and on the waves slew
The nickers by night, endured great distress,
Avenged Weders' sorrows (woes had they suffered),
Their foe-men destroyed, and now against Grendel,
Against the dread monster, alone shall decide
The fight 'gainst the giant. I of thee now then,
Prince of the Bright-Danes, desire to make,
Chief of the Scyldings, but one request,—
That do not thou refuse me, defender of warriors,
Dear friend of the people, now thus far am I come,—
That I may alone and my band of earls,
This company brave, Heorot cleanse.
Also have I heard that the dread monster
For boldness of mood recks not for weapons:
I that then do scorn—so be to me Hygelac,
My own people's-king, gracious in mind—
That I a sword bear or a broad shield
Yellow-rimmed to the battle; but I with grip shall
'Gainst my foe grapple and for life strive
Foe against foe: there shall confide
In the doom of the Lord he whom death takes.
I ween that he will, if he may prevail,
In the war-hall the folk of the Geats,

The fearless, devour, as he oft did
The might of the Hrethmen; thou needest
not then
My head conceal, but me he will have
Stainèd with gore, if death me take,
My bloody corpse bear, think to devour it,
Will eat it alone, unpityingly,
Will mark the moor-mounds: thou needest
not then
For my body's food longer take care.
Send thou to Hygelac, if battle me take,
Best one of war-weeds that covers my breast,
Noblest of burnies; 't is Hrædla's bequest,
Weland's skilled work. Goes aye Weird as
it will!'
Hrothgar then spoke, defence of the Scyld-
ings:
'For fight of protection, Beowulf my friend,
And for assistance, hast thou us sought.
Thy father fought a mighty contest;
He was of Heatholaf the slayer by hand
Among the Wylfings, when the kin of the
Waras
'Gainst the terror of war him might not have.
After that sought he the South-Danes' folk
Over the sea-waves, the Honor-Scyldings,
When I first ruled the folk of the Danes.
And in youth held the jewelled-rich
Hoard-city of heroes, when Heregar was
dead,
My elder brother bereft of life,
The son of Healfdene; he was better than I.
Afterwards the feud with money I set-
tled;
I sent to the Wylfings o'er the waters' ridge
Old-time treasures; he swore to me oaths.
Sorrow is in my mind for me to say
To any of men what to me Grendel hath
Of harm in Heorot with his hateful
thoughts,
Of sudden woes wrought; my hall-band is,
My war-heap, vanished; Weird swept them
away
Into Grendel's terror. God easily may
The mad foe restrain from his evil deeds.
Very often they boasted, drunken with
beer,
Over the ale-cup, the warriors bold,
That they in the beer-hall would then await
Grendel's contest with their terrible swords.
Then was this mead-hall in the morning-
time,
Lordly hall, stained with gore, when day-
light shone
All the bench-rows covered with blood,
The hall with sword-gore; I had the less
lieges,
Dearest companions, whom death took away.
Sit now at the feast and free from court-rules
The heroes victorious, as pleases thy
mind.'
Then was for the Geat-men all together
In the beer-hall a bench prepared,
Where the bold-minded hastened to sit,
Proud in their strength. The thane did his
service,
Who in his hands bore a gold-adorned ale-
cup.
Poured out the clear mead. Sometimes sang
the minstrel
With clear voice in Heorot: there was joy of
heroes,
No little band of Danes and Weders.

III

Hunferth's taunt. The swimming-match with Breca. Joy in Heorot.

Hunferth then spoke, the son of Ecglaf,
Who at the feet sat of the lord of the Scyld-
ings,
Unloosed his war-secret (was the coming of
Beowulf,
The proud sea-farer, to him mickle grief,
For that he granted not that any man else
Ever more honor of this mid-earth
Should gain under heavens than he him-
self):
'Art thou that Beowulf who strove with
Breca
On the broad sea in swimming-match,
When ye two for pride the billows tried
And for vain boasting in the deep water
Riskèd your lives? You two no man,
Nor friend nor foe, might then dissuade
From sorrowful venture, when ye on the sea
swam,
When ye the sea-waves with your arms
covered,
Measured the sea-ways, struck with your
hands,
Glided o'er ocean; with its great billows
Welled up winter's flood. In the power of
the water
Ye seven nights strove: he in swimming
thee conquered,
He had greater might. Then him in the
morning
On the Heathoremes' land the ocean bore up,
Whence he did seek his pleasant home,
Dear to his people, the land of the Brond-
ings,
His fair strong city, where he had people,
A city and rings. All his boast against thee
The son of Beanstan truly fulfilled.
Then ween I for thee a worse result,
Though thou in battle wert everywhere good,
A fiercer fight, if thou Grendel darest

The space of one night nigh to abide.'
Beowulf spoke, Ecgtheow's son:
'Lo! thou very much, Hunferth my friend,
Drunken with beer, hast spoken of Breca,
Hast said of his journey. I say the truth,
That I did the more sea-power possess,
Endurance 'mid waves, than any man else.
We two said this, when we were boys,
And we of this boasted (both were then still
In the prime of youth), that we out on the sea
Our lives would risk; and that we accomplished.
A naked sword had we, when we swam on the sea,
Boldly in hand: ourselves 'gainst the whales
We thought to defend. Not at all from me
On the flood-waves could he afar float,
On the sea quicker; I from him would not.
Then we two together were in the sea
The space of five nights, till flood apart drove us,
The swelling billows, coldest of storms,
Darkening night, and the north wind
Boisterous and fierce; rough were the waves.
The sea-fishes' spirit was then aroused:
There 'gainst the foes my body-sark,
Hard and hand-locked, to me help afforded;
The braided war-burnie on my breast lay,
With gold adorned. To the bottom me drew
The hostile foe; he held me fast,
Grim in his grip; yet was it granted me,
That I the monster with sword-point reached,
With battle-brand: the struggle took off
The mighty mere-beast by my own hand.
So often upon me the hateful foes
Powerfully pressed: I punished them
With my dear sword, as it behooved me.
Not at all did they have joy of their meal,
The evil-doers, that they me might devour,
'Round their banquet might sit nigh the sea-bottom,
But in the morning wounded with swords
Around the sea-strand and upon it they lay,
With swords put to sleep, that never thereafter
Upon the high ocean the farers-by-sea
Might they let on their journey. Light from the east came,
Bright beacon of God: still were the waves,
So that I the sea-nesses might now behold,
The windy walls. Weird often preserves
An unfated earl, when his might has availed!
Yet it granted to me that I with sword slew
Nine of the nickers. Ne'er heard I at night
Under heaven's vault of a harder fight,
Nor on the sea-billows of a more wretched man:
Yet I my foes' grip with life escaped
Weary of th' journey. Then me the sea bore,
The flood o'er the waves, upon the Finns' land,
The welling waters. Not at all about thee
Of such-like contests have I heard tell,
Of terror with swords. Breca ne'er yet
In battle-play, nor either of you,
So daring a deed ever has done,
With stainèd swords (not of that do I boast),
Though thou thine own brothers' murderer wast,
Thy blood-relations': for this shalt thou in hell
Curses endure, though thy wit may avail!
I tell thee in truth, son of Ecglaf,
That never had Grendel wrought so many horrors,
The terrible monster, to thine own prince,
Shame in Heorot, if thy mind were,
Thy temper, so fierce, as thou thyself reckonest:
But he hath found that he the feud need not,
The terrible contest of your own people,
Very much dread, of the Victor-Scyldings;
He taketh forced pledge, he spareth no one
Of the Danes' people, but he joy beareth,
Killeth and eateth, nor weeneth of contest
With the Spear-Danes. But I to him shall
The Geats' strength and might without delay now
Offer in battle. Then shall go he who may
Proudly to mead, when morning-light
Of the second day o'er the children of men,
The sun ether-clad, shall shine from the South.'
Then was in joy the giver of treasure,
Gray-haired and war-fierce; help he expected,
The ruler of Bright-Danes; in Beowulf heard
The people's shepherd the firm-set purpose.
There was laughter of heroes, the harp merry sounded,
Winsome were words. Went Wealhtheow forth,
The queen of Hrothgar, mindful of courtesies,
Gold-adorned greeted the men in the hall,
And the high-born woman then gave the cup
First to the East-Danes' home-protector,
Bade him be blithe at the beer-drinking,
Him dear to his people. In joy he received

The food and the hall-cup, victorious king.
Then around went the Helmings' lady
To every division of old and of young,
Costly gifts gave, until the time came
That she to Beowulf, the ring-adorned queen,
Noble in mind, the mead-cup bore:
She greeted the Geats' chief, thanks gave to God,
Wise in her words, that the wish to her fell,
That on any earl she might rely
For comfort in evils. Received he the cup,
The warrior fierce, at Wealhtheow's hands.
And then he spoke, ready for battle;
Beowulf spoke, Ecgtheow's son:
'This thought I then, when I on the sea stied,
Boarded my sea-boat with my warrior-band,
That I throughout of your own people
The will would work, or in battle fall,
Fast in fiend's grip. I shall perform
Deeds of valor, or end-day mine
In this mead-hall I shall await.'
To the woman these words well-pleasing were,
Boasts of the Geat: gold-adorned went
The high-born queen to sit by her lord.
Then was as before again in the hall
Mighty word spoken, in joy were the people,
The victor-folk's shout, until all at once
The son of Healfdene wished to seek out
His evening-rest; he knew for the monster
In the high hall was battle prepared,
[Because in this hall the Ring-Danes never
Dared to abide unless by day-time],
From the time that they the sun-light might see,
Till night spreading darkness over all things,
Night-wandering spirits, came advancing
Dark under the clouds. The crowd all arose:
Greeted then glad-minded one man another,
Hrothgar Beowulf, and offered him hail,
Power o'er the mead-hall, and this word spoke:
'Never to any man ere did I trust,
Since I could lift my hand and my shield,
Royal hall of the Danes except to thee now.
Have now and hold the noblest of houses,
Of glory be mindful, a hero's might show,
Watch 'gainst the foe. No wish shalt thou want,
If thou the great struggle escapest with life.'

IV

Beowulf and his men occupy Heorot. The coming of Grendel. The mighty contest. Beowulf's victory.

Then Hrothgar went with his warrior-band,
The prince of the Scyldings, out of the hall:
The war-prince would Wealhtheow seek,
His queen as companion. The glory of kings
Grendel against, as men heard say,
A hall-guard had set: he performed special service
For the prince of the Danes, he eoten-guard kept.
Now the prince of the Geats earnestly trusted
In his proud might, in the Creator's favor.
Then he laid him aside his iron burnie,
Helmet from head, his jewelled sword gave,
Choicest of weapons, to his servant-thane,
And bade him keep his armor of war.
Then spoke the hero some boastful words,
Beowulf the Geat, ere he on bed stied:
'I count not myself less good in war-might
For deeds of battle than Grendel himself:
Therefore with my sword I him will not kill,
Of life deprive, though I it all may.
He knows not these goods, so that he me may slay,
Hew down my shield, although he be fierce
In hostile deeds: but we at night shall
From swords refrain, if he dare to seek
War without weapons; and then the wise God,
The holy Lord, on whatever hand
May the glory adjudge, as seems to Him fit.'
Then lay down the warlike: the pillow received
The cheek of the earl, and him around many
A valiant sea-warrior sought his hall-rest.
No one of these thought that thence he should
Again his dear home ever seek out,
Folk or free-city where he was reared;
But they had heard that too many before
In this wine-hall bloody death carried off
Of the folk of the Danes. But to them the Lord gave
The web of war-speed, to the folk of the Weders
Comfort and help, so that they their foes
Through the craft of one all overcame,
By the might of one self: the truth is made known
That the mighty God the race of man
Has always ruled. — Came in wan night
The shadow-goer stepping. The warriors slept,
Who the horned hall then were to hold,
All except one. That was to men known,
That them he might not, whom the Creator would not,
The hostile demon drag into darkness;
But he keeping watch for his foe in anger
Awaited enraged the result of the battle.

Then came from the moor 'neath the misty slopes
Grendel going, God's anger he bore.
The wicked foe thought of the race of man
Some one to entrap in that high hall:
He went 'neath the clouds whither he the wine-hall,
The gold-hall of men, most thoroughly knew,
Shining with gold-plates: that was not the first time
That he of Hrothgar the home had sought.
Ne'er in his life-time before nor after
Bolder warriors, hall-thanes, did he find!
Then came to the hall the being approaching,
Of joys deprived. The door soon sprang open
Fast in its fire-bands, when he with hands touched it;
Then burst the bale-bringer, since he was enraged,
The door of the hall. Soon after that
On the many-colored floor the fiendish one trod,
Mad in mind went: from his eyes stood
A loathsome light likest to flame.
He saw in the hall many of warriors,
A band in peace sleeping all together,
A heap of kin-warriors. Then laughed his mood,
He thought that he would, ere day came, divide,
The terrible monster, of every one
The life from the body, since to him was fallen
A hope of much food. That no longer was fated,
That he might more of the race of man
Devour by night. The strong-in-might saw,
The kinsman of Hygelac, how the fell foe
With his swift attacks was going to act.
That did not the monster think to delay,
But quickly he seized for the first time
A sleeping warrior, him tore unresisting,
Bit his bone-frame, drank blood from his veins,
In great bites him swallowed: soon then he had,
Deprived of life, him all devoured,
Feet even and hands. Forth nearer he stepped,
Seized then with his hands the firm-in-mind
Warrior on bed. Him reached out against
The fiend with his hand: quickly he seized
The cunning-in-mind and on his arm sat.
Soon this perceived the worker of evil,
That he never found in this mid-earth,
In the regions of earth, in another man
A greater hand-grip: in mood he became
In his soul frightened; he could not sooner forth.
His mind was death-ready; into darkness would flee,
The devil-band seek: his course was not there,
As he in old-days before had found.
Remembered he then, good kinsman of Hygelac,
His evening-speech; upright he stood
And him fast seized: his fingers cracked.
The eoten would outwards: the earl further stepped;
The mighty one thought, whereso he might,
Afar to escape, and away thence
Flee into the marshes: he knew that his fingers
Were in his foe's grip: that was a bad journey
That the harm-bringing foe had taken to Heorot:
The royal hall sounded: for all the Danes was,
The city-dwellers, each one of the bold,
For earls the ale spilt. Angry were both
Furious contestants: the hall cracked aloud:
Then was it great wonder that the wine-hall
Withstood the fierce fighters, that it to ground fell not,
The fair folk-hall: but it was too fast
Within and without in its iron bands
By cunning skill forged. There from the sill fell
Many a mead-bench, as I have heard say,
Adorned with gold, where the foes fought.
Of this before weened not wise men of the Scyldings
That it ever with strength any of men,
Goodly and bone-adorned, to pieces might break,
With craft destroy, unless flame's embrace
In smoke should it swallow. The sound arose
Often repeated: to the North-Danes stood
Fearful terror, to every one
Of those who from the wall the weeping heard,
The terrible song sung of th' opposer of God,
The joyless song, his pain lament
The prisoner of hell. He held him too fast,
He who of men was strongest in might
In the day then of this mortal life.
The earl's defence would on no account
The bringer of woes let go alive,
Nor his life-days to any people
Did he count useful. There brandished many
An earl of Beowulf his good old sword;
His dear lord's life he would defend,

His noble chief's, whereso they might;
They knew not indeed, when they risked the contest,
The bold-in-mind heroes of battle,
And on each side they thought to hew,
To seek his soul, that the fiendish demon
Not any on earth choicest of weapons,
No one of war-swords, was able to touch,
But he had forsworn victorious weapons,
Each one of swords. His life-leaving should,
In the day then of this mortal life,
Miserably happen, and the strange-spirit
Into his foes' power afar depart.
Then that he perceived, he who oft before
In mirth of mind against mankind
His crimes had wrought, hostile to God,
That his body's frame him would not sustain,
But him the proud kinsman of Hygelac
Had by the hands: each was to other
Living a foe. Pain of body endured
The terrible monster: there was on his shoulder
An evident wound; apart sprang the sinews,
The bone-frame burst. To Beowulf was
Battle-fame given: Grendel should thence
Sick-of-life flee under the fen-slopes,
Seek his joyless abode; too surely he knew
That of his life the end was come,
The span of his days. To all of the Danes
By the bloody strife was the wish fulfilled;
He then had cleansed, who ere came from afar,
Wise and valiant, the hall of Hrothgar,
Saved it from sorrow, rejoiced in his night-work,
His glorious deeds. Then for the East-Danes
The prince of the Geats his boast had performed,
Likewise the sufferings all had removed,
Sorrows from foe, which they ere suffered,
And by compulsion had to endure,
No little distress. That was a clear proof,
After the battle-brave laid down the hand,
The arm and the shoulder (there all was together),
The claw of Grendel 'neath the wide roof.

V

Joy of the Danes. The minstrel's song of Sigemund and Fitela: of Heremod. Hrothgar's thanks to Beowulf.

Then was in the morning, as I have heard say,
Around the gift-hall many a warrior:
The people's leaders from far and near came
Through the wide ways the wonder to view,
The tracks of the foe. Ne'er did his life-severing
Sorrowful seem to any of men,
Of those who then viewed the track of the vanquished,
How weary in mind he away thence,
In fight overcome, to the mere of the nickers,
Doomed and driven, his life-tracks bore.
There was the surface welling in blood;
The frightful waves' lashing all commingled
Hot in gore boiled with the sword-blood;
The doomed-to-death dyed them, when of joys deprived
In his fen-refuge he laid down his life,
His heathen soul, where hell him received.
Thence back again came the old companions,
And many a young one from their glad course,
From the sea proudly riding on horses,
Heroes on steeds. There then was Beowulf's
Glory proclaimed: oft many said
That south nor north by the two seas
O'er the wide earth no other one
'Neath heaven's expanse was better than he
Of bearers of shields, more worthy of rule.
They did not now at all their dear lord blame,
The friendly Hrothgar, but that was a good king.
Sometimes the battle-famed permitted to leap,
In contest to go, their yellow horses
Where the land-roads seemed to them fair,
Known for their goodness. Sometimes a king's thane,
A man renowned, mindful of songs,
He who very many of old-time sagas,
A great number remembered, framed other words
Rightly connected: the scope then began
Beowulf's exploit with skill to tell,
And with art to relate well-composed tales,
Words to exchange; he told everything
That he of Sigemund had heard men say,
His noble deeds, much of the unknown,
The Wælsing's contest, his journeys wide,
Which the children of men did not well know,
The feuds and crimes, but Fitela with him,
When he some such thing wished to relate,
Uncle to nephew, as they ever were
In every fight comrades in need:
They had very many of the race of the eotens
Slain with their swords. To Sigemund came
After his death-day no little fame

Since he, brave in war, destroyed the dragon,
The guard of the hoard: he 'neath the gray stone,
The prince's son, had risked alone
The very bold deed; not with him was Fitela;
Yet it happened to him that the sword pierced through
The wonderful worm, that it in the wall stood,
The lordly weapon; in death lay the dragon.
The terrible one in strength had prevailed,
So that he the ring-hoard himself might enjoy
At his own will; he loaded his vessel,
Bore on the ship's bosom the ornaments bright,
The son of Wæls; the worm's heat melted *him*.
He was of exiles the greatest by far
Among the nations, the warriors' defence
In noble deeds; for that ere had he glory.
After of Heremod the battle-might failed,
His strength and prowess, he was 'mong the Jutes
Into his foe's power forthwith betrayed,
Sent away quickly: him waves of sorrow
Too long oppressed; he was to his people,
To all of his princes, a life-long distress:
Likewise oft lamented in former times
The brave one's journey many a wise churl,
Who trusted in him for help in misfortunes,
That the son of their prince was to grow up,
Take the place of his father, his people possess,
Hoard and head-city, kingdom of heroes,
Home of the Scyldings. *He* was there to all,
The kinsman of Hygelac, to the race of man,
To friends more beloved: *him* sorrow befell. —
Sometimes contending the yellow roads
With their horses they measured. Then was morning-light
Advanced and hastened: many a man went,
Brave now in mind, to the high hall
To see the rare wonder; the king himself also
From his bridal chamber, guardian of treasures,
Stepped strong in glory with a great crowd,
Famed for his virtues, and his queen with him
Measured the mead-path with her maiden-band.
Hrothgar then spoke (he went to the hall,
Stood by the column, looked at the high roof
Adorned with gold and at Grendel's hand):
'For this glad sight thanks to the Almighty
Quickly be given! Much evil I suffered,
Sorrows from Grendel: God may ever work
Wonder on wonder, King of glory.
Lately it was that I for myself
Of any of woes weened not my life long
Relief to obtain, since stained with blood
The noblest of houses drenched in gore stood;
Woe was brought down on every wise man,
Of those who weened not that they in their lives
The people's land-work from foes might defend,
From demons and devils. Now hath a hero,
Through the Lord's might, a deed performed,
Which we all before were not at all able
With wisdom to work. Lo! this may say
Even whatever woman brought forth this son
After man's nature, if she yet liveth,
That to her the eternal Creator was gracious
In her child-bearing. Now I thee, Beowulf,
Noblest of men, for myself as a son
Will love in life: keep well henceforth
The kinship new. To thee shall no lack be
Of earthly wishes o'er which I have power.
Very often for less have I fixed the reward,
The share of the treasure, to warrior less brave,
One worse in the fight. Thou hast for thyself
Effected by deeds that thy fame shall live
For ever and ever. May thee the Almighty
With good repay, as He heretofore did!'
Beowulf then spoke, Ecgtheow's son:
'That deed of might we, with great good-will,
That fight have fought, boldly encountered
The strength of the unknown: I rather would wish
That thou himself now mightest see,
The foe in his battle-dress wearied to death.
I quickly him with hardest grips
Thought then to bind on the death-bed,
That he by hand-grip of mine should lie
Striving for life, if his body escaped not:
I might not him, since the Creator willed not,
Cut off from escape: not so firm held I him,
The life-destroyer: too powerful was he,
The foe in his speed. Yet his hand did he let
For life-protection remain behind,
His arm and shoulder: not there, however,
Did the helpless man gain any comfort.
Not longer shall live the evil-doer
Burdened with sins, but him sore pain
In his strong grip sternly has seized,
In his bonds of bale: there shall abide

The sin-stained man the mickle doom,
How the glorious Creator to him will prescribe.'
Then was more silent the son of Ecglaf
In his boasting-speech of warlike deeds,
After the princes, by the earl's might,
Upon the high roof the hand had viewed,
The foe-man's fingers, each one before him:
Each place of the nails was likest to steel,
The heathen's hand-spurs, the battle-monster's
Horrible claw: each one then said
That him would touch of warlike men
No excellent weapon, so that the demon's
Bloody war-hand it would break off.

VI

Feasting and presents in Heorot. The minstrel's song of Finn, Hnæf, and Hengest. Wealhtheow's greeting to Beowulf. All retire to rest.

Then quickly was ordered Heorot within
By hands to adorn: there were many of those,
Of men and of women, who that wine-hall,
That guest-room prepared. Gold-adorned shone
The webs on the walls, many wondrous sights
To each one of men, who on such look.
That building bright was very much injured,
All the interior in its iron-bands fast;
The hinges were shivered; the roof alone saved
Entirely sound, when had the monster,
Condemned for his crimes, in flight escaped,
Hopeless of life. It will not be easy
Fate to escape, let do it who will;
But each shall obtain of soul-bearing men,
By necessity fixed for the children of men,
For dwellers on earth, the place prepared,
Where his dead body, fast in his death-bed,
Shall sleep after feast. Then was the fit time
That to the hall went Healfdene's son,
The king himself the feast would enjoy.
Ne'er heard I that folk in greater crowd
Around their ring-giver better behaved.
Went then to the benches the heroes renowned
Rejoiced at the plenty: courteously shared
Many a mead-cup the kinsmen of these,
The bold-minded ones in the high hall,
Hrothgar and Hrothulf. Heorot within
Was filled with friends: not at all deeds of guile
Did the Folk-Scyldings at this time prepare.
Gave then to Beowulf Healfdene's son
A golden banner as victory's reward,
A wreathèd standard, helmet and burnie;
A great jewelled sword many then saw
Before the chief borne. Beowulf received
The cup in the hall. Not of that treasure-giving
Before the warriors need he be ashamed:
Ne'er heard I, more courteously, that treasures four
With gold adorned, many of men
On the ale-bench to each other gave.
'Round the crown of the helmet head-protection
A boss wound with wires was keeping without,
That him the battle-swords boldly might not,
By file hardened, injure, when the shield-warrior
Against his foes in battle should go.
The earl's defence eight horses ordered,
With golden trappings, to lead in the hall
In under the barriers: on one of these stood
A saddle art-decked, with treasure adorned;
That was the battle-seat of the high king,
When in sword-play Healfdene's son
Wished to engage; ne'er at the front failed
The famed one's valor when corpses fell.
And then to Beowulf of each of the two
The prince of the Ingwins power delivered,
Of horses and weapons: bade him well use them.
So like a man the noble prince,
The hoard-keeper of heroes, contest repaid
With horses and treasures, such as never will blame
He who will speak truth according to right.
Then still on each one the prince of earls,
Of those who with Beowulf the watery waves traversed,
On the mead-bench a treasure bestowed,
A sword as an heir-loom, and bade for that one
To pay with gold, whom Grendel before
With evil killed, as he more of them would,
Had not the wise God weird averted,
And the man's courage: the Creator ruled all
Of the race of mankind, as He still doth:
Therefore is insight everywhere best,
Forethought of mind. He shall abide much
Of good and of ill, he who long here
In these days of sorrow useth the world.
There song and music was all together
About Healfdene's battle-leader;
The harp was played, the song oft rehearsed,
When joy in hall Hrothgar's minstrel

Along the mead-bench was to make known:
'He sang of Finn's sons when that danger befell
The heroes of Healfdene, when Hnæf of the Scyldings
In Frisian land was fated to fall.
Then indeed Hildeburh needed not praise
The faith of the Jutes: guiltless was she
Deprived of her dear ones in the shield-play,
Of sons and of brothers: by fate they fell
Wounded with spear: that was a sad woman.
Not without reason did the daughter of Hoc
Lament fate's decree, when morning came,
When she under heaven might then behold
The death-bale of kinsmen, where she before had
Most worldly joy. War took away all
The thanes of Finn except a few only,
So that he could not, on that meeting-place,
In fight with Hengest at all contend,
Nor even the remnant rescue by war
From the chief's thane: but they offered them terms,
That they for them other hall would provide,
Hall and high seat, that they power of half
With the Jutes' sons were to possess,
And at treasure-givings the son of Folcwalda
On every day would honor the Danes,
The band of Hengest with rings would enrich,
Even as much with costly jewels
Of plated gold, as he the Frisians
In the beer-hall would encourage.
Then they confirmed on either side
A firm peace-compact: Finn to Hengest,
In valor invincible, promised with oaths
That he the remnant, by the doom of his wise men,
In honor would hold, that no man there
By words nor works the compact should break,
Nor ever through cunning should violate it,
Though they their ring-giver's murderer followed,
Deprived of their prince, since so 't was appointed them:
If then of the Frisians any one with bold speech
Of that bloody feud mindful should be,
Then the edge of the sword it should avenge.
The oath was confirmed and treasure of gold
From the hoard taken. Of the warlike Scyldings
The best of the warriors was at the pyre ready;
At the funeral-pile was easily seen
The blood-stained sark, the all-golden swine,
The boar of hard iron, many a prince
Destroyed by wounds: some fell in slaughter.
Hildeburh bade then at Hnæf's funeral-pyre
To consign to the flame her own dear son,
The body to burn and on the pyre place.
The wretched woman wept on his shoulder,
Mourned him in songs. The fierce smoke arose,
Wound to the clouds the greatest of fires,
Before the mound roared: the heads were melted,
The wound-openings burst; then out sprang the blood
From the wound of the body. The flame swallowed all,
Greediest of spirits, of those whom war took
Of both of the peoples: gone was their breath. —
Then went the warriors to visit the dwellings,
Deprived of their friends, Friesland to see,
The homes and high city. Hengest then still
The slaughter-stained winter dwelt there with Finn,
In valor invincible; he remembered his land,
Though he might not on the sea drive
The ring-prowed ship: in storm rolled the ocean,
Fought with the wind: winter the waves locked
In its icy bond, until came another
Year in the dwellings, as now still do
(For they ever observe suitable seasons)
The clear-shining days. Then winter was gone,
Fair was the earth's bosom: strove the exile to go,
The guest from the dwellings; he then on vengeance
More eagerly thought than on the sea-voyage,
If he might effect a hostile meeting,
And in it remember the sons of the Jutes.
So he did not escape the fate of the world
When Hunlaf's son a battle-sword,
Best of weapons, thrust in his breast;
Well-known were its edges among the Jutes.
Also, bold-minded Finn afterwards befell
Death-bringing sword-bale at his own home,
When the fierce battle Guthlaf and Oslaf
After their sea-journey in sorrow lamented,
Blamed him for their woes: his flickering life might not
Keep itself in his breast. Then was the hall covered
With bodies of foes; also was Finn slain,
The king 'mong his band, and the queen taken.

The Scyldings' warriors bore to their ships
All the possessions of the king of the land,
Such as they might find at Finn's home
Of bright jewels and gems. They on the sea-road
The royal woman to the Danes bore,
Led to their people.' — The song was sung,
The gleeman's glee: the sport then arose,
Carousing resounded: the servants out-poured
Wine from the wondrous vessels. Then came Wealhtheow forth,
Going under her golden crown, where were the good ones two
Uncle and nephew sitting: then were they still at peace,
Each one true to the other. There also the orator Hunferth
Sat at the feet of the Scyldings' lord: each of them trusted his wisdom,
That he great courage had, tho' to his kinsmen he was not
Honest in play of the swords. Spoke then the queen of the Scyldings:
'Receive thou this cup, my dearest lord,
Giver of treasure. Be thou in health,
Gold-friend of men, and to the Geats speak
With mildest words, as a man shall do.
Be to the Geats kind, mindful of gifts;
Near and afar hast thou now peace.
One said to me thou for a son would
The warrior have. Heorot is cleansed,
The bright jewel-hall: use whilst thou mayest
Many rewards, and leave to thy kinsmen
Folk and kingdom, when thou shalt forth
Fate's decree see. I know well indeed
My friendly Hrothulf, that he the youth will
In honor hold, if thou sooner than he,
Friend of the Scyldings, leavest the world:
I ween that he with good will repay
Our own children, if he all remember,
What we, through good-will and also through honor,
Of kindnesses showed to him when a child.'
Turned she then to the bench where were her sons,
Hrethric and Hrothmund, and the warriors' children,
The youth together, where sat the good
Beowulf the Geat by the two brothers.
To him was a cup borne, and friendly greeting
Offered in words, and twisted gold
Gladly presented, arm-ornaments two,
A burnie and rings, the greatest of collars,
Of those which on earth I ever have heard of.
Under the heaven heard I of no better
Hoard-jewel of heroes, since Hama bore
To the bright city the Brosings' collar,
Bright jewel and costly; — he fell into the wiles
Of Eormenric, eternal fate chose.
This ring then had Higelac the Geat,
The grandson of Swerting, the very last time,
When he under his banner defended the treasure,
Battle-spoils guarded: Weird took him away,
When he for pride suffered great woes,
Feud from the Frisians: the jewels he bore,
The precious stones, o'er the wave-holder,
The mighty prince: he fell under his shield,
The life of the king into th' Franks' keeping went,
Breast-battle-weeds and the collar together:
Warriors inferior plundered the slain
After the overthrow of the Geats' people,
The battle-field held. — The hall resounded.
Wealhtheow then said, she before the crowd spoke:
'Use this collar, Beowulf dear,
Young man, with joy, and make use of this burnie,
People's treasures, and thrive thou well;
Bear thee with might and be to these youths
Friendly in counsel; thy reward I'll remember.
Thou hast now caused that thee far and near
All thy life long men shall honor,
Even so wide as the sea encircles,
Winds through its walls. Be, whilst thou livest,
Noble prince, happy. I grant to thee well
Precious treasures. Be thou to my sons
Friendly in deeds, thou joyful one:
Here is each earl true to the other,
Mild in his mood, loyal to his liege lord;
The thanes are at peace, the people all ready;
Warriors well-drunken, do as I bid.'
She went to the seat. There was choicest of feasts,
The men drank the wine: weird they knew not,
Destiny stern, as it did happen
To many of earls, when even came
And Hrothgar departed to go to his court,
The mighty to rest. The hall in-dwelt
A number of earls, as they oft before did;
They emptied the bench-space: it was over-spread
With beds and bolsters. A certain beer-servant,
Ready and fated, lay down to his rest.

They placed at their heads the battle-shields,
The bright wooden boards: there on the bench was
Over the warrior easily seen
The battle-high helmet, the ringèd burnie,
The mighty spear-shaft; their custom was
That they often were ready for combat
Both at home and in army, and in each one of them
Even at such a time as to their liege lord
Need there might be: that was a good folk.

VII

The coming of Grendel's mother. Sorrow is renewed. Hrothgar describes the mere. Beowulf's decision. His descent into the mere. The fight with Grendel's mother. Beowulf's return, bearing Grendel's head.

They went then to sleep: one sorely paid for
His evening-rest, as to them often happened
When the gold-hall Grendel in-dwelt,
Evil deeds wrought, until the end came,
Death for his crimes. That became plain,
To men widely known, that still an avenger
Lived for his foes. For a long time
After the war-sorrow Grendel's mother,
A terrible woman, nourished her grief
Who was said to inhabit the fearful waters,
The ice-cold streams, since Cain became
The murderer by sword of his only brother,
His father's son; then outlawed he went,
With murder marked, to flee human joy,
Dwelt in the waste. Thence many sprang
Of the demons of fate; of these one was Grendel,
Hateful and ravenous, who in Heorot found
A watching man awaiting the battle
Where the fell monster him was attacking:
Yet he remembered the strength of his might,
The powerful gift, which God to him gave,
And on the Lord's favor relied for himself
For comfort and help: so the fiend overcame he,
Felled the demon of hell, when he humbled departed,
Deprived of joy, his death-place to see,
The foe of mankind. And still his mother,
Greedy and raging, wished then to go
The sorrowful journey her son to avenge.
She came then to Heorot, where the Ring-Danes
Through the hall slept: then there was soon
A change to the earls, when within entered
Grendel's mother. The terror was less
Even by so much as is woman's strength,
A woman's war-terror, esteemed by a man,
When a bound sword, forged by the hammer,
The sword stained with gore, the boar on the helmet,
Strong in its edges, opposite cleaves.
Then was in the hall the hard-edged drawn,
The sword o'er the seats, many a broad shield
Raised firm in hand: of helmet one thought not,
Of burnie broad, when terror him seized.
She was in haste, would thence away,
Her life preserve, when she was discovered.
Quickly had she of one of the warriors
Firmly laid hold, when she to fen went:
He was to Hrothgar the dearest of men
In the office of comrade by the two seas,
A shield-warrior strong, whom she in bed killed,
A hero renowned. Not there was Beowulf,
But other room before was assigned,
After the treasure-giving, to the great Geat.
Noise was in Heorot: she in its gore took
The well-known hand. Grief was renewed
Again in the dwellings; 't was not a good trade,
That they on both sides payment should make
With the lives of their friends. Then was the old king,
The hoary warrior, in sorrowful mood,
When he his chief thane, deprived of life,
The dearest one, knew to be dead.
Quickly was Beowulf brought to the hall,
The victory-blest hero. At dawn of day
Went one of earls, the noble warrior,
Himself with his comrades, where the wise one awaited,
Whether for him the Almighty will ever,
After this woe-spell, a change of things work.
Went then on the floor the man war-renowned
With his band of men (the hall-wood resounded),
Until he addressed the wise one in words,
The lord of the Ingwins, asked if to him were,
As he had wished, the night undisturbed.
Hrothgar then spoke, the defence of the Scyldings:
'Ask not thou for health. Sorrow's renewed
To the Danes' people: dead is Æschere,
Of Yrmenlaf the elder brother,
My trusted counsellor and my adviser,

My right-hand man, when we in battle
Defended our heads, when warriors engaged,
When the boars clashed: such should an earl be,
An excellent prince, as Æschere was.
She was to him the murderer in Heorot,
The restless death-demon: I know not whither,
Proud of her prey, she frightful withdrew,
Well-known from her meal. The feud she avenged,
For that thou yester-night Grendel didst kill
In a powerful way by your hard grips,
Because he too long my own people
Lessened and killed: in battle he fell,
Of his life guilty, and now came another,
A mighty fell foe, her son would avenge,
And further has laid her feud upon us;
Wherefore it may seem to many a thane,
Who for his ring-giver mourns in his mind,
A bale hard to bear; now lies the hand helpless,
Which used to gratify all of your wishes.
I the land-dwellers, my own people,
Counsellors-in-hall, that have heard say
That they used to see a pair of such
Mickle mark-steppers holding the moors,
Spirits of elsewhere: one of these was,
As they most certainly might then perceive,
A woman's form: the other one wretched
In the likeness of man his exile trod —
Except he was greater than any man else —
Whom in yore-days Grendel they named,
The dwellers-on-earth: they know not their father,
Whether any to him was before born
Of wicked spirits. They in a dark land,
Cliffs of wolves, dwell, windy nesses,
Dangerous marshes, where mountain-stream
Under clouds of the nesses flows down below,
Lake under the earth. It is not far hence
In measure by miles that the mere stands,
Over which hang the rustling groves,
Wood firm in its roots; they cover the water.
There one every night a strange wonder may see,
Fire on the flood: so wise a one lives not
Of the children of men that knows its bottom:
Although the heath-stepper pressed by the dogs,
The stag, strong in horns, may seek the grove,
Pursued from afar, his life will he give,
His life on the shore, ere in it he will
Hide there his head. That's no unhaunted place;
Thence the boiling of waters rises up high
Wan to the clouds, when the wind rouses
The hateful storms, while dark grows the air,
The heavens weep. Now is ready counsel
Again in thee alone. The abode yet thou knowest not,
The terrible place, where thou mayest find
The much-sinning being: seek if thou dare.
I for the contest thee will repay
With old-time treasures, as I before did,
With twisted gold, if thou comest away.'
Beowulf then spoke, Ecgtheow's son:
'Sorrow not, wise man! It is better for each
That his friend he avenge than that he mourn much!
Each of us shall the end await
Of worldly life: let him who may gain
Honor ere death. That is for a warrior,
When he is dead, afterwards best.
Arise, kingdom's guardian! Let us quickly go
To view the track of Grendel's kinsman.
I promise it thee: he will not escape,
Nor in earth's bosom, nor in mountain-wood,
Nor in ocean's depths, go where he will.
Throughout this day do thou patience have
Of each of thy woes, as I ween of thee!'
Up leaped the agèd one, thanked he then God,
The mighty Lord, for what the man spoke.
Then was for Hrothgar a horse provided,
A steed with curled mane: the ruler wise
Well-equipped went; the band stepped forth
Of bearers of shields. The foot-tracks were
On the forest-paths widely perceived,
The course o'er the plain: she went straight ahead
O'er the murky moor, of knightly thanes bore
The noblest one deprived of life,
Of those who with Hrothgar defended his home.
Went he then over, the offspring of princes,
The steep, stony slopes, the narrow ways,
The strait single paths, the unknown course,
The headlands steep, many houses of nickers.
He one of few went on before,
Of the wise men, the plain to view,
Until he all at once the mountain-trees
O'er the gray stone found bending down,
The joyless wood: the water stood under
Gory and restless. To all the Danes 't was,
To the friends of the Scyldings, bitter in mood,
To many a thane sorrow to suffer,
To each one of earls, after of Æschere

On the holm-cliff the head they found.
The flood boiled with blood (the people looked on),
With the hot gore. The horn at times sang
The ready war-song. All the warriors sat down;
They saw then in the water many of worm-kind,
Strange sea-dragons, seeking the sea,
Such nickers lying out on the ness-slopes,
As at mid-day often prepare
A sorrowful voyage on the sail-road,
Worms and wild beasts: rushed they away
Fierce and angry; the noise they perceived,
The war-horn sound. The prince of the Geats
With his arrowed bow deprived one of life,
Of strife with the sea, so that stood in his vitals
The hard war-arrow: he was in the holm
The slower in swimming, whom death took away.
Quickly was in the waves with their boar-spears,
Their hookèd swords, fiercely attacked,
Pressed after with struggles and to the ness drawn,
The wonderful monster: the men looked upon
The terrible stranger. Beowulf girded him
With noble armor, not for life did he care:
The war-burnie should, woven with hands,
Wide and well-wrought, seek out the sea,
That which his body could well protect,
So that him battle-grip might not in breast,
The mad one's assault, injure in life:
But the bright helmet protected his head,
Which was to mingle with the depths of the sea,
Adorned with treasure seek the sea-waves,
Encircled with diadem, as in days of old
The weapon-smith wrought it, wondrously framed it,
Set with swine-bodies, so that it never after
The flaming war-swords might be able to bite.
That was not then the least of strong helps,
That to him in need Hrothgar's orator lent:
Of that hilted sword Hrunting was name;
That was a chief one of old-time treasures;
Its edge was of iron, with poison-twigs stained,
Hardened with battle-gore; ne'er failed it in fight
Any of men, who it wielded with hand,
He who durst tread the terrible paths,
The folk-place of foes: that was not the first time,
That deeds of valor it should perform.
The kinsman of Ecglaf remembered not now,
Mighty in strength, what he before spoke
Drunken with wine, when the weapon he lent
To a better sword-bearer; he himself durst not
Under waves' tumult venture his life,
Heroic deeds work; there he lost fame,
A name for valor; not so with the other,
When he for battle himself had prepared.
Beowulf then spoke, Ecgtheow's son:
'Bethink thyself now, great kinsman of Healfdene,
Thou ruler wise, now I'm for the way ready,
Gold-friend of men, of what we once spoke,
If I in thy service should at any time
Of my life be deprived, that thou wouldst ever be
To me when gone hence, in stead of a father.
Be thou a protector to my knightly thanes,
My trusty comrades, if war take me off:
Also the treasures, which thou gavest me,
Do thou, dear Hrothgar, to Hygelac send.
May then by the gold the Geat's lord perceive,
Hrethel's son see, when he looks on the treasure,
That I did one find in man's virtues good,
A giver of rings, him enjoyed while I might.
And do thou let Hunferth the ancient relic,
The wonderful sword, the widely-known man
The hard-edged have. I shall with Hrunting
Fame for me gain, or death will me take.'
After these words the prince of the Weder-Geats
Hastened with valor, not for an answer
Would he await. The water-flood took
The mighty warrior: then was a day's space
Ere the bottom-plain he might perceive.
Soon that discovered she who the flood's realm,
Eager for blood, for fifty years held,
Grim and greedy, that there some one of men
The monster's abode sought out from above.
She grasped then against him, the warrior seized
In her terrible claws; not sooner she injured
His body sound: the burnie him shielded,
So that she might not pierce through the corslet,

The locked linkèd sark, with fiendish fingers.
Bore then the sea-wolf, when she came to the bottom,
The giver of rings to her own abode,
So that he might not, tho' he was brave,
His weapons wield, but him many strange ones
Oppressed in the sea: many a sea-beast
With battle-tusks his war-sark brake;
The monsters harassed him. The earl then perceived
That he in sea-hall, he knew not what, was,
Where him no water in aught might harm,
Nor for the roofed hall might lay hold of him
Sudden grip of the flood: the fire-light he saw,
The brilliant beams brightly shining.
The good one perceived then the wolf of the bottom,
The mighty mere-woman; he gave a strong stroke
With his battle-bill, withheld not the blow,
So that on her head the ringèd blade sounded
A greedy war-song. Then the stranger perceived
That the war-weapon would not cleave through,
Injure her life, but the edge failed
The prince in his need: before it endured
Many hand-meetings, the helmet oft clave,
The fated one's corslet: that was the first time
To the dear treasure that power had failed.
Again was determined, not lacking in prowess,
Mindful of fame, the kinsman of Hygelac:
Then threw the etched brand, with jewels adorned,
The angry warrior, that it on the earth lay,
Strong and steel-edged; he trusted to strength,
The hand-grip of might: so shall a man do,
When he in war thinketh to gain
Praise everlasting, nor for his life careth.
Seized then by the shoulder (cared she not for the contest)
The War-Geats' prince Grendel's mother,
Threw then battle-brave, for he was enraged,
The life-destroyer, that she on the floor fell.
She him again quickly the hand-grip repaid
With her fierce claws, and seized him fast:
Then stumbled the weary one, strongest of warriors,
The fighter-on-foot, so that he fell.
She sat on the hall-guest and drew her short sword.
Broad and brown-edged, her son would avenge,
Her only child. On his shoulder lay
The braided breast-net: that his life saved,
Against point and edge entrance withstood.
Then had he perished, Ecgtheow's son,
'Neath the broad bottom, the chief of the Geats,
Had not the war-burnie lent help to him,
The hard battle-net, and had not holy God
Directed the victory, the all-knowing Lord;
The Ruler of heaven adjudged it aright;
Easily afterwards he again rose.
'Mongst the armor he saw then a victory-blessed weapon,
Old sword of the eotens strong in its edges,
Honor of warriors: that was choicest of weapons,
But it was greater than any man else
To the war-play was able to bear,
Good and ornate, the hand-work of giants.
He seized the chained hilt, the Scyldings' champion,
Raging and battle-fierce, the ringèd sword brandished,
Hopeless of life angrily struck,
So that 'gainst her neck it strongly grasped,
Broke the bone-rings; the bill pierced through
Her fated body: she on the floor fell;
The sword was bloody, in his deed he rejoiced.
The blade's beam shone, the light stood within,
Just as from heaven brightly doth shine
The firmament's candle. He looked through the hall
Turned then by the wall, uplifted the weapon
Strong by its hilts Higelac's thane,
Angry and firm: the edge was not useless
To the war-hero, but he quickly would
Grendel repay many warlike assaults
Of those which he wrought to the West-Danes
Oftener by far than for one time,
When he of Hrothgar the hearth-companions
Slew in their sleep, whilst sleeping ate
Of the Danes' folk fifteen of men,
And such another bore he away,
A sorrowful prey: he paid him for that,
The warrior fierce, as he on his bed saw
Weary of war Grendel there lying
Of life deprived, as him before injured
The combat at Heorot. His body sprang far,
When he after death suffered the blow,
The strong sword-stroke, that struck off his head. —

Soon that perceived the cunning churls,
Those who with Hrothgar gazed on the sea,
That the waves-stirring all was commingled,
The surge stained with blood. The hoary-haired elders
Concerning the good one together thus spoke,
That they for the prince looked not again,
That he, flushed with victory, would come to seek
Their mighty chief, since it seemed to so many
That the sea-wolf him had destroyed.
Then came the ninth hour; the ness forsook
The valiant Scyldings: he departed thence home,
The gold-friend of men. The strangers sat,
Sick in their mind, and stared on the sea:
They knew and weened not, that they their dear lord
Himself might see. — The sword then began
On account of the battle-gore in clots of blood
The war-bill to vanish (that was a wonder),
So that it all melted likest to ice,
When the frost's fetters the Father unlooses,
The ice-rope unwinds, He who has control
Of times and tides: that is true Creator.
Took he not in the dwelling, the Weder-Geats' prince,
More of rich treasures, though he many there saw,
But only the head and the hilts together,
With jewels adorned: the sword ere melted,
The etched brand burnt: the blood was so hot,
The strange-spirit poisonous, who therein died.
Soon was he swimming who lived through the strife,
The foes' fierce assault, dived he up through the water:
The stirrings of waves all were cleansed,
The regions wide, when the strange-spirit
Left his life-days and this fleeting creation.
Came then to the land the seamen's protector
Strong-minded swimming, joyed in his sea-booty,
The mighty burden of what he had with him.
They went then to meet him, gave thanks to God
The brave band of thanes, rejoiced in their chief,
For that they him safe might again see.
Then from the strong one helmet and burnie
Quickly was loosed: the lake became thick,
Water under the clouds stained with war-gore.
Forth went they thence on the foot-paths
Glad in their hearts, measured the land-ways,
The well-known roads; the very bold men
From the sea-cliff were bearing the head
With great exertion to each one of them:
Of the courageous four warriors should
On the spear-shaft with labor bear
To the gold-hall the head of Grendel,
Until forthwith to the hall came
Fourteen brave men and fierce in war
Of the Geats going: the lord of men with them,
Brave in the crowd, trod the mead-plains.

VIII

Beowulf's account of the fight. Hrothgar's moralizing speech. On the morrow Beowulf bids farewell to Hrothgar, receives presents, and returns to his ship.

Then entering came the prince of the thanes,
The man brave in deeds, honored in fame,
The battle-fierce warrior, Hrothgar to greet.
Then was by the hair on the floor borne
The head of Grendel, where the men drank,
Frightful to earls and the lady also,
A wonderful sight: the men on it gazed.
Beowulf then spoke, Ecgtheow's son:
'Lo! we thee this sea-booty, son of Healfdene,
Prince of the Scyldings, with joy have brought
As a token of fame, which thou gazest on here.
I that with my life scarcely escaped;
Under water in battle risked I the work
With great exertion; almost would have been
Ended the struggle, had not me God shielded.
I might not in battle with Hrunting the sword
Aught then perform, though that weapon is good:
But the Ruler of men granted to me
That I on the wall saw beautiful hanging
An old mighty sword (often has He directed
Those without friends), that I brandished the weapon.
Then I slew in the contest, when time favored me,
The house's keepers. Then did the battle-bill,

The etched brand, burn, as sprang forth the blood,
The hottest of battle-gore: I the hilt thence
Bore from my foes, avenged their ill-deeds,
Death-plague of the Danes, as it was right.
I promise thee then that thou mayest in Heorot,
Sorrowless sleep with thy warrior-band,
And each of the thanes of thine own people,
Of old and of young; thou needst not for them fear,
Chief of the Scyldings, from this direction
Life-bale for thy earls, as thou didst before.'
Then was the golden hilt to the old warrior,
The hoary war-chief, given in hand,
The old work of giants: it went into the keeping,
Since the fall of the devils, of the lord of the Danes,
The cunning smiths' work, when this world forsook
The bad-hearted being, the opposer of God,
Devoted to death, and his mother also.
It went into the power of the noblest one
Of the world-kings by the two seas,
Of those who in Sceden-ig treasure divided.
Hrothgar then spoke, on the hilt looked,
The old relic on which was the origin written
Of an old contest: the flood afterwards slew,
The rushing sea, the race of the giants;
Badly they fared: that people was hostile
To the Lord eternal; therefor a reward
Through waters' flood the Almighty them gave.
So was on the guard of purest gold
In runic letters rightly engraved,
Was set and said, for whom that sword,
Choicest of weapons, first had been wrought
With wreathed hilt snake-adorned. Then the chief spoke,
The son of Healfdene (kept silent all):
'Lo! that he may say who truth and right
Works for his people, the past all remembers,
An old home-guardian, that this earl was
One born of the best. Thy fame is wide-spread
Through distant ways, Beowulf my friend,
Over each nation: with patience thou holdest it all,
Thy might with prudence of mind. I shall to thee grant
My friendship, as we before spoke: thou shalt be for comfort,
All long-assured, to thine own people,
To heroes for help. Not so was Heremod
To the children of Ecgwela, the Honor-Scyldings;
He throve not for their pleasure, but for their slaughter,
And for death-plagues to the Danes' people:
Slew he enraged his table-companions,
His chosen comrades, till he went alone,
The mighty prince, from human joys:
Though him mighty God in joy of strength,
In power exalted, over all men
Him had uplifted, yet in his heart grew
A bloodthirsty feeling: he did not give rings
To the Danes by right: joyless abode he,
So that for this strife sorrow he suffered,
Misery lasting. By that teach thou thyself,
Practise man's virtues. This tale for thee
Have I, old in years, told. 'T is a wonder to say
How mighty God to the race of mankind,
Through His great mind, wisdom divides,
Homes and nobility: He rules over all.
Sometimes on love permits He to turn
The thoughts of the man of mighty race,
Gives him in his home the joy of earth,
A sheltering city of men to possess,
Makes subject to him parts of the world,
A kingdom wide, so that he of it may not,
For his lack of wisdom, think of the end:
He dwells in plenty, nor him does aught check,
Sickness nor age, nor for him does sorrow
Grow dark in his mind, nor a foe anywhere
Show him sword-hate, but for him all the world
Wends at his will. He knows not the worse,
Until him within a portion of pride
Waxes and grows, when sleeps the keeper,
The guard of the soul: that sleep is too firmly
Bound up with sorrows; very nigh is the slayer,
Who from arrowed bow spitefully shoots.
Then is he in his breast pierced under his helmet
With a sharp arrow: he cannot defend him
From the evil strange-orders of that cursed spirit:
Him seems it too little what he long held;
He with evil mind covets, gives not for boasting
Gold-plated rings, and he future fate
Forgets and neglects, for God gave him before,
The Ruler of glory, a share of earth's honors.
It at the end afterwards happens
That the frail body fleeting doth fail,
Fated doth fall: another succeeds,
He who undisturbed treasures divides,
The earl's former store, cares not for its owner.

Guard against wrong-doing, Beowulf dear,
Best one of heroes, and choose thou the better,
Counsels eternal. Care not for pride,
Mighty warrior. Now is thy strength's fame
Lasting a while: soon after it shall be
That sickness or sword shall rob thee of might,
Or clutch of the fire, or swell of the flood,
Or grip of the sword, or flight of the arrow,
Or fearful old age, or light of the eyes
Shall fail and grow dark: it suddenly shall be
That thee, great warrior, death shall overcome.
So I the Ring-Danes a hundred half-years
Ruled under heavens, and secured them by war
Against many tribes throughout this mid-earth,
With spears and with swords, so that any foe
Under circuit of heaven reckoned I not.
Lo! to me in my home a change of this came,
Sorrow for joy, after Grendel became
The foe of long years, my constant home-seeker:
I from this hostility continually suffered
Much sorrow of mind. Thanks to the Creator,
The Lord eternal, whilst in life I remained,
That I on this head drenchèd with gore,
After long sorrow, look with my eyes.
Go now to thy seat, partake of feast-joy,
Thou honored in war. To us shall be many
Of treasures in common, when morning shall come.'
The Geat was glad-minded: went he then soon
His seat to take, as the wise one bade.
Then was as before for the courageous
Sitters-in-hall fitly prepared
Another time. Night's canopy lowered
Dark o'er the warriors. The band all arose;
The white-haired one his bed would seek,
The agèd Scylding. The Geat beyond measure,
The brave shield-warrior, it pleased to rest:
Soon the hall-thane him of his way weary,
The comer-from-far, forth led to his couch,
He who through courtesy all would supply
Of the wants of the thane, as at that day
The farers-by-sea were wont to have.
The great-hearted rested: the hall arose
Wide and gold-decked: the guest slept within,
Until the black raven the joy of heaven
Blithe-hearted announced, when came the bright light
Shooting o'er shadows. The warriors hastened:
The æthelings were back to their people
Ready to go: he would far thence,
The high-minded guest, visit his vessel.
The brave one then bade Hrunting bear;
The son of Ecglaf, bade take his sword,
Precious weapon, thanked him for the loan,
Said that he counted the war-friend good,
Mighty in battle, not in words blamed he
The edge of the sword: that was a brave man.
When for their march ready, in armor equipped
The warriors were, went by the Danes honored
The prince to the throne, where was the other,
The battle-brave man: Hrothgar he greeted,
Beowulf spoke, Ecgtheow's son:
'Now we sea-goers desire to say,
Comers-from-far, that we intend
Hygelac to seek: we were here well
Supplied in our wishes: thou served'st us well.
If I then on earth may in any manner
More of thy heart's love gain for myself,
Ruler of men, than I have yet done,
For works of war I soon shall be ready.
If I that learn o'er the flood's course,
That thee thy neighbors with dread oppress,
As hating thee they sometimes have done,
To thee I shall bring thousands of thanes,
Of heroes for help. Of Hygelac I know,
Lord of the Geats, though he be young
Chief of his folk, that he me will aid
By words and by deeds that I may thee honor,
And to thee for help my spear-shaft bear,
The power of my might, if thou needest men.
If Hrethric then at the courts of the Geats,
The king's son, aid seeks, he may there many
Of his friends find: far countries will be
Better sought for by him who is worthy.'
Hrothgar then spoke to him in answer:
'These words to thee the all-wise Lord
Sent into thy mind: ne'er heard I more wisely
In so youthful age any man speak:
Thou art in might strong and in mind old,
A counsellor wise. I count on the hope,
If this may happen that the spear take,
Terrible battle, the son of Hrethel,
Sickness or weapon, thine own chieftain,
People's shepherd, and thou hast thy life,
That the Sea-Geats will not have a better,
To choose as their king, any one, than thee,

Hoard-keeper of heroes, if thou wilt hold
Thy kinsmen's kingdom. Me thy bold courage
Long pleases so well, Beowulf dear.
Thou hast now caused that to these nations shall,
To the Geats' people and to the Spear-Danes,
Peace be in common and strife shall cease,
The hostile contests which they ere suffered:
There shall be, whilst I wield the wide realm,
Treasures in common; many another
With presents shall greet o'er the swan's bath:
The ringèd ship shall o'er the sea bring
Presents and love-tokens. I know that the people
Towards foe and towards friend are firmly disposed,
In everything blameless after old custom.'
Then still to him the defence of earls gave,
The son of Healfdene, twelve jewels besides,
Bade him with these presents his own dear people
Seek in good health and quickly return.
Kissed him then the king noble in birth,
The prince of the Scyldings kissed the best thane,
And round the neck clasped; tears from him fell,
The gray-haired one: he had hope of both,
The agèd man, more of the latter,
That they might again each other see,
Courageous in council. The man was so dear
That he the breast-flood could not restrain,
But in his breast, fast in his mind's fetters,
For the dear man a secret longing
Burned through his blood. — Beowulf thence,
The gold-adorned warrior, the grassy plain trod,
Proud of his treasure: the sea-goer awaited
Its own possessor, which at anchor rode.
Then was on the way the gift of Hrothgar
Often extolled: that was a king
In everything blameless, till old age removed him
From his might's joys, which has oft oppressed many.

IX

Beowulf's arrival at home and welcome by Hygelac. The episode of Offa and Thrytho. Beowulf's account of his journey. Freaware and Ingeld. Presents of Beowulf and Hygelac.

Came then to the sea the very brave ones,
The band of attendants; their burnies they bore,
Their locked body-sarks. The land-guard perceived
The return of the earls, as he before did:
He did not with harm from the cliff's head
Greet then the guests, but towards them rode,
Quoth that as welcome the Weders' people,
The mail-clad warriors, went to their ship.
Then was on the shore the spacious boat,
The ring-prowed ship, with battle-weeds laden,
With horses and jewels; the mast arose
Over Hrothgar's hoard of treasures.
He to the boat-guard, bound with gold-work,
A sword then gave, so that after he was
On the mead-bench from the jewel more honored,
The costly heir-loom. He went in his sea-boat
To stir the deep water, the Danes' land forsook.
Then was to the mast one of sea-cloths,
Sail by rope fastened. The vessel groaned;
Not there the sea-floater did the wind o'er the waves
In its course hinder: the sea-goer went,
The foamy-necked floated forth o'er the water,
The curvèd-prowed went o'er the sea-waves,
Until the Geats' cliffs they might descry,
The well-known nesses. The keel pressed up,
Urged by the wind it stood on the land.
Quickly was at the sea the harbor-guard ready,
Who long time before for the dear men
Longing had gazed afar on the ocean:
He to the shore fastened the wide-bosomed ship
With anchor-chains fast, lest the waves' force
The winsome boat might carry away.
He bade then bear up the nobles' treasures,
Jewels and beaten gold; not for them far thence
Was it to seek the giver of rings:
Hygelac, Hrethel's son, there at home dwelt,
Himself with his comrades near the sea-wall.
The building was fine, the prince a good king,
High was the hall, Hygd very young,
Wise, well-instructed, although winters few
Under the city-locks she may have dwelt,
The daughter of Hæreth: she was not, though, niggardly,

Nor sparing in gifts, to the Geats' people,
In costly jewels. Modthrytho committed,
The great folk-queen, horrible crime:
No brave one durst that undertake,
Of dear companions, except her liege lord,
That on her by day he should look with his eyes:
But he wrought for himself death-fetters firm,
Twisted by hand: quickly afterwards was,
After the hand-grip, the sword appointed,
So that the carved weapon must it decide,
Tell the death-bale. Such is not queenly custom
For a woman to practise, though she be peerless,
That a peace-weaver of life should deprive,
On account of fierce anger, any dear man.
That indeed checked the kinsman of Heming.
The drinkers of ale other word said,
That she of folk-woes less did inflict,
Of hostile deeds, after she first was
Gold-adorned given to the young warrior,
The brave young noble, after she Offa's hall,
O'er the dark flood, by her father's command,
Sought in her journey, where she afterwards well,
On royal throne, by gifts renowned,
Her portion of life whilst living enjoyed,
Held her great love for the prince of heroes,
Of all mankind, as I have heard say,
The very best one by the two seas,
Of human race: for that Offa was
By gifts and war-deeds, the very brave man,
Widely renowned; with wisdom he ruled
His own possessions: thence Eomor sprang
For help to heroes, the kinsman of Heming,
Grandson of Garmund, crafty in contests. —
Went then the brave with his trusty band
Himself o'er the sand the sea-beach treading,
The wide-stretching shores: the world-candle shone,
Sun inclined from the south. They kept on their journey,
Went in their might, till the earls' defence,
The slayer of Ongentheow within in the city,
The good young war-king they then heard say
Rings was dividing. To Hygelac was
The journey of Beowulf quickly made known,
That there in the palace the warriors' defence,
His shield-companion, living was come,
Hale from the battle-play to the court going.
Quick was prepared, as the mighty one bade,
For the foot-guests the hall within.
Sat he then opposite, who 'scaped from the strife,
Kinsman with kinsman, after his lord
With courtly speech the loyal one greeted,
With mighty words. With mead-cups went
Through the high hall the daughter of Hæreth;
The people she served, the ale-cups she bore
To the men at hand. Hygelac began
His comrade-in-arms in the high hall
Kindly to ask (wish to know urged him),
What were the journeys of the Sea-Geats:
'How befell on your way, Beowulf dear,
When thou so suddenly thoughtest afar
The strife to seek o'er the salt water,
Battle at Heorot? But didst thou for Hrothgar
The widely-known woe in aught remove,
For the great chief? I for that in distress,
In sorrow-waves pined: the journey I trusted not
Of the dear man. Thee long I begged
That thou the death-spirit by no means wouldst seek,
Wouldst let the South-Danes themselves put an end to
Their war against Grendel. I give thanks to God,
For that I may see thee now safe and sound.'
Beowulf spoke, Ecgtheow's son:
'That is now plain, Hygelac lord,
Our great struggle, to many of men,
What a war-time of Grendel and me
Was in the place where he very many
Sorrows had wrought to the Victor-Scyldings,
Misery perpetual: all that I avenged,
So no kinsman of Grendel need now rejoice
At the morning-sound over the earth,
He who shall live longest of that evil race,
By danger surrounded! At first I came there
To the ringed hall Hrothgar to greet:
Soon for me the great son of Healfdene,
After he knew of my intention,
Near his own son a seat provided.
The crowd was in joy; ne'er saw I my life long
Under heaven's vault of sitters-in-hall
Greater mead-joy! Sometimes the great queen,
Peace-bringer of nations, went through all the hall,
Urged the young sons: oft she a bracelet
Gave to a warrior, ere she went to her seat.
Sometimes 'fore the court the daughter of Hrothgar
To the earls at the end the ale-cup bore,
Whom I Freaware the sitters-in-hall

Heard call by name, where she buckled treasure
Gave to the heroes. She had been promised,
Young, gold-adorned, to Froda's glad son:
Therefore it has happened to the friend of the Scyldings,
The kingdom's ruler, and he counts that a gain,
That he with the woman a part of fierce feuds,
Of quarrels appeased. Often the courtiers,
After folk's fall, in a little while
The deadly spear takes, though good be the bride.
It may therefore displease the prince of the Heathobards,
And each of the thanes of these peoples,
When he with the woman goes into the hall,
That a son of the Danes on her should attend:
For on him there shines the bequest of the agèd,
Hard and ring-decked, the Heathobards' treasure,
While they with weapons were able to rule,
Until they misled to the shield-play
Their dear companions and their own lives.
Then speaks at the beer-drinking he who sees the jewel,
An old spear-warrior, who all remembers,
Spear-death of men (fierce is his mind),
Begins, sad in mood, of the young warrior
The spirit to rouse by thoughts in his mind,
War-bale to excite, and this word speaks:
"Mayst thou, my friend, know now the sword,
Which thine own father bore into battle
Under his helmet for the last time,
The precious weapon, where the Danes slew him,
The battle-place held, when dead lay Withergyld,
After heroes' fall, the Scyldings brave?
Now here a son of some one of these murderers,
In his weapons rejoicing, goes into the hall,
Boasts of the murder and bears the jewel,
Which thou with right shouldest possess."
So he advises and each time reminds
With bitter words, until the time comes
That the woman's thane, for the deeds of his father,
After the sword's stroke blood-stained sleeps,
Guilty of his life: thence will the other
Warrior escape; he knows the land well.
Then are there broken on either side
The sword-oaths of earls, after in Ingeld
Are roused deadly feuds, and in him woman's love
After care-waves cooler becomes.
Therefore I count not on the faith of the Heathobards,
Folk-peace sincere, kept with the Danes,
Friendship confirmed. — I shall speak forth
Yet about Grendel, that thou mayst well know,
Giver of treasure, what was the result
Of the hand-fight of men. After heaven's gem
Glided over the earth, the angry fiend came,
The terrible even-guest, to make us a visit,
Where we unharmed guarded the hall.
There was Hondscio destined for fight,
Life-bale to the fated: he lay the first,
The belted warrior: to him was Grendel,
To the great war-thane, a mouth-destroyer,
The dear man's body all he swallowed.
Not sooner out then yet empty-handed,
The bloody-toothed murderer mindful of woes
From the gold-hall was willing to go,
But he, strong in might, made trial of me,
With ready hand grasped me. His glove was hanging,
Wide and wonderful, in cunning bands fast;
It was all wrought with curious skill
With devil's craft and dragon's skins;
He me therein, guiltless of crime,
The fierce deed-doer, wished to destroy,
One of many: it might not be so,
After in anger upright I stood.
Too long is to tell how I the folk's foe
For each of his ills a hand-reward paid,
Where I, my prince, thine own people
Honored by deeds. Away he escaped,
A little while life's joys enjoyed:
Yet of him a trace remained behind,
His right hand in Heorot, and he humbled thence,
Sorrowing in mind, to the sea-bottom sank.
Me for this contest the friend of the Scyldings
With plated gold much rewarded,
With many treasures, when morning came,
And we at the banquet had seated ourselves.
There was song and glee: the agèd Scylding,
Who much had heard, of past times related;
Sometimes the warrior the joy of the harp,
The play-wood touched; sometimes sang a song
True and sorrowful; sometimes a strange tale
Truthfully told the wide-hearted king;

Sometimes then began, burdened with age,
The hoary warrior to tell of his youth's
Prowess in battle; his breast swelled within,
When he old in years their number remembered.
So we therein the live-long day
Partook of hall-joys, until night came on,
Another to men. Then was again quickly
Ready for vengeance the mother of Grendel,
She sorrowful went: death took off her son,
War-hate of the Weders. The wondrous woman
Her son avenged, a warrior killed
Courageously; there was from Æschere,
The agèd counsellor, life departed.
Nor might they him, when morning came,
Delivered to death, the folk of the Danes
With fire consume, and on the pyre place
The dearly-loved man; the body she bore
In the fiend's embrace 'neath the mountain-stream.
That was to Hrothgar the greatest of sorrows,
Of those that long the prince befell.
Then the chief me by thine own life
Adjured, sad in mind, that I in the sea's flood
Should do valiant deeds, should risk my life,
Should honor gain; he promised reward.
I then of the water, which is widely known,
The grim and fearful guard of the deep found.
There a while was to us a hand-to-hand fight;
The sea welled with gore, and I of the head robbed
In the ground-hall the mother of Grendel
With a strong sword; I scarcely from thence
My life bore away; not yet was I fated;
But the earl's defence to me after gave
Many of treasures, the son of Healfdene.
So the folk-king lived as was right:
Not at all had I lost by these rewards,
This meed of might, but he gave me treasures,
The son of Healfdene, at mine own will,
Which I will to thee, warlike king, bring,
Willingly offer. Still on thee is all
Of favor dependent: I have very few
Of near relations save, Hygelac, thee.'
He bade then bring in the boar's-head-sign,
The battle-high helmet, the hoary burnie,
The war-sword ornate, his word then uttered:
'This cuirass to me Hrothgar then gave,
The crafty chief, bade with some words
That I of its origin first should thee tell,
Said that it had Hiorogar king,
Prince of the Scyldings, for a long while:
Not to his son sooner would he it give,
To the brave Heoroweard, though to him he were dear,
The defence of the breast. Use thou it well!'
I heard that to the armor four horses too,
Exactly alike, in their tracks followed,
Yellow as apples: he to him gave possession
Of horses and jewels. So shall a friend do,
Not at all cunning snares weave for another,
With secret craft death for him prepare,
His hand-companion. To Hygelac was,
In battle brave, his nephew devoted,
And each to the other mindful of kindness.
I heard that the necklace he to Hygd gave,
The curious treasure which Wealhtheow gave him,
The prince's daughter, three horses likewise,
Slender and saddle-bright: to her after was,
After the ring-giving, the breast adorned.
So bravely bore him Ecgtheow's son,
The man famed in wars, by his good deeds,
He did after right, not at all slew the drunken
Hearth-companions: his mind was not cruel,
But he of mankind with greatest power,
The mighty gift, which God him gave,
The warlike one kept. Long he was despised,
As him the Geats' children did not reckon good,
Nor him at the mead-bench as worthy of much
The lord of the people would then esteem;
They weened very strongly that he was slothful,
An unwarlike prince; a change after came
To the glory-blessed man of each of his sorrows.
The earl's defence bade then bring in,
The warlike king, Hrethel's bequest
Adorned with gold: there was not 'mong the Geats
A better treasure in the shape of a sword:
That did he place in Beowulf's keeping,
And to him gave seven thousand of gold,
A house and dominion. To them both together
Among the people was inherited land,
A home and its rights, more to the other,
A wide-spread kingdom, to him who was better.

BEOWULF AND THE DRAGON

X

Beowulf is king. The dragon's hoard robbed. The fiery vengeance of the dragon.

That happened after in later days
By battle-contests, when Hygelac died,
And to Heardred swords of battle
Under the shields were as a murderer,
When him there sought 'mong his victor-people
The warriors bold, the Battle-Scylfings,
By war oppressed the nephew of Hereric.
After to Beowulf the kingdom broad
Came into hand: he held it well
Fifty winters (then was the king agèd
The home-keeper old) until one began
On the dark nights, a dragon, to rule,
Who on the high heath a treasure protected,
A steep stony mountain: the path under lay,
To men unknown. There within went
Some one of men, who took his desire
From the heathen hoard: a certain hand-vessel,
Adorned with gold, he there then took,
Made of red gold, so that was robbed
By the fire sleeping the treasure's guardian
By a thief's craft: the prince after learnt,
The innocent warrior, that he was enraged.
Not at all of free-will the dragon-hoard's heap
Sought he of himself, who him sorely injured,
But through necessity the thane of some one
Of the children of men hateful blows fled,
Through dire compulsion, and therein entered
The innocent man. Soon it was at that time
That there to the stranger dread terror stood:
Yet miserable he there within took,
The frightened soul who terror suffered,
A costly-wrought vessel. There were many of such
In the earth-cave, of ancient treasures,
As them in old days some one of men,
The great bequest of a noble race,
With thoughtful mind there had concealed,
The precious treasures. Death them all took away
In former times, and the only one still
Of the people's nobles who there longest lived,
The friend-mourning guardian, wished that to delay,
So that he a short time longer the treasures
Might there enjoy. A mountain all ready
Stood on the plain near to the waters,
Steep by the ness, firm, inaccessible:
There within bore of noble treasures
The keeper of rings a part hard to carry
Of beaten gold, banning words spoke:
'Keep thou now, earth, since men may not,
The possession of earls. Lo! before it in thee
Good men obtained: war-death took away,
Fearful life-bale, each one of men,
Of mine own people, who gave up this life:
They saw hall-joy. I've not one to bear sword,
Or care for the cup of beaten gold,
The dear drinking-vessel: the chiefs elsewhere are gone.
The hard helmet shall, with gold adorned,
Be deprived of its jewels: the polishers sleep,
Those who the battle-mask should ever brighten;
And likewise the breast-plate, which in battle endured
O'er clash of shields the blows of weapons,
Crumbles after the warrior: nor may the ringed burnie
After the battle-chief go far and wide
By the side of heroes: there 's no harp's joy,
Play of the glee-wood, nor does the good hawk
Through the hall fly, nor the swift horse
The city-courts paw. Mighty death has
Many of mortals sent on their way.'
So sad in mind in sorrow mourned
One over all, miserable lived he
By day and night, until death's wave
Touched him at heart. The precious hoard found
The old twilight-foe open standing,
He who burning the mountains seeks,
The naked dragon, who flies by night
Surrounded by fire: him the earth-dwellers
Saw from afar. He shall inhabit
The hedge on the earth, where he heathen gold
Guards old in years: he shall not be the better.
So the folk-foe three hundred winters
Held in the earth one of hoard-halls
Wondrously great, until him one angered,
A man, in his mind: he bore to his lord
The jewelled cup, a peace-offering gave
To his own lord. Then was the hoard found,
Hoard of rings borne away; the prayer was granted
To the miserable man: his lord beheld
Men's ancient work for the first time.
When the dragon awoke, strife was renewed:
He went 'round o'er the stone, the brave-minded found

His enemy's foot-track: he forth had stepped
With secret craft near the head of the dragon.
So may one not fated easily escape
Woes and exile, who the Almighty's
Favor possesses. The hoard-keeper sought
O'er the ground eagerly, would find the man,
Who to him in sleep this harm had done:
Hot and fierce-minded oft he went 'round the cave
Wholly without: there was not any man
On the heath's waste. Yet in battle he joyed,
In hostile deeds: he returned to the mountain,
The precious cup sought: he that soon found,
That some one of men the gold had discovered,
The costly treasures. The hoard-keeper waited,
Angry in mind, until evening came:
Was then enraged the guard of the mountain,
Would many people with fire repay
For the dear drinking-cup. Then was the day gone
At the will of the dragon, nor in the cave longer
Would he abide, but with flame went he forth,
With fire provided. The beginning was fearful
To the folk in the land, as it too quickly
On their ring-giver sorely was ended.
Then the demon began to vomit with fire,
To burn the bright dwellings: the flame-light stood
For terror to men: not there aught living
The hateful air-flyer was willing to leave.
The worm's war-power widely was seen,
The hostile one's hate both near and far,
How the war-foe the folk of the Geats
Hated and harmed: to his hoard then he hastened,
The secret rich hall, before the day-time.
He had the land-dwellers with fire o'erwhelmed,
With flame and burning: to his mountain he trusted,
His war-might and wall: that hope him deceived.

XI

Beowulf prepares for the contest. The deaths of Hygelac and of Heardred recalled. Beowulf's reminiscences. The death of Herebeald and Hrethel's sorrow. Beowulf's slaying of Dæghrefn. Beowulf seeks the dragon alone. The fiery fight. Wiglaf goes to his help. The wounding of Beowulf. The death of the dragon. Wiglaf brings out the treasure. Beowulf's death.

Then was to Beowulf the terror made known
Quickly in truth, that of his own
The best of houses in fire-waves melted,
The gift-seat of the Geats. That was to the good one
Distress in mind, greatest of sorrows.
The wise one weened that he the Almighty
Against the old laws, the eternal Lord,
Had grievously angered: his breast within swelled
With gloomy thoughts, as to him was not usual.
The fire-drake had the people's fastness,
The island without, the landed possessions,
With fire destroyed: for him then the war-king,
The Weders' prince, revenge devised.
Bade then work for him the warriors' defence,
The lord of earls, all made of iron
A wonderful war-shield: he knew very well
That forest-wood him could not help,
The shield against fire. He of his fleeting days,
Excellent prince, the end should await
Of his worldly life, and the worm likewise,
Although his hoard-treasure he long had held.
Scorn did he then, the prince of rings,
That he the wide-flier with host should seek,
With a large army: he feared not the contest,
Nor did he for aught count the serpent's war-might,
His strength and prowess, for that he before many
Conflicts survived, though dangers encountering,
Clashings of battle, since he of Hrothgar,
A victory-blessed hero, the hall had cleansed,
And in battle destroyed the kinsmen of Grendel,
The hateful race. That was not the least
Of hand-encounters, where one Hygelac slew,
When the Geats' king in the contests of war,
Friendly lord of the folk, in the land of the Frisians,
The son of Hrethel, in sword-blood died,
Struck down with the brand. Thence Beowulf came
By his own might, swam through the sea:
He had on his arm thirty and one

Of battle-equipments, when he in the sea went.
The Hetwaras did not need to be boastful
Of their foot-contest, who against him before
Were bearing their shields: few again came
From the war-hero to visit their home.
Ecgtheow's son swam o'er the sea's surface,
Unhappy alone back to his people,
Where to him Hygd offered treasure and kingdom,
Rings and king's throne: she the child trusted not,
That 'gainst other peoples the nation's seats
He knew how to hold, when Hygelac was dead.
Not sooner might the forsaken ones find
At the hands of the prince in any respect,
That he to Heardred would be a lord,
Or he the kingdom was willing to choose:
Yet he him 'mong the people with friendly lore held,
Kindly with honor, until he was older,
And the Wedergeats ruled. Him did the banished ones
Seek o'er the sea, Ohthere's sons;
They had 'gainst the lord of the Scylfings rebelled,
The most excellent one of the sea-kings,
Who in the Swedes' kingdom treasure divided,
A mighty prince. That to him was life's end:
He there at the banquet the death-wound received
With blows of the sword, Hygelac's son,
And then he departed, Ongentheow's son,
To visit his home, when Heardred lay dead,
Let Beowulf hold the royal throne,
And rule the Geats: that was a good king!
He remembered reward for that people's loss
In later days; to Eadgils he was,
To the helpless a friend, with an army supported
O'er the wide sea Ohthere's son,
With war-might and weapons: he after avenged him
For the cold care-journeys, of life the king robbed. —
So he had survived each one of struggles,
Of dangerous contests, Ecgtheow's son,
Of mighty deeds, till that very day
That he 'gainst the serpent was going to fight.
He went one of twelve, swollen with rage,
The prince of the Geats, the dragon to view;
He had then learnt whence rose the feud,
Deadly hate to his warriors: into his keeping came
The great treasure-cup through the hand of the finder.
He was in the band the thirteenth man.
Who the beginning of this contest caused,
Sad in mind, fettered, despised he should thence
Point out the plain: he against his will went
For that he knew the earth-hall alone,
Cave under the earth near the sea-waves,
Near the rushing of waters, which was within full
Of jewels and wire-work: the monstrous guard,
The ready warrior, the gold-treasures held,
Old under the earth: that was no easy purchase
To be obtained for any of men.
Sat then on the ness the warlike king
Whilst farewell he bade to his hearth-companions,
The gold-friend of the Geats: his mind was sad,
Restless and death-ready, Weird very nigh,
Which should approach the agèd man,
Seek the soul's hoard, asunder divide
The life from the body; not then was long
The life of the prince in flesh enclosed.
Beowulf spoke, Ecgtheow's son:
'Many war-struggles in youth I survived,
Times of battle; I remember all that.
I was seven winters, when me lord of treasures,
Dear ruler of peoples, took from my father;
Supported and kept me Hrethel the king,
Gave me treasure and feast, remembered our kinship;
I was never to him at all a more hateful
Man in his palace than one of his sons,
Herebeald and Hæthcyn or Hygelac mine.
There was for the eldest contrary to right
By the deeds of his kinsman a death-bed prepared,
Since him did Hæthcyn from his hornèd bow,
His own dear lord, with arrow pierce,
Missed he the mark and his kinsman did shoot,
One brother the other, with bloody dart:
That was fee-less fight, wickedly sinned,
Sorrow-bringing to breast; should yet, however,
The lord unavenged from life depart.
So is it sorrowful to an agèd churl

To live to see that his son hang
Young on the gallows: then he utters a moan,
A sorrowful song, when his son hangs
For joy to the raven, and he him may not help,
Old and experienced, aught for him do.
Always is remembered on each one of mornings
His son's departure; he cares not another
To hope to see born in his own palace,
An heir to his throne, when this one has,
Through might of death, suffered such deeds.
He sorrowful sees in his son's dwelling
The wine-hall empty, the windy rest-place
Of merriment robbed; the warrior sleeps,
The prince in his grave; no sound of harp's there,
No sport in the courts, as there were once.
Then he goes to his chamber, sings sorrowful songs,
The one for the other: too empty all seemed,
Fields and dwelling. So the Weders' defence
For Herebeald sorrow of heart
Welling up bore: he might not at all
Upon that murderer the feud avenge;
Not sooner might he wreak his hate on the warrior
With evil deeds, though he was not to him dear.
He then with this sorrow, which befell him so sore,
Gave up human joy, God's light did choose,
Left to his sons, as a wealthy man does,
Land and chief city, when from life he departed.
Then was feud and strife of the Swedes and the Geats,
O'er the wide water contest in common,
A hard battle-struggle, after Hrethel was dead,
Whilst to them were Ongentheow's sons
Bold and warlike, friendship would not
O'er the sea keep, but around Hreosna-mount
Terrible inroads often did make.
For that mine own kinsmen vengeance did take,
For the feud and the wrong, as it was known,
Although the other it bought with his life,
A heavy price: to Hæthcyn was,
To the Geats' lord, the war destructive.
Then heard I that on th'morrow one kinsman the other
With edge of the sword avenged on the murderer,
When Ongentheow Eofor sought out:
The war-helmet split, the agèd Scylfing
Fell down sword-pale; his hand remembered
Of strife enough, the death-blow withheld not.—
I to him the treasures which he me gave
Repaid in war, as it was given me,
With the shining sword; he gave to me land,
A dwelling and home. There was not to him lack,
That he 'mong the Gifths, or 'mong the Spear-Danes,
Or in the Swedes' kingdom, needed to seek
A warrior worse, him buy with a price:
I always would go before him on foot,
Alone in front, and so for life shall I
Enmity work, while this sword permits,
Which often stood by me early and late.
Then 'fore the courtiers was I to Dæghrefn
For a hand-slayer, the Hugs' brave warrior:
Not he the jewels to the king of the Frisians,
The breast-adornment, was able to bring,
But in battle he fell, the standard's keeper,
The prince in his might; sword was not his slayer,
But for him battle-grip the swellings of heart,
The bone-house broke. Now shall the bill's edge,
Hand and hard sword, fight for the hoard.'
Beowulf said, with boastful words spoke
For the last time: 'I survived many
Wars in my youth; yet now I will,
Old people's guard, the contest seek,
With honor work, if me the fell foe
From his earth-hall dare to seek out.'
Greeted he then each one of men,
The brave helmet-bearers, for the last time,
His own dear comrades: 'I would not the sword bear,
Weapon 'gainst worm, if I knew how
Upon this monster I might otherwise
My boast maintain, as once upon Grendel.
But I there expect hot battle-fire,
Breath and poison: therefore I have on me
Shield and burnie. I will not the hill's guard,
The foe, flee from even part of one foot,
But at wall it shall be as for us Weird provides,
Each man's Creator: I am in mind brave,
So that 'gainst the war-flier from boast I refrain.
Await ye on mountain, clad in your burnies,
Heroes in armor, which one may better,
After the contest, from wounds escape
Of both of us. That is not your work,
Nor the might of a man but of me alone,
That he 'gainst the monster his strength should try,
Heroic deeds do. I shall with might

The gold obtain, or war shall take off,
Terrible life-bale, your own sovereign.'
Arose then by the rock the warrior fierce
Brave under his helmet, his battle-sark bore
'Neath the stone-cliffs, to the strength trusted
Of one man alone; such is no coward's work.
He saw then by the wall (he who very many,
In man's virtues good, of contest survived,
Struggles of battle, when warriors contended)
A stony arch stand, a stream out thence
Break from the mountain; the burn's flood was
With battle-fire hot; might not near the hoard
One without burning any while then
Endure the deep for the flame of the dragon.
Let then from his breast, since he was enraged,
The Wedergeats' prince his words go forth,
The strong-hearted stormed: his voice came in,
In battle clear-sounding, 'neath the hoar stone.
Strife was stirred up; the hoard-keeper knew
The voice of a man: there was not more time
Friendship to seek. First there came forth
The breath of the monster out of the rock,
Hot battle-sweat; the earth resounded.
The man 'neath the mountain his shield upraised
'Gainst the terrible demon, the lord of the Geats:
Then was the ring-bowed eager in heart
The contest to seek. The sword ere brandished
The good war-king, the ancient relic
Sharp in its edges: to each one was
Of those bent on bale dread from the other.
The strong-minded stood against the steep rock,
The prince of friends, when the worm bent
Quickly together: he in armor awaited.
Went he then burning advancing in curves,
To his fate hasting; the shield well protected
In life and in body a lesser while
The mighty chief than his wish sought,
If he that time, on the first day,
Was to control, as Weird did not permit him,
Triumph in battle. His hand he uplifted,
The prince of the Geats, the fearful foe struck
With the mighty relic, so that the edge softened
Brown on the bone, bit less strongly
Than the folk-king nèed of it had,
Oppressed with the fight. Then was the hill's keeper,
After the battle-blow, fierce in his mood,
Threw with death-fire; far and wide spread
The flame of the battle. Of triumphs he boasted not,
The gold-friend of the Geats: the war-bill failed
Naked in fight, as it should not,
Excellent weapon. That was no easy task,
So that the mighty kinsman of Ecgtheow
The plain of this earth was to forsake,
Must at the worm's will take up his abode
Elsewhere than here; so shall every man
His fleeting life leave. It was not then long
That the fierce ones again each other met.
The hoard-keeper raged, his breast swelled with breath:
A second time he suffered distress
Surrounded by fire, who before ruled his folk.
Not at all in a band did his companions,
Children of nobles, him stand around
With warlike virtues, but they to wood went,
Protected their lives. In one of them welled
His mind with sorrows; friendship may never
Be at all put aside by one who thinks well.
Wiglaf was named Weohstan's son,
The worthy warrior, prince of the Scylfings,
Kinsman of Ælfhere. He saw his lord
Under his helmet the heat endure;
He remembered the favor, that he once to him gave
The rich dwelling-place of the Wægmundings,
Each one of folk-rights which his father possessed.
He might not then refrain, his hand seized the shield,
The yellow wood, he drew his old sword:
That was among men Eanmund's bequest,
Ohthere's son, to whom in strife was,
To the friendless exile, Weohstan the slayer
By the edge of the sword, and he bore to his kinsmen
The brown-colored helmet, the ringèd burnie,
The old giant's sword that Onela gave him,
His own relation's war-equipments,
Ready war-weapons: he spoke not of the feud,
Though he had slain his brother's son.
He the ornaments held many half-years,
Bill and burnie, until his son might
Heroic deeds work, as his old father:
He gave to him then war-weeds 'mong the Geats,

Countless number of each, when he from life went
Old on his last journey. Then was the first time
To the young warrior that in storm of war
With his dear lord he should engage;
His courage failed not, nor his kinsman's bequest
Softened in battle: that the dragon perceived,
After they two together had gone.
Wiglaf then spoke many suitable words,
Said to his comrades (sad was his mind):
'I remember that time when we received mead,
When we did promise to our dear lord
In the beer-hall, who gave us these rings,
That we for the war-weeds him would repay,
If to him such need ever should happen,
For helmets and hard swords, since in host he us chose
For this expedition of his own will,
Thought of honors for us, and gave me these treasures,
Us whom he deemed spear-warriors good,
Brave helmet-bearers, although our lord
This noble work intended alone
To accomplish for us, ward of his folk,
Because he of men most noble deeds did,
Rashly-bold actions. Now is the day come
That our own chieftain has need of the strength
Of warriors good: let us to him go,
Help the war-prince whilst there is heat,
Fierce fiery terror. God knows in me,
That to me 't is far dearer that my own body
With my gold-giver the flame should embrace.
Not becoming, methinks, is 't that we should bear shields
Again to our home, unless we may sooner
Strike down the foe, the life protect
Of the Weders' chief. I know it well,
That he does not deserve that he alone shall
Of the Geats' nobles sorrow endure,
Fall in the battle: now shall sword and helmet,
Burnie and battle-dress, to us both be common.'
Went he then through the flame, his war-helmet bore
For help to his lord, spoke a few words:
'Beowulf dear! do thou all well,
As thou in thy youth long ago said'st,
That thou would'st not let for thyself living
Honor e'er cease; now shalt thou, strong in deeds,
Firm-minded prince, with all thy might
Thy life protect; I shall assist thee.'
After these words the angry worm came,
The terrible demon, a second time
With fire-waves shining to seek his foes,
The hostile men. With flame-billows burned
The shield to the rim: the burnie might not
To the young spear-warrior assistance afford.
But the young hero 'neath the shield of his kinsman
With courage went, when his own was
Destroyed by flames. Then still the war-king
Was mindful of fame, of his mighty strength,
Struck with his war-bill, that it stood in the head
Forcibly driven: broke in two Nægling,
Failed in battle Beowulf's sword,
Old and gray-etched. 'T was not granted to him,
That him of the sword the edges were able
To help in the battle: that hand was too strong,
Which any of swords, by my hearsay,
With its stroke tested, when to battle he bore
The sharp-wounding weapon: 't was not for him better.
Then was the folk-foe for the third time,
The bold fire-dragon, mindful of feuds,
Rushed on the strong one, since space him allowed,
Hot and war-fierce, clasped around all the neck
With his sharp bones: he was all bloodied
With the life-blood; gore welled in waves.
Then I heard say in the folk-king's need
The earl displayed unceasing bravery,
Strength and valor, as was natural to him:
He cared not for his head, but the hand burned
Of the brave man, where he helped with his strength,
So that the fell demon he struck somewhat lower,
The hero in armor, that the sword sank in,
Shining and gold-plated, that the fire began
After to lessen. Then still the king
His senses possessed, struck with his war-knife,
Cutting and battle-sharp, which he bore on his burnie:
The Weders' defence cut the serpent in two.
The foe they felled, force drove out life,
And they him then both had destroyed,
Kindred princes: such should a man be,
A thane in need. That was to the prince
The last of his victories by his own deeds,
Of work in the world. Then 'gan the wound,

Which on him the earth-drake before had inflicted,
To burn and to swell: that soon he perceived
That in his breast deadly ill welled,
Poison within. Then the prince went,
So that he by the rock, wise in his mind,
Sat on his seat, on the giants' work looked,
How the stone-arches, fast on their columns,
The earth-hall eternal held there within.
Then with his hands him bloody with gore,
The mighty prince, the excellent thane
His own dear lord with water laved,
Weary of battle, and his helmet unloosed.
Beowulf said: he spoke of his wound,
His deadly-pale wound (he knew very well
That he had spent his time allotted
Of the joy of earth; then was all gone
Of his days' number, death very nigh):
'Now I to my son would wish to give
These war-weeds of mine, if to me was granted
Any inheritor hereafter to be
The heir of my body. This people I ruled
Fifty of winters; there was not a folk-king,
Of those dwelling around any at all,
Who me durst meet with his war-friends,
With terror oppress. I awaited at home
The appointed time, kept mine own well,
Sought not hostilities, nor for myself swore
Many oaths falsely; I for all that,
With deadly wounds sick, now joy may have;
Hence the ruler of men need not to me charge
The murder of kinsmen, when shall depart
My life from my body. Now do thou quickly go
To see the hoard 'neath the hoar stone,
Wiglaf my dear one, now the serpent lies dead,
Sleeps sorely wounded, robbed of his treasure.
Be now in haste that I the old riches,
The treasure may view, thoroughly scan
The bright precious gems, that I may the easier,
On account of the treasure, give up mine own
Life and my people that I long held.'
Then heard I that quickly Weohstan's son,
After these words, his wounded lord
Sick from battle obeyed, bore his ringed net,
His battle-sark woven, 'neath the roof of the mountain.
Saw then victorious, when he by the seat went,
The brave kin-thane many of treasures,
Glittering gold on the ground lying,
Wonder on wall and the den of the worm,
The old air-flier, drinking-cups standing,
Vessels of old-time wanting the polisher,
Deprived of their ornaments. There was many a helmet
Old and rusty, many arm-bracelets
Curiously twisted. The treasure may easily,
The gold in the ground, each hoard of mankind
In value exceed, let him hide it who will.
Likewise he saw standing an all-golden banner
High over the hoard, greatest of wonders,
Wrought with hand-craft; from it light stood,
So that the ground-plain he might perceive,
Examine the treasures. There was not of the serpent
Any appearance, but sword took him off.
Then I heard say, in the cave the hoard robbed,
The old work of giants, one man alone,
Bore on his bosom the cups and the plates
At his own will; the banner he took,
Brightest of beacons, a bill sheathed with brass
(Its edge was of iron) of the old lord,
Who of these treasures was the protector
For a long while, bore fiery terror,
Hot, deadly-rolling, on account of the hoard
In the midst of the night, till he in death perished.
In haste was the messenger for return ready,
Provided with treasures; wonder him moved,
Whether he the high-minded alive would find
In that grassy spot, the prince of the Weders,
Deprived of strength, where he him before left.
He then with the treasures the mighty prince,
His own dear lord, bleeding did find
At the end of his life. He began him again
With water to sprinkle, until the word's point
Brake through his breast-hoard: Beowulf spoke,
The old man in sorrow (the gold he viewed):
'I for these treasures to the Lord of all thanks,
To the glorious King, in words do speak,
To the Lord eternal, — which I here look upon,
For this that I might for mine own people
Before my death-day such treasures obtain.
Now I for the hoard of jewels have paid
Mine own agèd life; do ye now supply

The needs of my people; I may not longer be here.
Bid ye the war-famed a mound to make
Bright after the pyre at the sea's point,
Which shall for remembrance to mine own people
Raise itself high on the Whale's ness,
That it the sea-farers hereafter may call
Beowulf's mound, who shall their high ships
O'er the sea's mists from afar drive.'
He put from his neck the golden ring,
The bold-minded prince, gave to the thane,
The young spear-warrior, his gold-adorned helm,
Collar and burnie, bade him use them well:
'Thou art the last left of our own kindred
Of the Wægmundings. Weird carried away all
Of mine own kinsmen at the time appointed,
Earls in their strength: I shall go after them.'
That was to the agèd the very last word
In his breast-thoughts, ere the pyre he chose,
The hot fiery waves: from his breast went
His soul to seek the doom of the saints.

XII

Wiglaf rebukes the thanes. Speech of the messenger. The death of Hæthcyn, pursuit of Hygelac, and death of Ongentheow. The warriors arrive. Wiglaf's speech. They enter the cave. The funeral-pyre. Beowulf's mound.

Then it had happened to the young man,
With sorrow of mind, that he on the earth saw
The dearest one at the end of his life
Livid become. The slayer too lay,
The fearful earth-drake, of life bereft,
Oppressed with bale: the ring-treasures longer
The twisted serpent might not control,
But the swords' edges took him away,
The hard battle-notched leavings of hammers,
So that the wide-flier, still from his wounds,
Fell on the earth nigh the hoard-hall;
Not at all through the air did he go springing
In the midst of the night, proud of his treasures
Showed he his form: but he to earth fell
On account of the handwork of this battle-prince.
Now that in the land to few of men throve
Of might-possessors, as I have heard say,
Though he were bold in every deed,
That one should meet the poison-foe's breath,
Or the ring-hall disturb with his hands,
If he were to find the waking guard
On the mount watching. By Beowulf was
The portion of treasures paid for with death:
It had for each the end obtained
Of fleeting life. — 'T was not then long after
That the cowardly ones the wood forsook,
The unwarlike truth-breakers, ten together,
Who durst not before fight with their spears
In their liege lord's very great need:
But they ashamed bore then their shields,
Their weeds of war, where the agèd one lay;
They gazed upon Wiglaf. He wearied sat,
The fighter-on-foot, near his lord's shoulders,
Refreshed him with water: it naught him availed.
He might not on earth, though he well would,
In the great prince his life retain,
Nor the Almighty's will could he change;
The doom of God in deeds would dispose
For each one of men, as He now doth.
Then was from the youth an answer grim
For him easy gotten, who before lost his valor.
Wiglaf then spoke, Weohstan's son,
The sorrowful man (he looked on the unloved):
'Lo! that may he say who will speak truth,
That the folk-king who gave you the treasures,
The war-equipments, in which ye there stand,
When he on the ale-bench often presented
To the hall-sitters helmet and burnie,
The prince to his thanes, such as anywhere bravest
From far or nigh he was able to find, —
That he without doubt the weeds of war
To no purpose wasted. When war him assailed,
Not at all did the folk-king of his comrades-in-war
Have cause to boast: yet God him granted,
The Ruler of victory, that himself he avenged
Alone with his sword, when he had need of strength.
I to him little life-defence might
In battle afford, and yet I undertook
Beyond my power my kinsman to help:
He was always the worse, when I with the sword struck

The life-destroyer: the fire ran stronger,
Welled from his breast. Too few defenders
Pressed round the prince, when the evil befell him.
Now taking of jewels and giving of swords,
All joy of home for your own kindred,
Comfort shall cease: of rights of land
Each one of men of this kindred tribe
Must be deprived, after the princes
From afar hear of your desertion,
Inglorious deed. Death shall be better
To each one of earls than a life of disgrace.'
He bade then the battle-work tell at the hedge
Upon the steep cliff, where the earl-band
The morning-long day sad in mind sat,
The warriors with shields, in expectance of both,
The final day and the return
Of the dear man. Little kept silent
Of the new tidings he who rode o'er the ness,
But he in truth spoke on all sides:
'Now is the joy-giver of the folk of the Weders,
The lord of the Geats, fast in his death-bed,
Fills his grave-rest by the deeds of the worm.
Along side of him lies the life-winner too
Dead from knife's wounds; with sword might he not
Upon the monster in any way
A wound inflict. Wiglaf sits there,
Sits over Beowulf Weohstan's son,
The earl o'er the other of life deprived,
With care attentive, keeps the death-watch
Of friend and of foe. Now the people expect
A time of strife, after well-known
To the Franks and the Frisians the fall of the king
Becomes far and wide. The contest was made
Strong 'gainst the Hugs, when Higelac came
With his ship-army going to the land of the Frisians,
Where the Hetwaras felled him in battle,
Bravely him conquered with their overmight,
So that the mailed-warrior was forced to bow,
Fell midst his warriors; no ornaments gave
The prince to his nobles. To us ever after
The Merwings' friendship was not to be granted.
Nor do I from the Swedes peace or good faith
At all expect; but it was widely known
That Ongentheow of life deprived
Hæthcyn, Hrethel's son, near Ravens' wood,
When through their pride at first did seek
The warlike Scylfings the folk of the Geats.
Soon to him the agèd father of Ohthere,
Old and terrible, gave a hand-stroke,
Hewed down the sea-chief, rescued his wife,
The old man his spouse, robbed of her gold,
The mother of Onela and of Ohthere,
And then he followed his deadly foes
Until they went in great distress
Into Ravens' wood, deprived of their lord.
Then besieged he with host those left by the sword,
Weary with wounds, woes oft he promised
To the miserable band the livelong night:
Said, he in the morning with the edge of the sword
Them would destroy, some on gallows hang
For sport to the fowls. Comfort afterwards came
To them sad in mind along with daylight,
After they Hygelac's horn and trumpets'
Sounding perceived, when the brave one came
In the track going of his peoples' earls.
There was bloody track of Swedes and of Geats,
The slaughter of men widely observed,
How the folk fought the feud one with another.
The good one then went with his companions
The agèd most sad, the fastness to seek,
The earl Ongentheow betook himself higher;
He had of Hygelac's prowess heard tell,
The proud one's war-craft; in resistance he trusted not,
That he the sea-men might then withstand,
His hoard protect from the sea-farers,
His children and wife; he went after thence
Old 'neath the earth-wall. Then was given pursuit
To the folk of the Swedes, their banner to Hygelac.
Forth then they went o'er the Peace-plain,
After the Hrethlings pressed into the hedge;
There Ongentheow was, with the edge of the sword,
The gray-haired one, forced to remain,
So that the folk-king had to submit
To Eofor's sole will; angrily him
Wulf, son of Wonred, attacked with his weapon,
So that for the blow blood spurted in streams

Forth under his hair. He was not though afraid,
The agèd Scylfing, but quickly repaid
In a worse way that fatal blow,
After the folk-king thither turned round:
Might not then the quick son of Wonred
To the old churl a hand-stroke give,
But he on his head his helmet first cleft,
So that, stained with blood, he had to bow,
Fell on the earth: he was not yet fated,
But he himself raised, though the wound pained him.
Then the brave thane of Hygelac let
With his broad sword, when his brother lay down,
The old sword of giants, the helmet of giants
Break over the shield-rim: then bowed the king,
The herd of the folk; he was struck to his life.
Then were there many who bound up his brother,
Quickly him lifted, when for them it was settled
That they the battle-place were to possess,
Whilst one warrior the other robbed,
From Ongentheow took his burnie of iron,
His hard hilted sword and his helmet besides,
The hoary one's armor to Hygelac bore.
The armor he took and to them fairly promised
Gifts to his people, and kept his word too.
The lord of the Geats paid for the contest,
The son of Hrethel, when he came to his home,
To Eofor and Wulf with very rich jewels,
To each of them gave a hundred thousand
Of land and locked rings (for the gifts him need not reproach
Any man on mid-earth, since they heroic deeds wrought),
And then to Eofor gave his sole daughter,
The home-adornment, as a pledge of his favor.
That is the feud and that the enmity,
Hate deadly of men, wherefore I expect
That the Swedes' people against us will seek,
After they learn that our own lord
Is 'reft of his life, him who before held
Against his foes his hoard and kingdom
After heroes' fall, the Scylfings brave,
Wrought his folk's good and further still
Heroic deeds did. — Now is haste best
That we the folk-king there should behold.
And him should bring who gave us rings
To the funeral-pyre. There shall not a part only
With the brave perish, but there's hoard of treasure,
Gold without number, bitterly purchased,
And now at the last with his own life
Rings has he bought: these fire shall devour,
The flame consume; no earl shall wear
A jewel in memory, nor the beautiful maid
Have on her neck a ring-adornment,
But she shall sad in mind, robbed of her gold,
Often not once tread a strange land.
Now that the war-chief laughter has left,
Mirth and enjoyment. For this shall the spear be,
Many a one morning-cold, clasped with the fingers,
Held in the hands; not at all shall harp's sound
Wake up the warriors, but the wan raven,
Eager over the fated, often shall speak,
Say to the eagle how he joyed in the eating,
When with the wolf he robbed the slain.'
So the brave warrior then was telling
Some tales of evil: he did not speak falsely
His facts nor words. — The band all arose;
Sadly they went 'neath the Eagles' ness,
With flowing tears, the wonder to see.
Then they found on the sand deprived of his life,
Holding his resting-place, him who rings them gave
In former times: then was the last day
Past to the good one, so that the war-king,
The prince of the Weders, a wondrous death died.
First there they saw a stranger being,
The worm on the plain opposite there,
The loathsome one lying; the fiery dragon,
The terror grim, was scorched with flames;
He was fifty feet, in his full measure,
Long as he lay; the air he enjoyed
Sometimes at night, down again went
To visit his den: he was then fast in death,
He had enjoyed the last of earth-caves.
By him there stood pitchers and cups,
Plates too lay there and precious swords,
Rusty and eaten-through, as in the earth's bosom
A thousand of winters there they had remained,
Since that bequest exceedingly great,
The gold of the ancients, was bewitched with a spell,
So that the ringed hall might one not touch,
Any of men, unless God himself,

True King of victories, to whom He would granted
To open the hoard, the charge of enchanters,
Even so to such man, as seemed to Him right.
Then was it seen that the way did not prosper
To him who with wrong had hid within
The hoard 'neath the wall. The keeper ere slew
Some one of his foes: then was the feud
With battle avenged. Is it a wonder
When a warlike earl the end approaches
Of his life-fate, when may no longer
A man with his kinsmen a mead-hall indwell?
So was it to Beowulf, when he the mount's keeper,
The contest sought: he himself knew not
How his world-severing was to take place;
How it against doom's-day deeply had cursed
The mighty princes who that put there,
That *that* man should be guilty of sins,
Shut up in cursed places, fast in hell-bonds,
Punished with plagues, who should that plain tread.
He was not gold-greedy; he rather would have
The owner's favor sooner looked on. —
Wiglaf then spoke, Weohstan's son:
'Oft many an earl for the sake of one
Sorrow shall suffer, as is happened to us.
We might not give to our dear prince,
The kingdom's ruler, any advice,
So that he might not that gold-keeper meet,
Might let him remain where he long was,
Dwell in his haunts until the world's end,
Fulfil his high fate. The hoard is looked on,
Bitterly gotten: that fate was too mighty
Which that folk-king thither enticed.
I was therein and looked through it all,
The treasures of hall, when 't was allowed me,
Not at all friendly a journey permitted
In 'neath the earth-wall. In haste I took
A great mighty burden with my own hands
Of the hoard-treasures, bore them out hither
To mine own king: he was then still alive,
Wise and still conscious: very much spoke
The agèd in sorrow and ordered to greet you,
Bade that ye should, for your friend's deeds, make
On the place of the pyre the lofty mound,
Mickle and mighty, as he of men was
The most worthy warrior through the wide earth,
While he city-treasures still could enjoy.
Let us now hasten a second time
To see and to seek that heap of treasures,
Wonder 'neath wall. I shall direct you,
That ye may once more see now enough
Of rings and broad gold. Be the bier ready,
Quickly prepared, when we come out,
And then let us bear our own dear lord,
The man beloved, where he shall long
In the Almighty's keeping patiently wait.'
Bade he then order, Weohstan's son,
The warrior brave, to many of men,
Of dwellers in houses, that they the fire-wood
Should bear from afar, the lords of the people,
To where lay the good one: 'Now shall fire eat
(The wan flame shall grow) the chief of warriors,
Him who oft awaited the iron-shower,
When the storm of arrows, loosed from the strings,
Leaped over the shield-wall, the shaft did its duty,
Fitted with feathers followed the barb.'
Now then the wise son of Weohstan
Called from the crowd of the king's thanes
Seven together, the choicest ones,
Went one of eight 'neath the hostile roof;
One warrior brave in his hands bore
A lighted torch, who went in front.
It was not then allotted who should plunder that hoard,
After unguarded any portion of it
The warriors saw remain in the hall,
Lie wasting away: little one sorrowed,
That they hastily carried without
The precious treasures. The dragon they shoved,
The worm, o'er the wall-cliff, let the waves take,
The flood embrace, the keeper of jewels.
There was twisted gold on a wain laden,
Of each countless heap: the prince was borne,
The hoary warrior, to the Whale's ness.
For him then prepared the folk of the Geats
A funeral-pyre on the earth firm,
Hung with helmets, with shields of war,
With burnies bright, as he had begged.
Laid they then in the midst the mighty prince,
The mourning warriors their lord beloved.
'Gan they then on the mountain the greatest of pyres
The warriors to kindle: the wood-smoke arose
From the burning pile black, the crackling flame
Mingled with mourning (the wind-roar was still),
Until it had broken the house of bone,

Hot in the breast. Sad in their minds
With sorrow they mourned their dear lord's death;
Also a sad song uttered the spouse,
Pained in her breast, grieved in her heart,
Mournful she frequently fettered her mind,
So that for her husband's most grievous blows
She wept, the grim fate of his bloody death,
. . . . . . terror of fire
. . . . . heaven swallowed the smoke.
Wrought they there then the folk of the Weders
A mound on the steep, which high was and broad,
For the sea-goers to see from afar,
And they built up within ten days,
The warlike one's beacon; the brightest of flames
They girt with a wall, as it most worthily
Very wise men might there devise.
They in the mound placed rings and bright jewels,
All such precious things as before in the hoard
Brave-minded men had taken away.
They let the earth hold the treasure of earls,
Gold in the ground, where it still lives
As useless to men as it before was.
Then 'round the mound the battle-brave rode,
Children of nobles (they were twelve in all),
Their sorrow would tell, grieve for their king,
Their mourning utter, and about the man speak;
His earlship they praised, and his noble deeds
They extolled to the courtiers, as it is right
That one his dear lord in word should praise,
With soul him love, when he shall forth
From his own body be severed by death.
So then lamented the folk of the Geats
The fall of their lord, the hearth-companions,
Said that he was a mighty king,
Mildest to men and most tender-hearted,
To his folk most kind and fondest of praise.

Cædmon (fl. ca. 670)

HYMN

Nu scylun hergan hefænricæs uard,
Metudes mæcti end his modgidanc,
Uerc uuldurfadur; sue he uundra gihuæs,
Eci Dryctin, or astelidæ.
He ærist scop ælda barnum
Heben til hrofe, haleg scepen;
Tha middungeard moncynnæs uard,
Eci Dryctin; æfter tiadæ
Firum foldu frea allmectig.

Now are we to praise the Guardian of heaven,
The Creator's might and his mind's most thought,
The glorious Father's work; how he each of wonders,
Lord everlasting, the beginning established.
He at first shaped for the off-spring of men
Heaven for a roof, Holy Creator;
The middle-yard then mankind's Warder,
Eternal God; and after arranged
Lands for men the Lord almighty.

JUDITH

. . . .

She doubted not the glorious Maker's gifts
In this wide earth; from the great Lord to find
Ready protection when she needed most
Grace from the highest Judge; that He, whose power
Is over all beginnings, with His peace
Would strengthen her against the highest terror.
Therefore the Heavenly Father, bright of mood,
Gave her her wish, because she ever had
Firm faith in the Almighty. .
Then heard I Holofernes bade prepare
Wine quickly, with all wonders gloriously
Prepare a feast, to which the chief of men
Bade all his foremost thanes, and with great haste,
Shield-warriors obeyed, came journeying
To the rich lord the leader of the people.
That was the fourth day after Judith, shrewd
Of thought, with elfin beauty, sought him first.

X

Then to the feast they went to sit in pride
At the wine-drinking, all his warriors
Bold in their war-shirts, comrades in his woe.
There were deep bowls oft to the benches borne,
Cups and full jugs to those who sat in hall.
The famed shield-warriors shared the feast, death-doomed,
Though that the chief, dread lord of earls, knew not.
Then Holofernes, the gold-friend of man,
Joyed in the pouring out, laughed, talked aloud.

Roared and uproared, that men from far might hear
How the stern-minded stormed and yelled in mirth,
Much bidding the bench sitters bear their part
Well in the feasting. So the wicked one
Through the day drenched his followers with wine,
The haughty Gift Lord, till they lay in swoon;
His nobles all o'er drenched as they were struck
To death, and every good poured out of them.
So bade the lord of men serve those in hall
Till the dark night drew near the sons of men.
Then bade the malice-blind to fetch with speed
The blessed maid, ring-wreathed, to his bed-rest.
The attendants quickly did as bade their lord,
Head of mailed warriors, in a twinkling went
To the guest chamber, where they Judith found
Prudent in soul, and then shield-warriors
Began to lead the pious, the bright maid
To the tent, the high one, where within at night
The chief at all times rested, Holofernes,
Hateful to God the Saviour. There was hung
All golden a fair fly-net round the bed
Of the folk-leader, that the baleful one,
The chief of warriors, might look through on each
Child of the brave who came therein, and none
Might look on him of mankind, save 't were one
Of his own ill-famed warriors whom the proud one
Bade to draw near, go in for secret council.
Then they brought quickly to his place of rest
The woman wise of wit; went rugged men
To make known to their lord that there was brought
The holy woman to his bower tent.
Then was the famed one blithe of mood, the chief
Of cities thought the bright maid to defile
With filth and stain, but that the glorious Judge
Would not allow, who kept the flock of fame,
The Lord, who guides the good, stayed him in that.
Then went the devilish one, with crowd of men,
Baleful, to seek his bed, where he should lose
His prosperous life, at once, within a night;
There had he to await his end, on earth
A bitter one, such as he in old time
Wrought for himself, while he, bold chief of men,
Dwelt on this earth under the roof of clouds.
So drunken then with wine the king fell down
In the midst of his bed, that counsel he knew none
Within the chamber of his thought. Out from within
Marched with all haste the warriors steeped in wine,
Who led the faithless, hated chief to bed
For the last time. The Saviour's hand-maid then
Gloried, intently mindful how she might
Take from the hateful one most easily
His life before the drunkard woke to shame.
Then she of braided locks, the Maker's maid,
Took a sharp sword, hard from the grinding, drew it
With strong palm from the sheath, and then by name
Began to name Heaven's Warden, Saviour
Of all who dwell on earth, and spake these words:
'God, first Creator, Spirit of Comfort, Son
Of the Almighty, glorious Trinity,
I will pray for Thy mercy upon me
Who need it. Strongly is my heart now stirred,
Distressed the mind sorely disturbed with care:
Give to me, Lord of Heaven, victory
And true belief, that with this sword I may
Hew at this giver of death. Grant me success,
Strong Lord of men, never had I more need
Of Thy compassion; now, O mighty Lord,
Bright-minded giver of renown, avenge
What stirs my mood to anger, mind to hate.'
He then, the highest Judge, encouraged her
At once with strength, so doth He to each one
Of those here dwelling who seek Him for help
With reason and with true belief. Her mood
Then became unoppressed and renovate
With holy hope; she took the heathen then
Fast by his hair, and drew him with her hands

Shamefully towards her, and laid with skill
The hateful man where she most easily
Might have the wicked one within her power.
She, braided-locked, then struck the scather-foe
With glittering sword, him in whose thought was hate,
That she cut half his neck through, and he lay
In swoon, drunk, with a death-wound, but not yet
Was dead, his soul all fled; the woman then,
Famous for strength, with vigour struck again
The heathen dog, so that his head went forth
Upon the floor. Then the foul carcase lay
Empty behind, while the soul went elsewhere
Under the abyss, and there it was condemned,
Tied down to torment ever after, wound
About with serpents, fixed to punishment,
Chained in hell's burning after it went hence.
Nor must he hope at all, in darkness whelmed,
That he can come thence from the serpents' hall,
But there shall dwell ever and ever more
Forth without end in the dark cavern-home,
Deprived for ever of the joys of light.

XI

Great glory Judith then had gained in strife,
As God, the Lord of Heaven, granted her,
Who gave her victory. The clear witted maid
Then quickly brought the leader's bleeding head
Into the bag that her attendant maid,
A pale-faced woman, trained to noble ways,
Had carried thither with the food of both,
And Judith, thoughtful minded, gave it then,
So gory, to her maid to carry home.
Then both the women went directly thence
Bold in their strength, exulting in success,
Out from that host, till they might clearly see
The glittering walls of fair Bethulia.
They then, adorned with bracelets, sped on foot
Forth until, glad of mood, they had gone on
To the wall gate. Sat warriors, men on watch,
Kept guard within the fortress, as before
Judith had bidden them in their distress,
The snare-devising maid, famed for her strength,
When she went forth upon her path of war.
Then she was come again, dear to her folk,
And then forthwith the prudent woman bade
Some of the men of the wide burgh go forth
To meet her, and to let her quickly in
Through the wall's gate, and to the victor folk
Spake thus: 'I now can tell you of a thing
Worth thanks, that ye no longer need to mourn.
Blithe to you is the Creator, Glory of kings:
Throughout the wide world that has been made known,
That glorious prosperity now shines
Brightly upon you, glory now is given
For all the evils that ye long have borne.'
Then were the burghers blithe when they had heard
Over the high wall how the holy maid
Spake to them. In the army there was joy;
The people hastened to the fortress gate,
Women and men together crush and crowd,
In bands, in bodies, thronged and ran, old, young,
Towards the handmaid of the Lord by thousands.
Within that festive city every man
Was gladdened in his spirit when they knew
That it was Judith come back to her home,
Quickly with reverence they then let her in.
The prudent one, adorned with gold, then bade
Her servant, grateful minded, to unwrap
The head of the war chieftain and to the eyes
Of the burghers show it, bloody, as a sign
How she had sped in the contest. Then to all
The people spake the noble woman: 'Here,
Men famed for victory, the people's leaders,
Here ye may plainly gaze upon the head
Of the most hated heathen warrior,
The lifeless Holofernes, of all men
He who for us most shaped sore care and death,
And worse would add, but God denied to him
A longer life to afflict us with his feuds.
Through help of God I forced his life from him.
Now my will is to bid each man of you,
Burghers, shield-warriors, that you instantly
Be ready for the fight. When from the east
God the Creator, Holy King, has sent
A ray of light, bear forth your shields on breast,

Fire hardened corslets and bright helms among
The horde of scathers, with your glittering swords
To slay the death-doomed leaders of the folk,
The fated chiefs. Your foes are doomed to death,
And ye have power and glory in the fight,
As through my hand the mighty Lord hath shown you.'
  Then a bold host was suddenly prepared
Of men keen for the conflict. Famed for courage
Soldiers and nobles marched, bore flags, straight forth
Helmeted men went from the holy burgh,
At the first reddening of dawn, to fight:
Loud stormed the din of shields.
For that rejoiced the lank wolf in the wood,
And the black raven, slaughter-greedy bird;
Both knew that men of the land thought to achieve
A slaughter of the fated ones: then flew
The eagle, dewy-feathered, on their track,
Eager for prey, the sallow-coated bird
Sang with its horny beak the song of war.
Warriors, brave men, marched to the battle,
They who not long before suffered reproach
From the foreigners, shame from the heathen. But all
That was hard was repaid at the play of the spears
To Assyria when under their war flags came
The Hebrews to the tents. Then boldly they
Let fly the showers of arrows, snakes of war,
From the horned bows the arrows firm in place;
Loud stormed the angry warriors, spears were sent
Amidst the throng of bold ones, men were wroth,
Men of the land against the hated race,
Marched stern of mood, rugged of mind, to take
Hard vengeance on old foes weary with mead.
The soldiers drew with hands their clear-marked swords,
Proved edges, slew the Assyrian warriors
Attempting evil, slew with zeal, spared none
Of all the army, whether wretch or rich,
Of living men whom they could overtake.

XII

So all the morning-time the kinsman troops
Pursued the stranger on their native soil,
Till the chief watchmen of the host, in wrath,
Saw that the Hebrews strongly showed to them
The swing of swords. They went to make that known
In words to the chief thanes. They roused the highest
And fearfully told him, mead-weary man,
The dreadful tale, the morning's quick alarm,
The cruel edge-play. Suddenly, I heard,
The hero doomed to slaughter leapt from sleep,
And hosts of men sought the pavilion
Of baleful Holofernes, thronged in crowds;
They only thought to offer him their help,
Their lord, before the terror came on him,
The power of the Hebrews. All supposed
The lord of men and the bright maid together
Were in the shining tent, the noble Judith
And he, the lustful, loathsome, terrible.
None was there of the earls who dared to wake
Or learn how it had been to the great chief
With the holy woman the handmaid of God.
Nearer the people of the Hebrews drew,
Fought stiffly with war weapons, hilts, bright swords,
Requited old assaults, all grievances.
In that day's work Assyria was subdued,
Its pride was bowed. Men stood about the tent
Of the chief, much stirred, and gloom was in their minds.
Then all together they cried noisily,
Began to clamour loudly, gnash their teeth,
Void of all good, setting their teeth in wrath:
Then was their glory, ease, power, at its end.
The earls thought so to waken their dear Lord,
But not a whit succeeded. Then was found
One of the warriors so resolute
That, hard in hate, within the bower-tent
He ventured, as need urged him; on the bed
Found his gold-giver lying pale, soul gone,
Deprived of life. Forthwith he, shuddering,
Fell to the ground, in fierce mood, tore his hair
And his robe too, and to the warriors
Who were outside there, joyless, thus he spake:
'Here we may plainly see our fate foreshown,
Sign given us the time presses near with ills,

When we shall perish all, destroyed in battle.
Here our support, hewn with the sword, lies headless.'
They then in bitter mood threw down their arms,
Turned themselves, faint of heart, to haste away
In flight.
Upon their track the folk enlarged in might
Fought till the most part of the army lay
In battle sacrificed, upon the field
Of victory, sword-hewn to please the wolves
And to content the birds that crave for slaughter.
They who yet lived fled from the foemen's arms,
The band of Hebrews followed on their track,
Honoured with victory, enriched with fame.
The Lord God, the Almighty, graciously
Gave them His help. They laboured piously,
The famous heroes, with bright swords to cut
A war path through the press of evil ones,
Hewed shields, cut the defence through, grim in fight
The Hebrew men were shooting, with desire
Strong in the thanes towards the strife of spears.
Here fell in dust the greatest part of all
The number of the nobles of Assyria,
Race of the enemy; few came alive
To their own country. Warriors renowned,
Within the place of slaughter, as they fled,
Turned them to reeking corpses. Room was there
For dwellers on the land to take red spoil
From their most hated foes, now dead, shields fair
Adorned, broad swords, brown helms, and costly cups.
The country's guardians, on the people's land,
Had gloriously overcome the foe
And silenced old oppressions with their swords.
They rested on the path who when alive
Of living men were their worst enemies.
Then for a month's space all men of the tribe,
Greatest of peoples, proud, with plaited locks,
Bore, drew to the bright town, Bethulia,
Helms, hip knives, corslets, the war dress of men
Gold-fretted, treasure more than cunning man
Can tell. All this the people of the land
Won with their strength in fight, bold under banners,
Through Judith's prudent teaching, noble maid.
They, the brave earls, brought from the raid for her,
As her own meed, the sword and bloody helm
Of Holofernes, his breast armour broad
And ornamented with red gold; and all
Of treasure that the haughty chief possessed,
His heritage of circlets and bright gems,
They gave to the bright woman prompt of thought.
For all this Judith gave to God the praise,
The glorious Lord of men who gave her honour,
Glory in Earth's kingdom, and reward in heaven,
In the bright skies reward of victory:
Because she had a true belief in God
Almighty, and at the end had not a doubt
Of the reward for which she long had yearned.
For this to latest ages evermore
Be glory unto the dear Lord who made
The wind and air, the heavens and wide earth,
And also the wild streams He made, and He
Through His own mercy made the joys of heaven.

PROSE

Adamnan (ca. 625–709)

LIFE OF COLUMBA [1]

In the course of a few days, while the solemnities of masses were being celebrated, according to custom, on the Lord's day; all on a sudden the face of the venerable man (Columba), as his eyes are lifted upward, is seen suffused with a ruddy glow, for, as it is written, 'When the heart is glad the face

[1] Translation by J. T. Fowler (1895), by permission of the Oxford University Press, Publishers.

blooms.' For in that same hour he alone saw an angel of the Lord hovering above within the walls of his oratory. And, because the lovely and tranquil aspect of the holy angels pours joy and gladness into the hearts of the elect, this was the cause of that sudden gladness imparted to the blessed man. And when those who were therein present inquired as to what, mark you, was the cause of the joy that was kindled within him, the Saint, looking upward, gave them this reply: 'Wonderful and incomparable is the subtilty of the nature of angels. For, behold, an angel of the Lord, sent to demand some deposit dear to God, looking down from above upon us within the church, and blessing us, has returned again through the vaulting of the church, and has left no traces of such an exit.' So far the Saint. But yet, as to the nature of that deposit for which the angel was sent to make inquiry, not one of those who were standing around was able to form an opinion. Our patron, however, gave the name of a holy deposit to his own soul, which had been entrusted to him by God; which soul, as will be narrated below, in the night of the next Lord's day, six days in succession coming between, passed away to the Lord.

And so the venerable man at the end of the same week, that is on the Sabbath day (Saturday), himself and his dutiful attendant Diormit, go to bless the granary, which was close at hand. On entering which, when he blessed both it and two heaps of corn there were stored therein, he uttered these words with giving of thanks, saying, 'I greatly congratulate the monks of my household that this year also, if I should have to depart from you to any place, ye will have enough for the year.' On hearing this saying, Diormit his attendant began to be sorrowful, and to speak thus: 'In the course of this year, Father, thou art often making us sorrowful, because thou so frequently makest mention of thy departure.' To whom the Saint gave this reply, 'I have some little secret discourse, and if thou wilt faithfully promise me not to disclose it to any one before my death, I shall be able to give thee some clearer intimation concerning my departure.' When the attendant, on bended knees, had completed some such promise, according to the wish of the Saint, the venerable man in the next place thus speaks: 'This day is in the sacred volumes called Sabbath, which is, being interpreted, Rest. And for me this day is a Sabbath indeed, because it is the last day of this my present laborious life, in which I take my rest after all the wearinesses of my labours. And in the middle of this most solemn night (eve) of the Lord's day that is now coming, according to the saying of the Scriptures, "I shall go the way of my fathers." For even now my Lord Jesus Christ deigneth to invite me, to Whom, I say, in the middle of this night, I shall depart, at His invitation. For thus it hath been revealed unto me by the Lord Himself.' The attendant on hearing these sad words began to weep bitterly, but the Saint endeavoured to console him as well as he could.

After this, the Saint goes out of the granary, and, returning to the monastery, sits down at the half-way, in which place a cross, afterwards fixed in a millstone, and standing at this day, is to be seen on the side of the road. And while the Saint, feeble with age, as I said before, sat down for a little while and rested in that place, behold! there comes up to him the white horse, that faithful servant, mark you, that used to carry the milk-pails between the cow-pasture (or byre?) and the monastery. This creature then coming up to the Saint, wonderful to say, putting its head in his bosom, as I believe under the inspiration of God, in Whose sight every animal is endowed with a sense of things, because the Creator Himself hath so ordered it; knowing that his master would soon depart from him, and that he would see his face no more, began to utter plaintive moans, and, as if a man, to shed tears in abundance into the Saint's lap, and so to weep, frothing greatly. Which when the attendant saw, he began to drive away that weeping mourner; but the Saint forbad him, saying, 'Let him alone! As he loves me so, let him alone; that into this my bosom he may pour out the tears of his most bitter lamentation. Behold! thou, even seeing that thou art a man, and hast a rational soul, couldest in no way know anything about my departure, except what I myself have lately shown to thee; but to this brute animal, destitute of reason, in what way soever the

Maker Himself hath willed, He hath revealed that his master is about to go away from him.' And, so saying, he blessed his sorrowing servant the horse, then turning about to go away from him.

And going forth thence, he ascended the little hill that overlooks the monastery, and stood for a little while on the top of it, and, standing with both hands lifted up, he blessed the monastery, saying, 'To this place, small and mean though it be, not only the Scotic kings (Irish and Dalriadic) with their peoples, but also the rulers of strange and foreign nations, with the people subject to them, shall bring great and extraordinary honour; by the Saints also of other churches shall no common reverence be shown.'

After these words, descending from that little hill, and returning to the monastery, he sat in his cell transcribing the Psalter; and coming to that verse of the thirty-third (34th) Psalm where it is written, 'But they who seek the Lord shall want no manner of thing that is good,' 'Here,' he says, 'at the end of the page, I must cease. What follows let Baithene write.' The last verse which he had written was very suitable for the Saint at his departure, to whom eternal things that are good shall never be wanting; while the following verse was most suitable for his successor, as a father and teacher of spiritual sons: 'Come, ye children, and hearken unto me; I will teach you the fear of the Lord.' And indeed he, as his predecessor enjoined, succeeded him not only in teaching, but also in transcribing.

After the transcription of the aforesaid verse, at the end of the page, the Saint enters the church for the evening mass (evensong) of the Lord's day night (eve), and as soon as this is over he returns to his cell, where he had bare rock for his bedding, and a stone for his pillow, which at this day is standing by his grave as a kind of sepulchral monument; and he sits on the bed through the night. And so, there sitting, he gives his last commands to the brethren, in the hearing of his attendant only; saying, 'These last words, O my children, I commend unto you; that ye have mutual and unfeigned charity among yourselves, with peace. And if, according to the example of the holy fathers, ye shall attend to this, God, the Comforter of good men, will help you; and I, abiding with Him, will intercede for you. And not only shall the necessaries of this present life be sufficiently supplied by Him, but He will also bestow those rewards of eternal riches, which are laid up for them that keep His Divine laws.' Thus far we have drawn up, recounted in a short paragraph, the last words of our venerable patron, spoken just as he was passing over from this weary pilgrimage unto the heavenly country.

Bede (673–735)

ECCLESIASTICAL HISTORY OF THE ENGLISH NATION

CONVERSION OF KING EDWIN

King Edwin, therefore, delaying to receive the word of God at the preaching of Paulinus, and using for some time, as has been said, to sit several hours alone, and seriously to ponder with himself what he was to do, and what religion he was to follow, the man of God came to him, laid his right hand on his head, and asked, 'Whether he knew that sign?' The king in a trembling condition, was ready to fall down at his feet, but he raised him up, and in a familiar manner said to him, 'Behold by the help of God you have escaped the hands of the enemies whom you feared. Behold you have of his gift obtained the kingdom which you desired. Take heed not to delay that which you promised to perform; embrace the faith, and keep the precepts of Him who, delivering you from temporal adversity, has raised you to the honour of a temporal kingdom; and if, from this time forward, you shall be obedient to his will, which through me He signifies to you, He will not only deliver you from the everlasting torments of the wicked, but also make you partaker with Him of his eternal kingdom in heaven.'

The king, hearing these words, answered, that he was both willing and bound to receive the faith which he taught; but that he would confer about it with his principal friends and counsellors, to the end that if they also were of his opinion, they might all together be cleansed in Christ the Fountain of Life. Paulinus consenting, the king did as he had said; for, holding a council with the wise men, he asked of every one in particular what he thought of the new doctrine, and the new worship that was preached? To which the chief of his own priests, Coifi, immediately answered, 'O king, consider what this is which is now preached to us; for I verily declare to you, that the religion which we have hitherto professed has, as far as I can learn, no virtue in it. For none of your people has applied himself more diligently to the worship of our gods than I: and yet there are many who receive greater favours from you, and are more preferred than I, and are more prosperous in all their undertakings. Now if the gods were good for anything, they would rather forward me, who have been more careful to serve them. It remains, therefore, that if upon examination you find those new doctrines, which are now preached to us, better and more efficacious, we immediately receive them without delay.'

Another of the king's chief men, approving of his words and exhortations, presently added: 'The present life of man, O king, seems to me, in comparison of that time which is unknown to us, like to the swift flight of a sparrow through the room wherein you sit at supper in winter, with your commanders and ministers, and a good fire in the midst, whilst the storms of rain and snow prevail abroad; the sparrow, I say, flying in at one door, and immediately out at another, whilst he is within, is safe from the wintry storm; but after a short space of fair weather, he immediately vanishes out of your sight, into the dark winter from which he had emerged. So this life of man appears for a short space, but of what went before, or what is to follow, we are utterly ignorant. If, therefore, this new doctrine contains something more certain, it seems justly to deserve to be followed.' The other elders and king's counsellors, by Divine inspiration, spoke to the same effect.

But Coifi added, that he wished more attentively to hear Paulinus discourse concerning the God whom he preached; which he having by the king's command performed, Coifi, hearing his words, cried out, 'I have long since been sensible that there was nothing in that which we worshipped; because the more diligently I sought after truth in that worship, the less I found it. But now I freely confess, that such truth evidently appears in this preaching as can confer on us the gifts of life, of salvation, and of eternal happiness. For which reason I advise, O king, that we instantly abjure and set fire to those temples and altars which we have consecrated without reaping any benefit from them.' In short, the king publicly gave his license to Paulinus to preach the Gospel, and renouncing idolatry, declared that he received the faith of Christ: and when he inquired of the high priest who should first profane the altars and temples of their idols, with the enclosures that were about them, he answered, 'I; for who can more properly than myself destroy those things which I worshipped through ignorance, for an example to all others, through the wisdom which has been given me by the true God?' Then immediately, in contempt of his former superstitions, he desired the king to furnish him with arms and a stallion; and mounting the same, he set out to destroy the idols; for it was not lawful before for the high priest either to carry arms, or to ride on any but a mare. Having, therefore, girt a sword about him, with a spear in his hand, he mounted the king's stallion and proceeded to the idols. The multitude beholding it, concluded he was distracted; but he lost no time, for as soon as he drew near the temple he profaned the same, casting into it the spear which he held; and rejoicing in the knowledge of the worship of the true God, he commanded his companions to destroy the temple, with all its enclosures, by fire. This place where the idols were is still shown, not far from York, to the eastward, beyond the river Derwent, and is now called Godmundingham, where the high priest, by the inspiration of the true God, profaned and destroyed the altars which he had himself consecrated.

THE POET CÆDMON

There was in this abbess's monastery a certain brother, particularly remarkable for the grace of God, who was wont to make pious and religious verses, so that whatever was interpreted to him out of Scripture, he soon after put the same into poetical expressions of much sweetness and humility, in English, which was his native language. By his verses the minds of many were often excited to despise the world, and to aspire to heaven. Others after him attempted, in the English nation, to compose religious poems, but none could ever compare with him, for he did not learn the art of poetry from men, but from God; for which reason he never could compose any trivial or vain poem, but only those which relate to religion suited his religious tongue; for having lived in a secular habit till he was well advanced in years, he had never learned anything of versifying; for which reason being sometimes at entertainments, when it was agreed for the sake of mirth that all present should sing in their turns, when he saw the instrument come towards him, he rose up from table and returned home.

Having done so at a certain time, and gone out of the house where the entertainment was, to the stable, where he had to take care of the horses that night, he there composed himself to rest at the proper time; a person appeared to him in his sleep, and saluting him by his name, said, 'Cædmon, sing some song to me.' He answered, 'I cannot sing; for that was the reason why I left the entertainment, and retired to this place, because I could not sing.' The other who talked to him, replied, 'However, you shall sing.' — 'What shall I sing?' rejoined he. 'Sing the beginning of created beings,' said the other. Hereupon he presently began to sing verses to the praise of God, which he had never heard, the purport whereof was thus: — We are now to praise the Maker of the heavenly kingdom, the power of the Creator and his counsel, the deeds of the Father of glory. How He, being the eternal God, became the author of all miracles, who first, as almighty preserver of the human race, created heaven for the sons of men as the roof of the house, and next the earth. This is the sense, but not the words in order as he sang them in his sleep; for verses, though never so well composed, cannot be literally translated out of one language into another, without losing much of their beauty and loftiness. Awaking from his sleep, he remembered all that he had sung in his dream, and soon added much more to the same effect in verse worthy of the Deity.

In the morning he came to the steward, his superior, and having acquainted him with the gift he had received, was conducted to the abbess, by whom he was ordered, in the presence of many learned men, to tell his dream, and repeat the verses, that they might all give their judgment what it was, and whence his verse proceeded. They all concluded that heavenly grace had been conferred on him by our Lord. They expounded to him a passage in holy writ, either historical, or doctrinal, ordering him, if he could, to put the same into verse. Having undertaken it, he went away, and returning the next morning, gave it to them composed in most excellent verse; whereupon the abbess, embracing the grace of God in the man, instructed him to quit the secular habit, and take upon him the monastic life; which being accordingly done, she associated him to the rest of the brethren in her monastery, and ordered that he should be taught the whole series of sacred history. Thus Cædmon, keeping in mind all he heard, and as it were chewing the cud, converted the same into most harmonious verse; and sweetly repeating the same, made his masters in their turn his hearers. He sang the creation of the world, the origin of man, and all the history of Genesis; and made many verses on the departure of the children of Israel out of Egypt, and their entering into the land of promise, with many other histories from holy writ; the incarnation, passion, resurrection of our Lord, and his ascension into heaven; the coming of the Holy Ghost, and the preaching of the apostles; also the terror of future judgment, the horror of the pains of hell, and the delights of heaven; besides many more about the Divine benefits and judgments, by which he endeavoured to turn away all men from the love of vice, and to excite in them the love of, and application to, good actions; for he was a very religious man, and humbly submissive to regular discipline, but full of zeal against those who behaved themselves otherwise; for which reason he ended his life happily.

For when the time of his departure drew near, he laboured for the space of fourteen days under a bodily infirmity which seemed to prepare the way, yet so moderate that he could talk and walk the whole time. In his neighbourhood was the house to which those that were sick, and like shortly to die, were carried. He desired the person that attended him, in the evening, as the night came on in which he was to depart this life, to make ready a place there for him to take his rest. This person, wondering why he should desire it, because there was as yet no sign of his dying soon, did what he had ordered. He accordingly went there, and conversing pleasantly in a joyful manner with the rest that were in the house before, when it was past midnight, he asked them, whether they had the Eucharist there? They answered, 'What need of the Eucharist? for you are not likely to die, since you talk so merrily with us, as if you were in perfect health.'—'However,' said he, 'bring me the Eucharist.' Having received the same into his hand, he asked, whether they were all in charity with him, and without any enmity or rancour? They answered, that they were all in perfect charity, and free from anger; and in their turn asked him, whether he was in the same mind towards them? He answered, 'I am in charity, my children, with all the servants of God.' Then strengthening himself with the heavenly viaticum, he prepared for the entrance into another life, and asked, how near the time was when the brothers were to be awakened to sing the nocturnal praises of our Lord? They answered, 'It is not far off.' Then he said, 'Well, let us wait that hour'; and signing himself with the sign of the cross, he laid his head on the pillow, and falling into a slumber, ended his life so in silence.

Thus it came to pass, that as he had served God with a simple and pure mind, and undisturbed devotion, so he now departed to his presence, leaving the world by a quiet death; and that tongue, which had composed so many holy words in praise of the Creator, uttered its last words whilst he was in the act of signing himself with the cross, and recommending himself into his hands, and by what has been here said, he seems to have had foreknowledge of his death.

AUTHOR'S ACCOUNT OF HIMSELF

Thus much of the Ecclesiastical History of Britain, and more especially of the English nation, as far as I could learn either from the writings of the ancients, or the tradition of our ancestors, or of my own knowledge, has, with the help of God, been digested by me, Bede, the servant of God, and priest of the monastery of the blessed apostles, Peter and Paul, which is at Weremouth and Jarrow; who being born in the territory of that same monastery, was given, at seven years of age, to be educated by the most reverend Abbot Benedict, and afterwards by Ceolfrid; and, spending all the remaining time of my life in that monastery, I wholly applied myself to the study of Scripture, and amidst the observance of regular discipline, and the daily care of singing in the church, I always took delight in learning, teaching, and writing. In the nineteenth year of my age, I received deacon's orders; in the thirtieth, those of the priesthood, both of them by the ministry of the most reverend Bishop John, and by the order of the Abbot Ceolfrid. From which time, till the fifty-ninth year of my age, I have made it my business, for the use of me and mine, to compile out of the works of the venerable Fathers, and to interpret and explain according to their meaning these following pieces. . . .

And now I beseech thee, good Jesus, that to whom thou hast graciously granted sweetly to partake of the words of thy wisdom and knowledge, thou wilt also vouchsafe that he may some time or other come to thee the fountain of all wisdom, and always appear before thy face, who livest and reignest world without end. Amen.

ANGLO-SAXON CHRONICLE

A.D. 435. This year the Goths sacked the city of Rome; and never since have the Romans reigned in Britain. This was about eleven hundred and ten winters after it was built. They reigned altogether in Britain four hundred and seventy winters since Gaius Julius first sought that land.

A.D. 449. This year Marcian and Valentinian assumed the empire, and reigned seven winters. In their days Hengest and Horsa, invited by Wurtgern king of the Britons to his assistance, landed in Britain in a place that is called Ipwinesfleet: first of all to support the Britons, but they afterwards fought against them. The king directed them to fight against the Picts; and they did so; and obtained the victory wheresoever they came. They then sent to the Angles, and desired them to send more assistance. They described the worthlessness of the Britons, and the richness of the land. They then sent them greater support. Then came the men from three powers of Germany; the Old Saxons, the Angles, and the Jutes. From the Jutes are descended the men of Kent, the Wightwarians (that is, the tribe that now dwelleth in the isle of Wight), and that kindred in Wessex that men yet call the kindred of the Jutes. From the Old Saxons came the people of Essex and Sussex and Wessex. From Anglia, which has ever since remained waste between the Jutes and the Saxons, came the East Angles, the Middle Angles, the Mercians, and all of those north of the Humber. Their leaders were two brothers, Hengest and Horsa; who were the sons of Wihtgils; Wihtgils was the son of Witta, Witta of Wecta, Wecta of Woden. From this Woden arose all our royal kindred, and that of the South-humbrians also.

A.D. 755. This year Cynewulf, with the consent of the West-Saxon council, deprived Sebright, his relative, for unrighteous deeds, of his kingdom, except Hampshire; which he retained, until he slew the alderman who remained the longest with him. Then Cynewulf drove him to the forest of Andred, where he remained, until a swain stabbed him at Privett, and revenged the alderman, Cumbra. The same Cynewulf fought many hard battles with the Welsh; and, about one and thirty winters after he had the kingdom, he was desirous of expelling a prince called Cyneard, who was the brother of Sebright. But he having understood that the king was gone, thinly attended, on a visit to a lady at Merton, rode after him, and beset him therein; surrounding the town without, ere the attendants of the king were aware of him. When the king found this, he went out of doors, and defended himself with courage; till, having looked on the etheling, he rushed out upon him, and wounded him severely. Then were they all fighting against the king, until they had slain him. As soon as the king's thanes in the lady's bower heard the tumult, they ran to the spot, whoever was then ready. The etheling immediately offered them life and rewards; which none of them would accept, but continued fighting together against him, till they all lay dead, except one British hostage, and he was severely wounded. When the king's thanes that were behind heard in the morning that the king was slain, they rode to the spot, Osric his alderman, and Wiverth his thane, and the men that he had left behind; and they met the etheling at the town, where the king lay slain. The gates, however, were locked against them, which they attempted to force; but he promised them their own choice of money and land, if they would grant him the kingdom; reminding them, that their relatives were already with him, who would never desert him. To which they answered, that no relative could be dearer to them than their lord, and that they would never follow his murderer. Then they besought their relatives to depart from him, safe and sound. They replied, that the same request was made to their comrades that were formerly with the king. 'And we are as regardless of the result,' they rejoined, 'as our comrades who with the king were slain.' Then they continued fighting at the gates, till they rushed in, and slew the etheling and all the men that were with him; except one, who was the godson of the alderman, and whose life he spared, though he was often wounded. This same Cynewulf reigned one and thirty winters. His body lies at Winchester, and that of the etheling at Axminster. Their paternal pedigree goeth in a direct line to Cerdic. — The same year Ethelbald, king of the Mercians, was slain at Seckington; and his body lies at Repton. He reigned one and forty years; and Bernred then succeeded to the kingdom, which he held but a little while, and unprosperously; for king Offa the same year put him to flight, and assumed the government; which he held nine and thirty winters. His son Everth held it a hundred and forty days. Offa was the son of Thingferth, Thingferth of Enwulf, Enwulf of Osmod, Osmod of Eawa, Eawa of Webba, Webba of Creoda, Creoda of Cenwald, Cenwald of Cnebba, Cnebba of Icel, Icel of Eomer, Eomer of Angelthew, Angelthew of Offa, Offa of Wermund, Wermund of Witley, Witley of Woden.

A.D. 897. In the summer of this year went the army, some into East Anglia, and some into Northumbria; and those that were penniless got themselves ships, and went south over sea to the Seine. The enemy had not, thank God, entirely destroyed the English nation; but they were much more weakened in these three years by the disease of cattle, and most of all of men; so that many of the mightiest of the king's thanes, that were in the land, died within the three years. Of these, one was Swithulf Bishop of Rochester, Ceolmund alderman in Kent, Bertulf alderman in Essex, Wulfred alderman in Hampshire, Elhard Bishop of Dorchester, Eadulf a king's thane in Sussex, Bernulf governor of Winchester, and Egulf the king's horse-thane; and many also with them; though I have named only the men of the highest rank. This same year the plunderers in East Anglia and Northumbria greatly harassed the land of the West Saxons by piracies on the southern coast, but most of all by the esks which they built many years before. Then King Alfred gave orders for building long ships against the esks, which were full-nigh twice as long as the others. Some had sixty oars, some more; and they were both swifter and steadier, and also higher than the others. They were not shaped either after the Frisian or the Danish model, but so as he himself thought that they might be most serviceable. Then, at a certain turn of this same year, came six of their ships to the isle of Wight; and going into Devonshire, they did much mischief both there and every where on the sea-coast. Then commanded the king his men to go out against them with nine of the new ships, and prevent their escape by the mouth of the river to the outer sea. Then came they out against them with three ships, and three others were standing upwards above the mouth on dry land; for the men were gone off upon shore. Of the first three ships they took two at the mouth outwards, and slew the men; the third veered off, but all the men were slain except five; and they too were severely wounded. Then came onward those who manned the other ships, which were also very uneasily situated. Three were stationed on that side of the deep where the Danish ships were aground, whilst the others were all on the opposite side; so that none of them could join the rest; for the water had ebbed many furlongs from them. Then went the Danes from their three ships to those other three that were on their side, be-ebbed; and there they then fought. There were slain Lucomon, the king's reve, and Wulfheard, a Frieslander; Ebb, a Frieslander, and Ethelere, a Frieslander; and Ethelferth, the king's neat-herd; and of all the men, Frieslanders and English, sixty-two; of the Danes a hundred and twenty. The tide, however, reached the Danish ships ere the Christians could shove theirs out; whereupon they rowed them out; but they were so crippled, that they could not row them beyond the coast of Sussex: there two of them the sea drove ashore; and the crew were led to Winchester to the king, who ordered them to be hanged. The men who escaped in the single ship came to East Anglia, severely wounded. This same year were lost no less than twenty ships, and the men withal, on the southern coast. Wulfric, the king's horse-thane, who was also vice-roy of Wales, died the same year.

A.D. 1137. This year went the king Stephen over sea to Normandy, and there was received; because they concluded that he should be all such as the uncle was, and because he had got his treasure: but he dealed it out, and scattered it foolishly. Much had king Henry gathered, gold and silver, but no good did he for his soul thereof. When the king Stephen came to England, he held his council at Oxford, and there he seized the bishop Roger of Sarum, and Alexander bishop of Lincoln, and the chancellor Roger his nephew; and threw all into prison till they gave up their castles. When the traitors understood that he was a mild man, and soft, and good, and no justice executed, then did they all wonders. They had done him homage, and sworn oaths, but they no truth maintained. They were all forsworn, and forgetful of their troth; for every rich man built his castles, which they held against him: and they filled the land full of castles. They cruelly oppressed the wretched men of the land with castle-works; and when the castles were made, they filled them with devils and evil men. Then took they those whom they supposed to have any goods, both by night and by day, men and women, and threw them into prison for their gold and silver, and inflicted on them unutterable tortures; for never were any martyrs so tortured as they were. Some they hanged up by the feet, and smoked them with foul smoke; and some by the thumbs, or by the head, and hung coats of mail on their feet. They tied knotted strings about their heads, and twisted them till the pain went to the brains. They put them into dungeons, wherein were adders, and snakes, and toads; and so destroyed them. Some they placed in a crucet-house; that is, in a chest that was short and narrow, and not deep; wherein they put sharp stones, and so thrust the man therein, that they broke all the limbs. In many of the castles were things loathsome and grim, called 'Rachenteges,' of which two or three men had enough to bear one. It was thus made: that is, fastened to a beam; and they placed a sharp iron [collar] about the man's throat and neck, so that he could in no direction either sit, or lie, or sleep, but bear all that iron. Many thousands they wore out with hunger. I neither can, nor may I tell all the wounds and all the pains which they inflicted on wretched men in this land. This lasted the 19 winters while Stephen was king; and it grew continually worse and worse. They constantly laid tribute on the towns, and called it 'tenserie'; and when the wretched men had no more to give, then they plundered and burned all the towns; that well thou mightest go a whole day's journey and never shouldest thou find a man sitting in a town, nor the land tilled. Then was corn dear, and flesh, and cheese, and butter; for none was there in the land. Wretched men starved of hunger. Some had recourse to alms, who were for a while rich men, and some fled out of the land. Never yet was there more wretchedness in the land; nor ever did heathen men worse than they did: for, after a time, they spared neither church nor churchyard, but took all the goods that were therein, and then burned the church and all together. Neither did they spare a bishop's land, or an abbot's or a priest's, but plundered both monks and clerks; and every man robbed another who could. If two men, or three, came riding to a town, all the township fled for them, concluding them to be robbers. The bishops and learned men cursed them continually, but the effect thereof was nothing to them; for they were all accursed, and forsworn, and abandoned. To till the ground was to plough the sea: the earth bare no corn, for the land was all laid waste by such deeds; and they said openly, that Christ slept, and his saints. Such things, and more than we can say, suffered we nineteen winters for our sins.

King Alfred (849–901)

PREFACE TO *CURA PASTORALIS*

King Alfred bids greet bishop Wærferth, lovingly and friendly in his words; and I bid thee to make it known that it hath very often come into my mind what wise men formerly were throughout the English race, both of the spiritual and of the secular condition, and how happy the times then were through the English race, and how the kings, who then had the government of this folk, obeyed God and his messengers, and how they held both their peace, their customs, and their government at home, and also increased their country abroad, and how they then sped both in war and in wisdom, and also the religious orders, how earnest they were, both about their doctrine and about their learning, and about all the services that they should do to God, and how men from abroad sought wisdom and instruction in this land, and how we must now get them from without, if we would have them. So clean was it [learning] now fallen off among the English race that there were very few on this side of the Humber that were able to understand their service in English, or even to turn a sent writing (an epistle) from Latin into English; and I think that there were not many beyond the Humber.—

So few there were of them that I cannot think of even one on the south of the Thames, when I first took to the kingdom. To God Almighty be thanks that we now have any teacher in the stall, and therefore I have commanded thee that thou do as I believe thou wilt — that thou, who from the things of this world art at leisure for this, as thou often mayest, that thou bestow the wisdom that God has given thee wherever thou mayest bestow it. Think what punishment shall come upon us for this world, when we have not ourselves loved it in the least degree, and also have not left it to other men to do so. We have had the name alone that we were Christians, and very few the virtues. When I then called to mind all this, then I remembered how I saw, ere that all in them was laid waste and burnt up, how the churches throughout all the English race stood filled with treasures and books, and also a great multitude of God's servants, but they knew very little use of those books, for that they could not understand anything of them, for that they were not written in their own language, such as they, our elders, spoke, who erewhile held these places; they loved wisdom, and through that got wealth, and left it to us. Here men may yet see their path, but we know not how to tread in their footsteps, inasmuch as we have both lost that wealth and wisdom, for that we would not with our minds stoop to their tracks. When I then called to mind all this, I then wondered greatly about those good and wise men that have been of old among the English race, and who had fully learned all the books, that they have not been willing to turn any part of them into their own language. But then I soon again answered myself and said, 'They did not think that men would ever become so reckless, and that learning should fall off in such a way. Of set purpose, then, they let it alone, and wished that there should be more wisdom in this land the more languages we knew.' Then I remembered how the Law was first found in the Hebrew tongue, and again, when the Greeks learnt it, then they turned the whole of it into their own language, and also all the other books. And again the Latins also in the same way, when they had learned it, turned it all through wise interpreters into their own language, and likewise all other Christian nations have translated some part into their own speech. Wherefore I think it better, if it also appears so to you, that we too should translate some books, which are the most necessary for all men to understand — that we should turn these into that tongue which we all can know, and so bring it about, as we very easily may, with God's help, if we have rest, that all the youth that now is among the English race, of free men, that have property, so that they can apply themselves to these things, may be committed to others for the sake of instruction, so long as they have no power for any other employments, until the time that they may know well how to read English writing. Let men afterwards further teach them Latin, those whom they are willing further to teach, and whom they wish to advance to a higher state.

When I then called to mind how the learning of the Latin tongue before this was fallen away throughout the English race, though many knew how to read writing in English — then began I, among other unlike and manifold businesses of this kingdom, to turn into English the book that is named in Latin *Pastoralis*, and in English the *Hind's book*, one-while word for word, another-while, meaning for meaning, so far as I learned it with Phlegmund, my archbishop, and with Asser, my bishop, and with Grimbold, my mass-priest, and with John, my mass-priest. After I had then learned them, so that I understood them, and so that I might read them with the fullest comprehension, I turned them into English, and to each bishop's see in my kingdom will send one, and on each is an 'æstel' that is, of [the value of] fifty mancuses, and I bid, in God's name, that no man undo the æstel from the books, nor the books from the minster. It is unknown how long there may be so learned bishops as now, thank God, are everywhere. For this, I would that they always should be at their place, unless the bishop will have them with him, or they be anywhere lent, or some one write others by them.

Aelfric (955?-1020?)

THE SECOND SUNDAY AFTER PENTECOST

Homo quidam erat dives: et reliqua.

The Sovereign Lord spake this parable to his disciples, thus saying, 'There was a certain rich man adorned with purple and fine linen, and daily lived sumptuously. A certain poor man lay at his gate, and his name was Lazarus, who was a leper,' etc.

This gospel is now simply said. The holy pope Gregory has revealed to us the mystery of this text. He said, 'The holy gospel did not express that the rich man was a robber, but that he was parsimonious, and exulted in his wealth.' By this it is to be considered how he will be punished who bereaves another, when he is condemned to hell, who would not give his own for love of God. This man's parsimony and pride sank him into quick torment, because he had no compassion, so that with his treasure he might have redeemed his own soul. Now some men will imagine that there is no peril in precious garments, but if there were no sin, the holy gospel would not have so evidently manifested with respect to the rich man, that he was adorned with purple and with fine linen. No man heeds precious garments save for vain pride, verily that he may through his splendour be accounted before other men. The Lord in another place praised John the Baptist for the rudeness of his garment, because he was clothed with camel's hair, poorly and ruggedly.

When Jesus spake of the rich man he said, 'There was a certain rich man.' Again, of the poor man, 'There was a certain poor man called Lazarus.' It is known to you that a rich man is more known by name among his people than a poor one; nevertheless Jesus named not the wealthy man, but the needy one; because the names of humble men are known to him through election, but he knows not the proud through their rejection. Some excuse the rich man might have had for his parsimony, if the leprous beggar had not lain before his sight: the mind of the poor man would also have been easier, if he had not seen the rich man's wealth. Divers afflictions he endured, seeing that he had neither nourishment, nor health, nor garments, and saw the rich man, hale and sumptuously decorated, enjoying his luxuries. For the beggar his infirmity had been enough, though he had had food; and again, his indigence had been enough for him, although he had been healthful. But the manifold hardship was the cleansing of his soul, and the parsimony and pride of the rich man were his condemnation; because he saw the other's misery, and with inflated mind despised him. But when he was despised of men, the dogs approached, and licked his wounds. The licking of a dog heals wounds.

It then happened that the beggar died, and angels bare his soul to the dwelling of the patriarch Abraham; and the rich man's spirit after death was sunk into hell; and he then wished to have him for protector, to whom he would not before give his crumbs. He then bade Abraham with piteous voice, that Lazarus might moisten his tongue; but that little favour was not granted to him, because Lazarus might not before in life gather the crumbs of his table. He particularly complained of his tongue, because it is usual that the wealthy in their feasting practise pernicious scoffing; therefore was his tongue, through righteous retribution, more harshly punished for his scoffing speech. The patriarch Abraham said to him, 'My son, be thou mindful that thou receivedst riches in thy life, and Lazarus misery.' This saying is rather to be feared than expounded. The rich man was requited with transitory prosperity, if he did aught of good; and the poor man was requited with misery, if he had perpetrated aught of evil. Then the wealthy man received his happiness in reward for short enjoyment, and the indigence of the needy one cleansed away his little sins. Poverty afflicted and purified him; his abundance enriched and deceived the other.

I pray you, men most beloved, despise not God's poor, though they perpetrate anything reprehensible; because their misery cleanses that which a little superfluity corrupts. Observe each one, for good often befalls the evil for life. The patriarch said to the wealthy man, 'Betwixt us and you is fixed a great vapour; though any-one will pass from us to you, he cannot; nor also from you to us.' With great eagerness the wicked desire to pass from the torment in which they suffer, but the fastening of the hellish enclosure never allows them to break out. Also the holy are so filled with their Creator's righteousness, that they in no wise lament the misery of the wicked; because they see the fordone ones as greatly estranged from them, as they are thrust away from their beloved Lord.

When the rich man became hopeless of his own deliverance, the remembrance of his brothers entered into his mind; for the punishment of the wicked very often uselessly stimulates their minds to love, so that they then love their relatives, who before in life loved neither themselves nor their kinsmen. He loves not himself who binds himself with sins. He recognized Lazarus, whom he had before despised, and he remembered his brothers, whom he had left behind; for the needy one would not have been fully avenged on the rich, if he in his punishment had not recognized him; and again, his punishment would not have been complete in the fire, unless he had expected the same torments for his relatives.

The sinful will now sometimes see the chosen in glory, whom they in the world despised, that the affliction of their minds may be the greater: and the righteous will ever see the unrighteous suffering in their torments, that their bliss and love to their Lord may be the greater, who rescued them from the power of the devil, and from the wicked band. That spectacle will excite no terror to the righteous, nor will their glory wane; for there will be no sorrowing for the misery of the wicked, but their torments will turn to the greater bliss of the chosen, as in a picture a dark likeness is provided, that the white may appear the brighter. The chosen will constantly see their Creator's brightness, and therefore there is nothing in creation concealed from him.

The rich man would not in life hear the teacher Moses, or God's prophets: then he thought that his brothers would also despise them as he did, and desired therefore that Lazarus might warn them, so that they came not to his torment. The patriarch answered him, 'If they despise the law of Moses and the preachings of the prophets, they will not believe, though one arose from death.' Those who neglect the easy commandments of the old law, how will they obey the sublime commandments of Christ's doctrine, who arose from death?

I pray you, my brethren, that ye be mindful of Lazarus's rest and of the rich man's punishment, and do as Christ himself taught, 'Gain to yourselves friends among God's poor, that they at your end may receive you into eternal dwelling-places.' Many Lazaruses ye have now lying at your gates, begging for your superfluity. Though they are esteemed as vile, they will, nevertheless, be hereafter your interceders with the Almighty. Verily we ought to enjoin the poor to pray for us, because they will be our protectors, who, now begging, desire sustenance of us. We should not despise their vileness, for Christ himself is served through reception of the poor, as he himself said, 'I was hungry, and ye fed me; I was thirsty, and ye gave me to drink; I was naked, and ye clothed me.'

Now says the holy Gregory, there was a reverend monk in the country of Lycaonia, very pious, his name was Martyrius. He went by order of his abbot to some other monastery, on his errand, when he found a leper lying by the way all chapped, and having no power of his feet: he said he wished to reach his hut, if he could. Then the monk was grieved for the helplessness of the leper, and he wrapt him in his cloak and bare him towards his monastery. Then it was disclosed to his abbot whom he was bearing, and he cried with a loud voice, and said, 'Run, run, and undo the gate of the monastery quickly, for our brother Martyrius bears Jesus on his back.' When the monk had reached the gate of the monastery, he who seemed a leper quitted his neck, and appeared in the likeness of Christ. The monk then looked up, and beheld how he ascended to heaven. Then said Jesus, while ascending, 'Martyrius, thou wast not ashamed of me on earth, nor will I be ashamed of thee in heaven.' Then the abbot hastened towards the monk, and eagerly said, 'My brother, where is he whom thou didst carry?' He said, 'If I had known who he was, I would have lain at his feet. When I bore him I felt no heaviness of any burthen.' How could he feel the heaviness of any weight, when he carried one who bore him? Now says the holy Gregory, Jesus verified the saying which he himself said, 'That which ye do for the poor in my name, that ye do for myself.'

What is there in human nature so glorious as the humanity of Christ, and what is esteemed more foul in human nature than the carcase of the leper, with tumours, and ulcers, and reeking stench? But he who is to be venerated above all creatures, vouchsafed to appear in that foul form, to the end that we might pity the misery of human beings, and according to our power comfort them, for love of the merciful and humble Jesus; that he may grant us a dwelling in his kingdom to eternal life, who rescued us from the devil's thraldom; who reigneth to eternity with the Almighty Father and the Holy Ghost, those three existing in one Godhead, without beginning and end, ever to eternity. Amen.

Anselm (1033–1109)

PROSLOGIUM, OR A DISCOURSE ON THE BEING OF GOD [1]

. . . This good thou art, thou, God the Father; this is thy Word, that is, thy Son. For nothing, other than what thou art, or greater or less than thou, can be in the Word by which thou dost express thyself; for thy Word is true, as thou art truthful. And hence it is truth itself, just as thou art; no other truth than thou; and thou art of so simple a nature, that of thee nothing can be born other than what thou art. This very good is the one love common to thee and to thy Son, that is, the Holy Spirit proceeding from both. For this love is not unequal to thee or to thy Son; seeing that thou dost love thyself and him, and he, thee, and himself, to the whole extent of thy being and his. Nor is there aught else proceeding from thee and from him, which is not unequal to thee and to him. Nor can anything proceed from the supreme simplicity, other than what this, from which it proceeds, is.

But what each is, separately, this is all the Trinity at once, Father, Son, and Holy Spirit; seeing that each separately is none other than the supremely simple unity, and the supremely unitary simplicity, which can neither be multiplied nor varied. Moreover, there is a single necessary Being. Now, this is that single, necessary Being, in which is every good; nay, which is every good, and a single entire good, and the only good.

And now, my soul, arouse and lift up all thy understanding, and conceive, so far as thou canst, of what character and how great is that good. For, if individual goods are delectable, conceive in earnestness how delectable is that good which contains the pleasantness of all goods; and not such as we have experienced in created objects, but as different as the Creator from the creature. For, if the created life is good, how good is the creative life! If the salvation given is delightful, how delightful is the salvation which has given all salvation! If wisdom in the knowledge of the created world is lovely, how lovely is the wisdom which has created all things from nothing! Finally, if there are many great delights in delectable things, what and how great is the delight in him who has made these delectable things!

Who shall enjoy this good? And what shall belong to him, and what shall not belong to him? At any rate, whatever he shall wish shall be his, and whatever he shall not wish shall not be his. For, these goods of body and soul will be such as eye hath not seen nor ear heard, neither has the heart of man conceived (Isaiah lxiv. 4; 1 Corinthians ii. 9).

Why, then, dost thou wander abroad, slight man, in thy search for the goods of thy soul and thy body? Love the one good in which are all goods, and it sufficeth. Desire the simple good which is every good, and it is enough. For, what dost thou love, my flesh? What dost thou desire, my soul? There, there is whatever ye love, whatever ye desire.

If beauty delights thee, there shall the righteous shine forth as the sun (Matthew xiii. 43). If swiftness or endurance, or freedom of body, which naught can withstand, delight thee, they shall be as angels of God,

[1] Translation by S. N. Deane (1903), by permission of the Open Court Publishing Co., Publishers.

— because it is sown a natural body; it is raised a spiritual body (1 Corinthians xv. 44) — in power certainly, though not in nature. If it is a long and sound life that pleases thee, there a healthful eternity is, and an eternal health. For the righteous shall live forever (Wisdom v. 15), and the salvation of the righteous is of the Lord (Psalms xxxvii. 39). If it is satisfaction of hunger, they shall be satisfied when the glory of the Lord hath appeared (Psalms xvii. 15). If it is quenching of thirst, they shall be abundantly satisfied with the fatness of thy house (Psalms xxxvi. 8). If it is melody, there the choirs of angels sing forever, before God. If it is any not impure, but pure, pleasure, thou shalt make them drink of the river of thy pleasures, O God (Psalms xxxvi. 8).

If it is wisdom that delights thee, the very wisdom of God will reveal itself to them. If friendship, they shall love God more than themselves, and one another as themselves. And God shall love them more than they themselves; for they love him, and themselves, and one another, through him, and he, himself and them, through himself. If concord, they shall all have a single will.

If power, they shall have all power to fulfil their will, as God to fulfil his. For, as God will have power to do what he wills, through himself, so they will have power, through him, to do what they will. For, as they will not will aught else than he, he shall will whatever they will; and what he shall will cannot fail to be. If honor and riches, God shall make his good and faithful servants rulers over many things (Luke xii. 42); nay, they shall be called sons of God, and gods; and where his Son shall be, there they shall be also, heirs indeed of God, and joint-heirs with Christ (Romans viii. 17).

If true security delights thee, undoubtedly they shall be as sure that those goods, or rather that good, will never and in no wise fail them; as they shall be sure that they will not lose it of their own accord; and that God, who loves them, will not take it away from those who love him against their will; and that nothing more powerful than God will separate him from them against his will and theirs.

But what, or how great, is the joy, where such and so great is the good! Heart of man, needy heart, heart acquainted with sorrows, nay, overwhelmed with sorrows, how greatly wouldst thou rejoice, if thou didst abound in all these things! Ask thy inmost mind whether it could contain its joy over so great a blessedness of its own.

Yet assuredly, if any other whom thou didst love altogether as thyself possessed the same blessedness, thy joy would be doubled, because thou wouldst rejoice not less for him than for thyself. But, if two, or three, or many more, had the same joy, thou wouldst rejoice as much for each one as for thyself, if thou didst love each as thyself. Hence, in that perfect love of innumerable blessed angels and sainted men, where none shall love another less than himself, every one shall rejoice for each of the others as for himself.

If, then, the heart of man will scarce contain his joy over his own so great good, how shall it contain so many and so great joys? And doubtless, seeing that every one loves another so far as he rejoices in the other's good, and as, in that perfect felicity, each one should love God beyond compare, more than himself and all the others with him; so he will rejoice beyond reckoning in the felicity of God, more than in his own and that of all the others with him.

But if they shall so love God with all their heart, and all their mind, and all their soul, that still all the heart, and all the mind, and all the soul shall not suffice for the worthiness of this love; doubtless they will so rejoice with all their hearts, and all their mind, and all their soul, that all the heart, and all the mind, and all the soul shall not suffice for the fulness of their joy.

My God and my Lord, my hope and the joy of my heart, speak unto my soul and tell me whether this is the joy of which thou tellest us through thy Son: Ask and ye shall receive, that your joy may be full (John xvi. 24). For I have found a joy that is full, and more than full. For when heart, and mind, and soul, and all the man, are full of that joy, joy beyond measure will still remain. Hence, not all of that joy shall enter into those who rejoice; but they who rejoice shall wholly enter into that joy.

Show me, O Lord, show thy servant in his heart whether this is the joy into which thy servants shall enter, who shall enter into the joy of their Lord. But that joy, surely, with which thy chosen ones shall rejoice, eye hath not seen nor ear heard, neither has it entered into the heart of man (Isaiah lxiv. 4; 1 Corinthians ii. 9). Not yet, then, have I told or conceived, O Lord, how greatly those blessed ones of thine shall rejoice. Doubtless they shall rejoice according as they shall love; and they shall love according as they shall know. How far they will know thee, Lord, then! and how much they will love thee! Truly, eye hath not seen, nor ear heard, neither has it entered into the heart of man in this life, how far they shall know thee, and how much they shall love thee in that life.

I pray, O God, to know thee, to love thee, that I may rejoice in thee. And if I cannot attain to full joy in this life, may I at least advance from day to day, until that joy shall come to the full. Let the knowledge of thee advance in me here, and there be made full. Let the love of thee increase, and there let it be full, that here my joy may be great in hope, and there full in truth. Lord, through thy Son thou dost command, nay, thou dost counsel us to ask; and thou dost promise that we shall receive, that our joy may be full. I ask, O Lord, as thou dost counsel through our wonderful Counsellor. I will receive what thou dost promise by virtue of thy truth, that my joy may be full. Faithful God, I ask. I will receive, that my joy may be full. Meanwhile, let my mind meditate upon it; let my tongue speak of it. Let my heart love it; let my mouth talk of it. Let my soul hunger for it; let my flesh thirst for it; let my whole being desire it, until I enter into thy joy, O Lord, who art the Three and the One God, blessed for ever and ever. Amen.

MIDDLE ENGLISH PERIOD

PARALLEL READINGS

Prose

1. *The Travels of Sir John Mandeville*
2. Malory — *Morte D'Arthur*

Drama

1. *The Play of Adam*
2. *Abraham and Isaac*
3. *Noah's Flood*
4. *The Second Shepherds' Play*
5. *Everyman*
6. Heywood — *The Four PP.*

MIDDLE ENGLISH PERIOD

ROMANCE AND BALLAD

After the Norman Conquest (1066) a great change took place in English society and literature. Among the outstanding features of the new social order were the establishment of Feudalism with its elaborate class distinctions, and of Chivalry with its emphasis upon courtly etiquette. At the top of the social ladder were the conquerors, who spoke and wrote in a dialect of French known as Anglo-Norman, and who, before their arrival in England, had become thoroughly embued with French culture. As a result the literature of England after 1066 was brought into closer touch than ever before with European culture; and consequently became more cosmopolitan in character.

From the Norman Conquest till the close of the Middle Ages the standards of culture and literature in England were largely French. Though Middle English, the descendant of Old English, more or less mixed with French, remained among the common people as a spoken language, writings regarded as important were generally composed in Anglo-Norman or in the more dignified Latin. Through Anglo-Norman or Latin the literature of England was enriched by numerous themes and ideas derived not only from classical antiquity but also from the Scandinavians and Celts. Since the literature of mediæval England is one of the great sources from which later writers, notably the poets and historical novelists of the eighteenth and nineteenth centuries, drew their inspiration, we cannot confine ourselves to strictly Middle English works if we are to appreciate fully the richness of the streams of tradition which poured into the great reservoir of mediæval literary culture.

The literary forms current in England during the Middle Ages were numerous. Among the most important were the romances of chivalry, ancestors of the modern novel, in which tales derived from classical or mediæval sources were retold in terms of chivalric society and with strong emphasis upon love and adventure. From the Breton, Welsh, or Irish Celts came wonder-tales of heroes, gods, and fairies, which furnished plots for short narrative poems known as Breton Lays and for a great body of romance dealing with exploits of King Arthur and the Knights of the Round Table. In Geoffrey of Monmouth's Latin *History of the Kings of Britain* Arthur appeared for the first time as a great king surrounded by a brilliant court where Anglo-Norman chivalry and courtly love replaced the barbaric manners of the ancient Celts. In Layamon's *Brut* the Arthurian story was adopted as the national epic of the English people. In the numerous Arthurian romances in prose or verse, the wistful charm of ancient Celtic literature is seen only through the eyes of the practical, courtly Norman. Other romances deal with themes derived from Oriental, Classical, or Scandinavian tradition.

The remaining types of mediæval literature include the drama (which grew out of the church service and dealt with Bible stories and saints' lives), satires on the abuses of society or the church (e.g., *Piers Plowman*), chronicles (from which we get many historical facts and an occasional glimpse of real life in a monastery), vast encyclopedias (which attempted to fit all knowledge sacred and secular into the framework of mediæval science and philosophy), a large body of lyric poems in Latin, French, or English (many of which reveal a keen enjoyment of life), and numerous ballads recording in simple language tales of popular heroes, of superstition, or of tragedy, which had impressed themselves upon the imagination of the common people.

Near the end of the Middle Ages Chaucer, with keen humor and inimitable genius, painted in his *Canterbury Tales* an unforgettable picture of fourteenth-century society and transmitted to posterity much of what was best in the literature of the Middle Ages.

WRITINGS IN CELTIC, FRENCH, AND LATIN

Irish

THE FEAST OF BRICRIU *

THE CHAMPION'S BARGAIN

Once upon a time as the Ulstermen were in Emain, fatigued after the gathering and the games, Conchobar and Fergus mac Roig, with Ulster's nobles as well, proceeded from the sporting field outside and seated themselves in the Royal Court (*lit.* Red Branch) of Conchobar. Neither Cuchulainn nor Conall the Victorious nor Loegaire the Triumphant were there that night. But the hosts of Ulster's valiant heroes were there. As they were seated, it being eventide, and the day drawing towards the close, they saw a bachlach (big uncouth fellow) of exceeding ugliness drawing nigh them into the hall. To them it seemed as if none of the Ulstermen would reach half his height. Horrible and ugly was the carle's guise. Next his skin he wore an old hide with a dark dun mantle around him, and over him a great spreading club-tree (branch) the size of a winter-shed under which thirty bullocks could find shelter. Ravenous yellow eyes he had, protruding from his head, each of the two the size of an ox-vat. Each finger as thick as another person's wrist. In his left hand a stick, a burden for twenty yoke of oxen. In his right hand an axe weighing thrice fifty glowing molten masses [of metal]. Its handle would require a plough-team (a yoke of six) to move it. Its sharpness such that it would lop off hairs, the wind blowing them against its edge.

In that guise he went and stood by the fork-beam beside the fire. 'Is the hall lacking in room for you,' quoth Duach of the Chafer Tongue to the uncouth clodhopper, 'that you find no other place than by the fork-beam, unless you wish to be domestic luminary? — only sooner will a blaze be to the house than brightness to the household.' 'What property soever may be mine, sooth you will agree, no matter how big I am, that the household as a whole will be enlightened, while the hall will not be burnt.

'That, however, is not my sole function; I have others as well. But neither in Erin nor in Alba nor in Europe nor in Africa nor in Asia, with Greece, Scythia, the Orkney Islands, the Pillars of Hercules, Bregon's Tower (Brigantium), and the Isles of Gades have I found the quest on which I have come, nor a man to do me fairplay regarding it. Since you Ulstermen have excelled all the folks of those lands in strength, prowess, valor; in rank, magnanimity, dignity; in truth, generosity and worth, get one among you to give me the boon I crave.'

'In sooth it is not just that the honor of a province be carried off,' quoth Fergus mac Roig, 'because of one man who fails in keeping his word of honor. Death, certainly, is not a whit nearer to him than to you.' 'Not that I shun it,' quoth he. 'Make thy quest known to us then,' quoth Fergus mac Roig. 'If but fairplay be vouchsafed me, I will tell it.' 'It is right to give fairplay,' quoth Sencha, son of Ailill, 'for it beseemeth not a great clannish folk to break a mutual covenant over any unknown individual. To us too it seems likely, if at long last you find such a person, you will find here one worthy of you.' 'Conchobar I put aside,' quoth he, 'for sake of his sovranty, and Fergus mac Roig also on account of his like privilege. These two excepted, come whosoever of you that may venture, that I may cut off his head to-night, he mine to-morrow night.'

'Sure then there is no warrior here,' quoth Duach, 'after these two.' 'By my troth there will be this moment,' quoth Munremar, son of Gercenn, as he sprang on to the floor of the hall. The strength then of that Munremar was as the strength of a hundred warriors, each arm having the might of a hundred 'centaurs.' 'Bend down, bachlach,' quoth Munremar, 'that I may cut your head off to-night, you to cut off mine to-morrow night.' 'Were that my quest, I could have got it anywhere,' quoth the bachlach. 'Let us act according to our covenant,' he quoth, 'I to cut off your head to-night, you to avenge it to-morrow night.' 'By my people's god,' quoth Duach of the Chafer

* Based on translation by George Henderson, Irish Texts Society, 1899. By permission of the Secretary.

Tongue, 'death is thus for thee no pleasant prospect should the man killed to-night attack thee on the morrow. It is given to you alone if you have the power, being killed night after night to avenge it next day.' 'Truly I will carry out what you all as a body agree upon by way of counsel, strange as it may seem to you,' quoth the bachlach. He then pledged the other to keep his troth in this contention as to fulfilling his tryst on the morrow.

With that Munremar took the axe from out of the bachlach's hand. Seven feet apart were its two angles. Then did the bachlach put his neck across the block. Munremar dealt a blow across it with the axe till it stuck in the block underneath, cutting off the head till it lay by the base of the fork-beam, the house being filled with the blood. Straightway the bachlach rose, recovered himself, clasped his head, block and axe to his breast, thus made his exit from the hall with blood streaming from his neck. It filled the Red Branch on every side. Great was the folk's horror, wondering at the marvel that had appeared to them. 'By my people's god,' quoth Duach of the Chafer Tongue, 'if the bachlach, having been killed to-night, come back to-morrow, he will not leave a man alive in Ulster.' The following night, however, he returned, and Munremar shirked him. Then began the bachlach to urge his pact with Munremar. 'Sooth it is not right for Munremar not to fulfil his covenant with me.'

That night, however, Loegaire the Triumphant was present. 'Who of the warriors that contest Ulster's Champion's Portion will carry out a bargain to-night with me? Where is Loegaire the Triumphant?' quoth he. 'Here,' said Loegaire. He pledged him too, yet Loegaire kept not his tryst. The bachlach returned on the morrow and similarly pledged Conall Cernach, who came not as he had sworn.

The fourth night the bachlach returned, and fierce and furious was he. All the ladies of Ulster came that night to see the strange marvel that had come into the Red Branch. That night Cuchulainn was there also. Then the fellow began to upbraid them. 'Ye men of Ulster, your valour and your prowess are gone. Your warriors greatly covet the Champion's Portion, yet are unable to contest it. Where is yon poor mad fellow that is called Cuchulainn? Fain would I know if *his* word be better than the others.' 'No covenant do I desire with you,' quoth Cuchulainn. 'Likely is that, you wretched fly; greatly dost thou fear to die.' Whereupon Cuchulainn sprang towards him and dealt him a blow with the axe, hurling his head to the top rafter of the Red Branch till the whole hall shook. Cuchulainn again caught up the head and gave it a blow with the axe and smashed it. Thereafter the bachlach rose up.

On the morrow the Ulstermen were watching Cuchulainn to see whether he would shirk the bachlach as the other heroes had done. As Cuchulainn was awaiting the bachlach, they saw that great dejection seized him. It had been fitting had they sung his dirge. They felt sure his life would last only till the bachlach came. Then said Cuchulainn with shame to Conchobar: 'Thou shall not go until my pledge to the bachlach is fulfilled; for death awaits me, and I would rather have death with honor.'

They were there as the day was closing when they saw the bachlach approaching. 'Where is Cuchulainn?' he quoth. 'Here am I,' he answered. 'You're dull of speech to-night, unhappy one; greatly you fear to die. Yet, though great your fear, death you have not shirked.' Thereafter Cuchulainn went up to him and stretched his neck across the block, which was of such size that his neck reached but half-way. 'Stretch out your neck, you wretch,' said the bachlach. 'You keep me in torment,' quoth Cuchulainn. 'Despatch me quickly; last night, by my troth, I tormented you not. Verily I swear if you torment me, I shall make myself as long as a crane above you.' 'I cannot slay you,' quoth the bachlach, 'what with the size of the block and the shortness of your neck and of your side.'

Then Cuchulainn stretched out his neck so that a warrior's full-grown foot would have fitted between any two of his ribs; his neck he distended till it reached the other side of the block. The bachlach raised his axe till it reached the roof-tree of the hall. The creaking of the old hide that was about the fellow and the crashing of the axe — both his arms being raised aloft with all his might — were as the loud noise of a wood tempest-tossed in a night of storm. Down it came then . . . on his neck, its blunt side below; all the nobles of Ulster were gazing upon them.

'O Cuchulainn, arise! . . . Of the warriors of Ulster and Erin, no matter what their mettle, none is found to be compared with thee in valor, bravery and truthfulness. The sovranty of the heroes of Erin to thee from this hour forth and the Champion's Portion undisputed, and to thy lady the precedence always of the ladies of Ulster in the Mead Hall. And whosoever shall lay wager against thee from now, as my folks swear I swear, while on life he will be in [sore danger].' Then the bachlach vanished.

9th c.?

CONNLA OF THE GOLDEN HAIR, AND THE FAIRY MAIDEN *

One day as Connla of the Golden Hair, son of Conn the Hundred-fighter, stood with his father on the royal Hill of Usna, he saw approaching a woman dressed in wonderful attire. "Whence comest thou, maiden," asked the prince.

The lady replied, 'I have come from the Land of the Living — a land where there is neither death nor sin. We pass our time pleasantly in feasting and harmless amusements; and we have no quarrels or contentions. We live in great peace (*sīd*); therefore we are called Side (Fairy-folk).'

'Who is this thou art talking to, my son?' said the king, for no one but Connla saw the woman.

She answered for the youth, 'Connla is speaking with a lovely, nobleborn maiden, who will never die, and who will never grow old. I love Connla of the Golden Hair, and I have come to bring him with me to Moy-mell, the plain of pleasure, where King Boadag rules for ever; his land knows neither grief nor woe. Come with me, O Connla of the ruddy cheek, the fair, freckled neck, and the blond hair! Come with me, and thou shalt retain the youth and beauty of thy form, free from the wrinkles of old age.

'Thy flowing golden hair, thy comely face,
Thy tall majestic form of peerless grace,
That show thee sprung from Conn's exalted
race.'

King Conn the Hundred-fighter, being much troubled, called then on his druid, Coran, to put forth his power against the witchery of the fairy woman —

'O Coran of the mystic arts and of the mighty incantations, here is a contest such as I have never been engaged in since I have been ruler — a contest with an invisible being. The witch-charms of a woman are taking away my son.

Then the druid sang a charm against the voice of the woman, so that no one, including the young prince heard her, and she disappeared.

As she was going away she gave an apple to Connla. Connla remained for a whole month without tasting food or drink, except the apple. And though he ate of it, it was never lessened, but remained whole. Moreover, in comparison with his apple he did not deem any other food worthy to be tasted. A longing seized him for the fairy-woman whom he had seen.

At the end of the month, Connla stood by his father's side on the Plain of Arcomin [on the seacoast], and he saw the same lady approaching. Then said she to him —

'A glorious seat, indeed, has Connla among wretched, short-lived mortals, awaiting dreadful death! But now, the ever-youthful people of Moy-mell, who never feel old age, seeing thee day by day among thy friends, in the assemblies of thy native land, invite thee to their land. A hero seemest thou to them!

When the king heard the words of the maiden, he said to his people —

'Bring my druid, Coran, to me; for I see that the fairy woman has this day regained the power of her voice.'

At this the lady said, 'O Conn, fighter of a hundred battles, put not your faith in the art of the druid. A just one with many noble attendants shall tread the wide strand. Full soon his law shall reach thee and shall break the druidic charms before the eyes of that black sorcerer the devil.'

Now Conn wondered that, as soon as the

* The verse is by P. W. Joyce, *Old Celtic Romances*, David Nutt, 1894.

woman had appeared Connla addressed no one else.

'Connla, my son,' asked the king, 'has thy mind been moved by the words of the lady?'

Connla replied, 'Father, I am troubled; though I love my people beyond all, yet I am filled with longing on account of this lady!'

Then sang the woman —

I

'A land of youth, a land of rest,
A land from sorrow free;
It lies far off in the golden west,
On the verge of the azure sea.
A swift canoe of crystal bright,
That never met mortal view —
We shall reach the land ere fall of night,
In that strong and swift canoe:
We shall reach the strand
Of that sunny land,
From druids and demons free;
The land of rest,
In the golden west,
On the verge of the azure sea!

II

'A pleasant land of winding vales, bright streams, and verdurous plains,
Where summer all the live-long year, in changeless splendor reigns;
A peaceful land of calm delight, of everlasting bloom;
Old age and death we never know, no sickness, care, or gloom;
The land of youth,
Of love and truth,
From pain and sorrow free;
The land of rest,
In the golden west,
On the verge of the azure sea!

III

'There are strange delights for mortal men in that island of the west;
The sun comes down each evening in its lovely vales to rest:
And though far and dim
On the ocean's rim
It seems to mortal view,
We shall reach its halls
Ere the evening falls,
In my strong and swift canoe:
And ever more
That verdant shore
Our happy home shall be;
The land of rest,
In the golden west,
On the verge of the azure sea.

IV

'It will guard thee, gentle Connla of the flowing golden hair,
It will guard thee from the druids, from the demons of the air;
My crystal boat will guard thee, till we reach that western shore,
Where thou and I in joy and love shall live for evermore:
From the druid's incantation,
From his black and deadly snare,
From the withering imprecation
Of the demon of the air,
It will guard thee, gentle Connla of the flowing golden hair:
My crystal boat will guard thee, till we reach that silver strand
Where thou shalt reign in endless joy, the king of the Fairy-land!'

When the maiden had ended her song, Connla sprang away from his father's side and into the glass boat, the gleaming, straight-gliding, strong curragh. The king and his people saw them in the distance, as far off as the eye could reach. The lovers fared forth across the sea and were never more seen; and no one can tell whither they went.

9th c.?

OSSIAN

Oisin mac Finn cecinit (Oisin, son of Finn, sang):*

'My hands have been withered,
My deeds have been quelled;
The tide has come, it has reached the shore
And has drowned my strength.

'I give thanks to the Creator;
I have found solace with great joy.
Long is my day in a wretched life:
There was a time when it was delightful with me.

'I was the beauty of the assembly,
I found stealthy women ready to yield.
Not loath am I to leave the world,
Gone is my sportive course.'

12th c.

* Revision of translation by K. Meyer, Royal Irish Acad., Todd Lect. Ser. XVI, p. xxviii.

'Once I had yellow, curly hair,
Now there grows on my head only a short gray crop.

I would like hair of the raven's color
Growing on my head rather than a short gray crop.

'Courting belongs not to me, for I deceive no women;
To-night my hair is hoar, it will not be as once it was.'

14th or 15th c.

Welsh

THE MABINOGION

PWYLL PRINCE OF DYVED

Once upon a time, Pwyll was at Narberth his chief palace, where a feast had been prepared for him, and with him was a great host of men. And after the first meal, Pwyll arose to walk, and he went to the top of a mound that was above the palace, and was called Gorsedd Arberth. 'Lord,' said one of the Court, 'it is peculiar to the mound that whosoever sits upon it cannot go thence, without either receiving wounds or blows, or else seeing a wonder.' 'I fear not to receive wounds and blows in the midst of such a host as this, but as to the wonder, gladly would I see it. I will go therefore and sit upon the mound.'

And upon the mound he sat. And while he sat there, they saw a lady, on a pure white horse of large size, with a garment of shining gold around her, coming along the highway that led from the mound; and the horse seemed to move at a slow and even pace, and to be coming up towards the mound. 'My men,' said Pwyll, 'is there any among you who knows yonder lady?' 'There is not, Lord,' said they. 'Go one of you and meet her, that we may know who she is.' And one of them arose, and as he came upon the road to meet her, she passed by, and he followed as fast as he could, being on foot; and the greater was his speed, the further was she from him. And when he saw that it profited him nothing to follow her, he returned to Pwyll, and said unto him, 'Lord, it is idle for any one in the world to follow her on foot.' 'Verily,' said Pwyll, 'go unto the palace, and take the fleetest horse that thou seest, and go after her.'

And he took a horse and went forward. And he came to an open level plain, and put spurs to his horse; and the more he urged his horse, the further was she from him. Yet she held the same pace as at first. And his horse began to fail; and when his horse's feet failed him, he returned to the place where Pwyll was. 'Lord,' said he, 'it will avail nothing for any one to follow yonder lady. I know of no horse in these realms swifter than this, and it availed me not to pursue her.' 'Of a truth,' said Pwyll, 'there must be some illusion here. Let us go towards the palace.' So to the palace they went, and they spent that day. And the next day they arose, and that also they spent until it was time to go to meat. And after the first meal, 'Verily,' said Pwyll, 'we will go the same party as yesterday to the top of the mound. And do thou,' said he to one of his young men, 'take the swiftest horse that thou knowest in the field.' And thus did the young man. And they went towards the mound, taking the horse with them. And as they were sitting down they beheld the lady on the same horse, and in the same apparel, coming along the same road. 'Behold,' said Pwyll, 'here is the lady of yesterday. Make ready, youth, to learn who she is.' 'My lord,' said he, 'that will I gladly do.' And thereupon the lady came opposite to them. So the youth mounted his horse; and before he had settled himself in his saddle, she passed by, and there was a clear space between them. But her speed was no greater than it had been the day before. Then he put his horse into an amble, and thought that notwithstanding the gentle pace at which his horse went, he should soon overtake her. But this availed him not; so he gave his horse the reins. And still he came no nearer to her than when he went at a foot's pace. And the more he urged his horse, the further was she from him. Yet she rode not faster than before. When he saw that it availed not to follow her, he returned to the place where Pwyll was. 'Lord,' said he, "the horse can no more than thou hast seen.' 'I see indeed that it avails not that any one should follow her. And by Heaven,' said he, 'she must needs have an errand to some one in this plain, if her haste would allow her to declare it. Let us go back to the palace.' And to the palace they went, and they spent that night in songs and feasting, as it pleased them.

And the next day they amused themselves until it was time to go to meat. And when meat was ended, Pwyll said, 'Where are the hosts that went yesterday and the day before to the top of the mound?' 'Behold, Lord, we are here,' said they. 'Let us go,' said he, 'to the mound, to sit there. And do thou,' said he to the page who tended his horse, 'saddle my horse well, and hasten with him to the road, and bring also my spurs with thee.' And the youth did thus. And they went and sat upon the mound; and ere they had been there but a short time, they beheld the lady coming by the same road, and in the same manner, and at the same pace. 'Young man,' said Pwyll, 'I see the lady coming; give me my horse.' And no sooner had he mounted his horse than she passed him. And he turned after her and followed her. And he let his horse go bounding playfully, and thought that at the second step or the third he should come up with her. But he came no nearer to her than at first. Then he urged his horse to his utmost speed, yet he found that it availed nothing to follow her. Then said Pwyll, 'O maiden, for the sake of him whom thou best lovest, stay for me.' 'I will stay gladly,' said she, 'and it were better for thy horse hadst thou asked it long since.' So the maiden stopped, and she threw back that part of her headdress which covered her face. And she fixed her eyes upon him, and began to talk with him. 'Lady,' asked he, 'whence comest thou, and whereunto dost thou journey?' 'I journey on mine own errand,' said she, 'and right glad am I to see thee.' 'My greeting be unto thee,' said he. Then he thought that the beauty of all the maidens, and all the ladies that he had ever seen, was as nothing compared to her beauty. 'Lady,' he said, 'wilt thou tell me aught concerning thy purpose?' 'I will tell thee,' said she. 'My chief quest was to seek thee.' 'Behold,' said Pwyll, 'this is to me the most pleasing quest on which thou couldst have come; and wilt thou tell me who thou art?' 'I will tell thee, Lord,' said she. 'I am Rhiannon, the daughter of Heveydd Hên, and they sought to give me to a husband against my will. But no husband would I have, and that because of my love for thee, neither will I yet have one unless thou reject me. And hither have I come to hear thy answer.' 'By Heaven,' said Pwyll, 'behold this is my answer. If I might choose among all the ladies and damsels in the world, thee would I choose.' 'Verily,' said she, 'if thou art thus minded, make a pledge to meet me ere I am given to another.' 'The sooner I may do so, the more pleasing will it be unto me,' said Pwyll, 'and wheresoever thou wilt, there will I meet with thee.' 'I will that thou meet me this day twelvemonth at the palace of Heveydd. And I will cause a feast to be prepared, so that it be ready against thou come.' 'Gladly,' said he, 'will I keep this tryst.' 'Lord,' said she, 'remain in health, and be mindful that thou keep thy promise; and now I will go hence.' So they parted, and he went back to his hosts and to them of his household. And whatsoever questions they asked him respecting the damsel, he always turned the discourse upon other matters. And when a year from that time was gone, he caused a hundred knights to equip themselves and to go with him to the palace of Heveydd Hên. And he came to the palace, and there was great joy concerning him, with much concourse of people and great rejoicing, and vast preparations for his coming. And the whole Court was placed under his orders.

And the hall was garnished and they went to meat, and thus did they sit; Heveydd Hên was on one side of Pwyll, and Rhiannon on the other. And all the rest according to their rank. And they ate and feasted and talked one with another, and at the beginning of the carousal after the meat, there entered a tall auburn-haired youth, of royal bearing, clothed in a garment of satin. And when he came into the hall, he saluted Pwyll and his companions. 'The greeting of Heaven be unto thee, my soul,' said Pwyll, 'come thou and sit down.' 'Nay,' said he, 'a suitor am I, and I will do mine errand.' 'Do so willingly,' said Pwyll. 'Lord,' said he, 'my errand is unto thee, and it is to crave a boon of thee that I come.' 'What boon soever thou mayest ask of me, as far as I am able, thou shalt have.' 'Ah,' said Rhiannon, 'wherefore didst thou give that answer?' 'Has he not given it before the presence of these nobles?' asked the youth. 'My soul,' said Pwyll, 'what is the boon thou askest?' 'The lady whom best I love is to be thy bride this night; I come to ask her of thee, with the feast and the banquet that are in this place.' And Pwyll was silent because of the answer which he had given. 'Be silent as long as thou wilt,' said Rhiannon. 'Never did man make worse use of his wits than thou hast done.' 'Lady,' said he, 'I knew not who he was.' 'Behold this is the man to whom they would have given me against my will,' said she. 'And he is Gwawl the son of Clud, a man of great power and wealth, and because of the word thou hast spoken, bestow me upon him lest shame befall thee.' 'Lady,' said he, 'I understand not thine answer. Never can I do as thou sayest.' 'Bestow me upon him,' said she [secretly], 'and I will cause that I shall never be his.' 'By what means will that be?' asked Pwyll. 'In thy hand will I give thee a small bag,' said she. 'See that thou keep it well, and he will ask of thee the banquet, and the feast, and the preparations which are not in thy power. Unto the hosts and the household will I give the feast. And such will be thy answer respecting this. And as concerns myself, I will engage to become his bride this night twelvemonth. And at the end of the year be thou here,' said she, 'and bring this bag with thee, and let thy hundred knights be in the orchard up yonder. And when he is in the midst of joy and feasting, come thou in by thyself, clad in ragged garments, and holding thy bag in thy hand, and ask nothing but a bagful of food, and I will cause that if all the meat and liquor that are in these seven Cantrevs were put into it, it would be no fuller than before. And after a great deal has been put therein, he will ask thee whether thy bag will ever be full. Say thou then that it never will, until a man of noble birth and of great wealth arise and press the food in the bag with both his feet, saying, "Enough has been put therein"; and I will cause him to go and tread down the food in the bag, and when he does so, turn thou the bag, so that he shall be up over his head in it, and then slip a knot upon the thongs of the bag. Let there be also a good bugle horn about thy neck, and as soon as thou hast bound him in the bag, wind thy horn, and let it be a signal between thee and thy knights. And when they hear the sound of the horn, let them come down upon the palace.' 'Lord,' said Gwawl, 'it is meet that I have an answer to my request.' 'As much of that thou hast asked as it is in my power to give, thou shalt have,' replied Pwyll. 'My soul,' said Rhiannon unto him, 'as for the feast and the banquet that are here, I have bestowed them upon the men of Dyved, and the household, and the warriors that are with us. These can I not suffer to be given to any. In a year from to-night a banquet shall be prepared for thee in this palace, that I may become thy bride.'

So Gwawl went forth to his possessions, and Pwyll went also back to Dyved. And they both spent that year until it was the time for the feast at the palace of Heveydd Hên. Then Gwawl the son of Clud set out to the feast that was prepared for him, and he came to the palace, and was received there with rejoicing. Pwyll, also, came to the orchard with his hundred knights, as Rhiannon had commanded him, having the bag with him. And Pwyll was clad in coarse and ragged garments, and wore large clumsy old shoes upon his feet. And when he knew that the carousal after the meat had begun, he went towards the hall, and when he came into the hall, he saluted Gwawl the son of Clud, and his company, both men and women. 'Heaven prosper thee,' said Gwawl, 'and the greeting of Heaven be unto thee.' 'Lord,' said he, 'may Heaven reward thee, I have an errand unto thee.' 'Welcome be thine errand, and if thou ask of me that which is just, thou shalt have it gladly.' 'It is fitting,' answered he. 'I crave but from want, and the boon that I ask is to have this small bag that thou seest filled with meat.' 'A request within reason is this,' said he, 'and gladly shalt thou have it. Bring him food.' A great number of attendants arose and began to fill the bag, but for all that they put into it, it was no fuller than at first.

'My soul,' said Gwawl, 'will thy bag be ever full?' 'It will not, I declare to Heaven,' said he, 'for all that may be put into it, unless one possessed of lands, and domains, and treasure, shall arise and tread down with both his feet the food that is within the bag, and shall say, "Enough has been put therein."' Then said Rhiannon unto Gwawl the son of Clud, 'Rise up quickly.' 'I will willingly arise,' said he. So he rose up, and put his two feet into the bag. And Pwyll turned up the sides of the bag, so that Gwawl was over his head in it. And he shut it up quickly and slipped a knot upon the thongs, and blew his horn. And thereupon behold his household came down upon the palace. And they seized all the host that had come with Gwawl, and cast them into his own prison. And Pwyll threw off his rags, and his old shoes, and his tattered array; and as they came in, every one of Pwyll's knights struck a blow upon the bag, and asked, 'What is here?' 'A Badger,' said they. And in this manner they played, each of them striking the bag, either with his foot or with a staff. And thus played they with the bag. Every one as he came in asked, 'What game are you playing at thus?' 'The game of Badger in the Bag,' said they. And then was the game of Badger in the Bag first played.

'Lord,' said the man in the bag, 'if thou wouldest but hear me, I merit not to be slain in a bag.' Said Heveydd Hên, 'Lord, he speaks truth. It were fitting that thou listen to him, for he deserves not this.' 'Verily,' said Pwyll, 'I will do thy counsel concerning him.' 'Behold this is my counsel then,' said Rhiannon; 'thou art now in a position in which it behoves thee to satisfy suitors and minstrels; let him give unto them in thy stead, and take a pledge from him that he will never seek to revenge that which has been done to him. And this will be punishment enough.' 'I will do this gladly,' said the man in the bag. 'And gladly will I accept it,' said Pwyll, 'since it is the counsel of Heveydd and Rhiannon.' 'Such then is our counsel,' answered they. 'I accept it,' said Pwyll. 'Seek thyself sureties.' 'We will be for him,' said Heveydd, 'until his men be free to answer for him.' And upon this he was let out of the bag, and his liegemen were liberated. 'Demand now of Gwawl his sureties,' said Heveydd, 'we know which should be taken for him.' And Heveydd numbered the sureties. Said Gwawl, 'Do thou thyself draw up the covenant.' 'It will suffice me that it be as Rhiannon said,' answered Pwyll. So unto that covenant were the sureties pledged. 'Verily, Lord,' said Gwawl, 'I am greatly hurt, and I have many bruises. I have need to be anointed; with thy leave I will go forth. I will leave nobles in my stead, to answer for me in all that thou shalt require.' 'Willingly,' said Pwyll, 'mayest thou do thus.' So Gwawl went towards his own possessions.

And the hall was set in order for Pwyll and the men of his host, and for them also of the palace, and they went to the tables and sat down. And as they had sat that time twelvemonth, so sat they that night. And they ate, and feasted, and spent the night in mirth and tranquillity. And the time came that they should sleep, and Pwyll and Rhiannon went to their chamber.

And next morning at the break of day, 'My Lord,' said Rhiannon, 'arise and begin to give thy gifts unto the minstrels. Refuse no one to-day that may claim thy bounty.' 'Thus shall it be gladly,' said Pwyll, 'both to-day and every day while the feast shall last.' So Pwyll arose, and he caused silence to be proclaimed, and desired all the suitors and the minstrels to show and to point out what gifts were to their wish and desire. And this being done, the feast went on, and he denied no one while it lasted. And when the feast was ended, Pwyll said unto Heveydd, 'My Lord, with thy permission I will set out for Dyved to-morrow.' 'Certainly,' said Heveydd, 'may Heaven prosper thee. Fix also a time when Rhiannon may follow thee.' 'By Heaven,' said Pwyll, 'we will go hence together.' 'Willest thou this, Lord?' said Heveydd. 'Yes, by Heaven,' answered Pwyll.

And the next day, they set forward towards Dyved, and journeyed to the palace of Narberth, where a feast was made ready for them. And there came to them great numbers of the chief men and the most noble ladies of the land, and of these there was none to whom Rhiannon did not give some rich gift, either a bracelet, or a ring, or a precious stone. And they ruled the land prosperously both that year and the next.

And in the third year the nobles of the land began to be sorrowful at seeing a man whom they loved so much, and who was moreover their lord and their foster-brother, without an heir. And they came to him. And the place where they met was Preseleu, in Dyved. 'Lord,' said they, 'we know that thou art not so young as some of the men of this country, and we fear that thou mayest not have an heir of the wife whom thou hast taken. Take therefore another wife of whom thou mayest have heirs. Thou canst not always continue with us, and though thou desire to remain as thou art, we will not suffer thee.' 'Truly,' said Pwyll, 'we have not long been joined together, and many things may yet befall. Grant me a year from this time, and for the space of a year we will abide together, and after that I will do according to your wishes.' So they granted it. And before the end of a year a son was born unto him. And in Narberth was he born; and on the night that he was born, women were brought to watch the mother and the boy. And the women slept, as did also Rhiannon, the mother of the boy. And the number of the women that were brought into the chamber was six. And they watched for a good portion of the night, and before midnight every one of them fell asleep, and towards break of day they awoke; and when they awoke, they looked where they had put the boy, and behold he was not there. 'Oh,' said one of the women, 'the boy is lost!' 'Yes,' said another, 'and it will be small vengeance if we are burnt or put to death because of the child.' Said one of the women, 'Is there any counsel for us in the world in this matter?' 'There is,' answered another, 'I offer you good counsel.' 'What is that?' asked they. 'There is here a stag-hound bitch, and she has a litter of whelps. Let us kill some of the cubs, and rub the blood on the face and hands of Rhiannon, and lay the bones before her, and assert that she herself hath devoured her son, and she alone will not be able to gainsay us six.' And according to this counsel it was settled. And towards morning Rhiannon awoke, and she said, 'Women, where is my son?' 'Lady,' said they, 'ask us not concerning thy son, we have nought but the blows and the bruises we got by struggling with thee, and of a truth we never saw any woman so violent as thou, for it was of no avail to contend with thee. Hast thou not thyself devoured thy son? Claim him not therefore of us.' 'For pity's sake,' said Rhiannon; 'the Lord God knows all things. Charge me not falsely. If you tell me this from fear, I assert before Heaven that I will defend you.' 'Truly,' said they, 'we would not bring evil on ourselves for any one in the world.' 'For pity's sake,' said Rhiannon, 'you will receive no evil by telling the truth.' But for all her words, whether fair or harsh, she received but the same answer from the women.

And Pwyll the chief of Dyved arose, and his household, and his hosts. And this occurrence could not be concealed, but the story went forth throughout the land, and all the nobles heard it. Then the nobles came to Pwyll, and besought him to put away his wife, because of the great crime which she had done. But Pwyll answered them, that they had no cause wherefore they might ask him to put away his wife, save for her having no children. 'But children has she now had, therefore will I not put her away; if she has done wrong, let her do penance for it.'

So Rhiannon sent for the teachers and the wise men, and as she preferred doing penance to contending with the women, she took upon her a penance. And the penance that was imposed upon her was, that she should remain in that palace of Narberth until the end of seven years, and that she should sit every day near unto a horse-block that was without the gate. And that she should relate the story to all who should come there, whom she might suppose not to know it already; and that she should offer the guests and strangers, if they would permit her, to carry them upon her back into the palace. But it rarely happened that any would permit. And thus did she spend part of the year.

Now at that time Teirnyon Twryv Vliant was Lord of Gwent Is Coed, and he was the best man in the world. And unto his house there belonged a mare, than which neither mare nor horse in the kingdom was more beautiful. And on the night of every first of May she foaled, and no one ever knew what became of the colt. And one night Teirnyon talked with his wife: 'Wife,' said he, 'it is very simple of us that our mare should foal every year, and that we should have none of her colts.' 'What can be done in the matter?' said she. 'This is the night of the first of May,' said he. 'The vengeance of Heaven be upon me, if I learn not what it is that takes away the colts.' So he caused the mare to be brought into a house, and he armed himself, and began to watch that night. And in the beginning of the night, the mare foaled a large and beautiful colt. And it was standing up in the place. And Teirnyon rose up and looked at the size of the colt, and as he did so he heard a great tumult, and after the tumult behold a claw came through the window into the house, and it seized the colt by the mane. Then Teirnyon drew his sword, and struck off the arm at the elbow, so that portion of the arm together with the colt was in the house with him. And then did he hear a tumult and wailing, both at once. And he opened the door, and rushed out in the direction of the noise, and he could not see the cause of the tumult because of the darkness of the night, but he rushed after it and followed it. Then he remembered that he had left the door open, and he returned. And at the door behold there was an infant boy in swaddling-clothes, wrapped around in a mantle of satin. And he took up the boy, and behold he was very strong for the age that he was.

Then he shut the door, and went into the chamber where his wife was. 'Lady,' said he, 'art thou sleeping?' 'No, lord,' said she, 'I was asleep, but as thou camest in I did awake.' 'Behold, here is a boy for thee if thou wilt,' said he, 'since thou hast never had one.' 'My lord,' said she, 'what adventure is this?' 'It was thus,' said Teirnyon; and he told her how it all befell. 'Verily, lord,' said she, 'what sort of garments are there upon the boy?' 'A mantle of satin,' said he. 'He is then a boy of gentle lineage,' she replied. 'My lord,' she said, 'if thou wilt, I shall have great diversion and mirth. I will call my women unto me, and tell them that I have been pregnant.' 'I will readily grant thee to do this,' he answered. And thus did they, and they caused the boy to be baptized, and the ceremony was performed there; and the name which they gave unto him was Gwri Wallt Euryn, because what hair was upon his head was as yellow as gold. And they had the boy nursed in the Court until he was a year old. And before the year was over he could walk stoutly. And he was larger than a boy of three years old, even one of great growth and size. And the boy was nursed the second year, and then he was as large as a child six years old. And before the end of the fourth year, he would bribe the grooms to allow him to take the horses to water. 'My lord,' said his wife unto Teirnyon, 'where is the colt which thou didst save on the night that thou didst find the boy?' 'I have commanded the grooms of the horses,' said he, 'that they take care of him.' 'Would it not be well, lord,' said she, 'if thou wert to cause him to be broken in, and given to the boy, seeing that on the same night that thou didst find the boy, the colt was foaled and thou didst save him?' 'I will not oppose thee in this matter,' said Teirnyon. 'I will allow thee to give him the colt.' 'Lord,' said she, 'may Heaven reward thee; I will give it him.' So the horse was given to the boy. Then she went to the grooms and those who tended the horses, and commanded them to be careful of the horse, so that he might be broken in by the time that the boy could ride him.

And while these things were going forward, they heard tidings of Rhiannon and her punishment. And Teirnyon Twryv Vliant, by reason of the pity that he felt on hearing this story of Rhiannon and her punishment, inquired closely concerning it, until he had heard from many of those who came to his court. Then did Teirnyon, often lamenting the sad history, ponder within himself, and he looked steadfastly on the boy, and as he looked upon him, it seemed to him that he had never beheld so great a likeness between father and son, as between the boy and Pwyll the Chief of Dyved. Now the semblance of Pwyll was well known to him, for he had of yore been one of his followers. And thereupon he became grieved for the wrong that he did, in keeping with him a boy whom he knew to be the son of another man. And the first time that he was alone with his wife, he told her that it was not right that they should keep the boy with them, and suffer so excellent a lady as Rhiannon to be punished so greatly on his account, whereas the boy was the son of Pwyll the Chief of Dyved. And Teirnyon's wife agreed with him, that they should send the boy to Pwyll. 'And three things, lord,' said she, 'shall we gain thereby. Thanks and gifts for releasing Rhiannon from her punishment; and thanks from Pwyll for nursing his son and restoring him unto him; and thirdly, if the boy is of gentle nature, he will be our foster-son, and he will do for us all the good in his power.' So it was settled according to this counsel.

And no later than the next day was Teirnyon equipped, and two other knights with him. And the boy, as a fourth in their company, went with them upon the horse which Teirnyon had given him. And they journeyed towards Narberth, and it was not long before they reached that place. And as they drew near to the palace, they beheld Rhiannon sitting beside the horse-block. And when they were opposite to her, 'Chieftain,' said she, 'go not further thus, I will bear every one of you into the palace, and this is my penance for slaying my own son and devouring him.' 'Oh, fair lady,' said Teirnyon, 'think not that I will be one to be carried upon thy back.' 'Neither will I,' said the boy. 'Truly, my soul,' said Teirnyon, 'we will not go.' So they went forward to the palace, and there was great joy at their coming. And at the palace a feast was prepared, because Pwyll was come back from the confines of Dyved. And they went into the hall and washed, and Pwyll rejoiced to see Teirnyon. And in this order they sat. Teirnyon between Pwyll and Rhiannon, and Teirnyon's two companions on the other side of Pwyll, with the boy between them. And after meat they began to carouse and to discourse. And Teirnyon's discourse was concerning the adventure of the mare and the boy, and how he and his wife had nursed and reared the child as their own. 'And behold here is thy son, lady,' said Teirnyon. 'And whosoever told that lie concerning thee, has done wrong. And when I heard of thy sorrow, I was troubled and grieved. And I believe that there is none of this host who will not perceive that the boy is the son of Pwyll,' said Teirnyon. 'There is none,' said they all, 'who is not certain thereof.' 'I declare to Heaven,' said Rhiannon, 'that if this be true, there is indeed an end to my trouble.' 'Lady,' said Pendaran Dyved,' well hast thou named thy son Pryderi, and well becomes him the name of Pryderi son of Pwyll Chief of Dyved.' 'Look you,' said Rhiannon, 'will not his own name become him better?' 'What name has he?' asked Pendaran Dyved. 'Gwri Wallt Euryn is the name that we gave him.' 'Pryderi,' said Pendaran, 'shall his name be.' 'It were more proper,' said Pwyll, 'that the boy should take his name from the word his mother spoke when she received the joyful tidings of him.' And thus was it arranged.

'Teirnyon,' said Pwyll, 'Heaven reward thee that thou hast reared the boy up to this time, and, being of gentle lineage, it were fitting that he repay thee for it.' 'My lord,' said Teirnyon, 'it was my wife who nursed him, and there is no one in the world so afflicted as she at parting with him. It were well that he should bear in mind what I and my wife have done for him.' 'I call Heaven to witness,' said Pwyll, 'that while I live I will support thee and thy possessions, as long as I am able to preserve my own. And when he shall have power, he will more fitly maintain them than I. And if this counsel be pleasing unto thee, and to my nobles, it shall be that, as thou hast reared him up to the present time, I will give him to be brought up by Pendaran Dyved, from henceforth. And you shall be companions, and shall both be foster-fathers unto him.' 'This is good counsel,' said they all. So the boy was given to Pendaran Dyved, and the nobles of the land were sent with him. And Teirnyon Twryv Vliant, and his companions, set out for his country, and his possessions, with love and gladness. And he went not without being offered the fairest jewels and the fairest horses, and the choicest dogs; but he would take none of them.

Thereupon they all remained in their own dominions. And Pryderi, the son of Pwyll the Chief of Dyved, was brought up carefully as was fit, so that he became the fairest youth, and the most comely, and the best skilled in all good games, of any in the kingdom. And thus passed years and years, until the end of Pwyll the Chief of Dyved's life came, and he died.

And Pryderi ruled the seven Cantrevs of Dyved prosperously, and he was beloved by his people, and by all around him. And at length he added unto them the three Cantrevs of Ystrad Tywi, and the four Cantrevs of Cardigan; and these were called the Seven Cantrevs of Seissyllwch. And when he made this addition, Pryderi the son of Pwyll the Chief of Dyved desired to take a wife. And the wife he chose was Kicva, the daughter of Gwynn Gohoyw, the son of Gloyw Wallt Lydan, the son of Prince Casnar, one of the nobles of this Island.

And thus ends this portion of the Mabinogion.

11th or early 12th c.?

Anglo-Norman French

THE LAY OF GUINGAMOR *

In Brittany of old time there reigned a king who held all the land in his sway, and was lord of many noble barons — his name I cannot tell ye. This king had a nephew who was both wise and courteous, a very brave and skilful knight, and Guingamor was he called. For his bravery and his beauty the king held him passing dear, and thought to make him his heir since he had no son. All men loved Guingamor; he knew how to promise, and how to give; knights and squires alike honoured him for his frankness and his courtesy; and his praises went abroad throughout all that land.

One day the king went forth to hunt and to disport himself in the forest. His nephew had that morn been bled and was still feeble, so might not go forth into the woodland, but would abide in his hostel, and with him were many of the king's companions.

At prime Guingamor arose and went forth to the castle to seek solace. The seneschal met him and threw his arm around his neck, and they spake together awhile, and then sat them down to play at chess. And as they sat there the queen came even to the door of the chamber, on her way to the chapel. She was tall and fair and graceful; and there she stood awhile to gaze on the knight whom she saw playing chess, and stayed her still and moved not.

Very fair did he seem to her in form and face and feature; he sat over against a window, and a ray of sunlight fell upon his face and illumined it with a fair colour. And the queen looked upon him till her thoughts were changed within her, and she was seized with love for him, for his beauty and his courtesy.

Then the queen turned her back, and called a maiden, and said: 'Go thou to the knight who sitteth within playing chess, Guingamor, the king's nephew, and bid him to come to me straightway.'

So the maiden went her way to the knight, and bare him her lady's greeting, and her prayer that he come forthwith and speak with her; and Guingamor let his game be, and went with the maiden.

The queen greeted him courteously, and bade him sit beside her; but little did he think wherefore she made such fair semblance to him.

The queen spake first: 'Guingamor, thou art very valiant, brave and courteous and winning — a fair adventure awaits thee — thou canst set thy love in high places! Thou hast a fair and courteous friend, I know neither dame nor damsel in the kingdom her equal! She loveth thee dearly, and thou canst have her for thy love.'

The knight answered: 'Lady, I know not how I can dearly love one whom I have never seen nor known; never have I heard speak of this aforetime, nor have I besought love from any.'

And the queen spake: 'Friend, be not so shamefaced; me canst thou very well love, for of a sooth I am not to be refused; I love thee well and will love thee all my days.'

Then Guingamor was much abashed and answered discreetly: 'Well do I know, lady, that I ought to love thee; thou art wife to my lord the king, and I am bound to honour thee as my liege lady.'

* Translation by Jessie L. Weston, David Nutt, 1904. By permission of Simpkin, Marshall, Hamilton, Kent & Company.

But the queen answered: 'I say not that thou shalt love me thus, but I would lőve thee as my lover, and be thy lady. Thou art fair, and I am gracious; if it be thy will to love me very joyful shall we both be,' and she drew him towards her and kissed him.

Guingamor understood well what she said, and what love she desired of him, and thereof had he great shame, and blushed rosy-red, and sprang up thinking to go forth from the chamber. The queen would fain keep him with her, and laid hold on his mantle, so that the clasp broke and he came forth without it.

Then Guingamor went back to the chess-board, and seated himself, much troubled at heart; so startled had he been that he had no thought for his mantle, but turned to his game without it.

The queen was much terrified when she thought of the king, for when Guingamor had so spoken, and showed her his mind she feared lest he should accuse her to his uncle. Then she called a maiden whom she trusted much, and gave her the mantle, and bade her bare it to the knight; and she laid it around his shoulders, but so troubled in mind was he that he knew not when she brought it to him; and the maiden returned to the queen.

So were the two in great fear till vesper-tide, when the king returned from the chase and sat him down to meat. They had had good sport that day, and he and his comrades were very joyful. After meat they laughed and made sport, and told their adventures, each spake of his deeds, who had missed, who had hit fair. Guingamor had not been with them, whereof he was sorrowful. So he held his peace, and spake no word.

But the queen watched him, and thinking to make him wrathful, she devised words of which each one should weigh heavily. She turned herself to the knights and spake: 'Much do I hear ye boast, and tell of your adventures, yet of all whom I see here is none brave enough (were one to give him a thousand pounds of gold) to dare hunt or wind horn in the forest here without, where the white boar wanders. Marvellous praise would he win who should take that boar!'

Then all the knights held their peace, for none would assay that venture. Guingamor knew well that it was for him she spake thus. Throughout the hall all were silent, there was no sound nor strife.

The king answered her first: 'Lady, thou hast often heard of the adventure of the forest, and this thou knowest; it displeaseth me much when in any place I hear it spoken of. No man may go thither to hunt the boar who may return therefrom, so adventurous is the land, and so perilous the river. Much mischief have I already suffered; ten knights, the best of the land, have I lost; they set forth to seek the boar and came never again.'

Then he said no more, but the company departed from each other, the knights went to their hostel to slumber and the king betook himself to his couch.

Guingamor did not forget the word which he had heard, but went his way to the king's chamber and knelt before him. 'Sire,' he said, 'I ask of thee somewhat whereof I have great need, and which I pray thee to grant me, nor in any wise to refuse the gift.'

The king said: "Fair nephew, I grant thee what thou prayest from me, ask securely, for in naught would I deny thy will.'

The knight thanked him, and said: 'This is that which I demanded, and the gift which thou hast given me. I go to hunt in the forest.' Then he prayed him to lend him his horse, his bloodhound, his brachet,[1] and his pack of hounds.

When the king heard what his nephew said, and knew the gift he had given, he was very sorrowful and knew not what to do. Fain would he have taken back his word and bade him let the matter be, for such a gift should he not have asked; never would he suffer him, even for his weight in gold, to go chase the white boar, for never might he return. And if he lent him his good brachet and his steed then would he lose them both and never see them again, and naught had he that he valued so highly; there was nothing on earth he would have taken for them — 'an I lose them I shall grieve all the days of my life.'

And Guingamor answered the king: 'Sire, by the faith I owe thee, for naught that thou

[1] a kind of female hound

could'st give me, were it the wide world, would I do other than I have said and chase the boar to-morrow. If thou wilt not lend me thy steed, and the brachet thou dost hold dear, thy hound and thine other dogs, then must I e'en take my own, such as they are.'

With that came the queen who had heard what Guingamor desired (and know ye that it pleased her well), and she prayed the king that he would do as the knight required, for she thought thus to be delivered from him, and never, in all her life, to see him again. So earnestly did she make her prayer that at length the king granted all she might ask. Then Guingamor prayed leave, and went joyful to his dwelling; naught might he sleep that night, but when he saw dawn he arose in haste and made ready, and called to him all his companions, the king's household, who were in much fear for him, and would gladly have hindered his going an they might. He bade them bring him the king's steed which he had lent him the night before, and his brachet, and his good horn, which he would not have given for its weight in gold. Two packs of the king's good dogs did Guingamor take with him, and forgat not the bloodhound. The king himself would accompany him forth from the town, and with him came the burghers and the courtiers, rich and poor, making great cry and lamentation, and with them too were many ladies sorrowing sorely.

To the thicket nearest the city went all the huntsmen, taking with them the bloodhound, and seeking for the track of the wild boar, for they knew well where he was wont to haunt. They found the track and knew it, for many a time had they seen it, and traced the beast to his lair in the thick bushes and loosed the bloodhound, and by force drove forth the boar.

Then Guingamor sounded his horn and bade them uncouple one pack of dogs and the other lead forward to await him near the forest, but they should not enter therein. Thus Guingamor began the chase and the boar fled before him, leaving his lair unwillingly. The dogs followed, giving tongue, and hunted him to the verge of the forest, but further might they not go, since they were weary, wherefore they uncoupled the others. Guingamor rode on winding his horn, and the pack ran yelping on the boar's track; return to his lair he might not, but plunged into the forest, and the knight followed after, carrying the brachet which he had borrowed from the king.

They who had borne him company, the king and his fellowship and the men of the city, stayed without the wood, nor would go further. There they abode so long as they might hear the blast of the horn and the barking of the dogs, and then they commended the knight to God and turned them back to the town.

The boar ran further and further till he had wearied out the dogs, then Guingamor took the brachet and loosened the leash, and set it on the track, which it followed of right good will, while the knight did what he might to aid and encourage his uncle's dog by blowing gaily on his horn. Much did the sounds of the chase please him, but ere long he had lost both brachet and boar, he heard neither yelp nor cry and became sorrowful and much displeased; he deemed he had lost the brachet through the thickness of the forest, and he was passing sorrowful for the sake of his uncle who loved the dog so well. So he went still forward into the forest, and coming to a high hill he stayed awhile, very sorrowful and much at a loss.

The sky was clear and the day fair, all around him sang the birds but he hearkened not to their song. Ere long he heard the brachet give tongue afar off and he began to wind his horn, troubled at heart till he saw the dog. Through a little plantation towards the open ground he saw the brachet and the boar come swiftly, and thought to reach them easily. He spurred his steed to a gallop, nor would delay, rejoicing much at heart and saying to himself that might he take the boar, and return whole and unharmed to court, he would win much fame, and his deed would be spoken of for all time.

In the joy of his heart he set the horn to his lips and blew a marvellous great blast. Afore him passed the boar with the brachet close upon its track. Guingamor rode after swiftly, through the adventurous land, across the perilous river, over the meadowland where the turf was green and flowery; well nigh had he overtaken his prey when he looked ahead and saw the walls of a great palace, well built, yet without mortar. 'T was all enclosed of green marble, and above the entry was a tower which seemed to him of silver, so great was the clearness it gave. The doors were of fine ivory, inlaid with golden trefoils, nor was there bar nor lock.

Guingamor came on swiftly, and when he saw the door stand wide and the entrance free, he thought him he would go within and find the goodman who kept the gate, for fain would he know who was lord of the palace, since 't was the fairest he had ever seen. Much it pleased him to look upon its beauties, for he thought he might lightly overtake the boar ere it had run far, since it was wearied by the chase. So he rode within and drew bridle in the palace, and looked around, but no man might he see, naught was there about him but fine gold; and the chambers which opened from the hall seemed of stones of Paradise. That he found neither man nor woman there pleased him not, else was he glad that he had found so fair an adventure to tell again in his own land.

Then he turned him back, and rode quickly through the meadows by the river, but naught did he see of his boar, quarry and dog were alike lost. Then was Guingamor wrathful. 'Of a truth,' he said, 'I am betrayed, men may well hold me for a fool. Methinks that to look upon a house have I lost all my labour. If I find not my dog and my boar little joy or pleasure shall I have henceforward, and never more may I return to my own land.' Much troubled, he betook himself to the high ground of the forest, and began to listen if he might hear the cry of the dog.

Then he heard the brachet give tongue afar off to his right hand, and he waited and hearkened till he surely heard both dog and boar. Then he began again to wind his horn, and rode towards them. The boar passed before him, and Guingamor rode after, encouraging the brachet with hue and cry.

Thus he came into the open country, and found a spring beneath an olive tree, widespreading, and covered with leaves. The water of the spring was clear and fair, and the gravel thereof gold and silver. In the water a maiden was bathing herself while another combed her hair and washed her feet and hands. Fair was she, long-limbed and softly rounded, in all the world was there nothing so fair, neither lily nor rose as that naked maiden.

As soon as Guingamor beheld her he was stirred by her beauty. He saw her garments on a bush, and turned his horse's bridle thither; he stayed not, but taking her robes, set them high in the fork of a great oak. When he had taken the boar, he thought to return and speak with the maiden, for he knew well that she would not go thence naked. But the maiden saw his deed, and called the knight to her, and spake proudly: 'Guingamor, let be my robes; an God will, never shall it be told among knights that thou didst so discourteous a deed as to hide the garments of a maiden in the fork of a tree! Come hither, and fear not. To-day shalt thou abide with me, thou hast laboured all day and hast had but ill success.'

Then Guingamor went towards her, and proffered her robe, and thanked her for her courtesy, and said he might not lodge with her, since he must seek the boar and the brachet which he had lost.

The maiden answered him: 'Friend, all the knights in the world let them labour as they might should not find those two, an I gave them not mine aid. Let that folly be, and make this covenant with me; come with me and I pledge thee loyally that I will give thee the boar as a prize, and the brachet shalt thou have again to take with thee into thine own land, on the third day hence.'

'Fair lady,' said the knight, 'by this covenant will I gladly abide even as thou hast spoken.'

Then he dismounted, and the maiden clad herself in a short space, and she who was with her brought her a mule well and richly harnessed, and a palfrey, better had never count nor king. Guingamor lifted the maiden to her saddle, and rode beside her, holding her bridle in his hand. Often did he look upon her, and seeing her so fair and tall and graceful, of good will would he become her lover. He looked upon her gently, and prayed her earnestly that she would grant him her love; never aforetime had his heart been troubled for any woman he had looked upon, nor had he thought of love.

The maiden, who was wise and courteous,

answered Guingamor that she would willingly grant him her love, whereof the knight was joyful, and since she had pledged herself to be his lady, he laid his arm around her and kissed her.

The waiting maiden had ridden on quickly to the palace wherein Guingamor had entered, and they had decked it richly, and bidden the knights mount and ride out to meet their lady, to do honour to the lover whom she brought with her. Three hundred or more of them there were, nor was there one but was clad in vest of silk wrought with gold thread. Each knight led with him his lady. 'T was a passing fair company. There were squires with hawks, and fair falcons that had passed their moulting. In the palace were there as many playing at chess and other games.

When Guingamor dismounted he beheld the ten knights who had gone forth to chase the boar, and been lost from his land. They rose from their seats to meet him, and greeted him right joyfully, and Guingamor kissed them each one. A fair lodging was his that night, great plenty of rich meats, with much rejoicing, and great state; there was the sound of harps and viols, the song of youths and maidens. Much did he marvel at the noble fare, the beauty and the richness of all around. He bethought him that he would abide there two days, and on the third would take his way homeward; the dog and the boar would he take, and make known to his uncle the adventure which had befallen him, then would he return again to his lady.

Yet otherwise than he deemed had it chanced to him; not three days but three hundred years had he been in that palace; dead was the king, and dead his household and the men of his lineage, and the cities he had known had fallen into destruction and ruin.

On the third day Guingamor prayed leave of his love that he might go to his own land, and that she would give him the brachet and the boar, according to her covenant; and the maiden answered:

'Friend, thou shalt have them, but know that thou wilt go hence for naught; 't is three hundred years past since thou camest hither, thine uncle and his folk are dead; neither friends nor kinsmen shalt thou find. One thing I tell thee, ask where thou wilt, nowhere shalt thou find a man so old that he may tell thee aught of those thou seekest.'

'Lady,' quoth Guingamor, 'I may not believe that thou sayest sooth, but if the thing be so then I swear to thee that I will straightway return hither.'

And she answered, 'I charge thee when thou hast passed the river to return to thine own land, that thou neither eat nor drink, however great may be thy need, till thou return once more to this land, otherwise art thou undone.'

Then she bade them bring his steed, and the great boar, and the brachet which she gave him in leash, and Guingamor took the boar's head (more might he not carry), and mounted his steed and went forth. His lady rode with him to the river, and had him put across in a boat, then she commended him to God and left him.

The knight rode forward and wandered till midday in the forest, nor might he find a way out. 'T was all so ill-looking and overgrown that he might know the way no longer. Then afar to the left he heard the axe of a woodcutter, who had made a fire and burnt charcoal, and he spurred towards the sound, and gave the man greeting, and asked where his uncle the king abode, and at what castle he should seek for him.

But the charcoal-burner answered: 'Of a faith, sire, I know naught; the king of whom thou speakest 't is over three hundred years since he died, he and all his folk, and the castles of which thou askest have long been in ruins. There are certain of the old folk who full oft tell tales of that king, and of his nephew who was a wondrous valiant knight, how he went one day to hunt within this forest and was seen no more.' Guingamor heard what he said, and a great pity seized him for the king his uncle, whom he had thus lost, and he spake to the charcoal-burner: 'Hearken what I say to thee, for I will tell thee what has befallen me. I am he who went hunting in this forest, and I thought to return and bring with me the white boar.' Then he began to tell of the palace he had found, and the maiden whom he had met, how she had lodged him royally for two days; 'and on the third did I depart, and she gave me my dog and the boar.'

Then he gave him the boar's head and bade him keep it well till he returned to his home, and might tell the folk of the land how he had seen and spoken with Guingamor the king's nephew.

The poor man thanked him, and Guingamor bade him farewell, and turned him back and left him. 'T was already past nones and the day drew towards vesper-tide; so great a hunger seized the knight that he became well-nigh ravening; by the roadside as he went there grew a wild apple tree, the boughs well laden with fruit; he drew near and plucked three and ate them. He did ill in that he forgat his lady's command, for even as he tasted the fruit he was aged and undone, so feeble of limb that he fell from his steed, and might move neither hand nor foot; when he might speak he began in a feeble voice to bemoan himself.

The charcoal-burner had followed him and seen what had chanced, and it seemed to him that he might scarce live till the evening. But as he would go to his aid there came riding two fair maidens, well and richly dressed, who dismounted beside Guingamor, and blamed him much, and reproached him for that he had so ill kept his lady's command. Gently they lifted the knight and set him on his horse, and led him to the river, where they placed him, his steed, and his dog, in a boat and rowed them over.

The peasant turned him back, and that night he sought his home bearing with him the boar's head; far and wide he told the tale, and affirmed it by his oath. The head he gave unto the king, who caused it to be shown at many a feast; and that none might forget the adventure the king bade make a lay which bare the name of Guingamor — and so do the Bretons call it.

ca. 1165

Latin

Geoffrey of Monmouth (1100?–1154)

HISTORY OF THE KINGS OF BRITAIN,* BK. IX

Chapter XI

Arthur invited unto him all soever of most prowess from far-off kingdoms and began to multiply his household retinue, and to hold such courtly fashion in his household as begat rivalry amongst peoples at a distance, insomuch as the noblest in the land, fain to vie with him, would hold himself as nought, save in the cut of his clothes and the manner of his arms he followed the pattern of Arthur's knights. . . .

Chapter XII

When the high festival of Whitsuntide began to draw nigh, Arthur, filled with exceeding great joy at having achieved so great success, was fain to hold high court, and to set the crown of the kingdom upon his head, to convene the Kings and Dukes that were his vassals to the festival so that he might the more worshipfully celebrate the same, and renew his peace more firmly amongst his barons. Howbeit, when he made known his desire unto his familiars, he, by their counsel, made choice of the City of Legions wherein to fulfil his design. For, situate in a passing pleasant position on the river Usk in Glamorgan, not far from the Severn sea, and abounding in wealth above all other cities, it was the place most meet for so high a solemnity. For on the one side thereof flowed the noble river aforesaid whereby the Kings and Princes that should come from oversea might be borne thither in their ships; and on the other side, girdled about with meadows and woods, passing fair was the magnificence of the kingly palaces thereof with the gilded verges of the roofs that imitated Rome. Howbeit, the chiefest glories thereof were the two churches, one raised in honour of the Martyr Julius, that was right fair graced by a convent of virgins that had dedicated them unto God, and the second, founded in the name of the blessed Aaron, his companion, the main pillars whereof were a brotherhood of canons regular, and this was the cathedral church of the third Metropolitan See of Britain. It had, moreover, a school of two hundred philosophers learned in astronomy and in the other arts, that did diligently observe the

* Translation by Sebastian Evans, J. M. Dent & Sons, London. By permission of the publishers.

courses of the stars, and did by true inferences foretell the prodigies which at that time were about to befall unto King Arthur. Such was the city, famed for such abundance of things delightsome, that was now busking her for the festival that had been proclaimed. Messengers were sent forth into the divers kingdoms, and all that owed allegiance throughout the Gauls and the neighbour islands were invited unto the court. . . .

Chapter XIII

When all at last were assembled in the city on the high day of the festival, the archbishops were conducted unto the palace to crown the King with the royal diadem. Dubric, therefore, upon whom the charge fell, for that the court was held within his diocese, was ready to celebrate the service. As soon as the King had been invested with the ensigns of kingship, he was led in right comely wise to the church of the Metropolitan See, two archbishops supporting him, the one upon his right hand side the other upon his left. Four Kings, moreover, to wit, those of Albany, Cornwall, and North and South Wales, went before him, bearing before him, as was their right, four golden swords. A company of clerics in holy orders of every degree went chanting music marvellous sweet in front. Of the other party, the archbishops and pontiffs led the Queen, crowned with laurel and wearing her own ensigns, unto the church of the virgins dedicate. The four Queens, moreover, of the four Kings already mentioned, did bear before her according to wont and custom four white doves, and the ladies that were present did follow after her rejoicing greatly. At last, when the procession was over, so manifold was the music of the organs and so many were the hymns that were chanted in both churches, that the knights who were there scarce knew which church they should enter first for the exceeding sweetness of the harmonies in both. First into the one and then into the other they flocked in crowds, nor, had the whole day been given up to the celebration, would any have felt a moment's weariness thereof. And when the divine services had been celebrated in both churches, the King and Queen put off their crowns, and doing on lighter robes of state, went to meat, he to his palace with the men, she to another palace with the women. For the Britons did observe the ancient custom of the Trojans, and were wont to celebrate their high festival days, the men with the men and the women with the women severally. And when all were set at table according as the rank of each did demand, Kay the Seneschal, in a doublet furred of ermines, and a thousand youths of full high degree in his company, all likewise clad in ermines, did serve the meats along with him. Of the other part, as many in doublets furred of vair did follow Bedevere the Butler, and along with him did serve the drinks from the divers ewers into the manifold-fashioned cups. In the palace of the Queen no less did numberless pages, clad in divers brave liveries, offer their service each after his office, the which were I to go about to describe I might draw out my history into an endless prolixity. For at that time was Britain exalted unto so high a pitch of dignity as that it did surpass all other kingdoms in plenty of riches, in luxury of adornment, and in the courteous wit of them that dwelt therein. Whatsoever knight in the land was of renown for his prowess did wear his clothes and his arms all of one same colour. And the dames, no less witty, would apparel them in like manner in a single colour, nor would they deign have the love of none save he had thrice approved him in the wars. Wherefore at that time did dames wax chaste and knights the nobler for their love.

Chapter XIV

Refreshed by their banqueting, they go forth into the fields without the city, and sundry among them fall to playing at sundry manner games. Presently the knights engage in a game on horseback, making show of fighting a battle whilst the dames and damsels looking on from the top of the walls, for whose sake the courtly knights make believe to be fighting, do cheer them on for the sake of seeing the better sport . . . And after the first three days had been spent on this wise, upon the fourth day all they that had done service in virtue of the office they held were summoned, and unto each was made grant of the honour of the office he held in possession, earldom, to wit, of city or castle, archbishopric, bishopric, abbacy, or whatsoever else it might be.

ca. 1135

Jocelin of Brakelond (fl. 1200)

CHRONICLE OF ST. EDMUNDSBURY*

HOW ABBOT SAMSON WAS RECEIVED AT THE MONASTERY

Now the lord abbot was thus received. The night before he had lain at Kentford, and at the proper moment we went to meet him in solemn procession, after leaving the chapter, as far as the gate of the graveyard, while bells were rung in the choir and outside it. But he was surrounded by a multitude of men, and when he saw the monastery, dismounted from his horse without the threshold of the gate, and causing his sandals to be removed, was received within the door barefooted, the prior and the sacristan supporting him on either side. And we chanted the responses 'Benedictus Dominus' from the service for Trinity Sunday, and afterwards the 'Martiri adhuc' from that for St. Edmund, and conducted the abbot as far as the high altar.

And when this had been done, the organs and bells were silenced, and the prior said the prayer 'Omnipotens sempiterne Deus, miserere huic,' over the prostrate abbot. Then the abbot made oblation and kissed the shrine, and returned to the choir. There Samson the precentor took him by the hand and led him to the abbot's chair on the western side of the choir, and while he stood there the precentor at once began 'Te Deum laudamus,' and while it was being chanted, the abbot was embraced by the prior and by the whole monastery.

And so, these ceremonies being completed, the abbot entered the chapter, the whole monastery and many others following. He said many times 'Benedicite,' and then he first returned thanks to the monastery that they had chosen him, the least of them all, as he said, not for his own merits but only by the will of God, to be their lord and pastor. And asking in a few words that they would pray for him, he addressed the clerks and knights, and asked them to advise him for the good of the monastery.

Then Wimer, the sheriff, answered for them all, and said, 'We also are ready to be with you in counsel and in helping you in every way, as with a dear lord whom the Lord has called for His honour, and for the honour of the holy martyr Edmund.'

Afterwards the charters of the king concerning the donation of the abbacy were brought forth, and were read in the hearing of all. The abbot himself also prayed that God would guide him according to His grace, and all answered 'Amen.' Then he went into his own chamber, and celebrated his day of festival with more than a thousand guests and with great joy.

HOW ABBOT SAMSON BEGAN TO RULE THE MONASTERY

In those days I was prior's chaplain, and within four months was made chaplain to the abbot. And I noted many things and committed them to memory. So, on the morrow of his feast, the abbot assembled the prior and some few others together, as if to seek advice from others, but he himself knew what he would do.

He said that a new seal must be made and adorned with a mitred effigy of himself, though his predecessors had not had such a seal. For a time, however, he used the seal of our prior, writing at the end of all letters that he did so for the time being because he had no seal of his own. And afterwards he ordered his household, and transferred various officials to other offices, saying that he proposed to maintain twenty-six horses in his court, and many times he declared that 'a child must first crawl, and afterwards he may stand upright and walk.' And he laid this special command upon his servants, that they should take care that he might not be laid open to the charge of not providing enough food and drink, but that they should assiduously provide for the maintenance of the hospitality of the house.

* Translation by L. C. Jane, "Medieval Library," American Branch Oxford University Press, 1922. By permission of Chatto and Windus, Publishers.

In these matters, and in all the things which he did and determined, he trusted fully in the help of God and his own good sense, holding it to be shameful to rely upon the counsel of another, and thinking he was sufficient unto himself. The monks marvelled and the knights were angered; they blamed his pride, and often defamed him at the court of the king, saying that he would not act in accordance with the advice of his freemen. He himself put away from his privy council all the great men of the abbey, both lay and literate, men without whose advice and assistance it seemed impossible that the abbey could be ruled. For this reason Ranulf de Glanville, justiciar of England, was at first offended with him, and was less well-disposed towards him than was expedient, until he knew well from definite proofs that the abbot acted providently and prudently, both in domestic and in external affairs.

HOW THE ABBOT DEALT WITH THE LANDS OF HIS HOUSE

When homage had been received, the abbot demanded an aid from the knights, and they promised twenty shillings from each fee of a knight. But they at once took counsel, and reduced the aid by twelve pounds from twelve knights, alleging that these twelve ought to assist the other forty to keep ward, and to make scutages, and also in assisting the abbey. When the abbot heard this, he was wroth, and said to his friends that should his life be spared, he would repay them like for like, and injury for injury.

After this, the abbot caused inquest to be made in every manor belonging to the abbacy as to the annual revenues of the free men, and the names of the villeins, and their holdings, and the services due from each, and caused all these details to be written down. Then he restored the old halls and ruined houses, through which kites and crows flew; he built new chapels, and rooms and seats in many places where there had never been buildings, save perhaps barns.

He also made many parks, which he filled with beasts, and had a huntsman and dogs. And whenever any important guest arrived, he used to sit with his monks in some retired grove, and watch the coursing for a while; but I never saw him interested in hunting. He made many clearings and brought land into cultivation, in everything regarding the advantage of the abbacy. But would that he had watched with equal care over the grants of the manors of the monastery. For he received our manors of Bradfield and Rougham for a while into his own hand, making good the loss of rent by the expenditure of forty pounds, which he afterwards handed over to us when he heard that the monastery murmured because he held our manors in his own hands.

For the management of the same manors and for the management of all other affairs, he appointed monks and laymen who were wiser than those who had previously held the posts, and who made careful provision for us and our lands.

Then he received eight hundreds into his own hands, and when Robert de Cokefield died, he took the hundred of Cosford. All these he handed over to the care of the servants of his own table. Matters of greater moment were kept for his own decision, and those which were of less import were decided by his agents; all things he turned to his advantage.

By his command, a general account was drawn up for every hundred of the leets and suits, of the hidages and customary supplies of fodder, of the hens which ought to be paid to him, and of all the other customary dues, revenues, and expenses, which the tenants had always concealed to a great extent. All these things he reduced to writing, so that within four years of his election, no one could deceive him as to the resources of the abbey even to a penny's value, whereas he had received nothing in writing from his predecessors concerning the management of the abbey, except a little schedule containing the names of the knights of St. Edmund and the names of the manors, and the rent which attached to each farm. Now he called this book of his, his Calendar, in the which also were written down all the debts which he had paid. And he consulted this book almost daily, as if in it he saw the image of his probity as in a glass.

OF THAT WHICH WAS DONE AT THE ABBOT'S FIRST CHAPTER

On the first day on the which he held a chapter he confirmed to us under his new seal the sixty shillings for Southrey, which his predecessors had in the first instance unjustly received from Edmund, called the golden monk, that the same might hold the said township to farm all the days of his life.

And he proposed an edict that no one should pledge the ornaments of the church henceforth without the assent of the monastery, as had been done formerly. He proposed also that no charter should be sealed with the seal of the monastery save in the chapter and in the presence of the whole community.

Then he made Hugh subsacristan, ordaining that William the sacristan should do nothing in the office of sacristan, either as to receipts or as to expenses, save by his assent. Afterwards, but on the same day, he removed the former custodians of the oblations to other offices. And last of all he deposed William himself, whereupon certain who loved William said, 'See the abbot! See the wolf of whom one dreamed! See how he ravens!'

HOW THE AUTHOR TALKED WITH THE ABBOT CONCERNING THE SADNESS OF HIS MANNER

But I noticed this, and taking a favourable occasion, as I was with him alone, said, 'There are two things in which you make me marvel greatly.' And when he asked what they were, I said, 'One is, that you, in the circumstances in which you are placed, favour the opinion of those of Melun who say that from a false premiss nothing can follow, and other foolish things.' And when he answered what he would to this, I added, 'The other thing at which I marvel is that you do not show a smiling face at home as you do elsewhere, nor remain among the brothers who cherish you, and love you, and have chosen you to be their lord, but are rarely with them, nor do you then rejoice with them, so they say.'

When he heard this, his expression changed, and he answered, with bowed head, 'You are a fool, and speak as a fool. You should know the saying of Solomon, Hast thou many daughters; show not thyself cheerful toward them.' Then I was silent, and from that time placed a guard on my lips.

Yet on another occasion I said, 'Lord, I heard you this night keeping watch after matins and breathing heavily contrary to your wont.' And he answered, 'Is it not strange? You share my good things, food, and drink, and riding, and the like. But you think little of the toil of providing for the house and household, of the many and arduous labours which are a pastor's care. These make me anxious, and cause me to groan and be troubled in spirit.' Thereupon I raised my hands to heaven and answered, 'From so great anxiety, almighty and merciful Lord, deliver me!'

I heard the abbot say that if he were in that condition in which he had been before he became a monk, and had five or six marks income wherewith he might support himself in the schools, he would never become either monk or abbot. And on another occasion, he said with an oath that had he known beforehand what care there was in ruling an abbey, and how great that care was, he would far rather have been almoner or librarian, than abbot and lord. And he declared that he had ever longed for the post of librarian above all others. Yet who would believe such things? Not I; no, not I; but that as I lived with him day and night for six years, I know fully the merit of his life and the wisdom of his mind.

CONCERNING THE APPEARANCE AND PRIVATE CHARACTER OF THE ABBOT

Abbot Samson was below the average height, almost bald; his face was neither round nor oblong; his nose was prominent and his lips thick; his eyes were clear and his glance penetrating; his hearing was excellent; his eyebrows arched, and frequently shaved; and a little cold soon made him hoarse. On the day of his election he was forty-seven, and had been a monk for seventeen years. In his ruddy beard there were a few grey hairs, and still fewer in his black and curling hair. But in the course of the first fourteen years after his election all his hair became white as snow.

He was an exceedingly temperate man; he possessed great energy and a strong constitution, and was fond both of riding and walking, until old age prevailed upon him and moderated his ardour in these respects. When he heard the news of the capture of the cross and the fall of Jerusalem, he began to wear under garments made of horse-hair, and a horse-hair shirt, and gave up the use of flesh and meat. None the less, he willed that flesh should be placed before him as he sat at table, that the alms might be increased. He ate sweet milk, honey, and similar sweet things far more readily than any other food.

He hated liars, drunkards, and talkative persons; for virtue ever loves itself and spurns that which is contrary to it. He blamed those who grumbled about their meat and drink, and especially monks who so grumbled, and personally kept to the same manners which he had observed when he was a cloistered monk. Moreover, he had this virtue in himself that he never desired to change the dish which was placed before him. When I was a novice, I wished to prove whether this was really true, and as I happened to serve in the refectory, I thought to place before him food which would have offended any other man, in a very dirty and broken dish. But when he saw this, he was as it were blind to it. Then, as there was some delay, I repented of what I had done, and straightway seized the dish, changed the food and dish for better, and carried it to him. He, however, was angry at the change, and disturbed.

He was an eloquent man, speaking both French and Latin, but rather careful of the good sense of that which he had to say than of the style of his words. He could read books written in English very well, and was wont to preach to the people in English, but in the dialect of Norfolk where he was born and bred. It was for this reason that he ordered a pulpit to be placed in the church, for the sake of those who heard him and for purposes of ornament.

The abbot further appeared to prefer the active to the contemplative life, and praised good officials more than good monks. He rarely commended anyone solely on account of his knowledge of letters, unless the man happened to have knowledge of secular affairs, and if he chanced to hear of any prelate who had given up his pastoral work and become a hermit, he did not praise him for this. He would not praise men who were too kindly, saying, 'He who strives to please all men, deserves to please none.'

HOW ABBOT SAMSON MANAGED HIS HOUSEHOLD

He laboured to secure a well-regulated house, and a household large, but not larger than was right, and he took care that the weekly allowance which in the time of his predecessor had not been enough for five days, should last him for eight days, or nine, or ten, if he were on his manors and there were no great coming of guests. Every week, moreover, he audited the expenses of his house, not through an agent, but in person, a thing which his predecessor had never been accustomed to do.

For his first seven years he had four dishes in his house, afterwards only three, if one excludes presents, and game from his parks and fish from his ponds. And if he happened to keep anyone for a while in his house at the request of some great man or of one of his friends, or messengers, or minstrels, or any such person, he used to take any opportunity of crossing the sea or going a long journey, and so prudently freed himself from so great expense.

CONCERNING IMPROVEMENTS WHICH THE ABBOT MADE IN THE ABBEY

Now when the abbot had built many different buildings in his townships throughout the abbacy, and had taken up his residence on them more often and more frequently than with us at home, at last he returned, as it were to himself. And making good, as it were, better, he said that he would stay at home more than had been his wont, and that he would build houses which were needed, regarding things within and without, and knowing that the presence of the master is the profit of the field.

Accordingly he ordered that the stables and offices in and around the court, which had previously been covered with reeds, should be covered with new roofs, made of slates, by means of Hugh the sacristan, that so all fear might be removed and all danger of fire. And behold the acceptable time, the day which had been desired! Of this I cannot write without joy, for that I had the care of the guests. Behold! by order of the abbot, the court resounded with spades and with the tools of masons, that the guest-house might be overthrown, and now was almost entirely razed, since the Highest planned its restoration!

The abbot built a new larder for himself in his court, and gave the old larder of the monastery for the use of the chamberlain, since it was unfittingly situated under the dormitory. The chapels of St. Andrew and St. Catherine and St. Faith were newly covered with lead. And many improvements were effected within and without the church. If you do not believe, open your eyes and behold!

And in his time also our stone almonry was constructed, which had before been out of repair and built of wood, and to the cost of this one of our brothers, Walter the physician, who was then almoner, contributed that which he had made from the practice of medicine.

Moreover, when the abbot saw that the silver table of the high altar, and many other precious ornaments, had been alienated for the recovery of Mildenhall and for the ransom of king Richard, he would not restore that table or other similar things, which for a like purpose might be torn away and distrained. But he turned his attention to the construction of a most valuable crest over the shrine of the glorious martyr Edmund, that his ornament might be placed there, whence for no reason could it be taken away, and where no man would dare to lay hands upon it. Indeed, when king Richard was taken captive in Germany, there was no treasure in England which was not given or for which redemption was not made, yet the shrine of St. Edmund remained intact.

For when there was a dispute for the justices in the exchequer court as to whether the shrine of St. Edmund should be partially dismantled for the ransom of the king, the abbot arose and said, 'Know it for the truth that this shall never be done by me, nor is there any man who can compel me to assent to this. But I will open the doors of the church; let him enter who will, let him approach who dares.' And all the justices answered with oaths, 'I will not come near it,' 'I will not come near it.' And they said, 'St. Edmund is even more angered against those who are far away and absent, than he is with those who are present and would take away his cloak.' And when this had been said, the shrine was not stripped, nor was a ransom paid for it. And for this cause the abbot omitted other things, and turned his mind with forethought and providence to the making of a crest for the shrine. And now the plates of gold and silver resounded between the hammer and the anvil, and the smiths worked with their tools.

Late 12th c.

Walter Map (ca. 1140–ca. 1210)

COURTIERS' TRIFLES *

THE STORY OF KING HERLA

That there was but one court similar to this of ours we learn from old stories. These tell us that Herla, the king of the very ancient Britons, was led into a compact by another king, seemingly a pigmy in the lowness of his stature, which did not exceed that of an ape. As the story hath it, this dwarf drew near, sitting on a huge goat — just such a man as Pan is pictured, with glowing face, enormous head, and a red beard so long that it touched his breast (which was brightly adorned with a dappled fawn skin), a hairy belly, and thighs which degenerated into goat-feet. Herla spake to him with no one by. Quoth the pigmy: 'I, the king of many kings and chiefs and of a people numerous beyond all count, come willingly, sent from them to thee, and though I am to thee unknown, yet I glory in the fame which hath raised thee high above other kings, since thou art the best and the nearest to me in

* Translation by Frederick Tupper and M. B. Ogle, the Macmillan Company, New York, 1924. By permission of the publishers.

place and blood, and art moreover worthy of having me grace with high honour thy wedding as a guest, when the King of the French giveth his daughter to thee — an arrangement concluded without thy knowledge, and lo, his messengers come this very day. Let there be an abiding compact between us, that I shall attend thy wedding, and thou mine a year later to the day.' With these words he turned his back with more than a tiger's swiftness and vanished from the king's sight. Then the king, returning in amazement, received the ambassadors and accepted their terms. As he was sitting in high state at the wedding feast, the pigmy entered before the first course with so great a multitude of his fellows that the tables were filled and more had to find places without than within, in the pigmy's own pavilions which were pitched in a moment. From these tents servants sprang forth with vases made of precious stones, perfect in form and fashioned with inimitable art, and they filled the palace and pavilions with gold and crystal vessels, nor did they serve any food or drink in silver or in wood. They were present wherever they were wanted, and offered nothing from the royal or other stores, but a bountiful entertainment only from their own, and thus, from the supplies brought with them, they outstripped the desires and requests of all.

Everything which Herla had prepared was left untouched. His servants sat in idleness, for they were not called upon and hence rendered no service. The pigmies were everywhere, winning everybody's thanks, aflame with the glory of their garments and gems, like the sun and moon before other stars, a burden to no one in word or deed, never in the way and never out of the way. Their king, in the midst of the ministrations of his servants, thus addressed King Herla: 'O best of kings, the Lord is my witness that, according to our compact, I am present at thy wedding. But if anything that thou cravest besides what thou seest here can be asked of me, I shall willingly supply it; but if not, thou must not put off thy requital of this high honour when I shall ask for it.' Without pausing for an answer to these words he suddenly returned to his pavilion and departed with his men about the time of cock-crow. But just a year later he suddenly appeared to Herla, and sought from him the discharge of his compact. Herla assented, and having provided himself with the wherewithal for the discharge of his debt, followed where he was led. He and his guide entered a cavern in a very lofty cliff, and after a space of darkness they passed into light, seemingly not of sun or of moon but of many lamps, to the home of the pigmies — a mansion in every way glorious, like the palace of the sun in Ovid's description. Having celebrated there the marriage, and having discharged fittingly his debt to the pigmy, Herla, with the sanction of his host, withdrew laden with gifts and with presents of horses, dogs, hawks, and all things befitting venery and falconry. The pigmy conducted his guests to the darkness and at parting gave to them a small bloodhound, to be carried in arms, strictly forbidding any one of Herla's whole company to dismount until the dog should leap forward from his bearer. Then, having said farewell, he returned to his country. When Herla in a short time was restored to sunlight and to his kingdom, he accosted an old shepherd and asked for news of his queen by name. Then the shepherd, regarding him with wonder, thus replied: 'My lord, I scarce understand thy language, since I am a Saxon and thou a Briton. But I have never heard of the name of that queen, save that men tell of one so called, a queen of the very ancient Britons, and wife of King Herla, who is reported in legends to have disappeared with a pigmy into this cliff and to have been seen nevermore on earth. The Saxons, having driven out the natives, have possessed this kingdom for full two hundred years.' The king, who had deemed his stay to be of three days only, could scarcely sit his horse for wonder. Some of his fellows, forsooth, heedless of the pigmy's warnings, dismounted before the descent of the dog, and were immediately changed to dust. But the king, understanding the reason for this change, prohibited, by threat of like death, any one to touch the earth before the descent of the dog. But the dog never descended.

Hence the story hath it that King Herla, in endless wandering, maketh mad marches with his army without stay or rest. Many have seen that army, as they declare. But finally, in the first year of the coronation of our King Henry, it ceased, so men say, to visit our kingdom frequently as in the past. And then it was seen by many Welsh sinking into the river Wye at Hereford.

THE STORY OF WILD EDRIC

Not unlike this story is that of Edric Wilde, that is, the man of the woods, so called from the agility of his body and the charm of his words and works, a man of great worth and lord of the manor of North Ledbury. When he was returning late from the hunt, he wandered in doubt about the ways until midnight, accompanied only by one boy. He chanced upon a great house on the edge of a grove, such a house as the English have in each parish for drinking, and call in their language 'guild-house' (ghildhus). When he drew near, attracted by a light in the house, and looked in, he saw a great band of many noble women. They were most beautiful in appearance and clad most elegantly in robes of the finest linen, and they were taller and more stately than our women. The soldier noted one among them far excelling the others in face and form, more to be desired than all the darlings of kings. They moved about with an airy motion, pleasing gesture, and restrained voice, and the sound, though melodious, was heard but faintly, and their speech was beyond his ken. At the sight of her, the soldier received a wound in his heart, and he could scarcely endure the fires kindled by Cupid's dart. He is wholly consumed by all the flames of love and winneth a mighty courage through the burning passion for this fairest of plagues, for this golden menace. He had heard of the wanderings of spirits, and the troops of demons who appear by night, and the sight of them which bringeth death, Dictinna, and bands of dryads and spectral squadrons, and he had learned of the vengeance inflicted by offended divinities upon those who came upon them suddenly. He had heard, too, how they preserve themselves undefiled and how they secretly inhabit unknown places apart from men and how they detest those who strive to explore their counsels that they may expose them and to pry into them that they may publish them, and with how great care they conceal themselves lest, once being visible, they should lose their value. He had heard of their revenge and of instances of men whom they had punished, but, because Cupid is rightly painted blind, Edric, recking naught of all this, doth not weigh the danger of the ghostly company, his eyes are closed to any avenger and, because he hath no sight, he rashly offendeth. He went around the house, and, finding an entrance, he rushed in and seized her by whom his heart had been seized; straightway he was seized by the others, and, being clutched close in the fiercest of contests, he escaped after a while only through the greatest of efforts of himself and his boy, not altogether without injury, but bearing on his feet and shins such marks as the teeth and nails of women could inflict. He carried away with him, however, the lady of his choice, and used her for his pleasure during three days and nights, but in all that time he was unable to get a word from her, though she passively submitted to his love. Finally, on the fourth day, she spake these words: 'Save thee, dearest! and safe thou shalt be and withal full of rejoicing in the happy lot of thee and thine, until thou shalt cast in my teeth either the sisters, from whom thou hast snatched me away, or that ground or grove whence thou carried me or anything else there anent these. From that day thou wilt fall from happiness, and, having lost me, thou wilt suffer from many other losses, and, because thou hast failed to regard times and seasons, thou wilt die before thy time.' He promised with all possible assurance to be firm and faithful in his love. He called together the noblest far and near, and, in the presence of a great throng of folk, solemnly married the lady. William the Bastard, recently crowned King of England, was then reigning; and the monarch, hearing of this marvel, and wishing to test openly its truth, summoned both the man and wife to fare together to London. They brought with them many witnesses, and also the evidence of many who could not be present; and indeed the woman herself, who was of a beauty hitherto unseen and unheard of, was the chief proof of her fairy nature. Amid the wonder of all, Edric and his wife were sent back to their home. After many years had passed, it happened that Edric, on his return from hunting about the third hour of the night, not finding her whom he sought, called and bade others call her. And when she came tardily, he looked angrily at her and said, 'Were you detained by your sisters?' and he spoke the rest of his reproof to the air, for she disappeared at the hearing of the word 'sisters.' Then the man regretted greatly his monstrous and calamitous error, and betook himself to the very spot where he had made her captive, but with no weepings nor wailings could he win her back. Day and night he cried aloud to his own undoing, for his life passed away there in never-ending sorrow.

THE THREE HERMITS AND THEIR WONDERFUL PENANCE

Philip of Naples, a man of mark, told me that when he was returning from hunting in Nigra Montana, he met a man of the woods, hairy and deformed, lying by a fountain to drink, and that he suddenly dragged him to his feet by his hair and asked him who he was and what he was doing there. The fellow begged in his humility to be released, saying, 'Three of us came to this solitude in order that, living here in penance, we might become imitators of the Fathers of old: the first and best of us was a Frank, the second, far braver and nobler than I, was an Englishman, I am a Scot. The Frank is of such perfection that I fear to speak of his life, for it passeth belief; the Angle, or rather angel, is bound with an iron chain only so long that it can be stretched seven feet. He always beareth with him an iron hammer and a stake with which he fasteneth his chain to the earth on the Sabbath, and within these narrow bounds he prayeth throughout the whole week, unfailing in hymns of joy. He is never complaining or sad; eating what he findeth there, he moveth his camp on the Sabbath, not wandering aimlessly, but seeking a place pleasant in its prospect, not plentiful in its products, a retreat not protected from the inclemency of the weather; and wherever he findeth any food with water near-by, there with joy in his heart he staketh out his possession. If you want to see this man, he is making his residence this week by the stream which floweth from this spring.' With these words he ran away with the speed of a wild animal. A little while after, the Neapolitan found the Englishman dead, and feeling such reverence for his virtues that he did not presume to touch him nor anything of his, he departed, entrusting to followers the due rites of burial. This Englishman bore in his heart Christ the fountain of joy, hence to him narrow circumstances could bring no sadness. So, as the Lord saith, let 'hypocrites be sad,' because 'perfect charity casteth out fear' together with sadness.

ADVICE OF VALERIUS TO RUFFINUS NOT TO MARRY

. . . The first wife of the first man (Adam) after the first creation of man, by the first sin, relieved her first hunger against God's direct command. Great hath been the spawn of Disobedience, which until the end of the world will never cease from assailing women and rendering them ever unwearied in carrying to the fell consequences their chief inheritance from their mother. O friend, a man's highest reproach is a disobedient wife. Beware!

The truth of God, which cannot err, saith of the blessed David: 'I have found a man after mine own heart.' Yet even he is a signal instance of descent, through the love of woman, from adultery to homicide, that 'offences may never come singly.' For every sin is rich in abundant company and surrendereth whatever home it entereth to the pollution of its fellow vices. O friend, Bathsheba spake not a word and maligned no man, yet she became the instigation of the overthrow of the perfect man and the dart of death to her innocent mate. Shall she be held guiltless who shall battle by her charm of speech as Samson's Delilah, and by her grace of form as Bathsheba, although her beauty alone may have triumphed without her will? If thou art not more after God's heart than David, doubt not that thou too mayst fall.

That sun of men, Solomon, treasure-house of the Lord's delights, chief dwelling-place of wisdom, was darkened by the inky blackness of shadows and lost the light of his soul, the fragrance of his fame, the glory of his home, by the witchery of women. At the last, having bowed his knee to Baal, he was degraded from a priest of the Lord to a limb of the devil, so that he seemed to be thrust over a yet greater precipice than Phoebus, who, after Phaeton's fall, was changed from the Apollo of Jove into the shepherd of Admetus. Friend, if thou art not wiser than Solomon — and no man is that — thou art not greater than he who can be bewitched by woman. 'Open thine eyes and see.'

Even the very good woman, who is rarer than the phoenix, cannot be loved without the loathsome bitterness of fear and worry and constant unhappiness. But bad women, of whom the swarm is so large that no spot is without their malice, punish bitterly the bestowal of love, and devote themselves utterly to dealing distress, 'to the division of soul and body.' O friend, a trite moral is, 'Look to whom thou givest.' True morality is, 'Look to whom thou givest thyself.'

Lucretia and Penelope, as well as the Sabine women, have borne aloft the banners of modesty and they have brought back trophies with but few in their following. Friend, there is now no Lucretia, no Penelope, no Sabine woman. Fear all the sex.

THE DECADENCE OF SOCIETY

What reason is there that we have fallen from our original estate in strength and virtue, and that all other living things in no way vary from their earliest endowment? Adam was created a giant in stature and in strength, he was made also an angel in mind until he was overthrown; although his immortality put on mortality, and his perfection imperfection, his life was much soothed by the solace of length of days. This happiness of morals, strength, virtue, and life lasted long unto his posterity; but in the time of the prophet of the Lord, David, he himself described as being of eighty years that life which had formerly been eight hundred or more without labour and sorrow. But we do not last seventy unharmed; nay, just as soon as we have begun to be wise, we are forced to die or lose our wits. Save man alone, all living things of earth, sea, and air enjoy the life and powers with which they were endowed at creation, as if they had not fallen from the grace of their Creator. What reason is there, unless it be that they observe the obedience enjoined them and we have refused it from the beginning? We have much the more reason for our sore distress in that, whereas all things still stand, the devils and we alone have fallen, in that we have our tempters as our allies, and in that our wickedness, arising from our imitation of the chief of sinners, hath found its punishment in the shortness of our day and strength.

Late 12th c.

ANONYMOUS LYRICS *

THE GLUTTON'S CONFESSION

In the public-house to die
  Is my resolution;
Let wine to my lips be nigh
  At life's dissolution:
That will make the angels cry,
  With glad elocution,
'Grant this toper, God on high,
  Grace and absolution!'

With the cup the soul lights up,
  Inspirations flicker;
Nectar lifts the soul on high
  With its heavenly ichor:
To my lips a sounder taste
  Hath the tavern's liquor
Than the wine a village clerk
  Waters for the vicar.

Nature gives to every man
  Some gift serviceable;
Write I never could nor can
  Hungry at the table;
Fasting, any stripling to
  Vanquish me is able;
Hunger, thirst, I liken to
  Death that ends the fable.

Nature gives to every man
  Gifts as she is willing;
I compose my verses when
  Good wine I am swilling,
Wine the best for jolly guest
  Jolly hosts are filling;
From such wine rare fancies fine
  Flow like dews distilling.

* From *Wine, Women, and Song*, translation by J. A. Symonds, Medieval Library, American Branch Oxford University Press, 1907. By permission of Chatto and Windus, Publishers.

Such my verse is wont to be
  As the wine I swallow;
No ripe thoughts enliven me
  While my stomach's hollow;
Hungry wits on hungry lips
  Like a shadow follow,
But when once I'm in my cups,
  I can beat Apollo.

12th c. or earlier

GAUDEAMUS IGITUR

Let us live, then, and be glad
  While young life's before us!
    After youthful pastime had,
    After old age hard and sad,
Earth will slumber o'er us.

Where are they who in this world,
  Ere we kept, were keeping?
    Go ye to the gods above;
    Go to hell; inquire thereof:
They are not; they're sleeping.

Brief is life, and brevity
  Briefly shall be ended:
    Death comes like a whirlwind strong,
    Bears us with his blast along;
None shall be defended.

Live this university,
  Men that learning nourish;
    Live each member of the same,
    Long live all that bear its name;
  Let them ever flourish!

Live the commonwealth also,
  And the men that guide it!
    Live our town in strength and health,
    Founders, patrons, by whose wealth
We are here provided!

Live all girls! A health to you
  Melting maids and beauteous!
    Live the wives and women too,
    Gentle, loving, tender, true,
Good, industrious, duteous!

Perish cares that pule and pine!
  Perish envious blamers!
    Die the Devil, thine and mine!
    Die the starch-necked Philistine!
Scoffers and defamers!

12th c. or earlier

Bartholomew (fl. ca. 1250)

A MEDIÆVAL ENCYCLOPEDIA *

MANNERS

Men behove to take heed of maidens: for they be tender of complexion; small, pliant and fair of disposition of body; shamefast,[1] fearful,[2] and merry. Touching outward disposition they be well nurtured, demure and soft of speech, and well ware of what they say: and delicate in their apparel. And for a woman is more meeker than a man, she weepeth sooner. And is more envious, and more laughing, and loving, and the malice of the soul is more in a woman than in a man. And she is of feeble kind, and she maketh more lesings,[3] and is more shamefast, and more slow in working and in moving than is a man.

A man is called Vir in Latin, and hath that name of might and strength. For in might and strength a man passeth a woman. A man is the head of a woman, as the apostle saith. And therefore a man is bound to rule his wife, as the head hath charge and rule of the body. And a man is called Maritus, as it were warding and defending Matrem, the mother, for he taketh ward and keeping of his wife, that is mother of the children. And is called Sponsus also, and hath that name of Spondere, for that he behoveth[4] and obligeth[4] himself. For in the contract of wedding he plighteth his troth to lead his life with his wife without departing, and to pay her his debt, and to keep her and love her afore all other. A man hath so great love to his wife that for her sake he adventureth himself to all perils; and setteth her love afore his mother's love; for he dwelleth with his wife, and forsaketh father and mother. Afore wedding, the spouse thinketh to win love of her that he wooeth with gifts, and certifieth of his will with letters and messengers, and with divers presents, and giveth many gifts, and much good and cattle, and promiseth much more. And to please her he putteth him to divers plays and games among gatherings of men, and useth oft deeds of arms, of might, and of

* From Robt. Steele's *Mediæval Lore*, 1905, Mediæval Library, Chatto and Windus (England) and Oxford University Press (America). By permission of the publishers.

[1] shamefaced [2] easily terrified [3] untruths [4] places under obligation

mastery. And maketh him gay and seemly in divers clothing and array. And all that he is prayed to give and to do for her love, he giveth and doth anon with all his might. And denieth no petition that is made in her name and for her love. He speaketh to her pleasantly, and beholdeth her cheer in the face with pleasing and glad cheer, and with a sharp eye, and at last assenteth to her, and telleth openly his will in presence of her friends, and spouseth her with a ring and giveth her gifts in token of contract of wedding, and maketh her charters, and deeds of grants and of gifts. He maketh revels and feasts and spousals, and giveth many good gifts to friends and guests, and comforteth and gladdeth his guests with songs and pipes and other minstrelsy of music. And afterward, when all this is done, he bringeth her to the privities of his chamber, and maketh her fellow at bed and at board. And then he maketh her lady of his money, and of his house and meinie.[1] And then he is no less diligent and careful for her than he is for himself: and specially lovingly he adviseth her if she do amiss, and taketh good heed to keep her well, and taketh heed of her bearing and going, of her speaking and looking, of her passing and ayencoming, out and home. No man hath more wealth, than he that hath a good woman to his wife, and no man hath more woe, than he that hath an evil wife, crying and jangling, chiding and scolding, drunken, lecherous, and unsteadfast, and contrary to him, costly, stout and gay, envious, noyful, leaping over lands, much suspicious, and wrathful. In a good spouse and wife behoveth these conditions, that she be busy and devout in God's service, meek and serviceable to her husband, and fair-speaking and goodly to her meinie, merciful and good to wretches that be needy, easy and peaceable to her neighbours, ready, wary, and wise in things that should be avoided, mightiful and patient in suffering, busy and diligent in her doing, mannerly in clothing, sober in moving, wary in speaking, chaste in looking, honest in bearing, sad[2] in going,[3] shamefast among the people, merry and glad with her husband, and chaste in privity. Such a wife is worthy to be praised, that entendeth more to please her husband with such womanly dues, than with her braided hairs, and desireth more to please him with virtues than with fair and gay clothes, and useth the goodness of matrimony more because of children than of fleshly liking, and hath more liking to have children of grace than of kind.

A man loveth his child and feedeth and nourisheth it, and setteth it at his own board when it is weaned. And teacheth him in his youth with speech and words, and chasteneth him with beating, and setteth him and putteth him to learn under ward and keeping of wardens and tutors. And the father sheweth him no glad cheer, lest he wax proud, and he loveth most the son that is like to him, and looketh oft on him. And giveth to his children clothing, meat and drink as their age requireth, and purchaseth lands and heritage for his children, and ceaseth not to make it more and more. And entaileth his purchase, and leaveth it to his heirs . . . The child cometh of the substance of father and mother, and taketh of them feeding and nourishing, and profiteth not, neither liveth, without help of them. The more the father loveth his child, the more busily he teacheth and chastiseth him and holdeth him the more strait under chastising and lore; and when the child is most loved of the father it seemeth that he loveth him not; for he beateth and grieveth him oft lest he draw to evil manners and tatches,[4] and the more the child is like the father, the better the father loveth him. The father is ashamed if he hear any foul thing told by his children. The father's heart is sore grieved, if his children rebel against him. In feeding and nourishing of their children stands the most business and charge of the parents.

Meat and drink be ordained and convenient to dinners and to feasts, for at feasts first meat is prepared and arrayed, guests be called together, forms and stools be set in the hall, and tables, cloths, and towels be ordained, disposed, and made ready. Guests be set with the lord in the chief place of the board, and they sit not down at the board before the guests wash their hands. Children be set in their place, and servants at a table by themselves.

[1] household [2] sedate [3] walking [4] tricks

First knives, spoons, and salts be set on the board, and then bread and drink, and many divers messes; household servants busily help each other to do everything diligently, and talk merrily together. The guests be gladded with lutes and harps. Now wine and now messes of meat be brought forth and departed.[1] At the last cometh fruit and spices, and when they have eaten, board, cloths, and relief[2] are borne away, and guests wash and wipe their hands again. Then grace is said, and guests thank the lord. Then for gladness and comfort drink is brought yet again. When all this is done at meat, men take their leave, and some go to bed and sleep, and some go home to their own lodgings.

MEDICINE

These be the signs of frenzy, woodness[3] and continual waking, moving and casting about the eyes, raging, stretching, and casting out of hands, moving and wagging of the head, grinding and gnashing together of the teeth; always they will arise out of their bed, now they sing, now they weep, and they bite gladly and rend their keeper and their leech[4]: seldom be they still, but cry much. And these be most perilously sick, and yet they wot not then that they be sick. Then they must be soon holpen lest they perish, and that both in diet and in medicine. The diet shall be full scarce, as crumbs of bread, which must many times be wet in water. The medicine is, that in the beginning the patient's head be shaven, and washed in lukewarm vinegar, and that he be well kept or bound in a dark place. Diverse shapes of faces and semblance of painting shall not be shewed tofore him, lest he be tarred[5] with woodness. All that be about him shall be commanded to be still and in silence; men shall not answer to his nice words. In the beginning of medicine he shall be let blood in a vein of the forehead, and bled as much as will fill an egg-shell. Afore all things (if virtue[6] and age suffereth) he shall bleed in the head vein. Over all things, with ointments and balming men shall labour to bring him asleep. The head that is shaven shall be plastered with lungs of a swine, or of a wether, or of a sheep; the temples and forehead shall be anointed with the juice of lettuce, or of poppy. If after these medicines are laid thus to, the woodness dureth three days without sleep, there is no hope of recovery.

GEOGRAPHY

England is the most island of Ocean, and is beclipped[7] all about by the sea, and departed[8] from the roundness of the world, and hight sometimes Albion: and had that name of white rocks, which were seen on the sea cliffs. And by continuance of time, lords and noble men of Troy, after that Troy was destroyed, went from thence, and were accompanied with a great navy, and fortuned to the cliffs of the foresaid island, and that by revelation of their feigned goddess Pallas, as it is said, and the Trojans fought with giants long time that dwelled therein, and overcame the giants, both with craft and with strength, and conquered the island, and called the land Britain, by the name of Brute that was prince of that host: and so the island hight Britain, as it were an island conquered of Brute that time, with arms and with might. Of this Brute's offspring came most mighty kings. And who that hath liking to know their deeds, let him read the story of Brute.

And long time after, the Saxons won the island with many and divers hard battles and strong, and their offspring had possession after them of the island, and the Britons were slain or exiled, and the Saxons departed[9] the island among them, and gave every province a name, by the property of its own name and nation, and therefore they cleped[10] the island Anglia, by the name of Engelia the queen, the worthiest duke of Saxony's daughter, that had the island in possession after many battles. Isidore saith, that this land hight Anglia, and hath that name of Angulus, a corner, as it were land set in the end, or a corner of the world. But saint Gregory, seeing English children to sell at Rome, when they were not christened, and hearing that they were called English: according with the name of the country, he answered and said: Truly they be English,

[1] apportioned out
[2] dessert
[3] madness
[4] physician
[5] provoked, incited
[6] strength
[7] embraced, surrounded
[8] separated
[9] shared
[10] called

for they shine in face right as angels: it is need to send them message, with word of salvation. For as Beda saith, the noble kind[1] of the land shone in their faces. Isidore saith, Britain, that now hight Anglia, is an island set afore France and Spain, and containeth about 48 times 75 miles. Also therein be many rivers and great and hot wells. There is great plenty of metals, there be enough of the stones Agates, and of pearls, the ground is special good, most apt to bear corn and other good fruit. There be, namely, many sheep with good wool, there be many harts and other wild beasts; there be few wolves or none, therefore there be many sheep, and may be securely left without ward, in pasture and in fields, as Beda saith.

England is a strong land and a sturdy, and the plenteousest corner of the world, so rich a land that unneth[2] it needeth help of any land, and every other land needeth help of England. England is full of mirth and of game, and men oft times able to mirth and game, free men of heart and with tongue, but the hand is more better and more free than the tongue.

NATURAL HISTORY

Phoenix is a bird, and there is but one of that kind in all the wide world. Therefore lewd[3] men wonder thereof, and among the Arabs, where this bird is bred, he is called singular — alone. The philosopher speaketh of this bird and saith that phoenix is a bird without make,[4] and liveth three hundred or five hundred years: when the which years are past, and he feeleth his own default and feebleness, he maketh a nest of right sweet-smelling sticks, that are full dry, and in summer when the western wind blows, the sticks and the nest are set on fire with burning heat of the sun, and burn strongly. Then this bird phoenix cometh wilfully[5] into the burning nest, and is there burnt to ashes among these burning sticks, and within three days a little worm is gendered of the ashes, and waxeth little and little, and taketh feathers and is shapen and turned to a bird. Ambrose saith the same in the Hexameron: Of the humours or ashes of phoenix ariseth a new bird and waxeth, and in space of time he is clothed with feathers and wings and restored into the kind[6] of a bird, and is the most fairest bird that is, most like to the peacock in feathers, and loveth the wilderness, and gathereth his meat of clean grains and fruits. Alan speaketh of this bird and saith, that when the highest bishop Onyas builded a temple in the city of Heliopolis in Egypt, to the likeness of the temple in Jerusalem, on the first day of Easter, when he had gathered much sweet-smelling wood, and set it on fire upon the altar to offer sacrifice, to all men's sight such a bird came suddenly, and fell into the middle of the fire, and was burnt anon to ashes in the fire of the sacrifice, and the ashes abode there, and were busily kept and saved by the commandments of the priests, and within three days, of these ashes was bred a little worm, that took the shape of a bird at the last, and flew into the wilderness.

Nothing is more busy and wittier[7] than a hound, for he hath more wit[8] than other beasts. And hounds know their own names, and love their masters, and defend the houses of their masters, and put themselves wilfully in peril of death for their masters, and run to take prey for their masters, and forsake not the dead bodies of their masters. We have known that hounds fought for their lords against thieves, and were sore wounded and that they kept away beasts and fowls from their masters' bodies dead. And that a hound compelled the slayer of his master with barking and biting to acknowledge his trespass and guilt. Also we read that Garamantus the king came out of exile, and brought with him two hundred hounds, and fought against his enemies with wondrous hardiness.[9]

Satyrs be somewhat like men, and have crooked nose and horns in the forehead, and like to goats in their feet. Saint Anthony saw such a one in the wilderness, as it is said, and he asked what he was and he answered Anthony, and said: 'I am deadly, and one of them that dwelleth in the wilderness.' These wonderful beasts be divers: for some of them be called Cynocephali, for they have heads as hounds, and seem by the

[1] nature, character
[2] hardly
[3] unlearned
[4] mate
[5] of set purpose
[6] nature
[7] more sensible, more knowing
[8] intelligence
[9] boldness

working, beasts rather than men, and some be called Cyclops, and have that name, for one of them hath but one eye, and that in the middle of the forehead, and some be all headless and noseless, and their eyen be in the shoulders, and some have plain faces without nostrils, and the nether lips of them stretch so, that they hele[1] therewith their faces when they be in the heat of the sun: and some of them have closed mouths, in their breasts only one hole, and breathe and such as it were with pipes and veins, and these be accounted tongueless, and use signs and becks instead of speaking. Also in Scythia be some with so great and large ears, that they spread their ears and cover all their bodies with them, and these be called Panchios. . . . And other be in Ethiopia, and each of them have only one foot so great and so large, that they beshadow themselves with the foot when they lie gaping on the ground in strong heat of the sun; and yet they be so swift, that they be likened to hounds in swiftness of running, and therefore among the Greeks they be called Cynopodes. Also some have the soles of their feet turned backward behind the legs, and in each foot eight toes, and such go about and stare in the desert of Lybia.

The mermaid is a sea beast wonderly shapen, and draweth shipmen to peril by sweetness of song. The Gloss on Is. xiii. saith that sirens are serpents with crests. And some men say, that they are fishes of the sea in likeness of women. Some men feign that there are three Sirens some-deal maidens, and some-deal fowls with claws and wings, and one of them singeth with voice, and another with a pipe, and the third with an harp, and they please so shipmen, with likeness of song, that they draw them to peril and to shipbreach,[2] but the sooth is, that they were strong hores, that drew men that passed by them to poverty and to mischief. And Physiologus saith it is a beast of the sea, wonderly shapen as a maid from the navel upward and a fish from the navel downward, and this wonderful beast is glad and merry in tempest, and sad and heavy in fair weather. With sweetness of song this beast maketh shipmen to sleep, and when she seeth that they are asleep, she goeth into the ship, and ravisheth which she may take with her, and bringeth him into a dry place, and maketh him first lie by her, and if he will not or may not, then she slayeth him and eateth his flesh. Of such wonderful beasts it is written in the great Alexander's story.

The sapphire is a precious stone, and is blue in colour, most like to heaven in fair weather, and clear, and is best among precious stones, and most apt and able to fingers of kings. Its virtue is contrary to venom and quencheth it every deal. And if thou put an addercop[3] in a box, and hold a very sapphire of Ind at the mouth of the box any while, by virtue thereof the addercop is overcome and dieth, as it were suddenly. And this same I have seen proved oft in many and divers places.

ca. 1250

Richard de Bury (1281–1345)

PHILOBIBLON, OR LOVE OF BOOKS *

Chapter I

THAT THE TREASURE OF WISDOM IS CHIEFLY CONTAINED IN BOOKS

The desirable treasure of wisdom and science which all men desire by an instinct of nature, infinitely surpasses all the riches of the world; in respect of which precious stones are worthless; in comparison with which silver is as clay and pure gold is as a little sand; at whose splendour the sun and moon are dark to look upon; compared with whose marvellous sweetness honey and manna are bitter to the taste. O value of wisdom that fadeth not away with time, virtue ever flourishing, that cleanseth its possessor from all venom! O heavenly gift of the divine bounty, descending from the Father of lights, that thou mayest exalt the rational soul to the very heavens! Thou art the celestial nourishment of the intellect,

* Translation by E. C. Thomas, Medieval Library, American Branch Oxford University Press. Chatto and Windus, London, Publishers, 1913. By permission of Kegan Paul, Trench, Trubner & Company.

[1] cover [2] shipwreck [3] spider

which those who eat shall still hunger and those who drink shall still thirst, and the gladdening harmony of the languishing soul which he that hears shall never be confounded. Thou art the moderator and rule of morals, which he who follows shall not sin. By thee kings reign and princes decree justice. By thee, rid of their native rudeness, their minds and tongues being polished, the thorns of vice being torn up by the roots, those men attain high places of honour, and become fathers of their country, and companions of princes, who without thee would have melted their spears into pruning-hooks and ploughshares, or would perhaps be feeding swine with the prodigal.

Where dost thou chiefly lie hidden, O most elect treasure! and where shall thirsting souls discover thee?

Certes, thou hast placed thy tabernacle in books, where the Most High, the Light of lights, the Book of Life, has established thee. There everyone who asks receiveth thee, and everyone who seeks finds thee, and to everyone that knocketh boldly it is speedily opened. Therein the cherubim spread out their wings, that the intellect of the students may ascend and look from pole to pole, from the east and west, from the north and from the south. Therein the mighty and incomprehensible God Himself is apprehensibly contained and worshipped; therein is revealed the nature of things celestial, terrestrial, and infernal; therein are discerned the laws by which every state is administered, the offices of the celestial hierarchy are distinguished, and the tyrannies of demons described, such as neither the ideas of Plato transcend, nor the chair of Crato contained.

In books I find the dead as if they were alive; in books I foresee things to come; in books warlike affairs are set forth; from books come forth the laws of peace. All things are corrupted and decay in time; Saturn ceases not to devour the children that he generates; all the glory of the world would be buried in oblivion, unless God had provided mortals with the remedy of books.

Alexander, the conqueror of the earth, Julius, the invader of Rome and of the world, who, the first in war and arts, assumed universal empire under his single rule, faithful Fabricius and stern Cato, would now have been unknown to fame, if the aid of books had been wanting. Towers have been razed to the ground; cities have been overthrown; triumphal arches have perished from decay; nor can either pope or king find any means of more easily conferring the privilege of perpetuity than by books. The book that he has made renders its author this service in return, that so long as the book survives its author remains immortal and cannot die, as Ptolemy declares in the Prologue to his Almagest: He is not dead, he says, who has given life to science.

Who wherefore will limit by anything of another kind the price of the infinite treasure of books, from which the scribe who is instructed bringeth forth things new and old? Truth that triumphs over all things, which overcomes the king, wine, and women, which it is reckoned holy to honour before friendship, which is the way without turning and the life without end, which holy Boethius considers to be three-fold in thought, speech, and writing, seems to remain more usefully and to fructify to greater profit in books. For the meaning of the voice perishes with the sound; truth latent in the mind is wisdom that is hid and treasure that is not seen; but truth which shines forth in books desires to manifest itself to every impressionable sense. It commends itself to the sight when it is read, to the hearing when it is heard, and moreover in a manner to the touch, when it suffers itself to be transcribed, bound, corrected, and preserved. The undisclosed truth of the mind, although it is the possession of the noble soul, yet because it lacks a companion, is not certainly known to be delightful, while neither sight nor hearing takes account of it. Further the truth of the voice is patent only to the ear and eludes the sight, which reveals to us more of the qualities of things, and linked with the subtlest of motions begins and perishes as it were in a breath. But the written truth of books, not transient but permanent, plainly offers itself to be observed, and by means of the previous spherules of the eyes, passing through the vestibule of perception and the courts of imagination, enters the chamber of intellect, taking its place in the couch of memory, where it engenders the eternal truth of the mind.

Finally we must consider what pleasantness of teaching there is in books, how easy, how secret! How safely we lay bare the poverty of human ignorance to books without feeling any shame! They are masters who instruct us without rod or ferule, without angry words, without clothes or money. If you come to them they are not asleep; if you ask and inquire of them they do not withdraw themselves; they do not chide if you make mistakes; they do not laugh at you if you are ignorant. O books, who alone are liberal and free, who give to all who ask of you and enfranchise all who serve you faithfully! by how many thousand types are ye commended to learned men in the Scriptures given us by inspiration of God! For ye are the minds of profoundest wisdom, to which the wise man sends his son that he may dig out treasures: Prov. ii. Ye are the wells of living waters, which father Abraham first digged, Isaac digged again, and which the Philistines strive to fill up: Gen. xxvi. Ye are indeed the most delightful ears of corn, full of grain, to be rubbed only by apostolic hands, that the sweetest food may be produced for hungry souls: Matt. xii. Ye are the golden pots in which manna is stored, and rocks flowing with honey, nay, combs of honey, most plenteous udders of the milk of life, garners ever full; ye are the tree of life and the fourfold river of Paradise, by which the human mind is nourished, and the thirsty intellect is watered and refreshed. Ye are the ark of Noah and the ladder of Jacob, and the troughs by which the young of those who look therein are coloured; ye are the stones of testimony and the pitchers holding the lamps of Gideon, the scrip of David, from which the smoothest stones are taken for the slaying of Goliath. Ye are the golden vessels of the temple, the arms of the soldiers of the Church with which to quench all the fiery darts of the wicked, fruitful olives, vines of Engadi, fig-trees that are never barren, burning lamps always to be held in readiness — and all the noblest comparisons of Scripture may be applied to books, if we choose to speak in figures.

Chapter XVII

OF SHOWING DUE PROPRIETY IN THE CUSTODY OF BOOKS

We are not only rendering service to God in preparing volumes of new books, but also exercising an office of sacred piety when we treat books carefully, and again when we restore them to their proper places and commend them to inviolable custody; that they may rejoice in purity while we have them in our hands, and rest securely when they are put back in their repositories. And surely next to the vestments and vessels dedicated to the Lord's body, holy books deserve to be rightly treated by the clergy, to which great injury is done so often as they are touched by unclean hands. Wherefore we deem it expedient to warn our students of various negligences, which might always be easily avoided and do wonderful harm to books.

And in the first place as to the opening and closing of books, let there be due moderation, that they be not unclasped in precipitate haste, nor when we have finished our inspection be put away without being duly closed. For it behoves us to guard a book much more carefully than a boot.

But the race of scholars is commonly badly brought up, and unless they are bridled in by the rules of their elders they indulge in infinite puerilities. They behave with petulance, and are puffed up with presumption, judging of everything as if they were certain, though they are altogether inexperienced.

You may happen to see some headstrong youth lazily lounging over his studies, and when the winter's frost is sharp, his nose running from the nipping cold drips down, nor does he think of wiping it with his pocket-handkerchief until he has bedewed the book before him with the ugly moisture. Would that he had before him no book, but a cobbler's apron! His nails are stuffed with fetid filth as black as jet, with which he marks any passage that pleases him. He distributes a multitude of straws, which he inserts to stick out in different places, so that the halm may remind him of what his memory cannot retain. These straws, because the book has no stomach to digest them, and no one takes them out, first distend the book from its wonted closing, and at length, being carelessly abandoned to oblivion, go to decay. He does not fear to eat fruit or cheese over an open book, or carelessly to carry a cup to and from his mouth; and because he has no wallet at hand he drops into books the fragments that are left. Continually chattering, he is never weary of disputing with his companions, and while he alleges a crowd of senseless arguments, he wets the book lying half open in his lap with sputtering showers. Aye, and then hastily folding his arms he leans forward on the book, and by a brief spell of study invites a prolonged nap; and then, by way of mending the wrinkles, he folds back the margin of the leaves, to the no small injury of the book. Now the rain is over and gone, and the flowers have appeared in our land. Then the scholar we are speaking of, a neglecter rather than an inspecter of books, will stuff his volume with violets, and primroses, with roses and quatrefoil. Then he will use his wet and perspiring hands to turn over the volumes; then he will thump the white vellum with gloves covered with all kinds of dust, and with his finger clad in long-used leather will hunt line by line through the page; then at the sting of the biting flea the sacred book is flung aside, and is hardly shut for another month, until it is so full of the dust that has found its way within, that it resists the effort to close it.

But the handling of books is specially to be forbidden to those shameless youths, who as soon as they have learned to form the shapes of letters, straightway, if they have the opportunity, become unhappy commentators, and wherever they find an extra margin about the text, furnish it with monstrous alphabets, or if any other frivolity strikes their fancy, at once their pen begins to write it. There the Latinist and sophister and every unlearned writer tries the fitness of his pen, a practice that we have frequently seen injuring the usefulness and value of the most beautiful books.

Again, there is a class of thieves shamefully mutilating books, who cut away the margins from the sides to use as material for letters, leaving only the text, or employ the leaves from the ends, inserted for the protection of the book, for various uses and abuses — a kind of sacrilege which should be prohibited by the threat of anathema.

Again, it is part of the decency of scholars that whenever they return from meals to their study, washing should invariably precede reading, and that no grease-stained finger should unfasten the clasps, or turn the leaves of a book. Nor let a crying child admire the pictures in the capital letters, lest he soil the parchment with wet fingers; for a child instantly touches whatever he sees. Moreover, the laity, who look at a book turned upside down just as if it were open in the right way, are utterly unworthy of any communion with books. Let the clerk take care also that the smutty scullion reeking from his stewpots does not touch the lily leaves of books, all unwashed, but he who walketh without blemish shall minister to the precious volumes. And, again, the cleanliness of decent hands would be of great benefit to books as well as scholars, if it were not that the itch and pimples are characteristic of the clergy.

Whenever defects are noticed in books, they should be promptly repaired, since nothing spreads more quickly then a tear and a rent which is neglected at the time will have to be repaired afterwards with usury.

Moses, the gentlest of men, teaches us to make bookcases most neatly, wherein they may be protected from any injury: Take, he says, this book of the law, and put it in the side of the ark of the covenant of the Lord your God. O fitting place and appropriate for a library, which was made of imperishable shittim-wood, and was all covered within and without with gold! But the Saviour also has warned us by His example against all unbecoming carelessness in the handling of books, as we read in S. Luke. For when He had read the scriptural prophecy of Himself in the book that was delivered to Him, He did not give it again to the minister, until He had closed it with his own most sacred hands. By which students are most clearly taught that in the care of books the merest trifles ought not to be neglected.

ca. 1345

RIMED CHRONICLE

Layamon (fl. ca. 1200)

BRUT

THE PASSING OF ARTHUR

THA[1] Modred hafde[2] his ferde[3]
isomned[4] of monnen,[5]
tha weoren[6] there italde[7]
sixti thusende
here-kempen[8] harde
of hethene folke,
tha heo[9] weoren icumen hidere
for Arthures hærme,
Modred to helpen,
forcuthest[10] monnen.
Tha the ferde wes isome[11]
of ælche mon-cunne[12]
tha heo weoren ther on hepe
an hundred thusende,
hethene and cristene,
mid Modrede kinge.
Arthur lai at Whitsond;
feouwertene niht him thuhte[13] to long.
And al Modred wuste[14]
wat[15] Arthur thær wolde;
ælche dai him comen sonde[16]
from thas kinges hirede.[17]
Tha ilomp[18] hit an one time
muchel rein[19] him gon[20] rine,[19]
and the wind him gon wende[21]
and stod of than æstende;
and Arthur him to scipe[22] fusde[23]
mid alle his ferde,
and hehte[24] that his scipmen
brohte hine to Romenel,
ther he thohte up wende
in to thissen londe.
Tha he to there havene com,
Modred him wes aforn on[25];
ase the dæi gon lihten
heo bigunnen to fihten
alle thene longe dæi;
moni mon ther ded læi,
summe hi fuhten a londe,
summe bi than stronde;
summe heo letten ut of scipen
scerpe[26] garen[27] scrithen.[28]
Walwain biforen wende
and thene wæi rumde,[29]
and sloh[30] ther a-neuste[31]
theines[32] elleovene[33];
he sloh Childriches sune,[34]
the was ther mid his fader icume.[35]
To reste eode[36] the sunne;
wæ[37] wes tha monnen.
Ther wes Walwain afslæge,[38]
and idon[39] of life-dage,
thurh an eorle[40] Sexisne:
særi wurthe[41] his saule.[42]
Tha wes Arthur særi
and sorhful an heorte forthi[43];
and thas word bodede,[44]
ricchest alre[45] Brutte:
'Nu ich[46] ileosed[47] habbe
mine sweines[48] leofe.[49]
Ich wuste bi mine swevene[50]
whæt soryen[51] me weoren yevethe.[52]
Islagen is Angel the king
the wes min ayen[53] deorling,
and Walwaine mi suster sune:
wa is me that ich was mon iboren.
Up nu of scipen bilive,[54]
mine beornes[55] ohte.'[56]
Æfne[57] than worde
wenden to fihte
sixti thusend anon:
selere[58] kempen,
and breken Modredes trume,[59]
and wel neh[60] him seolve wes inome.[61]
Modred bigon to fleon
and his folc after teon[62];
fluyen feondliche[63];
feldes beoveden[64] eke[65];
yurren[66] tha stanes
mid than blod-stremes.
Ther weore al that fiht idon,
ah[67] that niht to rathe[68] com;
yif tha niht neore,[69]
islayen hi weoren alle.
The niht heom todelde[70]

1 when, then
2 had
3 army
4 assembled
5 men
6 were
7 told, counted
8 warriors
9 they
10 wickedest
11 gathered
12 people
13 seemed
14 knew
15 what
16 messengers
17 army
18 happened
19 rain
20 did
21 turn
22 ship
23 proceeded
24 ordered
25 before
26 sharp
27 spears
28 go, fly
29 cleared
30 slew
31 quickly
32 thanes
33 eleven
34 son
35 come
36 went
37 woe
38 slain
39 deprived
40 earl
41 be
42 soul
43 for that
44 said
45 of all
46 I
47 lost
48 swains
49 dear
50 dream
51 sorrows
52 given
53 own
54 quickly
55 men
56 brave
57 even
58 good
59 troop, band
60 nigh
61 taken
62 follow
63 fiercely
64 trembled
65 also
66 resounded
67 but
68 quickly
69 had not been
70 separated

yeond[1] slades[2] and yeond dunen[3];
and Modred swa[4] forth com
that he wes at Lundene.
Iherden[5] tha burh-weren[6]
hu hit was al ifaren,[7]
and warnden[8] him inyeong[9]
and alle his folke.
Modred theone wende
toward Winchestre,
and heo hine underfengen[10]
mid alle his monnen.
And Arthur after wende
mid alle his mahte,[11]
that he com to Winchestre
mid muchelre ferde,
and tha burh[12] al biræd,[13]
and Modred therinne abeod.[14]
Tha Modred isæh[15]
that Arthur him wes swa neh,
ofte he hine bithohte
wæt he don mahte.
Tha a there ilke[16] niht
he hehte his cnihtes[17] alle,
mid alle heore iwepnen[18]
ut of burhye wenden,
and sæide that he weolde
mid fihte ther at-stonden.[19]
He bihehte there buryewere
aver mare freo laye[20]
with than tha heo him heolpen
at heyere[21] neoden.[22]
Tha hit wes dæi-liht
yaru[23] that wes heore fiht.
Arthur that bi-hedde,[24]
the king wes abolye[25];
he lette bemen[26] blawen,
and beonnen[27] men to fihten;
he hehte alle his theines
and athele[28] his cnihte
fon[29] somed[30] to fihten,
and his feond[31] afallen,[32]
and the burh alle fordon,[33]
and that burh-folc ahon.[34]
Heo togadere stopen[35]
and sturnliche fuhten.
Modred tha thohte
what he don mihte;
and he dude[36] there,
alse he dude elleswhare,
swikedom[37] mid than mæste[38];
for avere he dude unwraste[39];
he biswac[40] his iferen[41]
biforen Winchestren,
and lette him to cleopien[42]
his leofeste cnihtes anan,
and his leofeste freond alle
of allen his folke,
and bistal[43] from than fihte:
the feond hine aye[44]:
and that folc gode lette
al ther for-wurthe.[45]
Fuhten alle dæi;
wenden[46] that heore lauerd ther læi,
and weore heom a-neouste[47]
at muchelere neode.
Tha heold he thene wai
that touward Hamtone lai,
and heolde touward havene,
forcuthest hælethe[48];
and nom[49] alle tha scippen
tha ther oht weore,
and tha steormen[50] alle
to than scipen neode,
and ferden[51] into Cornwalen,
forcuthest kingen a than dayen.
And Arthur Winchestre
tha burh bilai[52] wel faste;
and al that moncun[53] of-sloh:
ther wes soryen inoh.[54]
Tha yeonge and tha alde,
alle he aqualde.[55]
Tha that folc wes al ded,
tha burh al for-swelde,[56]
tha lette he mid alle
tobreken tha walles alle.
Tha wes hit itimed[57] there
that Merlin seide while:
'Ærm[58] wurthest[59] thu Winchæstre,
tha eorthe the scal forswalye.[60]'
Swa Merlin sæide,
the witeye[61] wes mære.[62]
Tha quen[63] læi inne Eouwerwic,
næs[64] heo nævere swa sarlic;
that wes Wenhaver tha quene,
færyest wimmonne.
Heo iherde suggen[65]
sothere[66] worden,
hu ofte Modred flah,[67]
and hu Arthur hine bibah[68];
wa wes hire there while

1 through
2 grasslands
3 downs, hills
4 so
5 heard
6 citizens
7 gone
8 denied
9 entrance
10 received
11 might
12 city
13 besieged
14 abode
15 saw
16 same
17 knights
18 weapons
19 make a stand
20 laws
21 great
22 need
23 ready
24 watched
25 enraged
26 trumpets
27 assemble
28 noble
29 gather
30 together
31 enemy
32 fell, cut down
33 destroy
34 hang
35 stepped
36 did
37 treachery
38 most
39 weakly
40 deceived
41 companions
42 call
43 stole away
44 possess
45 perished
46 weened
47 near
48 men
49 took
50 steersmen
51 went
52 besieged
53 people
54 enough
55 killed
56 burnt up
57 befallen
58 wretched
59 becomest, art
60 swallow up
61 prophet
62 famous
63 queen
64 was not
65 say
66 sooth, true
67 fled
68 surrounded

that heo wes on life.
Ut of Eouerwike
bi nihte heo iwende,
and touward Karliun tuhte[1]
swa swithe[2] swa heo mahte.
Thider heo brohten bi nihte
of hire cnihten tweiye;
and me hire hafd[3] bi-wefde[4]
mid ane hali[5] rifte,[6]
and heo wes ther munechene,[7]
karefullest wife.
Tha nusten[8] men of there quene
war[9] heo bicumen weore,
no feole[10] yere seoththe[11]
nuste hit mon to sothe,
whather heo weore on dethe,
[and hu[12] heo[13] henne[14] wende]
tha heo hire seolf weore
isunken in the watere.
Modred wes i Cornwale
and somnede cnihtes feole;
to Irlonde he sende
a-neoste his sonde;
to Sex-londe he sende
a-neouste his sonde;
to Scotlonde he sende
a-neouste his sonde;
he hehten heom to cume alle anan
that wolde lond habben,
other seolver other gold,
other ahte[15] other lond;
on ælchere[16] wisen
he warnede hine seolven,
swa deth[17] ælc witer[18] mon
tha neode cum[an] wen[eth].
Arthur that iherde;
wrathest kinge,
that Modred waes in Cornwale
mid muchele monweorede,[19]
and ther wolde abiden
that Arthur come riden.
Arthur sende sonde
yeond al his kinelonde,[20]
and to cumen alle hehte
that quic[21] wes on londe,
tha to fihte oht weoren,
wepnen to beren;
and wha[22] swa hit for-sete[23]
that the king hete,[24]
the king hine wolde a-folden[25]
quic al forbernen.[26]
Hit læc[27] toward hirede,[28]
folc unimete,[29]
ridinde and ganninde,[30]
swa the rein falleth adune.
Arthur for[31] to Cornwale
mid unimete ferde.
Modred that iherde
and him togeines[32] heolde
mid unimete folke:
ther weore monie fæie.[33]
Uppen there Tambre
heo tuhten to-gadere,
the stude[34] hatte[35] Camelford:
ever mare ilast[36] that ilke weorde.
And at Camelforde wes isomned
sixti thusend,
and ma[37] thusend ther to:
Modred wes heore ælder.[38]
Tha thiderward gon ride
Arthur the riche
mid unimete folke,
fæie thah[39] it weore.
Uppe there Tambre
heo tuhte to-somne,[40]
heven[41] here-marken,[42]
halden to-gadere,
luken[43] sweord longe,
leiden[44] o the helmen;
fur[45] ut sprengen,
speren brastlien,[46]
sceldes[47] gonnen scanen,[48]
scaftes to-breken[49]:
ther faht al to-somne
folc unimete.
Tambre wes on flode
mid unimete blode.
Mon i than fihte non ther ne mihte
ikennen[50] nenne[51] kempe,
no wha dude wurse ne wha bet,
swa that withe[52] wes imenged,[53]
for ælc sloh adun riht,
weore he swein weore he cniht.
Ther wes Modred of-slaye
and idon of lif-daye,
[and alle his cnihtes
islaye] in than fihte.
Ther weoren of-slaye
alle tha snelle,[54]
Arthures hered-men[55]
heye [and lowe]
and tha Bruttes alle

[1] drew, moved
[2] quickly
[3] head
[4] covered
[5] holy
[6] veil
[7] nun
[8] knew not
[9] where
[10] many
[11] afterwards
[12] how
[13] she
[14] hence
[15] possessions
[16] each
[17] doth
[18] prudent
[19] army
[20] kingdom
[21] alive
[22] who
[23] declined
[24] commanded
[25] to the ground, completely
[26] burn up
[27] came
[28] army
[29] innumerable
[30] walking
[31] went
[32] against
[33] fated
[34] place
[35] called
[36] shall last
[37] more
[38] chief
[39] though
[40] together
[41] raise
[42] standards
[43] interlock
[44] smote
[45] fire
[46] crackle
[47] shields
[48] rend apart
[49] break to pieces
[50] recognize
[51] no
[52] conflict
[53] mingled
[54] brave
[55] retainers

of Arthures borde,[1]
and alle his fosterlinges
of feole kineriches.
And Arthur forwunded[2]
mid wal-spere[3] brade[4]:
fiftene he hafde
feondliche wunden;
mon mihte i thare lasten[5]
twa gloven ithraste.[6]
Tha nas ther na mare
i than fehte to lave,[7]
of twa hundred thusend monnen
tha ther leien to-hauwen,[8]
buten Arthur the king ane[9]
and of his cnihtes tweien.
Arthur wes for-wunded
wunder ane swithe[10]:
ther to him com a cnave[11]
the wes of his cunne[12];
he wes Cadores sune,
the eorles of Cornwaile.
Constantin hehte the cnave:
he wes than kinge deore.
Arthur him lokede on,
ther he lai on folden,
and thas word seide
mid sorhfulle heorte:
'Costætin, thu art wilcume;
thu weore Cadores sone:
ich the bitache[13] here
mine kineriche,
and wite[14] mine Bruttes
a[15] to thines lifes ende,
and hald heom alle tha layen
tha habbeoth istonden a mine dayen,
and alle tha layen gode
tha bi Utheres dayen stode.
And ich wulle faren to Avalun,
to fairest alre maidene,
to Argante there quene,
alven[16] swithe sceone[17];
and heo scal mine wunden
makien alle isunde,
al hal[18] me makien
mid haleweiye[19] drenchen.[20]
And seothe ich cumen wulle
to mine kineriche
and wunien[21] mid Brutten
mid muchelere wunne.[22]'
Æfne than worden
ther com of se wenden
that wes an sceort[23] bat[24] lithen,[25]
sceoven[26] mid uthen,[27]
and twa wimmen ther inne
wunderliche idihte[28];
and heo nomen Arthur anan
and aneouste hine fereden[29]
and softe hine adun leiden
and forth gunnen lithen.
Tha wes hit iwurthen[30]
that Merlin seide whilen,
that weore unimete care
of Arthures forth-fare.
Bruttes ileveth[31] yete
that he beo on live
and wunnie in Avalun
mid fairest alre alven;
and lokieth evere Bruttes yete
whan Arthur cume lithen.
Nis naver the mon iboren
of naver nane burde[32] icoren,[33]
the cunne[34] of than sothe
of Arthur sugen[35] mare.
ca. 1200

ROMANCES

SIR GAWAIN AND THE GREEN KNIGHT *

I

After the siege and the assault of Troy, when that burg was destroyed and burnt to ashes, and the traitor tried for his treason, the noble Æneas and his kin sailed forth to become princes and patrons of well-nigh all the Western Isles. Thus Romulus built Rome (and gave to the city his own name, which it bears even to this day); and Ticius turned him to Tuscany; and Langobard raised him up dwellings in Lombardy; and Felix Brutus sailed far over the French flood, and founded the kingdom of Britain, wherein have been war and waste and wonder, and bliss and bale, ofttimes since.

And in that kingdom of Britain have been wrought more gallant deeds than in

1 table
2 wounded
3 slaughter-spear
4 broad
5 least
6 thrust
7 leaving
8 cut to pieces
9 alone
10 much
11 boy
12 kin
13 give
14 keep
15 ever
16 elf
17 bright
18 whole
19 healing
20 draughts
21 dwell
22 joy
23 short
24 boat
25 gliding
26 moved
27 waves
28 dight
29 carried
30 befallen
31 believe
32 lady
33 chosen
34 knows
35 say

* Translation by Jessie L. Weston. David Nutt, 1903. By permission of Simpkin, Marshall, Hamilton, Kent, & Company.

any other; but of all British kings Arthur was the most valiant, as I have heard tell, therefore will I set forth a wondrous adventure that fell out in his time. And if ye will listen to me, but for a little while, I will tell it even as it stands in story stiff and strong, fixed in the letter, as it hath long been known in the land.

King Arthur lay at Camelot upon a Christmas-tide, with many a gallant lord and lovely lady, and all the noble brotherhood of the Round Table. There they held rich revels with gay talk and jest; one while they would ride forth to joust and tourney, and again back to the court to make carols; for there was the feast holden fifteen days with all the mirth that men could devise, song and glee, glorious to hear, in the daytime, and dancing at night. Halls and chambers were crowded with noble guests, the bravest of knights and the loveliest of ladies, and Arthur himself was the comeliest king that ever held a court. For all this fair folk were in their youth, the fairest and most fortunate under heaven, and the king himself of such fame that it were hard now to name so valiant a hero.

Now the New Year had but newly come in, and on that day a double portion was served on the high table to all the noble guests, and thither came the king with all his knights, when the service in the chapel had been sung to an end. And they greeted each other for the New Year, and gave rich gifts, the one to the other (and they that received them were not wroth, that may ye well believe!), and the maidens laughed and made mirth till it was time to get them to meat. Then they washed and sat them down to the feasting in fitting rank and order, and Guinevere the queen, gaily clad, sat on the high daïs. Silken was her seat, with a fair canopy over her head, of rich tapestries of Tars, embroidered, and studded with costly gems; fair she was to look upon, with her shining grey eyes, a fairer woman might no man boast himself of having seen.

But Arthur would not eat till all were served, so full of joy and gladness was he, even as a child; he liked not either to lie long, or to sit long at meat, so worked upon him his young blood and his wild brain. And another custom he had also, that came of his nobility, that he would never eat upon an high day till he had been advised of some knightly deed, or some strange and marvelous tale, of his ancestors, or of arms, or of other ventures. Or till some stranger knight should seek of him leave to joust with one of the Round Table, that they might set their lives in jeopardy, one against another, as fortune might favor them. Such was the king's custom when he sat in hall at each high feast with his noble knights, therefore on that New Year tide, he abode, fair of face, on the throne, and made much mirth withal.

Thus the king sat before the high tables, and spake of many things; and there good Sir Gawain was seated by Guinevere the queen, and on her other side sat Agravain, *à la dure main;* both were the king's sister's sons and full gallant knights. And at the end of the table was Bishop Bawdewyn, and Ywain, King Urien's son, sat at the other side alone. These were worthily served on the daïs, and at the lower tables sat many valiant knights. Then they bare the first course with the blast of trumpets and waving of banners, with the sound of drums and pipes, of song and lute, that many a heart was uplifted at the melody. Many were the dainties, and rare the meats; so great was the plenty they might scarce find room on the board to set on the dishes. Each helped himself as he liked best, and to each two were twelve dishes, with great plenty of beer and wine.

Now I will say no more of the service, but that ye may know there was no lack, for there drew near a venture that the folk might well have left their labour to gaze upon. As the sound of the music ceased, and the first course had been fitly served, there came in at the hall door one terrible to behold, of stature greater than any on earth; from neck to loin so strong and thickly made, and with limbs so long and so great that he seemed even as a giant. And yet he was but a man, only the mightiest that might mount a steed; broad of chest and shoulders and slender of waist, and all his features of like fashion; but men marveled much at his colour, for he rode even as a knight, yet was green all over.

For he was clad all in green, with a straight

coat, and a mantle above; all decked and lined with fur was the cloth and the hood that was thrown back from his locks and lay on his shoulders. Hose had he of the same green, and spurs of bright gold with silken fastenings richly worked; and all his vesture was verily green. Around his waist and his saddle were bands with fair stones set upon silken work, 't were too long to tell of all the trifles that were embroidered thereon — birds and insects in gay gauds of green and gold. All the trappings of his steed were of metal of like enamel, even the stirrups that he stood in stained of the same, and stirrups and saddle-bow alike gleamed and shone with green stones. Even the steed on which he rode was of the same hue, a green horse, great and strong, and hard to hold, with broidered bridle, meet for the rider.

The knight was thus gaily dressed in green, his hair falling around his shoulders, on his breast hung a beard, as thick and green as a bush, and the beard and the hair of his head were clipped all round above his elbows. The lower part of his sleeves was fastened with clasps in the same wise as a king's mantle. The horse's mane was crisp and plaited with many a knot folded in with gold thread about the fair green, here a twist of the hair, here another of gold. The tail was twined in like manner, and both were bound about with a band of bright green set with many a precious stone; then they were tied aloft in a cunning knot, whereon rang many bells of burnished gold. Such a steed might no other ride, nor had such ever been looked upon in that hall ere that time; and all who saw that knight spake and said that a man might scarce abide his stroke.

The knight bore no helm nor hauberk, neither gorget nor breast-plate, neither shaft nor buckler to smite nor to shield, but in one hand he had a holly-bough, that is greenest when the groves are bare, and in his other an axe, huge and uncomely, a cruel weapon in fashion, if one would picture it. The head was an ell-yard long, the metal all of green steel and gold, the blade burnished bright, with a broad edge, as well shapen to shear as a sharp razor. The steel was set into a strong staff, all bound round with iron, even to the end, and engraved with green in cunning work. A lace was twined about it, that looped at the head, and all adown the handle it was clasped with tassels on buttons of bright green richly broidered.

The knight rideth through the entrance of the hall, driving straight to the high daïs, and greeted no man, but looked ever upwards; and the first words he spake were, 'Where is the ruler of this folk? I would gladly look upon that hero, and have speech with him.' He cast his eyes on the knights, and mustered them up and down, striving ever to see who of them was of most renown.

Then was there great gazing to behold that chief, for each man marveled what it might mean that a knight and his steed should have even such a hue as the green grass; and that seemed even greener than green enamel on bright gold. All looked on him as he stood, and drew near unto him wondering greatly what he might be; for many marvels had they seen, but none such as this, and phantasm and faërie did the folk deem it. Therefore were the gallant knights slow to answer, and gazed astounded, and sat stone still in a deep silence through that goodly hall, as if a slumber were fallen upon them. I deem it was not all for doubt, but some for courtesy that they might give ear unto his errand.

Then Arthur beheld this adventurer before his high daïs, and knightly he greeted him, for fearful was he never. 'Sir,' he said, 'thou art welcome to this place — lord of this hall am I, and men call me Arthur. Light thee down, and tarry awhile, and what thy will is, that shall we learn after.'

'Nay,' quoth the stranger, 'so help me He that sitteth on high, 't was not mine errand to tarry any while in this dwelling; but the praise of this thy folk and thy city is lifted up on high, and thy warriors are holden for the best and the most valiant of those who ride mail-clad to the fight. The wisest and the worthiest of this world are they, and well proven in all knightly sports. And here, as I have heard tell, is fairest courtesy, therefore have I come hither as at this time. Ye may be sure by the branch that I bear here that I come in peace seeking no strife. For had I willed to journey in warlike guise I have at home both hauberk and helm, shield and shining spear, and other weapons to mine hand, but since I seek no war my raiment is that of peace. But if thou be as bold as all men tell thou wilt freely grant me the boon I ask.'

And Arthur answered, 'Sir Knight, if thou cravest battle here thou shalt not fail for lack of a foe.'

And the knight answered, 'Nay, I ask no fight, in faith here on the benches are but beardless children, were I clad in armor on my steed there is no man here might match me. Therefore I ask in this court but a Christmas jest, for that it is Yule-tide, and New Year, and there are here many fain for sport. If any one in this hall holds himself so hardy, so bold both of blood and brain, as to dare strike me one stroke for another, I will give him as a gift this axe, which is heavy enough, in sooth, to handle as he may list, and I will abide the first blow, unarmed as I sit. If any knight be so bold as to prove my words let him come swiftly to me here, and take this weapon, I quit claim to it, he may keep it as his own, and I will abide his stroke, firm on the floor. Then shalt thou give me the right to deal him another, the respite of a year and a day shall he have. Now haste, and let see whether any here dare say aught.'

Now if the knights had been astounded at the first, yet stiller were they all, high and low, when they had heard his words. The knight on his steed straightened himself in the saddle, and rolled his eyes fiercely round the hall, red they gleamed under his green and bushy brows. He frowned and twisted his beard, waiting to see who should rise, and when none answered he cried aloud in mockery, 'What, is this Arthur's hall, and these the knights whose renown hath run through many realms? Where are now your pride and your conquests, your wrath, and anger, and mighty words? Now are the praise and the renown of the Round Table overthrown by one man's speech, since all keep silence for dread ere ever they have seen a blow!'

With that he laughed so loudly that the blood rushed to the king's fair face for very shame; he waxed wroth, as did all his knights, and sprang to his feet, and drew near to the stranger and said, 'Now, by heaven, foolish is thy asking, and thy folly shall find its fitting answer. I know no man aghast at thy great words. Give me here thine axe and I shall grant thee the boon thou hast asked.' Lightly he sprang to him and caught at his hand, and the knight, fierce of aspect, lighted down from his charger.

Then Arthur took the axe and gripped the haft, and swung it round, ready to strike. And the knight stood before him, taller by the head than any in the hall; he stood, and stroked his beard, and drew down his coat, no more dismayed for the king's threats than if one had brought him a drink of wine.

Then Gawain, who sat by the queen, leaned forward to the king and spake, 'I beseech ye, my lord, let this venture be mine. Would ye but bid me rise from this seat, and stand by your side, so that my liege lady thought it not ill, then would I come to your counsel before this goodly court. For I think it not seemly when such challenges be made in your hall that ye yourself should undertake it, while there are many bold knights who sit beside ye, none are there, methinks, of readier will under heaven, or more valiant in open field. I am the weakest, I wot, and the feeblest of wit, and it will be the less loss of my life if ye seek sooth. For save that ye are mine uncle naught is there in me to praise, no virtue is there in my body save your blood, and since this challenge is such folly that it beseems ye not to take it, and I have asked it from ye first, let it fall to me, and if I bear myself ungallantly then let all this court blame me.'

Then they all spake with one voice that the king should leave this venture and grant it to Gawain.

Then Arthur commanded the knight to rise, and he rose up quickly and knelt down before the king, and caught hold of the weapon; and the king loosed his hold of it, and lifted up his hand, and gave him his blessing, and bade him be strong both of heart and hand. 'Keep thee well, nephew,' quoth Arthur, 'that thou give him but the one blow, and if thou redest him rightly I trow thou shalt well abide the stroke he may give thee after.'

Gawain stepped to the stranger, axe in hand, and he, never fearing, awaited his coming. Then the Green Knight spake to Sir Gawain, 'Make we our covenant ere we go further. First, I ask thee, knight, what is thy name? Tell me truly, that I may know thee.'

'In faith,' quoth the good knight, 'Gawain am I, who give thee this buffet, let what may come of it; and at this time twelvemonth will I take another at thine hand with whatsoever weapon thou wilt, and none other.'

Then the other answered again, 'Sir Gawain, so may I thrive as I am fain to take this buffet at thine hand,' and he quoth further, 'Sir Gawain, it liketh me well that I shall take at thy fist that which I have asked here, and thou hast readily and truly rehearsed all the covenant that I asked of the king, save that thou shalt swear me, by thy troth, to seek me thyself wherever thou hopest that I may be found, and win thee such reward as thou dealest me to-day, before this folk.'

'Where shall I seek thee?' quoth Gawain. 'Where is thy place? By Him that made me, I wot never where thou dwellest, nor know I thee, knight, thy court, nor thy name. But teach me truly all that pertaineth thereto, and tell me thy name, and I shall use all my wit to win my way thither, and that I swear thee for sooth, and by my sure troth.'

'That is enough in the New Year, it needs no more,' quoth the Green Knight to the gallant Gawain, 'if I tell thee truly when I have taken the blow, and thou hast smitten me; then will I teach thee of my house and home, and mine own name, then mayest thou ask thy road and keep covenant. And if I waste no words then farest thou the better, for thou canst dwell in thy land, and seek no further. But take now thy toll, and let see how thou strikest.'

'Gladly will I,' quoth Gawain, handling his axe.

Then the Green Knight swiftly made him ready, he bowed down his head, and laid his long locks on the crown that his bare neck might be seen. Gawain gripped his axe and raised it on high, the left foot he set forward on the floor, and let the blow fall lightly on the bare neck. The sharp edge of the blade sundered the bones, smote through the neck, and clave it in two, so that the edge of the steel bit on the ground, and the fair head fell to the earth that many struck it with their feet as it rolled forth. The blood spurted forth, and glistened on the green raiment, but the knight neither faltered nor fell; he started forward with out-stretched hand, and caught the head, and lifted it up; then he turned to his steed, and took hold of the bridle, set his foot in the stirrup, and mounted. His head he held by the hair, in his hand. Then he seated himself in his saddle as if naught ailed him, and he were not headless. He turned his steed about, the grim corpse bleeding freely the while, and they who looked upon him doubted them much for the covenant.

For he held up the head in his hand, and turned the face towards them that sat on the high daïs, and it lifted up the eyelids and looked upon them and spake as ye shall hear. 'Look, Gawain, that thou art ready to go as thou hast promised, and seek leally till thou find me, even as thou hast sworn in this hall in the hearing of these knights. Come thou, I charge thee, to the Green Chapel, such a stroke as thou hast dealt thou hast deserved, and it shall be promptly paid thee on New Year's morn. Many men know me as the knight of the Green Chapel, and if thou askest, thou shalt not fail to find me. Therefore it behoves thee to come, or to yield thee as recreant.'

With that he turned his bridle, and galloped out at the hall door, his head in his hands, so that the sparks flew from beneath his horse's hoofs. Whither he went none knew, no more than they wist whence he had come; and the king and Gawain they gazed and laughed, for in sooth this had proved a greater marvel than any they had known aforetime.

Though Arthur the king was astonished at his heart, yet he let no sign of it be seen, but spake in courteous wise to the fair queen: 'Dear lady, be not dismayed, such craft is well suited to Christmas-tide when we seek jesting, laughter, and song, and fair carols of knights and ladies. But now I may well get me to meat, for I have seen a marvel I may not forget.' Then he looked on Sir Gawain, and said gaily, 'Now, fair nephew, hang up thine axe, since it has hewn enough,' and they hung it on the dossal above the daïs, where all men might look on it for a marvel, and by its true token tell of the wonder. Then the twain sat them down together, the king and the good knight, and men served them with a double portion, as was the share of the noblest, with all manner of meat and of minstrelsy. And they spent that day in gladness, but Sir Gawain must well bethink him of the heavy venture to which he had set his hand.

II

This beginning of adventures had Arthur at the New Year; for he yearned to hear gallant tales, though his words were few when he sat at the feast. But now had they stern work on hand. Gawain was glad to begin the jest in the hall, but ye need have no marvel if the end be heavy. For though a man be merry in mind when he has well drunk, yet a year runs full swiftly, and the beginning but rarely matches the end.

For Yule was now over-past, and the year after, each season in its turn following the other. For after Christmas comes crabbed Lent, that will have fish for flesh and simpler cheer. But then the weather of the world chides with winter; the cold withdraws itself, the clouds uplift, and the rain falls in warm showers on the fair plains. Then the flowers come forth, meadows and groves are clad in green, the birds make ready to build, and sing sweetly for solace of the soft summer that follows thereafter. The blossoms bud and blow in the hedgerows rich and rank, and noble notes enough are heard in the fair woods.

After the season of summer, with the soft winds, when zephyr breathes lightly on seeds and herbs, joyous indeed is the growth that waxes thereout when the dew drips from the leaves beneath the blissful glance of the bright sun. But then comes harvest and hardens the grain, warning it to wax ripe ere the winter. The drought drives the dust on high, flying over the face of the land; the angry wind of the welkin wrestles with the sun; the leaves fall from the trees and light upon the ground, and all brown are the groves that but now were green, and ripe is the fruit that once was flower. So the year passes into many yesterdays, and winter comes again, as it needs no sage to tell us.

When the Michaelmas moon was come in with warnings of winter, Sir Gawain bethought him full oft of his perilous journey. Yet till All Hallows Day he lingered with Arthur, and on that day they made a great feast for the hero's sake, with much revel and richness of the Round Table. Courteous knights and comely ladies, all were in sorrow for the love of that knight, and though they spake no word of it, many were joyless for his sake.

And after meat, sadly Sir Gawain turned to his uncle, and spake of his journey, and said, 'Liege lord of my life, leave from you I crave. Ye know well how the matter stands without more words, to-morrow am I bound to set forth in search of the Green Knight.'

Then came together all the noblest knights, Ywain and Erec, and many another. Sir Dodinel le Sauvage, the Duke of Clarence, Launcelot and Lionel, and Lucan the Good, Sir Bors and Bedivere, valiant knights both, and many another hero, with Sir Mador de la Porte, and they all drew near, heavy at heart, to take counsel with Sir Gawain. Much sorrow and weeping was there in the hall to think that so worthy a knight as Gawain should wend his way to seek a deadly blow, and should no more wield his sword in fight. But the knight made ever good cheer, and said, 'Nay, wherefore should I shrink? What may a man do but prove his fate?'

He dwelt there all that day, and on the morn he arose and asked betimes for his armour; and they brought it unto him on this wise: first, a rich carpet was stretched on the floor (and brightly did the gold gear glitter upon it), then the knight stepped upon it, and handled the steel; clad he was in a doublet of silk, with a close hood, lined fairly throughout. Then they set the steel shoes upon his feet, and wrapped his legs with greaves, with polished knee-caps, fastened with knots of gold. Then they cased his thighs in cuisses closed with thongs, and brought him the byrny of bright steel rings sewn upon a fair stuff. Well burnished braces they set on each arm with good elbow-pieces, and gloves of mail, and all the goodly gear that should shield him in his need. And they cast over all a rich surcoat, and set the golden spurs on his heels, and girt him with a trusty sword fastened with a silken bawdrick. When he was thus clad his harness was costly, for the least loop or latchet gleamed with gold. So armed as he was he hearkened Mass and made his offering at the high altar. Then he came to the king, and the knights of his court, and courteously took leave of lords and ladies, and they kissed him, and commended him to Christ.

With that was Gringalet ready, girt with a saddle that gleamed gaily with many golden fringes, enriched and decked anew for the venture. The bridle was all barred about with bright gold buttons, and all the covertures and trappings of the steed, the crupper and the rich skirts, accorded with the saddle; spread fair with the rich red gold that glittered and gleamed in the rays of the sun.

Then the knight called for his helmet, which was well lined throughout, and set it high on his head, and hasped it behind. He wore a light kerchief over the vintail, that was broidered and studded with fair gems on a broad silken ribbon, with birds of gay colour, and many a turtle and true-lover's knot interlaced thickly, even as many a maiden had wrought diligently for seven winter long. But the circlet which crowned his helmet was yet more precious, being adorned with a device in diamonds. Then they brought him his shield, which was of bright red, with the pentangle painted thereon in gleaming gold. And why that noble prince bare the pentangle I am minded to tell you, though my tale tarry thereby. It is a sign that Solomon set ere-while, as betokening truth; for it is a figure with five points and each line overlaps the other, and nowhere hath it beginning or end, so that in English it is called 'the endless knot.' And therefore was it well suiting to this knight and to his arms, since Gawain was faithful in five and five-fold, for pure was he as gold, void of all villainy and endowed with all virtues. Therefore he bare the pentangle on shield and surcoat as truest of heroes and gentlest of knights.

For first he was faultless in his five senses; and his five fingers never failed him; and all his trust upon earth was in the five wounds that Christ bare on the cross, as the Creed tells. And wherever this knight found himself in stress of battle he deemed well that he drew his strength from the five joys which the Queen of Heaven had of her Child. And for this cause did he bear an image of Our Lady on the one half of his shield, that whenever he looked upon it he might not lack for aid. And the fifth five that the hero used were frankness and fellowship above all, purity and courtesy that never failed him, and compassion that surpasses all; and in these five virtues was that hero wrapped and clothed. And all these, five-fold, were linked one in the other, so that they had no end, and were fixed on five points that never failed, neither at any side were they joined or sundered, nor could ye find beginning or end. And therefore on his shield was the knot shapen, red-gold upon red, which is the pure pentangle. Now was Sir Gawain ready, and he took his lance in hand, and bade them all *Farewell*, he deemed it had been for ever.

Then he smote the steed with his spurs, and sprang on his way, so that sparks flew from the stones after him. All that saw him were grieved at heart, and said one to the other, 'By Christ, 't is great pity that one of such noble life should be lost! I' faith, 't were not easy to find his equal upon earth. The king had done better to have wrought more warily. Yonder knight should have been made a duke; a gallant leader of men is he, and such a fate had beseemed him better than to be hewn in pieces at the will of an elfish man, for mere pride. Who ever knew a king to take such counsel as to risk his knights on a Christmas jest?' Many were the tears that flowed from their eyes when that goodly knight rode from the hall. He made no delaying, but went his way swiftly, and rode many a wild road, as I heard say in the book.

So rode Sir Gawain through the realm of Logres, on an errand that he held for no jest. Often he lay companionless at night, and must lack the fare that he liked. No comrade had he save his steed, and none save God with whom to take counsel. At length he drew nigh to North Wales, and left the isles of Anglesey on his left hand, crossing over the fords by the foreland over at Holyhead, till he came into the wilderness of Wirral, where but few dwell who love God and man of true heart. And ever he asked, as he fared, of all whom he met, if they had heard any tidings of a Green Knight in the country thereabout, or of a Green Chapel? And all answered him, Nay, never in their lives had they seen any man of such a hue. And the knight wended his way by many a strange road and many a rugged path, and the fashion of his countenance changed full often ere he saw the Green Chapel.

Many a cliff did he climb in that unknown land, where afar from his friends he rode as a stranger. Never did he come to a stream or a ford but he found a foe before him, and that one so marvelous, so foul and fell, that it behoved him to fight. So many wonders did that knight behold, that it were too long to tell the tenth part of them. Sometimes he fought with dragons and wolves; sometimes with wild men that dwelt in the rocks; another while with bulls, and bears, and wild boars, or with giants of the high moorland that drew near to him. Had he not been a doughty knight, enduring, and of well-proved valour, and a servant of God, doubtless he had been slain, for he was oft in danger of death. Yet he cared not so much for the strife, what he deemed worse was when the cold clear water was shed from the clouds, and froze ere it fell on the fallow ground. More nights than enough he slept in his harness on the bare rocks, near slain with the sleet, while the stream leapt bubbling from the crest of the hills, and hung in hard icicles over his head.

Thus in peril and pain, and many a hardship, the knight rode alone till Christmas Eve, and in that tide he made his prayer to the Blessed Virgin that she would guide his steps and lead him to some dwelling. On that morning he rode by a hill, and came into a thick forest, wild and drear; on each side were high hills, and thick woods below them of great hoar oaks, a hundred together, of hazel and hawthorn with their trailing boughs interwined, and rough ragged moss spreading everywhere. On the bare twigs the birds chirped piteously, for pain of the cold. The knight upon Gringalet rode lonely beneath them, through marsh and mire, much troubled at heart lest he should fail to see the service of the Lord, who on that self-same night was born of a maiden for the cure of our grief; and therefore he said, sighing, 'I beseech thee, Lord, and Mary Thy gentle Mother, for some shelter where I may hear Mass, and Thy matins at morn. This I ask meekly, and thereto I pray my Paternoster, Ave, and Credo.' Thus he rode praying, and lamenting his misdeeds, and he crossed himself, and said, 'May the Cross of Christ speed me.'

Now that knight had crossed himself but thrice ere he was aware in the wood of a dwelling within a moat, above a lawn, on a mound surrounded by many mighty trees that stood round the moat. 'Twas the fairest castle that ever a knight owned; built in a meadow with a park all about it, and a spiked palisade, closely driven, that enclosed the trees for more than two miles. The knight was ware of the hold from the side, as it shone through the oaks. Then he lifted off his helmet, and thanked Christ and Saint Julian that they had courteously granted his prayer, and hearkened to his cry. 'Now,' quoth the knight, 'I beseech ye, grant me fair hostel.' Then he pricked Gringalet with his golden spurs, and rode gaily towards the great gate, and came swiftly to the bridge end.

The bridge was drawn up and the gates close shut; the walls were strong and thick, so that they might fear no tempest. The knight on his charger abode on the bank of the deep double ditch that surrounded the castle. The walls were set deep in the water, and rose aloft to a wondrous height; they were of hard hewn stone up to the corbels, which were adorned beneath the battlements with fair carvings, and turrets set in between with many a loophole; a better barbican Sir Gawain had never looked upon. And within he beheld the high hall, with its tower and many windows with carven cornices, and chalk-white chimneys on the turreted roofs that shone fair in the sun. And everywhere, thickly scattered on the castle battlements, were pinnacles, so many that it seemed as if it were all wrought out of paper, so white was it.

The knight on his steed deemed it fair enough, if he might come to be sheltered within it to lodge there while that the Holy-day lasted. He called aloud, and soon there came a porter of kindly countenance, who stood on the wall and greeted this knight and asked his errand.

'Good sir,' quoth Gawain, 'wilt thou go mine errand to the high lord of the castle, and crave for me lodging?'

'Yea, by Saint Peter,' quoth the porter. 'In sooth I trow that ye be welcome to dwell here so long as it may like ye.'

Then he went, and came again swiftly, and many folk with him to receive the knight. They let down the great drawbridge, and came forth and knelt on their knees on the cold earth to give him worthy welcome. They held wide open the great gates, and courteously he bid them rise, and rode over the bridge. Then men came to him and held his stirrup while he dismounted, and took and stabled his steed. There came down knights and squires to bring the guest with joy to the hall. When he raised his helmet there were many to take it from his hand, fain to serve him, and they took from him sword and shield.

Sir Gawain gave good greeting to the noble and the mighty men who came to do him honour. Clad in his shining armour they led him to the hall, where a great fire burnt brightly on the floor; and the lord of the household came forth from his chamber to meet the hero fitly. He spake to the knight, and said: 'Ye are welcome to do here as it likes ye. All that is here is your own to have at your will and disposal.'

'Gramercy!' quoth Gawain, 'may Christ requite ye.'

As friends that were fain each embraced the other; and Gawain looked on the knight who greeted him so kindly, and thought 't was a bold warrior that owned that burg.

Of mighty stature he was, and of high age; broad and flowing was his beard, and of a bright hue. He was stalwart of limb, and strong in his stride, his face fiery red, and his speech free: in sooth he seemed one well fitted to be a leader of valiant men.

Then the lord led Sir Gawain to a chamber, and commanded folk to wait upon him, and at his bidding there came men enough who brought the guest to a fair bower. The bedding was noble, with curtains of pure silk wrought with gold, and wondrous coverings of fair cloth all embroidered. The curtains ran on ropes with rings of red gold, and the walls were hung with carpets of Orient, and the same spread on the floor. There with mirthful speeches they took from the guest his byrny and all his shining armour, and brought him rich robes of the choicest in its stead. They were long and flowing, and became him well, and when he was clad in them all who looked on the hero thought that surely God had never made a fairer knight: he seemed as if he might be a prince without peer in the field where men strive in battle.

Then before the hearth-place, whereon the fire burned, they made ready a chair for Gawain, hung about with cloth and fair cushions; and there they cast around him a mantle of brown samite, richly embroidered and furred within with costly skins of ermine, with a hood of the same, and he seated himself in that rich seat, and warmed himself at the fire, and was cheered at heart. And while he sat thus the serving men set up a table on trestles, and covered it with a fair white cloth, and set thereon salt-cellar, and napkin, and silver spoons; and the knight washed at his will, and set him down to meat.

The folk served him courteously with many dishes seasoned of the best, a double portion. All kinds of fish were there, some baked in bread, some broiled on the embers, some sodden, some stewed and savored with spices, with all sorts of cunning devices to his taste. And often he called it a feast, when they spake gaily to him all together, and said, 'Now take ye this penance, and it shall be for your amendment.' Much mirth thereof did Sir Gawain make.

Then they questioned that prince courteously of whence he came; and he told them that he was of the court of Arthur, who is the rich royal king of the Round Table, and that it was Gawain himself who was within their walls, and would keep Christmas with them, as the chance had fallen out. And when the lord of the castle heard those tidings he laughed aloud for gladness, and all men in that keep were joyful that they should be in the company of him to whom belonged all fame, and valour, and courtesy, and whose honour was praised above that of all men on earth. Each said softly to his fellow, 'Now shall we see courteous bearing, and the manner of speech befitting courts. What charm lieth in gentle speech shall we learn without asking, since here we have welcomed the fine father of courtesy. God has surely shown us His grace since He sends us such a guest as Gawain! When men shall sit and sing, blithe for Christ's birth, this knight shall bring us to the knowledge of fair manners, and it may be that hearing him we may learn the cunning speech of love.'

By the time the knight had risen from dinner it was near nightfall. Then chaplains took their way to the chapel, and rang loudly, even as they should, for the solemn evensong of the high feast. Thither went the lord, and the lady also, and entered with her maidens into a comely closet, and thither also went Gawain. Then the lord took him by the sleeve and led him to a seat, and called him by his name, and told him he was of all men in the world the most welcome. And Sir Gawain thanked him truly, and each kissed the other, and they sat gravely together throughout the service.

Then was the lady fain to look upon that knight; and she came forth from her closet with many fair maidens. The fairest of ladies was she in face, and figure, and colouring, fairer even than Guinevere, so the knight thought. She came through the chancel to greet the hero, another lady held her by the left hand, older than she, and seemingly of high estate, with many nobles about her. But unlike to look upon were those ladies, for if the younger were fair, the elder was yellow. Rich red were the cheeks of the one, rough and wrinkled those of the other; the kerchiefs of the one were broidered with many glistening pearls, her throat and neck bare, and whiter than the snow that lies on the hills; the neck of the other was swathed in a gorget, with a white wimple over her black chin. Her forehead was wrapped in silk with many folds, worked with knots, so that naught of her was seen save her black brows, her eyes, her nose, and her lips, and those were bleared, and ill to look upon. A worshipful lady in sooth one might call her! In figure was she short and broad, and thickly made — far fairer to behold was she whom she led by the hand.

When Gawain beheld that fair lady, who looked at him graciously, with leave of the lord he went towards them, and, bowing low, he greeted the elder, but the younger and fairer he took lightly in his arms, and kissed her courteously, and greeted her in knightly wise. Then she hailed him as friend, and he quickly prayed to be counted as her servant, if she so willed. Then they took him between them, and talking, led him to the chamber, to the hearth, and bade them bring spices, and they brought them in plenty with the good wine that was wont to be drunk at such seasons. Then the lord sprang to his feet and bade them make merry, and took off his hood, and hung it on a spear, and bade him win the worship thereof who should make most mirth that Christmas-tide. 'And I shall try, by my faith, to fool it with the best, by the help of my friends, ere I lose my raiment.' Thus with gay words the lord made trial to gladden Gawain with jests that night, till it was time to bid them light the tapers, and Sir Gawain took leave of them and gat him to rest.

In the morn when all men call to mind how Christ our Lord was born on earth to die for us, there is joy, for His sake, in all dwellings of the world; and so was there here on that day. For high feast was held, with many dainties and cunningly cooked messes. On the daïs sat gallant men, clad in their best. The ancient dame sat on the high seat, with the lord of the castle beside her. Gawain and the fair lady sat together, even in the midst of the board, when the feast was served; and so throughout all the hall each sat in his degree, and was served in order. There was meat, there was mirth, there was much joy, so that to tell thereof would take me too long, though peradventure I might strive to declare it. But Gawain and that fair lady had much joy of each other's company through her sweet words and courteous converse. And there was music made before each prince, trumpets and drums, and merry piping; each man hearkened his minstrel, and they too hearkened theirs.

So they held high feast that day and the next, and the third day thereafter, and the joy on Saint John's Day was fair to hearken, for 't was the last of the feast and the guests would depart in the grey of the morning. Therefore they awoke early, and drank wine, and danced fair carols, and at last, when it was late, each man took his leave to wend early on his way. Gawain would bid his host farewell, but the lord took him by the hand, and led him to his own chamber beside the hearth, and there he thanked him for the favour he had shown him in honouring his dwelling at that high season, and gladdening his castle with his fair countenance. 'I wis, sir, that while I live I shall be held the worthier that Gawain has been my guest at God's own feast.'

'Gramercy, sir,' quoth Gawain, 'in good faith, all the honour is yours, may the High King give it you, and I am but at your will to work your behest, inasmuch as I am beholden to you in great and small by rights.'

Then the lord did his best to persuade the knight to tarry with him, but Gawain answered that he might in no wise do so. Then the host asked him courteously what stern behest had driven him at the holy season from the king's court, to fare all alone, ere yet the feast was ended?

'Forsooth,' quoth the knight, 'ye say but the truth: 't is a high quest and a pressing that hath brought me afield, for I am summoned myself to a certain place, and I know not whither in the world I may wend to find it; so help me Christ, I would give all the kingdom of Logres an I might find it by New Year's morn. Therefore, sir, I make request of you that ye tell me truly if ye ever heard word of the Green Chapel, where it may be found, and the Green Knight that keeps it. For I am pledged by solemn compact sworn between us to meet that knight at the New Year if so I were on life; and of that same New Year it wants but little — I' faith, I would look on that hero more joyfully than on any other fair sight! Therefore, by your will, it behoves me to leave you, for I have but barely three days, and I would as fain fall dead as fail of mine errand.'

Then the lord quoth, laughing, 'Now must ye needs stay, for I will show you your goal, the Green Chapel, ere your term be at an end, have ye no fear! But ye can take your ease, friend, in your bed, till the fourth day, and go forth on the first of the year and come to that place at mid-morn to do as ye will. Dwell here till New Year's Day, and then rise and set forth, and ye shall be set in the way; 't is not two miles hence.'

Then was Gawain glad, and he laughed gaily. 'Now I thank you for this above all else. Now my quest is achieved I will dwell here at your will, and otherwise do as ye shall ask.'

Then the lord took him, and set him beside him, and bade the ladies be fetched for their greater pleasure, 'tho' between themselves they had solace. The lord, for gladness, made merry jest, even as one who wist not what to do for joy; and he cried aloud to the knight, 'Ye have promised to do the thing I bid ye: will ye hold to this behest, here, at once?'

'Yea, forsooth,' said that true knight, 'while I abide in your burg I am bound by your behest.'

'Ye have traveled from far,' said the host, 'and since then ye have waked with me, ye are not well refreshed by rest and sleep, as I know. Ye shall therefore abide in your chamber, and lie at your ease to-morrow at Mass-tide, and go to meat when ye will with my wife, who shall sit with you, and comfort you with her company till I return; and I shall rise early and go forth to the chase.' And Gawain agreed to all this courteously.

'Sir knight,' quoth the host, 'we will make a covenant. Whatsoever I win in the wood shall be yours, and whatever may fall to your share, that shall ye exchange for it. Let us swear, friend, to make this exchange, however our hap may be, for worse or for better.'

'I grant ye your will,' quoth Gawain the good; 'if ye list so to do, it liketh me well.' 'Bring hither the wine-cup, the bargain is made,' so said the lord of that castle. They laughed each one, and drank of the wine, and made merry, these lords and ladies, as it pleased them. Then with gay talk and merry jest they arose, and stood, and spoke softly, and kissed courteously, and took leave of each other. With burning torches, and many a serving-man, was each led to his couch; yet ere they gat them to bed the old lord oft repeated their covenant, for he knew well how to make sport.

III

Full early, ere daylight, the folk rose up; the guests who would depart called their grooms, and they made them ready, and saddled the steeds, tightened up the girths, and trussed up their mails. The knights, all arrayed for riding, leapt up lightly, and took their bridles, and each rode his way as pleased him best.

The lord of the land was not the last. Ready for the chase, with many of his men, he ate a sop hastily when he had heard Mass, and then with blast of the bugle fared forth to the field. He and his nobles were to horse ere daylight glimmered upon the earth.

Then the huntsmen coupled their hounds, unclosed the kennel door, and called them out. They blew three blasts gaily on the bugles, the hounds bayed fiercely, and they that would go a-hunting checked and chastised them. A hundred hunters there were of the best, so I have heard tell. Then the trackers gat them to the trysting-place and uncoupled the hounds, and the forest rang again with their gay blasts.

At the first sound of the hunt the game quaked for fear, and fled, trembling, along the vale. They betook them to the heights, but the liers in wait turned them back with loud cries; the harts they let pass them, and the stags with their spreading antlers, for the lord had forbidden that they should be slain, but the hinds and the does they turned back, and drave down into the valleys. Then might ye see much shooting of arrows. As the deer fled under the boughs a broad whistling shaft smote and wounded each sorely, so that, wounded and bleeding, they fell dying on the banks. The hounds followed swiftly on their tracks, and hunters, blowing the horn, sped after them with ringing shouts as if the cliffs burst asunder. What game escaped those that shot was run down at the outer ring. Thus were they driven on the hills, and harassed at the waters, so well did the men know their work, and the greyhounds were so great and swift that they ran them down as fast as the hunters could slay them. Thus the lord passed the day in mirth and joyfulness, even to nightfall.

So the lord roamed the woods, and Gawain, that good knight, lay ever a-bed, curtained about, under the costly coverlet, while the daylight gleamed on the walls. And as he lay half slumbering, he heard a little sound at the door, and he raised his head, and caught back a corner of the curtain, and waited to see what it might be. It was the lovely lady, the lord's wife; she shut the door softly behind her, and turned towards the bed; and Gawain was shamed, laid him down softly and made as if he slept. And she came lightly to the bedside, within the curtain, and sat herself down beside him, to wait till he wakened. The knight lay there awhile, and marveled within himself what her coming might betoken; and he said to himself, ''T were more seemly if I asked her what hath brought her hither.' Then he made feint to waken, and turned towards her, and opened his eyes as one astonished, and crossed himself; and she looked on him laughing, with her cheeks red and white, lovely to behold, and small smiling lips.

'Good morrow, Sir Gawain,' said that fair lady; 'ye are but a careless sleeper, since one can enter thus. Now are ye taken unawares, and lest ye escape me I shall bind you in your bed; of that be ye assured!' Laughing, she spake these words.

'Good morrow, fair lady,' quoth Gawain blithely. 'I will do your will, as it likes me well. For I yield me readily, and pray your grace, and that is best, by my faith, since I needs must do so.' Thus he jested again, laughing. 'But an ye would, fair lady, grant me this grace that ye pray your prisoner to rise. I would get me from bed, and array me better, then could I talk with ye in more comfort.'

'Nay, forsooth, fair sir,' quoth the lady, 'ye shall not rise, I will rede ye better. I shall keep ye here, since ye can do no other, and talk with my knight whom I have captured. For I know well that ye are Sir Gawain, whom all the world worships, wheresoever ye may ride. Your honour and your courtesy are praised by lords and ladies, by all who live. Now ye are here and we are alone, my lord and his men are afield; the serving men in their beds, and my maidens also, and the door shut upon us. And since in this hour I have him that all men love, I shall use my time well with speech, while it lasts. Ye are welcome to my company, for it behoves me in sooth to be your servant.'

'In good faith,' quoth Gawain, 'I think me that I am not him of whom ye speak, for unworthy am I of such service as ye here proffer. In sooth, I were glad if I might set myself by word or service to your pleasure; a pure joy would it be to me!'

'In good faith, Sir Gawain,' quoth the gay lady, 'the praise and the prowess that pleases all ladies I lack them not, nor hold them light; yet are there ladies enough who would liever now have the knight in their hold, as I have ye here, to dally with your courteous words, to bring them comfort and to ease their cares, than much of the treasure and the gold that are theirs. And now, through the grace of Him who upholds the heavens, I have wholly in my power that which they all desire!'

Thus the lady, fair to look upon, made him great cheer, and Sir Gawain, with modest words, answered her again: 'Madam,' he quoth, 'may Mary requite ye, for in good faith I have found in ye a noble frankness. Much courtesy have other folk shown me, but the honour they have done me is naught to the worship of yourself, who knoweth but good.'

'By Mary,' quoth the lady, 'I think otherwise; for were I worth all the women alive, and had I the wealth of the world in my hand, and might choose me a lord to my liking, then, for all that I have seen in ye, Sir Knight, of beauty and courtesy and blithe semblance, and for all that I have hearkened and hold for true, there should be no knight on earth to be chosen before ye!'

'Well I wot,' quoth Sir Gawain, 'that ye have chosen a better; but I am proud that ye should so prize me, and as your servant do I hold ye my sovereign, and your knight am I, and may Christ reward ye.'

So they talked of many matters till midmorn was past, and ever the lady made as though she loved him, and the knight turned her speech aside. For though she were the brightest of maidens, yet had he forborne to show her love for the danger that awaited him, and the blow that must be given without delay.

Then the lady prayed her leave from him, and he granted it readily. And she gave him good-day, with laughing glance, but he must needs marvel at her words:

'Now He that speeds fair speech reward ye this disport; but that ye be Gawain my mind misdoubts me greatly.'

'Wherefore?' quoth the knight quickly, fearing lest he had lacked in some courtesy.

And the lady spake: 'So true a knight as Gawain is holden, and one so perfect in courtesy, would never have tarried so long with a lady but he would of his courtesy have craved a kiss at parting.'

Then quoth Gawain, 'I wot I will do even as it may please ye, and kiss at your commandment, as a true knight should who forbears to ask for fear of displeasure.'

At that she came near and bent down and kissed the knight, and each commended the other to Christ, and she went forth from the chamber softly.

Then Sir Gawain rose and called his chamberlain and chose his garments, and when he was ready he gat him forth to Mass, and then went to meat, and made merry all day till the rising of the moon, and never had a knight fairer lodging than had he with those two noble ladies, the elder and the younger.

And ever the lord of the land chased the hinds through holt and heath till eventide, and then with much blowing of bugles and baying of hounds they bore the game homeward; and by the time daylight was done all the folk had returned to that fair castle. And when the lord and Sir Gawain met together, then were they both well pleased. The lord commanded them all to assemble in the great hall, and the ladies to descend with their maidens, and there, before them all, he bade the men fetch in the spoil of the day's hunting, and he called unto Gawain, and counted the tale of the beasts, and showed them unto him, and said, 'What think ye of this game, Sir Knight? Have I deserved of ye thanks for my woodcraft?'

'Yea, I wis,' quoth the other, 'here is the fairest spoil I have seen this seven year in the winter season.'

'And all this do I give ye, Gawain,' quoth the host, 'for by accord of covenant ye may claim it as your own.'

'That in sooth,' quoth the other, 'I grant you that same; and I have fairly won this within walls, and with as good will do I yield it to ye.' With that he clasped his hands round the lord's neck and kissed him as courteously as he might. 'Take ye here my spoils, no more have I won; ye should have it freely, though it were greater than this.'

''T is good,' said the host, 'gramercy thereof. Yet were I fain to know where ye won this same favour, and if it were by your own wit?'

'Nay,' answered Gawain, 'that was not in the bond. Ask me no more: ye have taken what was yours by right, be content with that.'

They laughed and jested together, and sat them down to supper, where they were served with many dainties; and after supper they sat by the hearth, and wine was served out to them; and oft in their jesting they promised to observe on the morrow the same covenant that they had made before, and whatever chance might betide to exchange their spoil, be it much or little, when they met at night. Thus they renewed their bargain before the whole court, and then the night-drink was served, and each courteously took leave of the other and gat him to bed.

By the time the cock had crowed thrice the lord of the castle had left his bed; Mass was sung and meat fitly served. The folk were forth to the wood ere the day broke, with hound and horn they rode over the plain, and uncoupled their dogs among the thorns. Soon they struck on the scent, and the hunt cheered on the hounds who were first to seize it, urging them with shouts. The others hastened to the cry, forty at once, and there rose such a clamour from the pack that the rocks rang again. The huntsmen spurred them on with shouting and blasts of the horn; and the hounds drew together to a thicket betwixt the water and a high crag in the cliff beneath the hillside. There where the rough rock fell ruggedly they, the huntsmen, fared to the finding, and cast about round the hill and the thicket behind them. The knights wist well what beast was within, and would drive him forth with the bloodhounds. And as they beat the bushes, suddenly over the beaters there rushed forth a wondrous great and fierce boar, long since had he left the herd to roam by himself. Grunting, he cast many to the ground, and fled forth at his best speed, without more mischief. The men hallooed loudly and cried, '*Hay! Hay!*' and blew the horns to urge on the hounds, and rode swiftly after the boar. Many a time did he turn to bay and tare the hounds, and they yelped, and howled shrilly. Then the men made ready their arrows and shot at him, but the points were turned on his thick hide, and the barbs would not bite upon him, for the shafts shivered in pieces, and the head but leapt again wherever it hit.

But when the boar felt the stroke of the arrows he waxed mad with rage, and turned on the hunters and tare many, so that, affrightened, they fled before him. But the lord on a swift steed pursued him, blowing his bugle; as a gallant knight he rode through the woodland chasing the boar till the sun grew low.

So did the hunters this day, while Sir Gawain lay in his bed lapped in rich gear; and the lady forgat not to salute him, for early was she at his side, to cheer his mood.

She came to the bedside and looked on the knight, and Gawain gave her fit greeting, and she greeted him again with ready words, and sat her by his side and laughed, and with a sweet look she spoke to him:

'Sir, if ye be Gawain, I think it a wonder that ye be so stern and cold, and care not for the courtesies of friendship, but if one teach ye to know them ye cast the lesson out of your mind. Ye have soon forgotten what I taught ye yesterday, by all the truest tokens that I knew!'

'What is that?' quoth the knight. 'I trow I know not. If it be sooth that ye say, then is the blame mine own.'

'But I taught ye of kissing,' quoth the fair lady. 'Wherever a fair countenance is shown him, it behoves a courteous knight quickly to claim a kiss.'

'Nay, my dear,' said Sir Gawain, 'cease that speech; that durst I not do lest I were denied, for if I were forbidden I wot I were wrong did I further entreat.'

'I' faith,' quoth the lady merrily, 'ye may not be forbid, ye are strong enough to constrain by strength an ye will, were any so discourteous as to give ye denial.'

'Yea, by heaven,' said Gawain, 'ye speak well; but threats profit little in the land where I dwell, and so with a gift that is given not of good will! I am at your commandment to kiss when ye like, to take or to leave as ye list.'

Then the lady bent her down and kissed him courteously.

And as they spake together she said, 'I would learn somewhat from ye, an ye would not be wroth, for young ye are and fair, and so courteous and knightly as ye are known to be, the head of all chivalry, and versed in all wisdom of love and war — 't is ever told of true knights how they adventured their lives for their true love, and endured hardships for her favours, and avenged her with valour, and eased her sorrows, and brought joy to her bower; and ye are the fairest knight of your time, and your fame and your honour are everywhere, yet I have sat by ye here twice, and never a word have I heard of love! Ye who are so courteous and skilled in such love ought surely to teach one so young and unskilled some little craft of true love! Why are ye so unlearned who art otherwise so famous? Or is it that ye deemed me unworthy to hearken to your teaching? For shame, Sir Knight! I come hither alone and sit at your side to learn of ye some skill; teach me of your wit, while my lord is from home.'

'In good faith,' quoth Gawain, 'is my joy and my profit that so fair a lady as ye are should deign to come hither, and trouble ye with so poor a man, and make sport with your knight with kindly countenance, it pleaseth me much. But that I, in my turn, should take it upon me to tell of love and such like matters to ye who know more by half, or a hundred fold, of such craft than I do, or ever shall in all my lifetime, by my troth 't were folly indeed! I will work your will to the best of my might as I am bounden, and evermore will I be your servant, so help me Christ!'

Then often with guile she questioned that knight that she might win him to woo her, but he defended himself so fairly that none might in any wise blame him, and naught but bliss and harmless jesting was there between them. They laughed and talked together till at last she kissed him, and craved her leave of him, and went her way.

Then the knight arose and went forth to Mass, and afterward dinner was served and he sat and spake with the ladies all day. But the lord of the castle rode ever over the land chasing the wild boar, that fled through the thickets, slaying the best of his hounds and breaking their backs in sunder; till at last he was so weary he might run no longer, but made for a hole in a mound by a rock. He got the mound at his back and faced the hounds, whetting his white tusks and foaming at the mouth. The huntsmen stood aloof, fearing to draw nigh him; so many of them had been already wounded that they were loath to be torn with his tusks, so fierce he was and mad with rage. At length the lord himself came up, and saw the beast at bay, and the men standing aloof. Then quickly he sprang to the ground and drew out a bright blade, and waded through the stream to the boar.

When the beast was aware of the knight with weapon in hand, he set up his bristles and snorted loudly, and many feared for their lord lest he should be slain. Then the boar leapt upon the knight so that beast and man were one atop of the other in the water; but the boar had the worst of it, for the man had marked, even as he sprang, and set the point of his brand to the beast's chest, and drove it up to the hilt, so that the heart was split in twain, and the boar fell snarling, and was swept down by the water to where a hundred hounds seized on him, and the men drew him to shore for the dogs to slay.

Then was there loud blowing of horns and

baying of hounds, the huntsmen smote off the boar's head, and hung the carcase by the four feet to a stout pole, and so went on their way homewards. The head they bore before the lord himself, who had slain the beast at the ford by force of his strong hand.

It seemed him o'er long ere he saw Sir Gawain in the hall, and he called, and the guest came to take that which fell to his share. And when he saw Gawain the lord laughed aloud, and bade them call the ladies and the household together, and he showed them the game, and told them the tale, how they hunted the wild boar through the woods, and of his length and breadth and height; and Sir Gawain commended his deeds and praised him for his valour, well proven, for so mighty a beast had he never seen before.

Then they handled the huge head, and the lord said aloud, 'Now, Gawain, this game is your own by sure covenant, as ye right well know.'

''T is sooth,' quoth the knight, 'and as truly will I give ye all I have gained.' He took the host round the neck, and kissed him courteously twice. 'Now are we quits,' he said, 'this eventide, of all the covenants that we made since I came hither.'

And the lord answered, 'By Saint Giles, ye are the best I know; ye will be rich in a short space if ye drive such bargains!'

Then they set up the tables on trestles, and covered them with fair cloths, and lit waxen tapers on the walls. The knights sat and were served in the hall, and much game and glee was there round the hearth, with many songs, both at supper and after; song of Christmas, and new carols, with all the mirth one may think of. And ever that lovely lady sat by the knight, and with still stolen looks made such feint of pleasing him, that Gawain marveled much, and was wroth with himself, but he could not for his courtesy return her fair glances, but dealt with her cunningly, however she might strive to wrest the thing.

When they had tarried in the hall so long as it seemed them good, they turned to the inner chamber and the wide hearth-place, and there they drank wine, and the host proffered to renew the covenant for New Year's Eve; but the knight craved leave to depart on the morrow, for it was nigh to the term when he must fulfil his pledge. But the lord would withhold him from so doing, and prayed him to tarry, and said,

'As I am a true knight I swear my troth that ye shall come to the Green Chapel to achieve your task on New Year's morn, long before prime. Therefore abide ye in your bed, and I will hunt in this wood, and hold ye to the covenant to exchange with me against all the spoil I may bring hither. For twice have I tried ye, and found ye true, and the morrow shall be the third time and the best. Make we merry now while we may, and think on joy, for misfortune may take a man whensoever it wills.'

Then Gawain granted his request, and they brought them drink, and they gat them with lights to bed.

Sir Gawain lay and slept softly, but the lord, who was keen on woodcraft, was afoot early. After Mass he and his men ate a morsel, and he asked for his steed; all the knights who should ride with him were already mounted before the hall gates.

'T was a fair frosty morning, for the sun rose red in ruddy vapour, and the welkin was clear of clouds. The hunters scattered them by a forest side, and the rocks rang again with the blast of their horns. Some came on the scent of a fox, and a hound gave tongue; the huntsmen shouted, and the pack followed in a crowd on the trail. The fox ran before them, and when they saw him they pursued him with noise and much shouting, and he wound and turned through many a thick grove, often cowering and hearkening in a hedge. At last by a little ditch he leapt out of a spinney, stole away slily by a copse path, and so out of the wood and away from the hounds. But he went, ere he wist, to a chosen tryst, and three started forth on him at once, so he must needs double back, and betake him to the wood again.

Then was it joyful to hearken to the hounds; when all the pack had met together and had sight of their game they made as loud a din as if all the lofty cliffs had fallen clattering together. The huntsmen shouted and threatened, and followed close upon him so that he might scarce escape, but Reynard was wily, and he turned and doubled upon them, and led the lord and his men over the hills, now on the slopes, now in the vales, while the knight at home slept through the cold morning beneath his costly curtains.

But the fair lady of the castle rose betimes, and clad herself in a rich mantle that reached even to the ground, left her throat and her fair neck bare, and was bordered and lined with costly furs. On her head she wore no golden circlet, but a network of precious stones, that gleamed and shone through her tresses in clusters of twenty together. Thus she came into the chamber, closed the door after her, and set open a window, and called to him gaily, 'Sir Knight, how may ye sleep? The morning is so fair.'

Sir Gawain was deep in slumber, and in his dream he vexed him much for the destiny that should befall him on the morrow, when he should meet the knight at the Green Chapel, and abide his blow; but when the lady spake he heard her, and came to himself, and roused from his dream and answered swiftly. The lady came laughing, and kissed him courteously, and he welcomed her fittingly with a cheerful countenance. He saw her so glorious and gaily dressed, so faultless of features and complexion, that it warmed his heart to look upon her.

They spake to each other smiling, and all was bliss and good cheer between them. They exchanged fair words, and much happiness was therein, yet was there a gulf between them, and she might win no more of her knight, for that gallant prince watched well his words — he would neither take her love, nor frankly refuse it. He cared for his courtesy, lest he be deemed churlish, and yet more for his honour lest he be traitor to his host. 'God forbid,' quoth he to himself, 'that it should so befall.' Thus with courteous words did he set aside all the special speeches that came from her lips.

Then spake the lady to the knight, 'Ye deserve blame if ye hold not that lady who sits beside ye above all else in the world, if ye have not already a love whom ye hold dearer, and like better, and have sworn such firm faith to that lady that ye care not to loose it — and that am I now fain to believe. And now I pray ye straitly that ye tell me that in truth, and hide it not.'

And the knight answered, 'By Saint John' (and he smiled as he spake) 'no such love have I, nor do I think to have yet awhile.'

'That is the worst word I may hear,' quoth the lady, 'but in sooth I have mine answer; kiss me now courteously, and I will go hence; I can but mourn as a maiden that loves much.'

Sighing, she stooped down and kissed him, and then she rose up and spake as she stood, 'Now, dear, at our parting do me this grace: give me some gift, if it were but thy glove, that I may bethink me of my knight, and lessen my mourning.'

'Now, I wis,' quoth the knight, 'I would that I had here the most precious thing that I possess on earth that I might leave ye as love-token, great or small, for ye have deserved forsooth more reward than I might give ye. But it is not to your honour to have at this time a glove for reward as gift from Gawain, and I am here on a strange errand, and have no man with me, nor mails with goodly things — that mislikes me much, lady, at this time; but each man must fare as he is taken, if for sorrow and ill.'

'Nay, knight highly honoured,' quoth that lovesome lady, 'though I have naught of yours, yet shall ye have somewhat of mine.' With that she reached him a ring of red gold with a sparkling stone therein, that shone even as the sun (wit ye well, it was worth many marks); but the knight refused it, and spake readily,

'I will take no gift, lady, at this time. I have none to give, and none will I take.'

She prayed him to take it, but he refused her prayer, and sware in sooth that he would not have it.

The lady was sorely vexed, and said, 'If ye refuse my ring as too costly, that ye will not be so highly beholden to me, I will give you my girdle as a lesser gift.' With that she loosened a lace that was fastened at her side, knit upon her kirtle under her mantle. It was wrought of green silk, and gold, only braided by the fingers, and that she offered to the knight, and besought him though it were of little worth that he would take it, and he said nay, he would touch neither gold nor gear ere God give him grace to achieve the adventure for which he had come hither. 'And therefore, I pray ye, displease ye not, and ask me no longer, for I may not grant it. I am dearly beholden to ye for the favour ye have shown me, and ever, in heat and cold, will I be your true servant.'

'Now,' said the lady, 'ye refuse this silk, for it is simple in itself, and so it seems, indeed; lo, it is small to look upon and less in cost, but whoso knew the virtue that is knit therein he would, peradventure, value it more highly. For whatever knight is girded with this green lace, while he bears it knotted about him there is no man under heaven can overcome him, for he may not be slain for any magic on earth.'

Then Gawain bethought him, and it came into his heart that this were a jewel for the jeopardy that awaited him when he came to the Green Chapel to seek the return blow — could he so order it that he should escape unslain, 't were a craft worth trying. Then he bare with her chiding, and let her say her say, and she pressed the girdle on him and prayed him to take it, and he granted her prayer, and she gave it him with good will, and besought him for her sake never to reveal it but to hide it loyally from her lord; and the knight agreed that never should any man know it, save they two alone. He thanked her often and heartily, and she kissed him for the third time.

Then she took her leave of him, and when she was gone Sir Gawain rose, and clad him in rich attire, and took the girdle, and knotted it round him, and hid it beneath his robes. Then he took his way to the chapel, and sought out a priest privily and prayed him to teach him better how his soul might be saved when he should go hence; and there he shrived him, and showed his misdeeds, both great and small, and besought mercy and craved absolution; and the priest assoiled him, and set him as clean as if Doomsday had been on the morrow. And afterwards Sir Gawain made him merry with the ladies, with carols, and all kinds of joy, as never he did but that one day, even to nightfall; and all the men marveled at him, and said that never since he came thither had he been so merry.

Meanwhile the lord of the castle was abroad chasing the fox; awhile he lost him, and as he rode through a spinney he heard the hounds near at hand, and Reynard came creeping through a thick grove, with all the pack at his heels. Then the lord drew out his shining brand, and cast it at the beast, and the fox swerved aside for the sharp edge, and would have doubled back, but a hound was on him ere he might turn, and right before the horse's feet they all fell on him, and worried him fiercely, snarling the while.

Then the lord leapt from his saddle, and caught the fox from the jaws, and held it aloft over his head, and hallooed loudly, and many brave hounds bayed as they beheld it; and the hunters hied them thither, blowing their horns; all that bare bugles blew them at once, and all the others shouted. 'T was the merriest meeting that ever men heard, the clamour that was raised at the death of the fox. They rewarded the hounds, stroking them and rubbing their heads, and took Reynard and stripped him of his coat; then blowing their horns, they turned them homewards, for it was nigh nightfall.

The lord was gladsome at his return, and found a bright fire on the hearth, and the knight beside it, the good Sir Gawain, who was in joyous mood for the pleasure he had had with the ladies. He wore a robe of blue, that reached even to the ground, and a surcoat richly furred, that became him well. A hood like to the surcoat fell on his shoulders, and all alike were done about with fur. He met the host in the midst of the floor, and jesting, he greeted him, and said, 'Now shall I be first to fulfil our covenant which we made together when there was no lack of wine.' Then he embraced the knight, and kissed him thrice, as solemnly as he might.

'Of a sooth,' quoth the other, 'ye have good luck in the matter of this covenant, if ye made a good exchange!'

'Yea, it matters naught of the exchange,' quoth Gawain, 'since what I owe is swiftly paid.'

'Marry,' said the other, 'mine is behind, for I have hunted all this day, and naught have I got but this foul foxskin, and that is but poor payment for three such kisses as ye have here given me.'

'Enough,' quoth Sir Gawain, 'I thank ye, by the Rood.'

Then the lord told them of his hunting, and how the fox had been slain.

With mirth and minstrelsy, and dainties at their will, they made them as merry as a folk well might till 't was time for them to sever, for at last they must needs betake them to their beds. Then the knight took his leave of the lord, and thanked him fairly.

'For the fair sojourn that I have had here at this high feast may the High King give ye honour. I give ye myself, as one of your servants, if ye so like; for I must needs, as you know, go hence with the morn, and ye will give me, as ye promised, a guide to show me the way to the Green Chapel, an God will suffer me on New Year's Day to deal the doom of my weird.'

'By my faith,' quoth the host, 'all that ever I promised, that shall I keep with good will.' Then he gave him a servant to set him in the way, and lead him by the downs, that he should have no need to ford the stream, and should fare by the shortest road through the groves; and Gawain thanked the lord for the honour done him. Then he would take leave of the ladies, and courteously he kissed them, and spake, praying them to receive his thanks, and they made like reply; then with many sighs they commended him to Christ, and he departed courteously from that folk. Each man that he met he thanked him for his service and his solace, and the pains he had been at to do his will; and each found it as hard to part from the knight as if he had ever dwelt with him.

Then they led him with torches to his chamber, and brought him to his bed to rest. That he slept soundly I may not say, for the morrow gave him much to think on. Let him rest awhile, for he was near that which he sought, and if ye will but listen to me I will tell ye how it fared with him thereafter.

IV

Now the New Year drew nigh, and the night passed, and the day chased the darkness, as is God's will; but wild weather wakened therewith. The clouds cast the cold to the earth, with enough of the north to slay them that lacked clothing. The snow drave smartly, and the whistling wind blew from the heights, and made great drifts in the valleys. The knight, lying in his bed, listened, for though his eyes were shut, he might sleep but little, and hearkened every cock that crew.

He arose ere the day broke, by the light of a lamp that burned in his chamber, and called to his chamberlain, bidding him bring his armour and saddle his steed. The other gat him up, and fetched his garments, and robed Sir Gawain.

First he clad him in his clothes to keep off the cold, and then in his harness, which was well and fairly kept. Both hauberk and plates were well burnished, the rings of the rich byrny freed from rust, and all as fresh as at first, so that the knight was fain to thank them. Then he did on each piece, and bade them bring his steed, while he put the fairest raiment on himself; his coat with its fair cognizance, adorned with precious stones upon velvet, with broidered seams, and all furred within with costly skins. And he left not the lace, the lady's gift, that Gawain forgot not, for his own good. When he had girded on his sword he wrapped the gift twice about him, swathed around his waist. The girdle of green silk set gaily and well upon the royal red cloth, rich to behold, but the knight ware it not for pride of the pendants, polished though they were with fair gold that gleamed brightly on the ends, but to save himself from sword and knife, when it behoved him to abide his hurt without question. With that the hero went forth, and thanked that kindly folk full often.

Then was Gringalet ready, that was great and strong, and had been well cared for and tended in every wise; in fair condition was that proud steed, and fit for a journey. Then Gawain went to him, and looked on his coat, and said by his sooth, 'There is a folk in this place that thinketh on honour; much joy may they have, and the lord who maintains them, and may all good betide that lovely lady all her life long. Since they for charity cherish a guest, and hold honour in their hands, may He who holds the heaven on high requite them, and also ye all. And if I might live anywhile on earth, I would give ye full reward, readily, if so I might.' Then he set foot in the stirrup and bestrode his steed, and his squire gave him his shield, which he laid on his shoulder. Then he smote Gringalet with his golden spurs, and the steed pranced on the stones and would stand no longer.

By that his man was mounted, who bare his spear and lance, and Gawain quoth, 'I commend this castle to Christ, may he give it ever good fortune.' Then the drawbridge was let down, and the broad gates unbarred and opened on both sides; the knight crossed himself, and passed through the gateway, and praised the porter, who knelt before the prince, and gave him good-day, and commended him to God. Thus the knight went on his way with the one man who should guide him to that dread place where he should receive rueful payment.

The two went by hedges where the boughs were bare, and climbed the cliffs where the cold clings. Naught fell from the heavens, but 't was ill beneath them; mist brooded over the moor and hung on the mountains; each hill had a cap, a great cloak, of mist. The streams foamed and bubbled between their banks, dashing sparkling on the shores where they shelved downwards. Rugged and dangerous was the way through the woods, till it was time for the sun-rising. Then were they on a high hill; the snow lay white beside them, and the man who rode with Gawain drew rein by his master.

'Sir,' he said, 'I have brought ye hither, and now ye are not far from the place that ye have sought so specially. But I will tell ye for sooth, since I know ye well, and ye are such a knight as I well love, would ye follow my counsel ye would fare the better. The place whither ye go is accounted full perilous, for he who liveth in that waste is the worst on earth, for he is strong and fierce, and loveth to deal mighty blows; taller he is than any man on earth, and greater of frame than any four in Arthur's court, or in any other. And this is his custom at the Green Chapel; there may no man pass by that place, however proud his arms, but he does him to death by force of his hand, for he is a discourteous knight, and shows no mercy. Be he churl or chaplain who rides by that chapel, monk or mass priest, or any man else, he thinks it as pleasant to slay them as to pass alive himself. Therefore, I tell ye, as sooth as ye sit in saddle, if ye come there and that knight know it, ye shall be slain, though ye had twenty lives; trow me that truly! He has dwelt here full long and seen many a combat; ye may not defend ye against his blows. Therefore, good Sir Gawain, let the man be, and get ye away some other road; for God's sake seek ye another land, and there may Christ speed ye! And I will hie me home again, and I promise ye further that I will swear by God and the saints, or any other oath ye please, that I will keep counsel faithfully, and never let any wit the tale that ye fled for fear of any man.'

'Gramercy,' quoth Gawain, but ill-pleased. 'Good fortune be his who wishes me good, and that thou wouldst keep faith with me I will believe; but didst thou keep it never so truly, an I passed here and fled for fear as thou sayest, then were I a coward knight, and might not be held guiltless. So I will to the chapel let chance what may, and talk with that man, even as I may list, whether for weal or for woe as fate may have it. Fierce though he may be in fight, yet God knoweth well how to save His servants.'

'Well,' quoth the other, 'now that ye have said so much that ye will take your own harm on yourself, and ye be pleased to lose your life, I will neither let nor keep ye. Have here your helm and the spear in your hand, and ride down this same road beside the rock till ye come to the bottom of the valley, and there look a little to the left hand, and ye shall see in that vale the chapel, and the grim man who keeps it. Now fare ye well, noble Gawain; for all the gold on earth I would not go with ye nor bear ye fellowship one step further.' With that the man turned his bridle into the wood, smote the horse with his spurs as hard as he could, and galloped off, leaving the knight alone.

Quoth Gawain, 'I will neither greet nor groan, but commend myself to God, and yield me to His will.'

Then the knight spurred Gringalet, and rode adown the path close in by a bank beside a grove. So he rode through the rough thicket, right into the dale, and there he halted, for it seemed him wild enough. No sign of a chapel could he see, but high and burnt banks on either side and rough rugged crags with great stones above. An ill-looking place he thought it.

Then he drew in his horse and looked around to seek the chapel, but he saw none and thought it strange. Then he saw as it were a mound on a level space of land by a bank beside the stream where it ran swiftly, the water bubbled within as if boiling. The knight turned his steed to the mound, and lighted down and tied the rein to the branch of a linden; and he turned to the mound and walked round it, questioning with himself what it might be. It had a hole at the end and at either side, and was overgrown with clumps of grass, and it was hollow within as an old cave or the crevice of a crag; he knew not what it might be.

'Ah,' quoth Gawain, 'can this be the Green Chapel? Here might the devil say his matins at midnight! Now I wis there is wizardry here. 'T is an ugly oratory, all overgrown with grass, and 't would well beseem that fellow in green to say his devotions on devil's wise. Now feel I in five wits, 't is the foul fiend himself who hath set me this tryst, to destroy me here! This is a chapel of mischance: ill-luck betide it, 't is the cursedest kirk that ever I came in!'

Helmet on head and lance in hand, he came up to the rough dwelling, when he heard over the high hill beyond the brook, as it were in a bank, a wondrous fierce noise, that rang in the cliff as if it would cleave asunder. 'T was as if one ground a scythe on a grindstone, it whirred and whetted like water on a mill-wheel and rushed and rang, terrible to hear.

'By God,' quoth Gawain, 'I trow that gear is preparing for the knight who will meet me here. Alas! naught may help me, yet should my life be forfeit, I fear not a jot!' With that he called aloud. 'Who waiteth in this place to give me tryst? Now is Gawain come hither: if any man will aught of him let him hasten hither now or never.'

'Stay,' quoth one on the bank above his head, 'and ye shall speedily have that which I promised ye.' Yet for a while the noise of whetting went on ere he appeared, and then he came forth from a cave in the crag with a fell weapon, a Danish axe newly dight, wherewith to deal the blow. An evil head it had, four feet large, no less, sharply ground, and bound to the handle by the lace that gleamed brightly. And the knight himself was all green as before, face and foot, locks and beard, but now he was afoot. When he came to the water he would not wade it, but sprang over with the pole of his axe, and strode boldly over the brent that was white with snow.

Sir Gawain went to meet him, but he made no low bow. The other said, 'Now, fair sir, one may trust thee to keep tryst. Thou art welcome, Gawain, to my place. Thou hast timed thy coming as befits a true man. Thou knowest the covenant set between us: at this time twelve months agone thou didst take that which fell to thee, and I at this New Year will readily requite thee. We are in this valley, verily alone, here are no knights to sever us, do what we will. Have off thy helm from thine head, and have here thy pay; make me no more talking than I did then when thou didst strike off my head with one blow.'

'Nay,' quoth Gawain, 'by God that gave me life, I shall make no moan whatever befall me, but make thou ready for the blow and I shall stand still and say never a word to thee, do as thou wilt.'

With that he bent his head and showed his neck all bare, and made as if he had no fear, for he would not be thought adread.

Then the Green Knight made him ready, and grasped his grim weapon to smite Gawain. With all his force he bore it aloft with a mighty feint of slaying him: had it fallen as straight as he aimed he who was ever doughty of deed had been slain by the blow. But Gawain swerved aside as the axe came gliding down to slay him as he stood, and shrank a little with the shoulders, for the sharp iron. The other heaved up the blade and rebuked the prince with many proud words:

'Thou art not Gawain,' he said, 'who is held so valiant,. that never feared he man by hill or vale, but *thou* shrinkest for fear ere thou feelest hurt. Such cowardice did I never hear of Gawain! Neither did *I* flinch from thy blow, or make strife in King Arthur's hall. My head fell to my feet, and yet I fled not; but thou didst wax faint of heart ere any harm befell. Wherefore must I be deemed the braver knight.'

Quoth Gawain, 'I shrank once, but so will I no more; though an *my* head fall on the stones I cannot replace it. But haste, Sir Knight, by thy faith, and bring me to the point, deal me my destiny, and do it out of hand, for I will stand thee a stroke and move no more till thine axe have hit me — my troth on it.'

'Have at thee, then,' quoth the other, and heaved aloft the axe with fierce mien, as if he were mad. He struck at him fiercely but wounded him not, withholding his hand ere it might strike him.

Gawain abode the stroke, and flinched in no limb, but stood still as a stone or the stump of a tree that is fast rooted in the rocky ground with a hundred roots.

Then spake gaily the man in green, 'So now thou hast thine heart whole it behoves me to smite. Hold aside thy hood that Arthur gave thee, and keep thy neck thus bent lest it cover it again.'

Then Gawain said angrily, 'Why talk on thus? Thou dost threaten too long. I hope thy heart misgives thee.'

'For sooth,' quoth the other, 'so fiercely thou speakest I will no longer let thine errand wait its reward.' Then he braced himself to strike, frowning with lips and brow, 't was no marvel that it pleased but ill him who hoped for no rescue. He lifted the axe lightly and let it fall with the edge of the blade on the bare neck. Though he struck swiftly, it hurt him no more than on the one side where it severed the skin. The sharp blade cut into the flesh so that the blood ran over his shoulder to the ground. And when the knight saw the blood staining the snow, he sprang forth, swift-foot, more than a spear's length, seized his helmet and set it on his head, cast his shield over his shoulder, drew out his bright sword, and spake boldly (never since he was born was he half so blithe), 'Stop, Sir Knight, bid me no more blows. I have stood a stroke here without flinching, and if thou give me another, I shall requite thee, and give thee as good again. By the covenant made betwixt us in Arthur's hall but one blow falls to me here. Halt, therefore.'

Then the Green Knight drew off from him and leaned on his axe, setting the shaft on the ground, and looked on Gawain as he stood all armed and faced him fearlessly — at heart it pleased him well. Then he spake merrily in a loud voice, and said to the knight, 'Bold sir, be not so fierce, no man here hath done thee wrong, nor will do, save by covenant, as we made at Arthur's court. I promised thee a blow and thou hast it — hold thyself well paid! I release thee of all other claims. If I had been so minded I might perchance have given thee a rougher buffet. First I menaced thee with a feigned one, and hurt thee not for the covenant that we made in the first night, and which thou didst hold truly. All the gain didst thou give me as a true man should. The other feint I proffered thee for the morrow: my fair wife kissed thee, and thou didst give me her kisses — for both those days I gave thee two blows without scathe — true man, true return. But the third time thou didst fail, and therefore hadst thou that blow. For 't is *my* weed thou wearest, that same woven girdle, my own wife wrought it, that do I wot for sooth. Now know I well thy kisses, and thy conversation, and the wooing of my wife, for 't was mine own doing. I sent her to try thee, and in sooth I think thou art the most faultless knight that ever trode earth. As a pearl among white peas is of more worth than they, so is Gawain, i' faith, by other knights. But thou didst lack a little, Sir Knight, and wast wanting in loyalty, yet that was for no evil work, nor for wooing neither, but because thou lovedst thy life — therefore I blame thee the less.'

Then the other stood a great while, still sorely angered and vexed within himself; all the blood flew to his face, and he shrank for shame as the Green Knight spake; and the first words he said were, 'Cursed be ye, cowardice and covetousness, for in ye is the destruction of virtue.' Then he loosed the girdle, and gave it to the knight. 'Lo, take there the falsity, may foul befall it! For fear of thy blow cowardice bade me make friends with covetousness and forsake the customs of largess and loyalty, which befit all knights. Now am I faulty and false and have been afeared: from treachery and untruth come sorrow and care. I avow to thee, Sir Knight, that I have ill done; do then thy will. I shall be more wary hereafter.'

Then the other laughed and said gaily, 'I wot I am whole of the hurt I had, and thou hast made such free confession of thy misdeeds, and hast so borne the penance of mine axe edge, that I hold thee absolved from that sin, and purged as clean as if thou hadst never sinned since thou wast born. And this girdle that is wrought with gold and green, like my raiment, do I give thee, Sir Gawain, that thou mayest think upon this chance when thou goest forth among princes of renown, and keep this for a token of the adventure of the Green Chapel, as it chanced between chivalrous knights. And thou shalt come again with me to my dwelling and pass the rest of this feast in gladness.' Then the lord laid hold of him, and said, 'I wot we shall soon make peace with my wife, who was thy bitter enemy.'

'Nay, forsooth,' said Sir Gawain, and seized his helmet and took it off swiftly, and thanked the knight: 'I have fared ill, may bliss betide thee, and may He who rules all things reward thee swiftly. Commend me to that courteous lady, thy fair wife, and to the other my honoured ladies, who have beguiled their knight with skilful craft. But 't is no marvel if one be made a fool and brought to sorrow by women's wiles, for so was Adam beguiled by one, and Solomon by many, and Samson all too soon, for Delilah dealt him his doom; and David thereafter was wedded with Bathsheba, which brought him much sorrow — if one might love a woman and believe her not, 't were great gain! And since all they were beguiled by women, methinks 't is the less blame to me that I was misled! But as for thy girdle, that will I take with good will, not for gain of the gold, nor for samite, nor silk, nor the costly pendants, neither for weal nor for worship, but in sign of my frailty. I shall look upon it when I ride in renown and remind myself of the fault and faintness of the flesh; and so when pride uplifts me for prowess of arms, the sight of this lace shall humble my heart. But one thing would I pray, if it displease thee not: since thou art lord of yonder land wherein I have dwelt, tell me what thy rightful name may be, and I will ask no more.'

'That will I truly,' quoth the other. 'Bernlak de Hautdesert am I called in this land. Morgain le Fay dwelleth in mine house, and through knowledge of clerkly craft hath she taken many. For long time was she the mistress of Merlin, who knew well all you knights of the court. Morgain the goddess is she called therefore, and there is none so haughty but she can bring him low. She sent me in this guise to yon fair hall to test the truth of the renown that is spread abroad of the valour of the Round Table. She taught me this marvel to betray your wits, to vex Guinevere and fright her to death by the man who spake with his head in his hand at the high table. That is she who is at home, that ancient lady, she is even thine aunt, Arthur's half-sister, the daughter of the Duchess of Tintagel, who afterward married King Uther. Therefore I bid thee, knight, come to thine aunt, and make merry in thine house; my folk love thee, and I wish thee as well as any man on earth, by my faith, for thy true dealing.'

But Sir Gawain said nay, he would in no wise do so; so they embraced and kissed, and commended each other to the Prince of Paradise, and parted right there, on the cold ground. Gawain on his steed rode swiftly to the king's hall, and the Green Knight got him whithersoever he would.

Sir Gawain, who had thus won grace of his life, rode through wild ways on Gringalet; oft he lodged in a house, and oft without, and many adventures did he have and came off victor full often, as at this time I cannot relate in tale. The hurt that he had in his neck was healed, he bare the shining girdle as a baldric bound by his side, and made fast with a knot 'neath his left arm, in token that he was taken in a fault — and thus he came in safety again to the court.

Then joy awakened in that dwelling when the king knew that the good Sir Gawain was come, for he deemed it gain. King Arthur kissed the knight, and the queen also, and many valiant knights sought to embrace him. They asked him how he had fared, and he told them all that had chanced to him — the adventure of the chapel, the fashion of the knight, the love of the lady —

at last of the lace. He showed them the wound in the neck which he won for his disloyalty at the hand of the knight, the blood flew to his face for shame as he told the tale.

'Lo, lady,' he quoth, and handled the lace, 'this is the bond of the blame that I bear in my neck, this is the harm and the loss I have suffered, the cowardice and covetousness in which I was caught, the token of my covenant in which I was taken. And I must needs wear it so long as I live, for none may hide his harm, but undone it may not be, for if it hath clung to thee once, it may never be severed.'

Then the king comforted the knight, and the court laughed loudly at the tale, and all made accord that the lords and the ladies who belonged to the Round Table, each hero among them, should wear bound about him a baldric of bright green for the sake of Sir Gawain. And to this was agreed all the honour of the Round Table, and he who ware it was honoured the more thereafter, as it is testified in the best book of romance. That in Arthur's days this adventure befell, the book of Brutus bears witness. For since that bold knight came hither first, and the siege and the assault were ceased at Troy, I wis

Many a venture herebefore
  Hath fallen such as this:
May He that bare the crown of thorn
  Bring us unto His bliss.

ca. 1375 *Amen.*

THE SQUYR OF LOWE DEGRE

It was a squyer of lowe degre
That loved the kings doughter of Hungre.
The squir was curteous and hend,[1]
Ech man him loved and was his frend;
He served the kyng her father dere,
Fully the tyme of seven yere;
For he was marshall of his hall,
And set the lords both great and smal.
An hardy man he was, and wight,
Both in batayle and in fyght;
But ever he was styll mornyng,
And no man wyste[2] for what thyng;
And all was for that fayre lady,
The kynges doughter of Hungry.
There wyste no wyghte in Christente
Howe well he loved that lady fre;
He loved her more then seven yere,
Yet was of love never the nere.
He was not ryche of golde and fe,[3]
A gentyll man forsoth was he.
To no man durst he make his mone,
But syghed sore hymselfe alone.
  And evermore, whan he was wo,
Into his chambre would he goo;
And through the chambre he toke the waye,
Into the gardyn, that was full gaye;
And in the garden, as I wene,
Was an arber fayre and grene,
And in the arber was a tre,
A fayrer in the world might none be;
The tre it was of cypresse,
The fyrst tre that Jesu chese[4];
The sother-wood[5] and sykamoure,
The reed rose and the lyly-floure,
The boxe, the beche, and the larel-tre,
The date, also the damyse,[6]
The fylbyrdes hangyng to the ground,
The fygge-tre, and the maple round,
And other trees there was mane ane,
The pyany,[7] the popler, and the plane,
With brode braunches all aboute,
Within the arbar, and eke withoute;
On every braunche sate byrdes thre,
Syngynge with great melody,
The lavorocke[8] and the nightyngale,
The ruddocke[9] and the woodewale,[10]
The pee[11] and the popinjaye,[12]
The thrustele sange both nyght and daye,
The marlyn,[13] and the wrenne also,
The swalowe whippynge to and fro,
The jaye jangled them amonge,
The larke began that mery songe,
The sparowe spredde her on her spraye,
The mavys songe with notes full gaye,
The nuthake[14] with her notes newe,
The sterlynge set her notes full trewe,
The goldefynche made full mery chere,
Whan she was bente upon a brere,
And many other foules mo,
The osyll,[15] and the thrusshe also;
And they sange wyth notes clere,
In confortynge that squyere.
  And evermore, whan he was wo,
Into that arber wolde he go,
And under a bente he layde hym lowe,
Ryght even under her chambre wyndowe;
And lened his backe to a thorne,
And sayd, 'Alas, that I was borne!
That I were ryche of golde and fe,

[1] gracious
[2] knew
[3] wealth, money
[4] chose
[5] southernwood
[6] damson
[7] peony
[8] lark
[9] robin
[10] woodlark
[11] wryneck
[12] parrot
[13] merlin, a small hawk
[14] nuthatch
[15] ouzel, blackbird

That I might wedde that lady fre!
Of golde good, or some treasure,
That I myght wedde that lady floure!
Or elles come of so gentyll kynne,
The ladyes love that I myght wynne.
Wolde God that I were a kynges sonne,
That ladyes love that I myght wonne!
Or els so bolde in eche fyght,
As Syr Lybius that gentell knyght,
Or els so bolde in chyvalry,
As Syr Gawayne, or Syr Guy;
Or els so doughty of my hande
As was the gyaunte Syr Colbrande,
And it were put in jeopede[1]
What man shoulde wynne that lady fre,
Than should no man have her but I,
The Kynges doughter of Hungry.'
But ever he sayde, 'Wayle a waye!
For poverte passeth all my paye!'
And as he made thys rufull chere,
He sowned[2] downe in that arbere.
That lady herde his mournyng all,
Ryght under the chambre wall;
In her oryall there she was
Closed well with royall glas;
Fulfylled it was with ymagery,
Every wyndowe by and by,
On eche syde had there a gynne,[3]
Sperde with many a dyvers pynne.
Anone that lady, fayre and fre,
Undyd a pynne of yvere,
And wyd the windowes she open set,
The sunne shone in at her closet,
In that arber fayre and gaye,
She sawe where that squyre lay.
The lady sayd to hym anone,
'Syr, why makest thou that mone?
And whi thou mournest night and day
Now tell me, squyre, I thee pray;
And, as I am a true lady,
Thy counsayl shall I never dyscry;
And, yf it be no reprefe[4] to thee,
Thy bote[5] of bale yet shall I be.'
And often was he in wele and wo,
But never so well as he was tho.
The squyer set hym on hys kne,
And sayde, 'Lady, it is for thee,
I have loved this seven yere,
And bought thy love, lady, full dere.
Ye are so ryche in youre aray
That one word to you I dare not say,
And come ye be of so hye kynne,
No worde of love durst I begynne.
My wyll to you yf I had sayde,
And ye therwith not well apayde,[6]
Ye might have bewraied me to the kinge,
And brought me sone to my endynge.
Therfore, my lady fayre and fre,
I durst not shewe my harte to thee;
But I am here at your wyll,
Whether ye wyll me save or spyll[7];
For all the care I have in be,
A worde of you might comfort me;
And, yf ye wyll not do so,
Out of this land I must nedes go;
I wyll forsake both lande and lede,[8]
And become an hermyte in uncouth stede[9];
In many a lande to begge my bread,
To seke where Christ was quicke and dead;
A staffe I wyll make me of my spere,
Lynen cloth I shall none were;
Ever in travayle I shall wende,
Tyll I come to the worldes ende;
And, lady, but thou be my bote,
There shall no sho come on my fote;
Therfore, lady, I the praye,
For hym that dyed on Good Frydaye,
Let me not in daunger dwell,
For his love that harowed hell.'
Than sayd that lady milde of mode,
Ryght in her closet there she stode,
'By hym that dyed on a tre,
Thou shalt never be deceyved for me;
Though I for thee should be slayne,
Squyer, I shall the love agayne.
Go forth, and serve my father the kynge,
And let be all thy styll mournynge;
Let no man wete[10] that ye were here,
Thus all alone in my arbere;
If ever ye wyll come to your wyll,
Here and se, and holde you styll.
Beware of the stewarde, I you praye,
He wyll deceyve you and he maye;
For, if he wote of your woyng,
He wyl bewraye you to the kynge;
Anone for me ye shall be take,
And put in pryson for my sake;
Than must ye nedes abyde the lawe,
Peraventure both hanged and drawe.
That syght of you I would not se,
For all the golde in Christente.
For, and ye my love should wynne,
With chyvalry ye must begynne,
And other dedes of armes to done,
Through whiche ye may wynne your shone[11];
And ryde through many a peryllous place,
As a venterous man to seke your grace,
Over hylles and dales, and hye mountaines,
In wethers wete, both hayle and raynes,
And yf ye may no harbroughe se,
Than must ye lodge under a tre,
Among the beastes wyld and tame,

[1] chance [2] swooned [3] fastening [4] reproach [5] reward [6] pleased [7] destroy [8] people [9] place [10] know [11] shoes

And ever you wyll gette your name;
And in your armure must ye lye,
Every nyght than by and by,
And your meny[1] everychone,
Till seven yere be comen and gone;
And passe by many a peryllous see,
Squyer, for the love of me,
Where any war begynneth to wake,
And many a batayll undertake,
Throughout the land of Lumbardy,
In every cytie by and by.
And be avised, when thou shalt fight,
Loke that ye stand aye in the right;
And, yf ye wyll take good hede,
Yet all the better shall ye spede;
And whan the warre is brought to ende,
To the Rodes then must ye wende;
And, syr, I holde you not to prayes,
But ye there fyght thre Good Frydayes;
And if ye passe the batayles thre,
Than are ye worthy a knyght to be,
And to bere armes than are ye able
Of gold and goules[2] sete with sable;
Then shall ye were a shelde of blewe,
In token that ye shall be trewe,
With vines of golde set all aboute,
Within your shelde and eke without,
Fulfylled with ymagery,
And poudred with true loves by and by.
In the myddes of your sheld ther shal be set
A ladyes head, with many a frete,[3]
Above the head wrytten shall be
A reason for the love of me:
Both O and R shall be therin,
With A and M it shall begynne.
The baudryke, that shall hange therby,
Shall be of white sykerly,[4]
A crosse of reed therin shall be,
In token of the Trynyte.
Your basenette[5] shall be burnysshed bryght,
Your ventall[6] shalbe well dyght,
With starres of gold it shall be set,
And covered with good velvet.
A corenall[7] clene corven newe,
And oystryche fethers of dyvers hewe.
Your plates unto your body enbraste[8]
Sall syt full semely in your waste.
Your cote armoure of golde full fyne,
And poudred well with good armyne.[9]
Thus in your warres shall you ryde,
With syxe good yemen by your syde,
And whan your warres are brought to ende,
More ferther behoveth to you to wende,
And over many perellous streme,
Or ye come to Jerusalem,
Through feytes,[10] and feldes, and forestes thicke,
To seke where Christe were dead and quycke;
There must you drawe your swerde of were,
To the sepulchre ye must it bere,
And laye it there upon the stone,
Amonge the lordes everychone;
And offre there florences[11] fyve,
Whyles that ye are man on lyve;
And offre there florences thre,
In tokenyng of the Trynyte;
And whan that ye, syr, thus have done,
Than are ye worthy to were your shone;
Than may ye say, syr, by good ryght,
That you ar proved a venturous knyght.
I shall you geve to your rydinge
A thousande pounde to your spendinge;
I shall you geve hors and armure,
A thousande pounde of my treasure;
Where through that ye may honoure wynn,
And be the greatest of your kynne.
I pray to God and Our Lady,
Sende you the whele of vyctory,
That my father so fayne[12] may be,
That he wyll wede me unto thee,
And make the king of this countre,
To have and holde in honeste,
Wyth welth and wynne[13] to were the crowne,
And to be lorde of toure and towne;
That we might our dayes endure
In parfyte love that is so pure;
And if we may not so come to,
Other wyse then must we do;
And therfore, squyer, wende thy way,
And hye the fast on thy journay,
And take thy leve of kinge and quene,
And so to all the courte bydene.[14]
Ye shall not want at your goyng
Golde, nor sylver, nor other thyng.
This seven yere I shall you abyde,
Betyde of you what so betyde;
Tyll seven yere be comen and gone
I shall be mayde all alone.'
The squyer kneled on his kne,
And thanked that lady fayre and fre;
And thryes he kyssed that lady tho,
And toke his leve, and forth gan go.

The kinges steward stode full nye,
In a chambre fast them bye,
And hearde theyr wordes wonder wele,
And all the woyng every dele.
He made a vowe to heaven kynge,
For to bewraye that swete thynge,

[1] followers
[2] gules, red
[3] ornament
[4] surely
[5] bascinet, headpiece
[6] movable front of helmet
[7] circlet to helmet
[8] fastened
[9] ermine
[10] fights
[11] gold florins
[12] glad
[13] joy
[14] quickly

And that squyer taken shoulde be,
And hanged hye on a tre;
And that false stewarde full of yre,
Them to betraye was his desyre;
He bethought hym nedely,
Every daye by and by,
How he myght venged be
On that lady fayre and fre,
For he her loved pryvely,
And therfore dyd her great envye.[1]
Alas! it tourned to wrother-heyle[2]
That ever he wyste of theyr counsayle.
But leve we of the stewarde here,
And speke we more of that squyer,
Howe he to his chambre wente,
Whan he paste from that lady gente.
There he araied him in scarlet reed,
And set his chaplet upon his head,
A belte about his sydes two,
With brode barres to and fro;
A horne about his necke he caste,
And forth he went than at the last
To do hys office in the hall
Among the lordes both great and small.
He toke a white yeard[3] in his hande,
Before the kynge than gane he stande,
And sone he sate hym on his knee,
And served the kynge ryght royally,
With deynty meates that were dere,
With partryche, pecoke, and plovere,
With byrdes in bread ybake,
The tele, the ducke, and the drake,
The cocke, the curlewe, and the crane,
With fesauntes fayre, theyr were no wane,[4]
Both storkes and snytes[5] ther were also,
And venyson freshe of bucke and do,
And other deyntes many one,
For to set afore the kynge anone:
And when the squyer had done so,
He served the hall bothe to and fro.
Eche man hym loved in honeste,
Hye and lowe in theyr degre,
So dyd the kyng full sodenly,
And he wyst not wherfore nor why.
The kynge behelde the squyer wele,
And all his rayment every dele,
He thoughte he was the semylyest man
That ever in the worlde he sawe or than.
Thus sate the kyng and eate ryght nought,
But on his squyer was all his thought.
Anone the stewarde toke good hede,
And to the kyng full soone he yede,[6]
And soone he tolde unto the kynge
All theyr wordes and theyr woynge;
And how she hyght[7] hym lande and fe,
Golde and sylver great plentye,
And how he should his leve take,
And become a knight for her sake:
'And thus they talked bothe in-fere,[8]
And I drewe me nere and nere,
Had I not come in, verayly,
The squyer had layne her by,
But whan he was ware of me,
Full fast away can he fle;
That is sothe: here is my hand
To fight with him while I may stand.'
The kyng sayd to the steward tho,
'I may not beleve it should be so;
Hath he be so bonayre[9] and benyngne,
And served me syth he was yinge,
And redy with me in every nede,
Bothe true of word, and eke of dede,
I may not beleve, be nyght nor daye,
My doughter dere he wyll betraye,
Nor to come her chambre nye,
That fode[10] to longe with no foly;
Though she would to hym consente,
That lovely lady fayre and gente,
I truste hym so well withouten drede,
That he would never do that dede;
But yf he myght that lady wynne,
In wedlocke to welde withouten synne,
And yf she wyll assent him tyll,
The squyer is worthy to have none yll.
For I have sene that many a page
Have become men by mariage;
Than it is semely that squyer
To have my doughter by this manere,
And eche man in his degre
Become a lorde of ryaltye,
By fortune and by other grace,
By herytage and by purchase[11]:
Therfore, stewarde, beware hereby,
Defame hym not for no envy:
It were great reuth he should be spylte,
Or put to death withouten gylte;
And more ruthe of my doughter dere,
For chaungyng of that ladyes chere;
I woulde not for my crowne so newe,
That lady chaunge hyde or hewe;
Or for to put thyselfe in drede,
But thou myght take hym with the dede.
For yf it may be founde in thee
That thou them fame for enmyte,
Thou shalt be taken as a felon,
And put full depe in my pryson,
And fetered fast unto a stone,
Tyl .xii. yere were come and gone,
And drawen wyth hors throughe the cyte,
And soone hanged upon a tre;
And thou may not thy selfe excuse,
This dede thou shalt no wise refuse;

[1] harm, mischief
[2] calamity
[3] rod, staff
[4] lack
[5] snipes
[6] went
[7] promised
[8] together
[9] well-bred debonair
[10] child
[11] acquisition

And therfore, steward, take good hed,
How thou wilt answere to this ded.'
The stewarde answered with great envy,
'That I have sayd, I wyll stand therby;
To suffre death and endlesse wo,
Syr kynge, I wyl never go therfro;
For, yf that ye wyll graunt me here
Strength of men and great power,
I shall hym take this same nyght,
In chambre with your doughter bright;
For I shall never be gladde of chere,
Tyll I be venged of that squyer.'
 Than sayd the kynge full curteysly
Unto the stewarde, that stode hym by,
'Thou shalte have strength ynough with the,
Men of armes .xxx. and thre,
To watche that lady muche of pryce,
And her to kepe fro her enemyes.
For there is no knight in Chrystente,
That wolde betray that lady fre,
But he should dye under his shelde
And I myght se hym in the feldde;
And therfore, stewarde, I the pray,
Take hede what I shall to the say;
And if the squiere come to-night,
For to speke with that lady bryght,
Let hym say whatsoever he wyll,
And here and se and holde you styll;
And herken well what he wyll say,
Or thou with him make any fray
So he come not her chambre win,[1]
No bate[2] on hym loke thou begyn,
Though that he kysse that lady fre,
And take his leave ryght curteysly,
Let hym go, both hole and sounde,
Without wemme[3] or any wounde;
But yf he wyl her chamber breke,
No worde to hym that thou do speke.
But yf he come with company,
For to betraye that fayre lady,
Loke he be taken soone anone,
And all his meyne everychone,
And brought with strength to my pryson,
As traytour, thefe, and false felon;
And yf he make any defence,
Loke that he never go thence;
But loke thou hew hym al so small,
As flesshe whan it to the potte shall.
And yf he yelde hym to thee,
Brynge him both saufe and sounde to me.
I shall borowe,[4] for seven yere
He shall not wedde my doughter dere:
And therfore, stewarde, I thee praye,
Thou watche that lady nyght and daye.'
The stewarde sayde the kynge untyll,
'All your bidding I shall fulfyll.'
 The stewarde toke his leave to go,
The squyer came fro chambre tho:
Downe he went into the hall,
The officers sone can he call,
Both ussher, panter,[5] and butler,
And other that in office were;
There he them warned sone anone
To take up the bordes everychone.
Than they dyd his commaundement,
And sythe[6] unto the kyng he went;
Full lowe he set hym on his kne,
And voyded[7] his borde full gentely;
And whan the squyre had done so,
Anone he sayde the kynge unto,
'As ye are lorde of chyvalry,
Geve me leve to passe the sea,
To prove my strenthe with my ryght hande,
On Godes enemyes in uncouth land;
And to be knowe in chyvalry,
In Gascoyne, Spayne, and Lumbardy;
In eche batayle for to fyght,
To be proved a venterous knyght.'
The kyng sayd to the squyer tho,
'Thou shalt have good leve to go;
I shall the gyve both golde and fe,
And strength of men to wende with thee;
If thou be true in worde and dede,
I shall thee helpe in all thy nede.'
The squyer thanked the kyng anone,
And toke his leve and forth can gone,
With joye, and blysse, and muche pryde,
With all his meyny by his syde.
He had not ryden but a whyle,
Not the mountenaunce of a myle,
Or he was ware of a vyllage,
Anone he sayde unto a page,
'Our souper soone loke it be dyght,[8]
Here wyll we lodge all to-nyght.'
They toke theyr ynnes[9] in good intente,
And to theyr supper soone they wente.
Whan he was set, and served at meate,
Than he sayd he had forgete
To take leve of that lady fre,
The kynges doughter of Hungre.
 Anone the squyer made him yare,[10]
And by hymselfe forth can he fare;
Without strength of his meyne,
Unto the castell than went he.
Whan he came to the posterne gate,
Anone he entred in thereat,
And his drawen swerd in his hande,
There was no more with him wolde stande:
But it stode with hym full harde,
As ye shall here nowe of the stewarde.
He wende[11] in the worlde none had be

1 in or within?
2 strife
3 hurt
4 pledge
5 pantler, servant in charge of the pantry
6 afterwards
7 cleared
8 prepared
9 lodgings
10 ready
11 supposed

That had knowen of his pryvite;
Alas! it was not as he wende,
For all his counsayle the stewarde kende.[1]
He had bewrayed him to the kyng
Of all his love and his woyng;
And yet he laye her chambre by,
Armed with a great company,
And beset it one eche syde,
For treason walketh wonde wyde.
The squyer thought on no mystruste,
He wende no man in the worlde had wyste;
But yf he had knowen, by Saynt John,
He had not come theder by his owne;
Or yf that lady had knowen his wyll,
That he should have come her chamber tyll,
She would have taken hym golde and fe,
Strength of men and royalte;
But there ne wyst no man nor grome[2]
Where that squyer was become;
But forth he went hymselfe alone
Amonge his servauntes everychone.
Whan that he came her chambre to,
Anone he sayde, 'Your dore undo!
Undo,' he sayde, 'nowe, fayre lady!
I am beset with many a spy.
Lady, as whyte as whales bone,
There are thyrty agaynst me one.
Undo thy dore! my worthy wyfe,
I am besette with many a knyfe.
Undo your dore! my lady swete,
I am beset with enemyes great;
And, lady, but ye wyll aryse,
I shall be dead with myne enemyes.
Undo thy dore! my frely[3] floure,
For ye are myne, and I am your.'
  That lady with those wordes awoke,
A mantell of golde to her she toke;
She sayde, 'Go away, thou wicked wyght,
Thou shalt not come here this nyght;
For I wyll not my dore undo
For no man that cometh therto.
There is but one in Christente
That ever made that forwarde[4] with me;
There is but one that ever bare lyfe,
That ever I hight to be his wyfe;
He shall me wedde, by Mary bryght,
Whan he is proved a venterous knyght;
For we have loved this seven yere,
There was never love to me so dere.
There lyeth-on[5] me both kyng and knyght,
Dukes, erles, of muche might.
Wende forth, squyer, on your waye,
For here ye gette none other paye;
For I ne wote what ye should be,
That thus besecheth love of me.'
'I am your owne squyr,' he sayde,
'For me, lady, be not dismayde.
Come I am full pryvely
To take my leave of you, lady.'
'Welcome,' she sayd, 'my love so dere,
Myne owne dere heart and my squyer;
I shall you geve kysses thre,
A thousande pounde unto your fe,
And kepe I shall my maydenhode ryght,
Tyll ye be proved a venturous knyght.
For yf ye should me wede anone,
My father wolde make slee you soone.
I am the kynges doughter of Hungre,
And ye alone that have loved me,
And though you love me never so sore,
For me ye shall never be lore.[6]
Go forth, and aske me at my kynne,
And loke what graunt you may wynne;
Yf that ye gette graunte in faye,[7]
My selfe therto shall not say nay;
And yf ye may not do so,
Otherwyse ye shall come to.
Ye are bothe hardy, stronge, and wight,
Go forth and be a venterous knight.
I pray to God and our Lady,
To send you the whele of victory,
That my father so leve[8] he be,
That he wyll profer me to thee.
I wote well it is lyghtly sayd,
"Go forth, and be nothyng afrayde."
A man of worshyp may not do so,
He must have what neds him unto;
He must have gold, he must have fe,
Strength of men and royalte.
Golde and sylver spare ye nought,
Tyll to manhode ye be brought;
To what batayll soever ye go,
Ye shall have an hundreth pounde or two;
And yet to me, syr, ye may saye,
That I woulde fayne have you awaye,
That profered you golde and fe,
Out of myne eye syght for to be.
Neverthelesse it is not so,
It is for the worshyp of us two.
Though you be come of symple kynne,
Thus my love, syr, may ye wynne,
Yf ye have grace of victory,
As ever had Syr Lybyus, or Syr Guy,
Whan the dwarfe and mayde Ely
Came to Arthoure kyng so fre,
As a kyng of great renowne,
That wan the lady of Synadowne,
Lybius was graunted the batayle tho,
Therfore the dwarfe was full wo,
And sayd, "Arthur, thou arte to blame.
To bydde this chylde go [nurse] his dame
Better hym semeth, so mote I thryve,
Than for to do these batayles fyve
At the chapell of Salebraunce."

[1] knew [2] groom [3] lovely [4] agreement [5] importunes [6] lost [7] faith [8] dear

These wordes began great distaunce;
They sawe they had the victory,
They kneled downe and cryed mercy;
And afterward, syr, verament,[1]
They called hym knyght absolent[2];
Emperours, dukes, knyghtes, and quene,
At his commaundement for to bene.
Suche fortune with grace now to you fall,
To wynne the worthyest within the wall
And thynke on your love alone,
And for to love that ye chaunge none.'
Ryght as they talked thus in-fere,
Theyr enemyes approched nere and nere,
Foure and thyrty armed bryght
The steward had arayed hym to fyght.
The steward was ordeyned to spy,
And for to take him utterly.
He wende to death he should have gone,
He felled seven men agaynst hym one;
Whan he had them to grounde brought,
The stewarde at hym full sadly[3] fought,
So harde they smote together tho,
The stewardes throte he cut in two,
And sone he fell downe to the grounde,
As a traitour untrewe with many a wound.
The squyer sone in armes they hente,[4]
And of they dyd his good garmente,
And on the stewarde they it dyd,
And sone his body therin they hydde,
And with their swordes his face they share,
That she should not know what he ware;
They cast hym at her chambre dore,
The stewarde that was styffe and store,[5]
Whan they had made that great affraye,
Full pryvely they stale awaye;
In armes they take that squyer tho,
And to the kynges chambre can they go,
Without wemme or any wounde,
Before the kynge bothe hole and sounde.
As soone as the kynge him spyed with eye,
He sayd, 'Welcome, sonne, sykerly!
Thou hast cast thee my sonne to be,
This seven yere I shall let[6] thee.'
Leve we here of this squyer wight,
And speake we of that lady bryght,
How she rose, that lady dere,
To take her leve of that squyer.
Also [fresh] as she was borne,
She stod her chambre dore beforne.
'Alas,' she sayd, 'and weale away!
For all to long now have I lay';
She sayd, 'Alas, and all for wo!
Withouten men why came ye so?
Yf that ye wolde have come to me,
Other werninges there might have be.
Now all to dere my love is bought,
But it shall never be lost for nought';
And in her armes she toke hym there,
Into the chamber she dyd hym bere;
His bowels soone she dyd out drawe,
And buryed them in Goddes lawe.
She sered[7] that body with specery,[8]
With wyrgin[9] waxe and commendry[10];
And closed hym in a maser[11] tre,
And set on hym lockes thre.
She put him in a marble stone,
With quaynt gynnes many one;
And set hym at hir beddes head,
And every day she kyst that dead.
Soone at morne, whan she uprose,
Unto that dead body she gose,
There wold she knele downe on her kne,
And make her prayer to the Trynite,
And kysse that body twyse or thryse,
And fall in a swowne or she myght ryse.
Whan she had so done,
To chyrche than wolde she gone,
Than would she here masses fyve,
And offre to them whyle she myght lyve:
'There shall none knowe but heven kynge
For whome that I make myne offrynge.'
The kyng her father anone he sayde:
'My doughter, wy are you dysmayde?
So feare a lady as ye are one,
And so semely of fleshe and bone, —
Ye were whyte as whales bone,
Nowe are ye pale as any stone;
Your ruddy read as any chery,
With browes bent and eyes full mery;
Ye were wont to harpe and syng,
And be the meriest in chambre comyng;
Ye ware both golde and good velvet,
Clothe of damaske with saphyres set;
Ye ware the pery[12] on your head,
With stones full oryent, whyte and read;
Ye ware coronalles of golde,
With diamoundes set many a foulde;
And nowe ye were clothes of blacke,
Tell me, doughter, for whose sake?
If he be so poore of fame,
That ye may not be wedded for shame,
Brynge him to me anone ryght,
I shall hym make squyer and knight;
And, yf he be so great a lorde,
That your love may not accorde,
Let me, doughter, that lordynge se;
He shall have golde ynoughe with thee.'
'Gramercy, father, so mote I thryve,
For I mourne for no man alyve.
Ther is no man, by heven kyng,

[1] truly
[2] finished or perfect?
[3] firmly
[4] seized
[5] big
[6] prevent
[7] wrapped
[8] spicery
[9] virgin, pure
[10] cumin, an aromatic plant?
[11] maple
[12] gems

That shal knowe more of my mournynge.'
Her father knewe it every deale,
But he kept it in counsele:
'To-morowe ye shall on hunting fare,
And ryde, my doughter, in a chare,[1]
It shalbe covered with velvet reede,
And clothes of fyne golde al about your hed,
With damaske, white and asure blewe,
Wel dyapred[2] with lyllyes newe;
Your pomelles[3] shalbe ended with gold,
Your chaynes enameled many a folde;
Your mantel of ryche degre,
Purpyl palle[4] and armyne fre;
Jennettes[5] of Spayne, that ben so wyght,
Trapped to the ground with velvet bright;
Ye shall have harpe, sautry,[6] and songe,
And other myrthes you amonge;
Ye shall have rumney and malmesyne,
Both ypocrasse and vernage wyne,
Mountrose and wyne of Greke,
Both algrade and respice eke,
Antioche and bastarde,
Pyment also and garnarde;
Wyne of Greke and muscadell,
Both clare, pyment, and rochell.
The reed your stomake to defye,
And pottes of osey set you by.
You shall have venison ybake,
The best wylde foule that may be take.
A lese[7] of grehound with you to strike,
And hert and hynde and other lyke.
Ye shalbe set at such a tryst
That herte and hynde shall come to your fyst,
Your dysease[8] to dryve you fro,
To here the bugles there yblow,
With theyr begles[9] in that place,
And sevenscore braches[9] at his rechase.[10]
Homward thus shall ye ryde,
On haukyng by the ryvers syde,
With goshauke and with gentyll fawcon,
With egle horne and merlyon.[11]
Whan you come home, your men amonge,
Ye shall have revell, daunces, and songe;
Lytle chyldren, great and smale,
Shall syng, as doth the nyghtyngale.
Than shall ye go to your evensong,
With tenours and trebles among;
Threscore of copes, of damaske bryght,
Full of perles they shalbe pyght[12];
Your aulter clothes of taffata,
And your sicles[13] all of taffetra.[14]
Your sensours[15] shalbe of golde,
Endent with asure many a folde.
Your quere[16] nor organ songe shall wante
With countre note and dyscant,
The other halfe on orgayns playeng,
With yonge chyldren full fayre syngyng.
Than shall ye go to your suppere,
And sytte in tentes in grene arbere,
With clothes of Aras pyght to the grounde,
With saphyres set and dyamonde.
A cloth of golde abought your heade,
With popinjayes pyght with pery read,
And offycers all at your wyll,
All maner delightes to bryng you tyll.
The nightingale sitting on a thorne
Shall synge you notes both even and morne.
An hundreth knightes truly tolde
Shall play with bowles in alayes colde,
Your disease to drive awaie:
To se the fisshes in poles[17] plaie;
And then walke in arbere up and downe,
To se the floures of great renowne:
To a draw-brydge than shall ye,
The one halfe of stone, the other of tre;
A barge shall mete you full ryght
With .xxiiii. ores full bryght,
With trompettes and with claryowne,
The fresshe water to rowe up and downe;
Than shall ye go to the salte fome,
Your maner[18] to se, or ye come home,
With .lxxx. shyppes of large towre,
With dromedaryes[19] of great honour,
And carackes[19] with sayles two,
The sweftest that on water may goo,
With galyes good upon the haven,
With .lxxx. ores at the fore staven.[20]
Your maryners shall synge arowe[21]
"Hey how and rumbylawe."
Than shall ye, doughter, aske the wyne,
With spices that be good and fyne,
Gentyll pottes with genger grene,
With dates and deynties you betwene.
Forty torches brenynge bryght,
At your brydges to brynge you lyght.
Into your chambre they shall you brynge
With muche myrthe and more lykyng.
Your costerdes[22] covered with whyte and blewe,
And dyapred with lyles newe.
Your curtaines of camaca[23] all in folde,
Your felyoles[24] all of golde.
Your tester[25] pery at your heed,
Curtaines with popinjayes white and reed.
Your hyllynges[26] with furres of armyne,

1 chariot
2 adorned
3 knobs
4 fine cloth
5 small horses
6 psaltery
7 leash
8 sorrow
9 beagles, braches (kinds of hounds)
10 call
11 merlin
12 trimmed
13 tunics
14 taffeta?
15 censers
16 choir
17 pools
18 manor house
19 large vessels
20 prow
21 in a row
22 hangings for a bed, etc.
23 a fine fabric
24 columns?
25 canopy over a bed
26 coverings

Powdred with golde of hew full fyne.
Your blankettes shall be of fustyane,
Your shetes shall be of clothe of Rayne.
Your head shete shall be of pery pyght,
With dyamondes set and rubyes bryght.
Whan you are layde in bedde so softe,
A cage of golde shall hange alofte,
With longe peper[1] fayre burnning,
And cloves that be swete smellyng,
Frankensence and olibanum,[2]
That whan ye slepe the taste may come.
And yf ye no rest may take,
All night minstrelles for you shall wake.'
'Gramercy, father, so mote I the,[3]
For all these thinges lyketh not me.'
Unto her chambre she is gone,
And fell in sownyng sone anone,
With much sorow and sighing sore,
Yet seven yeare she kept hym thore.
  But leve we of that lady here,
And speake we more of that squyer,
That in pryson so was take
For the kinges doughters sake.
The kyng hym selfe upon a daye
Full pryvely he toke the waye,
Unto the pryson sone he came,
The squyer sone out he name,[4]
And anone he made hym swere
His counsayl he should never discure.[5]
The squyer there helde up his hande,
His byddyng never he should withstande.
The kyng him graunted ther to go
Upon his jorney to and fro,
And brefely to passe the sea,
That no man weste but he and he,
And whan he had his jurnay done,
That he wolde come full soone:
'And in my chambre for to be,
The whyles that I do ordayne for thee;
Than shalt thou wedde my doughter dere,
And have my landes both farre and nere.'
  The squyer was full mery tho,
And thanked the kynge, and forth gan go.
The kyng hym gave both lande and fe.
Anone the squyer passed the se.
In Tuskayne and in Lumbardy,
There he dyd great chyvalry.
In Portyngale nor yet in Spayne,
There myght no man stand hym agayne;
And where that ever that knyght gan fare,
The worshyp with hym away he bare:
And thus he travayled seven yere
In many a land bothe farre and nere;
Tyll on a day he thought hym tho
Unto the sepulture for to go;
And there he made his offerynge soone,
Right as the kinges doughter bad him don.
Than he thought hym on a day
That the kynge to hym dyd saye.
He toke his leve in Lumbardy,
And home he came to Hungry.
Unto the kynge soone he rade,
As he before his covenaunce made,
And to the kyng he tolde full soone,
Of batayles bolde that he had done,
And so he did the chyvalry
That he had sene in Lumbardy.
To the kynge it was good tydande[6];
Anone he toke him by the hande,
And he made him full royall chere,
And sayd, 'Welcome, my sonne so dere!
Let none wete of my meyne
That out of prison thou shuldest be,
But in my chamber holde the styll,
And I shall wete my doughters wyll.'
  The kynge wente forth hymselfe alone,
For to here his doughters mone,
Right under the chambre window.
There he might her counseyle knowe.
Had she wyst, that lady fre,
That her father there had be,
He shulde not withouten fayle
Have knowen so muche of her counsayle
Nor nothing she knew that he was there.
  Whan she began to carke[7] and care,
Unto that body she sayd tho,
'Alas that we should parte in two!'
Twyse or thryse she kyssed that body,
And fell in sownynge by and by.
'Alas!' than sayd that lady dere,
'I have the kept this seven yere,
And now ye be in powder small,
I may no lenger holde you with all.
My love, to the earth I shall the brynge,
And preestes for you to reade and synge.
Yf any man aske me what I have here,
I wyll say it is my treasure.
Yf any man aske why I do so,
"For no theves shall come therto":
And, squyer, for the love of the,
Fy on this worldes vanyte!
Farewell golde pure and fyne;
Farewell velvet and satyne;
Farewell castelles and maners also;
Farewell huntynge and hawkynge to;
Farewell revell, myrthe and play;
Farewell pleasure and garmentes gay;
Farewell perle and precyous stone;
Farewell my juielles everychone;
Farewell mantell and scarlet reed;
Farewell crowne unto my heed;
Farewell hawkes and farewell hounde;
Farewell markes and many a pounde;
Farewell huntynge at the hare;

[1] pepper [2] fragrant gum [3] thrive [4] took [5] reveal [6] tidings [7] sorrow

Farewell harte and hynde for evermare.
Nowe wyll I take the mantell and the rynge,
And become an ancresse[1] in my lyvynge:
And yet I am a mayden for thee,
And for all the men in Chrystente.
To Chryst I shall my prayers make,
Squyer, onely for thy sake;
And I shall never no masse heare
But ye shall have parte in-feare[2]:
And every daye whyles I lyve,
Ye shall have your masses fyve,
And I shall offre pence thre,
In tokenynge of the Trynyte.'
And whan this lady had this sayde,
In sownyng she fel at a brayde.[3]
The whyle she made this great mornynge,
Under the wall stode har father the kynge.
'Doughter,' he sayde, 'you must not do so,
For all those vowes thou must forgo.'
'Alas, father, and wele awaye!
Nowe have ye harde what I dyde saye.'
'Doughter, let be all thy mournynge,
Thou shalt be wedede to a kynge.'
'Iwys,[4] father, that shall not be
For all the golde in Christente;
Nor all the golde that ever God made
May not my harte glade.[5]'
'My doughter,' he sayde, 'dere derlynge,
I knowe the cause of your mournyng:
Ye wene this body your love should be,
It is not so, so mote I the.
It was my stewarde, Syr Maradose,
That ye so longe have kept in close.'
'Alas! father, why dyd ye so?'
'For he wrought you all thys wo.
He made revelation unto me,
That he knewe all your pryvyte;
And howe the squyer, on a day,
Unto your chambre toke the way,
And ther he should have leyen you bi,
Had he not come with company;
And howe ye hyght hym golde and fe,
Strengthe of men and royalte;
And than he watched your chambre bryght,
With men of armes hardy and wyght,
For to take that squyer,
That ye have loved this seven yere;
But as the stewarde strong and stout
Beseged your chambre rounde about,
To you your love came full ryght,
All alone about mydnight.
And whan he came your dore unto,
And "Lady," he sayde, "undo,"
And soone ye bade hym wende awaye,
Por there he gate none other paye:
And as ye talked thus in-fere,
Your enemyes drewe them nere and nere,
They smote to him full soone anone,
There were thyrty agaynst hym one:
But with a baslarde[6] large and longe
The squyer presed in to the thronge;
And so he bare hym in that stounde,
His enemyes gave he many a wounde.
With egre[7] mode[8] and herte full throwe,[9]
The stewardes throte he cut in two;
And than his meyne all in that place
With their swordes they hurte his face,
And than they toke him everichone
And layd him on a marble stone
Before your dore, that ye myght se,
Ryght as your love that he had be.
And sone the squier there they hent,
And they dyd of his good garment,
And did it on the stewarde there,
That ye wist not what he were:
Thus ye have kept your enemy here
Pallyng[10] more than seven yere,
And as the squyer there was take,
And done in pryson for your sake;
Therfore let be your mourning,
Ye shalbe wedded to a kyng,
Or els unto an emperoure,
With golde and sylver and great treasure.'
'Do awaye, father, that may not be,
For all the golde in Chrystente.
Alas! father,' anone she sayde,
'Why hath this traytour me betraid?
Alas!' she sayd, 'I have great wrong
That I have kept him here so long.
Alas! father, why dyd ye so?
Ye might have warned me of my fo;
And ye had tolde me who it had be,
My love had never be dead for me.'
Anone she tourned her fro the kyng,
And downe she fell in dead sownyng.
The kyng anone gan go,
And hente her in his armes two.
'Lady,' he sayd, 'be of good chere,
Your love lyveth and is here;
And he hath bene in Lombardy,
And done he hath great chyvalry;
And come agayne he is to me,
In lyfe and health ye shall him se.
He shall you wede, my doughter bryght,
I have hym made squier and knyght;
He shalbe a lorde of great renowne,
And after me to were the crowne.'
'Father,' she sayd, 'if it so be,
Let me soone that squyer se.'
The squyer forth than dyd he brynge,
Full fayre on lyve and in lykynge.

[1] anchoress, nun
[2] together
[3] in a moment
[4] certainly
[5] gladden
[6] dagger
[7] angry
[8] mood
[9] bold
[10] languishing

As sone as she saw him with her eye,
She fell in sownyng by and by.
The squyer her hente in armes two,
And kyssed her an hundreth tymes and mo.
There was myrth and melody
With harpe, getron, and sautry,
With rote, ribible, and clokarde,
With pypes, organs, and bumbarde,
With other mynstrelles them amonge,
With sytolphe and with sautry songe,
With fydle, recorde, and dowcemere,
With trompette and with claryon clere,
With dulcet pipes of many cordes.
In chambre revelyng all the lordes,
Unto morne that it was daye,
The kyng to his doughter began to saye,
'Have here thy love and thy lyking,
To lyve and ende in Gods blessinge;
And he that wyll departe[1] you two,
God geve him sorow and wo!
A trewer lover than ye are one
Was never yet of flesh ne bone;
And but he be as true to thee,
God let him never thryve ne thee.'
The kyng in herte he was full blithe,
He kissed his doughter many a sithe,[2]
With melody and muche chere;
Anone he called his messengere,
And commaunded him soone to go
Through his cities to and fro,
For to warne his chevalry
That they should come to Hungry,
That worthy wedding for to se,
And come unto that mangere.[3]
That messenger full sone he wente,
And did the kinges commaundemente.
Anone he commaunded bothe olde and yinge
For to be at that weddyng,
Both dukes and erles of muche myght,
And ladyes that were fayre and bryght.
As soone as ever they herde the crye,
The lordes were full soone redy;
With myrth and game and muche playe
They wedded them on a solempne[4] daye.
A royall feest there was holde,
With dukes and erles and barons bolde,
And knyghtes and squyers of that countre,
And sith with all the comunalte:
And certaynly, as the story sayes,
The revell lasted forty dayes;
Tyll on a day the kyng him selfe
To hym he toke his lordes twelfe,
And so he dyd the squyer
That wedded his doughter dere,
And even in the myddes of the hall
He made him kyng among them al;
And all the lordes everychone
They made him homage sone anon;
And sithen[5] they revelled all that day,
And toke theyr leve, and went theyr way,
Eche lorde unto his owne countre,
Where that hym thought best to be.
That yong man and the quene his wyfe,
With joy and blysse they led theyr lyfe,
For also farre as I have gone,
Suche two lovers sawe I none:
Therfore blessed may theyr soules be,
Amen, amen, for charyte!

ca. 1450 ?

Sir Thomas Malory (fl. ca. 1470)

LE MORTE DARTHUR*

BOOK XXI

Chapter I

As Sir Mordred was ruler of all England, he did do make letters as though that they came from beyond the sea, and the letters specified that King Arthur was slain in battle with Sir Launcelot. Wherefore Sir Mordred made a parliament, and called the lords together, and there he made them to choose him king; and so was he crowned at Canterbury, and held a feast there fifteen days; and afterward he drew him unto Winchester, and there he took the Queen Guenever, and said plainly that he would wed her which was his uncle's wife and his father's wife. And so he made ready for the feast, and a day prefixed that they should be wedded; wherefore Queen Guenever was passing heavy. But she durst not discover her heart, but spake fair, and agreed to Sir Mordred's will. Then she desired of Sir Mordred for to go to London, to buy all manner of things that longed unto the wedding. And because of her fair speech Sir Mordred trusted her well enough, and gave her leave to go. And so when she came to London she took the Tower of London, and suddenly in all haste possible she stuffed it with all manner of victual, and well garnished it with men, and so kept it. Then when Sir Mordred wist and understood how he was beguiled, he was passing

[1] separate [2] time [3] feast [4] festive [5] afterward

* Everyman's Library. By permission of E. P. Dutton & Company, Publishers.

wroth out of measure. And a short tale for to make, he went and laid a mighty siege about the Tower of London, and made many great assaults thereat, and threw many great engines unto them, and shot great guns. But all might not prevail Sir Mordred, for Queen Guenever would never for fair speech nor for foul, would never trust to come in his hands again. . . .

Chapter II

And so as Sir Mordred was at Dover with his host, there came King Arthur with a great navy of ships, and galleys, and carracks.[1] And there was Sir Mordred ready awaiting upon his landing, to let his own father to land upon the land that he was king over. Then there was launching of great boats and small, and full of noble men of arms; and there was much slaughter of gentle knights, and many a full bold baron was laid full low, on both parties. But King Arthur was so courageous that there might no manner of knights let him to land, and his knights fiercely followed him; and so they landed maugre Sir Mordred and all his power, and put Sir Mordred aback, that he fled and all his people. So when this battle was done, King Arthur let bury his people that were dead. And then was noble Sir Gawaine found in a great boat, lying more than half dead. When Sir Arthur wist that Sir Gawaine was laid so low, he went unto him; and there the king made sorrow out of measure, and took Sir Gawaine in his arms, and thrice he there swooned. And then when he awaked, he said: 'Alas, Sir Gawaine, my sister's son, here now thou liest, the man in the world that I loved most; and now is my joy gone, for now, my nephew Sir Gawaine, I will discover me unto your person: in Sir Launcelot and you I most had my joy, and mine affiance,[2] and now have I lost my joy of you both; wherefore all mine earthly joy is gone from me.' 'Mine uncle, King Arthur,' said Sir Gawaine, 'wit you well my death-day is come, and all is through mine own hastiness and wilfulness; for I am smitten upon the old wound the which Sir Launcelot gave me, on the which I feel well I must die; and had Sir Launcelot been with you as he was, this unhappy war had never begun; and of all this am I causer, for Sir Launcelot and his blood, through their prowess, held all your cankered[3] enemies in subjection and daunger.[4] And now,' said Sir Gawaine, 'ye shall miss Sir Launcelot. But alas, I would not accord with him, and therefore,' said Sir Gawaine, 'I pray you, fair uncle, that I may have paper, pen, and ink, that I may write to Sir Launcelot a cedle[5] with mine own hands.' And then when paper and ink was brought, then Gawaine was set up weakly by King Arthur, for he was shriven a little to-fore; and then he wrote thus, as the French book maketh mention: 'Unto Sir Launcelot, flower of all noble knights that ever I heard of or saw by my days, I, Sir Gawaine, King Lot's son of Orkney, sister's son unto the noble King Arthur, send thee greeting, and let thee have knowledge that the tenth day of May I was smitten upon the old wound that thou gavest me afore the city of Benwick, and through the same wound that thou gavest me I am come to my death-day. And I will that all the world wit, that I, Sir Gawaine, knight of the Table Round, sought my death, and not through thy deserving, but it was mine own seeking; wherefore I beseech thee, Sir Launcelot, to return again unto this realm, and see my tomb, and pray some prayer more or less for my soul. And this same day that I wrote this cedle, I was hurt to the death in the same wound, the which I had of thy hand, Sir Launcelot; for of a more nobler man might I not be slain. Also, Sir Launcelot, for all the love that ever was betwixt us, make no tarrying, but come over the sea in all haste, that thou mayest with thy noble knights rescue that noble king that made thee knight, that is my lord Arthur; for he is full straitly bestead with a false traitor, that is my half-brother, Sir Mordred; and he hath let crown him king, and would have wedded my lady Queen Guenever, and so had he done had she not put herself in the Tower of London. And so the tenth day of May last past, my lord Arthur and we all landed upon them at Dover; and there we put that false traitor, Sir Mordred, to

[1] large vessels [2] trust [3] inveterate [4] control [5] note

flight, and there it misfortuned me to be stricken upon thy stroke. And at the date of this letter was written, but two hours and a half afore my death, written with mine own hand, and so subscribed with part of my heart's blood. And I require thee, most famous knight of the world, that thou wilt see my tomb.' And then Sir Gawaine wept, and King Arthur wept: and then they swooned both. And when they awaked both, the king made Sir Gawaine to receive his Saviour. And then Sir Gawaine prayed the king for to send for Sir Launcelot, and to cherish him above all other knights. And so at the hour of noon Sir Gawaine yielded up the spirit; and then the king let inter him in a chapel within Dover Castle; and there yet all men may see the skull of him, and the same wound is seen that Sir Launcelot gave him in battle. Then was it told the king that Sir Mordred had pight[1] a new field upon Barham Down. And upon the morn the king rode thither to him, and there was a great battle betwixt them, and much people was slain on both parties; but at the last Sir Arthur's party stood best, and Sir Mordred and his party fled unto Canterbury.

Chapter III

And then the king let search all the towns for his knights that were slain, and interred them; and salved them with soft salves that so sore were wounded. Then much people drew unto King Arthur. And then they said that Sir Mordred warred upon King Arthur with wrong. And then King Arthur drew him with his host down by the seaside, westward toward Salisbury; and there was a day assigned betwixt King Arthur and Sir Mordred, that they should meet upon a down beside Salisbury, and not far from the seaside; and this day was assigned on a Monday after Trinity Sunday, whereof King Arthur was passing glad, that he might be avenged upon Sir Mordred. . . . So then [Arthur and his army] departed, and came to Sir Mordred, where he had a grim host of an hundred thousand men. And there they entreated Sir Mordred long time; and at the last Sir Mordred was agreed for to have Cornwall and Kent, by Arthur's days: after, all England, after the days of King Arthur.

Chapter IV

Then were they condescended that King Arthur and Sir Mordred should meet betwixt both their hosts, and everych of them should bring fourteen persons; and they came with this word unto Arthur. Then said he: 'I am glad that this is done': and so he went into the field. And when Arthur should depart, he warned all his host that an they see any sword drawn: 'Look ye come on fiercely, and slay that traitor, Sir Mordred, for I in no wise trust him.' In likewise Sir Mordred warned his host that: 'An ye see any sword drawn, look that ye come on fiercely, and so slay all that ever before you standeth; for in no wise I will not trust for this treaty, for I know well my father will be avenged on me.' And so they met as their appointment was, and so they were agreed and accorded thoroughly; and wine was fetched, and they drank. Right soon came an adder out of a little heath bush, and it stung a knight on the foot. And when the knight felt him stung, he looked down and saw the adder, and then he drew his sword to slay the adder, and thought of none other harm. And when the host on both parties saw that sword drawn, then they blew beams,[2] trumpets, and horns, and shouted grimly. And so both hosts dressed them together. And King Arthur took his horse, and said: 'Alas, this unhappy day!' and so rode to his party. And Sir Mordred in likewise. And never was there seen a more dolefuller battle in no Christian land; for there was but rushing and riding, foining[3] and striking, and many a grim word was there spoken either to other, and many a deadly stroke. But ever King Arthur rode throughout the battle of Sir Mordred many times, and did full nobly as a noble king should, and at all times he fainted never; and Sir Mordred that day put him in devoir, and in great peril. And thus they fought all the long day, and never stinted till the noble knights were laid to the cold earth; and ever they fought still till it was near night, and by that time was there an hundred thousand laid dead upon

[1] pitched, prepared [2] horns [3] thrusting

the down. Then was Arthur wood[1] wroth out of measure, when he saw his people so slain from him. Then the king looked about him, and then was he ware, of all his host and of all his good knights, were left no more alive but two knights; that one was Sir Lucan the Butler, and his brother Sir Bedivere, and they were full sore wounded. 'Jesu mercy,' said the king, 'where are all my noble knights become? Alas that ever I should see this doleful day, for now,' said Arthur, 'I am come to mine end. But would to God that I wist where were that traitor Sir Mordred, that hath caused all this mischief.' Then was King Arthur ware where Sir Mordred leaned upon his sword among a great heap of dead men. 'Now give me my spear,' said Arthur unto Sir Lucan, 'for yonder I have espied the traitor that all this woe hath wrought.' 'Sir, let him be,' said Sir Lucan, 'for he is unhappy; and if ye pass this unhappy day, ye shall be right well revenged upon him. Good lord, remember ye of your night's dream, and what the spirit of Sir Gawaine told you this night, yet God of his great goodness hath preserved you hitherto. Therefore, for God's sake, my lord, leave off by this; for, blessed be God, ye have won the field, for here we be three alive, and with Sir Mordred is none alive; and if ye leave off now, this wicked day of destiny is past.' 'Tide me death, betide me life,' saith the king, 'now I see him yonder alone he shall never escape mine hands, for at a better avail shall I never have him.' 'God speed you well,' said Sir Bedivere. Then the king gat his spear in both his hands, and ran toward Sir Mordred, crying: 'Traitor, now is thy death-day come.' And when Sir Mordred heard Sir Arthur, he ran until him with his sword drawn in his hand. And there King Arthur smote Sir Mordred under the shield, with a foin of his spear, throughout the body, more than a fathom. And when Sir Mordred felt that he had his death wound, he thrust himself with the might that he had up to the bur[2] of King Arthur's spear. And right so he smote his father Arthur, with his sword holden in both his hands, on the side of the head, that the sword pierced the helmet and the brain-pan, and therewithal Sir Mordred fell stark dead to the earth; and the noble Arthur fell in a swoon to the earth, and there he swooned ofttimes. And Sir Lucan the Butler and Sir Bedivere ofttimes heaved him up. And so weakly they led him betwixt them both, to a little chapel not far from the seaside. And when the king was there he thought him well eased. Then heard they people cry in the field. 'Now go, thou, Sir Lucan,' said the king, 'and do me to wit what betokens that noise in the field.' So Sir Lucan departed, for he was grievously wounded in many places. And so as he yede,[3] he saw and hearkened by the moonlight, how that pillers[4] and robbers were come into the field, to pill and to rob many a full noble knight of brooches, and beads, of many a good ring, and of many a rich jewel; and who that were not dead all out, there they slew them for their harness and their riches. When Sir Lucan understood this work, he came to the king as soon as he might, and told him all what he had heard and seen. 'Therefore by my rede,[5]' said Sir Lucan, 'it is best that we bring you to some town.' 'I would it were so,' said the king.

Chapter V

'But I may not stand, mine head works so. Ah, Sir Launcelot,' said King Arthur, 'this day have I sore missed thee: alas, that ever I was against thee, for now have I my death, whereof Sir Gawaine me warned in my dream.' Then Sir Lucan took up the king the one part, and Sir Bedivere the other part, and in the lifting the king swooned; and Sir Lucan fell in a swoon with the lift, that the part of his guts fell out of his body, and therewith the noble knight's heart brast.[6] And when the king awoke, he beheld Sir Lucan, how he lay foaming at the mouth, and part of his guts lay at his feet. 'Alas,' said the king, 'this is to me a full heavy sight, to see this noble duke so die for my sake, for he would have holpen me, that had more need of help than I. Alas, he would not complain him, his heart was so set to help me: now Jesu have mercy upon his soul!' Then Sir Bedivere wept for

[1] mad, insane
[2] a broad iron ring, to prevent the hand from slipping
[3] went
[4] pillagers
[5] advice
[6] burst

the death of his brother. 'Leave this mourning and weeping,' said the king, 'for all this will not avail me, for wit thou well an I might live myself, the death of Sir Lucan would grieve me evermore; but my time hieth fast,' said the king. 'Therefore,' said Arthur unto Sir Bedivere, 'take thou Excalibur, my good sword, and go with it to yonder water side, and when thou comest there I charge thee throw my sword in that water, and come again and tell me what thou there seest.' 'My lord,' said Bedivere, 'your commandment shall be done, and lightly bring you word again.' So Sir Bedivere departed, and by the way he beheld that noble sword, that the pommel and the haft was all of precious stones; and then he said to himself: 'If I throw this rich sword in the water, thereof shall never come good, but harm and loss.' And then Sir Bedivere hid Excalibur under a tree. And so, as soon as he might, he came again unto the king, and said he had been at the water, and had thrown the sword in the water. 'What saw thou there?' said the king. 'Sir,' he said, 'I saw nothing but waves and winds.' 'That is untruly said of thee,' said the king, 'therefore go thou lightly[1] again, and do my commandment; as thou art to me lief and dear, spare not, but throw it in.' Then Sir Bedivere returned again, and took the sword in his hand; and then him thought sin and shame to throw away that noble sword, and so eft[2] he hid the sword, and returned again, and told to the king that he had been at the water, and done his commandment. 'What saw thou there?' said the king. 'Sir,' he said, 'I saw nothing but the waters wappen[3] and waves wanne.[4] 'Ah, traitor untrue,' said King Arthur, 'now hast thou betrayed me twice. Who would have weened that, thou that hast been to me so lief and dear? and thou art named a noble knight, and would betray me for the richness of the sword. But now go again lightly, for thy long tarrying putteth me in great jeopardy of my life, for I have taken cold. And but if thou do now as I bid thee, if ever I may see thee, I shall slay thee with mine own hands; for thou wouldst for my rich sword see me dead.' Then Sir Bedivere departed, and went to the sword, and lightly took it up, and went to the water side; and there he bound the girdle about the hilts, and then he threw the sword as far into the water as he might; and there came an arm and an hand above the water and met it, and caught it, and so shook it thrice and brandished, and then vanished away the hand with the sword in the water. So Sir Bedivere came again to the king, and told him what he saw. 'Alas,' said the king, 'help me hence, for I dread me I have tarried over long.' Then Sir Bedivere took the king upon his back, and so went with him to that water side. And when they were at the water side, even fast by the bank hoved a little barge with many fair ladies in it, and among them all was a queen, and all they had black hoods, and all they wept and shrieked when they saw King Arthur. 'Now put me into the barge,' said the king. And so he did softly; and there received him three queens with great mourning; and so they set them down, and in one of their laps King Arthur laid his head. And then that queen said: 'Ah, dear brother, why have ye tarried so long from me? alas, this wound on your head hath caught over-much cold.' And so then they rowed from the land, and Sir Bedivere beheld all those ladies go from him. Then Sir Bedivere cried: 'Ah, my lord Arthur, what shall become of me, now ye go from me and leave me here alone among mine enemies?' 'Comfort thyself,' said the king, 'and do as well as thou mayest, for in me is no trust for to trust in; for I will into the vale of Avilion to heal me of my grievous wound: and if thou hear never more of me, pray for my soul.' But ever the queens and ladies wept and shrieked, that it was pity to hear. And as soon as Sir Bedivere had lost the sight of the barge, he wept and wailed, and so took the forest; and so he went all that night, and in the morning he was ware betwixt two holts[5] hoar,[6] of a chapel and an hermitage.

Chapter VI

Then was Sir Bedivere glad, and thither he went; and when he came into the chapel, he saw where lay an hermit groveling on all four, there fast by a tomb was new graven.[7] When the hermit saw Sir Bedi-

[1] quickly [2] again [3] lap [4] become wan [5] wooded hills [6] hoary with age [7] dug

vere he knew him well, for he was but little to-fore Bishop of Canterbury, that Sir Mordred flemed[1]. 'Sir,' said Bedivere, 'what man is there interred that ye pray so fast for?' 'Fair son,' said the hermit, 'I wot not verily, but by deeming. But this night, at midnight, here came a number of ladies, and brought hither a dead corpse, and prayed me to bury him; and here they offered an hundred tapers, and they gave me an hundred besaunts[2].' 'Alas,' said Sir Bedivere, 'that was my lord King Arthur, that here lieth buried in this chapel.' Then Sir Bedivere swooned; and when he awoke he prayed the hermit he might abide with him still there, to live with fasting and prayers. 'For from hence will I never go,' said Sir Bedivere, 'by my will, but all the days of my life here to pray for my lord Arthur.' 'Ye are welcome to me,' said the hermit, 'for I know ye better than ye ween that I do. Ye are the bold Bedivere, and the full noble duke, Sir Lucan the Butler, was your brother.' Then Sir Bedivere told the hermit all as ye have heard to-fore. So there bode Sir Bedivere with the hermit that was to-fore Bishop of Canterbury, and there Sir Bedivere put upon him poor clothes, and served the hermit full lowly in fasting and in prayers. Thus of Arthur I find never more written in books that be authorised, nor more of the very certainty of his death heard I never read[3], but thus was he led away in a ship wherein were three queens; that one was King Arthur's sister, Queen Morgan le Fay; the other was the Queen of Northgalis; the third was the Queen of the Waste Lands. Also there was Nimue, the chief lady of the lake, that had wedded Pelleas the good knight; and this lady had done much for King Arthur, for she would never suffer Sir Pelleas to be in no place where he should be in danger of his life; and so he lived to the uttermost of his days with her in great rest. More of the death of King Arthur could I never find, but that ladies brought him to his burials; and such one was buried there, that the hermit bare witness that sometime was Bishop of Canterbury, but yet the hermit knew not in certain that he was verily the body of King Arthur: for this tale Sir Bedivere, knight of the Table Round, made it to be written.

Chapter VII

Yet some men say in many parts of England that King Arthur is not dead, but had by the will of our Lord Jesu into another place; and men say that he shall come again, and he shall win the holy cross. I will not say it shall be so, but rather I will say: here in this world he changed his life. But many men say that there is written upon his tomb this verse: *Hic jacet Arthurus, Rex quondam Rexque futurus.*

1485

[1] put to flight [2] gold coins [3] tell

AGE OF CHAUCER

POETRY

[William Langland (1331?–1400?)]

PIERS THE PLOWMAN

THE PROLOGUE

In a somer seson, when soft was the sonne,
I shope[1] me in shroudes[2] as I a shepe[3] were,
In habite as an heremite unholy of workes,
Went wyde in this world wondres to here.
Ac[4] on a May mornynge, on Malverne hulles,[5]
Me byfel a ferly,[6] of fairy me thoughte;
I was wery, forwandred,[7] and wente me to reste
Under a brode banke, bi a bornes[8] side,
And as I lay and lened, and loked in the wateres,
I slombred in a slepyng, it sweyved[9] so merye.
Thanne gan I to meten a merveilouse swevene[10]
That I was in a wildernesse, wist I never where;
As I behelde in-to the est, an hiegh[11] to the sonne,
I seigh[12] a toure on a toft,[13] trieliche[14] ymaked;
A depe dale binethe, a dongeon there-inne,
With depe dyches and derke and dredful of sight.
A faire felde ful of folke fonde I there bytwene,
Of alle maner of men, the mene and the riche,
Worchyng and wandryng as the worlde asketh.
Some putten hem to the plow, pleyed ful selde,
In settyng and in sowyng swonken[15] ful harde,
And wonnen that wastours with glotonye destruyeth.
And some putten hem to pruyde,[16] apparailed hem thereafter,
In contenaunce[17] of clothyng comen disgisid.[18]
In prayers and in penance putten hem manye,
Al for love of owre lorde lyveden ful streyte,
In hope for to have hevene-riche blisse;
As ancres[19] and heremites, that holden hem in here selles,
And coveiten nought in contre to kairen[20] aboute,
For no likerous[21] liflode[22] her lykam[23] to plese.
And somme chosen chaffare,[24] they cheven[25] the bettere,
As it semeth to owre syght that suche men thryveth;
And somme murthes to make as mynstralles conneth,[26]
And geten gold with here glee, giltles, I leve.[27]
Ac japers[28] and jangelers,[29] Judas chylderen,
Feynen hem fantasies and foles hem maketh,
And han here witte at wille to worche yif thei sholde;
That Poule precheth of hem I nel nought preve it here;
Qui turpiloquium loquitur is Luciferes hyne.[30]
Bidders and beggeres fast aboute yede,[31]
With her belies and her bagges of bred ful ycrammed;
Fayteden[32] for here fode, foughten atte ale;

1 clad, shaped
2 (rough) garments
3 shepherd
4 but
5 hills
6 wonder
7 spent with wandering
8 brook
9 rippled
10 dream
11 on high
12 saw
13 elevation
14 choicely
15 worked
16 pride
17 display
18 tricked out
19 anchorites
20 wander
21 dainty
22 food
23 body
24 merchandise
25 thrive
26 know how
27 grant
28 jesters
29 babblers
30 servant
31 went
32 dissembled

In glotonye, God it wote, gon hii to bedde,
And risen with ribaudye tho roberdes-knaves[1];
Slepe and sori sleuthe[2] seweth[3] hem evre.
  Pilgrymes and palmers plighted hem togidere
For to seke Seynt James and seyntes in Rome;
Thei went forth in here way with many wise tales,
And hadden leve to lye al here lyf after.
I seigh somme that seiden thei had ysought seyntes:
To eche a tale that thei tolde here tonge was tempred to lye,
More than to sey soth,[4] it semed bi here speche.
  Heremites on an heep, with hoked staves,
Wenten to Walsyngham, and here wenches after;
Grete lobyes[5] and longe, that loth were to swynke,[6]
Clotheden hem in copis[7] to ben knowen fram othere;
And shopen hem heremites here ese to have.
  I fonde there freris,[8] alle the foure ordres,
Preched the peple for profit of hemselven,
Glosed the gospel as hem good lyked,
For coveitise[9] of copis construed it as thei wolde.
Many of this maistres freris mowe[10] clothen hem at lykyng,
For here money and marchandise marchen togideres.
For sith[11] charite hath be chapman,[12] and chief to shryve lordes,
Many ferlis han fallen in a fewe yeris.
But holychirche and hii holde better togideres,
The most myschief on molde[13] is mountyng wel faste.
  Ther preched a Pardoner, as he a prest were,
Broughte forth a bulle with bishopes seles,
And seide that hym-self myghte assoilen hem alle
Of falshed[14] of fastyng, of vowes ybroken.
  Lewed[15] men leved[16] hym wel and lyked his wordes,
Comen up knelyng to kissen his bulles;
He bonched[17] hem with his brevet[18] and blered here eyes,
And raughte[19] with his ragman[20] rynges and broches;
Thus they geven here golde glotones to kepe,
And leveth such loseles,[21] that lecherye haunten.
Were the bischop yblissed and worth bothe his eres,
His seel shulde nought be sent to deceyve the peple.
Ac it is naught by the bischop that the boy precheth,
For the parisch prest and the pardonere parten the silver,
That the poraille[22] of the parisch scholde have, yif thei nere.[23]
  Persones and parisch prestes pleyned hem to the bischop,
That here parisshes were pore sith the pestilence tyme,
To have a lycence and leve at London to dwelle,
And syngen there for symonye,[24] for silver is swete.
  Bischopes and bachelers, bothe maistres and doctours,
That han cure under Criste and crounyng [25] in tokne
And signe that thei sholden shryven here paroschienes,[26]
Prechen and prey for hem, and the pore fede,
Liggen[27] in London in Lenten, an elles.
Somme serven the kyng and his silver tellen,[28]
In cheker[29] and in chancerye chalengen his dettes
Of wardes and wardmotes,[30] weyves[31] and streyves.[32]
  And some serven as servantz lordes and ladyes,
And in stede of stuwardes sytten and demen.[33]
Here messe and here matynes, and many of here oures[34]
Arn don undevoutlych; drede is at the laste
Lest Crist in consistorie acorse ful manye.
I parceyved of the power that Peter had to kepe,
To bynde and to unbynde, as the boke telleth,

[1] lawless vagabonds
[2] sloth
[3] pursues
[4] truth
[5] lubbers
[6] work
[7] long cloaks
[8] friars
[9] avarice
[10] may
[11] since
[12] trader
[13] earth
[14] falsehood
[15] ignorant
[16] believed
[17] struck
[18] letter of indulgence
[19] got
[20] papal bull
[21] worthless fellows
[22] poor people
[23] were not
[24] trading preferments
[25] tonsure
[26] parishioners
[27] lie, dwell
[28] count
[29] exchequer
[30] meetings of a ward
[31] waifs
[32] estrays
[33] deem, judge
[34] 'hours' of the breviary

How he it lęft with love, as owre lorde hight,
Amonges foure vertues the best of all vertues,
That cardinales ben called and closyng gatis,
There Crist is in kyngdome, to close and to shutte,
And to opne it to hem and hevene blisse shewe.
Ac of the cardinales atte Courte that caught-of[1] that name,
And power presumed in hem a Pope to make,
To han that power that Peter hadde, inpugnen I nelle[2];
For in love and letterure[3] the eleccioun bilongeth,
For-thi[4] I can and can naughte of courte speke more.
Thanne come there a kyng. Knyghthod hym ladde,
Might of the comunes made hym to regne,
And thanne cam kynde[5] wytte, and clerkes he made,
For to conseille the kyng and the comune save.
The kyng and knyghthode and clergye bothe
Casten that the comune shulde hem-self fynde.
The comune contreved of kynde witte craftes,
And for profit of alle the poeple plowmen ordeygned,
To tilie and travaile as trewe lyf asketh.
The kynge and the comune and kynde witte the thridde[6]
Shope lawe and lewte,[7] eche man to knowe his owne.
Thanne loked up a lunatik, a lene thing with-alle,
And knelyng to the kyng clergealy[8] he seyde:
'Crist kepe the, Sire Kyng, and thi kyngriche,[9]
And leve[10] the lede[11] thi londe so leute the lovye,
And for thi rightful rewlyng be rewarded in hevene!'
And sithen in the eyre[12] an hiegh an angel of hevene
Lowed[13] to speke in Latyn — for lewed men ne coude
Jangle ne jugge[14] that justifie hem shulde,
But suffren and serven — for-thi seyde the angel:
'*Sum Rex, sum Princeps, neutrum fortasse deinceps;* —
O qui jura regis Christi specialia regis,
Hoc quod agas melius justus es, esto pius!
Nudum jus a te vestiri vult pietate;
Qualia vis metere talia grana sere.
Si jus nudatur, nudo de jure metatur;
Si seritur pietas, de pietate metas!'
Thanne greved[15] hym a Goliardeys, a glotoun of wordes,
And to the angel an heigh answered after,
'*Dum rex a regere dicatur nomen habere,*
Nomen habet sine re nisi studet jura tenere.'
And thanne gan alle the comune crye in vers of Latin,
To the kynges conseille construe ho-so wolde —
'*Precepta Regis sunt nobis vincula legis.*'
With that ran there a route of ratones[16] at ones,
And smale mys myd hem mo then a thousande,
And comen to a conseille for here comune profit;
For a cat of a courte cam whan hym lyked,
And overlepe hem lyghtlich and laughte hem at his wille,
And pleyde with hem perilouslych and possed[17] hem aboute.
'For doute[18] of dyverse dredes we dar noughte wel loke;
And yif we grucche[19] of his gamen,[20] he wil greve us alle,
Cracche[21] us, or clawe us, and in his cloches holde,
That us lotheth the lyf or he lete us passe.
Myghte we with any witte his wille withstonde,
We myghte be lordes aloft and lyven at owre ese.'
A raton of renon, most renable[22] of tonge,
Seide for a sovereygne help to hymselve; —
'I have ysein segges,[23]' quod he, 'in the cite of London
Beren bighes[24] ful brighte abouten here nekkes,
And some colers[25] of crafty werk; uncoupled thei wenden

[1] received
[2] will not
[3] learning
[4] therefore
[5] native
[6] third
[7] loyalty
[8] in a clerkly manner
[9] kingdom
[10] grant
[11] govern
[12] air
[13] stooped
[14] judge
[15] vexed
[16] small rats
[17] pushed
[18] fear
[19] complain
[20] play
[21] scratch
[22] eloquent
[23] men (dogs)
[24] neck-rings
[25] collars

Both in wareine[1] and in waste, where hem leve lyketh;
And otherwhile thei aren elles-where, as I here telle.
Were there a belle on here beighe, bi Jhesu, as me thynketh,
Men myghte wite where thei went, and awei renne!
And right so,' quod this raton, 'reson me sheweth
To bugge[2] a belle of brasse or of brighte sylver,
And knitten on a colere, for owre comune profit,
And hangen it upon the cattes hals[3]; thanne here we mowen
Where he ritt[4] or rest or renneth to playe.
And yif him list for to laike,[5] thenne loke we mowen,
And peren[6] in his presence ther-while hym plaie liketh,
And yif him wrattheth,[7] be ywar and his weye shonye.'
Alle this route of ratones to this reson thei assented.
Ac tho the belle was ybought and on the beighe hanged,
Ther ne was ratoun in alle the route, for alle the rewme of Fraunce,
That dorst have ybounden the belle aboute the cattis nekke,
Ne hangen it aboute the cattes hals, al Engelonde to wynne;
And helden hem unhardy and here conseille feble,
And leten here laboure lost and alle here longe studye.
A mous that moche good couthe,[8] as me thoughte,
Stroke forth sternly and stode biforn hem alle,
And to the route of ratones reherced these wordes:
'Though we culled[9] the catte, yut sholde ther come another,
To cracchy us and al owre kynde, though we croupe[10] under benches.
For-thi I conseille alle the comune to lat the catte worthe,[11]
And be we never so bolde the belle hym to shewe;
For I herde my sire seyn, is sevene yere ypassed,
There the catte is a kitoun[12] the courte is ful elyng[13];
That witnisseth holiwrite, who-so wil it rede,
Ve terre ubi puer rex est, etc.
For may no renke[14] there rest have, for ratones bi nyghte;
The while he caccheth conynges[15] he coveiteth nought owre caroyne,[16]
But fet[17] hym al with venesoun, defame we hym nevere.
For better is a litel losse than a longe sorwe,
The mase[18] amonge us alle though we mysse a shrewe.
For many mannes malt we mys wolde destruye,
And also ye route of ratones rende mennes clothes,
Nere that cat of that courte that can yow overlepe;
For had ye rattes yowre wille, ye couthe nought reule yowre-selve.
I sey for me,' quod the mous, 'I se so mykel after,
Shal never the cat ne the kitoun bi my conseille be greved,
Ne carpyng of this coler that costed me nevre.
And though it had coste me catel,[19] biknowen[20] it I nolde,
But suffre as hym-self wolde to do as hym liketh,
Coupled and uncoupled to cacche what thei mowe.
For-thi uche[21] a wise wighte I warne wite wel his owne.' —
What this meteles[22] bemeneth, ye men that be merye,
Devine ye, for I ne dar, bi dere God in hevene!
Yit hoved[23] there an hondreth in houves[24] of selke,
Serjauntz it semed that serveden atte barre,
Pleded for penyes and poundes the lawe,
And nought for love of owre lord unlese here lippes onis.
Thou myghtest better mete[25] the myste on Malverne hulles,
Then gete a momme[26] of here mouthe but money were shewed.
Barones and burgeis and bonde-men als

[1] warren
[2] buy
[3] neck
[4] rides, goes about
[5] play
[6] appear
[7] grows angry
[8] knew
[9] killed
[10] crept
[11] be
[12] kitten
[13] tedious, miserable
[14] man
[15] conies, rabbits
[16] flesh
[17] feeds
[18] confusion
[19] wealth
[20] acknowledge
[21] each
[22] dream
[23] hovered about
[24] coifs
[25] measure
[26] mumble

I seigh in this assemble, as ye schul here after.
Baxsteres[1] and brewesteres[2] and bocheres[3] manye,
Wollewebsteres[4] and weveres of lynnen,
Taillours and tynkeres and tolleres[5] in marketes,
Masons and mynours, and many other craftes,
Of alkin libbyng[6] laboreres lopen forth somme,
As dykers and delveres, that doth here dedes ille,
And dryven forth the longe day with '*Dieu vous save, Dame Emme!*'
Cokes and here knaves crieden 'Hote pies, hote!
Gode gris[7] and gees! Go we dyne, go we!'
Taverners un-til hem tolde the same,
'White wyn of Oseye and red wyn of Gascoigne,
Of the Ryne and of the Rochel, the roste to defye.[8]'
Al this I seigh slepyng, and sevene sythes[9] more.

1376–1377

Geoffrey Chaucer (1340?–1400)

THE CANTERBURY TALES

THE PROLOGUE

WHAN that Aprille with his shoures sote[10]
The droghte of Marche hath percèd to the rote,
And bathèd every veyne in swich[11] licour,[12]
Of which vertu[13] engendred is the flour;
Whan Zephirus eek[14] with his swete breeth
Inspirèd hath in every holt and heeth
The tendre croppes,[15] and the yonge sonne
Hath in the Ram his halfe cours y-ronne,
And smale fowles[16] maken melodye,
That slepen al the night with open yë,[17]
(So priketh hem nature in hir corages[18]):
Than longen folk to goon on pilgrimages
(And palmers for to seken straunge strondes[19])
To ferne[20] halwes,[21] couthe[22] in sondry londes;
And specially, from every shires ende
Of Engelond, to Caunterbury they wende,
The holy blisful martir for to seke,
That hem hath holpen, whan that they were seke.[23]
Bifel that, in that sesoun on a day,
In Southwerk at the Tabard as I lay
Redy to wenden on my pilgrimage
To Caunterbury with ful devout corage,
At night was come in-to that hostelrye
Wel nyne and twenty in a companye,
Of sondry folk, by aventure[24] y-falle
In felawshipe, and pilgrims were they alle,
That toward Caunterbury wolden ryde;
The chambres and the stables weren wyde,
And wel we weren esèd[25] atte[26] beste.
And shortly, whan the sonne was to reste,
So hadde I spoken with hem everichon,[27]
That I was of hir felawshipe, anon,
And made forward[28] erly for to ryse,
To take our wey, ther as I yow devyse.[29]
But natheles,[30] whyl I have tyme and space,
Er that I ferther in this tale pace,
Me thinketh it acordaunt to resoun,
To telle yow al the condicioun
Of ech of hem, so as it semèd me,
And whiche they weren, and of what degree;
And eek in what array that they were inne:
And at a knight than wol I first biginne.
A KNIGHT ther was, and that a worthy man,
That fro the tyme that he first bigan
To ryden out, he lovèd chivalrye,
Trouthe and honour, fredom and curteisye.
Ful worthy was he in his lordes werre,[31]
And therto hadde he riden (no man ferre[32])
As wel in cristendom as hethenesse,
And ever honoured for his worthinesse.
At Alisaundre he was, whan it was wonne;
Ful ofte tyme he hadde the bord[33] bigonne
Aboven alle nacioun in Pruce.
In Lettow hadde he reysèd[34] and in Ruce,
No cristen man so ofte of his degree.
In Gernade at the sege eek hadde he be
Of Algezir, and riden in Belmarye.
At Lyeys was he, and at Satalye,
Whan they were wonne; and in the Grete See
At many a noble aryve[35] hadde he be.
At mortal batailles hadde he been fiftene,
And foughten for our feith at Tramissene
In listes thryes, and ay slayn his foo.
This ilke[36] worthy knight hadde been also
Somtyme with the lord of Palatye,
Ageyn another hethen in Turkye:

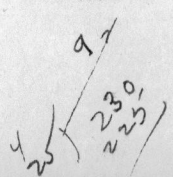

1 bakers
2 brewers
3 butchers
4 weavers
5 collectors
6 living
7 little pigs
8 digest
9 times
10 sweet
11 such
12 moisture, juice
13 power
14 also
15 buds
16 birds
17 eye
18 hearts
19 strands, shores
20 distant
21 shrines
22 known
23 sick
24 chance
25 entertained
26 at the
27 every one
28 agreement
29 tell, describe
30 nevertheless
31 war
32 farther
33 table
34 made expedition
35 arrival, landing
36 same

And everemore he hadde a sovereyn prys.[1]
And though that he were worthy, he was wys,[2]
And of his port[3] as meek as is a mayde.
He nevere yet no vileinye[4] ne sayde
In al his lyf, un-to no maner wight.
He was a verray parfit[5] gentil knight.
But for to tellen yow of his array,
His hors were gode, but he was nat gay.
Of fustian[6] he werèd a gipoun[7]
Al bismotered[8] with his habergeoun[9];
For he was late y-come from his viage,[10]
And wente for to doon his pilgrimage.
With him there was his sone, a yong Squyer,
A lovyere, and a lusty bacheler,
With lokkes crulle,[11] as they were leyd in presse.
Of twenty yeer of age he was, I gesse.
Of his stature he was of evene[12] lengthe,
And wonderly deliver,[13] and greet of strengthe.
And he had been somtyme in chivachye,[14]
In Flaundres, in Artoys, and Picardye,
And born him wel, as of so litel space,
In hope to stonden in his lady grace.
Embrouded[15] was he, as it were a mede[16]
Al ful of fresshe floures, whyte and rede.
Singinge he was, or floytinge,[17] al the day;
He was as fresh as is the month of May.
Short was his goune, with sleves longe and wyde.
Wel coude he sitte on hors, and faire ryde.
He coude songes make and wel endyte,[18]
Juste[19] and eek daunce, and wel purtreye[20] and wryte.
So hote he lovede, that by nightertale[21]
He sleep namore than doth a nightingale.
Curteys he was, lowly, and servisable,
And carf[22] biforn his fader at the table.
A Yeman hadde he, and servaunts namo[23]
At that tyme, for him liste[24] ryde so;
And he was clad in cote and hood of grene;
A sheef of pecok-arwes brighte and kene
Under his belt he bar ful thriftily;
(Wel coude he dresse his takel[25] yemanly:
His arwes drouped noght with fetheres lowe),
And in his hand he bar a mighty bowe.
A not-heed hadde he, with a broun visage.
Of wode-craft wel coude he al the usage.
Upon his arm he bar a gay bracer,[26]
And by his syde a swerd and a bokeler,[27]
And on that other syde a gay daggere,
Harneisèd[28] wel, and sharp as point of spere;
A Cristofre on his brest of silver shene.[29]
An horn he bar, the bawdrik[30] was of grene;
A forster was he, soothly, as I gesse.
Ther was also a Nonne, a Prioresse,
That of hir smyling was ful simple and coy;
Hir gretteste ooth was but by sëynt Loy;
And she was clepèd[31] madame Eglentyne.
Ful wel she song the service divyne,
Entunèd in hir nose ful semely;
And Frensh she spak ful faire and fetisly,[32]
After the scole[33] of Stratford atte Bowe,
For Frensh of Paris was to hir unknowe.
At mete wel y-taught was she with-alle;
She leet no morsel from hir lippes falle,
Ne wette hir fingres in hir sauce depe.
Wel coude she carie a morsel, and wel kepe,
That no drope ne fille up-on hir brest.
In curteisye was set ful muche hir lest.[34]
Hir over lippe wypèd she so clene,
That in hir coppe was no ferthing[35] sene
Of grece, whan she dronken hadde hir draughte.
Ful semely after hir mete she raughte,[36]
And sikerly[37] she was of greet disport,[38]
And ful plesaunt, and amiable of port,
And peynèd hir to countrefete chere
Of court, and been estatlich of manere,
And to ben holden digne[39] of reverence.
But, for to speken of hir conscience,
She was so charitable and so pitous,[40]
She wolde wepe, if that she sawe a mous
Caught in a trappe, if it were deed or bledde.
Of smale houndes had she, that she fedde
With rosted flesh, or milk and wastel[41] breed.
But sore weep she if oon of hem were deed,
Or if men smoot it with a yerde[42] smerte:
And al was conscience and tendre herte.
Ful semely hir wimpel[43] pinchèd[44] was;
Hir nose tretys[45]; hir eyen greye as glas;
Hir mouth ful smal, and ther-to softe and reed;
But sikerly she hadde a fair forheed;
It was almost a spanne brood, I trowe;
For, hardily,[46] she was nat undergrowe.
Ful fetis was hir cloke, as I was war.
Of smal coral aboute hir arm she bar
A peire of bedes, gauded[47] al with grene;

1 renown
2 wise
3 bearing, mien
4 ungentlemanly speech
5 perfect
6 coarse durable cloth
7 short coat
8 stained
9 coat of mail
10 voyage, journey
11 curly
12 average
13 active
14 military expedition
15 adorned
16 mead, meadow
17 playing on a flute
18 compose
19 joust
20 draw
21 night-time
22 carved
23 no more
24 pleased
25 arrows
26 arm-guard
27 small shield
28 equipped
29 bright
30 baldric, belt
31 called
32 neatly
33 school, style
34 pleasure
35 particle
36 reached
37 surely
38 sport
39 worthy
40 compassionate
41 of fine flour
42 rod
43 neck-cover
44 closely pleated
45 long and shapely
46 certainly
47 interspersed with large beads

And ther-on heng a broche of gold ful shene,
On which ther was first write a crownèd[1] A,
And after, *Amor vincit omnia.*
  Another NONNE with hir hadde she,
That was hir chapeleyne, and PREESTES three.
  A MONK ther was, a fair for the maistrye,
An out-rydere, that lovede venerye[2];
A manly man, to been an abbot able.
Ful many a deyntee hors hadde he in stable:
And, whan he rood, men mighte his brydel here
Ginglen in a whistling wynd as clere,
And eek as loude as doth the chapel-belle
Ther as this lord was keper of the celle.
The reule of seint Maure or of seint Beneit,
By-cause that it was old and som-del[3] streit,[4]
This ilke monk leet olde thinges pace,
And held after the newe world the space.[5]
He yaf[6] nat of that text a pullèd[7] hen,
That seith, that hunters been nat holy men;
Ne that a monk, whan he is cloisterlees,
Is lykned til a fish that is waterlees;
This is to seyn, a monk out of his cloistre.
But thilke text held he nat worth an oistre;
And I seyde, his opinioun was good.
What sholde he studie, and make him-selven wood,[8]
Upon a book in cloistre alwey to poure,
Or swinken[9] with his handes, and laboure,
As Austin bit[10]? How shal the world be servèd?
Lat Austin have his swink to him reservèd.
Therfore he was a pricasour[11] aright;
Grehoundes he hadde, as swifte as fowel in flight;
Of priking[12] and of hunting for the hare
Was al his lust, for no cost wolde he spare.
I seigh his sleves purfiled[13] at the hond
With grys,[14] and that the fyneste of a lond;
And, for to festne his hood under his chin,
He hadde of gold y-wroght a curious pin:
A love-knotte in the gretter ende ther was.
His heed was balled, that shoon as any glas,
And eek his face, as he had been anoint.
He was a lord ful fat and in good point;
His eyen stepe,[15] and rollinge in his heed,
That stemèd[16] as a forneys[17] of a leed[18];
His botes souple,[19] his hors in greet estat.
Now certeinly he was a fair prelat;
He was nat pale as a for-pynèd[20] goost.
A fat swan loved he best of any roost.
His palfrey was as broun as is a berye.
  A FRERE ther was, a wantown and a merye,
A limitour,[21] a ful solempne[22] man.
In alle the ordres foure is noon that can
So muche of daliaunce and fair langage.
He hadde maad ful many a mariage
Of yonge wommen, at his owne cost.
Un-to his ordre he was a noble post.
Ful wel biloved and famulier was he
With frankeleyns[23] over-al[24] in his contree,
And eek with worthy wommen of the toun:
For he had power of confessioun,
As seyde him-self, more than a curat,
For of his ordre he was licentiat.[25]
Ful swetely herde he confessioun,
And plesaunt was his absolucioun;
He was an esy man to yeve penaunce
Ther as he wiste to han a good pitaunce[26];
For unto a povre ordre for to yive
Is signe that a man is wel y-shrive.
For if he yaf, he dorste make avaunt,[27]
He wiste[28] that a man was repentaunt.
For many a man so hard is of his herte,
He may nat wepe al-thogh him sore smerte.
Therfore, in stede of weping and preyeres,
Men moot yeve silver to the povre freres.
His tipet[29] was ay farsèd[30] ful of knyves
And pinnes, for to yeven faire wyves.
And certeinly he hadde a mery note;
Wel coude he singe and pleyen on a rote.[31]
Of yeddinges[32] he bar utterly the prys.
His nekke whyt was as the flour-de-lys;
There-to he strong was as a champioun.
He knew the tavernes wel in every toun,
And everich hostiler[33] and tappestere[34]
Bet than a lazar[35] or a beggestere[36];
For un-to swich a worthy man as he
Acorded nat, as by his facultee,
To have with seke lazars aqueyntaunce.
It is nat honest, it may nat avaunce[37]
For to delen with no swich poraille,[38]
But al with riche and sellers of vitaille.[39]
And over-al, ther as profit sholde aryse,
Curteys he was, and lowly of servyse.
Ther nas no man nowher so vertuous.
He was the beste beggere in his hous;
For thogh a widwe hadde noght a sho,

[1] capital
[2] hunting
[3] somewhat
[4] narrow, strict
[5] course
[6] gave
[7] plucked
[8] mad
[9] work, toil
[10] bids
[11] hard rider
[12] spurring, riding
[13] fringed
[14] gray fur
[15] bright
[16] shone
[17] furnace
[18] cauldron
[19] soft, supple
[20] wasted away
[21] begging friar (within limits)
[22] important, festive
[23] freeholders
[24] everywhere
[25] licensed from Rome
[26] allowance (of food)
[27] boast
[28] knew
[29] hood
[30] stuffed
[31] a kind of fiddle
[32] songs
[33] inn keeper
[34] female tapster
[35] leper
[36] female beggar
[37] profit
[38] poor people
[39] victuals

So plesaunt was his '*In principio,*'
Yet wolde he have a ferthing, er he wente.
His purchas[1] was wel bettre than his rente.[2]
And rage[3] he coude, as it were right a whelpe.[4]
In love-dayes ther coude he muchel helpe.
For ther he was nat lyk a cloisterer,
With a thredbar cope,[5] as is a povre scoler,
But he was lyk a maister or a pope.
Of double worsted was his semi-cope,[6]
That rounded as a belle out of the presse.
Somwhat he lipsèd, for his wantownesse,
To make his English swete up-on his tonge;
And in his harping, whan that he had songe,
His eyen twinkled in his heed aright,
As doon the sterres in the frosty night.
This worthy limitour was clepèd Huberd.

A Marchant was ther with a forkèd berd,
In mottelee,[7] and hye on horse he sat,
Up-on his heed a Flaundrish bever hat;
His botes claspèd faire and fetisly.
His resons he spak ful solempnely,
Souninge[8] alway the'ncrees of his winning.
He wolde the see were kept for any thing
Bitwixe Middelburgh and Orewelle.
Wel coude he in eschaunge sheeldes[9] selle.
This worthy man ful wel his wit bisette[10];
Ther wiste no wight that he was in dette,
So estatly[11] was he of his governaunce,[12]
With his bargaynes, and with his chevisaunce.[13]
For sothe he was a worthy man with-alle,
But sooth to seyn, I noot[14] how men him calle.

A Clerk ther was of Oxenford also,
That un-to logik hadde longe y-go.[15]
As lene was his hors as is a rake,
And he nas nat right fat, I undertake;
But lokèd holwe, and ther-to soberly.
Ful thredbar was his overest[16] courtepy[17];
For he had geten him yet no benefyce,[18]
Ne was so worldly for to have offyce.
For him was lever[19] have at his beddes heed
Twenty bokes, clad in blak or reed,
Of Aristotle and his philosophye,
Than robes riche, or fithele,[20] or gay sautrye.[21]
But al be that he was a philosophre,
Yet hadde he but litel gold in cofre;
But al that he mighte of his freendes hente,[22]
On bokes and on lerninge he it spente,
And bisily gan for the soules preye
Of hem that yaf him wher-with to scoleye.[23]
Of studie took he most cure and most hede.
Noght o word spak he more than was nede,
And that was seyd in forme and reverence,
And short and quik, and ful of hy sentence.[24]
Souninge in moral vertu was his speche,
And gladly wolde he lerne, and gladly teche.

A Sergeant of the Lawe, war[25] and wys,
That often hadde been at the parvys,[26]
Ther was also, ful riche of excellence.
Discreet he was, and of greet reverence:
He semèd swich, his wordes weren so wyse,
Justyce he was ful often in assyse,[27]
By patente,[28] and by pleyn commissioun;
For his science,[29] and for his heigh renoun
Of fees and robes hadde he many oon.
So greet a purchasour[30] was nowher noon.
Al was fee simple to him in effect,
His purchasing mighte nat been infect.[31]
No-wher so bisy a man as he ther nas,
And yet he semèd bisier than he was.
In termes hadde he caas[32] and domes[33] alle,
That from the tyme of king William were falle.
Thereto he coude endyte, and make a thing,
Ther coude no wight pinche[34] at his wryting;
And every statut coude he pleyn[35] by rote.[36]
He rood but hoomly in a medlee[37] cote
Girt with a ceint[38] of silk, with barres smale;
Of his array telle I no lenger tale.

A Frankeleyn was in his companye;
Whyt was his berd, as is the dayesye.[39]
Of his complexioun he was sangwyn[40]
Wel loved he by the morwe a sop in wyn.
To liven in delyt was ever his wone,[41]
For he was Epicurus owne sone,
That heeld opinioun, that pleyn delyt
Was verraily felicitee parfyt.
An housholdere, and that a greet, was he;
Seynt Iulian he was in his contree.
His breed, his ale, was alwey after oon;
A bettre envynèd[42] man was nowher noon.
With-oute bake mete was never his hous,

[1] gain by begging
[2] income
[3] play, romp
[4] puppy
[5] cape, cloak
[6] short cape
[7] motley attire
[8] tending toward
[9] French crowns, coins
[10] used
[11] stately, orderly
[12] management
[13] borrowing
[14] know not
[15] gone
[16] uppermost
[17] outer coat
[18] clerical appointment, living
[19] dearer
[20] fiddle
[21] psaltery
[22] get
[23] go to school
[24] meaning
[25] cautious, wary
[26] church-porch
[27] county court
[28] letter patent
[29] knowledge, skill
[30] conveyancer
[31] invalid
[32] cases
[33] judgments
[34] find fault
[35] entirely
[36] by heart
[37] mixed color
[38] girdle
[39] daisy
[40] ruddy
[41] custom, habit
[42] stored with wine

Of fish and flesh, and that so plentevous,
It snewèd in his hous of mete and drinke,
Of alle deyntees that men coude thinke.
After the sondry sesons of the yeer,
So chaungèd he his mete and his soper.[1]
Ful many a fat partrich hadde he in mewe,[2]
And many a breem[3] and many a luce[3] in stewe.[4]
Wo was his cook, but-if his sauce were
Poynaunt[5] and sharp, and redy al his gere.[6]
His table dormant[7] in his halle alway
Stood redy covered al the longe day.
At sessiouns[8] ther was he lord and sire;
Ful ofte tyme he was knight of the shire.
An anlas[9] and a gipser[10] al of silk
Heng at his girdel, whyt as morne milk.
A shirreve[11] hadde he been, and a countour[12];
Was nowher such a worthy vavasour.[13]

An Haberdassher and a Carpenter,
A Webbe,[14] a Dyere, and a Tapicer,[15]
Were with us eek, clothed in o liveree,
Of a solempne and greet fraternitee.
Ful fresh and newe hir gere apykèd[16] was;
Hir knyves were y-chapèd[17] noght with bras,
But al with silver, wroght ful clene and weel,
Hir girdles and hir pouches every-deel.[18]
Wel semèd ech of hem a fair burgeys,[19]
To sitten in a yeldhalle[20] on a deys.[21]
Everich, for the wisdom that he can,
Was shaply[22] for to been an alderman.
For catel[23] hadde they y-nogh and rente,
And eek hir wyves wolde it wel assente;
And elles certein were they to blame.
It is ful fair to been y-clept '*ma dame*,'
And goon to vigilyës[24] al bifore,
And have a mantel royalliche y-bore.

A Cook they hadde with hem for the nones,
To boille chiknes with the mary-bones,
And poudre-marchant[25] tart,[26] and galingale.[27]
Wel coude he knowe a draughte of London ale.
He coude roste, and sethe, and broille, and frye,
Maken mortreux,[28] and wel bake a pye.
But greet harm was it, as it thoughte me,
That on his shine a mormal[29] hadde he;
For blankmanger,[30] that made he with the beste.

A Shipman was ther, woning[31] fer by weste:
For aught I woot, he was of Dertemouthe.
He rood up-on a rouncy,[32] as he couthe,
In a gowne of falding[33] to the knee.
A daggere hanging on a laas[34] hadde he
Aboute his nekke under his arm adoun.
The hote somer had maad his hewe al broun;
And, certeinly, he was a good felawe.
Ful many a draughte of wyn had he y-drawe
From Burdeux-ward, whyl that the chapman[35] sleep.
Of nyce conscience took he no keep.
If that he faught, and hadde the hyer hond,
By water he sente hem hoom to every lond.
But of his craft to rekene wel his tydes,
His stremes and his daungers him bisydes,[36]
His herberwe and his mone, his lodemenage,[37]
Ther nas noon swich from Hulle to Cartage.
Hardy he was, and wys to undertake;
With many a tempest hadde his berd been shake.
He knew wel alle the havenes, as they were,
From Gootlond to the cape of Finistere,
And every cryke[38] in Britayne and in Spayne;
His barge y-clepèd was the Maudelayne.

With us ther was a Doctour of Phisyk,
In al this worlde ne was ther noon him lyk
To speke of phisik and of surgerye;
For he was grounded in astronomye.[39]
He kepte his pacient a ful greet del
In houres,[40] by his magik naturel.
Wel coude he fortunen[41] the ascendent[42]
Of his images[43] for his pacient.
He knew the cause of everich maladye,
Were it of hoot or cold, or moiste, or drye,
And where engendred, and of what humour[44];
He was a verrey parfit practisour.
The cause y-knowe, and of his harm the rote,
Anon he yaf the seke man his bote.[45]
Ful redy hadde he his apothecaries,
To sende him drogges, and his letuaries,[46]
For ech of hem made other for to winne;
Hir frendschipe nas nat newe to biginne.
Wel knew he th'olde Esculapius,
And Deiscorides, and eek Rufus,
Old Ypocras, Haly, and Galien;
Serapion, Razis, and Avicen;
Averrois, Damascien, and Constantyn;
Bernard, and Gatesden, and Gilbertyn.
Of his diete mesurable[47] was he,
For it was of no superfluitee,

[1] supper, meals
[2] coop
[3] kinds of fish
[4] fish-pond
[5] pungent
[6] gear, utensils
[7] fixed, permanent
[8] sessions of the Peace
[9] knife
[10] pouch, purse
[11] governor of a shire, sheriff
[12] auditor
[13] sub-vassal
[14] weaver
[15] upholsterer
[16] trimmed
[17] capped (the sheath)
[18] every whit
[19] citizen
[20] guild-hall
[21] daïs
[22] fit
[23] property
[24] vigils
[25] a kind of spice
[26] pungent
[27] sweet cyperus
[28] a kind of soup
[29] cancer, sore
[30] a minced capon compound
[31] dwelling
[32] nag
[33] coarse cloth
[34] cord
[35] merchant
[36] near
[37] pilotage
[38] inlet, creek
[39] astrology
[40] astrological hours
[41] forecast
[42] planetary influence
[43] waxen images of his patient
[44] liquid in the body
[45] remedy, reward
[46] syrups
[47] moderate

But of greet norissing and digestible.
His studie was but litel on the bible.
In sangwin[1] and in pers[2] he clad was al,
Lynèd with taffata[3] and with sendal[3];
And yet he was but esy of dispence[4];
He kepte that he wan in pestilence.
For gold in phisik is a cordial,
Therfor he lovede gold in special.
A good WYF was ther of bisyde BATHE,
But she was som-del deef, and that was scathe.[5]
Of clooth-making she hadde swiche an haunt,[6]
She passèd hem of Ypres and of Gaunt.
In al the parisshe wyf ne was ther noon
That to th' offring bifore hir sholde goon;
And if ther dide, certeyn, so wrooth was she,
That she was out of alle charitee.
Hir coverchiefs[7] ful fyne were of ground;
I dorste swere they weyeden[8] ten pound
That on a Sonday were upon hir heed.
Hir hosen weren of fyn scarlet reed,
Ful streite y-teyd,[9] and shoos ful moiste and newe.
Bold was hir face, and fair, and reed of hewe.
She was a worthy womman al hir lyve,
Housbondes at chirche-dore she hadde fyve,
Withouten other companye in youthe;
But thereof nedeth nat to speke as nouthe.[10]
And thryes hadde she been at Jerusalem;
She hadde passèd many a straunge streem;
At Rome she hadde been, and at Boloigne,
In Galice at seint Jame, and at Coloigne.
She coude muche of wandring by the weye:
Gat-tothèd[11] was she, soothly for to seye.
Up-on an amblere[12] esily she sat,
Y-wimpled[13] wel, and on hir heed an hat
As brood as is a bokeler or a targe[14];
A foot-mantel aboute hir hipes large,
And on hir feet a paire of spores sharpe.
In felawschip wel coude she laughe and carpe.[15]
Of remedyes of love she knew perchaunce,
For she coude of that art the olde daunce.
A good man was ther of religioun,
And was a povre PERSOUN[16] of a toun;
But riche he was of holy thoght and werk.
He was also a lernèd man, a clerk,[17]
That Cristes gospel trewely wolde preche;
His parisshens[18] devoutly wolde he teche.
Benigne he was, and wonder diligent,
And in adversitee ful pacient;
And swich he was y-prevèd[19] ofte sythes.[20]
Ful looth were him to cursen[21] for his tythes,
But rather wolde he yeven, out of doute,
Un-to his povre parisshens aboute
Of his offring, and eek of his substaunce.
He coude in litel thing han suffisaunce.
Wyd was his parisshe, and houses fer a-sonder,
But he ne lafte nat, for reyn ne thonder,
In siknes nor in meschief,[22] to visyte
The ferreste in his parisshe, muche and lyte,
Up-on his feet, and in his hand a staf.
This noble ensample to his sheep he yaf,
That first he wroghte, and afterward he taughte;
Out of the gospel he tho wordes caughte;
And this figure he added eek ther-to,
That if gold ruste, what shal yren do?
For if a preest be foul, on whom we truste,
No wonder is a lewèd[23] man to ruste;
And shame it is, if a preest take keep,
A [filthy] shepherde and a clene sheep.
Wel oghte a preest ensample for to yive,
By his clennesse, how that his sheep shold live.
He sette nat his benefice to hyre,[24]
And leet his sheep encombred in the myre,
And ran to London, un-to sëynt Poules,
To seken him a chaunterie[25] for soules,
Or with a bretherhed to been withholde[26];
But dwelte at hoom, and kepte wel his folde,
So that the wolf ne made it nat miscarie;
He was a shepherde and no mercenarie.
And though he holy were, and vertuous,
He was to sinful man nat despitous,[27]
Ne of his speche daungerous[28] ne digne,[29]
But in his teching discreet and benigne.
To drawen folk to heven by fairnesse
By good ensample, was his bisinesse:
But it were any persone obstinat,
What so he were, of heigh or lowe estat,
Him wolde he snibben[30] sharply for the nones.
A bettre preest, I trowe that nowher noon is.
He wayted after no pompe and reverence,
Ne makèd him a spycèd[31] conscience,
But Cristes lore, and his apostles twelve,
He taughte, but first he folwed it him-selve.
With him ther was a PLOWMAN, was his brother,
That hadde y-lad[32] of dong ful many a fother,[33]

[1] red
[2] blue
[3] kinds of silk
[4] expenditures
[5] misfortune
[6] skill
[7] kerchiefs
[8] weighed
[9] tied
[10] just now
[11] gate-toothed
[12] ambling nag
[13] wearing a wimple
[14] shield
[15] talk
[16] parson
[17] scholar
[18] parishioners
[19] proved
[20] times
[21] excommunicate
[22] misfortune
[23] ignorant
[24] hire
[25] chantry
[26] maintained
[27] merciless
[28] severe
[29] haughty
[30] reprove
[31] sophisticated
[32] carried
[33] cart-load

A trewe swinker and a good was he,
Livinge in pees and parfit charitee.
God loved he best with al his hole herte
At alle tymes, thogh him gamed[1] or smerte,
And thanne his neighebour right as him-selve.
He wolde thresshe, and ther-to dyke and delve,
For Cristes sake, for every povre wight,
Withouten hyre, if it lay in his might.
His tythes payèd he ful faire and wel,
Bothe of his propre swink and his catel.
In a tabard[2] he rood upon a mere.[3]

Ther was also a Reve[4] and a Millere,
A Somnour[5] and a Pardoner[6] also,
A Maunciple,[7] and my-self; ther were namo.

The Miller was a stout carl,[8] for the nones,
Ful big he was of braun, and eek of bones;
That provèd wel, for over-al ther he cam,
At wrastling he wolde have alwey the ram.
He was short-sholdred, brood, a thikke knarre,[9]
Ther nas no dore that he nolde heve of harre,[10]
Or breke it, at a renning, with his heed.
His berd as any sowe or fox was reed,
And ther-to brood, as though it were a spade.
Up-on the cop[11] right of his nose he hade
A werte, and ther-on stood a tuft of heres,
Reed as the bristles of a sowes eres;
His nose-thirles[12] blake were and wyde.
A swerd and bokeler bar he by his syde;
His mouth as greet was as a greet forneys.
He was a janglere[13] and a goliardeys,[14]
And that was most of sinne and harlotryes.
Wel coude he stelen corn, and tollen thryes;
An yet he hadde a thombe of gold, pardee.
A whyt cote and a blew hood werèd he.
A baggepype wel coude he blowe and sowne,
And therwithal he broghte us out of towne.

A gentil Maunciple was ther of a temple,[15]
Of which achatours[16] mighte take exemple
For to be wyse in bying of vitaille.
For whether that he payde, or took by taille,[17]
Algate[18] he wayted so in his achat,
That he was ay biforn and in good stat.
Now is nat that of God a ful fair grace,
That swich a lewèd mannes wit shal pace
The wisdom of an heep of lernèd men?
Of maistres hadde he mo than thryes ten,
That were of lawe expert and curious;
Of which ther were a doseyn in that hous
Worthy to been stiwardes of rente and lond
Of any lord that is in Engelond,
To make him live by his propre good,[19]
In honour dettelees, but he were wood,
Or live as scarsly as him list desire;
And able for to helpen al a shire
In any cas that mighte falle or happe;
And yit this maunciple sette hir aller[20] cappe.[21]

The Reve was a sclendre colerik man,
His berd was shave as ny as ever he can.
His heer was by his eres round y-shorn.
His top was dokkèd[22] lyk a preest biforn.
Ful longe were his legges, and ful lene,
Y-lyk a staf, ther was no calf y-sene.
Wel coude he kepe a gerner[23] and a binne;
Ther was noon auditour coude on him winne.
Wel wiste he, by the droghte, and by the reyn,
The yeldyng of his seed, and of his greyn.
His lordes sheep, his neet,[24] his dayerye,[25]
His swyn, his hors, his stoor,[26] and his pultrye,
Was hoolly in this reves governing,
And by his covenaunt yaf the rekening,
Sin that his lord was twenty yeer of age;
Ther coude no man bringe him in arrerage.[27]
Ther nas baillif, ne herde,[28] ne other hyne,[29]
That he ne knew his sleighte[30] and his covyne[31];
They were adrad[32] of him, as of the deeth.
His woning was ful fair up-on an heeth,
With grene treës shadwed was his place.
He coude bettre than his lord purchace.
Ful riche he was astorèd[33] prively,
His lord wel coude he plesen subtilly,
To yeve and lene[34] him of his owne good,
And have a thank, and yet a cote, and hood.
In youthe he lernèd hadde a good mister[35];
He was a wel good wrighte,[36] a carpenter.
This reve sat up-on a ful good stot,[37]
That was al pomely[38] grey, and highte[39] Scot.
A long surcote[40] of pers up-on he hade,
And by his syde he bar a rusty blade.
Of Northfolk was this reve, of which I telle,
Bisyde a toun men clepen Baldeswelle.
Tukkèd[41] he was, as is a frere, aboute,
And ever he rood the hindreste[42] of our route.

1 pleased
2 sleeveless jacket
3 mare
4 steward, bailiff
5 summoner to ecclesiastical court
6 seller of indulgences
7 caterer for inn or college
8 churl
9 burly fellow
10 hinge
11 top, tip
12 nostrils
13 babbler
14 buffoon
15 inn of court
16 purchasers
17 tally, credit
18 always
19 goods
20 of all
21 caps
22 cut short
23 garner
24 cattle
25 dairy
26 stock (of a farm)
27 arrears
28 herd, keeper
29 hind, servant
30 craft
31 deceit
32 afraid
33 stored
34 lend
35 trade
36 workman
37 stallion
38 dappled
39 called
40 upper coat
41 tucked up
42 hindmost

A SOMNOUR was ther with us in that place,
That hadde a fyr-reed cherubinnes face,
For sawceflem[1] he was, with eyen narwe.
As hoot he was, and lecherous, as a sparwe;
With scallèd[2] browes blake, and pilèd[3] berd;
Of his visage children were aferd.
Ther nas quik-silver, litarge,[4] ne brimstoon,
Boras, ceruce,[4] ne oille of tartre noon,
Ne oynement that wolde clense and byte,
That him mighte helpen of his whelkes whyte,
Ne of the knobbes sittinge on his chekes.
Wel loved he garleek, oynons, and eek lekes,
And for to drinken strong wyn, reed as blood.
Thanne wolde he speke, and crye as he were wood.
And whan that he wel dronken hadde the wyn,
Than wolde he speke no word but Latyn.
A fewe termes hadde he, two or thre,
That he had lernèd out of som decree;
No wonder is, he herde it al the day;
And eek ye knowen wel, how that a jay
Can clepen 'Watte,' as well as can the pope.
But who-so coude in other thing him grope,[5]
Thanne hadde he spent al his philosophye;
Ay '*Questio quid iuris*' wolde he crye.
He was a gentil harlot[6] and a kynde[7];
A bettre felawe sholde men noght fynde.
He wolde suffre, for a quart of wyn,
A good felawe to have his concubyn
A twelf-month, and excuse him atte fulle:
And prively a finch eek coude he pulle.
And if he fond o-wher[8] a good felawe,
He wolde techen him to have non awe,
In swich cas, of the erchedeknes curs,
But-if a mannes soule were in his purs;
For in his purs he sholde y-punisshed be.
'Purs is the erchedeknes helle,' seyde he.
But wel I woot he lyèd right in dede;
Of cursing oghte ech gilty man him drede —
For curs wol slee, right as assoilling[9] saveth —
And also war him of a *significavit*.
In daunger[10] hadde he at his owne gyse[11]
The yonge girles[12] of the diocyse,
And knew hir counseil, and was al hir reed.
A gerland hadde he set up-on his heed,
As greet as it were for an ale-stake[13];
A bokeler hadde he maad him of a cake.

With him ther rood a gentil PARDONER
Of Rouncival, his freend and his compeer,
That streight was comen fro the court of Rome.
Ful loude he song, 'Com hider, love, to me.'
This somnour bar to him a stif burdoun,[14]
Was nevere trompe of half so greet a soun.
This pardoner hadde heer as yelow as wex,
But smothe it heng, as doth a strike[15] of flex;
By ounces[16] henge his lokkes that he hadde,
And there-with he his shuldres overspradde;
But thinne it lay, by colpons[17] oon and oon;
But hood, for jolitee, ne wered he noon,
For it was trussèd[18] up in his walet.
Him thoughte, he rood al of the newe jet[19];
Dischevele, save his cappe, he rood al bare.
Swiche glaringe eyen hadde he as an hare.
A vernicle[20] hadde he sowèd on his cappe.
His walet lay biforn him in his lappe,
Bret-ful[21] of pardoun come from Rome al hoot.
A voys he hadde as smal as hath a goot.
No berd hadde he, ne never sholde have.
As smothe it was as it were late y-shave;

. . . .

But of his craft, fro Berwik into Ware,
Ne was ther swich another pardoner.
For in his male[22] he hadde a pilwe-beer,[23]
Which that, he seyde, was our lady veyl:
He seyde, he hadde a gobet[24] of the seyl
That sëynt Peter hadde, whan that he wente
Up-on the see, til Jesu Crist him hente.
He hadde a croys[25] of latoun,[26] ful of stones,
And in a glas he hadde pigges bones.
But with thise relikes, whan that he fond
A povre person dwelling up-on lond,
Up-on a day he gat him more moneye
Than that the person gat in monthes tweye.
And thus with feynèd flaterye and japes,[27]
He made the person and the peple his apes.
But trewely to tellen, atte laste,
He was in chirche a noble ecclesiaste.
Wel coude he rede a lessoun or a storie,
But alderbest[28] he song an offertorie;
For wel he wiste, whan that song was songe,
He moste preche, and wel affyle[29] his tonge,
To winne silver, as he ful wel coude;
Therefore he song so meriely and loude.

Now have I told you shortly, in a clause,

1 pimpled
2 scurfy
3 scanty
4 white lead
5 test
6 ribald
7 natural
8 anywhere
9 absolution
10 jurisdiction
11 guise, fashion
12 young people
13 support for a sign
14 burden (of a song)
15 hank
16 small portions
17 shreds
18 packed
19 fashion
20 image of Christ
21 brimful
22 bag
23 pillow-case
24 fragment
25 cross
26 an alloy
27 tricks
28 best of all
29 polish

Th'estat, th'array, the nombre, and eek the cause
Why that assemblèd was this companye
In Southwerk, at this gentil hostelrye,
That highte the Tabard, faste by the Belle.
But now is tyme to yow for to telle
How that we baren us that ilke night,
Whan we were in that hostelrye alight.
And after wol I telle of our viage,
And al the remenaunt of our pilgrimage.
But first I pray yow, of your curteisye,
That ye n'arette[1] it nat my vileinye,
Thogh that I pleynly speke in this matere,
To telle yow hir wordes and hir chere;
Ne thogh I speke hir wordes proprely.
For this ye knowen al-so wel as I,
Who-so shal telle a tale after a man,
He moot reherce, as ny as ever he can,
Everich a word, if it be in his charge,
Al[2] speke he never so rudeliche and large;
Or elles he moot telle his tale untrewe,
Or feyne thing, or finde wordes newe.
He may nat spare, al-thogh he were his brother;
He moot as wel seye o word as another.
Crist spak him-self ful brode in holy writ,
And wel ye woot, no vileinye is it.
Eek Plato seith, who-so that can him rede,
The wordes mote be cosin to the dede.
Also I prey yow to foryeve it me,
Al have I nat set folk in hir degree
Here in this tale, as that they sholde stonde;
My wit is short, ye may wel understonde.

Greet chere made our hoste us everichon,
And to the soper sette he us anon;
And servèd us with vitaille at the beste.
Strong was the wyn, and wel to drinke us leste.
A semely man our hoste was with-alle
For to han been a marshal in an halle;
A large man he was with eyen stepe,
A fairer burgeys was ther noon in Chepe:
Bold of his speche, and wys, and wel y-taught,
And of manhood him lakkede right naught.
Eeek thereto he was right a mery man,
And after soper pleyen he bigan,
And spak of mirthe amonges othere thinges,
Whan that we hadde maad our rekeninges;
And seyde thus: 'Now, lordinges, trewely,
Ye ben to me right welcome hertely:
For by my trouthe, if that I shal nat lye,
I ne saugh this yeer so mery a companye
At ones in this herberwe as is now.
Fayn wolde I doon yow mirthe, wiste I how.
And of a mirthe I am right now bithoght,
To doon yow ese, and it shal coste noght.

Ye goon to Caunterbury; God yow spede,
The blisful martir quyte[3] yow your mede.[4]
And wel I woot, as ye goon by the weye,
Ye shapen[5] yow to talen[6] and to pleye;
For trewely, confort ne mirthe is noon
To ryde by the weye doumb as a stoon;
And therfore wol I maken yow disport,
As I seyde erst,[7] and doon yow som confort.
And if yow lyketh alle, by oon assent,
Now for to stonden at my jugement,
And for to werken as I shal yow seye,
To-morwe, whan ye ryden by the weye,
Now, by my fader soule, that is deed,
But ye be merye, I wol yeve yow myn heed.
Hold up your hond, withouten more speche.'

Our counseil was nat longe for to seche;
Us thoughte it was noght worth to make it wys,
And graunted him withouten more avys,[8]
And bad him seye his verdit, as him leste.

'Lordinges,' quod he, 'now herkneth for the beste;
But tak it not, I prey yow, in desdeyn;
This is the poynt, to speken short and pleyn,
That ech of yow, to shorte with your weye,
In this viage, shal telle tales tweye,[9]
To Caunterbury-ward, I mene it so,
And hom-ward he shal tellen othere two,
Of aventures that whylom han bifalle.
And which of yow that bereth him best of alle,
That is to seyn, that telleth in this cas
Tales of best sentence and most solas,[10]
Shal have a soper at our aller cost
Here in this place, sitting by this post,
Whan that we come agayn fro Caunterbury.
And for to make yow the more mery,
I wol my-selven gladly with yow ryde,
Right at myn owne cost, and be your gyde.
And who-so wol my jugement withseye[11]
Shal paye al that we spenden by the weye.
And if ye vouche-sauf[12] that it be so,
Tel me anon, with-outen wordes mo,
And I wol erly shape me therfore.'

This thing was graunted, and our othes swore
With ful glad herte, and preyden him also
That he wold vouche-sauf for to do so,
And that he wolde been our governour,
And of our tales juge and reportour,
And sette a soper at a certeyn prys;

1 ascribe
2 although
3 requite
4 reward
5 plan
6 tell tales
7 first
8 consideration
9 two
10 solace, mirth
11 gainsay
12 vouchsafe, grant

And we wold reulèd been at his devys,[1]
In heigh and lowe; and thus, by oon assent,
We been acorded to his jugement.
And ther-up-on the wyn was fet[2] anoon;
We dronken, and to reste wente echon,
With-outen any lenger taryinge.
A-morwe, whan that day bigan to springe,
Up roos our host, and was our aller cok,
And gadrede[3] us togidre, alle in a flok,
And forth we riden, a litel more than pas,[4]
Un-to the watering of seint Thomas.
And there our host bigan his hors areste,
And seyde; 'Lordinges, herkneth if yow leste.
Ye woot your forward, and I it yow recorde.[5]
If even-song and morwe-song acorde,
Lat se now who shal telle the firste tale.
As ever mote I drinke wyn or ale,
Who-so be rebel to my jugement
Shal paye for al that by the weye is spent.
Now draweth cut, er that we ferrer twinne[6];
He which that hath the shortest shal beginne.
Sire knight,' quod he, 'my maister and my lord,
Now draweth cut, for that is myn acord.
Cometh neer,' quod he, 'my lady prioresse;
And ye, sir clerk, lat be your shamfastnesse,[7]
Ne studieth noght; ley hond to, every man.'
Anon to drawen every wight bigan,
And shortly for to tellen, as it was,
Were it by aventure,[8] or sort,[9] or cas,[10]
The sothe is this, the cut fil to the kinght,
Of which ful blythe and glad was every wight;
And telle he moste his tale, as was resoun,
By forward and by composicioun,
As ye han herd; what nedeth wordes mo?
And whan this gode man saugh[11] it was so,
As he that wys was and obedient
To kepe his forward by his free assent,
He seyde: 'Sin I shal beginne the game,
What, welcome be the cut, a Goddes name!
Now lat us ryde, and herkneth what I seye.'
And with that word we riden forth our weye;
And he bigan with right a mery chere
His tale anon, and seyde in this manere.

THE NONNE PREESTES TALE

A povre widwe, somdel[12] stape[13] in age,
Was whylom dwelling in a narwe cotage,
Bisyde a grove, stonding in a dale.
This widwe, of which I telle yow my tale,
Sin thilke day that she was last a wyf,
In pacience ladde a ful simple lyf,
For litel was hir catel and hir rente;
By housbondrye, of such as god hir sente,
She fond[14] hir-self, and eek hir doghtren two.
Three large sowes hadde she, and namo,
Three kyn,[15] and eek a sheep that highte[16] Malle.
Ful sooty was hir bour, and eek hir halle,
In which she eet ful many a sclendre meel.
Of poynaunt[17] sauce hir neded never a deel.[18]
No deyntee morsel passèd thurgh hir throte;
Hir dyete was accordant to hir cote.
Repleccioun[19] ne made hir nevere syk;
Attempree[20] dyete was al hir phisyk,
And exercyse, and hertes suffisaunce.
The goute lette[21] hir no-thing for to daunce,
N'apoplexye shente[22] nat hir heed;
No wyn ne drank she, neither whyt ne reed;
Hir bord[23] was servèd most with whyt and blak,
Milk and broun breed, in which she fond no lak,
Seynd[24] bacoun, and somtyme an ey[25] or tweye,[26]
For she was as it were a maner deye.[27]
A yerd she hadde, enclosèd al aboute
With stikkes, and a drye dich with-oute,
In which she hadde a cok, hight Chauntecleer,
In al the land of crowing nas his peer.[28]
His vois was merier than the merye orgon
On messe[29] dayes that in the chirche gon;
Wel sikerer[30] was his crowing in his logge,[31]
Than is a clokke, or an abbey orlogge.[32]
By nature knew he ech ascencioun
Of equinoxial in thilke toun;
For whan degrees fiftene were ascended,
Thanne crew he, that it mighte nat ben amended.
His comb was redder than the fyn coral,
And batailed,[33] as it were a castel-wal.
His bile was blak, and as the jeet it shoon;
Lyk asur were his legges, and his toon;
His nayles whytter than the lilie flour,
And lyk the burnèd gold was his colour.
This gentil cok hadde in his governaunce

1 direction
2 fetched
3 gathered
4 foot-pace
5 remind
6 depart
7 modesty
8 luck
9 lot
10 chance
11 saw
12 somewhat
13 advanced
14 provided for
15 cows
16 was called
17 pungent
18 whit
19 over-eating
20 temperate
21 prevented
22 hurt
23 table
24 singed, broiled
25 egg
26 two
27 female servant
28 equal
29 mass
30 surer
31 lodging
32 clock
33 indented like a battlement

Sevene hennes, for to doon al his pleasaunce,
Whiche were his sustres and his paramours,
And wonder lyk to him, as of colours.
Of whiche the faireste hewèd on hir throte
Was clepèd faire damoysele[1] Pertelote.
Curteys she was, discreet, and debonaire,
And compaignable, and bar hir-self so faire,
Sin thilke day that she was seven night old,
That trewely she hath the herte in hold
Of Chauntecleer loken[2] in every lith[3];
He lovèd hir so, that wel him was therwith.
But such a joye was it to here hem singe,
Whan that the brighte sonne gan to springe,
In swete accord, 'my lief[4] is faren in londe.'
For thilke tyme, as I have understonde,
Bestes and briddes coude speke and singe.
  And so bifel, that in a dawenynge,
As Chauntecleer among his wyves alle
Sat on his perche, that was in the halle,
And next him sat this faire Pertelote,
This Chauntecleer gan gronen in his throte,
As man that in his dreem is drecchèd[5] sore.
And whan that Pertelote thus herde him rore,
She was agast, and seyde, 'O herte dere,
What eyleth[6] yow, to grone in this manere?
Ye been a verray sleper, fy for shame!'
And he answerde and seyde thus, 'Madame,
I pray yow, that ye take it nat a-grief[7]:
By god, me mette[8] I was in swich meschief[9]
Right now, that yet myn herte is sore afright.
Now god,' quod he, 'my swevene[10] recche[11] aright,
And keep my body out of foul prisoun!
Me mette, how that I romèd up and doun
Withinne our yerde, wher-as I saugh a beste,
Was lyk an hound, and wolde han maad areste
Upon my body, and wolde han had me deed.
His colour was bitwixe yelwe and reed;
And tippèd was his tail, and bothe his eres,
With blak, unlyk the remenant of his heres;
His snowte smal, with glowinge eyen tweye.
Yet of his look for fere almost I deye;
This causèd me my groning, douteles.'
  'Avoy[12]!' quod she, 'fy on yow, herteles[13]!
Allas!' quod she, 'for, by that god above,
Now han ye lost myn herte and al my love;
I can nat love a coward, by my feith.
For certes, what so any womman seith,
We alle desyren, if it mighte be,
To han housbondes hardy, wyse, and free,
And secree, and no nigard, ne no fool,
Ne him that is agast of every tool,
Ne noon avauntour,[14] by that god above!
How dorste ye seyn for shame unto your love,
That any thing mighte make yow aferd?
Have ye no mannes herte, and han a berd?
Allas! and conne ye been agast of swevenis?
No-thing, god wot, but vanitee, in sweven is.
Swevenes engendren[15] of repleccioups
And ofte of fume,[16] and of complecciouns,[17]
Whan humours[18] been to habundant in a wight.
Certes[19] this dreem, which ye han met to-night,
Cometh of the grete superfluitee
Of youre rede *colera*, pardee,
Which causeth folk to dremen in here dremes
Of arwes, and of fyr with rede lemes,[20]
Of grete bestes, that they wol hem byte,
Of contek,[21] and of whelpes grete and lyte;
Right as the humour of malencolye
Causeth ful many a man, in sleep, to crye,
For fere of blake beres, or boles[22] blake,
Or elles, blake develes wole hem take.
Of othere humours coude I telle also,
That werken many a man in sleep ful wo;
But I wol passe as lightly as I can.
  'Lo Catoun, which that was so wys a man,
Seyde he nat thus, ne do[23] no fors[24] of dremes?
Now, sire,' quod she, 'whan we flee fro the bemes,
For goddes love, as tak som laxatyf;
Up peril of my soule, and of my lyf,
I counseille yow the beste, I wol nat lye,
That both of colere,[25] and of malencolye
Ye purge yow; and for ye shul nat tarie,
Though in this toun is noon apotecarie,
I shal my-self to herbes techen yow,
That shul ben for your hele,[26] and for your prow[27];
And in our yerd tho herbes shal I fynde,
The whiche han of hir propretee, by kynde,
To purgen yow binethe, and eek above.
Forget not this, for goddes owene love!
Ye been ful colerik of compleccioun.
Ware the sonne in his ascencioun
Ne fynde yow nat repleet of humours hote;
And if it do, I dar wel leye a grote,[28]
That ye shul have a fevere terciane,

1 damsel
2 locked
3 limb
4 belovèd
5 troubled
6 ails
7 amiss
8 dreamed
9 misfortune
10 dream
11 interpret
12 fie
13 coward
14 boaster
15 are produced
16 vapor (from surfeiting)
17 temperament
18 liquids of the body
19 indeed
20 gleams
21 strife
22 bulls
23 make
24 force, matter
25 choler
26 health
27 profit
28 groat

Or an agu, that may be youre bane.[1]
A day or two ye shul have digestyves
Of wormes, er ye take your laxatyves,
Of lauriol,[2] centaure,[3] and fumetere,[4]
Or elles of ellebor,[5] that groweth there,
Of catapuce,[6] or of gaytres[7] beryis,
Of erbe yve, growing in our yerd, that mery is;
Pekke hem up right as they growe, and ete hem in.
Be mery, housbond, for your fader kyn!
Dredeth no dreem; I can say yow namore.'
'Madame,' quod he, '*graunt mercy* of your lore.
But nathelees, as touching daun[8] Catoun,
That hath of wisdom such a gret renoun,
Though that he bad no dremes for to drede,
By god, men may in olde bokes rede
Of many a man, more of auctoritee
Than ever Catoun was, so moot I thee,[9]
That al the revers seyn of this sentence,[10]
And han wel founden by experience,
That dremes ben significaciouns,
As wel of joye as tribulaciouns
That folk enduren in this lyf present.
Ther nedeth make of this noon argument;
The verray preve[11] sheweth it in dede.
'Oon of the gretteste auctours that men rede
Seith thus, that whylom two felawes wente
On pilgrimage, in a ful good entente;
And happèd so, thay come into a toun,
Wher as ther was swich congregacioun
Of peple, and eek so streit[12] of herbergage,[13]
That they ne founde as muche as o cotage,
In which they bothe mighte y-loggèd be.
Wherfor thay mosten, of necessitee,
As for that night, departen[14] compaignye;
And ech of hem goth to his hostelrye,
And took his logging as it wolde falle.
That oon of hem was loggèd in a stalle,
Fer in a yerd, with oxen of the plough;
That other man was loggèd wel y-nough,
As was his aventure,[15] or his fortune,
That us governeth alle as in commune.
'And so bifel, that, long er it were day,
This man mette in his bed, ther as he lay,
How that his felawe gan up-on him calle,
And seyde, "allas! for in an oxes stalle
This night I shal be mordred ther I lye.
Now help me, dere brother, er I dye;
In alle haste com to me," he sayde.
This man out of his sleep for fere abrayde[16];
But whan that he was wakned of his sleep,
He turnèd him, and took of this no keep;
Him thoughte his dreem nas but a vanitee.
Thus twyës in his sleping dremèd he.
And atte thridde tyme yet his felawe
Cam, as him thoughte, and seide, "I am now slawe[17];
Bihold my blody woundes, depe and wyde!
Arys up erly in the morwe-tyde,[18]
And at the west gate of the toun," quod he,
"A carte ful of donge ther shaltow see,
In which my body is hid ful prively;
Do thilke carte aresten boldely.
My gold causèd my mordre, sooth[19] to sayn";
And tolde him every poynt how he was slayn,
With a ful pitous face, pale of hewe.
And truste wel, his dreem he fond ful trewe;
For on the morwe, as sone as it was day,
To his felawes in[20] he took the way;
And whan that he cam to this oxes stalle,
After his felawe he bigan to calle.
'The hostiler answerde him anon,
And seyde, "sire, your felawe is agon,
As sone as day he wente out of the toun."
This man gan fallen in suspecioun,
Remembring on his dremes that he mette,
And forth he goth, no lenger wolde he lette,[21]
Unto the west gate of the toun, and fond
A dong-carte, as it were to donge lond,
That was arrayèd in that same wyse
As ye han herd the dede man devyse[22];
And with an hardy herte he gan to crye
Vengeaunce and justice of this felonye:—
"My felawe mordred is this same night,
And in this carte he lyth gapinge upright.
I crye out on the ministres,[23]" quod he,
"That sholden kepe and reulen this citee;
Harrow! allas! her lyth my felawe slayn!"
What sholde I more un-to this tale sayn?
The peple out-sterte, and caste the cart to grounde,
And in the middel of the dong they founde
The dede man, that mordred was al newe.
'O blisful god, that art so just and trewe!
Lo, how that thou biwreyest[24] mordre alway!
Mordre wol out, that se we day by day.
Mordre is so wlatsom[25] and abhominable
To god, that is so just and resonable,
That he ne wol nat suffre it helèd[26] be;
Though it abyde a yeer, or two, or three,
Mordre wol out, this my conclusioun.

1 death
2 spurge laurel
3 centaury
4 fumitory
5 hellebore
6 caper-spurge
7 dogwood
8 sir, Mr.
9 thrive
10 theme, subject
11 proof
12 scanty
13 lodging
14 separate
15 chance, luck
16 started up
17 slain
18 morning-time
19 truth
20 inn
21 delay
22 describe
23 officers
24 revealest
25 loathsome
26 concealed

And right anoon, ministres of that toun
Han hent[1] the carter, and so sore him pynèd,[2]
And eek the hostiler so sore engynèd,[3]
That thay biknewe[4] hir wikkednesse anoon,
And were an-hangèd by the nekke-boon.
'Here may men seen that dremes been to drede.
And certes, in the same book I rede,
Right in the nexte chapitre after this,
(I gabbe[5] nat, so have I joye or blis,)
Two men that wolde han passèd over see,
For certeyn cause, in-to a fer contree,
If that the wind ne hadde been contrarie,
That made hem in a citee for to tarie,
That stood ful mery upon an haven-syde.
But on a day, agayn[6] the even-tyde,
The wind gan chaunge, and blew right as hem leste.
Jolif and glad they wente un-to hir reste,
And casten hem ful erly for to saille;
But to that oo man fel a greet mervaille.
That oon of hem, in sleping as he lay,
Him mette a wonder dreem, agayn the day;
Him thoughte a man stood by his beddes syde,
And him comaunded, that he sholde abyde,
And seyde him thus, "if thou to-morwe wende,
Thou shalt be dreynt[7]; my tale is at an ende."
He wook, and tolde his felawe what he mette,
And preyde him his viage for to lette;
As for that day, he preyde him to abyde.
His felawe, that lay by his beddes syde,
Gan for to laughe, and scornèd him ful faste.
"No dreem," quod he, "may so myn herte agaste,[8]
That I wol lette for to do my thinges.
I sette not a straw by thy dreminges,
For swevenes been but vanitees and japes.[9]
Men dreme al-day of owles or of apes,
And eek of many a mase[10] therwithal;
Men dreme of thing that never was ne shal.
But sith[11] I see that thou wolt heer abyde,
And thus for-sleuthen[12] wilfully thy tyde,[13]
God wot it reweth[14] me; and have good day."
And thus he took his leve, and wente his way.
But er that he hadde halfe his cours y-seylèd,[15]
Noot I nat why, ne what mischaunce it eylèd,
But casuelly the shippes botme rente,
And ship and man under the water wente
In sighte of othere shippes it byside,
That with hem seylèd at the same tyde.
And therfor, faire Pertelote so dere,
By swiche ensamples olde maistow lere,
That no man sholde been to recchelees[16]
Of dremes, for I sey thee, doutelees,
That many a dreem ful sore is for to drede.
'Lo, in the lyf of seint Kenelm, I rede,
That was Kenulphus sone, the noble king
Of Mercenrike, how Kenelm mette a thing;
A lyte er he was mordred, on a day,
His mordre in his avisioun[17] he say.[18]
His norice[19] him expounèd every del[20]
His sweven, and bad him for to kepe him wel
For traisoun; but he nas but seven yeer old,
And therefore litel tale[21] hath he told[22]
Of any dreem, so holy was his herte.
By god, I hadde lever[23] than my sherte
That ye had rad his legende, as have I.
Dame Pertelote, I sey yow trewely,
Macrobeus, that writ th'avisioun
In Affrike of the worthy Cipioun,
Affermeth dremes, and seith that they been
Warning of thinges that men after seen.
'And forther-more, I pray yow loketh wel
In th'olde testament, of Daniel,
If he held dremes any vanitee.
Reed eek of Joseph, and ther shul ye see
Wher dremes ben somtyme (I set nat alle)
Warning of thinges that shul after falle.
Loke of Egipt the king, daun Pharao,
His bakere and his boteler also,
Wher they ne felte noon effect in dremes.
Who-so wol seken actes of sondry remes,[24]
May rede of dremes many a wonder thing.
'Lo Cresus, which that was of Lyde king,
Mette he nat that he sat upon a tree,
Which signified he sholde anhangèd be?
Lo heer Andromacha, Ectores wyf,
That day that Ector sholde lese[25] his lyf,
She dremèd on the same night biforn,
How that the lyf of Ector sholde be lorn,[26]
If thilke day he wente in-to bataille;
She warnèd him, but it mighte nat availle;
He wente for to fighte nathelees,
But he was slayn anoon of Achilles.
But thilke tale is al to long to telle,
And eek it is ny day, I may nat dwelle.
Shortly I seye, as for conclusioun,
That I shal han of this avisoun
Adversitee; and I seye forther-more,
That I ne telle of laxatyves no store,

[1] seized
[2] tortured
[3] racked
[4] confessed
[5] prate, jest
[6] toward
[7] drowned
[8] terrify
[9] tricks, jests
[10] maze
[11] since
[12] waste in sloth
[13] time
[14] makes sorry
[15] sailed
[16] careless
[17] vision
[18] saw
[19] nurse
[20] part
[21] account
[22] taken
[23] dearer, rather
[24] realms
[25] lose
[26] lost

For they ben venimous, I woot it wel;
I hem defye, I love hem nevere a del.
'Now let us speke of mirthe, and stinte[1] al this;
Madame Pertelote, so have I blis,
Of o thing god hath sent me large grace;
For whan I see the beautee of your face,
Ye ben so scarlet-reed about youre yën,
It maketh al my drede for to dyen;
For, also siker[2] as *In principio*,
Mulier est hominis confusio;
Madame, the sentence of this Latin is —
Womman is mannes joye and al his blis.
. . . .
I am so ful of joye and of solas
That I defye bothe sweven and dreem.'
And with that word he fley doun fro the beem,
For it was day, and eek his hennes alle;
And with a chuk he gan hem for to calle,
For he had founde a corn, lay in the yerd.
Royal he was, he was namore aferd;
He fethered Pertelote twenty tyme,
And trad as ofte, er that it was pryme.
He loketh as it were a grim leoun[3];
And on his toos he rometh up and doun,
Him deynèd not to sette his foot to grounde.
He chukketh, whan he hath a corn y-founde,
And to him rennen thanne his wyves alle.
Thus royal, as a prince is in his halle,
Leve I this Chauntecleer in his pasture;
And after wol I telle his aventure.
Whan that the month in which the world bigan,
That highte March, whan god first makèd man,
Was complet, and [y]-passèd were also,
Sin March bigan, thritty dayes and two,
Bifel that Chauntecleer, in al his pryde,
His seven wyves walking by his syde,
Caste up his eyen to the brighte sonne,
That in the signe of Taurus hadde y-ronne
Twenty degrees and oon, and somwhat more;
And knew by kynde,[4] and by noon other lore,
That it was pryme, and crew with blisful stevene.[5]
'The sonne,' he sayde, 'is clomben up on hevene
Fourty degrees and oon, and more, y-wis.[6]
Madame Pertelote, my worldes blis,
Herkneth thise blisful briddes how they singe,
And see the fresshe floures how they springe;
Ful is myn hert of revel[7] and solas.[8]'
But sodeinly him fil a sorweful cas;
For ever the latter ende of joye is wo.
Got woot that worldly joye is sone ago;
And if a rethor[9] coude faire endyte,[10]
He in a cronique[11] saufly mighte it write,
As for a sovereyn notabilitee.
Now every wys man, lat him herkne me;
This storie is al-so trewe, I undertake,
As is the book of Launcelot de Lake,
That wommen holde in ful gret reverence.
Now wol I torne agayn to my sentence.
A col-fox, ful of sly iniquitee,
That in the grove hadde wonèd[12] yeres three,
By heigh imaginacioun forn-cast,
The same night thurgh-out the hegges[13] brast[14]
Into the yerd, ther Chauntecleer the faire
Was wont,[15] and eek his wyves, to repaire;
And in a bed of wortes[16] stille he lay,
Til it was passèd undern[17] of the day,
Wayting his tyme on Chauntecleer to falle
As gladly doon thise homicydes alle,
That in awayt liggen[18] to mordre men.
O false mordrer, lurking in thy den!
O newe Scariot, newe Genilon!
False dissimilour, O Greek Sinon
That broghtest Troye al outrely[19] to sorwe!
O Chauntecleer, acursèd be that morwe,
That thou into that yerd flough[20] fro the bemes!
Thou were ful wel y-warnèd by thy dremes,
That thilke day was perilous to thee.
But what that god forwoot[21] mot nedes be,
After the opinioun of certeyn clerkis.
Witnesse on him, that any perfit clerk is,
That in scole is gret altercacioun
In this matere, and greet disputisoun,[22]
And hath ben of an hundred thousand men.
But I ne can not bulte[23] it to the bren,[24]
As can the holy doctour Augustyn,
Or Boëce, or the bishop Bradwardyn,
Whether that goddes worthy forwiting[25]
Streyneth[26] me nedely[27] for to doon a thing,
(Nedely clepe[28] I simple necessitee);
Or elles, if free choys be graunted me
To do that same thing, or do it noght,
Though god forwot it, er that it was wroght;
Or if his witing[29] streyneth nevere a del
But by necessitee condicionel.
I wol not han to do of swich matere;
My tale is of a cok, as ye may here,
That took his counseil of his wyf, with sorwe,
To walken in the yerd upon that morwe

1 cease
2 certain
3 lion
4 nature
5 voice
6 certainly
7 merry-making
8 mirth
9 rhetorician
10 compose
11 chronicle
12 dwelt
13 hedges
14 burst
15 accustomed
16 herbs
17 near 11 o'clock
18 lie
19 utterly
20 flew
21 foreknows
22 disputation
23 bolt
24 bran
25 foreknowledge
26 constrains
27 of necessity
28 call
29 knowledge

That he had met the dreem, that I yow tolde.
Wommennes counseils been ful ofte colde;
Wommannes counseil broghte us first to wo,
And made Adam fro paradys to go,
Ther-as he was ful mery, and wel at ese. —
But for I noot, to whom it mighte displese,
If I counseil of wommen wolde blame,
Passe over, for I seyde it in my game.[1]
Rede auctours, wher they trete of swich matere,
And what thay seyn of wommen ye may here.
Thise been the cokkes wordes, and nat myne;
I can noon harm of no womman divyne.[2]
Faire in the sond,[3] to bathe hir merily,
Lyth Pertelote, and alle hir sustres by,
Agayn the sonne; and Chauntecleer so free
Song merier than the mermayde in the see;
For Phisiologus seith sikerly,[4]
How that they singen wel and merily.
And so bifel that, as he caste his yë,
Among the wortes, on a boterflye,
He was war of this fox that lay ful lowe.
No-thing ne liste him thanne for to crowe,
But cryde anon, 'cok, cok,' and up he sterte,
As man that was affrayèd in his herte.
For naturelly a beest desyreth flee
Fro his contrarie, if he may it see,
Though he never erst[5] had seyn it with his yë.
This Chauntecleer, whan he gan him espye,
He wolde han fled, but that the fox anon
Seyde, 'Gentil sire, allas! wher wol ye gon?
Be ye affrayed of me that am your freend?
Now certes, I were worse than a feend,
If I to yow wolde harm or vileinye.[6]
I am nat come your counseil for t'espye;
But trewely, the cause of my cominge
Was only for to herkne how that ye singe.
For trewely ye have as mery a stevene,
As eny aungel hath, that is in hevene;
Therwith ye han in musik more felinge
Than hadde Boëce, or any that can singe.
My lord your fader (god his soule blesse!)
And eek your moder, of hir gentilesse,[7]
Han in myn hous y-been, to my gret ese;
And certes, sire, ful fayn wolde I yow plese.
But for men speke of singing, I wol saye,
So mote I brouke[8] wel myn eyen tweye,
Save yow, I herde never man so singe,
As dide your fader in the morweninge;
Certes, it was of herte, al that he song.
And for to make his voys the more strong,
He wolde so peyne[9] him, that with both his yën
He moste winke,[10] so loude he wolde cryen,
And stonden on his tiptoon ther-with-al,
And strecche forth his nekke long and smal.
And eek he was of swich discrecioun,
That ther nas no man in no regioun
That him in song or wisdom mighte passe.
I have wel rad in daun Burnel the Asse,
Among his vers, how that there was a cok,
For that a preestes sone yaf him a knok
Upon his leg, whyl he was yong and nyce,[11]
He made him for to lese his benefyce.
But certeyn, ther nis no comparisoun
Bitwix the wisdom and discrecioun
Of youre fader, and of his subtiltee.
Now singeth, sire, for seinte Charitee,
Let see, conne ye your fader countrefete[12]? '
This Chauntecleer his winges gan to bete,
As man that coude his tresoun nat espye,
So was he ravisshed with his flaterye.
Allas! ye lordes, many a fals flatour[13]
Is in your courtes, and many a losengeour,[14]
That plesen yow wel more, by my feith,
Than he that soothfastnesse[15] unto yow seith.
Redeth Ecclesiaste of flaterye;
Beth war, ye lordes, of hir trecherye.
This Chauntecleer stood hye up-on his toos,
Strecching his nekke, and heeld his eyen cloos,
And gan to crowe loude for the nones;
And daun Russel the fox sterte up at ones,
And by the gargat[16] hente Chauntecleer,
And on his bak toward the wode him beer,
For yet ne was ther no man that him sewèd.[17]
O destinee, that mayst nat been eschewèd[18]!
Allas, that Chauntecleer fleigh[19] fro the bemes!
Allas, his wyf ne roghte[20] nat of dremes!
And on a Friday fil al this meschaunce.
O Venus, that art goddesse of plesaunce,[21]
Sin that thy servant was this Chauntecleer,
And in thy service dide al his poweer,
More for delyt, than world to multiplye,
Why woldestow suffre him on thy day to dye?
O Gaufred, dere mayster soverayn,
That, whan thy worthy king Richard was slayn

[1] play
[2] predict, declare
[3] sand
[4] surely
[5] first, before
[6] aught low
[7] gentility
[8] enjoy
[9] take pains
[10] shut
[11] foolish
[12] imitate
[13] flatterer
[14] liar
[15] truth
[16] throat
[17] followed
[18] avoided
[19] flew
[20] cared for
[21] pleasure

With shot, compleynedest his deth so sore,
Why ne hadde I now thy sentence and thy lore,
The Friday for to chide, as diden ye?
(For on a Friday soothly slayn was he.)
Than wolde I shewe yow how that I coude pleyne[1]
For Chauntecleres drede, and for his peyne.
Certes, swich cry ne lamentacioun
Was never of ladies maad, whan Ilioun
Was wonne, and Pirrus with his streite[2] swerd,
Whan he hadde hent king Priam by the berd,
And slayn him (as saith us *Eneydos*),
As maden alle the hennes in the clos,[3]
Whan they had seyn of Chauntecleer the sighte.
But sovereynly dame Pertelote shrighte,[4]
Ful louder than dide Hasdrubales wyf,
Whan that hir housbond hadde lost his lyf,
And that the Romayns hadde brend[5] Cartage;
She was so ful of torment and of rage,[6]
That wilfully into the fyr she sterte,
And brende hir-selven with a stedfast herte.
O woful hennes, right so cryden ye,
As, whan that Nero brende the citee
Of Rome, cryden senatoures wyves,
For that hir housbondes losten alle hir lyves;
Withouten gilt this Nero hath hem slayn.
Now wol I torne to my tale agayn: —
This sely[7] widwe, and eek hir doghtres two,
Herden thise hennes crye and maken wo,
And out at dores sterten they anoon,
And syen[8] the fox toward the grove goon,
And bar upon his bak the cok away;
And cryden, 'Out! harrow! and weylaway!
Ha, ha, the fox!' and after him they ran,
And eek with staves many another man;
Ran Colle our dogge, and Talbot, and Gerland,
And Malkin, with a distaf in hir hand;
Ran cow and calf, and eek the verray hogges.
So were they fered[9] for berking of the dogges
And shouting of the men and wimmen eke,
They ronne so, hem thoughte hir herte breke.
They yelleden as feendes doon in helle;
The dokes[10] cryden as men wolde hem quelle[11];
The gees for fere flowen over the trees;
Out of the hyve cam the swarm of bees;
So hidous was the noyse, a! *benedicite!*
Certes, he Jakke Straw, and his meynee,[12]
Ne made never shoutes half so shrille,
Whan that they wolden any Fleming kille,
As thilke day was maad upon the fox.
Of bras thay broghten bemes,[13] and of box,[14]
Of horn, of boon, in whiche they blewe and poupèd,[15]
And therwithal thay shrykèd[16] and they houpèd[17];
It semèd as that heven sholde falle.
Now, gode men, I pray yow herkneth alle!
Lo, how fortune turneth sodeinly
The hope and pryde eek of hir enemy!
This cok, that lay upon the foxes bak,
In al his drede, un-to the fox he spak,
And seyde, 'sire, if that I were as ye,
Yet sholde I seyn (as wis god helpe me),
Turneth agayn, ye proude cherles[18] alle!
A verray pestilence up-on yow falle!
Now am I come un-to this wodes syde,
Maugree[19] your heed, the cok shal heer abyde;
I wol him ete in feith, and that anon.' —
The fox answerde, 'in feith, it shal be don,' —
And as he spak that word, al sodeinly
This cok brak from his mouth deliverly,[20]
And heighe up-on a tree he fleigh anon.
And whan the fox saugh[21] that he was y-gon,
'Allas!' quod he, 'O Chauntecleer, allas!
I have to yow,' quod he, 'y-doon trespas,
In-as-muche as I makèd yow aferd,
Whan I yow hente, and broghte out of the yerd;
But, sire, I dide it in no wikke[22] entente[23];
Com doun, and I shal telle yow what I mente.
I shal seye sooth to yow, god help me so.'
'Nay than,' quod he, 'I shrewe[24] us bothe two,
And first I shrewe my-self, bothe blood and bones,
If thou bigyle[25] me ofter[26] than ones.
Thou shalt namore, thurgh thy flaterye
Do me to singe and winke with myn yë.
For he that winketh, whan he sholde see,
Al wilfully, god lat him never thee!'
'Nay,' quod the fox, 'but god yive him meschaunce,
That is so undiscreet of governaunce,[27]
That jangleth[28] whan he sholde holde his pees.'
Lo, swich it is for to be recchelees,[29]
And necligent, and truste on flaterye.
But ye that holden this tale a folye,[30]
As of a fox, or of a cok and hen,

[1] complain
[2] drawn
[3] enclosure
[4] shrieked
[5] burned
[6] violent grief
[7] simple, poor
[8] see
[9] frightened
[10] ducks
[11] kill
[12] followers, rout
[13] horns, trumpets
[14] boxwood
[15] puffed
[16] shrieked
[17] whooped
[18] churls
[19] in spite of
[20] quickly
[21] saw
[22] wicked
[23] intention
[24] beshrew, curse
[25] beguile
[26] more often
[27] self-control
[28] prates
[29] careless
[30] piece of foolishness

Taketh the moralitee,[1] good men.
For seint Paul seith, that al that writen is,
To our doctryne[2] it is y-write, y-wis.
Taketh the fruyt, and lat the chaf be stille.
  Now, gode god, if that it be thy wille,
As seith my lord, so make us alle good men;
And bringe us to his heighe blisse. Amen.

THE PARDONERS TALE

  In Flaundres whylom was a companye
Of yongė folk, that haunteden folye,
As ryot,[3] hasard,[4] stewes,[5] and tavernes,
Wher-as, with harpes, lutes, and giternes,[6]
They daunce and pleye at dees[7] bothe day and night,
And ete also and drinken over hir might,
Thurgh which they doon the devel sacrifyse
With-in that develes temple, in cursèd wyse,
By superfluitee abhominable;
Hir othes been so grete and so dampnable,
That it is grisly for to here hem swere;
Our blissèd lordes body they to-tere[8];

. . . . . .

  Thise ryotoures three, of whiche I telle,
Longe erst er pryme rong of any belle,
Were set hem in a taverne for to drinke;
And as they satte, they herde a belle clinke
Biforn a cors was caried to his grave;
That oon of hem gan callen to his knave,
  'Go bet,'[9] quod he, 'and axe redily,
What cors is this that passeth heer forby;
And look that thou reporte his name wel.'
  'Sir,' quod this boy, 'it nedeth never-a-del.[10]
It was me told, er ye cam heer, two houres;
He was, pardee, an old felawe of youres;
And sodeynly he was y-slayn to-night,
For-dronke,[11] as he sat on his bench upright;
Ther cam a privee theef, men clepeth Deeth,
That in this contree al the peple sleeth,
And with his spere he smoot his herte atwo,[12]
And wente his wey with-outen wordes mo.
He hath a thousand slayn this pestilence:
And, maister, er ye come in his presence,
Me thinketh that it were necessarie
For to be war of swich an adversarie:
Beth redy for to mete him evermore.
Thus taughte me my dame, I sey namore.'
'By seinte Marie,' seyde this taverner,
'The child seith sooth, for he hath slayn this yeer,
Henne[13] over a myle, with-in a greet village,
Both man and womman, child ând hyne, and page.
I trowe his habitacioun be there;
To been avysèd[14] greet wisdom it were,
Er that he dide a man a dishonour.'
'Ye, goddes armes,' quod this ryotour,
'Is it swich peril with him for to mete?
I shal him seke by wey and eek by strete,
I make avow to goddes digne bones!
Herkneth, felawes, we three been al ones[15];
Lat ech of us holde up his hond til other,
And ech of us bicomen otheres brother,
And we wol sleen this false traytour Deeth;
He shal be slayn, which that so many sleeth,
By goddes dignitee, er it be night.'
  Togidres han thise three her trouthes plight,
To live and dyen ech of hem for other,
As though he were his owene y-boren brother.
And up they sterte al dronken, in this rage,
And forth they goon towardes that village,
Of which the taverner had spoke biforn,
And many a grisly ooth than han they sworn,
And Cristes blessèd body they to-rente —
'Deeth shal be deed, if that they may him hente.'
  Whan they han goon nat fully half a myle,
Right as they wolde han troden over a style,
An old man and a povre with hem mette.
This olde man ful mekely hem grette,[16]
And seyde thus, 'now, lordes, god yow see[17]!'
  The proudest of thise ryotoures three
Answerde agayn, 'what? carl, with sory grace,
Why artow[18] al forwrappèd[19] savė thy face?
Why livestow so longe in so greet age?'
  This olde man gan loke in his visage,
And seyde thus, 'for I ne can nat finde
A man, though that I walkèd in-to Inde,
Neither in citee nor in no village,
That wolde chaunge his youthe for myn age;
And therfore moot I han myn age stille,
As longe time as it is goddes wille.
'Ne deeth, allas! ne wol nat han my lyf;
Thus walke I, lyk a restelees caityf,[20]
And on the ground, which is my modres gate,
I knokke with my staf, bothe erly and late,
And seye, "leve[21] moder, leet me in!
Lo, how I vanish, flesh, and blood, and skin!
Allas! whan shul my bones been at reste?
Moder, with yow wolde I chaunge my cheste,
That in my chambre longe tyme hath be,
Ye! for an heyre clowt[22] to wrappe me!"

[1] moral
[2] instruction
[3] riotous living
[4] gambling
[5] brothels
[6] guitars
[7] dice
[8] tear to pieces
[9] quickly
[10] not a whit
[11] very drunk
[12] in two
[13] hence
[14] forewarned
[15] one, of one mind
[16] greeted
[17] see, protect
[18] art thou
[19] wrapped up
[20] wretch
[21] dear
[22] clout, piece of cloth

But yet to me she wol nat do that grace,
For which ful pale and welkėd[1] is my face.
'But, sirs, to yow it is no curteisye
To speken to an old man vileinye,
But he trespasse in worde, or elles in dede.
In holy writ ye may your-self wel rede,
"Agayns[2] an old man, hoor upon his heed,
Ye sholde aryse"; wherfor I yeve yow reed,
Ne dooth un-to an old man noon harm now,
Na-more than ye wolde men dide to yow
In age, if that ye so longe abyde;
And god be with yow, wher ye go[3] or ryde.
I moot go thider as I have to go.'
'Nay, olde cherl, by god, thou shalt nat so,'
Seyde this other hasardour anon;
'Thou partest nat so lightly, by seint John!
Thou spak right now of thilke traitour Deeth,
That in this contree alle our frendes sleeth.
Have heer my trouthe, as thou art his aspye,[4]
Tel wher he is, or thou shalt it abye,[5]
By god, and by the holy sacrament!
For soothly thou art oon of his assent,[6]
To sleen us yonge folk, thou false theef!'
'Now, sirs,' quod he, 'if that yow be so leef[7]
To finde Deeth, turne up this crokėd wey,
For in that grove I lafte him, by my fey,
Under a tree, and ther he wol abyde;
Nat for your boost[8] he wol him no-thing hyde.
See ye that ook? right ther ye shul him finde.
God save yow, that boghte agayn mankinde,
And yow amende!' — thus seyde this olde man.
And everich of thise ryotoures ran,
Til he cam to that tree, and ther they founde
Of florins fyne of golde y-coynėd rounde
Wel ny an eighte busshels, as hem thoughte.
No lenger thanne after Deeth they soughte,
But ech of hem so glad was of that sighte,
For that the florins been so faire and brighte,
That doun they sette hem by this precious hord.
The worste of hem he spak the firste word.
'Brethren,' quod he, 'tak kepe what I seye;
My wit is greet, though that I bourde[9] and pleye.
This tresor hath fortune un-to us yiven,
In mirthe and jolitee our lyf to liven,
And lightly as it comth, so wol we spende.
Ey! goddes precious dignitee! who wende[10]
To-day, that we sholde han so faire a grace?
But mighte this gold be caried fro this place
Hoom to myn hous, or elles un-to youres —
For wel ye woot that al this gold is oures —
Than were we in heigh felicitee.
But trewely, by daye it may nat be;
Men wolde seyn that we were theves stronge,
And for our owene tresor doon us honge.[11]
This tresor moste y-caried be by nighte
As wysly and as slyly as it mighte.
Wherfore I rede that cut among us alle
Be drawe, and lat se wher the cut wol falle;
And he that hath the cut with herte blythe
Shal renne to the toune, and that ful swythe,[12]
And bringe us breed and wyn ful prively.
And two of us shul kepen subtilly
This tresor wel; and, if he wol nat tarie,
Whan it is night, we wol this tresor carie
By oon assent, wher-as us thinketh best.'
That oon of hem the cut broughte in his fest,[13]
And bad hem drawe, and loke wher it wol falle;
And it fil on the yongeste of hem alle;
And forth toward the toun he wente anon.
And al-so sone as that he was gon,
That oon of hem spak thus un-to that other,
'Thou knowest wel thou art my sworne brother,
Thy profit wol I telle thee anon.
Thou woost wel that our felawe is agon;
And heer is gold, and that ful greet plentee,
That shal departed been among us three.
But natheles, if I can shape it so
That it departed were among us two,
Hadde I nat doon a frendes torn to thee?'
That other answerde, 'I noot how that may be;
He woot how that the gold is with us tweye,
What shal we doon, what shal we to him seye?'
'Shal it be conseil[14]?' seyde the firste shrewe,[15]
'And I shal tellen thee, in wordes fewe,
What we shal doon, and bringe it wel aboute.'
'I graunte,' quod that other, 'out of doute,
That, by my trouthe, I wol thee nat biwreye.[16]'
'Now,' quod the firste, 'thou woost wel we be tweye,
And two of us shul strenger be than oon.
Look whan that he is set, and right anoon
Arys, as though thou woldest with him pleye;
And I shal ryve him thurgh the sydes tweye
Whyl that thou strogelest with him as in game,

[1] withered
[2] in the presence of
[3] walk
[4] spy
[5] pay for
[6] agreement, plot
[7] desirous
[8] boasting
[9] jest
[10] thought
[11] hang
[12] quickly
[13] fist
[14] a secret understanding
[15] scoundrel
[16] betray

And with thy dagger look thou do the same;
And than shal al this gold departed be,
My dere freend, bitwixen me and thee;
Than may we bothe our lustes al fulfille,
And pleye at dees right at our owene wille.'
And thus acorded been thise shrewes tweye
To sleen the thridde, as ye han herd me seye.
  This yongest, which that wente un-to the toun,
Ful ofte in herte he rolleth up and doun
The beautee of thise florins newe and brighte.
'O lord!' quod he, 'if so were that I mighte
Have al this tresor to my-self allone,
Ther is no man that liveth under the trone[1]
Of god, that sholde live so mery as I!'
And atte laste the feend, our enemy,
Putte in his thought that he shold poyson beye,[2]
With which he mighte sleen his felawes tweye;
For-why[3] the feend fond him in swich lyvinge,
That he had leve[4] him to sorwe bringe,
For this was outrely[5] his fulle entente
To sleen hem bothe, and never to repente.
And forth he gooth, no lenger wolde he tarie,
Into the toun, un-to a pothecarie,
And preyèd him, that he him wolde selle
Some poyson, that he mighte his rattes quelle[6];
And eek ther was a polcat in his hawe,[7]
That, as he seyde, his capouns hadde y-slawe,[8]
And fayn he wolde wreke[9] him, if he mighte,
On vermin, that destroyèd him by nighte.
  The pothecarie answerde, 'and thou shalt have
A thing that, al-so god my soule save,
In al this world ther nis no creature,
That ete or dronke hath of this confiture[10]
Noght but the mountance[11] of a corn of whete,
That he ne shal his lyf anon forlete[12];
Ye, sterve[13] he shal, and that in lasse whyle
Than thou wolt goon a paas nat but a myle;
This poyson is so strong and violent.'
  This cursèd man hath in his hond y-hent
This poyson in a box, and sith[14] he ran
In-to the nexte strete, un-to a man,
And borwed [of] him large botels three;
And in the two his poyson pourèd he;
The thridde he kepte clene for his drinke.
For all the night he shoop[15] him for to swinke
In caryinge of the gold out of that place.
And whan this ryotour, with sory grace,
Had filled with wyn his grete botels three,
To his felawes agayn repaireth he.
  What nedeth it to sermone of it more?
For right as they had cast his deeth bifore,
Right so they han him slayn, and that anon.
And whan that this was doon, thus spak that oon,
'Now lat us sitte and drinke, and make us merie,
And afterward we wol his body berie.'
And with that word it happèd him, par cas,
To take the botel ther the poyson was,
And drank, and yaf his felawe drinke also,
For which anon they storven bothe the two.
  ca. 1385–1390

TRUTH

BALADE DE BON CONSEYL

FLEE fro the prees,[16] and dwelle with sothfastnesse,[17]
Suffyce unto thy good, though hit be smal;
For hord[18] hath hate, and climbing tikelnesse,[19]
Prees hath envye, and wele[20] blent[21] overal[22];
Savour[23] no more than thee bihove[24] shal;
Werk wel thy-self, that other folk canst rede[25];
And trouthe shal delivere, hit is no drede.[26]

Tempest[27] thee noght al crokèd to redresse,
In trust of hir[28] that turneth as a bal:
Gret reste stant[29] in litel besinesse;
And eek be war to sporne[30] ageyn an al[31];
Stryve noght, as doth the crokke[32] with the wal.
Daunte[33] thy-self, that dauntest otheres dede;
And trouthe shal delivere, hit is no drede.

That thee is sent, receyve in buxumnesse,[34]
The wrastling for this worlde axeth[35] a fal.
Her nis non hoom, her nis but wildernesse:
Forth, pilgrim, forth! Forth, beste,[36] out of thy stal!
Know thy contree, look up, thank God of al;
Hold the hye wey[37]; and lat thy gost[38] thee lede:
And trouthe shal delivere, hit is no drede.

[1] throne
[2] buy
[3] because
[4] permission
[5] utterly
[6] kill
[7] yard
[8] slain
[9] revenge
[10] mixture
[11] amount
[12] give up
[13] die
[14] afterwards
[15] planned
[16] press, crowd
[17] truth
[18] hoard, store
[19] insecurity
[20] prosperity
[21] blinds
[22] everywhere
[23] have relish for
[24] suit
[25] advise
[26] doubt
[27] distress
[28] *i.e.* Fortune
[29] stands, is
[30] spurn, kick
[31] awl
[32] earthenware pot
[33] subdue
[34] submissiveness
[35] asks, requires
[36] beast
[37] highway
[38] spirit

ENVOY

Therefore, thou vache,[1] leve thyn old wrecchednesse
Unto the worlde; leve[2] now to be thral;
Crye him mercy, that of his hy goodnesse
Made thee of noght, and in especial
Draw unto him, and pray in general
For thee, and eek for other, hevenlich mede[3];
And trouthe shal delivere, hit is no drede.

after 1386

THE COMPLEINT OF CHAUCER TO HIS EMPTY PURSE

To YOU, my purse, and to non other wight
Compleyne I, for ye be my lady dere!
I am so sory, now that ye be light;
For certes,[4] but[5] ye make me hevy chere,[6]
Me were as leef[7] be leyd up-on my bere[8];
For whiche un-to your mercy thus I crye:
Beth[9] hevy ageyn, or elles mot I dye!

Now voucheth-sauf[10] this day, or[11] hit be night,
That I of you the blisful soun may here,
Or see your colour lyk the sonne bright,
That of yelownesse hadde never pere.[12]
Ye be my lyf, ye be myn hertes stere,[13]
Quene of comfort and of good companye:
Beth hevy ageyn, or elles mot I dye!

Now purs, that be to me my lyves light,
And saveour, as doun in this worlde here,
Out of this toune help me through your might,
Sin that ye wole nat been my tresorere[14];
For I am shave as nye as any frere.
But yit I pray un-to your curtesye:
Beth hevy ageyn, or elles mot I dye!

LENVOY DE CHAUCER

O conquerour of Brutes Albioun!
Which that by lyne and free eleccioun
Ben verray king, this song to you I sende;
And ye, that mowen[15] al our harm amende,
Have minde up-on my supplicacioun!

1399?

John Gower (1325–1408)

CONFESSIO AMANTIS

PHILLIS AND DEMOPHON

Kynge Demophon whan he by ship
To Troiewarde with felauship,
Seylend[16] goth upon his weie,[17]
It hapneth hym at Rodopeie,
As Æolus hym had blowe
To londe, and rested for a throwe.[18]
And fell[19] that ylke[20] tyme thus,
The doughter of Licurgius,
Whiche quene was of the countree,
Was sojournèd in that Citee,
Within a castell nigh the stronde,[21]
Where Demophon cam up to londe:
Phillis she hight,[22] and of yonge age,
And of stature, and of visage
She had all that hir best besemeth.
Of Demophon right well hir quemeth,[23]
Whan he was come, and made hym chere,[24]
And he that was of his manere
A lustie knight, ne might asterte[25]
That he ne set on hir his herte:
So that within a daie or two
He thought, howe ever that it go,
He wolde assaie[26] the fortune,
And gan his herte to comune
With goodly wordes in hir ere.
And for to put hir out of fere,
He swore, and hath his trowthe plight
To be for ever hir owne knight.
And thus with hir he still abode
There, while his ship on anker[27] rode,
And had enough of tyme and space
To speke of love, and seke grace.
This ladie herde all that he saide,
Howe he swore, and howe he praide,
Whiche was as an enchantement
To hire, that was as innocent:
As though it were trouthe and feith,
She leveth[28] all that ever he seith:
And as hir infortune sholde,
She graunteth hym all that he wolde.
Thus was he for the time in joye
Till that he sholde go to Troye:
But tho[29] she made mochell[30] sorwe,
And he his trouthe leith to borwe[31]
To come, if that he live maie
Ageine, within a monthe daie,
And thereupon thei kisten bothe:
But were hym leef[32] or were hym loth,[33]
To ship he goth, and forth he went
To Troye, as was his first entent.
The daies go, the monthe passeth,
Hir love encreseth, and his lasseth.[34]
For hym she lefte slepe and mete,
And he his tyme hath all foryete,[35]
So that this wofull yonge quene,
Whiche wot[36] not what it mighte mene,
A letter sent, and prayd hym come,

1 cow, Sir Philip la Vache
2 cease
3 reward
4 indeed
5 unless
6 cheer, appearance
7 lief, pleasant
8 bier
9 be
10 vouchsafe, grant
11 ere
12 equal
13 rudder
14 treasurer
15 may, can
16 sailing
17 way
18 short while
19 befell
20 same
21 shore
22 was called
23 pleases
24 cheer, entertainment
25 escape, avoid
26 try
27 anchor
28 believeth
29 then
30 much, great
31 pledge
32 pleasing
33 disagreeable
34 decreases
35 forgotten
36 knew

And saith, howe she is overcome
With strength of love in suche a wise,
That she not longe maie suffise
To lyven out of his presence:
And put upon his conscience
The trouthe whiche he hath behote,[1]
Whereof she loveth hym so hote.
She saith, that if he lenger lette[2]
Of suche a daie as she hym sette,
She sholde sterven[3] in his slouthe,[4]
Whiche ware a shame unto his trouthe.
This letter is forth upon hir sonde,[5]
Wherof somdele[6] comfort on honde
She toke, as she that wolde abide
And wait upon that ylke tide[7]
Whiche she hath in hir letter write.
But nowe is pitee for to wite,[8]
As he did erst,[9] so he forgat
His tyme eftsoone and oversat.[10]
But she, which mighte not do so,
The tide awaiteth evermo,
And caste hir eie[11] upon the sea.
Somtyme naie, somtyme yea,
Somtyme he cam, somtyme nought:
Thus she disputeth in hir thought,
And wote not what she thynke mai;
But fastende[12] all the longe day
She was, in to the derke night,
And tho she hath do[13] set up light
In a lanterne on high alofte
Upon a tour, where she goth ofte
In hope that in his comynge
He sholde see the light brennynge[14]
Wherof he might his weies righte
To come where she was by nighte.
But all for nought, she was deceived,
For Venus hath hir hope weived,[15]
And shewèd hir upon the sky,
How that the daie was faste by,
So that within a littell throwe
The daies light she mighte knowe.
Tho she beheld the sea at large,
And whan she sih[16] there was no barge,
Ne ship, als[17] fer as she maie kenne,[18]
Down fro the tour she gan to renne[19]
Into an herber all hir owne,
Where many a wonder wofull mone
She made, that no life it wiste,[20]
As she whiche all hir joie miste,
That now she swouneth, now she pleineth,[21]
And all hir face she disteineth[22]
With teres, whiche as of a well
The stremes from hir eien fell;
So as she might, and ever in one
She clepede[23] upon Demophoon,
And saide: 'Allas thou slowe wight,
Wher was ther evere such a knight,
That so through his ungentilesse[24]
Of slouthe and of foryettilnesse[25]
Agein his trouthe brak his steven.[26]'
And tho hir eie up to the heven
She cast, and sayde: 'O thou unkynde,[27]
Here shalt thou through thy slouthe finde,
(If that the list[28] to come and see)
A lady dede for love of thee,
So as I shall myselve spille;
Whom, if it hadde be thy wille,
Thou mightest save well enough.'
With that upon a grene bough
A seynt[29] of sylk, whiche she there hadde
She knette, and so hireself she ladde,
That she about hir white swere[30]
It dede, and heng hirselfen there.
Wherof the goddes were amoved,[31]
And Demophon was so reproved,
That of the goddes providence
Was shape[32] such an evidence
Evere afterward ayein the slowe,
That Phillis in the same throwe
Was shape into a nutte tree
That alle men it mighte see;
And after Phillis Philliberd
This tree was clepèd in the yerd,[33]
And yet for Demophon to shame,
Into this daie it beareth the name.
This wofull chance howe that it ferde,[34]
Anone as Demophon it herde,
And every man it hadde in speche,
His sorowe was not tho to seche[35]:
He gan his slouthe for to banne,[36]
But it was all to late thanne.

CEIX AND ALCEONE

This fynde I writte in poesie:
Ceyx the kynge of Trocenie
Hadde Alceone to his wyf,
Whiche as hir owne hertes lyf
Hym loveth; and he hadde also
A brother, whiche was clepèd tho
Dedalion, and he per[37] cas,[38]
Fro kynde[39] of man forshape[40] was
In to a goshauk of likenes,
Whereof the kynge great heavinesse

[1] promised
[2] delayed
[3] die
[4] sloth
[5] message
[6] somewhat
[7] time
[8] know
[9] first
[10] overstayed
[11] eye
[12] fasting
[13] made, caused
[14] burning
[15] put aside, deferred
[16] saw
[17] as
[18] discern
[19] run
[20] knew
[21] complains
[22] stains
[23] called
[24] lack of gentleness
[25] forgetfulness
[26] promise
[27] unnatural one
[28] pleases
[29] girdle
[30] neck
[31] moved
[32] created
[33] yard; *here,* world
[34] fared, happened
[35] seek
[36] curse
[37] by
[38] chance
[39] nature
[40] changed

Hath take, and thoughte in his courage[1]
To gone upon a pelrinage
Into a strange region,
Where he hath his devocion
To don his sacrifice and preye,
If that he mighte in any weye
Towardes the goddes fynde grace,
His brother hele[2] to purchase,
So that he mighte be reformèd,
Of that he hadde be transformèd.
To this purpose and to this ende,
This kynge is redy for to wende,
As he which wolde go by shipe;
And for to don hym felaushipe,
His wife unto the sea hym broughte
With all hir herte, and hym besoughte,
That he the tyme hir wolde seyn,[3]
Whan that he thoughte come ageyn:
Within, he saith, two monethe daie.
And thus in all the haste he maie
He tok his leve, and forth he saileth
Wependde,[4] and she hirself bewaileth,
And torneth hom there she cam fro.
But whan the monethes were ago,
The whiche he sette of his comynge,
And that she herde no tydynge,
There was no care for to seche:
Whereof the goddes to beseche,
Tho she began in many wise,
And to Juno hir sacrifice
Above all other most she dede,
And for hir lord she hath so bede[5]
To witte[6] and knowe how that he ferde,[7]
That Juno the goddes hir herde
Anon, and upon this matiere
She bad[8] Iris hir massagyere,[9]
To Slepes hous that she shall wende,
And bydde hym that he make an ende
By sweven[10] and shewen all the cas
Unto this ladie, howe it was.
This Iris fro the highe stage
(Which undertake hath the message)
Hir reinie[11] cope[12] dede upon,
The which was wonderly begon[13]
With colours of dyverse hewe,
An honderd mo than men it knewe;
The hevene lych[14] unto a bowe
She bende, so she cam down lowe,
The god of Slep where that she fond.
And that was in a straunge lond,
Which marcheth[15] upon Chimerie:
For there, as seith the poesie,
The god of slep hath made his hous,
Which of entaylle[16] is mervailous.
Under an hille there is a cave,
Whiche of the sonne mai not have,
So that no man mai knowe aright
The poynt betwene the dai and night:
There is no fyr, there is no sparke,
There is no dore, which maie charke,[17]
Whereof an eie sholde unshette,[18]
So that inward there is no lette.[19]
And for to speke of that withoute,
There stant no great tree nigh aboute,
Whereon there might crowe or pie[20]
Alighte, for to clepe or crie:
There is no cocke to crowe day,
Ne beste[21] non, which noise[22] may
The hyll, but all aboute round
There is growende[23] upon the ground
Popi, which bear'th the sed of slep,
With othere herbes suche an hep.
A stille water for the nones
Rennende[24] upon the smalle stones,
Which highte[25] of Lethes the rivere,
Under that hill in such manere
There is, which yev'th great appetit
To slepe, and thus full of delit
Slep hath his hous; and of his couche
Withine his chambere if I shall touche,
Of Hebenus that slepie tree
The bordes all aboute bee.
And for he shuld slepe softe,
Upon a fethrebed alofte
He lieth with many a pilwe of down:
The chambre is strowèd up and down
With swevens many thousand fold.
Thus came Iris in to this hold,[26]
And to the bed, whiche is all black
So goth, and ther with Slepe she spak,
And in the wise as she was bede,
The massage of Juno she dede.
Full ofte hir wordes she reherseth,
Er she his slepie eares perseth.
With mochell wo but ate laste
His slomerende[27] yhen he upcaste,
And saide hir that it shall be do.
Wherof amonge a thousand tho
Withine his hous, that slepie were,
In speciall he ches[28] out there
Three, which sholden do this dede.
The firste of hem, so as I rede,
Was Morpheus, the whose nature
Is for to take the fygure
Of what persone that hym liketh,[29]
Wherof that he full ofte entriketh[30]
The lyf which slepe shall by nighte;
And Ithecus that other highte,
Which hath the voice of every soun,
The chere[31] and the condicioun

[1] heart [2] recovery [3] say, tell [4] weeping [5] prayed [6] learn [7] fared [8] bade [9] messenger [10] dream [11] rainy [12] cloak, covering [13] ornamented [14] like [15] borders [16] shape [17] creak [18] unclose [19] hindrance [20] magpie [21] beast [22] disturb [23] growing [24] running [25] is called [26] stronghold [27] slumbering [28] chose [29] pleases [30] ensnares [31] appearance

Of every life, what so it is:
  The thridde sewende[1] after this,
Is Panthasas, which may transforme
Of every thyng the righte forme,
And chaunge it in an other kynde.
Upon hem three, so as I fynde,
Of swevenes stant all th'apparence,[2]
Whiche other while is evidence,
And other while but a jape,[3]
But netheles[4] it is so shape,
That Morpheus by night allone
Appereth untill Alceone,
In lykenesse of hir husbonde,
All naked dead upon the stronde,
All how he dreinte[5] in speciall
These other two it shewen all.
The tempeste of the blacke clowde,
The woode[6] sea, the wyndes lowde,
All this she mette,[7] and sih hym dien;
Wherof that she began to crien
Slepende[8] abedde there she lay,
And with that noise of hire affray,[9]
Hir women sterten[10] up aboute,
Whiche of hir ladie were in doubte,
And asken hir howe that she ferde;
And she, right as she sigh[11] and herde,
Hir swevene hath told hem every del.[12]
And thei it halsen[13] alle wel
And seyn it is a tokne of gode;
But till she wiste how that it stode,
She hath no comfort in hire herte,
  Upon the morowe and up she sterte,
And to the sea (where that she mette
The bodi lay) withoute lette
She drough,[14] and whan that she cam nygh,
Stark dead, his armes sprad she syh
Hir lord fletende[15] upon the wawe.[16]
Wherof hire wittes ben withdrawe,
And she whiche tok of death no kepe,
Anone forth lepte in to the depe,
And wolde have caught hym in hir arm.
  This infortune of double harm
The goddes from the hevene above
Behelde, and for the trouthe of love,
Which in this worthie ladie stod[17]
Thei have upon the salt flod
Hir dreinte lord and hir also
Fro deth to life tornèd so,
That thei ben shapen in to briddes
Swimmende[18] upon the wave amiddes.
And whan she sih hir lord lyvende[19]
In lykenesse of a brid swymende,
And she was of the same sort,
So as she might do disport,
Upon the joie whiche she hadde
Hir winges both abrod she spradde,
And hym, so as she mai suffise,
Beclipte[20] and kiste in such a wise,
As she was whilome wont to do,
Hire winges for hire armes two
She tok, and for hire lippes softe
Hir harde bille, and so full ofte
She fondeth[21] in hir briddes forme,
If that she mighte hirself conforme
To do the plesance of a wif,
As she dide in that other lif:
For though she hade hir power lore,[22]
Her will stod as it was tofore,
And serveth hym so as she mai,
Wherof into this ylke dai
Togedre upon the sea thei wonne,[23]
Where many a doughter and sonne
Thei bringen forth of bryddes kynde;
And for men sholden take in mynde
This Alceon the trewe quene,
Hire briddes yet, as it is sene,
Of Alceon the name beare.

1390

[1] following
[2] appearance
[3] trick
[4] nevertheless
[5] drowned
[6] mad
[7] dreamed
[8] sleeping
[9] fright
[10] started
[11] saw
[12] part
[13] conjure, interpret
[14] drew
[15] floating
[16] wave
[17] existed
[18] swimming
[19] living
[20] embraced
[21] endeavors
[22] lost
[23] dwell

BALLADS

EDWARD

‘WHY dois[1] your brand[2] sae drap wi bluid,[3]
Edward, Edward,
Why dois your brand sae drap wi bluid,
And why sae sad gang[4] yee O?’
‘O I hae killed my hauke sae guid,
Mither, mither,
O I hae killed my hauke sae guid,
And I had nae mair[5] bot[6] hee O.’

‘Your haukis bluid was nevir sae reid,[7]
Edward, Edward,
Your haukis bluid was nevir sae reid,
My deir son I tell thee O.’
‘O I hae killed my reid-roan steid,
Mither, mither,
O I hae killed my reid-roan steid,
That erst[8] was sae fair and frie O.’

‘Your steid was auld, and ye hae got mair,
Edward, Edward,
Your steid was auld, and ye hae got mair,
Sum other dule[9] ye drie[10] O.’
‘O I hae killed my fadir deir,
Mither, mither,
O I hae killed my fadir deir,
Alas, and wae is mee O!’

‘And whatten penance wul ye drie for that,
Edward, Edward?
And whatten penance will ye drie for that?
My deir son, now tell me O.’
‘Ile set my feit in yonder boat,
Mither, mither,
Ile set my feit in yonder boat,
And Ile fare ovir the sea O.’

‘And what wul ye doe wi your towirs and your ha,[11]
Edward, Edward?
And what wul you doe wi your towirs and your ha,
That were sae fair to see O?’
‘Ile let thame stand tul they doun fa,
Mither, mither,
Ile let thame stand tul they down fa,
For here nevir mair maun[12] I bee O.’

‘And what wul ye leive to your bairns and your wife,
Edward, Edward?
And what wul ye leive to your bairns and your wife,
Whan ye gang ovir the sea O?’
‘The warldis room, late them beg thrae[13] life,
Mither, mither,
The warldis room, late them beg thrae life,
For thame nevir mair wul I see O.’

‘And what wul ye leive to your ain[14] mither deir,
Edward, Edward?
And what wul ye leive to your ain mither deir?
My deir son, now tell me O.’
‘The curse of hell frae me sall[15] ye beir,[16]
Mither, mither,
The curse of hell frae me sall ye beir,
Sic counseils ye gave to me O.’

THE THREE RAVENS

THERE were three ravens sat on a tree,
Downe a downe, hay down, hay downe;
There were three ravens sat on a tree,
With a downe;
There were three ravens sat on a tree,
They were as blacke as they might[17] be,
With a downe derrie, derrie, derrie, downe, downe.

The one of them said to his mate,
‘Where shall we our breakefast take?’

‘Downe in yonder greene field
There lies a knight slain under his shield.

‘His hounds they lie downe at his feete,
So well they can their master keepe.

‘His haukes they flie so eagerly
There's no fowle dare him come nie.’

Downe there comes a fallow[18] doe,
As great with yong as she might goe.

She lift up his bloudy hed,
And kist his wounds that were so red.

1 does
2 sword
3 blood
4 go
5 more
6 but
7 red
8 first, once
9 dole, sorrow
10 suffer, endure
11 hall
12 must
13 through
14 own
15 shall
16 bear
17 could
18 applied to a species of deer

She got him up upon her backe,
And carried him to earthen lake.[1]

She buried him before the prime,[2]
She was dead herselfe ere even-song time.

God send every gentleman,
Such haukes, such hounds, and such a leman.[3]

THOMAS RYMER

True Thomas lay oer yond grassy bank,
And he beheld a ladie gay,
A ladie that was brisk and bold,
Come riding oer the fernie[4] brae.[5]

Her skirt was of the grass-green silk,
Her mantel of the velvet fine,
At ilka[6] tett[7] of her horse's mane
Hung fifty silver bells and nine.

True Thomas he took off his hat,
And bowed him low down till his knee:
'All hail, thou mighty Queen of Heaven!
For your peer[8] on earth I never did see.'

'O no, O no, True Thomas,' she says,
'That name does not belong to me;
I am but the queen of fair Elfland,
And I'm come here for to visit thee.

. . . .

'But ye maun[9] go wi me now, Thomas,
True Thomas, ye maun go wi me,
For ye maun serve me seven years,
Thro weel or wae as may chance to be.'

She turned about her milk-white steed,
And took True Thomas up behind,
And aye wheneer her bridle rang,
The steed flew swifter than the wind.

For forty days and forty nights
He wade thro red blude to the knee,
And he saw neither sun nor moon,
But heard the roaring of the sea.

O they rade on and further on,
Until they came to a garden green:
'Light down, light down, ye ladie free,
Some of that fruit let me pull to thee.'

'O no, O no, True Thomas,' she says,
'That fruit maun not be touched by thee,
For a' the plagues that are in hell
Light on the fruit of this countrie.

'But I have a loaf here in my lap,
Likewise a bottle of claret wine,
And here ere we go farther on,
We'll rest a while, and ye may dine.'

When he had eaten and drunk his fill,
'Lay down your head upon my knee,'
The lady sayd, 'ere we climb yon hill,
And I will show you fairlies[10] three.

'O see ye not yon narrow road,
So thick beset wi thorns and briers?
That is the path of righteousness,
Tho after it but few enquires.

'And see not ye that braid[11] braid road,
That lies across yon lillie[12] leven[13]?
That is the path of wickedness,
Tho some call it the road to heaven.

'And see ye not that bonny road,
Which winds about the fernie brae?
That is the road to fair Elfland,
Where you and I this night maun gae.

'But Thomas, ye maun hold your tongue,
Whatever ye may hear or see,
For gin[14] ae word you should chance to speak,
You will neer get back to your ain countrie.'

He has gotten a coat of the even[15] cloth
And a pair of shoes of velvet green,
And till seven years were past and gone
True Thomas on earth was never seen.

SIR PATRICK SPENS

The king sits in Dumferling toune,
Drinking the blude-reid wine:
'O whar will I get guid[16] sailor,
To sail this schip of mine?'

Up and spak an eldern[17] knicht,
Sat at the kings richt kne:
'Sir Patrick Spence is the best sailor
That sails upon the se.'

The king has written a braid letter,
And signd it wi his hand,
And sent it to Sir Patrick Spence,
Was walking on the sand.

The first line that Sir Patrick red,
A loud lauch[18] lauchèd he;
The next line that Sir Patrick red,
The teir blinded his ee.

[1] pit, grave
[2] about 9 o'clock, A.M.
[3] lover
[4] full of fern
[5] hill
[6] each
[7] lock
[8] equal
[9] must
[10] wonders
[11] broad
[12] lovely
[13] lawn
[14] if
[15] smooth
[16] good
[17] old
[18] laugh

'O wha is this has don this deid,
This ill deid don to me,
To send me out this time o' the yeir,
To sail upon the se!

'Mak hast, mak haste, my mirry men all
Our guid schip sails the morne':
'O say na sae, my master deir,
For I feir a deadlie storme.

'Late, late yestreen[1] I saw the new moone,
Wi the auld moone in hir arme,
And I feir,[2] I feir, my deir master,
That we will cum to harme.'

O our Scots nobles wer richt laith[3]
To weet[4] their cork-heild schoone[5];
Bot lang owre[6] a' the play wer playd,
Thair hats they swam aboone.[7]

O lang, lang may their ladies sit,
Wi thair fans into their hand,
Or eir[8] they se Sir Patrick Spence
Cum sailing to the land.

O lang, lang may the ladies stand,
Wi thair gold kems[9] in their hair,
Waiting for thar ain deir lords,
For they'll se thame na mair

Haf owre,[10] haf owre to Aberdour,
It's fiftie fadom deip,
And thair lies guid Sir Patrick Spence,
Wi the Scots lords at his feit.

LORD THOMAS AND FAIR ANNET

Lord Thomas and Fair Annet
Sate a' day on a hill;
Whan night was cum, and sun was sett,
They had not talkt their fill.

Lord Thomas said a word in jest,
Fair Annet took it ill:
'A, I will nevir wed a wife
Against my ain friends' will.'

'Gif ye wull nevir wed a wife,
A wife wull neir wed yee.'
Sae he his hame to tell his mither,
And knelt upon his knee.

'O rede,[11] O rede, mither,' he says,
'A gude rede gie[12] to mee:
O sall I tak the nut-browne bride,
And let Faire Annet bee?'

'The nut-browne bride haes gowd and gear,[13]
Fair Annet she has gat nane;
And the little beauty Fair Annet haes,
O it wull soon be gane.'

And he has till his brother gane:
'Now, brother, rede ye mee;
A, sall I marrie the nut-browne bride,
And let Fair Annet bee?'

'The nut-browne bride has oxen, brother,
The nut-browne bride has kye[14];
I wad hae ye marrie the nut-browne bride,
And cast Fair Annet bye.'

'Her oxen may dye i the house, billie,[15]
And her kye into the byre[16];
And I sall hae nothing to mysell
Bot a fat fadge[17] by the fyre.'

And he has till his sister gane:
'Now, sister, rede ye mee;
O sall I marrie the nut-browne bride,
And set Fair Annet free?'

'I'se[18] rede ye tak Fair Annet, Thomas,
And let the browne bride alane,
Lest ye sould sigh, and say, Alace,[19]
What is this we brought hame!'

'No, I will tak my mither's counsel,
And marrie me owt o hand;
And I will tak the nut-browne bride:
Fair Annet may leive the land.'

Up then rose Fair Annet's father,
Twa hours or it were day,
And he is gane into the bower
Wherein Fair Annet lay.

'Rise up, rise up, Fair Annet,' he says;
'Put on your silken sheene[20]:
Let us gae to St. Marie's kirke,
And see that rich weddeen.'

'My maides, gae to my dressing-roome,
And dress to me my hair;
Whaireir[21] yee laid a plait before,
See yee lay ten times mair.

'My maides, gae to my dressing-room,
And dress to me my smock;
The one half is o the holland fine,
The other o needle-work.'

The horse fair Annet rade upon,
He amblit like the wind;
Wi siller[22] he was shod before,
Wi burning gowd behind.

[1] yesterday evening
[2] fear
[3] loth
[4] wet
[5] shoes
[6] ere
[7] above
[8] ever
[9] combs
[10] over
[11] counsel
[12] give
[13] property
[14] cows
[15] brother
[16] barn
[17] corpulent person
[18] I shall
[19] alas
[20] shoes
[21] wherever
[22] silver

Four and twanty siller bells
  Wer a' tyed till his mane,
And yae[1] tift[2] o the norland wind,
  They tinkled ane by ane.

Four and twanty gay gude knichts
  Rade by Fair Annet's side,
And four and twanty fair ladies,
  As gin she had bin a bride.

And whan she cam to Marie's kirk,
  She sat on Marie's stean[3]:
The cleading[4] that Fair Annet had on,
  It skinkled[5] in their een.[6]

And whan she cam into the kirk,
  She shimmered like the sun;
The belt that was about her waist,
  Was a' wi pearles bedone.

She sat her by the nut-browne bride,
  And her een they wer sae clear,
Lord Thomas he clean forgat the bride,
  Whan Fair Annet drew near.

He had a rose into his hand,
  He gae it kisses three,
And reaching by the nut-browne bride,
  Laid it on Fair Annet's knee.

Up than spak the nut-browne bride,
  She spak wi meikle[7] spite:
'And whair gat ye that rose-water,
  That does mak yee sae white?'

'O I did get the rose-water
  Whair ye wull neir get nane,
For I did get that very rose-water
  Into my mither's wame.[8]'

The bride she drew a long bodkin
  Frae out her gay head-gear,
And strake Fair Annet unto the heart,
  That word spak nevir mair.

Lord Thomas he saw Fair Annet wex pale,
  And marvelit what mote bee;
But whan he saw her dear heart's blude,
  A' wood[9]-wroth wexèd hee.

He drew his dagger, that was sae sharp,
  That was sae sharp and meet,
And drave it into the nut-browne bride,
  That fell deid at his feit.

'Now stay for me, dear Annet,' he sed,
  'Now stay, my dear,' he cry'd;
Then strake the dagger untill his heart,
  And fell deid by her side.

Lord Thomas was buried without kirk-wa,
  Fair Annet within the quiere[10];
And o the tane[11] thair grew a birk,
  The other a bonny briere.

And ay they grew, and ay they threw,[12]
  As they wad faine be neare;
And by this ye may ken right weil
  They were twa luvers deare.

SWEET WILLIAM'S GHOST

THERE came a ghost to Margret's door,
  With many a grievous groan,
And ay he tirled[13] at the pin,
  But answer made she none.

'Is that my father Philip,
  Or is't my brother John?
Or is't my true-love, Willy,
  From Scotland new come home?'

''T is not thy father Philip,
  Nor yet thy brother John;
But 't is thy true-love, Willy,
  From Scotland new come home.

'O sweet Margret, O dear Margret,
  I pray thee speak to me;
Give me my faith and troth, Margret,
  As I gave it to thee.'

'Thy faith and troth thou's never get,
  Nor yet will I thee lend,
Till that thou come within my bower
  And kiss my cheek and chin.'

'If I shoud come within thy bower,
  I am no earthly man;
And shoud I kiss thy rosy lips,
  Thy days will not be lang.

'O sweet Margret, O dear Margret,
  I pray thee speak to me;
Give me my faith and troth, Margret,
  As I gave it to thee.'

'Thy faith and troth thou's never get,
  Nor yet will I thee lend,
Till you take me to yon kirk
  And wed me with a ring.'

'My bones are buried in yon kirk-yard,
  Afar beyond the sea,
And it is but my spirit, Margret,
  That's now speaking to thee.'

1 every
2 puff
3 stone
4 clothing
5 sparkled
6 eyes
7 much, great
8 womb
9 mad
10 choir
11 the one
12 pressed close together, intertwined
13 rattled

She stretched out her lilly-white hand,
  And, for to do her best,
'Hae, there's your faith and troth, Willy,
  God send your soul good rest.'

Now she has kilted[1] her robes of green
  A piece below her knee,
And a' the live-lang winter night
  The dead corp followed she.

'Is there any room at your head, Willy?
  Or any room at your feet?
Or any room at your side, Willy,
  Wherein that I may creep?'

'There's no room at my head, Margret,
  There's no room at my feet;
There's no room at my side, Margret,
  My coffin's made so meet.'

Then up and crew the red, red cock,
  And up then crew the gray:
'T is time, 't is time, my dear Margret
  That you were going away.'

No more the ghost to Margret said,
  But, with a grievous groan,
Evanished in a cloud of mist,
  And left her all alone.

'O stay, my only true-love, stay,'
  The constant Margret cry'd;
Wan grew her cheeks, she closed her een,
  Stretched her soft limbs, and dy'd.

THE WIFE OF USHER'S WELL

There lived a wife at Usher's Well,
  And a wealthy wife was she;
She had three stout and stalwart sons,
  And sent them oer the sea.

They hadna been a week from her,
  A week but barely ane,
Whan word came to the carline[2] wife
  That her three sons were gane.

They hadna been a week from her,
  A week but barely three,
Whan word came to the carlin wife
  That her sons she'd never see.

'I wish the wind may never cease,
  Nor fashes[3] in the flood,
Till my three sons come hame to me,
  In earthly flesh and blood.'

It fell about the Martinmass,
  When nights are lang and mirk,[4]
The carlin wife's three sons came hame,
  And their hats were o the birk.[5]

It neither grew in syke[6] nor ditch,
  Nor yet in ony sheugh[7];
But at the gates o Paradise,
  That birk grew fair eneugh.

. . . . .

'Blow up the fire, my maidens,
  Bring water from the well;
For a' my house shall feast this night,
  Since my three sons are well.'

And she has made to them a bed,
  She's made it large and wide,
And she's taen her mantle her about,
  Sat down at the bed-side.

. . . . .

Up then crew the red, red cock,
  And up and crew the gray;
The eldest to the youngest said,
  ''T is time we were away.'

The cock he hadna crawd but once,
  And clappd his wings at a',
When the youngest to the eldest said,
  Brother, we must awa.[8]

'The cock doth craw, the day doth daw,[9]
  The channerin[10] worm doth chide;
Gin we be mist out o our place,
  A sair[11] pain we maun bide.

'Faer ye weel, my mother dear!
  Fareweel to barn and byre[12]!
And fare ye weel, the bonny lass
  That kindles my mother's fire!

BONNY BARBARA ALLAN

It was in and about the Martinmas time,
  When the green leaves were a falling,
That Sir John Græme, in the West Country,
  Fell in love with Barbara Allan.

He sent his man down through the town,
  To the place where she was dwelling:
'O haste and come to my master dear,
  Gin ye be Barbara Allan.'

O hooly,[13] hooly rose she up,
  To the place where he was lying,
And when she drew the curtain by,
  'Young man, I think you're dying.'

'O it's I'm sick, and very, very sick,
  And 't is a' for Barbara Allan':
'O the better for me ye's never be,
  Tho your heart's blood were a spilling.

[1] tucked up
[2] old
[3] troubles
[4] dark
[5] birch
[6] ditch, trench
[7] furrow
[8] away
[9] dawn
[10] fretting
[11] sore
[12] cow-house
[13] slowly, softly

'O dinna[1] ye mind, young man,' said she,
  'When ye was in the tavern a drinking,
That ye made the healths gae round and round,
  And slighted Barbara Allan?'

He turnd his face unto the wall,
  And death was with him dealing:
'Adieu, adieu, my dear friends all,
  And be kind to Barbara Allan.'

And slowly, slowly raise she up,
  And slowly, slowly left him,
And sighing said, she could not stay,
  Since death of life had reft him.

She had not gane a mile but twa,[2]
  When she heard the dead-bell ringing,
And every jow[3] that the dead-bell geid,[4]
  It cryd, Woe to Barbara Allan!

'O mother, mother, make my bed!
  O make it saft and narrow!
Since my love died for me to-day,
  I'll die for him to-morrow.'

ROBIN HOOD AND GUY OF GISBORNE

WHEN shawes[5] been sheene,[6] and shradds[7] full fayre,
  And leeves both large and longe,
It is merry, walking in the fayre fforrest,
  To heare the small birds' songe.

The woodweele[8] sang, and wold not cease,
  Amongst the leaves a lyne[9]:
And it is by two wight[10] yeomen,
  By deare God, that I meane.

. . . . . .

'Me thought they did mee beate and binde,
  And tooke my bowe mee froe;
If I bee Robin alive in this lande,
  I'le be wrocken[11] on both them towe.[12]'

'Sweavens[13] are swift, master,' quoth John,
  'As the wind that blowes ore a hill;
Ffor if itt be never soe lowde this night,
  To-morrow it may be still.'

'Buske[14] yee, bowne[15] yee, my merry men all,
  Ffor John shall goe with mee;
For I'le goe seeke yond wight yeomen
  In greenwood where the bee.'

The cast on their gowne of greene,
  A shooting gone are they,
Untill they came to the merry greenwood,
  Where they had gladdest bee;
There were they ware of a wight yeoman,
  His body leaned to a tree.

A sword and a dagger he wore by his side,
  Had beene many a mans bane,
And he was cladd in his capull-hyde,[16]
  Topp, and tayle, and mayne.

'Stand you still, master,' quoth Litle John,
  'Under this trusty tree,
And I will goe to yong wight yeoman,
  To know his meaning trulye.'

'A, John, by me thou setts noe store,
  And that's a ffarley[17] thinge;
How offt send I my men beffore,
  And tarry my-selfe behinde?

'It is noe cunning a knave to ken,[18]
  And a man but heare him speake;
And itt were not for bursting of my bowe,
  John, I wold thy head breake.'

But often words they breeden bale,[19]
  That parted Robin and John;
John is gone to Barnesdale,
  The gates he knowes eche one.

And when hee came to Barnesdale,
  Great heavinesse there hee hadd;
He ffound two of his fellowes
  Were slaine both in a slade,[20]

And Scarlett a ffoote flyinge was,
  Over stockes and stone,
For the sheriffe with seven score men
  Fast after him is gone.

'Yett one shoote I'le shoote,' sayes Litle John,
'With Crist his might and mayne[21];
I'le make yond fellow that flyes soe fast
  To be both glad and ffaine.'

John bent up a good veiwe[22] bow,
  And ffetteled[23] him to shoote;
The bow was made of a tender boughe,
  And fell downe to his foote.

'Woe worth[24] thee, wicked wood,' sayd Litle John,
  'That ere thou grew on a tree!
Ffor this day thou art my bale,
  My boote[25] when thou shold bee!'

[1] do not
[2] two
[3] stroke
[4] gave
[5] groves
[6] beautiful
[7] coppices, thickets
[8] woodlark
[9] linden
[10] stout
[11] avenged
[12] two
[13] dreams
[14] make ready
[15] prepare
[16] horse-hide
[17] strange
[18] know
[19] evil
[20] valley
[21] strength
[22] yew
[23] made ready
[24] be, come to
[25] help

This shoote it was but looselye shott,
The arrowè flew in vaine,
And it mett one of the sheriffes men;
Good William a Trent was slaine.

It had beene better for William a Trent
To hange upon a gallowe
Then for to lye in the greenwoode,
There slaine with an arrowe.

And it is sayd, when men be mett,
Six can doe more then three:
And they have tane[1] Litle John,
And bound him ffast to a tree.

'Thou shalt be drawen by dale and downe,' quoth the sheriffe,
'And hangèd hye on a hill':
'But thou may ffayle,' quoth Litle John,
'If itt be Christs owne will.'

Let us leave talking of Litle John,
For hee is bound fast to a tree,
And talke of Guy and Robin Hood
In the green woode where they bee.

How these two yeomen together they mett,
Under the leaves of lyne,
To see what marchandise they made
Even at that same time.

'Good morrow, good fellow,' quoth Sir Guy;
'Good morrow, good ffellow,' quoth hee;
'Methinkes by this bow thou beares in thy hand,
A good archer thou seems to bee.'

'I am wilfull[2] of my way,' quoth Sir Guye,
'And of my morning tyde[3]':
'I'le lead thee through the wood,' quoth Robin,
'Good ffellow, I'le be thy guide.'

'I seeke an outlaw,' quoth Sir Guye,
'Men call him Robin Hood;
I had rather meet with him upon a day
Then forty pound of golde.'

'If you tow mett, itt wold be seene whether were better
Afore yee did part awaye;
Let us some other pastime find,
Good ffellow, I thee pray.

'Let us some other masteryes[4] make,
And wee will walke in the woods even;
Wee may chance meet with Robin Hoode
Att some unsett[5] steven.[6]'

They cutt them downe the summer shroggs[7]
Which grew both under a bryar,
And sett them three score rood in twinn,[8]
To shoote the prickes[9] full neare.

'Leade on, good ffellow,' sayd Sir Guye,
'Lead on, I doe bidd thee':
'Nay, by my faith,' quoth Robin Hood,
'The leader thou shalt bee.'

The first good shoot that Robin ledd,
Did not shoote an inch the pricke ffroe;
Guy was an archer good enoughe,
But he cold neere shoote soe.

The second shoote Sir Guy shott,
He shott within the garlande[10];
But Robin Hoode shott it better then hee,
For he clove the good pricke-wande.[11]

'Gods blessing on thy heart!' sayes Guye,
'Goode ffellow, thy shooting is goode;
For an thy hart be as good as thy hands,
Thou were better then Robin Hood.

'Tell me thy name, good ffellow,' quoth Guy,
'Under the leaves of lyne':
'Nay, by my faith,' quoth good Robin,
'Till thou have told me thine.'

'I dwell by dale and downe,' quoth Guye,
'And I have done many a curst turne;
And he that calles me by my right name,
Calles me Guye of good Gysborne.'

'My dwelling is in the wood,' sayes Robin;
'By thee I set right nought;
My name is Robin Hood of Barnesdale,
A ffellow thou has long sought.'

He that had neither beene a kithe nor kin
Might have seene a full fayre sight,
To see how together these yeomen went,
With blades both browne and bright.

To have seene how these yeomen together fought,
Two howers of a summers day;
Itt was neither Guy nor Robin Hood
That ffettled them to flye away.

Robin was reacheles[12] on a roote,
And stumbled at that tyde,
And Guy was quicke and nimble withall,
And hitt him ore the left side.

'Ah, deere Lady!' sayd Robin Hoode,
'Thou art both mother and may[13]!
I thinke it was never man's destinye
To dye before his day.'

[1] taken
[2] astray
[3] time
[4] trials of skill
[5] not appointed, unexpected
[6] hour
[7] wands
[8] apart
[9] marks, targets
[10] circle around the mark
[11] target-rod
[12] heedless
[13] maid

Robin thought on Our Lady deere,
And soone leapt up againe,
And thus he came with an awkwarde[1] stroke;
Good Sir Guy hee has slayne.

He tooke Sir Guy's head by the hayre,
And sticked itt on his bowes end:
'Thou hast beene traytor all thy liffe,
Which thing must have an ende.'

Robin pulled forth an Irish kniffe,
And nicked Sir Guy in the fface,
That hee was never on a woman borne
Cold tell who Sir Guye was.

Saies, 'Lye there, lye there, good Sir Guye,
And with me be not wrothe;
If thou have had the worse stroakes at my hand,
Thou shalt have the better cloathe.'

Robin did off his gowne of greene,
Sir Guye hee did it throwe;
And hee put on that capull-hyde
That cladd him topp to toe.

'The bowe, the arrowes, and litle horne,
And with me now I'le beare;
Ffor now I will goe to Barnesdale
To see how my men doe ffare.'

Robin sett Guyes horne to his mouth,
A lowd blast in it he did blow;
That beheard the sheriffe of Nottingham,
As he leaned under a lowe.[2]

'Hearken! hearken!' sayd the sheriffe,
'I heard noe tydings but good;
For yonder I heare Sir Guyes horne blowe,
For he hath slaine Robin Hoode.

'For yonder I heare Sir Guyes horne blow,
Itt blowes soe well in tyde,
For yonder comes that wighty yeoman,
Cladd in his capull-hyde.

'Come hither, thou good Sir Guy,
Aske of mee what thou wilt have':
'I'le none of thy gold,' sayes Robin Hood,
'Nor I'le none of itt have.

'But now I have slaine the master,' he sayd,
'Let me goe strike the knave;
This is all the reward I aske,
Nor noe other will I have.'

'Thou art a madman,' said the shiriffe,
'Thou sholdest have had a knight's ffee;
Seeing thy asking hath beene soe badd,
Well granted it shall be.'

But Litle John heard his master speake,
Well he knew that was his steven[3];
'Now shall I be loset,[4]' quoth Litle John,
'With Christ's might in heaven.'

But Robin hee hyed him towards Litle John,
Hee thought hee wold loose him belive,[5]
The sheriffe and all his companye
Fast after him did drive.

'Stand abacke! stand abacke!' sayd Robin;
'Why draw you mee soe neere?
Itt was never the use in our countrye
Ones shrift another shold heere.'

But Robin pulled forth an Irysh kniffe,
And losed John hand and ffoote,
And gave him Sir Guyes bow in his hand,
And bade it be his boote.

But John tooke Guyes bow in his hand —
His arrowes were rawstye[6] by the roote —;
The sherriffe saw Litle John draw a bow
And ffettle him to shoote.

Towards his house in Nottingam
He ffled full fast away,
And soe did all his companye,
Not one behind did stay.

But he cold neither soe fast goe,
Nor away soe fast runn,
But Litle John, with an arrow broade,
Did cleave his heart in twinn.

ROBIN HOOD'S DEATH AND BURIAL

When Robin Hood and Little John
Down a down a down a down
Went oer yon bank of broom,
Said Robin Hood bold to Little John,
'We have shot for many a pound.'
Hey, etc.

'But I am not able to shoot one shot more,
My broad arrows will not flee;
But I have a cousin lives down below,
Please God, she will bleed me.'

Now Robin he is to fair Kirkly gone,
As fast as he can win[7];
But before he came there, as we do hear,
He was taken very ill.

And when he came to fair Kirkly-hall,
He knockd all at the ring,
But none was so ready as his cousin herself
For to let bold Robin in.

[1] back-handed [2] hill [3] voice [4] loosed [5] quickly [6] rusty [7] go

'Will you please to sit down, cousin Robin,' she said,
'And drink some beer with me?'
'No, I will neither eat nor drink,
Till I am blooded by thee.'

'Well, I have a room, cousin Robin,' she said,
'Which you did never see,
And if you please to walk therein,
You blooded by me shall be.'

She took him by the lyly-white hand,
And let him to a private room,
And there she blooded bold Robin Hood,
While one drop of blood would run down.

She blooded him in a vein of the arm,
And locked him up in the room;
Then did he bleed all the live-long day,
Until the next day at noon.

He then bethought him of a casement[1] there,
Thinking for to get down;
But was so weak he could not leap,
He could not get him down.

He then bethought him of his buglehorn,
Which hung low down to his knee;
He set his horn unto his mouth,
And blew out weak blasts three.

Then Little John, when hearing him,
As he sat under a tree,
'I fear my master is now near dead,
He blows so wearily.'

Then Little John to fair Kirkly is gone,
As fast as he can dree[2];
But when he came to Kirkly-hall,
He broke locks two or three:

Until he came bold Robin to see,
Then he fell on his knee;
'A boon, a boon,' cries Little John,
'Master, I beg of thee.'

'What is that boon,' said Robin Hood,
'Little John, thou begs of me?'
'It is to burn fair Kirkly-hall,
And all their nunnery.'

'Now nay, now nay,' quoth Robin Hood,
'That boon I'll not grant thee;
I never hurt woman in all my life,
Nor men in woman's company.

'I never hurt fair maid in all my time,
Nor at mine end shall it be;
But give me my bent bow in my hand,
And a broad arrow I'll let flee
And where this arrow is taken up,
There shall my grave digged be.

'Lay me a green sod under my head,
And another at my feet;
And lay my bent bow by my side,
Which was my music sweet;
And make my grave of gravel and green,
Which is most right and meet.

'Let me have length and breadth enough,
With a green sod under my head;
That they may say, when I am dead,
Here lies bold Robin Hood.'

These words they readily granted him,
Which did bold Robin please:
And there they buried bold Robin Hood,
Within the fair Kirkleys.

THE HUNTING OF THE CHEVIOT

The Perse owt off Northombarlonde,
And avowe[3] to God mayd he
That he wold hunte in the mowntayns
Off Chyviat within days thre,
In the magger[4] of doughte Dogles,
And all that ever with him be.

The fattiste hartes in all Cheviat
He sayd he wold kyll, and cary them away:
'Be my feth,' sayd the dougheti Doglas agayn,[5]
'I wyll let[6] that hontyng yf that I may.'

Then the Perse owt off Banborowe cam,
With him a myghtee meany,[7]
With fifteen hondrith archares bold off blood and bone;
The wear chosen owt of shyars thre.

This begane on a Monday at morn,
In Cheviat the hillys so he[8];
The chylde may rue that ys un-born,
It wos the mor pitte.

The dryvars thorowe the woodes went,
For to reas the dear;
Bomen[9] byckarte[10] uppone the bent[11]
With ther browd aros cleare.

Then the wyld[12] thorowe the woodes went,
On every syde shear[13];
Greahondes[14] thorowe the grevis[15] glent,[16]
For to kyll thear dear.

[1] window
[2] endure
[3] vow
[4] in spite of
[5] in return
[6] prevent
[7] rout, army
[8] high
[9] archers
[10] attacked
[11] field, moor
[12] wild ones, deer
[13] several
[14] greyhounds
[15] groves
[16] glided

This begane in Chyviat the hyls abone,[1]
  Yerly on a Monnyn-day;
Be that it drewe to the oware[2] off none,[3]
  A hondrith fat hartes ded ther lay.

The blewe a mort[4] uppone the bent,
  The semblyde[5] on sydis shear;
To the quyrry[6] then the Perse went,
  To se the bryttlynge[7] off the deare.

He sayd, 'It was the Duglas promys
  This day to met me hear;
But I wyste[8] he wolde faylle, verament[9]';
  A great oth the Perse swear.

At the laste a squyar off Northomberlonde
  Lokyde at his hand full ny;
He was war a the doughetie Doglas commynge,
  With him a myghtte meany.

Both with spear, bylle,[10] and brande,
  Yt was a myghtti sight to se;
Hardyar men, both off hart nor hande,
  Wear not in Cristiante.

The wear twenti hondrith spear-men good,
  Withoute any feale[11];
The wear borne along be the watter a Twyde,
  Yth[12] bowndes of Tividale.

'Leave of the brytlyng of the dear,' he sayd,
  'And to your boys[13] lock ye tayk good hede;
For never sithe[14] ye wear on your mothars borne
  Had ye never so mickle nede.'

The dougheti Dogglas on a stede,
  He rode alle his men beforne;
His armor glytteryde as dyd a glede[15];
  A boldar barne[16] was never born.

'Tell me whos men ye ar,' he says,
  'Or whos men that ye be:
Who gave youe leave to hunte in this Chyviat chays,[17]
  In the spyt of myn and of me.'

The first mane that ever him an answear mayd,
  Yt was the good lord Perse:
'We wyll not tell the whoys men we ar,' he says,
  'Nor whos men that we be;
But we wyll hounte hear in this chays,
  In the spyt of thyne and of the.

'The fattiste hartes in all Chyviat
  We have kyld, and cast[18] to carry them away.'
'Be my troth,' sayd the doughete Dogglas agayn,
  'Therfor the ton[19] of us shall de[20] this day.'

Then sayd the doughte Doglas
  Unto the lord Perse:
'To kyll alle thes giltles men,
  Alas, it wear great pitte!

'But, Perse, thowe art a lord of lande,
  I am a yerle[21] callyd within my contre;
Let all our men uppone a parti stande,
  And do the battell off the and of me.'

'Nowe Cristes cors[22] on his crowne,[23]' sayd the lord Perse,
  'Who-so-ever ther-to says nay!
Be my troth, doughtte Doglas,' he says,
  'Thow shalt never se that day,

'Nethar in Ynglonde, Skottlonde, nar France,
  Nor for no man of a woman born,
But, and fortune be my chance,
  I dar met him, on man for on.'

Then bespayke a squyar off Northombarlonde,
  Richard Wytharyngton was his nam;
'It shall never be told in Sothe-Ynglonde,' he says,
  'To Kyng Herry the Fourth for sham.

'I wat[24] youe byn great lordes twaw,[25]
  I am a poor squyar of lande;
I wylle never se my captayne fyght on a fylde,
  And stande my selffe and loocke on,
But whylle I may my weppone welde,
  I wylle not [fayle] both hart and hande.'

That day, that day, that dredfull day!
  The first fit[26] here I fynde;
And youe wyll here any mor a the hountynge a the Chyviat,
  Yet ys ther mor behynde.

The Ynglyshe men hade ther bowys yebent,
  Ther hartes were good yenoughe;
The first off arros that the shote off,
  Seven skore spear-men the sloughe.

[1] above
[2] hour
[3] noon
[4] death-note
[5] assembled
[6] quarry
[7] cutting up
[8] knew
[9] truly
[10] halberd
[11] fail
[12] in the
[13] bows
[14] since
[15] live coal
[16] man
[17] chase
[18] intend, plan
[19] the one
[20] die
[21] earl
[22] curse
[23] head
[24] know
[25] two
[26] canto, part of song

Yet byddys[1] the yerle Doglas uppon the bent,
A captayne good yenoughe,
And that was sene verament,
For he wrought hom both woo and wouche.[2]

The Dogglas partyd his ost in thre,
Lyk a cheffe cheften off pryde;
With suar[3] spears off myghtte tre,
The cum in on every syde;

Thrughe our Ynggglyshe archery
Gave many a wounde fulle wyde;
Many a doughete the garde[4] to dy,
Which ganyde[5] them no pryde.

The Ynglyshe men let ther boys be,
And pulde owt brandes that wer brighte;
It was a hevy syght to se
Bryght swordes on basnites[6] lyght.

Thorowe ryche male and myneyeple,[7]
Many sterne[8] the strocke done[9] streght;
Many a freyke[10] that was fulle fre,
Ther undar foot dyd lyght.

At last the Duglas and the Perse met,
Lyk to captayns of myght and of mayne;
The swapte[11] together tylle the both swat,[12]
With swordes that wear of fyn myllan.[13]

Thes worthe freckys for to fyght,
Ther-to the wear[14] fulle fayne,
Tylle the bloode owte off thear basnetes sprente,[15]
As ever dyd heal[16] or rayn.

'Yelde the, Perse,' sayde the Doglas,
'And i feth I shalle the brynge
Wher thowe shalte have a yerls wagis
Of Jamy our Skottish kynge.

'Thou shalte have thy ransom fre,
I hight[17] the hear this thinge;
For the manfullyste man yet art thowe
That ever I conqueryd in filde fighttynge.'

'Nay,' sayd the lord Perse,
'I tolde it the beforne,
That I wolde never yeldyde be
To no man of a woman born.'

With that ther cam an arrowe hastely,
Forthe off a myghtte wane[18];
Hit hathe strekene the yerle Duglas
In at the brest-bane.

Thorowe lyvar and longes bathe
The sharpe arrowe ys gane,
That never after in all his lyffe-days
He spayke mo wordes but ane:
That was, Fyghte ye, my myrry men, whyllys ye may,
For my lyff-days ben gan.

The Perse leanyde on his brande,
And sawe the Duglas de;
He tooke the dede mane by the hande,
And sayd, 'Wo ys me for the!

'To have savyde thy lyffe, I wolde have partyde with
My landes for years thre,
For a better man, of hart nare[19] of hande,
Was nat in all the north contre.'

Off all that se a Skottishe knyght,
Was callyd Ser Hewe the Monggombyrry;
He sawe the Duglas to the deth was dyght,[20]
He spendyd[21] a spear, a trusti tre.

He rod uppone a corsiare[22]
Throughe a hondrith archery:
He never stynttyde,[23] nar never blane,[24]
Tylle he cam to the good lord Perse.

He set uppone the lorde Perse
A dynte that was full soare;
With a suar spear of a myghtte tre
Clean thorow the body he the Perse ber,

A the tothar syde that a man myght se
A large cloth-yard and mare:
Towe bettar captayns wear nat in Cristiante
Then that day slan wear ther.

An archar off Northomberlonde
Say[25] slean was the lord Perse;
He bar a bende bowe in his hand,
Was made off trusti tre.

An arow, that a cloth-yarde was lang,
To the harde stele halyde[26] he;
A dynt that was both sad and soar
He sat on Ser Hewe the Monggombyrry.

The dynt yt was both sad and sar
That he of Monggomberry sete;
The swane-fethars that his arrowe bar
With his hart-blood the wear wete.

1 abides
2 harm
3 sure, trusty
4 made
5 gained
6 helmets
7 kind of gauntlet
8 stern ones
9 down
10 man
11 smote
12 sweated
13 Milan steel
14 were
15 spurted
16 hail
17 promise
18 number
19 nor
20 brought
21 grasped
22 courser
23 stopped
24 ceased
25 saw
26 pulled

Ther was never a freake wone[1] foot wolde fle,
But still in stour[2] dyd stand,
Heawyng on yche othar, whylle the myghte dre,[3]
With many a balfull brande.

This battell begane in Chyviat
An owar befor the none,
And when even-songe bell was rang,
The battell was nat half done.

The tocke . . . on ethar hande
Be the lyght off the mone;
Many hade no strenght for to stande,
In Chyviat the hillys abon.

Of fifteen hondrith archars of Ynglonde
Went away but seventi and thre;
Of twenti hondrith spear-men of Skotlonde,
But even five and fifti.

But all wear slayne Cheviat within;
The hade no strengthe to stand on hy[4];
The chylde may rue that ys unborne,
It was the mor pitte.

Thear was slayne, withe the lord Perse,
Sir Johan of Agerstone,
Ser Rogar, the hinde[5] Hartly,
Ser Wyllyam, the bolde Hearone.

Ser Jorg, the worthe Loumle,
A knyghte of great renowen,
Ser Raff, the ryche Rugbe,
With dyntes wear beaten dowene.

For Wetharryngton my harte was wo,
That ever he slayne shulde be;
For when both his leggis wear hewyne in to,[6]
Yet he knyled and fought on hys kny.

Ther was slayne, with the dougheti Duglas,
Ser Hewe the Monggombyrry,
Ser Davy Lwdale, that worthe was,
His sistars son was he.

Ser Charls a Murre in that place,
That never a foot wolde fle;
Ser Hewe Maxwelle, a lorde he was,
With the Doglas dyd he dey.

So on the morrowe the mayde them byears[7]
Off birch and hasell so gray;
Many wedous, with wepyng tears,
Cam to fache[8] ther makys[9] away.

Tivydale may carpe[10] off care,
Northombarlond may mayk great mon,
For towe such captayns as slayne wear thear
On the March-parti[11] shall never be non.

Word ys commen to Eddenburrowe,
To Jamy the Skottische kynge,
That dougheti Duglas, lyff-tenant[12] of the Marches,
He lay slean Chyviot within.

His handdes dyd he weal[13] and wryng,
He sayd, Alas, and woe ys me!
Such an othar captayn Skotland within,
He sayd, ye-feth[14] shuld never be.

Worde ys commyn to lovly Londone,
Till the fourth Harry our kynge,
That lord Perse, leyff-tenante of the Marchis,
He lay slayne Chyviat within.

'God have merci on his solle,' sayde Kyng Harry,
'Good Lord, yf thy will it be!
I have a hondrith captayns in Ynglonde,' he sayd,
'As good as ever was he:
But, Perse, and I brook[15] my lyffe,
Thy deth well quyte[16] shall be.'

As our noble kynge mayd his avowe,
Lyke a noble prince of renowen,
For the deth of the lord Perse
He dyde the battell of Hombylldown;

Wher syx and thritte Skottishe knyghtes
On a day wear beaten down;
Glendale glytteryde on ther armor bryght,
Over castille, towar, and town.

This was the hontynge off the Cheviat,
That tear[17] begane this spurn[18];
Old men that knowen the grownde well yenoughe
Call it the battell of Otterburn.

At Otterburn begane this spurne,
Uppone a Monnynday;
Ther was the doughte Doglas slean,
The Perse never went away.

Ther was never a tym on the Marche-partes
Sen the Doglas and the Perse met,
But yt ys mervele and the rede blude ronne not,
As the reane[19] doys in the stret.

1 one
2 combat
3 endure
4 upright
5 courteous
6 two
7 biers
8 fetch
9 mates
10 tell
11 border-parts
12 lieutenant
13 clench (?)
14 in faith
15 enjoy, keep
16 avenged
17 there (?)
18 conflict (?)
19 rain

Jhesue Crist our balys[1] bete,[2]
And to the blys us brynge!
Thus was the hountynge of the Chivyat:
God sent us alle good endyng!

JOHNIE ARMSTRONG

There dwelt a man in faire Westmerland,
Jonne Armestrong men did him call,
He had nither lands nor rents coming in,
Yet he kept eight score men in his hall.

He had horse and harness for them all,
Goodly steeds were all milke-white;
O the golden bands an about their necks,
And their weapons, they were all alike.

Newes then was brought unto the king
That there was sicke[3] a won[4] as hee,
That livèd lyke a bold out-law,
And robbèd all the north country.

The king he writt an a letter then,
A letter which was large and long;
He signèd it with his owne hand,
And he promised to doe him no wrong.

When this letter came Jonne untill,
His heart it was as blythe as birds on the tree:
'Never was I sent for before any king,
My father, my grandfather, nor none but mee.

'And if wee goe the king before,
I would we went most orderly;
Every man of you shall have his scarlet cloak,
Laced with silver laces three.

'Every won of you shall have his velvett coat,
Laced with silver lace so white;
O the golden bands an about your necks,
Black hatts, white feathers, all alyke.'

By the morrow morninge at ten of the clock,
Towards Edenburough gon was hee,
And with him all his eight score men;
Good lord, it was a goodly sight for to see!

When Jonne came befower the king,
He fell downe on his knee;
'O pardon, my soveraine leige,' he said,
'O pardon my eight score men and mee!'

'Thou shalt have no pardon, thou traytor strong,
For thy eight score men nor thee;
For to-morrow morning by ten of the clock,
Both thou and them shall hang on the gallow-tree.'

But Jonne looked over his left shoulder,
Good Lord, what a grevious look looked hee!
Saying, Asking grace of a graceles face —
Why there is none for you nor me.

But Jonne had a bright sword by his side,
And it was made of the mettle so free,
That had not the king stept his foot aside,
He had smitten his head from his faire bodde.

Saying, Fight on, my merry men all,
And see that none of you be taine[5];
For rather than men shall say we were hanged,
Let them report how we were slaine.

Then, God wott, faire Eddenburrough rose,
And so besett poore Jonne rounde,
That fowerscore and tenn of Jonnes best men
Lay gasping all upon the ground.

Then like a mad man Jonne laide about,
And like a mad man then fought hee,
Untill a falce Scot came Jonne behinde,
And runn him through the faire boddee.

Saying, Fight on, my merry men all,
And see that none of you be taine;
For I will stand by and bleed but awhile,
And then will I come and fight againe.

Newes then was brought to young Jonne Armestrong,
As he stood by his nurses knee,
Who vowed if ere he lived for to be a man,
O the treacherous Scots revengd hee'd be.

[1] troubles [2] relieve [3] such [4] one [5] taken

LYRICS

Anonymous

CUCKOO SONG

SUMER is icumen in:
  Lhude[1] sing cuccu[2]!
Groweth sed, and bloweth[3] med,[4]
  And springth the wude nu.[5]
    Sing cuccu!

Awe[6] bleteth after lomb;
  Lhouth[7] after calve cu[8];
Bulluc sterteth, bucke verteth.
  Murie[9] sing cuccu!

Cuccu, cuccu, well singes thu, cuccu:
  Ne swike[10] thu naver nu.
Sing cuccu, nu, sing cuccu!
  Sing cuccu, sing cuccu, nu!
  ca. 1300.

SPRINGTIME

LENTEN[11] ys come with love to toune,[12]
With blosmen and with briddes roune,[13]
  That al this blisse bryngeth;
Dayes-eyes[14] in this dales,
Notes suete[15] of nyhtegales,[16]
  Uch[17] foul song singeth.
The threstelcoc[18] him threteth[19] oo,[20]
Away is huere[21] wynter wo,
  When woderove[22] springeth;
This foules singeth ferly[23] fele,[24]
And wlyteth[25] on huere wynter wele,[26]
  That al the wode ryngeth.

The rose rayleth[27] hir rode,[28]
The leves on the lyhte[29] wode
  Waxen al with wille[30];
The mone mandeth[31] hire bleo,[32]
The lilie is lossom[33] to seo,
  The fenyl[34] and the fille[35];
Wowes[36] this wilde drakes;
Miles[37] murgeth[38] huere makes[39];
  Ase strem that striketh[40] stille,
Mody[41] meneth,[42] so doth mo,[43]
Ichot[44] ycham[45] on of tho,[46]
  For love that likes[47] ille.

The mone mandeth hire lyht,
So doth the semly sonne bryht,
  When briddes singeth breme[48];
Deawes donketh[49] the dounes,
Deores[50] with huere derne[51] rounes,
  Domes[52] forte[53] deme[54];
Wormes woweth under cloude,[55]
Wymmen waxeth wounder proude,
  So wel hit wol hem seme,[56]
Yef[57] me shal wonte[58] wille of on:
This wunne weole[59] I wole for-gon,
  And wyht in wode be fleme.[60]
  ca. 1300

A HYMN TO THE VIRGIN

OF on that is so fayr and bright,
  Velut maris stella,
Brighter than the day is light,
  Parens et puella:
Ic[61] crie to the, thou se to me,
Levedy,[62] preye thi sone for me,
  Tam pia,
That ic mote come to the,
  Maria.

Al this world was for-lore,[63]
  Eva peccatrice,
Tyl our lord was y-bore
  De te genetrice.
With *ave* it went away,
Thuster[64] nyth[65] and comz the day
  Salutis;
The welle springeth ut[66] of the
  Virtutis.

Levedi, flour of alle thing,
  Rosa sine spina,
Thu bere Jhesu, hevene king,
  Gratia divina;
Of alle thu berst the pris,[67]
Levedi, quene of parays[68]
  Electa.
Mayde milde, moder *es*
  Effecta.

1 loudly
2 cuckoo
3 blossometh
4 meadow
5 now
6 ewe
7 loweth
8 cow
9 merrily
10 cease
11 Lent, spring
12 to town, into the land
13 whisper,
14 daisies
15 sweet
16 nightingales
17 each
18 male thrush
19 chides
20 aye, ever
21 their
22 woodruff
23 wondrously
24 many
25 cry
26 weal
27 arrays, puts on
28 redness
29 light
30 a will
31 mends
32 complexion
33 lovely
34 fennel
35 thyme
36 woo
37 animals
38 make merry
39 mates
40 flows
41 The moody one
42 makes moan
43 more, others
44 I know
45 I am
46 those
47 pleases
48 loudly
49 make dank
50 lovers
51 secret
52 decisions (in love)
53 for to
54 deem, judge
55 serpents woo under clod
56 become
57 if
58 want, lack
59 this joyful boon
60 And be a banished wight in the woods
61 I
62 lady
63 lost
64 dark
65 night
66 out
67 highest fame
68 paradise

Of kare conseil thou ert best,
Felix fecundata,
Of alle wery thou ert rest,
Mater honorata.
Bisek him wiz[1] milde mod,[2]
That for ous alle sad[3] is[4] blod
In cruce,
That we moten comen til him
In luce.

Wel he wot[5] he is thi sone.
Ventre quem portasti;
He wyl nout werne[6] the thi bone,
Parvum quem lactasti;
So hende[7] and so god he his,[8]
He havet[9] brout ous to blis
Superni,
That havez[9] hi-dut[10] the foule put[11]
Inferni.
ca. 1300

ALYSOUN

BYTUENE Mershe and Averil
When spray biginneth to springe,
The lutel foul hath hire wyl
On hyre lud[12] to synge;
Ich[13] libbe[14] in love-longinge
For semlokest[15] of alle thynge,
He[16] may me blisse bringe,
Icham[17] in hire baundoun.[18]
An hendy hap ichabbe[19] yhent,[20]
Ichot from hevene it is me sent,
From alle wymmen mi love is lent[21]
Ant lyht[22] on Alysoun.

On heu hire her[23] is fayr ynoh,
Hire browe broune, hire eye blake,
With lossum[24] chere he on me loh[25];
With middel[26] smal and wel y-make;
Bote he me wolle to hire take
Forte[27] buen[28] hire owen make,[29]
Longe to lyven ichulle[30] forsake,
And feye[31] fallen adoun.
An hendy hap, etc.

Nihtes when I wende[32] and wake,
Forthi[33] myn wonges[34] waxeth won;
Levedi,[35] al for thine sake
Longinge is ylent[36] me on
In world nis non so wytermon[37]
That al hire bounte telle con;
Hire swyre[38] is whittore then the swon,
And feyrest may[39] in toune.
An hendy hap, etc.

Icham for wowyng[40] al forwake,[41]
Wery so water in wore[42];
Lest eny reve[43] me my make,
Ichabbe y-yernèd yore.[44]
Betere is tholien whyle sore[45]
Then mournen evermore.
Geynes[46] under gore,[47]
Herkne to my roun.
An hendy hap, etc.
ca. 1300

A PLEA FOR PITY

WITH longyng I am lad,
On molde[48] I waxe mad,
A maide marreth me;
I grede,[49] I grone, un-glad,
For selden I am sad[50]
That semly forte se;
Levedi, thou rewe[51] me!
To routhe thou havest me rad[52];
Be bote of that I bad,[53]
My lyf is long on the.

Levedy of alle londe,
Les[54] me out of bonde,
Broht icham in wo;
Have resting on honde,
And sent thou me thi sonde,[55]
Sone, er thou me slo[56];
My reste is with the ro[57]:
Thah men to me han onde,[58]
To love nuly[59] noht wonde,[60]
Ne lete[61] for non of tho.

Levedi, with al my miht
My love is on the liht,
To menske[62] when I may;
Thou rew and red[63] me ryht,
To dethe thou havest me diht,[64]
I deye longe er my day;
Thou leve[65] upon my lay.
Treuthe ichave the plyht,
To don that ich have hyht,[66]
Whil mi lif leste may.

1 with
2 mind
3 shed
4 his
5 knows
6 refuse
7 gracious
8 is
9 has
10 concealed
11 pit
12 language
13 I
14 live
15 the most beautiful
16 she
17 I am
18 power
19 I have
20 caught, received
21 departed
22 lighted
23 hair
24 lovesome
25 laughed
26 waist
27 for to
28 be
29 mate
30 I shall
31 ready to die
32 turn
33 therefore
34 cheeks
35 lady
36 come
37 wise man
38 neck
39 maid
40 wooing
41 worn with watching
42 weir
43 deprive
44 for a long time
45 endure hurt for a while
46 most gracious one
47 attire
48 earth
49 cry out
50 satisfied
51 pity
52 advised
53 asked
54 loose
55 message
56 slay
57 roe
58 jealousy
59 will I not
60 fear, hesitate
61 cease
62 honor
63 instruct
64 prepared
65 believe
66 promised

Lylie-whyt hue is,
Hire rode[1] so rose on rys,[2]
 That reveth[3] me mi rest.
Wymmon war[4] and wys,
Of prude hue bereth the pris,[5]
 Burde[6] on of the best;
 This wommon woneth[7] by west,
Brihtest under bys[8]:
Hevene I tolde[9] al his
 That o nyht were hire gest.
 ca. 1300

BLOW, NORTHERN WIND

Ichot[10] a burde[11] in boure bryht,
That fully semly is on syht,
Menskful[12] maiden of myht;
 Feir and fre to fonde[13];
In al this wurhliche[14] won[15]
A burde of blod and of bon
Never yete I nuste[16] non
 Lussomore[17] in londe.
  Blou northerne wynd!
  Send thou me my suetyng!
  Blou northerne wynd! blou, blou, blou!

With lokkes[18] lefliche[19] and longe,
With frount and face feir to fonge,[20]
With murthes monie mote heo monge,[21]
 That brid so breme[22] in boure.
With lossom[23] eye grete and gode,
With browen blysfol under hode,
He that reste him on the Rode,[24]
 That leflych lyf honoure.
  Blou northerne wynd! etc.

Hire lure[25] lumes[26] liht,
Ase a lanterne a nyht,
Hire bleo[27] blykyeth[28] so bryht,
 So feyr heo is and fyn.
A suetly swyre[29] heo hath to holde,
With armes shuldre ase mon wolde,
And fingres feyre forte folde,
 God wolde hue were myn!
  Blou northerne wynd! etc.

Heo is coral of godnesse,
Heo is rubie of ryhtfulnesse,
Heo is cristal of clannesse,
 And baner of bealte.[30]
Heo is lilie of largesse,
Heo is parvenke[31] of prouesse,[32]
Heo is solsecle[33] of suetnesse,
 And lady of lealte.[34]
  Blou northerne wynd! etc.

For hire love I carke[35] and care,
For hire love I droupne[36] and dare,[37]
For hire love my blisse is bare
 And al ich waxe won.
For hire love in slep I slake,[38]
For hire love al nyht ich wake,
For hire love mournynge I make
 More then eny mon.
  Blou northerne wynd!
  Send thou me my suetyng!
  Blou northerne wynd! blou, blou, blou!
 ca. 1300

Geoffrey Chaucer (1340?–1400)

BALADE

Hyd, Absolon, thy gilte tresses clere;
Ester, ley thou thy meknesse al a-doun;
Hyd, Jonathas, al thy frendly manere;
Penalopee, and Marcia Catoun,
Mak of your wyfhod no comparisoun;
Hyde ye your beautes, Isoude and Eleyne,
My lady cometh, that al this may disteyne.[39]

Thy faire body, lat hit nat appere,
Lavyne; and thou, Lucresse of Rome toun,
And Polixene, that boghten love so dere,
And Cleopatre, with al thy passioun,
Hyde ye your trouthe of love and your renoun;
And thou, Tisbe, that hast of love swich peyne;
My lady cometh, that al this may disteyne.

Herro, Dido, Laudomia, alle y-fere,[40]
And Phyllis, hanging for thy Demophoun,
And Canace, espyèd by thy chere,
Ysiphile, betraysèd with Jasoun,
Maketh of your trouthe neyther boost ne soun[41];
Nor Ypermistre or Adriane, ye tweyne;
My lady cometh, that al this may disteyne.
 1385?

[1] complexion
[2] spray
[3] deprives
[4] prudent
[5] prize
[6] lady
[7] dwells
[8] purple
[9] should count
[10] I know
[11] lady
[12] noble
[13] prove
[14] noble
[15] multitude
[16] knew not
[17] more lovable
[18] locks
[19] lovely
[20] take
[21] mingle
[22] lively
[23] loving
[24] Cross
[25] face
[26] beams
[27] color, hue
[28] shines
[29] neck
[30] beauty
[31] periwinkle
[32] excellence
[33] sunflower
[34] loyalty
[35] worry
[36] become dejected
[37] act like one half asleep
[38] I neglect to sleep
[39] bedim
[40] together
[41] vaunt

Robert Henryson (1425?–1506?)

ROBIN AND MAKYNE

ROBIN sat on gude green hill,
  Kepand[1] a flock of fe[2]:
Mirry Makyne said him till
  'Robin, thou rew[3] on me:
I haif thee luvit, loud and still,
  Thir yeiris twa or thre:
My dule[4] in dern[5] bot gif thou dill,[6]
  Doubtless but dreid[7] I de.'

Robin answerit, 'By the Rude[8]
  Na thing of luve I knaw,
But keipis my scheip undir yon wud:
  Lo, quhair[9] they raik[10] on raw.[11]
Quhat[12] has marrit[13] thee in thy mude,[14]
  Makyne, to me thou shaw;
Or quhat is luve, or to be lude[15]?
  Fain wad I leir[16] that law.'

'At luvis lair[17] gif thou will leir
  Tak thair ane A B C;
Be heynd,[18] courtass, and fair of feir.[19]
  Wyse, hardy, and free:
So that no danger do thee deir[20]
  Quhat dule in dern thou dre[21];
Preiss[22] thee with pain at all poweir
  Be patient and previe.[23]'

Robin answerit hir agane,
  'I wat nocht quhat is lufe;
But I haif mervel in certaine
  Quhat makis thee this wanrufe[24]:
The weddir is fair, and I am fain;
  My scheip gois haill[25] aboif[26];
And we wald pley us in this plane,
  They wald us baith reproif.'

'Robin, tak tent[27] unto my tale,
  And wirk all as I reid,
And thou sall haif my heart all haill,
  Eik[28] and my maiden-heid[29]:
Sen God sendis bute[30] for baill,[31]
  And for murnyng[32] remeid,[33]
In dern with thee bot gif I daill[34]
  Dowtles I am bot deid.'

'Makyne, to-morn this ilka[35] tyde
  And ye will meit me heir,
Peraventure my scheip may gang besyde,
  Quhyle we haif liggit[36] full neir:
But mawgre[37] haif I, and I byde
  Fra[38] they begin to steir[39];
Quhat lyis on heart I will nocht hyd;
  Makyn, then mak gude cheir.'

'Robin, thou reivis[40] me roiff[41] and rest;
  I luve bot thee allane.'
'Makyne, adieu! the sone gois west,
  The day is neir-hand gane.'
'Robin, in dule I am so drest
  That luve will be my bane.'
'Ga luve, Makyne, quhair-evir thow list,
  For lemman[42] I luve nane.'

'Robin, I stand in sic a styll,[43]
  I sicht and that full sair.'
'Makyne, I haif been here this quhyle;
  At hame God gif I wair.'
'My huny, Robin, talk ane quhyll,
  Gif thow will do no mair.'
'Makyn, sum uthir man begyle,
  For hamewart I will fair.'

Robin on his wayis went
  As light as leif of tre;
Makyne murnit in hir intent,
  And trowd[44] him nevir to se.
Robin brayd[45] attour[46] the bent[47]:
  Then Makyne cryit on hie,
'Now may thow sing, for I am schent[48]!
  Quhat alis[49] lufe at me?'

Makyne went hame withowttin fail,
  Full wery eftir cowth weip;
Then Robin in a ful fair daill
  Assemblit all his scheip.
Be that sum part of Makynis aill
  Out-throw his hairt cowd creip;
He fallowit hir fast thair till assaill,
  And till her tuke gude keip.

'Abyd, abyd, thow fair Makyne,
  A word for ony thing:
For all my luve, it sall be thyne,
  Withowttin departing.
Al haill thy hairt for till haif myne
  Is all my cuvating;
My scheip to-morn, quhyle hour is nyne,
  Will neid of no keping.'

'Robin, thow hes hard soung and say,
  In gestis[50] and storeis auld,
The man that will nocht quhen he may
  Sall haif nocht quhen he wald.

1 keeping
2 sheep, cattle
3 have pity
4 dole
5 secret
6 soothe
7 doubt, dread
8 Cross
9 where
10 range
11 row
12 what
13 marred
14 mind
15 loved
16 learn
17 lore
18 gracious
19 demeanor
20 daunt
21 endure
22 pursue
23 secret
24 unrest
25 whole
26 above
27 notice
28 also
29 maidenhood
30 remedy
31 bale
32 mourning
33 remedy
34 deal
35 same
36 lain
37 displeasure
38 from the time that
39 move
40 deprivest
41 quiet
42 lover, sweetheart
43 fix, plight
44 expected
45 strode
46 out-over
47 coarse grass
48 shamed
49 ails
50 tales

I pray to Jesu every day,
  Mot eik thair cairis cauld
That first preissis with thee to play
  Be firth, forrest, or fauld.'

'Makyne, the nicht is soft and dry,
  The weddir is warme and fair,
And the grene woid rycht neir us by
  To walk attour all quhair:
Thair ma na janglour[1] us espy.
  That is to lufe contrair;
Thairin, Makyne, baith ye and I,
  Unsene we ma repair.'

'Robin, that warld is all away,
  And quyt brocht till ane end:
And nevir agane thereto, perfay,[2]
  Sall it be as thow wend[3];
For of my pane thow maid it play;
  And all in vane I spend:
As thow hes done, sa sall I say,
  "Murne on, I think to mend."'

'Makyne, the howp of all my heill,[4]
  My hairt on thee is sett:
And evirmair to thee be leill[5]
  Quhill I may leif but lett;
Never to faill as utheris feill,
  Quhat grace that evir I gett.'
'Robin, with thee I will nocht deill;
  Adieu! for thus we mett.'

Makyne went hame blyth anneuche[6]
  Attour the holttis[7] hair[8];
Robin murnit, and Makyne leuche[9];
  Scho sang, he sichit sair:
And so left him baith wo and wreuch,[10]
  In dolour and in cair,
Kepand his hird under a huche[11]
  Amangis the holttis hair.
  1485?

William Dunbar (1465?–1520?)

TO A LADY

Sweet rois of vertew and of gentilness,
Delytsum lily of everie lustynes,
  Richest in bontie[12] and in bewtie clear,
  And everie vertew that is wenit[13] dear,
Except onlie that ye are mercyless.

Into your garth[14] this day I did persew;
There saw I flouris that fresche were of hew;
  Baith quhyte and reid most lusty were to seyne,
  And halesome herbis upon stalkis greene;
Yet leaf nor flowr find could I nane of rew.

I doubt that Merche, with his cauld blastis keyne,
Has slain this gentil herb, that I of mene[15];
  Quhois piteous death dois to my heart sic[16] paine
  That I would make to plant his root againe. —
So confortand[17] his levis unto me bene.[18]
  1500?

Anonymous

SONG OF WOMAN

Women, women, love of women
Make bare purs with some men.
Some be nyse[19] as a nunne[20] hene,[21]
  Yit al thei be nat so;
Some be lewde,[22] some all be shreude,[23]
  Go schrewes wher thei goo.

Sum be nyse, and some be fonde,[24]
And some be tame, I undirstonde,
And some cane take brede of a manys honde;
  Yit all thei be nat so.
Some be lewde, etc.

Some cane part[25] withouten hire,
And some make bate[26] in eviri chire,[27]
And some cheke-mate withoute sire[28];
  Yit all they be nat so.
Some be lewde, etc.

Some be browne, and some be whit,
And some be tender as accripe[29];
And some of theym be chiry ripe;
  Yit all thei be nat so.
Some be lewde, etc.

Some of them be treue of love,
Benethe the gerdelle, but nat above;
And in a hode above cane chove[30];
  Yit all thei do nat so.
Some be lewde, etc.

1 tattler
2 in faith
3 thought, hoped
4 health, well-being
5 faithful
6 enough
7 woodlands
8 hoar, gray
9 laughed
10 peevish
11 cliff
12 goodness
13 thought, esteemed
14 garden-close
15 that I refer to
16 such
17 comforting
18 be, are
19 foolish
20 nun's
21 hen
22 ignorant
23 wicked, accursed
24 foolish
25 divide, give
26 debate, trouble
27 in every shire, everywhere
28 sir, lord
29 a tripe
30 shove

Some cane whister,[1] and some cane crie;
Some cane flater, and some cane lye;
And some can sette the moke[2] awrie;
Yit all thei do nat so.
Some be lewde, etc.

He that made this song full good,
Came of the northe and of the sothern blode,
And somewhat kyne to Robyn Hode;
Yit all we be nat so.
Some be lewde, etc.

before 1500

CAROL

I SING of a maiden
That is makeles[3];
King of all kings
To her son she ches.[4]

He came al so still
There[5] his mother was,
As dew in April
That falleth on the grass.

He came al so still
To his mother's bour,
As dew in April
That falleth on the flour.

He came al so still
There his mother lay,
As dew in April
That falleth on the spray.

Mother and maiden
Was never none but she;
Well may such a lady
Goddes mother be.

ca. 1500

THE NUTBROWNE MAIDE

'BE it right or wrong, these men among on women do complaine,
Affermyng this, how that it is a labour spent in vaine
To love them wele, for never a dele[6] they love a man agayne[7];
For lete a man do what he can ther favour to attayne,
Yet yf a newe do them pursue, ther furst trew lover than
Laboureth for nought, and from her thought he is a bannished man.'

'I say not nay but that all day it is bothe writ and sayde
That woman's fayth is, as who saythe, all utterly decayed;
But nevertheless, right good witnes in this case might be layde,
That they love trewe and contynew, — recorde the Nutbrowne Maide,
Whiche from her love, whan, her to prove, he cam to make his mone,
Wolde not departe, for in her herte she lovyd but hym allone.'

'Than betwene us lete us discusse what was all the maner
Betwene them too,[8] we wyl also telle all the peyne infere[9]
That she was in. Now I begynne, see that ye me answere.
Wherefore [all] ye that present be, I pray you geve an eare.
I am a knyght, I cum be nyght, as secret as I can,
Sayng, "Alas! thus stondyth the case: I am a bannisshed man."'

'And I your wylle for to fulfylle, in this wyl not refuse,
Trusting to shewe, in wordis fewe, that men have an ille use,[10]
To ther owne shame wymen to blame, and causeles them accuse.
Therfore to you I answere now, alle wymen to excuse:
"Myn own hert dere, with you what chiere? I prey you telle anoon;
For in my mynde of all mankynde I love but you allon."'

'It stondith so, a deed is do wherof moche harme shal growe.
My desteny is for to dey a shamful dethe, I trowe,
Or ellis to fle; the ton[11] must bee, none other wey I knowe
But to withdrawe as an outlaw and take me to my bowe.
Wherfore, adew, my owne hert trewe, none other red[12] I can[13];
For I muste to the grene wode goo, alone, a bannysshed man.'

'O Lorde, what is this worldis blisse, that chaungeth as the mone?
My somers day in lusty May is derked before the none.
I here you saye "farwel"; nay, nay, we departe not soo sone.

[1] whisper [2] mark (?) [3] peerless [4] chose [5] where [6] bit [7] in return [8] two [9] together [10] custom [11] one [12] advice, course [13] know

Why say ye so? wheder wyl ye goo? alas! what have ye done?
Alle my welfare to sorow and care shulde chaunge if ye were gon;
For in my mynde of all mankynde I love but you alone.'

'I can beleve it shal you greve, and somwhat you distrayne[1];
But aftyrwarde your paynes harde within a day or tweyne
Shal sone aslake, and ye shal take confort to you agayne.
Why shuld ye nought? for to take thought, your labur were in vayne.
And thus I do, and pray you, too, as hertely as I can;
For I muste too the grene wode goo, alone, a bannysshed man.'

'Now syth[2] that ye have shewed to me the secret of your mynde,
I shalbe playne to you agayne, lyke as ye shal me fynde;
Syth it is so that ye wyll goo, I wol not leve[3] behynde;
Shal ne'er be sayd the Nutbrowne Mayd was to her love unkind.
Make you redy, for soo am I, all though it were anoon[4];
For in my mynde of all mankynde I love but you alone.'

'Yet I you rede to take good hede, what men wyl thinke and sey;
Of yonge and olde it shal be told that ye be gone away,
Your wanton wylle for to fulfylle, in grene wood you to play,
And that ye myght from your delyte noo lenger make delay.
Rather than ye shuld thus for me be called an ylle woman,
Yet wolde I to the grenewodde goo, alone, a banysshed man.'

'Though it be songe of olde and yonge that I shuld be to blame,
Theirs be the charge that speke so large in hurting of my name;
For I wyl prove that feythful love it is devoyd of shame,
In your distresse and hevynesse to parte[5] wyth you the same;
And sure all thoo[6] that doo not so, trewe lovers ar they noon;
But in my mynde of all mankynde I love but you alone.'

'I counsel yow, remembre how it is noo maydens lawe
Nothing to dought,[7] but to renne out to wod with an outlawe;
For ye must there in your hande bere a bowe redy and drawe,
And as a theef thus must ye lyve ever in drede and awe,
By whiche to yow gret harme myght grow; yet had I lever than[8]
That I had too the grenewod goo, alone, a banysshyd man.'

'I thinke not nay, but as ye saye, it is noo maydens lore;
But love may make me for your sake, as ye have said before,
To com on fote, to hunte and shote to gete us mete and store;
For soo that I your company may have, I aske noo more;
From whiche to parte, it makith myn herte as colde as ony ston;
For in my mynde of all mankynde I love but you alone.'

'For an outlawe this is the lawe, that men hym take and binde,
Wythout pytee hangèd to bee, and waver wyth the wynde.
Yf I had neede, as God forbede, what rescous[9] coude ye finde?
For sothe I trowe, you and your bowe shuld drawe for fere behynde;
And noo merveyle, for lytel avayle were in your councel than;
Wherfore I too the woode wyl goo, alone, a banysshed man.'

'Ful wel knowe ye that wymen bee ful febyl for to fyght;
Noo womanhed is it indeede to bee bolde as a knight;
Yet in suche fere yf that ye were, amonge enemys day and nyght,
I wolde wythstonde, with bowe in hande, to greeve them as I myght,
And you to save, as wymen have, from deth [ful] many one;
For in my mynde of all mankynde I love but you alone.'

'Yet take good hede, for ever I drede that ye coude not sustein
The thorney wayes, the depe valeis, the snowe, the frost, the reyn,
The colde, the hete; for, drye or wete, we must lodge on the playn,

[1] afflict
[2] since
[3] remain
[4] immediately
[5] share
[6] those
[7] doubt, fear
[8] then
[9] rescue

And, us aboove, noon other rove[1] but a brake, bussh, or twayne;
Whiche sone shulde greve you, I beleve, and ye wolde gladly than
That I had too the grenewode goo, alone, a banysshyd man.'

'Syth I have here been partynere with you of joy and blysse,
I muste also parte of your woo endure, as reason is;
Yet am I sure of oo[2] plesure, and shortly it is this,
That where ye bee, me semeth, perdé, I coude not fare amysse.
Wythout more speche, I you beseche that we were soon agone;
For in my mynde of all mankynde I love but you alone.'

'Yf ye goo thedyr, ye must consider, whan ye have lust[3] to dyne,
Ther shel no mete be fore to gete, nor drinke, bere, ale, ne wine,
Ne shetis clene to lye betwene, made of thred and twyne,
Noon other house but levys and bowes, to kever your hed and myn.
Loo! myn herte swete, this ylle dyet shuld make you pale and wan;
Wherfore I to the wood wyl goo, alone, a banysshid man.'

'Amonge the wylde dere suche an archier as men say that ye bee
Ne may not fayle of good vitayle, where is so grete plenté;
And watir cleere of the ryvere shal be ful swete to me,
Wyth whiche in hele[4] I shal right wele endure, as ye shal see;
And, er we goo, a bed or too I can provide anoon;
For in my mynde of all mankynde I love but you alone.'

'Loo! yet before ye must doo more, yf ye wyl goo with me, —
As cutte your here up by your ere, your kirtel by the knee,
Wyth bowe in hande, for to withstonde your enmys, yf nede be,
And this same nyght before daylight to woodward wyl I flee;
And if ye wyl all this fulfylle, doo it shortely as ye can;
Ellis[5] wil I to the grenewode goo, alone, a banysshyd man.'

'I shal, as now, do more for you than longeth to womanhede,
To short my here, a bowe to bere to shote in tyme of nede.
O my swete moder, before all other, for you have I most drede;
But now adiew! I must ensue, wher fortune duth me leede:
All this make ye; now lete us flee, the day cums fast upon;
For in my mynde of all mankynde I love but you alone.'

'Nay, nay, not soo, ye shal not goo! and I shal telle you why:
Your appetyte is to be lyght of love, I wele aspie;
For right as ye have sayd to me, in lykewise hardely
Ye wolde answere, whosoever it were, in way of company.
It is sayd of olde, "sone hote, sone colde," and so is a woman;
Wherfore I too the woode wyl goo, alone, a banysshid man.'

'Yef[6] ye take hede, yet is noo nede, suche wordis to say bee me,
For oft ye preyd, and longe assayed, or I you lovid, perdé!
And though that I of auncestry a baron's doughter bee,
Yet have you proved how I you loved, a squyer of lowe degree,
And ever shal, what so befalle, to dey therfore anoon;
For in my mynde of all mankynde I love but you alone.'

'A baron's childe to be begyled, it were a cursseèd dede,
To be felaw with an outlawe, almyghty God forbede!
Yet bettyr were the power[7] squyer alone to forest yede[8],
Than ye shal saye, another day, that be my wyked dede
Ye were betrayed; wherfore, good maide, the best red that I can,
Is that I too the greenewode goo, alone, a banysshed man.'

'Whatsoever befalle, I never shal of this thing you upbraid;
But yf ye goo and leve me so, than have ye me betraied.
Remembre you wele how that ye dele, for yf ye, as ye sayde,

[1] roof
[2] one
[3] desire
[4] health
[5] else
[6] if
[7] poor
[8] should go

Be so unkynde to leve behynd your love, the Notbrowne Maide,
Trust me truly that I shal dey sone after ye be gone;
For in my mynde of all mankynde I love but you alone.'

'Yef that ye went, ye shulde repent, for in the forest now
I have purveid[1] me of a maide, whom I love more than you, —
Another fayrer than ever ye were, I dare it wel avowe;
And of you bothe, eche shulde be wrothe with other, as I trowe.
It were myn ease to lyve in pease; so wyl I, yf I can;
Wherfore I to the wode wyl goo, alone, a banysshid man.'

'Though in the wood I undirstode ye had a paramour,
All this may nought remeve my thought, but that I wil be your;
And she shal fynde me soft and kynde, and curteis every our,
Glad to fulfylle all that she wylle commaunde me, to my power;
For had ye, loo! an hundred moo, yet wolde I be that one;
For in my mynde of all mankynde I love but you alone.'

'Myn oune dere love, I see the prove that ye be kynde and trewe;
Of mayde and wyf, in all my lyf, the best that ever I knewe!
Be mery and glad, be no more sad, the case is chaungèd newe;
For it were ruthe[2] that for your trouth you shuld have cause to rewe.
Be not dismayed, whatsoever I sayd, to you whan I began,
I wyl not too the grenewod goo, I am noo banysshyd man.'

'Theis tidingis be more glad to me than to be made a quene,
Yf I were sure they shuld endure; but it is often seen,
When men wyl breke promyse, they speke the wordis on the splene.
Ye shape some wyle, me to begyle, and stele fro me, I wene.
Then were the case wurs than it was, and I more woo-begone;
For in my mynde of all mankynde I love but you alone.'

'Ye shall not nede further to drede, I wyl not disparage
You, God defende,[3] sith you descende of so grete a lynage.
Nou understonde, to Westmerlande, whiche is my herytage,
I wyle you bringe, and wyth a rynge, be[4] wey of maryage,
I wyl you take, and lady make, as shortly as I can;
Thus have ye wone an erles son, and not a banysshyd man.'

Here may ye see that wymen be in love meke, kinde, and stable,
Late never man repreve them than, or calle them variable,
But rather prey God that we may to them be confortable,[5]
Whiche somtyme provyth suche as he loveth, yf they be charitable.
For sith men wolde that wymen sholde be meke to them echeon,[6]
Moche more ought they to God obey, and serve but hym alone.

ca. 1500

[1] provided [2] pity [3] forbid [4] by [5] comforting [6] each one

ELIZABETHAN AND PURITAN PERIODS

PARALLEL READINGS

RENAISSANCE

Drama

1. Mr. S. — *Gammer Gurton's Needle*
2. Udall — *Ralph Royster Doyster*
3. Sackville and Norton — *Gorboduc*

Prose

1. More — *Utopia*

ELIZABETHAN AGE

Drama

1. Lyly — *Campaspe*
2. Kyd — *Spanish Tragedy*
3. Marlowe — *Dr. Faustus*
4. Greene — *Friar Bacon and Friar Bungay*
5. Peele — *Old Wives Tale*
6. Shakespeare — A History, a Comedy, a Tragedy
7. Jonson — *Poetaster*
8. Beaumont and Fletcher — *Philaster*
9. Webster — *White Devil*
10. Middleton — *Changeling*

Prose Fiction

1. Lyly — *Euphues*
2. Greene — *Pandosto*
3. Lodge — *Rosalynde*
4. Nashe — *Unfortunate Traveler*
5. Sidney — *Arcadia*

PURITAN AGE

Prose

1. Taylor — *Holy Living* and *Holy Dying*
2. Walton — *Compleat Angler*

ELIZABETHAN AND PURITAN PERIODS

DRAMATIC NARRATIVE AND LYRIC

During the sixteenth century English life experienced a tremendous expansion. After the long and exhausting Wars of the Roses and the religious struggles of the Reformation, the return of peace and the triumph of Protestantism under Elizabeth stimulated patriotism and opened the way for important cultural influences from without. The Elizabethan age was characterized by a thirst for knowledge of the Greek and Latin Classics, an appetite for adventure and discovery, a love of beauty, and a longing for unlimited self-expression. The desire to make Classical culture prevail is called Humanism; the general broadening of interest, the Renaissance.

These aspects of life and thought are mirrored with fidelity in literature. The drama, the chief glory of Elizabethan literature, reflects both in form and in subject-matter the tendencies of the age. The new joy of living finds expression in a host of lyric poems scattered through the anthologies, plays, and prose romances that have survived, the remains doubtless of a larger number. Though preserving traces of the older native tradition, English lyric poetry of the Renaissance owes much to the love poetry of France and Italy, which had already taken up and elaborated the Classical conventions. Narrative verse, notably Spenser's *Faerie Queene,* also shows a blending of native elements with material derived from French, Italian, or directly from Classical sources. The English Renaissance was essentially a poetic age. In fact, much of the prose of Lyly, Sidney, and others is fundamentally poetic. Prose deals with more varied themes than formerly, and the style becomes less awkward as the English language increases in polish and flexibility. Elizabethan prose represents the highest development of the older tradition and is enriched by foreign devices in style, such as Euphuism, and in form, such as pastoralism.

Even during the Renaissance the strongly moral tone of the English character at times reacted against the unrestrained love of beauty in all its forms which marked the period, and although the rich and varied humanity of English life did not wholly disappear after the death of Elizabeth, the dominant note became more and more the serious and severe dignity of the Puritan, until the return of Charles II in 1660 inaugurated a new era. After 1600 the drama decays, and in 1642 the theaters are closed by act of Parliament. Lyric poetry falls more and more definitely into two groups — religious, composed under the influence of the spirited controversies between the Anglicans and the Puritans; and profane, carrying on, often with artificial elaboration, the themes of the preceding generation. Narrative poetry consists generally of long and usually uninspired romances or epics — insignificant predecessors of Milton's *Paradise Lost.* Prose abandons the worldly subjects popular during the reign of Elizabeth, and deals generally with various aspects of the Christian religion. In the hands of such writers as Sir Thomas Browne the form is more significant than the content, the style attaining a magnificence scarcely to be equalled elsewhere in English prose. Out of the prose of the Puritan age develop, especially in the side-current of journalism, the beginnings of modern prose, which were to take definite form during the Restoration.

RENAISSANCE

POETRY

Sir Thomas Wyatt (1503?–1542)

SONNETS

THE LOVER FOR SHAMEFASTNESS HIDETH HIS DESIRE WITHIN HIS FAITHFUL HEART

The longè love, that in my thought I harbor,
And in my heart doth keep his residence,
Into my face presseth with bold pretence,
And there campeth, displaying his banner.
She that me learns to love, and to suffer,
And wills that my trust, and lust's negligence
Be reined by reason, shame, and reverence,
With his hardiness takes displeasure.
Wherewith love to the heart's forest he fleeth,
Leaving his enterprise with pain and cry,
And there him hideth and not appeareth.
What may I do, when my master feareth,
But in the field with him to live and die?
For good is the life, ending faithfully.

1557

THE LOVER UNHAPPY BIDDETH HAPPY LOVERS REJOICE IN MAY, WHILE HE WAILETH THAT MONTH TO HIM MOST UNLUCKY

Ye that in love find luck and sweet abundance,
And live in lust of joyful jollity,
Arise, for shame, do way your sluggardy:
Arise, I say, do May some observance.
Let me in bed lie, dreaming of mischance;
Let me remember my mishaps unhappy,
That me betide in May most commonly;
As one whom love list little to advance.
Stephan said true, that my nativity
Mischancèd was with the ruler of May.
He guessed, I prove, of that the verity.
In May my wealth, and eke my wits, I say,
Have stood so oft in such perplexity:
Joy, let me dream of your felicity.

1557

THE LOVER COMPARETH HIS STATE TO A SHIP IN PERILOUS STORM TOSSED ON THE SEA

My galley chargèd with forgetfulness,
Through sharpè seas, in winter nights doth pass,
'Tween rock and rock; and eke my foe, alas,
That is my lord, steereth with cruelness,
And every hour, a thought in readiness,
As though that death were light in such a case.
An endless wind doth tear the sail apace
Of forcèd sighs, and trusty fearfulness.
A rain of tears, a cloud of dark disdain
Have done the wearied cords great hinderance.
Wreathèd with error, and with ignorance.
The stars be hid that led me to this pain,
Drownèd is reason that should me comfort,
And I remain, despairing of the port.

1557

THE LOVER LAMENTS THE DEATH OF HIS LOVE

The pillar perisht is whereto I leant,
The strongest stay of mine unquiet mind;
The like of it no man again can find,
From east to west still seeking though he went.
To mine unhap, for hap away hath rent
Of all my joy the very bark and rind,
And I, alas, by chance am thus assigned
Daily to mourn, till death do it relent.
But since that thus it is by destiny,
What can I more but have a woful heart,
My pen in plaint, my voice in careful cry,
My mind in woe, my body full of smart,
And I myself, myself always to hate,
Till dreadful death do ease my doleful state?

1557

A RENOUNCING OF LOVE

Farewell, Love, and all thy laws for ever,
Thy baited hooks shall tangle me no more;
Senec and Plato call me from thy lore
To perfect wealth, my wit for to endeavor.
In blind error when I did persèver,
Thy sharp repulse, that pricketh aye so sore,
Taught me in trifles that I set no store,
But 'scape forth thence, since liberty is lever.
Therefore, farewell, go trouble younger hearts,
And in me claim no more authority.
With idle youth go use thy property,
And thereon spend thy many brittle darts;
For, hitherto though I have lost my time,
Me list no longer rotten boughs to climb.

1557

THE LOVER DESPAIRING TO ATTAIN UNTO HIS LADY'S GRACE RELINQUISHETH THE PURSUIT

Whoso list to hunt, I know where is an hind!
But as for me, alas, I may no more,
The vain travail hath wearied me so sore;
I am of them that furthest come behind.
Yet may I by no means my wearied mind
Draw from the deer; but, as she fleeth afore,
Fainting I follow. I leave off therefore,
Since in a net I seek to hold the wind.
Who list her hunt, I put him out of doubt,
As well as I, may spend his time in vain.
And, graven with diamonds in letters plain,
There is written her fair neck round about:
'*Noli me tangere;* for Cæsar's I am,
And wildè for to hold, though I seem tame.'

1557

THE DESERTED LOVER CONSOLETH HIMSELF WITH REMEMBRANCE THAT ALL WOMEN ARE BY NATURE FICKLE

Divers doth use, as I have heard and know,
When that to change their ladies do begin,
To mourn, and wail, and never for to lynn,
Hoping thereby to 'pease their painful woe.
And some there be that when it chanceth so
That women change, and hate where love hath been,
They call them false, and think with words to win
The hearts of them which other where doth grow.
But as for me, though that by chance indeed
Change hath outworn the favour that I had,
I will not wail, lament, nor yet be sad,
Nor call her false that falsely did me feed;
But let it pass, and think it is of kind
That often change doth please a woman's mind.

DATE UNCERTAIN

THE LOVER TAUGHT, MISTRUSTETH ALLUREMENTS

It may be good, like it who list;
But I do doubt, who can me blame?
For oft assured, yet have I mist,
And now again I fear the same.
The words that from your mouth last came,
Of sudden change, make me aghast:
For dread to fall I stand not fast.

Alas, I tread an endless maze,
That seek t'accord two contraries,
And hope thus still, and nothing has,
Imprisonèd in liberties,
As one unheard, and still that cries,
Always thirsty, and nought doth taste:
For dread to fall I stand not fast.

Assured, I doubt I be not sure,
Should I then trust unto such surety,
That oft have put the proof in ure
And never yet have found it trusty?
Nay, sir, in faith, it were great folly.
And yet my life thus do I waste:
For dread to fall I stand not fast.

1557

THE LOVER SENDETH HIS COMPLAINTS AND TEARS TO SUE FOR GRACE

Pass forth, my wonted cries,
Those cruel ears to pierce,
Which in most hateful wise
Do still my plaints reverse.
Do you, my tears, also
So wet her barren heart,
That pity there may grow,
And cruelty depart.

For though hard rocks among
She seems to have been bred,
And of the tiger long
Been nourishèd and fed;
Yet shall that nature change,
If pity once win place,
Whom as unknown and strange
She now away doth chace.

And as the water soft,
Without forcing or strength,
Where that it falleth oft,
Hard stones doth pierce at length;
So in her stony heart
My plaints at last shall grave,
And, rigor set apart,
Win grant of that I crave.

Wherefore, my plaints, present
Still so to her my suit,
As ye, through her assent,
May bring to me some fruit.
And as she shall me prove,
So bid her me regard,
And render love for love,
Which is a just reward.

1557

THE LOVER COMPLAINETH THE UNKINDNESS OF HIS LOVE

My lute, awake, perform the last
Labour that thou and I shall waste,
And end that I have now begun;
And when this song is sung and past,
My lute, be still, for I have done.

As to be heard where ear is none,
As lead to grave in marble stone,
My song may pierce her heart as soon.
Should we then sigh, or sing, or moan?
No, no, my lute, for I have done.

The rocks do not so cruelly
Repulse the waves continually,
As she my suit and affection;
So that I am past remedy,
Whereby my lute and I have done.

Proud of the spoil that thou hast got
Of simple hearts through Lovès shot,
By whom unkind thou hast them won,
Think not he hath his bow forgot,
Although my lute and I have done.

Vengeance shall fall on thy disdain,
That makest but game on earnest pain;
Think not alone under the sun
Unquit to cause thy lovers playn,
Although my lute and I have done.

May chance thee lie withered and old,
In winter nights that are so cold,
Playning in vain unto the moon;
Thy wishes then dare not be told.
Care then who list, for I have done.

And then may chance thee to repent
The time that thou hast lost and spent
To cause thy lovers sigh and swoon;
Then shalt thou know beauty but lent,
And wish and want, as I have done.

Now cease, my lute, this is the last
Labour that thou and I shall waste,
And ended is that we begun;
Now is the song both sung and past,
My lute, be still, for I have done.

1557

THE LOVER'S LUTE CANNOT BE BLAMED, THOUGH IT SING OF HIS LADY'S UNKINDNESS

Blame not my lute, for he must sound
Of this or that as liketh me;
For lack of wit the lute is bound
To give such tunes as pleaseth me;
Though my songs be somewhat strange,
And speak such words as touch thy change,
Blame not my lute.

My lute, alas, doth not offend,
Though that perforce he must agree
To sound such tunes as I intend
To sing to them that heareth me;
Then though my songs be somewhat plain,
And toucheth some that use to feign,
Blame not my lute.

My lute and strings may not deny,
But as I strike they must obey;
Break not them then so wrongfully,
But break thyself some other way;
And though the songs which I indite
Do quit thy change with rightful spite,
Blame not my lute.

Spite asketh spite, and changing change,
And falsèd faith must needs be known;
And faults so great, the cause so strange;
Of right it must abroad be blown;
Then since that by thine own desert
My songs do tell how true thou art,
Blame not my lute.

Blame but thyself that hast misdone,
And well deservèd to have blame;
Change thou thy way, so evil begone,
And then my lute shall sound that same;
But if till then my fingers play,
By thy desert their wonted way,
Blame not my lute.

Farewell! unknown; for though thou break
My strings in spite with great disdain,
Yet have I found out, for thy sake,
Strings for to string my lute again:
And if perchance this silly rhyme
Do make thee blush, at any time,
Blame not my lute.

1524–1527?

THE LOVER BESEECHETH HIS MISTRESS NOT TO FORGET HIS STEADFAST FAITH AND TRUE INTENT

Forget not yet the tried intent
Of such a truth as I have meant;
My great travail so gladly spent,
Forget not yet!

Forget not yet when first began
The weary life ye know, since when
The suit, the service none tell can;
Forget not yet!

Forget not yet the great assays,
The cruel wrong, the scornful ways,
The painful patience in delays,
Forget not yet!

Forget not yet, forget not this! —
How long ago hath been, and is,
The mind that never meant amiss;
Forget not yet!

Forget not then thine own approved,
The which so long hath thee so loved,
Whose steadfast faith yet never moved:
Forget not this!

1524–1527?

HE COMPLAINETH TO HIS HEART THAT HAVING ONCE RECOVERED HIS FREEDOM HE HAD AGAIN BECOME THRALL TO LOVE

Ah, my heart, what aileth thee
To set so light my liberty,
Making me bond when I was free?
Ah, my heart, what aileth thee?

When thou were rid from all distress,
Void of all pain and pensiveness,
To choose again a new mistress,
Ah, my heart, what aileth thee?

When thou were well, thou could not hold;
To turn again, that were too bold;
Thus to renew my sorrows old,
Ah, my heart, what aileth thee?

Thou know'st full well that but of late
I was turned out of Lovès gate;
And now to guide me to this mate,
Ah, my heart, what aileth thee?

I hoped full well all had been done;
But now my hope is ta'en and won;
To my torment to yield so soon,
Ah, my heart, what aileth thee?

Date uncertain

OF HIS LOVE CALLED ANNA

What word is that, that changeth not,
Though it be turned and made in twain?
It is mine Anna, God it wot,
The only causer of my pain,
My love that meedeth with disdain.
Yet is it loved, what will you more?
It is my salve, and eke my sore.

1557

Henry Howard, Earl of Surrey (1516?–1547)

DESCRIPTION OF THE RESTLESS STATE OF A LOVER, WITH SUIT TO HIS LADY, TO RUE ON HIS DYING HEART

The sun hath twice brought forth his tender green,
And clad the earth in lively lustiness;
Once have the winds the trees despoilèd clean,
And new again begins their cruelness;
Since I have hid under my breast the harm
That never shall recover healthfulness.
The winter's hurt recovers with the warm,
The parchèd green restored is with the shade.
What warmth, alas, may serve for to disarm
The frozen heart that mine in flame hath made?
What cold again is able to restore
My fresh green years, that wither thus and fade?
Alas, I see, nothing hath hurt so sore,
But time in time reduceth a return;
In time my harm increaseth more and more,
And seems to have my cure always in scorn.
Strange kinds of death, in life that I do try,
At hand to melt, far off in flame to burn;
And like as time list to my cure apply,
So doth each place my comfort clean refuse.
All thing alive that seeth the heavens with eye
With cloak of night may cover and excuse
Itself from travail of the day's unrest,
Save I, alas, against all others' use,
That then stir up the torments of my breast,
And curse each star as causer of my fate.
And when the sun hath eke the dark opprest,
And brought the day, it doth nothing abate
The travails of mine endless smart and pain;
For then, as one that hath the light in hate,
I wish for night, more covertly to plain,
And me withdraw from every haunted place,
Lest by my cheer my chance appear too plain.
And in my mind I measure, pace by pace,
To seek the place where I myself had lost,
That day that I was tangled in the lace,
In seeming slack, that knitteth ever most.
But never yet the travail of my thought
Of better state could catch a cause to boast;
For if I found, sometime that I have sought,
Those stars by whom I trusted of the port,
My sails do fall, and I advance right nought,
As anchored fast, my spirits do all resort
To stand agazed, and sink in more and more
The deadly harm which she doth take in sport.
Lo, if I seek, how do I find my sore!
And if I flee I carry with me still
The venomed shaft, which doth his force restore
By haste of flight, and I may plain my fill
Unto myself, unless this careful song

Print in your heart some parcel of my teen;
For I, alas, in silence all too long
Of mine old hurt yet feel the wound but green.
Rue on my life, or else your cruel wrong
Shall well appear, and by my death be seen!

1557

PRISONED IN WINDSOR, HE RECOUNTETH HIS PLEASURE THERE PASSED

So cruel prison how could betide, alas,
As proud Windsor? where I, in lust and joy,
With a king's son, my childish years did pass,
In greater feast than Priam's sons of Troy:

Where each sweet place returns a taste full sour,
The large green courts where we were wont to hove,
With eyes cast up into the Maiden's Tower,
And easy sighs such as folk draw in love:

The stately seats, the ladies bright of hue,
The dances short, long tales of great delight,
With words and looks that tigers could but rue,
Where each of us did plead the other's right:

The palm-play, where, despoilèd for the game,
With dazèd eyes oft we by gleams of love,
Have missed the ball and got sight of our dame,
To bait her eyes, which kept the leads above:

The gravel ground, with sleeves tied on the helm,
On foaming horse, with swords and friendly hearts;
With cheer, as though one should another whelm,
Where we have fought, and chasèd oft with darts:

With silver drops the mead yet spread for ruth,
In active games of nimbleness and strength,
Where we did strain, trainèd with swarms of youth,
Our tender limbs that yet shot up in length:

The secret groves which oft we made resound
Of pleasant plaint, and of our ladies' praise,
Recording oft what grace each one had found,
What hope of speed, what dread of long delays:

The wild forest, the clothèd holts with green,
With reins availed and swift ybreathèd horse,
With cry of hounds, and merry blasts between,
Where we did chase the fearful hart of force:

The wide vales, eke, that harboured us each night,
Wherewith, alas, reviveth in my breast,
The sweet accord such sleeps as yet delight,
The pleasant dreams, the quiet bed of rest:

The secret thoughts imparted with such trust,
The wanton talk, the divers change of play,
The friendship sworn, each promise kept so just,
Wherewith we passed the winter nights away.

And with this thought, the blood forsakes the face;
The tears berain my cheeks of deadly hue,
The which, as soon as sobbing sighs, alas,
Upsuppèd have, thus I my plaint renew:

O place of bliss, renewer of my woes,
Give me accompt, where is my noble fere,
Whom in thy walls, thou dost each night inclose,
To other lief, but unto me most dear:

Echo, alas, that doth my sorrow rue,
Returns thereto a hollow sound of plaint.
Thus I alone, where all my freedom grew,
In prison pine with bondage and restraint

And with remembrance of the greater grief,
To banish the less, I find my chief relief.

1557

COMPLAINT OF THE ABSENCE OF HER LOVER BEING UPON THE SEA

O HAPPY dames, that may embrace
The fruit of your delight,
Help to bewail the woeful case,
And eke the heavy plight,
Of me, that wonted to rejoice
The fortune of my pleasant choice:
Good ladies, help to fill my mourning voice.

In ship, freight with rememberance
Of thoughts and pleasures past,
He sails that hath in governance
My life, while it will last;
With scalding sighs, for lack of gale,
Furthering his hope, that is his sail,
Toward me, the sweet port of his avail.

Alas, how oft in dreams I see
Those eyes that were my food,
Which sometime so delighted me
That yet they do me good;
Wherewith I wake with his return,
Whose absent flame did make me burn:
But when I find the lack, Lord, how I mourn!

When other lovers in arms across,
Rejoice their chief delight,
Drownèd in tears to mourn my loss,
I stand the bitter night
In my window, where I may see
Before the winds how the clouds flee:
Lo, what a mariner love hath made me!

And in green waves when the salt flood
Doth rise by rage of wind,
A thousand fancies in that mood
Assail my restless mind.
Alas, now drencheth my sweet foe,
That with the spoil of my heart did go,
And left me; but, alas, why did he so?

And when the seas wax calm again,
To chase from me annoy,
My doubtful hope doth cause me plain;
So dread cuts off my joy.
Thus is my wealth mingled with woe,
And of each thought a doubt doth grow;
Now he comes! will he come? alas, no, no!

1557

THE LOVER EXCUSETH HIMSELF OF SUSPECTED CHANGE

Though I regarded not
The promise made by me
Or passèd not to spot
My faith and honesty,
Yet were my fancy strange,
And wilful will to wite,
If I sought now to change
A falcon for a kite.

All men might well dispraise
My wit and enterprise,
If I esteemed a pease
Above a pearl in price,
Or judged the owl in sight
The sparhawk to excel,
Which flieth but in the night,
As all men know right well.

Or if I sought to sail
Into the brittle port,
Where anchor hold doth fail,
To such as do resort,
And leave the haven sure,
Where blows no blustering wind,
Nor fickleness in ure,
So far-forth as I find.

No, think me not so light,
Nor of so churlish kind,
Though it lay in my might
My bondage to unbind,
That I would leave the hind
To hunt the gander's foe.
No, no, I have no mind
To make exchanges so.

Nor yet to change at all;
For think, it may not be
That I should seek to fall
From my felicity,
Desirous for to win
And loth for to forego,
Or new change to begin —
How may all this be so?

The fire it cannot freeze,
For it is not his kind,
Nor true love cannot lese
The constance of the mind;
Yet as soon shall the fire
Want heat to blaze and burn,
As I in such desire
Have once a thought to turn.

1557

THE MEANS TO ATTAIN HAPPY LIFE

Martial, the things that do attain
The happy life, be these, I find:
The riches left, not got with pain,
The fruitful ground, the quiet mind;

The egall friend, no grudge, no strife,
No charge of rule, nor governance,
Without disease the healthful life,
The household of continuance;

The mean diet, no delicate fare,
True wisdom joined with simpleness,
The night dischargèd of all care,
Where wine the wit may not oppress;

The faithful wife, without debate,
Such sleeps as may beguile the night:
Contented with thine own estate,
Ne wish for death, ne fear his might.

1557

OF THE DEATH OF SIR T[HOMAS] W[YATT]

W. Resteth here, that quick could never rest;
Whose heavenly gifts encreasèd by disdain,
And virtue sank the deeper in his breast;
Such profit he by envy could obtain.

A head, where wisdom mysteries did frame,
Whose hammers beat still in that lively brain,
As on a stithe, where that some work of fame
Was daily wrought, to turn to Britain's gain.

A visage stern and mild, where both did grow,
Vice to contemn, in virtue to rejoice;
Amid great storms, whom grace assurèd so,
To live upright and smile at fortune's choice.

A hand that taught what might be said in rime,
That reft Chaucer the glory of his wit,
A mark, the which (unperfected, for time)
Some may approach, but never none shall hit.

A tongue that served in foreign realms his king,
Whose courteous talk to virtue did enflame
Each noble heart, a worthy guide to bring
Our English youth by travail unto fame.

An eye, whose judgment none affect could blind,
Friends to allure, and foes to reconcile,
Whose piercing look did represent a mind
With virtue fraught, reposèd, void of guile.

A heart, where dread was never so imprest,
To hide the thought that might the truth advance,
In neither fortune lost nor yet represt,
To swell in wealth or yield unto mischance.

A valiant corse, where force and beauty met,
Happy, alas, too happy, but for foes,
Livèd, and ran the race that Nature set,
Of manhood's shape, where she the mold did lose.

But to the heavens that simple soul is fled,
Which left, with such as covet Christ to know,
Witness of faith that never shall be dead,
Sent for our health, but not receivèd so.
Thus, for our guilt, this jewel have we lost;
The earth his bones, the heavens possess his ghost.

1557

HOW NO AGE IS CONTENT WITH HIS OWN ESTATE, AND HOW THE AGE OF CHILDREN IS THE HAPPIEST, IF THEY HAD SKILL TO UNDERSTAND IT

Laid in my quiet bed, in study as I were,
I saw within my troubled head a heap of thoughts appear;
And every thought did show so lively in mine eyes,
That now I sighed, and then I smiled, as cause of thought doth rise.
I saw the little boy in thought, how oft that he
Did wish of God to scape the rod, a tall young man to be;
The young man eke that feels his bones with pains opprest,
How he would be a rich old man, to live and lie at rest;
The rich old man that sees his end draw on so sore,
How he would be a boy again, to live so much the more.
Whereat full oft I smiled, to see how all these three,
From boy to man, from man to boy, would chop and change degree.
And musing thus I think, the case is very strange,
That man from wealth, to live in woe, doth ever seek to change.
Thus thoughtful as I lay, I saw my withered skin,
How it doth shew my dented chews, the flesh was worn so thin.
And eke my toothless chaps, the gates of my right way,
That opes and shuts as I do speak, do thus unto me say:
'Thy white and hoarish hairs, the messengers of age,
That shew, like lines of true belief, that this life doth assuage,
Bid thee lay hand, and feel them hanging on thy chin,
The which do write two ages past, the third now coming in.
Hang up therefore the bit of thy young wanton time,
And thou that therein beaten art, the happiest life define.'
Whereat I sighed and said: 'Farewell, my wonted joy,
Truss up thy pack, and trudge from me to every little boy,
And tell them thus from me, their time most happy is,
If, to their time, they reason had, to know the truth of this.'

1557

SONNETS

DESCRIPTION OF SPRING, WHEREIN EACH THING RENEWS, SAVE ONLY THE LOVER

The soote season, that bud and bloom forth brings,
With green hath clad the hill and eke the vale;
The nightingale with feathers new she sings;
The turtle to her make hath told her tale:
Summer is come, for every spray now springs;
The hart hath hung his old head on the pale;
The buck in brake his winter coat he flings;
The fishes flete with new repairèd scale;
The adder all her slough away she slings;
The swift swallow pursueth the flies smale;
The busy bee her honey now she mings;
Winter is worn, that was the flowers' bale.
And thus I see among these pleasant things
Each care decays, and yet my sorrow springs!

1557

DESCRIPTION AND PRAISE OF HIS LOVE GERALDINE

From Tuscan came my lady's worthy race;
Fair Florence was sometime her ancient seat;
The Western isle, whose pleasant shore doth face
Wild Camber's cliffs, did give her lively heat;
Fostered she was with milk of Irish breast,
Her sire an earl, her dame of princes' blood;
From tender years, in Britain she doth rest,
With king's child, where she tasteth costly food;
Hunsdon did first present her to mine eyen;
Bright is her hue, and Geraldine she hight;
Hampton me taught to wish her first for mine;
And Windsor, alas, doth chase me from her sight:
Her beauty of kind, her virtues from above,
Happy is he that can obtain her love!

1557

VOW TO LOVE FAITHFULLY HOWSOEVER HE BE REWARDED

Set me whereas the sun doth parch the green,
Or where his beams do not dissolve the ice;
In temperate heat, where he is felt and seen;
In presence prest of people, mad or wise:
Set me in high, or yet in low degree;
In longest night, or in the shortest day;
In clearest sky, or where clouds thickest be;
In lusty youth, or when my hairs are gray:
Set me in heaven, in earth, or else in hell;
In hill, or dale, or in the foaming flood;
Thrall, or at large, alive whereso I dwell;
Sick or in health, in evil fame or good:
Hers will I be, and only with this thought
Content myself, although my chance be naught.

1557

VIRGIL'S ÆNEID, BK. II

PRINCE ÆNEAS LOSES CREUSA

When I had said these words, my shoulders broad,
And laièd neck with garments gan I spread,
And thereon cast a yellow lion's skin;
And thereupon my burden I receive.
Young Iulus claspèd in my right hand,
Followeth me fast with unequal pace;
And at my back my wife. Thus did we pass
By places shadowèd most with the night.
And me, whom late the dart which enemies threw,
Nor press of Argive routs could make amazed,
Each whispering wind hath power now to fray,
And every sound to move my doubtful mind:
So much I dread my burden, and my fere.
And now we gan draw near unto the gate,
Right well escaped the danger, as me thought,
When that at hand a sound of feet we heard.
My father then, gazing throughout the dark,
Criėd on me, 'Flee, son! they are at hand.'
With that bright shields, and shene armours I saw.
But then I know not what unfriendly God
My troubled wit from me bereft for fear:
For while I ran by the most secret streets,
Eschewing still the common haunted track,
From me caitiff, alas! bereavèd was
Creusa then, my spouse, I wot not how;
Whether by fate, or missing of the way,
Or that she was by weariness retained:
But never sith these eyes might her behold;
Nor did I yet perceive that she was lost,
Ne never backward turnèd I my mind,
Till we came to the hill, whereas there stood
The old temple dedicate to Ceres.
And when that we were there assembled all,
She was only away, deceiving us
Her spouse, her son, and all her company.
What God or man did I not then accuse,
Near woode for ire? or what more cruel chance

Did hap to me, in all Troy's overthrow?
Ascanius to my feres I then betook,
With Anchises, and eke the Troyan Gods.
And left them hid within a valley deep.
And to the town I gan me hie again,
Clad in bright arms, and bent for to renew
Adventures past, to search throughout the town,
And yield my head to perils once again.
  And first the walls and dark entry I sought
Of the same gate whereat I issued out;
Holding backward the steps where we had come
In the dark night, looking all round about:
In every place the ugsome sights I saw;
The silence self of night aghast my sprite.
From hence again I passed unto our house,
If she by chance had been returnèd home.
The Greeks were there, and had it all beset:
The wasting fire, blown up by drift of wind,
Above the roofs the blazing flame sprang up;
The sound whereof with fury pierced the skies.
To Priam's palace, and the castle then
I made; and there at Juno's sanctuair,
In the void porches, Phenix, Ulysses eke
Stern guardians stood, watching of the spoil.
The riches here were set, reft from the brent
Temples of Troy: the tables of the Gods,
The vessels eke that were of massy gold,
And vestures spoiled, were gathered all in heap:
The children orderly, and mothers pale for fright,
Long rangèd on a row stood round about.
  So bold was I to show my voice that night
With clepes and cries to fill the streets throughout,
With Creuse' name in sorrow, with vain tears;
And often sithes the same for to repeat.
The town restless with fury as I sought,
Th' unlucky figure of Creusa's ghost,
Of stature more than wont, stood 'fore mine eyen.
Abashèd then I woxe: therewith my hair
Gan start right up: my voice stack in my throat:
When with such words she gan my heart remove:
'What helps, to yield unto such furious rage,
Sweet spouse?' quod she, 'Without will of the Gods
This chancèd not: ne lawful was for thee
To lead away Creusa hence with thee:
The King of the high heaven suffereth it not.
A long exile thou art assigned to bear,
Long to furrow large space of stormy seas:
So shalt thou reach at last Hesperian land,
Where Lidian Tiber with his gentle stream
Mildly doth flow along the fruitful fields.
There mirthful wealth, there kingdom is for thee;
There a king's child prepared to be thy make.
For thy beloved Creusa stint thy tears:
For now shall I not see the proud abodes
Of Myrmidons, nor yet of Dolopes:
Ne I, a Troyan lady, and the wife
Unto the son of Venus, the Goddess,
Shall go a slave to serve the Greekish dames.
Me here the God's great mother holds.
And now farewell: and keep in father's breast
The tender love of thy young son and mine.'
  Thus having said, she left me all in tears,
And minding much to speak; but she was gone,
And subtly fled into the weightless air.
Thrice raught I with mine arms t'accoll her neck:
Thrice did my hands vain hold th' image escape,
Like nimble winds, and like the flying dream.
So night spent out, return I to my feres;
And there wondering I find together swarmed
A new number of mates, mothers, and men,
A rout exiled, a wretched multitude,
From each-where flock together, prest to pass
With heart and goods, to whatsoever land
By sliding seas, me listed them to lead.
And now rose Lucifer above the ridge
Of lusty Ide, and brought the dawning light.
The Greeks held th' entries of the gates beset:
Of help there was no hope. Then gave I place,
Took up my sire, and hasted to the hill.

1557

Thomas Sackville, Lord Buckhurst
(1536–1608)

THE INDUCTION

TO *A Mirror for Magistrates*

The wrathful Winter, 'proaching on apace,
With blustering blasts had all ybared the treen,
And old Saturnus, with his frosty face,
With chilling cold had pierced the tender green;

The mantles rent, wherein enwrappèd been
The gladsome groves that now lay overthrown,
The tapets torn, and every bloom down blown.

The soil, that erst so seemly was to seen,
Was all despoilèd of her beauty's hue;
And soote fresh flowers, wherewith the summer's queen
Had clad the earth, now Boreas' blasts down blew;
And small fowls flocking, in their song did rue
The winter's wrath, wherewith each thing defaced
In woeful wise bewailed the summer past.

Hawthorn had lost his motley livery,
The naked twigs were shivering all for cold,
And dropping down the tears abundantly;
Each thing, methought, with weeping eye me told
The cruel season, bidding me withhold
Myself within; for I was gotten out
Into the fields, whereas I walked about.

When lo, the night with misty mantles spread,
Gan dark the day, and dim the azure skies;
And Venus in her message Hermes sped
To bloody Mars, to will him not to rise,
While she herself approached in speedy wise;
And Virgo hiding her disdainful breast,
With Thetis now had laid her down to rest.

Whiles Scorpio dreading Sagittarius' dart,
Whose bow prest bent in fight, the string had slipped,
Down slid into the ocean flood apart,
The Bear, that in the Irish seas had dipped
His grisly feet, with speed from thence he whipped:
For Thetis, hasting from the Virgin's bed,
Pursued the Bear, that ere she came was fled.

And Phaeton now, near reaching to his race
With glist'ring beams, gold streaming where they bent,
Was prest to enter in his resting place:
Erythius, that in the cart first went,
Had even now attained his journey's stent:
And, fast declining, hid away his head,
While Titan couched him in his purple bed.

And pale Cynthea, with her borrowed light,
Beginning to supply her brother's place,
Was past the noonstead six degrees in sight
When sparkling stars amid the heaven's face,
With twinkling light shone on the earth apace,
That, while they brought about the nightès chare,
The dark had dimmed the day ere I was ware.

And sorrowing I to see the summer flowers,
The lively green, the lusty leas forlorn,
The sturdy trees so shattered with the showers,
The fields so fade, that flourished so beforn,
It taught me well, all earthly things be born
To die the death, for naught long time may last;
The summer's beauty yields to winter's blast.

Then looking upward to the heaven's leams,
With nightes stars thick powdered everywhere,
Which erst so glistened with the golden streams
That cheerful Phœbus spread down from his sphere,
Beholding dark oppressing day so near:
The sudden sight reducèd to my mind,
The sundry changes that in earth we find.

That musing on this worldly wealth in thought,
Which comes, and goes, more faster than we see
The flickering flame that with the fire is wrought,
My busy mind presented unto me
Such fall of peers as in this realm had be;
That oft I wished some would their woes descrive,
To warn the rest whom fortune left alive.

And straight forth stalking with redoubled pace,
For that I saw the night drew on so fast,
In black all clad, there fell before my face
A piteous wight, whom woe had all forewaste;
Forth from her eyen the crystal tears out brast;
And sighing sore, her hands she wrung and fold,
Tare all her hair, that ruth was to behold.

Her body small, forewithered, and forespent,
As is the stalk that summer's drought oppressed;
Her welkèd face wih woeful tears besprent;

Her color pale; and, as it seemed her best.
In woe and plaint reposèd was her rest;
And, as the stone that drops of water wears,
So dented were her cheeks with fall of tears.

Her eyes swollen with flowing streams afloat,
Wherewith, her looks thrown up full piteously,
Her forceless hands together oft she smote,
With doleful shrieks, that echoed in the sky;
Whose plaint such sighs did straight accompany,
That, in my doom, was never man did see
A wight but half so woe-begone as she.

I stood aghast, beholding all her plight,
'Tween dread and dolor, so distrained in heart,
That, while my hairs upstarted with the sight,
The tears outstreamed for sorrow of her smart:
But, when I saw no end that could apart
The deadly dewle which she so sore did make,
With doleful voice then thus to her I spake:

'Unwrap thy woes, whatever wight thou be,
And stint in time to spill thyself with plaint:
Tell what thou art, and whence, for well I see
Thou canst not dure, with sorrow thus attaint':
And, with that word of sorrow, all forefaint
She lookèd up, and, prostrate as she lay,
With piteous sound, lo, thus she gan to say:

'Alas, I wretch, whom thus thou seest distrained
With wasting woes, that never shall aslake,
Sorrow I am, in endless torments pained
Among the Furies in the infernal lake,
Where Pluto, god of hell, so grisly black,
Doth hold his throne, and Lethe's deadly taste
Doth reave remembrance of each thing forepast:

'Whence come I am, the dreary destiny
And luckless lot for to bemoan of those
Whom fortune, in this maze of misery,
Of wretched chance, most woeful mirrors chose;
That, when thou seest how lightly they did lose
Their pomp, their power, and that they thought most sure,
Thou mayst soon deem no earthly joy may dure.'

Whose rueful voice no sooner had out brayed
Those woeful words wherewith she sorrowed so
But 'Out, alas!' she shright, and never stayed,
Fell down, and all to-dashed herself for woe:
The cold pale dread my limbs gan overgo,
And I so sorrowed at her sorrows eft,
That, what with grief and fear, my wits were reft.

I stretched myself, and straight my heart revives,
That dread and dolor erst did so appale;
Like him that with the fervent fever strives,
When sickness seeks his castle health to scale;
With gathered spirits so forced I fear to avale:
And, rearing her, with anguish all foredone,
My spirits returned, and then I thus begun:

'O Sorrow, alas, sith Sorrow is thy name,
And that to thee this drear doth well pertain,
In vain it were to seek to cease the same:
But, as a man himself with sorrow slain,
So I, alas, do comfort thee in pain,
That here in sorrow art foresunk so deep,
That at thy sight I can but sigh and weep.'

I had no sooner spoken of a stike,
But that the storm so rumbled in her breast,
As Æölus could never roar the like;
And showers down rained from her eyen so fast,
That all bedrent the place, till at the last,
Well easèd they the dolor of her mind,
As rage of rain doth swage the stormy wind:

For forth she pacèd in her fearful tale:
'Come, come,' quoth she, 'and see what I shall show,
Come, hear the plaining and the bitter bale
Of worthy men by Fortune overthrow:
Come thou, and see them ruing all in row,
They were but shades that erst in mind thou rolled:
Come, come with me, thine eyes shall them behold.'

What could these words but make me more aghast,
To hear her tell whereon I mused whilere?
So was I mazed therewith, till, at the last,
Musing upon her words, and what they were,

All suddenly well lessoned was my fear;
For to my mind returnèd, how she telled
Both what she was, and where her won she held.

Whereby I knew that she a goddess was,
And, therewithal, resorted to my mind
My thought, that late presented me the glass
Of brittle state, of cares that here we find,
Of thousand woes to silly men assigned:
And how she now bid me come and behold,
To see with eye that erst in thought I rolled.

Flat down I fell, and with all reverence
Adorèd her, perceiving now that she,
A goddess, sent by godly providence,
In earthly shape thus showed herself to me,
To wail and rue this world's uncertainty:
And, while I honored thus her godhead's might
With plaining voice these words to me she shright:

'I shall thee guide first to the grisly lake,
And thence unto the blissful place of rest,
Where thou shalt see, and hear, the plaint they make
That whilom here bare swing among the best:
This shalt thou see: but great is the unrest
That thou must bide, before thou canst attain
Unto the dreadful place where these remain.'

And, with these words, as I upraisèd stood,
And gan to follow her that straight forth paced,
Ere I was ware, into a desert wood
We now were come, where, hand in hand embraced,
She led the way, and through the thick so traced,
As, but I had been guided by her might,
It was no way for any mortal wight.

But lo, while thus amid the desert dark
We passèd on with steps and pace unmeet,
A rumbling roar, confused with howl and bark
Of dogs, shook all the ground under our feet,
And struck the din within our ears so deep,
As, half distraught, unto the ground I fell,
Besought return, and not to visit hell.

But she, forthwith, uplifting me apace,
Removed my dread, and, with a steadfast mind,
Bade me come on; for here was now the place,
The place where we our travail end should find:
Wherewith I rose, and to the place assigned
Astoined I stalk, when straight we approached near
The dreadful place, that you will dread to hear.

An hideous hole all vast, withouten shape,
Of endless depth, o'erwhelmed with ragged stone,
With ugly mouth, and grisly jaws doth gape,
And to our sight confounds itself in one:
Here entered we, and yeding forth, anon
An horrible loathly lake we might discern,
As black as pitch, that clepèd is Avern:

A deadly gulf, where naught but rubbish grows,
With foul black swelth in thickened lumps that lies,
Which up in th' air such stinking vapors throws,
That over there may fly no fowl but dies
Choked with the pestilent savors that arise:
Hither we come; whence forth we still did pace,
In dreadful fear amid the dreadful place:

And, first, within the porch and jaws of hell,
Sat deep Remorse of Conscience, all besprent
With tears; and to herself oft would she tell
Her wretchedness, and cursing never stent
To sob and sigh; but ever thus lament,
With thoughtful care, as she that, all in vain,
Would wear, and waste continually in pain.

Her eyes unsteadfast, rolling here and there,
Whirled on each place, as place that vengeance brought,
So was her mind continually in fear,
Tossed and tormented with the tedious thought
Of those detested crimes which she had wrought;
With dreadful cheer, and looks thrown to the sky,
Wishing for death, and yet she could not die.

Next saw we Dread, all trembling how he shook,
With foot uncertain, proffered here and there:
Benumbed of speech, and, with a ghastly look
Searched every place, all pale and dead for fear,

His cap borne up with staring of his hair,
'Stoined and amazed at his own shade for dread,
And fearing greater dangers than was need.

And next, within the entry of this lake,
Sat fell Revenge, gnashing her teeth for ire,
Devising means how she may vengeance take,
Never in rest, till she have her desire:
But frets within so farforth with the fire
Of wreaking flames, that now determines she
To die by death, or venged by death to be.

When fell Revenge, with bloody foul pretence
Had showed herself, as next in order set,
With trembling limbs we softly parted thence,
Till in our eyes another sight we met:
When from my heart a sigh forthwith I fet,
Ruing, alas! upon the woeful plight
Of Misery, that next appeared in sight.

His face was lean, and somedeal pined away,
And eke his hands consumèd to the bone,
But what his body was, I cannot say,
For on his carcass raiment had he none,
Save clouts and patches, piecèd one by one;
With staff in hand, and scrip on shoulders cast,
His chief defence against the winter's blast.

His food, for most, was wild fruits of the tree,
Unless sometimes some crumbs fell to his share,
Which in his wallet long, God wot, kept he,
As on the which full daint'ly would he fare:
His drink, the running stream; his cup, the bare
Of his palm closed; his bed, the hard cold ground:
To this poor life was Misery ybound.

Whose wretched state when we had well beheld,
With tender ruth on him, and on his fears,
In thoughtful cares forth then our pace we held;
And, by and by, another shape appears,
Of greedy Care, still brushing up the breres,
His knuckles knobbed, his flesh deep dented in,
With tawèd hands, and hard ytannèd skin.

The morrow gray no sooner hath begun
To spread his light, even peeping in our eyes,
When he is up, and to his work yrun:
But let the night's black misty mantles rise,
And with foul dark never so much disguise
The fair bright day, yet ceaseth he no while,
But hath his candles to prolong his toil.

By him lay heavy Sleep, the cousin of Death,
Flat on the ground, and still as any stone,
A very corpse, save yielding forth a breath:
Small keep took he, whom Fortune frownèd on,
Or whom she lifted up into the throne
Of high renown; but, as a living death,
So, dead alive, of life he drew the breath.

The body's rest, the quiet of the heart,
The travail's ease, the still night's fear was he,
And of our life in earth the better part;
Reaver of sight, and yet in whom we see
Things oft that tide, and oft that never be;
Without respect, esteeming equally
King Crœsus' pomp, and Irus' poverty.

And next, in order sad, Old Age we found:
His beard all hoar, his eyes hollow and blind,
With drooping cheer still poring on the ground,
As on the place where Nature him assigned
To rest, when that the Sisters had untwined
His vital thread, and ended with their knife
The fleeting course of fast declining life.

There heard we him with broke and hollow plaint
Rue with himself his end approaching fast,
And all for naught his wretched mind torment
With sweet remembrance of his pleasures past,
And fresh delights of lusty youth forewaste;
Recounting which, how would he sob and shriek,
And to be young again of Jove beseek!

But and the cruel fates so fixèd be,
That time forepast cannot return again,
This one request of Jove yet prayèd he:
That, in such withered plight, and wretched pain,
As eld, accompanied with his loathsome train,
Had brought on him, all were it woe and grief,
He might a while yet linger forth his life,

And not so soon descend into the pit,
Where Death, when he the mortal corpse hath slain,
With reckless hand in grave doth cover it,
Thereafter never to enjoy again
The gladsome light, but in the ground ylain,
In depth of darkness waste and wear to naught,
As he had never into the world been brought.

But who had seen him sobbing, how he stood
Unto himself, and how he would bemoan
His youth forepast, as though it wrought him good
To talk of youth, all were his youth foregone,
He would have mused, and marveled much, whereon
This wretched Age should life desire so fain,
And knows full well life doth but length his pain.

Crookbacked he was, tooth-shaken, and blear-eyed,
Went on three feet, and sometime crept on four,
With old lame bones that rattled by his side,
His scalp all pilled, and he with eld forlore:
His withered fist still knocking at Death's door,
Fumbling, and driveling, as he draws his breath:
For brief, the shape and messenger of Death.

And fast by him pale Malady was placed,
Sore sick in bed, her color all foregone,
Bereft of stomach, savor, and of taste,
Ne could she brook no meat, but broths alone:
Her breath corrupt, her keepers every one
Abhorring her, her sickness past recure,
Detesting physic, and all physic's cure.

But, oh, the doleful sight that then we see!
We turned our look, and, on the other side,
A grisly shape of Famine might we see,
With greedy looks, and gaping mouth that cried
And roared for meat, as she should there have died;
Her body thin and bare as any bone,
Whereto was left naught but the case alone.

And that, alas, was gnawn on every where,
All full of holes, that I ne might refrain
From tears, to see how she her arms could tear,
And with her teeth gnash on the bones in vain,
When, all for naught, she fain would so sustain
Her starven corpse, that rather seemed a shade,
Than any substance of a creature made.

Great was her force, whom stone wall could not stay,
Her tearing nails snatching at all she saw;
With gaping jaws, that by no means ymay
Be satisfied from hunger of her maw,
But eats herself as she that hath no law:
Gnawing, alas, her carcass all in vain,
Where you may count each sinew, bone, and vein.

On her while we thus firmly fixed our eyes,
That bled for ruth of such a dreary sight,
Lo, suddenly she shrieked in so huge wise,
As made hell-gates to shiver with the might:
Wherewith, a dart we saw, how it did light
Right on her breast, and, therewithal, pale Death
Enthrilling it, to reave her of her breath.

And by and by, a dumb dead corpse we saw,
Heavy, and cold, the shape of Death aright,
That daunts all earthly creatures to his law;
Against whose force in vain it is to fight:
Ne peers, ne princes, nor no mortal wight,
No towns, ne realms, cities, ne strongest tower,
But all, perforce, must yield unto his power.

His dart, anon, out of the corpse he took,
And in his hand (a dreadful sight to see)
With great triumph eftsoons the same he shook,
That most of all my fears affrayèd me:
His body dight with naught but bones, pardé.
The naked shape of man there saw I plain,
All save the flesh, the sinew, and the vein.

Lastly, stood War, in glittering arms yclad,
With visage grim, stern looks, and blackly hued;
In his right hand a naked sword he had,
That to the hilts was all with blood imbrued;
And in his left (that kings and kingdoms rued)
Famine and fire he held, and therewithal
He razèd towns, and threw down towers and all.

Cities he sacked, and realms that whilom flowered
In honor, glory, and rule, above the best,
He overwhelmed, and all their fame devoured,

Consumed, destroyed, wasted and never ceased,
Till he their wealth, their name, and all oppressed:
His face forehewed with wounds, and by his side
There hung his targe, with gashes deep and wide.

In mids of which, depainted there, we found
Deadly Debate, all full of snaky hair,
That with a bloody fillet was ybound,
Out breathing naught but discord everywhere:
And round about were portrayed, here and there,
The hugy hosts, Darius and his power,
His kings, princes, his peers, and all his flower,

Whom great Macedo vanquished there in sight,
With deep slaughter, despoiling all his pride,
Pierced through his realms, and daunted all his might:
Duke Hannibal beheld I there beside,
In Canna's field, victor how he did ride,
And woeful Romans that in vain withstood,
And consul Paulus covered all in blood.

Yet saw I more the fight at Thrasimene,
And Treby field, and eke when Hannibal
And worthy Scipio last in arms were seen
Before Carthago gate, to cry for all
The world's empire, to whom it should befall:
There saw I Pompey and Cæsar clad in arms,
Their hosts allied and all their civil harms:

With conquerors' hands, forebathed in their own blood,
And Cæsar weeping over Pompey's head;
Yet saw I Sulla and Marius where they stood,
Their great cruelty, and the deep bloodshed
Of friends: Cyrus I saw and his host dead,
And how the queen with great despite hath flung
His head in blood of them she overcome.

Xerxes, the Persian king, yet saw I there,
With his huge host, that drank the rivers dry,
Dismounted hills, and made the vales uprear,
His host and all yet saw I slain, pardé:
Thebes I saw, all razed how it did lie
In heaps of stones, and Tyrus put to spoil,
With walls and towers flat evened with the soil.

But Troy, alas, methought, above them all,
It made mine eyes in very tears consume:
When I beheld the woeful word befall,
That by the wrathful will of gods was come;
And Jove's unmovèd sentence and foredoom
On Priam king, and on his town so bent,
I could not lin, but I must there lament.

And that the more, sith destiny was so stern
As, force perforce, there might no force avail,
But she must fall: and, by her fall, we learn,
That cities, towers, wealth, world, and all shall quail:
No manhood, might, nor nothing might prevail;
All were there pressed full many a prince, and peer,
And many a knight that sold his death full dear.

Not worthy Hector, worthiest of them all,
Her hope, her joy, his force is now for naught:
O Troy, Troy, Troy, there is no boot but bale,
The hugy horse within thy walls is brought;
Thy turrets fall, thy knights, that whilom fought
In arms amid the field, are slain in bed,
Thy gods defiled, and all thy honor dead.

The flames up spring, and cruelly they creep
From wall to roof, till all to cinders waste:
Some fire the houses where the wretches sleep,
Some rush in here, some run in there as fast;
In every where or sword or fire they taste:
The walls are torn, the towers whirled to the ground;
There is no mischief but may there be found.

Cassandra yet there saw I how they haled
From Pallas' house, with spercled tress undone,
Her wrists fast bound, and with Greeks' rout empaled:
And Priam eke, in vain how he did run
To arms, whom Pyrrhus with despite hath done
To cruel death, and bathed him in the baign
Of his son's blood, before the altar slain.

But how can I describe the doleful sight,
That in the shield so livelike fair did shine?
Sith in this world, I think was never wight
Could have set forth the half, not half so fine:
I can no more, but tell how there is seen
Fair Ilium fall in burning red gledes down,
And, from the soil, great Troy, Neptunus' town.

Herefrom when scarce I could mine eyes withdraw,
That filled with tears as doth the springing well,
We passèd on so far forth till we saw
Rude Acheron, a loathsome lake to tell,
That boils and bubs up swelth as black as hell;
Where grisly Charon, at their fixèd tide,
Still ferries ghosts unto the farther side.

The agèd God no sooner Sorrow spied,
But, hasting straight unto the bank apace,
With hollow call unto the rout he cried,
To swerve apart, and give the goddess place:
Straight it was done, when to the shore we pace,
Where, hand in hand as we then linkèd fast,
Within the boat we are together placed.

And forth we launch full fraughted to the brink:
When, with the unwonted weight, the rusty keel
Began to crack as if the same should sink:
We hoise up mast and sail, that in a while
We fetched the shore, where scarcely we had while
For to arrive, but that we heard anon
A three-sound bark confounded all in one.

We had not long forth passed, but that we saw
Black Cerberus, the hideous hound of hell,
With bristles reared, and with a three-mouthed jaw
Foredinning the air with his horrible yell,
Out of the deep dark cave where he did dwell.
The goddess straight he knew, and by and by,
He peased and couched, while that we passèd by.

Thence come we to the horror and the hell,
The large great kingdoms, and the dreadful reign
Of Pluto in his throne where he did dwell,
The wide waste places, and the hugy plain,
The wailings, shrieks, and sundry sorts of pain,
The sighs, the sobs, the deep and deadly groan;
Earth, air, and all, resounding plaint and moan.

Here puled the babes, and here the maids unwed
With folded hands their sorry chance bewailed;
Here wept the guiltless slain, and lovers dead,
That slew themselves when nothing else availed;
A thousand sorts of sorrows here, that wailed
With sighs, and tears, sobs, shrieks, and all yfear,
That, oh, alas, it was a hell to hear.

We staid us straight, and with a rueful fear,
Beheld this heavy sight; while from mine eyes
The vapored tears down stillèd here and there,
And Sorrow eke, in far more woeful wise,
Took on with plaint, upheaving to the skies
Her wretched hands, that, with her cry, the rout
Gan all in heaps to swarm us round about.

'Lo here,' quoth Sorrow, 'princes of renown,
That whilom sat on top of Fortune's wheel,
Now laid full low; like wretches whirlèd down,
Even with one frown, that stayed but with a smile:
And now behold the thing that thou, erewhile,
Saw only in thought; and, what thou now shalt hear,
Recount the same to kesar, king, and peer.'

Then first came Henry, Duke of Buckingham,
His cloak of black all pilled and quite forworn,
Wringing his hands, and Fortune oft doth blame,
Which of a duke hath made him now her scorn:
With ghastly looks, as one in manner lorn,
Oft spread his arms, stretched hands he joins as fast
With rueful cheer, and vapored eyes upcast.

His cloak he rent, his manly breast he beat,
His hair all torn about the place it lay;
My heart so molt to see his grief so great
As feelingly, me thought, it dropped away:
His eyes they whirled about withouten stay,
With stormy sighs the place did so complain
As if his heart at each had burst in twain.

Thrice he began to tell his doleful tale.
And thrice the sighs did swallow up his voice,
At each of which he shriekèd so withal,
As though the heavens rivèd with the noise;
Till at the last recovering his voice,
Supping the tears that all his breast berained,
On cruel Fortune weeping thus he plained.

1563

LYRICS

Thomas, Lord Vaux (1510–1556)

OF A CONTENTED MIND

When all is done and said,
  In the end thus shall you find,
He most of all doth bathe in bliss
  That hath a quiet mind,
And, clear from worldly cares,
  To deem can be content
The sweetest time in all his life
  In thinking to be spent.

The body subject is
  To fickle Fortune's power,
And to a million of mishaps
  Is casual every hour;
And death in time doth change
  It to a clod of clay,
Whenas the mind, which is divine,
  Runs never to decay.

Companion none is like
  Unto the mind alone;
For many have been harmed by speech;
  Through thinking few or none:
Fear oftentimes restraineth words,
  But makes not thought to cease,
And he speaks best that hath the skill
  When for to hold his peace.

Our wealth leaves us at death;
  Our kinsmen at the grave;
But virtues of the mind unto
  The heavens with us we have.
Wherefore, for virtue's sake,
  I can be well content
The sweetest time of all my life
  To deem in thinking spent.

1576

Anonymous

A PRAISE OF HIS LADY

Give place, you ladies, and begone,
  Boast not yourselves at all;
For here at hand approacheth one
  Whose face will stain you all.

The virtue of her lively looks
  Excels the precious stone;
I wish to have none other books
  To read or look upon.

In each of her two crystal eyes
  Smileth a naked boy;
It would you all in heart suffice
  To see that lamp of joy.

I think nature hath lost the mould,
  Where she her shape did take;
Or else I doubt if nature could
  So fair a creature make.

She may be well compared
  Unto the Phenix kind,
Whose like was never seen or heard,
  That any man can find.

In life she is Diana chaste,
  In truth Penelope,
In word and eke in deed steadfast
  What will you more we say?

If all the world were sought so far,
  Who could find such a wight?
Her beauty twinketh like a star
  Within the frosty night.

Her rosial colour comes and goes
  With such a comely grace,
More redier too than doth the rose,
  Within her lively face.

At Bacchus' feast none shall her meet,
  Ne at no wanton play,
Nor gazing in an open street,
  Nor gadding as a stray.

The modest mirth that she doth use
  Is mixt with shamefastness;
All vice she doth wholly refuse,
  And hateth idleness.

O Lord, it is a world to see
  How virtue can repair,
And deck in her such honesty,
  Whom nature made so fair!

Truly she doth as far exceed
  Our women now-a-days
As doth the gilli-flower a weed,
  And more a thousand ways.

How might I do to get a graff
Of this unspotted tree?
For all the rest are plain but chaff,
Which seem good corn to be.

This gift alone I shall her give,
When Death doth what he can:
Her honest fame shall ever live
Within the mouth of man.

1557

THAT PETRARCH CANNOT BE PASSED BUT NOTWITHSTANDING THAT LAURA IS FAR SURPASSED

With Petrarch to compare there may no wight,
Nor yet attain unto so high a style,
But yet I wot full well where is a file,
To frame a learnèd man to praise aright.
Of stature mean, of seemly form and shape,
Each line of just proportion to her height;
Her colour fresh and mingled with such sleight,
As though the rose sat in the lily's lap;
In wit and tongue to show what may be said;
To every deed she joins a perfect grace.
If Laura lived she would her clean deface;
For I dare say and lay my life to wed
That Momus could not, if he down descended,
Once justly say, Lo, this may be amended.

1557

THE PROMISE OF A CONSTANT LOVER

As laurel leaves that cease not to be green,
From parching sun, nor yet from winter's threat,
As hardened oak that feareth no sword so keen,
As flint for tool in twain that will not fret,
As fast as rock or pillar surely set,
So fast am I to you and aye have been,
Assuredly, whom I cannot forget,
For joy, for pain, for torment, nor for teen,
For loss, for gain, for frowning, nor for threat,
But ever one, yea both in calm and blast,
Your faithful friend, and will be to my last.

1557

THAT EACH THING IS HURT OF ITSELF

Why fearest thou thy outward foe,
When thou thyself thy harm dost feed?
Of grief or hurt, of pain or woe,
Within each thing is sown a seed.

So fine was never yet the cloth,
No smith so hard his iron did beat,
But the one consumèd was with moth,
The other with canker all to-fret.

The knotty oak and wainscot old,
Within doth eat the silly worm;
Even so a mind in envy rolled
Always within itself doth burn.

Thus everything that nature wrought,
Within itself his hurt doth bear;
No outward harm need to be sought,
Where enemies be within so near.

1557

AN OLD LOVER TO A YOUNG GENTLEWOMAN

Ye are too young to bring me in,
And I too old to gape for flies;
I have too long a lover been,
If such young babes should blear mine eyes.
But trill the ball before my face,
I am content to make you play;
I will not see, I hide my face,
And turn my back and run away.

But if you follow on so fast
And cross the ways where I should go,
Ye may wax weary at the last
And then at length yourself o'erthrow:
I mean, where you and all your flock
Devise to pen men in the pound,
I know a key can pick your lock
And make you run yourselves on ground.

Some birds can eat the strawy corn
And flee the lime the fowlers set,
And some are feared of every thorn
And so thereby they scape the net;
But some do light and never look
And see not who doth stand in wait,
As fish that swallow up the hook
And is beguilèd through the bait.

But men can look before they leap
And be at price for every ware,
And pennyworths cast to buy good cheap,
And in each thing have eye and care;
But he that bluntly runs on head
And seeth not what the race shall be
Is like to bring a fool to bed,
And thus ye get no more of me.

1557

ALE SONG

I cannot eat but little meat,
My stomach is not good;
But, sure, I think that I can drink
With him that wears a hood.
Though I go bare, take ye no care,
I am nothing a-cold,
I stuff my skin so full within
Of jolly good ale and old.

Chorus —
Back and side, go bare, go bare;
Both foot and hand, go cold:
But, belly, God send thee good ale enough,
Whether it be new or old.

I love no roast, but a nut-brown toast
And a crab laid in the fire;
A little bread shall do me stead,
Much bread I not desire.
No frost nor snow, no wind, I trow,
Can hurt me if I would,
I am so wrapt and throughly lapt
Of jolly good ale and old.

And Tib my wife, that as her life
Loveth well good ale to seek,
Full oft drinks she till ye may see
The tears run down her cheek;
Then doth she trowl to me the bowl,
Even as a malt-worm should,
And saith, 'Sweetheart, I took my part
Of this jolly good ale and old.'

Now let them drink till they nod and wink,
Even as good fellows should do;
They shall not miss to have the bliss
Good ale doth bring men to.
And all poor souls that have scoured bowls,
Or have them lustily trowled,
God save the lives of them and their wives,
Whether they be young or old.

1575

Richard Edwardes (1523?–1566)

AMANTIUM IRA AMORIS REDINTEGRATIO EST

In going to my naked bed as one that would have slept,
I heard a wife sing to her child, that long before had wept;
She sighèd sore and sang full sweet, to bring the babe to rest,
That would not cease but criѐd still, in sucking at her breast.
She was full weary of her watch, and grievèd with her child,
She rockèd it, and rated it, till that on her it smiled.
Then did she say, Now have I found this proverb true to prove,
The falling out of faithful friends renewing is of love.

Then took I paper, pen, and ink, this proverb for to write,
In register for to remain of such a worthy wight:
As she proceeded thus in song unto her little brat,
Much matter uttered she of weight, in place whereas she sat:
And provèd plain there was no beast, nor creature bearing life,
Could well be known to live in love without discord and strife:
Then kissèd she her little babe, and sware by God above,
The falling out of faithful friends renewing is of love.

She said that neither king nor prince nor lord could live aright,
Until their puissance they did prove, their manhood and their might.
When manhood shall be matchèd so that fear can take no place,
Then weary works make warriors each other to embrace,
And left their force that failèd them, which did consume the rout,
That might before have lived their time, [their strength] and nature out:
Then did she sing as one that thought no man could her reprove,
The falling out of faithful friends renewing is of love.

She said she saw no fish nor fowl, nor beast within her haunt,
That met a stranger in their kind, but could give it a taunt:
Since flesh might not endure, but rest must wrath succeed,
And force the fight to fall to play in pasture where they feed,
So noble nature can well end the work she hath begun,
And bridle well that will not cease her tragedy in some:
Thus in song she oft rehearsed, as did her well behove,
The falling out of faithful friends renewing is of love.

I marvel much, pardy (quoth she) for to behold the rout,
To see man, woman, boy and beast, to toss the world about:
Some kneel, some crouch, some beck, some check, and some can smoothly smile,
And some embrace others in arm, and there think many a wile,
Some stand aloof at cap and knee, some humble and some stout,
Yet are they never friends indeed until they once fall out:
Thus ended she her song and said, before she did remove,
The falling out of faithful friends renewing is of love.

1576

George Gascoigne (1535?-1577)

THE LULLABY OF A LOVER

Sing lullaby, as women do,
Wherewith they bring their babes to rest,
And lullaby can I sing too,
As womanly as can the best.
With lullaby they still the child,
And if I be not much beguiled,
Full many wanton babes have I,
Which must be stilled with lullaby.

First, lullaby my youthful years,
It is now time to go to bed,
For crookèd age and hoary hairs,
Have won the haven within my head:
With lullaby then youth be still,
With lullaby content thy will,
Since courage quails and comes behind,
Go sleep, and so beguile thy mind.

Next lullaby my gazing eyes,
Which wonted were to glance apace;
For every glass may now suffice,
To shew the furrows in my face:
With lullaby then wink awhile,
With lullaby your looks beguile:
Let no fair face, nor beauty bright,
Entice you eft with vain delight.

And lullaby my wanton will,
Let Reason's rule now reign thy thought,
Since all too late I find by skill,
How dear I have thy fancies bought.
With lullaby now take thine ease,
With lullaby thy doubts appease:
For trust to this, if thou be still,
My body shall obey thy will.

. . . .

Thus lullaby my youth, mine eyes,
My will, my ware, and all that was,
I can no more delays devise,
But welcome pain, let pleasure pass:
With lullaby now take your leave,
With lullaby your dreams deceive,
And when you rise with waking eye,
Remember then this lullaby.

1573

A STRANGE PASSION OF A LOVER

Amid my bale I bathe in bliss,
I swim in heaven, I sink in hell:
I find amends for every miss,
And yet my moan no tongue can tell.
I live and love, what would you more?
As never lover lived before.

I laugh sometimes with little lust,
So jest I oft and feel no joy;
Mine eye is builded all on trust,
And yet mistrust breeds mine annoy.
I live and lack, I lack and have;
I have and miss the thing I crave.

These things seem strange, yet are they true.
Believe me, sweet, my state is such,
One pleasure which I would eschew,
Both slakes my grief and breeds my grutch.
So doth one pain which I would shun,
Renew my joys where grief begun.

Then like the lark that passed the night
In heavy sleep with cares opprest,
Yet when she spies the pleasant light,
She sends sweet notes from out her breast;
So sing I now because I think
How joys approach, when sorrows shrink.

And as fair Philomene again
Can watch and sing when others sleep,
And taketh pleasure in her pain,
To wray the woe that makes her weep;
So sing I now for to bewray
The loathsome life I lead alway.

The which to thee, dear wench, I write,
That know'st my mirth, but not my moan:
I pray God grant thee deep delight,
To live in joys when I am gone.
I cannot live; it will not be:
I die to think to part from thee.

1573

Edward de Vere, Earl of Oxford (1550–1604)

IF WOMEN COULD BE FAIR

If women could be fair, and yet not fond,
Or that their love were firm, not fickle, still,
I would not marvel that they make men bond
By service long to purchase their good will;
But when I see how frail those creatures are,
I muse that men forget themselves so far.

To mark the choice they make, and how they change,
How oft from Phœbus they do flee to Pan,
Unsettled still, like haggards wild, they range, —
These gentle birds that fly from man to man;
Who would not scorn and shake them from the fist,
And let them fly, fair fools, which way they list?

Yet, for disport, we fawn and flatter both,
To pass the time when nothing else can please;
And train them to our lure with subtle oath,
Till, weary of their wiles, ourselves we ease:
And then we say, when we their fancy try,
To play with fools, oh, what a fool was I!

1576

PROSE

William Caxton (ca. 1422–1491)

PREFACE TO *LE MORTE D'ARTHUR*

After that I had accomplished and finished divers histories, as well of contemplation as of other historial and worldly acts of great conquerors and princes, and also certain books of ensamples and doctrine, many noble and divers gentlemen of this realm of England came and demanded me many and oft-times, wherefore that I have not do made and imprint the noble history of the Saint Greal, and of the most renowned Christian king, first and chief of the three best Christian, and worthy, king Arthur, which ought most to be remembered amongst us Englishmen tofore all other Christian kings; for it is notoriously known through the universal world, that there be nine worthy and the best that ever were, that is to wit, three Paynims three Jews, and three Christian men. As for the Paynims, they were tofore the Incarnation of Christ, which were named, the first Hector of Troy, of whom the history is comen both in ballad and in prose, the second Alexander the Great, and the third, Julius Cæsar, Emperor of Rome, of whom the histories be well known and had. And as for the three Jews, which also were tofore the Incarnation of our Lord, of whom the first was duke Joshua which brought the children of Israel into the land of behest, the second David king of Jerusalem, and the third Judas Maccabæus. Of these three the Bible rehearseth all their noble histories and acts. And since the said Incarnation have been three noble Christian men, stalled and admitted through the universal world into the number of the nine best and worthy. Of whom was first the noble Arthur, whose noble acts I purpose to write in this present book here following. The second was Charlemain, or Charles the Great, of whom the history is had in many places, both in French and in English. And the third and last was Godfrey of Boloine, of whose acts and life I made a book unto the excellent prince and king of noble memory, king Edward the Fourth. The said noble gentlemen instantly required me to imprint the history of the said noble king and conqueror king Arthur, and of his knights, with the history of the Saint Greal, and of the death and ending of the said Arthur; affirming that I ought rather to imprint his acts and noble feats, than of Godfrey of Boloine, or any of the other eight, considering that he was a man born within this realm, and king and emperor of the same: and that there be in French divers and many noble volumes of his acts, and also of his knights. To whom I answered that divers men hold opinion that there was no such Arthur, and that all such books as been made of him, be feigned and fables, because that some chronicles make of him no mention, nor remember him nothing, nor of his knights. Whereto they answered, and one in special said, that in him that should say or think that there was never such a king called Arthur, might well be aretted great folly and blindness. For he said that there were many evidences of the contrary. First ye may see his sepulchre in the monastery of Glastonbury. And also in *Policronicon*, in the fifth book the sixth chapter, and in the seventh book the twenty-third chapter, where his body was buried, and after found, and translated into the said monastery. Ye shall see also in the history of Bochas, in his book *De Casu Principum* part of his noble acts, and also of his fall. Also Galfridus in his British book recounteth his life: and in divers places of England many remembrances be yet of him, and shall remain perpetually, and also of his knights. First in the abbey of Westminster, at Saint Edward's shrine, remaineth the print of his seal in red wax closed in beryl, in which is written *Patricius Arthurus, Britannie, Gallie, Germanie, Dacie, Imperator*. Item in the castle of Dover ye may see Gawaine's scull and Cradok's mantle: at Winchester the Round Table: in other places Launcelot's sword and many other things. Then all these things considered, there can no man reasonably gainsay but that there was a king of this land named Arthur. For in all places, Christian and heathen, he is reputed and taken for one of the nine worthy, and the first of the three Christian men. And also, he is more spoken of beyond the sea, more books made of his noble acts, than there be in England, as well in Dutch, Italian, Spanish, and Greekish, as in French. And yet of record remain in witness of him in Wales, in the town of Camelot, the great stones and the marvelous works of iron lying under the ground, and royal vaults, which divers now living have seen. Wherefore it is a marvel why he is no more renowned in his own country, save only it accordeth to the Word of God, which saith that no man is accepted for a prophet in his own country. Then all these things afore said alleged, I could not well deny but that there was such a noble king named Arthur, and reputed one of the nine worthy, and first and chief of the Christian men. And many noble volumes be made of him and of his noble knights in French, which I have seen and read beyond the sea, which be not had in our maternal tongue. But in Welsh be many and also in French, and some in English but no where nigh all. Wherefore, such as have late been drawn out briefly into English I have after the simple conning that God hath sent to me, under the favour and correction of all noble lords and gentlemen, enprised to imprint a book of the noble histories of the said king Arthur, and of certain of his knights, after a copy unto me delivered, which copy Sir Thomas Malorye did take out of certain books of French, and reduced it into English. And I, according to my copy, have done set it in print, to the intent that noble men may see and learn the noble acts of chivalry, the gentle and virtuous deeds that some knights used in those days, by which they came to honour, and how they that were vicious were punished and oft put to shame and rebuke; humbly beseeching all noble lords and ladies, with all other estates of what estate or degree they been of, that shall see and read in this said book and work, that they take the good and honest acts in their remembrance, and to follow the same. Wherein they shall find many joyous and pleasant histories, and noble and renowned acts of humanity, gentleness, and chivalry. For herein may be seen noble chivalry, courtesy, humanity, friendliness, hardiness, love, friendship, cowardice, murder, hate, virtue, and sin. Do after the good and leave the evil, and it shall bring you to good fame and renommee. And for to pass the time this book shall be pleasant to read in, but for to give faith and belief that all is true that is contained herein, ye be at your liberty: but all is written for our doctrine, and for to beware that we fall not to vice nor sin, but to exercise and follow virtue, by the which we may come and attain to good fame and renown in this life, and after this short and transitory life to come unto everlasting bliss in heaven; the which He grant us that reigneth in heaven, the blessed Trinity. Amen.

1485

PREFACE TO THE *ÆNEID*

After divers works made, translated, and achieved, having no work in hand, I sitting in my study, where lay many divers pamphlets and books, happened that to my hand came a little book in French, which late was translated out of Latin by some noble clerk of France; which book is named *Eneydos*, made in Latin by that noble poet and great clerk Virgil. Which book I saw over and read therein how, after the general destruction of the great Troy, Eneas departed, bearing his old father Anchises upon his shoulders, his little son Yolus on his hand, his wife with much other people following; and how he shipped and departed; with all the history of his adventures that he had ere he came to the achievement of his conquest of Italy, as all along shall be showed in this present book. In which book I had great pleasure because of the fair and honest terms and words in French; which I never saw tofore like, ne none so pleasant ne so well ordered. Which book, as me seemed, should be much requisite to noble men to see, as well for the eloquence as the histories; how well that, many hundred years past, was the said book of Eneydos with other works made and learned daily in schools, specially in Italy and other places; which history the said Virgil made in meter. And when I had advised me in this said book, I delibered and concluded to translate it into English, and forthwith took a pen and ink and wrote a leaf or twain, which I oversaw again to correct it; and when I saw the fair and strange terms therein, I doubted that it should not please some gentlemen which late blamed me, saying that in my translations I had over-curious terms, which could not be understood of common people, and desired me to use old and homely terms in my translations. And fain would I satisfy every man; and, so to do, took an old book and read therein; and certainly the English was so rude and broad that I could not well understand it; and also my lord abbot of Westminster did do show to me late certain evidences written in old English for to reduce it into our English now used, and certainly it was written in such wise that it was more like to Dutch than English; I could not reduce nor bring it to be understonden. And certainly our language now used varyeth far from that which was used and spoken when I was born. For we English men ben born under the domination of the moon, which is never steadfast but ever wavering, waxing one season and waneth and decreaseth another season. And that common English that is spoken in one shire varyeth from another, in so much that in my days happened that certain merchants were in a ship in Thames for to have sailed over the sea into Zealand, and, for lack of wind, they tarried at Forland, and went to land for to refresh them. And one of them named Sheffield, a mercer, came into an house and asked for meat and specially he asked after eggs, and the good wife answered that she could speke no French. And the merchant was angry, for he also could speak no French, but would have had eggs; and she understood him not. And then at last another said that he would have eyren. Then the good wife said that she understood him well. Lo, what should a man in these days now write, egges, or eyren? Certainly it is hard to please every man, because of diversity and change of language; for in these days every man that is in any reputation in his country will utter his communication and matters in such manners and terms that few men shall understand them. And some honest and great clerks have been with me and desired me to write the most curious terms that I could find. And thus, between plain rude, and curious, I stand abashed. But in my judgment the common terms that be daily used ben lighter to be understand than the old and ancient English. And, forasmuch as this present book is not for a rude uplondished man to labour therein ne read it, but only for a clerk and a noble gentleman that feeleth and understandeth in feats of arms, in love, and in noble chivalry; therefore in a mean between both I have reduced and translated this said book into our English, not over rude ne curious, but in such terms as shall be understanden, by God's grace according to my copy. And if any man will entermete in reading of it and findeth such terms that he cannot understand, let him go read and learn Virgil or the Epistles of Ovid, and there he shall see and understand lightly all, if he have a good reader and informer. For this book is not for every rude and uncunning man to see, but to clerks and very gentlemen, that understand gentleness and science. Then I pray all them that shall read in this little treatise, to hold me for excused for the translating of it, for I acknowledge myself ignorant of cunning to enprise on me so high and noble a work. But I pray Master John Skelton, late created poet-laureate in the university of Oxford, to oversee and correct this said book and to address and expown, where as shall be found fault, to them that shall require it, for him I know for sufficient to expown and English every difficulty that is therein, for he hath late translated the Epistles of Tully and the book of Diodorus Siculus and divers other works out of Latin into English, not in rude and old language, but in polished and ornate terms, craftily, as he that hath read Virgil, Ovid, Tully, and all the other noble poets and orators to me unknown; and also he hath read the IX muses and understands their musical sciences and to whom of them each science is appropred. I suppose he hath drunken of Helicon's well. Then I pray him and such other to correct, add or minish, where as he or they shall find fault, for I have but followed my copy in French as nigh as me is possible. And if any word be said therein well, I am glad; and if otherwise, I submit my said book to their correction. Which book I present unto the high-born my tocoming natural and sovereign lord, Arthur, by the grace of God Prince of Wales, Duke of Cornwall, and Earl of Chester, first begotten son and heir unto our most dread natural and sovereign lord and most Christian king, Henry VII, by the grace of God King of England and of France and lord of Ireland, beseeching his noble grace to receive it in thank of me, his most humble subject and servant. And I shall pray unto almighty God for his prosperous increasing in virtue, wisdom, and humanity, that he may be equal with the most renowned of all his noble progenitors, and so to live in this present life that after this transitory life he and we all may come to everlasting life in heaven. Amen!

1490

Roger Ascham (1515–1568)

TOXOPHILUS

TO ALL GENTLEMEN AND YEOMEN OF ENGLAND

Bias the wise man came to Crœsus the rich King, on a time when he was making new ships, purposing to have subdued by water the out-isles lying betwixt Greece and Asia Minor. 'What news now in Greece?' saith the King to Bias. 'None other news but these,' saith Bias: 'that the isles of Greece have prepared a wonderful company of horsemen to overrun Lydia withal.' 'There is nothing under heaven,' saith the King, 'that I would so soon wish, as that they durst be so bold to meet us on land with horse.' 'And think you,' saith Bias, 'that there is anything which they would sooner wish, than that you should be so fond to meet them on the water with ships?' And so Crœsus, hearing not the true news, but perceiving the wise man's mind and counsel, both gave then over making of his ships, and left also behind him a wonderful example for all commonwealths to follow: that is, evermore to regard and set most by that thing whereunto nature hath made them most apt, and use hath made them most fit.

By this matter I mean the shooting in the long bow, for Englishmen; which thing with all my heart I do wish, and if I were of authority, I would counsel all the gentlemen and yeomen of England, not to change it with any other thing, how good soever it seems to be; but that still, according to the old wont of England, youth should use it for the most honest pastime in peace, that men might handle it as a most sure weapon in war. Other strong weapons, which both experience doth prove to be good, and the wisdom of the King's Majesty and his council provides to be had, are not ordained to take away shooting; but that both, not compared together whether should be better than the other, but so joined together that the one should be always an aid and help for the other, might so strengthen the realm on all sides, that no kind of enemy, in any kind of weapon, might pass and go beyond us.

For this purpose I, partly provoked by

the counsel of some gentlemen, partly moved by the love which I have always borne toward shooting, have written this little treatise; wherein, if I have not satisfied any man, I trust he will the rather be content with my doing, because I am (I suppose) the first, which hath said anything in this matter, (and few beginnings be perfect, saith wise men) and also because, if I have said amiss, I am content that any man amend it: or, if I have said too little, any man that will, to add what him pleaseth to it.

My mind is, in profiting and pleasing every man, to hurt or displease no man, intending none other purpose, but that youth might be stirred to labour, honest pastime, and virtue, and as much as lieth in me, plucked from idleness, unthrifty games, and vice: which thing I have laboured only in this book, showing how fit shooting is for all kinds of men; how honest a pastime for the mind; how wholesome an exercise for the body; not vile for great men to use, not costly for poor men to sustain, not lurking in holes and corners for ill men at their pleasure to misuse it, but abiding in the open sight and face of the world, for good men, if it fault, by their wisdom to correct it.

And here I would desire all gentlemen and yeomen to use this pastime in such a mean, that the outrageousness of great gaming should not hurt the honesty of shooting, which, of his own nature, is always joined with honesty; yet for men's faults oftentimes blamed unworthily, as all good things have been, and evermore shall be.

If any man would blame me, either for taking such a matter in hand, or else for writing it in the English tongue, this answer I may make him, that when the best of the realm think it honest for them to use, I, one of the meanest sort, ought not to suppose it vile for me to write; and though to have written it in another tongue, had been both more profitable for my study, and also more honest for my name, yet I can think my labour well bestowed, if with a little hinderance of my profit and name, may come any furtherance to the pleasure or commodity of the gentlemen and yeomen of England, for whose sake I took this matter in hand. And as for the Latin or Greek tongue, every thing is so excellently done in them, that none can do better: in the English tongue, contrary, every thing in a manner so meanly both for the matter and handling, that no man can do worse. For therein the least learned, for the most part, have been always most ready to write. And they which had least hope in Latin, have been most bold in English: when surely every man that is most ready to talk, is not most able to write. He that will write well in any tongue, must follow this counsel of Aristotle, to speak as the common people do, to think as wise men do: and so should every man understand him, and the judgment of wise men allow him. Many English writers have not done so, but using strange words, as Latin, French, and Italian, do make all things dark and hard. Once I communed with a man which reasoned the English tongue to be enriched and increased thereby, saying 'Who will not praise that feast where a man shall drink at a dinner both wine, ale, and beer?' 'Truly (quoth I) they be all good, every one taken by himself alone, but if you put malmsey and sack, red wine and white, ale and beer, and all in one pot, you shall make a drink neither easy to be known, nor yet wholesome for the body.' Cicero, in following Isocrates, Plato, and Demosthenes, increased the Latin tongue after another sort. This way, because divers men that write do not know, they can neither follow it, because of their ignorance, nor yet will praise it for very arrogancy, two faults, seldom the one out of the other's company.

English writers by diversity of time have taken divers matters in hand. In our fathers' time nothing was read but books of feigned chivalry, wherein a man by reading should be led to none other end, but only to manslaughter and bawdry. If any man suppose they were good enough to pass the time withal, he is deceived. For surely vain words do work no small thing in vain, ignorant, and young minds, especially if they be given anything thereunto of their own nature. These books (as I have heard say) were made the most part in abbeys and monasteries, — a very likely and fit fruit of such an idle and blind kind of living. In our time now, when every man is given to know, much rather than to live well, very many do write, but after such a fashion as very many do shoot. Some shooters take in hand stronger bows than they be able to maintain. This thing maketh them sometime to outshoot the mark, sometime to shoot far wide, and perchance hurt some that look on. Other that never learned to shoot, nor yet knoweth good shaft nor bow, will be as busy as the best, but such one commonly plucketh down a side, and crafty archers which be against him, will be both glad of him, and also ever ready to lay and bet with him: it were better for such one to sit down than shoot. Other there be, which have very good bow and shafts, and good knowledge in shooting, but they have been brought up in such evil favoured shooting, that they can neither shoot fair nor yet near. If any man will apply these things together, he shall not see the one far differ from the other. And I also, amongst all other, in writing this little treatise, have followed some young shooters, which both will begin to shoot, for a little money, and also will use to shoot once or twice about the mark for nought, afore they begin a-good. And therefore did I take this little matter in hand, to assay myself, and hereafter, by the grace of God, if the judgment of wise men, that look on, think that I can do any good, I may perchance cast my shaft among other, for better game. Yet in writing this book, some man will marvel perchance, why that I, being an unperfect shooter, should take in hand to write of making a perfect archer: the same man, peradventure, will marvel how a whetstone, which is blunt, can make the edge of a knife sharp. I would the same man should consider also, that in going about any matter, there be four things to be considered, doing, saying, thinking, and perfectness: first, there is no man that doth so well, but he can say better, or else some men, which be now stark nought, should be too good: again, no man can utter with his tongue so well as he is able to imagine with his mind, and yet perfectness itself is far above all thinking: then, seeing that saying is one step nearer perfectness than doing, let every man leave marvelling why my word shall rather express, than my deed shall perform, perfect shooting.

I trust no man will be offended with this little book, except it be some fletchers and bowyers, thinking hereby that many that love shooting shall be taught to refuse such naughty wares as they would utter. Honest fletchers and bowyers do not so, and they that be unhonest, ought rather to amend themselves for doing ill, than being angry with me for saying well. A fletcher hath even as good a quarrel to be angry with an archer that refuseth an ill shaft, as a blade-smith hath to a fletcher that forsaketh to buy of him a naughty knife: for as an archer must be content that a fletcher know a good shaft in every point for the perfecter making of it; so an honest fletcher will also be content that a shooter know a good shaft in every point, for the perfecter using of it; because the one knoweth like a fletcher how to make it, the other knoweth like an archer how to use it. And seeing the knowledge is one in them both, yet the end divers, surely that fletcher is an enemy to archers and artillery which cannot be content that an archer know a shaft as well for his use in shooting, as he himself should know a shaft for his advantage in selling. And the rather, because shafts be not made so much to be sold, but chiefly to be used. And seeing that use and occupying is the end why a shaft is made, the making, as it were, a mean for occupying, surely the knowledge in every point of a good shaft, is more to be required in a shooter than a fletcher.

Yet, as I said before, no honest fletcher will be angry with me, seeing I do not teach how to make a shaft, which belongeth only to a good fletcher, but to know and handle a shaft, which belongeth to an archer. And this little book, I trust, shall please and profit both parties; for good bows and shafts shall be better known to the commodity of all shooters, and good shooting may, perchance, be the more occupied to the profit of all bowyers and fletchers. And this I pray God that all fletchers, getting their living truly, and all archers using shooting honestly, and all manner of men that favour artillery, may live continually in health and merriness, obeying their prince as they should, and loving God as they ought: to whom, for all things, be all honour and glory forever. Amen.

1545

John Foxe (1516-1587)

ACTS AND MONUMENTS (BOOK OF MARTYRS)

DEATH OF CRANMER

Cranmer at length cometh from the prison of Bocardo unto St. Mary's church (the chief church in the university), because it was a foul and rainy day, in this order: the mayor went before; next him the aldermen in their place and degree; after them was Cranmer brought between two friars, who, mumbling to and fro certain psalms in the streets, answered one another until they came to the church door, and there they began the song of Simeon, 'Nunc dimittis,' and entering into the church, the psalm-saying friars brought him to his standing, and there left him. There was a stage set over against the pulpit, of a mean height from the ground, where Cranmer had his standing, waiting until Cole made him ready to his sermon.

The lamentable case and sight of that man gave a sorrowful spectacle to all christian eyes that beheld him. He that late was archbishop, metropolitan, and primate of England, and the king's privy councillor, being now in a bare and ragged gown, and ill favouredly clothed, with an old square cap, exposed to the contempt of all men, did admonish men not only of his own calamity, but also of their state and fortune. For who would not pity his case, and bewail his fortune, and might not fear his own chance, to see such a prelate, so grave a councillor, and of so long continued honour, after so many dignities, in his old years to be deprived of his estate, adjudged to die, and in so painful a death to end his life, and now presently from such fresh ornaments, to descend to such vile and ragged apparel?

In this habit, when he stood a good space upon the stage, turning to a pillar near adjoining thereunto, he lifted up his hands to heaven, and prayed unto God once or twice, till at the length Dr. Cole coming into the pulpit, and beginning his sermon, entered first into mention of Tobias and Zachary. Whom after he had praised in the beginning of his sermon for their perseverance in the true worshiping of God, he then divided his whole sermon into three parts (according to the solemn custom of the schools), intending to speak, first, of the mercy of God: secondly, of his justice to be showed: and last of all, how the prince's secrets are not to be opened. And proceeding a little from the beginning, he took occasion by and by to turn his tale to Cranmer, and with many hot words reproved him, that once he, being indued with the favour and feeling of wholesome and catholic doctrine, fell into the contrary opinion of pernicious error; which he had not only defended by writings, and all his power, but also allured other men to do the like, with great liberality of gifts, as it were appointing rewards for error; and after he had allured them, by all means did cherish them. . . .

Here the standers-by were all astonied, marvelled, were amazed, did look one upon another, whose expectation he had so notably deceived. Some began to admonish him of his recantation, and to accuse him of falsehood. Briefly, it was a world to see the doctors beguiled of so great a hope. I think there was never cruelty more notably or better in time deluded and deceived; for it is not to be doubted but they looked for a glorious victory and a perpetual triumph by this man's retraction; who, as soon as they heard these things, began to let down their ears, to rage, fret, and fume; and so much the more, because they could not revenge their grief — for they could now no longer threaten or hurt him. For the most miserable man in the world can die but once; and whereas of necessity he must needs die that day, though the papists had been never so well pleased, now, being never so much offended with him, yet could he not be twice killed of them. And so, when they could do nothing else unto him, yet, lest they should say nothing, they ceased not to object unto him his falsehood and dissimulation.

Unto which accusation he answered, 'Ah! my masters,' quoth he, 'do not you take it so. Always since I lived hitherto, I have been a hater of falsehood, and a lover of simplicity, and never before this time have I dissembled': and in saying this, all the tears that remained in his body appeared in his eyes. And when he began to speak more of the sacrament and of the papacy, some of them began to cry out, yelp, and bawl, and specially Cole cried out upon him, 'Stop the heretic's mouth, and take him away.'

And then Cranmer being pulled down from the stage, was led to the fire, accompanied with those friars, vexing, troubling, and threatening him most cruelly, 'What madness,' say they, 'hath brought thee again into this error, by which thou wilt draw innumerable souls with thee into hell?' To whom he answered nothing, but directed all his talk to the people, saving that to one troubling him in the way, he spake, and exhorted him to get him home to his study, and apply his book diligently; saying, if he did diligently call upon God, by reading more he should get knowledge.

But the other Spanish barker, raging and foaming, was almost out of his wits, always having this in his mouth, 'Non fecisti?' 'Didst thou it not?'

But when he came to the place where the holy bishops and martyrs of God, Hugh Latimer and Nicholas Ridley, were burnt before him for the confession of the truth, kneeling down, he prayed to God; and not long tarrying in his prayers, putting off his garments to his shirt, he prepared himself to death. His shirt was made long, down to his feet. His feet were bare; likewise his head, when both his caps were off, was so bare, that one hair could not be seen upon it. His beard was long and thick, covering his face with marvellous gravity. Such a countenance of gravity moved the hearts both of his friends and of his enemies.

Then the Spanish friars, John and Richard, of whom mention was made before, began to exhort him, and play their parts with him afresh, but with vain and lost labour. Cranmer with steadfast purpose abiding in the profession of his doctrine, gave his hand to certain old men, and others that stood by, bidding them farewell.

And when he had thought to have done so likewise to Ely, the said Ely drew back his hand, and refused, saying, it was not lawful to salute heretics, and specially such a one as falsely returned unto the opinions that he had foresworn. And if he had known before, that he would have done so, he would never have used his company so familiarly: and chid those sergeants and citizens which had not refused to give him their hands. This Ely was a priest lately made, and student in divinity, being then one of the fellows of Brazennose.

Then was an iron chain tied about Cranmer, whom when they perceived to be more steadfast than that he could be moved from his sentence, they commanded the fire to be set unto him.

And when the wood was kindled, and the fire began to burn near him, stretching out his arm, he put his right hand into the flame, which he held so steadfast and immovable (saving that once with the same hand he wiped his face), that all men might see his hand burned before his body was touched. His body did so abide the burning of the flame with such constancy and steadfastness, that standing always in one place without moving his body, he seemed to move no more than the stake to which he was bound; his eyes were lifted up into heaven, and oftentimes he repeated 'his unworthy right hand,' so long as his voice would suffer him; and using often the words of Stephen, 'Lord Jesus, receive my spirit,' in the greatness of the flame he gave up the ghost.

CICELY ORMES OF NORWICH

About the 23d day of the said month of September, next after the other above mentioned, suffered at Norwich, Cicely Ormes, wife of Edmund Ormes, worsted-weaver, dwelling in St. Laurence's parish in Norwich. She, being of the age of thirty-two years or more, was taken at the death of Simon Miller and Elizabeth Cooper above mentioned, in a place called Lollards'-pit without Bishop's-gate, at the said Norwich, for that she said she would pledge them of the same cup that they drank on. For so saying, one master Corbet of Sprouston by Norwich, took her and sent her to the chancellor. When she came before him, he asked her what she said unto the sacrament of Christ's body; and she said, she did believe that it was the sacrament of the body of Christ. 'Yea,' said the chancellor, 'but what is that that the priest holdeth over his head?' She answered him and said, 'It is bread: and if you make it any better, it is worse.' At which words the chancellor sent her to the bishop's prison, to the keeper called Fellow, with many threatening and hot words, as a man being in a great chafe.

The 23d day of July she was called before the chancellor again, who sat in judgment with master Bridges and others. The chancellor offered her, if she would go to the church and keep her tongue, she should be at liberty, and believe as she would. But she told him she would not consent to his wicked desire therein, do with her what he would; for if she should, she said, God would surely plague her. Then, the chancellor told her, he had showed more favour to her, than ever he did to any, and that he was loth to condemn her, considering that she was an ignorant, unlearned, and foolish woman. But she, not weighing his words, told him, if he did, he should not be so desirous of her sinful flesh, as she would (God's grace) be content to give it in so good a quarrel. Then rose he and read the bloody sentence of condemnation against her; and so delivered her to the secular power of the sheriffs of the city, master Thomas Sutherton, and master Leonard Sutherton, brethren, who immediately carried her to the Guildhall in Norwich, where she remained until her death.

This Cicely Ormes was a very simple woman, but yet zealous in the Lord's cause, being born in East Dereham, and was there the daughter of one Thomas Haund, tailor. She was taken the 5th day of July, and did for a twelvemonth before she was taken, recant; but never after was she quiet in conscience, until she was utterly driven from all their popery. Between the time that she recanted, and that she was taken, she had gotten a letter made to give to the chancellor, to let know that she repented her recantation from the bottom of her heart, and would never do the like again while she lived: but before she exhibited her bill, she was taken and sent to prison, as is before said. She was burnt the 23d day of September, between seven and eight of the clock in the morning, the said two sheriffs being there, and of people to the number of two hundred. When she came to the stake, she kneeled down, and made her prayers to God: that being done, she rose up and said,

'Good people! I believe in God the Father, God the Son, and God the Holy Ghost, three persons and one God. This do I not, nor will I recant: but I recant utterly from the bottom of my heart the doings of the pope of Rome, and all his popish priests and shavelings. I utterly refuse and never will have to do with them again, by God's grace. And, good people! I would you should not think of me that I believe to be saved in that I offer myself here unto the death for the Lord's cause, but I believe to be saved by the death and passion of Christ; and this my death is and shall be a witness of my faith unto you all here present. Good people! as many of you as believe as I believe, pray for me.'

Then she came to the stake, and laid her hand on it, and said, 'Welcome the cross of Christ.' Which being done, she, looking on her hand, and seeing it blacked with the stake, wiped it upon her smock; for she was burnt at the same stake that Simon Miller and Elizabeth Cooper was burnt at. Then, after she had touched it with her hand, she came and kissed it, and said, 'Welcome the sweet cross of Christ'; and so gave herself to be bound thereto. After the tormentors had kindled the fire to her, she said, 'My soul doth magnify the Lord, and my spirit rejoiceth in God my Saviour.' And in so saying, she set her hands together right against her breast, casting her eyes and head upward; and so stood, heaving up her hands by little and little, till the very sinews of her arms did break asunder, and then they fell. But she yielded her life unto the Lord as quietly as if she had been in a slumber, or as one feeling no pain; so wonderfully did the Lord work with her: his name therefore be praised for evermore. Amen!

DEATH OF MARY

Now, then, after these so great afflictions falling upon this realm, from the first beginning of queen Mary's reign, wherein so many men, women, and children were burnt, many imprisoned, and in prison starved, divers exiled, some spoiled of goods and possessions, a great number driven from house and home, so many weeping eyes, so many sobbing hearts, so many children made fatherless, so many fathers bereft of their wives and children, so many vexed in conscience, and divers against conscience constrained to recant; and, in conclusion, never a good man almost in all the realm but suffered something during all the time of this bloody persecution: after all this (I say) now we are come at length (the Lord be praised!) to the 17th day of November, which day as it brought to the persecuted members of Christ rest from their careful mourning, so it easeth me somewhat likewise of my laborious writing, by the death I mean of queen Mary; who, being long sick before, upon the said 17th day of November, in the year above said, about three or four o'clock in the morning, yielded life to nature, and her kingdom to queen Elizabeth her sister. As touching the manner of whose death, some say that she died of a tympany, some (by her much sighing before her death) supposed she died of thought and sorrow. Whereupon her council, seeing her sighing, and desirous to know the cause, to the end they might minister the more ready consolation unto her, feared, as they said, that she took that thought for the king's majesty her husband, which was gone from her. To whom she answering again, 'Indeed,' said she, 'that may be one cause, but that is not the greatest wound that pierceth my oppressed mind': but what that was, she would not express to them. Albeit, afterward, she opened the matter more plainly to master Rise and mistress Clarencius (if it be true that they told me, which heard it of master Rise himself); who then, being most familiar with her, and most bold about her, told her, that they feared she took thought for king Philip's department from her. 'Not that only,' said she, 'but when I am dead and opened, you shall find Calais lying in my heart.' And here an end of queen Mary, and of her persecution.

Of queen Mary this truly may be affirmed, and left in story for a perpetual memorial or epitaph for all kings and queens that shall succeed her, to be noted — that before her, never was read in story of any king or queen of England, since the time of king Lucius, under whom, in time of peace, by hanging, beheading, burning, and prisoning, so much christian blood, so many Englishmen's lives, were spilled within this realm, as under the said queen Mary for the space of four years was to be seen, and I beseech the Lord never may be seen hereafter.

1563

ELIZABETHAN AGE

POETRY

NON-DRAMATIC

Edmund Spenser (1552?-1599)

THE FAERIE QUEENE, BOOK I

CANTO I

The patrone of true Holinesse
Foule Errour doth defeate:
Hypocrisie, him to entrappe,
Doth to his home entreate.

A GENTLE knight was pricking on the plaine,
Ycladd in mightie armes and silver shielde,
Wherein old dints of deepe woundes did remaine,
The cruell markes of many a bloody fielde;
Yet armes till that time did he never wield:
His angry steede did chide his foming bitt,
As much disdayning to the curbe to yield:
Full jolly knight he seemd, and faire did sitt,
As one for knightly giusts and fierce encounters fitt.

But on his brest a bloodie crosse he bore,
The deare remembrance of his dying Lord,
For whose sweete sake that glorious badge he wore,
And dead as living ever him adored:
Upon his shield the like was also scored,
For soveraine hope, which in his helpe he had:
Right faithfull true he was in deede and word,
But of his cheere did seeme too solemne sad;
Yet nothing did he dread, but ever was ydrad.

Upon a great adventure he was bond,
That greatest Gloriana to him gave,
That greatest glorious queene of Faery Lond,
To winne him worshippe, and her grace to have,
Which of all earthly thinges he most did crave;
And ever as he rode his hart did earne
To prove his puissance in battell brave
Upon his foe, and his new force to learne;
Upon his foe, a dragon horrible and stearne.

A lovely ladie rode him faire beside,
Upon a lowly asse more white then snow,
Yet she much whiter, but the same did hide
Under a vele, that wimpled was full low,
And over all a blacke stole shee did throw:
As one that inly mournd, so was she sad,
And heavie sate upon her palfrey slow:
Seemèd in heart some hidden care she had;
And by her in a line a milkewhite lambe she lad.

So pure and innocent, as that same lambe,
She was in life and every vertuous lore,
And by descent from royall lynage came
Of ancient kinges and queenes, that had of yore
Their scepters stretcht from east to westerne shore,
And all the world in their subjection held,
Till that infernall feend with foule uprore
Forwasted all their land, and them expeld:
Whom to avenge, she had this knight from far compeld.

Behind her farre away a dwarfe did lag,
That lasie seemd, in being ever last,
Or wearièd with bearing of her bag
Of needments at his backe. Thus as they past,
The day with cloudes was suddeine overcast,
And angry Jove an hideous storme of raine
Did poure into his lemans lap so fast,
That everie wight to shrowd it did constrain,
And this faire couple eke to shroud themselves were fain.

Enforst to seeke some covert nigh at hand,
A shadie grove not farr away they spide,
That promist ayde the tempest to withstand:
Whose loftie trees, yclad with sommers pride,
Did spred so broad, that heavens light did hide,
Not perceable with power of any starr;
And all within were pathes and alleies wide,
With footing worne, and leading inward farr;
Faire harbour that them seemes, so in they entred ar.

And foorth they passe, with pleasure forward led,
Joying to heare the birdes sweete harmony,
Which, therein shrouded from the tempest dred,
Seemd in their song to scorne the cruell sky.
Much can they praise the trees so straight and hy,
The sayling pine, the cedar proud and tall,
The vine-propp elme, the poplar never dry,
The builder oake, sole king of forrests all,
The aspine good for staves, the cypresse funerall,

The laurell, meed of mightie conquerours
And poets sage, the firre that weepeth still,
The willow worne of forlorne paramours,
The eugh obedient to the benders will,
The birch for shaftes, the sallow for the mill,
The mirrhe sweete bleeding in the bitter wound,
The warlike beech, the ash for nothing ill,
The fruitfull olive, and the platane round,
The carver holme, the maple seeldom inward sound.

Led with delight, they thus beguile the way,
Untill the blustring storme is overblowne;
When, weening to returne whence they did stray,
They cannot finde that path, which first was showne,
But wander too and fro in waies unknowne,
Furthest from end then, when they neerest weene,
That makes them doubt, their wits be not their owne:
So many pathes, so many turnings seene,
That which of them to take, in diverse doubt they been.

At last resolving forward still to fare,
Till that some end they finde, or in or out,
That path they take, that beaten seemd most bare,
And like to lead the labyrinth about;
Which when by tract they hunted had throughout,
At length it brought them to a hollowe cave,
Amid the thickest woods. The champion stout
Eftsoones dismounted from his courser brave,
And to the dwarfe a while his needlesse spere he gave.

'Be well aware,' quoth then that ladie milde,
'Least suddaine mischiefe ye too rash provoke:
The danger hid, the place unknowne and wilde,
Breedes dreadfull doubts: oft fire is without smoke,
And perill without show: therefore your stroke,
Sir knight, with-hold, till further tryall made.'
'Ah, ladie,' sayd he, 'shame were to revoke
The forward footing for an hidden shade:
Vertue gives her selfe light, through darkenesse for to wade.'

'Yea, but,' quoth she, 'the perill of this place
I better wot then you; though nowe too late
To wish you backe returne with foule disgrace,
Yet wisedome warnes, whilest foot is in the gate,
To stay the steppe, ere forcèd to retrate.
This is the wandring wood, this Errours den,
A monster vile, whom God and man does hate:
Therefore I read beware.' 'Fly, fly!' quoth then
The fearefull dwarfe: 'this is no place for living men.'

But full of fire and greedy hardiment,
The youthfull knight could not for ought be staide,
But forth unto the darksom hole he went,
And lookèd in: his glistring armor made
A litle glooming light, much like a shade,
By which he saw the ugly monster plaine,
Halfe like a serpent horribly displaide,
But th' other halfe did womans shape retaine,
Most lothsom, filthie, foule, and full of vile disdaine.

And as she lay upon the durtie ground,
Her huge long taile her den all overspred,
Yet was in knots and many boughtes upwound,
Pointed with mortall sting. Of her there bred
A thousand yong ones, which she dayly fed,
Sucking upon her poisnous dugs, eachone
Of sundrie shapes, yet all ill favorèd:
Soone as that uncouth light upon them shone,
Into her mouth they crept, and suddain all were gone.

Their dam upstart, out of her den effraide,
And rushèd forth, hurling her hideous taile
About her cursèd head, whose folds displaid
Were stretcht now forth at length without entraile.
She lookt about and seeing one in mayle
Armèd to point, sought backe to turne againe;
For light she hated as the deadly bale,

Ay wont in desert darknes to remaine,
Where plain none might her see, nor she see any plaine.

Which when the valiant Elfe perceived, he lept
As lyon fierce upon the flying pray,
And with his trenchand blade her boldly kept
From turning backe, and forcèd her to stay:
Therewith enraged she loudly gan to bray,
And turning fierce, her speckled taile advaunst,
Threatning her angrie sting, him to dismay:
Who, nought aghast, his mightie hand enhaunst:
The stroke down from her head unto her shoulder glaunst.

Much daunted with that dint, her sence was dazed,
Yet kindling rage her selfe she gathered round,
And all attonce her beastly bodie raizd
With doubled forces high above the ground:
Tho, wrapping up her wrethèd sterne arownd,
Lept fierce upon his shield, and her huge traine
All suddenly about his body wound,
That hand or foot to stirr he strove in vaine:
God helpe the man so wrapt in Errours endlesse traine.

His lady, sad to see his sore constraint,
Cride out, 'Now, now, sir knight, shew what ye bee:
Add faith unto your force, and be not faint:
Strangle her, els she sure will strangle thee.'
That when he heard, in great perplexitie,
His gall did grate for griefe and high disdaine;
And knitting all his force, got one hand free,
Wherewith he grypt her gorge with so great paine,
That soone to loose her wicked bands did her constraine.

Therewith she spewd out of her filthie maw
A floud of poyson horrible and blacke,
Full of great lumps of flesh and gobbets raw,
Which stunck so vildly, that it forst him slacke
His grasping hold, and from her turne him backe:
Her vomit full of bookes and papers was,
With loathly frogs and toades, which eyes did lacke,
And creeping sought way in the weedy gras:
Her filthie parbreake all the place defilèd has.

As when old father Nilus gins to swell
With timely pride above the Aegyptian vale,
His fattie waves doe fertile slime outwell,
And overflow each plaine and lowly dale:
But when his later spring gins to avale,
Huge heapes of mudd he leaves, wherin there breed
Ten thousand kindes of creatures, partly male
And partly femall, of his fruitful seed;
Such ugly monstrous shapes elswher may no man reed.

The same so sore annoyèd has the knight,
That, welnigh chokèd with the deadly stinke,
His forces faile, ne can no lenger fight.
Whose corage when the feend perceivd to shrinke,
She pourèd forth out of her hellish sinke
Her fruitfull cursèd spawne of serpents small,
Deformèd monsters, fowle, and blacke as inke,
Which swarming all about his legs did crall,
And him encombred sore, but could not hurt at all.

As gentle shepheard in sweete eventide,
When ruddy Phebus gins to welke in west,
High on an hill, his flocke to vewen wide,
Markes which doe byte their hasty supper best;
A cloud of cumbrous gnattes doe him molest,
All striving to infixe their feeble stinges,
That from their noyance he no where can rest,
But with his clownish hands their tender wings
He brusheth oft, and oft doth mar their murmurings.

Thus ill bestedd, and fearefull more of shame
Then of the certeine perill he stood in,
Halfe furious unto his foe he came,
Resolvd in minde all suddenly to win,
Or soone to lose, before he once would lin;
And stroke at her with more then manly force,
That from her body, full of filthie sin,
He raft her hatefull heade without remorse:
A streame of cole black blood forth gushèd from her corse.

Her scattred brood, soone as their parent deare
They saw so rudely falling to the ground,
Groning full deadly, all with troublous feare,
Gathred themselves about her body round,
Weening their wonted entrance to have found
At her wide mouth: but being there withstood,
They flockèd all about her bleeding wound,

And suckèd up their dying mothers bloud,
Making her death their life, and eke her hurt their good.

That detestable sight him much amazde,
To see th' unkindly impes, of heaven accurst,
Devoure their dam; on whom while so he gazd,
Having all satisfide their bloudy thurst,
Their bellies swolne he saw with fulnesse burst,
And bowels gushing forth; well worthy end
Of such as drunke her life, the which them nurst!
Now needeth him no lenger labour spend;
His foes have slaine themselves, with whom he should contend.

His lady, seeing all that chaunst, from farre,
Approcht in hast to greet his victorie,
And saide, 'Faire knight, borne under happie starre,
Who see your vanquisht foes before you lye,
Well worthie be you of that armory,
Wherein ye have great glory wonne this day,
And prooved your strength on a strong enimie,
Your first adventure: many such I pray,
And henceforth ever wish that like succeed it may.'

Then mounted he upon his steede againe,
And with the lady backward sought to wend;
That path he kept which beaten was most plaine,
Ne ever would to any by way bend,
But still did follow one unto the end,
The which at last out of the wood them brought.
So forward on his way (with God to frend)
He passèd forth, and new adventure sought:
Long way he traveilèd, before he heard of ought.

At length they chaunst to meet upon the way
An agèd sire, in long blacke weedes yclad,
His feete all bare, his beard all hoarie gray,
And by his belte his booke he hanging had;
Sober he seemde, and very sagely sad,
And to the ground his eyes were lowly bent,
Simple in shew, and voide of malice bad,
And all the way he prayèd as he went,
And often knockt his brest, as one that did repent.

He faire the knight saluted, louting low,
Who faire him quited, as that courteous was;
And after askèd him, if he did know
Of straunge adventures, which abroad did pas.
'Ah! my dear sonne,' quoth he, 'how should, alas!
Silly old man, that lives in hidden cell,
Bidding his beades all day for his trespas,
Tydings of warre and worldly trouble tell?
With holy father sits not with such thinges to mell.

'But if of daunger, which hereby doth dwell,
And homebredd evil ye desire to heare,
Of a straunge man I can you tidings tell,
That wasteth all his countrie farre and neare.'
'Of such,' saide he, 'I chiefly doe inquere,
And shall you well rewarde to shew the place,
In which that wicked wight his dayes doth weare:
For to all knighthood it is foule disgrace,
That such a cursèd creature lives so long a space.'

'Far hence,' quoth he, 'in wastfull wildernesse,
His dwelling is, by which no living wight
May ever passe, but thorough great distresse.'
'Now,' saide the ladie, 'draweth toward night,
And well I wote, that of your later fight
Ye all forwearied be: for what so strong,
But, wanting rest, will also want of might?
The Sunne, that measures heaven all day long,
At night doth baite his steedes the ocean waves emong.

'Then with the Sunne take, sir, your timely rest,
And with new day new worke at once begin:
Untroubled night, they say, gives counsell best.'
'Right well, sir knight, ye have advisèd bin,'
Quoth then that agèd man; 'the way to win
Is wisely to advise: now day is spent;
Therefore with me ye may take up your in
For this same night.' The knight was well content:
So with that godly father to his home they went.

A litle lowly hermitage it was,
Downe in a dale, hard by a forests side,
Far from resort of people, that did pas
In traveill to and froe: a litle wyde
There was an holy chappell edifyde,
Wherein the hermite dewly wont to say
His holy thinges each morne and even-tyde:
Thereby a christall streame did gently play,
Which from a sacred fountaine wellèd forth alway.

Arrivèd there, the litle house they fill,
Ne looke for entertainement, where none was:
Rest is their feast, and all thinges at their will;
The noblest mind the best contentment has.
With faire discourse the evening so they pas:
For that olde man of pleasing wordes had store,
And well could file his tongue as smooth as glas:
He told of saintes and popes, and evermore
He strowd an Ave-Mary after and before.

The drouping night thus creepeth on them fast,
And the sad humor loading their eye liddes,
As messenger of Morpheus, on them cast
Sweet slombring deaw, the which to sleep them biddes:
Unto their lodgings then his guestes he riddes:
Where when all drownd in deadly sleepe he findes,
He to his studie goes, and there amiddes
His magick bookes and artes of sundrie kindes,
He seekes out mighty charmes, to trouble sleepy minds.

Then choosing out few words most horrible,
(Let none them read) thereof did verses frame;
With which and other spelles like terrible,
He bad awake blacke Plutoes griesly dame,
And cursèd heven, and spake reproachful shame
Of highest God, the Lord of life and light:
A bold bad man, that dared to call by name
Great Gorgon, prince of darknes and dead night,
At which Cocytus quakes, and Styx is put to flight.

And forth he cald out of deepe darknes dredd
Legions of sprights, the which, like litle flyes
Fluttring about his ever damnèd hedd,
Awaite whereto their service he applyes,
To aide his friendes, or fray his enimies:
Of those he chose out two, the falsest twoo,
And fittest for to forge true-seeming lyes;
The one of them he gave a message too,
The other by him selfe staide, other worke to doo.

He, making speedy way through spersèd ayre,
And through the world of waters wide and deepe,
To Morpheus house doth hastily repaire.
Amid the bowels of the earth full steepe,
And low, where dawning day doth never peepe,
His dwelling is; there Tethys his wet bed
Doth ever wash, and Cynthia still doth steepe
In silver deaw his ever-drouping hed,
Whiles sad Night over him her mantle black doth spred.

Whose double gates he findeth lockèd fast,
The one faire framed of burnisht yvory,
The other all with silver overcast;
And wakeful dogges before them farre doe lye,
Watching to banish Care their enimy,
Who oft is wont to trouble gentle Sleepe.
By them the sprite doth passe in quietly,
And unto Morpheus comes, whom drownèd deepe
In drowsie fit he findes: of nothing he takes keepe.

And more, to lulle him in his slumber soft,
A trickling streame from high rock tumbling downe,
And ever drizling raine upon the loft,
Mixt with a murmuring winde, much like the sowne
Of swarming bees, did cast him in a swowne:
No other noyse, nor peoples troublous cryes,
As still are wont t'annoy the wallèd towne,
Might there be heard: but carelesse Quiet lyes,
Wrapt in eternall silence farre from enimyes.

The messenger approching to him spake,
But his waste wordes retourned to him in vaine:
So sound he slept, that nought mought him awake.
Then rudely he him thrust, and pusht with paine,
Whereat he gan to stretch: but he againe
Shooke him so hard, that forcèd him to speake.
As one then in a dreame, whose dryer braine
Is tost with troubled sights and fancies weake,
He mumbled soft, but would not all his silence breake.

The sprite then gan more boldly him to wake,
And threatened unto him the dreaded name
Of Hecate: whereat he gan to quake,
And, lifting up his lompish head, with blame
Halfe angrie askèd him, for what he came.
'Hether,' quoth he, 'me Archimago sent,
He that the stubborne sprites can wisely tame;

He bids thee to him send for his intent
A fit false dreame, that can delude the sleepers sent.'

The god obayde, and calling forth straight way
A diverse dreame out of his prison darke,
Delivered it to him, and downe did lay
His heavie head, devoide of careful carke;
Whose sences all were straight benumbd and starke.
He, backe returning by the yvorie dore,
Remounted up as light as cheareful larke,
And on his litle winges the dreame he bore
In hast unto his lord, where he him left afore.

Who all this while, with charmes and hidden artes,
Had made a lady of that other spright,
And framed of liquid ayre her tender partes,
So lively and so like in all mens sight,
That weaker sence it could have ravisht quight:
The maker selfe, for all his wondrous witt,
Was nigh beguilèd with so goodly sight:
Her all in white he clad, and over it
Cast a black stole, most like to seeme for Una fit.

Now when that ydle dreame was to him brought,
Unto that Elfin knight he bad him fly,
Where he slept soundly, void of evil thought,
And with false shewes abuse his fantasy,
In sort as he him schoolèd privily:
And that new creature, borne without her dew,
Full of the makers guyle, with usage sly
He taught to imitate that lady trew,
Whose semblance she did carrie under feignèd hew.

Thus well instructed, to their worke they haste,
And comming where the knight in slomber lay,
The one upon his hardie head him plaste,
And made him dreame of loves and lustfull play,
That nigh his manly hart did melt away,
Bathèd in wanton blis and wicked joy.
Then seemèd him his lady by him lay,
And to him playnd, how that false wingèd boy
Her chaste hart had subdewd to learne Dame Pleasures toy.

And she her selfe, of beautie soveraigne queene,
Fayre Venus, seemde unto his bed to bring
Her, whom he, waking, evermore did weene
To bee the chastest flowre that aye did spring
On earthly braunch, the daughter of a king,
Now a loose leman to vile service bound:
And eke the Graces seemèd all to sing
Hymen iö Hymen, dauncing all around,
Whylst freshest Flora her with yvie girlond crownd.

In this great passion of unwonted lust,
Or wonted feare of doing ought amis,
He started up, as seeming to mistrust
Some secret ill, or hidden foe of his:
Lo! there before his face his ladie is,
Under blacke stole hyding her bayted hooke,
And as halfe blushing offred him to kis,
With gentle blandishment and lovely looke,
Most like that virgin true, which for her knight him took.

All cleane dismayd to see so uncouth sight,
And halfe enragèd at her shamelesse guise,
He thought have slaine her in his fierce despight:
But hastie heat tempring with sufferance wise,
He stayde his hand, and gan himselfe advise
To prove his sense, and tempt her faignèd truth.
Wringing her hands in wemens pitteous wise,
Tho can she weepe, to stirre up gentle ruth,
Both for her noble blood, and for her tender youth.

And sayd, 'Ah sir, my liege lord and my love,
Shall I accuse the hidden cruell fate,
And mightie causes wrought in heaven above,
Or the blind god, that doth me thus amate,
For hopèd love to winne me certaine hate?
Yet thus perforce he bids me do, or die.
Die is my dew: yet rew my wretched state
You, whom my hard avenging destinie
Hath made judge of my life or death indifferently.

'Your owne deare sake forst me at first to leave
My fathers 'kingdom' — There she stopt with teares;
Her swollen hart her speech seemed to bereave;
And then againe begonne: 'My weaker yeares,
Captived to fortune and frayle worldly feares,
Fly to your fayth for succour and sure ayde:
Let me not die in languor and long teares.'
'Why, dame,' quoth he, 'what hath ye thus dismayd?
What frayes ye, that were wont to comfort me affrayd?'

'Love of your selfe,' she saide, 'and deare constraint,
Lets me not sleepe, but waste the wearie night
In secret anguish and unpittied plaint,
Whiles you in careless sleepe are drownèd quight.'
Her doubtfull words made that redoubted knight
Suspect her truth: yet since no' untruth he knew,
Her fawning love with foule disdainefull spight
He would not shend, but said, 'Deare dame, I rew,
That for my sake unknowne such griefe unto you grew.

'Assure your selfe, it fell not all to ground;
For all so deare as life is to my hart,
I deeme your love, and hold me to you bound;
Ne let vaine feares procure your needlesse smart,
Where cause is none, but to your rest depart.'
Not all content, yet seemd she to appease
Her mournfull plaintes, beguilèd of her art,
And fed with words, that could not chose but please;
So slyding softly forth, she turnd as to her ease.

Long after lay he musing at her mood,
Much grieved to thinke that gentle dame so light,
For whose defence he was to shed his blood.
At last dull wearines of former fight
Having yrockt asleepe his irkesome spright,
That troublous dreame gan freshly tosse his braine
With bowres, and beds, and ladies deare delight:
But when he saw his labour all was vaine,
With that misformèd spright he backe returnd againe.

CANTO II

The guilefull great enchaunter parts
The Redcrosse Knight from Truth:
Into whose stead faire Falshood steps,
And workes him woefull ruth.

By this the northerne wagoner had set
His sevenfold teme behind the stedfast starre,
That was in ocean waves yet never wet,
But firme is fixt, and sendeth light from farre
To al that in the wide deepe wandring arre:
And chearefull Chaunticlere with his note shrill
Had warnèd once, that Phoebus fiery carre
In hast was climbing up the easterne hill,
Full envious that night so long his roome did fill:

When those accursèd messengers of hell,
That feigning dreame, and that faire-forgèd spright,
Came to their wicked maister, and gan tel
Their bootelesse paines, and ill succeeding night:
Who, all in rage to see his skilfull might
Deluded so, gan threaten hellish paine
And sad Proserpines wrath, them to affright.
But when he saw his threatning was but vaine,
He cast about, and searcht his baleful bokes againe.

Eftsoones he tooke that miscreated faire,
And that false other spright, on whom he spred
A seeming body of the subtile aire,
Like a young squire, in loves and lustyhed
His wanton daies that ever loosely led,
Without regard of armes and dreaded fight:
Those twoo he tooke, and in a secrete bed,
Covered with darkenes and misdeeming night,
Them both together laid, to joy in vaine delight.

Forthwith he runnes with feignèd faithfull hast
Unto his guest, who, after troublous sights
And dreames, gan now to take more sound repast;
Whom suddenly he wakes with fearful frights,
As one aghast with feends or damnèd sprights,
And to him cals: 'Rise, rise, unhappy swaine,
That here wex old in sleepe, whiles wicked wights
Have knit themselves in Venus shameful chaine;
Come see, where your false lady doth her honor staine.'

All in amaze he suddenly up start
With sword in hand, and with the old man went;
Who soone him brought into a secret part,
Where that false couple were full closely ment
In wanton lust and leud embracement;
Which when he saw, he burnt with gealous fire,
The eie of reason was with rage yblent,
And would have slaine them in his furious ire,
But hardly was restreinèd of that agèd sire.

Retourning to his bed in torment great,
And bitter anguish of his guilty sight,
He could not rest, but did his stout heart eat,
And wast his inward gall with deepe despight,
Yrkesome of life, and too long lingring night.

At last faire Hesperus in highest skie
Had spent his lampe, and brought forth dawning light;
Then up he rose, and clad him hastily;
The dwarfe him brought his steed: so both away do fly.

Now when the rosy fingred Morning faire,
Weary of agèd Tithones saffron bed,
Had spred her purple robe through deawy aire,
And the high hils Titan discoverèd,
The royall virgin shooke of drousyhed,
And rising forth out of her baser bowre,
Lookt for her knight, who far away was fled,
And for her dwarfe, that wont to wait each howre:
Then gan she wail and weepe, to see that woeful stowre.

And after him she rode with so much speede,
As her slowe beast could make; but all in vaine:
For him so far had borne his light-foot steede,
Prickèd with wrath and fiery fierce disdaine,
That him to follow was but fruitlesse paine;
Yet she her weary limbes would never rest,
But every hil and dale, each wood and plaine,
Did search, sore grievèd in her gentle brest,
He so ungently left her, whome she lovèd best.

But subtill Archimago, when his guests
He saw divided into double parts,
And Una wandring in woods and forrests,
Th' end of his drift, he praisd his divelish arts,
That had such might over true meaning harts:
Yet rests not so, but other meanes doth make,
How he may worke unto her further smarts:
For her he hated as the hissing snake,
And in her many troubles did most pleasure take.

He then devisde himselfe how to disguise;
For by his mighty science he could take
As many formes and shapes in seeming wise,
As ever Proteus to himselfe could make:
Sometime a fowle, sometime a fish in lake,
Now like a foxe, now like a dragon fell,
That of himselfe he ofte for feare would quake,
And oft would flie away. O who can tell
The hidden powre of herbes, and might of magick spel?

But now seemde best, the person to put on
Of that good knight, his late beguilèd guest:
In mighty armes he was yclad anon,
And silver shield; upon his coward brest
A bloody crosse, and on his craven crest
A bounch of heares discolourd diversly:
Full jolly knight he seemde, and wel addrest,
And when he sate uppon his courser free,
Saint George himselfe ye would have deemèd him to be.

But he, the knight whose semblaunt he did beare,
The true Saint George, was wandred far away,
Still flying from his thoughts and gealous feare;
Will was his guide, and griefe led him astray.
At last him chaunst to meete upon the way
A faithlesse Sarazin, all armde to point,
In whose great shield was writ with letters gay
Sans foy: full large of limbe and every joint
He was, and carèd not for God or man a point.

Hee had a faire companion of his way,
A goodly lady clad in scarlot red,
Purfled with gold and pearle of rich assay;
And like a Persian mitre on her hed
Shee wore, with crowns and owches garnishèd,
The which her lavish lovers to her gave:
Her wanton palfrey all was overspred
With tinsell trappings, woven like a wave,
Whose bridle rung with golden bels and bosses brave.

With faire disport and courting dalliaunce
She intertainde her lover all the way:
But when she saw the knight his speare advaunce,
Shee soone left of her mirth and wanton play,
And bad her knight addresse him to the fray:
His foe was nigh at hand. He, prickte with pride
And hope to winne his ladies hearte that day,
Forth spurrèd fast: adowne his coursers side
The red bloud trickling staind the way, as he did ride.

The Knight of the Redcrosse, when him he spide
Spurring so hote with rage dispiteous,
Gan fairely couch his speare, and towards ride:
Soone meete they both, both fell and furious,
That, daunted with theyr forces hideous,
Their steeds doe stagger, and amazèd stand,
And eke themselves, too rudely rigorous,

Astonied with the stroke of their owne hand.
Doe backe rebutte, and ech to other yealdeth land.
As when two rams, stird with ambitious pride,
Fight for the rule of the rich fleecèd flocke,
Their hornèd fronts so fierce on either side
Doe meete, that, with the terror of the shocke
Astonied, both stand sencelesse as a blocke,
Forgetfull of the hanging victory:
So stood these twaine, unmovèd as a rocke,
Both staring fierce, and holding idely
The broken reliques of their former cruelty.

The Sarazin, sore daunted with the buffe,
Snatcheth his sword, and fiercely to him flies;
Who well it wards, and quyteth cuff with cuff:
Each others equall puissaunce envies,
And through their iron sides with cruell spies
Does seeke to perce: repining courage yields
No foote to foe. The flashing fier flies,
As from a forge, out of their burning shields,
And streams of purple bloud new dies the verdant fields.

'Curse on that Crosse,' quoth then the Sarazin,
'That keepes thy body from the bitter fitt!
Dead long ygoe, I wote, thou haddest bin,
Had not that charme from thee forwarnèd itt:
But yet I warne thee now assurèd sitt,
And hide thy head.' Therewith upon his crest
With rigor so outrageous he smitt,
That a large share it hewd out of the rest,
And glauncing downe his shield, from blame him fairely blest.

Who thereat wondrous wroth, the sleeping spark
Of native vertue gan eftsoones revive,
And at his haughty helmet making mark,
So hugely stroke, that it the steele did rive,
And cleft his head. He, tumbling downe alive,
With bloudy mouth his mother earth did kis,
Greeting his grave: his grudging ghost did strive
With the fraile flesh; at last it flitted is,
Whether the soules doe fly of men that live amis.

The lady, when she saw her champion fall,
Like the old ruines of a broken towre,
Staid not to waile his woefull funerall,
But from him fled away with all her powre;
Who after her as hastily gan scowre,
Bidding the dwarfe with him to bring away
The Sarazins shield, signe of the conquer-oure.
Her soone he overtooke, and bad to stay,
For present cause was none of dread her to dismay.

Shee, turning backe with ruefull countenaunce,
Cride, 'Mercy, mercy, sir, vouchsafe to showe
On silly dame, subject to hard mischaunce,
And to your mighty wil!' Her humblesse low,
In so ritch weedes and seeming glorious show,
Did much emmove his stout heroicke heart,
And said, 'Deare dame, your suddein overthrow
Much rueth me; but now put feare apart,
And tel, both who ye be, and who that tooke your part.'

Melting in teares, then gan shee thus lament:
'The wreched woman, whom unhappy howre
Hath now made thrall to your commandement,
Before that angry heavens list to lowre,
And Fortune false betraide me to your powre,
Was, (O what now availeth that I was?)
Borne the sole daughter of an emperour,
He that the wide west under his rule has,
And high hath set his throne where Tiberis doth pas.

'He, in the first flowre of my freshest age,
Betrothèd me unto the onely haire
Of a most mighty king, most rich and sage;
Was never prince so faithfull and so faire,
Was never prince so meeke and debonaire;
But ere my hopèd day of spousall shone,
My dearest lord fell from high honors staire,
Into the hands of hys accursèd fone,
And cruelly was slaine, that shall I ever mone.

'His blessèd body, spoild of lively breath,
Was afterward, I know not how, convaid
And fro me hid: of whose most innocent death
When tidings came to mee, unhappy maid,
O how great sorrow my sad soule assaid!
Then forth I went his woefull corse to find,

And many yeares throughout the world I straid,
A virgin widow, whose deepe wounded mind
With love, long time did languish as the striken hind.

'At last it chauncèd this proud Sarazin
To meete me wandring; who perforce me led
With him away, but yet could never win
The fort, that ladies hold in soveraigne dread.
There lies he now with foule dishonor dead,
Who, whilse he livde, was callèd proud Sansfoy:
The eldest of three brethren, all three bred
Of one bad sire, whose youngest is Sansjoy,
And twixt them both was born the bloudy bold Sansloy.

'In this sad plight, friendlesse, unfortunate,
Now miserable I Fidessa dwell,
Craving of you, in pitty of my state,
To doe none ill, if please ye not doe well.'
He in great passion al this while did dwell,
More busying his quicke eies, her face to view,
Then his dull eares, to heare what shee did tell:
And said, 'Faire lady, hard of flint would rew
The undeservèd woes and sorrows which ye shew.

'Henceforth in safe assuraunce may ye rest,
Having both found a new friend you to aid,
And lost an old foe, that did you molest:
Better new friend then an old foe is said.'
With chaunge of chear the seeming simple maid
Let fal her eien, as shamefast, to the earth,
And yeelding soft, in that she nought gainsaid,
So forth they rode, he feining seemely merth,
And shee coy lookes: so dainty, they say, maketh derth.

Long time they thus together traveilèd,
Til, weary of their way, they came at last
Where grew two goodly trees, that faire did spred
Their armes abroad, with gray mosse overcast,
And their greene leaves, trembling with every blast,
Made a calme shadowe far in compasse round:
The fearefull shepheard, often there aghast,
Under them never sat, ne wont there sound
His merry oaten pipe, but shund th' unlucky ground.

But this good knight, soone as he them can spie,
For the coole shade him thither hastly got:
For golden Phoebus, now ymounted hie,
From fiery wheeles of his faire chariot
Hurlèd his beame so scorching cruell hot,
That living creature mote it not abide;
And his new lady it endurèd not.
There they alight, in hope themselves to hide
From the fierce heat, and rest their weary limbs a tide.

Faire seemely pleasaunce each to other makes,
With goodly purposes, there as they sit:
And in his falsèd fancy he her takes
To be the fairest wight that livèd yit;
Which to expresse, he bends his gentle wit,
And thinking of those braunches greene to frame
A girlond for her dainty forehead fit,
He pluckt a bough; out of whose rifte there came
Smal drops of gory bloud, that trickled down the same.

Therewith a piteous yelling voice was heard,
Crying, 'O spare with guilty hands to teare
My tender sides in this rough rynd embard;
But fly, ah! fly far hence away, for feare
Least to you hap that happened to me heare,
And to this wretched lady, my deare love;
O too deare love, love bought with death too deare!'
Astond he stood, and up his heare did hove,
And with that suddein horror could no member move.

At last, whenas the dreadfull passion
Was overpast, and manhood well awake,
Yet musing at the straunge occasion,
And doubting much his sence, he thus bespake:
'What voice of damnèd ghost from Limbo lake,
Or guilefull spright wandring in empty aire,
Both which fraile men doe oftentimes mistake,

Sends to my doubtful eares these speaches rare,
And ruefull plaints, me bidding guiltlesse blood to spare?'

Then groning deep: 'Nor damnèd ghost,' quoth he,
'Nor guileful sprite to thee these words doth speake,
But once a man, Fradubio, now a tree;
Wretched man, wretched tree! whose nature weake
A cruell witch, her cursèd will to wreake,
Hath thus transformd, and plast in open plaines,
Where Boreas doth blow full bitter bleake,
And scorching sunne does dry my secret vaines:
For though a tree I seme, yet cold and heat me paines.'

'Say on, Fradubio, then, or man or tree,'
Quoth then the knight; 'by whose mischievous arts
Art thou misshapèd thus, as now I see?
He oft finds med'cine who his griefe imparts;
But double griefs afflict concealing harts,
As raging flames who striveth to suppresse.'
'The author then,' said he, 'of all my smarts,
Is one Duessa, a false sorceresse,
That many errant knights hath broght to wretchednesse.

'In prime of youthly yeares, when corage hott
The fire of love and joy of chevalree
First kindled in my brest, it was my lott
To love this gentle lady, whome ye see
Now not a lady, but a seeming tree;
With whome as once I rode accompanyde,
Me chauncèd of a knight encountred bee,
That had a like faire lady by his syde;
Lyke a faire lady, but did fowle Duessa hyde.

'Whose forgèd beauty he did take in hand
All other dames to have exceded farre;
I in defence of mine did likewise stand,
Mine, that did then shine as the morning starre:
So both to batteill fierce arraungèd arre;
In which his harder fortune was to fall
Under my speare; such is the dye of warre:
His lady, left as a prise martiall,
Did yield her comely person, to be at my call.

'So doubly loved of ladies unlike faire,
Th' one seeming such, the other such indeede
One day in doubt I cast for to compare,
Whether in beauties glorie did exceede;
A rosy girlond was the victors meede.
Both seemde to win, and both seemde won to bee,
So hard the discord was to be agreede:
Frælissa was as faire as faire mote bee,
And ever false Duessa seemde as faire as shee.

'The wicked witch, now seeing all this while
The doubtfull ballaunce equally to sway,
What not by right, she cast to win by guile;
And by her hellish science raisd streight way
A foggy mist, that overcast the day,
And a dull blast, that, breathing on her face,
Dimmèd her former beauties shining ray,
And with foule ugly forme did her disgrace:
Then was she fayre alone, when none was faire in place.

'Then cride she out, "Fye, fye! deformèd wight,
Whose borrowed beautie now appeareth plaine
To have before bewitchèd all mens sight;
O leave her soone, or let her soone be slaine."
Her loathly visage viewing with disdaine,
Eftsoones I thought her such as she me told,
And would have kild her; but with faignèd paine
The false witch did my wrathfull hand withhold:
So left her, where she now is turnd to treen mould.

'Thensforth I tooke Duessa for my dame,
And in the witch unweeting joyd long time,
Ne ever wist but that she was the same:
Till on a day (that day is everie prime,
When witches wont do penance for their crime)
I chaunst to see her in her proper hew,
Bathing her selfe in origane and thyme:
A filthy foule old woman I did vew,
That ever to have toucht her I did deadly rew.

'Her neather partes misshapen, monstruous,
Were hidd in water, that I could not see,
But they did seeme more foule and hideous,
Then womans shape man would beleeve to bee.
Thensforth from her most beastly companie
I gan refraine, in minde to slipp away,

Soone as appeard safe opportunitie:
For danger great, if not assurd decay,
I saw before mine eyes, if I were knowne to stray.

'The divelish hag, by chaunges of my cheare,
Perceived my thought; and drownd in sleepie night,
With wicked herbes and oyntments did besmeare
My body all, through charmes and magicke might,
That all my senses were bereavèd quight:
Then brought she me into this desert waste.
And by my wretched lovers side me pight,
Where now enclosd in wooden wals full faste,
Banisht from living wights, our wearie daies we waste.'

'But how long time,' said then the Elfin knight,
'Are you in this misformèd hous to dwell?'
'We may not chaunge,' quoth he, 'this evill plight
Till we be bathèd in a living well;
That is the terme prescribèd by the spell.'
'O how,' sayd he, 'mote I that well out find,
That may restore you to your wonted well?'
'Time and suffisèd fates to former kynd
Shall us restore; none else from hence may us unbynd.'

The false Duessa, now Fidessa hight,
Heard how in vaine Fradubio did lament,
And knew well all was true. But the good knight
Full of sad feare and ghastly dreriment,
When all this speech the living tree had spent,
The bleeding bough did thrust into the ground,
That from the blood he might be innocent,
And with fresh clay did close the wooden wound:
Then turning to his lady, dead with feare her fownd.

Her seeming dead he fownd with feignèd feare,
As all unweeting of that well she knew,
And paynd himselfe with busie care to reare
Her out of carelesse swowne. Her eyelids blew,
And dimmèd sight, with pale and deadly hew,
At last she up gan lift: with trembling cheare
Her up he tooke, too simple and too trew,
And oft her kist. At length, all passèd feare,
He set her on her steede, and forward forth did beare.

CANTO III

Forsaken Truth long seekes her love,
And makes the Lyon mylde;
Marres Blind Devotions mart, and fals
In hand of leachour vylde.

Nought is there under heav'ns wide hollownesse
That moves more deare compassion of mind
Then beautie brought t'unworthie wretchednesse
Through envies snares or fortunes freakes unkind:
I, whether lately through her brightnes blynd,
Or through alleageance and fast fealty
Which I do owe unto all womankynd,
Feele my hart perst with so great agony,
When such I see, that all for pitty I could dy.

And now it is empassionèd so deepe
For fairest Unaes sake, of whom I sing,
That my frayle eies these lines with teares do steepe,
To thinke how she through guyleful handeling,
Though true as touch, though daughter of a king,
Though faire as ever living wight was fayre,
Though nor in word nor deede ill meriting,
Is from her knight divorcèd in despayre,
And her dew loves deryved to that vile witches shayre.

Yet she, most faithfull ladie, all this while
Forsaken, wofull, solitarie mayd,
Far from all peoples preace, as in exile,
In wildernesse and wastfull deserts strayd
To seeke her knight; who, subtily betrayd
Through that late vision which th' enchaunter wrought,
Had her abandond. She, of nought affrayd,
Through woods and wastnes wide him daily sought;
Yet wishèd tydinges none of him unto her brought.

One day, nigh wearie of the yrkesome way,
From her unhastie beast she did alight,
And on the grasse her dainty limbs did lay

In secrete shadow, far from all mens sight:
From her fayre head her fillet she undight,
And layd her stole aside. Her angels face
As the great eye of heaven shynèd bright,
And made a sunshine in the shady place;
Did never mortall eye behold such heavenly grace.

It fortunèd, out of the thickest wood
A ramping lyon rushèd suddeinly,
Hunting full greedy after salvage blood:
Soone as the royall virgin he did spy,
With gaping mouth at her ran greedily,
To have attonce devourd her tender corse;
But to the pray when as he drew more ny,
His bloody rage aswagèd with remorse,
And, with the sight amazd, forgat his furious forse.

In stead thereof he kist her wearie feet,
And lickt her lilly hands with fawning tong,
As he her wrongèd innocence did weet.
O how can beautie maister the most strong,
And simple truth subdue avenging wrong!
Whose yielded pryde and proud submission,
Still dreading death, when she had markèd long,
Her hart gan melt in great compassion,
And drizling teares did shed for pure affection.

'The lyon, lord of everie beast in field,'
Quoth she, 'his princely puissance doth abate,
And mightie proud to humble weake does yield,
Forgetfull of the hungry rage, which late
Him prickt, in pittie of my sad estate:
But he, my lyon, and my noble lord,
How does he find in cruell hart to hate,
Her that him loved, and ever most adord,
As the god of my life? why hath he me abhord?'

Redounding teares did choke th' end of her plaint,
Which softly ecchoed from the neighbour wood;
And sad to see her sorrowfull constraint
The kingly beast upon her gazing stood;
With pittie calmd, downe fell his angry mood.
At last, in close hart shutting up her paine,
Arose the virgin borne of heavenly brood,
And to her snowy palfrey got agayne,
To seeke her strayèd champion if she might attayne.

The lyon would not leave her desolate,
But with her went along, as a strong gard
Of her chast person, and a faythfull mate
Of her sad troubles and misfortunes hard:
Still, when she slept, he kept both watch and ward,
And when she wakt, he wayted diligent,
With humble service to her will prepard:
From her fayre eyes he tooke commandement,
And ever by her lookes conceivèd her intent.

Long she thus traveilèd through deserts wyde,
By which she thought her wandring knight shold pas,
Yet never shew of living wight espyde;
Till that at length she found the troden gras,
In which the tract of peoples footing was,
Under the steepe foot of a mountaine hore;
The same she followes, till at last she has
A damzell spyde, slow footing her before,
That on her shoulders sad a pot of water bore.

To whom approching, she to her gan call,
To weet if dwelling place were nigh at hand;
But the rude wench her answerd nought at all;
She could not heare, nor speake, nor understand;
Till, seeing by her side the lyon stand,
With suddeine feare her pitcher downe she threw,
And fled away; for never in that land
Face of fayre lady she before did vew,
And that dredd lyons looke her cast in deadly hew.

Full fast she fled, ne ever lookt behynd,
As if her life upon the wager lay,
And home she came, whereas her mother blynd
Sate in eternall night: nought could she say,
But, suddeine catching hold, did her dismay
With quaking hands, and other signes of feare:
Who, full of ghastly fright and cold affray,
Gan shut the dore. By this arrivèd there
Dame Una, weary dame, and entrance did requere.

Which when none yielded, her unruly page
With his rude clawes the wicket open rent,
And let her in; where, of his cruell rage
Nigh dead with feare, and faint astonishment,
Shee found them both in darkesome corner pent;

Where that old woman day and night did pray
Upon her beads, devoutly penitent:
Nine hundred *Pater nosters* every day,
And thrise nine hundred *Aves*, she was wont to say.

And to augment her painefull penaunce more,
Thrise every weeke in ashes shee did sitt,
And next her wrinkled skin rough sackecloth wore,
And thrise three times did fast from any bitt:
But now for feare her beads she did forgett.
Whose needelesse dread for to remove away,
Faire Una framèd words and count'naunce fitt:
Which hardly doen, at length she gan them pray
That in their cotage small that night she rest her may.

The day is spent, and commeth drowsie night,
When every creature shrowded is in sleepe:
Sad Una downe her laies in weary plight,
And at her feete the lyon watch doth keepe:
In stead of rest, she does lament, and weepe
For the late losse of her deare lovèd knight,
And sighes, and grones, and ever more does steepe
Her tender brest in bitter teares all night;
All night she thinks too long, and often lookes for light.

Now when Aldeboran was mounted hye
Above the shinie Cassiopeias chaire,
And all in deadly sleepe did drownèd lye,
One knockèd at the dore, and in would fare;
He knockèd fast, and often curst, and sware,
That ready entraunce was not at his call:
For on his backe a heavy load he bare
Of nightly stelths and pillage severall,
Which he had got abroad by purchas criminall.

He was, to weete, a stout and sturdy thiefe,
Wont to robbe Churches of their ornaments,
And poore mens boxes of their due reliefe,
Which given was to them for good intents;
The holy saints of their rich vestiments
He did disrobe, when all men carelesse slept,
And spoild the priests of their habiliments;
Whiles none the holy things in safety kept,
Then he by conning sleights in at the window crept.

And all that he by right or wrong could find
Unto this house he brought, and did bestow
Upon the daughter of this woman blind,
Abessa, daughter of Corceca slow,
With whom he [lewdness] usd, that few did know,
And fed her fatt with feast of offerings,
And plenty, which in all the land did grow;
Ne sparèd he to give her gold and rings:
And now he to her brought part of his stolen things.

Thus, long the dore with rage and threats he bett,
Yet of those fearfull women none dorst rize,
(The lyon frayèd them,) him in to lett:
He would no lenger stay him to advize,
But open breakes the dore in furious wize,
And entring is; when that disdainfull beast,
Encountring fierce, him suddein doth surprize,
And seizing cruell clawes on trembling brest,
Under his lordly foot him proudly hath supprest.

Him booteth not resist, nor succour call,
His bleeding hart is in the vengers hand;
Who streight him rent in thousand peeces small,
And quite dismembred hath: the thirsty land
Dronke up his life; his corse left on the strand.
His fearefull freends weare out the wofull night,
Ne dare to weepe, nor seeme to understand
The heavie hap which on them is alight;
Affraid, least to themselves the like mishappen might.

Now when broad day the world discovered has,
Up Una rose, up rose the lyon eke,
And on their former journey forward pas,
In waies unknowne, her wandring knight to seeke,

With paines far passing that long wandring Greeke
That for his love refusèd deitye;
Such were the labours of this lady meeke,
Still seeking him that from her still did flye;
Then furthest from her hope, when most she weenèd nye.

Soone as she parted thence, the fearfull twayne,
That blind old woman and her daughter dear,
Came forth, and finding Kirkrapine there slayne,
For anguish great they gan to rend their heare,
And beat their brests, and naked flesh to teare.
And when they both had wept and wayld their fill,
Then forth they ran like two amazèd deare,
Halfe mad through malice and revenging will,
To follow her, that was the causer of their ill.

Whome overtaking, they gan loudly bray,
With hollow houling and lamenting cry,
Shamefully at her rayling all the way,
And her accusing of dishonesty,
That was the flowre of faith and chastity;
And still, amidst her rayling, she did pray
That plagues, and mischiefes, and long misery
Might fall on her, and follow all the way,
And that in endlesse error she might ever stray.

But when she saw her prayers nought prevaile,
Shee backe retournèd with some labour lost;
And in the way, as shee did weepe and waile,
A knight her mett in mighty armes embost,
Yet knight was not for all his bragging bost,
But subtill Archimag, that Una sought
By traynes into new troubles to have toste:
Of that old woman tidings he besought,
If that of such a ladie shee could tellen ought.

Therewith she gan her passion to renew,
And cry, and curse, and raile, and rend her heare,
Saying, that harlott she too lately knew,
That causd her shed so many a bitter teare,
And so forth told the story of her feare.
Much seemèd he to mone her haplesse chaunce,
And after for that lady did inquere;
Which being taught, he forward gan advaunce
His fair enchaunted steed, and eke his charmèd launce.

Ere long he came where Una traveild slow,
And that wilde champion wayting her besyde:
Whome seeing such, for dread hee durst not show
Him selfe too nigh at hand, but turnèd wyde
Unto an hil; from whence when she him spyde,
By his like seeming shield her knight by name
She weend it was, and towards him gan ride:
Approching nigh, she wist it was the same,
And with faire fearefull humblesse towards him shee came;

And weeping said, 'Ah! my long lackèd lord,
Where have ye bene thus long out of my sight?
Much fearèd I to have been quite abhord,
Or ought have done, that ye displeasen might,
That should as death unto my deare heart light:
For since mine eie your joyous sight did mis,
My chearefull day is turnd to chearelesse night,
And eke my night of death the shadow is;
But welcome now, my light, and shining lampe of blis.'

He thereto meeting said, 'My dearest dame,
Far be it from your thought and fro my wil
To thinke that knighthood I so much should shame,
As you to leave, that have me lovèd stil,
And chose in Faery court, of meere goodwil,
Where noblest knights were to be found on earth:
The earth shall sooner leave her kindly skil
To bring forth fruit, and make eternall derth,
Then I leave you, my liefe, yborn of hevenly berth.

'And sooth to say, why I lefte you so long,
Was for to seeke adventure in straunge place,
Where Archimago said a felon strong
To many knights did daily worke disgrace;
But knight he now shall never more deface:
Good cause of mine excuse, that mote ye please
Well to accept, and ever more embrace
My faithfull service, that by land and seas
Have vowd you to defend. Now then your plaint appease.'

His lovely words her seemd due recompence
Of all her passèd paines: one loving howre
For many yeares of sorrow can dispence:
A dram of sweete is worth a pound of sowre:
Shee has forgott how many a woeful stowre
For him she late endurd; she speakes no more
Of past: true is, that true love hath no powre
To looken backe; his eies be fixt before:
Before her stands her knight, for whom she toyld so sore.

Much like as when the beaten marinere,
That long hath wandred in the ocean wide,
Ofte soust in swelling Tethys saltish teare,
And long time having tand his tawney hide
With blustring breath of heaven, that none can bide,
And scorching flames of fierce Orions hound,
Soone as the port from far he has espide,
His chearfull whistle merily doth sound,
And Nereus crownes with cups; his mates him pledg around.

Such joy made Una, when her knight she found;
And eke th' enchaunter joyous seemde no lesse,
Then the glad marchant, that does vew from ground
His ship far come from watrie wildernesse;
He hurles out vowes, and Neptune oft doth blesse.
So forth they past, and all the way they spent
Discoursing of her dreadful late distresse,
In which he askt her, what the lyon ment:
Who told her all that fell in journey, as she went.

They had not ridden far, when they might see
One pricking towards them with hastie heat,
Full strongly armd, and on a courser free,
That through his fiersnesse fomèd all with sweat,
And the sharpe yron did for anger eat,
When his hot ryder spurd his chauffed side;
His looke was sterne, and seemèd still to threat
Cruell revenge, which he in hart did hyde;
And on his shield *Sans loy* in bloody lines was dyde.

When nigh he drew unto this gentle payre,
And saw the red-crosse, which the knight did beare,
He burnt in fire, and gan eftsoones prepare
Himselfe to batteill with his couchèd speare.
Loth was that other, and did faint through feare,
To taste th' untryèd dint of deadly steele;
But yet his lady did so well him cheare,
That hope of new good hap he gan to feele;
So bent his speare, and spurd his horse with yron heele.

But that proud Paynim forward came so ferce,
And full of wrath, that with his sharphead speare,
Through vainly crossèd shield he quite did perce,
And had his staggering steede not shronke for feare,
Through shield and body eke he should him beare:
Yet so great was the puissance of his push,
That from his sadle quite he did him beare:
He, tombling rudely downe, to ground did rush,
And from his gorèd wound a well of bloud did gush.

Dismounting lightly from his loftie steed,
He to him lept, in minde to reave his life,
And proudly said: 'Lo there the worthie meed
Of him that slew Sansfoy with bloody knife!
Henceforth his ghost, freed from repining strife,
In peace may passen over Lethe lake,
When mourning altars, purged with enimies life,

The black infernall Furies doen aslake:
Life from Sansfoy thou tookst, Sansloy shall from thee take.'

Therewith in haste his helmet gan unlace,
Till Una cride, 'O hold that heavie hand,
Deare sir, what ever that thou be in place!
Enough is, that thy foe doth vanquisht stand
Now at thy mercy: mercy not withstand:
For he is one the truest knight alive,
Though conquered now he lye on lowly land,
And whilest him fortune favourd, fayre did thrive
In bloudy field: therefore of life him not deprive.'

Her piteous wordes might not abate his rage,
But, rudely rending up his helmet, would
Have slayne him streight: but when he sees his age,
And hoarie head of Archimago old,
His hasty hand he doth amasèd hold,
And, halfe ashamèd, wondred at the sight:
For that old man well knew he, though untold,
In charmes and magick to have wondrous might;
Ne ever wont in field, ne in round lists, to fight.

And said, 'Why, Archimago, lucklesse syre,
What doe I see? what hard mishap is this,
That hath thee hether brought to taste mine yre?
Or thine the fault, or mine the error is,
In stead of foe to wound my friend amis?'
He answered nought, but in a traunce still lay,
And on those guilefull dazèd eyes of his
The cloude of death did sit. Which doen away,
He left him lying so, ne would no lenger stay;

But to the virgin comes; who all this while
Amasèd stands, her selfe so mockt to see
By him, who has the guerdon of his guile,
For so misfeigning her true knight to bee:
Yet is she now in more perplexitie,
Left in the hand of that same Paynim bold,
From whom her booteth not at all to flie;
Who, by her cleanly garment catching hold,
Her from her palfrey pluckt, her visage to behold.

But her fiers servant, full of kingly aw
And high disdaine, whenas his soveraine dame
So rudely handled by her foe he saw,
With gaping jawes full greedy at him came,
And, ramping on his shield, did weene the same
Have reft away with his sharp rending clawes:
But he was stout, and lust did now inflame
His corage more, that from his griping pawes
He hath his shield redeemd, and forth his swerd he drawes.

O then too weake and feeble was the forse
Of salvage beast, his puissance to withstand:
For he was strong, and of so mightie corse,
As ever wielded speare in warlike hand,
And feates of armes did wisely understand.
Eftsoones he percèd through his chaufèd chest
With thrilling point of deadly yron brand,
And launcht his lordly hart: with death opprest
He rored aloud, whiles life forsooke his stubborne brest.

Who now is left to keepe the forlorne maid
From raging spoile of lawlesse victors will?
Her faithfull gard removed, her hope dismaid,
Her selfe a yielded pray to save or spill.
He now, lord of the field, his pride to fill,
With foule reproches and disdaineful spight
Her vildly entertaines, and, will or nill,
Beares her away upon his courser light:
Her prayers nought prevaile; his rage is more of might.

And all the way, with great lamenting paine,
And piteous plaintes, she filleth his dull eares,
That stony hart could riven have in twaine,
And all the way she wetts with flowing teares:
But he, enraged with rancor, nothing heares.
Her servile beast yet would not leave her so,
But followes her far of, ne ought he feares,
To be partaker of her wandring woe.
More mild, in beastly kind, then that her beastly foe.

1590

Samuel Daniel (1562-1619)

THE CIVIL WARS

IMPRISONMENT AND DEATH OF RICHARD II

THE parliament, which now is held, decreed,
Whatever pleased the king but to propound,
Confirmes the crown to him, and to his seed,
And by their oath their due obedience bound;
Which was the power that stood him best in stead,
And made whatever broken courses sound.
For what he got by fortune, favour, might,
It was the state that now must make his right.

Here was agreed, to make all more secure,
That Richard should remain for evermore
Close prisoner; lest the realm might chance endure
Some new revolt, or any fresh uproar:
And that if any should such broil procure,
By him, or for him, he should die therefore.
So that a talk of tumult, and a breath,
Would serve him as his passing-bell to death.

Yet, reverend Carlile, thou didst there oppose
Thy holy voise to save thy prince's blood,
And freely check'dst this judgment and his foes:
When all were bad, yet thou dar'dst to be good.
Be it enrolled (that time may never lose
The memory) how firm thy courage stood,
When power, disgrace, nor death could ought divert
Thy glorious tongue thus to reveal thy heart.

'Grave, reverent lords, since that this sacred place,
Our Aventine-retire, our holy hill,
This place, soul of our state, the realm's best grace,
Doth privilege me speak what reason will:
Let me but say my conscience in this case:
Let sin of silence show my heart was ill:
And let these walls witness, if you will not,
I do discharge my soul of this foul blot.

'Never shall this poor breath of mine consent,
That he that two and twenty years hath reigned
As lawful lord, and king by just descent,
Should here be judged, unheard and unarraigned;
By subjects too, judges incompetent
To judge their king, unlawfully detained
And unbrought-forth to plead his guiltless cause;
Barring th' annointed liberty of laws.

'Have you not done enough with what is done?
Must needs disorder grow from bad to worse?
Can never mischief end as it begun;
But being once out, must further out, of force?
Think you that any means under the Sun,
Can assecure so indirect a course?
Or any broken cunning build so strong,
As can hold out the hand of vengeance long?'

Stopt there was his too vehement speech with speed,
And he sent close to ward from where he stood;
His zeal untimely, deemed too much t' exceed
The measure of his wit, and did no good.
They resolute, for all this, do proceed
Unto that judgment could not be withstood.
The king had all he craved, or could compel;
And all was done — let others judge how well.

Now, Muse, relate a woful accident,
And tell the bloodshed of these mighty peers,
Who (lately reconciled) rest discontent,
Grieved with disgrace, remaining in their fears:
However seeming outwardly content,
Yet th' inward touch that wounded honour bears,
Rests closely wrankling, and can find no ease,
Till death of one side cure this great disease.

Means how to feel and learn each other's heart,
By th' abbot's skill of Westminster is found;
Who, secretly disliking Henry's part,
Invites these lords, and those he meant to sound;
Feasts them with cost, and draws them on with art;
And dark and doubtful questions doth propound:
Then plainer speaks, and yet uncertain speaks:
Then wishes well — then off abruptly breaks.

'My lords,' saith he, 'I fear we shall not find
This long-desirèd king such as was thought.
But yet he may do well — God turn his mind:

'T is yet new days — but ill bodes new and nought.
Some yet speed well — though all men of my kind
Have cause to doubt. His speech is not forgot, —
That princes had too little, we too much.
God give him grace — but 't is ill trusting such.'

This open-close, apparent-dark discourse,
Drew on much speech: and every man replies:
And every man adds heat: and words enforce
And urge out words. For when one man espies
Another's mind like his, then ill breeds worse;
And out breaks all in th' end what closest lies.
For when men well have fed, th' blood being warm,
Then are they most improvident of harm.

Bewray they did their inward boiling spite;
Each stirring other to revenge their cause.
One says he never should endure the sight
Of that forsworn, that wrongs both land and laws.
Another vows the same; of his mind right.
A third t'a point more near the matter draws;
Swears if they would, he would attempt the thing,
To chase th' usurper, and replace their king.

Thus one by one kindling each other's fire,
Till all inflamed, they all in one agree;
All resolute to prosecute their ire,
Seeking their own and country's cause to free;
And have his first, that their blood did conspire.
For no way else, they said, but this, could be
Their wrong-detainèd honour to redeem,
Which true-bred blood should more than life esteem.

'And let not this our new-made faithless lord,'
Saith Surrey, 'think that we are left so bare
(Though bare enough) but we will find a sword
To kill him with, when he shall not be ware.'
For he that is with life and will enstored,
Hath (for revenge) enough, and needs not care:
For time brings means to furnish him withall;
Let him but wait th' occasions as they fall.

Then of the manner how t' effect the thing,
Consulted was, — and in the end agreed
That at a masque and common revelling,
Which was ordained, they should perform the deed:
For that would be least doubted of the king,
And fittest for their safety to proceed.
The night, their number, and the sudden act
Would dash all order, and protect their fact.

Besides, they might under the fair pretence
Of tilts and tournaments, which they intend,
Provide them horse and armour for defence,
And all things else convenient for their end.
Besides, they might hold sure intelligence
Among themselves, without suspect t' offend:
The king would think, they sought but grace in court,
With all their great preparing in this sort.

A solemn oath religiously they take,
By intermutual vows protesting there,
This never to reveal, nor to forsake
So good a cause, for danger, hope, or fear.
The sacrament, the pledge of faith, they take:
And every man upon his sword doth swear,
By knighthood, honour, or what else should bind;
To assecure the more each other's mind.

And when all this was done, and thought well done,
And every one assures him good success,
And easy seems the thing to every one,
That nought could cross their path, or them suppress;
Yet one among the rest (whose mind not won
With th' overweening thought of hot excess,
Nor headlong carried with the stream of will,
Nor by his own election led to ill),

Judicious Blount (whose learning, valour, wit,
Had taught true knowledge in the course of things;
Knew dangers as they were; and th' hum'rous fit
Of 'wareless discontent, what end it brings)
Counsels their heat with calm grave words, and fit,
(Words well fore-thought, that from experience springs)
And warns a warier carriage in the thing,
Lest blind presumption work their ruining.

'My lords,' saith he, 'I know your wisdom's such,
As that of mine advice you have no need;
I know you know how much the thing doth touch
The main of all your states, your blood, your seed;
Yet since the same concerns my life as much
As his whose hand is chiefest in this deed,
And that my foot must go as far as his;
I think my tongue may speak what needful is.

'The thing we enterprise, I know, doth bear
Great possibility of good effect;
For that so many men of might there are,
That venture here this action to direct;
Which meaner wights, of trust and credit bare,
Not so respected, could not look t' effect.
For none, without great hopes, will follow such,
Whose power and honour doth not promise much.

'Besides, this new and doubtful government,
The wavering faith of people vain and light;
The secret hopes of many discontent;
The natural affection to the right;
Our lawful sovereign's life, in prison pent,
Whom men begin to pity now, not spite;
Our well-laid plot and all, I must confess,
With our just cause, doth promise good success.

'But this is yet the outward, fairest side
Of our design — Within rests more of fear,
More dread of sad event yet undescried,
Than, my most worthy lords, I would there were.
But yet I speak not this, as to divide
Your thoughts from th' act, or to dismay your cheer;
Only to add unto your forward will
A moderate fear, to cast the worst of ill.

'Danger before, and in, and after th' act,
You needs must grant, is great, and to be weighed.
Before; lest, while we do the deed protract,
It be by any of ourselves bewrayed;
For, many being privy to the fact,
How hard it is to keep it unbetrayed,
When the betrayer shall have life and grace,
And rid himself of danger and disgrace.

'For though some few continue resolute,
Yet many shrink, which at the first would dare,
And be the foremost men to execute,
If th' act and motion at one instant were:
But intermission suffers men dispute
What dangers are, and cast with further care.
Cold doubt cavils with honour, scorneth fame;
And in the end, fear weighs down faith with shame.

'Then in the act what perils shall we find,
If either place, or time, or other course
Cause us to alter th' order now assigned,
Or that, than we expect, things happen worse?
If either errour, or a fainting mind,
An indiscreet amazement, or remorse,
In any at that instant should be found,
How much it might the act, and all confound?

'After the deed, the dangers are no less;
Lest that our forwardness not seconded
By our own followers and accomplices,
Being kept back, or slow, or hinderèd,
The hasty multitude rush on, t' oppress
Confusèd weakness, there unsuccorèd;
Or raise another head of that same race,
T' avenge his death, and prosecute the case.

'All this, my lords, must be considerèd
(The best and worst of that which may succeed),
That valour mixed with fear, boldness with dread,
May march more circumspect, with better heed.
And to prevent these mischiefs mentionèd,
Is by our faith, our secrecy, and speed:
For even already is the work begun;
And we rest all undone, till all be done.

'And though I could have wished another course,
In open field t' have hazarded my blood;
Yet some are here, whose love is of that force
To draw my life, whom zeal hath not withstood.
But like you not of your design the worse:
If the success be good, your course is good;
And ending well, our honour then begins:
No hand of strife is pure, but that which wins.'

This said, a sad still silence filled their minds,
Upon the fearful project of their woe;
But that not long, ere forward fury finds
Encouraging persuasions on to go.
'We must,' said they, 'we will; our honour binds;

Our safety bids; our faith must have it so.
We know the worst can come: 't is thought upon.
We cannot shift — being in, we must go on.'

And on indeed they went — But O! not far;
A fatal stop traversed their headlong course;
Their drift 'comes known, and they discovered are:
For some (of many) will be false, of force.
Aumarle became the man that all did mar,
Whether through indiscretion, chance, or worse;
He makes his peace with offering others' blood,
And shows the king how all the matter stood.

Then lo! dismayed confusion all possessed
Th' afflicted troop, hearing their plot descried.
Then runs amazed distress, with sad unrest,
To this, to that; to fly, to stand, to hide:
Distracted terror knew not what was best,
On what determination to abide.
At last despair would yet stand to the sword,
To try what friends would do, or fate afford.

Then this, then that man's aid, they crave, implore;
Post here for help, seek there their followers;
Conjure their friends they had, labour for more;
Solicit all reputed favourers
Who Richard's cause seemed to affect before:
And in his name write, pray, send messengers
To try what faith was left, if by this art
Any would step to take affliction's part.

And some were found — and some again drew back:
Uncertain power could not itself retain.
Entreat they may; authority they lack:
And here and there they march (but all in vain)
With desperate course; like those that see their wreck
Even on the rocks of death; and yet they strain,
That death may not them idly find t' attend
Their certain last, but work to meet their end.

And long they stand not, ere the chief, surprised,
Conclude with their dear blood their tragedy:
And all the rest dispersed, run, some disguised
To unknown coasts; some to the shores do fly;
Some to the woods, or whither fear advised:
But running from, all to destruction hie.
The breach once made upon a battered state,
Down goes distress: no shelter shrouds their fate.

And now what horrour in their souls doth grow!
What sorrows with their friends and near allies!
What mourning in their ruined houses now!
How many children's plaints, and mothers' cries!
How many woful widows left to bow
To sad disgrace! What perished families!
What heirs of high rich hopes their thoughts must frame
To base down-looking poverty and shame!

This slaughter and calamity foregoes
Thy eminent destruction, woful king:
This is the bloody comet of thy woes,
That doth foretell thy present ruining.
Here was thy end decreed, when these men rose;
And even with theirs this act thy death did bring,
Or hastened, at the least, upon this ground;
Yet if not this, another had been found.

Kings, (lords of times and of occasions) may
Take their advantage when and how they list:
For now the realm, he thought, in this dismay,
T' avoid like mischiefs, neither would resist,
Nor feel the wound at all: since by this way,
All future disturbations would desist.
The root cut off, from whence these tumults rose,
He should have rest, the commonwealth repose.

He knew this time: and yet he would not seem
Too quick to wrath, as if affecting blood;
But yet complains so far, that men might deem
He would 't were done, and that he thought it good:

And wished that some would so his life esteem,
As rid him of these fears wherein he stood.
And therewith eyes a knight that then was by,
Who soon could learn his lesson by his eye.

The man, he knew, was one that willingly
For one good look would hazard soul and all;
An instrument for any villainy,
That needed no commission more at all:
A great ease to the king, that should hereby
Not need in this a course of justice call,
Nor seem to will the act. For though what's wrought
Were his own deed, he grieves should so be thought.

'So foul a thing, O thou Injustice art,
That torturest both the doer and distrest,
For when a man hath done a wicked part,
How doth he strive t' excuse, to make the best,
To shift the fault, t' unburden his charged heart;
And glad to find the least surmise of rest!
And if he could make his seem other's sin,
What great repose, what ease he finds therein!'

This knight — But yet, why should I call him knight,
To give impiety this reverent style?
Title of honour, worth, and virtue's right,
Should not be given to a wretch so vile.
But pardon me if I do not aright;
It is because I will not here defile
My unstained verse with his opprobrious name,
And grace him so, to place him in the same.

This caitiff goes, and with him takes eight more
As desperate as himself, impiously bold,
(Such villains as he knew would not abhor
To execute what wicked act he would)
And hastes him down to Pomfret: where before,
The restless king conveyed, was laid in hold:
There would he do the deed he thought should bring
To him great grace and favour with his king.

Whether the soul receives intelligence,
By her near genius, of the body's end,
And so imparts a sadness to the sense,
Foregoing ruin whereto it doth tend:
Or whether nature else hath conference
With profound sleep, and so doth warning send,
By prophetising dreams, what hurt is near,
And gives the heavy careful heart to fear:

However, so it is, the now sad king,
(Tossed here and there his quiet to confound,)
Feels a strange weight of sorrows gathering
Upon his trembling heart, and sees no ground;
Feels sudden terror bring cold shivering;
Lists not to eat, still muses, sleeps unsound;
His senses droop, his steady eyes unquick,
And much he ails, and yet he is not sick.

The morning of that day which was his last,
After a weary rest, rising to pain,
Out at a little grate his eyes he cast
Upon those bordering hills and open plain,
And views the town, and sees how people passed;
Where others' liberty makes him complain
The more his own, and grieves his soul the more,
Conferring captive crowns with freedom poor.

'O happy man,' saith he, 'that lo I see,
Grazing his cattle in those pleasant fields!
If he but knew his good (how blessèd he
That feels not what affliction greatness yields!),
Other than what he is he would not be,
Nor change his state with him that sceptres wields.
Thine, thine is that true life; that is to live —
To rest secure, and not rise up to grieve.

'Thou sit'st at home safe by thy quiet fire,
And hear'st of others' harms but feelest none;
And there thou tell'st of kings, and who aspire,
Who fall, who rise, who triumph, who do moan.
Perhaps thou talk'st of me, and dost inquire
Of my restraint, why here I live alone;
And pitiest this my miserable fall,
For pity must have part, envy not all.

'Thrice happy you, that look as from the shore,
And have no venture in the wrack you see,
No int'rest, no occasion to deplore
Other men's travels while yourselves sit free.
How much doth your sweet rest make us the more

To see our misery and what we be!
Whose blinded greatness, ever in turmoil,
Still seeking happy life, makes life a toil.

'Great Diocletian (and more great therefore,
For yielding up that whereto pride aspires),
Reck'ning thy gardens in Illyria more
Than all the empire, all what th' earth admires,
Thou well didst teach that he is never poor
That little hath, but he that much desires;
Finding more true delight in that small ground
Than in possessing all the earth was found.

'Are kings, that freedom give, themselves not free
As meaner men to take what they may give?
What! are they of so fatal a degree
That they cannot descend from that and live?
Unless they still be kings, can they not be?
Nor may they their authority survive?
Will not my yielded crown redeem my breath?
Still am I feared? Is there no way but death?'

Scarce this word 'death' from sorrow did proceed,
When in rushed one and tells him such a knight
Is new arrived and comes from court in speed.
'What news,' said he, 'with him, that trait'rous wight?
What, more removing yet? alas! what need?
Are we not far enough sent out of sight?
Or is this place here not sufficient strong
To guard us in? Or must we have more wrong?'

By this the bloody troop were at the door,
Whenas a sudden and a strange dismay
Enforced them strain who should go in before.
One offers, and in off'ring makes a stay;
Another forward sets, and doth no more;
A third the like; and none durst make the way.
So much the horror of so vile a deed,
In vilest minds, deters them to proceed.

At length, as to some great advent'rous fight,
This bravo cheers these dastards all he can,
And valiantly their courage doth incite,
And all against one weak, unarmèd man.
A great exploit, and fit for such a knight;
Wherein so much renown his valour won!
But see how men that very presence fear
Which once they knew authority did bear!

Then on thrusts one, and he would foremost be
To shed another's blood, but lost his own:
For, ent'ring in, as soon as he did see
The face of majesty, to him well known,
Like Marius' soldier at Minternum, he
Stood still amazed, his courage overthrown;
The king, seeing this, starting from where he sate,
Out from his trembling hand his weapon gate.

Thus even his foes, who came to bring him death,
Bring him a weapon that before had none,
That yet he might not idly lose his breath,
But die revenged in action, not alone.
And this good chance, that thus much favoureth,
He slacks not, for he presently speeds on,
And lion-like upon the rest he flies:
And here falls one; — and there another lies.

And up and down he traverses his ground;
Now wards a felling blow, now strikes again;
Then nimbly shifts a thrust, then lends a wound,
Now back he gives, then rushes on amain.
His quick and ready hand doth so confound
These shameful beasts that four of them lie slain:
And all had perished happily and well,
But for one act that, oh, I grieve to tell.

This coward-knight, seeing with shame and fear
His men thus slain, and doubting his own end,
Leaps up into a chair that lo! was there;
The whilst the king did all his courage bend
Against those four which now before him were,
Doubting not who behind him doth attend;
And plies his hands undaunted, unafeared
And with good heart, and life for life he stirred.

And whilst he this and that and each man's blow
Doth eye, defend, and shift, being laid to sore;
Backward he bears for more advantage now,

Thinking the wall would safeguard him the more;
When lo! with impious hand, O wicked thou
That shameful durst not come to strike before,
Behind him gavest that lamentable wound,
Which laid that wretched prince flat on the ground.

Now proditorious wretch, what hast thou done,
To make this barbarous base assassinate
Upon the person of a prince; and one
Forespent with sorrow, and all desolate?
What great advancement hast thou hereby won,
By being the instrument to perpetrate
So foul a deed? Where is thy grace in court,
For such a service, acted in this sort?

First, he for whom thou dost this villainy,
Though pleased therewith, will not avouch thy fact,
But let the weight of thine own infamy
Fall on thee unsupported, and unbacked:
Then all men else will loathe thy treachery,
And thou thyself abhor thy proper act.
'So th' wolf, in hope the lion's grace to win,
Betraying other beasts, lost his own skin.'

But now, as this sweet prince distended lay,
And him nor life nor death their own could call;
(For life removing, rid not all away;
And death, though entering, had not seized on all)
That short-timed motion had a little stay,
The mover ceasing, though it were but small:
As th' organ-sound a time survives the stop,
Before it doth the dying note give up.

When lo! there streams a spring of blood so fast,
From those deep wounds, as all embrued the face
Of that accursèd caitiff, as he passed
(After the deed effected) through the place:
And therewithal, those dying eyes did cast
Such an upbraiding look on his disgrace,
Seeming to check so cowardly a part,
As left the impression even in his heart.

And this one king, most near in blood allied,
Is made th' oblation for the other's peace:
Which peace yet was not hereby ratified
So as it could all future fears release.
For though the other did forthwith provide
To have the rumour run of his decease,
By drawing the corpse to London, where it was
Laid, three days to be seen, with open face:

Yet so great was this execrable deed,
As men would scarce therein believe their eyes,
Much less their ears: and many sought to feed
The easy creditors of novelties,
By voicing him alive — how he was freed
By strange escape out of his miseries.
And many did conspire now to relieve
Him dead, who had forsaken him alive.

And many suffered for his cause, when now
He had none. Many wished for him again,
When they perceived th' exchange did not allow
Their hopes so much as they did look to gain
By trafficking of kings; and all saw how
Their full expectances were in the wain.
They had a king was more than him before;
But yet a king, where they were nought the more.

And sure this murdered prince, though weak he was,
He was not ill; nor yet so weak but that
He showed much martial valour in his place,
Adventuring oft his person for the state:
And might among our better princes pass;
Had not the flattery, rapine, and debate
Of factious lords, and greedy officers,
Disgraced his actions and abused his years.

Nor is it so much princes' weaknesses,
As the corruption of their ministers,
Whereby the commonwealth perceives distress.
For they attending their particulars,
Make imperfections their advantages,
To be themselves both kings and counsellors,
And sure this commonwealth can never take
Hurt by weak kings, but such as we do make.

Besides, he was (which people must respect
In princes, and which pleases vulgarly)
Of goodly personage, and of sweet aspect;
Of mild access and liberality;
And feasts, and shows, and triumphs did affect,
As the delights of youth and jollity.
But here the great profusion, and expense
Of his revenues, bred him much offence:

And gave advantage unto enmity,
This grievous accusation to prefer;
'That he consumed the common treasury;
Whereof he being the simple usager
But for the state, (not in propriety)
Did alien at his pleasure, and transfer
The same t' his minions, and to whom he list;
By which the commonwealth was to subsist.

'Whereby,' said they, 'the poor concussèd state,
Shall ever be exacted for supplies.'
Which accusation was th' occasion that
His successor by order nullifies
Many his patents, and did revocate
And reassume his liberalities.
And yet, for all these wastes, these gifts and feasts,
He was not found a bankrupt in his chests.

But they who took to Syndick in this sort
The actions of a monarch, knew those things
Wherein th' accompts were likely to fall short
Between the state of kingdoms and their kings:
Which president, of pestilent import,
Had not the Heavens blessed thy endeavourings,
Against thee, Henry, had been likewise brought,
Th' example made of thy example wrought.

For though this bounty and this liberalness
A glorious virtue be; it better fits
Great men than kings: who giving in excess,
Give not their own but others' benefits:
Which calls up many's hopes but pleasures less;
Destroying far more love than it begets.
For justice is their virtue — that alone
Makes them fit sure, and glorifies the throne.

1595

TO THE LADY MARGARET, COUNTESS OF CUMBERLAND

He that of such a height hath built his mind,
And reared the dwelling of his thoughts so strong,
As neither fear nor hope can shake the frame
Of his resolvèd powers; nor all the wind
Of vanity or malice pierce to wrong
His settled peace, or to disturb the same:
What a fair seat hath he, from whence he may
The boundless wastes and wilds of man survey!

And with how free an eye doth he look down
Upon these lower regions of turmoil!
Where all the storms of passions mainly beat
On flesh and blood: where honour, power, renown,
Are only gay afflictions, golden toil;
Where greatness stands upon as feeble feet
As frailty doth; and only great doth seem
To little minds, who do it so esteem.

He looks upon the mightiest monarch's wars
But only as on stately robberies;
Where evermore the fortune that prevails
Must be the right: the ill-succeeding mars
The fairest and the best-faced enterprise.
Great pirate Pompey lesser pirates quails:
Justice, he sees (as if seducèd) still
Conspires with power, whose cause must not be ill.

He sees the face of right t' appear as manifold
As are the passions of uncertain man;
Who puts it in all colours, all attires,
To serve his ends, and make his courses hold.
He sees, that let deceit work what it can,
Plot and contrive base ways to high desires;
That the all-guiding Providence doth yet
All disappoint, and mocks the smoke of wit.

Nor is he moved with all the thunder-cracks
Of tyrant's threats, or with the surly brow
Of Pow'r, that proudly sits on others' crimes:
Charged with more crying sins than those he checks.
The storms of sad confusion, that may grow
Up in the present for the coming times,
Appal not him, that hath no side at all,
But of himself, and knows the worst can fall.

Although his heart, so near allied to earth,
Cannot but pity the perplexèd state
Of troublous and distressed mortality,
That thus make way unto the ugly birth
Of their own sorrows, and do still beget
Affliction upon Imbecility,
Yet, seeing thus the course of things must run,
He looks thereon not strange, but as foredone.

And whilst distraught ambition compasses
And is encompassed; whilst as craft deceives
And is deceived; whilst man doth ransack man,
And builds on blood, and rises by distress,
And th' inheritance of desolation leaves
To great-expecting hopes; he looks thereon,
As from the shore of peace, with unwet eye,
And bears no venture in impiety.

Thus, madam, fares that man that hath prepared
A rest for his desires, and sees all things
Beneath him, and hath learned this book of man
Full of the notes of frailty, and compared
The best of Glory with her sufferings:
By whom, I see, you labour all you can
To plant your heart, and set your thoughts as near
His glorious mansion as your pow'rs can bear.

Which, madam, are so soundly fashionèd
By that clear judgment that hath carried you
Beyond the feeble limits of your kind,
As they can stand against the strongest head
Passion can make; inured to any hue
The world can cast; that cannot cast that mind
Out of her form of goodness, that doth see
Both what the best and worst of earth can be.

Which makes that, whatsoever here befalls,
You in the region of yourself remain,
Where no vain breath of th' impudent molests;
That hath secured within the brazen walls
Of a clear conscience, that, without all stain,
Rises in peace, in innocency rests;
Whilst all that Malice from without procures,
Shows her own ugly heart, but hurts not yours.

And whereas none rejoice more in revenge
Than women use to do; yet you well know,
That wrong is better checked by being contemned,
Than being pursued; leaving him t' avenge,
To whom it appertains. Wherein you show
How worthily your clearness hath condemned
Base malediction, living in the dark,
That at the rays of goodness still doth bark.

Knowing the heart of man is set to be
The centre of this world, about the which
These revolutions of disturbances
Still roll; where all th' aspects of misery
Predominate: whose strong effects are such,
As he must bear, being pow'rless to redress:
And that unless above himself he can
Erect himself, how poor a thing is man.

And how turmoiled they are that level lie
With earth, and cannot lift themselves from thence;
That never are at peace with their desires,
But work beyond their years, and even deny
Dotage her rest, and hardly will dispense
With death; that, when ability expires,
Desire lives still — so much delight they have
To carry toil and travail to the grave.

Whose ends you see, and what can be the best
They reach unto when they have cast the sum
And reckonings of their glory. And you know
This floating life hath but this port of rest —
A heart prepared, that fears no ill to come;
And that man's greatness rests but in his show,
The best of all whose days consumèd are
Either in war or peace conceiving war.

This concord, madam, of a well-tuned mind
Hath been so set by that all-working hand
Of Heaven, that though the world hath done his worst
To put it out by discords most unkind,
Yet doth it still in perfect union stand
With God and man, nor ever will be forced
From that most sweet accord, but still agree,
Equal in fortune's inequality.

And this note, madam, of your worthiness
Remains recorded in so many hearts
As time nor malice cannot wrong your right
In th' inheritance of fame you must possess;
You that have built you by your great deserts,
Out of small means, a far more exquisite
And glorious dwelling for your honoured name
Than all the gold that leaden minds can frame.

1603

Michael Drayton (1563–1631)

NYMPHIDIA

Old Chaucer doth of Topas tell,
Mad Rabelais of Pantagruel,
A later third of Dowsabel,
With such poor trifles playing;
Others the like have laboured at,
Some of this thing and some of that,
And many of them knew not what,
But what they may be saying.

Another sort there be, that will
Be talking of the Fairies still,
For never can they have their fill,
As they were wedded to them;
No tales of them their thirst can slake,
So much delight therein they take,
And some strange thing they fain would make,
Knew they the way to do them.

Then since no Muse hath been so bold,
Or of the later, or the old,
Those elvish secrets to enfold,
Which lie from others' reading:
My active Muse to light shall bring
The Court of that proud Fairy King,
And tell there of the revelling.
Joy prosper my proceeding!

And thou, Nymphidia, gentle Fay,
Which, meeting me upon the way,
These secrets didst to me bewray,
Which now I am in telling;
My pretty, light, fantastic maid,
I here invoke thee to my aid,
That I may speak what thou hast said,
In numbers smoothly swelling.

This palace standeth in the air,
By necromancy placèd there,
That it no tempest needs to fear,
Which way so'er it blow it.
And somewhat southward tow'rds the noon,
Whence lies a way up to the moon,
And thence the Fairy can as soon
Pass to the earth below it.

The walls of spiders' legs are made
Well mortisèd and finely laid;
It was the master of his trade
It curiously that builded;
The windows of the eyes of cats,
And for the roof, instead of slats,
Is covered with the skins of bats,
With moonshine that are gilded.

Hence Obe on him sport to make,
Their rest when weary mortals take,
And none but only fairies wake,
Descendeth for his pleasure;
And Mab, his merry Queen, by night
Bestrides young folks that lie upright,
(In elder times the mare that hight,)
Which plagues them out of measure.

Hence shadows, seeming idle shapes,
Of little frisking elves and apes
To earth do make their wanton scapes,
As hope of pastime hastes them;
Which maids think on the hearth they see
When fires well-nigh consumèd be,
There dancing hays by two and three,
Just as their fancy casts them.

These make our girls their sluttery rue,
By pinching them both black and blue,
And put a penny in their shoe
The house for cleanly sweeping;
And in their courses make that round
In meadows and in marshes found,
Of them so called the Fairy Ground,
Of which they have the keeping.

These when a child haps to be got
Which after proves an idiot
When folk perceive it thriveth not,
The fault therein to smother,
Some silly, doting, brainless calf
That understands things by the half,
Say that the Fairy left his oaf
And took away the other.

But listen, and I shall you tell
A chance in Faery that befell,
Which certainly may please some well
In love and arms delighting:
Of Oberon that jealous grew
Of one of his own Fairy crew;
Too well, he feared, his Queen that knew,
His love but ill requiting.

Pigwiggin was this Fairy Knight,
One wondrous gracious in the sight
Of fair Queen Mab, which day and night
He amorously observèd;
Which made King Oberon suspect
His service took too good effect,
His sauciness had often checkt
And could have wished him stervèd.

Pigwiggin gladly would commend
Some token to Queen Mab to send,
If sea or land him aught could lend
Were worthy of her wearing;
At length this lover doth devise
A bracelet made of emmet's eyes,
A thing he thought that she would prize,
No whit her state impairing.

And to the Queen a letter writes,
Which he most curiously indites,
Conjuring her by all the rites
  Of love, she would be pleasèd
To meet him, her true servant, where
They might, without suspect or fear,
Themselves to one another clear,
  And have their poor hearts easèd.

At midnight, the appointed hour;
'And for the Queen a fitting bower,'
Quoth he, 'is that fair cowslip flower
  On Hient hill that bloweth:
In all your train there's not a fay
That ever went to gather may
But she hath made it, in her way,
  The tallest there that groweth.'

When by Tom Thumb, a Fairy Page,
He sent it, and doth him engage
By promise of a mighty wage
  It secretly to carry;
Which done, the Queen her maids doth
    call,
And bids them to be ready all:
She would go see her summer hall,
  She could no longer tarry.

Her chariot ready straight is made,
Each thing therein is fitting laid,
That she by nothing might be stayed,
  For nought must be her letting;
Four nimble gnats the horses were,
Their harnesses of gossamere,
Fly Cranion her charioteer
  Upon the coach-box getting.

Her chariot of a snail's fine shell,
Which for the colours did excel,
The fair Queen Mab becoming well,
  So lively was the limning;
The seat the soft wool of the bee,
The cover, gallantly to see,
The wing of a pied butterfly;
  I trow 't was simple trimming.

The wheels composed of cricket's bones,
And daintily made for the nonce,
For fear of rattling on the stones
  With thistle-down they shod it;
For all her maidens much did fear
If Oberon had chance to hear
That Mab his Queen should have been there,
  He would not have abode it.

She mounts her chariot with a trice,
Nor would she stay, for no advice,
Until her maids that were so nice
  To wait on her were fitted;
But ran herself away alone,
Which when they heard, there was not one
But hasted after to be gone,
  As she had been diswitted.

Hop and Mop and Drop so clear,
Pip and Trip and Skip, that were
To Mab, their sovereign, ever dear,
  Her special maids of honour;
Fib and Tib and Pink and Pin,
Tick and Quick and Jill and Jin,
Tit and Nit and Wap and Win,
  The train that wait upon her.

Upon a grasshopper they got
And, what with amble what with trot,
For hedge and ditch they sparèd not,
  But after her they hie them;
A cobweb over them they throw,
To shield the wind if it should blow,
Themselves they wisely could bestow
  Lest any should espy them.

But let us leave Queen Mab awhile,
Through many a gate, o'er many a stile,
That now had gotten by this wile,
  Her dear Pigwiggin kissing;
And tell how Oberon doth fare,
Who grew as mad as any hare
When he had sought each place with care
  And found his Queen was missing.

By grisly Pluto he doth swear,
He rent his clothes and tore his hair,
And as he runneth here and there
  An acorn cup he greeteth,
Which soon he taketh by the stalk,
About his head he lets it walk,
Nor doth he any creature balk,
  But lays on all he meeteth.

The Tuscan poet doth advance
The frantic Paladin of France,
And those more ancient do enhance
  Alcides in his fury,
And others Ajax Telamon,
But to this time there hath been none
So Bedlam as our Oberon,
  Of which I dare assure ye.

And first encountering with a wasp,
He in his arms the fly doth clasp
As though his breath he forth would grasp,
  Him for Pigwiggin taking:
'Where is my wife, thou rogue?' quoth
    he;
'Pigwiggin, she is come to thee;
Restore her, or thou diest by me!'
  Whereat the poor Wasp quaking

Cries, 'Oberon, great Fairy King,
Content thee I am no such thing:
I am a Wasp, behold my sting!'
At which the Fairy started;
When soon away the Wasp doth go;
Poor wretch, was never frighted so;
He thought his wings were much too slow,
O'erjoyed they so were parted.

He next upon a Glow-worm light,
You must suppose it now was night,
Which, for her hinder part was bright,
He took to be a devil,
And furiously doth her assail
For carrying fire in her tail;
He thrashed her rough coat with his flail;
The mad King feared no evil.

'Oh!' quoth the Glow-worm, 'hold thy hand,
Thou puissant King of Fairy-land!
Thy mighty strokes who may withstand?
Hold, or of life despair I!'
Together then herself doth roll,
And tumbling down into a hole
She seemed as black as any coal;
Which vext away the Fairy.

From thence he ran into a hive:
Amongst the bees he letteth drive,
And down their combs begins to rive,
All likely to have spoilèd,
Which with their wax his face besmeared,
And with their honey daubed his beard:
It would have made a man afeared
To see how he was moilèd.

A new adventure him betides;
He met an Ant, which he bestrides,
And post thereon away he rides,
Which with his haste doth stumble;
And came full over on her snout,
Her heels so threw the dirt about,
For she by no means could get out,
But over him doth tumble.

And being in this piteous case,
And all be-slurrèd head and face,
On runs he in this wild-goose chase,
As here and there he rambles;
Half blind, against a molehole hit,
And for a mountain taking it,
For all he was out of his wit
Yet to top he scrambles.

And being gotten to the top,
Yet there himself he could not stop,
But down on the other side doth chop,
And to the foot came rumbling;
So that the grubs, therein that bred,
Hearing such turmoil overhead,
Thought surely they had all been dead;
So fearful was the jumbling.

And falling down into a lake,
Which him up to the neck doth take,
His fury somewhat it doth slake;
He calleth for a ferry:
Where you may some recovery note;
What was his club he made his boat,
And in his oaken cup doth float,
As safe as in a wherry.

Men talk of the adventures strange
Of Don Quixote and of their change
Through which he armèd oft did range,
Of Sancho Panza's travel;
But should a man tell everything
Done by this frantic Fairy King,
And them in lofty numbers sing,
It well his wits might gravel.

Scarce set on shore, but therewithal
He meeteth Puck, which most men call
Hobgoblin, and on him doth fall,
With words from frenzy spoken:
'Oh, oh,' quoth Hob, 'God save thy grace!
Who drest thee in this piteous case?
He thus that spoiled my sovereign's face,
I would his neck were broken!'

This Puck seems but a dreaming dolt,
Still walking like a ragged colt,
And oft out of a bush doth bolt,
Of purpose to deceive us;
And leading us makes us to stray,
Long winter's nights, out of the way;
And when we stick in mire and clay,
Hob doth with laughter leave us.

'Dear Puck,' quoth he, 'my wife is gone:
As e'er thou lovest King Oberon,
Let everything but this alone,
With vengeance and pursue her;
Bring her to me alive or dead,
Or that vile thief, Pigwiggin's head,
That villain hath [my Queen misled];
He to this folly drew her.'

Quoth Puck, 'My liege, I'll never lin,
But I will through thick and thin,
Until at length I bring her in;
My dearest lord, ne'er doubt it.'
Through brake, through briar,
Through muck, through mire,
Through water, through fire;
And thus goes Puck about it.

This thing Nymphidia overheard,
That on this mad king had a guard,
Not doubting of a great reward,
  For first this business broaching;
And through the air away doth go,
Swift as an arrow from the bow,
To let her sovereign Mab to know
  What peril was approaching.

The Queen, bound with love's powerful charm,
Sate with Pigwiggin arm in arm;
Her merry maids, that thought no harm,
  About the room were skipping;
A humble-bee, their minstrel, played
Upon his hautboy; every maid
Fit for this revel was arrayed,
  The hornpipe neatly tripping.

In comes Nymphidia, and doth cry,
'My sovereign, for your safety fly,
For there is danger but too nigh;
  I posted to forewarn you:
The King hath sent Hobgoblin out,
To seek you all the fields about,
And of your safety you may doubt,
  If he but once discern you.'

When, like an uproar in a town
Before them everything went down;
Some tore a ruff, and some a gown,
  'Gainst one another justling;
They flew about like chaff i' th' wind;
For haste some left their masks behind;
Some could not stay their gloves to find;
  There never was such bustling.

Forth ran they, by a secret way,
Into a brake that near them lay;
Yet much they doubted there to stay,
  Lest Hob should hap to find them; —
He had a sharp and piercing sight,
All one to him the day and night —
And therefore were resolved, by flight,
  To leave this place behind them.

At last one chanced to find a nut,
In the end of which a hole was cut,
Which lay upon a hazel root,
  There scattered by a squirrel
Which out the kernel gotten had;
When quoth this Fay, 'Dear Queen, be glad;
Let Oberon be ne'er so mad,
  I'll set you safe from peril.

'Come all into this nut,' quoth she,
'Come closely in; be ruled by me;
Each one may here a chooser be,
  For room ye need not wrastle:
Nor need ye be together heaped';
So one by one therein they crept,
And lying down they soundly slept,
  And safe as in a castle.

Nymphidia, that this while doth watch,
Perceived if Puck the Queen should catch
That he should be her over-match,
  Of which she well bethought her;
Found it must be some powerful charm,
The Queen against him that must arm,
Or surely he would do her harm,
  For throughly he had sought her.

And listening if she aught could hear,
That her might hinder, or might fear;
But finding still the coast was clear;
  Nor creature had descried her;
Each circumstance and having scanned,
She came thereby to understand,
Puck would be with them out of hand;
  When to her charms she hied her.

And first her fern-seed doth bestow,
The kernel of the mistletoe;
And here and there as Puck should go,
  With terror to affright him,
She night-shade strews to work him ill,
Therewith her vervain and her dill,
That hindereth witches of their will,
  Of purpose to despite him.

Then sprinkles she the juice of rue,
That groweth underneath the yew;
With nine drops of the midnight dew,
  From lunary distilling:
The molewarp's brain mixed therewithal;
And with the same the pismire's gall:
For she in nothing short would fall,
  The Fairy was so willing.

Then thrice under a briar doth creep,
Which at both ends was rooted deep,
And over it three times she leap;
  Her magic much availing:
Then on Proserpina doth call,
And so upon her spell doth fall,
Which here to you repeat I shall,
  Not in one tittle failing.

'By the croaking of a frog;
By the howling of the dog;
By the crying of the hog
  Against the storm arising;
By the evening curfew bell,
By the doleful dying knell,
O let this my direful spell,
  Hob, hinder my surprising!

'By the mandrake's dreadful groans;
By the lubrican's sad moans;
By the noise of dead men's bones
In charnel-houses rattling;
By the hissing of the snake,
The rustling of the fire-drake,
I charge thee thou this place forsake,
Nor of Queen Mab be prattling!

'By the whirlwind's hollow sound,
By the thunder's dreadful stound,
Yells of spirits underground,
I charge thee not to fear us;
By the screech-owl's dismal note,
By the black night-raven's throat,
I charge thee, Hob, to tear thy coat
With thorns, if thou come near us!'

Her spell thus spoke, she stept aside,
And in a chink herself doth hide,
To see thereof what would betide,
For she doth only mind him:
When presently she Puck espies,
And well she marked his gloating eyes,
How under every leaf he pries,
In seeking still to find them.

But once the circle got within,
The charms to work do straight begin,
And he was caught as in a gin;
For as he thus was busy,
A pain he in his head-piece feels,
Against a stubbèd tree he reels,
And up went poor Hobgoblin's heels,
Alas! his brain was dizzy!

At length upon his feet he gets,
Hobgoblin fumes, Hobgoblin frets;
And as again he forward sets,
And through the bushes scrambles,
A stump doth trip him in his pace;
Down comes poor Hob upon his face,
And lamentably tore his case,
Amongst the briars and brambles.

'A plague upon Queen Mab!' quoth he,
'And all her maids where'er they be:
I think the devil guided me,
To seek her so provokèd!'
Where stumbling at a piece of wood,
He fell into a ditch of mud,
Where to the very chin he stood,
In danger to be chokèd.

Now worse than e'er he was before,
Poor Puck doth yell, poor Puck doth roar,
That waked Queen Mab, who doubted sore
Some treason had been wrought her:
Until Nymphidia told the Queen,
What she had done, what she had seen,
Who then had well near cracked her spleen
With very extreme laughter.

But leave we Hob to clamber out,
Queen Mab and all her Fairy rout,
And come again to have a bout
With Oberon yet madding:
And with Pigwiggin now distraught,
Who much was troubled in his thought,
That he so long the Queen had sought,
And through the fields was gadding,

And as he runs he still doth cry,
'King Oberon, I thee defy,
And dare thee here in arms to try,
For my dear Lady's honour:
For that she is a Queen right good,
In whose defence I'll shed my blood,
And that thou in this jealous mood
Hast laid this slander on her.'

And quickly arms him for the field,
A little cockle-shell his shield,
Which he could very bravely wield;
Yet could it not be piercèd:
His spear a bent both stiff and strong,
And well near of two inches long:
The pile was of a horse-fly's tongue,
Whose sharpness nought reversèd.

And puts him on a coat of mail,
Which was of a fish's scale,
That when his foe should him assail,
No point should be prevailing:
His rapier was a hornet's sting,
For if he chanced to hurt the King,
It would be long in healing.

His helmet was a beetle's head,
Most horrible and full of dread,
That able was to strike one dead,
Yet did it well become him;
And for a plume a horse's hair
Which, being tossèd with the air,
Had force to strike his foe with fear,
And turn his weapon from him.

Himself he on an earwig set,
Yet scarce he on his back could get,
So oft and high he did curvet,
Ere he himself could settle:
He made him turn, and stop, and bound,
To gallop and to trot the round,
He scarce could stand on any ground,
He was so full of mettle.

When soon he met with Tomalin,
One that a valiant knight had been,
And to King Oberon of kin;
Quoth he, 'Thou manly Fairy,

Tell Oberon I come prepared,
Then bid him stand upon his guard;
This hand his baseness shall reward,
Let him be ne'er so wary.

'Say to him thus, that I defy
His slanders and his infamy,
And as a mortal enemy
Do publicly proclaim him:
Withal that if I had mine own,
He should not wear the Fairy crown,
But with a vengeance should come down,
Nor we a king should name him.'

This Tomalin could not abide,
To hear his sovereign vilified;
But to the Fairy Court him hied,
(Full furiously he posted,)
With everything Pigwiggin said:
How title to the crown he laid,
And in what arms he was arrayed,
As how himself he boasted.

'Twixt head and foot, from point to point,
He told the arming of each joint,
In every piece how neat and quoint,
For Tomalin could do it:
How fair he sat, how sure he rid,
As of the courser he bestrid,
How managed, and how well he did;
The King which listened to it,

Quoth he, 'Go, Tomalin, with speed,
Provide me arms, provide my steed,
And everything that I shall need;
By thee I will be guided;
To straight account call thou thy wit;
See there be wanting not a whit,
In everything see thou me fit,
Just as my foe's provided.'

Soon flew this news through Fairy-land,
Which gave Queen Mab to understand
The combat that was then in hand
Betwixt those men so mighty:
Which greatly she began to rue,
Perceiving that all Fairy knew
The first occasion from her grew
Of these affairs so weighty.

Wherefore attended with her maids,
Through fogs, and mists, and damps she wades,
To Proserpine the Queen of Shades,
To treat, that it would please her
The cause into her hands to take,
For ancient love and friendship's sake,
And soon thereof an end to make,
Which of much care would ease her.

A while there let we Mab alone,
And come we to King Oberon,
Who, armed to meet his foe, is gone,
For proud Pigwiggin crying:
Who sought the Fairy King as fast,
And had so well his journeys cast,
That he arrivèd at the last,
His puissant foe espying.

Stout Tomalin came with the King,
Tom Thumb doth on Pigwiggin bring,
That perfect were in everything
To single fights belonging:
And therefore they themselves engage,
To see them exercise their rage,
With fair and comely equipage,
Not one the other wronging.

So like in arms these champions were,
As they had been a very pair,
So that a man would almost swear
That either had been either;
Their furious steeds began to neigh,
That they were heard a mighty way;
Their staves upon their rests they lay;
Yet ere they flew together

Their seconds minister an oath,
Which was indifferent to them both,
That on their knightly faith and troth
No magic them supplièd;
And sought them that they had no charms,
Wherewith to work each other harms,
But came with simple open arms
To have their causes trièd.

Together furiously they ran,
That to the ground came horse and man,
The blood out of their helmets span,
So sharp were their encounters;
And though they to the earth were thrown,
Yet quickly they regained their own,
Such nimbleness was never shown,
They were two gallant mounters.

When in a second course again,
They forward came with might and main,
Yet which had better of the twain,
The seconds could not judge yet;
Their shields were into pieces cleft,
Their helmets from their heads were reft,
And to defend them nothing left,
These champions would not budge yet.

Away from them their staves they threw,
Their cruel swords they quickly drew,
And freshly they the fight renew,
They every stroke redoubled;
Which made Proserpina take heed,
And make to them the greater speed,
For fear lest they too much should bleed,
Which wondrously her troubled.

When to the infernal Styx she goes,
She takes the fogs from thence that rose,
And in a bag doth them enclose:
When well she had them blended,
She hies her then to Lethe spring,
A bottle and thereof doth bring,
Wherewith she meant to work the thing
Which only she intended.

Now Proserpine with Mab is gone,
Unto the place where Oberon
And proud Pigwiggin, one to one,
Both to be slain were likely:
And there themselves they closely hide,
Because they would not be espied;
For Proserpine meant to decide
The matter very quickly.

And suddenly unties the poke,
Which out of it sent such a smoke,
As ready was them all to choke,
So grievous was the pother;
So that the knights each other lost,
And stood as still as any post;
To Thumb nor Tomalin could boast
Themselves of any other.

But when the mist gan somewhat cease;
Proserpina commandeth peace;
And that awhile they should release
Each other of their peril:
'Which here,' quoth she, 'I do proclaim
To all in dreadful Pluto's name,
That as ye will eschew his blame,
You let me hear the quarrel:

'But here yourselves you must engage,
Somewhat to cool your spleenish rage;
Your grievous thirst and to assuage
That first you drink this liquor,
Which shall your understanding clear,
As plainly shall to you appear;
Those things from me that you shall hear,
Conceiving much the quicker.'

This Lethe water, you must know,
The memory destroyeth so,
That of our weal, or of our woe,
Is all remembrance blotted,
Of it nor can you ever think;
For they no sooner took this drink,
But nought into their brains could sink
Of what had them besotted.

King Oberon forgotten had
That he for jealousy ran mad,
But of his Queen was wondrous glad,
And asked how they came thither:
Pigwiggin likewise doth forget
That he Queen Mab had ever met,
Or that they were so hard beset,
When they were found together.

Nor neither of them both had thought
That e'er they each had other sought,
Much less that they a combat fought,
But such a dream were lothing.
Tom Thumb had got a little sup,
And Tomalin scarce kissed the cup,
Yet had their brains so sure locked up,
That they remembered nothing.

Queen Mab and her light maids, the while,
Amongst themselves do closely smile,
To see the King caught with this wile,
With one another jesting:
And to the Fairy Court they went,
With mickle joy and merriment,
Which thing was done with good intent,
And thus I left them feasting.

1627

LYRICS

Thomas Howell (fl. 1568)

WRITTEN TO A MOST EXCELLENT BOOK, FULL OF RARE INVENTION

Go, learned book, and unto Pallas sing,
Thy pleasant tunes that sweetly sound too high
For Pan to reach, though Zoylus thee doth sting,
And lower at thy laud, set nought thereby,
Thy maker's Muse in spight of envy's chin,
For wise device, deservèd praise shall win.

Who views thee well, and notes thy course aright,
And sifts each sense that couchèd is in thee:
Must needs extol the mind that did thee dight,
And wish the Muse may never weary be.
From whence doth flow such pith in filèd phrase,
As worthiest wit may joy on thee to gaze.

How much they err, thy rare event bewrays,
That stretch their skill the Fates to overthrow:
And how man's wisdom here in vain seeks ways,

To shun high powers that sway our states below.
Against whose rule, although we strive to run,
What Jove foresets, no human force may shun.

But all too long, thou hid'st so perfect work,
Seest not desire, how fain she seeks to find:
Thy light but lost, if thou in darkness lurk?
Then shew thy self and seem no more unkind.
Unfold thy fruit, and spread thy master's praise,
Whose prime of youth, grave deeds of age displays.

Go choice conceits, Minerva's mirrour bright,
With rubies rich y-fret, wrought by the wise:
Purfled with pearl, and deckèd with delight,
Where pleasure with profit, both in their guise.
Discourse of lovers, and such as fold sheep,
Whose saws well mixed, shrouds mysteries deep.

Go, yet I say, with speed thy charge deliver,
Thou needst not blush, nor fear the foil of blame:
The worthy Countess see thou follow ever;
Till Fates do fail, maintain her noble name.
Attend her will; if she vouchsafe to call,
Stoop to her state, down flat before her fall.

And ever thank thou him, that first such fruit did frame,
By whom thy praise shall live, to thy immortal fame.

1581

A DREAM

WHEN Phebus bright was settled in the West,
And darkness dim the earth had overspread;
When silent night, that moves each thing to rest,
With quiet pause, had placed me in my bed,
In slumbring dream, me thought I heard a wight,
His woes bewail, that grew through love's despight.

Whose wearing weed and vestures all were green,
Save that his loins with black were girded round:
And on his breast a badge of blue was seen,
In sign his faith and truth remainèd sound.
He sighèd oft and said, O blissful hire,
When hope with hap, may joy in his desire!

But still to hope, and find therein no fruit,
To be in bed, and restless there remain:
To seek to serve, and daily make pursuit,
To such as set but light of weary pain,
Doth breed such baleful dole within the breast,
As quite bereaves all joy and quiet rest.

Though taste of sour deserve the sweet to gain,
Yet cruel Fate I see the same denies:
So that desire and wisdom proves but vain,
Without accord and favour of the skies.
But steadfast hope, seem not (quoth he) to quail,
The heavens in time, may turn to thine avail.
Scarce had he thus his woful speech concluded,
When wake I did, and saw my self deluded.

1581

Sir Edward Dyer (1540?–1607)

MY MIND TO ME A KINGDOM IS

MY mind to me a kingdom is,
Such present joys therein I find,
That it excels all other bliss
That earth affords or grows by kind:
Though much I want which most would have,
Yet still my mind forbids to crave.

No princely pomp, no wealthy store,
No force to win the victory,
No wily wit to salve a sore,
No shape to feed a loving eye;
To none of these I yield as thrall:
For why? My mind doth serve for all.

I see how plenty [surfeits] oft,
And hasty climbers soon do fall;
I see that those which are aloft
Mishap doth threaten most of all;
They get with toil, they keep with fear:
Such cares my mind could never bear.

Content to live, this is my stay;
I seek no more than may suffice;
I press to bear no haughty sway;
Look, what I lack my mind supplies:
Lo, thus I triumph like a king,
Content with that my mind doth bring.

Some have too much, yet still do crave;
  I little have, and seek no more.
They are but poor, though much they have,
  And I am rich with little store:
They poor, I rich; they beg, I give;
They lack, I leave; they pine, I live.

I laugh not at another's loss;
  I grudge not at another's pain;
No worldly waves my mind can toss;
  My state at one doth still remain:
I fear no foe, I fawn no friend;
I loathe not life, nor dread my end.

Some weigh their pleasure by their lust,
  Their wisdom by their rage of will;
Their treasure is their only trust;
  A cloakèd craft their store of skill:
But all the pleasure that I find
Is to maintain a quiet mind.

My wealth is health and perfect ease:
  My conscience clear my chief defence;
I neither seek by bribes to please,
  Nor by deceit to breed offence:
Thus do I live; thus will I die;
Would all did so as well as I!

1588

Edmund Spenser (1552?–1599)

PROTHALAMION

Calme was the day, and through the trembling ayre
Sweete breathing Zephyrus did softly play,
A gentle spirit, that lightly did delay
Hot Titans beames, which then did glyster fayre:
When I, whom sullein care,
Through discontent of my long fruitlesse stay
In princes court, and expectation vayne
Of idle hopes, which still doe fly away,
Like empty shaddowes, did aflict my brayne,
Walkt forth to ease my payne
Along the shoare of silver streaming Themmes;
Whose rutty bancke, the which his river hemmes,
Was paynted all with variable flowers,
And all the meades adornd with daintie gemmes,
Fit to decke maydens bowres,
And crowne their paramours,
Against the brydale day, which is not long:
  Sweete Themmes, runne softly, till I end my song.

There, in a meadow, by the rivers side,
A flocke of nymphes I chauncèd to espy,
All lovely daughters of the flood thereby,
With goodly greenish locks all loose untyde,
As each had bene a bryde:
And each one had a little wicker basket,
Made of fine twigs entraylèd curiously,
In which they gathered flowers to fill their flasket;
And with fine fingers cropt full feateously
The tender stalkes on hye.
Of every sort, which in that meadow grew,
They gathered some; the violet pallid blew,
The little dazie, that at evening closes,
The virgin lillie, and the primrose trew,
With store of vermeil roses,
To decke their bridegromes posies
Against the brydale day, which was not long:
  Sweete Themmes, runne softly, till I end my song.

With that I saw two swannes of goodly hewe
Come softly swimming downe along the lee,
Two fairer birds I yet did never see:
The snow which doth the top of Pindus strew
Did never whiter shew,
Nor Jove himselfe, when he a swan would be
For love of Leda, whiter did appear:
Yet Leda was, they say, as white as he,
Yet not so white as these, nor nothing neare:
So purely white they were,
That even the gentle streame, the which them bare,
Seemed foule to them, and bad his billowes spare
To wet their silken feathers, least they might
Soyle their fayre plumes with water not so fayre,
And marre their beauties bright,
That shone as heavens light,
Against their brydale day, which was not long:
  Sweete Themmes, runne softly, till I end my song.

Eftsoones the nymphes, which now had flowers their fill,
Ran all in haste to see that silver brood,
As they came floating on the christal flood;
Whom when they sawe, they stood amazèd still,
Their wondring eyes to fill.
Them seemed they never saw a sight so fayre,

Of fowles so lovely, that they sure did deeme
Them heavenly borne, or to be that same payre
Which through the skie draw Venus silver teeme;
For sure they did not seeme
To be begot of any earthly seede,
But rather angels or of angels breede:
Yet were they bred of Somers-heat, they say,
In sweetest season, when each flower and weede
The earth did fresh aray;
So fresh they seemed as day,
Even as their brydale day, which was not long:
Sweete Themmes, runne softly, till I end my song.

Then forth they all out of their baskets drew
Great store of flowers, the honour of the field,
That to the sense did fragrant odours yield,
All which upon those goodly birds they threw,
And all the waves did strew,
That like old Peneus waters they did seeme,
When downe along by pleasant Tempes shore,
Scattred with flowres, through Thessaly they streeme,
That they appeare, through lillies plenteous store.
Like a brydes chamber flore.
Two of those nymphes, meane while, two garlands bound
Of freshest flowres which in that mead they found,
The which presenting all in trim array,
Their snowie foreheads therewithall they crownd,
Whil'st one did sing this lay,
Prepared against that day,
Against their brydale day, which was not long:
Sweete Themmes, runne softly, till I end my song.

'Ye gentle birdes, the worlds faire ornament,
And heavens glorie, whom this happie hower
Doth leade unto your lovers blissfull bower,
Joy may you have and gentle hearts content
Of your loves couplement:
And let faire Venus, that is Queene of Love,
With her heart-quelling sonne upon you smile,
Whose smile, they say, hath vertue to remove
All loves dislike, and friendships faultie guile
For ever to assoile.
Let endlesse peace your steadfast hearts accord,
And blessèd plentie wait upon your bord;
And let your bed with pleasures chast abound,
That fruitfull issue may to you afford,
Which may your foes confound,
And make your joyes redound,
Upon your brydale day, which is not long:
Sweete Themmes, run softlie, till I end my song.'

So ended she; and all the rest around
To her redoubled that her undersong,
Which said, their bridale daye should not be long.
And gentle Eccho from the neighbour ground
Their accents did resound.
So forth those joyous birdes did passe along,
Adowne the lee, that to them murmurde low,
As he would speake, but that he lackt a tong,
Yeat did by signes his glad affection show,
Making his streame run slow.
And all the foule which in his flood did dwell
Gan flock about these twaine, that did excell
The rest so far as Cynthia doth shend
The lesser starres. So they, enrangèd well,
Did on those two attend,
And their best service lend,
Against their wedding day, which was not long:
Sweete Themmes, run softly, till I end my song.

At length they all to mery London came,
To mery London, my most kyndly nurse,
That to me gave this lifes first native sourse;
Though from another place I take my name,
An house of auncient fame.
There when they came, whereas those bricky towres,
The which on Themmes brode agèd backe doe ryde,
Where now the studious lawyers have their bowers,
There whylome wont the Templer Knights to byde,
Till they decayd through pride:
Next whereunto there standes a stately place,

Where oft I gaynèd giftes and goodly grace
Of that great lord which therein wont to dwell,
Whose want too well now feeles my freendles case:
But ah! here fits not well
Olde woes, but joyes to tell,
Against the bridale daye, which is not long:
Sweete Themmes, runne softly, till I end my song.

Yet therein now doth lodge a noble peer,
Great Englands glory and the worlds wide wonder,
Whose dreadfull name late through all Spaine did thunder,
And Hercules two pillors standing neere
Did make to quake and feare.
Faire branch of honor, flower of chevalrie,
That fillest England with thy triumphes fame,
Joy have thou of thy noble victorie,
And endlesse happinesse of thine owne name
That promiseth the same:
That through thy prowesse and victorious armes
Thy country may be freed from forraine harmes;
And great Elisaes glorious name may ring
Through al the world, filed with thy wide alarmes,
Which some brave Muse may sing
To ages following,
Upon the brydale day, which is not long:
Sweete Themmes, runne softly, till I end my song.

From those high towers this noble lord issuing,
Like radiant Hesper when his golden hayre
In th' ocean billowes he hath bathèd fayre,
Descended to the rivers open vewing,
With a great traine ensuing,
Above the rest were goodly to bee seene
Two gentle knights of lovely face and feature,
Beseeming well the bower of anie queene,
With gifts of wit and ornaments of nature,
Fit for so goodly stature:
That like the twins of Jove they seemed in sight,
Which decke the bauldricke of the heavens bright.
They two, forth pacing to the rivers side,
Received those two faire brides, their loves delight,
Which, at th' appointed tyde,
Each one did make his bryde,
Against their brydale day which is not long:
Sweete Themmes, runne softly, till I end my song.

1596

Sir Walter Ralegh (1552?-1618)

A VISION UPON THIS CONCEIT OF THE FAIRY QUEEN

Methought I saw the grave where Laura lay,
Within that temple where the vestal flame
Was wont to burn: and, passing by that way,
To see that buried dust of living fame,
Whose tomb fair Love and fairer Virtue kept,
All suddenly I saw the Fairy Queen,
At whose approach the soul of Petrarch wept;
And from thenceforth those graces were not seen,
For they this Queen attended; in whose stead
Oblivion laid him down on Laura's hearse.
Hereat the hardest stones were seen to bleed,
And groans of buried ghosts the heavens did pierce:
Where Homer's spright did tremble all for grief,
And cursed the access of that celestial thief.

1590

REPLY TO MARLOWE'S PASSIONATE SHEPHERD

If all the world and love were young,
And truth in every shepherd's tongue,
These pretty pleasures might me move,
To live with thee and be thy love.

But time drives flocks from field to fold,
When rivers rage and rocks grow cold;
And Philomel becometh dumb;
The rest complains of cares to come.

The flowers do fade, and wanton fields
To wayward winter reckoning yields:
A honey tongue, a heart of gall,
Is fancy's spring, but sorrow's fall.

Thy gowns, thy shoes, thy beds of roses,
Thy cap, thy kirtle, and thy posies,
Soon break, soon wither, soon forgotten, —
In folly ripe, in reason rotten.

Thy belt of straw and ivy buds,
Thy coral clasps and amber studs, —
All those in me no means can move,
To come to thee and be thy love.

But could youth last, and love still breed,
Had joys no date, nor age no need;
Then those delights my mind might move
To live with thee and be thy love.

1600

IN THE GRACE OF WIT, OF TONGUE, AND FACE

Her face, her tongue, her wit, so fair, so sweet, so sharp,
First bent, then drew, now hit, mine eye, mine ear, my heart:
Mine eye, mine ear, my heart, to like, to learn, to love,
Her face, her tongue, her wit, doth lead, doth teach, doth move:
Her face, her tongue, her wit, with beams, with sound, with art,
Doth blind, doth charm, doth rule, mine eye, mine ear, my heart.

Mine eye, mine ear, my heart, with life, with hope, with skill,
Her face, her tongue, her wit, doth feed, doth feast, doth fill:
O face, O tongue, O wit, with frowns, with checks, with smart,
Wring not, vex not, wound not, mine eye, mine ear, my heart:
This eye, this ear, this heart, shall joy, shall bind, shall swear
Your face, your tongue, your wit, to serve, to love, to fear.

1602

THE LIE

Go, Soul, the body's guest,
Upon a thankless arrant:
Fear not to touch the best;
The truth shall be thy warrant:
Go, since I needs must die,
And give the world the lie.

Say to the court, it glows
And shines like rotten wood;
Say to the church, it shows
What's good, and doth no good:
If church and court reply,
Then give them both the lie.

Tell potentates, they live
Acting by others' action;
Not loved unless they give,
Not strong but by a faction:
If potentates reply,
Give potentates the lie.

Tell men of high condition
That manage the estate,
Their purpose is ambition,
Their practice only hate:
And if they once reply,
Then give them all the lie.

Tell them that brave it most,
They beg for more by spending,
Who, in their greatest cost,
Seek nothing but commending:
And if they make reply,
Then give them all the lie.

Tell zeal it wants devotion;
Tell love it is but lust;
Tell time it is but motion;
Tell flesh it is but dust:
And wish them not reply,
For thou must give the lie.

Tell age it daily wasteth;
Tell honour how it alters;
Tell beauty how she blasteth;
Tell favour how it falters:
And as they shall reply,
Give every one the lie.

Tell wit how much it wrangles
In tickle points of niceness;
Tell wisdom she entangles
Herself in over-wiseness:
And when they do reply,
Straight give them both the lie.

Tell physic of her boldness;
Tell skill it is pretension;
Tell charity of coldness;
Tell law it is contention:
And as they do reply,
So give them still the lie.

Tell fortune of her blindness;
Tell nature of decay;
Tell friendship of unkindness;
Tell justice of delay:
And if they will reply,
Then give them all the lie.

Tell arts they have no soundness,
But vary by esteeming;
Tell schools they want profoundness,
And stand too much on seeming:
If arts and schools reply,
Give arts and schools the lie.

Tell faith it's fled the city;
  Tell how the country erreth;
Tell manhood shakes off pity;
  Tell virtue least preferreth:
And if they do reply,
Spare not to give the lie.

So when thou hast, as I
  Commanded thee, done blabbing, —
Although to give the lie
  Deserves no less than stabbing, —
Stab at thee, he that will,
No stab the soul can kill.

1608

HIS PILGRIMAGE

Give me my scallop-shell of quiet,
  My staff of faith to walk upon,
My scrip of joy, immortal diet,
  My bottle of salvation,
My gown of glory, hope's true gauge;
And thus I'll take my pilgrimage.

Blood must be my body's balmer;
  No other balm will there be given;
Whilst my soul, like quiet palmer,
  Traveleth towards the land of heaven;
Over the silver mountains,
Where spring the nectar fountains:
    There will I kiss
    The bowl of bliss;
And drink mine everlasting fill
Upon every milken hill.
My soul will be a-dry before;
But after, it will thirst no more.

Then by that happy blissful day,
  More peaceful pilgrims I shall see,
That have cast off their rags of clay,
  And walk appareled fresh like me.
    I'll take them first,
    To quench their thirst
  And taste of nectar suckets,
    At those clear wells
    Where sweetness dwells,
  Drawn up by saints in crystal buckets.

  And when our bottles and all we
Are filled with immortality,
Then the blessèd paths we'll travel,
Strowed with rubies thick as gravel;
Ceilings of diamonds, sapphire floors,
High walls of coral, and pearly bowers.
From thence to heaven's bribeless hall,
Where no corrupted voices brawl;
No conscience molten into gold,
No forged accuser bought or sold,
No cause deferred, no vain-spent journey,
For there Christ is the king's attorney,
Who pleads for all without degrees,
And He hath angels, but no fees.
And when the grand twelve-million jury
Of our sins, with direful fury,
Against our souls black verdicts give,
Christ pleads His death, and then we live.

  Be Thou my speaker, taintless pleader,
Unblotted lawyer, true proceeder!
Thou givest salvation even for alms;
Not with a bribèd lawyer's palms.

  And this is mine eternal plea
To Him that made heaven, earth, and sea,
That, since my flesh must die so soon,
And want a head to dine next noon,
Just at the stroke, when my veins start and spread,
Set on my soul an everlasting head!
Then am I ready, like a palmer fit,
To tread those blest paths which before I writ.

Of death and judgment, heaven and hell,
Who oft doth think, must needs die well.

1604

THE CONCLUSION

Even such is time, that takes in trust
  Our youth, our joys, our all we have,
And pays us but with earth and dust;
  Who, in the dark and silent grave,
When we have wandered all our ways,
Shuts up the story of our days;
But from this earth, this grave, this dust,
My God shall raise me up, I trust!

1618

John Lyly (1553?-1606)

APELLES' SONG

Cupid and my Campaspe played
At cards for kisses; Cupid paid.
He stakes his quiver, bow and arrows,
His mother's doves and team of sparrows;
Loses them too. Then down he throws
The coral of his lip, the rose
Growing on's cheek, — but none knows how, —
With these the crystal of his brow,
And then the dimple of his chin;
All these did my Campaspe win.
At last he set her both his eyes;

She won, and Cupid blind did rise.
O Love, has she done this to thee?
What shall, alas! become of me?

1584

TRICO'S SONG

WHAT bird so sings, yet so does wail?
O 't is the ravished nightingale.
'Jug, jug, jug, jug, tereu,' she cries,
And still her woes at midnight rise.
Brave prick-song! who is 't now we hear?
None but the lark so shrill and clear.
Now at heaven's gates she claps her wings,
The morn not waking till she sings!
Hark, hark, with what a pretty throat
Poor Robin Red-breast tunes his note!
Hark how the jolly cuckoos sing,
'Cuckoo,' to welcome in the spring, —
'Cuckoo,' to welcome in the spring!

1584

Robert Greene (1558?–1592)

SEPHESTIA'S SONG TO HER CHILD

WEEP not, my wanton, smile upon my knee,
When thou art old there's grief enough for thee.
Mother's wag, pretty boy,
Father's sorrow, father's joy;
When thy father first did see
Such a boy by him and me,
He was glad, I was woe;
Fortune changèd made him so,
When he left his pretty boy,
Last his sorrow, first his joy.

Weep not, my wanton, smile upon my knee,
When thou art old there's grief enough for thee.
Streaming tears that never stint,
Like pearl drops from a flint,
Fell by course from his eyes,
That one another's place supplies;
Thus he grieved in every part,
Tears of blood fell from his heart,
When he left his pretty boy,
Father's sorrow, father's joy.

Weep not, my wanton, smile upon my knee,
When thou art old there's grief enough for thee.
The wanton smiled, father wept,
Mother cried, baby leapt;
More he crowed, more we cried,
Nature could not sorrow hide:
He must go, he must kiss
Child and mother, baby bless,
For he left his pretty boy,
Father's sorrow, father's joy.
Weep not, my wanton, smile upon my knee,
When thou art old there's grief enough for thee.

1587

THE SHEPHERD'S WIFE'S SONG

AH, what is love? It is a pretty thing,
As sweet unto a shepherd as a king;
And sweeter too,
For kings have cares that wait upon a crown,
And cares can make the sweetest love to frown:
Ah then, ah then,
If country loves such sweet desires do gain,
What lady would not love a shepherd swain?

His flocks are folded, he comes home at night,
As merry as a king in his delight;
And merrier too,
For kings bethink them what the state require,
Where shepherds careless carol by the fire:
Ah then, ah then,
If country loves such sweet desires do gain,
What lady would not love a shepherd swain?

He kisseth first, then sits as blithe to eat
His cream and curds, as doth the king his meat;
And blither too,
For kings have often fears when they do sup,
Where shepherds dread no poison in their cup:
Ah then, ah then,
If country loves such sweet desires do gain,
What lady would not love a shepherd swain?

To bed he goes, as wanton then, I ween,
As is a king in dalliance with a queen;
More wanton too,
For kings have many griefs affects to move,
Where shepherds have no greater grief than love:
Ah then, ah then,
If country loves such sweet desires do gain,
What lady would not love a shepherd swain?

Upon his couch of straw he sleeps as sound,
As doth the king upon his beds of down;
More sounder too,

For cares cause kings full oft their sleep to spill,
Where weary shepherds lie and snort their fill:
Ah then, ah then,
If country loves such sweet desires do gain,
What lady would not love a shepherd swain?

Thus with his wife he spends the year, as blithe
As doth the king at every tide or sithe;
And blither too,
For kings have wars and broils to take in hand
Where shepherds laugh and love upon the land:
Ah then, ah then,
If country loves such sweet desires do gain,
What lady would not love a shepherd swain?

1590

SONG

SWEET are the thoughts that savor of content;
The quiet mind is richer than a crown;
Sweet are the nights in careless slumber spent;
The poor estate scorns fortune's angry frown:
Such sweet content, such minds, such sleep, such bliss,
Beggars enjoy, when princes oft do miss.

The homely house that harbours quiet rest;
The cottage that affords no pride nor care;
The mean that 'grees with country music best;
The sweet consort of mirth and music's fare;
Obscurèd life sets down a type of bliss:
A mind content both crown and kingdom is.

1590

George Peele (1558?-1597)

CUPID'S CURSE

FAIR and fair, and twice so fair,
As fair as any may be;
The fairest shepherd on our green,
A love for any lady.
Fair and fair, and twice so fair,
As fair as any may be;
Thy love is fair for thee alone,
And for no other lady.
My love is fair, my love is gay,
As fresh as bin the flowers in May,
And of my love my roundelay,
My merry, merry roundelay,
Concludes with Cupid's curse, —
They that do change old love for new,
Pray gods they change for worse!

1584

Thomas Lodge (1558?-1625)

ROSALIND'S MADRIGAL

LOVE in my bosom like a bee
Doth suck his sweet:
Now with his wings he plays with me,
Now with his feet.
Within mine eyes he makes his nest,
His bed amidst my tender breast;
My kisses are his daily feast,
And yet he robs me of my rest.
Ah, wanton, will ye?

And if I sleep, then percheth he
With pretty flight,
And makes his pillow of my knee
The livelong night.
Strike I my lute, he tunes the string,
He music plays if so I sing,
He lends me every lovely thing;
Yet cruel he my heart doth sting.
Whist, wanton, still ye!

Else I with roses every day
Will whip you hence,
And bind you, when you long to play,
For your offence;
I'll shut mine eyes to keep you in,
I'll make you fast it for your sin,
I'll count your power not worth a pin.
Alas, what hereby shall I win,
If he gainsay me?

What if I beat the wanton boy
With many a rod?
He will repay me with annoy,
Because a god.
Then sit thou safely on my knee,
And let thy bower my bosom be;
Lurk in mine eyes, I like of thee.
O Cupid, so thou pity me,
Spare not, but play thee.

1590

ROSALIND'S DESCRIPTION

LIKE to the clear in highest sphere
Where all imperial glory shines,
Of selfsame colour is her hair,

Whether unfolded or in twines:
  Heigh ho, fair Rosalind!
Her eyes are sapphires set in snow,
Refining heaven by every wink;
The gods do fear whenas they glow,
And I do tremble when I think:
  Heigh ho, would she were mine!

Her cheeks are like the blushing cloud
That beautifies Aurora's face,
Or like the silver crimson shroud
That Phœbus' smiling looks doth grace:
  Heigh ho, fair Rosalind!
Her lips are like two budded roses,
Whom ranks of lilies neighbour nigh,
Within which bounds she balm encloses,
Apt to entice a deity:
  Heigh ho, would she were mine!

Her neck like to a stately tower
Where Love himself imprisoned lies,
To watch for glances every hour
From her divine and sacred eyes:
  Heigh ho, fair Rosalind!
Her paps are centres of delight,
Her breasts are orbs of heavenly frame,
Where Nature moulds the dew of light,
To feed perfection with the same:
  Heigh ho, would she were mine!

With orient pearl, with ruby red,
With marble white, with sapphire blue,
Her body every way is fed,
Yet soft in touch, and sweet in view:
  Heigh ho, fair Rosalind!
Nature herself her shape admires,
The gods are wounded in her sight,
And Love forsakes his heavenly fires
And at her eyes his brand doth light:
  Heigh ho, would she were mine!

Then muse not, nymphs, though I bemoan
The absence of fair Rosalind,
Since for her fair there's fairer none,
Nor for her virtues so divine:
  Heigh ho, fair Rosalind!
Heigh ho, my heart! would God that
  she were mine!

1590

Nicholas Breton (1545?–1626?)

A SWEET LULLABY

Come, little babe, come, silly soul,
  Thy father's shame, thy mother's grief,
Born, as I doubt, to all our dole,
  And to thyself unhappy chief:
Sing lullaby and lap it warm,
  Poor soul that thinks no creature harm.

Thou little think'st and less dost know
  The cause of this thy mother's moan;
Thou want'st the wit to wail her woe,
  And I myself am all alone:
    Why dost thou weep? why dost thou
      wail,
    And knowest not yet what thou dost ail?

Come, little wretch, ah silly heart,
  Mine only joy, what can I more?
If there be any wrong thy smart,
  That may the destinies implore:
    'Twas I, I say, against my will;
    I wail the time, but be thou still.

And dost thou smile? O, thy sweet face,
  Would God himself he might thee see!
No doubt thou wouldst soon purchase grace,
  I know right well, for thee and me:
    But come to mother, babe, and play,
    For father false is fled away.

Sweet boy, if it by fortune chance
  Thy father home again to send,
If death do strike me with his lance,
  Yet mayst thou me to him commend:
    If any ask thy mother's name,
    Tell how by love she purchased blame.

Then will his gentle heart soon yield,
  I know him of a noble mind;
Although a lion in the field,
  A lamb in town thou shalt him find:
    Ask blessing, babe, be not afraid,
    His sugared words hath me betrayed.

Then mayst thou joy and be right glad,
  Although in woe I seem to moan;
Thy father is no rascal lad,
  A noble youth of blood and bone:
    His glancing looks, if he once smile,
    Right honest women may beguile.

Come, little boy, and rock a-sleep,
  Sing lullaby and be thou still;
I that can do naught else but weep,
  Will sit by thee and wail my fill:
    God bless my babe, and lullaby,
    From this thy father's quality.

1594

PHYLLIDA AND CORYDON

In the merry month of May,
In a morn by break of day,
Forth I walked by the wood-side,
When as May was in her pride:

Then I spièd all alone
Phyllida and Corydon.
Much ado there was, God wot!
He would love and she would not.
She said, never man was true;
He said, none was false to you.
He said, he had loved her long;
She said, love should have no wrong.
Corydon would kiss her then;
She said, maids must kiss no men,
Till they did for good and all;
Then she made the shepherd call
All the heavens to witness truth:
Never loved a truer youth.
Thus with many a pretty oath,
Yea and nay, and faith and troth,
Such as silly shepherds use
When they will not love abuse,
Love, which had been long deluded,
Was with kisses sweet concluded;
And Phyllida, with garlands gay,
Was made the Lady of the May.

1600

Robert Southwell (1561?-1595)

THE BURNING BABE

As I in hoary winter's night stood shivering
    in the snow,
Surprised I was with sudden heat, which
    made my heart to glow;
And lifting up a fearful eye to view what fire
    was near,
A pretty babe, all burning bright, did in the
    air appear,
Who, scorchèd with excessive heat, such
    floods of tears did shed,
As though his floods should quench his
    flames which with his tears were fed.
'Alas!' quoth he, 'but newly born in fiery
    heats I fry;
Yet none approach to warm their hearts or
    feel my fire but I!
My faultless breast the furnace is, the fuel,
    wounding thorns,
Love is the fire, and sighs the smoke, the
    ashes, shame and scorns.
The fuel Justice layeth on, and Mercy blows
    the coals,
The metal in this furnace wrought are men's
    defilèd souls,
For which, as now on fire I am, to work them
    to their good,
So will I melt into a bath to wash them in
    my blood.'
With this he vanished out of sight, and
    swiftly shrunk away;
And straight I callèd unto mind that it was
    Christmas-day.

1595

Christopher Marlowe (1564-1593)

THE PASSIONATE SHEPHERD

Come live with me, and be my love;
And we will all the pleasures prove
That hills and valleys, dales and fields,
Woods, or steepy mountain yields.

And we will sit upon the rocks,
Seeing the shepherds feed their flocks
By shallow rivers, to whose falls
Melodious birds sing madrigals.

And I will make thee beds of roses,
And a thousand fragrant posies;
A cap of flowers, and a kirtle
Embroidered all with leaves of myrtle;

A gown made of the finest wool
Which from our pretty lambs we pull;
Fair-linèd slippers for the cold,
With buckles of the purest gold;

A belt of straw and ivy-buds,
With coral clasps and amber studs:
And, if these pleasures may thee move,
Come live with me, and be my love.

The shepherd-swains shall dance and sing
For thy delight each May-morning:
If these delights thy mind may move,
Then live with me, and be my love.

1599

Thomas Nashe (1567-1601)

DEATH'S SUMMONS

Adieu, farewell, earth's bliss,
This world uncertain is:
Fond are life's lustful joys,
Death proves them all but toys,
None from his darts can fly:
I am sick, I must die.
    Lord, have mercy on us!

Rich men, trust not in wealth,
Gold cannot buy you health;
Physic himself must fade,
All things to end are made;

The plague full swift goes by:
I am sick, I must die.
  Lord, have mercy on us!

Beauty is but a flower,
Which wrinkles will devour;
Brightness falls from the air,
Queens have died young and fair;
Dust hath closèd Helen's eye:
I am sick, I must die.
  Lord, have mercy on us!

Strength stoops unto the grave,
Worms feed on Hector brave,
Swords may not fight with fate,
Earth still holds ope her gate.
Come, come, the bells do cry:
I am sick, I must die.
  Lord, have mercy on us!

Wit with his wantonness,
Tasteth death's bitterness;
Hell's executioner
Hath no ears for to hear
What vain art can reply:
I am sick, I must die.
  Lord, have mercy on us!

Haste therefore each degree
To welcome destiny;
Heaven is our heritage,
Earth but a player's stage:
Mount we unto the sky:
I am sick, I must die.
  Lord, have mercy on us!

1600

William Shakespeare (1564–1616)

ON A DAY, ALACK THE DAY!

On a day, alack the day!
Love, whose month is ever May,
Spied a blossom passing fair
Playing in the wanton air:
Through the velvet leaves the wind,
All unseen, gan passage find;
That the lover, sick to death,
Wished himself the heaven's breath.
Air, quoth he, thy cheeks may blow;
Air, would I might triumph so!
But alack! my hand is sworn
Ne'er to pluck thee from thy thorn;
Vow, alack! for youth unmeet,
Youth so apt to pluck a sweet.
Do not call it sin in me,
That I am forsworn for thee;
Thou for whom e'en Jove would swear
Juno but an Ethiope were;
And deny himself for Jove,
Turning mortal for thy love.

1598

SPRING

I

When daisies pied and violets blue
  And lady-smocks all silver-white
And cuckoo-buds of yellow hue
  Do paint the meadows with delight,
The cuckoo then, on every tree,
Mocks married men; for thus sings he,
  Cuckoo;
Cuckoo, cuckoo, — O, word of fear,
Unpleasing to a married ear!

II

When shepherds pipe on oaten straws
  And merry larks are ploughmen's clocks,
When turtles tread, and rooks, and daws,
  And maidens bleach their summer smocks,
The cuckoo then on every tree
Mocks married men; for thus sings he,
  Cuckoo;
Cuckoo, cuckoo, — O word of fear,
Unpleasing to a married ear!

WINTER

III

When icicles hang by the wall,
  And Dick the shepherd blows his nail,
And Tom bears logs into the hall,
  And milk comes frozen home in pail,
When blood is nipped, and ways be foul,
Then nightly sings the staring owl,
  Tu-who;
Tu-whit, tu-who — a merry note,
While greasy Joan doth keel the pot.

IV

When all aloud the wind doth blow,
  And coughing drowns the parson's saw,
And birds sit brooding in the snow,
  And Marian's nose looks red and raw,
When roasted crabs hiss in the bowl,
Then nightly sings the staring owl,
  Tu-who;
Tu-whit, tu-who — a merry note,
While greasy Joan doth keel the pot.

1598

WHO IS SILVIA

Who is Silvia? what is she?
  That all our swains commend her?
Holy, fair, and wise is she;

The heaven such grace did lend her,
That she might admirèd be.

Is she kind as she is fair?
For beauty lives with kindness:
Love doth to her eyes repair,
To help him of his blindness;
And, being helped, inhabits there.

Then to Silvia let us sing,
That Silvia is excelling;
She excels each mortal thing
Upon the dull earth dwelling;
To her let us garlands bring.

1623

TELL ME WHERE IS FANCY BRED

Tell me where is fancy bred,
Or in the heart or in the head?
How begot, how nourishèd?
Reply, reply.
It is engendered in the eyes,
With gazing fed; and fancy dies
In the cradle where it lies.
Let us all ring fancy's knell:
I'll begin it, — Ding-dong, bell.

1600

UNDER THE GREENWOOD TREE

Under the greenwood tree
Who loves to lie with me,
And turn his merry note
Unto the sweet bird's throat,
Come hither, come hither, come hither:
Here shall he see
No enemy
But winter and rough weather.

Who doth ambition shun,
And loves to live i' the sun,
Seeking the food he eats,
And pleased with what he gets,
Come hither, come hither, come hither:
Here shall he see
No enemy
But winter and rough weather.

1623

BLOW, BLOW, THOU WINTER WIND

Blow, blow, thou winter wind,
Thou art not so unkind
As man's ingratitude;
Thy tooth is not so keen,
Because thou art not seen,
Although thy breath be rude.
Heigh-ho! sing, heigh-ho! unto the green holly:
Most friendship is feigning, most loving mere folly.
Then heigh-ho! the holly!
This life is most jolly.

Freeze, freeze, thou bitter sky,
That dost not bite so nigh
As benefits forgot:
Though thou the waters warp,
Thy sting is not so sharp
As friend remembered not.
Heigh-ho! sing, heigh-ho! etc.

1623

IT WAS A LOVER AND HIS LASS

It was a lover and his lass,
With a hey, and a ho, and a hey nonino,
That o'er the green corn-field did pass,
In the spring time, the only pretty ring time,
When birds do sing, hey ding a ding, ding;
Sweet lovers love the spring.

Between the acres of the rye,
With a hey, and a ho, and a hey nonino,
These pretty country folks would lie,
In the spring time, etc.

This carol they began that hour,
With a hey, and a ho, and a hey nonino,
How that a life was but a flower
In the spring time, etc.

And therefore take the present time,
With a hey, and a ho, and a hey nonino;
For love is crownèd with the prime
In the spring time, etc.

1623

O MISTRESS MINE

O mistress mine, where are you roaming?
O! stay and hear; your true love 's coming.
That can sing both high and low.
Trip no further, pretty sweeting;
Journeys end in lovers' meeting,
Every wise man's son doth know.

What is love? 't is not hereafter;
Present mirth hath present laughter;
What 's to come is still unsure:
In delay there lies no plenty;
Then come kiss me, sweet-and-twenty,
Youth's a stuff will not endure.

1623

COME AWAY, COME AWAY, DEATH

COME away, come away, death,
And in sad cypres let me be laid;
Fly away, fly away, breath;
I am slain by a fair cruel maid.
My shroud of white, stuck all with yew,
O! prepare it.
My part of death, no one so true
Did share it.

Not a flower, not a flower sweet,
On my black coffin let there be strown;
Not a friend, not a friend greet
My poor corpse, where my bones shall be thrown:
A thousand thousand sighs to save,
Lay me, O! where
Sad true lover never find my grave,
To weep there.

1623

FEAR NO MORE THE HEAT O' TH' SUN

FEAR no more the heat o' th' sun,
Nor the furious winter's rages;
Thou thy worldly task hast done,
Home art gone, and ta'en thy wages;
Golden lads and girls all must,
As chimney-sweepers, come to dust.

Fear no more the frown o' th' great,
Thou art past the tyrant's stroke:
Care no more to clothe and eat;
To thee the reed is as the oak:
The scepter, learning, physic, must
All follow this, and come to dust.

Fear no more the lightning-flash,
Nor the all-dreaded thunder-stone;
Fear not slander, censure rash;
Thou hast finished joy and moan:
All lovers young, all lovers must
Consign to thee, and come to dust.

No exorciser harm thee!
Nor no witchcraft charm thee!
Ghost unlaid forbear thee!
Nothing ill come near thee!
Quiet consummation have;
And renownèd be thy grave!

1623

COME UNTO THESE YELLOW SANDS

COME unto these yellow sands,
And then take hands:
Courtsied when you have, and kissed, —
The wild waves whist, —
Foot it featly here and there;
And, sweet sprites, the burden bear.
Hark, hark!
Bow, wow.
The watch-dogs bark:
Bow, wow.
Hark, hark! I hear
The strain of strutting Chanticleer
Cock-a-diddle-dow.

1623

FULL FATHOM FIVE THY FATHER LIES

FULL fathom five thy father lies;
Of his bones are coral made:
Those are pearls that were his eyes:
Nothing of him that doth fade,
But doth suffer a sea-change
Into something rich and strange.
Sea-nymphs hourly ring his knell;
Ding-dong.
Hark! now I hear them, — Ding-dong, bell.

1623

WHERE THE BEE SUCKS

WHERE the bee sucks, there suck I
In a cowslip's bell I lie;
There I couch when owls do cry.
On the bat's back I do fly
After summer merrily:
Merrily, merrily shall I live now
Under the blossom that hangs on the bough.

1623

CRABBED AGE AND YOUTH

CRABBÈD age and youth
Cannot live together:
Youth is full of pleasure,
Age is full of care;
Youth like summer morn,
Age like winter weather;
Youth like summer brave,
Age like winter bare.
Youth is full of sport,
Age's breath is short;
Youth is nimble, age is lame;
Youth is hot and bold,
Age is weak and cold;
Youth is wild, and age is tame.
Age, I do abhor thee,
Youth. I do adore thee;

O! my love, my love is young:
Age, I do defy thee:
O! sweet shepherd, hie thee,
For methinks thou stay'st too long!

1599

Thomas Campion (1567–1620)

TO LESBIA

My sweetest Lesbia, let us live and love;
And though the sager sort our deeds reprove,
Let us not weigh them: heaven's great lamps do dive
Into their west, and straight again revive:
But soon as once set is our little light,
Then must we sleep one ever-during night.

If all would lead their lives in love like me,
Then bloody swords and armour should not be;
No drum nor trumpet peaceful sleeps should move,
Unless alarm came from the camp of love:
But fools do live, and waste their little light,
And seek with pain their ever-during night.

When timely death my life and fortune ends,
Let not my hearse be vext with mourning friends;
But let all lovers, rich in triumph, come
And with sweet pastimes grace my happy tomb:
And, Lesbia, close up thou my little light,
And crown with love my ever-during night.

1601

THE MAN OF LIFE UPRIGHT

The man of life upright,
Whose guiltless heart is free
From all dishonest deeds,
Or thought of vanity;

The man whose silent days,
In harmless joys are spent,
Whom hopes cannot delude
Nor sorrow discontent;

That man needs neither towers
Nor armour for defence,
Nor secret vaults to fly
From thunder's violence:

He only can behold
With unaffrighted eyes
The horrors of the deep
And terrors of the skies.

Thus, scorning all the cares
That fate or fortune brings,
He makes the heaven his book,
His wisdom heavenly things;

Good thoughts his only friends,
His wealth a well-spent age,
And earth his sober inn
And quiet pilgrimage.

1601

JACK AND JOAN THEY THINK NO ILL

Jack and Joan they think no ill,
But loving live, and merry still;
Do their week-days' work, and pray
Devoutly on the holy-day:
Skip and trip it on the green,
And help to choose the Summer Queen;
Lash out, at a country feast,
Their silver penny with the best.

Well can they judge of nappy ale,
And tell at large a winter tale;
Climb up to the apple loft,
And turn the crabs till they be soft.
Tib is all the father's joy,
And little Tom the mother's boy.
All their pleasure is content;
And care, to pay their yearly rent.

Joan can call by name her cows,
And deck her window with green boughs;
She can wreaths and tutties make,
And trim with plums a bridal cake.
Jack knows what brings gain or loss,
And his long flail can stoutly toss:
Makes the hedge which others break;
And ever thinks what he doth speak.

Now, you courtly dames and knights,
That study only strange delights;
Though you scorn the homespun gray,
And revel in your rich array:
Though your tongues dissemble deep,
And can your heads from danger keep;
Yet, for all your pomp and train,
Securer lives the silly swain.

1613

THERE IS A GARDEN IN HER FACE

There is a garden in her face,
Where roses and white lilies grow;
A heavenly paradise is that place,
Wherein all pleasant fruits do flow.
There cherries grow, which none may buy
Till 'Cherry ripe' themselves do cry.

Those cherries fairly do enclose
Of orient pearl a double row;
Which when her lovely laughter shows,
They look like rosebuds filled with snow.
Yet them nor peer nor prince can buy
Till 'Cherry ripe' themselves do cry.

Her eyes like angels watch them still;
Her brows like bended bows do stand,
Threatening with piercing frowns to kill
All that attempt, with eye or hand,
Those sacred cherries to come nigh
Till 'Cherry ripe' themselves do cry.

1606

TURN ALL THY THOUGHTS TO EYES

Turn all thy thoughts to eyes,
Turn all thy hairs to ears,
Change all thy friends to spies,
And all thy joys to fears:
True love will yet be free,
In spite of jealousy.

Turn darkness into day,
Conjectures into truth,
Believe what th' envious say,
Let age interpret youth:
True love will yet be free,
In spite of jealousy.

Wrest every word and look,
Rack every hidden thought,
Or fish with golden hook;
True love cannot be caught.
For that will still be free,
In spite of jealousy!

ca. 1617

Michael Drayton (1563–1631)

AGINCOURT

Fair stood the wind for France,
When we our sails advance,
Nor now to prove our chance
  Longer will tarry;
But putting to the main
At Caux, the mouth of Seine,
With all his martial train
  Landed King Harry.

And taking many a fort,
Furnished in warlike sort,
Marcheth towards Agincourt
  In happy hour;
Skirmishing day by day
With those that stopped his way,
Where the French general lay
  With all his power.

Which, in his height of pride,
King Henry to deride,
His ransom to provide
  To the King sending;
Which he neglects the while,
As from a nation vile,
Yet, with an angry smile,
  Their fall portending.

And turning to his men,
Quoth our brave Henry then:
'Though they to one be ten
  Be not amazèd!
Yet have we well begun:
Battles so bravely won
Have ever to the sun
  By Fame been raisèd!

'And for myself,' quoth he,
'This my full rest shall be:
England ne'er mourn for me,
  Nor more esteem me!
Victor I will remain,
Or on this earth lie slain;
Never shall she sustain
  Loss to redeem me!

'Poitiers and Cressy tell,
When most their pride did swell,
Under our swords they fell.
  No less our skill is,
Than when our Grandsire great,
Claiming the regal seat,
By many a warlike feat
  Lopped the French lilies.'

The Duke of York so dread
The eager vanward led;
With the main, Henry sped
  Amongst his henchmen;
Exeter had the rear,
A braver man not there!
O Lord, how hot they were
  On the false Frenchmen!

They now to fight are gone;
Armor on armor shone;
Drum now to drum did groan:
  To hear, was wonder;
That, with the cries they make,
The very earth did shake;
Trumpet to trumpet spake;
  Thunder to thunder.

Well it thine age became,
O noble Erpingham,
Which didst the signal aim

To our hid forces!
When, from a meadow by,
Like a storm suddenly,
The English archery
Stuck the French horses.

With Spanish yew so strong;
Arrows a cloth-yard long,
That like to serpents stung,
Piercing the weather.
None from his fellow starts;
But, playing manly parts,
And like true English hearts,
Stuck close together.

When down their bows they threw,
And forth their bilboes drew,
And on the French they flew:
Not one was tardy.
Arms were from shoulders sent,
Scalps to the teeth were rent,
Down the French peasants went:
Our men were hardy.

This while our noble King,
His broad sword brandishing,
Down the French host did ding,
As to o'erwhelm it.
And many a deep wound lent;
His arms with blood besprent,
And many a cruel dent
Bruisèd his helmet.

Gloucester, that duke so good,
Next of the royal blood,
For famous England stood
With his brave brother.
Clarence, in steel so bright,
Though but a maiden knight,
Yet in that furious fight
Scarce such another!

Warwick in blood did wade;
Oxford, the foe invade,
And cruel slaughter made,
Still as they ran up.
Suffolk his axe did ply;
Beaumont and Willoughby
Bare them right doughtily;
Ferrers, and Fanhope.

Upon Saint Crispin's Day
Fought was this noble fray;
Which Fame did not delay
To England to carry.
O, when shall English men
With such acts fill a pen?
Or England breed again
Such a King Harry?

1605

Sir John Davies (1569-1626)

HYMNS OF ASTREA

III — TO SPRING

Earth now is green, and heaven is blue,
Lively spring which makes all new,
Jolly spring doth enter;
Sweet young sun-beams do subdue
Angry, agèd Winter.

Blasts are mild, and seas are calm,
Every meadow flows with balm,
The earth wears all her riches;
Harmonious birds sing such a psalm,
As ear and heart bewitches.

Reserve (sweet Spring) this nymph of ours,
Eternal garlands of thy flowers,
Green garlands never wasting;
In her shall last our state's fair spring,
Now and forever flourishing,
As long as Heaven is lasting.

V — TO THE LARK

Early cheerful mounting lark,
Light's gentle usher, morning's clark,
In merry notes delighting:
Stint awhile thy song and hark,
And learn my new enditing.

Bear up this hymn, to Heaven it bear,
E'en up to Heaven, and sing it there,
To Heaven each morning bear it;
Have it set to some sweet sphere,
And let the angels hear it!

Renowned Astrea, that great name,
Exceeding great in worth and fame,
Great worth hath so renowned it,
It is Astrea's name I praise,
Now then, sweet lark, do thou it raise,
And in high Heaven resound it.

XXVI — TO ENVY

Envy, go weep; my Muse and I
Laugh thee to scorn; thy feeble eye
Is dazzled with the glory
Shining in this gay poesy,
And little golden story.

Behold how my proud quill doth shed
Eternal nectar on her head:
The pomp of coronation
Hath not such power her fame to spread,
As this my admiration.

Respect my pen as free and frank,
Expecting not reward nor thank,
Great wonder only moves it;

I never made it mercenary,
Nor should my Muse this burthen carry
As hired but that she loves it.

1599

Thomas Dekker (1570?–1641)

O SWEET CONTENT

Art thou poor, yet hast thou golden slumbers?
O sweet content!
Art thou rich, yet is thy mind perplexed?
O punishment!
Dost thou laugh to see how fools are vexed
To add to golden numbers, golden numbers?
O sweet content! O sweet, O sweet content!
Work apace, apace, apace, apace;
Honest labor bears a lovely face;
Then hey nonny nonny, hey nonny nonny!

Canst drink the waters of the crispèd spring?
O sweet content!
Swimm'st thou in wealth, yet sink'st in thine own tears?
O punishment!
Then he that patiently want's burden bears
No burden bears, but is a king, a king!
O sweet content! O sweet, O sweet content!
Work apace, apace, apace, apace;
Honest labor bears a lovely face;
Then hey nonny nonny, hey nonny nonny!

1603

Richard Barnfield (1574–1627)

AS IT FELL UPON A DAY

As it fell upon a day
In the merry month of May,
Sitting in a pleasant shade
Which a group of myrtles made,
Beasts did leap and birds did sing,
Trees did grow and plants did spring;
Everything did banish moan
Save the nightingale alone:
She, poor bird, as all forlorn
Leaned her breast against a thorn,
And there sung the dolefull'st ditty
That to hear it was great pity.
'Fie, fie, fie?' now would she cry;
'Tereu, tereu?' by and by;
That to hear her so complain
Scarce I could from tears refrain;
For her griefs so lively shown
Made me think upon mine own.
Ah, thought I, thou mourn'st in vain,
None takes pity on thy pain:
Senseless trees they cannot hear thee,
Ruthless beasts they will not cheer thee:
King Pandion he is dead,
All thy friends are lapped in lead;
All thy fellow birds do sing
Careless of thy sorrowing:
Even so, poor bird, like thee,
None alive will pity me.

1600

Ben Jonson (1573?–1637)

HYMN TO DIANA

Queen and huntress, chaste and fair,
Now the sun is laid to sleep,
Seated in thy silver chair,
State in wonted manner keep:
Hesperus entreats thy light,
Goddess excellently bright.

Earth, let not thy envious shade
Dare itself to interpose;
Cynthia's shining orb was made
Heaven to clear when day did close:
Bless us then with wishèd sight,
Goddess excellently bright.

Lay thy bow of pearl apart
And thy crystal-shining quiver;
Give unto the flying hart
Space to breathe, how short soever:
Thou that makest a day of night,
Goddess excellently bright.

1600

EPITAPH ON S[ALATHIEL] P[AVY]

Weep with me all you that read
This little story;
And know, for whom a tear you shed,
Death's self is sorry.
'T was a child, that so did thrive
In grace and feature,
As heaven and nature seemed to strive
Which owned the creature.
Years he numbered scarce thirteen
When fates turned cruel;
Yet three filled zodiacs had he been
The stage's jewel;
And did act, what now we moan,

Old men so duly;
As, sooth, the Parcæ thought him one,
He played so truly.
So, by error, to his fate
They all consented;
But viewing him since, alas, too late!
They have repented;
And have sought, to give new birth,
In baths to steep him;
But, being so much too good for earth,
Heaven vows to keep him.

1616

TO CELIA

Drink to me only with thine eyes,
And I will pledge with mine;
Or leave a kiss but in the cup,
And I'll not look for wine.
The thirst that from the soul doth rise,
Doth ask a drink divine:
But might I of Jove's nectar sup,
I would not change for thine.

I sent thee late a rosy wreath,
Not so much honouring thee
As giving it a hope that there
It could not withered be.
But thou thereon didst only breathe,
And sent'st it back to me:
Since when it grows, and smells, I swear,
Not of itself, but thee.

1616

SONG: TO CELIA

Come, my Celia, let us prove,
While we may, the sports of love;
Time will not be ours for ever:
He at length our good will sever.
Spend not then his gifts in vain:
Suns that set, may rise again;
But if once we lose this light,
'T is with us perpetual night.
Why should we defer our joys?
Fame and rumour are but toys.
Cannot we delude the eyes
Of a few poor household spies?
Or his easier ears beguile,
Thus removèd by our wile?
'T is no sin love's fruits to steal,
But the sweet theft to reveal:
To be taken, to be seen,
These have crimes accounted been.

1607

SIMPLEX MUNDITIIS

Still to be neat, still to be drest,
As you were going to a feast;
Still to be powdered, still perfumed:
Lady, it is to be presumed,
Though art's hid causes are not found,
All is not sweet, all is not sound.

Give me a look, give me a face,
That makes simplicity a grace;
Robes loosely flowing, hair as free:
Such sweet neglect more taketh me
Than all the adulteries of art;
They strike mine eyes, but not my heart.

1609–10

EPITAPH ON ELIZABETH, L. H.

Would'st thou hear what man can say
In a little? Reader, stay.
Underneath this stone doth lie
As much beauty as could die;
Which in life did harbor give
To more virtue than doth live.
If, at all, she had a fault,
Leave it buried in this vault.
One name was Elizabeth,
The other let it sleep with death!
Fitter, where it died, to tell,
Than that it lived at all. Farewell.

1616

TO THE MEMORY OF MY BELOVED, MASTER WILLIAM SHAKSPERE

To draw no envy, Shakspere, on thy name,
Am I thus ample to thy book and fame;
While I confess thy writings to be such,
As neither man, nor muse, can praise too much.
'T is true, and all men's suffrage. But these ways
Were not the paths I meant unto thy praise;
For silliest ignorance on these may light,
Which, when it sounds at best, but echoes right;
Or blind affection, which doth ne'er advance
The truth, but gropes, and urgeth all by chance;
Or crafty malice might pretend this praise,
And think to ruin, where it seemed to raise.
These are, as some infamous bawd, or whore,
Should praise a matron; what would hurt her more?
But thou art proof against them, and, indeed,

Above the ill-fortune of them, or the need.
I, therefore, will begin. Soul of the age!
The applause! delight! and wonder of our stage!
My Shakspere, rise! I will not lodge thee by
Chaucer, or Spenser, or bid Beaumont lie
A little further off to make thee room:
Thou art a monument without a tomb,
And art alive still, while thy book doth live
And we have wits to read, and praise to give.
That I not mix thee so, my brain excuses,
I mean with great, but disproportioned Muses;
For if I thought my judgment were of years,
I should commit thee surely with thy peers,
And tell how far thou didst our Lyly outshine,
Or sporting Kyd, or Marlowe's mighty line.
And though thou hadst small Latin and less Greek,
From thence to honour thee, I will not seek
For names: but call forth thundering Æschylus,
Euripides, and Sophocles to us,
Pacuvius, Accius, him of Cordova dead,
To life again, to hear thy buskin tread,
And shake a stage; or, when thy socks were on,
Leave thee alone for the comparison
Of all that insolent Greece, or haughty Rome
Sent forth, or since did from their ashes come.
Triumph, my Britain, thou hast one to show,
To whom all scenes of Europe homage owe.
He was not of an age, but for all time!
And all the Muses still were in their prime,
When, like Apollo, he came forth to warm
Our ears, or like a Mercury to charm!
Nature herself was proud of his designs,
And joyed to wear the dressing of his lines,
Which were so richly spun, and woven so fit,
As, since, she will vouchsafe no other wit.
The merry Greek, tart Aristophanes,
Neat Terence, witty Plautus, now not please;
But antiquated and deserted lie,
As they were not of nature's family.
Yet must I not give nature all; thy art,
My gentle Shakspeare, must enjoy a part:
For though the poet's matter nature be,
His art doth give the fashion: and, that he
Who casts to write a living line, must sweat,
(Such as thine are) and strike the second heat
Upon the Muse's anvil; turn the same,
And himself with it, that he thinks to frame;
Or for the laurel, he may gain a scorn;
For a good poet's made, as well as born.
And such wert thou! Look how the father's face
Lives in his issue, even so the race
Of Shakspeare's mind and manners brightly shines
In his well turnèd, and true filèd lines;
In each of which he seems to shake a lance,
As brandished at the eyes of ignorance.
Sweet Swan of Avon! what a sight it were
To see thee in our water yet appear,
And make those flights upon the banks of Thames,
That so did take Eliza, and our James!
But stay, I see thee in the hemisphere
Advanced, and made a constellation there!
Shine forth, thou star of poets, and with rage,
Or influence, chide, or cheer the drooping stage,
Which, since thy flight from hence, hath mourned like night,
And despairs day, but for thy volume's light.

1623

Dr. John Donne (1573-1631)

SONG

Go and catch a falling star,
  Get with child a mandrake root,
Tell me where all years past are,
  Or who cleft the devil's foot;
Teach me to hear mermaids singing,
Or to keep off envy's stinging,
    And find,
    What wind
Serves to advance an honest mind.

If thou be'st born to strange sights,
  Things invisible go see,
Ride ten thousand days and nights,
  Till age snow white hairs on thee;
Thou, when thou return'st, wilt tell me
All strange wonders that befell thee,
    And swear,
    Nowhere
Lives a woman true and fair.

If thou find'st one, let me know,
  Such a pilgrimage were sweet;
Yet do not: I would not go,
  Though at next door we might meet;
Though she were true when you met her,
And last till you write your letter,

Yet she
Will be
False, ere I come, to two or three.

1633

THE INDIFFERENT

I CAN love both fair and brown;
Her whom abundance melts, and her whom want betrays;
Her who loves loneness best, and her who sports and plays;
Her whom the country formed, and whom the town;
Her who believes, and her who tries;
Her who still weeps with spongy eyes,
And her who is dry cork and never cries;
I can love her, and her, and you, and you,
I can love any, so she be not true.

Will no other vice content you?
Will it not serve your turn to do as did your mothers?
Or have you all old vices spent, and now would find out others?
Or doth a fear that men are true torment you?
Oh, we are not, be not you so;
Let me; and do you twenty know.
Rob me, but bind me not, and let me go;
Must I, who came to travel thorough you,
Grow your fixed subject, because you are true?

Venus heard me sing this song,
And by love's sweetest part, variety, she swore,
She heard not this till now; it should be so no more.
She went, examined, and returned ere long,
And said, Alas! some two or three
Poor heretics in love there be,
Which think to 'stablish dangerous constancy;
But I have told them, since you will be true,
You shall be true to them, who are false to you.

1633

A VALEDICTION FORBIDDING MOURNING

As virtuous men pass mildly away,
And whisper to their souls to go,
Whilst some of their sad friends do say,
The breath goes now, and some say no;

So let us melt, and make no noise,
No tear-floods, nor sigh-tempests move,
'T were profanation of our joys,
To tell the laity our love.

Moving of the earth brings harms and fears,
Men reckon what it did and meant;
But trepidation of the spheres,
Though greater far, is innocent.

Dull sublunary lover's love,
Whose soul is sense, cannot admit
Absence, because it doth remove
Those things which elemented it.

But we by a love so much refined
That ourselves know not what it is,
Inter-assurèd of the mind,
Care less eyes, lips, and hands to miss.

Our two souls, therefore, which are one,
Though I must go, endure not yet
A breach, but an expansion,
Like gold to airy thinness beat.

If they be two, they are two so
As stiff twin compasses are two;
Thy soul, the fixt foot, makes no show
To move, but doth if the other do.

And though it in the centre sit,
Yet when the other far doth roam,
It leans and hearkens after it,
And grows erect, as that comes home.

Such wilt thou be to me, who must,
Like the other foot, obliquely run.
Thy firmness makes my circle just,
And makes me end where I begun.

1633

LOVE'S DEITY

I LONG to talk with some old lover's ghost,
Who died before the god of Love was born:
I cannot think that he, who then loved most,
Sunk so low, as to love one which did scorn.
But since this god produced a destiny,
And that vice-nature, custom, lets it be,
I must love her that loves not me.

Sure they, which made him god, meant not so much,
Nor he in his young godhead practised it;
But when an even flame two hearts did touch,
His office was indulgently to fit
Actives to passives, correspondency
Only his subject was; it cannot be
Love, if I love who loves not me.

But every modern god will now extend
His vast prerogative as far as Jove;
To rage, to lust, to write to, to commend,
All is the purlieu of the god of Love.
Oh were we wakened by this tyranny
To ungod this child again, it could not be
I should love her, who loves not me.

Rebel and atheist too, why murmur I
As though I felt the worst that love could do?
Love may make me leave loving, or might try
A deeper plague, to make her love me too,
Which, since she loves before, I'm loath to see;
Falsehood is worse than hate; and that must be,
If she whom I love, should love me.

1633

THE COMPUTATION

For my first twenty years, since yesterday,
I scarce believed thou couldst be gone away;
For forty more I fed on favors past,
And forty on hopes, that thou wouldst they might last.
Tears drowned one hundred, and sighs blew out two;
A thousand I did neither think, nor do,
Or not divide, all being one thought of you:
Or in a thousand more forgot that too.
Yet call not this long life; but think, that I
Am, by being dead, immortal; can ghosts die?

1633

DEATH

Death, be not proud, though some have callèd thee
Mighty and dreadful, for thou art not so;
For those, whom thou think'st thou dost overthrow,
Die not, poor Death, nor yet canst thou kill me.
From rest and sleep, which but thy pictures be,
Much pleasure, then from thee much more must flow:
And soonest our best men with thee do go,
Rest of their bones, and souls' delivery.
Thou'rt slave to Fate, Chance, kings, and desperate men,
And dost with poison, war, and sickness dwell,
And poppy or charms can make us sleep as well,
And better than thy stroke, why swell'st thou then?
One short sleep past, we wake eternally,
And Death shall be no more; Death, thou shalt die.

1633

Sir Henry Wotton (1568–1639)

THE CHARACTER OF A HAPPY LIFE

How happy is he born and taught
That serveth not another's will;
Whose armour is his honest thought,
And simple truth his utmost skill;

Whose passions not his masters are;
Whose soul is still prepared for death,
Untied unto the world by care
Of public fame or private breath;

Who envies none that chance doth raise,
Nor vice; who never understood
How deepest wounds are given by praise:
Nor rules of state, but rules of good;

Who hath his life from rumours freed;
Whose conscience is his strong retreat;
Whose state can neither flatterers feed,
Nor ruin make oppressers great;

Who God doth late and early pray
More of his grace than gifts to lend;
And entertains the harmless day
With a religious book or friend.

This man is freed from servile bands
Of hope to rise or fear to fall:
Lord of himself, though not of lands,
And, having nothing, yet hath all.

1614?

ON HIS MISTRESS, THE QUEEN OF BOHEMIA

You meaner beauties of the night,
That poorly satisfy our eyes
More by your number than your light,
You common people of the skies;
What are you, when the moon shall rise?

You curious chanters of the wood
That warble forth Dame Nature's lays,
Thinking your passions understood

By your weak accents; what's your praise,
When Philomel her voice shall raise?

You violets that first appear,
By your pure purple mantles known
Like the proud virgins of the year,
As if the spring were all your own;
What are you when the rose is blown?

So, when my mistress shall be seen
In form and beauty of her mind,
By virtue first, then choice, a Queen,
Tell me if she were not designed
The eclipse and glory of her kind?

1624

Francis Beaumont (1584–1616)

ON THE LIFE OF MAN

Like to the falling of a star,
Or as the flights of eagles are,
Or like the fresh spring's gaudy hue,
Or silver drops of morning dew,
Or like a wind that chafes the flood,
Or bubbles which on water stood;
Even such is man, whose borrowed light
Is straight called in and paid to-night.
The wind blows out, the bubble dies,
The spring entombed in autumn lies,
The dew's dried up, the star is shot,
The flight is past, and man forgot.

1640

LINES ON THE TOMBS IN WESTMINSTER

Mortality, behold and fear!
What a change of flesh is here!
Think how many royal bones
Sleep within this heap of stones;
Here they lie, had realms and lands,
Who now want strength to stir their hands,
Where from their pulpits sealed with dust
They preach, 'In greatness is no trust.'
Here's an acre sown indeed
With the richest, royalest seed
That the earth did e'er suck in,
Since the first man died for sin:
Here the bones of birth have cried,
'Though gods they were, as men they died!'
Here are sands, ignoble things,
Dropt from the ruined sides of kings:
Here's a world of pomp and state
Buried in dust, once dead by fate.

1640

John Fletcher (1579–1625)

ASPATIA'S SONG

Lay a garland on my hearse
Of the dismal yew;
Maidens, willow branches bear;
Say I dièd true.

My love was false, but I was firm
From my hour of birth:
Upon my buried body lie
Lightly, gentle earth!

1619

WHAT IS LOVE?

Tell me, dearest, what is love?
'T is a lightning from above;
'T is an arrow, 't is a fire,
'T is a boy they call Desire.
'T is a grave,
Gapes to have
Those poor fools that long to prove.

Tell me more, are women true?
Yes, some are, and some as you.
Some are willing, some are strange,
Since you men first taught to change.
And till troth
Be in both,
All shall love, to love anew.

Tell me more yet, can they grieve?
Yes, and sicken sore, but live,
And be wise, and delay,
When you men are wise as they.
Then I see,
Faith will be,
Never till they both believe.

1647

CARE-CHARMING SLEEP

Care-charming Sleep, thou easer of all woes,
Brother to Death, sweetly thyself dispose
On this afflicted prince; fall like a cloud,
In gentle showers; give nothing that is loud,
Or painful to his slumbers; easy, light,
And as a purling stream, thou son of Night,
Pass by his troubled senses; sing his pain,
Like hollow murmuring wind or silver rain;
Into this prince gently, O gently slide,
And kiss him into slumbers like a bride.

1647

John Webster (1580?–1625?)

DIRGE

Call for the robin-red-breast and the wren,
Since o'er shady groves they hover,
And with leaves and flowers do cover
The friendless bodies of unburied men.
Call unto his funeral dole
The ant, the field-mouse, and the mole,
To rear him hillocks, that shall keep him warm,
And (when gay tombs are robbed) sustain no harm;
But keep the wolf far thence, that's foe to men,
For with his nails he'll dig them up again.

1612

DIRGE

Hark, now everything is still,
The screech-owl, and the whistler shrill
Call upon our dame aloud,
And bid her quickly don her shroud.
Much you had of land and rent,
Your length in clay's now competent.
A long war disturbed your mind,
Here your perfect peace is signed.
Of what is 't fools make such vain keeping?
Sin their conception, their birth weeping,
Their life, a general mist of error,
Their death, a hideous storm of terror.
Strew your hair with powders sweet,
Don clean linen, bathe your feet,
And (the foul fiend more to check)
A crucifix let bless your neck.
'T is now full tide, 'tween night and day;
End your groan, and come away.

1623

William Drummond (1585–1649)

EPITAPH

Stay, passenger, see where enclosèd lies
The paragon of princes, fairest frame
Time, nature, place could show to mortal eyes,
In worth, wit, virtue, miracle to fame:
At least that part the earth of him could claim
This marble holds, hard like the Destinies:
For as to his brave spirit and glorious name,
The one the world, the other fills the skies.
Th' immortal amaranthus, princely rose,
Sad violet, and that sweet flower that bears
In sanguine spots the tenor of our woes,
Spread on this stone, and wash it with thy tears:
Then go and tell, from Gades unto Ind,
Thou saw where earth's perfections were confined.

1613

MADRIGAL

This life, which seems so fair,
Is like a bubble blown up in the air
By sporting children's breath,
Who chase it every where,
And strive who can most motion it bequeath:
And though it sometime seem of its own might,
Like to an eye of gold, to be fixed there,
And firm to hover in that empty height,
That only is because it is so light.
But in that pomp it doth not long appear;
For even when most admired, it in a thought,
As swelled from nothing, doth dissolve in nought.

1616

William Browne (1591–1643)

ON THE COUNTESS DOWAGER OF PEMBROKE

Underneath this sable hearse
Lies the subject of all verse:
Sidney's sister, Pembroke's mother:
Death, ere thou hast slain another,
Fair, and learned, and good as she,
Time shall throw a dart at thee.

Marble piles let no man raise
To her name: for after days
Some kind woman born as she,
Reading this, like Niobe
Shall turn marble, and become
Both her mourner and her tomb.

1658

AN EPITAPH ON MRS. EL: Y

Underneath this stone there lies
More of beauty than are eyes;
Or to read that she is gone,
Or alive to gaze upon.
She in so much fairness clad,
To each grace a virtue had;
All her goodness cannot be
Cut in marble. Memory
Would be useless, ere we tell
In a stone her worth. Farewell!

[Date uncertain]

William Basse (1583–1653)

ELEGY ON SHAKESPEARE

Renowned Spenser lie a thought more nigh
To learnèd Chaucer, and rare Beaumont lie
A little nearer Spenser, to make room
For Shakespeare in your three-fold, four-fold tomb.
To lodge all four in one bed make a shift
Until Doomsday, for hardly will a fifth
Betwixt this day and that by Fate be slain,
For whom your curtains may be drawn again.

If your precedency in death doth bar
A fourth place in your sacred sepulcher,
Under this carvèd marble of thine own,
Sleep, rare tragedian, Shakespeare, sleep alone;
Thy unmolested peace, unsharèd cave,
Possess as lord, not tenant, of thy grave,
That unto us and others it may be
Honor hereafter to be laid by thee.

1633

George Wither (1588–1667)

SHALL I, WASTING IN DESPAIR

Shall I, wasting in despair,
Die, because a woman's fair?
Or make pale my cheeks with care,
'Cause another's rosy are?
Be she fairer than the day
Or the flowery meads in May,
If she be not so to me
What care I how fair she be?

Should my heart be grieved or pined,
'Cause I see a woman kind?
Or a well disposèd nature
Joinèd with a lovely feature?
Be she meeker, kinder than
Turtle-dove or pelican,
If she be not so to me
What care I how kind she be?

Shall a woman's virtues move
Me to perish for her love?
Or her well deserving, known,
Make me quite forget mine own?
Be she with that goodness blest
Which may gain her name of best,
If she be not such to me
What care I how good she be?

'Cause her fortune seems too high,
Shall I play the fool and die?
Those that bear a noble mind,
Where they want of riches find,
Think what, with them, they would do
That, without them, dare to woo!
And unless that mind I see,
What care I though great she be?

Great, or good, or kind, or fair,
I will ne'er the more despair.
If she love me (this believe!)
I will die ere she shall grieve.
If she slight me when I woo,
I can scorn, and let her go;
For if she be not for me,
What care I for whom she be?

1619

SONNET CYCLES

Sir Philip Sidney (1554–1586)

ASTROPHEL AND STELLA

I

Loving in truth, and fain in verse my love to show,
That she, dear She, might take some pleasure of my pain, —
Pleasure might cause her read, reading might make her know,
Knowledge might pity win, and pity grace obtain, —
I sought fit words to paint the blackest face of woe,
Studying inventions fine, her wits to entertain,
Oft turning others' leaves, to see if thence would flow
Some fresh and fruitful showers upon my sunburnt brain.
But words came halting out, wanting Invention's stay;
Invention, Nature's child, fled step-dame Study's blows;
And others' feet still seemed but strangers in my way.
Thus, great with child to speak, and helpless in my throes,

Biting my truant pen, beating myself for spite;
'Fool,' said my Muse to me, 'look in thy heart, and write.'

III

Let dainty wits cry on the Sisters nine,
That, bravely masked, their fancies may be told;
Or Pindar's apes flaunt in their phrases fine,
Enam'ling with pied flowers their thoughts of gold;
Or else let them in stately glory shine,
Ennobling new-found tropes with problems old;
Or with strange similes enrich each line,
Of herbs or beasts which Inde or Afric hold.
For me, in sooth, no Muse but one I know;
Phrases and problems from my reach do grow
And strange things cost too dear for my poor sprites:
How then? even thus, — In Stella's face I read
What Love and Beauty be; then all my deed
But copying is, what in her Nature writes.

VI

Some lovers speak, when they their Muses entertain,
Of hopes begot by fear, of wot not what desires,
Of force of heavenly beams infusing hellish pain,
Of living deaths, dear wounds, fair storms, and freezing fires:
Some one his song in Jove and Jove's strange tales attires,
Bordered with bulls and swans, powdered with golden rain:
Another, humbler wit, to shepherd's pipe retires.
Yet hiding royal blood full oft in rural vein,
To some a sweetest plaint a sweetest style affords,
While tears pour out his ink, and sighs breathe out his words,
His paper pale despair, and pain his pen doth move.
I can speak what I feel, and feel as much as they,
But think that all the map of my state I display
When trembling voice brings forth, that I do Stella love.

XV

You that do search for every purling spring
Which from the ribs of old Parnassus flows,
And every flower, not sweet perhaps, which grows
Near thereabouts, into your poesy wring;
You that do dictionary's method bring
Into your rimes, running in rattling rows;
You that poor Petrarch's long-deceasèd woes
With new-born sighs and denizened wit do sing;
You take wrong ways; those far-fet helps be such
As do bewray a want of inward touch,
And sure, at length stolen goods do come to light:
But if, both for your love and skill, your name
You seek to nurse at fullest breasts of Fame,
Stella behold, and then begin to endite.

XXI

Your words, my friend (right healthful caustics), blame
My young mind marred, whom Love doth windlass so;
That mine own writings, like bad servants, show
My wits quick in vain thoughts, in virtue lame;
That Plato I read for naught but if he tame
Such coltish years; that to my birth I owe
Nobler desires, lest else that friendly foe,
Great expectation, wear a train of shame:
For since mad Mars great promise made to me,
If now the May of my years much decline,
What can be hoped my harvest-time will be?
Sure, you say well, 'Your wisdom's golden mine
Dig deep with Learning's spade.' Now tell me this —
Hath this world aught so fair as Stella is?

XXXI

With how sad steps, O Moon, thou climb'st the skies!
How silently, and with how wan a face!
What, may it be that even in heavenly place
That busy archer his sharp arrows tries!
Sure, if that long-with-love-acquainted eyes
Can judge of love, thou feel'st a lover's case,
I read it in thy looks; thy languished grace,
To me that feel the like, my state descries.
Then, even of fellowship, O Moon, tell me,
Is constant love deemed there but want of wit?
Are beauties there as proud as here they be?
Do they above love to be loved, and yet

Those lovers scorn whom that love doth possess?
Do they call virtue there ungratefulness?

XXXIII

I might! — unhappy word — O me, I might,
And then would not, or could not, see my bliss;
Till now wrapt in a most infernal night,
I find how heav'nly day, wretch! I did miss.
Heart, rent thyself, thou dost thyself but right;
No lovely Paris made thy Helen his;
No force, no fraud robbed thee of thy delight,
No Fortune of thy fortune author is;
But to myself myself did give the blow,
While too much wit, forsooth, so troubled me
That I respects for both our sakes must show:
And yet could not, by rising morn foresee
How fair a day was near: O punished eyes,
That I had been more foolish, or more wise!

XXXIX

Come, Sleep! O Sleep, the certain knot of peace,
The baiting-place of wit, the balm of woe,
The poor man's wealth, the prisoner's release,
Th' indifferent judge between the high and low;
With shield of proof shield me from out the press
Of those fierce darts Despair at me doth throw;
O make in me those civil wars to cease;
I will good tribute pay, if thou do so.
Tak thou of me smooth pillows, sweetest bed,
A chamber deaf to noise and blind to light,
A rosy garland and a weary head:
And if these things, as being thine by right,
Move not thy heavy grace, thou shalt in me,
Livelier than elsewhere, Stella's image see.

XLI

Having this day my horse, my hand, my lance
Guided so well that I obtained the prize,
Both by the judgment of the English eyes
And of some sent from that sweet enemy France;
Horsemen my skill in horsemanship advance,
Town folks my strength; a daintier judge applies
His praise to sleight which from good use doth rise;
Some lucky wits impute it but to chance;
Others, because of both sides I do take
My blood from them who did excel in this,
Think Nature me a man-at-arms did make:
How far they shot awry! the true cause is,
Stella looked on, and from her heavenly face
Sent forth the beams which made so fair my race.

LXIX

O joy too high for my low style to show
O bliss fit for a nobler state than me!
Envy, put out thine eyes, lest thou do see
What oceans of delight in me do flow!
My friend, that oft saw through all masks my woe,
Come, come, and let me pour myself on thee.
Gone is the Winter of my misery!
My Spring appears; O see what here doth grow:
For Stella hath, with words where faith doth shine,
Of her high heart giv'n me the monarchy:
I, I, O I, may say that she is mine!
And though she give but thus conditionly,
This realm of bliss while virtuous course I take,
No kings be crowned but they some covenants make.

LXX

My Muse may well grudge at my heavenly joy,
If still I force her in sad rhymes to creep:
She oft hath drunk my tears, now hopes to enjoy
Nectar of mirth, since I love's cup do keep.
Sonnets be not bound prentice to annoy;
Trebles sing high, so well as bases deep;
Grief but Love's winter-livery is; the boy
Hath cheeks to smile, so well as eyes to weep.
Come then, my Muse, show thou height of delight
In well-raised notes; my pen, the best it may,
Shall paint out joy, though but in black and white.
Cease, eager Muse; peace, pen, for my sake stay,
I give you here my hand for truth of this, —
Wise silence is best music unto bliss.

LXXIV

I never drank of Aganippe well,
Nor ever did in shade of Tempe sit,

And Muses scorn with vulgar brains to dwell;
Poor layman I, for sacred rites unfit,
Some do I hear of poets' fury tell,
But, God wot, wot not what they mean by it;
And this I swear by blackest brook of hell,
I am no pick-purse of another's wit.
How falls it then, that with so smooth an ease
My thoughts I speak; and what I speak doth flow
In verse, and that my verse best wits doth please?
Guess we the cause? What, is it this? Fie, no.
Or so? Much less. How then? Sure thus it is,
My lips are sweet, inspired with Stella's kiss.

LXXXIV

Highway, since you my chief Parnassus be,
And that my Muse, to some ears not unsweet,
Tempers her words to trampling horses' feet
More oft than to a chamber-melody,
Now, blessèd you bear onward blessèd me
To her, where I my heart, safe-left, shall meet;
My Muse and I must you of duty greet
With thanks and wishes, wishing thankfully.
Be you still fair, honoured by public heed;
By no encroachment wronged, nor time forgot;
Nor blamed for blood, nor shamed for sinful deed;
And that you know I envy you no lot
O highest wish, I wish you so much bliss, —
Hundreds of years you Stella's feet may kiss.

XC

Stella, think not that I by verse seek fame,
Who seek, who hope, who love, who live but thee;
Thine eyes my pride, thy lips my history:
If thou praise not, all other praise is shame.
Nor so ambitious am I, as to frame
A nest for my young praise in laurel tree:
In truth, I swear I wish not there should be
Graved in my epitaph a Poet's name.
Nor, if I would, could I just title make,
That any laud thereof to me should grow,
Without my plumes from others' wings I take:
For nothing from my wit or will doth flow,
Since all my words thy beauty doth endite,
And Love doth hold my hand, and makes me write.

CIII

O happy Thames, that didst my Stella bear!
I saw thee with full many a smiling line
Upon thy cheerful face, joy's livery wear,
While those fair planets on thy streams did shine.
The boat for joy could not to dance forbear,
While wanton winds, with beauties so divine
Ravished, staid not, till in her golden hair
They did themselves, O sweetest prison, twine.
And fain those Æol's youth there would their stay
Have made, but forced by Nature still to fly,
First did with puffing kiss those locks display:
She, so dishevelled, blushed: from window I
With sight thereof cried out, 'O fair disgrace,
Let Honour's self to thee grant highest place.'

CIV

Envious wits, what hath been mine offence,
That with such poisonous care my looks you mark,
That to each word, nay sigh of mine, you hark,
As grudging me my sorrow's eloquence?
Ah, is it not enough, that I am thence,
Thence, so far thence, that scantly any spark
Of comfort dare come to this dungeon dark,
Where Rigour's exile locks up all my sense?
But if I by a happy window pass,
If I but stars upon mine armour bear;
Sick, thirsty, glad (though but of empty glass):
Your moral notes straight my hid meaning tear
From out my ribs, and, puffing, proves that I
Do Stella love: fools, who doth it deny?

1591

Samuel Daniel (1562–1619)

TO DELIA

II

Go, wailing verse, the infants of my love;
Minerva-like brought forth without a mother!
Present the image of the cares I prove;
Witness your father's grief exceeds all other.
Sigh out a story of her cruel deeds,

With interrupted accents of despair;
A monument that whosoever reads,
May justly praise, and blame my loveless fair.
Say her disdain hath drièd up my blood,
And starvèd you, in succors still denying:
Press to her eyes, importune me some good;
Waken her sleeping pity with your crying:
Knock at that hard heart; beg till you have moved her;
And tell th' unkind how dearly I have loved her.

VI

Fair is my love, and cruel as she 's fair;
Her brow shades frowns, although her eyes are sunny;
Her smiles are lightning, though her pride despair;
And her disdains are gall, her favours honey.
A modest maid, decked with a blush of honor;
Whose feet do tread green paths of youth and love!
The wonder of all eyes that look upon her:
Sacred on earth; designed a saint above!
Chastity and beauty, which were deadly foes,
Live reconcilèd friends within her brow:
And had she pity to conjoin with those;
Then who had heard the plaints I utter now?
For had she not been fair, and thus unkind,
My muse had slept, and none had known my mind.

XVII

Why should I sing in verse; why should I frame
These sad neglected notes for her dear sake?
Why should I offer up unto her name
The sweetest sacrifice my youth can make?
Why should I strive to make her live forever,
That never deigns to give me joy to live?
Why should m' afflicted Muse so much endeavour
Such honour unto cruelty to give?
If her defects have purchased her this fame,
What should her virtues do, her smiles, her love?
If this her worst, how should her best inflame?
What passions would her milder favours move?
Favours, I think, would sense quite overcome,
And that makes happy lovers ever dumb.

XIX

Restore thy tresses to the golden ore;
Yield Cytherea's son those arcs of love:
Bequeath the heavens the stars that I adore;
And to the orient do thy pearls remove.
Yield thy hands' pride unto the ivory white;
T' Arabian odors give thy breathing sweet;
Restore thy blush unto Aurora bright;
To Thetis give the honour of thy feet.
Let Venus have thy graces her resigned;
And thy sweet voice give back unto the spheres:
But yet restore thy fierce and cruel mind
To Hyrcan tigers and to ruthless bears.
Yield to the marble thy hard heart again;
So shalt thou cease to plague and I to pain.

XXXIII

Oft do I marvel whether Delia's eyes
Are eyes, or else two radiant stars that shine?
For how could Nature ever thus devise
Of earth, on earth, a substance so divine?
Stars, sure, they are, whose motions rule desires;
And calm and tempest follow their aspects:
Their sweet appearing still such power inspires,
That makes the world admire so strange effects.
Yet whether fixed or wandering stars are they,
Whose influence rules the orb of my poor heart?
Fixed, sure, they are, but wandering, make me stray
In endless errors, whence I cannot part.
Stars, then, not eyes, move you, with milder view,
Your sweet aspect on him that honors you!

XXXIX

Look, Delia, how w'esteem the half-blown rose,
The image of thy blush, and summer's honour,
Whilst yet her tender bud doth undisclose
That full of beauty Time bestows upon her:
No sooner spreads her glory in the air
But straight her wide-blown pomp comes to decline;
She then is scorned that late adorned the fair.
So fade the roses of those cheeks of thine:
No April can revive thy withered flowers

Whose springing grace adorns thy glory now;
Swift, speedy Time, feathered with flying hours,
Dissolves the beauty of the fairest brow.
Then do not thou such treasure waste in vain,
But love now whilst thou mayst be loved again.

XLI

When men shall find thy flower, thy glory, pass,
And thou, with careful brow sitting alone,
Receivèd hast this message from thy glass,
That tells the truth and says that all is gone;
Fresh shalt thou see in me the wounds thou madest,
Though spent thy flame, in me the heat remaining:
I that have loved thee thus before thou fadest,
My faith shall wax when thou art in thy waning:
The world shall find this miracle in me,
That fire can burn when all the matter's spent:
Then, what my faith hath been thyself shalt see;
And that thou wast unkind thou mayst repent.
Thou mayst repent that thou hast scorned my tears,
When winter snows upon thy sable hairs.

XLII

When winter snows upon thy sable hairs,
And frost of age hath nipt thy beauties near;
When dark shall seem thy day that never clears,
And all lies withered that was held so dear:
Then take this picture which I here present thee,
Limned with a pencil not all unworthy:
Here see the gifts that God and Nature lent thee,
Here read thyself, and what I suffered for thee.
This may remain thy lasting monument,
Which happily posterity may cherish;
These colors with thy fading are not spent,
These may remain when thou and I shall perish.
If they remain, then thou shalt live thereby;
They will remain, and so thou can'st not die.

LIV

Care-charmer Sleep, son of the sable Night,
Brother to Death, in silent darkness born:
Relieve my languish, and restore the light;
With dark forgetting of my care, return!
And let the day be time enough to mourn
The shipwreck of my ill-adventured youth:
Let waking eyes suffice to wail their scorn,
Without the torment of the night's untruth.
Cease, dreams, the images of day-desires,
To model forth the passions of the morrow;
Never let rising sun approve you liars,
To add more grief to aggravate my sorrow.
Still let me sleep, embracing clouds in vain;
And never wake to feel the day's disdain.

LVIII

None other fame mine unambitious Muse
Affected ever, but t' eternize thee:
All other honours do my hopes refuse,
Which meaner-prized and momentary be.
For God forbid I should my papers blot
With mercenary lines, with servile pen;
Praising virtues in them that have them not,
Basely attending on the hopes of men.
No, no; my verse respects not Thames nor theatres;
Nor seeks it to be known unto the great:
But Avon, rich in fame though poor in waters,
Shall have my song; where Delia hath her seat.
Avon shall be my Thames, and she my song;
No other prouder brooks shall hear my wrong.

1592

Edmund Spenser (1552?–1599)

AMORETTI

I

HAPPY ye leaves! when as those lilly hands,
Which hold my life in their dead doing might,
Shall handle you, and hold in loves soft bands,
Lyke captives trembling at the victors sight.
And happy lines! on which, with starry light,
Those lamping eyes will deigne sometimes to look,
And reade the sorrowes of my dying spright,

Written with teares in harts close bleeding book.
And happy rymes! bathed in the sacred brooke
Of Helicon, whence she derivèd is,
When ye behold that angels blessèd looke,
My soules long lackèd foode, my heavens blis.
Leaves, lines, and rymes, seeke her to please alone,
Whom if ye please, I care for other none.

IX

Long-while I sought to what I might compare
Those powerfull eies which lighten my dark spright;
Yet find I nought on earth to which I dare
Resemble th' ymage of their goodly light.
Not to the sun; for they doo shine by night:
Nor to the moone; for they are changèd never:
Nor to the starres; for they have purer sight:
Nor to the fire; for they consume not ever:
Nor to the lightning; for they still persèver:
Nor to the diamond; for they are more tender:
Nor unto christall; for nought may them sever:
Nor unto glasse; such basenesse mought offend her.
Then to the Maker selfe they likest be,
Whose light doth lighten all that here we see.

XV

Ye tradefull merchants, that with weary toyle
Do seeke most pretious things to make your gain,
And both the Indias of their treasures spoile,
What needeth you to seeke so farre in vaine?
For loe! my love doth in her selfe containe
All this worlds riches that may farre be found:
If saphyres, loe! her eies be saphyres plaine;
If rubies, loe! her lips be rubies sound;
If pearles, her teeth be pearles both pure and round;
If yvorie, her forhead yvory weene;
If gold, her locks are finest gold on ground;
If silver, her faire hands are silver sheene:
But that which fairest is but few behold,
Her mind, adornd with vertues manifold.

XXIV

When I behold that beauties wonderment,
And rare perfection of each goodly part,
Of Natures skill the onely complement,
I honor and admire the Makers art.
But when I feele the bitter balefull smart
Which her fayre eyes unwares doe worke in mee,
That death out of theyr shiny beames doe dart,
I thinke that I a new Pandora see;
Whom all the gods in councell did agree,
Into this sinfull world from heaven to send,
That she to wicked men a scourge should bee,
For all their faults with which they did offend.
But since ye are my scourge, I will intreat
That for my faults ye will me gently beat.

XXX

My love is lyke to yse, and I to fyre;
How comes it then that this her cold so great
Is not dissolved through my so hot desyre,
But harder growes the more I her intreat?
Or how comes it that my exceeding heat
Is not delayd by her hart frosen cold,
But that I burne much more in boyling sweat,
And feele my flames augmented manifold?
What more miraculous thing may be told,
That fire, which all things melts, should harden yse,
And yse, which is congeald with sencelesse cold,
Should kindle fyre by wonderful devyse?
Such is the powre of love in gentle mind,
That it can alter all the course of kynd.

XXXIII

Great wrong I doe, I can it not deny,
To that most sacred empresse, my dear dread,
Not finishing her Queene of Faëry.
That mote enlarge her living prayses, dead.
But Lodwick, this of grace to me aread:
Do ye not thinck th' accomplishment of it
Sufficient worke for one mans simple head,
All were it, as the rest, but rudely writ?
How then should I, without another wit,
Thinck ever to endure so tædious toyle,
Sins that this one is tost with troublous fit
Of a proud love, that doth my spirite spoyle?
Cease then, till she vouchsafe to grawnt me rest,
Or lend you me another living brest.

XXXIV

Lyke as a ship, that through the ocean wyde
By conduct of some star doth make her way,
Whenas a storme hath dimd her trusty guyde,
Out of her course doth wander far astray;
So I, whose star, that wont with her bright ray
Me to direct, with cloudes is overcast,
Doe wander now in darknesse and dismay,
Through hidden perils round about me plast.
Yet hope I well, that when this storme is past,
My Helice, the lodestar of my lyfe,
Will shine again, and looke on me at last,
With lovely light to cleare my cloudy grief.
Till then I wander carefull comfortlesse,
In secret sorrow and sad pensivenesse.

L

Long languishing in double malady,
Of my harts wound and of my bodies griefe,
There came to me a leach, that would apply
Fit medicines for my bodies best reliefe.
Vayne man! (quod I) that hast but little priefe
In deep discovery of the mynds disease,
Is not the hart of all the body chiefe,
And rules the members as it selfe doth please?
Then with some cordialls seeke first to appease
The inward languour of my wounded hart,
And then my body shall have shortly ease:
But such sweet cordialls passe physitions art;
Then, my lyfes leach, doe you your skill reveale,
And with one salve both hart and body heale.

LXIII

After long stormes and tempests sad assay,
Which hardly I endurèd heretofore,
In dread of death, and daungerous dismay,
With which my silly barke was tossèd sore,
I doe at length descry the happy shore,
In which I hope ere long for to arryve:
Fayre soyle it seemes from far, and fraught with store
Of all that deare and daynty is alyve.
Most happy he that can at last atchyve
The joyous safety of so sweet a rest;
Whose least delight sufficeth to deprive
Remembrance of all paines which him opprest.
All paines are nothing in respect of this,
All sorrowes short that gaine eternall blisse.

LXVII

Lyke as a huntsman, after weary chace,
Seeing the game from him escapt away,
Sits downe to rest him in some shady place,
With panting hounds beguilèd of their pray:
So, after long pursuit and vaine assay,
When I all weary had the chace forsooke,
The gentle deare returnd the selfe-same way,
Thinking to quench her thirst at the next brooke.
There she, beholding me with mylder looke,
Sought not to fly, but fearlesse still did bide:
Till I in hand her yet halfe trembling tooke,
And with her owne goodwill hir fyrmely tyde.
Strange thing, me seemd, to see a beast so wyld,
So goodly wonne, with her owne will beguyld.

LXXIV

Most happy letters! framed by skilfull trade,
With which that happy name was first desynd,
The which three times thrise happy hath me made,
With guifts of body, fortune, and of mind.
The first my being to me gave by kind,
From mothers womb derived by dew descent:
The second is my sovereigne Queene most kind,
That honour and large richesse to me lent:
The third, my love, my lives last ornament,
By whom my spirit out of dust was raysed,
To speake her prayse and glory excellent,
Of all alive most worthy to be praysed.
Ye three Elizabeths, for ever live,
That three such graces did unto me give.

LXXV

One day I wrote her name upon the strand,
But came the waves and washèd it away:
Agayne I wrote it with a second hand,
But came the tyde, and made my paynes his pray.
Vayne man, sayd she, that doest in vaine assay
A mortall thing so to immortalize!
For I my selve shall lyke to this decay,
And eek my name bee wypèd out lykewize.
Not so, (quod I) let baser things devize
To dy in dust, but you shall live by fame:
My verse your vertues rare shall eternize,
And in the hevens wryte your glorious name;
Where, whenas death shall all the world subdew,
Our love shall live, and later life renew.

1595

William Shakespeare (1564-1616)

SONNETS

I — THE FAIR FRIEND

I

From fairest creatures we desire increase,
That thereby beauty's rose might never die,
But as the riper should by time decease,
His tender heir might bear his memory:
But thou, contracted to thine own bright eyes,
Feed'st thy light's flame with self-substantial fuel,
Making a famine where abundance lies,
Thyself thy foe, to thy sweet self too cruel.
Thou that art now the world's fresh ornament
And only herald to the gaudy spring,
Within thine own bud buriest thy content
And, tender churl, mak'st waste in niggarding.
Pity the world, or else this glutton be,
To eat the world's due, by the grave and thee.

II

When forty winters shall besiege thy brow,
And dig deep trenches in thy beauty's field,
Thy youth's proud livery, so gazed on now,
Will be a tattered weed, of small worth held:
Then being asked where all thy beauty lies,
Where all the treasure of thy lusty days,
To say, within thine own deep-sunken eyes,
Were an all-eating shame and thriftless praise.
How much more praise deserved thy beauty's use,
If thou couldst answer, 'This fair child of mine
Shall sum my count, and make my old excuse,'
Proving his beauty by succession thine!
This were to be new made when thou art old,
And see thy blood warm when thou feel'st it cold.

XII

When I do count the clock that tells the time,
And see the brave day sunk in hideous night;
When I behold the violet past prime,
And sable curls, all silvered o'er with white;
When lofty trees I see barren of leaves,
Which erst from heat did canopy the herd,
And summer's green all girded up in sheaves,
Borne on the bier with white and bristly beard,
Then of thy beauty do I question make,
That thou among the wastes of time must go,
Since sweets and beauties do themselves forsake
And die as fast as they see others grow;
And nothing 'gainst Time's scythe can make defence
Save breed, to brave him when he takes thee hence.

XVII

Who will believe my verse in time to come,
If it were filled with your most high deserts?
Though yet, heaven knows, it is but as a tomb
Which hides your life and shows not half your parts.
If I could write the beauty of your eyes
And in fresh numbers number all your graces,
The age to come would say 'This poet lies;
Such heavenly touches ne'er touched earthly faces.'
So should my papers, yellowed with their age,
Be scorned, like old men of less truth than tongue,
And your true rights be termed a poet's rage
And stretchèd metre of an antique song:
But were some child of yours alive that time,
You should live twice, — in it and in my rhyme.

XVIII

Shall I compare thee to a summer's day?
Thou art more lovely and more temperate:
Rough winds do shake the darling buds of May,
And summer's lease hath all too short a date:
Sometime too hot the eye of heaven shines,
And often is his gold complexion dimmed;
And every fair from fair sometime declines,
By chance, or nature's changing course untrimmed;
But thy eternal summer shall not fade,
Nor lose possession of that fair thou ow'st,
Nor shall death brag thou wander'st in his shade,
When in eternal lines to time thou growest;
So long as men can breathe, or eyes can see,
So long lives this, and this gives life to thee.

XX

A woman's face with Nature's own hand painted
Hast thou, the master-mistress of my passion;

A woman's gentle heart, but not acquainted
With shifting change, as is false women's fashion;
An eye more bright than theirs, less false in rolling,
Gilding the object whereupon it gazeth;
A man in hue all hues in his controlling,
Which steals men's eyes and women's souls amazeth.
And for a woman wert thou first created;
Till Nature, as she wrought thee, fell a-doting,
And by addition me of thee defeated,
By adding one thing to my purpose nothing.
But since she pricked thee out for women's pleasure,
Mine by thy love, and thy love's use their treasure.

XXIX

When in disgrace with fortune and men's eyes,
I all alone beweep my outcast state,
And trouble deaf heaven with my bootless cries,
And look upon myself, and curse my fate,
Wishing me like to one more rich in hope,
Featured like him, like him with friends possessed,
Desiring this man's art, and that man's scope,
With what I most enjoy contented least;
Yet in these thoughts myself almost despising,
Haply I think on thee, — and then my state,
Like to the lark at break of day arising
From sullen earth, sings hymns at heaven's gate;
For thy sweet love remembered such wealth brings
That then I scorn to change my state with kings.

XXX

When to the sessions of sweet silent thought
I summon up remembrance of things past,
I sigh the lack of many a thing I sought,
And with old woes new wail my dear time's waste:
Then can I drown an eye, unused to flow,
For precious friends hid in death's dateless night,
And weep afresh love's long since canceled woe,
And moan the expense of many a vanished sight:
Then can I grieve at grievances foregone,
And heavily from woe to woe tell o'er
The sad account of fore-bemoanèd moan,
Which I new pay as if not paid before.
But if the while I think on thee, dear friend,
All losses are restored and sorrows end.

XXXII

If thou survive my well-contented day,
When that churl Death my bones with dust shall cover,
And shalt by fortune once more re-survey
These poor rude lines of thy deceasèd lover,
Compare them with the bettering of the time,
And though they be outstripped by every pen,
Reserve them for my love, not for their rhyme,
Exceeded by the height of happier men.
O! then vouchsafe me but this loving thought:
'Had my friend's Muse grown with this growing age,
A dearer birth than this his love had brought,
To march in ranks of better equipage:
But since he died, and poets better prove,
Theirs for their style I'll read, his for his love.'

XXXIII

Full many a glorious morning have I seen
Flatter the mountain-tops with sovereign eye,
Kissing with golden face the meadows green,
Gilding pale streams with heavenly alchemy;
Anon permit the basest clouds to ride
With ugly rack on his celestial face,
And from the forlorn world his visage hide,
Stealing unseen to west with this disgrace:
Even so my sun one early morn did shine,
With all-triumphant splendour on my brow;
But, out! alack! he was but one hour mine,
The region cloud hath masked him from me now.
Yet him for this my love no whit disdaineth;
Suns of the world may stain when heaven's sun staineth.

XLI

Those pretty wrongs that liberty commits,
When I am sometimes absent from thy heart,
Thy beauty and thy years full well befits,
For still temptation follows where thou art.
Gentle thou art, and therefore to be won,
Beauteous thou art, therefore to be assailed;
And when a woman woos, what woman's son

Will sourly leave her till she have prevailed?
Ay me! but yet thou mightst my seat forbear,
And chide thy beauty and thy straying youth,
Who lead thee in their riot even there
Where thou art forced to break a twofold truth; —
Hers, by thy beauty tempting her to thee,
Thine, by thy beauty being false to me.

LV

Not marble, nor the gilded monuments
Of princes, shall outlive this powerful rime;
But you shall shine more bright in these contents
Than unswept stone, besmeared with sluttish time.
When wasteful war shall statues overturn,
And broils root out the work of masonry,
Nor Mars his sword nor war's quick fire shall burn
The living record of your memory.
'Gainst death and all-oblivious enmity
Shall you pace forth; your praise shall still find room
Even in the eyes of all posterity
That wear this world out to the ending doom.
So, till the judgment that yourself arise,
You live in this, and dwell in lovers' eyes.

LX

Like as the waves make towards the pebbled shore,
So do our minutes hasten to their end;
Each changing place with that which goes before,
In sequent toil all forwards do contend.
Nativity, once in the main of light,
Crawls to maturity, wherewith being crowned,
Crookèd eclipses 'gainst his glory fight,
And Time that gave doth now his gift confound.
Time doth transfix the flourish set on youth
And delves the parallels in beauty's brow,
Feeds on the rarities of nature's truth,
And nothing stands but for his scythe to mow:
And yet to times in hope my verse shall stand,
Praising thy worth, despite his cruel hand.

LXIV

When I have seen by Time's fell hand defaced
The rich-proud cost of outworn buried age;
When sometime lofty towers I see downrazed
And brass eternal slave to mortal rage;
When I have seen the hungry ocean gain
Advantage on the kingdom of the shore,
And the firm soil win of the watery main,
Increasing store with loss, and loss with store;
When I have seen such interchange of state,
Or state itself confounded to decay;
Ruin hath taught me thus to ruminate —
That Time will come and take my love away.
This thought is as a death, which cannot choose
But weep to have that which it fears to lose.

LXV

Since brass, nor stone, nor earth, nor boundless sea,
But sad mortality o'er-sways their power,
How with this rage shall beauty hold a plea,
Whose action is no stronger than a flower?
O! how shall summer's honey breath hold out
Against the wreckful siege of battering days,
When rocks impregnable are not so stout,
Nor gates of steel so strong, but Time decays?
O fearful meditation! where, alack,
Shall Time's best jewel from Time's chest lie hid?
Or what strong hand can hold his swift foot back?
Or who his spoil of beauty can forbid?
O! none, unless this miracle have might,
That in black ink my love may still shine bright.

LXVI

Tired with all these, for restful death I cry,
As, to behold desert a beggar born,
And needy nothing trimmed in jollity,
And purest faith unhappily forsworn,
And gilded honor shamefully misplaced,
And maiden virtue rudely strumpeted,
And right perfection wrongfully disgraced,
And strength by limping sway disablèd,
And art made tongue-tied by authority,
And folly, doctor-like, controlling skill,
And simple truth miscalled simplicity,
And captive good attending captain ill:
Tired with all these, from these would I be gone,
Save that, to die, I leave my love alone.

LXXI

No longer mourn for me when I am dead
Than you shall hear the surly sullen bell

Give warning to the world that I am fled
From this vile world, with vilest worms to dwell:
Nay, if you read this line, remember not
The hand that writ it; for I love you so,
That I in your sweet thoughts would be forgot,
If thinking on me then should make you woe.
O! if, — I say, you look upon this verse,
When I perhaps compounded am with clay,
Do not so much as my poor name rehearse,
But let your love even with my life decay;
Lest the wise world should look into your moan,
And mock you with me after I am gone.

LXXIII

That time of year thou mayst in me behold
When yellow leaves, or none, or few, do hang
Upon those boughs which shake against the cold,
Bare ruin'd choirs, where late the sweet birds sang.
In me thou see'st the twilight of such day
As after sunset fadeth in the west;
Which by and by black night doth take away,
Death's second self, that seals up all in rest.
In me thou see'st the glowing of such fire
That on the ashes of his youth doth lie,
As the death-bed whereon it must expire,
Consum'd with that which it was nourish'd by.
This thou perceiv'st, which makes thy love more strong,
To love that well which thou must leave ere long.

LXXVIII

So oft have I invoked thee for my Muse
And found such fair assistance in my verse
As every alien pen hath got my use
And under thee their poesy disperse.
Thine eyes, that taught the dumb on high to sing
And heavy ignorance aloft to fly,
Have added feathers to the learned's wing
And given grace a double majesty.
Yet be most proud of that which I compile,
Whose influence is thine, and born of thee:
In others' works thou dost but mend the style,
And arts with thy sweet graces gracèd be;
But thou art all my art, and dost advance
As high as learning my rude ignorance.

XCVII

How like a winter hath my absence been
From thee, the pleasure of the fleeting year!
What freezings have I felt, what dark days seen!
What old December's bareness every where!
And yet this time remov'd was summer's time;
The teeming autumn, big with rich increase,
Bearing the wanton burden of the prime,
Like widowed wombs after their lords' decease:
Yet this abundant issue seem'd to me
But hope of orphans and unfather'd fruit;
For summer and his pleasures wait on thee.
And, thou away, the very birds are mute:
Or, if they sing, 'tis with so dull a cheer,
That leaves look pale, dreading the winter's near.

CIV

To me, fair friend, you never can be old,
For as you were when first your eye I eyed,
Such seems your beauty still. Three winters cold
Have from the forests shook three summers' pride,
Three beauteous springs to yellow autumn turned
In process of the seasons have I seen,
Three April perfumes in three hot Junes burned,
Since first I saw you fresh, which yet are green.
Ah! yet doth beauty, like a dial-hand,
Steal from his figure, and no pace perceived;
So your sweet hue, which methinks still doth stand,
Hath motion, and mine eye may be deceived:
For fear of which, hear this, thou age unbred:
Ere you were born was beauty's summer dead.

CVI

When in the chronicle of wasted time
I see descriptions of the fairest wights,
And beauty making beautiful old rime,
In praise of ladies dead and lovely knights,
Then, in the blazon of sweet beauty's best,
Of hand, of foot, of lip, of eye, of brow,
I see their antique pen would have expressed
Even such a beauty as you master now.
So all their praises are but prophecies
Of this our time, all you prefiguring,
And, for they looked but with divining eyes,

They had not skill enough your worth to sing:
For we, which now behold these present days,
Have eyes to wonder, but lack tongues to praise.

CXVI

Let me not to the marriage of true minds
Admit impediments. Love is not love
Which alters when it alteration finds,
Or bends with the remover to remove:
O, no! it is an ever-fixèd mark,
That looks on tempests and is never shaken;
It is the star to every wandering bark,
Whose worth 's unknown, although his height be taken.
Love 's not Time's fool, though rosy lips and cheeks
Within his bending sickle's compass come;
Love alters not with his brief hours and weeks,
But bears it out even to the edge of doom.
If this be error and upon me proved,
I never writ, nor no man ever loved.

CXXVI

O thou, my lovely boy, who in thy power
Dost hold Time's fickle glass, his sickle, hour;
Who hast by waning grown, and therein show'st
Thy lovers withering as thy sweet self grow'st;
If Nature, sovereign mistress over wrack,
As thou goest onwards, still will pluck thee back,
She keeps thee to this purpose, that her skill
May time disgrace and wretched minutes kill.
Yet fear her, O thou minion of her pleasure!
She may detain, but not still keep, her treasure:
Her audit, though delayed, answered must be,
And her quietus is to render thee.

II — THE DARK WOMAN

CXXVII

In the old age black was not counted fair,
Or if it were, it bore not beauty's name;
But now is black beauty's successive heir,
And beauty slandered with a bastard's shame:
For since each hand hath put on Nature's power,
Fairing the foul with Art's false borrowed face,
Sweet beauty hath no name, no holy bower,
But is profaned, if not lives in disgrace.
Therefore my mistress' brows are raven black,
Her eyes so suited, and they mourners seem
At such who, not born fair, no beauty lack,
Sland'ring creation with a false esteem:
Yet so they mourn, becoming of their woe,
That every tongue says beauty should look so.

CXXX

My mistress' eyes are nothing like the sun;
Coral is far more red than her lips' red:
If snow be white, why then her breasts are dun;
If hairs be wires, black wires grow on her head.
I have seen roses damasked, red and white,
But no such roses see I in her cheeks;
And in some perfumes is there more delight
Than in the breath that from my mistress reeks.
I love to hear her speak, yet well I know
That music hath a far more pleasing sound:
I grant I never saw a goddess go, —
My mistress, when she walks, treads on the ground:
And yet, by heaven, I think my love as rare
As any she belied with false compare.

CXXXVIII

When my love swears that she is made of truth,
I do believe her, though I know she lies,
That she might think me some untutored youth,
Unlearnèd in the world's false subtleties.
Thus vainly thinking that she thinks me young,
Although she knows my days are past the best,
Simply I credit her false-speaking tongue:
On both sides thus is simple truth suppressed.
But wherefore says she not she is unjust?
And wherefore say not I that I am old?
O! love's best habit is in seeming trust,
And age in love loves not to have years told:
Therefore I lie with her, and she with me,
And in our faults by lies we flattered be.

CXLIV

Two loves I have of comfort and despair,
Which like two spirits do suggest me still:
The better angel is a man right fair,
The worser spirit a woman coloured ill.
To win me soon to hell, my female evil
Tempteth my better angel from my side,

And would corrupt my saint to be a devil,
Wooing his purity with her foul pride.
And whether that my angel be turned fiend
Suspect I may, yet not directly tell;
But being both from me, both to each friend,
I guess one angel in another's hell:
Yet this shall I ne'er know, but live in doubt,
Till my bad angel fire my good one out.

CXLVI

Poor soul, the center of my sinful earth,
Fooled by these rebel powers that thee array,
Why dost thou pine within and suffer dearth,
Painting thy outward walls so costly gay?
Why so large cost, having so short a lease,
Dost thou upon thy fading mansion spend?
Shall worms, inheritors of this excess,
Eat up thy charge? Is this thy body's end?
Then, soul, live thou upon thy servant's loss,
And let that pine to aggravate thy store;
Buy terms divine in selling hours of dross;
Within be fed, without be rich no more:
So shalt thou feed on Death, that feeds on men,
And Death once dead, there 's no more dying then.

CLIV

The little Love-god lying once asleep
Laid by his side his heart-inflaming brand,
Whilst many nymphs that vowed chaste life to keep
Came tripping by; but in her maiden hand
The fairest votary took up that fire
Which many legions of true hearts had warmed;
And so the general of hot desire
Was, sleeping, by a virgin hand disarmed.
This brand she quenched in a cool well by,
Which from Love's fire took heat perpetual,
Growing a bath and healthful remedy
For men diseased; but I, my mistress' thrall,
Came there for cure, and this by that I prove,
Love's fire heats water, water cools not love.

1609

PROSE

CHRONICLE HISTORY AND BIOGRAPHY

Ralph Holinshed (–1580?)

CHRONICLES OF ENGLAND, SCOTLAND, AND IRELAND

MACBETH AND THE WEIRD SISTERS

Shortly after happened a strange and uncouth wonder, which afterward was the cause of much trouble in the realm of Scotland, as ye shall after hear. It fortuned as Macbeth and Banquo journeyed towards Fores, where the king then lay, they went sporting by the way together without other company, save only themselves, passing through the woods and fields, when suddenly in the midst of a land, there met them three women in strange and wild apparel, resembling creatures of elder world, whom when they attentively beheld, wondering much at the sight, the first of them spake and said: 'All hail Macbeth, thane of Glammis' (for he had lately entered into that dignity and office by the death of his father Sinell). The second of them said; 'Hail Macbeth, thane of Cawder.' But the third said: 'All hail Macbeth, that hereafter shalt be king of Scotland.'

Then Banquo; 'What manner of women (saith he) are you, that seem so little favourable unto me, whereas to my fellow here, besides high offices, ye assign also the kingdom, appointing forth nothing for me at all?' 'Yes (saith the first of them) we promise greater benefits unto thee, than unto him, for he shall reign indeed, but with an unlucky end: neither shall he leave any issue behind him to succeed in his place, where contrarily thou indeed shalt not reign at all, but of thee those shall be born which shall govern the

Scottish kingdom by long order of continual descent.' Herewith the foresaid women vanished immediately out of their sight. This was reputed at the first but some vain fantastical illusion by Macbeth and Banquo, insomuch that Banquo would call Macbeth in jest, king of Scotland; and Macbeth again would call him in sport likewise, the father of many kings. But afterwards the common opinion was, that these women were either the weird sisters, that is (as ye would say) the goddesses of destiny, or else some nymphs or fairies, indued with knowledge of prophecy by their necromantical science, because everything came to pass as they had spoken. For shortly after, the thane of Cawdor being condemned at Fores of treason against the king committed; his lands, livings, and offices were given of the king's liberality to Macbeth.

The same night after, at supper, Banquo jested with him and said; 'Now Macbeth, thou hast obtained those things which the two former sisters prophesied, there remaineth only for thee to purchase that which the third said should come to pass.' Whereupon Macbeth revolving the thing in his mind, began even then to devise how he might attain to the kingdom: but yet he thought with himself that he must tarry a time, which should advance him thereto (by the divine providence) as it had come to pass in his former preferment. But shortly after it chanced that king Duncan, having two sons by his wife, which was the daughter of Siward earl of Northumberland, he made the elder of them called Malcolm Prince of Cumberland, as it were thereby to appoint him his successor in the kingdom, immediately after his decease. Macbeth sore troubled herewith, for that he saw by this means his hope sore hindered (where, by the old laws of the realm, the ordinance was, that if he that should succeed were not of able age to take the charge upon himself, he that was next of blood unto him should be admitted) he began to take counsel how he might usurp the kingdom by force, having a just quarrel so to do (as he took the matter) for that Duncan did what in him lay to defraud him of all manner of title and claim, which he might in time to come, pretend unto the crown.

The words of the three weird sisters also (of whom before ye have heard) greatly encouraged him hereunto, but specially his wife lay sore upon him to attempt the thing, as she that was very ambitious, burning in unquenchable desire to bear the name of a queen. At length therefore, communicating his purposed intent with his trusty friends, amongst whom Banquo was the chiefest, upon confidence of their promised aid, he slew the king at Envernes, or (as some say) at Botgoswane, in the sixth year of his reign. Then having a company about him of such as he had made privy to his enterprise, he caused himself to be proclaimed king, and forthwith went unto Scone, where (by common consent) he received the investure of the kingdom according to the accustomed manner. The body of Duncan was first conveyed unto Elgin, and there buried in kingly wise; but afterwards it was removed and conveyed unto Colmkill, and there laid in a sepulture amongst his predecessors, in the year after the birth of our Saviour, 1046.

1577

Sir Thomas North (1535?-1601?)

TRANSLATION OF PLUTARCH'S LIVES

ASSASSINATION OF CÆSAR

Now all the Senators being entered first into this place or chapter-house where the council should be kept, all the other conspirators straight stood about Cæsar's chair, as if they had had something to have said unto him. And some say, that Cassius casting his eyes upon Pompey's image, made his prayer unto it, as if it had been alive. Trebonius on the other side, drew Antonius aside, as he came into the house where the Senate sat, and held him with a long talk without. When Cæsar was come into the house, all the Senate rose to honour him at his coming in. So when he was set, the conspirators flocked about him, and amongst them they presented one Tillius Cimber, who made humble suit for the calling home again of his brother that was banished. They all made as though they were intercessors for him, and took him by the hands, and kissed his head and breast. Cæsar at the first, simply refused their kindness and entreaties: but afterwards, perceiving they still pressed on him, he violently thrust them from him. Then Cimber with both his hands plucked Cæsar's gown over his shoulders, and Casca that stood behind him, drew his dagger first, and struck Cæsar upon the shoulder, but gave him no great wound. Cæsar feeling himself hurt, took him straight by the hand he held his dagger in, and cried out in Latin: O traitor, Casca, what doest thou? Casca on the other side cried in Greek, and called his brother to help him. So divers running on a heap together to fly upon Cæsar, he looking about him to have fled, saw Brutus with a sword drawn in his hand ready to strike at him: then he let Casca's hand go, and casting his gown over his face, suffered every man to strike at him that would. Then the conspirators thronging one upon another because every man was desirous to have a cut at him, so many swords and daggers lighting upon one body, one of them hurt another, and among them Brutus caught a blow on his hand, because he would make one in murthering of him, and all the rest also were every man of them bloodied. Cæsar being slain in this manner, Brutus standing in the midst of the house, would have spoken, and stayed the other Senators that were not of the conspiracy, to have told them the reason why they had done this fact. But they as men both afrayed and amazed, fled one upon another's neck in haste to get out at the door, and no man followed them. For it was set down, and agreed between them, that they should kill no man but Cæsar only, and should entreat all the rest to defend their liberty. All the conspirators, but Brutus, determining upon this matter, thought it good also to kill Antonius, because he was a wicked man, and that in nature favoured tyranny: besides also, for that he was in great estimation with soldiers, having been conversant of long time amongst them: and specially having a mind bent to great enterprises, he was also of great authority at that time, being Consul with Cæsar. But Brutus would not agree to it. First, for that he said it was not honest: secondly, because he told them there was hope of change in him. For he did not mistrust, but that Antonius being a noble-minded and courageous man (when he should know that Cæsar was dead) would willingly help his country to recover her liberty, having them an example unto him, to follow their courage and virtue. So Brutus by this means saved Antonius' life, who at that time disguised himself, and stale away. But Brutus and his consorts, having their swords bloody in their hands, went straight to the Capitol, persuading the Romans as they went, to take their liberty again. Now, at the first time when the murther was newly done, there were sudden outcries of people that ran up and down the city, the which indeed did the more increase the fear and tumult. But when they saw they slew no man, neither did spoil or make havoc of anything: then certain of the Senators, and many of the people emboldening themselves, went to the Capitol unto them. There a great number of men being assembled together one after another: Brutus made an oration unto them to win the favour of the people, and to justify that they had done. All those that were by, said they had done well, and cried unto them that they should boldly come down from the Capitol. Whereupon, Brutus and his companions came boldly down into the market-place. The rest followed in troop, but Brutus went foremost, very honourably compassed in round about with the noblest men of the city, which brought him from the Capitol, through the market-place, to the pulpit for orations. When the people saw him in the pulpit, although they were a multitude of rakehells of all sorts, and had a good will to make some stir: yet being ashamed to do it for the reverence they bore unto Brutus, they kept silence, to hear what he would say. When Brutus began to speak, they gave him quiet audience: howbeit immediately after, they shewed that they were not all contented with the murther. For when another called Cinna would have spoken, and began to accuse Cæsar: they fell into a great uproar among them, and marvellously reviled him. Insomuch that the conspirators returned again into the Capitol. There Brutus being affrayed to be besieged, sent back again the noblemen that came thither with him, thinking it no reason, that they which were no partakers of the murther, should be partakers of the danger. Then the next morning the Senate being assembled, and holden within the temple of the goddess Tellus, to wit the earth: and Antonius, Plancus, and Cicero, having made a motion to the Senate in that assembly, that they should take an order to pardon and forget all that was past, and to establish friendship and peace again: it was decreed, that they should not only be pardoned, but also that the Consuls should refer it to the Senate what honours should be appointed unto them. This being agreed upon, the Senate broke up, and Antonius the Consul, to put them in heart that were in the Capitol, sent them his son for a pledge. Upon this assurance, Brutus and his companions came down from the Capitol, where every man saluted and embraced each other, among the which, Antonius did bid Cassius to supper to him: and Lepidus also bade Brutus, and so one bade another, as they had friendship and acquaintance together. The next day following, the Senate being called again to council, did first of all commend Antonius, for that he had wisely stayed and quenched the beginning of a civil war: then they also gave Brutus and his consorts great praises, and lastly they appointed them several governments of provinces. For unto Brutus, they appointed Crete: Afric, unto Cassius: Asia, unto Trebonius: Bithynia, unto Cimber: and unto the other Decius Brutus Albinus, Gaul on this side the Alps. When this was done, they came to talk of Cæsar's will and testament, and of his funerals and tomb. Then Antonius thinking good his testament should be read openly, and also that his body should be honourably buried, and not in hugger-mugger, lest the people might thereby take occasion to be worse offended if they did otherwise: Cassius stoutly spake against it. But Brutus went with the motion, and agreed unto it: wherein it seemeth he committed a second fault. For the first fault he did was, when he would not consent to his fellow-conspirators, that Antonius should be slain. And therefore he was justly accused, that thereby he had saved and strengthened a strong and grievous enemy of their conspiracy. The second fault was, when he agreed that Cæsar's funerals should be as Antonius would have them: the which indeed marred all. For first of all, when Cæsar's testament was openly read among them, whereby it appeared that he bequeathed unto every citizen of Rome, seventy-five drachmas a man, and that he left his gardens and arbours unto the people, which he had on this side of the river of Tiber, in the place where now the temple of Fortune is built: the people then loved him, and were marvellous sorry for him. Afterwards when Cæsar's body was brought into the market-place, Antonius making his funeral oration in praise of the dead, according to the ancient custom of Rome, and perceiving that his words moved the common people to compassion: he framed his eloquence to make their hearts yearn the more, and taking Cæsar's gown all bloody in his hand, he laid it open to the sight of them all, showing what a number of cuts and holes it had upon it. Therewithal the people fell presently into such a rage and mutiny, that there was no more order kept amongst the common people. For some of them cried out, Kill the murtherers: others plucked up forms, tables, and stalls about the market-place, as they had done before at the funerals of Clodius, and having laid them all on a heap together, they set them on fire, and thereupon did put the body of Cæsar, and burnt it in the midst the most holy places. And furthermore, when the fire was throughly kindled, some here, some there, took burning firebrands, and ran with them to the murtherers' houses that had killed him, to set them afire. Howbeit the conspirators foreseeing the danger before, had wisely provided for themselves, and fled. But there was a poet called Cinna, who had been no partaker of the conspiracy, but was always one of Cæsar's chiefest friends: he dreamed the night before, that Cæsar bade him to supper with him, and that he refusing to go, Cæsar was very importunate with him, and compelled him, so that at length he led him by the hand into a great dark place, where being marvellously afraid, he was driven to follow him in spite of his heart. This dream put him all night into a fever, and yet notwithstanding, the next morning when he heard that they carried Cæsar's body to burial, being ashamed not to accompany his funerals: he went out of his house, and thrust himself into the press of the common people that were in a great uproar. And because some one called him by his name, Cinna: the people thinking he had been that Cinna, who in an oration he made had spoken very evil of Cæsar, they falling upon him in their rage, slew him outright in the market-place. This made Brutus and his companions more afraid, than any other thing, next unto the change of Antonius. Wherefore they got them out of Rome, and kept at the first in the city of Antium, hoping to return again to Rome, when the fury of the people were a little assuaged. The which they hoped would be quickly, considering that they had to deal with a fickle and unconstant multitude, easy to be carried, and that the Senate stood for them: who notwithstanding made no enquiry of them that had torn poor Cinna the Poet in pieces, but caused them to be sought for and apprehended, that went with firebrands to set fire of the conspirators' houses.

1579

CRITICISM

Sir Philip Sidney (1554–1586)

DEFENSE OF POESY

ITS SUPREMACY

Now therein of all sciences (I speak still of human, and according to the human conceits) is our poet the monarch. For he doth not only show the way, but giveth so sweet a prospect into the way, as will entice any man to enter into it. Nay, he doth as if your journey should lie through a fair vineyard, at the very first give you a cluster of grapes, that full of that taste you may long to pass further. He beginneth not with obscure definitions, which must blur the margent with interpretations, and load the memory with doubtfulness: but he cometh to you with words sent in delightful proportion, either accompanied with, or prepared for the well-enchanting skill of music; and with a tale forsooth he cometh unto you, with a tale which holdeth children from play, and old men from the chimney corner. And pretending no more, doth intend the winning of the mind from wickedness to virtue: even as the child is often brought to take most wholesome things, by hiding them in such other as have a pleasant taste, which, if one should begin to tell them the nature of aloes or rhubarb they should receive, would sooner take their physic at their ears than at their mouth. So it is in men (most of which are childish in the best things, till they be cradled in their graves) glad they will be to hear the tales of Hercules, Achilles, Cyrus, and Æneas; and, hearing them, must needs hear the right description of wisdom, valor, and justice; which, if they had been barely, that is to say, philosophically set out, they would swear they be brought to school again.

That imitation whereof poetry is, hath the most conveniency to nature of all other, insomuch, that as Aristotle saith, those things which in themselves are horrible, as cruel battles, unnatural monsters, are made in poetical imitation delightful. Truly I have known men, that even with reading *Amadis de Gaule* (which God knoweth wanteth much of a perfect poesy) have found their hearts moved to the exercise of courtesy, liberality, and especially courage.

Who readeth Æneas carrying old Anchises on his back, that wisheth not it were his fortune to perform so excellent an act? Whom do not the words of Turnus move (the tale of Turnus, having planted his image in his imagination)

— Fugientem hæc terra videbit,
Usque adeone mori miserum est? —

Where the philosophers, as they scorn to delight, so must they be content little to move: saving wrangling, whether virtue be the chief or the only good, whether the contemplative or the active life do excel, which Plato and

Boethius well knew, and therefore made Mistress Philosophy very often borrow the masking raiment of Poesy. For even those hard hearted evil men, who think virtue a school-name, and know no other good but *indulgere genio*, and therefore despise the austere admonitions of the philosopher, and feel not the inward reason they stand upon; yet will be content to be delighted, which is all the good-fellow poet seemeth to promise; and so steal to see the form of goodness (which seen they cannot but love) ere themselves be aware, as if they took a medicine of cherries. Infinite proofs of the strange effects of this poetical invention might be alleged, only two shall serve, which are so often remembered, as I think all men know them.

The one of Menenius Agrippa, who when the whole people of Rome had resolutely divided themselves from the Senate, with apparent show of utter ruin, though he were (for that time) an excellent Oratour, came not among them, upon trust of figurative speeches, or cunning insinuations, and much less, with far-set maxims of philosophy, which (especially if they were Platonic) they must have learned geometry before they could well have conceived: but forsooth he behaves himself, like a homely, and familiar Poet. He telleth them a tale, that there was a time, when all the parts of the body made a mutinous conspiracy against the belly, which they thought devoured the fruits of each others labour: they concluded they would let so unprofitable a spender starve. In the end, to be short (for the tale is notorious, and as notorious that it was a tale) with punishing the belly, they plagued themselves. This applied by him, wrought such effect in the people, as I never read, that ever words brought forth but then, so sudden and so good an alteration; for upon reasonable conditions, a perfect reconcilement ensued. The other is of Nathan the Prophet, who, when the holy David had so far forsaken God, as to confirm adultery with murther: when he was to do the tenderest office of a friend, in laying his own shame before his eyes, sent by God to call again so chosen a servant: how doth he it? but by telling of a man, whose beloved lamb was ungratefully taken from his bosom: the application most divinely true, but the discourse itself feigned: which made David (I speak of the second and instrumental cause) as in a glass, to see his own filthiness, as that heavenly Psalm of mercy well testifieth.

By these therefore examples and reasons, I think it may be manifest, that the Poet with that same hand of delight, doth draw the mind more effectually, than any other Art doth, and so a conclusion not unfitly ensueth: that as virtue is the most excellent resting place for all worldly learning to make his end of, so Poetry, being the most familiar to teach it, and most princely to move toward it, in the most excellent work, is the most excellent workman. But I am content, not only to decipher him by his works (although works in commendation or dispraise, must ever hold an high authority) but more narrowly will examine his parts: so that (as in a man) though all together may carry a presence full of majesty and beauty, perchance in some one defectious piece, we may find a blemish: now in his parts, kinds, or species (as you list to term them) it is to be noted, that some Poesies have coupled together two or three kinds, as Tragical and Comical, whereupon is risen, the Tragi-comical. Some in the like manner have mingled Prose and Verse, as Sanazzar and Boetius. Some have mingled matters Heroical and Pastoral. But that cometh all to one in this question, for if severed they be good, the conjunction cannot be hurtful. Therefore perchance forgetting some, and leaving some as needless to be remembered, it shall not be amiss in a word to cite the special kinds, to see what faults may be found in the right use of them.

Is it then the Pastoral Poem which is misliked? (for perchance, where the hedge is lowest, they will soonest leap over). Is the poor pipe disdained, which sometimes out of Melibeus mouth, can show the misery of people, under hard Lords and ravening Soldiers? And again, by Titirus, what blessedness is derived to them that lie lowest from the goodness of them that sit highest? Sometimes, under the pretty tales of Wolves and Sheep, can include the whole considerations of wrong doing and patience. Sometimes show, that contention for trifles, can get but a trifling victory. Where perchance a man may see, that even Alexander and Darius, when they strave who should be Cock of this worlds dunghill, the benefit they got, was, that the after-livers may say,

Hæc memini et victum frustra contendere
Thyrsin:
Ex illo Coridon, Coridon est tempore nobis.

Or is it the lamenting Elegiac, which in a kind heart would move rather pity than blame, who bewails with the great Philosopher Heraclitus, the weakness of mankind, and wretchedness of the world: who surely is to be praised, either for compassionate accompanying just causes of lamentation, or for rightly painting out how weak be the passions of wofulness. Is it the bitter, but wholesome Iambic, who rubs the galled mind, in making shame the trumpet of villainy, with bold and open crying out against naughtiness; or the Satiric? who

Omne vafer vitium, ridenti tangit amico?

Who sportingly never leaveth, until he make a man laugh at folly, and at length ashamed, to laugh at himself: which he cannot avoid, without avoiding the folly. Who while

Circum præcordia ludit

giveth us to feel, how many head-aches a passionate life bringeth us to. How when all is done,

Est Ulubris animus si nos non deficit æquus?

No perchance it is the Comic, whom naughty Play-makers and Stage-keepers, have justly made odious. To the argument of abuse, I will answer after. Only thus much now is to be said, that the Comedy is an imitation of the common errors of our life, which he representeth, in the most ridiculous and scornful sort that may be. So as it is impossible, that any beholder can be content to be such a one.

Now, as in Geometry, the oblique must be known as well as the right: and in Arithmetic, the odd as well as the even, so in the actions of our life, who seeth not the filthiness of evil, wanteth a great foil to perceive the beauty of virtue. This doth the Comedy handle so in our private and domestical matters, as with hearing it, we get as it were an experience, what is to be looked for of a niggardly Demea: of a crafty Danus: of a flattering Gnatho: of a vain glorious Thraso: and not only to know what effects are to be expected, but to know who be such, by the signifying badge given them by the Comedian. And little reason hath any man to say, that men learn evil by seeing it so set out: since as I have said before, there is no man living, but by the force truth hath in nature, no sooner seeth these men play their parts, but wisheth them in *Pistrinum:* although perchance the sack of his own faults, lie so behind his back, that he seeth not himself dance the same measure: whereto, yet nothing can more open his eyes, than to find his own actions contemptibly set forth. So that the right use of Comedy will (I think) by nobody be blamed, and much less of the high and excellent Tragedy, that openeth the greatest wounds, and showeth forth the ulcers, that are covered with Tissue: that maketh Kings fear to be Tyrants, and Tyrants manifest their tyrannical humours: that with stirring the effects of admiration and commiseration, teacheth, the uncertainty of this world, and upon how weak foundations gilden roofs are builded. That maketh us know,

Qui sceptra sævus, duro imperio regit,
Timet timentes, metus in authorem redit.

But how much it can move, Plutarch yieldeth a notable testimony, of the abominable Tyrant, Alexander Pheroeus; from whose eyes, a Tragedy well made, and represented, drew abundance of tears: who without all pity, had murdered infinite numbers, and some of his own blood. So as he, that was not ashamed to make matters for Tragedies, yet could not resist the sweet violence of a Tragedy.

And if it wrought no further good in him, it was, that he in despite of himself, withdrew himself from hearkening to that, which might mollify his hardened heart. But it is not the Tragedy they do mislike: for it were too absurd to cast out so excellent a representation of whatsoever is most worthy to be learned. Is it the Lyric that most displeaseth, who with his tuned Lyre, and well accorded voice, giveth praise, the reward of virtue, to virtuous acts? who gives moral precepts, and natural Problems, who sometimes raiseth up his voice to the height of the heavens, in singing the lauds of the immortal God? Certainly I must confess my own barbarousness, I never heard the old song of Percy and Douglas, that I found not my heart moved more than with a Trumpet: and yet is it sung but by some blind Crowder, with no rougher voice, than rude style: which being so evil apparelled in the dust and cobwebs of that uncivil age, what would it work trimmed in the gorgeous eloquence of Pindar? In Hungary I have seen it the manner at all Feasts, and other such meetings, to have songs of their Ancestors valour; which that right Soldier-like Nation think the chiefest kindlers of brave courage. The incomparable Lacedemonians, did not only carry that kind of Music ever with them to the field, but even at home, as such songs were made, so were they all content to be the singers of them, when the lusty men were to tell what they did, the old men, what they had done, and the young men what they would do. And where a man may say, that Pindar many times praiseth highly victories of small moment, matters rather of sport than virtue: as it may be answered, it was the fault of the Poet, and not of the Poetry; so indeed, the chief fault was in the time and custom of the Greeks, who set those toys at so high a price, that Philip of Macedon reckoned a horse-race won at Olympus, among his three fearful felicities. But as the unimitable Pindar often did, so is that kind most capable and most fit, to awake the thoughts from the sleep of idleness, to embrace honorable enterprises.

There rests the Heroical, whose very name (I think) should daunt all back-biters; for by what conceit can a tongue be directed to speak evil of that, which draweth with it, no less Champions than Achilles, Cyrus, Æneas, Turnus, Tideus, and Rinaldo? who doth not only teach and move to a truth, but teacheth and moveth to the most high and excellent truth. Who maketh magnanimity and justice shine, through all misty fearfulness and foggy desires. Who, if the saying of Plato and Tully be true, that who could see Virtue, would be wonderfully ravished with the love of her beauty: this man sets her out to make her more lovely in her holiday apparel, to the eye of any that will deign, not to disdain, until they understand. But if anything be already said in the defense of sweet Poetry, all concurreth to the maintaining the Heroical, which is not only a kind, but the best, and most accomplished kind of Poetry. For as the image of each action stirreth and instructeth the mind, so the lofty image of such Worthies, most inflameth the mind with desire to be worthy, and informs with counsel how to be worthy. Only let Æneas be worn in the tablet of your memory, how he governeth himself in the ruin of his Country, in the preserving his old Father, and carrying away his religious ceremonies: in obeying the Gods commandment to leave Dido, though not only all passionate kindness, but even the human consideration of virtuous gratefulness, would have craved other of him. How in storms, how in sports, how in war, how in peace, how a fugitive, how victorious, how besieged, how besieging, how to strangers, how to allies, how to enemies, how to his own: lastly, how in his inward self, and how in his outward government. And I think, in a mind not prejudiced with a prejudicating humor, he will be found in excellency fruitful: yea, even as Horace saith

Melius Chrisippo et Crantore.

But truly I imagine, it falleth out with these Poet-whippers, as with some good women, who often are sick, but in faith they cannot tell where. So the name of Poetry is odious to them, but neither his cause, nor effects, neither the sum that contains him, nor the particularities descending from him, give any fast handle to their carping dispraise.

Since then Poetry is of all human learning the most ancient, and of most fatherly antiquity, as from whence other learnings have taken their beginnings: since it is so universal, that no learned Nation doth despise it, nor barbarous Nation is without it: since both Roman and Greek gave divine names unto it: the one of prophesying, the other of making. And that indeed, that name of making is fit for him; considering, that where as other Arts retain themselves within their subject, and receive as it were, their being from it: the Poet only, bringeth his own stuff, and doth not learn a conceit out of a matter, but maketh matter for a conceit: since neither his description, nor his end, containeth any evil, the thing decribed cannot be evil: since his effects be so good as to teach goodness and delight the learners: since therein (namely in moral doctrine, the chief of all knowledges) he doth not only far pass the Historian, but for instructing, is well nigh comparable to the Philosopher: and for moving, leaves him behind him: since the Holy Scripture (wherein there is no uncleanness) hath whole parts in it poetical. And that even our Saviour Christ, vouchsafed to use the flowers of it: since all his kinds are not only in their united forms, but in their severed dissections fully commendable, I think (and think I think rightly) the Laurel crown appointed for triumphing Captains, doth worthily (of all other learnings) honor the Poet's triumph.

1595

Ben Jonson (1573?-1637)

TIMBER

Non nimium credendum antiquitati. — I know nothing can conduce more to letters, than to examine the writings of the ancients, and not to rest in their sole authority, or take all upon trust from them; provided the plagues of judgment and pronouncing against them be away; such as are envy, bitterness, precipitation, impudence, and scurril scoffing. For to all the observations of the ancients, we have our own experience; which if we will use, and apply, we have better means to pronounce. It is true they opened the gates, and made the way that went before us; but as guides, not commanders; *Non domini nostri, sed duces fuere.* Truth lies open to all; it is no man's several. *Patet omnibus veritas; nondum est occupata. Multum ex illa, etiam futuris relicta est.*

De Shakespeare nostrat. — Augustus in Hat. — I remember the players have often mentioned it as an honour to Shakespeare, that in his writing (whatsoever he penned) he never blotted out a line. My answer hath been, Would he had blotted a thousand. Which they thought a malevolent speech. I had not told posterity this, but for their ignorance, who chose that circumstance to commend their friend by, wherein he most faulted; and to justify mine own candour: for I loved the man, and do honour his memory, on this side idolatry, as much as any. He was (indeed) honest, and of an open and free nature; had an excellent phantasy, brave notions, and gentle expressions; wherein he flowed with that facility, that sometimes it was necessary he should be stopped. *Sufflaminandus erat,* as Augustus said of Haterius. His wit was in his own power, would the rule of it had been so too. Many times he fell into those things, could not escape laughter: as when he said in the person of Cæsar, one speaking to him, 'Cæsar, thou dost me wrong.' He replied, 'Cæsar did never wrong but with just cause,' and such like; which were ridiculous. But he redeemed his vices with his virtues. There was ever more in him to be praised than to be pardoned.

Dominus Verulamius. — One, though he be excellent, and the chief, is not to be imitated alone: for no imitator ever grew up to his author; likeness is always on this side truth. Yet there happened in my time one noble speaker, who was full of gravity in his speaking. His language (where he could spare or pass by a jest) was nobly censorious. No man ever spake more neatly, more pressly, more weightily, or suffered less emptiness, less idleness, in what he uttered. No member of his speech, but consisted of his own graces. His hearers could not cough, or look aside from him, without loss. He commanded where he spoke; and had his judges angry and pleased at his devotion. No man had their affections more in his power. The fear of every man that heard him was, lest he should make an end.

Consuetudo. — Perspicuitas, Venustas. — Authoritas. — Virgil. — Lucretius. — Chaucerism. — Paronomasia. — Custom is the most certain mistress of language, as the public stamp makes the current money. But we must not be too frequent with the mint, every day coming, nor fetch words from the extreme and utmost ages; since the chief virtue of a style is perspicuity, and nothing so vicious in it as to need an interpreter. Words borrowed of antiquity do lend a kind of majesty to style, and are not without their delight sometimes. For they have the authority of years, and out of their intermission do win themselves a kind of gracelike newness. But the eldest of the present, and newness of the past language, is the best. For what was the ancient language, which some men so dote upon, but the ancient custom? Yet when I name custom, I understand not the vulgar custom; for that were a precept no less dangerous to language than life, if we should speak or live after the manners of the vulgar: but that I call custom of speech, which is the consent of the learned; as custom of life, which is the consent of the good. Virgil was most loving of antiquity; yet how rarely doth he insert *aquai*, and *pictai!* Lucretius is scabrous and rough in these; he seeks them: as some do Chaucerisms with us, which were better expunged and banished. Some words are to be culled out for ornament and colour, as we gather flowers to strow houses, or make garlands; but they are better when they grow to our style; as in a meadow, where though the mere grass and greenness delight, yet the variety of flowers doth heighten and beautify. Marry we must not play or riot with them too much, as in Paronomasies; nor use too swelling or ill-sounding words; *Quæ per salebras, altaque saxa cadunt.* It is true there is no sound but shall find some lovers, as the bitterest confections are grateful to some palates. Our composition must be more accurate in the beginning and end than in the midst, and in the end more than in the beginning; for through the midst the stream bears us. And this is attained by custom more than care or diligence. We must express readily and fully not profusely. There is difference between a liberal and prodigal hand. As it is a great point of art, when our matter requires it, to enlarge and veer out all sail; so to take it in and contract it, is of no less praise, when the argument doth ask it. Either of them hath their fitness in the place. A good man always profits by his endeavour, by his help, yea, when he is absent, nay, when he is dead, by his example and memory. So good authors in their style: a strict and succinct style is that, where you can take away nothing without loss, and that loss to be manifest.

1641

LITERATURE OF TRAVEL AND THE SEA

Richard Hakluyt (1552?–1616)

VOYAGES

RALEGH'S LAST FIGHT OF THE REVENGE

Because the rumours are diversely spread, as well in England as in the low countries and elsewhere, of this late encounter between her Majesty's ships and the Armada of Spain; and that the Spaniards according to their usual manner, fill the world with their vainglorious vaunts, making great appearance of victories, when on the contrary, themselves are most commonly and shamefully beaten and dishonoured; thereby hoping to possess the ignorant multitude by anticipating and forerunning false reports: it is agreeable with all good reason, for manifestation of the truth, to overcome falsehood and untruth; that the beginning, continuance and success of this late honourable encounter of Sir Richard Grenville, and other her Majesty's captains, with the Armada of Spain; should be truly set down and published without partiality or false imaginations. And it is no marvel that the Spaniards should seek by false and slanderous pamphlets, advisos and letters, to cover their own loss, and to derogate from others their due honors, especially in this fight being performed far off: seeing they were not ashamed in the year 1588, when they purposed the invasion of this land, to publish in sundry languages, in print, great victories in words, which they pleaded to have obtained against this realm; and spread the same in a most false sort over all parts of France, Italy, and elsewhere. When shortly after it was happily manifested in very deed to all nations, how their navy which they termed invincible, consisting of two hundred and forty sail of ships, not only of their own kingdom, but strengthened by the greatest argosies, Portugal, Caracks, Florentines, and huge hulks of other countries, were by thirty of her Majesty's own ships of war, and a few of our own merchants, by the wise, valiant, and most advantageous conduction of the L. Charles Howard high Admiral of England, beaten and shuffled together; even from the Lizard in Cornwall first to Portland, where they shamefully left Don Pedro de Valdes, with his mighty ship; from Portland to Cales, where they lost Hugo de Moncado, with the gallies of which he was captain, and from Cales, driven with squibs from their anchors, were chased out of the sight of England, round about Scotland and Ireland. Where for the sympathy of their barbarous religion, hoping to find succour and assistance, a great part of them were crushed against the rocks, and those other that landed, being very many in number, were notwithstanding broken, slain, and taken, and so sent from village to village coupled in halters, to be shipped into England. Where her Majesty of her princely and invincible disposition, disdaining to put them to death, and scorning either to retain or entertain them: they were all sent back again to their countries, to witness and recount the worthy achievements of their invincible and dreadful navy: of which the number of soldiers, and fearful burthen of their ships, the commanders' names of every squadron, with all other their magazines of provisions, were put in print, as an army and navy unresistable, and disdaining prevention. With all which so great and terrible an ostentation, they did not in all their sailing round about England, so much as sink or take one ship, bark, pinnace, or cockboat of ours: or ever burnt so much as one sheepcote of this land. Whenas on the contrary, Sir Francis Drake, with only eight hundred soldiers not long before, landed in their Indies, and forced Sant-Iago, Santo Domingo, Cartagena, and the forts of Florida.

And after that, Sir John Norris marched from Peniche in Portugal, with a handful of soldiers, to the gates of Lisbon, being above forty English miles. Where the Earl of Essex himself and other valiant gentlemen braved the city of Lisbon, encamped at the very gates; from whence, after many days abode, finding neither promised party, nor provision to batter, made retreat by land, in despite of all their garrisons, both of horse and foot. In this sort I have a little digressed from my first purpose, only by the necessary comparison of theirs and our actions: the one covetous of honour without vaunt or ostentation; the other so greedy to purchase the opinion of their own affairs, and by false rumours to resist the blasts of their own dishonours, as they will not only not blush to spread all manner of untruths: but even for the least advantage, be it but for the taking of one poor adventurer of the English, will celebrate the victory with bonfires in every town, always spending more in fagots than the purchase was worth they obtained. When as we never thought it worth the consumption of two billets, when we have taken eight or ten of their Indian ships at one time, and twenty of the Brazil fleet. Such is the difference between true valour and ostentation: and between honourable actions and frivolous vainglorious vaunts. But now to return to my purpose.

The Lord Thomas Howard with six of her Majesty's ships, six victualers of London, the bark *Ralegh*, and two or three other pinnaces riding at anchor near unto Flores, one of the westerly islands of the Azores, the last of August in the afternoon, had intelligence by one Captain Middleton of the approach of the Spanish armada. Which Middleton being in a very good sailer, had kept them company three days before, of good purpose, both to discover their forces the more, as also to give advice to my Lord Thomas of their approach. He had no sooner delivered the news but the fleet was in sight; many of our ships' companies were on shore in the island; some providing ballast for their ships; others filling of water and refreshing themselves from the land with such things as they could either for money, or by force recover. By reason whereof our ships being all pestered and rummaging every thing out of order, very light for want of ballast, and that which was most to our disadvantage, the one half part of the men of every ship sick, and utterly unserviceable: for in the *Revenge* there were ninety diseased: in the *Bonaventure* not so many in health as could handle her mainsail. For had not twenty men been taken out of a bark of Sir George Carey's, his being commanded to be sunk, and those appointed to her, she had hardly ever recovered England. The rest, for the most part, were in little better state. The names of her Majesty's ships were these as followeth: the *Defiance*, which was admiral, the *Revenge*, viceadmiral, the *Bonaventure* commanded by Captain Cross, the *Lion* by George Fenner, the *Foresight* by M. Thomas Vavasour, and the *Crane* by Duffield. The *Foresight* and the *Crane* being but small ships; only the other were of the middle size; the rest, besides the bark *Ralegh*, commanded by Captain Thin, were victualers, and of small force or none. The Spanish fleet having shrouded their approach by reason of the island; were now so soon at hand, as our ships had scarce time to weigh their anchors, but some of them were driven to let slip their cables and set sail. Sir Richard Grenville was the last weighed, to recover the men that were upon the island, which otherwise had been lost. The Lord Thomas with the rest very hardly recovered the wind, which Sir Richard Grenville not being able to do, was persuaded by the master and others to cut his mainsail and cast about, and to trust to the sailing of the ship; for the squadron of Seville were on his weather bow. But Sir Richard utterly refused to turn from the enemy, alleging that he would rather choose to die, than to dishonour himself, his country, and her Majesty's ship, persuading his company that he would pass through the two squadrons, in despite of them, and enforce those of Seville to give him way. Which he performed upon divers of the foremost, who, as the mariners term it, sprang their luff, and fell under the lee of the *Revenge*. But the other course had been the better, and might right well have been answered in so great an impossibility of prevailing. Notwithstanding out of the greatness of his mind, he could not be persuaded. In the mean while as he attended those which were nearest him, the great *San Philip* being in the wind of him, and coming towards him, becalmed his sails in such sort, as the ship could neither make way, nor feel the helm; so huge and high carged was the Spanish ship, being of a thousand and five hundred tons. Who after laid the *Revenge* aboard. When he was thus bereft of his sails, the ships that were under his lee luffing up, also laid him aboard: of which the next was the admiral of the Biscayans, a very mighty and puissant ship commanded by Brittandona. The said *Philip* carried three tier of ordnance on a side, and eleven pieces in every tier. She shot eight forth right out of her chase, besides those of her stern ports.

After the *Revenge* was entangled with this *Philip*, four others boarded her; two on her larboard, and two on her starboard. The fight thus beginning at three of the clock in the afternoon, continued very terrible all that evening. But the great *San Philip* having received the lower tier of the *Revenge*, discharged with crossbar shot, shifted herself with all diligence from her sides, utterly misliking her first entertainment. Some say that the ship foundered, but we cannot report it for truth, unless we were assured. The Spanish ships were filled with companies of soldiers: in some two hundred besides the mariners; in some five, in others eight hundred. In ours there were none at all beside the mariners, but the servants of the commanders and some few voluntary gentlemen only. After many interchanged volleys of great ordnance and small shot, the Spaniards deliberated to enter the *Revenge*, and made divers attempts, hoping to force her by the multitudes of their armed soldiers and musketeers, but were still repulsed again and again, and at all times beaten back into their own ships, or into the seas. In the beginning of the fight, the *George Noble* of London having received some shot through her by the armadas, fell under the lee of the *Revenge*, and asked Sir Richard what he would command him, being but one of the victualers and of small force: Sir Richard bade him save himself, and leave him to his fortune. After the fight had thus, without intermission, continued while the day lasted and some hours of the night, many of our men were slain and hurt, and one of the great galleons of the armada, and the admiral of the hulks both sunk, and in many other of the Spanish ships great slaughter was made. Some write that Sir Richard was very dangerously hurt almost in the beginning of the fight, and lay speechless for a time ere he recovered. But two of the *Revenge's* own company, brought home in a ship of Lima from the islands, examined by some of the lords and others, affirmed that he was never so wounded as that he forsook the upper deck, till an hour before midnight: and then being shot into the body with a musket as he was a-dressing, was again shot into the head, and withal his surgeon wounded to death. This agreeth also with an examination taken by Sir Francis Godolphin, of four other mariners of the same ship being returned, which examination, the said Sir Francis sent unto Master William Killigrew, of her Majesty's privy chamber.

But to return to the fight, the Spanish ships which attempted to board the *Revenge*, as they were wounded and beaten off, so always others came in their places, she having never less than two mighty galleons by her sides, and aboard her: so that ere the morning, from three of the clock the day before, there had fifteen several armadas assailed her; and all so ill approved their entertainment, as they were by the break of day, far more willing to hearken to a composition than hastily to make any more assaults or entries. But as the day increased, so our men decreased: and as the light grew more and more, by so much more grew our discomforts. For none appeared in sight but enemies, saving one small ship called the *Pilgrim*, commanded by Jacob Whiddon, who hovered all night to see the success: but in the morning bearing with the *Revenge*, was hunted like a hare amongst many ravenous hounds, but escaped.

All the powder of the *Revenge* to the last barrel was now spent, all her pikes broken, forty of her best men slain, and the most part of the rest hurt. In the beginning of the fight she had but one hundred free from sickness, and fourscore and ten sick, laid in hold upon the ballast. A small troop to man such a ship, and a weak garrison to resist so mighty an army. By those hundred all was sustained, the volleys, boardings, and enterings of fifteen ships of war, besides those which beat her at large. On the contrary, the Spanish were always supplied with soldiers brought from every squadron: all manner of arms and powder at will. Unto ours there remained no comfort at all, no hope, no supply either of ships, men, or weapons; the masts all beaten overboard, all her tackle cut asunder, her upper work altogether razed, and in effect evened she was with the water, but the very foundation or bottom of a ship, nothing being left overhead either for flight or defence. Sir Richard finding himself in this distress, and unable any longer to make resistance, having endured in this fifteen hours' fight, the assault of fifteen several armadas, all by turns aboard him, and by estimation eight hundred shot of great artillery, besides many assaults and entries; and that himself and the ship must needs be possessed by the enemy, who were now all cast in a ring round about him. (The *Revenge* not able to move one way or other, but as she was moved with the waves and billow of the sea) commanded the master gunner, whom he knew to be a most resolute man, to split and sink the ship; that thereby nothing might remain of glory or victory to the Spaniards: seeing in so many hours fight, and with so great a navy they were not able to take her, having had fifteen hours time, fifteen thousand men, and fifty and three sail of men-of-war to perform it withal: and persuaded the company, or as many as he could induce, to yield themselves unto God, and to the mercy of none else; but as they had, like valiant resolute men, repulsed so many enemies, they should not now shorten the honour of their nation, by prolonging their own lives for a few hours, or a few days. The master gunner readily condescended and divers others; but the captain and the master were of another opinion, and besought Sir Richard to have care of them: alleging that the Spaniard would be as ready to entertain a composition, as they were willing to offer the same: and that there being divers sufficient and valiant men yet living, and whose wounds were not mortal, they might do their country and prince acceptable service hereafter. And (that where Sir Richard had alleged that the Spaniards should never glory to have taken one ship of her Majesty, seeing they had so long and so notably defended themselves); they answered, that the ship had six foot water in hold, three shot under water, which were so weakly stopped as with the first working of the sea, she must needs sink, and was besides so crushed and bruised, as she could never be removed out of the place.

And as the matter was thus in dispute, and Sir Richard refusing to hearken to any of those reasons: the master of the *Revenge* (while the captain won unto him the greater party) was convoyed aboard the General Don Alfonso Baçan. Who finding none over hasty to enter the *Revenge* again, doubting lest Sir Richard would have blown them up and himself, and perceiving by the report of the master of the *Revenge* his dangerous disposition, yielded that all their lives should be saved, the company sent for England, and the better sort to pay such reasonable ransom as their estate would bear, and in the mean season to be free from galley or imprisonment. To this he so much the rather condescended as well, as I have said, for fear of further loss and mischief to themselves, as also for the desire he had to recover Sir Richard Grenville; whom for his notable valor he seemed greatly to honour and admire.

When this answer was returned, and that safety of life was promised, the common sort being now at the end of their peril, the most drew back from Sir Richard and the master gunner, being no hard matter to dissuade men from death to life. The master gunner finding himself and Sir Richard thus prevented and mastered by the greater number, would have slain himself with a sword, had he not been by force withheld and locked into his cabin. Then the *General* sent many boats aboard the *Revenge,* and divers of our men fearing Sir Richard's dispositon, stole away aboard the *General* and other ships. Sir Richard thus overmatched, was sent unto by Alfonso Baçan to remove out of the *Revenge,* the ship being marvellous unsavory, filled with blood and bodies of dead, and wounded men like a slaughter-house. Sir Richard answered that he might do with his body what he list, for he esteemed it not, and as he was carried out of the ship he swooned, and reviving again desired the company to pray for him. The General used Sir Richard with all humanity, and left nothing unattempted that tended to his recovery, highly commending his valour and worthiness, and greatly bewailed the danger wherein he was, being unto them a rare spectacle, and a resolution seldom approved, to see one ship turn toward so many enemies, to endure the charge and boarding of so many huge armadas, and to resist and repel the assaults and entries of so many soldiers. All which and more is confirmed by a Spanish captain of the same Armada, and a present actor in the fight, who being severed from the rest in a storm, was by the *Lion* of London a small ship taken, and is now prisoner in London.

The general commander of the Armada was Don Alfonso Baçan, brother to the Marquis of Santa Cruz. The admiral of the Biscayan squadron, was Britan Dona. Of the squadron of Seville, the Marquis of Arumburch. The Hulks and Fly-boats were commanded by Luis Coutinho. There were slain and drowned in this fight, well near two thousand of the enemies, and two especial commanders Don Luis de Sant John, and Don George de Prunaria de Malaga, as the Spanish captain confesseth, besides divers others of special account, whereof as yet report is not made.

The Admiral of the Hulks and the *Ascension* of Seville were both sunk by the side of the *Revenge;* one other recovered the road of Saint Michaels, and sunk also there; a fourth ran herself with the shore to save her men. Sir Richard died, as it is said, the second or third day aboard the *General,* and was by them greatly bewailed. What became of his body, whether it was buried in the sea or on the land we know not: the comfort that remaineth to his friends is, that he hath ended his life honourably in respect of the reputation won to his nation and country, and of the same to his posterity, and that being dead, he hath not outlived his own honour.

For the rest of her Majesty's ships that entered not so far into the fight as the *Revenge*, the reasons and causes were these.

There were of them but six in all, whereof two but small ships; the *Revenge* engaged past recovery: the island of Flores was on the one side, fifty-three sail of the Spanish, divided into squadrons on the other, all as full filled with soldiers as they could contain: almost the one half of our men sick and not able to serve: the ships grown foul, unrummaged, and scarcely able to bear any sail for want of balast, having been six months at sea before. If all the rest had entered, all had been lost: for the very hugenes of the Spanish fleet, if no other violence had been offered, would have crushed them between them into shivers. Of which the dishonour and loss to the Queen had been far greater than the spoil or harme that the enemie could any way have received. Notwithstanding it is very true, that the Lord Thomas would have entered between the squadrons, but the rest would not condescend; and the master of his own ship offered to leap into the sea, rather than to conduct that her Majesty's ship and the rest to be a prey to the enemy, where there was no hope nor possibility either of defense or victory. Which also in my opinion had ill sorted or answered the discretion and trust of a general, to commit himself and his charge to an assured destruction, without hope or any likelihood of prevailing: thereby to diminish the strength of her Majesty's navy, and to enrich the pride and glory of the enemy. The *Foresight* of the Queen's commanded by M. Thomas Vavisour performed a very great fight, and staid two hours as near the *Revenge* as the weather would permit him, not forsaking the fight, till he was like to be encompassed by the squadrons, and with great difficulty cleared himself. The rest gave divers volleys of shot, and entered as far as the place permitted, and their own necessities, to keep the weather gage of the enemie, until they were parted by night. A few days after the fight was ended, and the English prisoners dispersed into the Spanish and Indian ships, there arose so great a storm from the west and northwest, that all the fleet was dispersed, as well the Indian fleet which were then come unto them, as the rest of the Armada which attended their arrival, of which, fourteen sail together with the *Revenge*, and in her two hundred Spaniards, were cast away upon the isle of St. Michaels. So it pleased them to honour the burial of that renowned ship the *Revenge*, not suffering her to perish alone, for the great honour she achieved in her lifetime. On the rest of the islands there were cast away in this storm, fifteen or sixteen more of the ships of war: and of an hundred and odd sail of the Indian fleet, expected this year in Spain, what in this tempest, and what before in the bay of Mexico, and about the Bermudas, there were seventy and odd consumed and lost, with those taken by our ships of London, besides one very rich Indian ship, which set herself on fire, being boarded by the Pilgrim, and five other taken by master Watts his ships of London, between the Havana and Cape St. Antonio. The fourth of this month of November we received letters from the Tercera, affirming that there are three thousand bodies of men remaining in that island, saved out of the perished ships: and that by the Spaniards' own confession, there are ten thousand cast away in this storm, besides those that are perished between the islands and the maine. Thus it hath pleased God to fight for us, and to defend the justice of our cause,. against the ambitious and bloody pretenses of the Spaniard, who seeking to devour all nations, are themselves devoured. A manifest testimony how unjust and displeasing, their attempts are in the sight of God, who hath pleased to witness by the success of their affairs, his mislike of their bloody and injurious designs, purposed and practised against all Christian princes, over whom they seek unlawful and ungodly rule and empery.

One day or two before this wreck happened to the Spanish fleet, when as some of our prisoners desired to be set on shore upon the islands, hoping to be from thence transported into England, which liberty was formerly by the general promised: one Morice Fitz John, son of old John of Desmond, a notable traitor, cousin german to the late Earl of Desmond, was sent to the English from ship to ship, to persuade them to serve the King of Spain. The arguments he used to induce them were these. The increase of pay which he promised to be trebled: advancement to the better sort:

and the exercise of the true Catholic Religion, and safety of their souls to all. For the first, even the beggarly and unnatural behavior of those English and Irish rebels, that served the King in that present action, was sufficient to answer that first argument of rich pay. For so poor and beggarly they were, as for want of apparel they stripped their poor countrymen prisoners out of their ragged garments, worn to nothing by six months service, and spared not to despoil them even of their bloody shirts, from their wounded bodies, and the very shoes from their feet: a notable testimony of their rich entertainment and great wages. The second reason was hope of advancement if they served well, and would continue faithful to the King. But what man can be so blockishly ignorant ever to expect place or honour from a foreign King, having no other argument or persuasion than his own disloyalty; to be unnatural to his own country that bred him; to his parents that begat him, and rebellious to his true prince, to whose obedience he is bound by oath, by nature, and by religion? No, they are only assured to be employed in all desperate enterprises, to be held in scorn and disdain ever among those whom they serve. And that ever traitour was either trusted or advanced I could never yet read, neither can I at this time remember any example. And no man could have less become the place of an orator for such a purpose, than this Morice of Desmond. For the Earl his cousin being one of the greatest subjects in that kingdom of Ireland, having almost whole countries in his possession; so many goodly manors, castles, and lordships; the Count Palatine of Kerry, five hundred gentlemen of his own name and family to follow him, besides others, all which he possessed in peace for three or four hundred years, was in less than three years after his adhering to the Spaniards and rebellion, beaten from all his holds, not so many as ten gentlemen of his name left living, himself taken and beheaded by a soldier of his own nation, and his land given by a Parliament to her Majesty, and possessed by the English: his other cousin Sir John of Desmond taken by Master John Zouch, and his body hanged over the gates of his native city to be devoured by ravens: the third brother Sir James hanged, drawn, and quartered in the same place. If he had withall vaunted of this success of his own house, no doubt the argument would have moved much, and wrought great effect: which because, he for that present forgot, I thought it good to remember in his behalf. For matter of religion it would require a particular volume, if I should set down how irreligiously they cover their greedy and ambitious pretences, with that veil of piety. But sure I am, that there is no kingdom or commonwealth in all Europe, but if they be reformed, they then invade it for religion sake: if it be, as they term Catholic, they pretend title; as if the Kings of Castile were the natural heirs of all the world: and so between both, no kingdom is unsought. Where they dare not with their own forces to invade, they basely entertain the traitors and vagabonds of all nations: seeking by those and by their runnagate Jesuits to win parts, and have by that mean ruined many noble houses and others in this land, and have extinguished both their lives and families. What good, honour, or fortune ever man yet by them achieved, is yet unheard of, or unwritten. And if our English Papists do but look into Portugal, against whom they have no pretence of religion, how the nobility are put to death, imprisoned, their rich men made a prey, and all sorts of people captived; they shall find that the obedience even of the Turk is easy and a liberty, in respect of the slavery and tyranny of Spain. What have they done in Sicily, in Naples, Milan, and in the low countries; who hath there been spared for religion at all? And it commeth to my remembrance of a certain Burger of Antwerp, whose house being entered by a company of Spanish soldiers, when they first sacked the city, he besought them to spare him and his goods, being a good Catholic, and one of their own party and faction. The Spaniards answered, that they knew him to be of a good conscience for himself, but his money, plate, jewels, and goods, were all heretical, and therefore good prize. So they abused and tormented the foolish Fleming, who hoped that an Agnus Dei had been a sufficient target against all force of that holy and charitable nation.

Neither have they at any time as they protest invaded the kingdoms of the Indies and Peru, and elsewhere, but only led thereunto, rather to reduce the people to Christianity, than for either gold or empery. When as in one only island called Hispaniola, they have wasted thirty hundred thousand of the natural people, besides many millions else in other places of the Indies: a poor and harmless people created of God, and might have been won to his knowledge, as many of them were, and almost as many as ever were persuaded thereunto. The story whereof is at large written by a bishop of their own nation called Bartholomew de las Casas, and translated into English and many other languages, entitled *The Spanish Cruelties*. Who would therefore repose trust in such a nation of ravenous strangers, and especially in those Spaniards which more greedily thirst after English blood, than after the lives of any other people of Europe, for the many overthrows and dishonours they have received at our hands, whose weakness we have discovered to the world, and whose forces at home, abroad, in Europe, in India, by sea and land, we have even with handfuls of men and ships, overthrown and dishonoured. Let not therefore any English man, of what religion soever, have other opinion of the Spaniards, but that those whom he seeketh to win of our nation, he esteemeth base and traitorous, unworthy persons, or unconstant fools: and that he useth his pretence of religion, for no other purpose but to bewitch us from the obedience of our natural prince, thereby hoping in time to bring us to slavery and subjection, and then none shall be unto them so odious, and disdained as the traitors themselves, who have sold their country to a stranger, and forsaken their faith and obedience contrary to nature and religion; and contrary to that human and general honour, not only of Christians, but of heathen and irreligious nations, who have always sustained what labour soever, and embraced even death itself, for their country, prince, or commonwealth. To conclude, it hath ever to this day pleased God to prosper and defend her Majesty, to break the purposes of malicious enemies, of forsworn traitors, and of unjust practises and invasions. She hath ever been honoured of the worthiest kings, served by faithful subjects, and shall by the favour of God resist, repel, and confound all whatsoever attempts against her sacred person or kingdom. In the meantime let the Spaniard and traitor vaunt of their success, and we her true and obedient vassals, guided by the shining light of her virtues, shall always love her, serve her, and obey her to the end of our lives.

1591, 1598

PAMPHLETS

Robert Greene (1558?–1592)

A GROATSWORTH OF WIT, BOUGHT WITH A MILLION OF REPENTANCE

To His Quondam Acquaintance:

If woeful experience may move you (Gentlemen) to beware, or unheard of wretchedness entreat you to take heed: I doubt not but you will look back with sorrow on your time past, and endeavor with repentance to spend that which is to come. Wonder not (for with thee will I first begin) thou famous gracer of tragedians, that *Greene*, who hath said with thee like the fool in his heart 'there is no God,' should now give glory unto his greatness: for penetrating is his power, his hand lies heavy upon me, he hath spoken unto me with a voice of thunder, and I have felt he is a God that can punish enemies. Why should thy excellent wit, his gift, be so blinded, that thou shouldst give no glory to the giver? Is it pestilent Machiavellian policy that thou hast studied? O peevish folly! What are his rules but mere confused mockeries, able to extirpate in small time the generation of mankind. For if *Sic volo, sic jubeo,* hold in those that are able to command: and if it be lawful *Fas et nefas* to do anything that is beneficial, only tyrants should possess the earth, and they striving to exceed in tyranny, should each to other be a slaughter man; till the mightiest outliving all, one stroke were left for Death, that in one age man's life should end. The brocher of this Diabolical atheism is dead, and in his life had never the felicity he aimed at; but as he began in craft, lived in fear, and ended in despair. *Quam inscrutabilia sunt Dei judicia!* This murderer of many brethren had his conscience seared like *Cain:* this betrayer of him that gave his life for him, inherited the portion of *Judas:* this *Apostata* perished as ill as *Julian:* and wilt thou, my friend, be his disciple? Look but to me, by him persuaded to that liberty, and thou shalt find it an infernal bondage. I know the least of my demerits merit this miserable death, but wilful striving against known truth, exceedeth all the terrors of my soul. Defer not (with me) till this last point of extremity; for little knowest thou how in the end thou shalt be visited.

With thee I join young Juvenal, that biting satyrist, that lastly with me together writ a comedy. Sweet boy, might I advise thee, be advised, and get not many enemies by bitter words: inveigh against vain men, for thou canst do it, no man better, no man so well: thou hast a liberty to reprove all and name none; for one being spoken to, all are offended, none being blamed, no man is injured. Stop shallow water still running, it will rage, or tread on a worm and it will turn: then blame not scholars vexed with sharp lines, if they reprove thy too much liberty of reproof.

And thou no less deserving than the other two, in some things rarer, in nothing inferior; driven (as myself) to extreme shifts, a little have I to say to thee; and were it not an idolatrous oath, I would swear by sweet St. George, thou art unworthy better hap, sith thou dependest on so mean a stay. Base minded men all three of you, if by my misery ye be not warned: for unto none of you (like me) sought those burrs to cleave, those puppets (I mean) that spake from our mouths, those anticks garnished in our colors. Is it not strange that I, to whom they all have been beholding: is it not like that you, to whom they all have been beholding, shall (were ye in that case as I am now) be both at once of them forsaken? Yes, trust them not: for there is an upstart Crow, beautified with our feathers that with his *Tigers heart wrapt in a Players hide,* supposes he is as well able to bombast out a blank verse as the best of you! and being an absolute *Johannes fac totum,* is in his own conceit the only Shake-scene in a country. O that I might entreat your rare wit to be employed in more profitable courses; and let those apes imitate your past excellence, and never more acquaint them with your admired inventions. I know the best husband of you all will never prove an usurer, and the kindest of them all will never prove a kind nurse: yet whilst you may, seek you better masters; for it is a pity men of such rare wits should be subject to the pleasures of such rude grooms.

In this I might insert two more, that both have writ against these buckram gentlemen: but let their own works serve to witness against their own wickedness, if they persevere to maintain any more such peasants. For other new comers, I leave them to the mercy of these painted monsters, who (I doubt not) will drive the best minded to despise them: for the rest, it skills not though they make a jest at them.

But now return I again to you three, knowing my misery is to you no news; and let me heartily entreat you to be warned by my harms. Delight not (as I have done) in irreligious oaths; for from the blasphemer's house, a curse shall not depart. Despise drunkenness, which wasteth the wit, and maketh men all equal unto beasts. Fly lust, as the deathsman of the soul, and defile not the Temple of the Holy Ghost. Abhor those epicures, whose loose life hath made religion loathsome to your ears; and when they soothe you with terms of mastership, remember *Robert Greene,* whom they have so often flattered, perishes now for want of comfort. Remember, Gentlemen, your lives are like so many lighted tapers, that are with care delivered to all of you to maintain;

these with wind-puffed wrath may be extinguished, which drunkenness put out, which negligence let fall: for man's time is not of itself so short, but it is more shortened by sin. The fire of my life is now at the last snuff, and for want of wherewith to sustain it, there is no substance left for life to feed on. Trust not then (I beseech ye) to such weak stays; for they are as changeable in mind as in many attires. Well, my hand is tired, and I am forced to leave where I would begin; for a whole book cannot contain their wrongs, which I am forced to knit up in some few lines of words.

Desirous that you should live, though himself be dying,

ROBERT GREENE.

1592

Thomas Dekker (1570?–1641)

THE GULL'S HORN-BOOK

HOW A GALLANT SHOULD BEHAVE HIMSELF IN A PLAY-HOUSE

The theatre is your poets' royal exchange, upon which their muses (that are now turned to merchants) meeting, barter away that light commodity of words for a lighter ware than words, *Plaudites*, and the breath of the great beast; which (like the threatenings of two cowards) vanish all into air. Players and their factors, who put away the stuff, and make the best of it they possibly can (as indeed 't is their parts so to do), your gallant, your courtier, and your captain, had wont to be the soundest paymasters; and I think are still the surest chapmen; and these, by means that their heads are well stocked, deal upon this comical freight by the gross: when your groundling and gallery-commoner buys his sport by the penny, and, like a haggler, is glad to utter it again by retailing.

Sithence then the place is so free in entertainment, allowing a stool as well to the farmer's son as to your templer: that your stinkard has the selfsame liberty to be there in his tobacco fumes, which your sweet courtier hath: and that your carman and tinker claim as strong a voice in their suffrage, and sit to give judgment on the play's life and death, as well as the proudest *Momus* among the tribes of critic: it is fit that he, whom the most tailors' bills do make room for, when he comes, should not be basely (like a viol) cased up in a corner.

Whether therefore the gatherers of the public or private playhouse stand to receive the afternoon's rent, let our gallant (having paid it) presently advance himself up to the throne of the stage. I mean not into the lord's room (which is now but the stage's suburbs): no, those boxes, by the iniquity of custom, conspiracy of waiting women and gentlemen ushers, that there sweat together, and the covetousness of sharers, are contemptibly thrust into the rear, and much new satin is there damned, by being smothered to death in darkness. But on the very rushes where the comedy is to dance, yea, and under the state of Cambises himself must our feathered estridge, like a piece of ordnance, be planted, valiantly (because impudently) beating down the mewes and hisses of the opposed rascality.

For do but cast up a reckoning, what large comings-in are pursed up by sitting on the stage. First, a conspicuous eminence is gotten; by which means, the best and most essential parts of a gallant (good clothes, a proportionable leg, white hand, the Persian lock, and a tolerable beard) are perfectly revealed.

By sitting on the stage, you have a signed patent to engross the whole commodity of censure; may lawfully presume to be a girder; and stand at the helm to steer the passage of scenes; yet no man shall once offer to hinder you from obtaining the title of an insolent, overweening coxcomb.

By sitting on the stage, you may (without travelling for it) at the very next door ask whose play it is: and, by that 'quest of inquiry,' the law warrants you to avoid much mistaking: if you know not the author, you may rail against him: and peradventure so behave yourself, that you may enforce the author to know you.

By sitting on the stage, if you be a knight, you may happily get you a mistress; if a mere Fleet street gentleman, a wife: but assure yourself, by continual residence, you are the first and principal man in election to begin the number of 'we three.'

By spreading your body on the stage

and by being a justice in examining of plays, you shall put yourself into such true scenical authority, that some poet shall not dare to present his muse rudely upon your eyes without having first unmasked her, rifled her, and discovered all her bare and most mystical parts before you at a tavern; when you most knightly shall, for his pains, pay for both their suppers.

By sitting on the stage, you may (with small cost) purchase the dear acquaintance of the boys, have a good stool for sixpence, at any time know what particular part any of the infants present, get your match lighted, examine the playsuits' lace, and perhaps win wagers upon laying 't is copper, etc. And to conclude, whether you be a fool or a justice of peace, a cuckold or a captain, a Lord Mayor's son or a dawcock, a knave or an under-sheriff, of what stamp soever you be, current or counterfeit, the stage, like time, will bring you to most perfect light and lay you open. Neither are you to be hunted from thence though the scarecrows in the yard hoot at you, hiss at you, spit at you, yea, throw dirt even in your teeth; 't is most gentlemanlike patience to endure all this and to laugh at the silly animals. But if the rabble, with a full throat, cry 'Away with the fool!' you were worse than a madman to tarry by it, for the gentleman and the fool should never sit on the stage together.

Marry, let this observation go hand in hand with the rest, or rather, like a country serving-man, some five yards before them. Present not yourself on the stage (especially at a new play) until the quaking Prologue hath (by rubbing) got colour into his cheeks and is ready to give the trumpets their cue that he's upon point to enter; for then it is time, as though you were one of the properties, or that you dropped out of the hangings, to creep from behind the arras, with your tripos or three-footed stool in one hand and a teston mounted between a forefinger and a thumb in the other; for, if you should bestow your person upon the vulgar when the belly of the house is but half full, your apparel is quite eaten up, the fashion lost, and the proportion of your body in more danger to be devoured than if it were served up in the Counter amongst the poultry: avoid that as you would the bastome. It shall crown you with rich commendation to laugh aloud in the midst of the most serious and saddest scene of the terriblest tragedy, and to let that clapper (your tongue) be tossed so high that all the house may ring of it: your lords use it; your knights are apes to the lords, and do so too; your inn-o'-court man is zany to the knights, and (marry, very scurvily) comes likewise limping after it. Be thou a beagle to them all and never lin snuffing till you have scented them; for by talking and laughing (like a ploughman in a morris) you heap Pelion upon Ossa, glory upon glory: as first, all the eyes in the galleries will leave walking after the players and only follow you, the simplest dolt in the house snatches up your name, and, when he meets you in the streets, or that you fall into his hands in the middle of a watch, his word shall be taken for you; he'll cry, 'He's such a gallant,' and you pass. Secondly, you publish your temperance to the world, in that you seem not to resort thither to taste vain pleasures with a hungry appetite, but only as a gentleman to spend a foolish hour or two because you can do nothing else. Thirdly, you mightily disrelish the audience, and disgrace the author; marry, you take up (though it be at the worst hand) a strong opinion of your own judgment and enforce the poet to take pity of your weakness, and, by some dedicated sonnet, to bring you into a better paradise, only to stop your mouth.

If you can (either for love or money) provide yourself a lodging by the waterside, for, above the convenience it brings to shun shoulder-clapping and to ship away your cockatrice betimes in the morning, it adds a kind of state unto you to be carried from thence to the stairs of your playhouse. Hate a sculler — remember that — worse than to be acquainted with one o' th' scullery. No, your oars are your only sea-crabs. Board them, and take heed you never go twice together with one pair; often shifting is a great credit to gentlemen, and that dividing of your fare will make the poor water-snakes be ready to pull you in pieces to enjoy your custom. No matter whether, upon landing, you have money or no; you may swim in twenty of their boats over the river upon ticket. Marry, when silver comes in, remember to pay treble their fare, and it will make your flounder-catchers to send more thanks after you when you do not draw than when you do, for they know it will be their own another day.

Before the play begins, fall to cards. You may win or lose (as fencers do in a prize) and beat one another by confederacy, yet share the money when you meet at supper. Notwithstanding, to gull the ragamuffins that stand aloof gaping at you, throw the cards (having first torn four or five of them) round about the stage, just, upon the third sound, as though you had lost. It skills not if the four knaves lie on their backs and outface the audience; there's none such fools as dare take exceptions at them, because, ere the play go off, better knaves than they will fall into the company.

Now, sir, if the writer be a fellow that hath either epigrammed you, or hath had a flirt at your mistress, or hath brought either your feather or your red beard, or your little legs, etc. on the stage, you shall disgrace him worse than by tossing him in a blanket or giving him the bastinado in a tavern if, in the middle of his play (be it pastoral or comedy, moral or tragedy) you rise with a screwed and discontented face from your stool to be gone. No matter whether the scenes be good or no; the better they are, the worse do you distaste them. And, being on your feet, sneak not away like a coward, but salute all your gentle acquaintance that are spread either on the rushes or on stools about you; and draw what troop you can from the stage after you. The mimics are beholden to you for allowing them elbow-room; their poet cries, perhaps, 'A pox go with you,' but care not you for that, — there's no music without frets.

Marry, if either the company or indisposition of the weather bind you to sit it out, my counsel is then that you turn plain ape: take up a rush and tickle the earnest ears of your fellow gallants to make other fools fall a laughing; mew at passionate speeches; blare at merry; find fault with the music; whew at the children's action; whistle at the songs; and, above all, curse the sharers, that whereas the same day you had bestowed forty shillings on an embroidered felt and feather (Scotch fashion) for your mistress in the court, or your punk in the city, within two hours after you encounter the very same block on the stage, when the haberdasher swore to you the impression was extant but that morning.

To conclude: hoard up the finest play-scraps you can get, upon which your lean wit may most savourly feed for want of other stuff, when the Arcadian and Euphuized gentlewomen have their tongues sharpened to set upon you. That quality (next to your shittlecock) is the only furniture to a courtier that's but a new beginner, and is but in his A B C of compliment. The next places that are filled, after the playhouses be emptied, are (or ought to be) taverns; into a tavern then let us next march, where the brains of one hogshead must be beaten out to make up another.

1609

ESSAYS

John Florio (1553?–1625)

TRANSLATION OF MONTAIGNE'S ESSAYS

OF IDLENESS

As we see some idle-fallow grounds, if they be fat and fertile, to bring forth store and sundry roots of wild and unprofitable weeds, and that to keep them in ure we must subject and imploy them with certain seeds for our use and service; and as we see some women, though single and alone, often to bring forth lumps of shapeless flesh, whereas to produce a perfect and natural generation, they must be manured with another kind of seed; so is it of minds, which except they be busied about some subject, that may bridle and keep them under, they will here and there wildly scatter themselves through the vast field of imaginations.

Sicut aquæ tremulum labris ubi lumen ahenis
Sole repercussum, aut radiantis imagine Lunæ,
Omnia pervolitat late loca, jamque sub auras
Erigitur, summique ferit laquearia tecti.

As trembling light reflected from the Sun,
Or radiant Moon on water-filled brass lavers,
Flies over all, in air unpraised soon,
Strikes house-top beams, betwixt both
 strangely wavers.

And there is no folly, or extravagant raving, they produce not in that agitation.

. . . *velut ægri somnia, vanæ*
Finguntur species.

Like sick men's dreams, that feign
Imaginations vain.

The mind that hath no fixed bound, will easily lose itself: For, as we say, 'To be everywhere, is to be nowhere.'

Quisquis ubique habitat, Maxime, nusquam
 habitat.

Good sir, he that dwells everywhere,
No where can say, that he dwells there.

It is not long since I retired myself unto mine own house, with full purpose, as much as lay in me, not to trouble myself with any business, but solitarily and quietly to wear out the remainder of my well-nigh-spent life; where me thought I could do my spirit no greater favour, than to give him the full scope of idleness, and entertain him as he best pleased, and withal, to settle himself as he best liked: which I hoped he might now, being by time become more settled and ripe, accomplish very easily: but I find,

Variam semper dant otia mentem.

Evermore idleness,
Doth wavering minds address.

That contrariwise playing the skittish and loose-broken jade, he takes a hundred times more cariere and liberty unto himself, than he did for others, and begets in me so many extravagant Chimeræs, and fantastical monsters, so orderless, and without any reason, one hudling upon another, that at leisure to view the foolishness and monstrous strangeness of them, I have begun to keep a register of them, hoping, if I live, one day to make him ashamed, and blush at himself.

OF THE CANNIBALS

At what time King Pyrrhus came into Italy, after he had surveyed the marshaling of the Army, which the Romans sent against him: 'I wot not,' said he, 'what barbarous men these are' (for so were the Grecians wont to call all strange nations) 'but the disposition of this Army, which I see, is nothing barbarous.' So said the Grecians of that which Flaminius sent into their country: And Philip viewing from a Tower the order and distribution of the Roman camp, in his kingdom under Publius Sulpitius Galba. Lo how a man ought to take heed, lest he over-weeningly follow vulgar opinions, which should be measured by the rule of reason, and not by the common report. I have had long time dwelling with me a man, who for the space of ten or twelve years had dwelt in that other world, which in our age was lately discovered in those parts where Villegaignon first landed, and surnamed Antarctic France. This discovery of so infinite and vast a country, seemeth worthy great consideration. I wot not whether I can warrant my self, that some other be not discovered hereafter, sithence so many worthy men, and better learned than we are, have so many ages been deceived in this. I fear me our eyes be greater than our bellies, and that we have more curiosity than capacity. We embrace all, but we fasten nothing but wind. Plato maketh Solon to report that he had learned of the Priests of the City of Says in Egypt, that whilom, and before the general Deluge, there was a great Island called Atlantis, situated at the mouth of the strait of Gibraltar, which contained more firm land than Africa and Asia together. And that the kings of that country did not only possess that Island, but had so far entered into the main land, that of the breadth of Africa, they held as far as Egypt; and of Europe's length, as far as Tuscany: and that they undertook to invade Asia, and to subdue all the nations that compass the Mediterranean Sea, to the gulf of Mare-Maggiore (the Black Sea), and to that end they traversed all Spain, France and Italy, so far as Greece, where the Athenians made head against them; but that a while after, both the Athenians themselves, and that great Island, were swallowed up by the Deluge. It is very likely this extreme ruin of waters wrought strange alterations in the habitations of the earth: as some hold that the Sea hath divided Sicily from Italy,

Hœc loca vi quandam, et vasta convulsa ruina
Dissiluisse ferunt, cùm protinus utraque tellus
Una foret.

Men say, sometimes this land by that forsaken,
And that by this, were split, and ruin-shaken,
Whereas till then both lands as one were taken.

Cypres from Suria, the Island of Negroponte from the main land of Beotia, and in other places joined lands that were sundered by the Sea, filling with mud and sand the channels between them.

. . . sterilisque diu palus aptaque remis
Vicinas urbes alit, et grave sentit aratrum.

The fen long barren, to be rowed in, now
Both feeds the neighbour, and feels the plow.

But there is no great appearance the said Island should be the new world we have lately discovered; for it well-nigh touched Spain, and it were an incredible effect of inundation to have removed the same more than twelve hundred leagues, as we see it is. Besides, our modern Navigations have now almost discovered that it is not an Island, but rather firm land, and a continent, with the East Indias on one side, and the countries lying under the two Poles on the other; from which if it be divided, it is with so narrow a strait and interval, that it no way deserveth to be named an Island: For, it seemeth there are certain motions in these vast bodies, some natural, and other some febricitant, as well as in ours. When I consider the impression my river of Dordoigne worketh in my time, toward the right shore of her descent, and how much it hath gained in twenty years, and how many foundations of divers houses it hath overwhelmed and violently carried away; I confess it to be an extraordinary agitation: for, should it always keep one course, or had it ever kept the same, the figure of the world had ere this been overthrown: But they are subject to changes and alterations. Sometimes they overflow and spread themselves on one side, sometimes on another; and other times they contain themselves in their natural beds or channels. I speak not of sudden inundations, whereof we now treat the causes. In Medoc alongst the Sea-coast, my brother the Lord of Arsacke, may see a town of his buried under the sands, which the sea casteth up before it: The tops of some buildings are yet to be discerned. His Rents and Domains have been changed into barren pastures. The inhabitants thereabouts affirm, that some years since, the Sea encroacheth so much upon them, that they have lost four leagues of firm land: These sands are her forerunners. And we see great hillocks of gravel moving, which march half a league before it, and usurp on the firm land. The other testimony of antiquity, to which some will refer this discovery, is in Aristotle (if at least that little book of unheard of wonders be his) where he reporteth that certain Carthaginians having sailed athwart the Atlantic Sea, without the strait of Gibraltar, after long time, they at last discovered a great fertile Island, all replenished with goodly woods, and watered with great and deep rivers, far distant from all land, and that both they and others, allured by the goodness and fertility of the soil, went thither with their wives, children, and household, and there began to inhabit and settle themselves. The Lords of Carthage seeing their country by little and little to be dispeopled, made a law and express inhibition, that upon pain of death no more men should go thither, and banished all that were gone thither to dwell, fearing (as they said) that in success of time, they would so multiply as they might one day supplant them, and overthrow their own estate. This narration of Aristotle hath no reference unto our new found countries. This servant I had, was a simple and rough-hewn fellow: a condition fit to yield a true testimony. For subtile people may indeed mark more curiously, and observe things more exactly, but they amplify and glose them: and the better to persuade, and make their interpretations of more validity, they cannot choose but somewhat alter the story. They never represent things truly, but fashion and mask them according to the visage they saw them in; and to purchase credit to their judgment, and draw you on to believe them, they commonly adorn, enlarge, yea, and hyperbolize the matter. Wherein is required either a most sincere Reporter, or a man so simple, that he may have no invention to build upon, and to give a true likelihood unto false devices, and be not wedded to his own will. Such a one was my man; who besides his own report, hath many times shewed me divers Marines and Merchants, whom he had known in that voyage. So am I pleased with his information, that I never enquire what Cosmographers say of it. We had need of Topographers to make us particular narrations of the places they have been in. For some of them, if they have the advantage of us, that they have seen Palestine, will challenge a privilege, to tell us news of all the world besides. I would have every man write what he knows, and no more: not only in that, but in all other subjects. For one may have particular knowledge of the nature of one river, and experience of the quality of one fountain, that in other things knows no more than another man: who nevertheless to publish this little scantling, will undertake to write of all the Physics. From which vice proceed divers great inconveniences. Now (to return to my purpose) I find (as far as I have been informed) there is nothing in that nation that is either barbarous or savage, unless men call that barbarism which is not common to them. As indeed, we have no other aim of truth and reason, than the example and idea of the opinions and customs of the country we live in. There is ever perfect religion, perfect policy, perfect and complete use of all things. They are even savage, as we call those fruits wild which nature of her self and of her ordinary progress hath produced: whereas indeed, they are those which our selves have altered by our artificial devices, and diverted from their common order, we should rather term savage. In those are the true and most profitable virtues, and natural properties most lively and vigorous, which in these we have bastardized, applying them to the pleasure of our corrupted taste. And if notwithstanding, in divers fruits of those countries that were never tilled, we shall find that in respect of ours they are most excellent, and as delicate unto our taste; there is no reason, art should gain the point of honour of our great and puissant mother Nature. We have so much by our inventions surcharged the beauties and riches of her works, that we have altogether overchoked her: yet where ever her purity shineth, she makes our vain and frivolous enterprises wonderfully ashamed.

Et veniunt hederæ sponte sua melius,
Surgit et in solis formosior arbutus antris,
Et volucres nulla dulcius arte canunt.

Ivies spring better of their own accord,
Unhaunted spots much fairer trees afford.
Birds by no art much sweeter notes record.

All our endeavour or wit cannot so much as reach to represent the nest of the least birdlet, its contexture, beauty, profit and use, no nor the web of a silly spider. All things (saith Plato) are produced either by nature, by fortune, or by art. The greatest and fairest by one or other of the two first, the least and imperfect by the last. Those nations seem therefore so barbarous unto me, because they have received very little fashion from human wit, and are yet near their original naturality. The laws of nature do yet command them which are but little bastardized by ours, and that with such purity, as I am sometimes grieved the knowledge of it came no sooner to light, at what time there were men that better than we could have judged of it. I am sorry, Lycurgus and Plato had it not: for me seemeth that what in those nations we see by experience, doth not only exceed all the pictures wherewith licentious Poesy hath proudly imbellished the golden age, and all her quaint inventions to feign a happy condition of man, but also the conception and desire of Philosophy. They could not imagine a genuity so pure and simple as we see it by experience; nor ever believe our society might be maintained with so little art and human combination. It is a nation, would I answer Plato, that hath no kind of traffick, no knowledge of letters, no intelligence of numbers, no name of magistrate, nor of politick superiority; no use of service, of riches or of poverty; no contracts, no successions, no partitions, no occupation but idle; no respect of kindred, but common, no apparel but natural, no manuring of lands, no use of wine, corn, or metal. The very words that import lying, falsehood, treason, dissimulations, covetousness, envy, detraction, and pardon, were never heard of amongst them. How dissonant would he find his imaginary commonwealth from this perfection?

Hos natura modos primùm dedit.

Nature at first uprise,
These manners did devise.

Furthermore, they live in a country of so exceeding pleasant and temperate situation, that as my testimonies have told me, it is very rare to see a sick body amongst them; and they have further assured me, they never saw any man there either shaking with the palsy, toothless, with eyes dropping, or crooked and stooping through age. They are seated alongst the sea-coast, encompassed toward the land with huge and steepy mountains, having between both, a hundred leagues or thereabout of open and champain ground. They have great abundance of fish and flesh, that have no resemblance at all with ours, and eat them without any sauces, or skill of cookery, but plain boiled or broiled. The first man that brought a horse thither, although he had in many other voyages conversed with them, bred so great a horror in the land, that before they could take notice of him, they slew him with arrows. Their buildings are very long, and able to contain two or three hundred souls, covered with barks of great trees, fastened in the ground at one end, enterlaced and joined close together by the tops, after the manner of some of our granges; the covering whereof hangs down to the ground, and steadeth them as a flank. They have a kind of wood so hard, that riving and cleaving the same, they make blades, swords, and grid-irons to broil their meat with. Their beds are of a kind of cotton cloth, fastened to the house roof, as our ship-cabins: every one hath his several couch; for the women lie from their husbands. They rise with the Sun, and feed for all day, as soon as they are up: and make no more meals after that. They drink not at meat, as Suidas reporteth, of some other people of the East, which drank after meals but drink many times a day, and are much given to pledge carouses. Their drink is made of a certain root, and of the colour of our Claret wines, which lasteth but two or three days; they drink it warm: It hath somewhat a sharp taste, wholesome for the stomach, nothing heady, but laxative for such as are not used unto it, yet very pleasing to such as are accustomed unto it. In stead of bread, they use a certain white composition, like unto Corianders confected. I have eaten some, the taste whereof is somewhat sweet and wallowish. They spend the whole day in dancing. Their young men go a hunting after wild beasts with bows and arrows. Their women busy themselves therewhilst with warming of their drink, which is their chiefest office. Some of their old men, in the morning before they go to eating, preach in common to all the household, walking from one end of the house to the other, repeating one selfsame sentence many times, till he have ended his turn (for their buildings are a hundred paces in length) he commends but two things unto his auditory, First, valour against their enemies, then lovingness unto their wives. They never miss (for their restraint) to put men in mind of this duty, that it is their wives which keep their drink lukewarm and well-seasoned. The form of their beds, cords, swords blades, and wooden bracelets, wherewith they cover their hand wrists, when they fight, and great canes open at one end, by the sound of which they keep time and cadence in their dancing, are in many places to be seen, and namely in mine own house. They are shaven all over, much more close and cleaner than we are, with no other razors than of wood or stone. They believe their souls to be eternal, and those that have deserved well of their Gods to be placed in that part of heaven where the Sun riseth, and the cursed toward the West in opposition. They have certain Prophets and Priests which commonly abide in the mountains, and very seldom shew themselves unto the people; but when they come down there is a great feast prepared, and a solemn assembly of many townships together (each Grange as I have described maketh a village, and they are about a French league one from another). The Prophet speaks to the people in public, exhorting them to embrace virtue, and follow their duty. All their moral discipline containeth but these two articles; first an undismayed resolution to war, then an inviolable affection to their wives. He doth also prognosticate of things to come, and what success they shall hope for in their enterprises: he either persuadeth or dissuadeth them from war; but if he chance to miss of his divination, and that it succeed otherwise than he foretold them, if he be taken, he is hewn in a thousand pieces, and condemned for a false prophet. And therefore he that hath once misreckoned himself is never seen again. Divination is the gift of God; the abusing whereof should be a punishable imposture. When the divines amongst the Scythians had foretold an untruth, they were couched along upon hurdles full of heath or brushwood, drawn by oxen, and so manacled hand and foot, burned to death. Those which manage matters subject to the conduct of man's sufficiency are excusable, although they shew the utmost of their skill. But those that gull and conicatch us with the assurance of an extraordinary faculty, and which is beyond our knowledge, ought to be double punished; first because they perform not the effect of their promise, then for the rashness of their imposture and unadvisedness of their fraud. They war against the nations that lie beyond their mountains, to which they go naked, having no other weapons than bows or wooden swords, sharp at one end, as our broaches are. It is an admirable thing to see the constant resolution of their combats, which never end but by effusion of blood and murther: for they know not what fear or routs are. Every victor brings home the head of the enemy he hath slain as a trophy of his victory, and fasteneth the same at the entrance of his dwelling place. After they have long time used and entreated their prisoners well, and with all commodities they can devise, he that is the master of them; summoning a great assembly of his acquaintance; tyeth a cord to one of the prisoners' arms, by the end whereof he holds him fast, with some distance from him, for fear he might offend him, and giveth the other arm, bound in like manner, to the dearest friend he hath, and both in the presence of all the assembly kill him with swords: which done, they roast and then eat him in common, and send some slices of him to such of their friends as are absent. It is not, as some imagine, to nourish themselves with it (as anciently the Scithians wont to do), but to represent an extreme and inexpiable revenge. Which we prove thus; some of them perceiving the Portugales, who had confederated themselves with their adversaries, to use another kind of death when they took them prisoners; which was, to bury them up to the middle, and against the upper part of the body to shoot arrows, and then being almost dead, to hang them up; they supposed, that these people of the other world (as they who had sowed the knowledge of many vices amongst their neighbours, and were much more cunning in all kinds of evils and mischief than they) undertook not this manner of revenge without cause, and that consequently it was more smartful and cruel than theirs, and thereupon began to leave their old fashion to follow this. I am not sorry we note the barbarous horror of such an action, but grieved, that prying so narrowly into their faults we are so blinded in ours. I think there is more barbarism in eating men alive, than to feed upon them being dead; to mangle by tortures and torments a body full of lively sense, to roast him in pieces, to make dogs and swine to gnaw and tear him in mammocks (as we have not only read, but seen very lately, yea and in our own memory, not amongst ancient enemies, but our neighbours and fellow-citizens; and which is worse, under pretence of piety and religion) than to roast and eat him after he is dead. Chrysippus and Zeno, arch-pillars of the Stoic sect, have supposed that it was no hurt at all in time of need, and to what end soever, to make use of our carrion bodies, and to feed upon them, as did our forefathers, who being besieged by Cæsar in the city of Alexia, resolved to sustain the famine of the siege, with the bodies of old men, women, and other persons unserviceable and unfit to fight.

Vascones (*fama est*) *alimentis talibus usi*
Produxere animas.

Gascoynes (as fame reports)
Lived with meats of such sorts.

And physicians fear not, in all kinds of compositions availful to our health, to make use of it, be it for outward or inward applications. But there was never any opinion found so unnatural and immodest, that would excuse treason, treachery, disloyalty, tyranny, cruelty, and such like, which are our ordinary faults. We may then well call them barbarous, in regard of reason's rules, but not in respect of us that exceed them in all kind of barbarism. Their wars are noble and generous, and have as much excuse and beauty as this human infirmity may admit: they aim at nought so much, and have no other foundation amongst them, but the mere jealousy of virtue. They contend not for the gaining of new lands; for to this day they yet enjoy that natural uberty and fruitfulness, which without labouring toil, doth in such plenteous abundance furnish them with all necessary things, that they need not enlarge their limits. They are yet in that happy estate as they desire no more than what their natural necessities direct them: whatsoever is beyond it, is to them superfluous. Those that are much about one age, do generally enter-call one another brethren, and such as are younger they call children, and the aged are esteemed as fathers to all the rest. These leave this full possession of goods in common, and without division to their heirs, without other claim or title but that which nature doth plainly impart unto all creatures, even as she brings them into the world. If their neighbours chance to come over the mountains to assail or invade them, and that they get the victory over them, the victors' conquest is glory, and the advantage to be and remain superior in valour and virtue: else have they nothing to do with the goods and spoils of the vanquished, and so return into their country, where they neither want any necessary thing, nor lack this great portion, to know how to enjoy their condition happily, and are contented with what nature affordeth them. So do these when their turn cometh. They require no other ransom of their prisoners, but an acknowledgment and confession that they are vanquished. And in a whole age, a man shall not find one that doth not rather embrace death, than either by word or countenance remissly to yield one jot of an invincible courage. There is none seen that would not rather be slain and devoured, than sue for life, or shew any fear: They use their prisoners with all liberty, that they may so much the more hold their lives dear and precious, and commonly entertain them with threats of future death, with the torments they shall endure, with the preparations intended for that purpose, with mangling and slicing of their members, and with the feast that shall be kept at their charge. All which is done, to wrest some remiss, and exact some faint-yielding speech of submission from them, or to possess them with a desire to escape or run away; that so they may have the advantage to have daunted and made them afraid, and to have forced their constancy. For certainly true victory consisteth in that only point.

> . . . *Victoria nulla est*
> *Quám quæ confessos animo quoque subjugat hostes.*

> No conquest such, as to suppress
> Foes' hearts, the conquest to confess.

The Hungarians, a most war-like nation, were whilom wont to pursue their prey no longer than they had forced their enemy to yield unto their mercy. For, having wrested this confession from him, they set him at liberty without offence or ransom, except it were to make him swear never after to bear arms against them. We get many advantages of our enemies, that are but borrowed and not ours: It is the quality of porterly-rascal, and not of virtue, to have stronger arms and sturdier legs: Disposition is a dead and corporal quality. It is a trick of fortune to make our enemy stoop, and to blear his eyes with the Sun's light: It is a prank of skill and knowledge to be cunning in the art of fencing, and which may happen unto a base and worthless man. The reputation and worth of a man consisteth in his heart and will: therein consists true honour: Constancy is valour, not of arms and legs, but of mind and courage; it consisteth not in the spirit and courage of our horse, nor of our arms, but in ours. He that obstinately faileth in his courage, *Si succiderit, de genu pugnat:* 'If he slip or fall, he fights upon his knee.' He that in danger of imminent death is no whit daunted in his assuredness; he that in yielding up his ghost beholding his enemy with a scornful and fierce look, he is vanquished, not by us, but by fortune: he is slain, but not conquered. The most valiant are often the most unfortunate. So are there triumphant losses in envy of victories. Not those four sister victories, the fairest that ever the Sun beheld with his all-seeing eye, of Salamis, of Platæa, of Mycale, and of Sicilia, durst ever dare to oppose all their glory together to the glory of the King Leonidas his discomfiture and of his men, at the passage of Thermopylæ: what man did ever run with so glorious an envy or more ambitious desire to the goal of a combat, than Captain Ischolas to an evident loss and overthrow? who so ingeniously or more politicly did ever assure himself of his welfare than he of his ruin? He was appointed to defend a certain passage of Peloponnesus against the Arcadians, which finding himself altogether unable to perform, seeing the nature of the place and inequality of the forces, and resolving that whatsoever should present it self unto his enemy, must necessarily be utterly defeated: On the other side, deeming it unworthy both his vertue and magnanimity, and the Lacedemonian name, to fail or faint in his charge, between these two extremities he resolved upon a mean and indifferent course, which was this. The youngest and best disposed of his troop he reserved for the service and defence of their country, to which he sent them back; and with those whose loss was least, and who might best be spared, he determined to maintain that passage, and by their death to force the enemy to purchase the entrance of it as dear as possibly he could; as indeed it followed. For being suddenly environed round by the Arcadians, after a great slaughter made of them, both himself and all his were put to the sword. Is any trophy assigned for conquerours that is not more duly due unto these conquered? A true conquest respecteth rather an undaunted resolution, an honourable end, than a fair escape, and the honour of vertue doth more consist in combating than in beating. But to return to our history, these prisoners, howsoever they are dealt withal, are so far from yielding, that contrariwise during two or three months that they are kept, they ever carry a cheerful countenance, and urge their keepers to hasten their trial, they outrageously defy and injure them. They upbraid them with their cowardliness, and with the number of battles they have lost against theirs. I have a song made by a prisoner, wherein is this clause, 'Let them boldly come altogether, and flock in multitudes, to feed on him; for with him they shall feed upon their fathers and grandfathers, that heretofore have served his body for food and nourishment: These muscles,' saith he, 'this flesh, and these veins, are your own; fond men as you are, know you not that the substance of your forefathers' limbs is yet tied unto ours? Taste them well, for in them shall you find the relish of your own flesh:' An invention that hath no shew of barbarism, those that paint them dying, and that represent this action, when they are put to execution, delineate the prisoners spitting in their executioners' faces, and making mows at them. Verily, so long as breath is in their body they never cease to brave and defy them, both in speech and countenance. Surely, in respect of us these are very savage men: for either they must be so in good sooth, or we must be so indeed: There is a wondrous distance between their form and ours. Their men have many wives, and by how much more they are reputed valiant so much the greater is their number. The manner and beauty of their marriages is wondrous strange and remarkable: For, the same jealousy our wives have to keep us from the love and affection of other women, the same have theirs to procure it. Being more careful for their husbands' honour and content than of any thing else, they endeavour and apply all their industry to have as many rivals as possibly they can, forasmuch as it is a testimony of their husbands' vertue. Our women would count it a wonder, but it is not so: It is virtue properly matrimonial, but of the highest kind. And in the Bible, Lea, Rachel, Sara, and Iacob's wives brought their fairest maiden servants into their husbands' beds. And Livia seconded the lustful appetites of Augustus to her great prejudice. And Stratonica, the wife of King Dejotarus did not only bring the most beauteous chamber-maid that served her to her husband's bed, but very carefully brought up the children he begot on her, and by all possible means aided and furthered them to succeed in their father's royalty. And lest a man should think that all this is done by a simple and servile or awful duty unto their custom, and by the impression of their ancient custom's authority, without discourse or judgment, and because they are so blockish and dull-spirited, that they can take no other resolution, it is not amiss we allege some evidence of their sufficiency. Besides what I have said of one of their warlike songs, I have another amorous canzonet, which beginneth in this sense: 'Adder stay, stay good adder, that my sister may by the pattern of thy party-coloured coat draw the fashion and work of a rich lace, for me to give unto my love; so may thy beauty, thy nimbleness or disposition be ever preferred before all other serpents.' The first couplet is the burthen of the song. I am so conversant with Poesie that I may judge this invention hath no barbarism at all in it, but is altogether Anacreontic. Their language is a kind of pleasant speech, and hath a pleasing sound, and some affinity with the Greek terminations. Three of that nation, ignorant how dear the knowledge of our corruptions will one day cost their repose, security, and happiness, and how their ruin shall proceed from this commerce, which I imagine is already well advanced (miserable as they are to have suffered themselves to be so cosened by a desire of new-fangled novelties, and to have quit the calmness of their climate to come and see ours), were at Rouen in the time of our late King Charles the ninth, who talked with them a great while. They were shewed our fashions, our pomp, and the form of a fair city; afterward some demanded their advice, and would needs know of them what things of note and admirable they had observed amongst us: they answered three things, the last of which I have forgotten, and am very sorry for it, the other two I yet remember. They said, 'First they found it very strange that so many tall men with long beards, strong and well armed, as it were about the King's person (it is very likely they meant the Switzers of his guard) would submit themselves to obey a beardless child, and that we did not rather choose one amongst them to command the rest.' Secondly (they have a manner of phrase whereby they call men but a moity one of another.) 'They had perceived there were men amongst us full gorged with all sorts of commodities, and others which, hunger-starved and bare with need and poverty, begged at their gates: and found it strange these moities so needy could endure such an injustice, and that they took not the others by the throat, or set fire on their houses.' I talked a good while with one of them, but I had so bad an interpreter, who did so ill apprehend my meaning, and who through his foolishness was so troubled to conceive my imaginations, that I could draw no great matter from him. Touching that point, wherein I demanded of him what good he received by the superiority he had amongst his countrymen (for he was a captain and our mariners called him King), he told me it was to march foremost in any charge of war: further, I asked him how many men did follow him, he shewed me a distance of place, to signify they were as many as might be contained in so much ground, which I guessed to be about four or five thousand men: moreover, I demanded if when wars were ended, all his authority expired; he answered, that he had only this left him, which was, that when he went on progress, and visited the villages depending of him, the inhabitants prepared paths and high-ways athwart the hedges of their woods, for him to pass through at ease. All this is not very ill; but what of that? They wear no kind of breeches nor hose.

1603

Francis Bacon (1561–1626)

ESSAYS

I. OF TRUTH

What is truth? said jesting Pilate; and would not stay for an answer. Certainly there be that delight in giddiness; and count it a bondage to fix a belief; affecting free-will in thinking, as well as in acting. And though the sects of philosophers of that kind be gone, yet there remain certain discoursing wits, which are of the same veins, though there be not so much blood in them as was in those of the ancients. But it is not only the difficulty and labor which men take in finding out of truth; nor again, that when it is found, it imposeth upon men's thoughts; that doth bring lies in favor: but a natural though corrupt love of the lie itself. One of the later school of the Grecians examineth the matter, and is at a stand to think what should be in it, that men should love lies; where neither they make for pleasure, as with poets; nor for advantage, as with the merchant; but for the lie's sake. But I cannot tell: this same truth is a naked and open day-light, that doth not show the masques, and mummeries, and triumphs of the world, half so stately and daintily as candle-lights. Truth may perhaps come to the price of a pearl, that showeth best by day: but it will not rise to the price of a diamond or carbuncle, that showeth best in varied lights. A mixture of a lie doth ever add pleasure. Doth any man doubt, that if there were taken out of men's minds, vain opinions, flattering hopes, false valuations, imaginations as one would, and the like; but it would leave the minds of a number of men, poor shrunken things; full of melancholy and indisposition, and unpleasing to themselves? One of the fathers, in great severity, called poesy *vinum dæmonum*, because it filleth the imagination, and yet it is but with the shadow of a lie. But it is not the lie that passeth through the mind, but the lie that sinketh in, and settleth in it, that doth the hurt, such as we spake of before. But howsoever these things are thus in men's depraved judgments and affections, yet truth, which only doth judge itself, teacheth, that the inquiry of truth, which is the love-making, or wooing of it; the knowledge of truth, which is the presence of it; and the belief of truth, which is the enjoying of it; is the sovereign good of human nature. The first creature of God, in the works of the days, was the light of the sense; the last was the light of reason; and his Sabbath work ever since is the illumination of his Spirit. First he breathed light upon the face of the matter, or chaos; then he breathed light into the face of man; and still he breatheth and inspireth light into the face of his chosen. The poet that beautified the sect, that was otherwise inferior to the rest, saith yet excellently well: 'It is a pleasure to stand upon the shore, and to see ships tost upon the sea: a pleasure to stand in the window of a castle, and to see a battle, and the adventures thereof below; but no pleasure is comparable to the standing upon the vantage ground of truth, a hill not to be commanded, and where the air is always clear and serene: and to see the errors, and wanderings, and mists, and tempests, in the vale below': so always, that this prospect be with pity, and not with swelling or pride. Certainly it is heaven upon earth, to have a man's mind move in charity, rest in Providence, and turn upon the poles of truth.

To pass from theological and philosophical truth, to the truth of civil business; it will be acknowledged, even by those that practice it not, that clear and round dealing is the honour of man's nature; and that mixture of falsehood is like alloy in coin of gold and silver; which may make the metal work the better, but it embaseth it. For these winding and crooked courses are the goings of the serpent; which goeth basely upon the belly, and not upon the feet. There is no vice that doth so cover a man with shame, as to be found false and perfidious. And therefore Montaigne saith prettily, when he inquired the reason why the word of the lie should be such a disgrace, and such an odious charge? Saith he, 'If it be well weighed, to say that a man lieth, is as much as to say that he is brave towards God, and a coward towards man. For a lie faces God, and shrinks from man.' Surely the wickedness of falsehood, and breach of faith, cannot possibly be so highly expressed, as in that it shall be the last peal to call the judgments of God upon the generations of men: it being foretold, that when Christ cometh *he shall not find faith upon the earth.*

V. OF ADVERSITY

It was a high speech of Seneca, after the manner of the Stoics, that the good things which belong to prosperity are to be wished, but the good things that belong to adversity are to be admired: *Bona rerum secundarum optabilia, adversarum mirabilia.* Certainly if miracles be the command over nature, they appear most in adversity. It is yet a higher speech of his than the other, much too high for a heathen, It is true greatness to have in one the frailty of a man, and the security of a God: *Vere magnum, habere fragilitatem hominis, securitatem Dei.* This would have done better in poesy, where transcendencies are more allowed. And the poets indeed have been busy with it; for it is in effect the thing which is figured in that strange fiction of the ancient poets, which seemeth not to be without mystery; nay, and to have some approach to the state of a Christian: that Hercules, when he went to unbind Prometheus, by whom human nature is represented, sailed the length of the great ocean in an earthen pot or pitcher; lively describing Christian resolution, that saileth in the frail bark of the flesh through the waves of the world. But to speak in a mean: the virtue of prosperity is temperance; the virtue of adversity is fortitude; which in morals is the more heroical virtue. Prosperity is the blessing of the Old Testament; adversity is the blessing of the New, which carrieth the greater benediction, and the clearer revelation of God's favour. Yet, even in the Old Testament, if you listen to David's harp, you shall hear as many hearse-like airs as carols: and the pencil of the Holy Ghost hath laboured more in describing the afflictions of Job than the felicities of Solomon. Prosperity is not without many fears and distastes; and adversity is not without comforts and hopes. We see in needle-works and embroideries, it is more pleasing to have a lively work upon a sad and solemn ground, than to have a dark and melancholy work upon a lightsome ground: judge therefore of the pleasure of the heart by the pleasure of the eye. Certainly virtue is like precious odours, most fragrant when they are incensed, or crushed; for prosperity doth best discover vice, but adversity doth best discover virtue.

VIII. OF MARRIAGE AND SINGLE LIFE

He that hath wife and children, hath given hostages to fortune; for they are impediments to great enterprises, either of virtue or mischief. Certainly the best works and of greatest merit for the public, have proceeded from the unmarried or childless men: which both in affection and means have married and endowed the public. Yet it were great reason, that those that have children should have greatest care of future times; unto which they know they must transmit their dearest pledges. Some there are, who though they lead a single life, yet their thoughts do end with themselves, and account future times impertinences. Nay, there are some other, that account wife and children but as bills of charges. Nay more, there are some foolish rich covetous men, that take a pride in having no children, because they may be thought so much the richer. For perhaps they have heard some talk, Such a one is a great rich man; and another except to it, Yea, but he hath a great charge of children: as if it were an abatement to his riches. But the most ordinary cause of a single life is liberty; especially in certain self-pleasing and humorous minds, which are so sensible of every restraint, as they will go near to think their girdles and garters to be bonds and shackles. Unmarried men are best friends, best masters, best servants, but not always best subjects; for they are light to run away; and almost all fugitives are of that condition. A single life doth well with churchmen: for charity will hardly water the ground, where it must first fill a pool. It is indifferent for judges and magistrates: for if they be facile and corrupt, you shall have a servant five times worse than a wife. For soldiers, I find the generals commonly, in their hortatives, put men in mind of their wives and children. And I think the despising of marriage amongst the Turks, maketh the vulgar soldiers more base. Certainly, wife and children are a kind of discipline of humanity: and single men, though they be many times more charitable, because their means are less exhaust; yet, on the other side, they are more cruel and hard-hearted, good to make severe inquisitors, because their tenderness is not so oft called upon. Grave natures, led by custom, and therefore constant, are commonly loving husbands; as was said of Ulysses, *vetulam suam praetulit immortalitati.* Chaste women are often proud and froward, as presuming upon the merit of their chastity. It is one of the best bonds, both of chastity and obedience, in the wife, if she think her husband wise; which she will never do if she find him jealous. Wives are young men's mistresses; companions for middle age; and old men's nurses. So as a man may have a quarrel to marry when he will. But yet he was reputed one of the wise men, that made answer to the question, when a man should marry? 'A young man not yet, an elder man not at all.' It is often seen, that bad husbands have very good wives; whether it be, that it raiseth the price of their husband's kindness when it comes; or that the wives take a pride in their patience. But this never fails if the bad husbands were of their own choosing, against their friends' consent; for then they will be sure to make good their own folly.

X. OF LOVE

The stage is more beholden to love, than the life of man. For as to the stage, love is ever a matter of comedies, and now and then of tragedies; but in life it doth much mischief, sometimes like a syren, sometimes like a fury. You may observe, that amongst all the great and worthy persons, whereof the memory remaineth, either ancient or recent, there is not one that hath been transported to the mad degree of love; which shows, that great spirits and great business do keep out this weak passion. You must except nevertheless Marcus Antonius the half-partner of the empire of Rome, and Appius Claudius the decemvir and lawgiver; whereof the former was indeed a voluptuous man and inordinate; but the latter was an austere and wise man: and therefore it seems, though rarely, that love can find entrance, not only into an open heart, but also into a heart well fortified, if watch be not well kept. It is a poor saying of Epicurus; *Satis magnum alter alteri theatrum sumus:* as if man, made for the contemplation of heaven, and all noble objects, should do nothing but kneel before a little idol, and make himself subject, though not of the mouth, as beasts are, yet of the eye, which was given him for higher purposes. It is a strange thing to note the excess of this passion; and how it braves the nature and value of things by this, that the speaking in a perpetual hyperbole is comely in nothing but in love. Neither is it merely in the phrase; for whereas it hath been well said, that the arch-flatterer, with whom all the petty flatterers have intelligence, is a man's self; certainly the lover is more. For there was never proud man thought so absurdly well of himself, as the lover doth of the person loved; and therefore it was well said, that it is impossible to love, and to be wise. Neither doth this weakness appear to others only, and not to the party loved, but to the loved most of all; except the love be reciproque. For it is a true rule, that love is ever rewarded either with the reciproque, or with an inward and secret contempt: by how much the more men ought to beware of this passion, which loseth not only other things, but itself. As for the other losses, the poet's relation doth well figure them; that he that preferred Helena, quitted the gifts of Juno and Pallas: for whosoever esteemeth too much of amorous affection quitteth both riches and wisdom. This passion hath its floods in the very times of weakness, which are great prosperity, and great adversity; though this latter hath been less observed; both which times kindle love, and make it more fervent, and therefore show it to be the child of folly. They do best, who, if they cannot but admit love, yet make it keep quarter; and sever it wholly from their serious affairs and actions of life: for if it check once with business, it troubleth men's fortunes, and maketh men that they can no ways be true to their own ends. I know not how, but martial men are given to love: I think it is, but as they are given to wine; for perils commonly ask to be paid in pleasures. There is in man's nature a secret inclination and motion towards love of others, which, if it be not spent upon some one or a few, doth naturally spread itself towards many, and maketh men become humane and charitable; as it is seen sometimes in friars. Nuptial love maketh mankind; friendly love perfecteth it; but wanton love corrupteth and embaseth it.

XI. OF GREAT PLACE

Men in great place are thrice servants: servants of the sovereign or state; servants of fame; and servants of business: so as they have no freedom, neither in their persons, nor in their actions, nor in their times. It is a strange desire, to seek power, and to lose liberty; or to seek power over others, and to lose power over a man's self. The rising unto place is laborious; and by pains men come to greater pains; and it is sometimes base; and by indignities men come to dignities. The standing is slippery, and the regress is either a downfall, or at least an eclipse, which is a melancholy thing. *Cum non sis qui fueris, non esse cur velis vivere.* Nay, retire men cannot when they would; neither will they when it were reason: but are impatient of privateness, even in age and sickness, which require the shadow: like old townsmen, that will be still sitting at their street door, though thereby they offer age to scorn. Certainly great persons had need to borrow other men's opinions to think themselves happy; for if they judge by their own feeling, they cannot find it; but if they think with themselves what other men think of them, and that other men would fain be as they are, then they are happy as it were by report, when perhaps they find the contrary within. For they are the first that find their own griefs; though they be the last that find their own faults. Certainly men in great fortunes are strangers to themselves, and while they are in the puzzle of business, they have no time to tend their health either of body or mind. *Illi mors gravis incubat, qui notus nimis omnibus, ignotus moritur sibi.* In place there is license to do good and evil; whereof the latter is a curse; for in evil the best condition is not to will; the second not to can. But power to do good is the true and lawful end of aspiring. For good thoughts, though God accept them, yet towards men are little better than good dreams, except they be put in act; and that cannot be without power and place; as the vantage and commanding ground. Merit and good works is the end of man's motion; and conscience of the same is the accomplishment of man's rest. For if a man can be partaker of God's theatre, he shall likewise be partaker of God's rest. *Et conversus Deus, ut aspiceret opera, quæ fecerunt manus suæ, vidit quod omnia essent bona nimis;* and then the Sabbath. In the discharge of thy place, set before thee the best examples; for imitation is a globe of precepts. And after a time set before thee thine own example; and examine thyself strictly, whether thou didst not best at first. Neglect not also the examples of those, that have carried themselves ill in the same place: not to set off thyself by taxing their memory; but to direct thyself what to avoid. Reform therefore, without bravery or scandal of former times and persons; but yet set it down to thyself, as well to create good precedents, as to follow them. Reduce things to the first institution, and observe wherein and how they have degenerated; but yet ask counsel of both times: of the ancient time what is best; and of the latter time what is fittest. Seek to make thy course regular; that men may know beforehand what they may expect: but be not too positive and peremptory; and express thyself well when thou digressest from thy rule. Preserve the right of thy place, but stir not questions of jurisdiction: and rather assume thy right in silence, and *de facto*, than voice it with claims and challenges. Preserve likewise the rights of inferior places; and think it more honour to direct in chief, than to be busy in all. Embrace and invite helps and advices touching the execution of thy place; and do not drive away such as bring thee information, as meddlers, but accept of them in good part. The vices of authority are chiefly four; delays, corruption, roughness, and facility. For delays; give easy access; keep times appointed; go through with that which is in hand; and interlace not business but of necessity. For corruption; do not only bind thine own hands, or thy servants' hands, from taking, but bind the hands of suitors also from offering. For integrity used doth the one; but integrity professed, and with a manifest detestation of bribery, doth the other: and avoid not only the fault, but the suspicion. Whosoever is found variable, and changeth manifestly without manifest cause, giveth suspicion of corruption. Therefore always when thou changest thine opinion or course, profess it plainly, and declare it, together with the reasons that move thee to change; and do not think to steal it. A servant or a favourite, if he be inward, and no other apparent cause of esteem, is commonly thought but a by-way to close corruption. For roughness, it is a needless cause of discontent; severity breedeth fear, but roughness breedeth hate. Even reproofs from authority ought to be grave, and not taunting. As for facility, it is worse than bribery. For bribes come but now and then; but if importunity or idle respects lead a man, he shall never be without. As Salomon saith; *to respect persons is not good; for such a man will transgress for a piece of bread.* It is most true that was anciently spoken, A place showeth the man: and it showeth some to the better, and some to the worse; *omnium consensu, capax imperii, nisi imperasset*, saith Tacitus of Galba: but of Vespasian he saith; *solus imperantium Vespasianus mutatus in melius.* Though the one was meant of sufficiency, the other of manners and affection. It is an assured sign of a worthy and generous spirit, whom honour amends. For honour is, or should be, the place of virtue: and as in nature things move violently to their place, and calmly in their place; so virtue in ambition is violent, in authority settled and calm. All rising to great place is by a winding-stair; and if there be factions, it is good to side a man's self whilst he is in the rising; and to balance himself when he is placed. Use the memory of thy predecessor fairly and tenderly; for if thou dost not, it is a debt will sure be paid when thou art gone. If thou have colleagues, respect them, and rather call them when they look not for it, than exclude them when they have reason to look to be called. Be not too sensible, or too remembering of thy place in conversation, and private answers to suitors; but let it rather be said, When he sits in place he is another man.

XLII. OF YOUTH AND AGE

A man that is young in years, may be old in hours, if he have lost no time. But that happeneth rarely. Generally youth is like the first cogitations, not so wise as the second. For there is a youth in thoughts, as well as in ages. And yet the invention of young men is more lively than that of old; and imaginations stream into their minds better, and as it were more divinely. Natures that have much heat, and great and violent desires and perturbations, are not ripe for action, till they have passed the meridian of their years: as it was with Julius Cæsar, and Septimius Severus. Of the latter of whom it is said, *Juventutem egit erroribus, imo furoribus, plenam.* And yet he was the ablest emperor almost of all the list. But reposed natures may do well in youth: as it is seen in Augustus Cæsar, Cosmos, duke of Florence, Gaston de Fois, and others. On the other side, heat and vivacity in age is an excellent composition for business. Young men are fitter to invent than to judge; fitter for execution than for counsel; and fitter for new projects than for settled business. For the experience of age, in things that fall within the compass of it, directeth them; but in new things abuseth them. The errors of young men are the ruin of business; but the errors of aged men amount but to this; that more might have been done, or sooner. Young men, in the conduct and manage of actions, embrace more than they can hold; stir more than they can quiet; fly to the end, without consideration of the means and degrees; pursue some few principles, which they have chanced upon, absurdly; care not to innovate, which draws unknown inconveniences; use extreme remedies at first; and, that which doubleth all errors, will not acknowledge or retract them; like an unready horse, that will neither stop nor turn. Men of age object too much, consult too long, adventure too little, repent too soon, and seldom drive business home to the full period; but content themselves with a mediocrity of success. Certainly it is good to compound employments of both; for that will be good for the present, because the virtues of either age may correct the defects of both: and good for succession, that young men may be learners, while men in age are actors: and, lastly, good for extern accidents, because authority followeth old men, and favour and popularity youth. But for the moral part, perhaps youth will have the pre-eminence, as age hath for the politic. A certain Rabbin upon the text, *Your young men shall see visions, and your old men shall dream dreams;* inferreth, that young men are admitted nearer to God than old; because vision is a clearer revelation than a dream. And certainly the more a man drinketh of the world, the more it intoxicateth; and age doth profit rather in the powers of understanding, than in the virtues of the will and affections. There be some have an over-early ripeness in their years, which fadeth betimes: these are, first, such as have brittle wits, the edge whereof is soon turned; such as was Hermogenes the rhetorician, whose books are exceeding subtile; who afterwards waxed stupid. A second sort, is of those that have some natural dispositions, which have better grace in youth than in age: such as is a fluent and luxuriant speech; which becomes youth well, but not age. So Tully saith of Hortensius; *idem manebat, neque idem decebat.* The third is, of such as take too high a strain at the first; and are magnanimous, more than tract of years can uphold. As was Scipio Africanus, of whom Livy saith in effect; *ultima primis cedebant.*

L. OF STUDIES

Studies serve for delight, for ornament, and for ability. Their chief use for delight, is in privateness and retiring; for ornament, is in discourse; and for ability, is in the judgment and disposition of business. For expert men can execute, and perhaps judge of particulars, one by one; but the general counsels, and the plots and marshalling of affairs, come best from those that are learned. To spend too much time in studies, is sloth; to use them too much for ornament, is affectation; to make judgment wholly by their rules, is the humor of a scholar. They perfect nature, and are perfected by experience: for natural abilities are like natural plants, that need pruning by study; and studies themselves do give forth directions too much at large, except they be bounded in by experience. Crafty men contemn studies; simple men admire them; and wise men use them: for they teach not their own use; but that is a wisdom without them, and above them, won by observation. Read not to contradict and confute; nor to believe and take for granted; nor to find talk and discourse; but to weigh and consider. Some books are to be tasted, others to be swallowed, and some few to be chewed and digested: that is, some books are to be read only in parts; others to be read, but not curiously; and some few to be read wholly, and with diligence and attention. Some books also may be read by deputy, and extracts made of them by others; but that would be only in the less important arguments, and the meaner sort of books: else distilled books are like common distilled waters, flashy things. Reading maketh a full man; conference a ready man; and writing an exact man. And therefore if a man write little, he had need have a great memory; if he confer little, he had need have a present wit; and if he read little, he had need have much cunning, to seem to know that he doth not. Histories make men wise; poets, witty; the mathematics, subtile; natural philosophy, deep; moral, grave; logic and rhetoric, able to contend: *Abeunt studia in mores.* Nay, there is no stond or impediment in the wit, but may be wrought out by fit studies; like as diseases of the body may have appropriate exercises: bowling is good for the stone and reins; shooting for the lungs and breast; gentle walking for the stomach; riding for the head; and the like. So if a man's wit be wandering, let him study the mathematics; for in demonstrations, if his wit be called away never so little, he must begin again: if his wit be not apt to distinguish or find differences, let him study the schoolmen; for they are *cymini sectores:* if he be not apt to beat over matters, and to call up one thing to prove and illustrate another, let him study the lawyer's cases: so every defect of the mind may have a special receipt.

1597, 1612, 1625

CHARACTERS

Joseph Hall (1574–1656)

CHARACTERS OF VIRTUES AND VICES

THE HONEST MAN

He looks not to what he might do, but what he should. Justice is his first guide: the second law of his actions, is Expedience. He would rather complain, than offend: and hates sin more for the indignity of it, than the danger. His simple uprightness works in him that confidence, which ofttimes wrongs him, and gives advantage to the subtle; when he rather pities their faithlessness, than repents of his credulity. He hath but one heart and that lies open sight; and, were it not for discretion, he never thinks ought, whereof he would avoid a witness. His word is his parchment and his yea his oath; which he will not violate, for fear, or for loss. The mishaps of following events may cause him to blame his providence, can never cause him to eat his promise: neither saith he, 'This I saw not,' but, 'This I said.' When he is made his friend's executor, he defrays debts, pays legacies; and scorneth to gain by orphans or to ransack graves: and therefore will be true to a dead friend, because he sees him not. All his dealings are square, and above the board: he bewrays the fault of what he sells, and restores the overseen gain of a false reckoning. He esteems a bribe venemous, though it comes gilded over with the colour of gratuity. His cheeks are never stained with the blushes of recantation; neither doth his tongue falter to make good a lie, with the secret glosses of double or reserved senses: and, when his name is traduced, his innocency bears him out with courage: then, lo, he goes on in the plain way of truth, and will either triumph in his integrity, or suffer with it. His conscience overrules his providence: so as, in all things, good or ill, he respects the nature of the actions, not the sequel. If he see what he must do, let God see what shall follow. He never loadeth himself with burdens above his strength, beyond his will; and, once bound, what he can he will do; neither doth he will, but what he can do. His ear is the sanctuary of his absent friend's name, of his present friend's secret: neither of them can miscarry, in his trust. He remembers the wrongs of his youth, and repays them with that usury, which he himself would not take. He would rather want than borrow, and beg than not pay. His fair conditions are without dissembling; and he loves actions above words. Finally, he hates falsehood worse than death: he is a faithful client of truth; no man's enemy; and, it is a question, whether more another man's friend, or his own. And, if there were no heaven, yet he would be virtuous.

THE HYPOCRITE

A Hypocrite is the worst kind of player, by so much as he acts the better part: which hath always two faces; oft times, two hearts: that can compose his forehead to sadness and gravity, while he bids his heart be wanton and careless within and in the meantime laughs within himself, to think how smoothly he hath cozened the beholder: in whose silent face are written the characters of religion, which his tongue and gestures pronounce but his hands recant: that hath a clean face and garment, with a foul soul: whose mouth belies his heart, and his fingers belie his mouth. Walking early up into the city, he turns into the great church, and salutes one of the pillars on one knee; worshipping that God, which, at home, he cares not for; while his eye is fixed on some window, or some passenger; and his heart knows not whither his lips go: he rises, and, looking about with admiration, complains of our frozen charity; commends the ancient. At church, he will ever sit where he may be seen best; and in the midst of the sermon, pulls out his tables in haste as if he feared to lose that note; when he writes either his forgotten errand or nothing: then, he turns his Bible with a noise to seek an omitted quotation; and folds the leaf, as if he had found it; and asks aloud the name of the preacher and repeats it; whom he publicly salutes, thanks, praises, invites, entertains with tedious good counsel, with good discourse, if it had come from an honester mouth. He can command tears when he speaks of his youth; indeed because it is past, not because it was sinful; himself is not better, but the times are worse. All other sins he reckons up with detestation, while he loves and hides his darling in his bosom. All his speech returns to himself, and every occurrent draws in a story to his own praise. When he should give, he looks about him, and says, 'Who sees me?' No alms, no prayers fall from him without a witness; belike lest God should deny that He hath received them; and when he hath done, lest the world should not know it, his own mouth is his trumpet to proclaim it. With the superfluity of his usury he builds a hospital; and harbours them whom his extortion hath spoiled: so, while he makes many beggars, he keeps some. He turneth all gnats into camels: and cares not to undo the world, for a circumstance: flesh on a Friday is more abomination to him than his neighbour's bed: he abhors more not to uncover at the name of Jesus than to swear by the name of God. When a rhymer reads his poem to him, he begs a copy, and persuades the press. There is nothing that he dislikes in presence; that, in absence, he censures not. He comes to the sick-bed of his stepmother and weeps; when he secretly fears her recovery. He greets his friend in the street, with so clear a countenance, so fast a closure, that the other thinks he reads his heart in his face; and shakes hands, with an indefinite invitation of 'When will you come?' and, when his back is turned, joys that he is so well rid of a guest: yet if that guest visit him unfeared, he counterfeits a smiling welcome; and excuses his cheer, when closely he frowns on his wife for too much. He shews well, and says well; and himself is the worst thing he hath. In brief, he is the stranger's saint; the neighbour's disease; the blot of goodness; a rotten stick in a dark night; the poppy in a cornfield; an ill tempered candle with a great snuff that in going out smells ill; an angel abroad, a devil at home; and worse when an angel than when a devil.

1608

Sir Thomas Overbury (1581–1613)

CHARACTERS

AN AMORIST

Is a man blasted or planet-stroken, and is the dog that leads blind Cupid; when he is at the best, his fashion exceeds the worth of his weight. He is never without verses and musk comfits, and sighs to the hazard of his buttons; his eyes are all white, either to wear the livery of his mistress' complexion, or to keep Cupid from hitting the black. He fights with passion, and loseth much of his blood by his weapon; dreams, then his paleness. His arms are carelessly used, as if their best use was nothing but embracements. He is untrussed, unbuttoned and ungartered, not out of carelessness, but care; his farthest end being but going to bed. Some times he wraps his petition in neatness, but he goeth not alone; for he makes some other quality moralise his affection, and his trimness is the grace of that grace. Her favour lifts him up, as the sun moisture; when she disfavours, unable to hold that happiness, it falls down in tears; his fingers are his orators, and he expresseth much of himself upon some instrument. He answers not, or not to the purpose; and no marvel, for he is not at home. He scotcheth time with dancing with his mistress, taking up of her glove, and wearing her feather; he is confined to her colour, and dares not pass out of the circuit of her memory. His imagination is a fool, and it goeth in a pied-coat of red and white: shortly, he is translated out of a man into folly; his imagination is the glass of lust, and himself the traitor to his own discretion.

A FAIR AND HAPPY MILK-MAID

Is a country wench, that is so far from making herself beautiful by art, that one look of hers is able to put all face-physic out of countenance. She knows a fair look is but a dumb orator to commend virtue, therefore minds it not. All her excellencies stand in her so silently, as if they had stolen upon her without her knowledge. The lining of her apparel (which is herself) is far better than outsides of tissue: for though she be not arrayed in the spoil of the silkworm, she is decked in innocency, a far better wearing. She doth not, with lying long abed, spoil both her complexion and conditions; nature hath taught her, too, immoderate sleep is rust to the soul: she rises therefore with chanticleer, her dame's cock, and at night makes the lamb her curfew. In milking a cow, and straining the teats through her fingers, it seems that so sweet a milk-press makes the milk the whiter or sweeter; for never came almond-glove, or aromatic ointment on her palm to taint it. The golden ears of corn fall and kiss her feet when she reaps them, as if they wished to be bound and led prisoners by the same hand that felled them. Her breath is her own, which scents all the year long of June, like a new-made hay-cock. She makes her hand hard with labour, and her heart soft with pity: and when winter evenings fall early (sitting at her merry wheel) she sings a defiance to the giddy wheel of fortune. She doth all things with so sweet a grace, it seems ignorance will not suffer her to do ill, being her mind is to do well. She bestows her year's wages at next fair; and in choosing her garments, counts no bravery in the world, like decency. The garden and bee-hive are all her physic and chirurgery, and she lives the longer for it. She dares go alone, and unfold sheep in the night, and fears no manner of ill, because she means none: yet, to say truth, she is never alone, for she is still accompanied with old songs, honest thoughts, and prayers, but short ones; yet they have their efficacy, in that they are not palled with ensuing idle cogitations. Lastly, her dreams are so chaste, that she dare tell them; only a Friday's dream is all her superstition: that she conceals for fear of anger. Thus lives she, and all her care is she may die in the springtime, to have store of flowers stuck upon her winding-sheet.

1614

John Earle (1601?–1665)

MICROCOSMOGRAPHY

A CHILD

Is a man in a small letter, yet the best copy of Adam before he tasted of Eve or the apple; and he is happy whose small practice in the world can only write his character. He is nature's fresh picture newly drawn in oil, which time, and much handling, dims and defaces. His soul is yet a white paper unscribbled with observations of the world, wherewith, at length, it becomes a blurred note-book. He is purely happy because he knows no evil, nor hath made means by sin to be acquainted with misery. He arrives not at the mischief of being wise, nor endures evils to come, by foreseeing them. He kisses and loves all, and when the smart of the rod is past, smiles on his beater. Nature and parents alike dandle him, and tice him on with a bait of sugar to a draught of wormwood. He plays yet, like a young prentice the first day, and is not come to his task of melancholy. All the language he speaks yet is tears, and they serve him well enough to express his necessity. His hardest labour is his tongue, as if he were loath to use so deceitful an organ; and he is best company with it when he can but prattle. We laugh at his foolish sports, but his game is our earnest; and his drums, rattles and hobby horses, but the emblems and mockings of man's business. His father hath writ him as his own little story, wherein he reads those days of his life that he cannot remember, and sighs to see what innocence he has outlived. The elder he grows he is a stair lower from God; and, like his first father, much worse in his breeches. He is the Christian's example, and the old man's relapse; the one imitates his pureness, and the other falls into his simplicity. Could he put off his body with his little coat, he had got eternity without a burthen, and exchanged but one heaven for another.

A PLAIN COUNTRY FELLOW

Is one that manures his ground well, but lets himself lie fallow and untilled. He has reason enough to do his business, and not enough to be idle or melancholy. He seems to have the punishment of Nebuchadnezzar, for his conversation is among beasts, and his talons none of the shortest, only he eats not grass, because he loves not sallets. His hand guides the plough, and the plough his thoughts, and his ditch and landmark is the very mound of his meditations. He expostulates with his oxen very understandingly, and speaks gee and ree, better than English. His mind is not much distracted with objects, but if a good fat cow come in his way, he stands dumb and astonisht, and though his haste be never so great, will fix here half an hour's contemplation. His habitation is some poor thatcht roof, distinguished from his barn by the loop-holes that let out smoke, which the rain had long since washed through, but for the double ceiling of bacon on the inside, which has hung there from his grandsire's time, and is yet to make rashers for posterity. His dinner is his other work, for he sweats at it as much as at his labour; he is a terrible fastner on a piece of beef, and you may hope to stave the guard off sooner. His religion is a part of his copyhold, which he takes from his landlord, and refers it wholly to his discretion. Yet if he give him leave, he is a good Christian to his power, (that is) comes to church in his best clothes, and sits there with his neighbours, where he is capable only of two prayers, for rain and fair weather. He apprehends God's blessings only in a good year, or a fat pasture, and never praises him but on good ground. Sunday he esteems a day to make merry in, and thinks a bagpipe as essential to it as evening prayer, where he walks very solemnly after service with his hands coupled behind him, and censures the dancing of his parish. His compliment with his neighbour is a good thump on the back, and his salutation some blunt curse. He thinks nothing to be vices, but pride and ill-husbandry, from which he will gravely dissuade the youth, and has some thrifty hobnail proverbs to clout his discourse. He is a niggard all the week, except only market-day, where, if his corn sell well, he thinks he may be drunk with a good conscience. His feet never stink so unbecomingly as when he trots after a lawyer in Westminster-hall, and even cleaves the ground with hard scraping in beseeching his worship to take his money. He is sensible of no calamity but the burning of a stack of corn or overflowing of a meadow, and thinks Noah's flood the greatest plague that ever was, not because it drowned the world, but spoiled the grass. For Death he is never troubled, and if he get in but his harvest before, let it come when it will, he cares not.

A CRITIC

Is one that has spelled over a great many books, and his observation is the orthography. He is the surgeon of old authors, and heals the wounds of dust and ignorance. He converses much in fragments and *desunt multa's*, and if he piece it up with two lines, he is more proud of that book than the author. He runs all over sciences to peruse their syntaxes, and thinks all learning comprised in writing Latin. He tastes styles as some discreeter palates do wine; and tells you which is genuine, which sophicate and bastard. His own phrase is a miscellany of old words, deceased long before the Cæsars, and entombed by Varro, and the modernest man he follows is Plautus. He writes *omneis* at length, and *quicquid*, and his gerund is most incomformable. He is a troublesome vexer of the dead, which after so long sparing must rise up to the judgment of his castigations. He is one that makes all books sell dearer, whilst he swells them into folios with his comments.

1628

THE BIBLE

ENGLISH AUTHORIZED VERSION

MARRIAGE OF SAMSON — JUDGES XIV

1 And Samson went down to Timnath, and saw a woman in Timnath of the daughters of the Philistines.

2 And he came up, and told his father and his mother, and said, I have seen a woman in Timnath of the daughters of the Philistines: now therefore get her for me to wife.

3 Then his father and his mother said unto him, *Is there* never a woman among the daughters of thy brethren, or among all my people, that thou goest to take a wife of the uncircumcised Philistines? And Samson said unto his father, Get her for me; for she pleaseth me well.

4 But his father and his mother knew not that it *was* of the LORD, that he sought an occasion against the Philistines: for at that time the Philistines had dominion over Israel.

5 ¶ Then went Samson down, and his father and his mother, to Timnath, and came to the vineyards of Timnath: and, behold, a young lion roared against him.

6 And the Spirit of the LORD came mightily upon him, and he rent him as he would have rent a kid, and *he had* nothing in his hand: but he told not his father or his mother what he had done.

7 And he went down, and talked with the woman; and she pleased Samson well.

8 ¶ And after a time he returned to take her, and he turned aside to see the carcase of the lion: and, behold, *there was* a swarm of bees and honey in the carcase of the lion.

9 And he took thereof in his hands, and went on eating, and came to his father and mother, and he gave them, and they did eat: but he told not them that he had taken the honey out of the carcase of the lion.

10 ¶ So his father went down unto the woman: and Samson made there a feast; for so used the young men to do.

11 And it came to pass, when they saw him, that they brought thirty companions to be with him.

12 ¶ And Samson said unto them, I will now put forth a riddle unto you: if ye can certainly declare it me within the seven days of the feast, and find *it* out, then I will give you thirty sheets and thirty change of garments:

13 But if ye cannot declare *it* me, then shall ye give me thirty sheets and thirty change of garments. And they said unto him, Put forth thy riddle, that we may hear it.

14 And he said unto them, Out of the eater came forth meat, and out of the strong came forth sweetness. And they could not in three days expound the riddle.

15 And it came to pass on the seventh day, that they said unto Samson's wife, Entice thy husband, that he may declare unto us the riddle, lest we burn thee and thy father's house with fire: have ye called us to take that we have? *is it* not *so?*

16 And Samson's wife wept before him, and said, Thou dost but hate me, and lovest me not: thou hast put forth a riddle unto the children of my people, and hast not told *it* me. And he said unto her, Behold, I have not told *it* my father nor my mother, and shall I tell *it* thee?

17 And she wept before him the seven days, while their feast lasted: and it came to pass on the seventh day, that he told her, because she lay sore upon him: and she told the riddle to the children of her people.

18 And the men of the city said unto him on the seventh day before the sun went down, What *is* sweeter than honey? and what *is* stronger than a lion? And he said unto them, If ye had not plowed with my heifer, ye had not found out my riddle.

19 ¶ And the Spirit of the LORD came upon him, and he went down to Ashkelon, and slew thirty men of them, and took their spoil, and gave change of garments unto them which expounded the riddle. And his anger was kindled, and he went up to his father's house.

20 But Samson's wife was *given* to his companion, whom he had used as his friend.

THE WOMAN AT THE WELL — ST. JOHN IV

1 When therefore the Lord knew how the Pharisees had heard that Jesus made and baptized more disciples than John,

2 (Though Jesus himself baptized not, but his disciples,)

3 He left Judæa, and departed again into Galilee.

4 And he must needs go through Samaria.

5 Then cometh he to a city of Samaria, which is called Sychar, near to the parcel of ground that Jacob gave to his son Joseph.

6 Now Jacob's well was there. Jesus therefore, being wearied with *his* journey, sat thus on the well: *and* it was about the sixth hour.

7 There cometh a woman of Samaria to draw water: Jesus saith unto her, Give me to drink.

8 (For his disciples were gone away unto the city to buy meat.)

9 Then saith the woman of Samaria unto him, How is it that thou, being a Jew, askest drink of me, which am a woman of Samaria? for the Jews have no dealings with the Samaritans.

10 Jesus answered and said unto her, If thou knewest the gift of God, and who it is that saith to thee, Give me to drink; thou wouldest have asked of him, and he would have given thee living water.

11 The woman saith unto him, Sir, thou hast nothing to draw with, and the well is deep: from whence then hast thou that living water?

12 Art thou greater than our father Jacob, which gave us the well, and drank thereof himself, and his children, and his cattle?

13 Jesus answered and said unto her, Whosoever drinketh of this water shall thirst again:

14 But whosoever drinketh of the water that I shall give him shall never thirst; but the water that I shall give him shall be in him a well of water springing up into everlasting life.

15 The woman saith unto him, Sir, give me this water, that I thirst not, neither come hither to draw.

16 Jesus saith unto her, Go, call thy husband, and come hither.

17 The woman answered and said, I have no husband. Jesus said unto her, Thou hast well said, I have no husband:

18 For thou hast had five husbands; and he whom thou now hast is not thy husband: in that saidst thou truly.

19 The woman saith unto him, Sir, I perceive that thou art a prophet.

20 Our fathers worshipped in this mountain; and ye say, that in Jerusalem is the place where men ought to worship.

21 Jesus saith unto her, Woman, believe me, the hour cometh, when ye shall neither in this mountain, nor yet at Jerusalem, worship the Father.

22 Ye worship ye know not what: we know what we worship: for salvation is of the Jews.

23 But the hour cometh, and now is, when the true worshippers shall worship the Father in spirit and in truth: for the Father seeketh such to worship him.

24 God *is* a Spirit: and they that worship him must worship *him* in spirit and in truth.

25 The woman saith unto him, I know that Messias cometh, which is called Christ: when he is come, he will tell us all things.

26 Jesus saith unto her, I that speak unto thee am *he*.

27 ¶ And upon this came his disciples, and marvelled that he talked with the woman: yet no man said, What seekest thou? or, Why talkest thou with her?

28 The woman then left her waterpot, and went her way into the city, and saith to the men,

29 Come, see a man, which told me all things that ever I did: is not this the Christ?

30 Then they went out of the city, and came unto him.

31 ¶ In the mean while his disciples prayed him, saying, Master, eat.

32 But he said unto them, I have meat to eat that ye know not of.

33 Therefore said the disciples one to another, Hath any man brought him *aught* to eat?

34 Jesus saith unto them, My meat is to do the will of him that sent me, and to finish his work.

35 Say not ye, There are yet four months, and *then* cometh harvest? behold, I say unto

you, Lift up your eyes, and look on the fields; for they are white already to harvest.

36 And he that reapeth receiveth wages, and gathereth fruit unto life eternal: that both he that soweth and he that reapeth may rejoice together.

37 And herein is that saying true, One soweth, and another reapeth.

38 I sent you to reap that whereon ye bestowed no labour: other men laboured, and ye are entered into their labours.

39 ¶ And many of the Samaritans of that city believed on him for the saying of the woman, which testified, He told me all that ever I did.

40 So when the Samaritans were come unto him, they besought him that he would tarry with them: and he abode there two days.

41 And many more believed because of his own word;

42 And said unto the woman, Now we believe, not because of thy saying: for we have heard *him* ourselves, and know that this is indeed the Christ, the Saviour of the world.

CHARITY — I CORINTHIANS XIII

1 Though I speak with the tongues of men and of angels, and have not charity, I am become *as* sounding brass, or a tinkling cymbal.

2 And though I have *the gift of* prophecy, and understand all mysteries, and all knowledge; and though I have all faith, so that I could remove mountains, and have not charity, I am nothing.

3 And though I bestow all my goods to feed *the poor*, and though I give my body to be burned, and have not charity, it profiteth me nothing.

4 Charity suffereth long, *and* is kind; charity envieth not; charity vaunteth not itself, is not puffed up,

5 Doth not behave itself unseemly, seeketh not her own, is not easily provoked, thinketh no evil;

6 Rejoiceth not in iniquity, but rejoiceth in the truth;

7 Beareth all things, believeth all things, hopeth all things, endureth all things.

8 Charity never faileth: but whether *there be* prophecies, they shall fail; whether *there be* tongues, they shall cease; whether *there be* knowledge, it shall vanish away.

9 For we know in part, and we prophesy in part.

10 But when that which is perfect is come, then that which is in part shall be done away.

11 When I was a child, I spake as a child, I understood as a child, I thought as a child: but when I became a man, I put away childish things.

12 For now we see through a glass, darkly; but then face to face: now I know in part; but then shall I know even as also I am known.

13 And now abideth faith, hope, charity, these three; but the greatest of these *is* charity.

1611

PURITAN AGE

POETRY

John Milton (1608–1674)

ON SHAKESPEARE

What needs my Shakespeare, for his honoured bones,
The labour of an age in pilèd stones?
Or that his hallowed relics should be hid
Under a star-ypointing pyramid?
Dear son of Memory, great heir of Fame,
What need'st thou such weak witness of thy name?
Thou, in our wonder and astonishment
Hast built thyself a livelong monument.
For whilst, to the shame of slow-endeavouring art,
Thy easy numbers flow, and that each heart
Hath, from the leaves of thy unvalued book,
Those Delphic lines with deep impression took;
Then thou, our fancy of itself bereaving,
Dost make us marble with too much conceiving;
And, so sepulchered, in such pomp dost lie,
That kings for such a tomb would wish to die.

1632

L'ALLEGRO

Hence, loathèd Melancholy,
Of Cerberus and blackest Midnight born,
In Stygian cave forlorn,
'Mongst horrid shapes, and shrieks, and sights unholy,
Find out some uncouth cell,
Where brooding Darkness spreads his jealous wings,
And the night-raven sings;
There under ebon shades and low-browed rocks,
As ragged as thy locks,
In dark Cimmerian desert ever dwell.
But come, thou Goddess fair and free,
In heaven ycleped Euphrosyne,
And by men, heart-easing Mirth,
Whom lovely Venus at a birth
With two sister Graces more
To ivy-crownèd Bacchus bore;
Or whether (as some sager sing)
The frolic Wind that breathes the spring,
Zephyr with Aurora playing,
As he met her once a-Maying,
There on beds of violets blue,
And fresh-blown roses washed in dew,
Filled her with thee, a daughter fair,
So buxom, blithe, and debonair.
Haste thee, Nymph, and bring with thee
Jest, and youthful Jollity,
Quips, and Cranks, and wanton Wiles,
Nods, and Becks, and wreathèd Smiles,
Such as hang on Hebe's cheek,
And love to live in dimple sleek;
Sport that wrinkled Care derides,
And Laughter holding both his sides,
Come, and trip it as ye go,
On the light fantastic toe;
And in thy right hand lead with thee
The mountain Nymph, sweet Liberty;
And, if I give thee honour due,
Mirth, admit me of thy crew,
To live with her, and live with thee,
In unreprovèd pleasures free;
To hear the lark begin his flight,
And singing startle the dull night,
From his watch-tower in the skies,
Till the dappled Dawn doth rise;
Then to come, in spite of sorrow,
And at my window bid good-morrow,
Through the sweet-briar or the vine,
Or the twisted eglantine;
While the cock with lively din,
Scatters the rear of Darkness thin;
And to the stack, or the barn-door,
Stoutly struts his dames before:
Oft listening how the hounds and horn
Cheerly rouse the slumbering Morn,
From the side of some hoar hill,
Through the high wood echoing shrill:
Sometime walking, not unseen,

By hedgerow elms, on hillocks green,
Right against the eastern gate,
Where the great Sun begins his state,
Robed in flames and amber light,
The clouds in thousand liveries dight;
While the ploughman, near at hand,
Whistles o'er the furrowed land,
And the milkmaid singeth blithe,
And the mower whets his scythe,
And every shepherd tells his tale
Under the hawthorn in the dale.
Straight mine eye hath caught new pleasures,
Whilst the landskip round it measures:
Russet lawns, and fallows gray,
Where the nibbling flocks do stray;
Mountains on whose barren breast
The labouring clouds do often rest;
Meadows trim with daisies pied;
Shallow brooks, and rivers wide.
Towers and battlements it sees
Bosomed high in tufted trees,
Where perhaps some Beauty lies,
The Cynosure of neighbouring eyes.
Hard by, a cottage chimney smokes
From betwixt two agèd oaks,
Where Corydon and Thyrsis met
Are at their savoury dinner set
Of herbs and other country messes,
Which the neat-handed Phillis dresses;
And then in haste her bower she leaves,
With Thestylis to bind the sheaves;
Or, if the earlier season lead,
To the tanned haycock in the mead.
Sometimes with secure delight
The upland hamlets will invite,
When the merry bells ring round,
And the jocund rebecks sound
To many a youth and many a maid
Dancing in the chequered shade;
And young and old come forth to play
On a sunshine holyday,
Till the livelong daylight fail:
Then to the spicy nut-brown ale,
With stories told of many a feat,
How fairy Mab the junkets eat:
She was pinched and pulled, she said;
And he, by Friar's lanthorn led,
Tells how the drudging Goblin sweat
To earn his cream-bowl duly set,
When in one night, ere glimpse of morn,
His shadowing flail hath threshed the corn
That ten day-labourers could not end;
Then lies him down the lubbar fiend,
And, stretched out all the chimney's length,
Basks at the fire his hairy strength,
And crop-full out of doors he flings,
Ere the first cock his matin rings.
Thus done the tales, to bed they creep,
By whispering winds soon lulled asleep.
Towered cities please us then,
And the busy hum of men,
Where throngs of Knights and Barons bold,
In weeds of peace, high triumphs hold,
With store of Ladies, whose bright eyes
Rain influence, and judge the prize
Of wit or arms, while both contend
To win her grace whom all commend.
There let Hymen oft appear
In saffron robe, with taper clear,
And pomp, and feast, and revelry,
With mask and antique pageantry;
Such sights as youthful Poets dream
On summer eves by haunted stream.
Then to the well-trod stage anon,
If Jonson's learnèd sock be on,
Or sweetest Shakespeare, Fancy's child,
Warble his native wood-notes wild.
And ever, against eating cares,
Lap me in soft Lydian airs,
Married to immortal verse,
Such as the meeting soul may pierce,
In notes with many a winding bout
Of linkèd sweetness long drawn out
With wanton heed and giddy cunning,
The melting voice through mazes running,
Untwisting all the chains that tie
The hidden soul of harmony;
That Orpheus' self may heave his head
From golden slumber on a bed
Of heaped Elysian flowers, and hear
Such strains as would have won the ear
Of Pluto to have quite set free
His half-regained Eurydice.
These delights if thou canst give,
Mirth, with thee I mean to live.

1645

IL PENSEROSO

Hence, vain deluding Joys,
The brood of Folly without father bred!
How little you bested,
Or fill the fixèd mind with all your toys!
Dwell in some idle brain,
And fancies fond with gaudy shapes possess,
As thick and numberless
As the gay motes that people the sunbeams,
Or likest hovering dreams,
The fickle pensioners of Morpheus' train.
But, hail! thou Goddess sage and holy!
Hail, divinest Melancholy!
Whose saintly visage is too bright
To hit the sense of human sight,
And, therefore to our weaker view
O'erlaid with black, staid Wisdom's hue;
Black, but such as in esteem

Prince Memnon's sister might beseem,
Or that starred Ethiop queen that strove
To set her beauty's praise above
The Sea-Nymphs, and their powers offended.
Yet thou art higher far descended;
Thee bright-haired Vesta long of yore
To solitary Saturn bore;
His daughter she; in Saturn's reign,
Such mixture was not held a stain.
Oft in glimmering bowers and glades
He met her, and in secret shades
Of woody Ida's inmost grove,
Whilst yet there was no fear of Jove.
Come, pensive Nun, devout and pure,
Sober, steadfast, and demure,
All in a robe of darkest grain,
Flowing with majestic train,
And sable stole of cypress lawn
Over thy decent shoulders drawn.
Come; but keep thy wonted state,
With even step, and musing gait,
And looks commércing with the skies,
Thy rapt soul sitting in thine eyes:
There, held in holy passion still,
Forget thyself to marble, till
With a sad leaden downward cast
Thou fix them on the earth as fast.
And join with thee calm Peace and Quiet,
Spare Fast, that oft with gods doth diet,
And hears the Muses in a ring
Aye round about Jove's altar sing;
And add to these retirèd Leisure,
That in trim gardens takes his pleasure;
But, first and chiefest, with thee bring
Him that yon soars on golden wing,
Guiding the fiery-wheelèd throne,
The cherub Contemplation;
And the mute Silence hist along,
'Less Philomel will deign a song,
In her sweetest saddest plight,
Smoothing the rugged brow of Night,
While Cynthia checks her dragon yoke
Gently o'er the accustomed oak.
Sweet bird, that shunn'st the noise of folly,
Most musical, most melancholy!
Thee, Chauntress, oft the woods among
I woo, to hear thy even-song;
And missing thee, I walk unseen
On the dry smooth-shaven green,
To behold the wandering Moon,
Riding near her highest noon,
Like one that had been led astray
Through the heaven's wide pathless way,
And oft, as if her head she bowed,
Stooping through a fleecy cloud.
Oft, on a plat of rising ground,
I hear the far-off curfew sound,
Over some wide-watered shore,
Swinging slow with sullen roar:
Or, if the air will not permit,
Some still removèd place will fit,
Where glowing embers through the room
Teach light to counterfeit a gloom,
Far from all resort of mirth,
Save the cricket on the hearth,
Or the Bellman's drowsy charm
To bless the doors from nightly harm.
Or let my lamp, at midnight hour,
Be seen in some high lonely tower,
Where I may oft outwatch the Bear,
With thrice great Hermes, or unsphere
The spirit of Plato, to unfold
What worlds or what vast regions hold
The immortal mind that hath forsook
Her mansion in this fleshly nook;
And of those Dæmons that are found
In fire, air, flood, or underground,
Whose power hath a true consent
With planet or with element.
Sometime let gorgeous Tragedy
In sceptered pall come sweeping by,
Presenting Thebes, or Pelops' line,
Or the tale of Troy divine,
Or what (though rare) of later age
Ennobled hath the buskined stage.
But, O sad Virgin! that thy power
Might raise Musæus from his bower;
Or bid the soul of Orpheus sing
Such notes as, warbled to the string,
Drew iron tears down Pluto's cheek,
And made Hell grant what love did seek;
Or call up him that left half-told
The story of Cambuscan bold,
Of Camball, and of Algarsife,
And who had Canacé to wife,
That owned the virtuous ring and glass,
And of the wondrous horse of brass
On which the Tartar King did ride;
And if aught else great Bards beside
In sage and solemn tunes have sung,
Of turneys, and of trophies hung,
Of forests, and enchantments drear,
Where more is meant than meets the ear.
Thus, Night, oft see me in thy pale career,
Till civil-suited Morn appear,
Not tricked and frounced as she was wont
With the Attic boy to hunt,
But kerchieft in a comely cloud,
While rocking winds are piping loud,
Or ushered with a shower still,
When the gust hath blown his fill,
Ending on the rustling leaves,
With minute-drops from off the eaves.
And, when the sun begins to fling
His flaring beams, me, Goddess, bring
To archèd walks of twilight groves,
And shadows brown, that Sylvan loves,
Of pine, or monumental oak.

Where the rude axe with heavèd stroke
Was never heard the Nymphs to daunt,
Or fright them from their hallowed haunt.
There in close covert, by some brook,
Where no profaner eye may look,
Hide me from Day's garish eye,
While the bee with honeyed thigh,
That at her flowery work doth sing,
And the waters murmuring,
With such consort as they keep,
Entice the dewy-feathered Sleep.
And let some strange mysterious dream
Wave at his wings, in airy stream
Of lively portraiture displayed,
Softly on my eyelids laid.
And as I wake, sweet music breathe
Above, about, or underneath,
Sent by some spirit to mortals good,
Or the unseen Genius of the wood.
But let my due feet never fail
To walk the studious cloister's pale,
And love the high embowèd roof,
With antick pillars massy proof,
And storied windows richly dight,
Casting a dim religious light.
There let the pealing organ blow,
To the full-voiced Quire below,
In service high and anthems clear,
As may with sweetness, through mine ear,
Dissolve me into ecstasies,
And bring all Heaven before mine eyes.
And may at last my weary age
Find out the peaceful hermitage,
The hairy gown and mossy cell,
Where I may sit and rightly spell
Of every star that Heaven doth shew,
And every herb that sips the dew;
Till old experience do attain
To something like prophetic strain.
These pleasures, Melancholy, give,
And I with thee will choose to live.

1645

COMUS

The first scene discovers a wild wood. The attendant spirit descends or enters.

Spirit. Before the starry threshold of Jove's court
My mansion is, where those immortal shapes
Of bright aerial Spirits live insphered
In regions mild of calm and serene air,
Above the smoke and stir of this dim spot
Which men call Earth, and, with low-thoughted care,
Confined and pestered in this pinfold here,
Strive to keep up a frail and feverish being,
Unmindful of the crown that Virtue gives,
After this mortal change, to her true servants
Amongst the enthronèd gods on sainted seats.
Yet some there be that by due steps aspire
To lay their just hands on that golden key
That opes the Palace of Eternity.
To such my errand is; and, but for such,
I would not soil these pure ambrosial weeds
With the rank vapours of this sin-worn mould.
But to my task. Neptune, besides the sway
Of every salt flood and each ebbing stream,
Took in, by lot, 'twixt high and nether Jove,
Imperial rule of all the sea-girt Isles
That, like to rich and various gems, inlay
The unadornèd bosom of the Deep;
Which he, to grace his tributary gods,
By course commits to several government,
And gives them leave to wear their sapphire crowns
And wield their little tridents. But this Isle,
The greatest and the best of all the main,
He quarters to his blue-haired deities;
And all this tract that fronts the falling sun
A noble Peer of mickle trust and power
Has in his charge, with tempered awe to guide
An old and haughty Nation, proud in arms:
Where his fair offspring, nursed in princely lore,
Are coming to attend their father's state,
And new-intrusted sceptre. But their way
Lies through the perplexed paths of this drear wood,
The nodding horror of whose shady brows
Threats the forlorn and wandering passenger;
And here their tender age might suffer peril,
But that, by quick command from sovran Jove,
I was dispatched for their defence and guard!
And listen why; for I will tell ye now
What never yet was heard in tale or song,
From old or modern bard, in hall or bower.
Bacchus, that first from out the purple grape
Crushed the sweet poison of misusèd wine,
After the Tuscan mariners transformed,
Coasting the Tyrrhene shore, as the winds listed,
On Circe's island fell. (Who knows not Circe,
The daughter of the Sun, whose charmèd cup
Whoever tasted lost his upright shape
And downward fell into a groveling swine?)
This Nymph that gazed upon his clustering locks,

With ivy berries wreathed, and his blithe youth,
Had by him, ere he parted thence, a Son
Much like his father, but his mother more,
Whom therefore she brought up, and Comus named:
Who, ripe and frolic of his full-grown age,
Roving the Celtic and Iberian fields,
At last betakes him to this ominous wood,
And, in thick shelter of black shades imbowered,
Excels his mother at her mighty art;
Offering to every weary traveller
His orient liquor in a crystal glass,
To quench the drouth of Phœbus; which as they taste
(For most do taste through fond intemperate thirst),
Soon as the potion works, their human count'nance,
The express resemblance of the gods, is changed
Into some brutish form of wolf or bear,
Or ounce or tiger, hog, or bearded goat,
All other parts remaining as they were.
And they, so perfect is their misery,
Not once perceive their foul disfigurement,
But boast themselves more comely than before,
And all their friends and native home forget,
To roll with pleasure in a sensual sty.
Therefore, when any favoured of high Jove,
Chances to pass through this adventurous glade,
Swift as the sparkle of a glancing star
I shoot from heaven, to give him safe convoy,
As now I do. But first I must put off
These my sky-robes, spun out of Iris' woof,
And take the weeds and likeness of a swain
That to the service of this house belongs,
Who, with his soft pipe and smooth-dittied song,
Well knows to still the wild winds when they roar,
And hush the waving woods; nor of less faith,
And in this office of his mountain watch
Likeliest, and nearest to the present aid
Of this occasion. But I hear the tread
Of hateful steps; I must be viewless now.

Comus enters, with a charming-rod in one hand, his glass in the other; with him a rout of Monsters, headed like sundry sorts of wild beasts, but otherwise like men and women, their apparel glistering. They come in making a riotous and unruly noise with torches in their hands.

Comus. The star that bids the shepherd fold
Now the top of heaven doth hold;
And the gilded car of Day
His glowing axle doth allay
In the steep Atlantic stream:
And the slope Sun his upward beam
Shoots against the dusky pole,
Pacing toward the other goal
Of his chamber in the east.
Meanwhile, welcome joy, and feast,
Midnight shout and revelry,
Tipsy Dance and Jollity.
Braid your locks with rosy twine,
Dropping odours, dropping wine.
Rigour now is gone to bed;
And Advice with scrupulous head,
Strict Age, and sour Severity,
With their grave saws, in slumber lie.
We, that are of purer fire,
Imitate the starry Quire,
Who, in their nightly watchful spheres,
Lead in swift round the months and years.
The sounds and seas, with all their finny drove,
Now to the Moon in wavering morrice move;
And on the tawny sands and shelves
Trip the pert Faeries and the dapper Elves.
By dimpled brook and fountain-brim,
The Wood-Nymphs, decked with daisies trim,
Their merry wakes and pastimes keep:
What hath night to do with sleep?
Night hath better sweets to prove;
Venus now wakes, and wakens Love.
Come, let us our rites begin;
'T is only daylight that makes sin,
Which these dun shades will ne'er report.
Hail, goddess of nocturnal sport,
Dark-veiled Cotytto, to whom the secret flame
Of midnight torches burns! mysterious Dame,
That ne'er art called but when the dragon womb
Of Stygian darkness spets her thickest gloom,
And makes one blot of all the air!
Stay thy cloudy ebon chair,
Wherein thou ridest with Hecat', and befriend
Us thy vowed priests, till utmost end
Of all thy dues be done, and none left out
Ere the blabbing eastern scout,
The nice Morn on the Indian steep
From her cabined loop-hole peep,
And to the tell-tale Sun descry
Our concealed solemnity.
Come, knit hands, and beat the ground
In a light fantastic round.

The Measure

Break off, break off! I feel the different pace
Of some chaste footing near about this ground.

Run to your shrouds within these brakes and trees;
Our number may affright. Some virgin sure
(For so I can distinguish by mine art)
Benighted in these woods! Now to my charms,
And to my wily trains: I shall ere long
Be well stocked with as fair a herd as grazed
About my mother Circe. Thus I hurl
My dazzling spells into the spongy air,
Of power to cheat the eye with blear illusion,
And give it false presentments, lest the place
And my quaint habits breed astonishment,
And put the Damsel to suspicious flight;
Which must not be, for that's against my course.
I, under fair pretence of friendly ends,
And well-placed words of glozing courtesy,
Baited with reasons not unplausible,
Wind me into the easy-hearted man,
And hug him into snares. When once her eye
Hath met the virtue of this magic dust
I shall appear some harmless villager,
Whom thrift keeps up about his country gear.
But here she comes; I fairly step aside,
And hearken, if I may her business hear.

The Lady enters

Lady. This way the noise was, if mine ear be true,
My best guide now. Methought it was the sound
Of riot and ill-managed merriment,
Such as the jocund flute or gamesome pipe
Stirs up among the loose unlettered hinds,
When, for their teeming flocks and granges full,
In wanton dance they praise the bounteous Pan,
And thank the gods amiss. I should be loth
To meet the rudeness and swilled insolence
Of such late wassailers; yet, oh! where else
Shall I inform my unacquainted feet
In the blind mazes of this tangled wood?
My brothers, when they saw me wearied out
With this long way, resolving here to lodge
Under the spreading favour of these pines,
Stepped, as they said, to the next thicket side
To bring me berries, or such cooling fruit
As the kind hospitable woods provide.
They left me then when the gray-hooded Even,
Like a sad Votarist in palmer's weed,
Rose from the hindmost wheels of Phœbus' wain.
But where they are, and why they came not back,
Is now the labour of my thoughts. 'T is likeliest
They had ingaged their wandering steps too far;
And envious darkness, ere they could return,
Had stole them from me. Else, O thievish Night,
Why shouldst thou, but for some felonious end,
In thy dark lantern thus close up the stars
That Nature hung in heaven, and filled their lamps
With everlasting oil, to give due light
To the misled and lonely travailler?
This is the place, as well as I may guess,
Whence even now the tumult of loud mirth
Was rife, and perfet in my list'ning ear;
Yet nought but single darkness do I find.
What might this be? A thousand fantasies
Begin to throng into my memory,
Of calling shapes, and beckoning shadows dire,
And airy tongues that syllable men's names
On sands and shores and desert wildernesses.
These thoughts may startle well, but not astound
The virtuous mind, that ever walks attended
By a strong siding champion, Conscience.
O welcome, pure-eyed Faith, white-handed Hope,
Thou hovering angel girt with golden wings,
And thou unblemished form of Chastity!
I see ye visibly, and now believe
That He, the Supreme Good, to whom all things ill
Are but as slavish officers of vengeance,
Would send a glistering guardian, if need were,
To keep my life and honour unassailed. . . .
Was I deceived, or did a sable cloud
Turn forth her silver lining on the night?
I did not err: there does a sable cloud
Turn forth her silver lining on the night,
And casts a gleam over this tufted grove.
I cannot hallo to my brothers, but
Such noise as I can make to be heard farthest
I'll venture; for my new-enlivened spirits
Prompt me, and they perhaps are not far off.

SONG

Sweet Echo, sweetest nymph, that liv'st unseen
Within thy airy shell
By slow Meander's margent green,
And in the violet-embroidered vale
Where the love-lorn Nightingale
Nightly to thee her sad song mourneth well:
Canst thou not tell me of a gentle pair

That likest thy Narcissus are?
O if thou have
Hid them in some flowery cave,
Tell me but where,
Sweet Queen of Parley, Daughter of the Sphere!
So may'st thou be translated to the skies,
And give resounding grace to all Heaven's harmonies!

Comus. Can any mortal mixture of earth's mould
Breathe such divine inchanting ravishment?
Sure something holy lodges in that breast,
And with these raptures moves the vocal air
To testify his hidden residence.
How sweetly did they float upon the wings
Of silence through the empty-vaulted night,
At every fall smoothing the raven down
Of darkness till it smiled! I have oft heard
My mother Circe with the Sirens three,
Amidst the flowery-kirtled Naiades,
Culling their potent herbs and baleful drugs,
Who, as they sung, would take the prisoned soul,
And lap it in Elysium: Scylla wept,
And chid her barking waves into attention,
And fell Charybdis murmured soft applause.
Yet they in pleasing slumber lulled the sense,
And in sweet madness robbed it of itself;
But such a sacred and home-felt delight,
Such sober certainty of waking bliss,
I never heard till now. I'll speak to her,
And she shall be my Queen. — Hail, foreign wonder!
Whom certain these rough shades did never breed,
Unless the Goddess that in rural shrine
Dwell'st here with Pan or Sylvan, by blest song
Forbidding every bleak unkindly fog
To touch the prosperous growth of this tall wood.
Lady. Nay, gentle shepherd, ill is lost that praise
That is addressed to unattending ears.
Not any boast of skill, but extreme shift
How to regain my severed company,
Compelled me to awake the courteous Echo
To give me answer from her mossy couch.
Comus. What chance, good Lady, hath bereft you thus?
Lady. Dim darkness and this leavy labyrinth.
Comus. Could that divide you from near-ushering guides?
Lady. They left me weary on a grassy turf.
Comus. By falsehood, or discourtesy, or why?
Lady. To seek i' the valley some cool friendly spring.
Comus. And left your fair side all unguarded, Lady?
Lady. They were but twain, and purposed quick return.
Comus. Perhaps forestalling night prevented them.
Lady. How easy my misfortune is to hit!
Comus. Imports their loss, beside the present need?
Lady. No less than if I should my brothers lose.
Comus. Were they of manly prime, or youthful bloom?
Lady. As smooth as Hebe's their unrazored lips.
Comus. Two such I saw, what time the laboured ox
In his loose traces from the furrow came,
And the swinked hedger at his supper sat.
I saw them under a green mantling vine
That crawls along the side of yon small hill,
Plucking ripe clusters from the tender shoots;
Their port was more than human, as they stood.
I took it for a faery vision
Of some gay creatures of the element,
That in the colours of the rainbow live,
And play i' the plighted clouds. I was awe-strook,
And, as I passed, I worshiped. If those you seek,
It were a journey like the path to Heaven,
To help you find them.
Lady. Gentle villager,
What readiest way would bring me to that place?
Comus. Due west it rises from this shrubby point.
Lady. To find out that, good Shepherd, I suppose,
In such a scant allowance of star-light,
Would overtask the best land-pilot's art,
Without the sure guess of well-practised feet.
Comus. I know each lane, and every alley green,
Dingle, or bushy dell, of this wild wood,
And every bosky bourn from side to side,
My daily walks and ancient neighbourhood;
And, if your stray attendance be yet lodged,
Or shroud within these limits, I shall know
Ere morrow wake, or the low-roosted lark
From her thatched pallet rouse. If otherwise,

I can conduct you, Lady, to a low
But loyal cottage, where you may be safe
Till further quest.
Lady. Shepherd, I take thy word,
And trust thy honest-offered courtesy,
Which oft is sooner found in lowly sheds,
With smoky rafters, than in tapestry halls
And courts of princes, where it first was named,
And yet is most pretended. In a place
Less warranted than this, or less secure,
I cannot be, that I should fear to change it.
Eye me, blest Providence, and square my trial
To my proportioned strength! Shepherd, lead on. . . .

The Two Brothers

Elder Brother. Unmuffle, ye faint stars; and thou, fair Moon,
That wont'st to love the traveller's benison,
Stoop thy pale visage through an amber cloud,
And disinherit Chaos, that reigns here
In double night of darkness and of shades;
Or, if your influence be quite dammed up
With black usurping mists, some gentle taper,
Though a rush-candle from the wicker hole
Of some clay habitation, visit us
With thy long levelled rule of streaming light,
And thou shalt be our star of Arcady,
Or Tyrian Cynosure.
Second Brother. Or, if our eyes
Be barred that happiness, might we but hear
The folded flocks, penned in their wattled cotes,
Or sound of pastoral reed with oaten stops,
Or whistle from the lodge, or village cock
Count the night-watches to his feathery dames,
'T would be some solace yet, some little cheering,
In this close dungeon of innumerous boughs.
But, Oh, that hapless virgin, our lost sister!
Where may she wander now, whither betake her
From the chill dew, amongst rude burs and thistles?
Perhaps some cold bank is her bolster now,
Or 'gainst the rugged bark of some broad elm
Leans her unpillowed head, fraught with sad fears.
What if in wild amazement and affright,
Or, while we speak, within the direful grasp
Of savage hunger, or of savage heat!
Elder Brother. Peace, brother: be not over-exquisite
To cast the fashion of uncertain evils;
For, grant they be so, while they rest unknown,
What need a man forestall his date of grief,
And run to meet what he would most avoid?
Or, if they be but false alarms of fear,
How bitter is such self-delusion!
I do not think my sister so to seek,
Or so unprincipled in virtue's book,
And the sweet peace that goodness bosoms ever,
As that the single want of light and noise
(Not being in danger, as I trust she is not)
Could stir the constant mood of her calm thoughts,
And put them into misbecoming plight.
Virtue could see to do what Virtue would
By her own radiant light, though sun and moon
Were in the flat sea sunk. And Wisdom's self
Oft seeks to sweet retirèd solitude,
Where, with her best nurse, Contemplation,
She plumes her feathers, and lets grow her wings,
That, in the various bustle of resort,
Were all to-ruffled, and sometimes impaired.
He that has light within his own clear breast
May sit i' th' centre, and enjoy bright day:
But he that hides a dark soul and foul thoughts
Benighted walks under the mid-day sun;
Himself is his own dungeon.
Second Brother. 'T is most true
That musing Meditation most affects
The pensive secrecy of desert cell,
Far from the cheerful haunt of men and herds,
And sits as safe as in a senate-house;
For who would rob a Hermit of his weeds,
His few books, or his beads, or maple dish,
Or do his gray hairs any violence?
But Beauty, like the fair Hesperian tree
Laden with blooming gold, had need the guard
Of dragon-watch with uninchanted eye
To save her blossoms, and defend her fruit,
From the rash hand of bold Incontinence.
You may as well spread out the unsunned heaps
Of miser's treasure by an outlaw's den,
And tell me it is safe, as bid me hope
Danger will wink on Opportunity,
And let a single helpless maiden pass
Uninjured in this wild surrounding waste.
Of night or loneliness it recks me not:
I fear the dread events that dog them both,
Lest some ill-greeting touch attempt the person
Of our unownèd sister.
Elder Brother. I do not, brother,
Infer as if I thought my sister's state

Secure without all doubt or controversy;
Yet, where an equal poise of hope and fear
Does arbitrate the event, my nature is
That I incline to hope rather than fear,
And gladly banish squint suspicion.
My sister is not so defenceless left
As you imagine; she has a hidden strength
Which you remember not.

Second Brother. What hidden strength,
Unless the strength of Heaven, if you mean that?

Elder Brother. I mean that too, but yet a hidden strength
Which, if Heaven gave it, may be termed her own:
'T is Chastity, my brother, Chastity:
She that has that is clad in complete steel,
And, like a quivered nymph with arrows keen,
May trace huge forests, and unharboured heaths,
Infamous hills, and sandy perilous wilds;
Where, through the sacred rays of chastity,
No savage fierce, bandite, or mountaineer
Will dare to soil her virgin purity.
Yea, there where very desolation dwells,
By grots and caverns shagged with horrid shades,
She may pass on with unblenched majesty,
Be it not done in pride, or in presumption.
Some say no evil thing that walks by night,
In fog or fire, by lake or moorish fen,
Blue meagre hag, or stubborn unlaid ghost,
That breaks his magic chains at curfew time,
No goblin or swart faery of the mine,
Hath hurtful power o'er true virginity.
Do ye believe me yet, or shall I call
Antiquity from the old schools of Greece
To testify the arms of Chastity?
Hence had the huntress Dian her dread bow,
Fair silver-shafted Queen forever chaste,
Wherewith she tamed the brinded lioness
And spotted mountain-pard, but set at naught
The frivolous bolt of Cupid; gods and men
Feared her stern frown, and she was queen o' th' woods.
What was that snaky-headed Gorgon shield
That wise Minerva wore, unconquered virgin,
Wherewith she freezed her foes to congealed stone,
But rigid looks of chaste austerity,
And noble grace that dashed brute violence
With sudden adoration and blank awe?
So dear to Heaven is saintly chastity
That, when a soul is found sincerely so,
A thousand liveried angels lackey her,
Driving far off each thing of sin and guilt,
And in clear dream and solemn vision
Tell her of things that no gross ear can hear;
Till oft converse with heavenly habitants
Begin to cast a beam on the outward shape,
The unpolluted temple of the mind,
And turns it by degrees to the soul's essence,
Till all be made immortal. But, when lust,
By unchaste looks, loose gestures, and foul talk,
But most by lewd and lavish act of sin,
Lets in defilement to the inward parts,
The soul grows clotted by contagion,
Imbodies and imbrutes, till she quite lose
The divine property of her first being.
Such are those thick and gloomy shadows damp
Oft seen in charnel vaults and sepulchres,
Lingering and sitting by a new-made grave,
As loth to leave the body that it loved,
And linked itself by carnal sensualty
To a degenerate and degraded state.

Second Brother. How charming is divine Philosophy!
Not harsh, and crabbèd, as dull fools suppose,
But musical as is Apollo's lute,
And a perpetual feast of nectared sweets,
Where no crude surfeit reigns.

Elder Brother. List, list! I hear
Some far-off halloo break the silent air.

Second Brother. Methought so too; what should it be?

Elder Brother. For certain,
Either some one, like us, night-foundered here,
Or else some neighbour woodman, or, at worst,
Some roving robber calling to his fellows.

Second Brother. Heaven keep my sister! Again, again, and near!
Best draw, and stand upon our guard.

Elder Brother. I 'll hallo.
If he be friendly, he comes well: if not,
Defence is a good cause, and Heaven be for us!

The Attendant Spirit, habited like a shepherd

That hallo I should know. What are you? speak.
Come not too near; you fall on iron stakes else.

Spirit. What voice is that? my young Lord! speak again.

Second Brother. O brother, 't is my father's Shepherd, sure.

Elder Brother. Thyrsis! whose artful strains have oft delayed
The huddling brook to hear his madrigal,
And sweetened every muskrose of the dale.
How camest thou here, good swain? Hath any ram
Slipped from the fold, or young kid lost his dam,

Or straggling wether the pent flock forsook?
How couldst thou find this dark sequestered nook?
Spirit. O my loved master's heir, and his next joy,
I came not here on such a trivial toy
As a strayed ewe, or to pursue the stealth
Of pilfering wolf; not all the fleecy wealth
That doth enrich these downs is worth a thought
To this my errand, and the care it brought.
But, oh! my virgin Lady, where is she?
How chance she is not in your company?
Elder Brother. To tell thee sadly, Shepherd, without blame,
Or our neglect, we lost her as we came.
Spirit. Ay me unhappy! then my fears are true.
Elder Brother. What fears, good Thyrsis? Prithee briefly shew.
Spirit. I'll tell ye. 'T is not vain or fabulous,
(Though so esteemed by shallow ignorance)
What the sage poets, taught the heavenly Muse,
Storied of old in high immortal verse,
Of dire Chimeras, and inchanted Isles,
And rifted rocks whose entrance leads to Hell;
For such there be, but unbelief is blind.
Within the navel of this hideous wood,
Immured in cypress shades, a Sorcerer dwells,
Of Bacchus and of Circe born, great Comus,
Deep skilled in all his mother's witcheries,
And here to every thirsty wanderer
By sly enticement gives his baneful cup,
With many murmurs mixed, whose pleasing poison
The visage quite transforms of him that drinks,
And the inglorious likeness of a beast
Fixes instead, unmoulding reason's mintage
Charactered in the face. This have I learnt
Tending my flocks hard by i' the hilly crofts
That brow this bottom glade; whence night by night
He and his monstrous rout are heard to howl
Like stabled wolves, or tigers at their prey,
Doing abhorred rites to Hecate
In their obscurèd haunts of inmost bowers.
Yet have they many baits and guileful spells
To inveigle and invite the unwary sense
Of them that pass unweeting by the way.
This evening late, by then the chewing flocks
Had ta'en their supper on the savoury herb
Of knot-grass dew-besprent, and were in fold, 542
I sat me down to watch upon a bank
With ivy canopied, and interwove
With flaunting honeysuckle, and began,
Wrapt in a pleasing fit of melancholy,
To meditate my rural minstrelsy,
Till fancy had her fill. But ere a close
The wonted roar was up amidst the woods,
And filled the air with barbarous dissonance;
At which I ceased, and listened them awhile,
Till an unusual stop of sudden silence
Gave respite to the drowsy-flighted steeds
That draw the litter of close-curtained Sleep.
At last a soft and solemn-breathing sound
Rose like a steam of rich distilled perfumes,
And stole upon the air, that even Silence 557
Was took ere she was ware, and wished she might
Deny her nature, and be never more,
Still to be so displaced. I was all ear,
And took in strains that might create a soul
Under the ribs of Death. But, oh! ere long
Too well I did perceive it was the voice
Of my most honoured Lady, your dear sister.
Amazed I stood, harrowed with grief and fear;
And 'O poor hapless Nightingale,' thought I,
'How sweet thou sing'st, how near the deadly snare!'
Then down the lawns I ran with headlong haste,
Through paths and turnings often trod by day, 569
Till, guided by mine ear, I found the place
Where that damned wisard, hid in sly disguise
(For so by certain signs I knew), had met
Already, ere my best speed could prevent,
The aidless innocent lady, his wished prey;
Who gently asked if he had seen such two,
Supposing him some neighbour villager.
Longer I durst not stay, but soon I guessed
Ye were the two she meant; with that I sprung 578
Into swift flight, till I had found you here;
But furder know I not.
Second Brother. O night and shades,
How are ye joined with hell in triple knot
Against the unarmed weakness of one virgin,
Alone and helpless! Is this the confidence
You gave me, brother?
Elder Brother. Yes, and keep it still;
Lean on it safely; not a period
Shall be unsaid for me. Against the threats
Of malice or of sorcery, or that power
Which erring men call Chance, this I hold firm:
Virtue may be assailed, but never hurt,
Surprised by unjust force, but not enthralled;

Yea, even that which Mischief meant most harm
Shall in the happy trial prove most glory.
But evil on itself shall back recoil,
And mix no more with goodness, when at last,
Gathered like scum, and settled to itself,
It shall be in eternal restless change
Self-fed and self-consumèd. If this fail,
The pillared firmament is rottenness,
And earth's base built on stubble. But come, let 's on!
Against the opposing will and arm of Heaven
May never this just sword be lifted up;
But, for that damned magician, let him be girt
With all the griesly legions that troop
Under the sooty flag of Acheron,
Harpies and Hydras, or all the monstrous forms
'Twixt Africa and Ind, I 'll find him out,
And force him to restore his purchase back,
Or drag him by the curls to a foul death,
Cursed as his life.

Spirit. Alas! good ventrous youth,
I love thy courage yet, and bold emprise;
But here thy sword can do thee little stead.
Far other arms and other weapons must
Be those that quell the might of hellish charms.
He with his bare wand can unthread thy joints,
And crumble all thy sinews.

Elder Brother. Why prithee, Shepherd,
How durst thou then thyself approach so near
As to make this relation?

Spirit. Care and utmost shifts
How to secure the Lady from surprisal
Brought to my mind a certain shepherd lad,
Of small regard to see to, yet well skilled
In every virtuous plant and healing herb
That spreads her verdant leaf to the morning ray.
He loved me well, and oft would beg me sing;
Which when I did, he on the tender grass
Would sit, and hearken even to ecstasy,
And in requital ope his leathern scrip
And show me simples of a thousand names,
Telling their strange and vigorous faculties.
Amongst the rest a small unsightly root,
But of divine effect, he culled me out.
The leaf was darkish, and had prickles on it,
But in another country, as he said,
Bore a bright golden flower, but not in this soil:
Unknown, and like esteemed, and the dull swain
Treads on it daily with his clouted shoon;
And yet more med'cinal is it than that Moly
That Hermes once to wise Ulysses gave.
He called it Hæmony, and gave it me,
And bade me keep it as of sovran use
'Gainst all inchantments, mildew blast, or damp,
Or ghastly Furies' apparition.
I pursed it up, but little reckoning made,
Till now that this extremity compelled.
But now I find it true; for by this means
I knew the foul inchanter, though disguised,
Entered the very lime-twigs of his spells,
And yet came off. If you have this about you
(As I will give you when we go), you may
Boldly assault the necromancer's hall;
Where if he be, with dauntless hardihood
And brandished blade rush on him: break his glass,
And shed the luscious liquor on the ground;
But seize his wand. Though he and his curst crew
Fierce sign of battail make, and menace high,
Or, like the sons of Vulcan, vomit smoke,
Yet will they soon retire, if he but shrink.

Elder Brother. Thyrsis, lead on apace; I 'll follow thee;
And some good angel bear a shield before us!

The Scene changes to a stately palace, set out with all manner of deliciousness: soft music, tables spread with all dainties. Comus appears with his rabble, and the Lady set in an inchanted chair; to whom he offers his glass; which she puts by, and goes about to rise.

Comus. Nay, Lady, sit. If I but wave this wand,
Your nerves are all chained up in alabaster,
And you a statue, or as Daphne was,
Root-bound, that fled Apollo.

Lady. Fool, do not boast.
Thou canst not touch the freedom of my mind
With all thy charms, although this corporal rind
Thou hast immanacled while Heaven sees good.

Comus. Why are you vexed, Lady? why do you frown?
Here dwell no frowns, nor anger; from these gates
Sorrow flies far. See, here be all the pleasures
That fancy can beget on youthful thoughts,
When the fresh blood grows lively, and returns
Brisk as the April buds in primrose season.
And first behold this cordial julep here,
That flames and dances in his crystal bounds,
With spirits of balm and fragrant syrups mixed.
Not that Nepenthes which the wife of Thone
In Egypt gave to Jove-born Helena
Is of such power to stir up joy as this,

To life so friendly, or so cool to thirst.
Why should you be so cruel to yourself,
And to those dainty limbs, which Nature lent
For gentle usage and soft delicacy?
But you invert the covenants of her trust,
And harshly deal, like an ill borrower,
With that which you received on other terms,
Scorning the unexempt condition
By which all mortal frailty must subsist,
Refreshment after toil, ease after pain,
That have been tired all day without repast,
And timely rest have wanted. But, fair virgin,
This will restore all soon.
Lady. 'T will not, false traitor!
'T will not restore the truth and honesty
That thou hast banished from thy tongue with lies.
Was this the cottage and the safe abode
Thou told'st me of? What grim aspects are these,
These roughly-headed monsters? Mercy guard me!
Hence with thy brewed enchantments, foul deceiver!
Hast thou betrayed my credulous innocence
With vizored falsehood and base forgery?
And wouldst thou seek again to trap me here
With lickerish baits, fit to ensnare a brute?
Were it a draught for Juno when she banquets,
I would not taste thy treasonous offer. None
But such as are good men can give good things;
And that which is not good is not delicious
To a well-governed and wise appetite.
Comus. O foolishness of men! that lend their ears
To those budge doctors of the Stoic fur,
And fetch their precepts from the Cynic tub,
Praising the lean and sallow Abstinence!
Wherefore did Nature pour her bounties forth
With such a full and unwithdrawing hand,
Covering the earth with odours, fruits, and flocks,
Thronging the seas with spawn innumerable,
But all to please and sate the curious taste?
And set to work millions of spinning worms,
That in their green shops weave the smooth-haired silk,
To deck her sons; and, that no corner might
Be vacant of her plenty, in her own loins
She hutched the all-worshipped ore and precious gems,
To store her children with. If all the world
Should, in a pet of temperance, feed on pulse,
Drink the clear stream, and nothing wear but frieze,
The All-giver would be unthanked, would be unpraised,
Not half his riches known, and yet despised;
And we should serve him as a grudging master,
As a penurious niggard of his wealth,
And live like Nature's bastards, not her sons,
Who would be quite surcharged with her own weight,
And strangled with her waste fertility:
The earth cumbered, and the winged air darked with plumes;
The herds would over-multitude their lords;
The sea o'erfraught would swell, and the unsought diamonds
Would so imblaze the forehead of the Deep
And so bestud with stars, that they below
Would grow inured to light, and come at last
To gaze upon the Sun with shameless brows.
List, Lady; be not coy, and be not cozened
With that same vaunted name, Virginity.
Beauty is Nature's coin; must not be hoarded,
But must be current; and the good thereof
Consists in mutual and partaken bliss,
Unsavoury in the enjoyment of itself.
If you let slip time, like a neglected rose
It withers on the stalk with languished head.
Beauty is Nature's brag, and must be shown
In courts, at feasts, and high solemnities,
Where most may wonder at the workmanship.
It is for homely features to keep home;
They had their name thence: coarse complexions
And cheeks of sorry grain, will serve to ply
The sampler, and to tease the huswife's wool.
What need a vermeil-tinctured lip for that,
Love-darting eyes, or tresses like the Morn?
There was another meaning in these gifts;
Think what, and be advised; you are but young yet.
Lady. I had not thought to have unlocked my lips
In this unhallowed air, but that this Juggler
Would think to charm my judgment, as mine eyes,
Obtruding false rules pranked in reason's garb.
I hate when Vice can bolt her arguments
And Virtue has no tongue to check her pride.
Impostor! do not charge most innocent Nature,
As if she would her children should be riotous
With her abundance. She, good Cateress,

Means her provision only to the good,
That live according to her sober laws,
And holy dictate of spare Temperance:
If every just man that now pines with want
Had but a moderate and beseeming share
Of that which lewdly-pampered Luxury
Now heaps upon some few with vast excess,
Nature's full blessings would be well-dispensed
In unsuperfluous even proportion,
And she no whit encumbered with her store;
And then the Giver would be better thanked,
His praise due paid: for swinish Gluttony
Ne'er looks to Heaven amidst his gorgeous feast,
But with besotted base ingratitude
Crams, and blasphemes his Feeder. Shall I go on?
Or have I said enow? To him that dares
Arm his profane tongue with contemptuous words
Against the sun-clad power of Chastity
Fain would I something say; — yet to what end?
Thou hast nor ear, nor soul, to apprehend
The sublime notion and high mystery
That must be uttered to unfold the sage
And serious doctrine of Virginity;
And thou art worthy that thou shouldst not know
More happiness than this thy present lot.
Enjoy your dear Wit, and gay Rhetoric,
That hath so well been taught her dazzling fence;
Thou art not fit to hear thyself convinced.
Yet, should I try, the uncontrollèd worth
Of this pure cause would kindle my rapt spirits
To such a flame of sacred vehemence
That dumb things would be moved to sympathize,
And the brute Earth would lend her nerves, and shake,
Till all thy magic structures, reared so high,
Were shattered into heaps o'er thy false head.

Comus. She fables not. I feel that I do fear
Her words set off by some superior power;
And, though not mortal, yet a cold shuddering dew
Dips me all o'er, as when the wrath of Jove
Speaks thunder and the chains of Erebus
To some of Saturn's crew. I must dissemble,
And try her yet more strongly. — Come, no more!
This is mere moral babble, and direct
Against the canon laws of our foundation.
I must not suffer this; yet 't is but the lees
And settlings of a melancholy blood.
But this will cure all straight; one sip of this
Will bathe the drooping spirits in delight
Beyond the bliss of dreams. Be wise and taste. . . .

The Brothers rush in with swords drawn, wrest his glass out of his hand, and break it against the ground: his rout make sign of resistance, but are all driven in. The attendant spirit comes in.

Spirit. What! have you let the false Enchanter scape?
O ye mistook; ye should have snatched his wand,
And bound him fast. Without his rod reversed,
And backward mutters of dissevering power,
We cannot free the Lady that sits here
In stony fetters fixed and motionless.
Yet stay; be not disturbed; now I bethink me,
Some other means I have which may be used,
Which once of Melibœus old I learnt,
The soothest Shepherd that ere piped on plains.

There is a gentle Nymph not far from hence,
That with moist curb sways the smooth Severn stream:
Sabrina is her name: a virgin pure;
Whilom she was the daughter of Locrine,
That had the sceptre from his father Brute.
She, guiltless damsel, flying the mad pursuit
Of her enragèd stepdame, Guendolen,
Commended her fair innocence to the flood
That stayed her flight with his cross-flowing course.
The water-Nymphs, that in the bottom played,
Held up their pearlèd wrists, and took her in,
Bearing her straight to aged Nereus' hall;
Who, piteous of her woes, reared her lank head,
And gave her to his daughters to imbathe
In nectared lavers strewed with asphodil,
And through the porch and inlet of each sense
Dropt in ambrosial oils, till she revived,
And underwent a quick immortal change,
Made Goddess of the river. Still she retains
Her maiden gentleness, and oft at eve
Visits the herds along the twilight meadows,
Helping all urchin blasts, and ill-luck signs

That the shrewd meddling Elf delights to
make,
Which she with pretious vialed liquors heals:
For which the Shepherds, at their festivals,
Carol her goodness loud in rustic lays,
And throw sweet garland wreaths into her
stream,
Of pansies, pinks, and gaudy daffadils.
And, as the old Swain said, she can unlock
The clasping charm, and thaw the numbing
spell,
If she be right invoked in warbled song;
For maidenhood she loves, and will be swift
To aid a virgin, such as was herself,
In hard-besetting need. This will I try,
And add the power of some adjuring
verse.

SONG

Sabrina fair,
Listen where thou art sitting
Under the glassy, cool, translucent wave,
In twisted braids of lilies knitting
The loose train of thy amber-dropping
hair;
Listen for dear honour's sake,
Goddess of the silver lake,
Listen and save!
Listen and appear to us
In name of great Oceanus,
By the earth-shaking Neptune's mace,
And Tethys' grave majestic pace;
By hoary Nereus' wrinkled look,
And the Carpathian wizard's hook;
By scaly Triton's winding shell,
And old soothsaying Glaucus' spell;
By Leucothea's lovely hands,
And her son that rules the strands;
By Thetis' tinsel-slippered feet,
And the songs of Sirens sweet;
By dead Parthenope's dear tomb,
And fair Ligea's golden comb,
Wherewith she sits on diamond rocks
Sleeking her soft alluring locks;
By all the nymphs that nightly dance
Upon thy streams with wily glance;
Rise, rise, and heave thy rosy head
From thy coral-paven bed,
And bridle in thy headlong wave,
Till thou our summons answered have.
Listen and save!

Sabrina rises, attended by Water-nymphs, and sings.

By the rushy-fringèd bank,
Where grows the willow and the osier dank,
My sliding chariot stays,
Thick set with agate, and the azurn sheen
Of turkis blue, and emerald green,
That in the channel strays;
Whilst from off the waters fleet
Thus I set my printless feet
O'er the cowslip's velvet head,
That bends not as I tread.
Gentle swain, at thy request
I am here!

Spirit. Goddess dear,
We implore thy powerful hand
To undo the charmèd band
Of true virgin here distressed
Through the force and through the wile
Of unblessed enchanter vile.

Sabrina. Shepherd, 't is my office best
To help ensnarèd Chastity.
Brightest Lady, look on me.
Thus I sprinkle on thy breast
Drops that from my fountain pure
I have kept of pretious cure;
Thrice upon thy finger's tip,
Thrice upon thy rubied lip.
Next this marble venomed seat,
Smeared with gums of glutinous heat,
I touch with chaste palms moist and cold.
Now the spell hath lost his hold;
And I must haste ere morning hour
To wait in Amphitrite's bower.

Sabrina descends, and the Lady rises out of her seat.

Spirit. Virgin, daughter of Locrine,
Sprung of old Anchises' line,
May thy brimmèd waves for this
Their full tribute never miss
From a thousand petty rills,
That tumble down the snowy hills:
Summer drouth, or singèd air
Never scorch thy tresses fair,
Nor wet October's torrent flood
Thy molten crystal fill with mud;
May thy billows roll ashore
The beryl and the golden ore;
May thy lofty head be crowned
With many a tower and terrace round,
And here and there thy banks upon
With groves of myrrh and cinnamon.
Come, Lady; while Heaven lends us
grace,
Let us fly this cursèd place,
Lest the Sorcerer us entice
With some other new device.
Not a waste or needless sound
Till we come to holier ground;
I shall be your faithful guide
Through this gloomy covert wide;
And not many furlongs thence
Is your Father's residence,
Where this night are met in state
Many a friend to gratulate
His wished presence, and beside

All the Swains that there abide
With jigs and rural dance resort.
We shall catch them at their sport,
And our sudden coming there
Will double all their mirth and cheer.
Come, let us haste; the stars grow high,
But Night sits monarch yet in the mid sky.

The Scene changes, presenting Ludlow Town, and the President's castle: then come in Country Dancers; after them the Attendant Spirit, with the two Brothers and the Lady.

SONG

Spirit. Back, Shepherds, back! Enough you play
Till next sun-shine holiday.
Here be, without duck or nod,
Other trippings to be trod
Of lighter toes, and such court guise
As Mercury did first devise
With the mincing Dryades
On the lawns and on the leas.

This second Song presents them to their Father and Mother.

Noble Lord and Lady bright,
I have brought ye new delight.
Here behold so goodly grown
Three fair branches of your own.
Heaven hath timely tried their youth,
Their faith, their patience, and their truth,
And sent them here through hard assays
With a crown of deathless praise,
To triumph in victorious dance
O'er sensual Folly and Intemperance.

The dances ended, the Spirit epiloguizes.

Spirit. To the ocean now I fly
And those happy climes that lie
Where day never shuts his eye,
Up in the broad fields of the sky.
There I suck the liquid air,
All amidst the Gardens fair
Of Hesperus, and his daughters three
That sing about the Golden Tree.
Along the crispèd shades and bowers
Revels the spruce and jocund Spring;
The Graces and the rosy-bosomed Hours
Thither all their bounties bring.
There eternal Summer dwells,
And west winds with musky wing
About the cedarn alleys fling
Nard and cassia's balmy smells.
Iris there with humid bow
Waters the odorous banks, that blow
Flowers of more mingled hue
Than her purfled scarf can shew,
And drenches with Elysian dew
(List mortals, if your ears be true)
Beds of hyacinth and roses,
Where young Adonis oft reposes,
Waxing well of his deep wound
In slumber soft, and on the ground
Sadly sits the Assyrian queen;
But far above in spangled sheen
Celestial Cupid, her famed son, advanced,
Holds his dear Psyche sweet entranced,
After her wandering labours long,
Till free consent the gods among
Make her his eternal Bride,
And from her fair unspotted side
Two blissful twins are to be born,
Youth and Joy; so Jove hath sworn.
But now my task is smoothly done,
I can fly, or I can run
Quickly to the green earth's end,
Where the bowed welkin slow doth bend,
And from thence can soar as soon
To the corners of the Moon.
Mortals that would follow me,
Love Virtue, she alone is free;
She can teach ye how to climb
Higher than the sphery chime:
Or, if Virtue feeble were,
Heaven itself would stoop to her.

1637

LYCIDAS

YET once more, O ye Laurels, and once more,
Ye Myrtles brown, with ivy never sere,
I come to pluck your berries harsh and crude,
And with forced fingers rude
Shatter your leaves before the mellowing year.
Bitter constraint and sad occasion dear
Compels me to disturb your season due;
For Lycidas is dead, dead ere his prime,
Young Lycidas, and hath not left his peer.
Who would not sing for Lycidas? he knew
Himself to sing, and build the lofty rhyme.
He must not float upon his watery bier
Unwept, and welter to the parching wind,
Without the meed of some melodious tear.
Begin, then, Sisters of the sacred well
That from beneath the seat of Jove doth spring;
Begin, and somewhat loudly sweep the string.
Hence with denial vain, and coy excuse:
So may some gentle Muse
With lucky words favour *my* destined urn,
And as he passes turn,
And bid fair peace be to my sable shroud!
For we were nursed upon the self-same hill,

Fed the same flock, by fountain, shade, and rill;
Together both, ere the high lawns appeared
Under the opening eyelids of the Morn,
We drove a-field, and both together heard
What time the gray-fly winds her sultry horn,
Battening our flocks with the fresh dews of night,
Oft till the star that rose at evening bright
Toward heaven's descent had sloped his westering wheel.
Meanwhile the rural ditties were not mute;
Tempered to the oaten flute
Rough Satyrs danced, and Fauns with cloven heel
From the glad sound would not be absent long;
And old Damœtas loved to hear our song.
But, oh! the heavy change, now thou art gone,
Now thou art gone and never must return!
Thee, Shepherd, thee the woods and desert caves,
With wild thyme and the gadding vine o'ergrown,
And all their echoes, mourn.
The willows, and the hazel copses green,
Shall now no more be seen
Fanning their joyous leaves to thy soft lays.
As killing as the canker to the rose,
Or taint-worm to the weanling herds that graze,
Or frost to flowers, that their gay wardrobe wear,
When first the white-thorn blows;
Such, Lycidas, thy loss to shepherd's ear.
Where were ye, Nymphs, when the remorseless deep
Closed o'er the head of your loved Lycidas?
For neither were ye playing on the steep
Where your old Bards, the famous Druids, lie,
Nor on the shaggy top of Mona high,
Nor yet where Deva spreads her wizard stream.
Ay me! I fondly dream
'Had ye been there,' . . . . for what could that have done?
What could the Muse herself that Orpheus bore,
The Muse herself, for her inchanting son,
Whom universal nature did lament,
When, by the rout that made the hideous roar,
His gory visage down the stream was sent,
Down the swift Hebrus to the Lesbian shore?
Alas! what boots it with incessant care
To tend the homely, slighted, Shepherd's trade,
And strictly meditate the thankless Muse?
Were it not better done, as others use,
To sport with Amaryllis in the shade,
Or with the tangles of Neæra's hair?
Fame is the spur that the clear spirit doth raise
(The last infirmity of noble mind)
To scorn delights and live laborious days;
But the fair guerdon when we hope to find,
And think to burst out into sudden blaze,
Comes the blind Fury with the abhorrèd shears,
And slits the thin-spun life. 'But not the praise,'
Phœbus replied, and touched my trembling ears:
'Fame is no plant that grows on mortal soil,
Nor in the glistering foil
Set off to the world, nor in broad rumour lies,
But lives and spreads aloft by those pure eyes
And perfect witness of all-judging Jove;
As he pronounces lastly on each deed,
Of so much fame in heaven expect thy meed.'
O fountain Arethuse, and thou honoured flood,
Smooth-sliding Mincius, crowned with vocal reeds,
That strain I heard was of a higher mood.
But now my oat proceeds,
And listens to the Herald of the Sea,
That came in Neptune's plea.
He asked the waves, and asked the felon winds,
What hard mishap hath doomed this gentle swain?
And questioned every gust of rugged wings,
That blows from off each beakèd promontory.
They know not of his story;
And sage Hippotades their answer brings,
That not a blast was from his dungeon strayed:
The air was calm, and on the level brine
Sleek Panopé with all her sisters played.
It was that fatal and perfidious bark,
Built in the eclipse, and rigged with curses dark,
That sunk so low that sacred head of thine.
Next, Camus, reverend Sire, went footing slow,
His mantle hairy, and his bonnet sedge

Not famous

Inwrought with figures dim, and on the edge
Like to that sanguine flower inscribed with woe.
'Ah! who hath reft,' quoth he, 'my dearest pledge?'
Last came, and last did go,
The Pilot of the Galilean Lake;
Two massy keys he bore of metals twain
(The golden opes, the iron shuts amain).
He shook his mitered locks, and stern bespake: —
'How well could I have spared for thee, young swain,
Anow of such as, for their bellies' sake,
Creep, and intrude, and climb into the fold!
Of other care they little reckoning make
Than how to scramble at the shearers' feast,
And shove away the worthy bidden guest.
Blind mouths! that scarce themselves know how to hold
A sheep-hook, or have learnt ought else the least
That to the faithful Herdsman's art belongs!
What recks it them? What need they? They are sped;
And, when they list, their lean and flashy songs
Grate on their scrannel pipes of wretched straw;
The hungry sheep look up, and are not fed,
But, swoln with wind and the rank mist they draw,
Rot inwardly, and foul contagion spread;
Besides what the grim Wolf with privy paw,
Daily devours apace, and nothing said.
But that two-handed engine at the door
Stands ready to smite once, and smite no more.'

Return, Alphëus; the dread voice is past
That shrunk thy streams; return, Sicilian Muse,
And call the vales, and bid them hither cast
Their bells and flowerets of a thousand hues.
Ye valleys low, where the mild whispers use
Of shades, and wanton winds, and gushing brooks,
On whose fresh lap the swart star sparely looks,
Throw hither all your quaint enameled eyes,
That on the green turf suck the honeyed showers,
And purple all the ground with vernal flowers.
Bring the rathe primrose that forsaken dies,
The tufted crow-toe, and pale gessamine,
The white pink, and the pansy freaked with jet,
The glowing violet,
The musk-rose, and the well-attired woodbine,
With cowslips wan that hang the pensive head,
And every flower that sad embroidery wears;
Bid amaranthus all his beauty shed,
And daffadillies fill their cups with tears,
To strew the laureate hearse where Lycid lies.
For so, to interpose a little ease,
Let our frail thoughts dally with false surmise.
Ay me! whilst thee the shores and sounding seas
Wash far away, where'er thy bones are hurled;
Whether beyond the stormy Hebrides,
Where thou perhaps under the whelming tide
Visit'st the bottom of the monstrous world;
Or whether thou, to our moist vows denied,
Sleep'st by the fable of Bellerus old,
Where the great Vision of the guarded mount
Looks toward Namancos and Bayona's hold.
Look homeward, Angel, now, and melt with ruth;
And, O ye dolphins, waft the hapless youth.

Weep no more, woeful shepherds, weep no more,
For Lycidas, your sorrow, is not dead,
Sunk though he be beneath the watery floor.
So sinks the day-star in the ocean-bed,
And yet anon repairs his drooping head,
And tricks his beams, and, with new-spangled ore,
Flames in the forehead of the morning sky:
So Lycidas sunk low, but mounted high,
Through the dear might of Him that walked the waves,
Where, other groves and other streams along,
With nectar pure his oozy locks he laves,
And hears the unexpressive nuptial song,
In the blest kingdoms meek of joy and love.
There entertain him all the Saints above,
In solemn troops, and sweet societies,
That sing, and, singing in their glory move,
And wipe the tears for ever from his eyes.
Now, Lycidas, the Shepherds weep no more;
Henceforth thou art the Genius of the shore,
In thy large recompense, and shalt be good
To all that wander in that perilous flood.

Thus sang the uncouth Swain to the oaks and rills,
While the still Morn went out with sandals grey:
He touched the tender stops of various quills,
With eager thought warbling his Doric lay:
And now the sun had stretched out all the hills,
And now was dropt into the western bay.
At last he rose, and twitched his mantle blue:
To-morrow to fresh woods, and pastures new.

1638

SONNETS

ON HIS BEING ARRIVED TO THE AGE OF TWENTY-THREE

How soon hath Time, the subtle thief of youth,
Stolen on his wing my three and twentieth year!
My hasting days fly on with full career,
But my late spring no bud nor blossom shew'th.
Perhaps my semblance might deceive the truth,
That I to manhood am arrived so near,
And inward ripeness doth much less appear,
That some more timely-happy spirits endu'th.
Yet be it less or more, or soon or slow,
It shall be still in strictest measure even
To that same lot, however mean or high,
Towards which Time leads me, and the will of Heaven.
All is, if I have grace to use it so,
As ever in my great Task-master's eye.

1645

TO THE LORD GENERAL CROMWELL, ON THE PROPOSALS OF CERTAIN MINISTERS AT THE COMMITTEE FOR PROPAGATION OF THE GOSPEL

Cromwell, our chief of men, who through a cloud
Not of war only, but detractions rude,
Guided by faith and matchless fortitude,
To peace and truth thy glorious way hast ploughed,
And on the neck of crownèd Fortune proud
Has reared God's trophies, and his work pursued,
While Darwen stream, with blood of Scots imbrued,
And Dunbar field, resounds thy praises loud,
And Worcester's laureate wreath: yet much remains
To conquer still; Peace hath her victories
No less renowned than War: new foes arise,
Threatening to bind our souls with secular chains.
Help us to save free conscience from the paw
Of hireling wolves, whose Gospel is their maw.

1694

ON THE LATE MASSACRE IN PIEMONT

Avenge, O Lord, thy slaughtered Saints, whose bones
Lie scattered on the Alpine mountains cold;
Even them who kept thy truth so pure of old,
When all our fathers worshiped stocks and stones,
Forget not: in thy book record their groans
Who were thy sheep, and in their ancient fold
Slain by the bloody Piemontese, that rolled
Mother with infant down the rocks. Their moans
The vales redoubled to the hills, and they
To heaven. Their martyred blood and ashes sow
O'er all the Italian fields, where still doth sway
The triple Tyrant; that from these may grow
A hundredfold, who, having learnt thy way,
Early may fly the Babylonian woe.

1672

ON HIS BLINDNESS

When I consider how my light is spent
Ere half my days in this dark world and wide,
And that one Talent which is death to hide
Lodged with me useless, though my soul more bent
To serve therewith my Maker, and present
My true account, lest He returning chide,
'Doth God exact day-labour, light denied?'
I fondly ask. But Patience, to prevent
That murmur, soon replies, 'God doth not need
Either man's work or his own gifts. Who best
Bear his mild yoke, they serve him best. His state
Is kingly: thousands at his bidding speed,
And post o'er land and ocean without rest;
They also serve who only stand and wait.'

1673

TO CYRIACK SKINNER

Cyriack, this three years' day these eyes, though clear,
To outward view, of blemish or of spot,
Bereft of light, their seeing have forgot;
Nor to their idle orbs doth sight appear
Of sun, or moon, or star, throughout the year,
Or man, or woman. Yet I argue not
Against Heaven's hand or will, nor bate a jot
Of heart or hope, but still bear up and steer
Right onward. What supports me, dost thou ask?
The conscience, friend, to have lost them over-plied
In Liberty's defence, my noble task,
Of which all Europe rings from side to side.
This thought might lead me through the world's vain mask,
Content, though blind, had I no better guide.

1694

ON HIS DECEASED WIFE

Methought I saw my late espousèd saint
Brought to me like Alcestis from the grave,
Whom Jove's great son to her glad husband gave,
Rescued from Death by force, though pale and faint.
Mine, as whom washed from spot of child-bed taint
Purification in the Old Law did save,
And such as yet once more I trust to have
Full sight of her in Heaven without restraint,
Came vested all in white, pure as her mind.
Her face was veiled; yet to my fancied sight
Love, sweetness, goodness, in her person shined
So clear as in no face with more delight.
But, oh! as to embrace me she inclined,
I waked, she fled, and day brought back my night.

1673

PARADISE LOST

BOOK I

THE ARGUMENT

This First Book proposes, first in brief, the whole subject — Man's disobedience, and the loss thereupon of Paradise, wherein he was placed: then touches the prime cause of his fall — the Serpent, or rather Satan in the Serpent, who, revolting from God, and drawing to his side many legions of Angels, was, by the command of God, driven out of Heaven, with all his crew, into the great Deep. Which action passed over, the Poem hastens into the midst of things; presenting Satan, with his Angels, now fallen into Hell — described here, not in the Center (for heaven and earth may be supposed as yet not made, certainly not yet accursed), but in a place of utter darkness, fitliest called Chaos. Here Satan, with his Angels lying on the burning lake, thunderstruck and astonished, after a certain space recovers, as from confusion; calls up him who, next in order and dignity, lay by him: they confer of their miserable fall. Satan awakens all his legions, who lay till then in the same manner confounded. They rise: their numbers; array of battle; their chief leaders named, according to the idols known afterwards in Canaan and the countries adjoining. To these Satan directs his speech; comforts them with hope yet of regaining Heaven; but tells them, lastly, of a new world and new kind of creature to be created, according to an ancient prophecy, or report, in Heaven — for that Angels were long before this visible creation was the opinion of many ancient Fathers. To find out the truth of this prophecy, and what to determine thereon, he refers to a full council. What his associates thence attempt. Pandemonium, the palace of Satan, rises, suddenly built out of the Deep: the infernal Peers there sit in council.

Of Man's first disobedience, and the fruit
Of that forbidden tree whose mortal taste
Brought death into the World, and all our woe,
With loss of Eden, till one greater Man
Restore us, and regain the blissful Seat,
Sing, Heavenly Muse, that on the secret top
Of Oreb, or of Sinai, didst inspire
That Shepherd who first taught the chosen seed
In the beginning how the heavens and earth
Rose out of Chaos: or, if Sion hill
Delight thee more, and Siloa's brook that flowed
Fast by the oracle of God, I thence
Invoke thy aid to my adventrous song,
That with no middle flight intends to soar
Above the Aonian mount, while it pursues
Things unattempted yet in prose or rhyme.
And chiefly Thou, O Spirit, that dost prefer
Before all temples the upright heart and pure,
Instruct me, for Thou know'st; Thou from the first
Wast present, and, with mighty wings outspread,
Dove-like sat'st brooding on the vast Abyss,
And mad'st it pregnant: what in me is dark
Illumine, what is low raise and support;
That, to the highth of this great argument,
I may assert Eternal Providence,
And justify the ways of God to men.
Say first — for Heaven hides nothing from thy view,
Nor the deep tract of Hell — say first what cause
Moved our grand Parents, in that happy state,
Favoured of Heaven so highly, to fall off
From their Creator, and transgress his will
For one restraint, lords of the World besides?

Who first seduced them to that foul revolt?
The infernal Serpent; he it was whose guile,
Stirred up with envy and revenge, deceived
The mother of mankind, what time his pride
Had cast him out from Heaven, with all his host
Of rebel Angels, by whose aid, aspiring
To set himself in glory above his peers,
He trusted to have equalled the Most High,
If he opposed, and with ambitious aim
Against the throne and monarchy of God,
Raised impious war in Heaven and battle proud,
With vain attempt. Him the Almighty Power
Hurled headlong flaming from the ethereal sky,
With hideous ruin and combustion, down
To bottomless perdition, there to dwell
In adamantine chains and penal fire,
Who durst defy the Omnipotent to arms.
Nine times the space that measures day and night
To mortal men, he, with his horrid crew,
Lay vanquisht, rowling in the fiery gulf,
Confounded, though immortal. But his doom
Reserved him to more wrath; for now the thought
Both of lost happiness and lasting pain
Torments him; round he throws his baleful eyes,
That witnessed huge affliction and dismay,
Mixed with obdurate pride and steadfast hate.
At once, as far as Angels ken, he views
The dismal situation waste and wilde.
A dungeon horrible, on all sides round,
As one great furnace flamed; yet from those flames
No light; but rather darkness visible
Served only to discover sights of woe,
Regions of sorrow, doleful shades, where peace
And rest can never dwell, hope never comes
That comes to all, but torture without end
Still urges, and a fiery deluge, fed
With ever-burning sulphur unconsumed.
Such place Eternal Justice had prepared
For those rebellious; here their prison ordained
In utter darkness, and their portion set,
As far removed from God and light of Heaven
As from the center thrice to the utmost pole.
Oh how unlike the place from whence they fell!
There the companions of his fall, o'erwhelmed
With floods and whirlwinds of tempestuous fire,
He soon discerns; and, weltring by his side,
One next himself in power, and next in crime,
Long after known in Palestine, and named
Beëlzebub. To whom the Arch-Enemy,
And thence in Heaven called Satan, with bold words
Breaking the horrid silence, thus began: —
'If thou beest he — but Oh how fallen! how changed
From him! — who, in the happy realms of light,
Clothed with transcendent brightness, didst outshine
Myriads, though bright — if he whom mutual league,
United thoughts and counsels, equal hope
And hazard in the glorious enterprise,
Joined with me once, now misery hath joined
In equal ruin; into what pit thou seest
From what highth fallen: so much the stronger proved
He with his thunder: and till then who knew
The force of those dire arms? Yet not for those,
Nor what the potent Victor in his rage
Can else inflict, do I repent, or change,
Though changed in outward lustre, that fixed mind,
And high disdain from sense of injured merit,
That with the Mightiest raised me to contend,
And to the fierce contention brought along
Innumerable force of Spirits armed,
That durst dislike his reign, and, me preferring,
His utmost power with adverse power opposed
In dubious battle on the plains of Heaven,
And shook his throne. What though the field be lost?
All is not lost — the unconquerable will,
And study of revenge, immortal hate,
And courage never to submit or yield:
And what is else not to be overcome;
That glory never shall his wrath or might
Extort from me. To bow and sue for grace
With suppliant knee, and deify his power
Who, from the terror of this arm, so late
Doubted his empire — that were low indeed;
That were an ignominy and shame beneath
This downfall; since, by fate, the strength of Gods,

And this empyreal substance, cannot fail;
Since, through experience of this great event,
In arms not worse, in foresight much advanced,
We may with more successful hope resolve
To wage by force or guile eternal war,
Irreconcilable to our grand Foe,
Who now triumphs, and in the excess of joy
Sole reigning holds the tyranny of Heaven.'
  So spake the apostate Angel, though in pain,
Vaunting aloud, but racked with deep despair;
And him thus answered soon his bold Compeer: —
  'O Prince, O Chief of many thronèd Powers
That led the imbattled Seraphim to war
Under thy conduct, and, in dreadful deeds
Fearless, endangered Heaven's perpetual King,
And put to proof his high supremacy,
Whether upheld by strength, or chance, or fate!
Too well I see and rue the dire event
That, with sad overthrow and foul defeat,
Hath lost us Heaven, and all this mighty host
In horrible destruction laid thus low,
As far as Gods and Heavenly Essences
Can perish: for the mind and spirit remains
Invincible, and vigour soon returns,
Though all our glory extinct, and happy state
Here swallowed up in endless misery.
But what if He our Conqueror (whom I now
Of force believe almighty, since no less
Than such could have o'erpowered such force as ours)
Have left us this our spirit and strength entire,
Strongly to suffer and support our pains,
That we may so suffice his vengeful ire,
Or do him mightier service as his thralls
By right of war, whate'er his business be,
Here in the heart of Hell to work in fire,
Or do his errands in the gloomy Deep?
What can it then avail though yet we feel
Strength undiminished, or eternal being
To undergo eternal punishment?'
  Whereto with speedy words the Arch-Fiend replied: —
'Fallen Cherub, to be weak is miserable,
Doing or suffering: but of this be sure —
To do aught good never will be our task,
But ever to do ill our sole delight,
As being the contrary to His high will
Whom we resist. If then his providence
Out of our evil seek to bring forth good,
Our labour must be to pervert that end,
And out of good still to find means of evil;
Which ofttimes may succeed so as perhaps
Shall grieve him, if I fail not, and disturb
His inmost counsels from their destined aim.
But see! the angry Victor hath recalled
His ministers of vengeance and pursuit
Back to the gates of Heaven: the sulphurous hail,
Shot after us in storm, o'erblown hath laid
The fiery surge that from the precipice
Of Heaven received us falling; and the thunder,
Winged with red lightning and impetuous rage,
Perhaps hath spent his shafts, and ceases now
To bellow through the vast and boundless Deep.
Let us not slip the occasion, whether scorn
Or satiate fury yield it from our Foe.
Seest thou yon dreary plain, forlorn and wild,
The seat of desolation, void of light,
Save what the glimmering of these livid flames
Casts pale and dreadful? Thither let us tend
From off the tossing of these fiery waves;
There rest, if any rest can harbour there;
And, re-assembling our afflicted powers,
Consult how we may henceforth most offend
Our Enemy, our own loss how repair,
How overcome this dire calamity,
What reinforcement we may gain from hope,
If not what resolution from despair.'
  Thus Satan, talking to his nearest Mate,
With head uplift above the wave, and eyes
That sparkling blazed; his other parts besides
Prone on the flood, extended long and large,
Lay floating many a rood, in bulk as huge
As whom the fables name of monstrous size,
Titanian or Earth-born, that warred on Jove,
Briareos or Typhon, whom the den
By ancient Tarsus held, or that sea-beast
Leviathan, which God of all his works
Created hugest that swim the ocean-stream.
Him, haply slumbering on the Norway foam,
The pilot of some small night-foundered skiff,
Deeming some island, oft, as seamen tell,
With fixèd anchor in his scaly rind,
Moors by his side under the lee, while night

Invests the sea, and wishèd morn delays.
So stretched out huge in length the Arch-Fiend lay,
Chained on the burning lake; nor ever thence
Had risen or heaved his head, but that the will
And high permission of all-ruling Heaven
Left him at large to his own dark designs,
That with reiterated crimes he might
Heap on himself damnation, while he sought
Evil to others, and enraged might see
How all his malice served but to bring forth
Infinite goodness, grace, and mercy, shewn
On Man by him seduced, but on himself
Treble confusion, wrath, and vengeance poured.
  Forthwith upright he rears from off the pool
His mighty stature; on each hand the flames
Driven backward slope their pointing spires, and, rowled
In billows, leave i' the midst a horrid vale.
Then with expanded wings he steers his flight
Aloft, incumbent on the dusky air,
That felt unusual weight; till on dry land
He lights — if it were land that ever burned
With solid, as the lake with liquid fire,
And such appeared in hue as when the force
Of subterranean wind transports a hill
Torn from Pelorus, or the shattered side
Of thundering Ætna, whose combustible
And fuelled entrails, thence conceiving fire,
Sublimed with mineral fury, aid the winds,
And leave a singèd bottom all involved
With stench and smoke. Such resting found the sole
Of unblest feet. Him followed his next Mate;
Both glorying to have scaped the Stygian flood
As gods, and by their own recovered strength,
Not by the sufferance of supernal power.
  'Is this the region, this the soil, the clime,'
Said then the lost Archangel, 'this the seat
That we must change for Heaven? — this mournful gloom
For that celestial light? Be it so, since He
Who now is sovran can dispose and bid
What shall be right: fardest from Him is best,
Whom reason hath equalled, force hath made supreme
Above his equals. Farewell, happy fields,
Where joy for ever dwells! Hail, horrors! hail,
Infernal World! and thou, profoundest Hell,
Receive thy new possessor — one who brings
A mind not to be changed by place or time.
The mind is its own place, and in itself
Can make a Heaven of Hell, a Hell of Heaven.
What matter where, if I be still the same,
And what I should be, all but less than he
Whom thunder hath made greater? Here at least
We shall be free; the Almighty hath not built
Here for his envy, will not drive us hence:
Here we may reign secure; and, in my choice,
To reign is worth ambition, though in Hell:
Better to reign in Hell than serve in Heaven.
But wherefore let we then our faithful friends,
The associates and co-partners of our loss,
Lie thus astonished on the oblivious pool,
And call them not to share with us their part
In this unhappy mansion, or once more
With rallied arms to try what may be yet
Regained in Heaven, or what more lost in Hell?'
  So Satan spake; and him Beëlzebub
Thus answered: — 'Leader of those armies bright
Which, but the Omnipotent, none could have foiled!
If once they hear that voice, their liveliest pledge
Of hope in fears and dangers — heard so oft
In worst extremes, and on the perilous edge
Of battle, when it raged, in all assaults
Their surest signal — they will soon resume
New courage and revive, though now they lie
Grovelling and prostrate on yon lake of fire,
As we erewhile, astounded and amazed;
No wonder, fallen such a pernicious highth!'
  He scarce had ceased when the superior Fiend
Was moving toward the shore; his ponderous shield,
Ethereal temper, massy, large, and round,
Behind him cast. The broad circumference
Hung on his shoulders like the moon, whose orb
Through optic glass the Tuscan artist views
At evening, from the top of Fesolè,
Or in Valdarno, to descry new lands,
Rivers, or mountains, in her spotty globe.

His spear — to equal which the tallest pine
Hewn on Norwegian hills, to be the mast
Of some great Ammiral, were but a wand —
He walked with, to support uneasy steps
Over the burning marle, not like those steps
On Heaven's azure; and the torrid clime
Smote on him sore besides, vaulted with fire.
Nathless he so endured, till on the beach
Of that inflamèd sea he stood, and called
His legions — Angel Forms, who lay entranced
Thick as autumnal leaves that strow the brooks
In Vallombrosa, where the Etrurian shades
High over-arched imbower; or scattered sedge
Afloat, when with fierce winds Orion armed
Hath vexed the Red-Sea coast, whose waves o'erthrew
Busiris and his Memphian chivalry,
While with perfidious hatred they pursued
The sojourners of Goshen, who beheld
From the safe shore their floating carcases
And broken chariot-wheels. So thick bestrown,
Abject and lost, lay these, covering the flood,
Under amazement of their hideous change.
He called so loud that all the hollow deep
Of Hell resounded: — 'Princes, Potentates,
Warriors, the Flower of Heaven — once yours; now lost,
If such astonishment as this can seize
Eternal Spirits! Or have ye chosen this place
After the toil of battle to repose
Your wearied virtue, for the ease you find
To slumber here, as in the vales of Heaven?
Or in this abject posture have ye sworn
To adore the Conquerour, who now beholds
Cherub and Seraph rowling in the flood
With scattered arms and ensigns, till anon
His swift pursuers from Heaven-gates discern
The advantage, and, descending, tread us down
Thus drooping, or with linkèd thunderbolts
Transfix us to the bottom of this gulf? —
Awake, arise, or be for ever fallen!'
They heard, and were abashed, and up they sprung
Upon the wing, as when men wont to watch,
On duty sleeping found by whom they dread,
Rouse and bestir themselves ere well awake.
Nor did they not perceive the evil plight
In which they were, or the fierce pains not feel;
Yet to their General's voice they soon obeyed
Innumerable. As when the potent rod
Of Amram's son, in Egypt's evil day,
Waved round the coast, up-called a pitchy cloud
Of locusts, warping on the eastern wind,
That o'er the realm of impious Pharaoh hung
Like Night, and darkened all the land of Nile;
So numberless were those bad Angels seen
Hovering on wing under the cope of Hell,
'Twixt upper, nether, and surrounding fires;
Till, as a signal given, the uplifted spear
Of their great Sultan waving to direct
Their course, in even balance down they light
On the firm brimstone, and fill all the plain:
A multitude like which the populous North
Poured never from her frozen loins to pass
Rhene or the Danaw, when her barbarous sons
Came like a deluge on the South, and spread
Beneath Gibralter to the Libyan sands.
Forthwith, from every squadron and each band,
The heads and leaders thither haste where stood
Their great Commander — godlike Shapes, and Forms
Excelling human; princely Dignities;
And Powers that erst in Heaven sat on thrones,
Though of their names in Heavenly records now
Be no memorial, blotted out and rased
By their rebellion from the Books of Life.
Nor had they yet among the sons of Eve
Got them new names, till, wandering o'er the earth,
Through God's high sufferance for the trial of man,
By falsities and lies the greatest part
Of mankind they corrupted to forsake
God their Creator, and the invisible
Glory of Him that made them to transform
Oft to the image of a brute, adorned
With gay religions full of pomp and gold,
And devils to adore for deities:
Then were they known to men by various names,
And various idols through the heathen world.
Say, Muse, their names then known, who first, who last,
Roused from the slumber on that fiery couch,
At their great Emperor's call, as next in worth
Came singly where he stood on the bare strand,
While the promiscuous crowd stood yet aloof.

The chief were those who, from the pit of Hell
Roaming to seek their prey on Earth, durst fix
Their seats, long after, next the seat of God,
Their altars by His altar, gods adored
Among the nations round, and durst abide
Jehovah thundering out of Sion, throned
Between the Cherubim; yea, often placed
Within His sanctuary itself their shrines,
Abominations; and with cursèd things
His holy rites and solemn feasts profaned,
And with their darkness durst affront His light.
First, *Moloch*, horrid King, besmeared with blood
Of human sacrifice, and parents' tears;
Though, for the noise of drums and timbrels loud,
Their children's cries unheard that passed through fire
To his grim idol. Him the Ammonite
Worshiped in Rabba and her watery plain,
In Argob and in Basan, to the stream
Of utmost Arnon. Nor content with such
Audacious neighbourhood, the wisest heart
Of Solomon he led by fraud to build
His temple right against the temple of God
On that opprobrious hill, and made his grove
The pleasant valley of Hinnom, Tophet thence
And black Gehenna called, the type of Hell.
Next *Chemos*, the obscene dread of Moab's sons,
From Aroar to Nebo and the wild
Of southmost Abarim; in Hesebon
And Horonaim, Seon's realm, beyond
The flowery dale of Sibma clad with vines,
And Elealè to the Asphaltick Pool:
Peor his other name, when he enticed
Israel in Sittim, on their march from Nile,
To do him wanton rites, which cost them woe.
Yet thence his lustful orgies he enlarged
Even to that hill of scandal, by the grove
Of Moloch homicide, lust hard by hate,
Till good Josiah drove them thence to Hell.
With these came they who, from the bordering flood
Of old Euphrates to the brook that parts
Egypt from Syrian ground, had general names
Of *Baalim* and *Ashtaroth* — those male,
These feminine. For Spirits, when they please,
Can either sex assume, or both; so soft
And uncompounded is their essence pure,
Not tied or manacled with joint or limb,
Nor founded on the brittle strength of bones,
Like cumbrous flesh; but, in what shape they choose,
Dilated or condensed, bright or obscure,
Can execute their aery purposes,
And works of love or enmity fulfil.
For those the race of Israel oft forsook
Their Living Strength, and unfrequented left
His righteous altar, bowing lowly down
To bestial gods; for which their heads, as low
Bowed down in battle, sunk before the spear
Of despicable foes. With these in troop
Came *Astoreth*, whom the Phœnicians called
Astarte, queen of Heaven, with crescent horns;
To whose bright image nightly by the moon
Sidonian virgins paid thir vows and songs;
In Sion also not unsung, where stood
Her temple on the offensive mountain, built
By that uxorious king whose heart, though large,
Beguiled by fair idolatresses, fell
To idols foul. *Thammuz* came next behind,
Whose annual wound in Lebanon allured
The Syrian damsels to lament his fate
In amorous ditties all a summer's day,
While smooth Adonis from his native rock
Ran purple to the sea, supposed with blood
Of Thammuz yearly wounded: the love-tale
Infected Sion's daughters with like heat,
Whose wanton passions in the sacred porch
Ezekiel saw, when, by the vision led,
His eye surveyed the dark idolatries
Of alienated Judah. Next came one
Who mourned in earnest, when the captive Ark
Maimed his brute image, head and hands lopt off,
In his own temple, on the grunsel-edge,
Where he fell flat, and shamed his worshipers:
Dagon his name, sea-monster, upward man
And downward fish; yet had his temple high
Reared in Azotus, dreaded through the coast
Of Palestine, in Gath and Ascalon,
And Accaron and Gaza's frontier bounds.
Him followed *Rimmon*, whose delightful seat
Was fair Damascus, on the fertile banks
Of Abbana and Pharphar, lucid streams.
He also against the house of God was bold:

A leper once he lost, and gained a king —
Ahaz, his sottish conqueror, whom he drew
God's altar to disparage and displace
For one of Syrian mode, whereon to burn
His odious offerings, and adore the gods
Whom he had vanquished. After these appeared
A crew who, under names of old renown —
Osiris, *Isis*, *Orus*, and their train —
With monstrous shapes and sorceries abused
Fanatic Egypt and her priests to seek
Their wandering gods disguised in brutish forms
Rather than human. Nor did Israel scape
The infection, when their borrowed gold composed
The calf in Oreb; and the rebel king
Doubled that sin in Bethel and in Dan,
Likening his Maker to the grazèd ox —
Jehovah, who, in one night, when he passed
From Egypt marching, equalled with one stroke
Both her first-born and all her bleating gods.
Belial came last; than whom a Spirit more lewd
Fell not from Heaven, or more gross to love
Vice for itself. To him no temple stood
Or altar smoked; yet who more oft than he
In temples and at altars, when the priest
Turns atheist, as did Eli's sons, who filled
With lust and violence the house of God?
In courts and palaces he also reigns,
And in luxurious cities, where the noise
Of riot ascends above their loftiest towers,
And injury and outrage; and when night
Darkens the streets, then wander forth the sons
Of Belial, flown with insolence and wine.
Witness the streets of Sodom, and that night
In Gibeah, when the hospitable door
Exposed a matron, to avoid worse rape.
These were the prime in order and in might:
The rest were long to tell; though far renowned
The Ionian gods — of Javan's issue held
Gods, yet confessed later than Heaven and Earth,
Their boasted parents; — *Titan*, Heaven's first-born,
With his enormous brood, and birthright seized
By younger *Saturn:* he from mightier Jove,
His own and Rhea's son, like measure found;
So *Jove* usurping reigned. These, first in Crete
And Ida known, thence on the snowy top
Of cold Olympus ruled the middle air,
Their highest heaven: or on the Delphian cliff,
Or in Dodona, and through all the bounds
Of Doric land; or who with Saturn old
Fled over Adria to the Hesperian fields,
And o'er the Celtic roamed the utmost Isles.
All these and more came flocking; but with looks
Downcast and damp; yet such wherein appeared
Obscure some glimpse of joy to have found their Chief
Not in despair, to have found themselves not lost
In loss itself; which on his countenance cast
Like doubtful hue. But he, his wonted pride
Soon recollecting, with high words, that bore
Semblance of worth, not substance, gently raised
Their fainting courage, and dispelled their fears;
Then straight commands that, at the warlike sound
Of trumpets loud and clarions, be upreared
His mighty standard. That proud honour claimed
Azazel as his right, a Cherub tall:
Who forthwith from the glittering staff unfurled
The imperial ensign; which, full high advanced,
Shon like a meteor streaming to the wind,
With gems and golden lustre rich imblazed,
Seraphic arms and trophies; all the while
Sonorous metal blowing martial sounds:
At which the universal host up-sent
A shout that tore Hell's concave, and beyond
Frighted the reign of Chaos and old Night.
All in a moment through the gloom were seen
Ten thousand banners rise into the air,
With orient colours waving: with them rose
A forest huge of spears; and thronging helms
Appeared, and serried shields in thick array
Of depth immeasurable. Anon they move
In perfect phalanx to the Dorian mood
Of flutes and soft recorders — such as raised
To highth of noblest temper heroes old
Arming to battle, and instead of rage
Deliberate valour breathed, firm, and unmoved
With dread of death to flight or foul retreat;
Nor wanting power to mitigate and swage
With solemn touches troubled thoughts, and chase

Anguish and doubt and fear and sorrow and pain
From mortal or immortal minds. Thus they,
Breathing united force with fixèd thought,
Moved on in silence to soft pipes that charmed
Their painful steps o'er the burnt soil. And now
Advanced in view they stand — a horrid front
Of dreadful length and dazzling arms, in guise
Of warriors old, with ordered spear and shield,
Awaiting what command their mighty Chief
Had to impose. He through the armèd files
Darts his experienced eye, and soon traverse
The whole battalion views — their order due,
Their visages and stature as of gods;
Their number last he sums. And now his heart
Distends with pride, and, hardening in his strength,
Glories; for never, since created Man,
Met such imbodied force as, named with these,
Could merit more than that small infantry
Warred on by cranes — though all the giant brood
Of Phlegra with the heroic race were joined
That fought at Thebes and Ilium, on each side
Mixed with auxiliar gods; and what resounds
In fable or romance of Uther's son,
Begirt with British and Armoric knights;
And all who since, baptized or infidel,
Jousted in Aspramont, or Montalban,
Damasco, or Marocco, or Trebisond,
Or whom Biserta sent from Afric shore
When Charlemain with all his peerage fell
By Fontarabbia. Thus far these beyond
Compare of mortal prowess, yet observed
Thir dread Commander. He, above the rest
In shape and gesture proudly eminent,
Stood like a tower. His form had yet not lost
All her original brightness, nor appeared
Less than Archangel ruined, and the excess
Of glory obscured: as when the sun new-risen
Looks through the horizontal misty air
Shorn of his beams, or, from behind the moon,
In dim eclipse, disastrous twilight sheds
On half the nations, and with fear of change
Perplexes monarchs. Darkened so, yet shon
Above them all the Archangel: but his face
Deep scars of thunder had intrenched, and care
Sat on his faded cheek, but under brows
Of dauntless courage, and considerate pride
Waiting revenge. Cruel his eye, but cast
Signs of remorse and passion, to behold
The fellows of his crime, the followers rather
(Far other once beheld in bliss), condemned
For ever now to have their lot in pain —
Millions of Spirits for his fault amerced
Of Heaven, and from eternal splendours flung
For his revolt — yet faithful how they stood,
Their glory withered; as, when heaven's fire
Hath scathed the forest oaks or mountain pines,
With singèd top their stately growth, though bare,
Stands on the blasted heath. He now prepared
To speak; whereat their doubled ranks they bend
From wing to wing, and half enclose him round
With all his peers: Attention held them mute.
Thrice he assayed, and thrice, in spite of scorn,
Tears, such as Angels weep, burst forth: at last
Words interwove with sighs found out their way: —
'O myriads of immortal Spirits! O Powers
Matchless, but with the Almighty! — and that strife
Was not inglorious, though the event was dire,
As this place testifies, and this dire change,
Hateful to utter. But what power of mind,
Foreseeing or presaging, from the depth
Of knowledge past or present, could have feared
How such united force of gods, how such
As stood like these, could ever know repulse?
For who can yet believe, though after loss,
That all these puissant legions, whose exile
Hath emptied Heaven, shall fail to re-ascend,
Self-raised, and re-possess their native seat?
For me, be witness all the host of Heaven,
If counsels different, or danger shunned
By me, have lost our hopes. But he who reigns
Monarch in Heaven till then as one secure

Sat on his throne, upheld by old repute,
Consent or custom, and his regal state
Put forth at full, but still his strength concealed —
Which tempted our attempt, and wrought our fall.
Henceforth his might we know, and know our own,
So as not either to provoke, or dread
New war provoked: our better part remains
To work in close design, by fraud or guile,
What force effected not; that he no less
At length from us may find, Who overcomes
By force hath overcome but half his foe.
Space may produce new Worlds; whereof so rife
There went a fame in Heaven that He ere long
Intended to create, and therein plant
A generation whom his choice regard
Should favour equal to the Sons of Heaven.
Thither, if but to pry, shall be perhaps
Our first eruption — thither, or elsewhere;
For this infernal pit shall never hold
Cælestial Spirits in bondage, nor the Abyss
Long under darkness cover. But these thoughts
Full counsel must mature. Peace is despaired;
For who can think submission? War, then, war
Open or understood, must be resolved.'
He spake; and, to confirm his words, outflew
Millions of flaming swords, drawn from the thighs
Of mighty Cherubim; the sudden blaze
Far round illumined Hell. Highly they raged
Against the Highest and fierce with graspèd arms
Clashed on their sounding shields the din of war,
Hurling defiance toward the vault of Heaven.
There stood a hill not far, whose griesly top
Belched fire and rowling smoke; the rest entire
Shon with a glossy scurf—undoubted sign
That in his womb was hid metallic ore,
The work of sulphur. Thither, winged with speed,
A numerous brigad hastened: as when bands
Of pioners, with spade and pickaxe armed,
Forerun the royal camp, to trench a field,
Or cast a rampart. Mammon led them on —
Mammon, the least erected Spirit that fell
From Heaven; for even in Heaven his looks and thoughts
Were always downward bent, admiring more
The riches of Heaven's pavement, trodden gold,
Than aught divine or holy else enjoyed
In vision beatific. By him first
Men also, and by his suggestion taught,
Ransacked the Centre, and with impious hands
Rifled the bowels of their mother Earth
For treasures better hid. Soon had his crew
Opened into the hill a spacious wound,
And digged out ribs of gold. Let none admire
That riches grow in Hell: that soil may best
Deserve the pretious bane. And here let those
Who boast in mortal things, and wondering tell
Of Babel, and the works of Memphian kings,
Learn how their greatest monuments of fame,
And strength, and art, are easily outdone
By Spirits reprobate, and in an hour
What in an age they, with incessant toil
And hands innumerable, scarce perform.
Nigh on the plain, in many cells prepared,
That underneath had veins of liquid fire
Sluiced from the lake, a second multitude
With wondrous art founded the massy ore,
Severing each kind, and scummed the bullion-dross.
A third as soon had formed within the ground
A various mould, and from the boiling cells
By strange conveyance filled each hollow nook;
As in an organ, from one blast of wind,
To many a row of pipes the sound-board breathes.
Anon out of the earth a fabric huge
Rose like an exhalation, with the sound
Of dulcet symphonies and voices sweet —
Built like a temple, where pilasters round
Were set, and Doric pillars overlaid
With golden architrave; nor did there want
Cornice or frieze, with bossy sculptures graven:
The roof was fretted gold. Not Babylon
Nor great Alcairo such magnificence
Equalled in all their glories, to inshrine
Belus or Serapis their gods, or seat
Their kings, when Ægypt with Assyria strove
In wealth and luxury. Th' ascending pile
Stood fixed her stately highth; and straight the doors,
Opening their brazen folds, discover, wide

Within, her ample spaces o'er the smooth
And level pavement: from the archèd roof,
Pendent by subtle magic, many a row
Of starry lamps and blazing cressets, fed
With naphtha and asphaltus, yielded light
As from a sky. The hasty multitude
Admiring entered; and the work some praise,
And some the Architect. His hand was known
In Heaven by many a towered structure high,
Where sceptered Angels held their residence,
And sat as Princes, whom the supreme King
Exalted to such power, and gave to rule,
Each in his hierarchy, the Orders bright.
Nor was his name unheard or unadored
In ancient Greece; and in Ausonian land
Men called him Mulciber; and how he fell
From Heaven they fabled, thrown by angry Jove
Sheer o'er the crystal battlements: from morn
To noon he fell, from noon to dewy eve,
A summer's day, and with the setting sun
Dropt from the zenith, like a falling star,
On Lemnos, the Ægæan isle. Thus they relate,
Erring; for he with this rebellious rout
Fell long before; nor aught availed him now
To have built in Heaven high towers; nor did he scape
By all his engines, but was headlong sent,
With his industrious crew, to build in Hell.
  Meanwhile the wingèd Haralds, by command
Of sovran power, with awful ceremony
And trumpet's sound, throughout the host proclaim
A solemn council forthwith to be held
At Pandæmonium, the high capital
Of Satan and his peers. Their summons called
From every band and squarèd regiment
By place or choice the worthiest: they anon
With hundreds and with thousands trooping came
Attended. All access was thronged; the gates
And porches wide, but chief the spacious hall
(Though like a covered field, where champions bold
Wont ride in armed, and at the Soldan's chair
Defied the best of Panim chivalry
To mortal combat, or carreer with lance),
Thick swarmed, both on the ground and in the air,
Brushed with the hiss of rustling wings. As bees
In spring-time, when the Sun with Taurus rides,
Pour forth their populous youth about the hive
In clusters; they among fresh dews and flowers
Fly to and fro, or on the smoothèd plank,
The suburb of their straw-built citadel,
New rubbed with balm, expatiate and confer
Their state-affairs: so thick the aerie crowd
Swarmed and were straitened; till, the signal given,
Behold a wonder! they but now who seemed
In bigness to surpass Earth's giant sons,
Now less than smallest dwarfs, in narrow room
Throng numberless — like that pygmean race
Beyond the Indian mount; or faery elves,
Whose midnight revels, by a forest-side
Or fountain, some belated peasant sees,
Or dreams he sees, while overhead the Moon
Sits arbitress, and nearer to the Earth
Wheels her pale course; they, on their mirth and dance
Intent, with jocond music charm his ear;
At once with joy and fear his heart rebounds.
Thus incorporeal Spirits to smallest forms
Reduced their shapes immense, and were at large,
Though without number still, amidst the hall
Of that infernal court. But far within,
And in their own dimensions like themselves,
The great Seraphic Lords and Cherubim
In close recess and secret conclave sat,
A thousand demi-gods on golden seats,
Frequent and full. After short silence then,
And summons read, the great consult began.

BOOK II

THE ARGUMENT

The consultation begun, Satan debates whether another battle be to be hazarded for the recovery of Heaven: some advise it, others dissuade. A third proposal is preferred, mentioned before by Satan — to search the truth of that prophecy or tradition in Heaven concerning another world, and another kind of creature, equal, or not much inferior, to themselves, about this time to be created. Their doubt who shall be sent on this difficult search: Satan, their chief, undertakes alone the voyage; is honoured and applauded. The council thus ended, the rest betake them several ways and to several imployments, as their inclinations lead them, to entertain the time till Satan return. He passes on his journey to Hell-gates; finds them shut, and who sat there to guard them; by whom at length they are opened, and discover to him the great gulf between Hell and Heaven. With what difficulty he passes through, directed by Chaos, the Power of that place, to the sight of this new World which he sought.

HIGH on a throne of royal state, which far
Outshon the wealth of Ormus and of Ind,

Or where the gorgeous East with richest hand
Showers on her kings barbaric pearl and gold,
Satan exalted sat, by merit raised
To that bad eminence; and, from despair
Thus high uplifted beyond hope, aspires
Beyond thus high, insatiate to pursue
Vain war with Heaven; and, by success untaught,
His proud imaginations thus displayed: —
'Powers and Dominions, Deities of Heaven! —
For, since no deep within her gulf can hold
Immortal vigour, though oppressed and fallen,
I give not Heaven for lost: from this descent
Celestial Virtues rising will appear
More glorious and more dread than from no fall,
And trust themselves to fear no second fate! —
Me though just right, and the fixed laws of Heaven,
Did first create your leader — next, free choice,
With what besides in council or in fight
Hath been achieved of merit — yet this loss,
Thus far at least recovered, hath much more
Established in a safe unenvied throne,
Yielded with full consent. The happier state
In Heaven, which follows dignity, might draw
Envy from each inferior; but who here
Will envy whom the highest place exposes
Foremost to stand against the Thunderer's aim
Your bulwark, and condemns to greatest share
Of endless pain? Where there is, then, no good
For which to strive, no strife can grow up there
From faction: for none sure will claim in Hell
Precedence; none whose portion is so small
Of present pain that with ambitious mind
Will covet more! With this advantage, then,
To union, and firm faith, and firm accord,
More than can be in Heaven, we now return
To claim our just inheritance of old,
Surer to prosper than prosperity
Could have assured us; and by what best way,
Whether of open war or covert guile,
We now debate. Who can advise may speak.'

He ceased; and next him Moloch, sceptred king,
Stood up — the strongest and the fiercest Spirit
That fought in Heaven, now fiercer by despair.
His trust was with the Eternal to be deemed
Equal in strength, and rather than be less
Cared not to be at all; with that care lost
Went all his fear: of God, or Hell, or worse,
He recked not, and these words thereafter spake: —
'My sentence is for open war. Of wiles,
More unexpert, I boast not: them let those
Contrive who need, or when they need; not now.
For, while they sit contriving, shall the rest —
Millions that stand in arms, and longing wait
The signal to ascend — sit lingering here,
Heaven's fugitives, and for their dwelling-place
Accept this dark opprobrious den of shame,
The prison of His tyranny who reigns
By our delay? No! let us rather choose,
Armed with Hell-flames and fury, all at once
O'er Heaven's high towers to force resistless way,
Turning our tortures into horrid arms
Against the Torturer; when, to meet the noise
Of his almighty engine, he shall hear
Infernal thunder, and, for lightning, see
Black fire and horror shot with equal rage
Among his Angels, and his throne itself
Mixed with Tartarean sulphur and strange fire,
His own invented torments. But perhaps
The way seems difficult, and steep to scale
With upright wing against a higher foe!
Let such bethink them, if the sleepy drench
Of that forgetful lake benumb not still,
That in our proper motion we ascend
Up to our native seat; descent and fall
To us is adverse. Who but felt of late,
When the fierce foe hung on our broken rear
Insulting, and pursued us through the Deep,
With what compulsion and laborious flight
We sunk thus low? The ascent is easy, then;
The event is feared! Should we again provoke
Our stronger, some worse way his wrath may find
To our destruction, if there be in Hell
Fear to be worse destroyed! What can be worse
Than to dwell here, driven out from bliss, condemned
In this abhorrèd deep to utter woe;
Where pain of unextinguishable fire

Must exercise us without hope of end
The vassals of his anger, when the scourge
Inexorably, and the torturing hour,
Calls us to penance? More destroyed than thus,
We should be quite abolished, and expire.
What fear we then? what doubt we to incense
His utmost ire? which, to the highth enraged,
Will either quite consume us, and reduce
To nothing this essential — happier far
Than miserable to have eternal being! —
Or, if our substance be indeed divine,
And cannot cease to be, we are at worst
On this side nothing; and by proof we feel
Our power sufficient to disturb his Heaven,
And with perpetual inroads to alarm,
Though inaccessible, his fatal Throne:
Which, if not victory, is yet revenge.'
He ended frowning, and his look denounced
Desperate revenge, and battle dangerous
To less than gods. On the other side up rose
Belial, in act more graceful and humane.
A fairer person lost not Heaven; he seemed
For dignity composed, and high exploit.
But all was false and hollow; though his tongue
Dropt manna, and could make the worse appear
The better reason, to perplex and dash
Maturest counsels: for his thoughts were low —
To vice industrious, but to nobler deeds
Timorous and slothful. Yet he pleased the ear,
And with persuasive accent thus began: —
'I should be much for open war, O Peers,
As not behind in hate, if what was urged
Main reason to persuade immediate war
Did not dissuade me most, and seem to cast
Ominous conjecture on the whole success;
When he who most excels in fact of arms,
In what he counsels and in what excels
Mistrustful, grounds his courage on despair
And utter dissolution, as the scope
Of all his aim, after some dire revenge.
First, what revenge? The towers of Heaven are filled
With armèd watch, that render all access
Impregnable: oft on the bordering Deep
Encamp their legions, or with obscure wing
Scout far and wide into the realm of Night,
Scorning surprise. Or, could we break our way
By force, and at our heels all Hell should rise
With blackest insurrection to confound
Heaven's purest light, yet our great Enemy,
All incorruptible, would on his throne
Sit unpolluted, and the ethereal mould,
Incapable of stain, would soon expel
Her mischief, and purge off the baser fire,
Victorious. Thus repulsed, our final hope
Is flat despair: we must exasperate
The Almighty Victor to spend all his rage;
And that must end us; that must be our cure —
To be no more. Sad cure! for who would lose,
Though full of pain, this intellectual being,
Those thoughts that wander through eternity,
To perish rather, swallowed up and lost
In the wide womb of uncreated Night,
Devoid of sense and motion? And who knows,
Let this be good, whether our angry Foe
Can give it, or will ever? How he can
Is doubtful; that he never will is sure.
Will He, so wise, let loose at once his ire,
Belike through impotence or unaware,
To give his enemies their wish, and end
Them in his anger whom his anger saves
To punish endless? "Wherefore cease we, then?"
Say they who counsel war; "we are decreed,
Reserved, and destined to eternal woe;
Whatever doing, what can we suffer more,
What can we suffer worse?" Is this, then, worst —
Thus sitting, thus consulting, thus in arms?
What when we fled amain, pursued and strook
With Heaven's afflicting thunder, and besought
The Deep to shelter us? This Hell then seemed
A refuge from those wounds. Or when we lay
Chained on the burning lake? That sure was worse.
What if the breath that kindled those grim fires,
Awaked, should blow them into sevenfold rage,
And plunge us in the flames; or from above
Should intermitted vengeance arm again
His red right hand to plague us? What if all
Her stores were opened, and this firmament
Of Hell should spout her cataracts of fire,
Impendent horrors, threatening hideous fall
One day upon our heads; while we perhaps,
Designing or exhorting glorious war,
Caught in a fiery tempest, shall be hurled,

Each on his rock transfixed, the sport and prey
Of racking whirlwinds, or for ever sunk
Under yon boiling ocean, wrapt in chains,
There to converse with everlasting groans,
Unrespited, unpitied, unreprieved,
Ages of hopeless end? This would be worse.
War, therefore, open or concealed, alike
My voice dissuades; for what can force or guile
With Him, or who deceive His mind, whose eye
Views all things at one view? He from Heaven's highth
All these our motions vain sees and derides,
Not more almighty to resist our might
Than wise to frustrate all our plots and wiles.
Shall we, then, live thus vile — the race of Heaven
Thus trampled, thus expelled to suffer here
Chains and these torments? Better these than worse,
By my advice; since fate inevitable
Subdues us, and omnipotent decree,
The Victor's will. To suffer, as to do,
Our strength is equal, nor the law unjust
That so ordains. This was at first resolved,
If we were wise, against so great a foe
Contending, and so doubtful what might fall.
I laugh when those who at the spear are bold
And ventrous, if that fail them, shrink, and fear
What yet they know must follow — to endure
Exile, or ignominy, or bonds, or pain,
The sentence of their conquerour. This is now
Our doom; which if we can sustain and bear,
Our Supreme Foe in time may much remit
His anger, and perhaps, thus far removed,
Not mind us not offending, satisfied
With what is punished; whence these raging fires
Will slacken, if his breath stir not their flames.
Our purer essence then will overcome
Their noxious vapour; or, inured, not feel;
Or, changed at length, and to the place conformed
In temper and in nature, will receive
Familiar the fierce heat; and, void of pain,
This horror will grow mild, this darkness light;
Besides what hope the never-ending flight
Of future days may bring, what chance, what change
Worth waiting — since our present lot appears
For happy though but ill, for ill not worst,
If we procure not to ourselves more woe.'
Thus Belial, with words clothed in reason's garb,
Counseled ignoble ease and peaceful sloth,
Not peace; and after him thus Mammon spake: —
'Either to disenthrone the King of Heaven
We war, if war be best, or to regain
Our own right lost. Him to unthrone we then
May hope, when everlasting Fate shall yield
To fickle Chance, and Chaos judge the strife.
The former, vain to hope, argues as vain
The latter; for what place can be for us
Within Heaven's bound, unless Heaven's Lord Supreme
We overpower? Suppose he should relent,
And publish grace to all, on promise made
Of new subjection; with what eyes could we
Stand in his presence humble, and receive
Strict laws imposed, to celebrate his throne
With warbled hymns, and to his Godhead sing
Forced Halleluiahs, while he lordly sits
Our envied sovran, and his altar breathes
Ambrosial odours and ambrosial flowers,
Our servile offerings? This must be our task
In Heaven, this our delight. How wearisome
Eternity so spent in worship paid
To whom we hate! Let us not then pursue,
By force impossible, by leave obtained
Unacceptable, though in Heaven, our state
Of splendid vassalage; but rather seek
Our own good from ourselves, and from our own
Live to ourselves, though in this vast recess,
Free and to none accountable, preferring
Hard liberty before the easy yoke
Of servile pomp. Our greatness will appear
Then most conspicuous when great things of small,
Useful of hurtful, prosperous of adverse,
We can create, and in what place soe'er
Thrive under evil, and work ease out of pain
Through labour and indurance. This deep world
Of darkness do we dread? How oft amidst
Thick clouds and dark doth Heaven's all-ruling Sire
Choose to reside, his glory unobscured,
And with the majesty of darkness round
Covers his throne, from whence deep thunders roar,

Mustering their rage, and Heaven resembles Hell!
As He our darkness, cannot we His light
Imitate when we please? This desart soil
Wants not her hidden lustre, gems and gold;
Nor want we skill or art, from whence to raise
Magnificence; and what can Heaven shew more?
Our torments also may, in length of time,
Become our elements, these piercing fires
As soft as now severe, our temper changed
Into their temper; which must needs remove
The sensible of pain. All things invite
To peaceful counsels, and the settled state
Of order, how in safety best we may
Compose our present evils, with regard
Of what we are and where, dismissing quite
All thoughts of war. Ye have what I advise.'
He scarce had finished, when such murmur filled
The assembly as when hollow rocks retain
The sound of blustering winds, which all night long
Had roused the sea, now with hoarse cadence lull
Seafaring men o'erwatched, whose bark by chance,
Or pinnace, anchors in a craggy bay
After the tempest. Such applause was heard
As Mammon ended, and his sentence pleased,
Advising peace: for such another field
They dreaded worse than Hell; so much the fear
Of thunder and the sword of Michaël
Wrought still within them; and no less desire
To found this nether empire, which might rise,
By policy and long process of time,
In emulation opposite to Heaven.
Which when Beëlzebub perceived — than whom,
Satan except, none higher sat — with grave
Aspect he rose, and in his rising seemed
A pillar of state. Deep on his front engraven
Deliberation sat, and public care;
And princely counsel in his face yet shon,
Majestic, though in ruin. Sage he stood,
With Atlantean shoulders, fit to bear
The weight of mightiest monarchies; his look
Drew audience and attention still as night
Or summer's noontide air, while thus he spake: —
'Thrones and Imperial Powers, Offspring of Heaven,
Ethereal Virtues! or these titles now
Must we renounce, and, changing style, be called
Princes of Hell? for so the popular vote
Inclines — here to continue, and build up here
A growing empire; doubtless! while we dream,
And know not that the King of Heaven hath doomed
This place our dungeon — not our safe retreat
Beyond his potent arm, to live exempt
From Heaven's high jurisdiction, in new league
Banded against his throne, but to remain
In strictest bondage, though thus far removed,
Under the inevitable curb, reserved
His captive multitude. For He, be sure,
In highth or depth, still first and last will reign
Sole king, and of his kingdom lose no part
By our revolt, but over Hell extend
His empire, and with iron sceptre rule
Us here, as with his golden those in Heaven.
What sit we then projecting peace and war?
War hath determined us and foiled with loss
Irreparable; terms of peace yet none
Vouchsafed or sought; for what peace will be given
To us enslaved, but custody severe,
And stripes and arbitrary punishment
Inflicted? and what peace can we return,
But, to our power, hostility and hate,
Untamed reluctance, and revenge, though slow,
Yet ever plotting how the Conquerour least
May reap his conquest, and may least rejoice
In doing what we most in suffering feel?
Nor will occasion want, nor shall we need
With dangerous expedition to invade
Heaven, whose high walls fear no assault or siege,
Or ambush from the Deep. What if we find
Some easier enterprise? There is a place
(If ancient and prophetic fame in Heaven
Err not) — another World, the happy seat
Of some new race, called Man, about this time
To be created like to us, though less
In power and excellence, but favoured more
Of Him who rules above; so was His will
Pronounced among the gods, and by an oath
That shook Heaven's whole circumference, confirmed.
Thither let us bend all our thoughts, to learn

What creatures there inhabit, of what mould
Or substance, how endued, and what their power
And where their weakness: how attempted best,
By force or subtlety. Though Heaven be shut,
And Heaven's high Arbitrator sit secure
In his own strength, this place may lie exposed,
The utmost border of his kingdom, left
To their defence who hold it: here, perhaps,
Some advantageous act may be achieved
By sudden onset — either with Hell-fire
To waste his whole creation, or possess
All as our own, and drive, as we are driven,
The puny habitants; or, if not drive,
Seduce them to our party, that their God
May prove their foe, and with repenting hand
Abolish his own works. This would surpass
Common revenge, and interrupt His joy
In our confusion, and our joy upraise
In his disturbance; when his darling sons,
Hurled headlong to partake with us, shall curse
Their frail original, and faded bliss —
Faded so soon! Advise if this be worth
Attempting, or to sit in darkness here
Hatching vain empires.' Thus Beëlzebub
Pleaded his devilish counsel — first devised
By Satan, and in part proposed: for whence,
But from the author of all ill, could spring
So deep a malice, to confound the race
Of mankind in one root, and Earth with Hell
To mingle and involve, done all to spite
The great Creator? But their spite still serves
His glory to augment. The bold design
Pleased highly those Infernal States, and joy
Sparkled in all their eyes: with full assent
They vote: whereat his speech he thus renews: —
'Well have ye judged, well ended long debate,
Synod of Gods, and, like to what ye are,
Great things resolved, which from the lowest deep
Will once more lift us up, in spite of fate,
Nearer our ancient Seat — perhaps in view
Of those bright confines, whence, with neighbouring arms,
And opportune excursion, we may chance
Re-enter Heaven; or else in some mild zone
Dwell, not unvisited of Heaven's fair light,
Secure, and at the brightening orient beam
Purge off this gloom: the soft delicious air,
To heal the scar of these corrosive fires,
Shall breathe her balm. But, first, whom shall we send
In search of this new World? whom shall we find
Sufficient? who shall tempt with wandering feet
The dark, unbottomed, infinite Abyss,
And through the palpable obscure find out
His uncouth way, or spread his aerie flight,
Upborne with indefatigable wings
Over the vast Abrupt, ere he arrive
The happy Isle? What strength, what art, can then
Suffice, or what evasion bear him safe
Through the strict senteries and stations thick
Of Angels watching round? Here he had need
All circumspection: and we now no less
Choice in our suffrage; for on whom we send
The weight of all, and our last hope, relies.'
This said, he sat; and expectation held
His look suspense, awaiting who appeared
To second, or oppose, or undertake
The perilous attempt. But all sat mute,
Pondering the danger with deep thoughts; and each
In other's countenance read his own dismay,
Astonished. None among the choice and prime
Of those Heaven-warring champions could be found
So hardy as to proffer or accept,
Alone, the dreadful voyage; till, at last,
Satan, whom now transcendent glory raised
Above his fellows, with monarchal pride
Conscious of highest worth, unmoved thus spake: —
'O Progeny of Heaven! Empyreal Thrones!
With reason hath deep silence and demur
Seized us, though undismayed. Long is the way
And hard, that out of Hell leads up to Light.
Our prison strong, this huge convex of fire,
Outrageous to devour, immures us round
Ninefold; and gates of burning adamant,
Barred over us, prohibit all egress.
These passed, if any pass, the void profound
Of unessential Night receives him next,
Wide-gaping, and with utter loss of being
Threatens him, plunged in that abortive gulf.
If thence he scape, into whatever world,

Or unknown region, what remains him less
Than unknown dangers, and as hard escape?
But I should ill become this throne, O Peers,
And this imperial sovranty, adorned
With splendour, armed with power, if aught proposed
And judged of public moment in the shape
Of difficulty or danger, could deter
Me from attempting. Wherefore do I assume
These royalties, and not refuse to reign,
Refusing to accept as great a share
Of hazard as of honour, due alike
To him who reigns, and so much to him due
Of hazard more as he above the rest
High honoured sits? Go, therefore, mighty Powers,
Terror of Heaven, though fallen; intend at home,
While here shall be our home, what best may ease
The present misery, and render Hell
More tolerable; if there be cure or charm
To respite, or deceive, or slack the pain
Of this ill mansion: intermit no watch
Against a wakeful Foe, while I abroad
Through all the coasts of dark destruction seek
Deliverance for us all. This enterprise
None shall partake with me.' Thus saying, rose
The Monarch, and prevented all reply;
Prudent lest, from his resolution raised,
Others among the chief might offer now,
Certain to be refused, what erst they feared,
And, so refused, might in opinion stand
His rivals, winning cheap the high repute
Which he through hazard huge must earn. But they
Dreaded not more the adventure than his voice
Forbidding; and at once with him they rose.
Their rising all at once was as the sound
Of thunder heard remote. Towards him they bend
With awful reverence prone, and as a God
Extol him equal to the Highest in Heaven.
Nor failed they to express how much they praised
That for the general safety he despised
His own: for neither do the Spirits damned
Lose all their virtue; lest bad men should boast
Their specious deeds on earth, which glory excites,
Or close ambition varnished o'er with zeal.
Thus they their doubtful consultations dark
Ended, rejoicing in thir matchless Chief:
As, when from mountain-tops the dusky clouds
Ascending, while the North-wind sleeps, o'erspread
Heaven's chearful face, the louring element
Scowls o'er the darkened landskip snow or shower,
If chance the radiant sun, with farewell sweet,
Extend his evening beam, the fields revive,
The birds their notes renew, and bleating herds
Attest their joy, that hill and valley rings.
O shame to men! Devil with devil damned
Firm concord holds; men only disagree
Of creatures rational, though under hope
Of heavenly grace, and, God proclaiming peace,
Yet live in hatred, enmity, and strife
Among themselves, and levy cruel wars
Wasting the earth, each other to destroy:
As if (which might induce us to accord)
Man had not hellish foes enow besides,
That day and night for his destruction wait!
The Stygian counsel thus dissolved; and forth
In order came the grand Infernal Peers:
Midst came their mighty Paramount, and seemed
Alone the Antagonist of Heaven, nor less
Than Hell's dread Emperor, with pomp supreme,
And god-like imitated state: him round
A globe of fiery Seraphim inclosed
With bright emblazonry, and horrent arms.
Then of their session ended they bid cry
With trumpet's regal sound the great result:
Toward the four winds four speedy Cherubim
Put to their mouths the sounding alchymy,
By harald's voice explained; the hollow Abyss
Heard far and wide, and all the host of Hell
With deafening shout returned them loud acclaim.
Thence more at ease their minds, and somwhat raised
By false presumptuous hope, the rangèd powers
Disband; and, wandering, each his several way

Pursues, as inclination or sad choice
Leads him perplexed, where he may likeliest find
Truce to his restless thoughts, and entertain
The irksome hours, till his great Chief return.
Part on the plain, or in the air sublime,
Upon the wing or in swift race contend,
As at the Olympian games or Pythian fields;
Part curb their fiery steeds, or shun the goal
With rapid wheels, or fronted brigads form:
As when, to warn proud cities, war appears
Waged in the troubled sky, and armies rush
To battle in the clouds; before each van
Prick forth the aerie knights, and couch their spears,
Till thickest legions close; with feats of arms
From either end of heaven the welkin burns.
Others, with vast Typhœan rage, more fell,
Rend up both rocks and hills, and ride the air
In whirlwind; Hell scarce holds the wild uproar: —
As when Alcides, from Œchalia crowned
With conquest, felt the envenomed robe, and tore
Through pain up by the roots Thessalian pines,
And Lichas from the top of Œta threw
Into the Euboic sea. Others more mild,
Retreated in a silent valley, sing
With notes angelical to many a harp
Their own heroic deeds, and hapless fall
By doom of battle, and complain that Fate
Free virtue should enthrall to Force or Chance.
Their song was partial; but the harmony
(What could it less when Spirits immortal sing?)
Suspended Hell, and took with ravishment
The thronging audience. In discourse more sweet
(For Eloquence the Soul, Song charms the Sense)
Others apart sat on a hill retired,
In thoughts more elevate, and reasoned high
Of Providence, Foreknowledge, Will, and Fate —
Fixed fate, free will, foreknowledge absolute —
And found no end, in wandering mazes lost.
Of good and evil much they argued then,
Of happiness and final misery,
Passion and apathy, and glory and shame:
Vain wisdom all, and false philosophie! —
Yet, with a pleasing sorcery, could charm
Pain for a while or anguish, and excite
Fallacious hope, or arm the obdurèd breast
With stubborn patience as with triple steel.
Another part, in squadrons and gross bands,
On bold adventure to discover wide
That dismal world, if any clime perhaps
Might yield them easier habitation, bend
Four ways their flying march, along the banks
Of four infernal rivers, that disgorge
Into the burning lake their baleful streams —
Abhorrèd Styx, the flood of deadly hate;
Sad Acheron of sorrow, black and deep;
Cocytus, named of lamentation loud
Heard on the rueful stream; fierce Phlegeton,
Whose waves of torrent fire inflame with rage.
Far off from these, a slow and silent stream,
Lethe, the river of oblivion, rowls
Her watery labyrinth, whereof who drinks
Forthwith his former state and being forgets —
Forgets both joy and grief, pleasure and pain.
Beyond this flood a frozen continent
Lies dark and wild, beat with perpetual storms
Of whirlwind and dire hail, which on firm land
Thaws not, but gathers heap, and ruin seems
Of ancient pile; all else deep snow and ice,
A gulf profound as that Serbonian bog
Betwixt Damiata and Mount Casius old
Where armies whole have sunk: the parching air
Burns frore, and cold performs the effect of fire.
Thither, by harpy-footed Furies haled,
At certain revolutions all the damned
Are brought; and feel by turns the bitter change
Of fierce extremes, extremes by change more fierce,
From beds of raging fire to starve in ice
Their soft ethereal warmth, and there to pine
Immovable, infixed, and frozen round,
Periods of time, — thence hurried back to fire.
They ferry over this Lethean sound
Both to and fro, their sorrow to augment,
And wish and struggle, as they pass, to reach
The tempting stream, with one small drop to lose
In sweet forgetfulness all pain and woe,
All in one moment, and so near the brink;

But Fate withstands, and, to oppose the attempt,
Medusa with Gorgonian terror guards
The ford, and of itself the water flies
All taste of living wight, as once it fled
The lip of Tantalus. Thus roving on
In confused march forlorn, the adventrous bands,
With shuddering horror pale, and eyes aghast,
Viewed first their lamentable lot, and found
No rest. Through many a dark and dreary vale
They passed, and many a region dolorous,
O'er many a frozen, many a fiery Alp,
Rocks, caves, lakes, fens, bogs, dens, and shades of death —
A universe of death, which God by curse
Created evil, for evil only good;
Where all life dies, death lives, and Nature breeds,
Perverse, all monstrous, all prodigious things,
Abominable, inutterable, and worse
Than fables yet have feigned or fear conceived,
Gorgons, and Hydras, and Chimæras dire.
Meanwhile the Adversary of God and Man,
Satan, with thoughts inflamed of highest design,
Puts on swift wings, and toward the gates of Hell
Explores his solitary flight: sometimes
He scours the right hand coast, somtimes the left;
Now shaves with level wing the Deep, then soars
Up to the fiery concave towering high.
As when far off at sea a fleet descried
Hangs in the clouds, by æquinoctial winds
Close sailing from Bengala, or the isles
Of Ternate and Tidore, whence merchants bring
Their spicy drugs; they on the trading flood,
Through the wide Ethiopian to the Cape,
Ply stemming nightly toward the pole: so seemed
Far off the flying Fiend. At last appear
Hell-bounds, high reaching to the horrid roof,
And thrice threefold the gates; three folds were brass,
Three iron, three of adamantine rock,
Impenetrable, impaled with circling fire,
Yet unconsumed. Before the gates there sat
On either side a formidable Shape.
The one seemed woman to the waist, and fair,
But ended foul in many a scaly fold,
Voluminous and vast — a serpent armed
With mortal sting. About her middle round
A cry of Hell-hounds never-ceasing barked
With wide Cerberean mouths full loud, and rung
A hideous peal; yet, when they list, would creep,
If ought disturbed their noise, into her womb,
And kennel there; yet there still barked and howled
Within unseen. Far less abhorred than these
Vexed Scylla, bathing in the sea that parts
Calabria from the hoarse Trinacrian shore;
Nor uglier follow the night-hag, when, called
In secret, riding through the air she comes,
Lured with the smell of infant blood, to dance
With Lapland witches, while the labouring moon
Eclipses at their charms. The other Shape —
If shape it might be called that shape had none
Distinguishable in member, joint, or limb;
Or substance might be called that shadow seemed,
For each seemed either — black it stood as Night,
Fierce as ten Furies, terrible as Hell,
And shook a dreadful dart: what seemed his head
The likeness of a kingly crown had on.
Satan was now at hand, and from his seat
The monster moving onward came as fast
With horrid strides; Hell trembled as he strode.
The undaunted Fiend what this might be admired —
Admired, not feared (God and his Son except,
Created thing naught valued he nor shunned),
And with disdainful look thus first began: —
'Whence and what art thou, execrable Shape,
That dar'st, though grim and terrible, advance
Thy miscreated front athwart my way
To yonder gates? Through them I mean to pass,

That be assured, without leave asked of thee.
Retire; or taste thy folly, and learn by proof,
Hell-born, not to contend with Spirits of Heaven.'
To whom the Goblin, full of wrauth, replied: —
'Art thou that Traitor-Angel, art thou he,
Who first broke peace in Heaven and faith, till then
Unbroken, and in proud rebellious arms
Drew after him the third part of Heaven's sons,
Conjured against the Highest — for which both thou
And they, outcast from God, are here condemned
To waste eternal days in woe and pain?
And reckon'st thou thyself with Spirits of Heaven,
Hell-doomed, and breath'st defiance here and scorn,
Where I reign king, and, to enrage thee more,
Thy king and lord? Back to thy punishment,
False fugitive; and to thy speed add wings,
Lest with a whip of scorpions I pursue
Thy lingering, or with one stroke of this dart
Strange horror seize thee, and pangs unfelt before.'
So spake the griesly Terror, and in shape,
So speaking and so threatening, grew tenfold
More dreadful and deform. On the other side,
Incensed with indignation, Satan stood
Unterrified, and like a comet burned,
That fires the length of Ophiuchus huge
In the arctic sky, and from his horrid hair
Shakes pestilence and war. Each at the head
Levelled his deadly aim; their fatal hands
No second stroke intend; and such a frown
Each cast at the other, as when two black clouds,
With Heaven's artillery fraught, come rattling on
Over the Caspian, then stand front to front
Hovering a space, till winds the signal blow
To join their dark encounter in mid-air.
So frowned the mighty combatants that Hell
Grew darker at their frown; so matched they stood;
For never but once more was either like
To meet so great a foe. And now great deeds
Had been achieved, whereof all Hell had rung,
Had not the snaky Sorceress, that sat
Fast by Hell-gate, and kept the fatal key,
Risen, and with hideous outcry rushed between.
'O father, what intends thy hand,' she cried,
'Against thy only son? What fury, O son,
Possesses thee to bend that mortal dart
Against thy father's head? And know'st for whom;
For him who sits above, and laughs the while
At thee, ordained his drudge to execute
Whate'er his wrauth, which He calls justice, bids —
His wrauth, which one day will destroy ye both!'
She spake, and at her words the hellish Pest
Forbore; then these to her Satan returned: —
'So strange thy outcry, and thy words so strange
Thou interposest, that my sudden hand,
Prevented, spares to tell thee yet by deeds
What it intends, till first I know of thee
What thing thou art, thus double-formed, and why,
In this infernal vale first met, thou call'st
Me father, and that fantasm call'st my son.
I know thee not, nor ever saw till now
Sight more detestable than him and thee.'
To whom thus the Portress of Hell-gate replied: —
'Hast thou forgot me, then; and do I seem
Now in thine eye so foul? — once deemed so fair
In Heaven, when at the assembly, and in sight
Of all the Seraphim with thee combined
In bold conspiracy against Heaven's King,
All on a sudden miserable pain
Surprised thee, dim thine eyes, and dizzy swum
In darkness, while thy head flames thick and fast
Threw forth, till on the left side opening wide,
Likest to thee in shape and countenance bright,
Then shining heavenly fair, a goddess armed,
Out of thy head I sprung. Amazement seized
All the host of Heaven; back they recoiled afraid
At first, and called me *Sin*, and for a sign
Portentous held me; but, familiar grown,

I pleased, and with attractive graces won
The most averse—thee chiefly, who full oft
Thyself in me thy perfect image viewing,
Becam'st enamoured; and such joy thou took'st
With me in secret that my womb conceived
A growing burden. Meanwhile war arose,
And fields were fought in Heaven: wherein remained
(For what could else?) to our Almighty Foe
Clear victory; to our part loss and rout
Through all the Empyrean. Down they fell,
Driven headlong from the pitch of Heaven, down
Into this Deep; and in the general fall
I also: at which time this powerful Key
Into my hands was given, with charge to keep
These gates for ever shut, which none can pass
Without my opening. Pensive here I sat
Alone; but long I sat not, till my womb,
Pregnant by thee, and now excessive grown,
Prodigious motion felt and rueful throes.
At last this odious offspring whom thou seest,
Thine own begotten, breaking violent way,
Tore through my entrails, that, with fear and pain
Distorted, all my nether shape thus grew
Transformed: but he my inbred enemy
Forth issued, brandishing his fatal dart,
Made to destroy. I fled, and cried out *Death!*
Hell trembled at the hideous name, and sighed
From all her caves, and back resounded *Death!*
I fled; but he pursued (though more, it seems,
Inflamed with lust than rage), and, swifter far,
Me overtook, his mother, all dismayed,
And, in embraces forcible and foul
Ingendering with me, of that rape begot
These yelling monsters, that with ceaseless cry
Surround me, as thou saw'st — hourly conceived
And hourly born, with sorrow infinite
To me: for, when they list, into the womb
That bred them they return, and howl, and gnaw
My bowels, their repast; then, bursting forth
Afresh, with conscious terrors vex me round,
That rest or intermission none I find.
Before mine eyes in opposition sits
Grim Death, my son and foe, who sets them on,
And me, his parent, would full soon devour
For want of other prey, but that he knows
His end with mine involved, and knows that I
Should prove a bitter morsel, and his bane,
Whenever that shall be: so Fate pronounced.
But thou, O father, I forewarn thee, shun
His deadly arrow; neither vainly hope
To be invulnerable in those bright arms,
Though tempered heavenly; for that mortal dint,
Save He who reigns above, none can resist.'

She finished; and the subtle Fiend his lore
Soon learned, now milder, and thus answered smooth: —

'Dear daughter — since thou claim'st me for thy sire,
And my fair son here show'st me, the dear pledge
Of dalliance had with thee in Heaven, and joys
Then sweet, now sad to mention, through dire change
Befallen us unforeseen, unthought-of — know,
I come no enemy, but to set free
From out this dark and dismal house of pain
Both him and thee, and all the Heavenly host
Of Spirits that, in our just pretences armed,
Fell with us from on high. From them I go
This uncouth errand sole, and one for all
Myself expose, with lonely steps to tread
The unfounded Deep, and through the void immense
To search, with wandering quest, a place foretold
Should be — and, by concurring signs, ere now
Created vast and round — a place of bliss
In the purlieus of Heaven; and therein placed
A race of upstart creatures, to supply
Perhaps our vacant room, though more removed,
Lest Heaven, surcharged with potent multitude,
Might hap to move new broils. Be this, or aught
Than this more secret, now designed, I haste

To know; and, this once known, shall soon return,
And bring ye to the place where thou and Death
Shall dwell at ease, and up and down unseen
Wing silently the buxom air, imbalmed
With odours. There ye shall be fed and filled
Immeasurably; all things shall be your prey.'
He ceased; for both seemed highly pleased, and Death
Grinned horrible a ghastly smile, to hear
His famine should be filled, and blessed his maw
Destined to that good hour. No less rejoiced
His mother bad, and thus bespake her Sire: —
'The key of this infernal Pit, by due
And by command of Heaven's all-powerful King,
I keep, by Him forbidden to unlock
These adamantine gates; against all force
Death ready stands to interpose his dart,
Fearless to be o'ermatched by living might.
But what owe I to His commands above,
Who hates me, and hath hither thrust me down
Into this gloom of Tartarus profound,
To sit in hateful office here confined,
Inhabitant of Heaven and heavenly-born —
Here in perpetual agony and pain,
With terrors and with clamours compassed round
Of mine own brood, that on my bowels feed?
Thou art my father, thou my author, thou
My being gav'st me; whom should I obey
But thee? whom follow? Thou wilt bring me soon
To that new world of light and bliss, among
The gods who live at ease, where I shall reign
At thy right hand voluptuous, as beseems
Thy daughter and thy darling, without end.'
Thus saying, from her side the fatal key,
Sad instrument of all our woe, she took;
And, toward the gate rowling her bestial train,
Forthwith the huge porcullis high up-drew,
Which, but herself, not all the Stygian Powers
Could once have moved; then in the key-hole turns
The intricate wards, and every bolt and bar
Of massy iron or solid rock with ease
Unfastens. On a sudden open fly,
With impetuous recoil and jarring sound,
The infernal doors, and on their hinges grate
Harsh thunder, that the lowest bottom shook
Of Erebus. She opened; but to shut
Excelled her power: the gates wide open stood,
That with extended wings a bannered host,
Under spread ensigns marching, might pass through
With horse and chariots ranked in loose array;
So wide they stood, and like a furnace-mouth
Cast forth redounding smoke and ruddy flame.
Before their eyes in sudden view appear
The secrets of the hoary Deep—a dark
Illimitable ocean, without bound,
Without dimension; where length, breadth, and highth,
And time, and place, are lost; where eldest Night
And Chaos, ancestors of Nature, hold
Eternal anarchy, amidst the noise
Of endless wars, and by confusion stand.
For Hot, Cold, Moist, and Dry, four champions fierce,
Strive here for maistrie, and to battle bring
Their embryon atoms: they around the flag
Of each his faction, in their several clans,
Light-armed or heavy, sharp, smooth, swift, or slow,
Swarm populous, unnumbered as the sands
Of Barca or Cyrene's torrid soil,
Levied to side with warring winds, and poise
Their lighter wings. To whom these most adhere
He rules a moment: Chaos umpire sits,
And by decision more imbroils the fray
By which he reigns: next him, high arbiter,
Chance governs all. Into this wild Abyss,
The womb of Nature, and perhaps her grave,
Of neither Sea, nor Shore, nor Air, nor Fire,
But all these in their pregnant causes mixed
Confusedly, and which thus must ever fight,
Unless the Almighty Maker them ordain
His dark materials to create more worlds —
Into this wild Abyss the wary Fiend
Stood on the brink of Hell and looked a while,
Pondering his voyage; for no narrow frith

He had to cross. Nor was his ear less pealed
With noises loud and ruinous (to compare
Great things with small) than when Bellona storms
With all her battering engines, bent to rase
Some capital city; or less than if this frame
Of heaven were falling, and these elements
In mutiny had from her axle torn
The steadfast Earth. At last his sail-broad vans
He spreads for flight, and, in the surging smoke
Uplifted, spurns the ground; thence many a league,
As in a cloudy chair, ascending rides
Audacious; but, that seat soon failing, meets
A vast vacuity. All unawares,
Fluttering his pennons vain, plumb-down he drops
Ten thousand fadom deep, and to this hour
Down had been falling, had not, by ill chance,
The strong rebuff of some tumultuous cloud,
Instinct with fire and nitre, hurried him
As many miles aloft. That fury stayed —
Quenched in a boggy Syrtis, neither sea,
Nor good dry land — nigh foundered, on he fares,
Treading the crude consistence, half on foot,
Half flying; behoves him now both oar and sail.
As when a gryfon through the wilderness
With wingèd course, o'er hill or moory dale,
Pursues the Arimaspian, who by stealth
Had from his wakeful custody purloined
The guarded gold; so eagerly the Fiend
O'er bog or steep, through strait, rough, dense, or rare,
With head, hands, wings, or feet, pursues his way,
And swims, or sinks, or wades, or creeps, or flies.
At length a universal hubbub wild
Of stunning sounds and voices all confused,
Borne through the hollow dark, assaults his ear
With loudest vehemence. Thither he plies
Undaunted, to meet there whatever Power
Or Spirit of the nethermost Abyss
Might in that noise reside, of whom to ask
Which way the nearest coast of darkness lies
Bordering on light; when straight behold the throne
Of *Chaos*, and his dark pavilion spread
Wide on the wasteful Deep! With him enthroned
Sat sable-vested *Night*, eldest of things,
The consort of his reign; and by them stood
Orcus and Ades, and the dreaded name
Of Demogorgon; Rumour next, and Chance,
And Tumult, and Confusion, all imbroiled,
And Discord with a thousand various mouths.
To whom Satan, turning boldly, thus: — 'Ye Powers
And Spirits of this nethermost Abyss,
Chaos and ancient Night, I come no spy
With purpose to explore or to disturb
The secrets of your realm; but, by constraint
Wandering this darksome desart, as my way
Lies through your spacious empire up to light,
Alone and without guide, half lost, I seek,
What readiest path leads where your gloomy bounds
Confine with Heaven; or, if some other place,
From your dominion won, the Ethereal King
Possesses lately, thither to arrive
I travel this profound. Direct my course:
Directed, no mean recompense it brings
To your behoof, if I that region lost,
All usurpation thence expelled, reduce
To her original darkness and your sway
(Which is my present journey), and once more
Erect the standard there of ancient Night.
Yours be the advantage all, mine the revenge!'
Thus Satan; and him thus the Anarch old,
With faltering speech and visage incomposed,
Answered: — 'I know thee, stranger, who thou art —
That mighty leading Angel, who of late
Made head against Heaven's King, though overthrown.
I saw and heard; for such a numerous host
Fled not in silence through the frighted Deep,
With ruin upon ruin, rout on rout,
Confusion worse confounded; and Heaven-gates
Poured out by millions her victorious bands,
Pursuing. I upon my frontiers here
Keep residence; if all I can will serve
That little which is left so to defend,
Encroached on still through our intestine broils
Weakening the sceptre of old Night: first, Hell,
Your dungeon, stretching far and wide beneath;

Now lately Heaven and Earth, another world
Hung o'er my realm, linked in a golden chain
To that side Heaven from whence your legions fell!
If that way be your walk, you have not far;
So much the nearer danger. Go, and speed;
Havoc, and spoil, and ruin, are my gain.'
He ceased; and Satan staid not to reply,
But, glad that now his sea should find a shore,
With fresh alacrity and force renewed
Springs upward, like a pyramid of fire,
Into the wild expanse, and through the shock
Of fighting elements, on all sides round
Environed, wins his way; harder beset
And more endangered than when Argo passed
Through Bosporus betwixt the justling rocks,
Or when Ulysses on the larboard shunned
Charybdis, and by the other Whirlpool steered.
So he with difficulty and labour hard
Moved on. With difficulty and labour he;
But, he once passed, soon after, when Man fell,
Strange alteration! Sin and Death amain,
Following his track (such was the will of Heaven)
Paved after him a broad and beaten way
Over the dark Abyss, whose boiling gulf
Tamely endured a bridge of wondrous length,
From Hell continued, reaching the utmost Orb
Of this frail World; by which the Spirits perverse
With easy intercourse pass to and fro
To tempt or punish mortals, except whom
God and good Angels guard by special grace.
But now at last the sacred influence
Of light appears, and from the walls of Heaven
Shoots far into the bosom of dim Night
A glimmering dawn. Here Nature first begins
Her fardest verge, and Chaos to retire,
As from her outmost works, a broken foe,
With tumult less and with less hostile din;
That Satan with less toil, and now with ease,
Wafts on the calmer wave by dubious light,
And, like a weather-beaten vessel, holds
Gladly the port, though shrouds and tackle torn;
Or in the emptier waste, resembling air,
Weighs his spread wings, at leisure to behold
Far off the empyreal Heaven, extended wide
In circuit, undetermined square or round,
With opal towers and battlements adorned
Of living sapphire, once his native seat,
And, fast by, hanging in a golden chain,
This pendent World, in bigness as a star
Of smallest magnitude close by the moon.
Thither, full fraught with mischievous revenge,
Accurst, and in a cursèd hour, he hies.

1667

LYRICS

George Herbert (1593–1633)

JORDAN

When first my verse of heavenly joys made mention,
Such was their lustre, they did so excel,
That I sought out quaint words and trim invention;
My thoughts began to burnish, sprout, and swell,
Curling with metaphors a plain intention,
Decking the sense as if it were to sell.

Thousands of notions in my brain did run,
Offering their service, if I were not sped:
I often blotted what I had begun —
This was not quick enough, and that was dead;
Nothing could seem too rich to clothe the sun,
Much less those joys which trample on his head.

As flames do work and wind when they ascend,
So did I weave myself into the sense;
But while I bustled I might hear a friend
Whisper, 'How wide is all this long pretence!
There is in love a sweetness ready penned;
Copy out only that, and save expense.'

1633

THE ALTAR

A BROKEN Altar, Lord, Thy servant rears,
Made of a heart, and cemented with tears,
Whose parts are as Thy hand did frame;
No workman's tool hath touched the same.
A heart alone
Is such a stone
As nothing but
Thy power doth cut.
Wherefore each part
Of my hard heart
Meets in this frame,
To praise thy name:
That, if I chance to hold my peace,
These stones to praise Thee may not cease.
O, let Thy blessèd Sacrifice be mine,
And sanctify this Altar to be Thine!

1633

EASTER WINGS

LORD, Who createdst man in wealth and store,
Though foolishly he lost the same,
Decaying more and more,
Till he became
Most poor:
With Thee
O let me rise,
As larks, harmoniously,
And sing this day Thy victories:
Then shall the fall further the flight in me.

My tender age in sorrow did begin;
And still with sicknesses and shame
Thou didst so punish sin,
That I became
Most thin.
With Thee
Let me combine,
And feel this day Thy victory;
For, if I imp my wing on thine,
Affliction shall advance the flight in me.

1633

VIRTUE

SWEET day, so cool, so calm, so bright,
The bridal of the earth and sky,
The dew shall weep thy fall to-night;
For thou must die.

Sweet rose, whose hue angry and brave
Bids the rash gazer wipe his eye,
Thy root is ever in its grave,
And thou must die.

Sweet spring, full of sweet days and roses,
A box where sweets compacted lie,
My music shows ye have your closes,
And all must die.

Only a sweet and virtuous soul,
Like seasoned timber, never gives;
But though the whole world turn to coal,
Then chiefly lives.

1633

THE QUIP

THE merry World did on a day
With his train-bands and mates agree
To meet together where I lay,
And all in sport to jeer at me.

First Beauty crept into a rose,
Which when I pluckt not, 'Sir,' said she,
'Tell me, I pray, whose hands are those?'
But Thou shalt answer, Lord, for me.

Then Money came, and chinking still,
'What tune is this, poor man?' said he;
'I heard in Music you had skill':
But Thou shalt answer, Lord, for me.

Then came brave Glory puffing by
In silks that whistled, who but he!
He scarce allowed me half an eye:
But Thou shalt answer, Lord, for me.

Then came quick Wit and Conversation,
And he would needs a comfort be,
And, to be short, make an oration:
But Thou shalt answer, Lord, for me.

Yet when the hour of Thy design
To answer these fine things shall come,
Speak not at large, say, I am Thine,
And then they have their answer home.

1633

THE COLLAR

I STRUCK the board, and cried, 'No more;
I will abroad.'
What, shall I ever sigh and pine?
My lines and life are free; free as the road,
Loose as the wind, as large as store.
Shall I be still in suit?
Have I no harvest but a thorn
To let me blood, and not restore
What I have lost with cordial fruit?
Sure there was wine

Before my sighs did dry it; there was corn
  Before my tears did drown it;
Is the year only lost to me?
  Have I no bays to crown it,
No flowers, no garlands gay? all blasted,
    All wasted?
  Not so, my heart; but there is fruit,
    And thou hast hands.
  Recover all thy sigh-blown age
On double pleasures; leave thy cold dispute
Of what is fit and not; forsake thy cage,
    Thy rope of sands
Which petty thoughts have made; and made to thee
  Good cable, to enforce and draw,
    And be thy law,
  While thou didst wink and wouldst not see.
    Away! take heed;
    I will abroad.
Call in thy death's head there, tie up thy fears;
    He that forbears
  To suit and serve his need
    Deserves his load.
But as I raved and grew more fierce and wild
    At every word,
  Methought I heard one calling, 'Child';
    And I replied, 'My Lord.'

1633

THE PULLEY

When God at first made man,
Having a glass of blessings standing by,
'Let us,' said He, 'pour on him all we can;
Let the world's riches, which dispersèd lie,
  Contract into a span.'

  So strength first made a way,
Then beauty flowed, then wisdom, honour, pleasure;
  When almost all was out, God made a stay,
Perceiving that, alone of all His treasure,
  Rest in the bottom lay.

  'For if I should,' said He,
'Bestow this jewel also on My creature,
  He would adore My gifts instead of Me,
And rest in Nature, not the God of Nature:
  So both should losers be.

  'Yet let him keep the rest,
But keep them with repining restlessness;
  Let him be rich and weary, that at least,
If goodness lead him not, yet weariness
  May toss him to My breast.'

1633

Thomas Carew (1598–1638)

A CRUEL MISTRESS

We read of kings and gods that kindly took
A pitcher filled with water from the brook;
But I have daily tendered without thanks
Rivers of tears that overflow their banks.
A slaughtered bull will appease angry Jove,
A horse the sun, a lamb the god of love,
But she disdains the spotless sacrifice
Of a pure heart, that at her altar lies.
Vesta is not displeased, if her chaste urn
Do with repairèd fuel ever burn;
But my saint frowns, though to her honoured name
I consecrate a never-dying flame.
The Assyrian king did none i' the furnace throw
But those that to his image did not bow;
With bended knees I daily worship her,
Yet she consumes her own idolater.
Of such a goddess no times leave record,
That burnt the temple where she was adored.

1640

DISDAIN RETURNED

He that loves a rosy cheek,
  Or a coral lip admires,
Or from star-like eyes doth seek
  Fuel to maintain his fires;
As old Time makes these decay,
So his flames must waste away.

But a smooth and steadfast mind,
  Gentle thoughts and calm desires,
Hearts with equal love combined,
  Kindle never-dying fires.
Where these are not, I despise
Lovely cheeks, or lips, or eyes.

No tears, Celia, now shall win
  My resolved heart to return;
I have searched thy soul within,
  And find naught but pride and scorn:
I have learned thy arts, and now
Can disdain as much as thou.

Some power in my revenge convey
That love to her I cast away.

1640

ASK ME NO MORE WHERE JOVE BESTOWS

Ask me no more where Jove bestows,
When June is past, the fading rose;
For in your beauty's orient deep
These flowers, as in their causes, sleep.

Ask me no more whither do stray
The golden atoms of the day;
For in pure love heaven did prepare
Those powders to enrich your hair.

Ask me no more whither doth haste
The nightingale, when May is past;
For in your sweet dividing throat
She winters, and keeps warm her note.

Ask me no more where those stars' light,
That downwards fall in dead of night;
For in your eyes they sit, and there
Fixèd become, as in their sphere.

Ask me no more if east or west
The phœnix builds her spicy nest;
For unto you at last she flies,
And in your fragrant bosom dies.

1640

Francis Quarles (1592–1644)

A GOOD-NIGHT

Close now thine eyes, and rest secure;
Thy soul is safe enough; thy body sure;
He that loves thee, he that keeps
And guards thee, never slumbers, never sleeps.
The smiling Conscience in a sleeping breast
Has only peace, has only rest;
The music and the mirth of kings,
Are all but very discords, when she sings:
Then close thine eyes and rest secure;
No sleep so sweet as thine, no rest so sure.

1632

SWEET PHOSPHOR, BRING THE DAY

Will 't ne'er be morning? Will that promised light
Ne'er break, and clear these clouds of night?
Sweet Phosphor, bring the day,
Whose conquering ray
May chase these fogs; sweet Phosphor, bring the day.
How long! how long shall these benighted eyes
Languish in shades, like feeble flies
Expecting Spring! How long shall darkness soil
The face of earth, and thus beguile
The souls of sprightful action; when will day
Begin to dawn, whose new-born ray
May gild the weathercocks of our devotion,
And give our unsouled souls new motion!
Sweet Phosphor, bring the day,
Thy light will fray
These horrid mists; sweet Phosphor, bring the day.

Let those have night that silly love t' immure
Their cloistered crimes, and sin secure;
Let those have night that blush to let men know
The baseness they ne'er blush to do;
Let those have night that love to take a nap
And loll in Ignorance's lap;
Let those whose eyes, like owls, abhor the light,
Let those have night that love the night!
Sweet Phosphor, bring the day;
How sad delay
Afflicts dull hopes! sweet Phosphor, bring the day.

Alas! my light-in-vain-expecting eyes
Can find no objects but what rise
From this poor mortal blaze, a dying spark
Of Vulcan's forge, whose flames are dark
And dangerous, a dull blue-burning light,
As melancholy as the night:
Here's all the suns that glisten in the sphere
Of earth: Ah me! what comfort's here?
Sweet Phosphor, bring the day;
Haste, haste away
Heaven's loitering lamp; sweet Phosphor, bring the day.

Blow, Ignorance: O thou, whose idle knee
Rocks earth into a lethargy,
And with thy sooty fingers hast bedight
The world's fair cheeks, blow, blow thy spite;
Since thou hast puffed our greater taper, do
Puff on, and out the lesser too;
If e'er that breath-exilèd flame return,
Thou hast not blown, as it will burn.
Sweet Phosphor, bring the day;
Light will repay
The wrongs of night; sweet Phosphor, bring the day.

1635

Robert Herrick (1591-1674)

THE ARGUMENT OF HIS BOOK

I SING of brooks, of blossoms, birds, and bowers;
Of April, May, of June, and July flowers.
I sing of May-poles, hock-carts, wassails, wakes;
Of bridegrooms, brides, and of their bridal-cakes.
I write of youth, of love, and have access
By these to sing of cleanly wantonness.
I sing of dews, of rains, and, piece by piece,
Of balm, of oil, of spice, and ambergris.
I sing of times trans-shifting; and I write
How roses first came red, and lilies white.
I write of groves, of twilights, and I sing
The court of Mab, and of the Fairy-king.
I write of hell; I sing, and ever shall,
Of heaven, and hope to have it after all.

1648

UPON THE LOSS OF HIS MISTRESSES

I HAVE lost, and lately, these
Many dainty mistresses:
Stately Julia, prime of all;
Sappho next, a principal;
Smooth Anthea, for a skin
White, and heaven-like crystalline;
Sweet Electra, and the choice
Myrha, for the lute and voice;
Next, Corinna, for her wit,
And the graceful use of it,
With Perilla: All are gone;
Only Herrick's left alone,
For to number sorrow by
Their departures hence, and die.

1648

DISCONTENTS IN DEVON

MORE discontents I never had
Since I was born than here,
Where I have been, and still am sad,
In this dull Devonshire.
Yet justly too I must confess,
I ne'er invented such
Ennobled numbers for the press,
Than where I loathed so much.

1648

CHERRY-RIPE

CHERRY-RIPE, ripe, ripe, I cry,
Full and fair ones; come and buy!
If so be you ask me where
They do grow, I answer, There,

Where my Julia's lips do smile;
There's the land, or cherry-isle,
Whose plantations fully show
All the year where cherries grow.

1648

DELIGHT IN DISORDER

A SWEET disorder in the dress
Kindles in clothes a wantonness.
A lawn about the shoulders thrown
Into a fine distraction;
An erring lace, which here and there
Enthrals the crimson stomacher;
A cuff neglectful, and thereby
Ribbands to flow confusedly;
A winning wave (deserving note)
In the tempestuous petticoat;
A careless shoe-string, in whose tie
I see a wild civility; —
Do more bewitch me than when art
Is too precise in every part.

1648

CORINNA'S GOING A MAYING

GET up, get up for shame, the blooming morn
Upon her wings presents the god unshorn.
  See how Aurora throws her fair
  Fresh-quilted colours through the air!
  Get up, sweet slug-a-bed, and see
  The dew-bespangling herb and tree.
Each flower has wept, and bowed toward the east,
Above an hour since; yet you not drest,
  Nay! not so much as out of bed?
  When all the birds have matins said,
  And sung their thankful hymns, 't is sin,
  Nay, profanation to keep in,
When as a thousand virgins on this day,
Spring, sooner than the lark, to fetch in May.

Rise, and put on your foliage, and be seen
To come forth, like the spring-time, fresh and green,
  And sweet as Flora. Take no care
  For jewels for your gown or hair.
  Fear not; the leaves will strew
  Gems in abundance upon you.
Besides, the childhood of the day has kept,
Against you come, some orient pearls unwept:
  Come, and receive them while the light
  Hangs on the dew-locks of the night,
  And Titan on the eastern hill
  Retires himself, or else stands still

Till you come forth. Wash, dress, be brief in praying:
Few beads are best when once we go a Maying.

Come, my Corinna, come; and coming, mark
How each field turns a street, each street a park
Made green, and trimmed with trees: see how
Devotion gives each house a bough
Or branch: each porch, each door, ere this,
An ark, a tabernacle is,
Made up of white-thorn neatly interwove;
As if here were those cooler shades of love.
Can such delights be in the street
And open fields, and we not see 't?
Come, we 'll abroad; and let 's obey
The proclamation made for May,
And sin no more, as we have done, by staying;
But, my Corinna, come, let 's go a Maying.

There 's not a budding boy, or girl, this day,
But is got up, and gone to bring in May.
A deal of youth, ere this, is come
Back, and with white-thorn laden home.
Some have dispatched their cakes and cream,
Before that we have left to dream:
And some have wept, and wooed, and plighted troth,
And chose their priest, ere we can cast off sloth.
Many a green-gown has been given;
Many a kiss, both odd and even;
Many a glance too has been sent
From out the eye, love's firmament;
Many a jest told of the keys betraying
This night, and locks picked, yet we 're not a Maying.

Come, let us go, while we are in our prime,
And take the harmless folly of the time.
We shall grow old apace, and die
Before we know our liberty.
Our life is short, and our days run
As fast away as does the sun;
And as a vapour, or a drop of rain,
Once lost, can ne'er be found again,
So when you or I are made
A fable, song, or fleeting shade,
All love, all liking, all delight,
Lies drowned with us in endless night.
Then while time serves, and we are but decaying;
Come, my Corinna, come, let's go a Maying.

1648

TO THE VIRGINS, TO MAKE MUCH OF TIME

Gather ye rose-buds while ye may,
Old time is still a flying,
And this same flower that smiles to-day,
To-morrow will be dying.

The glorious lamp of Heaven, the sun,
The higher he 's a getting,
The sooner will his race be run,
And nearer he 's to setting.

That age is best which is the first,
When youth and blood are warmer;
But being spent, the worse, and worst
Times still succeed the former.

Then be not coy, but use your time,
And while ye may, go marry;
For having lost but once your prime,
You may forever tarry.

1648

HIS POETRY HIS PILLAR

Only a little more
I have to write,
Then I 'll give o'er,
And bid the world good-night.

'T is but a flying minute
That I must stay,
Or linger in it;
And then I must away.

O time that cut'st down all!
And scarce leav'st here
Memorial
Of any men that were,

How many lie forgot
In vaults beneath,
And piece-meal rot
Without a fame in death!

Behold this living stone
I rear for me,
Ne'er to be thrown
Down, envious Time, by thee.

Pillars let some set up,
If so they please: —
Here is my hope,
And my Pyramides.

1648

HOW ROSES CAME RED

Roses at first were white,
Till they could not agree,

Whether my Sappho's breast,
Or they more white should be.

But being vanquished quite,
A blush their cheeks bespread;
Since which believe the rest,
The roses first came red.

1648

HOW VIOLETS CAME BLUE

Love on a day, wise poets tell,
Some time in wrangling spent,
Whether the violets should excel,
Or she, in sweetest scent.

But Venus having lost the day,
Poor girls, she fell on you,
And beat ye so, as some dare say,
Her blows did make ye blue.

1648

TO ANTHEA, WHO MAY COMMAND HIM ANYTHING

Bid me to live, and I will live
Thy protestant to be:
Or bid me love, and I will give
A loving heart to thee.

A heart as soft, a heart as kind,
A heart as sound and free
As in the whole world thou canst find,
That heart I 'll give to thee.

Bid that heart stay, and it will stay,
To honour thy decree:
Or bid it languish quite away,
And 't shall do so for thee.

Bid me to weep, and I will weep,
While I have eyes to see:
And, having none, yet I will keep
A heart to weep for thee.

Bid me despair, and I'll despair,
Under that cypress tree:
Or bid me die, and I will dare
E'en death, to die for thee.

Thou art my life, my love, my heart,
The very eyes of me,
And hast command of every part,
To live and die for thee.

1648

TO BACCHUS, A CANTICLE

Whither dost thou whorry me,
Bacchus, being full of thee?
This way, that way, that way, this,
Here and there a fresh love is.
That doth like me, this doth please;
Thus a thousand mistresses
I have now; yet I alone
Having all, injoy not one.

1648

HIS PRAYER TO BEN JONSON

When I a verse shall make,
Know I have prayèd thee
For old religion's sake,
Saint Ben, to aid me.

Make the way smooth for me,
When I, thy Herrick,
Honouring thee, on my knee
Offer my lyric.

Candles I'll give to thee,
And a new altar;
And thou, Saint Ben, shalt be
Writ in my Psalter.

1648

THE NIGHT PIECE, TO JULIA

Her eyes the glow-worm lend thee,
The shooting stars attend thee;
And the elves also,
Whose little eyes glow
Like the sparks of fire, befriend thee.

No Will-o'-th'-Wisp mis-light thee,
Nor snake or slow-worm bite thee;
But on, on thy way,
Not making a stay,
Since ghost there 's none to affright thee.

Let not the dark thee cumber,
What though the moon does slumber;
The stars of the night,
Will lend thee their light,
Like tapers clear without number.

Then, Julia, let me woo thee,
Thus, thus to come unto me;
And when I shall meet
Thy silvery feet,
My soul I 'll pour into thee.

1648

TO ELECTRA

I dare not ask a kiss;
I dare not beg a smile;
Lest having that or this,
I might grow proud the while.

Canticle liquefaction wassail

No, no, the utmost share
  Of my desire shall be,
Only to kiss that air
  That lately kissèd thee.

1648

UPON JULIA'S CLOTHES

Whenas in silks my Julia goes
Then, then, me thinks, how sweetly flows
The liquefaction of her clothes.

Next, when I cast mine eyes and see
That brave vibration, each way free,
O how that glittering taketh me!

1648

AN ODE FOR BEN JONSON

Ah Ben!
Say how or when
Shall we thy guests
Meet at those lyric feasts
Made at the Sun,
The Dog, the Triple Tun?
Where we such clusters had
As made us nobly wild, not mad;
And yet each verse of thine
Out-did the meat, out-did the frolic wine.

My Ben!
Or come again,
Or send to us
Thy wit's great over-plus;
But teach us yet
Wisely to husband it;
Lest we that talent spend,
And having once brought to an end
That precious stock, the store
Of such a wit the world should have no
  more.

1648

HIS PRAYER FOR ABSOLUTION

For those my unbaptizèd rimes,
Writ in my wild unhallowed times;
For every sentence, clause, and word,
That 's not inlaid with Thee, my Lord,
Forgive me, God, and blot each line
Out of my book, that is not thine.
But if, 'mongst all, thou find'st here one
Worthy thy benediction,
That one of all the rest shall be
The glory of my work and me.

1648

HIS LITANY TO THE HOLY SPIRIT

In the hour of my distress,
When temptations me oppress,
And when I my sins confess,
    Sweet Spirit, comfort me!

When I lie within my bed,
Sick in heart, and sick in head,
And with doubts discomforted,
    Sweet Spirit, comfort me!

When the house doth sigh and weep,
And the world is drowned in sleep,
Yet mine eyes the watch do keep,
    Sweet Spirit, comfort me!

When the artless doctor sees
No one hope, but of his fees,
And his skill runs on the lees,
    Sweet Spirit, comfort me!

When his potion and his pill,
His or none or little skill,
Meet for nothing, but to kill,
    Sweet Spirit, comfort me!

When the passing-bell doth toll,
And the furies in a shoal
Come to fright a parting soul,
    Sweet Spirit, comfort me!

When the tapers now burn blue,
And the comforters are few,
And that number more than true,
    Sweet Spirit, comfort me!

When the priest his last hath prayed,
And I nod to what is said,
'Cause my speech is now decayed,
    Sweet Spirit, comfort me!

When, God knows, I 'm tossed about,
Either with despair or doubt,
Yet before the glass be out,
    Sweet Spirit, comfort me!

When the Tempter me pursu'th
With the sins of all my youth,
And half damns me with untruth,
    Sweet Spirit, comfort me!

When the flames and hellish cries
Fright mine ears and fright mine eyes,
And all terrors me surprise,
    Sweet Spirit, comfort me!

When the judgment is revealed,
And that opened which was sealed,
When to thee I have appealed,
    Sweet Spirit, comfort me!

1648

A THANKSGIVING TO GOD FOR HIS HOUSE

Lord, thou hast given me a cell
Wherein to dwell,
A little house, whose humble roof
Is weather-proof,
Under the spars of which I lie
Both soft and dry;
Where thou, my chamber for to ward,
Hast set a guard
Of harmless thoughts, to watch and keep
Me while I sleep.
Low is my porch, as is my fate,
Both void of state;
And yet the threshold of my door
Is worn by the poor,
Who thither come, and freely get
Good words or meat.
Like as my parlour, so my hall
And kitchen 's small;
A little buttery, and therein
A little bin
Which keeps my little loaf of bread
Unchipped, unflead.
Some little sticks of thorn or briar
Make me a fire,
Close by whose living coal I sit,
And glow like it.
Lord, I confess too when I dine
The pulse is thine,
And all those other bits that be
There placed by thee;
The worts, the purslain, and the mess
Of water-cress,
Which of thy kindness thou hast sent;
And my content
Makes those, and my belovèd beet,
To be more sweet.
'T is thou that crown'st my glittering hearth
With guiltless mirth,
And giv'st me wassail bowls to drink,
Spiced to the brink.
Lord, 't is thy plenty-dropping hand
That soils my land,
And giv'st me, for my bushel sown,
Twice ten for one.
Thou mak'st my teeming hen to lay
Her egg each day,
Besides my healthful ewes to bear
Me twins each year;
The while the conduits of my kine
Run cream, for wine.
All these, and better, thou dost send
Me to this end,
That I should render, for my part,
A thankful heart;
Which, fired with incense, I resign
As wholly thine;
But the acceptance, that must be,
My Christ, by thee.

1648

THIS CROSS-TREE HERE

This cross-tree here
Doth Jesus bear,
Who sweetened first
The death accurst.
Here all things ready are, make haste, make haste away;
For long this work will be, and very short this day.
Why then, go on to act: here 's wonders to be done
Before the last least sand of thy ninth hour be run,
Or e'er dark clouds do dull or dead the mid-day's sun.
Act when thou wilt,
Blood will be spilt;
Pure balm that shall
Bring health to all.
Why then, begin
To pour first in
Some drops of wine,
In stead of brine,
To search the wound
So long unsound.
And when that 's done,
Let oil, next run,
To cure the sore
Sin made before.
And O! dear Christ,
E'en as thou di'st,
Look down and see
Us weep for thee.
And tho', love knows,
Thy dreadful woes
We cannot ease,
Yet do thou please,
Who mercy art,
T' accept each heart,
That gladly would
Help, if it could.
Mean while let me,
Beneath this tree,
This honour have,
To make my grave.

1648

ANOTHER GRACE FOR A CHILD

Here a little child I stand,
Heaving up my either hand:
Cold as paddocks though they be,

Here I lift them up to thee,
For a benison to fall
On our meat, and on us all. Amen.

1648

Sir John Suckling (1609–1642)

THE CONSTANT LOVER

Out upon it, I have loved
Three whole days together;
And am like to love three more,
If it prove fair weather.

Time shall moult away his wings,
Ere he shall discover
In the whole wide world again
Such a constant lover.

But the spite on 't is, no praise
Is due at all to me:
Love with me had made no stays,
Had it any been but she.

Had it any been but she,
And that very face,
There had been at least ere this
A dozen dozen in her place.

1659

WHY SO PALE AND WAN?

Why so pale and wan, fond lover?
Prithee, why so pale?
Will, when looking well can't move her,
Looking ill prevail?
Prithee, why so pale?

Why so dull and mute, young sinner?
Prithee, why so mute?
Will, when speaking well can't win her,
Saying nothing do 't?
Prithee, why so mute?

Quit, quit, for shame; this will not move:
This cannot take her.
If of herself she will not love,
Nothing can make her:
The devil take her!

1638

A BALLAD UPON A WEDDING

I tell thee, Dick, where I have been,
Where I the rarest things have seen;
O, things without compare!
Such sights again cannot be found
In any place on English ground,
Be it at wake or fair.

At Charing-Cross, hard by the way,
Where we (thou know'st) do sell our hay,
There is a house with stairs;
And there did I see coming down
Such folk, as are not in our town,
Forty at least, in pairs.

Amongst the rest, one pest'lent fine
(His beard no bigger, though, than thine)
Walked on before the rest:
Our landlord looks like nothing to him:
The king (God bless him) 't would undo him,
Should he go still so drest.

At Course-a-park, without all doubt,
He should have first been taken out
By all the maids i' the town:
Though lusty Roger there had been
Or little George upon the Green,
Or Vincent of the Crown.

But wot you what? the youth was going
To make an end of all his wooing;
The parson for him staid:
Yet by his leave (for all his haste)
He did not so much wish all past,
(Perchance) as did the maid.

The maid, (and thereby hangs a tale),
For such a maid no Whitsun-ale
Could ever yet produce:
No grape, that's kindly ripe, could be
So round, so plump, so soft as she,
Nor half so full of juice.

Her finger was so small, the ring
Would not stay on, which they did bring,
It was too wide a peck:
And to say truth (for out it must)
It looked like the great collar (just)
About our young colt's neck.

Her feet beneath her petticoat,
Like little mice, stole in and out,
As if they feared the light:
But oh! she dances such a way!
No sun upon an Easter-day
Is half so fine a sight.

Her cheeks so rare a white was on,
No daisy makes comparison;
(Who sees them is undone),
For streaks of red were mingled there,
Such as are on a Cath'rine pear,
(The side that's next the sun).

Her lips were red, and one was thin,
Compared to that was next her chin,
(Some bee had stung it newly);

But, (Dick) her eyes so guard her face,
I durst no more upon them gaze
Than on the sun in July.

Her mouth so small, when she does speak,
Thou 'dst swear her teeth her words did break,
That they might passage get;
But she so handled still the matter,
They came as good as ours, or better,
And are not spent a whit.

Passion o' me, how I run on!
There's that that would be thought upon,
I trow, besides the bride:
The business of the kitchen's great,
For it is fit that men should eat;
Nor was it there denied.

Just in the nick the cook knocked thrice,
And all the waiters in a trice
His summons did obey;
Each serving man, with dish in hand,
Marched boldly up, like our trained band,
Presented, and away.

When all the meat was on the table,
What man of knife, or teeth, was able
To stay to be entreated?
And this the very reason was,
Before the parson could say grace,
The company was seated.

Now hats fly off, and youths carouse;
Healths first go round, and then the house,
The bride's come thick and thick:
And when 't was named another's health,
Perhaps he made it hers by stealth;
And who could help it, Dick?

O' the sudden up they rise and dance;
Then sit again, and sigh, and glance;
Then dance again, and kiss:
Thus several ways the time did pass,
Till every woman wished her place,
And every man wished his.

By this time all were stolen aside
To counsel and undress the bride:
But that he must not know:
But yet 't was thought he guessed her mind,
And did not mean to stay behind
Above an hour or so.

When in he came, Dick, there she lay
Like new-fall'n snow melting away
('T was time, I trow, to part):
Kisses were now the only stay
Which soon she gave, as who would say,
Good boy! with all my heart.

1640

James Shirley (1596–1666)

NO ARMOUR AGAINST FATE

The glories of our blood and state
Are shadows, not substantial things;
There is no armour against fate;
Death lays his icy hand on kings:
Sceptre and crown
Must tumble down,
And in the dust be equal made
With the poor crookèd scythe and spade.

Some men with swords may reap the field,
And plant fresh laurels where they kill;
But their strong nerves at last must yield;
They tame but one another still:
Early or late
They stoop to fate
And must give up their murmuring breath
When they, pale captives, creep to Death.

The garlands wither on your brow.
Then boast no more your mighty deeds;
Upon Death's purple altar now
See where the victor-victim bleeds:
Your heads must come
To the cold tomb;
Only the actions of the just
Smell sweet, and blossom in their dust.

1659

poet of Cath. ecstatic + myst worship of Donne

Richard Crashaw (1613?–1649)

WISHES TO HIS (SUPPOSED) MISTRESS

Whoe'er she be,
That not impossible She
That shall command my heart and me;

Where'er she lie,
Locked up from mortal eye,
In shady leaves of destiny:

Till that ripe birth
Of studied fate stand forth,
And teach her fair steps tread our earth;

Till that divine
Idea take a shrine
Of crystal flesh, through which to shine:

Meet you her, my Wishes,
Bespeak her to my blisses,
And be ye called my absent kisses.

I wish her, beauty,
That owes not all its duty
To gaudy tire, or glist'ring shoe-tie, —

Something more than
Taffeta or tissue can,
Or rampant feather, or rich fan, —

More than the spoil
Of shop, or silkworm's toil,
Or a bought blush, or a set smile;

A face that's best
By its own beauty dressed,
And can alone command the rest, —

A face made up
Out of no other shop
Than what Nature's white hand sets ope;

A cheek where youth
And blood, with pen of truth
Write what their reader sweetly ru'th, —

A cheek where grows
More than a morning rose,
Which to no box his being owes;

Lips, where all day
A lover's kiss may play,
Yet carry nothing thence away;

Looks that oppress
Their richest tires, but dress
Themselves in simple nakedness;

Eyes, that displace
The neighbour diamond, and out-face
That sunshine by their own sweet grace;

Tresses, that wear
Jewels, but to declare
How much themselves more precious are, —

Whose native ray
Can tame the wanton day
Of gems that in their bright shades play, —

Each ruby there
Or pearl that dare appear,
Be its own blush, be its own tear;

A well-tamed heart
For whose more noble smart
Love may be long choosing a dart;

Eyes that bestow
Full quivers on Love's bow,
Yet pay less arrows than they owe;

Smiles that can warm
The blood, yet teach a charm,
That chastity shall take no harm;

Blushes that bin
The burnish of no sin,
Nor flames of aught too hot within;

Joys that confess
Virtue their mistress,
And have no other head to dress. . . .

Days that need borrow
No part of their good morrow
From a fore-spent night of sorrow;

Days that, in spite
Of darkness, by the light
Of a clear mind are day all night;

Nights sweet as they,
Made short by lovers' play,
Yet long by the absence of the day;

Life that dares send
A challenge to his end,
And when it comes say — Welcome, friend!

Sidneian showers
Of sweet discourse, whose powers
Can crown old Winter's head with flowers;

Soft silken hours,
Open suns, shady bowers;
'Bove all, nothing within that lowers;

Whate'er delight
Can make Day's forehead bright,
Or give down to the wings of Night.

In her whole frame,
Have Nature all the name,
Art and ornament the shame!

Her flattery
Picture and poesy:
Her counsel her own virtue be.

I wish her store
Of worth may leave her poor
Of wishes; and I wish — no more.

Now, if Time knows
That Her, whose radiant brows
Weave them a garland of my vows,

Her whose just bays
My future hopes can raise
A trophy to her present praise,

Her that dares be
What these lines wish to see:
I seek no further — it is She.

'T is She, and here
Lo! I unclothe and clear
My Wishes' cloudy character.

May she enjoy it
Whose merit dare apply it
But Modesty dares still deny it!

Such worth as this is
Shall fix my flying wishes,
And determine them to kisses.

Let her full glory,
My fancies! fly before ye!
Be you my fictions, but her Story!

1646

Edmund Waller (1606–1687)

ON A GIRDLE

That which her slender waist confined,
Shall now my joyful temples bind;
No monarch but would give his crown,
His arms might do what this has done.

It was my heaven's extremest sphere,
The pale which held that lovely deer.
My joy, my grief, my hope, my love,
Did all within this circle move!

A narrow compass! and yet there
Dwelt all that's good, and all that's fair;
Give me but what this riband bound,
Take all the rest the sun goes round.

1645

GO, LOVELY ROSE

Go, lovely Rose!
Tell her that wastes her time and me
That now she knows,
When I resemble her to thee,
How sweet and fair she seems to be.

Tell her that's young,
And shuns to have her graces spied,
That hadst thou sprung
In deserts, where no men abide,
Thou must have uncommended died.

Small is the worth
Of beauty from the light retired;
Bid her come forth,
Suffer herself to be desired,
And not blush so to be admired.

Then die! that she
The common fate of all things rare
May read in thee;
How small a part of time they share,
That are so wondrous sweet and fair!

1645

Richard Lovelace (1618–1658)

TO LUCASTA, ON GOING TO THE WARS

Tell me not, Sweet, I am unkind,
That from the nunnery
Of thy chaste breast and quiet mind
To war and arms I fly.

True, a new mistress now I chase,
The first foe in the field;
And with a stronger faith embrace
A sword, a horse, a shield.

Yet this inconstancy is such
As you too shall adore:
I could not love thee, dear, so much,
Loved I not honour more.

1649

TO ALTHEA, FROM PRISON

When Love with unconfinèd wings
Hovers within my gates,
And my divine Althea brings
To whisper at the grates;
When I lie tangled in her hair
And fettered to her eye,
The birds that wanton in the air
Know no such liberty.

When flowing cups run swiftly round
With no allaying Thames,
Our careless heads with roses bound,
Our hearts with loyal flames;
When thirsty grief in wine we steep,
When healths and draughts go free,
Fishes that tipple in the deep
Know no such liberty.

When, like committed linnets, I
With shriller throat shall sing
The sweetness, mercy, majesty,
And glories of my king;
When I shall voice aloud how good
He is, how great should be,
Enlargèd winds, that curl the flood,
Know no such liberty.

Stone walls do not a prison make,
Nor iron bars a cage;
Minds innocent and quiet take
That for an hermitage;
If I have freedom in my love
And in my soul am free,
Angels alone, that soar above,
Enjoy such liberty.

1649

Andrew Marvell (1621–1678)

TO HIS COY MISTRESS

Had we but world enough, and time,
This coyness, lady, were no crime.
We would sit down, and think which way
To walk, and pass our long love's day.
Thou by the Indian Ganges' side
Shouldst rubies find: I by the tide
Of Humber would complain. I would
Love you ten years before the flood,
And you should, if you please, refuse
Till the conversion of the Jews;
My vegetable love should grow
Vaster than empires and more slow;
An hundred years should go to praise
Thine eyes, and on thy forehead gaze;
Two hundred to adore each breast,
But thirty thousand to the rest;
An age at least to every part,
And the last age should show your heart.
For, lady, you deserve this state,
Nor would I love at lower rate.
  But at my back I always hear
Time's wingèd chariot hurrying near,
And yonder all before us lie
Deserts of vast eternity.
Thy beauty shall no more be found,
Nor, in thy marble vault, shall sound
My echoing song; then worms shall try
That long preserved virginity,
And your quaint honour turn to dust,
And into ashes all my lust:
The grave 's a fine and private place,
But none, I think, do there embrace.
  Now therefore, while the youthful hue
Sits on thy skin like morning dew,
And while thy willing soul transpires
At every pore with instant fires,
Now let us sport us while we may,
And now, like amorous birds of prey,
Rather at once our time devour,
Than languish in his slow-chapt power.
Let us roll all our strength and all
Our sweetness up into one ball,
And tear our pleasures with rough strife,
Thorough the iron gates of life;
Thus, though we cannot make our sun
Stand still, yet we will make him run.

1681

THE GARDEN

How vainly men themselves amaze,
To win the palm, the oak, or bays;
And their incessant labours see
Crowned from some single herb, or tree,
Whose short and narrow-vergèd shade
Does prudently their toils upbraid;
While all the flowers and trees do close,
To weave the garlands of repose!

Fair Quiet, have I found thee here,
And Innocence, thy sister dear?
Mistaken long, I sought you then
In busy companies of men.
Your sacred plants, if here below,
Only among the plants will grow;
Society is all but rude
To this delicious solitude.

No white nor red was ever seen
So amorous as this lovely green.
Fond lovers, cruel as their flame,
Cut in these trees their mistress' name:
Little, alas! they know or heed,
How far these beauties hers exceed!
Fair trees! wheres'e'r your bark I wound,
No name shall but your own be found.

When we have run our passion's heat,
Love hither makes his best retreat.
The gods, that mortal beauty chase,
Still in a tree did end their race;
Apollo hunted Daphne so,
Only that she might laurel grow;
And Pan did after Syrinx speed,
Not as a nymph, but for a reed.

What wondrous life is this I lead!
Ripe apples drop about my head;
The luscious clusters of the vine
Upon my mouth do crush their wine;
The nectarine, and curious peach,
Into my hands themselves do reach;
Stumbling on melons, as I pass,
Insnared with flowers, I fall on grass.

Meanwhile the mind, from pleasure less,
Withdraws into its happiness;
The mind, that ocean where each kind
Does straight its own resemblance find;
Yet it creates, transcending these,
Far other worlds, and other seas,
Annihilating all that 's made
To a green thought in a green shade.

Here at the fountain's sliding foot,
Or at some fruit-tree's mossy root,
Casting the body's vest aside,
My soul into the boughs does glide:
There, like a bird, it sits and sings,
Then whets and combs its silver wings,
And, till prepared for longer flight,
Waves in its plumes the various light.

Such was that happy garden-state,
While man there walked without a mate:
After a place so pure and sweet,
What other help could yet be meet!

But 't was beyond a mortal's share
To wander solitary there:
Two paradises 't were in one,
To live in paradise alone.

How well the skilful gardener drew
Of flowers, and herbs, this dial new;
Where, from above, the milder sun
Does through a fragrant zodiac run,
And, as it works, the industrious bee
Computes its time as well as we!
How could such sweet and wholesome hours
Be reckoned but with herbs and flowers?

1681

Henry Vaughan (1621?–1695)

THE RETREAT

HAPPY those early days, when I
Shined in my angel-infancy!
Before I understood this place
Appointed for my second race,
Or taught my soul to fancy ought
But a white, celestial thought;
When yet I had not walked above
A mile or two from my first love,
And looking back, at that short space,
Could see a glimpse of his bright face;
When on some gilded cloud or flower
My gazing soul would dwell an hour,
And in those weaker glories spy
Some shadows of eternity;
Before I taught my tongue to wound
My conscience with a sinful sound,
Or had the black art to dispense
A several sin to every sense,
But felt through all this fleshly dress
Bright shoots of everlastingness.
O how I long to travel back,
And tread again that ancient track!
That I might once more reach that plain,
Where first I left my glorious train;
From whence the enlightened spirit sees
That shady City of Palm trees.
But ah! my soul with too much stay
Is drunk, and staggers in the way!
Some men a forward motion love,
But I by backward steps would move;
And, when this dust falls to the urn,
In that state I came, return.

1650

THE WORLD

I SAW Eternity the other night,
Like a great Ring of pure and endless light,
All calm, as it was bright;
And round beneath it, Time, in hours, days, years,
Driven by the spheres,
Like a vast shadow moved, in which the world
And all her train were hurled.
The doting lover in his quaintest strain
Did there complain;
Near him, his lute, his fancy, and his flights,
Wit's sour delights;
With gloves, and knots the silly snares of pleasure,
Yet his dear treasure,
All scattered lay, while he his eyes did pour
Upon a flower.

The darksome statesman, hung with weights and woe,
Like a thick midnight-fog, moved there so slow,
He did nor stay, nor go;
Condemning thoughts (like sad eclipses) scowl
Upon his soul,
And clouds of crying witnesses without
Pursued him with one shout.
Yet digged the mole, and lest his ways be found,
Worked under ground,
Where he did clutch his prey. But one did see
That policy;
Churches and altars fed him; perjuries
Were gnats and flies;
It rained about him blood and tears; but he
Drank them as free.

The fearful miser on a heap of rust
Sat pining all his life there, did scarce trust
His own hands with the dust,
Yet would not place one piece above, but lives
In fear of thieves.
Thousands there were as frantic as himself,
And hugged each one his pelf;
The downright epicure placed heaven in sense,
And scorned pretence;
While others, slipt into a wide excess,
Said little less;
The weaker sort slight, trivial wares inslave,
Who think them brave,
And poor, despisèd Truth sat counting by
Their victory.

Yet some, who all this while did weep and sing,
And sing and weep, soared up into the Ring;
But most would use no wing.

O fools, said I, thus to prefer dark night
Before true light!
To live in grots and caves, and hate the day
Because it shows the way,
The way, which from this dead and dark abode
Leads up to God,
A way where you might tread the sun, and be
More bright than he!
But, as I did their madness so discuss,
One whispered thus,
'This Ring the Bridegroom did for none provide,
But for his bride.'

1650

DEPARTED FRIENDS

They are all gone into the world of light!
And I alone sit lingering here!
Their very memory is fair and bright,
And my sad thoughts doth clear.

It glows and glitters in my cloudy breast
Like stars upon some gloomy grove,
Or those faint beams in which this hill is drest
After the sun's remove.

I see them walking in an air of glory,
Whose light doth trample on my days;
My days, which are at best but dull and hoary,
Mere glimmering and decays.

O holy Hope! and high Humility!
High as the heavens above;
These are your walks, and you have shewed them me,
To kindle my cold love.

Dear, beauteous death! the jewel of the just!
Shining no where but in the dark;
What mysteries do lie beyond thy dust,
Could man outlook that mark!

He that hath found some fledged bird's nest may know
At first sight if the bird be flown;
But what fair dell or grove he sings in now,
That is to him unknown.

And yet, as angels in some brighter dreams
Call to the soul when man doth sleep,
So some strange thoughts transcend our wonted themes,
And into glory peep.

If a star were confined into a tomb,
Her captive flames must needs burn there;
But when the hand that locked her up gives room,
She'll shine through all the sphere.

O Father of eternal life, and all
Created glories under Thee!
Resume Thy spirit from this world of thrall
Into true liberty!

Either disperse these mists, which blot and fill
My perspective still as they pass;
Or else remove me hence unto that hill,
Where I shall need no glass.

1655

PROSE

Sir Thomas Browne (1605–1682)

RELIGIO MEDICI

THE SECOND PART

Now for [the] virtue of Charity, without which faith is a mere notion, and of no existence, I have ever endeavoured to nourish the merciful disposition and humane inclination I borrowed from my parents, and regulate it to the written and prescribed laws of Charity. And if I hold the true anatomy of myself, I am delineated and naturally framed to such a piece of virtue; for I am of a constitution so general, that it consorts and sympathiseth with all things. I have no antipathy, or rather idiosyncrasy, in diet, humor, air, anything. I wonder not at the French for their dishes of frogs, snails, and toadstools, nor at the Jews for locusts and grasshoppers; but being amongst them, make them my common viands, and I find they agree with my stomach as well as theirs. I could digest a salad gathered in a churchyard, as well as in a garden. I cannot start at the presence of a serpent, scorpion, lizard, or salamander: at the sight of a toad or viper, I find in me no desire to take up a stone to destroy them. I feel not in my self those common antipathies that I can discover in others: those national repugnances do not touch me, nor do I behold with prejudice the French, Italian, Spaniard, or Dutch: but where I find their actions in balance with my countrymen's, I honour, love, and embrace them in the same degree. I was born in the eighth climate, but seem for to be framed and constellated unto all. I am no plant that will not prosper out of a garden. All places, all airs, make unto me one country; I am in England every where, and under any meridian. I have been shipwrecked, yet am not enemy with the sea or winds; I can study, play, or sleep in a tempest. In brief, I am averse from nothing: my conscience would give me the lie if I should say I absolutely detest or hate any essence but the devil; or so at least abhor any thing, but that we might come to composition. If there be any among those common objects of hatred I do contemn and laugh at, it is that great enemy of reason, virtue and religion, the multitude: that numerous piece of monstrosity, which, taken asunder, seem men, and the reasonable creatures of God; but, confused together, make but one great beast, and a monstrosity more prodigious than Hydra. It is no breach of charity to call these fools; it is the style all holy writers have afforded them, set down by Solomon in canonical Scripture, and a point of our faith to believe so. Neither in the name of Multitude do I only include the base and minor sort of people; there is a rabble even amongst the gentry, a sort of plebeian heads, whose fancy moves with the same wheel as these; men in the same level with mechanics, though their fortunes do somewhat gild their infirmities, and their purses compound for their follies. But as, in casting account, three or four men together come short in account of one man placed by himself below them; so neither are a troop of these ignorant Doradoes of that true esteem and value, as many a forlorn person, whose condition doth place him below their feet. Let us speak like politicians: there is a nobility without heraldry, a natural dignity, whereby one man is ranked with another, another filed before him, according to the quality of his desert, and pre-eminence of his good parts. Though the corruption of these times and the bias of present practice wheel another way, thus it was in the first and primitive commonwealths, and is yet in the integrity and cradle of well-ordered polities, till corruption getteth ground; rudei desires labouring after that which wiser generations contemn, every one having a liberty to amass and heap up riches, and they a license or faculty to do or purchase anything.

This general and indifferent temper of mine doth more nearly dispose me to this noble virtue. It is a happiness to be born and framed unto virtue, and to grow up from the seeds of nature, rather than the inoculation and forced graffs of education; yet if we are directed only by our particular natures, and regulate our inclinations by no higher rule than that of our reasons, we are but moralists; divinity will still call us heathens. Therefore this great work of charity must have other motives, ends, and impulsions. I give no alms only to satisfy the hunger of my brother, but to fulfil and accomplish the will and command of my God: I draw not my purse for his sake that demands it, but His that enjoined it: I relieve no man upon the rhetoric of his miseries, nor to content mine own commiserating disposition; for this is still but moral charity, and an act that oweth more to passion than reason. He that relieves another upon the bare suggestion and bowels of pity, doth not this, so much for his sake as for his own; for by compassion we make others' misery our own, and so, by relieving them, we relieve our selves also. It is as erroneous a conceit to redress other men's misfortunes upon the common considerations of merciful natures, that it may be one day our own case; for this is a sinister and politic kind of charity, whereby we seem to bespeak the pities of men in the like occasions. And truly I have observed that those professed eleemosynaries, though in a crowd or multitude, do yet direct and place their petitions on a few and selected persons: there is surely a physiognomy, which those experienced and master mendicants observe, whereby they instantly discover a merciful aspect, and will single out a face wherein they spy the signatures and marks of mercy. For there are mystically in our faces certain characters which carry in them the motto of our souls, wherein he that cannot read A. B. C. may read our natures. I hold moreover that there is a phytognomy, or physiognomy, not only of men, but of plants and vegetables; and in every one of them some outward figures which hang as signs or bushes of their inward forms. The finger of God hath left an inscription upon all His works, not graphical or composed of letters, but of their several forms, constitutions, parts, and operations, which, aptly joined together, do make one word that doth express their natures. By these letters God calls the stars by their names; and by this alphabet Adam assigned to every creature a name peculiar to its nature. Now there are, besides these characters in our faces, certain mystical figures in our hands, which I dare not call mere dashes, strokes *à la volée*, or at random, because delineated by a pencil that never works in vain; and hereof I take more particular notice, because I carry that in mine own hand which I could never read of nor discover in another. Aristotle, I confess, in his acute and singular book of *Physiognomy*, hath made no mention of Chiromancy; yet I believe the Egyptians, who were nearer addicted to those abstruse and mystical sciences, had a knowledge therein, to which those vagabond and counterfeit Egyptians did after pretend, and perhaps retained a few corrupted principles, which sometimes might verify their prognostics.

It is the common wonder of all men, how among so many millions of faces, there should be none alike: now contrary, I wonder as much how there should be any. He that shall consider how many thousand several words have been carelessly and without study composed out of twenty-four letters; withal, how many hundred lines there are to be drawn in the fabric of one man, shall easily find that this variety is necessary; and it will be very hard that they shall so concur as to make one portrait like another. Let a painter carelessly limn out a million of faces, and you shall find them all different; yea, let him have his copy before him, yet after all his art there will remain a sensible distinction; for the pattern or example of everything is the perfectest in that kind, whereof we still come short, though we transcend or go beyond it, because herein it is wide, and agrees not in all points unto the copy. Nor doth the similitude of creatures disparage the variety of nature, nor any way confound the works of God. For even in things alike there is diversity; and those that do seem to accord do manifestly disagree. And thus is man like God; for in the same things that we resemble Him, we are utterly different from Him. There was never anything so like another as in all points to concur: there will ever some reserved difference slip in, to prevent the identity; without which, two several things would not be alike, but the same, which is impossible.

But to return from philosophy to charity: I hold not so narrow a conceit of this virtue, as to conceive that to give alms is only to be charitable, or think a piece of liberality can comprehend the total of charity. Divinity hath wisely divided the act thereof into many branches, and hath taught us in this narrow way many paths unto goodness; as many ways as we may do good, so many ways we may be charitable. There are infirmities not only of body, but of soul, and fortunes, which do require the merciful hand of our abilities. I cannot contemn a man for ignorance, but behold him with as much pity as I do Lazarus. It is no greater charity to clothe his body, than apparel the nakedness of his soul. It is an honourable object to see the reasons of other men wear our liveries, and their borrowed understandings do homage to the bounty of ours: it is the cheapest way of beneficence, and, like the natural charity of the sun, illuminates another without obscuring itself. To be reserved and caitiff in this part of goodness, is the sordidest piece of covetousness, and more contemptible than pecuniary avarice. To this (as calling myself a scholar,) I am obliged by the duty of my condition: I make not therefore my head a grave, but a treasury of knowledge; I intend no monopoly, but a community, in learning; I study not for my own sake only, but for theirs that study not for themselves. I envy no man that knows more than my self, but pity them that know less. I instruct no man as an exercise of my knowledge, or with an intent rather to nourish and keep it alive in mine own head than beget and propagate it in his: and in the midst of all my endeavours there is but one thought that dejects me, that my acquired parts must perish with my self, nor can be legacied among my honoured friends. I cannot fall out or contemn a man for an error, or conceive why a difference in opinion should divide an affection; for controversies, disputes, and argumentations, both in philosophy and in divinity, if they meet with discreet and peaceable natures, do not infringe the laws of charity. In all disputes, so much as there is of passion, so much there is of nothing to the purpose; for then reason, like a bad hound, spends upon a false scent, and forsakes the question first started. And this is one reason why controversies are never determined; for, though they be amply proposed, they are scarce at all handled, they do so swell with unnecessary digressions; and the parenthesis on the party is often as large as the main discourse upon the subject. The foundations of religion are already established, and the principles of salvation subscribed unto by all: there remain not many controversies worth a passion; and yet never any disputed without, not only in divinity, but inferior arts. What a Βατραχομυομαχία and hot skirmish is betwixt S. and T. in Lucian! How do grammarians hack and slash for the genitive case in *Jupiter!* How do they break their own pates to salve that of Priscian!

Si foret in terris, rideret Democritus.

Yea, even amongst wiser militants, how many wounds have been given, and credits slain, for the poor victory of an opinion, or beggarly conquest of a distinction! Scholars are men of peace, they bear no arms, but their tongues are sharper than Actius his razor; their pens carry farther, and give a louder report than thunder: I had rather stand the shock of a basilisco, than the fury of a merciless pen. It is not mere zeal to learning, or devotion to the Muses, that wiser princes patron the arts, and carry an indulgent aspect unto scholars; but a desire to have their names eternized by the memory of their writings, and a fear of the revengeful pen of succeeding ages; for these are the men, that, when they have played their parts, and had their *exits*, must step out and give the moral of their scenes, and deliver unto posterity an inventory of their virtues and vices. And surely there goes a great deal of conscience to the compiling of an history: there is no reproach to the scandal of a story; it is such an authentic kind of falsehood that with authority belies our good names to all nations and posterity.

There is another offence unto Charity, which no author hath ever written of, and few take notice of; and that's the reproach, not of whole professions, mysteries, and conditions, but of whole nations, wherein by opprobrious epithets we miscall each other, and by an uncharitable logic, from a disposition in a few, conclude a habit in all.

Le mutin Anglois, et le bravache Escossois,
Et le fol François,
Le poultron Romain, le larron de Gascongne,
L'Espagnol superbe, et l'Aleman yvrongne.

St. Paul, that calls the Cretans liars, doth it but indirectly, and upon quotation of their own poet. It is as bloody a thought in one way, as Nero's was in another; for by a word we wound a thousand, and at one blow assassine the honour of a nation. It is as complete a piece of madness to miscall and rave against the times, or think to recall men to reason by a fit of passion. Democritus, that thought to laugh the times into goodness, seems to me as deeply hypochondriac as Heraclitus, that bewailed them. It moves not my spleen to behold the multitude in their proper humours, that is, in their fits of folly and madness; as well understanding that wisdom is not profaned unto the world, and 't is the privilege of a few to be virtuous. They that endeavour to abolish vice, destroy also virtue; for contraries, though they destroy one another, are yet the life of one another. Thus virtue (abolish vice) is an idea. Again, the community of sin doth not disparage goodness; for when vice gains upon the major part, virtue, in whom it remains, becomes more excellent; and being lost in some, multiplies its goodness in others which remain untouched and persist intire in the general inundation. I can therefore behold vice without a Satyr, content only with an admonition, or instructive reprehension; for noble natures, and such as are capable of goodness, are railed into vice, that might as easily be admonished into virtue; and we should be all so far the orators of goodness, as to protect her from the power of vice, and maintain the cause of injured truth. No man can justly censure or condemn another, because indeed no man truly knows another. This I perceive in my self; for I am in the dark to all the world, and my nearest friends behold me but in a cloud. Those that know me but superficially, think less of me than I do of my self; those of my near acquaintance think more; God, Who truly knows me, knows that I am nothing; for He only beholds me and all the world, Who looks not on us through a derived ray, or a trajection of a sensible species, but beholds the substance without the helps of accidents, and the forms of things as we their operations. Further, no man can judge another, because no man knows himself: for we censure others but as they disagree from that humour which we fancy laudable in our selves, and commend others but for that wherein they seem to quadrate and consent with us. So that, in conclusion, all is but that we all condemn, self-love. 'T is the general complaint of these times, and perhaps of those past, that charity grows cold; which I perceive most verified in those which most do manifest the fires and flames of zeal; for it is a virtue that best agrees with coldest natures, and such as are complexioned for humility. But how shall we expect charity towards others, when we are uncharitable to our selves? *Charity begins at home,* is the voice of the world; yet is every man his greatest enemy, and, as it were, his own executioner. *Non occides,* is the commandment of God, yet scarce observed by any man; for I perceive every man is his own *Atropos,* and lends a hand to cut the thread of his own days. Cain was not therefore the first murderer, but Adam, who brought in death; whereof he beheld the practice and example in his own son Abel, and saw that verified in the experience of another, which faith could not persuade him in the theory of himself.

There is, I think, no man that apprehendeth his own miseries less than my self, and no man that so nearly apprehends another's. I could lose an arm without a tear, and with few groans, methinks, be quartered into pieces; yet can I weep most seriously at a play, and receive with a true passion the counterfeit griefs of those known and professed impostures. It is a barbarous part of inhumanity to add unto any afflicted party's misery, or endeavour to multiply in any man a passion whose single nature is already above his patience. This was the greatest affliction of Job, and those oblique expostulations of his friends a deeper injury than the downright blows of the devil. It is not the tears of our own eyes only, but of our friends also, that do exhaust the current of our sorrows; which, falling into many streams, runs more peaceably, and is contented with a narrower channel. It is an act within the power of charity, to translate a passion out of one breast into another, and to divide a sorrow almost out of it self; for an affliction, like a dimension, may be so divided, as, if not indivisible, at least to become insensible. Now with my friend I desire not to share or participate, but to engross, his sorrows; that, by making them mine own, I may more easily discuss them; for in mine own reason, and within my self, I can command that which I cannot intreat without my self, and within the circle of another. I have often thought those noble pairs and examples of friendship not so truly histories of what had been, as fictions of what should be; but I now perceive nothing in them but possibilities, nor any thing in the heroic examples of Damon and Pythias, Achilles and Patroclus, which methinks upon some grounds I could not perform within the narrow compass of my self. That a man should lay down his life for his friend, seems strange to vulgar affections, and such as confine themselves within that worldly principle, *Charity begins at home.* For mine own part I could never remember the relations that I held unto my self, nor the respect that I owe unto my own nature, in the cause of God, my country, and my friends. Next to these three, I do embrace my self. I confess I do not observe that order that the schools ordain our affections, to love our parents, wives, children, and then our friends; for, excepting the injunctions of religion, I do not find in my self such a necessary and indissoluble sympathy to all those of my blood. I hope I do not break the fifth commandment, if I conceive I may love my friend before the nearest of my blood, even those to whom I owe the principles of life. I never yet cast a true affection on a woman; but I have loved my friend as I do virtue, my soul, my God. From hence methinks I do conceive how God loves man, what happiness there is in the love of God. Omitting all other, there are three most mystical unions: two natures in one person; three persons in one nature; one soul in two bodies; for though indeed they be really divided, yet are they so united, as they seem but one, and make rather a duality than two distinct souls.

There are wonders in true affection: it is a body of enigmas, mysteries, and riddles; wherein two so become one, as they both become two. I love my friend before my self, and yet methinks I do not love him enough: some few months hence my multiplied affection will make me believe I have not loved him at all. When I am from him, I am dead till I be with him; when I am with him, I am not satisfied, but would still be nearer him. United souls are not satisfied with embraces, but desire to be truly each other; which being impossible, their desires are infinite, and must proceed without a possibility of satisfaction. Another misery there is in affection, that whom we truly love like our own selves, we forget their looks, nor can our memory retain the idea of their faces; and it is no wonder, for they are our selves, and our affection makes their looks our own. This noble affection falls not on vulgar and common constitutions, but on such as are marked for virtue: he that can love his friend with this noble ardour, will in a competent degree affect all. Now, if we can bring our affections to look beyond the body, and cast an eye upon the soul, we have found out the true object, not only of friendship, but Charity; and the greatest happiness that we can bequeath the soul, is that wherein we all do place our last felicity, Salvation; which though it be not in our power to bestow, it is in our charity and pious invocations to desire, if not procure and further. I cannot contentedly frame a prayer for my self in particular, without a catalogue for my friends; nor request a happiness, wherein my sociable disposition doth not desire the fellowship of my neighbour. I never hear the toll of a passing bell, though in my mirth, without my prayers and best wishes for the departing spirit; I cannot go to cure the body of my patient, but I forget my profession, and call unto God for his soul; I cannot see one say his prayers, but, in stead of imitating him, I fall into a supplication for him, who perhaps is no more to me than a common nature: and if God hath vouchsafed an ear to my supplications, there are surely many happy that never saw me, and enjoy the blessing of mine unknown devotions. To pray for enemies, that is, for their salvation, is no harsh precept, but the practice of our daily and ordinary devotions. I cannot believe the story of the Italian: our bad wishes and uncharitable desires proceed no further than this life; it is the devil, and the uncharitable votes of Hell, that desire our misery in the world to come.

To do no injury, nor take none, was a principle, which to my former years and impatient affections seemed to contain enough of morality; but my more settled years and christian constitution have fallen upon severer resolutions. I can hold there is no such thing as injury; that, if there be, there is no such injury as revenge, and no such revenge as the contempt of an injury; that to hate another, is to malign himself; that the truest way to love another, is to despise our selves. I were unjust unto mine own conscience, if I should say I am at variance with anything like my self. I find there are many pieces in this one fabric of man; this frame is raised upon a mass of antipathies. I am one methinks, but as the world; wherein notwithstanding there are a swarm of distinct essences, and in them another world of contrarieties; we carry private and domestic enemies within, public and more hostile adversaries without. The devil, that did but buffet St. Paul, plays methinks at sharp with me. Let me be nothing, if within the compass of my self I do not find the battle of Lepanto, passion against reason, reason against faith, faith against the devil, and my conscience against all. There is another man within me, that's angry with me, rebukes, commands, and dastards me. I have no conscience of marble to resist the hammer of more heavy offenses; nor yet so soft and waxen, as to take the impression of each single peccadillo or scrape of infirmity. I am of a strange belief, that it is as easy to be forgiven some sins, as to commit some others. For my original sin, I hold it to be washed away in my baptism: for my actual transgressions, I compute and reckon with God but from my last repentance, sacrament, or general absolution; and therefore am not terrified with the sins or madness of my youth. I thank the goodness of God, I have no sins that want a name; I am not singular in offenses; my transgressions are epidemical, and from the common breath of our corruption. For there are certain tempers of body, which, matched with a humourous depravity of mind, do hatch and produce vitiosities, whose newness and monstrosity of nature admits no name: this was the temper of that lecher that fell in love with a statua, and the constitution of Nero in his Spintrian recreations. For the heavens are not only fruitful in new and unheard-of stars, the earth in plants and animals, but men's minds also in villainy and vices. Now the dulness of my reason, and the vulgarity of my disposition, never prompted my invention, nor solicited my affection unto any of these; yet even those common and quotidian infirmities that so necessarily attend me, and do seem to be my very nature, have so dejected me, so broken the estimation that I should have otherwise of my self, that I repute my self the most abjectest piece of mortality. Divines prescribe a fit of sorrow to repentance: there goes indignation, anger, sorrow, hatred, into mine: passions of a contrary nature, which neither seem to suit with this action, nor my proper constitution. It is no breach of charity to our selves, to be at variance with our vices, nor to abhor that part of us which is an enemy to the ground of charity, our God; wherein we do but imitate our great selves, the world, whose divided antipathies and contrary faces do yet carry a charitable regard unto the whole by their particular discords preserving the common harmony, and keeping in fetters those powers, whose rebellions, once masters, might be the ruin of all.

I thank God, amongst those millions of vices I do inherit and hold from Adam, I have escaped one, and that a mortal enemy to charity, the first and father-sin, not only of man, but of the devil, Pride: a vice whose name is comprehended in a monosyllable, but in its nature not circumscribed with a world. I have escaped it in a condition that can hardly avoid it. Those petty acquisitions and reputed perfections that advance and elevate the conceits of other men, add no feathers unto mine. I have seen a grammarian tower and plume himself over a single line in Horace, and show more pride in the construction of one ode, than the author in the composure of the whole book. For my own part, besides the jargon and *patois* of several provinces, I understand no less than six languages; yet I protest I have no higher conceit of my self, than had our fathers before the confusion of Babel, when there was but one language in the world, and none to boast himself either linguist or critic. I have not only seen several countries, beheld the nature of their climes, the chorography of their provinces, topography of their cities, but understood their several laws, customs and policies; yet cannot all this persuade the dulness of my spirit unto such an opinion of my self, as I behold in nimbler and conceited heads, that never looked a degree beyond their nests. I know the names, and somewhat more, of all the constellations in my horizon; yet I have seen a prating mariner, that could only name the pointers and the north star, out-talk me, and conceit himself a whole sphere above me. I know most of the plants of my country, and of those about me; yet methinks I do not know so many as when I did but know a hundred, and had scarcely ever simpled further than Cheapside. For, indeed, heads of capacity, and such as are not full with a handful or easy measure of knowledge, think they know nothing till they know all; which being impossible, they fall upon the opinion of Socrates, and only know they know not any thing. I cannot think that Homer pined away upon the riddle of the fisherman; or that Aristotle, who understood the uncertainty of knowledge, and confessed so often the reason of man too weak for the works of nature, did ever drown himself upon the flux and reflux of Euripus. We do but learn to-day what our better advanced judgments will unteach to-morrow; and Aristotle doth but instruct us, as Plato did him; that is, to confute himself. I have run through all sorts, yet find no rest in any: though our first studies and junior endeavours may style us Peripatetics, Stoics, or Academics; yet I perceive the wisest heads prove, at last, almost all sceptics, and stand like Janus in the field of knowledge. I have therefore one common and authentic philosophy I learned in the schools, whereby I discourse and satisfy the reason of other men; another more reserved, and drawn from experience, whereby I content mine own. Solomon, that complained of ignorance in the height of knowledge, hath not only humbled my conceits, but discouraged my endeavours. There is yet another conceit that hath sometimes made me shut my books, which tells me it is a vanity to waste our days in the blind pursuit of knowledge; it is but attending a little longer, and we shall enjoy that by instinct and infusion, which we endeavour at here by labour and inquisition. It is better to sit down in a modest ignorance, and rest contented with the natural blessing of our own reasons, than buy the uncertain knowledge of this life with sweat and vexation, which death gives every fool gratis, and is an accessory of our glorification.

I was never yet once, and commend their resolutions who never marry twice: not that I disallow of second marriage; as neither, in all cases, of polygamy, which, considering some times, and the unequal number of both sexes, may be also necessary. The whole world was made for man, but the twelfth part of man for woman: man is the whole world, and the breath of God; woman the rib and crooked piece of man. I could be content that we might procreate like trees, without conjunction, or that there were any way to perpetuate the world without this trivial and vulgar way of union: it is the foolishest act a wise man commits in all his life; nor is there anything that will more deject his cooled imagination, when he shall consider what an odd and unworthy piece of folly he hath committed. I speak not in prejudice, nor am averse from that sweet sex, but naturally amorous of all that is beautiful. I can look a whole day with delight upon a handsome picture, though it be but of a horse. It is my temper, and I like it the better, to affect all harmony; and sure there is music even in the beauty, and the silent note which Cupid strikes, far sweeter than the sound of an instrument. For there is a music wherever there is a harmony, order, or proportion: and thus far we may maintain the music of the spheres; for those well-ordered motions, and regular paces, though they give no sound unto the ear, yet to the understanding they strike a note most full of harmony. Whosoever is harmonically composed delights in harmony; which makes me much distrust the symmetry of those heads which declaim against all church-music. For my self, not only from my obedience, but my particular genius, I do embrace it: for even that vulgar and tavern-music, which makes one man merry, another mad, strikes in me a deep fit of devotion, and a profound contemplation of the first composer. There is something in it of divinity more than the ear discovers: it is an hieroglyphical and shadowed lesson of the whole world, and creatures of God; such a melody to the ear, as the whole world, well understood, would afford the understanding. In brief, it is a sensible fit of that harmony which intellectually sounds in the ears of God. I will not say, with Plato, the soul is a harmony, but harmonical, and hath its nearest sympathy unto music: thus some, whose temper of body agrees, and humours the constitution of their souls, are born poets, though indeed all are naturally inclined unto rhythm. This made Tacitus, in the very first line of his story, fall upon a verse; and Cicero, the worst of poets, but declaiming for a poet, falls in the very first sentence upon a perfect hexameter. I feel not in me those sordid and unchristian desires of my profession; I do not secretly implore and wish for plagues, rejoice at famines, revolve ephemerides and almanacs in expectation of malignant aspects, fatal conjunctions, and eclipses. I rejoice not at unwholesome springs, nor unseasonable winters: my prayer goes with the husbandman's; I desire everything in its proper season, that neither men nor the times be put out of temper. Let me be sick my self, if sometimes the malady of my patient be not a disease unto me. I desire rather to cure his infirmities than my own necessities. Where I do him no good, methinks it is scarce honest gain; though I confess 't is but the worthy salary of our well-intended endeavours. I am not only ashamed, but heartily sorry, that, besides death, there are diseases incurable; yet not for my own sake, or that they be beyond my art, but for the general cause and sake of humanity, whose common cause I apprehend as mine own. And to speak more generally, those three noble professions which all civil commonwealths do honour, are raised upon the fall of Adam, and are not any way exempt from their infirmities; there are not only diseases incurable in physic, but cases indissolvable in laws, vices incorrigible in divinity. If general councils may err, I do not see why particular courts should be infallible: their perfectest rules are raised upon the erroneous reasons of man, and the laws of one do but condemn the rules of another; as Aristotle oft-times the opinions of his predecessors, because, though agreeable to reason, yet were not consonant to his own rules, and logic of his proper principles. Again, (to speak nothing of the sin against the Holy Ghost, whose cure not only, but whose nature is unknown,) I can cure the gout or stone in some, sooner than divinity, pride, or avarice in others. I can cure vices by physic when they remain incurable by divinity, and shall obey my pills when they contemn their precepts. I boast nothing, but plainly say, we all labour against our own cure; for death is the cure of all diseases. There is no *Catholicon* or universal remedy I know, but this; which, though nauseous to queasy stomachs, yet to prepared appetites is nectar, and a pleasant potion of immortality.

For my conversation, it is like the sun's, with all men, and with a friendly aspect to good and bad. Methinks there is no man bad, and the worst, best; that is, while they are kept within the circle of those qualities wherein they are good: there is no man's mind of such discordant and jarring a temper, to which a tunable disposition may not strike a harmony. *Magnæ virtutes, nec minora vitia;* it is the posie of the best natures, and may be inverted on the worst; there are in the most depraved and venemous dispositions, certain pieces that remain untouched, which by an *Antiperistasis* become more excellent, or by the excellency of their antipathies are able to preserve themselves from the contagion of their enemy vices, and persist entire beyond the general corruption. For it is also thus in nature: the greatest balsams do lie enveloped in the bodies of the most powerful corrosives. I say, moreover, and I ground upon experience, that poisons contain within themselves their own antidote, and that which preserves them from the venom of themselves, without which they were not deleterious to others only, but to themselves also. But it is the corruption that I fear within me, not the contagion of commerce without me. 'T is that unruly regiment within me, that will destroy me; 't is I that do infect my self; the man without a navel yet lives in me; I feel that original canker corrode and devour me; and therefore *Defenda me Dios de me*, 'Lord deliver me from my self,' is a part of my litany, and the first voice of my retired imaginations. There is no man alone, because every man is a microcosm, and carries the whole world about him. *Numquam minus solus quam cum solus*, though it be the apothegm of a wise man, is yet true in the mouth of a fool. Indeed, though in a wilderness, a man is never alone, not only because he is with himself and his own thoughts, but because he is with the devil, who ever consorts with our solitude, and is that unruly rebel that musters up those disordered motions which accompany our sequestered imaginations. And to speak more narrowly, there is no such thing as solitude, nor any thing that can be said to be alone and by itself, but God, Who is His own circle, and can subsist by Himself; all others, besides their dissimilarity and heterogeneous parts, which in a manner multiply their natures, cannot subsist without the concourse of God, and the society of that hand which doth uphold their natures. In brief, there can be nothing truly alone and by it self, which is not truly one; and such is only God: all others do transcend an unity, and so by consequence are many.

Now for my life, it is a miracle of thirty years, which to relate, were not a history, but a piece of poetry, and would sound to common ears like a fable. For the world, I count it not an inn, but an hospital; and a place not to live, but to die in. The world that I regard is my self; it is the microcosm of my own frame that I cast mine eye on; for the other, I use it but like my globe, and turn it round sometimes for my recreation. Men that look upon my outside, perusing only my condition and fortunes, do err in my altitude; for I am above Atlas his shoulders. The earth is a point not only in respect of the heavens above us, but of that heavenly and celestial part within us; that mass of flesh that circumscribes me, limits not my mind: that surface that tells the heavens it hath an end, cannot persuade me I have any: I take my circle to be above three hundred and sixty; though the number of the ark do measure my body, it comprehendeth not my mind: whilst I study to find how I am a microcosm, or little world, I find my self something more than the great. There is surely a piece of divinity in us, something that was before the elements, and owes no homage unto the sun. Nature tells me I am the image of God, as well as Scripture: he that understands not thus much, hath not his introduction or first lesson, and is yet to begin the alphabet of man. Let me not injure the felicity of others, if I say I am as happy as any: *Ruat cœlum, fiat voluntas Tua,* salveth all; so that whatsoever happens, it is but what our daily prayers desire. In brief, I am content; and what should Providence add more? Surely this is it we call happiness, and this do I enjoy; with this I am happy in a dream, and as content to enjoy a happiness in a fancy, as others in a more apparent truth and reality. There is surely a nearer apprehension of anything that delights us in our dreams, than in our waked senses: without this I were unhappy; for my awaked judgment discontents me, ever whispering unto me, that I am from my friend; but my friendly dreams in the night requite me, and make me think I am within his arms. I thank God for my happy dreams, as I do for my good rest; for there is a satisfaction in them unto reasonable desires, and such as can be content with a fit of happiness: and surely it is not a melancholy conceit to think we are all asleep in this world, and that the conceits of this life are as mere dreams to those of the next; as the phantasms of the night, to the conceits of the day. There is an equal delusion in both, and the one doth but seem to be the emblem or picture of the other: we are somewhat more than our selves in our sleeps, and the slumber of the body seems to be but the waking of the soul. It is the ligation of sense, but the liberty of reason; and our waking conceptions do not match the fancies of our sleeps. At my nativity my ascendant was the watery sign of Scorpius; I was born in the planetary hour of Saturn, and I think I have a piece of that leaden planet in me. I am no way facetious, nor disposed for the mirth and galliardize of company; yet in one dream I can compose a whole comedy, behold the action, apprehend the jests, and laugh my self awake at the conceits thereof. Were my memory as faithful as my reason is then fruitful, I would never study but in my dreams; and this time also would I choose for my devotions: but our grosser memories have then so little hold of our abstracted understandings, that they forget the story, and can only relate to our awaked souls, a confused and broken tale of that that hath passed. Aristotle, who hath written a singular tract *Of Sleep*, hath not, methinks, throughly defined it; nor yet Galen, though he seem to have corrected it; for those Noctambuloes and night-walkers, though in their sleep, do yet injoy the action of their senses. We must therefore say that there is something in us that is not in the jurisdiction of Morpheus; and that those abstracted and ecstatic souls do walk about in their own corps, as spirits with the bodies they assume, wherein they seem to hear, see, and feel, though indeed the organs are destitute of sense, and their natures of those faculties that should inform them. Thus it is observed, that men sometimes, upon the hour of their departure, do speak and reason above themselves; for then the soul, beginning to be freed from the ligaments of the body, begins to reason like her self, and to discourse in a strain above mortality.

We term sleep a death; and yet it is waking that kills us, and destroys those spirits that are the house of life. 'T is indeed a part of life that best expresseth death; for every man truly lives, so long as he acts his nature, or some way makes good the faculties of himself. Themistocles, therefore, that slew his soldier in his sleep, was a merciful executioner: 't is a kind of punishment the mildness of no laws hath invented: I wonder the fancy of Lucan and Seneca did not discover it. It is that death by which we may be literally said to die daily; a death which Adam died before his mortality; a death whereby we live a middle and moderating point between life and death: in fine, so like death, I dare not trust it without my prayers, and an half adieu unto the world, and take my farewell in a colloquy with God.

The night is come, like to the day,
Depart not Thou, great God, away.
Let not my sins, black as the night,
Eclipse the lustre of Thy light:
Keep still in my horizon; for to me
The sun makes not the day, but Thee.
Thou, Whose nature cannot sleep,
On my temples sentry keep;
Guard me 'gainst those watchful foes,
Whose eyes are open while mine close.
Let no dreams my head infest,
But such as Jacob's temples blest.
While I do rest, my soul advance;
Make my sleep a holy trance;
That I may, my rest being wrought,
Awake unto some holy thought;
And with as active vigour run
My course, as doth the nimble sun.
Sleep is a death; O make me try,
By sleeping what it is to die;
And as gently lay my head
On my grave, as now my bed.
Howe'er I rest, great God, let me
Awake again at last with Thee;
And thus assured, behold I lie
Securely, or to awake or die.
These are my drowsy days; in vain
I do now wake to sleep again:
O come that hour, when I shall never
Sleep again, but wake for ever.

This is the dormative I take to bedward; I need no other laudanum than this to make me sleep; after which I close mine eyes in security, content to take my leave of the sun, and sleep unto the Resurrection.

The method I should use in distributive justice, I often observe in commutative; and keep a geometrical proportion in both, whereby becoming equable to others, I become unjust to my self, and supererogate in that common principle, *Do unto others as thou wouldst be done unto thy self.* I was not born unto riches, neither is it, I think, my star to be wealthy; or, if it were, the freedom of my mind, and frankness of my disposition, were able to contradict and cross my fates: for to me, avarice seems not so much a vice, as a deplorable piece of madness; to conceive ourselves pipkins, or be persuaded that we are dead, is not so ridiculous, nor so many degrees beyond the power of Hellebore, as this. The opinions of theory, and positions of men, are not so void of reason as their practised conclusions. Some have held that snow is black, that the earth moves, that the soul is air, fire, water; but all this is philosophy, and there is no delirium, if we do but speculate the folly and indisputable dotage of avarice to that subterraneous idol, and God of the earth. I do confess I am an atheist; I cannot persuade myself to honour that the world adores; whatsoever virtue its prepared substance may have in my body, it hath no influence nor operation without. I would not entertain a base design, or an action that should call me villain, for the Indies; and for this only do I love and honour my own soul, and have methinks two arms too few to embrace myself. Aristotle is too severe, that will not allow us to be truly liberal without wealth, and the bountiful hand of fortune. If this be true, I must confess I am charitable only in my liberal intentions, and bountiful well-wishes; but if the example of the mite be not only an act of wonder, but an example of the noblest charity, surely poor men may also build hospitals, and the rich alone have not erected cathedrals. I have a private method which others observe not; I take the opportunity of my self to do good; I borrow occasion of charity from mine own necessities, and supply the wants of others, when

I am in most need my self: for it is an honest stratagem to take advantage of our selves, and so to husband the acts of virtue, that, where they are defective in one circumstance, they may repay their want and multiply their goodness in another. I have not Peru in my desires, but a competence, and ability to perform those good works to which He hath inclined my nature. He is rich, who hath enough to be charitable; and it is hard to be so poor, that a noble mind may not find a way to this piece of goodness. *He that giveth to the poor, lendeth to the Lord:* there is more rhetoric in that one sentence, than in a library of sermons; and indeed, if those sentences were understood by the reader, with the same emphasis as they are delivered by the author, we needed not those volumes of instructions, but might be honest by an epitome. Upon this motive only I cannot behold a beggar without relieving his necessities with my purse, or his soul with my prayers; these scenical and accidental differences between us, cannot make me forget that common and untouched part of us both: there is under these *Centoes* and miserable outsides, these mutilate and semi-bodies, a soul of the same alloy with our own, whose genealogy is God as well as ours, and in as fair a way to salvation as our selves. Statists that labour to contrive a commonwealth without poverty, take away the object of charity, not understanding only the commonwealth of a christian, but forgetting the prophesy of Christ.

Now, there is another part of charity, which is the basis and pillar of this, and that is the love of God, for Whom we love our neighbour; for this I think charity, to love God for Himself, and our neighbour for God. All that is truly amiable is God, or as it were a divided piece of Him, that retains a reflex or shadow of Himself. Nor is it strange that we should place affection on that which is invisible: all that we truly love is thus; what we adore under affection of our senses, deserves not the honour of so pure a title. Thus we adore virtue, though to the eye of sense she be invisible: thus that part of our noble friends that we love, is not that part that we embrace, but that insensible part that our arms cannot embrace. God, being all goodness, can love nothing but Himself; He loves us but for that part which is as it were Himself, and the traduction of His Holy Spirit. Let us call to assize the loves of our parents, the affection of our wives and children, and they are all dumb shows and dreams, without reality, truth, or constancy. For first there is a strong bond of affection between us and our parents; yet how easily dissolved! We betake our selves to a woman, forget our mother in a wife, and the womb that bare us, in that that shall bear our image. This woman blessing us with children, our affection leaves the level it held before, and sinks from our bed unto our issue and picture of posterity, where affection holds no steady mansion. They, growing up in years, desire our ends; or applying themselves to a woman, take a lawful way to love another better than our selves. Thus I perceive a man may be buried alive, and behold his grave in his own issue.

I conclude therefore, and say, there is no happiness under (or, as Copernicus will have it, *above*) the sun, nor any Crambe in that repeated verity and burthen of all the wisdom of Solomon, *All is vanity and vexation of spirit.* There is no felicity in that the world adores. Aristotle, whilst he labours to refute the ideas of Plato, falls upon one himself; for his *summum bonum* is a chimera, and there is no such thing as his felicity. That wherein God Himself is happy, the holy angels are happy, in whose defect the devils are unhappy, that dare I call happiness: whatsoever conduceth unto this, may with an easy metaphor deserve that name; whatsoever else the world terms happiness, is to me a story out of Pliny, a tale of Boccaccio or Malizspini, an apparition, or neat delusion, wherein there is no more of happiness than the name. Bless me in this life with but peace of my conscience, command of my affections, the love of Thy self and my dearest friends, and I shall be happy enough to pity Cæsar. These are, O Lord, the humble desires of my most reasonable ambition, and all I dare call happiness on earth; wherein I set no rule or limit to Thy hand or providence. Dispose of me according to the wisdom of Thy pleasure: Thy will be done, though in my own undoing.

(1642) 1643

John Milton (1608–1674)

LETTER ON EDUCATION

Master Hartlib,

I am long since persuaded, Master Hartlib, that to say or do aught worth memory and imitation, no purpose or respect should sooner move us than simply the love of God, and of mankind. Nevertheless to write now the reforming of education, though it be one of the greatest and noblest designs that can be thought on, and for the want whereof this nation perishes; I had not yet at this time been induced, but by your earnest entreaties and serious conjurements; as having my mind for the present half diverted in the pursuance of some other assertions, the knowledge and the use of which cannot but be a great furtherance both to the enlargement of truth, and honest living with much more peace. Nor should the laws of any private friendship have prevailed with me to divide thus, or transpose my former thoughts, but that I see those aims, those actions, which have won you with me the esteem of a person sent hither by some good providence from a far country to be the occasion and incitement of great good to this island.

And, as I hear, you have obtained the same repute with men of most approved wisdom, and some of the highest authority among us; not to mention the learned correspondence which you hold in foreign parts, and the extraordinary pains and diligence which you have used in this matter, both here and beyond the seas; either by the definite will of God so ruling, or the peculiar sway of nature, which also is God's working. Neither can I think that, so reputed and so valued as you are, you would, to the forfeit of your own discerning ability, impose upon me an unfit and over-ponderous argument; but that the satisfaction which you profess to have received, from those incidental discourses which we have wandered into, hath pressed and almost constrained you into a persuasion, that what you require from me in this point, I neither ought nor can in conscience defer beyond this time both of so much need at once, and so much opportunity to try what God hath determined.

I will not resist, therefore, whatever it is, either of divine or human obligement, that you lay upon me; but will forthwith set down in writing, as you request me, that voluntary idea, which hath long, in silence, presented itself to me, of a better education, in extent and comprehension far more large, and yet of time far shorter, and of attainment far more certain, than hath been yet in practice. Brief I shall endeavour to be; for that which I have to say, assuredly this nation hath extreme need should be done sooner than spoken. To tell you, therefore, what I have benefited herein among old renowned authors, I shall spare; and to search what many modern Januas and Didactics, more than ever I shall read, have projected, my inclination leads me not. But if you can accept of these few observations which have flowered off, and are as it were the burnishing of many studious and contemplative years, altogether spent in the search of religious and civil knowledge, and such as pleased you so well in the relating, I here give you them to dispose of.

The end then of learning is to repair the ruins of our first parents by regaining to know God aright, and out of that knowledge to love him, to imitate him, to be like him, as we may the nearest by possessing our souls of true virtue, which being united to the heavenly grace of faith, makes up the highest perfection. But because our understanding cannot in this body found itself but on sensible things, nor arrive so clearly to the knowledge of God and things invisible, as by orderly conning over the visible and inferior creature, the same method is necessarily to be followed in all discreet teaching. And seeing every nation affords not experience and tradition enough for all kinds of learning, therefore we are chiefly taught the languages of those people who have at any time been most industrious after wisdom; so that language is but the instrument conveying to us things useful to be known. And though a linguist should pride himself to have all the tongues that Babel cleft the world into, yet if he have not studied the solid things in them, as well as the words and lexicons, he were nothing so much to be esteemed a learned man, as any yeoman or tradesman competently wise in his mother dialect only.

Hence appear the many mistakes which have made learning generally so unpleasing and so unsuccessful; first, we do amiss to spend seven or eight years merely in scraping together so much miserable Latin and Greek, as might be learned otherwise easily and delightfully in one year. And that which casts our proficiency therein so much behind, is our time lost partly in too oft idle vacancies given both to schools and universities; partly in a preposterous exaction, forcing the empty wits of children to compose themes, verses, and orations, which are the acts of ripest judgment, and the final work of a head filled by long reading and observing, with elegant maxims and copious invention. These are not matters to be wrung from poor striplings, like blood out of the nose, or the plucking of untimely fruit. Besides the ill habit which they get of wretched barbarising against the Latin and Greek idiom, with their untutored Anglicisms, odious to be read, yet not to be avoided without a well-continued and judicious conversing among pure authors digested, which they scarce taste. Whereas, if after some preparatory grounds of speech by their certain forms got into memory, they were led to the praxis thereof in some chosen short book lessoned thoroughly to them, they might then forthwith proceed to learn the substance of good things, and arts in due order, which would bring the whole language quickly into their power. This I take to be the most rational and most profitable way of learning languages, and whereby we may best hope to give account to God of our youth spent herein.

And for the usual method of teaching arts, I deem it to be an old error of universities, not yet well recovered from the scholastic grossness of barbarous ages, that instead of beginning with arts most easy, (and those be such as are most obvious to the sense,) they present their young unmatriculated novices, at first coming, with the most intellective abstractions of logic and metaphysics; so that they having but newly left those grammatic flats and shallows, where they stuck unreasonably to learn a few words with lamentable construction, and now on the sudden transported under another climate, to be tossed and turmoiled with their unballasted wits in fathomless and unquiet deeps of controversy, do for the most part grow into hatred and contempt of learning, mocked and deluded all this while with ragged notions and babblements, while they expected worthy and delightful knowledge; till poverty or youthful years call them importunately their several ways, and hasten them, with the sway of friends, either to an ambitious and mercenary, or ignorantly zealous divinity: some allured to the trade of law, grounding their purposes not on the prudent and heavenly contemplation of justice and equity, which was never taught them, but on the promising and pleasing thoughts of litigious terms, fat contentions, and flowing fees; others betake them to state affairs, with souls so unprincipled in virtue and true generous breeding, that flattery and court-shifts and tyrannous aphorisms appear to them the highest points of wisdom; instilling their barren hearts with a conscientious slavery; if, as I rather think, it be not feigned. Others, lastly, of a more delicious and airy spirit, retire themselves (knowing no better) to the enjoyments of ease and luxury, living out their days in feast and jollity; which indeed is the wisest and safest course of all these, unless they were with more integrity undertaken. And these are the errors, and these are the fruits of misspending our prime youth at the schools and universities as we do, either in learning mere words, or such things chiefly as were better unlearned.

I shall detain you now no longer in the demonstration of what we should not do, but straight conduct you to a hill-side, where I will point you out the right path of a virtuous and noble education; laborious indeed at the first ascent, but else so smooth, so green, so full of goodly prospect, and melodious sounds on every side, that the harp of Orpheus was not more charming. I doubt not but ye shall have more ado to drive our dullest and laziest youth, our stocks and stubs, from the infinite desire of such a happy nurture, than we have now to hale and drag our choicest and hopefullest wits to that asinine feast of sow-thistles and brambles, which is commonly set before them as all the food and entertainment of their tenderest and most docible age. I call therefore a complete and generous education, that which fits a man to perform justly, skilfully, and magnanimously all the offices, both private and public, of peace and war. And how all this may be done between twelve and one and twenty, less time than is now bestowed in pure trifling at grammar and sophistry, is to be thus ordered.

First, to find out a spacious house and ground about it fit for an academy, and big enough to lodge a hundred and fifty persons, whereof twenty or thereabout may be attendants, all under the government of one, who shall be thought of desert sufficient, and ability either to do all, or wisely to direct and oversee it done. This place should be at once both school and university, not needing a remove to any other house of scholarship, except it be some peculiar college of law, or physic, where they mean to be practitioners; but as for those general studies which take up all our time from Lily to commencing, as they term it, master of art, it should be absolute. After this pattern, as many edifices may be converted to this use as shall be needful in every city throughout this land, which would tend much to the increase of learning and civility everywhere. This number, less or more thus collected, to the convenience of a foot company, or interchangeably two troops of cavalry, should divide their day's work into three parts as it lies orderly: their studies, their exercise, and their diet.

For their studies: first, they should begin with the chief and necessary rules of some good grammar, either that now used, or any better; and while this is doing, their speech is to be fashioned to a distinct and clear pronunciation, as near as may be to the Italian, especially in the vowels. For we Englishmen being far northerly, do not open our mouths in the cold air wide enough to grace a southern tongue; but are observed by all other nations to speak exceeding close and inward; so that to smatter Latin with an English mouth, is as ill a hearing as law French. Next, to make them expert in the usefullest points of grammar, and withal to season them and win them early to the love of virtue and true labour, ere any flattering seducement or vain principle seize them wandering, some easy and delightful book of education would be read to them, whereof the Greeks have store, as Cebes, Plutarch, and other Socratic discourses. But in Latin we have none of classic authority extant, except the two or three first books of Quintilian, and some select pieces elsewhere.

But here the main skill and groundwork will be, to temper them such lectures and explanations, upon every opportunity, as may lead and draw them in willing obedience, enflamed with the study of learning and the admiration of virtue; stirred up with high hopes of living to be brave men, and worthy patriots, dear to God, and famous to all ages. That they may despise and scorn all their childish and ill-taught qualities, to delight in manly and liberal exercises, which he who hath the art and proper eloquence to catch them with, what with mild and effectual persuasions, and that with the intimation of some fear, if need be, but chiefly by his own example, might in a short space gain them to an incredible diligence and courage, infusing into their young breasts such an ingenuous and noble ardour, as would not fail to make many of them renowned and matchless men. At the same time, some other hour of the day, might be taught them the rules of arithmetic; and soon after the elements of geometry, even playing, as the old manner was. After evening repast, till bedtime, their thoughts would be best taken up in the easy grounds of religion, and the story of Scripture.

The next step would be to the authors of agriculture, Cato, Varro, and Columella, for the matter is most easy; and, if the language be difficult, so much the better, it is not a difficulty above their years. And here will be an occasion of inciting, and enabling them hereafter to improve the tillage of their country, to recover the bad soil, and to remedy the waste that is made of good; for this was one of Hercules' praises. Ere half these authors be read (which will soon be with plying hard and daily) they cannot choose but be masters of any ordinary prose. So that it will be then seasonable for them to learn in any modern author the use of the globes, and all the maps, first, with the old names, and then with the new; or they might be then capable to read any compendious method of natural philosophy.

And at the same time might be entering into the Greek tongue, after the same manner as was before prescribed in the Latin; whereby the difficulties of grammar being soon overcome, all the historical physiology of Aristotle and Theophrastus are open before them, and, as I may say, under contribution. The like access will be to Vitruvius, to Seneca's natural questions, to Mela, Celsus, Pliny, or Solinus. And having thus passed the principles of arithmetic, geometry, astronomy, and geography, with a general compact of physics, they may descend in mathematics to the instrumental science of trigonometry, and from thence to fortification, architecture, enginery, or navigation. And in natural philosophy they may proceed leisurely from the history of meteors, minerals, plants, and living creatures, as far as anatomy.

Then also in course might be read to them, out of some not tedious writer, the institution of physic, that they may know the tempers, the humours, the seasons, and how to manage a crudity; which he who can wisely and timely do, is not only a great physician to himself and to his friends, but also may, at some time or other, save an army by this frugal and expenseless means only; and not let the healthy and stout bodies of young men rot away under him for want of this discipline; which is a great pity, and no less a shame to the commander. To set forward all these proceedings in nature and mathematics, what hinders but that they may procure, as oft as shall be needful, the helpful experiences of hunters, fowlers, fishermen, shepherds, gardeners, apothecaries; and in the other sciences, architects, engineers, mariners, anatomists; who doubtless would be ready, some for reward, and some to favour such a hopeful seminary. And this will give them such a real tincture of natural knowledge, as they shall never forget, but daily augment with delight. Then also those poets which are now counted most hard, will be both facile and pleasant, Orpheus, Hesiod, Theocritus, Aratus, Nicander, Oppian, Dionysius; and in Latin, Lucretius, Manilius, and the rural part of Virgil.

By this time, years and good general precepts will have furnished them more distinctly with that act of reason which in ethics is called Proairesis; that they may with some judgment contemplate upon moral good and evil. Then will be required a special reinforcement of constant and sound indoctrinating, to set them right and firm, instructing them more amply in the knowledge of virtue and the hatred of vice; while their young and pliant affections are led through all the moral works of Plato, Xenophon, Cicero, Plutarch, Laertius, and those Locrian remnants; but still to be reduced in their nightward studies wherewith they close the day's work, under the determinate sentence of David or Solomon, or the evangelists and apostolic scriptures. Being perfect in the knowledge of personal duty, they may then begin the study of economics. And either now or before this, they may have easily learned, at any odd hour, the Italian tongue. And soon after, but with wariness and good antidote, it would be wholesome enough to let them taste some choice comedies, Greek, Latin, or Italian; those tragedies also, that treat household matters, as Trachiniæ, Alcestis, and the like.

The next removal must be to the study of politics; to know the beginning, end, and reasons of political societies; that they may not, in a dangerous fit of the commonwealth, be such poor, shaken, uncertain reeds, of such a tottering conscience, as many of our great counsellors have lately shewn themselves, but steadfast pillars of the state. After this, they are to dive into the grounds of law, and legal justice; delivered first and with best warrant by Moses; and as far as human prudence can be trusted, in those extolled remains of Grecian lawgivers, Lycurgus, Solon, Zaleucus, Charondas, and thence to all the Roman edicts and tables with their Justinian: and so down to the Saxon and common laws of England, and the statutes.

Sundays also and every evening may be now understandingly spent in the highest matters of theology, and church history, ancient and modern; and ere this time the Hebrew tongue at a set hour might have been gained, that the Scriptures may be now read in their own original; whereto it would be no impossibility to add the Chaldee and the Syrian dialect. When all these employments are well conquered, then will the choice histories, heroic poems, and Attic tragedies of stateliest and most regal argument, with all the famous political orations, offer themselves; which if they were not only read, but some of them got by memory, and solemnly pronounced with right accent and grace, as might be taught, would endue them even with the spirit and vigour of Demosthenes or Cicero, Euripides or Sophocles.

And now, lastly, will be the time to read with them those organic arts which enable men to discourse and write perspicuously, elegantly, and according to the fittest style, of lofty, mean, or lowly. Logic, therefore, so much as is useful, is to be referred to this due place with all her well-couched heads and topics, until it be time to open her contracted palm into a graceful and ornate rhetoric, taught out of the rule of Plato, Aristotle, Phalereus, Cicero, Hermogenes, Longinus. To which poetry would be made subsequent, or indeed rather precedent, as being less subtile and fine, but more simple, sensuous, and passionate. I mean not here the prosody of a verse, which they could not but have hit on before among the rudiments of grammar; but that sublime art which in Aristotle's Poetics, in Horace, and the Italian commentaries of Castlevetro, Tasso, Mazzoni, and others, teaches what the laws are of a true epic poem, what of a dramatic, what of a lyric, what decorum is, which is the grand masterpiece to observe. This would make them soon perceive what despicable creatures our common rhymers and play-writers be; and show them what religious, what glorious and magnificent use might be made of poetry, both in divine and human things.

From hence, and not till now, will be the right season of forming them to be able writers and composers in every excellent matter, when they shall be thus fraught with an universal insight into things. Or whether they be to speak in parliament or council, honour and attention would be waiting on their lips. There would then also appear in pulpits other visage, other gestures, and stuff otherwise wrought than what we now sit under, oft-times to as great a trial of our patience as any other that they preach to us. These are the studies wherein our noble and our gentle youth ought to bestow their time, in a disciplinary way, from twelve to one and twenty: unless they rely more upon their ancestors dead, than upon themselves living. In which methodical course it is so supposed they must proceed by the steady pace of learning onward, as at convenient times, for memory's sake, to retire back into the middle ward, and sometimes into the rear of what they have been taught, until they have confirmed and solidly united the whole body of their perfected knowledge, like the embattling of a Roman legion. Now will be worth the seeing, what exercises and recreations may best agree, and become these studies.

The course of study hitherto briefly described is, what I can guess by reading, likest to those ancient and famous schools of Pythagoras, Plato, Isocrates, Aristotle, and such others, out of which were bred such a number of renowned philosophers, orators, historians, poets, and princes all over Greece, Italy, and Asia, besides the flourishing studies of Cyrene and Alexandria. But herein it shall exceed them, and supply a defect as great as that which Plato noted in the commonwealth of Sparta; whereas that city trained up their youth most for war, and these in their academies and Lycæum all for the gown, this institution of breeding which I here delineate shall be equally good both for peace and war. Therefore, about an hour and a half ere they eat at noon should be allowed them for exercise, and due rest afterwards; but the time for this may be enlarged at pleasure, according as their rising in the morning shall be early.

The exercise which I commend first, is the exact use of their weapon, to guard, and to strike safely with edge or point; this will keep them healthy, nimble, strong, and well in breath; is also the likeliest means to make them grow large and tall, and to inspire them with a gallant and fearless courage, which being tempered with seasonable lectures and precepts to them of true fortitude and patience, will turn into a native and heroic valour, and make them hate the cowardice of doing wrong. They must be also practised in all the locks and gripes of wrestling, wherein Englishmen were wont to excel, as need may often be in fight to tug, to grapple, and to close. And this perhaps will be enough, wherein to prove and heat their single strength.

The interim of unsweating themselves regularly, and convenient rest before meat, may, both with profit and delight, be taken up in recreating and composing their travailed spirits with the solemn and divine harmonies of music, heard or learned; either whilst the skilful organist plies his grave and fancied descant in lofty fugues, or the whole symphony with artful and unimaginable touches adorn and grace the well-studied chords of some choice composer; sometimes the lute or soft organ-stop waiting on elegant voices, either to religious, martial, or civil ditties; which, if wise men and prophets be not extremely out, have a great power over dispositions and manners, to smooth and make them gentle from rustic harshness and distempered passions. The like also would not be unexpedient after meat, to assist and cherish nature in her first concoction, and send their minds back to study in good tune and satisfaction. Where having followed it close under vigilant eyes, till about two hours before supper, they are, by a sudden alarum or watchword, to be called out to their military motions, under sky or covert, according to the season, as was the Roman wont; first on foot, then, as their age permits, on horseback, to all the art of cavalry; that having in sport, but with much exactness and daily muster, served out the rudiments of their soldiership, in all the skill of embattling, marching, encamping, fortifying, besieging, and battering, with all the helps of ancient and modern strategems, tactics, and warlike maxims, they may as it were out of a long war come forth renowned and perfect commanders in the service of their country. They would not then, if they were trusted with fair and hopeful armies, suffer them, for want of just and wise discipline, to shed away from about them like sick feathers, though they be never so oft supplied; they would not suffer their empty and unrecruitable colonels of twenty men in a company, to quaff out or convey into secret hoards, the wages of a delusive list, and miserable remnant; yet in the meanwhile to be overmastered with a score or two of drunkards, the only soldiery left about them, or else to comply with all rapines and violences. No, certainly, if they knew aught of that knowledge that belongs to good men or good governors, they would not suffer these things.

But to return to our own institute: besides these constant exercises at home, there is another opportunity of gaining experience to be won from pleasure itself abroad; in those vernal seasons of the year when the air is calm and pleasant, it were an injury and sullenness against nature, not to go out and see her riches, and partake in her rejoicing with heaven and earth. I should not therefore be a persuader to them of studying much then, after two or three years that they have well laid their grounds, but to ride out in companies, with prudent and staid guides, to all the quarters of the land: learning and observing all places of strength, all commodities of building and of soil, for towns and tillage, harbours and ports for trade. Sometimes taking sea as far as to our navy, to learn there also what they can in the practical knowledge of sailing and of sea-fight.

These ways would try all their peculiar gifts of nature; and if there were any secret excellence among them would fetch it out, and give it fair opportunities to advance itself by, which could not but mightily redound to the good of this nation, and bring into fashion again those old admired virtues and excellencies, with far more knowledge now in this purity of Christian knowledge. Nor shall we then need the monsieurs of Paris to take our hopeful youth into their slight and prodigal custodies, and send them over, back again, transformed into mimics, apes, and kickshaws. But if they desire to see other countries at three or four and twenty years of age, not to learn principles, but to enlarge experience, and make wise observation, they will by that time be such as shall deserve the regard and honour of all men where they pass, and the society and friendship of those in all places who are best and most eminent. And, perhaps, then other nations will be glad to visit us for their breeding, or else to imitate us in their own country.

Now, lastly, for their diet there cannot be much to say, save only that it would be best in the same house; for much time else would be lost abroad, and many ill habits got; and that it should be plain, healthful, and moderate, I suppose is out of controversy.

Thus, Mr. Hartlib, you have a general view in writing, as your desire was, of that which at several times I had discoursed with you concerning the best and noblest way of education; not beginning, as some have done, from the cradle, which yet might be worth many considerations, if brevity had not been my scope; many other circumstances also I could have mentioned, but this, to such as have the worth in them to make trial, for light and direction may be enough. Only I believe that this is not a bow for every man to shoot in, that counts himself a teacher; but will require sinews almost equal to those which Homer gave Ulysses; yet I am withal persuaded that it may prove much more easy in the assay, than it now seems at distance, and much more illustrious: howbeit, not more difficult than I imagine, and that imagination presents me with nothing but very happy, and very possible according to best wishes; if God have so decreed, and this age have spirit and capacity enought to apprehend.

1644

Thomas Fuller (1608–1661)

WORTHIES OF ENGLAND

JOHN TIPTOFT

John Tiptoft, son and heir of John Lord Tiptoft and Joyce his wife (daughter and co-heir of Edward Charlton Lord Powis by his wife Eleanor, sister and co-heir of Edmund Holland Earl of Kent) was born at Everton in this (but in the confines of Bedford) shire. He was bred in Baliol College in Oxford, where he attained to great learning; and by King Henry the Sixth was afterwards created first Vicecount, then Earl of Worcester, and Lord High Constable of England, and by King Edward the Fourth Knight of the Garter.

The skies began now to lower, and threaten Civil Wars; and the House of York fell sick of a relapse. Mean time this Earl could not be discourteous to Henry the Sixth, who had so much advanced him, nor disloyal to Edward the Fourth, in whom the right of the Crown lay. Consulting his own safety, he resolved on this expedient; for a time to quit his own, and visit the Holy-land. In his passage thither, or thence, he came to Rome, where he made a Latin speech before the Pope, Pius the Second, and converted the Italians into a better opinion than they had formerly of the Englishmen's learning, insomuch that his Holiness wept at the elegancy of the oration.

He returned from Christ's sepulcher to his own grave in England, coming home in a most unhappy juncture of time. If sooner, or later, he had found King Edward on that Throne, to which now Henry the Sixth was restored, and whose restitution was only remarkable for the death of this worthy Lord. Thus those who, when the house of the State is on fire, politicly hope to save their own chamber, are sometime burned therein.

Treason was charged upon him for secret siding with King Edward, who before and afterward *de facto*, and always *de jure*, was the lawful King of England. On this account he lost his life. Then did the axe at one blow cut off more learning in England than was left in the heads of all the surviving Nobility. His death happened on Saint Luke's day 1470.

THOMAS CORIAT

Thomas Coriat. Though some will censure him, as a person rather ridiculous than remarkable, he must not be omitted; for, first, few would be found to call him fool, might none do it save such who had as much learning as himself. Secondly, if others have more wisdom than he, thankfulness and humility is the way to preserve and increase it. He was born at Odcombe, nigh Evil, in this county; bred at Oxford, where he attained to admirable fluency in the Greek tongue. He carried folly (which the charitable called merriment) in his very face. The shape of his head had no promising form, being like a sugar-loaf inverted, with the little end before, as composed of fancy and memory, without any common-sense.

Such as conceived him fool *ad duo*, and something else *ad decem*, were utterly mistaken; for he drave on no design, carrying for coin and counters alike: so contented with what was present, that he accounted those men guilty of superfluity, who had more suits and shirts than bodies, seldom putting off either till they were ready to go away from him.

Prince Henry allowed him a pension, and kept him for his servant. Sweetmeats and Coriat made up the last course at all Court-entertainments. Indeed he was the courtiers' anvil to try their wits upon; and sometimes this anvil returned the hammers as hard knocks as it received, his bluntness repaying their abusiveness.

His book, known by the name of 'Coriat's Crudities,' nauseous to nice readers, for the rawness thereof, is not altogether useless; though the porch be more worth than the palace, I mean, the preface, of other men's mock-commending verses thereon.

At last he undertook to travail into the East Indies by land, mounted on an horse with ten toes, being excellently qualified for such a journey; for rare his dexterity (so properly as consisting most in manual signs) in interpreting and answering the dumb tokens of nations, whose language he did not understand. Besides, such his patience in all distresses, that in some sort he might seem, cooled with heat, fed with fasting, and refreshed with weariness. All expecting his return with more knowledge (though not more wisdom), he ended his earthly pilgrimage in the midst of his Indian travail, about (as I collect) the year of our Lord 1616.

WILLIAM SHAKESPEARE

William Shakespeare was born at Stratford on Avon in this county; in whom three eminent poets may seem in some sort to be compounded. 1. Martial, in the warlike sound of his surname (whence some may conjecture him of a military extraction) *Hastivibrans*, or *Shake-speare*. 2. Ovid, the most natural and witty of all poets; and hence it was that Queen Elizabeth, coming into a grammar-school, made this extemporary verse,

> 'Persius a crab-staff, bawdy Martial, Ovid a fine wag.'

3. Plautus, who was an exact comedian, yet never any scholar, as our Shakespeare (if alive) would confess himself. Add to all these, that though his genius generally was jocular, and inclining him to festivity, yet he could (when so disposed) be solemn and serious, as appears by his tragedies; so that Heraclitus himself (I mean if secret and unseen) might afford to smile at his comedies, they were so merry; and Democritus scarce forbear to sigh at his tragedies, they were so mournful.

He was an eminent instance of the truth of that rule, '*Poeta non fit, sed nascitur;*' one is not made, but born a poet. Indeed his learning was very little, so that, as Cornish diamonds are not polished by any lapidary, but are pointed and smoothed even as they are taken out of the earth, so Nature itself was all the art which was used upon him.

Many were the wit-combats betwixt him and Ben Jonson; which two I behold like a Spanish great galleon and an English man-of-war: Master Jonson (like the former) was built far higher in learning; solid, but slow, in his performances. Shake-speare, with the English man-of-war, lesser in bulk, but lighter in sailing, could turn with all tides, tack about, and take advantage of all winds, by the quickness of his wit and invention. He died *anno Domini* 16—, and was buried at Stratford upon Avon, the town of his nativity.

1662

RESTORATION AND EIGHTEENTH CENTURY

PARALLEL READINGS

RESTORATION

Drama

1. Dryden — *All for Love*
2. Otway — *Venice Preserved*
3. Congreve — *The Way of the World*

Allegory

1. Bunyan — *Pilgrim's Progress*

AGE OF POPE

Satire

1. Swift — *Gulliver's Travels*

Drama

1. Rowe — *The Fair Penitent*
2. Gay — *The Beggar's Opera*
3. Lillo — *The London Merchant*

Novel

1. Defoe — *Captain Singleton*
2. Richardson — *Pamela*
3. Fielding — *Joseph Andrews*

AGE OF JOHNSON

History and Oratory

1. Gibbon — *Decline and Fall,* selections
2. Burke — *On Conciliation with America, To a Noble Lord, On Warren Hastings*

Drama

1. Goldsmith — *She Stoops to Conquer*
2. Sheridan — *The Rivals*

Novel

1. Walpole — *Castle of Otranto*
2. Goldsmith — *Vicar of Wakefield*
3. Burney — *Evelina*
4. Beckford — *Vathek*

RESTORATION AND EIGHTEENTH CENTURY

SATIRE AND ESSAY

The Restoration of Charles II. to the English throne in 1660 marks the beginning of a new era. As a reaction against the social restraint and religious bigotry of the Puritan régime, the court, permeated as it was by French influences, became corrupt in morals and cynical and materialistic in temper. Following the lead of the court, polite society in general adopted sophisticated standards. Fearful of emotionalism, the upper classes sought for a test of human values that should be purely intellectual, and they found it in Rationalism, "common sense," Reason. The norm of humanity became the polished city man as opposed to the simple rustic, and the carefully trimmed garden ('Nature methodized') was admired at the expense of the wild, uncultivated landscape. The period was one of questioning and investigation in science and of satire and criticism in literature. It has been called the Age of Reason.

Late in the seventeenth century the rule of Reason associated itself with a body of critical principles known as Classicism. Applied to eighteenth-century literature, the term Classicism designates the imitation of the working principles of ancient Greek and Latin masterpieces as these principles were elaborated and reinterpreted by English and Continental, especially French, critics. In the eyes of the typical Classicist the supposed rules of the Ancients assumed an exaggerated authority. Toward the close of the seventeenth century the admiration of Classical models at the expense of more recent literature, including Shakespeare, resulted in a spirited controversy known as the "Quarrel of the Ancients and Moderns." Reason and Classicism, though overemphasizing the mechanical and intellectual elements in literary composition, performed a real service by urging the importance of clarity, order, and technical excellence.

With the subordination of emotion to intellect and of originality to imitation, the lyric poetry of the Restoration became less spontaneous. The ode, imitated from Pindar or Horace and adapted to English conditions, became a popular form. Social criticism and satire predominated in the non-dramatic poetry of the period, and prose began to rank with verse as an accepted vehicle of expression. The usual verse-form, at least for longer poems, was the couplet consisting of two ten-syllable rhyming lines and called Heroic because of its original employment in Heroic literature.

The new prose, originating in the pamphlet warfare and foreign news bulletins of the Puritan period, developed rapidly in the spirited journalism of the late seventeenth century. In the hands of men of literary talent associated with affairs of state (*e.g.*, Temple) it became a far more practical, if less ornamental, form than it had been previously. The specific literary types developed were the familiar essay, which reached its perfection in the work of Steele and Addison, and, early in the eighteenth century, the novel with its strong appeal to the new self-consciousness of the middle classes. From the beginning of the eighteenth century till the present day the history of English prose has been continuous.

The artificial suppression of the drama during the Puritan period was followed at the Restoration by a revival of dramatic interest. Of the various types of drama, in both verse and prose, that flourished during the late seventeenth century, the most characteristic was realistic comedy full of clever dialogue between personages drawn from the upper circles of society. Less democratic than the drama of the Elizabethan age, that of the Restoration was dominated by the Court and reflected its moral laxity and cold intellectuality. About the close of the seventeenth century an effort at reform was attempted in the sentimental drama, which emphasized virtuous conduct and the innate goodness of man.

The Age of Reason bore within itself the seeds of a new order of things. Even during the seventeenth century there were intimations that the so-called Rational view of the world was not entirely satisfactory. Science and philosophy revealed hitherto unsuspected beauties in the universe and in mankind, and the wilder aspects of Nature gained in favor as subjects of enthusiasm. With the rise of democratic ideas in government and society, greater emphasis was laid upon the virtues of the unsophisticated, and the simple peasant began to assume a new importance in the eyes of social theorists and poets. In religion and morals the true test of thought and conduct was found more and more in emotion rather than in intellect, in the heart rather than in the head. The conviction grew that luxury and sophistication were evils, and that poetry, along with the other arts, was doomed unless Rules were subordinated to spontaneous and original Genius. In short, the true solution of the human problem was found in a new Return to Nature.

As we progress through the eighteenth century, we find these ideas more and more clearly reflected in literature. Poets seek inspiration in simple country scenes (*e.g.*, Thomson, Goldsmith), in night and solitude (*e.g.*, Lady Winchilsea, Collins, Gray, Young, Blair), in the literature of the folk (see the ballad imitations), in Shakespeare, Spenser, and mediæval romance (*e.g.*, Thomson, Warton, Gray), and in writers such as Homer, the Celtic bards, and the Scandinavian skalds (*e.g.*, Gray), who were supposed to have lived in more primitive times and to have composed poetry by the aid of Original Genius rather than by Rules. Secular lyrics as well as hymns show a more profound sense of spiritual values and of the bond that unites man to his fellow-man and to the hereafter. In short, before Classicism had run its course, new forces, known as Romantic, were already at work in life and in literature.

18th cen prose

RESTORATION

POETRY

SATIRE

Samuel Butler (1612–1680)

HUDIBRAS, PART I, CANTO I

THE ARGUMENT

Sir Hudibras his passing worth,
The manner how he sallied forth,
His arms and equipage are shown,
His horse's virtues and his own:
Th' adventure of the bear and fiddle
Is sung, but breaks off in the middle.

When civil fury first grew high,
And men fell out, they knew not why;
When hard words, jealousies, and fears,
Set folks together by the ears,
And made them fight, like mad or drunk,
For Dame Religion as for punk;
Whose honesty they all durst swear for,
Though not a man of them knew wherefore;
When gospel-trumpeter, surrounded
With long-eared rout, to battle sounded;
And pulpit, drum ecclesiastic,
Was beat with fist instead of a stick;
Then did Sir Knight abandon dwelling,
And out he rode a colonelling.
A wight he was, whose very sight would
Entitle him Mirror of Knighthood,
That never bowed his stubborn knee
To any thing but chivalry,
Nor put up blow, but that which laid
Right Worshipful on shoulder-blade;
Chief of domestic knights and errant,
Either for chartel or for warrant;
Great on the bench, great in the saddle,
That could as well bind o'er as swaddle;
Mighty he was at both of these
And styled of War, as well as Peace:
(So some rats, of amphibious nature,
Are either for the land or water).
But here our authors make a doubt
Whether he were more wise or stout:
Some hold the one, and some the other,
But, howsoe'er they make a pother,
The diff'rence was so small, his brain
Outweighed his rage but half a grain;
Which made some take him for a tool
That knaves do work with, called a Fool.
For 't has been held by many, that
As Montaigne, playing with his cat,
Complains she thought him but an ass,
Much more she would Sir Hudibras:
(For that 's the name our valiant Knight
To all his challenges did write).
But they're mistaken very much;
'T is plain enough he was no such.
We grant, although he had much wit,
H' was very shy of using it,
As being loth to wear it out,
And therefore bore it not about,
Unless on holidays or so,
As men their best apparel do.
Beside, 't is known he could speak Greek
As naturally as pigs squeak;
That Latin was no more difficile,
Than to a blackbird 't is to whistle:
Being rich in both, he never scanted
His bounty unto such as wanted;
But much of either would afford
To many that had not one word.
For Hebrew roots, although they're found
To flourish most in barren ground,
He had such plenty as sufficed
To make some think him circumcised.
He was in logic a great critic,
Profoundly skilled in analytic;
He could distinguish, and divide
A hair 'twixt south and south-west side;
On either which he would dispute,
Confute, change hands, and still confute:
He'd undertake to prove, by force
Of argument, a man's no horse;
He'd prove a buzzard is no fowl,
And that a lord may be an owl;
A calf an alderman, a goose a justice.

And rocks Comittee-men and Trustees.
He 'd run in debt by disputation,
And pay with ratiocination:
All this by syllogism, true
In mood and figure he would do.
For rhetoric, he could not ope
His mouth, but out there flew a trope;
And when he happened to break off
I' th' middle of his speech, or cough,
H' had hard words ready to show why,
And tell what rules he did it by;
Else, when with greatest art he spoke,
You 'd think he talked like other folk;
For all a rhetorician's rules
Teach nothing but to name his tools.
But, when he pleased to show 't, his speech,
In loftiness of sound was rich;
A Babylonish dialect,
Which learnèd pedants much affect;
It was a party-coloured dress
Of patched and piebald languages;
'T was English cut on Greek and Latin,
Like fustian heretofore on satin;
It had an odd promiscuous tone,
As if h' had talked three parts in one;
Which made some think, when he did gabble,
Th' had heard three labourers of Babel,
Or Cerberus himself pronounce
A leash of languages at once.
This he as volubly would vent,
As if his stock would ne'er be spent:
And truly, to support that charge,
He had supplies as vast and large;
For he could coin or counterfeit
New words with little or no wit;
Words so debased and hard, no stone
Was hard enough to touch them on;
And when with hasty noise he spoke 'em,
The ignorant for current took 'em;
That, had the orator, who once
Did fill his mouth with pebble stones
When he harangued, but known his phrase,
He would have used no other ways.
In Mathematics he was greater
Than Tycho Brahe or Erra Pater;
For he, by geometric scale,
Could take the size of pots of ale;
Resolve by sines and tangents, straight
If bread or butter wanted weight;
And wisely tell what hour o' th' day
The clock does strike, by algebra.
Beside, he was a shrewd philosopher,
And had read every text and gloss over;
Whate'er the crabbed'st author hath,
He understood b' implicit faith:
Whatever sceptic could inquire for,
For every why he had a wherefore;
Knew more than forty of them do,
As far as words and terms could go;
All which he understood by rote,
And, as occasion served, would quote;
No matter whether right or wrong;
They might be either said or sung.
His notions fitted things so well,
That which was which he could not tell,
But oftentimes mistook the one
For th' other, as great clerks have done;
He could reduce all things to acts,
And knew their natures by abstracts;
Where Entity and Quiddity,
The ghosts of defunct bodies, fly;
Where truth in person does appear,
Like words congealed in northern air.
He knew what 's what, and that 's as high
As metaphysic wit can fly:
In school-divinity as able
As he that hight Irrefragable;
A second Thomas, or, at once,
To name them all, another Duns:
Profound in all the nominal
And real ways beyond them all;
And, with as delicate a hand,
Could twist as tough a rope of sand;
And weave fine cobwebs, fit for scull
That's empty when the moon is full;
Such as take lodgings in a head
That's to be let unfurnishèd.
He could raise scruples dark and nice,
And after solve 'em in a trice;
As if Divinity had catched
The itch, on purpose to be scratched;
Or, like a mountebank, did wound
And stab herself with doubts profound,
Only to show with how small pain
The sores of Faith are cured again;
Although by woful proof we find
They always leave a scar behind.
He knew the seat of Paradise,
Could tell in what degree it lies,
And, as he was disposed, could prove it
Below the moon, or else above it;
What Adam dreamt of, when his bride
Came from her closet in his side;
Whether the devil tempted her
By an high Dutch interpreter; . . .
Whether the Serpent, at the Fall,
Had cloven feet, or none at all:
All this, without a gloss or comment,
He could unriddle in a moment,
In proper terms, such as men smatter
When they throw out, and miss the matter.
For his religion, it was fit
To match his learning and his wit:
'T was Presbyterian true blue;
For he was of that stubborn crew
Of errant saints, whom all men grant
To be the true Church Militant;

Such as do build their faith upon
The holy text of pike and gun;
Decide all controversies by
Infallible artillery;
And prove their doctrine orthodox,
By apostolic blows and knocks;
Call fire and sword, and desolation,
A godly, thorough Reformation,
Which always must be carried on,
And still be doing, never done;
As if Religion were intended
For nothing else but to be mended:
A sect whose chief devotion lies
In odd perverse antipathies;
In falling out with that or this,
And finding somewhat still amiss;
More peevish, cross, and splenetic,
Than dog distract, or monkey sick:
That with more care keep holiday
The wrong, than others the right way;
Compound for sins they are inclined to,
By damning those they have no mind to:
Still so perverse and opposite,
As if they worshipped God for spite:
The self-same thing they will abhor
One way, and long another for:
Free-will they one way disavow,
Another, nothing else allow:
All piety consists therein
In them, in other men all sin:
Rather than fail, they will defy
That which they love most tenderly;
Quarrel with minced-pies, and disparage
Their best and dearest friend, plum-porridge;
Fat pig and goose itself oppose,
And blaspheme custard through the nose.
Th' apostles of this fierce religion,
Like Mahomet's, were ass and widgeon,
To whom our knight, by fast instinct
Of wit and temper, was so linkt,
As if hypocrisy and nonsense
Had got th' advowson of his conscience.
  Thus was he gifted and accoutred,
We mean on th' inside, not the outward:
That next of all we shall discuss;
Then listen, Sirs, it follows thus.
His tawny beard was th' equal grace
Both of his wisdom and his face;
In cut and die so like a tile,
A sudden view it would beguile;
The upper part whereof was whey,
The nether orange, mixed with gray.
This hairy meteor did denounce
The fall of sceptres and of crowns;
With grisly type did represent
Declining age of government,
And tell, with hieroglyphic spade,
Its own grave and the State's were made:
Like Samson's heart-breakers, it grew
In time to make a nation rue;
Though it contributed its own fall,
To wait upon the public downfall:
It was monastic, and did grow
In holy orders by strict vow.
Of rule as sullen and severe,
As that of rigid Cordeliere:
'T was bound to suffer persecution,
And martyrdom, with resolution;
T' oppose itself against the hate
And vengeance of th' incensèd state,
In whose defiance it was worn,
Still ready to be pulled and torn,
With red-hot irons to be tortured,
Reviled, and spit upon, and martyred;
Maugre all which 't was to stand fast
As long as monarchy should last;
But, when the state should hap to reel,
'T was to submit to fatal steel,
And fall, as it was consecrate,
A sacrifice to fall of state,
Whose thread of life the Fatal Sisters
Did twist together with its whiskers,
And twine so close that Time should never,
In life or death, their fortunes sever,
But with his rusty sickle mow
Both down together at a blow.
  So learnèd Taliacotius, from
The brawny part of porter's bum,
Cut supplemental noses, which
Would last as long as parent breech,
But when the date of Nock was out,
Off dropt the sympathetic snout.
His back, or rather burthen, showed
As if it stooped with its own load:
For as Æneas bore his sire
Upon his shoulders through the fire,
Our knight did bear no less a pack
Of his own buttocks on his back;
Which now had almost got the upper-
Hand of his head, for want of crupper.
To poise this equally, he bore
A paunch of the same bulk before,
Which still he had a special care
To keep well-crammed with thrifty fare,
As white-pot, butter-milk, and curds,
Such as a country-house affords;
With other victual, which anon
We farther shall dilate upon,
When of his hose we come to treat,
The cup-board where he kept his meat.
  His doublet was of sturdy buff,
And though not sword, yet cudgel-proof,
Whereby 't was fitter for his use
Who feared no blows but such as bruise.
  His breeches were of rugged woollen,
And had been at the siege of Bullen;
To Old King Harry so well known,

Some writers held they were his own:
Through they were lined with many a piece
Of ammunition bread and cheese,
And fat black-puddings, proper food
For warriors that delight in blood.
For, as we said, he always chose
To carry victual in his hose,
That often tempted rats and mice
The ammunition to surprise;
And when he put a hand but in
The one or t' other magazine,
They stoutly in defence on 't stood,
And from the wounded foe drew blood;
And till th' were stormed, and beaten out,
Ne'er left the fortified redoubt.
And though knights-errant, as some think,
Of old did neither eat nor drink,
Because when thorough deserts vast,
And regions desolate, they passed,
Where belly-timber above ground
Or under was not to be found,
Unless they grazed there's not one word
Of their provision on record;
Which made some confidently write,
They had no stomachs but to fight:
'T is false; for Arthur wore in hall
Round table like a farthingal,
On which, with shirt pulled out behind,
And eke before, his good knights dined:
Though 't was no table some suppose,
But a huge pair of round trunk-hose,
In which he carried as much meat
As he and all his knights could eat,
When, laying by their swords and truncheons,
They took their breakfasts or their nuncheons.
But let that pass at present, lest
We should forget where we digest,
As learnèd authors use, to whom
We leave it, and to th' purpose come.
His puissant sword unto his side,
Near his undaunted heart, was tied,
With basket-hilt that would hold broth,
And serve for fight and dinner both;
In it he melted lead for bullets,
To shoot at foes, and sometimes pullets,
To whom he bore so fell a grutch,
He ne'er gave quarter t' any such.
The trenchant blade, Toledo trusty,
For want of fighting was grown rusty,
And ate into itself for lack
Of somebody to hew and hack:
The peaceful scabbard where it dwelt,
The rancour of its edge had felt;
For of the lower end two handful
It had devoured, 't was so manful,
And so much scorned to lurk in case,
As if it durst not shew its face.
In many desperate attempts
Of warrants, exigents, contempts,
It had appeared with courage bolder
Than Serjeant Bum invading shoulder:
Oft had it ta'en possession,
And pris'ners too, or made them run.
This sword a dagger had, his page,
That was but little for his age,
And therefore waited on him so,
As dwarfs upon knights-errant do.
It was a serviceable dudgeon,
Either for fighting or for drudging:
When it had stabbed, or broke a head,
It would scrape trenchers, or chip bread;
Toast cheese or bacon; though it were
To bait a mouse-trap, 't would not care:
'T would make clean shoes, and in the earth
Set leeks and onions, and so forth:
It had been 'prentice to a brewer,
Where this and more it did endure,
But left the trade as many more
Have lately done on the same score.
In th' holsters, at his saddle-bow,
Two agèd pistols he did stow,
Among the surplus of such meat
As in his hose he could not get:
These would inveigle rats with th' scent,
To forage when the cocks were bent,
And sometimes catch 'em with a snap,
As cleverly as th' ablest trap.
They were upon hard duty still,
And every night stood centinel,
To guard the magazine in th' hose
From two-legged and from four-legged foes.
Thus clad and fortified, Sir Knight
From peaceful home set forth to fight.
But first with nimble active force
He got on th' outside of his horse:
For having but one stirrup tied
T' his saddle on the further side,
It was so short h' had much ado
To reach it with his desp'rate toe;
But after many strains and heaves,
He got upon the saddle eaves,
From whence he vaulted into th' seat
With so much vigour, strength, and heat,
That he had almost tumbled over
With his own weight, but did recover
By laying hold on tail and mane,
Which oft he used instead of rein.
But now we talk of mounting steed,
Before we further do proceed,
It doth behove us to say something
Of that which bore our valiant bumkin.
The beast was sturdy, large, and tall,
With mouth of meal and eyes of wall,
I would say eye, for h' had but one,
As most agree, though some say none.
He was well staid, and in his gait,

H Goes forth

Preserved a grave, majestic state;
At spur or switch no more he skipt
Or mended pace, than Spaniard whipt,
And yet so fiery, he would bound,
As if he grieved to touch the ground;
That Cæsar's horse, who, as fame goes,
Had corns upon his feet and toes,
Was not by half so tender hooft,
Nor trod upon the ground so soft:
And as that beast would kneel and stoop
(Some write) to take his rider up;
So Hudibras his ('t is well known)
Would often do to set him down.
We shall not need to say what lack
Of leather was upon his back,
For that was hidden under pad,
And breech of Knight, galled full as bad.
His strutting ribs on both sides showed
Like furrows he himself had ploughed;
For underneath the skirt of pannel,
'Twixt ev'ry two there was a channel.
His draggling tail hung in the dirt,
Which on his rider he would flirt,
Still as his tender side he pricked,
With armed heel, or with unarmed, kicked:
For Hudibras wore but one spur,
As wisely knowing could he stir
To active trot one side of 's horse,
Th' other would not hang [back, of course].
A Squire he had whose name was Ralph,
That in th' adventure went his half,
Though writers, for more stately tone,
Do call him Ralpho, 't is all one;
And when we can, with metre safe,
We'll call him so; if not, plain Raph,
(For rhyme the rudder is of verses,
With which, like ships, they steer their courses):
An equal stock of wit and valour
He had laid in, by birth a tailor.
The mighty Tyrian Queen, that gained
With subtle shreds a tract of land,
Did leave it with a castle fair
To his great ancestor, her heir;
From him descended cross-legged knights,
Famed for their faith, and warlike fights
Against the bloody Cannibal,
Whom they destroyed both great and small.
This sturdy Squire he had, as well
As the bold Trojan Knight, seen hell,
Not with a counterfeited pass
Of golden bough, but true gold-lace:
His knowledge was not far behind
The Knight's, but of another kind,
And he another way came by 't,
Some call it Gifts, and some New-light;
A lib'ral art, that costs no pains
Of study, industry, or brains.
His wit was sent him for a token,
But in the carriage cracked and broken;
Like commendation ninepence crooked
With — To and from my love — it looked.
He ne'er considered it, as loth
To look a gift-horse in the mouth,
And very wisely would lay forth
No more upon it than 't was worth;
But as he got it freely, so
He spent it frank and freely too:
For saints themselves will sometimes be,
Of gifts that cost them nothing, free.
By means of this, with hem and cough,
Prolongers to enlightened stuff,
He could deep mysteries unriddle,
As easily as thread a needle:
For as of vagabonds we say,
That they are ne'er beside their way,
Whate'er men speak by this new light,
Still they are sure to be i' th' right.
'T is a dark-lantern of the spirit,
Which none see by but those that bear it;
A light that falls down from on high,
For spiritual trades to cozen by;
An *ignis fatuus*, that bewitches,
And leads men into pools and ditches,
To make them dip themselves, and sound
For Christendom in dirty pond;
To dive like wild-fowl for salvation,
And fish to catch regeneration.
This light inspires and plays upon
The nose of saint, like bagpipe drone,
And speaks through hollow empty soul,
As through a trunk, or whisp'ring hole,
Such language as no mortal ear
But spiritual eaves-droppers can hear:
So Phœbus, or some friendly muse,
Into small poets song infuse;
Which they at second-hand rehearse,
Through reed or bagpipe, verse for verse.
Thus Ralph became infallible,
As three or four-legged oracle,
The ancient cup, or modern chair
Spoke truth point-blank, though unaware.
For mystic learning, wondrous able
In magic, talisman and cabal,
Whose primitive tradition reaches
As far as Adam's first green breeches;
Deep-sighted in intelligences,
Ideas, atoms, influences;
And much of *Terra Incognita*,
Th' intelligible world, could say;
A deep occult philosopher,
As learn'd as the wild Irish are,
Or Sir Agrippa, for profound
And solid lying much renowned:
He Anthroposophus, and Floud,
And Jacob Behmen understood;
Knew many an amulet and charm,

That would do neither good nor harm;
In Rosicrucian lore as learned
As he that *verè adeptus* earned:
He understood the speech of birds
As well as they themselves do words;
Could tell what subtlest parrots mean,
That speak and think contrary clean;
What member 't is of whom they talk,
When they cry Rope, and Walk, Knave,
  Walk.
He 'd extract numbers out of matter,
And keep them in a glass, like water,
Of sov'reign pow'r to make men wise;
For, dropt in blear, thick-sighted eyes,
They 'd make them see in darkest night,
Like owls, though purblind in the light.
By help of these (as he profest)
He had First Matter seen undrest:
He took her naked, all alone,
Before one rag of form was on.
The chaos, too, he had descried,
And seen quite through, or else he lied:
Not that of pasteboard, which men shew
For groats at fair of Barthol'mew;
But its great grandsire, first o' th' name,
Whence that and Reformation came,
Both cousin-germans, and right able
T' inveigle and draw in the rabble:
But Reformation was, some say,
O' th' younger house to puppet-play.
He could foretell whats'ever was
By consequence, to come to pass;
As death of great men, alterations,
Diseases, battles, inundations:
All this without th' eclipse of th' sun,
Or dreadful comet, he hath done
By inward light, a way as good,
And easy to be understood;
But with more lucky hit than those
That use to make the stars depose,
Like Knights o' th' Post, and falsely charge
Upon themselves what others forge;
As if they were consenting to
All mischiefs in the world men do,
Or, like the devil, did tempt and sway 'em
To rogueries, and then betray 'em.
They 'll search a planet's house, to know
Who broke and robbed a house below;
Examine Venus and the Moon,
Who stole a thimble or a spoon;
And though they nothing will confess,
Yet by their very looks can guess,
And tell what guilty aspect bodes,
Who stole, and who received the goods:
They 'll question Mars, and, by his look,
Detect who 't was that nimmed a cloak;
Make Mercury confess, and 'peach
Those thieves which he himself did teach.
They 'll find, i' th' physiognomies
O' th' planets, all men's destinies,
Like him that took the doctor's bill,
And swallowed it instead o' th' pill;
Cast the nativity o' th' question,
And from positions to be guessed on,
As sure as if they knew the moment
Of Native's birth, tell what will come on't.
They 'll feel the pulses of the stars,
To find out agues, coughs, catarrhs,
And tell what crisis does divine
The rot in sheep, or mange in swine;
In men, what gives or cures the itch,
What makes them cuckolds, poor, or
  rich;
What gains or loses, hangs or saves;
What makes men great, what fools or knaves,
But not what wise, for only of those
The stars (they say) cannot dispose,
No more than can the astrologians;
There they say right, and like true Trojans:
This Ralpho knew, and therefore took
The other course, of which we spoke.
  Thus was th' accomplished squire endued
With gifts and knowledge per'lous
  shrewd:
Never did trusty squire with knight,
Or knight with squire, e'er jump more right.
Their arms and equipage did fit,
As well as virtues, parts, and wit:
Their valors, too, were of a rate;
And out they sallied at the gate.
Few miles on horseback had they jogged
But fortune unto them turned dogged;
For they a sad adventure met,
Of which anon we mean to treat.
But ere we venture to unfold
Achievements so resolved and bold,
We should, as learned poets use,
Invoke th' assistance of some Muse,
However critics count it sillier,
Than jugglers talking to familiar;
We think 't is no great matter which,
They 're all alike, yet we shall pitch
On one that fits our purpose most,
Whom therefore thus we do accost: —
  Thou that with ale or viler liquors,
Didst inspire Withers, Pryn, and Vickars,
And force them, though it was in spite
Of Nature, and their stars, to write;
Who (as we find in sullen writs,
And cross-grained works of modern wits)
With vanity, opinion, want,
The wonder of the ignorant,
The praises of the author, penned
B' himself or wit-insuring friend,
The itch of picture in the front,
With bays and wicked rhyme upon 't,
(All that is left o' th' forked hill
To make men scribble without skill)

Canst make a poet, spite of Fate,
And teach all people to translate,
Though out of languages in which
They understand no part of speech;
Assist me but this once, I 'mplore,
And I shall trouble thee no more.
  In western clime there is a town,
To those that dwell therein well known,
Therefore there needs no more be said here,
We unto them refer our reader;
For brevity is very good,
When w' are, or are not understood.
To this town people did repair
On days of market, or of fair,
And to cracked fiddle, and hoarse tabor,
In merriment did drudge and labour:
But now a sport more formidable
Had raked together village rabble;
'T was an old way of recreating,
Which learnèd butchers call Bear-baiting;
A bold advent'rous exercise,
With ancient heroes in high prize;
For authors do affirm it came
From Isthmian or Nemean game;
Others derive it from the Bear
That's fixed in northern hemisphere,
And round about the pole does make
A circle, like a bear at stake,
That at the chain's end wheels about,
And overturns the rabble-rout:
For, after solemn proclamation
In the bear's name (as is the fashion
According to the law of arms,
To keep men from inglorious harms)
That none presume to come so near
As forty feet of stake of bear,
If any yet be so fool-hardy
T' expose themselves to vain jeopardy,
If they come wounded off and lame,
No honor's got by such a maim,
Although the bear gain much, being bound
In honour to make good his ground,
When he 's engaged, and take no notice,
If any press upon him, who 't is,
But lets them know, at their own cost,
That he intends to keep his post.
This to prevent and other harms
Which always wait on feats of arms
(For in the hurry of a fray
'T is hard to keep out of harm's way),
Thither the Knight his course did steer,
To keep the peace 'twixt dog and bear,
As he believed he was bound to do
In conscience and commission too;
And therefore thus bespoke the Squire: —
  We that are wisely mounted higher
Than constables in curule wit,
When on tribunal bench we sit,
Like speculators should foresee,
From Pharos of authority,
Portended mischiefs further than
Low Proletarian tithing-men;
And therefore, being informed by bruit
That Dog and Bear are to dispute,
For so of late men fighting name,
Because they often prove the same
(For where the first does hap to be,
The last does *coincidere*);
Quantum in nobis, have thought good
To save th' expense of Christian blood,
And try if we by mediation
Of treaty and accommodation,
Can end the quarrel, and compose
The bloody duel without blows.
Are not our liberties, our lives,
The laws, religion, and our wives,
Enough at once to lie at stake
For Cov'nant and the Cause's sake?
But in that quarrel Dogs and Bears,
As well as we, must venture theirs?
This feud, by Jesuits invented,
By evil counsel is fomented;
There is a Machiavellian plot
(Though ev'ry *nare olfact* it not)
And deep design in 't to divide
The well-affected that confide,
By setting brother against brother,
To claw and curry one another.
Have we not enemies *plus satis*,
That *cane et angue pejus* hate us?
And shall we turn our fangs and claws
Upon our own selves, without cause?
That some occult design doth lie
In bloody cynarctomachy,
Is plain enough to him that knows
How saints lead brothers by the nose.
I wish myself a pseudo-prophet,
But sure some mischief will come of it,
Unless by providential wit,
Or force, we averruncate it.
For what design, what interest,
Can beast have to encounter beast?
They fight for no espousèd cause,
Frail privilege, fundamental laws,
Nor for a thorough reformation,
Nor covenant, nor protestation,
Nor liberty of consciences,
Nor lords' and commons' ordinances;
Nor for the church, nor for church-lands,
To get them into their own hands;
Nor evil counsellers to bring
To justice, that seduce the King;
Nor for the worship of us men,
Though we have done as much for them.
Th' Egyptians worshipped dogs, and for
Their faith made internecine war;
Others adored a rat, and some

For that church suffered martyrdom;
The Indians fought for the truth
Of th' elephant and monkey's tooth,
And many, to defend the faith,
Fought it out *mordicus* to death;
But no beast ever was so slight,
For man, as for his God, to fight:
They have more wit, alas! and know
Themselves and us better than so.
But we, who only do infuse
The rage in them like *boute-feus*,
'T is our example that instils
In them the infection of our ills. . . .
Just so, by our example, cattle
Learn to give one another battle.
We read in Nero's time, the Heathen,
When they destroyed the Christian brethren,
They sewed them in the skins of bears,
And then set dogs about their ears;
From whence, no doubt, th' invention came
Of this lewd antichristian game.
  To this, quoth Ralpho, verily
The point seems very plain to me;
It is an antichristian game,
Unlawful both in thing and name.
First, for the name; the word bear-baiting
Is carnal, and of man's creating,
For certainly there's no such word
In all the Scripture on record;
Therefore unlawful, and a sin:
And so is (secondly) the thing;
A vile assembly 't is, that can
No more be proved by Scripture than
Provincial, Classic, National,
Mere human creature cobwebs all.
Thirdly, it is idolatrous;
For when men run a-[riot] thus
With their inventions, whatsoe'er
The thing be, whether Dog or Bear,
It is idolatrous and Pagan,
No less than worshipping of Dagon.
  Quoth Hudibras, I smell a rat;
Ralpho, thou dost prevaricate:
For though the thesis which thou lay'st
Be true *ad amussim*, as thou say'st
(For that Bear-baiting should appear
Jure divino lawfuller
Than Synods are, thou dost deny
Totidem verbis, so do I):
Yet there's a fallacy in this; . . .
Thou wouldst sophistically imply
Both are unlawful, I deny.
  And I, quoth Ralpho, do not doubt
But Bear-baiting may be made out,
In Gospel times, as lawful as is
Provincial, or Parochial Classis;
And that both are so near of kin,
And like in all, as well as sin,
That put 'em in a bag, and shake 'em,
Your self o' th' sudden would mistake 'em,
And not know which is which, unless
You measure by their wickedness;
For 't is not hard t' imagine whether
O' th' two is worst, though I name neither.
  Quoth Hudibras, thou offer'st much,
But art not able to keep touch;
Mira de lente, as 't is i' the adage,
Id est, to make a leek a cabbage:
Thou can'st at best but overstrain
A paradox, and th' own hot brain;
For what can synods have at all
With bear that's analogical?
Or what relation has debating
Of church-affairs with bear-baiting?
A just comparison still is
Of things *ejusdem generis;*
And then what *genus* rightly doth
Include and comprehend them both?
If animal, both of us may
As justly pass for bears as they;
For we are animals no less,
Although of diff'rent specieses.
But, Ralpho, this is no fit place,
Nor time, to argue out the case:
For now the field is not far off
Where we must give the world a proof
Of deeds, not words, and such as suit
Another manner of dispute:
A controversy that affords
Actions for arguments, not words;
Which we must manage at a rate
Of prowess and conduct adequate
To what our place and fame doth promise,
And all the godly expect from us.
Nor shall they be deceived, unless
We're slurred and outed by success;
Success, the mark no mortal wit,
Or surest hand, can always hit:
For whatsoe'er we perpetrate,
We do but row, we 're steered by Fate,
Which in success oft disinherits,
For spurious causes, noblest merits.
Great actions are not always true sons
Of great and mighty resolutions;
Nor do the bold'st attempts bring forth
Events still equal to their worth;
But sometimes fail, and in their stead,
Fortune and cowardice succeed.
Yet we have no great cause to doubt,
Our actions still have borne us out;
Which though they're known to be so ample,
We need not copy from example;
We're not the only person durst
Attempt this province, nor the first.
In northern clime a val'rous knight
Did whilom kill his bear in fight,
And wound a fiddler: we have both
Of these the objects of our wroth,

And equal fame and glory from
Th' attempt, or victory to come.
'T is sung there is a valiant Mamaluke
In foreign land, ycleped ———
To whom we have been oft compared
For person, parts, address, and beard;
Both equally reputed stout,
And in the same cause both have fought:
He oft in such attempts as these
Came off with glory and success;
Nor will we fail in th' execution,
For want of equal resolution.
Honour is like a widow, won
With brisk attempt and putting on;
With ent'ring manfully, and urging,
Not slow approaches, like a virgin.
  This said, as erst the Phrygian knight,
So ours with rusty steel did smite
His Trojan horse, and just as much
He mended pace upon the touch;
But from his empty stomach groaned,
Just as that hollow beast did sound,
And angry answered from behind
With brandished tail, [—] and [sluggish mind].
So have I seen, with armèd heel,
A wight bestride a Commonweal,
While still the more he kicked and spurred,
The less the sullen jade has stirred.

1663

John Wilmot, Earl of Rochester
(1647–1680)

A SATIRE AGAINST MANKIND

Were I, — who to my cost already am
One of those strange prodigious creatures man —
A spirit free, to choose for my own share,
What sort of flesh and blood I pleased to wear,
I'd be a dog, a monkey, or a bear,
Or any thing, but that vain animal,
Who is so proud of being rational.
The senses are too gross, and he'll contrive
A sixth, to contradict the other five;
And, before certain instinct, will prefer
Reason, which fifty times for one does err.
Reason, an *ignis fatuus* of the mind,
Which leaves the light of Nature, sense, behind:
Pathless and dangerous wandering ways it takes,
Through Errour's fenny bogs, and thorny brakes;
Whilst the misguided follower climbs with pain
Mountains of whimsies heapt in his own brain:
Stumbling from thought to thought, falls headlong down
Into Doubt's boundless sea, where, like to drown,
Books bear him up a while, and make him try
To swim with bladders of philosophy;
In hopes still to o'ertake the skipping light,
The vapour dances in his dazzled sight,
Till, spent, it leaves him to eternal night.
Then Old Age and Experience, hand in hand,
Lead him to Death, and make him understand,
After a search so painful and so long,
That all his life he has been in the wrong.
Huddled in dirt, this reasoning engine lies,
Who was so proud, so witty, and so wise:
Pride drew him in, as cheats their bubbles catch,
And made him venture to be made a wretch:
His wisdom did his happiness destroy,
Aiming to know the world he should enjoy:
And wit was his vain frivolous pretence,
Of pleasing others at his own expense. . . .
Women, and men of wit, are dangerous tools,
And ever fatal to admiring fools.
Pleasure allures; and when the fops escape,
'T is not that they are loved, but fortunate;
And therefore what they fear, at heart they hate,
But now, methinks, some formal band and beard
Takes me to task: 'Come on, sire I'm prepared.'
'Then, by your favour, any thing that's writ,
Against this gibing, gingling knack, called wit,
Likes me abundantly; but you'll take care,
Upon this point, not to be too severe;
Perhaps my Muse were fitter for this part;
For, I profess, I can be very smart
On wit, which I abhor with all my heart.
I long to lash it in some sharp essay,
But your grand indiscretion bids me stay,
And turns my tide of ink another way.
What rage ferments in your degenerate mind,
To make you rail at reason and mankind?
Blest glorious man, to whom alone kind Heaven
An everlasting soul hath freely given;
Whom his great Maker took such care to make,
That from himself he did the image take,

And this fair frame in shining reason drest,
To dignify his nature above beast:
Reason, by whose aspiring influence,
We take a flight beyond material sense,
Dive into mysteries, then, soaring, pierce
The flaming limits of the universe,
Search Heaven and Hell, find out what 's acted there,
And give the world true grounds of hope and fear.'
'Hold, mighty man,' I cry, 'all this we know
From the pathetic pen of Ingelo,
From Patrick's Pilgrim, Sibb's Soliloquies,
And 't is this very reason I despise
This supernatural gift, that makes a mite
Think he 's the image of the Infinite;
Comparing his short life, void of all rest,
To the Eternal and the Ever-blest:
This busy puzzling stirrer up of doubt,
That frames deep mysteries, then finds them out,
Filling with frantic crowds of thinking fools,
The reverend bedlams, colleges, and schools,
Borne on whose wings, each heavy sot can pierce
The limits of the boundless universe.
So charming ointments make an old witch fly
And bear a crippled carcass through the sky.
'T is this exalted power, whose business lies
In nonsense and impossibilities:
This made a whimsical philosopher,
Before the spacious world his tub prefer;
And we have many modern coxcombs, who
Retire to think, 'cause they have nought to do.
But thoughts were given for actions' government;
Where action ceases, thought 's impertinent.
Our sphere of action is life's happiness,
And he that thinks beyond, thinks like an ass.
Thus whilst against false reasoning I inveigh,
I own right reason, which I would obey;
That reason, which distinguishes by sense,
And gives us rules of good and ill from thence;
That bounds desires with a reforming will,
To keep them more in vigour, not to kill:
Your reason hinders, mine helps to enjoy,
Renewing appetites, yours would destroy.
My reason is my friend, yours is a cheat;
Hunger calls out, my reason bids me eat;
Perversely yours, your appetite does mock;
This asks for food; that answers, what 's o'clock?
'This plain distinction, sir, your doubt secures;
'T is not true reason I despise, but yours.
Thus I think reason righted: but for man,
I 'll ne'er recant, defend him if you can.
For all his pride, and his philosophy,
'T is evident beasts are, in their degree,
As wise at least, and better far than he.
Those creatures are the wisest, who attain,
By surest means, the ends at which they aim.
If therefore Jowler finds, and kills his hare,
Better than Meres supplies committee-chair;
Though one 's a statesman, th' other but a hound,
Jowler in justice will be wiser found.
You see how far man's wisdom here extends:
Look next if human nature makes amends;
Whose principles are most generous and just;
And to whose morals you would sooner trust:
Be judge yourself, I 'll bring it to the test,
Which is the basest creature, man or beast:
Birds feed on birds, beasts on each other prey,
But savage man alone does man betray.
Prest by necessity, they kill for food;
Man undoes man, to do himself no good;
With teeth and claws by Nature armed, they hunt
Nature's allowance, to supply their want.
But man, with smiles, embraces, friendships, praise,
Inhumanly his fellow's life betrays;
With voluntary pains works his distress;
Not through necessity, but wantonness.
For hunger or for love, they bite or tear,
Whilst wretched man is still in arms for fear:
For fear he arms, and is of arms afraid,
From fear to fear sucessively betrayed:
Base fear, the source whence his base passions came,
His boasted honour, and his dear-bought fame:
The lust of power, to which he 's such a slave,
And for the which alone he dares be brave;
To which his various projects are designed,
Which makes him generous, affable, and kind;
For which he takes such pains to be thought wise,
And screws his actions in a forced disguise;
Leads a most tedious life, in misery,
Under laborious, mean hypocrisy.
Look to the bottom of his vast design,
Wherein man's wisdom, power, and glory join;
The good he acts, the ill he does endure,
'T is all from fear to make himself secure.
Merely for safety, after fame they thirst;

For all men would be cowards if they durst:
And honesty 's against all common sense;
Men must be knaves; 't is in their own defence
Mankind 's dishonest; if you think it fair,
Amongst known cheats, to play upon the square,
You 'll be undone —
Nor can weak truth your reputation save;
The knaves will all agree to call you knave.
Wronged shall he live, insulted o'er, opprest,
Who dares be less a villain than the rest.
Thus here you see what human nature craves,
Most men are cowards, all men should be knaves.
The difference lies, as far as I can see,
Not in the thing itself, but the degree;
And all the subject-matter of debate,
Is only who 's a knave of the first-rate.'

POSTSCRIPT

All this with indignation have I hurled,
At the pretending part of the proud world,
Who, swoln with selfish vanity, devise
False freedoms, holy cheats, and formal lies,
Over their fellow-slaves to tyrannize.
But if in court so just a man there be,
(In court a just man, yet unknown to me)
Who does his needful flattery direct,
Not to oppress and ruin, but protect;
Since flattery, which way soever laid,
Is still a tax on that unhappy trade;
If so upright a statesman you can find,
Whose passions bend to his unbiased mind;
Who does his arts and policies apply,
To raise his country, not his family.
Is there a mortal who on God relies?
Whose life his faith and doctrine justifies?
Not one blown up with vain aspiring pride,
Who, for reproof of sins, does man deride:
Whose envious heart with saucy eloquence
Dares chide at kings, and rail at men of sense:
Who in his talking vents more peevish lies,
More bitter railings, scandals, calumnies,
Than at a gossiping are thrown about,
When the good wives drink free, and then fall out.
None of the sensual tribe, whose talents lie
In avarice, pride, in sloth, and gluttony;
Who hunt preferment, but abhor good lives.

. . . .

Nor doating — who would be adored,
For domineering at the council-board,
A greater fop, in business at fourscore,
Fonder of serious toys, affected more,
Than the gay glittering fool at twenty proves,
With all his noise, his tawdry clothes, and loves.
But a meek humble man of modest sense,
Who, preaching peace, does practice continence;
Whose pious life 's a proof he does believe
Mysterious truths, which no man can conceive.
If upon Earth there dwell such godlike men,
I 'll here recant my paradox to them;
Adore those shrines of virtue, homage pay,
And, with the thinking world, their laws obey.
If such there are, yet grant me this at least,
Man differs more from man, than man from beast.

1675

John Dryden (1631-1700)

ABSALOM AND ACHITOPHEL

In pious times, ere priestcraft did begin,
Before polygamy was made a sin,
When man on many multiplied his kind,
Ere one to one was cursedly confined;
When nature prompted, and no law denied
Promiscuous use of concubine and bride;
Then Israel's monarch after Heaven's own heart,
His vigorous warmth did variously impart
To wives and slaves: and, wide as his command,
Scattered his Maker's image through the land.
Michal, of royal blood, the crown did wear;
A soil ungrateful to the tiller's care:
Not so the rest: for several mothers bore
To godlike David several sons before.
But since like slaves his bed they did ascend,
No true succession could their seed attend.
Of all this numerous progeny was none
So beautiful, so brave, as Absalom . . .
Early in foreign fields he won renown,
With kings and states allied to Israel's crown;
In peace the thoughts of war he could remove,
And seemed as he were only born for love.
Whate'er he did, was done with so much ease,
In him alone 't was natural to please:
His motions all accompanied with grace;

And paradise was opened in his face.
With secret joy indulgent David viewed
His youthful image in his son renewed:
To all his wishes nothing he denied,
And made the charming Annabel his bride.
What faults he had (for who from faults is free?)
His father could not, or he would not see.
Some warm excesses, which the law forbore,
Were construed youth that purged by boiling o'er,
And Amnon's murder, by a specious name,
Was called a just revenge for injured fame.
Thus praised and loved, the noble youth remained,
While David, undisturbed, in Sion reigned.
But life can never be sincerely blest;
Heav'n punishes the bad, and proves the best.
The Jews, a headstrong, moody, murm'ring race,
As ever tried th' extent and stretch of grace;
God's pampered people, whom, debauched with ease,
No king could govern, nor no God could please;
(Gods they had tried of every shape and size,
That god-smiths could produce, or priests devise:)
These Adam-wits, too fortunately free,
Began to dream they wanted liberty;
And when no rule, no precedent was found,
Of men by laws less circumscribed and bound;
They led their wild desires to woods and caves,
And thought that all but savages were slaves.
They who, when Saul was dead, without a blow,
Made foolish Ishbosheth the crown forego;
Who banished David did from Hebron bring,
And with a general shout proclaimed him King;
Those very Jews, who, at their very best,
Their humor more than loyalty expressed,
Now wondered why so long they had obeyed
An idol monarch, which their hands had made;
Thought they might ruin him they could create,
Or melt him to that golden calf, a State.
But these were random bolts; no formed design,
Nor interest made the factious crowd to join:
The sober part of Israel, free from stain,
Well knew the value of a peaceful reign;
And, looking backward with a wise affright,
Saw seams of wounds, dishonest to the sight:
In contemplation of whose ugly scars
They cursed the memory of civil wars.
The moderate sort of men, thus qualified,
Inclined the balance to the better side;
And David's mildness managed it so well,
The bad found no occasion to rebel.
But when to sin our biassed nature leans,
The careful Devil is still at hand with means;
And providently pimps for ill desires.
The Good Old Cause revived, a plot requires:
Plots, true or false, are necessary things,
To raise up commonwealths, and ruin kings.

Th' inhabitants of old Jerusalem
Were Jebusites; the town so called from them;
And theirs the native right —
But when the chosen people grew more strong,
The rightful cause at length became the wrong;
And every loss the men of Jebus bore,
They still were thought God's enemies the more.
Thus worn and weakened, well or ill content,
Submit they must to David's government:
Impoverished and deprived of all command,
Their taxes doubled as they lost their land;
And, what was harder yet to flesh and blood,
Their gods disgraced, and burnt like common wood.
This set the heathen priesthood in a flame;
For priests of all religions are the same:
Of whatsoe'er descent their godhead be,
Stock, stone, or other homely pedigree,
In his defense his servants are as bold,
As if he had been born of beaten gold.
The Jewish rabbins, though their enemies,
In this conclude them honest men and wise:
For 't was their duty, all the learnèd think,
To espouse his cause, by whom they eat and drink.
From hence began that Plot, the nation's curse,
Bad in itself, but represented worse;
Raised in extremes, and in extremes decried;
With oaths affirmed, with dying vows denied;
Not weighed or winnowed by the multitude:

But swallowed in the mass, unchewed and crude.
Some truth there was, but dashed and brewed with lies,
To please the fools, and puzzle all the wise.
Succeeding times did equal folly call,
Believing nothing, or believing all.
Th' Egyptian rites the Jebusites embraced;
Where gods were recommended by their taste.
Such sav'ry deities must needs be good,
As served at once for worship and for food.
By force they could not introduce these gods,
For ten to one in former days was odds;
So fraud was used (the sacrificer's trade):
Fools are more hard to conquer then persuade.
Their busy teachers mingled with the Jews,
And raked for converts even the court and stews:
Which Hebrew priests the more unkindly took,
Because the fleece accompanies the flock.
Some thought they God's anointed meant to slay
By guns, invented since full many a day:
Our author swears it not; but who can know
How far the Devil and Jebusites may go?
This plot, which failed for want of common sense,
Had yet a deep and dangerous consequence:
For, as when raging fevers boil the blood,
The standing lake soon floats into a flood,
And ev'ry hostile humor, which before
Slept quiet in its channels, bubbles o'er;
So several factions from this first ferment
Work up to foam, and threat the government.
Some by their friends, more by themselves thought wise,
Opposed the power to which they could not rise.
Some had in courts been great, and thrown from thence,
Like fiends were hardened in impenitence.
Some, by their monarch's fatal mercy, grown
From pardoned rebels kinsmen to the throne,
Were raised in power and public office high;
Strong bands, if bands ungrateful men could tie.
Of these the false Achitophel was first;
A name to all succeeding ages curst:
For close designs and crookèd counsels fit;
Sagacious, bold, and turbulent of wit;
Restless, unfixed in principles and place;
In power unpleased, impatient of disgrace:
A fiery soul, which, working out its way,
Fretted the pigmy body to decay,
And o'er-informed the tenement of clay.
A daring pilot in extremity;
Pleased with the danger, when the waves went high,
He sought the storms; but, for a calm unfit,
Would steer too nigh the sands, to boast his wit.
Great wits are sure to madness near allied,
And thin partitions do their bounds divide;
Else why should he, with wealth and honor blest,
Refuse his age the needful hours of rest?
Punish a body which he could not please;
Bankrupt of life, yet prodigal of ease?
And all to leave what with his toil he won
To that unfeathered two-legged thing, a son;
Got, while his soul did huddled notions try;
And born a shapeless lump, like anarchy.
In friendship false, implacable in hate;
Resolved to ruin or to rule the State.
To compass this the triple bond he broke;
The pillars of the public safety shook;
And fitted Israel for a foreign yoke:
Then, seized with fear, yet still affecting fame,
Usurped a patriot's all-atoning name.
So easy still it proves in factious times
With public zeal to cancel private crimes.
How safe is treason, and how sacred ill,
Where none can sin against the people's will!
Where crowds can wink, and no offence be known,
Since in another's guilt they find their own!
Yet fame deserved no enemy can grudge;
The statesman we abhor, but praise the judge.
In Israel's courts ne'er sat an Abbethdin
With more discerning eyes, or hands more clean;
Unbribed, unsought, the wretched to redress;
Swift of despatch, and easy of access.
O, had he been content to serve the crown,
With virtues only proper to the gown;
Or had the rankness of the soil been freed
From cockle, that oppressed the noble seed;
David for him his tuneful harp had strung,
And Heav'n had wanted one immortal song.
But wild Ambition loves to slide, not stand,
And Fortune's ice prefers to Virtue's land.
Achitophel, grown weary to possess
A lawful fame, and lazy happiness,
Disdained the golden fruit to gather free,
And lent the crowd his arm to shake the tree.
Now, manifest of crimes contrived long since,

He stood at bold defiance with his prince;
Held up the buckler of the people's cause
Against the crown, and skulked behind the laws.
The wished occasion of the Plot he takes;
Some circumstances finds, but more he makes.
By buzzing emissaries fills the ears
Of listening crowds with jealousies and fears
Of arbitrary counsels brought to light,
And proves the king himself a Jebusite.
Weak arguments! which yet he knew full well
Were strong with people easy to rebel.
For, governed by the moon, the giddy Jews
Tread the same track when she the prime renews;
And once in twenty years, their scribes record,
By natural instinct they change their lord.
Achitophel still wants a chief, and none
Was found so fit as warlike Absalom:
Not that he wished his greatness to create,
(For politicians neither love nor hate,)
But, for he knew his title not allowed,
Would keep him still depending on the crowd:
That kingly power, thus ebbing out, might be
Drawn to the dregs of a democracy.
Him he attempts with studied arts to please,
And sheds his venom in such words as these:
'Auspicious prince, at whose nativity
Some royal planet ruled the southern sky;
Thy longing country's darling and desire;
Their cloudy pillar and their guardian fire:
Their second Moses, whose extended wand
Divides the seas and shows the promised land;
Whose dawning day in every distant age
Has exercised the sacred prophet's rage:
The people's prayer, the glad diviner's theme,
The young men's vision, and the old men's dream!
Thee, Savior, thee, the nation's vows confess,
And, never satisfied with seeing, bless:
Swift unbespoken pomps thy steps proclaim,
And stammering babes are taught to lisp thy name.
How long wilt thou the general joy detain,
Starve and defraud the people of thy reign?
Content ingloriously to pass thy days
Like one of Virtue's fools that feeds on praise;
Till thy fresh glories, which now shine so bright,
Grow stale and tarnish with our daily sight.
Believe me, royal youth, thy fruit must be
Or gathered ripe, or rot upon the tree.
Heav'n has to all allotted, soon or late,
Some lucky revolution of their fate;
Whose motions if we watch and guide with skill,
(For human good depends on human will,)
Our Fortune rolls as from a smooth descent,
And from the first impression takes the bent:
But, if unseized, she glides away like wind,
And leaves repenting Folly far behind.
Now, now she meets you with a glorious prize,
And spreads her locks before her as she flies.
Had thus old David, from whose loins you spring,
Not dared, when Fortune called him, to be king,
At Gath an exile he might still remain,
And Heaven's anointing oil had been in vain.
Let his successful youth your hopes engage;
But shun th' example of declining age:
Behold him setting in his western skies,
The shadows lengthening as the vapors rise.
He is not now, as when on Jordan's sand
The joyful people thronged to see him land,
Covering the beach and blackening all the strand;
But, like the Prince of Angels, from his height
Comes tumbling downward with diminished light;
Betrayed by one poor plot to public scorn,
(Our only blessing since his curst return;)
Those heaps of people which one sheaf did bind,
Blown off and scattered by a puff of wind.
What strength can he to your designs oppose,
Naked of friends, and round beset with foes?
If Pharaoh's doubtful succor he should use,
A foreign aid would more incense the Jews:
Proud Egypt would dissembled friendship bring;
Foment the war, but not support the king:
Nor would the royal party e'er unite
With Pharaoh's arms t' assist the Jebusite;
Or if they should, their interest soon would break,
And with such odious aid make David weak.
All sorts of men by my successful arts,

Abhorring kings, estrange their altered hearts
From David's rule: and 't is the general cry,
"Religion, commonwealth, and liberty."
If you, as champion of the public good,
Add to their arms a chief of royal blood,
What may not Israel hope, and what applause
Might such a general gain by such a cause?
Not barren praise alone, that gaudy flow'r,
Fair only to the sight, but solid pow'r;
And nobler is a limited command,
Giv'n by the love of all your native land,
Than a successive title, long and dark,
Drawn from the moldy rolls of Noah's ark.'
  What cannot praise effect in mighty minds,
When flattery soothes, and when ambition blinds?
Desire of pow'r, on earth a vicious weed,
Yet, sprung from high, is of celestial seed:
In God 't is glory; and when men aspire,
'T is but a spark too much of heavenly fire.
Th' ambitious youth, too covetous of fame,
Too full of angels' metal in his frame,
Unwarily was led from virtue's ways,
Made drunk with honor, and debauched with praise.
Half loth, and half consenting to the ill,
(For loyal blood within him struggled still,)
He thus replied: 'And what pretence have I
To take up arms for public liberty?
My father governs with unquestioned right;
The faith's defender, and mankind's delight;
Good, gracious, just, observant of the laws:
And Heav'n by wonders has espoused his cause.
Whom has he wronged in all his peaceful reign?
Who sues for justice to his throne in vain?
What millions has he pardoned of his foes,
Whom just revenge did to his wrath expose?
Mild, easy, humble, studious of our good;
Enclined to mercy, and averse from blood;
If mildness ill with stubborn Israel suit,
His crime is God's belovèd attribute.
What could he gain, his people to betray,
Or change his right for arbitrary sway?
Let haughty Pharaoh curse with such a reign
His fruitful Nile, and yoke a servile train.
If David's rule Jerusalem displease,
The Dog-star heats their brains to this disease.
Why then should I, encouraging the bad,
Turn rebel and run popularly mad?
Were he a tyrant, who, by lawless might
Oppressed the Jews, and raised the Jebusite,
Well might I mourn; but nature's holy bands
Would curb my spirits and restrain my hands;
The people might assert their liberty;
But what was right in them were crime in me.
His favor leaves me nothing to require,
Prevents my wishes, and outruns desire.
What more can I expect while David lives?
All but his kingly diadem he gives:
And that' — But here he paused; then sighing, said —
'Is justly destined for a worthier head.
For when my father from his toils shall rest,
And late augment the number of the blest,
His lawful issue shall the throne ascend,
Or the collat'ral line, where that shall end.
His brother, though oppressed with vulgar spite,
Yet dauntless and secure of native right,
Of every royal virtue stands possessed;
Still dear to all the bravest and the best.
His courage foes, his friends his truth proclaim,
His loyalty the king, the world his fame.
His mercy ev'n th' offending crowd will find;
For sure he comes of a forgiving kind.
Why should I then repine at Heaven's decree,
Which gives me no pretence to royalty?
Yet O that fate, propitiously inclined,
Had raised my birth, or had debased my mind;
To my large soul not all her treasure lent,
And then betrayed it to a mean descent!
I find, I find my mounting spirits bold,
And David's part disdains my mother's mold.
Why am I scanted by a niggard birth?
My soul disclaims the kindred of her earth;
And, made for empire, whispers me within,
Desire of greatness is a god-like sin.'
  Him staggering so when Hell's dire agent found,
While fainting Virtue scarce maintained her ground,
He pours fresh forces in, and thus replies:
'Th' eternal God, supremely good and wise,
Imparts not these prodigious gifts in vain:
What wonders are reserved to bless your reign!
Against your will, your arguments have shown,
Such virtue's only giv'n to guide a throne.

Not that your father's mildness I contemn;
But manly force becomes the diadem.
'T is true he grants the people all they crave;
And more, perhaps, than subjects ought to have:
For lavish grants suppose a monarch tame,
And more his goodness than his wit proclaim.
But when should people strive their bonds to break,
If not when kings are negligent or weak?
Let him give on till he can give no more,
The thrifty Sanhedrin shall keep him poor;
And every shekel which he can receive,
Shall cost a limb of his prerogative.
To ply him with new plots shall be my care;
Or plunge him deep in some expensive war;
Which when his treasure can no more supply,
He must, with the remains of kingship, buy.
His faithful friends, our jealousies and fears
Call Jebusites, and Pharaoh's pensioners;
Whom when our fury from his aid has torn,
He shall be naked left to public scorn.
The next successor, whom I fear and hate,
My arts have made obnoxious to the State;
Turned all his virtues to his overthrow,
And gained our elders to pronounce a foe.
His right, for sums of necessary gold,
Shall first be pawned, and afterwards be sold;
Till time shall ever-wanting David draw,
To pass your doubtful title into law:
If not, the people have a right supreme
To make their kings; for kings are made for them.
All empire is no more than pow'r in trust,
Which, when resumed, can be no longer just.
Succession, for the general good designed,
In its own wrong a nation cannot bind;
If altering that the people can relieve
Better one suffer than a nation grieve.
The Jews well know their pow'r: ere Saul they chose,
God was their king, and God they durst depose.
Urge now your piety, your filial name,
A father's right, and fear of future fame;
The public good, that universal call,
To which even Heav'n submitted, answers all.
Nor let his love enchant your generous mind;
'T is Nature's trick to propagate her kind.
Our fond begetters, who would never die,
Love but themselves in their posterity.
Or let his kindness by th' effects be tried,
Or let him lay his vain pretense aside.
God said he loved your father; could he bring
A better proof, than to anoint him king?
It surely shewed he loved the shepherd well,
Who gave so fair a flock as Israel.
Would David have you thought his darling son?
What means he then, to alienate the crown?
The name of godly he may blush to bear:
'T is after God's own heart to cheat his heir.
He to his brother gives supreme command,
To you a legacy of barren land,
Perhaps th' old harp, on which he thrums his lays,
Or some dull Hebrew ballad in your praise.
Then the next heir, a prince severe and wise,
Already looks on you with jealous eyes;
Sees through the thin disguises of your arts,
And marks your progress in the people's hearts.
Though now his mighty soul his grief contains,
He meditates revenge who least complains;
And, like a lion, slumb'ring in the way,
Or sleep dissembling, while he waits his prey,
His fearless foes within his distance draws,
Constrains his roaring, and contracts his paws;
Till at the last, his time for fury found,
He shoots with sudden vengeance from the ground;
The prostrate vulgar passes o'er and spares,
But with a lordly rage his hunter tears.
Your case no tame expedients will afford:
Resolve on death, or conquest by the sword,
Which for no less a stake than life you draw;
And self-defense is nature's eldest law.
Leave the warm people no considering time;
For then rebellion may be thought a crime.
Prevail yourself of what occasion gives,
But try your title while your father lives;
And that your arms may have a fair pretense,
Proclaim you take them in the king's defense;
Whose sacred life each minute would expose
To plots, from seeming friends and secret foes.
And who can sound the depth of David's soul?
Perhaps his fear his kindness may control.
He fears his brother, though he loves his son,
For plighted vows too late to be undone.
If so, by force he wishes to be gained;

Like women's lechery, to seem constrained.
Doubt not; but, when he most affects the frown,
Commit a pleasing rape upon the crown.
Secure his person to secure your cause:
They who possess the prince, possess the laws.'
He said, and this advice above the rest
With Absalom's mild nature suited best;
Unblamed of life, (ambition set aside,)
Not stained with cruelty, nor puffed with pride;
How happy had he been, if destiny
Had higher placed his birth, or not so high!
His kingly virtues might have claimed a throne,
And blest all other countries but his own.
But charming greatness since so few refuse,
'T is juster to lament him than accuse.
Strong were his hopes a rival to remove,
With blandishments to gain the public love;
To head the faction while their zeal was hot,
And popularly prosecute the Plot.
To farther this, Achitophel unites
The malcontents of all the Israelites;
Whose differing parties he could wisely join,
For several ends, to serve the same design:
The best, (and of the princes some were such,)
Who thought the pow'r of monarchy too much;
Mistaken men, and patriots in their hearts;
Not wicked, but seduced by impious arts.
By these the springs of property were bent,
And wound so high they cracked the government.
The next for interest sought t' embroil the State,
To sell their duty at a dearer rate;
And make their Jewish markets of the throne,
Pretending public good, to serve their own.
Others thought kings an useless heavy load,
Who cost too much, and did too little good.
These were for laying honest David by,
On principles of pure good husbandry.
With them joined all th' haranguers of the throng,
That thought to get preferment by the tongue.
Who follow next, a double danger bring,
Not only hating David, but the king:
The Solymæan rout, well-versed of old
In godly faction, and in treason bold;
Cow'ring and quaking at a conqu'ror's sword;
But lofty to a lawful prince restored;
Saw with disdain an Ethnic plot begun,
And scorned by Jebusites to be outdone.
Hot Levites headed these; who, pulled before
From th' ark, which in the Judges' days they bore,
Resumed their cant, and with a zealous cry
Pursued their old beloved Theocracy:
Where Sanhedrin and priest enslaved the nation,
And justified their spoils by inspiration:
For who so fit for reign as Aaron's race,
If once dominion they could found in grace?
These led the pack; though not of surest scent,
Yet deepest mouthed against the government.
A numerous host of dreaming saints succeed,
Of the true old enthusiastic breed:
'Gainst form and order they their pow'r imploy,
Nothing to build, and all things to destroy.
But far more numerous was the herd of such,
Who think too little, and who talk too much.
These, out of mere instinct, they knew not why,
Adored their fathers' God and property;
And, by the same blind benefit of fate,
The Devil and the Jebusite did hate:
Born to be saved, even in their own despite,
Because they could not help believing right.
Such were the tools; but a whole Hydra more
Remains, of sprouting heads too long to score.
Some of their chiefs were princes of the land:
In the first rank of these did Zimri stand;
A man so various, that he seemed to be
Not one, but all mankind's epitome:
Stiff in opinions, always in the wrong;
Was everything by starts, and nothing long;
But, in the course of one revolving moon,
Was chymist, fiddler, statesman, and buffoon:
Then all for women, painting, rhyming, drinking,
Besides ten thousand freaks that died in thinking.
Blest madman, who could every hour employ,
With something new to wish, or to enjoy!
Railing and praising were his usual themes;

And both (to show his judgment) in extremes:
So over-violent, or over-civil,
That every man, with him, was God or Devil.
In squand'ring wealth was his peculiar art:
Nothing went unrewarded but desert.
Beggared by fools, whom still he found too late,
He had his jest, and they had his estate.
He laughed himself from court; then sought relief
By forming parties, but could ne'er be chief;
For, spite of him, the weight of business fell
On Absalom and wise Achitophel:
Thus, wicked but in will, of means bereft,
He left not faction, but of that was left.
Titles and names 't were tedious to rehearse
Of lords, below the dignity of verse.
Wits, warriors, Commonwealth's-men, were the best;
Kind husbands, and mere nobles, all the rest,
And therefore, in the name of dulness, be
The [wanton] Balaam and cold Caleb, free;
And canting Nadab let oblivion damn,
Who made new porridge for the paschal lamb.
Let friendship's holy band some names assure;
Some their own worth, and some let scorn secure.
Nor shall the rascal rabble here have place,
Whom kings no titles gave, and God no grace:
Not bull-faced Jonas, who could statutes draw
To mean rebellion, and make treason law.
But he, though bad, is followed by a worse,
The wretch who Heav'n's anointed dared to curse:
Shimei, whose youth did early promise bring
Of zeal to God and hatred to his king,
Did wisely from expensive sins refrain,
And never broke the Sabbath, but for gain;
Nor ever was he known an oath to vent,
Or curse, unless against the government.
Thus heaping wealth, by the most ready way
Among the Jews, which was to cheat and pray,
The city, to reward his pious hate
Against his master, chose him magistrate.
His hand a vare of justice did uphold;
His neck was loaded with a chain of gold.
During his office, treason was no crime;
The sons of Belial had a glorious time;
For Shimei, though not prodigal of pelf,
Yet loved his wicked neighbor as himself.
When two or three were gathered to declaim
Against the monarch of Jerusalem,
Shimei was always in the midst of them;
And if they cursed the king when he was by,
Would rather curse than break good company.
If any durst his factious friends accuse,
He packed a jury of dissenting Jews;
Whose fellow-feeling in the godly cause
Would free the suffering saint from human laws.
For laws are only made to punish those
Who serve the king, and to protect his foes.
If any leisure time he had from pow'r,
(Because 't is sin to misimploy an hour,)
His bus'ness was, by writing to persuade
That kings were useless, and a clog to trade;
And, that his noble style he might refine,
No Rechabite more shunned the fumes of wine.
Chaste were his cellars, and his shrieval board
The grossness of a city feast abhorred:
His cooks, with long disuse, their trade forgot;
Cool was his kitchen, though his brains were hot.
Such frugal virtue malice may accuse,
But sure 't was necessary to the Jews;
For towns once burnt such magistrates require
As dare not tempt God's providence by fire.
With spiritual food he fed his servants well,
But free from flesh that made the Jews rebel;
And Moses' laws he held in more account,
For forty days of fasting in the mount.
To speak the rest, who better are forgot,
Would tire a well-breathed witness of the Plot.
Yet, Corah, thou shalt from oblivion pass:
Erect thyself, thou monumental brass,
High as the serpent of thy metal made,
While nations stand secure beneath thy shade.
What though his birth were base, yet comets rise
From earthly vapors, ere they shine in skies.
Prodigious actions may as well be done
By weaver's issue, as by prince's son.
This arch-attestor for the public good
By that one deed ennobles all his blood.
Who ever asked the witnesses' high race,
Whose oath with martyrdom did Stephen grace?

Ours was a Levite, and as times went then,
His tribe were God Almighty's gentlemen.
Sunk were his eyes, his voice was harsh and loud,
Sure signs he neither choleric was nor proud:
His long chin proved his wit; his saint-like grace
A church vermilion, and a Moses' face.
His memory, miraculously great,
Could plots, exceeding man's belief, repeat;
Which therefore cannot be accounted lies,
For human wit could never such devise.
Some future truths are mingled in his book;
But where the witness failed, the prophet spoke:
Some things like visionary flights appear;
The spirit caught him up, the Lord knows where;
And gave him his rabinnical degree
Unknown to foreign university.
His judgment yet his mem'ry did excel;
Which pieced his wondrous evidence so well,
And suited to the temper of the times,
Then groaning under Jebusitic crimes.
Let Israel's foes suspect his heav'nly call,
And rashly judge his writ apochryphal;
Our laws for such affronts have forfeits made:
He takes his life, who takes away his trade.
Were I myself in witness Corah's place,
The wretch who did me such a dire disgrace,
Should whet my memory, though once forgot,
To make him an appendix of my plot.
His zeal to Heav'n made him his prince despise,
And load his person with indignities;
But zeal peculiar privilege affords,
Indulging latitude to deeds and words;
And Corah might for Agag's murther call,
In terms as coarse as Samuel used to Saul.
What others in his evidence did join,
(The best that could be had for love or coin,)
In Corah's own predicament will fall;
For *witness* is a common name to all.
Surrounded thus with friends of every sort,
Deluded Absalom forsakes the court;
Impatient of high hopes, urged with renown,
And fired with near possession of a crown.
Th' admiring crowd are dazzled with surprise,
And on his goodly person feed their eyes.
His joy concealed, he sets himself to show,
On each side bowing popularly low;
His looks, his gestures, and his words he frames,
And with familiar ease repeats their names.
Thus formed by nature, furnished out with arts,
He glides unfelt into their secret hearts.
Then, with a kind compassionating look,
And sighs, bespeaking pity ere he spoke,
Few words he said; but easy those and fit,
More slow than Hybla-drops, and far more sweet.
'I mourn, my countrymen, your lost estate;
Though far unable to prevent your fate:
Behold a banished man, for your dear cause
Exposed a prey to arbitrary laws!
Yet O! that I alone could be undone,
Cut off from empire, and no more a son!
Now all your liberties a spoil are made;
Egypt and Tyrus intercept your trade,
And Jebusites your sacred rites invade.
My father, whom with reverence yet I name,
Charmed into ease, is careless of his fame;
And, bribed with petty sums of foreign gold,
Is grown in Bathsheba's embraces old;
Exalts his enemies, his friends destroys;
And all his pow'r against himself imploys.
He gives, and let him give, my right away;
But why should he his own and yours betray?
He, only he, can make the nation bleed,
And he alone from my revenge is freed.
Take then my tears, (with that he wiped his eyes,)
'T is all the aid my present pow'r supplies:
No court-informer can these arms accuse;
These arms may sons against their fathers use:
And 't is my wish, the next successor's reign
May make no other Israelite complain.'
Youth, beauty, graceful action seldom fail;
But common interest always will prevail;
And pity never ceases to be shown
To him who makes the people's wrongs his own.
The crowd, that still believe their kings oppress,
With lifted hands their young Messiah bless:
Who now begins his progress to ordain
With chariots, horsemen, and a num'rous train;
From east to west his glories he displays,
And, like the sun, the promised land surveys.
Fame runs before him as the morning star,
And shouts of joy salute him from afar:
Each house receives him as a guardian god,
And consecrates the place of his abode.

But hospitable treats did most commend
Wise Issachar, his wealthy western friend.
This moving court, that caught the people's eyes,
And seemed but pomp, did other ends disguise:
Achitophel had formed it, with intent
To sound the depths, and fathom, where it went,
The people's hearts; distinguish friends from foes,
And try their strength, before they came to blows.
It all was colored with a smooth pretense
Of specious love, and duty to their prince.
Religion, and redress of grievances,
Two names that always cheat and always please,
Are often urged; and good King David's life
Endangered by a brother and a wife.
Thus in a pageant shew a plot is made,
And peace itself is war in masquerade.
O foolish Israel! never warned by ill!
Still the same bait, and circumvented still!
Did ever men forsake their present ease,
In midst of health imagine a disease,
Take pains contingent mischiefs to foresee,
Make heirs for monarchs, and for God decree?
What shall we think! Can people give away,
Both for themselves and sons, their native sway?
Then they are left defenseless to the sword
Of each unbounded, arbitrary lord:
And laws are vain by which we right enjoy,
If kings unquestioned can those laws destroy.
Yet if the crowd be judge of fit and just,
And kings are only officers in trust,
Then this resuming cov'nant was declared
When kings were made, or is forever barred.
If those who gave the sceptre could not tie
By their own deed their own posterity,
How then could Adam bind his future race?
How could his forfeit on mankind take place?
Or how could heavenly justice damn us all,
Who ne'er consented to our father's fall?
Then kings are slaves to those whom they command,
And tenants to their people's pleasure stand.
Add that the pow'r, for property allowed,
Is mischievously seated in the crowd;
For who can be secure of private right,
If sovereign sway may be dissolved by might?
Nor is the people's judgment always true:
The most may err as grossly as the few;
And faultless kings run down, by common cry,
For vice, oppression, and for tyranny.
What standard is there in a fickle rout,
Which, flowing to the mark, runs faster out?
Not only crowds, but Sanhedrins may be
Infected with this public lunacy,
And share the madness of rebellious times,
To murther monarchs for imagined crimes.
If they may give and take whene'er they please,
Not kings alone, (the Godhead's images,)
But government itself at length must fall
To nature's state, where all have right to all.
Yet, grant our lords the people kings can make,
What prudent men a settled throne would shake?
For whatsoe'er their sufferings were before,
That change they covet makes them suffer more.
All other errors but disturb a state,
But innovation is the blow of fate.
If ancient fabrics nod, and threat to fall,
To patch the flaws, and buttress up the wall,
Thus far 't is duty: but here fix the mark;
For all beyond it is to touch our ark.
To change foundations, cast the frame anew,
Is work for rebels, who base ends pursue,
At once divine and human laws control,
And mend the parts by ruin of the whole.
The tamp'ring world is subject to this curse,
To physic their disease into a worse.

Now what relief can righteous David bring?
How fatal 't is to be too good a king!
Friends he has few, so high the madness grows:
Who dare be such, must be the people's foes.
Yet some there were, ev'n in the worst of days;
Some let me name, and naming is to praise.

In this short file Barzillai first appears;
Barzillai, crowned with honor and with years.
Long since, the rising rebels he withstood
In regions waste, beyond the Jordan's flood:
Unfortunately brave to buoy the State;
But sinking underneath his master's fate:
In exile with his godlike prince he mourned;
For him he suffered, and with him returned.

The court he practised, not the courtier's art:
Large was his wealth, but larger was his heart,
Which well the noblest objects knew to choose,
The fighting warrior, and recording Muse.
His bed could once a fruitful issue boast;
Now more than half a father's name is lost.
His eldest hope, with every grace adorned,
By me, (so Heav'n will have it) always mourned,
And always honored, snatched in manhood's prime
B' unequal fates, and Providence's crime;
Yet not before the goal of honor won,
All parts fulfilled of subject and of son:
Swift was the race, but short the time to run.
O narrow circle, but of pow'r divine,
Scanted in space, but perfect in thy line!
By sea, by land, thy matchless worth was known,
Arms thy delight, and war was all thy own:
Thy force, infused, the fainting Tyrians propped;
And haughty Pharaoh found his fortune stopped.
O ancient honor! O unconquered hand,
Whom foes unpunished never could withstand!
But Israel was unworthy of thy name;
Short is the date of all immoderate fame.
It looks as Heav'n our ruin had designed,
And durst not trust thy fortune and thy mind.
Now, free from earth, thy disencumbered soul
Mounts up, and leaves behind the clouds and starry pole:
From thence thy kindred legions mayst thou bring,
To aid the guardian angel of thy king.
Here stop, my Muse, here cease thy painful flight;
No pinions can pursue immortal height:
Tell good Barzillai thou canst sing no more,
And tell thy soul she should have fled before.
Or fled she with his life, and left this verse
To hang on her departed patron's hearse?
Now take thy steepy flight from heav'n, and see
If thou canst find on earth another *he:*
Another *he* would be too hard to find;
See then whom thou canst see not far behind.
Zadoc the priest, whom, shunning pow'r and place,
His lowly mind advanced to David's grace.
With him the Sagan of Jerusalem,
Of hospitable soul, and noble stem;
Him of the western dome, whose weighty sense
Flows in fit words and heavenly eloquence.
The prophet's sons, by such example led,
To learning and to loyalty were bred:
For colleges on bounteous kings depend,
And never rebel was to arts a friend.
To these succeed the pillars of the laws;
Who best could plead, and best can judge a cause.
Next them a train of loyal peers ascend;
Sharp-judging Adriel, the Muses' friend;
Himself a Muse — in Sanhedrin's debate
True to his prince, but not a slave to state:
Whom David's love with honors did adorn,
That from his disobedient son were torn.
Jothan of piercing wit, and pregnant thought;
Endued by nature, and by learning taught
To move assemblies, who but only tried
The worse a while, then chose the better side:
Nor chose alone, but turned the balance too;
So much the weight of one brave man can do.
Hushai, the friend of David in distress;
In public storms, of manly steadfastness:
By foreign treaties he informed his youth,
And joined experience to his native truth.
His frugal care supplied the wanting throne;
Frugal for that, but bounteous of his own:
'T is easy conduct when exchequers flow,
But hard the task to manage well the low;
For sovereign power is too depressed or high,
When kings are forced to sell, or crowds to buy.
Indulge one labor more, my weary Muse,
For Amiel: who can Amiel's praise refuse?
Of ancient race by birth, but nobler yet
In his own worth, and without title great:
The Sanhedrin long time as chief he ruled,
Their reason guided, and their passion cooled:
So dext'rous was he in the crown's defence,
So formed to speak a loyal nation's sense,
That, as their band was Israel's tribes in small,
So fit was he to represent them all.
Now rasher charioteers the seat ascend,
Whose loose careers his steady skill commend:
They, like th' unequal ruler of the day,
Misguide the seasons, and mistake the way;

While he withdrawn at their mad labor smiles,
And safe enjoys the sabbath of his toils.
These were the chief, a small but faithful band
Of worthies, in the breach who dared to stand,
And tempt th' united fury of the land.
With grief they viewed such powerful engines bent,
To batter down the lawful government:
A numerous faction, with pretended frights,
In Sanhedrins to plume the regal rights;
The true successor from the court removed;
The Plot, by hireling witnesses, improved.
These ills they saw, and, as their duty bound,
They showed the king the danger of the wound;
That no concessions from the throne would please,
But lenitives fomented the disease;
That Absalom, ambitious of the crown,
Was made the lure to draw the people down;
That false Achitophel's pernicious hate
Had turned the Plot to ruin Church and State;
The council violent, the rabble worse;
That Shimei taught Jerusalem to curse.
With all these loads of injuries oppressed,
And long revolving in his careful breast
Th' event of things, at last, his patience tired,
Thus from his royal throne, by Heav'n inspired,
The godlike David spoke: with awful fear
His train their Maker in their master hear.
'Thus long have I, by native mercy swayed,
My wrongs dissembled, my revenge delayed:
So willing to forgive th' offending age;
So much the father did the king assuage.
But now so far my clemency they slight,
Th' offenders question my forgiving right.
That one was made for many, they contend;
But 't is to rule; for that's a monarch's end.
They call my tenderness of blood, my fear;
Though manly tempers can the longest bear.
Yet, since they will divert my native course,
'T is time to show I am not good by force.
Those heaped affronts that haughty subjects bring,
Are burthens for a camel, not a king.
Kings are the public pillars of the State,
Born to sustain and prop the nation's weight;
If my young Samson will pretend a call
To shake the column, let him share the fall:
But O that yet he would repent and live!
How easy 't is for parents to forgive!
With how few tears a pardon might be won
From nature, pleading for a darling son!
Poor pitied youth, by my paternal care
Raised up to all the height his frame could bear!
Had God ordained his fate for empire born,
He would have giv'n his soul another turn:
Gulled with a patriot's name, whose modern sense
Is one that would by law supplant his prince;
The people's brave, the politician's tool;
Never was patriot yet, but was a fool.
Whence comes it that religion and the laws
Should more be Absalom's than David's cause?
His old instructor, ere he lost his place,
Was never thought endued with so much grace.
Good heav'ns, how faction can a patriot paint!
My rebel ever proves my people's saint.
Would they impose an heir upon the throne?
Let Sanhedrins be taught to give their own.
A king 's at least a part of government,
And mine as requisite as their consent;
Without my leave a future king to choose,
Infers a right the present to depose.
True, they petition me t' approve their choice;
But Esau's hands suit ill with Jacob's voice.
My pious subjects for my safety pray;
Which to secure, they take my pow'r away.
From plots and treasons Heav'n preserve my years,
But save me most from my petitioners!
Unsatiate as the barren womb or grave;
God cannot grant so much as they can crave.
What then is left, but with a jealous eye
To guard the small remains of royalty?
The law shall still direct my peaceful sway,
And the same law teach rebels to obey:
Votes shall no more established pow'r control —
Such votes as make a part exceed the whole:
No groundless clamors shall my friends remove,

Nor crowds have pow'r to punish ere they prove:
For gods and godlike kings their care express,
Still to defend their servants in distress.
O that my pow'r to saving were confined!
Why am I forced, like Heav'n, against my mind,
To make examples of another kind?
Must I at length the sword of justice draw?
O curst effects of necessary law!
How ill my fear they by my mercy scan!
Beware the fury of a patient man.
Law they require, let Law then shew her face;
They could not be content to look on Grace,
Her hinder parts, but with a daring eye
To tempt the terror of her front and die.
By their own arts, 't is righteously decreed,
Those dire artificers of death shall bleed.
Against themselves their witnesses will swear,
Till, viper-like, their mother Plot they tear;
And suck for nutriment that bloody gore,
Which was their principle of life before.
Their Belial with their Belzebub will fight;
Thus on my foes, my foes shall do me right.
Nor doubt th' event; for factious crowds engage,
In their first onset, all their brutal rage.
Then let 'em take an unresisted course;
Retire, and traverse, and delude their force;
But, when they stand all breathless, urge the fight,
And rise upon 'em with redoubled might;
For lawful pow'r is still superior found;
When long driv'n back, at length it stands the ground.'
He said. Th' Almighty, nodding, gave consent;
And peals of thunder shook the firmament.
Henceforth a series of new time began,
The mighty years in long procession ran:
Once more the godlike David was restored,
And willing nations knew their lawful lord.

1681

MAC FLECKNOE

OR, A SATIRE UPON THE TRUE-BLUE-PROTESTANT POET, T. S.

All human things are subject to decay,
And when fate summons, monarchs must obey.
This Flecknoe found, who, like Augustus, young
Was called to empire, and had governed long;
In prose and verse, was owned, without dispute,
Through all the realms of *Nonsense*, absolute.
This agèd prince, now flourishing in peace,
And blest with issue of a large increase;
Worn out with business, did at length debate
To settle the succession of the State;
And, pond'ring which of all his sons was fit
To reign, and wage immortal war with wit,
Cried: ''T is resolved; for nature pleads, that he
Should only rule, who most resembles me.
Sh—— alone my perfect image bears,
Mature in dulness from his tender years:
Sh—— alone, of all my sons, is he
Who stands confirmed in full stupidity.
The rest to some faint meaning make pretense,
But Sh—— never deviates into sense.
Some beams of wit on other souls may fall,
Strike through, and make a lucid interval;
But Sh——'s genuine night admits no ray,
His rising fogs prevail upon the day.
Besides, his goodly fabric fills the eye,
And seems designed for thoughtless majesty;
Thoughtless as monarch oaks that shade the plain,
And, spread in solemn state, supinely reign.
Heywood and Shirley were but types of thee,
Thou last great prophet of tautology.
Even I, a dunce of more renown than they,
Was sent before but to prepare thy way;
And, coarsely clad in Norwich drugget, came
To teach the nations in thy greater name.
My warbling lute, the lute I whilom strung,
When to King John of Portugal I sung,
Was but the prelude to that glorious day,
When thou on silver Thames didst cut thy way,
With well-timed oars before the royal barge,
Swelled with the pride of thy celestial charge;
And big with hymn, commander of a host,
The like was ne'er in Epsom blankets tossed.
Methinks I see the new Arion sail,
The lute still trembling underneath thy nail.
At thy well-sharpened thumb from shore to shore
The treble squeaks for fear, the basses roar; . . .
About thy boat the little fishes throng,
As at the morning toast that floats along.
Sometimes, as prince of thy harmonious band,

Thou wield'st thy papers in thy threshing hand.
St. André's feet ne'er kept more equal time,
Not ev'n the feet of thy own *Psyche's* rhyme;
Though they in number as in sense excel:
So just, so like tautology, they fell,
That, pale with envy, Singleton forswore
The lute and sword, which he in triumph bore,
And vowed he ne'er would act Villerius more.'
Here stopped the good old sire, and wept for joy
In silent raptures of the hopeful boy.
All arguments, but most his plays, persuade
That for anointed dulness he was made.
Close to the walls which fair Augusta bind,
(The fair Augusta much to fears inclined,)
An ancient fabric raised t' inform the sight,
There stood of yore, and Barbican it hight:
A watchtower once; but now, so fate ordains,
Of all the pile an empty name remains.
From its old ruins brothel-houses rise,
Scenes of lewd loves, and of polluted joys. . . .
Near these a Nursery erects its head,
Where queens are formed, and future heroes bred;
Where unfledged actors learn to laugh and cry,
Where infant [fools] their tender voices try,
And little Maximins the gods defy.
Great Fletcher never treads in buskins here,
Nor greater Jonson dares in socks appear;
But gentle Simkin just reception finds
Amidst this monument of vanished minds:
Pure clinches the suburbian Muse affords,
And Panton waging harmless war with words.
Here Flecknoe, as a place to fame well known,
Ambitiously designed his Sh——'s throne;
For ancient Dekker prophesied long since,
That in this pile should reign a mighty prince,
Born for a scourge of wit, and flail of sense;
To whom true dulness should some *Psyches* owe,
But worlds of *Misers* from his pen should flow;
Humorists and hypocrites it should produce,
Whole Raymond families, and tribes of Bruce.
Now Empress Fame had published the renown
Of Sh——'s coronation through the town.
Roused by report of Fame, the nations meet,
From near Bunhill, and distant Watling Street.
No Persian carpets spread th'imperial way,
But scattered limbs of mangled poets lay;
From dusty shops neglected authors come,
Martyrs of pies, and relics of the bum.
Much Heywood, Shirley, Ogleby there lay,
But loads of Sh—— almost choked the way.
Bilked stationers for yeomen stood prepared,
And Herringman was captain of the guard.
The hoary prince in majesty appeared,
High on a throne of his own labors reared.
At his right hand our young Ascanius sate,
Rome's other hope, and pillar of the State.
His brows thick fogs, instead of glories, grace,
And lambent dulness played around his face.
As Hannibal did to the altars come,
Sworn by his sire a mortal foe to Rome;
So Sh—— swore, nor should his vow be vain,
That he till death true dulness would maintain;
And, in his father's right, and realm's defense,
Ne'er to have peace with wit, nor truce with sense.
The king himself the sacred unction made,
As king by office, and as priest by trade.
In his sinister hand, instead of ball,
He placed a mighty mug of potent ale;
Love's Kingdom to his right he did convey,
At once his scepter, and his rule of sway;
Whose righteous lore the prince had practiced young,
And from whose loins recorded *Psyche* sprung.
His temples, last, with poppies were o'erspread,
That nodding seemed to consecrate his head.
Just at that point of time, if fame not lie,
On his left hand twelve reverend owls did fly.
So Romulus, 't is sung, by Tiber's brook,
Presage of sway from twice six vultures took.
Th' admiring throng loud acclamations make,
And omens of his future empire take.
The sire then shook the honors of his head,
And from his brows damps of oblivion shed
Full on the filial dulness: long he stood,
Repelling from his breast the raging god;

At length burst out in this prophetic mood:
'Heavens bless my son, from Ireland let him reign
To far Barbadoes on the western main;
Of his dominion may no end be known,
And greater than his father's be his throne;
Beyond *Love's Kingdom* let him stretch his pen!'
He paused, and all the people cried, 'Amen.'
Then thus continued he: 'My son, advance
Still in new impudence, new ignorance.
Success let others teach, learn thou from me
Pangs without birth, and fruitless industry.
Let *Virtuosos* in five years be writ;
Yet not one thought accuse thy toil of wit;
Let gentle George in triumph tread the stage,
Make Dorimant betray and Loveit rage;
Let Cully, Cockwood, Fopling, charm the pit,
And in their folly show the writer's wit.
Yet still thy fools shall stand in thy defense,
And justify their author's want of sense.
Let 'em be all by thy own model made
Of dulness, and desire no foreign aid;
That they to future ages may be known,
Not copies drawn, but issue of thy own.
Nay, let thy men of wit, too, be the same,
All full of thee, and differing but in name.
But let no alien Sedley interpose,
To lard with wit thy hungry Epsom prose.
And when false flowers of rhetoric thou wouldst cull,
Trust nature, do not labor to be dull;
But write thy best and top; and in each line
Sir Formal's oratory will be thine:
Sir Formal, though unsought, attends thy quill,
And does thy northern dedicaitons fill.
Nor let false friends seduce thy mind to fame,
By arrogating Jonson's hostile name.
Let father Flecknoe fire thy mind with praise,
And uncle Ogleby thy envy raise.
Thou art my blood, where Jonson has no part:
What share have we in nature, or in art?
Where did his wit on learning fix a brand,
And rail at arts he did not understand?
Where made he love in Prince Nicander's vein,
Or swept the dust in *Psyche's* humble strain? . . . .
When did his Muse from Fletcher scenes purloin,
As thou whole Eth'ridge dost transfuse to thine?
But so transfused, as oil on waters flow,
His always floats above, thine sinks below.
This is thy province, this thy wondrous way,
New humours to invent for each new play:
This is that boasted bias of thy mind,
By which one way, to dulness, 't is inclined;
Which makes thy writings lean on one side still,
And, in all changes, that way bends thy will.
Nor let thy mountain belly make pretense
Of likeness; thine's a tympany of sense.
A tun of man in thy large bulk is writ,
But sure thou 'rt but a kilderkin of wit.
Like mine, thy gentle numbers feebly creep;
Thy tragic Muse gives smiles, thy comic sleep.
With whate'er gall thou sett'st thyself to write,
Thy inoffensive satires never bite.
In thy felonious heart though venom lies,
It does but touch thy Irish pen, and dies.
Thy genius calls thee not to purchase fame
In keen iambics, but mild anagram.
Leave writing plays, and choose for thy command
Some peaceful province in acrostic land.
There thou mayst wings display and altars raise,
And torture one poor word ten thousand ways.
Or, if thou wouldst thy diff'rent talents suit,
Set thy own songs, and sing them to thy lute.'
He said; but his last words were scarcely heard;
For Bruce and Longville had a trap prepared,
And down they sent the yet declaiming bard.
Sinking he left his drugget robe behind
Borne upwards by a subterranean wind.
The mantle fell to the young prophet's part,
With double portion of his father's art.

1682

Daniel Defoe (1660?-1731)

THE TRUE-BORN ENGLISHMAN

PART I

Wherever God erects a house of prayer,
The Devil always builds a chapel there:
And 't will be found upon examination,
The latter has the largest congregation:
For ever since he first debauched the mind,
He made a perfect conquest of mankind.
With uniformity of service, he
Reigns with a general aristocracy.

No non-conforming sects disturb his reign,
For of his yoke, there's very few complain.
He knows the genius and the inclination,
And matches proper sins for ev'ry nation.
He needs no standing army government;
He always rules us by our own consent:
His laws are easy, and his gentle sway
Makes it exceeding pleasant to obey.
The list of his vicegerents and commanders,
Out-does your Cæsars, or your Alexanders.
They never fail of his infernal aid,
And he's as certain ne'er to be betrayed.
Through all the world they spread his vast command,
And death's eternal empire is maintained.
They rule so politicly and so well,
As if they were Lords Justices of hell;
Duly divided to debauch mankind,
And plant infernal dictates in their mind.

Pride, the first peer, and president of hell,
To his share, Spain, the largest province fell.
The subtle Prince thought fittest to bestow
On these the golden mines of Mexico,
With all the silver mountains of Peru;
Wealth which in wise hands would the world undo;
Because he knew their genius was such,
Too lazy and too haughty to be rich:
So proud a people, so above their fate,
That, if reduced to beg, they'll beg in state:
Lavish of money, to be counted brave,
And proudly starve, because they scorn to save;
Never was nation in the world before,
So very rich, and yet so very poor.

Lust chose the torrid zone of Italy,
Where blood ferments in rape and [felony],
Where swelling veins o'erflow with living streams,
With heat impregnate from Vesuvian flames;
Whose flowing sulphur forms infernal lakes,
And human body of the soil partakes.
There nature ever burns with hot desires,
Fanned with luxuriant air from subterranean fires:
Here undisturbed, in floods of scalding lust,
Th' infernal king reigns with infernal gust.

Drunkenness, the darling favourite of hell,
Chose Germany to rule; and rules so well,
No subjects more obsequiously obey,
None please so well, or are so pleased as they;
The cunning artist manages so well,
He lets them bow to heav'n, and drink to hell.
If but to wine and him they homage pay,
He cares not to what deity they pray;
What god they worship most, or in what way.
Whether by Luther, Calvin, or by Rome,
They sail for heaven, by wine he steers them home.

Ungoverned Passion settled first in France,
Where mankind lives in haste, and thrives by chance;
A dancing nation, fickle and untrue,
Have oft undone themselves, and others too;
Prompt the infernal dictates to obey,
And in hell's favour none more great than they.

The pagan world he blindly leads away,
And personally rules with arbitrary sway:
The mask thrown off, plain devil, his title stands;
And what elsewhere he tempts, he here commands;
There, with full gust, th' ambition of his mind,
Governs, as he of old in heaven designed:
Worshipped as God, his Paynim altars smoke,
Imbrued with blood of those that him invoke.

The rest by deputies he rules as well,
And plants the distant colonies of hell;
By them his secret power he well maintains,
And binds the world in his infernal chains.

By zeal the Irish, and the Russ by folly,
Fury the Dane, the Swede by melancholy;
By stupid ignorance, the Muscovite;
The Chinese, by a child of hell, called wit;
Wealth makes the Persian too effeminate;
And poverty the Tartar desperate:
The Turks and Moors, by Mah'met he subdues;
And God has given him leave to rule the Jews:
Rage rules the Portuguese, and fraud the Scotch;
Revenge the Pole, and avarice the Dutch.

Satire, be kind, and draw a silent veil,
Thy native England's vices to conceal:
Or, if that task 's impossible to do,
At least be just, and show her virtues too;
Too great the first, alas! the last too few.

England, unknown, as yet unpeopled lay,
Happy, had she remained so to this day,
And not to ev'ry nation been a prey.
Her open harbours, and her fertile plains,
The merchant's glory these, and those the swain's,
To ev'ry barbarous nation have betrayed her;
Who conquer her as oft as they invade her,
So beauty, guarded but by Innocence,
That ruins her which should be her defence.

Ingratitude, a devil of black renown,
Possessed her very early for his own:
An ugly, surly, sullen, selfish spirit,
Who Satan's worst perfections does inherit;
Second to him in malice and in force,
All devil without, and all within him worse.
He made her first-born race to be so rude,
And suffered her to be so oft subdued;
By several crowds of wandering thieves o'er-run,
Often unpeopled, and as oft undone;
While every nation that her powers reduced,
Their languages and manners introduced;
From whose mixed relics our compounded breed,
By spurious generation does succeed;
Making a race uncertain and uneven,
Derived from all the nations under heaven.
The Romans first with Julius Cæsar came,
Including all the nations of that name,
Gauls, Greeks, and Lombards; and, by computation,
Auxiliaries or slaves of every nation.
With Hengist, Saxons; Danes with Sweno came,
In search of plunder, not in search of fame.
Scots, Picts, and Irish from the Hibernian shore;
And conquering William brought the Normans o'er.
All these their barbarous offspring left behind,
The dregs of armies, they of all mankind;
Blended with Britons, who before were here,
Of whom the Welsh have blest the character.
From this amphibious, ill-born mob began,
That vain ill-natured thing, an Englishman.
The customs, sir-names, languages, and manners,
Of all these nations, are their own explainers;
Whose relics are so lasting and so strong,
They 've left a shibboleth upon our tongue;
By which, with easy search, you may distinguish
Your Roman, Saxon, Danish, Norman, English.
The great invading Norman let us know
What conquerors in after-times might do.
To every musqueteer he brought to town,
He gave the lands which never were his own;
When first the English crown he did obtain,
He did not send his Dutchmen home again.
No re-assumptions in his reign were known,
Davenant might there have let his book alone.
No parliament his army could disband;
He raised no money, for he paid in land.
He gave his legions their eternal station,
And made them all freeholders of the nation.
He canton'd out the country to his men,
And every soldier was a denizen.
The rascals thus enriched, he called them lords,
To please their upstart pride with new-made words,
And Doomsday Book his tyranny records.
And here begins the ancient pedigree
That so exalts our poor nobility.
'T is that from some French trooper they derive,
Who with the Norman bastard did arrive:
The trophies of the families appear;
Some show the sword, the bow, and some the spear,
Which their great ancestor, forsooth, did wear.
These in the herald's register remain,
Their noble mean extraction to explain,
Yet who the hero was, no man can tell,
Whether a drummer or a colonel:
The silent record blushes to reveal
Their undescended dark original.
But grant the best. How came the change to pass;
A true-born Englishman of Norman race?
A Turkish horse can show more history,
To prove his well-descended family.
Conquest, as by the moderns 't is expressed,
May give a title to the lands possessed;
But that the longest sword should be so civil,
To make a Frenchman English, that 's the devil.
These are the heroes that despise the Dutch,
And rail at new-come foreigners so much;
Forgetting that themselves are all derived
From the most scoundrel race that ever lived;
A horrid crowd of rambling thieves and drones
Who ransacked kingdoms and dispeopled towns;
The Pict and painted Briton, treacherous Scot,
By hunger, theft, and rapine, hither brought;
Norwegian pirates, buccaneering Danes,
Whose red-haired offspring everywhere remains;

Who, joined with Norman French, compound the breed
From whence your true-born Englishmen proceed.
And lest, by length of time, it be pretended,
The climate may this modern breed have mended;
Wise Providence, to keep us where we are,
Mixes us daily with exceeding care;
We have been Europe's sink, the [place] where she
Voids all her offal out-cast progeny;
From our fifth Henry's time the strolling bands,
Of banished fugitives from neighb'ring lands,
Have here a certain sanctuary found:
The eternal refuge of the vagabond,
Where in but half a common age of time,
Borrowing new blood and manners from the clime,
Proudly they learn all mankind to contemn,
And all their race are true-born Englishmen.
Dutch Walloons, Flemmings, Irishmen, and Scots,
Vaudois, and Valtolins, and Huguenots,
In good Queen Bess's charitable reign,
Supplied us with three hundred thousand men:
Religion — God, we thank thee! — sent them hither,
Priests, Protestants, the devil, and all together;
Of all professions, and of ev'ry trade,
All that were persecuted or afraid:
Whether for debt, or other crimes, they fled,
David at Hackelah was still their head.
The offspring of this miscellaneous crowd,
Had not their new plantations long enjoyed,
But they grew Englishmen, and raised their votes,
At foreign shoals of interloping Scots;
The royal branch from Pict-land did succeed,
With troops of Scots and scabs from North-by-Tweed;
The seven first years of his pacific reign,
Made him and half his nation Englishmen.
Scots from the northern frozen banks of Tay
With packs and plods came whigging all away,
Thick as the locusts which in Egypt swarmed,
With pride and hungry hopes completely armed;
With native truth, diseases, and no money,
Plundered our Canaan of the milk and honey;
Here they grew quickly lords and gentlemen,
And all their race are true-born Englishmen.
The civil wars, the common purgative,
Which always use to make the nation thrive,
Made way for all that strolling congregation,
Which thronged in pious Charles's restoration.
The royal refugee our breed restores,
With foreign courtiers, and with foreign [stores]:
And carefully re-peopled us again,
Throughout his lazy, long, lascivious reign,
With such a blest and true-born English fry,
As much illustrates our nobility.
A gratitude which will so black appear,
As future ages must abhor to hear:
When they look back on all that crimson flood,
Which streamed in Lindsey's, and Caernarvon's blood;
Bold Stafford, Cambridge, Capel, Lucas, Lisle,
Who crowned in death his father's fun'ral pile.
The loss of whom, in order to supply
With true-born English nobility,
Six bastard dukes survive his luscious reign,
The labours of Italian Castlemain,
French Portsmouth, Tabby Scott, and Cambrian;
Besides the num'rous bright and virgin throng,
Whose female glories shade them from my song.
This offspring if one age they multiply,
May half the house with English peers supply:
There with true English pride they may contemn
Schomberg and Portland, new-made noblemen. . . .
Beggars and bastards by this new creation
Much multiplied the peerage of the nation;
Who will be all, ere one short age runs o'er,
As true-born lords as those we had before.
Then to recruit the commons he prepares,
And heal the latent breaches of the wars;
The pious purpose better to advance,
He invites the banished Protestants of France;
Hither, for God's sake, and their own, they fled
Some for religion came, and some for bread:
Two hundred thousand pair of wooden shoes,
Who, God be thanked, had nothing left to lose;

To heaven's great praise did for religion fly,
To make us starve our poor in charity.
In ev'ry port they plant their fruitful train,
To get a race of true-born Englishmen;
Whose children will, when riper years they see,
Be as ill-natured, and as proud as we;
Call themselves English, foreigners despise,
Be surly like us all, and just as wise.
Thus from a mixture of all kinds began,
That heterogeneous thing, an Englishman:
In eager rapes, and furious lust begot,
Betwixt a painted Briton and a Scot:
Whose gend'ring offspring quickly learned to bow,
And yoke their heifers to the Roman plough;
From whence a mongrel half-bred race there came,
With neither name nor nation, speech nor fame,
In whose hot veins new mixtures quickly ran,
Infused betwixt a Saxon and a Dane. . . .
This nauseous brood directly did contain
The well-extracted blood of Englishmen.
Which medley, canton'd in a heptarchy,
A rhapsody of nations to supply,
Among themselves maintained eternal wars,
And still the ladies loved the conquerors.
The Western Angles all the rest subdued,
A bloody nation, barbarous and rude;
Who by the tenure of the sword possessed
One part of Britain, and subdued the rest:
And as great things denominate the small,
The conquering part gave title to the whole;
The Scot, Pict, Briton, Roman, Dane, submit,
And with the English Saxon all unite:
And these the mixture have so close pursued,
The very name and memory's subdued;
No Roman now, no Briton does remain;
Wales strove to separate, but strove in vain:
The silent nations undistinguished fall,
And Englishman 's the common name for all.
Fate jumbled them together, God knows how;
Whate'er they were, they 're true-born English now.
The wonder which remains is at our pride,
To value that which all wise men deride;
For Englishmen to boast of generation
Cancels their knowledge, and lampoons the nation.
A true-born Englishman 's a contradiction,
In speech an irony, in fact a fiction:
A banter made to be a test of fools,
Which those that use it justly ridicules;
A metaphor intended to express,
A man a-kin to all the universe.
For as the Scots, as learnèd men have said,
Throughout the world their wand'ring seed have spread,
So open-handed England, 't is believed,
Has all the gleanings of the world received.
Some think of England, 't was our Saviour meant,
The Gospel should to all the world be sent:
Since when the blessèd sound did hither reach,
They to all nations might be said to preach.
'T is well that virtue gives nobility;
How shall we else the want of birth supply?
Since scarce one family is left alive,
Which does not from some foreigner derive.
Of sixty thousand English gentlemen,
Whose names and arms in registers remain,
We challenge all our heralds to declare
Ten families which English Saxons are.
France justly boasts the ancient noble line
Of Bourbon, Montmorency, and Lorraine.
The Germans too, their house of Austria show,
And Holland, their invincible Nassau.
Lines which in heraldry were ancient grown,
Before the name of Englishman was known.
Even Scotland, too, her elder glory shows,
Her Gordons, Hamiltons, and her Monro's;
Douglas', Mackays, and Grahams, names well known,
Long before ancient England knew her own.
But England, modern to the last degree,
Borrows or makes her own nobility,
And yet she boldly boasts of pedigree;
Repines that foreigners are put upon her,
And talks of her antiquity and honour.
Her Sackvills, Savils, Cecils, Delamers,
Mohuns and Montagues, Duras and Veeres,
Not one have English names, yet all are English peers.
Your Houblons, Papillons, and Lethuliers,
Pass now for true-born English knights and squires,
And make good senate-members, or lord mayors.
Wealth, howsoever got, in England makes
Lords of mechanics, gentlemen of rakes.
Antiquity and birth are needless here;
'T is impudence and money makes a peer.
Innumerable city knights we know,
From Blue-coat Hospitals, and Bridewell flow.

Draymen and porters fill the city chair,
And foot-boys magisterial purple wear.
Fate has but very small distinction set
Betwixt the counter and the coronet.
Tarpaulin lords, pages of high renown,
Rise up by poor men's valour, not their own;
Great families of yesterday we show,
And lords, whose parents were the Lord knows who.

1701

ODES

Abraham Cowley (1618–1667)

ODE VI. UPON THE SHORTNESS OF MAN'S LIFE

Mark that swift arrow how it cuts the air,
How it outruns the hunting eye!
Use all persuasions now and try
If thou canst call it back or stay it there.
That way it went, but thou shalt find
No tract of 't left behind.

Fool, 't is thy life, and the fond archer, thou!
Of all the time thou'st shot away,
I'll bid thee fetch but yesterday,
And it shall be too hard a task to do.
Besides repentance, what canst find
That it hath left behind?

Our life is carried with too strong a tide,
A doubtful cloud our substance bears
And is the horse of all our years;
Each day doth on a wingèd whirlwind ride.
We and our glass run out, and must
Both render up our dust.

But his past life who without grief can see,
Who never thinks his end too near
But says to fame, 'Thou art mine heir,'
That man extends life's natural brevity:
This is, this is the only way
To outlive Nestor in a day.

1636

THE RESURRECTION

I

Not winds to voyagers at sea
Nor showers to earth more necessary be
(Heav'n's vital seed cast on the womb of earth
To give the fruitful year a birth)
Than verse to virtue, which can do
The midwife's office and the nurse's too:
It feeds it strongly, and it clothes it gay;
And when it dies, with comely pride
Embalms it, and erects a pyramide
That never will decay
Till heaven itself shall melt away
And naught behind it stay.

II

Begin the song, and strike the living lyre!
Lo, how the years to come, a numerous and well-fitted quire,
All hand in hand do decently advance,
And to my song with smooth and equal measures dance.
Whilst the dance lasts, how long soe'er it be,
My music's voice shall bear it company,
Till all gentle notes be drowned
In the last trumpet's dreadful sound.
That to the spheres themselves shall silence bring,
Untune the universal string:
Then all the wide extended sky,
And all th' harmonious worlds on high,
And Virgil's sacred work shall die;
And he himself shall see in one fire shine
Rich Nature's ancient Troy, though built by hands divine.

III

Whom thunder's dismal noise,
And all that prophets and apostles louder spake,
And all the creatures' plain conspiring voice,
Could not, whilst they lived, awake,
This mightier sound shall make,
When dead, t' arise,
And open tombs and open eyes
To the long sluggards of five thousand years.
This mightier sound shall make its hearers ears.

Then shall the scattered atoms crowding come
Back to their ancient home,
Some from birds, from fishes some,
Some from earth and some from seas,
Some from beasts and some from trees;
Some descend from clouds on high,
Some from metals upwards fly,
And, where th' attending soul naked and shivering stands,
Meet, salute, and join their hands,
As dispersed soldiers at the trumpet's call
Haste to their colours all:
Unhappy most, like tortured men,
Their joints new set, to be new racked again;
To mountains they for shelter pray,
The mountains shake, and run about no less confused than they.

IV

Stop, stop, my Muse! allay thy vig'rous heat,
Kindled at a hint so great.
Hold thy Pindaric Pegasus closely in,
Which does to rage begin,
And this steep hill would gallop up with violent course.
'T is an unruly and a hard-mouthed horse,
Fierce and unbroken yet,
Impatient of the spur or bit;
Now prances stately, and anon flies o'er the place,
Disdains the servile law of any settled pace;
Conscious and proud of his own natural force,
'T will no unskilful touch endure,
But flings writer and reader too that sits not sure.

1656

John Dryden (1631–1700)

TO THE PIOUS MEMORY OF THE ACCOMPLISHED YOUNG LADY

MRS. ANNE KILLIGREW

EXCELLENT IN THE TWO SISTER-ARTS OF POESY AND PAINTING

AN ODE

I

Thou youngest virgin-daughter of the skies,
Made in the last promotion of the blest;
Whose palms, new plucked from paradise,
In spreading branches more sublimely rise,
Rich with immortal green above the rest:
Whether, adopted to some neighboring star,
Thou roll'st above us, in thy wand'ring race,
Or, in procession fixed and regular,
Moved with the heavens' majestic pace;
Or, called to more superior bliss,
Thou tread'st, with seraphims, the vast abyss:
Whatever happy region is thy place,
Cease thy celestial song a little space;
(Thou wilt have time enough for hymns divine,
Since heav'n's eternal year is thine.)
Hear then a mortal Muse thy praise rehearse,
In no ignoble verse;
But such as thy own voice did practice here,
When thy first-fruits of poesy were giv'n,
To make thyself a welcome inmate there;
While yet a young probationer,
And candidate of heav'n.

II

If by traduction came thy mind,
Our wonder is the less to find
A soul so charming from a stock so good;
Thy father was transfused into thy blood:
So wert thou born into a tuneful strain,
(An early, rich, and inexhausted vein.)
But if thy pre-existing soul
Was formed, at first, with myriads more,
It did through all the mighty poets roll,
Who Greek or Latin laurels wore,
And was that Sappho last, which once it was before.
If so, then cease thy flight, O heaven-born mind!
Thou hast no dross to purge from thy rich ore;
Nor can thy soul a fairer mansion find,
Than was the beauteous frame she left behind:
Return, to fill or mend the choir of thy celestial kind.

III

May we presume to say, that at thy birth
New joy was sprung in heav'n, as well as here on earth?
For sure the milder planets did combine
On thy auspicious horoscope to shine,
And ev'n the most malicious were in trine.
Thy brother-angels at thy birth
Strung each his lyre, and tuned it high,
That all the people of the sky
Might know a poetess was born on earth.
And then, if ever, mortal ears
Had heard the music of the spheres!
And if no clust'ring swarm of bees

On thy sweet mouth distilled their golden dew,
'T was that such vulgar miracles
Heav'n had not leisure to renew:
For all the blest fraternity of love
Solemnized there thy birth, and kept thy holiday above.

IV

O gracious God! how far have we
Profaned thy heav'nly gift of poesy!
Made prostitute and profligate the Muse,
Debased to each obscene and impious use,
Whose harmony was first ordained above
For tongues of angels, and for hymns of love!
O wretched we! why were we hurried down
This lubric and adult'rate age,
(Nay, added fat pollutions of our own,)
T' increase the steaming ordures of the stage?
What can we say t' excuse our second fall?
Let this thy vestal, Heav'n, atone for all:
Her Arethusian stream remains unsoiled,
Unmixed with foreign filth, and undefiled;
Her wit was more than man, her innocence a child.

V

Art she had none, yet wanted none;
For nature did that want supply:
So rich in treasures of her own,
She might our boasted stores defy:
Such noble vigor did her verse adorn
That it seemed borrowed, where 't was only born.
Her morals too were in her bosom bred,
By great examples daily fed,
What in the best of books, her father's life, she read.
And to be read herself she need not fear;
Each test, and ev'ry light, her Muse will bear,
Though Epictetus with his lamp were there.
Ev'n love (for love sometimes her Muse expressed)
Was but a lambent flame which played about her breast,
Light as the vapors of a morning dream:
So cold herself, whilst she such warmth expressed,
'T was Cupid bathing in Diana's stream.

VI

Born to the spacious empire of the Nine,
One would have thought she should have been content
To manage well that mighty government;
But what can young ambitious souls confine?
To the next realm she stretched her sway,
For painture near adjoining lay,
A plenteous province, and alluring prey.
A chamber of dependences was framed,
(As conquerors will never want pretense,
When armed, to justify th' offense,)
And the whole fief in right of poetry she claimed.
The country open lay without defense;
For poets frequent inroads there had made,
And perfectly could represent
The shape, the face, with ev'ry lineament;
And all the large demains which the Dumb Sister swayed,
All bowed beneath her government;
Received in triumph wheresoe'er she went.
Her pencil drew whate'er her soul designed,
And oft the happy draught surpassed the image in her mind.
The sylvan scenes of herds and flocks,
And fruitful plains and barren rocks,
Of shallow brooks that flowed so clear
The bottom did the top appear;
Of deeper too and ampler floods,
Which, as in mirrors, showed the woods;
Of lofty trees, with sacred shades,
And perspectives of pleasant glades,
Where nymphs of brightest form appear,
And shaggy satyrs standing near,
Which them at once admire and fear:
The ruins too of some majestic piece,
Boasting the pow'r of ancient Rome, or Greece,
Whose statues, friezes, columns broken lie,
And, though defaced, the wonder of the eye:
What nature, art, bold fiction, e'er durst frame,
Her forming hand gave feature to the name.
So strange a concourse ne'er was seen before,
But when the peopled ark the whole creation bore.

VII

The scene then changed: with bold erected look
Our martial king the sight with reverence strook:

For, not content t' express his outward part,
Her hand called out the image of his heart:
His warlike mind, his soul devoid of fear,
His high-designing thoughts were figured there,
As when, by magic, ghosts are made appear.
Our Phœnix queen was portrayed too so bright,
Beauty alone could beauty take so right:
Her dress, her shape, her matchless grace,
Were all observed as well as heavenly face.
With such a peerless majesty she stands,
As in that day she took the crown from sacred hands;
Before a train of heroines was seen,
In beauty foremost, as in rank the queen.
Thus nothing to her genius was denied,
But like a ball of fire the further thrown,
Still with a greater blaze she shone,
And her bright soul broke out on ev'ry side.
What next she had designed, Heaven only knows;
To such immod'rate growth her conquest rose
That fate alone its progress could oppose.

VIII

Now all those charms, that blooming grace,
The well-proportioned shape, and beauteous face,
Shall never more be seen by mortal eyes:
In earth the much-lamented virgin lies!
Not wit, nor piety could fate prevent;
Nor was the cruel Destiny content
To finish all the murder at a blow,
To sweep at once her life and beauty too;
But, like a hardened felon, took a pride
To work more mischievously slow,
And plundered first, and then destroyed.
O double sacrilege on things divine,
To rob the relic, and deface the shrine!
But thus Orinda died:
Heaven, by the same disease, did both translate;
As equal were their souls, so equal was their fate.

IX

Meantime her warlike brother on the seas
His waving streamers to the winds displays,
And vows for his return, with vain devotion, pays.
Ah, generous youth, that wish forbear,
The winds too soon will waft thee here
Slack all thy sails, and fear to come,
Alas, thou know'st not, thou art wrecked at home!
No more shalt thou behold thy sister's face,
Thou hast already had her last embrace.
But look aloft, and if thou ken'st from far
Among the Pleiads a new-kindled star;
If any sparkles than the rest more bright,
'Tis she that shines in that propitious light.

X

When in mid-air the golden trump shall sound,
To raise the nations under ground;
When in the Valley of Jehosophat
The judging God shall close the book of fate,
And there the last assizes keep
For those who wake and those who sleep;
When rattling bones together fly
From the four corners of the sky;
When sinews o'er the skeletons are spread,
Those clothed with flesh, and life inspires the dead;
The sacred poets first shall hear the sound,
And foremost from the tomb shall bound,
For they are covered with the lightest ground;
And straight, with inborn vigor, on the wing,
Like mounting larks, to the new morning sing.
There thou, sweet saint, before the choir shalt go,
As harbinger of heav'n, the way to show,
The way which thou so well hast learned below.

1686

A SONG FOR ST. CECILIA'S DAY, 1687

I

FROM harmony, from heav'nly harmony
This universal frame began:
When Nature underneath a heap
Of jarring atoms lay,
And could not heave her head,
The tuneful voice was heard from high:
'Arise, ye more than dead.'
Then cold, and hot, and moist, and dry,
In order to their stations leap,
And Music's pow'r obey.
From harmony, from heav'nly harmony

This universal frame began:
From harmony to harmony
Through all the compass of the notes it ran,
The diapason closing full in Man.

II

What passion cannot Music raise and quell!
When Jubal struck the corded shell,
His list'ning brethren stood around,
And, wond'ring, on their faces fell
To worship that celestial sound.
Less than a god they thought there could not dwell
Within the hollow of that shell
That spoke so sweetly and so well.
What passion cannot Music raise and quell!

III

The Trumpet's loud clangor
Excites us to arms,
With shrill notes of anger,
And mortal alarms.
The double double double beat
Of the thund'ring drum
Cries: 'Hark! the foes come;
Charge, charge, 't is too late to retreat!'

IV

The soft complaining Flute
In dying notes discovers
The woes of hopeless lovers,
Whose dirge is whispered by the warbling Lute.

V

Sharp Violins proclaim
Their jealous pangs and desperation,
Fury, frantic indignation,
Depth of pains, and height of passion,
For the fair, disdainful dame.

VI

But O! what art can teach,
What human voice can reach,
The sacred Organ's praise?
Notes inspiring holy love,
Notes that wing their heav'nly ways
To mend the choirs above.

VII

Orpheus could lead the savage race;
And trees unrooted left their place,
Sequacious of the lyre;
But bright Cecilia raised the wonder high'r:
When to her Organ vocal breath was giv'n,
An angel heard, and straight appeared,
Mistaking earth for heav'n.

GRAND CHORUS

As from the pow'r of sacred lays
The spheres began to move,
And sung the great Creator's praise
To all the blest above;
So, when the last and dreadful hour
This crumbling pageant shall devour,
The Trumpet shall be heard on high,
The dead shall live, the living die,
And Music shall untune the sky.

1687

ALEXANDER'S FEAST

OR, THE POWER OF MUSIC; AN ODE IN HONOR OF ST. CECILIA'S DAY

I

'T WAS at the royal feast, for Persia won
By Philip's warlike son:
Aloft in awful state
The godlike hero sate
On his imperial throne:
His valiant peers were placed around;
Their brows with roses and with myrtles bound:
(So should desert in arms be crowned.)
The lovely Thais, by his side,
Sate like a blooming Eastern bride
In flow'r of youth and beauty's pride.
Happy, happy, happy pair!
None but the brave,
None but the brave,
None but the brave deserves the fair.

CHORUS

Happy, happy, happy pair!
None but the brave,
None but the brave,
None but the brave deserves the fair.

II

Timotheus, placed on high
Amid the tuneful choir,
With flying fingers touched the lyre:
The trembling notes ascend the sky,
And heav'nly joys inspire.
The song began from Jove,
Who left his blissful seats above,
(Such is the pow'r of mighty love.)
A dragon's fiery form belied the god:
Sublime on radiant spires he rode,
When he to fair Olympia pressed;
And while he sought her snowy breast:
Then, round her slender waist he curled,
And stamped an image of himself, a sov'reign of the world.
The list'ning crowd admire the lofty sound;

'A present deity,' they shout around;
'A present deity,' the vaulted roofs rebound:
With ravished ears
The monarch hears,
Assumes the god,
Affects to nod,
And seems to shake the spheres.

CHORUS

With ravished ears
The monarch hears,
Assumes the god,
Affects to nod,
And seems to shake the spheres.

III

The praise of Bacchus then the sweet musician sung,
Of Bacchus ever fair and ever young:
The jolly god in triumph comes;
Sound the trumpets; beat the drums;
Flushed with a purple grace
He shows his honest face:
Now give the hautboys breath; he comes, he comes.
Bacchus, ever fair and young,
Drinking joys did first ordain;
Bacchus' blessings are a treasure,
Drinking is the soldier's pleasure:
Rich the treasure,
Sweet the pleasure,
Sweet is pleasure after pain.

CHORUS

Bacchus' blessings are a treasure,
Drinking is the soldier's pleasure;
Rich the treasure,
Sweet the pleasure,
Sweet is pleasure after pain.

IV

Soothed with the sound, the king grew vain;
Fought all his battles o'er again;
And thrice he routed all his foes; and thrice he slew the slain.
The master saw the madness rise;
His glowing cheeks, his ardent eyes;
And, while he heav'n and earth defied,
Changed his hand, and checked his pride.
He chose a mournful Muse,
Soft pity to infuse:
He sung Darius great and good,
By too severe a fate,
Fallen, fallen, fallen, fallen,
Fallen from his high estate,
And welt'ring in his blood;
Deserted, at his utmost need,
By those his former bounty fed;
On the bare earth exposed he lies,
With not a friend to close his eyes.

With downcast looks the joyless victor sate,
Revolving in his altered soul
The various turns of chance below;
And, now and then, a sigh he stole;
And tears began to flow.

CHORUS

Revolving in his altered soul
The various turns of chance below;
And, now and then, a sigh he stole;
And tears began to flow.

V

The mighty master smiled to see
That love was in the next degree:
'T was but a kindred sound to move,
For pity melts the mind to love.
Softly sweet, in Lydian measures,
Soon he soothed his soul to pleasures.
'War,' he sung, 'is toil and trouble;
Honor, but an empty bubble;
Never ending, still beginning,
Fighting still, and still destroying:
If the world be worth thy winning,
Think, O think it worth enjoying;
Lovely Thais sits beside thee,
Take the good the gods provide thee.'

The many rend the skies with loud applause;
So Love was crowned, but Music won the cause.
The prince, unable to conceal his pain,
Gazed on the fair
Who caused his care,
And sighed and looked, sighed and looked,
Sighed and looked, and sighed again:
At length, with love and wine at once oppressed,
The vanquished victor sunk upon her breast.

CHORUS

The prince, unable to conceal his pain,
Gazed on the fair
Who caused his care,
And sighed and looked, sighed and looked,
Sighed and looked, and sighed again:
At length, with love and wine at once oppressed,
The vanquished victor sunk upon her breast.

VI

Now strike the golden lyre again:
A louder yet, and yet a louder strain.
Break his bands of sleep asunder,
And rouse him, like a rattling peal of thunder.
Hark, hark, the horrid sound
Has raised up his head:
As awaked from the dead,
And amazed, he stares around.
'Revenge, revenge!' Timotheus cries,
'See the Furies arise!
See the snakes that they rear,
How they hiss in their hair,
And the sparkles that flash from their eyes!
Behold a ghastly band,
Each a torch in his hand!
Those are Grecian ghosts, that in battle were slain,
And unburied remain
Inglorious on the plain:
Give the vengeance due
To the valiant crew.
Behold how they toss their torches on high,
How they point to the Persian abodes,
And glitt'ring temples of their hostile gods!'
The princes applaud, with a furious joy;
And the king seized a flambeau with zeal to destroy;
Thais led the way,
To light him to his prey,
And, like another Helen, fired another Troy.

CHORUS

And the king seized a flambeau with zeal to destroy;
Thais led the way,
To light him to his prey.
And, like another Helen, fired another Troy.

VII

Thus, long ago,
Ere heaving bellows learned to blow,
While organs yet were mute;
Timotheus, to his breathing flute,
And sounding lyre,
Could swell the soul to rage, or kindle soft desire.
At last, divine Cecilia came,
Inventress of the vocal frame;
The sweet enthusiast, from her sacred store,
Enlarged the former narrow bounds,
And added length to solemn sounds,
With nature's mother wit, and arts unknown before.
Let old Timotheus yield the prize,
Or both divide the crown;
He raised a mortal to the skies;
She drew an angel down.

GRAND CHORUS

At last, divine Cecilia came,
Inventress of the vocal frame;
The sweet enthusiast, from her sacred store,
Enlarged the former narrow bounds
And added length to solemn sounds,
With nature's mother wit, and arts unknown before.
Let old Timotheus yield the prize,
Or both divide the crown;
He raised a mortal to the skies;
She drew an angel down.

1697

William Congreve (1670–1729)

ODE

I

Daughter of Memory, immortal Muse,
Calliope; what poet wilt thou choose
Of Anna's name to sing?
To whom wilt thou thy fire impart,
Thy lyre, thy voice, and tuneful art;
Whom raise sublime on the ethereal wing,
And consecrate with dews of thy Castalian spring?

II

Without thy aid, the most aspiring mind
Must flag beneath, to narrow flights confined,
Striving to rise in vain:
Nor e'er can hope with equal lays
To celebrate bright Virtue's praise.
Thy aid obtained, even I, the humblest swain,
May climb Pierian heights, and quit the lowly plain.

III

High in the starry orb is hung,
And next Alcides' guardian arm,
That harp to which thy Orpheus sung,
Who woods, and rocks, and winds, could charm;
That harp which on Cyllene's shady Hill,
When first the vocal shell was found,
With more than mortal skill
Inventor Hermes taught to sound.
Hermes, on bright Latona's son,

By sweet persuasion won,
The wond'rous work bestowed;
Latona's son, to thine
Indulgent, gave the gift divine:
A god the gift, a god th' invention showed.

I

To that high-sounding lyre I tune my strains;
A lower note his lofty song disdains
Who sings of Anna's name.
The lyre is struck! the sounds I hear!
O muse, propitious to my pray'r!
O well known sounds! O Melody, the same
That kindled Mantuan fire, and raised Mæonian flame!

II

Nor are these sounds to British bards unknown,
Or sparingly revealed to one alone:
Witness sweet Spenser's lays:
And witness that immortal song,
As Spenser sweet, as Milton strong,
Which humble Boyn o'er Tiber's flood could raise,
And mighty William sing, with well proportioned praise.

III

Rise, fair Augusta, lift thy head,
With golden tow'rs thy front adorn;
Come forth, as comes from Tithon's bed,
With chearful ray, the ruddy morn.
Thy lovely form, and fresh reviving state,
In crystal flood of Thames survey;
Then bless thy better fate,
Bless Anna's most auspicious sway.
While distant realms and neighb'ring lands,
Armed troops and hostile bands
On ev'ry side molest,
Thy happier clime is free,
Fair Capital of Liberty!
And plenty knows, the days of Halcyon rest.

I

As Britain's isle, when old vexed ocean roars,
Unshaken sees, against her silver shores,
His foaming billows beat;
So Britain's Queen, amidst the jars
And tumults of a world of wars,
Fixed on the base of her well-founded state,
Serene and safe looks down, nor feels the shocks of fate.

II

But greatest souls, though blest with sweet repose,
Are soonest touched with sense of other's woes.
Thus Anna's mighty mind,
To mercy and soft pity prone,
And moved with sorrows not her own,
Has all her peace and downy rest resigned,
To wake for common good, and succor human-kind.

III

Fly, Tyranny, no more be known
Within Europa's blissful bound;
Far as th' unhabitable zone
Fly ev'ry hospitable ground.
To horrid Zembla's frozen realms repair,
There, with the baleful beldam, Night,
Unpeopled empire share,
And rob those lands of legal right.
For now is come the promised hour,
When justice shall have pow'r;
Justice to earth restored!
Again Astræa reigns!
Anna her equal scale maintains,
And Marlbro' wields her sure deciding sword.

I

Now, couldst thou soar, my Muse, to sing the man
In heights sublime, as when the Mantuan swan
Her tow'ring pinions spread;
Thou shouldst of Marlbro' sing, whose hand
Unerring from his Queen's command,
Far as the seven-mouthed Ister's secret head,
To save th' imperial state, her hardy Britons led.

II

Nor there thy song should end; though all the Nine
Might well their harps and heav'nly voices join
To sing that glorious day,
When bold Bavaria fled the field,
And veteran Gauls, unused to yield,
On Blenheim's plain, imploring mercy, lay;
And spoils and trophies won, perplexed the victor's way.

III

But could thy voice of Blenheim sing,
And with success that song pursue;
What art could aid thy wearied wing
To keep the victor still in view?
For as the sun ne'er stops his radiant flight,
Nor sets, but with impartial ray,
To all who want his light,
Alternately transfers the day:
So in the glorious round of fame,
Great Marlbro', still the same,
Incessant runs his course;
To climes remote, and near,
His conqu'ring arms by turns appear,
And universal is his aid and force.

I

Attempt not to proceed, unwary Muse,
For O! what notes, what numbers couldst thou choose,
Though in all numbers skilled;
To sing the hero's matchless deed,
Which Belgia saved, and Brabant freed;
To sing Ramilia's day! to which must yield
Cannæ's illustrious fight, and famed Pharsalia's field.

II

In the short course of diurnal sun,
Behold the work of many ages done!
What verse such worth can raise?
Lustre and life, the poet's art
To middle virtue may impart;
But deeds sublime, exalted high like these,
Transcend his utmost flight; and mock his distant praise.

III

Still would the willing Muse aspire,
With transport still her strains prolong;
But fear unstrings the trembling lyre,
And admiration stops her song.
Go on, great Chief, in Anna's cause proceed;
Nor sheath the terrors of thy sword,
Till Europe thou hast freed,
And universal peace restored.
This mighty work when thou shalt end,
Equal rewards attend,
Of value far above
Thy trophies and thy spoils;
Rewards even worthy of thy toils,
Thy Queen's just favor, and thy country's love.

1706

LYRICS

John Wilmot, Earl of Rochester
(1647-1680)

LOVE AND LIFE

All my past life is mine no more;
The flying hours are gone,
Like transitory dreams given o'er,
Whose images are kept in store
By memory alone.

The time that is to come is not;
How can it, then, be mine?
The present moment's all my lot;
And that, as fast as it is got,
Phyllis, is only thine.

Then talk not of inconstancy,
False hearts, and broken vows;
If I by miracle can be
This live-long minute true to thee,
'T is all that Heaven allows.

1680

UPON DRINKING IN A BOWL

Vulcan, contrive me such a cup
As Nestor used of old;
Show all thy skill to trim it up,
Damask it round with gold.

Make it so large that, filled with sack,
Up to the swelling brim,
Vast toasts on the delicious lake,
Like ships at sea may swim.

Engrave not battle on his cheek,
With war I've naught to do:
I'm none of those that took Mæstrick,
Nor Yarmouth leaguer knew.

Let it no name of planets tell,
Fixed stars or constellations;
For I am no Sir Sidrophel,
Nor none of his relations.

But carve thereon a spreading vine,
Then add two lovely boys;
Their limbs in amorous folds entwine,
The type of future joys.

Cupid and Bacchus my saints are;
May Drink and Love still reign!
With wine I wash away my care,
And then to love again.

1680

CONSTANCY

I CANNOT change as others do,
Though you unjustly scorn;
Since that poor swain that sighs for you,
For you alone was born.
No, Phillis, no; your heart to move
A surer way I'll try;
And, to revenge my slighted love,
Will still love on, will still love on, and die.

When, killed with grief, Amyntas lies,
And you to mind shall call
The sighs that now unpitied rise,
The tears that vainly fall;
That welcome hour that ends this smart
Will then begin your pain,
For such a faithful tender heart
Can never break, can never break in vain.

1680

John Oldham (1653–1683)

THE CARELESS GOOD FELLOW

A [plague] of this fooling and plotting of late,
What a pother and stir has it kept in the State;
Let the rabble run mad with suspicions and fears,
Let them scuffle and jar, till they go by the ears;
Their grievances never shall trouble my pate,
So I can enjoy my dear bottle at quiet.
What coxcombs were those who would barter their ease
And their necks for a toy, a thin wafer and mass;
At old Tyburn they never had needed to swing,
Had they been but true subjects to drink and their king;
A friend and a bottle is all my design;
He has no room for treason, that 's topfull of wine.

I mind not the members and makers of laws,
Let them sit or prorogue, as his majesty please;
Let them damn us to woollen, I 'll never repine
At my lodging when dead, so alive I have wine;
Yet oft, in my drink, I can hardly forbear
To curse them for making my claret so dear.

I mind not grave asses who idly debate
About right and succession, the trifles of state;
We 've a good king already; and he deserves laughter
That will trouble his head with who shall come after;
Come, here 's to his health, and I wish he may be
As free from all care and all trouble as we.

What care I how leagues with the Hollander go?
Or intrigues betwixt Sidney and Monsieur D'Avaux?
What concerns it my drinking, if Cassel be sold,
If the conqueror take it by storming, or gold?
Good Bordeaux alone is the place that I mind,
And when the fleet 's coming, I pray for a wind.

The bully of France, that aspires to renown
By dull cutting of throats, and venturing his own,
Let him fight and be damned, and make matches and treat,
To afford the newsmongers and coffee-house chat;
He 's but a brave wretch, while I am more free,
More safe, and a thousand times happier than he.

Come he, or the pope, or the devil to boot,
Or come faggot and stake, I care not a groat;
Never think that in Smithfield I porters will heat:
No, I swear, Mr. Fox, pray excuse me for that.
I'll drink in defiance of gibbet and halter,
This is the profession that never will alter.

1683

John Pomfret (1667–1702)

THE CHOICE

If Heaven the grateful liberty would give
That I might choose my method how to live;
And all those hours propitious fate should lend,
In blissful ease and satisfaction spend;
Near some fair town I 'd have a private seat,
Built uniform, not little, nor too great;
Better, if on a rising ground it stood;
On this side fields, on that a neighbouring wood.
It should within no other things contain
But what are useful, necessary, plain;
Methinks 't is nauseous, and I 'd ne'er endure
The needless pomp of gaudy furniture.
A little garden grateful to the eye,
And a cool rivulet run murmuring by;
On whose delicious banks a stately row
Of shady limes or sycamores should grow.
At the end of which a silent study placed,
Should be with all the noblest authors graced:
Horace and Virgil, in whose mighty lines
Immortal wit and solid learning shines;
Sharp Juvenal, and amorous Ovid too,
Who all the turns of love's soft passion knew:
He that with judgment reads his charming lines,
In which strong art with stronger nature joins,
Must grant his fancy does the best excel —
His thoughts so tender, and expressed so well:
With all those moderns, men of steady sense,
Esteemed for learning and for eloquence.
In some of these, as fancy should advise,
I 'd always take my morning exercise;
For sure no minutes bring us more content
Than those in pleasing useful studies spent.
  I 'd have a clear and competent estate,
That I might live genteelly, but not great;
As much as I could moderately spend;
A little more, sometimes to oblige a friend.
Nor should the sons of poverty repine
Too much at fortune; they should taste of mine;
And all that objects of true pity were,
Should be relieved with what my wants could spare;
For that our Maker has too largely given
Should be returned in gratitude to Heaven.
A frugal plenty should my table spread;
With healthy, not luxurious, dishes spread;
Enough to satisfy, and something more,
To feed the stranger, and the neighbouring poor.
Strong meat indulges vice, and pampering food
Creates diseases, and inflames the blood.
But what 's sufficient to make nature strong,
And the bright lamp of life continue long,
I 'd freely take; and, as I did possess,
The bounteous Author of my plenty bless.
  I 'd have a little vault, but always stored
With the best wines each vintage could afford.
Wine whets the wit, improves its native force,
And gives a pleasant flavour to discourse:
By making all our spirits debonair,
Throws off the lees, the sediment of care.
But as the greatest blessing Heaven lends
May be debauched, and serve ignoble ends;
So, but too oft, the grape's refreshing juice
Does many mischievous effects produce.
My house should no rude disorders know,
As from high drinking consequently flow;
Nor would I use what was so kindly given,
To the dishonour of indulgent Heaven.
If any neighbour came, he should be free,
Used with respect, and not uneasy be,
In my retreat, or to himself or me.
What freedom, prudence, and right reason give,
All men may, with impunity, receive:
But the least swerving from their rule 's too much;
For what 's forbidden us, 't is death to touch.
  That life may be more comfortable yet,
And all my joys refined, sincere, and great;
I 'd choose two friends, whose company would be
A great advance to my felicity:
Well-born, of humours suited to my own,
Discreet, and men as well as books have known;
Brave, generous, witty, and exactly free
From loose behaviour, or formality:
Airy and prudent; merry, but not light;
Quick in discerning, and in judgment right:
Secret they should be, faithful to their trust;
In reasoning cool, strong, temperate, and just;
Obliging, open, without huffing, brave;
Brisk in gay talking, and in sober, grave:
Close in dispute, but not tenacious; tryed
By solid reason, and let that decide:
Not prone to lust, revenge, or envious hate;
Nor busy meddlers with intrigues of state:
Strangers to slander, and sworn foes to spite;

Not quarrelsome, but stout enough to fight;
Loyal, and pious, friends to Cæsar; true
As dying martyrs to their Maker too.
In their society I could not miss
A permanent, sincere, substantial bliss.
Would bounteous Heaven once more indulge, I 'd choose
(For who would so much satisfaction lose
As witty nymphs, in conversation, give?)
Near some obliging modest fair to live:
For there 's that sweetness in a female mind,
Which in a man's we cannot hope to find;
That, by a secret, but a powerful art,
Winds up the springs of life, and does impart
Fresh vital heat to the transported heart.
I 'd have her reason all her passions sway:
Easy in company, in private gay:
Coy to a fop, to the deserving free;
Still constant to herself, and just to me.
A soul she should have for great actions fit;
Prudence and wisdom to direct her wit:
Courage to look bold danger in the face;
No fear, but only to be proud, or base;
Quick to advise, by an emergence prest,
To give good counsel, or to take the best.
I 'd have the expression of her thoughts be such,
She might not seem reserved, nor talk too much:
That shows a want of judgment, and of sense;
More than enough is but impertinence.
Her conduct regular, her mirth refined;
Civil to strangers, to her neighbours kind:
Averse to vanity, revenge, and pride;
In all the methods of deceit untryed:
So faithful to her friend, and good to all,
No censure might upon her actions fall:
Then would ev'n Envy be compelled to say
She goes the least of womankind astray.
To this fair creature I 'd sometimes retire;
Her conversation would new joys inspire;
Give life an edge so keen, no surly care
Would venture to assault my soul, or dare
Near my retreat, to hide one secret snare.
But so divine, so noble a repast
I 'd seldom, and with moderation, taste:
For highest cordials all their virtue lose,
By a too frequent and too bold an use;
And what would cheer the spirits in distress,
Ruins our health, when taken to excess.
I 'd be concerned in no litigious jar;
Beloved by all, not vainly popular.
Whate'er assistance I had power to bring
T' oblige my country, or to serve my king,
Whene'er they call, I 'd readily afford
My tongue, my pen, my counsel, or my sword.
Lawsuits I 'd shun, with as much studious care,
As I would dens where hungry lions are;
And rather put up injuries, than be
A plague to him, who 'd be a plague to me.
I value quiet at a price too great,
To give for my revenge so dear a rate:
For what do we by all our bustle gain,
But counterfeit delight for real pain?
If Heaven a date of many years would give,
Thus I 'd in pleasure, ease, and plenty live.
And as I near approached the verge of life,
Some kind relation (for I 'd have no wife)
Should take upon him all my worldly care,
Whilst I did for a better state prepare.
Then I 'd not be with any trouble vexed,
Nor have the evening of my days perplexed;
But by a silent and a peaceful death,
Without a sigh, resign my agèd breath.
And when committed to the dust, I 'd have
Few tears, but friendly, dropt into my grave,
Then would my exit so propitious be,
All men would wish to live and die like me.

1700

TO HIS FRIEND, INCLINED TO MARRY

I WOULD not have you, Strephon, choose a mate,
From too exalted, or too mean a state;
For in both these we may expect to find
A creeping spirit, or a haughty mind.
Who moves within the middle region, shares
The least disquiets, and the smallest cares.
Let her extraction with true lustre shine;
If something brighter, not too bright for thine:
Her education liberal, not great;
Neither inferior, nor above her state.
Let her have wit; but let that wit be free
From effectation, pride, and pedantry:
For the effect of woman's wit is such,
Too little is as dangerous as too much.
But chiefly let her humour close with thine,
Unless where yours does to a fault incline;
The least disparity in this destroys,
Like sulph'rous blasts, the very buds of joys.
Her person amiable, straight, and free
From natural, or chance, deformity.
Let not her years exceed, if equal thine,
For women past their vigour, soon decline:

Her fortune competent; and, if thy sight
Can reach so far, take care 't is gathered right.
If thine 's enough, then her's may be the less:
Do not aspire to riches in excess.
For that which makes our lives delightful prove,
Is a genteel sufficiency and love.

1700

PROSE

ESSAYS

Abraham Cowley (1618-1667)

OF OBSCURITY

Nam neque divitibus contingunt gaudia solis;
Nec vixit male, qui natus moriensque fefellit.

God made not pleasures only for the rich;
Nor have those men without their share too lived,
Who both in life and death the world deceived.

This seems a strange sentence, thus literally translated, and looks as if it were in vindication of the men of business (for who else can deceive the world?) whereas it is in commendation of those who live and die so obscurely, that the world takes no notice of them. This Horace calls deceiving the world; and in another place uses the same phrase.

—*Secretum iter et fallentis semita vitæ.*

The secret tracks of the deceiving life.

It is very elegant in Latin, but our English word will hardly bear up to that sense; and therefore Mr. Broom translates it very well—

Or from a life, led, as it were, by stealth.

Yet we say, in our language, a thing deceives our sight, when it passes before us unperceived: and we may say well enough, out of the same author,

Sometimes with sleep, sometimes with wine, we strive
The cares of life and troubles to deceive.

But that is not to deceive the world, but to deceive ourselves, as Quintilian says, '*Vitam fallere*,' to draw on still, and amuse, and deceive our life, till it be advanced insensibly to the fatal period, and fall into that pit which nature hath prepared for it. The meaning of all this is no more than that most vulgar saying, '*Bene qui latuit, bene vixit*,' he has lived well, who has lain well hidden. Which, if it be a truth, the world (I will swear) is sufficiently deceived: for my part, I think it is, and that the pleasantest condition of life is *in incognito*. What a brave privilege is it, to be free from all contentions, from all envying or being envied, from receiving or paying all kind of ceremonies! It is, in my mind, a very delightful pastime, for two good and agreeable friends to travel up and down together, in places where they are by nobody known, nor know anybody. It was the case of Æneas and his Achates, when they walked invisibly about the fields and streets of Carthage; Venus herself

A veil of thickened air around them cast,
That none might know, or see them, as they passed.

The common story of Demosthenes' confession, that he had taken great pleasure in hearing of a tanker-woman say, as he passed: 'This is that Demosthenes,' is wonderfully ridiculous from so solid an orator. I myself have often met with that temptation to vanity (if it were any); but am so far from finding it any pleasure, that it only makes me run faster from the place, till I get, as it were, out of sight-shot. Democritus relates, and in such a manner as if he gloried in the good fortune and commodity of it, that, when he came to Athens, nobody there did so much as take notice of him; and Epicurus lived there very well, that is, lay hid many years in his gardens, so famous since that time, with his friend Metrodorus: after whose death, making in one of his letters a kind commemoration of the happiness which they two had enjoyed together, he adds at last, that he thought it no disparagement to those great felicities of their life, that, in the midst of the most talked-of and talking country in the world, they had lived so long, not only without fame, but almost without being heard of. And yet, within a very few years afterward, there were no two names of men more known, or more generally celebrated. If we engage into a large acquaintance and various familiarities, we set open our gates to the invaders of most of our time: we expose our life to a quotidian ague of frigid impertinences, which would make a wise man tremble to think of. Now, as for being known much by sight, and pointed at, I cannot comprehend the honour that lies in that: whatsoever it be, every mountebank has it more than the best doctor, and the hangman more than the lord chief justice of a city. Every creature has it, both of nature and art, if it be anyways extraordinary. It was as often said, 'This is that Bucephalus,' or, 'This is that Incitatus,' when they were led prancing through the streets, as, 'This is that Alexander,' or, 'This is that Domitian'; and truly, for the latter, I take Incitatus to have been a much more honourable beast than his master, and more deserving the consulship, than he the empire.

I love and commend a true good fame, because it is the shadow of virtue; not that it doth any good to the body which it accompanies, but 't is an efficacious shadow, and, like that of St. Peter, cures the diseases of others. The best kind of glory, no doubt, is that which is reflected from honesty, such as was the glory of Cato and Aristides; but it was harmful to them both, and is seldom beneficial to any man, whilst he lives: what it is to him after his death I cannot say, because I love not philosophy merely notional and conjectural, and no man who has made the experiment has been so kind as to come back to inform us. Upon the whole matter, I account a person who has a moderate mind and fortune, and lives in the conversation of two or three agreeable friends, with little commerce in the world besides, who is esteemed well enough by his few neighbours that know him, and is truly irreproachable by anybody; and so, after a healthful quiet life, before the great inconveniences of old age, goes more silently out of it than he came in (for I would not have him so much as cry in the exit): this innocent deceiver of the world, as Horace calls him, this '*muta persona,*' I take to have been more happy in his part, than the greatest actors that fill the stage with show and noise, nay, even than Augustus himself, who asked with his last breath, whether he had not played his farce very well.

1668

OF MYSELF

It is a hard and nice subject for a man to write of himself; it grates his own heart to say anything of disparagement, and the reader's ears to hear anything of praise from him. There is no danger from me of offending him in this kind; neither my mind, nor my body, nor my fortune, allow me any materials for that vanity. It is sufficient for my own contentment, that they have preserved me from being scandalous, or remarkable on the defective side. But, besides that, I shall here speak of myself, only in relation to the subject of these precedent discourses and shall be likelier thereby to fall into the contempt, than rise up to the estimation, of most people.

As far as my memory can return back into my past life, before I knew, or was capable of guessing, what the world, or the glories or business of it, were, the natural affections of my soul gave me a secret bent of aversion from them, as some plants are said to turn away from others, by an antipathy imperceptible to themselves, and inscrutable to man's understanding. Even when I was a very young boy at school, instead of running about on holidays and playing with my fellows, I was wont to steal from them, and walk into the fields, either alone with a book, or with some one companion, if I could find any of the same temper. I was then, too, so much an enemy to all constraint, that my masters could never prevail on me, by any persuasions or encouragements, to learn without book the common rules of grammar; in which they dispensed with me alone, because they found I made a shift to do the usual exercise out of my own reading and observation. That I was then of the same mind as I am now (which, I confess, I wonder at, myself) may appear by the latter end of an ode, which I made when I was but thirteen years old, and which was then printed with many other verses. The beginning of it is boyish; but of this part, which I here set down (if a very little were corrected), I should hardly now be much ashamed.

This only grant me, that my means may lie
Too low for envy, for contempt too high.
  Some honour I would have,
Not from great deeds, but good alone;
The unknown are better, than ill known:
  Rumour can ope the grave.
Acquaintance I would have; but when 't depends
Not on the number, but the choice of friends.

Books should, not business, entertain the light,
And sleep, as undisturbed as death, the night.
  My house a cottage, more
Than palace; and should fitting be
For all my use, no luxury.
  My garden painted o'er
With nature's hand, nor art's; and pleasures yield,
Horace might envy in his Sabine field.

Thus would I double my life's fading space;
For he, that runs it well, twice runs his race.
  And in this true delight,
These unbought sports, that happy state,
I would not fear, nor wish, my fate;
  But boldly say each night,
To-morrow let my sun his beam display,
Or, in clouds hide them; I have lived, to-day.

You may see by it, I was even then acquainted with the poets (for the conclusion is taken out of Horace); and perhaps it was the immature and immoderate love of them, which stamped first, or rather engraved, the characters in me: they were like letters cut into the bark of a young tree, which with the tree still grow proportionably. But, how this love came to be produced in me so early, is a hard question: I believe, I can tell the particular little chance that filled my head first with such chimes of verse, as have never since left ringing there: for I remember, when I began to read, and take some pleasure in it, there was wont to lie in my mother's parlour (I know not by what accident, for she herself never in her life read any book but of devotion) but there was wont to lie Spenser's works: this I happened to fall upon, and was infinitely delighted with the stories of the knights, and giants, and monsters, and brave houses, which I found everywhere there (though my understanding had little to do with all this); and, by degrees, with the tinkling of the rhyme and dance of the numbers; so that, I think, I had read him all over before I was twelve years old.

With these affections of mind, and my heart wholly set upon letters, I went to the university; but was soon torn from thence by that violent public storm, which would suffer nothing to stand where it did, but rooted up every plant, even from the princely cedars to me the hyssop. Yet, I had as good fortune as could have befallen me in such a tempest; for I was cast by it into the family of one of the best persons, and into the court of one of the best princesses, of the world. Now, though I was here engaged in ways most contrary to the original design of my life, that is, into much company, and no small business, and into a daily sight of greatness, both militant and triumphant (for that was the state then of the English and the French courts); yet all this was so far from altering my opinion, that it only added the confirmation of reason to that which was before but natural inclination. I saw plainly all the paint of that kind of life, the nearer I came to it; and that beauty, which I did not fall in love with, when, for aught I knew, it was real, was not like to bewitch or entice me, when I saw it was adulterate. I met with several great persons, whom I liked very well; but could not perceive that any part of their greatness was to be liked or desired, no more than I would be glad or content to be in a storm, though I saw many ships which rid safely and bravely in it: a storm would not agree with my stomach, if it did with my courage. Though I was in a crowd of as good company as could be found anywhere, though I was in business of great and honourable trust, though I eat at the best table, and enjoyed the best conveniences for present subsistence that ought to be desired by a man of my condition in banishment and public distresses; yet I could not abstain from renewing my old school-boy's wish, in a copy of verses to the same effect:

Well then; I now do plainly see
This busy world and I shall ne'er agree.
The very honey of all earthly joy
Does of all meats the soonest cloy,
  And they (methinks) deserve my pity,
Who for it can endure the stings,
The crowd, and buzz, and murmurings
  Of this great hive, the city.

Ah, yet, ere I descend to the grave,
May I a small house and large garden have!
And a few friends, and many books, both true,
Both wise, and both delightful too!
  And since love ne'er will from me flee,
A mistress moderately fair,
And good as guardian-angels are,
  Only beloved, and loving me!

O fountains, when in you shall I
Myself, eased of unpeaceful thoughts espy?
O fields! O woods! when, when shall I be made,
The happy tenant of your shade?
  Here's the spring-head of pleasure's flood;
Here's wealthy Nature's treasury,
Where all the riches lie, that she
  Has coined and stamped for good.

Pride and ambition here
Only in far-fetched metaphors appear;
Here nought but winds can hurtful murmurs scatter,
And nought but echo flatter.
  The gods, when they descended hither
From heaven, did always choose their way;
And therefore we may boldly say,
  That 't is the way to thither.

How happy here should I
And one dear she live, and embracing die!
She who is all the world, and can exclude
In deserts solitude.
  I should have then this only fear,
Lest men, when they my pleasures see,
Should hither throng to live like me,
  And so make a city here.

And I never then proposed to myself any other advantage from his majesty's happy restoration, but the getting into some moderately convenient retreat in the country; which I thought, in that case, I might easily have compassed, as well as some others, who with no greater probabilities or pretences, have arrived to extraordinary fortunes: but I had before written a shrewd prophecy against myself; and I think Apollo inspired me in the truth, though not in the elegance of it:

Thou neither great at court, nor in the war,
Nor at the Exchange shalt be, nor at the wrangling bar.
Content thyself with the small barren praise,
Which thy neglected verse does raise.

She spake; and all my years to come
Took their unlucky doom.
Their several ways of life let others choose,
Their several pleasures let them use;
But I was born for love, and for a Muse.

With fate what boots it to contend?
Such I began, such am, and so must end.
The star, that did my being frame,
Was but a lambent flame,
And some small light it did dispence,
But neither heat nor influence.
No matter, Cowley; let proud Fortune see,
That thou canst her despise no less than she does thee.
Let all her gifts the portion be
Of folly, lust, and flattery,
Fraud, extortion, calumny,
Murder, infidelity,
Rebellion and hypocrisy.
Do thou not grieve nor blush to be,
As all the inspired tuneful men,
And all thy great forefathers were, from
Homer down to Ben.

However, by the failing of the forces which I had expected, I did not acquit the design which I had resolved on; I cast myself into it a *corps perdu*, without making capitulations, or taking counsel of fortune. But God laughs at a man who says to his soul, 'Take thy ease': I met presently not only with many little encumbrances and impediments, but with so much sickness (a new misfortune to me) as would have spoiled the happiness of an emperor as well as mine: yet I do neither repent, nor alter my course. *Non ego perfidum dixi sacramentum;* nothing shall separate me from a mistress, which I have loved so long, and have now at last married; though she neither has brought me a rich portion, nor lived yet so quietly with me as I hoped from her:

— Nec vos, dulcissima mundi
Nomina, vos Musæ, libertas, otia, libri,
Hortique sylvæque, animâ remanente relinquam.

  Nor by me e'er shall you,
You, of all names the sweetest, and the best,
You, Muses, books, and liberty, and rest;
You, gardens, fields, and woods, forsaken be,
As long as life itself forsakes not me.

1668

Sir William Temple (1628–1699)

OF HEROICK VIRTUE

Section III

'T is known enough, that about the year 1484, Alonzo Sanchez, master of a Spanish vessel, that usually traded from those coasts to the Canaries and Maderas, was, in his passage between these islands, surprised with a furious storm at East, so violent that he was forced to let his ship drive before it without any sail; and so black, that within twenty eight days he could not take the height of the sun. That he was at length cast upon a shore, but whether island or continent, he could not tell, but full of savage people. That after infinite toils, dangers, and miseries of hunger and sickness, he made at length one of the Tercera islands, with only five men left of seventeen he carried out; and meeting there with the famous Columbo, made him such relations, and so pertinent accounts of the voyage, as gave occasion for the discovery of America, or the West Indies, by this man so renowned in our modern story.

Whatever predictions have been since found out, or applied toward the discovery of this New World, or stories told of a certain prince in Wales, having run the same fortune, or of the ancient Carthaginians, I do not find, by all I have read upon this subject, any reason to believe that any mortals, from Europe or Africa, had ever traced these unknown paths of that Western Ocean, or left the least footsteps of having discovered those countries, before Alonzo Sanchez and his crew. Upon the arrival of the Spaniards there with Columbus, they found nature as naked as the inhabitants; in most parts no thought of business, further than the most natural pleasures or necessities of life; nations divided by natural bounds of rivers, rocks, or mountains, or difference of language; quarrels among them only for hunger or lust; the command in wars given to the strongest or the bravest; and in peace taken up or exercised by the boldest among them; and their lives commonly spent in the most innocent entertainments of hunting, fishing, feasting, or in the most careless leisure.

There were among them many principalities, that seemed to have grown up, from the original of paternal dominion, and some communities with orders and laws; but the two great dominions were those of Mexico and Peru, which had arrived to such extent of territory, power, and riches, that amazed those who had been enough acquainted with the greatness and splendour of the European kingdoms. And I never met with any story so entertaining, as the relations of the several learned Spanish Jesuits and others, concerning these countries and people, in their native innocence and simplicity. Mexico was so vast an empire, that it was well represented by the common answer of the Indians, all along that coast, to the Spaniards, when they came to any part, and asked the people whether they were under Montezuma, *Quien noes esclavo de Montezuma?* Or, *Who is not a slave of Montezuma?* As if they thought the whole world was so. They might truly call it slave, for no dominion was ever so absolute, so tyrannous, and so cruel as his. Among other tributes imposed on the people, one was of men to be sacrificed every year to an ugly deformed idol, in the great temple of Mexico. Such numbers as the king pleased of poor victims, were laid upon such extents of cities or villages, or numbers of inhabitants, and there chosen by lot, to satisfy such bloody and inhuman taxes. These were often influenced by the priests, who when they saw men grow negligent, either in respect to themselves, or devotion to their idols, would send to tell the king, that the gods were hungry, and thereupon the common tribute was raised; so as that year, the Spaniards landed and invaded Mexico, there had been above thirty thousand men sacrificed to this cruel superstition. And this was said to have given great occasion for the easy conquests of the Spaniards, by the willing revolts and submissions of the natives to any new dominion.

The same was observed to happen in Peru, by the general hatred and aversion of the people in that empire to Atahualpa, who being a bastard of the Incas family, had first by practices and subtility, and afterwards by cruelty and violence, raised himself to the throne of Peru, and cut off with merciless cruelty, all the masculine race of the true royal blood, that were at man's estate, or near it, after that line had lasted pure and sacred, and reigned with unspeakable felicity, both to themselves and their subjects, for above eight hundred years.

This kingdom is said to have extended near seven hundred leagues in length, from north to south, and about an hundred and twenty in breadth: 't is bounded on the west by the Pacific Ocean; on the east by mountains impassable for men or beasts, and as some write, even birds themselves; the height being such, as makes their tops always covered with snow, even in that warm region. On the north 't is bounded with a great river, and on the south with another, which separates it from the province of Chili, that reaches to the Magellan Straits.

The kingdom of Peru deduced its original from their great heroes, Mango Copac, and his wife and sister Coya Mama, who are said to have first appeared in that country, near a mighty lake, which is still sacred with them upon this occasion.

Before this time, the people of these countries are reported to have lived like the beasts among them, without any traces of orders, laws, or religion, without other food than from the trees or the herbs, or what game they could catch, without further provision than for present hunger, without any clothing or houses, but dwelt in rocks, of caves, or trees, to be secure from wild beasts, or in tops of hills, if they were in fear of fierce neighbours. When Mango Copac and his sister came first into these naked lands, as they were persons of excellent shape and beauty, so were they adorned with such clothes as continued afterwards the usual habit of the Incas, by which name they called themselves. They told the people who came first about them, that they were the son and daughter of the Sun, and that their father, taking pity of the miserable condition of mankind, had sent them down to reclaim them from those bestial lives, and to instruct them how to live happily and safely, by observing such laws, customs, and orders, as their father the Sun had commanded these his children to teach them. The great rule they first taught was, that every man should live according to reason, and consequently, neither say nor do anything to others, that they were not willing others should say or do to them, because it was against all common reason, to make one law for ourselves, and another for other people. And this was the great principle of all their morality. In the next place, that they should worship the Sun, who took care of the whole world, gave life to all creatures, and made the plants grow, and the herbs fit for food to maintain them; and was so careful and so good, as to spare no pains of his own, but to go round the world every day, to inspect and provide for all that was upon it, and had sent these his two children down on purpose, for the good and happiness of mankind, and to rule them with the same care and goodness that he did the world. After this, they taught them the arts most necessary for life, as Mango Copac, to sow maize (or the common Indian grain) at certain seasons, to preserve it against others, to build houses against inclemencies of air, and danger of wild beasts, to distinguish themselves by wedlock into several families, to clothe themselves, so as to cover at least the shame of nakedness, to tame and nourish such creatures as might be of common use and sustenance. Coya Mama taught the women to spin and weave, both cotton and certain coarse wools of some beasts among them.

With these instructions and inventions they were so much believed in all they said, and adored for what they did and taught of common utility, that they were followed by great numbers of people, observed and obeyed like sons of the Sun, sent down from heaven to instruct and to govern them. Mango Copac had in his hand a rod of gold, about two foot long and five inches round. He said that his father the Sun had given it him, and bid him when he traveled northward from the lake, he should every time he rested strike this wand down into the ground, and where at the first stroke it should go down to the very top, he should there build a temple to the Sun, and fix the seat of his government.

This fell out to be in the vale of Cozco, where he founded that city, which was head of this great kingdom of Peru.

He divided his company into two colonies

or plantations, and called one the high Casco, and t' other the low, and began here to be a lawgiver to these people. In each of these were at first a thousand families, which he caused all to be registered, with the numbers in each. This he did by strings of several colours, and knots of several kinds and colours upon them, by which both accounts were kept of things and times, and as much expressed of their minds, as was necessary in government, where neither letters nor money, nor consequently disputes or avarice, with their consequences, ever entered.

He instituted decurions through both these colonies, that is, one over every ten families, another over fifty, a third over a hundred, a fourth over five hundred, and a fifth over a thousand; and to this last they gave the name of Curaca or Governour. Every decurion was a censor, a patron, and a judge or arbiter in small controversies among those under his charge. They took care that every one clothed themselves, laboured, and lived according to the orders given them by the Incas, from their father the Sun; among which one was, that none who could work should be idle, more than to rest after labour; and that none who could not work, by age, sickness, or invalidity, should want, but be maintained by the others' pains. These were so much observed, that in the whole empire of Peru, and during the long race of the Inca kings, no beggar was ever known, and no woman ever so much as went to see a neighbour, but with their work in their hands, which they followed all the time the visit lasted. Upon this, I remember a strain of refined civility among them, which was, that when any woman went to see another of equal or ordinary birth, she worked at her own work in the other's house, but if she made a visit to any of the Pallas, (which was the name by which they called all the women of the true royal blood, as Incas was that of the men) then they immediately desired the Palla to give them a piece of her own work, and the visit passed in working for her. Idleness, sentenced by the decurions, was punished by so many stripes in public, and the disgrace was more sensible than the pain. Every colony had one supreme judge, to whom the lower decurions remitted great and difficult cases, or to whom (in such case) the criminals appealed. But every decurion that concealed any crime of those under his charge above a day and a night, became guilty of it, and liable to the same punishment. There were laws or orders likewise against theft, mutilations, murthers, disobedience to officers, and adulteries (for every man was to have one lawful wife, but had the liberty of keeping other women, as he could). The punishment of all crimes was either corporal pains or death, but commonly the last, upon these two reasons which they gave; first, that all crimes, whether great or small, were of the same nature, and deserved the same punishment, if they were committed against the divine commands, which were sent them down from the Sun; next, that to punish any man in his possessions or charges, and leave him alive, and in strength and liberty, was to leave an ill man more incensed, or necessitated to commit new crimes. On t' other side, they never forfeited the charge or possessions of a son for his father's offences, but the judges only remonstrated to him the guilt and punishment of them for his warning or example. These orders had so great force and effect, that many times a whole year passed without the execution of one criminal.

There is no doubt, but that which contributed much to this great order in the state, was the disuse of other possessions than what were necessary to life, and the eminent virtue of their first great hero, or legislator, which seemed to have been entailed upon their whole race, in the course of their reign: so as in the whole length of it 't is reported among them, that no true Inca was ever found guilty or punished for any crime. Thus particular qualities have been observed in old Rome, to be constant in the same families for several hundred years, as goodness, clemency, love of the people, in that of the Valerii, haughtiness, pride, cruelty, and hatred of the people, in that of the Apii, which may come from the force of blood, of education, or example. 'T is certain no government was ever established and continued by greater examples of virtue and severity, nor any ever gave greater testimonies, than the Incas, of an excellent institution, by the progresses and successes, both in the propagation and extent of empire, in force and plenty, in greatness and magnificence of all public works, as temples, palaces, highways, bridges, and in all provisions necessary to common ease, safety, and utility of human life: so as several of the Jesuits, and particularly Acosta, are either so just or so presuming as to prefer the civil constitutions of Mango Copac before those of Lycurgus, Numa, Solon, or any other lawgivers so celebrated in the more known parts of the world.

To every colony was assigned such a compass of land, whereof one part was appropriated to the Sun; a second to the widows, orphans, poor, old, or maimed; a third to the peculiar maintenance of every family, according to their number; and a fourth to the Inca. In this order the whole was tilled, and the harvest or product laid up in several granaries; out of which it was distributed by officers to that purpose, according to the several uses for which it was designed, and new seed issued out at the season for the new tillage.

Every decurion, besides the office of a censor and judge, had that likewise of a patron or solicitor, for relief of the necessities or wants of those under his charge. They were bound to give in, to the public registers, an account of all that were born, and of all that died under their charge. None was suffered to leave the colony, or people he was born in, without leave, nor to change the habit commonly used in it (by some parts or marks whereof those of each province were distinguished). None to marry out of it, no more than the Incas out of their own blood.

The Inca that reigned was called Capa Inca, which the Spaniards interpreted *Solo Sennor*, or *Only Lord*. He ever married the first of his female kindred, either sister, niece, or cousin, to preserve the line the purest they could. Once in two years he assembled all the unmarried Incas, men above twenty, and women above sixteen years old, and there in public married all such as he thought fit, by giving each of their hands one to the other. The same was done among the vulgar, by the Curaca of each people.

Every family at their time of meals, eat with their doors open, so that all might see their temperance and order.

By these and other such laws and institutions, Mango Copac first settled his government or kingdom in the colonies of Cozco, which were in time multiplied into many others, by the willing confluence and recourse of many several people round about him, allured by the divine authority of his orders, by the sweetness and clemency of his reign, and by the felicity of all that lived under it; and indeed, the whole government of this race of the Incas was rather like that of a tender father over his children, or a just, careful, and well-natured guardian over pupils, than of a lord or commander over slaves or subjects. By which they came to be so honoured or adored, that it was like sacrilege for any common person so much as to touch the Inca without his leave; which was given as a grace to those who served him well, or to new subjects that submitted to him.

After the extent of his kingdom into great compasses of territory round Cozco, by voluntary submission of the people, as to some evangelical rather than legal doctrines or institutions; Mango Copac assembled all his Curacas and told them, that his father the Sun had commanded him to extend his institutions and orders as far as he was able, for the good and happiness of mankind; and for that purpose, with armed troops to go to those remoter parts that had not received them, and to reduce them to their observance. That the Sun had commanded him to hurt or offend none that would submit to him, and thereby accept of the good and happiness that was offered him by such divine bounty, but to distress only such as refused, without killing any that did not assail them, and then to do it justly in their own defence.

For this design, he formed and assembled troops of men, armed both with offensive and chiefly with defensive weapons. He cast them into the order of decurions, in the same manner as he had done families; to every ten men was one officer, another to fifty, and another to one hundred, a fourth to five hundred, and a fifth to a thousand. There was a sixth over five thousand, and a seventh as a general over ten thousand;

of which number his first army was composed.

With this and other such armies, he reduced many new territories under his empire, declaring to every people he approached, the same things he had done first to those who came about him near the great lake; and offering them the benefit of the arts he had taught, the orders he had instituted, the protection he had given his subjects, and the felicity they enjoyed under it. Those who submitted were received into the same rights and enjoyments with the rest of his subjects. Those who refused were distressed, and pursued by his forces till they were necessitated to accept of his offers and conditions. He used no offensive weapons against any till they attacked them, and then defensive only at first, till the danger and slaughter of his men grew otherwise unavoidable; then he suffered his forces to fall upon them, and kill without mercy, and not to spare even those that yielded themselves, after having so long and obstinately resisted. Those who submitted after the first threats or distresses, or bloodless opposition, he received into grace, suffered them to touch his sacred person, made great and common feasts for them and his own soldiers together for several days, and then incorporated them into the body of his empire, and gave to each of them clothes to wear and corn to sow.

By these ways and such Heroick Virtue, and by the length of his reign, he so far extended his dominions, as to divide them into four provinces, over each whereof he appointed an Inca to be a viceroy (having many sons grown fit to command); and in each of them established three supreme councils, the first of justice, the second of war, and the third of the revenue, of which an Inca was likewise president, which continued ever after.

At the end of a long and adored reign, Mango Copac fell into the last period of his life; upon the approach whereof, he called together all his children and grand-children, with his eldest son, to whom he left his kingdom: and told them, that for his own part he was going to repose himself with his father the Sun, from whom he came; that he advised and charged them all, to go on in the paths of reason and virtue which he had taught them, till they followed him the same journey; and by this course only, they would prove themselves to be true sons of the Sun, and be as such honoured and esteemed. He gave the same charge more especially and more earnestly to the Inca his successor, and commanded him to govern his people according to his example, and the precepts he had received from the Sun; and to do it always with justice, mercy, piety, clemency, and care of the poor; and when he the Prince should go in time to rest with his father the Sun, that he should give the same instructions and exhortations to his successor. And this form was accordingly used in all the successions of the race of the Incas, which lasted eight hundred years with the same orders, and the greatest felicity that could be of any state.

I will say nothing of the greatness, magnificence, and riches of their buildings, palaces, or temples, especially those of the Sun; of the splendour of their court, their triumphs after victories, their huntings and feasts, their military exercises and honours. But as testimonies of their grandeur, mention only two of their highways, whereof one was five hundred leagues, plain and levelled through mountains, rocks and valleys, so that a carriage might drive through that whole length without difficulty. Another very long and large, paved all with cut or squared stone, fenced with low walls on each side, and set with trees, whose branches gave shade, and the fruits food, to all that passed.

I shall end this survey of their government, with one remark upon their religion, which is, that though the vulgar worshipped only the Sun, yet the Amantas, who were their sages or philosophers, taught, that the Sun was only the great minister of Pachacamac, whom they adored in the first place, and to whom a great and sumptuous temple was dedicated. This word is interpreted by the Spaniard, *Animador del Mundo:* or, *He that animates or enlivens the world*, and seems to be yet a more refined notion of the Deity, than that of the Chinese, who adored the spirit and soul of the world. By this principle of their religion, as all the others of their government and policy, it must I think, be allowed, that human nature is the same in these remote, as well as the other more known and celebrated parts of the world. That the different governments of it are framed and cultivated by as great reaches and strength of reason and of wisdom, as any of ours, and some of their frames less subject to be shaken by the passions, factions, and other corruptions, to which those in the middle scene of Europe and Asia have been so often and so much exposed. That the same causes produce every where the same effects, and that the same honours and obedience are in all places but consequences or tributes paid to the same Heroick Virtue, or Transcendent Genius, in what parts soever, or under what climates of the world it fortunes to appear.

1690

CRITICISM

John Dryden (1631-1700)

OF HEROIC PLAYS

Whether heroic verse ought to be admitted into serious plays is not now to be disputed: 't is already in possession of the stage; and I dare confidently affirm that very few tragedies, in this age, shall be received without it. All the arguments which are formed against it can amount to no more than this, that it is not so near conversation as prose, and therefore not so natural. But it is very clear to all who understand poetry, that serious plays ought not to imitate conversation too nearly. If nothing were to be raised above that level, the foundation of poetry would be destroyed. And if you once admit of a latitude, that thoughts may be exalted, and that images and actions may be raised above the life, and described in measure without rhyme, that leads you insensibly from your own principles to mine: you are already so far onward of your way, that you have forsaken the imitation of ordinary converse. You are gone beyond it; and to continue where you are is to lodge in the open fields betwixt two inns. You have lost that which you call natural, and have not acquired the last perfection of art. But it was only custom which cozened us so long; we thought, because Shakspeare and Fletcher went no further, that there the pillars of poetry were to be erected; that, because they excellently described passion without rhyme, therefore rhyme was not capable of describing it. But time has now convinced most men of that error. It is indeed so difficult to write verse that the adversaries of it have a good plea against many who undertook that task, without being formed by art or nature for it. Yet, even they who have written worst in it, would have written worse without it: they have cozened many with their sound, who never took the pains to examine their sense. In fine, they have succeeded; though, it is true, they have more dishonoured rhyme by their good success, than they have done by their ill. But I am willing to let fall this argument: it is free for every man to write, or not to write, in verse, as he judges it to be, or not to be, his talent; or as he imagines the audience will receive it.

For Heroic Plays (in which only I have used it without the mixture of prose), the first light we had of them, on the English theatre, was from the late Sir William D'Avenant. It being forbidden him in the rebellious times to act tragedies and comedies because they contained some matter of scandal to those good people, who could more easily dispossess their lawful sovereign than endure a wanton jest, he was forced to turn his thoughts another way, and to introduce the examples of moral virtue, writ in verse, and performed in recitative music. The original of this music, and of the scenes which adorned his work, he had from the Italian operas; but he heightened his characters (as I may probably imagine) from the example of Corneille and some French poets. In this condition did this part of poetry remain at his Majesty's return; when, growing bolder, as being now owned by a public authority, he reviewed his *Siege of Rhodes*, and caused it be acted as a just drama. But as few men have the happiness to begin and finish any new project, so neither did he live to make his design perfect: there wanted the fulness of a plot, and the variety of characters to form it as it ought; and, perhaps, something might have been added to the beauty of the style. All which he would have performed with more exactness had he pleased to have given us another work of the same nature. For myself and others, who come after him, we are bound, with all veneration to his memory, to acknowledge what advantage we received from that excellent groundwork which he laid: and, since it is an easy thing to add to what already is invented, we ought all of us, without envy to him, or partiality to ourselves, to yield him the precedence in it.

Having done him this justice, as my guide, I may do myself so much, as to give an account of what I have performed after him. I observed then, as I said, what was wanting to the perfection of his *Siege of Rhodes;* which was design, and variety of characters. And in the midst of this consideration, by mere accident, I opened the next book that lay by me, which was an Ariosto in Italian; and the very first two lines of that poem gave me light to all I could desire:

Le donne, i cavalier, l'arme, gli amori,
Le cortesie, l'audaci imprese io canto, etc.

For the very next reflection which I made was this, that an heroic play ought to be an imitation, in little, of an heroic poem; and, consequently, that love and valour ought to be the subject of it. Both these Sir William D'Avenant had begun to shadow; but it was so, as first discoverers draw their maps, with headlands, and promontories, and some few outlines of somewhat taken at a distance, and which the designer saw not clearly. The common drama obliged him to a plot well formed and pleasant, or, as the ancients call it, one entire and great action. But this he afforded not himself in a story, which he neither filled with persons, nor beautified with characters, nor varied with accidents. The laws of an heroic poem did not dispense with those of the other, but raised them to a greater height, and indulged him a further liberty of fancy, and of drawing all things as far above the ordinary proportion of the stage as that is beyond the common words and actions of human life; and, therefore, in the scanting of his images and design, he complied not enough with the greatness and majesty of an heroic poem.

I am sorry I cannot discover my opinion of this kind of writing, without dissenting much from his, whose memory I love and honour. But I will do it with the same respect to him, as if he were now alive, and overlooking my paper while I write. His judgment of an heroic poem was this: That it ought to be dressed in a more familiar and easy shape; more fitted to the common actions and passions of human life; and, in short, more like a glass of Nature, showing us ourselves in our ordinary habits, and figuring a more practicable virtue to us, than was done by the ancients or moderns. Thus he takes the image of an heroic poem from the drama, or stage poetry; and accordingly intended to divide it into five books, representing the same number of acts; and every book into several cantos, imitating the scenes which compose our acts.

But this, I think, is rather a play in narration, as I may call it, than an heroic poem; if at least you will not prefer the opinion of a single man to the practice of the most excellent authors, both of ancient and latter ages.

I am no admirer of quotations; but you shall hear, if you please, one of the ancients delivering his judgment on this question; it is Petronius Arbiter, the most elegant, and one of the most judicious authors of the Latin tongue; who, after he had given many admirable rules for the structure and beauties of an epic poem, concludes all in these following words: —

Non enim res gestæ versibus comprehendendæ sunt, quod longe melius historici faciunt: sed, per ambages, deorumque ministeria, præcipitandus est liber spiritus, ut potius furentis animi vaticinatio appareat, quam religiosæ orationis, sub testibus, fides.

In which sentence, and his own essay of a poem, which immediately he gives you, it is thought he taxes Lucan, who followed too much the truth of history, crowded sentences together, was too full of points, and too often offered at somewhat which had more of the sting of an epigram, than of the dignity and state of an heroic poem. Lucan used not much the help of his heathen deities: there was neither the ministry of the gods, nor the precipitation of the soul, nor the fury of a prophet (of which my author speaks), in his *Pharsalia;* he treats you more like a philosopher than a poet, and instructs you, in verse, with what he had been taught by his uncle Seneca in prose. In one word, he walks soberly afoot, when he might fly. Yet Lucan is not always this religious historian. The oracle of Appius, and the witchcraft of Erictho, will somewhat atone for him, who was, indeed, bound up by an ill-chosen and known argument, to follow truth with great exactness. For my part, I am of opinion that neither Homer, Virgil, Statius, Ariosto, Tasso, nor our English Spenser, could have formed their poems half so beautiful, without those gods and spirits, and those enthusiastic parts of poetry, which compose the most noble parts of all their writings. And I will ask any man who loves heroic poetry (for I will not dispute their tastes who do not), if the ghost of Polydorus in Virgil, the Enchanted Wood in Tasso, and the Bower of Bliss in Spenser (which he borrows from that admirable Italian) could have been omitted, without taking from their works some of the greatest beauties in them. And if any man object the improbabilities of a spirit appearing, or of a palace raised by magic, I boldly answer him, that an heroic poet is not tied to a bare representation of what is true, or exceeding probable; but that he may let himself loose to visionary objects, and to the representation of such things as depending not on sense, and therefore not to be comprehended by knowledge, may give him a freer scope for imagination. 'T is enough that, in all ages and religions, the greatest part of mankind have believed the power of magic, and that there are spirits or spectres which have appeared. This, I say, is foundation enough for poetry; and I dare further affirm that the whole doctrine of separated beings, whether those spirits are incorporeal substances (which Mr. Hobbs, with some reason, thinks to imply a contradiction), or that they are a thinner or more aërial sort of bodies (as some of the fathers have conjectured), may better be explicated by poets than by philosophers or divines. For their speculations on this subject are wholly poetical; they have only their fancy for their guide; and that, being sharper in an excellent poet, than it is likely it should in a phlegmatic, heavy gownman, will see further in its own empire, and produce more satisfactory notions on those dark and doubtful problems.

Some men think they have raised a great argument against the use of spectres and magic in heroic poetry by saying they are unnatural; but whether they or I believe there are such things is not material; 't is enough that, for aught we know, they may be in nature; and whatever is or may be, is not properly unnatural. Neither am I much concerned at Mr. Cowley's verses before *Gondibert* (though his authority is almost sacred to me): 't is true, he has resembled the epic poetry to a fantastic fairy-land; but he has contradicted himself by his own example. For he has himself made use of angels and visions in his *Davideis*, as well as Tasso in his *Godfrey*.

What I have written on this subject will not be thought a digression by the reader, if he please to remember what I said in the beginning of this essay, that I have modelled my heroic plays by the rules of an heroic poem. And if that be the most noble, the most pleasant, and the most instructive way of writing in verse, and withal the highest pattern of human life, as all poets have agreed, I shall need no other argument to justify my choice in this imitation. One advantage the drama has above the other, namely, that it represents to view what the poem only does relate: and, *Segnius irritant animum demissa per aures, quam quæ sunt oculis subjecta fidelibus*, as Horace tells us.

To those who object my frequent use of drums and trumpets, and my representations of battles, I answer, I introduced them not on the English stage: Shakspeare used them frequently; and though Jonson shows no battle in his *Catiline*, yet you hear from behind the scenes the sounding of trumpets, and the shouts of fighting armies. But I add farther, that these warlike instruments, and even their presentations of fighting on the stage, are no more than necessary to produce the effects of an heroic play; that is, to raise the imagination of the audience, and to persuade them, for the time, that what they behold on the theatre is really performed. The poet is then to endeavour an absolute dominion over the minds of the spectators; for, though our fancy will contribute to its own deceit, yet a writer ought to help its operation; and that the *Red Bull* has formerly done the same, is no more an argument against our practice, than it would be for a physician to forbear an approved medicine, because a mountebank has used it with success.

Thus I have given a short account of heroic plays. I might now, with the usual eagerness of an author, make a particular defence of this. But the common opinion (how unjust soever) has been so much to my advantage, that I have reason to be satisfied, and to suffer with patience all that can be urged against it.

For, otherwise, what can be more easy for me than to defend the character of Almanzor, which is one great exception that is made against the play? 'T is said, that Almanzor is no perfect pattern of heroic virtue, that he is a contemner of kings, and that he is made to perform impossibilities.

I must therefore avow, in the first place, from whence I took the character. The first image I had of him, was from the Achilles of Homer; the next from Tasso's Rinaldo (who was a copy of the former), and the third from the Artaban of Monsieur Calprenède, who has imitated both. The original of these, Achilles, is taken by Homer for his hero; and is described by him as one, who in strength and courage surpassed the rest of the Grecian army; but withal of so fiery a temper, so impatient of an injury, even from his king and general, that when his mistress was to be forced from him by the command of Agamemnon, he not only disobeyed it, but returned him an answer full of contumely, and in the most opprobrious terms he could imagine. They are Homer's words which follow, and I have cited but some few amongst a multitude:

Οἰνοβαρές, κυνὸς ὄμματ' ἔχων, κραδίην δ' ἐλάφοιο
— Il. A. v. 225.

Δημοβόρος βασιλεύς, etc. — Il. A. v. 231.

Nay, he proceeded so far in his insolence, as to draw out his sword, with intention to kill him:

Ἕλκετο δ' ἐκ κολεοῖο μέγα ξίφος.
— Il. A. v. 194.

And, if Minerva had not appeared, and held his hand, he had executed his design; and it was all she could do to dissuade him from it. The event was, that he left the army, and would fight no more. Agamemnon gives his character thus to Nestor:

Ἀλλ' ὅδ' ἀνὴρ ἐθέλει περὶ πάντων ἔμμεναι ἄλλων,
Πάντων μὲν κρατέειν ἐθέλει, πάντεσσι δ' ἀνάσσειν —.
— Il. A. v. 287, 288.

and Horace gives the same description of him in his *Art of Poetry:*

Honoratum si fortè reponis Achillem,
Impiger, iracundus, inexorabilis, acer,
Jura neget sibi nata, nihil non arroget armis.

Tasso's chief character, Rinaldo, was a man of the same temper; for, when he had slain Gernando in his heat of passion, he not only refused to be judged by Godfrey, his general, but threatened that if he came to seize him, he would right himself by arms upon him; witness these following lines of Tasso:

Venga egli, o mandi, io terrò fermo il piede:
Giudici fian tra noi la sorte, e l'arme;
Fera tragedia vuol che s'appresenti,
Per lor diporto, alle nemiche genti.

You see how little these great authors did esteem the *point of honour*, so much magnified by the French, and so ridiculously aped by us. They made their heroes men of honour; but so as not to divest them quite of human passions and frailties; they contented themselves to show you what men of great spirits would certainly do when they were provoked, not what they were obliged to do by the strict rules of moral virtue. For my own part, I declare myself for Homer and Tasso, and am more in love with Achilles and Rinaldo, than with Cyrus and Oroondates. I shall never subject my characters to the French standard, where love and honour are to be weighed by drachms and scruples. Yet, where I have designed the patterns of exact virtues, such as in this play are the parts of Almahide, of Ozmyn, and Benzayda, I may safely challenge the best of theirs.

But Almanzor is taxed with changing sides: and what tie has he on him to the contrary? He is not born their subject whom he serves, and he is injured by them to a very high degree. He threatens them, and speaks insolently of sovereign power; but so do Achilles and Rinaldo, who were subjects and soldiers to Agamemnon and Godfrey of Bulloigne. He talks extravagantly in his passion; but, if I would take the pains to quote an hundred passages of Ben Jonson's Cethegus, I could easily show you that the rodomontades of Almanzor are neither so irrational as his, nor so impossible to be put in execution; for Cethegus threatens to destroy Nature, and to raise a new one out of it; to kill all the Senate for his part of the action; to look Cato dead; and a thousand other things as extravagant he says, but performs not one action in the play.

But none of the former calumnies will stick: and, therefore, 't is at last charged upon me, that Almanzor does all things; or if you will have an absurd accusation, in their nonsense who make it, that he performs impossibilities. They say, that being a stranger, he appeases two fighting factions, when the authority of their lawful sovereign could not. This is indeed the most improbable of all his actions, but 't is far from being impossible. Their king had made himself contemptible to his people, as the history of Granada tells us; and Almanzor, though a stranger, yet was already known to them by his gallantry, in the *juego de toros*, his engagement on the weaker side, and more especially by the character of his person and brave actions, given by Abdalla just before; and, after all, the greatness of the enterprise consisted only in the daring, for he had the king's guards to second him. But we have read both of Cæsar, and many other generals, who have not only calmed a mutiny with a word, but have presented themselves single before an army of their enemies; which upon sight of them has revolted from their own leaders and come over to their trenches. In the rest of Almanzor's actions you see him for the most part victorious; but the same fortune has constantly attended many heroes who were not imaginary. Yet you see it no inheritance to him; for, in the first place, he is made a prisoner, and, in the last, defeated, and not able to preserve the city from being taken. If the history of the late Duke of Guise be true, he hazarded more, and performed not less in Naples, than Almanzor is feigned to have done in Granada.

I have been too tedious in this apology; but to make some satisfaction, I will leave the rest of my play exposed to the critics without defence.

The concernment of it is wholly passed from me, and ought to be in them who have been favourable to it, and are somewhat obliged to defend their own opinions. That there are errors in it, I deny not:

Ast opere in tanto fas est obrepere somnum.

But I have already swept the stakes; and, with the common good fortune of prosperous gamesters, can be content to sit quietly; to hear my fortune cursed by some, and my faults arraigned by others, and to suffer both without reply.

1672

JOURNALS

John Evelyn (1620-1706)

DIARY

March 9, 1652. — I went to Deptford, where I made preparation for my settlement, no more intending to go out of England, but endeavor a settled life, either in this or some other place, there being now so little appearance of any change for the better, all being entirely in the rebels' hands; and this particular habitation and the estate contiguous to it (belonging to my father-in-law, actually in his Majesty's service) very much suffering for want of some friend to rescue it out of the power of the usurpers, so as to preserve our interest, and take some care of my other concerns, by the advice and endeavor of my friends I was advised to reside in it, and compound with the soldiers. This I was besides authorised by his Majesty to do, and encouraged with a promise that what was in lease from the Crown, if ever it pleased God to restore him, he would secure to us in fee-farm. I had also addresses and cyphers, to correspond with his Majesty and Ministers abroad: upon all which inducements, I was persuaded to settle henceforth in England, having now run about the world, most part out on my own country, near ten years. I therefore now likewise meditated sending over for my wife, whom as yet I had left at Paris.

August 9, 1654. — To the old and ragged city of Leicester, large and pleasantly seated, but despicably built, the chimney-flues like so many smiths' forges; however, famous for the tomb of the tyrant, Richard the Third, which is now converted to a cistern, at which (I think) cattle drink. Also, here in one of the churches lies buried the magnificent Cardinal Wolsey. John of Gaunt has here also built a large but poor Hospital, near which a wretch has made him a house out of the ruins of a stately church. Saw the ruins of an old Roman Temple, thought to be of Janus. Entertained at a very fine collection of fruits, such as I did not expect to meet with so far north, especially very good melons. We returned to my uncle's.

September 3, 1658. — Died that arch-rebel, Oliver Cromwell, called Protector.

October 22. — Saw the superb funeral of the Protector. He was carried from Somerset House in a velvet bed of state, drawn by six horses, housed with the same; the pall held by his new Lords; Oliver lying in effigy, in royal robes, and crowned with a crown, sceptre, and globe, like a king. The pendants and guidons were carried by the officers of the army; the Imperial banners, achievements, &c. by the heralds in their coats; a rich caparisoned horse, embroidered all over with gold; a knight of honour, armed cap-a-pie, and, after all, his guards, soldiers, and innumerable mourners. In this equipage, they proceeded to Westminster: but it was the joyfullest funeral I ever saw; for there were none that cried but dogs, which the soldiers hooted away with a barbarous noise, drinking and taking tobacco in the streets as they went.

May 29, 1660. — This day, his Majesty, Charles the Second came to London, after a sad and long exile and calamitous suffering both of the King and Church, being seventeen years. This was also his birthday, and with a triumph of above 20,000 horse and foot, brandishing their swords, and shouting with inexpressible joy; the ways strewed with flowers, the bells ringing, the streets hung with tapestry, fountains running with wine; the Mayor, Aldermen, and all the Companies, in their liveries, chains of gold, and banners; Lords and Nobles, clad in cloth of silver, gold, and velvet; the windows and balconies, all set with ladies; trumpets, music, and myriads of people flocking, even so far as from Rochester, so as they were seven hours in passing the city, even from two in the afternoon till nine at night. I stood in the strand and beheld it, and blessed God. And all this was done without one drop of blood shed, and by that very army which rebelled against him: but it was the Lord's doing, for such a restoration was never mentioned in any history, ancient or modern, since the return of the Jews from their Babylonish captivity; nor so joyful a day and so bright ever seen in this nation, this happening when to expect or effect it was past all human policy.

September 2, 1666. — This fatal night about ten, began the deplorable fire, near Fish-street, in London.

3. I had public prayers at home. The fire continuing, after dinner, I took coach with my wife and son, and went to the Bankside in Southwark, where we beheld that dismal spectacle, the whole city in dreadful flames near the water-side; all the houses from the Bridge, all Thames-street, and upwards towards Cheapside, down to the Three Cranes, were now consumed; and so returned, exceeding astonished what would become of the rest.

The fire having continued all this night (if I may call that night which was light as day for ten miles round about, after a dreadful manner), when conspiring with a fierce eastern wind in a very dry season, I went on foot to the same place; and saw the whole south part of the city burning from Cheapside to the Thames, and all along Cornhill (for it likewise kindled back against the wind as well as forward), Tower-street, Fenchurch-street, Gracious-street, and so along to Baynard's Castle, and was now taking hold of St. Paul's Church, to which the scaffolds contributed exceedingly. The conflagration was so universal, and the people so astonished, that, from the beginning, I know not by what despondency, or fate, they hardly stirred to quench it; so that there was nothing heard, or seen, but crying out and lamentation, running about like distracted creatures, without at all attempting to save even their goods; such a strange consternation there was upon them, so as it burned both in breadth and length, the churches, public halls, Exchange, hospitals, monuments, and ornaments; leaping after a prodigious manner, from house to house, and street to street, at great distances one from the other. For the heat, with a long set of fair and warm weather, had even ignited the air, and prepared the materials to conceive the fire, which devoured, after an incredible manner, houses, furniture, and everything. Here, we saw the Thames covered with goods floating, all the barges and boats laden with what some had time and courage to save, as, on the other, the carts, &c., carrying out to the fields, which for many miles were strewed with moveables of all sorts, and tents erecting to shelter both people and what goods they could get away. Oh, the miserable and calamitous spectacle! such as haply the world had not seen since the foundation of it, nor can be outdone till the universal conflagration thereof. All the sky was of a fiery aspect, like the top of a burning oven, and the light seen above forty miles round about for many nights. God grant mine eyes may never behold the like, who now saw above 10,000 houses all in one flame! The noise and cracking and thunder of the impetuous flames, the shrieking of women and children, the hurry of people, the fall of towers, houses and churches, was like a hideous storm; and the air all about so hot and inflamed, that at the last one was not able to approach it, so that they were forced to stand still, and let the flames burn on, which they did, for near two miles in length and one in breadth. The clouds also of smoke were dismal, and reached, upon computation, near fifty miles in length. Thus, I left it this afternoon burning, a resemblance of Sodom, or the last day. It forcibly called to my mind that passage—*non enim hic habemus stabilem civitatem:* the ruins resembling the picture of Troy. London was, but it is no more! Thus, I returned.

May 26, 1703.— This day died Mr. Samuel Pepys, a very worthy, industrious and curious person, none in England exceeding him in knowledge of the navy, in which he had passed through all the most considerable offices, Clerk of the Acts and Secretary of the Admiralty, all which he performed with great integrity. When King James II went out of England, he laid down his office, and would serve no more; but withdrawing himself from all public affairs, he lived at Clapham with his partner, Mr. Hewer, formerly his clerk, in a very noble house and sweet place, where he enjoyed the fruit of his labours in great prosperity. He was universally beloved, hospitable, generous, learned in many things, skilled in music, a very great cherisher of learned men of whom he had the conversation. His library and collection of other curiosities were of the most considerable, the models of ships especially. Besides what he published of an account of the navy, as he found and left it, he had for divers years under his hand the History of the Navy, or *Navalia*, as he called it; but how far advanced, and what will follow of his, is left, I suppose, to his sister's son, Mr. Jackson, a young gentleman, whom Mr. Pepys had educated in all sorts of useful learning, sending him to travel abroad, from whence he returned with extraordinary accomplishments, and worthy to be heir. Mr. Pepys had been for near forty years so much my particular friend, that Mr. Jackson sent me complete mourning, desiring me to be one to hold up the pall at his magnificent obsequies; but my indisposition hindered me from doing him this last office.

October 31, 1706.— I am this day arrived to the 85th year of my age. Lord teach me so to number my days to come, that I may apply them to wisdom!

Samuel Pepys (1633–1703)

DIARY

January 1, 1660 (Lord's day). — This morning (we living lately in the garret), I rose, put on my suit with great skirts, having not lately worn any other clothes but them. Went to Mr. Gunning's chapel at Exeter House, where he made a very good sermon upon these words:— 'That in the fulness of time God sent his Son, made of a woman,' &c.; showing, that by 'made under the law' is meant the circumcision, which is solemnized this day. Dined at home in the garret, where my wife dressed the remains of a turkey, and in the doing of it she burned her hand. I stayed at home the whole afternoon, looking over my accounts; then went with my wife to my father's, and in going observed the great posts which the City workmen set up at the Conduit in Fleet Street.

May 25, 1660.— By the morning we were come close to the land, and everybody made ready to get on shore. The King and the two dukes did eat their breakfast before they went; and there being set some ship's diet before them, only to show them the manner of the ship's diet, they eat of nothing else but peas and pork, and boiled beef. I had Mr. Darcy in my cabin; and Dr. Clerke, who eat with me, told me how the King had given 50l. to Mr. Shepley for my Lord's servants, and 500l. among the officers and common men of the ship. I spoke to the Duke of York about business, who called me Pepys by name, and upon my desire did promise me his future favour. Great expectation of the King's making some knights, but there was none. About noon (though the brigantine that Beale made was there ready to carry him) yet he would go in my Lord's barge with the two Dukes. Our captain steered, and my Lord went along bare with him. I went, and Mr. Mansell, and one of the King's footmen, and a dog that the King loved, in a boat by ourselves, and so got on shore when the King did, who was received by General Monk with all imaginable love and respect at his entrance upon the land of Dover. Infinite the crowd of people and the gallantry of the horsemen, citizens, and noblemen of all sorts. The Mayor of the town came and gave him his white staff, the badge of his place, which the King did give him again. The Mayor also presented him from the town a very rich Bible, which he took, and said it was the thing that he loved above all things in the world. A canopy was provided for him to stand under, which he did, and talked awhile with General Monk and others, and so into a stately coach there set for him, and so away through the town towards Canterbury, without making any stay at Dover. The shouting and joy expressed by all is past imagination. Seeing that my Lord did not stir out of his barge, I got into a boat, and so into his barge, and we back to the ship, seeing a man almost drowned that fell into the sea. My Lord almost transported with joy that he had done all this without the least blur or obstruction in the world, that could give offence to any, and with the great honour he thought it would be to him. Being overtook by the brigantine, my Lord and we went out of our barge into it, and so went on board with Sir W. Batten and the Vice and Rear-Admirals. At night I supped with the captain, who told me what the King had given us. My Lord returned late, and at his coming did give me order to cause the mark to be gilded, and a Crown and C. R. to be made at the head of the coach table, where the King to-day with his own hand did mark his height, which accordingly I caused the painter to do, and is now done, as is to be seen.

January 3, 1661.— To the Theatre, where was acted 'Beggar's Bush,' it being very well done; and here the first time that ever I saw women come upon the stage.

January 1, 1662.— Waking this morning out of my sleep on a sudden, I did with my elbow hit my wife a great blow over her face and neck, which waked her with pain, at which I was sorry, and to sleep again. We went by coach to the play of the Spanish Curate; and a good play it is, only Diego the Sexton did overdo his part too much.

March 1, 1662.— My wife and I by coach, first to see my little picture that is a-drawing, and thence to the Opera, and there saw 'Romeo and Juliet,' the first time it was ever acted, but it is a play of itself the worst that ever I heard, and the worst acted that ever I saw these people do, and I am resolved to go no more to see the first time of acting, for they were all of them out more or less. I do find that I am 500l. beforehand in the world, which I was afraid I was not, but I find that I had spent above 250l. this last half year.

September 2, 1666 (Lord's day). — Some of our maids sitting up late last night to get things ready against our feast to-day, Jane called us up about three in the morning, to tell us of a great fire they saw in the City. So I rose and slipped on my night-gown, and went to her window; and thought it to be on the back-side of Marke-lane at the farthest; but, being unused to such fires as followed, I thought it far enough off; and so went to bed again, and to sleep. About seven rose again to dress myself, and there looked out at the window, and saw the fire not so much as it was, and further off. So to my closet to set things to rights, after yesterday's cleaning. By and by Jane comes and tells me that she hears that about 300 houses have been burned down to-night by the fire we saw, and that it is now burning down all Fish Street, by London Bridge. So I made myself ready presently, and walked to the Tower; and there got up upon one of the high places, Sir J. Robinson's little son going up with me; and there I did see the houses at that end of the bridge all on fire, and an infinite great fire on this and the other side the end of the bridge; which, among other people, did trouble me for poor little Michell and our Sarah on the bridge. So down with my heart full of trouble, to the Lieutenant of the Tower, who tells me that it begun this morning in the King's baker's house in Pudding-lane. and that it hath burned down St. Magnus's Church and most part of Fish Street already. So I down to the water-side, and there got a boat, and through bridge, and there saw a lamentable fire. Poor Michell's house, as far as the Old Swan, already burned that way, and the fire running further, that, in a very little time, it got as far as the Steele-yard, while I was there. Every body endeavouring to remove their goods, and flinging into the river, or bringing them into lighters that lay off; poor people staying in their houses as long as till the very fire touched them, and then running into boats, or clambering from one pair of stairs, by the water-side, to another. And, among other things, the poor pigeons, I perceive, were loth to leave their houses, but hovered about the windows and balconys, till they burned their wings and fell down. Having staid, and in an hour's time seen the fire rage every way; and nobody, to my sight, endeavouring to quench it, but to remove their goods, and leave all to the fire; and having seen it get as far as the Steele-yard, and the wind mighty high, and driving it into the City: and everything, after so long a drought, proving combustible, even the very stones of churches; and, among other things, the poor steeple by which pretty Mrs. —— lives, and whereof my old schoolfellow Elborough is parson, taken fire in the very top, and there burned till it fell down; I to White Hall, with a gentleman with me, who desired to go off from the Tower, to see the fire, in my boat; and there up to the King's closet in the Chapel, where people come about me, and I did give them an account dismayed them all, and word was carried into the King. So I was called for, and did tell the King and Duke of York what I saw; and, that unless his Majesty did command houses to be pulled down, nothing could stop the fire. They seemed much troubled, and the King commanded me to go to my Lord Mayor from him, and command him to spare no houses, but to pull down before the fire every way. The Duke of York bid me tell him, that if he would have any more soldiers, he shall; and so did my Lord Arlington afterwards, as a great secret. Here meeting with Captain Cocke, I in his coach, which he lent me, and Creed with me to Paul's; and there walked along Watling Street, as well as I could, every creature coming away loaden with goods to save, and, here and there, sick people carried away in beds. Extraordinary good goods carried in carts and on backs. At last met my Lord Mayor in Canning Street, like a man spent, with a hankercher about his neck. To the King's message, he cried like a fainting woman, 'Lord! what can I do? I am spent: people will not obey me. I have been pulling down houses; but the fire overtakes us faster than we can do it.' That he needed no more soldiers; and that, for himself, he must go and refresh himself, having been up all night. So he left me, and I him, and walked home: seeing people all almost distracted, and no manner of means used to quench the fire. The houses, too, so very thick thereabouts, and full of matter for burning, as pitch and tar, in Thames Street; and warehouses of oyle, and wines, and brandy, and other things. Here I saw Mr. Isaac Houblon, the handsome man, prettily dressed and dirty at his door at Dowgate, receiving some of his brothers' things, whose houses were on fire; and, as he says, have been removed twice already; and he doubts, as it soon proved, that they must be, in a little time, removed from his house also, which was a sad consideration. And to see the churches all filling with goods by people who themselves should have been quietly there at this time. By this time, it was about twelve o'clock; and so home, and there find my guests, who were Mr. Wood and his wife Barbary Shelden, and also Mr. Moone: she mighty fine, and her husband, for aught I see, a likely man. But Mr. Moone's design and mine, which was to look over my closet, and please him with the sight thereof, which he hath long desired, was wholly disappointed; for we were in great trouble and disturbance at this fire, not knowing what to think of it. However, we had an extraordinary good dinner, and as merry as at this time we could be. While at dinner, Mrs. Batelier come to enquire after Mr. Woolfe and Stanes, who, it seems, are related to them, whose houses in Fish Street are all burned, and they in a sad condition. She would not stay in the fright. Soon as dined, I and Moone away, and walked through the City, the streets full of nothing but people; and horses and carts loaden with goods, ready to run over one another, and removing goods from one burned house to another. They now removing out of Canning Street, which received goods in the morning, into Lumbard Street, and further: and among others, I now saw my little goldsmith Stokes receiving some friend's goods, whose house itself was burned the day after. We parted at Paul's; he home, and I to Paul's Wharf, where I had appointed a boat to attend me, and took in Mr. Carcasse and his brother, whom I met in the street, and carried them below and above bridge too. And again to see the fire, which was now got further, both below and above, and no likelihood of stopping it. Met with the King and Duke of York in their barge, and with them to Queenhithe, and there called Sir Richard Browne to them. Their order was only to pull down houses apace, and so below bridge at the waterside; but little was or could be done, the fire coming upon them so fast. Good hopes there was of stopping it at the Three Cranes above, and at Buttulph's Wharf below bridge, if care be used; but the wind carries it into the City, so as we know not, by the water-side, what it do there. River full of lighters and boats taking in goods, and good goods swimming in the water; and only I observed that hardly one lighter or boat in three that had the goods of a house in, but there was a pair of Virginall's in it. Having seen as much as I could now, I away to White Hall by appointment, and there walked to St. James's Park; and there met my wife, and Creed, and Wood, and his wife, and walked to my boat; and there upon the water again, and to the fire up and down, it still encreasing, and the wind great. So near the fire as we could for smoke; and all over the Thames, with one's faces in the wind, you were almost burned with a shower of fire-drops. This is very true: so as houses were burned by these drops and flakes of fire, three or four, nay, five or six houses, one from another. When we could endure no more upon the water, we to a little ale-house on the Bankside, over against the Three Cranes, and there staid till it was dark almost and saw the fire grow; and, as it grew darker, appeared more and more; and in corners and upon steeples, and between churches and houses, as far as we could see up the hill of the City, in a most horrid, malicious, bloody flame, not like the fine flame of an ordinary fire. Barbary and her husband away before us. We staid till, it being darkish, we saw the fire as only one entire arch of fire from this to the other side the bridge, and in a bow up the hill for an arch of above a mile long: it made me weep to see it. The churches, houses, and all on fire, and flaming at once; and a horrid noise the flames made, and the cracking of houses at their ruin. So home with a sad heart, and there find every body discoursing and lamenting the fire; and poor Tom Hater come with some few of his goods saved out of his house, which was burned upon Fish Street Hill. I invited him to lie at my house, and did receive his goods; but was deceived in his lying there, the news coming every moment of the growth of the fire; so as we were forced to begin to pack up our own goods, and prepare for their removal; and did by moonshine, it being brave, dry, and moonshine and warm weather, carry much of my goods into the garden; and Mr. Hater and I did remove my money and iron chests into my cellar, as thinking that the safest place. And got my bags of gold into my office, ready to carry away, and my chief papers of accounts also there, and my tallies into a box by themselves. So great was our fear, that Sir W. Batten hath carts come out of the country to fetch away his goods this night. We did put Mr. Hater, poor man! to bed a little; but he got but very little rest, so much noise being in my house, taking down of goods.

5.— I lay down in the office again upon W. Hewer's quilt, being mighty weary, and sore in my feet with going till I was hardly able to stand. About two in the morning my wife calls me up, and tells me of new cryes of fire, it being come to Barking Church, which is the bottom of our lane. I up; and finding it so, resolved presently to take her away, and did, and took my gold, which was about 2350l., W. Hewer and Jane down by Proundy's boat to Woolwich; but, Lord! what a sad sight it was by moonlight, to see the whole City almost on fire, that you might see it as plain at Woolwich, as if you were by it. There, when I come, I find the gates shut, but no guard kept at all; which troubled me, because of discourses now begun, that there is a plot in it, and that the French had done it. I got the gates open, and to Mr. Sheldon's, where I locked up my gold, and charged my wife and W. Hewer never to leave the room without one of them in it, night or day. So back again, by the way seeing my goods well in the lighters at Deptford, and watched well by people. Home, and whereas I expected to have seen our house on fire, it being now about seven o'clock, it was not. But to the fire, and there find greater hopes than I expected; for my confidence of finding our Office on fire was such, that I durst not ask any body how it was with us, till I come and saw it was not burned. But, going to the fire, I find, by the blowing up of houses, and the great help given by the workmen out of the King's yards, sent up by Sir W. Pen, there is a good stop given to it, as well at Marke Lane end as ours; it having only burned the dyall of Barking Church, and part of the porch, and was there quenched. I up to the top of Barking steeple, and there saw the saddest sight of desolation that ever I saw; everywhere great fires, oyle-cellars, and brimstone, and other things burning. I became afraid to stay there long, and therefore down again as fast as I could, the fire being spread as far as I could see; and to Sir W. Pen's, and there eat a piece of cold meat, having eaten nothing since Sunday, but the remains of Sunday's dinner. Here I met with Mr. Young and Whistler; and, having removed all my things, and received good hopes that the fire at our end is stopped, they and I walked into the town, and find Fenchurch Street, Gracious Street, and Lumbard Street all in dust. The Exchange a sad sight, nothing standing there, of all the statues or pillars, but Sir Thomas

Gresham's picture in the corner. Into Moorfields, our feet ready to burn, walking through the town among the hot coles, and find that full of people, and poor wretches carrying their goods there, and every body keeping his goods together by themselves; and a great blessing it is to them that it is fair weather for them to keep abroad night and day; drunk there, and paid twopence for a plain penny loaf. Thence homeward, having passed through Cheapside, and Newgate market, all burned; and seen Anthony Joyce's house in fire; and took up, which I keep by me, a piece of glass of the Mercers' chapel in the street, where much more was, so melted and buckled with the heat of the fire like parchment. I also did see a poor cat taken out of a hole in a chimney, joyning to the wall of the Exchange, with the hair all burned off the body, and yet alive. So home at night, and find there good hopes of saving our office; but great endeavours of watching all night, and having men ready; and so we lodged them in the office, and had drink and bread and cheese for them. And I lay down and slept a good night about midnight: though, when I rose, I heard that there had been a great alarm of French and Dutch being risen, which proved nothing. But it is a strange thing to see how long this time did look since Sunday, having been always full of variety of actions, and little sleep, that it looked like a week or more, and I had forgot almost the day of the week.

February 18, 1667. — To the King's house, to 'The Mayd's Tragedy'; but vexed all the while with two talking ladies and Sir Charles Sedley; yet pleased to hear their discourse, he being a stranger. And one of the ladies would, and did sit with her mask on, all the play, and, being exceeding witty as ever I heard woman, did talk most pleasantly with him; but was, I believe, a virtuous woman, and of quality. He would fain know who she was, but she would not tell; yet did give him many pleasant hints of her knowledge of him, by that means setting his brains at work to find out who she was, and did give him leave to use all means to find out who she was, but pulling off her mask. He was mighty witty, and she also making sport with him very inoffensively, that a more pleasant rencontre I never heard. But by that means lost the pleasure of the play wholly, to which now and then Sir Charles Sedley's exceptions against both words and pronouncing were very pretty.

May 31, 1669. — Up very betimes, and continued all the morning with W. Hewer, upon examining and stating my accounts, in order to the fitting myself to go abroad beyond sea, which the ill condition of my eyes and my neglect for a year or two, hath kept me behind-hand in, and so as to render it very difficult now, and troublesome to my mind to do it; but I this day made a satisfactory entrance therein. Had another meeting with the Duke of York, at White Hall, on yesterday's work, and made a good advance: and so, being called by my wife, we to the Park, Mary Batelier, and a Dutch gentleman, a friend of hers, being with us. Thence to 'The World's End,' a drinking-house by the Park; and there merry, and so home late.

And thus ends all that I doubt I shall ever be able to do with my own eyes in the keeping of my Journal, I being not able to do it any longer, having done now so long as to undo my eyes almost every time that I take a pen in my hand; and, therefore, whatever comes of it, I must forbear: and, therefore, resolve, from this time forward, to have it kept by my people in long-hand, and must be contented to set down no more than is fit for them and all the world to know; or, if there be anything, I must endeavour to keep a margin in my book open, to add, here and there, a note in short-hand with my own hand. And so I betake myself to that course, which is almost as much as to see myself go into my grave: for which and all the discomforts that will accompany my being blind, may God prepare me! S. P.

Jonathan Swift (1667–1745)

JOURNAL TO STELLA

January 16, 1711. — O faith, young women, I have sent my letter No. 13, without one crumb of an answer to any of MD's; there is for you now; and yet Presto ben't angry, faith, not a bit, only he will begin to be in pain next Irish post, except he sees MD's little handwriting in the glass frame at the bar of St. James's Coffee-house, where Presto would never go but for that purpose. Presto's at home, God help him, every night from six till bedtime, and has as little enjoyment or pleasure in life at present as anybody in the world, although in full favour with all the ministry. As hope saved, nothing gives Presto any sort of dream of happiness, but a letter now and then from his own dearest MD. I love the expectation of it, and when it does not come, I comfort myself, that I have it yet to be happy with. Yes, faith, and when I write to MD, I am happy too; it is just as if methinks you were here, and I prating to you, and telling you where I have been: Well, says you, Presto, come, where have you been to-day? come, let's hear now. And so then I answer; Ford and I were visiting Mr Lewis, and Mr Prior, and Prior has given me a fine Plautus, and then Ford would have me dine at his lodgings, and so I would not; and so I dined with him at an eating-house; which I have not done five times since I came here; and so I came home, after visiting Sir Andrew Fountaine's mother and sister, and Sir Andrew Fountaine is mending, though slowly.

January 26–30, 1711. — I have been so lazy and negligent these last four days, that I could not write to MD. My head is not in order, and yet it is not absolutely ill, but giddyish, and makes me listless. I walk every day, and take drops of Dr Cockburn, and I have just done a box of pills, and today Lady Kerry sent me some of her bitter drink, which I design to take twice a day, and hope I shall grow better. I wish I were with MD; I long for spring and good weather, and then I will come over. My riding in Ireland keeps me well. I am very temperate, and eat of the easiest meats, as I am directed, and hope the malignity will go off; but one fit shakes me a long time. I dined to-day with Lord Mountjoy, yesterday at Mr Stone's in the City, on Sunday at Vanhomrigh's, Saturday with Ford, and Friday I think at Vanhomrigh's, and that is all the journal I can send MD; for I was so lazy while I was well, that I could not write. I thought to have sent this to-night, but it is ten, and I will go to bed, and write on the other side to Parvisol to-morrow, and send it on Thursday; and so good night, my dears, and love Presto, and be healthy, and Presto will be so too, &c.

April 3, 1711. — I was this morning to see Mrs Barton; I love her better than any one here, and see her seldomer. Why, really now, so it often happens in the world, that where one loves a body best — pshah, pshah, you are so silly with your moral observations. — Well, but she told me a very good story. An old gentlewoman died here two months ago, and left in her will to have eight men and eight maids bearers, who should have two guineas apiece, ten guineas to the parson for a sermon, and two guineas to the clerk. But bearers, parson, and clerk must be all true virgins; and not to be admitted till they took their oaths of virginity: so the poor woman lies still unburied, and so must do till the general resurrection. I called at Mr Secretary, to see what the d—— ailed him on Sunday; I made him a very proper speech, told him 'I observed he was much out of temper; that I did not expect he would tell me the cause, but would be glad to see he was in better'; and one thing I warned him of, 'never to appear cold to me, for I would not be treated like a schoolboy; that I had felt too much of that in my life already (meaning Sir William Temple), that I expected every great minister, who honoured me with his acquaintance, if he heard or saw anything to my disadvantage, would let me know in plain words, and not put me in pain to guess by the change or coldness of his countenance or behaviour; for it was what I would hardly bear from a crowned head, and I thought no subject's favour was worth it; and that I designed to let my Lord Keeper and Mr Harley know the same thing, that they might use me accordingly.' He took all right; said 'I had reason'; vowed 'nothing ailed him but sitting up whole nights at business, and one night at drinking'; would have had me dine with him and Mrs Masham's brother, to make up matters, but I would not. I don't know, but I would not. But indeed I was engaged with my old friend Rollinson: you never heard of him before.

August 25, 1711. — I was with the Secretary this morning, who was in a mighty hurry, and went to Windsor in a chariot with Lord Keeper; so I was not invited, and am forced to stay at home, but not at all against my will; for I could have gone, and would not. I dined in the City with one of my printers, for whom I got *The Gazette*, and am come home early; and have nothing to say to you more, but finish this letter, and not send it by the bellman. Days grow short, and the weather grows bad, and the town is splenetic, and things are so oddly contrived, that I cannot be absent; otherwise I would go for a few days to Oxford, as I promised. They say, 't is certain that Prior has been in France; nobody doubts it: I had not time to ask the Secretary, he was in such haste. Well, I will take my leave of dearest MD for a while; for I must begin my next letter to-night: consider that, young women; and pray be merry, and good girls, and love Presto. There is now but one business the ministry wants me for; and when that is done, I will take my leave of them. I never got a penny from them, nor expect it. In my opinion, some things stand very ticklish; I dare say nothing at this distance. Farewell, dear sirrahs, dearest lives: there is peace and quiet with MD, and nowhere else. They have not leisure here to think of small things, which may ruin them; and I have been forward enough. Farewell again, dearest rogues: I am never happy but when I write or think of MD. I have enough of courts and ministers; and wish I were at Laracor; and if I could with honour come away this moment, I would. Bernage came to see me to-day; he is just landed from Portugal, and come to raise recruits; he looks very well, and seems pleased with his station and manner of life: he never saw London nor England before; he is ravished with Kent, which was his first prospect when he landed. Farewell again, &c., &c.

December 1, 1711. — Pish! sirrahs, put a date always at the bottom of your letter, as well as the top, that I may know when you send it; your last is of November 3, yet I had others at the same time, written a fortnight after. Whenever you would have any money, send me word three weeks before, and in that time you will certainly have an answer, with a bill on Parvisol: pray do this; for my head is full, and it will ease my memory. Why, I think I quoted to you some of ——'s letter, so you may imagine how witty the rest was; for it was all of a bunch, as goodman Peesley says. Pray let us have no more *bussiness*, but *busyness:* the deuce take me if I know how to spell it; your wrong spelling, Madam Stella, has put me out: it does not look right; let me see, *bussiness, busyness, business, bisyness, bisness, bysness;* faith, I know not which is right, I think the second; I believe I never writ the word in my life before; yes, sure I must, though; *business, busyness, bisyness.* ——I have perplexed myself, and can't do it. Prithee ask Walls. *Business*, I fancy that's right. Yes it is; I looked in my own pamphlet, and found it twice in ten lines, to convince you that I never writ it before. O, now I see it as plain as can be; so yours is only an *s* too much. The Parliament will certainly meet on Friday next; the Whigs will have a great majority in the House of Lords, no care is taken to prevent it; there is too much neglect; they are warned of it, and that signifies nothing: it was feared there would be some peevish address from the Lords against a peace. 'T is said about the town that several of the allies begin now to be content that a peace should be treated. This is all the news I have. The Queen is pretty well; and so now I bid poor dearest MD farewell till to-night, then I will talk with them again.

March 27, 1713. — Parnell's poem is mightily esteemed; but poetry sells ill. I am plagued with that — poor Harrison's mother; you would laugh to see how cautious I am of paying her the £100 I received for her son from the Treasury. I have asked every creature I know whether I may do it safely; yet durst not venture till my Lord Keeper assured me there was no danger. Yet I have not paid her, but will in a day or two: though I have a great mind to stay till Ppt sends me her opinion, because Ppt is a great lawyer. I dined to-day with a mixture of people at a Scotchman's, who made the invitation to Mr. Lewis and me, and has some design upon us, which we know very well. I went afterward to see a famous moving picture, and I never saw anything so pretty. You see a sea ten inches wide, a town at the other end, and ships sailing in the sea and discharging their cannon. You see a great sky, with moon and stars, etc. I am a fool. Night, dear MD.

April 15, 1713. — Lord Bolingbroke made me dine with him to-day; I was as good company as ever; and [he] told me the Queen would determine something for me to-night. The dispute is, Windsor or St Patrick's. I told him I would not stay for their disputes, and he thought I was in the right. Lord Masham told me that Lady Masham is angry I have not been to see her since this business, and desires I will come to-morrow. Night, dear MD.

April 16, 1713.— I was this noon at Lady Masham's, who was just come from Kensington, where her eldest son is sick. She said much to me of what she had talked to the Queen and Lord Treasurer. The poor lady fell a-shedding tears openly. She could not bear to think of my having St Patrick's, etc. I was never more moved than to see so much friendship. I would not stay with her, but went and dined with Dr Arbuthnot, with Mr Berkeley, one of your Fellows, whom I have recommended to the Doctor and to Lord Berkeley of Stratton. Mr Lewis tells me that the Duke of Ormond has been to-day with the Queen; and she was content that Dr Sterne should be Bishop of Dromore and I Dean of St Patrick's; but then out came Lord Treasurer, and said he would not be satisfied, but that I must be prebendary of Windsor. Thus he perplexes things. I expect neither; but I confess, as much as I love England, I am so angry at this treatment, that, if I had my choice, I would rather have St Patrick's. Lady Masham says she will speak to the purpose to the Queen to-morrow. Night, dear MD.

April 26, 1713. — I was at Court to-day, and a thousand people gave me joy; so I ran out. I dined with Lady Orkney. Yesterday I dined with Lord Treasurer and his Saturday people as usual; and was so bedeaned! The Archbishop of York says he will never more speak against me. Pray see that Parvisol stirs about getting my patent. I have given Tooke DD's note to prove she is alive.

AGE OF POPE

POETRY

Joseph Addison (1672–1719)

THE CAMPAIGN

While crowds of princes your deserts proclaim,
Proud in their number to enrol your name;
While emperors to you commit their cause,
And Anna's praises crown the vast applause;
Accept, great leader, what the Muse recites,
That in ambitious verse attempts your fights.
Fired and transported with a theme so new,
Ten thousand wonders opening to my view,
Shine forth at once; sieges and storms appear,
And wars and conquests fill the important year,
Rivers of blood I see, and hills of slain,
An Iliad rising out of one campaign.
The haughty Gaul beheld, with towering pride,
His ancient bounds enlarged on every side,
Pirene's lofty barriers were subdued,
And in the midst of his wide empire stood;
Ausonia's states, the victor to restrain,
Opposed their Alps and Apennines in vain,
Nor found themselves, with strength of rocks immured,
Behind their everlasting hills secured;
The rising Danube its long race began,
And half its course through the new conquests ran;
Amazed and anxious for her sovereign's fates,
Germania trembled through a hundred states;
Great Leopold himself was seized with fear;
He gazed around, but saw no succour near;
He gazed, and half abandoned to despair
His hopes on Heaven, and confidence in prayer.
To Britain's queen the nations turn their eyes,
On her resolves the Western world relies,
Confiding still, amidst its dire alarms,
In Anna's councils and in Churchill's arms.
Thrice happy Britain, from the kingdoms rent
To sit the guardian of the continent!
That sees her bravest son advanced so high,
And flourishing so near her prince's eye;
Thy favourites grow not up by fortune's sport,
Or from the crimes or follies of a court;
On the firm basis of desert they rise,
From long-tried faith, and friendship's holy ties:
Their sovereign's well-distinguished smiles they share,
Her ornaments in peace, her strength in war;
The nation thanks them with a public voice,
By showers of blessings Heaven approves their choice;
Envy itself is dumb, in wonder lost,
And factions strive who shall applaud them most.
Soon as soft vernal breezes warm the sky,
Britannia's colours in the zephyrs fly;
Her chief already has his march begun,
Crossing the provinces himself had won,
Till the Moselle, appearing from afar,
Retards the progress of the moving war.
Delightful stream, had Nature hid her fall
In distant climes, far from the perjured Gaul;
But now a purchase to the sword she lies,
Her harvests for uncertain owners rise,
Each vineyard doubtful of its master grows,
And to the victor's bowl each vintage flows.
The discontented shades of slaughtered hosts,
That wandered on her banks, her heroes' ghosts,
Hoped, when they saw Britannia's arms appear,
The vengeance due to their great deaths was near.

Our godlike leader, ere the stream he passed,
The mighty scheme of all his labours cast,
Forming the wondrous year within his thought;
His bosom glowed with battles yet unfought.
The long, laborious march he first surveys,
And joins the distant Danube to the Maese,
Between whose floods such pathless forests grow,
Such mountains rise, so many rivers flow:
The toil looks lovely in the hero's eyes,
And danger serves but to enhance the prize.

Big with the fate of Europe, he renews
His dreadful course, and the proud foe pursues:
Infected by the burning Scorpion's heat,
The sultry gales round his chafed temples beat,
Till on the borders of the Maine he finds
Defensive shadows and refreshing winds.
Our British youth, with inborn freedom bold,
Unnumbered scenes of servitude behold,
Nations of slaves, with tyranny debased,
(Their Maker's image more than half defaced,)
Hourly instructed, as they urge their toil,
To prize their queen, and love their native soil.

Still to the rising sun they take their way
Through clouds of dust, and gain upon the day;
When now the Neckar on its friendly coast,
With cooling streams revives the fainting host,
That cheerfully its labours past forgets,
The midnight watches, and the noonday heats.

O'er prostrate towns and palaces they pass,
(Now covered o'er with weeds and hid in grass,)
Breathing revenge; whilst anger and disdain
Fire every breast, and boil in every vein:
Here shattered walls, like broken rocks, from far
Rise up in hideous views, the guilt of war,
Whilst here the vine o'er hills of ruin climbs,
Industrious to conceal great Bourbon's crimes.

At length the fame of England's hero drew
Eugenio to the glorious interview.
Great souls by instinct to each other turn,
Demand alliance, and in friendship burn;
A sudden friendship, while with stretched-out rays
They meet each other, mingling blaze with blaze.
Polished in courts, and hardened in the field,
Renowned for conquest, and in council skilled.
Their courage dwells not in a troubled flood
Of mounting spirits, and fermenting blood:
Lodged in the soul, with virtue overruled,
Inflamed by reason, and by reason cooled,
In hours of peace content to be unknown,
And only in the field of battle shown:
To souls like these, in mutual friendship joined,
Heaven dares intrust the cause of humankind.

Britannia's graceful sons appear in arms,
Her harassed troops the hero's presence warms,
Whilst the high hills and rivers all around
With thundering peals of British shouts resound:
Doubling their speed, they march with fresh delight,
Eager for glory, and require the fight.
So the staunch hound the trembling deer pursues,
And smells his footsteps in the tainted dews,
The tedious track unravelling by degrees:
But when the scent comes warm in every breeze,
Fired at the near approach, he shoots away
On his full stretch, and bears upon his prey.

The march concludes, the various realms are past,
The immortal Schellenberg appears at last:
Like hills the aspiring ramparts rise on high,
Like valleys at their feet the trenches lie:
Batteries on batteries guard each fatal pass,
Threatening destruction; rows of hollow brass,
Tube behind tube, the dreadful entrance keep,
Whilst in their wombs ten thousand thunders sleep:
Great Churchill owns, charmed with the glorious sight,
His march o'erpaid by such a promised fight.

The western sun now shot a feeble ray,
And faintly scattered the remains of day;
Evening approached; but, oh! what hosts of foes
Were never to behold that evening close!
Thickening their ranks, and wedged in firm array,

The close-compacted Britons win their way:
In vain the cannon their thronged war defaced
With tracks of death, and laid the battle waste;
Still pressing forward to the fight, they broke
Through flames of sulphur, and a night of smoke,
Till slaughtered legions filled the trench below,
And bore their fierce avengers to the foe.
High on the works the mingling hosts engage;
The battle, kindled into tenfold rage
With showers of bullets and with storms of fire,
Burns in full fury; heaps on heaps expire;
Nations with nations mixed confusedly die,
And lost in one promiscuous carnage lie.
How many generous Britons meet their doom,
New to the field, and heroes in the bloom!
The illustrious youths, that left their native shore
To march where Britons never marched before,
(O fatal love of fame! O glorious heat,
Only destructive to the brave and great!)
After such toils o'ercome, such dangers past,
Stretched on Bavarian ramparts breathe their last.
But hold, my Muse, may no complaints appear,
Nor blot the day with an ungrateful tear:
While Marlborough lives, Britannia's stars dispense
A friendly light, and shine in innocence.
Plunging through seas of blood his fiery steed
Where'er his friends retire, or foes succeed;
Those he supports, these drives to sudden flight,
And turns the various fortune of the fight.
Forbear, great man, renowned in arms, forbear
To brave the thickest terrors of the war,
Nor hazard thus, confused in crowds of foes,
Britannia's safety, and the world's repose;
Let nations, anxious for thy life, abate
This scorn of danger and contempt of fate:
Thou livest not for thyself; thy queen demands
Conquest and peace from thy victorious hands;
Kingdoms and empires in thy fortune join,
And Europe's destiny depends on thine.
At length the long-disputed pass they gain,
By crowded armies fortified in vain;
The way breaks in, the fierce Bavarians yield,
And see their camp with British legions filled.
So Belgian mounds bear on their shattered sides
The sea's whole weight, increased with swelling tides;
But if the rushing wave a passage finds,
Enraged by watery moons, and warring winds,
The trembling peasant sees his country round
Covered with tempests, and in oceans drowned.
The few surviving foes dispersed in flight,
(Refuse of swords, and gleanings of a fight,)
In every rustling wind the victor hear,
And Marlborough's form in every shadow fear,
Till the dark cope of night with kind embrace
Befriends the rout, and covers their disgrace.
To Donawert, with unresisted force,
The gay, victorious army bends its course.
The growth of meadows, and the pride of fields,
Whatever spoils Bavaria's summer yields,
(The Danube's great increase,) Britannia shares,
The food of armies, and support of wars:
With magazines of death, destructive balls,
And cannons doomed to batter Landau's walls,
The victor finds each hidden cavern stored,
And turns their fury on their guilty lord.
Deluded prince! how is thy greatness crossed,
And all the gaudy dream of empire lost,
That proudly set thee on a fancied throne,
And made imaginary realms thy own!
Thy troops that now behind the Danube join,
Shall shortly seek for shelter from the Rhine,
Nor find it there: surrounded with alarms,
Thou hop'st the assistance of the Gallic arms;
The Gallic arms in safety shall advance,
And crowd thy standards with the power of France,
While to exalt thy doom, the aspiring Gaul
Shares thy destruction, and adorns thy fall.
Unbounded courage and compassion joined,
Tempering each other in the victor's mind,

Alternately proclaim him good and great,
And make the hero and the man complete.
Long did he strive the obdurate foe to gain
By proffered grace, but long he strove in vain:
Till fired at length, he thinks it vain to spare
His rising wrath, and gives a loose to war.
In vengeance roused, the soldier fills his hand
With sword and fire, and ravages the land,
A thousand villages to ashes turns,
In crackling flames a thousand harvests burns.
To the thick woods the woolly flocks retreat,
And mixed with bellowing herds confusedly bleat;
Their trembling lords the common shade partake,
And cries of infants sound in every brake:
The listening soldier fixed in sorrow stands,
Loth to obey his leader's just commands;
The leader grieves, by generous pity swayed,
To see his just commands so well obeyed.
  But now the trumpet, terrible from far,
In shriller clangors animates the war,
Confederate drums in fuller concert beat,
And echoing hills the loud alarm repeat:
Gallia's proud standards, to Bavaria's joined,
Unfurl their gilded lilies in the wind;
The daring prince his blasted hopes renews,
And while the thick embattled host he views
Stretched out in deep array, and dreadful length,
His heart dilates, and glories in his strength.
  The fatal day its mighty course began,
That the grieved world had long desired in vain:
States that their new captivity bemoaned,
Armies of martyrs that in exile groaned,
Sighs from the depth of gloomy dungeons heard,
And prayers in bitterness of soul preferred,
Europe's loud cries, that Providence assailed,
And Anna's ardent vows, at length prevailed;
The day was come when Heaven designed to show
His care and conduct of the world below.
  Behold, in awful march and dread array
The long-expected squadrons shape their way!
Death, in approaching terrible, imparts
An anxious horror to the bravest hearts;
Yet do their beating breasts demand the strife,
And thirst of glory quells the love of life.
No vulgar fears can British minds control:
Heat of revenge and noble pride of soul
O'erlook the foe, advantaged by his post,
Lessen his numbers, and contract his host.
Though fens and floods possessed the middle space,
That unprovoked they would have feared to pass,
Nor fens nor floods can stop Britannia's bands,
When her proud foe ranged on their borders stands.
  But, O my Muse, what numbers wilt thou find
To sing the furious troops in battle joined!
Methinks I hear the drum's tumultuous sound
The victor's shouts and dying groans confound,
The dreadful burst of cannon rend the skies,
And all the thunder of the battle rise.
'T was then great Marlborough's mighty soul was proved,
That, in the shock of charging hosts unmoved,
Amidst confusion, horror, and despair,
Examined all the dreadful scenes of war;
In peaceful thought the field of death surveyed,
To fainting squadrons sent the timely aid,
Inspired repulsed battalions to engage,
And taught the doubtful battle where to rage.
So when an angel by divine command
With rising tempests shakes a guilty land,
Such as of late o'er pale Britannia passed,
Calm and serene he drives the furious blast;
And, pleased the Almighty's orders to perform,
Rides in the whirlwind, and directs the storm.
  But see the haughty household-troops advance!
The dread of Europe, and the pride of France.
The war's whole art each private soldier knows,
And with a general's love of conquest glows;
Proudly he marches on, and, void of fear,
Laughs at the shaking of the British spear:
Vain insolence! with native freedom brave,
The meanest Briton scorns the highest slave:
Contempt and fury fire their souls by turns,
Each nation's glory in each warrior burns,
Each fights, as in his arm the important day

And all the fate of his great monarch lay:
A thousand glorious actions, that might claim
Triumphant laurels, and immortal fame,
Confused in clouds of glorious actions lie,
And troops of heroes undistinguished die.
O Dormer, how can I behold thy fate,
And not the wonders of thy youth relate!
How can I see the gay, the brave, the young,
Fall in the cloud of war and lie unsung!
In joys of conquest he resigns his breath,
And, filled with England's glory, smiles in death.

The rout begins, the Gallic squadrons run,
Compelled in crowds to meet the fate they shun;
Thousands of fiery steeds with wounds transfixed
Floating in gore, with their dead masters mixed,
Midst heaps of spears and standards driven around,
Lie in the Danube's bloody whirlpools drowned,
Troops of bold youths, born on the distant Soane,
Or sounding borders of the rapid Rhone.
Or where the Seine her flowery fields divides,
Or where the Loire through winding vineyards glides;
In heaps the rolling billows sweep away,
And into Scythian seas their bloated corps convey.
From Blenheim's towers the Gaul, with wild affright,
Beholds the various havoc of the fight;
His waving banners, that so oft had stood,
Planted in fields of death, and streams of blood,
So wont the guarded enemy to reach,
And rise triumphant in the fatal breach,
Or pierce the broken foe's remotest lines,
The hardy veteran with tears resigns.

Unfortunate Tallard! Oh, who can name
The pangs of rage, of sorrow, and of shame,
That with mixed tumult in thy bosom swelled!
When first thou sawest thy bravest troops repelled,
Thine only son pierced with a deadly wound,
Choked in his blood, and gasping on the ground,
Thyself in bondage by the victor kept!
The chief, the father, and the captive wept.
An English Muse is touched with generous woe,
And in the unhappy man forgets the foe.
Greatly distressed! thy loud complaints forbear,
Blame not the turns of fate, and chance of war;
Give thy brave foes their due, nor blush to own
The fatal field by such great leaders won,
The field whence famed Eugenio bore away
Only the second honours of the day.

With floods of gore that from the vanquished fell,
The marshes stagnate, and the rivers swell.
Mountains of slain lie heaped upon the ground,
Or 'midst the roarings of the Danube drowned;
Whole captive hosts the conqueror detains
In painful bondage and inglorious chains;
Even those who 'scape the fetters and the sword,
Nor seek the fortunes of a happier lord,
Their raging king dishonours, to complete
Marlborough's great work, and finish the defeat.

From Memminghen's high domes, and Augsburg's walls,
The distant battle drives the insulting Gauls;
Freed by the terror of the victor's name,
The rescued States his great protection claim;
Whilst Ulm the approach of her deliverer waits,
And longs to open her obsequious gates.

The hero's breast still swells with great designs,
In every thought the towering genius shines:
If to the foe his dreadful course he bends,
O'er the wide continent his march extends;
If sieges in his laboring thoughts are formed,
Camps are assaulted, and an army stormed;
If to the fight his active soul is bent,
The fate of Europe turns on its event.
What distant land, what region, can afford
An action worthy his victorious sword?
Where will he next the flying Gaul defeat,
To make the series of his toils complete?

Where the swoln Rhine, rushing with all its force,
Divides the hostile nations in its course,
While each contracts its bounds, or wider grows,
Enlarged or straitened as the river flows,
On Gallia's side a mighty bulwark stands,

That all the wide extended plain commands;
Twice, since the war was kindled, has it tried
The victor's rage, and twice has changed its side;
As oft whole armies, with the prize o'erjoyed,
Have the long summer on its walls employed.
Hither our mighty chief his arms directs,
Hence future triumphs from the war expects;
And though the dog-star had its course begun,
Carries his arms still nearer to the sun:
Fixed on the glorious action, he forgets
The change of seasons, and increase of heats:
No toils are painful that can danger show,
No climes unlovely that contain a foe.
The roving Gaul, to his own bounds restrained,
Learns to encamp within his native land,
But soon as the victorious host he spies,
From hill to hill, from stream to stream he flies:
Such dire impressions in his heart remain
Of Marlborough's sword, and Hochstet's fatal plain:
In vain Britannia's mighty chief besets
Their shady coverts, and obscure retreats;
They fly the conqueror's approaching fame,
That bears the force of armies in his name.
Austria's young monarch, whose imperial sway
Sceptres and thrones are destined to obey,
Whose boasted ancestry so high extends
That in the pagan gods his lineage ends,
Comes from afar, in gratitude to own
The great supporter of his father's throne;
What tides of glory to his bosom ran,
Clasped in the embraces of the godlike man!
How were his eyes with pleasing wonder fixed
To see such fire with so much sweetness mixed,
Such easy greatness, such a graceful port,
So turned and finished for the camp or court!
Achilles thus was formed with every grace,
And Nireus shone but in the second place;
Thus the great father of almighty Rome
(Divinely flushed with an immortal bloom,
That Cytherea's fragrant breath bestowed)
In all the charms of his bright mother glowed.
The royal youth by Marlborough's presence charmed,
Taught by his counsels, by his actions warmed,
On Landau with redoubled fury falls,
Discharges all his thunder on its walls,
O'er mines and caves of death provokes the fight,
And learns to conquer in the hero's sight.
The British chief, for mighty toils renowned,
Increased with titles, and with conquests crowned,
To Belgian coasts his tedious march renews,
And the long windings of the Rhine pursues,
Clearing its borders from usurping foes,
And blessed by rescued nations as he goes.
Treves fears no more, freed from its dire alarms;
And Traerbach feels the terror of his arms,
Seated on rocks her proud foundations shake,
While Marlborough presses to the bold attack,
Plants all his batteries, bids his cannon roar,
And shows how Landau might have fallen before.
Scared at his near approach, Great Louis fears
Vengeance reserved for his declining years,
Forgets his thirst of universal sway,
And scarce can teach his subjects to obey;
His arms he finds on vain attempts employed,
The ambitious projects for his race destroyed,
The work of ages sunk in one campaign,
And lives of millions sacrificed in vain.
Such are the effects of Anna's royal cares:
By her, Britannia, great in foreign wars,
Ranges through nations, wheresoe'er disjoined,
Without the wonted aid of sea and wind.
By her the unfettered Ister's states are free,
And taste the sweets of English liberty:
But who can tell the joys of those that lie
Beneath the constant influence of her eye!
Whilst in diffusive showers her bounties fall,
Like heaven's indulgence, and descend on all,
Secure the happy, succour the distressed,
Make every subject glad, and a whole people blessed.
Thus would I fain Britannia's wars rehearse,
In the smooth records of a faithful verse;

That, if such numbers can o'er time prevail,
May tell posterity the wondrous tale.
When actions, unadorned, are faint and weak,
Cities and countries must be taught to speak;
Gods may descend in factions from the skies,
And rivers from their oozy beds arise;
Fiction may deck the truth with spurious rays,
And round the hero cast a hallowed blaze.
Marlborough's exploits appear divinely bright,
And proudly shine in their own native light;
Raised of themselves, their genuine charms they boast,
And those who paint them truest praise them most.

1704

Alexander Pope (1688–1744)

AN ESSAY ON CRITICISM

I

'T is hard to say if greater want of skill
Appear in writing or in judging ill;
But of the two less dangerous is th' offense
To tire our patience than mislead our sense:
Some few in that, but numbers err in this;
Ten censure wrong for one who writes amiss;
A fool might once himself alone expose;
Now one in verse makes many more in prose.
'T is with our judgments as our watches, none
Go just alike, yet each believes his own.
In Poets as true Genius is but rare,
True Taste as seldom is the Critic's share;
Both must alike from Heav'n derive their light,
These born to judge, as well as those to write.
Let such teach others who themselves excel,
And censure freely who have written well;
Authors are partial to their wit, 't is true,
But are not Critics to their judgment too?
Yet if we look more closely, we shall find
Most have the seeds of judgment in their mind:
Nature affords at least a glimm'ring light;
The lines, though touched but faintly, are drawn right.
But as the slightest sketch, if justly traced,
Is by ill col'ring but the more disgraced,
So by false learning is good sense defaced:
Some are bewildered in the maze of schools,
And some made coxcombs Nature meant but fools:
In search of wit these lose their common sense,
And then turn Critics in their own defense:
Each burns alike, who can, or cannot write,
Or with a rival's or an eunuch's spite.
All fools have still an itching to deride,
And fain would be upon the laughing side.
If Mævius scribble in Apollo's spite,
There are who judge still worse than he can write.
Some have at first for Wits, then Poets passed,
Turned Critics next, and proved plain Fools at last.
Some neither can for Wits nor Critics pass,
As heavy mules are neither horse nor ass.
Those half-learned witlings, numerous in our isle,
As half-formed insects on the banks of Nile;
Unfinished things, one knows not what to call,
Their generation's so equivocal;
To tell them, would a hundred tongues require,
Or one vain Wit's, that might a hundred tire.
But you who seek to give and merit fame,
And justly bear a Critic's noble name,
Be sure yourself and your own reach to know,
How far your Genius, Taste, and Learning go,
Launch not beyond your depth, but be discreet,
And mark that point where Sense and Dulness meet.
Nature to all things fixed the limits fit,
And wisely curbed proud man's pretending wit.
As on the land while here the ocean gains,
In other parts it leaves wide sandy plains;
Thus in the soul while Memory prevails,
The solid power of Understanding fails;
Where beams of warm Imagination play,
The Memory's soft figures melt away.
One Science only will one genius fit;
So vast is Art, so narrow human wit:
Not only bounded to peculiar arts,
But oft in those confined to single parts.
Like Kings we lose the conquests gained before,
By vain ambition still to make them more:

Each might his sev'ral province well command,
Would all but stoop to what they understand.
First follow Nature, and your judgment frame
By her just standard, which is still the same;
Unerring Nature, still divinely bright,
One clear, unchanged, and universal light,
Life, force, and beauty, must to all impart,
At once the source, and end, and test of Art.
Art from that fund each just supply provides,
Works without show, and without pomp presides.
In some fair body thus th' informing soul
With spirits feeds, with vigour fills the whole;
Each motion guides, and every nerve sustains,
Itself unseen, but in th' effects remains.
Some, to whom Heav'n in wit has been profuse,
Want as much more to turn it to its use;
For Wit and Judgment often are at strife,
Though meant each other's aid, like man and wife.
'T is more to guide than spur the Muse's steed,
Restrain his fury than provoke his speed:
The wingèd courser, like a gen'rous horse,
Shows most true mettle when you check his course.
Those rules of old, discovered, not devised,
Are Nature still, but Nature methodized;
Nature, like Liberty, is but restrained
By the same laws which first herself ordained.
Hear how learned Greece her useful rules indites
When to repress and when indulge our flights:
High on Parnassus' top her sons she showed,
And pointed out those arduous paths they trod;
Held from afar, aloft, th' immortal prize,
And urged the rest by equal steps to rise.
Just precepts thus from great examples giv'n,
She drew from them what they derived from Heav'n.
The gen'rous Critic fanned the poet's fire,
And taught the world with reason to admire.
Then Criticism the Muses' handmaid proved,
To dress her charms, and make her more beloved:
But following Wits from that intention strayed:
Who could not win the mistress wooed the maid;
Against the Poets their own arms they turned,
Sure to hate most the men from whom they learned.
So modern 'pothecaries, taught the art
By doctors' bills to play the doctor's part,
Bold in the practice of mistaken rules,
Prescribe, apply, and call their masters fools.
Some on the leaves of ancient authors prey;
Nor time nor moths e'er spoiled so much as they;
Some drily plain, without invention's aid,
Write dull receipts how poems may be made;
These leave the sense their learning to display,
And those explain the meaning quite away.
You then whose judgment the right course would steer,
Know well each ancient's proper character;
His fable, subject, scope in every page;
Religion, country, genius of his age:
Without all these at once before your eyes,
Cavil you may, but never criticise.
Be Homer's works your study and delight,
Read them by day, and meditate by night;
Thence form your judgment, thence your maxims bring,
And trace the Muses upward to their spring.
Still with itself compared, his text peruse;
And let your comment be the Mantuan Muse.
When first young Maro in his boundless mind
A work t' outlast immortal Rome designed,
Perhaps he seemed above the critic's law,
And but from nature's fountains scorned to draw;
But when t' examine ev'ry part he came,
Nature and Homer were, he found, the same.
Convinced, amazed, he checks the bold design,
And rules as strict his laboured work confine
As if the Stagyrite o'erlooked each line.
Learn hence for ancient rules a just esteem;
To copy Nature is to copy them.
Some beauties yet no precepts can declare,
For there's a happiness as well as care.
Music resembles poetry; in each
Are nameless graces which no methods teach,
And which a master-hand alone can reach.
If, where the rules not far enough extend,
(Since rules were made but to promote their end)

Some lucky license answer to the full
Th' intent proposed, that license is a rule.
Thus Pegasus, a nearer way to take,
May boldly deviate from the common track;
From vulgar bounds with brave disorder part,
And snatch a grace beyond the reach of Art,
Which, without passing through the judgment, gains
The heart, and all its end at once attains.
In prospects thus some objects please our eyes,
Which out of Nature's common order rise,
The shapeless rock, or hanging precipice.
Great Wits sometimes may gloriously offend,
And rise to faults true Critics dare not mend.
But though the ancients thus their rules invade,
(As Kings dispense with laws themselves have made)
Moderns, beware! or if you must offend
Against the precept, ne'er transgress its end;
Let it be seldom, and compelled by need;
And have at least their precedent to plead;
The Critic else proceeds without remorse,
Seizes your fame, and puts his laws in force.
I know there are to whose presumptuous thoughts
Those freer beauties, ev'n in them, seem faults.
Some figures monstrous and misshaped appear,
Considered singly, or beheld too near,
Which, but proportioned to their light or place,
Due distance reconciles to form and grace.
A prudent chief not always must display
His powers in equal ranks and fair array,
But with th' occasion and the place comply,
Conceal his force, nay, seem sometimes to fly.
Those oft are stratagems which errors seem,
Nor is it Homer nods, but we that dream.
Still green with bays each ancient altar stands
Above the reach of sacrilegious hands,
Secure from flames, from Envy's fiercer rage,
Destructive war, and all-involving Age.
See from each clime the learned their incense bring!
Hear in all tongues consenting pæans ring!
In praise so just let ev'ry voice be joined,
And fill the gen'ral chorus of mankind.
Hail, Bards triumphant! born in happier days,
Immortal heirs of universal praise!
Whose honours with increase of ages grow,
As streams roll down, enlarging as they flow;
Nations unborn your mighty names shall sound,
And worlds applaud that must not yet be found!
Oh, may some spark of your celestial fire
The last, the meanest of your sons inspire,
(That on weak wings, from far, pursues your flights,
Glows while he reads, but trembles as he writes)
To teach vain Wits a science little known,
T' admire superior sense, and doubt their own!

II

Of all the causes which conspire to blind
Man's erring judgment, and misguide the mind,
What the weak head with strongest bias rules,
Is Pride, the never failing vice of fools.
Whatever Nature has in worth denied
She gives in large recruits of needful Pride:
For as in bodies, thus in souls, we find
What wants in blood and spirits swelled with wind:
Pride, where Wit fails, steps in to our defence,
And fills up all the mighty void of Sense:
If once right Reason drives that cloud away,
Truth breaks upon us with resistless day.
Trust not yourself; but your defects to know,
Make use of ev'ry friend — and ev'ry foe.
A little learning is a dangerous thing;
Drink deep, or taste not the Pierian spring:
There shallow draughts intoxicate the brain,
And drinking largely sobers us again.
Fired at first sight with what the Muse imparts,
In fearless youth we tempt the heights of arts,
While from the bounded level of our mind
Short views we take, nor see the lengths behind:
But more advanced, behold with strange surprise
New distant scenes of endless science rise!
So pleased at first the tow'ring Alps we try,
Mount o'er the vales, and seem to tread the sky;
Th' eternal snows appear already past,

And the first clouds and mountains seem the last:
But, those attained, we tremble to survey
The growing labours of the lengthened way;
Th' increasing prospect tires our wand'ring eyes,
Hills peep o'er hills, and Alps on Alps arise!
A perfect judge will read each work of wit
With the same spirit that its author writ;
Survey the whole, nor seek slight faults to find
Where Nature moves, and Rapture warms the mind:
Nor lose, for that malignant dull delight,
The gen'rous pleasure to be charmed with wit.
But in such lays as neither ebb nor flow,
Correctly cold, and regularly low,
That shunning faults one quiet tenor keep,
We cannot blame indeed — but we may sleep.
In Wit, as Nature, what affects our hearts
Is not th' exactness of peculiar parts;
'T is not a lip or eye we beauty call,
But the joint force and full result of all.
Thus when we view some well-proportioned dome,
(The world's just wonder, and ev'n thine, O Rome!)
No single parts unequally surprise,
All comes united to th' admiring eyes;
No monstrous height, or breadth, or length, appear;
The whole at once is bold, and regular.
Whoever thinks a faultless piece to see,
Thinks what ne'er was, nor is, nor e'er shall be.
In every work regard the writer's end,
Since none can compass more than they intend;
And if the means be just, the conduct true,
Applause, in spite of trivial faults, is due.
As men of breeding, sometimes men of wit,
T' avoid great errors must the less commit;
Neglect the rules each verbal critic lays,
For not to know some trifles is a praise.
Most critics, fond of some subservient art,
Still make the whole depend upon a part:
They talk of Principles, but Notions prize,
And all to one loved folly sacrifice.
Once on a time La Mancha's knight, they say,
A certain bard encount'ring on the way,
Discoursed in terms as just, with looks as sage,
As e'er could Dennis, of the Grecian stage;
Concluding all were desperate sots and fools
Who durst depart from Aristotle's rules.
Our author, happy in a judge so nice,
Produced his play, and begged the knight's advice;
Made him observe the Subject and the Plot,
The Manners, Passions, Unities; what not?
All which exact to rule were brought about,
Were but a combat in the lists left out.
'What! leave the combat out?' exclaims the knight.
'Yes, or we must renounce the Stagyrite.'
'Not so, by Heaven! (he answers in a rage)
Knights, squires, and steeds, must enter on the stage.'
'So vast a throng the stage can ne'er contain.'
'Then build a new, or act it in a plain.'
Thus critics of less judgment than caprice,
Curious, not knowing, not exact, but nice,
Form short ideas, and offend in Arts
(As most in Manners), by a love to parts.
Some to Conceit alone their taste confine,
And glitt'ring thoughts struck out at every line;
Pleased with a work where nothing's just or fit,
One glaring chaos and wild heap of wit.
Poets, like painters, thus unskilled to trace
The naked nature and the living grace,
With gold and jewels cover every part,
And hide with ornaments their want of Art.
True Wit is Nature to advantage dressed,
What oft was thought, but ne'er so well expressed;
Something whose truth convinced at sight we find,
That gives us back the image of our mind.
As shades more sweetly recommend the light,
So modest plainness sets off sprightly wit:
For works may have more wit than does 'em good,
As bodies perish through excess of blood.
Others for language all their care express,
And value books, as women men, for dress:
Their praise is still — the Style is excellent:
The Sense they humbly take upon content.
Words are like leaves; and where they most abound,
Much fruit of sense beneath is rarely found.
False eloquence, like the prismatic glass,
Its gaudy colours spreads on every place;

The face of Nature we no more survey,
All glares alike, without distinction gay;
But true expression, like th' unchanging sun,
Clears and improves whate'er it shines upon;
It gilds all objects, but it alters none.
Expression is the dress of thought, and still
Appears more decent as more suitable.
A vile Conceit in pompous words expressed,
Is like a clown in regal purple dressed:
For diff'rent styles with diff'rent subjects sort,
As sev'ral garbs with country, town, and court.
Some by old words to fame have made pretence,
Ancients in phrase, mere moderns in their sense;
Such laboured nothings, in so strange a style,
Amaze the unlearned, and make the learnèd smile;
Unlucky as Fungoso in the play,
These sparks with awkward vanity display
What the fine gentleman wore yesterday;
And but so mimic ancient wits at best,
As apes our grandsires in their doublets drest.
In words as fashions the same rule will hold,
Alike fantastic if too new or old:
Be not the first by whom the new are tried,
Nor yet the last to lay the old aside.
But most by Numbers judge a poet's song,
And smooth or rough with them is right or wrong.
In the bright Muse though thousand charms conspire,
Her voice is all these tuneful fools admire;
Who haunt Parnassus but to please their ear,
Not mend their minds; as some to church repair,
Not for the doctrine, but the music there.
These equal syllables alone require,
Though oft the ear the open vowels tire,
While expletives their feeble aid do join,
And ten low words oft creep in one dull line:
While they ring round the same unvaried chimes,
With sure returns of still expected rhymes;
Where'er you find 'the cooling western breeze,'
In the next line, it 'whispers through the trees';
If crystal streams 'with pleasing murmurs creep,'
The reader's threatened (not in vain) with 'sleep';
Then, at the last and only couplet, fraught
With some unmeaning thing they call a thought,
A needless Alexandrine ends the song,
That, like a wounded snake, drags its slow length along.
Leave such to tune their own dull rhymes, and know
What's roundly smooth, or languishingly slow;
And praise the easy vigour of a line
Where Denham's strength and Waller's sweetness join.
True ease in writing comes from Art, not Chance,
As those move easiest who have learned to dance.
'T is not enough no harshness gives offense;
The sound must seem an echo to the sense.
Soft is the strain when zephyr gently blows,
And the smooth stream in smoother numbers flows;
But when loud surges lash the sounding shore,
The hoarse rough verse should like the torrent roar.
When Ajax strives some rock's vast weight to throw,
The line, too, labours, and the words move slow;
Not so when swift Camilla scours the plain,
Flies o'er th' unbending corn, and skims along the main.
Hear how Timotheus' varied lays surprise,
And bid alternate passions fall and rise!
While at each change the son of Libyan Jove
Now burns with glory, and then melts with love;
Now his fierce eyes with sparkling fury glow,
Now sighs steal out, and tears begin to flow:
Persians and Greeks like turns of nature found,
And the world's Victor stood subdued by sound!
The power of music all our hearts allow,
And what Timotheus was is Dryden now.
Avoid extremes, and shun the fault of such
Who still are pleased too little or too much.
At every trifle scorn to take offence;
That always shows great pride or little sense:
Those heads, as stomachs, are not sure the best

Which nauseate all, and nothing can digest.
Yet let not each gay turn thy rapture move;
For fools admire, but men of sense approve:
As things seem large which we through mists descry,
Dulness is ever apt to magnify.
 Some foreign writers, some our own despise;
The ancients only, or the moderns prize.
Thus Wit, like Faith, by each man is applied
To one small sect, and all are damned beside.
Meanly they seek the blessing to confine,
And force that sun but on a part to shine,
Which not alone the southern wit sublimes,
But ripens spirits in cold northern climes;
Which from the first has shone on ages past,
Enlights the present, and shall warm the last;
Though each may feel increases and decays,
And see now clearer and now darker days.
Regard not then if wit be old or new,
But blame the False and value still the True.
 Some ne'er advance a judgment of their own,
But catch the spreading notion of the town;
They reason and conclude by precedent,
And own stale nonsense which they ne'er invent.
Some judge of authors' names, not works, and then
Nor praise nor blame the writings but the men.
Of all this servile herd, the worst is he
That in proud dullness joins with quality;
A constant critic at the great man's board,
To fetch and carry nonsense for my lord.
What woeful stuff this madrigal would be,
In some starved hackney sonneteer or me!
But let a lord once own the happy lines,
How the Wit brightens! how the Style refines!
Before his sacred name flies every fault,
And each exalted stanza teems with thought!
 The vulgar thus through imitation err,
As oft the learned by being singular;
So much they scorn the crowd, that if the throng
By chance go right, they purposely go wrong.
So schismatics the plain believers quit,
And are but damned for having too much wit.
Some praise at morning what they blame at night,
But always think the last opinion right.
A Muse by these is like a mistress used,
This hour she 's idolized, the next abused;
While their weak heads, like towns unfortified,
'Twixt sense and nonsense daily change their side.
Ask them the cause; they 're wiser still they say;
And still to-morrow 's wiser than to-day.
We think our fathers fools, so wise we grow;
Our wiser sons, no doubt, will think us so.
Once school-divines this zealous isle o'erspread;
Who knew most sentences was deepest read.
Faith, Gospel, all seemed made to be disputed,
And none had sense enough to be confuted.
Scotists and Thomists now in peace remain
Amidst their kindred cobwebs in Duck Lane.
If faith itself has diff'rent dresses worn,
What wonder modes in Wit should take their turn?
Oft, leaving what is natural and fit,
The current Folly proves the ready Wit;
And authors think their reputation safe,
Which lives as long as fools are pleased to laugh.
 Some, valuing those of their own side of mind,
Still make themselves the measure of mankind:
Fondly we think we honour merit then,
When we but praise ourselves in other men.
Parties in wit attend on those of state,
And public faction doubles private hate.
Pride, Malice, Folly, against Dryden rose,
In various shapes of parsons, critics, beaux;
But sense survived when merry jests were past;
For rising merit will buoy up at last.
Might he return and bless once more our eyes,
New Blackmores and new Milbourns must arise.
Nay, should great Homer lift his awful head,
Zoilus again would start up from the dead.
Envy will Merit as its shade pursue,
But like a shadow proves the substance true;
For envied Wit, like Sol eclipsed, makes known
Th' opposing body's grossness, not its own.

When first that sun too powerful beams displays,
It draws up vapours which obscure its rays;
But ev'n those clouds at last adorn its way,
Reflect new glories, and augment the day.
Be thou the first true merit to befriend;
His praise is lost, who stays till all commend.
Short is the date, alas! of modern rhymes,
And 't is but just to let them live betimes.
No longer now that Golden Age appears,
When patriarch wits survived a thousand years:
Now length of fame (our second life) is lost,
And bare threescore is all ev'n that can boast:
Our sons their fathers' failing language see,
And such as Chaucer is shall Dryden be.
So when the faithful pencil has designed
Some bright idea of the master's mind,
Where a new word leaps out at his command,
And ready Nature waits upon his hand;
When the ripe colours soften and unite,
And sweetly melt into just shade and light;
When mellowing years their full perfection give,
And each bold figure just begins to live,
The treach'rous colours the fair art betray,
And all the bright creation fades away!
Unhappy Wit, like most mistaken things,
Atones not for that envy which it brings:
In youth alone its empty praise we boast,
But soon the short-lived vanity is lost;
Like some fair flower the early Spring supplies,
That gaily blooms, but ev'n in blooming dies.
What is this Wit, which must our cares employ?
The owner's wife that other men enjoy;
Then most our trouble still when most admired,
And still the more we give, the more required;
Whose fame with pains we guard, but lose with ease,
Sure some to vex, but never all to please,
'T is what the vicious fear, the virtuous shun;
By fools 't is hated, and by knaves undone!
If Wit so much from Ignorance undergo,
Ah, let not Learning too commence its foe!
Of old those met rewards who could excel,
And such were praised who but endeavoured well;
Though triumphs were to gen'rals only due,
Crowns were reserved to grace the soldiers too.
Now they who reach Parnassus' lofty crown
Employ their pains to spurn some others down;
And while self-love each jealous writer rules,
Contending wits become the sport of fools;
But still the worst with most regret commend,
For each ill author is as bad a friend.
To what base ends, and by what abject ways,
Are mortals urged through sacred lust of praise!
Ah, ne'er so dire a thirst of glory boast,
Nor in the critic let the man be lost!
Good nature and good sense must ever join;
To err is human, to forgive divine.
But if in noble minds some dregs remain,
Not yet purged off, of spleen and sour disdain,
Discharge that rage on more provoking crimes,
Nor fear a dearth in these flagitious times.
No pardon vile obscenity should find,
Though Wit and Art conspire to move your mind;
But dulness with obscenity must prove
As shameful sure as impotence in love.
In the fat age of pleasure, wealth, and ease,
Sprung the rank weed, and thrived with large increase:
When love was all an easy monarch's care,
Seldom at council, never in a war;
Jilts ruled the state, and statesmen farces writ;
Nay wits had pensions, and young lords had wit;
The Fair sat panting at a courtier's play,
And not a mask went unimproved away;
The modest fan was lifted up no more,
And virgins smiled at what they blushed before.
The following license of a foreign reign
Did all the dregs of bold Socinus drain;
Then unbelieving priests reformed the nation,
And taught more pleasant methods of salvation;
Where Heav'n's free subjects might their rights dispute,
Lest God himself should seem too absolute;
Pulpits their sacred satire learned to spare,
And vice admired to find a flatt'rer there!
Encouraged thus, Wit's Titans braved the skies,
And the press groaned with licensed blasphemies.
These monsters, Critics! with your darts engage,

Here point your thunder, and exhaust your rage!
Yet shun their fault, who, scandalously nice,
Will needs mistake an author into vice:
All seems infected that th' infected spy,
As all looks yellow to the jaundiced eye.

III

Learn then what moral Critics ought to show,
For 't is but half a judge's task to know.
'T is not enough, Taste, Judgment, Learning join;
In all you speak, let Truth and Candour shine;
That not alone what to your Sense is due
All may allow, but seek your friendship too.
Be silent always when you doubt your Sense,
And speak, though sure, with seeming diffidence.
Some positive persisting fops we know,
Who if once wrong will needs be always so;
But you with pleasure own your errors past,
And make each day a critique on the last.
'T is not enough your counsel still be true;
Blunt truths more mischief than nice falsehoods do.
Men must be taught as if you taught them not,
And things unknown proposed as things forgot.
Without good breeding truth is disapproved;
That only makes superior Sense beloved.
Be niggards of advice on no pretence,
For the worst avarice is that of Sense.
With mean complacence ne'er betray your trust,
Nor be so civil as to prove unjust.
Fear not the anger of the wise to raise;
Those best can bear reproof who merit praise.
'T were well might critics still this freedom take,
But Appius reddens at each word you speak,
And stares tremendous, with a threat'ning eye,
Like some fierce tyrant in old tapestry.
Fear most to tax an honourable fool,
Whose right it is, uncensured to be dull:
Such without Wit, are poets when they please,
As without Learning they can take degrees.
Leave dangerous truths to unsuccessful satires,
And flattery to fulsome dedicators;
Whom, when they praise, the world believes no more
Than when they promise to give scribbling o'er.
'T is best sometimes your censure to restrain,
And charitably let the dull be vain;
Your silence there is better than your spite,
For who can rail so long as they can write?
Still humming on their drowsy course they keep,
And lashed so long, like tops, are lashed asleep.
False steps but help them to renew the race,
As, after stumbling, jades will mend their pace.
What crowds of these, impenitently bold,
In sounds and jingling syllables grown old,
Still run on poets, in a raging vein,
Ev'n to the dregs and squeezings of the brain,
Strain out the last dull droppings of their sense,
And rhyme with all the rage of impotence!
Such shameless bards we have; and yet 't is true
There are as mad abandoned critics too.
The bookful blockhead ignorantly read,
With loads of learnèd lumber in his head,
With his own tongue still edifies his ears,
And always list'ning to himself appears.
All books he reads, and all he reads assails,
From Dryden's Fables down to Durfey's Tales.
With him most authors steal their works, or buy;
Garth did not write his own Dispensary.
Name a new play, and he 's the poet's friend;
Nay, showed his faults — but when would poets mend?
No place so sacred from such fops is barred,
Nor is Paul's church more safe than Paul's churchyard:
Nay, fly to altars; there they 'll talk you dead,
For fools rush in where angels fear to tread.
Distrustful sense with modest caution speaks,
It still looks home, and short excursions makes;
But rattling nonsense in full volleys breaks
And never shocked, and never turned aside,
Bursts out, resistless, with a thund'ring tide.

But, where's the man who counsel can bestow,
Still pleased to teach, and yet not proud to know?
Unbiassed or by favour or by spite;
Not dully prepossessed nor blindly right;
Though learned, well bred; and though well bred sincere;
Modestly bold, and humanly severe;
Who to a friend his faults can freely show,
And gladly praise the merit of a foe;
Blessed with a taste exact, yet unconfined,
A knowledge both of books and human kind;
Gen'rous converse; a soul exempt from pride;
And love to praise, with reason on his side?
Such once were critics; such the happy few
Athens and Rome in better ages knew.
The mighty Stagyrite first left the shore,
Spread all his sails, and durst the deeps explore;
He steered securely, and discovered far,
Led by the light of the Mæonian star.
Poets, a race long unconfined and free,
Still fond and proud of savage liberty,
Received his laws, and stood convinced 't was fit,
Who conquered Nature, should preside o'er Wit.
  Horace still charms with graceful negligence,
And without method talks us into sense;
Will, like a friend, familiarly convey
The truest notions in the easiest way.
He who, supreme in judgment, as in wit,
Might boldly censure as he boldly writ,
Yet judged with coolness, though he sung with fire;
His precepts teach but what his works inspire.
Our critics take a contrary extreme,
They judge with fury, but they write with phlegm;
Nor suffers Horace more in wrong translations
By Wits, than Critics in as wrong quotations.
  See Dionysius Homer's thoughts refine,
And call new beauties forth from ev'ry line!
Fancy and art in gay Petronius please,
The Scholar's learning with the courtier's ease.
  In grave Quintilian's copious work we find
The justest rules and clearest method joined.
Thus useful arms in magazines we place,
All ranged in order, and disposed with grace:
But less to please the eye than arm the hand,
Still fit for use, and ready at command.
  Thee, bold Longinus! all the Nine inspire,
And bless their critic with a poet's fire:
An ardent judge, who, zealous in his trust,
With warmth gives sentence, yet is always just;
Whose own example strengthens all his laws,
And is himself that great sublime he draws.
  Thus long succeeding critics justly reigned,
Licence repressed, and useful laws ordained:
Learning and Rome alike in empire grew,
And arts still followed where her eagles flew;
From the same foes at last both felt their doom,
And the same age saw learning fall, and Rome.
With tyranny then superstition joined,
As that the body, this enslaved the mind;
Much was believed, but little understood,
And to be dull was construed to be good;
A second deluge learning thus o'errun,
And the monks finished what the Goths begun.
  At length Erasmus, that great injured name,
(The glory of the priesthood and the shame!)
Stemmed the wild torrent of a barb'rous age,
And drove those holy Vandals off the stage.
  But see! each muse in Leo's golden days
Starts from her trance, and trims her withered bays,
Rome's ancient genius, o'er its ruins spread,
Shakes off the dust, and rears his rev'rend head.
Then sculpture and her sister arts revive;
Stones leaped to form, and rocks began to live;
With sweeter notes each rising temple rung;
A Raphael painted and a Vida sung:
Immortal Vida! on whose honoured brow
The poet's bays and critic's ivy grow:
Cremona now shall ever boast thy name
As next in place to Mantua, next in fame!
  But soon by impious arms from Latium chased,
Their ancient bounds the banished Muses passed;
Thence arts o'er all the northern world advance,
But critic learning flourished most in France;
The rules a nation born to serve obeys,
And Boileau still in right of Horace sways.

But we, brave Britons, foreign laws despised,
And kept unconquered and uncivilized;
Fierce for the liberties of wit, and bold,
We still defied the Romans, as of old.
Yet some there were, among the sounder few
Of those who less presumed and better knew,
Who durst assert the juster ancient cause,
And here restored Wit's fundamental laws.
Such was the Muse whose rules and practice tell
'Nature's chief master-piece is writing well.'
Such was Roscommon, not more learned than good,
With manners gen'rous as his noble blood;
To him the wit of Greece and Rome was known,
And every author's merit but his own.
Such late was Walsh — the Muse's judge and friend,
Who justly knew to blame or to commend;
To failings mild but zealous to desert,
The clearest head, and the sincerest heart.
This humble praise, lamented Shade! receive;
This praise at least a grateful Muse may give:
The Muse whose early voice you taught to sing,
Prescribed her heights, and pruned her tender wing,
(Her guide now lost), no more attempts to rise,
But in low numbers short excursions tries;
Content if hence th' unlearned their wants may view,
The learned reflect on what before they knew;
Careless of censure, nor too fond of fame;
Still pleased to praise, yet not afraid to blame;
Averse alike to flatter or offend;
Not free from faults, nor yet too vain to mend.

1711

THE RAPE OF THE LOCK

CANTO I

What dire offence from am'rous causes springs,
What mighty contests rise from trivial things,
I sing — This verse to Caryll, muse! is due:
This, ev'n Belinda may vouchsafe to view:
Slight is the subject, but not so the praise,
If she inspire, and he approve my lays.
Say what strange motive, Goddess! could compel
A well-bred Lord t' assault a gentle Belle?
O say what stranger cause, yet unexplored,
Could make a gentle Belle reject a Lord?
In tasks so bold can little men engage,
And in soft bosoms dwells such mighty rage?
Sol through white curtains shot a tim'rous ray,
And oped those eyes that must eclipse the day.
Now lapdogs give themselves the rousing shake,
And sleepless lovers just at twelve, awake:
Thrice rung the bell, the slipper knocked the ground,
And the pressed watch returned a silver sound.
Belinda still her downy pillow prest,
Her guardian Sylph prolonged the balmy rest.
'T was he had summoned to her silent bed
The morning-dream that hovered o'er her head;
A youth more glitt'ring than a Birthnight Beau
(That ev'n in slumber caused her cheek to glow)
Seemed to her ear his winning lips to lay,
And thus in whispers said, or seemed to say:
'Fairest of mortals, thou distinguished care
Of thousand bright Inhabitants of Air!
If e'er one vision touched thy infant thought,
Of all the nurse and all the priest have taught—
Of airy elves by moonlight shadows seen,
The silver token, and the circled green,
Or virgins visited by Angel-powers,
With golden crowns and wreaths of heav'nly flowers;
Hear and believe! thy own importance know,
Nor bound thy narrow views to things below.
Some secret truths, from learnèd pride concealed,
To maids alone and children are revealed:
What though no credit doubting Wits may give?
The fair and innocent shall still believe.
Know, then, unnumbered Spirits round thee fly,
The light militia of the lower sky:
These, though unseen, are ever on the wing,
Hang o'er the Box, and hover round the Ring,
Think what an equipage thou hast in air,

And view with scorn two pages and a chair.
As now your own, our beings were of old,
And once enclosed in woman's beauteous mould;
Thence, by a soft transition, we repair
From earthly vehicles to these of air.
Think not, when woman's transient breath is fled,
That all her vanities at once are dead;
Succeeding vanities she still regards,
And, though she plays no more, o'erlooks the cards.
Her joy in gilded chariots, when alive,
And love of Ombre, after death survive.
For when the Fair in all their pride expire,
To their first elements their souls retire.
The sprites of fiery termagants in flame
Mount up, and take a Salamander's name.
Soft yielding minds to water glide away,
And sip, with Nymphs, their elemental tea.
The graver prude sinks downward to a Gnome,
In search of mischief still on earth to roam.
The light coquettes in Sylphs aloft repair,
And sport and flutter in the fields of air.
'Know further yet: whoever fair and chaste
Rejects mankind, is by some Sylph embraced;
For spirits, freed from mortal laws, with ease
Assume what sexes and what shapes they please.
What guards the purity of melting maids,
In courtly balls, and midnight masquerades,
Safe from the treach'rous friend, the daring spark,
The glance by day, the whisper in the dark;
When kind occasion prompts their warm desires,
When music softens, and when dancing fires?
'T is but their Sylph, the wise Celestials know,
Though Honor is the word with men below.
'Some nymphs there are, too conscious of their face,
For life predestined to the Gnome's embrace.
These swell their prospects and exalt their pride,
When offers are disdained, and love denied:
Then gay ideas crowd the vacant brain,
While peers, and dukes, and all their sweeping train,
And garters, stars, and coronets appear,
And in soft sounds, "Your Grace" salutes their ear.
'T is these that early taint the female soul,
Instruct the eyes of young coquettes to roll,
Teach infant cheeks a bidden blush to know,
And little hearts to flutter at a Beau.
'Oft, when the world imagine women stray,
The Sylphs through mystic mazes guide their way;
Through all the giddy circle they pursue,
And old impertinence expel by new.
What tender maid but must a victim fall
To one man's treat, but for another's ball?
When Florio speaks, what virgin could withstand,
If gentle Damon did not squeeze her hand?
With varying vanities, from every part,
They shift the moving toyshop of their heart;
Where wigs with wigs, with sword-knots sword-knots strive,
Beaux banish beaux, and coaches coaches drive.
This erring mortals levity may call;
Oh blind to truth! the Sylphs contrive it all.
'Of these am I, who thy protection claim,
A watchful sprite, and Ariel is my name.
Late, as I ranged the crystal wilds of air,
In the clear mirror of thy ruling star
I saw, alas! some dread event impend,
Ere to the main this morning sun descend,
But Heav'n reveals not what, or how or where.
Warned by the Sylph, O pious maid, beware!
This to disclose is all thy guardian can:
Beware of all, but most beware of man!'
He said; when Shock, who thought she slept too long,
Leaped up, and waked his mistress with his tongue.
'T was then, Belinda, if report say true,
Thy eyes first opened on a billet-doux;
Wounds, charms, and ardours were no sooner read,
But all the vision vanished from thy head.
And now, unveiled, the toilet stands displayed,
Each silver vase in mystic order laid.
First, robed in white, the nymph intent adores,
With head uncovered, the cosmetic powers.
A heav'nly image in the glass appears;
To that she bends, to that her eyes she rears.
Th' inferior priestess, at her altar's side,
Trembling begins the sacred rites of Pride.
Unnumbered treasures ope at once, and here
The various off'rings of the world appear;
From each she nicely culls with curious toil,

And decks the Goddess with the glitt'ring spoil.
This casket India's glowing gems unlocks,
And all Arabia breathes from yonder box.
The tortoise here and elephant unite,
Transformed to combs, the speckled, and the white.
Here files of pins extend their shining rows,
Puffs, powders, patches, bibles, billet-doux.
Now awful beauty puts on all its arms;
The Fair each moment rises in her charms,
Repairs her smiles, awakens every grace,
And calls forth all the wonders of her face;
Sees by degrees a purer blush arise,
And keener lightnings quicken in her eyes.
The busy Sylphs surround their darling care,
These set the head, and those divide the hair,
Some fold the sleeve, whilst others plait the gown;
And Betty's praised for labours not her own.

CANTO II

Not with more glories, in th' ethereal plain,
The sun first rises o'er the purpled main,
Than, issuing forth, the rival of his beams
Launched on the bosom of the silver Thames.
Fair nymphs, and well-dressed youths around her shone,
But every eye was fixed on her alone.
On her white breast a sparkling cross she wore,
Which Jews might kiss, and infidels adore.
Her lively looks a sprightly mind disclose,
Quick as her eyes, and as unfixed as those:
Favours to none, to all she smiles extends;
Oft she rejects, but never once offends.
Bright as the sun, her eyes the gazers strike,
And, like the sun, they shine on all alike.
Yet graceful ease, and sweetness void of pride,
Might hide her faults, if belles had faults to hide;
If to her share some female errors fall,
Look on her face, and you 'll forget 'em all.
This nymph, to the destruction of mankind,
Nourished two locks, which graceful hung behind
In equal curls, and well conspired to deck
With shining ringlets the smooth iv'ry neck.
Love in these labyrinths his slaves detains,
And mighty hearts are held in slender chains.
With hairy springes we the birds betray,
Slight lines of hair surprise the finny prey,
Fair tresses man's imperial race ensnare,
And beauty draws us with a single hair.
Th' adventurous baron the bright locks admired;
He saw, he wished, and to the prize aspired.
Resolved to win, he meditates the way,
By force to ravish, or by fraud betray;
For when success a lover's toil attends,
Few ask if fraud or force attained his ends.
For this, ere Phœbus rose, he had implored
Propitious Heav'n, and every Power adored,
But chiefly Love — to Love an altar built
Of twelve vast French romances, neatly gilt.
There lay three garters, half a pair of gloves,
And all the trophies of his former loves;
With tender billet-doux he lights the pyre,
And breathes three am'rous sighs to raise the fire.
Then prostrate falls, and begs with ardent eyes
Soon to obtain, and long possess the prize:
The Powers gave ear, and granted half his prayer,
The rest the winds dispersed in empty air.
But now secure the painted vessel glides,
The sunbeams trembling on the floating tides;
While melting music steals upon the sky,
And softened sounds along the waters die:
Smooth flow the waves, the zephyrs gently play,
Belinda smiled, and all the world was gay.
All but the Sylph — with careful thoughts opprest
Th' impending woe sat heavy on his breast.
He summons straight his denizens of air;
The lucid squadrons round the sails repair:
Soft o'er the shrouds aërial whispers breathe
That seemed but zephyrs to the train beneath.
Some to the sun their insect-wings unfold,
Waft on the breeze, or sink in clouds of gold;
Transparent forms too fine for mortal sight,
Their fluid bodies half dissolved in light,
Loose to the wind their airy garments flew,
Thin glitt'ring textures of the filmy dew,
Dipt in the richest tincture of the skies,
Where light disports in ever-mingling dyes,
While ev'ry beam new transient colours flings,
Colours that change whene'er they wave their wings.
Amid the circle, on the gilded mast,
Superior by the head was Ariel placed;
His purple pinions opening to the sun,
He raised his azure wand, and thus begun:
'Ye Sylphs and Sylphids, to your chief give ear.

Fays, Fairies, Genii, Elves, and Dæmons, hear!
Ye know the spheres and various tasks assigned
By laws eternal to the aërial kind.
Some in the fields of purest ether play,
And bask and whiten in the blaze of day:
Some guide the course of wand'ring orbs on high,
Or roll the planets through the boundless sky:
Some, less refined, beneath the moon's pale light
Pursue the stars that shoot athwart the night,
Or suck the mists in grosser air below,
Or dip their pinions in the painted bow,
Or brew fierce tempests on the wintry main,
Or o'er the glebe distil the kindly rain.
Others, on earth, o'er human race preside,
Watch all their ways, and all their actions guide:
Of these the chief the care of nations own,
And guard with arms divine the British Throne.
'Our humbler province is to tend the Fair,
Not a less pleasing, though less glorious care;
To save the Powder from too rude a gale;
Nor let th' imprisoned Essences exhale;
To draw fresh colours from the vernal flowers;
To steal from rainbows ere they drop in showers
A brighter Wash; to curl their waving hairs,
Assist their blushes and inspire their airs;
Nay oft, in dreams, invention we bestow,
To change a Flounce, or add a Furbelow.
'This day, black omens threat the brightest Fair,
That e'er deserved a watchful spirit's care;
Some dire disaster, or by force or slight;
But what, or where, the Fates have wrapped in night.
Whether the nymph shall break Diana's law,
Or some frail China jar receive a flaw;
Or stain her honour, or her new brocade,
Forget her prayers, or miss a masquerade,
Or lose her heart, or necklace, at a ball;
Or whether Heav'n has doomed that Shock must fall.
Haste, then, ye Spirits! to your charge repair;
The flutt'ring fan be Zephyretta's care;
The drops to thee, Brillante, we consign;
And, Momentilla, let the watch be thine;
Do thou, Crispissa, tend her fav'rite Lock;
Ariel himself shall be the guard of Shock.
'To fifty chosen sylphs, of special note,
We trust th' important charge, the petticoat;
Oft have we known that sev'n-fold fence to fail,
Though stiff with hoops, and armed with ribs of whale:
Form a strong line about the silver bound,
And guard the wide circumference around.
'Whatever spirit, careless of his charge,
His post neglects, or leaves the Fair at large,
Shall feel sharp vengeance soon o'ertake his sins:
Be stopped in vials, or transfixed with pins,
Or plunged in lakes of bitter washes lie,
Or wedged whole ages in a bodkin's eye;
Gums and pomatums shall his flight restrain,
While clogged he beats his silken wings in vain,
Or alum styptics with contracting power
Shrink his thin essence like a rivelled flower:
Or, as Ixion fixed, the wretch shall feel
The giddy motion of the whirling mill,
In fumes of burning chocolate shall glow,
And tremble at the sea that froths below!'
He spoke; the spirits from the sails descend;
Some, orb in orb, around the nymph extend;
Some thread the mazy ringlets of her hair;
Some hang upon the pendants of her ear;
With beating hearts the dire event they wait,
Anxious, and trembling for the birth of Fate.

CANTO III

Close by those meads, for ever crowned with flowers,
Where Thames with pride surveys his rising towers
There stands a structure of majestic frame,
Which from the neighb'ring Hampton takes its name.
Here Britain's statesmen oft the fall foredoom
Of foreign tyrants, and of nymphs at home;
Here thou, great ANNA! whom three realms obey,
Dost sometimes counsel take — and sometimes tea.
Hither the Heroes and the Nymphs resort,
To taste awhile the pleasures of a court;
In various talk th' instructive hours they past,
Who gave the ball, or paid the visit last;
One speaks the glory of the British Queen,
And one describes a charming Indian screen;
A third interprets motions, looks, and eyes;

At every word a reputation dies.
Snuff, or the fan, supply each pause of chat,
With singing, laughing, ogling, and all that.
Meanwhile, declining from the noon of day,
The sun obliquely shoots his burning ray;
The hungry judges soon the sentence sign,
And wretches hang that jurymen may dine;
The merchant from th' Exchange returns in peace,
And the long labours of the toilet cease.
Belinda now, whom thirst of fame invites,
Burns to encounter two adventurous knights,
At Ombre singly to decide their doom,
And swells her breast with conquests yet to come.
Straight the three bands prepare in arms to join,
Each band the number of the sacred Nine.
Soon as she spreads her hand, th' aërial guard
Descend, and sit on each important card:
First Ariel perched upon a Matadore,
Then each according to the rank they bore;
For Sylphs, yet mindful of their ancient race,
Are, as when women, wondrous fond of place.
Behold four Kings in majesty revered,
With hoary whiskers and a forky beard;
And four fair Queens, whose hands sustain a flower
Th' expressive emblem of their softer power;
Four Knaves, in garbs succinct, a trusty band,
Caps on their heads, and halberts in their hand
And party-coloured troops, a shining train,
Draw forth to combat on the velvet plain.
The skilful nymph reviews her force with care;
'Let spades be trumps!' she said, and trumps they were.
Now moved to war her sable Matadores,
In show like leaders of the swarthy Moors.
Spadillio first, unconquerable lord!
Led off two captive trumps, and swept the board.
As many more Manillio forced to yield,
And marched a victor from the verdant field.
Him Basto followed, but his fate more hard
Gained but one trump and one plebeian card.
With his broad sabre next, a chief in years,
The hoary Majesty of Spades appears,
Puts forth one manly leg, to sight revealed;
The rest his many coloured robe concealed.
The rebel Knave, who dares his prince engage,
Proves the just victim of his royal rage.
Ev'n mighty Pam, that kings and queens o'erthrew,
And mowed down armies in the fights of Loo,
Sad chance of war! now destitute of aid,
Falls undistinguished by the victor Spade!
Thus far both armies to Belinda yield;
Now to the Baron Fate inclines the field.
His warlike amazon her host invades,
Th' imperial consort of the crown of Spades.
The Club's black tyrant first her victim died,
Spite of his haughty mien and barb'rous pride:
What boots the regal circle on his head,
His giant limbs, in state unwieldy spread;
That long behind he trails his pompous robe,
And, of all monarchs only grasps the globe?
The Baron now his Diamonds pours apace;
Th' embroidered King who shows but half his face,
And his refulgent Queen, with powers combined,
Of broken troops an easy conquest find.
Clubs, Diamonds, Hearts, in wild disorder seen,
With throngs promiscuous strew the level green.
Thus when dispersed a routed army runs,
Of Asia's troops, and Afric's sable sons,
With like confusion diff'rent nations fly,
Of various habit, and of various dye;
The pierced battalions disunited fall,
In heaps on heaps; one fate o'erwhelms them all.
The Knave of Diamonds tries his wily arts,
And wins (oh shameful chance!) the Queen of Hearts.
At this, the blood the virgin's cheek forsook,
A livid paleness spreads o'er all her look;
She sees, and trembles at th' approaching ill,
Just in the jaws of ruin, and Codille.
And now (as oft in some distempered state)
On one nice trick depends the gen'ral fate!
An Ace of Hearts steps forth: the King unseen
Lurked in her hand, and mourned his captive Queen.
He springs to vengeance with an eager pace,
And falls like thunder on the prostrate Ace.
The nymph, exulting, fills with shouts the sky;
The walls, the woods, and long canals reply.

Oh thoughtless mortals! ever blind to fate,
Too soon dejected, and too soon elate:
Sudden these honours shall be snatched away,
And cursed for ever this victorious day.
For lo! the board with cups and spoons is crowned,
The berries crackle, and the mill turns round;
On shining altars of japan they raise
The silver lamp; the fiery spirits blaze:
From silver spouts the grateful liquors glide,
While China's earth receives the smoking tide.
At once they gratify their scent and taste,
And frequent cups prolong the rich repast.
Straight hover round the Fair her airy band;
Some, as she sipped, the fuming liquor fanned,
Some o'er her lap their careful plumes displayed,
Trembling, and conscious of the rich brocade.
Coffee (which makes the politician wise,
And see through all things with his half-shut eyes)
Sent up in vapours to the Baron's brain
New stratagems, the radiant Lock to gain.
Ah, cease, rash youth! desist ere 't is too late,
Fear the just Gods, and think of Scylla's fate!
Changed to a bird, and sent to flit in air,
She dearly pays for Nisus' injured hair!
But when to mischief mortals bend their will,
How soon they find fit instruments of ill!
Just then, Clarissa drew with tempting grace
A two-edged weapon from her shining case:
So ladies in romance assist their knight,
Present the spear, and arm him for the fight.
He takes the gift with rev'rence, and extends
The little engine on his finger's ends;
This just behind Belinda's neck he spread,
As o'er the fragrant steams she bends her head.
Swift to the Lock a thousand sprites repair;
A thousand wings, by turns, blow back the hair;
And thrice they twitched the diamond in her ear;
Thrice she looked back, and thrice the foe drew near.
Just in that instant, anxious Ariel sought
The close recesses of the virgin's thought:
As on the nosegay in her breast reclined,
He watched th' ideas rising in her mind,
Sudden he viewed, in spite of all her art,
An earthly Lover lurking at her heart.
Amazed, confused, he found his power expired,
Resigned to fate, and with a sigh retired.
The Peer now spreads the glitt'ring forfex wide,
T' inclose the Lock; now joins it, to divide.
Ev'n then, before the fatal engine closed,
A wretched Sylph too fondly interposed;
Fate urged the shears, and cut the Sylph in twain
(But airy substance soon unites again).
The meeting points the sacred hair dissever
From the fair head, for ever, and for ever!
Then flashed the living lightning from her eyes,
And screams of horror rend th' affrighted skies.
Not louder shrieks to pitying Heav'n are cast,
When husbands, or when lapdogs breathe their last;
Or when rich China vessels, fall'n from high,
In glitt'ring dust and painted fragments lie!
'Let wreaths of triumph now my temples twine,'
The Victor cried, 'the glorious prize is mine!
While fish in streams, or birds delight in air,
Or in a coach and six the British Fair,
As long as Atalantis shall be read,
Or the small pillow grace a lady's bed,
While visits shall be paid on solemn days,
When numerous wax-lights in bright order blaze:
While nymphs take treats, or assignations give,
So long my honour, name, and praise shall live!
What Time would spare, from Steel receives its date,
And monuments, like men, submit to Fate!
Steel could the labour of the Gods destroy,
And strike to dust th' imperial towers of Troy;
Steel could the works of mortal pride confound,
And hew triumphal arches to the ground.
What wonder, then, fair Nymph! thy hairs should feel
The conquering force of unresisted steel?'

CANTO IV

But anxious cares the pensive nymph opprest,
And secret passions laboured in her breast.
Not youthful kings in battle seized alive,
Not scornful virgins who their charms survive,
Not ardent lovers robbed of all their bliss,
Not ancient ladies when refused a kiss,
Not tyrants fierce that unrepenting die,
Not Cynthia when her mantua 's pinned awry,
E'er felt such rage, resentment, and despair,
As thou, sad Virgin! for thy ravished hair.
For, that sad moment, when the Sylphs withdrew,
And Ariel weeping from Belinda flew,
Umbriel, a dusky, melancholy sprite
As ever sullied the fair face of light,
Down to the central earth, his proper scene,
Repaired to search the gloomy cave of Spleen.
Swift on his sooty pinions flits the Gnome,
And in a vapour reached the dismal dome.
No cheerful breeze this sullen region knows,
The dreaded East is all the wind that blows.
Here in a grotto sheltered close from air,
And screened in shades from day's detested glare,
She sighs for ever on her pensive bed,
Pain at her side, and Megrim at her head.
Two handmaids wait the throne; alike in place,
But diff'ring far in figure and in face.
Here stood Ill-nature, like an ancient maid,
Her wrinkled form in black and white arrayed!
With store of prayers for mornings, nights, and noons,
Her hand is filled; her bosom with lampoons.
There Affectation, with a sickly mien,
Shows in her cheek the roses of eighteen,
Practiced to lisp, and hang the head aside,
Faints into airs, and languishes with pride;
On the rich quilt sinks with becoming woe,
Wrapped in a gown for sickness and for show.
The fair ones feel such maladies as these,
When each new night-dress gives a new disease.
A constant vapour o'er the palace flies,
Strange phantoms rising as the mists arise;
Dreadful, as hermits' dreams in haunted shades,
Or bright, as vision of expiring maids:
Now glaring fiends, and snakes on rolling spires,
Pale spectres, gaping tombs, and purple fires;
Now lakes of liquid gold, Elysian scenes,
And crystal domes, and angels in machines.
Unnumbered throngs on every side are seen,
Of bodies changed to various forms by Spleen.
Here living Teapots stand, one arm held out,
One bent; the handle this, and that the spout:
A Pipkin there, like Homer's Tripod walks;
Here sighs a Jar, and there a Goose-pie talks;
Men prove with child, as powerful fancy works,
And maids turned bottles call aloud for corks.
Safe passed the Gnome through this fantastic band,
A branch of healing spleenwort in his hand.
Then thus addressed the Power — 'Hail, wayward Queen!
Who rule the sex to fifty from fifteen:
Parent of Vapours and of female wit,
Who give th' hysteric or poetic fit,
On various tempers act by various ways,
Make some take physic, others scribble plays;
Who cause the proud their visits to delay,
And send the godly in a pet to pray.
A nymph there is that all your power disdains,
And thousands more in equal mirth maintains.
But oh! if e'er thy Gnome could spoil a grace,
Or raise a pimple on a beauteous face,
Like citron-waters matrons' cheeks inflame,
Or change complexions at a losing game;
If e'er with airy horns I planted heads,
Or rumpled petticoats, or tumbled beds,
Or caused suspicion when no soul was rude,
Or discomposed the head-dress of a prude,
Or e'er to costive lapdog gave disease,
Which not the tears of brightest eyes could ease,
Hear me, and touch Belinda with chagrin;
That single act gives half the world the spleen.'
The Goddess with a discontented air,
Seems to reject him though she grants his prayer.
A wondrous Bag with both her hands she binds,
Like that where once Ulysses held the winds;

There she collects the force of female lungs,
Sighs, sobs, and passions, and the war of tongues.
A Vial next she fills with fainting fears,
Soft sorrows, melting griefs, and flowing tears.
The Gnome rejoicing bears her gifts away,
Spreads his black wings, and slowly mounts to day.
Sunk in Thalestris' arms the nymph he found,
Her eyes dejected, and her hair unbound.
Full o'er their heads the swelling Bag he rent,
And all the Furies issued at the vent.
Belinda burns with more than mortal ire,
And fierce Thalestris fans the rising fire.
'O wretched maid!' she spread her hands, and cried
(While Hampton's echoes, 'Wretched maid!' replied),
'Was it for this you took such constant care
The bodkin, comb, and essence to prepare?
For this your locks in paper durance bound?
For this with torturing irons wreathed around?
For this with fillets strained your tender head,
And bravely bore the double loads of lead?
Gods! shall the ravisher display your hair,
While the fops envy, and the ladies stare!
Honour forbid! at whose unrivalled shrine
Ease, Pleasure, Virtue, all, our sex resign.
Methinks already I your tears survey,
Already hear the horrid things they say,
Already see you a degraded toast,
And all your honour in a whisper lost!
How shall I, then, your helpless fame defend?
'T will then be infamy to seem your friend!
And shall this prize, th' inestimable prize,
Exposed through crystal to the gazing eyes,
And heightened by the diamond's circling rays,
On that rapacious hand for ever blaze?
Sooner shall grass in Hyde Park Circus grow,
And Wits take lodgings in the sound of Bow;
Sooner let earth, air, sea, to chaos fall,
Men, monkeys, lapdogs, parrots, perish all!'
She said; then raging to Sir Plume repairs,
And bids her beau demand the precious hairs
(Sir Plume, of amber snuff-box justly vain,
And the nice conduct of a clouded cane):
With earnest eyes, and round unthinking face,
He first the snuff-box opened, then the case,
And thus broke out — 'My lord, why, what the devil!
Z —— ds! damn the Lock! 'fore Gad, you must be civil!
Plague on 't! 't is past a jest — nay, prithee, pox!
Give her the hair.' — He spoke, and rapped his box.
'It grieves me much,' replied the Peer again,
'Who speaks so well should ever speak in vain:
But by this Lock, this sacred Lock, I swear
(Which never more shall join its parted hair;
Which never more its honours shall renew,
Clipped from the lovely head where late it grew),
That, while my nostrils draw the vital air,
This hand, which won it, shall for ever wear.'
He spoke, and speaking, in proud triumph spread
The long-contended honours of her head.
But Umbriel, hateful Gnome, forbears not so;
He breaks the Vial whence the sorrows flow.
Then see! the nymph in beauteous grief appears,
Her eyes half-languishing, half drowned in tears;
On her heaved bosom hung her drooping head,
Which, with a sigh, she raised, and thus she said:
'For ever cursed be this detested day,
Which snatched my best, my fav'rite curl away!
Happy! ah, ten times happy had I been,
If Hampton Court these eyes had never seen!
Yet am not I the first mistaken maid,
By love of courts to numerous ills betrayed.
Oh, had I rather unadmired remained
In some lone isle, or distant northern land;
Where the gilt chariot never marks the way,
Where none learn Ombre, none e'er taste Bohea!
There kept my charms concealed from mortal eye,
Like roses, that in deserts bloom and die.
What moved my mind with youthful lords to roam?
O had I stayed, and said my prayers at home;

'T was this the morning omens seemed to tell,
Thrice from my trembling hand the patch-box fell;
The tott'ring china shook without a wind;
Nay, Poll sat mute, and Shock was most unkind!
A Sylph, too, warned me of the threats of fate,
In mystic visions, now believed too late!
See the poor remnants of these slighted hairs!
My hands shall rend what ev'n thy rapine spares.
These, in two sable ringlets taught to break,
Once gave new beauties to the snowy neck;
The sister-lock now sits uncouth alone,
And in its fellow's fate foresees its own;
Uncurled it hangs, the fatal shears demands,
And tempts once more thy sacrilegious hands.
Oh, hadst thou, cruel! been content to seize
Hairs less in sight, or any hairs but these!'

CANTO V

She said: the pitying audience melt in tears;
But Fate and Jove had stopped the Baron's ears.
In vain Thalestris with reproach assails,
For who can move when fair Belinda fails?
Not half so fixed the Trojan could remain,
While Anna begged and Dido raged in vain.
Then grave Clarissa graceful waved her fan;
Silence ensued, and thus the nymph began:
'Say, why are beauties praised and honoured most,
The wise man's passion, and the vain man's toast?
Why decked with all that land and sea afford,
Why angels called, and angel-like adored?
Why round our coaches crowd the white-gloved beaux?
Why bows the side-box from its inmost rows?
How vain are all these glories, all our pains,
Unless Good Sense preserve what Beauty gains;
That men may say, when we the front-box grace,
"Behold the first in virtue as in face!"
Oh! if to dance all night, and dress all day,
Charmed the smallpox, or chased old age away;
Who would not scorn what housewife's cares produce,
Or who would learn one earthly thing of use?
To patch, nay, ogle, might become a saint,
Nor could it sure be such a sin to paint.
But since, alas! frail beauty must decay,
Curled or uncurled, since locks will turn to gray;
Since painted, or not painted, all shall fade,
And she who scorns a man must die a maid;
What then remains, but well our power to use,
And keep good humour still whate'er we lose?
And trust me, dear, good humour can prevail,
When airs, and flights, and screams, and scolding fail.
Beauties in vain their pretty eyes may roll;
Charms strike the sight, but merit wins the soul.'
So spoke the dame, but no applause ensued;
Belinda frowned, Thalestris called her prude.
'To arms, to arms!' the fierce virago cries,
And swift as lightning to the combat flies.
All side in parties, and begin th' attack;
Fans clap, silks rustle, and tough whalebones crack;
Heroes' and heroines' shouts confusedly rise,
And bass and treble voices strike the skies.
No common weapons in their hands are found,
Like Gods they fight nor dread a mortal wound.
So when bold Homer makes the Gods engage,
And heav'nly breasts with human passions rage;
'Gainst Pallas, Mars; Latona, Hermes arms;
And all Olympus rings with loud alarms;
Jove's thunder roars, Heav'n trembles all around,
Blue Neptune storms, the bell'wing deeps resound:
Earth shakes her nodding towers, the ground gives way,
And the pale ghosts start at the flash of day!
Triumphant Umbriel, on a sconce's height,
Clapped his glad wings, and sat to view the fight:
Propped on their bodkin spears, the sprites survey
The growing combat, or assist the fray.
While through the press enraged Thalestris flies,

And scatters death around from both her eyes,
A Beau and Witling perished in the throng,
One died in metaphor, and one in song:
'O cruel Nymph! a living death I bear,'
Cried Dapperwit, and sunk beside his chair.
A mournful glance Sir Fopling upwards cast,
'Those eyes are made so killing' — was his last.
Thus on Mæander's flowery margin lies
Th' expiring swan, and as he sings he dies.
When bold Sir Plume had drawn Clarissa down,
Chloe stepped in, and killed him with a frown;
She smiled to see the doughty hero slain,
But, at her smile, the beau revived again.
Now Jove suspends his golden scales in air,
Weighs the men's wits against the lady's hair;
The doubtful beam long nods from side to side;
At length the wits mount up, the hairs subside.
See fierce Belinda on the Baron flies,
With more than usual lightning in her eyes;
Nor feared the chief th' unequal fight to try,
Who sought no more than on his foe to die.
But this bold lord, with manly strength endued,
She with one finger and a thumb subdued:
Just where the breath of life his nostrils drew,
A charge of snuff the wily virgin threw;
The Gnomes direct, to every atom just,
The pungent grains of titillating dust.
Sudden, with starting tears each eye o'erflows,
And the high dome reëchoes to his nose.
'Now meet thy fate,' incensed Belinda cried,
And drew a deadly bodkin from her side.
(The same, his ancient personage to deck,
Her great-great-grandsire wore about his neck,
In three seal-rings; which after, melted down,
Formed a vast buckle for his widow's gown:
Her infant grandame's whistle next it grew,
The bells she jingled, and the whistle blew;
Then in a bodkin graced her mother's hairs,
Which long she wore and now Belinda wears.)
'Boast not my fall,' he cried, 'insulting foe!
Thou by some other shalt be laid as low;
Nor think to die dejects my lofty mind:
All that I dread is leaving you behind!
Rather than so, ah, let me still survive,
And burn in Cupid's flames — but burn alive.'
'Restore the Lock!' she cries; and all around
'Restore the Lock!' the vaulted roofs rebound.
Not fierce Othello in so loud a strain
Roared for the handkerchief that caused his pain.
But see how oft ambitious aims are crossed,
And chiefs contend till all the prize is lost!
The lock, obtained with guilt, and kept with pain,
In ev'ry place is sought, but sought in vain:
With such a prize no mortal must be blessed.
So Heav'n decrees! with Heav'n who can contest?
Some thought it mounted to the lunar sphere,
Since all things lost on earth are treasured there.
There heroes' wits are kept in pond'rous vases,
And beaux' in snuffboxes and tweezer-cases.
There broken vows, and deathbed alms are found,
And lovers' hearts with ends of riband bound,
The courtier's promises, and sick man's prayers,
The smiles of harlots, and the tears of heirs,
Cages for gnats, and chains to yoke a flea,
Dried butterflies, and tomes of casuistry.
But trust the Muse — she saw it upward rise,
Though marked by none but quick poetic eyes
(So Rome's great founder to the heav'ns withdrew,
To Proculus alone confessed in view):
A sudden star, it shot through liquid air,
And drew behind a radiant trail of hair.
Not Berenice's locks first rose so bright,
The heav'ns bespangling with dishevelled light.
The Sylphs behold it kindling as it flies,
And pleased pursue its progress through the skies.
This the beau monde shall from the Mall survey,
And hail with music its propitious ray;
This the blest lover shall for Venus take,
And send up vows from Rosamonda's lake;
This Partridge soon shall view in cloudless skies,
When next he looks through Galileo's eyes;

And hence th' egregious wizard shall foredoom
The fate of Louis, and the fall of Rome.
Then cease, bright Nymph! to mourn thy ravished hair,
Which adds new glory to the shining sphere!
Not all the tresses that fair head can boast
Shall draw such envy as the Lock you lost.
For after all the murders of your eye,
When, after millions slain, yourself shall die;
When those fair suns shall set, as set they must,
And all those tresses shall be laid in dust,
This Lock the Muse shall consecrate to fame,
And 'midst the stars inscribe Belinda's name.

1712, 1714

EPISTLE TO DR. ARBUTHNOT

P. 'SHUT, shut the door, good John!' fatigued, I said.
'Tie up the knocker, say I'm sick, I'm dead.'
The Dog-star rages! nay, 't is past a doubt
All Bedlam or Parnassus is let out:
Fire in each eye, and papers in each hand,
They rave, recite, and madden round the land.
What walls can guard me, or what shades can hide?
They pierce my thickets, through my grot they glide,
By land, by water, they renew the charge,
They stop the chariot, and they board the barge.
No place is sacred, not the church is free,
Ev'n Sunday shines no Sabbath day to me:
Then from the Mint walks forth the man of rhyme,
Happy to catch me just at dinner time.
Is there a Parson much bemused in beer,
A maudlin Poetess, a rhyming Peer,
A clerk foredoomed his father's soul to cross,
Who pens a stanza when he should engross?
Is there who, locked from ink and paper, scrawls
With desp'rate charcoal round his darkened walls?
All fly to Twit'nam, and in humble strain
Apply to me to keep them mad or vain,
Arthur, whose giddy son neglects the laws,
Imputes to me and my damned works the cause:
Poor Cornus sees his frantic wife elope,
And curses Wit, and poetry, and Pope.
Friend to my life (which did not you prolong,
The world had wanted many an idle song)!
What Drop or Nostrum can this plague remove?
Or which must end me, a fool's wrath or love?
A dire dilemma! either way I'm sped;
If foes, they write, if friends, they read me dead.
Seized and tied down to judge, how wretched I!
Who can't be silent, and who will not lie.
To laugh were want of goodness and of grace,
And to be grave exceeds all power of face.
I sit with sad civility, I read
With honest anguish and an aching head,
And drop at last, but in unwilling ears,
This saving counsel, 'Keep your piece nine years.'
'Nine years!' cries he, who, high in Drury Lane,
Lulled by soft zephyrs through the broken pane,
Rhymes ere he wakes, and prints before Term ends,
Obliged by hunger and request of friends:
'The piece, you think, is incorrect? why, take it!
I'm all submission: what you 'd have it — make it.'
Three things another's modest wishes bound,
'My friendship, and a Prologue, and ten pound.'
Pitholeon sends to me: 'You know his Grace,
I want a patron; ask him for a place.'
Pitholeon libelled me — 'But here's a letter
Informs you, Sir, 't was when he knew no better.
Dare you refuse him? Curll invites to dine,
He 'll write a *Journal*, or he 'll turn Divine.'
Bless me! a packet. — 'T is a stranger sues,
A Virgin Tragedy, an Orphan Muse.
If I dislike it, 'Furies, death, and rage!'
If I approve, 'Commend it to the stage.'
There (thank my stars) my whole commission ends,
The players and I are, luckily, no friends.
Fired that the house reject him, ''Sdeath I'll print it,
And shame the fools — your int'rest, Sir, with Lintot.'
'Lintot, dull rogue, will think your price too much':
'Not, Sir, if you revise it, and retouch.'
All my demurs but double his attacks;
At last he whispers, 'Do, and we go snacks.'

Glad of a quarrel, straight I clap the door;
'Sir, let me see your works and you no more!'
'T is sung, when Midas' ears began to spring
(Midas, a sacred person and a king),
His very minister who spied them first
(Some say his Queen) was forced to speak or burst.
And is not mine, my friend, a sorer case,
When ev'ry coxcomb perks them in my face?
A. Good friend, forbear! you deal in dangerous things;
I'd never name Queens, Ministers, or Kings;
Keep close to ears, and those let asses prick,
'T is nothing——*P*. Nothing! if they bite and kick?
Out with it, DUNCIAD! let the secret pass,
That secret to each fool, that he's an ass:
The truth once told (and wherefore should we lie?)
The Queen of Midas slept, and so may I.
You think this cruel? Take it for a rule,
No creature smarts so little as a fool.
Let peals of laughter, Codrus! round thee break,
Thou unconcerned canst hear the mighty crack:
Pit, Box, and Gall'ry in convulsions hurled,
Thou stand'st unshook amidst a bursting world.
Who shames a Scribbler? break one cobweb through,
He spins the slight self-pleasing thread anew:
Destroy his fib, or sophistry — in vain!
The creature 's at his dirty work again,
Throned in the center of his thin designs,
Proud of a vast extent of flimsy lines.
Whom have I hurt? has Poet yet or Peer
Lost the arched eyebrow or Parnassian sneer? . . .
Does not one table Bavius still admit?
Still to one Bishop Philips seem a wit?
Still Sappho——*A*. Hold! for God's sake — you 'll offend.
No names — be calm — learn prudence of a friend.
I too could write, and I am twice as tall;
But foes like these— *P*. One flatt'rer's worse than all.
Of all mad creatures, if the learned are right,
It is the slaver kills, and not the bite.
A fool quite angry is quite innocent:
Alas! 't is ten times worse when they repent.
One dedicates in high heroic prose,
And ridicules beyond a hundred foes;
One from all Grub-street will my fame defend,
And, more abusive, calls himself my friend:
This prints my *Letters*, that expects a bribe,
And others roar aloud, 'Subscribe, subscribe!'
There are who to my person pay their court:
I cough like Horace; and though lean, am short;
Ammon's great son one shoulder had too high,
Such Ovid's nose, and 'Sir, you have an eye —'
Go on, obliging creatures! make me see
All that disgraced my betters met in me.
Say, for my comfort, languishing in bed,
'Just so immortal Maro held his head':
And when I die, be sure you let me know
Great Homer died three thousand years ago.
Why did I write? what sin to me unknown
Dipped me in ink, my parents', or my own?
As yet a child, nor yet a fool to fame,
I lisped in numbers, for the numbers came:
I left no calling for this idle trade,
No duty broke, no father disobeyed:
The Muse but served to ease some friend, not wife,
To help me through this long disease my life,
To second, Arbuthnot! thy art and care,
And teach the being you preserved, to bear.
A. But why then publish? *P*. Granville the polite,
And knowing Walsh, would tell me I could write;
Well-natured Garth inflamed with early praise,
And Congreve loved, and Swift endured my lays;
The courtly Talbot, Somers, Sheffield, read;
Ev'n mitred Rochester would nod the head,
And St. John's self (great Dryden's friends before)
With open arms received one poet more.
Happy my studies, when by these approved!
Happier their author, when by these beloved!
From these the world will judge of men and books,
Not from the Burnets, Oldmixons, and Cookes.
Soft were my numbers; who could take offence
While pure description held the place of sense?
Like gentle Fanny's was my flowery theme,
'A painted mistress or a purling stream.'

Yet then did Gildon draw his venal quill;
I wished the man a dinner, and sate still:
Yet then did Dennis rave in furious fret;
I never answered; I was not in debt.
If want provoked, or madness made them print,
I waged no war with Bedlam or the Mint.
Did some more sober critic come abroad;
If wrong, I smiled, if right, I kissed the rod.
Pains, reading, study, are their just pretence,
And all they want is spirit, taste, and sense.
Commas and points they set exactly right,
And 't were a sin to rob them of their mite.
Yet ne'er one sprig of laurel graced these ribalds,
From slashing Bentleys down to piddling Tibbalds.
Each wight who reads not, and but scans and spells,
Each word-catcher that lives on syllables,
Ev'n such small critics some regard may claim,
Preserved in Milton's or in Shakspeare's name.
Pretty! in amber to observe the forms
Of hairs, or straws, or dirt, or grubs, or worms!
The things, we know, are neither rich nor rare,
But wonder how the devil they got there.
Were others angry: I excused them too;
Well might they rage, I gave them but their due.
A man's true merit 't is not hard to find;
But each man's secret standard in his mind,
That casting-weight Pride adds to emptiness,
This, who can gratify? for who can guess?
The bard whom pilfered pastorals renown,
Who turns a Persian tale for half-a-crown,
Just writes to make his barrenness appear,
And strains from hard-bound brains eight lines a year;
He who still wanting, though he lives on theft,
Steals much, spends little, yet has nothing left;
And he who now to sense, now nonsense, leaning,
Means not, but blunders round about a meaning:
And he whose fustian's so sublimely bad,
It is not poetry, but prose run mad:
All these my modest satire bade translate,
And owned that nine such poets made a Tate.
How did they fume, and stamp, and roar, and chafe!
And swear not Addison himself was safe.
Peace to all such! But were there one whose fires
True genius kindles, and fair Fame inspires,
Blessed with each talent and each art to please,
And born to write, converse, and live with ease;
Should such a man, too fond to rule alone,
Bear, like the Turk, no brother near the throne;
View him with scornful, yet with jealous eyes,
And hate for arts that caused himself to rise;
Damn with faint praise, assent with civil leer,
And without sneering teach the rest to sneer;
Willing to wound, and yet afraid to strike,
Just hint a fault, and hesitate dislike;
Alike reserved to blame or to commend,
A tim'rous foe, and a suspicious friend;
Dreading ev'n fools; by flatterers besieged,
And so obliging that he ne'er obliged;
Like Cato, give his little Senate laws,
And sit attentive to his own applause:
While Wits and Templars ev'ry sentence raise,
And wonder with a foolish face of praise—
Who but must laugh if such a man there be?
Who would not weep, if Atticus were he?
What though my name stood rubric on the walls,
Or plastered posts, . . . in capitals?
Or smoking forth, a hundred hawkers' load,
On wings of winds came flying all abroad?
I sought no homage from the race that write;
I kept, like Asian Monarchs, from their sight:
Poems I heeded (now berhymed so long)
No more than thou, great George! a birth-day song.
I ne'er with Wits or Witlings passed my days
To spread about the itch of verse and praise;
Nor like a puppy daggled through the town
To fetch and carry sing-song up and down;
Nor at rehearsals sweat, and mouthed, and cried,
With handkerchief and orange at my side;
But sick of fops, and poetry, and prate,
To Bufo left the whole Castalian state.
Proud as Apollo on his forkèd hill,
Sat full-blown Bufo, puffed by every quill:
Fed with soft dedication all day long,
Horace and he went hand in hand in song.
His library (where busts of poets dead,
And a true Pindar stood without a head)
Received of Wits an undistinguished race,

Who first his judgment asked, and then a place:
Much they extolled his pictures, much his seat,
And flattered ev'ry day, and some days eat:
Till grown more frugal in his riper days,
He paid some bards with port, and some with praise;
To some a dry rehearsal was assigned,
And others (harder still) he paid in kind.
Dryden alone (what wonder?) came not nigh;
Dryden alone escaped this judging eye:
But still the great have kindness in reserve;
He helped to bury whom he helped to starve.
May some choice patron bless each grey goose quill!
May every Bavius have his Bufo still!
So when a statesman wants a day's defence,
Or Envy holds a whole week's war with Sense,
Or simple Pride for flatt'ry makes demands,
May dunce by dunce be whistled off my hands!
Blest be the great! for those they take away,
And those they left me — for they left me Gay;
Left me to see neglected Genius bloom,
Neglected die, and tell it on his tomb:
Of all thy blameless life the sole return
My Verse, and Queensb'ry weeping o'er thy urn!
Oh let me live my own, and die so too
(To live and die is all I have to do)!
Maintain a poet's dignity and ease,
And see what friends, and read what books I please;
Above a Patron, though I condescend
Sometimes to call a minister my Friend.
I was not born for courts or great affairs;
I pay my debts, believe, and say my prayers;
Can sleep without a poem in my head,
Nor know if Dennis be alive or dead.
Why am I asked what next shall see the light?
Heav'ns! was I born for nothing but to write?
Has life no joys for me? or (to be grave)
Have I no friend to serve, no soul to save?
'I found him close with Swift' — 'Indeed? no doubt
(Cries prating Balbus) something will come out.'
'T is all in vain, deny it as I will;
'No, such a genius never can lie still':
And then for mine obligingly mistakes
The first lampoon Sir Will or Bubo makes.
Poor guiltless I! and can I choose but smile,
When ev'ry coxcomb knows me by my style?
Curst be the verse, how well soe'er it flow,
That tends to make one worthy man my foe,
Give Virtue scandal, Innocence a fear,
Or from the soft-eyed virgin steal a tear!
But he who hurts a harmless neighbour's peace,
Insults fall'n Worth, or Beauty in distress,
Who loves a lie, lame Slander helps about,
Who writes a libel, or who copies out;
That fop whose pride affects a patron's name,
Yet, absent, wounds an author's honest fame;
Who can your merit selfishly approve,
And show the sense of it without the love;
Who has the vanity to call you friend,
Yet wants the honour, injured, to defend;
Who tells whate'er you think, whate'er you say,
And, if he lie not, must at least betray;
Who to the Dean and Silver Bell can swear,
And sees at Canons what was never there;
Who reads but with a lust to misapply,
Make satire a lampoon, and fiction lie:
A lash like mine no honest man shall dread,
But all such babbling blockheads in his stead.
Let Sporus tremble—— *A.* What? that thing of silk,
Sporus, that mere white curd of Ass's milk?
Satire or sense, alas! can Sporus feel?
Who breaks a butterfly upon a wheel?
P. Yet let me flap this bug with gilded wings,
This painted child of dirt, that stinks and stings;
Whose buzz the witty and the fair annoys,
Yet Wit ne'er tastes, and Beauty ne'er enjoys;
So well-bred spaniels civilly delight
In mumbling of the game they dare not bite.
Eternal smiles his emptiness betray,
As shallow streams run dimpling all the way,
Whether in florid impotence he speaks,
And, as the prompter breathes, the puppet squeaks,
Or at the ear of Eve, familiar toad,
Half froth, half venom, spits himself abroad,
In puns, or politics, or tales, or lies,
Or spite, or smut, or rhymes, or blasphemies;
His wit all see-saw between that and this,
Now high, now low, now master up, now miss,

And he himself one vile Antithesis.
Amphibious thing! that acting either part,
The trifling head, or the corrupted heart;
Fop at the toilet, flatt'rer at the board,
Now trips, a lady, and now struts, a lord.
Eve's tempter thus the Rabbins have exprest,
A cherub's face, a reptile all the rest;
Beauty that shocks you, Parts that none will trust,
Wit that can creep, and Pride that licks the dust.
  Not Fortune's worshipper, nor Fashion's fool,
Not Lucre's madman, nor Ambition's tool,
Not proud nor servile; — be one poet's praise,
That, if he pleased, he pleased by manly ways:
That flatt'ry ev'n to Kings, he held a shame,
And thought a lie in verse or prose the same;
That not in fancy's maze he wandered long,
But stooped to truth, and moralized his song;
That not for Fame, but Virtue's better end,
He stood the furious foe, the timid friend,
The damning critic, half approving wit,
The coxcomb hit, or fearing to be hit;
Laughed at the loss of friends he never had,
The dull, the proud, the wicked, and the mad;
The distant threats of vengeance on his head,
The blow unfelt, the tear he never shed;
The tale revived, the lie so oft o'erthrown,
Th' imputed trash and dullness not his own;
The morals blackened when the writings 'scape,
The libelled person, and the pictured shape;
Abuse on all he loved, or loved him, spread,
A friend in exile, or a father dead;
The whisper, that, to greatness still too near,
Perhaps yet vibrates on his Sov'reign's ear —
Welcome for thee, fair Virtue! all the past:
For thee, fair Virtue! welcome e'en the last!
  A. But why insult the poor? affront the great?
  P. A knave's a knave to me in ev'ry state;
Alike my scorn, if he succeed or fail,
Sporus at court, or Japhet in a jail;
A hireling scribbler, or a hireling peer,
Knight of the post corrupt, or of the shire;
If on a Pillory, or near a Throne,
He gain his prince's ear, or lose his own.
  Yet soft by nature, more a dupe than wit,
Sappho can tell you how this man was bit:
This dreaded Satirist Dennis will confess
Foe to his pride, but friend to his distress:
So humble, he has knocked at Tibbald's door,
Has drunk with Cibber, nay, has rhymed for Moore.
Full ten years slandered, did he once reply?
Three thousand suns went down on Welsted's lie.
To please a mistress one aspersed his life;
He lashed him not, but let her be his wife:
Let Budgell charge low Grub-street on his quill,
And write what'er he pleased, except his will;
Let the two Curlls of town and court abuse
His father, mother, body, soul, and muse:
Yet why? that father held it for a rule,
It was a sin to call our neighbour fool; . . .
Hear this, and spare his family, James Moore!
Unspotted names, and memorable long,
If there be force in Virtue, or in Song.
  Of gentle blood (part shed in honour's cause,
While yet in Britain honour had applause)
Each parent sprung— *A*. What fortune, pray?— *P*. Their own;
And better got than Bestia's from the throne.
Born to no pride, inheriting no strife,
Nor marrying discord in a noble wife,
Stranger to civil and religious rage,
The good man walked innoxious through his age.
No courts he saw, no suits would ever try,
Nor dared an oath, nor hazarded a lie.
Unlearned, he knew no schoolman's subtle art,
No language but the language of the heart.
By Nature honest, by Experience wise,
Healthy by Temp'rance and by Exercise;
His life, though long, to sickness passed unknown,
His death was instant and without a groan.
O grant me thus to live, and thus to die!
Who sprung from kings shall know less joy than I.
  O friend! may each domestic bliss be thine!
Be no unpleasing melancholy mine:
Me, let the tender office long engage
To rock the cradle of reposing Age,
With lenient arts extend a Mother's breath,
Make Languor smile, and smooth the bed of Death;
Explore the thought, explain the asking eye,

And keep a while one parent from the sky!
On cares like these if length of days attend,
May Heav'n, to bless those days, preserve my friend!
Preserve him social, cheerful, and serene,
And just as rich as when he served a Queen.
A. Whether that blessing be denied or giv'n,
Thus far was right; — the rest belongs to Heav'n.

1735

UNIVERSAL PRAYER

Father of all! in ev'ry age,
In ev'ry clime adored,
By saint, by savage, and by sage,
Jehovah, Jove, or Lord!

Thou Great First Cause, least understood,
Who all my sense confined
To know but this, that thou art good,
And that myself am blind;

Yet gave me, in this dark estate,
To see the good from ill;
And binding Nature fast in Fate,
Left free the human Will.

What Conscience dictates to be done,
Or warns me not to do;
This teach me more than Hell to shun,
That more than Heav'n pursue.

What blessings thy free bounty gives
Let me not cast away;
For God is paid when man receives;
T' enjoy is to obey.

Yet not to earth's contracted span
Thy goodness let me bound,
Or think thee Lord alone of man,
When thousand worlds are round.

Let not this weak unknowing hand
Presume thy bolts to throw,
And deal damnation round the land
On each I judge thy foe.

If I am right, thy grace impart,
Still in the right to stay;
If I am wrong, O teach my heart
To find that better way.

Save me alike from foolish Pride
Or impious Discontent,
At aught thy wisdom has denied,
Or aught thy goodness lent.

Teach me to feel another's woe,
To hide the fault I see:
That mercy I to others show,
That mercy show to me.

Mean though I am, not wholly so,
Since quickened by thy breath;
O lead me, wheresoe'er I go,
Through this day's life or death!

This day be bread and peace my lot:
All else beneath the sun
Thou know'st if best bestowed or not,
And let thy will be done.

To Thee, whose temple is all Space,
Whose altar earth, sea, skies,
One chorus let all Being raise,
All Nature's incense rise!

1738

Matthew Prior (1664–1721)

A SIMILE

Dear Thomas, didst thou never pop
Thy head into a tin-man's shop?
There, Thomas, didst thou never see
('T is but by way of simile)
A squirrel spend his little rage
In jumping round a rolling cage? —
The cage, as either side turned up,
Striking a ring of bells a-top? —
Moved in the orb, pleased with the chimes,
The foolish creature thinks he climbs:
But here or there, turn wood or wire,
He never gets two inches higher.
So fares it with those merry blades,
That frisk it under Pindus' shades.
In noble songs and lofty odes,
They tread on stars and talk with gods;
Still dancing in an airy round,
Still pleased with their own verses' sound;
Brought back, how fast soe'er they go,
Always aspiring, always low.

1707

AN ODE

The merchant, to secure his treasure,
Conveys it in a borrowed name:
Euphelia serves to grace my measure;
But Cloe is my real flame.

My softest verse, my darling lyre,
Upon Euphelia's toilet lay;
When Cloe noted her desire,
That I should sing, that I should play.

My lyre I tune, my voice I raise;
But with my numbers mix my sighs:

And whilst I sing Euphelia's praise,
I fix my soul on Cloe's eyes.

Fair Cloe blushed: Euphelia frowned:
I sung and gazed: I played and trembled:
And Venus to the Loves around
Remarked, how ill we all dissembled.

1718

Thomas Parnell (1679-1718)

A HYMN TO CONTENTMENT

Lovely, lasting peace of mind!
Sweet delight of human-kind!
Heavenly-born, and bred on high,
To crown the favourites of the sky
With more of happiness below,
Than victors in a triumph know!
Whither, O whither art thou fled,
To lay thy meek, contented head:
What happy region dost thou please
To make the seat of calms and ease!
Ambition searches all its sphere
Of pomp and state, to meet thee there.
Encreasing Avarice would find
Thy presence in its gold enshrined.
The bold adventurer ploughs his way
Through rocks amidst the foaming sea,
To gain thy love; and then perceives
Thou wert not in the rocks and waves.
The silent heart, which grief assails,
Treads soft and lonesome o'er the vales,
Sees daisies open, rivers run,
And seeks, as I have vainly done,
Amusing thought; but learns to know
That solitude 's the nurse of woe.
No real happiness is found
In trailing purple o'er the ground;
Or in a soul exalted high,
To range the circuit of the sky,
Converse with stars above, and know
All nature in its forms below;
The rest it seeks, in seeking dies,
And doubts at last, for knowledge, rise.
Lovely, lasting peace, appear!
This world itself, if thou art here,
Is once again with Eden blest,
And man contains it in his breast.
'T was thus, as under shade I stood,
I sung my wishes to the wood,
And lost in thought, no more perceived
The branches whisper as they waved:
It seemed, as all the quiet place
Confessed the presence of the Grace.
When thus she spoke — 'Go rule thy will,
Bid thy wild passions all be still,
Know God — and bring thy heart to know
The joys which from religion flow:
Then every Grace shall prove its guest,
And I 'll be there to crown the rest.'
Oh! by yonder mossy seat,
In my hours of sweet retreat,
Might I thus my soul employ,
With sense of gratitude and joy!
Raised as ancient prophets were,
In heavenly vision, praise, and prayer;
Pleasing all men, hurting none,
Pleased and blessed with God alone:
Then while the gardens take my sight,
With all the colours of delight;
While silver waters glide along,
To please my ear, and court my song;
I'll lift my voice, and tune my string,
And thee, great source of nature, sing.
The sun that walks his airy way,
To light the world, and give the day;
The moon that shines with borrowed light;
The stars that gild the gloomy night;
The seas that roll unnumbered waves;
The wood that spreads its shady leaves;
The field whose ears conceal the grain,
The yellow treasure of the plain;
All of these, and all I see,
Should be sung, and sung by me:
They speak their Maker as they can,
But want and ask the tongue of man.
Go search among your idle dreams,
Your busy or your vain extremes;
And find a life of equal bliss,
Or own the next begun in this.

1714

A NIGHT-PIECE ON DEATH

By the blue taper's trembling light,
No more I waste the wakeful night,
Intent with endless view to pore
The schoolmen and the sages o'er:
Their books from wisdom widely stray,
Or point at best the longest way.
I 'll seek a readier path, and go
Where wisdom 's surely taught below.
How deep yon azure dyes the sky,
Where orbs of gold unnumbered lie,
While through their ranks in silver pride
The nether crescent seems to glide!
The slumbering breeze forgets to breathe,
The lake is smooth and clear beneath,
Where once again the spangled show
Descends to meet our eyes below.
The grounds which on the right aspire,
In dimness from the view retire:
The left presents a place of graves,

Whose wall the silent water laves.
That steeple guides thy doubtful sight
Among the livid gleams of night.
There pass, with melancholy state,
By all the solemn heaps of fate,
And think, as softly-sad you tread
Above the venerable dead,
'Time was, like thee they life possest,
And time shall be, that thou shalt rest.'
  Those graves, with bending osier bound,
That nameless heave the crumbled ground,
Quick to the glancing thought disclose,
Where toil and poverty repose.
  The flat smooth stones that bear a name,
The chisel's slender help to fame,
(Which ere our set of friends decay
Their frequent steps may wear away,)
A middle race of mortals own,
Men, half ambitious, all unknown.
  The marble tombs that rise on high,
Whose dead in vaulted arches lie,
Whose pillars swell with sculptured stones,
Arms, angels, epitaphs, and bones,
These, all the poor remains of state,
Adorn the rich, or praise the great;
Who while on earth in fame they live,
Are senseless of the fame they give.
  Ha! while I gaze, pale Cynthia fades,
The bursting earth unveils the shades!
All slow, and wan, and wrapped with shrouds,
They rise in visionary crowds,
And all with sober accent cry,
'Think, mortal, what it is to die!'
  Now from yon black and funeral yew,
That bathes the charnel-house with dew,
Methinks I hear a voice begin;
(Ye ravens, cease your croaking din,
Ye tolling clocks, no time resound
O'er the long lake and midnight ground!)
It sends a peal of hollow groans,
Thus speaking from among the bones.
  'When men my scythe and darts supply,
How great a king of fears am I!
They view me like the last of things:
They make, and then they dread, my stings.
Fools! if you less provoked your fears,
No more my spectre form appears.
Death's but a path that must be trod,
If man would ever pass to God;
A port of calms, a state of ease
From the rough rage of swelling seas.
  'Why then thy flowing sable stoles,
Deep pendant cypress, mourning poles,
Loose scarfs to fall athwart thy weeds,
Long palls, drawn hearses, covered steeds,
And plumes of black, that, as they tread,
Nod o'er the 'scutcheons of the dead?
  'Nor can the parted body know,
Nor wants the soul, these forms of woe.
As men who long in prison dwell,
With lamps that glimmer round the cell,
Whene'er their suffering years are run,
Spring forth to greet the glittering sun:
Such joy, though far transcending sense,
Have pious souls at parting hence.
On earth, and in the body placed,
A few and evil years they waste;
But when their chains are cast aside,
See the glad scene unfolding wide,
Clap the glad wing, and tower away,
And mingle with the blaze of day.'

1722

John Gay (1685–1732)

A BALLAD

'T WAS when the seas were roaring
  With hollow blasts of wind;
A damsel lay deploring,
  All on a rock reclined.
Wide o'er the foaming billows
  She casts a wistful look;
Her head was crowned with willows,
  That tremble o'er the brook.

'Twelve months are gone and over,
  And nine long tedious days.
Why didst thou, vent'rous lover,
  Why didst thou trust the seas?
Cease, cease, thou cruel ocean,
  And let my lover rest:
Ah! what 's thy troubled motion
  To that within my breast?

'The merchant, robbed of pleasure,
  Sees tempests in despair:
But what 's the loss of treasure,
  To losing of my dear?
Should you some coast be laid on,
  Where gold and diamonds grow,
You 'd find a richer maiden,
  But none that loves you so.

'How can they say that nature
  Has nothing made in vain;
Why then beneath the water
  Should hideous rocks remain?
No eyes the rocks discover,
  That lurk beneath the deep,
To wreck the wand'ring lover,
  And leave the maid to weep.'

All melancholy lying,
  Thus wailed she for her dear:
Repaid each blast with sighing,

Each billow with a tear;
When o'er the white wave stooping,
His floating corpse she spied;
Then, like a lily drooping,
She bowed her head, and died.

1715

SWEET WILLIAM'S FAREWELL TO BLACK-EYED SUSAN

All in the Downs the fleet was moored,
The streamers waving in the wind,
When black-eyed Susan came aboard.
'Oh, where shall I my true love find?
Tell me, ye jovial sailors, tell me true,
If my sweet William sails among the crew.'

William, who high upon the yard
Rocked with the billow to and fro,
Soon as her well-known voice he heard,
He sighed, and cast his eyes below.
The cord slides swiftly through his glowing hands,
And, quick as lightning, on the deck he stands.

So the sweet lark, high poised in air,
Shuts close his pinions to his breast,
If chance his mate's shrill call he hear,
And drops at once into her nest.
The noblest captain in the British fleet
Might envy William's lip those kisses sweet.

'O Susan, Susan, lovely dear,
My vows shall ever true remain;
Let me kiss off that falling tear;
We only part to meet again.
Change, as ye list, ye winds; my heart shall be
The faithful compass that still points to thee.

'Believe not what the landmen say,
Who tempt with doubts thy constant mind:
They'll tell thee, sailors, when away,
In every port a mistress find:
Yes, yes, believe them when they tell thee so;
For thou art present wheresoe'er I go.

'If to fair India's coast we sail
Thy eyes are seen in diamonds bright,
Thy breath in Afric's spicy gale,
Thy skin is ivory so white.
Thus every beauteous object that I view,
Wakes in my soul some charm of lovely Sue.

'Though battle call me from thy arms,
Let not my pretty Susan mourn;
Though cannons roar, yet, safe from harms,
William shall to his dear return.
Love turns aside the balls that round me fly,
Lest precious tears should drop from Susan's eye.'

The boatswain gave the dreadful word,
The sails their swelling bosom spread;
No longer must she stay aboard:
They kissed, she sighed, he hung his head.
Her less'ning boat unwilling rows to land:
'Adieu!' she cries; and waved her lily hand.

1720

John Hughes (1677-1720)

THE PICTURE

Come, my Muse, a Venus draw;
Not the same the Grecians saw,
By the famed Apelles wrought,
Beauteous offspring of his thought.
No fantastic goddess mine,
Fiction far she does outshine.
Queen of fancy! hither bring
On thy gaudy-feathered wing
All the beauties of the spring.
Like the bee's industrious pains
To collect his golden gains,
So from every flower and plant
Gather first the immortal paint.
Fetch me lilies, fetch me roses,
Daisies, violets, cowslip-posies,
Amaranthus, parrot-pride,
Woodbines, pinks, and what beside
Does the embroidered meads adorn;
Where the fawns and satyrs play
In the merry month of May.
Steal the blush of opening morn;
Borrow Cynthia's silver white,
When she shines at noon of night,
Free from clouds to veil her light.
Juno's bird his tail shall spread,
Iris' bow its colours shed,
All to deck this charming piece,
Far surpassing ancient Greece.
First her graceful stature show,
Not too tall, nor yet too low.
Fat she must not be, nor lean;
Let her shape be straight and clean;
Small her waist, and thence increased,
Gently swells her rising breast.
Next in comely order trace
All the glories of her face.
Paint her neck of ivory,
Smiling cheeks and forehead high,
Ruby lips, and sparkling eyes.

Whence resistless lightning flies,
  Foolish Muse! what hast thou done!
Scarce th' outlines are yet begun,
Ere thy pencil 's thrown aside!
''T is no matter,' Love replied;
(Love's unlucky god stood by)
'At one stroke behold how I
Will th' unfinished draught supply.'
  Smiling then he took his dart,
And drew her picture in my heart.

1735

Henry Carey (1693?–1743)

SALLY IN OUR ALLEY

Of all the girls that are so smart
  There 's none like pretty Sally;
She is the darling of my heart,
  And she lives in our alley.
There is no lady in the land
  Is half so sweet as Sally;
She is the darling of my heart,
  And she lives in our alley.

Her father he makes cabbage-nets
  And through the streets does cry 'em;
Her mother she sells laces long
  To such as please to buy 'em:
But sure such folks could ne'er beget
  So sweet a girl as Sally!
She is the darling of my heart,
  And she lives in our alley.

When she is by, I leave my work,
  I love her so sincerely;
My master comes like any Turk,
  And bangs me most severely —
But let him bang his bellyful,
  I'll bear it all for Sally;
She is the darling of my heart,
  And she lives in our alley.

Of all the days that 's in the week
  I dearly love but one day —
And that 's the day that comes betwixt
  A Saturday and Monday;
For then I 'm drest all in my best
  To walk abroad with Sally;
She is the darling of my heart,
  And she lives in our alley.

My master carries me to church,
  And often am I blamed
Because I leave him in the lurch
  As soon as text is named;
I leave the church in sermon-time
  And slink away to Sally;
She is the darling of my heart,
  And she lives in our alley.

When Christmas comes about again
  O then I shall have money;
I'll hoard it up, and box it all,
  I'll give it to my honey:
I would it were ten thousand pound,
  I 'd give it all to Sally;
She is the darling of my heart,
  And she lives in our alley.

My master and the neighbours all
  Make game of me and Sally,
And, but for her, I 'd better be
  A slave and row a galley;
But when my seven long years are out
  O then I 'll marry Sally,—
O then we 'll wed, and then we 'll bed
  But not in our alley!

1713? 1724

Mark Akenside (1721–1770)

HYMN TO SCIENCE

Science! thou fair effusive ray
From the great source of mental day,
  Free, generous, and refined!
Descend with all thy treasures fraught,
Illumine each bewildered thought,
  And bless my labouring mind.

But first with thy resistless light
Disperse those phantoms from my sight,
  Those mimic shades of thee:
The scholiast's learning, sophist's cant,
The visionary bigots rant,
  The monk's philosophy.

Oh! let thy powerful charms impart
The patient head, the candid heart,
  Devoted to thy sway;
Which no weak passions e'er mislead,
Which still with dauntless steps proceed
  Where reason points the way.

Give me to learn each secret cause;
Let number's, figure's, motion's laws
  Revealed before me stand;
These to great Nature's scenes apply,
And round the globe, and through the sky,
  Disclose her working hand.

Next, to thy nobler search resigned,
The busy, restless, human mind
  Through every maze pursue;
Detect perception where it lies,

Catch the ideas as they rise,
  And all their changes view.

Say from what simple springs began
The vast ambitious thoughts of man,
  Which range beyond control,
Which seek eternity to trace,
Dive through the infinity of space,
  And strain to grasp the whole.

Her secret stores let memory tell,
Bid Fancy quit her fairy cell,
  In all her colours drest;
While, prompt her sallies to control,
Reason, the judge, recalls the soul
  To Truth's severest test.

Then launch through being's wide extent;
Let the fair scale with just ascent
  And cautious steps be trod;
And from the dead, corporeal mass,
Through each progressive order, pass
  To Instinct, Reason, God.

There, Science, veil thy daring eye;
Nor dive too deep, nor soar too high,
  In that divine abyss;
To faith content thy beams to lend,
Her hopes t'assure, her steps befriend
  And light her way to bliss.

Then downwards take thy flight again,
Mix with the policies of men,
  And social nature's ties;
The plan, the genius of each state,
Its interest and its powers relate,
  Its fortunes and its rise.

Through private life pursue thy course,
Trace every action to its source,
  And means and motives weigh:
Put tempers, passions, in the scale;
Mark what degrees in each prevail,
  And fix the doubtful sway.

That last best effort of thy skill,
To form the life, and rule the will,
  Propitious power! impart:
Teach me to cool my passion's fires,
Make me the judge of my desires,
  The master of my heart.

Raise me above the vulgar's breath,
Pursuit of fortune, fear of death,
  And all in life that's mean:
Still true to reason by my plan,
Still let my actions speak the man,
  Through every various scene.

Hail! queen of manners, light of truth;
Hail! charm of age, and guide of youth;
  Sweet refuge of distress:
In business, thou, exact, polite;
Thou giv'st retirement its delight,
  Prosperity its grace.

Of wealth, power, freedom, thou the cause;
Foundress of order, cities, laws;
  Of arts inventress thou:
Without thee, what were human-kind?
How vast their wants, their thoughts how blind!
  Their joys how mean, how few!

Sun of the soul! thy beams unveil:
Let others spread the daring sail,
  On Fortune's faithless sea:
While, undeluded, happier I
From the vain tumult timely fly,
  And sit in peace with thee.

1739

FOR A GROTTO

To me, whom, in their lays, the shepherds call
Actæa, daughter of the neighboring stream,
This cave belongs. The fig-tree and the vine,
Which o'er the rocky entrance downward shoot
Were placed by Glycon. He, with cowslips pale,
Primrose, and purple lychnis, decked the green
Before my threshold, and my shelving walls
With honeysuckle covered. Here, at noon,
Lulled by the murmur of my rising fount,
I slumber: here my clustering fruits I tend;
Or from the humid flowers at break of day,
Fresh garlands weave, and chase from all my bounds
Each thing impure or noxious. Enter in,
O stranger, undismayed. Nor bat, nor toad
Here lurks: and, if thy breast of blameless thoughts
Approve thee, not unwelcome shalt thou tread
My quiet mansion: chiefly, if thy name
Wise Pallas and the immortal Muses own.

1758

PROSE

SATIRE

Daniel Defoe (1660?–1731)

THE SHORTEST WAY WITH THE DISSENTERS

Sir Roger L'Estrange tells us a story in his collection of Fables, of the cock and the horses. The cock was gotten to roost in the stable among the horses; and there being no racks or other conveniences for him, it seems he was forced to roost upon the ground. The horses jostling about for room and putting the cock in danger of his life, he gives them this grave advice, 'Pray, gentlefolks! let us stand still! for fear we should tread upon one another!'

There are some people in the world, who, now they are unperched, and reduced to an equality with other people, and under strong and very just apprehensions of being further treated as they deserve, begin with Esop's cock, to preach up peace and union and the Christian duty of moderation; forgetting that when they had the power in their hands, those graces were strangers in their gates!

It is now near fourteen years, that the glory and peace of the purest and most flourishing church in the world has been eclipsed, buffeted, and disturbed by a sort of men whom God in his providence has suffered to insult over her, and bring her down. These have been the days of her humiliation and tribulation. She has borne with an invincible patience the reproach of the wicked; and God has at last heard her prayers, and delivered her from the oppression of the stranger.

And now, they find their day is over, their power gone, and the throne of this nation possessed by a royal, English, true, and ever constant member of, and friend to, the Church of England. Now they find that they are in danger of the Church of England's just resentments. Now, they cry out, 'Peace!' 'Union!' 'Forbearance!' and 'Charity!': as if the Church had not too long harbored her enemies under her wing, and nourished the viperous brood, till they hiss and fly in the face of the mother that cherished them!

No, gentlemen, the time of mercy is past, your day of grace is over, you should have practised peace, and moderation, and charity, if you expected any yourselves.

We have heard none of this lesson for fourteen years past. We have been huffed and bullied with your Act of Toleration. You have told us you are the Church established by law, as well as others; have set up your canting synagogues at our church doors; and the Church and her members have been loaded with reproaches, with oaths, associations, abjurations, and what not! Where has been the mercy, the forbearance, the charity you have shown to tender consciences of the Church of England that could not take oaths as fast as you made them; that, having sworn allegiance to their lawful and rightful king, could not dispense with that oath, their king being still alive, and swear to your new hodge-podge of a Dutch government? These have been turned out of their livings, and they and their families left to starve; their estates double taxed to carry on a war they had no hand in, and you got nothing by!

What account can you give of the multitudes you have forced to comply, against their consciences, with your new sophistical politics, who, like new converts in France, sin because they cannot starve? And now the tables are turned upon you, you must not be persecuted! It is not a Christian spirit!

You have butchered one king, deposed another king, and made a mock king of a third, and yet, you could have the face to expect to be employed and trusted by the fourth! Anybody that did not know the temper of your party, would stand amazed at the impudence as well as the folly to think of it!

Your management of your Dutch monarch, whom you reduced to a mere King of Clubs, is enough to give any future princes such an idea of your principles as to warn them sufficiently from coming into your clutches; and, God be thanked, the Queen is out of your hands, knows you, and will have a care of you!

There is no doubt but the supreme authority of a nation has in itself a power, and a right to that power, to execute the laws upon any part of that nation it governs. The execution of the known laws of the land, and that with but a gentle hand neither, was all that the fanatical party of this land have ever called persecution. This they have magnified to a height that the sufferings of the Huguenots in France were not to be compared with them. Now to execute the known laws of a nation upon those who transgress them, after having first been voluntarily consenting to the making of those laws, can never be called persecution, but justice. But justice is always violence to the party offending, for every man is innocent in his own eyes.

The first execution of the laws against Dissenters in England was in the days of King James I; and what did it amount to? Truly, the worst they suffered was, at their own request, to let them go to New England, and erect a new colony; and give them great privileges, grants, and suitable powers; keep them under protection, and defend them against all invaders; and receive no taxes or revenue from them!

This was the cruelty of the Church of England. Fatal lenity! It was the ruin of that excellent prince, King Charles I. Had King James sent all the Puritans in England away to the West Indies, we had been a national unmixed church. The Church of England had been kept undivided and entire!

To requite the lenity of the father, they take up arms against the son, conquer, pursue, take, imprison, and at last put to death the anointed of God, and destroy the very being and nature of government: setting up a sordid impostor, who had neither title to govern, nor understanding to manage, but supplied that want, with power, bloody and desperate counsels and craft, without conscience.

Had not King James I withheld the full execution of the laws: had he given them strict justice, he had cleared the nation of them! And the consequences had been plain; his son had never been murdered by them, nor the monarchy overwhelmed. It was too much mercy shown them that was the ruin of his posterity, and the ruin of the nation's peace. One would think the Dissenters should not have the face to believe that we are to be wheedled and canted into peace and toleration, when they know that they have once requited us with a civil war, and once with an intolerable and unrighteous persecution, for our former civility.

Nay, to encourage us to be easy with them, it is apparent that they never had the upper hand of the Church but they treated her with all the severity, with all the reproach and contempt as was possible! What peace and what mercy did they show the loyal gentry of the Church of England, in the time of their triumphant Commonwealth? How did they put all the gentry of England to ransom, whether they were actually in arms for the king or not, making people compound for their estates, and starve their families! How did they treat the clergy of the Church of England, sequester the ministers, devour the patrimony of the Church and divide the spoil, by sharing the Church lands among their soldiers, and turning her clergy out to starve! Just such measure as they have meted, should be measured to them again!

Charity and love is the known doctrine of the Church of England, and it is plain she has put it in practise towards the Dissenters, even beyond what they ought, till she has been wanting to herself, and in effect unkind to her own sons; particularly, in the too much lenity of King James I, mentioned before. Had he so rooted the Puritans from the face of the land, which he had an opportunity early to have done, they had not had the power to vex the Church, as since they have done.

In the days of King Charles II, how did the Church reward their bloody doings with lenity and mercy! Except the barbarous regicides of the pretended court of justice, not a soul suffered for all the blood in an unnatural war. King Charles came in all mercy and love, cherished them, preferred them, employed them, withheld the rigor of the law and oftentimes, even against the advice of his Parliament, gave them liberty of conscience; and how did they requite him? With the villainous contrivance to depose and murder him and his successor, at the Rye House Plot!

King James II, as if mercy was the inherent quality of the family, began his reign with unusual favor to them. Nor could their joining with the Duke of Monmouth against him, move him to do himself justice upon them. But that mistaken prince, thinking to win them by gentleness and love, proclaimed a universal liberty to them, and rather discountenanced the Church of England than them. How they requited him, all the world knows!

The late reign is too fresh in the memory of all the world to need a comment. How under pretense of joining with the Church in redressing some grievances, they pushed things to that extremity, in conjunction with some mistaken gentlemen, as to depose the late king; as if the grievance of the nation could not have been redressed but by the absolute ruin of the prince.

Here is an instance of their temper, their peace, and charity!

To what height they carried themselves during the reign of a king of their own, how they crope into all places of trust and profit; how they insinuated themselves into the favor of the king, and were at first preferred to the highest places in the nation, how they engrossed the ministry; and, above all, how pitifully they managed, is too plain to need any remarks.

But particularly, their mercy and charity, the spirit of union they tell us so much of, has been remarkable in Scotland. If any man would see the spirit of a Dissenter, let him look into Scotland. There, they made entire conquest of the Church, trampled down the sacred orders and suppressed the episcopal government, with an absolute, and, as they supposed, irretrievable victory; though it is possible they may find themselves mistaken!

Now it would be a very proper question to ask their impudent advocate, the *Observator*, 'Pray how much mercy and favor did the members of the Episcopal Church find in Scotland from the Scotch Presbyterian government?' And I shall undertake for the Church of England, that the Dissenters shall still receive as much here, though they deserve but little.

In a small treatise of *The Sufferings of the Episcopal Clergy in Scotland*, it will appear what usage they met with, how they not only lost their livings; but, in several places, were plundered and abused in their persons; the ministers that could not conform, turned out, with numerous families and no maintenance, and hardly charity enough left to relieve them with a bit of bread. The cruelties of the party were innumerable, and are not to be attempted in this short piece.

And now, to prevent the distant cloud which they perceive to hang over their heads from England, with a true Presbyterian policy, they put in for a union of nations — that England might unite their Church with the Kirk of Scotland, and their assembly of Scotch canting long-cloaks in our convocation. What might have been, if our fanatic Whiggish statesmen continued, God only knows; but we hope we are out of fear of that now.

It is alleged by some of the faction, and they have begun to bully us with it, that 'if we won't unite with them, they will not settle the Crown with us again; but when her Majesty dies, will choose a king for themselves!'

If they won't, we must make them; and it is not the first time we have let them know that we are able. The crowns of these kingdoms have not so far disowned the right of succession, but they may retrieve it again; and if Scotland thinks to come off from a successive to an elective state of government, England has not promised not to assist the right heir, and put him into possession, without any regards to their ridiculous settlements.

These are the gentlemen! these, their ways of treating the Church, both at home and abroad!

Now let us examine the reasons they pretend to give, why we should be favorable to them; why we should continue and tolerate them among us.

First. They are very numerous, they say. They are a great part of the nation, and we cannot suppress them!

To this, may be answered:

First. They are not so numerous as the Protestants in France: and yet the French king effectually cleared the nation of them at once; and we don't find he misses them at home!

But I am not of the opinion they are so numerous as is pretended. Their party is more numerous than their persons; and those mistaken people of the Church who are misled and deluded by their wheedling artifices to join with them, make their party the greater: but those will open their eyes when the government shall set heartily about the work, and come off from them, as some animals, which they say, always desert a house when it is likely to fall.

Secondly. The more numerous, the more dangerous; and therefore the more need to suppress them; and God has suffered us to bear them as goads in our sides, for not utterly extinguishing them long ago.

Thirdly. If we are to allow them, only because we cannot suppress them, then it ought to be tried, whether we can or no; and I am of opinion it is easy to be done, and could prescribe ways and means, if it were proper: but I doubt not the government will find effectual methods for the rooting of the contagion from the face of this land.

Another argument they use, which is this. That this is a time of war, and we have need to unite against the common enemy.

We answer, this common enemy had been no enemy, if they had not made him so. He was quiet, in peace, and no way disturbed and encroached upon us; and we know no reason we had to quarrel with him.

But further. We make no question but we are able to deal with this common enemy without their help: but why must we unite with them, because of the enemy? Will they go over to the enemy, if we do not prevent it, by a union with them? We are very well contented they should, and make no question, we shall be ready to deal with them and the common enemy too; and better without them than with them. Besides, if we have a common enemy, there is the more need to be secure against our private enemies. If there is one common enemy, we have the less need to have an enemy in our bowels!

It was a great argument some people used against suppressing the old money, that 'it was a time of war, and it was too great a risk for the nation to run. If we should not master it, we should be undone!' And yet the sequel proved the hazard was not so great but it might be mastered, and the success was answerable. The suppressing the Dissenters is not a harder work, nor a work of less necessity to the public. We can never enjoy a settled, uninterrupted union and tranquillity in this nation, till the spirit of Whiggism, faction, and schism is melted down like the old money!

To talk of difficulty is to frighten ourselves with chimeras and notions of a powerful party, which are indeed a party without power. Difficulties often appear greater at a distance than when they are searched into with judgment, and distinguished from the vapors and shadows that attend them.

We are not to be frightened with it! This age is wiser than that, by all our own experience, and theirs too! King Charles I had early suppressed this party, if he had taken more deliberate measures. In short, it is not worth arguing, to talk of their arms. Their Monmouths and Shaftesburys and Argyles are gone! Their Dutch sanctuary is at an end! Heaven has made way for their destruction, and if we do not close with the divine occasion, we are to blame ourselves! and may hereafter remember that we had, once, an opportunity to serve the Church of England, by extirpating her implacable enemies; and having let slip the minute that Heaven presented, may experimentally complain, *post est occasio calva.*

Here are some popular objections in the way.

As first, the queen has promised them to continue them in their tolerated liberty; and has told us she will be a religious observer of her word.

What her Majesty will do we cannot help, but what, as the head of the Church, she ought to do, is another case. Her Majesty has promised to protect and defend the

Church of England, and if she cannot effectually do that without the destruction of the Dissenters, she must, of course, dispense with one promise to comply with another.

But to answer this cavil more effectually. Her Majesty did never promise to maintain the toleration to the destruction of the Church; but it was upon supposition that it may be compatible with the well-being and safety of the Church, which she had declared she would take especial care of. Now if these two interests clash, it is plain her Majesty's intentions are to uphold, protect, defend, and establish the Church; and this, we conceive, is impossible.

Perhaps it may be said, that the Church is in no immediate danger from the Dissenters, and therefore it is time enough.

But this is a weak answer. For first: if the danger be real, the distance of it is no argument against, but rather a spur to quicken us to prevention, lest it be too late hereafter.

And secondly: here is the opportunity, and the only one, perhaps, that ever the Church had to secure herself and destroy her enemies.

The representatives of the nation have now an opportunity. The time is come which all good men have wished for, that the gentlemen of England may serve the Church of England, now they are protected and encouraged by a Church of England queen!

What will you do for your sister in the day that she shall be spoken for?

If ever you will establish the best Christian church in the world; if ever you will suppress the spirit of enthusiasm; if ever you will free the nation from the viperous brood that have so long sucked the blood of their mother; if ever you will leave your posterity free from faction and rebellion, this is the time! This is the time to pull up this heretical weed of sedition, that has so long disturbed the peace of the Church, and poisoned the good corn!

But, says another hot and cold objector, this is renewing fire and faggot, reviving the Act, *de heretico comburendo*. This will be cruelty in its nature, and barbarous to all the world.

I answer, it is cruelty to kill a snake or a toad in cold blood, but the poison of their nature makes it a charity to our neighbors to destroy those creatures, not for any personal injury received, but for prevention; not for the evil they have done, but the evil they may do. Serpents, toads, vipers, etc., are noxious to the body, and poison the sensitive life: these poison the soul, corrupt our posterity, ensnare our children, destroy the vitals of our happiness, our future felicity, and contaminate the whole mass!

Shall any law be given to such wild creatures? Some beasts are for sport, and the huntsmen give them the advantages of ground, but some are knocked on the head by all possible ways of violence and surprise.

I do not prescribe fire and faggot; but as Scipio said of Carthage, *Delenda est Carthago!* They are to be rooted out of this nation, if ever we will live in peace, serve God, or enjoy our own. As for the manner, I leave it to those hands who have a right to execute God's justice on the nation's and the Church's enemies.

But if we must be frighted from this justice, under these specious pretenses, and odious sense of cruelty, nothing will be effected. It will be more barbarous to our own children and dear posterity, when they shall reproach their fathers, as we ours, and tell us, 'You had an opportunity to root out this cursed race from the world under the favor and protection of a true Church of England queen, and out of your foolish pity, you spared them, because, forsooth, you would not be cruel! And now our Church is suppressed and persecuted, our religion trampled under foot, our estates plundered, our persons imprisoned, and dragged to gaols, gibbets, and scaffolds! Your sparing this Amalekite race is our destruction! Your mercy to them proves cruelty to your poor posterity!'

How just will such reflections be when our posterity shall fall under the merciless clutches of this uncharitable generation; when our Church shall be swallowed up in schism, faction, enthusiasm, and confusion; when our government shall be devolved upon foreigners, and our monarchy dwindled into a republic!

It would be more rational for us, if we

must spare this generation, to summon our own to a general massacre; and as we have brought them into the world free, to send them out so; and not betray them to destruction by our supine negligence, and then cry, 'It is mercy!'

Moses was a merciful meek man; and yet with what fury did he run through the camp, and cut the throats of three and thirty thousand of his dear Israelites that were fallen into idolatry. What was the reason? It was mercy to the rest, to make these examples, to prevent the destruction of the whole army.

How many millions of future souls we save from infection and delusion, if the present race of poisoned spirits were purged from the face of the land!

It is vain to trifle in this matter. The light foolish handling of them by mulcts, fines, etc.; 't is their glory and their advantage! If the gallows instead of the counter, and the galleys instead of the fines were the reward of going to a conventicle to preach or hear, there would not be so many sufferers. The spirit of martyrdom is over. They that will go to church to be chosen sheriffs and mayors, would go to forty churches rather than be hanged!

If one severe law were made and punctually executed that whoever was found at a conventicle should be banished the nation, and the preacher be hanged, we should soon see an end of the tale. They would all come to church again, and one age would make us all one again.

To talk of five shillings a month for not coming to the sacrament, and one shilling per week, for not coming to church: this is such a way of converting people as was never known. This is selling them a liberty to transgress, for so much money.

If it be not a crime, why don't we give them full license? And if it be, no price ought to compound for the committing of it, for that is selling a liberty to people to sin against God and the government.

If it be a crime of the highest consequence, both against the peace and welfare of the nation, the glory of God, the good of the Church, and the happiness of the soul, let us rank it among capital offenses, and let it receive a punishment in proportion to it.

We hang men for trifles, and banish them for things not worth naming; but that an offense against God and the Church, against the welfare of the world, and the dignity of religion shall be bought off for five shillings: this is such a shame to a Christian government that it is with regret I transmit it to posterity.

If men sin against God, affront his ordinances, rebel against his church, and disobey the precepts of their superiors; let them suffer, as such capital crimes deserve. So will religion flourish, and this divided nation be once again united.

And yet the title of barbarous and cruel will soon be taken off from this law too. I am not supposing that all the Dissenters in England should be hanged or banished. But as in case of rebellions and insurrections, if a few of the ringleaders suffer, the multitude are dismissed; so a few obstinate people being made examples, there is no doubt but the severity of the law would find a stop in the compliance of the multitude.

To make the reasonableness of this matter out of question, and more unanswerably plain, let us examine for what it is that this nation is divided into parties and factions; and let us see how they can justify a separation; or we of the Church of England can justify our bearing the insults and inconveniences of the party.

One of their leading pastors, and a man of as much learning as most among them, in his *Answer* to a pamphlet entitled *An Enquiry into the Occasional Conformity*, hath these words, p. 27:—'Do the religion of the Church and the meeting houses make two religions? Wherein do they differ? The substance of the same religion is common to them both, and the modes and accidents are the things in which only they differ.' P. 28:—'Thirty-nine Articles are given us for the summary of our religion; thirty-six contain the substance of it wherein we agree; three are additional appendices, about which we have some differences.'

Now, if, as by their own acknowledgment, the Church of England is a true church, and the difference is only in a few 'modes and accidents,' why should we expect that they will suffer the gallows and galleys, corporal punishment and banishment, for these trifles? There is no question, but they will be wiser. Even their own principles won't bear them out in it.

They will certainly comply with the laws, and with reason. And though, at the first, severity may seem hard, the next age will feel nothing of it; the contagion will be rooted out. The disease being cured, there will be no need of the operation. But if they should venture to transgress, and fall into the pit, all the world must condemn their obstinacy, as being without ground from their own principles.

Thus the pretense of cruelty will be taken off, and the party actually suppressed, and the disquiets they have so often brought upon the nation, prevented.

Their numbers and their wealth make them haughty; and that is so far from being an argument to persuade us to forbear them, that it is a warning to us, without any more delay, to reconcile them to the unity of the Church, or remove them from us.

At present, Heaven be praised! they are not so formidable as they have been, and it is our own fault if ever we suffer them to be so. Providence and the Church of England seem to join in this particular, that now the destroyers of the nation's peace may be overturned; and to this end, the present opportunity seems to put into our hands.

To this end, her present Majesty seems reserved to enjoy the crown, that the ecclesiastic as well as civil rights of the nation may be restored by her hand.

To this end, the face of affairs has received such a turn in the process of a few months as never has been before. The leading men of the nation, the universal cry of the people, the unanimous request of the clergy agree in this, that the deliverance of our Church is at hand!

For this end, has Providence given such a parliament, such a convocation, such a gentry, and such a queen, as we never had before.

And what may be the consequences of a neglect of such opportunities? The succession of the crown has but a dark prospect. Another Dutch turn may make the hopes of it ridiculous, and the practice impossible. Be the house of our future princes ever so well inclined, they will be foreigners. Many years will be spent in suiting the genius of strangers to this crown, and the interests of the nation; and how many ages it may be before the English throne be filled with so much zeal and candor, so much tenderness and hearty affection to the Church, as we see it now covered with, who can imagine?

It is high time, then, for the friends of the Church of England to think of building up and establishing her in such a manner that she may be no more invaded by foreigners, nor divided by factions, schisms, and error.

If this could be done by gentle and easy methods, I should be glad: but the wound is corroded, the vitals begin to mortify, and nothing but amputation of members can complete the cure. All the ways of tenderness and compassion, all persuasive arguments have been made use of in vain.

The humor of the Dissenters has so increased among the people, that they hold the Church in defiance, and the house of God is an abomination among them. Nay, they have brought up their posterity in such prepossessed aversion to our holy religion, that the ignorant mob think we are all idolators and worshippers of Baal, and account it a sin to come within the walls of our churches. The primitive Christians were not more shy of a heathen temple, or of meat offered to idols, nor the Jews of swine's flesh, than some of our Dissenters are of the church and the divine service solemnized therein.

The obstinacy must be rooted out, with the profession of it. While the generation are left at liberty daily to affront God Almighty, and dishonor his holy worship, we are wanting in our duty to God, and to our mother, the Church of England.

How can we answer it to God, to the Church, and to our posterity, to leave them entangled with fanaticism, error, and obstinacy, in the bowels of the nation; to leave them an enemy in their streets, that, in time, may involve them in the same crimes, and endanger the utter extirpation of the religion of the nation.

What is the difference betwixt this, and being subject to the power of the Church of Rome, from whence we have reformed? If one be an extreme to the one hand, and one on another, it is equally destructive to the truth to have errors settled among us, let them be of what nature they will. Both are enemies of our Church, and of our peace; and why should it not be as criminal to admit an enthusiast as a Jesuit? Why should the papist with his seven sacraments be worse than the Quaker with no sacraments at all? Why should religious houses be more intolerable than meeting houses?

Alas, the Church of England! What with popery on one hand, and schismatics on the other, how has she been crucified between two thieves. Now, let us crucify the thieves!

Let her foundations be established upon the destruction of her enemies! The doors of mercy being always open to the returning part of the deluded people, let the obstinate be ruled with the rod of iron!

Let all true sons of so holy and oppressed a mother, exasperated by her afflictions, harden their hearts against those who have oppressed her.

And may God Almighty put it into the hearts of all the friends of truth, to lift up a standard against pride and Antichrist, that the posterity of the sons of error may be rooted out from the face of this land, for ever!

1702

Jonathan Swift (1667–1745)

A MEDITATION UPON A BROOMSTICK

This single stick, which you now behold ingloriously lying in that neglected corner, I once knew in a flourishing state in a forest: it was full of sap, full of leaves, and full of boughs: but now, in vain does the busy art of man pretend to vie with nature, by tying that withered bundle of twigs to its sapless trunk; it is now, at best, but the reverse of what it was, a tree turned upside down, the branches on the earth, and the root in the air; it is now handled by every dirty wench, condemned to do her drudgery, and by a capricious kind of fate, destined to make other things clean, and be nasty itself: at length, worn to the stumps in the service of the maids, it is either thrown out of doors, or condemned to the last use, of kindling a fire. When I beheld this, I sighed, and said within myself, Surely man is a broomstick! Nature sent him into the world strong and lusty, in a thriving condition, wearing his own hair on his head, the proper branches of this reasoning vegetable, until the axe of intemperance has lopped off his green boughs, and left him a withered trunk: he then flies to art, and puts on a perriwig, valuing himself upon an unnatural bundle of hairs (all covered with powder) that never grew on his head; but now, should this our broomstick pretend to enter the scene, proud of those birchen spoils it never bore, and all covered with dust, though the sweepings of the finest lady's chamber, we should be apt to ridicule and despise its vanity. Partial judges that we are of our own excellencies, and other men's defaults!

But a broomstick, perhaps you will say, is an emblem of a tree standing on its head; and pray what is man, but a topsy-turvy creature, his animal faculties perpetually mounted on his rational, his head where his heels should be, grovelling on the earth! And yet, with all his faults, he sets up to be a universal reformer and corrector of abuses, a remover of grievances, rakes into every slut's corner of nature, bringing hidden corruption to the light, and raises a mighty dust where there was none before; sharing deeply all the while in the very same pollutions he pretends to sweep away: his last days are spent in slavery to women, and generally the least deserving; till worn out to the stumps, like his brother besom, he is either kicked out of doors, or made use of to kindle flames for others to warm themselves by.

1704

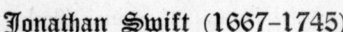

A MODEST PROPOSAL

FOR PREVENTING THE CHILDREN OF POOR PEOPLE IN IRELAND FROM BEING A BURDEN TO THEIR PARENTS OR COUNTRY, AND FOR MAKING THEM BENEFICIAL TO THE PUBLIC

It is a melancholy object to those, who walk through this great town, or travel in the country, when they see the streets, the roads, and cabin doors crowded with beggars of the female sex, followed by three, four, or six children, all in rags and importuning every passenger for an alms. These mothers, instead of being able to work for their honest livelihood, are forced to employ all their time in strolling to beg sustenance for their helpless infants; who as they grow up, either turn thieves, for want of work, or leave their dear native country to fight for the pretender in Spain, or sell themselves to the Barbadoes.

I think it is agreed by all parties, that this prodigious number of children in the arms, or on the backs, or at the heels of their mothers, and frequently of their fathers, is, in the present deplorable state of the kingdom, a very great additional grievance; and therefore whoever could find out a fair, cheap, and easy method of making these children sound useful members of the commonwealth, would deserve so well of the public, as to have his statue set up for a preserver of the nation.

But my intention is very far from being confined to provide only for the children of professed beggars: it is of a much greater extent, and shall take in the whole number of infants at a certain age, who are born of parents in effect as little able to support them, as those who demand our charity in the streets.

As to my own part, having turned my thoughts for many years upon this important subject, and maturely weighed the several schemes of our projectors, I have always found them grossly mistaken in their computation. It is true, a child just dropped from its dam may be supported by her milk for a solar year, with little other nourishment: at most not above the value of two shillings which the mother may certainly get, or the value in scraps, by her lawful occupation of begging; and it is exactly at one year old that I propose to provide for them in such a manner, as, instead of being a charge upon their parents or the parish, or wanting food and raiment for the rest of their lives, they shall, on the contrary, contribute to the feeding, and partly to the clothing of many thousands.

There is likewise another great advantage in my scheme, that it will prevent those voluntary abortions, and that horrid practice of women murdering their bastard children, alas! too frequent among us, sacrificing the poor innocent babes, I doubt more to avoid the expense than the shame, which would move tears and pity in the most savage and inhuman breast.

The number of souls in this kingdom being usually reckoned one million and a half, of these I calculate there may be about two hundred thousand couple, whose wives are breeders; from which number I subtract thirty thousand couple, who are able to maintain their own children, (although I apprehend there cannot be so many, under the present distresses of the kingdom) but this being granted, there will remain an hundred and seventy thousand breeders. I again subtract fifty thousand for those women who miscarry, or whose children die by accident or disease within the year. There only remains one hundred and twenty thousand children of poor parents annually born. The question therefore is, How this number shall be reared and provided for? which, as I have already said, under the present situation of affairs, is utterly impossible by all the methods hitherto proposed. For we can neither employ them in handicraft or agriculture; we neither build houses, (I mean in the country) nor cultivate land: they can very seldom pick up a livelihood by stealing, till they arrive at six years old, except where they are of towardly parts; although I confess they learn the rudiments much earlier; during which time they can however be properly looked upon only as probationers; as I have been informed by a principal gentleman in the county of Cavan, who protested to me, that he never knew above one or two instances under the age of six, even in a part of the kingdom so renowned for the quickest proficiency in that art.

I am assured by our merchants, that a boy or a girl before twelve years old is no salable commodity; and even when they come to this age, they will not yield above three pounds, or three pounds and half a crown at most, on the exchange; which cannot turn to account either to the parents or kingdom, the charge of nutriment and rags having been at least four times that value.

I shall now therefore humbly propose my own thoughts, which I hope will not be liable to the least objection.

I have been assured by a very knowing American of my acquaintance in London, that a young healthy child, well nursed, is at a year old a most delicious, nourishing, and wholesome food, whether stewed, roasted, baked, or boiled; and I make no doubt that it will equally serve in a fricassee, or a ragout.

I do therefore humbly offer it to public consideration, that of the hundred and twenty thousand children already computed, twenty thousand may be reserved for breed, whereof only one fourth part to be males; which is more than we allow to sheep, black cattle, or swine; and my reason is, that these children are seldom the fruits of marriage, a circumstance not much regarded by our savages, therefore one male will be sufficient to serve four females. That the remaining hundred thousand may, at a year old, be offered in sale to the persons of quality and fortune through the kingdom; always advising the mother to let them suck plentifully in the last month, so as to render them plump and fat for a good table. A child will make two dishes at an entertainment for friends; and when the family dines alone, the fore or hind quarter will make a reasonable dish, and seasoned with a little pepper or salt, will be very good boiled on the fourth day, especially in winter.

I have reckoned upon a medium, that a child just born will weigh 12 pounds, and in a solar year, if tolerably nursed, will increase to 28 pounds.

I grant this food will be somewhat dear, and therefore very proper for landlords, who, as they have already devoured most of the parents, seem to have the best title to the children.

Infant's flesh will be in season throughout the year, but more plentiful in March, and a little before and after; for we are told by a grave author, an eminent French physician, that fish being a prolific diet, there are more children born in Roman Catholic countries about nine months after Lent, than at any other season; therefore, reckoning a year after Lent, the markets will be more glutted than usual, because the number of popish infants is at least three to one in this kingdom; and therefore it will have one other collateral advantage, by lessening the number of papists among us.

I have already computed the charge of nursing a beggar's child (in which list I reckon all cottagers, labourers, and four fifths of the farmers) to be about two shillings per annum, rags included; and I believe no gentleman would repine to give ten shillings for the carcass of a good fat child, which, as I have said, will make four dishes of excellent nutritive meat, when he has only some particular friend or his own family to dine with him. Thus the squire will learn to be a good landlord, and grow popular among his tenants; the mother will have eight shillings net profit, and be fit for work, till she produces another child.

Those who are more thrifty (as I must confess the times require) may flay the carcass; the skin of which artificially dressed will make admirable gloves for ladies, and summer boots for fine gentlemen.

As to our city of Dublin, shambles may be appointed for this purpose in the most convenient parts of it, and butchers we may be assured will not be wanting; although I rather recommend buying the children alive, than dressing them hot from the knife, as we do roasting pigs.

A very worthy person, a true lover of his country, and whose virtues I highly esteem, was lately pleased in discoursing on this matter to offer a refinement upon my scheme. He said, that many gentlemen of this kingdom, having of late destroyed their deer, he conceived that the want of venison might be well supplied by the bodies of young lads and maidens, not exceeding fourteen years of age nor under twelve; so great a number of both sexes in every country being now ready to starve for want of work and service: and these to be disposed of by their parents if alive, or otherwise by their nearest relations. But with due deference to so excellent a friend, and so deserving a patriot, I cannot be altogether in his sentiments; for as to the males, my American acquaintance assured me from frequent experience, that their flesh was generally tough and lean, like that of our school-boys, by continual exercise, and their taste disagreeable, and to fatten them would not answer the charge. Then as to the females, it would, I think with humble submission, be a loss to the public, because they soon would become breeders themselves: and besides, it is not improbable that some scrupulous people might be apt to censure such a practice, (although indeed very unjustly) as a little bordering upon cruelty; which, I confess, has always been with me the strongest objection against any project, how well soever intended.

But in order to justify my friend, he confessed that this expedient was put into his head by the famous Psalmanaazar, a native of the island Formosa, who came from thence to London above twenty years ago; and in conversation told my friend, that in his country, when any young person happened to be put to death, the executioner sold the carcass to persons of quality as a prime dainty; and that in his time the body of a plump girl of fifteen, who was crucified for an attempt to poison the emperor, was sold to his imperial majesty's prime minister of state, and other great mandarins of the court, in joints from the gibbet, at four hundred crowns. Neither indeed can I deny, that if the same use were made of several plump young girls in this town, who, without one single groat to their fortunes, cannot stir abroad without a chair, and appear at a playhouse and assemblies in foreign fineries which they never will pay for, the kingdom would not be the worse.

Some persons of a desponding spirit are in great concern about that vast number of poor people, who are aged, diseased, or maimed; and I have been desired to employ my thoughts, what course may be taken to ease the nation of so grievous an incumbrance. But I am not in the least pain upon that matter, because it is very well known, that they are every day dying and rotting, by cold and famine, and filth and vermin, as fast as can be reasonably expected. And as to the young labourers, they are now in almost as hopeful a condition: they cannot get work, and consequently pine away for want of nourishment, to a degree that if at any time they are accidentally hired to common labour, they have not strength to perform it; and thus the country and themselves are happily delivered from the evils to come.

I have too long digressed, and therefore shall return to my subject. I think the advantages, by the proposal which I have made, are obvious and many, as well as of the highest importance.

For first, as I have already observed, it would greatly lessen the number of papists, with whom we are yearly overrun, being the principal breeders of the nation, as well as our most dangerous enemies; and who stay at home on purpose to deliver the kingdom to the pretender, hoping to take their advantage by the absence of so many good protestants, who have chosen rather to leave their country, than stay at home and pay tithes against their conscience to an episcopal curate.

Secondly, the poorer tenants will have something valuable of their own, which by law may be made liable to distress, and help to pay their landlord's rent; their corn and cattle being already seized, and money a thing unknown.

Thirdly, whereas the maintenance of a hundred thousand children, from two years old and upwards, cannot be computed at less than ten shillings a piece per annum, the nation's stock will be thereby increased fifty thousand pounds per annum, beside the profit of a new dish introduced to the tables of all gentlemen of fortune in the kingdom, who have any refinement in taste. And the money will circulate among ourselves, the goods being entirely of our own growth and manufacture.

Fourthly, the constant breeders, beside the gain of eight shillings sterling per annum by the sale of their children, will be rid of the charge of maintaining them after the first year.

Fifthly, this food would likewise bring great custom to taverns: where the vintners will certainly be so prudent as to procure the best receipts for dressing it to perfection, and consequently have their houses frequented by all the fine gentlemen, who justly value themselves upon their knowledge in good eating: and a skilful cook, who understands how to oblige his guests, will contrive to make it as expensive as they please.

Sixthly, this would be a great inducement to marriage, which all wise nations have either encouraged by rewards, or enforced by laws and penalties. It would increase the care and tenderness of mothers toward their children, when they were sure of a settlement for life to the poor babes, provided in some sort by the public, to their annual profit instead of expense. We should see an honest emulation among the married women, which of them could bring the fattest child to the market. Men would become as fond of their wives during the time of their pregnancy, as they are now of their mares in foal, their cows in calf, their sows when they are ready to farrow; nor offer to beat or kick them (as is too frequent a practice) for fear of a miscarriage.

Many other advantages might be enumerated. For instance, the addition of some thousand carcasses in our exportation of barreled beef: the propagation of swine's flesh, and improvement in the art of making good bacon, so much wanted among us by the great destruction of pigs, too frequent at our tables; which are no way comparable in taste or magnificence to a well grown, fat, yearling child, which roasted whole will make a considerable figure at a lord mayor's feast, or any other public entertainment. — But this and many others I omit, being studious of brevity.

Supposing that one thousand families in this city would be constant customers for infants' flesh, beside others who might have it at merry meetings, particularly at weddings and christenings, I compute that Dublin would take off annually about twenty thousand carcasses; and the rest of the kingdom (where probably they will be sold somewhat cheaper) the remaining eighty thousand.

I can think of no one objection, that will possibly be raised against this proposal, unless it should be urged, that the number of people will be thereby much lessened in the kingdom. This I freely own, and it was indeed one principal design in offering it to the world. I desire the reader will observe, that I calculate my remedy for this one individual kingdom of Ireland, and for no other that ever was, is, or, I think, ever can be upon earth. Therefore let no man talk to me of other expedients: of taxing our absentees at five shillings a pound; of using neither clothes, nor household furniture, except what is of our own growth and manufacture; of utterly rejecting the materials and instruments that promote foreign luxury; of curing the expensiveness of pride, vanity, idleness, and gaming in our women; of introducing a vein of parsimony, prudence, and temperance; of learning to love our country, in the want of which we differ even from Laplanders, and the inhabitants of Topinamboo; of quitting our animosities and factions, nor acting any longer like the Jews, who were murdering one another at the very moment their city was taken; of being a little cautious not to sell our country and conscience for nothing; of teaching landlords to have at least one degree of mercy toward their tenants; lastly, of putting a spirit of honesty, industry, and skill into our shopkeepers, who, if a resolution could now be taken to buy only our native goods, would immediately unite to cheat and exact upon us in the price, the measure, and the goodness, nor could ever yet be brought to make one fair proposal of just dealing, though often and earnestly invited to it.

Therefore I repeat, let no man talk to me of these and the like expedients, till he has at least some glimpse of hope, that there will ever be some hearty and sincere attempt to put them in practice.

But, as to myself, having been wearied out for many years with offering vain, idle, visionary thoughts, and at length utterly despairing of success, I fortunately fell upon this proposal; which, as it is wholly new, so it has something solid and real, of no expense and little trouble, full in our own power, and whereby we can incur no danger in disobliging England. For this kind of commodity will not bear exportation, the flesh being of too tender a consistence to admit a long continuance in salt, although perhaps I could name a country, which would be glad to eat up our whole nation without it.

After all, I am not so violently bent upon my own opinion as to reject any offer proposed by wise men, which shall be found equally innocent, cheap, easy, and effectual. But before something of that kind shall be advanced in contradiction to my scheme, and offering a better, I desire the author or authors will be pleased maturely to consider two points. First, as things now stand, how they will be able to find food and raiment for a hundred thousand useless mouths and backs. And secondly, there being a round million of creatures in human figure throughout this kingdom, whose whole subsistence put into a common stock would leave them in debt two millions of pounds sterling, adding those who are beggars by profession, to the bulk of farmers, cottagers, and labourers, with their wives and children, who are beggars in effect; I desire those politicians who dislike my overture, and may perhaps be so bold as to attempt an answer, that they will first ask the parents of these mortals, whether they would not at this day think it a great happiness to have been sold for food at a year old, in the manner I prescribe, and thereby have avoided such a perpetual scene of misfortunes, as they have since gone through, by the oppression of landlords, the impossibility of paying rent without money or trade, the want of common sustenance, with neither house nor clothes to cover them from the inclemencies of the weather, and the most inevitable prospect of entailing the like, or greater miseries, upon their breed for ever.

I profess, in the sincerity of my heart, that I have not the least personal interest in endeavouring to promote this necessary work, having no other motive than the public good of my country, by advancing our trade, providing for infants, relieving the poor, and giving some pleasure to the rich. I have no children, by which I can propose to get a single penny; the youngest being nine years old, and my wife past child-bearing.

1729

ESSAYS

Sir Richard Steele (1672–1729)

RECOLLECTIONS OF CHILDHOOD

There are those among mankind, who can enjoy no relish of their being, except the world is made acquainted with all that relates to them, and think everything lost that passes unobserved; but others find a solid delight in stealing by the crowd, and modelling their life after such a manner, as is as much above the approbation as the practice of the vulgar. Life being too short to give instances great enough of true friendship or good-will, some sages have thought it pious to preserve a certain reverence for the *names* of their deceased friends; and have withdrawn themselves from the rest of the world at certain seasons, to commemorate in their own thoughts such of their acquaintance who have gone before them out of this life. And indeed, when we are advanced in years, there is not a more pleasing entertainment, than to recollect in a gloomy moment the many we have parted with, that have been dear and agreeable to us, and to cast a melancholy thought or two after those, with whom, perhaps, we have indulged ourselves in whole nights of mirth and jollity. With such inclinations in my heart I went to my closet yesterday in the evening, and resolved to be sorrowful; upon which occasion I could not but look with disdain upon myself, that though all the reasons which I had to lament the loss of many of my friends are now as forcible as at the moment of their departure, yet did not my heart swell with the same sorrow which I felt at that time; but I could, without tears, reflect upon many pleasing adventures I have had with some, who have long been blended with common earth. Though it is by the benefit of nature, that length of time thus blots out the violence of afflictions; yet, with tempers too much given to pleasure, it is almost necessary to revive the old places of grief in our memory; and ponder step by step on past life, to lead the mind into that sobriety of thought which poises the heart, and makes it beat with due time, without being quickened with desire, or retarded with despair, from its proper and equal motion. When we wind up a clock that is out of order, to make it go well for the future, we do not immediately set the hand to the present instant, but we make it strike the round of all its hours, before it can recover the regularity of its time. Such, thought I, shall be my method this evening; and since it is that day of the year which I dedicate to the memory of such in another life as I much delighted in when living, an hour or two shall be sacred to sorrow and their memory, while I run over all the melancholy circumstances of this kind which have occurred to me in my whole life.

The first sense of sorrow I ever knew was upon the death of my father, at which time I was not quite five years of age; but was rather amazed at what all the house meant, than possessed with a real understanding why nobody was willing to play with me. I remember I went into the room where his body lay, and my mother sat weeping alone by it. I had my battledore in my hand and fell a beating the coffin, and calling Papa; for, I know not how, I had some slight idea that he was locked up there. My mother catched me in her arms, and, transported beyond all patience of the silent grief she was before in, she almost smothered me in her embraces; and told me in a flood of tears, 'Papa could not hear me, and would play with me no more, for they were going to put him under ground, whence he could never come to us again.' She was a very beautiful woman, of a noble spirit, and there was a dignity in her grief amidst all the wildness of her transport; which, methought, struck me with an instinct of sorrow, that, before I was sensible of what it was to grieve, seized my very soul, and has made pity the weakness of my heart ever since. The mind in infancy is, methinks, like the body in embryo; and receives impressions so forcible, that they are as hard to be removed by reason, as any mark with which a child is born is to be taken away by any future application. Hence it is, that good-nature in me is no merit; but having been so frequently overwhelmed with her tears before I knew the cause of any affliction, or could draw defences from my own judgement, I imbibed commiseration, remorse, and an unmanly gentleness of mind, which has since insnared me into ten thousand calamities; from whence I can reap no advantage, except it be, that, in such a humour as I am now in, I can the better indulge myself in the softnesses of humanity, and enjoy that sweet anxiety which arises from the memory of past afflictions.

We, that are very old, are better able to remember things which befell us in our distant youth, than the passages of later days. For this reason it is, that the companions of my strong and vigorous years present themselves more immediately to me in this office of sorrow. Untimely and unhappy deaths are what we are most apt to lament; so little are we able to make it indifferent when a thing happens, though we know it must happen. Thus we groan under life, and bewail those who are relieved from it. Every object that returns to our imagination raises different passions, according to the circumstance of their departure. Who can have lived in an army, and in a serious hour reflect upon the many gay and agreeable men that might long have flourished in the arts of peace, and not join with the imprecations of the fatherless and widow on the tyrant to whose ambition they fell sacrifices? But gallant men, who are cut off by the sword, move rather our veneration than our pity; and we gather relief enough from their own contempt of death, to make that no evil, which was approached with so much cheerfulness, and attended with so much honour. But when we turn our thoughts from the great parts of life on such occasions, and instead of lamenting those who stood ready to give death to those from whom they had the fortune to receive it; I say, when we let our thoughts wander from such noble objects, and consider the havoc which is made among the tender and the innocent, pity enters with an unmixed softness, and possesses all our souls at once.

Here (were there words to express such sentiments with proper tenderness) I should record the beauty, innocence, and untimely death, of the first object my eyes ever beheld with love. The beauteous virgin! how ignorantly did she charm, how carelessly excel! Oh Death! thou hast right to the bold, to the ambitious, to the high, and to the haughty; but why this cruelty to the humble, to the meek, to the undiscerning, to the thoughtless? Nor age, nor business, nor distress, can erase the dear image from my imagination. In the same week, I saw her dressed for a ball, and in a shroud. How ill did the habit of death become the pretty trifler! I still behold the smiling earth——A large train of disasters were coming on to my memory, when my servant knocked at my closet-door, and interrupted me with a letter, attended with a hamper of wine, of the same sort with that which is to be put to sale on Thursday next, at Garraway's coffee-house. Upon the receipt of it, I sent for three of my friends. We are so intimate, that we can be company in whatever state of mind we meet, and can entertain each other without expecting always to rejoice. The wine we found to be generous and warming, but with such a heat as moved us rather to be cheerful than frolicksome. It revived the spirits, without firing the blood. We commended it until two of the clock this morning; and having to-day met a little before dinner, we found, that though we drank two bottles a man, we had much more reason to recollect than forget what had passed the night before.

Tuesday, June 6, 1710

SIR ROGER IN LOVE

In my first description of the company in which I pass most of my time, it may be remembered, that I mentioned a great affliction which my friend Sir Roger had met with in his youth; which was no less than a disappointment in love. It happened this evening, that we fell into a very pleasing walk at a distance from his house. As soon as we came into it, 'It is,' quoth the good old man, looking round him with a smile, 'very hard that any part of my land should be settled upon one who has used me so ill as the perverse widow did; and yet I am sure I could not see a sprig of any bough of this whole walk of trees, but I should reflect upon her and her severity. She has certainly the finest hand of any woman in the world. You are to know, this was the place wherein I used to muse upon her: and by that custom I can never come into it, but the same tender sentiments revive in my mind, as if I had actually walked with that beautiful creature under these shades. I have been fool enough to carve her name on the bark of several of these trees; so unhappy is the condition of men in love, to attempt the removing of their passion by the methods which serve only to imprint it deeper. She has certainly the finest hand of any woman in the world.'

Here followed a profound silence; and I was not displeased to observe my friend falling so naturally into a discourse, which I had ever before taken notice he industriously avoided. After a very long pause, he entered upon an account of this great circumstance in his life, with an air which I thought raised my idea of him above what I had ever had before; and gave me the picture of that cheerful mind of his, before it received that stroke which has ever since affected his words and actions. But he went on as follows:

'I came to my estate in my twenty-second year, and resolved to follow the steps of the most worthy of my ancestors who have inhabited this spot of earth before me, in all the methods of hospitality and good neighbourhood, for the sake of my fame; and in country sports and recreations, for the sake of my health. In my twenty-third year I was obliged to serve as sheriff of the county; and in my servants, officers, and whole equipage, indulged the pleasure of a young man (who did not think ill of his own person) in taking that public occasion of showing my figure and behaviour to advantage. You may easily imagine to yourself what appearance I made, who am pretty tall, rode well, and was very well dressed, at the head of a whole county, with music before me, a feather in my hat, and my horse well bitted. I can assure you, I was not a little pleased with the kind looks and glances I had from all the balconies and windows as I rode to the hall where the assizes were held. But, when I came there, a beautiful creature in a widow's habit sat in a court, to hear the event of a cause concerning her dower. This commanding creature (who was born for the destruction of all who behold her) put on such a resignation in her countenance, and bore the whispers of all around the court with such a pretty uneasiness, I warrant you, and then recovered herself from one eye to another, until she was perfectly confused by meeting something so wistful in all she encountered, that at last, with a murrain to her, she cast her bewitching eye upon me. I no sooner met it, but I bowed like a great surprised booby; and knowing her cause to be the first which came on, I cried, like a captivated calf as I was, "Make way for the defendant's witnesses." This sudden partiality made all the county immediately see the sheriff also was become a slave to the fine widow. During the time her cause was upon trial, she behaved herself, I warrant you, with such a deep attention to her business, took opportunities to have little billets handed to her counsel, then would be in such a pretty confusion, occasioned, you must know, by acting before so much company, that not only I but the whole court was prejudiced in her favour; and all that the next heir to her husband had to urge, was thought so groundless and frivolous, that when it came to her counsel to reply, there was not half so much said as every one besides in the court thought he could have urged to her advantage. You must understand, sir, this perverse woman is one of those unaccountable creatures that secretly rejoice in the admiration of men, but indulge themselves in no farther consequences. Hence it is that she has ever had a train of admirers, and she removes from her slaves in town to those in the country, according to the seasons of the year. She is a reading lady, and far gone in the pleasures of friendship. She is always accompanied by a confidante, who is witness to her daily protestations against our sex, and consequently a bar to her first steps towards love, upon the strength of her own maxims and declarations.

'However, I must needs say, this accomplished mistress of mine has distinguished me above the rest, and has been known to declare Sir Roger de Coverley was the tamest and most humane of all the brutes in the country. I was told she said so, by one who thought he rallied me; but upon the strength of this slender encouragement of being thought least detestable, I made new liveries, new-paired my coach-horses, sent them all to town to be bitted, and taught to throw their legs well, and move all together, before I pretended to cross the country and wait upon her. As soon as I thought my retinue suitable to the character of my fortune and youth, I set out from hence to make my addresses. The particular skill of this lady has ever been to inflame your wishes, and yet command respect. To make her mistress of this art, she has a greater share of knowledge, wit, and good sense, than is usual even among men of merit; then she is beautiful beyond the race of women. If you will not let her go on with a certain artifice with her eyes, and the skill of beauty, she will arm herself with her real charms, and strike you with admiration instead of desire. It is certain that if you were to behold the whole woman, there is that dignity in her aspect, that composure in her motion, that complacency in her manner, that if her form makes you hope, her merit makes you fear. But then again, she is such a desperate scholar that no country gentleman can approach her without being a jest. As I was going to tell you, when I came to her house I was admitted to her presence with great civility; at the same time she placed herself to be first seen by me in such an attitude, as I think you call the posture of a picture, that she discovered new charms, and I at last came towards her with such an awe as made me speechless. This she no sooner observed but she made her advantage of it, and began a discourse to me concerning love and honour, as they both are followed by pretenders, and the real votaries to them. When she discussed these points in a discourse, which I verily believe was as learned as the best philosopher in Europe could possibly make, she asked me whether she was so happy as to fall in with my sentiments on these important particulars. Her confidante sat by her, and upon my being in the last confusion and silence, this malicious aid of hers turning to her, says, "I am very glad to observe Sir Roger pauses upon this subject, and seems resolved to deliver all his sentiments upon the matter when he pleases to speak." They both kept their countenances, and after I had sat half an hour meditating how to behave before such profound casuists, I rose up and took my leave. Chance has since that time thrown me very often in her way, and she as often has directed a discourse to me which I do not understand. This barbarity has kept me ever at a distance from the most beautiful object my eyes ever beheld. It is thus also she deals with all mankind, and you must make love to her, as you would conquer the sphinx, by posing her. But were she like other women, and that there were any talking to her, how constant must the pleasure of that man be, who could converse with a creature — But after all, you may be sure her heart is fixed on some one or other; and yet I have been credibly informed — but who can believe half that is said? — After she had done speaking to me, she put her hand to her bosom, and adjusted her tucker. Then she cast her eyes a little down, upon my beholding her too earnestly. They say she sings excellently: her voice in her ordinary speech has something in it inexpressibly sweet. You must know I dined with her at a public table the day after I first saw her, and she helped me to some tansy, in the eye of all the gentlemen in the country. She has certainly the finest hand of any woman in the world. I can assure you, sir, were you to behold her, you would be in the same condition; for as her speech is music, her form is angelic. But I find I grow irregular while I am talking of her; but indeed it would be stupidity to be unconcerned at such perfection. Oh the excellent creature! she is as inimitable to all women, as she is inaccessible to all men.'

I found my friend begin to rave, and insensibly led him towards the house, that we might be joined by some other company; and am convinced that the widow is the secret cause of all that inconsistency which appears in some parts of my friend's discourse: though he has so much command of himself as not directly to mention her, yet according to that of Martial, which one knows not how to render into English, *dum tacet hanc loquitur*.

Tuesday, July 10, 1711

Joseph Addison (1672-1719)

WESTMINSTER ABBEY

When I am in a serious humour, I very often walk by myself in Westminster Abbey; where the gloominess of the place, and the use to which it is applied, with the solemnity of the building, and the condition of the people who lie in it, are apt to fill the mind with a kind of melancholy, or rather thoughtfulness, that is not disagreeable. I yesterday passed a whole afternoon in the churchyard, the cloisters, and the church, amusing myself with the tombstones and inscriptions that I met with in those several regions of the dead. Most of them recorded nothing else of the buried person, but that he was born upon one day, and died upon another: the whole history of his life being comprehended in those two circumstances, that are common to all mankind. I could not but look upon these registers of existence, whether of brass or marble, as a kind of satire upon the departed persons; who had left no other memorial of them, but that they were born and that they died. They put me in mind of several persons mentioned in the battles of heroic poems, who have sounding names given them, for no other reason but that they may be killed, and are celebrated for nothing but being knocked on the head.

Γλαῦκόν τε Μέδοντά τε Θερσίλοχόν τε. Hom.
Glaucumque, Medontaque, Thersilochumque. Virg.

The life of these men is finely described in holy writ by 'the path of an arrow,' which is immediately closed up and lost.

Upon my going into the church, I entertained myself with the digging of a grave; and saw in every shovelful of it that was thrown up, the fragment of a bone or skull intermixt with a kind of fresh mouldering earth, that some time or other had a place in the composition of a human body. Upon this I began to consider with myself what innumerable multitudes of people lay confused together under the pavement of that ancient cathedral; how men and women, friends and enemies, priests and soldiers, monks and prebendaries, were crumbled amongst one another, and blended together in the same common mass; how beauty, strength, and youth, with old age, weakness and deformity, lay undistinguished in the same promiscuous heap of matter.

After having thus surveyed this great magazine of mortality, as it were, in the lump; I examined it more particularly by the accounts which I found on several of the monuments which are raised in every quarter of that ancient fabric. Some of them were covered with such extravagant epitaphs, that, if it were possible for the dead person to be acquainted with them, he would blush at the praises which his friends have bestowed upon him. There are others so excessively modest, that they deliver the character of the person departed in Greek or Hebrew, and by that means are not understood once in a twelvemonth. In the poetical quarter, I found there were poets who had no monuments, and monuments which had no poets. I observed, indeed, that the present war had filled the church with many of these uninhabited monuments, which had been erected to the memory of persons whose bodies were perhaps buried in the plains of Blenheim, or in the bosom of the ocean.

I could not but be very much delighted with several modern epitaphs, which are written with great elegance of expression and justness of thought, and therefore do honour to the living as well as to the dead. As a foreigner is very apt to conceive an idea of the ignorance or politeness of a nation, from the turn of their public monuments and inscriptions, they should be submitted to the perusal of men of learning and genius, before they are put in execution. Sir Cloudesly Shovel's monument has very often given me great offence: instead of the brave rough English Admiral, which was the distinguishing character of that plain gallant man, he is represented on his tomb by the figure of a beau, dressed in a long periwig, and reposing himself upon velvet cushions under a canopy of state. The inscription is answerable to the monument; for instead of celebrating the many remarkable actions he had performed in the service of his country, it acquaints us only with the manner of his death, in which it was impossible for him to reap any honour. The Dutch, whom we are apt to despise for want of genius, show an infinitely greater taste of antiquity and politeness in their buildings and works of this nature, than what we meet with in those of our own country. The monuments of their admirals, which have been erected at the public expense, represent them like themselves; and are adorned with rostral crowns and naval ornaments, with beautiful festoons of sea-weed, shells, and coral.

But to return to our subject. I have left the repository of our English kings for the contemplation of another day, when I shall find my mind disposed for so serious an amusement. I know that entertainments of this nature are apt to raise dark and dismal thoughts in timorous minds and gloomy imaginations; but for my own part, though I am always serious, I do not know what it is to be melancholy; and can therefore take a view of nature in her deep and solemn scenes, with the same pleasure as in her most gay and delightful ones. By this means I can improve myself with those objects which others consider with terror. When I look upon the tombs of the great, every emotion of envy dies in me; when I read the epitaphs of the beautiful, every inordinate desire goes out; when I meet with the grief of parents upon a tomb-stone, my heart melts with compassion; when I see the tomb of the parents themselves, I consider the vanity of grieving for those whom we must quickly follow: when I see kings lying by those who deposed them, when I consider rival wits placed side by side, or the holy men that divided the world with their contests and disputes, I reflect with sorrow and astonishment on the little competitions, factions, and debates of mankind. When I read the several dates of the tombs, of some that died yesterday, and some six hundred years ago, I consider that great day when we shall all of us be contemporaries, and make our appearance together.

Friday, March 30, 1711

A COUNTRY SUNDAY

I am always very well pleased with a country Sunday; and think, if keeping holy the seventh day were only a human institution, it would be the best method that could have been thought of for the polishing and civilizing of mankind. It is certain the country people would soon degenerate into a kind of savages and barbarians, were there not such frequent returns of a stated time, in which the whole village meet together with their best faces, and in their cleanliest habits, to converse with one another upon indifferent subjects, hear their duties explained to them, and join together in adoration of the Supreme Being. Sunday clears away the rust of the whole week, not only as it refreshes in their minds the notions of religion, but as it puts both the sexes upon appearing in their most agreeable forms, and exerting all such qualities as are apt to give them a figure in the eye of the village. A country fellow distinguishes himself as much in the churchyard as a citizen does upon the Change, the whole parish-politics being generally discussed in that place either after sermon or before the bell rings.

My friend Sir Roger, being a good churchman, has beautified the inside of his church with several texts of his own choosing: he has likewise given a handsome pulpit-cloth, and railed in the communion table at his own expense. He has often told me, that at his coming to his estate he found his parishioners very irregular; and that in order to make them kneel and join in the responses, he gave every one of them a hassock and a Common Prayer Book; and at the same time employed an itinerant singing-master, who goes about the country for that purpose, to instruct them rightly in the tunes of the psalms; upon which they now very much value themselves, and indeed outdo most of the country churches that I have ever heard.

As Sir Roger is landlord to the whole congregation, he keeps them in very good order, and will suffer nobody to sleep in it besides himself; for if by chance he has been surprised into a short nap at sermon, upon recovering out of it he stands up and looks about him, and if he sees anybody else nodding, either wakes them himself, or sends his servant to them. Several other of the old knight's particularities break out upon these occasions: sometimes he will be lengthening out a verse in the singing-psalms, half a minute after the rest of the congregation have done with it; sometimes, when he is pleased with the matter of his devotion, he pronounces Amen three or four times to the same prayer; and sometimes stands up when everybody else is upon their knees, to count the congregation, or see if any of his tenants are missing.

I was yesterday very much surprised to hear my old friend, in the midst of the service, calling out to one John Matthews to mind what he was about, and not disturb the congregation. This John Matthews, it seems, is remarkable for being an idle fellow, and at that time was kicking his heels for his diversion. This authority of the knight, though exerted in that odd manner which accompanies him in all circumstances of life, has a very good effect upon the parish, who are not polite enough to see anything ridiculous in his behaviour; besides that the general good sense and worthiness of his character, make his friends observe these little singularities as foils that rather set off than blemish his good qualities.

As soon as the sermon is finished, nobody presumes to stir till Sir Roger is gone out of the church. The knight walks down from his seat in the chancel between a double row of his tenants, that stand bowing to him on each side; and every now and then he inquires how such a one's wife, or mother, or son, or father do, whom he does not see at church; which is understood as a secret reprimand to the person that is absent.

The chaplain has often told me, that upon a catechising day, when Sir Roger has been pleased with a boy that answers well, he has ordered a Bible to be given him next day for his encouragement; and sometimes accompanies it with a flitch of bacon to his mother. Sir Roger has likewise added five pounds a year to the clerk's place; and that he may encourage the young fellows to make themselves perfect in the church-service, has promised, upon the death of the present incumbent, who is very old, to bestow it according to merit.

The fair understanding between Sir Roger and his chaplain, and their mutual concurrence in doing good, is the more remarkable, because the very next village is famous for the differences and contentions that rise between the parson and the squire, who live in a perpetual state of war. The parson is always preaching at the squire, and the squire, to be revenged on the parson, never comes to church. The squire has made all his tenants atheists and tithe-stealers; while the parson instructs them every Sunday in the dignity of his order, and insinuates to them, almost in every sermon, that he is a better man than his patron. In short, matters are come to such an extremity, that the squire had not said his prayers either in public or private this half year; and that the parson threatens him, if he does not mend his manners, to pray for him in the face of the whole congregation.

Feuds of this nature, though too frequent in the country, are very fatal to the ordinary people; who are so used to be dazzled with riches, that they pay as much deference to the understanding of a man of an estate, as of a man of learning; and are very hardly brought to regard any truth, how important soever it may be, that is preached to them, when they know there are several men of five hundred a year who do not believe it.

Monday, July 9, 1711

SIR ROGER AT THE ASSIZES

A man's first care should be to avoid the reproaches of his own heart; his next, to escape the censures of the world: if the last interferes with the former, it ought to be entirely neglected; but otherwise there cannot be a greater satisfaction to an honest mind, than to see those approbations which it gives itself seconded by the applauses of the public: a man is more sure of his conduct, when the verdict which he passes upon his own behaviour is thus warranted and confirmed by the opinion of all that know him.

My worthy friend Sir Roger is one of those who is not only at peace within himself, but beloved and esteemed by all about him. He receives a suitable tribute for his universal benevolence to mankind, in the returns of affection and good-will which are paid him by every one that lives within his neighbourhood. I lately met with two or three odd instances of that general respect which is shown to the good old knight. He would needs carry Will Wimble and myself with him to the country assizes: as we were upon the road, Will Wimble joined a couple of plain men who rid before us, and conversed with them for some time; during which my friend Sir Roger acquainted me with their characters.

The first of them, says he, that has a spaniel by his side, is a yeoman of about an hundred pounds a year, an honest man: he is just within the game act, and qualified to kill an hare or a pheasant: he knocks down a dinner with his gun twice or thrice a week; and by that means lives much cheaper than those who have not so good an estate as himself. He would be a good neighbour if he did not destroy so many partridges: in short, he is a very sensible man; shoots flying; and has been several times foreman of the petty jury.

The other that rides with him is Tom Touchy, a fellow famous for taking the law of everybody. There is not one in the town where he lives that he has not sued at a quarter-sessions. The rogue had once the impudence to go to law with the widow. His head is full of costs, damages, and ejectments: he plagued a couple of honest gentlemen so long for a trespass in breaking one of his hedges, till he was forced to sell the ground it enclosed to defray the charges of the prosecution. His father left him fourscore pounds a year; but he has cast and been cast so often, that he is not now worth thirty. I suppose he is going upon the old business of the willow-tree.

As Sir Roger was giving me this account of Tom Touchy, Will Wimble and his two companions stopped short till we came up to them. After having paid their respects to Sir Roger, Will told him that Mr. Touchy and he must appeal to him upon a dispute that arose between them. Will, it seems, had been giving his fellow-travelers an account of his angling one day in such a hole; when Tom Touchy, instead of hearing out his story, told him, that Mr. such an one, if he pleased, might take the law of him for fishing in that part of the river. My friend Sir Roger heard them both, upon a round trot, and after having paused some time, told them, with the air of a man who would not give his judgment rashly, that much might be said on both sides. They were neither of them dissatisfied with the knight's determination, because neither of them found himself in the wrong by it: upon which we made the best of our way to the assizes.

The court was sat before Sir Roger came, but notwithstanding all the justices had taken their places upon the bench, they made room for the old knight at the head of them; who, for his reputation in the country, took occasion to whisper in the judge's ear, that he was glad his lordship had met with so much good weather in his circuit. I was listening to the proceedings of the court with much attention, and infinitely pleased with that great appearance of solemnity which so properly accompanies such a public administration of our laws; when, after about an hour's sitting, I observed, to my great surprise, in the midst of a trial, that my friend Sir Roger was getting up to speak. I was in some pain for him, till I found he had acquitted himself of two or three sentences, with a look of much business and great intrepidity.

Upon his first rising the court was hushed, and a general whisper ran among the country people that Sir Roger was up. The speech he made was so little to the purpose, that I shall not trouble my readers with an account of it; and I believe was not so much designed by the knight himself to inform the court, as to give him a figure in my eye, and keep up his credit in the country.

I was highly delighted, when the court rose, to see the gentlemen of the country gathering about my old friend, and striving who should compliment him most; at the same time that the ordinary people gazed upon him at a distance, not a little admiring his courage, that was not afraid to speak to the judge.

In our return home we met with a very odd accident; which I cannot forbear relating, because it shows how desirous all who know Sir Roger are of giving him marks of their esteem. When we were arrived upon the verge of his estate, we stopped at a little inn to rest ourselves and our horses. The man of the house had, it seems, been formerly a servant in the knight's family; and to do honour to his old master, had some time since, unknown to Sir Roger, put him up in a sign-post before the door; so that The Knight's Head had hung out upon the road about a week before he himself knew anything of the matter. As soon as Sir Roger was acquainted with it, finding that his servant's indiscretion proceeded wholly from affection and good-will, he only told him that he had made him too high a compliment: and when the fellow seemed to think that could hardly be, added with a more decisive look, that it was too great an honour for any man under a duke; but told him at the same time, that it might be altered with a very few touches, and that he himself would be at the charge of it. Accordingly they got a painter by the knight's directions to add a pair of whiskers to the face, and by a little aggravation of the features to change it into the Saracen's Head. I should not have known this story, had not the inn-keeper, upon Sir Roger's alighting, told him in my hearing, that his Honour's head was brought back last night, with the alterations that he had ordered to be made in it. Upon this my friend, with his usual cheerfulness, related the particulars above-mentioned, and ordered the head to be brought into the room. I could not forbear discovering greater expressions of mirth than ordinary upon the appearance of this monstrous face, under which, notwithstanding it was made to frown and stare in the most extraordinary manner, I could still discover a distant resemblance of my old friend. Sir Roger, upon seeing me laugh, desired me to tell him truly if I thought it possible for people to know him in that disguise. I at first kept my usual silence; but upon the knight's conjuring me to tell him whether it was not still more like himself than a Saracen, I composed my countenance in the best manner I could, and replied 'That much might be said on both sides.'

These several adventures, with the knight's behaviour in them, gave me as pleasant a day as ever I met with in any of my travels.

Friday, July 20, 1711

THE VISION OF MIRZAH

When I was at Grand Cairo I picked up several oriental manuscripts, which I have still by me. Among others I met with one entitled, The Visions of Mirzah, which I have read over with great pleasure. I intend to give it to the public when I have no other entertainment for them; and shall begin with the first vision, which I have translated word for word as follows:

'On the fifth day of the moon, which according to the custom of my forefathers I always keep holy, after having washed myself, and offered up my morning devotions, I ascended the high hills of Bagdat, in order to pass the rest of the day in meditation and prayer. As I was here airing myself on the tops of the mountains, I fell into a profound contemplation on the vanity of human life; and passing from one thought to another, surely, said I, man is but a shadow, and life a dream. Whilst I was thus musing, I cast my eyes towards the summit of a rock that was not far from me, where I discovered one in the habit of a shepherd, with a musical instrument in his hand. As I looked upon him he applied it to his lips, and began to play upon it. The sound of it was exceeding sweet, and wrought into a variety of tunes that were inexpressibly melodious, and altogether different from anything I had ever heard. They put me in mind of those heavenly airs that are played to the departed souls of good men upon their first arrival in paradise, to wear out the impressions of their last agonies, and qualify them for the pleasures of that happy place. My heart melted away in secret raptures.

'I had been often told that the rock before me was the haunt of a Genius; and that several had been entertained with music who had passed by it, but never heard that the musician had before made himself visible. When he had raised my thoughts, by those transporting airs which he played, to taste the pleasures of his conversation, as I looked upon him like one astonished, he beckoned to me, and by the waving of his hand directed me to approach the place where he sat. I drew near with that reverence which is due to a superior nature; and as my heart was entirely subdued by the captivating strains I had heard, I fell down at his feet and wept. The Genius smiled upon me with a look of compassion and affability that familiarized him to my imagination, and at once dispelled all the fears and apprehensions with which I approached him. He lifted me from the ground, and taking me by the hand, Mirzah, said he, I have heard thee in thy soliloquies, follow me.

'He then led me to the highest pinnacle of the rock, and placed me on the top of it. Cast thy eyes eastward, said he, and tell me what thou seest. I see, said I, a huge valley, and a prodigious tide of water rolling through it. The valley that thou seest, said he, is the vale of misery, and the tide of water that thou seest is part of the great tide of eternity. What is the reason, said I, that the tide I see rises out of a thick mist at one end, and again loses itself in a thick mist at the other? What thou seest, said he, is that portion of eternity which is called time, measured out by the sun, and reaching from the beginning of the world to its consummation. Examine now, said he, this sea that is bounded with darkness at both ends, and tell me what thou discoverest in it. I see a bridge, said I, standing in the midst of the tide. The bridge thou seest, said he, is human life; consider it attentively. Upon a more leisurely survey of it, I found that it consisted of threescore and ten entire arches, with several broken arches, which added to those that were entire, made up the number about a hundred. As I was counting the arches the Genius told me that this bridge consisted at first of a thousand arches; but that a great flood swept away the rest, and left the bridge in the ruinous condition I now beheld it. But tell me further, said he, what thou discoverest on it. I see multitudes of people passing over it, said I, and a black cloud hanging on each end of it. As I looked more attentively, I saw several of the passengers dropping through the bridge, into the great tide that flowed underneath it; and upon farther examination, perceived there were innumerable trap-doors that lay concealed in the bridge, which the passengers no sooner trod upon, but they fell through them into the tide, and immediately disappeared. These hidden pit-falls were set very thick at the entrance of the bridge, so that throngs of people no sooner broke through the cloud, but many of them fell into them. They grew thinner towards the middle, but multiplied and lay closer together towards the end of the arches that were entire.

'There were indeed some persons, but their number was very small, that continued a kind of hobbling march on the broken arches, but fell through one after another, being quite tired and spent with so long a walk.

'I passed some time in the contemplation of this wonderful structure, and the great variety of objects which it presented. My heart was filled with a deep melancholy to see several dropping unexpectedly in the midst of mirth and jollity, and catching at everything that stood by them to save themselves. Some were looking up towards the heavens in a thoughtful posture, and in the midst of a speculation stumbled and fell out of sight. Multitudes were very busy in the pursuit of bubbles that glittered in their eyes and danced before them, but often when they thought themselves within the reach of them, their footing failed and down they sunk. In this confusion of objects, I observed some with scimetars in their hands, . . . who ran to and fro upon the bridge, thrusting several persons on trap-doors which did not seem to lie in their way, and which they might have escaped, had they not been thus forced upon them.

'The Genius seeing me indulge myself in this melancholy prospect, told me I had dwelt long enough upon it: take thine eyes off the bridge, said he, and tell me if thou yet seest anything thou dost not comprehend. Upon looking up, what mean, said I, those great flights of birds that are perpetually hovering about the bridge, and settling upon it from time to time? I see vultures, harpies, ravens, cormorants, and among many other feathered creatures, several little winged boys, that perch in great numbers upon the middle arches. These, said the Genius, are Envy, Avarice, Superstition, Despair, Love, with the like cares and passions, that infect human life.

'I here fetched a deep sigh; alas, said I, man was made in vain! How is he given away to misery and mortality! tortured in life, and swallowed up in death! The Genius, being moved with compassion towards me, bid me quit so uncomfortable a prospect. Look no more, said he, on man in the first stage of his existence, in his setting out for eternity; but cast thine eye on that thick mist into which the tide bears the several generations of mortals that fall into it. I directed my sight as I was ordered, and (whether or no the good Genius strengthened it with any supernatural force, or dissipated part of the mist that was before too thick for the eye to penetrate) I saw the valley opening at the farther end, and spreading forth into an immense ocean, that had a huge rock of adamant running through the midst of it, and dividing it into two equal parts. The clouds still rested on one half of it, insomuch that I could discover nothing in it: but the other appeared to me a vast ocean planted with innumerable islands, that were covered with fruits and flowers, and interwoven with a thousand little shining seas that ran among them. I could see persons dressed in glorious habits with garlands upon their heads, passing among the trees, lying down by the sides of fountains, or resting on beds of flowers; and could hear a confused harmony of singing birds, falling waters, human voices, and musical instruments. Gladness grew in me upon the discovery of so delightful a scene. I wished for the wings of an eagle, that I might fly away to those happy seats; but the Genius told me there was no passage to them, except through the gates of death that I saw opening every moment upon the bridge. The islands, said he, that lie so fresh and green before thee, and with which the whole face of the ocean appears spotted as far as thou canst see, are more in number than the sands on the sea-shore; there are myriads of islands behind those which thou here discoverest, reaching farther than thine eye, or even thine imagination, can extend itself. These are the mansions of good men after death, who, according to the degree and kinds of virtue in which they excelled, are distributed among these several islands, which abound with pleasures of different kinds and degrees, suitable to the relishes and perfections of those who are settled in them: every island is a paradise, accommodated to its respective inhabitants. Are not these, O Mirzah, habitations worth contending for? Does life appear miserable, that gives thee opportunities of earning such a reward? Is death to be feared, that will convey thee to so happy an existence? Think not man was made in vain, who has such an eternity reserved for him. I gazed with inexpressible pleasure on these happy islands. At length, said I, show me now, I beseech thee, the secrets that lie hid under those dark clouds which cover the ocean on the other side of the rock of adamant. The Genius making me no answer, I turned me about to address myself to him a second time, but I found that he had left me. I then turned again to the vision which I had been so long contemplating, but instead of the rolling tide, the arched bridge, and the happy islands, I saw nothing but the long hollow valley of Bagdat, with oxen, sheep, and camels grazing upon the sides of it.'

Saturday, September 1, 1711

THE DEATH OF SIR ROGER

We last night received a piece of ill news at our club, which very sensibly afflicted every one of us. I question not but my readers themselves will be troubled at the hearing of it. To keep them no longer in suspense, Sir Roger de Coverley is dead. He departed this life at his house in the country, after a few weeks' sickness. Sir Andrew Freeport has a letter from one of his correspondents in those parts, that informs him the old man caught a cold at the country sessions, as he was very warmly promoting an address of his own penning, in which he succeeded according to his wishes. But this particular comes from a Whig justice of peace, who was always Sir Roger's enemy and antagonist. I have letters both from the chaplain and Captain Sentry, which mention nothing of it, but are filled with many particulars to the honour of the good old man. I have likewise a letter from the butler, who took so much care of me last summer when I was at the knight's house. As my friend the butler mentions, in the simplicity of his heart, several circumstances the others have passed over in silence, I shall give my reader a copy of his letter, without any alteration or diminution.

'Honoured Sir,

'Knowing that you was my old master's good friend, I could not forbear sending you the melancholy news of his death, which has afflicted the whole country, as well as his poor servants, who loved him, I may say, better than we did our lives. I am afraid he caught his death the last county sessions, where he would go to see justice done to a poor widow woman, and her fatherless children, that had been wronged by a neighbouring gentleman; for you know, my good master was always the poor man's friend. Upon his coming home, the first complaint he made was, that he had lost his roast-beef stomach, not being able to touch a sirloin, which was served up according to custom: and you know he used to take great delight in it. From that time forward he grew worse and worse, but still kept a good heart to the last. Indeed we were once in great hope of his recovery, upon a kind message that was sent him from the widow lady whom he had made love to the forty last years of his life; but this only proved a lightning before his death. He has bequeathed to this lady, as a token of his love, a great pearl necklace, and a couple of silver bracelets set with jewels, which belonged to my good old lady his mother: he has bequeathed the fine white gelding, that he used to ride a hunting upon, to his chaplain, because he thought he would be kind to him, and has left you all his books. He has, moreover, bequeathed to the chaplain a very pretty tenement with good lands about it. It being a very cold day when he made his will, he left for mourning, to every man in the parish, a great frize coat, and to every woman a black riding-hood. It was a most moving sight to see him take leave of his poor servants, commending us all for our fidelity, whilst we were not able to speak a word for weeping. As we most of us are grown gray-headed in our dear master's service, he has left us pensions and legacies which we may live very comfortably upon the remaining part of our days. He has bequeathed a great deal more in charity, which is not yet come to my knowledge, and it is peremptorily said in the parish, that he has left money to build a steeple to the church: for he was heard to say some time ago, that if he lived two years longer, Coverley church should have a steeple to it. The chaplain tells everybody that he made a very good end, and never speaks of him without tears. He was buried, according to his own directions, among the family of the Coverleys, on the left hand of his father Sir Arthur. The coffin was carried by six of his tenants, and the pall held up by six of the quorum: the whole parish followed the corpse with heavy hearts, and in their mourning suits; the men in frize, and the women in riding-hoods. Captain Sentry, my master's nephew, has taken possession of the hall-house, and the whole estate. When my old master saw him, a little before his death, he shook him by the hand, and wished him joy of the estate which was falling to him, desiring him only to make a good use of it, and to pay the several legacies, and the gifts of charity, which he told him he had left as quit-rents upon the estate. The captain truly seems a courteous man, though says but little. He makes much of those whom my master loved, and shows great kindness to the old house-dog, that you know my poor master was so fond of. It would have gone to your heart to have heard the moans the dumb creature made on the day of my master's death. He has never joyed himself since; no more has any of us. It was the melancholiest day for the poor people that ever happened in Worcestershire. This being all from,

'Honoured sir, your most sorrowful servant,

Edward Biscuit.'

'P. S. My master desired, some weeks before he died, that a book which comes up to you by the carrier, should be given to Sir Andrew Freeport in his name.'

This letter, notwithstanding the poor butler's manner of writing it, gave us such an idea of our good old friend, that upon the reading of it, there was not a dry eye in the club. Sir Andrew opening the book, found it to be a collection of acts of parliament. There was, in particular, the act of uniformity, with some passages in it marked by Sir Roger's own hand. Sir Andrew found that they related to two or three points, which he had disputed with Sir Roger the last time he appeared at the club. Sir Andrew, who would have been merry at such an incident on another occasion, at the sight of the old man's hand-writing, burst into tears, and put the book into his pocket. Captain Sentry informs me, that the knight has left rings and mourning for every one in the club.

Thursday, October 23, 1712

ROMANTIC BEGINNINGS

Lady Winchilsea (1661-1720)

A NOCTURNAL REVERIE

In such a night, when every louder wind
Is to its distant cavern safe confined;
And only gentle zephyr fans his wings,
And lonely Philomel, still waking, sings;
Or from some tree, famed for the owl's delight,
She, hollowing clear, directs the wand'rer right:
In such a night, when passing clouds give place,
Or thinly veil the heav'ns mysterious face;
When in some river, overhung with green,
The waving moon and trembling leaves are seen;
When freshened grass now bears it self upright,
And makes cool banks to pleasing rest invite,
Whence springs the woodbind, and the bramble-rose,

And where the sleepy cowslip sheltered grows;
Whilst now a paler hue the foxglove takes,
Yet checquers still with red and dusky brakes
When scattered glow-worms, but in twilight fine,
Shew trivial beauties watch their hour to shine;
Whilst Salisbury stands the test of every light,
In perfect charms, and perfect virtue bright:
When odours, which declined repelling day,
Through temp'rate air uninterrupted stray;
When darkened groves their softest shadows wear,
And falling waters we distinctly hear;
When through the gloom more venerable shows
Some ancient fabrick, awful in repose,
While sunburnt hills their swarthy looks conceal,
And swelling haycocks thicken up the vale:
When the loosed horse now, as his pasture leads,
Comes slowly grazing through th' adjoining meads,
Whose stealing pace, and lengthened shade we fear,
Till torn up forage in his teeth we hear:
When nibbling sheep at large pursue their food,
And unmolested kine rechew the cud;
When curlews cry beneath the village-walls,
And to her straggling brood the partridge calls;
Their shortlived jubilee the creatures keep,
Which but endures, whilst Tyrant-Man does sleep;
When a sedate content the spirit feels,
And no fierce light disturb, whilst it reveals;
But silent musings urge the mind to seek
Something, too high for syllables to speak;
Till the free soul to a compos'dness charmed,
Finding the elements of rage disarmed,
O'er all below a solemn quiet grown,
Joys in th' inferiour world, and thinks it like her own;
In such a night let me abroad remain,
Till morning breaks, and all 's confused again;
Our cares, our toils, our clamours are renewed,
Or pleasures, seldom reached, again pursued.

1713

Lady Grizel Baillie (1665–1746)

WERENA MY HEART LICHT I WAD DEE

There was ance a may, and she loo'd na men:
She biggit her bonnie bower doun in yon glen;
But now she cries, Dool! and well-a-day!
Come doun the green gait and come here away!

When bonnie young Johnnie cam' ower the sea,
He said he saw naething sae lovely as me;
He hecht me baith rings and mony braw things, —
And werena my heart licht I wad dee.

He had a wee titty that loo'd na me,
Because I was twice as bonnie as she;
She raised such a pother 'twixt him and his mother
That werena my heart licht I wad dee.

The day it was set, and the bridal to be;
The wife took a dwam, and lay doun to dee;
She maned and she graned out o' dolour and pain,
Till he vowed he never wad see me again.

His kin was for ane of a higher degree,
Said, What had he to do wi' the like of me?
Albeit I was bonnie, I wasna for Johnnie, —
And werena my heart licht I wad dee.

They said I had neither cow nor calf,
Nor dribbles o' drink rins through the draff,
Nor pickles o' meal rins through the mill-e'e;
And werena my heart licht I wad dee.

His titty she was baith wylie and slee:
She spied me as I cam' ower the lea;
And then she ran in and made a loud din, —
Believe your ain een an' ye trow na me.

His bonnet stood aye fu' round on his brow, —
His auld ane looked aye as weel as some's new;
But now he lets 't wear ony gait it will hing,
And casts himself dowie upon the corn-bing.

And now he gaes daund'ring about the dykes,
And a' he dow do is to hund the tykes:
The live-lang nicht he ne'er steeks his e'e;
And werena my heart licht I wad dee.

Were I but young for thee, as I hae been,
We should hae been gallopin' doun on yon green,
And linkin' it on the lily-white lea, —
And wow! gin I were but young for thee!

1724

Lady Elizabeth Wardlaw
(1677–1727)

HARDYKNUTE

A FRAGMENT OF AN OLD HEROIC BALLAD

Stately stept he east the wa',
And stately stept he west;
Full seventy years he now had seen,
With scarce seven years of rest.
He lived when Britons' breach of faith
Wrought Scotland meikle wae;
And aye his sword tauld to their cost
He was their deadly fae.

Hie on a hill his castle stude,
With halls and towers a-hight,
And guidly chambers fair to see
Where he lodged mony a knight.
His dame, sae peirless anes and fair
For chaste and beauty deimt,
Nae marrow had in all the land
Save Elenor the Queen.

Full thirteen sons to him she bare,
All men of valour stout:
In bluidy fight, with sword in hand,
Nyne lost their lives bot doubt.
Four yet remain; — lang may they live
To stand by liege and land!
Hie was their fame, hie was their might,
And hie was their command.

Great love they bare to Fairly fair,
Their sister saft and deir:
Her girdle shaw'd her middle jimp,
And gowden glist her hair.
What waefu' wae her bewtie bred!
Waefu' to young and auld,
Waefu', I trow, to kyth and kin
As story ever tauld.

The King of Norse in summer-tide,
Puffed up with power and might,
Landed in fair Scotland the isle
With mony a hardy knight.
The tidings to our gude Scots King
Came as he sat at dyne
With noble chiefs in brave array,
Drinking the blude-red wyne.

'To horse, to horse, my royal liege; —
Your faes stand on the strand:
Full twenty thousand glittering spears
The King of Norse commands!'
'Bring me my steed Madge dapple-gray,'
Our gude King raise and cryed;
'A trustier beast in all the land
A Scots king never seyed!

'Go, little page, tell Hardyknute,
That lives on hill so hie,
To draw his sword, the dreid of faes,
And haste and follow me.'
The little page flew swift as dart
Flung by his master's arm:
'Come doun, come doun, Lord Hardyknute,
And redd your king frae harm!'

Then reid, reid grew his dark-brown cheiks,
Sae did his dark-brown brow;
His looks grew keen — as they were wont
In dangers great to do:
He has ta'en a horn as green as grass,
And gi'en five sounds sae shrill
That trees in greenwood shook thereat —
Sae loud rang ilka hill.

His sons in manly sport and glie
Had past the summer's morn;
When lo! down in a grassy dale,
They heard their father's horn.
'That horn,' quoth they, 'ne'er sounds in peace, —
We've other sport to byde.'
And soon they hied them up the hill,
And soon were at his syde.

'Late, late yestreen I weened in peace
To end my lengthened life, —
My age might weel excuse my arm
Frae manly feats of strife;
But now that Norse does proudly boast
Fair Scotland to enthrall,
It's ne'er be said of Hardyknute
He feared to fight or fall!

'Robin of Rothsay, bend thy bow, —
Thy arrows shoot so leal,
Mony a comely countenance
They have turned to deidly pale.
Brave Thomas, tak' ye but your lance,
Ye neid nae weapons mair
Gif ye fight wi't as ye did anes
'Gainst Westmoreland's fierce heir.

'And Malcom, light of foot as stag
That runs in forest wyld,
Get me my thousands three of men
Well bred to sword and shield.
Bring me my horse and harnisine,

My blade of metal cleir . . .'
(If faes kenned but the hand it bare
They soon had fled for fear.)

'Fareweil, my dame, sae pierless good,'
(And took her by the hand),
'Fairer to me in age you seem
Than maids for beauty famed.
My youngest son sall here remain,
To guard these stately towirs,
And shut the silver bolt that keips
Sae fast your painted bowirs.'

And first she wet her comely cheiks
And then her boddice green,
Her silken cords of twirtle twist
Weel plet with silver sheen,
And apron set with mony a dyce
Of needle-wark saw rare,
Wove by nae hand (as ye may guess)
Save that of Fairly fair.

And he has ridden owre muir and moss,
Owre hills and mony a glen,
When he came to a wounded knight
Making a heavy mane:
'Here maun I lye, here maun I dye,
By treachery's false guiles:
Witless I was that e'er gave faith
To wicked woman's smyles!'

'Sir Knight, gin ye were in my bowir,
To lean on silken seat,
My lady's kindly care you'd prove,
When ne'er kenned deidly hate:
Herself wad watch ye all the day,
Her maids at deid of nicht;
And Fairly fair your heart wad cheir
As she stands in your sight.

'Arise, young knight, and mount your steid, —
Full lowan's the shynand day:
Chuse frae my menzie whom ye please
To lead ye on the way!'
With smileless look, and visage wan,
The wounded knight replied,
'Kind chieftain, your intent pursue,
For here I maun abyde.

'To me nae after day nor night
Can e'ir be sweit or fair;
But soon, beneath some draping tree,
Cauld death sall end my care!'
With him nae pleading might prevail: —
Brave Hardyknute to gain,
With fairest words and reason strang,
Strave courteously in vain.

Syne he has gane far hyne — attour
Lord Chattan's land sae wyde; —
That lord a worthy wight was aye
When faes his courage seyed:
Of Pictish race by mother's syde,
When Picts ruled Caledon,
Lord Chattan claimed the princely maid
When he saved Pictish crown.

Now, with his fierce and stalwart train,
He reached a rising height,
Where — braid encampit on the dale —
Norse menzie lay in sight:
'Yonder, my valiant sons and feirs,
Our raging reevers wait,
On the unconquered Scottish swaird,
To try with us their fate!

'Mak' orisons to Him that saved
Our sauls upon the rood;
Syne bravely shaw your veins are filled
With Caledonian blude.'
Then furth he drew his trusty glaive, —
While thousands all around
Drawn frae their sheaths glanced in the sun,
And loud the bougles sound.

To join his king, adown the hill
In haste his march he made;
Whyle, playand pibrochs, minstrels meet
Afore him stately strade.
'Thrice welcome, valiant stoupe of weir,
Thy nation's shield and pryde!
Thy king nae reason has to feir
When thou art by his syde.'

When bows were bent and darts were thrawn,
For thrang scarce could they flie, —
The darts clove arrows as they met,
The arrows dart the trie.
Lang did they rage and fight full fierce
With little skaith to man;
But bluidy, bluidy was the field
Or that lang day was done!

The King of Scots, that sindle bruiked
The war that looked like play,
Drew his braid sword, and brake his bow —
Sen bows seimt but delay.
Quoth noble Rothsay, 'Myne I'll keip, —
I wot it's bled a score!'
'Haste up, my merry men!' cryed the King,
As he rade on before.

The King of Norse he sought to find,
With him to mense the faught;
But on his forehead there did light
A sharp unsonsie shaft.
As he his hand put up to find
The wound, an arrow keen
(O waefu' chance!) there pinned his hand,
In midst between his e'en.

'Revenge, revenge!' cryed Rothsay's heir,
'Your mail-coat sall nocht byde
The strength and sharpness of my dart,'—
Then sent it through his syde.
Another arrow weel he marked,—
It pierced his neck in twa:
His hands then quat the silver reins,
He laigh as eard did fa'.

'Sair bleeds my liege; sair, sair he bleeds!'
Again with might he drew,
And gesture dreid, his sturdy bow;—
Fast the braid arrow flew.
Wae to the knight he ettled at!
Lament now, Quene Elgried!
Hie dames, too, wail your darling's fall,
His youth and comely meid!

'Take aff, take aff his costly jupe!'
(Of gold weil was it twined—
Knit lyke the fowler's net—through which
His steilly harness shyned).
'Take Norse that gift frae me and bid
Him venge the bluid it beirs.'
'Say, if he face my bended bow
He sure nae weapon feirs!'

Proud Norse, with giant body tall,
Braid shoulders, and arms strong,
Cryed, 'Where is Hardyknute sae famed
And feired at Britain's throne?
The Britons tremble at his name;—
I soon shall make him wail
That e'ir my sword was made sae sharp,
Sae saft his coat of mail!'

That brag his stout heart couldna byde,
It lent him youthful might:
'I 'm Hardyknute!—This day,' he cryed,
'To Scotland's king I height
To lay thee low as horse's hufe:—
My word I mean to keip!'
Syne, with the first strake e'ir he strake,
He garred his body bleid.

Norse' e'en, lyke gray gosehawk's, stared wyld;
He sighed with shame and spyte:
'Disgraced is now my far-famed arm,
That left thee power to strike!'—
Then gave his head a blaw sae fell
It made him down to stoup
As laigh as he to ladies used
In courtly guise to lout.

Full soon he raised his bent body:
His bow he marvelled sair;—
Sen blaws till then on him but darred
As touch of Fairly fair.
Norse ferliet too, as sair as he,
To see his stately look,—
Sae soon as e'ir he strake a fae,
Sae soon his lyfe he took.

Whair, lyke a fyre to heather set,
Bauld Thomas did advance,
A sturdy fae, with look enraged,
Up towards him did prance:
He spurred his steid through thickest rank,
The hardy youth to quell;
Wha stood unmoved at his approach,
His fury to repell.

'That short brown shaft sae meanly trimmed
Looks lyke poor Scotland's gear,
But dreidful seims the rusty poynt!'
And loud he leugh in jeir.
'Aft Britons' bluid has dimmed its shyne—
This poynt cut short their vaunt:'—
Syne pierced the boaster's bearded cheik,—
Nae time he took to taunt.

Short while he in his saddle swang,—
His stirrup was nae stay;
Sae feible hung his unbent knee
Sure taken he was fey:
Swith on the hardened clay he fell,—
Right far was heard the thud;
But Thomas looked not as he lay
All waltering in his bluid:

With careless gesture, mynd unmoved,
On raid he north the plain;—
He seimt in thrang of fiercest strife
When winner, aye the same:
Nor yet his heart dame's dimpelit cheik
Could meise saft love to bruik,
Till vengeful Ann returned his scorn,—
Then languid grew his look.

In thrawis of death, with wailowit cheik,
All panting on the plain
The fainting corpse of warriors lay,
Ne'ir to aryse again,—
Ne'ir to return to native land,
Nae mair, with blythesome sounds,
To boast the glories of the day
And shaw their shyning wounds.

On Norway's coast the widowed dame
May wash the rocks with tears,
May lang look owre the shiples seas,
Before hir mate appeirs.
Ceise, Emma, ceise to hope in vain,—
Thy lord lyis in the clay:—
The valiant Scots nae reevers thole
To carry life away!

There, on a lee, whair stands a cross
Set up for monument,
Thousands full fierce that summer's day
Filled keen war's black intent.—

Let Scots, while Scots, praise Hardyknute;
Let Norse the name aye dreid:
Aye how he faught, aft how he spared,
Sall latest ages reid. —

Now loud and chill blew westlin' wind,
Sair beat the heavy showir,
Mirk grew the night e'ir Hardyknute
Wan near his stately tower.
His tower, that used with torches' bleise
To shine sae far at night,
Seimed now as black as mourning weed, —
Nae marvel sair he sigh't.

'There 's nae light in my lady's bouir,
There 's nae light in my hall;
Nae blink shynes round my Fairly fair,
Nor ward stands on my wall.
What bodes it? Robert, Thomas, say!'
Nae answer fits their dreid.
'Stand back, my sons, I'll be your guide . . .'
But by they passed with speid.

'As fast as I've sped owre Scotland's faes . . .'
There ceist his brag of weir,
Sair shamed to mynd aught but his dame
And maiden Fairly fair.
Black fear he felt — but what to fear
He wist not; yet with dreid
Sair shook his body, sair his limbs,
And all the warrior fled.

1719(?), 1724

Allan Ramsay (1686–1758)

MY PEGGY IS A YOUNG THING

My Peggy is a young thing,
Just entered in her teens,
Fair as the day, and sweet as May,
Fair as the day, and always gay;
My Peggy is a young thing,
And I 'm not very auld,
Yet well I like to meet her at
The wauking of the fauld.

My Peggy speaks sae sweetly,
Whene'er we meet alane,
I wish nae mair to lay my care,
I wish nae mair of a' that 's rare,
My Peggy speaks sae sweetly,
To a' the lave I'm cauld;
But she gars a' my spirits glow,
At wauking of the fauld.

My Peggy smiles sae kindly,
Whene'er I whisper love,
That I look down on a' the town,
That I look down upon a crown,
My Peggy smiles sae kindly,
It makes me blyth and bauld;
And naething gi'es me sic delight
As wauking of the fauld.

My Peggy sings sae saftly,
When on my pipe I play,
By a' the rest it is confest,
By a' the rest that she sings best,
My Peggy sings sae saftly,
And in her sangs are tald
With innocence the wale of sense,
At wauking of the fauld.

1725

THE LASS WITH A LUMP OF LAND

Gi'e me a lass with a lump of land,
And we for life shall gang thegither;
Though daft or wise I 'll never demand,
Or black or fair it maks na whether.
I 'm aff with wit, and beauty will fade,
And blood alane is no worth a shilling;
But she that 's rich, her market 's made,
For ilka charm about her is killing.

Gi'e me a lass with a lump of land,
And in my bosom I 'll hug my treasure;
Gin I had anes her gear in my hand,
Shou'd love turn dowf, it will find pleasure.
Laugh on wha likes, but there 's my hand,
I hate with poortith, though bonny, to meddle;
Unless they bring cash, or a lump of land,
They 'se never get me to dance to their fiddle.

There 's meikle good love in bands and bags,
And siller and gowd 's a sweet complexion;
But beauty, and wit, and virtue in rags,
Have tint the art of gaining affection.
Love tips his arrows with woods and parks,
And castles, and riggs, and moors, and meadows;
And naithing can catch our modern sparks,
But well-tochered lasses, or jointured widows.

1724

William Hamilton of Bangour (1704–1754)

THE BRAES OF YARROW

A. 'Busk ye, busk ye, my bonny bonny bride,
Busk ye, busk ye, my winsome marrow!

Busk ye, busk ye, my bonny bonny bride,
And think nae mair on the braes of Yarrow.'

B. 'Where got ye that bonny bonny bride,
Where got ye that winsome marrow?'
A. 'I got her where I durst not well be seen —
Pu'ing the birks on the braes of Yarrow.

Weep not, weep not, my bonny bonny bride,
Weep not, weep not, my winsome marrow;
Nor let thy heart lament to leave
Pu'ing the birks on the braes of Yarrow!'

B. 'Why does she weep, thy bonny bonny bride?
Why does she weep, thy winsome marrow?
And why dare ye nae mair weel be seen
Pu'ing the birks on the braes of Yarrow?'

A. 'Lang maun she weep, lang maun she, maun she weep,
Lang maun she weep with dule and sorrow;
And lang maun I nae mair weel be seen
Pu'ing the birks on the braes of Yarrow:

For she has tint her lover, lover dear —
Her lover dear, the cause of sorrow;
And I have slain the comeliest swain
That e'er pu'd birks on the braes of Yarrow!

Why runs thy stream, O Yarrow, Yarrow, reid?
Why on thy braes heard the voice of sorrow?
And why yon melancholious weeds,
Hung on the bonny birks of Yarrow?

What 's yonder floats on the rueful, rueful flood?
What 's yonder floats? O dule and sorrow!
'T is he, the comely swain I slew
Upon the duleful braes of Yarrow.

Wash, O wash his wounds, his wounds in tears,
His wounds in tears of dule and sorrow;
And wrap his limbs in mourning weeds,
And lay him on the braes of Yarrow.

Then build, then build, ye sisters, sisters sad,
Ye sisters sad, his tomb with sorrow;
And weep around, in woeful wise,
His hapless fate on the braes of Yarrow.

Curse ye, curse ye his useless, useless shield,
My arm that wrought the deed of sorrow,
The fatal spear that pierced his breast —
His comely breast on the braes of Yarrow!

Did I not warn thee, not to, not to luve?
And warn from fight? but to my sorrow
Too rashly bauld a stronger arm
Thou mett'st, and fell on the Braes of Yarrow.'

C. 'Sweet smells the birk, green grows, green grows the grass.
Yellow on Yarrow's bank the gowan,
Fair hangs the apple frae the rock,
Sweet the wave of Yarrow flowan.'

A. 'Flows Yarrow sweet? as sweet, as sweet flows Tweed,
As green its grass, its gowan as yellow,
As sweet smells on its braes the birk,
The apple frae its rock as mellow.

Fair was thy luve, fair, fair indeed thy luve,
In flow'ry bands thou didst him fetter;
Though he was fair, and weil beluved again
Than me he never luved thee better.

Busk ye, then busk, my bonny bonny bride,
Busk ye, busk ye, my winsome marrow,
Busk ye, and luve me on the banks of Tweed,
And think nae mair on the Braes of Yarrow.'

C. 'How can I busk, a bonny bonny bride?
How can I busk, a winsome marrow?

How luve him upon the banks of Tweed,
That slew my luve on the Braes of Yarrow?

O Yarrow fields, may never, never rain
Nor dew thy tender blossoms cover,
For there was basely slain my luve,
My luve, as he had not been a lover.

The boy put on his robes, his robes of green,
His purple vest — 't was my ain sewing:
Ah, wretched me! I little, little knew
He was in these to meet his ruin.

The boy took out his milk-white, milk-white steed,
Unheedful of my dule and sorrow;
But ere the to-fall of the night
He lay a corpse on the braes of Yarrow.

Much I rejoiced that woeful, woeful day;
I sang — my voice the woods returning; —
But lang ere night the spear was flown
That slew my love and left me mourning.

What can my barbarous, barbarous father do
But with his cruel rage pursue me?
My lover's blood is on thy spear;
How canst thou, barbarous man, then woo me?

My happy sisters may be, may be proud;
With cruel and ungentle scoffin',
May bid me seek on Yarrow's braes
My lover nailèd in his coffin:

My brother Douglas may upbraid,
And strive with threatening words to move me: —
My lover's blood is on thy spear,
How canst thou ever bid me love thee?

Yes, yes, prepare the bed, the bed of love;
With bridal sheets my body cover;
Unbar, ye bridal maids, the door,
Let in the expected husband lover.

But who the expected husband, husband is?
His hands, methinks, are bathed in slaughter.
Ah me! what ghastly spectre 's yon
Comes in his pale shroud, bleeding after?

Pale as he is, here lay him, lay him down,
O lay his cold head on my pillow;
Take aff, take aff, these bridal weids,
And crown my careful head with willow.

Pale though thou art, yet best, yet best beluved,
O could my warmth to life restore thee,
Ye 'd lye all night between my breists,
No youth lay ever there before thee.

Pale, pale indeed, O luvely, luvely youth!
Forgive, forgive so foul a slaughter:
And lye all night between my breists;
No youth shall ever lye there after.'

A. 'Return, return, O mournful, mournful bride,
Return, and dry thy useless sorrow:
Thy luver heeds none of thy sighs,
He lyes a corps on the Braes of Yarrow.'

1724

David Mallet (or Malloch) (1700?–1765?)

WILLIAM AND MARGARET

'T WAS at the fearful midnight hour
When all were fast asleep,
In glided Margaret's grimly ghost,
And stood at William's feet.

Her face was like April morn
Clad in a wintry cloud;
And clay-cold was her lily hand,
That held her sable shroud.

So shall the fairest face appear
When youth and years are flown:
Such is the robe that kings must wear,
When death has reft their crown.

Her bloom was like the springing flower,
That sips the silver dew;
The rose was budded in her cheek —
Just opening to the view.

But love had, like the canker-worm,
Consumed her early prime:
The rose grew pale, and left her cheek —
She died before her time.

'Awake!' she cried, 'thy true love calls —
 Come from her midnight grave:
Now let thy pity hear the maid
 Thy love refused to save.

'This is the dumb and dreary hour
 When injured ghosts complain,
And aid the secret fears of night,
 To fright the faithless man.

'Bethink thee, William, of thy fault,
 Thy pledge and broken oath!
And give me back my maiden-vow,
 And give me back my troth.

'How could you say my face was fair,
 And yet that face forsake?
How could you win my virgin heart,
 Yet leave that heart to break?

'Why did you promise love to me,
 And not that promise keep?
Why did you swear my eyes were bright —
 Yet leave those eyes to weep?

'How could you swear my lip was sweet,
 And made the scarlet pale?
And why did I, young witless maid!
 Believe the flattering tale?

'That face, alas! no more is fair,
 These lips no longer red:
Dark are my eyes, now closed in death,
 And every charm is fled.

'The hungry worm my sister is;
 This winding-sheet I wear:
And cold and weary lasts our night,
 Till that last morn appear.

'But hark! the cock has warned me hence —
 A long and late adieu!
Come see, false man, how low she lies,
 That died for love of you.'

The lark sung out; the morning smiled,
 And raised her glittering head;
Pale William quaked in every limb;
 Then raving left his bed.

He hied him to the fatal place
 Where Margaret's body lay;
And stretched him o'er the green-grass turf
 That wrapt her breathless clay.

And thrice he called on Margaret's name,
 And thrice he wept full sore;
Then laid his cheek on her cold grave,
 And word spoke never more!

1724

John Dyer (1699?–1758)

GRONGAR HILL

SILENT nymph with curious eye,
Who, the purple ev'ning, lie
On the mountain's lonely van
Beyond the noise of busy man,
Painting fair the form of things,
While the yellow linnet sings,
Or the tuneful nightingale
Charms the forest with her tale;
Come with all thy various hues,
Come, and aid thy sister Muse,
Now while Phœbus riding high
Gives lustre to the land and sky!
Grongar Hill invites my song, —
Draw the landskip bright and strong;
Grongar, in whose mossy cells
Sweetly musing Quiet dwells;
Grongar, in whose silent shade,
For the modest Muses made,
So oft I have, the evening still,
At the fountain of a rill,
Sate upon a flow'ry bed
With my hand beneath my head,
While strayed my eyes o'er Towy's flood,
Over mead and over wood,
From house to house, from hill to hill,
Till Contemplation had her fill.
 About his chequered sides I wind
And leave his brooks and meads behind,
And groves and grottoes where I lay,
And vistas shooting beams of day.
Wide and wider spreads the vale,
As circles on a smooth canal;
The mountains round, unhappy fate,
Sooner or later, of all height,
Withdraw their summits from the skies
And lessen as the others rise:
Still the prospect wider spreads,
Adds a thousand woods and meads;
Still it widens, widens still,
And sinks the newly-risen hill.
 Now I gain the mountain's brow —
What a landskip lies below!
No clouds, no vapours intervene,
But the gay, the open scene
Does the face of Nature show
In all the hues of heaven's bow,
And, swelling to embrace the light,
Spreads around beneath the sight.
 Old castles on the cliffs arise,
Proudly tow'ring in the skies;
Rushing from the woods, the spires
Seem from hence ascending fires;
Half his beams Apollo sheds
On the yellow mountain-heads,
Gilds the fleeces of the flocks,

And glitters on the broken rocks.
  Below me trees unnumbered rise,
Beautiful in various dyes:
The gloomy pine, the poplar blue,
The yellow beech, the sable yew,
The slender fir that taper grows,
The sturdy oak with broad-spread boughs.
And beyond the purple grove,
Haunt of Phyllis, queen of love,
Gaudy as the op'ning dawn
Lies a long and level lawn,
On which a dark hill, steep and high,
Holds and charms the wand'ring eye;
Deep are his feet in Towy's flood,
His sides are clothed with waving wood,
And ancient towers crown his brow
That cast an awful look below,
Whose ragged walls the ivy creeps
And with her arms from falling keeps —
So both a safety from the wind
On mutual dependence find.
'T is now the raven's bleak abode;
'T is now th' apartment of the toad;
And there the fox securely feeds;
And there the pois'nous adder breeds,
Concealed in ruins, moss, and weeds;
While, ever and anon, there falls
Huge heaps of hoary mouldered walls.
Yet Time has seen, that lifts the low
And level lays the lofty brow,
Has seen this broken pile complete,
Big with the vanity of state;
But transient is the smile of Fate:
A little rule, a little sway,
A sunbeam in a winter's day,
Is all the proud and mighty have
Between the cradle and the grave.
  And see the rivers, how they run
Through woods and meads, in shade and sun;
Sometimes swift, sometimes slow,
Wave succeeding wave, they go
A various journey to the deep,
Like human life to endless sleep:
Thus is Nature's vesture wrought
To instruct our wand'ring thought;
Thus she dresses green and gay
To disperse our cares away.
  Ever charming, ever new,
When will the landskip tire the view!
The fountain's fall, the river's flow,
The woody valleys, warm and low,
The windy summit, wild and high,
Roughly rushing on the sky,
The pleasant seat, the ruined tow'r,
The naked rock, the shady bow'r,
The town and village, dome and farm,
Each give each a double charm,
As pearls upon an Æthiop's arm.
  See on the mountain's southern side,
Where the prospect opens wide,
Where the evening gilds the tide,
How close and small the hedges lie,
What streaks of meadows cross the eye!
A step methinks may pass the stream.
So little distant dangers seem;
So we mistake the Future's face,
Eyed through Hope's deluding glass,
As yon summits soft and fair,
Clad in colours of the air,
Which to those who journey near
Barren, brown, and rough appear:
Still we tread the same coarse way;
The present's still a cloudy day.
  O may I with myself agree,
And never covet what I see;
Content me with an humble shade,
My passions tamed, my wishes laid:
For while our wishes wildly roll,
We banish quiet from the soul;
'T is thus the busy beat the air,
And misers gather wealth and care.
  Now, ev'n now, my joys run high,
As on the mountain-turf I lie;
While the wanton Zephyr sings,
And in the vale perfumes his wings;
While the waters murmur deep;
While the shepherd charms his sheep;
While the birds unbounded fly,
And with music fill the sky;
Now, ev'n now, my joys run high.
  Be full, ye courts; be great who will;
Search for Peace with all your skill:
Open wide the lofty door,
Seek her on the marble floor;
In vain you search, she is not there;
In vain ye search the domes of care!
Grass and flowers Quiet treads,
On the meads and mountain-heads,
Along with Pleasure, close allied,
Ever by each other's side;
And often, by the murm'ring rill,
Hears the thrush, while all is still,
Within the groves of Grongar Hill.

1726

James Thomson (1700–1748)

SEASONS

SUMMER

Now swarms the village o'er the joyful mead —
The rustic youth, brown with meridian toil,
Healthful and strong; full as the summer rose
Blown by prevailing suns, the ruddy maid,

Half naked, swelling on the sight, and all
Her kindled graces burning o'er her cheek.
Even stooping age is here; and infant hands
Trail the long rake, or, with the fragrant load
O'ercharged, amid the kind oppression roll.
Wide flies the tedded grain; all in a row
Advancing broad, or wheeling round the field,
They spread their breathing harvest to the sun,
That throws refreshful round a rural smell;
Or, as they rake the green-appearing ground,
And drive the dusky wave along the mead,
The russet hay-cock rises thick behind
In order gay: while heard from dale to dale,
Waking the breeze, resounds the blended voice
Of happy labour, love, and social glee.
Or, rushing thence, in one diffusive band
They drive the troubled flocks, by many a dog
Compelled, to where the mazy-running brook
Forms a deep pool, this bank abrupt and high,
And that fair-spreading in a pebbled shore.
Urged to the giddy brink, much is the toil,
The clamour much of men and boys and dogs
Ere the soft, fearful people to the flood
Commit their woolly sides. And oft the swain,
On some impatient seizing, hurls them in:
Emboldened then, nor hesitating more,
Fast, fast they plunge amid the flashing wave,
And, panting, labour to the farther shore.
Repeated this, till deep the well-washed fleece
Has drunk the flood, and from his lively haunt
The trout is banished by the sordid stream.
Heavy and dripping, to the breezy brow
Slow move the harmless race; where, as they spread
Their swelling treasures to the sunny ray,
Inly disturbed, and wondering what this wild
Outrageous tumult means, their loud complaints
The country fill; and, tossed from rock to rock,
Incessant bleatings run around the hills.
At last, of snowy white the gathered flocks
Are in the wattled pen innumerous pressed,
Head above head; and, ranged in lusty rows,
The shepherds sit, and whet the sounding shears.
The housewife waits to roll her fleecy stores,
With all her gay-drest maids attending round.
One, chief, in gracious dignity enthroned,
Shines o'er the rest, the pastoral queen, and rays
Her smiles, sweet-beaming on her shepherd-king;
While the glad circle round them yield their souls
To festive mirth, and wit that knows no gall.
Meantime, their joyous task goes on apace:
Some mingling stir the melted tar, and some,
Deep on the new-shorn vagrant's heaving side
To stamp his master's cipher ready stand;
Others the unwilling wether drag along;
And, glorying in his might, the sturdy boy
Holds by the twisted horns the indignant ram.
Behold where bound, and of its robe bereft
By needy man, that all-depending lord,
How meek, how patient, the mild creature lies!
What softness in its melancholy face,
What dumb complaining innocence appears!
Fear not, ye gentle tribes! 't is not the knife
Of horrid slaughter that is o'er you waved;
No, 't is the tender swain's well-guided shears,
Who having now, to pay his annual care,
Borrowed your fleece, to you a cumbrous load,
Will send you bounding to your hills again.
A simple scene! yet hence Britannia sees
Her solid grandeur rise: hence she commands
The exalted stores of every brighter clime,
The treasures of the sun without his rage:
Hence, fervent all with culture, toil, and arts,
Wide glows her land: her dreadful thunder hence
Rides o'er the waves sublime, and now, even now,
Impending hangs o'er Gallia's humbled coast;
Hence rules the circling deep, and awes the world.

1727

AUTUMN

But see the fading many-coloured woods,
Shade deepening over shade, the country round
Imbrown; a crowded umbrage, dusk and dun,

Of every hue from wan declining green
To sooty dark. These now the lonesome muse,
Low-whispering, lead into their leaf-strown walks,
And give the season in its latest view.
 Meantime, light shadowing all, a sober calm
Fleeces unbounded ether; whose least wave
Stands tremulous, uncertain where to turn
The gentle current; while, illumined wide,
The dewy-skirted clouds imbibe the sun,
And through their lucid veil his softened force
Shed o'er the peaceful world. Then is the time
For those whom wisdom and whom nature charm
To steal themselves from the degenerate crowd,
And soar above this little scene of things —
To tread low-thoughted vice beneath their feet,
To soothe the throbbing passions into peace,
And woo lone Quiet in her silent walks.
 Thus solitary, and in pensive guise,
Oft let me wander o'er the russet mead,
And through the saddened grove, where scarce is heard
One dying strain to cheer the woodman's toil.
Haply some widowed songster pours his plaint
Far in faint warblings through the tawny copse;
While congregated thrushes, linnets, larks,
And each wild throat whose artless strains so late
Swelled all the music of the swarming shades,
Robbed of their tuneful souls, now shivering sit
On the dead tree, a dull despondent flock,
With not a brightness waving o'er their plumes,
And nought save chattering discord in their note.
Oh, let not, aimed from some inhuman eye,
The gun the music of the coming year
Destroy, and harmless, unsuspecting harm,
Lay the weak tribes, a miserable prey,
In mingled murder fluttering on the ground!
 The pale descending year, yet pleasing still,
A gentler mood inspires; for now the leaf
Incessant rustles from the mournful grove,
Oft startling such as studious walk below,
And slowly circles through the waving air.
But, should a quicker breeze amid the boughs
Sob, o'er the sky the leafy deluge streams;
Till, choked and matted with the dreary shower,
The forest-walks, at every rising gale,
Roll wide the withered waste, and whistle bleak.
Fled is the blasted verdure of the fields;
And, shrunk into their beds, the flowery race
Their sunny robes resign. Even what remained
Of bolder fruits falls from the naked tree;
And — woods, fields, gardens, orchards, all around —
The desolated prospect thrills the soul.
 He comes! he comes! in every breeze the Power
Of Philosphic Melancholy comes!
His near approach the sudden-starting tear,
The glowing cheek, the mild dejected air,
The softened feature, and the beating heart,
Pierced deep with many a virtuous pang, declare.
O'er all the soul his sacred influence breathes;
Inflames imagination; through the breast
Infuses every tenderness; and far
Beyond dim earth exalts the swelling thought.
Ten thousand thousand fleet ideas, such
As never mingled with the vulgar dream,
Crowd fast into the mind's creative eye.
As fast the correspondent passions rise,
As varied, and as high — devotion raised
To rapture, and divine astonishment;
The love of nature unconfined, and, chief,
Of human race; the large ambitious wish
To make them blest; the sigh for suffering worth
Lost in obscurity; the noble scorn
Of tyrant pride; the fearless great resolve;
The wonder which the dying patriot draws,
Inspiring glory through remotest time;
The awakened throb for virtue and for fame;
The sympathies of love and friendship dear,
With all the social offspring of the heart.
 Oh! bear me then to vast embowering shades,
To twilight groves, and visionary vales,
To weeping grottoes, and prophetic glooms;
Where angel forms athwart the solemn dusk,
Tremendous, sweep, or seem to sweep along;
And voices more than human, through the void
Deep-sounding, seize the enthusiastic ear.

1730

WINTER

The keener tempests come: and, fuming dun
From all the livid east or piercing north,

Thick clouds ascend, in whose capacious womb
A vapoury deluge lies, to snow congealed.
Heavy they roll their fleecy world along,
And the sky saddens with the gathered storm.
Through the hushed air the whitening shower descends,
At first thin-wavering; till at last the flakes
Fall broad and wide and fast, dimming the day
With a continual flow. The cherished fields
Put on their winter-robe of purest white.
'T is brightness all; save where the new snow melts
Along the mazy current. Low the woods
Bow their hoar head; and, ere the languid sun
Faint from the west emits his evening ray,
Earth's universal face, deep-hid and chill,
Is one wide dazzling waste, that buries wide
The works of man. Drooping, the labourer-ox
Stands covered o'er with snow, and then demands
The fruit of all his toil. The fowls of heaven,
Tamed by the cruel season, crowd around
The winnowing store, and claim the little boon
Which Providence assigns them. One alone,
The redbreast, sacred to the household gods,
Wisely regardful of the embroiling sky,
In joyless fields and thorny thickets leaves
His shivering mates, and pays to trusted man
His annual visit. Half afraid, he first
Against the window beats; then brisk alights
On the warm hearth; then, hopping o'er the floor,
Eyes all the smiling family askance,
And pecks, and starts, and wonders where he is —
Till, more familiar grown, the table-crumbs
Attract his slender feet. The foodless wilds
Pour forth their brown inhabitants. The hare,
Though timorous of heart, and hard beset
By death in various forms, dark snares, and dogs,
And more unpitying men, the garden seeks,
Urged on by fearless want. The bleating kind
Eye the bleak heaven, and next the glistening earth,
With looks of dumb despair; then, sad-dispersed,
Dig for the withered herb through heaps of snow.
Now, shepherds, to your helpless charge be kind:
Baffle the raging year, and fill their pens
With food at will; lodge them below the storm,
And watch them strict: for, from the bellowing east,
In this dire season, oft the whirlwind's wing
Sweeps up the burden of whole wintry plains
In one wide waft, and o'er the hapless flocks,
Hid in the hollow of two neighbouring hills,
The billowy tempest whelms; till, upward urged,
The valley to a shining mountain swells,
Tipt with a wreath high-curling in the sky.
As thus the snows arise, and foul and fierce,
All Winter drives along the darkened air,
In his own loose-revolving fields the swain
Disastered stands; sees other hills ascend,
Of unknown joyless brow; and other scenes,
Of horrid prospect, shag the trackless plain;
Nor finds the river nor the forest, hid
Beneath the formless wild; but wanders on
From hill to dale, still more and more astray —
Impatient flouncing through the drifted heaps,
Stung with the thoughts of home: the thoughts of home
Rush on his nerves and call their vigour forth
In many a vain attempt. How sinks his soul!
What black despair, what horror fills his heart,.
When, for the dusky spot which fancy feigned
His tufted cottage rising through the snow,
He meets the roughness of the middle waste,
Far from the track and blest abode of man;
While round him night resistless closes fast,
And every tempest, howling o'er his head,
Renders the savage wilderness more wild.
Then throng the busy shapes into his mind
Of covered pits, unfathomably deep,
A dire descent! beyond the power of frost;
Of faithless bogs; of precipices huge,
Smoothed up with snow; and (what is land unknown,
What water) of the still unfrozen spring,
In the loose marsh or solitary lake,
Where the fresh fountain from the bottom boils.
These check his fearful steps; and down he sinks
Beneath the shelter of the shapeless drift,

Thinking o'er all the bitterness of death,
Mixed with the tender anguish nature shoots
Through the wrung bosom of the dying man —
His wife, his children, and his friends, unseen.
In vain for him the officious wife prepares
The fire fair-blazing and the vestment warm;
In vain his little children, peeping out
Into the mingling storm, demand their sire
With tears of artless innocence. Alas!
Nor wife nor children more shall he behold,
Nor friends, nor sacred home. On every nerve
The deadly Winter seizes, shuts up sense,
And, o'er his inmost vitals creeping cold,
Lays him along the snows a stiffened corse,
Stretched out, and bleaching in the northern blast.

1726

THE CASTLE OF INDOLENCE

In lowly dale, fast by a river's side,
With woody hill o'er hill encompassed round,
A most enchanting wizard did abide,
Than whom a fiend more fell is nowhere found.
It was, I ween, a lovely spot of ground;
And there a season atween June and May,
Half prankt with spring, with summer half imbrowned,
A listless climate made, where, sooth to say,
No living wight could work, ne carèd even for play.

Was nought around but images of rest:
Sleep-soothing groves, and quiet lawns between;
And flowery beds that slumbrous influence kest,
From poppies breathed; and beds of pleasant green,
Where never yet was creeping creature seen.
Meantime unnumbered glittering streamlets played,
And hurlèd everywhere their waters sheen,
That, as they bickered through the sunny glade,
Though restless still themselves, a lulling murmur made.

Joined to the prattle of the purling rills,
Were heard the lowing herds along the vale,
And flocks loud-bleating from the distant hills,
And vacant shepherds piping in the dale:
And now and then sweet Philomel would wail,
Or stock-doves plain amid the forest deep,
That drowsy rustled to the sighing gale;
And still a coil the grasshopper did keep:
Yet all these sounds yblent inclinèd all to sleep.

Full in the passage of the vale, above,
A sable, silent, solemn forest stood;
Where nought but shadowy forms were seen to move,
As Idless fancied in her dreaming mood.
And up the hills, on either side, a wood
Of blackening pines, ay waving to and fro,
Sent forth a sleepy horror through the blood;
And where this valley winded out, below,
The murmuring main was heard, and scarcely heard, to flow.

A pleasing land of drowsyhed it was:
Of dreams that wave before the half-shut eye:
And of gay castles in the clouds that pass,
Forever flushing round a summer sky:
There eke the soft delights, that witchingly
Instil a wanton sweetness through the breast,
And the calm pleasures always hovered nigh;
But whate'er smacked of noyance, or unrest,
Was far far off expelled from this delicious nest.

The landskip such, inspiring perfect ease;
Where Indolence (for so the wizard hight)
Close-hid his castle mid embowering trees,
That half shut out the beams of Phœbus bright,
And made a kind of checkered day and night.
Meanwhile, unceasing at the massy gate,
Beneath a spacious palm, the wicked wight
Was placed; and, to his lute, of cruel fate
And labour harsh complained, lamenting man's estate.

. . . .

The doors, that knew no shrill alarming bell,
Ne cursèd knocker plied by villain's hand,
Self-opened into halls, where, who can tell
What elegance and grandeur wide expand

The pride of Turkey and of Persia land?
Soft quilts on quilts, on carpets carpets spread,
And couches stretched around in seemly band;
And endless pillows rise to prop the head;
So that each spacious room was one full-swelling bed.

And everywhere huge covered tables stood,
With wines high-flavoured and rich viands crowned;
Whatever sprightly juice or tasteful food
On the green bosom of this Earth are found,
And all old Ocean genders in his round —
Some hand unseen these silently displayed,
Even undemanded by a sign or sound;
You need but wish, and, instantly obeyed,
Fair ranged the dishes rose, and thick the glasses played.

Here freedom reigned without the least alloy;
Nor gossip's tale, nor ancient maiden's gall,
Nor saintly spleen durst murmur at our joy,
And with envenomed tongue our pleasures pall.
For why? there was but one great rule for all;
To wit, that each should work his own desire,
And eat, drink, study, sleep, as it may fall,
Or melt the time in love, or wake the lyre,
And carol what, unbid, the Muses might inspire.

The rooms with costly tapestry were hung,
Where was inwoven many a gentle tale,
Such as of old the rural poets sung
Or of Arcadian or Sicilian vale:
Reclining lovers, in the lonely dale,
Poured forth at large the sweetly tortured heart;
Or, looking tender passion, swelled the gale,
And taught charmed echo to resound their smart;
While flocks, woods, streams around, repose and peace impart.

Those pleased the most, where, by a cunning hand,
Depeinten was the patriarchal age;
What time Dan Abraham left the Chaldee land,
And pastured on from verdant stage to stage,
Where fields and fountains fresh could best engage.
Toil was not then. Of nothing took they heed,
But with wild beasts the sylvan war to wage,
And o'er vast plains their herds and flocks to feed:
Blest sons of nature they! true golden age indeed!

Sometimes the pencil, in cool airy halls,
Bade the gay bloom of vernal landskips rise,
Or Autumn's varied shades imbrown the walls:
Now the black tempest strikes the astonished eyes;
Now down the steep the flashing torrent flies;
The trembling sun now plays o'er ocean blue,
And now rude mountains frown amid the skies;
Whate'er Lorraine light-touched with softening hue,
Or savage Rosa dashed, or learnèd Poussin drew.

Each sound too here to languishment inclined,
Lulled the weak bosom, and inducèd ease.
Aëreal music in the warbling wind,
At distance rising oft, by small degrees,
Nearer and nearer came, till o'er the trees
It hung, and breathed such soul-dissolving airs
As did, alas! with soft perdition please:
Intangled deep in its enchanting snares,
The listening heart forgot all duties and all cares.

A certain music, never known before,
Here soothed the pensive melancholy mind;
Full easily obtained. Behoves no more,
But sidelong to the gently-waving wind
To lay the well-tuned instrument reclined;
From which, with airy flying fingers light,
Beyond each mortal touch the most refined,
The god of winds drew sounds of deep delight:
Whence, with just cause, The Harp of Æolus it hight.

Ah me! what hand can touch the string so fine?
Who up the lofty diapason roll
Such sweet, such sad, such solemn airs divine,
Then let them down again into the soul?
Now rising love they fanned; now pleasing dole
They breathed, in tender musings, through the heart;
And now a graver sacred strain they stole,
As when seraphic hands an hymn impart:
Wild warbling Nature all, above the reach of Art!

Such the gay splendour, the luxurious state,
Of Caliphs old, who on the Tigris' shore,
In mighty Bagdat, populous and great,
Held their bright court, where was of ladies store;
And verse, love, music still the garland wore:
When sleep was coy, the bard in waiting there
Cheered the lone midnight with the muse's lore;
Composing music bade his dreams be fair,
And music lent new gladness to the morning air.

Near the pavilions where we slept, still ran
Soft-tinkling streams, and dashing waters fell,
And sobbing breezes sighed, and oft began
(So worked the wizard) wintry storms to swell,
As heaven and earth they would together mell:
At doors and windows, threatening, seemed to call
The demons of the tempest, growling fell;
Yet the least entrance found they none at all;
Whence sweeter grew our sleep, secure in massy hall.

1748

William Shenstone (1714–1763)

THE SCHOOLMISTRESS

Ah me! full sorely is my heart forlorn,
To think how modest worth neglected lies;
While partial fame doth with her blasts adorn
Such deeds alone, as pride and pomp disguise;
Deeds of ill sort, and mischievous emprize!
Lend me thy clarion, goddess! let me try
To sound the praise of merit, ere it dies;
Such as I oft have chaunced to espy,
Lost in the dreary shades of dull obscurity.

In every village marked with little spire,
Embowered in trees, and hardly known to fame,
There dwells, in lowly shed, and mean attire,
A matron old, whom we schoolmistress name;
Who boasts unruly brats with birch to tame;
They grieven sore, in piteous durance pent,
Awed by the power of this relentless dame;
And oft-times, on vagaries idly bent,
For unkempt hair, or talk unconned, are sorely shent.

And all in sight doth rise a birchen tree,
Which learning near her little dome did stowe;
Whilom a twig of small regard to see,
Though now so wide its waving branches flow;
And work the simple vassals mickle woe;
For not a wind might curl the leaves that blew,
But their limbs shuddered, and their pulse beat low;
And, as they looked, they found their horror grew,
And shaped it into rods, and tingled at the view.

So have I seen (who has not, may conceive)
A lifeless phantom near a garden placed;
So doth it wanton birds of peace bereave,
Of sport, of song, of pleasure, of repast;
They start, they stare, they wheel, they look aghast:
Sad servitude! such comfortless annoy
May no bold Briton's riper age e'er taste!
Ne superstition clog his dance of joy,
Ne vision empty, vain, his native bliss destroy.

Near to this dome is found a patch so green,
On which the tribe their gambols do display;

And at the door imprisoning board is
seen,
Lest weakly wights of smaller size should
stray;
Eager, perdie, to bask in sunny day!
The noises intermixed, which thence resound,
Do learning's little tenement betray:
Where sits the dame, disguised in look
profound,
And eyes her fairy throng, and turns her
wheel around.

Her cap, far whiter than the driven snow,
Emblem right meet of decency does yield:
Her apron dyed in grain, as blue, I
trow,
As is the hare-bell that adorns the field:
And in her hand, for scepter, she does
wield
Tway birchen sprays; with anxious fear
entwined,
With dark distrust, and sad repentance
filled;
And steadfast hate, and sharp affliction
joined,
And fury uncontrolled, and chastisement unkind.

Few have but kenned, in semblance meet
portrayed,
The childish faces, of old Eol's train;
Libs, Notus, Auster: these in frowns arrayed,
How then would fare on earth, or sky, or
main,
Were the stern god to give his slaves the
rein?
And were not she rebellious breasts to
quell,
And were not she her statutes to maintain,
The cot no more, I ween, were deemed the
cell,
Where comely peace of mind, and decent
order dwell.

A russet stole was o'er her shoulders
thrown;
A russet kirtle fenced the nipping air;
'T was simple russet, but it was her own;
'T was her own country bred the flock so
fair;
'T was her own labour did the fleece prepare;
And, sooth to say, her pupils ranged
around,
Through pious awe, did term it passing
rare;
For they in gaping wonderment abound,
And think, no doubt, she been the greatest
wight on ground.

Albeit ne flattery did corrupt her truth,
Ne pompous title did debauch her ear;
Goody, good-woman, gossip, n'aunt, forsooth,
Or dame, the sole additions she did hear;
Yet these she challenged, these she held
right dear:
Ne would esteem him act as mought behove,
Who should not honored eld with these
revere:
For never title yet so mean could prove,
But there was eke a mind which did that
title love.

One ancient hen she took delight to feed,
The plodding pattern of the busy dame;
Which, ever and anon, impelled by need,
Into her school, begirt with chickens,
came;
Such favour did her past deportment
claim;
And, if neglect had lavished on the
ground
Fragment of bread, she would collect the
same;
For well she knew, and quaintly could expound,
What sin it were to waste the smallest crumb
she found.

Herbs too she knew, and well of each could
speak
That in her garden sipped the silvery dew;
Where no vain flower disclosed a gaudy
streak,
But herbs for use and physic, not a few,
Of gray renown, within those borders
grew:
The tufted basil, pun-provoking thyme,
Fresh balm, and marigold of cheerful hue;
The lowly gill, that never dares to climb;
And more I fain would sing, disdaining here
to rhyme.

Yet euphrasy may not be left unsung,
That gives him dim eyes to wander leagues
around;
And pungent radish, biting infant's
tongue;
And plantain ribbed, that heals the reaper's wound;
And marjoram sweet, in shepherd's
posie found;
And lavender, whose spikes of azure
bloom
Shall be, ere-while, in arid bundles bound,

To lurk amidst the labours of her loom,
And crown her kerchiefs clean, with mickle rare perfume.

And here trim rosmarine, that whilom crowned
The daintiest garden of the proudest peer;
Ere, driven from its envied site, it found
A sacred shelter for its branches here;
Where edged with gold its glittering skirts appear.
Oh wassel days! O customs meet and well!
Ere this was banished from its lofty sphere:
Simplicity then sought this humble cell,
Nor ever would she more with thane and lordling dwell.

Here oft the dame, on Sabbath's decent eve,
Hymnèd such psalms as Sternhold forth did mete,
If winter 't were, she to her hearth did cleave;
But in her garden found a summer seat:
Sweet melody! to hear her then repeat
How Israel's sons, beneath a foreign king,
While taunting foemen did a song entreat,
All, for the nonce, untuning every string,
Uphung their useless lyres — small heart had they to sing.

For she was just, and friend to virtuous lore,
And passed much time in truly virtuous deed;
And, in those elfins' ears, would oft deplore
The times, when truth by popish rage did bleed;
And tort'rous death was true devotion's meed;
And simple faith in iron chains did mourn,
That nould on wooden image place her creed;
And lawny saints in smouldering flames did burn:
Ah! dearest Lord, forefend thilk days should e'er return.

In elbow chair, like that of Scottish stem
By the sharp tooth of cankering eld defaced,
In which, when he receives his diadem,
Our sovereign prince and liefest liege is placed,
The matron sate; and some with rank she graced,
(The source of children's and of courtier's pride!)
Redressed affronts, for vile affronts there passed;
And warned them not the fretful to deride,
But love each other dear, whatever them betide.

Right well she knew each temper to descry;
To thwart the proud, and the submiss to raise;
Some with vile copper prize exalt on high,
And some entice with pittance small of praise;
And other some with baleful sprig she 'frays:
Ev'n absent, she the reins of power doth hold,
While with quaint arts the giddy crowd she sways;
Forewarned, if little bird their pranks behold,
'T will whisper in her ear, and all the scene unfold.

Lo now with state she utters the command!
Eftsoons the urchins to their tasks repair;
Their books of stature small they take in hand,
Which with pellucid horn securèd are;
So save from finger wet the letters fair:
The work so gay, that on their back is seen,
St. George's high achievements does declare;
On which thilk wight that has y-gazing been,
Kens the forth-coming rod, unpleasing sight, I ween!

Ah luckless he, and born beneath the beam
Of evil star! it irks me whilst I write!
As erst the bard by Mulla's silver stream,
Oft, as he told of deadly dolorous plight,
Sighed as he sung, and did in tears indite.
For brandishing the rod, she doth begin
To loose the brogues, the stripling's late delight!
And down they drop; appears his dainty skin,
Fair as the furry coat of whitest ermilin.

O ruthful scene! when from a nook obscure,
His little sister doth his peril see:
All playful as she sate, she grows demure;

She finds full soon her wonted spirits flee;
She meditates a prayer to set him free:
Nor gentle pardon could this dame deny,
(If gentle pardon could with dames agree)
To her sad grief that swells in either eye,
And wrings her so that all for pïty she could die.

No longer can she now her shrieks command;
And hardly she forbears, through awful fear,
To rushen forth, and, with presumptuous hand,
To stay harsh justice in its mid career.
On thee she calls, on thee her parent dear!
(Ah! too remote to ward the shameful blow!)
She sees no kind domestic visage near,
And soon a flood of tears begins to flow;
And gives a loose at last to unavailing woe.

But ah! what pen his piteous plight may trace?
Or what device his loud laments explain?
The form uncouth of his diguisèd face?
The pallid hue that dyes his looks amain?
The plenteous shower that does his cheek distain?
When he, in abject wise, implores the dame,
Ne hopeth aught of sweet reprieve to gain;
Or when from high she levels well her aim,
And, through the thatch, his cries each falling stroke proclaim.

The other tribe, aghast, with sore dismay,
Attend, and conn their tasks with mickle care:
By turns, astonied, every twig survey,
And, from their fellow's hateful wounds, beware;
Knowing, I wist, how each the same may share;
Till fear has taught them a performance meet,
And to the well-known chest the dame repair;
Whence oft with sugared cates she doth 'em greet,
And ginger-bread y-rare; now, certes, doubly sweet!

See to their seats they hye with merry glee,
And in beseemly order sitten there;
All but the wight of bum y-gallèd, he
Abhorreth bench and stool, and form, and chair;
This hand in mouth y-fixed, that rends his hair;
And eke with snubs profound, and heaving breast,
Convulsions intermitting! does declare
His grievous wrong; his dame's unjust behest:
And scorns her offered love, and shuns to be caressed.

His face besprent with liquid crystal shines,
His blooming face that seems a purple flower,
Which low to earth its drooping head declines,
All smeared and sullied by a vernal shower.
O the hard bosoms of despotic power!
All, all, but she the author of his shame,
All, all, but she, regret this mournful hour:
Yet hence the youth, and hence the flower, shall claim,
If so I deem aright, transcending worth and fame.

Behind some door, in melancholy thought,
Mindless of food, he, dreary caitiff! pines;
Ne for his fellow's joyaunce careth aught,
But to the wind all merriment resigns;
And deems it shame, if he to peace inclines;
And many a sullen look askance is sent,
Which for his dame's annoyance he designs;
And still the more to pleasure him she's bent,
The more doth he, perverse, her haviour past resent.

Ah me! how much I fear lest pride it be!
But if that pride it be, which thus inspires,
Beware, ye dames, with nice discernment see,
Ye quench not too the sparks of nobler fires:
Ah! better far than all the muses' lyres,
All coward arts, is valour's generous heat;
The firm fixed breast which fit and right requires,
Like Vernon's patriot soul; more justly great
Than craft that pimps for ill, or flowery false deceit.

Yet nursed with skill, what dazzling fruits appear!
Even now sagacious foresight points to show
A little bench of heedless bishops here,
And there a chancellor in embryo,
Or bard sublime, if bard may e'er be so,
As Milton, Shakespeare, names that ne'er shall die!
Though now he crawl along the ground so low,
Nor weeting how the muse should soar on high,
Wisheth, poor starveling elf! his paper-kite may fly.

And this perhaps, who, censuring the design,
Low lays the house which that of cards doth build,
Shall Dennis be! if rigid fates incline,
And many an epic to his rage shall yield;
And many a poet quit the Aonian field;
And, soured by age, profound he shall appear,
As he who now with 'sdainful fury thrilled
Surveys mine work; and levels many a sneer,
And furls his wrinkly front, and cries, 'What stuff is here?'

But now Dan Phœbus gains the middle sky,
And liberty unbars her prison-door;
And like a rushing torrent out they fly,
And now the grassy cirque han covered o'er
With boistrous revel-rout and wild uproar;
A thousand ways in wanton rings they run,
Heaven shield their short-lived pastimes, I implore!
For well may freedom, erst so dearly won,
Appear to British elf more gladsome than the sun.

Enjoy, poor imps! enjoy your sportive trade;
And chase gay flies, and cull the fairest flowers;
For when my bones in grass-green sods are laid;
For never may ye taste more careless hours
In knightly castles, or in ladies' bowers.
O vain to seek delight in earthly thing!
But most in courts where proud ambition towers;
Deluded wight! who weens fair peace can spring
Beneath the pompous dome of kesar or of king.

See in each sprite some various bent appear!
These rudely carol most incondite lay;
Those sauntering on the green, with jocund leer
Salute the stranger passing on his way;
Some builden fragile tenements of clay;
Some to the standing lake their courses bend,
With pebbles smooth at duck and drake to play;
Thilk to the huxter's savory cottage tend,
In pastry kings and queens the allotted mite to spend.

Here, as each season yields a different store,
Each season's stores in order rangèd been;
Apples with cabbage-net y-covered o'er,
Galling full sore the unmoneyed wight, are seen;
And goose-b'rie clad in livery red or green;
And here of lovely dye, the catharine pear,
Fine pear! as lovely for thy juice, I ween:
O may no wight e'er pennyless come there,
Lest smit with ardent love he pine with hopeless care!

See! cherries here, ere cherries yet abound,
With thread so white in tempting posies tied,
Scattering like blooming maid their glances round,
With pampered look draw little eyes aside;
And must be bought, though penury betide.
The plumb all azure and the nut all brown,
And here each season do those cakes abide.
Whose honoured names the inventivè city own,
Rendering through Britain's isle Salopia's praises known.

Admired Salopia! that with venial pride
Eyes her bright form in Severn's ambient wave,
Famed for her loyal cares in perils tried,
Her daughters lovely, and her striplings brave:

Ah! midst the rest, may flowers adorn his grave,
Whose art did first these dulcet cates display!
A motive fair to learning's imps he gave,
Who cheerless o'er her darkling region stray;
Till reason's morn arise, and light them on their way.

1742

HOPE

My banks they are furnished with bees,
Whose murmur invites one to sleep;
My grottos are shaded with trees,
And my hills are white-over with sheep.
I seldom have met with a loss,
Such health do my fountains bestow;
My fountains all bordered with moss,
Where the hare-bells and violets grow.

Not a pine in my grove is there seen,
But with tendrils of woodbine is bound:
Not a beech's more beautiful green,
But a sweet-briar entwines it around.
Not my fields, in the prime of the year,
More charms than my cattle unfold:
Not a brook that is limpid and clear,
But it glitters with fishes of gold.

One would think she might like to retire
To the bower I have laboured to rear;
Not a shrub that I heard her admire,
But I hasted and planted it there.
O how sudden the jessamine strove
With the lilac to render it gay!
Already it calls for my love,
To prune the wild branches away.

From the plains, from the woodlands and groves,
What strains of wild melody flow!
How the nightingales warble their loves
From thickets of roses that blow!
And when her bright form shall appear,
Each bird shall harmoniously join
In a concert so soft and so clear,
As — she may not be fond to resign.

I have found out a gift for my fair;
I have found where the wood-pigeons breed:
But let me that plunder forbear,
She will say 't was a barbarous deed.
For he ne'er could be true, she averred,
Who would rob a poor bird of its young:
And I loved her the more, when I heard
Such tenderness fall from her tongue.

I have heard her with sweetness unfold
How that pity was due to — a dove:
That it ever attended the bold,
And she called it the sister of love.
But her words such a pleasure convey,
So much I her accents adore,
Let her speak, and whatever she say,
Methinks I should love her the more.

Can a bosom so gentle remain
Unmoved, when her Corydon sighs?
Will a nymph that is fond of the plain,
These plains and this valley despise?
Dear regions of silence and shade!
Soft scenes of contentment and ease!
Where I could have pleasingly strayed,
If aught, in her absence, could please.

But where does my Phyllida stray?
And where are her grots and her bowers?
Are the groves and the valleys as gay,
And the shepherds as gentle as ours?
The groves may perhaps be as fair,
And the face of the valleys as fine;
The swains may in manners compare,
But their love is not equal to mine.

1743

Edward Young (1683–1765)

THE COMPLAINT, OR NIGHT THOUGHTS ON LIFE, DEATH, AND IMMORTALITY

NIGHT I

Tired Nature's sweet restorer, balmy sleep!
He, like the world, his ready visit pays
Where fortune smiles; the wretched he forsakes;
Swift on his downy pinion flies from woe,
And lights on lids unsullied with a tear.
From short (as usual) and disturbed repose,
I wake: how happy they, who wake no more!
Yet that were vain, if dreams infest the grave.
I wake, emerging from a sea of dreams
Tumultuous; where my wrecked desponding thought,
From wave to wave of fancied misery,
At random drove, her helm of reason lost.
Though now restored, 't is only change of pain,
(A bitter change!) severer for severe.
The day too short for my distress; and night,
Even in the zenith of her dark domain,

Is sunshine to the colour of my fate.
Night, sable goddess! from her ebon throne,
In rayless majesty, now stretches forth
Her leaden scepter o'er a slumbering world.
Silence, how dead! and darkness, how profound!
Nor eye, nor list'ning ear, an object finds;
Creation sleeps. 'T is as the general pulse
Of life stood still, and nature made a pause;
An awful pause! prophetic of her end.
And let her prophecy be soon fulfilled;
Fate! drop the curtain; I can lose no more.
Silence and darkness! solemn sisters! twins
From ancient night, who nurse the tender thought
To reason, and on reason build resolve,
(That column of true majesty in man)
Assist me: I will thank you in the grave;
The grave, your kingdom: there this frame shall fall
A victim sacred to your dreary shrine.
But what are ye? —
Thou who didst put to flight
Primeval silence, when the morning stars,
Exulting, shouted o'er the rising ball;
O Thou, whose word from solid darkness struck
That spark, the sun; strike wisdom from my soul;
My soul, which flies to Thee, her trust, her treasure,
As misers to their gold, while others rest.
Through this opaque of nature, and of soul,
This double night, transmit one pitying ray,
To lighten, and to cheer. O lead my mind,
(A mind that fain would wander from its woe)
Lead it through various scenes of life and death;
And from each scene, the noblest truths inspire
Nor less inspire my conduct, than my song;
Teach my best reason, reason; my best will
Teach rectitude; and fix my firm resolve
Wisdom to wed, and pay her long arrear:
Nor let the vial of thy vengeance, poured
On this devoted head, be poured in vain.
The bell strikes one. We take no note of time
But from its loss. To give it then a tongue
Is wise in man. As if an angel spoke,
I feel the solemn sound. If heard aright,
It is the knell of my departed hours:
Where are they? With the years beyond the flood.
It is the signal that demands dispatch:
How much is to be done? My hopes and fears
Start up alarmed, and o'er life's narrow verge
Look down. — On what? a fathomless abyss;
A dread eternity! how surely mine!
And can eternity belong to me,
Poor pensioner on the bounties of an hour?
How poor, how rich, how abject, how august,
How complicate, how wonderful, is man!
How passing wonder He, who made him such!
Who centered in our make such strange extremes!
From diff'rent natures marvellously mixt,
Connexion exquisite of distant worlds!
Distinguished link in being's endless chain!
Midway from nothing to the deity!
A beam ethereal, sullied, and absorpt!
Though sullied and dishonoured, still divine!
Dim miniature of greatness absolute!
An heir of glory! a frail child of dust!
Helpless immortal! insect infinite!
A worm! a god! — I tremble at myself,
And in myself am lost! at home a stranger,
Thought wanders up and down, surprised, aghast,
And wond'ring at her own: how reason reels!
O what a miracle to man is man,
Triumphantly distressed! what joy, what dread!
Alternately transported, and alarmed!
What can preserve my life? or what destroy?
An angel's arm can't snatch me from the grave;
Legions of angels can't confine me there.
'T is past conjecture; all things rise in proof:
While o'er my limbs sleep's soft dominion spread:
What though my soul fantastic measures trod
O'er fairy fields; or mourned along the gloom
Of pathless woods; or down the craggy steep
Hurled headlong, swam with pain the mantled pool;
Or scaled the cliff; or danced on hollow winds,
With antic shapes, wild natives of the brain?
Her ceaseless flight, though devious, speaks her nature
Of subtler essence than the trodden clod;
Active, aërial, towering, unconfined,
Unfettered with her gross companion's fall.
Even silent night proclaims my soul immortal:
Even silent night proclaims eternal day.

For human weal, heaven husbands all events;
Dull sleep instructs, nor sport vain dreams in vain.
Why then their loss deplore, that are not lost?
Why wanders wretched thought their tombs around,
In infidel distress? Are angels there?
Slumbers, raked up in dust, ethereal fire?
They live! they greatly live a life on earth
Unkindled, unconceived; and from an eye
Of tenderness let heavenly pity fall
On me, more justly numbered with the dead.
This is the desert, this the solitude:
How populous, how vital, is the grave!
This is creation's melancholy vault,
The vale funereal, the sad cypress gloom;
The land of apparitions, empty shades!
All, all on earth is shadow, all beyond
Is substance; the reverse is folly's creed:
How solid all, where change shall be no more!
This is the bud of being, the dim dawn,
The twilight of our day, the vestibule;
Life's theater as yet is shut, and death,
Strong death, alone can heave the massy bar,
This gross impediment of clay remove,
And make us embryos of existence free.
From real life, but little more remote
Is he, not yet a candidate for light,
The future embryo, slumbering in his sire.
Embryos we must be, till we burst the shell,
Yon ambient azure shell, and spring to life,
The life of gods, O transport! and of man.
Yet man, fool man! here buries all his thoughts;
Inters celestial hopes without one sigh.
Prisoner of earth, and pent beneath the moon,
Here pinions all his wishes; winged by heaven
To fly at infinite; and reach it there,
Where seraphs gather immortality,
On life's fair tree, fast by the throne of God.
What golden joys ambrosial clustering glow,
In his full beam, and ripen for the just,
Where momentary ages are no more!
Where time, and pain, and chance, and death expire!
And is it in the flight of threescore years,
To push eternity from human thought,
And smother souls immortal in the dust?
A soul immortal, spending all her fires,
Wasting her strength in strenuous idleness,
Thrown into tumult, raptured, or alarmed,
At aught this scene can threaten or indulge,
Resembles ocean into tempest wrought,
To waft a feather, or to drown a fly.
Where falls this censure? it o'erwhelms myself;
How was my heart incrusted by the world!
O how self-fettered was my groveling soul!
How, like a worm, was I wrapt round and round
In silken thought, which reptile Fancy spun,
Till darkened Reason lay quite clouded o'er
With soft conceit of endless comfort here,
Nor yet put forth her wings to reach the skies!
Night-visions may befriend, (as sung above):
Our waking dreams are fatal. How I dreamt
Of things impossible! (Could sleep do more?)
Of joys perpetual in perpetual change!
Of stable pleasures on the tossing wave!
Eternal sunshine in the storms of life!
How richly were my noon-tide trances hung
With gorgeous tapestries of pictured joys!
Joy behind joy, in endless perspective!
Till at Death's toll, whose restless iron tongue
Calls daily for his millions at a meal,
Startling I woke, and found myself undone.
Where now my frenzy's pompous furniture?
The cobwebbed cottage, with its ragged wall
Of mouldering mud, is royalty to me!
The spider's most attenuated thread
Is cord, is cable, to man's tender tie
On earthly bliss; it breaks at every breeze.
O ye blest scenes of permanent delight!
Full above measure! lasting, beyond bound!
A perpetuity of bliss is bliss.
Could you, so rich in rapture, fear an end,
That ghastly thought would drink up all your joy,
And quite unparadise the realms of light.
Safe are you lodged above these rolling spheres;
The baleful influence of whose giddy dance
Sheds sad vicissitude on all beneath.
Here teems with revolutions every hour;
And rarely for the better; or the best,
More mortal than the common births of Fate.
Each Moment has its sickle, emulous
Of Time's enormous scythe, whose ample sweep

Strikes empires from the root; each Moment plays
His little weapon in the narrower sphere
Of sweet domestic comfort, and cuts down
The fairest bloom of sublunary bliss.
 Bliss! sublunary bliss! — proud words, and vain!
Implicit treason to divine decree!
A bold invasion of the rights of Heaven!
I clasped the phantoms, and I found them air.
O had I weighed it ere my fond embrace!
What darts of agony had missed my heart!
 Death! great proprietor of all! 't is thine
To tread out empire, and to quench the stars.
The sun himself by thy permission shines;
And, one day, thou shalt pluck him from his sphere.
Amid such mighty plunder, why exhaust
Thy partial quiver on a mark so mean?
Why thy peculiar rancour wreaked on me?
Insatiate archer! could not one suffice?
Thy shaft flew thrice; and thrice my peace was slain;
And thrice, ere thrice yon moon had filled her horn.
O Cynthia! why so pale? dost thou lament
Thy wretched neighbour? Grieve to see thy wheel
Of ceaseless change outwhirled in human life?
How wanes my borrowed bliss! from Fortune's smile
Precarious courtesy! not virtue's sure,
Self-given, solar ray of sound delight.
 In every varied posture, place, and hour,
How widowed every thought of every joy!
Thought, busy thought! too busy for my peace!
Through the dark postern of time long elapsed,
Led softly, by the stillness of the night,
Led, like a murderer, (and such it proves!)
Strays (wretched rover!) o'er the pleasing past;
In quest of wretchedness perversely strays;
And finds all desert now; and meets the ghosts
Of my departed joys; a numerous train!
I rue the riches of my former fate;
Sweet comfort's blasted clusters I lament;
I tremble at the blessings once so dear;
And every pleasure pains me to the heart.
 Yet why complain? or why complain for one?
Hangs out the sun his lustre but for me,
The single man? Are angels all beside?
I mourn for millions: 't is the common lot;
In this shape, or in that, has fate entailed
The mother's throes on all of woman born,
Not more the children, than sure heirs, of pain
 War, famine, pest, volcano, storm, and fire,
Intestine broils, oppression, with her heart
Wrapt up in triple brass, besiege mankind.
God's image disinherited of day,
Here, plunged in mines, forgets a sun was made.
There, beings deathless as their haughty lord,
Are hammered to the galling oar for life;
And plough the winter's wave, and reap despair.
Some, for hard masters, broken under arms,
In battle lopt away, with half their limbs,
Beg bitter bread through realms their valour saved,
If so the tyrant, or his minion, doom.
Want, and incurable disease, (fell pair!)
On hopeless multitudes remorseless seize
At once; and make a refuge of the grave.
How groaning hospitals eject their dead!
What numbers groan for sad admission there!
What numbers, once in fortune's lap high-fed,
Solicit the cold hand of charity!
To shock us more, solicit it in vain!
Ye silken sons of pleasure! since in pains
You rue more modish visits, visit here,
And breathe from your debauch: give, and reduce
Surfeit's dominion o'er you: but, so great
Your impudence, you blush at what is right.
 Happy! did sorrow seize on such alone.
Not prudence can defend, or virtue save;
Disease invades the chastest temperance;
And punishment the guiltless; and alarm,
Through thickest shades, pursues the fond of peace.
Man's caution often into danger turns,
And, his guard falling, crushes him to death.
Not happiness itself makes good her name!
Our very wishes give us not our wish.
How distant oft the thing we dote on most,
From that for which we dote, felicity!
The smoothest course of nature has its pains;
And truest friends, through error, wound our rest.
Without misfortune, what calamities!
And what hostilities, without a foe!
Nor are foes wanting to the best on earth.

But endless is the list of human ills,
And sighs might sooner fail, than cause to sigh.
A part how small of the terraqueous globe
Is tenanted by man! the rest a waste,
Rocks, deserts, frozen seas, and burning sands:
Wild haunts of monsters, poisons, stings, and death.
Such is earth's melancholy map! But, far
More sad! this earth is a true map of man.
So bounded are its haughty lord's delights
To woe's wide empire; where deep troubles toss,
Loud sorrows howl, envenomed passions bite,
Ravenous calamities our vitals seize,
And threatening Fate wide opens to devour.
What then am I, who sorrow for myself?
In age, in infancy, from others' aid
Is all our hope; to teach us to be kind.
That, Nature's first, last lesson to mankind;
The selfish heart deserves the pain it feels,
More generous sorrow, while it sinks, exalts;
And conscious virtue mitigates the pang.
Nor virtue, more than prudence, bids me give
Swoln thought a second channel; who divide,
They weaken too, the torrent of their grief.
Take then, O World! thy much-indebted tear:
How sad a sight is human happiness,
To those whose thought can pierce beyond an hour.
O thou! whate'er thou art, whose heart exults!
Wouldst thou I should congratulate thy fate?
I know thou wouldst; thy pride demands it from me.
Let thy pride pardon, what thy nature needs,
The salutary censure of a friend.
Thou happy wretch! by blindness thou art blessed;
By dotage dandled to perpetual smiles.
Know, smiler! at thy peril art thou pleased;
Thy pleasure is the promise of thy pain.
Misfortune, like a creditor severe,
But rises in demand for her delay;
She makes a scourge of past prosperity,
To sting thee more, and double thy distress.
Lorenzo, Fortune makes her court to thee,
Thy fond heart dances, while the syren sings.
Dear is thy welfare; think me not unkind:
I would not damp, but to secure thy joys.
Think not that fear is sacred to the storm:
Stand on thy guard against the smiles of Fate.
Is Heaven tremendous in its frowns? Most sure;
And in its favours formidable too:
Its favours here are trials, not rewards;
A call to duty, not discharge from care;
And should alarm us, full as much as woes;
Awake us to their cause and consequence;
And make us tremble, weighed with our desert;
Awe Nature's tumult, and chastise her joys,
Lest while we clasp, we kill them; nay, invert
To worse than simple misery, their charms.
Revolted joys, like foes in civil war,
Like bosom friendships to resentments soured,
With rage envenomed rise against our peace.
Beware what earth calls happiness; beware
All joys, but joys that never can expire.
Who builds on less than an immortal base,
Fond as he seems, condemns his joys to death.
Mine died with thee, Philander! thy last sigh
Dissolved the charm; the disenchanted earth
Lost all her lustre. Where her glittering towers?
Her golden mountains, where? all darkened down
To naked waste; a dreary vale of tears:
The great magician's dead! Thou poor, pale piece
Of outcast earth, in darkness! what a change
From yesterday! Thy darling hope so near,
(Long-laboured prize!) O how ambition flushed
Thy glowing cheek! Ambition truly great,
Of virtuous praise. Death's subtle seed within,
(Sly, treacherous miner!) working in the dark,
Smiled at thy well-concerted scheme, and beckoned
The worm to riot on that rose so red,
Unfaded ere it fell; one moment's prey!
Man's foresight is conditionally wise;
Lorenzo; wisdom into folly turns
Oft, the first instant, its idea fair
To laboring thought is born. How dim our eye!
The present moment terminates our sight;

Clouds, thick as those on doomsday, drown the next;
We penetrate, we prophesy in vain.
Time is dealt out by particles; and each,
Ere mingled with the streaming sands of life,
By fate's inviolable oath is sworn
Deep silence, 'Where eternity begins.'
By nature's law, what may be, may be now;
There 's no prerogative in human hours.
In human hearts what bolder thought can rise,
Than man's presumption on to-morrow's dawn?
Where is to-morrow? In another world.
For numbers this is certain; the reverse
Is sure to none; and yet on this perhaps,
This peradventure, infamous for lies,
As on a rock of adamant, we build
Our mountain hopes; spin our eternal schemes,
As we the fatal sisters could out-spin,
And, big with life's futurities, expire.
Not even Philander had bespoke his shroud.
Nor had he cause; a warning was denied:
How many fall as sudden, not as safe!
As sudden, though for years admonished home.
Of human ills the last extreme beware,
Beware, Lorenzo! a slow sudden death.
How dreadful that deliberate surprise!
Be wise to-day; 't is madness to defer;
Next day the fatal precedent will plead;
Thus on, till wisdom is pushed out of life.
Procrastination is the thief of time;
Year after year it steals, till all are fled,
And to the mercies of a moment leaves
The vast concerns of an eternal scene.
If not so frequent, would not this be strange?
That 't is so frequent, this is stranger still.
Of man's miraculous mistakes, this bears
The palm, 'That all men are about to live,'
For ever on the brink of being born.
All pay themselves the compliment to think
They one day shall not drivel: and their pride
On this reversion takes up ready praise;
At least, their own; their future selves applauds;
How excellent that life they ne'er will lead!
Time lodged in their own hands is folly's vails;
That lodged in Fate's, to wisdom they consign;
The thing they can't but purpose, they postpone;
'T is not in Folly, not to scorn a fool;
And scarce in human wisdom to do more.
All promise is poor dilatory man,
And that through every stage: when young, indeed
In full content we, sometimes, nobly rest,
Unanxious for ourselves; and only wish,
As duteous sons, our fathers were more wise.
At thirty man suspects himself a fool;
Knows it at forty, and reforms his plan;
At fifty chides his infamous delay,
Pushes his prudent purpose to resolve;
In all the magnanimity of thought
Resolves; and re-resolves; then dies the same.
And why? Because he thinks himself immortal.
All men think all men mortal, but themselves;
Themselves, when some alarming shock of Fate
Strikes through their wounded hearts the sudden dread;
But their hearts wounded, like the wounded air,
Soon close; where past the shaft, no trace is found.
As from the wing no scar the sky retains;
The parted wave no furrow from the keel;
So dies in human hearts the thought of death.
Even with the tender tear which nature sheds
O'er those we love, we drop it in their grave.
Can I forget Philander? That were strange!
O my full heart — But should I give it vent,
The longest night, though longer far, would fail,
And the lark listen to my midnight song.
The sprightly lark's shrill matin wakes the morn;
Grief's sharpest thorn hard pressing on my breast
I strive, with wakeful melody, to cheer
The sullen gloom, sweet Philomel! like thee,
And call the stars to listen: every star
Is deaf to mine, enamoured of thy lay.
Yet be not vain; there are, who thine excel,
And charm through distant ages: wrapt in shade,
Prisoner of darkness! to the silent hours,
How often I repeat their rage divine,
To lull my griefs, and steal my heart from woe!
In roll their raptures, but not catch their fire.

Dark, though not blind, like thee, Mæonides!
Or, Milton! thee; ah, could I reach your strain!
Or his, who made Mæonides our own.
Man too he sung: immortal man I sing;
Oft bursts my song beyond the bounds of life;
What, now, but immortality can please?
O had he pressed his theme, pursued the track,
Which opens out of darkness into day!
O had he, mounted on his wing of fire,
Soared where I sink, and sung immortal man!
How had it blessed mankind, and rescued me!

1742

Robert Blair (1699–1746)

THE GRAVE

WHILE some affect the sun, and some the shade,
Some flee the city, some the hermitage,
Their aims as various as the roads they take
In journeying through life, the task be mine
To paint the gloomy horrors of the tomb;
The appointed place of rendezvous, where all
These travellers meet. Thy succors I implore,
Eternal King! whose potent arm sustains
The keys of hell and death. — The Grave, dread thing!
Men shiver when thou 'rt named: nature, appalled,
Shakes off her wonted firmness. — Ah, how dark
Thy long-extended realms, and rueful wastes!
Where nought but silence reigns, and night, dark night,
Dark as was chaos, ere the infant sun
Was rolled together, or had tried his beams
Athwart the gloom profound. — The sickly taper
By glimmering through thy low-browed misty vaults,
Furred round with mouldy damps and ropy slime,
Lets fall a supernumerary horror,
And only serves to make thy night more irksome.
Well do I know thee by thy trusty yew,
Cheerless, unsocial plant! that loves to dwell
Midst skulls and coffins, epitaphs and worms:
Where light-heeled ghosts, and visionary shades,
Beneath the wan cold moon (as fame reports)
Embodied, thick, perform their mystic rounds.
No other merriment, dull tree! is thine.
See yonder hallowed fane; — the pious work
Of names once famed, now dubious or forgot,
And buried midst the wreck of things which were;
There lie interred the more illustrious dead.
The wind is up: hark! how it howls! Methinks
Till now I never heard a sound so dreary:
Doors creak, and windows clap, and night's foul bird,
Rooked in the spire, screams loud: the gloomy aisles,
Black-plastered, and hung round with shreds of 'scutcheons
And tattered coats of arms, send back the sound
Laden with heavier airs, from the low vaults,
The mansions of the dead. — Roused from their slumbers,
In grim array the grisly spectres rise,
Grin horrible, and, obstinately sullen,
Pass and repass, hushed as the foot of night.
Again the screech-owl shrieks: ungracious sound!
I'll hear no more; it makes one's blood run chill.
Quite round the pile, a row of reverend elms,
(Coeval near with that) all ragged show,
Long lashed by the rude winds. Some rift half down
Their branchless trunks; others so thin a-top,
That scarce two crows could lodge in the same tree.
Strange things, the neighbors say, have happened here:
Wild shrieks have issued from the hollow tombs;
Dead men have come again, and walked about;
And the great bell has tolled, unrung, untouched.
(Such tales their cheer, at wake or gossiping,
When it draws near the witching time of night.)
Oft in the lone church-yard at night I've seen,

By glimpse of moonshine chequering through the trees,
The school-boy, with his satchel in his hand,
Whistling aloud to bear his courage up,
And lightly tripping o'er the long flat stones,
(With nettles skirted, and with moss o'ergrown,)
That tell in homely phrase who lie below.
Sudden he starts, and hears, or thinks he hears,
The sound of something purring at his heels;
Full fast he flies, and dares not look behind him,
Till out of breath he overtakes his fellows;
Who gather round, and wonder at the tale
Of horrid apparition, tall and ghastly,
That walks at dead of night, or takes his stand
O'er some new-opened grave; and (strange to tell!)
Evanishes at crowing of the cock.
  The new-made widow, too, I've sometimes 'spied,
Sad sight! slow moving o'er the prostrate dead:
Listless, she crawls along in doleful black,
Whilst bursts of sorrow gush from either eye,
Fast falling down her now untasted cheek:
Prone on the lowly grave of the dear man
She drops; whilst busy, meddling memory,
In barbarous succession musters up
The past endearments of their softer hours,
Tenacious of its theme. Still, still she thinks
She sees him, and, indulging the fond thought,
Clings yet more closely to the senseless turf,
Nor heeds the passenger who looks that way.

. . . .

  Death's shafts fly thick: here falls the village swain,
And there his pampered lord. The cup goes round:
And who so artful as to put it by!
'T is long since Death had the majority;
Yet strange! the living lay it not to heart.
See yonder maker of the dead man's bed,
The sexton, hoary-headed chronicle,
Of hard, unmeaning face, down which ne'er stole
A gentle tear, with mattock in his hand,
Digs through whole rows of kindred and acquaintance,
By far his juniors. — Scarce a skull's cast up,
But well he knew its owner, and can tell
Some passage of his life. — Thus hand in hand
The sot has walked with Death twice twenty years,
And yet ne'er yonker on the green laughs louder
Or clubs a smuttier tale: when drunkards meet,
None sings a merrier catch, or lends a hand
More willing to his cup. — Poor wretch! he minds not,
That soon some trusty brother of the trade
Shall do for him, what he has done for thousands.
  On this side and on that, men see their friends
Drop off, like leaves in autumn, yet launch out
Into fantastic schemes, which the long livers
In the world's hale and undegenerate days
Could scarce have leisure for; fools that we are,
Never to think of death and of ourselves
At the same time! as if to learn to die
Were no concern of ours. O more than sottish!
For creatures of a day in gamesome mood
To frolic on eternity's dread brink,
Unapprehensive, when, for aught we know,
The very first swoln surge shall sweep us in!
Think we, or think we not, time hurries on
With a resistless unremitting stream,
Yet treads more soft than e'er did midnight thief,
That slides his hand under the miser's pillow
And carries off his prize. What is this world?
What but a spacious burial-field unwalled,
Strewed with Death's spoils, the spoils of animals
Savage and tame, and full of dead men's bones!
The very turf on which we tread once lived;
And we that live must lend our carcases
To cover our own offspring; in their turns
They too must cover theirs. 'T is here all meet:
The shiv'ring Icelander and sun-burnt Moor;
Men of all climes, that never met before,
And of all creeds, the Jew, the Turk, the Christian.
Here the proud prince, and favourite yet prouder,
His sov'reign's keeper and the people's scourge,
Are huddled out of sight! Here lie abashed
The great negotiators of the earth,

And celebrated masters of the balance,
Deep read in stratagems and wiles of courts:
Now vain their treaty-skill; Death scorns to treat.
Here the o'erloaded slave flings down his burden
From his galled shoulders; and when the stern tyrant,
With all his guards and tools of power about him,
Is meditating new unheard-of hardships,
Mocks his short arm, and, quick as thought, escapes
Where tyrants vex not and the weary rest.

. . . . . .

But know that thou must render up thy dead,
And with high interest too. — They are not thine;
But only in thy keeping for a season,
Till the great promised day of restitution;
When loud diffusive sound from brazen trump
Of strong-lunged cherub, shall alarm thy captives,
And rouse the long, long sleepers into life,
Day-light and liberty. —
Then must thy gates fly open, and reveal
The mines that lay long forming under ground,
In their dark cells immured; but now full ripe,
And pure as silver from the crucible,
That twice has stood the torture of the fire
And inquisition of the forge. — We know
The illustrious deliverer of mankind,
The Son of God, thee foiled, — Him in thy power
Thou couldst not hold: — self-vigorous he rose,
And shaking off thy fetters, soon retook
Those spoils his voluntary yielding lent:
(Sure pledge of our releasement from thy thrall!)
Twice twenty days he sojourned here on Earth,
And showed himself alive to chosen witnesses,
By proofs so strong, that the most slow assenting
Had not a scruple left. — This having done,
He mounted up to Heaven. — Methinks I see him
Climb the aërial heights, and glide along
Athwart the severing clouds: but the faint eye,
Flung backward in the chase, soon drops its hold,
Disabled quite, and jaded with pursuing.
Heaven's portals wide expand to let him in;
Nor are his friends shut out: as some great prince
Not for himself alone procures admission,
But for his train. — It was his royal will
That where he is, there should his followers be.
Death only lies between. — A gloomy path!
Made yet more gloomy by our coward fears:
But not untrod nor tedious; the fatigue
Will soon go off: besides, there 's no by-road
To bliss. — Then why, like ill-conditioned children,
Start we at transient hardships in the way
That leads to purer air, and softer skies,
And a ne'er setting sun? — Fools that we are!
We wish to be where sweets unwithering bloom;
But straight our wish revoke, and will not go.
So have I seen, upon a summer's even,
Fast by a rivulet's brink a youngster play:
How wishfully he looks to stem the tide!
This moment resolute, next unresolved:
At last he dips his foot; but as he dips,
His fears redouble, and he runs away
From the inoffensive stream, unmindful now
Of all the flowers that paint the further bank,
And smiled so sweet of late. — Thrice welcome Death!
That after many a painful bleeding step
Conducts us to our home, and lands us safe
On the long-wished-for shore. — Prodigious change!
Our bane turned to a blessing! — Death, disarmed,
Loses his fellness quite. — All thanks to Him
Who scourged the venom out. — Sure the last end
Of the good man is peace. How calm his exit!
Night-dews fall not more gently to the ground,
Nor weary worn-out winds expire so soft.
Behold him! in the evening tide of life,
A life well spent, whose early care it was
His riper years should not upbraid his green;
By unperceived degrees he wears away;
Yet like the sun seems larger at his setting!
High in his faith and hopes, look! how he reaches
After the prize in view! and, like a bird

That 's hampered, struggles hard to get away!
Whilst the glad gates of sight are wide expanded
To let new glories in, the first fair fruits
Of the fast-coming harvest! Then! O then!
Each earth-born joy grows vile, or disappears,
Shrunk to a thing of nought. O how he longs
To have his passport signed, and be dismissed!
'T is done, and now he 's happy! The glad soul
Has not a wish uncrowned. Even the lag flesh
Rests too in hope of meeting once again
Its better half, never to sunder more.
Nor shall it hope in vain: the time draws on
When not a single spot of burial-earth,
Whether on land, or in the spacious sea,
But must give back its long-committed dust
Inviolate: and faithfully shall these
Make up the full account; not the least atom
Embezzled, or mislaid, of the whole tale.
Each soul shall have a body ready-furnished;
And each shall have his own. Hence, ye profane:
Ask not how this can be. Sure the same power
That reared the piece at first, and took it down,
Can reassemble the loose scattered parts,
And put them as they were: Almighty God
Has done much more: Nor is his arm impaired
Through length of days; and what he can he will:
His faithfulness stands bound to see it done.
When the dread trumpet sounds, the slumbering dust,
Not unattentive to the call, shall wake;
And every joint possess its proper place,
With a new elegance of form, unknown
To its first state. Nor shall the conscious soul
Mistake its partner; but amidst the crowd,
Singling its other half, into its arms
Shall rush, with all the impatience of a man
That 's new come home, who having long been absent,
With haste runs over every different room,
In pain to see the whole. Thrice happy meeting!
Nor time, nor death, shall ever part them more.
'T is but a night, a long and moonless night;
We make the grave our bed, and then are gone.
Thus, at the shut of even, the weary bird
Leaves the wide air, and in some lonely brake
Cowers down, and dozes till the dawn of day;
Then claps his well-fledged wings and bears away.

1743

AGE OF JOHNSON

POETRY

Samuel Johnson (1709–1784)

THE VANITY OF HUMAN WISHES

Let observation with extensive view,
Survey mankind from China to Peru;
Remark each anxious toil, each eager strife,
And watch the busy scenes of crowded life;
Then say how hope and fear, desire and hate,
O'erspread with snares the clouded maze of fate,
Where wav'ring man betrayed by vent'rous pride,
To tread the dreary paths without a guide,
As treach'rous phantoms in the mist delude,
Shuns fancied ills, or chases airy good;
How rarely reason guides the stubborn choice,
Rules the bold hand or prompts the suppliant voice;
How nations sink, by darling schemes oppressed,
When Vengeance listens to the fool's request.
Fate wings with ev'ry wish th' afflictive dart,
Each gift of nature and each grace of art;
With fatal heat impetuous courage glows,
With fatal sweetness elocution flows;
Impeachment stops the speaker's pow'rful breath,
And restless fire precipitates on death.
  But, scarce observed, the knowing and the bold
Fall in the gen'ral massacre of gold;
Wide wasting pest! that rages unconfined,
And crowds with crimes the records of mankind;
For gold his sword the hireling ruffian draws,
For gold the hireling judge distorts the laws;
Wealth heaped on wealth, nor truth nor safety buys,
The dangers gather as the treasures rise.
  Let hist'ry tell, where rival kings command,
And dubious title shakes the madded land,
When statutes glean the refuse of the sword,
How much more safe the vassal than the lord;
Low sculks the hind beneath the rage of power,
And leaves the wealthy traitor in the tower,
Untouched his cottage, and his slumbers sound,
Though confiscation's vultures hover round.
  The needy traveller, serene and gay,
Walks the wild heath, and sings his toil away.
Does envy seize thee? crush th' upbraiding joy;
Increase his riches, and his peace destroy;
Now fears in dire vicissitude invade,
The rustling brake alarms, and quiv'ring shade;
Nor light nor darkness bring his pain relief,
One shows the plunder, and one hides the thief.
  Yet still one gen'ral cry the skies assails,
And gain and grandeur load the tainted gales;
Few know the toiling statesman's fear or care,
Th' insidious rival, and the gaping heir.
Once more, Democritus, arise on earth,
With cheerful wisdom and instructive mirth,
See motley life in modern trappings dressed,
And feed with varied fools th' eternal jest;
Thou who couldst laugh where want enchained caprice,
Toil crushed conceit, and man was of a piece;
Where wealth, unloved, without a mourner died;
And scarce a sycophant was fed by pride;
Where ne'er was known the form of mock debate;
Or seen a new made mayor's unwieldy state;
Where change of fav'rites made no change of laws,

And senates heard before they judged a cause;
How wouldst thou shake at Britain's modish tribe,
Dart the quick taunt, and edge the piercing gibe!
Attentive truth and nature to descry,
And pierce each scene with philosophic eye.
To thee were solemn toys, or empty show,
The robes of pleasure and the veils of woe;
All aid the farce, and all thy mirth maintain,
Whose joys are causeless, or whose griefs are vain.

Such was the scorn that filled the sage's mind,
Renewed at ev'ry glance on human kind;
How just that scorn ere yet thy voice declare,
Search every state, and canvass ev'ry prayer.

Unnumbered suppliants crowd Preferment's gate,
Athirst for wealth, and burning to be great,
Delusive Fortune hears th' incessant call,
They mount, they shine, evaporate, and fall.
On ev'ry stage the foes of peace attend,
Hate dogs their flight, and insult marks their end,
Love ends with hope, the sinking statesman's door
Pours in the morning worshipper no more;
For growing names the weekly scribbler lies,
To growing wealth the dedicator flies,
From ev'ry room descends the painted face,
That hung the bright palladium of the place;
And smoked in kitchens, or in auctions sold,
To better features yields the frame of gold;
For now no more we trace in ev'ry line
Heroic worth, benevolence divine;
The form distorted, justifies the fall,
And detestation rids th' indignant wall.

But will not Britain hear the last appeal,
Sign her foes' doom, or guard her fav'rites' zeal?
Through Freedom's sons no more remonstrance rings,
Degrading nobles and controlling kings;
Our supple tribes repress their patriot throats,
And ask no questions but the price of votes;
With weekly libels and septennial ale,
Their wish is full to riot and to rail.

In full-blown dignity see Wolsey stand,
Law in his voice, and fortune in his hand;
To him the church, the realm, their pow'rs consign,
Through him the rays of regal bounty shine,
Turned by his nod the stream of honour flows,
His smile alone security bestows;
Still to new heights his restless wishes tow'r,
Claim leads to claim, and pow'r advances pow'r;
Till conquest unresisted ceased to please,
And rights submitted left him none to seize.
At length his sov'reign frowns; — the train of state
Mark the keen glance, and watch the sign to hate.
Where'er he turns, he meets a stranger's eye,
His suppliants scorn him, and his followers fly;
Now drops at once the pride of awful state,
The golden canopy, the glitt'ring plate,
The regal palace, the luxurious board,
The liv'ried army, and the menial lord.
With age, with cares, with maladies oppressed,
He seeks the refuge of monastic rest.
Grief aids disease, remembered folly stings,
And his last sighs reproach the faith of kings.

Speak thou, whose thoughts at humble peace repine,
Shall Wolsey's wealth, with Wolsey's end, be thine?
Or liv'st thou now, with safer pride content,
The wisest justice on the banks of Trent?
For, why did Wolsey, near the steeps of fate,
On weak foundations raise th' enormous weight?
Why but to sink beneath misfortune's blow,
With louder ruin to the gulfs below?

What gave great Villiers to th' assassin's knife,
And fixed disease on Harley's closing life?
What murdered Wentworth, and what exiled Hyde,
By kings protected, and to kings allied?
What but their wish indulged in courts to shine,
And pow'r too great to keep, or to resign?

When first the college rolls receive his name,
The young enthusiast quits his ease for fame;
Resistless burns the fever of renown,
Caught from the strong contagion of the gown;
O'er Bodley's dome his future labours spread,
And Bacon's mansion trembles o'er his head.
Are these thy views? Proceed, illustrious youth,
And Virtue guard thee to the throne of Truth!
Yet, should thy soul indulge the gen'rous heat
Till captive Science yields her last retreat;

Should Reason guide thee with her brightest ray,
And pour on misty Doubt resistless day;
Should no false kindness lure to loose delight,
Nor praise relax, nor difficulty fright;
Should tempting Novelty thy cell refrain,
And Sloth effuse her opiate fumes in vain;
Should Beauty blunt on fops her fatal dart,
Nor claim the triumph of a lettered heart;
Should no Disease thy torpid veins invade,
Nor Melancholy's phantoms haunt thy shade;
Yet hope not life from grief or danger free,
Nor think the doom of man reversed for thee;
Deign on the passing world to turn thine eyes,
And pause awhile from letters, to be wise;
There mark what ills the scholar's life assail,
Toil, envy, want, the patron, and the gaol.
See nations, slowly wise and meanly just,
To buried merit raise the tardy bust.
If dreams yet flatter, once again attend,
Hear Lydiat's life and Galileo's end.

Nor deem, when learning her last prize bestows,
The glitt'ring eminence exempt from foes;
See, when the vulgar 'scapes, despised or awed,
Rebellion's vengeful talons seize on Laud.
From meaner minds, though smaller fines content
The plundered palace, or sequestered rent;
Marked out by dang'rous parts, he meets the shock,
And fatal Learning leads him to the block;
Around his tomb let Art and Genius weep,
But hear his death, ye blockheads, hear and sleep.

The festal blazes, the triumphal show,
The ravished standard, and the captive foe,
The Senate's thanks, the gazette's pompous tale,
With force resistless o'er the brave prevail.
Such bribes the rapid Greek o'er Asia whirled,
For such the steady Romans shook the world;
For such in distant lands the Britons shine,
And stain with blood the Danube or the Rhine;
This pow'r has praise, that virtue scarce can warm,
Till fame supplies the universal charm.
Yet Reason frowns on War's unequal game,
Where wasted nations raise a single name;
And mortgaged states their grandsires' wreaths regret,
From age to age in everlasting debt;
Wreaths which at last the dear-bought right convey
To rust on medals, or on stones decay.

On what foundations stands the warrior's pride,
How just his hopes, let Swedish Charles decide;
A frame of adamant, a soul of fire,
No dangers fright him, and no labours tire;
O'er love, o'er fear, extends his wide domain,
Unconquered lord of pleasure and of pain;
No joys to him pacific scepters yield,
War sounds the trump, he rushes to the field;
Behold surrounding kings their pow'rs combine,
And one capitulate, and one resign;
Peace courts his hand, but spreads her charms in vain;
'Think nothing gained,' he cries, 'till naught remain,
On Moscow's walls till Gothic standards fly,
And all be mine beneath the polar sky.'
The march begins in military state,
And nations on his eye suspended wait;
Stern Famine guards the solitary coast,
And Winter barricades the realms of Frost;
He comes, nor want nor cold his course delay; —
Hide, blushing Glory, hide Pultowa's day;
The vanquished hero leaves his broken bands,
And shows his miseries in distant lands;
Condemned a needy supplicant to wait,
While ladies interpose, and slaves debate.
But did not Chance at length her error mend?
Did no subverted empire mark his end?
Did rival monarchs give the fatal wound?
Or hostile millions press him to the ground?
His fall was destined to a barren strand,
A petty fortress, and a dubious hand;
He left the name, at which the world grew pale,
To point a moral, or adorn a tale.

All times their scenes of pompous woes afford,
From Persia's tyrant to Bavaria's lord.
In gay hostility and barbarous pride,
With half mankind embattled at his side,
Great Xerxes comes to seize the certain prey,
And starves exhausted regions in his way;
Attendant Flatt'ry counts his myriads o'er,
Till counted myriads sooth his pride no more;
Fresh praise is tried till madness fires his mind,

The waves he lashes, and enchains the wind.
New pow'rs are claimed, new pow'rs are still bestowed,
Till rude resistance lops the spreading god;
The daring Greeks deride the martial show,
And heap their vallies with the gaudy foe;
Th' insulted sea with humbler thought he gains,
A single skiff to speed his flight remains;
Th' encumbered oar scarce leaves the dreaded coast,
Through purple billows and a floating host.

The bold Bavarian, in a luckless hour,
Tries the dread summits of Cæsarean pow'r,
With unexpected legions bursts away,
And sees defenceless realms receive his sway.
Short sway! fair Austria spreads her mournful charms,
The queen, the beauty, sets the world in arms;
From hill to hill the beacon's rousing blaze
Spreads wide the hope of plunder and of praise;
The fierce Croatian, and the wild Hussar,
With all the sons of ravage crowd the war;
The baffled prince, in honour's flatt'ring bloom
Of hasty greatness, finds the fatal doom;
His foes' derision, and his subjects' blame,
And steals to death from anguish and from shame.

Enlarge my life with multitude of days!
In health, in sickness, thus the suppliant prays;
Hides from himself his state, and shuns to know,
That life protracted is protracted woe.
Time hovers o'er, impatient to destroy,
And shuts up all the passages of joy;
In vain their gifts the bounteous seasons pour,
The fruit autumnal, and the vernal flow'r;
With listless eyes the dotard views the store,
He views, and wonders that they please no more;
Now pall the tasteless meats, and joyless wines,
And Luxury with sighs her slave resigns.
Approach, ye minstrels, try the soothing strain,
Diffuse the tuneful lenitives of pain;
No sounds, alas! would touch th' impervious ear,
Though dancing mountains witnessed Orpheus near;
Nor lute nor lyre his feeble pow'rs attend,
Nor sweeter music of a virtuous friend;
But everlasting dictates crowd his tongue,
Perversely grave, or positively wrong.
The still returning tale, and ling'ring jest,
Perplex the fawning niece and pampered guest,
While growing hopes scarce awe the gath'ring sneer,
And scarce a legacy can bribe to hear;
The watchful guests still hint the last offence;
The daughter's petulance, the son's expense,
Improve his heady rage with treach'rous skill,
And mould his passions till they make his will.

Unnumbered maladies his joints invade,
Lay siege to life, and press the dire blockade;
But unextinguished Av'rice still remains,
And dreaded losses aggravate his pains;
He turns, with anxious heart and crippled hands,
His bonds of debt, and mortgages of lands;
Or views his coffers with suspicious eyes,
Unlocks his gold, and counts it till he dies.

But grant, the virtues of a temp'rate prime
Bless with an age exempt from scorn or crime;
An age that melts with unperceived decay,
And glides in modest innocence away;
Whose peaceful day Benevolence endears,
Whose night congratulating Conscience cheers;
The gen'ral fav'rite as the gen'ral friend;
Such age there is, and who shall wish its end?

Yet e'en on this her load Misfortune flings,
To press the weary minutes' flagging wings;
New sorrow rises as the day returns,
A sister sickens, or a daughter mourns.
Now kindred Merit fills the sable bier,
Now lacerated Friendship claims a tear;
Year chases year, decay pursues decay,
Still drops some joy from with'ring life away;
New forms arise, and diff'rent views engage,
Superfluous lags the vet'ran on the stage,
Till pitying Nature signs the last release,
And bids afflicted worth retire to peace.

But few there are whom hours like these await,
Who set unclouded in the gulfs of Fate.
From Lydia's monarch should the search descend,
By Solon cautioned to regard his end,
In life's last scene what prodigies surprise,

Fears of the brave, and follies of the wise!
From Marlborough's eyes the streams of dotage flow,
And Swift expires a driv'ler and a show.
The teeming mother, anxious for her race,
Begs for each birth the fortune of a face;
Yet Vane could tell what ills from beauty spring;
And Sedley cursed the form that pleased a king.
Ye nymphs of rosy lips and radiant eyes,
Whom Pleasure keeps too busy to be wise;
Whom joys with soft varieties invite,
By day the frolic, and the dance by night;
Who frown with vanity, who smile with art,
And ask the latest fashion of the heart;
What care, what rules, your heedless charms shall save,
Each nymph your rival, and each youth your slave?
Against your fame with fondness hate combines,
The rival batters, and the lover mines.
With distant voice neglected Virtue calls,
Less heard and less, the faint remonstrance falls;
Tired with contempt, she quits the slipp'ry reign,
And Pride and Prudence take her seat in vain.
In crowd at once, where none the pass defend,
The harmless freedom, and the private friend.
The guardians yield, by force superior plied;
To Int'rest, Prudence; and to Flatt'ry, Pride.
Here Beauty falls betrayed, despised, distressed,
And hissing Infamy proclaims the rest.
Where then shall Hope and Fear their objects find?
Must dull Suspense corrupt the stagnant mind?
Must helpless man, in ignorance sedate,
Roll darkling down the torrent of his fate?
Must no dislike alarm, no wishes rise,
No cries invoke the mercies of the skies?
Enquirer, cease; petitions yet remain
Which Heav'n may hear, nor deem Religion vain.
Still raise for good the supplicating voice,
But leave to Heav'n the measure and the choice.
Safe in his pow'r, whose eyes discern afar
The secret ambush of a specious pray'r;
Implore his aid, in his decisions rest,
Secure, whate'er he gives, he gives the best.
Yet, when the sense of sacred presence fires,
And strong devotion to the skies aspires,
Pour forth thy fervours for a healthful mind,
Obedient passions, and a will resigned;
For love, which scarce collective man can fill;
For patience, sov'reign o'er transmuted ill;
For faith, that, panting for a happier seat,
Counts death kind Nature's signal of retreat;
These goods for man the laws of Heav'n ordain,
These goods he grants, who grants the pow'r to gain;
With these celestial Wisdom calms the mind,
And makes the happiness she does not find.

1749

Oliver Goldsmith (1728–1774)

THE TRAVELLER

Remote, unfriended, melancholy, slow,
Or by the lazy Scheldt, or wandering Po;
Or onward, where the rude Carinthian boor,
Against the houseless stranger shuts the door;
Or where Campania's plain forsaken lies,
A weary waste expanding to the skies:
Where'er I roam, whatever realms to see,
My heart untravelled fondly turns to thee;
Still to my brother turns, with ceaseless pain,
And drags at each remove a lengthening chain.
Eternal blessings crown my earliest friend,
And round his dwelling guardian saints attend:
Blest be that spot, where cheerful guests retire
To pause from toil, and trim their ev'ning fire;
Blest that abode, where want and pain repair,
And every stranger finds a ready chair;
Blest be those feasts with simple plenty crowned,
Where all the ruddy family around
Laugh at the jests or pranks that never fail,
Or sigh with pity at some mournful tale,
Or press the bashful stranger to his food,
And learn the luxury of doing good.
But me, not destined such delights to share,
My prime of life in wand'ring spent and care,
Impelled, with steps unceasing, to pursue
Some fleeting good, that mocks me with the view;
That, like the circle bounding earth and skies,
Allures from far, yet, as I follow, flies;
My fortune leads to traverse realms alone,
And find no spot of all the world my own.

Even now, where Alpine solitudes ascend,
I sit me down a pensive hour to spend;
And, placed on high above the storm's career,
Look downward where an hundred realms appear;
Lakes, forests, cities, plains, extending wide,
The pomp of kings, the shepherd's humbler pride.
When thus Creation's charms around combine,
Amidst the store, should thankless pride repine?
Say, should the philosophic mind disdain
That good, which makes each humbler bosom vain?
Let school-taught pride dissemble all it can,
These little things are great to little man;
And wiser he, whose sympathetic mind
Exults in all the good of all mankind.
Ye glitt'ring towns, with wealth and splendour crowned,
Ye fields, where summer spreads profusion round,
Ye lakes, whose vessels catch the busy gale,
Ye bending swains, that dress the flow'ry vale;
For me your tributary stores combine;
Creation's heir, the world, the world is mine!
As some lone miser, visiting his store,
Bends at his treasure, counts, recounts it o'er;
Hoards after hoards his rising raptures fill,
Yet still he sighs, for hoards are wanting still:
Thus to my breast alternate passions rise,
Pleased with each good that Heaven to man supplies:
Yet oft a sigh prevails, and sorrows fall,
To see the hoard of human bliss so small;
And oft I wish, amidst the scene, to find
Some spot to real happiness consigned,
Where my worn soul, each wand'ring hope at rest,
May gather bliss to see my fellows blest.
But where to find that happiest spot below,
Who can direct, when all pretend to know?
The shudd'ring tenant of the frigid zone
Boldly proclaims that happiest spot his own,
Extols the treasures of his stormy seas,
And his long nights of revelry and ease;
The naked negro, panting at the line,
Boasts of his golden sands and palmy wine,
Basks in the glare, or stems the tepid wave,
And thanks his gods for all the good they gave.
Such is the patriot's boast, where'er we roam,
His first, best country ever is, at home.
And yet, perhaps, if countries we compare,
And estimate the blessings which they share,
Though patriots flatter, still shall wisdom find
An equal portion dealt to all mankind,
As different good, by Art or Nature given,
To different nations makes their blessings even.
Nature, a mother kind alike to all,
Still grants her bliss at Labour's earnest call;
With food as well the peasant is supplied
On Idra's cliffs as Arno's shelvy side;
And though the rocky-crested summits frown,
These rocks, by custom, turn to beds of down.
From Art more various are the blessings sent;
Wealth, commerce, honour, liberty, content.
Yet these each other's power so strong contest,
That either seems destructive of the rest.
Where wealth and freedom reign contentment fails,
And honour sinks where commerce long prevails.
Hence every state to one loved blessing prone,
Conforms and models life to that alone.
Each to the favourite happiness attends,
And spurns the plan that aims at other ends;
Till, carried to excess in each domain,
This favourite good begets peculiar pain.
But let us try these truths with closer eyes,
And trace them through the prospect as it lies;
Here for a while my proper cares resigned,
Here let me sit in sorrow for mankind,
Like yon neglected shrub at random cast,
That shades the steep, and sighs at every blast.
Far to the right, where Apennine ascends,
Bright as the summer, Italy extends;
Its uplands sloping deck the mountain's side,
Woods over woods in gay theatric pride;
While oft some temple's mould'ring tops between
With venerable grandeur mark the scene.
Could Nature's bounty satisfy the breast,
The sons of Italy were surely blest.
Whatever fruits in different climes were found,
That proudly rise, or humbly court the ground;
Whatever blooms in torrid tracts appear,
Whose bright succession decks the varied year;
Whatever sweets salute the northern sky
With vernal lives that blossom but to die;

These here disporting own the kindred soil,
Nor ask luxuriance from the planter's toil;
While sea-born gales their gelid wings expand
To winnow fragrance round the smiling land.
But small the bliss that sense alone bestows,
And sensual bliss is all the nation knows.
In florid beauty groves and fields appear,
Man seems the only growth that dwindles here.
Contrasted faults through all his manners reign,
Though poor, luxurious, though submissive, vain,
Though grave, yet trifling, zealous, yet untrue;
And e'en in penance planning sins anew.
All evils here contaminate the mind,
That opulence departed leaves behind;
For wealth was theirs, not far removed the date,
When Commerce proudly flourished through the state;
At her command the palace learned to rise,
Again the long-fall'n column sought the skies;
The canvas glowed beyond e'en Nature warm,
The pregnant quarry teemed with human form;
Till, more unsteady than the southern gale,
Commerce on other shores displayed her sail;
While nought remained of all that riches gave,
But towns unmanned, and lords without a slave;
And late the nation found with fruitless skill
Its former strength was but plethoric ill.
Yet still the loss of wealth is here supplied
By arts, the splendid wrecks of former pride;
From these the feeble heart and long-fall'n mind
An easy compensation seem to find.
Here may be seen, in bloodless pomp arrayed,
The paste-board triumph and the cavalcade;
Processions formed for piety and love,
A mistress or a saint in every grove.
By sports like these are all their cares beguiled,
The sports of children satisfy the child;
Each nobler aim, represt by long control,
Now sinks at last, or feebly mans the soul;
While low delights, succeeding fast behind,
In happier meanness occupy the mind:
As in those domes, where Cæsars once bore sway,
Defaced by time and tottering in decay,
There in the ruin, heedless of the dead,
The shelter-seeking peasant builds his shed,
And, wond'ring man could want the larger pile,
Exults, and owns his cottage with a smile.
My soul, turn from them, turn we to survey
Where rougher climes a nobler race display,
Where the bleak Swiss their stormy mansions tread,
And force a churlish soil for scanty bread;
No product here the barren hills afford,
But man and steel, the soldier and his sword.
No vernal blooms their torpid rocks array,
But winter ling'ring chills the lap of May;
No Zephyr fondly sues the mountain's breast,
But meteors glare, and stormy glooms invest.
Yet still, even here, content can spread a charm,
Redress the clime, and all its rage disarm.
Though poor the peasant's hut, his feasts though small,
He sees his little lot the lot of all;
Sees no contiguous palace rear its head
To shame the meanness of his humble shed;
No costly lord the sumptuous banquet deal,
To make him loath his vegetable meal;
But calm, and bred in ignorance and toil,
Each wish contracting, fits him to the soil.
Cheerful at morn he wakes from short repose,
Breasts the keen air, and carols as he goes;
With patient angle trolls the finny deep,
Or drives his venturous plow-share to the steep;
Or seeks the den where snow-tracks mark the way,
And drags the struggling savage into day.
At night returning, every labour sped,
He sits him down the monarch of a shed;
Smiles by his cheerful fire, and round surveys
His children's looks, that brighten at the blaze;
While his loved partner, boastful of her hoard,
Displays her cleanly platter on the board:
And haply too some pilgrim, thither led,
With many a tale repays the nightly bed.
Thus every good his native wilds impart,
Imprints the patriot passion on his heart,
And even those ills, that round his mansion rise,

Enhance the bliss his scanty fund supplies.
Dear is that shed to which his soul conforms,
And dear that hill which lifts him to the storms;
And as a child, when scaring sounds molest,
Clings close and closer to the mother's breast,
So the loud torrent, and the whirlwind's roar,
But bind him to his native mountains more.

Such are the charms to barren states assigned;
Their wants but few, their wishes all confined.
Yet let them only share the praises due,
If few their wants, their pleasures are but few;
For every want that stimulates the breast
Becomes a source of pleasure when redrest.
Whence from such lands each pleasing science flies,
That first excites desire, and then supplies;
Unknown to them, when sensual pleasures cloy,
To fill the languid pause with finer joy;
Unknown those powers that raise the soul to flame,
Catch every nerve, and vibrate through the frame.
Their level life is but a smould'ring fire,
Unquenched by want, unfanned by strong desire;
Unfit for raptures, or, if raptures cheer
On some high festival of once a year,
In wild excess the vulgar breast takes fire,
Till, buried in debauch, the bliss expire.

But not their joys alone thus coarsely flow:
Their morals, like their pleasures, are but low,
For, as refinement stops, from sire to son
Unaltered, unimproved, the manners run;
And love's and friendship's finely-pointed dart
Fall blunted from each indurated heart.
Some sterner virtues o'er the mountain's breast
May sit, like falcons cow'ring on the nest;
But all the gentler morals, such as play
Through life's more cultured walks and charm the way,
These far dispersed, on timorous pinions fly,
To sport and flutter in a kinder sky.

To kinder skies, where gentler manners reign,
I turn; and France displays her bright domain.
Gay sprightly land of mirth and social ease,
Pleased with thyself, whom all the world can please,
How often have I led thy sportive choir,
With tuneless pipe, beside the murmuring Loire,
Where shading elms along the margin grew,
And freshened from the wave the Zephyr flew!
And haply, though my harsh touch faltering still,
But mocked all tune, and marred the dancer's skill;
Yet would the village praise my wondrous power,
And dance, forgetful of the noon-tide hour.
Alike all ages. Dames of ancient days
Have led their children through the mirthful maze,
And the gay gransire, skilled in gestic lore,
Has frisked beneath the burthen of threescore.

So blest a life these thoughtless realms display,
Thus idly busy rolls their world away:
Theirs are those arts that mind to mind endear,
For honour forms the social temper here:
Honour, that praise which real merit gains,
Or even imaginary worth obtains,
Here passes current; paid from hand to hand,
It shifts in splendid traffic round the land:
From courts, to camps, to cottages it strays,
And all are taught an avarice of praise;
They please, are pleased, they give to get esteem,
Till, seeming blest, they grow to what they seem.

But while this softer art their bliss supplies,
It gives their follies also room to rise;
For praise too dearly loved, or warmly sought,
Enfeebles all internal strength of thought;
And the weak soul, within itself unblest,
Leans for all pleasure on another's breast.
Hence Ostentation here, with tawdry art,
Pants for the vulgar praise which fools impart;
Here Vanity assumes her pert grimace,
And trims her robes of frieze with copper-lace;
Here beggar Pride defrauds her daily cheer,
To boast one splendid banquet once a year;

The mind still turns where shifting fashion draws,
Nor weighs the solid worth of self-applause.
To men of other minds my fancy flies,
Embosomed in the deep where Holland lies.
Methinks her patient sons before me stand,
Where the broad ocean leans against the land,
And, sedulous to stop the coming tide,
Lift the tall rampire's artificial pride.
Onward, methinks, and diligently slow,
The firm-connected bulwark seems to grow;
Spreads its long arms amidst the wat'ry roar,
Scoops out an empire, and usurps the shore.
While the pent ocean rising o'er the pile,
Sees an amphibious world beneath him smile;
The slow canal, the yellow-blossomed vale,
The willow-tufted bank, the gliding sail,
The crowded mart, the cultivated plain,
A new creation rescued from his reign.
Thus, while around the wave-subjected soil
Impels the native to repeated toil,
Industrious habits in each bosom reign,
And industry begets a love of gain.
Hence all the good from opulence that springs,
With all those ills superfluous treasure brings,
Are here displayed. Their much-loved wealth imparts
Convenience, plenty, elegance, and arts;
But view them closer, craft and fraud appear,
Even liberty itself is bartered here.
At gold's superior charms all freedom flies,
The needy sell it, and the rich man buys;
A land of tyrants, and a den of slaves,
Here wretches seek dishonourable graves,
And calmly bent, to servitude conform,
Dull as their lakes that slumber in the storm.
Heavens! how unlike their Belgic sires of old!
Rough, poor, content, ungovernably bold;
War in each breast, and freedom on each brow;
How much unlike the sons of Britain now!
Fired at the sound, my genius spreads her wing,
And flies where Britain courts the western spring;
Where lawns extend that scorn Arcadian pride,
And brighter streams than famed Hydaspis glide.
There all around the gentlest breezes stray,
There gentle music melts on every spray;
Creation's mildest charms are there combined,
Extremes are only in the master's mind!
Stern o'er each bosom Reason holds her state.
With daring aims irregularly great,
Pride in their port, defiance in their eye,
I see the lords of human kind pass by,
Intent on high designs, a thoughtful band,
By forms unfashioned, fresh from Nature's hand;
Fierce in their native hardiness of soul,
True to imagined right, above control,
While even the peasant boasts these rights to scan,
And learns to venerate himself as man.
Thine, Freedom, thine the blessings pictured here,
Thine are those charms that dazzle and endear;
Too blest, indeed, were such without alloy,
But fostered even by Freedom ills annoy:
That independence Britons prize too high,
Keeps man from man, and breaks the social tie;
The self-dependent lordlings stand alone,
All claims that bind and sweeten life unknown;
Here, by the bonds of nature feebly held,
Minds combat minds, repelling and repelled.
Ferments arise, imprisoned factions roar,
Repressed ambition struggles round her shore,
Till over-wrought, the general system feels
Its motions stop, or phrenzy fire the wheels.
Nor this the worst. As nature's ties decay,
As duty, love, and honour fail to sway,
Fictitious bonds, the bonds of wealth and law,
Still gather strength, and force unwilling awe.
Hence all obedience bows to these alone,
And talent sinks, and merit weeps unknown;
Till time may come, when, stripped of all her charms,
The land of scholars, and the nurse of arms,
Where noble stems transmit the patriot flame,
Where kings have toiled, and poets wrote for fame,
One sink of level avarice shall lie,
And scholars, soldiers, kings, unhonoured die.
Yet think not, thus when Freedom's ills I state,
I mean to flatter kings, or court the great;
Ye Powers of truth, that bid my soul aspire,
Far from my bosom drive the low desire;

And thou, fair Freedom, taught alike to feel
The rabble's rage, and tyrant's angry steel;
Thou transitory flower, alike undone
By proud contempt, or favour's fostering sun,
Still may thy blooms the changeful clime endure,
I only would repress them to secure:
For just experience tells, in every soil,
That those who think must govern those that toil;
And all that Freedom's highest aims can reach,
Is but to lay proportioned loads on each.
Hence, should one order disproportioned grow,
Its double weight must ruin all below.
O then how blind to all that truth requires,
Who think it freedom when a part aspires!
Calm is my soul, nor apt to rise in arms,
Except when fast-approaching danger warms:
But when contending chiefs blockade the throne,
Contracting regal power to stretch their own,
When I behold a factious band agree
To call it freedom when themselves are free;
Each wanton judge new penal statutes draw,
Laws grind the poor, and rich men rule the law;
The wealth of climes, where savage nations roam,
Pillaged from slaves to purchase slaves at home;
Fear, pity, justice, indignation start,
Tear off reserve, and bare my swelling heart;
Till half a patriot, half a coward grown,
I fly from petty tyrants to the throne.
Yes, brother, curse with me that baleful hour,
When first ambition struck at regal power;
And thus polluting honour in its source,
Gave wealth to sway the mind with double force.
Have we not seen, round Britain's peopled shore,
Her useful sons exchanged for useless ore?
Seen all her triumphs but destruction haste,
Like flaring tapers brightening as they waste;
Seen Opulence, her grandeur to maintain,
Lead stern Depopulation in her train,
And over fields where scattered hamlets rose,
In barren solitary pomp repose?
Have we not seen at Pleasure's lordly call,
The smiling long-frequented village fall?
Beheld the duteous son, the sire decayed,
The modest matron, and the blushing maid,
Forced from their homes, a melancholy train,
To traverse climes beyond the western main;
Where wild Oswego spreads her swamps around,
And Niagàra stuns with thund'ring sound?
Even now, perhaps, as there some pilgrim strays
Through tangled forests, and through dangerous ways;
Where beasts with man divided empire claim,
And the brown Indian marks with murderous aim;
There, while above the giddy tempest flies,
And all around distressful yells arise,
The pensive exile, bending with his woe,
To stop too fearful, and too faint to go,
Casts a long look where England's glories shine,
And bids his bosom sympathize with mine.
Vain, very vain, my weary search to find
That bliss which only centres in the mind:
Why have I strayed from pleasure and repose,
To seek a good each government bestows?
In every government, though terrors reign,
Though tyrant kings, or tyrant laws restrain,
How small, of all that human hearts endure,
That part which laws or kings can cause or cure.
Still to ourselves in every place consigned,
Our own felicity we make or find:
With secret course, which no loud storms annoy,
Glides the smooth current of domestic joy.
The lifted ax, the agonizing wheel,
Luke's iron crown, and Damiens' bed of steel,
To men remote from power but rarely known,
Leave reason, faith, and conscience, all our own.

1764

THE DESERTED VILLAGE

Sweet Auburn, loveliest village of the plain,
Where health and plenty cheered the labouring swain,
Where smiling spring its earliest visit paid,
And parting summer's lingering blooms delayed:

Dear lovely bowers of innocence and ease,
Seats of my youth, when every sport could please,
How often have I loitered o'er thy green,
Where humble happiness endeared each scene;
How often have I paused on every charm,
The sheltered cot, the cultivated farm,
The never-failing brook, the busy mill,
The decent church that topped the neighbouring hill,
The hawthorn bush, with seats beneath the shade,
For talking age and whispering lovers made;
How often have I blessed the coming day,
When toil remitting lent its turn to play,
And all the village train, from labour free,
Led up their sports beneath the spreading tree;
While many a pastime circled in the shade,
The young contending as the old surveyed;
And many a gambol frolicked o'er the ground,
And sleights of art and feats of strength went round;
And still as each repeated pleasure tired,
Succeeding sports the mirthful band inspired;
The dancing pair that simply sought renown,
By holding out to tire each other down;
The swain mistrustless of his smutted face,
While secret laughter tittered round the place;
The bashful virgin's side-long looks of love,
The matron's glance that would those looks reprove:
These were thy charms, sweet village; sports like these,
With sweet succession, taught even toil to please;
These round thy bowers their cheerful influence shed,
These were thy charms — But all these charms are fled.
Sweet smiling village, loveliest of the lawn,
Thy sports are fled, and all thy charms withdrawn;
Amidst thy bowers the tyrant's hand is seen,
And desolation saddens all thy green:
One only master grasps the whole domain,
And half a tillage stints thy smiling plain:
No more thy glassy brook reflects the day,
But choked with sedges, works its weedy way.
Along thy glades, a solitary guest,
The hollow-sounding bittern guards its nest;
Amidst thy desert walks the lapwing flies,
And tires their echoes with unvaried cries.
Sunk are thy bowers, in shapeless ruin all,
And the long grass o'ertops the mouldering wall;
And, trembling, shrinking from the spoiler's hand,
Far, far away, thy children leave the land.
Ill fares the land, to hastening ills a prey,
Where wealth accumulates, and men decay:
Princes and lords may flourish, or may fade;
A breath can make them, as a breath has made;
But a bold peasantry, their country's pride,
When once destroyed, can never be supplied.
A time there was, ere England's griefs began,
When every rood of ground maintained its man;
For him light Labour spread her wholesome store,
Just gave what life required, but gave no more:
His best companions, innocence and health;
And his best riches, ignorance of wealth.
But times are altered; trade's unfeeling train
Usurp the land and dispossess the swain;
Along the lawn, where scattered hamlets rose,
Unwieldy wealth, and cumbrous pomp repose;
And every want to opulence allied,
And every pang that folly pays to pride.
Those gentle hours that plenty bade to bloom,
Those calm desires that asked but little room,
Those healthful sports that graced the peaceful scene,
Lived in each look, and brightened all the green;
These, far departing, seek a kinder shore,
And rural mirth and manners are no more.
Sweet Auburn! parent of the blissful hour,
Thy glades forlorn confess the tyrant's power.
Here as I take my solitary rounds,
Amidst thy tangling walks, and ruined grounds,
And, many a year elapsed, return to view
Where once the cottage stood, the hawthorn grew,
Remembrance wakes, with all her busy train,
Swells at my breast, and turns the past to pain.

In all my wanderings round this world of care,
In all my griefs — and God has given my share —
I still had hopes my latest hours to crown,
Amidst these humble bowers to lay me down;
To husband out life's taper at the close,
And keep the flame from wasting by repose.
I still had hopes, for pride attends us still,
Amidst the swains to show my book-learned skill,
Around my fire an evening group to draw,
And tell of all I felt, and all I saw;
And, as a hare, whom hounds and horns pursue,
Pants to the place from whence at first he flew,
I still had hopes, my long vexations passed,
Here to return — and die at home at last.
O blest retirement, friend to life's decline,
Retreats from care, that never must be mine,
How happy he who crowns in shades like these,
A youth of labour with an age of ease;
Who quits a world where strong temptations try,
And, since 't is hard to combat, learns to fly!
For him no wretches, born to work and weep,
Explore the mine, or tempt the dangerous deep;
No surly porter stands in guilty state
To spurn imploring famine from the gate;
But on he moves to meet his latter end,
Angels around befriending Virtue's friend;
Bends to the grave with unperceived decay,
While Resignation gently slopes the way;
And, all his prospects brightening to the last,
His Heaven commences ere the world be past!
Sweet was the sound, when oft at evening's close
Up yonder hill the village murmur rose;
There, as I passed with careless steps and slow,
The mingling notes came softened from below;
The swain responsive as the milkmaid sung,
The sober herd that lowed to meet their young,
The noisy geese that gabbled o'er the pool,
The playful children just let loose from school,
The watch-dog's voice that bayed the whispering wind,
And the loud laugh that spoke the vacant mind;
These all in sweet confusion sought the shade,
And filled each pause the nightingale had made.
But now the sounds of population fail,
No cheerful murmurs fluctuate in the gale,
No busy steps the grass-grown footway tread,
For all the bloomy flush of life is fled.
All but yon widowed, solitary thing,
That feebly bends beside the plashy spring;
She, wretched matron, forced, in age, for bread,
To strip the brook with mantling cresses spread,
To pick her wintry faggot from the thorn,
To seek her nightly shed, and weep till morn;
She only left of all the harmless train,
The sad historian of the pensive plain.
Near yonder copse, where once the garden smiled,
And still where many a garden-flower grows wild;
There, where a few torn shrubs the place disclose,
The village preacher's modest mansion rose.
A man he was to all the country dear,
And passing rich with forty pounds a year;
Remote from towns he ran his godly race,
Nor e'er had changed, nor wished to change his place;
Unpractised he to fawn, or seek for power,
By doctrines fashioned to the varying hour;
Far other aims his heart had learned to prize,
More skilled to raise the wretched than to rise.
His house was known to all the vagrant train,
He chid their wanderings, but relieved their pain;
The long remembered beggar was his guest,
Whose beard descending swept his agèd breast;
The ruined spendthrift, now no longer proud,
Claimed kindred there, and had his claims allowed;
The broken soldier, kindly bade to stay,
Sat by his fire, and talked the night away;
Wept o'er his wounds, or tales of sorrow done,
Shouldered his crutch, and showed how fields were won.
Pleased with his guests, the good man learned to glow,
And quite forgot their vices in their woe;
Careless their merits, or their faults to scan,

His pity gave ere charity began.
Thus to relieve the wretched was his pride,
And even his failings leaned to Virtue's side;
But in his duty prompt at every call,
He watched and wept, he prayed and felt, for all.
And, as a bird each fond endearment tries
To tempt its new-fledged offspring to the skies,
He tried each art, reproved each dull delay,
Allured to brighter worlds, and led the way.
Beside the bed where parting life was laid,
And sorrow, guilt, and pain, by turns dismayed,
The reverend champion stood. At his control
Despair and anguish fled the struggling soul;
Comfort came down the trembling wretch to raise,
And his last faltering accents whispered praise.
At church, with meek and unaffected grace,
His looks adorned the venerable place;
Truth from his lips prevailed with double sway,
And fools, who came to scoff, remained to pray.
The service passed, around the pious man,
With steady zeal, each honest rustic ran;
Even children followed with endearing wile,
And plucked his gown, to share the good man's smile.
His ready smile a parent's warmth expressed,
Their welfare pleased him, and their cares distressed;
To them his heart, his love, his griefs were given,
But all his serious thoughts had rest in Heaven.
As some tall cliff, that lifts its awful form,
Swells from the vale, and midway leaves the storm,
Though round its breast the rolling clouds are spread,
Eternal sunshine settles on its head.
Beside yon straggling fence that skirts the way,
With blossomed furze unprofitably gay,
There, in his noisy mansion, skilled to rule,
The village master taught his little school;
A man severe he was, and stern to view;
I knew him well, and every truant knew;
Well had the boding tremblers learned to trace
The day's disasters in his morning face;
Full well they laughed, with counterfeited glee,
At all his jokes, for many a joke had he;
Full well the busy whisper, circling round,
Conveyed the dismal tidings when he frowned;
Yet he was kind, or if severe in aught,
The love he bore to learning was in fault;
The village all declared how much he knew;
'T was certain he could write, and cipher too;
Lands he could measure, terms and tides presage,
And even the story ran that he could gauge.
In arguing too, the parson owned his skill,
For even though vanquished, he could argue still;
While words of learnèd length and thundering sound,
Amazed the gazing rustics ranged around;
And still they gazed, and still the wonder grew,
That one small head could carry all he knew.
But past is all his fame. The very spot,
Where many a time he triumphed, is forgot.
Near yonder thorn, that lifts its head on high,
Where once the sign-post caught the passing eye,
Low lies that house where nut-brown draughts inspired,
Where gray-beard Mirth and smiling Toil retired,
Where village statesmen talked with looks profound,
And news much older than their ale went round.
Imagination fondly stoops to trace
The parlour splendours of that festive place;
The white-washed wall, the nicely sanded floor,
The varnished clock that clicked behind the door;
The chest contrived a double debt to pay,
A bed by night, a chest of drawers by day;
The pictures placed for ornament and use,
The twelve good rules, the royal game of goose;
The hearth, except when winter chilled the day,
With aspen boughs, and flowers, and fennel gay;
While broken tea-cups, wisely kept for show,
Ranged o'er the chimney, glistened in a row.

Vain transitory splendours! could not all
Reprieve the tottering mansion from its fall!
Obscure it sinks, nor shall it more impart
An hour's importance to the poor man's heart;
Thither no more the peasant shall repair
To sweet oblivion of his daily care;
No more the farmer's news, the barber's tale,
No more the woodman's ballad shall prevail;
No more the smith his dusky brow shall clear,
Relax his ponderous strength, and lean to hear;
The host himself no longer shall be found
Careful to see the mantling bliss go round;
Nor the coy maid, half willing to be pressed,
Shall kiss the cup to pass it to the rest.
  Yes! let the rich deride, the proud disdain,
These simple blessings of the lowly train;
To me more dear, congenial to my heart,
One native charm, than all the gloss of art;
Spontaneous joys, where Nature has its play,
The soul adopts, and owns their first-born sway;
Lightly they frolic o'er the vacant mind,
Unenvied, unmolested, unconfined:
But the long pomp, the midnight masquerade,
With all the freaks of wanton wealth arrayed,
In these, ere triflers half their wish obtain,
The toiling pleasure sickens into pain;
And, even while Fashion's brightest arts decoy,
The heart distrusting asks, if this be joy.
  Ye friends to truth, ye statesmen, who survey
The rich man's joys increase, the poor's decay,
'T is yours to judge, how wide the limits stand
Between a splendid and a happy land.
Proud swells the tide with loads of freighted ore,
And shouting Folly hails them from her shore;
Hoards, even beyond the miser's wish abound,
And rich men flock from all the world around.
Yet count our gains. This wealth is but a name
That leaves our useful products still the same.
Not so the loss. The man of wealth and pride
Takes up a space that many poor supplied;
Space for his lake, his park's extended bounds,
Space for his horses, equipage, and hounds;
The robe that wraps his limbs in silken sloth
Has robbed the neighbouring fields of half their growth;
His seat, where solitary sports are seen,
Indignant spurns the cottage from the green;
Around the world each needful product flies,
For all the luxuries the world supplies:
While thus the land adorned for pleasure all
In barren splendour feebly waits the fall.
  As some fair female unadorned and plain,
Secure to please while youth confirms her reign,
Slights every borrowed charm that dress supplies,
Nor shares with art the triumph of her eyes:
But when those charms are passed, for charms are frail,
When time advances and when lovers fail,
She then shines forth, solicitous to bless,
In all the glaring impotence of dress.
Thus fares the land, by luxury betrayed,
In Nature's simplest charms at first arrayed;
But verging to decline, its splendours rise,
Its vistas strike, its palaces surprise;
While, scourged by famine, from the smiling land
The mournful peasant leads his humble band;
And while he sinks, without one arm to save,
The country blooms — a garden, and a grave.
  Where then, ah! where, shall poverty reside,
To 'scape the pressure of contiguous pride?
If to some common's fenceless limits strayed,
He drives his flock to pick the scanty blade,
Those fenceless fields the sons of wealth divide,
And even the bare-worn common is denied.
  If to the city sped — What waits him there?
To see profusion that he must not share;
To see ten thousand baneful arts combined
To pamper luxury, and thin mankind;
To see those joys the sons of pleasure know
Extorted from his fellow creatures' woe.
Here, while the courtier glitters in brocade,
There the pale artist plies the sickly trade;
Here, while the proud their long-drawn pomps display,
There the black gibbet glooms beside the way.

The dome where Pleasure holds her midnight reign,
Here, richly decked, admits the gorgeous train;
Tumultuous grandeur crowds the blazing square,
The rattling chariots clash, the torches glare.
Sure scenes like these no troubles e'er annoy!
Sure these denote one universal joy!
Are these thy serious thoughts? — Ah, turn thine eyes
Where the poor houseless shivering female lies.
She once, perhaps, in village plenty blessed,
Has wept at tales of innocence distressed;
Her modest looks the cottage might adorn,
Sweet as the primrose peeps beneath the thorn;
Now lost to all; her friends, her virtue fled,
Near her betrayer's door she lays her head,
And, pinched with cold, and shrinking from the shower,
With heavy heart deplores that luckless hour,
When idly first, ambitious of the town,
She left her wheel and robes of country brown.
Do thine, sweet Auburn, thine, the loveliest train,
Do thy fair tribes participate her pain?
Even now, perhaps, by cold and hunger led,
At proud men's doors they ask a little bread!
Ah, no! To distant climes, a dreary scene,
Where half the convex world intrudes between,
Through torrid tracts with fainting steps they go,
Where wild Altama murmurs to their woe.
Far different there from all that charmed before,
The various terrors of that horrid shore;
Those blazing suns that dart a downward ray,
And fiercely shed intolerable day;
Those matted woods where birds forget to sing,
But silent bats in drowsy clusters cling;
Those poisonous fields with rank luxuriance crowned,
Where the dark scorpion gathers death around;
Where at each step the stranger fears to wake
The rattling terrors of the vengeful snake;
Where crouching tigers wait their hapless prey,
And savage men more murderous still than they;
While oft in whirls the mad tornado flies,
Mingling the ravaged landscape with the skies.
Far different these from every former scene,
The cooling brook, the grassy-vested green,
The breezy covert of the warbling grove,
That only sheltered thefts of harmless love.
Good Heaven! what sorrows gloomed that parting day,
That called them from their native walks away,
When the poor exiles, every pleasure passed,
Hung round the bowers, and fondly looked their last,
And took a long farewell, and wished in vain
For seats like these beyond the western main;
And shuddering still to face the distant deep,
Returned and wept, and still returned to weep.
The good old sire the first prepared to go
To new-found worlds, and wept for others' woe;
But for himself, in conscious virtue brave,
He only wished for worlds beyond the grave.
His lovely daughter, lovelier in her tears,
The fond companion of his helpless years,
Silent went next, neglectful of her charms,
And left a lover's for a father's arms.
With louder plaints the mother spoke her woes,
And blessed the cot where every pleasure rose;
And kissed her thoughtless babes with many a tear,
And clasped them close, in sorrow doubly dear;
Whilst her fond husband strove to lend relief
In all the silent manliness of grief.
O Luxury! thou cursed by Heaven's decree,
How ill exchanged are things like these for thee!
How do thy potions, with insidious joy
Diffuse their pleasures only to destroy!
Kingdoms, by thee, to sickly greatness grown,
Boast of a florid vigour not their own;
At every draught more large and large they grow,
A bloated mass of rank unwieldy woe;
Till sapped their strength, and every part unsound,
Down, down they sink, and spread a ruin round.
Even now the devastation is begun,
And half the business of destruction done;
Even now, methinks, as pondering here I stand,

I see the rural Virtues leave the land:
Down where yon anchoring vessel spreads the sail,
That idly waiting flaps with every gale,
Downward they move, a melancholy band,
Pass from the shore, and darken all the strand.
Contented Toil, and hospitable Care,
And kind connubial Tenderness are there;
And Piety with wishes placed above,
And steady Loyalty, and faithful Love.
And thou, sweet Poetry, thou loveliest maid,
Still first to fly where sensual joys invade;
Unfit in these degenerate times of shame,
To catch the heart, or strike for honest fame;
Dear charming nymph, neglected and decried,
My shame in crowds, my solitary pride;
Thou source of all my bliss, and all my woe,
That found'st me poor at first, and keep'st me so;
Thou guide by which the nobler arts excel,
Thou nurse of every virtue, fare thee well!
Farewell! and O! where'er thy voice be tried,
On Torno's cliffs, or Pambamarca's side,
Whether where equinoctial fervours glow,
Or winter wraps the polar world in snow,
Still let thy voice, prevailing over time,
Redress the rigours of the inclement clime;
Aid slighted truth; with thy persuasive strain
Teach erring man to spurn the rage of gain;
Teach him, that states of native strength possessed,
Though very poor, may still be very blessed;
That trade's proud empire hastes to swift decay,
As ocean sweeps the laboured mole away;
While self-dependent power can time defy,
As rocks resist the billows and the sky.

1770

RETALIATION

Of old, when Scarron his companions invited,
Each guest brought his dish, and the feast was united;
If our landlord supplies us with beef, and with fish,
Let each guest bring himself, and he brings the best dish:
Our Dean shall be venison, just fresh from the plains;
Our Burke shall be tongue, with a garnish of brains;
Our Will shall be wild-fowl, of excellent flavour,
And Dick with his pepper shall heighten their savour:
Our Cumberland's sweet-bread its place shall obtain,
And Douglas is pudding, substantial and plain:
Our Garrick's a salad, for in him we see
Oil, vinegar, sugar, and saltness agree:
To make out the dinner, full certain I am,
That Ridge is anchovy, and Reynolds is lamb;
That Hickey's a capon, and, by the same rule,
Magnanimous Goldsmith, a gooseberry fool.
At a dinner so various, at such a repast,
Who'd not be a glutton, and stick to the last:
Here, waiter! more wine, let me sit while I'm able,
Till all my companions sink under the table;
Then, with chaos and blunders encircling my head,
Let me ponder, and tell what I think of the dead.

Here lies the good Dean, re-united to earth,
Who mixed reason with pleasure, and wisdom with mirth:
If he had any faults, he has left us in doubt,
At least, in six weeks, I could not find 'em out;
Yet some have declared, and it can't be denied 'em,
That Sly-boots was cursedly cunning to hide 'em.

Here lies our good Edmund, whose genius was such,
We scarcely can praise it, or blame it too much;
Who, born for the Universe, narrowed his mind,
And to party gave up what was meant for mankind.
Though fraught with all learning, yet straining his throat
To persuade Tommy Townshend to lend him a vote;
Who, too deep for his hearers, still went on refining,
And thought of convincing, while they thought of dining;
Though equal to all things, for all things unfit,
Too nice for a statesman, too proud for a wit:
For a patriot, too cool; for a drudge, disobedient;

And too fond of the right to pursue the expedient.
In short, 't was his fate, unemployed, or in place, sir,
To eat mutton cold, and cut blocks with a razor.
  Here lies honest William, whose heart was a mint,
While the owner ne'er knew half the good that was in't;
The pupil of impulse, it forced him along,
His conduct still right, with his argument wrong;
Still aiming at honour, yet fearing to roam,
The coachman was tipsy, the chariot drove home;
Would you ask for his merits? alas! he had none;
What was good was spontaneous, his faults were his own.
  Here lies honest Richard, whose fate I must sigh at,
Alas, that such frolic should now be so quiet!
What spirits were his, what wit and what whim,
Now breaking a jest, and now breaking a limb;
Now wrangling and grumbling to keep up the ball,
Now teasing and vexing, yet laughing at all!
In short, so provoking a devil was Dick,
That we wished him full ten times a day at Old Nick;
But missing his mirth and agreeable vein,
As often we wished to have Dick back again.
  Here Cumberland lies, having acted his parts,
The Terence of England, the mender of hearts;
A flattering painter, who made it his care
To draw men as they ought to be, not as they are.
His gallants are all faultless, his women divine,
And Comedy wonders at being so fine;
Like a tragedy queen he has dizened her out,
Or rather like Tragedy giving a rout.
His fools have their follies so lost in a crowd
Of virtues and feelings, that folly grows proud;
And coxcombs, alike in their failings alone,
Adopting his portraits, are pleased with their own.
Say, where has our poet this malady caught?
Or wherefore his characters thus without fault?
Say, was it that vainly directing his view
To find out men's virtues, and finding them few,
Quite sick of pursuing each troublesome elf,
He grew lazy at last, and drew from himself?
  Here Douglas retires from his toils to relax,
The scourge of imposters, the terror of quacks:
Come all ye quack bards, and ye quacking divines,
Come dance on the spot where your tyrant reclines;
When Satire and Censure encircled his throne,
I feared for your safety, I feared for my own;
But now he is gone, and we want a detector,
Our Dodds shall be pious, our Kenricks shall lecture;
Macpherson write bombast, and call it a style,
Our Townshend make speeches, and I shall compile;
New Lauders and Bowers the Tweed shall cross over,
No countryman living their tricks to discover;
Detection her taper shall quench to a spark,
And Scotchman meet Scotchman, and cheat in the dark.
  Here lies David Garrick, describe me, who can,
An abridgment of all that was pleasant in man;
As an actor, confessed without rival to shine:
As a wit, if not first, in the very first line:
Yet, with talents like these, and an excellent heart,
The man had his failings, a dupe to his art.
Like an ill-judging beauty, his colours he spread,
And beplastered with rouge his own natural red.
On the stage he was natural, simple, affecting;
'T was only that when he was off he was acting.
With no reason on earth to go out of his way,
He turned and he varied full ten times a day.
Though secure of our hearts, yet confoundedly sick,
If they were not his own by finessing and trick,
He cast off his friends, as a huntsman his pack,
For he knew when he pleased he could whistle them back.
Of praise a mere glutton, he swallowed what came,

And the puff of a dunce, he mistook it for fame;
Till his relish grown callous, almost to disease,
Who peppered the highest was surest to please.
But let us be candid, and speak out our mind,
If dunces applauded, he paid them in kind.
Ye Kenricks, ye Kellys, and Woodfalls so grave,
What a commerce was yours, while you got and you gave!
How did Grub-street re-echo the shouts that you raised,
While he was be-Rosciused, and you were be-praised!
But peace to his spirit, wherever it flies,
To act as an angel, and mix with the skies:
Those poets, who owe their best fame to his skill,
Shall still be his flatterers, go where he will.
Old Shakespeare, receive him, with praise and with love,
And Beaumonts and Bens be his Kellys above.
Here Hickey reclines, a most blunt, pleasant creature,
And slander itself must allow him good nature:
He cherished his friend, and he relished a bumper;
Yet one fault he had, and that one was a thumper.
Perhaps you may ask if the man was a miser?
I answer, no, no, for he always was wiser:
Too courteous, perhaps, or obligingly flat?
His very worst foe can't accuse him of that:
Perhaps he confided in men as they go,
And so was too foolishly honest? Ah no!
Then what was his failing? come tell it, and burn ye!
He was, could he help it? — a special attorney.
Here Reynolds is laid, and to tell you my mind,
He has not left a better or wiser behind:
His pencil was striking, resistless, and grand;
His manners were gentle, complying, and bland;
Still born to improve us in every part,
His pencil our faces, his manners our heart:
To coxcombs averse, yet most civilly steering,
When they judged without skill he was still hard of hearing:
When they talked of their Raphaels, Correggios, and stuff,
He shifted his trumpet, and only took snuff.

1774

ROMANTIC PROGRESS

William Collins (1721–1759)

DIRGE IN *CYMBELINE*

To fair Fidele's grassy tomb
Soft maids and village hinds shall bring
Each opening sweet of earliest bloom,
And rifle all the breathing spring.

No wailing ghost shall dare appear
To vex with shrieks this quiet grove;
But shepherd lads assemble here,
And melting virgins own their love.

No withered witch shall here be seen;
No goblins lead their nightly crew:
The female fays shall haunt the green,
And dress thy grave with pearly dew!

The redbreast oft, at evening hours,
Shall kindly lend his little aid,
With hoary moss, and gathered flowers,
To deck the ground where thou art laid.

When howling winds and beating rain
In tempests shake the sylvan cell,
Or 'midst the chase, on every plain,
The tender thought on thee shall dwell;

Each lonely scene shall thee restore;
For thee the tear be duly shed,
Beloved till life could charm no more,
And mourned till pity's self be dead.

1744

ODE TO SIMPLICITY

O THOU, by Nature taught
To breathe her genuine thought,
In numbers warmly pure, and sweetly strong;

Who first, on mountains wild,
In Fancy, loveliest child,
Thy babe, or Pleasure's, nursed the powers of song!

Thou, who, with hermit heart,
Disdain'st the wealth of art,
And gauds, and pageant weeds, and trailing pall;
But com'st a decent maid,
In Attic robe arrayed,
O chaste, unboastful nymph, to thee I call;

By all the honeyed store
On Hybla's thymy shore;
By all her blooms, and mingled murmurs dear;
By her whose lovelorn woe,
In evening musings slow,
Soothed sweetly sad Electra's poet's ear:

By old Cephisus deep,
Who spread his wavy sweep,
In warbled wanderings, round thy green retreat;
On whose enamelled side,
When holy Freedom died,
No equal haunt allured thy future feet.

O sister meek of Truth,
To my admiring youth,
Thy sober aid and native charms infuse!
The flowers that sweetest breathe,
Though Beauty culled the wreath,
Still ask thy hand to range their ordered hues.

While Rome could none esteem
But virtue's patriot theme,
You loved her hills, and led her laureat band:
But stayed to sing alone
To one distinguished throne;
And turned thy face, and fled her altered land.

No more, in hall or bower,
The passions own thy power;
Love, only love, her forceless numbers mean:
For thou hast left her shrine;
Nor olive more, nor vine,
Shall gain thy feet to bless the servile scene.

Though taste, though genius, bless
To some divine excess,
Faints the cold work till thou inspire the whole;
What each, what all supply,
May court, may charm, our eye;
Thou, only thou, canst raise the meeting soul!

Of these let others ask,
To aid some mighty task,
I only seek to find thy temperate vale;
Where oft my reed might sound
To maids and shepherds round,
And all thy sons, O Nature, learn my tale.

1746

ODE

How sleep the brave who sink to rest,
By all their country's wishes blessed!
When Spring, with dewy fingers cold,
Returns to deck their hallowed mould,
She there shall dress a sweeter sod
Than Fancy's feet have ever trod.

By fairy hands their knell is rung;
By forms unseen their dirge is sung;
There Honour comes, a pilgrim grey,
To bless the turf that wraps their clay;
And Freedom shall awhile repair,
To dwell, a weeping hermit, there!

1746

ODE TO EVENING

If aught of oaten stop, or pastoral song,
May hope, chaste Eve, to soothe thy modest ear,
Like thy own solemn springs,
Thy springs, and dying gales,

O nymph reserved, while now the bright-haired sun
Sits in yon western tent, whose cloudy skirts,
With brede ethereal wove,
O'erhang his wavy bed:

Now air is hushed, save where the weak-eyed bat
With short, shrill shriek, flits by on leathern wing;
Or where the beetle winds
His small but sullen horn,

As oft he rises 'midst the twilight path,
Against the pilgrim borne in heedless hum:
Now teach me, maid composed,
To breathe some softened strain,

Whose numbers, stealing through thy darkening vale,
May, not unseemly, with its stillness suit,
As, musing slow, I hail
Thy genial loved return!

For when thy folding star arising shows
His paly circlet, at his warning lamp

The fragrant Hours, and elves
Who slept in flowers the day,

And many a nymph who wreathes her brows with sedge,
And sheds the freshening dew, and, lovelier still,
The pensive Pleasures sweet
Prepare thy shadowy car.

Then lead, calm votaress, where some sheety lake
Cheers the lone heath, or some time-hallowed pile,
Or upland fallows grey
Reflect its last cool gleam.

But when chill blustering winds, or driving rain,
Forbid my willing feet, be mine the hut,
That from the mountain's side,
Views wilds, and swelling floods,

And hamlets brown, and dim-discovered spires;
And hears their simple bell, and marks o'er all
Thy dewy fingers draw
The gradual dusky veil.

While Spring shall pour his showers, as oft he wont,
And bathe thy breathing tresses, meekest Eve!
While Summer loves to sport
Beneath thy lingering light;

While sallow Autumn fills thy lap with leaves;
Or Winter, yelling through the troublous air,
Affrights thy shrinking train,
And rudely rends thy robes;

So long, sure-found beneath the sylvan shed,
Shall Fancy, Friendship, Science, rose-lipped Health,
Thy gentlest influence own,
And hymn thy favourite name!

1746

THE PASSIONS

AN ODE FOR MUSIC

When Music, heavenly maid, was young,
While yet in early Greece she sung,
The Passions oft, to hear her shell,
Thronged around her magic cell,
Exulting, trembling, raging, fainting,
Possest beyond the Muse's painting:
By turns they felt the glowing mind
Disturbed, delighted, raised, refined;
Till once, 't is said, when all were fired,
Filled with fury, rapt, inspired,
From the supporting myrtles round
They snatched her instruments of sound;
And, as they oft had heard apart
Sweet lessons of her forceful art,
Each (for madness ruled the hour)
Would prove his own expressive power.

First Fear, his hand, its skill to try,
Amid the chords bewildered laid,
And back recoiled, he knew not why,
Even at the sound himself had made.

Next Anger rushed; his eyes on fire,
In lightnings owned his secret stings:
In one rude clash he struck the lyre,
And swept, with hurried hand, the strings.

With woful measures wan Despair
Low, sullen sounds his grief beguiled;
A solemn, strange, and mingled air;
'T was sad by fits, by starts 't was wild.

But thou, O Hope, with eyes so fair,
What was thy delightful measure?
Still it whispered promised pleasure,
And bade the lovely scenes at distance hail!
Still would her touch the strain prolong;
And from the rocks, the woods, the vale,
She called on Echo still, through all the song;
And, where her sweetest theme she chose,
A soft responsive voice was heard at every close,
And Hope enchanted smiled, and waved her golden hair.

And longer had she sung; — but, with a frown,
Revenge impatient rose:
He threw his blood-stained sword, in thunder, down;
And with a withering look,
The war-denouncing trumpet took,
And blew a blast so loud and dread,
Were ne'er prophetic sounds so full of woe!
And, ever and anon, he beat
The doubling drum, with furious heat;
And though sometimes, each dreary pause between,
Dejected Pity, at his side,

Her soul-subduing voice applied,
Yet still he kept his wild unaltered mien,
While each strained ball of sight seemed bursting from his head.

Thy numbers, Jealousy, to naught were fixed;
Sad proof of thy distressful state;
Of differing themes the veering song was mixed;
And now it courted love, now raving called on hate.

With eyes upraised, as one inspired,
Pale Melancholy sat retired;
And, from her wild sequestered seat,
In notes by distance made more sweet,
Poured through the mellow horn her pensive soul:
And, dashing soft from rocks around,
Bubbling runnels joined the sound;
Through glades and glooms the mingled measure stole,
Or, o'er some haunted stream, with fond delay,
Round an holy calm diffusing,
Love of peace, and lonely musing,
In hollow murmurs died away.

But O! how altered was its sprightlier tone,
When Cheerfulness, a nymph of healthiest hue,
Her bow across her shoulder flung,
Her buskins gemmed with morning dew,
Blew an inspiring air, that dale and thicket rung,
The hunter's call, to faun and dryad known!
The oak-crowned sisters, and their chaste-eyed queen,
Satyrs and sylvan boys, were seen,
Peeping from forth their alleys green:
Brown Exercise rejoiced to hear;
And Sport leapt up, and seized his beechen spear.

Last came Joy's ecstatic trial:
He, with viny crown advancing,
First to the lively pipe his hand addrest;
But soon he saw the brisk awakening viol,
Whose sweet entrancing voice he loved the best;
They would have thought who heard the strain
They saw, in Tempe's vale, her native maids,
Amidst the festal sounding shades,
To some unwearied minstrel dancing,
While, as his flying fingers kissed the strings,
Love framed with Mirth a gay fantastic round;
Loose were her tresses seen, her zone unbound;
And he, amidst his frolic play,
As if he would the charming air repay,
Shook thousand odours from his dewy wings.

O Music! sphere-descended maid!
Friend of Pleasure, Wisdom's aid!
Why, goddess! why, to us denied,
Lay'st thou thy ancient lyre aside?
As, in that loved Athenian bower,
You learned an all-commanding power,
Thy mimic soul, O nymph endeared,
Can well recall what then it heard;
Where is thy native simple heart,
Devote to Virtue, Fancy, Art?
Arise, as in that elder time,
Warm, energetic, chaste, sublime!
Thy wonders, in that godlike age,
Fill thy recording sister's page —
'T is said, and I believe the tale,
Thy humblest reed could more prevail,
Had more of strength, diviner rage,
Than all which charms this laggard age;
E'en all at once together found,
Cecilia's mingled world of sound —
O bid our vain endeavours cease;
Revive the just designs of Greece:
Return in all thy simple state!
Confirm the tales her sons relate!

1746

ODE ON THE DEATH OF MR. THOMSON

In yonder grave a druid lies,
Where slowly winds the stealing wave;
The year's best sweets shall duteous rise
To deck its poet's sylvan grave.

In yon deep bed of whispering reeds
His airy harp shall now be laid,
That he, whose heart in sorrow bleeds,
May love through life the soothing shade.

Then maids and youths shall linger here,
And while its sounds at distance swell,
Shall sadly seem in pity's ear
To hear the woodland pilgrim's knell.

Remembrance oft shall haunt the shore
When Thames in summer wreaths is drest,
And oft suspend the dashing oar,
To bid his gentle spirit rest!

And oft, as ease and health retire
To breezy lawn, or forest deep,
The friend shall view yon whitening spire,
And 'mid the varied landscape weep.

But thou, who own'st that earthy bed,
Ah! what will every dirge avail;
Or tears, which love and pity shed,
That mourn beneath the gliding sail?

Yet lives there one whose heedless eye
Shall scorn thy pale shrine glimmering near?
With him, sweet bard, may fancy die,
And joy desert the blooming year.

But thou, lorn stream, whose sullen tide
No sedge-crowned sisters now attend,
Now waft me from the green hill's side,
Whose cold turf hides the buried friend!

And see — the fairy valleys fade;
Dun night has veiled the solemn view!
Yet once again, dear parted shade,
Meek nature's child, again adieu!

The genial meads, assigned to bless
Thy life, shall mourn thy early doom:
Their hinds and shepherd-girls shall dress,
With simple hands, thy rural tomb.

Long, long, thy stone and pointed clay
Shall melt the musing Briton's eyes:
O vales and wild woods! shall he say,
In yonder grave your druid lies!

1749

Thomas Gray (1716–1771)

ODE ON A DISTANT PROSPECT OF ETON COLLEGE

Ye distant spires, ye antique towers,
That crown the watery glade,
Where grateful Science still adores
Her Henry's holy shade;
And ye, that from the stately brow
Of Windsor's heights the expanse below
Of grove, of lawn, of mead survey,
Whose turf, whose shade, whose flowers among
Wanders the hoary Thames along
His silver-winding way.

Ah happy hills, ah pleasing shade,
Ah fields beloved in vain,
Where once my careless childhood strayed.
A stranger yet to pain!
I feel the gales, that from ye blow,
A momentary bliss bestow,
As waving fresh their gladsome wing
My weary soul they seem to soothe,
And, redolent of joy and youth,
To breathe a second spring.

Say, Father Thames, for thou hast seen
Full many a sprightly race
Disporting on thy margent green
The paths of pleasure trace,
Who foremost now delight to cleave
With pliant arm thy glassy wave?
The captive linnet which enthral?
What idle progeny succeed
To chase the rolling circle's speed,
Or urge the flying ball?

While some on earnest business bent
Their murmuring labours ply
'Gainst graver hours, that bring constraint
To sweeten liberty;
Some bold adventurers disdain
The limits of their little reign,
And unknown regions dare descry;
Still as they run they look behind,
They hear a voice in every wind,
And snatch a fearful joy.

Gay hope is theirs by fancy fed,
Less pleasing when possest;
The tear forgot as soon as shed,
The sunshine of the breast;
Theirs buxom health of rosy hue,
Wild wit, invention ever-new,
And lively cheer of vigour born;
The thoughtless day, the easy night,
The spirits pure, the slumbers light,
That fly the approach of morn.

Alas, regardless of their doom,
The little victims play!
No sense have they of ills to come,
Nor care beyond to-day;
Yet see how all around 'em wait
The ministers of human Fate,
And black Misfortune's baleful train!
Ah, show them where in ambush stand,
To seize their prey, the murtherous band!
Ah, tell them they are men!

These shall the fury Passions tear,
The vultures of the mind,
Disdainful Anger, pallid Fear,
And Shame that skulks behind;
Or pining Love shall waste their youth,
Or Jealousy with rankling tooth,
That inly gnaws the secret heart,
And Envy wan, and faded Care,
Grim-visaged comfortless Despair,
And Sorrow's piercing dart.

Ambition this shall tempt to rise,
Then whirl the wretch from high,
To bitter Scorn a sacrifice,
And grinning Infamy.
The stings of Falsehood those shall try,

And hard Unkindness' altered eye,
That mocks the tear it forced to flow;
And keen Remorse with blood defiled,
And moody Madness laughing wild
Amid severest woe.

Lo! in the vale of years beneath
A grisly troop are seen,
The painful family of Death,
More hideous than their queen.
This racks the joints, this fires the veins,
That every labouring sinew strains,
Those in the deeper vitals rage;
Lo, Poverty, to fill the band,
That numbs the soul with icy hand,
And slow-consuming Age.

To each his sufferings; all are men,
Condemned alike to groan,
The tender for another's pain,
The unfeeling for his own.
Yet ah! why should they know their fate?
Since sorrow never comes too late,
And happiness too swiftly flies,
Thought would destroy their paradise.
No more; where ignorance is bliss,
'T is folly to be wise.

1747

SONNET

ON THE DEATH OF RICHARD WEST

In vain to me the smiling mornings shine,
And reddening Phœbus lifts his golden fire;
The birds in vain their amorous descant join;
Or cheerful fields resume their green attire;
These ears, alas! for other notes repine,
A different object do these eyes require;
My lonely anguish melts no heart but mine;
And in my breast the imperfect joys expire.
Yet morning smiles the busy race to cheer,
And new-born pleasure brings to happier men;
The fields to all their wonted tribute bear;
To warm their little loves the birds complain;
I fruitless mourn to him that cannot hear,
And weep the more because I weep in vain.

1775

ELEGY WRITTEN IN A COUNTRY CHURCH-YARD

The curfew tolls the knell of parting day,
The lowing herd wind slowly o'er the lea,
The plowman homeward plods his weary way,
And leaves the world to darkness and to me.

Now fades the glimmering landscape on the sight,
And all the air a solemn stillness holds,
Save where the beetle wheels his droning flight,
And drowsy tinklings lull the distant folds;

Save that from yonder ivy-mantled tower
The moping owl does to the moon complain
Of such as, wandering near her secret bower,
Molest her ancient solitary reign.

Beneath those rugged elms, that yew-tree's shade,
Where heaves the turf in many a mouldering heap,
Each in his narrow cell forever laid,
The rude forefathers of the hamlet sleep.

The breezy call of incense-breathing Morn,
The swallow twittering from the straw-built shed,
The cock's shrill clarion, or the echoing horn,
No more shall rouse them from their lowly bed.

For them no more the blazing hearth shall burn,
Or busy housewife ply her evening care;
No children run to lisp their sire's return,
Or climb his knees the envied kiss to share.

Oft did the harvest to their sickle yield,
Their furrow oft the stubborn glebe has broke;
How jocund did they drive their team afield!
How bowed the woods beneath their sturdy stroke!

Let not Ambition mock their useful toil,
Their homely joys, and destiny obscure;
Nor Grandeur hear, with a disdainful smile
The short and simple annals of the poor.

The boast of heraldry, the pomp of power,
And all that beauty, all that wealth e'er gave,
Awaits alike the inevitable hour:
The paths of glory lead but to the grave.

Nor you, ye proud, impute to these the fault,
If Memory o'er their tomb no trophies raise,
Where through the long-drawn aisle and fretted vault
The pealing anthem swells the note of praise.

Can storied urn or animated bust
Back to its mansion call the fleeting breath?
Can Honour's voice provoke the silent dust,
Or Flattery soothe the dull cold ear of Death?

Perhaps in this neglected spot is laid
Some heart once pregnant with celestial fire;
Hands that the rod of empire might have swayed,
Or waked to ecstasy the living lyre.

But Knowledge to their eyes her ample page
Rich with the spoils of time did ne'er unroll;
Chill Penury repressed their noble rage,
And froze the genial current of the soul.

Full many a gem of purest ray serene
The dark unfathomed caves of ocean bear;
Full many a flower is born to blush unseen,
And waste its sweetness on the desert air.

Some village Hampden that with dauntless breast
The little tyrant of his fields withstood;
Some mute inglorious Milton here may rest,
Some Cromwell guiltless of his country's blood.

The applause of listening senates to command,
The threats of pain and ruin to despise,
To scatter plenty o'er a smiling land,
And read their history in a nation's eyes,

Their lot forbad; nor circumscribed alone
Their growing virtues, but their crimes confined;
Forbad to wade through slaughter to a throne,
And shut the gates of mercy on mankind,

The struggling pangs of conscious truth to hide,
To quench the blushes of ingenuous shame,
Or heap the shrine of Luxury and Pride
With incense kindled at the Muse's flame.

Far from the madding crowd's ignoble strife,
Their sober wishes never learned to stray;
Along the cool sequestered vale of life
They kept the noiseless tenor of their way.

Yet ev'n these bones from insult to protect
Some frail memorial still erected nigh,
With uncouth rhymes and shapeless sculpture decked,
Implores the passing tribute of a sigh.

Their name, their years, spelt by the unlettered Muse,
The place of fame and elegy supply;
And many a holy text around she strews,
That teach the rustic moralist to die.

For who, to dumb Forgetfulness a prey,
This pleasing anxious being e'er resigned,
Left the warm precincts of the cheerful day,
Nor cast one longing, lingering look behind?

On some fond breast the parting soul relies,
Some pious drops the closing eye requires;
Ev'n from the tomb the voice of Nature cries,
Ev'n in our ashes live their wonted fires.

For thee, who mindful of the unhonoured dead
Dost in these lines their artless tale relate;
If chance, by lonely Contemplation led,
Some kindred spirit shall inquire thy fate,

Haply some hoary-headed swain may say,
'Oft have we seen him at the peep of dawn
Brushing with hasty steps the dews away
To meet the sun upon the upland lawn.

'There at the foot of yonder nodding beech,
That wreathes its old fantastic roots so high,
His listless length at noontide would he stretch,
And pore upon the brook that babbles by.

'Hard by yon wood, now smiling as in scorn,
Muttering his wayward fancies he would rove,
Now drooping, woeful wan, like one forlorn,
Or crazed with care, or crossed in hopeless love.

'One morn I missed him on the customed hill,
Along the heath, and near his favourite tree;
Another came; nor yet beside the rill,
Nor up the lawn, nor at the wood was he;

'The next with dirges due in sad array
Slow through the church-way path we saw him borne.
Approach and read (for thou canst read) the lay,

Graved on the stone beneath yon aged thorn.'

THE EPITAPH

Here rests his head upon the lap of Earth
 A youth to Fortune and to Fame unknown.
Fair Science frowned not on his humble birth,
 And Melancholy marked him for her own.

Large was his bounty, and his soul sincere,
 Heaven did a recompense as largely send;
He gave to Misery all he had, a tear,
 He gained from Heaven ('t was all he wished) a friend.

No farther seek his merits to disclose,
 Or draw his frailties from their dread abode,
(There they alike in trembling hope repose),
 The bosom of his Father and his God.

1751

THE PROGRESS OF POESY

I. 1

Awake, Æolian lyre, awake,
And give to rapture all thy trembling strings.
 From Helicon's harmonious springs
A thousand rills their mazy progress take;
 The laughing flowers, that round them blow,
 Drink life and fragrance as they flow.
Now the rich stream of music winds along,
 Deep, majestic, smooth, and strong,
Through verdant vales, and Ceres' golden reign;
 Now rolling down the steep amain,
 Headlong, impetuous, see it pour;
The rocks and nodding groves rebellow to the roar.

I. 2

O! Sovereign of the willing soul,
Parent of sweet and solemn-breathing airs,
 Enchanting shell! the sullen Cares
And frantic Passions hear thy soft control.
 On Thracia's hills the Lord of War
 Has curbed the fury of his car,
And dropped his thirsty lance at thy command.
 Perching on the sceptred hand
Of Jove, thy magic lulls the feathered king
 With ruffled plumes and flagging wing;
 Quenched in dark clouds of slumber lie
The terror of his beak, and lightnings of his eye.

I. 3

Thee the voice, the dance, obey,
Tempered to thy warbled lay.
O'er Idalia's velvet-green
The rosy-crownèd Loves are seen,
 On Cytherea's day
With antic Sports and blue-eyed Pleasures,
Frisking light in frolic measures;
Now pursuing, now retreating,
 Now in circling troops they meet;
To brisk notes in cadence beating
 Glance their many-twinkling feet.
Slow melting strains their Queen's approach declare;
 Where'er she turns the Graces homage pay.
With arms sublime, that float upon the air,
 In gliding state she wins her easy way;
O'er her warm cheek, and rising bosom, move
The bloom of young Desire, and purple light of Love.

II. 1

Man's feeble race what ills await!
Labour, and Penury, the racks of Pain,
 Disease, and Sorrow's weeping train,
And Death, sad refuge from the storms of Fate!
 The fond complaint, my song, disprove,
 And justify the laws of Jove.
Say, has he given in vain the heav'nly Muse?
 Night, and all her sickly dews,
Her spectres wan, and birds of boding cry,
 He gives to range the dreary sky;
 Till down the eastern cliffs afar
Hyperion's march they spy, and glittering shafts of war.

II. 2

In climes beyond the solar road,
Where shaggy forms o'er ice-built mountains roam,
 The Muse has broke the twilight gloom
To cheer the shivering native's dull abode.
 And oft, beneath the odorous shade
 Of Chili's boundless forests laid,
She deigns to hear the savage youth repeat,
 In loose numbers wildly sweet,
Their feather-cinctured chiefs and dusky loves.
 Her track, where'er the goddess roves,
 Glory pursue, and generous Shame,

Th' unconquerable Mind, and Freedom's holy flame.

II. 3

Woods, that wave o'er Delphi's steep,
Isles, that crown the Ægean deep,
Fields, that cool Ilissus laves,
Or where Mæander's amber waves
In lingering labyrinths creep,
How do your tuneful echoes languish,
Mute, but to the voice of Anguish!
Where each old poetic mountain
Inspiration breathed around;
Every shade and hallowed fountain
Murmured deep a solemn sound;
Till the sad Nine in Greece's evil hour
Left their Parnassus for the Latian plains.
Alike they scorn the pomp of tyrant Power,
And coward Vice, that revels in her chains.
When Latium had her lofty spirit lost,
They sought, oh Albion! next thy sea-encircled coast.

III. 1

Far from the sun and summer-gale,
In thy green lap was Nature's darling laid,
What time, where lucid Avon strayed,
To him the mighty Mother did unveil
Her awful face. The dauntless child
Stretched forth his little arms, and smiled.
This pencil take (she said) whose colours clear
Richly paint the vernal year;
Thine too these golden keys, immortal boy!
This can unlock the gates of Joy,
Of Horror that, and thrilling Fears,
Or ope the sacred source of sympathetic tears.

III. 2

Nor second he, that rode sublime
Upon the seraph-wings of Ecstasy,
The secrets of the Abyss to spy.
He passed the flaming bounds of Place and Time;
The living throne, the sapphire blaze,
Where angels tremble, while they gaze,
He saw; but, blasted with excess of light,
Closed his eyes in endless night.
Behold, where Dryden's less presumptuous car
Wide o'er the fields of Glory bear
Two coursers of ethereal race,
With necks in thunder clothed, and long-resounding pace.

III. 3

Hark, his hands the lyre explore!
Bright-eyed Fancy hovering o'er
Scatters from her pictured urn
Thoughts that breathe, and words that burn.
But, ah! 't is heard no more —
Oh! Lyre divine, what daring spirit
Wakes thee now? Though he inherit
Nor the pride, nor ample pinion,
That the Theban Eagle bear
Sailing with supreme dominion
Through the azure deep of air;
Yet oft before his infant eyes would run
Such forms as glitter in the Muse's ray,
With orient hues unborrowed of the sun;
Yet shall he mount, and keep his distant way
Beyond the limits of a vulgar fate,
Beneath the good how far — but far above the great.

1757

THE BARD

I. 1

'Ruin seize thee, ruthless King!
Confusion on thy banners wait,
Though fanned by Conquest's crimson wing
They mock the air with idle state.
Helm, nor hauberk's twisted mail,
Nor even thy virtues, Tyrant, shall avail
To save thy secret soul from nightly fears,
From Cambria's curse, from Cambria's tears!'

Such were the sounds, that o'er the crested pride
Of the first Edward scattered wild dismay,
As down the steep of Snowdon's shaggy side
He wound with toilsome march his long array.
Stout Glo'ster stood aghast in speechless trance;
'To arms!' cried Mortimer, and couched his quivering lance.

I. 2

On a rock, whose haughty brow
Frowns o'er old Conway's foaming flood,

Robed in the sable garb of woe,
With haggard eyes the Poet stood;
(Loose his beard, and hoary hair
Streamed, like a meteor, to the troubled air)
And with a master's hand and prophet's fire,
Struck the deep sorrows of his lyre.

'Hark, how each giant oak, and desert cave,
Sighs to the torrent's awful voice beneath!
O'er thee, oh King! their hundred arms they wave,
Revenge on thee in hoarser murmurs breathe;
Vocal no more, since Cambria's fatal day,
To high-born Hoel's harp, or soft Llewellyn's lay.

I. 3

'Cold is Cadwallo's tongue,
That hushed the stormy main;
Brave Urien sleeps upon his craggy bed;
Mountains, ye mourn in vain
Modred, whose magic song
Made huge Plinlimmon bow his cloud-topped head.
On dreary Arvon's shore they lie,
Smeared with gore, and ghastly pale;
Far, far aloof the affrighted ravens sail;
The famished eagle screams, and passes by.
Dear lost companions of my tuneful art,
Dear, as the light that visits these sad eyes,
Dear, as the ruddy drops that warm my heart,
Ye died amidst your dying country's cries —
No more I weep. They do not sleep.
On yonder cliffs, a grisly band,
I see them sit, they linger yet,
Avengers of their native land;
With me in dreadful harmony they join,
And weave with bloody hands the tissue of thy line.

II. 1

'Weave the warp, and weave the woof,
The winding-sheet of Edward's race.
Give ample room, and verge enough
The characters of hell to trace.
Mark the year, and mark the night,
When Severn shall re-echo with affright
The shrieks of death, through Berkley's roofs that ring,
Shrieks of an agonizing King!
She-wolf of France, with unrelenting fangs,
That tear'st the bowels of thy mangled mate,
From thee be born, who o'er thy country hangs
The scourge of Heaven. What terrors round him wait!
Amazement in his van, with Flight combined,
And Sorrow's faded form, and Solitude behind.

II. 2

'Mighty victor, mighty lord!
Low on his funeral couch he lies!
No pitying heart, no eye, afford
A tear to grace his obsequies.
Is the Sable Warrior fled?
Thy son is gone. He rests among the dead.
The swarm, that in thy noon-tide beam were born?
Gone to salute the rising morn.
Fair laughs the morn, and soft the zephyr blows,
While proudly riding o'er the azure realm
In gallant trim the gilded vessel goes;
Youth on the prow, and Pleasure at the helm;
Regardless of the sweeping Whirlwind's sway,
That, hushed in grim repose, expects his evening prey.

II. 3

'Fill high the sparkling bowl,
The rich repast prepare,
Reft of a crown, he yet may share the feast;
Close by the regal chair
Fell Thirst and Famine scowl
A baleful smile upon their baffled guest.
Heard ye the din of battle bray,
Lance to lance, and horse to horse?
Long years of havoc urge their destined course,
And through the kindred squadrons mow their way.
Ye towers of Julius, London's lasting shame,
With many a foul and midnight murther fed,
Revere his consort's faith, his father's fame,

And spare the meek usurper's holy head.
Above, below, the rose of snow,
Twined with her blushing foe, we spread;
The bristled Boar in infant gore
Wallows beneath the thorny shade.
Now, brothers, bending o'er the accursed loom
Stamp we our vengeance deep, and ratify his doom.

III. 1

'Edward, lo! to sudden fate
(Weave we the woof. The thread is spun.)
Half of thy heart we consecrate.
(The web is wove. The work is done.)

Stay, oh stay! nor thus forlorn
Leave me unblessed, unpitied, here to mourn;
In yon bright track, that fires the western skies,
They melt, they vanish from my eyes.
But oh! what solemn scenes on Snowdon's height
Descending slow their glittering skirts unroll?
Visions of glory, spare my aching sight,
Ye unborn ages, crowd not on my soul!
No more our long-lost Arthur we bewail.
All hail, ye genuine kings, Britannia's issue, hail!

III. 2

'Girt with many a baron bold
Sublime their starry fronts they rear;
And gorgeous dames, and statesmen old
In bearded majesty, appear.
In the midst a form divine!
Her eye proclaims her of the Briton line;
Her lion-port, her awe commanding face,
Attempered sweet to virgin-grace.
What strings symphonious tremble in the air,
What strains of vocal transport round her play!
Hear from the grave, great Taliessin, hear;
They breathe a soul to animate thy clay.
Bright Rapture calls, and soaring, as she sings,
Waves in the eye of Heaven her many-coloured wings.

III. 3

'The verse adorn again
Fierce War, and faithful Love,
And Truth severe, by fairy Fiction drest.
In buskined measures move
Pale Grief and Pleasing Pain,
With Horror, tyrant of the throbbing breast.
A Voice, as of the Cherub-Choir,
Gales from blooming Eden bear;
And distant warblings lessen on my ear,
That lost in long futurity expire.
Fond impious man, think'st thou, yon sanguine cloud,
Raised by thy breath, has quenched the orb of day?
To-morrow he repairs the golden flood,
And warms the nations with redoubled ray.
Enough for me. With joy I see
The different doom our Fates assign.
Be thine Despair and sceptred Care,
To triumph, and to die, are mine.'

He spoke, and headlong from the mountain's height
Deep in the roaring tide he plunged to endless night.

1757

James Macpherson (1736–1796)

THE DEATH OF CUTHULLIN

'Is the wind on the shield of Fingal? Or is the voice of past times in my hall? Sing on, sweet voice! for thou art pleasant. Thou carriest away my night with joy. Sing on, O Bragela, daughter of car-borne Sorglan!

'It is the white wave of the rock, and not Cuthullin's sails. Often do the mists deceive me for the ship of my love! when they rise round some ghost, and spread their gray skirts on the wind. Why dost thou delay thy coming, son of the generous Semo? Four times has autumn returned with its winds, and raised the seas of Togorma, since thou hast been in the roar of battles, and Bragela distant far! Hills of the isle of mist! when will ye answer to his hounds? But ye are dark in your clouds. Sad Bragela calls in vain! Night comes rolling down. The face of ocean falls. The heath-cock's head is beneath his wing. The hind sleeps with the hart of the desert. They shall rise with morning's light, and feed by the mossy stream. But my tears return with the sun. My sighs come on with the night. When wilt thou come in thine arms, O chief of Erin's wars?'

Pleasant is thy voice in Ossian's ear, daughter of car-borne Sorglan! But retire to the hall of shells, to the beam of the burning oak. Attend to the murmur of the sea: it rolls at Dunscai's walls: let sleep descend on thy blue eyes. Let the hero arise in thy dreams!

Cuthullin sits at Lego's lake, at the dark rolling of waters. Night is around the hero. His thousands spread on the heath. A hundred oaks burn in the midst. The feast of shells is smoking wide. Carril strikes the harp beneath a tree. His gray locks glitter in the beam. The rustling blast of night is near, and lifts his aged hair. His song is of the blue Togorma, and of its chief, Cuthullin's friend! 'Why art thou absent, Connal, in the days of the gloomy storm? The chiefs of the south have convened against the car-borne Cormac. The winds detain thy sails. Thy blue waters roll around thee. But Cormac is not alone. The son of Semo fights his wars! Semo's son his battles fights! the terror of the stranger! He that is like the vapor of death, slowly borne by sultry winds. The sun reddens in its presence; the people fall around.'

Such was the song of Carril, when a son of the foe appeared. He threw down his pointless spear. He spoke the words of Torlath; Torlath, chief of heroes, from Lego's sable surge! He that led his thousands to battle, against car-borne Cormac. Cormac, who was distant far, in Temora's echoing halls: he learned to bend the bow of his fathers; and to lift the spear. Nor long didst thou lift the spear, mildly-shining beam of youth! death stands dim behind thee, like the darkened half of the moon behind its glowing light. Cuthullin rose before the bard, that came from generous Torlath. He offered him the shell of joy. He honored the son of songs. 'Sweet voice of Lego!' he said, 'what are the words of Torlath? Comes he to our feast or battle, the car-borne son of Cantela?'

'He comes to thy battle,' replied the bard, 'to the sounding strife of spears. When morning is gray on Lego, Torlath will fight on the plain. Wilt thou meet him, in thine arms, king of the isle of mist? Terrible is the spear of Torlath! it is a meteor of night. He lifts it, and the people fall! death sits in the lightning of his sword!' — 'Do I fear,' replied Cuthullin, 'the spear of car-borne Torlath? He is brave as a thousand heroes: but my soul delights in war! The sword rests not by the side of Cuthullin, bard of the times of old! Morning shall meet me on the plain, and the gleam on the blue arms of Semo's son. But sit thou on the heath, O bard, and let us hear thy voice. Partake of the joyful shell: and hear the songs of Temora!'

'This is no time,' replied the bard, 'to hear the song of joy: when the mighty are to meet in battle, like the strength of the waves of Lego. Why art thou so dark, Slimora! with all thy silent woods? No star trembles on thy top. No moonbeam on thy side. But the meteors of death are there: the gray watery forms of ghosts. Why art thou dark, Slimora! why thy silent woods?' He retired, in the sound of his song. Carril joined his voice. The music was like the memory of joys that are past, pleasant and mournful to the soul. The ghosts of departed bards heard on Slimora's side. Soft sounds spread along the wood. The silent valleys of night rejoice. So when he sits in the silence of the day, in the valley of his breeze, the humming of the mountain bee comes to Ossian's ear: the gale drowns it in its course: but the pleasant sound returns again! Slant looks the sun on the field! gradual grows the shade of the hill!

'Raise,' said Cuthullin to his hundred bards, 'the song of the noble Fingal: that song which he hears at night, when the dreams of his rest descend; when the bards strike the distant harp, and the faint light gleams on Selma's walls. Or let the grief of Lara rise: the sighs of the mother of Calmar, when he was sought, in vain, on his hills; when she beheld his bow in the hall. Carril, place the shield of Caithbat on that branch. Let the spear of Cuthullin be near; that the sound of my battle may rise, with the gray beam of the east.'

The hero leaned on his father's shield: the song of Lara rose! The hundred bards were distant far: Carril alone is near the chief. The words of the song were his: the sound of his harp was mournful.

'Alcletha with the aged locks! mother of car-borne Calmar! why dost thou look towards the desert, to behold the return of thy son? These are not his heroes, dark on the heath: nor is that the voice of Calmar. It is but the distant grove, Alcletha! but the roar of the mountain wind! — "Who bounds over Lara's stream, sister of the noble Calmar? Does not Alcletha behold his spear? But her eyes are dim! Is it not the son of Matha, daughter of my love?"

'"It is but an aged oak, Alcletha!" replied the lovely weeping Alona. "It is but an oak, Alcletha, bent over Lara's stream. But who comes along the plain? sorrow is in his speed. He lifts high the spear of Calmar. Alcletha, it is covered with blood!" —

'"But it is covered with the blood of foes, sister of car-borne Calmar! His spear never returned unstained with blood: nor his bow from the strife of the mighty. The battle is consumed in his presence: he is a flame of death, Alona! — Youth of the mournful speed! where is the son of Alcletha! Does he return with his fame, in the midst of his echoing shields? Thou art dark and silent! Calmar is then no more! Tell me not, warrior, how he fell. I must not hear of his wound!" Why dost thou look towards the desert, mother of low-laid Calmar?'

Such was the song of Carril, when Cuthullin lay on his shield. The bards rested on their harps. Sleep fell softly around. The son of Semo was awake alone. His soul fixed on war. The burning oaks began to decay. Faint red light is spread around. A feeble voice is heard! The ghost of Calmar came! He stalked dimly along the beam. Dark is the wound in his side. His hair is disordered and loose. Joy sits pale on his face. He seems to invite Cuthullin to his cave.

'Son of the cloudy night!' said the rising chief of Erin; 'why dost thou bend thy dark eyes on me, ghost of the noble Calmar? Wouldst thou frighten me, O Matha's son! from the battles of Cormac? Thy hand was not feeble in war: neither was thy voice for peace. How art thou changed, chief of Lara! if thou now dost advise to fly! But, Calmar, I never fled. I never feared the ghosts of night. Small is their knowledge, weak their hands; their dwelling is in the wind. But my soul grows in danger, and rejoices in the noise of steel. Retire thou to thy cave. Thou art not Calmar's ghost. He delighted in battle. His arm was like the thunder of heaven! He retired in his blast with joy, for he had heard the voice of his praise.'

The faint beam of the morning rose. The sound of Caithbat's buckler spread. Green Erin's warriors convened, like the roar of many streams. The horn of war is heard over Lego. The mighty Torlath came! 'Why dost thou come with thy thousands, Cuthullin,' said the chief of Lego. 'I know the strength of thy arm. Thy soul is an unextinguished fire. Why fight we not on the plain, and let our hosts behold our deeds? Let them behold us like roaring waves, that tumble round a rock; the mariners hasten away, and look on their strife with fear.'

'Thou risest like the sun, on my soul,' replied the son of Semo. 'Thine arm is mighty, O Torlath! and worthy of my wrath. Retire, ye men of Ullin, to Slimora's shady side. Behold the chief of Erin, in the day of his fame. Carril, tell to mighty Connal, if Cuthullin must fall, tell him I accused the winds, which roar on Togorma's waves. Never was he absent in battle, when the strife of my fame arose. Let his sword be before Cormac, like the beam of heaven. Let his counsel sound in Temora, in the day of danger!'

He rushed, in the sound of his arms, like the terrible spirit of Loda, when he comes, in the roar of a thousand storms, and scatters battles from his eyes. He sits on a cloud over Lochlin's seas. His mighty hand is on his sword. Winds lift his flaming locks! The waning moon half lights his dreadful face. His features blended in darkness arise to view. So terrible was Cuthullin in the day of his fame. Torlath fell by his hand. Lego's heroes mourned. They gather around the chief, like the clouds of the desert. A thousand swords rose at once; a thousand arrows flew; but he stood like a rock in the midst of a roaring sea. They fell around. He strode in blood. Dark Slimora echoed wide. The sons of Ullin came. The battle spread over Lego. The chief of Erin overcame. He returned over the field with his fame. But pale he returned! The joy of his face was dark. He rolled his eyes in silence. The sword hung, unsheathed, in his hand. His spear bent at every step!

'Carril,' said the chief in secret, 'the strength of Cuthullin fails. My days are with the years that are past. No morning of mine shall arise. They shall seek me at Temora, but I shall not be found. Cormac will weep in his hall, and say, Where is Erin's chief? But my name is renowned! my fame in the song of bards. The youth will say, in secret, O let me die as Cuthullin died! Renown clothed him like a robe. The light of his fame is great. — Draw the arrow from my side. Lay Cuthullin beneath that oak. Place the shield of Caithbat near, that they may behold me amidst the arms of my fathers!'

'And is the son of Semo fallen?' said Carril with a sigh. 'Mournful are Tura's walls. Sorrow dwells at Dunscai. Thy spouse is left alone in her youth. The son of thy love is alone! He shall come to Bragela and ask her why she weeps! He shall lift his eyes to the wall, and see his father's sword. Whose sword is that? he will say. The soul of his mother is sad. Who is that, like the hart of the desert, in the murmur of his course? His eyes look wildly round in search of his friend. Connal, son of Colgar, where hast thou been, when the mighty fell? Did the seas of Togorma roll around thee? Was the wind of the south in thy sails? The mighty have fallen in battle, and thou wast not there. Let none tell it in Selma, nor in Morven's woody land. Fingal will be sad, and the sons of the desert mourn!'

By the dark-rolling waves of Lego they raised the hero's tomb. Luath, at a distance, lies. The song of bards rose over the dead.

'Blest be thy soul, son of Semo! Thou wert mighty in battle. Thy strength was like the strength of a stream; thy speed like the eagle's wing. Thy path in battle was terrible: the steps of death were behind thy sword. Blest be thy soul, son of Semo, car-borne chief of Dunscai! Thou hast not fallen by the sword of the mighty, neither was thy blood on the spear of the brave. The arrow came, like the sting of death in a blast: nor did the feeble hand, which drew the bow, perceive it. Peace to thy soul, in thy cave, chief of the isle of mist!

'The mighty are dispersed at Temora; there is none in Cormac's hall. The king mourns in his youth. He does not behold thy return. The sound of thy shield is ceased: his foes are gathering round. Soft be thy rest in thy cave, chief of Erin's wars! Bragela will not hope for thy return, or see thy sails in ocean's foam. Her steps are not on the shore: nor her ear open to the voice of thy rowers. She sits in the hall of shells. She sees the arms of him that is no more. Thine eyes are full of tears, daughter of car-borne Sorglan! Blest be thy soul in death, O chief of shady Tura!'

1761

Thomas Chatterton (1752–1770)

BRISTOWE TRAGEDIE OR THE DETHE OF SYR CHARLES BAWDIN

THE featherd songster chaunticleer
  Han wounde hys bugle horne,
And tolde the earlie villager
  The commynge of the morne:

Kynge Edwarde sawe the ruddie streakes
  Of lyghte eclypse the greie;
And herde the raven's crokynge throte
  Proclayme the fated daie.

'Thou 'rt ryghte,' quod he, 'for, by the Godde
  That syttes enthroned on hyghe!
Charles Bawdin, and hys fellowes twaine,
  To-daie shall surelie die.'

Thenne wythe a jugge of nappy ale
  Hys knyghtes dydd onne hymm waite;
'Goe tell the traytour, thatt to-daie
  Hee leaves thys mortall state.'

Sir Canterlone thenne bendedd lowe,
  With harte brymm-fulle of woe;
Hee journeyed to the castle-gate,
  And to Syr Charles dydd goe.

Butt whenne hee came, hys children twaine,
  And eke hys lovynge wyfe,
Wythe brinie tears dydd wett the floore,
  For goode Syr Charleses lyfe.

'O, goode Syr Charles!' sayd Canterlone,
  'Badde tydyngs I doe brynge.'

'Speke boldlie, manne,' sayd brave Syr Charles,
'Whatte says the traytor kynge?'

'I greeve to telle; before yonne Sonne
Does fromme the welkinn flye,
Hee hathe uppon hys honour sworne,
Thatt thou shalt surelie die.'

'Wee all must die,' quod brave Syr Charles;
'Of thatte I'm not affearde;
Whatte bootes to lyve a little space?
Thanke Jesu, I'm prepared:

'Butt telle thye kynge, for myne hee's not,
I'de sooner die to-daie
Thanne lyve hys slave, as manie are,
Though I shoulde lyve for aie.'

Thenne Canterlone hee dydd goe out,
To telle the maior straite
To gett all thynges ynne redyness
For goode Syr Charleses fate.

Thenne Maister Canynge saughte the kynge,
And felle down onne hys knee;
'I'm come,' quod hee, 'unto your grace
To move your clemencye.'

Thenne quod the kynge, 'Youre tale speke out,
You have been much oure friende;
Whatever youre request may bee,
Wee wylle to ytte attende.

'My nobile liege! alle my request,
Ys for a nobile knyghte,
Who, though may hap hee has donne wronge,
Hee thoughte ytte stylle was ryghte:

'He has a spouse and children twaine,
Alle rewyned are for aie;
Yff that you are resolved to lett
Charles Bawdin die to-dai.'

'Speke not of such a traytour vile,'
The kynge ynn furie sayde;
'Before the evening starre doth sheene,
Bawdin shall loose hys hedde:

'Justice does loudlie for hym calle,
And hee shalle have hys meede:
Speke, maister Canynge! Whatte thynge else
Att present doe you neede?'

'My nobile liege!' goode Canynge sayde,
'Leave justice to our Godde,
And laye the yronne rule asyde;
Be thyne the olyve rodde.

'Was Godde to serche our hertes and reines,
The best were synners grete;
Christ's vycarr only knowes ne synne,
Ynne alle thys mortall state.

'Lett mercie rule thyne infante reigne,
'T wylle faste thye crowne fulle sure;
From race to race thye familie
Alle sov'reigns shall endure:

'But yff wythe bloode and slaughter thou
Beginne thy infante reigne,
Thy crowne upponne thy childrennes brows
Wylle never long remayne.'

'Canynge, awaie! thys traytour vile
Has scorned my power and mee;
Howe canst thou then for such a manne
Entreate my clemencye?'

'My nobile liege! the trulie brave
Wylle val'rous actions prize;
Respect a brave and nobile mynde,
Although ynne enemies.'

'Canynge, awaie! By Godde ynne Heav'n
That dydd mee beinge gyve,
I wylle nott taste a bitt of breade
Whilst thys Syr Charles dothe lyve.

'By Marie, and alle Seinctes ynne Heav'n,
Thys sunne shall be hys laste,'
Thenne Canynge dropt a brinie teare,
And from the presence paste.

With herte brymm-full of gnawynge grief,
Hee to Syr Charles dydd goe,
And sat hymm downe uponne a stoole,
And teares beganne to flowe.

'Wee all must die,' quod brave Syr Charles;
'Whatte bootes ytte howe or whenne;
Dethe ys the sure, the certaine fate
Of all wee mortall menne.

'Saye why, my friende, thie honest soul
Runns overr att thyne eye;
Is ytte for my most welcome doome
Thatt thou dost child-lyke crye?'

Quod godlie Canynge, 'I doe weepe,
Thatt thou soe soone must dye
And leave thy sonnes and helpless wyfe;
'T ys thys thatt wettes myne eye.'

'Thenne drie the tears thatt out thyne eye
From godlie fountaines sprynge;
Dethe I despise, and alle the power
Of Edwarde, traytour kynge.

'Whan through the tyrant's welcom means
I shall resigne my lyfe,

The Godde I serve wylle soone provyde
  For bothe mye soones and wyfe.

'Before I sawe the lyghtsome sunne,
  Thys was appointed mee;
Shall mortall manne repyne or grudge
  What Godde ordeynes to bee?

'Howe oft ynne battaile have I stood
  Whan thousands dyed arounde;
Whan smokynge streemes of crimson bloode
  Imbrewed the fattened grounde:

'Howe dydd I knowe thatt ev'ry darte,
  That cutte the airie waie,
Myghte nott fynde passage toe my harte,
  And close myne eyes for aie?

'And shall I nowe, forr feere of dethe,
  Looke wanne and bee dysmayde?
Ne! fromm my herte flie childyshe feere,
  Bee alle the manne displayed.

'Ah! goddelyke Henrie! Godde forefende,
  And guarde thee and thye sonne,
Yff 't is hys wylle; but yff 't is nott,
  Why thenne hys wylle bee donne.

'My honest friende, my faulte has beene
  To serve Godde and mye prynce;
And thatt I no tyme-server am,
  My dethe wylle soone convynce.

'Ynne Londonne citye was I borne,
  Of parents of grete note;
My fadre dydd a nobile armes
  Emblazon onne hys cote:

'I make ne doubte butt hee ys gone
  Where soone I hope to goe;
Where wee for ever shall bee blest,
  From oute the reech of woe.

'Hee taughte mee justice and the laws
  Wyth pitie to unite;
And eke hee taughte mee howe to knowe
  The wronge cause fromm the ryghte:

'Hee taughte mee with a prudent hande
  To feede the hungrie poore,
Ne lett mye sarvants dryve awaie
  The hungrie fromme my doore:

'And none can saye butt alle mye lyfe
  I have hys wordyes kept;
And summed the actyonns of the daie
  Eche nyght before I slept.

'I have a spouse, goe aske of her
  Yff I defyled her bedde?
I have a kynge, and none can laie
  Black treason onne my hedde.

'Ynne Lent, and onne the holie eve,
  Fromm fleshe I dydd refrayne;
Whie should I thenne appeare dismayed
  To leave thys worlde of payne?

'Ne, hapless Henrie! I rejoyce,
  I shall ne see thye dethe;
Moste willynglie ynne thye just cause
  Doe I resign my brethe.

'Oh, fickle people! rewyned londe!
  Thou wylt kenne peace ne moe;
Whyle Richard's sonnes exalt themselves,
  Thye brookes wythe bloude wylle flowe.

'Saie, were ye tyred of godlie peace,
  And godlie Henrie's reigne,
Thatt you dydd choppe your easie daies
  For those of bloude and peyne?

'Whatte though I onne a sledde be drawne,
  And mangled by a hynde,
I doe defye the traytor's pow'r,
  Hee can ne harm my mynd;

'Whatte though, uphoisted onne a pole,
  Mye lymbes shall rotte ynne ayre,
And ne ryche monument of brasse
  Charles Bawdin's name shall bear;

'Yett ynne the holie booke above,
  Whyche tyme can't eate awaie,
There wythe the sarvants of the Lord
  Mye name shall lyve for aie.

'Thenne welcome dethe! for lyfe eterne
  I leave thys mortall lyfe:
Farewell vayne world, and alle that's deare,
  Mye sonnes and lovynge wyfe!

'Nowe dethe as welcome to mee comes,
  As e'er the moneth of Maie;
Nor woulde I even wyshe to lyve,
  Wyth my dere wyfe to staie.'

Quod Canynge, ''T ys a goodlie thynge
  To bee prepared to die;
And from thys world of peyne and grefe
  To Godde ynne heav'n to flie.'

And nowe the belle began to tolle,
  And claryonnes to sound;
Syr Charles hee herde the horses feete
  A prauncyng onne the grounde:

And just before the officers
  His lovynge wyfe came ynne,
Weepynge unfeignèd teeres of woe,
  Wythe loude and dysmalle dynne.

'Sweet Florence! nowe I praie forbere,
  Ynn quiet lett mee die;

Praie Godde thatt ev'ry Christian soule
Maye looke onne dethe as I.

'Sweet Florence! why these brinie teers?
Theye washe my soule awaie,
And almost make mee wyshe for lyfe,
Wyth thee, sweete dame, to staie.

''Tys butt a journie I shalle goe
Untoe the lande of blysse;
Nowe, as a proofe of husbande's love,
Receive thys holie kysse.'

Thenne Florence, fault'ring ynne her saie,
Tremblynge these wordyes spoke,
'Ah, cruele Edwarde! bloudie kynge!
Mye herte ys welle nyghe broke:

'Ah, sweete Syr Charles! why wylt thou goe,
Wythoute thye lovynge wyfe?
The cruelle axe thatt cuttes thy necke,
Ytte eke shall ende mye lyfe.'

And nowe the officers came ynne
To brynge Syr Charles awaie,
Whoe turnedd toe hys lovynge wyfe,
And thus to her dydd saie:

'I goe to lyfe, and nott to dethe;
Truste thou ynne Godde above,
And teache thy sonnes to feare the Lorde,
And ynne theyre hertes hym love:

'Teache them to runne the nobile race
Thatt I theyre fader runne;
Florence! shou'd dethe thee take — adieu!
Yee officers leade onne.'

Thenne Florence raved as anie madde,
And dydd her tresses tere;
'Oh, staie, mye husbande, lorde, and lyfe!'
Syr Charles thenne dropt a teare.

'Tyll tyredd oute wythe ravynge loude,
Shee fellen onne the flore;
Syr Charles exerted alle hys myghte,
And marched fromm oute the dore.

Uponne a sledde hee mounted thenne,
Wythe lookes full brave and swete;
Lookes thatt enshone ne more concern
Thanne anie ynne the strete.

Before hym went the council-menne,
Ynne scarlett robes and golde,
And tassils spanglynge ynne the sunne,
Muche glorious to beholde:

The Freers of Seincte Augustyne next
Appearèd to the syghte,
Alle cladd ynne homelie russett weedes,
Of godlie monkysh plyghte:

Ynne diffraunt partes a godlie psaume
Moste sweetlie theye dydd chaunt;
Behynde theyre backes syx mynstrelles came,
Who tuned the strunge bataunt.

Thenne fyve-and-twentye archers came;
Echone the bowe dydd bende,
From rescue of Kynge Henries friends
Syr Charles forr to defend.

Bolde as a lyon came Syr Charles,
Drawne onne a cloth-layde sledde,
Bye two blacke stedes ynne trappynges white,
Wyth plumes uponne theyre hedde:

Behynde hym five-and-twenty moe
Of archers stronge and stoute,
Wyth bended bowe echone ynne hande,
Marchèd ynne goodlie route;

Seincte Jameses Freers marchèd next,
Echone hys parte dydd chaunt;
Behynde theyre backes syx mynstrelles came,
Who tuned the strunge bataunt:

Thenne came the maior and eldermenne,
Ynne clothe of scarlett deck't;
And theyre attendynge menne echone,
Lyke easterne princes trickt:

And after them, a multitude
Of citizens dydd thronge;
The wyndowes were alle fulle of heddes,
As hee dydd passe alonge.

And whenne hee came to the hyghe crosse,
Syr Charles dydd turne and saie,
'O, thou, thatt savest manne fromme synne,
Washe mye soule clean thys daie!'

Att the grete mynster wyndowe sat
The kynge ynne mycle state,
To see Charles Bawdin goe alonge
To hys most welcom fate.

Soone as the sledde drewe nyghe enowe,
Thatt Edwarde hee myghte heare,
The brave Syr Charles hee dydd stande uppe,
And thus hys wordes declare:

'Thou seest me, Edwarde! traytour vile!
Exposed to infamie;
Butt bee assured disloyall manne!
I'm greaterr nowe thanne thee.

'Bye foule proceedyngs, murdre, bloude,
Thou wearest nowe a crowne;
And hast appoynted mee to die,
By power nott thyne owne.

'Thou thynkest I shall die to-daie;
I have beene dede 'till nowe,
And soone shall lyve to weare a crowne
For aie uponne my browe:

'Whylst thou, perhapps, for som few yeares,
Shalt rule thys fickle lande,
To lett them knowe howe wyde the rule
'Twixt kynge and tyrant hande:

'Thye pow'r unjust, thou traytour slave!
Shall falle onne thye owne hedde' —
Fromm out of hearyng of the kynge
Departed thenne the sledde.

Kynge Edwarde's soule rushed to hys face,
Hee turned hys hedde awaie,
And to hys broder Gloucester
Hee thus dydd speke and saie:

'To hym that soe much dreaded dethe
Ne ghastlie terrors brynge,
Beholde the manne! hee spake the truthe,
Hee's greater thanne a kynge!'

'Soe let hym die!' Duke Richarde sayde;
'And maye echone oure foes
Bende downe theyre neckes to bloudie axe
And feede the carryon crowes.'

And nowe the horses gentlie drewe
Syr Charles uppe the hyghe hylle;
The axe dydd glysterr ynne the sunne,
His pretious bloude to spylle.

Syr Charles dydd uppe the scaffold goe,
As uppe a gilded carre
Of victory, bye val'rous chiefs
Gayned ynne the bloudie warre:

And to the people hee dyd saie,
'Beholde you see mee dye,
For servynge loyally mye kynge,
Mye kynge most ryghtfullie.

'As longe as Edwarde rules thys land,
Ne quiet you wylle knowe:
Your sonnes and husbandes shalle bee slayne
And brookes wythe bloude shall flowe.

'You leave youre goode and lawfulle kynge,
Whenne ynne adversitye;
Lyke mee, untoe the true cause stycke,
And for the true cause dye.'

Thenne, hee, wyth preestes, uponne hys knees,
A prayer to Godde dyd make,
Beseechynge hym unto hymselfe
Hys partynge soule to take.

Thenne, kneelynge downe, hee layd hys hedde
Most seemlie onne the blocke;
Whyche fromme hys bodie fayre at once
The able heddes-manne stroke:

And oute the bloude beganne to flowe,
And rounde the scaffolde twyne;
And teares, enow to washe 't awaie,
Dydd flowe fromme each mann's eyne.

The bloudie axe hys bodie fayre
Ynnto foure parties cutte;
And ev'rye parte, and eke hys hedde,
Uponne a pole was putte.

One parte dydd rotte onne Kynwulph-hylle
One onne the mynster-tower,
And one from off the castle-gate
The crowen dydd devoure;

The other onne Seyncte Powle's goode gate
A dreery spectacle;
Hys hedde was placed onne the hyghe crosse,
Ynne hyghe-streete most nobile.

Thus was the ende of Bawdin's fate:
Godde prosper longe oure kynge,
And grante hee maye, wyth Bawdin's soule,
Ynne heav'n Godd's mercie synge!

1772

MYNSTRELLES SONGE

O! SYNGE untoe mie roundelaie,
O! droppe the brynie teare wythe mee,
Daunce ne moe atte hallie daie,
Lycke a reynynge ryver bee;
Mie love ys dedde,
Gon to hys death-bedde,
Al under the wyllowe tree.

Blacke hys cryne as the wyntere nyghte,
Whyte hys rode as the sommer snowe,
Rodde hys face as the morynynge lyghte,
Cale he lyes ynne the grave belowe;
Mie love ys dedde,
Gon to hys death-bedde,
Al under the wyllowe tree.

Swote hys tyngue as the throstles note,
Quycke ynn daunce as thoughte canne bee,
Defte hys taboure, codgelle stote,
O! hee lyes bie the wyllowe tree:
Mie love ys dedde,
Gonne to hys death-bedde,
Alle under the wyllowe tree.

Harke! the ravenne flappes hys wynge,
In the briered delle belowe;
Harke! the dethe-owle loude dothe syngg,

To the nyghte-mares as heie goe;
Mie love ys dedde,
Gonne to hys death-bedde,
Al under the wyllowe tree.

See! the whyte moone sheenes onne hie;
Whyterre ys mie true loves shroude;
Whyterre thanne the mornynge skie,
Whyterre thanne the evenynge cloude;
Mie love ys dedde,
Gon to hys death-bedde,
Al under the wyllowe tree.

Heere, uponne mie true loves grave,
Schalle the baren fleurs be layde,
Nee one hallie Seyncte to save
Al the celness of a mayde.
Mie love ys dedde,
Gonne to hys death-bedde,
Alle under the wyllowe tree.

Wythe mie hondes I 'lle dente the brieres
Rounde his hallie corse to gre,
Ouphante fairie lyghte youre fyres,
Heere mie boddie stylle schalle bee.
Mie love ys dedde,
Gon to hys death-bedde,
Al under the wyllowe tree.

Comme, wythe acorne-coppe & thorne,
Drayne mie hartys blodde awaie;
Lyfe & all yttes goode I scorne,
Daunce bie nete, or feaste by daie.
Mie love ys dedde,
Gon to hys death-bedde,
Al under the wyllowe tree.

Waterre wytches, crownede wythe reytes,
Bere mee to yer leathalle tyde.
I die; I comme; mie true love waytes.
Thos the damselle spake, and dyed.

1777

Thomas Warton (1728–1790)

THE GRAVE OF KING ARTHUR

STATELY the feast, and high the cheer:
Girt with many an armèd peer,
And canopied with golden pall,
Amid Cilgarran's castle hall,
Sublime in formidable state,
And warlike splendour, Henry sate;
Prepared to stain the briny flood
Of Shannon's lakes with rebel blood.
Illumining the vaulted roof,
A thousand torches flamed aloof:
From massy cups, with golden gleam
Sparkled the red metheglin's stream:
To grace the gorgeous festival,
Along the lofty-windowed hall,
The storied tapestry was hung:
With minstrelsy the rafters rung
Of harps, that with reflected light
From the proud gallery glittered bright:
While gifted bards, a rival throng,
(From distant Mona, nurse of song,
From Teivi, fringed with umbrage brown,
From Elvy's vale, and Cader's crown,
From many a shaggy precipice
That shades Ierne's hoarse abyss,
And many a sunless solitude
Of Radnor's inmost mountains rude,)
To crown the banquet's solemn close,
Themes of British glory chose;
And to the strings of various chime
Attempered thus the fabling rhyme.
'O'er Cornwall's cliffs the tempest roared,
High the screaming sea-mew soared;
On Tintagell's topmost tower
Darksome fell the sleety shower;
Round the rough castle shrilly sung
The whirling blast, and wildly flung
On each tall rampart's thundering side
The surges of the tumbling tide:
When Arthur ranged his red-cross ranks
On conscious Camlan's crimsoned banks:
By Mordred's faithless guile decreed
Beneath a Saxon spear to bleed!
Yet in vain a paynim foe
Armed with fate the mighty blow;
For when he fell, an elfin queen,
All in secret, and unseen,
O'er the fainting hero threw
Her mantle of ambrosial blue;
And bade her spirits bear him far,
In Merlin's agate-axled car,
To her green isle's enamelled steep,
Far in the navel of the deep.
O'er his wounds she sprinkled dew
From flowers that in Arabia grew:
On a rich enchanted bed
She pillowed his majestic head;
O'er his brow, with whispers bland,
Thrice she waved an opiate wand;
And to soft music's airy sound,
Her magic curtains closed around.
There, renewed the vital spring,
Again he reigns a mighty king;
And many a fair and fragrant clime,
Blooming in immortal prime,
By gales of Eden ever fanned,
Owns the monarch's high command:
Thence to Britain shall return,
(If right prophetic rolls I learn)
Borne on Victory's spreading plume,
His ancient scepter to resume;
Once more, in old heroic pride,
His barbèd courser to bestride;

His knightly table to restore,
And brave the tournaments of yore.'
 They ceased: when on the tuneful stage
Advanced a bard, of aspect sage;
His silver tresses, thin besprent,
To age a graceful reverence lent;
His beard, all white as spangles frore
That clothe Plinlimmon's forests hoar,
Down to his harp descending flowed;
With Time's faint rose his features glowed;
His eyes diffused a softened fire,
And thus he waked the warbling wire.
 'Listen, Henry, to my read!
Not from fairy realms I lead
Bright-robed Tradition, to relate
In forgèd colours Arthur's fate;
Though much of old romantic lore
On the high theme I keep in store:
But boastful Fiction should be dumb,
Where Truth the strain might best become.
If thine ear may still be won
With songs of Uther's glorious son,
Henry, I a tale unfold,
Never yet in rime enrolled,
Nor sung nor harped in hall or bower;
Which in my youth's full early flower,
A minstrel, sprung of Cornish line,
Who spoke of kings from old Locrine,
Taught me to chaunt, one vernal dawn,
Deep in a cliff-encircled lawn,
What time the glistening vapours fled
From cloud-enveloped Clyder's head;
And on its sides the torrents gray
Shone to the morning's orient ray.
 'When Arthur bowed his haughty crest,
No princess, veiled in azure vest,
Snatched him, by Merlin's potent spell,
In groves of golden bliss to dwell;
Where, crowned with wreaths of mistletoe,
Slaughtered kings in glory go:
But when he fell, with wingèd speed,
His champions, on a milk-white steed,
From the battle's hurricane,
Bore him to Joseph's towered fane,
In the fair vale of Avalon:
There, with chaunted orison,
And the long blaze of tapers clear,
The stolèd fathers met the bier;
Through the dim isles, in order dread
Of martial woe, the chief they led,
And deep intombed in holy ground,
Before the altar's solemn bound.
Around no dusky banners wave,
No mouldering trophies mark the grave:
Away the ruthless Dane has torn
Each trace that Time's slow touch had worn;
And long, o'er the neglected stone,
Oblivion's veil its shade has thrown:
The faded tomb, with honour due,
'T is thine, O Henry, to renew!
Thither, when Conquest has restored
Yon recreant isle, and sheathed the sword,
When Peace with palm has crowned thy
  brows,
Haste thee, to pay thy pilgrim vows.
There, observant of my lore,
The pavement's hallowed depth explore;
And thrice a fathom underneath
Dive into the vaults of death.
There shall thine eye, with wild amaze,
On his gigantic stature gaze;
There shalt thou find the monarch laid,
All in warrior-weeds arrayed;
Wearing in death his helmet-crown,
And weapons huge of old renown.
Martial prince, 't is thine to save
From dark oblivion Arthur's grave!
So may thy ships securely stem
The western frith: thy diadem
Shine victorious in the van,
Nor heed the slings of Ulster's clan:
Thy Norman pike-men win their way
Up the dun rocks of Harald's bay:
And from the steeps of rough Kildare
Thy prancing hoofs the falcon scare:
So may thy bow's unerring yew
Its shafts in Roderick's heart imbrew.'
 Amid the pealing symphony
The spicèd goblets mantled high;
With passions new the song impressed
The listening king's impatient breast:
Flash the keen lightnings from his eyes;
He scorns awhile his bold emprise;
E'en now he seems, with eager pace,
The consecrated floor to trace,
And ope, from its tremendous gloom,
The treasure of the wondrous tomb:
E'en now he burns in thought to rear,
From its dark bed, the ponderous spear,
Rough with the gore of Pictish kings:
E'en now fond hope his fancy wings,
To poise the monarch's massy blade,
Of magic-tempered metal made;
And drag to day the dinted shield
That felt the storm of Camlan's field.
O'er the sepulchre profound
E'en now, with arching sculpture crowned,
He plans the chauntry's choral shrine,
The daily dirge, and rites divine.

1777

SONNETS

WRITTEN IN A BLANK LEAF OF DUGDALE'S *MONASTICON*

DEEM not, devoid of elegance, the sage,
By Fancy's genuine feelings unbeguiled,
Of painful pedantry the poring child;

Who turns, of these proud domes, the historic page,
Now sunk by Time, and Henry's fiercer rage.
Think'st thou the warbling muses never smiled
On his lone hours? Ingenuous views engage
His thoughts, on themes, unclassic falsely styled,
Intent. While cloistered Piety displays
Her mouldering roll, the piercing eye explores
New manners, and the pomp of elder days,
Whence culls the pensive bard his pictured stores.
Not rough, nor barren, are the winding ways
Of hoar Antiquity, but strown with flowers.

1777

WRITTEN AT STONEHENGE

Thou noblest monument of Albion's isle!
Whether by Merlin's aid from Scythia's shore,
To Amber's fatal plain Pendragon bore,
Huge frame of giant-hands, the mighty pile,
T' entomb his Britons slain by Hengist's guile:
Or Druid priests, sprinkled with human gore,
Taught mid thy massy maze their mystic lore:
Or Danish chiefs, enriched with savage spoil,
To Victory's idol vast, an unhewn shrine,
Reared the rude heap: or, in thy hallowed round,
Repose the kings of Brutus' genuine line;
Or here those kings in solemn state were crowned:
Studious to trace thy wondrous origine
We muse on many an ancient tale renowned.

1777

TO THE RIVER LODON

Ah! what a weary race my feet have run,
Since first I trod thy banks with alders crowned,
And thought my way was all through fairy ground,
Beneath thy azure sky, and golden sun:
Where first my Muse to lisp her notes begun!
While pensive Memory traces back the round,
Which fills the varied interval between;
Much pleasure, more of sorrow, marks the scene.
Sweet native stream! those skies and suns so pure
No more return, to cheer my evening road!
Yet still one joy remains, that not obscure,
Nor useless, all my vacant days have flowed,
From youth's gay dawn to manhood's prime mature;
Nor with the Muse's laurel unbestowed.

1777

Robert Fergusson (1750–1774)

THE DAFT DAYS

Now mirk December's dowie face
Glowrs owr the rigs wi' sour grimace,
While, through his minimum of space,
The bleer-eyed sun,
Wi' blinkin' light and stealing pace,
His race doth run.

From naked groves nae birdie sings;
To shepherd's pipe nae hillock rings;
The breeze nae od'rous flavour brings
From Borean cave;
And dwyning Nature droops her wings,
Wi' visage grave.

Mankind but scanty pleasure glean
Frae snawy hill or barren plain,
Whan Winter, 'midst his nipping train,
Wi' frozen spear,
Sends drift owr a' his bleak domain,
And guides the weir.

Auld Reikie! thou 'rt the canty hole,
A bield for mony a caldrife soul,
Wha snugly at thine ingle loll,
Baith warm and couth,
While round they gar the bicker roll
To weet their mouth.

When merry Yule Day comes, I trow,
You 'll scantlins find a hungry mou;
Sma' are our cares, our stamacks fou
O' gusty gear
And kickshaws, strangers to our view
Sin' fairn-year.

Ye browster wives, now busk ye bra,
And fling your sorrows far awa';
Then come and gie 's the tither blaw
O' reaming ale,
Mair precious than the Well of Spa,
Our hearts to heal.

Then, though at odds wi' a' the warl',
Amang oursells we 'll never quarrel;
Though Discord gie a cankered snarl
To spoil our glee,

As lang 's there 's pith into the barrel
We 'll drink and 'gree.

Fiddlers, your pins in temper fix,
And roset weel your fiddlesticks;
But banish vile Italian tricks
From out your quorum,
Nor *fortes* wi' *pianos* mix —
Gie 's 'Tullochgorum'!

For naught can cheer the heart sae weel
As can a canty Highland reel;
It even vivifies the heel
To skip and dance:
Lifeless is he wha canna feel
Its influence.

Let mirth abound; let social cheer
Invest the dawning of the year;
Let blithesome innocence appear,
To crown our joy;
Nor envy, wi' sarcastic sneer,
Our bliss destroy.

And thou, great god of *aqua vitæ!*
Wha sways the empire of this city, —
When fou we're sometimes capernoity, —
Be thou prepared
To hedge us frae that black banditti,
The City Guard.

1773

William Lisle Bowles (1762–1850)

SONNETS

BAMBOROUGH CASTLE

Ye holy Towers that shade the wave-worn steep,
Long may ye rear your agèd brows sublime,
Though, hurrying silent by, relentless Time
Assail you, and the winds of winter sweep
Round your dark battlements; for far from halls
Of Pride, here Charity hath fixed her seat,
Oft listening, tearful, when the tempests beat
With hollow bodings round your ancient walls;
And Pity, at the dark and stormy hour
Of midnight, when the moon is hid on high,
Keeps her lone watch upon the topmost tower,
And turns her ear to each expiring cry;
Blessed if her aid some fainting wretch may save,
And snatch him cold and speechless from the wave.

1789

INFLUENCE OF TIME ON GRIEF

O Time! who knowest a lenient hand to lay
Softest on Sorrow's wound, and slowly thence
(Lulling to sad repose the weary sense)
The faint pang stealest unperceived away;
On thee I rest my only hope at last,
And think, when thou hast dried the bitter tear
That flows in vain o'er all my soul held dear,
I may look back on every sorrow past,
And meet life's peaceful evening with a smile: —
As some lone bird, at day's departing hour,
Sings in the sunbeam, of the transient shower
Forgetful, though its wings are wet the while: —
Yet ah! how much must that poor heart endure,
Which hopes from thee, and thee alone, a cure!

1789

HOPE

As one who, long by wasting sickness worn,
Weary has watched the lingering night, and heard
Unmoved the carol of the matin bird
Salute his lonely porch; now first at morn
Goes forth, leaving his melancholy bed;
He the green slope and level meadow views,
Delightful bathed in slow-ascending dews;
Or marks the clouds that o'er the mountain's head
In varying forms fantastic wander white:
Or turns his ear to every random song,
Heard the green river's winding marge along,
The whilst each sense is steeped in still delight.
So o'er my breast young Summer's breath I feel,
Sweet Hope! thy fragrance pure and healing incense steal!

1789

DOVER CLIFFS

On these white cliffs, that calm above the flood,
Uprear their shadowing heads, and at their feet
Hear not the surge that has for ages beat,
How many a lonely wanderer has stood!
And, whilst the lifted murmur met his ear,
And o'er the distant billows the still eve
Sailed slow, has thought of all his heart must leave

Tomorrow; of the friends he loved most dear;
Of social scenes, from which he wept to part!
Oh! if, like me, he knew how fruitless all
The thoughts that would full fain the past recall,
Soon would he quell the risings of his heart,
And brave the wild winds and unhearing tide —
The World his country, and his God his guide.

1789

RETROSPECTION

I TURN these leaves with thronging thoughts, and say
Alas! how many friends of youth are dead;
How many visions of fair hope have fled,
Since first, my Muse, we met. — So speeds away
Life, and its shadows; yet we sit and sing,
Stretched in the noontide bower, as if the day
Declined not, and we yet might trill our lay
Beneath the pleasant morning's purple wing
That fans us; while aloft the gay clouds shine!
Oh, ere the coming of the long cold night,
Religion, may we bless thy purer light,
That still shall warm us, when the tints decline
O'er earth's dim hemisphere; and sad we gaze
On the vain visions of our passing days!

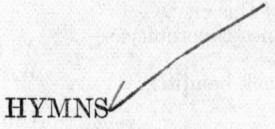

1789

HYMNS

Isaac Watts (1674–1748)

A CRADLE HYMN

HUSH! my dear, lie still and slumber,
Holy angels guard thy bed!
Heavenly blessings without number
Gently falling on thy head.

Sleep, my babe; thy food and raiment,
House and home, thy friends provide;
All without thy care or payment:
All thy wants are well supplied.

How much better thou'rt attended
Than the Son of God could be,
When from Heaven He descended
And became a child like thee!

Soft and easy is thy cradle:
Coarse and hard thy Saviour lay,
When His birthplace was a stable
And His softest bed was hay.

Blessèd babe! what glorious features —
Spotless fair, divinely bright!
Must He dwell with brutal creatures?
How could angels bear the sight?

Was there nothing but a manger
Cursèd sinners could afford
To receive the heavenly stranger?
Did they thus affront their Lord?

Soft, my child: I did not chide thee,
Though my song might sound too hard;
'T is thy mother sits beside thee,
And her arms shall be thy guard.

Yet to read the shameful story
How the Jews abused their King,
How they served the Lord of Glory,
Makes me angry while I sing.

See the kinder shepherds round Him,
Telling wonders from the sky!
Where they sought Him, there they found Him,
With His virgin mother by.

See the lovely babe a-dressing;
Lovely infant, how He smiled!
When He wept, the mother's blessing
Soothed and hushed the holy child.

Lo, He slumbers in His manger,
Where the hornèd oxen fed;
Peace, my darling; here's no danger,
Here's no ox a-near thy bed.

'T was to save thee, child, from dying,
Save my dear from burning flame,

Bitter groans and endless crying,
  That thy blest Redeemer came.

May'st thou live to know and fear Him,
  Trust and love Him all thy days;
Then go dwell forever near Him,
  See His face, and sing His praise!

1715

AM I A SOLDIER OF THE CROSS?

Am I a soldier of the cross,
  A follower of the Lamb?
And shall I fear to own His cause,
  Or blush to speak His name?

Must I be carried to the skies
  On flowery beds of ease,
While others fought to win the prize,
  And sailed through bloody seas?

Are there no foes for me to face?
  Must I not stem the flood?
Is this vile world a friend to grace,
  To help me on to God?

Sure I must fight, if I would reign;
  Increase my courage, Lord;
I'll bear the toil, endure the pain,
  Supported by Thy word.

1723

Charles Wesley (1707–1788)

IN TIME OF PRAYER AND TEMPTATION

Jesus, lover of my soul,
Let me to Thy bosom fly,
While the nearer waters roll,
While the tempest still is high!
Hide me, O my Saviour, hide,
Till the storm of life be past,
Safe into the haven guide;
O receive my soul at last!

Other refuge have I none;
Hangs my helpless soul on Thee;
Leave, ah! leave me not alone,
Still support and comfort me!
All my trust on Thee is stayed,
All my help from Thee I bring;
Cover my defenceless head
With the shadow of Thy wing!

Wilt Thou not regard my call?
Wilt Thou not accept my prayer?
Lo! I sink, I faint, I fall —
Lo! on Thee I cast my care!
Reach me out Thy gracious hand!
While I of Thy strength receive,
Hoping against hope I stand,
Dying, and behold I live!

Thou, O Christ, art all I want;
More than all in Thee I find:
Raise the fallen, cheer the faint,
Heal the sick, and lead the blind!
Just and holy is Thy name;
I am all unrighteousness;
False and full of sin I am,
Thou art full of truth and grace.

Plenteous grace with Thee is found,
Grace to cover all my sin;
Let the healing streams abound;
Make and keep me pure within!
Thou of Life the Fountain art,
Freely let me take of Thee;
Spring Thou up within my heart!
Rise to all eternity!

1740

A CHARGE TO KEEP

A charge to keep I have,
  A God to glorify;
A never-dying soul to save,
  And fit it for the sky.

To serve the present age,
  My calling to fulfill;
O may it all my powers engage,
  To do my Master's will!

Arm me with jealous care,
  As in Thy sight to live,
And O, Thy servant, Lord, prepare,
  A strict account to give!

Help me to watch and pray,
  And on Thyself rely,
Assured, if I my trust betray,
  I shall forever die.

1762

Augustus M. Toplady (1740–1778)

ROCK OF AGES

Rock of Ages, cleft for me,
  Let me hide myself in Thee;
Let the water and the blood,
  From Thy wounded side which flowed,
Be of sin the double cure,
  Save from wrath and make me pure.

Could my tears forever flow,
  Could my zeal no languor know,

These for sin could not atone;
  Thou must save, and Thou alone.
In my hand no price I bring;
  Simply to Thy cross I cling.

While I draw this fleeting breath,
  When my eyes shall close in death,
When I soar to worlds unknown,
  And behold Thee on Thy throne;
Rock of Ages, cleft for me,
  Let me hide myself in Thee.

1776

John Newton (1725–1807)

THE LORD'S DAY

Safely through another week
  God has brought us on our way;
Let us now a blessing seek,
  Waiting in His courts to-day;
Day of all the week the best,
  Emblem of eternal rest.

While we pray for pardoning grace,
  Through the dear Redeemer's name,
Show Thy reconcilèd face,
  Take away our sin and shame;
From our worldly cares set free,
  May we rest this day in Thee.

May Thy gospel's joyful sound
  Conquer sinners, comfort saints;
May the fruits of grace abound,
  Bring relief for all complaints:
Thus may all our Sabbaths prove
  Till we join the Church above.

1779

William Cowper (1731–1800)

WALKING WITH GOD

Oh! for a closer walk with God,
  A calm and heavenly frame;
A light to shine upon the road
  That leads me to the Lamb!

Where is the blessedness I knew
  When first I saw the Lord?
Where is the soul-refreshing view
  Of Jesus and his word?

What peaceful hours I once enjoyed!
  How sweet their memory still!
But they have left an aching void
  The world can never fill.

Return, O holy Dove, return,
  Sweet messenger of rest!
I hate the sins that made thee mourn,
  And drove thee from my breast.

The dearest idol I have known,
  Whate'er that idol be,
Help me to tear it from thy throne,
  And worship only thee.

So shall my walk be close with God,
  Calm and serene my frame;
So purer light shall mark the road
  That leads me to the Lamb.

1779

PRAISE FOR THE FOUNTAIN OPENED

There is a fountain filled with blood
  Drawn from Emmanuel's veins;
And sinners, plunged beneath that flood,
  Lose all their guilty stains.

The dying thief rejoiced to see
  That fountain in his day;
And there have I, as vile as he,
  Washed all my sins away.

Dear dying Lamb, thy precious blood
  Shall never lose its power,
Till all the ransomed church of God
  Be saved to sin no more.

E'er since, by faith, I saw the stream
  Thy flowing wounds supply,
Redeeming love has been my theme,
  And shall be till I die.

Then in a nobler, sweeter song,
  I'll sing thy power to save;
When this poor lisping stammering tongue
  Lies silent in the grave.

Lord, I believe thou hast prepared
  (Unworthy though I be)
For me a blood-bought free reward,
  A golden harp for me!

'T is strung, and tuned, for endless years,
  And formed by power divine,
To sound in God the Father's ears
  No other name but thine.

1779

PROSE

ESSAYS

Samuel Johnson (1709–1784)

THE GARRET

Nothing has more retarded the advancement of learning than the disposition of vulgar minds to ridicule and vilify what they cannot comprehend. All industry must be excited by hope; and as the student often proposes no other reward to himself than praise, he is easily discouraged by contempt and insult. He who brings with him into a clamorous multitude the timidity of recluse speculation, and has never hardened his front in public life, or accustomed his passions to the vicissitudes and accidents, the triumphs and defeats of mixed conversation, will blush at the stare of petulant incredulity, and suffer himself to be driven by a burst of laughter from the fortresses of demonstration. The mechanist will be afraid to assert before hardy contradiction, the possibility of tearing down bulwarks with a silkworm's thread; and the astronomer of relating the rapidity of light, the distance of the fixed stars, and the height of the lunar mountains.

If I could by any efforts have shaken off this cowardice, I had not sheltered myself under a borrowed name, nor applied to you for the means of communicating to the public the theory of a garret; a subject which, except some slight and transient strictures, has been hitherto neglected by those who were best qualified to adorn it, either for want of leisure to prosecute the various researches in which a nice discussion must engage them, or because it requires such diversity of knowledge, and such extent of curiosity, as is scarcely to be found in any single intellect; or perhaps others foresaw the tumults which would be raised against them, and confined their knowledge to their own breasts, and abandoned prejudice and folly to the direction of chance.

That the professors of literature generally reside in the highest stories, has been immemorially observed. The wisdom of the ancients was well acquainted with the intellectual advantages of an elevated situation: why else were the Muses stationed on Olympus or Parnassus by those who could with equal right have raised them bowers in the vale of Tempe, or erected their altars among the flexures of Meander? Why was Jove himself nursed upon a mountain? or why did the goddess, when the prize of beauty was contested, try the cause upon the top of Ida? Such were the fictions by which the great masters of the earlier ages endeavoured to inculcate to posterity the importance of a garret, which, though they had been long obscured by the negligence and ignorance of succeeding times, were well enforced by the celebrated symbol of Pythagoras, *ἀνεμῶν πνεόντων τὴν ἠχὼ προσκύνει*; 'when the wind blows, worship its echo.' This could not but be understood by his disciples as an inviolable injunction to live in a garret, which I have found frequently visited by the echo and the wind. Nor was the tradition wholly obliterated in the age of Augustus, for Tibullus evidently congratulates himself upon his garret, not without some allusion to the Pythagorean precept:

Quam juvat immites ventos audire cubantem —
Aut, gelidas hybernus aquas cum fuderit auster,
Securum somnos, imbre juvante, sequi!

How sweet in sleep to pass the careless hours,
Lulled by the beating winds and dashing showers!

And it is impossible not to discover the fondness of Lucretius, an earlier writer, for a garret, in his description of the lofty towers of serene learning, and of the pleasure with which a wise man looks down upon the confused and erratick state of the world moving below him:

Sed nil dulcius est, bene quam munita tenere
Edita doctrina sapientum templa serena;
Despicere unde queas alios, passimque videre
Errare, atque viam palanteis quœrere vitæ.

—'T is sweet thy labouring steps to guide
To virtue's heights, with wisdom well supplied,
And all the magazines of learning fortified:
From thence to look below on human kind,
Bewildered in the maze of life, and blind.
— Dryden

The institution has, indeed, continued to our own time; the garret is still the usual receptacle of the philosopher and poet, but this, like many ancient customs, is perpetuated only by an accidental imitation, without knowledge of the original reason for which it was established.

Causa latet; res est notissima.
The cause is secret, but the effect is known.
— Addison

Conjectures have, indeed, been advanced concerning these habitations of literature, but without much satisfaction to the judicious inquirer. Some have imagined that the garret is generally chosen by the wits as most easily rented; and concluded that no man rejoices in his aërial abode, but on the days of payment. Others suspect, that a garret is chiefly convenient, as it is remoter than any other part of the house from the outer door, which is often observed to be infested by visitants, who talk incessantly of beer, or linen, or a coat, and repeat the same sounds every morning, and sometimes again in the afternoon, without any variation, except that they grow daily more importunate and clamourous, and raise their voices in time from mournful murmurs to raging vociferations. This eternal monotony is always detestable to a man whose chief pleasure is to enlarge his knowledge, and vary his ideas. Others talk of freedom from noise, and abstraction from common business or amusements; and some, yet more visionary, tell us that the faculties are enlarged by open prospects, and that the fancy is more at liberty, when the eye ranges without confinement.

These conveniences may perhaps all be found in a well-chosen garret; but surely they cannot be supposed sufficiently important to have operated unvariably upon different climates, distant ages, and separate nations. Of an universal practice, there must still be presumed an universal cause, which, however recondite and abstruse, may be perhaps reserved to make me illustrious by its discovery, and you by its promulgation.

It is universally known that the faculties of the mind are invigorated or weakened by the state of the body, and that the body is in a great measure regulated by the various compressions of the ambient element.

The effects of the air in the production or cure of corporeal maladies have been acknowledged from the time of Hippocrates; but no man has yet sufficiently considered how far it may influence the operations of the genius, though every day affords instances of local understanding, of wits and reasoners, whose faculties are adapted to some single spot, and who, when they are removed to any other place, sink at once into silence and stupidity. I have discovered, by a long series of observations, that invention and elocution suffer great impediments from dense and impure vapours, and that the tenuity of a defecated air at a proper distance from the surface of the earth, accelerates the fancy, and sets at liberty those intellectual powers which were before shackled by too strong attraction, and unable to expand themselves under the pressure of a gross atmosphere. I have found dulness to quicken into sentiment in a thin ether, as water, though not very hot, boils in a receiver partly exhausted; and heads, in appearance empty, have teemed with notions upon rising ground, as the flaccid sides of a football would have swelled out into stiffness and extension.

For this reason I never think myself qualified to judge decisively of any man's faculties, whom I have only known in one degree of elevation; but take some opportunity of attending him from the cellar to the garret, and try upon him all the various degrees of rarefaction and condensation, tension and laxity. If he is neither vivacious aloft, nor serious below, I then consider him as hopeless; but as it seldom happens, that I do not find the temper to which the texture of his brain is fitted, I accommodate him in time with a tube of mercury, first marking the points most favourable to his intellects, according to rules which I have long studied, and which I may, perhaps, reveal to mankind in a complete treatise of barometrical pneumatology.

Another cause of the gaiety and sprightliness of the dwellers in garrets is probably the increase of that vertiginous motion, with which we are carried round by the diurnal revolution of the earth. The power of agitation upon the spirits is well known; every man has felt his heart lightened in a rapid vehicle, or on a galloping horse; and nothing is plainer, than that he who towers to the fifth story, is whirled through more space by every circumrotation, than another that grovels upon the ground floor. The nations between the tropicks are known to be fiery, inconstant, inventive, and fanciful; because, living at the utmost length of the earth's diameter, they are carried about with more swiftness than those whom nature has placed nearer to the poles; and therefore, as it becomes a wise man to struggle with the inconveniences of his country, whenever celerity and acuteness are requisite, we must actuate our languor by taking a few turns round the centre in a garret.

If you imagine that I ascribe to air and motion effects which they cannot produce, I desire you to consult your own memory, and consider whether you have never known a man acquire reputation in his garret, which, when fortune or a patron had placed him upon the first floor, he was unable to maintain; and who never recovered his former vigour of understanding, till he was restored to his original situation. That a garret will make every man a wit, I am very far from supposing; I know there are some who would continue blockheads even on the summit of the Andes, or on the peak of Teneriffe. But let not any man be considered as unimprovable till this potent remedy has been tried; for perhaps he was formed to be great only in a garret, as the joiner of Aretæus was rational in no other place but his own shop.

I think a frequent removal to various distances from the centre, so necessary to a just estimate of intellectual abilities, and consequently of so great use in education, that if I hoped that the publick could be persuaded to so expensive an experiment, I would propose, that there should be a cavern dug, and a tower erected, like those which Bacon describes in Solomon's house, for the expansion and concentration of understanding, according to the exigence of different employments or constitutions. Perhaps some that fume away in meditations upon time and space in the tower, might compose tables of interest at a certain depth; and he that upon level ground stagnates in silence, or creeps in narrative, might, at the height of half a mile, ferment into merriment, sparkle with repartee, and froth with declamation.

Addison observes, that we may find the heat of Virgil's climate, in some lines of his *Georgic:* so, when I read a composition, I immediately determine the height of the author's habitation. As an elaborate performance is commonly said to smell of the lamp, my commendation of a noble thought, a sprightly sally, or a bold figure, is to pronounce it fresh from the garret; an expression which would break from me upon the perusal of most of your papers, did I not believe, that you sometimes quit the garret, and ascend into the cockloft.

[Hypertatus]

Tuesday, April 30, 1751

Oliver Goldsmith (1728–1774)

JUSTICE AND GENEROSITY

Lysippus is a man whose greatness of soul the whole world admires. His generosity is such, that it prevents a demand, and saves the receiver the trouble and the confusion of a request. His liberality also, does not oblige more by its greatness, than by his inimitable grace in giving. Sometimes he even distributes his bounties to strangers, and has been known to do good offices to those who professed themselves his enemies. All the world are unanimous in the praise of his generosity; there is only one sort of people who complain of his conduct. Lysippus does not pay his debts.

It is no difficult matter to account for a conduct so seemingly incompatible with itself. There is greatness in being generous, and there is only simple justice in satisfying his creditors. Generosity is the part of a soul raised above the vulgar. There is in it something of what we admire in heroes, and praise with a degree of rapture. Justice, on the contrary, is a mere mechanic virtue, only fit for tradesmen, and what is practiced by every broker in Change Alley.

In paying his debts a man barely does his duty, and it is an action attended with no sort of glory. Should Lysippus satisfy his creditors, who would be at the pains of telling it to the world? Generosity is a virtue of a very different complexion. It is raised above duty, and from its elevation attracts the attention and the praises of us little mortals below.

In this manner do men generally reason upon justice and generosity. The first is despised, though a virtue essential to good society; and the other attracts our esteem, which too frequently proceeds from an impetuosity of temper, rather directed by vanity than reason. Lysippus is told that his banker asks a debt of forty pounds, and that a distressed acquaintance petitions for the same sum. He gives it, without hesitating, to the latter; for he demands as a favour what the fromer requires as a debt.

Mankind in general are not sufficiently acquainted with the import of the word justice: it is commonly believed to consist only in a performance of those duties to which the laws of society can oblige us. This I allow is sometimes the import of the word, and in this sense justice is distinquished from equity; but there is a justice still more extensive, and which can be shown to embrace all the virtues united.

Justice may be defined, that virtue which impels us to give to every person what is his due. In this extended sense of the word, it comprehends the practice of every virtue which reason prescribes, or society should expect. Our duty to our Maker, to each other, and to ourselves, is fully answered, if we give them what we owe them. Thus justice, properly speaking, is the only virtue, and all the rest have their origin in it.

The qualities of candour, fortitude, charity, and generosity, for instance, are not, in their own nature, virtues; and, if ever they deserve the title, it is owing only to justice, which impels and directs them. Without such a moderator, candour might become indiscretion, fortitude obstinacy, charity imprudence, and generosity mistaken profusion.

A disinterested action, if it be not conducted by justice, is at best indifferent in its nature, and not unfrequently even turns to vice. The expenses of society, of presents, of entertainment, and the other helps to cheerfulness, are actions merely indifferent, when not repugnant to a better method of disposing of our superfluities; but they become vicious when they obstruct or exhaust our abilities from a more virtuous disposition of our circumstances.

True generosity is a duty as indispensably necessary as those imposed upon us by law. It is a rule imposed upon us by reason, which should be the sovereign law of a rational being. But this generosity does not consist in obeying every impulse of humanity, in following blind passion for our guide, and impairing our circumstances by present benefactions, so as to render us incapable of future ones.

Misers are generally characterized as men without honour, or without humanity, who live only to accumulate, and to this passion sacrifice every other happiness. They have been described as madmen, who, in the midst of abundance, banish every pleasure, and make, from imaginary wants, real necessities. But few, very few, correspond to this exaggerated picture; and, perhaps, there is not one in whom all these circumstances are found united. Instead of this, we find the sober and the industrious branded by the vain and the idle, with this odious appellation; men who, by frugality and labour, raise themselves above their equals, and contribute their share of industry to the common stock.

Whatever the vain or the ignorant may say, well were it for society had we more of this character amongst us. In general, these close men are found at last the true benefactors of society. With an avaricious man we seldom lose in our dealings, but too frequently in our commerce with prodigality.

A French priest, whose name was Godinot, went for a long time by the name of the Griper. He refused to relieve the most apparent wretchedness, and by a skilful management of his vineyard, had the good fortune to acquire immense sums of money. The inhabitants of Rheims, who were his fellow-citizens, detested him, and the populace, who seldom love a miser, wherever he went, received him with contempt. He still, however, continued his former simplicity of life, his amazing and unremitted frugality. This good man had long perceived the wants of the poor in the city, particularly in having no water but what they were obliged to buy at an advanced price; wherefore that whole fortune which he had been amassing, he laid out in an aqueduct, by which he did the poor more useful and lasting service, than if he had distributed his whole income in charity every day at his door.

Among men long conversant with books, we too frequently find those misplaced virtues, of which I have been now complaining. We find the studious animated with a strong passion for the great virtues, as they are mistakenly called, and utterly forgetful of the ordinary ones. The declamations of philosophy are generally rather exhausted on these supererogatory duties, than on such as are indispensably necessary. A man, therefore, who has taken his ideas of mankind from study alone, generally comes into the world with a heart melting at every fictitious distress. Thus he is induced, by misplaced liberality, to put himself into the indigent circumstances of the person he relieves.

I shall conclude this paper with the advice of one of the ancients, to a young man whom he saw giving away all his substance to pretended distress. 'It is possible that the person you relieve may be an honest man; and I know that you who relieve him are such. You see, then, by your generosity, you only rob a man who is certainly deserving, to bestow it on one who may possibly be a rogue. And while you are unjust in rewarding uncertain merit, you are doubly guilty by stripping yourself.'

Saturday, October 20, 1759

ADVERSITIES OF POETS

I fancy the character of a poet is in every country the same: fond of enjoying the present, careless of the future; his conversation that of a man of sense, his actions those of a fool; of fortitude able to stand unmoved at the bursting of an earthquake, yet of sensibility to be affected by the breaking of a tea-cup; — such is his character, which, considered in every light, is the very opposite of that which leads to riches.

The poets of the west are as remarkable for their indigence as their genius, and yet, among the numerous hospitals designed to relieve the poor, I have heard of but one erected for the benefit of decayed authors. This was founded by Pope Urban the Eighth, and called the retreat of the incurables, intimating, that it was equally impossible to reclaim the patients, who sued for reception, from poverty or from poetry. To be sincere, were I to send you an account of the lives of the western poets, either ancient or modern, I fancy you would think me employed in collecting materials for an history of human wretchedness.

Homer is the first poet and beggar of note among the ancients: he was blind, and sang his ballads about the streets; but it is observed, that his mouth was more frequently filled with verses than with bread. Plautus the comic poet was better off; he had two trades, he was a poet for his diversion, and helped to turn a mill in order to gain a livelihood. Terence was a slave, and Boëthius died in jail.

Among the Italians, Paulo Borghese, almost as good a poet as Tasso, knew fourteen different trades, and yet died because he could get employment in none. Tasso himself, who had the most amiable character of all poets, has often been obliged to borrow a crown from some friend, in order to pay for a month's subsistence; he has left us a pretty sonnet, addressed to his cat, in which he begs the light of her eyes to write by, being too poor to afford himself a candle. But Bentivoglio, poor Bentivoglio! chiefly demands our pity. His comedies will last with the Italian language: he dissipated a noble fortune in acts of charity and benevolence; but, falling into misery in his old age, was refused to be admitted into an hospital which he himself had erected.

In Spain, it is said, the great Cervantes died of hunger; and it is certain, that the famous Camoëns ended his days in an hospital.

If we turn to France, we shall there find even stronger instances of the ingratitude of the public. Vaugelas, one of the politest writers, and one of the honestest men of his time, was surnamed the Owl, from his being obliged to keep within all day, and venture out only by night, through fear of his creditors. His last will is very remarkable. After having bequeathed all his worldly substance to the discharging his debts, he goes on thus: 'But as there still may remain some creditors unpaid, even after all that I have shall have been disposed of, in such a case, it is my last will, that my body should be sold to the surgeons to the best advantage, and that the purchase should go to the discharging those debts which I owe to society; so that if I could not, while living, at least when dead, I may be useful.'

Cassander was one of the greatest geniuses of his time, yet all his merit could not procure him a bare subsistence. Being by degrees driven into an hatred of all mankind, from the little pity he found amongst them, he even ventured at last ungratefully to impute his calamities to Providence. In his last agonies, when the priest entreated him to rely on the justice of Heaven, and ask mercy from him that made him — 'If God,' replies he, 'has shown me no justice here, what reason have I to expect any from him hereafter?' But being answered, that a suspension of justice was no argument that should induce us to doubt of its reality; 'Let me intreat you,' continued his confessor, 'by all that is dear, to be reconciled to God, your father, your maker, and friend.' 'No,' replied the exasperated wretch, 'you know the manner in which he left me to live; and,' pointing to the straw on which he was stretched, 'you see the manner in which he leaves me to die!'

But the sufferings of the poet in other countries is nothing when compared to his distresses here; the names of Spenser and Otway, Butler and Dryden, are every day mentioned as a national reproach: some of them lived in a state of precarious indigence, and others literally died of hunger.

At present, the few poets of England no longer depend on the great for subsistence; they have now no other patrons but the public, and the public collectively considered, is a good and a generous master. It is, indeed, too frequently mistaken as to the merits of every candidate for favour; but to make amends, it is never mistaken long. A performance indeed may be forced for a time into reputation, but, destitute of real merit, it soon sinks; time, the touchstone of what is truly valuable, will soon discover the fraud, and an author should never arrogate to himself any share of success, till his works have been read at least ten years with satisfaction.

A man of letters at present, whose works are valuable, is perfectly sensible of their value. Every polite member of the community, by buying what he writes, contributes to reward him. The ridicule, therefore, of living in a garret, might have been wit in the last age, but continues such no longer, because no longer true. A writer of real merit now may easily be rich, if his heart be set only on fortune: and for those who have no merit, it is but fit that such should remain in merited obscurity. He may now refuse an invitation to dinner, without fearing to incur his patron's displeasure, or to starve by remaining at home. He may now venture to appear in company with just such clothes as other men generally wear, and talk even to princes with all the conscious superiority of wisdom. Though he cannot boast of fortune here, yet he can bravely assert the dignity of independence.

1760

CRITICISM

Samuel Johnson (1709–1784)

PREFACE TO THE ENGLISH DICTIONARY

It is the fate of those who toil at the lower employments of life, to be rather driven by the fear of evil, than attracted by the prospect of good; to be exposed to censure, without hope of praise; to be disgraced by miscarriage, or punished for neglect, where success would have been without applause, and diligence without reward.

Among these unhappy mortals is the writer of dictionaries; whom mankind have considered, not as the pupil, but the slave of science, the pioneer of literature, doomed only to remove rubbish and clear obstructions from the paths through which Learning and Genius press forward to conquest and glory, without bestowing a smile on the humble drudge that facilitates their progress. Every other author may aspire to praise; the lexicographer can only hope to escape reproach, and even this negative recompense has been yet granted to very few.

I have, notwithstanding this discouragement, attempted a Dictionary of the English Language, which, while it was employed in the cultivation of every species of literature, has itself been hitherto neglected; suffered to spread, under the direction of chance, into wild exuberance; resigned to the tyranny of time and fashion; and exposed to the corruptions of ignorance, and caprices of innovation.

When I took the first survey of my undertaking, I found our speech copious without order, and energetick without rule: wherever I turned my view, there was perplexity to be disentangled and confusion to be regulated; choice was to be made out of boundless variety, without any established principle of selection; adulterations were to be detected, without a settled test of purity; and modes of expression to be rejected or received, without the suffrages of any writers of classical reputation or acknowledged authority.

Having therefore no assistance but from general grammar, I applied myself to the perusal of our writers; and noting whatever might be of use to ascertain or illustrate any word or phrase, accumulated in time the materials of a dictionary, which, by degrees, I reduced to method, establishing to myself, in the progress of the work, such rules as experience and analogy suggested to me; experience, which practice and observation were continually increasing; and analogy, which, though in some words obscure, was evident in others.

In adjusting the *Orthography*, which has been to this time unsettled and fortuitous, I found it necessary to distinguish those irregularities that are inherent in our tongue, and perhaps coëval with it, from others which the ignorance or negligence of later writers has produced. Every language has its anomalies, which though inconvenient, and in themselves once unnecessary, must be tolerated among the imperfections of human things, and which require only to be registered, that they may not be increased, and ascertained, that they may not be confounded: but every language has likewise its improprieties and absurdities, which it is the duty of the lexicographer to correct or proscribe.

As language was at its beginning merely oral, all words of necessary or common use were spoken before they were written; and while they were unfixed by any visible signs, must have been spoken with great diversity, as we now observe those who cannot read to catch sounds imperfectly, and utter them negligently. When this wild and barbarous jargon was first reduced to an alphabet, every penman endeavoured to express, as he could, the sounds which he was accustomed to pronounce or to receive, and vitiated in writing such words as were already vitiated in speech. The powers of the letters, when they were applied to a new language, must have been vague and unsettled, and therefore different hands would exhibit the same sound by different combinations.

From this uncertain pronunciation arise in great part the various dialects of the same country, which will always be observed to grow fewer, and less different, as books are multiplied; and from this arbitrary representation of sounds by letters, proceeds that diversity of spelling observable in the Saxon remains, and I suppose in the first books of every nation, which perplexes or destroys analogy, and produces anomalous formations, that, being once incorporated, can never be afterward dismissed or reformed.

Of this kind are the derivatives *length* from *long*, *strength* from *strong*, *darling* from *dear*, *breadth* from *broad*, from *dry*, *drought*, and from *high*, *height*, which Milton, in zeal for analogy, writes *highth: Quid te exempta juvat spinis de pluribus una?* to change all would be too much, and to change one is nothing.

This uncertainty is most frequent in the vowels, which are so capriciously pronounced, and so differently modified, by accident or affectation, not only in every province, but in every mouth, that to them, as is well known to etymologists, little regard is to be shown in the deduction of one language from another.

Such defects are not errours in orthography, but spots of barbarity impressed so deep in the English language, that criticism can never wash them away: these, therefore, must be permitted to remain untouched; but many words have likewise been altered by accident, or depraved by ignorance, as the pronunciation of the vulgar has been weakly followed; and some still continue to be variously written, as authors differ in their care or skill: of these it was proper to inquire the true orthography, which I have always considered as depending on their derivation, and have therefore referred them to their original languages: thus I write *enchant*, *enchantment*, *enchanter*, after the French, and *incantation* after the Latin; thus *entire* is chosen rather than *intire*, because it passed to us not from the Latin *integer*, but from the French *entier*.

Of many words it is difficult to say whether they were immediately received from the Latin or the French, since, at the time when we had dominions in France, we had Latin service in our churches. It is however, my opinion, that the French generally supplied us; for we have few Latin words among the terms of domestick use, which are not French; but many French, which are very remote from Latin.

Even in words of which the derivation is apparent, I have been often obliged to sacrifice uniformity to custom; thus I write, in compliance with a numberless majority, *convey* and *inveigh*, *deceit* and *receipt*, *fancy* and *phantom*, sometimes the derivative varies from the primitive, as *explain* and *explanation*, *repeat*, and *repetition*.

Some combinations of letters having the same power, are used indifferently without any discoverable reason of choice, as in *choak*, *choke; soap*, *sope; fewel*, *fuel*, and many others; which I have sometimes inserted twice, that those who search for them under either form, may not search in vain.

In examining the orthography of any doubtful word, the mode of spelling by which it is inserted in the series of the dictionary, is to be considered as that to which I give, perhaps not often rashly, the preference. I have left, in the examples, to every author his own practice unmolested, that the reader may balance suffrages, and judge between us: but this question is not always to be determined by reputed or by real learning; some men, intent upon greater things, have thought little on sounds and derivations; some, knowing in the ancient tongues, have neglected those in which our words are commonly to be sought. Thus Hammond writes *fecibleness*, for *feasibleness*, because I suppose he imagined it derived immediately from the Latin; and some words, such as *dependant*, *dependent; dependance*, *dependence*, vary their final syllable, as one or another language is present to the writer.

In this part of the work, where caprice has long wantoned without control, and vanity sought praise by petty reformation, I have endeavoured to proceed with a scholar's reverence for antiquity, and a grammarian's regard to the genius of our tongue. I have attempted few alterations, and among those few, perhaps the greater part is from the modern to the ancient practice; and I hope I may be allowed to recommend to those whose thoughts have been perhaps employed too anxiously on verbal singularities, not to disturb, upon narrow views, or for minute propriety, the orthography of their fathers. It has been asserted, that for the law to be *known*, is of more importance than to be *right.* 'Change,' says Hooker, 'is not made without inconvenience, even from worse to better.' There is in constancy and stability a general and lasting advantage, which will always overbalance the slow improvements of gradual correction. Much less ought our written language to comply with the corruptions of oral utterance, or copy that which every variation of time or place makes different from itself, and imitate those changes, which will again be changed, while imitation is employed in observing them.

This recommendation of steadiness and uniformity does not proceed from an opinion, that particular combinations of letters have much influence on human happiness; or that truth may not be successfully taught by modes of spelling fanciful and erroneous; I am not yet so lost in lexicography as to forget that *words are the daughters of earth, and that things are the sons of heaven.* Language is only the instrument of science, and words are but the signs of ideas: I wish, however, that the instrument might be less apt to decay, and that signs might be permanent, like the things which they denote.

In settling the orthography, I have not wholly neglected the pronunciation, which I have directed, by printing an accent upon the acute or elevated syllable. It will sometimes be found, that the accent is placed by the author quoted, on a different syllable from that marked in the alphabetical series: it is then to be understood, that custom has varied, or that the author has, in my opinion, pronounced wrong. Short directions are sometimes given where the sound of letters is irregular; and if they are sometimes omitted, defect in such minute observations will be more easily excused, than superfluity.

In the investigation both of the orthography and signification of words, their Etymology was necessarily to be considered, and they were therefore to be divided into primitives and derivatives. A primitive word, is that which can be traced no further to any English root; thus *circumspect, circumvent, circumstance, delude, concave,* and *complicate,* though compounds in the Latin, are to us primitives. Derivatives, are all those that can be referred to any word in English of greater simplicity.

The derivatives I have referred to their primitives, with an accuracy sometimes needless; for who does not see that *remcteness* comes from *remote, lovely* from *love, concavity* from *concave,* and *demonstrative* from *demonstrate?* But this grammatical exuberance the scheme of my work did not allow me to repress. It is of great importance, in examining the general fabrick of a language, to trace one word from another, by noting the usual modes of derivation and inflection; and uniformity must be preserved in systematical works, though sometimes at the expence of particular propriety.

Among other derivatives I have been careful to insert and elucidate the anomalous plurals of nouns and preterities of verbs, which in the Teutonick dialects are very frequent, and, though familiar to those who have always used them, interrupt and embarrass the learners of our language.

The two languages from which our primitives have been derived are the Roman and Teutonick: under the Roman I comprehend the French and provincial tongues; and under the Teutonick range the Saxon, German, and all their kindred dialects. Most of our polysyllables are Roman, and our words of one syllable are very often Teutonick.

In assigning the Roman original, it has perhaps sometimes happened that I have mentioned only the Latin, when the word was borrowed from the French; and considering myself as employed only in the illustration of my own language, I have not been very careful to observe whether the

Latin word be pure or barbarous, or the French elegant or obsolete.

For the Teutonick etymologies, I am commonly indebted to Junius and Skinner, the only names which I have forborne to quote when I copied their books; not that I might appropriate their labours or usurp their honours, but that I might spare a perpetual repetition by one general acknowledgment. Of these, whom I ought not to mention but with reverence due to instructors and benefactors, Junius appears to have excelled in extent of learning, and Skinner in rectitude of understanding. Junius was accurately skilled in all the northern languages, Skinner probably examined the ancient and remoter dialects only by occasional inspection into dictionaries; but the learning of Junius is often of no other use than to show him a track by which he may deviate from his purpose, to which Skinner always presses forward by the shortest way. Skinner is often ignorant, but never ridiculous: Junius is always full of knowledge; but his variety distracts his judgment, and his learning is very frequently disgraced by his absurdities.

The votaries of the northern muses will not perhaps easily restrain their indignation, when they find the name of Junius thus degraded by a disadvantageous comparison; but whatever reverence is due to his diligence, or his attainments, it can be no criminal degree of censoriousness to charge that etymologist with want of judgment, who can seriously derive *dream* from *drama*, because *life is a drama*, and *a drama is a dream;* and who declares with a tone of defiance, that no man can fail to derive *moan* from *μόνος*, *monos*, *single* or *solitary*, who considers that grief naturally loves to be alone.

Our knowledge of the northern literature is so scanty, that of words undoubtedly Teutonick, the original is not always to be found in any ancient language; and I have therefore inserted Dutch or German substitutes, which I consider not as radical, but parallel, not as the parents, but sisters of the English.

The words which are represented as thus related by descent or cognation, do not always agree in sense; for it is incident to words, as to their authors, to degenerate from their ancestors, and to change their manners when they change their country. It is sufficient, in etymological inquiries, if the senses of kindred words be found such as may easily pass into each other, or such as may both be referred to one general idea.

The etymology, so far as it is yet known, was easily found in the volumes where it is particularly and professedly delivered; and by proper attention to the rules of derivation, the orthography was soon adjusted. But to COLLECT the WORDS of our language was a task of greater difficulty: the deficiency of dictionaries was immediately apparent; and when they were exhausted, what was yet wanting must be sought by fortuitous and unguided excursions into books, and gleaned as industry should find, or chance should offer it, in the boundless chaos of a living speech. My search, however, has been either skilful or lucky; for I have much augmented the vocabulary.

As my design was a dictionary, common or appellative, I have omitted all words which have relation to proper names; such as *Arian*, *Socinian*, *Calvinist*, *Benedictine*, *Mahometan;* but have retained those of a more general nature, as *Heathen*, *Pagan*.

Of the terms of art I have received such as could be found either in books of science or technical dictionaries; and have often inserted, from philosophical writers, words which are supported perhaps only by a single authority, and which being not admitted into general use, stand yet as candidates or probationers, and must depend for their adoption on the suffrage of futurity.

The words which our authors have introduced by their knowledge of foreign languages, or ignorance of their own, by vanity or wantonness, by compliance with fashion or lust of innovation, I have registered as they occurred, though commonly only to censure them and warn others against the folly of naturalizing useless foreigners to the injury of the natives.

I have not rejected any by design, merely because they were unnecessary or exuberant; but have received those which by different writers have been differently formed, as *viscid, viscidity, viscous,* and *viscosity.*

Compounded or double words I have seldom noted, except when they obtain a signification different from that which the components have in their simple state. Thus *highwayman, woodman,* and *horsecourser,* require an explanation; but of *thieflike,* or *coachdriver* no notice was needed, because the primitives contain the meaning of the compounds.

Words arbitrarily formed by a constant and settled analogy, like diminutive adjectives in *ish,* as *greenish, bluish;* adverbs in *ly,* as *dully, openly;* substantives in *ness,* as *vileness, faultiness;* were less diligently sought, and sometimes have been omitted, when I had no authority that invited me to insert them; not that they are not genuine and regular offsprings of English roots, but because their relation to the primitive being always the same, their signification cannot be mistaken.

The verbal nouns in *ing,* such as the *keeping* of the *castle,* the *leading* of the *army,* are always neglected, or placed only to illustrate the sense of the verb, except when they signify things as well as actions, and have therefore a plural number, as *dwelling, living;* or have an absolute and abstract signification, as *colouring, painting, learning.*

The participles are likewise omitted, unless, by signifying rather habit or quality than action, they take the nature of adjectives; as a *thinking* man, a man of prudence; a *pacing* horse, a horse that can pace: these I have ventured to call *participial adjectives.* But neither are these always inserted, because they are commonly to be understood without any danger of mistake, by consulting the verb.

Obsolete words are admitted when they are found in authors not obsolete, or when they have any force or beauty that may deserve revival.

As composition is one of the chief characteristicks of a language, I have endeavoured to make some reparation for the universal negligence of my predecessors, by inserting great numbers of compounded words, as may be found under *after, fore, new, night, fair,* and many more. These, numerous as they are, might be multiplied, but that use and curiosity are here satisfied, and the frame of our language and modes of our combination amply discovered.

Of some forms of composition, such as that by which *re* is prefixed to note *repetition,* and *un* to signify *contrariety* or *privation,* all the examples cannot be accumulated, because the use of these particles, if not wholly arbitrary, is so little limited, that they are hourly affixed to new words as occasion requires, or is imagined to require them.

There is another kind of composition more frequent in our language than perhaps in any other, from which arises to foreigners the greatest difficulty. We modify the signification of many verbs by a particle subjoined; as to *come off,* to escape by a fetch; to *fall on,* to attack; to *fall off,* to apostatize; to *break off,* to stop abruptly; to *bear out,* to justify; to *fall in,* to comply; to *give over,* to cease; to *set off,* to embellish; to *set in,* to begin a continual tenour; to *set out,* to begin a course or journey; to *take off,* to copy; with innumerable expressions of the same kind, of which some appear wildly irregular, being so far distant from the sense of the simple words, that no sagacity will be able to trace the steps by which they arrived at the present use. These I have noted with great care; and though I cannot flatter myself that the collection is complete, I believe I have so far assisted the students of our language, that this kind of phraseology will be no longer insuperable; and the combinations of verbs and particles, by chance omitted, will be easily explained by comparison with those that may be found.

Many words yet stand supported only by the name of *Bailey, Ainsworth, Philips,* or the contracted *Dict.* for *Dictionaries* subjoined; of these I am not always certain that they are read in any book but the works of lexicographers. Of such I have omitted many, because I had never read them; and many I have inserted, because they may perhaps exist, though they have escaped my notice: they are, however, to be considered as resting only upon the credit of former dictionaries. Others, which I considered as useful, or know to be proper, though I could not at present support them by authorities, I have suffered to stand upon my own attestation, claiming the same privilege with my predecessors, of being sometimes credited without proof.

The words, thus selected and disposed, are grammatically considered; they are referred to the different parts of speech; traced, when they are irregularly inflected, through their various terminations; and illustrated by observations, not indeed of great or striking importance, separately considered, but necessary to the elucidation of our language, and hitherto neglected or forgotten by English grammarians.

That part of my work on which I expect malignity most frequently to fasten, is the *explanation;* in which I cannot hope to satisfy those, who are perhaps not inclined to be pleased, since I have not always been able to satisfy myself. To interpret a language by itself is very difficult; many words cannot be explained by synonimes, because the idea signified by them has not more than one appellation; nor by paraphrase, because simple ideas cannot be described. When the nature of things is unknown, or the notion unsettled and indefinite, and various in various minds, the words by which such notions are conveyed, or such things denoted, will be ambiguous and perplexed. And such is the fate of hapless lexicography, that not only darkness, but light, impedes and distresses it; things may be not only too little, but too much known, to be happily illustrated. To explain, requires the use of terms less abstruse than that which is to be explained, and such terms cannot always be found; for as nothing can be proved but by supposing something intuitively known, and evident without proof, so nothing can be defined but by the use of words too plain to admit a definition.

Other words there are, of which the sense is too subtle and evanescent to be fixed in a paraphrase; such are all those which are by the grammarians termed *expletives,* and, in dead languages, are suffered to pass for empty sounds, of no other use than to fill a verse, or to modulate a period, but which are easily perceived in living tongues to have power and emphasis, though it be sometimes such as no other form of expression can convey.

My labour has likewise been much increased by a class of verbs too frequent in the English language, of which the signification is so loose and general, the use so vague and indeterminate, and the senses detorted so widely from the first idea, that it is hard to trace them through the maze of variation, to catch them on the brink of utter inanity, to circumscribe them by any limitations, or interpret them by any words of distinct and settled meaning; such are *bear, break, come, cast, full, get, give, do, put, set, go, run, make, take, turn, throw.* If of these the whole power is not accurately delivered, it must be remembered, that while our language is yet living, and variable by the caprice of every one that speaks it, these words are hourly shifting their relations, and can no more be ascertained in a dictionary, than a grove, in the agitation of a storm, can be accurately delineated from its picture in the water.

The particles are among all nations applied with so great latitude, that they are not easily reducible under any regular scheme of explication: this difficulty is not less, nor perhaps greater, in English, than in other languages. I have laboured them with diligence, I hope with success; such at least as can be expected in a task, which no man, however learned or sagacious, has yet been able to perform.

Some words there are which I cannot explain, because I do not understand them; these might have been omitted very often with little inconvenience, but I would not so far indulge my vanity as to decline this confession: for when Tully owns himself ignorant whether *lessus,* in the twelve tables, means a *funeral song,* or *mourning garment;* and Aristotle doubts whether οὐρεύς in the Iliad, signifies a *mule,* or *muleteer,* I may surely, without shame, leave some obscurities to happier industry, or future information.

The rigour of interpretative lexicography requires that the explanation, and the word explained, should be always reciprocal; this I have always endeavoured, but could not always attain. Words are seldom exactly synonimous; a new term was not introduced, but because the former was thought inadequate: names, therefore, have often many ideas, but few ideas have many names. It was then necessary to use the proximate word, for the deficiency of single terms can very seldom be supplied by circumlocution; nor is the inconvenience great of such mutilated interpretations, because the sense may easily be collected entire from the examples.

In every word of extensive use, it was requisite to mark the progress of its meaning, and show by what gradations of intermediate sense it has passed from its primitive to its remote and accidental signification; so that every foregoing explanation should tend to that which follows, and the series be regularly concatenated from the first notion to the last.

This is specious, but not always practicable; kindred senses may be so interwoven, that the perplexity cannot be disentangled, nor any reason be assigned why one should be ranged before the other. When the radical idea branches out into parallel ramifications, how can a consecutive series be formed of senses in their nature collateral? The shades of meaning sometimes pass imperceptibly into each other, so that though on one side they apparently differ, yet it is impossible to mark the point of contact. Ideas of the same race, though not exactly alike, are sometimes so little different, that no words can express the dissimilitude, though the mind easily perceives it when they are exhibited together; and sometimes there is such a confusion of acceptations, that discernment is wearied, and distinction puzzled, and perseverance herself hurries to an end, by crowding together what she cannot separate.

These complaints of difficulty will, by those that have never considered words beyond their popular use, be thought only the jargon of a man willing to magnify his labours, and procure veneration to his studies by involution and obscurity. But every art is obscure to those that have not learned it: this uncertainty of terms, and commixture of ideas, is well known to those who have joined philosophy with grammar; and if I have not expressed them very clearly, it must be remembered that I am speaking of that which words are insufficient to explain.

The original sense of words is often driven out of use by their metaphorical acceptations, yet must be inserted for the sake of a regular origination. Thus I know not whether *ardour* is used for *material heat*, or whether *flagrant*, in English ever signifies the same with *burning;* yet such are the primitive ideas of these words, which are therefore set first, though without examples, that the figurative senses may be commodiously deduced.

Such is the exuberance of signification which many words have obtained, that it was scarcely possible to collect all their senses; sometimes the meaning of derivatives must be sought in the mother term, and sometimes deficient explanations of the primitive may be supplied in the train of derivation. In any case of doubt or difficulty, it will be always proper to examine all the words of the same race; for some words are slightly passed over to avoid repetition, some admitted easier and clearer explanation than others, and all will be better understood, as they are considered in greater variety of structures and relations.

All the interpretations of words are not written with the same skill, or the same happiness: things equally easy in themselves, are not all equally easy to any single mind. Every writer of a long work commits errours, where there appears neither ambiguity to mislead, nor obscurity to confound him; and in a search like this, many felicities of expression will be casually overlooked, many convenient parallels will be forgotten, and many particulars will admit improvement from a mind utterly unequal to the whole performance.

But many seeming faults are to be imputed rather to the nature of the undertaking, than the negligence of the performer. Thus some explanations are unavoidably reciprocal or circular, as *hind, the female of the stag; stag, the male of the hind:* sometimes easier words are changed into harder, as *burial*, into *sepulture*, or *interment*, *drier* into *desiccative*, *dryness* into *siccity* or *aridity*, *fit* into *paroxysm;* for the easiest word, whatever it be, can never be translated into one more easy. But easiness and difficulty are merely relative; and if the present prevalence of our language should invite foreigners to this Dictionary, many will be assisted by those words which now seem only to increase or produce obscurity. For this reason I have endeavoured frequently to join a Teutonick and Roman interpretation, as to *cheer*, to *gladden*, or *exhilarate*, that every learner of English may be assisted by his own tongue.

The solution of all difficulties, and the supply of all defects must be sought in the examples, subjoined to the various senses of each word, and ranged according to the time of their authors.

When I first collected these authorities, I was desirous that every quotation should be useful to some other end than the illustration of a word; I therefore extracted from philosophers principles of science; from historians remarkable facts; from chymists complete processes; from divines striking exhortations; and from poets beautiful descriptions. Such is design, while it is yet at a distance from execution. When the time called upon me to range this accumulation of elegance and wisdom into an alphabetical series, I soon discovered that the bulk of my volumes would fright away the student, and was forced to depart from my scheme of including all that was pleasing or useful in English literature, and reduce my transcripts very often to clusters of words, in which scarcely any meaning is retained; thus to the weariness of copying, I was condemned to add the vexation of expunging. Some passages I have yet spared, which may relieve the labour of verbal searches, and intersperse with verdure and flowers the dusty deserts of barren philology.

The examples, thus mutilated, are no longer to be considered as conveying the sentiments or doctrine of their authors; the word for the sake of which they are inserted, with all its appendant clauses, has been carefully preserved; but it may sometimes happen, by hasty detruncation, that the general tendency of the sentence may be changed: the divine may desert his tenets, or the philosopher his system.

Some of the examples have been taken from writers who were never mentioned as masters of elegance, or models of style; but words must be sought where they are used; and in what pages, eminent for purity, can terms of manufacture or agriculture be found? Many quotations serve no other purpose than that of proving the bare existence of words, and are therefore selected with less scrupulousness than those which are to teach their structures and relations.

My purpose was to admit no testimony of living authors, that I might not be misled by partiality, and that none of my contemporaries might have reason to complain; nor have I departed from this resolution, but when some performance of uncommon excellence excited my veneration, when my memory supplied me, from late books, with an example that was wanting, or when my heart, in the tenderness of friendship, solicited admission for a favourite name.

So far have I been from any care to grace my pages with modern decorations, that I have studiously endeavoured to collect examples and authorities from the writers before the restoration, whose works I regard as *the wells of English undefiled*, as the pure sources of genuine diction. Our language, for almost a century, has, by the concurrence of many causes, been gradually departing from its original Teutonick character, and deviating towards a Gallick structure and phraseology, from which it ought to be our endeavour to recall it, by making our ancient volumes the ground work of style, admitting among the additions of later times, only such as may supply real deficiencies, such as are readily adopted by the genius of our tongue, and incorporate easily with our native idioms.

But as every language has a time of rudeness antecedent to perfection, as well as of false refinement and declension, I have been cautious lest my zeal for antiquity might drive me into times too remote, and crowd my book with words now no longer understood. I have fixed Sidney's work for the boundary, beyond which I make few excursions. From the authors which rose in the time of Elizabeth, a speech might be formed adequate to all the purposes of use and elegance. If the language of theology were extracted from Hooker and the translation of the Bible; the terms of natural knowledge from Bacon; the phrases of policy, war, and navigation from Raleigh; the dialect of poetry and fiction from Spenser and Sidney; and the diction of common life from Shakespeare, few ideas would be lost to mankind, for want of English words, in which they might be expressed.

It is not sufficient that a word is found, unless it be so combined as that its meaning is apparently determined by the tract and tenour of the sentence; such passages I have therefore chosen, and when it happened that any author gave a definition of a term, or such an explanation as is equivalent to a definition, I have placed his authority as a supplement to my own, without regard to the chronological order, that is otherwise observed.

Some words, indeed, stand unsupported by any authority, but they are commonly derivative nouns or adverbs, formed from their primitives by regular and constant analogy, or names of things seldom occurring in books, or words of which I have reason to doubt the existence.

There is more danger of censure from the multiplicity than paucity of examples; authorities will sometimes seem to have been accumulated without necessity or use, and perhaps some will be found, which might, without loss, have been omitted. But a work of this kind is not hastily to be charged with superfluities; those quotations, which to careless or unskilful perusers appear only to repeat the same sense, will often exhibit, to a more accurate examiner, diversities of signification, or, at least, afford different shades of the same meaning: one will shew the word applied to persons, another to things; one will express an ill, another a good, and a third a neutral sense; one will prove the expression genuine from an ancient author; another will shew it elegant from a modern: a doubtful authority is corroborated by another of more credit; an ambiguous sentence is ascertained by a passage clear and determinate: the word, how often soever repeated, appears with new associates and in different combinations, and every quotation contributes something to the stability or enlargement of the language.

When words are used equivocally, I receive them in either sense; when they are metaphorical, I adopt them in their primitive acceptation.

I have sometimes, though rarely, yielded to the temptation of exhibiting a genealogy of sentiments, by shewing how one author copied the thoughts and diction of another: such quotations are indeed little more than repetitions, which might justly be censured, did they not gratify the mind, by affording a kind of intellectual history.

The various syntactical structures occurring in the examples have been carefully noted; the licence or negligence with which many words have been hitherto used, has made our style capricious and indeterminate; when the different combinations of the same word are exhibited together, the preference is readily given to propriety, and I have often endeavoured to direct the choice.

Thus have I laboured by settling the orthography, displaying the analogy, regulating the structures, and ascertaining the signification of English words, to perform all the parts of a faithful lexicographer: but I have not always executed my own scheme, or satisfied my own expectations. The work, whatever proofs of diligence and attention it may exhibit, is yet capable of many improvements: the orthography which I recommend is still controvertible; the etymology which I adopt is uncertain, and perhaps frequently erroneous; the explanations are sometimes too much contracted, and sometimes too much diffused, the significations are distinguished rather with subtility than skill, and the attention is harassed with unnecessary minuteness.

The examples are too often injudiciously truncated, and perhaps sometimes, I hope very rarely, alleged in a mistaken sense; for in making this collection I trusted more to memory, than, in a state of disquiet and embarrassment, memory can contain, and purposed to supply at the review what was left incomplete in the first transcription.

Many terms appropriated to particular occupations, though necessary and significant, are undoubtedly omitted; and of the words most studiously considered and exemplified, many senses have escaped observation.

Yet these failures, however frequent, may admit extenuation and apology. To have attempted much is always laudable, even when the enterprize is above the strength that undertakes it: To rest below his own aim is incident to every one whose fancy is active, and whose views are comprehensive; nor is any man satisfied with himself because he has done much, but because he can conceive little. When first I engaged in this work, I resolved to leave neither words nor things unexamined, and pleased myself with a prospect of the hours which I should revel away in feasts of literature, the obscure recesses of northern learning which I should enter and ransack, the treasures with which I expected every search into those neglected mines to reward my labour, and the triumph with which I should display my acquisitions to mankind. When I had thus enquired into the original of words, I resolved to shew likewise my attention to things; to pierce deep into every science, to enquire the nature of every substance of which I inserted the name, to limit every idea by a definition strictly logical, and exhibit every production of art or nature in an accurate description, that my book might be in place of all other dictionaries whether appellative or technical. But these were the dreams of a poet doomed at last to wake a lexicographer. I soon found that it is too late to look for instruments, when the work calls for execution, and that whatever abilities I had brought to my task, with those I must finally perform it. To deliberate whenever I doubted, to enquire whenever I was ignorant, would have protracted the undertaking without end, and, perhaps, without much improvement; for I did not find by my first experiments, that what I had not of my own was easily to be obtained: I saw that one enquiry only gave occasion to another, that book referred to book, that to search was not always to find, and to find was not always to be informed; and that thus to pursue perfection, was, like the first inhabitants of Arcadia, to chase the sun, which when they had reached the hill where he seemed to rest, was still beheld at the same distance from them.

I then contracted my design, determining to confide in myself, and no longer to solicit auxiliaries, which produced more incumbrance than assistance; by this I obtained at least one advantage, that I set limits to my work, which would in time be ended, though not completed.

Despondency has never so far prevailed as to depress me to negligence; some faults will at last appear to be the effects of anxious diligence and persevering activity. The nice and subtle ramifications of meaning were not easily avoided by a mind intent upon accuracy, and convinced of the necessity of disentangling combinations, and separating similitudes. Many of the distinctions which to common readers appear useless and idle, will be found real and important by men versed in the school of philosophy, without which no dictionary can ever be accurately compiled, or skilfully examined.

Some senses however there are, which, though not the same, are yet so nearly allied, that they are often confounded. Most men think indistinctly, and therefore cannot speak with exactness; and consequently some examples might be indifferently put to either signification: this uncertainty is not to be imputed to me, who do not form, but register the language; who do not teach men how they should think, but relate how they have hitherto expressed their thoughts.

The imperfect sense of some examples I lamented, but could not remedy, and hope they will be compensated by innumerable passages selected with propriety, and preserved with exactness; some shining with sparks of imagination, and some replete with treasures of wisdom.

The orthography and etymology, though imperfect, are not imperfect for want of care, but because care will not always be successful, and recollection or information come too late for use.

That many terms of art and manufacture are omitted, must be frankly acknowledged; but for this defect I may boldly allege that it was unavoidable; I could not visit caverns to learn the miner's language, nor take a voyage to perfect my skill in the dialect of navigation, nor visit the warehouses of merchants, and shops of artificers, to gain the names of wares, tools and operations, of which no mention is found in books; what favourable accident, or easy enquiry brought within my reach, has not been neglected; but it had been a hopeless labour to glean up words, by courting living information, and contesting with the sullenness of one, and the roughness of another.

To furnish the academicians *della Crusca* with words of this kind, a series of comedies called *la Fiera*, or *the Fair*, was professedly written by Buonaroti; but I had no such assistant, and therefore was content to want what they must have wanted likewise, had they not luckily been so supplied.

Nor are all words which are not found in the vocabulary, to be lamented as omissions. Of the laborious and mercantile part of the people, the diction is in a great measure casual and mutable; many of their terms are formed for some temporary or local convenience, and though current at certain times and places, are in others utterly unknown. This fugitive cant, which is always in a state of increase or decay, cannot be regarded as any part of the durable materials of a language, and therefore must be suffered to perish with other things unworthy of preservation.

Care will sometimes betray to the appearance of negligence. He that is catching opportunities which seldom occur, will suffer those to pass by unregarded, which he expects hourly to return; he that is searching for rare and remote things, will neglect those that are obvious and familiar; thus many of the most common and cursory words have been inserted with little illustration, because in gathering the authorities, I forbore to copy those which I thought likely to occur whenever they were wanted. It is remarkble that, in reviewing my collection, I found the word *sea* unexemplified.

Thus it happens, that in things difficult there is danger from ignorance, and in things easy from confidence; the mind, afraid of greatness, and disdainful of littleness, hastily withdraws herself from painful searches, and passes with scornful rapidity over tasks not adequate to her powers, sometimes too secure for caution, and again too anxious for vigorous effort; sometimes idle in a plain path, and sometimes distracted in labyrinths, and dissipated by different intentions.

A large work is difficult because it is large, even though all its parts might singly be performed with facility; where there are many things to be done, each must be allowed its share of time and labour, in the proportion only which it bears to the whole, nor can it be expected, that the stones which form the dome of a temple, should be squared and polished like the diamond of a ring.

Of the event of this work, for which, having laboured it with so much application, I cannot but have some degree of parental fondness, it is natural to form conjectures. Those who have been persuaded to think well of my design, will require that it should fix our language, and put a stop to those alterations which time and chance have hitherto been suffered to make in it without opposition. With this consequence I will confess that I flattered myself for a while; but now begin to fear that I have indulged expectation which neither reason nor experience can justify. When we see men grow old and die at a certain time one after another, from century to century, we laugh at the elixir that promises to prolong life to a thousand years; and with equal justice may the lexicographer be derided, who being able to produce no example of a nation that has preserved their words and phrases from mutability, shall imagine that his dictionary can embalm his language, and secure it from corruption and decay, that it is in his power to change sublunary nature, and clear the world at once from folly, vanity, and affectation.

With this hope, however, academies have been instituted, to guard the avenues of their languages, to retain fugitives, and repulse intruders; but their vigilance and activity have hitherto been vain; sounds are too volatile and subtile for legal restraints; to enchain syllables, and to lash the wind, are equally the undertakings of pride, unwilling to measure its desires by its strength. The French language has visibly changed under the inspection of the academy; the style of Amelot's translation of father Paul is observed by Le Courayer to be *un peu passé;* and no Italian will maintain, that the diction of any modern writer is not perceptibly different from that of Boccace, Machiavel, or Caro.

Total and sudden transformations of a language seldom happen; conquests and migrations are now very rare: but there are other causes of change, which, though slow in their operation, and invisible in their progress, are perhaps as much superior to human resistance, as the revolutions of the sky, or intumescence of the tide. Commerce, however necessary, however lucrative, as it depraves the manners corrupts the language; they that have frequent intercourse with strangers, to whom they endeavour to accommodate themselves, must in time learn a mingled dialect, like the jargon which serves the traffickers on the Mediterranean and Indian coasts. This will not always be confined to the exchange, the warehouse, or the port, but will be communicated by degrees to other ranks of the people, and be at last incorporated with the current speech.

There are likewise internal causes equally forcible. The language most likely to continue long without alteration, would be that of a nation raised a little, and but a little, above barbarity, secluded from strangers, and totally employed in procuring the conveniences of life; either without books, or, like some of the Mohometan countries, with very few: men thus busied and unlearned, having only such words as common use requires, would perhaps long continue to express the same notions by the same signs. But no such constancy can be expected in a people polished by arts, and classed by subordination, where one part of the community is sustained and accommodated by the labour of the other. Those who have much leisure to think, will always be enlarging the stock of ideas; and every increase of knowledge, whether real or fancied, will produce new words, or combinations of words. When the mind is unchained from necessity, it will range after convenience; when it is left at large in the field of speculation, it will shift opinions; as any custom is disused, the words that expressed it must perish with it; as any opinion grows popular, it will innovate speech in the same proportion as it alters practice.

As by the cultivation of various sciences, a language is amplified, it will be more furnished with words deflected from their original sense; the geometrician will talk of a courtier's zenith, or the eccentrick virtue of a wild hero, and the physician of sanguine expectations, and phlegmatic delays. Copiousness of speech will give opportunities to capricious choice, by which some words will be preferred, and others degraded; vicissitudes of fashion will enforce the use of new, or extend the signification of known terms. The tropes of poetry will make hourly encroachments, and the metaphorical will become the current sense; pronunciation will be varied by levity or ignorance, and the pen must at length comply with the tongue: illiterate writers will, at one time or other, by publick infatuation, rise into renown, who not knowing the original import of words, will use them with colloquial licentiousness, confound distinction, and forget propriety. As politeness increases, some expressions will be considered as too gross and vulgar for the delicate, others as too formal and ceremonious for the gay and airy; new phrases are therefore adopted, which must, for the same reasons, be in time dismissed. Swift, in his petty treatise on the English language, allows that new words must sometimes be introduced, but proposes that none should be suffered to become obsolete. But what makes a word obsolete, more than general agreement to forbear it? and how shall it be continued, when it conveys an offensive idea, or recalled again into the mouths of mankind, when it has once become unfamiliar by disuse, and unpleasing by unfamiliarity?

There is another cause of alteration more prevalent than any other, which yet in the present state of the world cannot be obviated. A mixture of two languages will produce a third distinct from both, and they will always be mixed, where the chief parts of education, and the most conspicuous accomplishment, is skill in ancient or in foreign tongues. He that has long cultivated another language, will find its words and combinations crowd upon his memory; and haste and negligence, refinement and affectation, will obtrude borrowed terms and exotic expressions.

The great pest of speech is frequency of translation. No book was ever turned from one language into another, without imparting something of its native idiom; this is the most mischievous and comprehensive innovation; single words may enter by thousands, and the fabrick of the tongue continue the same; but new phraseology changes much at once; it alters not the single stones of the building, but the order of the columns.

If an academy should be established for the cultivation of our style; which I, who can never wish to see dependence multiplied, hope the spirit of English liberty will hinder or destroy, let them, instead of compiling grammars and dictionaries, endeavour, with all their influence, to stop the licence of translators, whose idleness and ignorance, if it be suffered to proceed, will reduce us to babble a dialect of France.

If the changes that we fear be thus irresistible, what remains but to acquiesce with silence, as in the other insurmountable distresses of humanity? It remains that we retard what we cannot repel, that we palliate what we cannot cure. Life may be lengthened by care, though death cannot be ultimately defeated: tongues, like governments, have a natural tendency to degeneration; we have long preserved our constitution, let us make some struggles for our language.

In hope of giving longevity to that which its own nature forbids to be immortal, I have devoted this book, the labour of years, to the honour of my country, that we may no longer yield the palm of philology, without a contest, to the nations of the continent. The chief glory of every people arises from its authors: whether I shall add any thing by my own writings to the reputation of English literature, must be left to time: much of my life has been lost under the pressures of disease; much has been trifled away; and much has always been spent in provision for the day that was passing over me; but I shall not think my employment useless or ignoble, if by my assistance foreign nations, and distant ages, gain access to the propagators of knowledge, and understand the teachers of truth; if my labours afford light to the repositories of science, and add celebrity to Bacon, to Hooker, to Milton, and to Boyle.

When I am animated by this wish, I look with pleasure on my book, however defective, and deliver it to the world with the spirit of a man that has endeavoured well. That it will immediately become popular I have not promised to myself: a few wild blunders, and risible absurdities, from which no work of such multiplicity was ever free, may for a time furnish folly with laughter, and harden ignorance into contempt; but useful diligence will at last prevail, and there never can be wanting some who distinguish desert; who will consider that no dictionary of a living tongue ever can be perfect, since, while it is hastening to publication, some words are budding, and some falling away; that a whole life cannot be spent upon syntax and etymology, and that even a whole life would not be sufficient; that he, whose design includes whatever language can express, must often speak of what he does not understand; that a writer will sometimes be hurried by eagerness to the end, and sometimes faint with weariness under a task, which Scaliger compares to the labours of the anvil and the mine; that what is obvious is not always known, and what is known is not always present; that sudden fits of inadvertency will surprise vigilance, slight avocations will seduce attention, and casual eclipses of the mind will darken learning; and that the writer shall often in vain trace his memory at the moment of need, for that which yesterday he knew with intuitive readiness, and which will come uncalled into his thoughts to-morrow.

In this work, when it shall be found that much is omitted, let it not be forgotten that much likewise is performed; and though no book was ever spared out of tenderness to the author, and the world is little solicitous to know whence proceeded the faults of that which it condemns; yet it may gratify curiosity to inform it, that the *English Dictionary* was written with little assistance of the learned, and without any patronage of the great; not in the soft obscurities of retirement, or under the shelter of academick bowers, but amid inconvenience and distraction, in sickness and in sorrow. It may repress the triumph of malignant criticism to observe, that if our language is not here fully displayed, I have only failed in an attempt which no human powers have hitherto completed. If the lexicons of ancient tongues, now immutably fixed, and comprized in a few volumes, be yet, after the toil of successive ages, inadequate and delusive; if the aggregated knowledge, and coöperating diligence of the Italian academicians, did not secure them from the censure of Beni; if the embodied criticks of France, when fifty years had been spent upon their work, were obliged to change its economy, and give their second edition another form, I may surely be contented without the praise of perfection, which, if I could obtain, in this gloom of solitude, what would it avail me? I have protracted my work till most of those whom I wished to please have sunk into the grave, and success and miscarriage are empty sounds. I therefore dismiss it with frigid tranquillity, having little to fear or hope from censure or from praise.

1755

GRAY

Thomas Gray, the son of Mr. Philip Gray, a scrivener of London, was born in Cornhill, November 26, 1716. His grammatical education he received at Eton under the care of Mr. Antrobus, his mother's brother, then assistant to Dr. George; and when he left school, in 1734, entered a pensioner at Peterhouse in Cambridge.

The transition from the school to the college is, to most young scholars, the time from which they date their years of manhood, liberty, and happiness; but Gray seems to have been very little delighted with academical gratifications; he liked at Cambridge neither the mode of life nor the fashion of study, and lived sullenly on to the time when his attendance on lectures was no longer required. As he intended to profess the Common Law, he took no degree.

When he had been at Cambridge about five years, Mr. Horace Walpole, whose friendship he had gained at Eton, invited him to travel with him as his companion. They wandered through France into Italy; and Gray's Letters contain a very pleasing account of many parts of their journey. But unequal friendships are easily dissolved: at Florence they quarrelled, and parted; and Mr. Walpole is now content to have it told that it was by his fault. If we look, however, without prejudice on the world, we shall find that men, whose consciousness of their own merit sets them above the compliances of servility, are apt enough in their association with superiors to watch their own dignity with troublesome and punctilious jealousy, and in the fervour of independence to exact that attention which they refuse to pay. Part they did, whatever was the quarrel; and the rest of their travels was doubtless more unpleasant to them both. Gray continued his journey in a manner suitable to his own little fortune, with only an occasional servant.

He returned to England in September, 1741, and in about two months afterwards buried his father, who had, by an injudicious waste of money upon a new house, so much lessened his fortune, that Gray thought himself too poor to study the law. He therefore retired to Cambridge, where he soon after became Bachelor of Civil Law, and where, without liking the place or its inhabitants, or professing to like them, he passed, except a short residence at London, the rest of his life.

About this time he was deprived of Mr. West, the son of a chancellor of Ireland, a friend on whom he appears to have set a high value, and who deserved his esteem by the powers which he shews in his Letters, and in the *Ode to May*, which Mr. Mason has preserved, as well as by the sincerity with which, when Gray sent him part of *Agrippina*, a tragedy that he had just begun, he gave an opinion which probably intercepted the progress of the work, and which the judgment of every reader will confirm. It was certainly no loss to the English stage that *Agrippina* was never finished.

In this year (1742) Gray seems to have applied himself seriously to poetry; for in this year were produced the *Ode to Spring*, his *Prospect of Eton*, and his *Ode to Adversity*. He began likewise a Latin Poem, *De Principiis Cogitandi*.

It may be collected from the narrative of Mr. Mason, that his first ambition was to have excelled in Latin poetry: perhaps it were reasonable to wish that he had prosecuted his design; for, though there is at present some embarrassment in his phrase, and some harshness in his lyrick numbers, his copiousness of language is such as very few possess; and his lines, even when imperfect, discover a writer whom practice would have made skilful.

He now lived on at Peterhouse, very little solicitous what others did or thought, and cultivated his mind and enlarged his views without any other purpose than of improving and amusing himself; when Mr. Mason, being elected Fellow of Pembroke Hall, brought him a companion who was afterwards to be his editor, and whose fondness and fidelity has kindled in him a zeal of admiration which cannot be reasonably expected from the neutrality of a stranger, and the coldness of a critick.

In his retirement he wrote (1747) an ode on the *Death of Mr. Walpole's Cat;* and the year afterwards attempted a poem, of more importance, on *Government and Education,* of which the fragments which remain have many excellent lines.

His next production (1750) was his far-famed *Elegy in the Church-yard*, which, finding its way into a Magazine, first, I believe, made him known to the publick.

An invitation from Lady Cobham about this time gave occasion to an odd composition called *A Long Story,* which adds little to Gray's character.

Several of his pieces were published (1753), with designs by Mr. Bentley; and, that they might in some form or other make a book, only one side of each leaf was printed. I believe the poems and the plates recommended each other so well, that the whole impression was soon bought. This year he lost his mother.

Some time afterwards (1756) some young men of the college, whose chambers were near his, diverted themselves with disturbing him by frequent and troublesome noises, and, as is said, by pranks yet more offensive and contemptuous. This insolence, having endured it a while, he represented to the governors of the society, among whom perhaps he had no friends; and, finding his complaint little regarded, removed himself to Pembroke Hall.

In 1757 he published *The Progress of Poetry,* and *The Bard,* two compositions at which the readers of poetry were at first content to gaze in mute amazement. Some that tried them confessed their inability to understand them, though Warburton said that they were understood as well as the works of Milton and Shakspeare, which it is the fashion to admire. Garrick wrote a few lines in their praise. Some hardy champions undertook to rescue them from neglect; and in a short time many were content to be shewn beauties which they could not see.

Gray's reputation was now so high, that, after the death of Cibber, he had the honour of refusing the laurel, which was then bestowed on Mr. Whitehead.

His curiosity, not long after, drew him away from Cambridge to a lodging near the Museum, where he resided near three years, reading and transcribing; and, so far as can be discovered, very little affected by two odes on 'Oblivion' and 'Obscurity,' in which his lyrick performances were ridiculed with much contempt and much ingenuity.

When the Professor of Modern History at Cambridge died, he was, as he says, 'cockered and spirited up,' till he asked it of Lord Bute, who sent him a civil refusal; and the place was given to Mr. Brocket, the tutor of Sir James Lowther.

His constitution was weak, and, believing that his health was promoted by exercise and change of place, he undertook (1765) a journey into Scotland, of which his account, so far as it extends, is very curious and elegant: for, as his comprehension was ample, his curiosity extended to all the works of art, all the appearances of nature, and all the monuments of past events. He naturally contracted a friendship with Dr. Beattie, whom he found a poet, a philosopher, and a good man. The Mareschal College at Aberdeen offered him the degree of Doctor of Laws, which, having omitted to take it at Cambridge, he thought it decent to refuse.

What he had formerly solicited in vain was at last given him without solicitation. The Professorship of History became again vacant, and he received (1768) an offer of it from the Duke of Grafton. He accepted, and retained it to his death; always designing lectures, but never reading them; uneasy at his neglect of duty, and appeasing his uneasiness with designs of reformation, and with a resolution which he believed himself to have made of resigning the office, if he found himself unable to discharge it.

Ill health made another journey necessary, and he visited (1769) Westmoreland and Cumberland. He that reads his epistolary narration wishes, that to travel, and to tell his travels, had been more of his employment; but it is by studying at home that we must obtain the ability of travelling with intelligence and improvement.

His travels and his studies were now near their end. The gout, of which he had sustained many weak attacks, fell upon his stomach, and, yielding to no medicines, produced strong convulsions, which (July 30, 1771,) terminated in death.

His character I am willing to adopt, as Mr. Mason has done, from a Letter written to my friend Mr. Boswell, by the Rev. Mr. Temple, rector of St. Gluvias in Cornwall; and am as willing as his warmest well-wisher to believe it true.

'Perhaps he was the most learned man in Europe. He was equally acquainted with the elegant and profound parts of science, and that not superficially, but thoroughly. He knew every branch of history, both natural and civil; had read all the original historians of England, France, and Italy; and was a great antiquarian. Criticism, metaphysicks, morals, politicks, made a principal part of his study; voyages and travels of all sorts were his favourite amusements; and he had a fine taste in painting, prints, architecture, and gardening. With such a fund of knowledge, his conversation must have been equally instructing and entertaining; but he was also a good man, a man of virtue and humanity. There is no character without some speck, some imperfection; and I think the greatest defect in his was an affectation in delicacy, or rather effeminacy, and a visible fastidiousness, or contempt and disdain of his inferiors in science. He also had, in some degree, that weakness which disgusted Voltaire so much in Mr. Congreve: though he seemed to value others chiefly according to the progress that they had made in knowledge, yet he could not bear to be considered merely as a man of letters; and, though without birth, or fortune, or station, his desire was to be looked upon as a private independent gentleman, who read for his amusement. Perhaps it may be said, What signifies so much knowledge, when it produced so little? Is it worth taking so much pains to leave no memorials but a few poems? But let it be considered that Mr. Gray was to others at least innocently employed; to himself certainly beneficially. His time passed agreeably: he was every day making some new acquisition in science; his mind was enlarged, his heart softened, his virtue strengthened; the world and mankind were shewn to him without a mask; and he was taught to consider every thing as trifling, and unworthy of the attention of a wise man, except the pursuit of knowledge and practice of virtue, in that state wherein God hath placed us.'

To this character Mr. Mason has added a more particular account of Gray's skill in zoölogy. He has remarked, that Gray's effeminacy was affected most 'before those whom he did not wish to please'; and that he is unjustly charged with making knowledge his sole reason of preference, as he paid his esteem to none whom he did not likewise believe to be good.

What has occurred to me from the slight inspection of his Letters in which my undertaking has engaged me is, that his mind had a large grasp; that his curiosity was unlimited, and his judgment cultivated; that he was a man likely to love much where he loved at all; but that he was fastidious and hard to please. His contempt, however, is often employed where I hope it will be approved, upon scepticism and infidelity. His short account of Shaftesbury I will insert.

'You say you cannot conceive how Lord Shaftesbury came to be a philosopher in vogue; I will tell you; first, he was a lord; secondly, he was as vain as any of his readers; thirdly, men are very prone to believe what they do not understand; fourthly, they will believe any thing at all, provided they are under no obligation to believe it; fifthly, they love to take a new road, even when that road leads no where; sixthly, he was reckoned a fine writer, and seems always to mean more than he said. Would you have any more reasons? An interval of above forty years has pretty well destroyed the charm. A dead lord ranks with commoners; vanity is no longer interested in the matter; for a new road has become an old one.'

Mr. Mason has added, from his own knowledge, that, though Gray was poor, he was not eager of money; and that, out of the little that he had, he was very willing to help the necessitous.

As a writer he had this peculiarity, that

he did not write his pieces first rudely, and then correct them, but laboured every line as it arose in the train of composition; and he had a notion not very peculiar, that he could not write but at certain times, or at happy moments; a fantastick foppery, to which my kindness for a man of learning and virtue wishes him to have been superior.

Gray's Poetry is now to be considered; and I hope not to be looked on as an enemy to his name, if I confess that I contemplate it with less pleasure than his life.

His ode *On Spring* has something poetical, both in the language and the thought; but the language is too luxuriant, and the thoughts have nothing new. There has of late arisen a practice of giving to adjectives derived from substantives the termination of participles; such as the *cultured* plain, the *daisied* bank; but I was sorry to see, in the lines of a scholar like Gray, the *honied* Spring. The morality is natural, but too stale; the conclusion is pretty.

The poem *On the Cat* was doubtless by its author considered as a trifle; but it is not a happy trifle. In the first stanza, 'the azure flowers *that* blow' shew resolutely a rhyme is sometimes made when it cannot easily be found. Selima, the Cat, is called a nymph, with some violence both to language and sense; but there is no good use made of it when it is done; for of the two lines,

'What female heart can gold despise?
What cat 's averse to fish?'

the first relates merely to the nymph, and the second only to the cat. The sixth stanza contains a melancholy truth, that 'a favourite has no friend'; but the last ends in a pointed sentence of no relation to the purpose; if *what glistered* had been *gold*, the cat would not have gone into the water; and, if she had, would not less have been drowned.

The *Prospect of Eton College* suggests nothing to Gray which every beholder does not equally think and feel. His supplication to Father Thames, to tell him who drives the hoop or tosses the ball, is useless and puerile. Father Thames has no better means of knowing than himself. His epithet 'buxom health' is not elegant; he seems not to understand the word. Gray thought his language more poetical as it was more remote from common use: finding in Dryden 'honey redolent of Spring,' an expression that reaches the utmost limits of our language, Gray drove it a little more beyond common apprehension, by making 'gales' to be 'redolent of joy and youth.'

Of the *Ode on Adversity* the hint was at first taken from '*O Diva, gratum quæ regis Antium*': but Gray has excelled his original by the variety of his sentiments, and by their moral application. Of this piece, at once poetical and rational, I will not, by slight objections, violate the dignity.

My process has now brought me to the *wonderful* 'Wonder of Wonders,' the two Sister Odes; by which, though either vulgar ignorance or common sense at first universally rejected them, many have been since persuaded to think themselves delighted. I am one of those that are willing to be pleased, and therefore would gladly find the meaning of the first stanza of *The Progress of Poetry*.

Gray seems in his rapture to confound the images of 'spreading sound and running water.' A 'stream of musick' may be allowed; but where does 'musick,' however 'smooth and strong,' after having visited the 'verdant vales, rowl down the steep amain,' so as that 'rocks and nodding groves rebellow to the roar'? If this be said of Musick, it is nonsense; if it be said of Water, it is nothing to the purpose.

The second stanza, exhibiting Mars' car and Jove's eagle, is unworthy of further notice. Criticism disdains to chase a schoolboy to his commonplaces.

To the third it may likewise be objected, that it is drawn from mythology, though such as may be more easily assimilated to real life. Idalia's 'velvet green' has something of cant. An epithet or metaphor drawn from Nature enobles Art; an epithet or metaphor drawn from Art degrades Nature. Gray is too fond of words arbitrarily compounded. 'Many-twinkling' was formerly censured as not analogical; we may say 'many spotted,' but scarcely 'many-spotting.' This stanza, however, has something pleasing.

Of the second ternary of stanzas, the first endeavours to tell something, and would have told it, had it not been crossed by Hyperion: the second describes well enough the universal prevalence of Poetry; but I am afraid that the conclusion will not arise from the premises. The caverns of the North and the plains of Chili are not the residences of 'Glory and generous Shame.' But that Poetry and Virtue go always together is an opinion so pleasing, that I can forgive him who resolves to think it true.

The third stanza sounds big with 'Delphi,' and 'Egean,' and 'Ilissus,' and 'Meander,' and 'hallowed fountains,' and 'solemn sound'; but in all Gray's odes there is a kind of cumbrous splendour which we wish away. His position is at last false: in the time of Dante and Petrarch, from whom we derive our first school of Poetry, Italy was overrun by 'tyrant power' and 'coward vice'; nor was our state much better when we first borrowed the Italian arts.

Of the third ternary, the first gives a mythological birth of Shakspeare. What is said of that mighty genius is true; but it is not said happily: the real effects of this poetical power are put out of sight by the pomp of machinery. Where truth is sufficient to fill the mind, fiction is worse than useless; the counterfeit debases the genuine.

His account of Milton's blindness, if we suppose it caused by study in the formation of his poem, a supposition surely allowable, is poetically true, and happily imagined. But the *car* of Dryden, with his *two coursers*, has nothing in it peculiar; it is a car in which any other rider may be placed.

The Bard appears, at the first view, to be, as Algarotti and others have remarked, an imitation of the prophecy of Nereus. Algarotti thinks it superior to its original; and, if preference depends only on the imagery and animation of the two poems, his judgment is right. There is in *The Bard* more force, more thought, and more variety. But to copy is less than to invent, and the copy has been unhappily produced at a wrong time. The fiction of Horace was to the Romans credible; but its revival disgusts us with apparent and unconquerable falsehood. *Incredulus odi.*

To select a singular event, and swell it to a giant's bulk by fabulous appendages of spectres and predictions, has little difficulty; for he that forsakes the probable may always find the marvellous. And it has little use; we are affected only as we believe; we are improved only as we find something to be imitated or declined. I do not see that *The Bard* promotes any truth, moral or political.

His stanzas are too long, especially his epodes; the ode is finished before the ear has learned its measures, and consequently before it can receive pleasure from their consonance and recurrence.

Of the first stanza the abrupt beginning has been celebrated; but technical beauties can give praise only to the inventor. It is in the power of any man to rush abruptly upon his subject, that has read the ballad of *Johnny Armstrong*.

'Is there ever a man in all Scotland —'

The initial resemblances, or alliterations, 'ruin, ruthless, helm or hauberk,' are below the grandeur of a poem that endeavours at sublimity.

In the second stanza the Bard is well described; but in the third we have the puerilities of obsolete mythology. When we are told that 'Cadwallo hushed the stormy main,' and that 'Modred made huge Plinlimmon bow his cloud-topped head,' attention recoils from the repetition of a tale that, even when it was first heard, was heard with scorn.

The *weaving* of the *winding-sheet* he borrowed, as he owns, from the Northern Bards; but their texture, however, was very properly the work of female powers, as the act of spinning the thread of life is another mythology. Theft is always dangerous; Gray has made weavers of slaughtered bards by a fiction outrageous and incongruous. They are then called upon to 'Weave the warp, and weave the woof,' perhaps with no great propriety; for it is by crossing the woof with the warp that men weave the web or piece; and the first line was dearly bought by the admission of its wretched correspondent, 'Give ample room and verge enough.' He has, however, no other line as bad.

The third stanza of the second ternary is commended, I think, beyond its merit. The personification is indistinct. *Thrift* and *Hunger* are not alike; and their features, to make the imagery perfect, should have been discriminated. We are told, in the same stanza, how 'towers are fed.' But I will no longer look for particular faults; yet let it be observed that the ode might have been concluded with an action of better example; but suicide is always to be had, without expence of thought.

These odes are marked by glittering accumulations of ungraceful ornaments; they strike, rather than please; the images are magnified by affectation; the language is laboured into harshness. The mind of the writer seems to work with unnatural violence. 'Double, double, toil and trouble.' He has a kind of strutting dignity, and is tall by walking on tiptoe. His art and his struggle are too visible, and there is too little appearance of ease and nature.

To say that he has no beauties, would be unjust: a man like him, of great learning and great industry, could not but produce something valuable. When he pleases least, it can only be said that a good design was ill directed.

His translations of Northern and Welsh Poetry deserve praise; the imagery is preserved, perhaps often improved; but the language is unlike the language of other poets.

In the character of his Elegy I rejoice to concur with the common reader; for by the common sense of readers, uncorrupted with literary prejudices, after all the refinements of subtility and the dogmatism of learning, must be finally decided all claim to poetical honours. The *Church-yard* abounds with images which find a mirrour in every mind, and with sentiments to which every bosom returns an echo. The four stanzas, beginning 'Yet even these bones,' are to me original: I have never seen the notions in any other place; yet he that reads them here persuades himself that he has always felt them. Had Gray written often thus, it had been vain to blame, and useless to praise him.

1781

BIOGRAPHY

James Boswell (1740–1795)

THE LIFE OF JOHNSON

THE FIRST MEETING

Mr. Thomas Davies the actor, who then kept a bookseller's shop in Russell Street, Covent Garden, told me that Johnson was very much his friend, and came frequently to his house, where he more than once invited me to meet him; but by some unlucky accident or other he was prevented from coming to us.

Mr. Thomas Davies was a man of good understanding and talents, with the advantage of a liberal education. Though somewhat pompous, he was an entertaining companion; and his literary performances have no inconsiderable share of merit. He was a friendly and very hospitable man. Both he and his wife, (who has been celebrated for her beauty,) though upon the stage for many years, maintained an uniform decency of character; and Johnson esteemed them, and lived in as easy an intimacy with them, as with any family which he used to visit. Mr. Davies recollected several of Johnson's remarkable sayings, and was one of the best of the many imitators of his voice and manner, while relating them. He increased my impatience more and more to see the extraordinary man whose works I highly valued, and whose conversation was reported to be so peculiarly excellent.

At last, on Monday the 16th of May, when I was sitting in Mr. Davies's back-parlour, after having drunk tea with him and Mrs. Davies, Johnson unexpectedly came into the shop; and Mr. Davies having perceived him through the glass-door in the room in which we were sitting, advancing towards us, — he announced his awful approach to me, somewhat in the manner of an actor in the part of Horatio, when he addresses Hamlet on the appearance of his father's ghost, 'Look, my lord, it comes.' I found that I had a very perfect idea of Johnson's figure, from the portrait of him painted by Sir Joshua Reynolds soon after he had published his Dictionary, in the attitude of sitting in his easy chair in deep meditation; which was the first picture his friend did for him, which Sir Joshua very kindly presented to me, and from which an engraving has been made for this work. Mr. Davies mentioned my name, and respectfully introduced me to him. I was much agitated; and recollecting his prejudice against the Scotch, of which I had heard much, I said to Davies, 'Don't tell where I come from.' — 'From Scotland,' cried Davies, roguishly. 'Mr. Johnson, (said I) I do indeed come from Scotland, but I cannot help it.' I am willing to flatter myself that I meant this as light pleasantry to soothe and conciliate him, and not as an humiliating abasement at the expense of my country. But however that might be, this speech was somewhat unlucky; for with that quickness of wit for which he was so remarkable, he seized the expression 'come from Scotland,' which I used in the sense of being of that country; and, as if I had said that I had come away from it, or left it, retorted, 'That, Sir, I find, is what a very great many of your countrymen cannot help.' This stroke stunned me a good deal; and when we had sat down, I felt myself not a little embarrassed, and apprehensive of what might come next. He then addressed himself to Davies: 'What do you think of Garrick? He has refused me an order for the play for Miss Williams, because he knows the house will be full, and that an order would be worth three shillings.' Eager to take any opening to get into conversation with him, I ventured to say, 'O, Sir, I cannot think Mr. Garrick would grudge such a trifle to you.' 'Sir, (said he, with a stern look,) I have known David Garrick longer than you have done: and I know no right you have to talk to me on the subject.' Perhaps I deserved this check; for it was rather presumptuous in me, an entire stranger, to express any doubt of the justice of his animadversion upon his old acquaintance and pupil. I now felt myself much mortified, and began to think that the hope which I had long indulged of obtaining his acquaintance was blasted. And, in truth, had not my ardour been uncommonly strong, and my resolution uncommonly persevering, so rough a reception might have deterred me for ever from making any further attempts. Fortunately, however, I remained upon the field not wholly discomfited; and was soon rewarded by hearing some of his conversation.

THE FIRST CALL

A few days afterwards I called on Davies, and asked him if he thought I might take the liberty of waiting on Mr. Johnson at his chambers in the Temple. He said I certainly might, and that Mr. Johnson would take it as a compliment. So upon Tuesday the 24th of May, after having been enlivened by the witty sallies of Messieurs Thornton, Wilkes, Churchill, and Lloyd, with whom I had passed the morning, I boldly repaired to Johnson. His chambers were on the first floor of No. 1, Inner-Temple-lane, and I entered them with an impression given me by the Reverend Dr. Blair, of Edinburgh, who had been introduced to him not long before, and described his having 'found the Giant in his den'; an expression which, when I came to be pretty well acquainted with Johnson, I repeated to him, and he was diverted at this picturesque account of himself. Dr. Blair had been presented to him by Dr. James Fordyce. At this time the controversy concerning the pieces published by Mr. James Macpherson, as translations of Ossian, was at its height. Johnson had all along denied their authenticity; and, what was still more provoking to their admirers, maintained that they had no merit. The subject having been introduced by Dr. Fordyce, Dr. Blair, relying on the internal evidence of their antiquity, asked Dr. Johnson whether he thought any man of a modern age could have written such poems? Johnson replied, 'Yes, Sir, many men, many women, and many children.' Johnson, at this time, did not know that Dr. Blair had just published a Dissertation, not only defending their authenticity, but seriously ranking them with the poems of Homer and Virgil; and when he was afterwards informed of this circumstance, he expressed some displeasure at Dr. Fordyce's having suggested the topic, and said, 'I am not sorry that they got thus much for their pains

Sir, it was like leading one to talk of a book, when the author is concealed behind the door.'

He received me very courteously; but it must be confessed that his apartment, and furniture, and morning dress, were sufficiently uncouth. His brown suit of clothes looked very rusty; he had on a little old shriveled unpowdered wig, which was too small for his head; his shirt-neck and knees of his breeches were loose; his black worsted stockings ill drawn up; and he had a pair of unbuckled shoes by way of slippers. But all these slovenly particularities were forgotten the moment that he began to talk. Some gentlemen, whom I do not recollect, were sitting with him; and when they went away, I also rose; but he said to me, 'Nay, don't go.' — 'Sir, (said I,) I am afraid that I intrude upon you. It is benevolent to allow me to sit and hear you.' He seemed pleased with this compliment, which I sincerely paid him, and answered, 'Sir, I am obliged to any man who visits me.'

THE POET GRAY

'Sir, I do not think Gray a first-rate poet. He has not a bold imagination, nor much command of words. The obscurity in which he has involved himself will not persuade us that he is sublime. His Elegy in a Churchyard has a happy selection of images, but I don't like what are called his great things. His Ode which begins

'Ruin seize thee, ruthless King,
Confusion on thy banners wait!'

has been celebrated for its abruptness, and plunging into the subject all at once. But such arts as these have no merit, unless when they are original. We admire them only once; and this abruptness has nothing new in it. We have had it often before. Nay, we have it in the old song of Johnny Armstrong:

'Is there ever a man in all Scotland
From the highest estate to the lowest degree,'

And then, Sir,

'Yes, there is a man in Westmoreland
And Johnny Armstrong they do him call.'

There, now, you plunge at once into the subject. You have no previous narration to lead you to it. — The two next lines in that Ode are, I think, very good:

'Though fanned by conquest's crimson wing,
They mock the air with idle state.'

Here let it be observed, that although his opinion of Gray's poetry was widely different from mine, and I believe from that of most men of taste, by whom it is with justice highly admired, there is certainly much absurdity in the clamour which has been raised, as if he had been culpably injurious to the merit of that bard, and had been actuated by envy. Alas! ye little short-sighted critics, could JOHNSON be envious of the talents of any of his contemporaries? That his opinion on this subject was what in private and in public he uniformly expressed, regardless of what others might think, we may wonder, and perhaps regret; but it is shallow and unjust to charge him with expressing what he did not think.

DR. GOLDSMITH

As Dr. Oliver Goldsmith will frequently appear in this narrative, I shall endeavour to make my readers in some degree acquainted with his singular character. He was a native of Ireland, and a contemporary with Mr. Burke, at Trinity College, Dublin, but did not then give much promise of future celebrity. He, however, observed to Mr. Malone, that 'though he made no great figure in mathematics, which was a study in much repute there, he could turn an Ode of Horace into English better than any of them.' He afterwards studied physic at Edinburgh, and upon the Continent; and I have been informed, was enabled to pursue his travels on foot, partly by demanding at Universities to enter the lists as a disputant, by which, according to the custom of many of them, he was entitled to the premium of a crown, when luckily for him his challenge was not accepted; so that, as I once observed to Dr. Johnson, he *disputed* his passage through Europe. He then came to England, and was employed successively in the capacities of an usher to an academy, a corrector of the press, a reviewer, and a writer for a newspaper. He had sagacity enough to cultivate assiduously the acquaintance of Johnson, and his faculties were gradually enlarged by the contemplation of such a model. To me and many others it appeared that he studiously copied the manner of Johnson, though, indeed, upon a smaller scale.

At this time I think he had published nothing with his name, though it was pretty generally known that *one Dr. Goldsmith* was the author of 'An Inquiry into the present State of polite Learning in Europe,' and of 'The Citizen of the World,' a series of letters supposed to be written from London by a Chinese. No man had the art of displaying with more advantage as a writer, whatever literary acquisitions he made. '*Nihil quod tetigit non ornavit.*' His mind resembled a fertile, but thin soil. There was a quick, but not a strong vegetation, of whatever chanced to be thrown upon it. No deep root could be struck. The oak of the forest did not grow there; but the elegant shrubbery and the fragrant parterre appeared in gay succession. It has been generally circulated and believed that he was a mere fool in conversation; but, in truth, this has been greatly exaggerated. He had, no doubt, a more than common share of that hurry of ideas which we often find in his countrymen, and which sometimes produces a laughable confusion in expressing them. He was very much what the French call *un étourdi*, and from vanity and an eager desire of being conspicuous wherever he was, he frequently talked carelessly without knowledge of the subject, or even without thought. His person was short, his countenance coarse and vulgar, his deportment that of a scholar awkwardly affecting the easy gentleman. Those who were in any way distinguished, excited envy in him to so ridiculous an excess, that the instances of it are hardly credible. When accompanying two beautiful young ladies with their mother on a tour in France, he was seriously angry that more attention was paid to them than to him; and once at the exhibition of the *Fantoccini* in London, when those who sat next him observed with what dexterity a puppet was made to toss a pike, he could not bear that it should have such praise, and exclaimed, with some warmth, 'Pshaw! I can do it better myself.'

He, I am afraid, had no settled system of any sort, so that his conduct must not be strictly scrutinized; but his affections were social and generous, and when he had money he gave it away very liberally. His desire of imaginary consequence predominated over his attention to truth. When he began to rise into notice, he said he had a brother who was Dean of Durham, a fiction so easily detected, that it is wonderful how he should have been so inconsiderate as to hazard it. He boasted to me at this time of the power of his pen in commanding money, which I believe was true in a certain degree, though in the instance he gave he was by no means correct. He told me that he had sold a novel for four hundred pounds. This was his 'Vicar of Wakefield.' But Johnson informed me, that he had made the bargain for Goldsmith, and the price was sixty pounds. 'And, Sir, (said he,) a sufficient price too, when it was sold; for then the fame of Goldsmith had not been elevated, as it afterwards was, by his 'Traveller'; and the bookseller had such faint hopes of profit by his bargain, that he kept the manuscript by him a long time, and did not publish it till after 'The Traveller' had appeared. Then, to be sure, it was accidentally worth more money.'

Mrs. Piozzi and Sir John Hawkins have strangely misstated the history of Goldsmith's situation and Johnson's friendly interference, when this novel was sold. I shall give it authentically from Johnson's own exact narration:

'I received one morning a message from poor Goldsmith that he was in great distress, and as it was not in his power to come to me, begging that I would come to him as soon as possible. I sent him a guinea, and promised to come to him directly. I accordingly went as soon as I was drest, and found that his landlady had arrested him for his rent, at which he was in a violent passion. I perceived that he had already changed my guinea, and had got a bottle of Madeira and a glass before him. I put the cork into the bottle, desired he would be calm, and began to talk to him of the means by which he might be extricated. He then told me that he had a novel ready for the press, which he produced to me. I looked into it, and saw its merit; told the landlady I should soon return, and having gone to a bookseller, sold it for sixty pounds. I brought Goldsmith the money, and he discharged his rent, not without rating his landlady in a high tone for having used him so ill.'

JOHNSON'S WATCH

At this time I observed upon the dial-plate of his watch a short Greek inscription, taken from the New Testament, Νὺξ γὰρ ἔρχεται, being the first words of our SAVIOUR'S solemn admonition to the improvement of that time which is allowed us to prepare for eternity; 'the night cometh when no man can work.' He sometime afterwards laid aside this dial-plate; and when I asked him the reason, he said, 'It might do very well upon a clock which a man keeps in his closet; but to have it upon his watch which he carries about with him, and which is often looked at by others, might be censured as ostentatious.' Mr. Steevens is now possessed of the dial-plate inscribed as above.

REARING A CHILD

I know not how so whimsical a thought came into my mind, but I asked, 'If, Sir, you were shut up in a castle, and a new-born child with you, what would you do?' JOHNSON. 'Why, Sir, I should not much like my company.' BOSWELL. 'But would you take the trouble of rearing it?' He seemed, as may well be supposed, unwilling to pursue the subject: but upon my persevering in my question, replied, 'Why yes, Sir, I would; but I must have all conveniencies. If I had no garden, I would make a shed on the roof, and take it there for fresh air. I should feed it, and wash it much, and with warm water to please it, not with cold water to give it pain.' BOSWELL. 'But, Sir, does not heat relax?' JOHNSON. 'Sir, you are not to imagine the water is to be very hot. I would not *coddle* the child. No, Sir, the hardy method of treating children does no good. I 'll take you five children from London, who shall cuff five Highland children. Sir, a man bred in London will carry a burthen, or run, or wrestle, as well as a man brought up in the hardest manner in the country.' BOSWELL. 'Good living, I suppose, makes the Londoners strong.' JOHNSON. 'Why, Sir, I don't know that it does. Our chairmen from Ireland, who are as strong men as any, have been brought up upon potatoes. Quantity makes up for quality.' BOSWELL. 'Would you teach this child that I have furnished you with, any thing?' JOHNSON. 'No, I should not be apt to teach it.' BOSWELL. 'Would not you have a pleasure in teaching it?' JOHNSON. 'No, Sir, I should *not* have a pleasure in teaching it.' BOSWELL. 'Have you not a pleasure in teaching men! — *There* I have you. You have the same pleasure in teaching men, that I should have in teaching children.' JOHNSON. 'Why, something about that.'

BOLT COURT

Having arrived in London late on Friday, the 15th of March, I hastened next morning to wait on Dr. Johnson, at his house; but found he was removed from Johnson's-court, No. 7, to Bolt-court, No. 8, still keeping to his favourite Fleet-street. My reflection at the time upon this change as marked in my Journal, is as follows: 'I felt a foolish regret that he had left a court which bore his name; but it was not foolish to be affected with some tenderness of regard for a place in which I had seen him a great deal, from whence I had often issued a better and a happier man than when I went in, and which had often appeared to my imagination while I trod its pavement, in the solemn darkness of the night, to be sacred to wisdom and piety.' Being informed that he was at Mr. Thrale's, in the Borough, I hastened thither, and found Mrs. Thrale and him at breakfast. I was kindly welcomed. In a moment he was in a full glow of conversation, and I felt myself elevated as if brought into another state of being. Mrs. Thrale and I looked to each other while he talked, and our looks expressed our congenial admiration and affection for him. I shall ever recollect this scene with great pleasure. I exclaimed to her, 'I am now, intellectually, *Hermippus redivivus*, I am quite restored by him, by transfusion of *mind*.' 'There are many (she replied) who admire and respect Mr. Johnson; but you and I *love* him.'

TITTERING REBUKED

Talking of a very respectable authour, he told us a curious circumstance in his life, which was, that he had married a printer's devil. REYNOLDS. 'A printer's devil, Sir! Why, I thought a printer's devil was a creature with a black face and in rags.' JOHNSON. 'Yes, Sir. But I suppose, he had her face washed, and put clean clothes on her. (Then looking very serious, and very earnest.) And she did not disgrace him; the woman had a bottom of good sense.' The word *bottom* thus introduced, was so ludicrous when contrasted with his gravity, that most of us could not forbear tittering and laughing; though I recollect that the Bishop of Killaloe kept his countenance with perfect steadiness, while Miss Hannah More slyly hid her face behind a lady's back who sat on the same settee with her. His pride could not bear that any expression of his should excite ridicule, when he did not intend it; he therefore resolved to assume and exercise despotick power, glanced sternly around, and called out in a strong tone, 'Where's the merriment?' Then collecting himself, and looking aweful, to make us feel how he could impose restraint, and as it were searching his mind for a still more ludicrous word, he slowly pronounced, 'I say the *woman* was *fundamentally* sensible'; as if he had said, hear this now, and laugh if you dare. We all sat composed as at a funeral.

JOHNSON'S FUNERAL

A few days before his death, he had asked Sir John Hawkins, as one of his executors, where he should be buried; and on being answered, 'Doubtless, in Westminster-Abbey,' seemed to feel a satisfaction, very natural to a Poet; and indeed in my opinion very natural to every man of any imagination, who has no family sepulchre in which he can be laid with his fathers. Accordingly, upon Monday, December 20, his remains were deposited in that noble and renowned edifice; and over his grave was placed a large blue flag-stone, with this inscription:

'SAMUEL JOHNSON, LL.D.
Obiit XIII *die Decembris,*
Anno Domini
M.DCC.LXXXIV.
Ætatis suæ LXXV.'

His funeral was attended by a respectable number of his friends, particularly such of the members of the Literary Club as were then in town; and was also honoured with the presence of several of the Reverend Chapter of Westminster. Mr. Burke, Sir Joseph Banks, Mr. Windham, Mr. Langton, Sir Charles Bunbury, and Mr. Colman, bore his pall. His school-fellow, Dr. Taylor, performed the mournful office of reading the burial service.

I trust, I shall not be accused of affectation, when I declare, that I find myself unable to express all that I felt upon the loss of such a 'Guide, Philosopher, and Friend.' I shall, therefore, not say one word of my own, but adopt those of an eminent friend, which he uttered with an abrupt felicity, superior to all studied compositions: — 'He has made a chasm, which not only nothing can fill up, but which nothing has a tendency to fill up. — Johnson is dead. — Let us go to the next best: — there is nobody; no man can be said to put you in mind of Johnson.'

1791

PRIVATE LETTERS

Philip Dormer Stanhope, Earl of Chesterfield, (1694–1773)

TO HIS SON

Spa, July 25, N. S. 1741

Dear Boy,

I have often told you in my former letters (and it is most certainly true) that the strictest and most scrupulous honour and virtue can alone make you esteemed and valued by mankind; that parts and learning can alone make you admired and celebrated by them; but that the possession of lesser talents was most absolutely necessary towards making you liked, beloved, and sought after in private life. Of these lesser talents, good-breeding is the principal and most necessary one, not only as it is very important in itself; but as it adds great lustre to the more solid advantages both of the heart and the mind. I have often touched upon good-breeding to you before; so that this letter shall be upon the next necessary qualification to it, which is a genteel, easy manner and carriage, wholly free from those odd tricks, ill habits, and awkwardnesses, which even very many worthy and sensible people have in their behaviour. However trifling a genteel manner may sound, it is of very great consequence towards pleasing in private life, especially the women; which, one time or other, you will think worth pleasing; and I have known many a man, from his awkwardness, give people such a dislike of him at first, that all his merit could not get the better of it afterwards. Whereas a genteel manner prepossesses people in your favour, bends them towards you, and makes them wish to like you. Awkwardness can proceed but from two causes; either from not having kept good company, or from not having attended to it. As for your keeping good company, I will take care of that; do you take care to observe their ways and manners, and to form your own upon them. Attention is absolutely necessary for this, as indeed it is for everything else; and a man without attention is not fit to live in the world. When an awkward fellow first comes into a room, it is highly probable that his sword gets between his legs, and throws him down, or makes him stumble at least; when he has recovered this accident, he goes and places himself in the very place of the whole room where he should not; there he soon lets his hat fall down; and, taking it up again, throws down his cane; in recovering his cane, his hat falls a second time; so that he is a quarter of an hour before he is in order again. If he drinks tea or coffee, he certainly scalds his mouth, and lets either the cup or the saucer fall, and spills the tea or coffee in his breeches. At dinner, his awkwardness distinguishes itself particularly, as he has more to do: there he holds his knife, fork, and spoon differently from other people; eats with his knife to the great danger of his mouth, picks his teeth with his fork, and puts his spoon, which has been in his throat twenty times, into the dishes again. If he is to carve, he can never hit the joint; but, in his vain efforts to cut through the bone, scatters the sauce in everybody's face. He generally daubs himself with soup and grease, though his napkin is commonly stuck through a button-hole, and tickles his chin. When he drinks, he infallibly coughs in his glass, and besprinkles the company. Besides all this, he has strange tricks and gestures; such as snuffing up his nose, making faces, putting his fingers in his nose, or blowing it and looking afterwards in his handkerchief, so as to make the company sick. His hands are troublesome to him, when he has not something in them, and he does not know where to put them; but they are in perpetual motion between his bosom and his breeches: he does not wear his clothes, and in short does nothing, like other people. All this, I own, is not in any degree criminal; but it is highly disagreeable and ridiculous in company, and ought most carefully to be avoided by whoever desires to please.

From this account of what you should not do, you may easily judge what you should do; and a due attention to the manners of people of fashion, and who have seen the world, will make it habitual and familiar to you.

There is, likewise, an awkwardness of expression and words, most carefully to be avoided; such as false English, bad pronunciation, old sayings, and common proverbs; which are so many proofs of having kept bad and low company. For example; if, instead of saying that tastes are different, and that every man has his own peculiar one, you should let off a proverb, and say That what is one man's meat is another man's poison; or else, Every one as they like, as the good man said when he kissed his cow; everybody would be persuaded that you had never kept company with anybody above footmen and housemaids.

Attention will do all this; and without attention nothing is to be done: want of attention, which is really want of thought, is either folly or madness. You should not only have attention to everything, but a quickness of attention, so as to observe, at once, all the people in the room; their motions, their looks, and their words; and yet without staring at them, and seeming to be an observer. This quick and unobserved observation is of infinite advantage in life, and is to be acquired with care; and, on the contrary, what is called absence, which is a thoughtlessness, and want of attention about what is doing, makes a man so like either a fool or a madman, that, for my part, I see no real difference. A fool never has thought; a madman has lost it; and an absent man is, for the time, without it.

Adieu! Direct your next to me, *chez Monsieur Chabert, Banquier, à Paris;* and take care that I find the improvements I expect at my return.

TO HIS SON

London, December 9, O. S. 1749

Dear Boy,

It is now above forty years since I have never spoken nor written one single word, without giving myself at least one moment's time to consider, whether it was a good one or a bad one, and whether I could not find out a better in its place. An unharmonious and rugged period, at this time, shocks my ears; and I, like all the rest of the world, will willingly exchange, and give up some degree of rough sense, for a good degree of pleasing sound. I will freely and truly own to you, without either vanity or false modesty, that whatever reputation I have acquired as a speaker, is more owing to my constant attention to my diction, than to my matter, which was necessarily just the same as other people's. When you come into Parliament, your reputation as a speaker will depend much more upon your words, and your periods, than upon the subject. The same matter occurs equally to everybody of common sense, upon the same question; the dressing it well, is what excites the attention and admiration of the audience.

It is in Parliament that I have set my heart upon your making a figure; it is there that I want to have you justly proud of yourself, and to make me justly proud of you. This means that you must be a good speaker there; I use the word *must*, because I know you may if you will. The vulgar, who are always mistaken, look upon a speaker and a comet with the same astonishment and admiration, taking them both for preternatural phenomena. This error discourages many young men from attempting that character; and good speakers are willing to have their talent considered as something very extraordinary, if not a peculiar gift of God to his elect. But let you and I analyse and simplify this good speaker; let us strip him of those adventitious plumes, with which his own pride, and the ignorance of others have decked him, and we shall find the true definition of him to be no more than this:—A man of good common sense, who reasons justly, and expresses himself elegantly on that subject upon which he speaks. There is, surely, no witchcraft in this. A man of sense, without a superior and astonishing degree of parts, will not talk nonsense upon any subject; nor will he, if he has the least taste or application, talk inelegantly. What then does all this mighty art and mystery of speaking in Parliament amount to? Why, no more than this, That the man who speaks in the House of Commons, speaks in that House, and to four hundred people, that opinion, upon a given subject, which he would make no difficulty of speaking in any house in England, round the fire, or at table, to any fourteen people whatsoever; better judges, perhaps, and severer critics of what he says, than any fourteen gentlemen of the House of Commons.

I have spoken frequently in Parliament, and not always without some applause; and therefore I can assure you, from my experience, that there is very little in it. The elegancy of the style, and the turn of the periods, make the chief impression upon the hearers. Give them but one or two round and harmonious periods in a speech, which they will retain and repeat, and they will go home as well satisfied, as people do from an opera, humming all the way one or two favourite tunes that have struck their ears and were easily caught. Most people have ears, but few have judgment; tickle those ears, and, depend upon it, you will catch their judgments, such as they are.

Cicero, conscious that he was at the top of his profession, (for in his time Eloquence was a profession) in order to set himself off, defines, in his Treatise *de Oratore*, an Orator to be such a man as never was, or never will be; and by this fallacious argument, says, that he must know every art and science whatsoever, or how shall he speak upon them? But with submission to so great an authority, my definition of an Orator is extremely different from, and, I believe, much truer than his. I call that man an Orator, who reasons justly, and expresses himself elegantly upon whatever subject he treats. Problems in Geometry, Equations in Algebra, Processes in Chymistry, and Experiments in Anatomy, are never, that I have heard of, the objects of Eloquence; and therefore I humbly conceive, that a man may be a very fine speaker, and yet know nothing of Geometry, Algebra, Chymistry, or Anatomy. The subjects of all Parliamentary debates, are subjects of common sense singly.

Thus I write whatever occurs to me, that I may contribute either to form or inform you. May my labour not be in vain! and it will not, if you will but have half the concern for yourself, that I have for you. Adieu.

Thomas Gray (1716–1771)

TO HORACE WALPOLE

Cambridge, February 11, 1751

As you have brought me into a little sort of distress, you must assist me, I believe, to get out of it as well as I can. Yesterday I had the misfortune of receiving a letter from certain gentlemen (as their bookseller expresses it), who have taken the Magazine of Magazines into their hands. They tell me that an *ingenious* Poem, called reflections in a Country Church-yard, has been communicated to them, which they are printing forthwith; that they are informed that the *excellent* author of it is I by name, and that they beg not only his *indulgence*, but the *honour* of his correspondence, etc. As I am not at all disposed to be either so indulgent, or so correspondent, as they desire, I have but one bad way left to escape the honour they would inflict upon me; and therefore am obliged to desire you would make Dodsley print it immediately (which may be done in less than a week's time) from your copy, but without my name, in what form is most convenient for him, but on his best paper and character; he must correct the press himself, and print it without any interval between the stanzas, because the sense is in some places continued beyond them; and the title must be, — Elegy, written in a Country Church-yard. If he would add a line or two to say it came into his hands by accident, I should like it better. If you behold the Magazine of Magazines in the light that I do, you will not refuse to give yourself this trouble on my account, which you have taken of your own accord before now. If Dodsley do not do this immediately, he may as well let it alone.

TO THE REV. WILLIAM MASON

Dec. 19, 1757

Though I very well know the bland emollient saponaceous qualities both of sack and silver, yet if any great man would say to me, 'I make you rat-catcher to his Majesty, with a salary of £300 a year and two butts of the best Malaga; and though it has been usual to catch a mouse or two, for form's sake, in public once a year, yet to you, sir, we shall not stand upon these things,' I cannot say I should jump at it; nay, if they would drop the very name of the office, and call me Sinecure to the King's Majesty, I should still feel a little awkward, and think everybody I saw smelt a rat about me; but I do not pretend to blame any one else that has not the same sensations; for my part I would rather be sergeant trumpeter or pinmaker to the palace. Nevertheless I interest myself a little in the history of it, and rather wish somebody may accept it that will retrieve the credit of the thing, if it be retrievable, or ever had any credit. Rowe was, I think, the last man of character that had it. As to Settle, whom you mention, he belonged to my lord mayor not to the king. Eusden was a person of great hopes in his youth, though at last he turned out a drunken parson. Dryden was as disgraceful to the office, from his character, as the poorest scribbler could have been from his verses. The office itself has always humbled the professor hitherto (even in an age when kings were somebody), if he were a poor writer by making him more conspicuous, and if he were a good one by setting him at war with the little fry of his own profession, for there are poets little enough to envy even a poet-laureat.

I am obliged to you for your news; pray send me some more, and better of the sort. I can tell you nothing in return; so your generosity will be the greater; — only Dick is going to give up his rooms, and live at Ashwell. Mr. Treasurer sets Sir M. Lamb at nought, and says he has sent him reasons half a sheet at a time; and Mr. Brown attests his veracity as an eye-witness. I have had nine pages of criticism on the 'Bard' sent me in an anonymous letter, directed to the Reverend Mr. G. at Strawberry Hill; and if I have a mind to hear as much more on the other Ode, I am told where I may direct. He seems a good sensible man, and I dare say a clergyman. He is very frank, and indeed much ruder than he means to be. Adieu, dear Mason, and believe me that I am too.

TO HORACE WALPOLE

[June 28 (?), 1760]

I am so charmed with the two specimens of Erse poetry, that I cannot help giving you the trouble to enquire a little farther about them, and should wish to see a few lines of the original, that I may form some slight idea of the language, the measures, and the rhythm.

Is there anything known of the author or authors, and of what antiquity are they supposed to be? Is there any more to be had of equal beauty, or at all approaching to it? I have been often told that the poem called 'Hardicanute' (which I always admired and still admire) was the work of somebody that lived a few years ago. This I do not at all believe, though it has evidently been retouched in places by some modern hand: but however, I am authorized by this report to ask, whether the two Poems in question are certainly antique and genuine. I make this enquiry in quality of an antiquary, and am not otherwise concerned about it: for, if I were sure that any one now living in Scotland had written them to divert himself, and laugh at the credulity of the world, I would undertake a journey into the Highlands only for the pleasure of seeing him.

TO THE REV. NORTON NICHOLLS

Pembroke Hall, August 26, 1766

It is long since that I heard you were gone in hast into Yorkshire on account of your mother's illness; and the same letter informed me that she was recovered; otherwise I had then wrote to you, only to beg you would take care of her, and to inform you that I had discovered a thing very little known, which is, that in one's whole life one never can have any more than a single mother. You may think this is obvious, and (what you call) a trite observation. You are a green gosling! I was at the same age (very near) as wise as you, and yet I never discovered this (with full evidence and conviction, I mean) till it was too late. It is thirteen years ago, and seems but yesterday; and every day I live it sinks deeper into my heart. Many a corollary could I draw from this axiom for your use (not for my own) but I will leave you the merit of doing it yourself. Pray tell me how your own health is. I conclude it perfect, as I hear you offered yourself for a guide to Mr. Palgrave, into the Sierra-Morena of Yorkshire. For me, I passed the end of May and all June in Kent not disagreeably; the country is all a garden, gay, rich, and fruitful, and (from the rainy season) had preserved, till I left it, all that emerald verdure, which commonly one only sees for the first fortnight of spring. In the west part of it from every eminence the eye catches some long winding reach of the Thames or Medway, with all their navigation; in the east, the sea breaks in upon you, and mixes its white transient sails and glittering blue expanse with the deeper and brighter greens of the woods and corn. This last sentence is so fine, I am quite ashamed; but, no matter! you must translate it into prose. Palgrave, if he heard it, would cover his face with his pudding sleeve. I went to Margate for a day; one would think it was Bartholomew fair that had *flown* down from Smithfield to Kent in the London machine, like my Lady Stuffdamask (to be sure you have read the *New Bath Guide*, the most fashionable of books): so then I did *not* go to Kingsgate, because it belonged to my Lord Holland; but to Ramsgate I did, and so to Sandwich, and Deal, and Dover, and Folkestone, and Hythe, all along the coast, very delightful. I do not tell you of the great and small beasts, and creeping things innumerable that I met with, because you do not suspect that this world is inhabited by anything but men and women and clergy, and such two-legged cattle. Now I am here again very disconsolate and all alone, even Mr. Brown is gone; and the cares of this world are coming thick upon me; I do not mean children. You, I hope, are better off, riding and walking in the woods of Studley with Mr. Aislaby, singing duets with my cousin Fanny, improving with Mr. Weddell, conversing with Mr. Harry Duncomb. I must not wish for you here; besides, I am going to town at Michaelmas, by no means for amusement. Do you remember how we are to go into Wales next year? well! — Adieu, I am sincerely yours.

Samuel Johnson (1709–1784)

TO THE RIGHT HONOURABLE THE EARL OF CHESTERFIELD

February 7, 1755

My Lord,

I have lately been informed, by the proprietor of the World, that two papers, in which my Dictionary is recommended to the public, were written by your Lordship. To be so distinguished, is an honour, which, being very little accustomed to favours from the great, I know not well how to receive, or in what terms to acknowledge.

When, upon some slight encouragement, I first visited your Lordship, I was overpowered, like the rest of mankind, by the enchantment of your address; and could not forbear to wish that I might boast myself *Le vainqueur du vainqueur de la terre;* — that I might obtain that regard for which I saw the world contending; but I found my attendance so little encouraged, that neither pride nor modesty would suffer me to continue it. When I had once addressed your Lordship in public, I had exhausted all the art of pleasing which a retired and uncourtly scholar can possess. I had done all that I could; and no man is well pleased to have his all neglected, be it ever so little.

Seven years, my Lord, have now past, since I waited in your outward rooms, or was repulsed from your door; during which time I have been pushing on my work through difficulties, of which it is useless to complain, and have brought it, at last, to the verge of publication, without one act of assistance, one word of encouragement, or one smile of favour. Such treatment I did not expect, for I never had a Patron before.

The shepherd in Virgil grew at last acquainted with Love, and found him a native of the rocks.

Is not a Patron, my Lord, one who looks

with unconcern on a man struggling for life in the water, and, when he has reached ground, encumbers him with help? The notice which you have been pleased to take of my labours, had it been early, had been kind; but it has been delayed till I am indifferent, and cannot enjoy it; till I am solitary, and cannot impart it; till I am known, and do not want it. I hope it is no very cynical asperity not to confess obligations where no benefit has been received, or to be unwilling that the Public should consider me as owing that to a Patron, which Providence has enabled me to do for myself.

Having carried on my work thus far with so little obligation to any favourer of learning, I shall not be disappointed though I should conclude it, if less be possible, with less; for I have been long wakened from that dream of hope, in which I once boasted myself with so much exultation,

My Lord,
Your Lordship's most humble
Most obedient servant,
SAM. JOHNSON

TO BENNET LANGTON

July 5, 1774

DEAR SIR, — You have reason to reproach me that I have left your last letter so long unanswered, but I had nothing particular to say. Chambers, you find, is gone far, and poor Goldsmith is gone much further. He died of a fever, exasperated, as I believe, by the fear of distress. He had raised money and squandered it by every artifice of acquisition, and folly of expence. But let not his frailties be remembered; he was a very great man.

I have just begun to print my Journey to the Hebrides, and am leaving the press to take another journey into Wales, whither Mr. Thrale is going, to take possession of, at least, five hundred a year, fallen to his lady. All at Streatham, that are alive, are well.

I have never recovered from the last dreadful illness, but flatter myself that I grow gradually better; much, however, yet remains to mend. Κύριε ἐλέησον.

If you have the Latin version of *Busy, curious, thirsty, fly*, be so kind as to transcribe and send it; but you need not be in haste, for I shall be I know not where, for at least five weeks. I wrote the following tetrastick on poor Goldsmith:

Τὸν τάφον εἰσοράας τὸν 'Ολιβαρίοιο, κονίην
"Αφροσι μὴ σεμνὴν, Ξεῖνε , πόδεσσι πάτει.
Οἷσι μέμηλε φύσις, μέτρων χάρις, ἔργα παλαιῶν
Κλαίετε ποιητήν, ἱστορικόν, φυσικόν.

Please to make my most respectful compliments to all the ladies, and remember me to young George and his sisters. I reckon George begins to shew a pair of heels.

Do not be sullen now, but let me find a letter when I come back. I am, dear Sir,

Your affectionate, humble servant,
SAM. JOHNSON

TO JAMES MACPHERSON

[before February, 1775]

MR. JAMES MACPHERSON,

I received your foolish and impudent letter. Any violence offered me I shall do my best to repel; and what I cannot do for myself, the law shall do for me. I hope I shall never be deterred from detecting what I think a cheat, by the menaces of a ruffian.

What would you have me retract? I thought your book an imposture; I think it an imposture still. For this opinion I have given my reasons to the public, which I here dare you to refute. Your rage I defy. Your abilities, since your Homer, are not so formidable; and what I hear of your morals, inclines me to pay regard not to what you shall say, but to what you shall prove. You may print this if you will.

SAM. JOHNSON

TO MRS. BOSWELL

May 16, 1776

MADAM, — You must not think me uncivil in omitting to answer the letter with which you favoured me some time ago. I imagined it to have been written without Mr. Boswell's knowledge, and therefore supposed the answer to require, what I could not find, a private conveyance.

The difference with Lord Auchinleck is now over; and since young Alexander has appeared, I hope no more difficulties will arise among you; for I sincerely wish you all happy. Do not teach the young ones to dislike me, as you dislike me yourself; but let me at least have Veronica's kindness, because she is my acquaintance.

You will now have Mr. Boswell home; it is well that you have him; he has led a wild life. I have taken him to Lichfield, and he has followed Mr. Thrale to Bath. Pray take care of him, and tame him. The only thing in which I have the honour to agree with you is, in loving him; and while we are so much of a mind in a matter of so much importance, our other quarrels will, I hope, produce no great bitterness. I am, Madam,

Your most humble servant,

SAM. JOHNSON

TO MRS. PIOZZI (THRALE)

July 2, 1784

MADAM, — If I interpret your letter right, you are ignominiously married: if it is yet undone, let us once more talk together. If you have abandoned your children and your religion, God forgive your wickedness; if you have forfeited your fame and your country, may your folly do no further mischief! If the last act is yet to do, I who have loved you, esteemed you, reverenced you, and served you, I who long thought you the first of womankind, entreat that, before your fate is irrevocable, I may once more see you.

I was, I once was, Madam, most truly yours,

SAM. JOHNSON

Horace Walpole (1717–1797)

TO GEORGE MONTAGU, ESQ.

Arlington Street, Dec. 8, 1761

I return you the list of prints, and shall be glad you will bring me all to which I have affixed this mark x. The rest I have; yet the expense of the whole list would not ruin me. Lord Farnham, who, I believe, departed this morning, brings you the list of the Duke of Devonshire's pictures.

I have been told that Mr. Bourk's history was of England, not of Ireland; I am glad it is the latter, for I am now in Mr. Hume's England, and would fain read no more. I not only know what has been written, but what would be written. Our story is so exhausted, that to make it new, they really *make* it *new*. Mr. Hume has exalted Edward the Second, and depressed Edward the Third. The next historian, I suppose, will make James the First a hero, and geld Charles the Second.

Fingal is come out; I have not yet got through it; not but it is very fine — yet I cannot at once compass an epic poem now. It tires me to death to read how many ways a warrior is like the moon, or the sun, or a rock, or a lion, or the ocean. Fingal is a brave collection of similes, and will serve all the boys at Eton and Westminster for these twenty years. I will trust you with a secret, but you must not disclose it; I should be ruined with my Scotch friends; in short, I cannot believe it genuine; I cannot believe a regular poem of six books has been preserved, uncorrupted, by oral tradition, from times before Christianity was introduced into the island. What! preserved unadulterated by savages dispersed among mountains, and so often driven from their dens, so wasted by wars civil and foreign! Has one man ever got all by heart? I doubt it; were parts preserved by some, other parts by others? Mighty lucky, that the tradition was never interrupted, nor any part lost — not a verse, not a measure, not the sense! luckier and luckier. I have been extremely qualified myself lately for this Scotch memory; we have had nothing but a coagulation of rains, fogs, and frosts, and though they have clouded all understanding, I suppose, if I had tried, I should have found that they thickened, and gave great consistence to my remembrance.

You want news — I must make it, if I send it. To change the dullness of the scene I went to the play [at Drury Lane], where I had not been this winter. They are so crowded, that though I went before six, I got no better place than a fifth row, where I heard very ill, and was pent for five hours without a soul near me that I knew. It was Cymbeline, and appeared to me as long as if everybody in it went really to Italy in every act, and came back again. With a few pretty passages and a scene or two, it is so absurd and tiresome, that I am persuaded Garrick * * *

TO THOMAS CHATTERTON

Arlington Street, March 28, 1769

I cannot but think myself singularly obliged by a gentleman with whom I have not the pleasure of being acquainted, when I read your very curious and kind letter, which I have this minute received. I give you a thousand thanks for it, and for the very obliging offer you make me, of communicating your MSS. to me. What you have already sent me is very valuable, and full of information; but instead of correcting you, Sir, you are far more able to correct me. I have not the happiness of understanding the Saxon language, and without your learned notes should not have been able to comprehend Rowley's text.

As a second edition of my Anecdotes was published but last year, I must not flatter myself that a third will be wanted soon; but I shall be happy to lay up any notices you will be so good as to extract for me, and send me at your leisure; for, as it is uncertain when I may use them, I would by no means borrow and detain your MSS.

Give me leave to ask you where Rowley's poems are to be found? I should not be sorry to print them; or at least, a specimen of them, if they have never been printed.

The Abbot John's verses that you have given me, are wonderful for their harmony and spirit, though there are some words I do not understand.

You do not point out exactly the time when he lived, which I wish to know, as I suppose it was long before John Ab Eyck's discovery of oil-painting. If so, it confirms what I had guessed, and have hinted in my Anecdotes, that oil-painting was known here much earlier than that discovery or revival.

I will not trouble you with more questions now, Sir, but flatter myself from the humanity and politeness you have already shown me, that you will sometimes give me leave to consult you. I hope, too, you will forgive the simplicity of my direction, as you have favoured me with no other.

I am, Sir,
Your much obliged
And obedient humble servant,
Hor. Walpole

TO THE REV. WILLIAM COLE

Strawberry Hill, June 19, 1777

I thank you for your notices, dear Sir, and shall remember that on Prince William. I did see the 'Monthly Review,' but hope one is not guilty of the death of every man who does not make one the dupe of a forgery. I believe M'Pherson's success with 'Ossian' was more the ruin of Chatterton than I. Two years passed between my doubting the authenticity of Rowley's poems and his death. I never knew he had been in London till some time after he had undone and poisoned himself there. The poems he sent me were transcripts in his own hand, and even in that circumstance he told a lie: he said he had them from the very person at Bristol to whom he had given them. If any man was to tell you that monkish rhymes had been dug up at Herculaneum, which was destroyed several centuries before there was any such poetry, should you believe it? Just the reverse is the case of Rowley's pretended poems. They have all the elegance of Waller and Prior, and more than Lord Surrey — but I have no objection to anybody believing what he pleases. I think poor Chatterton was an astonishing genius — but I cannot think that Rowley foresaw metres that were invented long after he was dead, or that our language was more refined at Bristol in the reign of Henry V. than it was at Court under Henry VIII. One of the chaplains of the Bishop of Exeter has found a line of Rowley in Hudibras — the monk might foresee that too! The prematurity of Chatterton's genius is, however, full as wonderful, as that such a prodigy as Rowley should never have been heard of till the eighteenth century. The youth and industry of the former are miracles, too, yet still more credible. There is not a symptom in the poems, but the old words, that savours of Rowley's age — change the old words for modern, and the whole construction is of yesterday.

TO THE COUNTESS OF [OSSORY]

January 13, 1797

You distress me infinitely by showing my idle notes, which I cannot conceive can amuse anybody. My old-fashioned breeding impels me every now and then to reply to the letters you honour me with writing; but in truth very unwillingly, for I seldom can have anything particular to say. I scarce go out of my own house, and then only to two or three very private places, where I see nobody that really knows anything — and what I learn comes from newspapers, that collect intelligence from coffee-houses — consequently, what I neither believe nor report. At home I see only a few charitable elders, except about fourscore nephews and nieces of various ages, who are each brought to me once a year, to stare at me as the Methusalem of the family; and they can only speak of their own contemporaries, which interest no more than if they talked of their dolls, or bats and balls. Must not the result of all this, madam, make me a very entertaining correspondent? — and can such letters be worth showing? — or can I have any spirit when so old, and reduced to dictate? Oh! my good madam, dispense with me from such a task, and think how it must add to it to apprehend such letters being shown. Pray send me no more such laurels, which I desire no more than their leaves when decked with a scrap of tinsel, and stuck on twelfth-cakes that lie on the shop-boards of pastry-cooks at Christmas. I shall be quite content with a sprig of rosemary thrown after me, when the parson of the parish commits my dust to dust. Till then, pray, madam, accept the resignation of

Your ancient servant

William Cowper (1731–1800)

TO THE REV. WILLIAM UNWIN

Olney, October 31, 1779

My Dear Friend, — I wrote my last letter merely to inform you that I had nothing to say, in answer to which you have said nothing. I admire the propriety of your conduct, though I am a loser by it. I will endeavour to say something now, and shall hope for something in return.

I have been well entertained with Johnson's biography, for which I thank you: with one exception, and that a swinging one, I think he has acquitted himself with his usual good sense and sufficiency. His treatment of Milton is unmerciful to the last degree. A pensioner is not likely to spare a republican, and the Doctor, in order, I suppose, to convince his royal patron of the sincerity of his monarchical principles, has belaboured that great poet's character with the most industrious cruelty. As a man, he has hardly left him the shadow of one good quality. Churlishness in his private life, and a rancorous hatred of everything royal in his public, are the two colours with which he has smeared all the canvas. If he had any virtues, they are not to be found in the Doctor's picture of him; and it is well for Milton that some sourness in his temper is the only vice with which his memory has been charged; it is evident enough that, if his biographer could have discovered more, he would not have spared him. As a poet, he has treated him with severity enough, and has plucked one or two of the most beautiful feathers out of his Muse's wing, and trampled them under his great foot. He has passed sentence of condemnation upon Lycidas, and has taken occasion, from that charming poem, to expose to ridicule (what is indeed ridiculous enough) the childish prattlement of pastoral compositions, as if Lycidas was the prototype and pattern of them all. The liveliness of the description, the sweetness of the numbers, the classical spirit of antiquity that prevails in it, go for nothing. I am convinced, by the way, that he has no ear for poetical numbers, or that it was stopped, by prejudice, against the harmony of Milton's. Was there ever anything so delightful as the music of the Paradise Lost? It is like that of a fine organ; has the fullest and deepest tones of majesty, with all the softness and elegance of the Dorian flute, variety without end, and never equalled, unless, perhaps, by Virgil. Yet the Doctor has little or nothing to say upon this copious theme, but talks something about the unfitness of the English language for blank verse, and how apt it is in the mouth of some readers, to degenerate into declamation. Oh! I could thrash his old jacket till I made his pension jingle in his pockets.

I could talk a good while longer, but I have no room. Our love attends yourself, Mrs. Unwin, and Miss Shuttleworth, not forgetting the two miniature pictures at your elbow.

Yours affectionately,

W. C.

TO THE REV. WILLIAM UNWIN

Olney, August 6, 1780

My dear Friend, — You like to hear from me — this is a very good reason why I should write — but I have nothing to say — this seems equally a good reason why I should not; yet if you had alighted from your horse at our door this morning, and at this present writing, being five o'clock in the afternoon, had found occasion to say to me — 'Mr. Cowper, you have not spoke since I came in; have you resolved never to speak again?' — it would be but a poor reply, if, in answer to the summons, I should plead inability as my best and only excuse. And this, by the way, suggests to me a seasonable piece of instruction, and reminds me of what I am very apt to forget when I have any epistolary business in hand; that a letter may be written upon anything or nothing, just as that anything or nothing happens to occur. A man that has a journey before him twenty miles in length, which he is to perform on foot, will not hesitate and doubt whether he shall set out or not, because he does not readily conceive how he shall ever reach the end of it; for he knows that, by the simple operation of moving one foot forward first and then the other, he shall be sure to accomplish it. So it is in the present case, and so it is in every similar case. A letter is written, as a conversation is maintained or a journey performed, not by preconcerted or premeditated means, a new contrivance, or an invention never heard of before; but merely by maintaining a progress, and resolving, as a postilion does, having once set out, never to stop till we reach the appointed end. If a man may talk without thinking, why may he not write upon the same terms? A grave gentleman of the last century, a tie-wig, square-toe, Steinkirk figure, would say, 'My good sir, a man has no right to do either.' But it is to be hoped that the present century has nothing to do with the moldy opinions of the last; and so, good Sir Launcelot, or St. Paul, or whatever be your name, step into your picture-frame again, and look as if you thought for another century, and leave us moderns in the mean time to think when we can, and to write whether we can or not, else we might as well be dead as you are.

When we look back upon our forefathers, we seem to look back upon the people of another nation, almost upon creatures of another species. Their vast rambling mansions, spacious halls, and painted casements, the gothic porch, smothered with honeysuckles, their little gardens and high walls, their box-edgings, balls of holly, and yew-tree statues, are become so entirely unfashionable now, that we can hardly believe it possible that a people who resembled us so little in their taste should resemble us in anything else. But in everything else I suppose they were our counterparts exactly, and time, that has sewed up the slashed sleeve, and reduced the large trunk hose to a neat pair of silk stockings, has left human nature just where it found it. The inside of the man at least has undergone no change. His passions, appetites, and aims, are just what they ever were. They wear perhaps a handsomer disguise than they did in the days of yore, for philosophy and literature will have their effect upon the exterior; but in every other respect a modern is only an ancient in a different dress.

Yours,

W. C.

TO THE REV. JOHN NEWTON

Olney, July 12, 1781

My very dear Friend, — I am going to send, what when you have read, you may scratch your head, and say, I suppose, there's nobody knows whether what I have got be verse or not; — by the tune and the time, it ought to be rhyme, but if it be, did you ever see, of late or of yore, such a ditty before?

I have writ Charity, not for popularity, but as well as I could, in hopes to do good; and if the Reviewer should say 'to be sure the gentleman's Muse wears Methodist shoes, you may know by her pace and talk about grace, that she and her bard have little regard for the taste and fashions, and ruling passions, and hoidening play, of the modern day; and though she assume a borrowed plume, and now and then wear a tittering air, 'tis only her plan to catch, if she can, the giddy and gay, as they go that way, by a production on a new construction: she has baited her trap, in hopes to snap all that may come with a sugar-plum.' —— His opinion in this will not be amiss; 'tis what I intend, my principal end, and, if I succeed, and folks should read, till a few are brought to a serious thought, I shall think I am paid for all I have said and all I have done, though I have run many a time, after a rhyme, as far as from hence to the end of my sense, and by hook or crook, write another book, if I live and am here, another year.

I have heard before, of a room with a floor laid upon springs, and such like things, with so much art in every part, that when you went in you was forced to begin a minuet pace, with an air and a grace, swimming about, now in and now out, with a deal of state, in a figure of eight, without pipe, or string, or any such thing; and now I have writ, in a rhyming fit, what will make you dance, and as you advance, will keep you still, though against your will, dancing away, alert and gay, till you come to an end of what I have penned, which that you may do, ere Madam and you are quite worn out with jigging about, I take my leave, and here you receive a bow profound, down to the ground, from your humble me —

W. C.

TO THE REV. JOHN NEWTON

Dec. 10, 1785

My dear Friend, — What you say of my last volume gives me the sincerest pleasure. I have heard a like favourable report of it from several different quarters, but never any (for obvious reasons) that has gratified me more than yours. I have a relish for moderate praise, because it bids fair to be judicious; but praise excessive, such as our poor friend ——'s, (I have an uncle also who celebrates me exactly in the same language,) — such praise is rather too big for an ordinary swallow. I set down nine-tenths of it to the account of family partiality. I know no more than you what kind of a market my book has found; but this I believe, that had not Henderson died, and had it been worth my while to have given him a hundred pounds to have read it in public, it would have been more popular than it is. I am at least very unwilling to esteem John Gilpin as better worth than all the rest that I have written, and he has been popular enough.

Your sentiments of Pope's Homer agree perfectly with those of every competent judge with whom I have at any time conversed about it. I never saw a copy so unlike the original. There is not I believe in all the world to be found an uninspired poem so simple as those of Homer, nor in all the world a poem more bedizened with ornaments than Pope's translation of them. Accordingly, the sublime of Homer in the hands of Pope becomes bloated and tumid, and his description tawdry. Neither had Pope the faintest conception of those exquisite discriminations of character for which Homer is so remarkable. All his persons, and equally upon all occasions, speak in an inflated and strutting phraseology, as Pope has managed them; although in the original the dignity of their utterance, even when they are most majestic, consists principally in the simplicity of their sentiments and their language. Another censure I must needs pass upon our Anglo-Grecian, out of many that obtrude themselves upon me, but for which I have neither time to spare, nor room, which is, that with all his great abilities he was defective in his feelings to a degree that some passages in his own poems make it difficult to account for. No writer more pathetic than Homer, because none more natural; and because none less natural than Pope in his version of Homer, therefore than he none less pathetic. But I shall tire you with a theme with which I would not wish to cloy you beforehand.

If the great change in my experience, of which you express so lively an expectation, should take place, and whenever it shall take place, you may securely depend upon receiving the first notice of it. But, whether you come with congratulations, or whether without them, I need not say that you and yours will always be most welcome here. Mrs. Unwin's love both to yourself and to Mrs. Newton joins itself as usual, and as warmly as usual, to that of

Yours, my dear friend,
Affectionately and faithfully,
Wm. Cowper

TO THE REV. JOHN NEWTON

June 12, 1793

My dear Friend, — You promise to be contented with a line, and a short one you must have, hurried over in the little interval I have happened to find between the conclusion of my morning task and breakfast. Study has this good effect, at least: it makes me an early riser, who might otherwise, perhaps, be as much given to dozing as my readers.

The scanty opportunity I have, I shall employ in telling you what you principally wish to be told — the present state of mine and Mrs. Unwin's health. In her I cannot perceive any alteration for the better; and must be satisfied, I believe, as indeed I have great reason to be, if she does not alter for the worse. She uses the orchard-walk daily, but always supported between two, and is still unable to employ herself as formerly. But she is cheerful, seldom in much pain, and has always strong confidence in the mercy and faithfulness of God.

As to myself, I have always the same song to sing — Well in body, but sick in spirit; sick, nigh unto death.

Seasons return, but not to me returns
God, or the sweet approach of heavenly day,
Or sight of cheering truth, or pardon sealed,
Or joy, or hope, or Jesus' face divine;
But cloud, &c.

I could easily set my complaint to Milton's tone, and accompany him through the whole passage, on the subject of a blindness more deplorable than his; but time fails me.

I feel great desire to see your intended publication; a desire which the manner in which Mr. Bull speaks of it, who called here lately, has no tendency to allay. I believe I forgot to thank you for your last poetical present; not because I was not much pleased with it, but I write always in a hurry, and in a hurry must now conclude myself, with our united love,

Yours, my dear friend,
Most sincerely,
Wm. Cowper

NINETEENTH CENTURY

PARALLEL READINGS

AGE OF ROMANTICISM

Biography

1. Southey — *Life of Nelson*
2. Lockhart — *Life of Scott*, Selections

Novel

1. Austen — *Pride and Prejudice*
2. Scott — *Bride of Lammermoor*, or *Redgauntlet*
3. Lytton — *Harold*, or *Last Days of Pompeii*

Drama

1. Knowles — *Virginius*
2. Lytton — *Lady of Lyons*, or *Richelieu*

VICTORIAN AGE

Novel

1. Dickens — *David Copperfield*
2. Thackeray — *Vanity Fair*
3. Eliot — *Mill on the Floss*
4. Stevenson — *Master of Ballantrae*
5. Meredith — *Ordeal of Richard Feverel*
6. Hardy — *Return of the Native*

Drama

1. Browning — *Blot in the 'Scutcheon*
2. Robertson — *Society*, or *Caste*
3. Tennyson — *Becket*

MODERN PERIOD

Novel

1. De Morgan — *Joseph Vance*
2. Conrad — *Nigger of the Narcissus*

Drama

1. Barrie — *Peter Pan*
2. Shaw — *Man and Superman*
3. Galsworthy — *Silver Box*
4. Masefield — *Tragedy of Nan*

NINETEENTH CENTURY

THE NEWER POETRY AND CRITICISM AND THE NOVEL

Reaction against conventionality, emphasis upon spontaneity and emotion, interest in the past, in Nature, in solitude, in the remote or exotic, in unspoiled humanity, and in children and childlike simplicity were, as indicated above (p. 404*f*), characteristics of eighteenth-century English opinion which foreshadow a new order. Stimulated by the transformation of English industrial life, the rise of Methodism, and the French Revolution, this body of thought grew more and more influential as the century progressed, and resulted in what is known as the Romantic Movement. Though too complex for exact definition, Romanticism has as its chief characteristics emphasis upon the emotional life and an enthusiastic idealism.

In literature Romanticism finds its fullest expression in the *Lyrical Ballads*, published by Wordsworth and Coleridge in 1798. In literary theory the Preface to the *Lyrical Ballads* has been called the Declaration of Independence of the Romantic Movement.

Under the influence of the Romantic spirit all literary types showed a renewed vigor, but the chief glory of the movement was poetry. No other period of English literature can boast a greater wealth of distinguished names than this, which produced almost simultaneously Wordsworth, Coleridge, Byron, Shelley, and Keats, along with a multitude of minor though nevertheless inspired writers. In prose fiction the preëminent figure is Scott, whose novels form the culmination of a long line of historical and Gothic romances. Jane Austen painted with realistic fidelity the country society of her own day. The familiar essay attained a high degree of perfection in the delicately humorous personal revelations of Lamb. Longer prose exposition was admirably represented in the imaginative compositions of De Quincey and the stirring appeals of Carlyle. In the drama alone is there a dearth of significant productions. The best plays of the Romantic era are significant for their poetry or their philosophy of life rather than for their acting qualities.

As the nineteenth century progressed the emotionalism and the intensely personal attitude of the romanticist yielded gradually to a more detached and disciplined view of the world. Though the Romantic spirit by no means disappeared, the Victorian Era, covering roughly the last three-quarters of the nineteenth century, tended to become conservative in its attitude toward society and art. Coupled with the development of the new scientific spirit, prose fiction, especially the novel, became dominated by Realism, which may be defined as the attempt to present truth objectively, even scientifically, without suppression or sentimental bias. The mild Realism of Dickens, Thackeray, and George Eliot is gradually replaced by the more profound and mordant criticism of life in Meredith and Hardy. During the late nineteenth and the first quarter of the twentieth century, Naturalism ("an acute form of Realism") and "psychological analysis" become increasingly common as methods of literary treatment. Socialism and other remedies for the ills of society also appear in the work of late nineteenth and early twentieth century writers, notably Shaw and Wells. Among the shorter prose forms, the most significant are the short-story, with its highly developed special technique, and the critical essay, which latter reached a high degree of perfection in the hands of Arnold, Ruskin, Swinburne, and other writers. A crowning achievement of the age was the perfection of the modern prose sentence by Macaulay, Arnold, Newman, and Pater. That poetry was not stultified by the prevailing scientific spirit of the Victorian period is evinced by the presence of two of the greatest English poets, Browning and Tennyson, along with a number of slightly less gifted writers. During the latter part of the nineteenth and the beginning of the twentieth century a new romantic reaction against conventionality and materialism manifested itself in a multitude of ways — in the splendid optimism and high spirit of adventure of Stevenson, in the "religion of beauty" of Pater, in the decadent æstheticism of Oscar Wilde, in the mystical search for the Celtic spirit by the poets of the Irish Renaissance.

In its combination of tradition with contemporary interests, the Victorian era, when the present unjust prejudice has passed, will stand out as one of the richest and greatest in the history of English literature. The beginning of the twentieth century reveals little new or significant in any branch of literature; even Free Verse is largely a recombination of old features. Hence we feel justified in concluding that another great literary era closed with the beginning of the World War.

AGE OF ROMANTICISM

POETRY

William Cowper (1731–1800)

THE DIVERTING HISTORY OF JOHN GILPIN

John Gilpin was a citizen
Of credit and renown,
A trainband captain eke was he
Of famous London town.

John Gilpin's spouse said to her dear,
'Though wedded we have been
These twice ten tedious years, yet we
No holiday have seen.

'To-morrow is our wedding-day,
And we will then repair
Unto The Bell at Edmonton,
All in a chaise and pair.

'My sister, and my sister's child,
Myself, and children three,
Will fill the chaise; so you must ride
On horseback after we.'

He soon replied, — 'I do admire
Of womankind but one,
And you are she, my dearest dear,
Therefore it shall be done.

'I am a linendraper bold,
As all the world doth know,
And my good friend the calender
Will lend his horse to go.'

Quoth Mistress Gilpin, — 'That 's well said;
And for that wine is dear,
We will be furnished with our own,
Which is both bright and clear.'

John Gilpin kissed his loving wife;
O'erjoyed was he to find,
That, though on pleasure she was bent,
She had a frugal mind.

The morning came, the chaise was brought,
But yet was not allowed
To drive up to the door, lest all
Should say that she was proud.

So three doors off the chaise was stayed,
Where they did all get in;
Six precious souls, and all agog
To dash through thick and thin.

Smack went the whip, round went the wheels,
Were never folk so glad,
The stones did rattle underneath
As if Cheapside were mad.

John Gilpin at his horse's side
Seized fast the flowing mane,
And up he got, in haste to ride,
But soon came down again;

For saddletree scarce reached had he,
His journey to begin,
When, turning round his head, he saw
Three customers come in.

So down he came; for loss of time,
Although it grieved him sore,
Yet loss of pence, full well he knew,
Would trouble him much more.

'T was long before the customers
Were suited to their mind,
When Betty screaming came down stairs,
'The wine is left behind!'

'Good lack!' quoth he, 'yet bring it me,
My leathern belt likewise,
In which I bear my trusty sword
When I do exercise.'

Now Mistress Gilpin (careful soul!)
Had two stone bottles found,
To hold the liquor that she loved,
And keep it safe and sound.

Each bottle had a curling ear,
Through which the belt he drew,
And hung a bottle on each side,
To make his balance true.

Then over all, that he might be
  Equipped from top to toe,
His long red cloak, well brushed and neat
  He manfully did throw.

Now see him mounted once again
  Upon his nimble steed,
Full slowly pacing o'er the stones
  With caution and good heed.

But finding soon a smoother road
  Beneath his well shod feet,
The snorting beast began to trot,
  Which galled him in his seat.

So, 'Fair and softly,' John he cried,
  But John he cried in vain;
That trot became a gallop soon,
  In spite of curb and rein.

So stooping down, as needs he must
  Who cannot sit upright,
He grasped the mane with both his hands,
  And eke with all his might.

His horse, who never in that sort
  Had handled been before,
What thing upon his back had got
  Did wonder more and more.

Away went Gilpin, neck or naught;
  Away went hat and wig;
He little dreamt, when he set out
  Of running such a rig.

The wind did blow, the cloak did fly,
  Like streamer long and gay,
Till, loop and button failing both,
  At last it flew away.

Then might all people well discern
  The bottles he had slung;
A bottle swinging at each side,
  As hath been said or sung.

The dogs did bark, the children screamed,
  Up flew the windows all;
And every soul cried out, 'Well done!'
  As loud as he could bawl.

Away went Gilpin — who but he?
  His fame soon spread around;
'He carries weight!' 'he rides a race!'
  ''T is for a thousand pound!'

And still, as fast as he drew near,
  'T was wonderful to view,
How in a trice the turnpike men
  Their gates wide open threw.

And now, as he went bowing down
  His reeking head full low,
The bottles twain behind his back
  Were shattered at a blow.

Down ran the wine into the road,
  Most piteous to be seen,
Which made his horse's flanks to smoke
  As they had basted been.

But still he seemed to carry weight,
  With leathern girdle braced;
For all might see the bottle-necks
  Still dangling at his waist.

Thus all through merry Islington
  These gambols he did play,
And till he came unto the Wash
  Of Edmonton so gay;

And there he threw the wash about,
  On both sides of the way,
Just like unto a trundling mop,
  Or a wild goose at play.

At Edmonton, his loving wife
  From the balcony spied
Her tender husband, wondering much
  To see how he did ride.

'Stop, stop, John Gilpin! — here's the house!'
  They all at once did cry;
'The dinner waits, and we are tired': —
  Said Gilpin — 'So am I!'

But yet his horse was not a whit
  Inclined to tarry there;
For why? — his owner had a house
  Full ten miles off, at Ware.

So like an arrow swift he flew,
  Shot by an archer strong;
So did he fly — which brings me to
  The middle of my song.

Away went Gilpin, out of breath,
  And sore against his will,
Till, at his friend the calender's,
  His horse at last stood still.

The calender, amazed to see
  His neighbour in such trim,
Laid down his pipe, flew to the gate
  And thus accosted him: —

'What news? what news? your tidings tell;
  Tell me you must and shall —
Say why bareheaded you are come,
  Or why you come at all?'

Now Gilpin had a pleasant wit,
  And loved a timely joke;

And thus unto the calender
  In merry guise, he spoke:

'I came because your horse would come;
  And, if I well forebode,
My hat and wig will soon he here, —
  They are upon the road.'

The calender, right glad to find
  His friend in merry pin,
Returned him not a single word,
  But to the house went in;

Whence straight he came with hat and wig;
  A wig that flowed behind,
A hat not much the worse for wear,
  Each comely in its kind.

He held them up, and in his turn,
  Thus showed his ready wit; —
'My head is twice as big as yours,
  They therefore needs must fit.

'But let me scrape the dirt away
  That hangs upon your face;
And stop and eat, for well you may
  Be in a hungry case.'

Says John —'It is my wedding-day,
  And all the world would stare,
If wife should dine at Edmonton,
  And I should dine at Ware.'

So turning to his horse, he said,
  'I am in haste to dine;
'T was for your pleasure you came here,
  You shall go back for mine.'

Ah! luckless speech, and bootless boast!
  For which he paid full dear;
For while he spake, a braying ass
  Did sing most loud and clear;

Whereat his horse did snort, as he
  Had heard a lion roar,
And galloped off with all his might,
  As he had done before.

Away went Gilpin, and away
  Went Gilpin's hat and wig:
He lost them sooner than at first,
  For why? — they were too big.

Now Mistress Gilpin, when she saw
  Her husband posting down
Into the country far away,
  She pulled out half-a-crown;

And thus unto the youth she said,
  That drove them to The Bell,
'This shall be yours when you bring back
  My husband safe and well.'

The youth did ride, and soon did meet
  John coming back amain;
Whom in a trice he tried to stop
  By catching at his rein;

But not performing what he meant,
  And gladly would have done,
The frighted steed he frighted more,
  And made him faster run.

Away went Gilpin, and away
  Went postboy at his heels,
The postboy's horse right glad to miss
  The lumbering of the wheels.

Six gentlemen upon the road,
  Thus seeing Gilpin fly,
With postboy scampering in the rear,
  They raised the hue and cry: —

'Stop thief! stop thief! — a highwayman!'
  Not one of them was mute;
And all and each that passed that way
  Did join in the pursuit.

And now the turnpike-gates again
  Flew open in short space,
The toll-men thinking as before,
  That Gilpin rode a race.

And so he did, and won it too,
  For he got first to town;
Nor stopped till where he had got up
  He did again get down.

Now let us sing, Long live the king,
  And Gilpin, long live he;
And when he next doth ride abroad,
  May I be there to see!

1782

THE TASK, BOOK IV

THE WINTER EVENING

HARK! 't is the twanging horn! O'er yonder bridge
That with its wearisome but needful length
Bestrides the wintry flood, in which the moon
Sees her unwrinkled face reflected bright,
He comes, the herald of a noisy world,
With spattered boots, strapped waist, and frozen locks,
News from all nations lumbering at his back.
True to his charge, the close-packed load behind,
Yet careless what he brings, his one concern
Is to conduct it to the destined inn,
And, having dropped the expected bag, pass on.

He whistles as he goes, light-hearted wretch,
Cold and yet cheerful; messenger of grief
Perhaps to thousands, and of joy to some;
To him indifferent whether grief or joy.
Houses in ashes, and the fall of stocks,
Births, deaths, and marriages, epistles wet
With tears that trickled down the writer's cheeks
Fast as the periods from his fluent quill,
Or charged with amorous sighs of absent swains,
Or nymphs responsive, equally affect
His horse and him, unconscious of them all.
But oh the important budget! ushered in
With such heart-shaking music, who can say
What are its tidings? have our troops awaked?
Or do they still, as if with opium drugged,
Snore to the murmurs of the Atlantic wave?
Is India free? and does she wear her plumed
And jewelled turban with a smile of peace?
Or do we grind her still? The grand debate,
The popular harangue, the tart reply,
The logic, and the wisdom, and the wit,
And the loud laugh — I long to know them all;
I burn to set the imprisoned wranglers free,
And give them voice and utterance once again.
  Now stir the fire, and close the shutters fast,
Let fall the curtains, wheel the sofa round,
And while the bubbling and loud-hissing urn
Throws up a steamy column, and the cups
That cheer but not inebriate, wait on each,
So let us welcome peaceful evening in.
Not such his evening, who with shining face
Sweats in the crowded theatre, and squeezed
And bored with elbow-points through both his sides,
Outscolds the ranting actor on the stage:
Nor his, who patient stands till his feet throb
And his head thumps, to feed upon the breath
Of patriots bursting with heroic rage,
Or placemen all tranquillity and smiles.
This folio of four pages, happy work!
Which not even critics criticise; that holds
Inquisitive attention while I read,
Fast bound in chains of silence, which the fair,
Though eloquent themselves, yet fear to break;
What is it but a map of busy life,
Its fluctuations and its vast concerns?
Here runs the mountainous and craggy ridge
That tempts Ambition. On the summit, see
The seals of office glitter in his eyes;
He climbs, he pants, he grasps them! At his heels,
Close at his heels, a demagogue ascends,
And with a dextrous jerk soon twists him down
And wins them, but to lose them in his turn.
Here rills of oily eloquence in soft
Meanders lubricate the course they take;
The modest speaker is ashamed and grieved
To engross a moment's notice, and yet begs,
Begs a propitious ear for his poor thoughts,
However trivial all that he conceives.
Sweet bashfulness! it claims at least this praise;
The dearth of information and good sense
That it foretells us, always comes to pass.
Cataracts of declamation thunder here,
There forests of no meaning spread the page,
In which all comprehension wanders lost;
While fields of pleasantry amuse us there
With merry descants on a nation's woes.
The rest appears a wilderness of strange
But gay confusion; roses for the cheeks
And lilies for the brows of faded age,
Teeth for the toothless, ringlets for the bald,
Heaven, earth, and ocean, plundered of their sweets.
Nectareous essences, Olympian dews,
Sermons, and city feasts, and favorite airs,
Ethereal journeys, submarine exploits,
And Katterfelto, with his hair on end
At his own wonders, wondering for his bread.
  'T is pleasant through the loopholes of retreat
To peep at such a world; to see the stir
Of the great Babel, and not feel the crowd;
To hear the roar she sends through all her gates
At a safe distance, where the dying sound
Falls a soft murmur on the uninjured ear.
Thus sitting, and surveying thus at ease
The globe and its concerns, I seem advanced
To some secure and more than mortal height,
That liberates and exempts me from them all.
It turns submitted to my view, turns round
With all its generations; I behold
The tumult, and am still. The sound of war
Has lost its terrors ere it reaches me;
Grieves, but alarms me not. I mourn the pride
And avarice that makes man a wolf to man;
Hear the faint echo of those brazen throats
By which he speaks the language of his heart,

And sigh, but never tremble at the sound.
He travels and expatiates, as the bee
From flower to flower so he from land to land;
The manners, customs, policy of all
Pay contribution to the store he gleans;
He sucks intelligence in every clime,
And spreads the honey of his deep research
At his return, a rich repast for me.
He travels, and I too. I tread his deck,
Ascend his topmast, through his peering eyes
Discover countries, with a kindred heart
Suffer his woes and share in his escapes;
While fancy, like the finger of a clock,
Runs the great circuit, and is still at home.
Oh Winter, ruler of the inverted year,
Thy scattered hair with sleetlike ashes filled,
Thy breath congealed upon thy lips, thy cheeks
Fringed with a beard made white with other snows
Than those of age, thy forehead wrapped in clouds,
A leafless branch thy sceptre, and thy throne
A sliding car indebted to no wheels,
But urged by storms along its slippery way,
I love thee, all unlovely as thou seemest,
And dreaded as thou art! Thou holdest the sun
A prisoner in the yet undawning east,
Shortening his journey between morn and noon,
And hurrying him, impatient of his stay,
Down to the rosy west; but kindly still
Compensating his loss with added hours
Of social converse and instructive ease,
And gathering at short notice, in one group
The family dispersed, and fixing thought,
Not less dispersed by daylight and its cares.
I crown thee king of intimate delights,
Fireside enjoyments, homeborn happiness,
And all the comforts that the lowly roof
Of undisturbed Retirement, and the hours
Of long uninterrupted evening know.
No rattling wheels stop short before these gates;
No powdered pert proficient in the art
Of sounding an alarm, assaults these doors
Till the street rings; no stationary steeds
Cough their own knell, while, heedless of the sound
The silent circle fan themselves, and quake;
But here the needle plies its busy task,
The pattern grows, the well-depicted flower,
Wrought patiently into the snowy lawn,
Unfolds its bosom; buds, and leaves, and sprigs,
And curly tendrils, gracefully disposed,
Follow the nimble finger of the fair;
A wreath that cannot fade, of flowers that blow
With most success when all besides decay.
The poet's or historian's page, by one
Made vocal for the amusement of the rest;
The sprightly lyre, whose treasure of sweet sounds
The touch from many a trembling chord shakes out;
And the clear voice, symphonious yet distinct,
And in the charming strife triumphant still,
Beguile the night, and set a keener edge
On female industry; the threaded steel
Flies swiftly, and unfelt the task proceeds.
The volume closed, the customary rites
Of the last meal commence: a Roman meal,
Such as the mistress of the world once found
Delicious, when her patriots of high note,
Perhaps by moonlight, at their humble doors,
And under an old oak's domestic shade,
Enjoyed, spare feast! a radish and an egg.
Discourse ensues, not trivial, yet not dull,
Nor such as with a frown forbids the play
Of fancy, or proscribes the sound of mirth:
Nor do we madly, like an impious world,
Who deem religion frenzy, and the God
That made them an intruder on their joys,
Start at his awful name, or deem his praise
A jarring note. Themes of a graver tone
Exciting oft our gratitude and love,
While we retrace with Memory's pointing wand,
That calls the past to our exact review,
The dangers we have 'scaped, the broken snare,
The disappointed foe, deliverance found
Unlooked for, life preserved, and peace restored,
Fruits of omnipotent eternal love.
'Oh evenings worthy of the gods!' exclaimed
The Sabine bard. Oh evenings, I reply,
More to be prized and coveted than yours,
As more illumined and with nobler truths,
That I, and mine, and those we love, enjoy.
Is winter hideous in a garb like this?
Needs he the tragic fur, the smoke of lamps,
The pent-up breath of an unsavoury throng,
To thaw him into feeling, or the smart
And snappish dialogue, that flippant wits
Call comedy, to prompt him with a smile?
The self-complacent actor, when he views
(Stealing a sidelong glance at a full house)

The slope of faces from the floor to the roof,
(As if one master-spring controlled them all)
Relaxed into an universal grin,
Sees not a countenance there that speaks of joy
Half so refined or so sincere as ours.
Cards were superfluous here, with all the tricks
That idleness has ever yet contrived
To fill the void of an unfurnished brain,
To palliate dulness and give time a shove.
Time as he passes us has a dove's wing,
Unsoiled and swift, and of a silken sound,
But the World's Time, is Time in masquerade.
Theirs, should I paint him, has his pinions fledged
With motley plumes, and, where the peacock shows
His azure eyes, is tinctured black and red,
With spots quadrangular of diamond form,
Ensanguined hearts, clubs typical of strife,
And spades the emblem of untimely graves.
What should be and what was an hourglass once,
Becomes a dicebox, and a billiard-mast
Well does the work of his destructive scythe.
Thus decked, he charms a world whom Fashion blinds
To his true worth, most pleased when idle most;
Whose only happy are their wasted hours.
Even misses, at whose age their mothers wore
The backstring and the bib, assume the dress
Of womanhood, sit pupils in the school
Of card-devoted Time, and night by night
Placed at some vacant corner of the board,
Learn every trick, and soon play all the game.
But truce with censure. Roving as I rove,
Where shall I find an end, or how proceed?
As he that travels far, oft turns aside
To view some rugged rock or mouldering tower,
Which seen delights him not; then coming home,
Describes and prints it, that the world may know
How far he went for what was nothing worth;
So I, with brush in hand and pallet spread,
With colours mixed for a far different use,
Paint cards and dolls, and every idle thing
That Fancy finds in her excursive flights.
  Come, Evening, once again, season of peace;
Return, sweet Evening, and continue long!
Methinks I see thee in the streaky west,
With matronstep slow moving, while the Night
Treads on thy sweeping train; one hand employed
In letting fall the curtain of repose
On bird and beast, the other charged for man
With sweet oblivion of the cares of day:
Not sumptuously adorned, nor needing aid,
Like homely-featured Night, of clustering gems;
A star or two, just twinkling on thy brow,
Suffices thee; save that the moon is thine
No less than hers, not worn indeed on high
With ostentatious pageantry, but set
With modest grandeur in thy purple zone,
Resplendent less, but of an ampler round.
Come, then, and thou shalt find thy votary calm,
Or make me so. Composure is thy gift:
And whether I devote thy gentle hours
To books, to music, or the poet's toil;
To weaving nets for bird-alluring fruit;
Or twining silken threads round ivory reels,
When they command whom man was born to please;
I slight thee not, but make thee welcome still.
  Just when our drawingrooms begin to blaze
With lights, by clear reflection multiplied
From many a mirror, in which he of Gath,
Goliath, might have seen his giant bulk
Whole without stooping, towering crest and all,
My pleasures too begin. But me, perhaps,
The glowing hearth may satisfy a while
With faint illumination, that uplifts
The shadow to the ceiling, there by fits
Dancing uncouthly to the quivering flame.
Not undelightful is an hour to me
So spent in parlour twilight; such a gloom
Suits well the thoughtful or unthinking mind,
The mind contemplative, with some new theme
Pregnant, or indisposed alike to all.
Laugh ye, who boast your more mercurial powers
That never feel a stupor, know no pause,
Nor need one; I am conscious and confess,
Fearless, a soul that does not always think.
Me oft has Fancy ludicrous and wild,
Soothed with a waking dream of houses, towers,
Trees, churches, and strange visages expressed
In the red cinders, while with poring eye
I gazed, myself creating what I saw.

Nor less amused, have I quiescent watched
The sooty films that play upon the bars,
Pendulous, and foreboding, in the view
Of superstition, prophesying still
Though still deceived, some stranger's near approach.
'T is thus the understanding takes repose
In indolent vacuity of thought,
And sleeps and is refreshed. Meanwhile the face
Conceals the mood lethargic with a mask
Of deep deliberation, as the man
Were tasked to his full strength, absorbed and lost.
Thus oft, reclined at ease, I lose an hour
At evening, till at length the freezing blast,
That sweeps the bolted shutter, summons home
The recollected powers, and snapping short
The glassy threads with which the Fancy weaves
Her brittle toys, restores me to myself.
How calm is my recess, and how the frost,
Raging abroad, and the rough wind, endear
The silence and the warmth enjoyed within.
I saw the woods and fields at close of day
A variegated show; the meadows green
Though faded; and the lands where lately waved
The golden harvest, of a mellow brown,
Upturned so lately by the forceful share.
I saw far off the weedy fallows smile
With verdure not unprofitable, grazed
By flocks, fast feeding and selecting each
His favourite herb; while all the leafless groves
That skirt the horizon, wore a sable hue,
Scarce noticed in the kindred dusk of eve.
To-morrow brings a change, a total change!
Which even now, though silently performed
And slowly, and by most unfelt, the face
Of universal nature undergoes.
Fast falls a fleecy shower; the downy flakes
Descending, and with never-ceasing lapse
Softly alighting upon all below,
Assimilate all objects. Earth receives
Gladly the thickening mantle, and the green
And tender blade, that feared the chilling blast,
Escapes unhurt beneath so warm a veil.
In such a world, so thorny, and where none
Finds happiness unblighted, or if found,
Without some thistly sorrow at its side,
It seems the part of wisdom, and no sin
Against the law of love, to measure lots
With less distinguished than ourselves, that thus
We may with patience bear our moderate ills,
And sympathise with others suffering more.
Ill fares the traveller now, and he that stalks
In ponderous boots beside his reeking team.
The wain goes heavily, impeded sore
By congregating loads adhering close
To the clogged wheels; and in its sluggish pace
Noiseless, appears a moving hill of snow.
The toiling steeds expand the nostril wide,
While every breath, by respiration strong
Forced downward, is consolidated soon
Upon their jutting chests. He, formed to bear
The pelting brunt of the tempestuous night,
With half-shut eyes, and puckered cheeks, and teeth
Presented bare against the storm, plods on.
One hand secures his hat, save when with both
He brandishes his pliant length of whip,
Resounding oft, and never heard in vain.
Oh happy! and, in my account, denied
That sensibility of pain with which
Refinement is endued, thrice happy thou!
Thy frame, robust and hardy, feels indeed
The piercing cold, but feels it unimpaired.
The learnèd finger never need explore
Thy vigorous pulse, and the unhealthful East,
That breathes the spleen, and searches every bone
Of the infirm, is wholesome air to thee.
Thy days roll on exempt from household care:
Thy waggon is thy wife, and the poor beasts
That drag the dull companion to and fro,
Thine helpless charge, dependent on thy care.
Ah, treat them kindly! rude as thou appearest,
Yet show that thou hast mercy, which the great,
With needless hurry whirled from place to place,
Humane as they would seem, not always show.
Poor, yet industrious, modest, quiet, neat,
Such claim compassion in a night like this,
And have a friend in every feeling heart.
Warmed, while it lasts, by labour, all day long
They brave the season, and yet find at eve,
Ill-clad and fed but sparely, time to cool.

The frugal housewife trembles when she lights
Her scanty stock of brushwood, blazing clear,
But dying soon, like all terrestrial joys.
The few small embers left she nurses well;
And while her infant race, with outspread hands
And crowded knees, sit cowering o'er the sparks,
Retires, content to quake, so they be warmed.
The man feels least, as more inured than she
To winter, and the current in his veins
More briskly moved by his severer toil;
Yet he too finds his own distress in theirs.
The taper soon extinguished, which I saw
Dangled along at the cold finger's end
Just when the day declined, and the brown loaf
Lodged on the shelf, half-eaten without sauce
Of savoury cheese, or butter costlier still,
Sleep seems their only refuge: for, alas!
Where penury is felt the thought is chained,
And sweet colloquial pleasures are but few.
With all this thrift they thrive not. All the care
Ingenious parsimony takes, but just
Saves the small inventory, bed and stool,
Skillet and old carved chest, from public sale.
They live, and live without extorted alms
From grudging hands, but other boast have none
To soothe their honest pride, that scorns to beg;
Nor comfort else, but in their mutual love.
I praise you much, ye meek and patient pair,
For ye are worthy; choosing rather far
A dry but independent crust, hard earned
And eaten with a sigh, than to endure
The rugged frowns and insolent rebuffs
Of knaves in office, partial in their work
Of distribution; liberal of their aid
To clamorous importunity in rags,
But oft-times deaf to suppliants who would blush
To wear a tattered garb however coarse,
Whom famine cannot reconcile to filth;
These ask with painful shyness, and, refused
Because deserving, silently retire.
But be ye of good courage. Time itself
Shall much befriend you. Time shall give increase,
And all your numerous progeny, well trained,
But helpless, in few years shall find their hands,
And labour too. Meanwhile ye shall not want
What, conscious of your virtues, we can spare,
Nor what a wealthier than ourselves may send.
I mean the man who, when the distant poor
Need help, denies them nothing but his name.
But poverty with most, who whimper forth
Their long complaints, is self-inflicted woe,
The effect of laziness or sottish waste.
Now goes the nightly thief prowling abroad
For plunder, much solicitous how best
He may compensate for a day of sloth,
By works of darkness and nocturnal wrong.
Woe to the gardener's pale, the farmer's hedge
Plashed neatly, and secured with driven stakes
Deep in the loamy bank. Uptorn by strength,
Resistless in so bad a cause, but lame
To better deeds, he bundles up the spoil,
An ass's burden, and when laden most
And heaviest, light of foot steals fast away.
Nor does the boarded hovel better guard
The well-stacked pile of riven logs and roots
From his pernicious force. Nor will he leave
Unwrenched the door, however well secured,
Where chanticleer amidst his harem sleeps
In unsuspecting pomp. Twitched from the perch,
He gives the princely bird, with all his wives,
To his voracious bag, struggling in vain,
And loudly wondering at the sudden change.
Nor this to feed his own! 'T were some excuse,
Did pity of their sufferings warp aside
His principle, and tempt him into sin
For their support, so destitute. But they
Neglected pine at home, themselves, as more
Exposed than others, with less scruple made
His victims, robbed of their defenceless all.
Cruel is all he does. 'T is quenchless thirst
Of ruinous ebriety that prompts
His every action, and imbrutes the man.
Oh for a law to noose the villain's neck
Who starves his own, who persecutes the blood
He gave them in his children's veins, and hates
And wrongs the woman he has sworn to love.
Pass where we may, through city or through town,
Village or hamlet, of this merry land,
Though lean and beggared, every twentieth pace

Conducts the unguarded nose to such a whiff
Of stale debauch, forth-issuing from the styes
That law has licensed, as makes Temperance reel.
There sit involved and lost in curling clouds
Of Indian fume, and guzzling deep, the boor,
The lackey, and the groom; the craftsman there
Takes a Lethean leave of all his toil;
Smith, cobbler, joiner, he that plies the shears,
And he that kneads the dough; all loud alike,
All learnèd, and all drunk. The fiddle screams
Plaintive and piteous, as it wept and wailed
Its wasted tones, and harmony unheard:
Fierce the dispute, whate'er the theme; while she,
Fell Discord, arbitress of such debate,
Perched on the signpost, holds with even hand
Her undecisive scales. In this she lays
A weight of ignorance; in that, of pride;
And smiles delighted with the eternal poise.
Dire is the frequent curse, and its twin sound
The cheek-distending oath, not to be praised
As ornamental, musical, polite,
Like those which modern senators employ,
Whose oath is rhetoric, and who swear for fame.
Behold the schools in which plebeian minds,
Once simple, are initiated in arts,
Which some may practise with politer grace,
But none with readier skill! — 'T is here they learn
The road that leads from competence and peace
To indigence and rapine; till at last
Society, grown weary of the load,
Shakes her encumbered lap, and casts them out.
But censure profits little: vain the attempt
To advertise in verse a public pest,
That like the filth with which the peasant feeds
His hungry acres, stinks and is of use.
The excise is fattened with the rich result
Of all this riot; and ten thousand casks,
For ever dribbling out their base contents,
Touched by the Midas finger of the state,
Bleed gold for ministers to sport away.
Drink and be mad then; 't is your country bids!
Gloriously drunk, obey the important call!
Her cause demands the assistance of your throats;
Ye all can swallow, and she asks no more.

Would I had fallen upon those happier days
That poets celebrate; those golden times
And those Arcadian scenes that Maro sings,
And Sidney, warbler of poetic prose.
Nymphs were Dianas then, and swains had hearts
That felt their virtues; Innocence, it seems,
From courts dismissed, found shelter in the groves;
The footsteps of simplicity, impressed
Upon the yielding herbage (so they sing),
Then were not all effaced; then speech profane,
And manners profligate, were rarely found,
Observed as prodigies, and soon reclaimed.
Vain wish! those days were never: airy dreams
Sat for the picture; and the poet's hand,
Imparting substance to an empty shade,
Imposed a gay delirium for a truth.
Grant it: — I still must envy them an age
That favoured such a dream, in days like these
Impossible, when Virtue is so scarce,
That to suppose a scene where she presides
Is tramontane, and stumbles all belief.
No: we are polished now! The rural lass,
Whom once her virgin modesty and grace,
Her artless manners, and her neat attire,
So dignified, that she was hardly less
Than the fair shepherdess of old romance,
Is seen no more. The character is lost!
Her head adorned with lappets pinned aloft
And ribbons streaming gay, superbly raised,
And magnified beyond all human size,
Indebted to some smart wig-weaver's hand
For more than half the tresses it sustains;
Her elbows ruffled, and her tottering form
Ill propped upon French heels; she might be deemed
But that the basket dangling on her arm
Interprets her more truly) of a rank
Too proud for dairy work, or sale of eggs.
Expect her soon with footboy at her heels,
No longer blushing for her awkward load,
Her train and her umbrella all her care.

The town has tinged the country; and the stain

Appears a spot upon a vestal's robe,
The worse for what it soils. The fashion runs
Down into scenes still rural; but, alas,
Scenes rarely graced with rural manners now!
Time was when in the pastoral retreat
The unguarded door was safe; men did not watch
To invade another's right, or guard their own.
Then sleep was undisturbed by Fear, unscared
By drunken howlings; and the chilling tale
Of midnight murder was a wonder heard
With doubtful credit, told to frighten babes.
But farewell now to unsuspicious nights,
And slumbers unalarmed! Now, ere you sleep,
See that your polished arms be primed with care,
And drop the night-bolt; — ruffians are abroad;
And the first larum of the cock's shrill throat
May prove a trumpet, summoning your ear
To horrid sounds of hostile feet within.
Even daylight has its dangers; and the walk
Through pathless wastes and woods, unconscious once
Of other tenants than melodious birds
Or harmless flocks, is hazardous and bold.
Lamented change! to which full many a cause
Inveterate, hopeless of a cure, conspires.
The course of human things from good to ill,
From ill to worse, is fatal, never fails.
Increase of power begets increase of wealth;
Wealth luxury, and luxury excess;
Excess, the scrofulous and itchy plague
That seizes first the opulent, descends
To the next rank contagious, and in time
Taints downward all the graduated scale
Of order, from the chariot to the plough.
The rich, and they that have an arm to check
The licence of the lowest in degree,
Desert their office; and themselves intent
On pleasure, haunt the capital, and thus
To all the violence of lawless hands
Resign the scenes their presence might protect.
Authority herself not seldom sleeps,
Though resident, and witness of the wrong.
The plump convivial parson often bears
The magisterial sword in vain, and lays
His reverence and his worship both to rest
On the same cushion of habitual sloth.
Perhaps timidity restrains his arm;
When he should strike, he trembles and sets free,
Himself enslaved by terror of the band,
The audacious convict, whom he dares not bind.
Perhaps, though by profession ghostly pure,
He too may have his vice, and sometimes prove
Less dainty than becomes his grave outside,
In lucrative concerns. Examine well
His milkwhite hand; the palm is hardly clean
But here and there an ugly smutch appears.
Foh! 't was a bribe that left it: he has touched
Corruption! Whoso seeks an audit here
Propitious, pays his tribute, game or fish,
Wildfowl or venison, and his errand speeds.
  But faster far, and more than all the rest,
A noble cause, which none who bears a spark
Of public virtue ever wished removed,
Works the deplored and mischievous effect.
'T is universal soldiership has stabbed
The heart of merit in the meaner class.
Arms, through the vanity and brainless rage
Of those that bear them, in whatever cause,
Seem most at variance with all moral good,
And incompatible with serious thought.
The clown, the child of nature, without guile,
Blest with an infant's ignorance of all
But his own simple pleasures, now and then
A wrestling match, a footrace, or a fair,
Is balloted, and trembles at the news:
Sheepish he doffs his hat, and mumbling swears
A Bible-oath to be whate'er they please,
To do he knows not what. The task performed,
That instant he becomes the serjeant's care,
His pupil, and his torment, and his jest.
His awkward gait, his introverted toes,
Bent knees, round shoulders, and dejected looks,
Procure him many a curse. By slow degrees,
Unapt to learn, and formed of stubborn stuff,
He yet by slow degrees puts off himself,
Grows conscious of a change, and likes it well:
He stands erect, his slouch becomes a walk;
He steps right onward, martial in his air,
His form and movement; is as smart above
As meal and larded locks can make him; wears
His hat, or his plumed helmet with a grace;
And his three years of heroship expired,

Returns indignant to the slighted plough.
He hates the field in which no fife or drum
Attends him, drives his cattle to a march,
And sighs for the smart comrades he has left.
'T were well if his exterior change were all,
But with his clumsy port the wretch has lost
His ignorance and harmless manners too.
To swear, to game, to drink; to show at home
By lewdness, idleness, and sabbath-breach,
The great proficiency he made abroad;
To astonish and to grieve his gazing friends;
To break some maiden's and his mother's heart;
To be a pest where he was useful once;
Are his sole aim, and all his glory now.
  Man in society is like a flower
Blown in its native bed; 't is there alone
His faculties, expanded in full bloom,
Shine out; there only reach their proper use.
But man associated and leagued with man
By regal warrant, or self-joined by bond
For interest sake, or swarming into clans
Beneath one head for purposes of war,
Like flowers selected from the rest, and bound
And bundled close to fill some crowded vase,
Fades rapidly, and by compression marred,
Contracts defilement not to be endured.
Hence chartered boroughs are such public plagues;
And burghers, men immaculate perhaps
In all their private functions, once combined,
Become a loathsome body, only fit
For dissolution, hurtful to the main.
Hence merchants, unimpeachable of sin
Against the charities of domestic life,
Incorporated, seem at once to lose
Their nature, and, disclaiming all regard
For mercy and the common rights of man,
Build factories with blood, conducting trade
At the sword's point, and dyeing the white robe
Of innocent commercial Justice red.
Hence, too, the field of glory, as the world
Misdeems it, dazzled by its bright array,
With all its majesty of thundering pomp,
Enchanting music, and immortal wreaths,
Is but a school where thoughtlessness is taught
On principle, where foppery atones
For folly, gallantry for every vice.
  But slighted as it is, and by the great
Abandoned, and which still I more regret,
Infected with the manners and the modes
It knew not once, the country wins me still.
I never framed a wish, or formed a plan,
That flattered me with hopes of earthly bliss,
But there I laid the scene. There early strayed
My Fancy, ere yet liberty of choice
Had found me, or the hope of being free.
My very dreams were rural; rural too
The firstborn efforts of my youthful Muse,
Sportive, and jingling her poetic bells,
Ere yet her ear was mistress of their powers.
No bard could please me but whose lyre was tuned
To Nature's praises. Heroes and their feats
Fatigued me, never weary of the pipe
Of Tityrus, assembling, as he sang,
The rustic throng beneath his favourite beech.
Then Milton had indeed a poet's charms:
New to my taste his Paradise surpassed
The struggling efforts of my boyish tongue
To speak its excellence; I danced for joy;
I marvelled much that, at so ripe an age
As twice seven years, his beauties had then first
Engaged my wonder, and admiring still,
And still admiring, with regret supposed
The joy half lost, because not sooner found.
Thee too enamoured of the life I loved,
Pathetic in its praise, in its pursuit
Determined, and possessing it at last
With transports such as favoured lovers feel,
I studied, prized, and wished that I had known,
Ingenious Cowley! and though now re-claimed
By modern lights from an erroneous taste,
I cannot but lament thy splendid wit
Entangled in the cobwebs of the schools,
I still revere thee, courtly though retired;
Though stretched at ease in Chertsey's silent bowers,
Not unemployed, and finding rich amends
For a lost world in solitude and verse.
'T is born with all: the love of Nature's works
Is an ingredient in the compound, man,
Infused at the creation of the kind.
And though the Almighty Maker has throughout
Discriminated each from each, by strokes
And touches of his hand, with so much art
Diversified, that two were never found
Twins at all points — yet this obtains in all,
That all discern a beauty in his works,
And all can taste them: minds that have been formed
And tutored with a relish more exact,

But none without some relish, none unmoved.
It is a flame that dies not even there
Where nothing feeds it. Neither business, crowds,
Nor habits of luxurious city-life,
Whatever else they smother of true worth
In human bosoms, quench it or abate.
The villas with which London stands begirt,
Like a swarth Indian with his belt of beads,
Prove it. A breath of unadulterate air,
The glimpse of a green pasture, how they cheer
The citizen, and brace his languid frame!
Even in the stifling bosom of the town,
A garden in which nothing thrives, has charms
That soothe the rich possessor; much consoled
That here and there some sprigs of mournful mint,
Of nightshade, or valerian, grace the well
He cultivates. These serve him with a hint
That Nature lives; that sight-refreshing green
Is still the livery she delights to wear,
Though sickly samples of the exuberant whole.
What are the casements lined with creeping herbs,
The prouder sashes fronted with a range
Of orange, myrtle, or the fragrant weed
The Frenchman's darling? are they not all proofs
That man immured in cities, still retains
His inborn inextinguishable thirst
Of rural scenes, compensating his loss
By supplemental shifts, the best he may?
The most unfurnished with the means of life,
And they that never pass their brick-wall bounds
To range the fields and treat their lungs with air,
Yet feel the burning instinct: over-head
Suspend their crazy boxes, planted thick,
And watered duly. There the pitcher stands
A fragment, and the spoutless teapot there;
Sad witnesses how close-pent man regrets
The country, with what ardour he contrives
A peep at Nature, when he can no more.
Hail, therefore, patroness of health and ease
And contemplation, heart-consoling joys
And harmless pleasures, in the thronged abode
Of multitudes unknown! hail, rural life!
Address himself who will to the pursuit
Of honours, or emolument, or fame,
I shall not add myself to such a chase,
Thwart his attempts, or envy his success.
Some must be great. Great offices will have
Great talents: and God gives to every man
The virtue, temper, understanding, taste,
That lifts him into life, and lets him fall
Just in the niche he was ordained to fill.
To the deliverer of an injured land
He gives a tongue to enlarge upon, a heart
To feel, and courage to redress her wrongs;
To monarchs dignity; to judges sense;
To artists ingenuity and skill;
To me an unambitious mind, content
In the low vale of life, that early felt
A wish for ease and leisure, and ere long
Found here that leisure and that ease I wished.

1785

ON THE RECEIPT OF MY MOTHER'S PICTURE

Oh that those lips had language! Life has passed
With me but roughly since I heard thee last.
Those lips are thine — thy own sweet smile I see,
The same that oft in childhood solaced me;
Voice only fails, else how distinct they say,
'Grieve not, my child, chase all thy fears away!'
The meek intelligence of those dear eyes
(Blessed be the Art that can immortalize, —
The Art that baffles Time's tyrannic claim
To quench it) here shines on me still the same.
Faithful remembrancer of one so dear,
O welcome guest, though unexpected, here!
Who bidst me honor with an artless song,
Affectionate, a mother lost so long,
I will obey, not willingly alone,
But gladly, as the precept were her own:
And while that face renews my filial grief,
Fancy shall weave a charm for my relief, —
Shall steep me in Elysian reverie,
A momentary dream, that thou art she.
My mother! when I learned that thou wast dead,
Say, wast thou conscious of the tears I shed?
Hovered thy spirit o'er thy sorrowing son,
Wretch even then, life's journey just begun?
Perhaps thou gavest me, though unfelt, a kiss;
Perhaps a tear, if souls can weep in bliss —
Ah, that maternal smile! It answers — 'Yes.'

I heard the bell tolled on thy burial day,
I saw the hearse that bore thee slow away,
And, turning from my nursery window, drew
A long, long sigh, and wept a last adieu!
But was it such? — It was. — Where thou art gone
Adieus and farewells are a sound unknown;
May I but meet thee on that peaceful shore,
The parting word shall pass my lips no more!
Thy maidens grieved themselves at my concern,
Oft gave me promise of thy quick return.
What ardently I wished, I long believed,
And, disappointed still, was still deceived;
By expectation every day beguiled,
Dupe of to-morrow even from a child.
Thus many a sad to-morrow came and went,
Till, all my stock of infant sorrow spent,
I learned at last submission to my lot,
But, though I less deplored thee, ne'er forgot.

Where once we dwelt our name is heard no more,
Children not thine have trod my nursery floor;
And where the gardener Robin, day by day,
Drew me to school along the public way,
Delighted with my bauble coach, and wrapped
In scarlet mantle warm, and velvet capped,
'T is now become a history little known,
That once we called the pastoral house our own.
Shortlived possession! but the record fair,
That memory keeps of all thy kindness there,
Still outlives many a storm that has effaced
A thousand other themes less deeply traced.
Thy nightly visits to my chamber made,
That thou mightest know me safe and warmly laid;
Thy morning bounties ere I left my home,
The biscuit, or confectionary plum;
The fragrant waters on my cheeks bestowed
By thy own hand, till fresh they shone and glowed:
All this, and more endearing still than all,
Thy constant flow of love, that knew no fall,
Ne'er roughened by those cataracts and brakes,
That humor interposed too often makes;
All this still legible in Memory's page,
And still to be so to my latest age,
Adds joy to duty, makes me glad to pay
Such honors to thee as my numbers may;
Perhaps a frail memorial, but sincere,
Not scorned in Heaven, though little noticed here.

Could Time, his flight reversed, restore the hours
When, playing with thy vesture's tissued flowers,
The violet, the pink, and jassamine,
I pricked them into paper with a pin,
(And thou wast happier than myself the while,
Wouldst softly speak, and stroke my head and smile),
Could those few pleasant days again appear,
Might one wish bring them, would I wish them here?
I would not trust my heart — the dear delight
Seems so to be desired, perhaps I might. —
But no — what here we call our life is such,
So little to be loved, and thou so much,
That I should ill requite thee, to constrain
Thy unbound spirit into bonds again.

Thou, as a gallant bark from Albion's coast
(The storms all weathered and the ocean crossed)
Shoots into port at some well-havened isle,
Where spices breathe, and brighter seasons smile,
There sits quiescent on the floods that show
Her beauteous form reflected clear below,
While airs impregnated with incense play
Around her, fanning light her streamers gay; —
So thou, with sails how swift! hast reached the shore,
'Where tempests never beat nor billows roar';
And thy loved consort on the dangerous tide
Of life, long since has anchored by thy side.
But me, scarce hoping to attain that rest,
Always from port withheld, always distressed —
Me howling blasts drive devious, tempest-tost,
Sails ripped, seams opening wide, and compass lost,
And day by day some current's thwarting force
Sets me more distant from a prosperous course.
Yet, oh the thought, that thou art safe, and he!
That thought is joy, arrive what may to me.
My boast is not, that I deduce my birth
From loins enthroned, and rulers of the earth;

But higher far my proud pretensions rise —
The son of parents passed into the skies.
And now, Farewell. — Time unrevoked has run
His wonted course, yet what I wished is done.
By Contemplation's help, not sought in vain,
I seem to have lived my childhood o'er again;
To have renewed the joys that once were mine,
Without the sin of violating thine;
And while the wings of Fancy still are free,
And I can view this mimic show of thee,
Time has but half succeeded in his theft —
Thyself removed, thy power to soothe me left.

1798

ON THE LOSS OF THE ROYAL GEORGE

Toll for the brave!
The brave that are no more!
All sunk beneath the wave,
Fast by their native shore!

Eight hundred of the brave,
Whose courage well was tried,
Had made the vessel heel,
And laid her on her side.

A land-breeze shook the shrouds,
And she was overset;
Down went the Royal George,
With all her crew complete!

Toll for the brave!
Brave Kempenfelt is gone;
His last sea-fight is fought;
His work of glory done.

It was not in the battle;
No tempest gave the shock;
She sprang no fatal leak;
She ran upon no rock.

His sword was in the sheath;
His fingers held the pen,
When Kempenfelt went down
With twice four hundred men.

Weigh the vessel up,
Once dreaded by our foes,
And mingle with our cup
The tears that England owes.

Her timbers yet are sound,
And she may float again,
Full charged with England's thunder,
And plough the distant main.

But Kempenfelt is gone,
His victories are o'er;
And He and his Eight Hundred
Must plough the wave no more.

1803

SONNET TO MRS. UNWIN

Mary! I want a lyre with other strings,
Such aid from heaven as some have feigned they drew,
An eloquence scarce given to mortals, new,
And undebased by praise of meaner things,
That, ere through age or woe I shed my wings,
I may record thy worth with honor due,
In verse as musical as thou art true,
Verse that immortalizes whom it sings!
But thou hast little need. There is a book
By seraphs writ with beams of heavenly light,
On which the eyes of God not rarely look,
A chronicle of actions just and bright;
There all thy deeds, my faithful Mary, shine,
And, since thou ownest that praise, I spare thee mine.

1803

THE CASTAWAY

Obscurest night involved the sky,
The Atlantic billows roared,
When such a destined wretch as I,
Washed headlong from on board,
Of friends, of hope, of all bereft,
His floating home forever left.

No braver chief could Albion boast
Than he with whom he went,
Nor ever ship left Albion's coast
With warmer wishes sent.
He loved them both, but both in vain,
Nor him beheld, nor her again.

Not long beneath the whelming brine,
Expert to swim, he lay;
Nor soon he felt his strength decline,
Or courage die away:
But waged with Death a lasting strife,
Supported by despair of life.

He shouted; nor his friends had failed
To check the vessel's course,
But so the furious blast prevailed,
That, pitiless perforce,
They left their outcast mate behind,
And scudded still before the wind.

Some succor yet they could afford;
  And, such as storms allow,
The cask, the coop, the floated cord,
  Delayed not to bestow:
But he, they knew, nor ship nor shore,
Whate'er they gave, should visit more.

Nor, cruel as it seemed, could he
  Their haste himself condemn,
Aware that flight, in such a sea,
  Alone could rescue them:
Yet bitter felt it still to die
Deserted, and his friends so nigh.

He long survives, who lives an hour
  In ocean, self-upheld:
And so long he, with unspent power,
  His destiny repelled:
And ever, as the minutes flew,
Entreated 'Help!' or cried — 'Adieu!'

At length, his transient respite past,
  His comrades, who before
Had heard his voice in every blast,
  Could catch the sound no more:
For then, by toil subdued, he drank
The stifling wave, and then he sank.

No poet wept him; but the page
  Of narrative sincere,
That tells his name, his worth, his age,
  Is wet with Anson's tear:
And tears by bards or heroes shed
Alike immortalize the dead.

I therefore purpose not, or dream,
  Descanting on his fate,
To give the melancholy theme
  A more enduring date:
But misery still delights to trace
Its semblance in another's case.

No voice divine the storm allayed,
  No light propitious shone:
When, snatched from all effectual aid,
  We perished, each alone:
But I beneath a rougher sea,
And whelmed in deeper gulfs than he.

1803

George Crabbe (1754–1832)

THE VILLAGE

BOOK I

THE Village Life, and every care that reigns
O'er youthful peasants and declining swains;
What labor yields, and what, that labor past,
Age, in its hour of languor, finds at last;
What form the real Picture of the Poor,
Demand a song — the Muse can give no more.
  Fled are those times, when, in harmonious strains,
The rustic poet praised his native plains:
No shepherds now, in smooth alternate verse,
Their country's beauty or their nymphs' rehearse;
Yet still for these we frame the tender strain,
Still in our lays fond Corydons complain,
And shepherds' boys their amorous pains reveal,
The only pains, alas! they never feel.
  On Mincio's banks, in Cæsar's bounteous reign,
If Tityrus found the Golden Age again,
Must sleepy bards the flattering dream prolong,
Mechanic echoes of the Mantuan song?
From Truth and Nature shall we widely stray,
Where Virgil, not where Fancy, leads the way?
  Yes, thus the Muses sing of happy swains,
Because the Muses never knew their pains:
They boast their peasant's pipes; but peasants now
Resign their pipes and plod behind the plough;
And few, amid the rural-tribe, have time
To number syllables, and play with rime;
Save honest Duck, what son of verse could share
The poet's rapture, and the peasant's care?
Or the great labors of the field degrade,
With the new peril of a poorer trade?
  From this chief cause these idle praises spring,
That themes so easy few forbear to sing;
For no deep thought the trifling subjects ask;
To sing of shepherds is an easy task:
The happy youth assumes the common strain,
A nymph his mistress, and himself a swain;
With no sad scenes he clouds his tuneful prayer,
But all, to look like her, is painted fair.
  I grant indeed that fields and flocks have charms
For him that grazes or for him that farms;
But when amid such pleasing scenes I trace
The poor laborious natives of the place,
And see the mid-day sun, with fervid ray,
On their bare heads and dewy temples play;

While some, with feebler heads, and fainter hearts
Deplore their fortune, yet sustain their parts:
Then shall I dare these real ills to hide
In tinsel trappings of poetic pride?
No; cast by Fortune on a frowning coast,
Which neither groves nor happy valleys boast;
Where other cares than those the Muse relates,
And other shepherds dwell with other mates;
By such examples taught, I paint the Cot,
As Truth will paint it, and as Bards will not:
Nor you, ye poor, of lettered scorn complain,
To you the smoothest song is smooth in vain;
O'ercome by labor, and bowed down by time,
Feel you the barren flattery of a rime?
Can poets soothe you, when you pine for bread,
By winding myrtles round your ruined shed?
Can their light tales your weighty griefs o'erpower,
Or glad with airy mirth the toilsome hour?
Lo! where the heath, with withering brake grown o'er,
Lends the light turf that warms the neighboring poor;
From thence a length of burning sand appears,
Where the thin harvest waves its withered ears;
Rank weeds, that every art and care defy,
Reign o'er the land, and rob the blighted rye:
There thistles stretch their prickly arms afar,
And to the ragged infant threaten war;
There poppies nodding, mock the hope of toil;
There the blue bugloss paints the sterile soil;
Hardy and high, above the slender sheaf,
The slimy mallow waves her silky leaf;
O'er the young shoot the charlock throws a shade,
And clasping tares cling round the sickly blade;
With mingled tints the rocky coasts abound,
And a sad splendor vainly shines around.
So looks the nymph whom wretched arts adorn,
Betrayed by man, then left for man to scorn;
Whose cheek in vain assumes the mimic rose,
While her sad eyes the troubled breast disclose;
Whose outward splendor is but folly's dress,
Exposing most when most it gilds distress.
Here joyless roam a wild amphibious race,
With sullen woe displayed in every face;
Who, far from civil arts and social fly,
And scowl at strangers with suspicious eye.
Here too the lawless merchant of the main
Draws from his plough the intoxicated swain;
Want only claimed the labor of the day,
But vice now steals his nightly rest away.
Where are the swains, who, daily labor done,
With rural games played down the setting sun;
Who struck with matchless force the bounding ball,
Or made the pond'rous quoit obliquely fall;
While some huge Ajax, terrible and strong,
Engaged some artful stripling of the throng,
And fell beneath him, foiled, while far around
Hoarse triumph rose, and rocks returned the sound?
Where now are these? — Beneath yon cliff they stand,
To show the freighted pinnace where to land;
To load the ready steed with guilty haste,
To fly in terror o'er the pathless waste,
Or, when detected, in their straggling course,
To foil their foes by cunning or by force;
Or, yielding part (which equal knaves demand),
To gain a lawless passport through the land.
Here, wand'ring long, amid these frowning fields,
I sought the simple life that Nature yields;
Rapine and Wrong and Fear usurped her place,
And a bold, artful, surly, savage race;
Who, only skilled to take the finny tribe,
The yearly dinner, or septennial bribe,
Wait on the shore, and, as the waves run high,
On the tossed vessel bend their eager eye,
Which to their coast directs its vent'rous way;
Theirs or the ocean's miserable prey.
As on their neighbouring beach yon swallows stand,
And wait for favoring winds to leave the land;
While still for flight the ready wing is spread:
So waited I the favoring hour, and fled;
Fled from these shores where guilt and famine reign,
And cried, Ah! hapless they who still remain;
Who still remain to hear the ocean roar,

Whose greedy waves devour the lessening shore;
Till some fierce tide, with more imperious sway
Sweeps the low hut and all it holds away;
When the sad tenant weeps from door to door,
And begs a poor protection from the poor!
But these are scenes where Nature's niggard hand
Gave a spare portion to the famished land;
Hers is the fault, if here mankind complain
Of fruitless toil and labor spent in vain;
But yet in other scenes more fair in view,
When Plenty smiles — alas! she smiles for few —
And those who taste not, yet behold her store,
Are as the slaves that dig the golden ore, —
The wealth around them makes them doubly poor.
Or will you deem them amply paid in health,
Labor's fair child, that languishes with wealth?
Go then! and see them rising with the sun,
Through a long course of daily toil to run;
See them beneath the Dog-star's raging heat,
When the knees tremble and the temples beat;
Behold them, leaning on their scythes, look o'er
The labor past, and toils to come explore;
See them alternate suns and showers engage,
And hoard up aches and anguish for their age;
Through fens and marshy moors their steps pursue,
When their warm pores imbibe the evening dew;
Then own that labor may as fatal be
To these thy slaves, as thine excess to thee.
Amid this tribe too oft a manly pride
Strives in strong toil the fainting heart to hide;
There may you see the youth of slender frame
Contend with weakness, weariness, and shame;
Yet, urged along, and proudly loth to yield,
He strives to join his fellows of the field.
Till long-contending nature droops at last,
Declining health rejects his poor repast,
His cheerless spouse the coming danger sees,
And mutual murmurs urge the slow disease.
Yet grant them health, 't is not for us to tell,
Though the head droops not, that the heart is well;
Or will you praise that homely, healthy fare,
Plenteous and plain, that happy peasants share!
Oh! trifle not with wants you cannot feel,
Nor mock the misery of a stinted meal;
Homely, not wholesome, plain, not plenteous, such
As you who praise, would never deign to touch.
Ye gentle souls, who dream of rural ease,
Whom the smooth stream and smoother sonnet please;
Go! if the peaceful cot your praises share,
Go look within, and ask if peace be there;
If peace be his — that drooping weary sire,
Or theirs, that offspring round their feeble fire;
Or hers, that matron pale, whose trembling hand
Turns on the wretched hearth the expiring brand!
Nor yet can Time itself obtain for these
Life's latest comforts, due respect and ease;
For yonder see that hoary swain, whose age
Can with no cares except its own engage;
Who, propped on that rude staff, looks up to see
The bare arms broken from the withering tree,
On which, a boy, he climbed the loftiest bough,
Then his first joy, but his sad emblem now.
He once was chief in all the rustic trade;
His steady hand the straightest furrow made;
Full many a prize he won, and still is proud
To find the triumphs of his youth allowed;
A transient pleasure sparkles in his eyes,
He hears and smiles, then thinks again and sighs:
For now he journeys to his grave in pain;
The rich disdain him; nay, the poor disdain:
Alternate masters now their slave command,
Urge the weak efforts of his feeble hand,
And, when his age attempts its task in vain,
With ruthless taunts, of lazy poor complain.
Oft may you see him, when he tends the sheep,
His winter charge, beneath the hillock weep;
Oft hear him murmur to the winds that blow
O'er his white locks and bury them in snow,
When, roused by rage and muttering in the morn,

He mends the broken hedge with icy thorn: —
'Why do I live, when I desire to be
At once from life and life's long labour free?
Like leaves in spring, the young are blown away,
Without the sorrows of a slow decay;
I, like yon withered leaf, remain behind,
Nipped by the frost, and shivering in the wind;
There it abides till younger buds come on,
As I, now all my fellow-swains are gone;
Then, from the rising generation thrust,
It falls, like me, unnoticed to the dust.
'These fruitful fields, these numerous flocks I see,
Are others' gain, but killing cares to me;
To me the children of my youth are lords,
Cool in their looks, but hasty in their words:
Wants of their own demand their care; and who
Feels his own want and succours others too?
A lonely, wretched man, in pain I go,
None need my help, and none relieve my wo;
Then let my bones beneath the turf be laid,
And men forget the wretch they would not aid.'
Thus groan the old, till, by disease oppressed,
They taste a final wo, and then they rest.
Theirs is yon house that holds the parish-poor,
Whose walls of mud scarce bear the broken door;
There, where the putrid vapours, flagging, play,
And the dull wheel hums doleful through the day; —
There children dwell who know no parents' care;
Parents, who know no children's love, dwell there!
Heartbroken matrons on their joyless bed,
Forsaken wives, and mothers never wed;
Dejected widows with unheeded tears,
And crippled age with more than childhood fears;
The lame, the blind, and, far the happiest they!
The moping idiot and the madman gay.
Here too the sick their final doom receive,
Here brought, amid the scenes of grief, to grieve,
Where the loud groans from some sad chamber flow,
Mixed with the clamours of the crowd below;
Here, sorrowing, they each kindred sorrow scan,
And the cold charities of man to man:
Whose laws indeed for ruined age provide,
And strong compulsion plucks the scrap from pride;
But still that scrap is bought with many a sigh,
And pride embitters what it can't deny.
Say ye, oppressed by some fantastic woes,
Some jarring nerve that baffles your repose;
Who press the downy couch, while slaves advance
With timid eye, to read the distant glance;
Who with sad prayers the weary doctor tease,
To name the nameless ever-new disease;
Who with mock patience dire complaints endure,
Which real pain and that alone can cure;
How would ye bear in real pain to lie,
Despised, neglected, left alone to die?
How would ye bear to draw your latest breath,
Where all that's wretched paves the way for death?
Such is that room which one rude beam divides,
And naked rafters form the sloping sides;
Where the vile bands that bind the thatch are seen,
And lath and mud are all that lie between;
Save one dull pane, that, coarsely patched, gives way
To the rude tempest, yet excludes the day:
Here, on a matted flock, with dust o'erspread,
The drooping wretch reclines his languid head;
For him no hand the cordial cup applies,
Or wipes the tear that stagnates in his eyes;
No friends with soft discourse his pain beguile,
Or promise hope till sickness wears a smile.
But soon a loud and hasty summons calls,
Shakes the thin roof, and echoes round the walls;
Anon, a figure enters, quaintly neat,
All pride and business, bustle and conceit;
With looks unaltered by these scenes of wo,
With speed that, entering, speaks his haste to go,
He bids the gazing throng around him fly,
And carries fate and physic in his eye:
A potent quack, long versed in human ills
Who first insults the victim whom he kills,

Whose murd'rous hand a drowsy Bench protect,
And whose most tender mercy is neglect.
Paid by the parish for attendance here,
He wears contempt upon his sapient sneer;
In haste he seeks the bed where Misery lies,
Impatience marked in his averted eyes;
And, some habitual queries hurried o'er,
Without reply, he rushes on the door:
His drooping patient, long inured to pain,
And long unheeded, knows remonstrance vain;
He ceases now the feeble help to crave
Of man; and silent sinks into the grave.
But ere his death some pious doubts arise,
Some simple fears, which 'bold bad' men despise;
Fain would he ask the parish-priest to prove
His title certain to the joys above:
For this he sends the murmuring nurse, who calls
The holy stranger to these dismal walls:
And doth not he, the pious man, appear,
He, 'passing rich with forty pounds a year'?
Ah! no; a shepherd of a different stock,
And far unlike him, feeds this little flock:
A jovial youth, who thinks his Sunday's task
As much as God or man can fairly ask;
The rest he gives to loves and labors light,
To fields the morning, and to feasts the night;
None better skilled the noisy pack to guide,
To urge their chase, to cheer them or to chide;
A sportsman keen, he shoots through half the day,
And, skilled at whist, devotes the night to play:
Then, while such honors bloom around his head,
Shall he sit sadly by the sick man's bed,
To raise the hope he feels not, or with zeal
To combat fears that e'en the pious feel?
Now once again the gloomy scene explore,
Less gloomy now; the bitter hour is o'er,
The man of many sorrows sighs no more. —
Up yonder hill, behold how sadly slow
The bier moves winding from the vale below:
There lie the happy dead, from trouble free,
And the glad parish pays the frugal fee:
No more, O Death! thy victim starts to hear
Churchwarden stern, or kingly overseer;
No more the farmer claims his humble bow,
Thou art his lord, the best of tyrants thou!
Now to the church behold the mourners come,
Sedately torpid and devoutly dumb;
The village children now their games suspend,
To see the bier that bears their ancient friend;
For he was one in all their idle sport,
And like a monarch ruled their little court;
The pliant bow he formed, the flying ball,
The bat, the wicket, were his labours all;
Him now they follow to his grave, and stand
Silent and sad, and gazing, hand in hand;
While bending low, their eager eyes explore
The mingled relics of the parish poor:
The bell tolls late, the moping owl flies round,
Fear marks the flight and magnifies the sound;
The busy priest, detained by weightier care,
Defers his duty till the day of prayer;
And, waiting long, the crowd retire distressed,
To think a poor man's bones should lie unblessed.

1783

Robert Burns (1759–1796)

THE COTTER'S SATURDAY NIGHT

My loved, my honoured, much respected friend!
No mercenary bard his homage pays;
With honest pride, I scorn each selfish end,
My dearest meed, a friend's esteem and praise:
To you I sing, in simple Scottish lays,
The lowly train in life's sequestered scene;
The native feelings strong, the guileless ways;
What Aiken in a cottage would have been;
Ah, though his worth unknown, far happier there I ween!

November chill blaws loud wi' angry sugh;
The short'ning winter-day is near a close;
The miry beasts retreating frae the pleugh;
The black'ning trains o' craws to their repose:
The toil-worn Cotter frae his labour goes —
This night his weekly moil is at an end,
Collects his spades, his mattocks, and his hoes,
Hoping the morn in ease and rest to spend,
And weary, o'er the moor, his course does hameward bend.

At length his lonely cot appears in view,
Beneath the shelter of an agèd tree;
Th' expectant wee-things, toddlin, stacher through
To meet their dad, wi' flichterin' noise and glee.
His wee bit ingle, blinkin bonilie,
His clean hearth-stane, his thrifty wifie's smile,
The lisping infant, prattling on his knee,
Does a' his weary kiaugh and care beguile,
And makes him quite forget his labour and his toil.

Belyve, the elder bairns come drapping in,
At service out, amang the farmers roun';
Some ca' the pleugh, some herd, some tentie rin
A cannie errand to a neebor town:
Their eldest hope, their Jenny, woman-grown,
In youthfu' bloom, love sparkling in her e'e,
Comes hame; perhaps, to shew a braw new gown,
Or deposite her sair-won penny-fee,
To help her parents dear, if they in hardship be.

With joy unfeigned, brothers and sisters meet,
And each for other's weelfare kindly spiers:
The social hours, swift-winged, unnoticed fleet;
Each tells the uncos that he sees or hears.
The parents partial eye their hopeful years;
Anticipation forward points the view;
The mother, wi' her needle and her sheers,
Gars auld claes look amaist as weel 's the new;
The father mixes a' wi' admonition due.

Their master's and their mistress's command
The younkers a' are warnèd to obey;
And mind their labours wi' an eydent hand,
And ne'er, though out o' sight, to jauk or play:
'And O be sure to fear the Lord alway,
And mind your duty, duly, morn and night;
Lest in temptation's path ye gang astray,
Implore His counsel and assisting might:
They never sought in vain that sought the Lord aright.'

But hark! a rap comes gently to the door;
Jenny, wha kens the meaning o' the same,
Tells how a neebor lad came o'er the moor,
To do some errands, and convoy her hame.
The wily mother sees the conscious flame
Sparkle in Jenny's e'e, and flush her cheek;
With heart-struck anxious care, enquires his name,
While Jenny hafflins is afraid to speak;
Weel-pleased the mother hears, it 's nae wild, worthless rake.

With kindly welcome, Jenny brings him ben;
A strappin' youth, he takes the mother's eye;
Blythe Jenny sees the visit 's no ill taen;
The father cracks of horses, pleughs, and kye.
The youngster's artless heart o'erflows wi' joy,
But blate and laithfu', scarce can weel behave;
The mother, wi' a woman's wiles, can spy
What makes the youth sae bashfu' and sae grave;
Weel-pleased to think her bairn 's respected like the lave.

O happy love! where love like this is found:
O heart-felt raptures! bliss beyond compare!
I've pacèd much this weary, mortal round,
And sage experience bids me this declare:—
'If Heaven a draught of heavenly pleasure spare,
One cordial in this melancholy vale,
'T is when a youthful, loving, modest pair,
In other's arms, breathe out the tender tale
Beneath the milk-white thorn that scents the evening gale.'

Is there, in human form, that bears a heart,
A wretch! a villain! lost to love and truth!
That can, with studied, sly, ensnaring art,
Betray sweet Jenny's unsuspecting youth?
Curse on his perjured arts! dissembling, smooth!
Are honour, virtue, conscience, all exiled?
Is there no pity, no relenting ruth,
Points to the parents fondling o'er their child?
Then paints the ruined maid, and their distraction wild?

But now the supper crowns their simple board,
The healsome parrich, chief o' Scotia's food;
The soupe their only hawkie does afford,

That 'yont the hallan snugly chows her cood;
The dame brings forth, in complimental mood,
To grace the lad, her weel-hained kebbuck, fell;
And aft he 's prest, and aft he ca's it guid;
The frugal wifie, garrulous, will tell,
How 't was a towmond auld, sin' lint was i' the bell.

The chearfu' supper done, wi' serious face,
They, round the ingle, form a circle wide;
The sire turns o'er, wi' patriarchal grace,
The big ha'-Bible, ance his father's pride.
His bonnet rev'rently is laid aside,
His lyart haffets wearing thin and bare;
Those strains that once did sweet in Zion glide,
He wales a portion with judicious care,
And 'Let us worship God!' he says, with solemn air.

They chant their artless notes in simple guise,
They tune their hearts, by far the noblest aim;
Perhaps *Dundee's* wild-warbling measures rise,
Or plaintive *Martyrs*, worthy of the name;
Or noble *Elgin* beets the heaven-ward flame,
The sweetest far of Scotia's holy lays:
Compared with these, Italian trills are tame;
The tickled ears no heart-felt raptures raise;
Nae unison hae they, with our Creator's praise.

The priest-like father reads the sacred page,
How Abram was the friend of God on high;
Or Moses bade eternal warfare wage
With Amalek's ungracious progeny;
Or, how the royal Bard did groaning lie
Beneath the stroke of Heaven's avenging ire;
Or Job's pathetic plaint, and wailing cry;
Or rapt Isaiah's wild, seraphic fire;
Or other holy Seers that tune the sacred lyre.

Perhaps the Christian volume is the theme:
How guiltless blood for guilty man was shed;
How He, who bore in Heaven the second name,
Had not on earth whereon to lay His head;
How His first followers and servants sped;
The precepts sage they wrote to many a land:
How he, who lone in Patmos banishèd,
Saw in the sun a mighty angel stand,
And heard great Bab'lon's doom pronounced by Heaven's command.

Then kneeling down to Heaven's Eternal King,
The saint, the father, and the husband prays:
Hope 'springs exulting on triumphant wing,'
That thus they all shall meet in future days,
There, ever bask in uncreated rays,
No more to sigh or shed the bitter tear,
Together hymning their Creator's praise,
In such society, yet still more dear;
While circling Time moves round in an eternal sphere.

Compared with this, how poor Religion's pride,
In all the pomp of method, and of art;
When men display to congregations wide
Devotion's ev'ry grace, except the heart,
The Power, incensed, the pageant will desert,
The pompous strain, the sacerdotal stole;
But haply, in some cottage far apart,
May hear, well-pleased, the language of the soul,
And in His Book of Life the inmates poor enroll.

Then homeward all take off their sev'ral way;
The youngling cottagers retire to rest:
The parent-pair their secret homage pay,
And proffer up to Heaven the warm request,
That He who stills the raven's clam'rous nest,
And decks the lily fair in flow'ry pride,
Would, in the way His wisdom sees the best,
For them and for their little ones provide;
But, chiefly in their hearts with Grace Divine preside.

From scenes like these, old Scotia's grandeur springs,
That makes her loved at home, revered abroad:
Princes and lords are but the breath of kings,
'An honest man 's the noblest work of God';
And certes, in fair Virtue's heavenly road,
The cottage leaves the palace far behind;

What is a lordling's pomp? a cumbrous load,
Disguising oft the wretch of human kind,
Studied in arts of Hell, in wickedness refined!

O Scotia! my dear, my native soil!
For whom my warmest wish to Heaven is sent!
Long may thy hardy sons of rustic toil
Be blest with health, and peace, and sweet content!
And O may Heaven their simple lives prevent
From Luxury's contagion, weak and vile!
Then, howe'er crowns and coronets be rent,
A virtuous populace may rise the while,
And stand a wall of fire around their much-loved Isle.

O Thou, who poured the patriotic tide,
That streamed through Wallace's undaunted heart,
Who dared to, nobly, stem tyrannic pride,
Or nobly die, the second glorious part:
(The patriot's God, peculiarly Thou art,
His friend, inspirer, guardian, and reward!)
O never, never Scotia's realm desert;
But still the patriot, and the patriot-bard
In bright succession raise, her ornament and guard!

1786

TO A MOUSE

Wee, sleekit, cowrin, tim'rous beastie,
O, what a panic 's in thy breastie!
Thou need na start awa sae hasty
Wi' bickering brattle!
I wad be laith to rin an' chase thee,
Wi' murdering pattle!

I'm truly sorry man's dominion
Has broken Nature's social union,
An' justifies that ill opinion
Which makes thee startle
At me, thy poor, earth-born companion
An' fellow-mortal!

I doubt na, whyles, but thou may thieve;
What then? poor beastie, thou maun live:
A daimen icker in a thrave
'S a sma' request;
I 'll get a blessin wi' the lave,
An' never miss 't!

Thy wee-bit housie, too, in ruin!
Its silly wa's the win's are strewin!
An' naething, now, to big a new ane,
O' foggage green!
An' bleak December's win's ensuin,
Baith snell an' keen!

Thou saw the fields laid bare an' waste,
An' weary winter comin fast,
An' cozie here, beneath the blast,
Thou thought to dwell,
Till, crash! the cruel coulter passed
Out through thy cell.

That wee bit heap o' leaves an' stibble,
Has cost thee monie a weary nibble!
Now thou 's turned out, for a' thy trouble,
But house or hald,
To thole the winter's sleety dribble,
An' cranreuch cauld!

But Mousie, thou art no thy lane,
In proving foresight may be vain:
The best-laid schemes o' mice an' men
Gang aft agley,
An' lea'e us naught but grief an' pain,
For promised joy!

Still thou art blest, compared wi' me!
The present only toucheth thee:
But och! I backward cast my e'e,
On prospects drear!
An' forward, though I canna see,
I guess an' fear!

1786

TO A MOUNTAIN DAISY

Wee, modest, crimson-tippèd flow'r,
Thou 's met me in an evil hour;
For I maun crush amang the stoure
Thy slender stem:
To spare thee now is past my pow'r,
Thou bonie gem.

Alas! it 's no thy neebor sweet,
The bonie lark, companion meet,
Bending thee 'mang the dewy weet,
Wi' spreckled breast!
When upward-springing, blythe, to greet
The purpling east.

Cauld blew the bitter-biting north
Upon thy early, humble birth;
Yet cheerfully thou glinted forth
Amid the storm,
Scarce reared above the parent-earth
Thy tender form.

The flaunting flow'rs our gardens yield,
High shelt'ring woods and wa's maun shield;
But thou, beneath the random bield

O' clod or stane,
Adorns the histie stibble-field,
Unseen, alane.

There, in thy scanty mantle clad,
Thy snawie bosom sunward spread,
Thou lifts thy unassuming head
In humble guise;
But now the share uptears thy bed,
And low thou lies!

Such is the fate of artless maid,
Sweet flow'ret of the rural shade!
By love's simplicity betrayed,
And guileless trust;
Till she, like thee, all soiled, is laid
Low i' the dust.

Such is the fate of simple Bard,
On Life's rough ocean luckless starred!
Unskilful he to note the card
Of prudent lore,
Till billows rage, and gales blow hard,
And whelm him o'er!

Such fate to suffering Worth is giv'n,
Who long with wants and woes has striv'n,
By human pride or cunning driv'n
To mis'ry's brink;
Till, wrenched of ev'ry stay but Heav'n,
He, ruined, sink!

Ev'n thou who mourn'st the Daisy's fate,
That fate is thine — no distant date;
Stern Ruin's plough-share drives elate,
Full on thy bloom,
Till crushed beneath the furrow's weight
Shall be thy doom!

1786

EPISTLE TO JOHN LAPRAIK, AN OLD SCOTTISH BARD

While briers an' woodbines budding green,
And paitricks scraichin loud at e'en,
An' morning poussie whiddin seen,
Inspire my Muse,
This freedom, in an unknown frien'
I pray excuse.

On Fasten-e'en we had a rockin,
To ca' the crack and weave our stockin;
And there was muckle fun and jokin,
Ye need na doubt;
At length we had a hearty yokin,
At 'sang about.'

There was ae sang, amang the rest,
Aboon them a' it pleased me best,
That some kind husband had addrest
To some sweet wife:
It thirled the heart-strings through the breast,
A' to the life.

I've scarce heard ought described sae weel,
What gen'rous, manly bosoms feel;
Thought I, 'Can this be Pope or Steele,
Or Beattie's wark?'
They tauld me 't was an odd kind chiel
About Muirkirk.

It pat me fidgin-fain to hear't,
An' sae about him there I spier't;
Then a' that kent him round declared
He had ingine;
That name excelled it, few cam near't,
It was sae fine:

That, set him to a pint of ale,
An' either douce or merry tale,
Or rhymes an' sangs he'd made himsel,
Or witty catches,
'Tween Inverness an' Teviotdale,
He had few matches.

Then up I gat, an' swoor an aith,
Though I should pawn my pleugh an' graith,
Or die a cadger pownie's death,
At some dyke-back,
A pint an' gill I'd gie them baith,
To hear your crack.

But, first an' foremost, I should tell,
Amaist as soon as I could spell,
I to the crambo-jingle fell;
Though rude an' rough —
Yet crooning to a body's sel,
Does weel eneugh.

I am nae poet, in a sense;
But just a rhymer like by chance,
An' hae to learning nae pretence;
Yet, what the matter?
Whene'er my Muse does on me glance,
I jingle at her.

Your critic-folk may cock their nose,
And say, 'How can you e'er propose,
You wha ken hardly verse frae prose,
To mak a sang?'
But, by your leaves, my learnèd foes,
Ye're maybe wrang.

What's a' your jargon o' your Schools,
Your Latin names for horns an' stools?
If honest Nature made you fools,
What sairs your grammars?
Ye'd better taen up spades and shools,
Or knappin-hammers.

A set o' dull, conceited hashes
Confuse their brains in college-classes,

They gang in stirks, and come out asses,
Plain truth to speak;
An' syne they think to climb Parnassus
By dint o' Greek!

Gie me ae spark o' Nature's fire,
That's a' the learning I desire;
Then, though I drudge through dub an' mire
At pleugh or cart,
My Muse, though hamely in attire,
May touch the heart.

O for a spunk o' Allan's glee,
Or Fergusson's, the bauld an' slee,
Or bright Lapraik's, my friend to be,
If I can hit it!
That would be lear eneugh for me,
If I could get it.

Now, sir, if ye hae friends enow,
Though real friends I b'lieve are few;
Yet, if your catalogue be fow,
I' se no insist:
But, gif ye want ae friend that 's true,
I'm on your list.

I winna blaw about mysel,
As ill I like my fauts to tell;
But friends, an' folks that wish me well,
They sometimes roose me;
Though, I maun own, as monie still
As far abuse me.

There's ae wee faut they whyles lay to me,
I like the lasses — Gude forgie me!
For monie a plack they wheedle frae me
At dance or fair;
Maybe some ither thing they gie me,
They weel can spare.

But Mauchline Race or Mauchline Fair,
I should be proud to meet you there;
We 'se gie ae night's discharge to care,
If we forgather;
And hae a swap o' rhymin-ware
Wi' ane anither.

The four-gill chap, we 'se gar him clatter,
An' kirsen him wi' reekin' water;
Syne we 'll sit down an' tak our whitter,
To cheer our heart;
An' faith, we 'se be acquainted better
Before we part.

Awa ye selfish warly race,
Wha think that havins, sense, an' grace,
Ev'n love an' friendship should give place
To Catch-the-Plack!
I dinna like to see your face,
Nor hear your crack.

But ye whom social pleasure charms,
Whose hearts the tide of kindness warms,
Who hold your being on the terms,
'Each aid the others,'
Come to my bowl, come to my arms,
My friends, my brothers!

But, to conclude my lang epistle,
As my auld pen 's worn to the grissle,
Twa lines frae you wad gar me fissle,
Who am most fervent,
While I can either sing or whistle,
Your friend and servant.

1786

OF A' THE AIRTS

Of a' the airts the wind can blaw
I dearly like the west,
For there the bonie lassie lives,
The lassie I lo'e best.
There wild woods grow, and rivers row,
And monie a hill between,
But day and night my fancy's flight
Is ever wi' my Jean.

I see her in the dewy flowers —
I see her sweet and fair.
I hear her in the tunefu' birds —
I hear her charm the air:
There's not a bonie flower that springs
By fountain, shaw, or green,
There's not a bonie bird that sings,
But minds me o' my Jean.

1790

MY HEART'S IN THE HIGHLANDS

My heart 's in the Highlands, my heart is not here,
My heart's in the Highlands a-chasing the deer,
A-chasing the wild deer and following the roe —
My heart's in the Highlands, wherever I go!

Farewell to the Highlands, farewell to the North,
The birthplace of valour, the country of worth!
Wherever I wander, wherever I rove,
The hills of the Highlands for ever I love.

Farewell to the mountains high covered with snow,
Farewell to the straths and green valleys below,

Farewell to the forests and wild-hanging woods,
Farewell to the torrents and loud-pouring floods!
My heart 's in the Highlands, my heart is not here,
My heart 's in the Highlands a-chasing the deer,
A-chasing the wild deer and following the roe —
My heart 's in the Highlands, wherever I go!

1790

JOHN ANDERSON, MY JO

John Anderson my jo, John,
When we were first acquent,
Your locks were like the raven,
Your bonie brow was brent;
But now your brow is beld, John,
Your locks are like the snaw,
But blessings on your frosty pow,
John Anderson my jo!

John Anderson my jo, John,
We clamb the hill thegither,
And monie a cantie day, John,
We 've had wi' ane anither;
Now we maun totter down, John,
And hand in hand we'll go,
And sleep thegither at the foot,
John Anderson my jo!

1790

AULD LANG SYNE

Should auld acquaintance be forgot,
And never brought to mind?
Should auld acquaintance be forgot,
And auld lang syne!

Chorus. — For auld lang syne, my dear,
For auld lang syne,
We 'll tak a cup o' kindness yet,
For auld lang syne!

And surely ye 'll be your pint-stowp,
And surely I 'll be mine,
And we 'll tak a cup o' kindness yet
For auld lang syne!

We twa hae run about the braes,
And pou'd the gowans fine,
But we 've wandered monie a weary fit
Sin' auld lang syne.

We twa hae paidled in the burn
Frae morning sun till dine,
But seas between us braid hae roared
Sin' auld lang syne.

And there 's a hand, my trusty fiere,
And gie 's a hand o' thine,
And we 'll tak a right guid-willie waught
For auld lang syne.

1796

TAM O' SHANTER

When chapman billies leave the street,
And drouthy neebors neebors meet;
As market-days are wearing late,
An' folk begin to tak the gate;
While we sit bousing at the nappy,
An' getting fou and unco happy,
We think na on the lang Scots miles,
The mosses, waters, slaps, and styles,
That lie between us and our hame,
Whare sits our sulky, sullen dame,
Gathering her brows like gathering storm,
Nursing her wrath to keep it warm.
This truth fand honest Tam o' Shanter,
As he frae Ayr ae night did canter:
(Auld Ayr, wham ne'er a town surpasses,
For honest men and bonie lasses).
O Tam, had'st thou but been sae wise,
As taen thy ain wife Kate's advice!
She tauld thee weel thou was a skellum,
A blethering, blustering, drunken blellum;
That frae November till October,
Ae market-day thou was nae sober;
That ilka melder wi' the miller,
Thou sat as lang as thou had siller;
That ev'ry naig was ca'd a shoe on,
The smith and thee gat roaring fou on;
That at the Lord's house, even on Sunday,
Thou drank wi' Kirkton Jean till Monday.
She prophesied, that, late or soon,
Thou would be found deep drowned in Doon,
Or catched wi' warlocks in the mirk
By Alloway's auld, haunted kirk.
Ah! gentle dames, it gars me greet,
To think how monie counsels sweet,
How monie lengthened, sage advices
The husband frae the wife despises!
But to our tale: Ae market-night,
Tam had got planted unco right,
Fast by an ingle, bleezing finely,
Wi' reaming swats, that drank divinely;
And at his elbow, Souter Johnie,
His ancient, trusty, drouthy cronie:
Tam lo'ed him like a very brither;
They had been fou for weeks thegither.
The night drave on wi' sangs and clatter;
And ay the ale was growing better:
The landlady and Tam grew gracious
Wi' secret favours, sweet and precious:

The Souter tauld his queerest stories;
The landlord's laugh was ready chorus:
The storm without might rair and rustle,
Tam did na mind the storm a whistle.
 Care, mad to see a man sae happy,
E'en drowned himsel amang the nappy.
As bees flee hame wi' lades o' treasure,
The minutes winged their way wi' pleasure:
Kings may be blest but Tam was glorious,
O'er a' the ills o' life victorious!
 But pleasures are like poppies spread:
You seize the flow'r, its bloom is shed;
Or like the snow falls in the river,
A moment white — then melts forever;
Or like the borealis race,
That flit ere you can point their place;
Or like the rainbow's lovely form
Evanishing amid the storm.
Nae man can tether time or tide;
The hour approaches Tam maun ride:
That hour, o' night's black arch the key-stane,
That dreary hour Tam mounts his beast in;
And sic a night he taks the road in,
As ne'er poor sinner was abroad in.
 The wind blew as 't wad blawn its last;
The rattling showers rose on the blast;
The speedy gleams the darkness swallowed;
Loud, deep, and lang the thunder bellowed:
That night, a child might understand,
The Deil had business on his hand.
 Weel mounted on his gray mare Meg,
A better never lifted leg,
Tam skelpit on through dub and mire,
Despising wind, and rain, and fire;
Whiles holding fast his guid blue bonnet,
Whiles crooning o'er some auld Scots sonnet,
Whiles glow'ring round wi' prudent cares,
Lest bogles catch him unawares:
Kirk-Alloway was drawing nigh,
Whare ghaists and houlets nightly cry.
 By this time he was cross the ford,
Whare in the snaw the chapman smoored;
And past the birks and meikle stane,
Whare drunken Charlie brak's neck-bane;
And through the whins, and by the cairn,
Whare hunters fand the murdered bairn;
And near the thorn, aboon the well,
Whare Mungo's mither hanged hersel.
Before him Doon pours all his floods;
The doubling storm roars through the woods;
The lightnings flash from pole to pole;
Near and more near the thunders roll:
When, glimmering through the groaning trees,
Kirk-Alloway seemed in a bleeze,
Through ilka bore the beams were glancing,
And loud resounded mirth and dancing.
 Inspiring bold John Barleycorn,
What dangers thou canst make us scorn!
Wi' tippenny, we fear nae evil;
Wi' usquebae, we 'll face the Devil!
The swats sae reamed in Tammie's noddle,
Fair play, he cared na deils a boddle.
But Maggie stood, right sair astonished,
Till, by the heel and hand admonished,
She ventured forward on the light;
And, vow! Tam saw an unco sight!
 Warlocks and witches in a dance:
Nae cotillion, brent new frae France,
But hornpipes, jigs, strathspeys, and reels,
Put life and mettle in their heels.
A winnock-bunker in the east,
There sat Auld Nick, in shape o' beast;
A tousie tyke, black, grim, and large,
To gie them music was his charge:
He screwed the pipes and gart them skirl,
Till roof and rafters a' did dirl.
Coffins stood round, like open presses,
That shawed the dead in their last dresses;
And, by some devilish cantraip sleight,
Each in its cauld hand held a light:
By which heroic Tam was able
To note upon the haly table,
A murderer's banes, in gibbet-airns;
Twa span-lang, wee, unchristened bairns;
A thief, new-cutted frae a rape —
Wi' his last gasp his gab did gape;
Five tomahawks wi' bluid red-rusted;
Five scimitars wi' murder crusted;
A garter which a babe had strangled;
A knife a father's throat had mangled —
Whom his ain son o' life bereft —
The grey-hairs yet stack to the heft;
Wi' mair of horrible and awefu',
Which even to name wad be unlawfu'.
 As Tammie glowered, amazed, and curious,
The mirth and fun grew fast and furious;
The piper loud and louder blew,
The dancers quick and quicker flew,
They reeled, they set, they crossed, they cleekit,
Till ilka carlin swat and reekit,
And coost her duddies to the wark,
And linket at it in her sark!
 Now Tam, O Tam! had thae been queans,
A' plump and strapping in their teens!
Their sarks, instead o' creeshie flannen,
Been snaw-white seventeen-hunder linen! —
Thir breeks o' mine, my only pair,
That ance were plush, o' guid blue hair,
I wad hae gi'en them off my hurdies
For ae blink o' the bonie burdies!
 But withered beldams, auld and droll,
Rigwoodie hags wad spean a foal,

ping and flinging on a crummock,
onder didna turn thy stomach!
But Tam kend what was what fu' brawlie:
ere was ae winsome wench and wawlie,
hat night enlisted in the core,
ng after kend on Carrick shore
'or monie a beast to dead she shot,
n' perished monie a bonie boat,
nd shook baith meikle corn and bear,
nd kept the country-side in fear).
er cutty sark, o' Paisley harn,
hat while a lassie she had worn,
 longitude though sorely scanty,
 was her best, and she was vauntie. . . .
h! little kend thy reverend grannie,
hat sark she coft for her wee Nannie,
i' twa pund Scots ('t was a' her riches),
ad ever graced a dance o' witches!
But here my Muse her wing maun cour,
 flights are far beyond her power:
 sing how Nannie lap and flang
souple jad she was and strang),
d how Tam stood like ane bewitched,
nd thought his very een enriched;
Even Satan glowered, and fidged fu' fain,
And hotched and blew wi' might and main;
Till first ae caper, syne anither,
Tam tint his reason a' thegither,
And roars out: 'Weel done, Cutty-sark!'
And in an instant all was dark;
And scarcely had he Maggie rallied,
When out the hellish legion sallied.
As bees bizz out wi' angry fyke,
When plundering herds assail their byke;
As open pussie's mortal foes,
When, pop! she starts before their nose;
As eager runs the market-crowd,
When 'Catch the thief!' resounds aloud:
So Maggie runs, the witches follow,
Wi' monie an eldritch skriech and hollo.
Ah, Tam! ah, Tam! thou'll get thy fairin!
In hell they'll roast thee like a herrin!
In vain thy Kate awaits thy comin!
Kate soon will be a woefu' woman!
Now, do thy speedy utmost, Meg,
And win the key-stane of the brig;
There, at them thou thy tail may toss,
A running stream they dare na cross!
But ere the key-stane she could make,
The fient a tail she had to shake;
For Nannie, far before the rest,
Hard upon noble Maggie prest,
And flew at Tam wi' furious ettle;
But little wist she Maggie's mettle!
Ae spring brought off her master hale,
But left behind her ain grey tail:
The carlin claught her by the rump,
And left poor Maggie scarce a stump.
Now, wha this tale o' truth shall read,
Ilk man, and mother's son, take heed:
Whene'er to drink you are inclined,
Or cutty sarks run in your mind,
Think! ye may buy the joys o'er dear:
Remember Tam o' Shanter's mare.

1791

SWEET AFTON

Flow gently, sweet Afton, among thy green braes!
Flow gently, I'll sing thee a song in thy praise!
My Mary's asleep by thy murmuring stream —
Flow gently, sweet Afton, disturb not her dream!

Thou stock-dove whose echo resounds through the glen,
Ye wild whistling blackbirds in yon thorny den,
Thou green-crested lapwing, thy screaming forbear —
I charge you disturb not my slumbering fair!

How lofty, sweet Afton, thy neighbouring hills,
Far marked with the courses of clear, winding rills!
There daily I wander, as noon rises high,
My flocks and my Mary's sweet cot in my eye.

How pleasant thy banks and green valleys below,
Where wild in the woodlands the primroses blow!
There oft, as mild Evening weeps over the lea,
The sweet-scented birk shades my Mary and me.

Thy crystal stream, Afton, how lovely it glides,
And winds by the cot where my Mary resides!
How wanton thy waters her snowy feet lave,
As, gathering sweet flowerets, she stems thy clear wave!

Flow gently, sweet Afton, among thy green braes!
Flow gently, sweet river, the theme of my lays!
My Mary's asleep by thy murmuring stream —
Flow gently, sweet Afton, disturb not her dream!

1792

AE FOND KISS

Ae fond kiss, and then we sever!
Ae farewell, and then forever!
Deep in heart-wrung tears I 'll pledge thee,
Warring sighs and groans I 'll wage thee.
Who shall say that Fortune grieves him,
While the star of hope she leaves him?
Me, nae cheerfu' twinkle lights me,
Dark despair around benights me.

I 'll ne'er blame my partial fancy:
Naething could resist my Nancy!
But to see her was to love her,
Love but her, and love forever.
Had we never loved sae kindly,
Had we never loved sae blindly,
Never met — or never parted —
We had ne'er been broken-hearted.

Fare-thee-weel, thou first and fairest!
Fare-thee-weel, thou best and dearest!
Thine be ilka joy and treasure,
Peace, Enjoyment, Love, and Pleasure!
Ae fond kiss, and then we sever!
Ae farewell, alas, for ever!
Deep in heart-wrung tears I 'll pledge thee,
Warring sighs and groans I 'll wage thee.

1792

HIGHLAND MARY

Ye banks, and braes, and streams around
The castle o' Montgomery,
Green be your woods and fair your flowers,
Your waters never drumlie!
There simmer first unfauld her robes,
And there the langest tarry;
For there I took the last fareweel,
O' my sweet Highland Mary.

How sweetly bloomed the gay green birk,
How rich the hawthorn's blossom,
As underneath their fragrant shade
I clasped her to my bosom!
The golden hours, on angel wings,
Flew o'er me and my dearie;
For dear to me as light and life,
Was my sweet Highland Mary.

Wi' monie a vow and locked embrace
Our parting was fu' tender;
And, pledging aft to meet again,
We tore oursels asunder;
But O! fell death's untimely frost,
That nipt my flower sae early!
Now green's the sod, and cauld's the clay,
That wraps my Highland Mary!

O pale, pale now, those rosy lips,
I aft hae kissed sae fondly!
And closed for aye the sparkling glance,
That dwelt on me sae kindly!
And mould'ring now in silent dust,
That heart that lo'ed me dearly!
But still within my bosom's core
Shall live my Highland Mary.

1799

YE FLOWERY BANKS

Ye flowery banks o' bonie Doon,
How can ye blume sae fair?
How can ye chant, ye little birds,
And I sae fu' o' care?

Thou 'll break my heart, thou bonie bird
That sings upon the bough:
Thou minds me o' the happy days
When my fause Luve was true!

Thou 'll break my heart, thou bonie bird
That sings beside thy mate:
For sae I sat, and sae I sang,
And wist na o' my fate!

Aft hae I roved by bonie Doon
To see the woodbine twine,
And ilka bird sang o' its luve,
And sae did I o' mine.

Wi' lightsome heart I pu'd a rose
Frae aff its thorny tree,
And my fause luver staw my rose,
But left the thorn wi' me.

1792

A RED, RED ROSE

O, my luve is like a red, red rose,
That 's newly sprung in June.
O, my luve is like the melodie,
That 's sweetly played in tune.

As fair art thou, my bonie lass,
So deep in luve am I,
And I will luve thee still, my dear,
Till a' the seas gang dry.

Till a' the seas gang dry, my dear,
And the rocks melt wi' the sun!
And I will luve thee still, my dear,
While the sands o' life shall run.

And fare thee weel, my only luve,
And fare thee weel awhile!
And I will come again, my luve,
Though it were ten thousand mile!

1796

SCOTS, WHA HAE

Scots, wha hae wi' Wallace bled,
Scots, wham Bruce has aften led,
Welcome to your gory bed,
Or to victorie!

Now 's the day, and now 's the hour:
See the front o' battle lour,
See approach proud Edward's power —
Chains and slaverie!

Wha will be a traitor knave?
Wha can fill a coward's grave?
Wha sae base as be a slave? —
Let him turn, and flee!

Wha for Scotland's King and Law
Freedom's sword will strongly draw,
Freeman stand or freeman fa',
Let him follow me!

By Oppression's woes and pains,
By your sons in servile chains,
We will drain our dearest veins
But they shall be free!

Lay the proud usurpers low!
Tyrants fall in every foe!
Liberty 's in every blow!
Let us do, or die!

1794

A MAN'S A MAN FOR A' THAT

Is there for honest poverty
That hings his head, an' a' that?
The coward slave, we pass him by —
We dare be poor for a' that!
For a' that, an' a' that,
Our toils obscure, an' a' that,
The rank is but the guinea's stamp,
The man 's the gowd for a' that.

What though on hamely fare we dine,
Wear hoddin grey, an' a' that?
Gie fools their silks, and knaves their wine —
A man 's a man for a' that,
For a' that, an' a' that,
Their tinsel show, an' a' that,
The honest man, though e'er sae poor,
Is king o' men for a' that.

Ye see yon birkie ca'd a lord,
Wha struts, an' stares, an' a' that?
Though hundreds worship at his word,
He 's but a cuif for a' that.
For a' that, an' a' that,
His ribband, star, an' a' that,
The man o' independent mind,
He looks an' laughs at a' that.

A prince can mak a belted knight,
A marquis, duke, an' a' that!
But an honest man 's aboon his might —
Guid faith, he mauna fa' that!
For a' that, an' a' that,
Their dignities, an' a' that,
The pith o' sense an' pride o' worth
Are higher rank than a' that.

Then let us pray that come it may
(As come it will for a' that)
That Sense and Worth o'er a' the earth
Shall bear the gree an' a' that!
For a' that, an' a' that,
It 's comin yet for a' that,
That man to man the world o'er
Shall brithers be for a' that.

1795

William Blake (1757–1827)

SONG

How sweet I roamed from field to field,
And tasted all the summer's pride,
Till I the Prince of Love beheld
Who in the sunny beams did glide.

He showed me lilies for my hair,
And blushing roses for my brow;
He led me through his gardens fair,
Where all his golden pleasures grow.

With sweet May-dews my wings were wet,
And Phœbus fired my vocal rage;
He caught me in his silken net,
And shut me in his golden cage.

He loves to sit and hear me sing,
Then, laughing, sports and plays with me;
Then stretches out my golden wing,
And mocks my loss of liberty.

1783

PIPING DOWN THE VALLEYS WILD

Piping down the valleys wild,
Piping songs of pleasant glee,
On a cloud I saw a child,
And he laughing said to me:

'Pipe a song about a Lamb!'
So I piped with merry cheer.
'Piper, pipe that song again';
So I piped: he wept to hear.

'Drop thy pipe, thy happy pipe;
Sing thy songs of happy cheer!'

So I sang the same again,
While he wept with joy to hear.

'Piper, sit thee down and write
In a book, that all may read.'
So he vanished from my sight;
And I plucked a hollow reed,

And I made a rural pen,
And I stained the water clear,
And I wrote my happy songs
Every child may joy to hear.

1789

INFANT JOY

'I have no name;
I am but two days old.'
What shall I call thee?
'I happy am,
Joy is my name.'
Sweet joy befall thee!

Pretty joy!
Sweet joy, but two days old.
Sweet joy I call thee:
Thou dost smile,
I sing the while;
Sweet joy befall thee!

1789

A DREAM

Once a dream did weave a shade
O'er my angel-guarded bed,
That an emmet lost its way
Where on grass methought I lay.

Troubled, wildered, and forlorn,
Dark, benighted, travel-worn,
Over many a tangled spray,
All heart-broke, I heard her say:

'Oh my children! do they cry,
Do they hear their father sigh?
Now they look abroad to see,
Now return and weep for me.'

Pitying, I dropped a tear;
But I saw a glow-worm near,
Who replied, 'What wailing wight
Calls the watchman of the night?

'I am set to light the ground,
While the beetle goes his round:
Follow now the beetle's hum;
Little wanderer, hie thee home!'

1789

A CRADLE SONG

Sleep, sleep, beauty bright,
Dreaming in the joys of night;
Sleep, sleep; in thy sleep
Little sorrows sit and weep.

Sweet babe, in thy face
Soft desires I can trace,
Secret joys and secret smiles,
Little pretty infant wiles.

As thy softest limbs I feel,
Smiles as of the morning steal
O'er thy cheek, and o'er thy breast
Where thy little heart does rest.

Oh the cunning wiles that creep
In thy little heart asleep!
When thy little heart does wake,
Then the dreadful light shall break.

1794

THE TIGER

Tiger, Tiger, burning bright
In the forest of the night,
What immortal hand or eye
Framed thy fearful symmetry?

In what distant deeps or skies
Burned that fire within thine eyes?
On what wings dared he aspire?
What the hand dared seize the fire?

And what shoulder, and what art,
Could twist the sinews of thy heart?
When thy heart began to beat,
What dread hand formed thy dread feet?

What the hammer, what the chain,
Knit thy strength and forged thy brain?
What the anvil? What dread grasp
Dared thy deadly terrors clasp?

When the stars threw down their spears,
And watered heaven with their tears,
Did he smile his work to see?
Did he who made the lamb make thee?

1794

THE DEFILED SANCTUARY

I saw a chapel all of gold,
That none did dare to enter in,
And many weeping stood without,
Weeping, mourning, worshipping.

I saw a serpent rise between
The white pillars of the door,

And he forced and forced and forced
  Till he the golden hinges tore:

And along the pavement sweet,
  Set with pearls and rubies bright,
All his shining length he drew, —
  Till upon the altar white

He vomited his poison out
  On the bread and on the wine.
So I turned into a sty,
  And laid me down among the swine.

1863

AUGURIES OF INNOCENCE

To see a world in a grain of sand,
  And a heaven in a wild flower;
Hold infinity in the palm of your hand,
  And eternity in an hour.

A Robin Redbreast in a cage
Puts all Heaven in a rage;
A dove-house filled with doves and pigeons
Shudders hell through all its regions.
A dog starved at his master's gate
Predicts the ruin of the state;
A game-cock clipped and armed for fight
Doth the rising sun affright;
A horse misused upon the road
Calls to Heaven for human blood.
Every wolf's and lion's howl
Raises from hell a human soul;
Each outcry of the hunted hare
A fibre from the brain doth tear;
A skylark wounded on the wing
Doth make a cherub cease to sing.

He who shall hurt the little wren
Shall never be beloved by men;
He who the ox to wrath has moved
Shall never be by woman loved;
He who shall train the horse to war
Shall never pass the Polar Bar.
The wanton boy that kills the fly
Shall feed the spider's enmity;
He who torments the chafer's sprite
Weaves a bower in endless night.
The caterpillar on the leaf
Repeats to thee thy mother's grief;
The wild deer wandering here and there
Keep the human soul from care:
The lamb misused breeds public strife,
And yet forgives the butcher's knife.
Kill not the moth nor butterfly,
For the last judgment draweth nigh;
The beggar's dog and widow's cat,
Feed them and thou shalt grow fat.
Every tear from every eye
Becomes a babe in eternity;
The bleat, the bark, bellow, and roar,
Are waves that beat on heaven's shore.

The bat that flits at close of eve
Has left the brain that won't believe;
The owl that calls upon the night
Speaks the unbeliever's fright.
The gnat that sings his summer song
Poison gets from Slander's tongue;
The poison of the snake and newt
Is the sweat of Envy's foot;
The poison of the honey-bee
Is the artist's jealousy;
The strongest poison ever known
Came from Cæsar's laurel crown.

Nought can deform the human race
Like to the armourer's iron brace;
The soldier armed with sword and gun
Palsied strikes the summer's sun.
When gold and gems adorn the plough,
To peaceful arts shall Envy bow.
The beggar's rags fluttering in the air
Do to rags the heavens tear;
The prince's robes and beggar's rags
Are toadstools on the miser's bags.
One mite wrung from the labourer's hands
Shall buy and sell the miser's lands,
Or, if protected from on high,
Shall that whole nation sell and buy;
The poor man's farthing is worth more
Than all the gold on Afric's shore.
The [bawd] and gambler, by the state
Licensed, build that nation's fate;
The harlot's cry from street to street
Shall weave old England's winding sheet;
The winner's shout, the loser's curse,
Shall dance before dead England's hearse.

He who mocks the infant's faith
Shall be mocked in age and death;
He who shall teach the child to doubt
The rotting grave shall ne'er get out;
He who respects the infant's faith
Triumphs over hell and death.
The babe is more than swaddling-bands
Throughout all these human lands;
Tools were made, and born were hands,
Every farmer understands.
The questioner who sits so sly
Shall never know how to reply.
He who replies to words of doubt
Doth put the light of knowledge out;
A puddle, or the cricket's cry,
Is to doubt a fit reply.
The child's toys and the old man's reasons
Are the fruits of the two seasons.
The emmet's inch and eagle's mile
Make lame philosophy to smile.
A truth that's told with bad intent

Beats all the lies you can invent.
He who doubts from what he sees
Will ne'er believe, do what you please;
If the sun and moon should doubt,
They'd immediately go out.

Every night and every morn
Some to misery are born;
Every morn and every night
Some are born to sweet delight;
Some are born to sweet delight,
Some are born to endless night.
Joy and woe are woven fine,
A clothing for the soul divine;
Under every grief and pine
Runs a joy with silken twine.
It is right it should be so;
Man was made for joy and woe;
And, when this we rightly know,
Safely through the world we go.

We are led to believe a lie
When we see *with* not *through* the eye,
Which was born in a night to perish in a night
When the soul slept in beams of light.
God appears and God is light
To those poor souls who dwell in night;
But doth a human form display
To those who dwell in realms of day.

1863

William Wordsworth (1770-1850)

WE ARE SEVEN

——A SIMPLE child,
That lightly draws its breath,
And feels its life in every limb,
What should it know of death?

I met a little cottage girl:
She was eight years old, she said;
Her hair was thick with many a curl
That clustered round her head.

She had a rustic, woodland air,
And she was wildly clad:
Her eyes were fair, and very fair;
— Her beauty made me glad.

'Sisters and brothers, little maid,
How many may you be?'
'How many? Seven in all,' she said,
And wondering looked at me.

'And where are they? I pray you tell.'
She answered, 'Seven are we;
And two of us at Conway dwell,
And two are gone to sea.

'Two of us in the church-yard lie,
My sister and my brother;
And, in the church-yard cottage, I
Dwell near them with my mother.'

'You say that two at Conway dwell,
And two are gone to sea,
Yet ye are seven! — I pray you tell,
Sweet maid, how this may be.'

Then did the little maid reply,
'Seven boys and girls are we;
Two of us in the church-yard lie,
Beneath the church-yard tree.'

'You run about, my little maid,
Your limbs they are alive;
If two are in the church-yard laid,
Then ye are only five.'

'Their graves are green, they may be seen,'
The little maid replied,
'Twelve steps or more from my mother's door,
And they are side by side.

'My stockings there I often knit,
My kerchief there I hem;
And there upon the ground I sit,
And sing a song to them.

'And often after sunset, sir,
When it is light and fair,
I take my little porringer,
And eat my supper there.

'The first that died was sister Jane;
In bed she moaning lay,
Till God released her of her pain;
And then she went away.

'So in the church-yard she was laid;
And, when the grass was dry,
Together round her grave we played,
My brother John and I.

'And when the ground was white with snow,
And I could run and slide,
My brother John was forced to go,
And he lies by her side.'

'How many are you, then,' said I,
'If they two are in heaven?'
Quick was the little maid's reply,
'O master! we are seven.'

'But they are dead; those two are dead!
Their spirits are in heaven!'
'T was throwing words away; for still
The little maid would have her will,
And said, 'Nay, we are seven!'

1800

LINES WRITTEN IN EARLY SPRING

I HEARD a thousand blended notes,
While in a grove I sate reclined,
In that sweet mood when pleasant thoughts
Bring sad thoughts to the mind.

To her fair works did Nature link
The human soul that through me ran;
And much it grieved my heart to think
What man has made of man.

Through primrose tufts, in that green bower,
The periwinkle trailed its wreaths;
And 't is my faith that every flower
Enjoys the air it breathes.

The birds around me hopped and played,
Their thoughts I cannot measure: —
But the least motion which they made,
It seemed a thrill of pleasure.

The budding twigs spread out their fan,
To catch the breezy air;
And I must think, do all I can,
That there was pleasure there.

If this belief from heaven be sent,
If such be Nature's holy plan,
Have I not reason to lament
What man has made of man?

1798

EXPOSTULATION AND REPLY

'WHY, William, on that old grey stone,
Thus for the length of half a day,
Why, William, sit you thus alone,
And dream your time away?

'Where are your books? — that light bequeathed
To Beings else forlorn and blind!
Up! up! and drink the spirit breathed
From dead men to their kind.

'You look round on your Mother Earth,
As if she for no purpose bore you;
As if you were her first-born birth,
And none had lived before you!'

One morning thus, by Esthwaite lake,
When life was sweet, I knew not why,
To me my good friend Matthew spake,
And thus I made reply:

'The eye — it cannot choose but see;
We cannot bid the ear be still;
Our bodies feel, where'er they be,
Against or with our will.

'Nor less I deem that there are Powers
Which of themselves our minds impress;
That we can feed this mind of ours
In a wise passiveness.

'Think you, 'mid all this mighty sum
Of things for ever speaking,
That nothing of itself will come,
But we must still be seeking?

'— Then ask not wherefore, here, alone,
Conversing as I may,
I sit upon this old grey stone,
And dream my time away.'

1798

THE TABLES TURNED

UP! up! my Friend, and quit your books;
Or surely you 'll grow double:
Up! up! my Friend, and clear your looks;
Why all this toil and trouble?

The sun, above the mountain's head,
A freshening lustre mellow
Through all the long green fields has spread,
His first sweet evening yellow.

Books! 't is a dull and endless strife:
Come, hear the woodland linnet,
How sweet his music! on my life,
There 's more of wisdom in it.

And hark! how blithe the throstle sings!
He, too, is no mean preacher:
Come forth into the light of things,
Let Nature be your Teacher.

She has a world of ready wealth,
Our minds and hearts to bless —
Spontaneous wisdom breathed by health,
Truth breathed by cheerfulness.

One impulse from a vernal wood
May teach you more of man,
Of moral evil and of good,
Than all the sages can.

Sweet is the lore which Nature brings;
Our meddling intellect
Mis-shapes the beauteous forms of things: —
We murder to dissect.

Enough of Science and of Art;
Close up those barren leaves;
Come forth, and bring with you a heart
That watches and receives.

1798

LINES

COMPOSED A FEW MILES ABOVE TINTERN ABBEY

Five years have past; five summers, with the length
Of five long winters! and again I hear
These waters, rolling from their mountain-springs
With a soft inland murmur. — Once again
Do I behold these steep and lofty cliffs,
That on a wild secluded scene impress
Thoughts of more deep seclusion; and connect
The landscape with the quiet of the sky.
The day is come when I again repose
Here, under this dark sycamore, and view
These plots of cottage-ground, these orchard-tufts,
Which at this season, with their unripe fruits,
Are clad in one green hue, and lose themselves
'Mid groves and copses. Once again I see
These hedge-rows, hardly hedge-rows, little lines
Of sportive wood run wild: these pastoral farms,
Green to the very door; and wreaths of smoke
Sent up, in silence, from among the trees!
With some uncertain notice, as might seem
Of vagrant dwellers in the houseless woods,
Or of some Hermit's cave, where by his fire
The Hermit sits alone.
These beauteous forms,
Through a long absence, have not been to me
As is a landscape to a blind man's eye:
But oft, in lonely rooms, and 'mid the din
Of towns and cities, I have owed to them,
In hours of weariness, sensations sweet,
Felt in the blood, and felt along the heart;
And passing even into my purer mind,
With tranquil restoration: — feelings too
Of unremembered pleasure: such, perhaps,
As have no slight or trivial influence
On that best portion of a good man's life,
His little, nameless, unremembered, acts
Of kindness and of love. Nor less, I trust,
To them I may have owed another gift,
Of aspect more sublime; that blessèd mood,
In which the burthen of the mystery,
In which the heavy and the weary weight
Of all this unintelligible world,
Is lightened: — that serene and blessèd mood,
In which the affections gently lead us on, —
Until, the breath of this corporeal frame
And even the motion of our human blood
Almost suspended, we are laid asleep
In body, and become a living soul:
While with an eye made quiet by the power
Of harmony, and the deep power of joy,
We see into the life of things.
If this
Be but a vain belief, yet, oh! how oft —
In darkness and amid the many shapes
Of joyless daylight; when the fretful stir
Unprofitable, and the fever of the world,
Have hung upon the beatings of my heart —
How oft, in spirit, have I turned to thee,
O sylvan Wye! thou wanderer through the woods,
How often has my spirit turned to thee!
And now, with gleams of half-extinguished thought,
With many recognitions dim and faint,
And somewhat of a sad perplexity,
The picture of the mind revives again:
While here I stand, not only with the sense
Of present pleasure, but with pleasing thoughts
That in this moment there is life and food
For future years. And so I dare to hope,
Though changed, no doubt, from what I was when first
I came among these hills; when like a roe
I bounded o'er the mountains, by the sides
Of the deep rivers, and the lonely streams,
Wherever nature led: more like a man
Flying from something that he dreads than one
Who sought the thing he loved. For nature then
(The coarser pleasures of my boyish days,
And their glad animal movements all gone by)
To me was all in all. — I cannot paint
What then I was. The sounding cataract
Haunted me like a passion: the tall rock,
The mountain, and the deep and gloomy wood,
Their colours and their forms, were then to me
An appetite; a feeling and a love,
That had no need of a remoter charm,
By thought supplied, nor any interest
Unborrowed from the eye. — That time is past,
And all its aching joys are now no more,
And all its dizzy raptures. Not for this
Faint I, nor mourn nor murmur; other gifts
Have followed; for such loss, I would believe,
Abundant recompense. For I have learned
To look on nature, not as in the hour
Of thoughtless youth; but hearing oftentimes

The still, sad music of humanity,
Nor harsh nor grating, though of ample power
To chasten and subdue. And I have felt
A presence that disturbs me with the joy
Of elevated thoughts; a sense sublime
Of something far more deeply interfused,
Whose dwelling is the light of setting suns,
And the round ocean and the living air,
And the blue sky, and in the mind of man:
A motion and a spirit, that impels
All thinking things, all objects of all thought,
And rolls through all things. Therefore am I still
A lover of the meadows and the woods,
And mountains; and of all that we behold
From this green earth; of all the mighty world
Of eye, and ear, — both what they half create,
And what perceive; well pleased to recognise
In nature and the language of the sense
The anchor of my purest thoughts, the nurse,
The guide, the guardian of my heart, and soul
Of all my moral being.
Nor perchance,
If I were not thus taught, should I the more
Suffer my genial spirits to decay:
For thou art with me here upon the banks
Of this fair river; thou my dearest Friend,
My dear, dear Friend; and in thy voice I catch
The language of my former heart, and read
My former pleasures in the shooting lights
Of thy wild eyes. Oh! yet a little while
May I behold in thee what I was once,
My dear, dear Sister! and this prayer I make,
Knowing that Nature never did betray
The heart that loved her; 't is her privilege,
Through all the years of this our life, to lead
From joy to joy: for she can so inform
The mind that is within us, so impress
With quietness and beauty, and so feed
With lofty thoughts, that neither evil tongues,
Rash judgments, nor the sneers of selfish men,
Nor greetings where no kindness is, nor all
The dreary intercourse of daily life,
Shall e'er prevail against us, or disturb
Our cheerful faith, that all which we behold
Is full of blessings. Therefore let the moon
Shine on thee in thy solitary walk;
And let the misty mountain-winds be free
To blow against thee: and, in after years,
When these wild ecstasies shall be matured
Into a sober pleasure; when thy mind
Shall be a mansion for all lovely forms,
Thy memory be as a dwelling-place
For all sweet sounds and harmonies; oh! then,
If solitude, or fear, or pain, or grief,
Should be thy portion, with what healing thoughts
Of tender joy wilt thou remember me,
And these my exhortations! Nor, perchance —
If I should be where I no more can hear
Thy voice, nor catch from thy wild eyes these gleams
Of past existence — wilt thou then forget
That on the banks of this delightful stream
We stood together; and that I, so long
A worshipper of Nature, hither came
Unwearied in that service: rather say
With warmer love — oh! with far deeper zeal
Of holier love. Nor wilt thou then forget
That after many wanderings, many years
Of absence, these steep woods and lofty cliffs,
And this green pastoral landscape, were to me
More dear, both for themselves and for thy sake!

1798

LUCY POEMS

STRANGE FITS OF PASSION HAVE I KNOWN

Strange fits of passion have I known:
And I will dare to tell,
But in the Lover's ear alone,
What once to me befell.

When she I loved looked every day
Fresh as a rose in June,
I to her cottage bent my way,
Beneath an evening-moon.

Upon the moon I fixed my eye,
All over the wide lea;
With quickening pace my horse drew nigh
Those paths so dear to me.

And now we reached the orchard-plot;
And, as we climbed the hill,
The sinking moon to Lucy's cot
Came near, and nearer still.

In one of those sweet dreams I slept,
Kind Nature's gentlest boon!
And all the while my eyes I kept
On the descending moon.

My horse moved on; hoof after hoof
He raised, and never stopped:
When down behind the cottage roof,
At once, the bright moon dropped.

What fond and wayward thoughts will slide
Into a Lover's head!
'O mercy!' to myself I cried,
'If Lucy should be dead!'

1800

SHE DWELT AMONG THE UNTRODDEN WAYS

She dwelt among the untrodden ways
Beside the springs of Dove,
A Maid whom there were none to praise
And very few to love:

A violet by a mossy stone
Half hidden from the eye!
— Fair as a star, when only one
Is shining in the sky.

She lived unknown, and few could know
When Lucy ceased to be;
But she is in her grave, and, oh,
The difference to me!

1800

I TRAVELLED AMONG UNKNOWN MEN

I travelled among unknown men,
In lands beyond the sea;
Nor, England! did I know till then
What love I bore to thee.

'T is past, that melancholy dream!
Nor will I quit thy shore
A second time; for still I seem
To love thee more and more.

Among thy mountains did I feel
The joy of my desire;
And she I cherished turned her wheel
Beside an English fire.

Thy mornings showed, thy nights concealed,
The bowers where Lucy played;
And thine too is the last green field
That Lucy's eyes surveyed.

1807

THREE YEARS SHE GREW

Three years she grew in sun and shower,
Then Nature said, 'A lovelier flower
On earth was never sown;
This Child I to myself will take;
She shall be mine, and I will make
A Lady of my own.

'Myself will to my darling be
Both law and impulse: and with me
The Girl, in rock and plain,
In earth and heaven, in glade and bower,
Shall feel an overseeing power
To kindle or restrain.

'She shall be sportive as the fawn
That wild with glee across the lawn
Or up the mountain springs;
And hers shall be the breathing balm,
And hers the silence and the calm
Of mute insensate things.

'The floating clouds their state shall lend
To her; for her the willow bend;
Nor shall she fail to see
Even in the motions of the Storm
Grace that shall mould the Maiden's form
By silent sympathy.

'The stars of midnight shall be dear
To her; and she shall lean her ear
In many a secret place
Where rivulets dance their wayward round,
And beauty born of murmuring sound
Shall pass into her face.

'And vital feelings of delight
Shall rear her form to stately height,
Her virgin bosom swell;
Such thoughts to Lucy I will give
While she and I together live
Here in this happy dell.'

Thus Nature spake — The work was done —
How soon my Lucy's race was run!
She died, and left to me
This heath, this calm, and quiet scene;
The memory of what has been,
And never more will be.

1800

A SLUMBER DID MY SPIRIT SEAL

A slumber did my spirit seal;
I had no human fears:
She seemed a thing that could not feel
The touch of earthly years.

No motion has she now, no force;
She neither hears nor sees;
Rolled round in earth's diurnal course,
With rocks, and stones, and trees.

1800

LUCY GRAY

OR, SOLITUDE

Oft I had heard of Lucy Gray:
And, when I crossed the wild,

I chanced to see at break of day
The solitary child.

No mate, no comrade Lucy knew;
She dwelt on a wide moor,
— The sweetest thing that ever grew
Beside a human door!

You yet may spy the fawn at play,
The hare upon the green;
But the sweet face of Lucy Gray
Will never more be seen.

'To-night will be a stormy night —
You to the town must go;
And take a lantern, Child, to light
Your mother through the snow.'

'That, Father! will I gladly do:
'T is scarcely afternoon —
The minster-clock has just struck two,
And yonder is the moon!'

At this the Father raised his hook,
And snapped a faggot-band;
He plied his work; — and Lucy took
The lantern in her hand.

Not blither is the mountain roe:
With many a wanton stroke
Her feet disperse the powdery snow,
That rises up like smoke.

The storm came on before its time:
She wandered up and down;
And many a hill did Lucy climb:
But never reached the town.

The wretched parents all that night
Went shouting far and wide;
But there was neither sound nor sight
To serve them for a guide.

At day-break on a hill they stood
That overlooked the moor;
And thence they saw the bridge of wood,
A furlong from their door.

They wept — and, turning homeward, cried,
'In heaven we all shall meet';
— When in the snow the mother spied
The print of Lucy's feet.

Then downwards from the steep hill's edge
They tracked the footmarks small;
And through the broken hawthorn hedge,
And by the long stone-wall;

And then an open field they crossed:
The marks were still the same;
They tracked them on, nor ever lost;
And to the bridge they came.

They followed from the snowy bank
Those footmarks, one by one,
Into the middle of the plank;
And further there were none!

— Yet some maintain that to this day
She is a living child;
That you may see sweet Lucy Gray
Upon the lonesome wild.

O'er rough and smooth she trips along,
And never looks behind;
And sings a solitary song
That whistles in the wind.

1800

MICHAEL

If from the public way you turn your steps
Up the tumultuous brook of Green-head Ghyll,
You will suppose that with an upright path
Your feet must struggle; in such bold ascent
The pastoral mountains front you, face to face.
But, courage! for around that boisterous brook
The mountains have all opened out themselves,
And made a hidden valley of their own.
No habitation can be seen; but they
Who journey thither find themselves alone
With a few sheep, with rocks and stones, and kites
That overhead are sailing in the sky.
It is in truth an utter solitude;
Nor should I have made mention of this Dell
But for one object which you might pass by,
Might see and notice not. Beside the brook
Appears a straggling heap of unhewn stones!
And to that simple object appertains
A story — unenriched with strange events,
Yet not unfit, I deem, for the fireside,
Or for the summer shade. It was the first
Of those domestic tales that spake to me
Of Shepherds, dwellers in the valleys, men
Whom I already loved; — not verily
For their own sakes, but for the fields and hills
Where was their occupation and abode.
And hence this Tale, while I was yet a Boy
Careless of books, yet having felt the power
Of Nature, by the gentle agency
Of natural objects, led me on to feel
For passions that were not my own, and think
(At random and imperfectly indeed)
On man, the heart of man, and human life.

Therefore, although it be a history
Homely and rude, I will relate the same
For the delight of a few natural hearts;
And, with yet fonder feeling, for the sake
Of youthful Poets, who among these hills
Will be my second self when I am gone.
Upon the forest-side in Grasmere Vale
There dwelt a Shepherd, Michael was his name;
An old man, stout of heart, and strong of limb.
His bodily frame had been from youth to age
Of an unusual strength: his mind was keen,
Intense, and frugal, apt for all affairs,
And in his shepherd's calling he was prompt
And watchful more than ordinary men.
Hence had he learned the meaning of all winds,
Of blasts of every tone; and oftentimes,
When others heeded not, He heard the South
Make subterraneous music, like the noise
Of bagpipers on distant Highland hills.
The Shepherd, at such warning, of his flock
Bethought him, and he to himself would say,
'The winds are now devising work for me!'
And, truly, at all times, the storm, that drives
The traveller to a shelter, summoned him
Up to the mountains: he had been alone
Amid the heart of many thousand mists,
That came to him, and left him, on the heights.
So lived he till his eightieth year was past.
And grossly that man errs, who should suppose
That the green valleys, and the streams and rocks,
Were things indifferent to the Shepherd's thoughts.
Fields, where with cheerful spirits he had breathed
The common air; hills, which with vigorous step
He had so often climbed; which had impressed
So many incidents upon his mind
Of hardship, skill or courage, joy or fear;
Which, like a book, preserved the memory
Of the dumb animals, whom he had saved,
Had fed or sheltered, linking to such acts
The certainty of honourable gain;
Those fields, those hills — what could they less? had laid
Strong hold on his affections, were to him
A pleasurable feeling of blind love,
The pleasure which there is in life itself.
His days had not been passed in singleness.
His Helpmate was a comely matron, old —
Though younger than himself full twenty years.
She was a woman of a stirring life,
Whose heart was in her house: two wheels she had
Of antique form; this large, for spinning wool;
That small, for flax; and, if one wheel had rest,
It was because the other was at work.
The Pair had but one inmate in their house,
An only Child, who had been born to them
When Michael, telling o'er his years, began
To deem that he was old, — in shepherd's phrase,
With one foot in the grave. This only Son,
With two brave sheep-dogs tried in many a storm,
The one of an inestimable worth,
Made all their household. I may truly say,
That they were as a proverb in the vale
For endless industry. When day was gone,
And from their occupations out of doors
The Son and Father were come home, even then,
Their labour did not cease; unless when all
Turned to the cleanly supper-board, and there,
Each with a mess of pottage and skimmed milk,
Sat round the basket piled with oaten cakes,
And their plain home-made cheese. Yet when the meal
Was ended, Luke (for so the Son was named)
And his old Father both betook themselves
To such convenient work as might employ
Their hands by the fire-side; perhaps to card
Wool for the Housewife's spindle, or repair
Some injury done to sickle, flail, or scythe,
Or other implement of house or field.
Down from the ceiling, by the chimney's edge,
That in our ancient uncouth country style
With huge and black projection overbrowed
Large space beneath, as duly as the light
Of day grew dim the Housewife hung a lamp;
An aged utensil, which had performed
Service beyond all others of its kind.
Early at evening did it burn — and late,
Surviving comrade of uncounted hours,
Which, going by from year to year, had found,
And left, the couple neither gay perhaps

Nor cheerful, yet with objects and with hopes,
Living a life of eager industry.
And now, when Luke had reached his eighteenth year,
There by the light of this old lamp they sate,
Father and Son, while far into the night
The Housewife plied her own peculiar work,
Making the cottage through the silent hours
Murmur as with the sound of summer flies.
This light was famous in its neighbourhood,
And was a public symbol of the life
That thrifty Pair had lived. For, as it chanced,
Their cottage on a plot of rising ground
Stood single, with large prospect, north and south,
High into Easedale, up to Dunmail-Raise,
And westward to the village near the lake;
And from this constant light, so regular,
And so far seen, the House itself, by all
Who dwelt within the limits of the vale,
Both old and young, was named The Evening Star.
  Thus living on through such a length of years,
The Shepherd, if he loved himself, must needs
Have loved his Helpmate; but to Michael's heart
This son of his old age was yet more dear —
Less from instinctive tenderness, the same
Fond spirit that blindly works in the blood of all —
Than that a child, more than all other gifts
That earth can offer to declining man,
Brings hope with it, and forward-looking thoughts,
And stirrings of inquietude, when they
By tendency of nature needs must fail.
Exceeding was the love he bare to him,
His heart and his heart's joy! For oftentimes
Old Michael, while he was a babe in arms,
Had done him female service, not alone
For pastime and delight, as is the use
Of fathers, but with patient mind enforced
To acts of tenderness; and he had rocked
His cradle, as with a woman's gentle hand.
  And in a later time, ere yet the Boy
Had put on boy's attire, did Michael love,
Albeit of a stern unbending mind,
To have the Young-one in his sight, when he
Wrought in the field, or on his shepherd's stool
Sate with a fettered sheep before him stretched
Under the large old oak, that near his door
Stood single, and, from matchless depth of shade,
Chosen for the Shearer's covert from the sun,
Thence in our rustic dialect was called
The Clipping Tree, a name which yet it bears.
There, while they two were sitting in the shade,
With others round them, earnest all and blithe,
Would Michael exercise his heart with looks
Of fond correction and reproof bestowed
Upon the Child, if he disturbed the sheep
By catching at their legs, or with his shouts
Scared them, while they lay still beneath the shears.
  And when by Heaven's good grace the boy grew up
A healthy Lad, and carried in his cheek
Two steady roses that were five years old;
Then Michael from a winter coppice cut
With his own hand a sapling, which he hooped
With iron, making it throughout in all
Due requisites a perfect shepherd's staff,
And gave it to the Boy; wherewith equipt
He as a watchman oftentimes was placed
At gate or gap, to stem or turn the flock;
And, to his office prematurely called,
There stood the urchin, as you will divine,
Something between a hindrance and a help;
And for this cause not always, I believe,
Receiving from his Father hire of praise;
Though nought was left undone which staff, or voice,
Or looks, or threatening gestures, could perform.
  But soon as Luke, full ten years old, could stand
Against the mountain blasts; and to the heights,
Not fearing toil, nor length of weary ways,
He with his Father daily went, and they
Were as companions, why should I relate
That objects which the Shepherd loved before
Were dearer now? that from the Boy there came
Feelings and emanations — things which were
Light to the sun and music to the wind;
And that the old Man's heart seemed born again?
  Thus in his Father's sight the Boy grew up:
And now, when he had reached his eighteenth year,

He was his comfort and his daily hope.
While in this sort the simple household lived
From day to day, to Michael's ear there came
Distressful tidings. Long before the time
Of which I speak, the Shepherd had been bound
In surety for his brother's son, a man
Of an industrious life, and ample means;
But unforeseen misfortunes suddenly
Had prest upon him; and old Michael now
Was summoned to discharge the forfeiture,
A grievous penalty, but little less
Than half his substance. This unlooked-for claim,
At the first hearing, for a moment took
More hope out of his life than he supposed
That any old man ever could have lost.
As soon as he had armed himself with strength
To look his trouble in the face, it seemed
The Shepherd's sole resource to sell at once
A portion of his patrimonial fields.
Such was his first resolve; he thought again,
And his heart failed him. 'Isabel,' said he,
Two evenings after he had heard the news,
'I have been toiling more than seventy years,
And in the open sunshine of God's love
Have we all lived; yet, if these fields of ours
Should pass into a stranger's hand, I think
That I could not lie quiet in my grave.
Our lot is a hard lot; the sun himself
Has scarcely been more diligent than I;
And I have lived to be a fool at last
To my own family. An evil man
That was, and made an evil choice, if he
Were false to us; and, if he were not false,
There are ten thousand to whom loss like this
Had been no sorrow. I forgive him; — but
'T were better to be dumb than to talk thus.
'When I began, my purpose was to speak
Of remedies and of a cheerful hope.
Our Luke shall leave us, Isabel; the land
Shall not go from us, and it shall be free;
He shall possess it, free as is the wind
That passes over it. We have, thou know'st,
Another kinsman — he will be our friend
In this distress. He is a prosperous man,
Thriving in trade — and Luke to him shall go,
And with his kinsman's help and his own thrift
He quickly will repair this loss, and then
He may return to us. If here he stay,
What can be done? Where every one is poor,
What can be gained?'
At this the old Man paused,
And Isabel sat silent, for her mind
Was busy, looking back into past times.
There's Richard Bateman, thought she to herself,
He was a parish-boy — at the church-door
They made a gathering for him, shillings, pence,
And halfpennies, wherewith the neighbours bought
A basket, which they filled with pedlar's wares;
And, with this basket on his arm, the lad
Went up to London, found a master there,
Who, out of many, chose the trusty boy
To go and overlook his merchandise
Beyond the seas; where he grew wondrous rich,
And left estates and monies to the poor,
And, at his birth-place, built a chapel floored
With marble, which he sent from foreign lands.
These thoughts, and many others of like sort,
Passed quickly through the mind of Isabel,
And her face brightened. The old Man was glad,
And thus resumed: — 'Well, Isabel! this scheme
These two days has been meat and drink to me.
Far more than we have lost is left us yet.
'We have enough — I wish indeed that I
Were younger; — but this hope is a good hope.
Make ready Luke's best garments, of the best
Buy for him more, and let us send him forth
To-morrow, or the next day, or to-night:
If he *could* go, the Boy should go to-night.'
Here Michael ceased, and to the fields went forth
With a light heart. The Housewife for five days
Was restless morn and night, and all day long
Wrought on with her best fingers to prepare
Things needful for the journey of her son.
But Isabel was glad when Sunday came
To stop her in her work: for, when she lay
By Michael's side, she through the last two nights
Heard him, how he was troubled in his sleep:
And when they rose at morning she could see

That all his hopes were gone. That day at noon
She said to Luke, while they two by themselves
Were sitting at the door, 'Thou must not go:
We have no other Child but thee to lose,
None to remember — do not go away,
For if thou leave thy Father he will die.'
The Youth made answer with a jocund voice;
And Isabel, when she had told her fears,
Recovered heart. That evening her best fare
Did she bring forth, and all together sat
Like happy people round a Christmas fire.
With daylight Isabel resumed her work;
And all the ensuing week the house appeared
As cheerful as a grove in Spring: at length
The expected letter from their kinsman came,
With kind assurances that he would do
His utmost for the welfare of the Boy;
To which, requests were added, that forthwith
He might be sent to him. Ten times or more
The letter was read over; Isabel
Went forth to show it to the neighbours round;
Nor was there at that time on English land
A prouder heart than Luke's. When Isabel
Had to her house returned, the old Man said,
'He shall depart to-morrow.' To this word
The Housewife answered, talking much of things
Which, if at such short notice he should go,
Would surely be forgotten. But at length
She gave consent, and Michael was at ease.
Near the tumultuous brook of Green-head Ghyll,
In that deep valley, Michael had designed
To build a Sheep-fold; and, before he heard
The tidings of his melancholy loss,
For this same purpose he had gathered up
A heap of stones, which by the streamlet's edge
Lay thrown together, ready for the work.
With Luke that evening thitherward he walked:
And soon as they had reached the place he stopped,
And thus the old Man spake to him: — 'My son,
To-morrow thou wilt leave me: with full heart
I look upon thee, for thou art the same
That wert a promise to me ere thy birth,
And all thy life hast been my daily joy.
I will relate to thee some little part
Of our two histories; 't will do thee good
When thou art from me, even if I should touch
On things thou canst not know of. — After thou
First cam'st into the world — as oft befalls
To new-born infants — thou didst sleep away
Two days, and blessings from thy Father's tongue
Then fell upon thee. Day by day passed on,
And still I loved thee with increasing love.
Never to living ear came sweeter sounds
Than when I heard thee by our own fireside
First uttering, without words, a natural tune;
While thou, a feeding babe, didst in thy joy
Sing at thy Mother's breast. Month followed month,
And in the open fields my life was passed
And on the mountains; else I think that thou
Hadst been brought up upon thy Father's knees.
But we were playmates, Luke: among these hills,
As well thou knowest, in us the old and young
Have played together, nor with me didst thou
Lack any pleasure which a boy can know.'
Luke had a manly heart; but at these words
He sobbed aloud. The old Man grasped his hand,
And said, 'Nay, do not take it so — I see
That these are things of which I need not speak.
— Even to the utmost I have been to thee
A kind and a good Father: and herein
I but repay a gift which I myself
Received at others' hands; for, though now old
Beyond the common life of man, I still
Remember them who loved me in my youth.
Both of them sleep together: here they lived,
As all their Forefathers had done; and, when
At length their time was come, they were not loth
To give their bodies to the family mould.
I wished that thou shouldst live the life they lived,
But 't is a long time to look back, my Son,
And see so little gain from threescore years.

These fields were burthened when they came to me;
Till I was forty years of age, not more
Than half of my inheritance was mine.
I toiled and toiled; God blessed me in my work,
And till these three weeks past the land was free.
— It looks as if it never could endure
Another Master. Heaven forgive me, Luke,
If I judge ill for thee, but it seems good
That thou shouldst go.'
At this the old Man paused;
Then, pointing to the stones near which they stood,
Thus, after a short silence, he resumed:
'This was a work for us; and now, my Son,
It is a work for me. But, lay one stone —
Here, lay it for me, Luke, with thine own hands.
Nay, Boy, be of good hope; — we both may live
To see a better day. At eighty-four
I still am strong and hale; — do thou thy part;
I will do mine. — I will begin again
With many tasks that were resigned to thee:
Up to the heights, and in among the storms,
Will I without thee go again, and do
All works which I was wont to do alone,
Before I knew thy face. — Heaven bless thee, Boy!
Thy heart these two weeks has been beating fast
With many hopes; it should be so — yes — yes —
I knew that thou couldst never have a wish
To leave me, Luke: thou hast been bound to me
Only by links of love: when thou art gone,
What will be left to us! — But I forget
My purposes. Lay now the corner-stone,
As I requested; and hereafter, Luke,
When thou art gone away, should evil men
Be thy companions, think of me, my Son,
And of this moment; hither turn thy thoughts,
And God will strengthen thee: amid all fear
And all temptation, Luke, I pray that thou
May'st bear in mind the life thy Fathers lived,
Who, being innocent, did for that cause
Bestir them in good deeds. Now, fare thee well —
When thou return'st, thou in this place wilt see
A work which is not here: a covenant
'T will be between us; but, whatever fate
Befall thee, I shall love thee to that last,
And bear thy memory with me to the grave.'
The Shepherd ended here; and Luke stooped down,
And, as his Father had requested, laid
The first stone of the Sheep-fold. At the sight
The old Man's grief broke from him; to his heart
He pressed his Son, he kissèd him and wept;
And to the house together they returned.
— Hushed was that House in peace, or seeming peace,
Ere the night fell: — with morrow's dawn the Boy
Began his journey, and, when he had reached
The public way, he put on a bold face;
And all the neighbours, as he passed their doors,
Came forth with wishes and with farewell prayers,
That followed him till he was out of sight.
A good report did from their Kinsman come,
Of Luke and his well-doing: and the Boy
Wrote loving letters, full of wondrous news,
Which, as the Housewife phrased it, were throughout
'The prettiest letters that were ever seen.'
Both parents read them with rejoicing hearts.
So, many months passed on: and once again
The Shepherd went about his daily work
With confident and cheerful thoughts; and now
Sometimes when he could find a leisure hour
He to that valley took his way, and there
Wrought at the Sheep-fold. Meantime Luke began
To slacken in his duty; and, at length,
He in the dissolute city gave himself
To evil courses: ignominy and shame
Fell on him, so that he was driven at last
To seek a hiding-place beyond the seas.
There is a comfort in the strength of love;
'T will make a thing endurable, which else
Would overset the brain, or break the heart:
I have conversed with more than one who well
Remember the old Man, and what he was
Years after he had heard this heavy news.
His bodily frame had been from youth to age

Of an unusual strength. Among the rocks
He went, and still looked up to sun and cloud,
And listened to the wind; and, as before,
Performed all kinds of labour for his sheep,
And for the land, his small inheritance.
And to that hollow dell from time to time
Did he repair, to build the Fold of which
His flock had need. 'T is not forgotten yet
The pity which was then in every heart
For the old Man — and 'tis believed by all
That many and many a day he thither went,
And never lifted up a single stone.
  There, by the Sheep-fold, sometimes was he seen
Sitting alone, or with his faithful Dog,
Then old, beside him, lying at his feet.
The length of full seven years, from time to time,
He at the building of this Sheep-fold wrought,
And left the work unfinished when he died.
Three years, or little more, did Isabel
Survive her Husband: at her death the estate
Was sold, and went into a stranger's hand.
The Cottage which was named the Evening Star
Is gone — the ploughshare has been through the ground
On which it stood; great changes have been wrought
In all the neighbourhood: — yet the oak is left
That grew beside their door; and the remains
Of the unfinished Sheep-fold may be seen
Beside the boisterous brook of Green-head Ghyll.

1800

MY HEART LEAPS UP

My heart leaps up when I behold
  A rainbow in the sky:
So was it when my life began;
So is it now I am a man;
So be it when I shall grow old,
  Or let me die!
The Child is father of the Man;
And I could wish my days to be
Bound each to each by natural piety.

1807

RESOLUTION AND INDEPENDENCE

There was a roaring in the wind all night;
The rain came heavily and fell in floods;
But now the sun is rising calm and bright;
The birds are singing in the distant woods;
Over his own sweet voice the Stock-dove broods;
The Jay makes answer as the Magpie chatters;
And all the air is filled with pleasant noise of waters.

All things that love the sun are out of doors;
The sky rejoices in the morning's birth;
The grass is bright with rain-drops; — on the moors
The hare is running races in her mirth;
And with her feet she from the plashy earth
Raises a mist; that, glittering in the sun,
Runs with her all the way, wherever she doth run.

I was a Traveller then upon the moor;
I saw the hare that raced about with joy;
I heard the woods and distant waters roar;
Or heard them not, as happy as a boy:
The pleasant season did my heart employ:
My old remembrances went from me wholly;
And all the ways of men, so vain and melancholy.

But, as it sometimes chanceth, from the might
Of joy in minds that can no further go,
As high as we have mounted in delight
In our dejection do we sink as low;
To me that morning did it happen so;
And fears and fancies thick upon me came;
Dim sadness — and blind thoughts, I knew not, nor could name.

I heard the sky-lark warbling in the sky;
And I bethought me of the playful hare:
Even such a happy Child of earth am I;
Even as these blissful creatures do I fare;
Far from the world I walk, and from all care;
But there may come another day to me —
Solitude, pain of heart, distress, and poverty.

My whole life I have lived in pleasant thought,
As if life's business were a summer mood;
As if all needful things would come unsought
To genial faith, still rich in genial good;
But how can He expect that others should

Build for him, sow for him, and at his call
Love him, who for himself will take no heed at all?

I thought of Chatterton, the marvellous Boy,
The sleepless Soul that perished in his pride;
Of Him who walked in glory and in joy
Following his plough, along the mountain-side:
By our own spirits are we deified:
We Poets in our youth begin in gladness;
But thereof come in the end despondency and madness.

Now, whether it were by peculiar grace,
A leading from above, a something given,
Yet it befell that, in this lonely place,
When I with these untoward thoughts had striven,
Beside a pool bare to the eye of heaven
I saw a Man before me unawares:
The oldest man he seemed that ever wore grey hairs.

As a huge stone is sometimes seen to lie
Couched on the bald top of an eminence;
Wonder to all who do the same espy,
By what means it could thither come, and whence;
So that it seems a thing endued with sense:
Like a sea-beast crawled forth, that on a shelf
Of rock or sand reposeth, there to sun itself;

Such seemed this Man, not all alive nor dead,
Nor all asleep — in his extreme old age:
His body was bent double, feet and head
Coming together in life's pilgrimage;
As if some dire constraint of pain, or rage
Of sickness felt by him in times long past,
A more than human weight upon his frame had cast.

Himself he propped, limbs, body, and pale face,
Upon a long grey staff of shaven wood:
And, still as I drew near with gentle pace,
Upon the margin of that moorish flood
Motionless as a cloud the old Man stood,
That heareth not the loud winds when they call;
And moveth all together, if it move at all.

At length, himself unsettling, he the pond
Stirred with his staff, and fixedly did look
Upon the muddy water, which he conned,
As if he had been reading in a book:
And now a stranger's privilege I took;
And, drawing to his side, to him did say,
'This morning gives us promise of a glorious day.'

A gentle answer did the old Man make,
In courteous speech which forth he slowly drew:
And him with further words I thus bespake,
'What occupation do you there pursue?
This is a lonesome place for one like you.'
Ere he replied, a flash of mild surprise
Broke from the sable orbs of his yet-vivid eyes.

His words came feebly, from a feeble chest,
But each in solemn order followed each,
With something of a lofty utterance drest —
Choice word and measured phrase, above the reach
Of ordinary men; a stately speech;
Such as grave Livers do in Scotland use,
Religious men, who give to God and man their dues.

He told, that to these waters he had come
To gather leeches, being old and poor:
Employment hazardous and wearisome!
And he had many hardships to endure:
From pond to pond he roamed, from moor to moor;
Housing, with God's good help, by choice or chance;
And in this way he gained an honest maintenance.

The old Man still stood talking by my side;
But now his voice to me was like a stream
Scarce heard; nor word from word could I divide;
And the whole body of the Man did seem
Like one whom I had met with in a dream;
Or like a man from some far region sent,
To give me human strength, by apt admonishment.

My former thoughts returned: the fear that kills;
And hope that is unwilling to be fed;
Cold, pain, and labour, and all fleshly ills;
And mighty Poets in their misery dead.
— Perplexed, and longing to be comforted,
My question eagerly did I renew,
'How is it that you live, and what is it you do?'

He with a smile did then his words repeat;
And said that, gathering leeches, far and wide
He travelled; stirring thus about his feet
The waters of the pools where they abide.
'Once I could meet with them on every side;

But they have dwindled long by slow decay;
Yet still I persevere, and find them where I may.'

While he was talking thus, the lonely place,
The old Man's shape, and speech — all troubled me:
In my mind's eye I seemed to see him pace
About the weary moors continually,
Wandering about alone and silently.
While I these thoughts within myself pursued,
He, having made a pause, the same discourse renewed.

And soon with this he other matter blended,
Cheerfully uttered, with demeanour kind,
But stately in the main; and, when he ended,
I could have laughed myself to scorn to find
In that decrepit Man so firm a mind.
'God,' said I, 'be my help and stay secure;
I 'll think of the Leech-gatherer on the lonely moor!'

1807

TO H. C.

SIX YEARS OLD

O thou! whose fancies from afar are brought;
Who of thy words dost make a mock apparel,
And fittest to unutterable thought
The breeze-like motion and the self-born carol;
Thou faery voyager! that dost float
In such clear water, that thy boat
May rather seem
To brood on air than on an earthly stream;
Suspended in a stream as clear as sky,
Where earth and heaven do make one imagery;
O blessèd vision! happy child!
Thou art so exquisitely wild,
I think of thee with many fears
For what may be thy lot in future years.

I thought of times when Pain might be thy guest,
Lord of thy house and hospitality;
And Grief, uneasy lover! never rest
But when she sate within the touch of thee.
O too industrious folly!
O vain and causeless melancholy!
Nature will either end thee quite;
Or, lengthening out thy season of delight,
Preserve for thee, by individual right,
A young lamb's heart among the full-grown flocks.
What hast thou to do with sorrow,
Or the injuries of to-morrow?
Thou art a dew-drop, which the morn brings forth,
Ill fitted to sustain unkindly shocks,
Or to be trailed along the soiling earth;
A gem that glitters while it lives,
And no forewarning gives;
But, at the touch of wrong, without a strife
Slips in a moment out of life.

1807

AT THE GRAVE OF BURNS

I shiver, Spirit fierce and bold,
At thought of what I now behold:
As vapours breathed from dungeons cold
Strike pleasure dead,
So sadness comes from out the mould
Where Burns is laid.

And have I then thy bones so near,
And thou forbidden to appear?
As if it were thyself that 's here
I shrink with pain;
And both my wishes and my fear
Alike are vain.

Off weight — nor press on weight! — away
Dark thoughts! — they came, but not to stay;
With chastened feelings would I pay
The tribute due
To him, and aught that hides his clay
From mortal view.

Fresh as the flower, whose modest worth
He sang, his genius 'glinted' forth,
Rose like a star that touching earth,
For so it seems,
Doth glorify its humble birth
With matchless beams.

The piercing eye, the thoughtful brow,
The struggling heart, where be they now? —
Full soon the Aspirant of the plough,
The prompt, the brave,
Slept, with the obscurest, in the low
And silent grave.

I mourned with thousands, but as one
More deeply grieved, for He was gone
Whose light I hailed when first it shone,
And showed my youth
How Verse may build a princely throne
On humble truth.

Alas! where'er the current tends,
Regret pursues and with it blends, —
Huge Criffel's hoary top ascends

By Skiddaw seen, —
Neighbours we were, and loving friends
We might have been;

True friends though diversely inclined;
But heart with heart and mind with mind,
Where the main fibres are entwined,
Through Nature's skill,
May even by contraries be joined
More closely still.

The tear will start, and let it flow;
Thou 'poor Inhabitant below,'
At this dread moment — even so —
Might we together
Have sate and talked where gowans blow,
Or on wild heather.

What treasures would have then been placed
Within my reach; of knowledge graced
By fancy what a rich repast!
But why go on? —
Oh! spare to sweep, thou mournful blast,
His grave grass-grown.

There, too, a Son, his joy and pride,
(Not three weeks past the Stripling died,)
Lies gathered to his Father's side,
Soul-moving sight!
Yet one to which is not denied
Some sad delight.

For *he* is safe, a quiet bed
Hath early found among the dead,
Harboured where none can be misled,
Wronged, or distrest;
And surely here it may be said
That such are blest.

And oh for Thee, by pitying grace
Checked oft-times in a devious race,
May He, who halloweth the place
Where Man is laid,
Receive thy Spirit in the embrace
For which it prayed!

Sighing I turned away; but ere
Night fell I heard, or seemed to hear,
Music that sorrow comes not near,
A ritual hymn,
Chanted in love that casts out fear
By Seraphim.

1842

TO A HIGHLAND GIRL

Sweet Highland Girl, a very shower
Of beauty is thy earthly dower!
Twice seven consenting years have shed
Their utmost bounty on thy head:
And these grey rocks; that household lawn;
Those trees, a veil just half withdrawn;
This fall of water that doth make
A murmur near the silent lake;
This little bay; a quiet road
That holds in shelter thy Abode —
In truth together do ye seem
Like something fashioned in a dream;
Such Forms as from their covert peep
When earthly cares are laid asleep!
But, O fair Creature! in the light
Of common day, so heavenly bright,
I bless Thee, Vision as thou art,
I bless thee with a human heart;
God shield thee to thy latest years!
Thee, neither know I, nor thy peers;
And yet my eyes are filled with tears.
With earnest feeling I shall pray
For thee when I am far away:
For never saw I mien, or face,
In which more plainly I could trace
Benignity and home-bred sense
Ripening in perfect innocence.
Here scattered, like a random seed,
Remote from men, Thou dost not need
The embarrassed look of shy distress,
And maidenly shamefacedness:
Thou wear'st upon thy forehead clear
The freedom of a Mountaineer:
A face with gladness overspread!
Soft smiles, by human kindness bred!
And seemliness complete, that sways
Thy courtesies, about thee plays;
With no restraint, but such as springs
From quick and eager visitings
Of thoughts that lie beyond the reach
Of thy few words of English speech:
A bondage sweetly brooked, a strife
That gives thy gestures grace and life!
So have I, not unmoved in mind,
Seen birds of tempest-loving kind —
Thus beating up against the wind.
What hand but would a garland cull
For thee who art so beautiful?
O happy pleasure! here to dwell
Beside thee in some heathy dell;
Adopt your homely ways, and dress,
A Shepherd, thou a Shepherdess!
But I could frame a wish for thee
More like a grave reality:
Thou art to me but as a wave
Of the wild sea; and I would have
Some claim upon thee, if I could,
Though but of common neighbourhood.
What joy to hear thee, and to see!
Thy elder Brother I would be,
Thy Father — anything to thee!

Now thanks to Heaven! that of its grace
Hath led me to this lonely place.
Joy have I had; and going hence
I bear away my recompense.
In spots like these it is we prize
Our Memory, feel that she hath eyes:
Then, why should I be loth to stir?
I feel this place was made for her;
To give new pleasure like the past,
Continued long as life shall last.
Nor am I loth, though pleased at heart,
Sweet Highland Girl! from thee to part;
For I, methinks, till I grow old,
As fair before me shall behold,
As I do now, the cabin small,
The lake, the bay, the waterfall;
And Thee, the Spirit of them all!

1807

THE SOLITARY REAPER

Behold her, single in the field,
Yon solitary Highland Lass!
Reaping and singing by herself;
Stop here, or gently pass!
Alone she cuts and binds the grain,
And sings a melancholy strain;
O listen! for the Vale profound
Is overflowing with the sound.

No Nightingale did ever chaunt
More welcome notes to weary bands
Of travellers in some shady haunt,
Among Arabian sands:
A voice so thrilling ne'er was heard
In spring-time from the Cuckoo-bird,
Breaking the silence of the seas
Among the farthest Hebrides.

Will no one tell me what she sings?—
Perhaps the plaintive numbers flow
For old, unhappy, far-off things,
And battles long ago:
Or is it some more humble lay,
Familiar matter of to-day?
Some natural sorrow, loss, or pain,
That has been, and may be again?

Whate'er the theme, the Maiden sang
As if her song could have no ending;
I saw her singing at her work,
And o'er the sickle bending;—
I listened, motionless and still;
And, as I mounted up the hill,
The music in my heart I bore,
Long after it was heard no more.

1807

TO THE CUCKOO

O blithe New-comer! I have heard,
I hear thee and rejoice.
O Cuckoo! shall I call thee Bird,
Or but a wandering Voice?

While I am lying on the grass
Thy twofold shout I hear;
From hill to hill it seems to pass
At once far off, and near.

Though babbling only to the Vale,
Of sunshine and of flowers,
Thou bringest unto me a tale
Of visionary hours.

Thrice welcome, darling of the Spring!
Even yet thou art to me
No bird, but an invisible thing,
A voice, a mystery;

The same whom in my schoolboy days
I listened to; that Cry
Which made me look a thousand ways
In bush, and tree, and sky.

To seek thee did I often rove
Through woods and on the green;
And thou wert still a hope, a love;
Still longed for, never seen.

And I can listen to thee yet;
Can lie upon the plain
And listen, till I do beget
That golden time again.

O blessèd Bird! the earth we pace
Again appears to be
An unsubstantial, faery place;
That is fit home for Thee!

1807

SHE WAS A PHANTOM OF DELIGHT

She was a Phantom of delight
When first she gleamed upon my sight;
A lovely Apparition, sent
To be a moment's ornament;
Her eyes as stars of Twilight fair;
Like Twilight's, too, her dusky hair;
But all things else about her drawn
From May-time and the cheerful Dawn;
A dancing Shape, an Image gay,
To haunt, to startle, and way-lay.

I saw her upon nearer view,
A Spirit, yet a Woman too!
Her household motions light and free,
And steps of virgin-liberty;

A countenance in which did meet
Sweet records, promises as sweet;
A Creature not too bright or good
For human nature's daily food;
For transient sorrows, simple wiles,
Praise, blame, love, kisses, tears, and smiles.

And now I see with eye serene
The very pulse of the machine;
A Being breathing thoughtful breath,
A Traveller between life and death;
The reason firm, the temperate will,
Endurance, foresight, strength, and skill;
A perfect Woman, nobly planned,
To warn, to comfort, and command;
And yet a Spirit still, and bright
With something of angelic light.

1807

I WANDERED LONELY AS A CLOUD

I WANDERED lonely as a cloud
That floats on high o'er vales and hills,
When all at once I saw a crowd,
A host, of golden daffodils;
Beside the lake, beneath the trees,
Fluttering and dancing in the breeze.

Continuous as the stars that shine
And twinkle on the milky way,
They stretched in never-ending line
Along the margin of a bay:
Ten thousand saw I at a glance,
Tossing their heads in sprightly dance.

The waves beside them danced; but they
Out-did the sparkling waves in glee:
A poet could not but be gay,
In such a jocund company:
I gazed — and gazed — but little thought
What wealth the show to me had brought:

For oft, when on my couch I lie
In vacant or in pensive mood,
They flash upon that inward eye
Which is the bliss of solitude;
And then my heart with pleasure fills,
And dances with the daffodils.

1807

ODE TO DUTY

STERN Daughter of the Voice of God!
O Duty! if that name thou love
Who art a light to guide, a rod
To check the erring, and reprove;
Thou, who art victory and law
When empty terrors overawe;
From vain temptations dost set free;
And calm'st the weary strife of frail humanity!

There are who ask not if thine eye
Be on them; who, in love and truth,
Where no misgiving is, rely
Upon the genial sense of youth:
Glad Hearts! without reproach or blot;
Who do thy work, and know it not:
Oh! if through confidence misplaced
They fail, thy saving arms, dread Power! around them cast.

Serene will be our days and bright,
And happy will our nature be,
When love is an unerring light,
And joy its own security.
And they a blissful course may hold
Even now, who, not unwisely bold,
Live in the spirit of this creed;
Yet seek thy firm support, according to their need.

I, loving freedom, and untried;
No sport of every random gust,
Yet being to myself a guide,
Too blindly have reposed my trust:
And oft, when in my heart was heard
Thy timely mandate, I deferred
The task, in smoother walks to stray;
But thee I now would serve more strictly, if I may.

Through no disturbance of my soul,
Or strong compunction in me wrought,
I supplicate for thy control;
But in the quietness of thought:
Me this unchartered freedom tires;
I feel the weight of chance-desires:
My hopes no more must change their name,
I long for a repose that ever is the same.

Stern Lawgiver! yet thou dost wear
The Godhead's most benignant grace;
Nor know we anything so fair
As is the smile upon thy face:
Flowers laugh before thee on their beds
And fragrance in thy footing treads;
Thou dost preserve the stars from wrong;
And the most ancient heavens, through Thee, are fresh and strong.

To humbler functions, awful Power!
I call thee: I myself commend
Unto thy guidance from this hour;
Oh, let my weakness have an end!
Give unto me, made lowly wise,
The spirit of self-sacrifice;

The confidence of reason give;
And in the light of truth thy Bondman let me live!

1807

ELEGIAC STANZAS

SUGGESTED BY A PICTURE OF PEELE CASTLE, IN A STORM, PAINTED BY SIR GEORGE BEAUMONT

I WAS thy neighbour once, thou rugged Pile!
Four summer weeks I dwelt in sight of thee:
I saw thee every day; and all the while
Thy Form was sleeping on a glassy sea.

So pure the sky, so quiet was the air!
So like, so very like, was day to day!
Whene'er I looked, thy Image still was there;
It trembled, but it never passed away.

How perfect was the calm! it seemed no sleep;
No mood, which season takes away, or brings:
I could have fancied that the mighty Deep
Was even the gentlest of all gentle Things.

Ah! then, if mine had been the Painter's hand,
To express what then I saw; and add the gleam,
The light that never was, on sea or land,
The consecration, and the Poet's dream;

I would have planted thee, thou hoary Pile
Amid a world how different from this!
Beside a sea that could not cease to smile;
On tranquil land, beneath a sky of bliss.

Thou shouldst have seemed a treasure-house divine
Of peaceful years; a chronicle of heaven;—
Of all the sunbeams that did ever shine
The very sweetest had to thee been given.

A Picture had it been of lasting ease,
Elysian quiet, without toil or strife;
No motion but the moving tide, a breeze,
Or merely silent Nature's breathing life.

Such, in the fond illusion of my heart,
Such Picture would I at that time have made:
And seen the soul of truth in every part,
A steadfast peace that might not be betrayed.

So once it would have been,—'t is so no more;
I have submitted to a new control:
A power is gone, which nothing can restore;
A deep distress hath humanised my Soul.

Not for a moment could I now behold
A smiling sea, and be what I have been:
The feeling of my loss will ne'er be old;
This, which I know, I speak with mind serene.

Then, Beaumont, Friend! who would have been the Friend,
If he had lived, of Him whom I deplore,
This work of thine I blame not, but commend;
This sea in anger, and that dismal shore.

O 't is a passionate Work!—yet wise and well,
Well chosen is the spirit that is here;
That Hulk which labours in the deadly swell,
This rueful sky, this pageantry of fear!

And this huge Castle, standing here sublime,
I love to see the look with which it braves,
Cased in the unfeeling armour of old time,
The lightning, the fierce wind, and trampling waves.

Farewell, farewell the heart that lives alone,
Housed in a dream, at distance from the Kind!
Such happiness, wherever it be known,
Is to be pitied; for 't is surely blind.

But welcome fortitude, and patient cheer,
And frequent sights of what is to be borne!
Such sights, or worse, as are before me here.—
Not without hope we suffer and we mourn.

1807

ODE

INTIMATIONS OF IMMORTALITY FROM RECOLLECTIONS OF EARLY CHILDHOOD

THERE was a time when meadow, grove, and stream,
The earth, and every common sight,
To me did seem
Apparelled in celestial light,
The glory and the freshness of a dream.
It is not now as it hath been of yore;—
Turn wheresoe'er I may,
By night or day,
The things which I have seen I now can see no more.

The Rainbow comes and goes,
And lovely is the Rose,
The Moon doth with delight
Look round her when the heavens are bare,
Waters on a starry night
Are beautiful and fair;
The sunshine is a glorious birth;
But yet I know, where'er I go,
That there hath past away a glory from the earth.

Now, while the birds thus sing a joyous song,
And while the young lambs bound
As to the tabor's sound,
To me alone there came a thought of grief:
A timely utterance gave that thought relief,
And I again am strong:
The cataracts blow their trumpets from the steep;
No more shall grief of mine the season wrong;
I hear the Echoes through the mountains throng,
The Winds come to me from the fields of sleep,
And all the earth is gay;
Land and sea
Give themselves up to jollity,
And with the heart of May
Doth every Beast keep holiday;—
Thou Child of Joy,
Shout round me, let me hear thy shouts, thou happy Shepherd-boy!

Ye blessèd Creatures, I have heard the call
Ye to each other make; I see
The heavens laugh with you in your jubilee;
My heart is at your festival,
My head hath its coronal,
The fulness of your bliss, I feel—I feel it all.
Oh evil day! if I were sullen
While Earth herself is adorning,
This sweet May-morning,
And the Children are culling
On every side,
In a thousand valleys far and wide,
Fresh flowers; while the sun shines warm,
And the Babe leaps up on his Mother's arm:—
I hear, I hear, with joy I hear!
—But there's a Tree, of many, one,
A single Field which I have looked upon,
Both of them speak of something that is gone:
The Pansy at my feet
Doth the same tale repeat:
Whither is fled the visionary gleam?
Where is it now, the glory and the dream?

Our birth is but a sleep and a forgetting:
The Soul that rises with us, our life's Star,
Hath had elsewhere its setting,
And cometh from afar:
Not in entire forgetfulness,
And not in utter nakedness,
But trailing clouds of glory do we come
From God, who is our home:
Heaven lies about us in our infancy!
Shades of the prison-house begin to close
Upon the growing Boy,
But He beholds the light, and whence it flows,
He sees it in his joy;
The Youth, who daily farther from the east
Must travel, still is Nature's Priest,
And by the vision splendid
Is on his way attended;
At length the Man perceives it die away,
And fade into the light of common day.

Earth fills her lap with pleasures of her own;
Yearnings she hath in her own natural kind,
And, even with something of a Mother's mind,
And no unworthy aim,
The homely Nurse doth all she can
To make her Foster-child, her Inmate Man,
Forget the glories he hath known,
And that imperial palace whence he came.

Behold the Child among his new-born blisses,
A six years' Darling of a pigmy size!
See, where 'mid work of his own hand he lies,
Fretted by sallies of his mother's kisses,
With light upon him from his father's eyes!
See, at his feet, some little plan or chart,
Some fragment from his dream of human life,
Shaped by himself with newly-learned art;
A wedding or a festival,
A mourning or a funeral;
And this hath now his heart,
And unto this he frames his song:
Then will he fit his tongue
To dialogues of business, love, or strife;
But it will not be long
Ere this be thrown aside,
And with new joy and pride
The little Actor cons another part;
Filling from time to time his 'humorous stage'
With all the Persons, down to palsied Age,
That Life brings with her in her equipage;
As if his whole vocation
Were endless imitation.

Thou, whose exterior semblance doth belie
Thy Soul's immensity;
Thou best Philosopher, who yet dost keep
Thy heritage, thou Eye among the blind,
That, deaf and silent, read'st the eternal deep,
Haunted for ever by the eternal mind, —
Mighty Prophet! Seer blest!
On whom those truths do rest,
Which we are toiling all our lives to find,
In darkness lost, the darkness of the grave;
Thou, over whom thy Immortality
Broods like the Day, a Master o'er a Slave,
A Presence which is not to be put by;
Thou little Child, yet glorious in the might
Of heaven-born freedom on thy being's height,
Why with such earnest pains dost thou provoke
The years to bring the inevitable yoke,
Thus blindly with thy blessedness at strife?
Full soon thy Soul shall have her earthly freight,
And custom lie upon thee with a weight,
Heavy as frost, and deep almost as life!

O joy! that in our embers
Is something that doth live,
That nature yet remembers
What was so fugitive!
The thought of our past years in me doth breed
Perpetual benediction: not indeed
For that which is most worthy to be blest;
Delight and liberty, the simple creed
Of Childhood, whether busy or at rest,
With new-fledged hope still fluttering in his breast: —
Not for these I raise
The song of thanks and praise;
But for those obstinate questionings
Of sense and outward things,
Fallings from us, vanishings;
Blank misgivings of a Creature
Moving about in worlds not realised,
High instincts before which our mortal Nature
Did tremble like a guilty Thing surprised:
But for those first affections,
Those shadowy recollections,
Which, be they what they may,
Are yet the fountain-light of all our day,
Are yet a master-light of all our seeing;
Uphold us, cherish, and have power to make
Our noisy years seem moments in the being
Of the eternal Silence: truths that wake,
To perish never:
Which neither listlessness, nor mad endeavour,
Nor Man nor Boy,
Nor all that is at enmity with joy,
Can utterly abolish or destroy!
Hence in a season of calm weather
Though inland far we be,
Our Souls have sight of that immortal sea
Which brought us hither,
Can in a moment travel thither,
And see the Children sport upon the shore,
And hear the mighty waters rolling evermore.

Then sing, ye Birds, sing, sing a joyous song!
And let the young Lambs bound
As to the tabor's sound!
We in thought will join your throng,
Ye that pipe and ye that play,
Ye that through your hearts to-day
Feel the gladness of the May!
What though the radiance which was once so bright
Be now for ever taken from my sight,
Though nothing can bring back the hour
Of splendour in the grass, of glory in the flower;
We will grieve not, rather find
Strength in what remains behind;
In the primal sympathy
Which having been must ever be;
In the soothing thoughts that spring
Out of human suffering;
In the faith that looks through death,
In years that bring the philosophic mind.

And O, ye Fountains, Meadows, Hills, and Groves,
Forebode not any severing of our loves!
Yet in my heart of hearts I feel your might;
I only have relinquished one delight
To live beneath your more habitual sway.
I love the Brooks which down their channels fret,
Even more than when I tripped lightly as they;
The innocent brightness of a new-born Day
Is lovely yet;
The Clouds that gather round the setting sun
Do take a sober colouring from an eye
That hath kept watch o'er man's mortality;
Another race hath been, and other palms are won.
Thanks to the human heart by which we live,

Thanks to its tenderness, its joys, and fears,
To me the meanest flower that blows can give
Thoughts that do often lie too deep for tears.

1807

COMPOSED UPON AN EVENING OF EXTRAORDINARY SPLENDOUR AND BEAUTY

Had this effulgence disappeared
With flying haste, I might have sent,
Among the speechless clouds, a look
Of blank astonishment;
But 't is endued with power to stay,
And sanctify one closing day,
That frail Mortality may see —
What is? — ah no, but what *can* be!
Time was when field and watery cove
With modulated echoes rang,
While choirs of fervent Angels sang
Their vespers in the grove;
Or, crowning, star-like, each some sovereign height,
Warbled, for heaven above and earth below,
Strains suitable to both. — Such holy rite,
Methinks, if audibly repeated now
From hill or valley, could not move
Sublimer transport, purer love,
Than doth this silent spectacle — the gleam —
The shadow — and the peace supreme!

No sound is uttered, — but a deep
And solemn harmony pervades
The hollow vale from steep to steep,
And penetrates the glades.
Far-distant images draw nigh,
Called forth by wondrous potency
Of beamy radiance, that imbues
Whate'er it strikes with gem-like hues!
In vision exquisitely clear,
Herds range along the mountain side;
And glistening antlers are descried;
And gilded flocks appear.
Thine is the tranquil hour, purpureal Eve!
But long as god-like wish, or hope divine,
Informs my spirit, ne'er can I believe
That this magnificence is wholly thine!
— From worlds not quickened by the sun
A portion of the gift is won;
An intermingling of Heaven's pomp is spread
On ground which British shepherds tread!

And if there be whom broken ties
Afflict, or injuries assail,
Yon hazy ridges to their eyes
Present a glorious scale,
Climbing suffused with sunny air,
To stop — no record hath told where!
And tempting Fancy to ascend,
And with immortal Spirits blend!
— Wings at my shoulders seem to play;
But, rooted here, I stand and gaze
On those bright steps that heavenward raise
Their practicable way.
Come forth, ye drooping old men, look abroad,
And see to what fair countries ye are bound!
And if some traveller, weary of his road,
Hath slept since noon-tide on the grassy ground,
Ye Genii! to his covert speed;
And wake him with such gentle heed
As may attune his soul to meet the dower
Bestowed on this transcendent hour!

Such hues from their celestial Urn
Were wont to stream before mine eye,
Where'er it wandered in the morn
Of blissful infancy.
This glimpse of glory, why renewed?
Nay, rather speak with gratitude;
For, if a vestige of those gleams
Survived, 't was only in my dreams.
Dread Power! whom peace and calmness serve
No less than Nature's threatening voice,
If aught unworthy be my choice,
From Thee if I would swerve;
Oh, let Thy grace remind me of the light
Full early lost, and fruitlessly deplored;
Which, at this moment, on my waking sight
Appears to shine, by miracle restored;
My soul, though yet confined to earth,
Rejoices in a second birth!
—'T is past, the visionary splendour fades;
And night approaches with her shades.

1820

TO A SKYLARK

Ethereal minstrel! pilgrim of the sky!
Dost thou despise the earth where cares abound?
Or, while the wings aspire, are heart and eye
Both with thy nest upon the dewy ground?
Thy nest which thou canst drop into at will,
Those quivering wings composed, that music still!

Leave to the nightingale her shady wood;
A privacy of glorious light is thine;
Whence thou dost pour upon the world a flood

Of harmony, with instinct more divine;
Type of the wise who soar, but never roam;
True to the kindred points of Heaven and Home!

1827

EXTEMPORE EFFUSION UPON THE DEATH OF JAMES HOGG

When first, descending from the moorlands,
I saw the Stream of Yarrow glide
Along a bare and open valley,
The Ettrick Shepherd was my guide.

When last along its banks I wandered,
Through groves that had begun to shed
Their golden leaves upon the pathways,
My steps the Border-minstrel led.

The mighty Minstrel breathes no longer,
'Mid mouldering ruins low he lies;
And death upon the braes of Yarrow,
Has closed the Shepherd-poet's eyes:

Nor has the rolling year twice measured,
From sign to sign, its steadfast course,
Since every mortal power of Coleridge
Was frozen at its marvellous source;

The rapt One, of the godlike forehead,
The heaven-eyed creature sleeps in earth:
And Lamb, the frolic and the gentle,
Has vanished from his lonely hearth.

Like clouds that rake the mountain-summits,
Or waves that own no curbing hand,
How fast has brother followed brother,
From sunshine to the sunless land!

Yet I, whose lids from infant slumber
Were earlier raised, remain to hear
A timid voice, that asks in whispers,
'Who next will drop and disappear?'

Our haughty life is crowned with darkness,
Like London with its own black wreath,
On which with thee, O Crabbe! forthlooking,
I gazed from Hampstead's breezy heath.

As if but yesterday departed,
Thou too art gone before; but why,
O'er ripe fruit, seasonably gathered,
Should frail survivors heave a sigh?

Mourn rather for that holy Spirit,
Sweet as the spring, as ocean deep;
For Her who, ere her summer faded,
Has sunk into a breathless sleep.

No more of old romantic sorrows,
For slaughtered Youth or love-lorn Maid!
With sharper grief is Yarrow smitten,
And Ettrick mourns with her their Poet dead.

1835

SONNETS

COMPOSED UPON WESTMINSTER BRIDGE, SEPTEMBER 3, 1802

Earth has not anything to show more fair:
Dull would he be of soul who could pass by
A sight so touching in its majesty:
This City now doth, like a garment, wear
The beauty of the morning; silent, bare,
Ships, towers, domes, theatres, and temples lie
Open unto the fields, and to the sky;
All bright and glittering in the smokeless air.
Never did sun more beautifully steep
In his first splendour, valley, rock, or hill;
Ne'er saw I, never felt, a calm so deep!
The river glideth at his own sweet will:
Dear God! the very houses seem asleep;
And all that mighty heart is lying still!

1807

IT IS A BEAUTEOUS EVENING

It is a beauteous evening, calm and free,
The holy time is quiet as a Nun
Breathless with adoration; the broad sun
Is sinking down in its tranquillity;
The gentleness of heaven broods o'er the Sea:
Listen! the mighty Being is awake,
And doth with his eternal motion make
A sound like thunder — everlastingly.
Dear Child! dear Girl! that walkest with me here,
If thou appear untouched by solemn thought,
Thy nature is not therefore less divine:
Thou liest in Abraham's bosom all the year;
And worshipp'st at the Temple's inner shrine,
God being with thee when we know it not.

1807

LONDON, 1802

Milton! thou shouldst be living at this hour:
England hath need of thee: she is a fen
Of stagnant waters: altar, sword, and pen,
Fireside, the heroic wealth of hall and bower,

Have forfeited their ancient English dower
Of inward happiness. We are selfish men;
Oh! raise us up, return to us again;
And give us manners, virtue, freedom, power.
Thy soul was like a Star, and dwelt apart;
Thou hadst a voice whose sound was like the sea:
Pure as the naked heavens, majestic, free,
So didst thou travel on life's common way,
In cheerful godliness; and yet thy heart
The lowliest duties on herself did lay.

1807

THE WORLD IS TOO MUCH WITH US

The world is too much with us; late and soon,
Getting and spending, we lay waste our powers:
Little we see in Nature that is ours;
We have given our hearts away, a sordid boon!
This Sea that bares her bosom to the moon;
The winds that will be howling at all hours,
And are up-gathered now like sleeping flowers;
For this, for everything, we are out of tune;
It moves us not. — Great God! I'd rather be
A Pagan suckled in a creed outworn;
So might I, standing on this pleasant lea,
Have glimpses that would make me less forlorn;
Have sight of Proteus rising from the sea;
Or hear old Triton blow his wreathèd horn.

1807

TO SLEEP

A flock of sheep that leisurely pass by,
One after one; the sound of rain, and bees
Murmuring; the fall of rivers, winds and seas,
Smooth fields, white sheets of water, and pure sky;
I have thought of all by turns, and yet do lie
Sleepless! and soon the small birds' melodies
Must hear, first uttered from my orchard trees;
And the first cuckoo's melancholy cry.
Even thus last night, and two nights more, I lay
And could not win thee, Sleep! by any stealth:
So do not let me wear to-night away:
Without Thee what is all the morning's wealth?
Come, blessèd barrier between day and day,
Dear mother of fresh thoughts and joyous health!

1807

NUNS FRET NOT

Nuns fret not at their convent's narrow room;
And hermits are contented with their cells;
And students with their pensive citadels;
Maids at the wheel, the weaver at his loom,
Sit blithe and happy; bees that soar for bloom,
High as the highest Peak of Furness-fells,
Will murmur by the hour in foxglove bells:
In truth the prison, unto which we doom
Ourselves, no prison is: and hence for me,
In sundry moods, 'twas pastime to be bound
Within the Sonnet's scanty plot of ground;
Pleased if some Souls (for such there needs must be)
Who have felt the weight of too much liberty,
Should find brief solace there, as I have found.

1807

SCORN NOT THE SONNET

Scorn not the Sonnet; Critic, you have frowned,
Mindless of its just honours; with this key
Shakspeare unlocked his heart; the melody
Of this small lute gave ease to Petrarch's wound;
A thousand times this pipe did Tasso sound;
With it Camöens soothed an exile's grief;
The Sonnet glittered a gay myrtle leaf
Amid the cypress with which Dante crowned
His visionary brow: a glow-worm lamp,
It cheered mild Spenser, called from Faery-land
To struggle through dark ways; and when a damp
Fell round the path of Milton, in his hand
The Thing became a trumpet; whence he blew
Soul-animating strains — alas, too few!

1827

AFTER-THOUGHT

I thought of Thee, my partner and my guide,
As being past away. — Vain sympathies!

For, backward, Duddon! as I cast my eyes,
I see what was, and is, and will abide;
Still glides the Stream, and shall forever
glide;
The Form remains, the Function never dies;
While we, the brave, the mighty, and the
wise,
We Men, who in our morn of youth defied
The elements, must vanish; — be it so!
Enough, if something from our hands have
power
To live, and act, and serve the future hour;
And if, as toward the silent tomb we go,
Through love, through hope, and faith's
transcendent dower,
We feel that we are greater than we know.

1820

Samuel Taylor Coleridge (1772-1834)

DOMESTIC PEACE

Tell me, on what holy ground
May Domestic Peace be found?
Halcyon daughter of the skies,
Far on fearful wings she flies,
From the pomp of Sceptered State,
From the Rebel's noisy hate.
In a cottaged vale She dwells,
Listening to the Sabbath bells!
Still around her steps are seen
Spotless Honour's meeker mien,
Love, the sire of pleasing fears,
Sorrow smiling through her tears,
And conscious of the past employ
Memory, bosom-spring of joy.

1794

TO A FRIEND WHO ASKED, HOW I FELT WHEN THE NURSE FIRST PRESENTED MY INFANT TO ME

Charles! my slow heart was only sad, when
first
I scanned that face of feeble infancy:
For dimly on my thoughtful spirit burst
All I had been, and all my child might be!
But when I saw it on its mother's arm,
And hanging at her bosom (she the while
Bent o'er its features with a tearful smile)
Then I was thrilled and melted, and most
warm
Impressed a father's kiss: and all beguiled
Of dark remembrance and presageful fear,
I seemed to see an angel-form appear —
'T was even thine, belovèd woman mild!
So for the mother's sake the child was dear,
And dearer was the mother for the child.

1797

THE RIME OF THE ANCIENT MARINER

PART I

It is an ancient Mariner,
And he stoppeth one of three.
'By thy long grey beard and glittering eye,
Now wherefore stopp'st thou me?

The Bridegroom's doors are opened wide,
And I am next of kin;
The guests are met, the feast is set:
May'st hear the merry din.'

He holds him with his skinny hand,
'There was a ship,' quoth he.
'Hold off! unhand me, grey-beard loon!'
Eftsoons his hand dropt he.

He holds him with his glittering eye —
The Wedding-Guest stood still,
And listens like a three years' child:
The Mariner hath his will.

The Wedding-Guest sat on a stone:
He cannot choose but hear;
And thus spake on that ancient man,
The bright-eyed Mariner.

'The ship was cheered, the harbour cleared,
Merrily did we drop
Below the kirk, below the hill,
Below the lighthouse top.

The Sun came up upon the left,
Out of the sea came he!
And he shone bright, and on the right
Went down into the sea.

Higher and higher every day,
Till over the mast at noon —'
The Wedding-Guest here beat his breast,
For he heard the loud bassoon.

The bride hath paced into the hall,
Red as a rose is she;
Nodding their heads before her goes
The merry minstrelsy.

The Wedding-Guest he beat his breast,
Yet he cannot choose but hear;
And thus spake on that ancient man,
The bright-eyed Mariner.

'And now the Storm-blast came, and he
Was tyrannous and strong:

He struck with his o'ertaking wings,
And chased us south along.

With sloping masts and dipping prow,
As who pursued with yell and blow
Still treads the shadow of his foe,
And forward bends his head,
The ship drove fast, loud roared the blast,
And southward aye we fled.

And now there came both mist and snow,
And it grew wondrous cold:
And ice, mast-high, came floating by,
As green as emerald.

And through the drifts the snowy clifts
Did send a dismal sheen:
Nor shapes of men nor beasts we ken —
The ice was all between.

The ice was here, the ice was there,
The ice was all around:
It cracked and growled, and roared and howled,
Like noises in a swound!

At length did cross an Albatross,
Thorough the fog it came;
As if it had been a Christian soul,
We hailed it in God's name.

It ate the food it ne'er had eat,
And round and round it flew.
The ice did split with a thunder-fit;
The helmsman steered us through!

And a good south wind sprung up behind;
The Albatross did follow,
And every day, for food or play,
Came to the mariner's hollo!

In mist or cloud, on mast or shroud,
It perched for vespers nine;
Whiles all the night, through fog-smoke white,
Glimmered the white Moon-shine.'

'God save thee, ancient Mariner!
From the fiends, that plague thee thus! —
Why look'st thou so?' — With my cross-bow
I shot the Albatross.

PART II

The Sun now rose upon the right:
Out of the sea came he,
Still hid in mist, and on the left
Went down into the sea.

And the good south wind still blew behind,
But no sweet bird did follow,
Nor any day for food or play
Came to the mariners' hollo!

And I had done a hellish thing,
And it would work 'em woe:
For all averred, I had killed the bird
That made the breeze to blow.
Ah wretch! said they, the bird to slay,
That made the breeze to blow!

Nor dim nor red, like God's own head,
The glorious Sun uprist:
Then all averred, I had killed the bird
That brought the fog and mist.
'T was right, said they, such birds to slay,
That bring the fog and mist.

The fair breeze blew, the white foam flew,
The furrow followed free;
We were the first that ever burst
Into that silent sea.

Down dropt the breeze, the sails dropt down,
'T was sad as sad could be;
And we did speak only to break
The silence of the sea!

All in a hot and copper sky,
The bloody Sun, at noon,
Right up above the mast did stand,
No bigger than the Moon.

Day after day, day after day,
We stuck, nor breath nor motion;
As idle as a painted ship
Upon a painted ocean.

Water, water, every where,
And all the boards did shrink;
Water, water, every where,
Nor any drop to drink.

The very deep did rot: O Christ!
That ever this should be!
Yea, slimy things did crawl with legs
Upon the slimy sea.

About, about, in reel and rout
The death-fires danced at night;
The water, like a witch's oils,
Burnt green, and blue and white.

And some in dreams assurèd were
Of the Spirit that plagued us so;
Nine fathom deep he had followed us
From the land of mist and snow.

And every tongue, through utter drought,
Was withered at the root;
We could not speak, no more than if
We had been choked with soot.

Ah! well a-day! what evil looks
Had I from old and young!
Instead of the cross, the Albatross
About my neck was hung.

PART III

There passed a weary time. Each throat
Was parched, and glazed each eye.
A weary time! a weary time!
How glazed each weary eye,
When looking westward, I beheld
A something in the sky.

At first it seemed a little speck,
And then it seemed a mist;
It moved and moved, and took at last
A certain shape, I wist.

A speck, a mist, a shape, I wist!
And still it neared and neared:
As if it dodged a water-sprite,
It plunged and tacked and veered.

With throats unslaked, with black lips baked,
We could nor laugh nor wail;
Through utter drought all dumb we stood!
I bit my arm, I sucked the blood,
And cried, A sail! a sail!

With throats unslaked, with black lips baked,
Agape they heard me call:
Gramercy! they for joy did grin,
And all at once their breath drew in,
As they were drinking all.

See! see! (I cried) she tacks no more!
Hither to work us weal;
Without a breeze, without a tide,
She steadies with upright keel!

The western wave was all a-flame.
The day was well nigh done!
Almost upon the western wave
Rested the broad bright Sun;
When that strange shape drove suddenly
Betwixt us and the Sun.

And straight the Sun was flecked with bars,
(Heaven's Mother send us grace!)
As if through a dungeon-grate he peered
With broad and burning face.

Alas! (thought I, and my heart beat loud)
How fast she nears and nears!
Are those *her* sails that glance in the Sun,
Like restless gossameres?

Are those *her* ribs through which the Sun
Did peer, as through a grate?
And is that Woman all her crew?
Is that a Death? and are there two?
Is Death that woman's mate?

Her lips were red, *her* looks were free,
Her locks were yellow as gold:
Her skin was as white as leprosy,
The Night-mare Life-in-Death was she,
Who thicks man's blood with cold.

The naked hulk alongside came,
And the twain were casting dice;
'The game is done! I've won! I've won!'
Quoth she, and whistles thrice.

The Sun's rim dips; the stars rush out:
At one stride comes the dark;
With far-heard whisper, o'er the sea,
Off shot the spectre-bark.

We listened and looked sideways up!
Fear at my heart, as at a cup,
My life-blood seemed to sip!
The stars were dim, and thick the night,
The steersman's face by his lamp gleamed white;
From the sails the dew did drip —
Till clomb above the eastern bar
The hornèd Moon, with one bright star
Within the nether tip.

One after one, by the star-dogged Moon,
Too quick for groan or sigh,
Each turned his face with a ghastly pang,
And cursed me with his eye.

Four times fifty living men,
(And I heard nor sigh nor groan)
With heavy thump, a lifeless lump,
They dropped down one by one.

The souls did from their bodies fly, —
They fled to bliss or woe!
And every soul, it passed me by,
Like the whizz of my cross-bow!

PART IV

'I fear thee, ancient Mariner!
I fear thy skinny hand!
And thou art long, and lank, and brown,
As is the ribbed sea-sand.

I fear thee and thy glittering eye,
And thy skinny hand, so brown.' —
Fear not, fear not, thou Wedding-Guest!
This body dropt not down.

Alone, alone, all, all alone,
Alone on a wide wide sea!
And never a saint took pity on
My soul in agony.

The many men, so beautiful!
And they all dead did lie:
And a thousand thousand slimy things
Lived on; and so did I.

I looked upon the rotting sea,
And drew my eyes away;
I looked upon the rotting deck,
And there the dead men lay.

I looked to heaven, and tried to pray;
But or ever a prayer had gusht,
A wicked whisper came, and made
My heart as dry as dust.

I closed my lids, and kept them close,
And the balls like pulses beat;
For the sky and the sea, and the sea and the sky
Lay like a load on my weary eye,
And the dead were at my feet.

The cold sweat melted from their limbs,
Nor rot nor reek did they:
The look with which they looked on me
Had never passed away.

An orphan's curse would drag to hell
A spirit from on high;
But oh! more horrible than that
Is the curse in a dead man's eye!
Seven days, seven nights, I saw that curse,
And yet I could not die.

The moving Moon went up the sky,
And no where did abide:
Softly she was going up,
And a star or two beside —

Her beams bemocked the sultry main,
Like April hoar-frost spread;
But where the ship's huge shadow lay,
The charmèd water burnt alway
A still and awful red.

Beyond the shadow of the ship,
I watched the water-snakes:
They moved in tracks of shining white,
And when they reared, the elfish light
Fell off in hoary flakes.

Within the shadow of the ship
I watched their rich attire:
Blue, glossy green, and velvet black,
They coiled and swam; and every track
Was a flash of golden fire.

O happy living things! no tongue
Their beauty might declare:
A spring of love gushed from my heart,
And I blessed them unaware:
Sure my kind saint took pity on me,
And I blessed them unaware.

The self-same moment I could pray;
And from my neck so free
The Albatross fell off, and sank
Like lead into the sea.

PART V

Oh sleep! it is a gentle thing,
Beloved from pole to pole!
To Mary Queen the praise be given!
She sent the gentle sleep from Heaven,
That slid into my soul.

The silly buckets on the deck,
That had so long remained,
I dreamt that they were filled with dew;
And when I awoke, it rained.

My lips were wet, my throat was cold,
My garments all were dank;
Sure I had drunken in my dreams,
And still my body drank.

I moved, and could not feel my limbs:
I was so light — almost
I thought that I had died in sleep,
And was a blessèd ghost.

And soon I heard a roaring wind:
It did not come anear;
But with its sound it shook the sails,
That were so thin and sere.

The upper air burst into life!
And a hundred fire-flags sheen,
To and fro they were hurried about!
And to and fro, and in and out,
The wan stars danced between.

And the coming wind did roar more loud,
And the sails did sigh like sedge;
And the rain poured down from one black cloud;
The Moon was at its edge.

The thick black cloud was cleft, and still
The Moon was at its side:
Like waters shot from some high crag,
The lightning fell with never a jag,
A river steep and wide.

The loud wind never reached the ship,
Yet now the ship moved on!
Beneath the lightning and the Moon
The dead men gave a groan.

They groaned, they stirred, they all uprose,
Nor spake, nor moved their eyes;

It had been strange, even in a dream,
To have seen those dead men rise.

The helmsman steered, the ship moved on;
Yet never a breeze up-blew;
The mariners all 'gan work the ropes,
Where they were wont to do;
They raised their limbs like lifeless tools —
We were a ghastly crew.

The body of my brother's son
Stood by me, knee to knee:
The body and I pulled at one rope,
But he said nought to me.

'I fear thee, ancient Mariner!'
Be calm, thou Wedding-Guest!
'T was not those souls that fled in pain,
Which to their corses came again,
But a troop of spirits blest:

For when it dawned — they dropped their arms,
And clustered round the mast;
Sweet sounds rose slowly through their mouths,
And from their bodies passed.

Around, around, flew each sweet sound,
Then darted to the Sun;
Slowly the sounds came back again,
Now mixed, now one by one.

Sometimes a-dropping from the sky
I heard the sky-lark sing;
Sometimes all little birds that are,
How they seemed to fill the sea and air
With their sweet jargoning!

And now 't was like all instruments,
Now like a lonely flute;
And now it is an angel's song,
That makes the heavens be mute.

It ceased; yet still the sails made on
A pleasant noise till noon,
A noise like of a hidden brook
In the leafy month of June,
That to the sleeping woods all night
Singeth a quiet tune.

Till noon we quietly sailed on,
Yet never a breeze did breathe:
Slowly and smoothly went the ship,
Moved onward from beneath.

Under the keel nine fathom deep,
From the land of mist and snow,
The spirit slid: and it was he
That made the ship to go.
The sails at noon left off their tune,
And the ship stood still also.

The Sun, right up above the mast,
Had fixed her to the ocean:
But in a minute she 'gan stir,
With a short uneasy motion —
Backwards and forwards half her length
With a short uneasy motion.

Then like a pawing horse let go,
She made a sudden bound:
It flung the blood into my head,
And I fell down in a swound.

How long in that same fit I lay,
I have not to declare;
But ere my living life returned,
I heard and in my soul discerned
Two voices in the air.

'Is it he?' quoth one, 'Is this the man?
By him who died on cross,
With his cruel bow he laid full low
The harmless Albatross.

The spirit who bideth by himself
In the land of mist and snow,
He loved the bird that loved the man
Who shot him with his bow.'

The other was a softer voice,
As soft as honey-dew:
Quoth he, 'The man hath penance done,
And penance more will do.'

PART VI

First voice

'But tell me, tell me! speak again,
Thy soft response renewing —
What makes that ship drive on so fast?
What is the ocean doing?'

Second voice

'Still as a slave before his lord,
The ocean hath no blast;
His great bright eye most silently
Up to the Moon is cast —

If he may know which way to go;
For she guides him smooth or grim.
See, brother, see! how graciously
She looketh down on him.'

First voice

'But why drives on that ship so fast,
Without or wave or wind?'

Second Voice

'The air is cut away before,
And closes from behind.

Fly, brother, fly! more high, more high!
Or we shall be belated:
For slow and slow that ship will go,
When the Mariner's trance is abated.'

I woke, and we were sailing on
As in a gentle weather:
'T was night, calm night, the moon was high;
The dead men stood together.

All stood together on the deck,
For a charnel-dungeon fitter:
All fixed on me their stony eyes,
That in the Moon did glitter.

The pang, the curse, with which they died,
Had never passed away:
I could not draw my eyes from theirs,
Nor turn them up to pray.

And now this spell was snapt: once more
I viewed the ocean green,
And looked far forth, yet little saw
Of what had else been seen —

Like one, that on a lonesome road
Doth walk in fear and dread,
And having once turned round walks on,
And turns no more his head;
Because he knows, a frightful fiend
Doth close behind him tread.

But soon there breathed a wind on me,
Nor sound nor motion made:
Its path was not upon the sea,
In ripple or in shade.

It raised my hair, it fanned my cheek
Like a meadow-gale of spring —
It mingled strangely with my fears,
Yet it felt like a welcoming.

Swiftly, swiftly flew the ship,
Yet she sailed softly too:
Sweetly, sweetly blew the breeze —
On me alone it blew.

Oh! dream of joy! is this indeed
The light-house top I see?
Is this the hill? is this the kirk?
Is this mine own countree?

We drifted o'er the harbour-bar,
And I with sobs did pray —
O let me be awake, my God!
Or let me sleep alway.

The harbour-bay was clear as glass,
So smoothly it was strewn!
And on the bay the moonlight lay,
And the shadow of the Moon.

The rock shone bright, the kirk no less,
That stands above the rock:
The moonlight steeped in silentness
The steady weathercock.

And the bay was white with silent light,
Till rising from the same,
Full many shapes, that shadows were,
In crimson colours came.

A little distance from the prow
Those crimson shadows were:
I turned my eyes upon the deck —
Oh, Christ! what saw I there!

Each corse lay flat, lifeless and flat,
And, by the holy rood!
A man all light, a seraph-man,
On every corse there stood.

This seraph-band, each waved his hand:
It was a heavenly sight!
They stood as signals to the land,
Each one a lovely light;

This seraph-band, each waved his hand,
No voice did they impart —
No voice; but oh! the silence sank
Like music on my heart.

But soon I heard the dash of oars,
I heard the Pilot's cheer;
My head was turned perforce away
And I saw a boat appear.

The Pilot and the Pilot's boy,
I heard them coming fast:
Dear Lord in Heaven! it was a joy
The dead men could not blast.

I saw a third — I heard his voice:
It is the Hermit good!
He singeth loud his godly hymns
That he makes in the wood.
He'll shrieve my soul, he'll wash away
The Albatross's blood.

PART VII

This Hermit good lives in that wood
Which slopes down to the sea.
How loudly his sweet voice he rears!
He loves to talk with marineres
That come from a far countree.

He kneels at morn, and noon, and eve —
He hath a cushion plump:

It is the moss that wholly hides
The rotted old oak-stump.

The skiff-boat neared: I heard them talk,
'Why, this is strange, I trow!
Where are those lights so many and fair,
That signal made but now?'

'Strange, by my faith!' the Hermit said —
'And they answered not our cheer!
The planks looked warped! and see those sails,
How thin they are and sere!
I never saw aught like to them,
Unless perchance it were

Brown skeletons of leaves that lag
My forest-brook along;
When the ivy-tod is heavy with snow,
And the owlet whoops to the wolf below,
That eats the she-wolf's young.'

'Dear Lord! it hath a fiendish look —
(The Pilot made reply)
I am a-feared' — 'Push on, push on!'
Said the Hermit cheerily.

The boat came closer to the ship,
But I nor spake nor stirred;
The boat came close beneath the ship,
And straight a sound was heard.

Under the water it rumbled on,
Still louder and more dread:
It reached the ship, it split the bay;
The ship went down like lead.

Stunned by that loud and dreadful sound,
Which sky and ocean smote,
Like one that hath been seven days drowned
My body lay afloat;
But swift as dreams, myself I found
Within the Pilot's boat.

Upon the whirl, where sank the ship,
The boat spun round and round;
And all was still, save that the hill
Was telling of the sound.

I moved my lips — the Pilot shrieked
And fell down in a fit;
The holy Hermit raised his eyes,
And prayed where he did sit.

I took the oars: the Pilot's boy,
Who now doth crazy go,
Laughed loud and long, and all the while
His eyes went to and fro.
'Ha! ha!' quoth he, 'full plain I see,
The Devil knows how to row.'

And now, all in my own countree,
I stood on the firm land!
The Hermit stepped forth from the boat,
And scarcely he could stand.

'O shrieve me, shrieve me, holy man!'
The Hermit crossed his brow.
'Say quick,' quoth he, 'I bid thee say —
What manner of man art thou?'

Forthwith this frame of mine was wrenched
With a woful agony,
Which forced me to begin my tale;
And then it left me free.

Since then, at an uncertain hour,
That agony returns:
And till my ghastly tale is told,
This heart within me burns.

I pass, like night, from land to land;
I have strange power of speech;
That moment that his face I see,
I know the man that must hear me:
To him my tale I teach.

What loud uproar bursts from that door!
The wedding-guests are there:
But in the garden-bower the bride
And bride-maids singing are:
And hark the little vesper bell,
Which biddeth me to prayer!

O Wedding-Guest! this soul hath been
Alone on a wide wide sea:
So lonely 't was, that God himself
Scarce seemèd there to be.

O sweeter than the marriage-feast,
'T is sweeter far to me,
To walk together to the kirk
With a goodly company! —

To walk together to the kirk,
And all together pray,
While each to his great Father bends,
Old men, and babes, and loving friends
And youths and maidens gay!

Farewell, farewell! but this I tell
To thee, thou Wedding-Guest!
He prayeth well, who loveth well
Both man and bird and beast.

He prayeth best, who loveth best
All things both great and small;
For the dear God who loveth us,
He made and loveth all.

The Mariner, whose eye is bright,
Whose beard with age is hoar,

Is gone: and now the Wedding-Guest
Turned from the bridegroom's door.

He went like one that hath been stunned,
And is of sense forlorn:
A sadder and a wiser man,
He rose the morrow morn.

1798

CHRISTABEL

PART I

'T is the middle of night by the castle clock,
And the owls have awakened the crowing cock;
Tu — whit! —— Tu — whoo!
And hark, again! the crowing cock,
How drowsily it crew.

Sir Leoline, the Baron rich,
Hath a toothless mastiff bitch;
From her kennel beneath the rock
She maketh answer to the clock,
Four for the quarters, and twelve for the hour;
Ever and aye, by shine and shower,
Sixteen short howls, not over loud;
Some say, she sees my lady's shroud.

Is the night chilly and dark?
The night is chilly, but not dark.
The thin gray cloud is spread on high,
It covers but not hides the sky.
The moon is behind, and at the full;
And yet she looks both small and dull.
The night is chill, the cloud is gray:
'T is a month before the month of May,
And the Spring comes slowly up this way.

The lovely lady, Christabel,
Whom her father loves so well,
What makes her in the wood so late,
A furlong from the castle gate?
She had dreams all yesternight
Of her own betrothèd knight;
And she in the midnight wood will pray
For the weal of her lover that 's far away.

She stole along, she nothing spoke,
The sighs she heaved were soft and low,
And naught was green upon the oak
But moss and rarest misletoe:
She kneels beneath the huge oak tree,
And in silence prayeth she.

The lady sprang up suddenly,
The lovely lady, Christabel!
It moaned as near, as near can be,
But what it is she cannot tell. —
On the other side it seems to be,
Of the huge, broad-breasted, old oak tree.

The night is chill; the forest bare;
Is it the wind that moaneth bleak?
There is not wind enough in the air
To move away the ringlet curl
From the lovely lady's cheek —
There is not wind enough to twirl
The one red leaf, the last of its clan,
That dances as often as dance it can,
Hanging so light, and hanging so high,
On the topmost twig that looks up at the sky.

Hush, beating heart of Christabel!
Jesu, Maria, shield her well!
She folded her arms beneath her cloak,
And stole to the other side of the oak.
What sees she there?

There she sees a damsel bright,
Drest in a silken robe of white,
That shadowy in the moonlight shone:
The neck that made that white robe wan,
Her stately neck, and arms were bare;
Her blue-veined feet unsandaled were,
And wildly glittered here and there
The gems entangled in her hair.
I guess, 't was frightful there to see
A lady so richly clad as she —
Beautiful exceedingly!

Mary mother, save me now!
(Said Christabel,) And who art thou?

The lady strange made answer meet,
And her voice was faint and sweet: —
Have pity on my sore distress,
I scarce can speak for weariness:
Stretch forth thy hand, and have no fear!
Said Christabel, How camest thou here?
And the lady, whose voice was faint and sweet,
Did thus pursue her answer meet: —

My sire is of a noble line,
And my name is Geraldine:
Five warriors seized me yestermorn,
Me, even me, a maid forlorn:
They choked my cries with force and fright,
And tied me on a palfrey white.
The palfrey was as fleet as wind,
And they rode furiously behind.

They spurred amain, their steeds were white:
And once we crossed the shade of night.
As sure as Heaven shall rescue me,
I have no thought what men they be;
Nor do I know how long it is
(For I have lain entranced I wis)

Since one, the tallest of the five,
Took me from the palfrey's back,
A weary woman, scarce alive.
Some muttered words his comrades spoke:
He placed me underneath this oak;
He swore they would return with haste;
Whither they went I cannot tell —
I thought I heard, some minutes past,
Sounds as of a castle bell.
Stretch forth thy hand (thus ended she),
And help a wretched maid to flee.

Then Christabel stretched forth her hand,
And comforted fair Geraldine:
O well, bright dame! may you command
The service of Sir Leoline;
And gladly our stout chivalry
Will he send forth and friends withal
To guide and guard you safe and free
Home to your noble father's hall.

She rose: and forth with steps they passed
That strove to be, and were not, fast.

Her gracious stars the lady blest,
And thus spake on sweet Christabel:
All our household are at rest,
The hall as silent as the cell;
Sir Leoline is weak in health,
And may not well awakened be,
But we will move as if in stealth,
And I beseech your courtesy,
This night, to share your couch with me.

They crossed the moat, and Christabel
Took the key that fitted well;
A little door she opened straight,
All in the middle of the gate;
The gate that was ironed within and without,
Where an army in battle array had marched out.
The lady sank, belike through pain,
And Christabel with might and main
Lifted her up, a weary weight,
Over the threshold of the gate:
Then the lady rose again,
And moved, as she were not in pain.

So free from danger, free from fear,
They crossed the court: right glad they were.
And Christabel devoutly cried
To the lady by her side,
Praise we the Virgin all divine
Who hath rescued thee from thy distress!
Alas, alas! said Geraldine,
I cannot speak for weariness.
So free from danger, free from fear,
They crossed the court: right glad they were.

Outside her kennel, the mastiff old
Lay fast asleep, in moonshine cold.
The mastiff old did not awake,
Yet she an angry moan did make!
And what can ail the mastiff bitch?
Never till now she uttered yell
Beneath the eye of Christabel.
Perhaps it is the owlet's scritch:
For what can ail the mastiff bitch?

They passed the hall, that echoes still,
Pass as lightly as you will!
The brands were flat, the brands were dying,
Amid their own white ashes lying;
But when the lady passed, there came
A tongue of light, a fit of flame;
And Christabel saw the lady's eye,
And nothing else saw she thereby,
Save the boss of the shield of Sir Leoline tall,
Which hung in a murky old niche in the wall.
O softly tread, said Christabel,
My father seldom sleepeth well.

Sweet Christabel her feet doth bare,
And jealous of the listening air
They steal their way from stair to stair,
Now in glimmer, and now in gloom,
And now they pass the Baron's room,
As still as death, with stifled breath!
And now have reached her chamber door;
And now doth Geraldine press down
The rushes of the chamber floor.

The moon shines dim in the open air,
And not a moonbeam enters here.
But they without its light can see
The chamber carved so curiously,
Carved with figures strange and sweet,
All made out of the carver's brain,
For a lady's chamber meet:
The lamp with twofold silver chain
Is fastened to an angel's feet.

The silver lamp burns dead and dim;
But Christabel the lamp will trim.
She trimmed the lamp, and made it bright,
And left it swinging to and fro,
While Geraldine, in wretched plight,
Sank down upon the floor below.

O weary lady, Geraldine,
I pray you, drink this cordial wine!
It is a wine of virtuous powers;
My mother made it of wild flowers.

And will your mother pity me,
Who am a maiden most forlorn?
Christabel answered — Woe is me!
She died the hour that I was born.
I have heard the grey-haired friar tell
How on her death-bed she did say,

That she should hear the castle-bell
Strike twelve upon my wedding-day.
O mother dear! that thou wert here!
I would, said Geraldine, she were!

But soon with altered voice, said she —
'Off, wandering mother! Peak and pine!
I have power to bid thee flee.'
Alas! what ails poor Geraldine?
Why stares she with unsettled eye?
Can she the bodiless dead espy?
And why with hollow voice cries she,
'Off, woman, off! this hour is mine —
Though thou her guardian spirit be,
Off, woman, off! 't is given to me.'

Then Christabel knelt by the lady's side,
And raised to heaven her eyes so blue —
Alas! said she, this ghastly ride —
Dear lady! it hath wildered you!
The lady wiped her moist cold brow,
And faintly said, ''t is over now!'

Again the wild-flower wine she drank:
Her fair large eyes 'gan glitter bright,
And from the floor whereon she sank,
The lofty lady stood upright:
She was most beautiful to see,
Like a lady of a far countrée.

And thus the lofty lady spake —
'All they who live in the upper sky,
Do love you, holy Christabel!
And you love them, and for their sake
And for the good which me befel,
Even I in my degree will try,
Fair maiden, to requite you well.
But now unrobe yourself; for I
Must pray, ere yet in bed I lie.'

Quoth Christabel, So let it be!
And as the lady bade, did she.
Her gentle limbs did she undress,
And lay down in her loveliness.

But through her brain of weal and woe
So many thoughts moved to and fro,
That vain it were her lids to close;
So half-way from the bed she rose,
And on her elbow did recline
To look at the lady Geraldine.

Beneath the lamp the lady bowed,
And slowly rolled her eyes around;
Then drawing in her breath aloud,
Like one that shuddered, she unbound
The cincture from beneath her breast:
Her silken robe, and inner vest,
Dropt to her feet, and full in view,
Behold! her bosom and half her side —
A sight to dream of, not to tell!
O shield her! shield sweet Christabel!

Yet Geraldine nor speaks nor stirs;
Ah! what a stricken look was hers!
Deep from within she seems half-way
To lift some weight with sick assay,
And eyes the maid and seeks delay;
Then suddenly, as one defied,
Collects herself in scorn and pride,
And lay down by the Maiden's side! —
And in her arms the maid she took,
Ah wel-a-day!
And with low voice and doleful look
These words did say:
'In the touch of this bosom there worketh a spell,
Which is lord of thy utterance, Christabel!
Thou knowest to-night, and wilt know to-morrow,
This mark of my shame, this seal of my sorrow;

But vainly thou warrest,
For this is alone in
Thy power to declare,
That in the dim forest
Thou heard'st a low moaning,
And found'st a bright lady, surpassingly fair;
And didst bring her home with thee in love and in charity,
To shield her and shelter her from the damp air.'

THE CONCLUSION TO PART I

It was a lovely sight to see
The lady Christabel, when she
Was praying at the old oak tree.
Amid the jaggèd shadows
Of mossy leafless boughs,
Kneeling in the moonlight,
To make her gentle vows;
Her slender palms together prest,
Heaving sometimes on her breast;
Her face resigned to bliss or bale —
Her face, oh call it fair not pale,
And both blue eyes more bright than clear,
Each about to have a tear.

With open eyes (ah woe is me!)
Asleep, and dreaming fearfully,
Fearfully dreaming, yet, I wis,
Dreaming that alone, which is —
O sorrow and shame! Can this be she,
The lady, who knelt at the old oak tree?
And lo! the worker of these harms,
That holds the maiden in her arms,

Seems to slumber still and mild,
As a mother with her child.

A star hath set, a star hath risen,
O Geraldine! since arms of thine
Have been the lovely lady's prison.
O Geraldine! one hour was thine —
Thou 'st had thy will! By tairn and rill,
The night-birds all that hour were still.
But now they are jubilant anew,
From cliff and tower, tu — whoo! tu — whoo!
Tu — whoo! tu — whoo! from wood and fell!

And see! the lady Christabel
Gathers herself from out her trance;
Her limbs relax, her countenance
Grows sad and soft; the smooth thin lids
Close o'er her eyes; and tears she sheds —
Large tears that leave the lashes bright!
And oft the while she seems to smile
As infants at a sudden light!

Yea, she doth smile, and she doth weep,
Like a youthful hermitess,
Beauteous in a wilderness,
Who, praying always, prays in sleep.
And, if she move unquietly,
Perchance, 't is but the blood so free
Comes back and tingles in her feet.
No doubt, she hath a vision sweet.
What if her guardian spirit 't were,
What if she knew her mother near?
But this she knows, in joys and woes,
That saints will aid if men will call:
For the blue sky bends over all!

PART II

Each matin bell, the Baron saith,
Knells us back to a world of death.
These words Sir Leoline first said,
When he rose and found his lady dead:
These words Sir Leoline will say
Many a morn to his dying day!

And hence the custom and law began
That still at dawn the sacristan,
Who duly pulls the heavy bell,
Five and forty beads must tell
Between each stroke — a warning knell,
Which not a soul can choose but hear
From Bratha Head to Wyndermere.

Saith Bracy the bard, So let it knell!
And let the drowsy sacristan
Still count as slowly as he can!
There is no lack of such, I ween,
As well fill up the space between.
In Langdale Pike and Witch's Lair,
And Dungeon-ghyll so foully rent,
With ropes of rock and bells of air
Three sinful sextons' ghosts are pent,
Who all give back, one after t' other,
The death-note to their living brother;
And oft too, by the knell offended,
Just as their one! two! three! is ended,
The devil mocks the doleful tale
With a merry peal from Borodale.

The air is still! through mist and cloud
That merry peal comes ringing loud;
And Geraldine shakes off her dread,
And rises lightly from the bed;
Puts on her silken vestments white,
And tricks her hair in lovely plight,
And nothing doubting of her spell
Awakens the lady Christabel.
'Sleep you, sweet lady Christabel?
I trust that you have rested well.'

And Christabel awoke and spied
The same who lay down by her side —
O rather say, the same whom she
Raised up beneath the old oak tree!
Nay, fairer yet! and yet more fair!
For she belike hath drunken deep
Of all the blessedness of sleep!
And while she spake, her looks, her air
Such gentle thankfulness declare,
That (so it seemed) her girded vests
Grew tight beneath her heaving breasts.
'Sure I have sinned!' said Christabel,
'Now heaven be praised if all be well!'
And in low faltering tones, yet sweet,
Did she the lofty lady greet
With such perplexity of mind
As dreams too lively leave behind.

So quickly she rose, and quickly arrayed
Her maiden limbs, and having prayed
That He, who on the cross did groan,
Might wash away her sins unknown,
She forthwith led fair Geraldine
To meet her sire, Sir Leoline.

The lovely maid and the lady tall
Are pacing both into the hall,
And pacing on through page and groom,
Enter the Baron's presence-room.

The Baron rose, and while he prest
His gentle daughter to his breast,
With cheerful wonder in his eyes
The lady Geraldine espies,
And gave such welcome to the same,
As might beseem so bright a dame!

But when he heard the lady's tale,
And when she told her father's name,

Why waxed Sir Leoline so pale,
Murmuring o'er the name again,
Lord Roland de Vaux of Tryermaine?

Alas! they had been friends in youth;
But whispering tongues can poison truth;
And constancy lives in realms above;
And life is thorny; and youth is vain;
And to be wroth with one we love
Doth work like madness in the brain.
And thus it chanced, as I divine,
With Roland and Sir Leoline.
Each spake words of high disdain
And insult to his heart's best brother:
They parted — ne'er to meet again!
But never either found another
To free the hollow heart from paining —
They stood aloof, the scars remaining,
Like cliffs which had been rent asunder;
A dreary sea now flows between; —
But neither heat, nor frost, nor thunder,
Shall wholly do away, I ween,
The marks of that which once hath been.

Sir Leoline, a moment's space,
Stood gazing on the damsel's face:
And the youthful Lord of Tryermaine
Came back upon his heart again.
O then the Baron forgot his age,
His noble heart swelled high with rage;
He swore by the wounds in Jesu's side
He would proclaim it far and wide,
With trump and solemn heraldry,
That they, who thus had wronged the dame,
Were base as spotted infamy!
'And if they dare deny the same,
My herald shall appoint a week,
And let the recreant traitors seek
My tourney court — that there and then
I may dislodge their reptile souls
From the bodies and forms of men!'
He spake: his eye in lightning rolls!
For the lady was ruthlessly seized; and he kenned
In the beautiful lady the child of his friend!

And now the tears were on his face,
And fondly in his arms he took
Fair Geraldine, who met the embrace,
Prolonging it with joyous look.
Which when she viewed, a vision fell
Upon the soul of Christabel,
The vision of fear, the touch and pain!
She shrunk and shuddered, and saw again —
(Ah, woe is me! Was it for thee,
Thou gentle maid! such sights to see?)

Again she saw that bosom old,
Again she felt that bosom cold,
And drew in her breath with a hissing sound:
Whereat the Knight turned wildly round,
And nothing saw, but his own sweet maid
With eyes upraised, as one that prayed.

The touch, the sight, had passed away,
And in its stead that vision blest,
Which comforted her after-rest
While in the lady's arms she lay,
Had put a rapture in her breast,
And on her lips and o'er her eyes
Spread smiles like light!
With new surprise,
'What ails then my belovèd child?'
The Baron said — His daughter mild
Made answer, 'All will yet be well!'
I ween, she had no power to tell
Aught else: so mighty was the spell.

Yet he, who saw this Geraldine,
Had deemed her sure a thing divine:
Such sorrow with such grace she blended,
As if she feared she had offended
Sweet Christabel, that gentle maid!
And with such lowly tones she prayed
She might be sent without delay
Home to her father's mansion.
'Nay!
Nay, by my soul!' said Leoline.
'Ho! Bracy the bard, the charge be thine!
Go thou, with music sweet and loud,
And take two steeds with trappings proud,
And take the youth whom thou lov'st best
To bear thy harp, and learn thy song,
And clothe you both in solemn vest,
And over the mountains haste along,
Lest wandering folk, that are abroad,
Detain you on the valley road.

'And when he has crossed the Irthing flood,
My merry bard! he hastes, he hastes
Up Knorren Moor, through Halegarth Wood,
And reaches soon that castle good
Which stands and threatens Scotland's wastes.

'Bard Bracy! bard Bracy! your horses are fleet,
Ye must ride up the hall, your music so sweet,
More loud than your horses' echoing feet!
And loud and loud to Lord Roland call,
Thy daughter is safe in Langdale hall!
Thy beautiful daughter is safe and free —
Sir Leoline greets thee thus through me!
He bids thee come without delay
With all thy numerous array
And take thy lovely daughter home:

And he will meet thee on the way
With all his numerous array
White with their panting palfreys' foam:
And, by mine honour! I will say,
That I repent me of the day
When I spake words of fierce disdain
To Roland de Vaux of Tryermaine! —
— For since that evil hour hath flown,
Many a summer's sun hath shone;
Yet ne'er found I a friend again
Like Roland de Vaux of Tryermaine.'

The lady fell, and clasped his knees,
Her face upraised, her eyes o'erflowing;
And Bracy replied, with faltering voice,
His gracious Hail on all bestowing! —
'Thy words, thou sire of Christabel,
Are sweeter than my harp can tell;
Yet might I gain a boon of thee,
This day my journey should not be,
So strange a dream hath come to me,
That I had vowed with music loud
To clear yon wood from thing unblest,
Warned by a vision in my rest!
For in my sleep I saw that dove,
That gentle bird, whom thou dost love,
And call'st by thy own daughter's name —
Sir Leoline! I saw the same
Fluttering, and uttering fearful moan,
Among the green herbs in the forest alone.
Which when I saw and when I heard,
I wondered what might ail the bird;
For nothing near it could I see,
Save the grass and green herbs underneath the old tree.

'And in my dream methought I went
To search out what might there be found;
And what the sweet bird's trouble meant,
That thus lay fluttering on the ground.
I went and peered, and could descry
No cause for her distressful cry;
But yet for her dear lady's sake
I stooped, methought, the dove to take,
When lo! I saw a bright green snake
Coiled around its wings and neck.
Green as the herbs on which it couched,
Close by the dove's its head it crouched;
And with the dove it heaves and stirs,
Swelling its neck as she swelled hers!
I woke; it was the midnight hour,
The clock was echoing in the tower;
But though my slumber was gone by,
This dream it would not pass away —
It seems to live upon my eye!
And thence I vowed this self-same day
With music strong and saintly song
To wander through the forest bare,
Lest aught unholy loiter there.'

Thus Bracy said: the Baron, the while,
Half-listening heard him with a smile;
Then turned to Lady Geraldine,
His eyes made up of wonder and love;
And said in courtly accents fine,
'Sweet maid, Lord Roland's beauteous dove,
With arms more strong than harp or song,
Thy sire and I will crush the snake!'
He kissed her forehead as he spake,
And Geraldine in maiden wise
Casting down her large bright eyes,
With blushing cheek and courtesy fine
She turned her from Sir Leoline;
Softly gathering up her train,
That o'er her right arm fell again;
And folded her arms across her chest,
And couched her head upon her breast,
And looked askance at Christabel ——
Jesu, Maria, shield her well!

A snake's small eye blinks dull and shy;
And the lady's eyes they shrunk in her head,
Each shrunk up to a serpent's eye,
And with somewhat of malice, and more of dread,
At Christabel she looked askance! —
One moment — and the sight was fled!
But Christabel in dizzy trance
Stumbling on the unsteady ground
Shuddered aloud, with a hissing sound;
And Geraldine again turned round,
And like a thing, that sought relief,
Full of wonder and full of grief,
She rolled her large bright eyes divine
Wildly on Sir Leoline.

The maid, alas! her thoughts are gone,
She nothing sees — no sight but one!
The maid, devoid of guile and sin,
I know not how, in fearful wise,
So deeply had she drunken in
That look, those shrunken serpent eyes,
That all her features were resigned
To this sole image in her mind:
And passively did imitate
That look of dull and treacherous hate!
And thus she stood, in dizzy trance,
Still picturing that look askance
With forced unconscious sympathy
Full before her father's view ——
As far as such a look could be
In eyes so innocent and blue!

And when the trance was o'er, the maid
Paused awhile, and inly prayed:
Then falling at the Baron's feet,
'By my mother's soul do I entreat
That thou this woman send away!'

She said: and more she could not say:
For what she knew she could not tell,
O'er-mastered by the mighty spell.

Why is thy cheek so wan and wild,
Sir Leoline? Thy only child
Lies at thy feet, thy joy, thy pride,
So fair, so innocent, so mild;
The same, for whom thy lady died!
O by the pangs of her dear mother
Think thou no evil of thy child!
For her, and thee, and for no other,
She prayed the moment ere she died:
Prayed that the babe for whom she died,
Might prove her dear lord's joy and pride!
That prayer her deadly pangs beguiled,
Sir Leoline!
And wouldst thou wrong thy only child,
Her child and thine?

Within the Baron's heart and brain
If thoughts, like these, had any share,
They only swelled his rage and pain,
And did but work confusion there.
His heart was cleft with pain and rage,
His cheeks they quivered, his eyes were wild,
Dishonoured thus in his old age;
Dishonoured by his only child,
And all his hospitality
To the wronged daughter of his friend
By more than woman's jealousy
Brought thus to a disgraceful end —
He rolled his eye with stern regard
Upon the gentle minstrel bard,
And said in tones abrupt, austere —
'Why, Bracy! dost thou loiter here?
I bade thee hence!' The bard obeyed;
And turning from his own sweet maid,
The agèd knight, Sir Leoline,
Led forth the lady Geraldine!

THE CONCLUSION TO PART II

A little child, a limber elf,
Singing, dancing to itself,
A fairy thing with red round cheeks,
That always finds, and never seeks,
Makes such a vision to the sight
As fills a father's eyes with light;
And pleasures flow in so thick and fast
Upon his heart, that he at last
Must needs express his love's excess
With words of unmeant bitterness.
Perhaps 't is pretty to force together
Thoughts so all unlike each other;
To mutter and mock a broken charm,
To dally with wrong that does no harm.
Perhaps 't is tender too and pretty
At each wild word to feel within
A sweet recoil of love and pity.
And what, if in a world of sin
(O sorrow and shame should this be true!)
Such giddiness of heart and brain
Comes seldom save from rage and pain,
So talks as it 's most used to do.

1816

KUBLA KHAN

In Xanadu did Kubla Khan
A stately pleasure-dome decree:
Where Alph, the sacred river, ran
Through caverns measureless to man
Down to a sunless sea.
So twice five miles of fertile ground
With walls and towers were girdled round:
And there were gardens bright with sinuous rills,
Where blossomed many an incense-bearing tree;
And here were forests ancient as the hills,
Enfolding sunny spots of greenery.
But oh! that deep romantic chasm which slanted
Down the green hill athwart a cedarn cover!
A savage place! as holy and enchanted
As e'er beneath a waning moon was haunted
By woman wailing for her demon-lover!
And from this chasm, with ceaseless turmoil seething,
As if this earth in fast thick pants were breathing,
A mighty fountain momently was forced:
Amid whose swift half-intermitted burst
Huge fragments vaulted like rebounding hail,
Or chaffy grain beneath the thresher's flail:
And 'mid these dancing rocks at once and ever
It flung up momently the sacred river.
Five miles meandering with a mazy motion
Through wood and dale the sacred river ran,
Then reached the caverns measureless to man,
And sank in tumult to a lifeless ocean:
And 'mid this tumult Kubla heard from far
Ancestral voices prophesying war!
The shadow of the dome of pleasure
Floated midway on the waves;
Where was heard the mingled measure
From the fountain and the caves.
It was a miracle of rare device,
A sunny pleasure-dome with caves of ice!

A damsel with a dulcimer
In a vision once I saw:
It was an Abyssinian maid,

And on her dulcimer she played,
Singing of Mount Abora.
Could I revive within me
Her symphony and song,
To such a deep delight 't would win me,
That with music loud and long,
I would build that dome in air,
That sunny dome! those caves of ice!
And all who heard should see them there,
And all should cry, Beware! Beware!
His flashing eyes, his floating hair!
Weave a circle round him thrice,
And close your eyes with holy dread,
For he on honey-dew hath fed,
And drunk the milk of Paradise.

1816

FROST AT MIDNIGHT

The Frost performs its secret ministry,
Unhelped by any wind. The owlet's cry
Came loud — and hark, again! loud as before.
The inmates of my cottage, all at rest,
Have left me to that solitude, which suits
Abstruser musings: save that at my side
My cradled infant slumbers peacefully.
'T is calm indeed! so calm, that it disturbs
And vexes meditation with its strange
And extreme silentness. Sea, hill, and wood,
This populous village! Sea, and hill, and wood,
With all the numberless goings-on of life,
Inaudible as dreams! the thin blue flame
Lies on my low-burnt fire, and quivers not;
Only that film, which fluttered on the grate,
Still flutters there, the sole unquiet thing.
Methinks, its motion in this hush of nature
Gives it dim sympathies with me who live,
Making it a companionable form,
Whose puny flaps and freaks the idling Spirit
By its own moods interprets, every where
Echo or mirror seeking of itself,
And makes a toy of Thought.
But O! how oft,
How oft, at school, with most believing mind,
Presageful, have I gazed upon the bars,
To watch that fluttering *stranger!* and as oft
With unclosed lids, already had I dreamt
Of my sweet birth-place, and the old church-tower,
Whose bells, the poor man's only music, rang
From morn to evening, all the hot Fair-day,
So sweetly, that they stirred and haunted me
With a wild pleasure, falling on mine ear
Most like articulate sounds of things to come!
So gazed I, till the soothing things, I dreamt,
Lulled me to sleep, and sleep prolonged my dreams!
And so I brooded all the following morn,
Awed by the stern preceptor's face, mine eye
Fixed with mock study on my swimming book:
Save if the door half opened, and I snatched
A hasty glance, and still my heart leaped up,
For still I hoped to see the *stranger's* face,
Townsman, or aunt, or sister more beloved,
My play-mate when we both were clothed alike!
Dear Babe, that sleepest cradled by my side,
Whose gentle breathings, heard in this deep calm,
Fill up the interspersèd vacancies
And momentary pauses of the thought!
My babe so beautiful! it thrills my heart
With tender gladness, thus to look at thee,
And think that thou shalt learn far other lore,
And in far other scenes! For I was reared
In the great city, pent 'mid cloisters dim,
And saw nought lovely but the sky and stars.
But *thou*, my babe! shalt wander like a breeze
By lakes and sandy shores, beneath the crags
Of ancient mountain, and beneath the clouds,
Which image in their bulk both lakes and shores
And mountain crags: so shalt thou see and hear
The lovely shapes and sounds intelligible
Of that eternal language, which thy God
Utters, who from eternity doth teach
Himself in all, and all things in himself.
Great universal Teacher! he shall mould
Thy spirit, and by giving make it ask.
Therefore all seasons shall be sweet to thee,
Whether the summer clothe the general earth
With greenness, or the redbreast sit and sing
Betwixt the tufts of snow on the bare branch
Of mossy apple-tree, while the nigh thatch
Smokes in the sun-thaw; whether the eave-drops fall
Heard only in the trances of the blast,
Or if the secret ministry of frost
Shall hang them up in silent icicles,
Quietly shining to the quiet Moon.

1798

FRANCE: AN ODE

Ye Clouds! that far above me float and pause,
Whose pathless march no mortal may controul!
Ye Ocean-Waves! that, wheresoe'er ye roll,
Yield homage only to eternal laws!
Ye Woods! that listen to the night-birds singing,
Midway the smooth and perilous slope reclined,
Save when your own imperious branches swinging,
Have made a solemn music of the wind!
Where, like a man beloved of God,
Through glooms, which never woodman trod,
How oft, pursuing fancies holy,
My moonlight way o'er flowering weeds I wound,
Inspired, beyond the guess of folly,
By each rude shape and wild unconquerable sound!
O ye loud Waves! and O ye Forests high!
And O ye Clouds that far above me soared!
Thou rising Sun! thou blue rejoicing Sky!
Yea, every thing that is and will be free!
Bear witness for me, wheresoe'er ye be,
With what deep worship I have still adored
The spirit of divinest Liberty.

When France in wrath her giant-limbs upreared,
And with that oath, which smote air, earth, and sea,
Stamped her strong foot and said she would be free,
Bear witness for me, how I hoped and feared!
With what a joy my lofty gratulation
Unawed I sang, amid a slavish band:
And when to whelm the disenchanted nation,
Like fiends embattled by a wizard's wand,
The Monarchs marched in evil day,
And Britain joined the dire array;
Though dear her shores and circling ocean,
Though many friendships, many youthful loves
Had swoln the patriot emotion
And flung a magic light o'er all her hills and groves;
Yet still my voice, unaltered, sang defeat
To all that braved the tyrant-quelling lance,
And shame too long delayed and vain retreat!
For ne'er, O Liberty! with partial aim
I dimmed thy light or damped thy holy flame;
But blessed the pæans of delivered France,
And hung my head and wept at Britain's name.

'And what,' I said, 'though Blasphemy's loud scream
With that sweet music of deliverance strove!
Though all the fierce and drunken passions wove
A dance more wild than e'er was maniac's dream!
Ye storms, that round the dawning East assembled,
The Sun was rising, though ye hid his light!'
And when, to soothe my soul, that hoped and trembled,
The dissonance ceased, and all seemed calm and bright;
When France her front deep-scarred and gory
Concealed with clustering wreaths of glory;
When, insupportably advancing,
Her arm made mockery of the warrior's ramp;
While timid looks of fury glancing,
Domestic treason, crushed beneath her fatal stamp,
Writhed like a wounded dragon in his gore;
Then I reproached my fears that would not flee;
'And soon,' I said, 'shall Wisdom teach her lore
In the low huts of them that toil and groan!
And, conquering by her happiness alone,
Shall France compel the nations to be free,
Till Love and Joy look round, and call the Earth their own.'

Forgive me, Freedom! O forgive those dreams!
I hear thy voice, I hear thy loud lament,
From bleak Helvetia's icy caverns sent —
I hear thy groans upon her blood-stained streams!
Heroes, that for your peaceful country perished,
And ye that, fleeing, spot your mountain-snows
With bleeding wounds; forgive me, that I cherished

One thought that ever blessed your cruel foes!
To scatter rage, and traitorous guilt,
Where Peace her jealous home had built;
A patriot-race to disinherit
Of all that made their stormy wilds so dear;
And with inexpiable spirit
To taint the bloodless freedom of the mountaineer —
O France, that mockest Heaven, adulterous, blind,
And patriot only in pernicious toils!
Are these thy boasts, Champion of human kind?
To mix with Kings in the low lust of sway,
Yell in the hunt, and share the murderous prey;
To insult the shrine of Liberty with spoils
From freemen torn; to tempt and to betray?

The Sensual and the Dark rebel in vain,
Slaves by their own compulsion! In mad game
They burst their manacles and wear the name
Of Freedom, graven on a heavier chain!
O Liberty! with profitless endeavour
Have I pursued thee, many a weary hour;
But thou nor swell'st the victor's strain, nor ever
Didst breathe thy soul in forms of human power.
Alike from all, howe'er they praise thee,
(Nor prayer, nor boastful name delays thee)
Alike from Priestcraft's harpy minions,
And factious Blasphemy's obscener slaves,
Thou speedest on thy subtle pinions,
The guide of homeless winds, and playmate of the waves!
And there I felt thee! — on that sea-cliff's verge,
Whose pines, scarce travelled by the breeze above,
Had made one murmur with the distant surge!
Yes, while I stood and gazed, my temples bare,
And shot my being through earth, sea, and air,
Possessing all things with intensest love,
O Liberty! my spirit felt thee there.

1798

DEJECTION: AN ODE

Late, late yestreen I saw the new Moon,
With the old Moon in her arms;
And I fear, I fear, my Master dear!
We shall have a deadly storm.
—*Ballad of Sir Patrick Spence*

Well! If the Bard was weather-wise, who made
The grand old ballad of Sir Patrick Spence,
This night, so tranquil now, will not go hence
Unroused by winds, that ply a busier trade
Than those which mould yon cloud in lazy flakes,
Or the dull sobbing draft, that moans and rakes
Upon the strings of this Æolian lute,
Which better far were mute.
For lo! the New-moon winter-bright!
And overspread with phantom light,
(With swimming phantom light o'erspread
But rimmed and circled by a silver thread)
I see the old Moon in her lap, foretelling
The coming-on of rain and squally blast.
And oh! that even now the gust were swelling,
And the slant night-shower driving loud and fast!
Those sounds which oft have raised me, whilst they awed,
And sent my soul abroad,
Might now perhaps their wonted impulse give,
Might startle this dull pain, and make it move and live!

A grief without a pang, void, dark, and drear,
A stifled, drowsy, unimpassioned grief,
Which finds no natural outlet, no relief,
In word, or sigh, or tear —
O Lady! in this wan and heartless mood,
To other thoughts by yonder throstle wooed,
All this long eve, so balmy and serene,
Have I been gazing on the western sky,
And its peculiar tint of yellow green:
And still I gaze — and with how blank an eye!
And those thin clouds above, in flakes and bars,
That give away their motion to the stars;
Those stars, that glide behind them or between,
Now sparkling, now bedimmed, but always seen:
Yon crescent Moon, as fixed as if it grew

In its own cloudless, starless lake of blue;
I see them all so excellently fair,
I see, not feel, how beautiful they are!

My genial spirits fail;
And what can these avail
To lift the smothering weight from off my breast?
It were a vain endeavour,
Though I should gaze for ever
On that green light that lingers in the west:
I may not hope from outward forms to win
The passion and the life, whose fountains are within.

O Lady! we receive but what we give,
And in our life alone does Nature live:
Ours is her wedding garment, ours her shroud!
And would we aught behold, of higher worth,
Than that inanimate cold world allowed
To the poor loveless ever-anxious crowd,
Ah! from the soul itself must issue forth
A light, a glory, a fair luminous cloud
Enveloping the Earth —
And from the soul itself must there be sent
A sweet and potent voice, of its own birth,
Of all sweet sounds the life and element!

O pure of heart! thou need'st not ask of me
What this strong music in the soul may be!
What, and wherein it doth exist,
This light, this glory, this fair luminous mist,
This beautiful and beauty-making power.
Joy, virtuous Lady! Joy that ne'er was given,
Save to the pure, and in their purest hour,
Life, and Life's effluence, cloud at once and shower,
Joy, Lady! is the spirit and the power,
Which wedding Nature to us gives in dower
A new Earth and new Heaven,
Undreamt of by the sensual and the proud —
Joy is the sweet voice, Joy the luminous cloud —
We in ourselves rejoice!
And thence flows all that charms or ear or sight,
All melodies the echoes of that voice,
All colours a suffusion from that light.

There was a time when, though my path was rough,
This joy within me dallied with distress,
And all misfortunes were but as the stuff
Whence Fancy made me dreams of happiness:
For hope grew round me, like the twining vine,
And fruits, and foliage, not my own, seemed mine.
But now afflictions bow me down to earth:
Nor care I that they rob me of my mirth;
But oh! each visitation
Suspends what nature gave me at my birth,
My shaping spirit of Imagination.
For not to think of what I needs must feel,
But to be still and patient, all I can;
And haply by abstruse research to steal
From my own nature all the natural man —
This was my sole resource, my only plan:
Till that which suits a part infects the whole,
And now is almost grown the habit of my soul.

Hence, viper thoughts, that coil around my mind,
Reality's dark dream!
I turn from you, and listen to the wind,
Which long has raved unnoticed. What a scream
Of agony by torture lengthened out
That lute sent forth! Thou Wind, that rav'st without,
Bare crag, of mountain-tairn, or blasted tree,
Or pine-grove whither woodman never clomb,
Or lonely house, long held the witches' home,
Methinks were fitter instruments for thee,
Mad Lutanist! who in this month of showers,
Of dark-brown gardens, and of peeping flowers,
Mak'st Devils' yule, with worse than wintry song,
The blossoms, buds, and timorous leaves among.
Thou Actor, perfect in all tragic sounds!
Thou mighty Poet, e'en to frenzy bold!
What tell'st thou now about?
'T is of the rushing of an host in rout,
With groans, of trampled men, with smarting wounds —
At once they groan with pain, and shudder with the cold!
But hush! there is a pause of deepest silence!
And all that noise, as of a rushing crowd,
With groans, and tremulous shudderings — all is over —
It tells another tale, with sounds less deep and loud!

A tale of less affright,
And tempered with delight,
As Otway's self had framed the tender lay, —
'T is of a little child
Upon a lonesome wild,
Not far from home, but she hath lost her way:
And now moans low in bitter grief and fear,
And now screams loud, and hopes to make her mother hear.

'T is midnight, but small thoughts have I of sleep:
Full seldom may my friend such vigils keep!
Visit her, gentle Sleep! with wings of healing,
And may this storm be but a mountain-birth,
May all the stars hang bright above her dwelling,
Silent as though they watched the sleeping Earth!
With light heart may she rise,
Gay fancy, cheerful eyes,
Joy lift her spirit, joy attune her voice;
To her may all things live, from pole to pole,
Their life the eddying of her living soul!
O simple spirit, guided from above,
Dear Lady! friend devoutest of my choice,
Thus mayest thou ever, evermore rejoice.

1802

HYMN BEFORE SUN-RISE, IN THE VALE OF CHAMOUNI

HAST thou a charm to stay the morning-star
In his steep course? So long he seems to pause
On thy bald awful head, O sovran Blanc,
The Arve and Arveiron at thy base
Rave ceaselessly; but thou, most awful Form!
Risest from forth thy silent sea of pines,
How silently! Around thee and above
Deep is the air and dark, substantial, black,
An ebon mass: methinks thou piercest it,
As with a wedge! But when I look again,
It is thine own calm home, thy crystal shrine,
Thy habitation from eternity!
O dread and silent Mount! I gazed upon thee,
Till thou, still present to the bodily sense,
Didst vanish from my thought: entranced in prayer
I worshipped the Invisible alone.
Yet, like some sweet beguiling melody,
So sweet, we know not we are listening to it,
Thou, the meanwhile, wast blending with my Thought,
Yea, with my Life and Life's own secret joy:
Till the dilating Soul, enrapt, transfused,
Into the mighty vision passing — there
As in her natural form, swelled vast to Heaven!
Awake, my soul! not only passive praise
Thou owest! not alone these swelling tears,
Mute thanks and secret ecstasy! Awake,
Voice of sweet song! Awake, my heart, awake!
Green vales and icy cliffs, all join my Hymn.
Thou first and chief, sole sovereign of the Vale!
O struggling with the darkness all the night,
And visited all night by troops of stars,
Or when they climb the sky or when they sink:
Companion of the morning-star at dawn,
Thyself Earth's rosy star, and of the dawn
Co-herald: wake, O wake, and utter praise!
Who sank thy sunless pillars deep in Earth?
Who filled thy countenance with rosy light?
Who made thee parent of perpetual streams?
And you, ye five wild torrents fiercely glad!
Who called you forth from night and utter death,
From dark and icy caverns called you forth,
Down those precipitous, black, jaggèd rocks,
For ever shattered and the same for ever?
Who gave you your invulnerable life,
Your strength, your speed, your fury, and your joy,
Unceasing thunder and eternal foam?
And who commanded (and the silence came),
Here let the billows stiffen, and have rest?
Ye Ice-falls! ye that from the mountain's brow
Adown enormous ravines slope amain —
Torrents, methinks, that heard a mighty voice,
And stopped at once amid their maddest plunge!
Motionless torrents! silent cataracts!
Who made you glorious as the Gates of Heaven
Beneath the keen full moon? Who bade the sun
Clothe you with rainbows? Who, with living flowers
Of loveliest blue, spread garlands at your feet? —
God! let the torrents, like a shout of nations,

Answer! and let the ice-plains echo, God!
God! sing ye meadow-streams with gladsome voice!
Ye pine-groves, with your soft and soul-like sounds!
And they too have a voice, yon piles of snow,
And in their perilous fall shall thunder, God!
  Ye living flowers that skirt the eternal frost!
Ye wild goats sporting round the eagle's nest!
Ye eagles, play-mates of the mountain-storm!
Ye lightnings, the dread arrows of the clouds!
Ye signs and wonders of the element!
Utter forth God, and fill the hills with praise!
  Thou too, hoar Mount! with thy sky-pointing peaks,
Oft from whose feet the avalanche, unheard,
Shoots downward, glittering through the pure serene
Into the depth of clouds, that veil thy breast —
Thou too again, stupendous Mountain! thou
That as I raise my head, awhile bowed low
In adoration, upward from thy base
Slow travelling with dim eyes suffused with tears,
Solemnly seemest, like a vapoury cloud,
To rise before me — Rise, O ever rise,
Rise like a cloud of incense from the Earth!
Thou kingly Spirit throned among the hills,
Thou dread ambassador from Earth to Heaven,
Great Hierarch! tell thou the silent sky,
And tell the stars, and tell yon rising sun
Earth, with her thousand voices, praises God.

1802

THE PAINS OF SLEEP

Ere on my bed my limbs I lay,
It hath not been my use to pray
With moving lips or bended knees;
But silently, by slow degrees,
My spirit I to Love compose,
In humble trust mine eye-lids close,
With reverential resignation,
No wish conceived, no thought exprest,
Only a sense of supplication;
A sense o'er all my soul imprest
That I am weak, yet not unblest,
Since in me, round me, every where
Eternal Strength and Wisdom are.

But yester-night I prayed aloud
In anguish and in agony,
Up-starting from the fiendish crowd
Of shapes and thoughts that tortured me:
A lurid light, a trampling throng,
Sense of intolerable wrong,
And whom I scorned, those only strong!
Thirst of revenge, the powerless will
Still baffled, and yet burning still!
Desire with loathing strangely mixed
On wild or hateful objects fixed.
Fantastic passions! maddening brawl!
And shame and terror over all!
Deeds to be hid which were not hid,
Which all confused I could not know
Whether I suffered, or I did:
For all seemed guilt, remorse or woe,
My own or others still the same
Life-stifling fear, soul-stifling shame.

So two nights passed: the night's dismay
Saddened and stunned the coming day.
Sleep, the wide blessing, seemed to me
Distemper's worst calamity.
The third night, when my own loud scream
Had waked me from the fiendish dream,
O'ercome with sufferings strange and wild,
I wept as I had been a child;
And having thus by tears subdued
My anguish to a milder mood,
Such punishments, I said, were due
To natures deepliest stained with sin, —
For aye entempesting anew
The unfathomable hell within,
The horror of their deeds to view,
To know and loathe, yet wish and do!

1816

YOUTH AND AGE

Verse, a breeze mid blossoms straying,
Where Hope clung feeding, like a bee —
Both were mine! Life went a-maying
    With Nature, Hope, and Poesy,
        When I was young!

When I was young? — Ah, woful When!
Ah! for the change 'twixt Now and Then!
This breathing house not built with hands,
This body that does me grievous wrong,
O'er aery cliffs and glittering sands,
How lightly then it flashed along: —
Like those trim skiffs, unknown of yore,
On winding lakes and rivers wide,
That ask no aid of sail or oar,
That fear no spite of wind or tide!
Nought cared this body for wind or weather
When Youth and I lived in't together.

Flowers are lovely; Love is flower-like;
Friendship is a sheltering tree;
O! the joys, that came down shower-like,
Of Friendship, Love, and Liberty,
Ere I was old!

Ere I was old? Ah woful Ere,
Which tells me, Youth 's no longer here!
O Youth! for years so many and sweet,
'T is known, that Thou and I were one,
I'll think it but a fond conceit —
It cannot be that Thou art gone!
Thy vesper-bell hath not yet tolled: —
And thou wert aye a masker bold!
What strange disguise hast now put on,
To make believe, that thou art gone?
I see these locks in silvery slips,
This drooping gait, this altered size:
But Spring-tide blossoms on thy lips,
And tears take sunshine from thine eyes!
Life is but thought: so think I will
That Youth and I are house-mates still.

Dew-drops are the gems of morning,
But the tears of mournful eve!
Where no hope is, life 's a warning
That only serves to make us grieve,
When we are old:

That only serves to make us grieve
With oft and tedious taking-leave,
Like some poor nigh-related guest,
That may not rudely be dismist;
Yet hath outstayed his welcome while,
And tells the jest without the smile.

1828

WORK WITHOUT HOPE

All Nature seems at work. Slugs leave their lair —
The bees are stirring — birds are on the wing —
And Winter slumbering in the open air,
Wears on his smiling face a dream of Spring!
And I the while, the sole unbusy thing,
Nor honey make, nor pair, nor build, nor sing.

Yet well I ken the banks where amaranths blow,
Have traced the fount whence streams of nectar flow.
Bloom, O ye amaranths! bloom for whom ye may,
For me ye bloom not! Glide, rich streams, away!
With lips unbrightened, wreathless brow, I stroll:
And would you learn the spells that drowse my soul?
Work without Hope draws nectar in a sieve,
And Hope without an object cannot live.

1828

EPITAPH

Stop, Christian passer-by! — Stop, child of God,
And read with gentle breast. Beneath this sod
A poet lies, or that which once seemed he.
O, lift one thought in prayer for S. T. C.;
That he who many a year with toil of breath
Found death in life, may here find life in death!
Mercy for praise — to be forgiven for fame
He asked, and hoped, through Christ. Do thou the same!

1834

Walter Scott (1771-1832)

LOCHINVAR

O, young Lochinvar is come out of the west,
Through all the wide Border his steed was the best;
And save his good broadsword he weapons had none,
He rode all unarmed, and he rode all alone.
So faithful in love, and so dauntless in war,
There never was knight like the young Lochinvar.

He stayed not for brake, and he stopped not for stone,
He swam the Eske river where ford there was none;
But ere he alighted at Netherby gate,
The bride had consented, the gallant came late:
For a laggard in love, and a dastard in war,
Was to wed the fair Ellen of brave Lochinvar.

So boldly he entered the Netherby Hall,
Among bride's-men, and kinsmen, and brothers, and all:
Then spoke the bride's father, his hand on his sword,
(For the poor craven bridegroom said never a word,)
'O come ye in peace here, or come ye in war,
Or to dance at our bridal, young Lord Lochinvar?'

'I long wooed your daughter, my suit you denied; —
Love swells like the Solway, but ebbs like its tide —
And now am I come, with this lost love of mine,
To lead but one measure, drink one cup of wine.
There are maidens in Scotland more lovely by far,
That would gladly be bride to the young Lochinvar.'

The bride kissed the goblet: the knight took it up,
He quaffed off the wine, and he threw down the cup.
She looked down to blush, and she looked up to sigh,
With a smile on her lips, and a tear in her eye.
He took her soft hand, ere her mother could bar, —
'Now tread we a measure!' said young Lochinvar.

So stately his form, and so lovely her face,
That never a hall such a galliard did grace;
While her mother did fret, and her father did fume,
And the bridegroom stood dangling his bonnet and plume;
And the bride-maidens whispered, ''T were better by far,
To have matched our fair cousin with young Lochinvar.'

One touch to her hand, and one word in her ear,
When they reached the hall-door, and the charger stood near;
So light to the croupe the fair lady he swung,
So light to the saddle before her he sprung!
'She is won! we are gone, over bank, bush, and scaur;
They 'll have fleet steeds that follow,' quoth young Lochinvar.

There was mounting 'mong Graemes of the Netherby clan;
Forsters, Fenwicks, and Musgraves, they rode and they ran:
There was racing and chasing on Cannobie Lee,
But the lost bride of Netherby ne'er did they see.
So daring in love, and so dauntless in war,
Have ye e'er heard of gallant like young Lochinvar?

1808

MARMION

CANTO VI. — THE BATTLE

WHILE great events were on the gale,
And each hour brought a varying tale,
And the demeanour, changed and cold,
Of Douglas, fretted Marmion bold,
And, like the impatient steed of war,
He snuffed the battle from afar;
And hopes were none, that back again
Herald should come from Terouenne,
Where England's king in leaguer lay,
Before decisive battle-day;
Whilst these things were, the mournful Clare
Did in the Dame's devotions share:
For the good Countess ceaseless prayed
To Heaven and Saints, her sons to aid,
And, with short interval, did pass
From prayer to book, from book to mass,
And all in high Baronial pride, —
A life both dull and dignified;
Yet as Lord Marmion nothing pressed
Upon her intervals of rest,
Dejected Clara well could bear
The formal state, the lengthened prayer,
Though dearest to her wounded heart
The hours that she might spend apart.

I said, Tantallon's dizzy steep
Hung o'er the margin of the deep.
Many a rude tower and rampart there
Repelled the insult of the air,
Which, when the tempest vexed the sky,
Half breeze, half spray, came whistling by.
Above the rest, a turret square
Did o'er its Gothic entrance bear,
Of sculpture rude, a stony shield;
The Bloody Heart was in the Field,
And in the chief three mullets stood,
The cognizance of Douglas blood.
The turret held a narrow stair,
Which, mounted, gave you access where
A parapet's embattled row
Did seaward round the castle go.
Sometimes in dizzy steps descending,
Sometimes in narrow circuit bending,
Sometimes in platform broad extending,
Its varying circle did combine
Bulwark, and bartizan, and line,
And bastion, tower, and vantage-coign;
Above the booming ocean leant
The far-projecting battlement;
The billows burst, in ceaseless flow,
Upon the precipice below.
Where'er Tantallon faced the land,
Gate-works, and walls, were strongly manned;
No need upon the sea-girt side;

The steepy rock, and frantic tide,
Approach of human step denied;
And thus these lines and ramparts rude
Were left in deepest solitude.

And, for they were so lonely, Clare
Would to these battlements repair,
And muse upon her sorrows there,
  And list the sea-bird's cry;
Or slow, like noontide ghost, would glide
Along the dark-grey bulwarks' side,
And ever on the heaving tide
  Look down with weary eye.
Oft did the cliff and swelling main
Recall the thoughts of Whitby's fane, —
A home she ne'er might see again;
  For she had laid adown,
So Douglas bade, the hood and veil,
And frontlet of the cloister pale,
  And Benedictine gown:
It were unseemly sight, he said,
A novice out of convent shade.
Now her bright locks, with sunny glow,
Again adorned her brow of snow;
Her mantle rich, whose borders, round,
A deep and fretted broidery bound,
In golden foldings sought the ground;
Of holy ornament, alone
Remained a cross with ruby stone;
  And often did she look
On that which in her hand she bore,
With velvet bound, and broidered o'er,
  Her breviary book.
In such a place, so lone, so grim,
At dawning pale, or twilight dim,
  It fearful would have been
To meet a form so richly dressed
With book in hand, and cross on breast,
And such a woful mien.
Fitz-Eustace, loitering with his bow,
To practise on the gull and crow,
Saw her, at distance, gliding slow,
  And did by Mary swear
Some love-lorn Fay she might have been,
Or, in Romance, some spell-bound Queen;
For ne'er in work-day world was seen
  A form so witching fair.

Once walking thus, at evening tide,
It chanced a gliding sail she spied,
And, sighing, thought — 'The Abbess, there,
Perchance, does to her home repair;
Her peaceful rule, where Duty, free,
Walks hand in hand with Charity;
Where oft Devotion's trancèd glow
Can such a glimpse of heaven bestow,
That the enraptured sisters see
High vision and deep mystery;
The very form of Hilda fair,
Hovering upon the sunny air,
And smiling on her votaries' prayer.
O! wherefore, to my duller eye,
Did still the Saint her form deny!
Was it, that, seared by sinful scorn,
My heart could neither melt nor burn?
Or lie my warm affections low,
With him, that taught them first to glow?
Yet, gentle Abbess, well I knew,
To pay thy kindness grateful due,
And well could brook the mild command,
That ruled thy simple maiden band.
How different now! condemned to bide
My doom from this dark tyrant's pride.
But Marmion has to learn, ere long,
That constant mind, and hate of wrong,
Descended to a feeble girl,
From Red De Clare, stout Gloster's Earl:
Of such a stem, a sapling weak,
He ne'er shall bend, although he break.

'But see! what makes this armour here?' —
  For in her path there lay
Targe, corslet, helm; she viewed them near.
'The breast-plate pierced! — Ay, much I fear,
Weak fence wert thou 'gainst foeman's spear,
That hath made fatal entrance here,
  As these dark blood-gouts say.
Thus Wilton — oh! not corslet's ward,
Nor truth, as diamond pure and hard,
Could be thy manly bosom's guard,
  On yon disastrous day!'
She raised her eyes in mournful mood, —
Wilton himself before her stood!
It might have seemed his passing ghost,
For every youthful grace was lost;
And joy unwonted, and surprise,
Gave their strange wildness to his eyes.
Expect not, noble dames and lords,
That I can tell such scene in words:
What skilful limner e'er would choose
To paint the rainbow's varying hues,
Unless to mortal it were given
To dip his brush in dyes of heaven?
Far less can my weak line declare
  Each changing passion's shade;
Brightening to rapture from despair,
Sorrow, surprise, and pity there,
And joy, with her angelic air,
And hope, that paints the future fair,
  Their varying hues displayed:
Each o'er its rival's ground extending,
Alternate conquering, shifting, blending,
Till all, fatigued, the conflict yield,
And mighty Love retains the field.
Shortly I tell what then he said,
By many a tender word delayed,

And modest blush, and bursting sigh,
And question kind, and fond reply: —

'Forget we that disastrous day,
When senseless in the lists I lay.
Thence dragged, — but how I cannot know,
For sense and recollection fled, —
I found me on a pallet low,
Within my ancient beadsman's shed.
Austin, — remember'st thou, my Clare,
How thou didst blush, when the old man,
When first our infant love began,
Said we would make a matchless pair? —
Menials, and friends, and kinsmen fled
From the degraded traitor's bed, —
He only held my burning head,
And tended me for many a day,
While wounds and fever held their sway.
But far more needful was his care,
When sense returned to wake despair;
For I did tear the closing wound,
And dash me frantic on the ground,
If e'er I heard the name of Clare.
At length, to calmer reason brought,
Much by his kind attendance wrought,
With him I left my native strand,
And, in a Palmer's weeds arrayed,
My hated name and form to shade,
I journeyed many a land;
No more a lord of rank and birth,
But mingled with the dregs of earth.
Oft Austin for my reason feared,
When I would sit, and deeply brood
On dark revenge, and deeds of blood,
Or wild mad schemes upreared.
My friend at length fell sick, and said,
God would remove him soon:
And, while upon his dying bed,
He begged of me a boon —
If e'er my deadliest enemy
Beneath my brand should conquered lie,
Even then my mercy should awake,
And spare his life for Austin's sake.

'Still restless as a second Cain,
To Scotland next my route was ta'en,
Full well the paths I knew.
Fame of my fate made various sound,
That death in pilgrimage I found,
That I had perished of my wound, —
None cared which tale was true:
And living eye could never guess
De Wilton in his Palmer's dress;
For now that sable slough is shed,
And trimmed my shaggy beard and head,
I scarcely know me in the glass.
A chance most wondrous did provide,
That I should be that baron's guide —
I will not name his name!
Vengeance to God alone belongs;
But, when I think on all my wrongs,
My blood is liquid flame!
And ne'er the time shall I forget,
When, in a Scottish hostel set,
Dark looks we did exchange:
What were his thoughts I cannot tell;
But in my bosom mustered Hell
Its plans of dark revenge.

'A word of vulgar augury,
That broke from me, I scarce knew why,
Brought on a village tale;
Which wrought upon his moody sprite,
And sent him armèd forth by night.
I borrowed steed and mail,
And weapons, from his sleeping band;
And, passing from a postern door,
We met, and countered hand to hand, —
He fell on Gifford moor.
For the death-stroke my brand I drew,
(O then my helmèd head he knew,
The Palmer's cowl was gone,)
Then had three inches of my blade
The heavy debt of vengeance paid;
My hand the thought of Austin staid;
I left him there alone.
O good old man! even from the grave
Thy spirit could thy master save:
If I had slain my foeman, ne'er
Had Whitby's Abbess, in her fear,
Given to my hand this packet dear,
Of power to clear my injured fame,
And vindicate De Wilton's name.
Perchance you heard the Abbess tell
Of the strange pageantry of Hell,
That broke our secret speech —
It rose from the infernal shade,
Or featly was some juggle played,
A tale of peace to teach.
Appeal to Heaven I judged was best,
When my name came among the rest.

'Now here, within Tantallon Hold,
To Douglas late my tale I told,
To whom my house was known of old.
Won by my proofs, his falchion bright
This eve anew shall dub me knight.
These were the arms that once did turn
The tide of fight on Otterburne,
And Harry Hotspur forced to yield,
When the Dead Douglas won the field.
These Angus gave — his armourer's care,
Ere morn shall every breach repair;
For nought, he said, was in his halls,
But ancient armour on the walls,
And agèd chargers in the stalls,
And women, priests, and grey-haired men,

The rest were all in Twisel glen.
And now I watch my armour here,
By law of arms, till midnight's near;
Then, once again a belted knight,
Seek Surrey's camp with dawn of light.

'There soon again we meet, my Clare!
This Baron means to guide thee there:
Douglas reveres his King's command,
Else would he take thee from his band.
And there thy kinsman, Surrey, too,
Will give De Wilton justice due.
Now meeter far for martial broil,
Firmer my limbs, and strung by toil,
Once more' — 'O Wilton! must we then
Risk new-found happiness again,
  Trust fate of arms once more?
And is there not an humble glen,
  Where we, content and poor,
Might build a cottage in the shade,
A shepherd thou, and I to aid
  Thy task on dale and moor?
That reddening brow! — too well I know,
Not even thy Clare can peace bestow,
  While falsehood stains thy name:
Go then to fight! Clare bids thee go!
Clare can a warrior's feelings know,
  And weep a warrior's shame,
Can Red Earl Gilbert's spirit feel,
Buckle the spurs upon thy heel,
And belt thee with thy brand of steel,
  And send thee forth to fame!'

That night, upon the rocks and bay,
The midnight moonbeam slumbering lay,
And poured its silver light, and pure,
Through loop-hole, and through embrazure
  Upon Tantallon's tower and hall;
But chief where archèd windows wide
Illuminate the chapel's pride,
  The sober glances fall.
Much was there need; though, seamed with scars,
Two veterans of the Douglas' wars,
  Though two grey priests were there,
And each a blazing torch held high,
You could not by their blaze descry
  The chapel's carving fair.
Amid that dim and smoky light,
Chequering the silvery moonshine bright,
  A bishop by the altar stood,
  A noble lord of Douglas blood,
With mitre sheen, and rocquet white.
Yet showed his meek and thoughtful eye
But little pride of prelacy;
More pleased that, in a barbarous age,
He gave rude Scotland Virgil's page,
Than that beneath his rule he held
The bishopric of fair Dunkeld.

Beside him ancient Angus stood,
Doffed his furred gown, and sable hood:
O'er his huge form and visage pale,
He wore a cap and shirt of mail;
And leaned his large and wrinkled hand
Upon the huge and sweeping brand
Which wont of yore, in battle fray,
His foeman's limbs to shred away,
As wood-knife lops the sapling spray.
  He seemed as, from the tombs around
    Rising at judgment-day,
  Some giant Douglas may be found
    In all his old array;
So pale his face, so huge his limb,
So old his arms, his look so grim.

Then at the altar Wilton kneels,
And Clare the spurs bound on his heels;
And think what next he must have felt,
At buckling of the falchion belt!
  And judge how Clara changed her hue,
While fastening to her lover's side
A friend, which, though in danger tried,
  He once had found untrue!
Then Douglas struck him with his blade:
'Saint Michael and Saint Andrew aid,
    I dub thee knight.
Arise, Sir Ralph, De Wilton's heir!
For King, for Church, for Lady fair,
    See that thou fight.' —
And Bishop Gawain, as he rose,
Said — 'Wilton! grieve not for thy woes,
    Disgrace, and trouble;
For He who honour best bestows,
    May give thee double.' —
De Wilton sobbed, for sob he must —
'Where'er I meet a Douglas, trust
  That Douglas is my brother!' —
  'Nay, nay,' old Angus said, 'not so;
To Surrey's camp thou now must go,
  Thy wrongs no longer smother.
I have two sons in yonder field;
And, if thou meet'st them under shield,
Upon them bravely — do thy worst;
And foul fall him that blenches first!'

Not far advanced was morning day,
When Marmion did his troop array
  To Surrey's camp to ride;
He had safe conduct for his band,
Beneath the royal seal and hand,
  And Douglas gave a guide:
The ancient Earl, with stately grace,
Would Clara on her palfrey place,
And whispered in an under tone,
'Let the hawk stoop, his prey is flown.'
The train from out the castle drew,
But Marmion stopped to bid adieu: —
  'Though something I might plain,' he said,

'Of cold respect to stranger guest,
Sent hither by your king's behest,
While in Tantallon's towers I staid;
Part we in friendship from your land,
And, noble Earl, receive my hand.'
But Douglas round him drew his cloak,
Folded his arms, and thus he spoke:
'My manors, halls, and bowers shall still
Be open, at my Sovereign's will,
To each one whom he lists, howe'er
Unmeet to be the owner's peer.
My castles are my King's alone,
From turret to foundation-stone —
The hand of Douglas is his own;
And never shall in friendly grasp
The hand of such as Marmion clasp.'

Burned Marmion's swarthy cheek like fire,
And shook his very frame for ire,
And 'This to me!' he said;
'An 't were not for thy hoary beard,
Such hand as Marmion's had not spared
To cleave the Douglas' head!
And, first I tell thee, haughty Peer,
He who does England's message here,
Although the meanest in her state,
May well, proud Angus, be thy mate:
And, Douglas, more I tell thee here,
Even in thy pitch of pride,
Here in thy hold, thy vassals near —
(Nay, never look upon your lord,
And lay your hands upon your sword!)
I tell thee, thou 'rt defied!
And if thou said'st I am not peer
To any lord in Scotland here,
Lowland or Highland, far or near,
Lord Angus, thou hast lied!'
On the Earl's cheek the flush of rage
O'ercame the ashen hue of age:
Fierce he broke forth, 'And dar'st thou then
To beard the lion in his den,
The Douglas in his hall?
And hop'st thou hence unscathed to go?
No, by Saint Bride of Bothwell, no!
Up drawbridge, grooms — what, warder, ho!
Let the portcullis fall.'
Lord Marmion turned, — well was his need,
And dashed the rowels in his steed,
Like arrow through the archway sprung,
The ponderous grate behind him rung:
To pass there was such scanty room,
The bars, descending, razed his plume.

The steed along the drawbridge flies,
Just as it trembled on the rise;
Not lighter does the swallow skim
Along the smooth lake's level brim:
And when Lord Marmion reached his band,
He halts, and turns with clenchèd hand,
And shout of loud defiance pours,
And shook his gauntlet at the towers.
'Horse! horse!' the Douglas cried, 'and chase!'
But soon he reined his fury's pace:
'A royal messenger he came,
Though most unworthy of the name. —
A letter forged! Saint Jude to speed!
Did ever knight so foul a deed!
At first in heart it liked me ill,
When the king praised his clerkly skill.
Thanks to Saint Bothan, son of mine,
Save Gawain, ne'er could pen a line:
So swore I, and I swear it still,
Let my boy-bishop fret his fill.
Saint Mary mend my fiery mood!
Old age ne'er cools the Douglas blood,
I thought to slay him where he stood.
'T is pity of him too,' he cried:
'Bold can he speak, and fairly ride,
I warrant him a warrior tried.'
With this his mandate he recalls,
And slowly seeks his castle halls.

The day in Marmion's journey wore;
Yet, ere his passion's gust was o'er,
They crossed the heights of Stanrig-moor.
His troop more closely there he scanned,
And missed the Palmer from the band.
'Palmer or not,' young Blount did say,
'He parted at the peep of day;
Good sooth, it was in strange array.'
'In what array?' said Marmion quick.
'My lord, I ill can spell the trick;
But all night long, with clink and bang,
Close to my couch did hammers clang;
At dawn the falling drawbridge rang,
And from a loop-hole while I peep,
Old Bell-the-Cat came from the Keep,
Wrapped in a gown of sables fair,
As fearful of the morning air;
Beneath, when that was blown aside,
A rusty shirt of mail I spied,
By Archibald won in bloody work,
Against the Saracen and Turk:
Last night it hung not in the hall;
I thought some marvel would befall.
And next I saw them saddled lead
Old Cheviot forth, the Earl's best steed,
A matchless horse, though something old,
Prompt in his paces, cool and bold.
I heard the Sheriff Sholto say,
The Earl did much the Master pray
To use him on the battle-day;
But he preferred' — 'Nay, Henry, cease!
Thou sworn horse-courser, hold thy peace.
Eustace, thou bear'st a brain — I pray,
What did Blount see at break of day?'

'In brief, my lord, we both descried
(For then I stood by Henry's side)
The Palmer mount, and outwards ride,
Upon the Earl's own favourite steed:
All sheathed he was in armour bright,
And much resembled that same knight,
Subdued by you in Cotswold fight:
Lord Angus wished him speed.'
The instant that Fitz-Eustace spoke,
A sudden light on Marmion broke; —
'Ah! dastard fool, to reason lost!'
He muttered; ''t was nor fay nor ghost
I met upon the moonlight wold,
But living man of earthly mould.
O dotage blind and gross!
Had I but fought as wont, one thrust
Had laid De Wilton in the dust,
My path no more to cross.
How stand we now? — he told his tale
To Douglas; and with some avail;
'T was therefore gloomed his rugged brow.
Will Surrey dare to entertain,
'Gainst Marmion, charge disproved and vain?
Small risk of that, I trow.
Yet Clare's sharp questions must I shun,
Must separate Constance from the Nun —
O what a tangled web we weave,
When first we practise to deceive!
A Palmer too! — no wonder why
I felt rebuked beneath his eye:
I might have known there was but one,
Whose look could quell Lord Marmion.'

Stung with these thoughts, he urged to speed
His troop, and reached at eve the Tweed,
Where Lennel's convent closed their march;
(There now is left but one frail arch,
Yet mourn thou not its cells;
Our time a fair exchange has made;
Hard by, in hospitable shade,
A reverend pilgrim dwells,
Well worth the whole Bernardine brood,
That e'er wore sandal, frock, or hood.)
Yet did Saint Bernard's Abbot there
Give Marmion entertainment fair,
And lodging for his train and Clare.
Next morn the Baron climbed the tower,
To view afar the Scottish power,
Encamped on Flodden edge:
The white pavilions made a show,
Like remnants of the winter snow,
Along the dusky ridge.
Long Marmion looked: at length his eye
Unusual movement might descry
Amid the shifting lines:
The Scottish host drawn out appears,
For, flashing on the hedge of spears
The eastern sunbeam shines.
Their front now deepening, now extending;
Their flank inclining, wheeling, bending,
Now drawing back, and now descending,
The skilful Marmion well could know
They watched the motions of some foe,
Who traversed on the plain below.

Even so it was. From Flodden ridge
The Scots beheld the English host
Leave Barmore-wood, their evening post,
And heedful watched them as they crossed
The Till by Twisel Bridge.
High sight it is and haughty, while
They dive into the deep defile;
Beneath the caverned cliff they fall,
Beneath the castle's airy wall;
By rock, by oak, by hawthorn-tree,
Troop after troop are disappearing;
Troop after troop their banners rearing,
Upon the eastern bank you see;
Still pouring down the rocky den,
Where flows the sullen Till,
And rising from the dim-wood glen,
Standards on standards, men on men,
In slow succession still,
And, sweeping o'er the Gothic arch,
And pressing on, in ceaseless march,
To gain the opposing hill.
That morn, to many a trumpet clang,
Twisel! thy rock's deep echo rang;
And many a chief of birth and rank,
Saint Helen! at thy fountain drank.
Thy hawthorn glade, which now we see
In spring-tide bloom so lavishly,
Had then from many an axe its doom,
To give the marching columns room.

And why stands Scotland idly now,
Dark Flodden! on thy airy brow,
Since England gains the pass the while,
And struggles through the deep defile?
What checks the fiery soul of James?
Why sits that champion of the dames
Inactive on his steed,
And sees, between him and his land,
Between him and Tweed's southern strand,
His host Lord Surrey lead?
What 'vails the vain knight-errant's brand?
O, Douglas, for thy leading wand!
Fierce Randolph, for thy speed!
O! for one hour of Wallace wight,
Or well-skilled Bruce, to rule the fight,
And cry, 'Saint Andrew and our right!'
Another sight had seen that morn,
From Fate's dark book a leaf been torn,

And Flodden had been Bannockbourne!
The precious hour has passed in vain,
And England's host has gained the plain;
Wheeling their march, and circling still,
Around the base of Flodden hill.

Ere yet the bands met Marmion's eye
Fitz-Eustace shouted loud and high,
'Hark! hark! my lord, an English drum!
And see ascending squadrons come
Between Tweed's river and the hill,
Foot, horse, and cannon: hap what hap,
My basnet to a prentice cap,
Lord Surrey 's o'er the Till!
Yet more! yet more! — how fair arrayed
They file from out the hawthorn shade,
And sweep so gallant by!
With all their banners bravely spread,
And all their armour flashing high,
Saint George might waken from the dead,
To see fair England's standards fly.'
'Stint in thy prate,' quoth Blount, 'thou 'dst best,
And listen to our lord's behest.'
With kindling brow Lord Marmion said,
'This instant be our band arrayed;
The river must be quickly crossed,
That we may join Lord Surrey's host.
If fight King James, — as well I trust,
That fight he will, and fight he must, —
The Lady Clare behind our lines
Shall tarry, while the battle joins.'

Himself he swift on horseback threw,
Scarce to the Abbot bade adieu;
Far less would listen to his prayer
To leave behind the helpless Clare.
Down to the Tweed his band he drew,
And muttered as the flood they view,
'The pheasant in the falcon's claw,
He scarce will yield to please a daw:
Lord Angus may the Abbot awe,
So Clare shall bide with me.'
Then on that dangerous ford, and deep,
Where to the Tweed Leat's eddies creep,
He ventured desperately:
And not a moment will he bide,
Till squire, or groom, before him ride;
Headmost of all he stems the tide,
And stems it gallantly.
Eustace held Clare upon her horse,
Old Hubert led her rein,
Stoutly they braved the current's course,
And, though far downward driven per force,
The southern bank they gain;
Behind them, straggling, came to shore,
As best they might, the train:
Each o'er his head his yew-bow bore,
A caution not in vain;
Deep need that day that every string,
By wet unharmed, should sharply ring.
A moment then Lord Marmion staid,
And breathed his steed, his men arrayed,
Then forward moved his band,
Until, Lord Surrey's rear-guard won,
He halted by a Cross of Stone,
That, on a hillock standing lone,
Did all the field command.

Hence might they see the full array
Of either host, for deadly fray;
Their marshaled lines stretched east and west,
And fronted north and south,
And distant salutation passed
From the loud cannon mouth;
Not in the close successive rattle,
That breathes the voice of modern battle,
But slow and far between.
The hillock gained, Lord Marmion staid:
'Here, by this Cross,' he gently said,
'You well may view the scene.
Here shalt thou tarry, lovely Clare:
O! think of Marmion in thy prayer!
Thou wilt not? — well, no less my care
Shall, watchful, for thy weal prepare.
You, Blount and Eustace, are her guard,
With ten picked archers of my train;
With England if the day go hard,
To Berwick speed amain.
But if we conquer, cruel maid,
My spoils shall at your feet be laid,
When here we meet again.'
He waited not for answer there,
And would not mark the maid's despair,
Nor heed the discontented look
From either squire; but spurred amain,
And, dashing through the battle plain,
His way to Surrey took.

'The good Lord Marmion, by my life!
Welcome to danger's hour!
Short greeting serves in time of strife:
Thus have I ranged my power:
Myself will rule this central host,
Stout Stanley fronts their right,
My sons command the va'ward post,
With Brian Tunstall, stainless knight;
Lord Dacre, with his horsemen light,
Shall be in rearward of the fight,
And succour those that need it most.
Now, gallant Marmion, well I know,
Would gladly to the vanguard go;
Edmund, the Admiral, Tunstall there,
With thee their charge will blithely share;
There fight thine own retainers too,
Beneath De Burg, thy steward true.'

'Thanks, noble Surrey!' Marmion said,
Nor farther greeting there he paid;
But, parting like a thunderbolt,
First in the vanguard made a halt,
  Where such a shout there rose
Of Marmion! Marmion! that the cry,
Up Flodden mountain shrilling high,
  Startled the Scottish foes.

Blount and Fitz-Eustace rested still
With Lady Clare upon the hill!
On which (for far the day was spent),
The western sunbeams now were bent.
The cry they heard, its meaning knew,
Could plain their distant comrades view:
Sadly to Blount did Eustace say,
'Unworthy office here to stay!
No hope of gilded spurs to-day.
But see! look up — on Flodden bent
The Scottish foe has fired his tent.'
  And sudden, as he spoke,
From the sharp ridges of the hill,
All downward to the banks of Till,
  Was wreathed in sable smoke.
Volumed and fast, and rolling far,
The cloud enveloped Scotland's war,
  As down the hill they broke;
Nor martial shout, nor minstrel tone,
Announced their march; their tread alone,
At times one warning trumpet blown,
  At times a stifled hum,
Told England, from his mountain-throne
  King James did rushing come.
Scarce could they hear, or see their foes,
Until at weapon-point they close.
They close, in clouds of smoke and dust,
With sword-sway, and with lance's thrust;
  And such a yell was there,
Of sudden and portentous birth,
As if men fought upon the earth,
  And fiends in upper air;
O life and death were in the shout,
Recoil and rally, charge and rout,
  And triumph and despair.
Long looked the anxious squires; their eye
Could in the darkness nought descry.

At length the freshening western blast
Aside the shroud of battle cast;
And, first, the ridge of mingled spears
Above the brightening cloud appears;
And in the smoke the pennons flew,
As in the storm the white sea-mew.
Then marked they, dashing broad and far,
The broken billows of the war,
And plumèd crests of chieftains brave
Floating like foam upon the wave;
  But nought distinct they see:
Wide raged the battle on the plain;
Spears shook, and falchions flashed amain;
Fell England's arrow-flight like rain;
Crests rose, and stooped, and rose again,
  Wild and disorderly.
Amid the scene of tumult, high
They saw Lord Marmion's falcon fly:
And stainless Tunstall's banner white,
And Edmund Howard's lion bright,
Still bear them bravely in the fight:
  Although against them come,
Of gallant Gordons many a one,
And many a stubborn Badenoch-man,
And many a rugged Border clan,
  With Huntly, and with Home.

Far on the left, unseen the while,
Stanley broke Lennox and Argyle;
Though there the western mountaineer
Rushed with bare bosom on the spear,
And flung the feeble targe aside,
And with both hands the broadsword plied.
'T was vain: — But Fortune, on the right,
With fickle smile, cheered Scotland's fight.
Then fell that spotless banner white,
  The Howard's lion fell;
Yet still Lord Marmion's falcon flew
With wavering flight, while fiercer grew
  Around the battle-yell.
The Border slogan rent the sky!
A Home! a Gordon! was the cry:
  Loud were the clanging blows;
Advanced, forced back, now low, now high,
  The pennon sunk and rose;
As bends the bark's mast in the gale,
When rent are rigging, shrouds, and sail,
  It wavered mid the foes.
No longer Blount the view could bear:
'By Heaven, and all its saints! I swear
  I will not see it lost!
Fitz-Eustace, you with Lady Clare
May bid your beads, and patter prayer, —
  I gallop to the host.'
And to the fray he rode amain,
Followed by all the archer train.
The fiery youth, with desperate charge,
Made for a space an opening large,
  The rescued banner rose,
But darkly closed the war around,
Like pine-tree rooted from the ground,
  It sank among the foes.
Then Eustace mounted too: — yet staid
As loath to leave the helpless maid,
  When, fast as shaft can fly,
Bloodshot his eyes, his nostrils spread,
The loose rein dangling from his head,
Housing and saddle bloody red,
  Lord Marmion's steed rushed by;

And Eustace, maddening at the sight,
  A look and sign to Clara cast
  To mark he would return in haste,
Then plunged into the fight.

Ask me not what the maiden feels,
  Left in that dreadful hour alone:
Perchance her reason stoops or reels;
  Perchance a courage, not her own,
  Braces her mind to desperate tone.
The scattered van of England wheels;
  She only said, as loud in air
  The tumult roared, 'Is Wilton there?'
  They fly, or, maddened by despair,
  Fight but to die, — 'Is Wilton there?'
With that, straight up the hill there rode
  Two horsemen drenched with gore,
And in their arms, a helpless load,
  A wounded knight they bore.
His hand still strained the broken brand;
His arms were smeared with blood and sand:
Dragged from among the horses' feet,
With dinted shield, and helmet beat,
The falcon-crest and plumage gone,
Can that be haughty Marmion!
Young Blount his armour did unlace,
And, gazing on his ghastly face,
  Said, 'By Saint George, he 's gone!
That spear-wound has our master sped,
And see the deep cut on his head!
  Good-night to Marmion.'
'Unnurtured Blount! thy brawling cease:
He opes his eyes,' said Eustace; 'peace!'

When, doffed his casque, he felt free air,
Around 'gan Marmion wildly stare: —
'Where's Harry Blount? Fitz-Eustace where?
Linger ye here, ye hearts of hare!
Redeem my pennon, — charge again!
Cry 'Marmion to the rescue!' — Vain!
Last of my race, on battle-plain
That shout shall ne'er be heard again!
  Yet my last thought is England's; fly,
To Dacre bear my signet-ring:
Tell him his squadrons up to bring.
  Fitz-Eustace, to Lord Surrey hie;
Tunstall lies dead upon the field,
His lifeblood stains the spotless shield:
Edmund is down; — my life is reft;
The Admiral alone is left.
Let Stanley charge with spur of fire, —
With Chester charge, and Lancashire,
Full upon Scotland's central host,
Or victory and England's lost.
Must I bid twice? — hence, varlets! fly!
Leave Marmion here alone — to die.'
They parted, and alone he lay;
Clare drew her from the sight away,
Till pain wrung forth a lowly moan,
And half he murmured, 'Is there none,
  Of all my halls have nurst,
Page, squire, or groom, one cup to bring
Of blessèd water from the spring,
  To slake my dying thirst!'

O Woman! in our hours of ease,
Uncertain, coy, and hard to please,
And variable as the shade
By the light quivering aspen made;
When pain and anguish wring the brow,
A ministering angel thou!
Scarce were the piteous accents said,
When, with the Baron's casque, the maid
  To the nigh streamlet ran:
Forgot were hatred, wrongs, and fears;
The plaintive voice alone she hears,
  Sees but the dying man.
She stooped her by the runnel's side,
  But in abhorrence backward drew;
For, oozing from the mountain's side,
Where raged the war, a dark-red tide
  Was curdling in the streamlet blue.
Where shall she turn? — behold her mark
  A little fountain cell,
Where water, clear as diamond spark,
  In a stone basin fell.
Above, some half-worn letters say,

Drink. weary. pilgrim. drink. and. pray.
For. the. kind. soul. of. Sibyl. Grey.
  Who. built. this. cross. and. well.

She filled the helm, and back she hied,
And with surprise and joy espied
  A monk supporting Marmion's head:
A pious man, whom duty brought
To dubious verge of battle fought,
  To shrieve the dying, bless the dead.

Deep drank Lord Marmion of the wave,
And, as she stooped his brow to lave —
'Is it the hand of Clare,' he said,
'Or injured Constance, bathes my head?'
  Then, as remembrance rose, —
'Speak not to me of shrift or prayer!
  I must redress her woes.
Short space, few words, are mine to spare:
Forgive and listen, gentle Clare!'
  'Alas!' she said, 'the while, —
O, think of your immortal weal!
In vain for Constance is your zeal;
  She — died at Holy Isle.'
Lord Marmion started from the ground,
As light as if he felt no wound;
Though in the action burst the tide,
In torrents, from his wounded side.
'Then it was truth,' he said; 'I knew

That the dark presage must be true.
I would the Fiend, to whom belongs
The vengeance due to all her wrongs,
  Would spare me but a day!
For wasting fire, and dying groan,
And priests slain on the altar stone,
  Might bribe him for delay.
It may not be! this dizzy trance —
Curse on yon base marauder's lance,
And doubly cursed my failing brand!
A sinful heart makes feeble hand.'
Then, fainting, down on earth he sunk,
Supported by the trembling monk.

With fruitless labour, Clara bound,
And strove to stanch the gushing wound:
The Monk, with unavailing cares,
Exhausted all the Church's prayers.
Ever, he said, that, close and near,
A lady's voice was in his ear,
And that the priest he could not hear;
  For that she ever sung,
'*In the lost battle, borne down by the flying,*
Where mingles war's rattle with groans of the dying!'
  So the notes rung; —
'Avoid thee, Fiend! with cruel hand,
Shake not the dying sinner's sand!
O, look, my son, upon yon sign
Of the Redeemer's grace divine;
  O, think on faith and bliss!
By many a death-bed I have been,
And many a sinner's parting seen,
  But never aught like this.'
The war, that for a space did fail,
Now trebly thundering swelled the gale,
  And — Stanley! was the cry;
A light on Marmion's visage spread,
  And fired his glazing eye:
With dying hand above his head,
He shook the fragment of his blade,
  And shouted 'Victory!
Charge, Chester, charge! On, Stanley, on!'
Were the last words of Marmion.

By this though deep the evening fell,
Still rose the battle's deadly swell,
For still the Scots, around their King,
Unbroken, fought in desperate ring.
Where 's now their victor va'ward wing,
  Where Huntly, and where Home? —
O, for a blast of that dread horn,
On Fontarabian echoes borne,
  That to King Charles did come,
When Rowland brave, and Olivier,
And every paladin and peer,
  On Roncesvalles died!
Such blast might warn them, not in vain,
To quit the plunder of the slain,
And turn the doubtful day again,
  While yet on Flodden side,
Afar, the Royal Standard flies,
And round it toils, and bleeds, and dies,
  Our Caledonian pride!
In vain the wish — for far away,
While spoil and havoc mark their way,
Near Sybil's Cross the plunderers stray.
'Oh, lady,' cried the monk, 'away!'
  And placed her on her steed,
And led her to the chapel fair,
  Of Tilmouth upon Tweed.
There all the night they spent in prayer,
And at the dawn of morning, there
She met her kinsman, Lord Fitz-Clare.

But as they left the dark'ning heath,
More desperate grew the strife of death.
The English shafts in volleys hailed,
In headlong charge their horse assailed;
Front, flank, and rear, the squadrons sweep
To break the Scottish circle deep,
  That fought around their King.
But yet, though thick the shafts as snow,
Though charging knights like whirlwinds go,
Though bill-men ply the ghastly blow,
  Unbroken was the ring;
The stubborn spear-men still made good
Their dark impenetrable wood,
Each stepping where his comrade stood,
  The instant that he fell.
No thought was there of dastard flight;
Linked in the serried phalanx tight,
Groom fought like noble, squire like knight,
  As fearlessly and well;
Till utter darkness closed her wing
O'er their thin host and wounded King.
Then skilful Surrey's sage commands
Led back from strife his shattered bands;
  And from the charge they drew,
As mountain-waves, from wasted lands,
  Sweep back to ocean blue.
Then did their loss his foemen know;
Their King, their Lords, their mightiest low,
They melted from the field as snow,
When streams are swoln and south winds blow,
  Dissolves in silent dew.
Tweed's echoes heard the ceaseless plash,
  While many a broken band,
Disordered, through her currents dash,
  To gain the Scottish land;
To town and tower, to down and dale,
To tell red Flodden's dismal tale,
And raise the universal wail.
Tradition, legend, tune, and song,

Shall many an age that wail prolong:
Still from the sire the son shall hear
Of the stern strife, and carnage drear,
  Of Flodden's fatal field,
Where shivered was fair Scotland's spear,
  And broken was her shield!

Day dawns upon the mountain's side:
There, Scotland! lay thy bravest pride,
Chiefs, knights, and nobles, many a one:
The sad survivors all are gone.
View not that corpse mistrustfully,
Defaced and mangled though it be;
Nor to yon Border castle high
Look northward with upbraiding eye:
  Nor cherish hope in vain,
That, journeying far on foreign strand,
The Royal Pilgrim to his land
  May yet return again.
He saw the wreck his rashness wrought;
Reckless of life, he desperate fought,
  And fell on Flodden plain:
And well in death his trusty brand,
Firm clenched within his manly hand,
  Beseemed the Monarch slain.
But, O! how changed since yon blithe night!
Gladly I turn me from the sight,
  Unto my tale again.

Short is my tale: Fitz-Eustace' care
A pierced and mangled body bare
To moated Lichfield's lofty pile;
And there, beneath the southern aisle,
A tomb, with Gothic sculpture fair,
Did long Lord Marmion's image bear.
(Now vainly for its sight you look;
'T was levelled when fanatic Brook
The fair cathedral stormed and took;
But, thanks to Heaven and good Saint Chad,
A guerdon meet the spoiler had!)
There erst was martial Marmion found,
His feet upon a couchant hound,
  His hands to heaven upraised;
And all around, on scutcheon rich,
And tablet carved, and fretted niche,
  His arms and feats were blazed.
And yet, though all was carved so fair,
And priest for Marmion breathed the prayer,
The last Lord Marmion lay not there.
From Ettrick woods a peasant swain
Followed his lord to Flodden plain,—
One of those flowers, whom plaintive lay
In Scotland mourns as 'wede away':
Sore wounded, Sybil's Cross he spied,
And dragged him to its foot, and died,
Close by the noble Marmion's side.
The spoilers stripped and gashed the slain,
And thus their corpses were mista'en;
And thus, in the proud Baron's tomb,
The lowly woodsman took the room.

Less easy task it were, to show
Lord Marmion's nameless grave, and low.
  They dug his grave e'en where he lay,
    But every mark is gone;
  Time's wasting hand has done away
  The simple cross of Sybil Grey,
    And broke her font of stone;
But yet out from the little hill
Oozes the slender springlet still;
  Oft halts the stranger there,
For thence may best his curious eye
The memorable field descry;
  And shepherd boys repair
To seek the water-flag and rush,
And rest them by the hazel bush,
  And plait their garlands fair;
Nor dream they sit upon the grave,
That holds the bones of Marmion brave.
When thou shalt find the little hill,
With thy heart commune, and be still.
If ever, in temptation strong,
Thou left'st the right path for the wrong;
If every devious step, thus trod,
Still led thee farther from the road;
Dread thou to speak presumptuous doom
On noble Marmion's lowly tomb;
But say, 'He died a gallant knight,
With sword in hand, for England's right.'

I do not rhyme to that dull elf,
Who cannot image to himself,
That all through Flodden's dismal night,
Wilton was foremost in the fight;
That, when brave Surrey's steed was slain,
'T was Wilton mounted him again;
'T was Wilton's brand that deepest hewed,
Amid the spearmen's stubborn wood:
Unnamed by Holinshed or Hall,
He was the living soul of all:
That, after fight, his faith made plain,
He won his rank and lands again;
And charged his old paternal shield
With bearings won on Flodden Field.
Nor sing I to that simple maid,
To whom it must in terms be said,
That King and kinsmen did agree,
To bless fair Clara's constancy;
Who cannot, unless I relate,
Paint to her mind the bridal's state;
That Wolsey's voice the blessing spoke,

More, Sands, and Denny, passed the joke:
That bluff King Hal the curtain drew,
And Catherine's hand the stocking threw;
And afterwards, for many a day,
That it was held enough to say,
In blessing to a wedded pair,
'Love they like Wilton and like Clare!'

1808

SOLDIER, REST!

Soldier, rest! thy warfare o'er,
Sleep the sleep that knows not breaking;
Dream of battled fields no more,
Days of danger, nights of waking.
In our isle's enchanted hall,
Hands unseen thy couch are strewing,
Fairy strains of music fall,
Every sense in slumber dewing.
Soldier, rest! thy warfare o'er,
Dream of fighting fields no more:
Sleep the sleep that knows not breaking,
Morn of toil, nor night of waking.

No rude sound shall reach thine ear,
Armour's clang, or war-steed champing,
Trump nor pibroch summon here
Mustering clan, or squadron tramping.
Yet the lark's shrill fife may come
At the day-break from the fallow,
And the bittern sound his drum,
Booming from the sedgy shallow.
Ruder sounds shall none be near,
Guards nor warders challenge here,
Here 's no war-steed's neigh and champing,
Shouting clans, or squadrons stamping.

Huntsman, rest! thy chase is done;
While our slumbrous spells assail ye,
Dream not, with the rising sun,
Bugles here shall sound reveillé.
Sleep! the deer is in his den;
Sleep! thy hounds are by thee lying;
Sleep! nor dream in yonder glen,
How thy gallant steed lay dying.
Huntsman, rest! thy chase is done,
Think not of the rising sun,
For at dawning to assail ye,
Here no bugles sound reveillé.

1810

CORONACH

He is gone on the mountain,
He is lost to the forest,
Like a summer-dried fountain,
When our need was the sorest.
The font, reappearing,
From the rain-drops shall borrow,
But to us comes no cheering,
To Duncan no morrow!

The hand of the reaper
Takes the ears that are hoary,
But the voice of the weeper
Wails manhood in glory.
The autumn winds rushing
Waft the leaves that are searest,
But our flower was in flushing,
When blighting was nearest.

Fleet foot on the correi,
Sage counsel in cumber,
Red hand in the foray,
How sound is thy slumber!
Like the dew on the mountain,
Like the foam on the river,
Like the bubble on the fountain,
Thou art gone, and forever!

1810

BRIGNAL BANKS

O, Brignal banks are wild and fair,
And Greta woods are green,
And you may gather garlands there
Would grace a summer queen.
And as I rode by Dalton-hall,
Beneath the turrets high,
A maiden on the castle wall
Was singing merrily, —
'O, Brignal banks are fresh and fair,
And Greta woods are green;
I 'd rather rove with Edmund there,
Than reign our English queen.'

'If, maiden, thou wouldst wend with me,
To leave both tower and town,
Thou first must guess what life lead we,
That dwell by dale and down.
And if thou canst that riddle read,
As read full well you may,
Then to the greenwood shalt thou speed,
As blithe as Queen of May.'
Yet sung she, 'Brignal banks are fair,
And Greta woods are green;
I 'd rather rove with Edmund there,
Than reign our English queen.

'I read you, by your bugle-horn,
And by your palfrey good,
I read you for a ranger sworn,
To keep the king's greenwood.'

'A ranger, lady, winds his horn,
And 't is at peep of light;
His blast is heard at merry morn,
And mine at dead of night.'
Yet sung she, 'Brignal banks are fair,
And Greta woods are gay;
I would I were with Edmund there,
To reign his Queen of May!

'With burnished brand and musketoon,
So gallantly you come,
I read you for a bold dragoon,
That lists the tuck of drum.'
'I list no more the tuck of drum,
No more the trumpet hear;
But when the beetle sounds his hum,
My comrades take the spear.
And O! though Brignal banks be fair,
And Greta woods be gay,
Yet mickle must the maiden dare,
Would reign my Queen of May!

'Maiden! a nameless life I lead,
A nameless death I 'll die;
The fiend, whose lantern lights the mead,
Were better mate than I!
And when I 'm with my comrades met
Beneath the greenwood bough,
What once we were we all forget,
Nor think what we are now.
Yet Brignal banks are fresh and fair,
And Greta woods are green,
And you may gather garlands there
Would grace a summer queen.'

1812

PROUD MAISIE

PROUD Maisie is in the wood,
Walking so early;
Sweet Robin sits on the bush,
Singing so rarely.

'Tell me, thou bonny bird,
When shall I marry me?'
'When six braw gentlemen
Kirkward shall carry ye.'

'Who makes the bridal bed,
Birdie, say truly?'
'The grey-headed sexton
That delves the grave duly.

'The glow-worm o'er grave and stone
Shall light thee steady.
The owl from the steeple sing,
"Welcome, proud lady."'

1818

George Gordon (Lord) Byron
(1788–1824)

THE PRAYER OF NATURE

FATHER of Light! great God of Heaven!
Hear'st thou the accents of despair?
Can guilt like man's be e'er forgiven?
Can vice atone for crimes by prayer?

Father of Light, on thee I call!
Thou seest my soul is dark within;
Thou who canst mark the sparrow's fall,
Avert from me the death of sin.

No shrine I seek, to sects unknown;
Oh, point to me the path of truth!
Thy dread omnipotence I own;
Spare, yet amend, the faults of youth.

Let bigots rear a gloomy fane,
Let superstition hail the pile,
Let priests, to spread their sable reign,
With tales of mystic rites beguile.

Shall man confine his Maker's sway
To Gothic domes of mouldering stone?
Thy temple is the face of day;
Earth, ocean, heaven, thy boundless throne.

Shall man condemn his race to hell,
Unless they bend in pompous form?
Tell us that all, for one who fell,
Must perish in the mingling storm?

Shall each pretend to reach the skies,
Yet doom his brother to expire,
Whose soul a different hope supplies,
Or doctrines less severe inspire?

Shall these, by creeds they can't expound,
Prepare a fancied bliss or woe?
Shall reptiles, grovelling on the ground,
Their great Creator's purpose know?

Shall those, who live for self alone,
Whose years float on in daily crime —
Shall they by Faith for guilt atone,
And live beyond the bounds of Time?

Father! no prophet's laws I seek, —
Thy laws in Nature's works appear; —
I own myself corrupt and weak,
Yet will I pray, for thou wilt hear!

Thou, who canst guide the wandering star
Through trackless realms of æther's space;
Who calm'st the elemental war,
Whose hand from pole to pole I trace:

Thou, who in wisdom placed me here,
Who, when thou wilt, canst take me hence,
Ah! whilst I tread this earthly sphere,
Extend to me thy wide defence.

To Thee, my God, to thee I call!
Whatever weal or woe betide,
By thy command I rise or fall,
In thy protection I confide.

If, when this dust to dust 's restored,
My soul shall float on airy wing,
How shall thy glorious name adored
Inspire her feeble voice to sing!

But, if this fleeting spirit share
With clay the grave's eternal bed,
While life yet throbs I raise my prayer,
Though doomed no more to quit the dead.

To Thee I breathe my humble strain,
Grateful for all thy mercies past,
And hope, my God, to thee again
This erring life may fly at last.

1830

WHEN WE TWO PARTED

When we two parted
In silence and tears,
Half broken-hearted
To sever for years,
Pale grew thy cheek and cold,
Colder thy kiss;
Truly that hour foretold
Sorrow to this.

The dew of the morning
Sunk chill on my brow —
It felt like the warning
Of what I feel now.
Thy vows are all broken,
And light is thy fame:
I hear thy name spoken,
And share in its shame.

They name thee before me,
A knell to mine ear;
A shudder comes o'er me —
Why wert thou so dear?
They know not I knew thee,
Who knew thee too well: —
Long, long shall I rue thee,
Too deeply to tell.

In secret we met —
In silence I grieve,
That thy heart could forget,
Thy spirit deceive.
If I should meet thee
After long years,
How should I greet thee? —
With silence and tears.

1816

MAID OF ATHENS, ERE WE PART

Ζώη μοῦ, σᾶς ἀγαπῶ

Maid of Athens, ere we part,
Give, oh give me back my heart!
Or, since that has left my breast,
Keep it now, and take the rest!
Hear my vow before I go,
Ζώη μοῦ, σᾶς ἀγαπῶ.

By those tresses unconfined,
Wooed by each Ægean wind;
By those lids whose jetty fringe
Kiss thy soft cheeks' blooming tinge;
By those wild eyes like the roe,
Ζώη μοῦ, σᾶς ἀγαπῶ.

By that lip I long to taste;
By that zone-encircled waist;
By all the token-flowers that tell
What words can never speak so well;
By love's alternate joy and woe,
Ζώη μοῦ, σᾶς ἀγαπῶ.

Maid of Athens! I am gone:
Think of me, sweet! when alone.
Though I fly to Istambol,
Athens holds my heart and soul:
Can I cease to love thee? No!
Ζώη μοῦ, σᾶς ἀγαπῶ.

1812

SHE WALKS IN BEAUTY

She walks in beauty, like the night
Of cloudless climes and starry skies;
And all that 's best of dark and bright
Meet in her aspect and her eyes:
Thus mellowed to that tender light
Which heaven to gaudy day denies.

One shade the more, one ray the less,
Had half impaired the nameless grace
Which waves in every raven tress,
Or softly lightens o'er her face;
Where thoughts serenely sweet express
How pure, how dear their dwelling-place.

And on that cheek, and o'er that brow,
So soft, so calm, yet eloquent,
The smiles that win, the tints that glow,

But tell of days in goodness spent,
A mind at peace with all below,
A heart whose love is innocent!

1815

THE DESTRUCTION OF SENNACHERIB

The Assyrian came down like the wolf on the fold,
And his cohorts were gleaming in purple and gold;
And the sheen of their spears was like stars on the sea,
When the blue wave rolls nightly on deep Galilee.

Like the leaves of the forest when Summer is green,
That host with their banners at sunset were seen:
Like the leaves of the forest when Autumn hath blown,
That host on the morrow lay withered and strown.

For the Angel of Death spread his wings on the blast,
And breathed in the face of the foe as he passed;
And the eyes of the sleepers waxed deadly and chill,
And their hearts but once heaved, and for ever grew still!

And there lay the steed with his nostril all wide,
But through it there rolled not the breath of his pride;
And the foam of his gasping lay white on the turf,
And cold as the spray of the rock-beating surf.

And there lay the rider distorted and pale,
With the dew on his brow, and the rust on his mail:
And the tents were all silent, the banners alone,
The lances unlifted, the trumpet unblown.

And the widows of Ashur are loud in their wail,
And the idols are broke in the temple of Baal;
And the might of the Gentile, unsmote by the sword,
Hath melted like snow in the glance of the Lord!

1815

STANZAS FOR MUSIC

There 's not a joy the world can give like that it takes away,
When the glow of early thought declines in feeling's dull decay;
'T is not on youth's smooth cheek the blush alone, which fades so fast,
But the tender bloom of heart is gone, ere youth itself be past.

Then the few whose spirits float above the wreck of happiness
Are driven o'er the shoals of guilt or ocean of excess:
The magnet of their course is gone, or only points in vain
The shore to which their shivered sail shall never stretch again.

Then the mortal coldness of the soul like death itself comes down;
It cannot feel for others' woes, it dare not dream its own;
That heavy chill has frozen o'er the fountain of our tears,
And though the eye may sparkle still, 't is where the ice appears.

Though wit may flash from fluent lips, and mirth distract the breast,
Through midnight hours that yield no more their former hope of rest;
'T is but as ivy-leaves around the ruined turret wreath,
All green and wildly fresh without, but worn and grey beneath.

Oh could I feel as I have felt, — or be what I have been,
Or weep as I could once have wept o'er many a vanished scene;
As springs in deserts found seem sweet, all brackish though they be,
So, midst the withered waste of life, those tears would flow to me.

1816

FARE THEE WELL

Fare thee well! and if for ever,
Still for ever, fare thee well:
Even though unforgiving, never
'Gainst thee shall my heart rebel.

Would that breast were bared before thee
Where thy head so oft hath lain,
While that placid sleep came o'er thee
Which thou ne'er canst know again:

Would that breast, by thee glanced over,
  Every inmost thought could show!
Then thou wouldst at last discover
  'T was not well to spurn it so.

Though the world for this commend thee —
  Though it smile upon the blow,
Even its praises must offend thee,
  Founded on another's woe:

Though my many faults defaced me,
  Could no other arm be found,
Than the one which once embraced me,
  To inflict a cureless wound?

Yet, oh yet, thyself deceive not;
  Love may sink by slow decay,
But by sudden wrench, believe not
  Hearts can thus be torn away:

Still thine own its life retaineth,
  Still must mine, though bleeding, beat;
And the undying thought which paineth
  Is — that we no more may meet.

These are words of deeper sorrow
  Than the wail above the dead;
Both shall live, but every morrow
  Wake us from a widowed bed.

And when thou wouldst solace gather,
  When our child's first accents flow,
Wilt thou teach her to say 'Father!'
  Though his care she must forego?

When her little hands shall press thee,
  When her lip to thine is pressed,
Think of him whose prayer shall bless thee,
  Think of him thy love had blessed!

Should her lineaments resemble
  Those thou never more may'st see,
Then thy heart will softly tremble
  With a pulse yet true to me.

All my faults perchance thou knowest,
  All my madness none can know;
All my hopes, where'er thou goest,
  Wither, yet with *thee* they go.

Every feeling hath been shaken;
  Pride, which not a world could bow,
Bows to thee — by thee forsaken,
  Even my soul forsakes me now:

But 't is done — all words are idle —
  Words from me are vainer still;
But the thoughts we cannot bridle
  Force their way without the will.

Fare thee well! thus disunited,
  Torn from every nearer tie,
Seared in heart, and lone, and blighted,
  More than this I scarce can die.

1816

SO, WE'LL GO NO MORE A ROVING

So, we'll go no more a roving
  So late into the night,
Though the heart be still as loving,
  And the moon be still as bright.

For the sword outwears its sheath,
  And the soul wears out the breast,
And the heart must pause to breathe,
  And love itself have rest.

Though the night was made for loving,
  And the day returns too soon,
Yet we'll go no more a roving
  By the light of the moon.

1830

TO THOMAS MOORE

My boat is on the shore,
  And my bark is on the sea;
But, before I go, Tom Moore,
  Here's a double health to thee!

Here's a sigh to those who love me,
  And a smile to those who hate;
And, whatever sky's above me,
  Here's a heart for every fate.

Though the ocean roar around me,
  Yet it still shall bear me on;
Though a desert should surround me,
  It hath springs that may be won.

Were 't the last drop in the well,
  As I gasped upon the brink,
Ere my fainting spirit fell,
  'T is to thee that I would drink.

With that water, as this wine,
  The libation I would pour
Should be — peace with thine and mine,
  And a health to thee, Tom Moore.

1821

STANZAS WRITTEN ON THE ROAD BETWEEN FLORENCE AND PISA

Oh, talk not to me of a name great in story;
The days of our youth are the days of our
  glory;

And the myrtle and ivy of sweet two-and-twenty
Are worth all your laurels, though ever so plenty.

What are garlands and crowns to the brow that is wrinkled?
'T is but as a dead-flower with May-dew besprinkled.
Then away with all such from the head that is hoary!
What care I for the wreaths that can *only* give glory!

Oh Fame! — if I e'er took delight in thy praises,
'T was less for the sake of thy high-sounding phrases,
Than to see the bright eyes of the dear one discover,
She thought that I was not unworthy to love her.

There chiefly I sought thee, *there* only I found thee;
Her glance was the best of the rays that surround thee;
When it sparkled o'er aught that was bright in my story,
I knew it was love, and I felt it was glory.

1830

CHILDE HAROLD'S PILGRIMAGE

CANTO III

Is thy face like thy mother's, my fair child!
Ada! sole daughter of my house and heart?
When last I saw thy young blue eyes they smiled,
And then we parted, — not as now we part,
But with a hope. —
Awaking with a start,
The waters heave around me; and on high
The winds lift up their voices: I depart,
Whither I know not; but the hour's gone by,
When Albion's lessening shores could grieve or glad mine eye.

Once more upon the waters! yet once more!
And the waves bound beneath me as a steed
That knows his rider. Welcome to their roar!
Swift be their guidance, wheresoe'er it lead!
Though the strained mast should quiver as a reed,
And the rent canvas fluttering strew the gale,
Still must I on; for I am as a weed,
Flung from the rock, on Ocean's foam to sail
Where'er the surge may sweep, the tempest's breath prevail.

In my youth's summer I did sing of One,
The wandering outlaw of his own dark mind;
Again I seize the theme, then but begun,
And bear it with me, as the rushing wind
Bears the cloud onwards: in that Tale I find
The furrows of long thought, and dried-up tears,
Which, ebbing, leave a sterile track behind,
O'er which all heavily the journeying years
Plod the last sands of life, — where not a flower appears.

Since my young days of passion — joy, or pain,
Perchance my heart and harp have lost a string,
And both may jar: it may be, that in vain
I would essay as I have sung to sing.
Yet, though a dreary strain, to this I cling;
So that it wean me from the weary dream
Of selfish grief or gladness — so it fling
Forgetfulness around me — it shall seem
To me, though to none else, a not ungrateful theme.

He, who grown agèd in this world of woe,
In deeds, not years, piercing the depths of life,
So that no wonder waits him; nor below
Can love or sorrow, fame, ambition, strife,
Cut to his heart again with the keen knife
Of silent, sharp endurance: he can tell
Why thought seeks refuge in lone caves, yet rife
With airy images, and shapes which dwell
Still unimpaired, though old, in the soul's haunted cell.

'T is to create, and in creating live
A being more intense that we endow
With form our fancy, gaining as we give
The life we image, even as I do now.
What am I? Nothing: but not so art thou,
Soul of my thought! with whom I traverse earth,
Invisible but gazing, as I glow
Mixed with thy spirit, blended with thy birth,
And feeling still with thee in my crushed feelings' dearth.

Yet must I think less wildly: — I *have* thought
Too long and darkly, till my brain became,
In its own eddy boiling and o'erwrought,
A whirling gulf of phantasy and flame:
And thus, untaught in youth my heart to tame,
My springs of life were poisoned. 'T is too late!
Yet am I changed; though still enough the same
In strength to bear what time cannot abate,
And feed on bitter fruits without accusing Fate.

Something too much of this: — but now 't is past,
And the spell closes with its silent seal.
Long absent Harold re-appears at last;
He of the breast which fain no more would feel,
Wrung with the wounds which kill not, but ne'er heal;
Yet Time, who changes all, had altered him
In soul and aspect as in age: years steal
Fire from the mind as vigour from the limb;
And life's enchanted cup but sparkles near the brim.

His had been quaffed too quickly, and he found
The dregs were wormwood; but he filled again,
And from a purer fount, on holier ground,
And deemed its spring perpetual; but in vain!
Still round him clung invisibly a chain
Which galled for ever, fettering though unseen,
And heavy though it clanked not; worn with pain,
Which pined although it spoke not, and grew keen,
Entering with every step he took through many a scene.

Secure in guarded coldness, he had mixed
Again in fancied safety with his kind,
And deemed his spirit now so firmly fixed
And sheathed with an invulnerable mind,
That, if no joy, no sorrow lurked behind;
And he, as one, might 'midst the many stand
Unheeded, searching through the crowd to find
Fit speculation; such as in strange land
He found in wonder-works of God and Nature's hand.

But who can view the ripened rose, nor seek
To wear it? who can curiously behold
The smoothness and the sheen of beauty's cheek,
Nor feel the heart can never all grow old?
Who can contemplate Fame through clouds unfold
The star which rises o'er her steep, nor climb?
Harold, once more within the vortex, rolled
On with the giddy circle, chasing Time,
Yet with a nobler aim than in his youth's fond prime.

But soon he knew himself the most unfit
Of men to herd with Man; with whom he held
Little in common; untaught to submit
His thoughts to others, though his soul was quelled
In youth by his own thoughts; still uncompelled,
He would not yield dominion of his mind
To spirits against whom his own rebelled;
Proud though in desolation; which could find
A life within itself, to breathe without mankind.

Where rose the mountains, there to him were friends;
Where rolled the ocean, thereon was his home;
Where a blue sky, and glowing clime, extends,
He had the passion and the power to roam;
The desert, forest, cavern, breaker's foam,
Were unto him companionship; they spake
A mutual language, clearer than the tome
Of his land's tongue, which he would oft forsake
For Nature's pages glassed by sunbeams on the lake.

Like the Chaldean, he could watch the stars,
Till he had peopled them with beings bright
As their own beams; and earth, and earth-born jars,
And human frailties, were forgotten quite:
Could he have kept his spirit to that flight
He had been happy; but this clay will sink
Its spark immortal, envying it the light
To which it mounts, as if to break the link
That keeps us from yon heaven which woos us to its brink.

But in Man's dwellings he became a thing
Restless and worn, and stern and wearisome,
Drooped as a wild-born falcon with clipt wing,
To whom the boundless air alone were home:
Then came his fit again, which to o'ercome,

As eagerly the barred-up bird will beat
His breast and beak against his wiry dome
Till the blood tinge his plumage, so the heat
Of his impeded soul would through his bosom eat.

Self-exiled Harold wanders forth again,
With nought of hope left, but with less of gloom;
The very knowledge that he lived in vain,
That all was over on this side the tomb,
Had made Despair a smilingness assume,
Which, though 't were wild, — as on the plundered wreck
When mariners would madly meet their doom
With draughts intemperate on the sinking deck, —
Did yet inspire a cheer, which he forbore to check.

Stop! — for thy tread is on an Empire's dust!
An Earthquake's spoil is sepulchred below!
Is the spot marked with no colossal bust?
Nor column trophied for triumphal show?
None; but the moral's truth tells simpler so,
As the ground was before, thus let it be; —
How that red rain hath made the harvest grow!
And is this all the world has gained by thee,
Thou first and last of fields! king-making Victory?

And Harold stands upon this place of skulls,
The grave of France, the deadly Waterloo!
How in an hour the power which gave annuls
Its gifts, transferring fame as fleeting too!
In 'pride of place' here last the eagle flew,
Then tore with bloody talon the rent plain,
Pierced by the shaft of banded nations through;
Ambition's life and labours all were vain;
He wears the shattered links of the world's broken chain.

Fit retribution! Gaul may champ the bit
And foam in fetters; — but is Earth more free?
Did nations combat to make *One* submit;
Or league to teach all kings true sovereignty?
What! shall reviving Thraldom again be
The patched-up idol of enlightened days?
Shall we, who struck the Lion down, shall we
Pay the Wolf homage? proffering lowly gaze
And servile knees to thrones? No; *prove* before ye praise!

If not, o'er one fallen despot boast no more!
In vain fair cheeks were furrowed with hot tears
For Europe's flowers long rooted up before
The trampler of her vineyards; in vain years
Of death, depopulation, bondage, fears,
Have all been borne, and broken by the accord
Of roused-up millions; all that most endears
Glory, is when the myrtle wreathes a sword
Such as Harmodius drew on Athens' tyrant lord.

There was a sound of revelry by night,
And Belgium's capital had gathered then
Her Beauty and her Chivalry, and bright
The lamps shone o'er fair women and brave men;
A thousand hearts beat happily; and when
Music arose with its voluptuous swell,
Soft eyes looked love to eyes which spake again,
And all went merry as a marriage bell;
But hush! hark! a deep sound strikes like a rising knell!

Did ye not hear it? — No; 't was but the wind,
Or the car rattling o'er the stony street;
On with the dance! let joy be unconfined;
No sleep till morn, when Youth and Pleasure meet
To chase the glowing Hours with flying feet —
But hark! — that heavy sound breaks in once more,
As if the clouds its echo would repeat;
And nearer, clearer, deadlier than before!
Arm! Arm! it is — it is — the cannon's opening roar!

Within a windowed niche of that high hall
Sate Brunswick's fated chieftain; he did hear
That sound the first amidst the festival,
And caught its tone with Death's prophetic ear;
And when they smiled because he deemed it near,
His heart more truly knew that peal too well
Which stretched his father on a bloody bier,
And roused the vengeance blood alone could quell;
He rushed into the field, and, foremost fighting, fell.

Ah! then and there was hurrying to and fro,
And gathering tears, and tremblings of distress,
And cheeks all pale, which but an hour ago
Blushed at the praise of their own loveliness;
And there were sudden partings, such as press
The life from out young hearts, and choking sighs
Which ne'er might be repeated; who could guess
If ever more should meet those mutual eyes,
Since upon night so sweet such awful morn could rise!

And there was mounting in hot haste: the steed,
The mustering squadron, and the clattering car,
Went pouring forward with impetuous speed,
And swiftly forming in the ranks of war;
And the deep thunder peal on peal afar;
And near, the beat of the alarming drum
Roused up the soldier ere the morning star;
While thronged the citizens with terror dumb,
Or whispering, with white lips — 'The foe! they come! they come!'

And wild and high the 'Cameron's gathering' rose!
The war-note of Lochiel, which Albyn's hills
Have heard, and heard, too, have her Saxon foes: —
How in the noon of night that pibroch thrills,
Savage and shrill! But with the breath which fills
Their mountain-pipe, so fill the mountaineers
With the fierce native daring which instils
The stirring memory of a thousand years,
And Evan's, Donald's fame rings in each clansman's ears!

And Ardennes waves above them her green leaves,
Dewy with nature's tear-drops as they pass,
Grieving, if aught inanimate e'er grieves,
Over the unreturning brave, — alas!
Ere evening to be trodden like the grass
Which now beneath them, but above shall grow
In its next verdure, when this fiery mass
Of living valour, rolling on the foe
And burning with high hope shall moulder cold and low.

Last noon beheld them full of lusty life,
Last eve in Beauty's circle proudly gay,
The midnight brought the signal-sound of strife,
The morn the marshalling in arms, — the day
Battle's magnificently stern array!
The thunder-clouds close o'er it, which when rent
The earth is covered thick with other clay,
Which her own clay shall cover, heaped and pent,
Rider and horse, — friend, foe, — in one red burial blent!

Their praise is hymned by loftier harps than mine:
Yet one I would select from that proud throng,
Partly because they blend me with his line,
And partly that I did his sire some wrong,
And partly that bright names will hallow song;
And his was of the bravest, and when showered
The death-bolts deadliest the thinned files along,
Even where the thickest of war's tempest lowered,
They reached no nobler breast than thine, young gallant Howard!

There have been tears and breaking hearts for thee,
And mine were nothing had I such to give;
But when I stood beneath the fresh green tree,
Which living waves where thou didst cease to live,
And saw around me the wide field revive
With fruits and fertile promise, and the Spring
Came forth her work of gladness to contrive,
With all her reckless birds upon the wing,
I turned from all she brought to those she could not bring.

I turned to thee, to thousands, of whom each
And one as all a ghastly gap did make
In his own kind and kindred, whom to teach
Forgetfulness were mercy for their sake;
The Archangel's trump, not Glory's, must awake
Those whom they thirst for; though the sound of Fame
May for a moment soothe, it cannot slake
The fever of vain longing, and the name
So honoured but assumes a stronger, bitterer claim.

They mourn, but smile at length; and, smiling,
The tree will wither long before it fall;
The hull drives on, though mast and sail be torn;
The roof-tree sinks, but moulders on the hall
In massy hoariness; the ruined wall
Stands when its wind-worn battlements are gone;
The bars survive the captive they enthral;
The day drags through, though storms keep out the sun;
And thus the heart will break, yet brokenly live on:

Even as a broken mirror, which the glass
In every fragment multiplies; and makes
A thousand images of one that was,
The same, and still the more, the more it breaks;
And thus the heart will do which not forsakes,
Living in shattered guise; and still, and cold,
And bloodless, with its sleepless sorrow aches,
Yet withers on till all without is old,
Showing no visible sign, for such things are untold.

There is a very life in our despair,
Vitality of poison, — a quick root
Which feeds these deadly branches; for it were
As nothing did we die; but Life will suit
Itself to Sorrow's most detested fruit,
Like to the apples on the Dead Sea's shore,
All ashes to the taste: Did man compute
Existence by enjoyment, and count o'er
Such hours 'gainst years of life, — say, would he name threescore?

The Psalmist numbered out the years of man:
They are enough; and if thy tale be *true*,
Thou, who didst grudge him even that fleeting span,
More than enough, thou fatal Waterloo!
Millions of tongues record thee, and anew
Their children's lips shall echo them, and say —
'Here, where the sword united nations drew,
Our countrymen were warring on that day!'
And this is much, and all which will not pass away.

There sunk the greatest, nor the worst of men,
Whose spirit, antithetically mixt,
One moment of the mightiest, and again
On little objects with like firmness fixt;
Extreme in all things! hadst thou been betwixt,
Thy throne had still been thine, or never been;
For daring made thy rise as fall: thou seek'st
Even now to re-assume the imperial mien,
And shake again the world, the Thunderer of the scene!

Conqueror and captive of the earth art thou!
She trembles at thee still, and thy wild name
Was ne'er more bruited in men's minds than now
That thou art nothing, save the jest of Fame,
Who wooed thee once, thy vassal, and became
The flatterer of thy fierceness, till thou wert
A god unto thyself; nor less the same
To the astounded kingdoms all inert,
Who deemed thee for a time whate'er thou didst assert.

Oh, more or less than man — in high or low,
Battling with nations, flying from the field;
Now making monarchs' necks thy footstool, now
More than thy meanest soldier taught to yield;
An empire thou couldst crush, command, rebuild,
But govern not thy pettiest passion, nor,
However deeply in men's spirits skilled,
Look through thine own, nor curb the lust of war,
Nor learn that tempted Fate will leave the loftiest star.

Yet well thy soul hath brooked the turning tide
With that untaught innate philosophy,
Which, be it wisdom, coldness, or deep pride,
Is gall and wormwood to an enemy.
When the whole host of hatred stood hard by,
To watch and mock thee shrinking, thou hast smiled
With a sedate and all-enduring eye; —
When Fortune fled her spoiled and favourite child,
He stood unbowed beneath the ills upon him piled.

Sager than in thy fortunes; for in them
Ambition steeled thee on too far to show
That just habitual scorn, which could contemn

Men and their thoughts; 't was wise to feel, not so
To wear it ever on thy lip and brow,
And spurn the instruments thou wert to use
Till they were turned unto thine overthrow:
'T is but a worthless world to win or lose;
So hath it proved to thee, and all such lot who choose.

If, like a tower upon a headland rock,
Thou hast been made to stand or fall alone,
Such scorn of man had helped to brave the shock;
But men's thoughts were the steps which paved thy throne,
Their admiration thy best weapon shone;
The part of Philip's son was thine, not then
(Unless aside thy purple had been thrown)
Like stern Diogenes to mock at men;
For sceptred cynics earth were far too wide a den.

But quiet to quick bosoms is a hell,
And *there* hath been thy bane; there is a fire
And motion of the soul which will not dwell
In its own narrow being, but aspire
Beyond the fitting medium of desire;
And, but once kindled, quenchless evermore,
Preys upon high adventure, nor can tire
Of aught but rest; a fever at the core,
Fatal to him who bears, to all who ever bore.

This makes the madmen who have made men mad
By their contagion; Conquerors and Kings,
Founders of sects and systems, to whom add
Sophists, Bards, Statesmen, all unquiet things
Which stir too strongly the soul's secret springs,
And are themselves the fools to those they fool;
Envied, yet how unenviable! what stings
Are theirs! One breast laid open were a school
Which would unteach mankind the lust to shine or rule:

Their breath is agitation, and their life
A storm whereon they ride, to sink at last,
And yet so nursed and bigoted to strife,
That should their days, surviving perils past,
Melt to calm twilight, they feel overcast
With sorrow and supineness, and so die;
Even as a flame unfed, which runs to waste
With its own flickering, or a sword laid by,
Which eats into itself, and rusts ingloriously.

He who ascends to mountain-tops, shall find
The loftiest peaks most wrapt in clouds and snow;
He who surpasses or subdues mankind,
Must look down on the hate of those below.
Though high *above* the sun of glory glow,
And far *beneath* the earth and ocean spread,
Round him are icy rocks, and loudly blow
Contending tempests on his naked head,
And thus reward the toils which to those summits led.

Away with these! true Wisdom's world will be
Within its own creation, or in thine,
Maternal Nature! for who teems like thee,
Thus on the banks of thy majestic Rhine?
There Harold gazes on a work divine,
A blending of all beauties; streams and dells,
Fruit, foliage, crag, wood, cornfield, mountain, vine,
And chiefless castles breathing stern farewells
From gray but leafy walls, where Ruin greenly dwells.

And there they stand, as stands a lofty mind,
Worn, but unstooping to the baser crowd,
All tenantless, save to the crannying wind,
Or holding dark communion with the crowd.
There was a day when they were young and proud;
Banners on high, and battles passed below;
But they who fought are in a bloody shroud,
And those which waved are shredless dust ere now,
And the bleak battlements shall bear no future blow.

Beneath those battlements, within those walls,
Power dwelt amidst her passions; in proud state
Each robber chief upheld his armèd halls,
Doing his evil will, nor less elate
Than mightier heroes of a longer date.
What want these outlaws conquerors should have
But history's purchased page to call them great?
A wider space, an ornamented grave?
Their hopes were not less warm, their souls were full as brave.

In their baronial feuds and single fields,
What deeds of prowess unrecorded died!
And Love, which lent a blazon to their
shields,
With emblems well devised by amorous
pride,
Through all the mail of iron hearts would
glide;
But still their flame was fierceness, and drew
on
Keen contest and destruction near allied,
And many a tower for some fair mischief
won,
Saw the discoloured Rhine beneath its ruin
run.

But Thou, exulting and abounding river!
Making thy waves a blessing as they flow
Through banks whose beauty would endure
for ever
Could man but leave thy bright creation
so,
Nor its fair promise from the surface mow
With the sharp scythe of conflict, — then to
see
Thy valley of sweet waters, were to know
Earth paved like Heaven; and to seem such
to me,
Even now what wants thy stream? — that
it should Lethe be.

A thousand battles have assailed thy banks,
But these and half their fame have passed
away,
And Slaughter heaped on high his weltering
ranks;
Their very graves are gone, and what are
they?
Thy tide washed down the blood of yester-
day,
And all was stainless, and on thy clear stream
Glassed, with its dancing light, the sunny
ray;
But o'er the blackened memory's blighting
dream
Thy waves would vainly roll, all sweeping as
they seem.

Thus Harold inly said, and passed along,
Yet not insensible to all which here
Awoke the jocund birds to early song
In glens which might have made even exile
dear:
Though on his brow were graven lines austere,
And tranquil sternness, which had ta'en the
place
Of feelings fierier far but less severe,
Joy was not always absent from his face,
But o'er it in such scenes would steal with
transient trace.

Nor was all love shut from him, though his
days
Of passion had consumed themselves to
dust.
It is in vain that we would coldly gaze
On such as smile upon us; the heart must
Leap kindly back to kindness, though disgust
Hath weaned it from all worldlings: thus he
felt,
For there was soft remembrance, and sweet
trust
In one fond breast, to which his own would
melt,
And in its tenderer hour on that his bosom
dwelt.

And he had learned to love, — I know not
why,
For this in such as him seems strange of
mood, —
The helpless looks of blooming infancy,
Even in its earliest nurture; what subdued,
To change like this, a mind so far imbued
With scorn of man, it little boots to know;
But thus it was; and though in solitude
Small power the nipped affections have to
grow,
In him this glowed when all beside had
ceased to glow.

And there was one soft breast, as hath been
said,
Which unto his was bound by stronger ties
Than the church links withal; and, though
unwed,
That love was pure, and, far above dis-
guise,
Had stood the test of mortal enmities
Still undivided, and cemented more
By peril, dreaded most in female eyes;
But this was firm, and from a foreign shore
Well to that heart might his these absent
greetings pour!

The castled crag of Drachenfels
Frowns o'er the wide and winding Rhine,
Whose breast of waters broadly swells
Between the banks which bear the vine,
And hills all rich with blossomed trees,
And fields which promise corn and wine,
And scattered cities crowning these,
Whose far white walls along them shine,
Have strewed a scene, which I should
see
With double joy wert *thou* with me.

And peasant girls, with deep blue eyes,
And hands which offer early flowers,
Walk smiling o'er this paradise;
Above, the frequent feudal towers

Through green leaves lift their walls of gray;
And many a rock which steeply lowers,
And noble arch in proud decay,
Look o'er this vale of vintage-bowers;
But one thing want these banks of Rhine,—
Thy gentle hand to clasp in mine!

I send the lilies given to me;
Though long before thy hand they touch,
I know that they must withered be,
But yet reject them not as such;
For I have cherished them as dear,
Because they yet may meet thine eye,
And guide thy soul to mine even here,
When thou behold'st them drooping nigh,
And know'st them gathered by the Rhine,
And offered from my heart to thine!

The river nobly foams and flows,
The charm of this enchanted ground,
And all its thousand turns disclose
Some fresher beauty varying round:
The haughtiest breast its wish might bound
Through life to dwell delighted here;
Nor could on earth a spot be found
To nature and to me so dear,
Could thy dear eyes in following mine
Still sweeten more these banks of Rhine!

By Coblentz, on a rise of gentle ground,
There is a small and simple pyramid,
Crowning the summit of the verdant mound;
Beneath its base are heroes' ashes hid,
Our enemy's — but let not that forbid
Honour to Marceau! o'er whose early tomb
Tears, big tears, gushed from the rough soldier's lid,
Lamenting and yet envying such a doom,
Falling for France, whose rights he battled to resume.

Brief, brave, and glorious was his young career, —
His mourners were two hosts, his friends and foes;
And fitly may the stranger lingering here
Pray for his gallant spirit's bright repose;
For he was Freedom's champion, one of those,
The few in number, who had not o'erstept
The charter to chastise which she bestows
On such as wield her weapons; he had kept
The whiteness of his soul, and thus men o'er him wept.

Here Ehrenbreitstein, with her shattered wall
Black with the miner's blast, upon her height
Yet shows of what she was, when shell and ball
Rebounding idly on her strength did light:
A tower of victory! from whence the flight
Of baffled foes was watched along the plain:
But Peace destroyed what War could never blight,
And laid those proud roofs bare to Summer's rain —
On which the iron shower for years had poured in vain.

Adieu to thee, fair Rhine! How long delighted
The stranger fain would linger on his way!
Thine is a scene alike where souls united
Or lonely Contemplation thus might stray;
And could the ceaseless vultures cease to prey
On self-condemning bosoms, it were here,
Where Nature, nor too sombre nor too gay,
Wild but not rude, awful yet not austere,
Is to the mellow Earth as Autumn to the year.

Adieu to thee again! a vain adieu!
There can be no farewell to scene like thine;
The mind is coloured by thy every hue;
And if reluctantly the eyes resign
Their cherished gaze upon thee, lovely Rhine!
'T is with the thankful heart of parting praise;
More mighty spots may rise, more glaring shine,
But none unite in one attaching maze
The brilliant, fair, and soft, — the glories of old days.

The negligently grand, the fruitful bloom
Of coming ripeness, the white city's sheen,
The rolling stream, the precipice's gloom,
The forest's growth, and Gothic walls between,
The wild rocks shaped as they had turrets been,
In mockery of man's art; and these withal
A race of faces happy as the scene,
Whose fertile bounties here extend to all,
Still springing o'er thy banks, though Empires near them fall.

But these recede. Above me are the Alps,
The palaces of Nature, whose vast walls
Have pinnacled in clouds their snowy scalps,

And throned Eternity in icy halls
Of cold sublimity, where forms and falls
The avalanche — the thunderbolt of snow!
All that expands the spirit, yet appals,
Gather around these summits, as to show
How Earth may pierce to Heaven, yet leave vain man below.

But ere these matchless heights I dare to scan,
There is a spot should not be passed in vain, —
Morat! the proud, the patriot field! where man
May gaze on ghastly trophies of the slain,
Nor blush for those who conquered on that plain;
Here Burgundy bequeathed his tombless host,
A bony heap, through ages to remain,
Themselves their monument; — the Stygian coast
Unsepulchred they roamed, and shrieked each wandering ghost.

While Waterloo with Cannæ's carnage vies,
Morat and Marathon twin names shall stand;
They were true Glory's stainless victories,
Won by the unambitious heart and hand
Of a proud, brotherly, and civic band,
All unbought champions in no princely cause
Of vice-entailed Corruption; they no land
Doomed to bewail the blasphemy of laws
Making kings' rights divine, by some Draconic clause.

By a lone wall a lonelier column rears
A gray and grief-worn aspect of old days;
'T is the last remnant of the wreck of years,
And looks as with the wild-bewildered gaze
Of one to stone converted by amaze,
Yet still with consciousness; and there it stands
Making a marvel that it not decays,
When the coeval pride of human hands,
Levelled Adventicum, hath strewed her subject lands.

And there — oh! sweet and sacred be the name! —
Julia — the daughter, the devoted — gave
Her youth to Heaven; her heart, beneath a claim
Nearest to Heaven's, broke o'er a father's grave.
Justice is sworn 'gainst tears, and hers would crave
The life she lived in; but the judge was just,
And then she died on him she could not save.
Their tomb was simple, and without a bust,
And held within their urn one mind, one heart, one dust.

But these are deeds which should not pass away,
And names that must not wither, though the earth
Forgets her empires with a just decay,
The enslavers and the enslaved, their death and birth;
The high, the mountain-majesty of worth
Should be, and shall, survivor of its woe,
And from its immortality look forth
In the sun's face, like yonder Alpine snow,
Imperishably pure beyond all things below.

Lake Leman woos me with its crystal face,
The mirror where the stars and mountains view
The stillness of their aspect in each trace
Its clear depth yields of their far height and hue:
There is too much of man here, to look through
With a fit mind the might which I behold;
But soon in me shall Loneliness renew
Thoughts hid, but not less cherished than of old,
Ere mingling with the herd had penned me in their fold.

To fly from, need not be to hate, mankind:
All are not fit with them to stir and toil,
Nor is it discontent to keep the mind
Deep in its fountain, lest it overboil
In the hot throng, where we become the spoil
Of our infection, till too late and long
We may deplore and struggle with the coil,
In wretched interchange of wrong for wrong
Midst a contentious world, striving where none are strong.

There, in a moment we may plunge our years
In fatal penitence, and in the blight
Of our own soul turn all our blood to tears,
And colour things to come with hues of Night;
The race of life becomes a hopeless flight
To those that walk in darkness: on the sea
The boldest steer but where their ports invite;
But there are wanderers o'er Eternity
Whose bark drives on and on, and anchored ne'er shall be.

Is it not better, then, to be alone,
And love Earth only for its earthly sake?
By the blue rushing of the arrowy Rhone,
Or the pure bosom of its nursing lake,
Which feeds it as a mother who doth make
A fair but froward infant her own care,
Kissing its cries away as these awake; —
Is it not better thus our lives to wear,
Than join the crushing crowd, doomed to inflict or bear?

I live not in myself, but I become
Portion of that around me; and to me
High mountains are a feeling, but the hum
Of human cities torture: I can see
Nothing to loathe in nature, save to be
A link reluctant in a fleshly chain,
Classed among creatures, when the soul can flee,
And with the sky, the peak, the heaving plain
Of ocean, or the stars, mingle, and not in vain.

And thus I am absorbed, and this is life:
I look upon the peopled desert past,
As on a place of agony and strife,
Where, for some sin, to sorrow I was cast,
To act and suffer, but remount at last
With a fresh pinion; which I feel to spring,
Though young, yet waxing vigorous as the blast
Which it would cope with, on delighted wing,
Spurning the clay-cold bonds which round our being cling.

And when, at length, the mind shall be all free
From what it hates in this degraded form,
Reft of its carnal life, save what shall be
Existent happier in the fly and worm, —
When elements to elements conform,
And dust is as it should be, shall I not
Feel all I see, less dazzling, but more warm?
The bodiless thought? the Spirit of each spot?
Of which, even now, I share at times the immortal lot?

Are not the mountains, waves, and skies, a part
Of me and of my soul, as I of them?
Is not the love of these deep in my heart
With a pure passion? should I not contemn
All objects, if compared with these? and stem
A tide of suffering, rather than forego
Such feelings for the hard and worldly phlegm
Of those whose eyes are only turned below,
Gazing upon the ground, with thoughts which dare not glow?

But this is not my theme; and I return
To that which is immediate, and require
Those who find contemplation in the urn,
To look on One, whose dust was once all fire,
A native of the land where I respire
The clear air for a while — a passing guest,
Where he became a being, — whose desire
Was to be glorious; 't was a foolish quest,
The which to gain and keep, he sacrificed all rest.

Here the self-torturing sophist, wild Rousseau,
The apostle of affliction, he who threw
Enchantment over passion, and from woe
Wrung overwhelming eloquence, first drew
The breath which made him wretched; yet he knew
How to make madness beautiful, and cast
O'er erring deeds and thoughts a heavenly hue
Of words, like sunbeams, dazzling as they past
The eyes, which o'er them shed tears feelingly and fast.

His love was passion's essence: — as a tree
On fire by lightning, with ethereal flame
Kindled he was, and blasted; for to be
Thus, and enamoured, were in him the same.
But his was not the love of living dame,
Nor of the dead who rise upon our dreams,
But of ideal beauty, which became
In him existence, and o'erflowing teems
Along his burning page, distempered though it seems.

This breathed itself to life in Julie, *this*
Invested her with all that 's wild and sweet;
This hallowed, too, the memorable kiss
Which every morn his fevered lip would greet,
From hers, who but with friendship his would meet;
But to that gentle touch through brain and breast
Flashed the thrilled spirit's love-devouring heat;
In that absorbing sigh perchance more blest
Than vulgar minds may be with all they seek possest.

His life was one long war with self-sought foes,
Or friends by him self-banished; for his mind
Had grown Suspicion's sanctuary, and chose,
For its own cruel sacrifice, the kind,
'Gainst whom he raged with fury strange and blind.
But he was phrensied, — wherefore, who may know?
Since cause might be which skill could never find;
But he was phrensied by disease or woe,
To that worst pitch of all, which wears a reasoning show.

For then he was inspired, and from him came,
As from the Pythian's mystic cave of yore,
Those oracles which set the world in flame,
Nor ceased to burn till kingdoms were no more:
Did he not this for France? which lay before
Bowed to the inborn tyranny of years?
Broken and trembling to the yoke she bore,
Till by the voice of him and his compeers
Roused up to too much wrath, which follows o'ergrown fears?

They made themselves a fearful monument!
The wreck of old opinions — things which grew,
Breathed from the birth of time: the veil they rent,
And what behind it lay, all earth shall view.
But good with ill they also overthrew,
Leaving but ruins, wherewith to rebuild
Upon the same foundation, and renew
Dungeons and thrones, which the same hour refilled,
As heretofore, because ambition was self-willed.

But this will not endure, nor be endured!
Mankind have felt their strength, and made it felt.
They might have used it better, but, allured
By their new vigour, sternly have they dealt
On one another; pity ceased to melt
With her once natural charities. But they,
Who in oppression's darkness caved had dwelt,
They were not eagles, nourished with the day;
What marvel then, at times, if they mistook their prey?

What deep wounds ever closed without a scar?
The heart's bleed longest, and but heal to wear
That which disfigures it; and they who war
With their own hopes, and have been vanquished, bear
Silence, but not submission: in his lair
Fixed Passion holds his breath, until the hour
Which shall atone for years; none need despair:
It came, it cometh, and will come, — the power
To punish or forgive — in *one* we shall be slower.

Clear, placid Leman! thy contrasted lake,
With the wild world I dwelt in, is a thing
Which warns me, with its stillness, to forsake
Earth's troubled waters for a purer spring.
This quiet sail is as a noiseless wing
To waft me from distraction; once I loved
Torn ocean's roar, but thy soft murmuring
Sounds sweet as if a Sister's voice reproved,
That I with stern delights should e'er have been so moved.

It is the hush of night, and all between
Thy margin and the mountains, dusk, yet clear,
Mellowed and mingling, yet distinctly seen,
Save darkened Jura, whose capt heights appear
Precipitously steep; and drawing near,
There breathes a living fragrance from the shore,
Of flowers yet fresh with childhood; on the ear
Drops the light drip of the suspended oar,
Or chirps the grasshopper one good-night carol more;

He is an evening reveller, who makes
His life an infancy, and sings his fill;
At intervals, some bird from out the brakes
Starts into voice a moment, then is still.
There seems a floating whisper on the hill,
But that is fancy, for the starlight dews
All silently their tears of love instil,
Weeping themselves away, till they infuse
Deep into nature's breast the spirit of her hues.

Ye stars! which are the poetry of heaven!
If in your bright leaves we would read the fate
Of men and empires, — 't is to be forgiven,
That in our aspirations to be great,
Our destinies o'erleap their mortal state,
And claim a kindred with you; for ye are
A beauty and a mystery, and create

In us such love and reverence from afar,
That fortune, fame, power, life, have named themselves a star.

All heaven and earth are still — though not in sleep,
But breathless, as we grow when feeling most;
And silent, as we stand in thoughts too deep: —
All heaven and earth are still: From the high host
Of stars, to the lulled lake and mountain-coast,
All is concentered in a life intense,
Where not a beam, nor air, nor leaf is lost,
But hath a part of being, and a sense
Of that which is of all Creator and defence.

Then stirs the feeling infinite, so felt
In solitude, where we are *least* alone;
A truth, which through our being then doth melt,
And purifies from self: it is a tone,
The soul and source of music, which makes known
Eternal harmony, and sheds a charm
Like to the fabled Cytherea's zone,
Binding all things with beauty; — 't would disarm
The spectre Death, had he substantial power to harm.

Not vainly did the early Persian make
His altar the high places, and the peak
Of earth-o'ergazing mountains, and thus take
A fit and unwalled temple, there to seek
The Spirit, in whose honour shrines are weak,
Upreared of human hands. Come, and compare
Columns and idol-dwellings, Goth or Greek,
With Nature's realms of worship, earth and air,
Nor fix on fond abodes to circumscribe thy pray'r!

The sky is changed! — and such a change! Oh night,
And storm, and darkness, ye are wondrous strong,
Yet lovely in your strength, as is the light
Of a dark eye in woman! Far along,
From peak to peak, the rattling crags among
Leaps the live thunder! Not from one lone cloud,
But every mountain now hath found a tongue,
And Jura answers, through her misty shroud,
Back to the joyous Alps, who call to her aloud!

And this is in the night: — Most glorious night!
Thou wert not sent for slumber! let me be
A sharer in thy fierce and far delight, —
A portion of the tempest and of thee!
How the lit lake shines, a phosphoric sea,
And the big rain comes dancing to the earth!
And now again 't is black, — and now, the glee
Of the loud hills shakes with its mountain-mirth,
As if they did rejoice o'er a young earth-quake's birth.

Now, where the swift Rhone cleaves his way between
Heights which appear as lovers who have parted
In hate, whose mining depths so intervene,
That they can meet no more, though broken-hearted;
Though in their souls, which thus each other thwarted,
Love was the very root of the fond rage
Which blighted their life's bloom, and then departed:
Itself expired, but leaving them an age
Of years all winters, — war within themselves to wage.

Now, where the quick Rhone thus hath cleft his way,
The mightiest of the storms hath ta'en his stand:
For here, not one, but many, make their play,
And fling their thunder-bolts from hand to hand,
Flashing and cast around; of all the band,
The brightest through these parted hills hath forked
His lightnings, — as if he did understand,
That in such gaps as desolation worked,
There the hot shaft should blast whatever therein lurked.

Sky, mountains, river, winds, lake, lightnings! ye!
With night, and clouds, and thunder, and a soul
To make these felt and feeling, well may be
Things that have made me watchful; the far roll
Of your departing voices, is the knoll
Of what in me is sleepless, — if I rest.
But where of ye, O tempests! is the goal?
Are ye like those within the human breast?
Or do ye find, at length, like eagles, some high nest?

Could I embody and unbosom now
That which is most within me, — could I wreak
My thoughts upon expression, and thus throw
Soul, heart, mind, passions, feelings, strong or weak,
All that I would have sought, and all I seek,
Bear, know, feel, and yet breathe — into *one* word,
And that one word were Lightning, I would speak;
But as it is, I live and die unheard,
With a most voiceless thought, sheathing it as a sword.

The morn is up again, the dewy morn,
With braeth all incense, and with cheek all bloom,
Laughing the clouds away with playful scorn,
And living as if earth contained no tomb, —
And glowing into day: we may resume
The march of our existence: and thus I,
Still on thy shores, fair Leman! may find room
And food for meditation, nor pass by
Much, that may give us pause, if pondered fittingly.

Clarens! sweet Clarens, birthplace of deep Love!
Thine air is the young breath of passionate thought;
Thy trees take root in Love; the snows above
The very Glaciers have his colours caught,
And sun-set into rose-hues sees them wrought
By rays which sleep there lovingly: the rocks,
The permanent crags, tell here of Love, who sought
In them a refuge from the worldly shocks,
Which stir and sting the soul with hope that woos, then mocks.

Clarens! by heavenly feet thy paths are trod, —
Undying Love's, who here ascends a throne
To which the steps are mountains; where the god
Is a pervading life and light, — so shown
Not on those summits solely, nor alone
In the still cave and forest; o'er the flower
His eye is sparkling, and his breath hath blown,
His soft and summer breath, whose tender power
Passes the strength of storms in their most desolate hour.

All things are here of *him;* from the black pines,
Which are his shade on high, and the loud roar
Of torrents, where he listeneth, to the vines
Which slope his green path downward to the shore,
Where the bowed waters meet him, and adore,
Kissing his feet with murmurs; and the wood,
The covert of old trees, with trunks all hoar,
But light leaves, young as joy, stands where it stood,
Offering to him, and his, a populous solitude.

A populous solitude of bees and birds,
And fairy-formed and many-coloured things,
Who worship him with notes more sweet than words,
And innocently open their glad wings,
Fearless and full of life: the gush of springs,
And fall of lofty fountains, and the bend
Of stirring branches, and the bud which brings
The swiftest thought of beauty, here extend,
Mingling, and made by Love, unto one mighty end.

He who hath loved not, here would learn that lore,
And make his heart a spirit; he who knows
That tender mystery, will love the more;
For this is Love's recess, where vain men's woes,
And the world's waste, have driven him far from those,
For 't is his nature to advance or die;
He stands not still, but or decays, or grows
Into a boundless blessing, which may vie
With the immortal lights, in its eternity!

'T was not for fiction chose Rousseau this spot,
Peopling it with affections; but he found
It was the scene which Passion must allot
To the mind's purified beings; 't was the ground
Where early Love his Psyche's zone unbound,
And hallowed it with loveliness: 't is lone,
And wonderful, and deep, and hath a sound,
And sense, and sight of sweetness; here the Rhone
Hath spread himself a couch, the Alps have reared a throne.

Lausanne! and Ferney! ye have been the abodes
Of names which unto you bequeathed a name;
Mortals, who sought and found, by dangerous roads,
A path to perpetuity of fame:
They were gigantic minds, and their steep aim
Was, Titan-like, on daring doubts to pile
Thoughts which should call down thunder, and the flame
Of Heaven again assailed, if Heaven the while
On man and man's research could deign do more than smile.

The one was fire and fickleness, a child
Most mutable in wishes, but in mind
A wit as various, — gay, grave, sage, or wild, —
Historian, bard, philosopher, combined;
He multiplied himself among mankind,
The Proteus of their talents: But his own
Breathed most in ridicule, — which, as the wind,
Blew where it listed, laying all things prone, —
Now to o'erthrow a fool, and now to shake a throne.

The other, deep and slow, exhausting thought,
And hiving wisdom with each studious year,
In meditation dwelt, with learning wrought,
And shaped his weapon with an edge severe,
Sapping a solemn creed with solemn sneer;
The lord of irony, — that master-spell,
Which stung his foes to wrath, which grew from fear,
And doomed him to the zealot's ready Hell,
Which answers to all doubts so eloquently well.

Yet, peace be with their ashes, — for by them,
If merited, the penalty is paid;
It is not ours to judge, — far less condemn;
The hour must come when such things shall be made
Known unto all, or hope and dread allayed
By slumber, on one pillow, in the dust,
Which, thus much we are sure, must lie decayed;
And when it shall revive, as is our trust,
'T will be to be forgiven, or suffer what is just.

But let me quit man's works, again to read
His Maker's, spread around me, and suspend
This page, which from my reveries I feed,
Until it seems prolonging without end.
The clouds above me to the white Alps tend,
And I must pierce them, and survey whate'er
May be permitted, as my steps I bend
To their most great and growing region, where
The earth to her embrace compels the powers of air.

Italia! too, Italia! looking on thee,
Full flashes on the soul the light of ages,
Since the fierce Carthaginian almost won thee,
To the last halo of the chiefs and sages
Who glorify thy consecrated pages;
Thou wert the throne and grave of empires; still,
The fount at which the panting mind assuages
Her thirst of knowledge, quaffing there her fill,
Flows from the eternal source of Rome's imperial hill.

Thus far have I proceeded in a theme
Renewed with no kind auspices: — to feel
We are not what we have been, and to deem
We are not what we should be, and to steel
The heart against itself; and to conceal,
With a proud caution, love, or hate, or aught, —
Passion or feeling, purpose, grief or zeal, —
Which is the tyrant spirit of our thought,
Is a stern task of soul: — No matter, — it is taught.

And for these words, thus woven into song,
It may be that they are a harmless wile, —
The colouring of the scenes which fleet along,
Which I would seize, in passing, to beguile
My breast, or that of others, for a while.
Fame is the thirst of youth, but I am not
So young as to regard men's frown or smile,
As loss or guerdon of a glorious lot;
I stood and stand alone, — remembered or forgot.

I have not loved the world, nor the world me;
I have not flattered its rank breath, nor bowed
To its idolatries a patient knee,
Nor coined my cheek to smiles, nor cried aloud
In worship of an echo; in the crowd
They could not deem me one of such; I stood
Among them, but not of them; in a shroud

Of thoughts which were not their thoughts, and still could,
Had I not filed my mind, which thus itself subdued.

I have not loved the world, nor the world me, —
But let us part fair foes; I do believe,
Though I have found them not, that there may be
Words which are things, hopes which will not deceive,
And virtues which are merciful, nor weave
Snares for the failing; I would also deem
O'er others' griefs that some sincerely grieve;
That two, or one, are almost what they seem,
That goodness is no name, and happiness no dream.

My daughter! with thy name this song begun;
My daughter! with thy name thus much shall end;
I see thee not, I hear thee not, but none
Can be so wrapt in thee; thou art the friend
To whom the shadows of far years extend:
Albeit my brow thou never shouldst behold,
My voice shall with thy future visions blend,
And reach into thy heart, when mine is cold,
A token and a tone, even from thy father's mould.

To aid thy mind's development, to watch
Thy dawn of little joys, to sit and see
Almost thy very growth, to view thee catch
Knowledge of objects, — wonders yet to thee!
To hold thee lightly on a gentle knee,
And print on thy soft cheek a parent's kiss, —
This, it should seem, was not reserved for me;
Yet this was in my nature: as it is,
I know not what is there, yet something like to this.

Yet, though dull Hate as duty should be taught,
I know that thou wilt love me; though my name
Should be shut from thee, as a spell still fraught
With desolation, and a broken claim:
Though the grave closed between us, — 't were the same,
I know that thou wilt love me; though to drain
My blood from out thy being were an aim,
And an attainment, — all would be in vain, —
Still thou wouldst love me, still that more than life retain.

The child of love, though born in bitterness,
And nurtured in convulsion. Of thy sire
These were the elements, and thine no less.
As yet such are around thee, but thy fire
Shall be more tempered, and thy hope far higher.
Sweet be thy cradled slumbers! O'er the sea
And from the mountains where I now respire,
Fain would I waft such blessing upon thee,
As, with a sigh, I deem thou might'st have been to me.

1816

THE PRISONER OF CHILLON

My hair is grey, but not with years,
Nor grew it white
In a single night,
As men's have grown from sudden fears:
My limbs are bowed, though not with toil,
But rusted with a vile repose,
For they have been a dungeon's spoil,
And mine has been the fate of those
To whom the goodly earth and air
Are banned, and barred — forbidden fare:
But this was for my father's faith
I suffered chains and courted death;
That father perished at the stake
For tenets he would not forsake;
And for the same his lineal race
In darkness found a dwelling-place;
We were seven — who now are one,
Six in youth, and one in age,
Finished as they had begun,
Proud of Persecution's rage;
One in fire, and two in field,
Their belief with blood have sealed,
Dying as their father died,
For the God their foes denied;
Three were in a dungeon cast,
Of whom this wreck is left the last.

There are seven pillars of Gothic mould,
In Chillon's dungeons deep and old,
There are seven columns, massy and grey,
Dim with a dull imprisoned ray,
A sunbeam which hath lost its way,
And through the crevice and the cleft
Of the thick wall is fallen and left;
Creeping o'er the floor so damp,

Like a marsh's meteor lamp:
And in each pillar there is a ring,
And in each ring there is a chain;
That iron is a cankering thing,
For in these limbs its teeth remain,
With marks that will not wear away,
Till I have done with this new day,
Which now is painful to these eyes,
Which have not seen the sun so rise
For years — I cannot count them o'er,
I lost their long and heavy score,
When my last brother drooped and died,
And I lay living by his side.

They chained us each to a column stone,
And we were three — yet, each alone;
We could not move a single pace,
We could not see each other's face,
But with that pale and livid light
That made us strangers in our sight:
And thus together — yet apart,
Fettered in hand, but joined in heart,
'T was still some solace, in the dearth
Of the pure elements of earth,
To hearken to each other's speech,
And each turn comforter to each
With some new hope, or legend old,
Or song heroically bold;
But even these at length grew cold.
Our voices took a dreary tone,
An echo of the dungeon stone,
A grating sound, not full and free,
As they of yore were wont to be:
It might be fancy, but to me
They never sounded like our own.

I was the eldest of the three,
And to uphold and cheer the rest
I ought to do — and did my best —
And each did well in his degree.
The youngest, whom my father loved,
Because our mother's brow was given
To him, with eyes as blue as heaven —
For him my soul was sorely moved;
And truly might it be distressed
To see such bird in such a nest;
For he was beautiful as day —
(When day was beautiful to me
As to young eagles, being free) —
A polar day, which will not see
A sunset till its summer 's gone,
Its sleepless summer of long light,
The snow-clad offspring of the sun:
And thus he was as pure and bright,
And in his natural spirit gay,
With tears for nought but others' ills,
And then they flowed like mountain rills,
Unless he could assuage the woe
Which he abhorred to view below.

The other was as pure of mind,
But formed to combat with his kind;
Strong in his frame, and of a mood
Which 'gainst the world in war had stood,
And perished in the foremost rank
With joy: — but not in chains to pine:
His spirit withered with their clank,
I saw it silently decline —
And so perchance in sooth did mine:
But yet I forced it on to cheer
Those relics of a home so dear.
He was a hunter of the hills,
Had followed there the deer and wolf;
To him his dungeon was a gulf,
And fettered feet the worst of ills.

Lake Leman lies by Chillon's walls:
A thousand feet in depth below
Its massy waters meet and flow;
Thus much the fathom-line was sent
From Chillon's snow-white battlement,
Which round about the wave inthrals:
A double dungeon wall and wave
Have made — and like a living grave
Below the surface of the lake
The dark vault lies wherein we lay,
We heard it ripple night and day;
Sounding o'er our heads it knocked;
And I have felt the winter's spray
Wash through the bars when winds were high
And wanton in the happy sky;
And then the very rock hath rocked,
And I have felt it shake, unshocked,
Because I could have smiled to see
The death that would have set me free.

I said my nearer brother pined,
I said his mighty heart declined,
He loathed and put away his food;
It was not that 't was coarse and rude,
For we were used to hunter's fare,
And for the like had little care:
The milk drawn from the mountain goat
Was changed for water from the moat,
Our bread was such as captives' tears
Have moistened many a thousand years,
Since man first pent his fellow men
Like brutes within an iron den;
But what were these to us or him?
These wasted not his heart or limb;
My brother's soul was of that mould
Which in a palace had grown cold,
Had his free breathing been denied
The range of the steep mountain's side;
But why delay the truth? — he died.
I saw, and could not hold his head,
Nor reach his dying hand — nor dead, —
Though hard I strove, but strove in vain,

To rend and gnash my bonds in twain.
He died, and they unlocked his chain,
And scooped for him a shallow grave
Even from the cold earth of our cave,
I begged them as a boon to lay
His corse in dust whereon the day
Might shine — it was a foolish thought,
But then within my brain it wrought,
That even in death his freeborn breast
In such a dungeon could not rest.
I might have spared my idle prayer —
They coldly laughed, and laid him there:
The flat and turfless earth above
The being we so much did love;
His empty chain above it leant,
Such murder's fitting monument!

But he, the favourite and the flower,
Most cherished since his natal hour,
His mother's image in fair face,
The infant love of all his race,
His martyred father's dearest thought,
My latest care, for whom I sought
To hoard my life, that his might be
Less wretched now, and one day free;
He, too, who yet had held untired
A spirit natural or inspired —
He, too, was struck, and day by day
Was withered on the stalk away.
Oh, God! it is a fearful thing
To see the human soul take wing
In any shape, in any mood:
I've seen it rushing forth in blood,
I've seen it on the breaking ocean
Strive with a swoln convulsive motion,
I've seen the sick and ghastly bed
Of Sin delirious with its dread;
But these were horrors — this was woe
Unmixed with such — but sure and slow:
He faded, and so calm and meek,
So softly worn, so sweetly weak,
So tearless, yet so tender, kind,
And grieved for those he left behind;
With all the while a cheek whose bloom
Was as a mockery of the tomb,
Whose tints as gently sunk away
As a departing rainbow's ray;
An eye of most transparent light,
That almost made the dungeon bright,
And not a word of murmur, not
A groan o'er his untimely lot, —
A little talk of better days,
A little hope my own to raise,
For I was sunk in silence — lost
In this last loss, of all the most;
And then the sighs he would suppress
Of fainting nature's feebleness,
More slowly drawn, grew less and less:
I listened, but I could not hear;
I called, for I was wild with fear;
I knew 't was hopeless, but my dread
Would not be thus admonishèd;
I called, and thought I heard a sound —
I burst my chain with one strong bound,
And rushed to him: — I found him not,
I only stirred in this black spot,
I only lived, *I* only drew
The accursèd breath of dungeon-dew;
The last, the sole, the dearest link
Between me and the eternal brink,
Which bound me to my failing race,
Was broken in this fatal place.
One on the earth, and one beneath —
My brothers — both had ceased to breathe:
I took that hand which lay so still,
Alas! my own was full as chill;
I had not strength to stir, or strive,
But felt that I was still alive —
A frantic feeling, when we know
That what we love shall ne'er be so.
I know not why
I could not die,
I had no earthly hope but faith,
And that forbade a selfish death.

What next befell me then and there
I know not well — I never knew —
First came the loss of light, and air,
And then of darkness too:
I had no thought, no feeling — none —
Among the stones I stood a stone,
And was, scarce conscious what I wist,
As shrubless crags within the mist;
For all was blank, and bleak, and grey;
It was not night, it was not day;
It was not even the dungeon-light,
So hateful to my heavy sight,
But vacancy absorbing space,
And fixedness without a place;
There were no stars, no earth, no time,
No check, no change, no good, no crime,
But silence, and a stirless breath
Which neither was of life nor death;
A sea of stagnant idleness,
Blind, boundless, mute, and motionless!

A light broke in upon my brain, —
It was the carol of a bird;
It ceased, and then it came again,
The sweetest song ear ever heard,
And mine was thankful till my eyes
Ran over with the glad surprise,
And they that moment could not see
I was the mate of misery;
But then by dull degrees came back
My senses to their wonted track;
I saw the dungeon walls and floor

Close slowly round me as before,
I saw the glimmer of the sun
Creeping as it before had done,
But through the crevice where it came
That bird was perched, as fond and tame,
  And tamer than upon the tree;
A lovely bird, with azure wings,
And song that said a thousand things,
  And seemed to say them all for me!
I never saw its like before,
I ne'er shall see its likeness more:
It seemed like me to want a mate,
But was not half so desolate,
And it was come to love me when
None lived to love me so again,
And cheering from my dungeon's brink,
Had brought me back to feel and think.
I know not if it late were free,
  Or broke its cage to perch on mine,
But knowing well captivity,
  Sweet bird! I could not wish for thine!
Or if it were, in wingèd guise,
A visitant from Paradise;
For — Heaven forgive that thought! the while
Which made me both to weep and smile —
I sometimes deemed that it might be
My brother's soul come down to me;
But then at last away it flew,
And then 't was mortal well I knew,
For he would never thus have flown,
And left me twice so doubly lone,
Lone as the corse within its shroud,
Lone as a solitary cloud, —
  A single cloud on a sunny day,
While all the rest of heaven is clear,
A frown upon the atmosphere,
That hath no business to appear
  When skies are blue, and earth is gay.

A kind of change came in my fate,
My keepers grew compassionate;
I know not what had made them so,
They were inured to sights of woe,
But so it was: — my broken chain
With links unfastened did remain,
And it was liberty to stride
Along my cell from side to side,
And up and down, and then athwart,
And tread it over every part;
And round the pillars one by one,
Returning where my walk begun,
Avoiding only, as I trod,
My brothers' graves without a sod;
For if I thought with heedless tread
My step profaned their lowly bed,
My breath came gaspingly and thick,
And my crushed heart fell blind and sick.
I made a footing in the wall,
  It was not therefrom to escape,
For I had buried one and all
  Who loved me in a human shape;
And the whole earth would henceforth be
A wider prison unto me:
No child, no sire, no kin had I,
No partner in my misery;
I thought of this, and I was glad,
For thought of them had made me mad;
But I was curious to ascend
To my barred windows, and to bend
Once more, upon the mountains high,
The quiet of a loving eye.

I saw them, and they were the same,
They were not changed like me in frame;
I saw their thousand years of snow
On high — their wide long lake below,
And the blue Rhone in fullest flow;
I heard the torrents leap and gush
O'er channelled rock and broken bush;
I saw the white-walled distant town,
And whiter sails go skimming down;
And then there was a little isle,
Which in my very face did smile,
    The only one in view;
A small green isle, it seemed no more,
Scarce broader than my dungeon floor,
But in it there were three tall trees,
And o'er it blew the mountain breeze,
And by it there were waters flowing,
And on it there were young flowers growing
    Of gentle breath and hue.
The fish swam by the castle wall,
And they seemed joyous each and all;
The eagle rode the rising blast,
Methought he never flew so fast
As then to me he seemed to fly;
And then new tears came in my eye,
And I felt troubled — and would fain
I had not left my recent chain;
And when I did descend again,
The darkness of my dim abode
Fell on me as a heavy load;
It was as is a new-dug grave,
Closing o'er one we sought to save, —
And yet my glance, too much opprest,
Had almost need of such a rest.

It might be months, or years, or days,
  I kept no count, I took no note,
I had no hope my eyes to raise,
  And clear them of their dreary mote;
At last men came to set me free;
  I asked not why, and recked not where;
It was at length the same to me,
Fettered or fetterless to be,
  I learned to love despair.

And thus when they appeared at last,
And all my bonds aside were cast,
These heavy walls to me had grown
A hermitage — and all my own!
And half I felt as they were come
To tear me from a second home:
With spiders I had friendship made,
And watched them in their sullen trade,
Had seen the mice by moonlight play,
And why should I feel less than they?
We were all inmates of one place,
And I, the monarch of each race,
Had power to kill — yet, strange to tell!
In quiet we had learned to dwell;
My very chains and I grew friends,
So much a long communion tends
To make us what we are: — even I
Regained my freedom with a sigh.

1816

THE ISLES OF GREECE

The isles of Greece, the isles of Greece!
  Where burning Sappho loved and sung,
Where grew the arts of war and peace,
  Where Delos rose, and Phœbus sprung!
Eternal summer gilds them yet,
But all, except their sun, is set.

The Scian and the Teian muse,
  The hero's harp, the lover's lute,
Have found the fame your shores refuse:
  Their place of birth alone is mute
To sounds which echo further west
Than your sires' 'Islands of the Blest.'

The mountains look on Marathon —
  And Marathon looks on the sea;
And musing there an hour alone,
  I dreamed that Greece might still be free;
For standing on the Persians' grave,
I could not deem myself a slave.

A king sate on the rocky brow
  Which looks o'er sea-born Salamis;
And ships, by thousands, lay below,
  And men in nations; — all were his!
He counted them at break of day —
And when the sun set where were they?

And where are they? and where art thou,
  My country? On thy voiceless shore
The heroic lay is tuneless now —
  The heroic bosom beats no more!
And must thy lyre, so long divine,
Degenerate into hands like mine?

'T is something, in the dearth of fame,
  Though linked among a fettered race,
To feel at least a patriot's shame,
  Even as I sing, suffuse my face;
For what is left the poet here?
For Greeks a blush — for Greece a tear.

Must *we* but weep o'er days more blest?
  Must *we* but blush? — Our fathers bled.
Earth! render back from out thy breast
  A remnant of our Spartan dead!
Of the three hundred grant but three,
To make a new Thermopylæ!

What, silent still? and silent all?
  Ah! no; — the voices of the dead
Sound like a distant torrent's fall,
  And answer, 'Let one living head,
But one arise, — we come, we come!'
'T is but the living who are dumb.

In vain — in vain: strike other chords;
  Fill high the cup with Samian wine!
Leave battles to the Turkish hordes,
  And shed the blood of Scio's vine!
Hark! rising to the ignoble call —
How answers each bold Bacchanal!

You have the Pyrrhic dance as yet;
  Where is the Pyrrhic phalanx gone?
Of two such lessons, why forget
  The nobler and the manlier one?
You have the letters Cadmus gave —
Think ye he meant them for a slave?

Fill high the bowl with Samian wine!
  We will not think of themes like these!
It made Anacreon's song divine:
  He served — but served Polycrates —
A tyrant; but our masters then
Were still, at least, our countrymen.

The tyrant of the Chersonese
  Was freedom's best and bravest friend;
That tyrant was Miltiades!
  Oh! that the present hour would lend
Another despot of the kind!
Such chains as his were sure to bind.

Fill high the bowl with Samian wine!
  On Suli's rock, and Parga's shore,
Exists the remnant of a line
  Such as the Doric mothers bore;
And there, perhaps, some seed is sown,
The Heracleidan blood might own.

Trust not for freedom to the Franks —
  They have a king who buys and sells;
In native swords, and native ranks,
  The only hope of courage dwells:
But Turkish force, and Latin fraud,
Would break your shield, however broad.

Fill high the bowl with Samian wine!
  Our virgins dance beneath the shade —

I see their glorious black eyes shine;
  But gazing on each glowing maid,
My own the burning tear-drop laves,
To think such breasts must suckle slaves.

Place me on Sunium's marbled steep,
  Where nothing, save the waves and I,
May hear our mutual murmurs sweep;
  There, swan-like, let me sing and die:
A land of slaves shall ne'er be mine —
Dash down yon cup of Samian wine!

1821

DON JUAN

CANTO IV, STANZAS I-LXXII

NOTHING so difficult as a beginning
  In poesy, unless perhaps the end;
For oftentimes when Pegasus seems winning
  The race, he sprains a wing, and down we tend,
Like Lucifer when hurled from heaven for sinning;
  Our sin the same, and hard as his to mend,
Being pride, which leads the mind to soar too far,
Till our own weakness shows us what we are.

But time, which brings all beings to their level,
  And sharp Adversity, will teach at last
Man, — and, as we would hope, — perhaps the devil,
  That neither of their intellects are vast:
While youth's hot wishes in our red veins revel,
  We know not this — the blood flows on too fast:
But as the torrent widens towards the ocean,
We ponder deeply on each past emotion.

As boy, I thought myself a clever fellow,
  And wished that others held the same opinion;
They took it up when my days grew more mellow,
  And other minds acknowledged my dominion:
Now my sere fancy 'falls into the yellow
  Leaf,' and Imagination droops her pinion,
And the sad truth which hovers o'er my desk
Turns what was once romantic to burlesque.

And if I laugh at any mortal thing,
  'T is that I may not weep; and if I weep,
'T is that our nature cannot always bring
  Itself to apathy, for we must steep
Our hearts first in the depths of Lethe's spring,
  Ere what we least wish to behold will sleep:
Thetis baptized her mortal son in Styx;
A mortal mother would on Lethe fix.

Some have accused me of a strange design
  Against the creed and morals of the land,
And trace it in this poem every line;
  I don't pretend that I quite understand
My own meaning when I would be *very* fine;
  But the fact is that I have nothing planned,
Unless it were to be a moment merry,
A novel word in my vocabulary.

To the kind reader of our sober clime
  This way of writing will appear exotic;
Pulci was sire of the half-serious rhyme,
  Who sang when chivalry was more Quixotic,
And revelled in the fancies of the time,
  True knights, chaste dames, huge giant kings despotic:
But all these, save the last, being obsolete,
I chose a modern subject as more meet.

How I have treated it, I do not know;
  Perhaps no better than they have treated me,
Who have imputed such designs as show
  Not what they saw, but what they wished to see;
But if it gives them pleasure, be it so,
  This is a liberal age, and thoughts are free:
Meantime Apollo plucks me by the ear,
And tells me to resume my story here.

Young Juan and his lady-love were left
  To their own hearts' most sweet society;
Even Time the pitiless in sorrow cleft
  With his rude scythe such gentle bosoms; he
Sighed to behold them of their hours bereft,
  Though foe to love; and yet they could not be
Meant to grow old, but die in happy spring,
Before one charm or hope had taken wing.

Their faces were not made for wrinkles, their
  Pure blood to stagnate, their great hearts to fail;
The blank grey was not made to blast their hair,
  But like the climes that know nor snow nor hail,
They were all summer; lightning might assail

And shiver them to ashes, but to trail
A long and snake-like life of dull decay
Was not for them — they had too little clay.

They were alone once more; for them to be
Thus was another Eden; they were never
Weary, unless when separate: the tree
Cut from its forest root of years — the river
Dammed from its fountain — the child from the knee
And breast maternal weaned at once for ever, —
Would wither less than these two torn apart;
Alas! there is no instinct like the heart —

The heart — which may be broken: happy they!
Thrice fortunate! who of that fragile mould,
The precious porcelain of human clay,
Break with the first fall: they can ne'er behold
The long year linked with heavy day on day,
And all which must be borne, and never told;
While life's strange principle will often lie
Deepest in those who long the most to die.

'Whom the gods love die young' was said of yore,
And many deaths do they escape by this:
The death of friends, and that which slays even more —
The death of friendship, love, youth, all that is,
Except mere breath; and since the silent shore
Awaits at last even those who longest miss
The old archer's shafts, perhaps the early grave
Which men weep over may be meant to save.

Haidée and Juan thought not of the dead.
The heavens, and earth, and air, seemed made for them:
They found no fault with Time, save that he fled;
They saw not in themselves aught to condemn;
Each was the other's mirror, and but read
Joy sparkling in their dark eyes like a gem,
And knew such brightness was but the reflection
Of their exchanging glances of affection.

The gentle pressure, and the thrilling touch,
The least glance better understood than words,
Which still said all, and ne'er could say too much;
A language, too, but like to that of birds,
Known but to them, at least appearing such
As but to lovers a true sense affords;
Sweet playful phrases, which would seem absurd
To those who have ceased to hear such, or ne'er heard.

All these were theirs, for they were children still,
And children still they should have ever been;
They were not made in the real world to fill
A busy character in the dull scene,
But like two beings born from out a rill,
A nymph and her beloved, all unseen
To pass their lives in fountains and on flowers,
And never know the weight of human hours.

Moons changing had rolled on, and changeless found
Those their bright rise had lighted to such joys
As rarely they beheld throughout their round;
And these were not of the vain kind which cloys,
For theirs were buoyant spirits, never bound
By the mere senses; and that which destroys
Most love, possession, unto them appeared
A thing which each endearment more endeared.

Oh beautiful! and rare as beautiful!
But theirs was love in which the mind delights
To lose itself, when the old world grows dull,
And we are sick of its hack sounds and sights,
Intrigues, adventures of the common school,
Its petty passions, marriages, and flights,
Where Hymen's torch but brands one strumpet more,
Whose husband only knows her not a wh—re.

Hard words; harsh truth; a truth which many know.
Enough. — The faithful and the fairy pair,

Who never found a single hour too slow,
  What was it made them thus exempt from care?
Young innate feelings all have felt below,
  Which perish in the rest, but in them were
Inherent; what we mortals call romantic,
And always envy, though we deem it frantic.

This is in others a factitious state,
  An opium dream of too much youth and reading,
But was in them their nature or their fate:
  No novels e'er had set their young hearts bleeding,
For Haidée's knowledge was by no means great,
  And Juan was a boy of saintly breeding;
So that there was no reason for their loves
More than for those of nightingales or doves.

They gazed upon the sunset; 't is an hour
  Dear unto all, but dearest to *their* eyes,
For it had made them what they were: the power
  Of love had first o'erwhelmed them from such skies,
When happiness had been their only dower,
  And twilight saw them linked in passion's ties;
Charmed with each other, all things charmed that brought
The past still welcome as the present thought.

I know not why, but in that hour to-night,
  Even as they gazed, a sudden tremor came,
And swept, as 't were, across their hearts' delight,
  Like the wind o'er a harp-string, or a flame,
When one is shook in sound, and one in sight:
  And thus some boding flashed through either frame,
And called from Juan's breast a faint low sigh,
While one new tear arose in Haidée's eye.

That large black prophet eye seemed to dilate
  And follow far the disappearing sun,
As if their last day of a happy date
  With his broad, bright, and dropping orb were gone.
Juan gazed on her as to ask his fate —
  He felt a grief, but knowing cause for none,
His glance inquired of hers for some excuse
For feelings causeless, or at least abstruse.

She turned to him, and smiled, but in that sort
  Which makes not others smile; then turned aside:
Whatever feeling shook her, it seemed short,
  And mastered by her wisdom or her pride;
When Juan spoke, too — it might be in sport —
  Of this their mutual feeling, she replied —
'If it should be so, — but — it cannot be —
Or I at least shall not survive to see.'

Juan would question further, but she pressed
  His lips to hers, and silenced him with this,
And then dismissed the omen from her breast,
  Defying augury with that fond kiss;
And no doubt of all methods 't is the best:
  Some people prefer wine — 't is not amiss;
I have tried both; so those who would a part take
May choose between the headache and the heartache.

One of the two according to your choice,
  Woman or wine, you 'll have to undergo;
Both maladies are taxes on our joys:
  But which to choose, I really hardly know;
And if I had to give a casting voice,
  For both sides I could many reasons show,
And then decide, without great wrong to either,
It were much better to have both than neither.

Juan and Haidée gazed upon each other
  With swimming looks of speechless tenderness,
Which mixed all feelings, friend, child, lover, brother;
  All that the best can mingle and express
When two pure hearts are poured in one another,
  And love too much, and yet cannot love less;
But almost sanctify the sweet excess
By the immortal wish and power to bless.

Mixed in each other's arms, and heart in heart,
  Why did they not then die? — they had lived too long
Should an hour come to bid them breathe apart;
  Years could but bring them cruel things or wrong;

The world was not for them, nor the world's art
For beings passionate as Sappho's song;
Love was born *with* them, *in* them, so intense,
It was their very spirit — not a sense.

They should have lived together deep in woods,
Unseen as sings the nightingale; they were
Unfit to mix in these thick solitudes
Called social, haunts of Hate, and Vice, and Care;
How lonely every freeborn creature broods!
The sweetest song-birds nestle in a pair;
The eagle soars alone; the gull and crow
Flock o'er their carrion, just like men below.

Now pillowed cheek to cheek, in loving sleep,
Haidée and Juan their siesta took,
A gentle slumber, but it was not deep,
For ever and anon a something shook
Juan, and shuddering o'er his frame would creep;
And Haidèe's sweet lips murmured like a brook
A wordless music, and her face so fair
Stirred with her dream, as rose-leaves with the air;

Or as the stirring of a deep clear stream
Within an Alpine hollow, when the wind
Walks o'er it, was she shaken by the dream,
The mystical usurper of the mind —
O'erpowering us to be whate'er may seem
Good to the soul which we no more can bind:
Strange state of being! (for 't is still to be),
Senseless to feel, and with sealed eyes to see.

She dreamed of being alone on the sea-shore,
Chained to a rock; she knew not how, but stir
She could not from the spot, and the loud roar
Grew, and each wave rose roughly, threatening her;
And o'er her upper lip they seemed to pour,
Until she sobbed for breath, and soon they were
Foaming o'er her lone head, so fierce and high —
Each broke to drown her, yet she could not die.

Anon — she was released, and then she strayed
O'er the sharp shingles with her bleeding feet,
And stumbled almost every step she made;
And something rolled before her in a sheet,
Which she must still pursue howe'er afraid:
'T was white and indistinct, nor stopped to meet
Her glance nor grasp, for still she gazed and grasped,
And ran, but it escaped her as she clasped.

The dream changed: — in a cave she stood, its walls
Were hung with marble icicles; the work
Of ages on its water-fretted halls,
Where waves might wash, and seals might breed and lurk;
Her hair was dripping, and the very balls
Of her black eyes seemed turned to tears, and mirk
The sharp rocks looked below each drop they caught,
Which froze to marble as it fell, — she thought.

And wet, and cold, and lifeless at her feet,
Pale as the foam that frothed on his dead brow,
Which she essayed in vain to clear, (how sweet
Were once her cares, how idle seemed they now!)
Lay Juan, nor could aught renew the beat
Of his quenched heart; and the sea dirges low
Rang in her sad ears like a mermaid's song,
And that brief dream appeared a life too long.

And gazing on the dead, she thought his face
Faded, or altered into something new —
Like to her father's features, till each trace
More like and like to Lambro's aspect grew —
With all his keen worn look and Grecian grace;
And starting, she awoke, and what to view?
Oh! Powers of Heaven! what dark eye meets she there?
'T is — 't is her father's — fixed upon the pair!

Then shrieking, she arose, and shrieking fell,
With joy and sorrow, hope and fear, to see
Him whom she deemed a habitant where dwell

The ocean-buried, risen from death, to be
Perchance the death of one she loved too well:
Dear as her father had been to Haidée,
It was a moment of that awful kind ——
I have seen such — but must not call to mind.

Up Juan sprang to Haidée's bitter shriek,
And caught her falling, and from off the wall
Snatched down his sabre, in hot haste to wreak
Vengeance on him who was the cause of all:
Then Lambro, who till now forebore to speak,
Smiled scornfully, and said, 'Within my call,
A thousand scimitars await the word;
Put up, young man, put up your silly sword.'

And Haidée clung around him; 'Juan, 't is —
'T is Lambro — 't is my father! Kneel with me —
He will forgive us — yes — it must be — yes.
Oh! dearest father, in this agony
Of pleasure and of pain — even while I kiss
Thy garment's hem with transport, can it be
That doubt should mingle with my filial joy?
Deal with me as thou wilt, but spare this boy.'

High and inscrutable the old man stood,
Calm in his voice, and calm within his eye —
Not always signs with him of calmest mood:
He looked upon her, but gave no reply;
Then turned to Juan, in whose cheek the blood
Oft came and went, as there resolved to die;
In arms, at least, he stood, in act to spring
On the first foe whom Lambro's call might bring.

'Young man, your sword'; so Lambro once more said:
Juan replied, 'Not while this arm is free.'
The old man's cheek grew pale, but not with dread,
And drawing from his belt a pistol, he
Replied, 'Your blood be then on your own head.'
Then looked close at the flint, as if to see
'T was fresh — for he had lately used the lock —
And next proceeded quietly to cock.

It has a strange quick jar upon the ear,
That cocking of a pistol, when you know
A moment more will bring the sight to bear
Upon your person, twelve yards off, or so;
A gentlemanly distance, not too near,
If you have got a former friend for foe;
But after being fired at once or twice,
The ear becomes more Irish, and less nice.

Lambro presented, and one instant more
Had stopped this Canto, and Don Juan's breath,
When Haidée threw herself her boy before;
Stern as her sire: 'On me,' she cried, 'let death
Descend — the fault is mine; this fatal shore
He found — but sought not. I have pledged my faith;
I love him — I will die with him: I knew
Your nature's firmness — know your daughter's too.'

A minute past, and she had been all tears,
And tenderness, and infancy; but now
She stood as one who championed human fears —
Pale, statue-like, and stern, she wooed the blow;
And tall beyond her sex, and their compeers,
She drew up to her height, as if to show
A fairer mark; and with a fixed eye scanned
Her father's face — but never stopped his hand.

He gazed on her, and she on him; 't was strange
How like they looked! the expression was the same;
Serenely savage, with a little change
In the large dark eye's mutual-darted flame;
For she, too, was as one who could avenge,
If cause should be — a lioness, though tame;
Her father's blood before her father's face
Boiled up, and proved her truly of his race.

I said they were alike, their features and
Their stature, differing but in sex and years:
Even to the delicacy of their hand
There was resemblance, such as true blood wears;
And now to see them, thus divided, stand
In fixed ferocity, when joyous tears,
And sweet sensations, should have welcomed both,
Show what the passions are in their full growth.

The father paused a moment, then withdrew
His weapon, and replaced it; but stood still,
And looking on her, as to look her through,
'Not *I*,' he said, 'have sought this stranger's ill;
Not *I* have made this desolation: few
Would bear such outrage, and forbear to kill;
But I must do my duty — how thou hast
Done thine, the present vouches for the past.

'Let him disarm; or, by my father's head,
His own shall roll before you like a ball!'
He raised his whistle as the word he said,
And blew; another answered to the call,
And rushing in disorderly, though led,
And armed from boot to turban, one and all,
Some twenty of his train came, rank on rank;
He gave the word, 'Arrest or slay the Frank.'

Then, with a sudden movement, he withdrew
His daughter; while compressed within his clasp,
'Twixt her and Juan interposed the crew;
In vain she struggled in her father's grasp —
His arms were like a serpent's coil: then flew
Upon their prey, as darts an angry asp,
The file of pirates: save the foremost, who
Had fallen, with his right shoulder half cut through.

The second had his cheek laid open; but
The third, a wary, cool old sworder, took
The blows upon his cutlass, and then put
His own well in; so well, ere you could look,
His man was floored, and helpless at his foot,
With the blood running like a little brook
From two smart sabre gashes, deep and red —
One on the arm, the other on the head.

And then they bound him where he fell, and bore
Juan from the apartment: with a sign
Old Lambro bade them take him to the shore,
Where lay some ships which were to sail at nine.
They laid him in a boat, and plied the oar
Until they reached some galliots, placed in line;
On board of one of these, and under hatches,
They stowed him, with strict orders to the watches.

The world is full of strange vicissitudes,
And here was one exceedingly unpleasant:
A gentleman so rich in the world's goods,
Handsome and young, enjoying all the present,
Just at the very time when he least broods
On such a thing, is suddenly to sea sent,
Wounded and chained, so that he cannot move,
And all because a lady fell in love.

Here I must leave him, for I grow pathetic,
Moved by the Chinese nymph of tears, green tea!
Than whom Cassandra was not more prophetic;
For if my pure libations exceed three,
I feel my heart become so sympathetic,
That I must have recourse to black Bohea:
'T is pity wine should be so deleterious,
For tea and coffee leave us much more serious,

Unless when qualified with thee, Cogniac!
Sweet Naïad of the Phlegethontic rill!
Ah! why the liver wilt thou thus attack,
And make, like other nymphs, thy lovers ill?
I would take refuge in weak punch, but *rack*
(In each sense of the word), whene'er I fill
My mild and midnight beakers to the brim.
Wakes me next morning with its synonym.

I leave Don Juan for the present, safe —
Not sound, poor fellow, but severely wounded;
Yet could his corporal pangs amount to half
Of those with which his Haidée's bosom bounded!
She was not one to weep, and rave, and chafe,
And then give way, subdued because surrounded;
Her mother was a Moorish maid from Fez,
Where all is Eden, or a wilderness.

There the large olive rains its amber store
In marble fonts; there grain, and flour, and fruit,
Gush from the earth until the land runs o'er;
But there, too, many a poison-tree has root,
And midnight listens to the lion's roar,
And long, long deserts scorch the camel's foot,
Or heaving whelm the helpless caravan;
And as the soil is, so the heart of man.

Afric is all the sun's, and as her earth
Her human clay is kindled; full of power
For good or evil, burning from its birth,
The Moorish blood partakes the planet's hour,
And like the soil beneath it will bring forth:
Beauty and love were Haidée's mother's dower;
But her large dark eye showed deep Passion's force,
Though sleeping like a lion near a source.

Her daughter, tempered with a milder ray,
Like summer clouds all silvery, smooth, and fair,
Till slowly charged with thunder they display
Terror to earth, and tempest to the air,
Had held till now her soft and milky way;
But overwrought with passion and despair,
The fire burst forth from her Numidian veins,
Even as the Simoom sweeps the blasted plains.

The last sight which she saw was Juan's gore,
And he himself o'ermastered and cut down;
His blood was running on the very floor
Where late he trod, her beautiful, her own;
Thus much she viewed an instant and no more, —
Her struggles ceased with one convulsive groan;
On her sire's arm, which until now scarce held
Her writhing, fell she like a cedar felled.

A vein had burst, and her sweet lips' pure dyes
Were dabbled with the deep blood which ran o'er;
And her head drooped, as when the lily lies
O'ercharged with rain: her summoned handmaids bore
Their lady to her couch with gushing eyes;
Of herbs and cordials they produced their store,
But she defied all means they could employ,
Like one life could not hold, nor death destroy.

Days lay she in that state unchanged, though chill —
With nothing livid, still her lips were red;
She had no pulse, but death seemed absent still;
No hideous sign proclaimed her surely dead;
Corruption came not in each mind to kill
All hope; to look upon her sweet face bred
New thoughts of life, for it seemed full of soul —
She had so much, earth could not claim the whole.

The ruling passion, such as marble shows
When exquisitely chiselled, still lay there,
But fixed as marble's unchanged aspect throws
O'er the fair Venus, but for ever fair;
O'er the Laocoön's all eternal throes,
And ever-dying Gladiator's air,
Their energy like life forms all their fame,
Yet looks not life, for they are still the same.

She woke at length, but not as sleepers wake,
Rather the dead, for life seemed something new,
A strange sensation which she must partake
Perforce, since whatsoever met her view
Struck not on memory, though a heavy ache
Lay at her heart, whose earliest beat still true
Brought back the sense of pain without the cause,
For, for a while, the furies made a pause.

She looked on many a face with vacant eye,
On many a token without knowing what;
She saw them watch her without asking why,
And recked not who around her pillow sat;
Not speechless, though she spoke not; not a sigh
Relieved her thoughts; dull silence and quick chat
Were tried in vain by those who served; she gave
No sign, save breath, of having left the grave.

Her handmaids tended, but she heeded not;
Her father watched, she turned her eyes away;
She recognised no being, and no spot,
However dear or cherished in their day;
They changed from room to room, but all forgot,
Gentle, but without memory she lay;
At length those eyes, which they would fain be weaning
Back to old thoughts, waxed full of fearful meaning.

And then a slave bethought her of a harp;
The harper came, and tuned his instrument;
At the first notes, irregular and sharp,
On him her flashing eyes a moment bent,

Then to the wall she turned as if to warp
Her thoughts from sorrow through her heart re-sent;
And he began a long low island song
Of ancient days, ere tyranny grew strong.

Anon her thin wan fingers beat the wall
In time to his old tune; he changed the theme,
And sung of love; the fierce name struck through all
Her recollection; on her flashed the dream
Of what she was, and is, if ye could call
To be so being; in a gushing stream
The tears rushed forth from her o'erclouded brain,
Like mountain mists at length dissolved in rain.

Short solace, vain relief! — thought came too quick,
And whirled her brain to madness; she arose
As one who ne'er had dwelt among the sick,
And flew at all she met, as on her foes;
But no one ever heard her speak or shriek,
Although her paroxysm drew towards its close; —
Hers was a phrensy which disdained to rave,
Even when they smote her, in the hope to save.

Yet she betrayed at times a gleam of sense;
Nothing could make her meet her father's face,
Though on all other things with looks intense
She gazed, but none she ever could retrace;
Food she refused, and raiment; no pretence
Availed for either; neither change of place,
Nor time, nor skill, nor remedy, could give her
Senses to sleep — the power seemed gone for ever.

Twelve days and nights she withered thus; at last,
Without a groan, or sigh, or glance, to show
A parting pang, the spirit from her passed:
And they who watched her nearest could not know
The very instant, till the change that cast
Her sweet face into shadow, dull and slow,
Glazed o'er her eyes — the beautiful, the black —
Oh! to possess such lustre — and then lack!

She died, but not alone; she held within
A second principle of life, which might
Have dawned a fair and sinless child of sin;
But closed its little being without light,
And went down to the grave unborn, wherein
Blossom and bough lie withered with one blight;
In vain the dews of Heaven descend above
The bleeding flower and blasted fruit of Love.

Thus lived — thus died she; never more on her
Shall sorrow light, or shame. She was not made
Through years or moons the inner weight to bear,
Which colder hearts endure till they are laid
By age in earth; her days and pleasures were
Brief but delightful — such as had not stayed
Long with her destiny; but she sleeps well
By the sea-shore, whereon she loved to dwell.

The isle is now all desolate and bare,
Its dwellings down, its tenants passed away;
None but her own and father's grave is there,
And nothing outward tells of human clay:
Ye could not know where lies a thing so fair,
No stone is there to show, no tongue to say
What was: no dirge, except the hollow sea's,
Mourns o'er the beauty of the Cyclades.

1821

ON THIS DAY I COMPLETE MY THIRTY-SIXTH YEAR

'T is time this heart should be unmoved,
Since others it hath ceased to move;
Yet, though I cannot be beloved,
Still let me love!

My days are in the yellow leaf;
The flowers and fruits of love are gone;
The worm, the canker, and the grief
Are mine alone!

The fire that on my bosom preys
Is lone as some volcanic isle;
No torch is kindled at its blaze —
A funeral pile.

The hope, the fear, the jealous care,
The exalted portion of the pain
And power of love, I cannot share,
But wear the chain.

But 't is not *thus* — and 't is not *here* —
Such thoughts should shake my soul, nor *now*,
Where glory decks the hero's bier,
Or binds his brow.

The sword, the banner, and the field,
Glory and Greece, around me see!
The Spartan, borne upon his shield,
Was not more free.

Awake! (not Greece — she *is* awake!)
Awake, my spirit! Think through *whom*
Thy life-blood tracks its parent lake,
And then strike home!

Tread those reviving passions down,
Unworthy manhood! — unto thee
Indifferent should the smile or frown
Of beauty be.

If thou regrett'st thy youth, *why live?*
The land of honourable death
Is here: — up to the field, and give
Away thy breath!

Seek out — less often sought than found —
A soldier's grave, for thee the best;
Then look around, and choose thy ground,
And take thy rest.

1824

Percy Bysshe Shelley (1792–1822)

HYMN TO INTELLECTUAL BEAUTY

THE awful shadow of some unseen Power
Floats though unseen among us, — visiting
This various world with as inconstant wing
As summer winds that creep from flower to flower, —
Like moonbeams that behind some piny mountain shower,
It visits with inconstant glance
Each human heart and countenance;
Like hues and harmonies of evening, —
Like clouds in starlight widely spread, —
Like memory of music fled, —
Like aught that for its grace may be
Dear, and yet dearer for its mystery.

Spirit of Beauty, that dost consecrate
With thine own hues all thou dost shine upon
Of human thought or form, — where art thou gone?
Why dost thou pass away and leave our state,
This dim vast vale of tears, vacant and desolate?
Ask why the sunlight not for ever
Weaves rainbows o'er yon mountain-river,
Why aught should fail and fade that once is shown,
Why fear and dream and death and birth
Cast on the daylight of this earth
Such gloom, — why man has such a scope
For love and hate, despondency and hope?

No voice from some sublimer world hath ever
To sage or poet these responses given —
Therefore the names of Demon, Ghost, and Heaven,
Remain the records of their vain endeavour,
Frail spells — whose uttered charm might not avail to sever,
From all we hear and all we see,
Doubt, chance, and mutability.
Thy light alone — like mist o'er mountains driven,
Or music by the night-wind sent
Through strings of some still instrument,
Or moonlight on a midnight stream,
Gives grace and truth to life's unquiet dream.

Love, Hope, and Self-esteem, like clouds depart
And come, for some uncertain moments lent.
Man were immortal, and omnipotent,
Didst thou, unknown and awful as thou art,
Keep with thy glorious train firm state within his heart.
Thou messenger of sympathies,
That wax and wane in lovers' eyes —
Thou — that to human thought art nourishment,
Like darkness to a dying flame!
Depart not as thy shadow came,
Depart not — lest the grave should be,
Like life and fear, a dark reality.

While yet a boy I sought for ghosts, and sped
Through many a listening chamber, cave and ruin,

And starlight wood, with fearful steps pursuing
Hopes of high talk with the departed dead.
I called on poisonous names with which our youth is fed;
I was not heard — I saw them not —
When musing deeply on the lot
Of life, at that sweet time when winds are wooing
All vital things that wake to bring
News of birds and blossoming, —
Sudden, thy shadow fell on me;
I shrieked, and clasped my hands in ecstasy!

I vowed that I would dedicate my powers
To thee and thine — have I not kept the vow?
With beating heart and streaming eyes, even now
I called the phantoms of a thousand hours
Each from his voiceless grave: they have in visioned bowers
Of studious zeal or love's delight
Outwatched with me the envious night —
They know that never joy illumed my brow
Unlinked with hope that thou wouldst free
This world from its dark slavery,
That thou — O awful Loveliness,
Wouldst give whate'er these words cannot express.

The day becomes more solemn and serene
When noon is past — there is a harmony
In autumn, and a lustre in its sky,
Which through the summer is not heard or seen,
As if it could not be, as if it had not been!
Thus let thy power, which like the truth
Of nature on my passive youth
Descended, to my onward life supply
Its calm — to one who worships thee,
And every form containing thee,
Whom, Spirit fair, thy spells did bind
To fear himself, and love all human kind.

1819

OZYMANDIAS

I MET a traveller from an antique land
Who said: Two vast and trunkless legs of stone
Stand in the desert . . . Near them, on the sand,
Half sunk, a shattered visage lies, whose frown,
And wrinkled lip, and sneer of cold command,
Tell that its sculptor well those passions read
Which yet survive, stamped on these lifeless things,
The hand that mocked them, and the heart that fed:
And on the pedestal these words appear:
'My name is Ozymandias, king of kings:
Look on my works, ye Mighty, and despair!'
Nothing beside remains. Round the decay
Of that colossal wreck, boundless and bare
The lone and level sands stretch far away.

1819

STANZAS

WRITTEN IN DEJECTION, NEAR NAPLES

THE sun is warm, the sky is clear,
The waves are dancing fast and bright,
Blue isles and snowy mountains wear
The purple noon's transparent might,
The breath of the moist earth is light,
Around its unexpanded buds;
Like many a voice of one delight,
The winds, the birds, the ocean floods,
The City's voice itself, is soft like Solitude's.

I see the Deep's untrampled floor
With green and purple seaweeds strown;
I see the waves upon the shore,
Like light dissolved in star-showers, thrown:
I sit upon the sands alone, —
The lightning of the noontide ocean
Is flashing round me, and a tone
Arises from its measured motion,
How sweet! did any heart now share in my emotion.

Alas! I have nor hope nor health,
Nor peace within nor calm around,
Nor that content surpassing wealth
The sage in meditation found,
And walked with inward glory crowned —
Nor fame, nor power, nor love, nor leisure.
Others I see whom these surround —
Smiling they live, and call life pleasure; —
To me that cup has been dealt in another measure.

Yet now despair itself is mild,
Even as the winds and waters are;
I could lie down like a tired child,
And weep away the life of care
Which I have borne and yet must bear,
Till death like sleep might steal on me,

And I might feel in the warm air
My cheek grow cold, and hear the sea
Breathe o'er my dying brain its last monotony.

Some might lament that I were cold,
As I, when this sweet day is gone,
Which my lost heart, too soon grown old,
Insults with this untimely moan;
They might lament — for I am one
Whom men love not, — and yet regret,
Unlike this day, which, when the sun
Shall on its stainless glory set,
Will linger, though enjoyed, like joy in memory yet.

1824

ODE TO THE WEST WIND

O WILD West Wind, thou breath of Autumn's being,
Thou, from whose unseen presence the leaves dead
Are driven, like ghosts from an enchanter fleeing,

Yellow, and black, and pale, and hectic red,
Pestilence-stricken multitudes: O thou,
Who chariotest to their dark wintry bed

The wingèd seeds, where they lie cold and low,
Each like a corpse within its grave, until
Thine azure sister of the Spring shall blow

Her clarion o'er the dreaming earth, and fill
(Driving sweet buds like flocks to feed in air)
With living hues and odours plain and hill:

Wild Spirit, which art moving everywhere;
Destroyer and preserver; hear, oh, hear!

Thou on whose stream, mid the steep sky's commotion,
Loose clouds like earth's decaying leaves are shed,
Shook from the tangled boughs of Heaven and Ocean,

Angels of rain and lightning: there are spread
On the blue surface of thine aëry surge,
Like the bright hair uplifted from the head

Of some fierce Maenad, even from the dim verge
Of the horizon to the zenith's height,
The locks of the approaching storm. Thou dirge

Of the dying year, to which this closing night
Will be the dome of a vast sepulchre,
Vaulted with all thy congregated might

Of vapours, from whose solid atmosphere
Black rain, and fire, and hail will burst: oh, hear!

Thou who didst waken from his summer dreams
The blue Mediterranean, where he lay,
Lulled by the coil of his crystalline streams,

Beside a pumice isle in Baiae's bay,
And saw in sleep old palaces and towers
Quivering within the wave's intenser day,

All overgrown with azure moss and flowers
So sweet, the sense faints picturing them! Thou
For whose path the Atlantic's level powers

Cleave themselves into chasms, while far below
The sea-blooms and the oozy woods which wear
The sapless foliage of the ocean, know

Thy voice, and suddenly grow gray with fear,
And tremble and despoil themselves: oh, hear!

If I were a dead leaf thou mightest bear,
If I were a swift cloud to fly with thee;
A wave to pant beneath thy power, and share

The impulse of thy strength, only less free
Than thou, O uncontrollable! If even
I were as in my boyhood, and could be

The comrade of thy wanderings over Heaven,
As then, when to outstrip thy skiey speed
Scarce seemed a vision; I would ne'er have striven

As thus with thee in prayer in my sore need.
Oh, lift me as a wave, a leaf, a cloud!
I fall upon the thorns of life! I bleed!

A heavy weight of hours has chained and bowed
One too like thee: tameless, and swift, and proud.

Make me thy lyre, even as the forest is:
What if my leaves are falling like its own!
The tumult of thy mighty harmonies

Will take from both a deep, autumnal tone,
Sweet though in sadness. Be thou, Spirit fierce,
My spirit! Be thou me, impetuous one!

Drive my dead thoughts over the universe
Like withered leaves to quicken a new birth!
And, by the incantation of this verse,

Scatter, as from an unextinguished hearth
Ashes and sparks, my words among mankind!
Be through my lips to unawakened earth

The trumpet of a prophecy! O, Wind,
If Winter comes, can Spring be far behind?

1820

THE CLOUD

I BRING fresh showers for the thirsting flowers,
From the seas and the streams;
I bear light shade for the leaves when laid
In their noonday dreams.
From my wings are shaken the dews that waken
The sweet buds every one,
When rocked to rest on their mother's breast,
As she dances about the sun.
I wield the flail of the lashing hail,
And whiten the green plains under,
And then again I dissolve it in rain,
And laugh as I pass in thunder.

I sift the snow on the mountains below,
And their great pines groan aghast;
And all the night 't is my pillow white,
While I sleep in the arms of the blast.
Sublime on the towers of my skiey bowers,
Lightning my pilot sits;
In a cavern under is fettered the thunder,
It struggles and howls at fits;
Over earth and ocean, with gentle motion,
This pilot is guiding me,
Lured by the love of the genii that move
In the depths of the purple sea;
Over the rills, and the crags, and the hills,
Over the lakes and the plains,
Wherever he dream, under mountain or stream,
The Spirit he loves remains;
And I all the while bask in Heaven's blue smile,
Whilst he is dissolving in rains.

The sanguine Sunrise, with his meteor eyes,
And his burning plumes outspread,
Leaps on the back of my sailing rack,
When the morning star shines dead;
As on the jag of a mountain crag,
Which an earthquake rocks and swings,
An eagle alit one moment may sit
In the light of its golden wings.
And when Sunset may breathe, from the lit sea beneath,
Its ardours of rest and of love,
And the crimson pall of eve may fall
From the depth of Heaven above,
With wings folded I rest, on mine aëry nest,
As still as a brooding dove.

That orbèd maiden with white fire laden,
Whom mortals call the Moon,
Gildes glimmering o'er my fleece-like floor,
By the midnight breezes strewn;
And wherever the beat of her unseen feet,
Which only the angels hear,
May have broken the woof of my tent's thin roof,
The stars peep behind her and peer;
And I laugh to see them whirl and flee,
Like a swarm of golden bees,
When I widen the rent in my wind-built tent,
Till the calm rivers, lakes, and seas,
Like strips of the sky fallen through me on high,
Are each paved with the moon and these.

I bind the Sun's throne with a burning zone,
And the Moon's with a girdle of pearl;
The volcanoes are dim, and the stars reel and swim,
When the whirlwinds my banner unfurl.
From cape to cape, with a bridge-like shape,
Over a torrent sea,
Sunbeam-proof, I hang like a roof, —
The mountains its columns be.
The triumphal arch through which I march
With hurricane, fire, and snow,
When the Powers of the air are chained to my chair,
Is the million-coloured bow;
The sphere-fire above its soft colours wove,
While the moist Earth was laughing below.

I am the daughter of Earth and Water,
And the nursling of the Sky;
I pass through the pores of the ocean and shores;
I change, but I cannot die.
For after the rain when with never a stain
The pavilion of Heaven is bare,
And the winds and sunbeams with their convex gleams

Build up the blue dome of air,
I silently laugh at my own cenotaph,
And out of the caverns of rain,
Like a child from the womb, like a ghost from the tomb,
I arise and unbuild it again.

1820

TO A SKYLARK

Hail to thee, blithe Spirit!
Bird thou never wert,
That from Heaven, or near it,
Pourest thy full heart
In profuse strains of unpremeditated art.

Higher still and higher
From the earth thou springest
Like a cloud of fire;
The blue deep thou wingest,
And singing still dost soar, and soaring ever singest.

In the golden lightning
Of the sunken sun,
O'er which clouds are bright'ning,
Thou dost float and run;
Like an unbodied joy whose race is just begun.

The pale purple even
Melts around thy flight;
Like a star of Heaven,
In the broad daylight
Thou art unseen, but yet I hear thy shrill delight,

Keen as are the arrows
Of that silver sphere,
Whose intense lamp narrows
In the white dawn clear
Until we hardly see — we feel that it is there.

All the earth and air
With thy voice is loud,
As, when night is bare,
From one lonely cloud
The moon rains out her beams, and Heaven is overflowed.

What thou art we know not;
What is most like thee?
From rainbow clouds there flow not
Drops so bright to see
As from thy presence showers a rain of melody.

Like a Poet hidden
In the light of thought,
Singing hymns unbidden,
Till the world is wrought
To sympathy with hopes and fears it heeded not:

Like a high-born maiden
In a palace-tower,
Soothing her love-laden
Soul in secret hour
With music sweet as love, which overflows her bower:

Like a glow-worm golden
In a dell of dew,
Scattering unbeholden
Its aëreal hue
Among the flowers and grass, which screen it from the view!

Like a rose embowered
In its own green leaves,
By warm winds deflowered,
Till the scent it gives
Makes faint with too much sweet those heavy-wingèd thieves:

Sound of vernal showers
On the twinkling grass,
Rain-awakened flowers,
All that ever was
Joyous, and clear, and fresh, thy music doth surpass:

Teach us, Sprite or Bird,
What sweet thoughts are thine:
I have never heard
Praise of love or wine
That panted forth a flood of rapture so divine.

Chorus Hymeneal,
Or triumphal chant,
Matched with thine would be all
But an empty vaunt,
A thing wherein we feel there is some hidden want.

What objects are the fountains
Of thy happy strain?
What fields, or waves, or mountains?
What shapes of sky or plain?
What love of thine own kind? what ignorance of pain?

With thy clear keen joyance
Languor cannot be:
Shadow of annoyance
Never came near thee:
Thou lovest — but ne'er knew love's sad satiety.

Waking or asleep,
Thou of death must deem
Things more true and deep
Than we mortals dream,
Or how could thy notes flow in such a crystal stream?

We look before and after,
And pine for what is not:
Our sincerest laughter
With some pain is fraught;
Our sweetest songs are those that tell of saddest thought.

Yet if we could scorn
Hate, and pride, and fear;
If we were things born
Not to shed a tear,
I know not how thy joy we ever should come near.

Better than all measures
Of delightful sound,
Better than all treasures
That in books are found,
Thy skill to poet were, thou scorner of the ground!

Teach me half the gladness
That thy brain must know,
Such harmonious madness
From my lips would flow
The world should listen then — as I am listening now.

1820

TIME LONG PAST

LIKE the ghost of a dear friend dead
Is Time long past.
A tone which is now forever fled,
A hope which is now forever past,
A love so sweet it could not last,
Was Time long past.

There were sweet dreams in the night
Of Time long past:
And, was it sadness or delight,
Each day a shadow onward cast
Which made us wish it yet might last —
That Time long past.

There is regret, almost remorse,
For Time long past.
'T is like a child's belovèd corse
A father watches, till at last
Beauty is like remembrance, cast
From Time long past.

1824

TO NIGHT

SWIFTLY walk o'er the western wave,
Spirit of Night!
Out of the misty eastern cave,
Where, all the long and lone daylight,
Thou wovest dreams of joy and fear,
Which make thee terrible and dear,—
Swift be thy flight!

Wrap thy form in a mantle gray,
Star-inwrought!
Blind with thine hair the eyes of Day;
Kiss her until she be wearied out,
Then wander o'er city, and sea, and land,
Touching all with thine opiate wand —
Come, long-sought!

When I arose and saw the dawn,
I sighed for thee;
When light rode high, and the dew was gone,
And noon lay heavy on flower and tree,
And the weary Day turned to his rest,
Lingering like an unloved guest,
I sighed for thee.

Thy brother Death came, and cried,
Wouldst thou me?
Thy sweet child Sleep, the filmy-eyed,
Murmured like a noontide bee,
Shall I nestle near thy side?
Wouldst thou me? — And I replied,
No, not thee!

Death will come when thou art dead,
Soon, too soon —
Sleep will come when thou art fled;
Of neither would I ask the boon
I ask of thee, belovèd Night —
Swift be thine approaching flight,
Come soon, soon!

1824

TIME

UNFATHOMABLE Sea! whose waves are years,
Ocean of Time, whose waters of deep woe
Are brackish with the salt of human tears!
Thou shoreless flood, which in thy ebb and flow
Claspest the limits of mortality,
And sick of prey, yet howling on for more,
Vomitest thy wrecks on its inhospitable shore;
Treacherous in calm, and terrible in storm,
Who shall put forth on thee,
Unfathomable Sea?

1824

TO ———

Music, when soft voices die,
Vibrates in the memory —
Odours, when sweet violets sicken,
Live within the sense they quicken.

Rose leaves, when the rose is dead,
Are heaped for the belovèd's bed;
And so thy thoughts, when thou art gone,
Love itself shall slumber on.

1824

SONG

Rarely, rarely, comest thou,
Spirit of Delight!
Wherefore hast thou left me now
Many a day and night?
Many a weary night and day
'T is since thou art fled away.

How shall ever one like me
Win thee back again?
With the joyous and the free
Thou wilt scoff at pain.
Spirit false! thou hast forgot
All but those who need thee not.

As a lizard with the shade
Of a trembling leaf,
Thou with sorrow art dismayed;
Even the sighs of grief
Reproach thee, that thou art not near,
And reproach thou wilt not hear.

Let me set my mournful ditty
To a merry measure;
Thou wilt never come for pity,
Thou wilt come for pleasure;
Pity then will cut away
Those cruel wings, and thou wilt stay.

I love all that thou lovest,
Spirit of Delight!
The fresh Earth in new leaves dressed,
And the starry night;
Autumn evening, and the morn
When the golden mists are born.

I love snow, and all the forms
Of the radiant frost;
I love waves, and winds, and storms,
Everything almost
Which is Nature's, and may be
Untainted by man's misery.

I love tranquil solitude,
And such society
As is quiet, wise, and good;
Between thee and me
What difference? but thou dost possess
The things I seek, not love them less.

I love Love — though he has wings,
And like light can flee,
But above all other things,
Spirit, I love thee —
Thou art love and life! Oh, come,
Make once more my heart thy home.

1824

MUTABILITY

The flower that smiles to-day
To-morrow dies;
All that we wish to stay
Tempts and then flies.
What is this world's delight?
Lightning that mocks the night,
Brief even as bright.

Virtue, how frail it is!
Friendship how rare!
Love, how it sells poor bliss
For proud despair!
But we, though soon they fall,
Survive their joy, and all
Which ours we call.

Whilst skies are blue and bright,
Whilst flowers are gay,
Whilst eyes that change ere night
Make glad the day;
Whilst yet the calm hours creep,
Dream thou — and from thy sleep
Then wake to weep.

1824

A LAMENT

O world! O life! O time!
On whose last steps I climb,
Trembling at that where I had stood before;
When will return the glory of your prime?
No more — Oh, never more!

Out of the day and night
A joy has taken flight;
Fresh spring, and summer, and winter hoar,
Move my faint heart with grief, but with delight
No more — Oh. never more!

1824

REMEMBRANCE

Swifter far than summer's flight —
Swifter far than youth's delight —
Swifter far than happy night,
    Art thou come and gone —
As the earth when leaves are dead,
As the night when sleep is sped,
As the heart when joy is fled,
    I am left lone, alone.

The swallow summer comes again —
The owlet night resumes her reign —
But the wild-swan youth is fain
    To fly with thee, false as thou. —
My heart each day desires the morrow;
Sleep itself is turned to sorrow;
Vainly would my winter borrow
    Sunny leaves from any bough.

Lilies for a bridal bed —
Roses for a matron's head —
Violets for a maiden dead —
    Pansies let *my* flowers be:
On the living grave I bear
Scatter them without a tear —
Let no friend, however dear,
    Waste one hope, one fear for me.

1824

TO ——

One word is too often profaned
    For me to profane it,
One feeling too falsely disdained
    For thee to disdain it;
One hope is too like despair
    For prudence to smother,
And pity from thee more dear
    Than that from another.

I can give not what men call love,
    But wilt thou accept not
The worship the heart lifts above
    And the Heavens reject not, —
The desire of the moth for the star,
    Of the night for the morrow,
The devotion to something afar
    From the sphere of our sorrow?

1824

ADONAIS

I weep for Adonais — he is dead!
O, weep for Adonais! though our tears
Thaw not the frost which binds so dear a
    head!
And thou, sad Hour, selected from all years
To mourn our loss, rouse thy obscure com-
    peers,
And teach them thine own sorrow, say:
    'With me
Died Adonais; till the Future dares
Forget the Past, his fate and fame shall be
An echo and a light unto eternity!'

Where wert thou, mighty Mother, when he
    lay,
When thy Son lay, pierced by the shaft which
    flies
In darkness? where was lorn Urania
When Adonais died? With veilèd eyes,
'Mid listening Echoes, in her Paradise
She sate, while one, with soft enamoured
    breath,
Rekindled all the fading melodies,
With which, like flowers that mock the corse
    beneath,
He had adorned and hid the coming bulk of
    Death.

Oh, weep for Adonais — he is dead!
Wake, melancholy Mother, wake and
    weep!
Yet wherefore? Quench within their burn-
    ing bed
Thy fiery tears, and let thy loud heart keep
Like his, a mute and uncomplaining sleep;
For he is gone, where all things wise and fair
Descend; — oh, dream not that the amorous
    Deep
Will yet restore him to the vital air;
Death feeds on his mute voice, and laughs
    at our despair.

Most musical of mourners, weep again!
Lament anew, Urania! — He died,
Who was the Sire of an immortal strain,
Blind, old, and lonely, when his country's
    pride,
The priest, the slave, and the liberticide,
Trampled and mocked with many a loathèd
    rite
Of lust and blood; he went, unterrified,
Into the gulf of death; but his clear Sprite
Yet reigns o'er earth; the third among the
    sons of light.

Most musical of mourners, weep anew!
Not all to that bright station dared to climb;
And happier they their happiness who knew,
Whose tapers yet burn through that night of
    time
In which suns perished; others more sub-
    lime,
Struck by the envious wrath of man or god,
Have sunk, extinct in their refulgent prime;
And some yet live, treading the thorny road,
Which leads, through toil and hate, to
    Fame's serene abode.

But now, thy youngest, dearest one, has perished —
The nursling of thy widowhood, who grew,
Like a pale flower by some sad maiden cherished,
And fed with true-love tears, instead of dew;
Most musical of mourners, weep anew!
Thy extreme hope, the loveliest and the last,
The bloom, whose petals nipped before they blew
Died on the promise of the fruit, is waste;
The broken lily lies — the storm is overpast.

To that high Capital, where kingly Death
Keeps his pale court in beauty and decay,
He came; and bought, with price of purest breath,
A grave among the eternal. — Come away!
Haste, while the vault of blue Italian day
Is yet his fitting charnel-roof! while still
He lies, as if in dewy sleep he lay;
Awake him not! surely he takes his fill
Of deep and liquid rest, forgetful of all ill.

He will awake no more, oh, never more! —
Within the twilight chamber spreads apace
The shadow of white Death, and at the door
Invisible Corruption waits to trace
His extreme way to her dim dwelling-place;
The eternal Hunger sits, but pity and awe
Soothe her pale rage, nor dares she to deface
So fair a prey, till darkness, and the law
Of change, shall o'er his sleep the mortal curtain draw.

Oh, weep for Adonais! — The quick Dreams,
The passion-wingèd Ministers of thought,
Who were his flocks, whom near the living streams
Of his young spirit he fed, and whom he taught
The love which was its music, wander not, —
Wander no more, from kindling brain to brain,
But droop there, whence they sprung; and mourn their lot
Round the cold heart, where, after their sweet pain,
They ne'er will gather strength, or find a home again.

And one with trembling hands clasps his cold head,
And fans him with her moonlight wings, and cries;
'Our love, our hope, our sorrow, is not dead;
See, on the silken fringe of his faint eyes,
Like dew upon a sleeping flower, there lies
A tear some Dream has loosened from his brain.'
Lost Angel of a ruined Paradise!
She knew not 't was her own; as with no stain
She faded, like a cloud which had outwept its rain.

One from a lucid urn of starry dew
Washed his light limbs as if embalming them;
Another clipped her profuse locks, and threw
The wreath upon him, like an anadem,
Which frozen tears instead of pearls begem;
Another in her wilful grief would break
Her bow and wingèd reeds, as if to stem
A greater loss with one which was more weak;
And dull the barbèd fire against his frozen cheek.

Another Splendour on his mouth alit,
That mouth, whence it was wont to draw the breath
Which gave it strength to pierce the guarded wit,
And pass into the panting heart beneath
With lightning and with music: the damp death
Quenched its caress upon his icy lips;
And, as a dying meteor stains a wreath
Of moonlight vapour, which the cold night clips,
It flushed through his pale limbs, and passed to its eclipse.

And others came . . . Desires and Adorations,
Wingèd Persuasions and veiled Destinies,
Splendours, and Glooms, and glimmering Incarnations
Of hopes and fears, and twilight Phantasies;
And Sorrow, with her family of Sighs,
And Pleasure, blind with tears, led by the gleam
Of her own dying smile instead of eyes,
Came in slow pomp; — the moving pomp might seem
Like pageantry of mist on an autumnal stream.

All he had loved, and moulded into thought,
From shape, and hue, and odour, and sweet sound,
Lamented Adonais. Morning sought
Her eastern watch-tower, and her hair unbound,
Wet with the tears which should adorn the ground,
Dimmed the aëreal eyes that kindle day;

Afar the melancholy thunder moaned,
Pale Ocean in unquiet slumber lay,
And the wild Winds flew round, sobbing in their dismay.

Lost Echo sits amid the voiceless mountains,
And feeds her grief with his remembered lay,
And will no more reply to winds or fountains,
Or amorous birds perched on the young green spray,
Or herdsman's horn, or bell at closing day;
Since she can mimic not his lips, more dear
Than those for whose disdain she pined away
Into a shadow of all sounds: — a drear
Murmur, between their songs, is all the woodmen hear.

Grief made the young Spring wild, and she threw down
Her kindling buds, as if she Autumn were,
Or they dead leaves; since her delight is flown,
For whom should she have waked the sullen year?
To Phoebus was not Hyacinth so dear
Nor to himself Narcissus, as to both
Thou, Adonais: wan they stand and sere
Amid the faint companions of their youth,
With dew all turned to tears; odour, to sighing ruth.

Thy spirit's sister, the lorn nightingale
Mourns not her mate with such melodious pain;
Not so the eagle, who like thee could scale
Heaven, and could nourish in the sun's domain
Her mighty youth with morning, doth complain,
Soaring and screaming round her empty nest,
As Albion wails for thee: the curse of Cain
Light on his head who pierced thy innocent breast,
And scared the angel soul that was its earthly guest!

Ah, woe is me! Winter is come and gone,
But grief returns with the revolving year;
The airs and streams renew their joyous tone;
The ants, the bees, the swallows reappear;
Fresh leaves and flowers deck the dead Seasons' bier;
The amorous birds now pair in every brake,
And build their mossy homes in field and brere;
And the green lizard, and the golden snake,
Like unimprisoned flames, out of their trance awake.

Through wood and stream and field and hill and Ocean
A quickening life from the Earth's heart has burst
As it has ever done, with change and motion,
From the great morning of the world when first
God dawned on Chaos; in its stream immersed,
The lamps of Heaven flash with a softer light;
All baser things pant with life's sacred thirst;
Diffuse themselves; and spend in love's delight,
The beauty and the joy of their renewèd might.

The leprous corpse, touched by this spirit tender,
Exhales itself in flowers of gentle breath;
Like incarnations of the stars, when splendour
Is changed to fragrance, they illumine death
And mock the merry worm that wakes beneath;
Nought we know, dies. Shall that alone which knows
Be as a sword consumed before the sheath
By sightless lightning? — the intense atom glows
A moment, then is quenched in a most cold repose.

Alas! that all we loved of him should be,
But for our grief, as if it had not been,
And grief itself be mortal! Woe is me!
Whence are we, and why are we? of what scene
The actors or spectators? Great and mean
Meet massed in death, who lends what life must borrow.
As long as skies are blue, and fields are green,
Evening must usher night, night urge the morrow,
Month follow month with woe, and year wake year to sorrow.

He will awake no more, oh, never more!
'Wake thou,' cried Misery, 'childless Mother, rise
Out of thy sleep, and slake, in thy heart's core,
A wound more fierce than his, with tears and sighs.'
And all the Dreams that watched Urania's eyes,

And all the Echoes whom their sister's song
Had held in holy silence, cried: 'Arise!'
Swift as a Thought by the snake Memory stung,
From her ambrosial rest the fading Splendour sprung.

She rose like an autumnal Night, that springs
Out of the East, and follows wild and drear
The golden Day, which, on eternal wings,
Even as a ghost abandoning a bier,
Had left the Earth a corpse. Sorrow and fear
So struck, so roused, so rapped Urania;
So saddened round her like an atmosphere
Of stormy mist; so swept her on her way
Even to the mournful place where Adonais lay.

Out of her secret Paradise she sped,
Through camps and cities rough with stone, and steel,
And human hearts, which to her aery tread
Yielding not, wounded the invisible
Palms of her tender feet where'er they fell:
And barbèd tongues, and thoughts more sharp than they,
Rent the soft Form they never could repel,
Whose sacred blood, like the young tears of May,
Paved with eternal flowers that undeserving way.

In the death-chamber for a moment Death,
Shamed by the presence of that living Might,
Blushed to annihilation, and the breath
Revisited those lips, and Life's pale light
Flashed through those limbs, so late her dear delight.
'Leave me not wild and drear and comfortless,
As silent lightning leaves the starless night!
Leave me not!' cried Urania: her distress
Roused Death: Death rose and smiled, and met her vain caress.

'Stay yet awhile! speak to me once again;
Kiss me, so long but as a kiss may live;
And in my heartless breast and burning brain
That word, that kiss, shall all thoughts else survive,
With food of saddest memory kept alive,
Now thou art dead, as if it were a part
Of thee, my Adonais! I would give
All that I am to be as thou now art!
But I am chained to Time, and cannot thence depart!

'O gentle child, beautiful as thou wert,
Why didst thou leave the trodden paths of men
Too soon, and with weak hands though mighty heart
Dare the unpastured dragon in his den?
Defenceless as thou wert, oh, where was then
Wisdom the mirrored shield, or scorn the spear?
Or hadst thou waited the full cycle, when
Thy spirit should have filled its crescent sphere,
The monsters of life's waste had fled from thee like deer.

'The herded wolves, bold only to pursue;
The obscene ravens, clamorous o'er the dead;
The vultures to the conqueror's banner true
Who feed where Desolation first has fed,
And whose wings rain contagion; — how they fled,
When, like Apollo, from his golden bow
The Pythian of the age one arrow sped
And smiled! — The spoilers tempt no second blow,
They fawn on the proud feet that spurn them lying low.

'The sun comes forth, and many reptiles spawn;
He sets, and each ephemeral insect then
Is gathered into death without a dawn,
And the immortal stars awake again;
So is it in the world of living men:
A godlike mind soars forth, in its delight
Making earth bare and veiling heaven, and when
It sinks, the swarms that dimmed or shared its light
Leave to its kindred lamps the spirit's awful night.'

Thus ceased she: and the mountain shepherds came,
Their garlands sere, their magic mantles rent;
The Pilgrim of Eternity, whose fame
Over his living head like Heaven is bent,
An early but enduring monument,
Came, veiling all the lightnings of his song
In sorrow; from her wilds Ierne sent
The sweetest lyrist of her saddest wrong,
And Love taught Grief to fall like music from his tongue.

Midst others of less note, came one frail Form,
A phantom among men; companionless
As the last cloud of an expiring storm
Whose thunder is its knell; he, as I guess,
Had gazed on Nature's naked loveliness,
Actaeon-like, and now he fled astray
With feeble steps o'er the world's wilderness,
And his own thoughts, along that rugged way,
Pursued, like raging hounds, their father and their prey.

A pardlike Spirit beautiful and swift —
A Love in desolation masked; — a Power
Girt round with weakness; — it can scarce uplift
The weight of the superincumbent hour;
It is a dying lamp, a falling shower,
A breaking billow; — even whilst we speak
Is it not broken? On the withering flower
The killing sun smiles brightly: on a cheek
The life can burn in blood, even while the heart may break.

His head was bound with pansies overblown,
And faded violets, white, and pied, and blue;
And a light spear topped with a cypress cone,
Round whose rude shaft dark ivy-tresses grew
Yet dripping with the forest's noonday dew,
Vibrated, as the ever-beating heart
Shook the weak hand that grasped it; of that crew
He came the last, neglected and apart;
A herd-abandoned deer struck by the hunter's dart.

All stood aloof, and at his partial moan
Smiled through their tears; well knew that gentle band
Who in another's fate now wept his own,
As in the accents of an unknown land
He sung new sorrow; sad Urania scanned
The Stranger's mien, and murmured: 'Who art thou?'
He answered not, but with a sudden hand
Made bare his branded and ensanguined brow,
Which was like Cain's or Christ's — oh! that it should be so!

What softer voice is hushed over the dead?
Athwart what brow is that dark mantle thrown?
What form leans sadly o'er the white death-bed,
In mockery of monumental stone,
The heavy heart heaving without a moan?
If it be He, who, gentlest of the wise,
Taught, soothed, loved, honoured the departed one,
Let me not vex, with inharmonious sighs,
The silence of that heart's accepted sacrifice.

Our Adonais has drunk poison — oh!
What deaf and viperous murderer could crown
Life's early cup with such a draught of woe?
The nameless worm would now itself disown:
It felt, yet could escape, the magic tone
Whose prelude held all envy, hate, and wrong,
But what was howling in one breast alone,
Silent with expectation of the song,
Whose master's hand is cold, whose silver lyre unstrung.

Live thou, whose infamy is not thy fame!
Live! fear no heavier chastisement from me,
Thou noteless blot on a remembered name!
But be thyself, and know thyself to be!
And ever at thy season be thou free
To spill the venom when thy fangs o'erflow:
Remorse and Self-contempt shall cling to thee;
Hot Shame shall burn upon thy secret brow,
And like a beaten hound tremble thou shalt — as now.

Nor let us weep that our delight is fled
Far from these carrion kites that scream below;
He wakes or sleeps with the enduring dead;
Thou canst not soar where he is sitting now —
Dust to the dust! but the pure spirit shall flow
Back to the burning fountain whence it came,
A portion of the Eternal, which must glow
Through time and change, unquenchably the same,
Whilst thy cold embers choke the sordid hearth of shame.

Peace, peace! he is not dead, he doth not sleep —
He hath awakened from the dream of life —
'T is we, who lost in stormy visions, keep
With phantoms an unprofitable strife,
And in mad trance, strike with our spirit's knife

Invulnerable nothings. — *We* decay
Like corpses in a charnel; fear and grief
Convulse us and consume us day by day,
And cold hopes swarm like worms within our living clay.

He has outsoared the shadow of our night;
Envy and calumny and hate and pain,
And that unrest which men miscall delight,
Can touch him not and torture not again;
From the contagion of the world's slow stain
He is secure, and now can never mourn
A heart grown cold, a head grown gray in vain;
Nor, when the spirit's self has ceased to burn,
With sparkless ashes load an unlamented urn.

He lives, he wakes — 't is Death is dead, not he;
Mourn not for Adonais. — Thou young Dawn,
Turn all thy dew to splendour, for from thee
The spirit thou lamentest is not gone;
Ye caverns and ye forests, cease to moan!
Cease, ye faint flowers and fountains, and thou Air,
Which like a mourning veil thy scarf hadst thrown
O'er the abandoned Earth, now leave it bare
Even to the joyous stars which smile on its despair!

He is made one with Nature: there is heard
His voice in all her music, from the moan
Of thunder, to the song of night's sweet bird;
He is a presence to be felt and known
In darkness and in light, from herb and stone,
Spreading itself where'er that Power may move
Which has withdrawn his being to its own;
Which wields the world with never-wearied love,
Sustains it from beneath, and kindles it above.

He is a portion of the loveliness
Which once he made more lovely: he doth bear
His part, while the one Spirit's plastic stress
Sweeps through the dull dense world, compelling there,
All new successions to the forms they wear;
Torturing th' unwilling dross that checks its flight
To its own likeness, as each mass may bear;
And bursting in its beauty and its might
From trees and beasts and men into the Heaven's light.

The splendours of the firmament of time
May be eclipsed, but are extinguished not;
Like stars to their appointed height they climb,
And death is a low mist which cannot blot
The brightness it may veil. When lofty thought
Lifts a young heart above its mortal lair,
And love and life contend in it, for what
Shall be its earthly doom, the dead live there
And move like winds of light on dark and stormy air.

The inheritors of unfulfilled renown
Rose from their thrones, built beyond mortal thought,
Far in the Unapparent. Chatterton
Rose pale, — his solemn agony had not
Yet faded from him; Sidney, as he fought
And as he fell and as he lived and loved
Sublimely mild, a Spirit without spot,
Arose; and Lucan, by his death approved:
Oblivion as they rose shrank like a thing reproved.

And many more, whose names on Earth are dark,
But whose transmitted effluence cannot die
So long as fire outlives the pȧrent spark,
Rose, robed in dazzling immortality.
'Thou art become as one of us,' they cry,
'It was for thee yon kingless sphere has long
Swung blind in unascended majesty,
Silent alone amid an Heaven of Song.
Assume thy wingèd throne, thou Vesper of our throng!'

Who mourns for Adonais? Oh, come forth,
Fond wretch! and know thyself and him aright.
Clasp with thy panting soul the pendulous Earth;
As from a centre, dart thy spirit's light
Beyond all worlds, until its spacious might
Satiate the void circumference: then shrink
Even to a point within our day and night;
And keep thy heart light lest it make thee sink
When hope has kindled hope, and lured thee to the brink.

Or go to Rome, which is the sepulchre,
Oh, not of him, but of our joy: 't is nought
That ages, empires, and religions there
Lie buried in the ravage they have wrought;
For such as he can lend, — they borrow not
Glory from those who made the world their prey;
And he is gathered to the kings of thought
Who waged contention with their time's decay,
And of the past are all that cannot pass away.

Go thou to Rome, — at once the Paradise,
The grave, the city, and the wilderness;
And where its wrecks like shattered mountains rise,
And flowering weeds, and fragrant copses dress
The bones of Desolation's nakedness
Pass, till the spirit of the spot shall lead
Thy footsteps to a slope of green access
Where, like an infant's smile, over the dead
A light of laughing flowers along the grass is spread;

And gray walls moulder round, on which dull Time
Feeds, like slow fire upon a hoary brand;
And one keen pyramid with wedge sublime,
Pavilioning the dust of him who planned
This refuge for his memory, doth stand
Like flame transformed to marble; and beneath,
A field is spread, on which a newer band
Have pitched in Heaven's smile their camp of death,
Welcoming him we lose with scarce extinguished breath.

Here pause: these graves are all too young as yet
To have outgrown the sorrow which consigned
Its charge to each; and if the seal is set,
Here, on one fountain of a mourning mind,
Break it not thou! too surely shalt thou find
Thine own well full, if thou returnest home,
Of tears and gall. From the world's bitter wind
Seek shelter in the shadow of the tomb.
What Adonais is, why fear we to become?

The One remains, the many change and pass;
Heaven's light forever shines, Earth's shadows fly;
Life, like a dome of many-coloured glass,
Stains the white radiance of Eternity,
Until Death tramples it to fragments. — Die,
If thou wouldst be with that which thou dost seek!
Follow where all is fled! — Rome's azure sky,
Flowers, ruins, statues, music, words, are weak
The glory they tranfuse with fitting truth to speak.

Why linger, why turn back, why shrink, my Heart?
Thy hopes are gone before: from all things here
They have departed; thou shouldst now depart!
A light is passed from the revolving year,
And man, and woman; and what still is dear
Attracts to crush, repels to make thee wither.
The soft sky smiles, — the low wind whispers near:
'T is Adonais calls! oh, hasten thither,
No more let Life divide what Death can join together.

That Light whose smile kindles the Universe,
That Beauty in which all things work and move,
That Benediction which the eclipsing Curse
Of birth can quench not, that sustaining Love
Which through the web of being blindly wove
By man and beast and earth and air and sea,
Burns bright or dim, as each are mirrors of
The fire for which all thirst; now beams on me,
Consuming the last clouds of cold mortality.

The breath whose might I have invoked in song
Descends on me; my spirit's bark is driven,
Far from the shore, far from the trembling throng
Whose sails were never to the tempest given;
The massy earth and spherèd skies are riven!
I am borne darkly, fearfully, afar;
Whilst, burning through the inmost veil of Heaven,
The soul of Adonais, like a star,
Beacons from the abode where the Eternal are.

1821

WITH A GUITAR, TO JANE

Ariel to Miranda: — Take
This slave of Music, for the sake
Of him who is the slave of thee,
And teach it all the harmony
In which thou canst, and only thou.
Make the delighted spirit glow,
Till joy denies itself again,
And, too intense, is turned to pain;
For by permission and command
Of thine own Prince Ferdinand,
Poor Ariel sends this silent token
Of more than ever can be spoken;
Your guardian spirit, Ariel, who,
From life to life, must still pursue
Your happiness; — for thus alone
Can Ariel ever find his own.
From Prospero's enchanted cell,
As the mighty verses tell,
To the throne of Naples, he
Lit you o'er the trackless sea,
Flitting on, your prow before,
Like a living meteor.
When you die, the silent Moon,
In her interlunar swoon,
Is not sadder in her cell
Than deserted Ariel.
When you live again on earth,
Like an unseen star of birth,
Ariel guides you o'er the sea
Of life from your nativity.
Many changes have been run
Since Ferdinand and you begun
Your course of love, and Ariel still
Has tracked your steps, and served your will;
Now, in humbler, happier lot,
This is all remembered not;
And now, alas! the poor sprite is
Imprisoned, for some fault of his.
In a body like a grave; —
From you he only dares to crave,
For his service and his sorrow,
A smile to-day, a song to-morrow.

The artist who this idol wrought,
To echo all harmonious thought,
Felled a tree, while on the steep
The woods were in their winter sleep,
Rocked in that repose divine
On the wind-swept Apennine;
And dreaming, some of Autumn past,
And some of Spring approaching fast,
And some of April buds and showers,
And some of songs in July bowers,
And all of love; and so this tree, —
O that such our death may be! —
Died in sleep, and felt no pain,
To live in happier form again:
From which, beneath Heaven's fairest star,
The artist wrought this loved Guitar,
And taught it justly to reply,
To all who question skilfully,
In language gentle as thine own;
Whispering in enamoured tone
Sweet oracles of woods and dells,
And summer winds in sylvan cells;
For it had learned all harmonies
Of the plains and of the skies,
Of the forests and the mountains,
And the many-voicèd fountains;
The clearest echoes of the hills,
The softest notes of falling rills,
The melodies of birds and bees,
The murmuring of summer seas,
And pattering rain, and breathing dew,
And airs of evening; and it knew
That seldom-heard mysterious sound,
Which, driven on its diurnal round,
As it floats through boundless day,
Our world enkindles on its way. —
All this it knows, but will not tell
To those who cannot question well
The Spirit that inhabits it;
It talks according to the wit
Of its companions; and no more
Is heard than has been felt before,
By those who tempt it to betray
These secrets of an elder day:
But, sweetly as its answers will
Flatter hands of perfect skill,
It keeps its highest, holiest tone
For our belovèd Jane alone.

1832

A DIRGE

Rough wind, that moanest loud
  Grief too sad for song;
Wild wind, when sullen cloud
  Knells all the night long;
Sad storm, whose tears are vain,
Bare woods, whose branches strain,
Deep caves and dreary main, —
  Wail, for the world's wrong!

1824

John Keats (1795–1821)

SONNETS

KEEN, FITFUL GUSTS

Keen, fitful gusts are whisp'ring here and there
Among the bushes half leafless, and dry;
The stars look very cold about the sky,

And I have many miles on foot to fare.
Yet feel I little of the cool bleak air,
Or of the dead leaves rustling drearily,
Or of those silver lamps that burn on high,
Or of the distance from home's pleasant lair:
For I am brimfull of the friendliness
That in a little cottage I have found;
Of fair-haired Milton's eloquent distress,
And all his love for gentle Lycid drowned;
Of lovely Laura in her light green dress,
And faithful Petrarch gloriously crowned.

1817

TO ONE WHO HAS BEEN LONG IN CITY PENT

To one who has been long in city pent,
'T is very sweet to look into the fair
And open face of heaven, — to breathe a prayer
Full in the smile of the blue firmament.
Who is more happy, when, with heart's content,
Fatigued he sinks into some pleasant lair
Of wavy grass, and reads a debonair
And gentle tale of love and languishment?
Returning home at evening, with an ear
Catching the notes of Philomel, — an eye
Watching the sailing cloudlet's bright career,
He mourns that day so soon has glided by:
E'en like the passage of an angel's tear
That falls through the clear ether silently.

1817

ON FIRST LOOKING INTO CHAPMAN'S HOMER

Much have I travelled in the realms of gold,
And many goodly states and kingdoms seen;
Round many western islands have I been
Which bards in fealty to Apollo hold.
Oft of one wide expanse had I been told
That deep-browed Homer ruled as his demesne;
Yet did I never breathe its pure serene
Till I heard Chapman speak out loud and bold:
Then felt I like some watcher of the skies
When a new planet swims into his ken;
Or like stout Cortez when with eagle eyes
He stared at the Pacific — and all his men
Looked at each other with a wild surmise —
Silent, upon a peak in Darien.

1817

ON LEAVING SOME FRIENDS AT AN EARLY HOUR

Give me a golden pen, and let me lean
On heaped up flowers, in regions clear, and far;
Bring me a tablet whiter than a star,
Or hand of hymning angel, when 't is seen
The silver strings of heavenly harp atween:
And let there glide by many a pearly car,
Pink robes, and wavy hair, and diamond jar,
And half discovered wings, and glances keen.
The while let music wander round my ears,
And as it reaches each delicious ending,
Let me write down a line of glorious tone,
And full of many wonders of the spheres:
For what a height my spirit is contending!
'T is not content so soon to be alone.

1817

ADDRESSED TO [HAYDON]

Great spirits now on earth are sojourning;
He of the cloud, the cataract, the lake,
Who on Helvellyn's summit, wide awake,
Catches his freshness from Archangel's wing:
He of the rose, the violet, the spring,
The social smile, the chain for Freedom's sake:
And lo! — whose stedfastness would never take
A meaner sound than Raphael's whispering.
And other spirits there are standing apart
Upon the forehead of the age to come;
These, these will give the world another heart,
And other pulses. Hear ye not the hum
Of mighty workings? —
Listen awhile ye nations, and be dumb.

1817

WHEN I HAVE FEARS

When I have fears that I may cease to be
Before my pen has gleaned my teeming brain,
Before high-pilèd books, in charactery,
Hold like rich garners the full ripened grain;
When I behold, upon the night's starred face,
Huge cloudy symbols of a high romance,
And think that I may never live to trace
Their shadows, with the magic hand of chance;
And when I feel, fair creature of an hour,
That I shall never look upon thee more,
Never have relish in the faery power
Of unreflecting love; — then on the shore
Of the wide world I stand alone, and think
Till love and fame to nothingness do sink.

1848

BRIGHT STAR

BRIGHT star, would I were stedfast as thou art —
Not in lone splendour hung aloft the night
And watching, with eternal lids apart,
Like nature's patient, sleepless Eremite,
The moving waters at their priestlike task
Of pure ablution round earth's human shores,
Or gazing on the new soft-fallen mask
Of snow upon the mountains and the moors —
No — yet still stedfast, still unchangeable,
Pillowed upon my fair love's ripening breast,
To feel for ever its soft fall and swell,
Awake for ever in a sweet unrest,
Still, still to hear her tender-taken breath,
And so live ever — or else swoon to death.

1846

THE EVE OF ST. AGNES

ST. AGNES' Eve — Ah, bitter chill it was!
The owl, for all his feathers, was a-cold;
The hare limped trembling through the frozen grass,
And silent was the flock in woolly fold:
Numb were the Beadsman's fingers, while he told
His rosary, and while his frosted breath,
Like pious incense from a censer old,
Seemed taking flight for heaven, without a death,
Past the sweet Virgin's picture, while his prayer he saith.

His prayer he saith, this patient, holy man;
Then takes his lamp, and riseth from his knees,
And back returneth, meagre, barefoot, wan,
Along the chapel aisle by slow degrees:
The sculptured dead, on each side, seem to freeze,
Emprisoned in black, purgatorial rails:
Knights, ladies, praying in dumb orat'ries,
He passeth by; and his weak spirit fails
To think how they may ache in icy hoods and mails.

Northward he turneth through a little door,
And scarce three steps, ere Music's golden tongue
Flattered to tears this agèd man and poor;
But no — already had his deathbell rung:
The joys of all his life were said and sung:
His was harsh penance on St. Agnes' Eve:
Another way he went, and soon among
Rough ashes sat he for his soul's reprieve,
And all night kept awake, for sinners' sake to grieve.

That ancient Beadsman heard the prelude soft;
And so it chanced, for many a door was wide,
From hurry to and fro. Soon, up aloft,
The silver, snarling trumpets 'gan to chide:
The level chambers, ready with their pride,
Were glowing to receive a thousand guests:
The carvèd angels, ever eager-eyed,
Stared, where upon their heads the cornice rests,
With hair blown back, and wings put crosswise on their breasts.

At length burst in the argent revelry,
With plume, tiara, and all rich array,
Numerous as shadows haunting faerily
The brain, new stuffed, in youth, with triumphs gay
Of old romance. These let us wish away,
And turn, sole-thoughted, to one Lady there,
Whose heart had brooded, all that wintry day,
On love, and winged St. Agnes' saintly care,
As she had heard old dames full many times declare.

They told her how, upon St. Agnes' Eve,
Young virgins might have visions of delight,
And soft adorings from their loves receive
Upon the honeyed middle of the night,
If ceremonies due they did aright;
As, supperless to bed they must retire,
And couch supine their beauties, lily white;
Nor look behind, nor sideways, but require
Of Heaven with upward eyes for all that they desire.

Full of this whim was thoughtful Madeline:
The music, yearning like a God in pain,
She scarcely heard: her maiden eyes divine,
Fixed on the floor, saw many a sweeping train
Pass by — she heeded not at all: in vain
Came many a tiptoe, amorous cavalier,
And back retired; not cooled by high disdain,
But she saw not: her heart was otherwhere:
She sighed for Agnes' dreams, the sweetest of the year.

She danced along with vague, regardless eyes,
Anxious her lips, her breathing quick and short:

The hallowed hour was near at hand: she sighs
Amid the timbrels, and the thronged resort
Of whisperers in anger, or in sport;
'Mid looks of love, defiance, hate, and scorn,
Hoodwinked with faery fancy; all amort,
Save to St. Agnes and her lambs unshorn,
And all the bliss to be before to-morrow morn.

So, purposing each moment to retire,
She lingered still. Meantime, across the moors,
Had come young Porphyro, with heart on fire
For Madeline. Beside the portal doors,
Buttressed from moonlight, stands he, and implores
All saints to give him sight of Madeline,
But for one moment in the tedious hours,
That he might gaze and worship all unseen;
Perchance speak, kneel, touch, kiss — in sooth such things have been.

He ventures in: let no buzzed whisper tell:
All eyes be muffled, or a hundred swords
Will storm his heart, Love's fev'rous citadel:
For him, those chambers held barbarian hordes,
Hyena foemen, and hot-blooded lords,
Whose very dogs would execrations howl
Against his lineage: not one breast affords
Him any mercy, in that mansion foul,
Save one old beldame, weak in body and in soul.

Ah, happy chance! the agèd creature came,
Shuffling along with ivory-headed wand,
To where he stood, hid from the torch's flame,
Behind a broad hall-pillar, far beyond
The sound of merriment and chorus bland:
He startled her; but soon she knew his face,
And grasped his fingers in her palsied hand,
Saying, 'Mercy, Porphyro! hie thee from this place:
They are all here to-night, the whole blood-thirsty race!

'Get hence! get hence! there 's dwarfish Hildebrand;
He had a fever late, and in the fit
He cursèd thee and thine, both house and land:
Then there 's that old Lord Maurice, not a whit
More tame for his gray hairs — Alas me! flit!
Flit like a ghost away.' — 'Ah, Gossip dear,
We 're safe enough; here in this arm-chair sit,
And tell me how' — 'Good Saints! not here, not here;
Follow me, child, or else these stones will be thy bier.'

He followed through a lowly archèd way,
Brushing the cobwebs with his lofty plume,
And as she muttered 'Well-a — well-a-day!'
He found him in a little moonlight room,
Pale, latticed, chill, and silent as a tomb.
'Now tell me where is Madeline,' said he,
'O tell me, Angela, by the holy loom
Which none but secret sisterhood may see,
When they St. Agnes' wool are weaving piously.'

'St. Agnes! Ah! it is St. Agnes' Eve —
Yet men will murder upon holy days:
Thou must hold water in a witch's sieve,
And be liege-lord of all the Elves and Fays,
To venture so: it fills me with amaze
To see thee, Porphyro! — St. Agnes' Eve!
God's help! my lady fair the conjuror plays
This very night: good angels her deceive!
But let me laugh awhile, I 've mickle time to grieve.'

Feebly she laugheth in the languid moon,
While Porphyro upon her face doth look,
Like puzzled urchin on an agèd crone
Who keepeth closed a wond'rous riddle-book,
As spectacled she sits in chimney nook.
But soon his eyes grew brilliant, when she told
His lady's purpose; and he scarce could brook
Tears, at the thought of those enchantments cold,
And Madeline asleep in lap of legends old.

Sudden a thought came like a full-blown rose,
Flushing his brow, and in his painèd heart
Made purple riot: then doth he propose
A stratagem, that makes the beldame start:
'A cruel man and impious thou art:
Sweet lady, let her pray, and sleep, and dream
Alone with her good angels, far apart
From wicked men like thee. Go, go! — I deem
Thou canst not surely be the same that thou didst seem.'

'I will not harm her, by all saints I swear,'
Quoth Porphyro: 'O may I ne'er find grace
When my weak voice shall whisper its last prayer,
If one of her soft ringlets I displace,
Or look with ruffian passion in her face:
Good Angela, believe me by these tears;
Or I will, even in a moment's space,
Awake, with horrid shout, my foemen's ears,
And beard them, though they be more fanged than wolves and bears.'

'Ah! why wilt thou affright a feeble soul?
A poor, weak, palsy-stricken, churchyard thing,
Whose passing-bell may ere the midnight toll;
Whose prayers for thee, each morn and evening,
Were never missed.' — Thus plaining, doth she bring
A gentler speech from burning Porphyro;
So woful, and of such deep sorrowing,
That Angela gives promise she will do
Whatever he shall wish, betide her weal or woe.

Which was, to lead him, in close secrecy,
Even to Madeline's chamber, and there hide
Him in a closet, of such privacy
That he might see her beauty unespied,
And win perhaps that night a peerless bride,
While legioned faeries paced the coverlet,
And pale enchantment held her sleepy-eyed.
Never on such a night have lovers met,
Since Merlin paid his Demon all the monstrous debt.

'It shall be as thou wishest,' said the Dame:
'All cates and dainties shall be storèd there
Quickly on this feast-night: by the tambour frame
Her own lute thou wilt see: no time to spare,
For I am slow and feeble, and scarce dare
On such a catering trust my dizzy head.
Wait here, my child, with patience; kneel in prayer
The while: Ah! thou must needs the lady wed,
Or may I never leave my grave among the dead.'

So saying, she hobbled off with busy fear.
The lover's endless minutes slowly passed;
The dame returned, and whispered in his ear
To follow her; with agèd eyes aghast
From fright of dim espial. Safe at last,
Through many a dusky gallery, they gain
The maiden's chamber, silken, hushed, and chaste;
Where Porphyro took covert, pleased amain.
His poor guide hurried back with agues in her brain.

Her falt'ring hand upon the balustrade,
Old Angela was feeling for the stair,
When Madeline, St. Agnes' charmèd maid,
Rose, like a missioned spirit, unaware:
With silver taper's light, and pious care,
She turned, and down the agèd gossip led
To a safe level matting. Now prepare,
Young Porphyro, for gazing on that bed;
She comes, she comes again, like ring-dove frayed and fled.

Out went the taper as she hurried in;
Its little smoke, in pallid moonshine, died:
She closed the door, she panted, all akin
To spirits of the air, and visions wide:
No uttered syllable, or, woe betide!
But to her heart, her heart was voluble,
Paining with eloquence her balmy side;
As though a tongueless nightingale should swell
Her throat in vain, and die, heart-stifled, in her dell.

A casement high and triple-arched there was,
All garlanded with carven imag'ries
Of fruits, and flowers, and bunches of knot-grass,
And diamonded with panes of quaint device,
Innumerable of stains and splendid dyes,
As are the tiger-moth's deep-damasked wings;
And in the midst, 'mong thousand heraldries,
And twilight saints, and dim emblazonings,
A shielded scutcheon blushed with blood of queens and kings.

Full on this casement shone the wintry moon,
And threw warm gules on Madeline's fair breast,
As down she knelt for heaven's grace and boon;
Rose-bloom fell on her hands, together prest,
And on her silver cross soft amethyst,
And on her hair a glory, like a saint:
She seemed a splendid angel, newly drest,
Save wings, for heaven: — Porphyro grew faint:
She knelt, so pure a thing, so free from mortal taint.

Anon his heart revives: her vespers done,
Of all its wreathèd pearls her hair she frees;
Unclasps her warmèd jewels one by one;
Loosens her fragrant boddice; by degrees
Her rich attire creeps rustling to her knees:
Half-hidden, like a mermaid in sea-weed,
Pensive awhile she dreams awake, and sees,
In fancy, fair St. Agnes in her bed,
But dares not look behind, or all the charm is fled.

Soon, trembling in her soft and chilly nest,
In sort of wakeful swoon, perplexed she lay,
Until the poppied warmth of sleep oppressed
Her soothèd limbs, and soul fatigued away;
Flown, like a thought, until the morrow-day;
Blissfully havened both from joy and pain;
Clasped like a missal where swart Paynims pray;
Blinded alike from sunshine and from rain,
As though a rose should shut, and be a bud again.

Stol'n to this paradise, and so entranced,
Porphyro gazed upon her empty dress,
And listened to her breathing, if it chanced
To wake into a slumberous tenderness;
Which when he heard, that minute did he bless,
And breathed himself: then from the closet crept,
Noiseless as fear in a wide wilderness,
And over the hushed carpet, silent, stept,
And 'tween the curtains peeped, where, lo! — how fast she slept.

Then by the bed-side, where the faded moon
Made a dim, silver twilight, soft he set
A table, and, half anguished, threw thereon
A cloth of woven crimson, gold, and jet: —
O for some drowsy Morphean amulet!
The boisterous, midnight, festive clarion,
The kettle-drum, and far-heard clarinet,
Affray his ears, though but in dying tone: —
The hall door shuts again, and all the noise is gone.

And still she slept an azure-lidded sleep,
In blanchèd linen, smooth, and lavendered,
While he from forth the closet brought a heap
Of candied apple, quince, and plum, and gourd;
With jellies soother than the creamy curd,
And lucent syrops, tinct with cinnamon;
Manna and dates, in argosy transferred
From Fez; and spicèd dainties, every one,
From silken Samarcand to cedared Lebanon.

These delicates he heaped with glowing hand
On golden dishes and in baskets bright
Of wreathèd silver: sumptuous they stand
In the retirèd quiet of the night,
Filling the chilly room with perfume light. —
'And now, my love, my seraph fair, awake!
Thou art my heaven, and I thine eremite:
Open thine eyes, for meek St. Agnes' sake,
Or I shall drowse beside thee, so my soul doth ache.'

Thus whispering, his warm, unnervèd arm
Sank in her pillow. Shaded was her dream
By the dusk curtains: — 't was a midnight charm
Impossible to melt as icèd stream:
The lustrous salvers in the moonlight gleam;
Broad golden fringe upon the carpet lies:
It seemed he never, never could redeem
From such a stedfast spell his lady's eyes;
So mused awhile, entoiled in woofèd phantasies.

Awakening up, he took her hollow lute, —
Tumultuous, — and, in chords that tenderest be,
He played an ancient ditty, long since mute,
In Provence called, 'La belle dame sans mercy':
Close to her ear touching the melody; —
Wherewith disturbed, she uttered a soft moan:
He ceased — she panted quick — and suddenly
Her blue affrayèd eyes wide open shone:
Upon his knees he sank, pale as smooth-sculptured stone.

Her eyes were open, but she still beheld,
Now wide awake, the vision of her sleep:
There was a painful change, that nigh expelled
The blisses of her dream so pure and deep
At which fair Madeline began to weep,
And moan forth witless words with many a sigh;
While still her gaze on Porphyro would keep;
Who knelt, with joinèd hands and piteous eye,
Fearing to move or speak, she looked so dreamingly.

'Ah, Porphyro!' said she, 'but even now
Thy voice was at sweet tremble in mine ear,
Made tuneable with every sweetest vow;
And those sad eyes were spiritual and clear:
How changed thou art! how pallid, chill, and drear!
Give me that voice again, my Porphyro,
Those looks immortal, those complainings dear!
Oh leave me not in this eternal woe,
For if thou diest, my Love, I know not where to go.'

Beyond a mortal man impassioned far
At these voluptuous accents, he arose,
Ethereal, flushed, and like a throbbing star
Seen mid the sapphire heaven's deep repose;
Into her dream he melted, as the rose
Blendeth its odour with the violet, —
Solution sweet: meantime the frost-wind blows
Like Love's alarum pattering the sharp sleet
Against the window-panes; St. Agnes' moon hath set.

'T is dark: quick pattereth the flaw-blown sleet:
'This is no dream, my bride, my Madeline!'
'T is dark: the icèd gusts still rave and beat:
'No dream, alas! alas! and woe is mine!
Porphyro will leave me here to fade and pine. —
Cruel! what traitor could thee hither bring?
I curse not, for my heart is lost in thine,
Though thou forsakest a deceivèd thing; —
A dove forlorn and lost with sick unprunèd wing.'

'My Madeline! sweet dreamer! lovely bride!
Say, may I be for aye thy vassal blest?
Thy beauty's shield, heart-shaped and vermeil dyed?
Ah, silver shrine, here will I take my rest
After so many hours of toil and quest,
A famished pilgrim, — saved by miracle.
Though I have found, I will not rob thy nest
Saving of thy sweet self; if thou think'st well
To trust, fair Madeline, to no rude infidel.

'Hark! 't is an elfin-storm from faery land,
Of haggard seeming, but a boon indeed:
Arise — arise! the morning is at hand; —
The bloated wassaillers will never heed: —
Let us away, my love, with happy speed;
There are no ears to hear, or eyes to see, —
Drowned all in Rhenish and the sleepy mead:
Awake! arise! my love, and fearless be,
For o'er the southern moors I have a home for thee.'

She hurried at his words, beset with fears,
For there were sleeping dragons all around,
At glaring watch, perhaps, with ready spears —
Down the wide stairs a darkling way they found.—
In all the house was heard no human sound.
A chain-drooped lamp was flickering by each door;
The arras, rich with horseman, hawk, and hound,
Fluttered in the besieging wind's uproar;
And the long carpets rose along the gusty floor.

They glide, like phantoms, into the wide hall;
Like phantoms, to the iron porch, they glide;
Where lay the Porter, in uneasy sprawl,
With a huge empty flaggon by his side:
The wakeful bloodhound rose, and shook his hide,
But his sagacious eye an inmate owns:
By one, and one, the bolts full easy slide: —
The chains lie silent on the footworn stones; —
The key turns, and the door upon its hinges groans.

And they are gone: aye, ages long ago
These lovers fled away into the storm.
That night the Baron dreamt of many a woe,
And all his warrior-guests, with shade and form
Of witch, and demon, and large coffin-worm,
Were long be-nightmared. Angela the old
Died palsy-twitched, with meagre face deform;
The Beadsman, after thousand aves told,
For aye unsought for slept among his ashes cold.

1820

ODE TO A NIGHTINGALE

My heart aches, and a drowsy numbness pains
My sense, as though of hemlock I had drunk,
Or emptied some dull opiate to the drains
One minute past, and Lethe-wards had sunk:

'T is not through envy of thy happy lot,
But being too happy in thine happiness, —
That thou, light-wingèd Dryad of the trees,
In some melodious plot
Of beechen green, and shadows numberless,
Singest of summer in full-throated ease.

O, for a draught of vintage! that hath been
Cooled a long age in the deep-delvèd earth,
Tasting of Flora and the country green,
Dance, and Provençal song, and sunburnt mirth!
O for a beaker full of the warm South,
Full of the true, the blushful Hippocrene,
With beaded bubbles winking at the brim,
And purple-stainèd mouth;
That I might drink, and leave the world unseen,
And with thee fade away into the forest dim:

Fade far away, dissolve, and quite forget
What thou among the leaves hast never known,
The weariness, the fever, and the fret
Here, where men sit and hear each other groan;
Where palsy shakes a few, sad, last gray hairs,
Where youth grows pale, and spectre-thin, and dies;
Where but to think is to be full of sorrow
And leaden-eyed despairs,
Where Beauty cannot keep her lustrous eyes,
Or new Love pine at them beyond to-morrow.

Away! away! for I will fly to thee,
Not charioted by Bacchus and his pards,
But on the viewless wings of Poesy,
Though the dull brain perplexes and retards:
Already with thee! tender is the night,
And haply the Queen-Moon is on her throne,
Clustered around by all her starry Fays;
But here there is no light,
Save what from heaven is with the breezes blown
Through verdurous glooms and winding mossy ways.

I cannot see what flowers are at my feet,
Nor what soft incense hangs upon the boughs,
But, in embalmèd darkness, guess each sweet
Wherewith the seasonable month endows
The grass, the thicket, and the fruit-tree wild;
White hawthorn, and the pastoral eglantine;
Fast fading violets covered up in leaves;
And mid-May's eldest child,
The coming musk-rose, full of dewy wine,
The murmurous haunt of flies on summer eves.

Darkling I listen; and, for many a time
I have been half in love with easeful Death,
Called him soft names in many a musèd rhyme,
To take into the air my quiet breath;
Now more than ever seems it rich to die,
To cease upon the midnight with no pain,
While thou art pouring forth thy soul abroad
In such an ecstasy!
Still wouldst thou sing, and I have ears in vain —
To thy high requiem become a sod.

Thou wast not born for death, immortal Bird!
No hungry generations tread thee down;
The voice I hear this passing night was heard
In ancient days by emperor and clown:
Perhaps the self-same song that found a path
Through the sad heart of Ruth, when, sick for home,
She stood in tears amid the alien corn;
The same that oft-times hath
Charmed magic casements, opening on the foam
Of perilous seas, in faery lands forlorn.

Forlorn! the very word is like a bell
To toll me back from thee to my sole self,
Adieu! the fancy cannot cheat so well
As she is famed to do, deceiving elf.
Adieu! adieu! thy plaintive anthem fades
Past the near meadows, over the still stream,
Up the hill-side; and now 't is buried deep
In the next valley-glades:
Was it a vision, or a waking dream?
Fled is that music: — Do I wake or sleep?

1820

ODE ON A GRECIAN URN

THOU still unravished bride of quietness,
Thou foster-child of silence and slow time,
Sylvan historian, who canst thus express
A flowery tale more sweetly than our rhyme:
What leaf-fringed legend haunts about thy shape
Of deities or mortals, or of both,
In Tempe or the dales of Arcady?
What men or gods are these? What maidens lōth?
What mad pursuit? What struggle to escape?
What pipes and timbrels? What wild ecstasy?

Heard melodies are sweet, but those unheard
Are sweeter; therefore, ye soft pipes, play on;
Not to the sensual ear, but, more endeared,
Pipe to the spirit ditties of no tone:
Fair youth, beneath the trees, thou canst not leave
Thy song, nor ever can those trees be bare;
Bold Lover, never, never canst thou kiss,
Though winning near the goal — yet, do not grieve;
She cannot fade, though thou hast not thy bliss,
For ever wilt thou love, and she be fair!

Ah, happy, happy boughs! that cannot shed
Your leaves, nor ever bid the Spring adieu;
And, happy melodist, unwearièd,
For ever piping songs for ever new;
More happy love! more happy, happy love!
For ever warm and still to be enjoyed,
For ever panting, and for ever young;
All breathing human passion far above,
That leaves a heart high-sorrowful and cloyed,
A burning forehead, and a parching tongue.

Who are these coming to the sacrifice?
To what green altar, O mysterious priest,
Lead'st thou that heifer lowing at the skies,
And all her silken flanks with garlands drest?
What little town by river or sea shore,
Or mountain-built with peaceful citadel,
Is emptied of this folk, this pious morn?
And, little town, thy streets for evermore
Will silent be; and not a soul to tell
Why thou art desolate, can e'er return.

O Attic shape! Fair attitude! with brede
Of marble men and maidens overwrought,
With forest branches and the trodden weed;
Thou, silent form, dost tease us out of thought
As doth eternity: Cold Pastoral!
When old age shall this generation waste,
Thou shalt remain, in midst of other woe
Than ours, a friend to man, to whom thou say'st,
'Beauty is truth, truth beauty,' — that is all
Ye know on earth, and all ye need to know.

1820

ODE TO PSYCHE

O GODDESS! hear these tuneless numbers, wrung
By sweet enforcement and remembrance dear,
And pardon that thy secrets should be sung
Even into thine own soft-conchèd ear:
Surely I dreamt to-day, or did I see
The wingèd Psyche with awakened eyes?
I wandered in a forest thoughtlessly,
And, on the sudden, fainting with surprise,
Saw two fair creatures, couchèd side by side
In deepest grass, beneath the whisp'ring roof
Of leaves and trembled blossoms, where there ran
A brooklet, scarce espied:

'Mid hushed, cool-rooted flowers, fragrant-eyed,
Blue, silver-white, and budded Tyrian,
They lay calm-breathing on the bedded grass;
Their arms embracèd, and their pinions too;
Their lips touched not, but had not bade adieu,
As if disjoinèd by soft-handed slumber,
And ready still past kisses to outnumber
At tender eye-dawn of aurorean love:
The wingèd boy I knew;
But who wast thou, O happy, happy dove?
His Psyche true!

O latest born and loveliest vision far
Of all Olympus' faded hierarchy!
Fairer than Phœbe's sapphire-regioned star,
Or Vesper, amorous glow-worm of the sky;
Fairer than these, though temple thou hast none,

Nor altar heaped with flowers;
Nor virgin-choir to make delicious moan
Upon the midnight hours;
No voice, no lute, no pipe, no incense sweet
From chain-swung censer teeming;
No shrine, no grove, no oracle, no heat
Of pale-mouthed prophet dreaming.

O brightest! though too late for antique vows,
Too, too late for the fond believing lyre,
When holy were the haunted forest boughs,
Holy the air, the water, and the fire;
Yet even in these days so far retired
From happy pieties, thy lucent fans,
Fluttering among the faint Olympians,
I see, and sing, by my own eyes inspired.
So let me be thy choir, and make a moan
Upon the midnight hours;
Thy voice, thy lute, thy pipe, thy incense sweet
From swingèd censer teeming;
Thy shrine, thy grove, thy oracle, thy heat
Of pale-mouthed prophet dreaming.

Yes, I will be thy priest, and build a fane
In some untrodden region of my mind,
Where branchèd thoughts, new grown with pleasant pain,
Instead of pines shall murmur in the wind:
Far, far around shall those dark-clustered trees
Fledge the wild-ridgèd mountains steep by steep;
And there by zephyrs, streams, and birds, and bees,
The moss-lain Dryads shall be lulled to sleep;
And in the midst of this wide quietness
A rosy sanctuary will I dress
With the wreathed trellis of a working brain,
With buds, and bells, and stars without a name,
With all the gardener Fancy e'er could feign,
Who breeding flowers, will never breed the same:
And there shall be for thee all soft delight
That shadowy thought can win,
A bright torch, and a casement ope at night,
To let the warm Love in!

1820

TO AUTUMN

Season of mists and mellow fruitfulness,
Close bosom-friend of the maturing sun;
Conspiring with him how to load and bless
With fruit the vines that round the thatch-eves run;
To bend with apples the mossed cottage-trees,
And fill all fruit with ripeness to the core;
To swell the gourd, and plump the hazel shells
With a sweet kernel; to set budding more,
And still more, later flowers for the bees,
Until they think warm days will never cease,
For Summer has o'er-brimmed their clammy cells.

Who hath not seen thee oft amid thy store?
Sometimes whoever seeks abroad may find
Thee sitting careless on a granary floor,
Thy hair soft-lifted by the winnowing wind;
Or on a half-reaped furrow sound asleep,
Drowsed with the fume of poppies, while thy hook
Spares the next swath and all its twinèd flowers:
And sometimes like a gleaner thou dost keep
Steady thy laden head across a brook;
Or by a cyder-press, with patient look,
Thou watchest the last oozings hours by hours.

Where are the songs of Spring? Ay, where are they?
Think not of them, thou hast thy music too, —
While barrèd clouds bloom the soft-dying day,
And touch the stubble-plains with rosy hue;
Then in a wailful choir the small gnats mourn
Among the river sallows, borne aloft
Or sinking as the light wind lives or dies;
And full-grown lambs loud bleat from hilly bourn;
Hedge-crickets sing; and now with treble soft
The red-breast whistles from a garden-croft;
And gathering swallows twitter in the skies.

1820

ODE ON MELANCHOLY

No, no, go not to Lethe, neither twist
Wolf's-bane, tight-rooted, for its poisonous wine;
Nor suffer thy pale forehead to be kissed
By nightshade, ruby grape of Proserpine;
Make not your rosary of yew-berries,

Lethe

Nor let the beetle, nor the death-moth be
Your mournful Psyche, nor the downy owl
A partner in your sorrow's mysteries;
For shade to shade will come too drowsily,
And drown the wakeful anguish of the soul.

But when the melancholy fit shall fall
Sudden from heaven like a weeping cloud,
That fosters the droop-headed flowers all,
And hides the green hill in an April shroud;
Then glut thy sorrow on a morning rose,
Or on the rainbow of the salt sand-wave,
Or on the wealth of globèd peonies;
Or if thy mistress some rich anger shows,
Emprison her soft hand, and let her rave,
And feed deep, deep upon her peerless eyes.

She dwells with Beauty — Beauty that must die;
And Joy, whose hand is ever at his lips
Bidding adieu; and aching Pleasure nigh,
Turning to Poison while the bee-mouth sips:
Ay, in the very temple of delight
Veiled Melancholy has her sovran shrine,
Though seen of none save him whose strenuous tongue
Can burst Joy's grape against his palate fine;
His soul shall taste the sadness of her might,
And be among her cloudy trophies hung.

1820

BARDS OF PASSION AND OF MIRTH

Bards of Passion and of Mirth,
Ye have left your souls on earth!
Have ye souls in heaven too,
Double-lived in regions new?
Yes, and those of heaven commune
With the spheres of sun and moon;
With the noise of fountains wond'rous,
And the parle of voices thund'rous;
With the whisper of heaven's trees
And one another, in soft ease
Seated on Elysian lawns
Browsed by none but Dian's fawns;
Underneath large blue-bells tented,
Where the daisies are rose-scented,
And the rose herself has got
Perfume which on earth is not;
Where the nightingale doth sing
Not a senseless, trancèd thing,
But divine melodious truth;
Philosophic numbers smooth;
Tales and golden histories
Of heaven and its mysteries.

Thus ye live on high, and then
On the earth ye live again;
And the souls ye left behind you
Teach us, here, the way to find you,
Where your other souls are joying,
Never slumbered, never cloying.
Here, your earth-born souls still speak
To mortals, of their little week;
Of their sorrows and delights;
Of their passions and their spites;
Of their glory and their shame;
What doth strengthen and what maim.
Thus ye teach us, every day,
Wisdom, though fled far away.

Bards of Passion and of Mirth,
Ye have left your souls on earth!
Ye have souls in heaven too,
Doubled-lived in regions new!

1820

LINES ON THE MERMAID TAVERN

Souls of Poets dead and gone,
What Elysium have ye known,
Happy field or mossy cavern,
Choicer than the Mermaid Tavern?
Have ye tippled drink more fine
Than mine host's Canary wine?
Or are fruits of Paradise
Sweeter than those dainty pies
Of venison? O generous food!
Drest as though bold Robin Hood
Would, with his maid Marian,
Sup and bowse from horn and can.

I have heard that on a day
Mine host's sign-board flew away,
Nobody knew whither, till
An astrologer's old quill
To a sheepskin gave the story,
Said he saw you in your glory,
Underneath a new old sign
Sipping beverage divine,
And pledging with contented smack
The Mermaid in the Zodiac.

Souls of Poets dead and gone,
What Elysium have ye known,
Happy field or mossy cavern,
Choicer than the Mermaid Tavern?

1820

LA BELLE DAME SANS MERCI

Ah, what can ail thee, wretched wight,
  Alone and palely loitering;
The sedge is withered from the lake,
  And no birds sing.

Ah, what can ail thee, wretched wight,
  So haggard and so woe-begone?
The squirrel's granary is full,
  And the harvest 's done.

I see a lilly on thy brow,
  With anguish moist and fever dew;
And on thy cheek a fading rose
  Fast withereth too.

I met a lady in the meads
  Full beautiful, a faery's child;
Her hair was long, her foot was light,
  And her eyes were wild.

I set her on my pacing steed,
  And nothing else saw all day long;
For sideways would she lean, and sing
  A faery's song.

I made a garland for her head,
  And bracelets too, and fragrant zone;
She looked at me as she did love,
  And made sweet moan.

She found me roots of relish sweet,
  And honey wild, and manna dew;
And sure in language strange she said,
  I love thee true.

She took me to her elfin grot,
  And there she gazed and sighèd deep,
And there I shut her wild sad eyes —
  So kissed to sleep.

And there we slumbered on the moss,
  And there I dreamed, ah woe betide,
The latest dream I ever dreamed
  On the cold hill side.

I saw pale kings, and princes too,
  Pale warriors, death-pale were they all;
Who cried — 'La belle Dame sans merci
  Hath thee in thrall!'

I saw their starved lips in the gloam
  With horrid warning gapèd wide,
And I awoke, and found me here
  On the cold hill side.

And this is why I sojourn here
  Alone and palely loitering,
Though the sedge is withered from the lake,
  And no birds sing.

1820

HYPERION

BOOK I

Deep in the shady sadness of a vale
Far sunken from the healthy breath of morn,
Far from the fiery noon, and eve's one star,
Sat gray-haired Saturn, quiet as a stone,
Still as the silence round about his lair;
Forest on forest hung about his head
Like cloud on cloud. No stir of air was there,
Not so much life as on a summer's day
Robs not one light seed from the feathered grass,
But where the dead leaf fell, there did it rest.
A stream went voiceless by, still deadened more
By reason of his fallen divinity
Spreading a shade: the Naiad 'mid her reeds
Pressed her cold finger closer to her lips.
  Along the margin-sand large foot-marks went,
No further than to where his feet had strayed,
And slept there since. Upon the sodden ground
His old right hand lay nerveless, listless, dead,
Unsceptred; and his realmless eyes were closed;
While his bowed head seemed list'ning to the Earth,
His ancient mother, for some comfort yet.
  It seemed no force could wake him from his place;
But there came one, who with a kindred hand
Touched his wide shoulders, after bending low
With reverence, though to one who knew it not.
She was a Goddess of the infant world;
By her in stature the tall Amazon
Had stood a pigmy's height: she would have ta'en
Achilles by the hair and bent his neck;
Or with a finger stayed Ixion's wheel.
Her face was large as that of Memphian sphinx,
Pedestaled haply in a palace court,
When sages looked to Egypt for their lore.
But oh! how unlike marble was that face:
How beautiful, if sorrow had not made
Sorrow more beautiful than Beauty's self.
There was a listening fear in her regard,
As if calamity had but begun;
As if the vanward clouds of evil days
Had spent their malice, and the sullen rear

Was with its storèd thunder labouring up.
One hand she pressed upon that aching spot
Where beats the human heart, as if just there,
Though an immortal, she felt cruel pain:
The other upon Saturn's bended neck
She laid, and to the level of his ear
Leaning with parted lips, some words she spake
In solemn tenour and deep organ tone:
Some mourning words, which in our feeble tongue
Would come in these like accents; O how frail
To that large utterance of the early Gods!
'Saturn, look up! — though wherefore, poor old King?
I have no comfort for thee, no not one:
I cannot say, "O wherefore sleepest thou?"
For heaven is parted from thee, and the earth
Knows thee not, thus afflicted, for a God;
And ocean too, with all its solemn noise,
Has from thy sceptre passed; and all the air
Is emptied of thine hoary majesty.
Thy thunder, conscious of the new command,
Rumbles reluctant o'er our fallen house;
And thy sharp lightning in unpractised hands
Scorches and burns our once serene domain.
O aching time! O moments big as years!
All as ye pass swell out the monstrous truth,
And press it so upon our weary griefs
That unbelief has not a space to breathe.
Saturn, sleep on: — O thoughtless, why did I
Thus violate thy slumbrous solitude?
Why should I ope thy melancholy eyes?
Saturn, sleep on! while at thy feet I weep.'
As when, upon a trancèd summer-night,
Those green-robed senators of mighty woods,
Tall oaks, branch-charmèd by the earnest stars,
Dream, and so dream all night without a stir,
Save from one gradual solitary gust
Which comes upon the silence, and dies off,
As if the ebbing air had but one wave;
So came these words and went; the while in tears
She touched her fair large forehead to the ground,
Just where her falling hair might be outspread
A soft and silken mat for Saturn's feet.
One moon, with alteration slow, had shed
Her silver seasons four upon the night,
And still these two were postured motionless,
Like natural sculpture in cathedral cavern;
The frozen God still couchant on the earth,
And the sad Goddess weeping at his feet:
Until at length old Saturn lifted up
His faded eyes, and saw his kingdom gone,
And all the gloom and sorrow of the place,
And that fair kneeling Goddess; and then spake,
As with a palsied tongue, and while his beard
Shook horrid with such aspen-malady:
'O tender spouse of gold Hyperion,
Thea, I feel thee ere I see thy face;
Look up, and let me see our doom in it;
Look up, and tell me if this feeble shape
Is Saturn's; tell me, if thou hear'st the voice
Of Saturn; tell me, if this wrinkling brow,
Naked and bare of its great diadem,
Peers like the front of Saturn. Who had power
To make me desolate? whence came the strength?
How was it nurtured to such bursting forth,
While Fate seemed strangled in my nervous grasp?
But it is so; and I am smothered up,
And buried from all godlike exercise
Of influence benign on planets pale,
Of admonitions to the winds and seas,
Of peaceful sway above man's harvesting,
And all those acts which Deity supreme
Doth ease its heart of love in. — I am gone
Away from my own bosom: I have left
My strong identity, my real self,
Somewhere between the throne, and where I sit
Here on this spot of earth. Search, Thea, search!
Open thine eyes eterne, and sphere them round
Upon all space: space starred, and lorn of light;
Space regioned with life-air; and barren void;
Spaces of fire, and all the yawn of hell. —
Search, Thea, search! and tell me, if thou seest
A certain shape or shadow, making way
With wings or chariot fierce to repossess
A heaven he lost erewhile: it must — it must
Be of ripe progress — Saturn must be King.
Yes, there must be a golden victory;
There must be Gods thrown down, and trumpets blown
Of triumph calm, and hymns of festival
Upon the gold clouds metropolitan,

Voices of soft proclaim, and silver stir
Of strings in hollow shells; and there shall be
Beautiful things made new, for the surprise
Of the sky-children; I will give command:
Thea! Thea! Thea! where is Saturn?'
This passion lifted him upon his feet,
And made his hands to struggle in the air,
His Druid locks to shake and ooze with sweat,
His eyes to fever out, his voice to cease.
He stood, and heard not Thea's sobbing deep;
A little time, and then again he snatched
Utterance thus. — 'But cannot I create?
Cannot I form? Cannot I fashion forth
Another world, another universe,
To overbear and crumble this to naught?
Where is another chaos? Where?' — That word
Found way unto Olympus, and made quake
The rebel three. — Thea was startled up,
And in her bearing was a sort of hope,
As thus she quick-voiced spake, yet full of awe.
'This cheers our fallen house: come to our friends,
O Saturn! come away, and give them heart;
I know the covert, for thence came I hither.'
Thus brief; then with beseeching eyes she went
With backward footing through the shade a space:
He followed, and she turned to lead the way
Through agèd boughs, that yielded like the mist
Which eagles cleave upmounting from their nest.
Meanwhile in other realms big tears were shed,
More sorrow like to this, and such like woe,
Too huge for mortal tongue or pen of scribe:
The Titans fierce, self-hid, or prison-bound,
Groaned for the old allegiance once more,
And listened in sharp pain for Saturn's voice.
But one of the whole mammoth-brood still kept
His sov'reignty, and rule, and majesty; —
Blazing Hyperion on his orbèd fire
Still sat, still snuffed the incense, teeming up
From man to the sun's God; yet unsecure:
For as among us mortals omens drear
Fright and perplex, so also shuddered he —
Not at dog's howl, or gloom-bird's hated screech,
Or the familiar visiting of one
Upon the first toll of his passing-bell,
Or prophesyings of the midnight lamp;
But horrors, portioned to a giant nerve,
Oft made Hyperion ache. His palace bright
Bastioned with pyramids of glowing gold,
And touched with shade of bronzèd obelisks,
Glared a blood-red through all its thousand courts,
Arches, and domes, and fiery galleries;
And all its curtains of Aurorian clouds
Flushed angerly: while sometimes eagle's wings,
Unseen before by Gods or wondering men,
Darkened the place; and neighing steeds were heard,
Not heard before by Gods or wondering men.
Also, when he would taste the spicy wreaths
Of incense, breathed aloft from sacred hills,
Instead of sweets, his ample palate took
Savour of poisonous brass and metal sick:
And so, when harboured in the sleepy west,
After the full completion of fair day, —
For rest divine upon exalted couch
And slumber in the arms of melody,
He paced away the pleasant hours of ease
With stride colossal, on from hall to hall;
While far within each aisle and deep recess,
His wingèd minions in close clusters stood,
Amazed and full of fear; like anxious men
Who on wide plains gather in panting troops,
When earthquakes jar their battlements and towers.
Even now, while Saturn, roused from icy trance,
Went step for step with Thea through the woods,
Hyperion, leaving twilight in the rear,
Came slope upon the threshold of the west;
Then, as was wont, his palace-door flew ope
In smoothest silence, save what solemn tubes,
Blown by the serious Zephyrs, gave of sweet
And wandering sounds, slow-breathèd melodies;
And like a rose in vermeil tint and shape,
In fragrance soft, and coolness to the eye,
That inlet to severe magnificence
Stood full blown, for the God to enter in.
He entered, but he entered full of wrath;
His flaming robes streamed out beyond his heels,
And gave a roar, as if of earthly fire,
That scared away the meek ethereal Hours

And made their dove-wings tremble. On he flared,
From stately nave to nave, from vault to vault,
Through bowers of fragrant and enwreathèd light,
And diamond-pavèd lustrous long arcades,
Until he reached the great main cupola;
There standing fierce beneath, he stamped his foot,
And from the basements deep to the high towers
Jarred his own golden region; and before
The quavering thunder thereupon had ceased,
His voice leapt out, despite of godlike curb,
To this result: 'O dreams of day and night!
O monstrous forms! O effigies of pain!
O spectres busy in a cold, cold gloom!
O lank-eared Phantoms of black-weeded pools!
Why do I know ye? why have I seen ye? why
Is my eternal essence thus distraught
To see and to behold these horrors new?
Saturn is fallen, am I too to fall?
Am I to leave this haven of my rest,
This cradle of my glory, this soft clime,
This calm luxuriance of blissful light,
These crystalline pavilions, and pure fanes,
Of all my lucent empire? It is left
Deserted, void, nor any haunt of mine.
The blaze, the splendor, and the symmetry,
I cannot see — but darkness, death and darkness.
Even here, into my centre of repose,
The shady visions come to domineer,
Insult, and blind, and stifle up my pomp. —
Fall! — No, by Tellus and her briny robes!
Over the fiery frontier of my realms
I will advance a terrible right arm
Shall scare that infant thunderer, rebel Jove,
And bid old Saturn take his throne again.' —
He spake, and ceased, the while a heavier threat
Held struggle with his throat but came not forth;
For as in theatres of crowded men
Hubbub increases more they call out 'Hush!'
So at Hyperion's words the Phantoms pale
Bestirred themselves, thrice horrible and cold;
And from the mirrored level where he stood
A mist arose, as from a scummy marsh.
At this, through all his bulk an agony
Crept gradual, from the feet unto the crown,
Like a lithe serpent vast and muscular
Making slow way, with head and neck convulsed
From over-strainèd might. Released, he fled
To the eastern gates, and full six dewy hours
Before the dawn in season due should blush,
He breathed fierce breath against the sleepy portals,
Cleared them of heavy vapours, burst them wide
Suddenly on the ocean's chilly streams.
The planet orb of fire, whereon he rode
Each day from east to west the heavens through,
Spun round in sable curtaining of clouds;
Not therefore veilèd quite, blindfold, and hid,
But ever and anon the glancing spheres,
Circles, and arcs, and broad-belting colure,
Glowed through, and wrought upon the muffling dark
Sweet-shapèd lightnings from the nadir deep
Up to the zenith, — hieroglyphics old
Which sages and keen-eyed astrologers
Then living on the earth, with labouring thought
Won from the gaze of many centuries:
Now lost, save what we find on remnants huge
Of stone, or marble swart; their import gone,
Their wisdom long since fled. — Two wings this orb
Possessed for glory, two fair argent wings,
Ever exalted at the God's approach:
And now, from forth the gloom their plumes immense
Rose, one by one, till all outspreaded were;
While still the dazzling globe maintained eclipse,
Awaiting for Hyperion's command.
Fain would he have commanded, fain took throne
And bid the day begin, if but for change.
He might not: — No, though a primeval God:
The sacred seasons might not be disturbed.
Therefore the operations of the dawn
Stayed in their birth, even as here 't is told.
Those silver wings expanded sisterly,
Eager to sail their orb; the porches wide
Opened upon the dusk demesnes of night;
And the bright Titan, phrenzied with new woes,
Unused to bend, by hard compulsion bent

His spirit to the sorrow of the time;
And all along a dismal rack of clouds,
Upon the boundaries of day and night,
He stretched himself in grief and radiance faint.
There as he lay, the Heaven with its stars
Looked down on him with pity, and the voice
Of Cœlus, from the universal space,
Thus whispered low and solemn in his ear.
'O brightest of my children dear, earth-born
And sky-engendered, Son of Mysteries
All unrevealèd even to the powers
Which met at thy creating; at whose joys
And palpitations sweet, and pleasures soft,
I, Cœlus, wonder, how they came and whence;
And at the fruits thereof what shapes they be,
Distinct, and visible; symbols divine,
Manifestations of that beauteous life
Diffused unseen throughout eternal space:
Of these new-formed art thou, oh brightest child!
Of these, thy brethren and the Goddesses!
There is sad feud among ye, and rebellion
Of son against his sire. I saw him fall,
I saw my first-born tumbled from his throne!
To me his arms were spread, to me his voice
Found way from forth the thunders round his head!
Pale wox I, and in vapours hid my face.
Art thou, too, near such doom? vague fear there is:
For I have seen my sons most unlike Gods.
Divine ye were created, and divine
In sad demeanour, solemn, undisturbed,
Unruffled, like high Gods, ye lived and ruled:
Now I behold in you fear, hope, and wrath;
Actions of rage and passion; even as
I see them, on the mortal world beneath,
In men who die. — This is the grief, O Son!
Sad sign of ruin, sudden dismay, and fall!
Yet do thou strive; as thou art capable,
As thou canst move about, an evident God;
And canst oppose to each malignant hour
Ethereal presence: — I am but a voice;
My life is but the life of winds and tides,
No more than winds and tides can I avail: —
But thou canst. — Be thou therefore in the van
Of circumstance; yea, seize the arrow's barb
Before the tense string murmur. — To the earth!
For there thou wilt find Saturn, and his woes.
Meantime I will keep watch on thy bright sun,
And of thy seasons be a careful nurse.' —
Ere half this region-whisper had come down,
Hyperion arose, and on the stars
Lifted his curved lids, and kept them wide
Until it ceased; and still he kept them wide:
And still they were the same bright, patient stars.
Then with a slow incline of his broad breast,
Like to a diver in the pearly seas,
Forward he stooped over the airy shore,
And plunged all noiseless into the deep night.

1820

James Hogg (1770–1835)

WHEN THE KYE COMES HAME

Come, all ye jolly shepherds
That whistle through the glen,
I 'll tell ye of a secret
That courtiers dinna ken:
What is the greatest bliss
That the tongue o' man can name?
'T is to woo a bonnie lassie
When the kye comes hame,
When the kye comes hame,
When the kye comes hame,
'Tween the gloaming and the mirk,
When the kye comes hame.

'T is not beneath the coronet,
Nor canopy of state,
'T is not on couch of velvet,
Nor arbour of the great —
'T is beneath the spreading birk,
In the glen without the name,
Wi' a bonnie, bonnie lassie,
When the kye comes hame,
When the kye comes hame, etc.

There the blackbird bigs her nest
For the mate he lo'es to see,
And on the topmost bough,
Oh, a happy bird is he;
Where he pours his melting ditty,
And love is a' the theme,
And he 'll woo his bonnie lassie
When the kye comes hame,
When the kye comes hame, etc.

When the blewart bears a pearl,
And the daisy turns a pea,
And the bonnie lucken-gowan
Has fauldit up her ee,
Then the laverock frae the blue lift
Drops down, an' thinks nae shame
To woo his bonnie lassie
When the kye comes hame,
When the kye comes hame, etc.

See yonder pawkie shepherd,
That lingers on the hill,
His ewes are in the fauld,
An' his lambs are lying still;
Yet he downa gang to bed,
For his heart is in a flame
To meet his bonnie lassie
When the kye comes hame,
When the kye comes hame, etc.

When the little wee bit heart
Rises high in the breast,
An' the little wee bit starn
Rises red in the east,
Oh there 's a joy sae dear,
That the heart can hardly frame,
Wi' a bonnie, bonnie lassie,
When the kye comes hame!
When the kye comes hame, etc.

Then since all nature joins
In this love without alloy,
Oh, wha wad prove a traitor
To Nature's dearest joy?
Or wha wad choose a crown,
Wi' its perils and its fame,
And miss his bonnie lassie
When the kye comes hame,
When the kye comes hame,
When the kye comes hame,
'Tween the gloaming and the mirk,
When the kye comes hame!

1810

THE SKYLARK

BIRD of the wilderness,
Blithesome and cumberless,
Sweet be thy matin o'er moorland and lea!
Emblem of happiness,
Blest is thy dwelling-place —
Oh, to abide in the desert with thee!

Wild is thy lay and loud,
Far in the downy cloud,
Love gives it energy, love gave it birth.
Where on thy dewy wing,
Where art thou journeying?
Thy lay is in heaven, thy love is on earth.

O'er fell and fountain sheen,
O'er moor and mountain green,
O'er the red streamer that heralds the day,
Over the cloudlet dim,
Over the rainbow's rim,
Musical cherub, soar, singing, away!

Then when the gloaming comes,
Low in the heather blooms
Sweet will thy welcome and bed of love be!
Emblem of happiness,
Blest is thy dwelling-place —
Oh, to abide in the desert with thee!

1810

KILMENY

BONNIE Kilmeny gaed up the glen;
But it wasna to meet Duneira's men,
Nor the rosy monk of the isle to see,
For Kilmeny was pure as pure could be.
It was only to hear the yorlin sing,
And pu' the cress-flower round the spring;
The scarlet hypp and the hind-berrye,
And the nest that hung frae the hazel tree;
For Kilmeny was pure as pure could be.
But lang may her minny look o'er the wa';
And lang may she seek i' the greenwood shaw;
Lang the laird o' Duneira blame,
And lang, lang greet or Kilmeny come hame!

When many lang day had come and fled,
When grief grew calm, and hope was dead,
When mass for Kilmeny's soul had been sung,
When the bedesman had prayed and the dead-bell rung,
Late, late in a gloaming, when all was still,
When the fringe was red on the westlin hill,
The wood was sere, the moon i' the wane,
The reek o' the cot hung o'er the plain,
Like a little wee cloud in the world its lane;
When the ingle lowed wi' an eiry leme —
Late, late in the gloaming Kilmeny came hame!

'Kilmeny, Kilmeny, where have you been?
Lang hae we sought baith holt and dean;
By burn, by ford, by greenwood tree,
Yet you are halesome and fair to see.
Where gat ye that joup o' the lily sheen?
That bonnie snood o' the birk sae green?
And those roses, the fairest that ever were seen?
Kilmeny, Kilmeny, where have you been?'

Kilmeny looked up wi' a lovely grace,
But nae smile was seen on Kilmeny's face;
As still was her look, and as still was her e'e,
As the stillness that lay on the emerant lea,
Or the mist that sleeps on a waveless sea.
For Kilmeny had been, she kenned not where,
And Kilmeny had seen what she could not declare;

Kilmeny had been where the cock never crew,
Where the rain never fell, and the wind never blew.

But it seemed as the harp of the sky had rung,
And the airs of heaven played round her tongue,
When she spoke of the lovely forms she had seen,
And a land where sin had never been;
A land of love and a land of light,
Withouten sun, or moon, or night;
Where the river swa'd a living stream;
And the light a pure and cloudless beam;
The land of vision, it would seem,
A still, an everlasting dream.

In yon green wood there is a waik,
And in that waik there is a wene,
And in that wene there is a maike;
That neither has flesh, nor blood, nor bane;
And down in yon greenwood he walks his lane.

In that green wene Kilmeny lay,
Her bosom hap'd wi' flowerets gay;
But the air was soft, and the silence deep,
And bonny Kilmeny fell sound asleep.
She kenned nae mair, nor opened her e'e,
Till waked by the hymns of a far countrye.

She woke on a couch of silk sae slim,
All striped wi' the bars of the rainbow's rim;
And lovely beings round were rife,
Who erst had travelled mortal life;
And aye they smiled and 'gan to speer,
'What spirit has brought this mortal here?'

'Lang have I ranged the world wide,'
A meek and reverend fere replied;
'Baith night and day I have watched the fair,
Eident a thousand years and mair.
Yes, I have watched o'er ilk degree,
Wherever blooms feminitye;
And sinless virgin, free of stain
In mind and body, found I nane.
Never since the banquet of time
Found I a virgin in her prime,
Till late this bonnie maiden I saw
As spotless as the morning snaw;
Full twenty years she has lived as free
As the spirits that sojourn in this countrye:
I have brought her away from the snares of men,
That sin or death she never may ken.'

They clasped her waist, and her hands sae fair,
They kissed her cheeks, and they kemmed her hair;
And round came many a blooming fere,
Saying, 'Bonnie Kilmeny, ye're welcome here!
Women are freed of the littand scorn,
O blessed be the day Kilmeny was born!
Now shall the land of the spirits see,
Now shall it ken what a woman may be!
Many lang year, in sorrow and pain,
Many lang year through the world we've gane,
Commissioned to watch fair woman-kind,
For it's they who nurse the immortal mind.
We have watched their steps as the dawning shone,
And deep in the greenwood walks alone;
By lily bower and silken bed,
The viewless tears have been o'er them shed;
Have soothed their ardent minds to sleep,
Or left the couch of love to weep.
We have seen, we have seen! but the time maun come,
And the angels will weep at the day of doom!

'O would the fairest of mortal kind
Aye keep these holy truths in mind,
That kindred spirits their motions see,
Who watch their ways with anxious e'e,
And grieve for the guilt of humanitye!
O, sweet to Heaven the maiden's prayer,
And the sigh that heaves a bosom sae fair!
And dear to Heaven the words of truth
And the praise of virtue frae beauty's mouth!
And dear to the viewless forms of air,
The mind that kythes as the body fair!

'O, bonny Kilmeny! free frae stain,
If ever you seek the world again,
That world of sin, of sorrow, and fear,
O tell of the joys that are waiting here;
And tell of the signs you shall shortly see;
Of the times that are now, and the times that shall be.'

They lifted Kilmeny, they led her away,
And she walked in the light of a sunless day;
The sky was a dome of crystal bright,
The fountain of vision, and fountain of light;
The emerant fields were of dazzling glow,
And the flowers of everlasting blow.
Then deep in the stream her body they laid,
That her youth and her beauty never might fade;
And they smiled on Heaven, when they saw her lie

In the stream of life that wandered by.
And she heard a song, she heard it sung,
She kenned not where, but sae sweetly it rung,
It fell on the ear like a dream of the morn, —
'O blest be the day Kilmeny was born!
Now shall the land of the spirits see,
Now shall it ken what a woman may be!
The sun that shines on the world sae bright,
A borrowed gleid frae the fountain of light;
And the moon that sleeks the sky sae dun,
Like a gouden bow or a beamless sun,
Shall wear away and be seen nae mair,
And the angels shall miss them travelling the air.
But lang, lang after, baith nicht and day,
When the sun and the world have fled away;
When the sinner has gane to his waesome doom,
Kilmeny shall smile in eternal bloom!'

They bore her away, she wist not how,
For she felt not arm nor rest below;
But so swift they wained her through the light,
'T was like the motion of sound or sight;
They seemed to split the gales of air,
And yet nor gale nor breeze was there.
Unnumbered groves below them grew,
They came, they passed, and backward flew,
Like floods of blossoms gliding on,
A moment seen, in a moment gone.
Ah! never vales to mortal view
Appeared like those o'er which they flew,
That land to human spirits given,
The lowermost vales of the storied heaven;
From thence they can view the world below,
And heaven's blue gates with sapphires glow.
More glory yet unmeet to know.

They bore her far to a mountain green,
To see what mortal never had seen,
And they seated her high on a purple sward,
And bade her heed what she saw and heard,
And note the changes the spirits wrought,
For now she lived in the land of thought.
She looked, and she saw nor sun nor skies,
But a crystal dome of a thousand dyes:
She looked, and she saw nae land aright,
But an endless whirl of glory and light,
And radiant beings went and came,
Far swifter than wind, or the linkèd flame.
She hid her e'en frae the dazzling view;
She looked again, and the scene was new.

She saw a sun in a summer sky,
And clouds of amber sailing by;
A lovely land beneath her lay,
And that land had lakes and mountains grey;
And that land had valleys and hoary piles,
And marlèd seas and a thousand isles.
Its fields were speckled, its forests green,
And its lakes were all of the dazzling sheen,
Like magic mirrors, where shining lay
The sun, and the sky, and the cloudlet grey;
Which heaved and trembled and gently swung,
On every shore they seemed to be hung:
For there they were seen on their downward plain
A thousand times and a thousand again;
In winding lake, and placid firth,
Little peaceful heavens in the bosom of earth.

Kilmeny sighed and seemed to grieve,
For she found her heart to that land did cleave;
She saw the corn wave on the vale;
She saw the deer run down the dale;
She saw the plaid and the broad claymore,
And the brows that the badge of freedom bore, —
And she thought she had seen the land before.

She saw a lady sit on a throne,
The fairest that ever the sun shone on;
A lion licked her hand of milk,
And she held him in a leish of silk;
And a leifu' maiden stood at her knee,
With a silver wand and melting e'e;
Her sovereign shield till love stole in,
And poisoned all the fount within.

Then a gruff, untoward bedesman came,
And hundit the lion on his dame;
And the guardian maid wi' the dauntless e'e,
She dropped a tear, and left her knee;
And she saw till the queen frae the lion fled,
Till the bonniest flower o' the world lay dead;
A coffin was set on a distant plain,
And she saw the red blood fall like rain;
Then bonnie Kilmeny's heart grew sair,
And she turned away, and could look nae mair.

Then the gruff, grim carle girned amain,
And they trampled him down, but he rose again;
And he baited the lion to deeds of weir,
Till he lapped the blood to the kingdom dear;
And weening his head was danger preef,
When crowned with the rose and clover leaf,

He gowled at the carle, and chased him away,
To feed wi' the deer on the mountain grey.
He gowled at the carle, and he gecked at heaven,
But his mark was set and his arles given.
Kilmeny a while her een withdrew;
She looked again, and the scene was new.

She saw before her fair unfurled
One-half of all the glowing world,
Where oceans rolled, and rivers ran,
To bound the aims of sinful man.
She saw a people, fierce and fell,
Burst frae their bounds like fiends of hell;
There lilies grew, and the eagle flew;
And she herkèd on her ravening crew,
Till the cities and towers were wrapt in a blaze,
And the thunder it roared o'er the lands and the seas.
The widows wailed, and the red blood ran,
And she threatened an end to the race of man;
She never lened, nor stood in awe,
Till caught by the lion's deadly paw.
Oh! then the eagle swinked for life,
And brainzelled up a mortal strife;
But flew she north, or flew she south,
She met wi' the gowl o' the lion's mouth.

With a mooted wing and waefu' maen,
The eagle sought her eiry again;
But lang may she cower in her bloody nest,
And lang, lang sleek her wounded breast,
Before she sey another flight,
To play wi' the norland lion's might.

But to sing the sights Kilmeny saw,
So far surpassing nature's law,
The singer's voice wad sink away,
And the string of his harp wad cease to play.
But she saw till the sorrows of man were by,
And all was love and harmony;—
Till the stars of heaven fell calmly away,
Like flakes of snaw on a winter day.

Then Kilmeny begged again to see
The friends she had left in her ain countrie,
To tell of the place where she had been,
And the glories that lay in the land unseen;
To warn the living maidens fair,
The loved of heaven, the spirits' care,
That all whose minds unmeled remain
Shall bloom in beauty when time is gane.

With distant music, soft and deep,
They lulled Kilmeny sound asleep;
And when she awakened, she lay her lane,
All happed with flowers, in the greenwood wene.
When seven long years had come and fled,
When grief was calm, and hope was dead,
Whence scarce was remembered Kilmeny's name,
Late, late in a gloamin' Kilmeny came hame.
And O, her beauty was fair to see,
But still and steadfast was her e'e!
Such beauty bard may never declare,
For there was no pride nor passion there;
And the soft desire of maiden's een
In that mild face could never be seen.
Her seymar was the lily flower,
And her cheek the moss-rose in the shower;
And her voice like the distant melodye,
That floats along the twilight sea.
But she loved to raike the lanely glen,
And keep afar frae the haunts of men,
Her holy hymns unheard to sing,
To suck the flowers, and drink the spring;
But wherever her peaceful form appeared,
The wild beasts of the hill were cheered;
The wolf played blythely round the field,
The lordly byson lowed, and kneeled;
The dun deer wooed with manner bland,
And cowered beneath her lily hand.
And when at eve the woodlands rung,
When hymns of other worlds she sung
In ecstasy of sweet devotion,
O, then the glen was all in motion!
The wild beasts of the forest came,
Broke from their boughts and faulds the tame,
And goved around, charmed and amazed;
Even the dull cattle crooned and gazed,
And murmured, and looked with anxious pain
For something the mystery to explain.
The buzzard came with the throstle-cock;
The corby left her houf in the rock;
The blackbird alang wi' the eagle flew;
The hind came tripping o'er the dew;
The wolf and the kid their raike began,
And the kid and the lamb and the leveret ran;
The hawk and the hern attour them hung,
And the merle and the mavis forhooyed their young;
And all in a peaceful ring were hurled —
It was like an eve in a sinless world!

When a month and a day had come and gane,
Kilmeny sought the greenwood wene;
There laid her down on the leaves sae green,
And Kilmeny on earth was never mair seen.
But O! the words that fell frae her mouth

Were words of wonder, and words of
truth!
But all the land were in fear and dread,
For they kendna whether she was living or
dead.
It wasna her hame, and she couldna remain;
She left this world of sorrow and pain,
And returned to the land of thought
again.

1813

Robert Southey (1774-1843)

THE BATTLE OF BLENHEIM

It was a summer evening,
Old Kaspar's work was done,
And he before his cottage door
Was sitting in the sun,
And by him sported on the green
His little grandchild Wilhelmine.

She saw her brother Peterkin
Roll something large and round,
Which he beside the rivulet
In playing there had found;
He came to ask what he had found,
That was so large, and smooth, and round.

Old Kaspar took it from the boy,
Who stood expectant by;
And then the old man shook his head,
And, with a natural sigh,
''T is some poor fellow's skull,' said he,
'Who fell in the great victory.

'I find them in the garden,
For there 's many here about;
And often when I go to plough,
The ploughshare turns them out!
For many thousand men,' said he,
'Were slain in that great victory.'

'Now tell me what 't was all about,'
Young Peterkin, he cries;
And little Wilhelmine looks up
With wonder-waiting eyes;
'Now tell us all about the war,
And what they fought each other for.'

'It was the English,' Kaspar cried,
'Who put the French to rout;
But what they fought each other for,
I could not well make out;
But everybody said,' quoth he,
'That 't was a famous victory.

'My father lived at Blenheim then,
Yon little stream hard by;
They burnt his dwelling to the ground,
And he was forced to fly;
So with his wife and child he fled,
Nor had he where to rest his head.

'With fire and sword the country round
Was wasted far and wide,
And many a childing mother then,
And new-born baby died;
But things like that, you know, must be
At every famous victory.

'They say it was a shocking sight
After the field was won;
For many thousand bodies here
Lay rotting in the sun;
But things like that, you know, must be
After a famous victory.

'Great praise the Duke of Marlbro' won,
And our good Prince Eugene.'
'Why 't was a very wicked thing!'
Said little Wilhelmine.
'Nay, nay, my little girl,' quoth he,
'It was a famous victory.

'And everybody praised the Duke
Who this great fight did win.'
'But what good came of it at last?'
Quoth little Peterkin.
'Why that I cannot tell,' said he,
'But 't was a famous victory.'

1798

MY DAYS AMONG THE DEAD ARE PAST

My days among the Dead are past;
Around me I behold,
Where'er these casual eyes are cast,
The mighty minds of old;
My never-failing friends are they,
With whom I converse day by day.

With them I take delight in weal,
And seek relief in woe;
And while I understand and feel
How much to them I owe,
My cheeks have often been bedewed
With tears of thoughtful gratitude.

My thoughts are with the Dead, with them
I live in long-past years,
Their virtues love, their faults condemn,
Partake their hopes and fears,
And from their lessons seek and find
Instruction with an humble mind.

My hopes are with the Dead, anon
My place with them will be,
And I with them will travel on

Through all Futurity;
Yet leaving here a name, I trust,
That will not perish in the dust.

1823

THE CATARACT OF LODORE

'How does the water
Come down at Lodore?'
My little boy asked me
Thus, once on a time;
And moreover he tasked me
To tell him in rhyme.
Anon at the word,
There first came one daughter
And then came another,
To second and third
The request of their brother,
And to hear how the water
Comes down at Lodore,
With its rush and its roar,
As many a time
They had seen it before.
So I told them in rhyme,
For of rhymes I had store:
And 't was in my vocation
For their recreation
That so I should sing;
Because I was Laureate
To them and the King.

From its sources which well
In the tarn on the fell;
From its fountains
In the mountains,
Its rills and its gills;
Through moss and through brake,
It runs and it creeps
For awhile, till it sleeps
In its own little lake.
And thence at departing,
Awakening and starting,
It runs through the reeds
And away it proceeds,
Through meadow and glade,
In sun and in shade,
And through the wood-shelter,
Among crags in its flurry,
Helter-skelter,
Hurry-scurry.
Here it comes sparkling,
And there it lies darkling;
Now smoking and frothing
Its tumult and wrath in,
Till in this rapid race
On which it is bent,
It reaches the place
Of its steep descent.
The cataract strong
Then plunges along,
Striking and raging
As if a war waging
Its caverns and rocks among:
Rising and leaping,
Sinking and creeping,
Swelling and sweeping,
Showering and springing,
Flying and flinging,
Writhing and ringing,
Eddying and whisking,
Spouting and frisking,
Turning and twisting,
Around and around
With endless rebound!
Smiting and fighting,
A sight to delight in;
Confounding, astounding,
Dizzying and deafening the ear with its sound.

Collecting, projecting,
Receding and speeding,
And shocking and rocking,
And darting and parting,
And threading and spreading,
And whizzing and hissing,
And dripping and skipping,
And hitting and splitting,
And shining and twining,
And rattling and battling,
And shaking and quaking,
And pouring and roaring,
And waving and raving,
And tossing and crossing,
And flowing and going,
And running and stunning,
And foaming and roaming,
And dinning and spinning,
And dropping and hopping,
And working and jerking,
And guggling and struggling,
And heaving and cleaving,
And moaning and groaning;
And glittering and frittering,
And gathering and feathering,
And whitening and brightening,
And quivering and shivering,
And hurrying and skurrying,
And thundering and floundering;

Dividing and gliding and sliding,
And falling and brawling and sprawling,
And driving and riving and striving,
And sprinkling and twinkling and wrinkling,
And sounding and bounding and rounding,
And bubbling and troubling and doubling,

And grumbling and rumbling and tumbling,
And clattering and battering and shattering;
Retreating and beating and meeting and sheeting,
Delaying and straying and playing and spraying,
Advancing and prancing and glancing and dancing,
Recoiling, turmoiling and toiling and boiling,
And gleaming and streaming and steaming and beaming,
And rushing and flushing and brushing and gushing,
And flapping and rapping and clapping and slapping,
And curling and whirling and purling and twirling,
And thumping and plumping and bumping and jumping,
And dashing and flashing and splashing and clashing;
And so never ending, but always descending,
Sounds and motions for ever and ever are blending,
All at once and all o'er, with a mighty uproar;
And this way the water comes down at Lodore.

1823

Thomas Campbell (1777–1844)

YE MARINERS OF ENGLAND

A NAVAL ODE

Ye mariners of England!
That guard our native seas,
Whose flag has braved a thousand years
The battle and the breeze!
Your glorious standard launch again
To match another foe!
And sweep through the deep,
While the stormy winds do blow;
While the battle rages loud and long,
And the stormy winds do blow.

The spirits of your fathers
Shall start from every wave! —
For the deck it was their field of fame,
And Ocean was their grave:
Where Blake and mighty Nelson fell,
Your manly hearts shall glow,
As ye sweep through the deep,
While the stormy winds do blow;
While the battle rages loud and long,
And the stormy winds do blow.

Britannia needs no bulwarks,
No towers along the steep;
Her march is o'er the mountain waves,
Her home is on the deep.
With thunders from her native oak
She quells the floods below —
As they roar on the shore,
When the stormy winds do blow;
When the battle rages loud and long,
And the stormy winds do blow.

The meteor flag of England
Shall yet terrific burn,
Till danger's troubled night depart,
And the star of peace return.
Then, then, ye ocean-warriors!
Our song and feast shall flow
To the fame of your name,
When the storm has ceased to blow;
When the fiery fight is heard no more,
And the storm has ceased to blow.

1801

THE EXILE OF ERIN

There came to the beach a poor Exile of Erin,
The dew on his thin robes was heavy and chill:
For his country he sighed, when at twilight repairing
To wander alone by the wind-beaten hill.
But the day-star attracted his eye's sad devotion,
For it rose o'er his own native isle of the ocean,
Where once in the fire of his youthful emotion,
He sang the bold anthem of 'Erin go bragh!'

'Sad is my fate!' said the heart-broken stranger;
'The wild deer and wolf to a covert can flee,
But I have no refuge from famine and danger,
A home and a country remain not to me.
Never again, in the green sunny bowers,
Where my forefathers lived, shall I spend the sweet hours,
Or cover my harp with the wild-woven flowers,
And strike to the numbers of "Erin go bragh!"

'Erin, my country! though sad and forsaken,
In dreams I revisit thy sea-beaten shore;
But, alas! in a far foreign land I awaken,

And sigh for the friends who can meet me no more!
Oh cruel fate! wilt thou never replace me
In a mansion of peace — where no perils can chase me?
Never again shall my brothers embrace me?
They die to defend me, or live to deplore!

'Where is my cabin-door, fast by the wild wood?
Sisters and sire! did ye weep for its fall?
Where is the mother that looked on my childhood?
And where is the bosom-friend, dearer than all?
Oh! my sad heart! long abandoned by pleassure,
Why did it dote on a fast-fading treasure?
Tears, like the rain-drop, may fall without measure,
But rapture and beauty they cannot recall.

'Yet all its sad recollections suppressing,
One dying wish my lone bosom can draw:
Erin! an exile bequeaths thee his blessing!
Land of my forefathers! "Erin go bragh!"
Buried and cold, when my heart stills her motion,
Green be thy fields — sweetest isle of the ocean!
And thy harp-striking bards sing aloud with devotion —
"Erin mavournin — Erin go bragh!"'

1801

HOHENLINDEN

On Linden, when the sun was low,
All bloodless lay the untrodden snow,
And dark as winter was the flow
Of Iser, rolling rapidly.

But Linden saw another sight,
When the drum beat at dead of night,
Commanding fires of death to light
The darkness of her scenery.

By torch and trumpet fast arrayed,
Each horseman drew his battle-blade,
And furious every charger neighed,
To join the dreadful revelry.

Then shook the hills with thunder riven,
Then rushed the steed to battle driven,
And louder than the bolts of heaven,
Far flashed the red artillery.

But redder yet that light shall glow
On Linden's hills of stainèd snow,
And bloodier yet the torrent flow
Of Iser, rolling rapidly.

'T is morn, but scarce yon level sun
Can pierce the war-clouds, rolling dun,
Where furious Frank and fiery Hun
Shout in their sulphurous canopy.

The combat deepens. On, ye brave,
Who rush to glory, or the grave!
Wave, Munich! all thy banners wave,
And charge with all thy chivalry!

Few, few shall part where many meet!
The snow shall be their winding-sheet,
And every turf beneath their feet
Shall be a soldier's sepulchre.

1802

LOCHIEL'S WARNING

Wizard

Lochiel, Lochiel! beware of the day
When the Lowlands shall meet thee in battle array!
For a field of the dead rushes red on my sight,
And the clans of Culloden are scattered in fight.
They rally, they bleed, for their kingdom and crown;
Woe, woe to the riders that trample them down!
Proud Cumberland prances, insulting the slain,
And their hoof-beaten bosoms are trod to the plain.
But hark! through the fast-flashing lightning of war,
What steed to the desert flies frantic and far?
'T is thine, oh Glenullin! whose bride shall await,
Like a love-lighted watch-fire, all night at the gate.
A steed comes at morning: no rider is there;
But its bridle is red with the sign of despair.
Weep, Albin! to death and captivity led!
O weep! but thy tears cannot number the dead:
For a merciless sword on Culloden shall wave,
Culloden! that reeks with the blood of the brave.

Lochiel

Go, preach to the coward, thou death-telling seer!
Or, if gory Culloden so dreadful appear,
Draw, dotard, around thy old wavering sight
This mantle, to cover the phantoms of fright.

Wizard

Ha! laugh'st thou, Lochiel, my vision to scorn?
Proud bird of the mountain, thy plume shall be torn!
Say, rushed the bold eagle exultingly forth,
From his home, in the dark rolling clouds of the north?
Lo! the death-shot of foemen outspeeding, he rode
Companionless, bearing destruction abroad;
But down let him stoop from his havoc on high!
Ah! home let him speed — for the spoiler is nigh.
Why flames the far summit? Why shoot to the blast
Those embers, like stars from the firmament cast?
'T is the fire-shower of ruin, all dreadfully driven
From his eyrie, that beacons the darkness of heaven.
Oh, crested Lochiel! the peerless in might,
Whose banners arise on the battlement's height,
Heaven's fire is around thee, to blast and to burn;
Return to thy dwelling! all lonely return!
For the blackness of ashes shall mark where it stood,
And a wild mother scream o'er her famishing brood.

Lochiel

False Wizard, avaunt! I have marshalled my clan,
Their swords are a thousand, their bosoms are one!
They are true to the last of their blood and their breath,
And like reapers descend to the harvest of death.
Then welcome be Cumberland's steed to the shock!
Let him dash his proud foam like a wave on the rock!
But woe to his kindred, and woe to his cause,
When Albin her claymore indignantly draws;
When her bonneted chieftains to victory crowd,
Clanronald the dauntless, and Moray the proud,
All plaided and plumed in their tartan array ——

Wizard

— Lochiel, Lochiel! beware of the day;
For, dark and despairing, my sight I may seal,
But man cannot cover what God would reveal;
'T is the sunset of life gives me mystical lore,
And coming events cast their shadows before.
I tell thee, Culloden's dread echoes shall ring
With the bloodhounds that bark for thy fugitive king.
Lo! anointed by Heaven with the vials of wrath,
Behold, where he flies on his desolate path!
Now in darkness and billows, he sweeps from my sight:
Rise, rise! ye wild tempests, and cover his flight!
'T is finished. Their thunders are hushed on the moors:
Culloden is lost, and my country deplores.
But where is the iron-bound prisoner? Where?
For the red eye of battle is shut in despair.
Say, mounts he the ocean-wave, banished forlorn,
Like a limb from his country cast bleeding and torn?
Ah no! for a darker departure is near;
The war-drum is muffled, and black is the bier;
His death-bell is tolling: oh! mercy dispel
Yon sight, that it freezes my spirit to tell!
Life flutters convulsed in his quivering limbs,
And his blood-streaming nostril in agony swims.
Accursed be the fagots, that blaze at his feet,
Where his heart shall be thrown, ere it ceases to beat,
With the smoke of its ashes to poison the gale ——

Lochiel

— Down, soothless insulter! I trust not the tale:
For never shall Albin a destiny meet,
So black with dishonour, so foul with retreat.
Though my perishing ranks should be strewed in their gore,
Like ocean-weeds heaped on the surf-beaten shore,
Lochiel, untainted by flight or by chains,
While the kindling of life in his bosom remains,

Shall victor exult, or in death be laid low,
With his back to the field, and his feet to the foe!
And leaving in battle no blot on his name,
Look proudly to Heaven from the deathbed of fame.

1802

THE BATTLE OF THE BALTIC

Of Nelson and the North,
Sing the glorious day's renown,
When to battle fierce came forth
All the might of Denmark's crown,
And her arms along the deep proudly shone;
By each gun the lighted brand,
In a bold determined hand,
And the Prince of all the land
Led them on.

Like leviathans afloat
Lay their bulwarks on the brine;
While the sign of battle flew
On the lofty British line;
It was ten of April morn by the chime;
As they drifted on their path,
There was silence deep as death;
And the boldest held his breath,
For a time.

But the might of England flushed
To anticipate the scene;
And her van the fleeter rushed
O'er the deadly space between.
'Hearts of oak!' our captain cried; when each gun
From its adamantine lips
Spread a death-shade round the ships,
Like the hurricane eclipse
Of the sun.

Again! again! again!
And the havoc did not slack,
Till a feeble cheer the Dane
To our cheering sent us back —
Their shots along the deep slowly boom —
Then ceased — and all is wail,
As they strike the shattered sail;
Or, in conflagration pale,
Light the gloom.

Out spoke the victor then,
As he hailed them o'er the wave;
'Ye are brothers! ye are men!
And we conquer but to save —
So peace instead of death let us bring;
But yield, proud foe, thy fleet,
With the crews, at England's feet,
And make submission meet
To our King.'

Then Denmark blessed our chief,
That he gave her wounds repose;
And the sounds of joy and grief
From her people wildly rose,
As death withdrew his shades from the day,
While the sun looked smiling bright
O'er a wide and woeful sight,
Where the fires of funeral light
Died away.

Now joy, Old England, raise!
For the tidings of thy might,
By the festal cities' blaze,
While the wine cup shines in light;
And yet amidst that joy and uproar,
Let us think of them that sleep,
Full many a fathom deep,
By thy wild and stormy steep,
Elsinore!

Brave hearts! to Britain's pride
Once so faithful and so true,
On the deck of fame that died;
With the gallant good Riou:
Soft sigh the winds of Heaven o'er their grave!
While the billow mournful rolls
And the mermaid's song condoles,
Singing glory to the souls
Of the brave!

1809

LORD ULLIN'S DAUGHTER

A chieftain to the Highlands bound
  Cries, 'Boatman, do not tarry!
And I'll give thee a silver pound
  To row us o'er the ferry.'

'Now who be ye would cross Lochgyle,
  This dark and stormy water?'
'O, I'm the chief of Ulva's isle,
  And this Lord Ullin's daughter.

'And fast before her father's men
  Three days we've fled together,
For should he find us in the glen,
  My blood would stain the heather.

'His horsemen hard behind us ride;
  Should they our steps discover,
Then who will cheer my bonnie bride
  When they have slain her lover?'

Out spoke the hardy Highland wight,
  'I'll go, my chief — I'm ready;
It is not for your silver bright,
  But for your winsome lady:

'And by my word! the bonny bird
  In danger shall not tarry;
So though the waves are raging white,
  I 'll row you o'er the ferry.'

By this the storm grew loud apace,
  The water-wraith was shrieking;
And in the scowl of heaven each face
  Grew dark as they were speaking.

But still as wilder blew the wind,
  And as the night grew drearer,
Adown the glen rode armèd men,
  Their trampling sounded nearer.

'Oh, haste thee, haste!' the lady cries,
  'Though tempests round us gather;
I 'll meet the raging of the skies,
  But not an angry father.'

The boat has left a stormy land,
  A stormy sea before her —
When, oh! too strong for human hand,
  The tempest gathered o'er her.

And still they rowed amidst the roar
  Of waters fast prevailing:
Lord Ullin reached that fatal shore,
  His wrath was changed to wailing.

For sore dismayed, through storm and shade,
  His child he did discover:
One lovely hand she stretched for aid,
  And one was round her lover.

'Come back! come back!' he cried in grief,
  'Across this stormy water:
And I 'll forgive your Highland chief,
  My daughter! — oh, my daughter!'

'T was vain: the loud waves lashed the shore,
  Return or aid preventing:
The waters wild went o'er his child —
  And he was left lamenting.

1809

Thomas Moore (1779-1852)

THE LAKE OF THE DISMAL SWAMP

'They made her a grave, too cold and damp
  For a soul so warm and true;
And she 's gone to the Lake of the Dismal Swamp,
Where, all night long, by a fire-fly lamp,
  She paddles her white canoe.

'And her fire-fly lamp I soon shall see,
  And her paddle I soon shall hear;
Long and loving our life shall be,
And I 'll hide the maid in a cypress tree,
  When the footstep of death is near.'

Away to the Dismal Swamp he speeds —
  His path was rugged and sore,
Through tangled juniper, beds of reeds,
Through many a fen where the serpent feeds,
  And man never trod before.

And, when on the earth he sunk to sleep,
  If slumber his eyelids knew,
He lay where the deadly vine doth weep
Its venomous tear and nightly steep
  The flesh with blistering dew!

And near him the she-wolf stirred the brake,
  And the copper-snake breathed in his ear,
Till he starting cried, from his dream awake,
'Oh! when shall I see the dusky Lake,
  And the white canoe of my dear?'

He saw the Lake, and a meteor bright
  Quick over its surface played —
'Welcome,' he said, 'my dear one's light!'
And the dim shore echoed, for many a night,
  The name of the death-cold maid.

Till he hollowed a boat of the birchen bark,
  Which carried him off from shore;
Far, far he followed the meteor spark,
The wind was high and the clouds were dark,
  And the boat returned no more.

But oft, from the Indian hunter's camp
  This lover and maid so true
Are seen at the hour of midnight damp
To cross the Lake by a fire-fly lamp,
  And paddle their white canoe!

1806

THE HARP THAT ONCE THROUGH TARA'S HALLS

The harp that once through Tara's halls
  The soul of music shed,
Now hangs as mute on Tara's walls,
  As if that soul were fled. —
So sleeps the pride of former days,
  So glory's thrill is o'er,
And hearts, that once beat high for praise,
  Now feel that pulse no more!

No more to chiefs and ladies bright
  The harp of Tara swells;
The chord alone, that breaks at night,
  Its tale of ruin tells.
Thus Freedom now so seldom wakes,

The only throb she gives,
Is when some heart indignant breaks,
To show that still she lives.

1808

SHE IS FAR FROM THE LAND

She is far from the land where her young hero sleeps,
And lovers are round her, sighing:
But coldly she turns from their gaze, and weeps,
For her heart in his grave is lying.

She sings the wild song of her dear native plains,
Every note which he loved awaking; —
Ah! little they think who delight in her strains,
How the heart of the Minstrel is breaking.

He had lived for his love, for his country he died,
They were all that to life had entwined him;
Nor soon shall the tears of his country be dried,
Nor long will his love stay behind him.

Oh! make her a grave where the sun-beams rest,
When they promise a glorious morrow;
They 'll shine o'er her sleep, like a smile from the West,
From her own loved island of sorrow.

1808

'T IS THE LAST ROSE OF SUMMER

'T is the last rose of summer
Left blooming alone;
All her lovely companions
Are faded and gone;
No flower of her kindred,
No rose-bud is nigh,
To reflect back her blushes,
Or give sigh for sigh.

I 'll not leave thee, thou lone one!
To pine on the stem;
Since the lovely are sleeping,
Go, sleep thou with them.
Thus kindly I scatter
Thy leaves o'er the bed,
Where thy mates of the garden
Lie scentless and dead.

So soon may *I* follow,
When friendships decay,
And from Love's shining circle
The gems drop away.
When true hearts lie withered,
And fond ones are flown,
Oh! who would inhabit
This bleak world alone?

1808

OFT IN THE STILLY NIGHT

Oft in the stilly night,
Ere Slumber's chain has bound me,
Fond Memory brings the light
Of other days around me;
The smiles, the tears,
Of boyhood's years,
The words of love then spoken;
The eyes that shone,
Now dimmed and gone,
The cheerful hearts now broken!
Thus, in the stilly night,
Ere Slumber's chain has bound me,
Sad Memory brings the light
Of other days around me.

When I remember all
The friends, so linked together,
I 've seen around me fall,
Like leaves in wintry weather;
I feel like one,
Who treads alone
Some banquet-hall deserted,
Whose lights are fled,
Whose garland's dead,
And all but he departed!
Thus, in the stilly night,
Ere Slumber's chain has bound me,
Sad Memory brings the light
Of other days around me.

1816

Charles Wolfe (1791–1823)

THE BURIAL OF SIR JOHN MOORE AT CORUNNA

Not a drum was heard, not a funeral note,
As his corse to the rampart we hurried;
Not a soldier discharged his farewell shot
O'er the grave where our hero we buried.

We buried him darkly at dead of night,
The sods with our bayonets turning;
By the struggling moonbeam's misty light,
And the lantern dimly burning.

No useless coffin enclosed his breast,
Not in sheet nor in shroud we wound him;

But he lay like a warrior taking his rest,
With his martial cloak around him.

Few and short were the prayers we said,
And we spoke not a word of sorrow;
But we steadfastly gazed on the face that was dead,
And we bitterly thought of the morrow.

We thought, as we hollowed his narrow bed,
And smoothed down his lonely pillow,
That the foe and the stranger would tread o'er his head,
And we far away on the billow!

Lightly they 'll talk of the spirit that 's gone,
And o'er his cold ashes upbraid him, —
But little he 'll reck, if they let him sleep on
In the grave where a Briton has laid him.

But half of our heavy task was done,
When the clock struck the hour for retiring;
And we heard the distant and random gun
That the foe was sullenly firing.

Slowly and sadly we laid him down,
From the field of his fame fresh and gory;
We carved not a line, and we raised not a stone —
But we left him alone with his glory.

1817

Thomas Love Peacock (1785–1866)

THE FRIAR'S SONG

Though I be now a gray, gray friar,
Yet I was once a hale young knight:
The cry of my dogs was the only choir
In which my spirit did take delight.

Little I recked of matin bell,
But drowned its toll with my clanging horn
And the only beads I loved to tell
Were the beads of dew on the spangled thorn.

An archer keen I was withal,
As ever did lean on greenwood tree;
And could make the fleetest roebuck fall,
A good three hundred yards from me.

Though changeful time, with hand severe,
Has made me now these joys forego,
Yet my heart bounds whene'er I hear
Yoicks! hark away! and tally ho!

1822

THE WAR-SONG OF DINAS VAWR

The mountain sheep are sweeter,
But the valley sheep are fatter;
We therefore deemed it meeter
To carry off the latter.
We made an expedition;
We met an host, and quelled it;
We forced a strong position,
And killed the men who held it.

On Dyfed's richest valley,
Where herds of kine were browsing,
We made a mighty sally,
To furnish our carousing.
Fierce warriors rushed to meet us;
We met them, and o'erthrew them:
They struggled hard to beat us;
But we conquered them, and slew them.

As we drove our prize at leisure,
The king marched forth to catch us;
His rage surpassed all measure,
But his people could not match us.
He fled to his hall-pillars;
And, ere our force we led off,
Some sacked his house and cellars,
While others cut his head off.

We there, in strife bewildering,
Spilt blood enough to swim in:
We orphaned many children,
And widowed many women.
The eagles and the ravens
We glutted with our foemen;
The heroes and the cravens,
The spearmen and the bowmen.

We brought away from battle,
And much their land bemoaned them,
Two thousand head of cattle,
And the head of him who owned them:
Ednyfed, King of Dyfed,
His head was borne before us;
His wine and beasts supplied our feasts,
And his overthrow, our chorus.

1829

Leigh Hunt (1784–1859)

ABOU BEN ADHEM

Abou Ben Adhem (may his tribe increase!)
Awoke one night from a deep dream of peace,
And saw, within the moonlight in his room,
Making it rich, and like a lily in bloom,
An angel writing in a book of gold: —

Exceeding peace had made Ben Adhem bold,
And to the presence in the room he said,
'What writest thou?' — The vision raised its head,
And with a look made of all sweet accord,
Answered, 'The names of those who love the Lord.'
'And is mine one?' said Abou. 'Nay, not so,'
Replied the angel. Abou spoke more low,
But cheerly still; and said, 'I pray thee, then,
Write me as one that loves his fellow-men.'

The angel wrote, and vanished. The next night
It came again with a great wakening light,
And showed the names whom love of God had blessed,
And, lo! Ben Adhem's name led all the rest!

1844

RONDEAU

Jenny kissed me when we met,
Jumping from the chair she sat in;
Time, you thief, who love to get
Sweets into your list, put that in:
Say I 'm weary, say I 'm sad,
Say that health and wealth have missed me,
Say I 'm growing old, but add,
Jenny kissed me.

1838

George Darley (1795–1846)

THE CALL OF THE MORNING

Vale of the waterfalls!
Glen of the streams!
Wake from your slumbering!
Wake from your dreams!

Wild sings the mountain-lark,
Bird of the air!
Calling the valley-birds
Up to him there!

Sweet ring the mountain-bells
High o'er the dale,
Waking the little bells
Down in the vale.

Fresh breathes the morning-wind,
Bright looks the day, —
Up to the heather-hills,
Lilian, away!

1822

PRAYER AT BURIAL

TO A HAREBELL GROWING BY A GRAVE

Pretty flower! mourn for me:
I 'd rather hear thee sigh
Than friends that counterfeit a grief,
They feel no more than I!

Pretty flower! mourn for me:
I 'd rather have thy tear,
Than all a hypocritic world
Could waste upon my bier!

Pretty flower! mourn for me:
And dirger's time to save,
Hang down thy little passing-bell
And ring me to my grave!

1822

THE FALLEN STAR

A star is gone! a star is gone!
There is a blank in Heaven,
One of the cherub choir has done
His airy course this even.

He sat upon the orb of fire
That hung for ages there,
And lent his music to the choir
That haunts the nightly air.

But when his thousand years were passed,
With a cherubic sigh
He vanished with his car at last,
For even cherubs die!

Hear how his angel-brothers mourn —
The minstrels of the spheres —
Each chiming sadly in his turn
And dropping splendid tears.

The planetary Sisters all
Join in the fatal song,
And weep this hapless brother's fall
Who sang with them so long.

But deepest of the choral band
The Lunar Spirit sings,
And with a bass according hand
Sweeps all her sullen strings.

From the deep chambers of the dome
Where sleepless Uriel lies,
His rude harmonic thunders come
Mingled with mighty sighs.

The thousand car-borne cherubim,
The wandering Eleven,
All join to chant the dirge of him
Who fell just now from Heaven.

1822

Thomas Hood (1799–1845)

FAIR INES

O SAW ye not fair Ines?
She 's gone into the West,
To dazzle when the sun is down,
And rob the world of rest:
She took our daylight with her,
The smiles that we love best,
With morning blushes on her cheek,
And pearls upon her breast.

O turn again, fair Ines,
Before the fall of night,
For fear the Moon should shine alone,
And stars unrivaled bright;
And blessèd will the lover be
That walks beneath their light,
And breathes the love against thy cheek
I dare not even write!

Would I had been, fair Ines,
That gallant cavalier,
Who rode so gaily by thy side,
And whispered thee so near! —
Were there no bonny dames at home,
Or no true lovers here,
That he should cross the seas to win
The dearest of the dear?

I saw thee, lovely Ines,
Descend along the shore,
With bands of noble gentlemen,
And banners waved before:
And gentle youth and maidens gay,
And snowy plumes they wore; —
It would have been a beauteous dream,
— If it had been no more!

Alas, alas! fair Ines,
She went away with song,
With music waiting on her steps,
And shoutings of the throng;
But some were sad and felt no mirth,
But only music's wrong,
In sounds that sang farewell, farewell
To her you 've loved so long.

Farewell, farewell, fair Ines!
That vessel never bore
So fair a lady on its deck,
Nor danced so light before, —
Alas for pleasure on the sea,
And sorrow on the shore!
The smile that blest one lover's heart
Has broken many more!

1827

THE DEATH-BED

WE watched her breathing through the night,
Her breathing soft and low,
As in her breast the wave of life
Kept heaving to and fro.

So silently we seemed to speak,
So slowly moved about,
As we had lent her half our powers
To eke her living out.

Our very hopes belied our fears,
Our fears our hopes belied —
We thought her dying when she slept,
And sleeping when she died.

For when the morn came dim and sad,
And chill with early showers,
Her quiet eyelids closed — she had
Another morn than ours.

1825

THE BRIDGE OF SIGHS

ONE more unfortunate
Weary of breath,
Rashly importunate,
Gone to her death!

Take her up tenderly,
Lift her with care;
Fashioned so slenderly,
Young, and so fair!

Look at her garments
Clinging like cerements;
Whilst the wave constantly
Drips from her clothing;
Take her up instantly,
Loving, not loathing.

Touch her not scornfully;
Think of her mournfully,
Gently and humanly;
Not of the stains of her,
All that remains of her
Now is pure womanly.

Make no deep scrutiny
Into her mutiny
Rash and undutiful:
Past all dishonor,
Death has left on her
Only the beautiful.

Still, for all slips of hers,
One of Eve's family —
Wipe those poor lips of hers
Oozing so clammily.

Loop up her tresses
  Escaped from the comb,
Her fair auburn tresses;
Whilst wonderment guesses
  Where was her home?

Who was her father?
  Who was her mother?
Had she a sister?
  Had she a brother?
Or was there a dearer one
Still, and a nearer one
  Yet, than all other?

Alas! for the rarity
Of Christian charity
  Under the sun!
O, it was pitiful!
Near a whole city full,
  Home she had none.

Sisterly, brotherly,
Fatherly, motherly
  Feelings had changed:
Love, by harsh evidence,
Thrown from its eminence;
Even God's providence
  Seeming estranged.

Where the lamps quiver
So far in the river,
  With many a light
From window and casement,
From garret to basement,
She stood with amazement,
  Houseless by night.

The bleak wind of March
  Made her tremble and shiver;
But not the dark arch,
  Or the black flowing river:
Mad from life's history,
Glad to death's mystery,
  Swift to be hurled —
Anywhere, anywhere
  Out of the world!

In she plunged boldly,
No matter how coldly
  The rough river ran;
Over the brink of it,
Picture it, think of it,
  Dissolute man!
Lave in it, drink of it,
  Then, if you can!

Take her up tenderly,
  Lift her with care;
Fashioned so slenderly,
  Young, and so fair!

Ere her limbs frigidly
Stiffen too rigidly,
  Decently, kindly
Smooth and compose them;
And her eyes, close them,
  Staring so blindly!

Dreadfully staring
  Through muddy impurity,
As when with the daring
Last look of despairing
  Fixed on futurity.

Perishing gloomily,
Spurred by contumely,
Cold inhumanity,
Burning insanity,
  Into her rest —
Cross her hands humbly,
As if praying dumbly,
  Over her breast!

Owning her weakness,
  Her evil behaviour,
And leaving, with meekness,
  Her sins to her Saviour!

1844

Hartley Coleridge (1796–1849)

SONNETS

IX

LONG time a child, and still a child, when years
Had painted manhood on my cheek, was I,—
For yet I lived like one not born to die;
A thriftless prodigal of smiles and tears,
No hope I needed, and I knew no fears.
But sleep, though sweet, is only sleep, and waking,
I waked to sleep no more, at once o'ertaking
The vanguard of my age, with all arrears
Of duty on my back. Nor child, nor man,
Nor youth, nor sage, I find my head is grey,
For I have lost the race I never ran:
A rathe December blights my lagging May;
And still I am a child, though I be old,
Time is my debtor for my years untold.

XI

How long I sailed, and never took a thought
To what port I was bound! Secure as sleep,
I dwelt upon the bosom of the deep
And perilous sea. And though my ship was fraught

With rare and precious fancies, jewels brought
From fairy-land, no course I cared to keep,
Nor changeful wind nor tide I heeded aught,
But joyed to feel the merry billows leap,
And watch sunbeams dallying with the waves;
Or haply dream what realms beneath may lie
Where the clear ocean is an emerald sky,
And mermaids warble in their coral caves,
Yet vainly woo me to their secret home; —
And sweet it were for ever so to roam.

XXII

Youth, thou art fled, — but where are all the charms
Which, though with thee they came, and passed with thee,
Should leave a perfume and sweet memory
Of what they have been? — All thy boons and harms
Have perished quite. — Thy oft-renewed alarms
Forsake the fluttering echo. — Smiles and tears
Die on my cheek, or, petrified with years,
Shew the dull woe which no compassion warms,
The mirth none shares. Yet could a wish, a thought,
Unravel all the complex web of age, —
Could all the characters that Time hath wrought
Be clean effaced from my memorial page
By one short word, the word I would not say: —
I thank my God, because my hairs are grey.

XXIII

I thank my God because my hairs are grey!
But have grey hairs brought wisdom? Doth the flight
Of summer birds, departed while the light
Of life is lingering on the middle way,
Predict the harvest nearer by a day?
Will the rank weeds of hopeless appetite
Droop at the glance and venom of the blight
That made the vermeil bloom, the flush so gay,
Dim and unlovely as a dead worm's shroud?
Or is my heart, that, wanting hope, has lost
The strength and rudder of resolve, at peace?
Is it no longer wrathful, vain, and proud?
Is it a Sabbath, or untimely frost,
That makes the labour of the soul to cease?

1833

Thomas Babington Macaulay
(1800–1859)

IVRY

Now glory to the Lord of Hosts, from whom all glories are!
And glory to our Sovereign Liege, King Henry of Navarre!
Now let there be the merry sound of music and the dance,
Through thy corn-fields green, and sunny vines, O pleasant land of France!
And thou, Rochelle, our own Rochelle, proud city of the waters,
Again let rapture light the eyes of all thy mourning daughters.
As thou wert constant in our ills, be joyous in our joy,
For cold, and stiff, and still are they who wrought thy walls annoy.
Hurrah! Hurrah! a single field hath turned the chance of war,
Hurrah! Hurrah! for Ivry, and King Henry of Navarre.

Oh! how our hearts were beating, when, at the dawn of day,
We saw the army of the League drawn out in long array;
With all its priest-led citizens, and all its rebel peers,
And Appenzel's stout infantry, and Egmont's Flemish Spears.
There rode the blood of false Lorraine, the curses of our land;
And dark Mayenne was in the midst, a truncheon in his hand:
And, as we looked on them, we thought of Seine's empurpled flood,
And good Coligni's hoary hair all dabbled with his blood;
And we cried unto the living God, who rules the fate of war,
To fight for His own holy name, and Henry of Navarre.

The King is come to marshal us, in all his armour drest,
And he has bound a snow-white plume upon his gallant crest.
He looked upon his people, and a tear was in his eye;
He looked upon the traitors, and his glance was stern and high.
Right graciously he smiled on us, as rolled from wing to wing,
Down all our line, in deafening shout, 'God save our lord, the King!'

'And if my standard-bearer fall, as fall full well he may,
For never saw I promise yet of such a bloody fray,
Press where ye see my white plume shine, amidst the ranks of war,
And be your oriflamme to-day the helmet of Navarre.'

Hurrah! the foes are moving. Hark to the mingled din
Of fife, and steed, and trump, and drum, and roaring culverin.
The fiery duke is pricking fast across St. Andre's plain,
With all the hireling chivalry of Guelders and Almayne.
Now by the lips of those ye love, fair gentlemen of France,
Charge for the golden lilies, — upon them with the lance.
A thousand spurs are striking deep, a thousand spears in rest,
A thousand knights are pressing close behind the snow-white crest;
And in they burst, and on they rushed, while, like a guiding star,
Amidst the thickest carnage blazed the helmet of Navarre.

Now, God be praised, the day is ours. Mayenne hath turned his rein.
D'Aumale hath cried for quarter. The Flemish count is slain.
Their ranks are breaking like thin clouds before a Biscay gale;
The field is heaped with bleeding steeds, and flags, and cloven mail.
And then we thought on vengeance, and, all along our van,
'Remember Saint Bartholomew,' was passed from man to man.
But out spake gentle Henry, 'No Frenchman is my foe:
Down, down, with every foreigner, but let your brethren go.'
Oh! was there ever such a knight, in friendship or in war,
As our Sovereign Lord, King Henry, the soldier of Navarre?

Right well fought all the Frenchmen who fought for France to-day;
And many a lordly banner God gave them for a prey.
But we of the religion have borne us best in fight;
And the good Lord of Rosny hath ta'en the cornet white.
Our own true Maximilian the cornet white hath ta'en,
The cornet white with crosses black, the flag of false Lorraine.
Up with it high; unfurl it wide; that all the host may know
How God hath humbled the proud house which wrought His Church such woe.
Then on the ground, while trumpets sound their loudest point of war,
Fling the red shreds, a footcloth meet for Henry of Navarre.

Ho! maidens of Vienna; ho! matrons of Lucerne;
Weep, weep, and rend your hair for those who never shall return.
Ho! Philip, send, for charity, thy Mexican pistoles,
That Antwerp monks may sing a mass for thy poor spearmen's souls.
Ho! gallant nobles of the League, look that your arms be bright;
Ho! burghers of St. Genevieve, keep watch and ward to-night.
For our God hath crushed the tyrant, our God hath raised the slave,
And mocked the counsel of the wise, and the valour of the brave:
Then glory to his holy name, from whom all glories are;
And glory to our Sovereign Lord, King Henry of Navarre.

1824

Thomas Lovell Beddoes (1803–1849)

DIRGE

If thou wilt ease thine heart
Of love and all its smart,
Then sleep, dear, sleep;
And not a sorrow
Hang any tear on your eyelashes;
Lie still and deep,
Sad soul, until the sea-wave washes
The rim o' the sun to-morrow,
In eastern sky.

But wilt thou cure thine heart
Of love and all its smart,
Then die, dear, die;
'T is deeper, sweeter,
Than on a rose bank to lie dreaming
With folded eye;
And then alone, amid the beaming
Of love's stars, thou 'lt meet her
In eastern sky.

1850

SONG

How many times do I love thee, dear?
  Tell me how many thoughts there be
      In the atmosphere
      Of a new-fall'n year,
Whose white and sable hours appear
  The latest flake of Eternity:
So many times do I love thee, dear.

How many times do I love again?
  Tell me how many beads there are
      In a silver chain
      Of evening rain,
Unravelled from the tumbling main,
  And threading the eye of a yellow star:
So many times do I love again.

1851

DREAM-PEDLARY

If there were dreams to sell,
  What would you buy?
Some cost a passing bell;
  Some a light sigh,
That shakes from Life's fresh crown
Only a rose-leaf down.
If there were dreams to sell,
Merry and sad to tell,
And the crier rang the bell,
  What would you buy?

A cottage lone and still,
  With bowers nigh,
Shadowy, my woes to still,
  Until I die.
Such pearl from Life's fresh crown
Fain would I shake me down.
Were dreams to have at will,
This would best heal my ill,
  This would I buy.

But there were dreams to sell
  Ill didst thou buy;
Life is a dream, they tell,
  Waking, to die.
Dreaming a dream to prize,
Is wishing ghosts to rise;
And if I had the spell
To call the buried well,
  Which one would I?

If there are ghosts to raise,
  What shall I call,
Out of hell's murky haze,
  Heaven's blue pall?
Raise my loved long-lost boy,
To lead me to his joy.
There are no ghosts to raise;
Out of death lead no ways;
  Vain is the call.

Know'st thou not ghosts to sue?
  No love thou hast.
Else lie, as I will do,
  And breathe thy last.
So out of Life's fresh crown
Fall like a rose-leaf down.
Thus are the ghosts to woo;
Thus are all dreams made true,
  Ever to last!

1851

Walter Savage Landor (1775–1864)

ROSE AYLMER

Ah, what avails the sceptered race,
  Ah, what the form divine!
What every virtue, every grace!
  Rose Aylmer, all were thine.
Rose Aylmer, whom these wakeful eyes
  May weep, but never see,
A night of memories and of sighs
  I consecrate to thee.

1806

YES; I WRITE VERSES

Yes; I write verses now and then,
But blunt and flaccid is my pen,
No longer talkt of by young men
      As rather clever:

In the last quarter are my eyes,
You see it by their form and size;
Is it not time then to be wise?
      Or now or never.

Fairest that ever sprang from Eve!
While Time allows the short reprieve,
Just look at me! would you believe
      'T was once, a lover?

I can not clear the five-bar gate,
But, trying first its timber's state,
Climb stiffly up, take breath, and wait
      To trundle over.

Through gallopade I cannot swing
The entangling blooms of Beauty's spring:
I can not say the tender thing,
      Be 't true or false,

And am beginning to opine
Those girls are only half-divine
Whose waists yon wicked boys entwine
      In giddy waltz.

I fear that arm above that shoulder,
I wish them wiser, graver, older,
Sedater, and no harm if colder
And panting less.

Ah! people were not half so wild
In former days, when starchly mild,
Upon her high-heeled Essex smiled
The Brave Queen Bess.

1846

TO ROBERT BROWNING

There is delight in singing, though none hear
Beside the singer; and there is delight
In praising, though the praiser sit alone
And see the praised far off him, far above.
Shakespeare is not our poet, but the world's,
Therefore on him no speech! and brief for thee,
Browning! Since Chaucer was alive and hale,
No man hath walkt along our roads with step
So active, so inquiring eye, or tongue
So varied in discourse. But warmer climes
Give brighter plumage, stronger wing: the breeze
Of Alpine heights thou playest with, borne on
Beyond Sorrento and Amalfi, where
The Siren waits thee, singing song for song.

1846

TO YOUTH

Where art thou gone, light-ankled Youth?
With wing at either shoulder,
And smile that never left thy mouth
Until the Hours grew colder:

Then somewhat seemed to whisper near
That thou and I must part;
I doubted it: I felt no fear,
No weight upon the heart:

If aught befell it, Love was by
And rolled it off again;
So, if there ever was a sigh,
'T was not a sigh of pain.

I may not call thee back; but thou
Returnest when the hand
Of gentle Sleep waves o'er my brow
His poppy-crested wand;

Then smiling eyes bend over mine,
Then lips once prest invite;
But Sleep hath given a silent sign,
And both, alas! take flight.

1853

TO AGE

Welcome, old friend! These many years
Have we lived door by door:
The Fates have laid aside their shears
Perhaps for some few more.

I was indocile at an age
When better boys were taught,
But thou at length hast made me sage,
If I am sage in aught.

Little I know from other men,
Too little they from me,
But thou hast pointed well the pen
That writes these lines to thee.

Thanks for expelling Fear and Hope,
One vile, the other vain;
One's scourge, the other's telescope,
I shall not see again:

Rather what lies before my feet
My notice shall engage —
He who hath braved Youth's dizzy heat
Dreads not the frost of Age.

1853

ON HIS SEVENTY-FIFTH BIRTHDAY

I strove with none, for none was worth my strife,
Nature I loved, and next to Nature, Art;
I warmed both hands before the fire of life,
It sinks, and I am ready to depart.

1853

TO MY NINTH DECADE

To my ninth decade I have tottered on,
And no soft arm bends now my steps to steady;
She, who once led me where she would, is gone,
So when he calls me, Death shall find me ready.

1863

PROSE

CRITICISM

William Wordsworth (1770–1850)

PREFACE TO THE 'LYRICAL BALLADS'

THE first Volume of these Poems has already been submitted to general perusal. It was published, as an experiment, which, I hoped, might be of some use to ascertain, how far, by fitting to metrical arrangement a selection of the real language of men in a state of vivid sensation, that sort of pleasure and that quantity of pleasure may be imparted, which a Poet may rationally endeavour to impart.

I had formed no very inaccurate estimate of the probable effect of those Poems: I flattered myself that they who should be pleased with them would read them with more than common pleasure: and, on the other hand, I was well aware, that by those who should dislike them, they would be read with more than common dislike. The result has differed from my expectation in this only, that a greater number have been pleased than I ventured to hope I should please.

Several of my Friends are anxious for the success of these Poems, from a belief, that, if the views with which they were composed were indeed realised, a class of Poetry would be produced, well adapted to interest mankind permanently, and not unimportant in the quality, and in the multiplicity of its moral relations: and on this account they have advised me to prefix a systematic defence of the theory upon which the Poems were written. But I was unwilling to undertake the task, knowing that on this occasion the Reader would look coldly upon my arguments, since I might be suspected of having been principally influenced by the selfish and foolish hope of *reasoning* him into an approbation of these particular Poems: and I was still more unwilling to undertake the task, because, adequately to display the opinions, and fully to enforce the arguments, would require a space wholly disproportionate to a preface. For, to treat the subject with the clearness and coherence of which it is susceptible, it would be necessary to give a full account of the present state of the public taste in this country, and to determine how far this taste is healthy or depraved; which, again, could not be determined, without pointing out in what manner language and the human mind act and re-act on each other, and without retracing the revolutions, not of literature alone, but likewise of society itself. I have therefore altogether declined to enter regularly upon this defence; yet I am sensible, that there would be something like impropriety in abruptly obtruding upon the Public, without a few words of introduction, Poems so materially different from those upon which general approbation is at present bestowed.

It is supposed, that by the act of writing in verse an Author makes a formal engagement that he will gratify certain known habits of association; that he not only thus apprises the Reader that certain classes of ideas and expressions will be found in his book, but that others will be carefully excluded. This exponent or symbol held forth by metrical language must in different eras of literature have excited very different expectations: for example, in the age of Catullus, Terence, and Lucretius, and that of Statius or Claudian; and in our own country, in the age of Shakspeare and Beaumont and Fletcher, and that of Donne and Cowley, or Dryden, or Pope. I will not take upon me to determine the exact import of the promise which, by the act of writing in verse, an Author in the present day makes to his reader: but it will undoubtedly appear to many persons that I have not fulfilled the terms of an engagement thus voluntarily contracted. They who have been accustomed to the gaudiness and inane phraseology of many modern writers, if they persist in reading this book to its conclusion, will, no doubt, frequently have to struggle with feelings of strangeness and awkwardness: they will look round for poetry, and will be induced to inquire by what species of courtesy these attempts can be permitted to assume that title. I hope therefore the Reader will not censure me for attempting to state what I have proposed to myself to perform; and also (as far as the limits of a preface will permit) to explain some of the chief reasons which have determined me in the choice of my purpose: that at least he may be spared any unpleasant feeling of disappointment, and that I myself may be protected from one of the most dishonourable accusations which can be brought against an Author; namely, that of an indolence which prevents him from endeavouring to ascertain what is his duty, or, when his duty is ascertained, prevents him from performing it.

The principal object, then, proposed in these Poems was to choose incidents and situations from common life, and to relate or describe them, throughout, as far as was possible in a selection of language really used by men, and, at the same time, to throw over them a certain colouring of imagination, whereby ordinary things should be presented to the mind in an unusual aspect; and, further, and above all, to make these incidents and situations interesting by tracing in them, truly though not ostentatiously, the primary laws of our nature: chiefly, as far as regards the manner in which we associate ideas in a state of excitement. Humble and rustic life was generally chosen, because, in that condition, the essential passions of the heart find a better soil in which they can attain their maturity, are less under restraint, and speak a plainer and more emphatic language; because in that condition of life our elementary feelings coexist in a state of greater simplicity, and, consequently, may be more accurately contemplated, and more forcibly communicated; because the manners of rural life germinate from those elementary feelings, and, from the necessary character of rural occupations, are more easily comprehended, and are more durable; and, lastly, because in that condition the passions of men are incorporated with the beautiful and permanent forms of nature. The language, too, of these men has been adopted (purified indeed from what appear to be its real defects, from all lasting and rational causes of dislike or disgust) because such men hourly communicate with the best objects from which the best part of language is originally derived; and because, from their rank in society and the sameness and narrow circle of their intercourse, being less under the influence of social vanity, they convey their feelings and notions in simple and unelaborated expressions. Accordingly, such a language, arising out of repeated experience and regular feelings, is a more permanent, and a far more philosophical language, than that which is frequently substituted for it by Poets, who think that they are conferring honour upon themselves and their art, in proportion as they separate themselves from the sympathies of men, and indulge in arbitrary and capricious habits of expression, in order to furnish food for fickle tastes, and fickle appetites, of their own creation.

I cannot, however, be insensible to the present outcry against the triviality and meanness, both of thought and language, which some of my contemporaries have occasionally introduced into their metrical compositions; and I acknowledge that this defect, where it exists, is more dishonourable to the Writer's own character than false refinement or arbitrary innovation, though I should contend at the same time, that it is far less pernicious in the sum of its consequences. From such verses the Poems in these volumes will be found distinguished at least by one mark of difference, that each of them has a worthy *purpose.* Not that I always began to write with a distinct purpose formally conceived; but habits of meditation have, I trust, so prompted and regulated my feelings, that my descriptions of such objects as strongly excite those feelings, will be found to carry along with them a *purpose.* If this opinion be erroneous, I can have little right to the name of a Poet. For all good poetry is the spontaneous overflow of powerful feelings: and though this be true, Poems to which any value can be attached were never produced on any variety of subjects but by a man who, being possessed of more than usual organic sensibility, had also thought long and deeply. For our continued influxes of feeling are modified and directed by our thoughts, which are indeed the representatives of all our past feelings; and, as by contemplating the relation of these general representatives to each other, we discover what is really important to men, so, by the repetition and continuance of this act, our feelings will be connected with important subjects, till at length, if we be originally possessed of much sensibility, such habits of mind will be produced, that, by obeying blindly and mechanically the impulses of those habits, we shall describe objects, and utter sentiments, of such a nature, and in such connection with each other, that the understanding of the Reader must necessarily be in some degree enlightened, and his affections strengthened and purified.

It has been said that each of these poems has a purpose. Another circumstance must be mentioned which distinguishes these Poems from the popular Poetry of the day; it is this, that the feeling therein developed gives importance to the action and situation, and not the action and situation to the feeling.

A sense of false modesty shall not prevent me from asserting, that the Reader's attention is pointed to this mark of distinction, far less for the sake of these particular Poems than from the general importance of the subject. The subject is indeed important! For the human mind is capable of being excited without the application of gross and violent stimulants; and he must have a very faint perception of its beauty and dignity who does not know this, and who does not further know, that one being is elevated above another, in proportion as he possesses this capability. It has therefore appeared to me, that to endeavour to produce or enlarge this capability is one of the best services in which, at any period, a Writer can be engaged; but this service, excellent at all times, is especially so at the present day. For a multitude of causes, unknown to former times, are now acting with a combined force to blunt the discriminating powers of the mind, and, unfitting it for all voluntary exertion, to reduce it to a state of almost savage torpor. The most effective of these causes are the great national events which are daily taking place, and the increasing accumulation of men in cities, where the uniformity of their occupations produces a craving for extraordinary incident, which the rapid communication of intelligence hourly gratifies. To this tendency of life and manners the literature and theatrical exhibitions of the country have conformed themselves. The invaluable works of our elder writers, I had almost said the works of Shakspeare and Milton, are driven into neglect by frantic novels, sickly and stupid German Tragedies, and deluges of idle and extravagant stories in verse. — When I think upon this degrading thirst after outrageous stimulation, I am almost ashamed to have spoken of the feeble endeavour made in these volumes to counteract it; and, reflecting upon the magnitude of the general evil, I should be oppressed with no dishonourable melancholy, had I not a deep impression of certain inherent and indestructible qualities of the human mind, and likewise of certain powers in the great and permanent objects that act upon it, which are equally inherent and indestructible; and were there not added to this impression a belief, that the time is approaching when the evil will be systematically opposed, by men of greater powers, and with far more distinguished success.

Having dwelt thus long on the subjects and aim of these Poems, I shall request the Reader's permission to apprise him of a few circumstances relating to their *style*, in order, among other reasons, that he may not censure me for not having performed what I never attempted. The Reader will find that personifications of abstract ideas rarely occur in these volumes; and are utterly rejected, as an ordinary device to elevate the style, and raise it above prose. My purpose was to imitate, and, as far as possible, to adopt the very language of men; and assuredly such personifications do not make any natural or regular part of that language. They are, indeed, a figure of speech occasionally prompted by passion, and I have made use of them as such; but have endeavoured utterly to reject them as a mechanical device of style, or as a family language which Writers in metre seem to lay claim to by prescription. I have wished to keep the Reader in the company of flesh and blood, persuaded that by so doing I shall interest him. Others who pursue a different track will interest him likewise; I do not interfere with their claim, but wish to prefer a claim of my own. There will also be found in these volumes little of what is usually called poetic diction; as much pains has been taken to avoid it as is ordinarily taken to produce it; this has been done for the reason already alleged, to bring my language near to the language of men; and further, because the pleasure which I have proposed to myself to impart, is of a kind very different from that which is supposed by many persons to be the proper object of poetry. Without being culpably particular, I do not know how to give my Reader a more exact notion of the style in which it was my wish and intention to write, than by informing him that I have at all times endeavoured to look steadily at my subject; consequently, there is I hope in these Poems little falsehood of description, and my ideas are expressed in language fitted to their respective importance. Something must have been gained by this practice, as it is friendly to one property of all good poetry, namely, good sense: but it has necessarily cut me off from a large portion of phrases and figures of speech which from father to son have long been regarded as the common inheritance of Poets. I have also thought it expedient to restrict myself still further, having abstained from the use of many expressions, in themselves proper and beautiful, but which have been foolishly repeated by bad Poets, till such feelings of disgust are connected with them as it is scarcely possible by any art of association to overpower.

If in a poem there should be found a series of lines, or even a single line, in which the language, though naturally arranged, and according to the strict laws of metre, does not differ from that of prose, there is a numerous class of critics, who, when they stumble upon these prosaisms, as they call them, imagine that they have made a notable discovery, and exult over the Poet as over a man ignorant of his own profession. Now these men would establish a canon of criticism which the Reader will conclude he must utterly reject, if he wishes to be pleased with these volumes. And it would be a most easy task to prove to him, that not only the language of a large portion of every good poem, even of the most elevated character, must necessarily, except with reference to the metre, in no respect differ from that of good prose, but likewise that some of the most interesting parts of the best poems will be found to be strictly the language of prose when prose is well written. The truth of this assertion might be demonstrated by innumerable passages from almost all the poetical writings, even of Milton himself. To illustrate the subject in a general manner, I will here adduce a short composition of Gray, who was at the head of those who, by their reasonings, have attempted to widen the space of separation betwixt Prose and Metrical composition, and was more than any other man curiously elaborate in the structure of his own poetic diction.

'In vain to me the smiling mornings shine,
And reddening Phœbus lifts his golden fire:
The birds in vain their amorous descant join,
Or cheerful fields resume their green attire.
These ears, alas! for other notes repine;
A different object do these eyes require;
My lonely anguish melts no heart but mine;
And in my breast the imperfect joys expire;
Yet morning smiles the busy race to cheer,
And new-born pleasure brings to happier men;
The fields to all their wonted tribute bear;
To warm their little loves the birds complain.
I fruitless mourn to him that cannot hear,
And weep the more because I weep in vain.'

It will easily be perceived, that the only part of this Sonnet which is of any value is the lines printed in Italics; it is equally obvious, that, except in the rhyme, and in the use of the single word 'fruitless' for fruitlessly, which is so far a defect, the language of these lines does in no respect differ from that of prose.

By the foregoing quotation it has been shown that the language of Prose may yet be well adapted to Poetry; and it was previously asserted, that a large portion of the language of every good poem can in no respect differ from that of good Prose. We will go further. It may be safely affirmed, that there neither is, nor can be, any *essential* difference between the language of prose and metrical composition. We are fond of tracing the resemblance between Poetry and Painting, and, accordingly, we call them Sisters: but where shall we find bonds of connection sufficiently strict to typify the affinity betwixt metrical and prose composition? They both speak by and to the same organs; the bodies in which both of them are clothed may be said to be of the same substance, their affections are kindred, and almost identical, not necessarily differing even in degree; Poetry sheds no tears 'such as Angels weep,' but natural and human tears; she can boast of no celestial ichor that distinguishes her vital juices from those of prose; the same human blood circulates through the veins of them both.

If it be affirmed that rhyme and metrical arrangement of themselves constitute a distinction which overturns what has just been said on the strict affinity of metrical language with that of prose, and paves the way for other artificial distinctions which the mind voluntarily admits, I answer that the language of such Poetry as is here recommended is, as far as is possible, a selection of the language really spoken by men; that this selection, wherever it is made with true taste and feeling, will of itself form a distinction far greater than would at first be imagined, and will entirely separate the composition from the vulgarity and meanness of ordinary life; and, if metre be superadded thereto, I believe that a dissimilitude will be produced altogether sufficient for the gratification of a rational mind. What other distinction would we have? Whence is it to come? And where is it to exist? Not, surely, where the Poet speaks through the mouths of his characters: it cannot be necessary here, either for elevation of style, or any of its supposed ornaments: for, if the Poet's subject be judiciously chosen, it will naturally, and upon fit occasion, lead him to passions the language of which, if selected truly and judiciously, must necessarily be dignified and variegated, and alive with metaphors and figures. I forbear to speak of an incongruity which would shock the intelligent Reader, should the Poet interweave any foreign splendour of his own with that which the passion naturally suggests: it is sufficient to say that such addition is unnecessary. And, surely, it is more probable that those passages, which with propriety abound with metaphors and figures, will have their due effect, if, upon other occasions where the passions are of a milder character, the style also be subdued and temperate.

But, as the pleasure which I hope to give by the Poems now presented to the Reader must depend entirely on just notions upon this subject, and, as it is in itself of high importance to our taste and moral feelings, I cannot content myself with these detached remarks. And if, in what I am about to say, it shall appear to some that my labour is unnecessary, and that I am like a man fighting a battle without enemies, such persons may be reminded, that, whatever be the language outwardly holden by men, a practical faith in the opinions which I am wishing to establish is almost unknown. If my conclusions are admitted, and carried as far as they must be carried if admitted at all, our judgments concerning the works of the greatest Poets both ancient and modern will be far different from what they are at present, both when we praise, and when we censure: and our moral feelings influencing and influenced by these judgments will, I believe, be corrected and purified.

Taking up the subject, then, upon general grounds, let me ask, what is meant by the word Poet? What is a Poet? To whom does he address himself? And what language is to be expected from him? — He is a man speaking to men: a man, it is true, endowed with more lively sensibility, more enthusiasm and tenderness, who has a greater knowledge of human nature, and a more comprehensive soul, than are supposed to be common among mankind; a man pleased with his own passions and volitions, and who rejoices more than other men in the spirit of life that is in him; delighting to contemplate similar volitions and passions as manifested in the goings-on of the Universe, and habitually impelled to create them where he does not find them. To these qualities he has added a disposition to be affected more than other men by absent things as if they were present; an ability of conjuring up in himself passions, which are indeed far from being the same as those produced by real events, yet (especially in those parts of the general sympathy which are pleasing and delightful) do more nearly resemble the passions produced by real events, than anything which, from the motions of their own minds merely, other men are accustomed to feel in themselves: — whence, and from practice, he has acquired a greater readiness and power in expressing what he thinks and feels, and especially those thoughts and feelings which, by his own choice, or from the structure of his own mind, arise in him without immediate external excitement.

But whatever portion of this faculty we may suppose even the greatest Poet to possess, there cannot be a doubt that the language which it will suggest to him, must often, in liveliness and truth, fall short of that which is uttered by men in real life, under the actual pressure of those passions, certain shadows of which the Poet thus produces, or feels to be produced, in himself.

However exalted a notion we would wish to cherish of the character of a Poet, it is obvious, that while he describes and imitates passions, his employment is in some degree mechanical, compared with the freedom and power of real and substantial action and suffering. So that it will be the wish of the Poet to bring his feelings near to those of the persons whose feelings he describes, nay, for short spaces of time, perhaps, to let himself slip into an entire delusion, and even confound and identify his own feelings with theirs; modifying only the language which is thus suggested to him by a consideration that he describes for a particular purpose, that of giving pleasure. Here, then, he will apply the principle of selection which has been already insisted upon. He will depend upon this for removing what would otherwise be painful or disgusting in the passion; he will feel that there is no necessity to trick out or to elevate nature: and, the more industriously he applies this principle, the deeper will be his faith that no words, which *his* fancy or imagination can suggest, will be to be compared with those which are the emanations of reality and truth.

But it may be said by those who do not object to the general spirit of these remarks, that, as it is impossible for the Poet to produce upon all occasions language as exquisitely fitted for the passion as that which the real passion itself suggests, it is proper that he should consider himself as in the situation of a translator, who does not scruple to substitute excellencies of another kind for those which are unattainable by him; and endeavours occasionally to surpass his original, in order to make some amends for the general inferiority to which he feels that he must submit. But this would be to encourage idleness and unmanly despair. Further, it is the language of men who speak of what they do not understand; who talk of Poetry as of a matter of amusement and idle pleasure; who will converse with us as gravely about a *taste* for Poetry, as they express it, as if it were a thing as indifferent as a taste for rope-dancing, or Frontiniac or Sherry. Aristotle, I have been told, has said, that Poetry is the most philosophic of all writing: it is so: its object is truth, not individual and local, but general, and operative; not standing upon external testimony, but carried alive into the heart by passion; truth which is its own testimony, which gives competence and confidence to the tribunal to which it appeals, and receives them from the same tribunal. Poetry is the image of man and nature. The obstacles which stand in the way of the fidelity of the Biographer and Historian, and of their consequent utility, are incalculably greater than those which are to be encountered by the Poet who comprehends the dignity of his art. The Poet writes under one restriction only, namely, the necessity of giving immediate pleasure to a human Being possessed of that information which may be expected from him, not as a lawyer, a physician, a mariner, an astronomer, or a natural philosopher, but as a Man. Except this one restriction, there is no object standing between the Poet and the image of things; between this, and the Biographer and Historian, there are a thousand.

Nor let this necessity of producing immediate pleasure be considered as a degradation of the Poet's art. It is far otherwise. It is an acknowledgment of the beauty of the universe, an acknowledgment the more sincere, because not formal, but indirect; it is a task light and easy to him who looks at the world in the spirit of love: further, it is a homage paid to the native and naked dignity of man, to the grand elementary principle of pleasure, by which he knows, and feels, and lives, and moves. We have no sympathy but what is propagated by pleasure: I would not be misunderstood; but wherever we sympathise with pain, it will be found that the sympathy is produced and carried on by subtle combinations with pleasure. We have no knowledge, that is, no general principles drawn from the contemplation of particular facts, but what has been built up by pleasure, and exists in us by pleasure alone. The Man of science, the Chemist and Mathematician, whatever difficulties and disgusts they may have had to struggle with, know and feel this. However painful may be the objects with which the Anatomist's knowledge is connected, he feels that his knowledge is pleasure; and where he has no pleasure he has no knowledge. What then does the Poet? He considers man and the objects that surround him as acting and re-acting upon each other, so as to produce an infinite complexity of pain and pleasure; he considers man in his own nature and in his ordinary life as contemplating this with a certain quantity of immediate knowledge, with certain convictions, intuitions, and deductions, which from habit acquire the quality of intuitions; he considers him as looking upon this complex scene of ideas and sensations, and finding everywhere objects that immediately excite in him sympathies which, from the necessities of his nature, are accompanied by an overbalance of enjoyment.

To this knowledge which all men carry about with them, and to these sympathies in which, without any other discipline than that of our daily life, we are fitted to take delight, the Poet principally directs his attention. He considers man and nature as essentially adapted to each other, and the mind of man as naturally the mirror of the fairest and most interesting properties of nature. And thus the Poet, prompted by this feeling of pleasure, which accompanies him through the whole course of his studies, converses with general nature, with affections akin to those, which, through labour and length of time, the Man of science has raised up in himself, by conversing with those particular parts of nature which are the objects of his studies. The knowledge both of the Poet and the Man of science is pleasure; but the knowledge of the one cleaves to us as a necessary part of our existence, our natural and unalienable inheritance; the other is a personal and individual acquisition, slow to come to us, and by no habitual and direct sympathy connecting us with our fellow-beings. The Man of science seeks truth as a remote and unknown benefactor; he cherishes and loves it in his solitude: the Poet, singing a song in which all human beings join with him, rejoices in the presence of truth as our visible friend and hourly companion. Poetry is the breath and finer spirit of all knowledge; it is the impassioned expression which is in the countenance of all Science. Emphatically may it be said of the Poet, as Shakspeare hath said of man, 'that he looks before and after.' He is the rock of defence for human nature; an upholder and preserver, carrying everywhere with him relationship and love. In spite of difference of soil and climate, of language and manners, of laws and customs: in spite of things silently gone out of mind, and things violently destroyed; the Poet binds together by passion and knowledge the vast empire of human society, as it is spread over the whole earth, and over all time. The objects of the Poet's thoughts are everywhere; though the eyes and senses of man are, it is true, his favourite guides, yet he will follow wheresoever he can find an atmosphere of sensation in which to move his wings. Poetry is the first and last of all knowledge — it is as immortal as the heart of man. If the labours of Men of science should ever create any material revolution, direct or indirect, in our condition, and in the impressions which we habitually receive, the Poet will sleep then no more than at present; he will be ready to follow the steps of the Man of science, not only in those general indirect effects, but he will be at his side, carrying sensation into the midst of the objects of the science itself. The remotest discoveries of the Chemist, the Botanist, or Mineralogist, will be as proper objects of the Poet's art as any upon which it can be employed, if the time should ever come when these things shall be familiar to us, and the relations under which they are contemplated by the followers of these respective sciences shall be manifestly and palpably material to us as enjoying and suffering beings. If the time should ever come when what is now called science, thus familiarised to men, shall be ready to put on, as it were, a form of flesh and blood, the Poet will lend his divine spirit to aid the transfiguration, and will welcome the Being thus produced, as a dear and genuine inmate of the household of man. — It is not, then, to be supposed that any one, who holds that sublime notion of Poetry which I have attempted to convey, will break in upon the sanctity and truth of his pictures by transitory and accidental ornaments, and endeavour to excite admiration of himself by arts, the necessity of which must manifestly depend upon the assumed meanness of his subject.

What has been thus far said applies to Poetry in general; but especially to those parts of composition where the Poet speaks through the mouths of his characters; and upon this point it appears to authorise the conclusion that there are few persons of good sense, who would not allow that the dramatic parts of composition are defective, in proportion as they deviate from the real language of nature, and are coloured by a diction of the Poet's own, either peculiar to him as an individual Poet or belonging simply to Poets in general; to a body of men who, from the circumstance of their compositions being in metre, it is expected will employ a particular language.

It is not, then, in the dramatic parts of composition that we look for this distinction of language; but still it may be proper and necessary where the Poet speaks to us in his own person and character. To this I answer by referring the Reader to the description before given of a Poet. Among the qualities there enumerated as principally conducing to form a Poet, is implied nothing differing in kind from other men, but only in degree. The sum of what was said is, that the Poet is chiefly distinguished from other men by a greater promptness to think and feel without immediate external excitement, and a greater power in expressing such thoughts and feelings as are produced in him in that manner. But these passions and thoughts and feelings are the general passions and thoughts and feelings of men. And with what are they connected? Undoubtedly with our moral sentiments and animal sensations, and with the causes which excite these; with the operations of the elements, and the appearances of the visible universe; with storm and sunshine, with the revolutions of the seasons, with cold and heat, with loss of friends and kindred, with injuries and resentments, gratitude and hope, with fear and sorrow. These, and the like, are the sensations and objects which the Poet describes, as they are the sensations of other men, and the objects which interest them. The Poet thinks and feels in the spirit of human passions. How, then, can his language differ in any material degree from that of all other men who feel vividly and see clearly? It might be *proved* that it is impossible. But supposing that this were not the case, the Poet might then be allowed to use a peculiar language when expressing his feelings for his own gratification, or that of men like himself. But Poets do not write for Poets alone, but for men. Unless therefore we are advocates for that admiration which subsists upon ignorance, and that pleasure which arises from hearing what we do not understand, the Poet must descend from this supposed height; and, in order to excite rational sympathy, he must express himself as other men express themselves. To this it may be added, that while he is only selecting from the real language of men, or, which amounts to the same thing, composing accurately in the spirit of such selection, he is treading upon safe ground, and we know what we are to expect from him. Our feelings are the same with respect to metre; for, as it may be proper to remind the Reader, the distinction of metre is regular and uniform, and not, like that which is produced by what is usually called POETIC DICTION, arbitrary, and subject to infinite caprices upon which no calculation whatever can be made. In the one case, the Reader is utterly at the mercy of the Poet, respecting what imagery or diction he may choose to connect with the passion; whereas, in the other, the metre obeys certain laws, to which the Poet and Reader both willingly submit because they are certain, and because no interference is made by them with the passion, but such as the concurring testimony of ages has shown to heighten and improve the pleasure which co-exists with it.

It will now be proper to answer an obvious question, namely, Why, professing these opinions, have I written in verse? To this, in addition to such answer as is included in what has been already said, I reply, in the first place, Because, however I may have restricted myself, there is still left open to me what confessedly constitutes the most valuable object of all writing, whether in prose or verse; the great and universal passions of men, the most general and interesting of their occupations, and the entire world of nature before me — to supply endless combinations of forms and imagery. Now, supposing for a moment that whatever is interesting in these objects may be as vividly described in prose, why should I be condemned for attempting to superadd to such description the charm which, by the consent of all nations, is acknowledged to exist in metrical language? To this, by such as are yet unconvinced, it may be answered that a very small part of the pleasure given by Poetry depends upon the metre, and that it is injudicious to write in metre, unless it be accompanied with the other artificial distinctions of style with which metre is usually accompanied, and that, by such deviation, more will be lost from the shock which will thereby be given to the Reader's associations than will be counterbalanced by any pleasure which he can derive from the general power of numbers. In answer to those who still contend for the necessity of accompanying metre with certain appropriate colours of style in order to the accomplishment of its appropriate end, and who also, in my opinion, greatly underrate the power of metre in itself, it might, perhaps, as far as relates to these Volumes, have been almost sufficient to observe, that poems are extant, written upon more humble subjects, and in a still more naked and simple style, which have continued to give pleasure from generation to generation. Now, if nakedness and simplicity be a defect, the fact here mentioned affords a strong presumption that poems somewhat less naked and simple are capable of affording pleasure at the present day; and, what I wished *chiefly* to attempt, at present, was to justify myself for having written under the impression of this belief.

But various causes might be pointed out why, when the style is manly, and the subject of some importance, words metrically arranged will long continue to impart such a pleasure to mankind as he who proves the extent of that pleasure will be desirous to impart. The end of Poetry is to produce excitement in co-existence with an overbalance of pleasure; but, by the supposition, excitement is an unusual and irregular state of the mind; ideas and feelings do not, in that state, succeed each other in accustomed order. If the words, however, by which this excitement is produced be in themselves powerful, or the images and feelings have an undue proportion of pain connected with them, there is some danger that the excitement may be carried beyond its proper bounds. Now the co-presence of something regular, something to which the mind has been accustomed in various moods and in a less excited state, cannot but have great efficacy in tempering and restraining the passion by an intertexture of ordinary feeling, and of feeling not strictly and necessarily connected with the passion. This is unquestionably true; and hence, though the opinion will at first appear paradoxical, from the tendency of metre to divest language, in a certain degree, of its reality, and thus to throw a sort of half-consciousness of unsubstantial existence over the whole composition, there can be little doubt but that more pathetic situations and sentiments, that is, those which have a greater proportion of pain connected with them, may be endured in metrical composition, especially in rhyme, than in prose. The metre of the old ballads is very artless; yet they contain many passages which would illustrate this opinion; and, I hope, if the following Poems be attentively perused, similar instances will be found in them. This opinion may be further illustrated by appealing to the Reader's own experience of the reluctance with which he comes to the re-perusal of the distressful parts of 'Clarissa Harlowe,' or the 'Gamester'; while Shakspeare's writings, in the most pathetic scenes, never act upon us, as pathetic, beyond the bounds of pleasure — an effect which, in a much greater degree than might at first be imagined, is to be ascribed to small, but continual and regular impulses of pleasurable surprise from the metrical arrangement. — On the other hand (what it must be allowed will much more frequently happen) if the Poet's words should be incommensurate with the passion, and inadequate to raise the Reader to a height of desirable excitement, then, (unless the Poet's choice of his metre has been grossly injudicious) in the feelings of pleasure which the Reader has been accustomed to connect with metre in general, and in the feeling, whether cheerful or melancholy, which he has been accustomed to connect with that particular movement of metre, there will be found something which will greatly contribute to impart passion to the words, and to effect the complex end which the Poet proposes to himself.

If I had undertaken a Systematic defence of the theory here maintained, it would have been my duty to develope the various causes upon which the pleasure received from metrical language depends. Among the chief of these causes is to be reckoned a principle which must be well known to those who have made any of the Arts the object of accurate reflection; namely, the pleasure which the mind derives from the perception of similitude in dissimilitude. This principle is the great spring of the activity of our minds, and their chief feeder. From this principle the direction of the sexual appetite, and all the passions connected with it, take their origin: it is the life of our ordinary conversation; and upon the accuracy with which similitude in dissimilitude, and dissimilitude in similitude are perceived, depend our taste and our moral feelings. It would not be a useless employment to apply this principle to the consideration of metre, and to show that metre is hence enabled to afford much pleasure, and to point out in what manner that pleasure is produced. But my limits will not permit me to enter upon this subject, and I must content myself with a general summary.

I have said that poetry is the spontaneous overflow of powerful feelings: it takes its origin from emotion recollected in tranquillity: the emotion is contemplated till, by a species of reaction, the tranquillity gradually disappears, and an emotion, kindred to that which was before the subject of contemplation, is gradually produced, and does itself actually exist in the mind. In this mood successful composition generally begins, and in a mood similar to this it is carried on; but the emotion, of whatever kind, and in whatever degree, from various causes, is qualified by various pleasures, so that in describing any passions whatsoever, which are voluntarily described, the mind will, upon the whole, be in a state of enjoyment. If Nature be thus cautious to preserve in a state of enjoyment a being so employed, the Poet ought to profit by the lesson held forth to him, and ought especially to take care, that, whatever passions he communicates to his Reader, those passions, if his Reader's mind be sound and vigorous, should always be accompanied with an overbalance of pleasure. Now the music of harmonious metrical language, the sense of difficulty overcome, and the blind association of pleasure which has been previously received from works of rhyme or metre of the same or similar construction, an indistinct perception perpetually renewed of language closely resembling that of real life, and yet, in the circumstance of metre, differing from it so widely — all these imperceptibly make up a complex feeling of delight, which is of the most important use in tempering the painful feeling always found intermingled with powerful descriptions of the deeper passions. This effect is always produced in pathetic and impassioned poetry; while, in lighter compositions, the ease and gracefulness with which the Poet manages his numbers are themselves confessedly a principal source of the gratification of the Reader. All that it is *necessary* to say, however, upon this subject, may be effected by affirming, what few persons will deny, that, of two descriptions, either of passions, manners, or characters, each of them equally well executed, the one in prose and the other in verse, the verse will be read a hundred times where the prose is read once.

Having thus explained a few of my reasons for writing in verse, and why I have chosen subjects from common life, and endeavoured to bring my language near to the real language of men, if I have been too minute in pleading my own cause, I have at the same time been treating a subject of general interest; and for this reason a few words shall be added with reference solely to these particular poems, and to some defects which will probably be found in them. I am sensible that my associations must have sometimes been particular instead of general, and that, consequently, giving to things a false importance, I may have sometimes written upon unworthy subjects; but I am less apprehensive on this account, than that my language may frequently have suffered from those arbitrary connections of feelings and ideas with particular words and phrases, from which no man can altogether protect himself. Hence I have no doubt, that, in some instances, feelings, even of the ludicrous, may be given to my Readers by expressions which appeared to me tender and pathetic. Such faulty expressions, were I convinced they were faulty at present, and that they must necessarily continue to be so, I would willingly take all reasonable pains to correct. But it is dangerous to make these alterations on the simple authority of a few individuals, or even of certain classes of men; for where the understanding of an Author is not convinced, or his feelings altered, this cannot be done without great injury to himself: for his own feelings are his stay and support; and, if he set them aside in one instance, he may be induced to repeat this act till his mind shall lose all confidence in itself, and become utterly debilitated. To this it may be added, that the critic ought never to forget that he is himself exposed to the same errors as the Poet, and, perhaps, in a much greater degree: for there can be no presumption in saying of most readers, that it is not probable they will be so well acquainted with the various stages of meaning through which words have passed, or with the fickleness or stability of the relations of particular ideas to each other; and, above all, since they are so much less interested in the subject, they may decide lightly and carelessly.

Long as the Reader has been detained, I hope he will permit me to caution him against a mode of false criticism which has been applied to Poetry, in which the language closely resembles that of life and nature. Such verses have been triumphed over in parodies, of which Dr. Johnson's stanza is a fair specimen: —

'I put my hat upon my head
And walked into the Strand,
And there I met another man
Whose hat was in his hand.'

Immediately under these lines let us place one of the most justly-admired stanzas of the 'Babes in the Wood.'

'These pretty Babes with hand in hand
Went wandering up and down;
But never more they saw the Man
Approaching from the Town.'

In both these stanzas the words, and the order of the words, in no respect differ from the most unimpassioned conversation. There are words in both, for example, 'the Strand,' and 'the Town,' connected with none but the most familiar ideas; yet the one stanza we admit as admirable, and the other as a fair example of the superlatively contemptible. Whence arises this difference? Not from the metre, not from the language, not from the order of the words; but the *matter* expressed in Dr. Johnson's stanza is contemptible. The proper method of treating trivial and simple verses, to which Dr. Johnson's stanza would be a fair parallelism, is not to say, this is a bad kind of poetry, or, this is not poetry; but, this wants sense; it is neither interesting in itself, nor can *lead* to anything interesting; the images neither originate in that sane state of feeling which arises out of thought, nor can excite thought or feeling in the Reader. This is the only sensible manner of dealing with such verses. Why trouble yourself about the species till you have previously decided upon the genus? Why take pains to prove that an ape is not a Newton, when it is self-evident that he is not a man?

One request I must make of my reader, which is, that in judging these Poems he would decide by his own feelings genuinely, and not by reflection upon what will probably be the judgment of others. How common is it to hear a person say, I myself do not object to this style of composition, or this or that expression, but, to such and such classes of people it will appear mean or ludicrous! This mode of criticism, so destructive of all sound unadulterated judgment, is almost universal: let the Reader then abide, independently, by his own feelings, and, if he finds himself affected, let him not suffer such conjectures to interfere with his pleasure.

If an Author, by any single composition, has impressed us with respect for his talents, it is useful to consider this as affording a presumption, that on other occasions where we have been displeased, he, nevertheless, may not have written ill or absurdly; and further, to give him so much credit for this one composition as may induce us to review what has displeased us, with more care than we should otherwise have bestowed upon it. This is not only an act of justice, but, in our decisions upon poetry especially, may conduce, in a high degree, to the improvement of our own taste; for an *accurate* taste in poetry, and in all the other arts, as Sir Joshua Reynolds has observed, is an *acquired* talent, which can only be produced by thought and a long-continued intercourse with the best models of composition. This is mentioned, not with so ridiculous a purpose as to prevent the most inexperienced Reader from judging for himself, (I have already said that I wish him to judge for himself;) but merely to temper the rashness of decision, and to suggest, that, if Poetry be a subject on which much time has not been bestowed, the judgment may be erroneous; and that, in many cases, it necessarily will be so.

Nothing would, I know, have so effectually contributed to further the end which I have in view, as to have shown of what kind the pleasure is, and how that pleasure is produced, which is confessedly produced by metrical composition essentially different from that which I have here endeavoured to recommend: for the Reader will say that he has been pleased by such composition; and what more can be done for him? The power of any art is limited; and he will suspect, that, if it be proposed to furnish him with new friends, that can be only upon condition of his abandoning his old friends. Besides, as I have said, the Reader is himself conscious of the pleasure which he has received from such composition, composition to which he has peculiarly attached the endearing name of Poetry; and all men feel an habitual gratitude, and something of an honourable bigotry, for the objects which have long continued to please them: we not only wish to be pleased, but to be pleased in that particular way in which we have been accustomed to be pleased. There is in these feelings enough to resist a host of arguments; and I should be the less able to combat them successfully, as I am willing to allow, that, in order entirely to enjoy the Poetry which I am recommending, it would be necessary to give up much of what is ordinarily enjoyed. But, would my limits have permitted me to point out how this pleasure is produced, many obstacles might have been removed, and the Reader assisted in perceiving that the powers of language are not so limited as he may suppose; and that it is possible for poetry to give other enjoyments, of a purer, more lasting, and more exquisite nature. This part of the subject has not been altogether neglected, but it has not been so much my present aim to prove, that the interest excited by some other kinds of poetry is less vivid, and less worthy of the nobler powers of the mind, as to offer reasons for presuming, that if my purpose were fulfilled, a species of poetry would be produced, which is genuine poetry; in its nature well adapted to interest mankind permanently, and likewise important in the multiplicity and quality of its moral relations.

From what has been said, and from a perusal of the Poems, the Reader will be able clearly to perceive the object which I had in view: he will determine how far it has been attained; and, what is a much more important question, whether it be worth attaining: and upon the decision of these two questions will rest my claim to the approbation of the Public.

1800

Samuel Taylor Coleridge
(1772–1834)

BIOGRAPHIA LITERARIA

Chapter XIV

During the first year that Mr. Wordsworth and I were neighbors, our conversations turned frequently on the two cardinal points of poetry, the power of exciting the sympathy of the reader by a faithful adherence to the truth of nature, and the power of giving the interest of novelty by the modifying colors of imagination. The sudden charm which accidents of light and shade, which moonlight or sunset diffused over a known and familiar landscape, appeared to represent the practicability of combining both. These are the poetry of nature. The thought suggested itself — (to which of us I do not recollect) — that a series of poems might be composed of two sorts. In the one, the incidents and agents were to be, in part at least, supernatural; and the excellence aimed at was to consist in the interesting of the affections by the dramatic truth of such emotions, as would naturally accompany such situations, supposing them real. And real in this sense they have been to every human being who, from whatever source of delusion, has at any time believed himself under supernatural agency. For the second class, subjects were to be chosen from ordinary life; the characters and incidents were to be such as will be found in every village and its vicinity, where there is a meditative and feeling mind to seek after them, or to notice them, when they present themselves.

In this idea originated the plan of the *Lyrical Ballads;* in which it was agreed, that my endeavors should be directed to persons and characters supernatural, or at least romantic; yet so as to transfer from our inward nature a human interest and a semblance of truth sufficient to procure for these shadows of imagination that willing suspension of disbelief for the moment, which constitutes poetic faith. Mr. Wordsworth, on the other hand, was to propose to himself as his object, to give the charm of novelty to things of every day, and to excite a feeling analogous to the supernatural, by awakening the mind's attention to the lethargy of custom, and directing it to the loveliness and the wonders of the world before us; an inexhaustible treasure, but for which, in consequence of the film of familiarity and selfish solicitude we have eyes, yet see not, ears that hear not, and hearts that neither feel nor understand.

With this view I wrote the *Ancient Mariner*, and was preparing among other poems, *The Dark Ladie*, and the *Christabel*, in which I should have more nearly realized my ideal than I had done in my first attempt. But Mr. Wordsworth's industry had proved so much more successful, and the number of his poems so much greater, that my compositions, instead of forming a balance, appeared rather an interpolation of heterogeneous matter. Mr. Wordsworth added two or three poems written in his own character, in the impassioned, lofty, and sustained diction, which is characteristic of his genius. In this form the *Lyrical Ballads* were published; and were presented by him, as an experiment, whether subjects, which from their nature rejected the usual ornaments and extra-colloquial style of poems in general, might not be so managed in the language of ordinary life as to produce the pleasurable interest, which it is the peculiar business of poetry to impart. To the second edition he added a preface of considerable length; in which, notwithstanding some passages of apparently a contrary import, he was understood to contend for the extension of this style to poetry of all kinds, and to reject as vicious and indefensible all phrases and forms of speech that were not included in what he (unfortunately, I think, adopting an equivocal expression) called the language of real life. From this preface, prefixed to poems in which it was impossible to deny the presence of original genius, however mistaken its direction might be deemed, arose the whole long-continued controversy. For from the conjunction of perceived power with supposed heresy I explain the inveteracy and in some instances, I grieve to say, the acrimonious passions, with which the controversy has been conducted by the assailants.

Had Mr. Wordsworth's poems been the silly, the childish things, which they were for a long time described as being; had they been really distinguished from the compositions of other poets merely by meanness of language and inanity of thought; had they indeed contained nothing more than what is found in the parodies and pretended imitations of them; they must have sunk at once, a dead weight, into the slough of oblivion, and have dragged the preface along with them. But year after year increased the number of Mr. Wordsworth's admirers. They were found too not in the lower classes of the reading public, but chiefly among young men of strong sensibility and meditative minds; and their admiration (inflamed perhaps in some degree by opposition) was distinguished by its intensity, I might almost say, by its religious fervor. These facts, and the intellectual energy of the author, which was more or less consciously felt, where it was outwardly and even boisterously denied, meeting with sentiments of aversion to his opinions, and of alarm at their consequences, produced an eddy of criticism, which would of itself have borne up the poems by the violence with which it whirled them round and round. With many parts of this preface in the sense attributed to them and which the words undoubtedly seem to authorize, I never concurred; but on the contrary objected to them as erroneous in principle, and as contradictory (in appearance at least) both to other parts of the same preface, and to the author's own practice in the greater part of the poems themselves. Mr. Wordsworth in his recent collection has, I find, degraded this prefatory disquisition to the end of his second volume, to be read or not at the reader's choice. But he has not, as far as I can discover, announced any change in his poetic creed. At all events, considering it as the source of a controversy, in which I have been honored more than I deserve by the frequent conjunction of my name with his, I think it expedient to declare once for all, in what points I coincide with the opinions supported in that preface, and in what points I altogether differ. But in order to render myself intelligible I must previously, in as few words as possible, explain my views, first, of a Poem; and secondly, of Poetry itself, in kind, and in essence.

The office of philosophical disquisition consists in just distinction; while it is the privilege of the philosopher to preserve himself constantly aware, that distinction is not division. In order to obtain adequate notions of any truth, we must intellectually separate its distinguishable parts; and this is the technical process of philosophy. But having so done, we must then restore them in our conceptions to the unity, in which they actually co-exist; and this is the result of philosophy. A poem contains the same elements as a prose composition; the difference therefore must consist in a different combination of them, in consequence of a different object being proposed. According to the difference of the object will be the difference of the combination. It is possible, that the object may be merely to facilitate the recollection of any given facts or observations by artificial arrangement; and the composition will be a poem, merely because it is distinguished from prose by metre, or by rhyme, or by both conjointly. In this, the lowest sense, a man might attribute the name of a poem to the well-known enumeration of the days in the several months:

'Thirty days hath September,
April, June, and November,' &c.

and others of the same class and purpose. And as a particular pleasure is found in anticipating the recurrence of sound and quantities, all compositions that have this charm superadded, whatever be their contents, *may* be entitled poems.

So much for the superficial form. A difference of object and contents supplies an additional ground of distinction. The immediate purpose may be the communication of truths; either of truth absolute and demonstrable, as in works of science; or of facts experienced and recorded, as in history. Pleasure, and that of the highest and most permanent kind, may result from the attainment of the end; but it is not itself the immediate end. In other works the communication of pleasure may be the immediate purpose; and though truth, either moral or intellectual, ought to be the ultimate end, yet this will distinguish the character of the author, not the class to which the work belongs. Blest indeed is that state of society, in which the immediate purpose would be baffled by the perversion of the proper ultimate end; in which no charm of diction or imagery could exempt the

Bathyllus even of an Anacreon, or the Alexis of Virgil, from disgust and aversion!

But the communication of pleasure may be the immediate object of a work not metrically composed; and that object may have been in a high degree attained, as in novels and romances. Would then the mere superaddition of metre, with or without rhyme, entitle these to the name of poems? The answer is, that nothing can permanently please, which does not contain in itself the reason why it is so, and not otherwise. If metre be superadded, all other parts must be made consonant with it. They must be such, as to justify the perpetual and distinct attention to each part, which an exact corrrespondent recurrence of accent and sound are calculated to excite. The final definition then, so deduced, may be thus worded. A poem is that species of composition, which is opposed to works of science, by proposing for its *immediate* object pleasure, not truth; and from all other species — (having *this* object in common with it) — it is discriminated by proposing to itself such delight from the *whole*, as is compatible with a distinct gratification from each component *part*.

Controversy is not seldom excited in consequence of the disputants attaching each a different meaning to the same word; and in few instances has this been more striking, than in disputes concerning the present subject. If a man chooses to call every composition a poem, which is rhyme, or measure, or both, I must leave his opinion uncontroverted. The distinction is at least competent to characterize the writer's intention. If it were subjoined, that the whole is likewise entertaining or affecting, as a tale, or as a series of interesting reflections, I of course admit this as another fit ingredient of a poem, and an additional merit. But if the definition sought for be that of a *legitimate* poem, I answer, it must be one, the parts of which mutually support and explain each other; all in their proportion harmonizing with, and supporting the purpose and known influences of metrical arrangement. The philosophic critics of all ages coincide with the ultimate judgment of all countries, in equally denying the praises of a just poem, on the one hand, to a series of striking lines or distichs, each of which, absorbing the whole attention of the reader to itself, becomes disjoined from its context, and forms a separate whole, instead of a harmonizing part; and on the other hand, to an unsustained composition, from which the reader collects rapidly the general result unattracted by the component parts. The reader should be carried forward, not merely or chiefly by the mechanical impulse of curiosity, or by a restless desire to arrive at the final solution; but by the pleasurable activity of mind excited by the attractions of the journey itself. Like the motion of a serpent, which the Egyptians made the emblem of intellectual power; or like the path of sound through the air: — at every step he pauses and half recedes, and from the retrogressive movement collects the force which again carries him onward, *Praecipitandus est liber spiritus*, says Petronius most happily. The epithet, *liber*, here balances the preceding verb; and it is not easy to conceive more meaning condensed in fewer words.

But if this should be admitted as a satisfactory character of a poem, we have still to seek for a definition of poetry. The writings of Plato and Jeremy Taylor, and Burnet's Theory of the Earth, furnish undeniable proofs that poetry of the highest kind may exist without metre, and even without the contra-distinguishing objects of a poem. The first chapter of Isaiah — (indeed a very large proportion of the whole book) — is poetry in the most emphatic sense; yet it would be not less irrational than strange to assert, that pleasure, and not truth was the immediate object of the prophet. In short, whatever specific import we attach to the word Poetry, there will be found involved in it, as a necessary consequence, that a poem of any length neither can be, nor ought to be, all poetry. Yet if an harmonious whole is to be produced, the remaining parts must be preserved in keeping with the poetry; and this can be no otherwise effected than by such a studied selection and artificial arrangement, as will partake of one, though not a peculiar property of poetry. And this again can be no other than the property of exciting a more continuous and equal attention than the language of prose aims at, whether colloquial or written.

My own conclusions on the nature of poetry, in the strictest use of the word, have been in part anticipated in some of the remarks on the Fancy and Imagination in the first part of this work. What is poetry? — is so nearly the same question with, what is a poet? — that the answer to the one is involved in the solution of the other. For it is a distinction resulting from the poetic genius itself, which sustains and modifies the images, thoughts, and emotions of the poet's own mind.

The poet, described in ideal perfection, brings the whole soul of man into activity, with the subordination of its faculties to each other according to their relative worth and dignity. He diffuses a tone and spirit of unity, that blends, and (as it were) *fuses*, each into each, by that synthetic and magical power, to which I would exclusively appropriate the name of Imagination. This power, first put in action by the will and understanding, and retained under their irremissive, though gentle and unnoticed, control, *laxis effertur habenis*, reveals itself in the balance or reconcilement of opposite or discordant qualities: of sameness with difference; of the general with the concrete; the idea with the image; the individual with the representative; the sense of novelty and freshness with old and familiar objects; a more than usual state of emotion with more than usual order; judgment ever awake and steady self-possession with enthusiasm and feeling profound or vehement; and while it blends and harmonizes the natural and the artificial, still subordinates art to nature; the manner to the matter; and our admiration of the poet to our sympathy with the poetry. Doubtless, as Sir John Davies observes of the soul — (and his words may with slight alteration be applied, and even more appropriately, to the poetic Imagination) —

'Doubtless this could not be, but that she turns
Bodies to *spirit* by sublimation strange,
As fire converts to fire the things it burns,
As we our food into our nature change.

From their gross matter she abstracts *their* forms,
And draws a kind of quintessence from things;
Which to her proper nature she transforms
To bear them light on her celestial wings.

Thus does she, when from *individual states*
She doth abstract the universal kinds;
Which then re-clothed in divers names and fates
Steal access through our senses to our minds.'

Finally, Good Sense is the Body of poetic genius, Fancy its Drapery, Motion its Life, and Imagination the Soul that is everywhere, and in each; and forms all into one graceful and intelligent whole.

1817

William Hazlitt (1778–1830)

ON FAMILIAR STYLE

It is not easy to write a familiar style. Many people mistake a familiar for a vulgar style, and suppose that to write without affectation is to write at random. On the contrary, there is nothing that requires more precision, and, if I may so say, purity of expression, than the style I am speaking of. It utterly rejects not only all unmeaning pomp, but all low, cant phrases, and loose, unconnected, *slipshod* allusions. It is not to take the first word that offers, but the best word in common use; it is not to throw words together in any combinations we please, but to follow and avail ourselves of the true idiom of the language. To write a genuine familiar or truly English style, is to write as any one would speak in common conversation who had a thorough command and choice of words, or who could discourse with ease, force, and perspicuity, setting aside all pedantic and oratorical flourishes. Or to give another illustration, to write naturally is the same thing in regard to common conversation as to read naturally is in regard to common speech. It does not follow that it is an easy thing to give the true accent and inflection to the words you utter, because you do not attempt to rise above the level of ordinary life and colloquial speaking. You do not assume, indeed, the solemnity of the pulpit, or the tone of stage-declamation: neither are you at liberty to gabble on at a venture, without emphasis or discretion, or to resort to vulgar dialect or clownish pronunciation. You must steer a middle course. You are tied down to a given and appropriate articulation, which is determined by the habitual associations between sense and sound, and which you can only hit by entering into the author's meaning, as you must find the proper words and style to express yourself by fixing your thoughts on the subject you have to write about. Any one may mouth out a passage with a theatrical cadence, or get upon stilts to tell his thoughts; but to write or speak with propriety and simplicity is a more difficult task. Thus it is easy to affect a pompous style, to use a word twice as big as the thing you want to express: it is not so easy to pitch upon the very word that exactly fits it. Out of eight or ten words equally common, equally intelligible, with nearly equal pretensions, it is a matter of some nicety and discrimination to pick out the very one the preferableness of which is scarcely perceptible, but decisive. The reason why I object to Dr. Johnson's style is, that there is no discrimination, no selection, no variety in it. He uses none but 'tall, opaque words,' taken from the 'first row of the rubric'; — words with the greatest number of syllables, or Latin phrases with merely English terminations. If a fine style depended on this sort of arbitrary pretension, it would be fair to judge of an author's elegance by the measurement of his words, and the substitution of foreign circumlocutions (with no precise associations) for the mother-tongue. How simple it is to be dignified without ease, to be pompous without meaning! Surely, it is but a mechanical rule for avoiding what is low, to be always pedantic and affected. It is clear you cannot use a vulgar English word, if you never use a common English word at all. A fine tact is shown in adhering to those which are perfectly common, and yet never falling into any expressions which are debased by disgusting circumstances, or which owe their signification and point to technical or professional allusions. A truly natural or familiar style can never be quaint or vulgar, for this reason, that it is of universal force and applicability, and that quaintness and vulgarity arise out of the immediate connection of certain words with coarse and disagreeable or with confined ideas. The last form what we understand by *cant* or *slang* phrases. — To give an example of what is not very clear in the general statement. I should say that the phrase *To cut with a knife*, or *To cut a piece of wood*, is perfectly free from vulgarity, because it is perfectly common: but *To cut an acquaintance* is not quite unexceptionable, because it is not perfectly common or intelligible, and has hardly yet escaped out of the limits of slang phraseology. I should hardly therefore use the word in this sense without putting it in italics as a license of expression, to be received *cum grano salis*. All provincial or bye-phrases come under the same mark of reprobation — all such as the writer transfers to the page from his fireside or a particular *coterie*, or that he invents for his own sole use and convenience. I conceive that words are like money, not the worse for being common, but that it is the stamp of custom alone that gives them circulation or value. I am fastidious in this respect, and would almost as soon coin the currency of the realm as counterfeit the King's English. I never invented or gave a new and unauthorised meaning to any word but one single one (the term *impersonal* applied to feelings), and that was in an abstruse metaphysical discussion to express a very difficult distinction. I have been (I know) loudly accused of revelling in vulgarisms and broken English. I cannot speak to that point: but so far I plead guilty to the determined use of acknowledged idioms and common elliptical expressions. I am not sure that the critics in question know the one from the other, that is, can distinguish any medium between formal pedantry and the most barbarous solecism. As an author, I endeavor to employ plain words and popular modes of construction, as, were I a chapman and dealer, I should common weights and measures.

The proper force of words lies not in the words themselves, but in their application. A word may be a fine-sounding word, of an unusual length, and very imposing from its learning and novelty, and yet in the connection in which it is introduced may be quite pointless and irrelevant. It is not pomp or pretension, but the adaptation of the expression to the idea that clenches a writer's meaning: — as it is not the size or glossiness of the materials, but their being fitted each to its place, that gives strength to the arch;

or as the pegs and nails are as necessary to the support of the building as the larger timbers, and more so than the mere showy, unsubstantial ornaments. I hate anything that occupies more space than it is worth. I hate to see a load of band-boxes go along the street, and I hate to see a parcel of big words without anything in them. A person who does not deliberately dispose of all his thoughts alike in cumbrous draperies and flimsy disguises, may strike out twenty varieties of familiar everyday language, each coming somewhat nearer to the feeling he wants to convey, and at last not hit upon that particular and only one, which may be said to be identical with the exact impression in his mind. This would seem to show that Mr. Cobbett is hardly right in saying that the first word that occurs is always the best. It may be a very good one; and yet a better may present itself on reflection or from time to time. It should be suggested naturally, however, and spontaneously, from a fresh and lively conception of the subject. We seldom succeed by trying at improvement, or by merely substituting one word for another that we are not satisfied with, as we cannot recollect the name of a place or person by merely plaguing ourselves about it. We wander farther from the point by persisting in a wrong scent; but it starts up accidentally in the memory when we least expect it, by touching some link in the chain of previous association.

There are those who hoard up and make a cautious display of nothing but rich and rare phraseology; ancient medals, obscure coins, and Spanish pieces of eight. They are very curious to inspect; but I myself would neither offer nor take them in the course of exchange. A sprinkling of archaisms is not amiss; but a tissue of obsolete expressions is more fit *for keep than wear*. I do not say I would not use any phrase that had been brought into fashion before the middle or the end of the last century; but I should be shy of using any that had not been employed by any approved author during the whole of that time. Words, like clothes, get old-fashioned, or mean and ridiculous, when they have been for some time laid aside. Mr. Lamb is the only imitator of old English style I can read with pleasure; and he is so thoroughly imbued with the spirit of his authors that the idea of imitation is almost done away. There is an inward unction, a marrowy vein both in the thought and feeling, an intuition, deep and lively, of his subject, that carries off any quaintness or awkwardness arising from an antiquated style and dress. The matter is completely his own, though the manner is assumed. Perhaps his ideas are altogether so marked and individual, as to require their point and pungency to be neutralised by the affectation of a singular but traditional form of conveyance. Tricked out in the prevailing costume, they would probably seem more startling and out of the way. The old English authors, Burton, Fuller, Coryate, Sir Thomas Browne, are a kind of mediators between us and the more eccentric and whimsical modern, reconciling us to his peculiarities. I do not, however, know how far this is the case or not, till he condescends to write like one of us. I must confess that what I like best of his papers under the signature of Elia (still I do not presume, amidst such excellence, to decide what is most excellent) is the account of 'Mrs. Battle's Opinions on Whist,' which is also the most free from obsolete allusions and turns of expression —

'A well of native English undefiled.'

To those acquainted with his admired prototypes, these Essays of the ingenious and highly gifted author have the same sort of charm and relish that Erasmus's Colloquies or a fine piece of modern Latin have to the classical scholar. Certainly, I do not know any borrowed pencil that has more power of felicity of execution than the one of which I have here been speaking.

It is as easy to write a gaudy style without ideas, as it is to spread a pallet of showy colors, or to smear in a flaunting transparency. 'What do you read?' — 'Words, words, words.' — 'What is the matter?' — '*Nothing*,' it might be answered. The florid style is the reverse of the familiar. The last is employed as an unvarnished medium to convey ideas; the first is resorted to as a spangled veil to conceal the want of them. When there is nothing to be set down but words, it costs little to have them fine.

Look through the dictionary, and cull out a *florilegium*, rival the *tulipomania*. *Rouge* high enough, and never mind the natural complexion. The vulgar, who are not in the secret, will admire the look of preternatural health and vigor; and the fashionable, who regard only appearances, will be delighted with the imposition. Keep to your sounding generalities, your tinkling phrases, and all will be well. Swell out an unmeaning truism to a perfect tympany of style. A thought, a distinction, is the rock on which all this brittle cargo of verbiage splits at once. Such writers have merely *verbal* imaginations, that retain nothing but words. Or their puny thoughts have dragon-wings, all green and gold. They soar far above the vulgar failing of the *Sermo humi abrepens* — their most ordinary speech is never short of an hyperbole, splendid, imposing, vague, incomprehensible, magniloquent, a cento of sounding commonplaces. If some of us, whose 'ambition is more lowly,' pry a little too narrowly into nooks and corners to pick up a number of 'unconsidered trifles,' they never once direct their eyes or lift their hands to seize on any but the most gorgeous, tarnished, threadbare, patchwork set of phrases, the left-off finery of poetic extravagance, transmitted down through successive generations of barren pretenders. If they criticise actors and actresses, a huddled phantasmagoria of feathers, spangles, floods of light, and oceans of sound float before their morbid sense, which they paint in the style of Ancient Pistol. Not a glimpse can you get of the merits or defects of the performers: they are hidden in a profusion of barbarous epithets and wilful rhodomontade. Our hypercritics are not thinking of these little fantoccini beings —

'That strut and fret their hour upon the
stage' —

but of tall phantoms of words, abstractions, *genera* and *species*, sweeping clauses, periods that unite the Poles, forced alliterations, astounding antitheses —

'And on their pens *Fustian* sits plumed.'

If they describe kings and queens, it is an Eastern pageant. The Coronation at either House is nothing to it. We get at four repeated images — a curtain, a throne, a sceptre, and a foot-stool. These are with them the wardrobe of a lofty imagination; and they turn their servile strains to servile uses. Do we read a description of pictures? It is not a reflection of tones and hues which 'nature's own sweet and cunning hand laid on,' but piles of precious stones, rubies, pearls, emeralds, Golconda's mines, and all the blazonry of art. Such persons are in fact besotted with words, and their brains are turned with the glittering, but empty and sterile phantoms of things. Personifications, capital letters, seas of sunbeams, visions of glory, shining inscriptions, the figures of a transparency, Britannia with her shield, or Hope leaning on an anchor, make up their stock in trade. They may be considered as *hieroglyphical* writers. Images stand out in their minds isolated and important merely in themselves, without any groundwork of feeling — there is no context in their imaginations. Words affect them in the same way, by the mere sound, that is, by their possible, not by their actual application to the subject in hand. They are fascinated by first appearances, and have no sense of consequences. Nothing more is meant by them than meets the ear: they understand or feel nothing more than meets their eye. The web and texture of the universe, and of the heart of man, is a mystery to them: they have no faculty that strikes a chord in unison with it. They cannot get beyond the daubings of fancy, the varnish of sentiment. Objects are not linked to feelings, words to things, but images revolve in splendid mockery, words represent themselves in their strange rhapsodies. The categories of such a mind are pride and ignorance. Pride in outside show, to which they sacrifice everything, and ignorance of the true worth and hidden structure both of words and things. With a sovereign contempt for what is familiar and natural, they are the slaves of vulgar affectation — of a routine of high-flown phrases. Scorning to imitate realities, they are unable to invent anything, to strike out one original idea. They are not copyists of nature, it is true; but they are the poorest of all plagiarists, the plagiarists of words. All is far-fetched, dear-bought, artificial, oriental in subject and allusion; all is mechanical, conventional, vapid, formal, pedantic in style and execution. They startle and confound the understanding of the reader, by the remoteness and obscurity of their illustrations; they soothe the ear by the monotony of the same everlasting round of circuitous metaphors. They are the *mock-school* in poetry and prose. They flounder about between fustian in expression and bathos in sentiment. They tantalise the fancy, but never reach the head nor touch the heart. Their Temple of Fame is like a shadowy structure raised by Dulness to Vanity, or like Cowper's description of the Empress of Russia's palace of ice, 'as worthless as in show 't was glittering' —

'It smiled, and it was cold!'

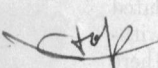

1821

MR. WORDSWORTH

Mr. Wordsworth's genius is a pure emanation of the Spirit of the Age. Had he lived in any other period of the world, he would never have been heard of. As it is, he has some difficulty to contend with the *hebetude* of his intellect, and the meanness of his subject. With him 'lowliness is young ambition's ladder': but he finds it a toil to climb in this way the steep of Fame. His homely Muse can hardly raise her wing from the ground, nor spread her hidden glories to the sun. He has 'no figures nor no fantasies, which busy passion draws in the brains of men': neither the gorgeous machinery of mythologic lore, nor the splendid colours of poetic diction. His style is vernacular: he delivers household truths. He sees nothing loftier than human hopes; nothing deeper than the human heart. This he probes, this he tampers with, this he poises, with all its incalculable weight of thought and feeling, in his hands; and at the same time calms the throbbing pulses of his own heart, by keeping his eye ever fixed on the face of nature. If he can make the life-blood flow from the wounded breast, this is the living colouring with which he paints his verse: if he can assuage the pain or close up the wound with the balm of solitary musing, or the healing power of plants and herbs and 'skyey influences,' this is the sole triumph of his art. He takes the simplest elements of nature and of the human mind, the mere abstract conditions inseparable from our being, and tries to compound a new system of poetry from them; and has perhaps succeeded as well as any one could. '*Nihil humani a me alienum puto*' — is the motto of his works. He thinks nothing low or indifferent of which this can be affirmed: every thing that professes to be more than this, that is not an absolute essence of truth and feeling, he holds to be vitiated, false, and spurious. In a word, his poetry is founded on setting up an opposition (and pushing it to the utmost length) between the natural and the artificial; between the spirit of humanity, and the spirit of fashion and of the world!

It is one of the innovations of the time. It partakes of, and is carried along with, the revolutionary movement of our age: the political changes of the day were the model on which he formed and conducted his poetical experiments. His Muse (it cannot be denied, and without this we cannot explain its character at all) is a levelling one. It proceeds on a principle of equality, and strives to reduce all things to the same standard. It is distinguished by a proud humility. It relies upon its own resources, and disdains external show and relief. It takes the commonest events and objects, as a test to prove that nature is always interesting from its inherent truth and beauty, without any of the ornaments of dress or pomp of circumstances to set it off. Hence the unaccountable mixture of seeming simplicity and real abstruseness in the *Lyrical Ballads*. Fools have laughed at, wise men scarcely understand them. He takes a subject or a story merely as pegs or loops to hang thought and feeling on; the incidents are trifling, in proportion to his contempt for imposing appearances; the reflections are profound, according to the gravity and the aspiring pretensions of his mind.

His popular, inartificial style gets rid (at a blow) of all the trappings of verse, of all the high places of poetry: 'the cloud-capt towers, the solemn temples, the gorgeous palaces,' are swept to the ground, and 'like the baseless fabric of a vision, leave not a wreck behind.' All the traditions of learning, all the superstitions of age, are obliterated and effaced. We begin *de novo*, on a *tabula rasa* of poetry. The purple pall, the nodding plume of tragedy are exploded as mere pantomime and trick, to return to the simplicity of truth and nature. Kings, queens, priests, nobles, the altar and the throne, the distinctions of rank, birth, wealth, power, 'the judge's robe, the marshal's truncheon, the ceremony that to great ones 'longs,' are not to be found here. The author tramples on the pride of art with greater pride. The Ode and Epode, the Strophe and the Antistrophe, he laughs to scorn. The harp of Homer, the trump of Pindar and of Alcæus are still. The decencies of costume, the decorations of vanity are stripped off without mercy as barbarous, idle, and Gothic. The jewels in the crisped hair, the diadem on the polished brow are thought meretricious, theatrical, vulgar; and nothing contents his fastidious taste beyond a simple garland of flowers. Neither does he avail himself of the advantages which nature or accident holds out to him. He chooses to have his subject a foil to his invention, to owe nothing but to himself. He gathers manna in the wilderness, he strikes the barren rock for the gushing moisture. He elevates the mean by the strength of his own aspirations; he clothes the naked with beauty and grandeur from the stores of his own recollections. No cypress grove loads his verse with funeral pomp; but his imagination lends a sense of joy

> 'To the bare trees and mountains bare,
> And grass in the green field.'

No storm, no shipwreck startles us by its horrors: but the rainbow lifts its head in the cloud, and the breeze sighs through the withered fern. No sad vicissitude of fate, no overwhelming catastrophe in nature deforms his page: but the dew-drop glitters on the bending flower, the tear collects in the glistening eye.

> 'Beneath the hills, along the flowery vales,
> The generations are prepared; the pangs,
> The internal pangs are ready; the dread strife
> Of poor humanity's afflicted will,
> Struggling in vain with ruthless destiny.'

As the lark ascends from its low bed on fluttering wing, and salutes the morning skies, Mr. Wordsworth's unpretending Muse, in russet guise, scales the summits of reflection, while it makes the round earth its footstool, and its home!

Possibly a good deal of this may be regarded as the effect of disappointed views and an inverted ambition. Prevented by native pride and indolence from climbing the ascent of learning or greatness, taught by political opinions to say to the vain pomp and glory of the world, 'I hate ye,' seeing the path of classical and artificial poetry blocked up by the cumbrous ornaments of style and turgid *common-places*, so that nothing more could be achieved in that direction but by the most ridiculous bombast or the tamest servility; he has turned back partly from the bias of his mind, partly perhaps from a judicious policy—has struck into the sequestered vale of humble life, sought out the Muse among sheep-cotes and hamlets and the peasant's mountain-haunts, has discarded all the tinsel pageantry of verse, and endeavoured (not in vain) to aggrandise the trivial and add the charm of novelty to the familiar. No one has shown the same imagination in raising trifles into importance: no one has displayed the same pathos in treating of the simplest feelings of the heart. Reserved, yet haughty, having no unruly or violent passions, (or those passions having been early suppressed,) Mr. Wordsworth has passed his life in solitary musing, or in daily converse with the face of nature. He exemplifies in an eminent degree the power of *association;* for his poetry has no other source or character. He has dwelt among pastoral scenes, till each object has become connected with a thousand feelings, a link in the chain of thought, a fibre of his own heart. Every one is by habit and familiarity strongly attached to the place of his birth, or to objects that recall the most pleasing and eventful circumstances of his life. But to the author of the *Lyrical*

Ballads, nature is a kind of home; and he may be said to take a personal interest in the universe. There is no image so insignificant that it has not in some mood or other found the way into his heart: no sound that does not awaken the memory of other years. —

'To him the meanest flower that blows can give
Thoughts that do often lie too deep for tears.'

The daisy looks up to him with sparkling eyes as an old acquaintance: the cuckoo haunts him with sounds of early youth not to be expressed: a linnet's nest startles him with boyish delight: an old withered thorn is weighed down with a heap of recollections: a gray cloak, seen on some wild moor, torn by the wind, or drenched in the rain, afterwards becomes an object of imagination to him: even the lichens on the rock have a life and being in his thoughts. He has described all these objects in a way and with an intensity of feeling that no one else had done before him, and has given a new view or aspect of nature. He is in this sense the most original poet now living, and the one whose writings could the least be spared: for they have no substitute elsewhere. The vulgar do not read them, the learned, who see all things through books, do not understand them, the great despise, the fashionable may ridicule them; but the author has created himself an interest in the heart of the retired and lonely student of nature, which can never die. Persons of this class will still continue to feel what he has felt: he has expressed what they might in vain wish to express except with glistening eye and faltering tongue! There is a lofty philosophic tone, a thoughtful humanity, infused into his pastoral vein. Remote from the passions and events of the great world, he has communicated interest and dignity to the primal movements of the heart of man, and ingrafted his own conscious reflections on the casual thoughts of hinds and shepherds. Nursed amidst the grandeur of mountain scenery, he has stooped to have a nearer view of the daisy under his feet, or plucked a branch of white-thorn from the spray: but in describing it, his mind seems imbued with the majesty and solemnity of the objects around him — the tall rock lifts its head in the erectness of his spirit; the cataract roars in the sound of his verse; and in its din and mysterious meaning, the mists seem to gather in the hollows of Helvellyn, and the forked Skiddaw hovers in the distance. There is little mention of mountainous scenery in Mr. Wordsworth's poetry; but by internal evidence one might be almost sure that it was written in a mountainous country, from its bareness, its simplicity, its loftiness and its depth!

His later philosophic productions have a somewhat different character. They are a departure from, a dereliction of his first principles. They are classical and courtly. They are polished in style, without being gaudy; dignified in subject without affectation. They seem to have been composed not in a cottage at Grasmere, but among the half-inspired groves and stately recollections of Cole-Orton. We might allude in particular, for examples of what we mean, to the lines on a Picture by Claude Lorraine, and to the exquisite poem, entitled *Laodamia*. The last of these breathes the pure spirit of the finest fragments of antiquity — the sweetness, the gravity, the strength, the beauty and the languor of death —

'Calm contemplation and majestic pains.'

Its glossy brilliancy arises from the perfection of the finishing, like that of careful sculpture, not from gaudy colouring — the texture of the thoughts has the smoothness and solidity of marble. It is a poem that might be read aloud in Elysium, and the spirits of departed heroes and sages would gather round to listen to it! Mr. Wordsworth's philosophic poetry, with a less glowing aspect and less tumult in the veins than Lord Byron's on similar occasions, bends a calmer and keener eye on mortality; the impression, if less vivid, is more pleasing and permanent; and we confess it (perhaps it is a want of taste and proper feeling) that there are lines and poems of our author's that we think of ten times for once that we recur to any of Lord Byron's. Or if there are any of the latter's writings, that we can dwell upon in the same way, that is, as lasting and heart-felt sentiments, it is when laying aside his usual pomp and pretension, he descends with Mr. Wordsworth to the common ground of a disinterested humanity. It may be considered as characteristic of our poet's writings, that they either make no impression on the mind at all, seem mere *nonsense-verses*, or that they leave a mark behind them that never wears out. They either

'Fall blunted from the indurated breast' —

without any perceptible result, or they absorb it like a passion. To one class of readers he appears sublime, to another (and we fear the largest) ridiculous. He has probably realised Milton's wish, — 'and fit audience found, though few': but we suspect he is not reconciled to the alternative. There are delightful passages in the *Excursion*, both of natural description and of inspired reflection (passages of the latter kind that in the sound of the thoughts and of the swelling language resemble heavenly symphonies, mournful requiems over the grave of human hopes;) but we must add, in justice and in sincerity, that we think it impossible that this work should ever become popular, even in the same degree as the *Lyrical Ballads*. It affects a system without having any intelligible clue to one; and instead of unfolding a principle in various and striking lights, repeats the same conclusions till they become flat and insipid. Mr. Wordsworth's mind is obtuse, except as it is the organ and the receptacle of accumulated feelings: it is not analytic, but synthetic; it is reflecting, rather than theoretical. The *Excursion*, we believe, fell stillborn from the press. There was something abortive, and clumsy, and ill-judged in the attempt. It was long and laboured. The personages, for the most part, were low, the fare rustic: the plan raised expectations which were not fulfilled, and the effect was like being ushered into a stately hall and invited to sit down to a splendid banquet in the company of clowns, and with nothing but successive courses of apple-dumplings served up. It was not even *toujours perdrix!*

Mr. Wordsworth, in his person, is above the middle size, with marked features, and an air somewhat stately and Quixotic. He reminds one of some of Holbein's heads, grave, saturnine, with a slight indication of sly humour, kept under by the manners of the age or by the pretensions of the person. He has a peculiar sweetness in his smile, and great depth and manliness and a rugged harmony, in the tones of his voice. His manner of reading his own poetry is particularly imposing; and in his favourite passages his eye beams with preternatural lustre, and the meaning labours slowly up from his swelling breast. No one who has seen him at these moments could go away with an impression that he was a 'man of no mark or likelihood.' Perhaps the comment of his face and voice is necessary to convey a full idea of his poetry. His language may not be intelligible, but his manner is not to be mistaken. It is clear that he is either mad or inspired. In company, even in a *tête-à-tête*, Mr. Wordsworth is often silent, indolent, and reserved. If he is become verbose and oracular of late years, he was not so in his better days. He threw out a bold or an indifferent remark without either effort or pretension, and relapsed into musing again. He shone most (because he seemed most roused and animated) in reciting his own poetry, or in talking about it. He sometimes gave striking views of his feelings and trains of association in composing certain passages; or if one did not always understand his distinctions, still there was no want of interest — there was a latent meaning worth inquiring into, like a vein of ore that one cannot exactly hit upon at the moment, but of which there are sure indications. His standard of poetry is high and severe, almost to exclusiveness. He admits of nothing below, scarcely of any thing above himself. It is fine to hear him talk of the way in which certain subjects should have been treated by eminent poets, according to his notions of the art. Thus he finds fault with Dryden's description of Bacchus in the *Alexander's Feast*, as if he were a mere good-looking youth, or boon companion —

'Flushed with a purple grace,
He shows his honest face' —

instead of representing the God returning from the conquest of India, crowned with vine-leaves, and drawn by panthers, and followed by troops of satyrs, of wild men and animals that he had tamed. You would think, in hearing him speak on this subject, that you saw Titian's picture of the meeting of *Bacchus and Ariadne* — so classic were his conceptions, so glowing his style. Milton is his great idol, and he sometimes dares to compare himself with him. His Sonnets, indeed, have something of the same high-raised tone and prophetic spirit. Chaucer is another prime favourite of his, and he has been at the pains to modernize some of the Canterbury Tales. Those persons who look upon Mr. Wordworth as a merely puerile writer, must be rather at a loss to account for his strong predilection for such geniuses as Dante and Michael Angelo. We do not think our author has any very cordial sympathy with Shakspeare. How should he? Shakspeare was the least of an egotist of any body in the world. He does not much relish the variety and scope of dramatic composition. 'He hates those interlocutions between Lucius and Caius.' Yet Mr. Wordsworth himself wrote a tragedy when he was young; and we have heard the following energetic lines quoted from it, as put into the mouth of a person smit with remorse for some rash crime:

——'Action is momentary,
The motion of a muscle this way or that;
Suffering is long, obscure, and infinite!'

Perhaps for want of light and shade, and the unshackled spirit of the drama, this performance was never brought forward. Our critic has a great dislike to Gray, and a fondness for Thomson and Collins. It is mortifying to hear him speak of Pope and Dryden, who, because they have been supposed to have all the possible excellences of poetry, he will allow to have none. Nothing, however, can be fairer, or more amusing, than the way in which he sometimes exposes the unmeaning verbiage of modern poetry. Thus, in the beginning of Dr. Johnson's *Vanity of Human Wishes* —

'Let observation with extensive view,
Survey mankind from China to Peru' —

he says there is a total want of imagination accompanying the words, the same idea is repeated three times under the disguise of a different phraseology: it comes to this — 'let *observation*, with extensive *observation*, *observe* mankind'; or take away the first line, and the second,

'Survey mankind from China to Peru,'

literally conveys the whole. Mr. Wordsworth is, we must say, a perfect Drawcansir as to prose writers. He complains of the dry reasoners and matter-of-fact people for their want of *passion;* and he is jealous of the rhetorical declaimers and rhapsodists as trenching on the province of poetry. He condemns all French writers (as well of poetry as prose) in the lump. His list in this way is indeed small. He approves of Walton's Angler, Paley, and some other writers of an inoffensive modesty of pretension. He also likes books of voyages and travels, and Robinson Crusoe. In art, he greatly esteems Bewick's woodcuts, and Waterloo's sylvan etchings. But he sometimes takes a higher tone, and gives his mind fair play. We have known him enlarge with a noble intelligence and enthusiasm on Nicolas Poussin's fine landscape-compositions, pointing out the unity of design that pervades them, the superintending mind, the imaginative principle that brings all to bear on the same end; and declaring he would not give a rush for any landscape that did not express the time of day, the climate, the period of the world it was meant to illustrate, or had not this character of *wholeness* in it. His eye also does justice to Rembrandt's fine and masterly effects. In the way in which that artist works something out of nothing, and transforms the stump of a tree, a common figure into an ideal object, by the gorgeous light and shade thrown upon it, he perceives an analogy to his own mode of investing the minute details of nature with an atmosphere of sentiment: and in pronouncing Rembrandt to be a man of genius, feels that he strengthens his own claim to the title. It has been said of Mr. Wordsworth, that 'he hates conchology, that he hates the Venus of Medicis.' But these, we hope, are mere epigrams and *jeux-d'esprit*, as far from truth as they are free from malice; a sort of running satire or critical clenches —

'Where one for sense and one for rhyme,
Is quite sufficient at one time.'

We think, however, that if Mr. Wordsworth had been a more liberal and candid critic, he would have been a more sterling writer. If a greater number of sources of pleasure had been open to him, he would have communicated pleasure to the world more frequently. Had he been less fastidious in pronouncing sentence on the works of others, his own would have been received more favourably, and treated more leniently. The current of his feelings is deep, but narrow; the range of his understanding is lofty and aspiring rather than discursive. The force, the originality, the absolute truth and identity with which he feels some things, makes him indifferent to so many others. The simplicity and enthusiasm of his feelings, with respect to nature, renders him bigoted and intolerant in his judgments of men and things. But it happens to him, as to others, that his strength lies in his weakness; and perhaps we have no right to complain. We might get rid of the cynic and the egotist, and find in his stead a commonplace man. We should 'take the good the Gods provide us': a fine and original vein of poetry is not one of their most contemptible gifts, and the rest is scarcely worth thinking of, except as it may be a mortification to those who expect perfection from human nature; or who have been idle enough at some period of their lives, to deify men of genius as possessing claims above it. But this is a chord that jars, and we shall not dwell upon it.

Lord Byron we have called, according to the old proverb, 'the spoiled child of fortune': Mr. Wordsworth might plead, in mitigation of some peculiarities, that he is 'the spoiled child of disappointment.' We are convinced, if he had been early a popular poet, he would have borne his honours meekly, and would have been a person of great *bonhommie* and frankness of disposition. But the sense of injustice and of undeserved ridicule sours the temper and narrows the views. To have produced works of genius, and to find them neglected or treated with scorn, is one of the heaviest trials of human patience. We exaggerate our own merits when they are denied by others, and are apt to grudge and cavil at every particle of praise bestowed on those to whom we feel a conscious superiority. In mere self-defence we turn against the world, when it turns against us; brood over the undeserved slights we receive; and thus the genial current of the soul is stopped, or vents itself in effusions of petulance and self-conceit. Mr. Wordsworth has thought too much of contemporary critics and criticism; and less than he ought of the award of posterity, and of the opinion, we do not say of private friends, but of those who were made so by their admiration of his genius. He did not court popularity by a conformity to established models, and he ought not to have been surprised that his originality was not understood as a matter of course. He has *gnawed too much on the bridle;* and has often thrown out crusts to the critics, in mere defiance or as a point of honour when he was challenged, which otherwise his own good sense would have withheld. We suspect that Mr. Wordsworth's feelings are a little morbid in this respect, or that he resents censure more than he is gratified by praise. Otherwise, the tide has turned much in his favour of late years — he has a large body of determined partisans — and is at present sufficiently in request with the public to save or relieve him from the last necessity to which a man of genius can be reduced — that of becoming the God of his own idolatry!

1825

ESSAYS

Charles Lamb (1775–1834)

DREAM-CHILDREN: A REVERIE

Children love to listen to stories about their elders, when *they* were children; to stretch their imagination to the conception of a traditionary great-uncle or grandame whom they never saw. It was in this spirit that my little ones crept about me the other evening to hear about their great-grandmother Field, who lived in a great house in Norfolk, (a hundred times bigger than that in which they and papa lived,) which had been the scene (so at least it was generally believed in that part of the country) of the tragic incidents which they had lately become familiar with from the ballad of the Children in the Wood. Certain it is that the whole story of the children and their cruel uncle was to be seen fairly carved out in wood upon the chimney-piece of the great hall, the whole story down to the Robin Redbreasts; till a foolish rich person pulled it down to set up a marble one of modern invention in its stead, with no story upon it. Here Alice put out one of her dear mother's looks, too tender to be called upbraiding. Then I went on to say how religious and how good their great-grandmother Field was, how beloved and respected by everybody, though she was not indeed the mistress of this great house, but had only the charge of it (and yet in some respects she might be said to be the mistress of it too) committed to her by the owner, who preferred living in a newer and more fashionable mansion which he had purchased somewhere in the adjoining county; but still she lived in it in a manner as if it had been her own, and kept up the dignity of the great house in a sort while she lived, which afterwards came to decay, and was nearly pulled down, and all its old ornaments stripped and carried away to the owner's other house, where they were set up, and looked as awkward as if some one were to carry away the old tombs they had seen lately at the Abbey, and stick them up in Lady C.'s tawdry gilt drawing-room. Here John smiled, as much as to say, 'that would be foolish indeed.' And then I told how, when she came to die, her funeral was attended by a concourse of all the poor, and some of the gentry too, of the neighborhood for many miles round, to show their respect for her memory, because she had been such a good and religious woman; so good indeed that she knew all the Psaltery by heart, ay, and a great part of the Testament besides. Here little Alice spread her hands. Then I told what a tall, upright, graceful person their great-grandmother Field once was; and how in her youth she was esteemed the best dancer, (here Alice's little right foot played an involuntary movement, till, upon my looking grave, it desisted,) the best dancer, I was saying, in the county, till a cruel disease, called a cancer, came, and bowed her down with pain; but it could never bend her good spirits, or make them stoop, but they were still upright, because she was so good and religious. Then I told how she was used to sleep by herself in a lone chamber of the great lone house; and how she believed that an apparition of two infants was to be seen at midnight gliding up and down the great staircase near where she slept, but she said 'those innocents would do her no harm'; and how frightened I used to be, though in those days I had my maid to sleep with me, because I was never half so good or religious as she; and yet I never saw the infants. Here John expanded all his eyebrows and tried to look courageous. Then I told how good she was to all her grandchildren, having us to the great house in the holidays, where I in particular used to spend many hours by myself, in gazing upon the old busts of the twelve Cæsars, that had been Emperors of Rome, till the old marble heads would seem to live again, or I to be turned into marble with them; how I never could be tired with roaming about that huge mansion, with its vast empty rooms, with their worn-out hangings, fluttering tapestry, and carved oaken panels, with the gilding almost rubbed out; sometimes in the spacious old-fashioned gardens, which I had almost to myself, unless when now and then a solitary gardening man would cross me; and how the nectarines and peaches hung upon the walls, without my ever offering to pluck them, because they were forbidden fruit, unless now and then; and because I had more pleasure in strolling about among the old melancholy-looking yew-trees, or the firs, and picking up the red berries, and the fir-apples, which were good for nothing but to look at — or in lying about upon the fresh grass with all the fine garden smells around me — or basking in the orangery, till I could almost fancy myself ripening too along with the oranges and the limes in that grateful warmth — or in watching the dace that darted to and fro in the fishpond at the bottom of the garden, with here and there a great sulky pike hanging midway down the water in silent state, as if it mocked at their impertinent friskings, — I had more pleasure in these busy-idle diversions than in all the sweet flavours of peaches, nectarines, oranges, and such-like common baits for children. Here John slyly deposited back upon the plate a bunch of grapes, which, not unobserved by Alice, he had meditated dividing with her, and both seemed willing to relinquish them for the present as irrelevant. Then, in somewhat a more heightened tone, I told how, though their great-grandmother Field loved all her grandchildren, yet in an especial manner she might be said to love their uncle, John L——, because he was so handsome and spirited a youth, and a king to the rest of us; and, instead of moping about in solitary corners, like some of us, he would mount the most mettlesome horse he could get, when but an imp no bigger than themselves, and make it carry him half over the county in a morning, and join the hunters when there were any out; (and yet he loved the old great house and gardens too, but had too much spirit to be always pent up within their boundaries;) and how their uncle grew up to man's estate as brave as he was handsome, to the admiration of every body, but of their great-grandmother Field most especially; and how he used to carry me upon his back when I was a lame-footed boy, (for he was a good bit older than I,) many a mile when I could not walk for pain; and how in after-life he became lame-footed too, and I did not always, I fear, make allowances enough for him when he was impatient, and in pain, nor remember sufficiently how considerate he had been to me when I was lame-footed; and how when he died, though he had not been dead an hour, it seemed as if he had died a great while ago, such a distance there is betwixt life and death; and how I bore his death as I thought pretty well at first, but afterwards it haunted and haunted me; and though I did not cry or take it to heart as some do, and as I think he would have done if I had died, yet I missed him all day long, and knew not till then how much I had loved him. I missed his kindness, and I missed his crossness, and wished him to be alive again, to be quarreling with him, (for we quarreled sometimes,) rather than not have him again, and was as uneasy without him, as he, their poor uncle, must have been when the doctor took off his limb. — Here the children fell a crying, and asked if their little mourning which they had on was not for Uncle John, and they looked up, and prayed me not to go on about their uncle, but to tell them some stories about their pretty dead mother. Then I told how for seven long years, in hope sometimes, sometimes in despair, yet persisting ever, I courted the fair Alice W——n; and, as much as children could understand, I explained to them what coyness, and difficulty, and denial, meant in maidens — when suddenly, turning to Alice, the soul of the first Alice looked out at her eyes with such a reality of re-presentment, that I became in doubt which of them stood there before me, or whose that bright hair was; and while I stood gazing, both the children gradually grew fainter to my view, receding, and still receding, till nothing at last but two mournful features were seen in the uttermost distance, which, without speech, strangely impressed upon me the effects of speech: 'We are not of Alice, nor of thee, nor are we children at all. The children of Alice call Bartrum father. We are nothing; less than nothing, and dreams. We are only what might have been, and must wait upon the tedious shores of Lethe millions of ages before we have existence and a name'—— and immediately awaking, I found myself quietly seated in my bachelor arm-chair, where I had fallen asleep, with the faithful Bridget unchanged by my side; but John L. (or James Elia) was gone for ever.

1822

A DISSERTATION UPON ROAST PIG

Mankind, says a Chinese manuscript, which my friend M—— was obliging enough to read and explain to me, for the first seventy thousand ages ate their meat raw, clawing or biting it from the living animal, just as they do in Abyssinia to this day. This period is not obscurely hinted at by their great Confucius in the second chapter of his Mundane Mutations, where he designates a kind of golden age by the term Cho-fang, literally the Cooks' Holiday. The manuscript goes on to say, that the art of roasting, or rather broiling (which I take to be the elder brother) was accidentally discovered in the manner following. The swine-herd Ho-ti, having gone out into the woods one morning, as his manner was, to collect mast for his hogs, left his cottage in the care of his eldest son Bo-bo, a great lubberly boy, who being fond of playing with fire, as younkers of his age commonly are, let some sparks escape into a bundle of straw, which kindling quickly, spread the conflagration over every part of their poor mansion, till it was reduced to ashes. Together with the cottage (a sorry antediluvian makeshift of a building, you may think it,) what was of much more importance, a fine litter of new-farrowed pigs, no less than nine in number, perished. China pigs have been esteemed a luxury all over the East, from the remotest periods that we read of. Bo-bo was in the utmost consternation, as you may think, not so much for the sake of the tenement, which his father and he could easily build up again with a few dry branches, and the labour of an hour or two at any time, as for the loss of the pigs. While he was thinking what he should say to his father, and wringing his hands over the smoking remnants of one of those untimely sufferers, an odour assailed his nostrils, unlike any scent which he had before experienced. What could it proceed from? Not from the burnt cottage: he had smelt that smell before; indeed this was by no means the first accident of the kind which had occurred through the negligence of this unlucky young fire-brand. Much less did it resemble that of any known herb, weed, or flower. A premonitory moistening at the same time overflowed his nether lip. He knew not what to think. He next stooped down to feel the pig, if there were any signs of life in it. He burnt his fingers, and to cool them he applied them in his booby fashion to his mouth. Some of the crumbs of the scorched skin had come away with his fingers, and for the first time in his life, (in the world's life indeed, for before him no man had known it,) he tasted *crackling!* Again he felt and fumbled at the pig. It did not burn him so much now, still he licked his fingers from a sort of habit. The truth at length broke into his slow understanding, that it was the pig that smelt so, and the pig that tasted so delicious; and surrendering himself up to the new-born pleasure, he fell to tearing up whole handfuls of the scorched skin with the flesh next it, and was cramming it down his throat in his beastly fashion, when his sire entered amid the smoking rafters, armed with retributory cudgel, and finding how affairs stood, began to rain blows upon the young rogue's shoulders as thick as hail-stones, which Bo-bo heeded not any more than if they had been flies. The tickling pleasure which he experienced in his lower regions had rendered him quite callous to any inconveniences he might feel in those remote quarters. His father might lay on, but he could not beat him from his pig, till he had fairly made an end of it, when, becoming a little more sensible of his situation, something like the following dialogue ensued: —

'You graceless whelp, what have you got there devouring? Is it not enough that you have burnt me down three houses with your dog's tricks, and be hanged to you!

but you must be eating fire, and I know not what. What have you got there, I say?'

'O father, the pig, the pig! do come and taste how nice the burnt pig eats.'

The ears of Ho-ti tingled with horror. He cursed his son, and he cursed himself that ever he should beget a son that should eat burnt pig.

Bo-bo, whose scent was wonderfully sharpened since morning, soon raked out another pig, and fairly rending it asunder, thrust the lesser half by main force into the fists of Ho-ti, still shouting out, 'Eat, eat, eat the burnt pig, father, only taste, — O Lord,' — with such-like barbarous ejaculations, cramming all the while as if he would choke.

Ho-ti trembled in every joint while he grasped the abominable thing, wavering whether he should not put his son to death for an unnatural young monster, when the crackling scorching his fingers, as it had done his son's, and applying the same remedy to them, he in his turn tasted some of its flavour, which, make what sour mouths he would for a pretence, proved not altogether displeasing to him. In conclusion, (for the manuscript here is a little tedious,) both father and son fairly sat down to the mess, and never left off till they had despatched all that remained of the litter.

Bo-bo was strictly enjoined not to let the secret escape, for the neighbours would certainly have stoned them for a couple of abominable wretches, who could think of improving upon the good meat which God had sent them. Nevertheless, strange stories got about. It was observed that Ho-ti's cottage was burnt down now more frequently than ever. Nothing but fires from this time forward. Some would break out in broad day, others in the night-time. As often as the sow farrowed, so sure was the house of Ho-ti to be in a blaze; and Ho-ti himself, which was the more remarkable, instead of chastising his son, seemed to grow more indulgent to him than ever. At length they were watched, the terrible mystery discovered, and father and son summoned to take their trial at Pekin, then an inconsiderable assize town. Evidence was given, the obnoxious food itself produced in court, and verdict about to be pronounced, when the foreman of the jury begged that some of the burnt pig, of which the culprits stood accused, might be handed into the box. He handled it, and they all handled it; and burning their fingers, as Bo-bo and his father had done before them, and nature prompting to each of them the same remedy, against the face of all the facts, and the clearest charge which judge had ever given, — to the surprise of the whole court, townsfolk, strangers, reporters, and all present — without leaving the box, or any manner of consultation whatever, they brought in a simultaneous verdict of Not Guilty.

The judge, who was a shrewd fellow, winked at the manifest iniquity of the decision: and, when the court was dismissed, went privily and bought up all the pigs that could be had for love or money. In a few days his lordship's town house was observed to be on fire. The thing took wing, and now there was nothing to be seen but fires in every direction. Fuel and pigs grew enormously dear all over the district. The insurance offices, one and all, shut up shop. People built slighter and slighter every day, until it was feared that the very science of architecture would in no long time be lost to the world. Thus this custom of firing houses continued, till in process of time, says my manuscript, a sage arose, like our Locke, who made a discovery that the flesh of swine, or indeed of any other animal, might be cooked (*burnt*, as they called it,) without the necessity of consuming a whole house to dress it. Then first began the rude form of a gridiron. Roasting by the string or spit came in a century or two later, I forget in whose dynasty. By such slow degrees, concludes the manuscript, do the most useful, and seemingly the most obvious, arts make their way among mankind.

Without placing too implicit faith in the account above given, it must be agreed that if a worthy pretext for so dangerous an experiment as setting houses on fire (especially in these days) could be assigned in favour of any culinary object, that pretext and excuse might be found in ROAST PIG.

Of all the delicacies in the whole *mundus*

edibilis, I will maintain it to be the most delicate — *princeps obsoniorum.*

I speak not of your grown porkers — things between pig and pork, those hobbydehoys — but a young and tender suckling, under a moon old, guiltless as yet of the sty, with no original speck of the *amor immunditiæ*, the hereditary failing of the first parent, yet manifest — his voice as yet not broken, but something between a childish treble and a grumble — the mild forerunner or *præludium* of a grunt.

He must be roasted. I am not ignorant that our ancestors ate them seethed, or boiled; but what a sacrifice of the exterior tegument!

There is no flavour comparable, I will contend, to that of the crisp, tawny, well-watched, not over-roasted, *crackling*, as it is well called. The very teeth are invited to their share of the pleasure at this banquet in overcoming the coy, brittle resistance — with the adhesive oleaginous — O call it not fat! but an indefinable sweetness growing up to it — the tender blossoming of fat — fat cropped in the bud — taken in the shoot — in the first innocence — the cream and quintessence of the child-pig's yet pure food — the lean, no lean, but a kind of animal manna — or, rather, fat and lean (if it must be so) so blended and running into each other, that both together make but one ambrosian result, or common substance.

Behold him, while he is 'doing' — it seemeth rather a refreshing warmth than a scorching heat that he is so passive to. How equably he twirleth round the string! — Now he is just done. To see the extreme sensibility of that tender age! he hath wept out his pretty eyes — radiant jellies — shooting stars. —

See him in the dish, his second cradle, how meek he lieth! — Wouldst thou have had this innocent grow up to the grossness and indocility which too often accompany maturer swinehood? Ten to one he would have proved a glutton, a sloven, an obstinate, disagreeable animal, wallowing in all manner of filthy conversation. From these sins he is happily snatched away.

'Ere sin could blight or sorrow fade,
Death came with timely care.'

His memory is odoriferous. No clown curseth, while his stomach half rejecteth, the rank bacon; no coal-heaver bolteth him in reeking sausages; he hath a fair sepulchre in the grateful stomach of the judicious epicure, and for such a tomb might be content to die.

He is the best of sapors. Pineapple is great. She is indeed almost too transcendent, — a delight, if not sinful, yet so like to sinning, that really a tender-conscienced person would do well to pause, — too ravishing for mortal taste, she woundeth and excoriateth the lips that approach her. Like lovers' kisses, she biteth: she is a pleasure bordering on pain from the fierceness and insanity of her relish; but she stoppeth at the palate; she meddleth not with the appetite; and the coarsest hunger might barter her consistently for a mutton chop.

Pig (let me speak his praise) is no less provocative of the appetite than he is satisfactory to the criticalness of the censorious palate. The strong man may batten on him, and the weakling refuseth not his mild juices.

Unlike to mankind's mixed characters, a bundle of virtues and vices, inexplicably intertwisted, and not to be unraveled without hazard, he is good throughout. No part of him is better or worse than another. He helpeth, as far as his little means extend, all around. He is the least envious of banquets. He is all neighbours' fare.

I am one of those who freely and ungrudgingly impart a share of the good things of this life which fall to their lot (few as mine are in this kind) to a friend. I protest I take as great an interest in my friend's pleasures, his relishes, and proper satisfactions, as in mine own. 'Presents,' I often say, 'endear Absents.' Hares, pheasants, partridges, snipes, barndoor chickens (those 'tame villatic fowl,') capons, plovers, brawn, barrels of oysters, I dispense as freely as I receive them. I love to taste them, as it were, upon the tongue of my friend. But a stop must be put somewhere. One would not, like Lear, 'give everything.' I make my stand upon pig. Methinks it is an ingratitude to the giver of all good flavours, to extra-domiciliate, or send out of the house slightingly (under pretext of friendship, or I know not what,) a blessing so particularly adapted, predestined, I may say, to my individual palate. — It argues an insensibility.

I remember a touch of conscience in this kind at school. My good old aunt, who never parted from me at the end of a holiday without stuffing a sweetmeat, or some nice thing into my pocket, had dismissed me one evening with a smoking plum-cake, fresh from the oven. In my way to school (it was over London Bridge) a grey-headed old beggar saluted me. (I have no doubt, at this time of day, that he was a counterfeit). I had no pence to console him with, and in the vanity of self-denial, and the very coxcombry of charity, schoolboy-like, I made him a present of the whole cake. I walked on a little, buoyed up, as one is on such occasions, with a sweet soothing of self-satisfaction; but before I had got to the end of the bridge my better feelings returned, and I burst into tears, thinking how ungrateful I had been to my good aunt, to go and give her good gift away to a stranger that I had never seen before, and who might be a bad man for aught I knew; and then I thought of the pleasure my aunt would be taking in thinking that I (I myself, and not another) would eat her nice cake. And what should I say to her the next time I saw her? — how naughty I was to part with her pretty present! — and the odour of that spicy cake came back upon my recollection, and the pleasure and the curiosity I had taken in seeing her make it, and her joy when she sent it to the oven, and how disappointed she would feel that I had never had a bit of it in my mouth at last. And I blamed my impertinent spirit of alms-giving, and out-of-place hypocrisy of goodness; and above all, I wished never to see the face again of that insidious, good-for-nothing, old grey impostor.

Our ancestors were nice in their method of sacrificing these tender victims. We read of pigs whipt to death with something of a shock, as we hear of any other obsolete custom. The age of discipline is gone by, or it would be curious to inquire (in a philosophical light merely) what effect this process might have towards intenerating and dulcifying a substance naturally so mild and dulcet as the flesh of young pigs. It looks like refining a violet. Yet we should be cautious, while we condemn the inhumanity, how we censure the wisdom of the practice. It might impart a gusto.

I remember an hypothesis, argued upon by the young students when I was at St. Omer's, and maintained with much learning and pleasantry on both sides, 'Whether, supposing that the flavour of a pig who obtained his death by whipping (*per flagellationem extremam*) superadded a pleasure upon the palate of a man more intense than any possible suffering we can conceive in the animal, is man justified in using that method of putting the animal to death?' I forget the decision.

His sauce should be considered: decidedly, a few bread crumbs, done up with his liver and brains, and a dash of mild sage. But, banish, dear Mrs. Cook, I beseech you, the whole onion tribe. Barbecue your whole hogs to your palate, steep them in shalots, stuff them out with plantations of the rank and guilty garlic; you cannot poison them, or make them stronger than they are; but consider, he is a weakling, — a flower.

1822

POOR RELATIONS

A Poor Relation is the most irrelevant thing in nature, — a piece of impertinent correspondency, — an odious approximation, — a haunting conscience, — a preposterous shadow, lengthening in the noontide of our prosperity, — an unwelcome remembrancer, — a perpetually recurring mortification, — a drain on your purse, a more intolerable dun upon your pride, — a drawback upon success, — a rebuke to your rising, — a stain in your blood, — a blot on your 'scutcheon, — a rent in your garment, — a death's head at your banquet, — Agathocles's pot, — a Mordecai in your gate, a Lazarus at your door, — a lion in your path, — a frog in your chamber, — a fly in your ointment, — a mote in your eye, — a triumph to your enemy, an apology to your friends, — the one thing not needful, — the hail in harvest, — the ounce of sour in a pound of sweet.

He is known by his knock. Your heart telleth you 'That is Mr. ——.' A rap between familiarity and respect, that demands, and at the same time seems to despair of, entertainment. He entereth smiling and embarrassed. He holdeth out his hand to you to shake, and draweth it back again. He casually looketh in about dinner-time, when the table is full. He offereth to go away, seeing you have company, but is induced to stay. He filleth a chair, and your visitor's two children are accommodated at a side table. He never cometh upon open days, when your wife says, with some complacency, 'My dear, perhaps Mr. —— will drop in to-day.' He remembereth birthdays, and professeth he is fortunate to have stumbled upon one. He declareth against fish, the turbot being small, yet suffereth himself to be importuned into a slice, against his first resolution. He sticketh by the port, yet will be prevailed upon to empty the remainder glass of claret, if a stranger press it upon him. He is a puzzle to the servants, who are fearful of being too obsequious or not civil enough to him. The guests think 'they have seen him before.' Everyone speculateth upon his condition; and the most part take him to be a tide waiter. He calleth you by your Christian name, to imply that his other is the same with your own. He is too familiar by half, yet you wish he had less diffidence. With half the familiarity, he might pass for a casual dependant; with more boldness, he would be in no danger of being taken for what he is. He is too humble for a friend; yet taketh on him more state than befits a client. He is a worse guest than a country tenant, inasmuch as he bringeth up no rent; yet 't is odds, from his garb and demeanour, that your guests take him for one. He is asked to make one at the whist table; refuseth on the score of poverty, and resents being left out. When the company break up, he proffereth to go for a coach, and lets the servant go. He recollects your grandfather; and will thrust in some mean and quite unimportant anecdote of the family. He knew it when it was not quite so flourishing as 'he is blest in seeing it now.' He reviveth past situations, to institute what he calleth 'favorable comparisons.' With a reflecting sort of congratulation he will inquire the price of your furniture, and insults you with a special commendation of your window-curtains. He is of opinion that the urn is the more elegant shape; but, after all, there was something more comfortable about the old tea-kettle, which you must remember. He dares say you must find a great convenience in having a carriage of your own, and appealeth to your lady if it is not so. Inquireth if you have had your arms done on vellum yet; and did not know, till lately, that such-and-such had been the crest of the family. His memory is unseasonable; his compliments perverse; his talk a trouble; his stay pertinacious; and when he goeth away, you dismiss his chair into a corner, as precipitately as possible, and feel fairly rid of two nuisances.

There is a worse evil under the sun, and that is a female Poor Relation. You may do something with the other; you may pass him off tolerably well; but your indigent she-relative is hopeless. 'He is an old humorist,' you may say, 'and affects to go threadbare. His circumstances are better than folks would take them to be. You are fond of having a Character at your table, and truly he is one.' But in the indications of female poverty there can be no disguise. No woman dresses below herself from caprice. The truth must out without shuffling. 'She is plainly related to the L——s; or what does she at their house?' She is, in all probability, your wife's cousin. Nine times out of ten, at least, this is the case. Her garb is something between a gentlewoman's and a beggar's, yet the former evidently predominates. She is most provokingly humble, and ostentatiously sensible to her inferiority. He may require to be repressed sometimes — *aliquando sufflaminandus erat* — but there is no raising her. You send her soup at dinner, and she begs to be helped after the gentlemen. Mr. —— requests the honour of taking wine with her; she hesitates between Port and Madeira, and chooses the former, because he does. She calls the servant *Sir;* and insists on not troubling him to hold her plate. The housekeeper patronises her. The children's governess takes upon her to correct her when she has mistaken the piano for a harpsichord.

Richard Amlet, Esq., in the play, is a noticeable instance of the disadvantages to which this chimerical notion of *affinity constituting a claim to an acquaintance,* may subject the spirit of a gentleman. A little foolish blood is all that is betwixt him and a lady with a great estate. His stars are perpetually crossed by the malignant maternity of an old woman, who persists in calling him 'her son Dick.' But she has wherewithal in the end to recompense his indignities, and float him again upon the brilliant surface, under which it had been her seeming business and pleasure all along to sink him. All men, besides, are not of Dick's temperament. I knew an Amlet in real life, who wanting Dick's buoyancy, sank indeed. Poor W—— was of my own standing at Christ's, a fine classic, and a youth of promise. If he had a blemish, it was too much pride; but its quality was inoffensive; it was not of that sort which hardens the heart, and serves to keep inferiors at a distance; it only sought to ward off derogation from itself. It was the principle of self-respect carried as far as it could go, without infringing upon that respect which he would have every one else equally maintain for himself. He would have you to think alike with him on this topic. Many a quarrel have I had with him, when we were rather older boys, and our tallness made us more obnoxious to observation in the blue clothes, because I would not thread the alleys and blind ways of the town with him to elude notice, when we have been out together on a holiday in the streets of this sneering and prying metropolis. W—— went, sore with these notions, to Oxford, where the dignity and sweetness of a scholar's life, meeting with the alloy of an humble introduction, wrought in him a passionate devotion to the place, with a profound aversion from the society. The servitor's gown (worse than his school array) clung to him with Nessian venom. He thought himself ridiculous in a garb under which Latimer must have walked erect, and in which Hooker, in his young days, possibly flaunted in a vein of no discommendable vanity. In the depth of college shades, or in his lonely chamber, the poor student shrunk from observation. He found shelter among books, which insult not; and studies, that ask no questions of a youth's finances. He was lord of his library, and seldom cared for looking out beyond his domains. The healing influence of studious pursuits was upon him, to soothe and to abstract. He was almost a healthy man, when the waywardness of his fate broke out against him with a second and worse malignity. The father of W—— had hitherto exercised the humble profession of house-painter at N——, near Oxford. A supposed interest with some of the heads of colleges had now induced him to take up his abode in that city, with the hope of being employed upon some public works which were talked of. From that moment I read in the countenance of the young man the determination which at length tore him from academical pursuits for ever. To a person unacquainted with our universities, the distance between the gownsmen and the townsmen, as they are called — the trading part of the latter especially — is carried to an excess that would appear harsh and incredible. The temperament of W——'s father was diametrically the reverse of his own. Old W—— was a little, busy, cringing tradesman, who, with his son upon his arm, would stand bowing and scraping, cap in hand, to anything that wore the semblance of a gown — insensible to the winks and opener remonstrances of the young man, to whose chamber-fellow, or equal in standing, perhaps, he was thus obsequiously and gratuitously ducking. Such a state of things could not last. W—— must change the air of Oxford, or be suffocated. He chose the former; and let the sturdy moralist, who strains the point of the filial duties as high as they can bear, censure the dereliction; he cannot estimate the struggle. I stood with W——, the last afternoon I ever saw him, under the eaves of his paternal dwelling.

It was in the fine lane leading from the High Street to the back of **** college, where W—— kept his rooms. He seemed thoughtful and more reconciled. I ventured to rally him — finding him in a better mood — upon a representation of the Artist Evangelist, which the old man, whose affairs were beginning to flourish, had caused to be set up in a splendid sort of frame over his really handsome shop, either as a token of prosperity or badge of gratitude to his saint. W—— looked up at the Luke, and, like Satan, 'knew his mounted sign — and fled.' A letter on his father's table, the next morning, announced that he had accepted a commission in a regiment about to embark for Portugal. He was among the first who perished before the walls of St. Sebastian.

Upon a subject which I began with treating half seriously, I do not know how I should have fallen upon a recital so eminently painful; but this theme of poor relationship is replete with so much matter for tragic as well as comic associations, that it is difficult to keep the account distinct without blending. The earliest impressions which I received on this matter are certainly not attended with anything painful, or very humiliating, in the recalling. At my father's table (no very splendid one) was to be found, every Saturday, the mysterious figure of an aged gentleman, clothed in neat black, of a sad yet comely appearance. His deportment was of the essence of gravity; his words were few or none; and I was not to make a noise in his presence. I had little inclination to do so, for my cue was to admire in silence. A particular elbow chair was appropriated to him, which was in no case to be violated. A peculiar sort of sweet pudding, which appeared on no other occasion, distinguished the days of his coming. I used to think him a prodigiously rich man. All I could make out of him was, that he and my father had been schoolfellows, a world ago, at Lincoln, and that he came from the Mint. The Mint I knew to be a place where all the money was coined, and I thought he was the owner of all that money. Awful ideas of the Tower twined themselves about his presence. He seemed above human infirmities and passions. A sort of melancholy grandeur invested him. From some inexplicable doom I fancied him obliged to go about in an eternal suit of mourning; a captive; a stately being let out of the Tower on Saturdays. Often have I wondered at the temerity of my father, who, in spite of an habitual general respect which we all in common manifested toward him, would venture now and then to stand up against him in some argument touching their youthful days. The houses of the ancient city of Lincoln are divided (as most of my readers know) between the dwellers on the hill and in the valley. This marked distinction formed an obvious division between the boys who lived above (however brought together in a common school) and the boys whose paternal residence was on the plain; a sufficient cause of hostility in the code of these young Grotiuses. My father had been a leading Mountaineer; and would still maintain the general superiority, in skill and hardihood, of the *Above Boys* (his own faction) over the *Below Boys* (so were they called), of which party his contemporary had been a chieftain. Many and hot were the skirmishes on this topic, the only one upon which the old gentleman was ever brought out; and bad blood bred, even sometimes almost to the recommencement (so I expected) of actual hostilities. But my father, who scorned to insist upon advantages, generally contrived to turn the conversation upon some adroit by-commendation of the old Minster; in the general preference of which, before all other cathedrals in the island, the dweller on the hill, and the plain-born, could meet on a conciliating level, and lay down their less important differences. Once only I saw the old gentleman really ruffled, and I remembered with anguish the thought that came over me: 'perhaps he will never come here again.' He had been pressed to take another plate of the viand, which I have already mentioned as the indispensable concomitant of his visits. He had refused with a resistance amounting to rigour when my aunt, an old Lincolnian, but who had something of this, in common with my cousin Bridget, that she would sometimes press civility out of season, uttered the following memorable application:

'Do take another slice, Mr. Billet, for you do not get pudding every day.' The old gentleman said nothing at the time; but he took occasion in the course of the evening, when some argument had intervened between them, to utter with an emphasis which chilled the company, and which chills me now as I write it, 'Woman, you are superannuated!' John Billet did not survive long after the digesting of this affront: but he survived long enough to assure me that peace was actually restored! and, if I remember aright, another pudding was discreetly substituted in the place of that which had occasioned the offence. He died at the Mint, (anno 1781,) where he had long held, what he accounted, a comfortable independence; and with five pounds, fourteen shillings, and a penny, which were found in his escritoire after his decease, he left the world, blessing God that he had enough to bury him, and that he had never been obliged to any man for a sixpence. This was a Poor Relation.

1823

THE SUPERANNUATED MAN

Sera tamen respexit
Libertas. — VIRGIL

A Clerk I was in London gay. — O'KEEFE

If peradventure, Reader, it has been thy lot to waste the golden years of thy life, thy shining youth, in the irksome confinement of an office; to have thy prison days prolonged through middle age down to decrepitude and silver hairs, without hope of release or respite; to have lived to forget that there are such things as holidays, or to remember them but as the prerogatives of childhood; then, and then only, will you be able to appreciate my deliverance.

It is now six-and-thirty years since I took my seat at the desk in Mincing Lane. Melancholy was the transition at fourteen from the abundant playtime, and the frequently intervening vacations of school days, to the eight, nine, and sometimes ten hours a-day attendance at the counting-house. But time partially reconciles us to any thing. I gradually became content; doggedly contented, as wild animals in cages.

It is true I had my Sundays to myself; but Sundays, admirable as the institution of them is for purposes of worship, are for that very reason the very worst adapted for days of unbending and recreation. In particular, there is a gloom for me attendant upon a city Sunday, a weight in the air. I miss the cheerful cries of London, the music, and the ballad-singers, the buzz and stirring murmur of the streets. Those eternal bells depress me. The closed shops repel me. Prints, pictures, all the glittering and endless succession of knacks and gewgaws, and ostentatiously displayed wares of tradesmen, which make a week-day saunter through the less busy parts of the metropolis so delightful, are shut out. No book-stalls deliciously to idle over; no busy faces to recreate the idle man who contemplates them ever passing by; the very face of business a charm by contrast to his temporary relaxation from it. Nothing to be seen but unhappy countenances — or half-happy at best — of emancipated 'prentices and little tradesfolk, with here and there a servant maid that has got leave to go out, who, slaving all the week, with the habit has lost almost the capacity of enjoying a free hour, and livelily expressing the hollowness of a day's pleasuring. The very strollers in the fields on that day looked any thing but comfortable.

But besides Sundays, I had a day at Easter, and a day at Christmas, with a full week in the summer to go and air myself in my native fields of Hertfordshire. This last was a great indulgence; and the prospect of its recurrence, I believe, alone kept me up through the year, and made my durance tolerable. But when the week came around, did the glittering phantom of the distance keep touch with me? or rather was it not a series of seven uneasy days, spent in restless pursuit of pleasure, and a wearisome anxiety to find out how to make the most of them? Where was the quiet? where the promised rest? Before I had a taste of it, it was vanished. I was at the desk again, counting upon the fifty-one tedious weeks that must intervene before such another snatch would come. Still the prospect of its coming threw something of an illumination upon the darker side of my captivity. Without it, as I have said, I could scarcely have sustained my thraldom.

Independently of the rigours of attendance, I have ever been haunted with a sense (perhaps a mere caprice) of incapacity for business. This, during my latter years, had increased to such a degree, that it was visible in all the lines of my countenance. My health and my good spirits flagged. I had perpetually a dread of some crisis, to which I should be found unequal. Besides my daylight servitude, I served over again all night in my sleep, and would awake with terrors of imaginary false entries, errors in my accounts, and the like. I was fifty years of age, and no prospect of emancipation presented itself. I had grown to my desk, as it were; and the wood had entered into my soul.

My fellows in the office would sometimes rally me upon the trouble legible in my countenance; but I did not know that it had raised the suspicions of any of my employers, when, on the fifth of last month, a day ever to be remembered by me, L——, the junior partner in the firm, calling me on one side, directly taxed me with my bad looks, and frankly inquired the cause of them. So taxed, I honestly made confession of my infirmity, and added that I was afraid I should eventually be obliged to resign his service. He spoke some words of course to hearten me, and there the matter rested. A whole week I remained labouring under the impression that I had acted imprudently in my disclosure; that I had foolishly given a handle against myself, and had been anticipating my own dismissal. A week passed in this manner, the most anxious one, I verily believe, in my whole life, when on the evening of the twelfth of April, just as I was about quitting my desk to go home, (it might be about eight o'clock,) I received an awful summons to attend the presence of the whole assembled firm in the formidable back parlour. I thought now my time was surely come, I have done for myself, I am going to be told that they have no longer occasion for me. L——, I could see, smiled at the terror I was in, which was a little relief to me, — when to my utter astonishment B——, the eldest partner, began a formal harangue to me on the length of my services, my very meritorious conduct during the whole of the time, (the deuce, thought I, how did he find out that? I protest I never had the confidence to think as much). He went on to descant on the expediency of retiring at a certain time of life, (how my heart panted!) and asking me a few questions as to the amount of my own property, of which I have a little, ended with a proposal, to which his three partners nodded a grave assent, that I should accept from the house, which I had served so well, a pension for life to the amount of two-thirds of my accustomed salary, — a magnificent offer! I do not know what I answered between surprise and gratitude, but it was understood that I accepted their proposal, and I was told that I was free from that hour to leave their service. I stammered out a bow, and at just ten minutes after eight I went home — for ever. This noble benefit (gratitude forbids me to conceal their names) I owe to the kindness of the most munificent firm in the world, — the house of Boldero, Merryweather, Bosanquet, and Lacy.

Esto perpetua!

For the first day or two I felt stunned, overwhelmed. I could only apprehend my felicity; I was too confused to taste it sincerely. I wandered about, thinking I was happy, and knowing that I was not. I was in the condition of a prisoner in the Old Bastile, suddenly let loose after a forty years' confinement. I could scarce trust myself with myself. It was like passing out of Time into Eternity, for it is a sort of Eternity for a man to have his Time all to himself. It seemed to me that I had more time on my hands than I could ever manage. From a poor man, poor in Time, I was suddenly lifted up into a vast revenue; I could see no end of my possessions: I wanted some steward, or judicious bailiff, to manage my estates in Time for me. And here let me caution persons grown old in active business, not lightly, nor without weighing their own resources, to forego their customary employment all at once, for there may be danger in it. I feel it by myself, but I know that my resources are sufficient; and now that those first giddy raptures have subsided, I have a quiet home feeling of the blessedness of my condition. I am in no hurry. Having all holidays, I am as though I had none. If Time hung heavy upon me, I could walk it away; but I do *not* walk all day long, as I used to do in those transient holidays, thirty miles a day, to make the most of them. If Time were troublesome, I could read it away; but I do *not* read in that violent measure, with which, having no Time my own but candlelight Time, I used to weary out my head and eye-sight in bygone winters. I walk, read, or scribble, (as now,) just when the fit seizes me. I no longer hunt after pleasure; I let it come to me. I am like the man

> — 'that's born, and has his years come
> to him,
> In some green desert.'

'Years!' you will say; 'what is that superannuated simpleton calculating upon? He has already told us he is past fifty.'

I have indeed lived nominally fifty years; but deduct out of them the hours which I have lived to other people, and not to myself, and you will find me still a young fellow: for *that* is the only true Time which a man can properly call his own, that which he has all to himself; the rest, though in some sense he may be said to live it, is other people's Time, not his. The remnant of my poor days, long or short, is at least multiplied for me threefold. My ten next years, if I stretch so far, will be as long as any preceding thirty. 'T is a fair Rule-of-Three sum.

Among the strange fantasies which beset me at the commencement of my freedom, and of which all traces are not yet gone, one was, that a vast tract of time had intervened since I quitted the Counting House. I could not conceive of it as an affair of yesterday. The partners, and the clerks, with whom I had for so many years and for so many hours in each day of the year been closely associated, being suddenly removed from them, they seemed as dead to me. There is a fine passage, which may serve to illustrate this fancy, in a tragedy by Sir Robert Howard, speaking of a friend's death:—

> —— ''T was but just now he went away;
> I have not since had time to shed a tear;
> And yet the distance does the same appear
> As if he had been a thousand years from
> me!
> Time takes no measure in Eternity.'

To dissipate this awkward feeling, I have been fain to go among them once or twice since; to visit my old desk-fellows — my co-brethren of the quill — that I had left below in the state militant. Not all the kindness with which they received me could quite restore to me that pleasant familiarity which I had hitherto enjoyed among them. We cracked some of our old jokes, but methought they went off but faintly. My old desk, the peg where I hung my hat, were appropriated to another. I knew it must be, but I could not take it kindly. D——l take me, if I did not feel some remorse — beast, if I had not — at quitting my old compeers, the faithful partners of my toils for six-and-thirty years, that smoothed for me with their jokes and conundrums the ruggedness of my professional road. Had it been so rugged then, after all? or was I simply a coward? Well, it is too late to repent; and I also know that these suggestions are a common fallacy of the mind on such occasions. But my heart smote me. I had violently broken the bands betwixt us. It was at least not courteous. I shall be some time before I get quite reconciled to the separation. Farewell, old cronies; yet not for long, for again and again I will come among ye, if I shall have your leave. Farewell, Ch——, dry, sarcastic, and friendly! Do——, mild, slow to move, and gentlemanly! Pl——, officious to do and to volunteer, good services! — and thou, thou dreary pile, fit mansion for a Gresham or a Whittington of old, stately house of Merchants; with thy labyrinthine passages, and light-excluding, pent-up offices, where candles for one half the year supplied the place of the sun's light; unhealthy contributor to my weal, stern fosterer of my living, farewell! In thee remain, and not in the obscure collection of some wandering bookseller, my 'works!' There let them rest, as I do from my labours, piled on thy massy shelves, more MSS. in folio than ever Aquinas left, and full as useful! My mantle I bequeath among ye.

A fortnight has passed since the date of my first communication. At that period I was approaching to tranquillity, but had not reached it. I boasted of a calm indeed, but it was comparative only. Something of the first flutter was left; an unsettling sense of novelty; the dazzle to weak eyes of unaccustomed light. I missed my old chains, forsooth, as if they had been some necessary part of my apparel. I was a poor Carthusian, from strict cellular discipline suddenly by some revolution returned upon the world. I am now as if I had never been other than my own master. It is natural to me to go where I please, to do what I please. I find myself at eleven o'clock in the day in Bond Street, and it seems to me that I have been sauntering there at that very hour for years past. I digress into Soho, to explore a bookstall. Methinks I have been thirty years a collector. There is nothing strange nor new in it. I find myself before a fine picture in the morning. Was it ever otherwise? What is become of Fish Street Hill? Where is Fenchurch Street? Stones of old Mincing Lane, which I have worn with my daily pilgrimage for six-and-thirty years, to the footsteps of what toil-worn clerk are your everlasting flints now vocal? I indent the gayer flags of Pall Mall. It is 'Change time, and I am strangely among the Elgin marbles. It was no hyperbole when I ventured to compare the change in my condition to a passing into another world. Time stands still in a manner to me. I have lost all distinction of season. I do not know the day of the week or of the month. Each day used to be individually felt by me in its reference to the foreign post days; in its distance from, or propinquity to, the next Sunday. I had my Wednesday feelings, my Saturday nights' sensations. The genius of each day was upon me distinctly during the whole of it, affecting my appetite, spirits, &c. The phantom of the next day, with the dreary five to follow, sate as a load upon my poor Sabbath recreations. What charm has washed that Ethiop white? What is gone of Black Monday? All days are the same. Sunday itself — that unfortunate failure of a holiday, as it too often proved, what with my sense of its fugitiveness, and overcare to get the greatest quantity of pleasure out of it — is melted down into a week day. I can spare time to go to church now, without grudging the huge cantle which it used to seem to cut out of the holiday. I have Time for everything. I can visit a sick friend. I can interrupt the man of much occupation when he is busiest. I can insult over him with an invitation to take a day's pleasure with me to Windsor this fine May morning. It is Lucretian pleasure to behold the poor drudges, whom I have left behind in the world, carking and caring; like horses in a mill, drudging on in the same eternal round: and what is it all for? A man can never have too much Time to himself, nor too little to do. Had I a little son, I would christen him Nothing-to-Do; he should do nothing. Man, I verily believe, is out of his element as long as he is operative. I am altogether for the life contemplative. Will no kindly earthquake come and swallow up those accursed cotton mills? Take me that lumber of a desk there, and bowl it down

'As low as to the fiends.'

I am no longer ——, clerk to the Firm of, &c. I am Retired Leisure. I am to be met with in trim gardens. I am already come to be known by my vacant face and careless gesture, perambulating at no fixed pace, nor with any settled purpose. I walk about; not to and from. They tell me, a certain *cum dignitate* air, that has been buried so long with my other good parts, has begun to shoot forth in my person. I perceptibly grow into gentility. When I take up a newspaper, it is to read the state of the opera. *Opus operatum est.* I have done all that I came into this world to do. I have worked task-work, and have the rest of the day to myself.

1825

Leigh Hunt (1784–1859)

GETTING UP ON COLD MORNINGS

An Italian author — Giulio Cordara, a Jesuit — has written a poem upon insects, which he begins by insisting, that those troublesome and abominable little animals were created for our annoyance, and that they were certainly not inhabitants of Paradise. We of the north may dispute this piece of theology; but on the other hand, it is as clear as the snow on the house-tops, that Adam was not under the necessity of shaving; and that when Eve walked out of her delicious bower, she did not step upon ice three inches thick.

Some people say it is a very easy thing to get up of a cold morning. You have only, they tell you, to take the resolution; and the thing is done. This may be very true; just as a boy at school has only to take a flogging, and the thing is over. But we have not at all made up our minds upon it; and we find it a very pleasant exercise to discuss the matter, candidly, before we get up. This at least is not idling, though it may be lying. It affords an excellent answer to those, who ask how lying in bed can be indulged in by a reasoning being — a rational creature. How? Why with the argument calmly at work in one's head, and the clothes over one's shoulder. Oh — it is a fine way of spending a sensible, impartial half-hour.

If these people would be more charitable, they would get on with their argument better. But they are apt to reason so ill, and to assert so dogmatically, that one could wish to have them stand round one's bed of a bitter morning, and *lie* before their faces. They ought to hear both sides of the bed, the inside and out. If they cannot entertain themselves with their own thoughts for half an hour or so, it is not the fault of those who can. If their will is never pulled aside by the enticing arms of imagination, so much the luckier for the stage-coachman.

Candid inquiries into one's decumbency, besides the greater or less privileges to be allowed a man in proportion to his ability of keeping early hours, the work given his faculties, etc., will at least concede their due merits to such representations as the following. In the first place, says the injured but calm appealer, I have been warm all night, and find my system in a state perfectly suitable to a warm-blooded animal. To get out of this state into the cold, besides the inharmonious and uncritical abruptness of the transition, is so unnatural to such a creature, that the poets, refining upon the tortures of the damned, make one of their greatest agonies consist in being suddenly transported from heat to cold, — from fire to ice. They are 'haled' out of their 'beds,' says Milton, by 'harpy-footed furies,' — fellows who come to call them. On my first movement towards the anticipation of getting up, I find that such parts of the sheets and bolster, as are exposed to the air of the room, are stone-cold. On opening my eyes, the first thing that meets them is my own breath rolling forth, as if in the open air, like smoke out of a cottage chimney.

Think of this symptom. Then I turn my eyes sideways and see the window all frozen over. Think of that. Then the servant comes in. 'It is very cold this morning, is it not?' — 'Very cold, Sir.' — 'Very cold indeed, isn't it?' — 'Very cold indeed, Sir.' — 'More than usually so, isn't it, even for this weather?' (Here the servant's wit and good-nature are put to a considerable test, and the inquirer lies on thorns for the answer.) 'Why, Sir . . . I think it *is*.' (Good creature! There is not a better, or more truth-telling servant going.) 'I must rise, however — get me some warm water.' — Here comes a fine interval between the departure of the servant and the arrival of the hot water; during which, of course, it is of 'no use' to get up. The hot water comes. 'Is it quite hot?' — 'Yes, Sir.' — 'Perhaps too hot for shaving: I must wait a little?' — 'No, Sir; it will just do.' (There is an over-nice propriety sometimes, an officious zeal of virtue, a little troublesome.) 'Oh — the shirt — you must air my clean shirt — linen gets very damp this weather.' — 'Yes, Sir.' Here another delicious five minutes. A knock at the door. 'Oh, the shirt — very well. My stockings — I think the stockings had better be aired too.' —'Very well, Sir.' — Here another interval. At length everything is ready, except myself. I now, continues our incumbent (a happy word, by the bye, for a country vicar) — I now cannot help thinking a good deal — who can? — upon the unnecessary and villainous custom of shaving: it is a thing so unmanly (here I nestle closer) — so effeminate (here I recoil from an unlucky step into the colder part of the bed.) — No wonder that the Queen of France took part with the rebels against the degenerate King, her husband, who first affronted her smooth visage with a face like her own. The Emperor Julian never showed the luxuriancy of his genius to better advantage than in reviving the flowing beard. Look at Cardinal Bembo's picture — at Michael Angelo's — at Titian's — at Shakespeare's — at Fletcher's — at Spenser's — at Chaucer's — at Alfred's — at Plato's — I could name a great man for every tick of my watch. — Look at the Turks, a grave and otiose people. —Think of Haroun Al Raschid and Bed-ridden Hassan. — Think of Wortley Montague, the worthy son of his mother, a man above the prejudice of his time. — Look at the Persian gentlemen, whom one is ashamed of meeting about the suburbs, their dress and appearance are so much finer than our own. — Lastly, think of the razor itself — how totally opposed to every sensation of bed — how cold, how edgy, how hard! how utterly different from anything like the warm and circling amplitude, which

> 'Sweetly recommends itself
> Unto our gentle senses.'

Add to this, benumbed fingers, which may help you to cut yourself, a quivering body, a frozen towel, and a ewer full of ice; and he that says there is nothing to oppose in all this, only shows, at any rate, that he has no merit in opposing it.

Thomson the poet, who exclaims in his Seasons —

> 'Falsely luxurious! Will not man awake?'

used to lie in bed till noon, because he said he had no motive in getting up. He could imagine the good of rising; but then he could also imagine the good of lying still; and his exclamation, it must be allowed, was made upon summer-time, not winter. We must proportion the argument to the individual character. A money-getter may be drawn out of his bed by three and four pence; but this will not suffice for a student. A proud man may say, 'What shall I think of myself, if I don't get up?' but the more humble one will be content to waive this prodigious notion of himself, out of respect to his kindly bed. The mechanical man shall get up without any ado at all; and so shall the barometer. An ingenious lier in bed will find hard matter of discussion even on the score of health and longevity. He will ask us for our proofs and precedents of the ill effects of lying later in cold weather; and sophisticate much on the advantages of an even temperature of body; of the natural propensity (pretty universal) to have one's way; and of the animals that roll themselves up, and sleep all the winter. As to longevity, he will ask whether the longest life is of necessity the best; and whether Holborn is the handsomest street in London.

We only know of one confounding, not to say confounded argument, fit to overturn the huge luxury, the 'enormous bliss' — of the vice in question. A lier in bed may be allowed to profess a disinterested indifference for his health or longevity; but while he is showing the reasonableness of consulting his own or one person's comfort, he must admit the proportionate claim of more than one; and the best way to deal with him is this, especially for a lady; for we earnestly recommend the use of that sex on such occasions, if not somewhat *over*-persuasive; since extremes have an awkward knack of meeting. First then, admit all the ingeniousness of what he says, telling him that the bar has been deprived of an excellent lawyer. Then look at him in the most good-natured manner in the world, with a mixture of assent and appeal in your countenance, and tell him that you are waiting breakfast for him; that you never like to breakfast without him; that you really want it too; that the servants want theirs; that you shall not know how to get the house into order, unless he rises; and that you are sure he would do things twenty times worse, even than getting out of his warm bed, to put them all into good humour and a state of comfort. Then, after having said this, throw in the comparatively indifferent matter, to *him*, about his health; but tell him that it is no indifferent matter to you; that the sight of his illness makes more people suffer than one; but that if, nevertheless, he really does feel so very sleepy and so very much refreshed by — Yet stay; we hardly know whether the frailty of a — Yes, yes; say that too, especially if you say it with sincerity; for if the weakness of human nature on the one hand and the *vis inertiæ* on the other, should lead him to take advantage of it once or twice, good-humour and sincerity form an irresistible junction at last; and are still better and warmer things than pillows and blankets.

Other little helps of appeal may be thrown in, as occasion requires. You may tell a lover, for instance, that lying in bed makes people corpulent; a father, that you wish him to complete the fine manly example he sets his children; a lady, that she will injure her bloom or her shape, which M. or W. admires so much; and a student or artist, that he is always so glad to have done a good day's work, in his best manner.

Reader. And pray, Mr. Indicator, how do *you* behave yourself in this respect?

Indic. Oh, Madam, perfectly, of course; like all advisers.

Reader. Nay, I allow that your mode of argument does not look quite so suspicious as the old way of sermonizing and severity, but I have my doubts, especially from that laugh of yours. If I should look in to-morrow morning——

Indic. Ah, Madam, the look in of a face like yours does anything with me. It shall fetch me up at nine, if you please — *six*, I meant to say.

1820

Thomas De Quincey (1785–1859)

SUSPIRIA DE PROFUNDIS

LEVANA AND OUR LADIES OF SORROW

Oftentimes at Oxford I saw Levana in my dreams. I knew her by her Roman symbols. Who is Levana? Reader, that do not pretend to have leisure for very much scholarship, you will not be angry with me for telling you. Levana was the Roman goddess that performed for the new-born infant the earliest office of ennobling kindness, — typical, by its mode, of that grandeur which belongs to man everywhere, and of that benignity in powers invisible which even in Pagan worlds sometimes descends to sustain it. At the very moment of birth, just as the infant tasted for the first time the atmosphere of our troubled planet, it was laid on the ground. *That* might bear different interpretations. But immediately, lest so grand a creature should grovel there for more than one instant, either the paternal hand, as proxy for the goddess Levana, or some near kinsman, as proxy for the father, raised it upright, bade it look erect as the king of all this world, and presented its forehead to the stars, saying, perhaps, in his heart, 'Behold what is greater than yourselves!' This symbolic act represented the function of Levana. And that mysterious lady, who never revealed her face (except to me in dreams), but always acted by delegation, had her name from the Latin verb (as still it is the Italian verb) *levare*, to raise aloft.

This is the explanation of Levana. And hence it has arisen that some people have understood by Levana the tutelary power that controls the education of the nursery. She, that would not suffer at his birth even a prefigurative or mimic degradation for her awful ward, far less could be supposed to suffer the real degradation attaching to the non-development of his powers. She therefore watches over human education. Now, the word *edŭco*, with the penultimate short, was derived (by a process often exemplified in the crystallization of languages) from the word *edūco*, with the penultimate long. Whatsoever *educes*, or develops, *educates*. By the education of Levana, therefore, is meant, — not the poor machinery that moves by spelling-books and grammars, but that mighty system of central forces hidden in the deep bosom of human life, which by passion, by strife, by temptation, by the energies of resistance, works forever upon children, — resting not day or night, any more than the mighty wheel of day and night themselves, whose moments, like restless spokes, are glimmering for ever as they revolve.

If, then, *these* are the ministries by which Levana works, how profoundly must she reverence the agencies of grief! But you, reader! think, — that children generally are not liable to grief such as mine. There are two senses in the word *generally*, — the sense of Euclid, where it means *universally* (or in the whole extent of the *genus*), and a foolish sense of this world, where it means *usually*. Now, I am far from saying that children universally are capable of grief like mine. But there are more than you ever heard of who die of grief in this island of ours. I will tell you a common case. The rules of Eton require that a boy on the *foundation* should be there twelve years: he is superannuated at eighteen, consequently he must come at six. Children torn away from mothers and sisters at that age not unfrequently die. I speak of what I know. The complaint is not entered by the registrar as grief; but *that* it is. Grief of that sort, and at that age, has killed more than ever have been counted amongst its martyrs.

Therefore it is that Levana often communes with the powers that shake man's heart: therefore it is that she dotes upon grief. 'These ladies,' said I softly to myself, on seeing the ministers with whom Levana was conversing, 'these are the Sorrows; and they are three in number, as the *Graces* are three, who dress man's life with beauty; the *Parcæ* are three, who weave the dark arras of man's life in their mysterious loom always with colors sad in part, sometimes angry with tragic crimson and black; the *Furies* are three, who visit with retributions called from the other side of the grave offences that walk upon this; and once even the *Muses* were but three, who fit the harp, the trumpet, or the lute, to the great burdens of man's impassioned creations. These are the Sorrows, all three of whom I know.' The last words I say *now;* but in Oxford I said, 'One of whom I know, and the others too surely I *shall* know.' For already, in my fervent youth, I saw (dimly relieved upon the dark back-ground of my dreams) the imperfect lineaments of the awful sisters. These sisters — by what name shall we call them?

If I say simply, 'The Sorrows,' there will be a chance of mistaking the term; it might be understood of individual sorrow, — separate cases of sorrow, — whereas I want a term expressing the mighty abstractions that incarnate themselves in all individual sufferings of man's heart; and I wish to have these abstractions presented as impersonations, that is, as clothed with human attributes of life, and with functions pointing to flesh. Let us call them, therefore, *Our Ladies of Sorrow.* I know them thoroughly, and have walked in all their kingdoms. Three sisters they are, of one mysterious household; and their paths are wide apart; but of their dominion there is no end. Them I saw often conversing with Levana, and sometimes about myself. Do they talk, then? Oh, no! Mighty phantoms like these disdain the infirmities of language. They may utter voices through the organs of man when they dwell in human hearts, but amongst themselves is no voice nor sound; eternal silence reigns in *their* kingdoms. *They* spoke not, as they talked with Levana; *they* whispered not; *they* sang not; though oftentimes methought they *might* have sung: for I upon earth had heard their mysteries oftentimes deciphered by harp and timbrel, by dulcimer and organ. Like God, whose servants they are, they utter their pleasure not by sounds that perish, or by words that go astray, but by signs in heaven, by changes on earth, by pulses in secret rivers, heraldries painted on darkness, and hieroglyphics written on the tablets of the brain. *They* wheeled in mazes; *I* spelled the steps. *They* telegraphed from afar; *I* read the signals. *They* conspired together; and on the mirrors of darkness *my* eye traced the plots. *Theirs* were the symbols; *mine* are the words.

What is it the sisters are? What is it that they do? Let me describe their form, and their presence; if form it were that still fluctuated in its outline; or presence it were that forever advanced to the front, or forever receded amongst shades.

The eldest of the three is named *Mater Lachrymarum*, Our Lady of Tears. She it is that night and day raves and moans, calling for vanished faces. She stood in Rama, where a voice was heard of lamentation, — Rachel weeping for her children, and refused to be comforted. She it was that stood in Bethlehem on the night when Herod's sword swept its nurseries of Innocents, and the little feet were stiffened forever, which, heard at times as they tottered along floors overhead, woke pulses of love in household hearts that were not unmarked in heaven.

Her eyes are sweet and subtile, wild and sleepy, by turns; oftentimes rising to the clouds, oftentimes challenging the heavens. She wears a diadem round her head. And I knew by childish memories that she could go abroad upon the winds, when she heard that sobbing of litanies, or the thundering of organs, and when she beheld the mustering of summer clouds. This sister, the elder, it is that carries keys more than papal at her girdle, which open every cottage and every palace. She, to my knowledge, sat all last summer by the bedside of the blind beggar, him that so often and so gladly I talked with, whose pious daughter, eight years old with the sunny countenance, resisted the temptations of play and village mirth to travel all day long on dusty roads with her afflicted father. For this did God send her a great reward. In the spring-time of the year, and whilst yet her own spring was budding, he recalled her to himself. But her blind father mourns for ever over *her;* still he dreams at midnight that the little guiding hand is locked within his own; and still he wakens to a darkness that is *now* within a second and a deeper darkness. This *Mater Lachrymarum* also has been sitting all this winter of 1844–1845 within the bed-chamber of the Czar, bringing before his eyes a daughter (not less pious) that vanished to God not less suddenly, and left behind her a darkness not less profound. By the power of her keys it is that Our Lady of Tears glides a ghostly intruder into the chambers of sleepless men, sleepless women, sleepless children, from Ganges to the Nile, from Nile to Mississippi. And her, because she is the first-born of her house, and has the widest empire, let us honor with the title of 'Madonna.'

The second sister is called *Mater Suspiriorum,* Our Lady of Sighs. She never scales the clouds, nor walks abroad upon the winds. She wears no diadem. And her eyes if they were ever seen, would be neither sweet nor subtile; no man could read their story; they would be found filled with perishing dreams, and with wrecks of forgotten delirium. But she raises not her eyes; her head, on which sits a dilapidated turban, droops forever, forever fastens on the dust. She weeps not. She groans not. But she sighs inaudibly at intervals. Her sister Madonna is oftentimes stormy and frantic, raging in the highest against heaven, and demanding back her darlings. But Our Lady of Sighs never clamors, never defies, dreams not of rebellious aspirations. She is humble to abjectness. Hers is the meekness that belongs to the hopeless. Murmur she may, but it is in her sleep. Whisper she may, but it is to herself in the twilight. Mutter she does at times, but it is in solitary places that are desolate as she is desolate, in ruined cities, and when the sun has gone down to his rest. This sister is the visitor of the Pariah, of the Jew, of the bondsman to the oar in the Mediterranean galleys; and of the English criminal in Norfolk Island, blotted out from the books of remembrance in sweet far-off England; of the baffled penitent reverting his eyes forever upon a solitary grave, which to him seems the altar overthrown of some past and bloody sacrifice, on which altar no oblations can now be availing, whether towards pardon that he might implore, or towards reparation that he might attempt. Every slave that at noonday looks up to the tropical sun with timid reproach, as he points with one hand to the earth, our general mother, but for *him* a stepmother, — as he points with the other hand to the Bible, our general teacher, but against *him* sealed and sequestered; — every woman sitting in darkness, without love to shelter her head, or hope to illumine her solitude, because the heaven-born instincts kindling in her nature germs of holy affections, which God implanted in her womanly bosom, having been stifled by social necessities, now burn sullenly to waste, like sepulchral lamps amongst the ancients; every nun defrauded of her unreturning

May-time by wicked kinsman, whom God will judge; every captive in every dungeon; all that are betrayed, and all that are rejected; outcasts by traditionary law, and children of *hereditary* disgrace, — all these walk with Our Lady of Sighs. She also carries a key; but she needs it little. For her kingdom is chiefly amongst the tents of Shem, and the houseless vagrant of every clime. Yet in the very highest ranks of man she finds chapels of her own; and even in glorious England there are some that, to the world, carry their heads as proudly as the reindeer, who yet secretly have received her mark upon their foreheads.

But the third sister, who is also the youngest ——! Hush! whisper whilst we talk of *her!* Her kingdom is not large, or else no flesh should live; but within that kingdom all power is hers. Her head, turreted like that of Cybele, rises almost beyond the reach of sight. She droops not; and her eyes rising so high *might* be hidden by distance. But, being what they are, they cannot be hidden; through the treble veil of crape which she wears, the fierce light of a blazing misery, that rests not for matins or for vespers, for noon of day or noon of night, for ebbing or for flowing tide, may be read from the very ground. She is the defier of God. She also is the mother of lunacies, and the suggestress of suicides. Deep lie the roots of her power; but narrow is the nation that she rules. For she can approach only those in whom a profound nature has been upheaved by central convulsions; in whom the heart trembles and the brain rocks under conspiracies of tempest from without and tempest from within. Madonna moves with uncertain steps, fast or slow, but still with tragic grace. Our Lady of Sighs creeps timidly and stealthily. But this youngest sister moves with incalculable motions, bounding, and with a tiger's leaps. She carries no key; for, though coming rarely amongst men, she storms all doors at which she is permitted to enter at all. And *her* name is *Mater Tenebrarum*, — Our Lady of Darkness.

These were the *Semnai Theai*, or Sublime Goddesses, these were the *Eumenides*, or Gracious Ladies (so called by antiquity in shuddering propitiation) of my Oxford dreams. Madonna spoke. She spoke by her mysterious hand. Touching my head, she beckoned to Our Lady of Sighs; and *what* she spoke, translated out of the signs which (except in dreams) no man reads, was this:

'Lo! here is he, whom in childhood I dedicated to my altars. This is he that once I made my darling. Him I led astray, him I beguiled, and from heaven I stole away his young heart to mine. Through me did he become idolatrous; and through me it was, by languishing desires, that he worshipped the worm, and prayed to the wormy grave. Holy was the grave to him; lovely was its darkness; saintly its corruption. Him, this young idolator, I have seasoned for thee, dear gentle Sister of Sighs! Do thou take him now to *thy* heart, and season him for our dreadful sister. And thou,' — turning to the *Mater Tenebrarum*, she said, — 'wicked sister, that temptest and hatest, do thou take him from *her*. See that thy sceptre lie heavy on his head. Suffer not woman and her tenderness to sit near him in his darkness. Banish the frailties of hope, wither the relenting of love, scorch the fountains of tears, curse him as only thou canst curse. So shall he be accomplished in the furnace, so shall he see the things that ought *not* to be seen, sights that are abominable, and secrets that are unutterable. So shall he read elder truths, sad truths, grand truths, fearful truths. So shall he rise again *before* he dies. And so shall our commission be accomplished which from God we had, — to plague his heart until we had unfolded the capacities of his spirit.'

1845

THE ENGLISH MAIL-COACH

DREAM-FUGUE

'Whence the sound
Of instruments, that made melodious chime,
Was heard, of harp and organ; and who moved
Their stops and chords, was seen; his volant touch
Instinct through all proportions, low and high,
Fled and pursued transverse the resonant fugue.'

Par. Lost, Bk. XI

Tumultuosissimamente

Passion of sudden death! that once in youth I read and interpreted by the shadows of thy averted signs! — rapture of panic taking the shape (which amongst tombs in churches I have seen) of woman bursting her sepulchral bonds — of woman's Ionic form bending from the ruins of her grave with arching foot, with eyes upraised, with clasped adoring hands — waiting, watching, trembling, praying for the trumpet's call to rise from dust for ever! Ah, vision too fearful of shuddering humanity on the brink of almighty abysses! — vision that didst start back, that didst reel away, like a shrivelling scroll from before the wrath of fire racing on the wings of the wind! Epilepsy so brief of horror, wherefore is it that thou canst not die? Passing so suddenly into darkness, wherefore is it that still thou sheddest thy sad funeral blights upon the gorgeous mosaics of dreams? Fragment of music too passionate, heard once, and heard no more, what aileth thee, that thy deep rolling chords come up at intervals through all the worlds of sleep, and after forty years, have lost no element of horror?

I

Lo, it is summer — almighty summer! The everlasting gates of life and summer are thrown open wide: and on the ocean, tranquil and verdant as a savannah, the unknown lady from the dreadful vision and I myself are floating — she upon a fairy pinnace, and I upon an English three-decker. Both of us are wooing gales of festal happiness within the domain of our common country, within that ancient watery park, within that pathless chase of ocean, where England takes her pleasure as a huntress through winter and summer, from the rising to the setting sun. Ah, what a wilderness of floral beauty was hidden, or was suddenly revealed, upon the tropic islands through which the pinnace moved! And upon her deck what a bevy of human flowers — young women how lovely, young men how noble, that were dancing together, and slowly drifting towards *us* amidst music and incense, amidst blossoms from forests and gorgeous corymbi from vintages, amidst natural carolling and the echoes of sweet girlish laughter. Slowly the pinnace nears us, gaily she hails us, and silently she disappears beneath the shadow of our mighty bows. But then, as at some signal from heaven, the music, and the carols, and the sweet echoing of girlish laughter — all are hushed. What evil has smitten the pinnace, meeting or overtaking her? Did ruin to our friends couch within our own dreadful shadow? Was our shadow the shadow of death? I looked over the bow for an answer, and, behold! the pinnace was dismantled; the revel and the revellers were found no more; the glory of the vintage was dust; and the forests with their beauty were left without a witness upon the seas. 'But where,' and I turned to our crew — 'where are the lovely women that danced beneath the awning of flowers and clustering corymbi! Whither have fled the noble young men that danced with *them?*' Answer there was none. But suddenly the man at the masthead, whose countenance darkened with alarm, cried out, 'Sail on the weather beam! Down she comes upon us: in seventy seconds she also will founder.'

II

I looked to the weather side, and the summer had departed. The sea was rocking, and shaken with gathering wrath. Upon its surface sat mighty mists, which grouped themselves into arches and long cathedral aisles. Down one of these, with the fiery pace of a quarrel from a cross-bow, ran a frigate right athwart our course. 'Are they mad?' some voice exclaimed from our deck. 'Do they woo their ruin?' But in a moment, as she was close upon us, some impulse of a heady current or local vortex gave a wheeling bias to her course, and off she forged without a shock. As she ran past us, high aloft amongst the shrouds stood the lady of the pinnace. The deeps opened ahead in malice to receive her, towering surges of foam ran after her, the billows were fierce to catch her. But far away she was borne into desert spaces of the sea: whilst still by sight I followed her as she ran before the howling gale, chased by angry sea-birds and by maddening billows; still I saw her, as at the moment when she ran past us, standing amongst the shrouds, with her white draperies streaming before the wind. There she stood, with hair dishevelled, one hand clutched amongst the tackling — rising, sinking, fluttering, trembling, praying — there for leagues I saw her as she stood, raising at intervals one hand to heaven, amidst the fiery crests of the pursuing waves and the raving of the storm; until at last, upon a sound from afar of malicious laughter and mockery, all was hidden forever in driving showers; and afterwards, but when I knew not, nor how.

III

Sweet funeral bells from some incalculable distance, wailing over the dead that die before the dawn, awakened me as I slept in a boat moored to some familiar shore. The morning twilight even then was breaking; and, by the dusky revelations which it spread, I saw a girl, adorned with a garland of white roses about her head for some great festival, running along the solitary strand in extremity of haste. Her running was the running of panic; and often she looked back as to some dreadful enemy in the rear. But when I leaped ashore, and followed on her steps to warn her of a peril in front, alas! from me she fled as from another peril, and vainly I shouted to her of quicksands that lay ahead. Faster and faster she ran; round a promontory of rocks she wheeled out of sight; in an instant I also wheeled round it, but only to see the treacherous sands gathering above her head. Already her person was buried; only the fair young head and the diadem of white roses around it were still visible to the pitying heavens: and, last of all, was visible one white marble arm. I saw by the early twilight this fair young head, as it was sinking down to darkness — saw this marble arm, as it rose above her head and her treacherous grave, tossing, faltering, rising, clutching as at some false deceiving hand stretched out from the clouds — saw this marble arm uttering her dying hope, and then uttering her dying despair. The head, the diadem, the arm — these all had sunk; at last over these also the cruel quicksand had closed; and no memorial of the fair young girl remained on earth, except my own solitary tears, and the funeral bells from the desert seas, that, rising again more softly, sang a requiem over the grave of the buried child, and over her blighted dawn.

I sat, and wept in secret the tears that men have ever given to the memory of those that died before the dawn, and by the treachery of earth, our mother. But suddenly the tears and funeral bells were hushed by a shout as of many nations, and by a roar as from some great king's artillery, advancing rapidly along the valleys, and heard afar by echoes from the mountains. 'Hush!' I said, as I bent my ear earthwards to listen — 'hush! — this either is the very anarchy of strife, or else' — and then I listened more profoundly, and whispered as I raised my head — 'or else, oh heavens! it is *victory* that is final, victory that swallows up all strife.'

IV

Immediately, in trance, I was carried over land and sea to some distant kingdom, and placed upon a triumphal car, amongst companions crowned with laurel. The darkness of gathering midnight, brooding over all the land, hid from us the mighty crowds that were weaving restlessly about ourselves as a centre: we heard them, but saw them not. Tidings had arrived, within an hour, of a grandeur that measured itself against centuries; too full of pathos they were, too full of joy, to utter themselves by other language than by tears, by restless anthems, and *Te Deums* reverberated from the choirs and orchestras of earth. These tidings we that sat upon the laurelled car had it for our privilege to publish amongst all nations. And already, by signs audible through the darkness, by snortings and tramplings, our angry horses, that knew no fear of fleshly weariness, upbraided us with delay. Wherefore *was* it that we delayed? We waited for a secret word that should bear witness to the hope of nations, as now accomplished for ever. At midnight the secret word arrived; which word was — Waterloo and Recovered Christendom! The dreadful word shone by its own light; before us it went; high above our leaders' heads it rode, and spread a golden light over the paths which we traversed. Every city, at the presence of the secret word, threw open its gates. The rivers were conscious as we crossed. All the forests, as we ran along their margins, shivered in homage to the secret word. And the darkness comprehended it.

Two hours after midnight we approached a mighty Minster. Its gates, which rose to the clouds, were closed. But when the dreadful word, that rode before us, reached them with its golden light, silently they moved back upon their hinges; and at a flying gallop our equipage entered the grand aisle of the cathedral. Headlong was our pace; and at every altar, in the little chapels and oratories to the right hand and left of our course, the lamps, dying or sickening, kindled anew in sympathy with the secret word that was flying past. Forty leagues we might have run in the cathedral, and as yet no strength of morning light had reached us when before us we saw the aerial galleries of organ and choir. Every pinnacle of the fretwork, every station of advantage amongst the traceries, was crested by white-robed choristers, that sang deliverance; that wept no more tears, as once their fathers had wept; but at intervals that sang together to the generations, saying,

'Chant the deliverer's praise in every tongue,'

and receiving answers from afar,

'Such as once in heaven and earth were sung.'

And of their chanting was no end; of our headlong pace was neither pause nor slackening.

Thus, as we ran like torrents — thus, as we swept with bridal rapture over the Campo Santo of the cathedral graves — suddenly we became aware of a vast necropolis rising upon the far-off horizon — a city of sepulchres, built within the saintly cathedral for the warrior dead that rested from their feuds on earth. Of purple granite was the necropolis; yet, in the first minute, it lay like a purple stain upon the horizon, so mighty was the distance. In the second minute it trembled through many changes, growing into terraces and towers of wondrous altitude, so mighty was the pace. In the third minute already, with our dreadful gallop, we were entering its suburbs. Vast sarcophagi rose on every side, having towers and turrets that, upon the limits of the central aisle, strode forward with haughty intrusion, that ran back with mighty shadows into answering recesses. Every sarcophagus showed many bas-reliefs — bas-reliefs of battles and of battle-fields; battles from forgotten ages — battles from yesterday — battle-fields that, long since, nature had healed and reconciled to herself with the sweet oblivion of flowers — battle-fields that were yet angry and crimson with carnage. Where the terraces ran, there did *we* run; where the towers curved, there did *we* curve. With the flight of swallows our horses swept round every angle. Like rivers in flood, wheeling round headlands — like hurricanes that ride into the secrets of forests — faster than ever light unwove the mazes of darkness, our flying equipage carried earthly passions, kindled warrior instincts, amongst the dust that lay around us — dust oftentimes of our noble fathers that had slept in God from Créci to Trafalgar. And now had we reached the last sarcophagus, now were we abreast of the last bas-relief, already had we recovered the arrow-like flight of the illimitable central aisle, when coming up this aisle to meet us we beheld afar off a female child, that rode in a carriage as frail as flowers. The mists, which went before her, hid the fawns that drew her, but could not hide the shells and tropic flowers with which she played — but could not hide the lovely smiles by which she uttered her trust in the mighty cathedral, and in the cherubim that looked down upon her from the mighty shafts of its pillars. Face to face she was meeting us; face to face she rode, as if danger there were none. 'Oh, baby!' I exclaimed, 'shalt thou be the ransom for Waterloo? Must we, that carry tidings of great joy to every people, be messengers of ruin to thee!' In horror I rose at the thought; but then also, in horror at the thought, rose one that was sculptured on a bas-relief — a Dying Trumpeter. Solemnly from the field of battle he rose to his feet; and, unslinging his stony trumpet, carried it, in his dying anguish, to his stony lips — sounding once, and yet once again; proclamation that, in *thy* ears, oh baby! spoke from the battlements of death. Immediately deep shadows fell between us, and aboriginal silence. The choir had ceased to sing. The hoofs of our horses, the dreadful rattle of our harness, the groaning of our wheels, alarmed the graves no more. By horror the bas-relief had been unlocked unto life. By horror we, that were so full of life, we men and our horses, with their fiery fore-legs rising in mid air to their everlasting gallop, were frozen to a bas-relief. Than a third time the trumpet sounded; the seals were taken off all pulses; life, and the frenzy of life, tore into their channels again; again the choir burst forth in sunny grandeur, as from the muffling of storms and darkness; again the thunderings of our horses carried temptation into the graves. One cry burst from our lips, as the clouds, drawing off from the aisle, showed it empty before us. — 'Whither has the infant fled? — is the young child caught up to God?' Lo! afar off, in a vast recess, rose three mighty windows to the clouds; and on a level with their summits, at height insuperable to man, rose an altar of purest alabaster. On its eastern face was trembling a crimson glory. A glory was it from the reddening dawn that now streamed *through* the windows? Was it from the crimson robes of the martyrs painted *on* the windows? Was it from the bloody bas-reliefs of earth? There, suddenly, within that crimson radiance, rose the apparition of a woman's head, and then of a woman's figure. The child it was — grown up to woman's height. Clinging to the horns of the altar, voiceless she stood — sinking, rising, raving, despairing; and behind the volume of incense, that, night and day, streamed upwards from the altar, dimly was seen the fiery font, and the shadow of that dreadful being who should have baptized her with the baptism of death. But by her side was kneeling her better angel, that hid his face with wings; that wept and pleaded for *her;* that prayed when *she* could *not;* that fought with Heaven by tears for *her* deliverance; which also, as he raised his immortal countenance from his wings, I saw, by the glory in his eye, that from Heaven he had won at last.

V

Then was completed the passion of the mighty fugue. The golden tubes of the organ, which as yet had but muttered at intervals — gleaming amongst clouds and surges of incense — threw up, as from fountains unfathomable, columns of heart-shattering music. Choir and anti-choir were filling fast with unknown voices. Thou also, Dying Trumpeter! — with thy love that was victorious, and thy anguish that was finishing — didst enter the tumult; trumpet and echo — farewell love, and farewell anguish — rang through the dreadful *sanctus.* Oh, darkness of the grave! that from the crimson altar and from the fiery font wert visited and searched by the effulgence in the angel's eye — were these indeed thy children? Pomps of life, that, from the burials of centuries, rose again to the voice of perfect joy, did ye indeed mingle with the festivals of Death? Lo! as I looked back for seventy leagues through the mighty cathedral, I saw the quick and the dead that sang together to God, together that sang to the generations of man. All the hosts of jubilation, like armies that ride in pursuit, moved with one step. Us, that, with laurelled heads, were passing from the cathedral, they overtook, and, as with a garment, they wrapped us round with thunders greater than our own. As brothers we moved together; to the dawn that advanced — to the stars that fled; rendering thanks to God in the highest — that, having hid his face through one generation behind the thick clouds of War, once again was ascending — from the Campo Santo of Waterloo was ascending — in the visions of Peace; rendering thanks for thee, young girl! whom, having overshadowed with his ineffable passion of death, suddenly did God relent; suffered thy angel to turn aside his arm; and even in thee, sister unknown! shown to me for a moment only to be hidden forever, found an occasion to glorify his goodness. A thousand times, amongst the phantoms of sleep, have I seen thee entering the gates of the golden dawn — with the secret word riding before thee — with the armies of the grave behind thee: seen thee sinking, rising, raving, despairing; a thousand times in the worlds of sleep have seen thee followed by God's angel through storms; through desert seas; through the darkness of quicksands; through dreams, and the dreadful revelations that are in dreams — only that at the last, with one sling of his victorious arm, he might snatch thee back from ruin, and might emblazon in thy deliverance the endless resurrections of his love!

1849

BIOGRAPHY

Thomas Carlyle (1795–1881)

DEATH OF GOETHE

In the Obituary of these days stands one article of quite peculiar import; the time, the place and particulars of which will have to be often repeated and rewritten, and continue in remembrance many centuries: this namely, that Johann Wolfgang von Goethe died at Weimar, on the 22d March, 1832. It was about eleven in the morning; 'he expired,' says the record, 'without any apparent suffering, having, a few minutes previously, called for paper for the purpose of writing, and expressed his delight at the arrival of spring.' A beautiful death; like that of a soldier found faithful at his post, and in the cold hand his arms still grasped! The Poet's last words are a greeting of the new-awakened Earth; his last movement is to work at his appointed task. Beautiful; what we might call a Classic sacred-death; if it were not rather an Elijah-translation, — in a chariot, not of fire and terror, but of hope and soft vernal sunbeams! It was at Frankfort-on-Mayn, on the 28th of August, 1749, that this man entered the world; and now, gently welcoming the birthday of his eighty-second spring, he closes his eyes, and takes farewell.

So, then, our Greatest has departed. That melody of life, with its cunning tones, which took captive ear and heart, has gone silent; the heavenly force that dwelt here victorious over so much, is here no longer; thus far, not farther, by speech and by act, shall the wise man utter himself forth. The End! What solemn meaning lies in that sound, as it peals mournfully through the soul, when a living friend has passed away! All now is closed, irrevocable; the changeful life-picture, growing daily into new coherence, under new touches and hues, has suddenly become completed and unchangeable; there as it lay, it is dipped, from this moment, in the æther of the heavens, and shines transfigured, to endure even so — forever. Time and Time's Empire; stern, wide-devouring, yet not without their grandeur! The week-day man, who was one of us, has put on the garment of Eternity, and become radiant and triumphant; the Present is all at once the Past; Hope is suddenly cut away, and only the backward vistas of Memory remain, shone on by a light that proceeds not from this earthly sun.

The death of Goethe, even for the many hearts that personally loved him, is not a thing to be lamented over; is to be viewed, in his own spirit, as a thing full of greatness and sacredness. For all men it is appointed once to die. To this man the full measure of a man's life had been granted, and a course and task such as to only a few in the whole generations of the world: what else could we hope or require but that now he should be called hence, and have leave to depart, having finished the work that was given him to do? If his course, as we may say of him more justly than of any other, was like the Sun's, so also was his going down. For, indeed, as the material Sun is the eye and revealer of all things, so is Poetry, so is the World-Poet in a spiritual sense. Goethe's life, too, if we examine it, is well represented in that emblem of a solar Day. Beautifully rose our summer sun, gorgeous in the red fervid east, scattering the spectres and sickly damps (of both of which there were enough to scatter); strong, benignant in his noonday clearness, walking triumphant through the upper realms; and now, mark also how he sets! '*So stirbt ein Held; anbetungsvoll*, So dies a hero; sight to be worshipped!'

And yet, when the inanimate material sun has sunk and disappeared, it will happen that we stand to gaze into the still-glowing west; and there rise great pale motionless clouds, like coulisses or curtains, to close the flame-theatre within; and then, in that death-pause of the Day, an unspeakable feeling will come over us: it is as if the poor sounds of Time, those hammerings of tired Labour on his anvils, those voices of simple men, had become awful and supernatural; as if in listening, we could hear them 'mingle with the everpealing tone of old Eternity.' In such moments the secrets of Life lie opener to us; mysterious things flit over the soul; Life itself seems holier, wonderful and fearful. How much more when our sunset was of a living sun; and *its* bright countenance and shining return to us, not on the morrow, but 'no more again, at all, for-ever'! In such a scene, silence, as over the mysterious great, is for him that has some feeling there of the fittest mood. Nevertheless, by silence the distant is not brought into communion; the feeling of each is without response from the bosom of his brother. There are now, what some years ago there were not, English hearts that know something of what those three words, 'Death of Goethe,' mean; to such men, among their many thoughts on the event, which are not to be translated into speech, may these few, through that imperfect medium, prove acceptable.

'Death,' says the philosopher, 'is a commingling of Eternity with Time; in the death of a good man Eternity is seen looking through Time.' With such a sublimity here offered to eye and heart, it is not unnatural to look with new earnestness before and behind, and ask, What space in those years and æons of computed Time, this man with his activity may influence; what relation to the world of change and mortality, which the earthly name Life, he who is even now called to the Immortals has borne and may bear.

Goethe, it is commonly said, made a New Era in Literature; a Poetic Era began with him, the end or ulterior tendencies of which are yet nowise generally visible. This common saying is a true one; and true with a far deeper meaning than, to the most, it conveys. Were the Poet but a sweet sound and singer, solacing the ear of the idle with pleasant songs; and the new Poet one who could sing his idle pleasant song to a new air, — we should account him a small matter, and his performance small. But this man, it is not unknown to many, was a Poet in such a sense as the late generations have witnessed no other; as it is, in this generation, a kind of distinction to believe in the existence of, in the possibility of. The true Poet is ever, as of old, the Seer; whose eye has been gifted to discern the godlike Mystery of God's Universe, and decipher some new lines of its celestial writing; we can still call him a *Vates* and Seer; for he *sees* into this greatest of secrets, 'the open secret'; hidden things become clear; how the Future (both resting on Eternity) is but another phasis of the Present: thereby are his words in very truth prophetic; what he has spoken shall be done.

It begins now to be everywhere surmised that the real Force, which in this world all things must obey, is Insight, Spiritual Vision and Determination. The Thought is parent of the Deed, nay is living soul of it, and last and continual, as well as first mover of it; is the foundation and beginning and essence, therefore, of man's whole existence here below. In this sense, it has been said, the Word of man (the uttered Thought of man) is still a magic formula, whereby he rules the world. Do not the winds and waters, and all tumultuous powers, inanimate and animate, obey him? A poor, quite mechanical Magician speaks; and fire-winged ships cross the Ocean at his bidding. Or mark, above all, that 'raging of the nations,' wholly in contention, desperation and dark chaotic fury; how the meek voice of a Hebrew Martyr and Redeemer stills it into order, and a savage Earth becomes kind and beautiful, and the habitation of horrid cruelty a temple of peace. The true Sovereign of the world, who moulds the world like soft wax, according to his pleasure, is he who lovingly *sees* into the world; the 'inspired Thinker,' whom in these days we name Poet. The true Sovereign is the Wise Man.

However, as the Moon, which can heave up the Atlantic, sends not in her obedient billows at once, but gradually; and the Tide, which swells today on our shores, and washes every creek, rose in the bosom of the great Ocean (astronomers assure us) eight-and-forty hours ago; and indeed, all world-movements, by nature deep, are by nature calm, and flow and swell onwards with a certain majestic slowness: so too with the Impulse of a Great Man, and the effect he has to manifest on other men. To such a one we may grant some generation or two, before the celestial Impulse he impressed on the world will universally proclaim itself, and become (like the working of the Moon) if still not intelligible, yet palpable, to all men; some generation or two more, wherein it has to grow, and expand, and envelop all things, before it can reach its acme; and thereafter mingling with other movements and new impulses, at length cease to require a specific observation or designation. Longer or shorter such period may be, according to the nature of the Impulse itself, and of the elements it works in; according, above all, as the Impulse was intrinsically great and deep-reaching, or only wide-spread, superficial and transient. Thus, if David Hume is at this hour pontiff of the world, and rules most hearts, and guides most tongues (the hearts and tongues even of those that in vain rebel against him), there are nevertheless symptoms that his task draws towards completion; and now in the distance his successor becomes visible. On the other hand, we have seen a Napoleon, like some gunpowder force (with which sort, indeed, he chiefly worked), explode his whole virtue suddenly, and thunder himself out and silent, in a space of five-and-twenty years. While again, for a man of true greatness, working with spiritual implements, two centuries is no uncommon period; nay, on this Earth of ours, there have been men whose Impulse has not completed its development till after fifteen hundred years and might perhaps be seen still individually subsistent after two thousand.

But, as was once written, 'though our clock strikes when there is a change from hour to hour, no hammer in the Horologe of Time peals through the Universe to proclaim that there is a change from era to era.' The true Beginning is oftenest unnoticed and unnoticeable. Thus do men go wrong in their reckoning; and grope hither and thither, not knowing where they are, in what course their history runs. Within this last century, for instance, with its wild doings and destroyings, what hope, grounded on miscalculation, ending in disappointment! How many world-famous victories were gained and lost, dynasties founded and subverted, revolutions accomplished, constitutions sworn to; and ever the 'new era' was come, was coming, yet still it came not, but the time continued sick! Alas, all these were but spasmodic convulsions of the death-sick time: the crisis of cure and regeneration to the time was not there indicated. The real new era was when a Wise Man came into the world, with clearness of vision and greatness of soul to accomplish this old high enterprise, amid these new difficulties, yet again: A Life of Wisdom. Such a man became, by Heaven's pre-appointment, in very deed the Redeemer of the time. Did he not bear the curse of the time? He was filled full with its scepticism, bitterness, hollowness and thousandfold contradictions, till his heart was like to break; but he subdued all this, rose victorious over this, and manifoldly by word and act showed others that come after, how to do the like. Honour to him who first 'through the impassable paves a road'! Such, indeed, is the task of every great man; nay of every good man in one or the other sphere, since goodness is greatness, and the good man, high or humble, is ever a martyr and 'spiritual hero that ventures forward into the gulf for our deliverance.' The gulf into which this man ventured, which he tamed and rendered habitable, was the greatest and most perilous of all, wherein truly all others lie included: *The whole distracted Existence of man is an age of Unbelief.* Whoso lives, whoso with earnest mind studies to live wisely in that mad element, may yet know, perhaps too well, what an enterprise was here; and for the Chosen Man of our time who could prevail in it, have the higher reverence, and a gratitude such as belongs to no other.

How far he prevailed in it, and by what means, with what endurances and achievements, will in due season be estimated. Those volumes called *Goethe's Works* will now receive no farther addition or alteration; and the record of his whole spiritual Endeavour lies written there,—were the man or men but ready that could read it rightly! A glorious record; wherein he who would understand himself and his environment, who struggles for escape out of darkness into light as for the one thing needful, will long thankfully study. For the whole chaotic Time, what it has suffered, attained, and striven after, stands imaged there: interpreted, ennobled into poetic clearness. From the passionate longings and wailings of *Werter*, spoken as from the heart of all Europe; onwards through the wild unearthly melody of *Faust*, like the spirit-song of falling worlds; to that serenely smiling wisdom of *Meisters Lehrjahre*, and the *German Hafiz*, — what an interval; and all enfolded in an ethereal music, as from unknown spheres, harmoniously uniting all! A long interval; and wide as well as long; for this was a universal man. History, Science, Art, human Activity under every aspect; the laws of Light in his *Farbenlehre;* the laws of wild Italian Life in his *Benvenuto Cellini;* — nothing escaped him; nothing that he did not look into, that he did not see into. Consider, too, the genuineness of whatsoever he did; his hearty, idiomatic way; simplicity with loftiness, and nobleness, and aërial grace! Pure works of Art, completed with an antique Grecian polish, as *Torquato Tasso*, as *Iphigenie*; Proverbs; *Xenien;* Patriarchal Sayings, which, since the Hebrew Scriptures were closed, we know not where to match; in whose homely depths lie often the materials for volumes.

To measure and estimate all this, as we said, the time is not come; a century hence will be the fitter time. He who investigates it best will find its meaning greatest, and be the readiest to acknowledge that it transcends him. Let the reader have *seen*, before he attempts to *oversee*. A poor reader, in the mean while, were he who discerned not here the authentic rudiments of that same New Era, whereof we have so often had false warning. Wondrously, the wrecks and pulverised rubbish of ancient things, institutions, religions, forgotten noblenesses, made alive again by the breath of Genius, lie here in new coherence and incipient union, the spirit of Art working creative through the mass; that *chaos*, into which the eighteenth century with its wild war of hypocrites and sceptics had reduced the Past, begins here to be once more a *world*. — This, the highest that can be said of written Books, is to be said of these: there is in them a New Time, the prophecy and beginning of a New Time. The corner-stone of a new social edifice for mankind is laid there; firmly, as before, on the natural rock: far-extending traces of a ground-plan we can also see; which future centuries may go on to enlarge, to amend, and work into reality. These sayings seem strange to some; nevertheless they are not empty exaggerations, but expressions, in their way, of a belief, which is not now of yesterday; perhaps when Goethe has been read and meditated for another generation, they will not seem so strange.

Precious is the new light of Knowledge which our Teacher conquers for us; yet small to the new light of Love which also we derive from him: the most important element of any man's performance is the Life he has accomplished. Under the intellectual union of man and man, which works by precept, lies a holier union of affection, working by example; the influences of which latter, mystic, deep-reaching, all-embracing, can still less be computed. For Love is ever the beginning of Knowledge, as fire is of light; and works also more in the manner of *fire*. That Goethe was a great Teacher of men means already that he was a good man; that he had himself learned; in the school of experience had striven and proved victorious. To how many hearers, languishing, nigh dead, in the airless dungeon of Unbelief (a true vacuum and nonentity), has the assurance that there was such a man, that such a man was still possible, come like tidings of great joy! He who would learn to reconcile reverence with clearness; to deny and defy what is False, yet believe and worship what is True; amid raging factions, bent on what is either altogether empty or has substance in it only for a day, which stormfully convulse and tear hither and thither a distracted expiring system of society, to adjust himself aright; and, working for the world and in the world, keep himself unspotted from the world, — let him look here. This man, we may say, became morally great, by being in his own age, what in some other ages many might have been, a genuine man. His grand excellency was this, that he was genuine. As his primary faculty, the foundation of all others, was Intellect, depth and force of Vision; so his primary virtue was Justice, was the courage to be just. A giant's strength we admired in him; yet strength ennobled into softest mildness; even like that 'silent rock-bound strength of a world,' on whose bosom, which rests on the adamant, grow flowers. The greatest of hearts was also the bravest; fearless, unwearied, peacefully invincible. A completed man: the trembling sensibility, the wild enthusiasm of a Mignon can assort with the scornful world-mockery of a Mephistopheles; and each side of many-sided life receives its due from him.

Goethe reckoned Schiller happy that he died young, in the full vigour of his days; that we could 'figure him as a youth forever.' To himself a different, higher destiny was appointed. Through all the changes of man's life, onwards to its extreme verge he was to go; and through them all nobly. In youth, flatterings of fortune, uninterrupted outward prosperity cannot corrupt him; a wise observer has to remark: 'None but a Goethe, at the Sun of earthly happiness, can keep his phœnix-wings unsinged.' — Through manhood, in the most complex relation, as poet, courtier, politician, man of business, man of speculation; in the middle of revolutions and counter-revolutions, outward and spiritual; with the world loudly for him, with the world loudly or silently against him; in all seasons and situations, he holds equally on his way. Old age itself, which is called dark and feeble, he was to render lovely: who that looked upon him there, venerable in himself, and in the world's reverence ever the clearer, the purer, but could have prayed that he too were such an old man? And did not the kind Heavens continue kind, and grant to a career so glorious a worthiest end?

Such was Goethe's life; such has his departure been. He sleeps now beside his Schiller and his Carl August of Weimar: so had the Prince willed it, that between these two should be his own final rest. In life they were united, in death they are not divided. The unwearied Workman now rests from his labours; the fruit of these is left growing, and to grow. His earthly years have been numbered and ended: but of his Activity, for it stood rooted in the Eternal, there is no end. All that we mean by the higher Literature of Germany, which is the higher Literature of Europe, already gathers round this man, as its creator; of which grand object, dawning mysterious on a world that hoped not for it, who is there that can measure the significance and far-reaching influences? The Literature of Europe will pass away; Europe itself, the Earth itself will pass away: this little life-boat of an Earth, with its noisy crew of a Mankind, and all their troubled History, will one day have vanished; faded like a cloud-speck from the azure of the All! What, then, is man! What, then, is man! He endures but for an hour, and is crushed before the moth. Yet in the being and in the working of a faithful man is there already (as all faith, from the beginning, gives assurance) a something that pertains not to this wild death-element of Time; that triumphs over Time, and *is*, and will be, when Time shall be no more.

And now we turn back into the world, withdrawing from this new-made grave. The man whom we love lies there: but glorious, worthy; and his spirit yet lives in us with an authentic life. Could each here vow to do his little task, even as the Departed did his great one; in the manner of a true man, not for a Day, but for Eternity! To live, as he counselled and commanded, not commodiously in the Reputable, the Plausible, the Half, but resolutely in the Whole, the Good, the True:

'Im Ganzen, Guten, Wahren resolut zu leben!'

1832

Thomas Babington Macaulay
(1800–1859)

OLIVER GOLDSMITH

Oliver Goldsmith [was] one of the most pleasing English writers of the eighteenth century. He was of a Protestant and Saxon family which had been long settled in Ireland, and which had, like most other Protestant and Saxon families, been, in troubled times, harassed and put in fear by the native population. His father, Charles

Goldsmith, studied in the reign of Queen Anne at the diocesan school of Elphin, became attached to the daughter of the schoolmaster, married her, took orders, and settled at a place called Pallas in the county of Longford. There he with difficulty supported his wife and children on what he could earn, partly as a curate and partly as a farmer.

At Pallas Oliver Goldsmith was born in November, 1728. That spot was then, for all practical purposes, almost as remote from the busy and splendid capital in which his later years were passed, as any clearing in Upper Canada or any sheep-walk in Australasia now is. Even at this day those enthusiasts who venture to make a pilgrimage to the birthplace of the poet are forced to perform the latter part of their journey on foot. The hamlet lies far from any high road, on a dreary plain which, in wet weather, is often a lake. The lanes would break any jaunting car to pieces; and there are ruts and sloughs through which the most strongly built wheels cannot be dragged.

When Oliver was still a child, his father was presented to a living worth about 200 *l.* a year, in the county of Westmeath. The family accordingly quitted their cottage in the wilderness for a spacious house on a frequented road, near the village of Lissoy. Here the boy was taught his letters by a maid-servant, and was sent in his seventh year to a village school kept by an old quartermaster on half-pay, who professed to teach nothing but reading, writing and arithmetic, but who had an inexhaustible fund of stories about ghosts, banshees and fairies, about the great Rapparee chiefs, Baldearg O'Donnell and galloping Hogan, and about the exploits of Peterborough and Stanhope, the surprise of Monjuich, and the glorious disaster of Brihuega. This man must have been of the Protestant religion; but he was of the aboriginal race, and not only spoke the Irish language, but could pour forth unpremeditated Irish verses. Oliver early became, and through life continued to be, a passionate admirer of the Irish music, and especially of the compositions of Carolan, some of the last notes of whose harp he heard. It ought to be added that Oliver, though by birth one of the Englishry, and though connected by numerous ties with the Established Church, never showed the least sign of that contemptuous antipathy with which, in his days, the ruling minority in Ireland too generally regarded the subject majority. So far indeed was he from sharing in the opinions and feelings of the caste to which he belonged, that he conceived an aversion to the Glorious and Immortal Memory, and, even when George the Third was on the throne, maintained that nothing but the restoration of the banished dynasty could save the country.

From the humble academy kept by the old soldier Goldsmith was removed in his ninth year. He went to several grammar schools, and acquired some knowledge of the ancient languages. His life at this time seems to have been far from happy. He had, as appears from the admirable portrait of him at Knowle, features harsh even to ugliness. The small-pox had set its mark on him with more than usual severity. His stature was small, and his limbs ill put together. Among boys little tenderness is shown to personal defects; and the ridicule excited by poor Oliver's appearance was heightened by a peculiar simplicity and a disposition to blunder which he retained to the last. He became the common butt of boys and masters, was pointed at as a fright in the playground, and flogged as a dunce in the schoolroom. When he had risen to eminence, those who had once derided him ransacked their memory for the events of his early years, and recited repartees and couplets which had dropped from him, and which, though little noticed at the time, were supposed, a quarter of a century later, to indicate the powers which produced 'The Vicar of Wakefield' and 'The Deserted Village.'

In his seventeenth year Oliver went up to Trinity College, Dublin, as a sizar. The sizars paid nothing for food and tuition, and very little for lodging; but they had to perform some menial services from which they have long been relieved. They swept the court: they carried up the dinner to the fellows' table, and changed the plates and poured out the ale of the rulers of the society. Goldsmith was quartered, not alone, in a garret, on the window of which his name, scrawled by himself, is still read with interest. From such garrets many men of less parts than his have made their way to the woolsack or to the episcopal bench. But Goldsmith, while he suffered all the humiliations, threw away all the advantages, of his situation. He neglected the studies of the place, stood low at the examinations, was turned down to the bottom of his class for playing the buffoon in the lecture room, was severely reprimanded for pumping on a constable, and was caned by a brutal tutor for giving a ball in the attic story of the college to some gay youths and damsels from the city.

While Oliver was leading at Dublin a life divided between squalid distress and squalid dissipation, his father died, leaving a mere pittance. The youth obtained his bachelor's degree, and left the university. During some time the humble dwelling to which his widowed mother had retired was his home. He was now in his twenty-first year; it was necessary that he should do something; and his education seemed to have fitted him to do nothing but to dress himself in gaudy colours, of which he was as fond as a magpie, to take a hand at cards, to sing Irish airs, to play the flute, to angle in summer, and to tell ghost stories by the fire in winter. He tried five or six professions in turn without success. He applied for ordination; but, as he applied in scarlet clothes, he was speedily turned out of the episcopal palace. He then became tutor in an opulent family, but soon quitted his situation in consequence of a dispute about play. Then he determined to emigrate to America. His relations, with much satisfaction, saw him set out for Cork on a good horse, with thirty pounds in his pocket. But in six weeks he came back on a miserable hack, without a penny, and informed his mother that the ship in which he had taken his passage, having got a fair wind while he was at a party of pleasure, had sailed without him. Then he resolved to study the law. A generous kinsman advanced fifty pounds. With this sum Goldsmith went to Dublin, was enticed into a gaming-house, and lost every shilling. He then thought of medicine. A small purse was made up; and in his twenty-fourth year he was sent to Edinburgh. At Edinburgh he passed eighteen months in nominal attendance on lectures, and picked up some superficial information about chemistry and natural history. Thence he went to Leyden, still pretending to study physic. He left that celebrated university, the third university at which he had resided, in his twenty-seventh year, without a degree, with the merest smattering of medical knowledge, and with no property but his clothes and his flute. His flute, however, proved a useful friend. He rambled on foot through Flanders, France, and Switzerland, playing tunes which everywhere set the peasantry dancing, and which often procured for him a supper and a bed. He wandered as far as Italy. His musical performances, indeed, were not to the taste of the Italians; but he contrived to live on the alms which he obtained at the gates of convents. It should, however, be observed that the stories which he told about this part of his life ought to be received with great caution; for strict veracity was never one of his virtues; and a man who is ordinarily inaccurate in narration is likely to be more than ordinarily inaccurate when he talks about his own travels. Goldsmith, indeed, was so regardless of truth as to assert in print that he was present at a most interesting conversation between Voltaire and Fontenelle, and that this conversation took place at Paris. Now it is certain that Voltaire never was within a hundred leagues of Paris during the whole time which Goldsmith passed on the Continent.

In 1756 the wanderer landed at Dover, without a shilling, without a friend, and without a calling. He had, indeed, if his own unsupported evidence may be trusted, obtained from the University of Padua a doctor's degree; but this dignity proved utterly useless to him. In England his flute was not in request; there were no convents; and he was forced to have recourse to a series of desperate expedients. He turned strolling player; but his face and figure were ill suited to the boards even of the humblest theatre. He pounded drugs and ran about London with phials for charitable chemists. He joined a swarm of beggars, which made its nest in Axe Yard. He was for a time usher of a school, and felt the miseries and humiliations of this situation so keenly that he thought it a promotion to be permitted to earn his bread as a bookseller's hack; but he soon found the new yoke more galling than the old one, and was glad to become an usher again. He obtained a medical appointment in the service of the East India Company; but the appointment was speedily revoked. Why it was revoked we are not told. The subject was one on which he never liked to talk. It is probable that he was incompetent to perform the duties of the place. Then he presented himself at Surgeons' Hall for examination, as mate to a naval hospital. Even to so humble a post he was found unequal. By this time the schoolmaster whom he had served for a morsel of food and the third part of a bed was no more. Nothing remained but to return to the lowest drudgery of literature. Goldsmith took a garret in a miserable court, to which he had to climb from the brink of Fleet Ditch by a dizzy ladder of flagstones called Breakneck Steps. The court and the ascent have long disappeared; but old Londoners well remember both. Here, at thirty, the unlucky adventurer sat down to toil like a galley slave.

In the succeeding six years he sent to the press some things which have survived, and many which have perished. He produced articles for reviews, magazines, and newspapers; children's books which, bound in gilt paper and adorned with hideous woodcuts, appeared in the window of the once far-famed shop at the corner of St. Paul's Churchyard; 'An Inquiry into the State of Polite Learning in Europe,' which, though of little or no value, is still reprinted among his works; a 'Life of Beau Nash,' which is not reprinted, though it well deserves to be so; a superficial and incorrect, but very readable, 'History of England,' in a series of letters purporting to be addressed by a nobleman to his son; and some very lively and amusing 'Sketches of London Society,' in a series of letters purporting to be addressed by a Chinese traveler to his friends. All these works were anonymous; but some of them were well known to be Goldsmith's; and he gradually rose in the estimation of the booksellers for whom he drudged. He was, indeed, emphatically a popular writer. For accurate research or grave disquisition he was not well qualified by nature or by education. He knew nothing accurately: his reading had been desultory; nor had he meditated deeply on what he had read. He had seen much of the world; but he had noticed and retained little more of what he had seen than some grotesque incidents and characters which happened to strike his fancy. But, though his mind was very scantily stored with materials, he used what materials he had in such a way as to produce a wonderful effect. There have been many greater writers; but perhaps no writer was ever more uniformly agreeable. His style was always pure and easy, and, on proper occasions, pointed and energetic. His narratives were always amusing, his descriptions always picturesque, his humour rich and joyous, yet not without an occasional tinge of amiable sadness. About everything that he wrote, serious or sportive, there was a certain natural grace and decorum, hardly to be expected from a man a great part of whose life had been passed among thieves and beggars, street-walkers and merry andrews, in those squalid dens which are the reproach of great capitals.

As his name gradually became known, the circle of his acquaintance widened. He was introduced to Johnson, who was then considered as the first of living English writers; to Reynolds, the first of English painters; and to Burke, who had not yet entered Parliament, but had distinguished himself greatly by his writings and by the eloquence of his conversation. With these eminent men Goldsmith became intimate. In 1763 he was one of the nine original members of that celebrated fraternity which has sometimes been called the Literary Club, but which has always disclaimed that epithet, and still glories in the simple name of The Club.

By this time Goldsmith had quitted his miserable dwelling at the top of Breakneck Steps, and had taken chambers in the more civilized region of the Inns of Court. But he was still often reduced to pitiable shifts. Towards the close of 1764 his rent was so long in arrear that his landlady one morning called in the help of a sheriff's officer. The debtor, in great perplexity, dispatched a messenger to Johnson; and Johnson, always friendly though often surly, sent back the messenger with a guinea, and promised to follow speedily. He came, and found that Goldsmith had changed the guinea, and was railing at the landlady over a bottle of Madeira. Johnson put the cork into the bottle, and entreated his friend to consider calmly how money was to be procured. Goldsmith said that he had a novel ready for the press. Johnson glanced at the manuscript, saw that there were good things in it, took it to a bookseller, sold it for 60 *l.*, and soon returned with the money. The rent was paid, and the sheriff's officer withdrew. According to one story, Goldsmith gave his landlady a sharp reprimand for her treatment of him; according to another, he insisted on her joining him in a bowl of punch. Both stories are probably true. The novel which was thus ushered into the world was 'The Vicar of Wakefield.'

But, before 'The Vicar of Wakefield' appeared in print, came the great crisis of Goldsmith's literary life. In Christmas week, 1764, he published a poem, entitled 'The Traveller.' It was the first work to which he had put his name; and it at once raised him to the rank of a legitimate English classic. The opinion of the most skilful critics was, that nothing finer had appeared in verse since the fourth book of 'The Dunciad.' In one respect 'The Traveller' differs from all Goldsmith's other writings. In general his designs were bad, and his execution good. In 'The Traveller,' the execution, though deserving of much praise, is far inferior to the design. No philosophical poem, ancient or modern, has a plan so noble, and at the same time so simple. An English wanderer, seated on a crag among the Alps, near the point where three great countries meet, looks down on the boundless prospect, reviews his long pilgrimage, recalls the varieties of scenery, of climate, of government, of religion, of national character, which he has observed, and comes to the conclusion, just or unjust, that our happiness depends little on political institutions, and much on the temper and regulation of our minds.

While the fourth edition of 'The Traveller' was on the counters of the booksellers, 'The Vicar of Wakefield' appeared, and rapidly obtained a popularity which has lasted down to our own time, and which is likely to last as long as our language. The fable is indeed one of the worst that ever was constructed. It wants, not merely that probability which ought to be found in a tale of common English life, but that consistency which ought to be found even in the wildest fiction about witches, giants, and fairies. But the earlier chapters have all the sweetness of pastoral poetry, together with all the vivacity of comedy. Moses and his spectacles, the vicar and his monogamy, the sharper and his cosmogony, the squire proving from Aristotle that relatives are related, Olivia preparing herself for the arduous task of converting a rakish lover by studying the controversy between Robinson Crusoe and Friday, the great ladies with their scandal about Sir Tomkyn's amours and Dr. Burdock's verses, and Mr. Burchell with his 'Fudge,' have caused as much harmless mirth as has ever been caused by matter packed into so small a number of pages. The latter part of the tale is unworthy of the beginning. As we approach the catastrophe, the absurdities lie thicker and thicker; and the gleams of pleasantry become rarer and rarer.

The success which had attended Goldsmith as a novelist emboldened him to try his fortune as a dramatist. He wrote 'The Good-natured Man,' a piece which had a worse fate than it deserved. Garrick refused to produce it at Drury Lane. It was acted at Covent Garden in 1768, but was coldly received. The author, however, cleared by his benefit nights, and by the sale of the copyright, not less than 500 *l.*, five times as much as he had made by 'The Traveller' and 'The Vicar of Wakefield' together. The plot of 'The Good natured Man' is, like almost all Goldsmith's plots, very ill constructed. But some passages are exquisitely ludicrous; much more ludicrous, indeed, than suited the taste of the town at that time. A canting, mawkish play, entitled 'False Delicacy,' had just had an immense run. Sentimentality was all the mode. During some years, more tears were shed at comedies than at tragedies; and a pleasantry which moved the audience to anything more than a grave smile was reprobated as low. It is not strange, therefore, that the very best scene in 'The Good-natured Man,' that in which Miss Richland finds her lover attended by the bailiff and the bailiff's follower in full court-dresses, should have been mercilessly hissed, and should have been omitted after the first night.

In 1770 appeared 'The Deserted Village.' In mere diction and versification, this celebrated poem is fully equal, perhaps superior, to 'The Traveller'; and it is generally preferred to 'The Traveller' by that large class of readers who think, with Bayes in 'The Rehearsal,' that the only use of a plan is to bring in fine things. More discerning judges, however, while they admire the beauty of the details, are shocked by one unpardonable fault which pervades the whole. The fault which we mean is not that theory about wealth and luxury which has so often been censured by political economists. The theory is indeed false: but the poem, considered merely as a poem, is not necessarily the worse on that account. The finest poem in the Latin language, indeed, the finest didactic poem in any language, was written in defense of the silliest and meanest of all systems of natural and moral philosophy. A poet may easily be pardoned for reasoning ill; but he cannot be pardoned for describing ill, for observing the world in which he lives so carelessly that his portraits bear no resemblance to the originals, for exhibiting as copies from real life monstrous combinations of things which never were and never could be found together. What would be thought of a painter who should mix August and January in one landscape, who should introduce a frozen river into a harvest scene? Would it be a sufficient defense of such a picture to say that every part was exquisitely coloured, that the green hedges, the apple-trees loaded with fruit, the wagons reeling under the yellow sheaves, and the sunburned reapers wiping their foreheads, were very fine, and that the ice and the boys sliding were also very fine? To such a picture 'The Deserted Village' bears a great resemblance. It is made up of incongruous parts. The village in its happy days is a true English village. The village in its decay is an Irish village. The felicity and the misery which Goldsmith has brought close together belong to two different countries, and to two different stages in the progress of society. He had assuredly never seen in his native island such a rural paradise, such a seat of plenty, content, and tranquillity, as his 'Auburn.' He had assuredly never seen in England all the inhabitants of such a paradise turned out of their homes in one day and forced to emigrate in a body to America. The hamlet he had probably seen in Kent; the ejectment he had probably seen in Munster; but, by joining the two, he has produced something which never was and never will be seen in any part of the world.

In 1773 Goldsmith tried his chance at Covent Garden with a second play, 'She Stoops to Conquer.' The manager was not without great difficulty induced to bring this piece out. The sentimental comedy still reigned; and Goldsmith's comedies were not sentimental. 'The Good-natured Man' had been too funny to succeed; yet the mirth of 'The Good-natured Man' was sober when compared with the rich drollery of 'She Stoops to Conquer,' which is, in truth, an incomparable farce in five acts. On this occasion, however, genius triumphed. Pit, boxes, and galleries were in a constant roar of laughter. If any bigoted admirer of Kelly and Cumberland ventured to hiss or groan, he was speedily silenced by a general cry of 'turn him out' or 'throw him over.' Two generations have since confirmed the verdict which was pronounced on that night.

While Goldsmith was writing 'The Deserted Village' and 'She Stoops to Conquer,' he was employed on works of a very different kind, works from which he derived little reputation but much profit. He compiled for the use of schools a 'History of Rome,' by which he made 300 *l.*, a 'History of England,' by which he made 600 *l.*, a 'History of Greece,' for which he received 250 *l.*, a 'Natural History,' for which the booksellers covenanted to pay him 800 guineas. These works he produced without any elaborate research, by merely selecting, abridging, and translating into his own clear, pure, and flowing language what he found in books well known to the world, but too bulky or too dry for boys and girls. He committed some strange blunders; for he knew nothing with accuracy. Thus, in his 'History of England' he tells us that Naseby is in Yorkshire; nor did he correct this mistake when the book was reprinted. He was very nearly hoaxed into putting into the 'History of Greece' an account of a battle between Alexander the Great and Montezuma. In his 'Animated Nature' he relates, with faith and with perfect gravity, all the most absurd lies which he could find in books of travels about gigantic Patagonians, monkeys that preach sermons, nightingales that repeat long conversations. 'If he can tell a horse from a cow,' says Johnson, 'that is the extent of his knowledge of zoölogy.' How little Goldsmith was qualified to write about the physical sciences is sufficiently proved by two anecdotes. He on one occasion denied that the sun is longer in the northern than in the southern signs. It was vain to cite the authority of Maupertuis. 'Maupertuis!' he cried, 'I understand those matters better than Maupertuis.' On another occasion he, in defiance of the evidence of his own senses, maintained obstinately, and even angrily, that he chewed his dinner by moving his upper jaw.

Yet, ignorant as Goldsmith was, few writers have done more to make the first steps in the laborious road to knowledge easy and pleasant. His compilations are widely distinguished from the compilations of ordinary book-makers. He was a great, perhaps an unequalled, master of the arts of selection and condensation. In these respects his histories of Rome and of England, and still more his own abridgments of these histories, well deserve to be studied. In general nothing is less attractive than an epitome: but the epitomes of Goldsmith, even when most concise, are always amusing; and to read them is considered by intelligent children, not as a task, but as a pleasure.

Goldsmith might now be considered as a prosperous man. He had the means of living in comfort, and even in what to one who had so often slept in barns and on bulks must have been luxury. His fame was great and was constantly rising. He lived in what was intellectually far the best society of the kingdom, in a society in which no talent or accomplishment was wanting, and in which the art of conversation was cultivated with splendid success. There probably were never four talkers more admirable in four different ways than Johnson, Burke, Beauclerk, and Garrick; and Goldsmith was on terms of intimacy with all the four. He aspired to share in their colloquial renown; but never was amibition more unfortunate. It may seem strange that a man who wrote with so much perspicuity, vivacity, and grace, should have been, whenever he took a part in conversation, an empty, noisy, blundering rattle. But on this point the evidence is overwhelming. So extraordinary was the contrast between Goldsmith's published works and the silly things which he said, that Horace Walpole described him as an inspired idiot. 'Noll,' said Garrick, 'wrote like an angel, and talked like poor Pol.' Chamier declared that it was a hard exercise of faith to believe that so foolish a chatterer could have really written 'The Traveller.' Even Boswell could say, with contemptuous compassion, that he liked very well to hear honest Goldsmith run on. 'Yes, sir,' said Johnson, 'but he should not like to hear himself.' Minds differ as rivers differ. There are transparent and sparkling rivers from which it is delightful to drink as they flow; to such rivers the minds of such men as Burke and Johnson may be compared. But there are rivers of which the water when first drawn is turbid and noisome, but becomes pellucid as crystal, and delicious to the taste, if it be suffered to stand till it has deposited a sediment; and such a river is a type of the mind of Goldsmith. His first thoughts on every subject were confused even to absurdity; but they required only a little time to work themselves clear. When he wrote they had that time; and therefore his readers pronounced him a man of genius: but when he talked he talked nonsense, and made himself the laughingstock of his hearers. He was painfully sensible of his inferiority in conversation; he felt every failure keenly; yet he had not sufficient judgment and self-command to hold his tongue. His animal spirits and vanity were always impelling him to try to do the one thing which he could not do. After every attempt he felt that he had exposed himself, and writhed with shame and vexation; yet the next moment he began again.

His associates seem to have regarded him with kindness, which, in spite of their admiration of his writings, was not unmixed with contempt. In truth, there was in his character much to love, but very little to respect. His heart was soft even to weakness: he was so generous that he quite forgot to be just; he forgave injuries so readily that he might be said to invite them; and was so liberal to beggars that he had nothing left for his tailor and his butcher. He was vain, sensual, frivolous, profuse, improvident. One vice of a darker shade was imputed to him, envy. But there is not the least reason to believe that this bad passion, though it sometimes made him wince and utter fretful exclamations, ever impelled him to injure by wicked arts the reputation of any of his rivals. The truth probably is, that he was not more envious, but merely less prudent, than his neighbours. His heart was on his lips. All those small jealousies, which are but too common among men of letters, but which a man of letters who is also a man of the world does his best to conceal, Goldsmith avowed with the simplicity of a child. When he was envious, instead of affecting indifference, instead of damning with faint praise, instead of doing injuries slyly and in the dark, he told everybody that he was envious. 'Do not, pray, do not talk of Johnson in such terms,' he said to Boswell; 'you harrow up my very soul.' George Steevens and Cumberland were men far too cunning to say such a thing. They would have echoed the praises of the man whom they envied, and then have sent to the newspapers anonymous libels upon him. Both what was good and what was bad in Goldsmith's character was to his associates a perfect security that he would never commit such villany. He was neither ill-natured enough, nor long-headed enough, to be guilty of any malicious act which required contrivance and disguise.

Goldsmith has sometimes been represented as a man of genius, cruelly treated by the world, and doomed to struggle with difficulties which at last broke his heart. But no representation can be more remote from the truth. He did, indeed, go through much sharp misery before he had done anything considerable in literature. But, after his name had appeared on the title-page of 'The Traveller,' he had none but himself to blame for his distresses. His average income, during the last seven years of his life, certainly exceeded 400 *l.* a year; and 400 *l.* a year ranked, among the incomes of that day, at least as high as 800 *l.* a year would rank at present. A single man living in the Temple with 400 *l.* a year might then be called opulent. Not one in ten of the young gentlemen of good families who were studying the law there had so much. But all the wealth which Lord Clive had brought from Bengal, and Sir Lawrence Dundas from Germany, joined together, would not have sufficed for Goldsmith. He spent twice as much as he had. He wore fine clothes, gave dinners of several courses, paid court to venal beauties. He had also, it should be remembered, to the honour of his heart, though not of his head, a guinea, or five, or ten, according to the state of his purse, ready for any tale of distress, true or false. But it was not in dress or feasting, in promiscuous amours or promiscuous charities, that his chief expense lay. He had been from boyhood a gambler, and at once the most sanguine and the most unskilful of gamblers. For a time he put off the day of inevitable ruin by temporary expedients. He obtained advances from booksellers, by promising to execute works which he never began. But at length this source of supply failed. He owed more than 2000 *l.*, and he saw no hope of extrication from his embarrassments. His spirits and health gave way. He was attacked by a nervous fever, which he thought himself competent to treat. It would have been happy for him if his medical skill had been appreciated as justly by himself as by others. Notwithstanding the degree which he pretended to have received at Padua, he could procure no patients. 'I do not practice,' he once said; 'I make it a rule to prescribe only for my friends.' 'Pray, dear Doctor,' said Beauclerk, 'alter your rule; and prescribe only for your enemies.' Goldsmith now, in spite of this excellent advice, prescribed for himself. The remedy aggravated the malady. The sick man was induced to call in real physicians; and they at one time imagined that they had cured the disease. Still his weakness and restlessness continued. He could get no sleep. He could take no food. 'You are worse,' said one of his medical attendants, 'than you should be from the degree of fever which you have. Is your mind at ease?' 'No, it is not,' were the last recorded words of Oliver Goldsmith. He died on the third of April 1774, in his forty-sixth year. He was laid in the churchyard of the Temple; but the spot was not marked by any inscription, and is now forgotten. The coffin was followed by Burke and Reynolds. Both these great men were sincere mourners. Burke, when he heard of Goldsmith's death, had burst into a flood of tears. Reynolds had been so much moved by the news that he had flung aside his brush and palette for the day.

A short time after Goldsmith's death, a little poem appeared, which will, as long as our language lasts, associate the names of his two illustrious friends with his own. It has already been mentioned that he sometimes felt keenly the sarcasm which his wild blundering talk brought upon him. He was, not long before his last illness, provoked into retaliating. He wisely betook himself to his pen; and at that weapon he proved himself a match for all his assailants together. Within a small compass he drew with a singularly easy and vigorous pencil the characters of nine or ten of his intimate associates. Though this little work did not receive his last touches, it must always be regarded as a masterpiece. It is impossible, however, not to wish that four or five likenesses which have no interest for posterity were wanting to that noble gallery, and that their places were supplied by sketches of Johnson and Gibbon, as happy and vivid as the sketches of Burke and Garrick.

Some of Goldsmith's friends and admirers honoured him with a cenotaph in Westminster Abbey. Nollekens was the sculptor; and Johnson wrote the inscription. It is much to be lamented that Johnson did not leave to posterity a more durable and a more valuable memorial of his friend. A life of Goldsmith would have been an inestimable addition to the Lives of the Poets. No man appreciated Goldsmith's writings more justly than Johnson: no man was better acquainted with Goldsmith's character and habits; and no man was more competent to delineate with truth and spirit the peculiarities of a mind in which great powers were found in company with great weaknesses. But the list of poets to whose works Johnson was requested by the booksellers to furnish prefaces ended with Lyttelton, who died in 1773. The line seems to have been drawn expressly for the purpose of excluding the person whose portrait would have most fitly closed the series. Goldsmith, however, has been fortunate in his biographers. Within a few years his life has been written by Mr. Prior, by Mr. Washington Irving, and by Mr. Forster. The diligence of Mr. Prior deserves great praise; the style of Mr. Washington Irving is always pleasing; but the highest place must, in justice, be assigned to the eminently interesting work of Mr. Forster.

1843

VICTORIAN AGE

POETRY

Alfred (Lord) Tennyson (1809–1892)

CLARIBEL

A MELODY

Where Claribel low-lieth
The breezes pause and die,
Letting the rose-leaves fall:
But the solemn oak-tree sigheth,
Thick-leaved, ambrosial,
With an ancient melody
Of an inward agony,
Where Claribel low-lieth.

At eve the beetle boometh
Athwart the thicket lone:
At noon the wild bee hummeth
About the mossed headstone:
At midnight the moon cometh,
And looketh down alone.
Her song the lintwhite swelleth,
The clear-voiced mavis dwelleth,
The callow throstle lispeth,
The slumbrous wave outwelleth,
The babbling runnel crispeth,
The hollow grot replieth
Where Claribel low-lieth.

1830

MARIANA

With blackest moss the flower-plots
Were thickly crusted, one and all:
The rusted nails fell from the knots
That held the pear to the gable-wall.
The broken sheds looked sad and strange:
Unlifted was the clinking latch;
Weeded and worn the ancient thatch
Upon the lonely moated grange.
She only said, 'My life is dreary,
He cometh not,' she said;
She said, 'I am aweary, aweary,
I would that I were dead!'

Her tears fell with the dews at even;
Her tears fell ere the dews were dried;
She could not look on the sweet heaven,
Either at morn or eventide.
After the flitting of the bats,
When thickest dark did trance the sky,
She drew her casement curtain by,
And glanced athwart the glooming flats.
She only said, 'The night is dreary,
He cometh not,' she said;
She said, 'I am aweary, aweary,
I would that I were dead!'

Upon the middle of the night,
Waking she heard the night-fowl crow:
The cock sung out an hour ere light:
From the dark fen the oxen's low
Came to her: without hope of change,
In sleep she seemed to walk forlorn,
Till cold winds woke the gray-eyed morn
About the lonely moated grange.
She only said, 'The day is dreary,
He cometh not,' she said;
She said, 'I am aweary, aweary,
I would that I were dead!'

About a stone-cast from the wall
A sluice with blackened waters slept,
And o'er it many, round and small,
The clustered marish-mosses crept.
Hard by a poplar shook alway,
All silver-green with gnarlèd bark:
For leagues no other tree did mark
The level waste, the rounding gray.
She only said, 'My life is dreary,
He cometh not,' she said;
She said, 'I am aweary, aweary,
I would that I were dead!'

And ever when the moon was low,
And the shrill winds were up and away,
In the white curtain, to and fro,
She saw the gusty shadow sway.
But when the moon was very low,
And wild winds bound within their cell,
The shadow of the poplar fell

Upon her bed, across her brow.
She only said, 'The night is dreary,
He cometh not,' she said;
She said, 'I am aweary, aweary,
I would that I were dead!'

All day within the dreamy house,
The doors upon their hinges creaked;
The blue fly sung in the pane; the mouse
Behind the mouldering wainscot shrieked,
Or from the crevice peered about.
Old faces glimmered through the doors,
Old footsteps trod the upper floors,
Old voices called her from without.
She only said, 'My life is dreary,
He cometh not,' she said;
She said, 'I am aweary, aweary,
I would that I were dead!'

The sparrow's chirrup on the roof,
The slow clock ticking, and the sound
Which to the wooing wind aloof
The poplar made, did all confound
Her sense; but most she loathed the hour
When the thick-moted sunbeam lay
Athwart the chambers, and the day
Was sloping toward his western bower.
Then, said she, 'I am very dreary,
He will not come,' she said;
She wept, 'I am aweary, aweary,
Oh God, that I were dead!'

1830

THE LADY OF SHALOTT

PART I

On either side the river lie
Long fields of barley and of rye,
That clothe the wold and meet the sky;
And through the field the road runs by
To many-towered Camelot;
And up and down the people go,
Gazing where the lilies blow
Round an island there below,
The island of Shalott.

Willows whiten, aspens quiver,
Little breezes dusk and shiver
Through the wave that runs for ever
By the island in the river
Flowing down to Camelot.
Four gray walls, and four gray towers,
Overlook a space of flowers,
And the silent isle imbowers
The Lady of Shalott.

By the margin, willow-veiled
Slide the heavy barges trailed
By slow horses; and unhailed
The shallop flitteth silken-sailed
Skimming down to Camelot:
But who hath seen her wave her hand?
Or at the casement seen her stand?
Or is she known in all the land,
The Lady of Shalott?

Only reapers, reaping early
In among the bearded barley,
Hear a song that echoes cheerly
From the river winding clearly,
Down to towered Camelot:
And by the moon the reaper weary,
Piling sheaves in uplands airy,
Listening, whispers ''T is the fairy
Lady of Shalott.'

PART II

There she weaves by night and day
A magic web with colours gay.
She has heard a whisper say,
A curse is on her if she stay
To look down to Camelot.
She knows not what the curse may be,
And so she weaveth steadily,
And little other care hath she,
The Lady of Shalott.

And moving through a mirror clear
That hangs before her all the year,
Shadows of the world appear.
There she sees the highway near
Winding down to Camelot:
There the river eddy whirls,
And there the surly village-churls,
And the red cloaks of market girls,
Pass onward from Shalott.

Sometimes a troop of damsels glad,
An abbot on an ambling pad,
Sometimes a curly shepherd-lad,
Or long-haired page in crimson clad,
Goes by to towered Camelot:
And sometimes through the mirror blue
The knights come riding two and two:
She hath no loyal knight and true,
The Lady of Shalott.

But in her web she still delights
To weave the mirror's magic sights,
For often through the silent nights
A funeral, with plumes and lights
And music, went to Camelot:
Or when the moon was overhead,
Came two young lovers lately wed;
'I am half sick of shadows,' said
The Lady of Shalott.

PART III

A bow-shot from her bower-eaves,
He rode between the barley-sheaves,
The sun came dazzling through the leaves,
And flamed upon the brazen greaves
Of bold Sir Lancelot.
A red-cross knight for ever kneeled
To a lady in his shield,
That sparkled on the yellow field,
Beside remote Shalott.

The gemmy bridle glittered free,
Like to some branch of stars we see
Hung in the golden Galaxy.
The bridle bells rang merrily
As he rode down to Camelot:
And from his blazoned baldric slung
A mighty silver bugle hung,
And as he rode his armour rung,
Beside remote Shalott.

All in the blue unclouded weather
Thick-jewelled shone the saddle-leather,
The helmet and the helmet-feather
Burned like one burning flame together,
As he rode down to Camelot.
As often through the purple night,
Below the starry clusters bright,
Some bearded meteor, trailing light,
Moves over still Shalott.

His broad clear brow in sunlight glowed;
On burnished hooves his war-horse trode;
From underneath his helmet flowed
His coal-black curls as on he rode,
As he rode down to Camelot.
From the bank and from the river
He flashed into the crystal mirror,
'Tirra lirra,' by the river
Sang Sir Lancelot.

She left the web, she left the loom,
She made three paces through the room,
She saw the water-lily bloom,
She saw the helmet and the plume,
She looked down to Camelot.
Out flew the web and floated wide;
The mirror cracked from side to side;
'The curse is come upon me,' cried
The Lady of Shalott.

PART IV

In the stormy east-wind straining,
The pale yellow woods were waning,
The broad stream in his banks complaining,
Heavily the low sky raining
Over towered Camelot;
Down she came and found a boat
Beneath a willow left afloat,
And round about the prow she wrote
The Lady of Shalott.

And down the river's dim expanse
Like some bold seër in a trance,
Seeing all his own mischance —
With a glassy countenance
Did she look to Camelot.
And at the closing of the day
She loosed the chain, and down she lay;
The broad stream bore her far away,
The Lady of Shalott.

Lying, robed in snowy white
That loosely flew to left and right —
The leaves upon her falling light —
Through the noises of the night
She floated down to Camelot:
And as the boat-head wound along
The willowy hills and fields among,
They heard her singing her last song,
The Lady of Shalott.

Heard a carol, mournful, holy,
Chanted loudly, chanted lowly,
Till her blood was frozen slowly,
And her eyes were darkened wholly,
Turned to towered Camelot.
For ere she reached upon the tide
The first house by the water-side,
Singing in her song she died,
The Lady of Shalott.

Under tower and balcony,
By garden-wall and gallery,
A gleaming shape she floated by,
Dead-pale between the houses high,
Silent into Camelot.
Out upon the wharfs they came,
Knight and burgher, lord and dame,
And round the prow they read her name,
The Lady of Shalott.

Who is this? and what is here?
And in the lighted palace near
Died the sound of royal cheer;
And they crossed themselves for fear,
All the knights at Camelot:
But Lancelot mused a little space;
He said, 'She has a lovely face;
God in his mercy lend her grace,
The Lady of Shalott.'

1832–3

THE PALACE OF ART

I BUILT my soul a lordly pleasure-house,
Wherein at ease for aye to dwell.
I said, 'O Soul, make merry and carouse,
Dear soul, for all is well.'

A huge crag-platform, smooth as burnished brass
I chose. The rangèd ramparts bright
From level meadow-bases of deep grass
Suddenly scaled the light.

Thereon I built it firm. Of ledge or shelf
The rock rose clear, or winding stair.
My soul would live alone unto herself
In her high palace there.

And 'While the world runs round and round,' I said,
'Reign thou apart, a quiet king,
Still as, while Saturn whirls, his stedfast shade
Sleeps on his luminous ring.'

To which my soul made answer readily:
'Trust me, in bliss I shall abide
In this great mansion, that is built for me,
So royal-rich and wide.'

. . . .
. . . .

Four courts I made, East, West and South and North,
In each a squarèd lawn, wherefrom
The golden gorge of dragons spouted forth
A flood of fountain-foam.

And round the cool green courts there ran a row
Of cloisters, branched like mighty woods,
Echoing all night to that sonorous flow
Of spouted fountain-floods.

And round the roofs a gilded gallery
That lent broad verge to distant lands,
Far as the wild swan wings, to where the sky
Dipt down to sea and sands.

From those four jets four currents in one swell
Across the mountain streamed below
In misty folds, that floating as they fell
Lit up a torrent-bow.

And high on every peak a statue seemed
To hang on tiptoe, tossing up
A cloud of incense of all odour steamed
From out a golden cup.

So that she thought, 'And who shall gaze upon
My palace with unblinded eyes,
While this great bow will waver in the sun,
And that sweet incense rise?'

For that sweet incense rose and never failed,
And, while day sank or mounted higher,
The light aërial gallery, golden-railed,
Burnt like a fringe of fire.

Likewise the deep-set windows, stained and traced,
Would seem slow-flaming crimson fires
From shadowed grots of arches interlaced,
And tipt with frost-like spires.

. . . .
. . . .

Full of long-sounding corridors it was,
That over-vaulted grateful gloom,
Through which the livelong day my soul did pass,
Well-pleased, from room to room.

Full of great rooms and small the palace stood,
All various, each a perfect whole
From living Nature, fit for every mood
And change of my still soul.

For some were hung with arras green and blue,
Showing a gaudy summer-morn,
Where with puffed cheek the belted hunter blew
His wreathèd bugle-horn.

One seemed all dark and red — a tract of sand,
And some one pacing there alone,
Who paced for ever in a glimmering land,
Lit with a low large moon.

One showed an iron coast and angry waves.
You seemed to hear them climb and fall
And roar rock-thwarted under bellowing caves,
Beneath the windy wall.

And one, a full-fed river winding slow
By herds upon an endless plain,
The ragged rims of thunder brooding low,
With shadow-streaks of rain.

And one, the reapers at their sultry toil.
In front they bound the sheaves. Behind
Were realms of upland, prodigal in oil,
And hoary to the wind.

And one a foreground black with stones and slags,
Beyond, a line of heights, and higher

All barred with long white cloud the scornful crags,
And highest, snow and fire.

And one, an English home — gray twilight poured
On dewy pastures, dewy trees,
Softer than sleep — all things in order stored,
A haunt of ancient Peace.

Nor these alone, but every landscape fair,
As fit for every mood of mind,
Or gay, or grave, or sweet, or stern, was there
Not less than truth designed.

. . . .
. . . .

Or the maid-mother by a crucifix,
In tracts of pasture sunny-warm,
Beneath branch-work of costly sardonyx
Sat smiling, babe in arm.

Or in a clear-walled city on the sea,
Near gilded organ-pipes, her hair
Wound with white roses, slept St. Cecily;
An angel looked at her.

Or thronging all one porch of Paradise
A group of Houris bowed to see
The dying Islamite, with hands and eyes
That said, We wait for thee.

Or mythic Uther's deeply-wounded son
In some fair space of sloping greens
Lay, dozing in the vale of Avalon,
And watched by weeping queens.

Or hollowing one hand against his ear,
To list a foot-fall, ere he saw
The wood-nymph, stayed the Ausonian king to hear
Of wisdom and of law.

Or over hills with peaky tops engrailed,
And many a tract of palm and rice,
The throne of Indian Cama slowly sailed
A summer fanned with spice.

Or sweet Europa's mantle blew unclasped,
From off her shoulder backward borne:
From one hand drooped a crocus: one hand grasped
The mild bull's golden horn.

Or else flushed Ganymede, his rosy thigh
Half-buried in the Eagle's down,
Sole as a flying star shot through the sky
Above the pillared town.

Nor these alone: but every legend fair
Which the supreme Caucasian mind
Carved out of Nature for itself, was there,
Not less than life, designed.

. . . .
. . . .

Then in the towers I placed great bells that swung,
Moved of themselves, with silver sound;
And with choice paintings of wise men I hung
The royal dais round.

For there was Milton like a seraph strong,
Beside him Shakespeare bland and mild;
And there the world-worn Dante grasped his song,
And somewhat grimly smiled.

And there the Ionian father of the rest;
A million wrinkles carved his skin;
A hundred winters snowed upon his breast,
From cheek and throat and chin.

Above, the fair hall-ceiling stately-set
Many an arch high up did lift,
And angels rising and descending met
With interchange of gift.

Below was all mosaic choicely planned
With cycles of the human tale
Of this wide world, the times of every land
So wrought, they will not fail.

The people here, a beast of burden slow,
Toiled onward, pricked with goads and stings;
Here played, a tiger, rolling to and fro
The heads and crowns of kings;

Here rose, an athlete, strong to break or bind
All force in bonds that might endure,
And here once more like some sick man declined,
And trusted any cure.

But over these she trod: and those great bells
Began to chime. She took her throne:
She sat betwixt the shining Oriels,
To sing her songs alone.

And through the topmost Oriels' coloured flame
Two godlike faces gazed below;
Plato the wise, and large-browed Verulam,
The first of those who know.

And all those names, that in their motion were
Full-welling fountain-heads of change,
Betwixt the slender shafts were blazoned fair
In diverse raiment strange:

Through which the lights, rose, amber, emerald, blue,
Flushed in her temples and her eyes,
And from her lips, as morn from Memnon, drew
Rivers of melodies.

No nightingale delighteth to prolong
Her low preamble all alone,
More than my soul to hear her echoed song
Throb through the ribbèd stone;

Singing and murmuring in her feastful mirth,
Joying to feel herself alive,
Lord over Nature, Lord of the visible earth,
Lord of the senses five;

Communing with herself: 'All these are mine,
And let the world have peace or wars,
'T is one to me.' She — when young night divine
Crowned dying day with stars,

Making sweet close of his delicious toils —
Lit light in wreaths and anadems,
And pure quintessences of precious oils
In hollowed moons of gems,

To mimic heaven; and clapt her hands and cried,
'I marvel if my still delight
In this great house so royal-rich, and wide,
Be flattered to the height.

'O all things fair to sate my various eyes!
O shapes and hues that please me well!
O silent faces of the Great and Wise,
My Gods, with whom I dwell!

'O God-like isolation which art mine,
I can but count thee perfect gain,
What time I watch the darkening droves of swine
That range on yonder plain.

'In filthy sloughs they roll a prurient skin,
They graze and wallow, breed and sleep;
And oft some brainless devil enters in,
And drives them to the deep.'

Then of the moral instinct would she prate
And of the rising from the dead,
As hers by right of full-accomplished Fate;
And at the last she said:

'I take possession of man's mind and deed.
I care not what the sects may brawl.
I sit as God holding no form of creed,
But contemplating all.'

. . . . .
. . . . .

Full oft the riddle of the painful earth
Flashed through her as she sat alone,
Yet not the less held she her solemn mirth,
And intellectual throne.

And so she throve and prospered: so three years
She prospered: on the fourth she fell,
Like Herod, when the shout was in his ears,
Struck through with pangs of hell.

Lest she should fail and perish utterly,
God, before whom ever lie bare
The abysmal deeps of Personality,
Plagued her with sore despair.

When she would think, where'er she turned her sight
The airy hand confusion wrought,
Wrote, 'Mene, mene,' and divided quite
The kingdom of her thought.

Deep dread and loathing of her solitude
Fell on her, from which mood was born
Scorn of herself; again, from out that mood
Laughter at her self-scorn.

'What! is not this my place of strength,' she said,
'My spacious mansion built for me,
Whereof the strong foundation-stones were laid
Since my first memory?'

But in dark corners of her palace stood
Uncertain shapes; and unawares
On white-eyed phantasms weeping tears of blood,
And horrible nightmares,

And hollow shades, enclosing hearts of flame,
And, with dim fretted foreheads all,
On corpses three-months-old at noon she came,
That stood against the wall.

A spot of dull stagnation, without light
Or power of movement, seemed my soul,
'Mid onward-sloping motions infinite
Making for one sure goal.

A still salt pool, locked in with bars of sand,
Left on the shore; that hears all night
The plunging seas draw backward from the land
Their moon-led waters white.

A star that with the choral starry dance
Joined not, but stood, and standing saw
The hollow orb of moving Circumstance
Rolled round by one fixed law.

Back on herself her serpent pride had curled.
'No voice,' she shrieked in that lone hall,
'No voice breaks through the stillness of this world:
One deep, deep silence all!'

She, mouldering with the dull earth's mouldering sod,
Inwrapt tenfold in slothful shame,
Lay there exiled from eternal God,
Lost to her place and name;

And death and life she hated equally,
And nothing saw, for her despair,
But dreadful time, dreadful eternity,
No comfort anywhere;

Remaining utterly confused with fears,
And ever worse with growing time,
And ever unrelieved by dismal tears,
And all alone in crime:

Shut up as in a crumbling tomb, girt round
With blackness as a solid wall,
Far off she seemed to hear the dully sound
Of human footsteps fall.

As in strange lands a traveller walking slow,
In doubt and great perplexity,
A little before moon-rise hears the low
Moan of an unknown sea;

And knows not if it be thunder, or a sound
Of rocks thrown down, or one deep cry
Of great wild beasts; then thinketh, 'I have found
A new land, but I die.'

She howled aloud, 'I am on fire within.
There comes no murmur of reply.
What is it that will take away my sin,
And save me lest I die?'

So when four years were wholly finished,
She threw her royal robes away.
'Make me a cottage in the vale,' she said,
'Where I may mourn and pray.

'Yet pull not down my palace towers, that are
So lightly, beautifully built:
Perchance I may return with others there
When I have purged my guilt.'

1832–3

A DREAM OF FAIR WOMEN

I READ, before my eyelids dropt their shade,
'The Legend of Good Women,' long ago
Sung by the morning star of song, who made
His music heard below;

Dan Chaucer, the first warbler, whose sweet breath
Preluded those melodious bursts that fill
The spacious times of great Elizabeth
With sounds that echo still.

And, for a while, the knowledge of his art
Held me above the subject, as strong gales
Hold swollen clouds from raining, tho' my heart,
Brimful of those wild tales,

Charged both mine eyes with tears. In every land
I saw, wherever light illumineth,
Beauty and anguish walking hand in hand
The downward slope to death.

Those far-renownèd brides of ancient song
Peopled the hollow dark, like burning stars,
And I heard sounds of insult, shame, and wrong,
And trumpets blown for wars;

And clattering flints battered with clanging hoofs;
And I saw crowds in columned sanctuaries;
And forms that passed at windows and on roofs
Of marble palaces;

Corpses across the threshold; heroes tall
Dislodging pinnacle and parapet
Upon the tortoise creeping to the wall;
Lances in ambush set;

And high shrine-doors burst through with heated blasts
That run before the fluttering tongues of fire;
White surf wind-scattered over sails and masts,
And ever climbing higher;

Squadrons and squares of men in brazen plates,
Scaffolds, still sheets of water, divers woes,
Ranges of glimmering vaults with iron grates,
And hushed seraglios.

So shape chased shape as swift as, when to land
Bluster the winds and tides the self-same way,
Crisp foam-flakes scud along the level sand,
Torn from the fringe of spray.

I started once, or seemed to start in pain,
Resolved on noble things, and strove to speak,
As when a great thought strikes along the brain,
And flushes all the cheek.

And once my arm was lifted to hew down
A cavalier from off his saddle-bow,
That bore a lady from a leaguered town;
And then, I know not how,

All those sharp fancies, by down-lapsing thought
Streamed onward, lost their edges, and did creep
Rolled on each other, rounded, smoothed, and brought
Into the gulfs of sleep.

At last methought that I had wandered far
In an old wood: fresh-washed in coolest dew
The maiden splendours of the morning star
Shook in the stedfast blue.

Enormous elm-tree-boles did stoop and lean
Upon the dusky brushwood underneath
Their broad curved branches, fledged with clearest green,
New from its silken sheath.

The dim red morn had died, her journey done,
And with dead lips smiled at the twilight plain,
Half-fall'n across the threshold of the sun,
Never to rise again.

There was no motion in the dumb dead air,
Not any song of bird or sound of rill;
Gross darkness of the inner sepulchre
Is not so deadly still

As that wide forest. Growths of jasmine turned
Their humid arms festooning tree to tree,
And at the root through lush green grasses burned
The red anemone.

I knew the flowers, I knew the leaves, I knew
The tearful glimmer of the languid dawn
On those long, rank, dark wood-walks drenched in dew,
Leading from lawn to lawn.

The smell of violets, hidden in the green,
Poured back into my empty soul and frame
The times when I remember to have been
Joyful and free from blame.

And from within me a clear under-tone
Thrilled through mine ears in that unblissful clime,
'Pass freely through: the wood is all thine own,
Until the end of time.'

At length I saw a lady within call,
Stiller than chiselled marble, standing there;
A daughter of the gods, divinely tall,
And most divinely fair.

Her loveliness with shame and with surprise
Froze my swift speech: she turning on my face
The star-like sorrows of immortal eyes,
Spoke slowly in her place.

'I had great beauty: ask thou not my name:
No one can be more wise than destiny.
Many drew swords and died. Where'er I came
I brought calamity.'

'No marvel, sovereign lady: in fair field
Myself for such a face had boldly died,'
I answered free; and turning I appealed
To one that stood beside.

But she, with sick and scornful looks averse,
To her full height her stately stature draws;
'My youth,' she said, 'was blasted with a curse:
This woman was the cause.

'I was cut off from hope in that sad place,
Which men called Aulis in those iron years:
My father held his hand upon his face;
I, blinded with my tears,

'Still strove to speak: my voice was thick with sighs
As in a dream. Dimly I could descry
The stern black-bearded kings with wolfish eyes,
Waiting to see me die.

'The high masts flickered as they lay afloat;
The crowds, the temples, wavered, and the shore;

The bright death quivered at the victim's
throat;
Touched; and I knew no more.'

Whereto the other with a downward brow:
'I would the white cold heavy-plunging
foam,
Whirled by the wind, had rolled me deep be-
low,
Then when I left my home.'

Her slow full words sank through the silence
drear,
As thunder-drops fall on a sleeping sea:
Sudden I heard a voice that cried, 'Come
here,
That I may look on thee.'

I turning saw, throned on a flowery rise,
One sitting on a crimson scarf unrolled;
A queen, with swarthy cheeks and bold black
eyes,
Brow-bound with burning gold.

She, flashing forth a haughty smile, began:
'I governed men by change, and so I
swayed
All moods. 'T is long since I have seen a man.
Once, like the moon, I made

'The ever-shifting currents of the blood
According to my humour ebb and flow.
I have no men to govern in this wood:
That makes my only woe.

'Nay — yet it chafes me that I could not
bend
One will; nor tame and tutor with mine
eye
That dull cold-blooded Cæsar. Prythee,
friend,
Where is Mark Antony?

'The man, my lover, with whom I rode sub-
lime
On Fortune's neck: we sat as God by God:
The Nilus would have risen before his time
And flooded at our nod.

'We drank the Libyan Sun to sleep, and
lit
Lamps which out-burned Canopus. O my
life
In Egypt! O the dalliance and the wit,
The flattery and the strife,

'And the wild kiss, when fresh from war's
alarms,
My Hercules, my Roman Antony,
My mailed Bacchus leapt into my arms,
Contented there to die!

'And there he died: and when I heard my
name
Sighed forth with life I would not brook
my fear
Of the other: with a worm I balked his
fame.
What else was left? look here!'

(With that she tore her robe apart, and
half
The polished argent of her breast to
sight
Laid bare. Thereto she pointed with a laugh,
Showing the aspick's bite.)

'I died a Queen. The Roman soldier found
Me lying dead, my crown about my
brows,
A name for ever! — lying robed and crowned,
Worthy a Roman spouse.

Her warbling voice, a lyre of widest range
Struck by all passion, did fall down and
glance
From tone to tone, and glided through all
change
Of liveliest utterance.

When she made pause I knew not for delight;
Because with sudden motion from the
ground
She raised her piercing orbs, and filled with
light
The interval of sound.

Still with their fires Love tipt his keenest
darts;
As once they drew into two burning rings
All beams of Love, melting the mighty
hearts
Of captains and of kings.

Slowly my sense undazzled. Then I heard
A noise of some one coming through the
lawn,
And singing clearer than the crested bird
That claps his wings at dawn.

'The torrent brooks of hallowed Israel
From craggy hollows pouring, late and
soon,
Sound all night long, in falling through the
dell,
Far-heard beneath the moon.

'The balmy moon of blessèd Israel
Floods all the deep-blue gloom with beams
divine:
All night the splintered crags that wall the
dell
With spires of silver shine.'

As one that museth where broad sunshine laves
  The lawn by some cathedral, through the door
Hearing the holy organ rolling waves
  Of sound on roof and floor

Within, and anthem sung, is charmed and tied
  To where he stands, — so stood I, when that flow
Of music left the lips of her that died
  To save her father's vow;

The daughter of the warrior Gileadite,
  A maiden pure; as when she went along
From Mizpeh's towered gate with welcome light,
  With timbrel and with song.

My words leapt forth: 'Heaven heads the count of crimes
  With that wild oath.' She rendered answer high:
'Not so, nor once alone; a thousand times
  I would be born and die.

'Single I grew, like some green plant, whose root
  Creeps to the garden water-pipes beneath,
Feeding the flower; but ere my flower to fruit
  Changed, I was ripe for death.

'My God, my land, my father — these did move
  Me from my bliss of life, that Nature gave,
Lowered softly with a threefold cord of love
  Down to a silent grave.

'And I went mourning, "No fair Hebrew boy
  Shall smile away my maiden blame among
The Hebrew mothers" — emptied of all joy,
  Leaving the dance and song,

'Leaving the olive-gardens far below,
  Leaving the promise of my bridal bower,
The valleys of grape-loaded vines that glow
  Beneath the battled tower.

'The light white cloud swam over us. Anon
  We heard the lion roaring from his den;
We saw the large white stars rise one by one,
  Or, from the darkened glen,

'Saw God divide the night with flying flame,
  And thunder on the everlasting hills.
I heard Him, for He spake, and grief became
  A solemn scorn of ills.

'When the next moon was rolled into the sky,
  Strength came to me that equalled my desire.
How beautiful a thing it was to die
  For God and for my sire!

'It comforts me in this one thought to dwell,
  That I subdued me to my father's will;
Because the kiss he gave me, ere I fell,
  Sweetens the spirit still.

'Moreover it is written that my race
  Hewed Ammon, hip and thigh, from Aroer
On Arnon unto Minneth.' Here her face
  Glowed, as I looked at her.

She locked her lips: she left me where I stood:
  'Glory to God,' she sang, and past afar,
Thridding the sombre boskage of the wood,
  Toward the morning-star.

Losing her carol I stood pensively,
  As one that from a casement leans his head,
When midnight bells cease ringing suddenly,
  And the old year is dead.

'Alas! alas!' a low voice, full of care,
  Murmured beside me: 'Turn and look on me:
I am that Rosamond, whom men call fair,
  If what I was I be.

'Would I had been some maiden coarse and poor!
  O me, that I should ever see the light!
Those dragon eyes of angered Eleanor
  Do hunt me, day and night.'

She ceased in tears, fallen from hope and trust:
  To whom the Egyptian: 'Oh, you tamely died!
You should have clung to Fulvia's waist, and thrust
  The dagger through her side.'

With that sharp sound the white dawn's creeping beams,
  Stol'n to my brain, dissolved the mystery
Of folded sleep. The captain of my dreams
  Ruled in the eastern sky.

Morn broadened on the borders of the dark,
  Ere I saw her, who clasped in her last trance
Her murdered father's head, or Joan of Arc,
  A light of ancient France;

Or her who knew that Love can vanquish Death,
  Who kneeling, with one arm about her king,
Drew forth the poison with her balmy breath,
  Sweet as new buds in Spring.

No memory labours longer from the deep
  Gold-mines of thought to lift the hidden ore
That glimpses, moving up, than I from sleep
  To gather and tell o'er

Each little sound and sight. With what dull pain
  Compassed, how eagerly I sought to strike
Into that wondrous track of dreams again!
  But no two dreams are like.

As when a soul laments, which hath been blest,
  Desiring what is mingled with past years,
In yearnings that can never be exprest
  By sighs or groans or tears;

Because all words, though culled with choicest art,
  Failing to give the bitter of the sweet,
Wither beneath the palate, and the heart
  Faints, faded by its heat.

1832-3

ULYSSES

It little profits that an idle king,
By this still hearth, among these barren crags,
Matched with an agèd wife, I mete and dole
Unequal laws unto a savage race,
That hoard, and sleep, and feed, and know not me.
I cannot rest from travel: I will drink
Life to the lees: all times I have enjoyed
Greatly, have suffered greatly, both with those
That loved me, and alone; on shore, and when
Through scudding drifts the rainy Hyades
Vext the dim sea: I am become a name;
For always roaming with a hungry heart
Much have I seen and known: cities of men,
And manners, climates, councils, governments,
Myself not least, but honoured of them all;
And drunk delight of battle with my peers,
Far on the ringing plains of windy Troy.
I am a part of all that I have met;
Yet all experience is an arch wherethrough
Gleams that untravelled world, whose margin fades
For ever and for ever when I move.
How dull it is to pause, to make an end,
To rust unburnished, not to shine in use!
As though to breathe were life. Life piled on life
Were all too little, and of one to me
Little remains: but every hour is saved
From that eternal silence, something more,
A bringer of new things; and vile it were
For some three suns to store and hoard myself,
And this gray spirit yearning in desire
To follow knowledge like a sinking star,
Beyond the utmost bound of human thought.
  This is my son, mine own Telemachus,
To whom I leave the sceptre and the isle —
Well-loved of me, discerning to fulfil
This labour, by slow prudence to make mild
A rugged people, and through soft degrees
Subdue them to the useful and the good.
Most blameless is he, centred in the sphere
Of common duties, decent not to fail
In offices of tenderness, and pay
Meet adoration to my household gods,
When I am gone. He works his work, I mine.
  There lies the port; the vessel puffs her sail:
There gloom the dark broad seas. My mariners,
Souls that have toiled, and wrought, and thought with me —
That ever with a frolic welcome took
The thunder and the sunshine, and opposed
Free hearts, free foreheads — you and I are old;
Old age hath yet his honour and his toil;
Death closes all: but something ere the end,
Some work of noble note, may yet be done,
Not unbecoming men that strove with Gods.
The lights begin to twinkle from the rocks:
The long day wanes: the slow moon climbs: the deep
Moans round with many voices. Come, my friends,
'T is not too late to seek a newer world.
Push off, and sitting well in order smite
The sounding furrows; for my purpose holds
To sail beyond the sunset, and the baths
Of all the western stars, until I die.
It may be that the gulfs will wash us down:
It may be we shall touch the Happy Isles,
And see the great Achilles, whom we knew.
Though much is taken, much abides; and though
We are not now that strength which in old days

Moved earth and heaven; that which we are, we are;
One equal temper of heroic hearts,
Made weak by time and fate, but strong in will
To strive, to seek, to find, and not to yield.

1842

LOCKSLEY HALL

Comrades, leave me here a little, while as yet 't is early morn:
Leave me here, and when you want me, sound upon the bugle-horn.

'T is the place, and all around it, as of old, the curlews call,
Dreary gleams about the moorland flying over Locksley Hall;

Locksley Hall, that in the distance overlooks the sandy tracts,
And the hollow ocean-ridges roaring into cataracts.

Many a night from yonder ivied casement, ere I went to rest,
Did I look on great Orion sloping slowly to the West.

Many a night I saw the Pleiads, rising through the mellow shade,
Glitter like a swarm of fire-flies tangled in a silver braid.

Here about the beach I wandered, nourishing a youth sublime
With the fairy tales of science, and the long result of Time;

When the centuries behind me like a fruitful land reposed;
When I clung to all the present for the promise that it closed:

When I dipt into the future far as human eye could see;
Saw the Vision of the world, and all the wonder that would be. —

In the Spring a fuller crimson comes upon the robin's breast;
In the Spring the wanton lapwing gets himself another crest;

In the Spring a livelier iris changes on the burnished dove;
In the Spring a young man's fancy lightly turns to thoughts of love.

Then her cheek was pale and thinner than should be for one so young,
And her eyes on all my motions with a mute observance hung.

And I said, 'My cousin Amy, speak, and speak the truth to me,
Trust me, cousin, all the current of my being sets to thee.'

On her pallid cheek and forehead came a color and a light,
As I have seen the rosy red flushing in the northern night.

And she turned — her bosom shaken with a sudden storm of sighs —
All the spirit deeply dawning in the dark of hazel eyes —

Saying, 'I have hid my feelings, fearing they should do me wrong';
Saying, 'Dost thou love me, cousin?' weeping, 'I have loved thee long.'

Love took up the glass of Time, and turned it in his glowing hands;
Every moment, lightly shaken, ran itself in golden sands.

Love took up the harp of Life, and smote on all the chords with might;
Smote the chord of Self, that, trembling, passed in music out of sight.

Many a morning on the moorland did we hear the copses ring,
And her whisper thronged my pulses with the fullness of the Spring.

Many an evening by the waters did we watch the stately ships,
And our spirits rushed together at the touching of the lips.

O my cousin, shallow-hearted! O my Amy, mine no more!
O the dreary, dreary moorland! O the barren, barren shore!

Falser than all fancy fathoms, falser than all songs have sung,
Puppet to a father's threat, and servile to a shrewish tongue!

Is it well to wish thee happy? — having known me — to decline
On a range of lower feelings and a narrower heart than mine!

Yet it shall be: thou shalt lower to his level day by day,
What is fine within thee growing coarse to sympathise with clay.

As the husband is, the wife is: thou art mated with a clown,
And the grossness of his nature will have weight to drag thee down.

He will hold thee, when his passion shall have spent its novel force,
Something better than his dog, a little dearer than his horse.

What is this? his eyes are heavy: think not they are glazed with wine.
Go to him: it is thy duty: kiss him: take his hand in thine.

It may be my lord is weary, that his brain is overwrought:
Soothe him with thy finer fancies, touch him with thy lighter thought.

He will answer to the purpose, easy things to understand —
Better thou wert dead before me, though I slew thee with my hand!

Better thou and I were lying, hidden from the heart's disgrace,
Rolled in one another's arms, and silent in a last embrace.

Cursèd be the social wants that sin against the strength of youth!
Cursèd be the social lies that warp us from the living truth!

Cursèd be the sickly forms that err from honest Nature's rule!
Cursèd be the gold that gilds the straitened forehead of the fool!

Well — 't is well that I should bluster! — Hadst thou less unworthy proved —
Would to God — for I had loved thee more than ever wife was loved.

Am I mad, that I should cherish that which bears but bitter fruit?
I will pluck it from my bosom, though my heart be at the root.

Never, though my mortal summers to such length of years should come
As the many-wintered crow that leads the clanging rookery home.

Where is comfort? in division of the records of the mind?
Can I part her from herself, and love her, as I knew her, kind?

I remember one that perished: sweetly did she speak and move:
Such a one do I remember, whom to look at was to love.

Can I think of her as dead, and love her for the love she bore?
No — she never loved me truly: love is love for evermore.

Comfort? comfort scorned of devils! this is truth the poet sings,
That a sorrow's crown of sorrow is remembering happier things.

Drug thy memories, lest thou learn it, lest thy heart be put to proof,
In the dead unhappy night, and when the rain is on the roof.

Like a dog, he hunts in dreams, and thou art staring at the wall,
Where the dying night-lamp flickers, and the shadows rise and fall.

Then a hand shall pass before thee, pointing to his drunken sleep,
To thy widowed marriage-pillows, to the tears that thou wilt weep.

Thou shalt hear the 'Never, never,' whispered by the phantom years,
And a song from out the distance in the ringing of thine ears;

And an eye shall vex thee, looking ancient kindness on thy pain.
Turn thee, turn thee on thy pillow: get thee to thy rest again.

Nay, but Nature brings thee solace; for a tender voice will cry.
'T is a purer life than thine; a lip to drain thy trouble dry.

Baby lips will laugh me down: my latest rival brings thee rest.
Baby fingers, waxen touches, press me from the mother's breast.

O, the child too clothes the father with a dearness not his due.
Half is thine and half is his: it will be worthy of the two.

O, I see thee old and formal, fitted to thy petty part,
With a little hoard of maxims preaching down a daughter's heart.

'They were dangerous guides the feelings — she herself was not exempt —
Truly, she herself had suffered' — Perish in thy self-contempt!

Overlive it — lower yet — be happy! wherefore should I care?
I myself must mix with action, lest I wither by despair.

What is that which I should turn to, lighting upon days like these?
Every door is barred with gold, and opens but to golden keys.

Every gate is thronged with suitors, all the markets overflow.
I have but an angry fancy: what is that which I should do?

I had been content to perish, falling on the foeman's ground,
When the ranks are rolled in vapour, and the winds are laid with sound.

But the jingling of the guinea helps the hurt that Honour feels,
And the nations do but murmur, snarling at each other's heels.

Can I but relive in sadness? I will turn that earlier page.
Hide me from my deep emotion, O thou wondrous Mother-Age!

Make me feel the wild pulsation that I felt before the strife,
When I heard my days before me, and the tumult of my life;

Yearning for the large excitement that the coming years would yield,
Eager-hearted as a boy when first he leaves his father's field,

And at night along the dusky highway near and nearer drawn,
Sees in heaven the light of London flaring like a dreary dawn;

And his spirit leaps within him to be gone before him then,
Underneath the light he looks at, in among the throngs of men:

Men, my brothers, men the workers, ever reaping something new:
That which they have done but earnest of the things that they shall do:

For I dipt into the future, far as human eye could see,
Saw the Vision of the world, and all the wonder that would be;

Saw the heavens fill with commerce, argosies of magic sails,
Pilots of the purple twilight, dropping down with costly bales;

Heard the heavens fill with shouting, and there rained a ghastly dew
From the nations' airy navies grappling in the central blue;

Far along the world-wide whisper of the south-wind rushing warm,
With the standards of the peoples plunging through the thunder-storm;

Till the war-drum throbbed no longer, and the battle-flags were furled
In the Parliament of man, the Federation of the world.

There the common sense of most shall hold a fretful realm in awe,
And the kindly earth shall slumber, lapt in universal law.

So I triumphed ere my passion sweeping through me left me dry,
Left me with the palsied heart, and left me with the jaundiced eye;

Eye, to which all order festers, all things here are out of joint:
Science moves, but slowly, slowly, creeping on from point to point:

Slowly comes a hungry people, as a lion creeping nigher,
Glares at one that nods and winks behind a slowly-dying fire.

Yet I doubt not through the ages one increasing purpose runs.
And the thoughts of men are widened with the process of the suns.

What is that to him that reaps not harvest of his youthful joys,
Though the deep heart of existence beat for ever like a boy's?

Knowledge comes, but wisdom lingers, and I linger on the shore,
And the individual withers, and the world is more and more.

Knowledge comes, but wisdom lingers, and he bears a laden breast,
Full of sad experience, moving toward the stillness of his rest.

Hark, my merry comrades call me, sounding on the bugle-horn,
They to whom my foolish passion were a target for their scorn:

Shall it not be scorn to me to harp on such a mouldered string?
I am shamed through all my nature to have loved so slight a thing.

Weakness to be wroth with weakness! woman's pleasure, woman's pain —
Nature made them blinder motions bounded in a shallower brain:

Woman is the lesser man, and all thy passions, matched with mine,
Are as moonlight unto sunlight, and as water unto wine —

Here at least, where nature sickens, nothing. Ah, for some retreat
Deep in yonder shining Orient, where my life began to beat;

Where in wild Mahratta-battle fell my father evil-starred; —
I was left a trampled orphan, and a selfish uncle's ward.

Or to burst all links of habit — there to wander far away,
On from island unto island at the gateways of the day.

Larger constellations burning, mellow moons and happy skies,
Breadths of tropic shade and palms in cluster, knots of Paradise.

Never comes the trader, never floats an European flag,
Slides the bird o'er lustrous woodland, swings the trailer from the crag;

Droops the heavy-blossomed bower, hangs the heavy-fruited tree —
Summer isles of Eden lying in dark-purple spheres of sea.

There methinks would be enjoyment more than in this march of mind,
In the steamship, in the railway, in the thoughts that shake mankind.

There the passions cramped no longer shall have scope and breathing space:
I will take some savage woman, she shall rear my dusky race.

Iron-jointed, supple-sinewed, they shall dive, and they shall run,
Catch the wild goat by the hair, and hurl their lances in the sun;

Whistle back the parrot's call, and leap the rainbows of the brooks,
Not with blinded eyesight poring over miserable books —

Fool, again the dream, the fancy! but I *know* my words are wild,
But I count the gray barbarian lower than the Christian child.

I, to herd with narrow foreheads, vacant of our glorious gains,
Like a beast with lower pleasures, like a beast with lower pains!

Mated with a squalid savage — what to me were sun or clime?
I the heir of all the ages, in the foremost files of time —

I that rather held it better men should perish one by one,
Than that earth should stand at gaze like Joshua's moon in Ajalon!

Not in vain the distance beacons. Forward, forward let us range,
Let the great world spin for ever down the ringing grooves of change.

Through the shadow of the globe we sweep into the younger day:
Better fifty years of Europe than a cycle of Cathay.

Mother-Age (for mine I knew not) help me as when life begun:
Rift the hills, and roll the waters, flash the lightnings, weigh the Sun.

O, I see the crescent promise of my spirit hath not set.
Ancient founts of inspiration well through all my fancy yet.

Howsoever these things be, a long farewell to Locksley Hall!
Now for me the woods may wither, now for me the roof-tree fall.

Comes a vapour from the margin, blackening over heath and holt,
Cramming all the blast before it, in its breast a thunderbolt.

Let it fall on Locksley Hall, with rain or hail, or fire or snow;
For the mighty wind arises, roaring seaward, and I go.

1842

SIR GALAHAD

My good blade carves the casques of men,
My tough lance thrusteth sure,
My strength is as the strength of ten,
Because my heart is pure.
The shattering trumpet shrilleth high,
The hard brands shiver on the steel,
The splintered spear-shafts crack and fly,
The horse and rider reel:
They reel, they roll in clanging lists,
And when the tide of combat stands,
Perfume and flowers fall in showers,
That lightly rain from ladies' hands.

How sweet are looks that ladies bend
On whom their favours fall!
For them I battle till the end,
To save from shame and thrall:
But all my heart is drawn above,
My knees are bowed in crypt and shrine:
I never felt the kiss of love,
Nor maiden's hand in mine.
More bounteous aspects on me beam,
Me mightier transports move and thrill;
So keep I fair through faith and prayer
A virgin heart in work and will.

When down the stormy crescent goes,
A light before me swims,
Between dark stems the forest glows,
I hear a noise of hymns:
Then by some secret shrine I ride;
I hear a voice but none are there;
The stalls are void, the doors are wide,
The tapers burning fair.
Fair gleams the snowy altar-cloth,
The silver vessels sparkle clean,
The shrill bell rings, the censer swings,
And solemn chaunts resound between.

Sometimes on lonely mountain-meres
I find a magic bark;
I leap on board: no helmsman steers:
I float till all is dark.
A gentle sound, an awful light!
Three angels bear the holy Grail:
With folded feet, in stoles of white,
On sleeping wings they sail.
Ah, blessèd vision! blood of God!
My spirit beats her mortal bars,
As down dark tides the glory slides,
And star-like mingles with the stars.

When on my goodly charger borne
Through dreaming towns I go,
The cock crows ere the Christmas morn,
The streets are dumb with snow.
The tempest crackles on the leads,
And, ringing, springs from brand and mail;
But o'er the dark a glory spreads,
And gilds the driving hail.
I leave the plain, I climb the height;
No branchy thicket shelter yields;
But blessèd forms in whistling storms
Fly o'er waste fens and windy fields.

A maiden knight — to me is given
Such hope, I know not fear;
I yearn to breathe the airs of heaven
That often meet me here.
I muse on joy that will not cease,
Pure spaces clothed in living beams,
Pure lilies of eternal peace,
Whose odours haunt my dreams;
And, stricken by an angel's hand,
This mortal armour that I wear,
This weight and size, this heart and eyes,
Are touched, are turned to finest air.

The clouds are broken in the sky,
And through the mountain-walls
A rolling organ-harmony
Swells up, and shakes and falls.
Then move the trees, the copses nod,
Wings flutter, voices hover clear:
'O just and faithful knight of God!
Ride on! the prize is near.'
So pass I hostel, hall, and grange;
By bridge and ford, by park and pale,
All-armed I ride, whate'er betide,
Until I find the holy Grail.

1842

BREAK, BREAK, BREAK

Break, break, break,
On thy cold gray stones, O Sea!
And I would that my tongue could utter
The thoughts that arise in me.

O well for the fisherman's boy,
That he shouts with his sister at play!
O well for the sailor lad,
That he sings in his boat on the bay!

And the stately ships go on
To their haven under the hill;
But O for the touch of a vanished hand,
And the sound of a voice that is still!

Break, break, break,
At the foot of thy crags, O Sea!
But the tender grace of a day that is dead
Will never come back to me.

1842

SONGS FROM THE PRINCESS

THE SPLENDOUR FALLS

The splendour falls on castle walls
And snowy summits old in story:
The long light shakes across the lakes,
And the wild cataract leaps in glory.
Blow, bugle, blow, set the wild echoes flying,
Blow, bugle; answer, echoes, dying, dying, dying.

O hark, O hear! how thin and clear,
And thinner, clearer, farther going!
O sweet and far from cliff and scar
The horns of Elfland faintly blowing!
Blow, let us hear the purple glens replying:
Blow, bugle; answer, echoes, dying, dying, dying.

O love, they die in yon rich sky,
They faint on hill or field or river:
Our echoes roll from soul to soul,
And grow for ever and for ever.
Blow, bugle, blow, set the wild echoes flying,
And answer, echoes, answer, dying, dying, dying.

1850

TEARS, IDLE TEARS

'Tears, idle tears, I know not what they mean,
Tears from the depth of some divine despair
Rise in the heart, and gather to the eyes,
In looking on the happy Autumn-fields,
And thinking of the days that are no more.

'Fresh as the first beam glittering on a sail,
That brings our friends up from the underworld,
Sad as the last which reddens over one
That sinks with all we love below the verge;
So sad, so fresh, the days that are no more.

'Ah, sad and strange as in dark summer dawns
The earliest pipe of half-awakened birds
To dying ears, when unto dying eyes
The casement slowly grows a glimmering square;
So sad, so strange, the days that are no more.

'Dear as remembered kisses after death,
And sweet as those by hopeless fancy feigned
On lips that are for others; deep as love,
Deep as first love, and wild with all regret;
O Death in Life, the days that are no more.'

1850

HOME THEY BROUGHT HER WARRIOR DEAD

Home they brought her warrior dead:
She nor swooned, nor uttered cry:
All her maidens, watching, said,
'She must weep or she will die.'

Then they praised him, soft and low,
Called him worthy to be loved,
Truest friend and noblest foe;
Yet she neither spoke nor moved.

Stole a maiden from her place,
Lightly to the warrior stept,
Took the face-cloth from the face;
Yet she neither moved nor wept.

Rose a nurse of ninety years,
Set his child upon her knee —
Like summer tempest came her tears —
'Sweet my child, I live for thee.'

1850

IN MEMORIAM A. H. H.

Strong Son of God, immortal Love,
Whom we, that have not seen thy face,
By faith, and faith alone, embrace,
Believing where we cannot prove;

Thine are these orbs of light and shade;
Thou madest Life in man and brute;
Thou madest Death; and lo, thy foot
Is on the skull which thou hast made.

Thou wilt not leave us in the dust:
Thou madest man, he knows not why,
He thinks he was not made to die;
And thou hast made him: thou art just.

Thou seemest human and divine,
The highest, holiest manhood, thou:
Our wills are ours, we know not how;
Our wills are ours, to make them thine.

Our little systems have their day;
They have their day and cease to be:
They are but broken lights of thee,
And thou, O Lord, art more than they.

We have but faith: we cannot know;
For knowledge is of things we see;
And yet we trust it comes from thee,
A beam in darkness: let it grow.

Let knowledge grow from more to more,
But more of reverence in us dwell;
That mind and soul, according well,
May make one music as before,

But vaster. We are fools and slight;
We mock thee when we do not fear:
But help thy foolish ones to bear;
Help thy vain worlds to bear thy light.

Forgive what seemed my sin in me;
What seemed my worth since I began;
For merit lives from man to man,
And not from man, O Lord, to thee.

Forgive my grief for one removed,
Thy creature, whom I found so fair.
I trust he lives in thee, and there
I find him worthier to be loved.

Forgive these wild and wandering cries,
Confusions of a wasted youth;
Forgive them where they fail in truth,
And in thy wisdom make me wise.

I

I held it truth, with him who sings
To one clear harp in divers tones,
That men may rise on stepping-stones
Of their dead selves to higher things.

But who shall so forecast the years
And find in loss a gain to match?
Or reach a hand through time to catch
The far-off interest of tears?

Let Love clasp Grief lest both be drowned,
Let darkness keep her raven gloss:
Ah, sweeter to be drunk with loss,
To dance with death, to beat the ground,

Than that the victor Hours should scorn
The long result of Love, and boast,
'Behold the man that loved and lost,
But all he was is overworn.'

V

I sometimes hold it half a sin
To put in words the grief I feel;
For words, like Nature, half reveal
And half conceal the Soul within.

But, for the unquiet heart and brain,
A use in measured language lies;
The sad mechanic exercise,
Like dull narcotics, numbing pain.

In words, like weeds, I'll wrap me o'er,
Like coarsest clothes against the cold:
But that large grief which these enfold
Is given in outline and no more.

IX

Fair ship, that from the Italian shore
Sailest the placid ocean-plains
With my lost Arthur's loved remains,
Spread thy full wings, and waft him o'er.

So draw him home to those that mourn
In vain; a favourable speed
Ruffle thy mirrored mast, and lead
Through prosperous floods his holy urn.

All night no ruder air perplex
Thy sliding keel, till Phosphor, bright
As our pure love, through early light
Shall glimmer on the dewy decks.

Sphere all your lights around, above;
Sleep, gentle heavens, before the prow;
Sleep, gentle winds, as he sleeps now,
My friend, the brother of my love;

My Arthur, whom I shall not see
Till all my widowed race be run;
Dear as the mother to the son,
More than my brothers are to me.

XXII

The path by which we twain did go,
Which led by tracts that pleased us well,
Through four sweet years arose and fell,
From flower to flower, from snow to snow:

And we with singing cheered the way,
And, crowned with all the season lent,
From April on to April went,
And glad at heart from May to May:

But where the path we walked began
To slant the fifth autumnal slope,
As we descended following Hope
There sat the Shadow feared of man;

Who broke our fair companionship,
And spread his mantle dark and cold,
And wrapt thee formless in the fold,
And dulled the murmur on thy lip,

And bore thee where I could not see
Nor follow, though I walk in haste,
And think, that somewhere in the waste
The Shadow sits and waits for me.

XXVII

I envy not in any moods
The captive void of noble rage,
The linnet born within the cage,
That never knew the summer woods:

I envy not the beast that takes
His license in the field of time,
Unfettered by the sense of crime,
To whom a conscience never wakes;

Nor, what may count itself as blest,
The heart that never plighted troth
But stagnates in the weeds of sloth;
Nor any want-begotten rest.

I hold it true, whate'er befall;
I feel it, when I sorrow most;
'T is better to have loved and lost
Than never to have loved at all.

XLVIII

If these brief lays, of Sorrow born,
Were taken to be such as closed
Grave doubts and answers here proposed,
Then these were such as men might scorn:

Her care is not to part and prove;
She takes, when harsher moods remit,
What slender shade of doubt may flit,
And makes it vassal unto love:

And hence, indeed, she sports with words,
But better serves a wholesome law,
And holds it sin and shame to draw
The deepest measure from the chords:

Nor dare she trust a larger lay,
But rather loosens from the lip
Short swallow-flights of song, that dip
Their wings in tears, and skim away.

LIV

Oh yet we trust that somehow good
Will be the final goal of ill,
To pangs of nature, sins of will,
Defects of doubt, and taints of blood;

That nothing walks with aimless feet;
That not one life shall be destroyed,
Or cast as rubbish to the void,
When God hath made the pile complete;

That not a worm is cloven in vain;
That not a moth with vain desire
Is shrivelled in a fruitless fire,
Or but subserves another's gain.

Behold, we know not anything;
I can but trust that good shall fall
At last — far off — at last, to all,
And every winter change to spring.

So runs my dream: but what am I?
An infant crying in the night:
An infant crying for the light:
And with no language but a cry.

LV

The wish, that of the living whole
No life may fail beyond the grave,
Derives it not from what we have
The likest God within the soul?

Are God and Nature then at strife,
That Nature lends such evil dreams?
So careful of the type she seems,
So careless of the single life;

That I, considering everywhere
Her secret meaning in her deeds,
And finding that of fifty seeds
She often brings but one to bear,

I falter where I firmly trod,
And falling with my weight of cares
Upon the great world's altar-stairs
That slope through darkness up to God,

I stretch lame hands of faith, and grope,
And gather dust and chaff, and call
To what I feel is Lord of all,
And faintly trust the larger hope.

XCVI

You say, but with no touch of scorn,
Sweet-hearted, you, whose light-blue eyes
Are tender over drowning flies,
You tell me, doubt is Devil-born.

I know not: one indeed I knew
In many a subtle question versed,
Who touched a jarring lyre at first,
But ever strove to make it true:

Perplext in faith, but pure in deeds,
At last he beat his music out.
There lives more faith in honest doubt,
Believe me, than in half the creeds.

He fought his doubts and gathered strength,
He would not make his judgment blind,
He faced the spectres of the mind
And laid them: thus he came at length

To find a stronger faith his own;
And Power was with him in the night,
Which makes the darkness and the light,
And dwells not in the light alone,

But in the darkness and the cloud,
As over Sinaï's peaks of old,
While Israel made their gods of gold,
Although the trumpet blew so loud.

CVI

Ring out, wild bells, to the wild sky,
The flying cloud, the frosty light:
The year is dying in the night;
Ring out, wild bells, and let him die.

Ring out the old, ring in the new,
Ring, happy bells, across the snow:
The year is going, let him go;
Ring out the false, ring in the true.

Ring out the grief that saps the mind,
For those that here we see no more;
Ring out the feud of rich and poor,
Ring in redress to all mankind.

Ring out a slowly dying cause,
And ancient forms of party strife;
Ring in the nobler modes of life,
With sweeter manners, purer laws.

Ring out the want, the care, the sin,
The faithless coldness of the times;
Ring out, ring out my mournful rhymes,
But ring the fuller minstrel in.

Ring out false pride in place and blood,
The civic slander and the spite;
Ring in the love of truth and right,
Ring in the common love of good.

Ring out old shapes of foul disease;
Ring out the narrowing lust of gold;
Ring out the thousand wars of old,
Ring in the thousand years of peace.

Ring in the valiant man and free,
The larger heart, the kindlier hand;
Ring out the darkness of the land,
Ring in the Christ that is to be.

CXXX

Thy voice is on the rolling air;
I hear thee where the waters run;
Thou standest in the rising sun,
And in the setting thou art fair.

What art thou then? I cannot guess;
But though I seem in star and flower
To feel thee some diffusive power,
I do not therefore love thee less:

My love involves the love before;
My love is vaster passion now;
Though mixed with God and Nature thou,
I seem to love thee more and more.

Far off thou art, but ever nigh;
I have thee still, and I rejoice;
I prosper, circled with thy voice;
I shall not lose thee though I die.

CXXXI

O living will that shalt endure
When all that seems shall suffer shock,
Rise in the spiritual rock,
Flow through our deeds and make them pure,

That we may lift from out of dust
A voice as unto him that hears,
A cry above the conquered years
To one that with us works, and trust,

With faith that comes of self-control,
The truths that never can be proved
Until we close with all we loved,
And all we flow from, soul in soul.

1850

ODE ON THE DEATH OF THE DUKE OF WELLINGTON

Bury the Great Duke
 With an empire's lamentation,
Let us bury the Great Duke
 To the noise of the mourning of a mighty nation,
Mourning when their leaders fall,
Warriors carry the warrior's pall,
And sorrow darkens hamlet and hall.

Where shall we lay the man whom we deplore?
Here, in streaming London's central roar.
Let the sound of those he wrought for,
And the feet of those he fought for,
Echo round his bones for evermore.

Lead out the pageant: sad and slow,
As fits an universal woe,
Let the long, long procession go,
And let the sorrowing crowd about it grow,
And let the mournful martial music blow;
The last great Englishman is low.

Mourn, for to us he seems the last,
Remembering all his greatness in the Past.
No more in soldier fashion will he greet
With lifted hand the gazer in the street.
O friends, our chief state-oracle is mute:
Mourn for the man of long-enduring blood,
The statesman-warrior, moderate, resolute,
Whole in himself, a common good.
Mourn for the man of amplest influence,
Yet clearest of ambitious crime,
Our greatest yet with least pretence,
Great in council and great in war,
Foremost captain of his time,
Rich in saving common-sense,
And, as the greatest only are,
In his simplicity sublime.
O good gray head which all men knew,
O voice from which their omens all men drew,
O iron nerve to true occasion true,
O fall'n at length that tower of strength
Which stood four-square to all the winds that blew!
Such was he whom we deplore.
The long self-sacrifice of life is o'er.
The great World-victor's victor will be seen no more.

All is over and done:
Render thanks to the Giver,
England, for thy son.
Let the bell be tolled.
Render thanks to the Giver,
And render him to the mould.
Under the cross of gold
That shines over city and river,
There he shall rest for ever
Among the wise and the bold.
Let the bell be tolled:
And a reverent people behold
The towering car, the sable steeds:
Bright let it be with its blazoned deeds,
Dark in its funeral fold.
Let the bell be tolled:
And a deeper knell in the heart be knolled;
And the sound of the sorrowing anthem rolled
Through the dome of the golden cross;
And the volleying cannon thunder his loss;
He knew their voices of old.
For many a time in many a clime
His captain's-ear has heard them boom
Bellowing victory, bellowing doom:
When he with those deep voices wrought,
Guarding realms and kings from shame;
With those deep voices our dead captain taught
The tyrant, and asserts his claim
In that dread sound to the great name,
Which he has worn so pure of blame,
In praise and in dispraise the same,
A man of well-tempered frame.
O civic muse, to such a name,
To such a name for ages long,
To such a name,
Preserve a broad approach of fame,
And ever-echoing avenues of song.

Who is he that cometh, like an honoured guest,
With banner and with music, with soldier and with priest,
With a nation weeping, and breaking on my rest?
Mighty Seaman, this is he
Was great by land as thou by sea.
Thine island loves thee well, thou famous man,
The greatest sailor since our world began.
Now, to the roll of muffled drums,
To thee the greatest soldier comes;
For this is he
Was great by land as thou by sea;
His foes were thine; he kept us free;
O give him welcome, this is he
Worthy of our gorgeous rites,
And worthy to be laid by thee;
For this is England's greatest son,
He that gained a hundred fights,
Nor ever lost an English gun;
This is he that far away
Against the myriads of Assaye

Clashed with his fiery few and won;
And underneath another sun,
Warring on a later day,
Round affrighted Lisbon drew
The treble works, the vast designs
Of his laboured rampart-lines,
Where he greatly stood at bay,
Whence he issued forth anew,
And ever great and greater grew,
Beating from the wasted vines
Back to France her banded swarms,
Back to France with countless blows,
Till o'er the hills her eagles flew
Beyond the Pyrenean pines,
Followed up in valley and glen
With blare of bugle, clamour of men,
Roll of cannon and clash of arms,
And England pouring on her foes.
Such a war had such a close.
Again their ravening eagle rose
In anger, wheeled on Europe-shadowing wings,
And barking for the thrones of kings;
Till one that sought but Duty's iron crown
On that loud sabbath shook the spoiler down;
A day of onsets of despair!
Dashed on every rocky square
Their surging charges foamed themselves away;
Last, the Prussian trumpet blew;
Through the long-tormented air
Heaven flashed a sudden jubilant ray,
And down we swept and charged and overthrew.
So great a soldier taught us there,
What long-enduring hearts could do
In that world-earthquake, Waterloo!
Mighty Seaman, tender and true,
And pure as he from taint of craven guile,
O saviour of the silver-coasted isle,
O shaker of the Baltic and the Nile,
If aught of things that here befall
Touch a spirit among things divine,
If love of country move thee there at all,
Be glad, because his bones are laid by thine!
And through the centuries let a people's voice
In full acclaim,
A people's voice,
The proof and echo of all human fame,
A people's voice, when they rejoice
At civic revel and pomp and game,
Attest their great commander's claim
With honour, honour, honour, honour to him,
Eternal honour to his name.

A people's voice! we are a people yet.
Though all men else their nobler dreams forget,
Confused by brainless mobs and lawless Powers;
Thank Him who isled us here, and roughly set
His Briton in blown seas and storming showers,
We have a voice, with which to pay the debt
Of boundless love and reverence and regret
To those great men who fought, and kept it ours.
And keep it ours, O God, from brute control;
O Statesmen, guard us, guard the eye, the soul
Of Europe, keep our noble England whole,
And save the one true seed of freedom sown
Betwixt a people and their ancient throne,
That sober freedom out of which there springs
Our loyal passion for our temperate kings;
For, saving that, ye help to save mankind
Till public wrong be crumbled into dust,
And drill the raw world for the march of mind,
Till crowds at length be sane and crowns be just.
But wink no more in slothful overtrust.
Remember him who led your hosts;
He bade you guard the sacred coasts.
Your cannons moulder on the seaward wall;
His voice is silent in your council-hall
For ever; and whatever tempests lour
For ever silent; even if they broke
In thunder, silent; yet remember all
He spoke among you, and the Man who spoke;
Who never sold the truth to serve the hour,
Nor paltered with Eternal God for power;
Who let the turbid streams of rumour flow
Through either babbling world of high and low;
Whose life was work, whose language rife
With rugged maxims hewn from life;
Who never spoke against a foe;
Whose eighty winters freeze with one rebuke
All great self-seekers trampling on the right:
Truth-teller was our England's Alfred named;
Truth-lover was our English Duke;
Whatever record leap to light
He never shall be shamed.

Lo, the leader in these glorious wars
Now to glorious burial slowly borne,
Followed by the brave of other lands,
He, on whom from both her open hands
Lavish Honour showered all her stars,

And affluent Fortune emptied all her horn.
Yea, let all good things await
Him who cares not to be great,
But as he saves or serves the state.
Not once or twice in our rough island-story,
The path of duty was the way to glory:
He that walks it, only thirsting
For the right, and learns to deaden
Love of self, before his journey closes,
He shall find the stubborn thistle bursting
Into glossy purples, which outredden
All voluptuous garden-roses.
Not once or twice in our fair island-story,
The path of duty was the way to glory:
He, that ever following her commands,
On with toil of heart and knees and hands,
Through the long gorge to the far light has won
His path upward, and prevailed,
Shall find the toppling crags of Duty scaled
Are close upon the shining table-lands
To which our God Himself is moon and sun.
Such was he: his work is done.
But while the races of mankind endure,
Let his great example stand
Colossal, seen of every land,
And keep the soldier firm, the statesman pure:
Till in all lands and through all human story
The path of duty be the way to glory:
And let the land whose hearths he saved from shame
For many and many an age proclaim
At civic revel and pomp and game,
And when the long-illumined cities flame,
Their ever-loyal iron leader's fame,
With honour, honour, honour, honour to him,
Eternal honour to his name.
Peace, his triumph will be sung
By some yet unmoulded tongue
Far on in summers that we shall not see:
Peace, it is a day of pain
For one about whose patriarchal knee
Late the little children clung:
O peace, it is a day of pain
For one, upon whose hand and heart and brain
Once the weight and fate of Europe hung.
Ours the pain, be his the gain!
More than is of man's degree
Must be with us, watching here
At this, our great solemnity.
Whom we see not we revere;
We revere, and we refrain
From talk of battles loud and vain,
And brawling memories all too free
For such a wise humility
As befits a solemn fane:
We revere, and while we hear
The tides of Music's golden sea
Setting toward eternity,
Uplifted high in heart and hope are we,
Until we doubt not that for one so true
There must be other nobler work to do
Than when he fought at Waterloo,
And Victor he must ever be.
For though the Giant Ages heave the hill
And break the shore, and evermore
Make and break, and work their will;
Though world on world in myriad myriads roll
Round us, each with different powers,
And other forms of life than ours,
What know we greater than the soul?
On God and Godlike men we build our trust.
Hush, the Dead March wails in the people's ears:
The dark crowd moves, and there are sobs and tears:
The black earth yawns: the mortal disappears;
Ashes to ashes, dust to dust;
He is gone who seemed so great.—
Gone; but nothing can bereave him
Of the force he made his own
Being here, and we believe him
Something far advanced in State,
And that he wears a truer crown
Than any wreath that man can weave him.
Speak no more of his renown,
Lay your earthly fancies down,
And in the vast cathedral leave him,
God accept him, Christ receive him.

1852

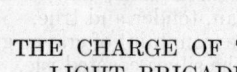

THE CHARGE OF THE LIGHT BRIGADE

Half a league, half a league,
Half a league onward,
All in the valley of Death
Rode the six hundred.
'Forward, the Light Brigade!
Charge for the guns!' he said:
Into the valley of Death
Rode the six hundred.

'Forward, the Light Brigade!'
Was there a man dismayed?
Not though the soldier knew
Some one had blundered:
Theirs not to make reply,
Theirs not to reason why,
Theirs but to do and die:
Into the valley of Death
Rode the six hundred.

Cannon to right of them,
Cannon to left of them,
Cannon in front of them
 Volleyed and thundered;
Stormed at with shot and shell,
Boldly they rode and well,
Into the jaws of Death,
Into the mouth of Hell
 Rode the six hundred.

Flashed all their sabres bare,
Flashed as they turned in air
Sabring the gunners there,
Charging an army, while
 All the world wondered:
Plunged in the battery-smoke
Right through the line they broke;
Cossack and Russian
Reeled from the sabre-stroke
Shattered and sundered.
Then they rode back, but not —
 Not the six hundred.

Cannon to right of them,
Cannon to left of them,
Cannon behind them
 Volleyed and thundered;
Stormed at with shot and shell,
While horse and hero fell,
They that had fought so well
Came through the jaws of Death,
Back from the mouth of Hell,
All that was left of them,
 Left of six hundred.

When can their glory fade?
O the wild charge they made!
 All the world wondered.
Honour the charge they made!
Honour the Light Brigade,
 Noble six hundred!

1854

MAUD; A MONODRAMA

XI

O LET the solid ground
 Not fail beneath my feet
Before my life has found
 What some have found so sweet;
Then let come what come may,
What matter if I go mad,
I shall have had my day.

Let the sweet heavens endure,
 Not close and darken above me
Before I am quite quite sure
 That there is one to love me;
Then let come what come may
To a life that has been so sad,
I shall have had my day.

XVII

Go not, happy day,
 From the shining fields,
Go not, happy day,
 Till the maiden yields.
Rosy is the West,
 Rosy is the South,
Roses are her cheeks,
And a rose her mouth
When the happy Yes
Falters from her lips,
Pass and blush the news
Over glowing ships;
Over blowing seas,
Over seas at rest,
Pass the happy news,
 Blush it through the West;
Till the red man dance
By his red cedar-tree,
And the red man's babe,
 Leap, beyond the sea.
Blush from West to East,
Blush from East to West,
Till the West is East,
 Blush it through the West.
Rosy is the West,
 Rosy is the South,
Roses are her cheeks,
 And a rose her mouth.

XXII

Come into the garden, Maud,
 For the black bat, night, has flown,
Come into the garden, Maud,
 I am here at the gate alone;
And the woodbine spices are wafted abroad,
 And the musk of the rose is blown.

For a breeze of morning moves,
 And the planet of Love is on high,
Beginning to faint in the light that she loves
 On a bed of daffodil sky,
To faint in the light of the sun she loves,
 To faint in his light, and to die.

All night have the roses heard
 The flute, violin, bassoon;
All night has the casement jessamine stirred
 To the dancers dancing in tune;
Till a silence fell with the waking bird,
 And a hush with the setting moon.

I said to the lily, 'There is but one
 With whom she has heart to be gay.
When will the dancers leave her alone?

She is weary of dance and play.'
Now half to the setting moon are gone,
And half to the rising day;
Low on the sand and loud on the stone
The last wheel echoes away.

I said to the rose, 'The brief night goes
In babble and revel and wine.
O young lord-lover, what sighs are those,
For one that will never be thine?
But mine, but mine,' so I sware to the rose,
'For ever and ever, mine.'

And the soul of the rose went into my blood,
As the music clashed in the hall;
And long by the garden lake I stood,
For I heard your rivulet fall
From the lake to the meadow and on to the wood,
Our wood, that is dearer than all;

From the meadow your walks have left so sweet
That whenever a March-wind sighs
He sets the jewel-print of your feet
In violets blue as your eyes,
To the woody hollows in which we meet
And the valleys of Paradise.

The slender acacia would not shake
One long milk-bloom on the tree;
The white lake-blossom fell into the lake
As the pimpernel dozed on the lea;
But the rose was awake all night for your sake,
Knowing your promise to me;
The lilies and roses were all awake,
They sighed for the dawn and thee.

Queen rose of the rosebud garden of girls,
Come hither, the dances are done,
In gloss of satin and glimmer of pearls,
Queen lily and rose in one;
Shine out, little head, sunning over with curls,
To the flowers, and be their sun.

There has fallen a splendid tear
From the passion-flower at the gate.
She is coming, my dove, my dear;
She is coming, my life, my fate;
The red rose cries, 'She is near, she is near';
And the white rose weeps, 'She is late';
The larkspur listens, 'I hear, I hear';
And the lily whispers, 'I wait.'

She is coming, my own, my sweet;
Were it ever so airy a tread,
My heart would hear her and beat,
Were it earth in an earthy bed;
My dust would hear her and beat,
Had I lain for a century dead;
Would start and tremble under her feet,
And blossom in purple and red.

1855

SONG OF THE BROOK

I COME from haunts of coot and hern,
I make a sudden sally,
And sparkle out among the fern,
To bicker down a valley.

By thirty hills I hurry down,
Or slip between the ridges,
By twenty thorps, a little town,
And half a hundred bridges.

Till last by Philip's farm I flow
To join the brimming river,
For men may come and men may go,
But I go on for ever.

I chatter over stony ways,
In little sharps and trebles,
I bubble into eddying bays,
I babble on the pebbles.

With many a curve my banks I fret
By many a field and fallow,
And many a fairy foreland set
With willow-weed and mallow.

I chatter, chatter, as I flow
To join the brimming river,
For men may come and men may go,
But I go on for ever.

I wind about, and in and out,
With here a blossom sailing,
And here and there a lusty trout,
And here and there a grayling,

And here and there a foamy flake
Upon me, as I travel
With many a silvery waterbreak
Above the golden gravel,

And draw them all along, and flow
To join the brimming river,
For men may come and men may go,
But I go on for ever.

1855

GUINEVERE

QUEEN GUINEVERE had fled the court, and sat
There in the holy house at Almesbury
Weeping, none with her save a little maid,

A novice: one low light betwixt them burned
Blurred by the creeping mist, for all abroad,
Beneath a moon unseen albeit at full,
The white mist, like a face-cloth to the face,
Clung to the dead earth, and the land was still.

For hither had she fled, her cause of flight
Sir Modred; he that like a subtle beast
Lay couchant with his eyes upon the throne,
Ready to spring, waiting a chance: for this
He chilled the popular praises of the King
With silent smiles of slow disparagement;
And tampered with the Lords of the White Horse,
Heathen, the brood by Hengist left; and sought
To make disruption in the Table Round
Of Arthur, and to splinter it into feuds
Serving his traitorous end; and all his aims
Were sharpened by strong hate for Lancelot.

For thus it chanced one morn when all the court,
Green-suited, but with plumes that mocked the may,
Had been, their wont, a-maying and returned,
That Modred still in green, all ear and eye,
Climbed to the high top of the garden-wall
To spy some secret scandal if he might,
And saw the Queen who sat betwixt her best
Enid, and lissome Vivien, of her court
The wiliest and the worst; and more than this
He saw not, for Sir Lancelot passing by
Spied where he couched, and as the gardener's hand
Picks from the colewort a green caterpillar,
So from the high wall and the flowering grove
Of grasses Lancelot plucked him by the heel,
And cast him as a worm upon the way;
But when he knew the Prince though marred with dust,
He, reverencing king's blood in a bad man,
Made such excuses as he might, and these
Full knightly without scorn; for in those days
No knight of Arthur's noblest dealt in scorn;
But, if a man were halt or hunched, in him
By those whom God had made full-limbed and tall,
Scorn was allowed as part of his defect,
And he was answered softly by the King
And all his Table. So Sir Lancelot holp
To raise the Prince, who rising twice or thrice
Full sharply smote his knees, and smiled, and went:
But, ever after, the small violence done
Rankled in him and ruffled all his heart,
As the sharp wind that ruffles all day long
A little bitter pool about a stone
On the bare coast.
But when Sir Lancelot told
This matter to the Queen, at first she laughed
Lightly, to think of Modred's dusty fall,
Then shuddered, as the village wife who cries
'I shudder, some one steps across my grave';
Then laughed again, but faintlier, for indeed
She half-foresaw that he, the subtle beast,
Would track her guilt until he found, and hers
Would be for evermore a name of scorn.
Henceforward rarely could she front in hall,
Or elsewhere, Modred's narrow foxy face,
Heart-hiding smile, and gray persistent eye:
Henceforward too, the Powers that tend the soul,
To help it from the death that cannot die,
And save it even in extremes, began
To vex and plague her. Many a time for hours,
Beside the placid breathings of the King,
In the dead night, grim faces came and went
Before her, or a vague spiritual fear —
Like to some doubtful noise of creaking doors,
Heard by the watcher in a haunted house,
That keeps the rust of murder on the walls —
Held her awake: or if she slept, she dreamed
An awful dream; for then she seemed to stand
On some vast plain before a setting sun,
And from the sun there swiftly made at her
A ghastly something, and its shadow flew
Before it, till it touched her, and she turned —
When lo! her own, that broadening from her feet,
And blackening, swallowed all the land, and in it
Far cities burnt, and with a cry she woke.
And all this trouble did not pass but grew;
Till ev'n the clear face of the guileless King,
And trustful courtesies of household life,
Became her bane; and at the last she said,
'O Lancelot, get thee hence to thine own land,
For if thou tarry we shall meet again,
And if we meet again, some evil chance
Will make the smouldering scandal break and blaze
Before the people, and our lord the King.'
And Lancelot ever promised, but remained,
And still they met and met. Again she said,
'O Lancelot, if thou love me get thee hence.'
And then they were agreed upon a night

(When the good King should not be there) to meet
And part for ever. Vivien, lurking, heard.
She told Sir Modred. Passion-pale they met
And greeted. Hands in hands, and eye to eye,
Low on the border of her couch they sat
Stammering and staring. It was their last hour,
A madness of farewells. And Modred brought
His creatures to the basement of the tower
For testimony; and crying with full voice
'Traitor, come out, ye are trapt at last,' aroused
Lancelot, who rushing outward lionlike
Leapt on him, and hurled him headlong, and he fell
Stunned, and his creatures took and bare him off,
And all was still: then she, 'The end is come,
And I am shamed for ever'; and he said,
'Mine be the shame; mine was the sin: but rise,
And fly to my strong castle overseas:
There will I hide thee, till my life shall end,
There hold thee with my life against the world.'
She answered, 'Lancelot, wilt thou hold me so?
Nay, friend, for we have taken our farewells.
Would God that thou couldst hide me from myself!
Mine is the shame, for I was wife, and thou
Unwedded: yet rise now, and let us fly,
For I will draw me into sanctuary,
And bide my doom.' So Lancelot got her horse,
Set her thereon, and mounted on his own,
And then they rode to the divided way,
There kissed, and parted weeping: for he past,
Love-loyal to the least wish of the Queen,
Back to his land; but she to Almesbury
Fled all night long by glimmering waste and weald,
And heard the Spirits of the waste and weald
Moan as she fled, or thought she heard them moan:
And in herself she moaned, 'Too late, too late!'
Till in the cold wind that foreruns the morn,
A blot in heaven, the Raven, flying high,
Croaked, and she thought, 'He spies a field of death;
For now the Heathen of the Northern Sea,
Lured by the crimes and frailties of the court,
Begin to slay the folk, and spoil the land.'

And when she came to Almesbury she spake
There to the nuns, and said, 'Mine enemies
Pursue me, but, O peaceful Sisterhood,
Receive, and yield me sanctuary, nor ask
Her name to whom ye yield it, till her time
To tell you': and her beauty, grace and power,
Wrought as a charm upon them, and they spared
To ask it.

So the stately Queen abode
For many a week, unknown, among the nuns;
Nor with them mixed, nor told her name, nor sought,
Wrapt in her grief, for housel or for shrift,
But communed only with the little maid,
Who pleased her with a babbling heedlessness
Which often lured her from herself; but now,
This night, a rumour wildly blown about
Came, that Sir Modred had usurped the realm,
And leagued him with the heathen, while the King
Was waging war on Lancelot: then she thought,
'With what a hate the people and the King
Must hate me,' and bowed down upon her hands
Silent, until the little maid, who brooked
No silence, brake it, uttering, 'Late! so late!
What hour, I wonder, now?' and when she drew
No answer, by and by began to hum
An air the nuns had taught her, 'Late, so late!'
Which when she heard, the Queen looked up, and said,
'O maiden, if indeed ye list to sing,
Sing, and unbind my heart that I may weep.'
Whereat full willingly sang the little maid.

'Late, late, so late! and dark the night and chill!
Late, late, so late! but we can enter still.
Too late, too late! ye cannot enter now.

'No light had we: for that we do repent;
And learning this, the bridegroom will relent.
Too late, too late! ye cannot enter now.

'No light: so late! and dark and chill the night!
O let us in, that we may find the light!
Too late, too late: ye cannot enter now.

'Have we not heard the bridegroom is so sweet?
O let us in, though late, to kiss his feet!
No, no, too late! ye cannot enter now.'

So sang the novice, while full passionately,
Her head upon her hands, remembering
Her thought when first she came, wept the sad Queen.
Then said the little novice prattling to her,
'O pray you, noble lady, weep no more;
But let my words, the words of one so small,
Who knowing nothing knows but to obey,
And if I do not there is penance given —
Comfort your sorrows; for they do not flow
From evil done; right sure am I of that,
Who see your tender grace and stateliness.
But weigh your sorrows with our lord the King's,
And weighing find them less; for gone is he
To wage grim war against Sir Lancelot there,
Round that strong castle where he holds the Queen;
And Modred whom he left in charge of all,
The traitor — Ah sweet lady, the King's grief
For his own self, and his own Queen, and realm,
Must needs be thrice as great as any of ours.
For me, I thank the saints, I am not great.
For if there ever come a grief to me
I cry my cry in silence, and have done.
None knows it, and my tears have brought me good:
But even were the griefs of little ones
As great as those of great ones, yet this grief
Is added to the griefs the great must bear,
That howsoever much they may desire
Silence, they cannot weep behind a cloud:
As even here they talk at Almesbury
About the good King and his wicked Queen,
And were I such a King with such a Queen,
Well might I wish to veil her wickedness,
But were I such a King, it could not be.'
Then to her own sad heart muttered the Queen,
'Will the child kill me with her innocent talk?'
But openly she answered, 'Must not I,
If this false traitor have displaced his lord,
Grieve with the common grief of all the realm?'
'Yea,' said the maid, 'this is all woman's grief,
That *she* is woman, whose disloyal life
Hath wrought confusion in the Table Round
Which good King Arthur founded, years ago,
With signs and miracles and wonders, there
At Camelot, ere the coming of the Queen.'
Then thought the Queen within herself again,
'Will the child kill me with her foolish prate?'
But openly she spake and said to her,
'O little maid, shut in by nunnery walls,
What canst thou know of Kings and Tables Round,
Or what of signs and wonders, but the signs
And simple miracles of thy nunnery?'

To whom the little novice garrulously,
'Yea, but I know: the land was full of signs
And wonders ere the coming of the Queen.
So said my father, and himself was knight
Of the great Table — at the founding of it;
And rode thereto from Lyonesse, and he said
That as he rode, an hour or maybe twain
After the sunset, down the coast, he heard
Strange music, and he paused, and turning — there,
All down the lonely coast of Lyonesse,
Each with a beacon-star upon his head,
And with a wild sea-light about his feet,
He saw them — headland after headland flame
Far on into the rich heart of the west:
And in the light the white mermaiden swam,
And strong man-breasted things stood from the sea,
And sent a deep sea-voice through all the land,
To which the little elves of chasm and cleft
Made answer, sounding like a distant horn.
So said my father — yea, and furthermore,
Next morning, while he passed the dim-lit woods,
Himself beheld three spirits mad with joy
Come dashing down on a tall wayside flower,
That shook beneath them, as the thistle shakes
When three gray linnets wrangle for the seed:
And still at evenings on before his horse
The flickering fairy-circle wheeled and broke
Flying, and linked again, and wheeled and broke
Flying, for all the land was full of life.
And when at last he came to Camelot,
A wreath of airy dancers hand-in-hand
Swung round the lighted lantern of the hall;
And in the hall itself was such a feast
As never man had dreamed; for every knight
Had whatsoever meat he longed for served

By hands unseen; and even as he said
Down in the cellars merry bloated things
Shouldered the spigot, straddling on the butts
While the wine ran: so glad were spirits and men
Before the coming of the sinful Queen.'
Then spake the Queen and somewhat bitterly,
'Were they so glad? ill prophets were they all,
Spirits and men: could none of them foresee,
Not even thy wise father with his signs
And wonders, what has fall'n upon the realm?'
To whom the novice garrulously again,
'Yea, one, a bard; of whom my father said,
Full many a noble war-song had he sung,
Ev'n in the presence of an enemy's fleet,
Between the steep cliff and the coming wave;
And many a mystic lay of life and death
Had chanted on the smoky mountain-tops,
When round him bent the spirits of the hills
With all their dewy hair blown back like flame:
So said my father — and that night the bard
Sang Arthur's glorious wars, and sang the King
As wellnigh more than man, and railed at those
Who called him the false son of Gorloïs:
For there was no man knew from whence he came;
But after tempest, when the long wave broke
All down the thundering shores of Bude and Bos,
There came a day as still as heaven, and then
They found a naked child upon the sands
Of dark Tintagil by the Cornish sea;
And that was Arthur; and they fostered him
Till he by miracle was approven King:
And that his grave should be a mystery
From all men, like his birth; and could he find
A woman in her womanhood as great
As he was in his manhood, then, he sang,
The twain together well might change the world.
But even in the middle of his song
He faltered, and his hand fell from the harp,
And pale he turned, and reeled, and would have fall'n,
But that they stayed him up; nor would he tell
His vision; but what doubt that he foresaw
This evil work of Lancelot and the Queen?'
Then thought the Queen, 'Lo! they have set her on,
Our simple-seeming Abbess and her nuns,
To play upon me,' and bowed her head nor spake.
Whereat the novice crying, with clasped hands,
Shame on her own garrulity garrulously,
Said the good nuns would check her gadding tongue
Full often, 'and, sweet lady, if I seem
To vex an ear too sad to listen to me,
Unmannerly, with prattling and the tales
Which my good father told me, check me too
Nor let me shame my father's memory, one
Of noblest manners, though himself would say
Sir Lancelot had the noblest; and he died,
Killed in a tilt, come next, five summers back,
And left me; but of others who remain,
And of the two first-famed for courtesy —
And pray you check me if I ask amiss —
But pray you, which had noblest, while you moved
Among them, Lancelot or our lord the King?'
Then the pale Queen looked up and answered her,
'Sir Lancelot, as became a noble knight,
Was gracious to all ladies, and the same
In open battle or the tilting-field
Forbore his own advantage, and the King
In open battle or the tilting-field
Forbore his own advantage, and these two
Were the most nobly-mannered men of all;
For manners are not idle, but the fruit
Of loyal nature, and of noble mind.'
'Yea,' said the maid, 'be manners such fair fruit?
Then Lancelot's needs must be a thousand-fold
Less noble, being, as all rumour runs,
The most disloyal friend in all the world.'
To which a mournful answer made the Queen:
'O closed about by narrowing nunnery-walls,
What knowest thou of the world, and all its lights
And shadows, all the wealth and all the woe?
If ever Lancelot, that most noble knight,
Were for one hour less noble than himself,
Pray for him that he scape the doom of fire,
And weep for her who drew him to his doom.'
'Yea,' said the little novice, 'I pray for both;

But I should all as soon believe that his,
Sir Lancelot's, were as noble as the King's,
As I could think, sweet lady, yours would be
Such as they are, were you the sinful Queen.'
So she, like many another babbler, hurt
Whom she would soothe, and harmed where she would heal;
For here a sudden flush of wrathful heat
Fired all the pale face of the Queen, who cried,
'Such as thou art be never maiden more
For ever! thou their tool, set on to plague
And play upon, and harry me, petty spy
And traitress.' When that storm of anger brake
From Guinevere, aghast the maiden rose,
White as her veil, and stood before the Queen
As tremulously as foam upon the beach
Stands in a wind, ready to break and fly,
And when the Queen had added 'Get thee hence,'
Fled frighted. Then that other left alone
Sighed, and began to gather heart again,
Saying in herself, 'The simple, fearful child
Meant nothing, but my own too-fearful guilt,
Simpler than any child, betrays itself.
But help me, heaven, for surely I repent.
For what is true repentance but in thought —
Not ev'n in inmost thought to think again
The sins that made the past so pleasant to us:
And I have sworn never to see him more,
To see him more.'
And ev'n in saying this,
Her memory from old habit of the mind
Went slipping back upon the golden days
In which she saw him first, when Lancelot came,
Reputed the best knight and goodliest man,
Ambassador, to lead her to his lord
Arthur, and led her forth, and far ahead
Of his and her retinue moving, they,
Rapt in sweet talk or lively, all on love
And sport and tilts and pleasure, (for the time
Was maytime, and as yet no sin was dreamed,)
Rode under groves that looked a paradise
Of blossom, over sheets of hyacinth
That seemed the heavens upbreaking through the earth,
And on from hill to hill, and every day
Beheld at noon in some delicious dale
The silk pavilions of King Arthur raised
For brief repast or afternoon repose
By couriers gone before; and on again,
Till yet once more ere set of sun they saw
The Dragon of the great Pendragonship,
That crowned the state pavilion of the King,
Blaze by the rushing brook or silent well.
But when the Queen immersed in such a trance,
And moving through the past unconsciously,
Came to that point where first she saw the King
Ride toward her from the city, sighed to find
Her journey done, glanced at him, thought him cold,
High, self-contained, and passionless, not like him,
'Not like my Lancelot' — while she brooded thus
And grew half-guilty in her thoughts again,
There rode an armèd warrior to the doors.
A murmuring whisper through the nunnery ran,
Then on a sudden a cry, 'The King.' She sat
Stiff-stricken, listening; but when armèd feet
Through the long gallery from the outer doors
Rang coming, prone from off her seat she fell,
And grovelled with her face against the floor:
There with her milkwhite arms and shadowy hair
She made her face a darkness from the King:
And in the darkness heard his armèd feet
Pause by her; then came silence, then a voice,
Monotonous and hollow like a Ghost's
Denouncing judgment, but though changed, the King's:
'Liest thou here so low, the child of one
I honoured, happy, dead before thy shame?
Well is it that no child is born of thee.
The children born of thee are sword and fire,
Red ruin, and the breaking up of laws,
The craft of kindred and the Godless hosts
Of heathen swarming o'er the Northern Sea;
Whom I, while yet Sir Lancelot, my right arm,
The mightiest of my knights, abode with me,
Have everywhere about this land of Christ
In twelve great battles ruining overthrown.
And knowest thou now from whence I come — from him,
From waging bitter war with him: and he,
That did not shun to smite me in worse way,
Had yet that grace of courtesy in him left,
He spared to lift his hand against the King
Who made him knight: but many a knight was slain;
And many more, and all his kith and kin
Clave to him, and abode in his own land.
And many more when Modred raised revolt,

Forgetful of their troth and fealty, clave
To Modred, and a remnant stays with me.
And of this remnant will I leave a part,
True men who love me still, for whom I live,
To guard thee in the wild hour coming on,
Lest but a hair of this low head be harmed.
Fear not: thou shalt be guarded till my death.
Howbeit I know, if ancient prophecies
Have erred not, that I march to meet my doom.
Thou hast not made my life so sweet to me,
That I the King should greatly care to live;
For thou hast spoilt the purpose of my life.
Bear with me for the last time while I show,
Ev'n for thy sake, the sin which thou hast sinned.
For when the Roman left us, and their law
Relaxed its hold upon us, and the ways
Were filled with rapine, here and there a deed
Of prowess done redressed a random wrong.
But I was first of all the kings who drew
The Knighthood-errant of this realm and all
The realms together under me, their Head,
In that fair Order of my Table Round,
A glorious company, the flower of men,
To serve as model for the mighty world,
And be the fair beginning of a time.
I made them lay their hands in mine and swear
To reverence the King, as if he were
Their conscience, and their conscience as their King,
To break the heathen and uphold the Christ,
To ride abroad redressing human wrongs,
To speak no slander, no, nor listen to it,
To honour his own word as if his God's,
To lead sweet lives in purest chastity,
To love one maiden only, cleave to her,
And worship her by years of noble deeds,
Until they won her; for indeed I knew
Of no more subtle master under heaven
Than is the maiden passion for a maid,
Not only to keep down the base in man,
But teach high thought, and amiable words
And courtliness, and the desire of fame,
And love of truth, and all that makes a man.
And all this throve before I wedded thee,
Believing, "lo mine helpmate, one to feel
My purpose and rejoicing in my joy."
Then came thy shameful sin with Lancelot;
Then came the sin of Tristram and Isolt;
Then others, following these my mightiest knights,
And drawing foul ensample from fair names,
Sinned also, till the loathsome opposite
Of all my heart had destined did obtain,
And all through thee! so that this life of mine
I guard as God's high gift from scathe and wrong,
Not greatly care to lose; but rather think
How sad it were for Arthur, should he live,
To sit once more within his lonely hall,
And miss the wonted number of my knights,
And miss to hear high talk of noble deeds
As in the golden days before thy sin.
For which of us, who might be left, could speak
Of the pure heart, nor seem to glance at thee?
And in thy bowers of Camelot or of Usk
Thy shadow still would glide from room to room,
And I should evermore be vext with thee
In hanging robe or vacant ornament,
Or ghostly footfall echoing on the stair.
For think not, though thou wouldst not love thy lord,
Thy lord has wholly lost his love for thee.
I am not made of so slight elements.
Yet must I leave thee, woman, to thy shame.
I hold that man the worst of public foes
Who either for his own or children's sake,
To save his blood from scandal, lets the wife
Whom he knows false, abide and rule the house:
For being through his cowardice allowed
Her station, taken everywhere for pure,
She like a new disease, unknown to men,
Creeps, no precaution used, among the crowd,
Makes wicked lightnings of her eyes, and saps
The fealty of our friends, and stirs the pulse
With devil's leaps, and poisons half the young.
Worst of the worst were that man he that reigns!
Better the King's waste hearth and aching heart
Than thou reseated in thy place of light,
The mockery of my people, and their bane.'
He paused, and in the pause she crept an inch
Nearer, and laid her hands about his feet.
Far off a solitary trumpet blew.
Then waiting by the doors the warhorse neighed
As at a friend's voice, and he spake again:
'Yet think not that I come to urge thy crimes,
I did not come to curse thee, Guinevere,
I, whose vast pity almost makes me die

To see thee, laying there thy golden head,
My pride in happier summers, at my feet.
The wrath which forced my thoughts on that fierce law,
The doom of treason and the flaming death
(When first I learnt thee hidden here), is past.
The pang — which while I weighed thy heart with one
Too wholly true to dream untruth in thee,
Made my tears burn — is also past — in part.
And all is past, the sin is sinned and I,
Lo! I forgive thee, as Eternal God
Forgives: do thou for thine own soul the rest.
But how to take last leave of all I loved?
O golden hair, with which I used to play
Not knowing! O imperial-moulded form,
And beauty such as never woman wore,
Until it came a kingdom's curse with thee —
I cannot touch thy lips, they are not mine,
But Lancelot's: nay, they never were the King's.
I cannot take thy hand; that too is flesh,
And in the flesh thou hast sinned; and mine own flesh,
Here looking down on thine polluted, cries
"I loathe thee": yet not less, O Guinevere,
For I was ever virgin save for thee,
My love through flesh hath wrought into my life
So far, that my doom is, I love thee still.
Let no man dream but that I love thee still.
Perchance, and so thou purify thy soul,
And so thou lean on our fair father Christ,
Hereafter in that world where all are pure
We two may meet before high God, and thou
Wilt spring to me, and claim me thine, and know
I am thine husband — not a smaller soul,
Nor Lancelot, nor another. Leave me that,
I charge thee, my last hope. Now must I hence.
Through the thick night I hear the trumpet blow:
They summon me their King to lead mine hosts
Far down to that great battle in the west,
Where I must strike against the man they call
My sister's son — no kin of mine, who leagues
With Lords of the White Horse, heathen, and knights,
Traitors — and strike him dead, and meet myself
Death, or I know not what mysterious doom.
And thou remaining here wilt learn the event;
But hither shall I never come again,
Never lie by thy side; see thee no more —
Farewell!'

And while she grovelled at his feet,
She felt the King's breath wander o'er her neck,
And in the darkness o'er her fallen head,
Perceived the waving of his hands that blest.

Then, listening till those armèd steps were gone,
Rose the pale Queen, and in her anguish found
The casement: 'peradventure,' so she thought,
'If I might see his face, and not be seen.'
And lo, he sat on horseback at the door!
And near him the sad nuns with each a light
Stood, and he gave them charge about the Queen,
To guard and foster her for evermore.
And while he spake to these his helm was lowered,
To which for crest the golden dragon clung
Of Britain; so she did not see the face,
Which then was as an angel's, but she saw,
Wet with the mists and smitten by the lights,
The Dragon of the great Pendragonship
Blaze, making all the night a steam of fire.
And even then he turned; and more and more
The moony vapour rolling round the King,
Who seemed the phantom of a Giant in it,
Enwound him fold by fold, and made him gray
And grayer, till himself became as mist
Before her, moving ghostlike to his doom.

Then she stretched out her arms and cried aloud
'O Arthur!' there her voice brake suddenly,
Then — as a stream that spouting from a cliff
Fails in mid-air, but gathering at the base
Re-makes itself, and flashes down the vale —
Went on in passionate utterance:

'Gone — my lord!
Gone through my sin to slay and to be slain!
And he forgave me, and I could not speak.
Farewell? I should have answered his farewell.
His mercy choked me. Gone, my lord the King,
My own true lord! how dare I call him mine?
The shadow of another cleaves to me,
And makes me one pollution: he, the King,

Called me poluted: shall I kill myself?
What help in that? I cannot kill my sin,
If soul be soul; nor can I kill my shame;
No, nor by living can I live it down.
The days will grow to weeks, the weeks to months,
The months will add themselves and make the years,
The years will roll into the centuries,
And mine will ever be a name of scorn.
I must not dwell on that defeat of fame.
Let the world be; that is but of the world.
What else? what hope? I think there was a hope,
Except he mocked me when he spake of hope;
His hope he called it; but he never mocks,
For mockery is the fume of little hearts.
And blessèd be the King, who hath forgiven
My wickedness to him, and left me hope
That in mine own heart I can live down sin
And be his mate hereafter in the heavens
Before high God. Ah, great and gentle lord,
Who wast, as is the conscience of a saint
Among his warring senses, to thy knights —
To whom my false voluptuous pride, that took
Full easily all impressions from below,
Would not look up, or half-despised the height
To which I would not or I could not climb —
I thought I could not breathe in that fine air
That pure severity of perfect light —
I yearned for warmth and colour which I found
In Lancelot — now I see thee what thou art,
Thou art the highest and most human too,
Not Lancelot nor another. Is there none
Will tell the King I love him though so late?
Now — ere he goes to the great Battle? none:
Myself must tell him in that purer life,
But now it were too daring. Ah my God,
What might I not have made of thy fair world,
Had I but loved thy highest creature here?
It was my duty to have loved the highest:
It surely was my profit had I known:
It would have been my pleasure had I seen.
We needs must love the highest when we see it,
Not Lancelot, nor another.'
Here her hand
Grasped, made her vail her eyes: she looked and saw
The novice, weeping, suppliant, and said to her,
'Yea, little maid, for am *I* not forgiven?'
Then glancing up beheld the holy nuns
All round her, weeping; and her heart was loosed
Within her, and she wept with these and said,
'Ye know me then, that wicked one, who broke
The vast design and purpose of the King.
O shut me round with narrowing nunnery-walls,
Meek maidens, from the voices crying "shame."
I must not scorn myself: he loves me still.
Let no one dream but that he loves me still.
So let me, if you do not shudder at me,
Nor shun to call me sister, dwell with you;
Wear black and white, and be a nun like you,
Fast with your fasts, not feasting with your feasts;
Grieve with your griefs, not grieving at your joys,
But not rejoicing; mingle with your rites;
Pray and be prayed for; lie before your shrines;
Do each low office of your holy house;
Walk your dim cloister, and distribute dole
To poor sick people, richer in His eyes
Who ransomed us, and haler too than I;
And treat their loathsome hurts and heal mine own;
And so wear out in almsdeed and in prayer
The sombre close of that voluptuous day,
Which wrought the ruin of my lord the King.'
She said: they took her to themselves; and she
Still hoping, fearing, 'is it yet too late?'
Dwelt with them, till in time their Abbess died.
Then she, for her good deeds and her pure life,
And for the power of ministration in her,
And likewise for the high rank she had borne,
Was chosen Abbess, there, an Abbess, lived
For three brief years, and there, an Abbess, past
To where beyond these voices there is peace.

1859

THE PASSING OF ARTHUR

THAT story which the bold Sir Bedivere,
First made and latest left of all the knights,
Told, when the man was no more than a voice
In the white winter of his age, to those
With whom he dwelt, new faces, other minds.
For on their march to westward, Bedivere,

Who slowly paced among the slumbering host,
Heard in his tent the moanings of the King:
'I found Him in the shining of the stars,
I marked Him in the flowering of His fields,
But in His ways with men I find Him not.
I waged His wars, and now I pass and die.
O me! for why is all around us here
As if some lesser god had made the world,
But had not force to shape it as he would,
Till the High God behold it from beyond,
And enter it, and make it beautiful?
Or else as if the world were wholly fair,
But that these eyes of men are dense and dim,
And have not power to see it as it is:
Perchance, because we see not to the close; —
For I, being simple, thought to work His will,
And have but stricken with the sword in vain;
And all whereon I leaned in wife and friend
Is traitor to my peace, and all my realm
Reels back into the beast, and is no more.
My God, thou hast forgotten me in my death:
Nay — God my Christ — I pass but shall not die.'
Then, ere that last weird battle in the west,
There came on Arthur sleeping, Gawain killed
In Lancelot's war, the ghost of Gawain blown
Along a wandering wind, and past his ear
Went shrilling, 'Hollow, hollow all delight!
Hail, King! to-morrow thou shalt pass away.
Farewell! there is an isle of rest for thee.
And I am blown along a wandering wind,
And hollow, hollow, hollow all delight.'
And fainter onward, like wild birds that change
Their season in the night and wail their way
From cloud to cloud, down the long wind the dream
Shrilled; but in going mingled with dim cries
Far in the moonlit haze among the hills,
As of some lonely city sacked by night,
When all is lost, and wife and child with wail
Pass to new lords; and Arthur woke and called,
'Who spake? A dream. O light upon the wind,
Thine, Gawain, was the woice — are these dim cries
Thine? or doth all that haunts the waste and wild
Mourn, knowing it will go along with me?'
This heard the bold Sir Bedivere and spake:
'O me, my King, let pass whatever will,
Elves, and the harmless glamour of the field;
But in their stead thy name and glory cling
To all high places like a golden cloud
For ever: but as yet thou shalt not pass.
Light was Gawain in life, and light in death
Is Gawain, for the ghost is as the man;
And care not thou for dreams from him, but rise —
I hear the steps of Modred in the west,
And with him many of thy people, and knights
Once thine, whom thou hast loved, but grosser grown
Than heathen, spitting at their vows and thee.
Right well in heart they know thee for the King.
Arise, go forth and conquer as of old.'
Then spake King Arthur to Sir Bedivere:
'Far other is this battle in the west
Whereto we move, than when we strove in youth,
And brake the petty kings, and fought with Rome,
Or thrust the heathen from the Roman wall,
And shook him through the north. Ill doom is mine
To war against my people and my knights.
The king who fights his people fights himself.
And they my knights, who loved me once, the stroke
That strikes them dead is as my death to me.
Yet let us hence, and find or feel a way
Through this blind haze, which ever since I saw
One lying in the dust at Almesbury,
Hath folded in the passes of the world.'
Then rose the King and moved his host by night,
And ever pushed Sir Modred, league by league,
Back to the sunset bound of Lyonesse —
A land of old upheaven from the abyss
By fire, to sink into the abyss again;
Where fragments of forgotten peoples dwelt,
And the long mountains ended in a coast
Of ever-shifting sand, and far away
The phantom circle of a moaning sea.
There the pursuer could pursue no more,
And he that fled no further fly the King;
And there, that day when the great light of heaven
Burned at his lowest in the rolling year,
On the waste sand by the waste sea they closed.
Nor ever yet had Arthur fought a fight
Like this last, dim, weird battle of the west.
A deathwhite mist slept over sand and sea:

Whereof the chill, to him who breathed it, drew
Down with his blood, till all his heart was cold
With formless fear; and ev'n on Arthur fell
Confusion, since he saw not whom he fought.
For friend and foe were shadows in the mist,
And friend slew friend not knowing whom he slew;
And some had visions out of golden youth,
And some beheld the faces of old ghosts
Look in upon the battle; and in the mist
Was many a noble deed, many a base,
And chance and craft and strength in single fights,
And ever and anon with host to host
Shocks, and the splintering spear, the hard mail hewn,
Shield-breakings, and the clash of brands, the crash
Of battleaxes on shattered helms, and shrieks
After the Christ, of those who falling down
Looked up for heaven, and only saw the mist;
And shouts of heathen and the traitor knights,
Oaths, insult, filth, and monstrous blasphemies,
Sweat, writhings, anguish, labouring of the lungs
In that close mist, and cryings for the light,
Moans of the dying, and voices of the dead.
  Last, as by some one deathbed after wail
Of suffering, silence follows, or through death
Or deathlike swoon, thus over all that shore,
Save for some whisper of the seething seas,
A dead hush fell; but when the dolorous day
Grew drearier toward twilight falling, came
A bitter wind, clear from the North, and blew
The mist aside, and with that wind the tide
Rose, and the pale King glanced across the field
Of battle: but no man was moving there;
Nor any cry of Christian heard thereon,
Nor yet of heathen; only the wan wave
Brake in among dead faces, to and fro
Swaying the helpless hands, and up and down
Tumbling the hollow helmets of the fallen,
And shivered brands that once had fought with Rome,
And rolling far along the gloomy shores
The voice of days of old and days to be.
  Then spake King Arthur to Sir Bedivere,
And whiter than the mist that all day long
Had held the field of battle was the King:
'Hearest thou this great voice that shakes the world,
And wastes the narrow realm whereon we move,
And beats upon the faces of the dead,
My dead, as though they had not died for me?—
O Bedivere, for on my heart hath fall'n
Confusion, till I know not what I am,
Nor whence I am, nor whether I be King,
Behold, I seem but King among the dead.'
  Then spake the bold Sir Bedivere: 'My King,
King everywhere! and so the dead have kings,
There also will I worship thee as King.
Yet still thy life is whole, and still I live
Who love thee; but who hates thee, he that brought
The heathen back among us, yonder stands,
Modred unharmed, the traitor of thine house.'
  Then spake the King: 'My house hath been my doom.
But call not thou this traitor of my house
Who hath but dwelt beneath one roof with me.
My house are rather they who sware my vows,
Yea, even while they brake them, owned me King.
And well for thee, saying in my dark hour,
When all the purport of my throne hath failed,
That quick or dead thou holdest me for King.
King am I, whatsoever be their cry;
And one last act of kinghood shalt thou see
Yet, ere I pass.' And uttering this the King
Made at the man: then Modred smote his liege
Hard on that helm which many a heathen sword
Had beaten thin; while Arthur at one blow,
Striking the last stroke with Excalibur,
Slew him, and all but slain himself, he fell.
  So all day long the noise of battle rolled
Among the mountains by the winter sea;
Until King Arthur's Table, man by man,
Had fall'n in Lyonesse about their lord,
King Arthur. Then, because his wound was deep,
The bold Sir Bedivere uplifted him,
And bore him to a chapel nigh the field,
A broken chancel with a broken cross,
That stood on a dark strait of barren land:
On one side lay the Ocean, and on one
Lay a great water, and the moon was full.
  Then spake King Arthur tc Sir Bedivere:
'The sequel of to-day unsolders all

The goodliest fellowship of famous knights
Whereof this world holds record. Such a sleep
They sleep — the men I loved. I think that we
Shall never more, at any future time,
Delight our souls with talk of knightly deeds,
Walking about the gardens and the halls
Of Camelot, as in the days that were.
I perish by this people which I made, —
Though Merlin sware that I should come again
To rule once more; but, let what will be, be,
I am so deeply smitten through the helm
That without help I cannot last till morn.
Thou therefore take my brand Excalibur,
Which was my pride: for thou rememberest how
In those old days, one summer noon, an arm
Rose up from out the bosom of the lake,
Clothed in white samite, mystic, wonderful,
Holding the sword — and how I rowed across
And took it, and have worn it, like a king;
And, wheresoever I am sung or told
In aftertime, this also shall be known:
But now delay not: take Excalibur,
And fling him far into the middle mere:
Watch what thou seëst, and lightly bring me word.'

To him replied the bold Sir Bedivere:
'It is not meet, Sir King, to leave thee thus,
Aidless, alone, and smitten through the helm —
A little thing may harm a wounded man;
Yet I thy hest will all perform at full,
Watch what I see, and lightly bring thee word.'

So saying, from the ruined shrine he stept,
And in the moon athwart the place of tombs,
Where lay the mighty bones of ancient men,
Old knights, and over them the sea-wind sang
Shrill, chill, with flakes of foam. He, stepping down
By zigzag paths, and juts of pointed rock,
Came on the shining levels of the lake.

There drew he forth the brand Excalibur,
And o'er him, drawing it, the winter moon,
Brightening the skirts of a long cloud, ran forth
And sparkled keen with frost against the hilt:
For all the haft twinkled with diamond sparks,
Myriads of topaz-lights, and jacinth-work
Of subtlest jewellery. He gazed so long
That both his eyes were dazzled as he stood,
This way and that dividing the swift mind,
In act to throw: but at the last it seemed
Better to leave Excalibur concealed
There in the many-knotted waterflags,
That whistled stiff and dry about the marge.
So strode he back slow to the wounded King.

Then spake King Arthur to Sir Bedivere:
'Hast thou performed my mission which I gave?
What is it thou hast seen? or what hast heard?'

And answer made the bold Sir Bedivere:
'I heard the ripple washing in the reeds,
And the wild water lapping on the crag.'

To whom replied King Arthur, faint and pale:
'Thou hast betrayed thy nature and thy name,
Not rendering true answer, as beseemed
Thy fëalty, nor like a noble knight:
For surer sign had followed, either hand,
Or voice, or else a motion of the mere.
This is a shameful thing for men to lie.
Yet now, I charge thee, quickly go again,
As thou art lief and dear, and do the thing
I bade thee, watch, and lightly bring me word.'

Then went Sir Bedivere the second time
Across the ridge, and paced beside the mere,
Counting the dewy pebbles, fixed in thought;
But when he saw the wonder of the hilt,
How curiously and strangely chased, he smote
His palms together, and he cried aloud:

'And if indeed I cast the brand away,
Surely a precious thing, one worthy note,
Should thus be lost for ever from the earth,
Which might have pleased the eyes of many men.
What good should follow this, if this were done?
What harm, undone? Deep harm to disobey,
Seeing obedience is the bond of rule.
Were it well to obey then, if a king demand
An act unprofitable, against himself?
The King is sick, and knows not what he does.
What record, or what relic of my lord
Should be to aftertime, but empty breath
And rumours of a doubt? But were this kept,
Stored in some treasure-house of mighty kings,
Some one might show it at a joust of arms,
Saying, "King Arthur's sword, Excalibur,

Wrought by the lonely maiden of the Lake.
Nine years she wrought it, sitting in the deeps
Upon the hidden bases of the hills."
So might some old man speak in the aftertime
To all the people, winning reverence.
But now much honour and much fame were lost.'
So spake he, clouded with his own conceit,
And hid Excalibur the second time,
And so strode back slow to the wounded King.
Then spoke King Arthur, breathing heavily:
'What is it thou hast seen? or what hast heard?'
And answer made the bold Sir Bedivere:
'I heard the water lapping on the crag,
And the long ripple washing in the reeds.'
To whom replied King Arthur, much in wrath:
'Ah, miserable and unkind, untrue,
Unknightly, traitor-hearted! Woe is me!
Authority forgets a dying king,
Laid widowed of the power in his eye
That bowed the will. I see thee what thou art,
For thou, the latest-left of all my knights,
In whom should meet the offices of all,
Thou wouldst betray me for the precious hilt;
Either from lust of gold, or like a girl
Valuing the giddy pleasure of the eyes.
Yet, for a man may fail in duty twice,
And the third time may prosper, get thee hence:
But, if thou spare to fling Excalibur,
I will arise and slay thee with my hands.'
Then quickly rose Sir Bedivere, and ran,
And, leaping down the ridges lightly, plunged
Among the bulrush beds, and clutched the sword,
And strongly wheeled and threw it. The great brand
Made lightnings in the splendour of the moon,
And flashing round and round, and whirled in an arch,
Shot like a streamer of the northern morn,
Seen where the moving isles of winter shock
By night, with noises of the Northern Sea.
So flashed and fell the brand Excalibur:
But ere he dipt the surface, rose an arm
Clothed in white samite, mystic, wonderful,
And caught him by the hilt, and brandished him
Three times, and drew him under in the mere.
And lightly went the other to the King.
Then spoke King Arthur, drawing thicker breath:
'Now see I by thine eyes that this is done.
Speak out: what is it thou has heard, or seen?'
And answer made the bold Sir Bedivere:
'Sir King, I closed mine eyelids, lest the gems
Should blind my purpose, for I never saw,
Nor shall see, here or elsewhere, till I die,
Not though I live three lives of mortal men,
So great a miracle as yonder hilt.
Then with both hands I flung him, wheeling him;
But when I looked again, behold an arm,
Clothed in white samite, mystic, wonderful,
That caught him by the hilt, and brandished him
Three times, and drew him under in the mere.'
And answer made King Arthur, breathing hard:
'My end draws nigh; 't is time that I were gone.
Make broad thy shoulders to receive my weight,
And bear me to the margin; yet I fear
My wound hath taken cold, and I shall die.'
So saying, from the pavement he half rose,
Slowly, with pain, reclining on his arm,
And looking wistfully with wide blue eyes
As in a picture. Him Sir Bedivere
Remorsefully regarded through his tears,
And would have spoken, but he found not words;
Then took with care, and kneeling on one knee,
O'er both his shoulders drew the languid hands,
And rising bore him through the place of tombs.
But, as he walked, King Arthur panted hard,
Like one that feels a nightmare on his bed
When all the house is mute. So sighed the King
Muttering and murmuring at his ear, 'Quick, quick!
I fear it is too late, and I shall die.'
But the other swiftly strode from ridge to ridge,
Clothed with his breath, and looking, as he walked,
Larger than human on the frozen hills.
He heard the deep behind him, and a cry

Before. His own thought drove him like a goad.
Dry clashed his harness in the icy caves
And barren chasms, and all to left and right
The bare black cliff clanged round him, as he based
His feet on juts of slippery crag that rang
Sharp-smitten with the dint of armed heels —
And on a sudden, lo! the level lake,
And the long glories of the winter moon.
Then saw they how there hove a dusky barge,
Dark as a funeral scarf from stem to stern,
Beneath them; and descending they were ware
That all the decks were dense with stately forms,
Black-stoled, black-hooded, like a dream — by these
Three Queens with crowns of gold: and from them rose
A cry that shivered to the tingling stars,
And, as it were one voice, an agony
Of lamentation, like a wind that shrills
All night in a waste land, where no one comes,
Or hath come, since the making of the world.
Then murmured Arthur, 'Place me in the barge.'
So to the barge they came. There those three Queens
Put forth their hands, and took the King, and wept.
But she, that rose the tallest of them all
And fairest, laid his head upon her lap,
And loosed the shattered casque, and chafed his hands,
And called him by his name, complaining loud,
And dropping bitter tears against a brow
Striped with dark blood: for all his face was white
And colourless, and like the withered moon
Smote by the fresh beam of the springing east;
And all his greaves and cuisses dashed with drops
Of onset; and the light and lustrous curls —
That made his forehead like a rising sun
High from the daïs-throne — were parched with dust;
Or clotted into points and hanging loose,
Mixed with the knightly growth that fringed his lips.
So like a shattered column lay the King;
Not like that Arthur who, with lance in rest,
From spur to plume a star of tournament,
Shot through the lists at Camelot, and charged
Before the eyes of ladies and of kings.
Then loudly cried the bold Sir Bedivere:
'Ah! my Lord Arthur, whither shall I go?
Where shall I hide my forehead and my eyes?
For now I see the true old times are dead,
When every morning brought a noble chance,
And every chance brought out a noble knight.
Such times have been not since the light that led
The holy Elders with the gift of myrrh.
But now the whole Round Table is dissolved
Which was an image of the mighty world,
And I, the last, go forth companionless,
And the days darken round me, and the years,
Among new men, strange faces, other minds.'
And slowly answered Arthur from the barge:
'The old order changeth, yielding place to new,
And God fulfils himself in many ways,
Lest one good custom should corrupt the world,
Comfort thyself: what comfort is in me?
I have lived my life, and that which I have done
May He within himself make pure! but thou,
If thou shouldst never see my face again,
Pray for my soul. More things are wrought by prayer
Than this world dreams of. Wherefore, let thy voice
Rise like a fountain for me night and day.
For what are men better than sheep or goats
That nourish a blind life within the brain,
If, knowing God, they lift not hands of prayer
Both for themselves and those who call them friend?
For so the whole round earth is every way
Bound by gold chains about the feet of God.
But now farewell. I am going a long way
With these thou seëst — if indeed I go
(For all my mind is clouded with a doubt) —
To the island-valley of Avilion;
Where falls not hail, or rain, or any snow.
Nor ever wind blows loudly; but it lies
Deep-meadowed, happy, fair with orchard lawns
And bowery hollows crowned with summer sea,
Where I will heal me of my grievous wound.'
So said he, and the barge with oar and sail
Moved from the brink, like some full-breasted swan
That, fluting a wild carol ere her death,

Ruffles her pure cold plume, and takes the flood
With swarthy webs. Long stood Sir Bedivere
Revolving many memories, till the hull
Looked one black dot against the verge of dawn,
And on the mere the wailing died away.
But when that moan had past for evermore,
The stillness of the dead world's winter dawn
Amazed him, and he groaned, 'The King is gone.'
And therewithal came on him the weird rhyme,
'From the great deep to the great deep he goes.'
Whereat he slowly turned and slowly clomb
The last hard footstep of that iron crag;
Thence marked the black hull moving yet, and cried,
'He passes to be King among the dead,
And after healing of his grievous wound
He comes again; but—if he come no more—
O me, be yon dark Queens in yon black boat,
Who shrieked and wailed, the three whereat we gazed
On that high day, when, clothed with living light,
They stood before his throne in silence, friends
Of Arthur, who should help him at his need?'
Then from the dawn it seemed there came, but faint
As from beyond the limit of the world,
Like the last echo born of a great cry,
Sounds, as if some fair city were one voice
Around a king returning from his wars.
Thereat once more he moved about, and clomb
Ev'n to the highest he could climb, and saw,
Straining his eyes beneath an arch of hand,
Or thought he saw, the speck that bare the king,
Down that long water opening on the deep
Somewhere far off, pass on and on, and go
From less to less and vanish into light.
And the new sun rose bringing the new year.

1842, 1869

FLOWER IN THE CRANNIED WALL

Flower in the crannied wall,
I pluck you out of the crannies,
I hold you here, root and all, in my hand,
Little flower — but *if* I could understand
What you are, root and all, and all in all,
I should know what God and man is.

1869

RIZPAH

Wailing, wailing, wailing, the wind over land and sea —
And Willy's voice in the wind, 'O mother come out to me.'
Why should he call me to-night, when he knows that I cannot go?
For the downs are as bright as day, and the full moon stares at the snow.

We should be seen, my dear; they would spy us out of the town.
The loud black nights for us, and the storm rushing over the down,
When I cannot see my own hand, but am led by the creak of the chain,
And grovel and grope for my son till I find myself drenched with the rain.

Anything fallen again? nay — what was there left to fall?
I have taken them home, I have numbered the bones, I have hidden them all.
What am I saying? and what are *you*? do you come as a spy?
Falls? what falls? who knows? As the tree falls so must it lie.

Who let her in? how long has she been? you — what have you heard?
Why did you sit so quiet? you never have spoken a word.
O — to pray with me — yes — a lady — none of their spies —
But the night has crept into my heart, and begun to darken my eyes.

Ah — you, that have lived so soft, what should *you* know of the night,
The blast and the burning shame and the bitter frost and the fright?
I have done it, while you were asleep — you were only made for the day.
I have gathered my baby together — and now you may go your way.

Nay — for it's kind of you, Madam, to sit by an old dying wife.
But say nothing hard of my boy, I have only an hour of life.
I kissed my boy in the prison, before he went out to die.
'They dared me to do it,' he said, and he never has told me a lie.
I whipt him for robbing an orchard once when he was but a child —
'The farmer dared me to do it,' he said; he was always so wild —

And idle — and couldn't be idle — my Willy — he never could rest.
The King should have made him a soldier, he would have been one of his best.

But he lived with a lot of wild mates, and they never would let him be good;
They swore that he dare not rob the mail, and he swore that he would;
And he took no life, but he took one purse, and when all was done
He flung it among his fellows — I'll none of it, said my son.

I came into court to the Judge and the lawyers. I told them my tale,
God's own truth — but they killed him, they killed him for robbing the mail.
They hanged him in chains for a show — we had always borne a good name —
To be hanged for a thief — and then put away — isn't that enough shame?
Dust to dust — low down — let us hide! but they set him so high
That all the ships of the world could stare at him, passing by.
God 'ill pardon the hell-black raven and horrible fowls of the air,
But not the black heart of the lawyer who killed him and hanged him there.

And the jailer forced me away. I had bid him my last goodbye;
They had fastened the door of his cell. 'O mother!' I heard him cry.
I couldn't get back though I tried, he had something further to say,
And now I never shall know it. The jailer forced me away.

Then since I couldn't but hear that cry of my boy that was dead,
They seized me and shut me up: they fastened me down on my bed.
'Mother, O mother!' — he called in the dark to me year after year —
They beat me for that, they beat me — you know that I couldn't but hear;
And then at the last they found I had grown so stupid and still
They let me abroad again — but the creatures had worked their will.

Flesh of my flesh was gone, but bone of my bone was left —
I stole them all from the lawyers — and you, will you call it a theft? —
My baby, the bones that had sucked me, the bones that had laughed and had cried —
Theirs? O no! they are mine — not theirs — they had moved in my side.

Do you think I was scared by the bones? I kissed 'em, I buried 'em all —
I can't dig deep, I am old — in the night by the churchyard wall.
My Willy 'ill rise up whole when the trumpet of judgment 'ill sound;
But I charge you never to say that I laid him in holy ground.

They would scratch him up — they would hang him again on the cursèd tree.
Sin? O yes — we are sinners, I know — let all that be,
And read me a Bible verse of the Lord's good will toward men —
'Full of compassion and mercy, the Lord' — let me hear it again;
'Full of compassion and mercy — long-suffering.' Yes, O yes!
For the lawyer is born but to murder — the Saviour lives but to bless.
He'll never put on the black cap except for the worst of the worst,
And the first may be last — I have heard it in church — and the last may be first.
Suffering — O long-suffering — yes, as the Lord must know,
Year after year in the mist and the wind and the shower and the snow.

Heard, have you? what? they have told you he never repented his sin.
How do they know it? are *they* his mother? are *you* of his kin?
Heard! have you ever heard, when the storm on the downs began,
The wind that 'ill wail like a child and the sea that 'ill moan like a man?

Election, Election and Reprobation — it's all very well.
But I go to-night to my boy, and I shall not find him in Hell.
For I cared so much for my boy that the Lord has looked into my care,
And He means me I'm sure to be happy with Willy, I know not where.

And if *he* be lost — but to save *my* soul, that is all your desire:
Do you think that I care for *my* soul if my boy be gone to the fire?
I have been with God in the dark — go, go, you may leave me alone —
You never have borne a child — you are just as hard as a stone.

Madam, I beg your pardon! I think that you mean to be kind,
But I cannot hear what you say for my Willy's voice in the wind —

The snow and the sky so bright — he used but to call in the dark,
And he calls to me now from the church and not from the gibbet — for hark!
Nay — you can hear it yourself — it is coming — shaking the walls —
Willy — the moon's in a cloud — Goodnight. I am going. He calls.

1880

'FRATER AVE ATQUE VALE'

Row us out from Desenzano, to your Sirmione row!
So they rowed, and there we landed — 'O venusta Sirmio!'
There to me through all the groves of olive in the summer glow,
There beneath the Roman ruin where the purple flowers grow,
Came that 'Ave atque Vale' of the Poet's hopeless woe,
Tenderest of Roman poets nineteen hundred years ago,
'Frater Ave atque Vale,' — as we wandered to and fro,
Gazing at the Lydian laughter of the Garda Lake below,
Sweet Catullus's all-but-island, olive-silvery Sirmio!

1883

MERLIN AND THE GLEAM

O YOUNG Mariner,
You from the haven
Under the sea-cliff,
You that are watching
The gray Magician
With eyes of wonder,
I am Merlin,
And *I* am dying,
I am Merlin
Who follow The Gleam.

Mighty the Wizard
Who found me at sunrise
Sleeping, and woke me
And learned me Magic!
Great the Master,
And sweet the Magic,
When over the valley,
In early summers,
Over the mountain,
On human faces,
And all around me,
Moving to melody,
Floated The Gleam.

Once at the croak of a Raven
who crost it,
A barbarous people,
Blind to the magic,
And deaf to the melody,
Snarled at and cursed me.
A demon vext me,
The light retreated,
The landskip darkened,
The melody deadened,
The Master whispered,
'Follow The Gleam.'

Then to the melody,
Over a wilderness
Gliding, and glancing at
Elf of the woodland,
Gnome of the cavern,
Griffin and Giant,
And dancing of Fairies
In desolate hollows,
And wraiths of the mountain,
And rolling of dragons
By warble of water,
Or cataract music
Of falling torrents,
Flitted The Gleam.

Down from the mountain
And over the level,
And streaming and shining on
Silent river,
Silvery willow,
Pasture and plowland,
Innocent maidens,
Garrulous children,
Homestead and harvest,
Reaper and gleaner,
And rough-ruddy faces
Of lowly labour,
Slided The Gleam —

Then, with a melody
Stronger and statelier,
Led me at length
To the city and palace
Of Arthur the king;
Touched at the golden
Cross of the churches,
Flashed on the Tournament,
Flickered and bickered
From helmet to helmet,
And last on the forehead
Of Arthur the blameless
Rested The Gleam.

Clouds and darkness
Closed upon Camelot;
Arthur had vanished
I knew not whither,
The king who loved me,

And cannot die;
For out of the darkness
Silent and slowly
The Gleam, that had waned to a
  wintry glimmer
On icy fallow
And faded forest,
Drew to the valley
Named of the shadow,
And slowly brightening
Out of the glimmer,
And slowly moving again to a melody
Yearningly tender,
Fell on the shadow,
No longer a shadow,
But clothed with The Gleam.

And broader and brighter
The Gleam flying onward,
Wed to the melody,
Sang through the world;
And slower and fainter,
Old and weary,
But eager to follow,
I saw, whenever
In passing it glanced upon
Hamlet or city,
That under the Crosses
The dead man's garden,
The mortal hillock,
Would break into blossom
And so to the land's
Last limit I came —
And can no longer,
But die rejoicing,
For through the Magic
Of Him the Mighty,
Who taught me in childhood,
There on the border
Of boundless Ocean,
And all but in Heaven
Hovers The Gleam.

Not of the sunlight,
Not of the moonlight,
Not of the starlight!
O young Mariner,
Down to the haven,
Call your companions,
Launch your vessel,
And crowd your canvas,
And, ere it vanishes
Over the margin,
After it, follow it,
Follow The Gleam.

1889

CROSSING THE BAR

SUNSET and evening star,
  And one clear call for me!
And may there be no moaning of the bar,
  When I put out to sea,

But such a tide as moving seems asleep,
  Too full for sound and foam,
When that which drew from out the boundless deep
  Turns again home.

Twilight and evening bell,
  And after that the dark!
And may there be no sadness of farewell,
  When I embark;

For though from out our bourne of Time and Place
  The flood may bear me far,
I hope to see my Pilot face to face
  When I have crost the bar.

1889

Robert Browning (1812–1889)

SONG FROM *PIPPA PASSES*

THE year 's at the spring,
And day 's at the morn;
Morning 's at seven;
The hill-side 's dew-pearled;
The lark 's on the wing;
The snail 's on the thorn;
God 's in His heaven —
All 's right with the world!

1841

CAVALIER TUNES

I. MARCHING ALONG

KENTISH Sir Byng stood for his King,
Bidding the crop-headed Parliament swing:
And, pressing a troop unable to stoop
And see the rogues flourish and honest folk
  droop,
Marched them along, fifty-score strong,
Great-hearted gentlemen, singing this song.

God for King Charles! Pym and such carles
To the Devil that prompts 'em their treasonous parles!
Cavaliers, up! Lips from the cup,
Hands from the pasty, nor bite take nor
  sup
Till you 're —
  (*Chorus*) *Marching along, fifty-score strong,*
    Great-hearted gentlemen, singing
    this song.

Hampden to Hell, and his obsequies' knell
Serve Hazelrig, Fiennes, and young Harry as well!
England, good cheer! Rupert is near!
Kentish and loyalists, keep we not here
(*Chorus*) *Marching along, fifty-score strong,*
Great-hearted gentlemen, singing this song?

Then, God for King Charles! Pym and his snarls
To the Devil that pricks on such pestilent carles!
Hold by the right, you double your might;
So, onward to Nottingham, fresh for the fight,
(*Chorus*) *March we along, fifty-score strong,*
Great-hearted gentlemen, singing this song!

II. Give a Rouse

King Charles, and who 'll do him right now?
King Charles, and who 's ripe for fight now?
Give a rouse: here 's, in Hell's despite now,
King Charles!

Who gave me the goods that went since?
Who raised me the house that sank once?
Who helped me to gold I spent since?
Who found me in wine you drank once?
(*Chorus*) *King Charles, and who 'll do him right now?*
King Charles, and who 's ripe for fight now?
Give a rouse: here 's, in Hell's despite now,
King Charles!

To whom used my boy George quaff else,
By the old fool's side that begot him?
For whom did he cheer and laugh else,
While Noll's damned troopers shot him?
(*Chorus*) *King Charles, and who 'll do him right now?*
King Charles, and who 's ripe for fight now?
Give a rouse: here 's, in Hell's despite now,
King Charles!

III. Boot and Saddle

Boot, saddle, to horse, and away!
Rescue my Castle, before the hot day
Brightens to blue from its silvery grey,
(*Chorus*) *Boot, saddle, to horse, and away!*

Ride past the suburbs, asleep as you 'd say;
Many 's the friend there, will listen and pray
'God's luck to gallants that strike up the lay —
(*Chorus*) *Boot, saddle, to horse, and away!'*

Forty miles off, like a roebuck at bay,
Flouts Castle Brancepeth the Roundheads' array:
Who laughs, 'Good fellows ere this, by my fay,
(*Chorus*) *Boot, saddle, to horse, and away?'*

Who? My wife Gertrude; that, honest and gay,
Laughs when you talk of surrendering, 'Nay!
I've better counsellors; what counsel they?
(*Chorus*) *Boot, saddle, to horse, and away!'*

1842

INCIDENT OF THE FRENCH CAMP

You know, we French stormed Ratisbon:
A mile or so away
On a little mound, Napoleon
Stood on our storming-day;
With neck out-thrust, you fancy how,
Legs wide, arms locked behind,
As if to balance the prone brow
Oppressive with its mind.

Just as perhaps he mused 'My plans
That soar, to earth may fall,
Let once my army-leader Lannes
Waver at yonder wall,' —
Out 'twixt the battery-smokes there flew
A rider, bound on bound
Full-galloping; nor bridle drew
Until he reached the mound.

Then off there flung in smiling joy,
And held himself erect
By just his horse's mane, a boy:
You hardly could suspect —
(So tight he kept his lips compressed,
Scarce any blood came through)
You looked twice ere you saw his breast
Was all but shot in two.

'Well,' cried he, 'Emperor, by God's grace
We 've got you Ratisbon!
The Marshal 's in the market-place,
And you 'll be there anon
To see your flag-bird flap his vans
Where I, to heart's desire,
Perched him!' The Chief's eye flashed; his plans
Soared up again like fire.

The Chief's eye flashed; but presently
Softened itself, as sheathes
A film the mother-eagle's eye

When her bruised eaglet breathes:
'You 're wounded!' 'Nay,' his soldier's pride
Touched to the quick, he said:
'I 'm killed, Sire!' And his Chief beside,
Smiling the boy fell dead.

1842

MY LAST DUCHESS

FERRARA

That 's my last Duchess painted on the wall,
Looking as if she were alive; I call
That piece a wonder, now: Frà Pandolf's hands
Worked busily a day, and there she stands.
Will 't please you sit and look at her? I said
'Frà Pandolf' by design, for never read
Strangers like you that pictured countenance,
The depth and passion of its earnest glance,
But to myself they turned (since none puts by
The curtain I have drawn for you, but I)
And seemed as they would ask me, if they durst,
How such a glance came there; so, not the first
Are you to turn and ask thus. Sir, 't was not
Her husband's presence only, called that spot
Of joy into the Duchess' cheek: perhaps
Frà Pandolf chanced to say 'Her mantle laps
Over my Lady's wrist too much,' or 'Paint
Must never hope to reproduce the faint
Half-flush that dies along her throat'; such stuff
Was courtesy, she thought, and cause enough
For calling up that spot of joy. She had
A heart . . . how shall I say? . . . too soon made glad,
Too easily impressed; she liked whate'er
She looked on, and her looks went everywhere.
Sir, 't was all one! My favour at her breast,
The dropping of the daylight in the West,
The bough of cherries some officious fool
Broke in the orchard for her, the white mule
She rode with round the terrace — all and each
Would draw from her alike the approving speech,
Or blush, at least. She thanked men, — good; but thanked
Somehow . . . I know not how . . . as if she ranked
My gift of a nine-hundred-years-old name
With anybody's gift. Who 'd stoop to blame
This sort of trifling? Even had you skill
In speech — (which I have not) — to make your will
Quite clear to such an one, and say 'Just this
Or that in you disgusts me; here you miss,
Or there exceed the mark' — and if she let
Herself be lessoned so, nor plainly set
Her wits to yours, forsooth, and made excuse,
— E'en then would be some stooping, and I chuse
Never to stoop. Oh, Sir, she smiled, no doubt,
Whene'er I passed her; but who passed without
Much the same smile? This grew; I gave commands;
Then all smiles stopped together. There she stands
As if alive. Will 't please you rise? We 'll meet
The company below, then. I repeat,
The Count your Master's known munificence
Is ample warrant that no just pretence
Of mine for dowry will be disallowed;
Though his fair daughter's self, as I avowed
At starting, is my object. Nay, we 'll go
Together down, Sir! Notice Neptune, though,
Taming a sea-horse, thought a rarity,
Which Claus of Innsbruck cast in bronze for me.

1842

THE LABORATORY

Now that I, tying thy glass mask tightly,
May gaze through these faint smokes curling whitely,
As thou pliest thy trade in this devil's-smithy —
Which is the poison to poison her, prithee?

He is with her; and they know that I know
Where they are, what they do: they believe my tears flow
While they laugh, laugh at me, at me fled to the drear
Empty church, to pray God in, for them! — I am here.

Grind away, moisten and mash up thy paste,
Pound at thy powder, — I am not in haste!
Better sit thus, and observe thy strange things,
Than go where men wait me and dance at the King's.

That in the mortar — you call it a gum?
Ah, the brave tree whence such gold oozings come!
And yonder soft phial, the exquisite blue,
Sure to taste sweetly, — is that poison too?

Had I but all of them, thee and thy treasures,
What a wild crowd of invisible pleasures!
To carry pure death in an earring, a casket,
A signet, a fan-mount, a filigree-basket!

Soon, at the King's, a mere lozenge to give
And Pauline should have just thirty minutes to live!
But to light a pastille, and Elise, with her head
And her breast and her arms and her hands, should drop dead!

Quick — is it finished? The colour's too grim!
Why not soft like the phial's, enticing and dim?
Let it brighten her drink, let her turn it and stir,
And try it and taste, ere she fix and prefer!

What a drop! She 's not little, no minion like me —
That 's why she ensnared him: this never will free
The soul from those masculine eyes, — say, 'no!'
To that pulse's magnificent come-and-go.

For only last night, as they whispered, I brought
My own eyes to bear on her so, that I thought
Could I keep them one half minute fixed, she would fall,
Shrivelled; she fell not; yet this does it all!

Not that I bid you spare her the pain!
Let death be felt and the proof remain;
Brand, burn up, bite into its grace —
He is sure to remember her dying face!

Is it done? Take my mask off! Nay, be not morose;
It kills her, and this prevents seeing it close:
The delicate droplet, my whole fortune's fee —
If it hurts her, beside, can it ever hurt me?

Now, take all my jewels, gorge gold to your fill,
You may kiss me, old man, on my mouth if you will!
But brush this dust off me, lest horror it brings
Ere I know it — next moment I dance at the King's!

1844

THE LOST LEADER

Just for a handful of silver he left us,
Just for a riband to stick in his coat —
Found the one gift of which fortune bereft us,
Lost all the others she lets us devote;
They, with the gold to give, doled him out silver,
So much was theirs who so little allowed:
How all our copper had gone for his service!
Rags — were they purple, his heart had been proud!
We that had loved him so, followed him, honoured him,
Lived in his mild and magnificent eye,
Learned his great language, caught his clear accents,
Made him our pattern to live and to die!
Shakespeare was of us, Milton was for us,
Burns, Shelley, were with us, — they watch from their graves!
He alone breaks from the van and the freemen,
He alone sinks to the rear and the slaves!

We shall march prospering, — not through his presence;
Songs may inspirit us, — not from his lyre;
Deeds will be done, — while he boasts his quiescence,
Still bidding crouch whom the rest bade aspire:
Blot out his name, then, record one lost soul more,
One task more declined, one more footpath untrod,
One more triumph for devils and sorrow for angels,
One wrong more to man, one more insult to God!
Life's night begins: let him never come back to us!
There would be doubt, hesitation and pain,
Forced praise on our part — the glimmer of twilight,
Never glad confident morning again!
Best fight on well, for we taught him, — strike gallantly,

Menace our heart ere we master his own;
Then let him receive the new knowledge and wait us,
Pardoned in Heaven, the first by the throne!

1845

'HOW THEY BROUGHT THE GOOD NEWS FROM GHENT TO AIX'

I SPRANG to the stirrup, and Joris, and he;
I galloped, Dirck galloped, we galloped all three;
'Good speed!' cried the watch, as the gate-bolts undrew;
'Speed!' echoed the wall to us galloping through;
Behind shut the postern, the lights sank to rest,
And into the midnight we galloped abreast.

Not a word to each other; we kept the great pace
Neck by neck, stride by stride, never changing our place;
I turned in my saddle and made its girths tight,
Then shortened each stirrup, and set the pique right,
Rebuckled the cheek-strap, chained slacker the bit,
Nor galloped less steadily Roland a whit.

'T was moonset at starting; but while we drew near
Lokeren, the cocks crew and twilight dawned clear;
At Boom, a great yellow star came out to see;
At Düffeld, 't was morning as plain as could be;
And from Mecheln church-steeple we heard the half-chime,
So Joris broke silence with, 'Yet there is time!'

At Aerschot, up leaped of a sudden the sun,
And against him the cattle stood black every one,
To stare through the mist at us galloping past,
And I saw my stout galloper Roland at last,
With resolute shoulders, each butting away
The haze, as some bluff river headland its spray.
And his low head and crest, just one sharp ear bent back
For my voice, and the other pricked out on his track;
And one eye's black intelligence, — ever that glance
O'er its white edge at me, his own master, askance!
And the thick heavy spume-flakes which aye and anon
His fierce lips shook upwards in galloping on.

By Hasselt, Dirck groaned; and cried Joris, 'Stay spur!
Your Roos galloped bravely, the fault 's not in her,
We 'll remember at Aix' — for one heard the quick wheeze
Of her chest, saw the stretched neck and staggering knees,
And sunk tail, and horrible heave of the flank,
As down on her haunches she shuddered and sank.

So we were left galloping, Joris and I,
Past Looz and past Tongres, no cloud in the sky;
The broad sun above laughed a pitiless laugh,
'Neath our feet broke the brittle bright stubble like chaff;
Till over by Dalhem a dome-spire sprang white,
And 'Gallop,' gasped Joris, 'for Aix is in sight!'

'How they 'll greet us!' — and all in a moment his roan
Rolled neck and croup over, lay dead as a stone;
And there was my Roland to bear the whole weight
Of the news which alone could save Aix from her fate,
With his nostrils like pits full of blood to the brim,
And with circles of red for his eye-sockets' rim.

Then I cast loose my buffcoat, each holster let fall,
Shook off both my jack-boots, let go belt and all,
Stood up in the stirrup, leaned, patted his ear,
Called my Roland his pet-name, my horse without peer;

Clapped my hands, laughed and sang, any noise, bad or good,
Till at length into Aix Roland galloped and stood.

And all I remember is, friends flocking round
As I sat with his head 'twixt my knees on the ground;
And no voice but was praising this Roland of mine,
As I poured down his throat our last measure of wine,
Which (the burgesses voted by common consent)
Was no more than his due who brought good news from Ghent.

1845

MEETING AT NIGHT

The grey sea and the long black land;
And the yellow half-moon large and low;
And the startled little waves that leap
In fiery ringlets from their sleep,
As I gain the cove with pushing prow,
And quench its speed in the slushy sand.

Then a mile of warm sea-scented beach;
Three fields to cross till a farm appears;
A tap at the pane, the quick sharp scratch
And blue spurt of a lighted match,
And a voice less loud, through its joys and fears,
Than the two hearts beating each to each!

1845

PARTING AT MORNING

Round the cape of a sudden came the sea,
And the sun looked over the mountain's rim:
And straight was a path of gold for him,
And the need of a world of men for me.

1845

HOME-THOUGHTS, FROM ABROAD

Oh, to be in England
Now that April 's there,
And whoever wakes in England
Sees, some morning, unaware,
That the lowest boughs and the brushwood sheaf
Round the elm-tree bole are in tiny leaf,
While the chaffinch sings on the orchard bough
In England — now!

And after April, when May follows,
And the whitethroat builds, and all the swallows!
Hark, where my blossomed pear-tree in the hedge
Leans to the field and scatters on the clover
Blossoms and dewdrops — at the bent spray's edge —
That 's the wise thrush; he sings each song twice over,
Lest you should think he never could recapture
The first fine careless rapture!
And though the fields look rough with hoary dew,
All will be gay when noontide wakes anew
The buttercups, the little children's dower
— Far brighter than this gaudy melon-flower!

1845

HOME-THOUGHTS, FROM THE SEA

Nobly, nobly Cape Saint Vincent to the North-West died away;
Sunset ran, one glorious blood-red, reeking into Cadiz Bay;
Bluish mid the burning water, full in face Trafalgar lay;
In the dimmest North-East distance, dawned Gibraltar grand and gray;
'Here and here did England help me: how can I help England?' — say,
Whoso turns as I, this evening, turn to God to praise and pray,
While Jove's planet rises yonder, silent over Africa.

1845

THE BISHOP ORDERS HIS TOMB AT SAINT PRAXED'S CHURCH

Vanity, saith the preacher, vanity!
Draw round my bed: is Anselm keeping back?
Nephews — sons mine . . . ah God, I know not! Well —
She, men would have to be your mother once,
Old Gandolf envied me, so fair she was!
What 's done is done, and she is dead beside,
Dead long ago, and I am Bishop since,
And as she died so must we die ourselves,
And thence ye may perceive the world's a dream.
Life, how and what is it? As here I lie
In this state-chamber, dying by degrees,
Hours and long hours in the dead night, I ask

'Do I live, am I dead?' Peace, peace seems all.
Saint Praxed's ever was the church for peace;
And so, about this tomb of mine. I fought
With tooth and nail to save my niche, ye know:
— Old Gandolf cozened me, despite my care;
Shrewd was that snatch from out the corner South
He graced his carrion with, God curse the same!
Yet still my niche is not so cramped but thence
One sees the pulpit o' the epistle-side,
And somewhat of the choir, those silent seats,
And up into the aery dome where live
The angels, and a sunbeam 's sure to lurk:
And I shall fill my slab of basalt there,
And 'neath my tabernacle take my rest,
With those nine columns round me, two and two,
The odd one at my feet where Anselm stands:
Peach-blossom marble all, the rare, the ripe
As fresh-poured red wine of a mighty pulse
— Old Gandolf with his paltry onion-stone,
Put me where I may look at him! True peach,
Rosy and flawless: how I earned the prize!
Draw close: that conflagration of my church
— What then? So much was saved if aught were missed!
My sons, ye would not be my death? Go dig
The white-grape vineyard where the oil-press stood,
Drop water gently till the surface sinks,
And if ye find . . . Ah, God I know not, I! . . .
Bedded in store of rotten figleaves soft,
And corded up in a tight olive-frail,
Some lump, ah God, of *lapis lazuli*,
Big as a Jew's head cut off at the nape,
Blue as a vein o'er the Madonna's breast . . .
Sons, all have I bequeathed you, villas, all,
That brave Frascati villa with its bath,
So, let the blue lump poise between my knees,
Like God the Father's globe on both His hands
Ye worship in the Jesu Church so gay,
For Gandolf shall not choose but see and burst!
Swift as a weaver's shuttle fleet our years:
Man goeth to the grave, and where is he?
Did I say basalt for my slab, sons? Black —
'T was ever antique-black I meant! How else
Shall ye contrast my frieze to come beneath?
The bas-relief in bronze ye promised me,
Those Pans and Nymphs ye wot of, and perchance
Some tripod, thyrsus, with a vase or so,
The Saviour at his sermon on the mount,
Saint Praxed in a glory, and one Pan
Ready to twitch the Nymph's last garment off,
And Moses with the tables . . . but I know
Ye mark me not! What do they whisper thee,
Child of my bowels, Anselm? Ah, ye hope
To revel down my villas while I gasp
Bricked o'er with beggar's mouldy travertine
Which Gandolf from his tomb-top chuckles at!
Nay, boys, ye love me — all of jasper, then!
'T is jasper ye stand pledged to, lest I grieve.
My bath must needs be left behind, alas!
One block, pure green as a pistachio-nut,
There 's plenty jasper somewhere in the world —
And have I not Saint Praxed's ear to pray
Horses for ye, and brown Greek manuscripts,
And mistresses with great smooth marbly limbs?
— That 's if ye carve my epitaph aright,
Choice Latin, picked phrase, Tully's every word,
No gaudy ware like Gandolf's second line —
Tully, my masters? Ulpian serves his need!
And then how I shall lie through centuries,
And hear the blessèd mutter of the mass,
And see God made and eaten all day long,
And feel the steady candle-flame, and taste
Good strong thick stupefying incense-smoke!
For as I lie here, hours of the dead night,
Dying in state and by such slow degrees,
I fold my arms as if they clasped a crook,
And stretch my feet forth straight as stone can point,
And let the bedclothes for a mortcloth drop
Into great laps and folds of sculptor's-work:
And as yon tapers dwindle, and strange thoughts
Grow, with a certain humming in my ears,
About the life before I lived this life,
And this life too, Popes, Cardinals and Priests,
Saint Praxed at his sermon on the mount,
Your tall pale mother with her talking eyes,
And new-found agate urns as fresh as day,
And marble's language, Latin pure, discreet,
— Aha, ELUCESCEBAT quoth our friend?
No Tully, said I, Ulpian at the best!
Evil and brief hath been my pilgrimage.
All *lapis*, all, sons! Else I give the Pope

My villas: will ye ever eat my heart?
Ever your eyes were as a lizard's quick,
They glitter like your mother's for my soul,
Or ye would heighten my impoverished frieze,
Piece out its starved design, and fill my vase
With grapes, and add a vizor and a Term,
And to the tripod ye would tie a lynx
That in his struggle throws the thyrsus down,
To comfort me on my entablature
Whereon I am to lie till I must ask
'Do I live, am I dead?' There, leave me, there!
For ye have stabbed me with ingratitude
To death — ye wish it — God, ye wish it! Stone —
Gritstone, a-crumble! Clammy squares which sweat
As if the corpse they keep were oozing through —
And no more *lapis* to delight the world!
Well, go! I bless ye. Fewer tapers there,
But in a row: and, going, turn your backs
— Ay, like departing altar-ministrants,
And leave me in my church, the church for peace,
That I may watch at leisure if he leers —
Old Gandolf, at me, from his onion-stone,
As still he envied me, so fair she was!

1845

A WOMAN'S LAST WORD

LET 's contend no more, Love,
Strive nor weep:
All be as before, Love,
— Only sleep!

What so wild as words are?
I and thou
In debate, as birds are,
Hawk on bough!

See the creature stalking
While we speak!
Hush and hide the talking,
Cheek on cheek!

What so false as truth is,
False to thee?
Where the serpent's tooth is,
Shun the tree —

Where the apple reddens
Never pry —
Lest we lose our Edens,
Eve and I!

Be a god and hold me
With a charm!
Be a man and fold me
With thine arm!

Teach me, only teach, Love!
As I ought
I will speak thy speech, Love,
Think thy thought —

Meet, if thou require it,
Both demands,
Laying flesh and spirit
In thy hands.

That shall be to-morrow
Not to-night:
I must bury sorrow
Out of sight:

— Must a little weep, Love,
(Foolish me!)
And so fall asleep, Love,
Loved by thee.

1855

EVELYN HOPE

BEAUTIFUL Evelyn Hope is dead!
Sit and watch by her side an hour.
That is her book-shelf, this her bed;
She plucked that piece of geranium-flower,
Beginning to die too, in the glass;
Little has yet been changed, I think:
The shutters are shut, no light may pass
Save two long rays through the hinge's chink.

Sixteen years old when she died!
Perhaps she had scarcely heard my name;
It was not her time to love; beside,
Her life had many a hope and aim,
Duties enough and little cares,
And now was quiet, now astir,
Till God's hand beckoned unawares, —
And the sweet white brow is all of her.

Is it too late then, Evelyn Hope?
What, your soul was pure and true,
The good stars met in your horoscope,
Made you of spirit, fire and dew —
And, just because I was thrice as old
And our paths in the world diverged so wide,
Each was nought to each, must I be told?
We were fellow mortals, nought beside?

No, indeed! for God above
Is great to grant, as mighty to make,
And creates the love to reward the love:

I claim you still, for my own love's sake!
Delayed it may be for more lives yet,
Through worlds I shall traverse, not a few:
Much is to learn and much to forget
Ere the time be come for taking you.

But the time will come, — at last it will,
When, Evelyn Hope, what meant, I shall say,
In the lower earth, in the years long still,
That body and soul so pure and gay?
Why your hair was amber, I shall divine,
And your mouth of your own geranium's red —
And what you would do with me, in fine,
In the new life come in the old one's stead.

I have lived, I shall say, so much since then,
Given up myself so many times,
Gained me the gains of various men,
Ransacked the ages, spoiled the climes;
Yet one thing, one, in my soul's full scope,
Either I missed or itself missed me:
And I want and find you, Evelyn Hope!
What is the issue? let us see!

I loved you, Evelyn, all the while!
My heart seemed full as it could hold —
There was place and to spare for the frank young smile
And the red young mouth and the hair's young gold.
So, hush, — I will give you this leaf to keep —
See, I shut it inside the sweet cold hand.
There, that is our secret! go to sleep;
You will wake, and remember, and understand.

1855

LOVE AMONG THE RUINS

WHERE the quiet-coloured end of evening smiles
Miles and miles
On the solitary pastures where our sheep
Half-asleep
Tinkle homeward through the twilight, stray or stop
As they crop —

Was the site once of a city great and gay,
(So they say)
Of our country's very capital, its prince
Ages since
Held his court in, gathered councils, wielding far
Peace or war.

Now — the country does not even boast a tree,
As you see,
To distinguish slopes of verdure, certain rills
From the hills
Intersect and give a name to, (else they run
Into one)
Where the domed and daring palace shot its spires
Up like fires
O'er the hundred-gated circuit of a wall
Bounding all,
Made of marble, men might march on nor be prest,
Twelve abreast.

And such plenty and perfection, see, of grass
Never was!
Such a carpet as, this summer-time, o'erspreads
And embeds
Every vestige of the city, guessed alone,
Stock or stone —
Where a multitude of men breathed joy and woe
Long ago;
Lust of glory pricked their hearts up, dread of shame
Struck them tame;
And that glory and that shame alike, the gold
Bought and sold.

Now, — the single little turret that remains
On the plains,
By the caper overrooted, by the gourd
Overscored,
While the patching houseleek's head of blossom winks
Through the chinks —
Marks the basement whence a tower in ancient time
Sprang sublime,
And a burning ring, all round, the chariots traced
As they raced,
And the monarch and his minions and his dames
Viewed the games.

And I know, while thus the quiet-coloured eve
Smiles to leave
To their folding, all our many-tinkling fleece
In such peace,

And the slopes and rills in undistinguished grey
Melt away —
That a girl with eager eyes and yellow hair
Waits me there
In the turret whence the charioteers caught soul
For the goal,
When the king looked, where she looks now, breathless, dumb
Till I come.

But he looked upon the city, every side,
Far and wide,
All the mountains topped with temples, all the glades'
Colonnades,
All the causeys, bridges, aqueducts, — and then,
All the men!

When I do come, she will speak not, she will stand,
Either hand
On my shoulder, give her eyes the first embrace
Of my face,
Ere we rush, ere we extinguish sight and speech
Each on each.

In one year they sent a million fighters forth
South and North,
And they built their gods a brazen pillar high
As the sky,
Yet reserved a thousand chariots in full force —
Gold, of course.

Oh, heart! oh, blood that freezes, blood that burns!
Earth's returns
For whole centuries of folly, noise and sin!
Shut them in,
With their triumphs and their glories and the rest.
Love is best!

1855

A TOCCATA OF GALUPPI'S

Oh, Galuppi, Baldassaro, this is very sad to find!
I can hardly misconceive you; it would prove me deaf and blind;
But although I take your meaning, 't is with such a heavy mind!

Here you come with your old music, and here 's all the good it brings.
What, they lived once thus at Venice where the merchants were the kings,
Where St. Mark's is, where the Doges used to wed the sea with rings?

Ay, because the sea 's the street there; and 't is arched by . . . what you call
. . . Shylock's bridge with houses on it, where they kept the carnival:
I was never out of England — it 's as if I saw it all!

Did young people take their pleasure when the sea was warm in May?
Balls and masks begun at midnight, burning ever to mid-day
When they made up fresh adventures for the morrow, do you say?

Was a lady such a lady, cheeks so round and lips so red, —
On her neck the small face buoyant, like a bell-flower on its bed,
O'er the breast's superb abundance where a man might base his head?

Well, (and it was graceful of them) they 'd break talk off and afford
— She, to bite her mask's black velvet, he, to finger on his sword,
While you sat and played Toccatas, stately at the clavichord?

What? Those lesser thirds so plaintive, sixths diminished, sigh on sigh,
Told them something? Those suspensions, those solutions — 'Must we die?'
Those commiserating sevenths — 'Life might last! we can but try!'

'Were you happy?' — 'Yes.' — 'And are you still as happy?' — 'Yes. And you?'
— 'Then, more kisses!' — 'Did *I* stop them, when a million seemed so few?'
Hark! the dominant's persistence, till it must be answered to!

So an octave struck the answer. Oh, they praised you, I dare say!
'Brave Galuppi! that was music! good alike at grave and gay!
I can always leave off talking, when I hear a master play.'

Then they left you for their pleasure: till in due time, one by one,
Some with lives that came to nothing, some with deeds as well undone,
Death came tacitly and took them where they never see the sun.

But when I sit down to reason, think to take my stand nor swerve,
While I triumph o'er a secret wrung from nature's close reserve,
In you come with your cold music, till I creep through every nerve.

Yes, you, like a ghostly cricket, creaking where a house was burned —
'Dust and ashes, dead and done with, Venice spent what Venice earned!
The soul, doubtless, is immortal — where a soul can be discerned.

Yours for instance, you know physics, something of geology,
Mathematics are your pastime; souls shall rise in their degree;
Butterflies may dread extinction, — you'll not die, it cannot be!

As for Venice and its people, merely born to bloom and drop,
Here on earth they bore their fruitage, mirth and folly were the crop:
What of soul was left, I wonder, when the kissing had to stop?

'Dust and ashes!' So you creak it, and I want the heart to scold.
Dear dead women, with such hair, too — what 's become of all the gold
Used to hang and brush their bosoms? I feel chilly and grown old.

1855

'DE GUSTIBUS —'

Your ghost will walk, you lover of trees,
(If our loves remain)
In an English lane,
By a cornfield-side a-flutter with poppies.
Hark, those two in the hazel coppice —
A boy and a girl, if the good fates please,
Making love, say, —
The happier they!
Draw yourself up from the light of the moon,
And let them pass, as they will too soon,
With the beanflowers' boon,
And the blackbird's tune,
And May, and June!

What I love best in all the world,
Is, a castle, precipice-encurled,
In a gash of the wind-grieved Apennine.
Or look for me, old fellow of mine,
(If I get my head from out the mouth
O' the grave, and loose my spirit's bands,
And come again to the land of lands) —
In a sea-side house to the farther South,
Where the baked cicalas die of drouth,
And one sharp tree — 't is a cypress — stands,
By the many hundred years red-rusted,
Rough iron-spiked, ripe fruit-o'er-crusted,
My sentinel to guard the sands
To the water's edge. For, what expands
Before the house, but the great opaque
Blue breadth of sea without a break?
While, in the house, for ever crumbles
Some fragment of the frescoed walls,
From blisters where a scorpion sprawls.
A girl bare-footed brings, and tumbles
Down on the pavement, green-flesh melons,
And says there's news to-day — the king
Was shot at, touched in the liver-wing,
Goes with his Bourbon arm in a sling:
— She hopes they have not caught the felons.
Italy, my Italy!
Queen Mary's saying serves for me —
(When fortune's malice
Lost her, Calais)
Open my heart and you will see
Graved inside of it, 'Italy.'
Such lovers old are I and she;
So it always was, so shall ever be!

1855

MY STAR

All that I know
Of a certain star,
Is, it can throw
(Like the angled spar)
Now a dart of red,
Now a dart of blue,
Till my friends have said
They would fain see, too,
My star that dartles the red and the blue!
Then it stops like a bird; like a flower, hangs furled:
They must solace themselves with the Saturn above it.
What matter to me if their star is a world?
Mine has opened its soul to me; therefore I love it.

1855

THE LAST RIDE TOGETHER

I said — Then, Dearest, since 't is so,
Since now at length my fate I know,
Since nothing all my love avails,
Since all, my life seemed meant for, fails,
Since this was written and needs must be —
My whole heart rises up to bless
Your name in pride and thankfulness!

Take back the hope you gave, — I claim
Only a memory of the same,
— And this beside, if you will not blame,
Your leave for one more last ride with me.

My mistress bent that brow of hers;
Those deep dark eyes where pride demurs
When pity would be softening through,
Fixed me a breathing-while or two
With life or death in the balance: right!
The blood replenished me again;
My last thought was at least not vain:
I and my mistress, side by side
Shall be together, breathe and ride,
So one day more am I deified —
Who knows but the world may end to-night.

Hush! if you saw some western cloud
All billowy-bosomed, over-bowed
By many benedictions — sun's
And moon's and evening-star's at once —
And so, you, looking and loving best,
Conscious grew, your passion drew
Cloud, sunset, moonrise, star-shine too,
Down on you, near and yet more near,
Till flesh must fade for heaven was here! —
Thus leant she and lingered — joy and fear!
Thus lay she a moment on my breast.

Then we began to ride. My soul
Smoothed itself out — a long-cramped scroll
Freshening and fluttering in the wind.
Past hopes already lay behind.
What need to strive with a life awry?
Had I said that, had I done this,
So might I gain, so might I miss.
Might she have loved me? just as well
She might have hated, — who can tell?
Where had I been now if the worst befell?
And here we are riding, she and I.

Fail I alone, in words and deeds?
Why, all men strive and who succeeds?
We rode; it seemed my spirit flew,
Saw other regions, cities new,
As the world rushed by on either side.
I thought, — All labour, yet no less
Bear up beneath their unsuccess.
Look at the end of work, contrast
The petty Done, the Undone vast,
This Present of theirs with the hopeful Past!
I hoped she would love me: here we ride.

What hand and brain went ever paired?
What heart alike conceived and dared?
What act proved all its thought had been?
What will but felt the fleshly screen?
We ride and I see her bosom heave.
There 's many a crown for who can reach.
Ten lines, a statesman's life in each!
The flag stuck on a heap of bones,
A soldier's doing! what atones?
They scratch his name on the Abbey-stones.
My riding is better, by their leave.

What does it all mean, poet? well,
Your brains beat into rhythm — you tell
What we felt only; you expressed
You hold things beautiful the best,
And pace them in rhyme so, side by side.
'T is something, nay 't is much — but then,
Have you yourself what 's best for men?
Are you — poor, sick, old ere your time —
Nearer one whit your own sublime
Than we who never have turned a rhyme?
Sing, riding 's a joy! For me, I ride.

And you, great sculptor — so, you gave
A score of years to Art, her slave,
And that 's your Venus — whence we turn
To yonder girl that fords the burn!
You acquiesce, and shall I repine?
What, man of music, you, grown grey
With notes and nothing else to say,
Is this your sole praise from a friend,
'Greatly his opera's strains intend,
But in music we know how fashions end!'
I gave my youth — but we ride, in fine.

Who knows what 's fit for us? Had fate
Proposed bliss here should sublimate
My being; had I signed the bond —
Still one must lead some life beyond,
— Have a bliss to die with, dim-descried.
This foot once planted on the goal,
This glory-garland round my soul,
Could I descry such? Try and test!
I sink back shuddering from the quest —
Earth being so good, would Heaven seem best?
Now, Heaven and she are beyond this ride.

And yet — she has not spoke so long!
What if Heaven be that, fair and strong
At life's best, with our eyes upturned
Whither life's flower is first discerned,
We, fixed so, ever should so abide?
What if we still ride on, we two,
With life for ever old yet new,
Changed not in kind but in degree,
The instant made eternity, —
And Heaven just prove that I and she
Ride, ride together, for ever ride?

1855

A GRAMMARIAN'S FUNERAL

Let us begin and carry up this corpse,
Singing together.
Leave we the common crofts, the vulgar thorpes,
Each in its tether
Sleeping safe on the bosom of the plain,
Cared-for till cock-crow:
Look out if yonder be not day again
Rimming the rock-row!
That 's the appropriate country; there, man's thought,
Rarer, intenser,
Self-gathered for an outbreak, as it ought,
Chafes in the censer!
Leave we the unlettered plain its herd and crop;
Seek we sepulture
On a tall mountain, citied to the top,
Crowded with culture!
All the peaks soar, but one the rest excels;
Clouds overcome it;
No, yonder sparkle is the citadel's
Circling its summit!
Thither our path lies; wind we up the heights:
Wait ye the warning?
Our low life was the level's and the night's;
He 's for the morning!
Step to a tune, square chests, erect the head,
'Ware the beholders!
This is our master, famous, calm, and dead,
Borne on our shoulders.

Sleep, crop and herd! sleep, darkling thorpe and croft,
Safe from the weather!
He, whom we convoy to his grave aloft,
Singing together,
He was a man born with thy face and throat,
Lyric Apollo!
Long he lived nameless: how should spring take note
Winter would follow?
Till lo, the little touch, and youth was gone!
Cramped and diminished,
Moaned he, 'New measures, other feet anon!
My dance is finished?'
No, that 's the world's way! (keep the mountain-side,
Make for the city,)
He knew the signal, and stepped on with pride
Over men's pity;
Left play for work, and grappled with the world
Bent on escaping:
'What 's in the scroll,' quoth he, 'thou keepest furled?
Show me their shaping,
Theirs, who most studied man, the bard and sage, —
Give!' — So he gowned him,
Straight got by heart that book to its last page:
Learnèd, we found him!
Yea, but we found him bald too — eyes like lead,
Accents uncertain:
'Time to taste life,' another would have said,
'Up with the curtain!' —
This man said rather, 'Actual life comes next?
Patience a moment!
Grant I have mastered learning's crabbèd text,
Still, there 's the comment.
Let me know all! Prate not of most or least,
Painful or easy:
Even to the crumbs I'd fain eat up the feast,
Ay, nor feel queasy!'
Oh, such a life as he resolved to live,
When he had learned it,
When he had gathered all books had to give!
Sooner, he spurned it.
Image the whole, then execute the parts —
Fancy the fabric
Quite, ere you build, ere steel strike fire from quartz,
Ere mortar dab brick!

(Here 's the town-gate reached: there 's the market-place
Gaping before us.)
Yea, this in him was the peculiar grace
(Hearten our chorus)
That before living he 'd learn how to live —
No end to learning:
Earn the means first — God surely will contrive
Use for our earning.
Others mistrust and say — 'But time escapes!
Live now or never!'
He said, 'What 's time? leave Now for dogs and apes!
Man has Forever.'
Back to his book then: deeper drooped his head:
Calculus racked him:
Leaden before, his eyes grew dross of lead:
Tussis attacked him.
'Now, Master, take a little rest!' — not he!
(Caution redoubled!
Step two a-breast, the way winds narrowly)
Not a whit troubled,

Back to his studies, fresher than at first,
Fierce as a dragon
He (soul-hydroptic with a sacred thirst)
Sucked at the flagon.
Oh, if we draw a circle premature,
Heedless of far gain,
Greedy for quick returns of profit, sure,
Bad is our bargain!
Was it not great? did not he throw on God,
(He loves the burthen) —
God's task to make the heavenly period
Perfect the earthen?
Did not he magnify the mind, show clear
Just what it all meant?
He would not discount life, as fools do here,
Paid by instalment!
He ventured neck or nothing — Heaven's success
Found, or earth's failure:
'Wilt thou trust death or not?' He answered 'Yes!
Hence with life's pale lure!'
That low man seeks a little thing to do,
Sees it and does it:
This high man, with a great thing to pursue,
Dies ere he knows it.
That low man goes on adding one to one,
His hundred 's soon hit:
This high man, aiming at a million,
Misses an unit.
That, has the world here — should he need the next,
Let the world mind him!
This, throws himself on God, and unperplext
Seeking shall find Him.
So, with the throttling hands of Death at strife,
Ground he at grammar;
Still, through the rattle, parts of speech were rife:
While he could stammer
He settled *Hoti's* business — let it be! —
Properly based *Oun* —
Gave us the doctrine of the enclitic *De*,
Dead from the waist down.
Well, here 's the platform, here 's the proper place.
Hail to your purlieus,
All ye highfliers of the feathered race,
Swallows and curlews!
Here 's the top-peak! the multitude below
Live, for they can, there.
This man decided not to Live but Know —
Bury this man there?
Here — here 's his place, where meteors shoot, clouds form,
Lightnings are loosened,
Stars come and go! let joy break with the storm,
Peace let the dew send!
Lofty designs must close in like effects:
Loftily lying,
Leave him — still loftier than the world suspects,
Living and dying.

1855

CHILDE ROLAND TO THE DARK TOWER CAME'

My first thought was, he lied in every word,
That hoary cripple, with malicious eye
Askance to watch the working of his lie
On mine, and mouth scarce able to afford
Suppression of the glee that pursed and scored
Its edge at one more victim gained thereby.

What else should he be set for, with his staff?
What, save to waylay with his lies, ensnare
All travellers that might find him posted there,
And ask the road? I guessed what skull-like laugh
Would break, what crutch 'gin write my epitaph
For pastime in the dusty thoroughfare,

If at his counsel I should turn aside
Into that ominous tract which, all agree,
Hides the Dark Tower. Yet acquiescingly
I did turn as he pointed; neither pride
Nor hope rekindling at the end descried,
So much as gladness that some end might be.

For, what with my whole world-wide wandering,
What with my search drawn out through years, my hope
Dwindled into a ghost not fit to cope
With that obstreperous joy success would bring, —
I hardly tried now to rebuke the spring
My heart made, finding failure in its scope.

As when a sick man very near to death
Seems dead indeed, and feels begin and end
The tears and takes the farewell of each friend,
And hears one bid the other go, draw breath

Freelier outside, ('since all is o'er,' he saith,
'And the blow fallen no grieving can amend';)

While some discuss if near the other graves
Be room enough for this, and when a day
Suits best for carrying the corpse away,
With care about the banners, scarves and staves, —
And still the man hears all, and only craves
He may not shame such tender love and stay.

Thus, I had so long suffered in this quest,
Heard failure prophesied so oft, been writ
So many times among 'The Band' — to wit,
The knights who to the Dark Tower's search addressed
Their steps — that just to fail as they, seemed best,
And all the doubt was now — should I be fit.

So, quiet as despair, I turned from him,
That hateful cripple, out of his highway
Into the path he pointed. All the day
Had been a dreary one at best, and dim
Was settling to its close, yet shot one grim
Red leer to see the plain catch its estray.

For mark! no sooner was I fairly found
Pledged to the plain, after a pace or two,
Than, pausing to throw backward a last view
To the safe road, 't was gone; grey plain all round:
Nothing but plain to the horizon's bound.
I might go on; nought else remained to do.

So, on I went. I think I never saw
Such starved ignoble nature; nothing throve:
For flowers — as well expect a cedar grove!
But cockle, spurge, according to their law
Might propagate their kind, with none to awe,
You 'd think; a burr had been a treasure-trove.

No! penury, inertness and grimace,
In some strange sort, were the land's portion. 'See
Or shut your eyes,' said Nature peevishly,
'It nothing skills: I cannot help my case:
'T is the Last Judgment's fire must cure this place,
Calcine its clods and set my prisoners free.'

If there pushed any ragged thistle-stalk
Above its mates, the head was chopped — the bents
Were jealous else. What made those holes and rents
In the dock's harsh swarth leaves — bruised as to baulk
All hope of greenness? 't is a brute must walk
Pashing their life out, with a brute's intents.

As for the grass, it grew as scant as hair
In leprosy; thin dry blades pricked the mud
Which underneath looked kneaded up with blood.
One stiff blind horse, his every bone a-stare,
Stood stupefied, however he came there:
Thrust out past service from the devil's stud!

Alive? he might be dead for aught I know,
With that red, gaunt and colloped neck a-strain,
And shut eyes underneath the rusty mane;
Seldom went such grotesqueness with such woe;
I never saw a brute I hated so;
He must be wicked to deserve such pain.

I shut my eyes and turned them on my heart.
As a man calls for wine before he fights,
I asked one draught of earlier, happier sights,
Ere fitly I could hope to play my part.
Think first, fight afterwards — the soldier's art:
One taste of the old time sets all to rights!

Not it! I fancied Cuthbert's reddening face
Beneath its garniture of curly gold,
Dear fellow, till I almost felt him fold
An arm in mine to fix me to the place,
That way he used. Alas, one night's disgrace!
Out went my heart's new fire and left it cold.

Giles, then, the soul of honour — there he stands
Frank as ten years ago when knighted first.
What honest men should dare (he said) he durst.
Good — but the scene shifts — faugh! what hangman's hands
Pin to his breast a parchment? his own bands
Read it. Poor traitor, spit upon and curst!

Better this Present than a Past like that;
Back therefore to my darkening path again.
No sound, no sight as far as eye could strain.
Will the night send a howlet or a bat?
I asked: when something on the dismal flat
Came to arrest my thoughts and change their train.

A sudden little river crossed my path
As unexpected as a serpent comes.
No sluggish tide congenial to the glooms —
This, as it frothed by, might have been a bath
For the fiend's glowing hoof — to see the wrath
Of its black eddy bespate with flakes and spumes.

So petty yet so spiteful! all along,
Low scrubby alders kneeled down over it;
Drenched willows flung them headlong in a fit
Of mute despair, a suicidal throng:
The river which had done them all the wrong,
Whate'er that was, rolled by, deterred no whit.

Which, while I forded, — good saints, how I feared
To set my foot upon a dead man's cheek,
Each step, or feel the spear I thrust to seek
For hollows, tangled in his hair or beard!
— It may have been a water-rat I speared,
But, ugh! it sounded like a baby's shriek.

Glad was I when I reached the other bank.
Now for a better country. Vain presage!
Who were the strugglers, what war did they wage
Whose savage trample thus could pad the dank
Soil to a plash? toads in a poisoned tank,
Or wild cats in a red-hot iron cage —

The fight must so have seemed in that fell cirque.
What penned them there, with all the plain to choose?
No foot-print leading to that horrid mews,
None out of it. Mad brewage set to work
Their brains, no doubt, like galley-slaves the Turk
Pits for his pastime, Christians against Jews.

And more than that — a furlong on — why, there!
What bad use was that engine for, that wheel,
Or brake, not wheel — that harrow fit to reel
Men's bodies out like silk? with all the air
Of Tophet's tool, on earth left unaware,
Or brought to sharpen its rusty teeth of steel.

Then came a bit of stubbed ground, once a wood,
Next a marsh, it would seem, and now mere earth
Desperate and done with; (so a fool finds mirth,
Makes a thing and then mars it, till his mood
Changes and off he goes!) within a rood —
Bog, clay and rubble, sand and stark black dearth.

Now blotches rankling, coloured gay and grim,
Now patches where some leanness of the soil's
Broke into moss or substances like boils;
Then came some palsied oak, a cleft in him
Like a distorted mouth that splits its rim
Gaping at death, and dies while it recoils.

And just as far as ever from the end!
Nought in the distance but the evening, nought
To point my footstep further! At the thought,
A great black bird, Apollyon's bosom-friend,
Sailed past, nor beat his wide wing dragon-penned
That brushed my cap — perchance the guide I sought.

For, looking up, aware I somehow grew,
'Spite of the dusk, the plain had given place
All round to mountains — with such name to grace
Mere ugly heights and heaps now stolen in view.
How thus they had surprised me, — solve it, you!
How to get from them was no clearer case.

Yet half I seemed to recognise some trick
Of mischief happened to me, God knows when —
In a bad dream perhaps. Here ended, then,
Progress this way. When, in the very nick
Of giving up, one time more, came a click
As when a trap shuts — you 're inside the den!

Burningly it came on me all at once,
This was the place! those two hills on the right,
Crouched like two bulls locked horn in horn in fight;
While to the left, a tall scalped mountain . . . Dunce,
Fool, to be dozing at the very nonce,
After a life spent training for the sight!

What in the midst lay but the Tower itself?
The round squat turret, blind as the fool's heart,
Built of brown stone, without a counterpart
In the whole world. The tempest's mocking elf
Points to the shipman thus the unseen shelf
He strikes on, only when the timbers start.

Not see? because of night perhaps? — Why, day
Came back again for that! before it left,
The dying sunset kindled through a cleft:
The hills, like giants at a hunting, lay,
Chin upon hand, to see the game at bay, —
'Now stab and end the creature — to the heft!'

Not hear? when noise was everywhere! it tolled
Increasing like a bell. Names in my ears,
Of all the lost adventurers my peers, —
How such a one was strong, and such was bold,
And such was fortunate, yet each of old
Lost, lost! one moment knelled the woe of years.

There they stood, ranged along the hillsides, met
To view the last of me, a living frame
For one more picture! in a sheet of flame
I saw them and I knew them all. And yet
Dauntless the slug-horn to my lips I set,
And blew. *'Childe Roland to the Dark Tower came.'*

1855

FRA LIPPO LIPPI

I AM poor brother Lippo, by your leave!
You need not clap your torches to my face.
Zooks, what 's to blame? you think you see a monk!
What, it 's past midnight, and you go the rounds,
And here you catch me at an alley's end
Where sportive ladies leave their doors ajar?
The Carmine 's my cloister: hunt it up,
Do, — harry out, if you must show your zeal,
Whatever rat, there, haps on his wrong hole,
And nip each softling of a wee white mouse,
Weke, weke, that 's crept to keep him company!
Aha, you know your betters? Then, you'll take
Your hand away that 's fiddling on my throat,
And please to know me likewise. Who am I?
Why, one, sir, who is lodging with a friend
Three streets off — he 's a certain . . . how d' ye call?
Master — a . . . Cosimo of the Medici,
In the house that caps the corner. Boh! you were best!
Remember and tell me, the day you 're hanged,
How you affected such a gullet's-gripe!
But you, sir, it concerns you that your knaves
Pick up a manner nor discredit you.
Zooks, are we pilchards, that they sweep the streets
And count fair prize what comes into their net?
He 's Judas to a tittle, that man is!
Just such a face! why, sir, you make amends.
Lord, I'm not angry! Bid your hang-dogs go
Drink out this quater-florin to the health
Of the munificent House that harbours me
(And many more beside, lads! more beside!)
And all 's come square again. I 'd like his face —
His, elbowing on his comrade in the door
With the pike and lantern, — for the slave that holds
John Baptist's head a-dangle by the hair
With one hand ('look you, now,' as who should say)
And his weapon in the other, yet unwiped!
It 's not your chance to have a bit of chalk,
A wood-coal or the like? or you should see!
Yes, I'm the painter, since you style me so.
What, brother Lippo's doings, up and down,
You know them and they take you? like enough!
I saw the proper twinkle in your eye —
'Tell you, I liked your looks at very first.
Let 's sit and set things straight now, hip to haunch.
Here 's spring come, and the nights one makes up bands
To roam the town and sing out carnival,

And I've been three weeks shut within my mew,
A-painting for the great man, saints and saints
And saints again. I could not paint all night —
Ouf! I leaned out of window for fresh air.
There came a hurry of feet and little feet,
A sweep of lute-strings, laughs, and whifts of song, —
Flower o' the broom,
Take away love, and our earth is a tomb!
Flower o' the quince,
I let Lisa go, and what good 's in life since?
Flower o' the thyme — and so on. Round they went.
Scarce had they turned the corner when a titter
Like the skipping of rabbits by moonlight, — three slim shapes —
And a face that looked up . . . zooks, sir, flesh and blood,
That 's all I 'm made of! Into shreds it went,
Curtain and counterpane and coverlet,
All the bed-furniture — a dozen knots,
There was a ladder! down I let myself,
Hands and feet, scrambling somehow, and so dropped,
And after them. I came up with the fun
Hard by Saint Laurence, hail fellow, well met, —
Flower o' the rose,
If I 've been merry, what matter who knows?
And so as I was stealing back again
To get to bed and have a bit of sleep
Ere I rise up to-morrow and go to work
On Jerome knocking at his poor old breast
With his great round stone to subdue the flesh,
You snap me of the sudden. Ah, I see!
Though your eye twinkles still, you shake your head —
Mine 's shaved, — a monk, you say — the sting 's in that!
If Master Cosimo announced himself,
Mum 's the word naturally; but a monk!
Come, what am I a beast for? tell us, now!
I was a baby when my mother died
And father died and left me in the street.
I starved there, God knows how, a year or two
On fig skins, melon-parings, rinds and shucks,
Refuse and rubbish. One fine frosty day
My stomach being empty as your hat,
The wind doubled me up and down I went.
Old Aunt Lapaccia trussed me with one hand,
(Its fellow was a stinger as I knew)
And so along the wall, over the bridge,
By the straight cut to the convent. Six words, there,
While I stood munching my first bread that month:
'So, boy, you're minded,' quoth the good fat father
Wiping his own mouth, 't was refection-time, —
'To quit this very miserable world?
Will you renounce' . . . The mouthful of bread? thought I;
By no means! Brief, they made a monk of me;
I did renounce the world, its pride and greed,
Palace, farm, villa, shop and banking-house,
Trash, such as these poor devils of Medici
Have given their hearts to — all at eight years old.
Well, sir, I found in time, you may be sure,
'T was not for nothing — the good bellyful,
The warm serge and the rope that goes all round,
And day-long blessèd idleness beside!
'Let 's see what the urchin 's fit for' — that came next.
Not overmuch their way, I must confess.
Such a to-do! they tried me with their books.
Lord, they 'd have taught me Latin in pure waste!
Flower o' the clove,
All the Latin I construe is, 'amo' I love!
But, mind you, when a boy starves in the streets
Eight years together, as my fortune was,
Watching folk's faces to know who will fling
The bit of half-stripped grape-bunch he desires,
And who will curse or kick him for his pains —
Which gentleman processional and fine,
Holding a candle to the Sacrament
Will wink and let him lift a plate and catch
The droppings of the wax to sell again,
Or holla for the Eight and have him whipped, —
How say I? — nay, which dog bites, which lets drop
His bone from the heap of offal in the street, —
Why, soul and sense of him grow sharp alike,
He learns the look of things, and none the less
For admonitions from the hunger-pinch.
I had a store of such remarks, be sure,
Which, after I found leisure, turned to use:
I drew men's faces on my copy-books,
Scrawled them within the antiphonary's marge,

Joined legs and arms to the long music-notes,
Found nose and eyes and chin for A.s and B.s,
And made a string of pictures of the world
Betwixt the ins and outs of verb and noun,
On the wall, the bench, the door. The monks looked black.
'Nay,' quoth the Prior, 'turn him out, d' ye say?
In no wise. Lose a crow and catch a lark.
What if at last we get our man of parts,
We Carmelites, like those Camaldolese
And Preaching Friars, to do our church up fine
And put the front on it that ought to be!'
And hereupon they bade me daub away.
Thank you! my head being crammed, their walls a blank,
Never was such prompt disemburdening.
First, every sort of monk, the black and white,
I drew them, fat and lean: then, folks at church,
From good old gossips waiting to confess
Their cribs of barrel-droppings, candle-ends, —
To the breathless fellow at the altar-foot,
Fresh from his murder, safe and sitting there
With the little children round him in a row
Of admiration, half for his beard and half
For that white anger of his victim's son
Shaking a fist at him with one fierce arm,
Signing himself with the other because of Christ
(Whose sad face on the cross sees only this
After the passion of a thousand years)
Till some poor girl, her apron o'er her head
Which the intense eyes looked through, came at eve
On tip-toe, said a word, dropped in a loaf,
Her pair of earrings and a bunch of flowers
The brute took growling, prayed, and then was gone.
I painted all, then cried, 't is ask and have —
Choose, for more 's ready!' — laid the ladder flat,
And showed my covered bit of cloister-wall.
The monks closed in a circle and praised loud
Till checked, — taught what to see and not to see,
Being simple bodies, — 'that 's the very man!
Look at the boy who stoops to pat the dog!
That woman 's like the Prior's niece who comes
To care about his asthma: it 's the life!'
But there my triumph's straw-fire flared and funked —
Their betters took their turn to see and say:
The Prior and the learnèd pulled a face
And stopped all that in no time. 'How? what 's here?
Quite from the mark of painting, bless us all!
Faces, arms, legs and bodies like the true
As much as pea and pea! it 's devil's-game!
Your business is not to catch men with show,
With homage to the perishable clay,
But lift them over it, ignore it all,
Make them forget there 's such a thing as flesh.
Your business is to paint the souls of men—
Man's soul, and it 's a fire, smoke . . . no it 's not . . .
It 's vapour done up like a new-born babe —
(In that shape when you die it leaves your mouth)
It 's . . . well, what matters talking, it 's the soul!
Give us no more of body than shows soul!
Here 's Giotto, with his Saint a-praising God,
That sets you praising, — why not stop with him?
Why put all thoughts of praise out of our heads
With wonder at lines, colours, and what not?
Paint the soul, never mind the legs and arms!
Rub all out, try at it a second time.
Oh, that white smallish female with the breasts,
She 's just my niece . . . Herodias, I would say, —
Who went and danced and got men's heads cut off —
Have it all out!' Now, is this sense, I ask?
A fine way to paint soul, by painting body
So ill, the eye can't stop there, must go further
And can't fare worse! Thus, yellow does for white
When what you put for yellow 's simply black,
And any sort of meaning looks intense
When all beside itself means and looks nought.
Why can't a painter lift each foot in turn,
Left foot and right foot, go a double step,
Make his flesh liker and his soul more like,
Both in their order? Take the prettiest face,
The Prior's niece . . . patron-saint — is it so pretty
You can't discover if it means hope, fear,
Sorrow or joy? won't beauty go with these?
Suppose I 've made her eyes all right and blue,

Can't I take breath and try to add life's flash,
And then add soul and heighten them three-fold?
Or say there's beauty with no soul at all —
(I never saw it — put the case the same —)
If you get simple beauty and nought else,
You get about the best thing God invents, —
That's somewhat. And you'll find the soul you have missed,
Within yourself when you return Him thanks,
'Rub all out!' Well, well, there's my life, in short.
And so the thing has gone on ever since.
I'm grown a man no doubt, I've broken bounds —
You should not take a fellow eight years old
And make him swear to never kiss the girls.
I'm my own master, paint now as I please —
Having a friend, you see, in the Corner-house!
Lord, it's fast holding by the rings in front —
Those great rings serve more purposes than just
To plant a flag in, or tie up a horse!
And yet the old schooling sticks, the old grave eyes
Are peeping o'er my shoulder as I work,
The heads shake still — 'It's Art's decline, my son!
You're not of the true painters, great and old;
Brother Angelico's the man, you'll find;
Brother Lorenzo stands his single peer:
Fag on at flesh, you'll never make the third!'
Flower o' the pine,
You keep your mistr . . . manners, and I'll stick to mine!
I'm not the third, then: bless us, they must know!
Don't you think they're the likeliest to know,
They with their Latin? so, I swallow my rage,
Clench my teeth, suck my lips in tight, and paint
To please them — sometimes do, and sometimes don't,
For, doing most, there's pretty sure to come
A turn, some warm eve finds me at my saints —
A laugh, a cry, the business of the world —
(*Flower o' the peach,*
Death for us all, and his own life for each!)
And my whole soul revolves, the cup runs over,
The world and life's too big to pass for a dream,
And I do these wild things in sheer despite,
And play the fooleries you catch me at,
In pure rage! the old mill-horse, out at grass
After hard years, throws up his stiff heels so,
Although the miller does not preach to him
The only good of grass is to make chaff.
What would men have? Do they like grass or no —
May they or mayn't they? all I want's the thing
Settled for ever one way: as it is,
You tell too many lies and hurt yourself.
You don't like what you only like too much,
You do like what, if given you at your word,
You find abundantly detestable.
For me, I think I speak as I was taught —
I always see the Garden and God there
A-making man's wife — and, my lesson learned,
The value and significance of flesh,
I can't unlearn ten minutes afterwards.

You understand me: I'm a beast, I know.
But see, now — why, I see as certainly
As that the morning-star's about to shine,
What will hap some day. We've a youngster here
Comes to our convent, studies what I do,
Slouches and stares and lets no atom drop —
His name is Guidi — he'll not mind the monks —
They call him Hulking Tom, he lets them talk —
He picks my practice up — he'll paint apace,
I hope so — though I never live so long,
I know what's sure to follow. You be judge!
You speak no Latin more than I, belike —
However, you're my man, you've seen the world
— The beauty and the wonder and the power,
The shapes of things, their colours, lights and shades,
Changes, surprises, — and God made it all!
— For what? do you feel thankful, ay or no,
For this fair town's face, yonder river's line,
The mountain round it and the sky above,
Much more the figures of man, woman, child,
These are the frame to? What's it all about?
To be passed over, despised? or dwelt upon,

Wondered at? oh, this last of course! — you say.
But why not do as well as say, — paint these
Just as they are, careless what comes of it?
God's works — paint anyone, and count it crime
To let a truth slip. Don't object, 'His works
Are here already — nature is complete:
Suppose you reproduce her — (which you can't)
There's no advantage! you must beat her, then.'
For, don't you mark, we're made so that we love
First when we see them painted, things we have passed
Perhaps a hundred times nor cared to see;
And so they are better, painted — better to us,
Which is the same thing. Art was given for that —
God uses us to help each other so,
Lending our minds out. Have you noticed, now,
Your cullion's hanging face? A bit of chalk,
And trust me but you should, though! How much more,
If I drew higher things with the same truth!
That were to take the Prior's pulpit-place,
Interpret God to all of you! oh, oh,
It makes me mad to see what men shall do
And we in our graves! This world's no blot for us,
Nor blank — it means intensely, and means good:
To find its meaning is my meat and drink.
'Ay, but you don't so instigate to prayer!'
Strikes in the Prior: 'when your meaning's plain
It does not say to folks — remember matins,
Or, mind you fast next Friday.' Why, for this
What need of art at all? A skull and bones
Two bits of stick nailed cross-wise, or, what's best,
A bell to chime the hour with, does as well.
I painted a Saint Laurence six months since
At Prato, splashed the fresco in fine style:
'How looks my painting, now the scaffold's down?'
I ask a brother: 'Hugely,' he returns —
'Already not one phiz of your three slaves
That turn the Deacon off his toasted side,
But's scratched and prodded to our heart's content,
The pious people have so eased their own
When coming to say prayers there in a rage:
We get on fast to see the bricks beneath.
Expect another job this time next year,
For pity and religion grow i' the crowd —
Your painting serves its purpose!' Hang the fools!
— That is — you'll not mistake an idle word
Spoke in a huff by a poor monk, God wot,
Tasting the air this spicy night which turns
The unaccustomed head like Chianti wine!
Oh, the church knows! don't misreport me, now!
It's natural a poor monk out of bounds
Should have his apt word to excuse himself:
And hearken how I plot to make amends.
I have bethought me: I shall paint a piece
. . . There's for you! Give me six months, then go, see
Something in Sant' Ambrogio's! Bless the nuns!
They want a cast of my office. I shall paint
God in the midst, Madonna and her babe,
Ringed by a bowery, flowery angel-brood,
Lilies and vestments and white faces, sweet
As puff on puff of grated orris-root
When ladies crowd to church at midsummer.
And then in the front, of course a saint or two —
Saint John, because he saves the Florentines,
Saint Ambrose, who puts down in black and white
The convent's friends and gives them a long day,
And Job, I must have him there past mistake,
The man of Uz, (and Us without the z,
Painters who need his patience.) Well, all these
Secured at their devotions, up shall come
Out of a corner when you least expect,
As one by a dark stair into a great light,
Music and talking, who but Lippo! I! —
Mazed, motionless and moon-struck — I'm the man!
Back I shrink — what is this I see and hear?
I, caught up with my monk's things by mistake,
My old serge gown and rope that goes all round,
I, in this presence, this pure company!
Where's a hole, where's a corner for escape?
Then steps a sweet angelic slip of a thing
Forward, puts out a soft palm — 'Not so fast!'
— Addresses the celestial presence, 'nay —
He made you and devised you, after all,

Though he's none of you! Could Saint John there, draw —
His camel-hair make up a painting-brush?
We come to brother Lippo for all that,
Iste perfecit opus!' So, all smile —
I shuffle sideways with my blushing face
Under the cover of a hundred wings
Thrown like a spread of kirtles when you're gay
And play hot cockles, all the doors being shut,
Till, wholly unexpected, in there pops
The hothead husband! Thus I scuttle off
To some safe bench behind, not letting go
The palm of her, the little lily thing
That spoke the good word for me in the nick,
Like the Prior's niece . . . Saint Lucy, I would say.
And so all's saved for me, and for the church
A pretty picture gained. Go, six months hence!
Your hand, sir, and good-bye: no lights, no lights!
The street's hushed, and I know my own way back,
Don't fear me! There's the grey beginning. Zooks!

1855

ANDREA DEL SARTO

But do not let us quarrel any more,
No, my Lucrezia; bear with me for once:
Sit down and all shall happen as you wish.
You turn your face, but does it bring your heart?
I'll work then for your friend's friend, never fear,
Treat his own subject after his own way,
Fix his own time, accept too his own price,
And shut the money into this small hand
When next it takes mine. Will it? tenderly?
Oh, I'll content him, — but to-morrow, Love!
I often am much wearier than you think,
This evening more than usual, and it seems
As if — forgive now — should you let me sit
Here by the window with your hand in mine
And look a half hour forth on Fiesole,
Both of one mind, as married people use,
Quietly, quietly, the evening through,
I might get up to-morrow to my work
Cheerful and fresh as ever. Let us try.
To-morrow how you shall be glad for this!
Your soft hand is a woman of itself,
And mine the man's bared breast she curls inside.
Don't count the time lost, either; you must serve
For each of the five pictures we require —
It saves a model. So! keep looking so —
My serpentining beauty, rounds on rounds!
— How could you ever prick those perfect ears,
Even to put the pearl there! oh, so sweet —
My face, my moon, my everybody's moon,
Which everybody looks on and calls his,
And, I suppose, is looked on by in turn,
While she looks — no one's: very dear, no less!
You smile? why, there's my picture ready made.
There's what we painters call our harmony!
A common greyness silvers everything, —
All in a twilight, you and I alike
— You, at the point of your first pride in me
(That's gone you know), — but I, at every point;
My youth, my hope, my art, being all toned down
To yonder sober pleasant Fiesole.
There's the bell clinking from the chapel-top;
That length of convent-wall across the way
Holds the trees safer, huddled more inside;
The last monk leaves the garden; days decrease
And autumn grows, autumn in everything.
Eh? the whole seems to fall into a shape
As if I saw alike my work and self
And all that I was born to be and do,
A twilight-piece. Love, we are in God's hand.
How strange now, looks the life He makes us lead!
So free we seem, so fettered fast we are!
I feel He laid the fetter: let it lie!
This chamber for example — turn your head —
All that's behind us! you don't understand
Nor care to understand about my art,
But you can hear at least when people speak;
And that cartoon, the second from the door
— It is the thing, Love! so such things should be —
Behold Madonna, I am bold to say.
I can do with my pencil what I know,
What I see, what at bottom of my heart
I wish for, if I ever wish so deep —
Do easily, too — when I say perfectly
I do not boast, perhaps: yourself are judge
Who listened to the Legate's talk last week,
And just as much they used to say in France.

At any rate 't is easy, all of it,
No sketches first, no studies, that 's long past —
I do what many dream of all their lives
— Dream? strive to do, and agonise to do,
And fail in doing. I could count twenty such
On twice your fingers, and not leave this town,
Who strive — you don't know how the others strive
To paint a little thing like that you smeared
Carelessly passing with your robes afloat, —
Yet do much less, so much less, Someone says,
(I know his name, no matter) so much less!
Well, less is more, Lucrezia! I am judged.
There burns a truer light of God in them,
In their vexed, beating, stuffed and stopped-up brain,
Heart, or whate'er else, than goes on to prompt
This low-pulsed forthright craftsman's hand of mine.
Their works drop groundward, but themselves, I know,
Reach many a time a heaven that 's shut to me,
Enter and take their place there sure enough,
Though they come back and cannot tell the world.
My works are nearer heaven, but I sit here.
The sudden blood of these men! at a word —
Praise them, it boils, or blame them, it boils too.
I, painting from myself and to myself,
Know what I do, am unmoved by men's blame
Or their praise either. Somebody remarks
Morello's outline there is wrongly traced,
His hue mistaken — what of that? or else,
Rightly traced and well ordered — what of that?
Speak as they please, what does the mountain care?
Ah, but a man's reach should exceed his grasp,
Or what 's a Heaven for? all is silver-grey
Placid and perfect with my art — the worse!
I know both what I want and what might gain —
And yet how profitless to know, to sigh
'Had I been two, another and myself,
Our head would have o'erlooked the world!' No doubt.
Yonder 's a work, now, of that famous youth
The Urbinate who died five years ago.
('T is copied, George Vasari sent it me.)
Well, I can fancy how he did it all,
Pouring his soul, with kings and popes to see,
Reaching, that Heaven might so replenish him,
Above and through his art — for it gives way;
That arm is wrongly put — and there again —
A fault to pardon in the drawing's lines,
Its body, so to speak: its soul is right,
He means right — that, a child may understand.
Still, what an arm! and I could alter it.
But all the play, the insight and the stretch —
Out of me! out of me! And wherefore out?
Had you enjoined them on me, given me soul,
We might have risen to Rafael, I and you.
Nay, Love, you did give all I asked, I think —
More than I merit, yes, by many times.
But had you — oh, with the same perfect brow,
And perfect eyes, and more than perfect mouth,
And the low voice my soul hears, as a bird
The fowler's pipe, and follows to the snare —
Had you, with these the same, but brought a mind!
Some women do so. Had the mouth there urged
'God and the glory! never care for gain.
The Present by the Future, what is that?
Live for fame, side by side with Angelo —
Rafael is waiting. Up to God all three!'
I might have done it for you. So it seems —
Perhaps not. All is as God over-rules.
Beside, incentives come from the soul's self;
The rest avail not. Why do I need you?
What wife had Rafael, or has Angelo?
In this world, who can do a thing, will not —
And who would do it, cannot, I perceive:
Yet the will 's somewhat — somewhat, too, the power —
And thus we half-men struggle. At the end,
God, I conclude, compensates, punishes.
'T is safer for me, if the award be strict,
That I am something underrated here,
Poor this long while, despised, to speak the truth.
I dared not, do you know, leave home all day,
For fear of chancing on the Paris lords.
The best is when they pass and look aside;
But they speak sometimes; I must bear it all.

Well may they speak! That Francis, that first time,
And that long festal year at Fontainebleau!
I surely then could sometimes leave the ground,
Put on the glory, Rafael's daily wear,
In that humane great monarch's golden look,—
One finger in his beard or twisted curl
Over his mouth's good mark that made the smile,
One arm about my shoulder, round my neck,
The jingle of his gold chain in my ear,
I painting proudly with his breath on me,
All his court round him, seeing with his eyes,
Such frank French eyes, and such a fire of souls
Profuse, my hand kept plying by those hearts,—
And, best of all, this, this, this face beyond,
This in the background, waiting on my work,
To crown the issue with a last reward!
A good time, was it not, my kingly days?
And had you not grown restless — but I know —
'T is done and past; 't was right, my instinct said;
Too live the life grew, golden and not grey,
And I 'm the weak-eyed bat no sun should tempt
Out of the grange whose four walls make his world.
How could it end in any other way?
You called me, and I came home to your heart.
The triumph was, to have ended there; then if
I reached it ere the triumph, what is lost?
Let my hands frame your face in your hair's gold,
You beautiful Lucrezia that are mine!
'Rafael did this, Andrea painted that —
The Roman's is the better when you pray,
But still the other's Virgin was his wife —'
Men will excuse me. I am glad to judge
Both pictures in your presence; clearer grows
My better fortune, I resolve to think.
For, do you know, Lucrezia, as God lives,
Said one day Angelo, his very self,
To Rafael . . . I have known it all these years . . .
(When the young man was flaming out his thoughts
Upon a palace-wall for Rome to see,
Too lifted up in heart because of it)
'Friend, there 's a certain sorry little scrub
Goes up and down our Florence, none cares how,
Who, were he set to plan and execute
As you are, pricked on by your popes and kings,
Would bring the sweat into that brow of yours!'
To Rafael's! — And indeed the arm is wrong.
I hardly dare — yet, only you to see,
Give the chalk here — quick, thus the line should go!
Ay, but the soul! he 's Rafael! rub it out!
Still, all I care for, if he spoke the truth,
(What he? why, who but Michale Angelo?
Do you forget already words like those?)
If really there was such a chance, so lost, —
Is, whether you 're — not grateful — but more pleased.
Well, let me think so. And you smile indeed!
This hour has been an hour! Another smile?
If you would sit thus by me every night
I should work better, do you comprehend?
I mean that I should earn more, give you more.
See, it is settled dusk now; there 's a star;
Morello 's gone, the watch-lights show the wall,
The cue-owls speak the name we call them by.
Come from the window, Love, — come in, at last,
Inside the melancholy little house
We built to be so gay with. God is just.
King Francis may forgive me. Oft at nights
When I look up from painting, eyes tired out,
The walls become illumined, brick from brick
Distinct, instead of mortar, fierce bright gold,
That gold of his I did cement them with!
Let us but love each other. Must you go?
That Cousin here again? he waits outside?
Must see you — you, and not with me? Those loans?
More gaming debts to pay? you smiled for that?
Well, let smiles buy me! have you more to spend?
While hand and eye and something of a heart
Are left me, work 's my ware, and what 's it worth?
I 'll pay my fancy. Only let me sit
The grey remainder of the evening out,
Idle, you call it, and muse perfectly

How I could paint, were I but back in France,
One picture, just one more — the Virgin's face,
Not yours this time! I want you at my side
To hear them — that is, Michael Angelo —
Judge all I do and tell you of its worth.
Will you? To-morrow, satisfy your friend.
I take the subjects for his corridor,
Finish the portrait out of hand — there, there,
And throw him in another thing or two
If he demurs; the whole should prove enough
To pay for this same Cousin's freak. Beside,
What's better and what's all I care about,
Get you the thirteen scudi for the ruff.
Love, does that please you? Ah, but what does he,
The Cousin! what does he to please you more?
  I am grown peaceful as old age tonight.
I regret little, I would change still less.
Since there my past life lies, why alter it?
The very wrong to Francis! — it is true
I took his coin, was tempted and complied,
And built this house and sinned, and all is said.
My father and my mother died of want.
Well, had I riches of my own? you see
How one gets rich! Let each one bear his lot.
They were born poor, lived poor, and poor they died:
And I have laboured somewhat in my time
And not been paid profusely. Some good son
Paint my two hundred pictures — let him try!
No doubt, there's something strikes a balance. Yes,
You loved me quite enough, it seems tonight.
This must suffice me here. What would one have?
In Heaven, perhaps, new chances, one more chance —
Four great walls in the New Jerusalem
Meted on each side by the angel's reed,
For Leonard, Rafael, Angelo and me
To cover — the three first without a wife,
While I have mine! So — still they overcome
Because there's still Lucrezia, — as I choose.
Again the Cousin's whistle! Go, my Love.

1855

PROSPICE

Fear death? — to feel the fog in my throat,
  The mist in my face,
When the snows begin, and the blasts denote
  I am nearing the place,
The power of the night, the press of the storm,
  The post of the foe;
Where he stands, the Arch Fear in a visible form,
  Yet the strong man must go:
For the journey is done and the summit attained,
  And the barriers fall,
Though a battle's to fight ere the guerdon be gained,
  The reward of it all.
I was ever a fighter, so — one fight more,
  The best and the last!
I would hate that death bandaged my eyes, and forbore,
  And bade me creep past.
No! let me taste the whole of it, fare like my peers
  The heroes of old,
Bear the brunt, in a minute pay glad life's arrears
  Of pain, darkness and cold.
For sudden the worst turns the best to the brave,
  The black minute's at end,
And the element's rage, the fiend-voices that rave,
  Shall dwindle, shall blend,
Shall change, shall become first a peace out of pain,
  Then a light, then thy breast,
O thou soul of my soul! I shall clasp thee again,
  And with God be the rest!

1864

ABT VOGLER

Would that the structure brave, the manifold music I build,
  Bidding my organ obey, calling its keys to their work,
Claiming each slave of the sound, at a touch, as when Solomon willed
  Armies of angels that soar, legions of demons that lurk,
Man, brute, reptile, fly, — alien of end and of aim,
  Adverse, each from the other heaven-high, hell-deep removed, —

Should rush into sight at once as he named the ineffable Name,
And pile him a palace straight, to pleasure the princess he loved!

Would it might tarry like his, the beautiful building of mine,
This which my keys in a crowd pressed and importuned to raise!
Ah, one and all, how they helped, would dispart now and now combine,
Zealous to hasten the work, heighten their master his praise!
And one would bury his brow with a blind plunge down to hell,
Burrow awhile and build, broad on the roots of things,
Then up again swim into sight, having based me my palace well,
Founded it, fearless of flame, flat on the nether springs.

And another would mount and march, like the excellent minion he was,
Ay, another and yet another, one crowd but with many a crest,
Raising my rampired walls of gold as transparent as glass,
Eager to do and die, yield each his place to the rest:
For higher still and higher (as a runner tips with fire,
When a great illumination surprises a festal night —
Outlining round and round Rome's dome from space to spire)
Up, the pinnacled glory reached, and the pride of my soul was in sight.

In sight? Not half! for it seemed, it was certain, to match man's birth,
Nature in turn conceived, obeying an impulse as I;
And the emulous heaven yearned down, made effort to reach the earth,
As the earth had done her best, in my passion, to scale the sky:
Novel splendours burst forth, grew familiar and dwelt with mine,
Not a point nor peak but found and fixed its wandering star;
Meteor-moons, balls of blaze: and they did not pale nor pine,
For earth had attained to heaven, there was no more near nor far.

Nay more; for there wanted not who walked in the glare and glow,
Presences plain in the place; or, fresh from the Protoplast,
Furnished for ages to come, when a kindlier wind should blow,
Lured now to begin and live, in a house to their liking at last;
Or else the wonderful Dead who have passed through the body and gone,
But were back once more to breathe in an old world worth their new:
What never had been, was now; what was, as it shall be anon;
And what is, — shall I say, matched both? for I was made perfect too.

All through my keys that gave their sounds to a wish of my soul,
All through my soul that praised as its wish flowed visibly forth,
All through music and me! For think, had I painted the whole,
Why, there it had stood, to see, nor the process so wonder-worth:
Had I written the same, made verse — still, effect proceeds from cause,
Ye know why the forms are fair, ye hear how the tale is told;
It is all triumphant art, but art in obedience to laws,
Painter and poet are proud in the artist-list enrolled: —

But here is the finger of God, a flash of the will that can,
Existent behind all laws, that made them and, lo, they are!
And I know not if, save in this, such gift be allowed to man,
That out of three sounds he frame, not a fourth sound, but a star.
Consider it well: each tone of our scale in itself is nought;
It is everywhere in the world — loud, soft, and all is said:
Give it to me to use! I mix it with two in my thought;
And, there! Ye have heard and seen: consider and bow the head!

Well, it is gone at last, the palace of music I reared;
Gone! and the good tears start, the praises that come too slow;
For one is assured at first, one scarce can say that he feared,
That he even gave it a thought, the gone thing was to go.
Never to be again! But many more of the kind
As good, nay, better perchance: is this your comfort to me?

To me, who must be saved because I cling with my mind
To the same, same self, same love, same God: ay, what was shall be.

Therefore to whom turn I but to Thee, the ineffable Name?
Builder and maker, Thou, of houses not made with hands!
What, have fear of change from Thee who art ever the same?
Doubt that Thy power can fill the heart that Thy power expands?
There shall never be one lost good!
What was, shall live as before;
The evil is null, is nought, is silence implying sound;
What was good, shall be good, with, for evil, so much good more;
On the earth the broken arcs; in the heaven, a perfect round.

All we have willed or hoped or dreamed of good, shall exist;
Not its semblance, but itself; no beauty, nor good, nor power
Whose voice has gone forth, but each survives for the melodist
When eternity affirms the conception of an hour.
The high that proved too high, the heroic for earth too hard,
The passion that left the ground to lose itself in the sky,
Are music sent up to God by the lover and the bard;
Enough that He heard it once: we shall hear it by and by.

And what is our failure here but a triumph's evidence
For the fullness of the days? Have we withered or agonized?
Why else was the pause prolonged but that singing might issue thence?
Why rushed the discords in, but that harmony should be prized?
Sorrow is hard to bear, and doubt is slow to clear,
Each sufferer says his say, his scheme of the weal and woe:
But God has a few of us whom He whispers in the ear;
The rest may reason and welcome: 't is we musicians know.

Well, it is earth with me; silence resumes her reign:
I will be patient and proud, and soberly acquiesce.
Give me the keys. I feel for the common chord again,
Sliding by semitones, till I sink to the minor, — yes,
And I blunt it into a ninth, and I stand on alien ground,
Surveying a while the heights I rolled from into the deep;
Which, hark, I have dared and done, for my resting-place is found,
The C Major of this life: so, now I will try to sleep.

1864

RABBI BEN EZRA

Grow old along with me!
The best is yet to be,
The last of life, for which the first was made:
Our times are in His hand
Who saith 'A whole I planned,
Youth shows but half; trust God: see all, nor be afraid!'

Not that, amassing flowers,
Youth sighed 'Which rose make ours,
Which lily leave and then as best recall?'
Not that, admiring stars,
It yearned 'Nor Jove, nor Mars;
Mine be some figured flame which blends, transcends them all!'

Not for such hopes and fears
Annulling youth's brief years,
Do I remonstrate: folly wide the mark!
Rather I prize the doubt
Low kinds exist without,
Finished and finite clods, untroubled by a spark.

Poor vaunt of life indeed,
Were man but formed to feed
On joy, to solely seek and find and feast:
Such feasting ended, then
As sure an end to men;
Irks care the crop-full bird? Frets doubt the maw-crammed beast?

Rejoice we are allied
To That which doth provide
And not partake, effect and not receive!
A spark disturbs our clod;
Nearer we hold of God
Who gives, than of His tribes that take, I must believe.

Then, welcome each rebuff
That turns earth's smoothness rough,
Each sting that bids nor sit nor stand but go!

Be our joys three-parts pain!
Strive, and hold cheap the strain;
Learn, nor account the pang; dare, never grudge the throe!

For thence, — a paradox
Which comforts while it mocks, —
Shall life succeed in that it seems to fail:
What I aspired to be,
And was not, comforts me:
A brute I might have been, but would not sink i' the scale.

What is he but a brute
Whose flesh hath soul to suit,
Whose spirit works lest arms and legs want play?
To man, propose this test —
Thy body at its best,
How far can that project thy soul on its lone way?

Yet gifts should prove their use:
I own the Past profuse
Of power each side, perfection every turn:
Eyes, ears took in their dole,
Brain treasured up the whole;
Should not the heart beat once 'How good to live and learn?'

Not once beat 'Praise be Thine!
I see the whole design,
I, who saw Power, see now Love perfect too:
Perfect I call Thy plan:
Thanks that I was a man!
Maker, remake, complete, — I trust what Thou shalt do!'

For pleasant is this flesh;
Our soul in its rose-mesh
Pulled ever to the earth, still yearns for rest:
Would we some prize might hold
To match those manifold
Possessions of the brute, — gain most, as we did best!

Let us not always say
'Spite of this flesh to-day
I strove, made head, gained ground upon the whole!'
As the bird wings and sings,
Let us cry 'All good things
Are ours, nor soul helps flesh more, now, than flesh helps soul!'

Therefore I summon age
To grant youth's heritage,
Life's struggle having so far reached its term:
Thence shall I pass, approved
A man, for ay removed
From the developed brute; a God though in the germ.

And I shall thereupon
Take rest, ere I be gone
Once more on my adventure brave and new:
Fearless and unperplexed,
When I wage battle next,
What weapons to select, what armour to indue.

Youth ended, I shall try
My gain or loss thereby;
Be the fire ashes, what survives is gold:
And I shall weigh the same,
Give life its praise or blame:
Young, all lay in dispute; I shall know, being old.

For note, when evening shuts,
A certain moment cuts
The deed off, calls the glory from the grey:
A whisper from the west
Shoots — 'Add this to the rest,
Take it and try its worth: here dies another day.'

So, still within this life,
Though lifted o'er its strife,
Let me discern, compare, pronounce at last,
'This rage was right i' the main,
That acquiescence vain:
The Future I may face now I have proved the Past.'

For more is not reserved
To man, with soul just nerved
To act to-morrow what he learns to-day:
Here, work enough to watch
The Master work, and catch
Hints of the proper craft, tricks of the tool's true play.

As it was better, youth
Should strive, through acts uncouth,
Toward making, than repose on aught found made;
So, better, age, exempt
From strife, should know, than tempt
Further. Thou waitedst age; wait death nor be afraid!

Enough now, if the Right
And Good and Infinite
Be named here, as thou callest thy hand thine own,
With knowledge absolute,
Subject to no dispute
From fools that crowded youth, nor let thee feel alone.

Be there, for once and all,
Severed great minds from small,
Announced to each his station in the Past!
Was I, the world arraigned,
Were they, my soul disdained,
Right? Let age speak the truth and give us peace at last!

Now, who shall arbitrate?
Ten men love what I hate,
Shun what I follow, slight what I receive;
Ten, who in ears and eyes
Match me: we all surmise,
They, this thing, and I, that: whom shall my soul believe?

Not on the vulgar mass
Called 'work,' must sentence pass,
Things done, that took the eye and had the price;
O'er which, from level stand,
The low world laid its hand,
Found straightway to its mind, could value in a trice:

But all, the world's coarse thumb
And finger failed to plumb,
So passed in making up the main account;
All instincts immature,
All purposes unsure,
That weighed not as his work, yet swelled the man's amount:

Thoughts hardly to be packed
Into a narrow act,
Fancies that broke through language and escaped;
All I could never be,
All, men ignored in me,
This, I was worth to God, whose wheel the pitcher shaped.

Ay, note that Potter's wheel,
That metaphor! and feel
Why time spins fast, why passive lies our clay,—
Thou, to whom fools propound,
When the wine makes its round,
'Since life fleets, all is change; the Past gone, seize to-day!'

Fool! All that is, at all,
Lasts ever, past recall;
Earth changes, but thy soul and God stand sure:
What entered into thee,
That was, is, and shall be:
Time's wheel runs back or stops; Potter and clay endure.

He fixed thee mid this dance
Of plastic circumstance,
This Present, thou, forsooth, wouldst fain arrest:
Machinery just meant
To give thy soul its bent,
Try thee and turn thee forth, sufficiently impressed.

What though the earlier grooves
Which ran the laughing loves
Around thy base, no longer pause and press?
What though, about thy rim,
Skull-things in order grim
Grow out, in graver mood, obey the sterner stress?

Look not thou down but up!
To uses of a cup,
The festal board, lamp's flash and trumpet's peal,
The new wine's foaming flow,
The Master's lips aglow!
Thou, heaven's consummate cup, what needst thou with earth's wheel?

But I need, now as then,
Thee, God, who mouldest men;
And since, not even while the whirl was worst,
Did I,—to the wheel of life
With shapes and colours rife,
Bound dizzily,—mistake my end, to slake Thy thirst:

So, take and use Thy work!
Amend what flaws may lurk,
What strain o' the stuff, what warpings past the aim!
My times be in Thy hand!
Perfect the cup as planned!
Let age approve of youth, and death complete the same!

1864

CALIBAN UPON SETEBOS

['Will sprawl, now that the heat of day is best,
Flat on his belly in the pit's much mire,
With elbows wide, fists clenched to prop his chin;
And, while he kicks both feet in the cool slush,
And feels about his spine small eft-things course,
Run in and out each arm, and make him laugh;
And while above his head a pompion-plant,
Coating the cave-top as a brow its eye,
Creeps down to touch and tickle hair and beard,

And now a flower drops with a bee inside,
And now a fruit to snap at, catch and crunch:
He looks out o'er yon sea which sunbeams cross
And recross till they weave a spider-web
(Meshes of fire, some great fish breaks at times),
And talks to his own self, howe'er he please,
Touching that other, whom his dam called God.
Because to talk about Him, vexes — ha,
Could He but know! and time to vex is now,
When talk is safer than in winter-time.
Moreover Prosper and Miranda sleep
In confidence he drudges at their task,
And it is good to cheat the pair, and gibe,
Letting the rank tongue blossom into speech.]

Setebos, Setebos, and Setebos!
'Thinketh, He dwelleth i' the cold o' the moon.
'Thinketh He made it, with the sun to match,
But not the stars; the stars came otherwise;
Only made clouds, winds, meteors, such as that:
Also this isle, what lives and grows thereon,
And snaky sea which rounds and ends the same.

'Thinketh, it came of being ill at ease:
He hated that He cannot change His cold,
Nor cure its ache. 'Hath spied an icy fish
That longed to 'scape the rock-stream where she lived,
And thaw herself within the lukewarm brine
O' the lazy sea her stream thrusts far amid,
A crystal spike 'twixt two warm walls of wave;
Only she ever sickened, found repulse
At the other kind of water, not her life,
(Green-dense and dim-delicious, bred o' the sun)
Flounced back from bliss she was not born to breathe,
And in her old bounds buried her despair,
Hating and loving warmth alike: so He.

'Thinketh, He made thereat the sun, this isle,
Trees and the fowls here, beast and creeping thing.
Yon otter, sleek-wet, black, lithe as a leech;
Yon auk, one fire-eye in a ball of foam,
That floats and feeds; a certain badger brown
He hath watched hunt with that slant white-wedge eye
By moonlight; and the pie with the long tongue
That pricks deep into oakwarts for a worm,
And says a plain word when she finds her prize,
But will not eat the ants; the ants themselves
That build a wall of seeds and settled stalks
About their hole — He made all these and more,
Made all we see, and us, in spite: how else?
He could not, Himself, make a second self
To be His mate; as well have made Himself.
He would not make what He mislikes or slights,
An eyesore to Him, or not worth His pains:
But did, in envy, listlessness or sport,
Make what Himself would fain, in a manner, be —
Weaker in most points, stronger in a few,
Worthy, and yet mere playthings all the while,
Things He admires and mocks too, — that is it.
Because, so brave, so better though they be,
It nothing skills if He begin to plague.
Look now, I melt a gourd-fruit into mash,
Add honeycomb and pods, I have perceived,
Which bite like finches when they bill and kiss, —
Then, when froth rises bladdery, drink up all,
Quick, quick, till maggots scamper through my brain;
And throw me on my back i' the seeded thyme,
And wanton, wishing I were born a bird.
Put case, unable to be what I wish,
I yet could make a live bird out of clay:
Would not I take clay, pinch my Caliban
Able to fly? — for, there, see, he hath wings,
And great comb like the hoopoe's to admire,
And there, a sting to do his foes offence,
There, and I will that he begin to live,
Fly to yon rock-top, nip me off the horns
Of grigs high up that make the merry din,
Saucy through their veined wings, and mind me not.
In which feat, if his leg snapped, brittle clay,
And he lay stupid-like, — why, I should laugh;
And if he, spying me, should fall to weep,
Beseech me to be good, repair his wrong,
Bid his poor leg smart less or grow again, —
Well, as the chance were, this might take or else
Not take my fancy: I might hear his cry,
And give the manikin three legs for his one,
Or pluck the other off, leave him like an egg,

And lessoned he was mine and merely clay.
Were this no pleasure, lying in the thyme,
Drinking the mash, with brain become alive,
Making and marring clay at will? So He.
'Thinketh, such shows nor right nor wrong in Him,
Nor kind, nor cruel: He is strong and Lord.
'Am strong myself compared to yonder crabs
That march now from the mountain to the sea;
'Let twenty pass, and stone the twenty-first,
Loving not, hating not, just choosing so.
'Say, the first straggler that boasts purple spots
Shall join the file, one pincer twisted off;
'Say, this bruised fellow shall receive a worm,
And two worms he whose nippers end in red;
As it likes me each time, I do: so He.
Well then, 'supposeth He is good i' the main,
Placable if His mind and ways were guessed.
But rougher than His handiwork, be sure!
Oh, He hath made things worthier than Himself,
And envieth that, so helped, such things do more
Than He who made them! What consoles but this?
That they, unless through Him, do nought at all,
And must submit: what other use in things?
'Hath cut a pipe of pithless elder-joint
That, blown through, gives exact the scream o' the jay
When from her wing you twitch the feathers blue:
Sound this, and little birds that hate the jay
Flock within stone's throw, glad their foe is hurt:
Put case such pipe could prattle and boast forsooth
'I catch the birds, I am the crafty thing,
I make the cry my maker cannot make
With his great round mouth; he must blow through mine!'
Would not I smash it with my foot? So He.
But wherefore rough, why cold and ill at ease?
Aha, that is a question! Ask, for that,
What knows, — the something over Setebos
That made Him, or He, may be, found and fought,
Worsted, drove off and did to nothing, perchance.
There may be something quiet o'er His head,
Out of His reach, that feels nor joy nor grief,
Since both derive from weakness in some way.
I joy because the quails come; would not joy
Could I bring quails here when I have a mind:
This Quiet, all it hath a mind to, doth.
'Esteemeth stars the outposts of its couch,
But never spends much thought nor care that way.
It may look up, work up, — the worse for those
It works on! 'Careth but for Setebos
The many-handed as a cuttle-fish,
Who, making Himself feared through what He does,
Looks up, first, and perceives He cannot soar
To what is quiet and hath happy life;
Next looks down here, and out of very spite
Makes this a bauble-world to ape yon real,
These good things to match those as hips do grapes.
'T is solace making baubles, ay, and sport.
Himself peeped late, eyed Prosper at his books
Careless and lofty, lord now of the isle:
Vexed, 'stitched a book of broad leaves, arrow-shaped,
Wrote thereon, he knows what, prodigious words;
Has peeled a wand and called it by a name;
Weareth at whiles for an enchanter's robe
The eyed skin of a supple oncelot;
And hath an ounce sleeker than youngling mole,
A four-legged serpent he makes cower and couch,
Now snarl, now hold its breath and mind his eye,
And saith she is Miranda and my wife:
'Keeps for his Ariel a tall pouch-bill crane
He bids go wade for fish and straight disgorge;
Also a sea-beast, lumpish, which he snared,
Blinded the eyes of, and brought somewhat tame,
And split its toe-webs, and now pens the drudge
In a hole o' the rock and calls him Caliban;
A bitter heart, that bides its time and bites,
'Plays thus at being Prosper in a way,
Taketh his mirth with make-believes: so He.
His dam held that the Quiet made all things
Which Setebos vexed only: 'holds not so.
Who made them weak, meant weakness He might vex.
Had He meant other, while His hand was in,

Why not make horny eyes no thorn could prick,
Or plate my scalp with bone against the snow,
Or overscale my flesh 'neath joint and joint,
Like an orc's armour? Ay, — so spoil His sport!
He is the One now: only He doth all.
'Saith, He may like, perchance, what profits Him.
Ay, himself loves what does him good; but why?
'Gets good no otherwise. This blinded beast
Loves whoso places flesh-meat on his nose,
But, had he eyes, would want no help, but hate
Or love, just as it liked him: He hath eyes.
Also it pleaseth Setebos to work,
Use all His hands, and exercise much craft,
By no means for the love of what is worked.
'Tasteth, himself, no finer good i' the world
When all goes right, in this safe summer-time,
And he wants little, hungers, aches not much,
Than trying what to do with wit and strength.
'Falls to make something: 'piled yon pile of turfs,
And squared and stuck there squares of soft white chalk,
And, with a fish-tooth, scratched a moon on each,
And set up endwise certain spikes of tree,
And crowned the whole with a sloth's skull a-top,
Found dead i' the woods, too hard for one to kill.
No use at all i' the work, for work's sole sake;
'Shall some day knock it down again: so He.
'Saith He is terrible: watch His feats in proof!
One hurricane will spoil six good months' hope.
He hath a spite against me, that I know,
Just as He favours Prosper, who knows why?
So it is, all the same, as well I find.
'Wove wattles half the winter, fenced them firm
With stone and stake to stop she-tortoises
Crawling to lay their eggs here: well, one wave,
Feeling the foot of Him upon its neck,
Gaped as a snake does, lolled out its large tongue,
And licked the whole labour flat: so much for spite.
'Saw a ball flame down late (yonder it lies)
Where, half an hour before, I slept i' the shade:
Often they scatter sparkles: there is force!
'Dug up a newt He may have envied once
And turned to stone, shut up inside a stone.
Please Him and hinder this? — What Prosper does?
Aha, if He would tell me how! Not He!
There is the sport: discover how or die!
All need not die, for of the things o' the isle
Some flee afar, some dive, some run up trees;
Those at His mercy, — why, they please Him most
When . . when . . well, never try the same way twice!
Repeat what act has pleased, He may grow wroth.
You must not know His ways, and play Him off,
Sure of the issue. 'Doth the like himself:
'Spareth a squirrel that it nothing fears
But steals the nut from underneath my thumb,
And when I threat, bites stoutly in defence:
'Spareth an urchin that, contrariwise,
Curls up into a ball, pretending death
For fright at my approach: the two ways please.
But what would move my choler more than this,
That either creature counted on its life
To-morrow and next day and all days to come,
Saying forsooth in the inmost of its heart,
'Because he did so yesterday with me,
And otherwise with such another brute,
So must he do henceforth and always.' — Ay?
'Would teach the reasoning couple what 'must' means!
'Doth as he likes, or wherefore Lord? So He.
'Conceiveth all things will continue thus,
And we shall have to live in fear of Him
So long as He lives, keeps His strength: no change,
If He have done His best, make no new world
To please Him more, so leave off watching this, —
If He surprise not even the Quiet's self
Some strange day, — or, suppose, grow into it
As grubs grow butterflies: else, here are we,
And there is He, and nowhere help at all.
'Believeth with the life, the pain shall stop.

His dam held different, that after death
He both plagued enemies and feasted friends:
Idly! He doth His worst in this our life,
Giving just respite lest we die through pain,
Saving last pain for worst, — with which, an end.
Meanwhile, the best way to escape His ire
Is, not to seem too happy. Sees, himself,
Yonder two flies, with purple films and pink,
Bask on the pompion-bell above: kills both.
'Sees two black painful beetles roll their ball
On head and tail as if to save their lives:
Moves them the stick away they strive to clear.
  Even so, 'would have Him misconceive, suppose
This Caliban strives hard and ails no less,
And always, above all else, envies Him.
Wherefore he mainly dances on dark nights,
Moans in the sun, gets under holes to laugh,
And never speaks his mind save housed as now:
Outside, 'groans, curses. If He caught me here,
O'erheard this speech, and asked 'What chucklest at?'
'Would, to appease Him, cut a finger off,
Or of my three kid yearlings burn the best,
Or let the toothsome apples rot on tree,
Or push my tame beast for the orc to taste:
While myself lit a fire, and made a song
And sung it, '*What I hate, be consecrate*
To celebrate Thee and Thy state, no mate
For Thee; what see for envy in poor me?'
Hoping the while, since evils sometimes mend,
Warts rub away, and sores are cured with slime,
That some strange day, will either the Quiet catch
And conquer Setebos, or likelier He
Decrepit may doze, doze, as good as die.
  [What, what? A curtain o'er the world at once!
Crickets stop hissing; not a bird — or, yes,
There scuds His raven that hath told Him all!
It was fool's play, this prattling! Ha! The wind
Shoulders the pillared dust, death's house o' the move,
And fast invading fires begin! White blaze —
A tree's head snaps — and there, there, there, there, there, there,
His thunder follows! Fool to gibe at Him!
Lo! 'Lieth flat and loveth Setebos!
'Maketh his teeth meet through his upper lip,
Will let those quails fly, will not eat this month
One little mess of whelks, so he may 'scape!]

1864

APPARENT FAILURE

No, for I 'll save it! Seven years since,
  I passed through Paris, stopped a day
To see the baptism of your Prince;
  Saw, made my bow, and went my way:
Walking the heat and headache off,
  I took the Seine-side, you surmise,
Thought of the Congress, Gortschakoff,
  Cavour's appeal and Buol's replies,
So sauntered till — what met my eyes?

Only the Doric little Morgue!
  The dead-house where you show your drowned:
Petrarch's Vaucluse makes proud the Sorgue,
  Your Morgue has made the Seine renowned.
One pays one's debt in such a case;
  I plucked up heart and entered, — stalked,
Keeping a tolerable face
  Compared with some whose cheeks were chalked:
Let them! No Briton 's to be baulked!

First came the silent gazers; next,
  A screen of glass, we 're thankful for;
Last, the sight's self, the sermon's text,
  The three men who did most abhor
Their life in Paris yesterday,
  So killed themselves: and now, enthroned
Each on his copper couch, they lay
  Fronting me, waiting to be owned.
I thought, and think, their sin 's atoned.

Poor men, God made, and all for that!
  The reverence struck me; o'er each head
Religiously was hung his hat,
  Each coat dripped by the owner's bed,
Sacred from touch: each had his berth,
  His bounds, his proper place of rest,
Who last night tenanted on earth
  Some arch, where twelve such slept abreast, —
Unless the plain asphalte seemed best.

How did it happen, my poor boy?
  You wanted to be Buonaparte
And have the Tuileries for toy,
  And could not, so it broke your heart?

You, old one by his side, I judge,
Were, red as blood, a socialist,
A leveller! Does the Empire grudge
You 've gained what no Republic missed?
Be quiet, and unclench your fist!

And this — why, he was red in vain,
Or black, — poor fellow that is blue!
What fancy was it, turned your brain?
Oh, women were the prize for you!
Money gets women, cards and dice
Get money, and ill-luck gets just
The copper couch and one clear nice
Cool squirt of water o'er your bust,
The right thing to extinguish lust!

It 's wiser being good than bad;
It 's safer being meek than fierce:
It 's fitter being sane than mad.
My own hope is, a sun will pierce
The thickest cloud earth ever stretched;
That, after Last, returns the First,
Though a wide compass round be fetched;
That what began best, can't end worst,
Nor what God blessed once, prove accurst.

1864

EPILOGUE

At the midnight in the silence of the sleep-time,
When you set your fancies free,
Will they pass to where — by death, fools think, imprisoned —
Low he lies who once so loved you, whom you loved so,
— Pity me?

Oh to love so, be so loved, yet so mistaken!
What had I on earth to do
With the slothful, with the mawkish, the unmanly?
Like the aimless, helpless, hopeless, did I drivel
— Being — who?

One who never turned his back but marched breast forward,
Never doubted clouds would break,
Never dreamed, though right were worsted, wrong would triumph,
Held we fall to rise, are baffled to fight better,
Sleep to wake.

No, at noonday in the bustle of man's work-time
Greet the unseen with a cheer!
Bid him forward, breast and back as either should be,
'Strive and thrive!' cry, 'Speed, — fight on, fare ever
There as here!'

1889

Elizabeth Barrett Browning
(1806–1861)

LADY GERALDINE'S COURTSHIP

Dear my friend and fellow student, I would lean my spirit o'er you!
Down the purple of this chamber, tears should scarcely run at will.
I am humbled who was humble. Friend, — I bow my head before you.
You should lead me to my peasants, — but their faces are too still.

There 's a lady — an earl's daughter, — she is proud and she is noble,
And she treads the crimson carpet, and she breathes the perfumed air,
And a kingly blood sends glances up her princely eye to trouble,
And the shadow of a monarch's crown is softened in her hair.

She has halls among the woodlands, she has castles by the breakers,
She has farms and she has manors, she can threaten and command,
And the palpitating engines snort in steam across her acres,
As they mark upon the blasted heaven the measure of the land.

There are none of England's daughters who can show a prouder presence;
Upon princely suitors praying, she has looked in her disdain.
She was sprung of English nobles, I was born of English peasants;
What was *I* that I should love her — save for competence to pain?

I was only a poor poet, made for singing at her casement,
As the finches or the thrushes, while she thought of other things.
Oh, she walked so high above me, she appeared to my abasement,
In her lovely silken murmur, like an angel clad in wings!

Many vassals bow before her as her carriage sweeps their doorways;
She has blest their little children, — as a priest or queen were she.
Far too tender, or too cruel far, her smile upon the poor was,
For I thought it was the same smile which she used to smile on *me*.

She has voters in the Commons, she has lovers in the palace;
And of all the fair court-ladies, few have jewels half as fine;
Oft the prince has named her beauty 'twixt the red wine and the chalice.
Oh, and what was *I* to love her? my beloved, my Geraldine!

Yet I could not choose but love her. I was born to poet-uses,
To love all things set above me, all of good and all of fair:
Nymphs of mountain, not of valley, we are wont to call the Muses
And in nympholeptic climbing, poets pass from mount to star.

And because I was a poet, and because the public praised me,
With a critical deduction for the modern writer's fault,
I could sit at rich men's tables, — though the courtesies that raised me,
Still suggested clear between us the pale spectrum of the salt.

And they praised me in her presence; — 'Will your book appear this summer?'
Then returning to each other — 'Yes, our plans are for the moors.'
Then with whisper dropped behind me — 'There he is! the latest comer!
Oh, she only likes his verses! what is over, she endures.

'Quite low-born! self-educated! somewhat gifted though by nature, —
And we make a point of asking him, — of being very kind.
You may speak, he does not hear you! and besides, he writes no satire, —
All these serpents kept by charmers leave the natural sting behind.'

I grew scornfuller, grew colder, as I stood up there among them,
Till as frost intense will burn you, the cold scorning scorched my brow;
When a sudden silver speaking, gravely cadenced, over-rung them,
And a sudden silken stirring touched my inner nature through.

I looked upward and beheld her. With a calm and regnant spirit,
Slowly round she swept her eyelids, and said clear before them all —
'Have you such superfluous honour, sir, that able to confer it
You will come down, Mister Bertram, as my guest to Wycombe Hall?'

Here she paused, — she had been paler at the first word of her speaking,
But because a silence followed it, blushed somewhat, as for shame,
Then, as scorning her own feeling, resumed calmly — 'I am seeking
More distinction than these gentlemen think worthy of my claim.

'Ne'ertheless, you see, I seek it — not because I am a woman'
(Here her smile sprang like a fountain, and, so, overflowed her mouth),
'But because my woods in Sussex have some purple shades at gloaming
Which are worthy of a king in state, or poet in his youth.

'I invite you, Mister Bertram, to no scene for worldly speeches —
Sir, I scarce should dare — but only where God asked the thrushes first —
And if *you* will sing beside them, in the covert of my beeches,
I will thank you for the woodlands, . . . for the human world, at worst.'

Then she smiled around right childly, then she gazed around right queenly,
And I bowed — I could not answer; alternated light and gloom —
While as one who quells the lions, with a steady eye serenely,
She, with level fronting eyelids, passed out stately from the room.

Oh, the blessèd woods of Sussex, I can hear them still around me,
With their leafy tide of greenery still rippling up the wind.
Oh, the cursèd woods of Sussex! where the hunter's arrow found me,
When a fair face and a tender voice had made me mad and blind!

In that ancient hall of Wycombe, thronged the numerous guests invited,
And the lovely London ladies trod the floors with gliding feet;
And their voices low with fashion, not with feeling, softly freighted
All the air about the windows, with elastic laughters sweet.

For at eve, the open windows flung their light out on the terrace,
Which the floating orbs of curtains did with gradual shadow sweep,
While the swans upon the river, fed at morning by the heiress,
Trembled downward through their snowy wings at music in their sleep.

And there evermore was music, both of instrument and singing,
Till the finches of the shrubberies grew restless in the dark;
But the cedars stood up motionless, each in a moonlight ringing,
And the deer, half in the glimmer, strewed the hollows of the park.

And though sometimes she would bind me with her silver-corded speeches
To commix my words and laughter with the converse and the jest,
Oft I sate apart, and gazing on the river through the beeches,
Heard, as pure the swans swam down it, her pure voice o'erfloat the rest.

In the morning, horn of huntsman, hoof of steed, and laugh of rider,
Spread out cheery from the court-yard till we lost them in the hills,
While herself and other ladies, and her suitors left beside her,
Went a-wandering up the gardens through the laurels and abeles.

Thus, her foot upon the new-mown grass, bareheaded, with the flowing
Of the virginal white vesture gathered closely to her throat,—
And the golden ringlets in her neck just quickened by her going,
And appearing to breathe sun for air, and doubting if to float,—

With a branch of dewy maple, which her right hand held above her,
And which trembled a green shadow in betwixt her and the skies,
As she turned her face in going, thus, she drew me on to love her,
And to worship the divineness of the smile hid in her eyes.

For her eyes alone smile constantly: her lips have serious sweetness,
And her front is calm — the dimple rarely ripples on the cheek;
But her deep blue eyes smile constantly, as if they in discreetness
Kept the secret of a happy dream she did not care to speak.

Thus she drew me the first morning, out across into the garden,
And I walked among her noble friends and could not keep behind.
Spake she unto all and unto me — 'Behold, I am the warden
Of the song-birds in these lindens, which are cages to their mind.

'But within this swarded circle, into which the lime-walk brings us,
Whence the beeches, rounded greenly, stand away in reverent fear,
I will let no music enter, saving what the fountain sings us,
Which the lilies round the basin may seem pure enough to hear.

'The live air that waves the lilies waves the slender jet of water
Like a holy thought sent feebly up from soul of fasting saint:
Whereby lies a marble Silence, sleeping! (Lough the sculptor wrought her)
So asleep she is forgetting to say Hush! — a fancy quaint.

'Mark how heavy white her eyelids! not a dream between them lingers,
And the left hand's index droppeth from the lips upon the cheek;
While the right hand, — with the symbol rose held slack within the fingers, —
Has fallen backward in the basin — yet this Silence will not speak!

'That the essential meaning growing may exceed the special symbol,
Is the thought as I conceive it: it applies more high and low.
Our true noblemen will often through right nobleness grow humble,
And assert an inward honour by denying outward show.'

'Nay, your Silence,' said I, 'truly, holds her symbol rose but slackly,
Yet *she holds it* — or would scarcely be a Silence to our ken;
And your nobles wear their ermine on the outside, or walk blackly
In the presence of the social law as mere ignoble men.

'Let the poets dream such dreaming! madam, in these British islands
'T is the substance that wanes ever, 't is the symbol that exceeds.
Soon we shall have nought but symbol! and, for statues like this Silence,
Shall accept the rose's image — in another case, the weed's.'

'Not so quickly,' she retorted, — 'I confess, where'er you go, you
Find for things, names — shows for actions, and pure gold for honour clear;
But when all is run to symbol in the Social, I will throw you
The world's book which now reads dryly, and sit down with Silence here.'

Half in playfulness she spoke, I thought, and half in indignation;
Friends who listened, laughed her words off, while her lovers deemed her fair:
A fair woman, flushed with feeling, in her noble-lighted station
Near the statue's white reposing — and both bathed in sunny air! —

With the trees round, not so distant but you heard their vernal murmur,
And beheld in light and shadow the leaves in and outward move,
And the little fountain leaping toward the sun-heart to be warmer,
Then recoiling in a tremble from the too much light above.

'T is a picture for remembrance. And thus, morning after morning,
Did I follow as she drew me by the spirit to her feet.
Why, her greyhound followed also! dogs — we both were dogs for scorning —
To be sent back when she pleased it and her path lay through the wheat.

And thus, morning after morning, spite of vows and spite of sorrow,
Did I follow at her drawing, while the week-days passed along,
Just to feed the swans this noontide, or to see the fawns to-morrow,
Or to teach the hill-side echo some sweet Tuscan in a song.

Aye, for sometimes on the hill-side, while we sate down in the gowans,
While the forest green behind us, and its shadow cast before,
And the river running under, and across it from the rowans
A brown partridge whirring near us, till we felt the air it bore, —

There, obedient to her praying, did I read aloud the poems
Made to Tuscan flutes, or instruments more various of our own;
Read the pastoral parts of Spenser — or the subtle interflowings
Found in Petrarch's sonnets — here 's the book — the leaf is folded down!

Or at times a modern volume — Wordsworth's solemn-thoughted idyl,
Howitt's ballad-verse, or Tennyson's enchanted reverie, —
Or from Browning some 'Pomegranate,' which, if cut deep down the middle,
Shows a heart within blood-tinctured, of a veined humanity.

Or at times I read there, hoarsely, some new poem of my making:
Poets ever fail in reading their own verses to their worth, —
For the echo in you breaks upon the words which you are speaking,
And the chariot-wheels jar in the gate through which you drive them forth.

After, when we were grown tired of books, the silence round us flinging
A slow arm of sweet compression, felt with beatings at the breast,
She would break out, on a sudden, in a gush of woodland singing,
Like a child's emotion in a god — a naiad tired of rest.

Oh, to see or hear her singing! scarce I know which is divinest —
For her looks sing too — she modulates her gestures on the tune;
And her mouth stirs with the song, like song; and when the notes are finest,
'T is the eyes that shoot out vocal light and seem to swell them on.

Then we talked — oh, how we talked! her voice, so cadenced in the talking,
Made another singing — of the soul! a music without bars;
While the leafy sounds of woodlands, humming round where we were walking,
Brought interposition worthy-sweet, — as skies about the stars.

And she spake such good thoughts natural, as if she always thought them;
She had sympathies so rapid, open, free as bird on branch,
Just as ready to fly east as west, whichever way besought them,
In the birchen-wood a chirrup, or a cock-crow in the grange.

In her utmost lightness there is truth — and often she speaks lightly,
Has a grace in being gay, which even mournful souls approve,
For the root of some grave earnest thought is understruck so rightly
As to justify the foliage and the waving flowers above.

And she talked on — *we* talked, rather! upon all things, substance, shadow,
Of the sheep that browsed the grasses, of the reapers in the corn,
Of the little children from the schools, seen winding through the meadow —
Of the poor rich world beyond them, still kept poorer by its scorn.

So, of men, and so, of letters — books are men of higher stature,
And the only men that speak aloud for future times to hear;
So, of mankind in the abstract, which grows slowly into nature,
Yet will lift the cry of 'progress,' as it trod from sphere to sphere.

And her custom was to praise me when I said, — 'The Age culls simples,
With a broad clown's back turned broadly to the glory of the stars.
We are gods by our own reck'ning, and may well shut up the temples,
And wield on, amid the incense-steam, the thunder of our cars.

'For we throw out acclamations of self-thanking, self-admiring,
With, at every mile run faster, — "O the wondrous, wondrous age,"
Little thinking if we work our souls as nobly as our iron,
Or if angels will commend us at the goal of pilgrimage.

'Why, what *is* this patient entrance into nature's deep resources,
But the child's most gradual learning to walk upright without bane?
When we drive out, from the cloud of steam, majestical white horses,
Are we greater than the first men who led black ones by the mane?

'If we trod the deeps of ocean, if we struck the stars in rising,
If we wrapped the globe intensely with one hot electric breath,
'T were but power within our tether, no new spirit-power comprising,
And in life we were not greater men, nor bolder men in death.'

She was patient with my talking; and I loved her, loved her, certes,
As I loved all heavenly objects, with uplifted eyes and hands!
As I loved pure inspirations, loved the graces, loved the virtues,
In a Love content with writing his own name on desert sands.

Or at least I thought so, purely! — thought no idiot Hope was raising
Any crown to crown Love's silence — silent Love that sate alone.
Out, alas! the stag is like me — he, that tries to go on grazing
With the great gun-wound in his neck, then reels with sudden moan.

It was thus I reeled. I told you that her hand had many suitors;
But she smiles them down imperially, as Venus did the waves,
And with such a gracious coldness, that they cannot press their futures
On the present of her courtesy, which yieldingly enslaves.

And this morning, as I sate alone within the inner chamber,
With the great saloon beyond it, lost in pleasant thought serene,
For I had been reading Camoëns — that poem you remember,
Which his lady's eyes are praised in, as the sweetest ever seen.

And the book lay open, and my thought flew from it, taking from it
A vibration and impulsion to an end beyond its own,
As the branch of a green osier, when a child would overcome it,
Springs up freely from his clasping and goes swinging in the sun.

As I mused I heard a murmur, — it grew deep as it grew longer —
Speakers using earnest language — 'Lady Geraldine, you *would!*'
And I heard a voice that pleaded ever on, in accents stronger
As a sense of reason gave it power to make its rhetoric good.

Well I knew that voice — it was an earl's, of soul that matched his station,
Soul completed into lordship — might and right read on his brow;
Very finely courteous — far too proud to doubt his domination
Of the common people, he atones for grandeur by a bow.

High straight forehead, nose of eagle, cold blue eyes, of less expression
Than resistance, coldly casting off the looks of other men,
As steel, arrows, — unelastic lips, which seem to taste possession,
And be cautious lest the common air should injure or distrain.

For the rest, accomplished, upright, — aye, and standing by his order
With a bearing not ungraceful; fond of art and letters too;
Just a good man made a proud man, — as the sandy rocks that border
A wild coast, by circumstances, in a regnant ebb and flow.

Thus, I knew that voice — I heard it, and I could not help the hearkening.
In the room I stood up blindly, and my burning heart within
Seemed to seethe and fuse my senses, till they ran on all sides darkening,
And scorched, weighed, like melted metal round my feet that stood therein.

And that voice, I heard it pleading, for love's sake, for wealth, position,
For the sake of liberal uses, and great actions to be done —
And she interrupted gently, 'Nay, my lord, the old tradition
Of your Normans, by some worthier hand than mine is, should be won.'

'Ah, that white hand!' he said quickly, — and in his he either drew it
Or attempted — for with gravity and instance she replied,
'Nay, indeed, my lord, this talk is vain, and we had best eschew it,
And pass on, like friends, to other points less easy to decide.'

What he said again, I know not. It is likely that his trouble
Worked his pride up to the surface, for she answered in slow scorn,
'And your lordship judges rightly. Whom I marry, shall be noble,
Aye, and wealthy. I shall never blush to think how he was born.'

There, I maddened! her words stung me. Life swept through me into fever,
And my soul sprang up astonished, sprang, full-statured in an hour.
Know you what it is when anguish, with apocalyptic NEVER,
To a Pythian height dilates you, — and despair sublimes to power?

From my brain, the soul-wings budded, — waved a flame about my body,
Whence conventions coiled to ashes. I felt self-drawn out, as man,
From amalgamate false natures, and I saw the skies grow ruddy
With the deepening feet of angels, and I knew what spirits can.

I was mad — inspired — say either! (anguish worketh inspiration)
Was a man, or beast — perhaps so, for the tiger roars, when speared;
And I walked on, step by step, along the level of my passion —
Oh my soul! and passed the doorway to her face, and never feared.

He had left her, peradventure, when my footstep proved my coming —
But for *her* — she half arose, then sate — grew scarlet and grew pale.
Oh, she trembled! — 't is so always with a worldly man or woman
In the presence of true spirits — what else *can* they do but quail?

Oh, she fluttered like a tame bird, in among its forest-brothers
Far too strong for it; then drooping, bowed her face upon her hands —
And I spake out wildly, fiercely, brutal truths of her and others:
I, she planted in the desert, swathed her, windlike, with my sands.

I plucked up her social fictions, bloody-rooted though leaf-verdant, —
Trod them down with words of shaming, — all the purple and the gold,
All the 'landed stakes' and lordships, all, that spirits pure and ardent
Are cast out of love and honour because chancing not to hold.

'For myself I do not argue,' said I, 'though I love you, madam,
But for better souls that nearer to the height of yours have trod;
And this age shows, to my thinking, still more infidels to Adam,
Than directly, by profession, simple infidels to God.

'Yet, O God,' I said, 'O grave,' I said, 'O mother's heart and bosom,
With whom first and last are equal, saint and corpse and little child!
We are fools to your deductions, in these figments of heart-closing;
We are traitors to your causes, in these sympathies defiled.

'Learn more reverence, madam, not for rank or wealth — *that* needs no learning,
That comes quickly — quick as sin does, aye, and culminates to sin;
But for Adam's seed, MAN! Trust me, 't is a clay above your scorning,
With God's image stamped upon it, and God's kindling breath within.

'What right have you, madam, gazing in your palace mirror daily,
Getting so by heart your beauty which all others must adore,
While you draw the golden ringlets down your fingers, to vow gaily
You will wed no man that 's only good to God, and nothing more?

'Why, what right have you, made fair by that same God — the sweetest woman
Of all women He has fashioned — with your lovely spirit-face,
Which would seem too near to vanish if its smile were not so human,
And your voice of holy sweetness, turning common words to grace,

'What right *can* you have, God's other works to scorn, despise, revile them
In the gross, as mere men, broadly — not as *noble* men, forsooth, —
As mere Parias of the outer world, forbidden to assoil them
In the hope of living, dying, near that sweetness of your mouth?

'Have you any answer, madam? If my spirit were less earthly,
If its instrument were gifted with a better silver string,
I would kneel down where I stand, and say — Behold me! I am worthy
Of thy loving, for I love thee! I am worthy as a king.

'As it is — your ermined pride, I swear, shall feel this stain upon her,
That *I*, poor, weak, tost with passion, scorned by me and you again,
Love you, madam — dare to love you — to my grief and your dishonour,
To my endless desolation, and your impotent disdain!'

More mad words like these — mere madness! friend, I need not write them fuller,
For I hear my hot soul dropping on the lines in showers of tears.
Oh, a woman! friend, a woman! why, a beast had scarce been duller
Than roar bestial loud complaints against the shining of the spheres.

But at last there came a pause. I stood all vibrating with thunder
Which my soul had used. The silence drew her face up like a call.
Could you guess what word she uttered? She looked up, as if in wonder,
With tears beaded on her lashes, and said 'Bertram!' — it was all.

If she had cursed me, and she might have — or if even, with queenly bearing
Which at need is used by women, she had risen up and said,
'Sir, you are my guest, and therefore I have given you a full hearing,
Now, beseech you, choose a name exacting somewhat less, instead,' —

I had borne it! — but that 'Bertram' — why it lies there on the paper
A mere word, without her accent, — and you cannot judge the weight
Of the calm which crushed my passion: I seemed drowning in a vapour, —
And her gentleness destroyed me whom her scorn made desolate.

So, struck backward and exhausted by that inward flow of passion
Which had rushed on, sparing nothing, into forms of abstract truth,
By a logic agonizing through unseemly demonstration,
And by youth's own anguish turning grimly grey the hairs of youth, —

By the sense accursed and instant, that if even I spake wisely
I spake basely — using truth, if what I spake, indeed was true,
To avenge wrong on a woman — *her*, who sate there weighing nicely
A poor manhood's worth, found guilty of such deeds as I could do! —

By such wrong and woe exhausted — what I suffered and occasioned, —
As a wild horse through the city runs with lightning in his eyes,
And then dashing at a church's cold and passive wall, impassioned,
Strikes the death into his burning brain, and blindly drops and dies —

So I fell, struck down before her! do you blame me, friend, for weakness?
'T was my strength of passion slew me! — fell before her like a stone.
Fast the dreadful world rolled from me, on its roaring wheels of blackness —
When the light came, I was lying in this chamber, and alone.

Oh, of course, she charged her lacqueys to bear out the sickly burden,
And to cast it from her scornful sight — but not *beyond* the gate;
She is too kind to be cruel, and too haughty not to pardon
Such a man as I! 't were something to be level to her hate.

But for me — you now are conscious why, my friend, I write this letter,
How my life is read all backward, and the charm of life undone:
I shall leave her house at dawn; I would to-night, if I were better —
And I charge my soul to hold my body strengthened for the sun.

When the sun has dyed the oriel, I depart, with no last gazes,
No weak moanings (one word only, left in writing for her hands),
Out of reach of all derision, and some unavailing praises,
To make front against this anguish in the far and foreign lands.

Blame me not. I would not squander life in grief — I am abstemious:
I but nurse my spirit's falcon, that its wing may soar again.
There 's no room for tears of weakness in the blind eyes of a Phemius!
Into work the poet kneads them, — and he does not die *till then*.

CONCLUSION

Bertram finished the last pages, while along the silence ever
Still in hot and heavy splashes, fell the tears on every leaf:
Having ended he leans backward in his chair, with lips that quiver
From the deep unspoken, aye, and deep unwritten thoughts of grief.

Soh! how still the lady standeth! 't is a dream — a dream of mercies!
'Twixt the purple lattice-curtains, how she standeth still and pale!
'T is a vision, sure, of mercies, sent to soften his self-curses —
Sent to sweep a patient quiet o'er the tossing of his wail.

'Eyes,' he said, 'now throbbing through me! are ye eyes that did undo me?
Shining eyes, like antique jewels set in Parian statue-stone!
Underneath that calm white forehead, are ye ever burning torrid
O'er the desolate sand-desert of my heart and life undone?'

With a murmurous stir uncertain, in the air, the purple curtain
Swelleth in and swelleth out around her motionless pale brows,
While the gliding of the river sends a rippling noise for ever
Through the open casement whitened by the moonlight's slant repose.

Said he — 'Vision of a lady! stand there silent, stand there steady!
Now I see it plainly, plainly; now I cannot hope or doubt —
There, the brows of mild repression — there, the lips of silent passion,
Curvèd like an archer's bow to send the bitter arrows out.'

Ever, evermore the while in a slow silence she kept smiling,
And approached him slowly, slowly, in a gliding measured pace;
With her two white hands extended, as if praying one offended,
And a look of supplication, gazing earnest in his face.

Said he — 'Wake me by no gesture, — sound of breath, or stir of vesture!
Let the blessèd apparition melt not yet to its divine!
No approaching — hush, no breathing! or my heart must swoon to death in
The too utter life thou bringest — O thou dream of Geraldine!'

Ever, evermore the while in a slow silence she kept smiling —
But the tears ran over lightly from her eyes, and tenderly;
'Dost thou, Bertram, truly love me? Is no woman far above me
Found more worthy of thy poet-heart than such a one as *I*?'

Said he — 'I would dream so ever, like the flowing of that river,
Flowing ever in a shadow greenly onward to the sea!
So, thou vision of all sweetness — princely to a full completeness, —
Would my heart and life flow onward — deathward — through this dream of THEE!'

Ever, evermore the while in a slow silence she kept smiling,
While the silver tears ran faster down the blushing of her cheeks;
Then with both her hands enfolding both of his, she softly told him,
'Bertram, if I say I love thee, . . . 't is the vision only speaks.'

Softened, quickened to adore her, on his knee he fell before her —
And she whispered low in triumph, 'It shall be as I have sworn!
Very rich he is in virtues, — very noble — noble, certes;
And I shall not blush in knowing that men call him lowly born.'

1844

THE CRY OF THE CHILDREN

Do ye hear the children weeping, O my brothers,
Ere the sorrow comes with years?
They are leaning their young heads against their mothers,
And *that* cannot stop their tears.
The young lambs are bleating in the meadows,
The young birds are chirping in the nest,
The young fawns are playing with the shadows,
The young flowers are blowing toward the west —
But the young, young children, O my brothers,
They are weeping bitterly!
They are weeping in the playtime of the others,
In the country of the free.

Do you question the young children in the sorrow
Why their tears are falling so?
The old man may weep for his to-morrow
Which is lost in Long Ago;
The old tree is leafless in the forest,
The old year is ending in the frost,
The old wound, if stricken, is the sorest,
The old hope is hardest to be lost:
But the young, young children, O my brothers,
Do you ask them why they stand
Weeping sore before the bosoms of their mothers,
In our happy Fatherland?

They look up with their pale and sunken faces,
And their looks are sad to see,
For the man's hoary anguish draws and presses
Down the cheeks of infancy.
'Your old earth,' they say, 'is very dreary;
Our young feet,' they say, 'are very weak!
Few paces have we taken, yet are weary —
Our grave-rest is very far to seek.
Ask the agèd why they weep, and not the children;
For the outside earth is cold;
And we young ones stand without, in our bewildering,
And the graves are for the old.'

'True,' say the children, 'it may happen
That we die before our time;
Little Alice died last year — her grave is shapen
Like a snowball, in the rime.
We looked into the pit prepared to take her:
Was no room for any work in the close clay!
From the sleep wherein she lieth none will wake her,
Crying, "Get up, little Alice! it is day."
If you listen by that grave, in sun and shower,
With your ear down, little Alice never cries;
Could we see her face, be sure we should not know her,
For the smile has time for growing in her eyes:
And merry go her moments, lulled and stilled in
The shroud by the kirk-chime!
It is good when it happens,' say the children,
'That we die before our time.'

Alas, alas, the children! they are seeking
Death in life, as best to have;
They are binding up their hearts away from breaking,
With a cerement from the grave.
Go out, children, from the mine and from the city,
Sing out, children, as the little thrushes do;
Pluck you handfuls of the meadow cowslips pretty,
Laugh aloud, to feel your fingers let them through!
But they answer, 'Are your cowslips of the meadows
Like our weeds anear the mine?
Leave us quiet in the dark of the coal-shadows,
From your pleasures fair and fine!

'For oh,' say the children, 'we are weary,
And we cannot run or leap;
If we cared for any meadows, it were merely
To drop down in them and sleep.
Our knees tremble sorely in the stooping,
We fall upon our faces, trying to go;
And, underneath our heavy eyelids drooping,

The reddest flower would look as pale as snow;
For, all day, we drag our burden tiring
Through the coal-dark, underground —
Or, all day, we drive the wheels of iron
In the factories, round and round.

'For, all day, the wheels are droning, turning, —
Their wind comes in our faces, —
Till our hearts turn, — our heads with pulses burning,
And the walls turn in their places:
Turns the sky in the high window blank and reeling,
Turns the long light that drops adown the wall,
Turn the black flies that crawl along the ceiling,
All are turning, all the day, and we with all.
And all day, the iron wheels are droning,
And sometimes we could pray,
"O ye wheels" (breaking out in a mad moaning),
"Stop! be silent for to-day!"'

Aye! be silent! Let them hear each other breathing
For a moment, mouth to mouth!
Let them touch each other's hands, in a fresh wreathing
Of their tender human youth!
Let them feel that this cold metallic motion
Is not all the life God fashions or reveals:
Let them prove their living souls against the notion
That they live in you, or under you, O wheels! —
Still, all day, the iron wheels go onward,
Grinding life down from its mark;
And the children's souls, which God is calling sunward,
Spin on blindly in the dark.

Now tell the poor young children, O my brothers,
To look up to Him and pray;
So the blessèd One who blesseth all the others,
Will bless them another day.
They answer, 'Who is God that He should hear us,
While the rushing of the iron wheels is stirred?
When we sob aloud, the human creatures near us
Pass by, hearing not, or answer not a word.
And *we* hear not (for the wheels in their resounding)
Strangers speaking at the door:
Is it likely God, with angels singing round Him,
Hears our weeping any more?

'Two words, indeed, of praying we remember,
And at midnight's hour of harm,
"Our Father," looking upward in the chamber,
We say softly for a charm.
We know no other words, except "Our Father,"
And we think that, in some pause of angel's song,
God may pluck them with the silence sweet to gather,
And hold both within His right hand which is strong.
"Our Father!" If He heard us, He would surely
(For they call Him good and mild)
Answer, smiling down the steep world very purely,
"Come and rest with Me, My child."

'But, no!' say the children, weeping faster,
'He is speechless as a stone;
And they tell us, of His image is the master
Who commands us to work on.
Go to!' say the children, — 'up in Heaven,
Dark, wheel-like, turning clouds are all we find.
Do not mock us; grief has made us unbelieving —
We look up for God, but tears have made us blind.'
Do you hear the children weeping and disproving,
O my brothers, what ye preach?
For God's possible is taught by His world's loving,
And the children doubt of each.

And well may the children weep before you!
They are weary ere they run;
They have never seen the sunshine, nor the glory
Which is brighter than the sun.
They know the grief of man, without its wisdom;
They sink in man's despair, without its calm;
And slaves, without the liberty in Christdom,
Are martyrs, by the pang without the palm, —
Are worn, as if with age, yet unretrievingly

The harvest of its memories cannot reap, —
Are orphans of the earthly love and heavenly.
Let them weep! let them weep!

They look up, with their pale and sunken faces,
And their look is dread to see,
For they mind you of their angels in high places,
With eyes turned on Deity! —
'How long,' they say, 'how long, O cruel nation,
Will you stand, to move the world, on a child's heart, —
Stifle down with a mailed heel its palpitation,
And tread onward to your throne amid the mart?
Our blood splashes upward, O gold-heaper,
And your purple shows your path!
But the child's sob in the silence curses deeper
Than the strong man in his wrath.'

1844

SONNETS FROM THE PORTUGUESE

I

I THOUGHT once how Theocritus had sung
Of the sweet years, the dear and wished-for years,
Who each one in a gracious hand appears
To bear a gift for mortals, old or young:
And, as I mused it in his antique tongue,
I saw, in gradual vision through my tears,
The sweet, sad years, the melancholy years,
Those of my own life, who by turns had flung
A shadow across me. Straightway I was 'ware,
So weeping, how a mystic Shape did move
Behind me, and drew me backward by the hair,
And a voice said in mastery while I strove, . .
'Guess now who holds thee?' — 'Death,' I said. But, there,
The silver answer rang, . . 'Not Death, but Love.'

VII

THE face of all the world is changed, I think,
Since first I heard the footsteps of thy soul
Move still, oh, still, beside me, as they stole
Betwixt me and the dreadful outer brink
Of obvious death, where I, who thought to sink,
Was caught up into love, and taught the whole
Of life in a new rhythm. The cup of dole
God gave for baptism, I am fain to drink,
And praise its sweetness, Sweet, with thee anear.
The names of country, heaven, are changed away
For where thou art or shalt be, there or here;
And this . . . this lute and song . . . loved yesterday
(The singing angels know) are only dear,
Because thy name moves right in what they say.

XIV

IF thou must love me, let it be for nought
Except for love's sake only. Do not say
'I love her for her smile . . . her look . . . her way
Of speaking gently, . . for a trick of thought
That falls in well with mine, and certes brought
A sense of pleasant ease on such a day' —
For these things in themselves, Belovèd, may
Be changed, or change for thee, — and love, so wrought,
May be unwrought so. Neither love me for
Thine own dear pity's wiping my cheeks dry, —
A creature might forget to weep, who bore
Thy comfort long, and lose thy love thereby!
But love me for love's sake, that evermore
Thou mayst love on, through love's eternity.

XVII

MY poet, thou canst touch on all the notes
God set between His After and Before,
And strike up and strike off the general roar
Of the rushing worlds, a melody that floats
In a serene air purely. Antidotes
Of medicated music, answering for
Mankind's forlornest uses, thou canst pour
From thence into their ears. God's will devotes
Thine to such ends, and mine to wait on thine.
How, Dearest, wilt thou have me for most use?
A hope, to sing by gladly? . . or a fine
Sad memory, with thy songs to interfuse?
A shade, in which to sing . . . of palm or pine?
A grave, on which to rest from singing? . . Choose.

XXXIX

BECAUSE thou hast the power and own'st the grace
To look through and behind this mask of me
(Against which years have beat thus blanchingly

With their rains) and behold my soul's true face,
The dim and weary witness of life's race! —
Because thou hast the faith and love to see,
Through that same soul's distracting lethargy,
The patient angel waiting for a place
In the new heavens! because nor sin nor woe,
Nor God's infliction, nor death's neighbourhood,
Nor all which others viewing, turn to go, . .
Nor all which makes me tired of all, self viewed, . .
Nothing repels thee, . . dearest, teach me so
To pour out gratitude, as thou dost, good.

XLII

'*My future will not copy fair my past*' —
I wrote that once; and thinking at my side
My ministering life-angel justified
The word by his appealing look upcast
To the white throne of God, I turned at last,
And there, instead, saw thee, not unallied
To angels in thy soul! Then I, long tried
By natural ills, received the comfort fast,
While budding, at thy sight, my pilgrim's staff
Gave out green leaves with morning dews impearled.
I seek no copy now of life's first half:
Leave here the pages with long musing curled,
And write me new my future's epigraph,
New angel mine, unhoped for in the world!

XLIII

How do I love thee? Let me count the ways.
I love thee to the depth and breadth and height
My soul can reach, when feeling out of sight
For the ends of Being and ideal Grace.
I love thee to the level of every day's
Most quiet need, by sun and candlelight.
I love thee freely, as men strive for Right;
I love thee purely, as they turn from Praise.
I love thee with the passion put to use
In my old griefs, and with my childhood's faith.
I love thee with a love I seemed to lose
With my lost saints, — I love thee with the breath,
Smiles, tears, of all my life! — and, if God choose,
I shall but love thee better after death.

1850

Matthew Arnold (1822–1888)

SONNETS

TO A FRIEND

Who prop, thou ask'st, in these bad days, my mind?
He much, the old man, who, clearest-souled of men,
Saw The Wide Prospect, and the Asian Fen,
And Tmolus' hill, and Smyrna bay, though blind.
Much he, whose friendship I not long since won,
That halting slave, who in Nicopolis
Taught Arrian, when Vespasian's brutal son
Cleared Rome of what most shamed him. But be his
My special thanks, whose even-balanced soul,
From first youth tested up to extreme old age,
Business could not make dull, nor Passion wild:
Who saw life steadily, and saw it whole;
The mellow glory of the Attic stage;
Singer of sweet Colonus, and its child.

1849

SHAKESPEARE

Others abide our question. Thou art free.
We ask and ask: Thou smilest and art still,
Out-topping knowledge. For the loftiest hill
That to the stars uncrowns his majesty,
Planting his steadfast footsteps in the sea,
Making the Heaven of Heavens his dwelling-place,
Spares but the cloudy border of his base
To the foiled searching of mortality:
And thou, who didst the stars and sunbeams know,
Self-schooled, self-scanned, self-honoured, self-secure,
Didst tread on Earth unguessed at. Better so!
All pains the immortal spirit must endure,
All weakness that impairs, all griefs that bow,
Find their sole voice in that victorious brow.

1849

A PICTURE AT NEWSTEAD

What made my heart, at Newstead, fullest swell? —
'T was not the thought of Byron, of his cry
Stormily sweet, his Titan agony;

It was the sight of that Lord Arundel
Who struck, in heat, the child he loved so well,
And the child's reason flickered, and did die.
Painted (he willed it) in the gallery
They hang; the picture doth the story tell.
Behold the stern, mailed father, staff in hand!
The little fair-haired son, with vacant gaze,
Where no more lights of sense or knowledge are!
Methinks the woe which made that father stand
Baring his dumb remorse to future days,
Was woe than Byron's woe more tragic far.

1867

THE FORSAKEN MERMAN

COME, dear children, let us away;
Down and away below.
Now my brothers call from the bay;
Now the great winds shorewards blow;
Now the salt tides seawards flow;
Now the wild white horses play,
Champ, and chafe and toss in the spray.
Children dear, let us away.
This way, this way.

Call her once before you go.
Call once yet.
In a voice that she will know:
'Margaret! Margaret!'
Children's voices should be dear
(Call once more) to a mother's ear:
Children's voices, wild with pain.
Surely she will come again.
Call her once and come away.
This way, this way.
'Mother dear, we cannot stay.'
The wild white horses foam and fret.
Margaret! Margaret!

Come, dear children, come away down.
Call no more.
One last look at the white-walled town,
And the little grey church on the windy shore,
Then come down.
She will not come though you call all day.
Come away, come away.

Children dear, was it yesterday
We heard the sweet bells over the bay?
In the caverns where we lay,
Through the surf and through the swell,
The far-off sound of a silver bell?
Sand-strewn caverns, cool and deep,
Where the winds are all asleep;
Where the spent lights quiver and gleam;
Where the salt weed sways in the stream;
Where the sea-beasts ranged all round
Feed in the ooze of their pasture-ground;
Where the sea-snakes coil and twine,
Dry their mail and bask in the brine;
Where great whales come sailing by,
Sail and sail, with unshut eye,
Round the world for ever and aye?
When did music come this way?
Children dear, was it yesterday?

Children dear, was it yesterday
(Call yet once) that she went away?
Once she sate with you and me,
On a red gold throne in the heart of the sea,
And the youngest sate on her knee.
She combed its bright hair, and she tended it well,
When down swung the sound of a far-off bell.
She sighed, she looked up through the clear green sea.
She said; 'I must go, for my kinsfolk pray
In the little grey church on the shore to-day.
'T will be Easter-time in the world — ah me!
And I lose my poor soul, Merman, here with thee.'
I said; 'Go up, dear heart, through the waves;
Say thy prayer, and come back to the kind sea-caves.'
She smiled, she went up through the surf in the bay.
Children dear, was it yesterday?

Children dear, were we long alone?
'The sea grows stormy, the little ones moan.
Long prayers,' I said, 'in the world they say.
Come,' I said, and we rose through the surf in the bay.
We went up the beach, by the sandy down
Where the sea-stocks bloom, to the white-walled town.
Through the narrow paved streets, where all was still,
To the little grey church on the windy hill.
From the church came a murmur of folk at their prayers,
But we stood without in the cold blowing airs.
We climbed on the graves, on the stones, worn with rains,
And we gazed up the aisle through the small leaded panes.
She sate by the pillar; we saw her clear:
'Margaret, hist! come quick, we are here.

Dear heart,' I said, 'we are long alone.
The sea grows stormy, the little ones moan.'
But, ah, she gave me never a look,
For her eyes were sealed to the holy book.
'Loud prays the priest; shut stands the door.'
Come away, children, call no more.
Come away, come down, call no more.

Down, down, down.
Down to the depths of the sea.
She sits at her wheel in the humming town,
Singing most joyfully.
Hark, what she sings; 'O joy, O joy,
For the humming street, and the child with its toy.
For the priest, and the bell, and the holy well.
For the wheel where I spun,
And the blessèd light of the sun.'
And so she sings her fill,
Singing most joyfully,
Till the shuttle falls from her hand,
And the whizzing wheel stands still.
She steals to the window, and looks at the sand;
And over the sand at the sea;
And her eyes are set in a stare;
And anon there breaks a sigh,
And anon there drops a tear,
From a sorrow-clouded eye,
And a heart sorrow-laden,
A long, long sigh,
For the cold strange eyes of a little Mermaiden,
And the gleam of her golden hair.

Come away, away children.
Come children, come down.
The hoarse wind blows colder;
Lights shine in the town.
She will start from her slumber
When gusts shake the door;
She will hear the winds howling,
Will hear the waves roar.
We shall see, while above us
The waves roar and whirl,
A ceiling of amber,
A pavement of pearl.
Singing, 'Here came a mortal,
But faithless was she.
And alone dwell for ever
The kings of the sea.'

But, children, at midnight,
When soft the winds blow;
When clear falls the moonlight;
When spring-tides are low:
When sweet airs come seaward
From heaths starred with broom;
And high rocks throw mildly
On the blanched sands a gloom:
Up the still, glistening beaches,
Up the creeks we will hie;
Over banks of bright seaweed
The ebb-tide leaves dry.
We will gaze, from the sand-hills,
At the white, sleeping town;
At the church on the hill-side —
And then come back down.
Singing, 'There dwells a loved one,
But cruel is she.
She left lonely for ever
The kings of the sea.'

1849

SOHRAB AND RUSTUM

AN EPISODE

And the first gray of morning filled the east,
And the fog rose out of the Oxus stream.
But all the Tartar camp along the stream
Was hushed, and still the men were plunged in sleep;
Sohrab alone, he slept not: all night long
He had lain wakeful, tossing on his bed;
But when the gray dawn stole into his tent,
He rose, and clad himself, and girt his sword,
And took his horseman's cloak, and left his tent,
And went abroad into the cold wet fog,
Through the dim camp to Peran-Wisa's tent.
Through the black Tartar tents he passed, which stood
Clustering like bee-hives on the low flat strand
Of Oxus, where the summer floods o'erflow
When the sun melts the snows in high Pamere:
Through the black tents he passed, o'er that low strand,
And to a hillock came, a little back
From the stream's brink, the spot where first a boat,
Crossing the stream in summer, scrapes the land.
The men of former times had crowned the top
With a clay fort: but that was fall'n; and now
The Tartars built there Peran-Wisa's tent,
A dome of laths, and o'er it felts were spread.
And Sohrab came there, and went in, and stood
Upon the thick-piled carpets in the tent,
And found the old man sleeping on his bed
Of rugs and felts, and near him lay his arms.
And Peran-Wisa heard him, though the step

Was dulled; for he slept light, an old man's sleep;
And he rose quickly on one arm, and said: —
'Who art thou? for it is not yet clear dawn.
Speak! is there news, or any night alarm?'
But Sohrab came to the bedside, and said: —
'Thou know'st me, Peran-Wisa: it is I.
The sun is not yet risen, and the foe
Sleep; but I sleep not; all night long I lie
Tossing and wakeful, and I come to thee.
For so did King Afrasiab bid me seek
Thy counsel, and to heed thee as thy son,
In Samarcand, before the army marched;
And I will tell thee what my heart desires.
Thou know'st if, since from Ader-baijan first
I came among the Tartars, and bore arms,
I have still served Afrasiab well, and shown,
At my boy's years, the courage of a man.
This too thou know'st, that, while I still bear on
The conquering Tartar ensigns through the world,
And beat the Persians back on every field,
I see one man, one man, and one alone —
Rustum, my father; who, I hoped, should greet,
Should one day greet, upon some well-fought field,
His not unworthy, not inglorious son.
So I long hoped, but him I never find.
Come then, hear now, and grant me what I ask.
Let the two armies rest to-day: but I
Will challenge forth the bravest Persian lords
To meet me, man to man: if I prevail,
Rustum will surely hear it; if I fall —
Old man, the dead need no one, claim no kin.
Dim is the rumour of a common fight,
Where host meets host, and many names are sunk:
But of a single combat Fame speaks clear.'
He spoke: and Peran-Wisa took the hand
Of the young man in his, and sighed, and said: —
'O Sohrab, an unquiet heart is thine!
Canst thou not rest among the Tartar chiefs,
And share the battle's common chance with us
Who love thee, but must press forever first,
In single fight incurring single risk,
To find a father thou hast never seen?
That were far best, my son, to stay with us
Unmurmuring; in our tents, while it is war,
And when 't is truce, then in Afrasiab's towns.
But, if this one desire indeed rules all,
To seek out Rustum — seek him not through fight:
Seek him in peace, and carry to his arms,
O Sohrab, carry an unwounded son!
But far hence seek him, for he is not here.
For now it is not as when I was young,
When Rustum was in front of every fray:
But now he keeps apart, and sits at home,
In Seïstan, with Zal, his father old.
Whether that his own mighty strength at last
Feels the abhorred approaches of old age;
Or in some quarrel with the Persian King.
There go: — Thou wilt not? Yet my heart forebodes
Danger or death awaits thee on this field.
Fain would I know thee safe and well, though lost
To us: fain therefore send thee hence, in peace
To seek thy father, not seek single fights
In vain: — but who can keep the lion's cub
From ravening? and who govern Rustum's son?
Go: I will grant thee what thy heart desires.'
So said he, and dropped Sohrab's hand, and left
His bed, and the warm rugs whereon he lay,
And o'er his chilly limbs his woolen coat
He passed, and tied his sandals on his feet,
And threw a white cloak round him, and he took
In his right hand a ruler's staff, no sword;
And on his head he placed his sheep-skin cap,
Black, glossy, curled, the fleece of Kara-Kul;
And raised the curtain of his tent, and called
His herald to his side, and went abroad.
The sun, by this, had risen, and cleared the fog
From the broad Oxus and the glittering sands:
And from their tents the Tartar horsemen filed
Into the open plain; so Haman bade;
Haman, who next to Peran-Wisa ruled
The host, and still was in his lusty prime.
From their black tents, long files of horse, they streamed:
As when, some gray November morn, the files,
In marching order spread, of long-necked cranes
Stream over Casbin, and the southern slopes
Of Elburz, from the Aralian estuaries,
Or some frore Caspian reed-bed, southward bound

For the warm Persian sea-board: so they streamed.
The Tartars of the Oxus, the King's guard,
First, with black sheep-skin caps and with long spears;
Large men, large steeds; who from Bokhara come
And Khiva, and ferment the milk of mares.
Next the more temperate Toorkmuns of the south,
The Tukas, and the lances of Salore,
And those from Attruck and the Caspian sands;
Light men, and on light steeds, who only drink
The acrid milk of camels, and their wells.
And then a swarm of wandering horse, who came
From far, and a more doubtful service owned;
The Tartars of Ferghana, from the banks
Of the Jaxartes, men with scanty beards
And close-set skull-caps; and those wilder hordes
Who roam o'er Kipchak and the northern waste,
Kalmuks and unkempt Kuzzaks, tribes who stray
Nearest the Pole, and wandering Kirghizzes,
Who come on shaggy ponies from Pamere.
These all filed out from camp into the plain.
And on the other side the Persians formed:
First a light cloud of horse, Tartars they seemed,
The Ilyats of Khorassan: and behind,
The royal troops of Persia, horse and foot,
Marshaled battalions bright in burnished steel.
But Peran-Wisa with his herald came
Threading the Tartar squadrons to the front,
And with his staff kept back the foremost ranks.
And when Ferood, who led the Persians, saw
That Peran-Wisa kept the Tartars back,
He took his spear, and to the front he came,
And checked his ranks, and fixed them where they stood.
And the old Tartar came upon the sand
Betwixt the silent hosts, and spake, and said: —
'Ferood, and ye, Persians and Tartars, hear!
Let there be truce between the hosts to-day.
But choose a champion from the Persian lords
To fight our champion Sohrab, man to man.'
As, in the country, on a morn in June,
When the dew glistens on the pearlèd ears,
A shiver runs through the deep corn for joy —
So, when they heard what Peran-Wisa said,
A thrill through all the Tartar squadrons ran
Of pride and hope for Sohrab, whom they loved.
But as a troop of peddlers, from Cabool,
Cross underneath the Indian Caucasus,
That vast sky-neighbouring mountain of milk snow;
Winding so high, that, as they mount, they pass
Long flocks of traveling birds dead on the snow,
Choked by the air, and scarce can they themselves
Slake their parched throats with sugared mulberries —
In single file they move, and stop their breath,
For fear they should dislodge the o'erhanging snows —
So the pale Persians held their breath with fear.
And to Ferood his brother chiefs came up
To counsel: Gudurz and Zoarrah came,
And Feraburz, who ruled the Persian host
Second, and was the uncle of the King:
These came and counseled; and then Gudurz said: —
'Ferood, shame bids us take their challenge up,
Yet champion have we none to match this youth.
He has the wild stag's foot, the lion's heart.
But Rustum came last night; aloof he sits
And sullen, and has pitched his tents apart:
Him will I seek, and carry to his ear
The Tartar challenge, and this young man's name.
Haply he will forget his wrath, and fight.
Stand forth the while, and take their challenge up.'
So spake he; and Ferood stood forth and said: —
'Old man, be it agreed as thou hast said.
Let Sohrab arm, and we will find a man.'
He spoke; and Peran-Wisa turned, and strode
Back through the opening squadrons to his tent.
But through the anxious Persians Gudurz ran,
And crossed the camp which lay behind, and reached.

Out on the sands beyond it, Rustum's tents.
Of scarlet cloth they were, and glittering gay,
Just pitched: the high pavilion in the midst
Was Rustum's, and his men lay camped around.
And Gudurz entered Rustum's tent, and found
Rustum: his morning meal was done, but still
The table stood beside him, charged with food:
A side of roasted sheep, and cakes of bread,
And dark green melons; and there Rustum sate
Listless, and held a falcon on his wrist,
And played with it; but Gudurz came and stood
Before him; and he looked, and saw him stand;
And with a cry sprang up, and dropped the bird,
And greeted Gudurz with both hands, and said: —
'Welcome! these eyes could see no better sight.
What news? but sit down first, and eat and drink.'
But Gudurz stood in the tent door, and said: —
'Not now: a time will come to eat and drink,
But not to-day: to-day has other needs.
The armies are drawn out, and stand at gaze:
For from the Tartars is a challenge brought
To pick a champion from the Persian lords
To fight their champion — and thou know'st his name —
Sohrab men call him, but his birth is hid.
O Rustum, like thy might is this young man's!
He has the wild stag's foot, the lion's heart.
And he is young, and Iran's chiefs are old,
Or else too weak; and all eyes turn to thee.
Come down and help us, Rustum, or we lose.'
He spoke: but Rustum answered with a smile: —
'Go to! if Iran's chiefs are old, then I
Am older: if the young are weak, the King
Errs strangely: for the King, for Kai-Khosroo,
Himself is young, and honours younger men,
And lets the agèd moulder to their graves.
Rustum he loves no more, but loves the young —
The young may rise at Sohrab's vaunts, not I.
For what care I, though all speak Sohrab's fame?
For would that I myself had such a son,
And not that one slight helpless girl I have,
A son so famed, so brave, to send to war,
And I to tarry with the snow-haired Zal,
My father, whom the robber Afghans vex,
And clip his borders short, and drive his herds,
And he has none to guard his weak old age.
There would I go, and hang my armour up,
And with my great name fence that weak old man,
And spend the goodly treasures I have got,
And rest my age, and hear of Sohrab's fame,
And leave to death the hosts of thankless kings,
And with these slaughterous hands draw sword no more.'
He spoke, and smiled; and Gudurz made reply: —
'What then, O Rustum, will men say to this,
When Sohrab dares our bravest forth, and seeks
Thee most of all, and thou, whom most he seeks,
Hidest thy face? Take heed, lest men should say,
"Like some old miser, Rustum hoards his fame,
And shuns to peril it with younger men."'
And, greatly moved, then Rustum made reply: —
'O Gudurz, wherefore dost thou say such words?
Thou knowest better words than this to say.
What is one more, one less, obscure or famed,
Valiant or craven, young or old, to me?
Are not they mortal, am not I myself?
But who for men of naught would do great deeds?
Come, thou shall see how Rustum hoards his fame.
But I will fight unknown, and in plain arms;
Let not men say of Rustum, he was matched
In single fight with any mortal man.'
He spoke, and frowned; and Gudurz turned, and ran
Back quickly through the camp in fear and joy,
Fear at his wrath, but joy that Rustum came.
But Rustum strode to his tent door, and called
His followers in, and bade them bring his arms,
And clad himself in steel: the arms he chose

Were plain, and on his shield was no device,
Only his helm was rich, inlaid with gold,
And from the fluted spine atop a plume
Of horsehair waved, a scarlet horsehair plume.
So armed, he issued forth; and Ruksh, his horse,
Followed him, like a faithful hound, at heel,
Ruksh, whose renown was noised through all the earth,
The horse, whom Rustum on a foray once
Did in Bokhara by the river find
A colt beneath its dam, and drove him home,
And reared him; a bright bay, with lofty crest;
Dight with a saddle-cloth of broidered green
Crusted with gold, and on the ground were worked
All beasts of chase, all beasts which hunters know:
So followed, Rustum left his tents, and crossed
The camp, and to the Persian host appeared.
And all the Persians knew him, and with shouts
Hailed; but the Tartars knew not who he was.
And dear as the wet diver to the eyes
Of his pale wife who waits and weeps on shore,
By sandy Bahrein, in the Persian Gulf,
Plunging all day in the blue waves, at night,
Having made up his tale of precious pearls,
Rejoins her in their hut upon the sands —
So dear to the pale Persians Rustum came.

And Rustum to the Persian front advanced,
And Sohrab armed in Haman's tent, and came.
And as afield the reapers cut a swathe
Down through the middle of a rich man's corn,
And on each side are squares of standing corn,
And in the midst a stubble, short and bare;
So on each side were squares of men, with spears
Bristling, and in the midst, the open sand.
And Rustum came upon the sand, and cast
His eyes toward the Tartar tents, and saw
Sohrab come forth, and eyed him as he came.

As some rich woman, on a winter's morn,
Eyes through her silken curtains the poor drudge
Who with numb blackened fingers makes her fire —
At cock-crow on a starlit winter's morn,
When the frost flowers the whitened window-panes —
And wonders how she lives, and what the thoughts
Of that poor drudge may be; so Rustum eyed
The unknown adventurous Youth, who from afar
Came seeking Rustum, and defying forth
All the most valiant chiefs: long he perused
His spirited air, and wondered who he was.
For very young he seemed, tenderly reared;
Like some young cypress, tall, and dark, and straight,
Which in a queen's secluded garden throws
Its slight dark shadow on the moonlit turf,
By midnight, to a bubbling fountain's sound —
So slender Sohrab seemed, so softly reared.
And a deep pity entered Rustum's soul
As he beheld him coming; and he stood,
And beckoned to him with his hand, and said: —

'O thou young man, the air of Heaven is soft,
And warm, and pleasant; but the grave is cold.
Heaven's air is better than the cold dead grave.
Behold me: I am vast, and clad in iron,
And tried; and I have stood on many a field
Of blood, and I have fought with many a foe:
Never was that field lost, or that foe saved.
O Sohrab, wherefore wilt thou rush on death?
Be governed: quit the Tartar host, and come
To Iran, and be as my son to me,
And fight beneath my banner till I die.
There are no youths in Iran brave as thou.'

So he spake, mildly: Sohrab heard his voice,
The mighty voice of Rustum; and he saw
His giant figure planted on the sand,
Sole, like some single tower, which a chief
Has builded on the waste in former years
Against the robbers; and he saw that head,
Streaked with its first gray hairs: hope filled his soul;
And he ran forwards and embraced his knees,
And clasped his hand within his own and said: —

'Oh, by thy father's head! by thine own soul!
Art thou not Rustum? Speak! art thou not he?'

But Rustum eyed askance the kneeling youth,
And turned away, and spake to his own soul: —
'Ah me, I muse what this young fox may mean.
False, wily, boastful, are these Tartar boys.
For if I now confess this thing he asks,
And hide it not, but say — *Rustum is here* —
He will not yield indeed, nor quit our foes,
But he will find some pretext not to fight,
And praise my fame, and proffer courteous gifts,
A belt or sword perhaps, and go his way.
And on a feast-tide, in Afrasiab's hall,
In Samarcand, he will arise and cry —
"I challenged once, when the two armies camped
Beside the Oxus, all the Persian lords
To cope with me in single fight; but they
Shrank; only Rustum dared: then he and I
Changed gifts, and went on equal terms away."
So will he speak, perhaps, while men applaud.
Then were the chiefs of Iran shamed through me.'
And then he turned, and sternly spake aloud: —
'Rise! wherefore dost thou vainly question thus
Of Rustum? I am here, whom thou hast called
By challenge forth: make good thy vaunt, or yield.
Is it with Rustum only thou wouldst fight?
Rash boy, men look on Rustum's face and flee.
For well I know, that did great Rustum stand
Before thy face this day, and were revealed,
There would be then no talk of fighting more.
But being what I am, I tell thee this;
Do thou record it in thine inmost soul:
Either thou shalt renounce thy vaunt, and yield;
Or else thy bones shall strew this sand, till winds
Bleach them, or Oxus with his summer floods,
Oxus in summer wash them all away.'
He spoke: and Sohrab answered, on his feet: —
'Art thou so fierce? Thou wilt not fright me so.
I am no girl, to be made pale by words.
Yet this thou hast said well, did Rustum stand
Here on this field, there were no fighting then.
But Rustum is far hence, and we stand here.
Begin: thou art more vast, more dread than I,
And thou art proved, I know, and I am young —
But yet Success sways with the breath of Heaven.
And though thou thinkest that thou knowest sure
Thy victory, yet thou canst not surely know.
For we are all, like swimmers in the sea,
Poised on the top of a huge wave of Fate,
Which hangs uncertain to which side to fall.
And whether it will heave us up to land,
Or whether it will roll us out to sea,
Back out to sea, to the deep waves of death,
We know not, and no search will make us know:
Only the event will teach us in its hour.'
He spoke; and Rustum answered not, but hurled
His spear: down from the shoulder, down it came,
As on some partridge in the corn a hawk
That long has towered in the airy clouds
Drops like a plummet: Sohrab saw it come,
And sprang aside, quick as a flash: the spear
Hissed, and went quivering down into the sand,
Which it sent flying wide: — then Sohrab threw
In turn, and full struck Rustum's shield: sharp rang,
The iron plates rang sharp, but turned the spear.
And Rustum seized his club, which none but he
Could wield: an unlopped trunk it was, and huge,
Still rough; like those which men in treeless plains
To build them boats fish from the flooded rivers,
Hyphasis or Hydaspes, when, high up
By their dark springs, the wind in winter-time
Has made in Himalayan forests wrack,
And strewn the channels with torn boughs; so huge
The club which Rustum lifted now, and struck
One stroke; but again Sohrab sprang aside
Lithe as the glancing snake, and the club came

Thundering to earth, and leapt from Rustum's hand.
And Rustum followed his own blow, and fell
To his knees, and with his fingers clutched the sand:
And now might Sohrab have unsheathed his sword,
And pierced the mighty Rustum while he lay
Dizzy, and on his knees, and choked with sand:
But he looked on, and smiled, nor bared his sword,
But courteously drew back, and spoke, and said: —
'Thou strik'st too hard: that club of thine will float
Upon the summer-floods, and not my bones.
But rise, and be not wroth; not wroth am I:
No, when I see thee, wrath forsakes my soul.
Thou say'st thou art not Rustum: be it so.
Who art thou then, that canst so touch my soul?
Boy as I am, I have seen battles too;
Have waded foremost in their bloody waves,
And heard their hollow roar of dying men;
But never was my heart thus touched before.
Are they from Heaven, these softenings of the heart?
O thou old warrior, let us yield to Heaven!
Come, plant we here in earth our angry spears,
And make a truce, and sit upon this sand,
And pledge each other in red wine, like friends,
And thou shalt talk to me of Rustum's deeds.
There are enough foes in the Persian host
Whom I may meet, and strike, and feel no pang;
Champions enough Afrasiab has, whom thou
Mayst fight; fight them, when they confront thy spear.
But oh, let there be peace 'twixt thee and me!'
He ceased: but while he spake, Rustum had risen,
And stood erect, trembling with rage: his club
He left to lie, but had regained his spear,
Whose fiery point now in his mailed right-hand
Blazed bright and baleful, like that autumn Star,
The baleful sign of fevers: dust had soiled
His stately crest, and dimmed his glittering arms.
His breast heaved; his lips foamed; and twice his voice
Was choked with rage: at last these words broke way: —
'Girl! nimble with thy feet, not with thy hands!
Curled minion, dancer, coiner of sweet words!
Fight; let me hear thy hateful voice no more!
Thou art not in Afrasiab's gardens now
With Tartar girls, with whom thou art wont to dance;
But on the Oxus sands, and in the dance
Of battle, and with me, who make no play
Of war: I fight it out, and hand to hand.
Speak not to me of truce, and pledge, and wine!
Remember all thy valour; try thy feints
And cunning: all the pity I had is gone:
Because thou hast shamed me before both the hosts
With thy light skipping tricks, and thy girl's wiles.'
He spoke: and Sohrab kindled at his taunts,
And he too drew his sword: at once they rushed
Together, as two eagles on one prey
Come rushing down together from the clouds,
One from the east, one from the west: their shields
Dashed with a clang together, and a din
Rose, such as that the sinewy woodcutters
Make often in the forest's heart at morn,
Of hewing axes, crashing trees: such blows
Rustum and Sohrab on each other hailed.
And you would say that sun and stars took part
In that unnatural conflict; for a cloud
Grew suddenly in Heaven, and darked the sun
Over the fighters' heads; and a wind rose
Under their feet, and moaning swept the plain,
And in a sandy whirlwind wrapped the pair.
In gloom they twain were wrapped, and they alone;
For both the on-looking hosts on either hand
Stood in broad daylight, and the sky was pure,
And the sun sparkled on the Oxus stream.
But in the gloom they fought, with bloodshot eyes
And labouring breath; first Rustum struck the shield
Which Sohrab held stiff out: the steel-spiked spear

Rent the tough plates, but failed to reach the skin,
And Rustum plucked it back with angry groan.
Then Sohrab with his sword smote Rustum's helm,
Nor clove its steel quite through; but all the crest
He shore away, and that proud horsehair plume,
Never till now defiled, sank to the dust;
And Rustum bowed his head; but then the gloom
Grew blacker: thunder rumbled in the air,
And lightnings rent the cloud; and Ruksh, the horse,
Who stood at hand, uttered a dreadful cry:
No horse's cry was that, most like the roar
Of some pained desert lion, who all day
Hath trailed the hunter's javelin in his side,
And comes at night to die upon the sand: —
The two hosts heard that cry, and quaked for fear,
And Oxus curdled as it crossed his stream.
But Sohrab heard, and quailed not, but rushed on,
And struck again; and again Rustum bowed
His head; but this time all the blade, like glass,
Sprang in a thousand shivers on the helm,
And in his hand the hilt remained alone.
Then Rustum raised his head; his dreadful eyes
Glared, and he shook on high his menacing spear,
And shouted, *Rustum!* Sohrab heard that shout,
And shrank amazed: back he recoiled one step,
And scanned with blinking eyes the advancing Form:
And then he stood bewildered; and he dropped
His covering shield, and the spear pierced his side.
He reeled, and staggering back, sunk to the ground.
And then the gloom dispersed, and the wind fell,
And the bright sun broke forth, and melted all
The cloud; and the two armies saw the pair;
Saw Rustum standing, safe upon his feet,
And Sohrab, wounded, on the bloody sand.

Then, with a bitter smile, Rustum began: —
'Sohrab, thou thoughtest in thy mind to kill
A Persian lord this day, and strip his corpse,
And bear thy trophies to Afrasiab's tent.
Or else that the great Rustum would come down
Himself to fight, and that thy wiles would move
His heart to take a gift, and let thee go.
And then that all the Tartar host would praise
Thy courage or thy craft, and spread thy fame,
To glad thy father in his weak old age.
Fool! thou art slain, and by an unknown man!
Dearer to the red jackals shalt thou be,
Than to thy friends, and to thy father old.'

And, with a fearless mien, Sohrab replied: —
'Unknown thou art; yet thy fierce vaunt is vain.
Thou dost not slay me, proud and boastful man!
No! Rustum slays me, and this filial heart.
For were I matched with ten such men as thou,
And I were he who till to-day I was,
They should be lying here, I standing there.
But that belovèd name unnerved my arm —
That name, and something, I confess, in thee,
Which troubles all my heart, and made my shield
Fall; and thy spear transfixed an unarmed foe.
And now thou boastest, and insult'st my fate.
But hear thou this, fierce Man, tremble to hear!
The mighty Rustum shall avenge my death!
My father, whom I seek through all the world,
He shall avenge my death, and punish thee!'

As when some hunter in the spring hath found
A breeding eagle sitting on her nest,
Upon the craggy isle of a hill lake,
And pierced her with an arrow as she rose,
And followed her to find her where she fell
Far off; — anon her mate comes winging back
From hunting, and a great way off descries
His huddling young left sole; at that, he checks
His pinion, and with short uneasy sweeps

Circles above his eyry, with loud screams
Chiding his mate back to her nest; but she
Lies dying, with the arrow in her side,
In some far stony gorge out of his ken,
A heap of fluttering feathers: never more
Shall the lake glass her, flying over it;
Never the black and dripping precipices
Echo her stormy scream as she sails by: —
As that poor bird flies home, nor knows his loss —
So Rustum knew not his own loss, but stood
Over his dying son, and knew him not.

But with a cold, incredulous voice, he said: —
'What prate is this of fathers and revenge?
The mighty Rustum never had a son.'

And, with a failing voice, Sohrab replied: —
'Ah, yes, he had! and that lost son am I.
Surely the news will one day reach his ear,
Reach Rustum, where he sits, and tarries long,
Somewhere, I know not where, but far from here;
And pierce him like a stab, and make him leap
To arms, and cry for vengeance upon thee.
Fierce Man, bethink thee, for an only son!
What will that grief, what will that vengeance be!
Oh, could I live, till I that grief had seen!
Yet him I pity not so much, but her,
My mother, who in Ader-baijan dwells
With that old King, her father, who grows grey
With age, and rules over the valiant Koords.
Her most I pity, who no more will see
Sohrab returning from the Tartar camp,
With spoils and honour, when the war is done.
But a dark rumour will be bruited up,
From tribe to tribe, until it reach her ear;
And then will that defenceless woman learn
That Sohrab will rejoice her sight no more;
But that in battle with a nameless foe,
By the far-distant Oxus, he is slain.'

He spoke; and as he ceased he wept aloud,
Thinking of her he left, and his own death.
He spoke; but Rustum listened, plunged in thought.
Nor did he yet believe it was his son
Who spoke, although he called back names he knew;
For he had had sure tidings that the babe,
Which was in Ader-baijan born to him,
Had been a puny girl, no boy at all:
So that sad mother sent him word, for fear
Rustum should take the boy, to train in arms;
And so he deemed that either Sohrab took,
By a false boast, the style of Rustum's son;
Or that men gave it him, to swell his fame.
So deemed he; yet he listened, plunged in thought;
And his soul set to grief, as the vast tide
Of the bright rocking Ocean sets to shore
At the full moon: tears gathered in his eyes;
For he remembered his own early youth,
And all its bounding rapture; as, at dawn,
The Shepherd from his mountain-lodge descries
A far bright City, smitten by the sun,
Through many rolling clouds; — so Rustum saw
His youth; saw Sohrab's mother, in her bloom;
And that old King, her father, who loved well
His wandering guest, and gave him his fair child
With joy; and all the pleasant life they led,
They three, in that long-distant summer-time —
The castle, and the dewy woods, and hunt
And hound, and morn on those delightful hills
In Ader-baijan. And he saw that Youth,
Of age and looks to be his own dear son,
Piteous and lovely, lying on the sand,
Like some rich hyacinth, which by the scythe
Of an unskilful gardener has been cut,
Mowing the garden grass-plots near its bed,
And lies, a fragrant tower of purple bloom,
On the mown, dying grass; — so Sohrab lay,
Lovely in death, upon the common sand.
And Rustum gazed on him with grief, and said: —

'O Sohrab, thou indeed art such a son
Whom Rustum, wert thou his, might well have loved!
Yet here thou errest, Sohrab, or else men
Have told thee false; — thou art not Rustum's son.
For Rustum had no son: one child he had —
But one — a girl: who with her mother now
Plies some light female task, nor dreams of us —
Of us she dreams not, nor of wounds, nor war.'

But Sohrab answered him in wrath; for now
The anguish of the deep-fixed spear grew fierce,

And he desirèd to draw forth the steel,
And let the blood flow free, and so to die;
But first he would convince his stubborn foe —
And, rising sternly on one arm, he said: —
'Man, who art thou who dost deny my words?
Truth sits upon the lips of dying men,
And Falsehood, while I lived, was far from mine.
I tell thee, pricked upon this arm I bear
That seal which Rustum to my mother gave,
That she might prick it on the babe she bore.'
He spoke: and all the blood left Rustum's cheeks;
And his knees tottered, and he smote his hand
Against his breast, his heavy mailèd hand,
That the hard iron corslet clanked aloud:
And to his heart he pressed the other hand,
And in a hollow voice he spake, and said: —
'Sohrab, that were a proof which could not lie.
If thou show this, then art thou Rustum's son.'
Then, with weak hasty fingers, Sohrab loosed
His belt, and near the shoulder bared his arm,
And shewed a sign in faint vermilion points
Pricked: as a cunning workman, in Pekin,
Pricks with vermilion some clear porcelain vase,
An emperor's gift — at early morn he paints,
And all day long, and, when night comes, the lamp
Lights up his studious forehead and thin hands: —
So delicately pricked the sign appeared
On Sohrab's arm, the sign of Rustum's seal.
It was that Griffin, which of old reared Zal,
Rustum's great father, whom they left to die,
A helpless babe, among the mountain rocks.
Him that kind Creature found, and reared, and loved —
Then Rustum took it for his glorious sign.
And Sohrab bared that figure on his arm,
And himself scanned it long with mournful eyes,
And then he touched it with his hand and said: —
'How say'st thou? Is that sign the proper sign
Of Rustum's son, or of some other man's?'
He spoke: but Rustum gazed, and gazed, and stood
Speechless; and then he uttered one sharp cry —
O Boy — thy Father! — and his voice choked there.
And then a dark cloud passed before his eyes,
And his head swam, and he sank down to earth.
But Sohrab crawled to where he lay, and cast
His arms about his neck, and kissed his lips,
And with fond faltering fingers stroked his cheeks,
Trying to call him back to life: and life
Came back to Rustum, and he oped his eyes,
And they stood wide with horror; and he seized
In both his hands the dust which lay around,
And threw it on his head, and smirched his hair,
His hair, and face, and beard, and glittering arms:
And strong convulsive groanings shook his breast,
And his sobs choked him; and he clutched his sword,
To draw it, and forever let life out.
But Sohrab saw his thought, and held his hands,
And with a soothing voice he spake, and said: —
'Father, forbear: for I but meet to-day
The doom that at my birth was written down
In Heaven, and thou art Heaven's unconscious hand.
Surely my heart cried out that it was thou,
When first I saw thee; and thy heart spoke too,
I know it: but Fate trod those promptings down
Under its iron heel; Fate, Fate engaged
The strife, and hurled me on my father's spear.
But let us speak no more of this: I find
My father; let me feel that I have found.
Come, sit beside me on this sand, and take
My head betwixt thy hands, and kiss my cheeks,
And wash them with thy tears, and say: *My son!*
Quick! quick! for numbered are my sands of life,
And swift; for like the lightning to this field
I came, and like the wind I go away —
Sudden, and swift, and like a passing wind.
But it was writ in Heaven that this should be.'

So said he: and his voice released the heart
Of Rustum, and his tears broke forth; he cast
His arms round his son's neck, and wept aloud,
And kissed him. And awe fell on both the hosts
When they saw Rustum's grief: and Ruksh, the horse,
With his head bowing to the ground, and mane
Sweeping the dust, came near, and in mute woe
First to the one, then to the other moved
His head, as if inquiring what their grief
Might mean; and from his dark, compassionate eyes,
The big warm tears rolled down, and caked the sand.
But Rustum chid him with stern voice, and said: —
'Ruksh, now thou grievest; but, O Ruksh, thy feet
Should then have rotted on thy nimble joints,
When first they bore thy Master to this field.'
But Sohrab looked upon the horse and said: —
'Is this then Ruksh? How often, in past days,
My mother told me of thee, thou brave Steed!
My terrible father's terrible horse; and said,
That I should one day find thy lord and thee.
Come, let me lay my hand upon thy mane.
O Ruksh, thou art more fortunate than I;
For thou hast gone where I shall never go,
And snuffed the breezes of my father's home.
And thou hast trod the sands of Seïstan,
And seen the River of Helmund, and the Lake
Of Zirrah; and the agèd Zal himself
Has often stroked thy neck, and given thee food,
Corn in a golden platter soaked with wine,
And said — "O Ruksh! bear Rustum well!" — but I
Have never known my grandsire's furrowed face,
Nor seen his lofty house in Seïstan,
Nor slaked my thirst at the clear Helmund stream:
But lodged among my father's foes, and seen
Afrasiab's cities only, Samarcand,
Bokhara, and lone Khiva in the waste,
And the black Toorkmun tents; and only drunk
The desert rivers, Moorghab and Tejend,
Kohik, and where the Kalmuks feed their sheep,
The northern Sir; and this great Oxus stream —
The yellow Oxus, by whose brink I die.'
And, with a heavy groan, Rustum replied: —
'Oh that its waves were flowing over me!
Oh that I saw its grains of yellow silt
Roll tumbling in the current o'er my head!'
And, with a grave mild voice, Sohrab replied: —
'Desire not that, my father; thou must live.
For some are born to do great deeds, and live,
As some are born to be obscured, and die.
Do thou the deeds I die too young to do,
And reap a second glory in thine age.
Thou art my father, and thy gain is mine.
But come: thou seest this great host of men
Which follow me; I pray thee, slay not these:
Let me entreat for them: what have they done?
They followed me, my hope, my fame, my star.
Let them all cross the Oxus back in peace.
But me thou must bear hence, not send with them,
But carry me with thee to Seïstan,
And place me on a bed, and mourn for me,
Thou, and the snow-haired Zal, and all thy friends.
And thou must lay me in that lovely earth,
And heap a stately mound above my bones,
And plant a far-seen pillar over all:
That so the passing horseman on the waste
May see my tomb a great way off, and say —
Sohrab, the mighty Rustum's son, lies there,
Whom his great father did in ignorance kill —
And I be not forgotten in my grave.'
And, with a mournful voice, Rustum replied: —
'Fear not; as thou hast said, Sohrab, my son,
So shall it be; for I will burn my tents,
And quit the host, and bear thee hence with me,
And carry thee away to Seïstan,
And place thee on a bed, and mourn for thee,
With the snow-headed Zal, and all my friends,
And I will lay thee in that lovely earth,
And heap a stately mound above thy bones,
And plant a far-seen pillar over all:

And men shall not forget thee in thy grave.
And I will spare thy host: yea, let them go:
Let them all cross the Oxus back in peace.
What should I do with slaying any more?
For would that all whom I have ever slain
Might be once more alive; my bitterest foes,
And they who were called champions in their time,
And through whose death I won that fame I have;
And I were nothing but a common man,
A poor, mean soldier, and without renown;
So thou mightest live too, my Son, my Son!
Or rather would that I, even I myself,
Might now be lying on this bloody sand,
Near death, and by an ignorant stroke of thine,
Not thou of mine; and I might die, not thou;
And I, not thou, be borne to Seïstan;
And Zal might weep above my grave, not thine;
And say — *O son, I weep thee not too sore,*
For willingly, I know, thou met'st thine end —
But now in blood and battles was my youth,
And full of blood and battles is my age;
And I shall never end this life of blood.'
Then, at the point of death, Sohrab replied: —
'A life of blood indeed, thou dreadful Man!
But thou shalt yet have peace; only not now:
Not yet: but thou shalt have it on that day,
When thou shalt sail in a high-masted Ship,
Thou and the other peers of Kai Khosroo,
Returning home over the salt blue sea,
From laying thy dear Master in his grave.'
And Rustum gazed in Sohrab's face, and said: —
'Soon be that day, my Son, and deep that sea!
Till then, if Fate so wills, let me endure.'
He spoke; and Sohrab smiled on him, and took
The spear, and drew it from his side, and eased
His wound's imperious anguish: but the blood
Came welling from the open gash, and life
Flowed with the stream: all down his cold white side
The crimson torrent ran, dim now, and soiled,
Like the soiled tissue of white violets
Left, freshly gathered, on their native bank,
By romping children, whom their nurses call
From the hot fields at noon: his head drooped low,
His limbs grew slack: motionless, white, he lay —
White, with eyes closed; only when heavy gasps,
Deep, heavy gasps, quivering through all his frame,
Convulsed him back to life, he opened them,
And fixed them feebly on his father's face:
Till now all strength was ebbed, and from his limbs
Unwillingly the spirit fled away,
Regretting the warm mansion which it left,
And youth, and bloom, and this delightful world.
So, on the bloody sand, Sohrab lay dead.
And the great Rustum drew his horseman's cloak
Down o'er his face, and sate by his dead son.
As those black granite pillars, once high-reared,
By Jemshid in Persepolis, to bear
His house, now mid their broken flights of steps,
Lie prone, enormous, down the mountain side —
So, in the sand lay Rustum by his son.
And night came down over the solemn waste,
And the two gazing hosts, and that sole pair,
And darkened all; and a cold fog, with night,
Crept from the Oxus. Soon a hum arose,
As of a great assembly loosed, and fires
Began to twinkle through the fog: for now
Both armies moved to camp, and took their meal:
The Persians took it on the open sands
Southward: the Tartars by the river marge:
And Rustum and his son were left alone.
But the majestic River floated on,
Out of the mist and hum of that low land,
Into the frosty starlight, and there moved,
Rejoicing, through the hushed Chorasmian waste,
Under the solitary moon: he flowed
Right for the Polar Star, past Orgunjè,
Brimming, and bright, and large: then sands begin
To hem his watery march, and dam his streams,
And split his currents, that for many a league
The shorn and parceled Oxus strains along
Through beds of sand and matted rushy isles —
Oxus, forgetting the bright speed he had
In his high mountain cradle in Pamere,
A foiled circuitous wanderer: — till at last

The longed-for dash of waves is heard, and wide
His luminous home of waters opens, bright
And tranquil, from whose floor the new-bathed stars
Emerge, and shine upon the Aral Sea.

1853

REQUIESCAT

STREW on her roses, roses,
And never a spray of yew.
In quiet she reposes:
Ah, would that I did too.

Her mirth the world required:
She bathed it in smiles of glee.
But her heart was tired, tired,
And now they let her be.

Her life was turning, turning,
In mazes of heat and sound.
But for peace her soul was yearning,
And now peace laps her round.

Her cabined, ample Spirit,
It fluttered and failed for breath.
To-night it doth inherit
The vasty Hall of Death.

1853

RUGBY CHAPEL

COLDLY, sadly descends
The autumn evening. The Field
Strewn with its dank yellow drifts
Of withered leaves, and the elms,
Fade into dimness apace,
Silent; — hardly a shout
From a few boys late at their play!
The lights come out in the street,
In the school-room windows; but cold,
Solemn, unlighted, austere,
Through the gathering darkness, arise
The Chapel walls, in whose bound
Thou, my father! art laid.

There thou dost lie, in the gloom
Of the autumn evening. But ah!
That word, *gloom*, to my mind
Brings thee back, in the light
Of thy radiant vigour again!
In the gloom of November we passed
Days not of gloom at thy side;
Seasons impaired not the ray
Of thine even cheerfulness clear.
Such thou wast; and I stand
In the autumn evening, and think
Of bygone autumns with thee.

Fifteen years have gone round
Since thou arosest to tread,
In the summer morning, the road
Of death, at a call unforeseen,
Sudden. For fifteen years,
We who till then in thy shade
Rested as under the boughs
Of a mighty oak, have endured
Sunshine and rain as we might,
Bare, unshaded, alone,
Lacking the shelter of thee.

O strong soul, by what shore
Tarriest thou now? For that force,
Surely, has not been left vain!
Somewhere, surely, afar,
In the sounding labour-house vast
Of being, is practised that strength,
Zealous, beneficent, firm!

Yes, in some far-shining sphere,
Conscious or not of the past,
Still thou performest the word
Of the Spirit in whom thou dost live,
Prompt, unwearied, as here!
Still thou upraisest with zeal
The humble good from the ground,
Sternly repressest the bad.
Still, like a trumpet, dost rouse
Those who with half-open eyes
Tread the border-land dim
'Twixt vice and virtue; reviv'st,
Succourest! — this was thy work,
This was thy life upon earth.

What is the course of the life
Of mortal men on the earth?
Most men eddy about
Here and there — eat and drink,
Chatter and love and hate,
Gather and squander, are raised
Aloft, are hurled in the dust,
Striving blindly, achieving
Nothing; and, then they die —
Perish; and no one asks
Who or what they have been,
More than he asks what waves
In the moonlit solitudes mild
Of the midmost Ocean, have swelled,
Foamed for a moment, and gone.

And there are some, whom a thirst
Ardent, unquenchable, fires,
Not with the crowd to be spent,
Not without aim to go round
In an eddy of purposeless dust,
Effort unmeaning and vain.
Ah, yes, some of us strive
Not without action to die
Fruitless, but something to snatch

From dull oblivion, nor all
Glut the devouring grave!
We, we have chosen our path —
Path to a clear-purposed goal,
Path of advance! but it leads
A long, steep journey, through sunk
Gorges, o'er mountains in snow!
Cheerful, with friends, we set forth;
Then, on the height, comes the storm!
Thunder crashes from rock
To rock, the cataracts reply;
Lightnings dazzle our eyes;
Roaring torrents have breached
The track, the stream-bed descends
In the place where the wayfarer once
Planted his footstep — the spray
Boils o'er its borders; aloft,
The unseen snow-beds dislodge
Their hanging ruin; — alas,
Havoc is made in our train!
Friends who set forth at our side
Falter, are lost in the storm!
We, we only are left!
With frowning foreheads, with lips
Sternly compressed, we strain on,
On — and at nightfall, at last,
Come to the end of our way,
To the lonely inn 'mid the rocks;
Where the gaunt and taciturn Host
Stands on the threshold, the wind
Shaking his thin white hairs —
Holds his lantern to scan
Our storm-beat figures, and asks:
Whom in our party we bring,
Whom we have left in the snow?

Sadly we answer: We bring
Only ourselves; we lost
Sight of the rest in the storm.
Hardly ourselves we fought through,
Stripped, without friends, as we are.
Friends, companions, and train,
The avalanche swept from our side.

But thou would'st not *alone*
Be saved, my father! *alone*
Conquer and come to thy goal,
Leaving the rest in the wild.
We were weary, and we
Fearful, and we, in our march,
Fain to drop down and to die.
Still thou turnedst, and still
Beckonedst the trembler, and still
Gavest the weary thy hand!
If, in the paths of the world,
Stones might have wounded thy feet,
Toil or dejection have tried
Thy spirit, of that we saw
Nothing! to us thou wert still
Cheerful, and helpful, and firm.
Therefore to thee it was given
Many to save with thyself;
And, at the end of thy day,
O, faithful shepherd! to come,
Bringing thy sheep in thy hand.

And through thee I believe
In the noble and great who are gone;
Pure souls honoured and blest
By former ages, who else —
Such, so soulless, so poor,
Is the race of men whom I see —
Seemed but a dream of the heart,
Seemed but a cry of desire.
Yes! I believe that there lived
Others like thee in the past,

Not like the men of the crowd
Who all round me to-day
Bluster or cringe, and make life
Hideous, and arid, and vile;
But souls tempered with fire,
Fervent, heroic, and good,
Helpers and friends of mankind.

Servants of God! — or sons
Shall I not call you? because
Not as servants ye knew
Your Father's innermost mind,
His, who unwillingly sees
One of his little ones lost —
Yours is the praise, if mankind
Hath not as yet in its march
Fainted, and fallen, and died!

See! In the rocks of the world
Marches the host of mankind,
A feeble, wavering line.
Where are they tending? — A God
Marshaled them, gave them their goal. —
Ah, but the way is so long!
Years they have been in the wild!
Sore thirst plagues them; the rocks,
Rising all round, overawe.
Factions divide them; their host
Threatens to break, to dissolve.
Ah, keep, keep them combined!
Else, of the myriads who fill
That army, not one shall arrive!
Sole they shall stray; in the rocks
Labour for ever in vain,
Die one by one in the waste.

Then, in such hour of need
Of your fainting, dispirited race,
Ye, like angels, appear,
Radiant with ardour divine.
Beacons of hope, ye appear!
Languor is not in your heart,

Weakness is not in your word,
Weariness not on your brow.
Ye alight in our van: at your voice,
Panic, despair, flee away.
Ye move through the ranks, recall
The stragglers, refresh the outworn,
Praise, re-inspire the brave.
Order, courage, return.
Eyes rekindling, and prayers,
Follow your steps as ye go.
Ye fill up the gaps in our files,
Strengthen the wavering line,
Stablish, continue our march,
On, to the bound of the waste,
On, to the City of God.

1867

THYRSIS

How changed is here each spot man makes or fills!
In the two Hinkseys nothing keeps the same;
The village-street its haunted mansion lacks,
And from the sign is gone Sibylla's name,
And from the roofs the twisted chimney-stacks;
Are ye too changed, ye hills?
See, 't is no foot of unfamiliar men
To-night from Oxford up your pathway strays.
Here came I often, often, in old days;
Thyrsis and I; we still had Thyrsis then.

Runs it not here, the track by Childsworth Farm,
Up past the wood, to where the elm-tree crowns
The hill behind whose ridge the sunset flames?
The signal-elm, that looks on Ilsley Downs,
The Vale, the three lone weirs, the youthful Thames? —
This winter-eve is warm,
Humid the air; leafless, yet soft as spring,
The tender purple spray on copse and briers;
And that sweet City with her dreaming spires,
She needs not June for beauty's heightening.

Lovely all times she lies, lovely to-night!
Only, methinks, some loss of habit's power
Befalls me wandering through this upland dim;
Once passed I blindfold here, at any hour,
Now seldom come I, since I came with him.
That single elm-tree bright
Against the west — I miss it! is it gone?
We prized it dearly; while it stood, we said,
Our friend, the Scholar-Gipsy, was not dead;
While the tree lived, he in these fields lived on.

Too rare, too rare, grow now my visits here!
But once I knew each field, each flower, each stick;
And with the country-folk acquaintance made
By barn in threshing-time, by new-built rick.
Here, too, our shepherd-pipes we first assayed.
Ah me! this many a year,
My pipe is lost, my shepherd's-holiday!
Needs must I lose them, needs with heavy heart
Into the world and wave of men depart;
But Thyrsis of his own will went away.

It irked him to be here, he could not rest.
He loved each simple joy the country yields,
He loved his mates; but yet he could not keep,
For that a shadow lowered on the fields,
Here with the shepherds and the silly sheep.
Some life of men unblest
He knew, which made him droop, and filled his head.
He went; his piping took a troubled sound
Of storms that rage outside our happy ground;
He could not wait their passing, he is dead!

So, some tempestuous morn in early June,
When the year's primal burst of bloom is o'er,
Before the roses and the longest day —
When garden-walks, and all the grassy floor,
With blossoms, red and white, of fallen May,
And chestnut-flowers are strewn —
So have I heard the cuckoo's parting cry,
From the wet field, through the vext garden-trees,

Come with the volleying rain and tossing breeze:
The bloom is gone, and with the bloom go I.

Too quick despairer, wherefore wilt thou go?
Soon will the high Midsummer pomps come on,
Soon will the musk carnations break and swell,
Soon shall we have gold-dusted snapdragon,
Sweet-William with its homely cottage-smell,
And stocks in fragrant blow;
Roses that down the alleys shine afar,
And open, jasmine-muffled lattices,
And groups under the dreaming garden-trees,
And the full moon, and the white evening-star.

He hearkens not! light comer, he is flown!
What matters it? next year he will return,
And we shall have him in the sweet spring-days,
With whitening hedges, and uncrumpling fern,
And blue-bells trembling by the forest-ways,
And scent of hay new-mown.
But Thyrsis never more we swains shall see!
See him come back, and cut a smoother reed,
And blow a strain the world at last shall heed—
For Time, not Corydon, hath conquered thee.

Alack, for Corydon no rival now!—
But when Sicilian shepherds lost a mate,
Some good survivor with his flute would go,
Piping a ditty sad for Bion's fate,
And cross the unpermitted ferry's flow,
And relax Pluto's brow,
And make leap up with joy the beauteous head
Of Proserpine, among whose crownèd hair
Are flowers, first opened on Sicilian air,
And flute his friend, like Orpheus, from the dead.

O easy access to the hearer's grace
When Dorian shepherds sang to Proserpine!
For she herself had trod Sicilian fields,
She knew the Dorian water's gush divine,
She knew each lily white which Enna yields,
Each rose with blushing face;
She loved the Dorian pipe, the Dorian strain.
But ah, of our poor Thames she never heard!
Her foot the Cumner cowslips never stirred!
And we should tease her with our plaint in vain.

Well! wind-dispersed and vain the words will be,
Yet, Thyrsis, let me give my grief its hour
In the old haunt, and find our tree-topped hill!
Who, if not I, for questing here hath power?
I know the wood which hides the daffodil,
I know the Fyfield tree,
I know what white, what purple fritillaries
The grassy harvest of the river-fields,
Above by Ensham, down by Sandford, yields,
And what sedged brooks are Thames's tributaries;

I know these slopes; who knows them if not I?—
But many a dingle on the loved hill-side,
With thorns once studded, old, white-blossomed trees,
Where thick the cowslips grew, and far descried,
High towered the spikes of purple orchises,
Hath since our day put by
The coronals of that forgotten time.
Down each green bank hath gone the ploughboy's team,
And only in the hidden brookside gleam
Primroses, orphans of the flowery prime.

Where is the girl, who, by the boatman's door,
Above the locks, above the boating throng,
Unmoored our skiff, when, through the Wytham flats,
Red loosestrife and blond meadow-sweet among,
And darting swallows, and light water-gnats,
We tracked the shy Thames shore?
Where are the mowers, who, as the tiny swell

Of our boat passing heaved the river-grass,
Stood with suspended scythe to see us pass? —
They all are gone, and thou art gone as well.

Yes, thou art gone! and round me too the night
In ever-nearing circle weaves her shade.
I see her veil draw soft across the day,
I feel her slowly chilling breath invade
The cheek grown thin, the brown hair sprent with grey;
I feel her finger light
Laid pausefully upon life's headlong train;
The foot less prompt to meet the morning dew,
The heart less bounding at emotion new,
And hope, once crushed, less quick to spring again.

And long the way appears, which seemed so short
To the unpractised eye of sanguine youth;
And high the mountain-tops, in cloudy air,
The mountain-tops where is the throne of Truth,
Tops in life's morning-sun so bright and bare!
Unbreachable the fort
Of the long-battered world uplifts its wall.
And strange and vain the earthly turmoil grows,
And near and real the charm of thy repose,
And night as welcome as a friend would fall.

But hush! the upland hath a sudden loss
Of quiet; — Look! adown the dusk hill-side,
A troop of Oxford hunters going home,
As in old days, jovial and talking, ride!
From hunting with the Berkshire hounds they come —
Quick let me fly, and cross
Into yon further field! — 'T is done; and see,
Backed by the sunset, which doth glorify
The orange and pale violet evening-sky,
Bare on its lonely ridge, the Tree! the Tree!

I take the omen! Eve lets down her veil,
The white fog creeps from bush to bush about,
The west unflushes, the high stars grow bright,
And in the scattered farms the lights come out.
I cannot reach the Signal-Tree to-night.
Yet, happy omen, hail!
Hear it from thy broad lucent Arno vale
(For there thine earth-forgetting eyelids keep
The morningless and unawakening sleep
Under the flowery oleanders pale),

Hear it, O Thyrsis, still our Tree is there!
Ah, vain! These English fields, this upland dim,
These brambles pale with mist engarlanded,
That lone, sky-pointing tree, are not for him.
To a boon southern country he is fled,
And now in happier air,
Wandering with the great Mother's train divine
(And purer or more subtle soul than thee,
I trow, the mighty Mother doth not see!)
Within a folding of the Apennine,

Thou hearest the immortal strains of old.
Putting his sickle to the perilous grain
In the hot cornfield of the Phrygian king,
For thee the Lityerses song again
Young Daphnis with his silver voice doth sing;
Sings his Sicilian fold,
His sheep, his hapless love, his blinded eyes;
And how a call celestial round him rang
And heavenward from the fountain-brink he sprang,
And all the marvel of the golden skies.

There thou art gone, and me thou leavest here
Sole in these fields; yet will I not despair;
Despair I will not, while I yet descry
'Neath the soft canopy of English air
That lonely Tree against the western sky.
Still, still these slopes, 't is clear,
Our Gipsy-Scholar haunts, outliving thee!
Fields where soft sheep from cages pull the hay,
Woods with anemonies in flower till May,
Know him a wanderer still; then why not me?

A fugitive and gracious light he seeks,
Shy to illumine; and I seek it too.
This does not come with houses or with gold,
With place, with honour, and a flattering crew;
'T is not in the world's market bought and sold.
But the smooth-slipping weeks
Drop by, and leave its seeker still untired;
Out of the heed of mortals he is gone,
He wends unfollowed, he must house alone;
Yet on he fares, by his own heart inspired.

Thou too, O Thyrsis, on like quest wert bound,
Thou wanderedst with me for a little hour;
Men gave thee nothing, but this happy quest,
If men esteemed thee feeble, gave thee power,
If men procured thee trouble, gave thee rest.
And this rude Cumner ground,
Its fir-topped Hurst, its farms, its quiet fields,
Here cam'st thou in thy jocund youthful time,
Here was thine height of strength, thy golden prime;
And still the haunt beloved a virtue yields.

What though the music of thy rustic flute
Kept not for long its happy, country tone,
Lost it too soon, and learnt a stormy note
Of men contention-tost, of men who groan,
Which tasked thy pipe too sore, and tired thy throat —
It failed, and thou wast mute;
Yet hadst thou alway visions of our light,
And long with men of care thou couldst not stay,
And soon thy foot resumed its wandering way,
Left human haunt, and on alone till night.

Too rare, too rare, grow now my visits here!
'Mid city-noise, not, as with thee of yore,
Thyrsis, in reach of sheep-bells is my home!
Then through the great town's harsh, heart-wearying roar,
Let in thy voice a whisper often come,
To chase fatigue and fear:
Why faintest thou? I wandered till I died.
Roam on! the light we sought is shining still.
Dost thou ask proof? Our Tree yet crowns the hill,
Our Scholar travels yet the loved hillside.

1866

DOVER BEACH

THE sea is calm to-night,
The tide is full, the moon lies fair
Upon the Straits; — on the French coast, the light
Gleams, and is gone; the cliffs of England stand,
Glimmering and vast, out in the tranquil bay.
Come to the window, sweet is the night air!
Only, from the long line of spray
Where the sea meets the moon-blanched sand,
Listen! you hear the grating roar
Of pebbles which the waves suck back, and fling,
At their return, up the high strand,
Begin, and cease, and then again begin,
With tremulous cadence slow, and bring
The eternal note of sadness in.

Sophocles long ago
Heard it on the Ægean, and it brought
Into his mind the turbid ebb and flow
Of human misery; we
Find also in the sound a thought,
Hearing it by this distant northern sea.

The sea of faith
Was once, too, at the full, and round earth's shore
Lay like the folds of a bright girdle furled;
But now I only hear
Its melancholy, long, withdrawing roar,
Retreating to the breath
Of the night-wind down the vast edges drear
And naked shingles of the world.

Ah, love, let us be true
To one another! for the world, which seems
To lie before us like a land of dreams,
So various, so beautiful, so new,
Hath really neither joy, nor love, nor light,
Nor certitude, nor peace, nor help for pain;
And we are here as on a darkling plain
Swept with confused alarms of struggle and flight,
Where ignorant armies clash by night.

1867

Dante Gabriel Rossetti (1828-1882)

THE BLESSED DAMOZEL

The blessèd damozel leaned out
From the golden bar of Heaven;
Her eyes were deeper than the depth
Of waters stilled at even;
She had three lilies in her hand,
And the stars in her hair were seven.

Her robe, ungirt from clasp to hem,
No wrought flowers did adorn,
But a white rose of Mary's gift,
For service meetly worn;
Her hair that lay along her back
Was yellow like ripe corn.

Her seemed she scarce had been a day
One of God's choristers;
The wonder was not yet quite gone
From that still look of hers;
Albeit, to them she left, her day
Had counted as ten years.

(To one, it is ten years of years.
. . . Yet now, and in this place,
Surely she leaned o'er me — her hair
Fell all about my face. . . .
Nothing: the autumn-fall of leaves.
The whole year sets apace.)

It was the rampart of God's house
That she was standing on;
By God built over the sheer depth
The which is Space begun;
So high, that looking downward thence
She scarce could see the sun.

It lies in Heaven, across the flood
Of ether, as a bridge.
Beneath, the tides of day and night
With flame and darkness ridge
The void, as low as where this earth
Spins like a fretful midge.

Around her, lovers, newly met
'Mid deathless love's acclaims,
Spoke evermore among themselves
Their heart-remembered names;
And the souls mounting up to God
Went by her like thin flames.

And still she bowed herself and stooped
Out of the circling charm;
Until her bosom must have made
The bar she leaned on warm,
And the lilies lay as if asleep
Along her bended arm.

From the fixed place of Heaven she saw
Time like a pulse shake fierce
Through all the world. Her gaze still strove
Within the gulf to pierce
Its path; and now she spoke as when
The stars sang in their spheres.

The sun was gone now; the curled moon
Was like a little feather
Fluttering far down the gulf; and now
She spoke through the still weather.
Her voice was like the voice the stars
Had when they sang together.

(Ah, sweet! Even now, in that bird's song,
Strove not her accents there,
Fain to be hearkened? When those bells
Possessed the mid-day air,
Strove not her steps to reach my side
Down all the echoing stair?)

'I wish that he were come to me,
For he will come,' she said.
'Have I not prayed in Heaven? — on earth,
Lord, Lord, has he not prayed?
Are not two prayers a perfect strength?
And shall I feel afraid?

'When round his head the aureole clings,
And he is clothed in white,
I 'll take his hand and go with him
To the deep wells of light;
As unto a stream we will step down,
And bathe there in God's sight.

'We two will stand beside that shrine,
Occult, withheld, untrod.
Whose lamps are stirred continually
With prayer sent up to God;
And see our old prayers, granted, melt
Each like a little cloud.

'We two will lie i' the shadow of
That living mystic tree
Within whose secret growth the Dove
Is sometimes felt to be,
While every leaf that His plumes touch
Saith His Name audibly.

'And I myself will teach to him,
I myself, lying so,
The songs I sing here; which his voice
Shall pause in, hushed and slow,
And find some knowledge at each pause,
Or some new thing to know.'

(Alas! We two, we two, thou say'st!
Yea, one wast thou with me
That once of old. But shall God lift
To endless unity
The soul whose likeness with thy soul
Was but its love for thee?)

'We two,' she said, 'will seek the groves
Where the lady Mary is,
With her five handmaidens, whose names

Are five sweet symphonies,
Cecily, Gertrude, Magdalen,
Margaret and Rosalys.

'Circlewise sit they, with bound locks
And foreheads garlanded;
Into the fine cloth white like flame
Weaving the golden thread,
To fashion the birth-robes for them
Who are just born, being dead.

'He shall fear, haply, and be dumb:
Then will I lay my cheek
To his, and tell about our love,
Not once abashed or weak:
And the dear Mother will approve
My pride, and let me speak.

'Herself shall bring us, hand in hand,
To Him round whom all souls
Kneel, the clear-ranged unnumbered heads
Bowed with their aureoles:
And angels meeting us shall sing
To their citherns and citoles.

'There will I ask of Christ the Lord
Thus much for him and me: —
Only to live as once on earth
With Love, only to be,
As then awhile, for ever now
Together, I and he.'

She gazed and listened and then said,
Less sad of speech than mild, —
'All this is when he comes.' She ceased.
The light thrilled towards her, filled
With angels in strong level flight.
Her eyes prayed, and she smiled.

(I saw her smile.) But soon their path
Was vague in distant spheres:
And then she cast her arms along
The golden barriers,
And laid her face between her hands,
And wept. (I heard her tears.)

1850

MY SISTER'S SLEEP

She fell asleep on Christmas Eve:
At length the long-ungranted shade
Of weary eyelids overweighed
The pain naught else might yet relieve.

Our mother, who had leaned all day
Over the bed from chime to chime,
Then raised herself for the first time,
And as she sat her down, did pray.

Her little work-table was spread
With work to finish. For the glare
Made by her candle, she had care
To work some distance from the bed.

Without there was a cold moon up,
Of winter radiance sheer and thin;
The hollow halo it was in
Was like an icy crystal cup.

Through the small room, with subtle sound
Of flame, by vents the fireshine drove
And reddened. In its dim alcove
The mirror shed a clearness round.

I had been sitting up some nights,
And my tired mind felt weak and blank;
Like a sharp strengthening wine it drank
The stillness and the broken lights.

Twelve struck. That sound, by dwindling years
Heard in each hour, crept off; and then
The ruffled silence spread again,
Like water that a pebble stirs.

Our mother rose from where she sat:
Her needles, as she laid them down,
Met lightly, and her silken gown
Settled: no other noise than that.

'Glory unto the Newly Born!'
So, as said angels, she did say;
Because we were in Christmas Day
Though it would still be long till morn.

Just then in the room over us
There was a pushing back of chairs,
As some who had sat unawares
So late, now heard the hour, and rose.

With anxious softly-stepping haste
Our mother went where Margaret lay,
Fearing the sounds o'er head — should they
Have broken her long watched-for rest!

She stooped an instant, calm, and turned,
But suddenly turned back again;
And all her features seemed in pain
With woe, and her eyes gazed and yearned.

For my part, I but hid my face,
And held my breath, and spoke no word:
There was none spoken; but I heard
The silence for a little space.

Our mother bowed herself and wept:
And both my arms fell, and I said,
'God knows I knew that she was dead.'
And there, all white, my sister slept.

Then kneeling upon Christmas morn
A little after twelve o'clock,
We said, ere the first quarter struck,
'Christ's blessing on the newly born!'

1580

SUDDEN LIGHT

I HAVE been here before,
But when or how I cannot tell:
I know the grass beyond the door,
The sweet keen smell,
The sighing sound, the lights around the shore.

You have been mine before, —
How long ago I may not know:
But just when at that swallow's soar
Your neck turned so,
Some veil did fall, — I knew it all of yore.

Has this been thus before?
And shall not thus time's eddying flight
Still with our lives our loves restore
In death's despite,
And day and night yield one delight once more?

1863

THE WOODSPURGE

THE wind flapped loose, the wind was still,
Shaken out dead from tree and hill:
I had walked on at the wind's will, —
I sat now, for the wind was still.

Between my knees my forehead was, —
My lips, drawn in, said not Alas!
My hair was over in the grass,
My naked ears heard the day pass.

My eyes, wide open, had the run
Of some ten weeds to fix upon;
Among those few, out of the sun,
The woodspurge flowered, three cups in one.

From perfect grief there need not be
Wisdom or even memory:
One thing then learnt remains to me, —
The woodspurge has a cup of three.

1870

THE KING'S TRAGEDY

I CATHERINE am a Douglas born,
A name to all Scots dear;
And Kate Barlass they 've called me now
Through many a waning year.

This old arm 's withered now. 'T was once
Most deft 'mong maidens all
To rein the steed, to wing the shaft,
To smite the palm-play ball.

In hall adown the close-linked dance
It has shone most white and fair;
It has been the rest for a true lord's head,
And many a sweet babe's nursing-bed,
And the bar to a King's chambère.

Aye, lasses, draw round Kate Barlass,
And hark with bated breath
How good King James, King Robert's son,
Was foully done to death.

Through all the days of his gallant youth
The princely James was pent,
By his friends at first and then by his foes,
In long imprisonment.

For the elder Prince, the kingdom's heir,
By treason's murderous brood
Was slain; and the father quaked for the child
With the royal mortal blood.

I' the Bass Rock fort, by his father's care,
Was his childhood's life assured;
And Henry the subtle Bolingbroke,
Proud England's King, 'neath the southron yoke
His youth for long years immured.

Yet in all things meet for a kingly man
Himself did he approve;
And the nightingale through his prison-wall
Taught him both lore and love.

For once, when the bird's song drew him close
To the opened window-pane,
In her bower beneath a lady stood,
A light of life to his sorrowful mood,
Like a lily amid the rain.

And for her sake, to the sweet bird's note,
He framed a sweeter Song,
More sweet than ever a poet's heart
Gave yet to the English tongue.

She was a lady of royal blood;
And when, past sorrow and teen
He stood where still through his crownless years
His Scottish realm had been,
At Scone were the happy lovers crowned,
A heart-wed King and Queen.

But the bird may fall from the bough of youth,
And song be turned to moan,
And Love's storm-cloud be the shadow of Hate,
When the tempest-waves of a troubled State
Are beating against a throne.

Yet well they loved; and the god of Love,
  Whom well the King had sung,
Might find on the earth no truer hearts
  His lowliest swains among.

From the days when first she rode abroad
  With Scotish maids in her train,
I Catherine Douglas won the trust
  Of my mistress sweet Queen Jane.

And oft she sighed, 'To be born a King!'
  And oft along the way
When she saw the homely lovers pass
  She has said, 'Alack the day!'

Years waned, — the loving and toiling years:
  Till England's wrong renewed
Drove James, by outrage cast on his crown,
  To the open field of feud.

'T was when the King and his host were met
  At the leaguer of Roxbro' hold,
The Queen o' the sudden sought his camp
  With a tale of dread to be told.

And she showed him a secret letter writ
  That spoke of treasonous strife,
And how a band of his noblest lords
  Were sworn to take his life.

'And it may be here or it may be there,
  In the camp or the court,' she said:
'But for my sake come to your people's arms
  And guard your royal head.'

Quoth he, ''T is the fifteenth day of the siege,
  And the castle's nigh to yield.'
'O face your foes on your throne,' she cried,
  'And show the power you wield;
And under your Scotish people's love
  You shall sit as under your shield.'

At the fair Queen's side I stood that day
  When he bade them raise the siege,
And back to his Court he sped to know
  How the lords would meet their Liege.

But when he summoned his Parliament,
  The louring brows hung round,
Like clouds that circle the mountain-head
  Ere the first low thunders sound.

For he had tamed the nobles' lust
  And curbed their power and pride,
And reached out an arm to right the poor
  Through Scotland far and wide;
And many a lordly wrong-doer
  By the headsman's axe had died.

'T was then upspoke Sir Robert Græme,
  The bold o'ermastering man: —
'O King, in the name of your Three Estates
  I set you under their ban!

'For, as your lords made oath to you
  Of service and fealty,
Even in like wise you pledged your oath
  Their faithful sire to be: —

'Yet all we here that are nobly sprung
  Have mourned dear kith and kin
Since first for the Scotish Barons' curse
  Did your bloody rule begin.'

With that he laid his hands on his King: —
  'Is this not so, my lords?'
But of all who had sworn to league with him
  Not one spake back to his words.

Quoth the King: — 'Thou speak'st but for one Estate,
  Nor doth it avow thy gage.
Let my liege lords hale this traitor hence!'
  The Græme fired dark with rage: —
'Who works for lesser men than himself,
  He earns but a witness wage!'

But soon from the dungeon where he lay
  He won by privy plots,
And forth he fled with a price on his head
  To the country of the Wild Scots.

And word there came from Sir Robert Græme
  To the King of Edinbro': —
'No Liege of mine thou art; but I see
From this day forth alone in thee
  God's creature, my mortal foe.

'Through thee are my wife and children lost,
  My heritage and lands;
And when my God shall show me a way,
Thyself my mortal foe will I slay
  With these my proper hands.'

Against the coming of Christmastide
  That year the King bade call
I' the Black Friars' Charterhouse of Perth
  A solemn festival.

And we of his household rode with him
  In a close-ranked company;
But not till the sun had sunk from his throne
  Did we reach the Scotish Sea.

That eve was clenched for a boding storm,
  'Neath a toilsome moon, half seen;
The cloud stooped low and the surf rose high;
And where there was a line of the sky,
  Wild wings loomed dark between.

And on a rock of the black beach-side
  By the veiled moon dimly lit,
There was something seemed to heave with life
  As the King drew nigh to it.

And was it only the tossing furze
  Or brake of the waste sea-wold?
Or was it an eagle bent to the blast?
When near we came, we knew it at last
  For a woman tattered and old.

But it seemed as though by a fire within
  Her writhen limbs were wrung;
And as soon as the King was close to her,
  She stood up gaunt and strong.

'T was then the moon sailed clear of the rack
  On high in her hollow dome;
And still as aloft with hoary crest
  Each clamorous wave rang home,
Like fire in snow the moonlight blazed
  Amid the champing foam.

And the woman held his eyes with her eyes: —
  'O King, thou art come at last;
But thy wraith has haunted the Scotish Sea
  To my sight for four years past.

'Four years it is since first I met,
  'Twixt the Duchray and the Dhu,
A shape whose feet clung close in a shroud,
  And that shape for thine I knew.

'A year again, and on Inchkeith Isle
  I saw thee pass in the breeze,
With the cerecloth risen above thy feet
  And wound about thy knees.

'And yet a year, in the Links of Forth,
  As a wanderer without rest,
Thou cam'st with both thine arms i' the shroud
  That clung high up thy breast.

'And in this hour I find thee here,
  And well mine eyes may note
That the winding-sheet hath passed thy breast
  And risen around thy throat.

'And when I meet thee again, O King,
  That of death hast such sore drouth, —
Except thou turn again on this shore, —
The winding-sheet shall have moved once more
  And covered thine eyes and mouth.

'O King, whom poor men bless for their King,
  Of thy fate be not so fain;
But these my words for God's message take,
And turn thy steed, O King, for her sake
  Who rides beside thy rein!'

While the woman spoke, the King's horse reared
  As if it would breast the sea,
And the Queen turned pale as she heard on the gale
  The voice die dolorously.

When the woman ceased, the steed was still,
  But the King gazed on her yet,
And in silence save for the wail of the sea
  His eyes and her eyes met.

At last he said: — 'God's ways are His own;
  Man is but shadow and dust.
Last night I prayed by His altar-stone;
To-night I wend to the Feast of His Son;
  And in Him I set my trust.

'I have held my people in sacred charge,
  And have not feared the sting
Of proud men's hate, — to His will resigned
Who has but one same death for a hind
  And one same death for a King.

'And if God in His wisdom have brought close
  The day when I must die,
That day by water or fire or air
My feet shall fall in the destined snare
  Wherever my road may lie.

'What man can say but the Fiend hath set
  Thy sorcery on my path,
My heart with the fear of death to fill,
And turn me against God's very will
  To sink in His burning wrath?'

The woman stood as the train rode past,
  And moved nor limb nor eye;
And when we were shipped, we saw her there
  Still standing against the sky.

As the ship made way, the moon once more
  Sank slow in her rising pall;
And I thought of the shrouded wraith of the King,
  And I said, 'The Heavens know all.'

And now, ye lasses, must ye hear
  How my name is Kate Barlass: —
But a little thing, when all the tale
  Is told of the weary mass
Of crime and woe which in Scotland's realm
  God's will let come to pass.

'T was in the Charterhouse of Perth
That the King and all his Court
Were met, the Christmas Feast being done,
For solace and disport.

'T was a wind-wild eve in February,
And against the casement-pane
The branches smote like summoning hands
And muttered the driving rain.

And when the wind swooped over the lift
And made the whole heaven frown,
It seemed a grip was laid on the walls
To tug the housetop down.

And the Queen was there, more stately fair
Than a lily in garden set;
And the King was loth to stir from her side;
For as on the day when she was his bride,
Even so he loved her yet.

And the Earl of Athole, the King's false friend,
Sat with him at the board;
And Robert Stuart the chamberlain
Who had sold his sovereign Lord.

Yet the traitor Christopher Chaumber there
Would fain have told him all,
And vainly four times that night he strove
To reach the King through the hall.

But the wine is bright at the goblet's brim
Though the poison lurk beneath;
And the apples still are red on the tree
Within whose shade may the adder be
That shall turn thy life to death.

There was a knight of the King's fast friends
Whom he called the King of Love;
And to such bright cheer and courtesy
That name might best behove.

And the King and Queen both loved him well
For his gentle knightliness;
And with him the King, as that eve wore on,
Was playing at the chess.

And the King said, (for he thought to jest
And soothe the Queen thereby;) —
'In a book 't is writ that this same year
A King shall in Scotland die.

'And I have pondered the matter o'er,
And this have I found, Sir Hugh, —
There are but two Kings on Scotish ground,
And those Kings are I and you.

'And I have a wife and a newborn heir,
And you are yourself alone;
So stand you stark at my side with me
To guard our double throne.

'For here sit I and my wife and child,
As well your heart shall approve,
In full surrender and soothfastness,
Beneath your Kingdom of Love.'

And the Knight laughed, and the Queen too smiled;
But I knew her heavy thought,
And I strove to find in the good King's jest
What cheer might thence be wrought.

And I said, 'My Liege, for the Queen's dear love
Now sing the song that of old
You made, when a captive Prince you lay,
And the nightingale sang sweet on the spray,
In Windsor's castle-hold.'

Then he smiled the smile I knew so well
When he thought to please the Queen;
The smile which under all bitter frowns
Of hate that rose between,
For ever dwelt at the poet's heart
Like the bird of love unseen.

And he kissed her hand and took his harp,
And the music sweetly rang;
And when the song burst forth, it seemed
'T was the nightingale that sang.

'Worship, ye lovers, on this May:
Of bliss your kalends are begun:
Sing with us, Away, Winter, away!
Come, Summer, the sweet season and sun!
Awake for shame, — your heaven is won, —
And amorously your heads lift all:
Thank Love, that you to his grace doth call!'

But when he bent to the Queen and sang
The speech whose praise was hers,
It seemed his voice was the voice of the Spring
And the voice of the bygone years.

'The fairest and the freshest flower
That ever I saw before that hour,
The which o' the sudden made to start
The blood of my body to my heart.

. . . .

Ah sweet, are ye a worldly creature
Or heavenly thing in form of nature?'

And the song was long, and richly stored
With wonder and beauteous things;
And the harp was tuned to every change

Of minstrel ministerings;
But when he spoke of the Queen at the last,
Its strings were his own heart-strings.

'*Unworthy but only of her grace,*
Upon Love's rock that's easy and sure,
In guerdon of all my love's space
She took me her humble creäture.
Thus fell my blissful aventure
In youth of love that from day to day
Flowereth aye new, and further I say,

'*To reckon all the circumstance*
As it happed when lessen gan my sore,
Of my rancor and woful chance,
It were too long, — I have done therefor.
And of this flower I say no more
But unto my help her heart hath tended
And even from death her man defended.'

'Aye, even from death,' to myself I said;
For I thought of the day when she
Had borne him the news, at Roxbro' siege,
Of the fell confederacy.

But Death even then took aim as he sang
With an arrow deadly bright;
And the grinning skull lurked grimly aloof,
And the wings were spread far over the roof
More dark than the winter night.

Yet truly along the amorous song
Of Love's high pomp and state,
There were words of Fortune's rackless doom
And the dreadful face of Fate.

And oft have I heard again in dreams
The voice of dire appeal
In which the King then sang of the pit
That is under Fortune's wheel.

'*And under the wheel beheld I there*
An ugly Pit as deep as hell,
That to behold I quaked for fear:
And this I heard, that who therein fell
Came no more up, tidings to tell:
Whereat, astound of the fearful sight,
I wist not what to do for fright.'

And oft has my thought called up again
These words of the changeful song: —
'*Wist thou thy pain and thy trvaial*
To come, well might'st thou weep and wail!'
And our wail, O God! is long.

But the song's end was all of his love;
And well his heart was graced
With her smiling lips and her tear-bright eyes
As his arm went round her waist.

And on the swell of her long fair throat
Close clung the necklet-chain
As he bent her pearl-tired head aside,
And in the warmth of his love and pride
He kissed her lips full fain.

And her true face was a rosy red,
The very red of the rose
That, couched on the happy garden-bed,
In the summer sunlight glows.

And all the wondrous things of love
That sang so sweet through the song
Were in the look that met in their eyes,
And the look was deep and long.

'T was then a knock came at the outer gate,
And the usher sought the King.
'The woman you met by the Scotish Sea,
My Liege, would tell you a thing;
And she says that her present need for speech
Will bear no gainsaying.'

And the King said: 'The hour is late;
To-morrow will serve, I ween.'
Then he charged the usher strictly, and said:
'No word of this to the Queen.'

But the usher came again to the King.
'Shall I call her back?' quoth he:
'For as she went on her way, she cried,
"Woe! woe! then the thing must be!"'

And the king paused, but he did not speak.
Then he called for the Voidee-cup:
And as we heard the twelfth hour strike,
There by true lips and false lips alike
Was the draught of trust drained up.

So with reverence meet to King and Queen,
To bed went all from the board;
And the last to leave of the courtly train
Was Robert Stuart the chamberlain
Who had sold his sovereign lord.

And all the locks of the chamber-door
Had the traitor riven and brast;
And that Fate might win sure way from afar,
He had drawn out every bolt and bar
That made the entrance fast.

And now at midnight he stole his way
To the moat of the outer wall,
And laid strong hurdles closely across
Where the traitor's tread should fall.

But we that were the Queen's bower-maids
Alone were left behind;
And with heed we drew the curtains close
Against the winter wind.

And now that all was still through the hall,
  More clearly we heard the rain
That clamored ever against the glass
  And the boughs that beat on the pane.

But the fire was bright in the ingle-nook,
  And through empty space around
The shadows cast on the arrased wall
'Mid the pictured kings stood sudden and tall
  Like specters sprung from the ground.

And the bed was dight in a deep alcove;
  And as he stood by the fire
The King was still in talk with the Queen
  While he doffed his goodly attire.

And the song had brought the image back
  Of many a bygone year;
And many a loving word they said
With hand in hand and head laid to head;
  And none of us went anear.

But Love was weeping outside the house,
  A child in the piteous rain;
And as he watched the arrow of Death,
He wailed for his own shafts close in the
    sheath
  That never should fly again.

And now beneath the window arose
  A wild voice suddenly:
And the King reared straight, but the Queen
    fell back
  As for bitter dule to dree;
And all of us knew the woman's voice
  Who spoke by the Scottish Sea.

'O King,' she cried, 'in an evil hour
  They drove me from thy gate;
And yet my voice must rise to thine ears;
  But alas! it comes too late!

'Last night at mid-watch, by Aberdour,
  When the moon was dead in the skies,
O King, in a death-light of thine own
  I saw thy shape arise.

'And in full season, as erst I said,
  The doom had gained its growth;
And the shroud had risen above thy neck
  And covered thine eyes and mouth.

'And no moon woke, but the pale dawn
    broke,
  And still thy soul stood there;
And I thought its silence cried to my soul
  As the first rays crowned its hair.

'Since then have I journeyed fast and fain
  In very despite of Fate,
Lest Hope might still be found in God's will:
  But they drove me from thy gate.

'For every man on God's ground, O King,
  His death grows up from his birth
In a shadow-plant perpetually;
And thine towers high, a black yew-tree,
  O'er the Charterhouse of Perth!'

That room was built far out from the
    house;
  And none but we in the room
Might hear the voice that rose beneath,
  Nor the tread of the coming doom.

For now there came a torchlight-glare,
  And a clang of arms there came;
And not a soul in that space but thought
  Of the foe Sir Robert Græme.

Yea, from the country of the Wild Scots,
  O'er mountain, valley, and glen,
He had brought with him in murderous
    league
  Three hundred armèd men.

The King knew all in an instant's flash,
  And like a King did he stand;
But there was no armor in all the room,
  Nor weapon lay to his hand.

And all we women flew to the door
  And thought to have made it fast;
But the bolts were gone and the bars were
    gone
  And the locks were riven and brast.

And he caught the pale pale Queen in his
    arms
  As the iron footsteps fell, —
Then loosed her, standing alone, and said,
  'Our bliss was our farewell!'

And 'twixt his lips he murmured a prayer,
  And he crossed his brow and breast;
And proudly in royal hardihood
Even so with folded arms he stood, —
  The prize of the bloody quest.

Then on me leaped the Queen like a deer: —
  'O Catherine, help!' she cried.
And low at his feet we clasped his knees
  Together side by side.
'Oh! even a king, for his people's sake,
  From treasonous death must hide!'

'For *her* sake most!' I cried, and I
    marked
  The pang that my words could wring.
And the iron tongs from the chimney-nook
  I snatched and held to the King: —
'Wrench up the plank! and the vault be-
    neath
  Shall yield safe harboring.'

With brows low-bent, from my eager hand
  The heavy heft did he take;
And the plank at his feet he wrenched and tore;
And as he frowned through the open floor,
  Again I said, 'For her sake!'

Then he cried to the Queen, 'God's will be done!'
  For her hands were clasped in prayer.
And down he sprang to the inner crypt;
And straight we closed the plank he had ripped,
  And toiled to smooth it fair.

(Alas! in that vault a gap once was
  Wherethrough the King might have fled:
But three days since close-walled had it been
By his will; for the ball would roll therein
  When without at the palm he played.)

Then the Queen cried, 'Catherine, keep the door,
  And I to this will suffice!'
At her word I rose all dazed to my feet,
  And my heart was fire and ice.

And louder ever the voices grew,
  And the tramp of men in mail;
Until to my brain it seemed to be
As though I tossed on a ship at sea
  In the teeth of a crashing gale.

Then back I flew to the rest; and hard
  We strove with sinews knit
To force the table against the door
  But we might not compass it.

Then my wild gaze sped far down the hall
  To the place of the hearthstone-sill;
And the Queen bent ever above the floor,
  For the plank was rising still.

And now the rush was heard on the stair,
  And 'God, what help?' was our cry.
And was I frenzied or was I bold?
I looked at each empty stanchion-hold,
  And no bar but my arm had I!

Like iron felt my arm, as through
  The staple I made it pass: —
Alack! it was flesh and bone — no more!
'T was Catherine Douglas sprang to the door,
  But I fell back Kate Barlass.

With that they all thronged into the hall,
  Half dim to my failing ken;
And the space that was but a void before
  Was a crowd of wrathful men.

Behind the door I had fall'n and lay,
  Yet my sense was widely aware,
And for all the pain of my shattered arm
  I never fainted there.

Even as I fell, my eyes were cast
  Where the King leaped down to the pit;
And lo! the plank was smooth in its place,
  And the Queen stood far from it.

And under the litters and through the bed
  And within the presses all
The traitors sought for the King, and pierced
  The arras around the wall.

And through the chamber they ramped and stormed
  Like lions loose in the lair,
And scarce could trust to their very eyes, —
  For behold! no King was there.

Then one of them seized the Queen, and cried, —
  'Now tell us, where is thy lord?'
And he held the sharp point over her heart:
She drooped not her eyes nor did she start,
  But she answered never a word.

Then the sword half pierced the true true breast:
  But it was the Græme's own son
Cried, 'This is a woman, — we seek a man!'
  And away from her girdle-zone
He struck the point of the murderous steel;
  And that foul deed was not done.

And forth flowed all the throng like a sea,
  And 't was empty space once more;
And my eyes sought out the wounded Queen
  As I lay behind the door.

And I said: 'Dear Lady, leave me here,
  For I cannot help you now;
But fly while you may, and none shall reck
  Of my place here lying low.'

And she said, 'My Catherine, God help thee!'
  Then she looked to the distant floor,
And clasping her hands, 'O God help *him*,'
  She sobbed, 'for we can no more!'

But God he knows what help may mean,
  If it mean to live or to die;
And what sore sorrow and mighty moan
On earth it may cost ere yet a throne
  Be filled in His house on high.

And now the ladies fled with the Queen;
And thorough the open door
The night-wind wailed round the empty room
And the rushes shook on the floor.

And the bed drooped low in the dark recess
Whence the arras was rent away;
And the firelight still shone over the space
Where our hidden secret lay.

And the rain had ceased, and the moonbeams lit
The window high in the wall, —
Bright beams that on the plank that I knew
Through the painted pane did fall
And gleamed with the splendor of Scotland's crown
And shield armorial.

But then a great wind swept up the skies,
And the climbing moon fell back;
And the royal blazon fled from the floor,
And nought remained on its track;
And high in the darkened window-pane
The shield and the crown were black,

And what I say next I partly saw
And partly I heard in sooth,
And partly since from the murderers' lips
The torture wrung the truth.

For now again came the armèd tread,
And fast through the hall it fell;
But the throng was less: and ere I saw,
By the voice without I could tell
That Robert Stuart had come with them
Who knew that chamber well.

And over the space the Græme strode dark
With his mantle round him flung;
And in his eye was a flaming light
But not a word on his tongue.

And Stuart held a torch to the floor,
And he found the thing he sought;
And they slashed the plank away with their swords;
And O God! I fainted not!

And the traitor held his torch in the gap,
All smoking and smoldering;
And through the vapor and fire, beneath
In the dark crypt's narrow ring,
With a shout that pealed to the room's high roof
They saw their naked King.

Half naked he stood, but stood as one
Who yet could do and dare:
With the crown, the King was stript away, —
The Knight was reft of his battle-array, —
But still the Man was there.

From the rout then stepped a villain forth, —
Sir John Hall was his name;
With a knife unsheathed he leapt to the vault
Beneath the torchlight-flame.

Of his person and stature was the King
A man right manly strong,
And mightily by the shoulder-blades
His foe to his feet he flung.

Then the traitor's brother, Sir Thomas Hall,
Sprang down to work his worst;
And the King caught the second man by the neck
And flung him above the first.

And he smote and trampled them under him;
And a long month thence they bare
All black their throats with the grip of his hands
When the hangman's hand came there.

And sore he strove to have had their knives,
But the sharp blades gashed his hands.
Oh James! so armed, thou hadst battled there
Till help had come of thy bands;
And oh! once more thou hadst held our throne
And ruled thy Scotish lands!

But while the King o'er his foes still raged
With a heart that naught could tame,
Another man sprang down to the crypt;
And with his sword in his hand hard-gripped,
There stood Sir Robert Græme.

(Now shame on the recreant traitor's heart
Who durst not face his King,
Till the body unarmed was wearied out
With two-fold combating!

Ah! well might the people sing and say,
As oft ye have heard aright: —
O Robert Græme, O Robert Græme,
Who slew our King, God give thee shame!'
For he slew him not as a knight.)

And the naked King turned round at bay,
But his strength had passed the goal,
And he could but gasp: — 'Mine hour is come;
But oh! to succor thine own soul's doom,
Let a priest now shrive my soul!'

And the traitor looked on the King's spent strength
And said: — 'Have I kept my word? —
Yea, King, the mortal pledge that I gave?
No black friar's shrift thy soul shall have,
But the shrift of this red sword!'

With that he smote his King through the breast;
And all they three in the pen
Fell on him and stabbed and stabbed him there
Like merciless murderous men.

Yet seemed it now that Sir Robert Græme,
Ere the King's last breath was o'er,
Turned sick at heart with the deadly sight
And would have done no more.

But a cry came from the troop above: —
'If him thou do not slay,
The price of his life that thou dost spare
Thy forfeit life shall pay!'

O God! what more did I hear or see,
Or how should I tell the rest,
But there at length our King lay slain
With sixteen wounds in his breast.

O God! and now did a bell boom forth,
And the murderers turned and fled; —
Too late, too late, O God, did it sound! —
And I heard the true men mustering round,
And the cries and the coming tread.

But ere they came, to the black death-gap
Somewise did I creep and steal;
And lo! or ever I swooned away,
Through the dusk I saw where the white face lay
In the Pit of Fortune's Wheel.

And now, ye Scotish maids who have heard
Dread things of the days grown old, —
Even at the last, of true Queen Jane
May somewhat yet be told,
And how she dealt for her dear lord's sake
Dire vengeance manifold.

'T was in the Charterhouse of Perth,
In the fair-lit Death-chapelle,
That the slain King's corpse on bier was laid
With chaunt and requiem-knell.

And all with royal wealth of balm
Was the body purified;
And none could trace on the brow and lips
The death that he had died.

In his robes of state he lay asleep
With orb and scepter in hand;
And by the crown he wore on his throne
Was his kingly forehead spanned.

And, girls, 't was a sweet sad thing to see
How the curling golden hair,
As in the day of the poet's youth,
From the King's crown clustered there.

And if all had come to pass in the brain
That throbbed beneath those curls,
Then Scots had said in the days to come
That this their soul was a different home
And a different Scotland, girls!

And the Queen sat by him night and day,
And oft she knelt in prayer,
All wan and pale in the widow's veil
That shrouded her shining hair.

And I had got good help of my hurt:
And only to me some sign
She made; and save the priests that were there
No face would she see but mine.

And the month of March wore on apace;
And now fresh couriers fared
Still from the country of the Wild Scots
With news of the traitors snared.

And still as I told her day by day,
Her pallor changed to sight,
And the frost grew to a furnace-flame,
That burnt her visage white.

And evermore as I brought her word,
She bent to her dead King James,
And in the cold ear with fire-drawn breath,
She spoke the traitors' names.

But when the name of Sir Robert Græme
Was the one she had to give,
I ran to hold her up from the floor;
For the froth was on her lips, and sore
I feared that she could not live.

And the month of March wore nigh to its end,
And still was the death-pall spread;
For she would not bury her slaughtered lord
Till his slayers all were dead.

And now of their dooms dread tidings came
And of torments fierce and dire;
And naught she spake, — she had ceased to speak, —
But her eyes were a soul on fire.

But when I told her the bitter end
  Of the stern and just award,
She leaned o'er the bier, and thrice three times
  She kissed the lips of her lord.

And then she said, — 'My King, they are dead!'
  And she knelt on the chapel-floor,
And whispered low with a strange proud smile, —
  'James, James, they suffered more!'

Last she stood up to her queenly height,
  But she shook like an autumn leaf,
As though the fire wherein she burned
Then left the body, and all were turned
  To winter of life-long grief.

And 'O James!' she said, — 'My James!' she said, —
  'Alas for the woful thing,
That a poet true and a friend of man,
In desperate days of bale and ban,
  Should needs be born a King!'

1881

SONNETS

THE HOUSE OF LIFE

A SONNET is a moment's monument, —
Memorial from the Soul's eternity
To one dead deathless hour. Look that it be,
Whether for lustral rite or dire portent,
Of its own arduous fulness reverent:
Carve it in ivory or in ebony,
As Day or Night may rule; and let Time see
Its flowering crest impearled and orient.
A Sonnet is a coin: its face reveals
The soul, — its converse, to what Power 't is due: —
Whether for tribute to the august appeals
Of Life, or dower in Love's high retinue,
It serve; or, 'mid the dark wharf's cavernous breath,
In Charon's palm it pay the toll to Death.

I. — YOUTH AND CHANGE

I. — LOVE ENTHRONED

I MARKED all kindred Powers the heart finds fair: —
Truth, with awed lips; and Hope, with eyes upcast;
And Fame, whose loud wings fan the ashen Past
To signal-fires, Oblivion's flight to scare;
And Youth, with still some single golden hair
Unto his shoulder clinging, since the last
Embrace wherein two sweet arms held him fast;
And Life, still wreathing flowers for Death to wear.
Love's throne was not with these; but far above
All passionate wind of welcome and farewell
He sat in breathless bowers they dream not of;
Though Truth foreknow Love's heart, and Hope foretell,
And Fame be for Love's sake desirable,
And Youth be dear and Life be sweet to Love.

IV. LOVESIGHT

WHEN do I see thee most, belovèd one?
When in the light the spirits of mine eyes
Before thy face, their altar, solemnize
The worship of that Love through thee made known?
Or when in the dusk hours (we two alone,)
Close-kissed and eloquent of still replies,
Thy twilight-hidden glimmering visage lies,
And my soul only sees thy soul its own?
O love, my love! if I no more should see
Thyself, nor on the earth the shadow of thee,
Nor image of thine eyes in any spring, —
How then should sound upon Life's darkening slope
The ground-whirl of the perished leaves of Hope,
The wind of Death's imperishable wing?

XV. THE BIRTH-BOND

HAVE you not noted, in some family
Where two were born of a first marriage-bed,
How still they own their gracious bond, though fed
And nursed on the forgotten breast and knee? —
How to their father's children they shall be
In act and thought of one goodwill; but each
Shall for the other have, in silence speech,
And in a word complete community?
Even so, when first I saw you, seemed it, love,
That among souls allied to mine was yet
One nearer kindred than life hinted of.
O born with me somewhere that men forget,

And though in years of sight and sound unmet,
Known for my soul's birth-partner well enough!

XVIII. GENIUS IN BEAUTY

Beauty like hers is genius. Not the call
Of Homer's or of Dante's heart sublime, —
Not Michael's hand furrowing the zones of time, —
Is more with compassed mysteries musical;
Nay, not in Spring's or Summer's sweet footfall
More gathered gifts exuberant Life bequeathes
Than doth this sovereign face, whose love-spell breathes
Even from its shadowed contour on the wall.
As many men are poets in their youth,
But for one sweet-strung soul the wires prolong
Even through all change the indomitable song;
So in likewise the envenomed years, whose tooth
Rends shallower grace with ruin void of ruth,
Upon this beauty's power shall wreak no wrong.

XXVI. MID-RAPTURE

Thou lovely and belovèd, thou my love;
Whose kiss seems still the first; whose summoning eyes,
Even now, as for our love-world's new sunrise,
Shed very dawn; whose voice, attuned above
All modulation of the deep-bowered dove,
Is like a hand laid softly on the soul;
Whose hand is like a sweet voice to control
Those worn tired brows it hath the keeping of: —
What word can answer to thy word, — what gaze
To thine, which now absorbs within its sphere
My worshipping face, till I am mirrored there
Light-circled in a heaven of deep-drawn rays?
What clasp, what kiss mine inmost heart can prove,
O lovely and belovèd, O my love?

XXVII. SOUL-LIGHT

What other woman could be loved like you,
Or how of you should love possess his fill?
After the fulness of all rapture, still, —
As at the end of some deep avenue
A tender glamour of day, — there comes to view
Far in your eyes a yet more hungering thrill, —
Such fire as Love's soul-winnowing hands distil
Even from his inmost ark of light and dew.
And as the traveller triumphs with the sun,
Glorying in heat's mid-height, yet startide brings
Wonder new-born, and still fresh transport springs
From limpid lambent hours of day begun: —
Even so, through eyes and voice, your soul doth move
My soul with changeful light of infinite love.

XLIII. LOVE AND HOPE

Bless love and hope. Full many a withered year
Whirled past us, eddying to its chill doomsday;
And clasped together where the blown leaves lay,
We long have knelt and wept full many a tear.
Yet lo! one hour at last, the Spring's compeer,
Flutes softly to us from some green byway:
Those years, those tears are dead, but only they: —
Bless love and hope, true soul; for we are here.
Cling heart to heart; nor of this hour demand
Whether in very truth, when we are dead,
Our hearts shall wake to know Love's golden head
Sole sunshine of the imperishable land;
Or but discern, through night's unfeatured scope,
Scorn-fired at length the illusive eyes of Hope.

XLIX–LII. WILLOWWOOD

1

I sat with Love upon a woodside well,
Leaning across the water, I and he;
Nor ever did he speak nor looked at me,
But touched his lute, wherein was audible
The certain secret thing he had to tell:
Only our mirrored eyes met silently
In the low wave; and that sound came to be
The passionate voice I knew; and my tears fell.
And at their fall, his eyes beneath grew hers;

And with his foot and with his wing-feathers
He swept the spring that watered my heart's drouth.
Then the dark ripples spread to waving hair,
And as I stooped, her own lips rising there
Bubbled with brimming kisses at my mouth.

2

And now Love sang: but his was such a song,
So meshed with half-remembrance hard to free,
As souls disused in death's sterility
May sing when the new birthday tarries long.
And I was made aware of a dumb throng
That stood aloof, one form by every tree,
All mournful forms, for each was I or she,
The shades of those our days that had no tongue.
They looked on us, and knew us and were known;
While fast together, alive from the abyss,
Clung the soul-wrung implacable close kiss;
And pity of self through all made broken moan
Which said, 'For once, for once, for once alone!'
And still Love sang, and what he sang was this: —

3

'O ye, all ye that walk in Willowwood,
That walk with hollow faces burning white;
What fathom-depth of soul-struck widowhood,
What long, what longer hours, one lifelong night,
Ere ye again, who so in vain have wooed
Your last hope lost, who so in vain invite
Your lips to that their unforgotten food,
Ere ye, ere ye again shall see the light.
Alas! the bitter banks in Willowwood,
With tear-spurge wan, with blood-wort burning red:
Alas! if ever such a pillow could
Steep deep the soul in sleep till she were dead. —
Better all life forget her than this thing,
That Willowwood should hold her wandering!'

4

So sang he: and as meeting rose and rose
Together cling through the wind's wellaway
Nor change at once, yet near the end of day
The leaves drop loosened where the heart-stain glows, —
So when the song died did the kiss unclose;
And her face fell back drowned, and was as gray
As its gray eyes; and if it ever may
Meet mine again I know not if Love knows.
Only I know that I leaned low and drank
A long draught from the water where she sank,
Her breath and all her tears and all her soul:
And as I leaned, I know I felt Love's face
Pressed on my neck with moan of pity and grace,
Till both our heads were in his aureole.

LV. STILLBORN LOVE

THE hour which might have been yet might not be,
Which man's and woman's heart conceived and bore
Yet whereof life was barren, — on what shore
Bides it the breaking of Time's weary sea?
Bondchild of all consummate joys set free,
It somewhere sighs and serves, and mute before
The house of Love, hears through the echoing door
His hours elect in choral consonancy.
But lo! what wedded souls now hand in hand
Together tread at last the immortal strand
With eyes where burning memory lights love home?
Lo! how the little outcast hour has turned
And leaped to them and in their faces yearned: —
'I am your child: O parents, ye have come!'

II. Change and Fate

LX. TRANSFIGURED LIFE

As growth of form or momentary glance
In a child's features will recall to mind
The father's with the mother's face combined, —
Sweet interchange that memories still enhance:
And yet, as childhood's years and youth's advance,
The gradual mouldings leave one stamp behind,
Till in the blended likeness now we find
A separate man's or woman's countenance: —

So in the Song, the singer's Joy and Pain,
Its very parents, evermore expand
To bid the passion's fullgrown birth remain,
By Art's transfiguring essence subtly spanned;
And from that song-cloud shaped as a man's hand
There comes the sound as of abundant rain.

LXI. THE SONG-THROE

By thine own tears thy song must tears beget,
O Singer! Magic mirror thou hast none
Except thy manifest heart; and save thine own
Anguish or ardor, else no amulet.
Cisterned in Pride, verse is the feathery jet
Of soulless air-flung fountains; nay, more dry
Than the Dead Sea for throats that thirst and sigh,
That song o'er which no singer's lids grew wet.
The Song-god — He the Sun-god — is no slave
Of thine: thy Hunter he, who for thy soul
Fledges his shaft: to no august control
Of thy skilled hand his quivered store he gave:
But if thy lips' loud cry leap to his smart,
The inspired recoil shall pierce thy brother's heart.

LXIII. INCLUSIVENESS

The changing guests, each in a different mood,
Sit at the roadside table and arise:
And every life among them in likewise
Is a soul's board set daily with new food.
What man has bent o'er his son's sleep, to brood
How that face shall watch his when cold it lies? —
Or thought, as his own mother kissed his eyes,
Of what her kiss was when his father wooed?
May not this ancient room thou sit'st in dwell
In separate living souls for joy or pain?
Nay, all its corners may be painted plain
Where Heaven shows pictures of some life spent well;
And may be stamped, a memory all in vain,
Upon the sight of lidless eyes in Hell.

LXXIII. THE CHOICE

Think thou and act; to-morrow thou shalt die.
Outstretched in the sun's warmth upon the shore,
Thou say'st: 'Man's measured path is all gone o'er;
Up all his years, steeply, with strain and sigh,
Man clomb until he touched the truth; and I,
Even I, am he whom it was destined for.'
How should this be? Art thou then so much more
Than they who sowed, that thou shouldst reap thereby?
Nay, come up hither. From this wave-washed mound
Unto the furthest flood-brim look with me;
Then reach on with thy thought till it be drowned.
Miles and miles distant though the last line be,
And though thy soul sail leagues and leagues beyond, —
Still, leagues beyond those leagues, there is more sea.

XCIX–C. NEWBORN DEATH

1

To-day Death seems to me an infant child
Which her worn mother Life upon my knee
Has set to grow my friend and play with me;
If haply so my heart might be beguiled
To find no terrors in a face so mild, —
If haply so my weary heart might be
Unto the newborn milky eyes of thee,
O Death, before resentment reconciled.
How long, O Death? And shall thy feet depart
Still a young child's with mine, or wilt thou stand
Fullgrown the helpful daughter of my heart,
What time with thee indeed I reach the strand
Of the pale wave which knows thee what thou art,
And drink it in the hollow of thy hand?

2

And thou, O Life, the lady of all bliss,
With whom, when our first heart beat full and fast,
I wandered till the haunts of men were passed,

And in fair places found all bowers amiss
Till only woods and waves might hear our kiss,
While to the winds all thought of Death we cast: —
Ah, Life! and must I have from thee at last
No smile to greet me and no babe but this?
Lo! Love, the child once ours; and Song, whose hair
Blew like a flame and blossomed like a wreath;
And Art, whose eyes were worlds by God found fair;
These o'er the book of Nature mixed their breath
With neck-twined arms, as oft we watched them there:
And did these die that thou mightst bear me Death?

1881

CHIMES

Honey-flowers to the honey-comb
And the honey-bees from home.

A honey-comb and a honey-flower,
And the bee shall have his hour.

A honeyed heart for the honey-comb,
And the humming bee flies home.

A heavy heart in the honey-flower,
And the bee has had his hour.

A honey-cell 's in the honeysuckle,
And the honey-bee knows it well.

The honey-comb has a heart of honey
And the humming bee 's so bonny.

A honey-flower 's the honeysuckle,
And the bee 's in the honey-bell.

The honeysuckle is sucked of honey,
And the bee is heavy and bonny.

Brown shell first for the butterfly
And a bright wing by and by.

Butterfly, good-bye to your shell,
And, bright wings, speed you well.

Bright lamplight for the butterfly
And a burnt wing by and by.

Butterfly, alas for your shell,
And, bright wings, fare you well.

Lost love-labor and lullaby,
And lowly let love lie.

Lost love-morrow and love-fellow
And love's life lying low.

Lovelorn labor and life laid by
And lowly let love lie.

Late love-longing and life-sorrow
And love's life lying low.

Beauty's body and benison
With a bosom-flower new-blown.

Bitter beauty and blessing banned
With a breast to burn and brand.

Beauty's bower in the dust o'erblown
With a bare white breast of bone.

Barren beauty and bower of sand
With a blast on either hand.

Buried bars in the breakwater
And bubble of the brimming weir.

Body's blood in the breakwater
And a buried body's bier.

Buried bones in the breakwater
And bubble of the brawling weir.

Bitter tears in the breakwater
And a breaking heart to bear.

Hollow heaven and the hurricane
And hurry of the heavy rain.

Hurried clouds in the hollow heaven
And a heavy rain hard-driven.

The heavy rain it hurries amain
And heaven and the hurricane.

Hurrying wind o'er the heaven's hollow
And the heavy rain to follow.

1881

William Morris (1834–1896)

SHAMEFUL DEATH

There were four of us about that bed;
 The mass-priest knelt at the side,
I and his mother stood at the head,
 Over his feet lay the bride;
We were quite sure that he was dead,
 Though his eyes were open wide.

He did not die in the night,
He did not die in the day,
But in the morning twilight
His spirit passed away,
When neither sun nor moon was bright,
And the trees were merely grey.

He was not slain with the sword,
Knight's axe, or the knightly spear,
Yet spoke he never a word
After he came in here;
I cut away the cord
From the neck of my brother dear.

He did not strike one blow,
For the recreants came behind,
In a place where the hornbeams grow,
A path right hard to find,
For the hornbeam boughs swing so,
That the twilight makes it blind.

They lighted a great torch then,
When his arms were pinioned fast,
Sir John the knight of the Fen,
Sir Guy of the Dolorous Blast,
With knights threescore and ten,
Hung Brave Lord Hugh at last.

I am threescore and ten,
And my hair is all turned grey,
But I met Sir John of the Fen
Long ago on a summer day,
And am glad to think of the moment when
I took his life away.

I am threescore and ten,
And my strength is mostly passed,
But long ago I and my men,
When the sky was overcast,
And the smoke rolled over the reeds of the fen,
Slew Guy of the Dolorous Blast.

And now, knights all of you,
I pray you pray for Sir Hugh,
A good knight and a true,
And for Alice, his wife, pray too.

1858

AN APOLOGY

Of Heaven or Hell I have no power to sing,
I cannot ease the burden of your fears,
Or make quick-coming death a little thing,
Or bring again the pleasure of past years,
Nor for my words shall ye forget your tears,
Or hope again for aught that I can say,
The idle singer of an empty day.

But rather, when aweary of your mirth,
From full hearts still unsatisfied ye sigh,
And, feeling kindly unto all the earth,
Grudge every minute as it passes by,
Made the more mindful that the sweet days die —
Remember me a little then, I pray,
The idle singer of an empty day.

The heavy trouble, the bewildering care
That weighs us down who live and earn our bread,
These idle verses have no power to bear;
So let me sing of names rememberèd,
Because they, living not, can ne'er be dead,
Or long time take their memory quite away
From us poor singers of an empty day.

Dreamer of dreams, born out of my due time,
Why should I strive to set the crookèd straight?
Let it suffice me that my murmuring rhyme
Beats with light wing against the ivory gate,
Telling a tale not too importunate
To those who in the sleepy region stay,
Lulled by the singer of an empty day.

Folk say, a wizard to a northern king
At Christmas-tide such wondrous things did show,
That through one window men beheld the spring,
And through another saw the summer glow,
And through a third the fruited vines a-row,
While still, unheard, but in its wonted way,
Piped the drear wind of that December day.

So with this Earthly Paradise it is,
If ye will read aright, and pardon me,
Who strive to build a shadowy isle of bliss
Midmost the beating of the steely sea,
Where tossed about all hearts of men must be;
Whose ravening monsters mighty men shall slay,
Not the poor singer of an empty day.

1868

ATALANTA'S RACE

Through thick Arcadian woods a hunter went,
Following the beasts up, on a fresh spring day;
But since his horn-tipped bow but seldom bent

Now at the noontide naught had happed to slay,
Within a vale he called his hounds away,
Hearkening the echoes of his lone voice cling
About the cliffs and through the beech-trees ring.

But when they ended, still awhile he stood,
And but the sweet familiar thrush could hear,
And all the day-long noises of the wood,
And o'er the dry leaves of the vanished year
His hounds' feet pattering as they drew anear,
And heavy breathing from their heads low hung,
To see the mighty cornel bow unstrung.

Then smiling did he turn to leave the place,
But with his first step some new fleeting thought
A shadow cast across his sun-burnt face:
I think the golden net that April brought
From some warm world his wavering soul had caught;
For, sunk in vague sweet longing, did he go
Betwixt the trees with doubtful steps and slow.

Yet howsoever slow he went, at last
The trees grew sparser, and the wood was done;
Whereon one farewell backward look he cast,
Then, turning round to see what place was won,
With shaded eyes looked underneath the sun,
And o'er green meads and new-turned furrows brown
Beheld the gleaming of King Schœneus' town.

So thitherward he turned, and on each side
The folk were busy on the teeming land,
And man and maid from the brown furrows cried,
Or midst the newly blossomed vines did stand,
And as the rustic weapon pressed the hand
Thought of the nodding of the well-filled ear,
Or how the knife the heavy bunch should shear.

Merry it was: about him sung the birds,
The spring flowers bloomed along the firm dry road,
The sleek-skinned mothers of the sharp-horned herds
Now for the barefoot milking-maidens lowed;
While from the freshness of his blue abode,
Glad his death-bearing arrows to forget,
The broad sun blazed, nor scattered plagues as yet.

Through such fair things unto the gates he came,
And found them open, as though peace were there;
Wherethrough, unquestioned of his race or name,
He entered, and along the streets 'gan fare,
Which at the first of folk were well-nigh bare;
But pressing on, and going more hastily,
Men hurrying too he 'gan at last to see.

Following the last of these, he still pressed on,
Until an open space he came unto,
Where wreaths of fame had oft been lost and won,
For feats of strength folk there were wont to do.
And now our hunter looked for something new,
Because the whole wide space was bare, and stilled
The high seats were, with eager people filled.

There with the others to a seat he gat,
Whence he beheld a broidered canopy,
'Neath which in fair array King Schœneus sat
Upon his throne with councilors thereby;
And underneath his well-wrought seat and high,
He saw a golden image of the sun,
A silver image of the Fleet-foot One.

A brazen altar stood beneath their feet
Whereon a thin flame flickered in the wind,
Nigh this a herald clad in raiment meet
Made ready even now his horn to wind,
By whom a huge man held a sword, entwined
With yellow flowers; these stood a little space
From off the altar, nigh the starting-place.

And there two runners did the sign abide
Foot set to foot, — a young man slim and fair,
Crisp-haired, well-knit, with firm limbs often tried
In places where no man his strength may spare;
Dainty his thin coat was, and on his hair
A golden circlet of renown he wore,
And in his hand an olive garland bore.

But on this day with whom shall he contend?
A maid stood by him like Diana clad
When in the woods she lists her bow to bend,
Too fair for one to look on and be glad,
Who scarcely yet has thirty summers had,
If he must still behold her from afar;
Too fair to let the world live free from war.

She seemed all earthly matters to forget;
Of all tormenting lines her face was clear,
Her wide gray eyes upon the goal were set
Calm and unmoved as though no soul were near;
But her foe trembled as a man in fear,
Nor from her loveliness one moment turned
His anxious face with fierce desire that burned.

Now through the hush there broke the trumpet's clang
Just as the setting sun made eventide.
Then from light feet a spurt of dust there sprang,
And swiftly were they running side by side;
But silent did the thronging folk abide
Until the turning-post was reached at last,
And round about it still abreast they passed.

But when the people saw how close they ran,
When half-way to the starting-point they were,
A cry of joy broke forth, whereat the man
Headed the white-foot runner, and drew near
Unto the very end of all his fear;
And scarce his straining feet the ground could feel,
And bliss unhoped-for o'er his heart 'gan steal.

But midst the loud victorious shouts he heard
Her footsteps drawing nearer, and the sound
Of fluttering raiment, and thereat afeard
His flushed and eager face he turned around,
And even then he felt her past him bound
Fleet as the wind, but scarcely saw her there
Till on the goal she laid her fingers fair.

There stood she breathing like a little child
Amid some warlike clamour laid asleep,
For no victorious joy her red lips smiled,
Her cheek its wonted freshness did but keep;
No glance lit up her clear gray eyes and deep,
Though some divine thought softened all her face
As once more rang the trumpet through the place.

But her late foe stopped short amidst his course,
One moment gazed upon her piteously,
Then with a groan his lingering feet did force
To leave the spot whence he her eyes could see;
And, changed like one who knows his time must be
But short and bitter, without any word
He knelt before the bearer of the sword;

Then high rose up the gleaming deadly blade,
Bared of its flowers, and through the crowded place
Was silence now, and midst of it the maid
Went by the poor wretch at a gentle pace,
And he to hers upturned his sad white face;
Nor did his eyes behold another sight
Ere on his soul there fell eternal night.

So was the pageant ended, and all folk
Talking of this and that familiar thing
In little groups from that sad concourse broke,
For now the shrill bats were upon the wing,
And soon dark night would slay the evening,
And in dark gardens sang the nightingale
Her little-heeded, oft-repeated tale.

And with the last of all the hunter went,
Who, wondering at the strange sight he had seen,
Prayed an old man to tell him what it meant,
Both why the vanquished man so slain had been,
And if the maiden were an earthly queen,
Or rather what much more she seemed to be,
No sharer in the world's mortality.

'Stranger,' said he, 'I pray she soon may die
Whose lovely youth has slain so many an one!
King Schœneus' daughter is she verily,
Who when her eyes first looked upon the sun
Was fain to end her life but new begun,
For he had vowed to leave but men alone
Sprung from his loins when he from earth was gone.

'Therefore he bade one leave her in the wood,
And let wild things deal with her as they might,
But this being done, some cruel god thought good
To save her beauty in the world's despite:
Folk say that her, so delicate and white
As now she is, a rough root-grubbing bear
Amidst her shapeless cubs at first did rear.

'In course of time the woodfolk slew her nurse,
And to their rude abode the youngling brought,
And reared her up to be a kingdom's curse;
Who, grown a woman, of no kingdom thought,
But armed and swift, 'mid beasts destruction wrought,
Nor spared two shaggy centaur kings to slay
To whom her body seemed an easy prey.

'So to this city, led by fate, she came,
Whom, known by signs, whereof I cannot tell,
King Schœneus for his child at last did claim,
Nor otherwhere since that day doth she dwell
Sending too many a noble soul to hell —
What! thine eyes glisten? what then, thinkest thou
Her shining head unto the yoke to bow?

'Listen, my son, and love some other maid
For she the saffron gown will never wear,
And on no flower-strewn couch shall she be laid,
Nor shall her voice make glad a lover's ear:
Yet if of Death thou hast not any fear,
Yea, rather, if thou lov'st him utterly,
Thou still may'st woo her ere thou com'st to die,

'Like him that on this day thou sawest lie dead;
For, fearing as I deem the sea-born one,
The maid has vowed e'en such a man to wed
As in the course her swift feet can outrun,
But whoso fails herein, his days are done:
He came the nighest that was slain to-day,
Although with him I deem she did but play.

'Behold, such mercy Atalanta gives
To those that long to win her loveliness;
Be wise! be sure that many a maid there lives
Gentler than she, of beauty little less,
Whose swimming eyes thy loving words shall bless,
When in some garden, knee set close to knee,
Thou sing'st the song that love may teach to thee.'

So to the hunter spake that ancient man,
And left him for his own home presently:
But he turned round, and through the moonlight wan
Reached the thick wood, and there 'twixt tree and tree
Distraught he passed the long night feverishly,
'Twixt sleep and waking, and at dawn arose
To wage hot war against his speechless foes.

There to the hart's flank seemed his shaft to grow,
As panting down the broad green glades he flew,
There by his horn the Dryads well might know
His thrust against the bear's heart had been true,
And there Adonis' bane his javelin slew,
But still in vain through rough and smooth he went,
For none the more his restlessness was spent.

So wandering, he to Argive cities came,
And in the lists with valiant men he stood,
And by great deeds he won him praise and fame,
And heaps of wealth for little-valued blood;
But none of all these things, or life, seemed good
Unto his heart, where still unsatisfied
A ravenous longing warred with fear and pride.

Therefore it happed when but a month had gone
Since he had left King Schœneus' city old,
In hunting-gear again, again alone
The forest-bordered meads did he behold,
Where still mid thoughts of August's quivering gold
Folk hoed the wheat, and clipped the vine in trust
Of faint October's purple-foaming must.

And once again he passed the peaceful gate,
While to his beating heart his lips did lie,
That owning not victorious love and fate,
Said, half aloud, 'And here too must I try
To win of alien men the mastery,
And gather for my head fresh meed of fame
And cast new glory on my father's name.'

In spite of that, how beat his heart, when first
Folk said to him, 'And art thou come to see
That which still makes our city's name accurst
Among all mothers for its cruelty?

Then know indeed that fate is good to thee
Because to-morrow a new luckless one
Against the whitefoot maid is pledged to run.'

So on the morrow with no curious eyes
As once he did, that piteous sight he saw,
Nor did that wonder in his heart arise
As toward the goal the conquering maid 'gan draw,
Nor did he gaze upon her eyes with awe,
Too full the pain of longing filled his heart
For fear or wonder there to have a part.

But O, how long the night was ere it went!
How long it was before the dawn begun
Showed to the wakening birds the sun's intent
That not in darkness should the world be done!
And then, and then, how long before the sun
Bade silently the toilers of the earth
Get forth to fruitless cares or empty mirth!

And long it seemed that in the market-place
He stood and saw the chaffering folk go by,
Ere from the ivory throne King Schœneus' face
Looked down upon the murmur royally,
But then came trembling that the time was nigh
When he midst pitying looks his love must claim,
And jeering voices must salute his name.

But as the throng he pierced to gain the throne,
His alien face distraught and anxious told
What hopeless errand he was bound upon,
And, each to each, folk whispered to behold
His godlike limbs; nay, and one woman old
As he went by must pluck him by the sleeve
And pray him yet that wretched love to leave.

For sidling up she said, 'Canst thou live twice,
Fair son? canst thou have joyful youth again,
That thus thou goest to the sacrifice
Thyself the victim? Nay then, all in vain
Thy mother bore her longing and her pain,
And one more maiden on the earth must dwell
Hopeless of joy, nor fearing death and hell.

'O fool, thou knowest not the compact then
That with the threeformed goddess she has made
To keep her from the loving lips of men,
And in no saffron gown to be arrayed,
And therewithal with glory to be paid,
And love of her the moonlit river sees
White 'gainst the shadow of the formless trees.

'Come back, and I myself will pray for thee
Unto the sea-born framer of delights,
To give thee her who on the earth may be
The fairest stirrer up to death and fights,
To quench with hopeful days and joyous nights
The flame that doth thy youthful heart consume:
Come back, nor give thy beauty to the tomb.'

How should he listen to her earnest speech?
Words such as he not once or twice had said
Unto himself, whose meaning scarce could reach
The firm abode of that sad hardihead —
He turned about, and through the marketstead
Swiftly he passed, until before the throne
In the cleared space he stood at last alone.

Then said the king, 'Stranger, what dost thou here?
Have any of my folk done ill to thee?
Or art thou of the forest men in fear?
Or art thou of the sad fraternity
Who still will strive my daughter's mates to be,
Staking their lives to win to earthly bliss
The lonely maid, the friend of Artemis?'

'O King,' he said, 'thou sayest the word indeed;
Nor will I quit the strife till I have won
My sweet delight, or death to end my need.
And know that I am called Milanion,
Of King Amphidamas the well-loved son:
So fear not that to thy old name, O King,
Much loss or shame my victory will bring.'

'Nay, Prince,' said Schœneus, 'welcome to this land
Thou wert indeed, if thou wert here to try
Thy strength 'gainst some one mighty of his hand;
Nor would we grudge thee well-won mastery.
But now, why wilt thou come to me to die,
And at my door lay down thy luckless head,
Swelling the band of the unhappy dead,

'Whose curses even now my heart doth fear?
Lo, I am old, and know what life can be,
And what a bitter thing is death anear.
O Son! be wise, and hearken unto me,

And if no other can be dear to thee,
At least as now, yet is the world full wide,
And bliss in seeming hopeless hearts may hide:

'But if thou losest life, then all is lost.'
'Nay, King,' Milanion said, 'thy words are vain.
Doubt not that I have counted well the cost.
But say, on what day wilt thou that I gain
Fulfilled delight, or death to end my pain?
Right glad were I if it could be to-day,
And all my doubts at rest forever lay.'

'Nay,' said King Schœneus, 'thus it shall not be,
But rather shalt thou let a month go by,
And weary with thy prayers for victory
What god thou know'st the kindest and most nigh.
So doing, still perchance thou shalt not die:
And with my good-will wouldst thou have the maid,
For of the equal gods I grow afraid.

'And until then, O Prince, be thou my guest,
And all these troublous things awhile forget.'
'Nay,' said he, 'couldst thou give my soul good rest,
And on mine head a sleepy garland set,
Then had I 'scaped the meshes of the net,
Nor shouldst thou hear from me another word;
But now, make sharp thy fearful heading-sword.

'Yet will I do what son of man may do,
And promise all the gods may most desire,
That to myself I may at least be true;
And on that day my heart and limbs so tire,
With utmost strain and measureless desire,
That, at the worst, I may but fall asleep
When in the sunlight round that sword shall sweep.'

He went therewith, nor anywhere would bide,
But unto Argos restlessly did wend;
And there, as one who lays all hope aside,
Because the leech has said his life must end,
Silent farewell he bade to foe and friend,
And took his way unto the restless sea,
For there he deemed his rest and help might be.

Upon the shore of Argolis there stands
A temple to the goddess that he sought,
That, turned unto the lion-bearing lands,
Fenced from the east, of cold winds hath no thought,
Though to no homestead there the sheaves are brought,
No groaning press torments the close-clipped murk,
Lonely the fane stands, far from all men's work.

Pass through a close, set thick with myrtle-trees,
Through the brass doors that guard the holy place,
And, entering, hear the washing of the seas
That twice a-day rise high above the base,
And, with the south-west urging them, embrace
The marble feet of her that standeth there
That shrink not, naked though they be and fair.

Small is the fane through which the seawind sings
About Queen Venus' well-wrought image white,
But hung around are many precious things,
The gifts of those who, longing for delight,
Have hung them there within the goddess' sight,
And in return have taken at her hands
The living treasures of the Grecian lands.

And thither now has come Milanion,
And showed unto the priests' wide open eyes
Gifts fairer than all those that there have shown,
Silk cloths, inwrought with Indian fantasies,
And bowls inscribed with sayings of the wise
Above the deeds of foolish living things;
And mirrors fit to be the gifts of kings.

And now before the Sea-born One he stands,
By the sweet veiling smoke made dim and soft,
And while the incense trickles from his hands,
And while the odorous smoke-wreaths hang aloft,
Thus doth he pray to her: 'O thou who oft
Hast holpen man and maid in their distress
Despise me not for this my wretchedness!

'O goddess, among us who dwell below,
Kings and great men, great for a little while,
Have pity on the lowly heads that bow,
Nor hate the hearts that love them without guile;

Wilt thou be worse than these, and is thy smile
A vain device of him who set thee here,
An empty dream of some artificer?

'O great one, some men love, and are ashamed;
Some men are weary of the bonds of love;
Yea, and by some men lightly art thou blamed,
That from thy toils their lives they cannot move,
And 'mid the ranks of men their manhood prove.
Alas! O goddess, if thou slayest me
What new immortal can I serve but thee?

'Think then, will it bring honour to thy head
If folk say, "Everything aside he cast
And to all fame and honour was he dead,
And to his one hope now is dead at last,
Since all unholpen he is gone and past:
Ah, the gods love not man, for certainly,
He to his helper did not cease to cry."

'Nay, but thou wilt help; they who died before
Not single-hearted as I deem came here,
Therefore unthanked they laid their gifts before
Thy stainless feet, still shivering with their fear,
Lest in their eyes their true thought might appear,
Who sought to be the lords of that fair town,
Dreaded of men and winners of renown.

'O Queen, thou knowest I pray not for this:
O, set us down together in some place
Where not a voice can break our heaven of bliss,
Where naught but rocks and I can see her face,
Softening beneath the marvel of thy grace,
Where not a foot our vanished steps can track—
The golden age, the golden age come back!

'O fairest, hear me now who do thy will,
Plead for thy rebel that she be not slain,
But live and love and be thy servant still;
Ah, give her joy and take away my pain,
And thus two long-enduring servants gain.
An easy thing this is to do for me,
What need of my vain words to weary thee?

'But none the less this place will I not leave
Until I needs must go my death to meet,
Or at thy hands some happy sign receive
That in great joy we twain may one day greet
Thy presence here and kiss thy silver feet,
Such as we deem thee, fair beyond all words,
Victorious o'er our servants and our lords.'

Then from the altar back a space he drew
But from the Queen turned not his face away,
But 'gainst a pillar leaned, until the blue
That arched the sky, at ending of the day,
Was turned to ruddy gold and changing grey,
And clear, but low, the nigh-ebbed windless sea
In the still evening murmured ceaselessly.

And there he stood when all the sun was down,
Nor had he moved, when the dim golden light,
Like the far lustre of a godlike town,
Had left the world to seeming hopeless night,
Nor would he move the more when wan moonlight
Streamed through the pillars for a little while,
And lighted up the white Queen's changeless smile.

Naught noted he the shallow-flowing sea
As step by step it set the wrack a-swim;
The yellow torchlight nothing noted he
Wherein with fluttering gown and half-bared limb
The temple damsels sung their midnight hymn;
And naught the doubled stillness of the fane
When they were gone and all was hushed again.

But when the waves had touched the marble base,
And steps the fish swim over twice a-day,
The dawn beheld him sunken in his place
Upon the floor; and sleeping there he lay,
Not heeding aught the little jets of spray
The roughened sea brought nigh, across him cast,
For as one dead all thought from him had passed.

Yet long before the sun had showed his head,
Long ere the varied hangings on the wall
Had gained once more their blue and green and red,

He rose as one some well-known sign doth call
When war upon the city's gates doth fall,
And scarce like one fresh risen out of sleep,
He 'gan again his broken watch to keep.

Then he turned round; not for the seagull's cry
That wheeled above the temple in his flight,
Not for the fresh south wind that lovingly
Breathed on the new-born day and dying night,
But some strange hope 'twixt fear and great delight
Drew round his face, now flushed, now pale and wan,
And still constrained his eyes the sea to scan.

Now a faint light lit up the southern sky,
Not sun or moon, for all the world was grey,
But this a bright cloud seemed, that drew anigh,
Lighting the dull waves that beneath it lay
As toward the temple still it took its way,
And still grew greater, till Milanion
Saw nought for dazzling light that round him shone.

But as he staggered with his arms outspread,
Delicious unnamed odours breathed around,
For languid happiness he bowed his head,
And with wet eyes sank down upon the ground,
Nor wished for aught, nor any dream he found
To give him reason for that happiness,
Or make him ask more knowledge of his bliss.

At last his eyes were cleared, and he could see
Through happy tears the goddess face to face
With that faint image of Divinity,
Whose well-wrought smile and dainty changeless grace
Until that morn so gladdened all the place;
Then he, unwitting cried aloud her name,
And covered up his eyes for fear and shame.

But through the stillness he her voice could hear
Piercing his heart with joy scarce bearable,
That said, 'Milanion, wherefore dost thou fear?
I am not hard to those who love me well;
List to what I a second time will tell,
And thou mayest hear perchance, and live to save
The cruel maiden from a loveless grave.

'See, by my feet three golden apples lie —
Such fruit among the heavy roses falls,
Such fruit my watchful damsels carefully
Store up within the best loved of my walls,
Ancient Damascus, where the lover calls
Above my unseen head, and faint and light
The rose-leaves flutter round me in the night.

'And note, that these are not alone most fair
With heavenly gold, but longing strange they bring
Unto the hearts of men, who will not care
Beholding these, for any once-loved thing
Till round the shining sides their fingers cling.
And thou shalt see the well-girt swiftfoot maid
By sight of these amidst her glory stayed.

'For bearing these within a scrip with thee,
When first she heads thee from the starting-place
Cast down the first one for her eyes to see,
And when she turns aside make on apace,
And if again she heads thee in the race
Spare not the other two to cast aside
If she not long enough behind will bide.

'Farewell, and when has come the happy time
That she Diana's raiment must unbind
And all the world seems blessed with Saturn's clime,
And thou with eager arms about her twined
Beholdest first her grey eyes growing kind,
Surely, O trembler, thou shalt scarcely then
Forget the helper of unhappy men.'

Milanion raised his head at this last word,
For now so soft and kind she seemed to be
No longer of her Godhead was he feared;
Too late he looked; for nothing could he see
But the white image glimmering doubtfully
In the departing twilight cold and grey,
And those three apples on the steps that lay.

These then he caught up quivering with delight,
Yet fearful lest it all might be a dream;
And though aweary with the watchful night,
And sleepless nights of longing, still did deem

He could not sleep; but yet the first sunbeam
That smote the fane across the heaving deep
Shone on him laid in calm untroubled sleep.

But little ere the noontide did he rise,
And why he felt so happy scarce could tell
Until the gleaming apples met his eyes.
Then, leaving the fair place where this befell
Oft he looked back as one who loved it well,
Then homeward to the haunts of men 'gan wend
To bring all things unto a happy end.

Now has the lingering month at last gone by,
Again are all folk around the running place,
Nor other seems the dismal pageantry
Than heretofore, but that another face
Looks o'er the smooth course ready for the race,
For now, beheld of all, Milanion
Stands on the spot he twice has looked upon.

But yet — what change is this that holds the maid?
Does she indeed see in his glittering eye
More than disdain of the sharp shearing blade,
Some happy hope of help and victory?
The others seemed to say, 'We come to die,
Look down upon us for a little while,
That dead, we may bethink us of thy smile.'

But he — what look of mastery was this
He cast on her? why were his lips so red?
Why was his face so flushed with happiness?
So looks not one who deems himself but dead,
E'en if to death he bows a willing head;
So rather looks a god well pleased to find
Some earthly damsel fashioned to his mind.

Why must she drop her lids before his gaze,
And even as she casts adown her eyes
Redden to note his eager glance of praise,
And wish that she were clad in other guise?
Why must the memory to her heart arise
Of things unnoticed when they first were heard,
Some lover's song, some answering maiden's word?

What makes these longings, vague, without a name,
And this vain pity never felt before,
This sudden languor, this contempt of fame,
This tender sorrow for the time past o'er,
These doubts that grow each minute more and more?
Why does she tremble as the time grows near,
And weak defeat and woeful victory fear?

But while she seemed to hear her beating heart,
Above their heads the trumpet blast rang out
And forth they sprang; and she must play her part.
Then flew her white feet, knowing not a doubt,
Though, slackening once, she turned her head about,
But then she cried aloud and faster fled
Than e'er before, and all men deemed him dead.

But with no sound he raised aloft his hand,
And thence what seemed a ray of light there flew
And past the maid rolled on along the sand;
Then trembling she her feet together drew
And in her heart a strong desire there grew
To have the toy; some god she thought had given
That gift to her, to make of earth a heaven.

Then from the course with eager steps she ran,
And in her odorous bosom laid the gold.
But when she turned again, the great-limbed man
Now well ahead she failed not to behold,
And mindful of her glory waxing cold,
Sprang up and followed him in hot pursuit,
Though with one hand she touched the golden fruit.

Note, too, the bow that she was wont to bear
She laid aside to grasp the glittering prize,
And o'er her shoulder from the quiver fair
Three arrows fell and lay before her eyes
Unnoticed, as amidst the people's cries
She sprang to head the strong Milanion,
Who now the turning-post had well-nigh won.

But as he set his mighty hand on it,
White fingers underneath his own were laid,
And white limbs from his dazzled eyes did flit,
Then he the second fruit cast by the maid:

But she ran awhile, then as one afraid
Wavered and stopped, and turned and made no stay,
Until the globe with its bright fellow lay.

Then, as a troubled glance she cast around
Now far ahead the Argive could she see,
And in her garment's hem one hand she wound
To keep the double prize, and strenuously
Sped o'er the course, and little doubt had she
To win the day, though now but scanty space
Was left betwixt him and the winning-place.

Short was the way unto such wingèd feet,
Quickly she gained upon him till at last
He turned about her eager eyes to meet
And from his hand the third fair apple cast.
She wavered not, but turned and ran so fast
After the prize that should her bliss fulfil,
That in her hand it lay ere it was still.

Nor did she rest, but turned about to win
Once more, an unblest woeful victory —
And yet — and yet — why does her breath begin
To fail her, and her feet drag heavily?
Why fails she now to see if far or nigh
The goal is? Why do her grey eyes grow dim?
Why do these tremors run through every limb?

She spreads her arms abroad some stay to find
Else must she fall, indeed, and findeth this,
A strong man's arms about her body twined.
Nor may she shudder now to feel his kiss,
So wrapped she is in new unbroken bliss:
Made happy that the foe the prize hath won,
She weeps glad tears for all her glory done.

Shatter the trumpet, hew adown the posts!
Upon the brazen altar break the sword,
And scatter incense to appease the ghosts
Of those who died here by their own award.
Bring forth the image of the mighty Lord,
And her who unseen o'er the runners hung,
And did a deed forever to be sung.

Here are the gathered folk; make no delay,
Open King Schœneus' well-filled treasury,
Bring out the gifts long hid from light of day,
The golden bowls o'erwrought with imagery,
Gold chains, and unguents brought from over sea,
The saffron gown the old Phœnician brought,
Within the temple of the goddess wrought.

O ye, O damsels, who shall never see
Her, that Love's servant bringeth now to you,
Returning from another victory,
In some cool bower do all that now is due!
Since she in token of her service new
Shall give to Venus offerings rich enow,
Her maiden zone, her arrows, and her bow.

1868

Algernon Charles Swinburne
(1837–1909)

A SONG IN TIME OF ORDER

Push hard across the sand,
For the salt wind gathers breath;
Shoulder and wrist and hand,
Push hard as the push of death.

The wind is as iron that rings,
The foam-heads loosen and flee;
It swells and welters and swings,
The pulse of the tide of the sea.

And up on the yellow cliff
The long corn flickers and shakes;
Push, for the wind holds stiff,
And the gunwale dips and rakes.

Good hap to the fresh fierce weather,
The quiver and beat of the sea!
While three men hold together,
The kingdoms are less by three.

Out to the sea with her there,
Out with her over the sand,
Let the kings keep the earth for their share!
We have done with the sharers of land.

They have tied the world in a tether,
They have bought over God with a fee;
While three men hold together,
The kingdoms are less by three.

We have done with the kisses that sting,
The thief's mouth red from the feast,
The blood on the hands of the king,
And the lie at the lips of the priest.

Will they tie the winds in a tether,
Put a bit in the jaws of the sea?
While three men hold together,
The kingdoms are less by three.

Let our flag run out straight in the wind!
The old red shall be floated again
When the ranks that are thin shall be thinned,
When the names that were twenty are ten;

When the devil's riddle is mastered,
  And the galley-bench creaks with a Pope,
We shall see Buonaparte the bastard
  Kick heels with his throat in a rope.

While the shepherd sets wolves on his sheep,
  And the emperor halters his kine,
While Shame is a watchman asleep,
  And Faith is a keeper of swine, —

Let the wind shake our flag like a feather,
  Like the plumes of the foam of the sea!
While three men hold together,
  The kingdoms are less by three.

All the world has its burdens to bear,
  From Cayenne to the Austrian whips;
Forth, with the rain in our hair
  And the salt sweet foam in our lips;

In the teeth of the hard glad weather,
  In the blown wet face of the sea;
While three men hold together,
  The kingdoms are less by three.

1862

BEFORE THE BEGINNING OF YEARS

Before the beginning of years
  There came to the making of man
Time, with a gift of tears;
  Grief, with a glass that ran;
Pleasure, with pain for leaven;
  Summer, with flowers that fell;
Remembrance fallen from heaven,
  And madness risen from hell;
Strength without hands to smite;
  Love that endures for a breath;
Night, the shadow of light,
  And life, the shadow of death.

And the high gods took in hand
  Fire, and the falling of tears,
And a measure of sliding sand
  From under the feet of the years;
And froth and drift of the sea;
  And dust of the laboring earth;
And bodies of things to be
  In the houses of death and of birth;
And wrought with weeping and laughter,
  And fashioned with loathing and love,
With life before and after
  And death beneath and above,
For a day and a night and a morrow,
  That his strength might endure for a span
With travail and heavy sorrow,
  The holy spirit of man.

From the winds of the north and the south
  They gathered as unto strife;
They breathed upon his mouth,
  They filled his body with life;
Eyesight and speech they wrought
  For the veils of the soul therein,
A time for labour and thought,
  A time to serve and to sin;
They gave him light in his ways,
  And love, and a space for delight,
And beauty and length of days,
  And night, and sleep in the night.
His speech is a burning fire;
  With his lips he travaileth;
In his heart is a blind desire,
  In his eyes foreknowledge of death;
He weaves, and is clothed with derision;
  Sows, and he shall not reap;
His life is a watch or a vision
  Between a sleep and a sleep.

1865

A LEAVE-TAKING

Let us go hence, my songs; she will not hear;
Let us go hence together without fear.
Keep silence now, for singing-time is over,
And over all old things and all things dear.
She loves not you nor me as all we love her:
Yea, though we sang as angels in her ear,
  She would not hear.

Let us rise up and part: she will not know.
Let us go seaward as the great winds go,
Full of blown sand and foam. What help is here?
There is no help, for all these things are so,
And all the world is bitter as a tear.
And how these things are, though ye strove to show,
  She would not know.

Let us go home and hence: she will not weep.
We gave love many dreams and days to keep,
Flowers without scent, and fruits that would not grow,
Saying, 'If thou wilt, thrust in thy sickle, and reap.'
All is reaped now; no grass is left to mow:
And we that sowed, though all we fell on sleep,
  She would not weep.

Let us go hence and rest: she will not love.
She shall not hear us if we sing hereof,
Nor see love's ways, how sore they are and steep.

Come hence, let be, lie still; it is enough.
Love is a barren sea, bitter and deep;
And, though she saw all heaven in flower above,
She would not love.

Let us give up, go down: she will not care.
Though all the stars made gold of all the air,
And the sea moving saw before it move
One moon-flower making all the foam-flowers fair;
Though all those waves went over us, and drove
Deep down the stifling lips and drowning hair, —
She would not care.

Let us go hence, go hence: she will not see.
Sing all once more together; surely she,
She too, remembering days and words that were,
Will turn a little toward us, sighing; but we,
We are hence, we are gone, as though we had not been there.
Nay, and though all men seeing had pity on me,
She would not see.

1866

A MATCH

If love were what the rose is,
And I were like the leaf,
Our lives would grow together
In sad or singing weather,
Blown fields or flowerful closes,
Green pleasure or gray grief;
If love were what the rose is,
And I were like the leaf.

If I were what the words are,
And love were like the tune,
With double sound and single
Delight our lips would mingle,
With kisses glad as birds are
That get sweet rain at noon;
If I were what the words are,
And love were like the tune.

If you were life, my darling,
And I your love were death,
We 'd shine and snow together
Ere March made sweet the weather
With daffodil and starling
And hours of fruitful breath;
If you were life, my darling,
And I your love were death.

If you were thrall to sorrow,
And I were page to joy,
We 'd play for lives and seasons
With loving looks and treasons
And tears of night and morrow
And laughs of maid and boy;
If you were thrall to sorrow,
And I were page to joy.

If you were April's lady,
And I were lord in May,
We 'd throw with leaves for hours
And draw for days with flowers,
Till day like night were shady
And night were bright like day;
If you were April's lady,
And I were lord in May.

If you were queen of pleasure,
And I were king of pain,
We 'd hunt down love together,
Pluck out his flying-feather,
And teach his feet a measure,
And find his mouth a rein;
If you were queen of pleasure,
And I were king of pain.

1866

ROCOCO

Take hands, and part with laughter;
Touch lips, and part with tears;
Once more and no more after,
Whatever comes with years.
We twain shall not re-measure
The ways that left us twain,
Nor crush the lees of pleasure
From sanguine grapes of pain.

We twain once well in sunder,
What will the mad gods do
For hate with me, I wonder,
Or what for love with you?
Forget them till November,
And dream there 's April yet;
Forget that I remember,
And dream that I forget.

Time found our tired love sleeping,
And kissed away his breath;
But what should we do weeping,
Though light love sleep to death?
We have drained his lips at leisure,
Till there 's not left to drain
A single sob of pleasure,
A single pulse of pain.

Dream that the lips once breathless
Might quicken if they would;
Say that the soul is deathless;

Dream that the gods are good;
Say March may wed September,
And time divorce regret:
But not that you remember,
And not that I forget.

We have heard from hidden places
What love scarce lives and hears;
We have seen on fervent faces
The pallor of strange tears;
We have trod the wine-vat's treasure,
Whence, ripe to steam and stain,
Foams round the feet of pleasure
The blood-red must of pain.

Remembrance may recover,
And time bring back to time
The name of your first lover,
The ring of my first rhyme;
But rose-leaves of December
The frosts of June shall fret,
The day that you remember,
The day that I forget.

The snake that hides and hisses
In heaven, we twain have known
The grief of cruel kisses,
The joy whose mouth makes moan;
The pulse's pause and measure,
Where in one furtive vein
Throbs through the heart of pleasure
The purpler blood of pain.

We have done with tears and treasons
And love for treason's sake;
Room for the swift new seasons,
The years that burn and break.
Dismantle and dismember
Men's days and dreams, Juliette:
For love may not remember,
But time will not forget.

Life treads down love in flying,
Time withers him at root;
Bring all dead things and dying,
Reaped sheaf and ruined fruit,
Where, crushed by three days' pressure,
Our three days' love lies slain;
And earlier leaf of pleasure,
And latter flower of pain.

Breathe close upon the ashes,
It may be flame will leap;
Unclose the soft close lashes,
Lift up the lids, and weep.
Light love's extinguished ember,
Let one tear leave it wet,
For one that you remember,
And ten that you forget.

1866

THE GARDEN OF PROSERPINE

HERE, where the world is quiet,
Here, where all trouble seems
Dead winds' and spent waves' riot
In doubtful dreams of dreams;
I watch the green field growing
For reaping folk and sowing,
For harvest-time and mowing,
A sleepy world of streams.

I am tired of tears and laughter,
And men that laugh and weep,
Of what may come hereafter
For men that sow to reap:
I am weary of days and hours,
Blown buds of barren flowers,
Desires and dreams and powers,
And every thing but sleep.

Here life has death for neighbor,
And far from eye or ear
Wan waves and wet winds labor,
Weak ships and spirits steer;
They drive adrift, and whither
They wot not who make thither;
But no such winds blow hither,
And no such things grow here.

No growth of moor or coppice,
No heather-flower or vine,
But bloomless buds of poppies,
Green grapes of Proserpine,
Pale beds of blowing rushes
Where no leaf blooms or blushes
Save this whereout she crushes
For dead men deadly wine.

Pale, without name or number,
In fruitless fields of corn,
They bow themselves and slumber
All night till light is born;
And like a soul belated,
In hell and heaven unmated,
By cloud and mist abated
Comes out of darkness morn.

Though one were strong as seven,
He too with death shall dwell,
Nor wake with wings in heaven,
Nor weep for pains in hell;
Though one were fair as roses,
His beauty clouds and closes;
And well though love reposes,
In the end it is not well.

Pale, beyond porch and portal,
Crowned with calm leaves, she stands
Who gathers all things mortal
With cold immortal hands;

Her languid lips are sweeter
Than love's who fears to greet her
To men that mix and meet her
From many times and lands.

She waits for each and other,
She waits for all men born;
Forgets the earth her mother,
The life of fruits and corn;
And spring and seed and swallow
Take wing for her, and follow
Where summer song rings hollow,
And flowers are put to scorn.

There go the loves that wither,
The old loves with wearier wings;
And all dead years draw thither,
And all disastrous things;
Dead dreams of days forsaken,
Blind buds that snows have shaken,
Wild leaves that winds have taken,
Red strays of ruined springs.

We are not sure of sorrow,
And joy was never sure;
To-day will die to-morrow;
Time stoops to no man's lure;
And love, grown faint and fretful,
With lips but half regretful
Sighs, and with eyes forgetful
Weeps that no loves endure.

From too much love of living,
From hope and fear set free,
We thank with brief thanksgiving
Whatever gods may be
That no life lives for ever;
That dead men rise up never;
That even the weariest river
Winds somewhere safe to sea.

Then star nor sun shall waken,
Nor any change of light;
Nor sound of waters shaken,
Nor any sound or sight;
Nor wintry leaves nor vernal,
Nor days nor things diurnal:
Only the sleep eternal
In an eternal night.

1866

HERTHA

I AM that which began;
Out of me the years roll;
Out of me God and man;
I am equal and whole;
God changes, and man, and the form of them bodily; I am the soul.

Before ever land was,
Before ever the sea,
Or soft hair of the grass,
Or fair limbs of the tree,
Or the flesh-colored fruit of my branches, I was, and thy soul was in me.

First life on my sources
First drifted and swam;
Out of me are the forces
That save it or damn;
Out of me, man and woman, and wild-beast and bird; before God was, I am.

Beside or above me
Naught is there to go;
Love or unlove me,
Unknow me or know,
I am that which unloves me and loves; I am stricken, and I am the blow.

I the mark that is missed
And the arrows that miss,
I the mouth that is kissed
And the breath in the kiss,
The search, and the sought, and the seeker, the soul and the body that is.

I am that thing which blesses
My spirit elate;
That which caresses
With hands uncreate
My limbs unbegotten that measure the length of the measure of fate.

But what thing dost thou now,
Looking Godward, to cry
'I am I, thou art thou,
I am low, thou art high'?
I am thou, whom thou seekest to find him; find thou but thyself, thou art I.

I the grain and the furrow,
The plough-cloven clod
And the plough-share drawn thorough,
The germ and the sod,
The deed and the doer, the seed and the sower, the dust which is God.

Hast thou known how I fashioned thee,
Child, underground?
Fire that impassioned thee,
Iron that bound,
Dim changes of water, what thing of all these hast thou known of or found?

Canst thou say in thine heart
Thou hast seen with thine eyes
With what cunning of art
Thou wast wrought in what wise,

By what force of what stuff thou wast shapen, and shown on my breast to the skies?

Who hath given, who hath sold it thee,
Knowledge of me?
Hath the wilderness told it thee?
Hast thou learnt of the sea?
Hast thou communed in spirit with night? have the winds taken counsel with thee?

Have I set such a star
To show light on thy brow
That thou sawest from afar
What I show to thee now?
Have ye spoken as brethren together, the sun and the mountains and thou?

What is here, dost thou know it?
What was, hast thou known?
Prophet nor poet
Nor tripod nor throne
Nor spirit nor flesh can make answer, but only thy mother alone.

Mother, not maker,
Born, and not made;
Though her children forsake her,
Allured or afraid,
Praying prayers to the God of their fashion, she stirs not for all that have prayed.

A creed is a rod,
And a crown is of night;
But this thing is God,
To be man with thy might,
To grow straight in the strength of thy spirit, and live out thy life as the light.

I am in thee to save thee,
As my soul in thee saith;
Give thou as I gave thee,
Thy life-blood and breath,
Green leaves of thy labor, white flowers of thy thought, and red fruit of thy death.

Be the ways of thy giving
As mine were to thee;
The free life of thy living,
Be the gift of it free;
Not as servant to lord, nor as master to slave, shalt thou give thee to me.

O children of banishment,
Souls overcast,
Were the lights ye see vanish meant
Always to last,
Ye would know not the sun overshining the shadows and stars overpast.

I that saw where ye trod
The dim paths of the night
Set the shadow called God
In your skies to give light;
But the morning of manhood is risen, and the shadowless soul is in sight.

The tree many-rooted
That swells to the sky
With frondage red-fruited
The life-tree am I;
In the buds of your lives is the sap of my leaves: ye shall live and not die.

But the gods of your fashion
That take and that give,
In their pity and passion
That scourge and forgive,
They are worms that are bred in the bark that falls off, they shall die and not live.

My own blood is what stanches
The wounds in my bark;
Stars caught in my branches
Make day of the dark,
And are worshipped as suns till the sunrise shall tread out their fires as a spark.

Where dead ages hide under
The live roots of the tree,
In my darkness the thunder
Makes utterance of me;
In the clash of my boughs with each other ye hear the waves sound of the sea.

That noise is of Time,
As his feathers are spread
And his feet set to climb
Through the boughs overhead,
And my foliage rings round him and rustles, and branches are bent with his tread.

The storm-winds of ages
Blow through me and cease,
The war-wind that rages,
The spring-wind of peace,
Ere the breath of them roughen my tresses, ere one of my blossoms increase.

All sounds of all changes,
All shadows and lights

On the world's mountain-ranges,
And stream-riven heights,
Whose tongue is the wind's tongue and language of storm-clouds on earth-shaking nights;

All forms of all faces,
All works of all hands
In unsearchable places
Of time-stricken lands,
All death and all life, and all reigns and all ruins, drop through me as sands.

Though sore be my burden
And more than ye know,
And my growth have no guerdon
But only to grow,
Yet I fail not of growing for lightnings above me or death-worms below.

These too have their part in me,
As I too in these;
Such fire is at heart in me,
Such sap is this tree's,
Which hath in it all sounds and all secrets of infinite lands and of seas.

In the spring-colored hours
When my mind was as May's,
There brake forth of me flowers
By centuries of days,
Strong blossoms with perfume of manhood, shot out from my spirit as rays.

And the sound of them springing
And smell of their shoots
Were as warmth and sweet singing,
And strength to my roots;
And the lives of my children made perfect with freedom of soul were my fruits.

I bid you but be;
I have need not of prayer;
I have need of you free
As your mouths of mine air;
That my heart may be greater within me, beholding the fruits of me fair.

More fair than strange fruit is
Of faiths ye espouse;
In me only the root is
That blooms in your boughs;
Behold now your god that ye made you, to feed him with faith of your vows.

In the darkening and whitening
Abysses, adored,
With dayspring and lightning
For lamp and for sword,
God thunders in heaven, and his angels are red with the wrath of the Lord.

O my sons, O too dutiful
Towards gods not of me,
Was not I enough beautiful?
Was it hard to be free?
For behold, I am with you, am in you and of you; look forth now and see.

Lo, winged with world's wonders,
With miracles shod,
With the fires of his thunders
For raiment and rod,
God trembles in heaven, and his angels are white with the terror of God.

For his twilight is come on him,
His anguish is here;
And his spirits gaze dumb on him,
Grown gray from his fear;
And his hour taketh hold on him stricken, the last of his infinite year.

Thought made him and breaks him,
Truth slays and forgives;
But to you, as time takes him,
This new thing it gives,
Even love, the belovèd Republic, that feeds upon freedom and lives.

For truth only is living,
Truth only is whole,
And the love of his giving
Man's polestar and pole;
Man, pulse of my center, and fruit of my body, and seed of my soul.

One birth of my bosom;
One beam of mine eye;
One topmost blossom
That scales the sky;
Man, equal and one with me, man that is made of me, man that is I.

1871

A FORSAKEN GARDEN

In a coign of the cliff between lowland and highland,
At the sea-down's edge between windward and lee,
Walled round with rocks as an inland island,
The ghost of a garden fronts the sea.
A girdle of brushwood and thorn encloses
The steep square slope of the blossomless bed
Where the weeds that grew green from the graves of its roses
Now lie dead.

The fields fall southward, abrupt and broken,
To the low last edge of the long lone land.
If a step should sound or a word be spoken,
Would a ghost not rise at the strange guest's hand?
So long have the gray bare walks lain guestless,
Through branches and briers if a man make way,
He shall find no life but the sea-wind's restless
Night and day.

The dense hard passage is blind and stifled
That crawls by a track none turn to climb
To the strait waste place that the years have rifled
Of all but the thorns that are touched not of time.
The thorns he spares when the rose is taken;
The rocks are left when he wastes the plain;
The wind that wanders, the weeds wind-shaken,
These remain.

Not a flower to be pressed of the foot that falls not;
As the heart of a dead man the seed-plots are dry;
From the thicket of thorns whence the nightingale calls not,
Could she call, there were never a rose to reply.
Over the meadows that blossom and wither,
Rings but the note of a sea-bird's song.
Only the sun and the rain come hither
All year long.

The sun burns sear, and the rain dishevels
One gaunt bleak blossom of scentless breath,
Only the wind here hovers and revels
In a round where life seems barren as death.
Here there was laughing of old, there was weeping,
Haply, of lovers none ever will know,
Whose eyes went seaward a hundred sleeping
Years ago.

Heart handfast in heart as they stood, 'Look thither,'
Did he whisper? 'Look forth from the flowers to the sea;
For the foam-flowers endure when the rose-blossoms wither,
And men that love lightly may die — but we?'
And the same wind sang, and the same waves whitened,
And or ever the garden's last petals were shed,
In the lips that had whispered, the eyes that had lightened,
Love was dead.

Or they loved their life through, and then went whither?
And were one to the end — but what end who knows?
Love deep as the sea as a rose must wither,
As the rose-red seaweed that mocks the rose.
Shall the dead take thought for the dead to love them?
What love was ever as deep as a grave?
They are loveless now as the grass above them
Or the wave.

All are at one now, roses and lovers,
Not known of the cliffs and the fields and the sea.
Not a breath of the time that has been hovers
In the air now soft with a summer to be.
Not a breath shall there sweeten the seasons hereafter
Of the flowers or the lovers that laugh now or weep,
When as they that are free now of weeping and laughter
We shall sleep.

Here death may deal not again for ever;
Here change may come not till all change end.
From the graves they have made they shall rise up never,
Who have left naught living to ravage and rend.
Earth, stones, and thorns of the wild ground growing,
While the sun and the rain live, these shall be;
Till a last wind's breath, upon all these blowing,
Roll the sea.

Till the slow sea rise, and the sheer cliff crumble,
Till terrace and meadow the deep gulfs drink,
Till the strength of the waves of the high tides humble
The fields that lessen, the rocks that shrink,

Here now in his triumph where all things falter,
Stretched out on the spoils that his own hand spread,
As a god self-slain on his own strange altar,
Death lies dead.

1876

Arthur Hugh Clough (1819–1861)

QUA CURSUM VENTUS

As ships, becalmed at eve, that lay
With canvas drooping, side by side,
Two towers of sail at dawn of day
Are scarce long leagues apart descried;

When fell the night, upsprung the breeze,
And all the darkling hours they plied,
Nor dreamt but each the self-same seas
By each was cleaving, side by side:

E'en so — but why the tale reveal
Of those whom, year by year unchanged,
Brief absence joined anew to feel,
Astounded, soul from soul estranged?

At dead of night their sails were filled,
And onward each rejoicing steered —
Ah, neither blame, for neither willed,
Or wist, what first with dawn appeared!

To veer, how vain! On, onward strain,
Brave barks! In light, in darkness too,
Through winds and tides one compass guides —
To that, and your own selves, be true.

But O blithe breeze; and O great seas,
Though ne'er, that earliest parting past,
On your wide plain they join again,
Together lead them home at last.

One port, methought, alike they sought,
One purpose hold where'er they fare, —
O bounding breeze, O rushing seas!
At last, at last, unite them there.

1843

SAY NOT THE STRUGGLE NOUGHT AVAILETH

Say not the struggle nought availeth,
The labour and the wounds are vain,
The enemy faints not, nor faileth,
And as things have been they remain.

If hopes were dupes, fears may be liars;
It may be, in yon smoke concealed,
Your comrades chase e'en now the fliers,
And, but for you, possess the field.

For while the tired waves, vainly breaking,
Seem here no painful inch to gain,
Far back, through creeks and inlets making,
Comes silent, flooding in, the main.

And not by eastern windows only,
When daylight comes, comes in the light,
In front, the sun climbs slow, how slowly,
But westward, look, the land is bright.

1862

Charles Kingsley (1819–1875)

THE SANDS OF DEE

'O Mary, go and call the cattle home,
And call the cattle home,
And call the cattle home
Across the sands of Dee';
The western wind was wild and dank with foam,
And all alone went she.

The western tide crept up along the sand,
And o'er and o'er the sand,
And round and round the sand,
As far as eye could see.
The rolling mist came down and hid the land:
And never home came she.

'Oh! is it weed, or fish, or floating hair —
A tress of golden hair,
A drownèd maiden's hair
Above the nets at sea?
Was never salmon yet that shone so fair
Among the stakes on Dee.'

They rowed her in across the rolling foam,
The cruel crawling foam,
The cruel hungry foam,
To her grave beside the sea:
But still the boatmen hear her call the cattle home
Across the sands of Dee.

1849

THE THREE FISHERS

Three fishers went sailing away to the West,
Away to the West as the sun went down;
Each thought on the woman who loved him the best,
And the children stood watching them out of the town;

For men must work, and women must weep,
And there 's little to earn, and many to keep,
Though the harbour bar be moaning.

Three wives sat up in the lighthouse tower,
And they trimmed the lamps as the sun went down;
They looked at the squall, and they looked at the shower,
And the night-rack came rolling up ragged and brown.
But men must work, and women must weep,
Though storms be sudden, and waters deep,
And the harbour bar be moaning.

Three corpses lay out on the shining sands
In the morning gleam as the tide went down,
And the women are weeping and wringing their hands
For those who will never come home to the town;
For men must work, and women must weep,
And the sooner it 's over, the sooner to sleep;
And good-bye to the bar and its moaning.

1851

WHEN ALL THE WORLD IS YOUNG

When all the world is young, lad,
And all the trees are green;
And every goose a swan, lad,
And every lass a queen;
Then hey for boot and horse, lad,
And round the world away;
Young blood must have its course, lad,
And every dog his day.

When all the world is old, lad,
And all the trees are brown;
And all the sport is stale, lad,
And all the wheels run down;
Creep home, and take your place there,
The spent and maimed among:
God grant you find one face there,
You loved when all was young.

1863

Sydney Dobell (1824–1874)

AMERICA

I

Men say, Columbia, we shall hear thy guns.
But in what tongue shall be thy battle-cry?
Not that our sires did love in years gone by,
When all the Pilgrim Fathers were little sons
In merrie homes of Englaunde? Back, and see
Thy satchelled ancestor! Behold, he runs
To mine, and, clasped, they tread the equal lea
To the same village-school, where side by side
They spell 'our Father.' Hard by, the twin-pride
Of that grey hall whose ancient oriel gleams
Through yon baronial pines, with looks of light
Our sister-mothers sit beneath one tree.
Meanwhile our Shakspere wanders past and dreams
His Helena and Hermia. Shall we fight?

II

Nor force nor fraud shall sunder us! O ye
Who north or south, on east or western land,
Native to noble sounds, say truth for truth,
Freedom for freedom, love for love, and God
For God; O ye who in eternal youth
Speak with a living and creative flood
This universal English, and do stand
Its breathing book; live worthy of that grand
Heroic utterance — parted, yet a whole,
Far, yet unsevered, — children brave and free
Of the great Mother-tongue, and ye shall be
Lords of an Empire wide as Shakspere's soul,
Sublime as Milton's immemorial theme,
And rich as Chaucer's speech, and fair as Spenser's dream.

1855

THE SAILOR'S RETURN

This morn I lay a-dreaming,
This morn, this merry morn,
When the cock crew shrill from over the hill,
I heard a bugle horn.

And through the dream I was dreaming,
There sighed the sigh of the sea,
And through the dream I was dreaming,
This voice came singing to me.

'High over the breakers,
Low under the lee,
Sing ho
The billow,
And the lash of the rolling sea!

'Boat, boat, to the billow,
Boat, boat, to the lee!
Love, on thy pillow,
Art thou dreaming of me?

'Billow, billow, breaking,
Land us low on the lee!
For, sleeping or waking,
Sweet love, I am coming to thee!

'High, high, o'er the breakers,
Low, low, on the lee,
Sing ho!
The billow
That brings me back to thee!'

1856

HOME, WOUNDED

Wheel me into the sunshine,
Wheel me into the shadow,
There must be leaves on the woodbine,
Is the king-cup crowned in the meadow?

Wheel me down to the meadow,
Down to the little river,
In sun or in shadow
I shall not dazzle or shiver,
I shall be happy anywhere,
Every breath of the morning air
Makes me throb and quiver.

Stay wherever you will,
By the mount or under the hill,
Or down by the little river:
Stay as long as you please,
Give me only a bid from the trees,
Or a blade of grass in morning dew,
Or a cloudy violet clearing to blue,
I could look on it for ever.

Wheel, wheel through the sunshine,
Wheel, wheel through the shadow;
There must be odours round the pine,
There must be balm of breathing kine
Somewhere down in the meadow.
Must I choose? Then anchor me there
Beyond the beckoning poplars, where
The larch is snooding her flowery hair
With wreaths of morning shadow.

Among the thicket hazels of the brake
Perchance some nightingale doth shake
His feathers, and the air is full of song;
In those old days when I was young and strong,
He used to sing on yonder garden tree,
Beside the nursery.
Ah, I remember how I loved to wake,
And find him singing on the self-same bough
(I know it even now)
Where, since the flit of bat,
In ceaseless voice he sat,
Trying the spring night over, like a tune,
Beneath the vernal moon;
And while I listed long,
Day rose, and still he sang,
And all his stanchless song,
As something falling unaware,
Fell out of the tall trees he sang among,
Fell ringing down the ringing morn, and rang —
Rang like a golden jewel down a golden stair.
Is it too early? I hope not.
But wheel me to the ancient oak,
On this side of the meadow;
Let me hear the raven's croak
Loosened to an amorous note
In the hollow shadow.
Let me see the winter snake
Thawing all his frozen rings
On the bank where the wren sings.
Let me hear the little bell,
Where the red-wing, top-mast high,
Looks towards the northern sky,
And jangles his farewell.
Let us rest by the ancient oak,
And see his net of shadow,
His net of barren shadow,
Like those wrestlers' nets of old,
Hold the winter dead and cold,
Hoary winter, white and cold,
While all is green in the meadow.

And when you 've rested, brother mine,
Take me over the meadow;
Take me along the level crown
Of the bare and silent down,
And stop by the ruined tower.
On its green scarp, by and by,
I shall smell the flowering thyme,
On its wall the wall-flower.

In the tower there used to be
A solitary tree.
Take me there, for the dear sake
Of those old days wherein I loved to lie
And pull the melilote,
And look across the valley to the sky,
And hear the joy that filled the warm wide hour
Bubble from the thrush's throat,
As into a shining mere
Rills some rillet trebling clear,
And speaks the silent silver of the lake
There mid cloistering tree-roots, year by year,
The hen-thrush sat, and he, her lief and dear,
Among the boughs did make
A ceaseless music of her married time,

And all the ancient stones grew sweet to hear,
And answered him in the unspoken rhyme
Of gracious forms most musical
That tremble on the wall
And trim its age with airy fantasies
That flicker in the sun, and hardly seem
As if to be beheld were all,
And only to our eyes
They rise and fall,
And fall and rise,
Sink down like silence, or a-sudden stream
As wind-blown on the wind, as streams a wedding-chime.

But you are wheeling me while I dream,
And we 've almost reached the meadow!
You may wheel me fast through the sunshine,
You may wheel me fast through the shadow,
But wheel me slowly, brother mine,
Through the green of the sappy meadow;
For the sun, these days have been so fine,
Must have touched it over with celandine,
And the southern hawthorn, I divine,
Sheds a muffled shadow.

There blows
The first primrose,
Under the bare bank roses:
There is but one,
And the bank is brown,
But soon the children will come down,
The ringing children come singing down,
To pick their Easter posies,
And they 'll spy it out, my beautiful,
Among the bare brier-roses;
And when I sit here again alone,
The bare brown bank will be blind and dull,
Alas for Easter posies!
But when the din is over and gone,
Like an eye that opens after pain,
I shall see my pale flower shining again;
Like a fair star after a gust of rain
I shall see my pale flower shining again;
Like a glow-worm after the rolling wain
Hath shaken darkness down the lane
I shall see my pale flower shining again;
And it will blow here for two months more,
And it will blow here again next year,
And the year past that, and the year beyond;
And through all the years till my years are o'er
I shall always find it here.
Shining across from the bank above,
Shining up from the pond below,
Ere a water-fly wimple the silent pond,
Or the first green weed appear.
And I shall sit here under the tree,
And as each slow bud uncloses,
I shall see it brighten and brighten to me,
From among the leafing brier-roses,
The leaning leafing roses,
As at eve the leafing shadows grow,
And the star of light and love
Draweth near o'er her airy glades,
Draweth near through her heavenly shades,
As a maid through a myrtle grove.
And the flowers will multiply,
As the stars come blossoming over the sky,
The bank will blossom, the waters blow,
Till the singing children hitherward hie
To gather May-day posies;
And the bank will be bare wherever they go,
As dawn, the primrose-girl, goes by,
And alas for heaven's primroses!

Blare the trumpet, and boom the gun,
But, oh, to sit here thus in the sun,
To sit here, feeling my work is done,
While the sands of life so golden run,
And I watch the children's posies,
And my idle heart is whispering,
'Bring whatever the years may bring,
The flowers will blossom, the birds will sing,
And there 'll always be primroses.'

Looking before me here in the sun,
I see the Aprils one after one,
Primrosed Aprils one by one,
Primrosed Aprils on and on,
Till the floating prospect closes
In golden glimmers that rise and rise,
And perhaps are gleams of Paradise,
And perhaps — too far for mortal eyes —
New years of fresh primroses,
Years of earth's primroses,
Springs to be, and springs for me
Of distant dim primroses.

My soul lies out like a basking hound,
A hound that dreams and dozes;
Along my life my length I lay,
I fill to-morrow and yesterday,
I am warm with the suns that have long since set,
I am warm with the summers that are not yet,
And like one who dreams and dozes
Softly afloat on a sunny sea,
Two worlds are whispering over me,
And there blows a wind of roses
From the backward shore to the shore before,
From the shore before to the backward shore,
And like two clouds that meet and pour
Each through each, till core in core

A single self reposes,
The nevermore with the evermore
Above me mingles and closes:
As my soul lies out like the basking
hound,
And wherever it lies seems happy ground,
And when, awakened by some sweet sound,
A dreamy eye uncloses,
I see a blooming world around,
And I lie amid primroses —
Years of sweet primroses,
Springs of fresh primroses,
Springs to be, and springs for me
Of distant dim primroses.

Oh to lie a-dream, a-dream,
To feel I may dream and to know you deem
My work is done for ever,
And the palpitating fever
That gains and loses, loses and gains,
And beats the hurrying blood on the brunt of
a thousand pains
Cooled at once by that blood-let
Upon the parapet;
And all the tedious taskèd toil of the difficult
long endeavour
Solved and quit by no more fine
Than these limbs of mine,
Spanned and measured once for all
By that right hand I lost,
Bought up at so light a cost
As one bloody fall
On the soldier's bed,
And three days on the ruined wall
Among the thirstless dead.
Oh to think my name is crost
From duty's muster-roll;
That I may slumber though the clarion
call,
And live the joy of an embodied soul
Free as a liberated ghost.

Oh to feel a life of deed
Was emptied out to feed
That fire of pain that burned so brief a
while —
That fire from which I come, as the dead
come
Forth from the irreparable tomb,
Or as a martyr on his funeral pile
Heaps up the burdens other men do bear
Through years of segregated care,
And takes the total load
Upon his shoulders broad,
And steps from earth to God.

Oh to think, through good or ill,
Whatever I am you'll love me still;
Oh to think, though dull I be,
You that are so grand and free,
You that are so bright and gay,
Will pause to hear me when I will,
As though my head were grey;
And though there's little I can say,
Each will look kind with honour while he
hears.
And to your loving ears
My thoughts will halt with honourable scars,
And when my dark voice stumbles with the
weight
Of what it doth relate
(Like that blind comrade — blinded in the
wars —
Who bore the one-eyed brother that was
lame),
You'll remember, 't is the same
That cried 'Follow me,'
Upon a summer's day;
And I shall understand with unshed tears
This great reverence that I see,
And bless the day — and Thee,
Lord God of victory!

And she,
Perhaps, oh, even she
May look as she looked when I knew her
In those old days of childish sooth,
Ere my boyhood dared to woo her.
I will not seek nor sue her,
For I'm neither fonder nor truer
Than when she slighted my love-lorn youth,
My giftless, graceless, guinealess truth,
And I only lived to rue her.
But I'll never love another,
And, in spite of her lovers and lands,
She shall love me yet, my brother!
As a child that holds by his mother,
While his mother speaks his praises,
Holds with eager hands,
And ruddy and silent stands
In the ruddy and silent daisies,
And hears her bless her boy,
And lifts a wondering joy,
So I'll not seek nor sue her,
But I'll leave my glory to woo her,
And I'll stand like a child beside,
And from behind the purple pride
I'll lift my eyes unto her,
And I shall not be denied.
And you will love her, brother dear,
And perhaps next year you'll bring me here
All through the balmy April-tide,
And she will trip like spring by my side,
And be all the birds to my ear.
And here all three we'll sit in the sun,
And see the Aprils one by one,
Primrosed Aprils on and on,
Till the floating prospect closes
In golden glimmers that rise and rise,

And perhaps are gleams of Paradise,
And perhaps, too far for mortal eyes,
New springs of fresh primroses,
Springs of earth's primroses,
Springs to be and springs to me,
Of distant dim primroses.

1856

A NUPTIAL EVE (Keith of Ravelston)

Oh, happy, happy maid,
In the year of war and death
She wears no sorrow!
By her face so young and fair,
By the happy wreath
That rules her happy hair,
She might be a bride to-morrow!
She sits and sings within her moonlit bower,
Her moonlit bower in rosy June,
Yet, ah, her bridal breath,
Like fragrance from some sweet high-blowing flower,
Moves from her moving lips in many a mournful tune!
She sings no song of love's despair,
She sings no lover lowly laid,
No fond peculiar grief
Has ever touched or bud or leaf
Of her unblighted spring.
She sings because she needs must sing:
She sings the sorrow of the air
Whereof her voice is made.
That night in Britain howso'er
On any chords the finger strayed,
They gave the notes of care.
A dim sad legend old
Long since in some pale shade
Of some fair twilight told,
She knows not when or where,
She sings, with trembling hand on trembling lute-strings laid: —

The murmur of the mourning ghost
That keeps the shadowy kine,
'Oh, Keith of Ravelston,
The sorrows of thy line!'

Ravelston, Ravelston,
The merry path that leads
Down the golden morning hill,
And through the silver meads;

Ravelston, Ravelston,
The stile beneath the tree,
The maid that kept her mother's kine,
The song that sang she!

She sang her song, she kept her kine,
She sat beneath the thorn,
When Andrew Keith of Ravelston
Rode through the Monday morn.

His henchmen sing, his hawk-bells ring,
His belted jewels shine!
Oh, Keith of Ravelston,
The sorrows of thy line!

Year after year, where Andrew came,
Comes evening down the glade,
And still there sits a moonshine ghost
Where sat the sunshine maid.

Her misty hair is faint and fair,
She keeps the shadowy kine;
Oh, Keith of Ravelston,
The sorrows of thy line!

I lay my hand upon the stile,
The stile is lone and cold,
The burnie that goes babbling by
Says nought that can be told.

Yet, stranger! here, from year to year,
She keeps her shadowy kine;
Oh, Keith of Ravelston,
The sorrows of thy line!

Step out three steps, where Andrew stood —
Why blanch thy cheeks for fear?
The ancient stile is not alone,
'T is not the burn I hear!

She makes her immemorial moan,
She keeps her shadowy kine;
Oh, Keith of Ravelston,
The sorrows of thy line!

1856

FAREWELL

Hear me, hear me, now!
By this heaven less pure than thou,
Fare thee well!
By this living light,
Less bright,
Fare thee well!

By the boundless sea
Of mine agony,
Fare thee well!
That unfathomed sea
Which must roll from me to thee,
Must roll from thee to me,
Fare thee well!

By the tears that I have bled for thee,
Farewell!
By the life's-blood I will shed for thee,
Farewell!

By that field of death and fear
Where I 'll fight with sword and spear
The fight I 'm fighting here,
Fare thee well!

By a form amid the storm,
Fare thee well!
By a sigh above the cry,
Fare thee well!
By the war-cloud and the shout
That shall wrap me round about,
But can never shut thee out,
Fare thee well!

By the wild and bloody close,
When I loose this hell of woes,
And these fires shall eat our foes,
Fare thee well!

By all thou 'lt not forget,
Fare thee well!
By the joy when first we met,
Fare thee well!

By the mighty love and pain
Of the frantic arms that strain
What they ne'er shall clasp again,
Fare thee well!

By the bliss of our first kiss,
Fare thee well!
By the locked love of our last,
Till a passion like a blast
Tore the future from the past,
Fare thee well!

By the nights that I shall weep for thee,
Farewell!
By the vigils I shall keep for thee,
Farewell!
By the memories that will beam of thee,
Farewell!
By the dreams that I shall dream of thee,
Farewell!

By the passion when I wake
Of this heart that will not break,
That can bleed, but cannot break,
Fare thee well!

By that holier woe of thine,
Fare thee well!
By thy love more pure than mine,
Fare thee well!

By the days thou shalt hold dear for me,
The lone life thou shalt bear for me,
The grey hairs thou shalt wear for me,
Farewell!

By thy good deeds offered up for me,
Farewell!
When thou fillest the wanderer's cup for me,
Farewell!
When thou givest the hungry bread for me,
Farewell!
When thou watchest by the dead for me,
Farewell!

By the faith of thy pure eyes,
By the hopes that shall arise
Day and night to the deaf skies,
Fare thee well!

By that faith I cannot share,
Fare thee well!
By this hopeless heart's despair,
Fare thee well!

By the days I have been glad for thee,
The years I shall be sad for thee,
The hours I shall be mad for thee,
Farewell!

1856

Edward Fitzgerald (1809-1883)

THE RUBÁIYÁT OF OMAR KHAYYÁM

WAKE! For the Sun who scattered into flight
The Stars before him from the Field of Night,
Drives Night along with them from Heav'n and strikes
The Sultán's Turret with a Shaft of Light.

Before the phantom of False morning died,
Methought a Voice within the Tavern cried,
'When all the Temple is prepared within,
Why nods the drowsy Worshipper outside?'

And, as the cock crew, those who stood before
The Tavern shouted—'Open then the Door!
You know how little while we have to stay,
And, once departed, may return no more.'

Now the New Year reviving old Desires,
The thoughtful Soul to Solitude retires,
Where the WHITE HAND OF MOSES on the Bough
Puts out, and Jesus from the Ground suspires.

Iram indeed is gone with all his Rose,
And Jamshyd's Sev'n-ringed Cup where no one knows;
But still a Ruby kindles in the Vine,
And many a Garden by the Water blows.

And David's lips are lockt; but in divine
High-piping Pehleví, with 'Wine! Wine! Wine!
Red Wine!' — the Nightingale cries to the Rose
That sallow cheek of hers to incarnadine.

Come, fill the Cup, and in the fire of Spring
Your Winter-garment of Repentance fling:
The Bird of Time has but a little way
To flutter — and the Bird is on the Wing.

Whether at Naishápúr or Babylon,
Whether the Cup with sweet or bitter run,
The Wine of Life keeps oozing drop by drop,
The Leaves of Life keep falling one by one.

Each morn a thousand Roses brings, you say:
Yes, but where leaves the Rose of Yester-day?
And this first Summer month that brings the Rose
Shall take Jamshyd and Kaikobád away.

Well, let it take them! What have we to do
With Kaikobád the Great, or Kaikhosrú?
Let Zál and Rustum bluster as they will,
Or Hátim call to supper — heed not you.

With me along the strip of Herbage strown
That just divides the desert from the sown,
Where name of Slave and Sultán is for-got —
And Peace to Mahmúd on his golden Throne!

A Book of Verses underneath the Bough,
A Jug of Wine, a Loaf of Bread — and Thou
Beside me singing in the Wilderness —
Oh, Wilderness were Paradise enow!

Some for the Glories of This World; and some
Sigh for the Prophet's Paradise to come;
Ah, take the Cash, and let the Credit go,
Nor heed the rumble of a distant Drum!

Look to the blowing Rose about us — 'Lo,
Laughing,' she says, 'into the world I blow,
At once the silken tassel of my Purse
Tear, and its Treasure on the Garden throw.'

And those who husbanded the Golden grain,
And those who flung it to the winds like Rain,
Alike to no such aureate Earth are turned
As, buried once, Men want dug up again.

The Worldly Hope men set their Hearts upon
Turns Ashes — or it prospers; and anon,
Like Snow upon the Desert's dusty Face,
Lighting a little hour or two — is gone.

Think, in this battered Caravanserai
Whose Portals are alternate Night and Day,
How Sultán after Sultán with his Pomp
Abode his destined Hour, and went his way.

They say the Lion and the Lizard keep
The Courts where Jamshyd gloried and drank deep:
And Bahrám, that great Hunter — the Wild Ass
Stamps o'er his Head, but cannot break his Sleep.

I sometimes think that never blows so red
The Rose as where some buried Cæsar bled;
That every Hyacinth the Garden wears
Dropt in her Lap from some once lovely Head.

And this reviving Herb whose tender Green
Fledges the River-Lip on which we lean —
Ah, lean upon it lightly! for who knows
From what once lovely Lip it springs un-seen!

Ah, my Belovèd, fill the Cup that clears
TO-DAY of past Regret and future Fears:
To-morrow! — Why, To-morrow I may be
Myself with Yesterday's Sev'n thousand Years.

For some we loved, the loveliest and the best
That from his Vintage rolling Time hath prest,
Have drunk their Cup a Round or two before,
And one by one crept silently to rest.

And we, that now make merry in the Room
They left, and Summer dresses in new bloom,
Ourselves must we beneath the Couch of Earth
Descend — ourselves to make a Couch — for whom?

Ah, make the most of what we yet may spend,
Before we too into the Dust descend;
Dust into Dust, and under Dust to lie,
Sans Wine, sans Song, sans Singer, and — sans End!

Alike for those who for TO-DAY prepare,
And those that after some TO-MORROW stare,
A Muezzín from the Tower of Darkness cries,
'Fools, your Reward is neither Here nor There.'

Why, all the Saints and Sages who discussed
Of the Two Worlds so wisely — they are thrust
Like foolish Prophets forth; their Words to Scorn
Are scattered, and their Mouths are stopt with Dust.

Myself when young did eagerly frequent
Doctor and Saint, and heard great argument
About it and about: but evermore
Came out by the same Door where in I went.

With them the seed of Wisdom did I sow,
And with mine own hand wrought to make it grow;
And this was all the Harvest that I reaped —
'I came like Water, and like Wind I go.'

Into this Universe, and *Why* not knowing
Nor *Whence*, like Water willy-nilly flowing;
And out of it, as Wind along the Waste,
I know not *Whither*, willy-nilly blowing.

What, without asking, hither hurried *Whence?*
And, without asking, *Whither* hurried hence!
Oh, many a Cup of this forbidden Wine
Must drown the memory of that insolence!

Up from Earth's Centre through the Seventh Gate
I rose, and on the Throne of Saturn sate,
And many a Knot unraveled by the Road;
But not the Master-knot of Human Fate.

There was the Door to which I found no Key;
There was the Veil through which I might not see:
Some little talk awhile of ME and THEE
There was — and then no more of THEE and ME.

Earth could not answer; nor the Seas that mourn
In flowing Purple, of their Lord forlorn;
Nor rolling Heaven, with all his Signs revealed
And hidden by the sleeve of Night and Morn.

Then of the THEE IN ME who works behind
The Veil, I lifted up my hands to find
A Lamp amid the Darkness; and I heard,
As from Without — 'THE ME WITHIN THEE BLIND!'

Then to the Lip of this poor earthen Urn
I leaned, the Secret of my Life to learn:
And Lip to Lip it murmured — 'While you live,
Drink! — for, once dead, you never shall return.'

I think the Vessel, that with fugitive
Articulation answered, once did live,
And drink; and Ah! the passive Lip I kissed,
How many Kisses might it take — and give!

For I remember stopping by the way
To watch a Potter thumping his wet Clay:
And with its all-obliterated Tongue
It murmured — 'Gently, Brother, gently, pray!'

And has not such a Story from of Old
Down Man's successive generations rolled
Of such a clod of saturated Earth
Cast by the Maker into Human mould?

And not a drop that from our Cups we throw
For Earth to drink of, but may steal below
To quench the fire of Anguish in some Eye
There hidden — far beneath, and long ago.

As then the Tulip for her morning sup
Of Heav'nly Vintage from the soil looks up,
Do you devoutly do the like, till Heav'n
To Earth invert you — like an empty Cup.

Perplext no more with Human or Divine,
To-morrow's tangle to the winds resign,
And lose your fingers in the tresses of
The Cypress-slender Minister of Wine.

And if the Wine you drink, the Lip you press,
End in what All begins and ends in — Yes;
Think then you are TO-DAY what YESTERDAY
You were — TO-MORROW you shall not be less.

So when the Angel of the darker Drink
At last shall find you by the river-brink,
And offering his Cup, invite your Soul
Forth to your Lips to quaff — you shall not shrink.

Why, if the Soul can fling the Dust aside,
And naked on the Air of Heaven ride,
Were 't not a Shame — were 't not a Shame for him
In this clay carcase crippled to abide?

'T is but a Tent where takes his one day's rest
A Sultán to the realm of Death addrest;
The Sultán rises, and the dark Ferrásh
Strikes, and prepares it for another Guest.

And fear not lest Existence closing your
Account, and mine, should know the like no more;
The Eternal Sákí from the Bowl has poured
Millions of Bubbles like us, and will pour.

When You and I behind the Veil are past,
Oh, but the long, long while the World shall last,
Which of our Coming and Departure heeds
As the Sea's self should heed a pebble-cast.

A Moment's Halt — a momentary taste
Of Being from the Well amid the Waste —
And Lo! — the phantom Caravan has reached
The Nothing it set out from — Oh, make haste!

Would you that spangle of Existence spend
About the secret — quick about it, Friend!
A Hair perhaps divides the False and True —
And upon what, prithee, does life depend?

A Hair perhaps divides the False and True;
Yes; and a single Alif were the clue —
Could you but find it — to the Treasure-house,
And peradventure to The Master too;

Whose secret Presence, through Creation's veins
Running Quicksilver-like, eludes your pains;
Taking all shapes from Máh to Máhi; and
They change and perish all — but He remains;

A moment guessed — then back behind the Fold
Immerst of Darkness round the Drama rolled
Which, for the Pastime of Eternity,
He doth himself contrive, enact, behold.

But if in vain, down on the stubborn floor
Of Earth, and up to Heav'n's unopening Door,
You gaze To-day, while You are You — how then
To-morrow, when You shall be You no more?

Waste not your Hour, nor in the vain pursuit
Of This and That endeavour and dispute;
Better be jocund with the fruitful Grape
Than sadden after none, or bitter, Fruit.

You know, my Friends, with what a brave Carouse
I made a Second Marriage in my house;
Divorced old barren Reason from my Bed,
And took the Daughter of the Vine to Spouse.

For 'Is' and 'Is-not' though with Rule and Line
And 'Up-and-down' by Logic I define,
Of all that one should care to fathom, I
Was never deep in anything but — Wine.

Ah, but my Computations, People say,
Reduced the Year to better reckoning? — Nay,
'T was only striking from the Calendar
Unborn To-morrow, and dead Yesterday.

And lately, by the Tavern Door agape,
Came shining through the Dusk an Angel Shape
Bearing a Vessel on his Shoulder; and
He bid me taste of it; and 't was — the Grape!

The Grape that can with Logic Absolute
The Two and Seventy jarring Sects confute:
The sovereign Alchemist that in a trice
Life's leaden metal into Gold transmute:

The mighty Mahmúd, Allah-breathing Lord,
That all the misbelieving and black Horde
Of Fears and Sorrows that infest the Soul
Scatters before him with his whirlwind Sword.

Why, be this Juice the growth of God, who dare
Blaspheme the twisted tendril as a Snare?
A Blessing, we should use it, should we not?
And if a Curse — why, then, Who set it there?

I must abjure the Balm of Life, I must,
Scared by some After-reckoning ta'en on trust,
Or lured with Hope of some Diviner Drink,
To fill the Cup — when crumbled into Dust!

Oh threats of Hell and Hopes of Paradise!
One thing at least is certain — *This* Life flies;

One thing is certain and the rest is Lies;
The Flower that once has blown for ever dies.

Strange, is it not? that of the myriads who
Before us passed the door of Darkness through,
Not one returns to tell us of the Road,
Which to discover we must travel too.

The Revelations of Devout and Learned
Who rose before us, and as Prophets burned,
Are all but Stories, which, awoke from Sleep
They told their comrades, and to Sleep returned.

I sent my soul through the Invisible,
Some letter of that After-life to spell:
And by and by my Soul returned to me,
And answered 'I Myself am Heav'n and Hell':

Heav'n but the Vision of fulfilled Desire,
And Hell the Shadow from a Soul on fire,
Cast on the Darkness into which Ourselves,
So late emerged from, shall so soon expire.

We are no other than a moving row
Of Magic Shadow-shapes that come and go
Round with the Sun-illumined Lantern held
In Midnight by the Master of the Show;

But helpless Pieces of the Game He plays
Upon this Checker-board of Nights and Days;
Hither and thither moves, and checks, and slays,
And one by one back in the Closet lays.

The Ball no question makes of Ayes and Noes,
But Here or There as strikes the Player goes;
And He that tossed you down into the Field,
He knows about it all — HE knows — HE knows!

The Moving Finger writes; and, having writ,
Moves on: nor all your Piety nor Wit
Shall lure it back to cancel half a Line,
Nor all your Tears wash out a Word of it.

And that inverted Bowl they call the Sky,
Whereunder crawling cooped we live and die,
Lift not your hands to *It* for help — for It
As impotently moves as you or I.

With Earth's first Clay They did the Last Man knead,
And there of the Last Harvest sowed the Seed:
And the first Morning of Creation wrote
What the Last Dawn of Reckoning shall read.

YESTERDAY *This* Day's Madness did prepare;
TO-MORROW's Silence, Triumph, or Despair:
Drink! for you know not whence you came, nor why:
Drink! for you know not why you go, nor where.

I tell you this — When, started from the Goal,
Over the flaming shoulders of the Foal,
Of Heav'n Parwin and Mushtarí they flung,
In my predestined Plot of Dust and Soul

The Vine had struck a fibre: which about
If clings my Being — let the Dervish flout;
Of my Base metal may be filed a Key
That shall unlock the Door he howls without.

And this I know: whether the one True Light
Kindle to Love, or Wrath consume me quite,
One Flash of It within the Tavern caught
Better than in the Temple lost outright.

What! out of senseless Nothing to provoke
A conscious Something to resent the yoke
Of unpermitted Pleasure, under pain
Of Everlasting Penalties, if broke!

What! from his helpless Creature be repaid
Pure Gold for what he lent him dross-allayed —
Sue for a Debt we never did contract,
And cannot answer — Oh the sorry trade!

O Thou, who didst with pitfall and with gin
Beset the Road I was to wander in,
Thou wilt not with Predestined Evil round
Enmesh, and then impute my Fall to Sin!

Oh Thou, who Man of Baser Earth didst make,
And ev'n with Paradise devise the Snake:
For all the Sin wherewith the Face of Man
Is blackened — Man's forgiveness give — and take!

. . . .

As under cover of departing Day
Slunk hunger-stricken Ramazán away,
Once more within the Potter's house alone
I stood, surrounded by the Shapes of Clay.

Shapes of all Sorts and Sizes, great and small,
That stood along the floor and by the wall;
And some loquacious Vessels were; and some
Listened perhaps, but never talked at all.

Said one among them — 'Surely not in vain
My substance of the common Earth was ta'en
And to this Figure moulded, to be broke,
Or trampled back to shapeless Earth again.'

Then said a Second — 'Ne'er a peevish Boy
Would break the Bowl from which he drank in joy;
And He that with his hand the Vessel made
Will surely not in after Wrath destroy.'

After a momentary silence spake
Some Vessel of a more ungainly Make;
'They sneer at me for leaning all awry:
What! did the Hand then of the Potter shake?'

Whereat someone of the loquacious Lot —
I think a Súfi pipkin — waxing hot —
'All this of Pot and Potter — Tell me then,
Who is the Potter, pray, and who the Pot?'

'Why,' said another, 'Some there are who tell
Of one who threatens he will toss to Hell
The luckless Pots he marred in making — Pish!
He 's a Good Fellow, and 't will all be well.'

'Well,' murmured one, 'Let whoso make or buy,
My Clay with long Oblivion is gone dry:
But fill me with the old familiar Juice,
Methinks I might recover by and by.'

So while the Vessels one by one were speaking,
The little Moon looked in that all were seeking:
And then they jogged each other, 'Brother! Brother!
Now for the Porter's shoulder-knot a-creaking!'

. . . .

Ah, with the Grape my fading Life provide,
And wash the Body whence the Life has died,
And lay me, shrouded in the living Leaf,
By some not unfrequented Garden-side.

That ev'n my buried Ashes such a snare
Of Vintage shall fling up into the Air
As not a True believer passing by
But shall be overtaken unaware.
Indeed the Idols I have loved so long
Have done my credit in this World much wrong:
Have drowned my Glory in a shallow Cup,
And sold my Reputation for a Song.

Indeed, indeed, Repentance oft before
I swore — but was I sober when I swore?
And then and then came Spring, and Rose-in-hand
My thread-bare Penitence apieces tore.

And much as Wine has played the Infidel,
And robbed me of my Robe of Honour — Well,
I wonder often what the Vintners buy,
One-half so precious as the stuff they sell.

Yet Ah, that Spring should vanish with the Rose!
That Youth's sweet scented manuscript should close!
The Nightingale that in the branches sang,
Ah whence, and whither flown again, who knows!

Would but the Desert of the Fountain yield
One glimpse — if dimly, yet indeed, revealed,
To which the fainting Traveler might spring,
As springs the trampled herbage of the field!

Would but some wingèd Angel ere too late
Arrest the yet unfolded Roll of Fate,
And made the stern Recorder otherwise
Enregister, or quite obliterate!

Ah Love! could you and I with Him conspire
To grasp this sorry Scheme of Things entire,
Would not we shatter it to bits — and then
Remould it nearer to the Heart's Desire!

. . . .

Yon rising Moon that looks for us again —
How oft hereafter will she wax and wane;
How oft hereafter rising look for us
Through this same Garden — and for *one* in vain!

And when like her, O Sáki, you shall pass
Among the Guests Star-scattered on the Grass,
And in your joyous errand reach the spot
Where I made One — turn down an empty Glass!

1859, 1879

Christina Rossetti * (1830-1894)

SONG

When I am dead, my dearest,
Sing no sad songs for me;
Plant thou no roses at my head,
Nor shady cypress-tree:
Be the green grass above me
With showers and dewdrops wet:
And if thou wilt, remember,
And if thou wilt, forget.

I shall not see the shadows,
I shall not feel the rain;
I shall not hear the nightingale
Sing on, as if in pain:
And dreaming through the twilight
That doth not rise nor set,
Haply I may remember,
And haply may forget.

1862

THREE SEASONS

'A cup for hope!' she said,
In springtime ere the bloom was old;
The crimson wine was poor and cold
By her mouth's richer red.

'A cup for love!' how low,
How soft the words; and all the while
Her blush was rippling with a smile
Like summer after snow.

'A cup for memory!'
Cold cup that one must drain alone:
While autumn winds are up and moan
Across the barren sea.

Hope, memory, love:
Hope for fair morn, and love for day,
And memory for the evening grey
And solitary dove.

1862

UP-HILL

Does the road wind up-hill all the way?
Yes, to the very end.
Will the day's journey take the whole long day?
From morn to night, my friend.

But is there for the night a resting-place?
A roof for when the slow dark hours begin.
May not the darkness hide it from my face?
You cannot miss that inn.

Shall I meet other wayfarers at night?
Those who have gone before.
Then must I knock, or call when just in sight?
They will not keep you standing at that door.

Shall I find comfort, travel-sore and weak?
Of labour you shall find the sum.
Will there be beds for me and all who seek?
Yea, beds for all who come.

1862

THE SUMMER IS ENDED

Wreathe no more lilies in my hair,
For I am dying, Sister sweet:
Or, if you will for the last time
Indeed, why make me fair
Once for my winding-sheet.

Pluck no more roses for my breast,
For I, like them, fade in my prime:
Or, if you will, why pluck them still,
That they may share my rest
Once more for the last time.

Weep not for me when I am gone,
Dear tender one, but hope and smile:
Or, if you cannot choose but weep,
A little while weep on,
Only a little while.

1896

SLEEPING AT LAST

Sleeping at last, the trouble and tumult over,
Sleeping at last, the struggle and horror past,
Cold and white, out of sight of friend and of lover,
Sleeping at last.

No more a tired heart downcast or overcast,
No more pangs that wring or shifting fears that hover,
Sleeping at last in a dreamless sleep locked fast.

*Poetical Works, Globe Edition, The Macmillan Company, 1924. By permission of the Publishers.

Fast asleep. Singing birds in their leafy cover
Cannot wake her, nor shake her the gusty blast.
Under the purple thyme and the purple clover
Sleeping at last.

1896

James Thomson (1834-1882)

THE CITY OF DREADFUL NIGHT

PROEM

Lo, THUS, as prostrate, 'In the dust I write
My heart's deep languor and my soul's sad tears.'
Yet why evoke the spectres of black night
To blot the sunshine of exultant years?
Why disinter dead faith from mouldering hidden?
Why break the seals of mute despair unbidden,
And wail life's discords into careless ears?

Because a cold rage seizes one at whiles
To show the bitter old and wrinkled truth
Stripped naked of all vesture that beguiles,
False dreams, false hopes, false masks and modes of youth;
Because it gives some sense of power and passion
In helpless impotence to try to fashion
Our woe in living words howe'er uncouth.

Surely I write not for the hopeful young,
Or those who deem their happiness of worth,
Or such as pasture and grow fat among
The shows of life and feel nor doubt nor dearth,
Or pious spirits with a God above them
To sanctify and glorify and love them,
Or sages who foresee a heaven on earth.

For none of these I write, and none of these
Could read the writing if they deigned to try:
So may they flourish, in their due degrees,
On our sweet earth and in their unplaced sky.
If any cares for the weak words here written,
It must be some one desolate, Fate-smitten,
Whose faith and hope are dead, and who would die.

Yes, here and there some weary wanderer
In that same city of tremendous night,
Will understand the speech, and feel a stir
Of fellowship in all-disastrous fight;
'I suffer mute and lonely, yet another
Uplifts his voice to let me know a brother
Travels the same wild paths though out of sight.'

O sad Fraternity, do I unfold
Your dolorous mysteries shrouded from of yore?
Nay, be assured; no secret can be told
To any who divined it not before:
None uninitiate by many a presage
Will comprehend the language of the message,
Although proclaimed aloud for evermore.

I

The City is of Night; perchance of Death,
But certainly of Night; for never there
Can come the lucid morning's fragrant breath
After the dewy dawning's cold grey air;
The moon and stars may shine with scorn or pity;
The sun has never visited that city,
For it dissolveth in the daylight fair.

Dissolveth like a dream of night away;
Though present in distempered gloom of thought
And deadly weariness of heart all day.
But when a dream night after night is brought
Throughout a week, and such weeks few or many
Recur each year for several years, can any
Discern that dream from real life in aught?

For life is but a dream whose shapes return,
Some frequently, some seldom, some by night
And some by day, some night and day: we learn,
The while all change and many vanish quite,
In their recurrence with recurrent changes
A certain seeming order; where this ranges
We count things real; such is memory's might.

A river girds the city west and south,
The main north channel of a broad lagoon,
Regurging with the salt tides from the mouth;
Waste marshes shine and glister to the moon

For leagues, then moorland black, then stony ridges;
Great piers and causeways, many noble bridges,
  Connect the town and islet suburbs strewn.

Upon an easy slope it lies at large,
  And scarcely overlaps the long curved crest
Which swells out two leagues, from the river marge.
  A trackless wilderness rolls north and west,
Savannahs, savage woods, enormous mountains,
Bleak uplands, black ravines with torrent fountains;
  And eastward rolls the shipless sea's unrest.

The city is not ruinous, although
  Great ruins of an unremembered past,
With others of a few short years ago
  More sad, are found within its precincts vast.
The street-lamps always burn; but scarce a casement
In house or palace front from roof to basement
  Doth glow or gleam athwart the mirk air cast.

The street-lamps burn amidst the baleful glooms,
  Amidst the soundless solitudes immense
Of rangèd mansions dark and still as tombs.
  The silence which benumbs or strains the sense
Fulfils with awe the soul's despair unweeping:
Myriads of habitants are ever sleeping,
  Or dead, or fled from nameless pestilence!

Yet as in some necropolis you find
  Perchance one mourner to a thousand dead,
So there; worn faces that look deaf and blind
  Like tragic masks of stone. With weary tread,
Each wrapt in his own doom, they wander, wander,
Or sit foredone and desolately ponder
  Through sleepless hours with heavy drooping head.

Mature men chiefly, few in age or youth,
  A woman rarely, now and then a child:
A child! If here the heart turns sick with ruth
  To see a little one from birth defiled,
Or lame or blind, as preordained to languish
Through youthless life, think how it bleeds with anguish
  To meet one erring in that homeless wild.

They often murmur to themselves, they speak
  To one another seldom, for their woe
Broods maddening inwardly and scorns to wreak
  Itself abroad; and if at whiles it grow
To frenzy which must rave, none heeds the clamour,
Unless there waits some victim of like glamour,
  To rave in turn, who lends attentive show.

The City is of Night, but not of Sleep;
  There sweet sleep is not for the weary brain;
The pitiless hours like years and ages creep,
  A night seems termless hell. This dreadful strain
Of thought and consciousness which never ceases,
Or which some moments' stupor but increases,
  This, worse than woe, makes wretches there insane.

They leave all hope behind who enter there:
  One certitude while sane they cannot leave,
One anodyne for torture and despair;
  The certitude of Death, which no reprieve
Can put off long; and which, divinely tender,
But waits the outstretched hand to promptly render
  That draught whose slumber nothing can bereave.

II

Because he seemed to walk with an intent
  I followed him; who shadowlike and frail,
Unswervingly though slowly onward went,
  Regardless, wrapt in thought as in a veil:
Thus step for step with lonely sounding feet
We travelled many a long dim silent street.

At length he paused: a black mass in the gloom
  A tower that merged into the heavy sky;
Around, the huddled stones of grave and tomb:
  Some old God's-acre now corruption's sty:

He murmured to himself with dull despair,
Here Faith died, poisoned by this charnel air.

Then turning to the right went on once more,
And travelled weary roads without suspense;
And reached at last a low wall's open door,
Whose villa gleamed beyond the foliage dense:
He gazed, and muttered with a hard despair,
Here Love died, stabbed by its own worshipped pair.

Then turning to the right resumed his march,
And travelled streets and lanes with wondrous strength,
Until on stooping through a narrow arch
We stood before a squalid house at length:
He gazed, and whispered with a cold despair,
Here Hope died, starved out in its utmost lair.

When he had spoken thus, before he stirred,
I spoke, perplexed by something in the signs
Of desolation I had seen and heard
In this drear pilgrimage to ruined shrines:
When Faith and Love and Hope are dead indeed,
Can Life still live? By what doth it proceed?

As whom his one intense thought overpowers,
He answered coldly, Take a watch, erase
The signs and figures of the circling hours,
Detach the hands, remove the dial-face;
The works proceed until run down; although
Bereft of purpose, void of use, still go.

Then turning to the right paced on again,
And traversed squares and travelled streets whose glooms
Seemed more and more familiar to my ken;
And reached that sullen temple of the tombs;
And paused to murmur with the old despair,
Here Faith died, poisoned by this charnel air.

I ceased to follow, for the knot of doubt
Was severed sharply with a cruel knife:
He circled thus for ever tracing out
The series of the fraction left of Life;
Perpetual recurrence in the scope
Of but three terms, dead Faith, dead Love, dead Hope.

IV

He stood alone within the spacious square
Declaiming from the central grassy mound,
With head uncovered and with streaming hair,
As if large multitudes were gathered round:
A stalwart shape, the gestures full of might,
The glances burning with unnatural light: —

As I came through the desert thus it was,
As I came through the desert: All was black,
In heaven no single star, on earth no track;
A brooding hush without a stir or note,
The air so thick it clotted in my throat;
And thus for hours; then some enormous things
Swooped past with savage cries and clanking wings:
But I strode on austere;
No hope could have no fear.

As I came through the desert thus it was,
As I came through the desert: Eyes of fire
Glared at me throbbing with a starved desire;
The hoarse and heavy and carnivorous breath
Was hot upon me from deep jaws of death;
Sharp claws, swift talons, fleshless fingers cold
Plucked at me from the bushes, tried to hold:
But I strode on austere;
No hope could have no fear.

As I came through the desert thus it was,
As I came through the desert: Lo you, there,
That hillock burning with a brazen glare;
Those myriad dusky flames with points a-glow
Which writhed and hissed and darted to and fro;
A Sabbath of the Serpents, heaped pell-mell
For Devil's roll-call and some *fête* of Hell:
Yet I strode on austere;
No hope could have no fear.

As I came through the desert thus it was,
As I came through the desert: Meteors ran
And crossed their javelins on the black sky-span;

The zenith opened to a gulf of flame,
The dreadful thunderbolts jarred earth's fixed frame:
The ground all heaved in waves of fire that surged
And weltered round me sole there unsubmerged:
Yet I strode on austere;
No hope could have no fear.

As I came through the desert thus it was,
As I came through the desert: Air once more,
And I was close upon a wild sea-shore;
Enormous cliffs arose on either hand,
The deep tide thundered up a league-broad strand;
White foambelts seethed there, wan spray swept and flew;
The sky broke, moon and stars and clouds and blue:
And I strode on austere;
No hope could have no fear.

As I came through the desert thus it was,
As I came through the desert: On the left
The sun arose and crowned a broad crag-cleft;
There stopped and burned out black, except a rim,
A bleeding eyeless socket, red and dim;
Whereon the moon fell suddenly southwest,
And stood above the right-hand cliffs at rest:
Still I strode on austere;
No hope could have no fear.

As I came through the desert thus it was,
As I came through the desert: From the right
A shape came slowly with a ruddy light;
A woman with a red lamp in her hand,
Bareheaded and barefooted on that strand;
O desolation moving with such grace!
O anguish with such beauty in thy face!
I fell as on my bier,
Hope travailed with such fear.

As I came through the desert thus it was,
As I came through the desert: I was twain,
Two selves distinct that cannot join again;
One stood apart and knew but could not stir,
And watched the other stark in swoon and her;
And she came on, and never turned aside,
Between such sun and moon and roaring tide:
And as she came more near
My soul grew mad with fear.

As I came through the desert thus it was,
As I came through the desert: Hell is mild
And piteous matched with that accursèd wild;
A large black sign was on her breast that bowed,
A broad black band ran down her snowwhite shroud;
That lamp she held was her own burning heart,
Whose blood-drops trickled step by step apart;
The mystery was clear;
Mad rage had swallowed fear.

As I came through the desert thus it was,
As I came through the desert: By the sea
She knelt and bent above that senseless me;
Those lamp-drops fell upon my white brow there,
She tried to cleanse them with her tears and hair;
She murmured words of pity, love, and woe,
She heeded not the level rushing flow:
And mad with rage and fear,
I stood stonebound so near.

As I came through the desert thus it was,
As I came through the desert: When the tide
Swept up to her there kneeling by my side,
She clasped that corpse-like me, and they were borne
Away, and this vile me was left forlorn;
I know the whole sea cannot quench that heart,
Or cleanse that brow, or wash those two apart:
They love; their doom is drear,
Yet they nor hope nor fear;
But I, what do I here?

VI

I sat forlornly by the river-side,
And watched the bridge-lamps glow like golden stars
Above the blackness of the swelling tide,
Down which they struck rough gold in ruddier bars;
And heard the heave and plashing of the flow
Against the wall a dozen feet below.

Large elm-trees stood along that river-walk;
And under one, a few steps from my seat,
I heard strange voices join in stranger talk,
Although I had not heard approaching feet;

These bodiless voices in my waking dream
Flowed dark words blending with the sombre stream: —

And you have after all come back; come back.
I was about to follow on your track.
And you have failed: our spark of hope is black.

That I have failed is proved by my return:
The spark is quenched, nor ever more will burn.
But listen: and the story you shall learn.

I reached the portal common spirits fear,
And read the words above it, dark and clear,
'Leave hope behind, all ye who enter here':

And would have passed in, gratified to gain
That positive eternity of pain,
Instead of this insufferable inane.

A demon warder clutched me, Not so fast;
First leave your hopes behind! — But years have passed
Since I left all behind me, to the last:

You cannot count for hope, with all your wit,
This bleak despair that drives me to the Pit:
How could I seek to enter void of it?

He snarled, What thing is this which apes a soul,
And would find entrance to our gulf of dole
Without the payment of the settled toll?

Outside the gate he showed an open chest:
Here pay their entrance fees the souls unblest;
Cast in some hope, you enter with the rest.

This is Pandora's box; whose lid shall shut,
And Hell-gate too, when hopes have filled it; but
They are so thin that it will never glut.

I stood a few steps backwards, desolate;
And watched the spirits pass me to their fate,
And fling off hope, and enter at the gate.

When one casts off a load he springs upright,
Squares back his shoulders, breathes with all his might,
And briskly paces forward strong and light:

But these, as if they took some burden, bowed;
The whole frame sank; however strong and proud
Before, they crept in quite infirm and cowed.

And as they passed me, earnestly from each
A morsel of his hope I did beseech,
To pay my entrance; but all mocked my speech.

Not one would cede a tittle of his store
Though knowing that in instants three or four
He must resign the whole for evermore.

So I returned. Our destiny is fell;
For in this Limbo we must ever dwell,
Shut out alike from Heaven and Earth and Hell.

The others sighed back, Yea; but if we grope
With care through all this Limbo's dreary scope,
We yet may pick up some minute lost hope;

And, sharing it between us, entrance win,
In spite of fiends so jealous for gross sin:
Let us without delay our search begin.

VIII

While I still lingered on that river-walk,
And watched the tide as black as our black doom,
I heard another couple join in talk,
And saw them to the left hand in the gloom
Seated against an elm bole on the ground,
Their eyes intent upon the stream profound.

'I never knew another man on earth
But had some joy and solace in his life,
Some chance of triumph in the dreadful strife:
My doom has been unmitigated dearth.'

'We gaze upon the river, and we note
The various vessels large and small that float,
Ignoring every wrecked and sunken boat.'

'And yet I asked no splendid dower, no spoil
Of sway or fame or rank or even wealth;
But homely love with common food and health,
And nightly sleep to balance daily toil.'

'This all-too humble soul would arrogate
Unto itself some signalising hate
From the supreme indifference of Fate!'

'Who is most wretched in this dolorous place?
I think myself; yet I would rather be
My miserable self than He, than He
Who formed such creatures to His own disgrace.

'The vilest thing must be less vile than Thou
From whom it had its being, God and Lord!
Creator of all woe and sin! abhorred,
Malignant and implacable! I vow

'That not for all Thy power furled and unfurled,
For all the temples to Thy glory built,
Would I assume the ignominious guilt
Of having made such men in such a world.'

'As if a Being, God or Fiend, could reign,
At once so wicked, foolish, and insane,
As to produce men when He might refrain!

'The world rolls round for ever like a mill;
It grinds out death and life and good and ill;
It has no purpose, heart or mind or will.

'While air of Space and Time's full river flow
The mill must blindly whirl unresting so:
It may be wearing out, but who can know?

'Man might know one thing were his sight less dim;
That it whirls not to suit his petty whim,
That it is quite indifferent to him.

'Nay, does it treat him harshly as he saith?
It grinds him some slow years of bitter breath,
Then grinds him back into eternal death.'

X

The mansion stood apart in its own ground;
In front thereof a fragrant garden-lawn,
High trees about it, and the whole walled round:
The massive iron gates were both withdrawn;
And every window of its front shed light,
Portentous in that City of the Night.

But though thus lighted it was deadly still
As all the countless bulks of solid gloom:
Perchance a congregation to fulfil
Solemnities of silence in this doom,
Mysterious rites of dolour and despair
Permitting not a breath of chant or prayer?

Broad steps ascended to a terrace broad
Whereon lay still light from the open door;
The hall was noble, and its aspect awed,
Hung round with heavy black from dome to floor;
And ample stairways rose to left and right
Whose balustrades were also draped with night.

I paced from room to room, from hall to hall,
Nor any life throughout the maze discerned;
But each was hung with its funereal pall,
And held a shrine, around which tapers burned,
With picture or with statue or with bust,
All copied from the same fair form of dust:

A woman very young and very fair;
Beloved by bounteous life and joy and youth,
And loving these sweet lovers, so that care
And age and death seemed not for her in sooth:
Alike as stars, all beautiful and bright,
These shapes lit up that mausolean night.

At length I heard a murmur as of lips,
And reached an open oratory hung
With heaviest blackness of the whole eclipse;
Beneath the dome a fuming censer swung;
And one lay there upon a low white bed,
With tapers burning at the foot and head:

The Lady of the images: supine,
Deathstill, lifesweet, with folded palms she lay:
And kneeling there as at a sacred shrine
A young man wan and worn who seemed to pray;
A crucifix of dim and ghostly white
Surmounted the large altar left in night:—

The chambers of the mansion of my heart,
In every one whereof thine image dwells,
Are black with grief eternal for thy sake.

The inmost oratory of my soul,
Wherein thou ever dwellest quick or dead,
Is black with grief eternal for thy sake.

I kneel beside thee and I clasp the cross
With eyes for ever fixed upon that face,
So beautiful and dreadful in its calm.

I kneel here patient as thou liest there;
As patient as a statue carved in stone,
Of adoration and eternal grief.

Whilst thou dost not awake I cannot move;
And something tells me thou wilt never wake
And I alive feel turning into stone.

Most beautiful were Death to end my grief,
Most hateful to destroy the sight of thee,
Dear vision better than all death or life.

But I renounce all choice of life or death,
For either shall be ever at thy side,
And thus in bliss or woe be ever well.—

He murmured thus and thus in monotone,
  Intent upon that uncorrupted face,
Entranced except his moving lips alone:
  I glided with hushed footsteps from the place.
This was the festival that filled with light
That palace in the City of the Night.

XII

Our isolated units could be brought
  To act together for some common end?
For one by one, each silent with his thought,
  I marked a long loose line approach and wend
Athwart the great cathedral's cloistered square,
And slowly vanish from the moonlit air.

Then I would follow in among the last:
  And in the porch a shrouded figure stood,
Who challenged each one pausing ere he passed,
  With deep eyes burning through a blank white hood:
Whence come you in the world of life and light
To this our City of Tremendous Night?—

From pleading in a senate of rich lords
For some scant justice to our countless hordes
Who toil half-starved with scarce a human right:
I wake from daydreams to this real night.

From wandering through many a solemn scene
Of opium visions, with a heart serene
And intellect miraculously bright:
I wake from daydreams to this real night.

From making hundreds laugh and roar with glee
By my transcendent feats of mimicry,
And humour wanton as an elfish sprite:
I wake from daydreams to this real night.

From prayer and fasting in a lonely cell,
Which brought an ecstasy ineffable
Of love and adoration and delight:
I wake from daydreams to this real night.

From ruling on a splendid kingly throne
A nation which beneath my rule has grown
Year after year in wealth and arts and might:
I wake from daydreams to this real night.

From preaching to an audience fired with faith
The Lamb who died to save our souls from death,
Whose blood hath washed our scarlet sins wool-white:
I wake from daydreams to this real night.

From drinking fiery poison in a den
Crowded with tawdry girls and squalid men,
Who hoarsely laugh and curse and brawl and fight:
I wake from daydreams to this real night.

From picturing with all beauty and all grace
First Eden and the parents of our race,
A luminous rapture unto all men's sight:
I wake from daydreams to this real night.

From writing a great work with patient plan
To justify the ways of God to man,
And show how ill must fade and perish quite:
I wake from daydreams to this real night.

From desperate fighting with a little band
Against the powerful tyrants of our land,
To free our brethren in their own despite:
I wake from daydreams to this real night.

Thus, challenged by that warder sad and stern,
  Each one responded with his countersign,
Then entered the cathedral; and in turn
  I entered also, having given mine;
But lingered near until I heard no more,
And marked the closing of the massive door.

XIV

Large glooms were gathered in the mighty fane,
  With tinted moongleams slanting here and there,
And all was hush: no swelling organ-strain,
  No chant, no voice or murmuring of prayer;
No priests came forth, no tinkling censers fumed,
And the high altar space was unillumed.

Around the pillars and against the walls
  Leaned men and shadows; others seemed to brood
Bent or recumbent in secluded stalls.
  Perchance they were not a great multitude
Save in that city of so lonely streets
Where one may count up every face he meets.

All patiently awaited the event
Without a stir or sound, as if no less
Self-occupied, doomstricken, while attent.
And then we heard a voice of solemn stress
From the dark pulpit, and our gaze there met
Two eyes which burned as never eyes burned yet.

Two steadfast and intolerable eyes
Burning beneath a broad and rugged brow;
The head behind it of enormous size,
And as black fir-groves in a large wind bow,
Our rooted congregation, gloom-arrayed,
By that great sad voice deep and full were swayed: —

O melancholy Brothers, dark, dark, dark!
O battling in black floods without an ark!
O spectral wanderers of unholy Night!
My soul hath bled for you these sunless years,
With bitter blood-drops running down like tears:
Oh, dark, dark, dark, withdrawn from joy and light!

My heart is sick with anguish for your bale!
Your woe hath been my anguish; yea, I quail
And perish in your perishing unblest.
And I have searched the heights and depths, the scope
Of all our universe, with desperate hope
To find some solace for your wild unrest.

And now at last authentic word I bring,
Witnessed by every dead and living thing;
Good tidings of great joy for you, for all:
There is no God; no Fiend with names divine
Made us and tortures us; if we must pine,
It is to satiate no Being's gall.

It was the dark delusion of a dream,
That living Person conscious and supreme,
Whom we must curse for cursing us with life;
Whom we must curse because the life He gave
Could not be buried in the quiet grave,
Could not be killed by poison or by knife.

This little life is all we must endure,
The grave's most holy peace is ever sure,
We fall asleep and never wake again;
Nothing is of us but the mouldering flesh,
Whose elements dissolve and merge afresh
In earth, air, water, plants, and other men.

We finish thus; and all our wretched race
Shall finish with its cycle, and give place
To other beings, with their own time-doom
Infinite æons ere our kind began;
Infinite æons after the last man
Has joined the mammoth in earth's tomb and womb.

We bow down to the universal laws,
Which never had for man a special clause
Of cruelty or kindness, love or hate:
If toads and vultures are obscene to sight,
If tigers burn with beauty and with might,
Is it by favour or by wrath of fate?

All substance lives and struggles evermore
Through countless shapes continually at war,
By countless interactions interknit:
If one is born a certain day on earth,
All times and forces tended to that birth,
Not all the world could change or hinder it.

I find no hint throughout the Universe
Of good or ill, of blessing or of curse;
I find alone Necessity Supreme;
With infinite Mystery, abysmal, dark,
Unlighted ever by the faintest spark
For us the flitting shadows of a dream.

O Brothers of sad lives! they are so brief;
A few short years must bring us all relief:
Can we not bear these years of labouring breath?
But if you would not this poor life fulfil,
Lo, you are free to end it when you will,
Without the fear of waking after death. —

The organ-like vibrations of his voice
Thrilled through the vaulted aisles and died away;
The yearning of the tones which bade rejoice
Was sad and tender as a requiem lay:
Our shadowy congregation rested still
As brooding on that 'End it when you will.'

XVI

Our shadowy congregation rested still,
As musing on that message we had heard
And brooding on that 'End it when you will';
Perchance awaiting yet some other word;
When keen as lightning through a muffled sky
Sprang forth a shrill and lamentable cry: —

The man speaks sooth, alas! the man speaks sooth:
We have no personal life beyond the grave;

There is no God; Fate knows nor wrath nor ruth:
Can I find here the comfort which I crave?

In all eternity I had one chance,
One few years' term of gracious human life:
The splendours of the intellect's advance,
The sweetness of the home with babes and wife;

The social pleasures with their genial wit;
The fascination of the worlds of art,
The glories of the worlds of nature, lit
By large imagination's glowing heart;

The rapture of mere being, full of health;
The careless childhood and the ardent youth,
The strenuous manhood winning various wealth,
The reverend age serene with life's long truth:

All the sublime prerogatives of Man;
The storied memories of the times of old,
The patient tracking of the world's great plan
Through sequences and changes myriadfold.

This chance was never offered me before;
For me the infinite Past is blank and dumb:
This chance recurreth never, nevermore;
Blank, blank for me the infinite To-come.

And this sole chance was frustrate from my birth,
A mockery, a delusion; and my breath
Of noble human life upon this earth
So racks me that I sigh for senseless death.

My wine of life is poison mixed with gall,
My noonday passes in a nightmare dream,
I worse than lose the years which are my all:
What can console me for the loss supreme?

Speak not of comfort where no comfort is,
Speak not at all: can words make foul things fair?
Our life's a cheat, our death a black abyss:
Hush and be mute envisaging despair. —

This vehement voice came from the northern aisle
Rapid and shrill to its abrupt harsh close;
And none gave answer for a certain while,
For words must shrink from these most wordless woes;

At last the pulpit speaker simply said,
With humid eyes and thoughtful drooping head: —

My Brother, my poor Brothers, it is thus;
This life itself holds nothing good for us,
But it ends soon and nevermore can be;
And we knew nothing of it ere our birth,
And shall know nothing when consigned to earth:
I ponder these thoughts and they comfort me.

XVIII

I wandered in a suburb of the north,
And reached a spot whence three close lanes led down,
Beneath thick trees and hedge rows winding forth
Like deep brook channels, deep and dark and lown:
The air above was wan with misty light,
The dull grey south showed one vague blur of white.

I took the left-hand lane and slowly trod
Its earthen footpath, brushing as I went
The humid leafage; and my feet were shod
With heavy languor, and my frame downbent,
With infinite sleepless weariness outworn,
So many nights I thus had paced forlorn.

After a hundred steps I grew aware
Of something crawling in the lane below;
It seemed a wounded creature prostrate there
That sobbed with pangs in making progress slow,
The hind limbs stretched to push, the fore limbs then
To drag; for it would die in its own den.

But coming level with it I discerned
That it had been a man; for at my tread
It stopped in its sore travail and half-turned,
Leaning upon its right, and raised its head,
And with the left hand twitched back as in ire
Long grey unreverend locks befouled with mire.

A haggard filthy face with bloodshot eyes,
An infamy for manhood to behold.
He gasped all trembling, What, you want my prize?
You leave, to rob me, wine and lust and gold

And all that men go mad upon, since you
Have traced my sacred secret of the clue?

You think that I am weak and must submit;
Yet I but scratch you with this poisoned blade,
And you are dead as if I clove with it
That false fierce greedy heart. Betrayed! betrayed
I fling this phial if you seek to pass,
And you are forthwith shrivelled up like grass.

And then with sudden change, Take thought! take thought!
Have pity on me! it is mine alone.
If you could find, it would avail you naught;
Seek elsewhere on the pathway of your own:
For who of mortal or immortal race
The lifetrack of another can retrace?

Did you but know my agony and toil!
Two lanes diverge up yonder from this lane;
My thin blood marks the long length of their soil;
Such clue I left, who sought my clue in vain:
My hands and knees are worn both flesh and bone;
I cannot move but with continual moan.

But I am in the very way at last
To find the long-lost broken golden thread
Which reunites my present with my past,
If you but go your own way. And I said,
I will retire as soon as you have told
Whereunto leadeth this lost thread of gold.

And so you know it not! he hissed with scorn;
I feared you, imbecile! It leads me back
From this accursèd night without a morn,
And through the deserts which have else no track,
And through vast wastes of horror-haunted time,
To Eden innocence in Eden's clime:

And I become a nursling soft and pure,
An infant cradled on its mother's knee,
Without a past, love-cherished and secure;
Which if it saw this loathsome present Me,
Would plunge its face into the pillowing breast,
And scream abhorrence hard to lull to rest.

He turned to grope; and I retiring brushed
Thin shreds of gossamer from off my face,
And mused, His life would grow, the germ uncrushed;
He should to antenatal night retrace,
And hide his elements in that large womb
Beyond the reach of man-evolving Doom.

And even thus, what weary way were planned,
To seek oblivion through the far-off gate
Of birth, when that of death is close at hand!
For this is law, if law there be in Fate:
What never has been, yet may have its when;
The thing which has been, never is again.

XIX

The mighty river flowing dark and deep,
With ebb and flood from the remote sea-tides
Vague-sounding through the City's sleepless sleep,
Is named the River of the Suicides;
For night by night some lorn wretch over-weary,
And shuddering from the future yet more dreary,
Within its cold secure oblivion hides.

One plunges from a bridge's parapet,
As by some blind and sudden frenzy hurled;
Another wades in slow with purpose set
Until the waters are above him furled;
Another in a boat with dreamlike motion
Glides drifting down into the desert ocean,
To starve or sink from out the desert world.

They perish from their suffering surely thus,
For none beholding them attempts to save,
The while each thinks how soon, solicitous,
He may seek refuge in the self-same wave;
Some hour when tired of ever-vain endurance
Impatience will forerun the sweet assurance
Of perfect peace eventual in the grave.

When this poor tragic-farce has palled us long,
Why actors and spectators do we stay? —
To fill our so-short *rôles* out right or wrong;
To see what shifts are yet in the dull play
For our illusion; to refrain from grieving
Dear foolish friends by our untimely leaving:
But those asleep at home, how blest are they!

Yet it is but for one night after all:
What matters one brief night of dreary pain?

When after it the weary eyelids fall
Upon the weary eyes and wasted brain;
And all sad scenes and thoughts and feelings vanish
In that sweet sleep no power can ever banish,
That one best sleep which never wakes again.

XX

I sat me weary on a pillar's base,
And leaned against the shaft; for broad moonlight
O'erflowed the peacefulness of cloistered space,
A shore of shadow slanting from the right:
The great cathedral's western front stood there,
A wave-worn rock in that calm sea of air.

Before it, opposite my place of rest,
Two figures faced each other, large, austere;
A couchant sphinx in shadow to the breast,
An angel standing in the moonlight clear;
So mighty by magnificence of form,
They were not dwarfed beneath that mass enorm.

Upon the cross-hilt of a naked sword
The angel's hands, as prompt to smite, were held;
His vigilant, intense regard was poured
Upon the creature placidly unquelled,
Whose front was set at level gaze which took
No heed of aught, a solemn trance-like look.

And as I pondered these opposèd shapes
My eyelids sank in stupor, that dull swoon
Which drugs and with a leaden mantle drapes
The outworn to worse weariness. But soon
A sharp and clashing noise the stillness broke,
And from the evil lethargy I woke.

The angel's wings had fallen, stone on stone,
And lay there shattered; hence the sudden sound:
A warrior leaning on his sword alone
Now watched the sphinx with that regard profound;
The sphinx unchanged looked forthright, as aware
Of nothing in the vast abyss of air.

Again I sank in that repose unsweet,
Again a clashing noise my slumber rent;
The warrior's sword lay broken at his feet:
An unarmed man with raised hands impotent
Now stood before the sphinx, which ever kept
Such mien as if with open eyes it slept.

My eyelids sank in spite of wonder grown;
A louder crash upstartled me in dread:
The man had fallen forward, stone on stone,
And lay there shattered, with his trunkless head
Between the monster's large quiescent paws,
Beneath its grand front changeless as life's laws.

The moon had circled westward full and bright,
And made the temple-front a mystic dream,
And bathed the whole enclosure with its light,
The sworded angel's wrecks, the sphinx supreme:
I pondered long that cold majestic face
Whose vision seemed of infinite void space.

XXI

Anear the centre of that northern crest
Stands out a level upland bleak and bare,
From which the city east and south and west
Sinks gently in long waves; and thronèd there
An Image sits, stupendous, superhuman,
The bronze colossus of a wingèd Woman,
Upon a graded granite base foursquare.

Low-seated she leans forward massively,
With cheek on clenched left hand, the forearm's might
Erect, its elbow on her rounded knee;
Across a clasped book in her lap the right
Upholds a pair of compasses; she gazes
With full set eyes, but wandering in thick mazes
Of sombre thought beholds no outward sight.

Words cannot picture her; but all men know
That solemn sketch the pure sad artist wrought
Three centuries and threescore years ago,
With phantasies of his peculiar thought:
The instruments of carpentry and science
Scattered about her feet, in strange alliance
With the keen wolf-hound sleeping undistraught;

Scales, hour-glass, bell, and magic-square above;
The grave and solid infant perched beside,

With open winglets that might bear a dove,
Intent upon its tablets, heavy-eyed;
Her folded wings as of a mighty eagle,
But all too impotent to lift the regal
Robustness of her earth-born strength and pride;
And with those wings, and that light wreath which seems
To mock her grand head and the knotted frown
Of forehead charged with baleful thoughts and dreams,
The household bunch of keys, the housewife's gown
Voluminous, indented, and yet rigid
As if a shell of burnished metal frigid;
The feet thick-shod to tread all weakness down;
The comet hanging o'er the waste dark seas,
The massy rainbow curved in front of it,
Beyond the village with the masts and trees;
The snaky imp, dog-headed, from the Pit,
Bearing upon its batlike leathern pinions
Her name unfolded in the sun's dominions,
The 'MELENCOLIA' that transcends all wit.

Thus has the artist copied her, and thus
Surrounded to expound her form sublime,
Her fate heroic and calamitous;
Fronting the dreadful mysteries of Time,
Unvanquished in defeat and desolation,
Undaunted in the hopeless conflagration
Of the day setting on her baffled prime.

Baffled and beaten back she works on still,
Weary and sick of soul she works the more,
Sustained by her indomitable will:
The hands shall fashion and the brain shall pore
And all her sorrow shall be turned to labour,
Till death the friend-foe piercing with his sabre
That mighty heart of hearts ends bitter war.

But as if blacker night could dawn on night,
With tenfold gloom on moonless night unstarred,
A sense more tragic than defeat and blight,
More desperate than strife with hope debarred,
More fatal than the adamantine Never
Encompassing her passionate endeavour,
Dawns glooming in her tenebrous regard:

The sense that every struggle brings defeat
Because Fate holds no prize to crown success;
That all the oracles are dumb or cheat
Because they have no secret to express;
That none can pierce the vast black veil uncertain
Because there is no light beyond the curtain;
That all is vanity and nothingness.

Titanic from her high throne in the north,
That City's sombre Patroness and Queen,
In bronze sublimity she gazes forth
Over her Capital of teen and threne,
Over the river with its isles and bridges,
The marsh and moorland, to the stern rock-ridges,
Confronting them with a coëval mien.

The moving moon and stars from east to west
Circle before her in the sea of air;
Shadows and gleams glide round her solemn rest.
Her subjects often gaze up to her there:
The strong to drink new strength of iron endurance,
The weak new terrors; all, renewed assurance
And confirmation of the old despair.

1874

NIGHT

HE cried out through the night:
'Where is the light?
Shall nevermore
Open Heaven's door?
Oh, I am left
Lonely, bereft!'

He cried out through the night:
It spread vaguely white,
With its ghost of a moon
Above the dark swoon
Of the earth lying chill,
Breathless, grave still.

He cried out through the night:
His voice in its might
Rang forth far and far,
And then like a star
Dwindled from sense
In the Immense.

He cried out through the night:
No answering light,
No syllabled sound;
Beneath and around
A long shuddering thrill
Then all again still.

1881

Thomas Edward Brown * (1830–1897)

IBANT OBSCURAE

To-night I saw three maidens on the beach,
Dark-robed descending to the sea,
So slow, so silent of all speech,
And visible to me
Only by that strange drift-light, dim, forlorn,
Of the sun's wreck and clashing surges born.
Each after other went,
And they were gathered to his breast —
It seemed to me a sacrament
Of some stern creed unblest:
As when to rocks, that cheerless girt the bay,
They bound thy holy limbs, Andromeda.

1868

SONG

Look at me, sun, ere thou set
In the far sea;
From the gold and the rose and the jet
Look full at me!

Leave on my brow a trace
Of tenderest light;
Kiss me upon the face,
Kiss for good-night.

1893

THE LAUGH

An empty laugh, I heard it on the road
Shivering the twilight with its lance of mirth;
And yet why empty? Knowing not its birth,
This much I know, that it goes up to God;
And if to God, from God it surely starts,
Who has within Himself the secret springs
Of all the lovely, causeless, unclaimed things,
And loves them in His very heart of hearts.
A girl of fifteen summers, pure and free,
Æolian, vocal to the lightest touch
Of fancy's winnowed breath — Ah, happy such
Whose life is music of the eternal sea!
Laugh on, laugh loud and long, O merry child,
And be not careful to unearth a cause:
Thou art serenely placed above our laws,
And we in thee with God are reconciled.

1893

OPIFEX

As I was carving images from clouds,
And tinting them with soft ethereal dyes
Pressed from the pulp of dreams, one comes, and cries: —
'Forbear!' and all my heaven with gloom enshrouds.

'Forbear! Thou hast no tools wherewith to essay
The delicate waves of that elusive grain:
Wouldst have due recompense of vulgar pain?
The potter's wheel for thee, and some coarse clay!

'So work, if work thou must, O humbly skilled!
Thou hast not known the Master; in thy soul
His spirit moves not with a sweet control;
Thou art outside, and art not of the guild.'

Thereat I rose, and from his presence passed,
But, going, murmured: — 'To the God above,
Who holds my heart, and knows its store of love,
I turn from thee, thou proud iconoclast.'

Then on the shore God stooped to me, and said: —
'He spake the truth: even so the springs are set
That move thy life, nor will they suffer let,
Nor change their scope; else, living, thou wert dead.

'This is thy life: indulge its natural flow,
And carve these forms. They yet may find a place
On shelves for them reserved. In any case,
I bid thee carve them, knowing what I know.'

1893

A WISH

Of two things one: with Chaucer let me ride,
And hear the Pilgrims' tales; or, that denied,
Let me with Petrarch in a dew-sprent grove
Ring endless changes on the bells of love.

1893

THE VOICES OF NATURE

This cluck of water in the tangles —
What said it to the Angles?

* *Collected Poems*, The Macmillan Company, 1900. By permission of the Publishers.

What to the Jutes,
This wave sip-sopping round the salt sea-
roots?
With what association did it hit on
The tympanum of a Damnonian Briton?
To tender Guinevere, to Britomart,
The stout of heart,
Along the guarded beach
Spoke it the same speech
It speaks to me —
This sopping of the sea?

Surely the plash
Of water upon stones,
Encountering in their ears the tones
Of dominant passions masterful,
Made but a bourdon for the chord
Of a great key, that rested lord
Of all the music, straining not the bones
Of Merlin's scull;
And in the ear of Vivian its frets
Were silver castanets
That tinkled 'mong the vanities, and quick-
ened
The free, full-blooded pulse,
Nor sickened
Her soul, nor stabbed her to the heart.
Strange! that to me this gurgling of the dulse
Allays no smart,
Consoles no nerve,
Rounds off no curve —
Alack!
Comes rather like a sigh,
A question that has no reply —
Opens a deep misgiving
What is this life I'm living —
Our fathers were not so —
Silence, thou moaning wrack!
And yet . . . I do not know.
And yet . . . I would go back.

1893

JUVENTA PERENNIS

If youth be thine,
Spare not to drink its wine;
If youth be fled,
Hold up
The golden cup —
God's grapes are always red.

1901

I BENDED UNTO ME

I bended unto me a bough of May,
That I might see and smell:
It bore it in a sort of way,
It bore it very well.
But, when I let it backward sway,
Then it were hard to tell
With what a toss, with what a swing,
The dainty thing
Resumed its proper level,
And sent me to the devil.
I know it did — you doubt it?
I turned, and saw them whispering about it.

1901

Arthur O'Shaughnessy (1844–1881)

ODE

We are the music-makers,
And we are the dreamers of dreams,
Wandering by lone sea-breakers,
And sitting by desolate streams;
World-losers and world-forsakers,
On whom the pale moon gleams:
Yet we are the movers and shakers
Of the world for ever, it seems.

With wonderful deathless ditties
We build up the world's great cities,
And out of a fabulous story
We fashion an empire's glory:
One man with a dream, at pleasure,
Shall go forth and conquer a crown;
And three with a new song's measure
Can trample a kingdom down.

We, in the ages lying
In the buried past of the earth,
Built Nineveh with our sighing,
And Babel itself in our mirth;
And o'erthrew them with prophesying
To the Old of the New World's worth;
For each age is a dream that is dying,
Or one that is coming to birth.

A breath of our inspiration
Is the life of each generation;
A wondrous thing of our dreaming
Unearthly, impossible seeming —
The soldier, the king, and the peasant
Are working together in one,
Till our dream shall become their present,
And their work in the world be done.

They had no vision amazing
Of the goodly house they are raising;
They had no divine foreshowing
Of the land to which they are going:
But on one man's soul it hath broken,
A light that doth not depart;
And his look, or a word he hath spoken,
Wrought flame in another man's heart.

And therefore to-day is thrilling
With a past day's late fulfilling;
And the multitudes are enlisted
In the faith that their fathers resisted,
And, scorning the dream of to-morrow,
Are bringing to pass, as they may,
In the world, for its joys or its sorrow,
The dream that was scorned yesterday.

But we, with our dreaming and singing,
Ceaseless and sorrowless we!
The glory about us clinging
Of the glorious futures we see,
Our souls with high music ringing:
O men! it must ever be
That we dwell, in our dreaming and singing,
A little apart from ye.

For we are afar with the dawning
And the suns that are not yet high,
And out of the infinite morning
Intrepid you hear us cry —
How, spite of your human scorning,
Once more God's future draws nigh,
And already goes forth the warning
That ye of the past must die.

Great hail! we cry to the comers
From the dazzling unknown shore;
Bring us hither your sun and your summers,
And renew our world as of yore;
You shall teach us your song's new numbers,
And things that we dreamed not before:
Yea, in spite of a dreamer who slumbers,
And a singer who sings no more.

1874

SONG

I MADE another garden, yea,
For my new love;
I left the dead rose where it lay,
And set the new above.
Why did the summer not begin?
Why did my heart not haste?
My old love came and walked therein,
And laid the garden waste.

She entered with her weary smile,
Just as of old;
She looked around a little while,
And shivered at the cold.
Her passing touch was death to all,
Her passing look a blight:
She made the white rose-petals fall,
And turned the red rose white.

Her pale robe, clinging to the grass,
Seemed like a snake
That bit the grass and ground, alas!
And a sad trail did make.
She went up slowly to the gate;
And there, just as of yore,
She turned back at the last to wait,
And say farewell once more.

1874

A LOVE SYMPHONY

ALONG the garden ways just now
I heard the flowers speak;
The white rose told me of your brow,
The red rose of your cheek,
The lily of your bended head,
The bindweed of your hair:
Each looked its loveliest and said
You were more fair.

I went into the wood anon,
And heard the wild birds sing,
How sweet you were; they warbled on,
Piped, trilled the self-same thing.
Thrush, blackbird, linnet, without pause,
The burden did repeat,
And still began again because
You were more sweet.

And then I went down to the sea,
And heard it murmuring too,
Part of an ancient mystery,
All made of me and you.
How many a thousand years ago
I loved, and you were sweet, —
Longer I could not stay, and so
I fled back to your feet.

1881

Robert Louis Stevenson * (1850–1894)

REQUIEM

UNDER the wide and starry sky,
Dig the grave and let me lie.
Glad did I live and gladly die,
And I laid me down with a will.

This be the verse you grave for me:
Here he lies where he longed to be;
Home is the sailor, home from the sea,
And the hunter home from the hill.

1887

* *Poems.* By permission of Charles Scribner's Sons, publishers.

IN THE STATES

WITH half a heart I wander here
  As from an age gone by
A brother — yet though young in years,
  An elder brother, I.

You speak another tongue than mine,
  Though both were English born.
I towards the night of time decline,
  You mount into the morn.

Youth shall grow great and strong and free,
  But age must still decay:
To-morrow for the States — for me,
  England and Yesterday.

1887

HEATHER ALE

FROM the bonny bells of heather
  They brewed a drink long-syne,
Was sweeter far than honey,
  Was stronger far than wine.
They brewed it and they drank it,
  And lay in a blessèd swound
For days and days together
  In their dwellings underground.

There rose a king in Scotland,
  A fell man to his foes,
He smote the Picts in battle,
  He hunted them like roes.
Over miles of the red mountain
  He hunted as they fled,
And strewed the dwarfish bodies
  Of the dying and the dead.

Summer came in the country,
  Red was the heather bell;
But the manner of the brewing
  Was none alive to tell.
In graves that were like children's
  On many a mountain head,
The Brewsters of the Heather
  Lay numbered with the dead.

The king in the red moorland
  Rode on a summer's day;
And the bees hummed, and the curlews
  Cried beside the way.
The king rode, and was angry,
  Black was his brow and pale,
To rule in a land of heather
  And lack the Heather Ale.

It fortuned that his vassals,
  Riding free on the heath,
Came on a stone that was fallen
  And vermin hid beneath.
Rudely plucked from their hiding,
  Never a word they spoke:
A son and his agèd father —
  Last of the dwarfish folk.

And the king sat high on his charger,
  He looked on the little men;
And the dwarfish and swarthy couple
  Looked at the king again.
Down by the shore he had them;
  And there on the giddy brink —
'I will give you life, ye vermin,
  For the secret of the drink.'

There stood the son and father
  And they looked high and low;
The heather was red around them,
  The sea rumbled below.
And up and spoke the father,
  Shrill was his voice to hear:
'I have a word in private,
  A word for the royal ear.

'Life is dear to the agèd,
  And honour a little thing;
I would gladly sell the secret,'
  Quoth the Pict to the king.
His voice was small as a sparrow's,
  And shrill and wonderful clear:
'I would gladly sell my secret,
  Only my son I fear.

'For life is a little matter,
  And death is nought to the young;
And I dare not sell my honour
  Under the eye of my son.
Take *him*, O king, and bind him,
  And cast him far in the deep;
And it 's I will tell the secret
  That I have sworn to keep.'

They took the son and bound him,
  Neck and heels in a thong,
And a lad took him and swung him,
  And flung him far and strong,
And the sea swallowed his body,
  Like that of a child of ten; —
And there on the cliff stood the father,
  Last of the dwarfish men.

'True was the word I told you:
  Only my son I feared;
For I doubt the sapling courage
  That goes without the beard.
But now in vain is the torture,
  Fire shall never avail:
Here dies in my bosom
  The secret of Heather Ale.'

1891

William Ernest Henley (1849–1903)

BALLADE OF TRUISMS

GOLD or silver, every day,
Dies to gray.
There are knots in every skein.
Hours of work and hours of play
Fade away
Into one immense Inane.
Shadow and substance, chaff and grain,
Are as vain
As the foam or as the spray.
Life goes crooning, faint and fain,
One refrain: —
'If it could be always May!'

Though the earth be green and gay,
Though, they say,
Man the cup of heaven may drain;
Though, his little world to sway,
He display
Hoard on hoard of pith and brain:
Autumn brings a mist and rain
That constrain
Him and his to know decay,
Where undimmed the lights that wane
Would remain,
If it could be always May.

Yea, alas, must turn to *Nay*
Flesh to clay.
Chance and Time are ever twain.
Men may scoff, and men may pray,
But they pay
Every pleasure with a pain.
Life may soar, and Fortune deign
To explain
Where her prizes hide and stray;
But we lack the lusty train
We should gain,
If it could be always May.

Envoy

Time, the pedagogue, his cane
Might retain,
But his charges all would stray
Truanting in every lane —
Jack with Jane —
If it could be always May.

1888

TO MY MOTHER

CHIMING a dream by the way
With ocean's rapture and roar,
I met a maiden to-day
Walking alone on the shore:
Walking in maiden wise,
Modest and kind and fair,
The freshness of spring in her eyes
And the fulness of spring in her hair.

Cloud-shadow and scudding sun-burst
Were swift on the floor of the sea,
And a mad wind was romping its worst,
But what was their magic to me?
Or the charm of the midsummer skies?
I only saw she was there,
A dream of the sea in her eyes
And the kiss of the sea in her hair.

I watched her vanish in space;
She came where I walked no more;
But something had passed of her grace
To the spell of the wave and the shore;
And now, as the glad stars rise,
She comes to me, rosy and rare,
The delight of the wind in her eyes
And the hand of the wind in her hair.

1888

O, GATHER ME THE ROSE

O, GATHER me the rose, the rose,
While yet in flower we find it,
For summer smiles, but summer goes,
And winter waits behind it!

For with the dream foregone, foregone,
The deed forborne forever,
The worm, regret, will canker on,
And Time will turn him never.

So well it were to love, my love,
And cheat of any laughter
The fate beneath us and above,
The dark before and after.

The myrtle and the rose, the rose,
The sunshine and the swallow,
The dream that comes, the wish that goes,
The memories that follow!

1888

OUT OF THE NIGHT THAT COVERS ME

OUT of the night that covers me,
Black as the Pit from pole to pole,
I thank whatever gods may be
For my unconquerable soul.

In the fell clutch of circumstance
I have not winced nor cried aloud.
Under the bludgeonings of chance
My head is bloody, but unbowed.

Beyond this place of wrath and tears
  Looms but the Horror of the shade,
And yet the menace of the years
  Finds, and shall find, me unafraid.

It matters not how strait the gate,
  How charged with punishments the scroll,
I am the master of my fate:
  I am the captain of my soul.

1888

PROSE

ESSAYS

John Henry Newman (1801-1890)

WHAT IS A UNIVERSITY

If I were asked to describe as briefly and popularly as I could, what a University was, I should draw my answer from its ancient designation of a *Studium Generale,* or 'School of Universal Learning.' This description implies the assemblage of strangers from all parts in one spot; — *from all parts;* else, how will you find professors and students for every department of knowledge? and *in one spot;* else, how can there be any school at all? Accordingly, in its simple and rudimental form, it is a school of knowledge of every kind, consisting of teachers and learners from every quarter. Many things are requisite to complete and satisfy the idea embodied in this description; but such a University seems to be in its essence a place for the communication and circulation of thought, by means of personal intercourse, through a wide extent of country.

There is nothing far-fetched or unreasonable in the idea thus presented to us; and if this be a University, then a University does but contemplate a necessity of our nature, and is but one specimen in a particular department out of many which might be adduced in others, of a provision for that necessity. Mutual education, in a large sense of the word, is one of the great and incessant occupations of human society, carried on partly with set purpose, and partly not. One generation forms another; and the existing generation is ever acting and reacting upon itself in the persons of its individual members. Now, in this process, books, I need scarcely say, that is, the *litera scripta,* are one special instrument. It is true; and emphatically so in this age. Considering the prodigious powers of the press, and how they are developed at this time in the never-intermitting issue of periodicals, tracts, pamphlets, works in series, and light literature, we must allow there never was a time which promised fairer for dispensing with every other means of information and instruction. What can we want more, you will say, for the intellectual education of the whole man, and for every man, than so exuberant and diversified and persistent a promulgation of all kinds of knowledge? Why, you will ask, need we go up to knowledge, when knowledge comes down to us? The Sibyl wrote her prophecies upon the leaves of the forest, and wasted them; but here such careless profusion might be prudently indulged, for it can be afforded without loss, in consequence of the almost fabulous fecundity of the instrument which these latter ages have invented. We have sermons in stones, and books in the running brooks; works larger and more comprehensive than those which have gained for ancients an immortality, issue forth every morning, and are projected onward to the ends of the earth at the rate of hundreds of miles a day. Our seats are strewed, our pavements are powdered, with swarms of little tracts; and the very bricks of our city walls preach wisdom, by largely informing us where we can at once cheaply purchase it.

I allow all this, and much more; such certainly is our popular education, and its effects are remarkable. Nevertheless, after all, even in this age, when men are really serious about getting what, in the language of trade, is called 'a good article,' when they aim at something precise, something refined, something really luminous, something really large, something choice, they go to another market; they avail themselves, in some shape or other, of the rival method, the ancient method, of oral instruction, of present communication between man and man, of teachers instead of teaching, of the personal influence of a master, and the humble initiation of a disciple, and, in consequence, of great centres of pilgrimage and throng, which such a method of education necessarily involves. This, I think, will be found good in all those departments or aspects of society, which possess an interest sufficient to bind men together, or to constitute what is called 'a world.' It holds in the political world, and in the high world, and in the religious world; and it holds also in the literary and scientific world.

If the actions of men may be taken as any test of their convictions, then we have reason for saying this, viz.; — that the province and the inestimable benefit of the *litera scripta* is that of being a record of truth, and an authority of appeal, and an instrument of teaching in the hands of a teacher; but that, if we wish to become exact and fully furnished in any branch of knowledge which is diversified and complicated, we must consult the living man and listen to his living voice. I am not bound to investigate the cause of this, and anything I may say will, I am conscious, be short of its full analysis; — perhaps we may suggest that no books can get through the number of minute questions which it is possible to ask on any extended subject, or hit upon the very difficulties which are respectively felt by each reader in succession. Or again, that no book can convey the special spirit and delicate peculiarities of its subject with that rapidity and certainty which attend on the sympathy of mind with mind, through the eyes, the look, the accent, and the manner, in casual expressions thrown off at the moment, and the unstudied turns of familiar conversation. But I am already dwelling too long on what is but an incidental portion of my main subject. Whatever be the cause, the fact is undeniable. The general principles of any study you may learn by books at home; but the detail, the colour, the tone, the air, the life which makes it live in us, you must catch all these from those in whom it lives already. You must imitate the student in French or German, who is not content with his grammar, but goes to Paris or Dresden; you must take example from the young artist, who aspires to visit the great Masters in Florence and in Rome. Till we have discovered some intellectual daguerreotype, which takes off the course of thought, and the form, lineaments, and features of truth, as completely and minutely as the optical instrument produces the sensible object, we must come to the teachers of wisdom to learn wisdom, we must repair to the fountain, and drink there. Portions may go from thence to the ends of the earth by means of books, but the fulness is in one place alone. It is in such assemblages and congregations of intellect that books themselves, the masterpieces of human genius, are written, or at least originated.

The principle on which I have been insisting is so obvious, and instances in point so ready, that I should think it tiresome to proceed with the subject, except that one or two illustrations may serve to explain my own language about it, which may not have been as clear as the subject on which it has been employed.

For instance, the polished manners and highbred behaviour which are so difficult of attainment, and so strictly personal when attained, which are so much admired in society, from society are obtained. All that goes to constitute a gentleman, — the carriage, gait, address, gestures, voice; the ease, the self-possession, the courtesy, the power of conversing, the success in not offending; the lofty principle, the delicacy of thought, the happiness of expression, the taste and propriety, the generosity and forbearance, the candour and consideration, the openness of hand; — these qualities, some of them come by nature, some of them may be found in any rank, some of them are a direct precept of Christianity; but the full assemblage of them, bound up in the unity of an individual character, do we expect they can be learned from books? are they not necessarily acquired, where they are to be found, in high society? The very nature of the case leads us to say so; you cannot fence without an antagonist, nor challenge all comers in disputation before you have supported a thesis; and in like manner, it stands to reason, you cannot learn to converse till you have the world to converse with; you cannot unlearn your natural bashfulness, or awkwardness, or stiffness, or other besetting deformity, till you serve your time in some school of manners. Well, and is it not so in matter of fact? The metropolis, the court, the great houses of the land, are the centres to which at stated times the country comes up, as to shrines of refinement and good taste; and then in due time the country goes back again home, enriched with a portion of those social accomplishments which those very visits serve to call out and heighten in the gracious dispensers of them. We are unable to conceive how the 'gentlemanlike' can otherwise be maintained; and maintained in this way it is.

And now a second instance, and here too I am going to speak without personal experience of the subject I am introducing. I admit I have not been in Parliament, any more than I have figured in the *beau monde;* yet I cannot but think that statesmanship, as well as high breeding, is learned, not by books, but in certain centres of education. If it be not presumption to say so, Parliament puts a clever man *au courant* with politics and affairs of state in a way surprising to himself. A member of the Legislature, if tolerably observant, begins to see things with new eyes, even though his views undergo no change. Words have a meaning now, and ideas a reality, such as they had not before. He hears a vast deal in public speeches and private conversation which is never put into print. The bearing of measures and events, the action of parties, and the persons of friends and enemies, are brought out to the man who is in the midst of them with a distinctness which the most diligent perusal of newspapers will fail to throw around them. It is access to the fountain-heads of political wisdom and experience, it is daily intercourse, of one kind or another, with the multitude who go up to them, it is familiarity with business, it is access to the contributions of fact and opinion thrown together by many witnesses from many quarters, which does this for him. However, I need not account for a fact to which it is sufficient to appeal; that the Houses of Parliament and the atmosphere around them are a sort of University of politics.

As regards the world of science, we find a remarkable instance of the principle which I am illustrating, in the periodical meetings for its advance which have arisen in the course of the last twenty years, such as the British Association. Such gatherings would to many persons appear at first sight simply preposterous. Above all subjects of study, Science is conveyed, is propagated, by books, or by private teaching; experiments and investigations are conducted in silence; discoveries are made in solitude. What have philosophers to do with festive celebrities, and panegyrical solemnities with mathematical and physical truth? Yet on a closer attention to the subject, it is found that not even scientific thought can dispense with the suggestions, the instruction, the stimulus, the sympathy, the intercourse with mankind on a large scale, which such meetings secure. A fine time of year is chosen, when days are long, skies are bright, the earth smiles, and all nature rejoices; a city or town is taken by turns, of ancient name or modern opulence, where buildings are spacious and hospitality hearty. The novelty of place and circumstance, the excitement of strange, or the refreshment of well-known faces, the majesty of rank or of genius, the amiable charities of men pleased both with themselves and with each other; the elevated spirits, the circulation of thought, the curiosity; the morning sections, the outdoor exercise, the well-furnished, well-earned board, the not ungraceful hilarity, the evening circle; the brilliant lecture, the discussions or collisions or guesses of great men one with another, the narratives of scientific processes, of hopes, disappointments, conflicts, and successes, the splendid eulogistic orations; these and the like constituents of the annual celebration, are considered to do something real and substantial for the advance of knowledge which can be done in no other way. Of course they can but be occasional; they answer to the annual Act, or Commencement, or Commemoration of a University, not to its ordinary condition; but they are of a

University nature; and I can well believe in their utility. They issue in the promotion of a certain living and, as it were, bodily communication of knowledge from one to another, of a general interchange of ideas, and a comparison and adjustment of science with science, of an enlargement of mind, intellectual and social, of an ardent love of the particular study which may be chosen by each individual, and a noble devotion to its interests.

Such meetings, I repeat, are but periodical, and only partially represent the idea of a University. The bustle and whirl which are their usual concomitants are in ill keeping with the order and gravity of earnest intellectual education. We desiderate the means of instruction without the interruption of our ordinary habits; nor need we seek it long, for the natural course of things brings it about, while we debate over it. In every great country, the metropolis itself becomes a sort of necessary University, whether we will or no. As the chief city is the seat of the court, of high society, of politics, and of law, so, as a matter of course, is it the seat of letters also; and at this time, for a long term of years, London and Paris are in fact and in operation Universities, though in Paris its famous University is no more, and in London a University scarcely exists except as a board of management. The newspapers, magazines, reviews, journals, and periodicals of all kinds, the publishing trade, the libraries, museums, and academies there found, the learned and scientific societies, necessarily invest it with the functions of a University; and that atmosphere of intellect, which in a former age hung over Oxford or Bologna or Salamanca, has, with the change of time, moved away to the centre of civil government. Thither come up youths from all parts of the country, the students of law, medicine, and the fine arts, and the *employés* and *attachés* of literature. There they live, as chance determines; and they are satisfied with their temporary home, for they find in it all that was promised to them there. They have not come in vain, as far as their own object in coming is concerned. They have not learned any particular religion, but they have learned their own particular profession well. They have, moreover, become acquainted with the habits, manners, and opinions of their place of sojourn, and done their part in maintaining the tradition of them. We cannot then be without virtual Universities; a metropolis is such: the simple question is, whether the education sought and given should be based on principle, formed upon rule, directed to the highest ends, or left to the random succession of masters and schools, one after another, with a melancholy waste of thought and an extreme hazard of truth.

Religious teaching itself affords us an illustration of our subject to a certain point. It does not indeed seat itself merely in centres of the world; this is impossible from the nature of the case. It is intended for the many, not the few; its subject-matter is truth necessary, not truth recondite and rare; but it concurs in the principle of a University so far as this, that its great instrument, or rather organ, has ever been that which nature prescribes in all education, the personal presence of a teacher, or, in theological language, Oral Tradition. It is the living voice, the breathing form, the expressive countenance, which preaches, which catechises. Truth, a subtle, invisible, manifold spirit, is poured into the mind of the scholar by his eyes and ears, through his affections, imagination, and reason; it is poured into his mind and is sealed up there in perpetuity, by propounding and repeating it, by questioning and requestioning, by correcting and explaining, by progressing, and then recurring to first principles, by all those ways which are implied in the word 'catechising.' In the first ages it was a work of long time; months, sometimes years, were devoted to the arduous task of disabusing the mind of the incipient Christian of its pagan errors, and of moulding it upon the Christian faith. The Scriptures indeed were at hand for the study of those who could avail themselves of them; but St. Irenæus does not hesitate to speak of whole races who had been converted to Christianity, without being able to read them. To be unable to read or write was in those times no evidence of want of learning: the hermits of the deserts were, in this sense of the word, illiterate; yet the great St. Anthony, though he knew not letters, was a match in disputation for the learned philosophers who came to try him. Didymus again, the great Alexandrian theologian, was blind. The ancient discipline, called the *Disciplina Arcani*, involved the same principle. The more sacred doctrines of Revelation were not committed to books, but passed on by successive tradition. The doctrines of the Blessed Trinity and the Eucharist appear to have been so handed down for some hundred years; and when at length reduced to writing, they have filled many folios, which after all have left much unsaid.

But I have said more than enough in illustration; I end as I began; — a University is a place of concourse, whither students come from every quarter for every kind of knowledge. You cannot have the best of every kind everywhere; you must go to some great city or emporium for it. There you have all the choicest productions of nature and art all together, which you find each in its own separate place elsewhere. All the riches of the land, and of the world, are carried up thither; there are the best markets, and there the best workmen. It is the centre of trade, the supreme court of fashion, the umpire of rival skill, and the standard of things rare and precious. It is the place for seeing galleries of first-rate pictures, and for hearing wonderful voices and miraculous performers. It is the place for great preachers, great orators, great nobles, great statesmen. In the nature of things, greatness and unity go together; excellence implies a centre. Such, then, for the third or fourth time, is a University; I hope I do not weary out the reader by repeating it. It is the place to which a thousand schools make contributions; in which the intellect may safely range and speculate, sure to find its equal in some antagonist activity, and its judge in the tribunal of truth. It is a place where inquiry is pushed forward, and discoveries verified and perfected, and rashness rendered innocuous, and error exposed, by the collision of mind with mind, and knowledge with knowledge. It is the place where the professor becomes eloquent, and a missionary and preacher of science, displaying it in its most complete and most winning form, pouring it forth with the zeal of enthusiasm, and lighting up his own love of it in the breasts of his hearers. It is the place where the catechist makes good his ground as he goes, treading in the truth day by day into the ready memory, and wedging and tightening it into the expanding reason. It is a place which attracts the affections of the young by its fame, wins the judgment of the middle-aged by its beauty, and rivets the memory of the old by its associations. It is a seat of wisdom, a light of the world, a minister of the faith, an Alma Mater of the rising generation. It is this and a great deal more, and demands a somewhat better head and hand than mine to describe it well.

Such is it in its idea and in its purpose; such in good measure has it before now been in fact. Shall it ever be again? We are going forward in the strength of the Cross, under the patronage of Mary, in the name of Patrick, to attempt it.

1854

John Ruskin (1819–1900)

TRAFFIC

My good Yorkshire friends, you asked me down here among your hills that I might talk to you about this Exchange you are going to build: but earnestly and seriously asking you to pardon me, I am going to do nothing of the kind. I cannot talk, or at least can say very little, about this same Exchange. I must talk of quite other things, though not willingly; — I could not deserve your pardon, if, when you invited me to speak on one subject, I *wilfully* spoke on another. But I cannot speak, to purpose, of anything about which I do not care; and most simply and sorrowfully I have to tell you, in the outset, that I do *not* care about this Exchange of yours.

If, however, when you sent me your invitation, I had answered, 'I won't come, I don't care about the Exchange of Bradford,' you would have been justly offended with me, not knowing the reasons of so blunt a carelessness. So I have come down, hoping that you will patiently let me tell you why, on this, and many other such occasions, I now remain silent, when formerly I should have caught at the opportunity of speaking to a gracious audience.

In a word, then, I do not care about this Exchange, — because *you* don't; and because you know perfectly well I cannot make you. Look at the essential conditions of the case, which you, as business men, know perfectly well, though perhaps you think I forget them. You are going to spend £30,000, which to you, collectively, is nothing; the buying a new coat is, as to the cost of it, a much more important matter of consideration to me, than building a new Exchange is to you. But you think you may as well have the right thing for your money. You know there are a great many odd styles of architecture about; you don't want to do anything ridiculous; you hear of me, among others, as a respectable architectural man-milliner; and you send for me, that I may tell you the leading fashion; and what is, in our shops, for the moment, the newest and sweetest thing in pinnacles.

Now, pardon me for telling you frankly, you cannot have good architecture merely by asking people's advice on occasion. All good architecture is the expression of national life and character; and it is produced by a prevalent and eager national taste, or desire for beauty. And I want you to think a little of the deep significance of this word 'taste'; for no statement of mine has been more earnestly or oftener controverted than that good taste is essentially a moral quality. 'No,' say many of my antagonists, 'taste is one thing, morality is another. Tell us what is pretty: we shall be glad to know that; but we need no sermons even were you able to preach them, which may be doubted.'

Permit me, therefore, to fortify this old dogma of mine somewhat. Taste is not only a part and an index of morality — it is the ONLY morality. The first, and last, and closest trial question to any living creature is, 'What do you like?' Tell me what you like, and I'll tell you what you are. Go out into the street, and ask the first man or woman you meet, what their 'taste' is; and if they answer candidly, you know them, body and soul. 'You, my friend in the rags, with the unsteady gait, what do *you* like?' 'A pipe and a quartern of gin.' I know you. 'You, good woman, with the quick step and tidy bonnet, what do you like?' 'A swept hearth, and a clean tea-table; and my husband opposite me, and a baby at my breast.' Good, I know you also. 'You, little girl with the golden hair and the soft eyes, what do you like?' 'My canary, and a run among the wood hyacinths.' 'You, little boy with the dirty hands, and the low forehead, what do you like?' 'A shy at the sparrows, and a game at pitch farthing.' Good; we know them all now. What more need we ask?

'Nay,' perhaps you answer: 'we need rather to ask what these people and children do, than what they like. If they *do* right, it is no matter that they like what is wrong; and if they *do* wrong, it is no matter that they like what is right. Doing is the great thing; and it does not matter that the man likes drinking, so that he does not drink; nor that the little girl likes to be kind to her canary, if she will not learn her lessons; nor that the little boy likes throwing stones at the sparrows, if he goes to the Sunday School.' Indeed, for a short time, and in a provisional sense, this is true. For if, resolutely, people do what is right, in time they come to like doing it. But they only are in a right moral state when they *have* come to like doing it; and as long as they don't like it, they are still in a vicious state. The man is not in health of body who is always thinking of the bottle in the cupboard, though he bravely bears his thirst; but the man who heartily enjoys water in the morning, and wine in the evening, each in its proper quantity and time. And the entire object of true education is to make people not merely *do* the right things, but *enjoy* the right things: — not merely industrious, but to love industry — not merely learned, but to love knowledge — not merely pure, but to love purity — not merely just, but to hunger and thirst after justice.

But you may answer or think, 'Is the liking for outside ornaments, — for pictures, or statues, or furniture, or architecture, a moral quality?' Yes, most surely, if a rightly set liking. Taste for *any* pictures or statues is not a moral quality, but taste for good ones is. Only here again we have to define the word 'good.' I don't mean by 'good,' clever — or learned — or difficult in the doing. Take a picture by Teniers, of sots quarreling over their dice; it is an entirely clever picture; so clever that nothing in its kind has ever been done equal to it; but it is also an entirely base and evil picture. It is an expression of delight in the prolonged contemplation of a vile thing, and delight in that is an 'unmannered,' or 'immoral' quality. It is 'bad taste' in the profoundest sense — it is the taste of the devils. On the other hand, a picture of Titian's, or a Greek statue, or a Greek coin, or a Turner landscape, expresses delight in the perpetual contemplation of a good and perfect thing. That is an entirely moral quality — it is the taste of the angels. And all delight in fine art, and all love of it, resolve themselves into simple love of that which deserves love. That deserving is the quality which we call 'loveliness' — (we ought to have an opposite word, hateliness, to be said of the things which deserve to be hated); and it is not an indifferent nor optional thing whether we love this or that; but it is just the vital function of all our being. What we *like* determines what we *are*, and is the sign of what we are; and to teach taste is inevitably to form character.

As I was thinking over this, in walking up Fleet Street the other day, my eye caught the title of a book standing open in a bookseller's window. It was — 'On the necessity of the diffusion of taste among all classes.' 'Ah,' I thought to myself, 'my classifying friend, when you have diffused your taste, where will your classes be? The man who likes what you like, belongs to the same class with you, I think. Inevitably so. You may put him to other work if you choose; but, by the cߋndition you have brought him into, he will dislike the work as much as you would yourself. You get hold of a scavenger, or a costermonger, who enjoyed the Newgate Calendar for literature, and 'Pop goes the Weasel' for music. You think you can make him like Dante and Beethoven? I wish you joy of your lessons; but if you do, you have made a gentleman of him: — he won't like to go back to his costermongering.'

And so completely and unexceptionally is this so, that, if I had time to-night, I could show you that a nation cannot be affected by any vice, or weakness, without expressing it, legibly, and forever, either in bad art, or by want of art; and that there is no national virtue, small or great, which is not manifestly expressed in all the art which circumstances enable the people possessing that virtue to produce. Take, for instance, your great English virtue of enduring and patient courage. You have at present in England only one art of any consequence — that is, iron-working. You know thoroughly well how to cast and hammer iron. Now, do you think in those masses of lava which you build volcanic cones to melt, and which you forge at the mouths of the Infernos you have created; do you think, on those iron plates, your courage and endurance are not written forever — not merely with an iron pen, but on iron parchment? And take also your great English vice — European vice — vice of all the world — vice of all other worlds that roll or shine in heaven, bearing with them yet the atmosphere of hell — the vice of jealousy, which brings competition into your commerce, treachery into your councils, and dishonor into your wars — that vice which has rendered for you, and for your next neighboring nation, the daily occupations of existence no longer possible, but with the mail upon your breasts and the sword loose in its sheath; so that at last, you have realized for all the multitudes of the two great peoples who lead the so-called civilization of the earth, — you have realized for them all, I say, in person and in policy, what was once true only of the rough Border riders of your Cheviot hills —

'They carved at the meal
With gloves of steel,
And they drank the red wine through the helmet barred;' —

do you think that this national shame and dastardliness of heart are not written as legibly on every rivet of your iron armor as the strength of the right hands that forged it?

Friends, I know not whether this thing be the more ludicrous or the more melancholy. It is quite unspeakably both. Suppose, instead of being now sent for by you, I had been sent for by some private gentleman, living in a suburban house, with his garden separated only by a fruit wall from his next door neighbor's; and he had called me to consult with him on the furnishing of his drawing room. I begin looking about me, and find the walls rather bare; I think such and such a paper might be desirable — perhaps a little fresco here and there on the ceiling — a damask curtain or so at the windows. 'Ah,' says my employer, 'damask curtains, indeed! That 's all very fine, but you know I can't afford that kind of thing just now!' 'Yet the world credits you with a splendid income!' 'Ah, yes,' says my friend, 'but do you know, at present, I am obliged to spend it nearly all in steel-traps?' 'Steel-traps! for whom?' 'Why, for that fellow on the other side of the wall, you know: we 're very good friends, capital friends, but we are obliged to keep our traps set on both sides of the wall; we could not possibly keep on friendly terms without them, and our spring guns. The worst of it is, we are both clever fellows enough; and there 's never a day passes that we don't find out a new trap, or a new gun-barrel, or something; we spend about fifteen millions a year each in our traps, take it all together; and I don't see how we 're to do with less.' A highly comic state of life for two private gentlemen! but for two nations, it seems to me, not wholly comic? Bedlam would be comic, perhaps, if there were only one madman in it; and your Christmas pantomime is comic, when there is only one clown in it; but when the whole world turns clown, and paints itself red with its own heart's blood instead of vermilion, it is something else than comic, I think.

Mind, I know a great deal of this is play, and willingly allow for that. You don't know what to do with yourselves for a sensation: fox-hunting and cricketing will not carry you through the whole of this unendurably long mortal life: you liked pop-guns when you were schoolboys, and rifles and Armstrongs are only the same things better made: but then the worst of it is, that what was play to you when boys, was not play to the sparrows; and what is play to you now, is not play to the small birds of State neither; and for the black eagles, you are somewhat shy of taking shots at them, if I mistake not.

I must get back to the matter in hand, however. Believe me, without farther instance, I could show you, in all time, that every nation's vice, or virtue, was written in its art: the soldiership of early Greece; the sensuality of late Italy; the visionary religion of Tuscany; the splendid human energy of Venice. I have no time to do this tonight (I have done it elsewhere before now); but I proceed to apply the principle to ourselves in a more searching manner.

I notice that among all the new buildings which cover your once wild hills, churches and schools are mixed in due, that is to say, in large proportion, with your mills and mansions; and I notice also that the churches and schools are almost always Gothic, and the mansions and mills are never Gothic. May I ask the meaning of this; for, remember, it is peculiarly a modern phenomenon? When Gothic was invented, houses were Gothic as well as churches; and when the Italian style superseded the Gothic, churches were Italian as well as houses. If there is a Gothic spire to the cathedral of Antwerp, there is a Gothic belfry to the Hôtel de Ville at Brussels; if Inigo Jones builds an Italian Whitehall, Sir Christopher Wren builds an Italian St. Paul's. But now you live under one school of architecture, and worship under another. What do you mean by doing this? Am I to understand that you are thinking of changing your architecture back to Gothic; and that you treat your churches experimentally, because it does not matter what mistakes you make in a church? Or am I to understand that you consider Gothic a pre-eminently sacred and beautiful mode of building, which you think, like the fine frankincense, should be mixed for the tabernacle only, and reserved for your religious services? For if this be the feeling, though it may seem at first as if it were graceful and reverent, at the root of the matter, it signifies neither more nor less than that you have separated your religion from your life.

For consider what a wide significance this fact has; and remember that it is not you only, but all the people of England, who are behaving thus, just now.

You have all got into the habit of calling the church 'the house of God.' I have seen, over the doors of many churches, the legend actually carved, '*This* is the house of God, and this is the gate of heaven.' Now, note where that legend comes from, and of what place it was first spoken. A boy leaves his father's house to go on a long journey on foot, to visit his uncle: he has to cross a wild hill-desert; just as if one of your own boys had to cross the wolds to visit an uncle at Carlisle. The second or third day your boy finds himself somewhere between Hawes and Brough, in the midst of the moors, at sunset. It is stony ground, and boggy; he cannot go one foot farther that night. Down he lies, to sleep, on Wharnside, where best he may, gathering a few of the stones together to put under his head; — so wild the place is, he cannot get anything but stones. And there, lying under the broad night, he has a dream; and he sees a ladder set up on the earth, and the top of it reaches to heaven, and the angels of God are seen ascending and descending upon it. And when he wakes out of his sleep, he says, 'How dreadful is this place; surely, this is none other than the house of God, and this is the gate of heaven.' This PLACE, observe; not this church; not this city; not this stone, even, which he puts up for a memorial — the piece of flint on which his head has lain. But this *place;* this windy slope of Wharnside; this moorland hollow, torrent-bitten, snow-blighted! this *any* place where God lets down the ladder. And how are you to know where that will be? or how are you to determine where it may be, but by being ready for it always? Do you know where the lightning is to fall next? You *do* know that, partly; you can guide the lightning; but you cannot guide the going forth of the Spirit, which is as that lightning when it shines from the east to the west.

But the perpetual and insolent warping of that strong verse to serve a merely ecclesiastical purpose, is only one of the thousand instances in which we sink back into gross Judaism. We call our churches 'temples.' Now, you know perfectly well they are *not* temples. They have never had, never can have, anything whatever to do with temples. They are 'synagogues' — 'gathering places' — where you gather yourselves together as an assembly; and by not calling them so, you again miss the force of another mighty text — 'Thou, when thou prayest, shalt not be as the hypocrites are; for they love to pray standing in the *churches*' (we should translate it), 'that they may be seen of men. But thou, when thou prayest, enter into thy closet, and when thou hast shut thy door, pray to thy Father,' — which is, not in chancel nor in aisle, but 'in secret.'

Now you feel, as I say this to you — I know you feel — as if I were trying to take away the honor of your churches. Not so; I am trying to prove to you the honor of your houses and your hills; not that the Church is not sacred — but that the whole Earth is. I would have you feel what careless, what constant, what infectious sin there is in all modes of thought, whereby, in calling your churches only 'holy,' you call your hearths and homes 'profane'; and have separated yourselves from the heathen by casting all your household gods to the ground, instead of recognizing, in the place of their many and feeble Lares, the presence of your One and Mighty Lord and Lar.

'But what has all this to do with our Exchange?' you ask me, impatiently. My dear friends, it has just everything to do with it; on these inner and great questions depend all the outer and little ones; and if you have asked me down here to speak to you, because you had before been interested in anything I have written, you must know that all I have yet said about architecture was to show this. The book I called *The Seven Lamps* was to show that certain right states of temper and moral feeling were the magic powers by which all good architecture, without exception, had been produced. *The Stones of Venice* had, from beginning to end, no other aim than to show that the Gothic architecture of Venice had arisen out of, and indicated in all its features, a state of pure national faith, and of domestic virtue; and that its Renaissance architecture had arisen out of, and in all its features indicated, a state of concealed national infidelity, and of domestic corruption. And now, you ask me what style is best to build in, and how can I answer, knowing the meaning of the two styles, but by another question — do you mean to build as Christians or as infidels? And still more — do you mean to build as honest Christians or as honest infidels? as thoroughly and confessedly either one or the other? You don't like to be asked such rude questions. I cannot help it; they are of much more importance than this Exchange business; and if they can be at once answered, the Exchange business settles itself in a moment. But before I press them farther, I must ask leave to explain one point clearly.

In all my past work, my endeavor has been to show that good architecture is essentially religious — the production of a faithful and virtuous, not of an infidel and corrupted people. But in the course of doing this, I have had also to show that good architecture is not *ecclesiastical*. People are so apt to look upon religion as the business of the clergy, not their own, that the moment they hear of anything depending on 'religion,' they think it must also have depended on the priesthood; and I have had to take what place was to be occupied between these two errors, and fight both, often with seeming contradiction. Good architecture is the work of good and believing men; therefore, you say, at least some people say, 'Good architecture must essentially have been the work of the clergy, not of the laity.' No — a thousand times no; good architecture has always been the work of the commonalty, *not* of the clergy. What, you say, those glorious cathedrals — the pride of Europe — did their builders not form Gothic architecture? No; they corrupted Gothic architecture. Gothic was formed in the baron's castle, and the burgher's street. It was formed by the thoughts, and hands, and powers of laboring citizens and warrior kings. By the monk it was used as an instrument for the aid of his superstition: when that superstition became a beautiful madness, and the best hearts of Europe vainly dreamed and pined in the cloister, and vainly raged and perished in the crusade — through that fury of perverted faith and wasted war, the Gothic rose also to its loveliest, most fantastic, and, finally, most foolish dreams; and, in those dreams, was lost.

I hope, now, that there is no risk of your misunderstanding me when I come to the gist of what I want to say tonight; — when I repeat, that every great national architecture has been the result and exponent of a great national religion. You can't have bits of it here, bits there — you must have it everywhere or nowhere. It is not the monopoly of a clerical company — it is not the exponent of a theological dogma — it is not the hieroglyphic writing of an initiated priesthood; it is the manly language of a people inspired by resolute and common purpose, and rendering resolute and common fidelity to the legible laws of an undoubted God.

Now there have as yet been three distinct schools of European architecture. I say, European, because Asiatic and African architectures belong so entirely to other races and climates, that there is no question of them here; only, in passing, I will simply assure you that whatever is good or great in Egypt, and Syria, and India, is just good or great for the same reasons as the buildings on our side of the Bosphorus. We Europeans, then, have had three great religions: the Greek, which was the worship of the God of Wisdom and Power; the Mediæval, which was the Worship of the God of Judgment and Consolation; the Renaissance, which was the worship of the God of Pride and Beauty: these three we have had — they are past, — and now, at last, we English have got a fourth religion, and a God of our own, about which I want to ask you. But I must explain these three old ones first.

I repeat, first, the Greeks essentially worshipped the God of Wisdom; so that whatever contended against their religion, — to the Jews a stumbling block, — was, to the Greeks — *Foolishness*.

The first Greek idea of deity was that expressed in the word, of which we keep the remnant in our words '*Di*-urnal' and '*Di*-vine' — the god of *Day*, Jupiter the revealer. Athena is his daughter, but especially daughter of the Intellect, springing armed from the head. We are only with the help of recent investigation beginning to penetrate the depth of meaning couched under the Athenaic symbols; but I may note rapidly, that her ægis, the mantle with the serpent fringes, in which she often, in the best statues, is represented as folding up her left hand, for better guard; and the Gorgon, on her shield, are both representative mainly of the chilling horror and sadness (turning men to stone, as it were,) of the outmost and superficial spheres of knowledge — that knowledge which separates, in bitterness, hardness, and sorrow, the heart of the full-grown man from the heart of the child. For out of imperfect knowledge spring terror, dissension, danger, and disdain; but from perfect knowledge, given by the full-revealed Athena, strength and peace, in sign of which she is crowned with the olive spray, and bears the resistless spear.

This, then, was the Greek conception of purest Deity; and every habit of life, and every form of his art developed themselves from the seeking this bright, serene, resistless wisdom; and setting himself, as a man, to do things evermore rightly and strongly; not with any ardent affection or ultimate hope; but with a resolute and continent energy of will, as knowing that for failure there was no consolation, and for sin there was no remission. And the Greek architecture rose unerring, bright, clearly defined, and self-contained.

Next followed in Europe the great Christian faith, which was essentially the religion of Comfort. Its great doctrine is the remission of sins; for which cause, it happens, too often, in certain phases of Christianity, that sin and sickness themselves are partly glorified, as if, the more you had to be healed of, the more divine was the healing. The practical result of this doctrine, in art, is a continual contemplation of sin and disease, and of imaginary states of purification from them; thus we have an architecture conceived in a mingled sentiment of melancholy and aspiration, partly severe, partly luxuriant, which will bend itself to every one of our needs, and every one of our fancies, and be strong or weak with us, as we are strong or weak ourselves. It is, of all architecture, the basest, when base people build it — of all, the noblest, when built by the noble.

And now note that both these religions — Greek and Mediæval — perished by falsehood in their own main purpose. The Greek religion of Wisdom perished in a false philosophy — 'Oppositions of science, falsely so called.' The Mediæval religion of Consolation perished in false comfort; in remission of sins given lyingly. It was the selling of absolution that ended the Mediæval faith; and I can tell you more, it is the selling of absolution which, to the end of time, will mark false Christianity. Pure Christianity gives her remission of sins only by *ending* them; but false Christianity gets her remission of sins by *compounding for* them. And there are many ways of compounding for them. We English have beautiful little quiet ways of buying absolution, whether in low Church or high, far more cunning than any of Tetzel's trading.

Then, thirdly, there followed the religion of Pleasure, in which all Europe gave itself to luxury, ending in death. First, *bals masqués* in every saloon, and then guillotines in every square. And all these three worships issue in vast temple building. Your Greek worshiped Wisdom, and built you the Parthenon — the Virgin's temple. The Mediæval worshiped Consolation, and built you Virgin temples also — but to our Lady of Salvation. Then the Revivalist worshiped beauty, of a sort, and built you Versailles and the Vatican. Now, lastly, will you tell me what *we* worship, and what *we* build?

You know we are speaking always of the real, active, continual, national worship; that by which men act, while they live; not that which they talk of, when they die. Now, we have, indeed, a nominal religion, to which we pay tithes of property and sevenths of time; but we have also a practical and earnest religion, to which we devote nine-tenths of our property, and six-sevenths of our time. And we dispute a great deal about the nominal religion: but we are all unanimous about this practical one; of which I think you will admit that the ruling goddess may be best generally described as the 'Goddess of Getting-on,' or 'Britannia of the Market.' The Athenians had an 'Athena Agoraia,' or Athena of the Market; but she was a subordinate type of their goddess, while our Britannia Agoraia is the principal type of ours. And all your great architectural works are, of course, built to her. It is long since you built a great cathedral; and how you would laugh at me if I proposed building a cathedral on the top of one of these hills of yours, to make it an Acropolis! But your railroad mounds, vaster than the walls of Babylon; your railroad stations, vaster than the temple of Ephesus, and innumerable; your chimneys, how much more mighty and costly than cathedral spires! your harbor piers; your warehouses; your exchanges! — all these are built to your great Goddess of 'Getting-on'; and she has formed, and will continue to form, your architecture, as long as you worship her; and it is quite vain to ask me to tell you how to build to *her;* you know far better than I.

There might indeed, on some theories, be a conceivably good architecture for Exchanges — that is to say, if there were any heroism in the fact or deed of exchange, which might be typically carved on the outside of your building. For, you know, all beautiful architecture must be adorned with sculpture or painting; and for sculpture or painting, you must have a subject. And hitherto it has been a received opinion among the nations of the world that the only right subjects for either, were *heroisms* of some sort. Even on his pots and his flagons, the Greek put a Hercules slaying lions, or an Apollo slaying serpents, or Bacchus slaying melancholy giants, and earthborn despondencies. On his temples, the Greek put contests of great warriors in founding states, or of gods with evil spirits. On his houses and temples alike, the Christian put carvings of angels conquering devils; or of hero-martyrs exchanging this world for another: subject inappropriate, I think, to our direction of exchange here. And the Master of Christians not only left his followers without any orders as to the sculpture of affairs of exchange on the outside of buildings, but gave some strong evidence of his dislike of affairs of exchange within them. And yet there might surely be a heroism in such affairs; and all commerce become a kind of selling of doves, not impious. The wonder has always been great to me, that heroism has never been supposed to be in anywise consistent with the practice of supplying people with food, or clothes; but rather with that of quartering one's self upon them for food, and stripping them of their clothes. Spoiling of armor is an heroic deed in all ages; but the selling of clothes, old, or new, has never taken any color of magnanimity. Yet one does not see why feeding the hungry and clothing the naked should ever become base business, even when engaged in on a large scale. If one could contrive to attach the notion of conquest to them anyhow! so that, supposing there were anywhere an obstinate race, who refused to be comforted, one might take some pride in giving them compulsory comfort! and as it were, '*occupying* a country' with one's gifts, instead of one's armies? If one could only consider it as much a victory to get a barren field sown, as to get an eared field stripped; and contend who should build villages, instead of who should 'carry' them! Are not all forms of heroism conceivable in doing these serviceable deeds? You doubt who is strongest? It might be ascertained by push of spade, as well as push of sword. Who is wisest? There are witty things to be thought of in planning other business than campaigns. Who is bravest? There are always the elements to fight with, stronger than men; and nearly as merciless.

The only absolutely and unapproachably heroic element in the soldier's work seems to be — that he is paid little for it — and regularly: while you traffickers, and exchangers, and others occupied in presumably benevolent business, like to be paid much for it — and by chance. I never can make out how it is that a *knight*-errant does not expect to be paid for his trouble, but a *peddler*-errant always does; — that people are willing to take hard knocks for nothing, but never to sell ribbons cheap; that they are ready to go on fervent crusades, to recover the tomb of a buried God, but never on any travels to fulfil the orders of a living one; — that they will go anywhere barefoot to preach their faith, but must be well bribed to practise it, and are perfectly ready to give the Gospel gratis, but never the loaves and fishes.

If you choose to take the matter up on any such soldierly principle; to do your commerce, and your feeding of nations, for fixed salaries; and to be as particular about giving people the best food, and the best cloth, as soldiers are about giving them the best gunpowder, I could carve something for you on your exchange worth looking at. But I can only at present suggest decorating its frieze with pendant purses; and making its pillars broad at the base, for the sticking of bills. And in the innermost chambers of it there might be a statue of Britannia of the Market, who may have, perhaps advisably, a partridge for her crest, typical at once of her courage in fighting for noble ideas, and of her interest in game; and round its neck, the inscription in golden letters, *Perdix fovit quae non peperit.* Then, for her spear, she might have a weaver's beam; and on her shield, instead of St. George's Cross, the Milanese boar, semi-fleeced, with the town of Gennesaret proper, in the field; and the legend 'In the best market,' and her corselet, of leather, folded over her heart in the shape of a purse, with thirty slits in it, for a piece of money to go in at, on each day of the month. And I doubt not but that people would come to see your exchange, and its goddess, with applause.

Nevertheless, I want to point out to you certain strange characters in this goddess of yours. She differs from the great Greek and Mediæval deities essentially in two things — first, as to the continuance of her presumed power; secondly, as to the extent of it.

Ist, as to the Continuance.

The Greek Goddess of Wisdom gave continual increase of wisdom; as the Christian Spirit of Comfort (or Comforter) continual increase of comfort. There was no question, with these, of any limit or cessation of function. But with your Agora Goddess, that is just the most important question. Getting on — but where to? Gathering together — but how much? Do you mean to gather always — never to spend? If so I wish you joy of your goddess, for I am just as well off as you, without the trouble of worshiping her at all. But if you do not spend, somebody else will — somebody else must. And it is because of this (among many other such errors) that I have fearlessly declared your so-called science of Political Economy to be no science; because, namely, it has omitted the study of exactly the most important branch of the business — the study of *spending*. For spend you must, and as much as you make, ultimately. You gather corn: — will you bury England under a heap of grain; or will you, when you have gathered, finally eat? You gather gold: — will you make your house-roofs of it, or pave your streets with it? That is still one way of spending it. But if you keep it, that you may get more, I 'll give you more; I 'll give you all the gold you want — all you can imagine — if you can tell me what you 'll do with it. You shall have thousands of gold pieces; — thousands of thousands — millions — mountains, of gold; where will you keep them? Will you put an Olympus of silver upon a golden Pelion — make Ossa like a wart? Do you think the rain and dew would then come down to you, in the streams from such mountains, more blessedly than they will down the mountains which God has made for you, of moss and whinstone? But it is not gold that you want to gather! What is it? greenbacks? No; not those neither. What is it then — is it ciphers after a capital I? Cannot you practise writing ciphers, and write as many as you want! Write ciphers for an hour every morning, in a big book, and say every evening, I am worth all those naughts more than I was yesterday. Won't that do? Well, what in the name of Plutus is it you want? Not gold, not greenbacks, not ciphers after a capital I? You will have to answer, after all, 'No; we want, somehow or other, money's *worth.*' Well, what is that? Let your Goddess of Getting-on discover it, and let her learn to stay therein.

II. But there is yet another question to be asked respecting this Goddess of Getting-on. The first was of the continuance of her power; the second is of its extent.

Pallas and the Madonna were supposed to be all the world's Pallas, and all the world's Madonna. They could teach all men, and they could comfort all men. But, look strictly into the nature of the power of your Goddess of Getting-on; and you will find she is the Goddess — not of everybody's getting on — but only of somebody's getting on. This is a vital, or rather deathful, distinction. Examine it in your own ideal of the state of national life which this Goddess is to evoke and maintain. I asked you what it was, when I was last here; — you have never told me. Now, shall I try to tell you?

Your ideal of human life then is, I think, that it should be passed in a pleasant undulating world, with iron and coal everywhere underneath it. On each pleasant bank of this world is to be a beautiful mansion, with two wings; and stables, and coach-houses; a moderately sized park; a large garden and hothouses; and pleasant carriage drives through the shrubberies. In this mansion are to live the favored votaries of the Goddess; the English gentleman, with his gracious wife, and his beautiful family; he always able to have the boudoir and the jewels for the wife, and the beautiful ball dresses for the daughters, and hunters for the sons, and a shooting in the Highlands for himself. At the bottom of the bank, is to be the mill; not less than a quarter of a mile long, with a steam engine at each end, and two in the middle, and a chimney three hundred feet high. In this mill are to be in constant employment from eight hundred to a thousand workers, who never drink, never strike, always go to church on Sunday, and always express themselves in respectful language.

Is not that, broadly, and in the main features, the kind of thing you propose to yourselves? It is very pretty indeed, seen from above; not at all so pretty, seen from below. For, observe, while to one family this deity is indeed the Goddess of Getting-on, to a thousand families she is the Goddess of *not* Getting-on. 'Nay,' you say, 'they have all their chance.' Yes, so has every one in a lottery, but there must always be the same number of blanks. 'Ah! but in a lottery it is not skill and intelligence which take the lead, but blind chance.' What then! do you think the old practice, that 'they should take who have the power, and they should keep who can,' is less iniquitous, when the power has become power of brains instead of fist? and that, though we may not take advantage of a child's or a woman's weakness, we may of a man's foolishness? 'Nay, but finally, work must be done, and some one must be at the top, some one at the bottom.' Granted, my friends. Work must always be, and captains of work must always be; and if you in the least remember the tone of any of my writings, you must know that they are thought unfit for this age, because they are always insisting on need of government, and speaking with scorn of liberty. But I beg you to observe that there is a wide difference between being captains or governors of work, and taking the profits of it. It does not follow, because you are general of an army, that you are to take all the treasure, or land, it wins; (if it fight for treasure or land;) neither, because you are king of a nation, that you are to consume all the profits of the nation's work. Real kings, on the contrary, are known invariably by their doing quite the reverse of this, — by their taking the least possible quantity of the nation's work for themselves. There is no test of real kinghood so infallible as that. Does the crowned creature live simply, bravely, unostentatiously? probably he *is* a King. Does he cover his body with jewels, and his table with delicates? in all probability he is *not* a King. It is possible he may be, as Solomon was; but that is when the nation shares his splendor with him. Solomon made gold, not only to be in his own palace as stones, but to be in Jerusalem as stones. But, even so, for the most part, these splendid kinghoods expire in ruin, and only the true kinghoods live, which are of royal laborers governing loyal laborers; who, both leading rough lives, establish the true dynasties. Conclusively, you will find that because you are king of a nation, it does not follow that you are to gather for yourself all the wealth of that nation; neither, because you are king of a small part of the nation, and lord over the means of its maintenance — over field, or mill, or mine, — are you to take all the produce of that piece of the foundation of national existence for yourself.

You will tell me I need not preach against these things, for I cannot mend them. No, good friends, I cannot; but you can, and you will; or something else can and will. Even good things have no abiding power — and shall these evil things persist in victorious evil? All history shows, on the contrary, that to be the exact thing they never can do. Change *must* come; but it is ours to determine whether change of growth, or change of death. Shall the Parthenon be in ruins on its rock, and Bolton priory in its meadow, but these mills of yours be the consummation of the buildings of the earth, and their wheels be as the wheels of eternity? Think you that 'men may come, and men may go,' but — mills — go on forever? Not so; out of these, better or worse shall come; and it is for you to choose which.

I know that none of this wrong is done with deliberate purpose. I know, on the contrary, that you wish your workmen well; that you do much for them, and that you desire to do more for them, if you saw your way to such benevolence safely. I know that even all this wrong and misery are brought about by a warped sense of duty, each of you striving to do his best; but, unhappily, not knowing for whom this best should be done. And all our hearts have been betrayed by the plausible impiety of the modern economist, telling us that, 'To do the best for ourselves, is finally to do the best for others.' Friends, our great Master said not so; and most absolutely we shall find this world is not made so. Indeed, to do the best for others, is finally to do the best for ourselves; but it will not do to have our eyes fixed on that issue. The Pagans had got beyond that. Hear what a Pagan says of this matter; hear what were, perhaps, the last written words of Plato, — if not the last actually written (for this we cannot know), yet assuredly in fact and power his parting words — in which, endeavoring to give full crowning and harmonious close to all his thoughts, and to speak the sum of them by the imagined sentence of the Great Spirit, his strength and his heart fail him, and the words cease, broken off forever.

They are at the close of the dialogue called 'Critias,' in which he describes, partly from real tradition, partly in ideal dream, the early state of Athens; and the genesis, and order, and religion, of the fabled isle of Atlantis; in which genesis he conceives the same first perfection and final degeneracy of man, which in our own Scriptural tradition is expressed by saying that the Sons of God intermarried with the daughters of men, for he supposes the earliest race to have been indeed the children of God; and to have corrupted themselves, until 'their spot was not the spot of his children.' And this, he says, was the end; that indeed 'through many generations, so long as the God's nature in them yet was full, they were submissive to the sacred laws, and carried themselves lovingly to all that had kindred with them in divineness; for their uttermost spirit was faithful and true, and in every wise great; so that, in *all meekness of wisdom, they dealt with each other*, and took all the chances of life; and despising all things except virtue, they cared little what happened day by day, and *bore lightly the burden* of gold and of possessions; for they saw that, if *only their common love and virtue increased, all these things would be increased together with them;* but to set their esteem and ardent pursuit upon material possession would be to lose that first, and their virtue and affection together with it. And by such reasoning, and what of the divine nature remained in them, they gained all this greatness of which we have already told; but when the God's part of them faded and became extinct, being mixed again and again, and effaced by the prevalent mortality; and the human nature at last exceeded, they then became unable to endure the courses of fortune; and fell into shapelessness of life, and baseness in the sight of him who could see, having lost everything that was fairest of their honor; while to the blind hearts which could not discern the true life, tending to happiness, it seemed that they were then chiefly noble and happy, being filled with all iniquity of inordinate possession and power. Whereupon, the God of gods, whose Kinghood is in laws, beholding a once just nation thus cast into misery, and desiring to lay such punishment upon them as might make them repent into restraining, gathered together all the gods into his dwelling place, which from heaven's center overlooks whatever has part in creation; and having assembled them, he said' —

The rest is silence. Last words of the chief wisdom of the heathen, spoken of this idol of riches; this idol of yours; this golden image, high by measureless cubits, set up where your green fields of England are furnace-burnt into the likeness of the plain of Dura; this idol, forbidden to us, first of all idols, by our own Master and faith; forbidden to us also by every human lip that has ever, in any age or people, been accounted of as able to speak according to the purposes of God. Continue to make that forbidden deity your principal one, and soon no more art, no more science, no more pleasure will be possible. Catastrophe will come; or, worse than catastrophe, slow moldering and withering into Hades. But if you can fix some conception of a true human state of life to be striven for — life, good for all men, as for yourselves; if you can determine some honest and simple order of existence; following those trodden ways of wisdom, which are pleasantness, and seeking her quiet and withdrawn paths, which are peace; — then, and so sanctifying wealth into 'commonwealth,' all your art, your literature, your daily labors, your domestic affection, and citizen's duty, will join and increase into one magnificent harmony. You will know then how to build, well enough; you will build with stone well, but with flesh better; temples not made with hands, but riveted of hearts; and that kind of marble, crimson-veined, is indeed eternal.

1866

Robert Louis Stevenson (1850–1894)

ÆS TRIPLEX

The changes wrought by death are in themselves so sharp and final, and so terrible and melancholy in their consequences, that the thing stands alone in man's experience, and has no parallel upon earth. It outdoes all other accidents because it is the last of them. Sometimes it leaps suddenly upon its victims, like a Thug; sometimes it lays a regular siege and creeps upon their citadel during a score of years. And when the business is done, there is sore havoc made in other people's lives, and a pin knocked out by which many subsidiary friendships hung together. There are empty chairs, solitary walks, and single beds at night. Again, in taking away our friends, death does not take them away utterly, but leaves behind a mocking, tragical, and soon intolerable residue, which must be hurriedly concealed. Hence a whole chapter of sights and customs striking to the mind, from the pyramids of Egypt to the gibbets and dule trees of mediæval Europe. The poorest persons have a bit of pageant going towards the tomb; memorial stones are set up over the least memorable; and, in order to preserve some show of respect for what remains of our old loves and friendships, we must accompany it with much grimly ludicrous ceremonial, and the hired undertaker parades before the door. All this, and much more of the same sort, accompanied by the eloquence of poets, has gone a great way to put humanity in error; nay, in many philosophies the error has been embodied and laid down with every circumstance of logic; although in real life the bustle and swiftness, in leaving people little time to think, have not left them time enough to go dangerously wrong in practice.

As a matter of fact, although few things are spoken of with more fearful whisperings than this prospect of death, few have less influence on conduct under healthy circumstances. We have all heard of cities in South America built upon the side of fiery mountains, and how, even in this tremendous neighborhood, the inhabitants are not a jot more impressed by the solemnity of mortal conditions than if they were delving gardens in the greenest corner of England. There are serenades and suppers and much gallantry among the myrtles overhead; and meanwhile the foundation shudders underfoot, the bowels of the mountain growl, and at any moment living ruin may leap sky-high into the moonlight, and tumble man and his merry-making in the dust. In the eyes of very young people, and very dull old ones, there is something indescribably reckless and desperate in such a picture. It seems not credible that respectable married people, with umbrellas, should find appetite for a bit of supper within quite a long distance of a fiery mountain; ordinary life begins to smell of high-handed debauch when it is carried on so close to a catastrophe; and even cheese and salad, it seems, could hardly be relished in such circumstances without something like a defiance of the Creator. It should be a place for nobody but hermits dwelling in prayer and maceration, or mere born-devils drowning care in a perpetual carouse.

And yet, when one comes to think upon it calmly, the situation of these South American citizens forms only a very pale figure for the state of ordinary mankind. This world itself, travelling blindly and swiftly in overcrowded space, among a million other worlds travelling blindly and swiftly in contrary directions, may very well come by a knock that would set it into explosion like a penny squib. And what, pathologically looked at, is the human body with all its organs, but a mere bagful of petards? The least of these is as dangerous to the whole economy as the ship's powder-magazine to the ship; and with every breath we breathe, and every meal we eat, we are putting one or more of them in peril. If we clung as devotedly as some philosophers pretend we do to the abstract idea of life, or were half as frightened as they make out we are, for the subversive accident that ends it all, the trumpets might sound by the hour and no one would follow them into battle — the blue-peter might fly at the truck, but who would climb into a sea-going ship? Think (if these philosophers were right) with what a preparation of spirit we should affront the daily peril of the dinner-table: a deadlier spot than any battle-field in history, where the far greater proportion of our ancestors have miserably left their bones! What woman would ever be lured into marriage, so much more dangerous than the wildest sea? And what would it be to grow old? For, after a certain distance, every step we take in life we find the ice growing thinner below our feet, and all around us and behind us we see our contemporaries going through. By the time a man gets well into the seventies, his continued existence is a mere miracle; and when he lays his old bones in bed for the night, there is an overwhelming probability that he will never see the day. Do the old men mind it, as a matter of fact? Why, no. They were never merrier; they have their grog at night, and tell the raciest stories; they hear of the death of people about their own age, or even younger, not as if it was a grisly warning, but with a simple childlike pleasure at having outlived some one else; and when a draught might puff them out like a guttering candle, or a bit of a stumble shatter them like so much glass, their old hearts keep sound and unaffrighted, and they go on, bubbling with laughter, through years of man's age compared to which the valley at Balaclava was as safe and peaceful as a village cricket-green on Sunday. It may fairly be questioned (if we look to the peril only) whether it was a much more daring feat for Curtius to plunge into the gulf, than for any old gentleman of ninety to doff his clothes and clamber into bed.

Indeed, it is a memorable subject for consideration, with what unconcern and gaiety mankind pricks on along the Valley of the Shadow of Death. The whole way is one wilderness of snares, and the end of it, for those who fear the last pinch, is irrevocable ruin. And yet we go spinning through it all, like a party for the Derby. Perhaps the reader remembers one of the humorous devices of the deified Caligula: how he encouraged a vast concourse of holiday-makers on to his bridge over Baiæ bay; and when they were in the height of their enjoyment, turned loose the Prætorian guards among the company, and had them tossed into the sea. This is no bad miniature of the dealings of nature with the transitory race of man. Only, what a chequered picnic we have of it, even while it lasts! and into what great waters, not to be crossed by any swimmer, God's pale Prætorian throws us over in the end!

We live the time that a match flickers; we pop the cork of a ginger-beer bottle, and the earthquake swallows us on the instant. Is it not odd, is it not incongruous, is it not, in the highest sense of human speech, incredible, that we should think so highly of the ginger-beer, and regard so little the devouring earthquake? The love of Life and the fear of Death are two famous phrases that grow harder to understand the more we think about them. It is a well-known fact that an immense proportion of boat accidents would never happen if people held the sheet in their hands instead of making it fast; and yet, unless it be some martinet of a professional mariner or some landsman with shattered nerves, every one of God's creatures makes it fast. A strange instance of man's unconcern and brazen boldness in the face of death!

We confound ourselves with metaphysical phrases, which we import into daily talk with noble inappropriateness. We have no idea of what death is, apart from its circumstances and some of its consequences to others; and although we have some experience of living there is not a man on earth who has flown so high into abstraction as to have any practical guess at the meaning of the word *life*. All literature, from Job and Omar Khayyám to Thomas Carlyle or Walt Whitman, is but an attempt to look upon the human state with such largeness of view as shall enable us to rise from the consideration of living to the Definition of Life. And our sages give us about the best satisfaction in their power when they say that it is a vapour, or a show, or made out of the same stuff with dreams. Philosophy, in its more rigid sense, has been at the same work for ages; and after a myriad bald heads have wagged over the problem, and piles of words have been heaped one upon another into dry and cloudy volumes without end; philosophy has the honour of laying before us, with modest pride, her contribution towards the subject: that life is a Permanent Possibility of Sensation. Truly a fine result! A man may very well love beef, or hunting, or a woman; but surely, surely, not a Permanent Possibility of Sensation! He may be afraid of a precipice, or a dentist, or a large enemy with a club, or even an undertaker's man; but not certainly of abstract death. We may trick with the word life in its dozen senses until we are weary of tricking; we may argue in terms of all the philosophies on earth, but one fact remains true throughout — that we do not love life, in the sense that we are greatly preoccupied about its conservation; that we do not, properly speaking, love life at all, but living. Into the views of the least careful there will enter some degree of providence; no man's eyes are fixed entirely on the passing hour; but although we have some anticipation of good health, good weather, wine, active employment, love, and self-approval, the sum of these anticipations does not amount to anything like a general view of life's possibilities and issues; nor are those who cherish them most vividly, at all the most scrupulous of their personal safety. To be deeply interested in the accidents of our existence, to enjoy keenly the mixed texture of human experience, rather leads a man to disregard precautions, and risk his neck against a straw. For surely the love of living is stronger in an Alpine climber roping over a peril, or a hunter riding merrily at a stiff fence, than in a creature who lives upon a diet and walks a measured distance in the interest of his constitution.

There is a great deal of very vile nonsense talked upon both sides of the matter: tearing divines reducing life to the dimensions of a mere funeral procession, so short as to be hardly decent; and melancholy unbelievers yearning for the tomb as if it were a world too far away. Both sides must feel a little ashamed of their performances now and again when they draw in their chairs to dinner. Indeed, a good meal and a bottle of wine is an answer to most standard works upon the question. When a man's heart warms to his viands, he forgets a great deal of sophistry, and soars into a rosy zone of contemplation. Death may be knocking at the door, like the Commander's statue; we have something else in hand, thank God, and let him knock. Passing bells are ringing all the world over. All the world over, and every hour, some one is parting company with all his aches and ecstasies. For us also the trap is laid. But we are so fond of life that we have no leisure to entertain the terror of death. It is a honeymoon with us all through, and none of the longest. Small blame to us if we give our whole hearts to this glowing bride of ours, to the appetites, to honour, to the hungry curiosity of the mind, to the pleasure of the eyes in nature, and the pride of our own nimble bodies.

We all of us appreciate the sensations; but as for caring about the Permanence of the Possibility, a man's head is generally very bald, and his senses very dull, before he comes to that. Whether we regard life as a lane leading to a dead wall — a mere bag's end, as the French say — or whether we think of it as a vestibule or gymnasium, where we wait our turn and prepare our faculties for some more noble destiny; whether we thunder in a pulpit, or pule in little atheistic poetry-books, about its vanity and brevity; whether we look justly for years of health and vigour, or are about to mount into a Bath-chair, as a step towards the hearse; in each and all of these views and situations there is but one conclusion possible: that a man should stop his ears against paralysing terror, and run the race that is set before him with a single mind. No one surely could have recoiled with more heartache and terror from the thought of death than our respected lexicographer; and yet we know how little it affected his conduct, how wisely and boldly he walked, and in what a fresh and lively vein he spoke of life. Already an old man, he ventured on his Highland tour; and his heart, bound with triple brass, did not recoil before twenty-seven individual cups of tea. As courage and intelligence are the two qualities best worth a good man's cultivation, so it is the first part of intelligence to recognize our precarious estate in life, and the first part of courage to be not at all abashed before the fact. A frank and somewhat headlong carriage, not looking too anxiously before, not dallying in maudlin regret over the past, stamps the man who is well armoured for this world.

And not only well armoured for himself, but a good friend and a good citizen to boot. We do not go to cowards for tender dealing; there is nothing so cruel as panic; the man who has least fear for his own carcass, has most time to consider others. That eminent chemist who took his walks abroad in tin shoes, and subsisted wholly upon tepid milk, had all his work cut out for him in considerate dealings with his own digestion. So soon as prudence has begun to grow up in the brain, like a dismal fungus, it finds its first expression in a paralysis of generous acts. The victim begins to shrink spiritually; he develops a fancy for parlours with a regulated temperature, and takes his morality on the principle of tin shoes and tepid milk. The care of one important body or soul becomes so engrossing, that all the noises of the outer world begin to come thin and faint into the parlour with the regulated temperature; and the tin shoes go equably forward over blood and rain. To be otherwise is to ossify; and the scruple-monger ends by standing stock-still. Now the man who has his heart on his sleeve, and a good whirling weathercock of a brain, who reckons his life as a thing to be dashingly used and cheerfully hazarded, makes a very different acquaintance of the world, keeps all his pulses going true and fast, and gathers impetus as he runs, until, if he be running towards anything better than wildfire, he may shoot up and become a constellation in the end. Lord look after his health, Lord have a care of his soul, says he; and he has at the key of the position, and swashes through incongruity and peril towards his aim. Death is on all sides of him with pointed batteries, as he is on all sides of all of us; unfortunate surprises gird him round; mim-mouthed friends and relations hold up their hands in quite a little elegiacal synod about his path: and what cares he for all this? Being a true lover of living, a fellow with something pushing and spontaneous in his inside, he must, like any other soldier, in any other stirring, deadly warfare, push on at his best pace until he touch the goal. 'A peerage or Westminster Abbey!' cried Nelson in his bright, boyish, heroic manner. These are great incentives; not for any of these, but for the plain satisfaction of living, of being about their business in some sort or other, do the brave, serviceable men of every nation tread down the nettle danger, and pass flyingly over all the stumbling-blocks of prudence. Think of the heroism of Johnson, think of that superb indifference to mortal limitation that set him upon his dictionary, and carried him through triumphantly until the end! Who, if he were wisely considerate of things at large, would ever embark upon any work much more considerable than a half-penny post card? Who would project a serial novel, after Thackeray and Dickens had each fallen in mid-course? Who would find heart enough to begin to live, if he dallied with the consideration of death?

And, after all, what sorry and pitiful quibbling all this is! To forego all the issues of living in a parlour with a regulated temperature — as if that were not to die a hundred times over, and for ten years at a stretch! As if it were not to die in one's own lifetime, and without even the sad immunities of death! As if it were not to die, and yet be the patient spectators of our own pitiable change! The Permanent Possibility is preserved, but the sensations carefully held at arm's length, as if one kept a photographic plate in a dark chamber. It is better to lose health like a spendthrift than to waste it like a miser. It is better to live and be done with it, than to die daily in the sick-room. By all means begin your folio; even if the doctor does not give you a year, even if he hesitates about a month, make one brave push and see what can be accomplished in a week. It is not only in finished undertakings that we ought to honour useful labour. A spirit goes out of the man who means execution, which outlives the most untimely ending. All who have meant good work with their whole hearts, have done good work, although they may die before they have the time to sign it. Every heart that has beat strong and cheerfully has left a hopeful impulse behind it in the world, and bettered the tradition of mankind. And even if death catch people, like an open pitfall, and in mid-career, laying out vast projects, and planning monstrous foundations, flushed with hope, and their mouths full of boastful language, they should be at once tripped up and silenced: is there not something brave and spirited in such a termination? and does not life go down with a better grace, foaming in full body over a precipice, than miserably straggling to an end in sandy deltas? When the Greeks made their fine saying that those whom the gods love die young, I cannot help believing they had this sort of death also in their eye. For surely, at whatever age it overtake the man, this is to die young. Death has not been suffered to take so much as an illusion from his heart. In the hot-fit of life, a-tiptoe on the highest point of being, he passes at a bound on to the other side. The noise of the mallet and chisel is scarcely quenched, the trumpets are hardly done blowing, when, trailing with him clouds of glory, this happy-starred, full-blooded spirit shoots into the spiritual land.

1881

PULVIS ET UMBRA *

We look for some reward of our endeavours and are disappointed; not success, not happiness, not even peace of conscience, crowns our ineffectual efforts to do well. Our frailties are invincible, our virtues barren; the battle goes sore against us to the going down of the sun. The canting moralist tells us of right and wrong; and we look abroad, even on the face of our small earth, and find them change with every climate, and no country where some action is not honoured for a virtue and none where it is not branded for a vice; and we look in our experience, and find no vital congruity in the wisest rules, but at the best a municipal fitness. It is not strange if we are tempted to despair of good. We ask too much. Our religions and moralities have been trimmed to flatter us, till they are all emasculate and sentimentalised, and only please and weaken. Truth is of a rougher strain. In the harsh face of life, faith can read a bracing gospel. The human race is a thing more ancient than the ten commandments; and the bones and revolutions of the Kosmos, in whose joints we are but moss and fungus, more ancient still.

1

Of the Kosmos in the last resort, science reports many doubtful things and all of them appalling. There seems no substance on this solid globe on which we stamp: nothing but symbols and ratios. Symbols and ratios carry us and bring us forth and beat us down; gravity that swings the incommensurable suns and worlds through space, is but a figment varying inversely as the squares of distances; and the suns and worlds themselves, imponderable figures of abstractions, NH_3 and H_2O. Consideration dares not dwell upon this view; that way madness lies; science carries us into zones of speculation, where there is no habitable city for the mind of man.

But take the Kosmos with a grosser faith, as our senses give it us. We behold space sown with rotary islands, suns and worlds and the shards and wrecks of systems: some, like the sun, still blazing; some rotting, like the earth; others, like the moon, stable in desolation. All of these we take to be made of something we call matter: a thing no analysis can help us to conceive; to whose incredible properties no familiarities can reconcile our minds. This stuff, when not purified by the lustration of fire, rots uncleanly into something we call life; seized through all its atoms with a pediculous malady; swelling in tumours that become independent, sometimes even (by an abhorrent prodigy) locomotory; one splitting into millions, millions cohering into one, as the malady proceeds through varying stages. This vital putrescence of the dust, used as we are to it, yet strikes us with occasional disgust, and the profusion of worms in a piece of ancient turf, or the air of a marsh darkened with insects, will sometimes check our breathing so that we aspire for cleaner places. But none is clean: the moving sand is infected with lice; the pure spring, where it bursts out of the mountain, is a mere issue of worms; even in the hard rock the crystal is forming.

In two main shapes this eruption covers the countenance of the earth: the animal and

* *Across the Plains.* By permission of Charles Scribner's Sons, publishers.

the vegetable: one in some degree the inversion of the other: the second rooted to the spot; the first coming detached out of its natal mud, and scurrying abroad with the myriad feet of insects or towering into the heavens on the wings of birds: a thing so inconceivable that, if it be well considered, the heart stops. To what passes with the anchored vermin, we have little clue: doubtless they have their joys and sorrows, their delights and killing agonies: it appears not how. But of the locomotory, to which we ourselves belong, we can tell more. These share with us a thousand miracles: the miracles of sight, of hearing, of the projection of sound, things that bridge space; the miracles of memory and reason, by which the present is conceived, and when it is gone, its image kept living in the brains of man and brute; the miracle of reproduction, with its imperious desires and staggering consequences. And to put the last touch upon this mountain mass of the revolting and the inconceivable, all these prey upon each other, lives tearing other lives in pieces, cramming them inside themselves, and by that summary process, growing fat: the vegetarian, the whale, perhaps the tree, not less than the lion of the desert; for the vegetarian is only the eater of the dumb.

Meanwhile our rotary island loaded with predatory life, and more drenched with blood, both animal and vegetable, than ever mutinied ship, scuds through space with unimaginable speed, and turns alternate cheeks to the reverberation of a blazing world, ninety million miles away.

II

What a monstrous spectre is this man, the disease of agglutinated dust, lifting alternate feet or lying drugged with slumber; killing, feeding, growing, bringing forth small copies of himself; grown upon with hair like grass, fitted with eyes that move and glitter in his face; a thing to set children screaming; — and yet looked at nearlier, known as his fellows know him, how surprising are his attributes! Poor soul, here for so little, cast among so many hardships, filled with desires so incommensurate and so inconsistent, savagely surrounded, savagely descended, irremediably condemned to prey upon his fellow lives: who should have blamed him had he been of a piece with his destiny and a being merely barbarous? And we look and behold him instead filled with imperfect virtues: infinitely childish, often admirably valiant, often touchingly kind; sitting down, amidst his momentary life, to debate of right and wrong and the attributes of the deity; rising up to do battle for an egg or die for an idea; singling out his friends and his mate with cordial affection; bringing forth in pain, rearing with long-suffering solicitude, his young. To touch the heart of his mystery, we find in him one thought, strange to the point of lunacy: the thought of duty; the thought of something owing to himself, to his neighbour, to his God: an ideal of decency, to which he would rise if it were possible; a limit of shame, below which, if it be possible, he will not stoop. The design in most men is one of conformity; here and there, in picked natures, it transcends itself and soars on the other side, arming martyrs with independence; but in all, in their degrees, it is a bosom thought: — Not in man alone, for we trace it in dogs and cats whom we know fairly well, and doubtless some similar point of honour sways the elephant, the oyster, and the louse, of whom we know so little: — But in man, at least, it sways with so complete an empire that merely selfish things come second, even with the selfish: that appetites are starved, fears are conquered, pains supported; that almost the dullest shrinks from the reproof of a glance, although it were a child's; and all but the most cowardly stand amid the risks of war; and the more noble, having strongly conceived an act as due to their ideal, affront and embrace death. Strange enough if, with their singular origin and perverted practice, they think they are to be rewarded in some future life: stranger still, if they are persuaded of the contrary, and think this blow, which they solicit, will strike them senseless for eternity. I shall be reminded what a tragedy of misconception and misconduct man at large presents: of organised injustice, cowardly violence, and treacherous crime; and of the damning imperfections of the best. They cannot be too darkly drawn. Man is indeed marked for failure in his efforts to do right. But where the best consistently miscarry, how tenfold more remarkable that all should continue to strive; and surely we should find it both touching and inspiriting, that in a field from which success is banished, our race should not cease to labour.

If the first view of this creature, stalking in his rotatory isle, be a thing to shake the courage of the stoutest, on this nearer sight, he startles us with an admiring wonder. It matters not where we look, under what climate we observe him, in what stage of society, in what depth of ignorance, burthened with what erroneous morality; by camp-fires in Assiniboia, the snow powdering his shoulders, the wind plucking his blanket, as he sits, passing the ceremonial calumet and uttering his grave opinions like a Roman senator; in ships at sea, a man inured to hardship and vile pleasures, his brightest hope a fiddle in a tavern and a bedizened trull who sells herself to rob him, and he for all that simple, innocent, cheerful, kindly like a child, constant to toil, brave to drown, for others; in the slums of cities, moving among indifferent millions to mechanical employments, without hope of change in the future, with scarce a pleasure in the present, and yet true to his virtues, honest up to his lights, kind to his neighbours, tempted perhaps in vain by the bright gin-palace, perhaps long-suffering with the drunken wife that ruins him; in India (a woman this time) kneeling with broken cries and streaming tears, as she drowns her child in the sacred river; in the brothel, the discard of society, living mainly on strong drink, fed with affronts, a fool, a thief, the comrade of thieves, and even here keeping the point of honour and the touch of pity, often repaying the world's scorn with service, often standing firm upon a scruple, and at a certain cost, rejecting riches: — everywhere some virtue cherished or affected, everywhere some decency of thought and carriage, everywhere the ensign of man's ineffectual goodness: — ah! if I could show you this! if I could show you these men and women, all the world over, in every stage of history, under every abuse of error, under every circumstance of failure, without hope, without help, without thanks, still obscurely fighting the lost fight of virtue, still clinging, in the brothel or on the scaffold, to some rag of honour, the poor jewel of their souls! They may seek to escape, and yet they cannot; it is not alone their privilege and glory, but their doom; they are condemned to some nobility; all their lives long, the desire of good is at their heels, the implacable hunter.

Of all earth's meteors, here at least is the most strange and consoling: That this ennobled lemur, this hair-crowned bubble of the dust, this inheritor of a few years and sorrows, should yet deny himself his rare delights, and add to his frequent pains, and live for an ideal, however misconceived. Nor can we stop with man. A new doctrine, received with screams a little while ago by canting moralists, and still not properly worked into the body of our thoughts, lights us a step farther into the heart of this rough but noble universe. For nowadays the pride of man denies in vain his kinship with the original dust. He stands no longer like a thing apart. Close at his heels we see the dog, prince of another genus: and in him too, we see dumbly testified the same cultus of an unattainable ideal, the same constancy in failure. Does it stop with the dog? We look at our feet where the ground is blackened with the swarming ant: a creature so small, so far from us in the hierarchy of brutes, that we can scarce trace and scarce comprehend his doings; and here also, in his ordered polities and rigorous justice, we see confessed the law of duty and the fact of individual sin. Does it stop, then, with the ant? Rather this desire of well-doing and this doom of frailty run through all the grades of life: rather is this earth, from the frosty top of Everest to the next margin of the internal fire, one stage of ineffectual virtues and one temple of pious tears and perseverance. The whole creation groaneth and travaileth together. It is the common and the god-like law of life. The browsers, the biters, the barkers, the hairy coats of field and forest, the squirrel in the oak, the thousand-footed creeper in the dust, as they share with us the gift of life, share with us the love of an ideal: strive like us — like us are tempted to grow weary of the struggle — to do well; like us receive at times unmerited refreshment, visitings of support, returns of courage; and are condemned like us to be crucified between that double law of the members and the will. Are they like us, I wonder, in the timid hope of some reward, some sugar with the drug? do they, too, stand aghast at unrewarded virtues, at the sufferings of those whom, in our partiality, we take to be just, and the prosperity of such as, in our blindness we call wicked? It may be, and yet God knows what they should look for. Even while they look, even while they repent, the foot of man treads them by thousands in the dust, the yelping hounds burst upon their trail, the bullet speeds, the knives are heating in the den of the vivisectionist; or the dew falls, and the generation of a day is blotted out. For these are creatures, compared with whom our weakness is strength, our ignorance wisdom, our brief span eternity.

And as we dwell, we living things, in our isle of terror and under the imminent hand of death, God forbid it should be man the erected, the reasoner, the wise in his own eyes — God forbid it should be man that wearies in well-doing, that despairs of unrewarded effort, or utters the language of complaint. Let it be enough for faith, that the whole creation groans in mortal frailty, strives with unconquerable constancy: surely not all in vain.

1892

CRITICISM

Matthew Arnold (1822–1888)

THE STUDY OF POETRY

'The future of poetry is immense, because in poetry, where it is worthy of its high destinies, our race, as time goes on, will find an ever surer and surer stay. There is not a creed which is not shaken, not an accredited dogma which is not shown to be questionable, not a received tradition which does not threaten to dissolve. Our religion has materialized itself in the fact, in the supposed fact; it has attached its emotion to the fact, and now the fact is failing it. But for poetry the idea is everything; the rest is a world of illusion, of divine illusion. Poetry attaches its emotion to the idea; the idea *is* the fact. The strongest part of our religion to-day is its unconscious poetry.'

Let me be permitted to quote these words of my own, as uttering the thought which should, in my opinion, go with us and govern us in all our study of poetry. In the present work it is the course of one great contributory stream to the world-river of poetry that we are invited to follow. We are here invited to trace the stream of English poetry. But whether we set ourselves, as here, to follow only one of the several streams that make the mighty river of poetry, or whether we seek to know them all, our governing thought should be the same. We should conceive of poetry worthily, and more highly than it has been the custom to conceive of it. We should conceive of it as capable of higher uses, and called to higher destinies, than those which in general men have assigned to it hitherto. More and more mankind will discover that we have to turn to poetry to interpret life for us, to console us, to sustain us. Without poetry, our science will appear incomplete; and most of what now passes with us for religion and philosophy will be replaced by poetry. Science, I say, will appear incomplete without it. For finely and truly does Wordsworth call poetry 'the impassioned expression which is in the countenance of all science'; and what is a countenance without its expression? Again, Wordsworth finely and truly calls poetry 'the breath and finer spirit of all knowledge': our religion, parading evidences such as those on which the popular mind relies now; our philosophy, pluming itself on its reasonings about causation and finite and infinite being; what are they but the shadows and dreams and false shows of knowledge? The day will come when we shall wonder at ourselves for having trusted to them, for having taken them seriously; and the more we perceive their hollowness, the more we shall prize 'the breath and finer spirit of knowledge' offered to us by poetry.

But if we conceive thus highly of the destinies of poetry, we must also set our standard for poetry high, since poetry, to be capable of fulfilling such high destinies, must be poetry of a high order of excellence. We must accustom ourselves to a high standard and to a strict judgment. Sainte-Beuve relates that Napoleon one day said, when somebody was spoken of in his presence as a charlatan: 'Charlatan as much as you please; but where is there *not* charlatanism?' — 'Yes,' answers Sainte-Beuve, 'in politics, in the art of governing mankind, that is perhaps true. But in the order of thought, in art, the glory, the eternal honour is that charlatanism shall find no entrance; herein lies the inviolableness of that noble portion of man's being.' It is admirably said, and let us hold fast to it. In poetry, which is thought and art in one, it is the glory, the eternal honour, that charlatanism shall find no entrance; that this noble sphere be kept inviolate and inviolable. Charlatanism is for confusing or obliterating the distinctions between excellent and inferior, sound and unsound or only half-sound, true and untrue or only half-true. It is charlatanism, conscious or unconscious, whenever we confuse or obliterate these. And in poetry, more than anywhere else, it is unpermissible to confuse or obliterate them. For in poetry the distinction between excellent and inferior, sound and unsound or only half-sound, true and untrue or only half-true, is of paramount importance. It is of paramount importance because of the high destinies of poetry. In poetry, as a criticism of life under the conditions fixed for such a criticism by the laws of poetic truth and poetic beauty, the spirit of our race will find, we have said, as time goes on and as other helps fail, its consolation and stay. But the consolation and stay will be of power in proportion to the power of the criticism of life. And the criticism of life will be of power in proportion as the poetry conveying it is excellent rather than inferior, sound rather than unsound or half-sound, true rather than untrue or half-true.

The best poetry is what we want; the best poetry will be found to have a power of forming, sustaining, and delighting us, as nothing else can. A clearer, deeper sense of the best in poetry, and of the strength and joy to be drawn from it, is the most precious benefit which we can gather from a poetical collection such as the present. And yet in the very nature and conduct of such a collection there is inevitably something which tends to obscure in us the consciousness of what our benefit should be, and to distract us from the pursuit of it. We should therefore steadily set it before our minds at the outset, and should compel ourselves to revert constantly to the thought of it as we proceed.

Yes; constantly in reading poetry, a sense for the best, the really excellent, and of the strength and joy to be drawn from it, should be present in our minds and should govern our estimate of what we read. But this real estimate, the only true one, is liable to be superseded, if we are not watchful, by two other kinds of estimate, the historic estimate and the personal estimate, both of which are fallacious. A poet or a poem may count to us historically, they may count to us on grounds personal to ourselves, and they may count to us really. They may count to us historically. The course of development of a nation's language, thought, and poetry, is profoundly interesting; and by regarding a poet's work as a stage in this course of development we may easily bring ourselves to make it of more importance as poetry than in itself it really is, we may come to use a language of quite exaggerated praise in criticising it; in short, to over-rate it. So arises in our poetic judgments the fallacy caused by the estimate which we may call historic. Then, again, a poet or a poem may count to us on grounds personal to ourselves. Our personal affinities, likings, and circumstances, have great power to sway our estimate of this or that poet's work, and to make us attach more importance to it as poetry than in itself it really possesses, because to us it is, or has been, of high importance. Here also we over-rate the object of our interest, and apply to it a language of praise which is quite exaggerated. And thus we get the source of a second fallacy in our poetic judgments — the fallacy caused by an estimate which we may call personal.

Both fallacies are natural. It is evident how naturally the study of the history and development of a poetry may incline a man to pause over reputations and works once conspicuous but now obscure, and to quarrel with a careless public for skipping, in obedience to mere tradition and habit, from one famous name or work in its national poetry to another, ignorant of what it misses, and of the reason for keeping what it keeps, and of the whole process of growth in its poetry. The French have become diligent students of their own early poetry, which they long neglected; the study makes many of them dissatisfied with this so-called classical poetry, the court-tragedy of the seventeenth century, a poetry which Pellisson long ago reproached with its want of the true poetic stamp, with its *politesse stérile et rampante*, but which nevertheless has reigned in France as absolutely as if it had been the perfection of classical poetry indeed. The dissatisfaction is natural; yet a lively and accomplished critic, M. Charles d'Héricault, the editor of Clément Marot, goes too far when he says that 'the cloud of glory playing round a classic is a mist as dangerous to the future of a literature as it is intolerable for the purposes of history.' 'It hinders,' he goes on, 'it hinders us from seeing more than one single point, the culminating and exceptional point; the summary, fictitious and arbitrary, of a thought and of a work. It substitutes a halo for a physiognomy, it puts a statue where there was once a man, and hiding from us all trace of the labour, the attempts, the weaknesses, the failures, it claims not study but veneration; it does not show us how the thing is done, it imposes upon us a model. Above all, for the historian this creation of classic personages is inadmissible; for it withdraws the poet from his time, from his proper life, it breaks historical relationships, it blinds criticism by conventional admiration, and renders the investigation of literary origins unacceptable. It gives us a human personage no longer, but a God seated immovable amidst His perfect work, like Jupiter on Olympus; and hardly will it be possible for the young student, to whom such work is exhibited at such a distance from him, to believe that it did not issue ready made from that divine head.'

All this is brilliantly and tellingly said, but we must plead for a distinction. Everything depends on the reality of a poet's classic character. If he is a dubious classic, let us sift him; if he is a false classic, let us explode him. But if he is a real classic, if his work belongs to the class of the very best (for this is the true and right meaning of the word *classic, classical*), then the great thing for us is to feel and enjoy his work as deeply as ever we can, and to appreciate the wide difference between it and all work which has not the same high character. This is what is salutary, this is what is formative; this is the great benefit to be got from the study of poetry. Everything which interferes with it, which hinders it, is injurious. True, we must read our classic with open eyes, and not with eyes blinded with superstition; we must perceive when his work comes short, when it drops out of the class of the very best, and we must rate it, in such cases, at its proper value. But the use of this negative criticism is not in itself, it is entirely in its enabling us to have a clearer sense and a deeper enjoyment of what is truly excellent. To trace the labour, the attempts, the weaknesses, the failures of a genuine classic, to acquaint oneself with his time and his life and his historical relationships, is mere literary dilettantism unless it has that clear sense and deeper enjoyment for its end. It may be said that the more we know about a classic the better we shall enjoy him; and, if we lived as long as Methuselah and had all of us heads of perfect clearness and wills of perfect steadfastness, this might be true in fact as it is plausible in theory. But the case here is much the same as the case with the Greek and Latin studies of our schoolboys. The elaborate philological groundwork which we require them to lay is in theory an admirable preparation for appreciating the Greek and Latin authors worthily. The more thoroughly we lay the groundwork, the better we shall be able, it may be said, to enjoy the authors. True, if time were not so short, and schoolboys' wits not so soon tired and their power of attention exhausted; only, as it is, the elaborate philological preparation goes on, but the authors are little known and less enjoyed. So with the investigator of 'historic origins' in poetry. He ought to enjoy the true classic all the better for his investigations; he often is distracted from the enjoyment of the best, and with the less good he overbusies himself, and is prone to over-rate it in proportion to the trouble which it has cost him.

The idea of tracing historic origins and historical relationships cannot be absent from a compilation like the present. And naturally the poets to be exhibited in it will be assigned to those persons for exhibition who are known to prize them highly, rather than to those who have no special inclination towards them. Moreover the very occupation with an author, and the business of exhibiting him, disposes us to affirm and amplify his importance. In the present work, therefore, we are sure of frequent temptation to adopt the historic estimate, or the personal estimate, and to forget the real estimate; which latter, nevertheless, we must employ if we are to make poetry yield us its full benefit. So high is that benefit, the benefit of clearly feeling and of deeply enjoying the really excellent, the truly classic in poetry, that we do well, I say, to set it fixedly before our minds as our object in studying poets and poetry, and to make the desire of attaining it the one principle to which, as the *Imitation* says, whatever we may read or come to know, we always return. *Cum multa legeris et cognoveris, ad unum semper oportet redire principium.*

The historic estimate is likely in especial to affect our judgment and our language when we are dealing with ancient poets; the personal estimate when we are dealing with poets our contemporaries, or at any rate modern. The exaggerations due to the historic estimate are not in themselves, perhaps, of very much gravity. Their report hardly enters the general ear; probably they do not always impose even on the literary men who adopt them. But they lead to a dangerous abuse of language. So we hear Cædmon, amongst our own poets, compared to Milton. I have already noticed the enthusiasm of one accomplished French critic for 'historic origins.' Another eminent French critic, M. Vitet, comments upon that famous document of the early poetry of his nation, the *Chanson de Roland*. It is indeed a most interesting document. The *joculator* or *jongleur* Taillefer, who was with William the Conqueror's army at Hastings, marched before the Norman troops, so said the tradition, singing 'of Charlemagne and of Roland and of Oliver, and of the vassals who died at Roncevaux'; and it is suggested that in the *Chanson de Roland* by one Turoldus or Théroulde, a poem preserved in a manuscript of the twelfth century in the Bodleian Library at Oxford, we have certainly the matter, perhaps even some of the words of the chant which Taillefer sang. The poem has vigour and freshness; it is not without pathos. But M. Vitet is not satisfied with seeing in it a document of some poetic value, and of very high historic and linguistic value; he sees in it a grand and beautiful work, a monument of epic genius. In its general design he finds the grandiose conception, in its details he finds the constant union of simplicity with greatness, which are the marks, he truly says, of the genuine epic, and distinguish it from the artificial epic of literary ages. One thinks of Homer; this is the sort of praise which is given to Homer, and justly given. Higher praise there cannot well be, and it is the praise due to epic poetry of the highest order only, and to no other. Let us try, then, the *Chanson de Roland* at its best. Roland, mortally wounded, lays himself down under a pine-tree, with his face turned toward Spain and the enemy—

'De plusurs choses à remembrer li prist,
De tantes teres cume li bers cunquist,
De dulce France, des humes de sun lign,
De Carlemagne sun seignor ki l'nurrit.'

That is primitive work, I repeat, with an undeniable poetic quality of its own. It deserves such praise, and such praise is sufficient for it. But now turn to Homer—

Ὣς φάτο, τοὺς δ ἤδη κατέχεν φυσίζοος αἶα
ἐν Λακεδαίμονι αὖθι, φίλῃ ἐν πατρίδι γαίῃ.

We are here in another world, another order of poetry altogether; here is rightly due such supreme praise as that which M. Vitet gives to the *Chanson de Roland*. If our words are to have any meaning, if our judgments are to have any solidity, we must not heap that supreme praise upon poetry of an order immeasurably inferior.

Indeed there can be no more useful help for discovering what poetry belongs to the class of the truly excellent, and can therefore do us most good, than to have always in one's mind lines and expressions of the great masters, and to apply them as a touchstone to other poetry. Of course we are not to require this other poetry to resemble them; it may be very dissimilar. But if we have any tact we shall find them, when we have lodged them well in our minds, an infallible touchstone for detecting the presence or absence of high poetic quality, and also the degree of this quality, in all other poetry which we may place beside them. Short passages, even single lines, will serve our turn quite sufficiently. Take the two lines which I have just quoted from Homer, the poet's comment on Helen's mention of her brothers; — or take his

Ἆ δειλὼ τί σφῶϊ δόμεν Πηλῆϊ ἄνακτι
θνητῷ; ὑμεῖς δ' ἐστὸν ἀγήρω τ' ἀθανάτω τε.
ἦ ἵνα δυστήνοισι μετ' ἀνδράσιν ἄλγε' ἔχητον;

the address of Zeus to the horses of Peleus; — or take finally his

Καὶ *σέ, γέρον, τὸ πρὶν μὲν ἀκούομεν ὄλβιον εἶναι*

the words of Achilles to Priam, a suppliant before him. Take that incomparable line and a half of Dante, Ugolino's tremendous words—

'Io no piangeva; sì dentro impietrai.
Piangevan elli . . .'

take the lovely words of Beatrice to Virgil—

'Io son fatta da Dio, sua mercè, tale,
Che la vostra miseria non mi tange,
Nè fiamma d'esto incendio non m'assale . . .'

take the simple, but perfect, single line —

'In la sua volontade è nostra pace.'

Take of Shakespeare a line or two of Henry the Fourth's expostulation with sleep—

'Wilt thou upon the high and giddy mast
Seal up the ship-boy's eyes, and rock his brains
In cradle of the rude imperious surge . . .'

and take, as well, Hamlet's dying request to Horatio —

'If thou didst ever hold me in thy heart,
Absent thee from felicity awhile,
And in this harsh world draw thy breath in pain
To tell my story . . .'

Take of Milton that Miltonic passage —

'Darkened so, yet shone
Above them all the archangel; but his face
Deep scars of thunder had intrenched, and care
Sat on his faded cheek . . .'

add two such lines as —

'And courage never to submit or yield
And what is else not to be overcome . . .'

and finish with the exquisite close to the loss of Proserpine, the loss

'. . . which cost Ceres all that pain
To seek her through the world.'

These few lines, if we have tact and can use them, are enough even of themselves to keep clear and sound our judgments about poetry, to save us from fallacious estimates of it, to conduct us to a real estimate.

The specimens I have quoted differ widely from one another, but they have in common this: the possession of the very highest poetical quality. If we are thoroughly penetrated by their power, we shall find that we have acquired a sense enabling us, whatever poetry may be laid before us, to feel the degree in which a high poetical quality is present or wanting there. Critics give themselves great labour to draw out what in the abstract constitutes the characters of a high quality of poetry. It is much better simply to have recourse to concrete examples; — to take specimens of poetry of the high, the very highest quality, and to say: The characters of a high quality of poetry are what is expressed *there*. They are far better recognized by being felt in the verse of the master, than by being perused in the prose of the critic. Nevertheless if we are urgently pressed to give some critical account of them, we may safely, perhaps, venture on laying down, not indeed how and why the characters arise, but where and in what they arise. They are in the matter and substance of the poetry, and they are in its manner and style. Both of these, the substance and matter on the one hand, the style and manner on the other, have a mark, an accent, of high beauty, worth, and power. But if we are asked to define this mark and accent in the abstract, our answer must be: No, for we should thereby be darkening the question, not clearing it. The mark and accent are as given by the substance and matter of that poetry, by the style and manner of that poetry, and of all other poetry which is akin to it in quality.

Only one thing we may add as to the substance and matter of poetry, guiding ourselves by Aristotle's profound observation that the superiority of poetry over history consists in its possessing a higher truth and a higher seriousness (φιλοσοφώτερον καὶ σπουδαιότερον). Let us add, therefore, to what we have said, this: that the substance and matter of the best poetry acquire their special character from possessing, in an eminent degree, truth and seriousness. We may add yet further, what is in itself evident, that to the style and manner of the best poetry their special character, their accent, is given by their diction, and, even yet more, by their movement. And though we distinguish between the two characters, the two accents, of superiority, yet they are nevertheless vitally connected one with the other. The superior character of truth and seriousness, in the matter and substance of the best poetry, is inseparable from the superiority of diction and movement marking its style and manner. The two superiorities are closely related, and are in steadfast proportion one to the other. So far as high poetic truth and seriousness are wanting to a poet's matter and substance, so far also, we may be sure, will a high poetic stamp of diction and movement be wanting to his style and manner. In proportion as this high stamp of diction and movement, again, is absent from a poet's style and manner, we shall find, also, that high poetic truth and seriousness are absent from his substance and matter.

So stated, these are but dry generalities; their whole force lies in their application. And I could wish every student of poetry to make the application of them for himself. Made by himself, the application would impress itself upon his mind far more deeply than made by me. Neither will my limits allow me to make any full application of the generalities above propounded; but in the hope of bringing out, at any rate, some significance in them, and of establishing an important principle more firmly by their means, I will, in the space which remains to me, follow rapidly from the commencement the course of our English poetry with them in my view.

Once more I return to the early poetry of France, with which our own poetry, in its origins, is indissolubly connected. In the twelfth and thirteenth centuries, that seed-time of all modern language and literature, the poetry of France had a clear predominance in Europe. Of the two divisions of that poetry, its productions in the *langue d' oïl* and its productions in the *langue d' oc*, the poetry of the *langue d' oc*, of southern France, of the troubadours, is of importance because of its effect on Italian literature; — the first literature of modern Europe to strike the true and grand note, and to bring forth, as in Dante and Petrarch it brought forth, classics. But the predominance of French poetry in Europe, during the twelfth and thirteenth centuries, is due to its poetry of the *langue d' oïl*, the poetry of northern France and of the tongue which is now the French language. In the twelfth century the bloom of this romance-poetry was earlier and stronger in England, at the court of our Anglo-Norman kings, than in France itself. But it was a bloom of French poetry; and as our native poetry formed itself, it formed itself out of this. The romance-poems which took possession of the heart and imagination of Europe in the twelfth and thirteenth centuries are French; 'they are,' as Southey justly says, 'the pride of French literature, nor have we anything which can be placed in competition with them.' Themes were supplied from all quarters; but the romance-setting which was common to them all, and which gained the ear of Europe, was French. This constituted for the French poetry, literature, and language, at the height of the Middle Age, an unchallenged predominance. The Italian Brunetto Latini, the master of Dante, wrote his *Treasure* in French because, he says, '*la parleure en est plus délitable et plus commune à toutes gens*.' In the same century, the thirteenth, the French romance-writer, Christian of Troyes, formulates the claims, in chivalry and letters, of France, his native country, as follows: —

'Or vous ert par ce livre apris,
Que Gresse ot de chevalerie
Le premier los et de clergie;

Puis vint chevalerie à Rome,
Et de la clergie la some,
Qui ore est en France venue.
Diex doinst qu'ele i soit retenue,
Et que li lius li abelisse
Tant que de France n'isse
L'onor qui s'i est arestée!'

'Now by this book you will learn that first Greece had the renown for chivalry and letters: then chivalry and the primacy in letters passed to Rome, and now it is come to France. God grant it may be kept there; and that the place may please it so well, that the honour which has come to make stay in France may never depart thence!'

Yet it is now all gone, this French romance-poetry, of which the weight of substance and the power of style are not unfairly represented by this extract from Christian of Troyes. Only by means of the historic estimate can we persuade ourselves now to think that any of it is of poetical importance.

But in the fourteenth century there comes an Englishman nourished on this poetry, taught his trade by this poetry, getting words, rhyme, metre from this poetry; for even of that stanza which the Italians used, and which Chaucer derived immediately from the Italians, the basis and suggestion was probably given in France. Chaucer (I have already named him) fascinated his contemporaries, but so too did Christian of Troyes and Wolfram of Eschenbach. Chaucer's power of fascination, however, is enduring; his poetical importance does not need the assistance of the historic estimate; it is real. He is a genuine source of joy and strength, which is flowing still for us and will flow always. He will be read, as time goes on, far more generally than he is read now. His language is a cause of difficulty for us; but so also, and I think in quite as great a degree, is the language of Burns. In Chaucer's case, as in that of Burns, it is a difficulty to be unhesitatingly accepted and overcome.

If we ask ourselves wherein consists the immense superiority of Chaucer's poetry over the romance-poetry — why it is that in passing from this to Chaucer we suddenly feel ourselves to be in another world, we shall find that his superiority is both in the substance of his poetry and in the style of his poetry. His superiority in substance is given by his large, free, simple, clear yet kindly view of human life, — so unlike the total want, in the romance-poets, of all intelligent command of it. Chaucer has not their helplessness; he has gained the power to survey the world from a central, a truly human point of view. We have only to call to mind the Prologue to *The Canterbury Tales*. The right comment upon it is Dryden's: 'It is sufficient to say, according to the proverb, that *here is God's plenty*.' And again: 'He is a perpetual fountain of good sense.' It is by a large, free, sound representation of things, that poetry, this high criticism of life, has truth of substance; and Chaucer's poetry has truth of substance.

Of his style and manner, if we think first of the romance-poetry and then of Chaucer's divine liquidness of diction, his divine fluidity of movement, it is difficult to speak temperately. They are irresistible, and justify all the rapture with which his successors speak of his 'gold dew-drops of speech.' Johnson misses the point entirely when he finds fault with Dryden for ascribing to Chaucer the first refinement of our numbers, and says that Gower also can show smooth numbers and easy rhymes. The refinement of our numbers means something far more than this. A nation may have versifiers with smooth numbers and easy rhymes, and yet may have no real poetry at all. Chaucer is the father of our splendid English poetry; he is our 'well of English undefiled,' because by the lovely charm of his diction, the lovely charm of his movement, he makes an epoch and founds a tradition. In Spenser, Shakspere, Milton, Keats, we can follow the tradition of the liquid diction, the fluid movement, of Chaucer; at one time it is his liquid diction of which in these poets we feel the virtue, and at another time it is his fluid movement. And the virtue is irresistible.

Bounded as is my space, I must yet find room for an example of Chaucer's virtue, as I have given examples to show the virtue of the great classics. I feel disposed to say that a single line is enough to show the charm of Chaucer's verse; that merely one line like this

'O martyr souded in virginitee!'

has a virtue of manner and movement such as we shall not find in all the verse of romance-poetry; — but this is saying nothing. The virtue is such as we shall not find, perhaps, in all English poetry, outside the poets whom I have named as the special inheritors of Chaucer's tradition. A single line, however, is too little if we have not the strain of Chaucer's verse well in our memory; let us take a stanza. It is from *The Prioress's Tale*, the story of the Christian child murdered in a Jewry —

'My throte is cut unto my nekke-bone,
Saidè this child, and as by way of kinde
I should have deyd, yea, longè time agone;
But Jesu Christ, as ye in bookès finde,
Will that his glory last and be in minde,
And for the worship of his mother dere
Yet may I sing *O Alma* loud and clere.'

Wordsworth has modernized this Tale, and to feel how delicate and evanescent is the charm of verse, we have only to read Wordsworth's first three lines of this stanza after Chaucer's —

'My throat is cut unto the bone, I trow,
Said this young child, and by the law of kind
I should have died, yea, many hours ago.'

The charm is departed. It is often said that the power of liquidness and fluidity in Chaucer's verse was dependent upon a free, a licentious dealing with language, such as is now impossible; upon a liberty, such as Burns too enjoyed, of making words like *neck*, *bird*, into a dissyllable by adding to them, and words like *cause*, *rhyme*, into a dissyllable by sounding the *e* mute. It is true that Chaucer's fluidity is conjoined with this liberty, and is admirably served by it; but we ought not to say that it was dependent upon it. It was dependent upon his talent. Other poets with a like liberty do not attain to the fluidity of Chaucer; Burns himself does not attain to it. Poets, again, who have a talent akin to Chaucer's, such as Shakspere or Keats, have known how to attain to his fluidity without the like liberty.

And yet Chaucer is not one of the great classics. His poetry transcends and effaces, easily and without effort, all the romance-poetry of Catholic Christendom; it transcends and effaces all the English poetry contemporary with it, it transcends and effaces all the English poetry subsequent to it down to the age of Elizabeth. Of such avail is poetic truth of substance, in its natural and necessary union with poetic truth of style. And yet, I say, Chaucer is not one of the great classics. He has not their accent. What is wanting to him is suggested by the mere mention of the name of the first great classic of Christendom, the immortal poet who died eighty years before Chaucer, — Dante. The accent of such verse as

'In la sua volontade è nostra pace . . .'

is altogether beyond Chaucer's reach; we praise him, but we feel that this accent is out of the question for him. It may be said that it was necessarily out of the reach of any poet in the England of that stage of growth. Possibly; but we are to adopt a real, not a historic, estimate of poetry. However we may account for its absence, something is wanting, then, to the poetry of Chaucer, which poetry must have before it can be placed in the glorious class of the best. And there is no doubt what that something is. It is the σπουδαιότης, the high and excellent seriousness, which Aristotle assigns as one of the grand virtues of poetry. The substance of Chaucer's poetry, his view of things and his criticism of life, has largeness, freedom, shrewdness, benignity; but it has not this high seriousness. Homer's criticism of life has it, Dante's has it, Shakspere's has it. It is this chiefly which gives to our spirits what they can rest upon; and with the increasing demands of our modern ages upon poetry, this virtue of giving us what we can rest upon will be more and more highly esteemed. A voice from the slums of Paris, fifty or sixty years after Chaucer, the voice of poor Villon out of his life of riot and crime, has at its happy moments (as, for instance, in the last stanza of *La Belle Heaulmière*) more of this important poetic virtue of seriousness than all the productions of Chaucer. But its apparition in Villon, and in men like Villon, is fitful; the greatness of the great poets, the power of their criticism of life, is that their virtue is sustained.

To our praise, therefore, of Chaucer as a poet there must be this limitation; he lacks the high seriousness of the great classics, and therewith an important part of their virtue. Still, the main fact for us to bear in mind about Chaucer is his sterling value according to that real estimate which we firmly adopt for all poets. He has poetic truth of substance, though he has not high poetic seriousness, and corresponding to his truth of substance he has an exquisite virtue of style and manner. With him is born our real poetry.

But for my present purpose I need not dwell on our Elizabethan poetry, or on the continuation and close of this poetry in Milton. We all of us profess to be agreed in the estimate of this poetry; we all of us recognize it as great poetry, our greatest, and Shakspere and Milton as our poetical classics. The real estimate, here, has universal currency. With the next age of our poetry divergency and difficulty begin. An historic estimate of that poetry has established itself; and the question is, whether it will be found to coincide with the real estimate.

The age of Dryden, together with our whole eighteenth century which followed it, sincerely believed itself to have produced poetical classics of its own, and even to have made advance, in poetry, beyond all its predecessors. Dryden regards as not seriously disputable the opinion 'that the sweetness of English verse was never understood or practised by our fathers.' Cowley could see nothing at all in Chaucer's poetry. Dryden heartily admired it, and, as we have seen, praised its matter admirably; but of its exquisite manner and movement all he can find to say is that 'there is the rude sweetness of a Scotch tune in it, which is natural and pleasing, though not perfect.' Addison, wishing to praise Chaucer's numbers, compares them with Dryden's own. And all through the eighteenth century, and down even into our own times, the stereotyped phrase of approbation for good verse found in our early poetry has been, that it even approached the verse of Dryden, Addison, Pope, and Johnson.

Are Dryden and Pope poetical classics? Is the historic estimate, which represents them as such, and which has been so long established that it cannot easily give way, the real estimate? Wordsworth and Coleridge, as is well known, denied it; but the authority of Wordsworth and Coleridge does not weigh much with the young generation, and there are many signs to show that the eighteenth century and its judgments are coming into favour again. Are the favourite poets of the eighteenth century classics?

It is impossible within my present limits to discuss the question fully. And what man of letters would not shrink from seeming to dispose dictatorially of the claims of two men who are, at any rate, such masters in letters as Dryden and Pope; two men of such admirable talent, both of them, and one of them, Dryden, a man, on all sides, of such energetic and genial power? And yet, if we are to gain the full benefit from poetry, we must have the real estimate of it. I cast about for some mode of arriving, in the present case, at such an estimate without offence. And perhaps the best way is to begin, as it is easy to begin, with cordial praise.

When we find Chapman, the Elizabethan translator of Homer, expressing himself in his preface thus: 'Though truth in her very nakedness sit in so deep a pit, that from Gades to Aurora and Ganges few eyes can sound her, I hope yet those few here will so discover and confirm, that, the date being out of her darkness in this morning of our poet, he shall now gird his temples with the sun,' — we pronounce that such a prose is intolerable. When we find Milton writing: 'And long it was not after, when I was confirmed in this opinion, that he, who would not be frustrate of his hope to write well hereafter in laudable things, ought himself to be a true poem,' — we pronounce that such a prose has its own grandeur, but that it is obsolete and inconvenient. But when we find Dryden telling us: 'What Virgil wrote in the vigour of his age, in plenty and at ease, I have undertaken to translate in my declining years; struggling with wants, oppressed with sickness, curbed in my genius, liable to be misconstrued in all I write,' — then we exclaim that here at last we have the true English prose, a prose such as we would all gladly use if we only knew how. Yet Dryden was Milton's contemporary.

But after the Restoration the time had come when our nation felt the imperious need of a fit prose. So, too, the time had likewise come when our nation felt the imperious need of freeing itself from the absorbing preoccupation which religion in the Puritan age had exercised. It was impossible that this freedom should be brought about without some negative excess, without some neglect and impairment of the religious life of the soul; and the spiritual history of the eighteenth century shows us that the freedom was not achieved without them. Still, the freedom was achieved; the preoccupation, an undoubtedly baneful and retarding one if it had continued, was got rid of. And as with religion amongst us at that period, so it was also with letters. A fit prose was a necessity; but it was impossible that a fit prose should establish itself amongst us without some touch of frost to the imaginative life of the soul. The needful qualities for a fit prose are regularity, uniformity, precision, balance. The men of letters, whose destiny it may be to bring their nation to the attainment of a fit prose, must of necessity, whether they work in prose or in verse, give a predominating, an almost exclusive attention to the qualities of regularity, uniformity, precision, balance. But an almost exclusive attention to these qualities involves some repression and silencing of poetry.

We are to regard Dryden as the puissant and glorious founder, Pope as the splendid high-priest, of our age of prose and reason, of our excellent and indispensable eighteenth century. For the purposes of their mission and destiny their poetry, like their prose, is admirable. Do you ask me whether Dryden's verse, take it almost where you will, is not good?

'A milk-white Hind, immortal and unchanged,
Fed on the lawns and in the forest ranged.'

I answer: Admirable for the purposes of the inaugurator of an age of prose and reason. Do you ask me whether Pope's verse, take it almost where you will, is not good?

'To Hounslow Heath I point, and Banstead Down;
Thence comes your mutton, and these chicks my own.'

I answer: Admirable for the purposes of the high-priest of an age of prose and reason. But do you ask me whether such verse proceeds from men with an adequate poetic criticism of life, from men whose criticism of life has a high seriousness, or even, without that high seriousness, has poetic largeness, freedom, insight, benignity? Do you ask me whether the application of ideas to life in the verse of these men, often a powerful application, no doubt, is a powerful *poetic* application? Do you ask me whether the poetry of these men has either the matter or the inseparable manner of such an adequate poetic criticism; whether it has the accent of

'Absent thee from felicity awhile . . .'

or of

'And what is else not to be overcome . . .'

or of

'O martyr souded in virginitee!'

I answer: It has not and cannot have them; it is the poetry of the builders of an age of prose and reason. Though they may write in verse, though they may in a certain sense be masters of the art of versification, Dryden and Pope are not classics of our poetry, they are classics of our prose.

Gray is our poetical classic of that literature and age; the position of Gray is singular, and demands a word of notice here. He has not the volume or the power of poets who, coming in times more favourable, have attained to an independent criticism of life. But he lived with the great poets, he lived, above all, with the Greeks, through perpetually studying and enjoying them; and he caught their poetic point of view for regarding life, caught their poetic manner. The point of view and the manner are not self-sprung in him, he caught them of others; and he had not the free and abundant use of them. But whereas Addison and Pope never had the use of them, Gray had the use of them at times. He is the scantiest and frailest of classics in our poetry, but he is a classic.

And now, after Gray, we are met, as we draw towards the end of the eighteenth century, we are met by the great name of Burns. We enter now on times where the personal estimate of poets begins to be rife, and where the real estimate of them is not reached without difficulty. But in spite of the disturbing pressures of personal partiality, of national partiality, let us try to reach a real estimate of the poetry of Burns.

By his English poetry Burns in general belongs to the eighteenth century, and has little importance for us.

'Mark ruffian Violence, distained with crimes,
Rousing elate in these degenerate times;
View unsuspecting Innocence a prey,
As guileful Fraud points out the erring way;
While subtle Litigation's pliant tongue
The life-blood equal sucks of Right and
Wrong!'

Evidently this is not the real Burns, or his name and fame would have disappeared long ago. Nor is Clarinda's love poet, Sylvander, the real Burns either. But he tells us himself: 'These English songs gravel me to death. I have not the command of the language that I have of my native tongue. In fact, I think that my ideas are more barren in English than in Scotch. I have been at *Duncan Gray* to dress it in English, but all I can do is desperately stupid.' We English turn naturally, in Burns, to the poems in our own language, because we can read them easily; but in those poems we have not the real Burns.

The real Burns is of course in his Scotch poems. Let us boldly say that of much of this poetry, a poetry dealing perpetually with Scotch drink, Scotch religion, and Scotch manners, a Scotchman's estimate is apt to be personal. A Scotchman is used to this world of Scotch drink, Scotch religion, and Scotch manners; he has a tenderness for it; he meets its poet half way. In this tender mood he reads pieces like the *Holy Fair* or *Halloween*. But this world of Scotch drink, Scotch religion, and Scotch manners is against a poet, not for him, when it is not a partial countryman who reads him; for in itself it is not a beautiful world, and no one can deny that it is of advantage to a poet to deal with a beautiful world. Burns' world of Scotch drink, Scotch religion, and Scotch manners, is often a harsh, a sordid, a repulsive world: even the world of his *Cotter's Saturday Night* is not a beautiful world. No doubt a poet's criticism of life may have such truth and power that it triumphs over its world and delights us. Burns may triumph over his world, often he does triumph over his world, but let us observe how and where. Burns is the first case we have had where the bias of the personal estimate tends to mislead; let us look at him closely, he can bear it.

Many of his admirers will tell us that we have Burns, convivial, genuine, delightful, here —

'Leeze me on drink! it gies us mair
Than either school or college;
It kindles wit, it waukens lair,
It pangs us fou o' knowledge.
Be 't whiskey gill or penny wheep
Or ony stronger potion,
It never fails, on drinking deep,
To kittle up our notion
By night or day.'

There is a great deal of that sort of thing in Burns, and it is unsatisfactory, not because it is bacchanalian poetry, but because it has not that accent of sincerity which bacchanalian poetry, to do it justice, very often has. There is something in it of bravado, something which makes us feel that we have not the man speaking to us with his real voice; something, therefore, poetically unsound.

With still more confidence will his admirers tell us that we have the genuine Burns, the great poet, when his strain asserts the independence, equality, dignity, of men, as in the famous song *For a' that and a' that* —

'A prince can mak' a belted knight,
A marquis, duke, and a' that;
But an honest man's aboon his might,
Guid faith he mauna fa' that!
For a' that and a' that,
Their dignities, and a' that,
The pith o' sense, and pride o' worth,
Are higher rank than a' that.'

Here they find his grand, genuine touches; and still more, when this puissant genius, who so often set morality at defiance, falls moralizing —

'The sacred lowe o' weel-placed love
Luxuriantly indulge it;
But never tempt th' illicit rove,
Tho' naething should divulge it.
I waive the quantum o' the sin,
The hazard o' concealing,
But och! it hardens a' within,
And petrifies the feeling.'

Or in a higher strain —

'Who made the heart, 't is He alone
Decidedly can try us;
He knows each chord, its various tone;
Each spring, its various bias.
Then at the balance let 's be mute,
We never can adjust it;
What 's *done* we partly may compute,
But know not what 's resisted.'

Or in a better strain yet, a strain, his admirers will say, unsurpassable —

'To make a happy fire-side clime
To weans and wife,
That 's the true pathos and sublime
Of human life.'

There is criticism of life for you, the admirers of Burns will say to us; there is the application of ideas to life! There is, undoubtedly. The doctrine of the last-quoted lines coincides almost exactly with what was the aim and end, Xenophon tells us, of all the teaching of Socrates. And the application is a powerful one; made by a man of vigourous understanding, and (need I say?) a master of language.

But for supreme poetical success more is required than the powerful application of ideas to life; it must be an application under the conditions fixed by the laws of poetic truth and poetic beauty. Those laws fix as an essential condition, in the poet's treatment of such matters as are here in question, high seriousness; — the high seriousness which comes from absolute sincerity. The accent of high seriousness, born of absolute sincerity, is what gives to such verse as

'In la sua volontade è nostra pace . . .'

to such criticism of life as Dante's, its power. Is this accent felt in the passages which I have been quoting from Burns? Surely not; surely, if our sense is quick, we must perceive that we have not in those passages a voice from the very inmost soul of the genuine Burns; he is not speaking to us from these depths, he is more or less preaching. And the compensation for admiring such passages less, from missing the perfect poetic accent in them, will be that we shall admire more the poetry where that accent is found.

No; Burns, like Chaucer, comes short of the high seriousness of the great classics, and the virtue of matter and manner which goes with that high seriousness is wanting to his work. At moments he touches it in a profound and passionate melancholy, as in those four immortal lines taken by Byron as a motto for *The Bride of Abydos*, but which have in them a depth of poetic quality such as resides in no verse of Byron's own —

'Had we never loved sae kindly,
Had we never loved sae blindly,
Never met, or never parted,
We had ne'er been broken-hearted.'

But a whole poem of that quality Burns cannot make; the rest, in the *Farewell to Nancy*, is verbiage.

We arrive best at the real estimate of Burns, I think, by conceiving his work as having truth of matter and truth of manner, but not the accent or the poetic virtue of the highest masters. His genuine criticism of life, when the sheer poet in him speaks, is ironic; it is not —

'Thou Power Supreme, whose mighty scheme
These woes of mine fulfil,
Here firm I rest, they must be best
Because they are Thy will!'

It is far rather: *Whistle owre the lave o' t!* Yet we may say of him as of Chaucer, that of life and the world, as they come before him, his view is large, free, shrewd, benignant, — truly poetic, therefore; and his manner of rendering what he sees is to match. But we must note, at the same time, his great difference from Chaucer. The freedom of Chaucer is heightened, in Burns, by a fiery, reckless energy; the benignity of Chaucer deepens, in Burns, into an overwhelming sense of the pathos of things; — of the pathos of human nature, the pathos, also, of non-human nature. Instead of the fluidity of Chaucer's manner, the manner of Burns has spring, bounding swiftness. Burns is by far the greater force, though he has perhaps less charm. The world of Chaucer is fairer, richer, more significant than that of Burns; but when the largeness and freedom of Burns get full sweep, as in *Tam o' Shanter*, or still more in that puissant and splendid production, *The Jolly Beggars*, his world may be what it will, his poetic genius triumphs over it. In the world of *The Jolly Beggars* there is more than hideousness and squalor, there is bestiality; yet the piece is a superb poetic success. It has a breadth, truth, and power which make the famous scene in Auerbach's Cellar, of Goethe's *Faust*, seem artificial and tame beside it, and which are only matched by Shakspeare and Aristophanes.

Here, where his largeness and freedom serve him so admirably, and also in those poems and songs where to shrewdness he adds infinite archness and wit, and to benignity infinite pathos, where his manner is flawless, and a perfect poetic whole is the result, — in things like the address to the Mouse whose home he had ruined, in things like *Duncan Gray*, *Tam Glen*, *Whistle and I'll come to you, my lad*, *Auld Lang Syne* (this list might be made much longer), — here we have the genuine Burns, of whom the real estimate must be high indeed. Not a classic, nor with the excellent σπουδαιότης of the great classics, nor with a verse rising to a criticism of life and a virtue like theirs; but a poet with thorough truth of substance and an answering truth of style, giving us a poetry sound to the core. We all of us have a leaning towards the pathetic, and may be inclined perhaps to prize Burns most for his touches of piercing, sometimes almost intolerable, pathos; for verse like —

'We twa hae paidl't i' the burn
From mornin' sun till dine;
But seas between us braid hae roared,
Sin auld lang syne . . .'

where he is as lovely as he is sound. But perhaps it is by the perfection of soundness of his lighter and archer masterpieces that he is poetically most wholesome for us. For the votary misled by a personal estimate of Shelley, as so many of us have been, are, and will be, — of that beautiful spirit building his many-coloured haze of words and images

'Pinnacled dim in the intense inane' —

no contact can be wholesomer than the contact with Burns at his archest and soundest. Side by side with the

'On the brink of the night and the morning
My coursers are wont to respire,
But the Earth has just whispered a warning,
That their flight must be swifter than fire . . .'

of *Prometheus Unbound*, how salutary, how very salutary, to place this from *Tam Glen* —

'My minnie does constantly deave me
And bids me beware o' young men;
They flatter, she says, to deceive me;
But wha can think sae o' Tam Glen?'

But we enter on burning ground as we approach the poetry of times so near to us — poetry like that of Byron, Shelley, and Wordsworth — of which the estimates are so often not only personal, but personal with passion. For my purpose, it is enough to have taken the single case of Burns, the first poet we come to of whose work the estimate formed is evidently apt to be personal, and to have suggested how we may proceed, using the poetry of the great classics as a sort of touchstone, to correct this estimate, as we had previously corrected by the same means the historic estimate where we met with it. A collection like the present, with its succession of celebrated names and celebrated poems, offers a good opportunity to us for resolutely endeavouring to make our estimates of poetry real. I have sought to point out a method which will help us in making them so, and to exhibit it in use so far as to put any one who likes in a way of applying it for himself.

At any rate the end to which the method and the estimate are designed to lead, and from leading to which, if they do lead to it, they get their whole value, — the benefit of being able clearly to feel and deeply to enjoy the best, the truly classic, in poetry, — is an end, let me say it once more at parting, of supreme importance. We are often told that an era is opening in which we are to see multitudes of a common sort of readers, and masses of a common sort of literature; that such readers do not want and could not relish anything better than such literature, and that to provide it is becoming a vast and profitable industry. Even if good literature entirely lost currency with the world, it would still be abundantly worth while to continue to enjoy it by oneself. But it never will lose currency with the world, in spite of momentary appearances; it never will lose supremacy. Currency and supremacy are insured to it, not indeed by the world's deliberate and conscious choice, but by something far deeper, — by the instinct of self-preservation in humanity.

1880

Walter Pater (1839–1894)

STYLE

Since all progress of mind consists for the most part in differentiation, in the resolution of an obscure and complex object into its component aspects, it is surely the stupidest of losses to confuse things which right reason has put asunder, to lose the sense of achieved distinctions, the distinction between poetry and prose, for instance, or, to speak more exactly, between the laws and characteristic excellences of verse and prose composition. On the other hand, those who have dwelt most emphatically on the distinction between prose and verse, prose and poetry, may sometimes have been tempted to limit the proper functions of prose too narrowly; and this again is at least false economy, as being, in effect, the renunciation of a certain means or faculty, in a world where after all we must needs make the most of things. Critical efforts to limit art *a priori*, by anticipations regarding the natural incapacity of the material with which this or that artist works, as the sculptor with solid form, or the prose-writer with the ordinary language of men, are always liable to be discredited by the facts of artistic production; and while prose is actually found to be a coloured thing with Bacon, picturesque with Livy and Carlyle, musical with Cicero and Newman, mystical and intimate with Plato and Michelet and Sir Thomas Browne, exalted or florid, it may be, with Milton and Taylor, it will be useless to protest that it can be nothing at all, except something very tamely and narrowly confined to mainly practical ends — a kind of 'good round-hand'; as useless as the protest that poetry might not touch prosaic subjects as with Wordsworth, or an abstruse matter as with Browning, or treat contemporary life nobly as with Tennyson. In subordination to one essential beauty in all good literary style, in all literature as a fine art, as there are many beauties of poetry so the beauties of prose are many, and it is the business of criticism to estimate them as such; as it is good in the criticism of verse to look for those hard, logical and quasi-prosaic excellences which that too has, or needs. To find in the poem, amid the flowers, the allusions, the mixed perspectives, of *Lycidas* for instance, the thought, the logical structure: — how wholesome! how delightful! as to identify in prose what we call the poetry, the imaginative power, not treating it as out of place and a kind of vagrant intruder, but by way of an estimate of its rights, that is, of its achieved powers, there.

Dryden, with the characteristic instinct of his age, loved to emphasize the distinction between poetry and prose, the protest against their confusion with each other, coming with somewhat diminished effect from one whose poetry was so prosaic. In truth, his sense of prosaic excellence affected his verse rather than his prose, which is not only fervid, richly figured, poetic, as we say, but vitiated, all unconsciously, by many a scanning line. Setting up correctness, that humble merit of prose, as the central literary excellence, he is really a less correct writer than he may seem, still with an imperfect mastery of the relative pronoun. It might have been foreseen that, in the rotations of mind, the province of poetry in prose would find its assertor; and, a century after Dryden, amid very different intellectual needs, and with the need therefore of great modifications in literary form, the range of the poetic force in literature was effectively enlarged by Wordsworth. The true distinction between prose and poetry he regarded as the almost technical or accidental one of the absence or presence of metrical beauty, or, say! metrical restraint; and for him the opposition came to be between verse and prose of course; but, as the essential dichotomy in this matter, between imaginative and unimaginative writing, parallel to De Quincey's distinction between 'the literature of power and the literature of knowledge,' in the former of which the composer gives us not fact, but his peculiar sense of fact, whether past or present.

Dismissing then, under sanction of Wordsworth, that harsher opposition of poetry to prose, as savouring in fact of the arbitrary psychology of the last century, and with it the prejudice that there can be but one only beauty of prose style, I propose here to point out certain qualities of all literature as a fine art, which, if they apply to the literature of fact, apply still more to the literature of the imaginative sense of fact, while they apply indifferently to verse and prose, so far as either is really imaginative — certain conditions of true art in both alike, which conditions may also contain in them the secret of the proper discrimination and guardianship of the peculiar excellences of either.

The line between fact and something quite different from external fact is, indeed, hard to draw. In Pascal, for instance, in the persuasive writers generally, how difficult to define the point where, from time to time, argument which, if it is to be worth anything at all, must consist of facts or groups of facts, becomes a pleading — a theorem no longer, but essentially an appeal to the reader to catch the writer's spirit, to think with him, if one can or will — an expression no longer of fact but of his sense of it, his peculiar intuition of a world, prospective, or discerned below the faulty conditions of the present, in either case changed somewhat from the actual world. In science, on the other hand, in history so far as it conforms to scientific rule, we have a literary domain where the imagination may be thought to be always an intruder. And as, in all science, the functions of literature reduce themselves eventually to the transcribing of fact, so all the excellences of literary form in regard to science are reducible to various kinds of painstaking; this good quality being involved in all 'skilled work' whatever, in the drafting of an act of parliament, as in sewing. Yet here again, the writer's sense of fact, in history especially, and in all those complex subjects which do but lie on the borders of science, will still take the place of fact, in various degrees. Your historian, for instance, with absolutely truthful intention, amid the multitude of facts presented to him must needs select, and in selecting assert something of his own humour, something that comes not of the world without but of a vision within. So Gibbon moulds his unwieldy material to a preconceived view. Livy, Tacitus, Michelet, moving full of poignant sensibility amid the records of the past, each, after his own sense, modifies — who can tell where and to what degree? — and becomes something else than a transcriber; each, as he thus modifies, passing into the domain of art proper. For just in proportion as the writer's aim, consciously or unconsciously, comes to be the transcribing, not of the world, not of mere fact, but of his sense of it, he becomes an artist, his work *fine* art; and good art (as I hope ultimately to show) in proportion to the truth of his presentment of that sense; as in those humbler or plainer functions of literature also, truth — truth to bare fact, there — is the essence of such artistic quality as they may have. Truth! there can be no merit, no craft at all, without that. And further, all beauty is in the long run only *fineness* of truth, or what we call expression, the finer accommodation of speech to that vision within.

— The transcript of his sense of fact rather than the fact, as being preferable, pleasanter, more beautiful to the writer himself. In literature, as in every other product of human skill, in the moulding of a bell or a platter for instance, wherever this sense asserts itself, wherever the producer so modifies his work as, over and above its primary use or intention, to make it pleasing (to himself, of course, in the first instance) there, 'fine' as opposed to merely serviceable art, exists. Literary art, that is, like all art which is in any way imitative or reproductive of fact — form, or colour, or incident — is the representation of such fact as connected with soul, of a specific personality, in its preferences, its volition and power.

Such is the matter of imaginative or artistic literature — this transcript, not of mere fact, but of fact in its infinite variety, as modified by human preference in all its infinitely varied forms. It will be good literary art not because it is brilliant or sober, or rich, or impulsive, or severe, but just in proportion as its representation of that sense, that soul-fact, is true, verse being only one department of such literature, and imaginative prose, it may be thought, being the special art of the modern world. That imaginative prose should be the special and opportune art of the modern world results from two important facts about the latter: first, the chaotic variety and complexity of its interests, making the intellectual issue, the really master currents of the present time incalculable — a condition of mind little susceptible of the restraint proper to verse form, so that the most characteristic verse of the nineteenth century has been lawless verse; and secondly, an all-pervading naturalism, a curiosity about everything whatever as it really is, involving a certain humility of attitude, cognate to what must, after all, be the less ambitious form of literature. And prose thus asserting itself as the special and privileged artistic faculty of the present day, will be, however critics may try to narrow its scope, as varied in its excellence as humanity itself reflecting on the facts of its latest experience — an instrument of many stops, meditative, observant, descriptive, eloquent, analytic, plaintive, fervid. Its beauties will be not exclusively 'pedestrian': it will exert, in due measure, all the varied charms of poetry, down to the rhythm which, as in Cicero, or Michelet, or Newman, at their best, gives its musical value to every syllable.

The literary artist is of necessity a scholar, and in what he proposes to do will have in mind, first of all, the scholar and the scholarly conscience — the male conscience in this matter, as we must think it, under a system of education which still to so large an extent limits real scholarship to men. In his self-criticism, he supposes always that sort of reader who will go (full of eyes) warily, considerately, though without consideration for him, over the ground which the female conscience traverses so lightly, so amiably. For the material in which he works is no more a creation of his own than the sculptor's marble. Product of a myriad various minds and contending tongues, compact of obscure and minute association, a language has its own abundant and often recondite laws, in the habitual and summary recognition of which scholarship consists. A writer, full of a matter he is before all things anxious to express, may think of those laws, the limitations of vocabulary, structure, and the like, as a restriction, but if a real artist will find in them an opportunity. His punctilious observance of the proprieties of his medium will diffuse through all he writes a general air of sensibility, of refined usage. *Exclusiones debitae naturae* — the exclusions, or rejections, which nature demands — we know how large a part these play, according to Bacon, in the science of nature. In a somewhat changed sense, we might say that the art of the scholar is summed up in the observance of those rejections demanded by the nature of his medium, the material he must use. Alive to the value of an atmosphere in which every term finds its utmost degree of expression, and with all the jealousy of a lover of words, he will resist a constant tendency on the part of the majority of those who use them to efface the distinctions of language, the facility of writers often reinforcing in this respect the work of the vulgar. He will feel the obligation not of the laws only, but of those affinities, avoidances, those mere preferences, of his language, which through the associations of literary history have become a part of its nature, prescribing the rejection of many a neology, many a license, many a gipsy phrase which might present itself as actually expressive. His appeal, again, is to the scholar, who has great experience in literature, and will show no favour to short-cuts, or hackneyed illustration, or an affectation of learning designed for the unlearned. Hence a contention, a sense of self-restraint and renunciation, having for the susceptible reader the effect of a challenge for minute consideration; the attention of the writer, in every minutest detail, being a pledge that it is worth the reader's while to be attentive too, that the writer is dealing scrupulously with his instrument, and therefore, indirectly, with the reader himself also, that he has the science of the instrument he plays on, perhaps, after all, with a freedom which in such case will be the freedom of a master.

For meanwhile, braced only by those restraints, he is really vindicating his liberty in the making of a vocabulary, an entire system of composition, for himself, his own true manner; and when we speak of the manner of a true master we mean what is essential in his art. Pedantry being only the scholarship of *le cuistre* (we have no English equivalent) he is no pedant, and does but show his intelligence of the rules of language in his freedoms with it, addition or expansion, which like the spontaneities of manner in a well-bred person will still further illustrate good taste. — The right vocabulary! Translators have not invariably seen how all-important that is in the work of translation, driving for the most part at idiom or construction; whereas, if the original be first-rate, one's first care should be with its elementary particles, Plato, for instance, being often reproducible by an exact following, with no variation in structure, of word after word, as the pencil follows a drawing under tracing-paper, so only each word or syllable be not of false colour, to change my illustration a little.

Well! that is because any writer worth translating at all has winnowed and searched through his vocabulary, is conscious of the words he would select in systematic reading of a dictionary, and still more of the words he would reject were the dictionary other than Johnson's; and doing this with his peculiar sense of the world ever in view, in search of an instrument for the adequate expression of that, he begets a vocabulary faithful to the colouring of his own spirit, and in the strictest sense original. That living authority which language needs lies, in truth, in its scholars, who recognizing always that every language possesses a genius, a very fastidious genius, of its own, expand at once and purify its very elements, which must needs change along with the changing thoughts of living people. Ninety years ago, for instance, great mental force, certainly, was needed by Wordsworth, to break through the consecrated poetic associations of a century, and speak the language that was his, that was to become in a measure the language of the next generation. But he did it with the tact of a scholar also. English, for a quarter of a century past, has been assimilating the phraseology of pictorial art; for half a century, the phraseology of the great German metaphysical movement of eighty years ago; in part also the language of mystical theology: and none but pedants will regret a great consequent increase of its resources. For many years to come its enterprise may well lie in the naturalisation of the vocabulary of science, so only it be under the eye of sensitive scholarship — in a liberal naturalisation of the ideas of science too, for after all the chief stimulus of good style is to possess a full, rich, complex matter to grapple with. The literary artist, therefore, will be well aware of physical science; science also attaining, in its turn, its true literary ideal. And then, as the scholar is nothing without the historic sense, he will be apt to restore not really obsolete or really worn-out words, but the finer edge of words still in use: *ascertain*, *communicate*, *discover* — words like these it has been part of our 'business' to misuse. And still, as language was made for man, he will be no authority for correctnesses which, limiting freedom of utterance, were yet but accidents in their origin; as if one vowed not to say '*its*,' which ought to have been in Shakspere; '*his*' and '*hers*,' for inanimate objects, being but a barbarous and really inexpressive survival. Yet we have known many things like this. Racy Saxon monosyllables, close to us as touch and sight, he will intermix readily with those long, savoursome, Latin words, rich in 'second intention.' In this late day certainly, no critical process can be conducted reasonably without eclecticism. Of such eclecticism we have a justifying example in one of the first poets of our time. How illustrative of monosyllabic effect, of sonorous Latin, of the phraseology of science, of metaphysic, of colloquialism even, are the writings of Tennyson; yet with what a fine, fastidious scholarship throughout!

A scholar writing for the scholarly, he will of course leave something to the willing intelligence of his reader. 'To go preach to the first passer-by,' says Montaigne, 'to become tutor to the ignorance of the first I meet, is a thing I abhor'; a thing, in fact, naturally distressing to the scholar, who will therefore ever be shy of offering uncomplimentary assistance to the reader's wit. To really strenuous minds there is a pleasurable stimulus in the challenge for a continuous effort on their part, to be rewarded by securer and more intimate grasp of the author's sense. Self-restraint, a skilful economy of means, *ascêsis*, that too has a beauty of its own; and for the reader supposed there will be an æsthetic satisfaction in that frugal closeness of style which makes the most of a word, in the exaction from every sentence of a precise relief, in the just spacing out of word to thought, in the logically filled space connected always with the delightful sense of difficulty overcome.

Different classes of persons, at different times, make, of course, very various demands upon literature. Still, scholars, I suppose, and not only scholars, but all disinterested lovers of books, will always look to it, as to all other fine art, for a refuge, a sort of cloistral refuge, from a certain vulgarity in the actual world. A perfect poem like *Lycidas*, a perfect fiction like *Esmond*, the perfect handling of a theory like Newman's *Idea of a University*, has for them something of the uses of a religious 'retreat.' Here, then, with a view to the central need of a select few, those 'men of a finer thread' who have formed and maintain the literary ideal, everything, every component element will have undergone exact trial, and, above all, there will be no uncharacteristic or tarnished or vulgar decoration, permissible ornament being for the most part structural, or necessary. As the painter in his picture, so the artist in his book, aims at the production by honourable artifice of a peculiar atmosphere. 'The artist,' says Schiller, 'may be known rather by what he *omits'*; and in literature, too, the true artist may be best recognized by his tact of omission. For to the grave reader words too are grave; and the ornamental word, the figure, the accessory form or colour or reference, is rarely content to die to thought precisely at the right moment, but will inevitably linger awhile, stirring a long 'brain-wave' behind it of perhaps quite alien associations.

Just there, it may be, is the detrimental tendency of the sort of scholarly attentiveness of mind I am recommending. But the true artist allows for it. He will remember that, as the very word ornament indicates what is in itself non-essential, so the 'one beauty' of all literary style is of its very essence, and independent, in prose and verse alike, of all removable decoration; that it may exist in its fullest luster, as in Flaubert's *Madame Bovary*, for instance, or in Stendhal's *Le Rouge et Le Noir*, in a composition utterly unadorned, with hardly a single suggestion of visibly beautiful things. Parallel, allusion, the allusive way generally, the flowers in the garden: — he knows the narcotic force of these upon the negligent intelligence to which any *diversion*, literally, is welcome, any vagrant intruder, because one can go wandering away with it from the immediate subject. Jealous, if he have a really quickening motive within, of all that does not hold directly to that, of the facile, the otiose, he will never depart from the strictly pedestrian process, unless he gains a ponderable something thereby. Even assured of its congruity, he will still question its serviceableness. Is it worth while, can we afford, to attend to just that, to just that figure or literary reference, just then? — Surplusage! he will dread that, as the runner on his muscles. For in truth all art does but consist in the removal of surplusage, from the last finish of the gem-engraver blowing away the last particle of invisible dust, back to the earliest divination of the finished work to be, lying somewhere, according to Michelangelo's fancy, in the rough-hewn block of stone.

And what applies to figure or flower must be understood of all other accidental or removable ornaments of writing whatever; and not of specific ornament only, but of all that latent colour and imagery which language as such carries in it. A lover of words for their own sake, to whom nothing about them is unimportant, a minute and constant observer of their physiognomy, he will be on the alert not only for obviously mixed metaphors of course, but for the metaphor that is mixed in all our speech, though a rapid use may involve no cognition of it. Currently recognizing the incident, the colour, the physical elements or particles in words like *absorb*, *consider*, *extract*, to take the first that occur, he will avail himself of them, as further adding to the resources of expression. The elementary particles of language will be realized as colour and light and shade through his scholarly living in the full sense of them. Still opposing the constant degradation of language by those who use it carelessly, he will not treat coloured glass as if it were clear; and while half the world is using figure unconsciously, will be fully aware not only of all that latent figurative texture in speech, but of the vague, lazy, half-formed personification — a rhetoric, depressing, and worse than nothing, because it has no really rhetorical motive — which plays so large a part there, and, as in the case of more ostentatious ornament, scrupulously exact of it, from syllable to syllable, its precise value.

So far I have been speaking of certain conditions of the literary art arising out of the medium or material in or upon which it works, the essential qualities of language and its aptitudes for contingent ornamentation, matters which define scholarship as science and good taste respectively. They are both subservient to a more intimate quality of good style: more intimate, as coming nearer to the artist himself. The otiose, the facile, surplusage: why are these abhorrent to the true literary artist, except because, in literary as in all other art, structure is all-important, felt, or painfully missed, everywhere? — that architectural conception of work, which foresees the end in the beginning and never loses sight of it, and in every part is conscious of all the rest, till the last sentence does but, with undiminished vigour, unfold and justify the first — a condition of literary art, which, in contradistinction to another quality of the artist himself, to be spoken of later, I shall call the necessity of *mind* in style.

An acute philosophical writer, the late Dean Mansel (a writer whose works illustrate the literary beauty there may be in closeness, and with obvious repression or economy of a fine rhetorical gift) wrote a book, of fascinating precision in a very obscure subject, to show that all the technical laws of logic are but means of securing, in each and all of its apprehensions, the unity, the strict identity with itself, of the apprehending mind. All the laws of good writing aim at a similar unity or identity of the mind in all the processes by which the word is associated to its import. The term is right, and has its essential beauty, when it becomes, in a manner, what it signifies, as with the names of simple sensations. To give the phrase, the sentence, the structural member, the entire composition, song, or essay, a similar unity with its subject and with itself: — style is in the right way when it tends towards that. All depends upon the original unity, the vital wholeness and identity, of the initiatory apprehension or view. So much is true of all art, which therefore requires always its logic, its comprehensive reason — insight, foresight, retrospect, in simultaneous action — true, most of all, of the literary art, as being of all the arts most closely cognate to the abstract intelligence. Such logical coherency may be evidenced not merely in the lines of composition as a whole, but in the choice of a single word, while it by no means interferes with, but may even prescribe, much variety, in the building of the sentence for instance, or in the manner, argumentative, descriptive, discursive, of this or that part or member of the entire design. The blithe, crisp sentence, decisive as a child's expression of its needs, may alternate with the long-contending, victoriously intricate sentence; the sentence, born with the integrity of a single word, relieving the sort of sentence in which, if you look closely, you can see much contrivance, much adjustment, to bring a highly qualified matter into compass at one view. For the literary architecture, if it is to be rich and expressive, involves not only foresight of the end in the beginning, but also development or growth of design, in the process of execution, with many irregularities, surprises, and afterthoughts; the contingent as well as the necessary being subsumed under the unity of the whole. As truly, to the lack of such architectural design, of a single, almost visual, image, vigorously informing an entire, perhaps very intricate, composition, which shall be austere, ornate, argumentative, fanciful, yet true from first to last to that vision within, may be attributed those weaknesses of conscious or unconscious repetition of word, phrase, motive, or member of the whole matter, indicating, as Flaubert was aware, an original structure in thought not organically complete. With such foresight, the actual conclusion will most often get itself written out of hand, before, in the more obvious sense, the work is finished. With some strong and leading sense of the world, the tight hold of which secures true *composition* and not mere loose accretion, the literary artist, I suppose, goes on considerately, setting joint to joint, sustained by yet restraining the productive ardour, retracing the negligences of his first sketch, repeating his steps only that he may give the reader a sense of secure and restful progress, readjusting mere assonances even, that they may soothe the reader, or at least not interrupt him on his way; and then, somewhere before the end comes, is burdened, inspired, with his conclusion, and betimes delivered of it, leaving off, not in weariness and because he finds *himself* at an end, but in all the freshness of volition. His work now structurally complete, with all the accumulating effect of secondary shades of meaning, he finishes the whole up to the just proportion of that antepenultimate conclusion, and all becomes expressive. The house he has built is rather a body he has informed. And so it happens, to its greater credit, that the better interest even of a narrative to be recounted, a story to be told, will often be in its second reading. And though there are instances of great writers who have been no artists, an unconscious tact sometimes directing work in which we may detect, very pleasurably, many of the effects of conscious art, yet one of the greatest pleasures of really good prose literature is in the critical tracing out of that conscious artistic structure, and the pervading sense of it as we read. Yet of poetic literature too; for, in truth, the kind of constructive intelligence here supposed is one of the forms of the imagination.

That is the special function of mind, in style. Mind and soul: — hard to ascertain philosophically, the distinction is real enough practically, for they often interfere, are sometimes in conflict, with each other. Blake, in the last century, is an instance of preponderating soul, embarrassed, at a loss, in an era of preponderating mind. As a quality of style, at all events, soul is a fact, in certain writers — the way they have of absorbing language, of attracting it into the peculiar spirit they are of, with a subtlety which makes the actual result seem like some inexplicable inspiration. By mind, the literary artist reaches us, through static and objective indications of design in his work, legible to all. By soul, he reaches us, somewhat capriciously perhaps, one and not another, through vagrant sympathy and a kind of immediate contact. Mind we cannot choose but approve where we recognize it; soul may repel us, not because we misunderstand it. The way in which theological interests sometimes avail themselves of language is perhaps the best illustration of the force I mean to indicate generally in literature, by the word *soul*. Ardent religious persuasion may exist, may make its way, without finding any equivalent heat in language: or, again, it may enkindle words to various degrees, and when it really takes hold of them doubles its force. Religious history presents many remarkable instances in which, through no mere phrase-worship, an unconscious literary tact has, for the sensitive, laid open a privileged pathway from one to another. 'The altar-fire,' people say, 'has touched those lips!' The Vulgate, the English Bible, the English Prayer-Book, the writings of Swedenborg, the Tracts for the Times: — there, we have instances of widely different and largely diffused phases of religious feeling in operation as soul in style. But something of the same kind acts with similar power in certain writers of quite other than theological literature, on behalf of some wholly personal and peculiar sense of theirs. Most easily illustrated by theological literature, this quality lends to profane writers a kind of religious influence. At their best, these writers become, as we say sometimes, 'prophets'; such character depending on the effect not merely of their matter, but of their matter as allied to, in 'electric affinity' with, peculiar form, and working in all cases by an immediate sympathetic contact, on which account it is that it may be called soul, as opposed to mind, in style. And this, too, is a faculty of choosing and rejecting what is congruous or otherwise, with a drift towards unity — unity of atmosphere here, as there of design — soul securing colour (or perfume, might we say?) as mind secures form, the latter being essentially finite, the former vague or infinite, as the influence of a living person is practically infinite. There are some to whom nothing has any real interest, or real meaning, except as operative in a given person; and it is they who best appreciate the quality of soul in literary art. They seem to know a *person*, in a book, and make way by intuition: yet, although they thus enjoy the completeness of a personal information, it is still a characteristic of soul, in this sense of the word, that it does but suggest what can never be uttered, not as being different from, or more obscure than, what actually gets said, but as containing that plenary substance of which there is only one phase or facet in what is there expressed.

If all high things have their martyrs, Gustave Flaubert might perhaps rank as the martyr of literary style. In his printed correspondence, a curious series of letters, written in his twenty-fifth year, records what seems to have been his one other passion — a series of letters which, with its fine casuistries, its firmly repressed anguish, its tone of harmonious gray, and the sense of disillusion in which the whole matter ends, might have been, a few slight changes supposed, one of his own fictions. Writing to Madame X. certainly he does display, by 'taking thought' mainly, by constant and delicate pondering, as in his love for literature, a heart really moved, but still more, and as the pledge of that emotion, a loyalty to his work. Madame X., too, is a literary artist, and the best gifts he can send her are precepts of perfection in art, counsels for the effectual pursuit of that better love. In his love-letters it is the pains and pleasures of art he insists on, its solaces: he communicates secrets, reproves, encourages, with a view to that. Whether the lady was dissatisfied with such divided or indirect service, the reader is not enabled to see; but sees that, on Flaubert's part at least, a living person could be no rival of what was, from first to last, his leading passion, a somewhat solitary and exclusive one.

'I must scold you (he writes) for one thing, which shocks, scandalises me, the small concern, namely, you show for art just now. As regards glory be it so: there, I approve. But for art! — the one thing in life that is good and real — can you compare with it an earthly love? — prefer the adoration of a relative beauty to the *cultus* of the true beauty? Well! I tell you the truth. That is the one thing good in me: the one thing I have, to me estimable. For yourself, you blend with the beautiful a heap of alien things, the useful, the agreeable, what not? —

'The only way not to be unhappy is to shut yourself up in art, and count everything else as nothing. Pride takes the place of all beside when it is established on a large basis. Work! God wills it. That, it seems to me, is clear. —

'I am reading over again the *Æneid*, certain verses of which I repeat to myself to satiety. There are phrases there which stay in one's head, by which I find myself beset, as with those musical airs which are forever returning, and cause you pain, you love them so much. I observe that I no longer laugh much, and am no longer depressed. I am ripe. You talk of my serenity, and envy me. It may well surprise you. Sick, irritated, the prey a thousand times a day of cruel pain, I continue my labour like a true working-man, who, with sleeves turned up, in the sweat of his brow, beats away at his anvil, never troubling himself whether it rains or blows, for hail or thunder. I was not like that formerly. The change has taken place naturally, though my will has counted for something in the matter. —

'Those who write in good style are sometimes accused of a neglect of ideas, and of the moral end, as if the end of the physician were something else than healing, of the painter than painting — as if the end of art were not, before all else, the beautiful.'

What, then, did Flaubert understand by beauty, in the art he pursued with so much fervour, with so much self-command? Let us hear a sympathetic commentator: —

'Possessed of an absolute belief that there exists but one way of expressing one thing, one word to call it by, one adjective to qualify, one verb to animate it, he gave himself to superhuman labour for the discovery, in every phrase, of that word, that verb, that epithet. In this way, he believed in some mysterious harmony of expression, and when a true word seemed to him to lack euphony still went on seeking another, with invincible patience, certain that he had not yet got hold of the *unique* word. . . . A thousand preoccupations would beset him at the same moment, always with this desperate certitude fixed in his spirit: Among all the expressions in the world, all forms and turns of expression, there is but *one* — one form, one mode — to express what I want to say.'

The one word for the one thing, the one thought, amid the multitude of words, terms, that might just do: the problem of style was there! — the unique word, phrase, sentence, paragraph, essay, or song, absolutely proper to the single mental presentation or vision within. In that perfect justice, over and above the many contingent and removable beauties with which beautiful style may charm us, but which it can exist without, independent of them yet dexterously availing itself of them, omnipresent in good work, in function at every point, from single epithets to the rhythm of a whole book, lay the specific, indispensable, very intellectual, beauty of literature, the possibility of which constitutes it a fine art.

One seems to detect the influence of a philosophic idea there, the idea of a natural economy, of some pre-existent adaptation, between a relative, somewhere in the world of thought, and its correlative, somewhere in the world of language — both alike, rather, somewhere in the mind of the artist, desiderative, expectant, inventive — meeting each other with the readiness of 'soul and body reunited,' in Blake's rapturous design; and, in fact, Flaubert was fond of giving his theory philosophical expression. —

'There are no beautiful thoughts (he would say) without beautiful forms, and conversely. As it is impossible to extract from a physical body the qualities which really constitute it — colour, extension, and the like — without reducing it to a hollow abstraction, in a word, without destroying it; just so it is impossible to detach the form from the idea, for the idea only exists by virtue of the form.'

All the recognized flowers, the removable ornaments of literature (including harmony and ease in reading aloud, very carefully considered by him) counted, certainly; for these too are part of the actual value of what one says. But still, after all, with Flaubert, the search, the unwearied research, was not for the smooth, or winsome, or forcible word, as such, as with false Ciceronians, but quite simply and honestly, for the word's adjustment to its meaning. The first condition of this must be, of course, to know yourself, to have ascertained your own sense exactly. Then, if we suppose an artist, he says to the reader, — I want you to see precisely what I see. Into the mind sensitive to 'form,' a flood of random sounds, colours, incidents, is ever penetrating from the world without, to become, by sympathetic selection, a part of its very structure, and, in turn, the visible vesture and expression of that other world it sees so steadily within, nay, already with a partial conformity thereto, to be refined, enlarged, corrected, at a hundred points; and it is just there, just at those doubtful points that the function of style, as tact or taste, intervenes. The unique term will come more quickly to one than another, at one time than another, according also to the kind of matter in question. Quickness and slowness, ease and closeness alike, have nothing to do with the artistic character of the true word found at last. As there is a charm of ease, so there is also a special charm in the signs of discovery, of effort and contention towards a due end, as so often with Flaubert himself — in the style which has been pliant, as only obstinate, durable metal can be, to the inherent perplexities and recusancy of a certain difficult thought.

If Flaubert had not told us, perhaps we should never have guessed how tardy and painful his own procedure really was, and after reading his confession may think that his almost endless hesitation had much to do with diseased nerves. Often, perhaps, the felicity supposed will be the product of a happier, a more exuberant nature than Flaubert's. Aggravated, certainly, by a morbid physical condition, that anxiety in 'seeking the phrase,' which gathered all the other small *ennuis* of a really quiet existence into a kind of battle, was connected with his lifelong contention against facile poetry, facile art — art, facile and flimsy; and what constitutes the true artist is not the slowness or quickness of the process, but the absolute success of the result. As with those labourers in the parable, the prize is independent of the mere length of the actual day's work. 'You talk,' he writes, odd, trying lover, to Madame X. —

'You talk of the exclusiveness of my literary tastes. That might have enabled you to divine what kind of a person I am in the matter of love. I grow so hard to please as a literary artist, that I am driven to despair. I shall end by not writing another line.'

'Happy,' he cries, in a moment of discouragement at that patient labour, which for him, certainly, was the condition of a great success. —

'Happy those who have no doubts of themselves! who lengthen out, as the pen runs on, all that flows forth from their brains. As for me, I hesitate, I disappoint myself, turn round upon myself in despite: my taste is augmented in proportion as my natural vigour decreases, and I afflict my soul over some dubious word out of all proportion to the pleasure I get from a whole page of good writing. One would have to live two centuries to attain a true idea of any matter whatever. What Buffon said is a big blasphemy: genius is not long-continued patience. Still, there is some truth in the statement, and more than people think, especially as regards our own day. Art! art! art! bitter deception! phantom that glows with light, only to lead one on to destruction.'

Again —

'I am growing so peevish about my writing. I am like a man whose ear is true but who plays falsely on the violin: his fingers refuse to reproduce precisely those sounds of which he has the inward sense. Then the tears come rolling down from the poor scraper's eyes and the bow falls from his hand.'

Coming slowly or quickly, when it comes, as it came with so much labour of mind, but also with so much luster, to Gustave Flaubert, this discovery of the word will be, like all artistic success and felicity, incapable of strict analysis: effect of an intuitive condition of mind, it must be recognized by like intuition on the part of the reader, and a sort of immediate sense. In every one of those masterly sentences of Flaubert there was, below all mere contrivance, shaping and afterthought, by some happy instantaneous concourse of the various faculties of the mind with each other, the exact apprehension of what was *needed* to carry the meaning. And that it fits with absolute justice will be a judgment of immediate sense in the appreciative reader. We all feel this in what may be called inspired translation. Well! all language involves translation from inward to outward. In literature, as in all forms of art, there are the absolute and the merely relative or accessory beauties; and precisely in that exact proportion of the term to its purpose is the absolute beauty of style, prose or verse. All the good qualities, the beauties, of verse also, are such, only as precise expression.

In the highest as in the lowliest literature, then, the one indispensable beauty is, after all, truth: — truth to bare fact in the latter, as to some personal sense of fact, diverted somewhat from men's ordinary sense of it, in the former; truth there as accuracy, truth here as expression, that finest and most intimate form of truth, the *vraie vérité*. And what an eclectic principle this really is! employing for its one sole purpose — that absolute accordance of expression to idea — all other literary beauties and excellences whatever: how many kinds of style it covers, explains, justifies, and at the same time safeguards! Scott's facility, Flaubert's deeply pondered evocation of 'the phrase,' are equally good art. Say what you have to say, what you have a will to say, in the simplest, the most direct and exact manner possible, with no surplusage: — there, is the justification of the sentence so fortunately born, 'entire, smooth, and round,' that it needs no punctuation, and also (that is the point!) of the most elaborate period, if it be right in its elaboration. Here is the office of ornament: here also the purpose of restraint in ornament. As the exponent of truth, that austerity (the beauty, the function, of which in literature Flaubert understood so well) becomes not the correctness or purism of the mere scholar, but a security against the otiose, a jealous exclusion of what does not really tell towards the pursuit of relief, of life and vigour in the portraiture of one's sense. License again, the making free with rule, if it be indeed, as people fancy, a habit of genius, flinging aside or transforming all that opposes the liberty of beautiful production, will be but faith to one's own meaning. The seeming baldness of *Le Rouge et Le Noir* is nothing in itself; the wild ornament of *Les Misérables* is nothing in itself; and the restraint of Flaubert, amid a real natural opulence, only redoubled beauty — the phrase so large and so precise at the same time, hard as bronze, in service to the more perfect adaptation of words to their matter. Afterthoughts, retouchings, finish, will be of profit only so far as they too really serve to bring out the original, initiative, generative, sense in them.

In this way, according to the well-known saying, 'The style is the man,' complex or simple, in his individuality, his plenary sense of what he really has to say, his sense of the world; all cautions regarding style arising out of so many natural scruples as to the medium through which alone he can expose that inward sense of things, the purity of this medium, its laws or tricks of refraction: nothing is to be left there which might give conveyance to any matter save that. Style in all its varieties, reserved or opulent, terse, abundant, musical, stimulant, academic, so long as each is really characteristic or expressive, finds thus its justification, the sumptuous good taste of Cicero being as truly the man himself, and not another, justified, yet insured inalienably to him, thereby, as would have been his portrait by Raffaelle, in full consular splendour, on his ivory chair.

A relegation, you may say perhaps — a relegation of style to the subjectivity, the mere caprice, of the individual, which must soon transform it into mannerism. Not so! since there is, under the conditions supposed, for those elements of the man, for every lineament of the vision within, the one word, the one acceptable word, recognisable by the sensitive, by others 'who have intelligence' in the matter, as absolutely as ever anything can be in the evanescent and delicate region of human language. The style, the manner, would be the man, not in his unreasoned and really uncharacteristic caprices, involuntary or affected, but in absolutely sincere apprehension of what is most real to him. But let us hear our French guide again. —

'Styles (says Flaubert's commentator), *Styles*, as so many peculiar moulds, each of which bears the mark of a particular writer, who is to pour into it the whole content of his ideas, were no part of his theory. What he believed in was *Style:* that is to say, a certain absolute and unique manner of expressing a thing, in all its intensity and colour. For him the *form* was the work itself. As in living creatures, the blood, nourishing the body, determines its very contour and external aspect, just so, to his mind, the *matter*, the basis, in a work of art, imposed, necessarily, the unique, the just expression, the measure, the rhythm — the *form* in all its characteristics.'

If the style be the man, in all the colour and intensity of a veritable apprehension, it will be in a real sense 'impersonal.'

I said, thinking of books like Victor Hugo's *Les Misérables*, that prose literature was the characteristic art of the nineteenth century, as others, thinking of its triumphs since the youth of Bach, have assigned that place to music. Music and prose literature are, in one sense, the opposite terms of art; the art of literature presenting to the imagination, through the intelligence, a range of interests, as free and various as those which music presents to it through sense. And certainly the tendency of what has been here said is to bring literature too under those conditions, by conformity to which music takes rank as the typically perfect art. If music be the ideal of all art whatever, precisely because in music it is impossible to distinguish the form from the substance or matter, the subject from the expression, then, literature, by finding its specific excellence in the absolute correspondence of the term to its import, will be but fulfilling the condition of all artistic quality in things everywhere, of all good art.

Good art, but not necessarily great art; the distinction between great art and good art depending immediately, as regards literature at all events, not on its form, but on the matter. Thackeray's *Esmond*, surely, is greater art than *Vanity Fair*, by the greater dignity of its interests. It is on the quality of the matter it informs or controls, its compass, its variety, its alliance to great ends, or the depth of the note of revolt, or the largeness of hope in it, that the greatness of literary art depends, as *The Divine Comedy*, *Paradise Lost*, *Les Misérables*, *The English Bible*, are great art. Given the conditions I have tried to explain as constituting good art; — then, if it be devoted further to the increase of men's happiness, to the redemption of the oppressed, or the enlargement of our sympathies with each other, or to such presentment of new or old truth about ourselves and our relation to the world as may ennoble and fortify us in our sojourn here, or immediately, as with Dante, to the glory of God, it will be also great art; if, over and above those qualities I summed up as mind and soul — that colour and mystic perfume, and that reasonable structure, it has something of the soul of humanity in it, and finds its logical, its architectural place, in the great structure of human life.

1888

Algernon Charles Swinburne (1837-1909)

KING LEAR*

If nothing were left of Shakespeare but the single tragedy of *King Lear*, it would still be as plain as it is now that he was the greatest man that ever lived. As a poet, the author of this play can only be compared with Æschylus: the Hebrew prophets and the creator of Job are sometimes as sublime in imagination and in passion, but always quite incomparably inferior in imaginative intelligence. Sophocles is as noble, as beautiful, and as kindly a thinker and a writer: but the gentle Shakespeare could see farther and higher and wider and deeper at a glance than ever could the gentle Sophocles. Aristophanes had as magnificent a power of infinitely joyous wit and infinitely inexhaustible humour: but whom can he show us or offer us to be set against Falstaff or the Fool? It is true that Shakespeare has neither the lyric nor the prophetic power of the Greeks and the Hebrews: but then it must be observed and remembered that he, and he alone among poets and among men, could well afford to dispense even with such transcendent gifts as these. Freedom of thought and sublimity of utterance came hand in hand together into English speech: our first great poet, if loftiness and splendour of spirit and of word be taken as the test of greatness, was Christopher Marlowe. From his dead hand the one man born to excel him, and to pay a due and a deathless tribute to his deathless memory, took up the heritage of dauntless thought, of daring imagination, and of since unequalled song.

The tragedy of *King Lear*, like the trilogy of the Oresteia, is a thing imcomparable and unique. To compare it with *Othello* is as inevitable a temptation as to compare the *Agamemnon* with the *Prometheus* of the one man comparable with Shakespeare. And the result, for any reader of human intelligence and decent humility in sight of what is highest in the spiritual world, must always be a sense of adoring doubt and exulting hesitation. In *Othello* and in *Prometheus* a single figure, an everlasting and godlike type of heroic and human agony, dominates and dwarfs all others but those of the traitor Iago and the tyrant God. There is no Clytæmnestra in the one, and there is no Cordelia in the other. 'The gentle lady married to the Moor' is too gentle for comparison with the most glorious type of womanhood which even Shakespeare ever created before he conceived and brought forth Imogen. No one could have offered to Cordelia the tribute of so equivocal a compliment as was provoked by the submissive endurance of Desdemona — 'Truly, an obedient lady.' Antigone herself — and with Antigone alone can we imagine the meeting of Cordelia in the heaven of heavens — is not so divinely human as Cordelia. We love her all the more, with a love that at once tempers and heightens our worship, for the rough and abrupt repetition of her nobly unmerciful reply to her father's fond and fatuous appeal. Almost cruel and assuredly severe in its uncompromising self-respect, this brief and natural word of indignantly reticent response is the key-note of all that follows — the spark which kindles into eternal life the most tragic of all tragedies in the world. All the yet unimaginable horror of the future becomes at once inevitable and assured when she shows herself so young and so untender — so young and true. And what is the hereditary horror of doom once imminent over the house of Atreus to this instant imminence of no supernatural but a more awfully natural fate? Cursed and cast out, she leaves him and knows that she leaves him in the hands of Goneril and Regan.

Coleridge, the greatest though not the first great critic and apostle or interpreter of Shakespeare, has noted 'these daughters and these sisters' as the only characters in Shakespeare whose wickedness is ultranatural — something outside and beyond the presumable limits of human evil. It would be well for human nature if it were so; but is it? They are 'remorseless, treacherous,

*Three Plays of Shakespeare, Harper and Brothers, 1909. By permission of the Publishers.

lecherous, kindless'; hot and hard, cold and cunning, savage and subtle as a beast of the field or the wilderness or the jungle. But such dangerous and vicious animals are not more exceptional than the noblest and purest of their kind. An Iago is abnormal: his wonderful intelligence, omnipotent and infallible within its limit and its range, gives to the unclean and maleficent beast that he is the dignity and the mystery of a devil. Goneril and Regan would be almost vulgarly commonplace by comparison with him if the conditions of their life and the circumstances of their story were not so much more extraordinary than their instincts and their acts. 'Regan,' according to Coleridge, 'is not, in fact, a greater monster than Goneril, but she has the power of casting more venom.' A champion who should wish to enter the lists on behalf of Goneril might plead that Regan was so much more of a Gadarean sow than her elder sister as to be, for all we know, incapable of such passion as flames out in Goneril at the thought of foreign banners spread in a noiseless land.

'Where's thy drum?
France spreads his banners in our noiseless land;
With plumèd helm thy slayer begins [his] threats;
Whiles thou, a moral fool, sit'st still, and criest
'Alack, why does he so?'

Beast and she-devil as she is, she rises in that instant to the level of an unclean and a criminal Joan of Arc. Her advocate might also invoke as an extenuating circumstance the fact that she poisoned Regan.

François-Victor Hugo, the author of the best and fullest commentary ever written on the text of which he gave us the most wonderful and masterly of all imaginable translations, has perhaps unwittingly enforced and amplified the remark of Coleridge on the difference between the criminality of the one man chosen by chance and predestined by nature as the proper paramour of either sister and the monstrosity of the creatures who felt towards him as women feel towards the men they love. Edmund is not a more true-born child of hell than a true-born son of his father. Goneril and Regan are legitimate daughters of the pit; the man who excites in them such emotion as in such as they are may pass as the substitute for love is but a half-blooded fellow from the infernal as well as the human point of view. His last wish is to undo the last and most monstrous of his crimes. Such a wish would have been impossible to either of the sisters by whom he can boast with his dying breath that Edmund was beloved.

'I pant for life: some good I mean to do,
Despite of mine own nature. Quickly send,
Be brief in it, to the castle; for my writ
Is on the life of Lear and on Cordelia;
Nay, send in time.'

The incomparable genius of the greatest among all poets and all men approved itself incomparable for ever by the possibly unconscious instinct which in this supreme work induced or compelled him to set side by side the very lowest and the very highest types of imaginable humanity. Kent and Oswald, Regan and Cordelia, stand out in such relief against each other that Shakespeare alone could have wrought their several figures into one perfect scheme of spiritual harmony. Setting aside for a moment the reflection that outside the work of Æschylus there is no such poetry in the world, we must remember that there is no such realism. And there is no discord between the supreme sublimities of impassioned poetry and the humblest realities of photographic prose. Incredible and impossible as it seems, the impression of the one is enhanced and intensified by the impression of the other.

That Shakespeare's judgment was as great and almost as wonderful as his genius has been a commonplace of criticism ever since the days of Coleridge; questionable only by such dirty and dwarfish creatures of simian intellect and facetious idiocy as mistake it for a sign of wit instead of dullness, and of distinction instead of degradation, to deny the sun in heaven and affirm the fragrance of a sewer. But I do not know whether his equally unequalled skill in the selection and composition of material for the construction of a masterpiece has or has not been as all but universally recognized. No more happy and no more terrible inspiration ever glorified the genius of a poet than was that which bade the greatest of them all inweave or fuse together the legend of Lear and his daughters with the story of Gloucester and his sons.

It is possible that an episode in Sidney's *Arcadia* may have suggested, as is usually supposed or usually repeated, the notion or conception of this more than tragic underplot; but the student will be disappointed who thinks to find in the sweet and sunbright work of Sidney's pure and happy genius a touch or a hint of such tragic horror as could only be conceived and made endurable by the deeper as well as higher, and darker as well as brighter, genius of Shakespeare. And this fearful understudy in terror is a necessary, an indispensable, part of the most wonderful creation ever imagined and realized by man. The author of the Book of Job, the author of the Eumenides, can show nothing to be set beside the third act of *King Lear*. All that is best and all that is worst in man might have been brought together and flashed together upon the mind's eye of the spectator or the student without the intervention of such servile ministers as take part with Goneril and Regan against their father. Storm and lightning, thunder and rain, become to us, even as they became to Lear, no less conscious and responsible partners in the superhuman inhumanity of an unimaginable crime. The close of the *Prometheus* itself seems less spiritually and overpoweringly fearful by comparison with a scene which is not the close and is less terrible than the close of *King Lear*. And it is no whit more terrible than it is beautiful. The splendour of the lightning and the menace of the thunder serve only or mainly to enhance the effect of suffering and the potency of passion on the spirit and the conscience of a man. The sufferer is transfigured: but he is not transformed. Mad or sane, living or dying, he is passionate and vehement, single-hearted and self-willed. And therefore it is that the fierce appeal, the fiery protest against the social iniquities and the legal atrocities of civilized mankind, which none before the greatest of all Englishmen had ever dreamed of daring to utter in song or set forth upon the stage, comes not from Hamlet, but from Lear. The young man whose infinite capacity of thought and whose delicate scrupulosity of conscience at once half disabled and half deified him could never have seen what was revealed by suffering to an old man who had never thought or felt more deeply or more keenly than an average labourer or an average king. Lear's madness, at all events, was assuredly not his enemy, but his friend.

The rule of Elizabeth and her successor may have been more arbitrary than we can now understand how the commonwealth of England could accept and could endure; but how far it was from a monarchy, from a government really deserving of that odious and ignominious name, we may judge by the fact that this play could be acted and published. Among all its other great qualities, among all the many other attributes which mark it for ever as matchless among the works of man, it has this above all, that it is the first great utterance of a cry from the heights and the depths of the human spirit on behalf of the outcasts of the world — on behalf of the social sufferer, clean or unclean, innocent or criminal, thrall or free. To satisfy the sense of righteousness, the craving for justice, as unknown and unimaginable by Dante as by Chaucer, a change must come upon the social scheme of things which shall make an end of the actual relations between the judge and the cutpurse, the beadle and the prostitute, the beggar and the king. All this could be uttered, could be prophesied, could be thundered from the English stage at the dawn of the seventeenth century. Were it within the power of omnipotence to create a German or a Russian Shakespeare, could anything of the sort be whispered or muttered or hinted or suggested from the boards of a Russian or a German theatre at the dawn of the twentieth? When a Tolstoi or a Sudermann can do this, and can do it with impunity in success, it will be allowed that his country is not more than three centuries behind England in civilization and freedom. Not political reform, but social revolution as beneficent and as bloodless, as absolute and as radical, as enkindled the aspiration and the faith of Victor Hugo, is the key-note of the creed and the watchword of the gospel according to Shakespeare. Not, of course, that it was not his first and last aim to follow the impulse which urged him to do good work for its own sake and for love of his own art: but this he could not do without delivery of the word that was in him — the word of witness against wrong done by oversight as well as by cruelty, by negligence as surely as by crime. These things were hidden from the marvellous wisdom of Hamlet, and revealed to the more marvellous insanity of Lear.

There is nothing of the miraculous in this marvel: the mere presence and companionship of the Fool should suffice to account for it; Cordelia herself is but a little more adorably worthy of our love than the poor fellow who began to pine away after her going into France and before his coming into sight of the reader or spectator. Here again the utmost humiliation imaginable of social state and daily life serves only to exalt and to emphasize the nobility and the manhood of the natural man. The whip itself cannot degrade him; the threat of it cannot change his attitude towards Lear; the dread of it cannot modify his defiance of Goneril. Being, if not half-witted, not altogether as other men are, he urges Lear to return and ask his daughters' blessing rather than brave the midnight and the storm: but he cleaves to his master with the divine instinct of fidelity and love which is not, though it should be, as generally recognized in the actual nature of a cat as in the proverbial nature of a dog. And when the old man is trembling on the very verge of madness, he sees and understands the priceless worth of such devotion and the godlike wisdom of such folly. In the most fearfully pathetic of all poems the most divinely pathetic touch of all is the tender thought of the houseless king for the suffering of such a fellow-sufferer as his fool. The whirlwind of terror and pity in which we are living as we read may at first confuse and obscure to the sight of a boyish reader the supreme significance and the unutterable charm of it. But if any elder does not feel it too keenly and too deeply for tears, it is a pity that he should waste his time and misuse his understanding in the study of Shakespeare.

There is nothing in all poetry so awful, so nearly unendurable by the reader who is compelled by a natural instinct of imagination to realize and believe it, as the close of the *Choephorœ*, except only the close of *King Lear*. The cry of Ugolino to the earth that would not open to swallow and to save is not quite so fearful in its pathos. But the skill which made use of the stupid old chronicle or tradition to produce this final masterpiece of tragedy is coequal with the genius which created it. The legendary Cordelia hanged herself in prison, long after her father's death, when defeated in battle by the sons of Goneril. And this most putrid and contemptible tradition suggested to Shakespeare the most dramatic and the most poetic of all scenes and all events that ever bade all men not devoid of understanding understand how much higher is the genius of man than the action of chance: how far the truth of imagination exceeds and transcends at all points the accident of fact. That an event may have happened means nothing and matters nothing; that a man such as Æschylus or Shakespeare imagined it means this: that it endures and bears witness what man may be, at the highest of his powers and the noblest of his nature, for ever.

1902

CHRISTOPHER MARLOWE *

The first great English poet was the father of English tragedy and the creator of English blank verse. Chaucer and Spenser were great writers and great men: they shared between them every gift which goes to the making of a poet except the one which alone can make a poet, in the proper sense of the word, great. Neither pathos nor humour nor fancy nor invention will suffice for that: no poet is great as a poet whom no one could ever pretend to recognize as sublime. Sublimity is the test of imagination as distinguished from invention or from fancy: and the first English poet whose powers can be called sublime was Christopher Marlowe.

The majestic and exquisite excellence of various lines and passages in Marlowe's first play must be admitted to relieve, if it cannot be allowed to redeem, the stormy monotony of Titanic truculence which blusters like a simoom; through the noisy course of its ten fierce acts. With many and heavy faults there is something of genuine greatness in *Tamburlaine the Great;* and for two grave reasons it must always be remembered with

**The Age of Shakespeare*, Harper and Brothers, 1908. By permission of the Publishers.

distinction and mentioned with honour. It is the first poem ever written in English blank verse, as distinguished from mere rhymeless decasyllabics; and it contains one of the noblest passages — perhaps, indeed, the noblest in the literature of the world — ever written by one of the greatest masters of poetry in loving praise of the glorious delights and sublime submission to the everlasting limits of his art. In its highest and most distinctive qualities, in unfaltering and infallible command of the right note of music and the proper tone of colour for the finest touches of poetic execution, no poet of the most elaborate modern school, working at ease upon every consummate resource of luxurious learning and leisurely refinement, has ever excelled the best and most representative work of a man who had literally no models before him, and probably or evidently was often, if not always, compelled to write against time for his living.

The just and generous judgment passed by Goethe on the *Faustus* of his English predecessor in tragic treatment of the same subject is somewhat more than sufficient to counterbalance the slighting or the sneering references to that magnificent poem which might have been expected from the ignorance of Byron or the incompetence of Hallam. And the particular note of merit observed, the special point of the praise conferred, by the great German poet should be no less sufficient to dispose of the vulgar misconception yet lingering among sciolists and pretenders to criticism, which regards a writer than whom no man was ever born with a finer or a stronger instinct for perfection of excellence in execution as a mere noble savage of letters, a rough self-taught sketcher or scribbler of crude and rude genius, whose unhewn blocks of verse had in them some veins of rare enough metal to be quarried and polished by Shakespeare. What most impressed the author of *Faust* in the work of Marlowe was a quality the want of which in the author of *Manfred* is proof enough to consign his best work to the second or third class at most. 'How greatly it is all planned!' the first requisite of all great work, and one of which the highest genius possible to a greatly gifted barbarian could by no possibility understand the nature or conceive the existence. That Goethe 'had thought of translating it' is perhaps hardly less precious a tribute to its greatness than the fact that it has been actually and admirably translated by the matchless translator of Shakespeare — the son of Victor Hugo, whose labour of love may thus be said to have made another point in common, and forged as it were another link of union, between Shakespeare and the young master of Shakespeare's youth. Of all great poems in dramatic form it is perhaps the most remarkable for absolute singleness of aim and simplicity of construction; yet is it wholly free from all possible imputation of monotony or aridity. *Tamburlaine* is monotonous in the general roll and flow of its stately and sonorous verse through a noisy wilderness of perpetual bluster and slaughter; but the unity of tone and purpose in *Doctor Faustus* is not unrelieved by change of manner and variety of incident. The comic scenes, written evidently with as little labour as of relish, are for the most part scarcely more than transcripts, thrown into the form of dialogue, from a popular prose History of Dr. Faustus, and therefore should be set down as little to the discredit as to the credit of the poet. Few masterpieces of any age in any language can stand beside this tragic poem — it has hardly the structure of a play — for the qualities of terror and splendour, for intensity of purpose and sublimity of note. In the vision of Helen, for example, the intense perception of loveliness gives actual sublimity to the sweetness and radiance of mere beauty in the passionate and spontaneous selection of words the most choice and perfect; and in like manner the sublimity of simplicity in Marlowe's conception and expression of the agonies endured by Faustus under the immediate imminence of his doom gives the highest note of beauty, the quality of absolute fitness and propriety, to the sheer straightforwardness of speech in which his agonizing horror finds vent ever more and more terrible from the first to the last equally beautiful and fearful verse of that tremendous monologue which has no parallel in all the range of tragedy.

It is now a commonplace of criticism to observe and regret the decline of power and interest after the opening acts of *The Jew of Malta.* This decline is undeniable, though even the latter part of the play is not wanting in rough energy and a coarse kind of interest; but the first two acts would be sufficient foundation for the durable fame of a dramatic poet. In the blank verse of Milton alone, who perhaps was hardly less indebted than Shakespeare was before him to Marlowe as the first English master of word-music in its grander forms, has the glory or the melody of passages in the opening soliloquy of Barabas been possibly surpassed. The figure of the hero before it degenerates into caricature is as finely touched as the poetic execution is excellent; and the rude and rapid sketches of the minor characters show at least some vigour and vivacity of touch.

In *Edward II* the interest rises and the execution improves as visibly and as greatly with the course of the advancing story as they decline in *The Jew of Malta.* The scene of the king's deposition at Kenilworth is almost as much finer in tragic effect and poetic quality as it is shorter and less elaborate than the corresponding scene in Shakespeare's *King Richard II.* The terror of the death scene undoubtedly rises into horror; but this horror is with skilful simplicity of treatment preserved from passing into disgust. In pure poetry, in sublime and splendid imagination, this tragedy is excelled by *Doctor Faustus;* in dramatic power and positive impression of natural effect it is as certainly the masterpiece of Marlowe. It was almost inevitable, in the hands of any poet but Shakespeare, that none of the characters represented should be capable of securing or even exciting any finer sympathy or more serious interest than attends on the mere evolution of successive events or the mere display of emotions (except always in the great scene of the deposition) rather animal than spiritual in their expression of rage or tenderness or suffering. The exact balance of mutual effect, the final note of scenic harmony between ideal conception and realistic execution, is not yet struck with perfect accuracy of touch and security of hand; but on this point also Marlowe has here come nearer by many degrees to Shakespeare than any of his other predecessors have ever come near to Marlowe.

Of *The Massacre at Paris* it is impossible to judge fairly from the garbled fragment of its genuine text, which is all that has come down to us. To Mr. Collier, among numberless other obligations, we owe the discovery of a striking passage excised in the piratical edition which gives us the only version extant of this unlucky play; and which, it must be allowed, contains nothing of quite equal value. This is obviously an occasional and polemical work, and being as it is overcharged with the anti-Catholic passion of the time, has a typical quality which gives it some empirical significance and interest. That anti-papal ardour is indeed the only note of unity in a rough and ragged chronicle which shambles and stumbles onward from the death of Queen Jeanne of Navarre to the murder of the last Valois. It is possible to conjecture what it would be fruitless to affirm, that it gave a hint in the next century to Nathaniel Lee for his far superior and really admirable tragedy on the same subject, issued ninety-seven years after the death of Marlowe.

The tragedy of *Dido, Queen of Carthage,* was probably completed for the stage after that irreparable and incalculable loss to English letters by Thomas Nash, the worthiest English precursor of Swift in vivid, pure, and passionate prose, embodying the most terrible and splendid qualities of a personal and social satirist; a man gifted also with some fair faculty of elegiac and even lyric verse, but in nowise qualified to put on the buskin left behind him by the 'famous gracer of tragedians,' as Marlowe had already been designated by their common friend Greene from among the worthiest of his fellows. In this somewhat thin-spun and evidently hasty play a servile fidelity to the text of Virgil's narrative has naturally resulted in the failure which might have been expected from an attempt at once to transcribe what is essentially inimitable and to reproduce it under the hopelessly alien conditions of dramatic adaptation. The one really noble passage in a generally feeble and incomposite piece of work is, however, uninspired by the unattainable model to which the dramatists have been only too obsequious in their subservience.

It is as nearly certain as anything can be

which depends chiefly upon cumulative and collateral evidence that the better part of what is best in the serious scenes of *King Henry VI* is mainly the work of Marlowe. That he is, at any rate, the principal author of the second and third plays passing under that name among the works of Shakespeare, but first and imperfectly printed as *The Contention between the Two Famous Houses of York and Lancaster*, can hardly be now a matter of debate among competent judges. The crucial difficulty of criticism in this matter is to determine, if indeed we should not rather say to conjecture, the authorship of the humourous scenes in prose, showing as they generally do a power of comparatively high and pure comic realism to which nothing in the acknowledged works of any pre-Shakespearean dramatist is even remotely comparable. Yet, especially in the original text of these scenes as they stand unpurified by the ultimate revision of Shakespeare, there are tones and touches which recall rather the clownish horseplay and homely ribaldry of his predecessors than anything in the lighter interludes of his very earliest plays. We find the same sort of thing which we find in their writings, only better done than they usually do it, rather than such work as Shakespeare's a little worse done than usual. And even in the final text of the tragic or metrical scenes the highest note struck is always, with one magnificent and unquestionable exception, rather in the key of Marlowe at his best than of Shakespeare while yet in great measure his disciple.

It is another commonplace of criticism to affirm that Marlowe had not a touch of comic genius, not a gleam of wit in him or a twinkle of humour: but it is an indisputable fact that he had. In *The Massacre at Paris*, the soliloquy of the soldier lying in wait for the minion of Henri III has the same very rough but very real humour as a passage in the *Contention* which was cancelled by the reviser. The same hand is unmistakable in both these broad and boyish outbreaks of unseemly but undeniable fun: and if we might wish it rather less indecorous, we must admit that the tradition which denies all sense of humour and all instinct of wit to the first great poet of England is no less unworthy of serious notice or elaborate refutation than the charges and calumnies of an informer who was duly hanged the year after Marlowe's death. For if the same note of humour is struck in an undoubted play of Marlowe's and in a play of disputed authorship, it is evident that the rest of the scene in the latter play must also be Marlowe's. And in that unquestionable case the superb and savage humour of the terribly comic scenes which represent with such rough magnificence of realism the riot of Jack Cade and his ruffians through the ravaged streets of London must be recognizable as no other man's than his. It is a pity we have not before us for comparison the comic scenes or burlesque interludes of *Tamburlaine* which the printer or publisher, as he had the impudence to avow in his prefatory note, purposely omitted and left out.

The author of *A Study of Shakespeare* was therefore wrong, and utterly wrong, when in a book issued some quarter of a century ago he followed the lead of Mr. Dyce in assuming that because the author of *Doctor Faustus* and *The Jew of Malta* 'was as certainly' — and certainly it is difficult to deny that whether as a mere transcriber or as an original dealer in pleasantry he sometimes was — 'one of the least and worst among jesters as he was one of the best and greatest among poets,' he could not have had a hand in the admirable comic scenes of *The Taming of the Shrew*. For it is now, I should hope, unnecessary to insist that the able and conscientious editor to whom his fame and his readers owe so great a debt was over-hasty in assuming and asserting that he was a poet 'to whom, we have reason to believe, nature had denied even a moderate talent for the humourous.' The serious or would-be poetical scenes of the play are as unmistakably the work of an imitator as are most of the better passages in *Titus Andronicus* and *King Edward III*. Greene or Peele may be responsible for the bad poetry, but there is no reason to suppose that the great poet whose mannerisms he imitated with so stupid a servility was incapable of the good fun.

Had every copy of Marlowe's boyish version or perversion of Ovid's *Elegies* deservedly perished in the flames to which it was judicially condemned by the sentence of a brace of prelates, it is possible that an occasional bookworm, it is certain that no poetical student, would have deplored its destruction, if its demerits — hardly relieved, as his first competent editor has happily remarked, by the occasional incidence of a fine and felicitous couplet — could in that case have been imagined. His translation of the first book of Lucan alternately rises above the original and falls short of it; often inferior to the Latin in point and weight of expressive rhetoric, now and then brightened by a clearer note of poetry and lifted into a higher mood of verse. Its terseness, vigour, and purity of style would in any case have been praiseworthy, but are nothing less than admirable, if not wonderful, when we consider how close the translator has on the whole (in spite of occasional slips into inaccuracy) kept himself to the most rigid limit of literal representation, phrase by phrase and often line by line. The really startling force and felicity of occasional verses are worthier of remark than the inevitable stiffness and heaviness of others, when the technical difficulty of such a task is duly taken into account.

One of the most faultless lyrics and one of the loveliest fragments in the whole range of descriptive and fanciful poetry would have secured a place for Marlowe among the memorable men of his epoch, even if his plays had perished with himself. His *Passionate Shepherd* remains ever since unrivalled in its way — a way of pure fancy and radiant melody without break or lapse. The untitled fragment, on the other hand, has been very closely rivalled, perhaps very happily imitated, but only by the greatest lyric poet of England — by Shelley alone. Marlowe's poem of *Hero and Leander*, closing with the sunrise which closes the night of the lover's union, stands alone in its age, and far ahead of the work of any possible competitor between the death of Spenser and the dawn of Milton. In clear mastery of narrative and presentation, in melodious ease and simplicity of strength, it is not less preeminent than in the adorable beauty and impeccable perfection of separate lines or passages.

The place and the value of Christopher Marlowe as a leader among English poets it would be almost impossible for historical criticism to over-estimate. To none of them all, perhaps, have so many of the greatest among them been so deeply and so directly indebted. Nor was ever any great writer's influence upon his fellows more utterly and unmixedly an influence for good. He first, and he alone, guided Shakespeare into the right way of work; his music, in which there is no echo of any man's before him, found its own echo in the more prolonged but hardly more exalted harmony of Milton's. He is the greatest discoverer, the most daring and inspired pioneer, in all our poetic literature. Before him there was neither genuine blank verse nor genuine tragedy in our language. After his arrival the way was prepared, the paths were made straight, for Shakespeare.

1908

MODERN PERIOD

POETRY

Edmund Gosse (1849–)

IMPRESSION

In these restrained and careful times
Our knowledge petrifies our rhymes;
Ah! for that reckless fire men had
When it was witty to be mad,

When wild conceits were piled in scores,
And lit by flaring metaphors,
When all was crazed and out of tune, —
Yet throbbed with music of the moon.

If we could dare to write as ill
As some whose voices haunt us still,
Even we, perchance, might call our own
Their deep enchanting undertone.

We are too diffident and nice,
Too learnèd and too over-wise,
Too much afraid of faults to be
The flutes of bold sincerity.

For, as this sweet life passes by,
We blink and nod with critic eye;
We've no words rude enough to give
Its charm so frank and fugitive.

The green and scarlet of the Park,
The undulating streets at dark,
The brown smoke blown across the blue,
This colored city we walk through; —

The pallid faces full of pain,
The field-smell of the passing wain,
The laughter, longing, perfume, strife,
The daily spectacle of life; —

Ah! how shall this be given to rhyme,
By rhymesters of a knowing time?
Ah! for the age when verse was glad,
Being godlike, to be bad and mad.

1894

Eugene Lee-Hamilton* (1845–1907)

WHAT THE SONNET IS

Fourteen small broidered berries on the hem
Of Circe's mantle, each of magic gold;
Fourteen of lone Calypso's tears that rolled
Into the sea, for pearls to come of them;
Fourteen clear signs of omen in the gem
With which Medea human fate foretold;
Fourteen small drops, which Faustus, growing old,
Craved of the Fiend, to water Life's dry stem.
It is the pure white diamond Dante brought
To Beatrice; the sapphire Laura wore
When Petrarch cut it sparkling out of thought;
The ruby Shakespeare hewed from his heart's core;
The dark, deep emerald that Rossetti wrought
For his own soul, to wear for evermore.

1894

ON HIS 'SONNETS OF THE WINGLESS HOURS'

I wrought them like a targe of hammered gold
On which all Troy is battling round and round;
Or Circe's cup, embossed with snakes that wound
Through buds and myrtles, fold on scaly fold;
Or like gold coins, which Lydian tombs may hold,
Stamped with winged racers, in the old red ground;
Or twined gold armlets from the funeral mound
Of some great viking, terrible of old.
I know not in what metal I have wrought;
Nor whether what I fashioned will be thrust
Beneath the clods that hide forgotten thought;
But if it is of gold it will not rust;
And when the time is ripe it will be brought
Into the sun and glitter through its dust.

1894

* *Poems*, Canterbury Poets, Walter Scott Publishing Company. By Permission.

Alfred Austin * (1835-1913)

AT SHELLEY'S HOUSE AT LERICI

Maiden, with English hair and eyes
The colour of Italian skies,
What seek you by this shore?
'I seek, sir, for the latest home
Where Shelley dwelt, and, o'er the foam
Speeding, returned no more.'

Come, then with me: I seek it, too.
Are you his kith? For strangely you
Resemble him in mien.
'No, save it be that all are kin
Who cherish the same thoughts within,
And gaze on things unseen.'

It should be easy, sure, to find.
Waves close in front, woods close behind,
Green shutters, whitewashed walls;
A little space of rocky ground,
Where climbs the wave, and, round and round,
The seagull curves and calls.

Lo! there it stands. A quiet spot,
Untenanted, it seems forgot,
Like shrine from which the God
Hath vanished, and but left behind
A something in the air, the wind,
Recalling where he trod.

Upon this balcony how oft,
When waves were smooth and winds were soft,
As now, he must have stood,
And dreamed of days when men should be
Bondless as this unfettered sea,
And peaceful as that wood.

What would he find if came he now?
A phantom crown on kingly brow,
Veiled sceptre, trembling throne;
Pulpits where threat and curse have ceased,
And shrines whereat half-sceptic priest
Worships, too oft, alone.

With muffled psalm and whispered hymn,
At secret dawn or twilight dim,
A pious remnant pray;
For their maimed rites indulgence plead,
And, half uncertain of their creed,
Explain their God away.

Gone the conventions Shelley cursed:
The first are last, the last are first;
The lame, the halt, the blind,
Now in the seat of power, along
With the far-seeing and the strong,
Mould mandates for mankind.

No longer doth man's will decide,
And woman's feebler impulse guide;
He yields to her his might:
Duty hath grown an old-world tale,
And chaste Obedience rends her veil,
For epicene delight.

Where now do towering despots reign
Over lithe knee and servile brain,
The sacred, the base, the bought?
Monarchs themselves now bend with awe
Before the kingliness of Law,
The majesty of Thought.

Yes, Kings have gone, or reign as slaves;
Religion mumbles round our graves,
But shapes our lives no more:
Tradition, thrice-spurned Sibyl, burns
The leaves mob Sovereignty spurns,
Contemptuous of her lore.

Fair Maiden with the sea-blue eyes,
With whom, beneath these sea-blue skies,
Shelley had loved to live,
Forgive me if his dream, unborn
Then, but not adult, moves my scorn:
Would He too not forgive?

For where both Crown and Cowl defied
Sue for the ruth they once denied,
What would he find instead?
A fiercer despot, fouler creed,
The Rule of Gold, the Rites of Greed,
And a bitterer cry for bread.

Wake, poet! and retune your strings.
The earth now swarms with petty kings,
Seated on self-made thrones,
And altar-tables richly spread,
Where Roguery consecrates the bread,
And Opulence atones.

Here Shelley prayed that War might cease
From earth, and Pentecostal Peace
Descend with dovelike breath.
Look round this bay! each treeless gorge,
Each scarred ravine, incessant forge
The instruments of death.

From Salterbrand's unfreezing peaks
To sunny Manfredonia's creeks,
Have alien satraps gone;
But, guarding Italy the Free,
Her murderous mammoth-monsters, see,
Come grimly wallowing on.

Yes, here He dwelt and dreamed: and there,
Gleams *Porto Venere* the fair,
The mockery of a name.
Where fervent Venus once was Queen,
Hot Mars now ravishes the scene,
And fans a fiercer flame.

* *Narrative Poems*, The Macmillan Company, 1891. By permission of the Publishers.

Fair Maiden with the English brow,
Although from me, who shortly now
Must tread life's downward slope,
Illusions one by one depart,
Still foster in your virgin heart
The embryo of Hope.

The hills remain, the woods, the waves;
And they alone are dupes or slaves
Who, spurning Nature's breast,
Too high would soar, too deep would sound,
And madden vainly round and round
The orbit of unrest.

Pity, too, lingers. As I speak,
The teardrops tremble on your cheek,
Too silent to deceive;
And with assuaging hand you show
How tenderness still tempers woe,
And none need singly grieve.

Yes! sweet it were, with you for guide,
To float across that dimpling tide,
And on its farther shore,
To prove if Venus still holds sway,
And, wandering with you round the bay,
Tempt back one's youth once more.

But, child! it is not Shelley's world.
Fancy's light sails had best be furled,
Before they surge and swell,
What helm can steer the heart? or who
Keep moored, inspired by such as You?
Heaven prosper you! Farewell.

1891

IN THE MONTH WHEN SINGS THE CUCKOO

HARK! Spring is coming. Her herald sings
Cuckoo!
The air resounds and the woodland rings,
Cuckoo! Cuckoo!
Leave the milking pail and the mantling cream,
And down by the meadow, and up by the stream,
Where movement is music and life a dream,
In the month when sings the cuckoo.

Away with old Winter's frowns and fears,
Cuckoo! Cuckoo!
Now May with a smile dries April's tears,
Cuckoo!
When the bees are humming in bloom and bud,
And the kine sit chewing the moist green cud,
Shall the snow not melt in a maiden's blood,
In the month when sings the cuckoo?

The popinjay mates and the lapwing woos;
Cuckoo!
In the lane is a footstep. I wonder Whose?
Cuckoo! Cuckoo!
How sweet are low whispers! and sweet, so sweet,
When the warm hands touch and the shy lips meet,
And sorrel and woodruff are round our feet,
In the month when sings the cuckoo.

Your face is as fragrant as moist musk-rose;
Cuckoo! Cuckoo!
All the year in your cheek the windflower blows;
Cuckoo! Cuckoo!
You flit as blithely as bird on wing;
And when you answer, and when they sing,
I know not if they, or You, be Spring,
In the month when pairs the cuckoo.

Will you love me still when the blossom droops?
Cuckoo!
When the cracked husk falls and the field-fare troops?
Cuckoo!
Let sere leaf or snowdrift shade your brow,
By the soul of the Spring, sweet-heart, I vow,
I will love you then as I love you now,
In the month when sings the cuckoo.

Smooth, smooth is the sward where the loose-strife grows,
Cuckoo! Cuckoo!
As we lie and hear in a dreamy doze,
Cuckoo! Cuckoo! Cuckoo!
And smooth is the curve of a maiden's cheek,
When she loves to listen but fears to speak,
And we yearn but we know not what we seek,
In the month when sings the cuckoo.

But in warm mid summer we hear no more,
Cuckoo!
And August brings not, with all its store,
Cuckoo!
When Autumn shivers on Winter's brink,
And the wet wind wails through crevice and chink,
We gaze at the logs, and sadly think
Of the month when called the cuckoo.

But the cuckoo comes back and shouts once more,
Cuckoo!
And the world is as young as it was before;
Cuckoo! Cuckoo!

It grows not older for mortal tears,
For the falsehood of men or for women's fears;
'T is as young as it was in the bygone years,
When first was heard the cuckoo.

I will love you then as I love you now,
Cuckoo!
What cares the Spring for a broken vow?
Cuckoo! Cuckoo!
The broods of last year are pairing, this;
And there will never lack, while love is bliss,
Fresh ears to cozen, fresh lips to kiss,
In the month when sings the cuckoo.

O cruel bird! will you never have done?
Cuckoo! Cuckoo! Cuckoo!
You sing for the cloud, as you sang for the sun;
Cuckoo! Cuckoo!
You mock me now as you mocked me then,
When I knew not yet that the loves of men
Are as brief as the glamour of glade and glen,
And the glee of the fleeting cuckoo.

O, to lie once more in the long fresh grass,
Cuckoo!
And dream of the sounds and scents that pass;
Cuckoo! Cuckoo!
To savour the woodbine, surmise the dove,
With no roof save the far-off sky above,
And a curtain of kisses round couch of love,
While distantly called the cuckoo.

But if now I slept, I should sleep to wake
To the sleepless pang and the dreamless ache,
To the wild babe blossom within my heart,
To the darkening terror and swelling smart,
To the searching look and the words apart,
And the hint of the tell-tale cuckoo.

The meadow grows thick, and the stream runs deep,
Cuckoo!
Where the aspens quake and the willows weep;
Cuckoo! Cuckoo!
The dew of the night and the morning heat
Will close up the track of my farewell feet: —
So good-bye to the life that once was sweet,
When so sweetly called the cuckoo.

The kine are unmilked, and the cream unchurned,
Cuckoo!
The pillow unpressed, and the quilt unturned,
Cuckoo! Cuckoo!
'T was easy to gibe at a beldame's fear
For the quick brief blush and the sidelong-tear;
But if maids will gad in the youth of the year,
They should heed what says the cuckoo.

There are marks in the meadow laid up for hay,
Cuckoo!
And the tread of a foot where no foot should stray:
Cuckoo! Cuckoo!
The banks of the pool are broken down,
Where the water is quiet and deep and brown; —
The very spot, if one longed to drown,
And no more to hear the cuckoo.

'T is a full taut net and heavy haul,
Cuckoo! Cuckoo!
Look! her auburn hair and her trim new shawl!
Cuckoo! Cuckoo!
Draw a bit this way where 't is not so steep;
There, cover her face! She but seems asleep;
While the swallows skim and the graylings leap,
And joyously sings the cuckoo.

1891

See Arnold 975

Oscar Wilde* (1856–1900)

REQUIESCAT

TREAD lightly, she is near
Under the snow,
Speak gently, she can hear
The daisies grow.

All her bright golden hair
Tarnished with rust,
She that was young and fair
Fallen to dust.

Lily-like, white as snow,
She hardly knew
She was a woman, so
Sweetly she grew.

Coffin-board, heavy stone,
Lie on her breast,
I vex my heart alone,
She is at rest.

* *Poems*, The Modern Library, Inc. By permission of the Publishers.

Peace, Peace, she cannot hear
Lyre or sonnet,
All my life 's buried here,
Heap earth upon it.

1881

THE BALLAD OF READING GAOL

I

He did not wear his scarlet coat,
For blood and wine are red,
And blood and wine were on his hands
When they found him with the dead,
The poor dead woman whom he loved,
And murdered in her bed.

He walked amongst the Trial Men
In a suit of shabby grey;
A cricket cap was on his head,
And his step seemed light and gay;
But I never saw a man who looked
So wistfully at the day.

I never saw a man who looked
With such a wistful eye
Upon that little tent of blue
Which prisoners call the sky,
And at every drifting cloud that went
With sails of silver by.

I walked, with other souls in pain,
Within another ring,
And was wondering if the man had done
A great or little thing,
When a voice behind me whispered low,
'*That fellow's got to swing.*'

Dear Christ! the very prison walls
Suddenly seemed to reel,
And the sky above my head became
Like a casque of scorching steel;
And, though I was a soul in pain,
My pain I could not feel.

I only knew what hunted thought
Quickened his step, and why
He looked upon the garish day
With such a wistful eye;
The man had killed the thing he loved
And so he had to die.

. . . .

Yet each man kills the thing he loves,
By each let this be heard,
Some do it with a bitter look,
Some with a flattering word,
The coward does it with a kiss,
The brave man with a sword!

Some kill their love when they are young,
And some when they are old;
Some strangle with the hands of Lust,
Some with the hands of Gold:
The kindest use a knife, because
The dead so soon grow cold.

Some love too little, some too long,
Some sell, and others buy;
Some do the deed with many tears,
And some without a sigh:
For each man kills the thing he loves,
Yet each man does not die.

He does not die a death of shame
On a day of dark disgrace,
Nor have a noose about his neck,
Nor a cloth upon his face,
Nor drop feet foremost through the floor
Into an empty space.

. . . .

He does not sit with silent men
Who watch him night and day;
Who watch him when he tries to weep,
And when he tries to pray;
Who watch him lest himself should rob
The prison of its prey.

He does not wake at dawn to see
Dread figures throng his room,
The shivering Chaplain robed in white,
The Sheriff stern with gloom,
And the Governor all in shiny black,
With the yellow face of Doom.

He does not rise in piteous haste
To put on convict-clothes,
While some coarse-mouthed Doctor gloats, and notes
Each new and nerve-twitched pose,
Fingering a watch whose little ticks
Are like horrible hammer-blows.

He does not know that sickening thirst
That sands one's throat, before
The hangman with his gardener's gloves
Slips through the padded door,
And binds one with three leathern thongs,
That the throat may thirst no more.

He does not bend his head to hear
The Burial Office read,
Nor, while the terror of his soul
Tells him he is not dead,
Cross his own coffin, as he moves
Into the hideous shed.

He does not stare upon the air
Through a little roof of glass:

He does not pray with lips of clay
  For his agony to pass;
Nor feel upon his shuddering cheek
  The kiss of Caiaphas.

II

Six weeks our guardsman walked the yard,
  In the suit of shabby grey:
His cricket cap was on his head,
  And his step seemed light and gay,
But I never saw a man who looked
  So wistfully at the day.

I never saw a man who looked
  With such a wistful eye
Upon that little tent of blue
  Which prisoners call the sky,
And at every wandering cloud that trailed
  Its ravelled fleeces by.

He did not wring his hands, as do
  Those witless men who dare
To try to rear the changeling Hope
  In the cave of black Despair:
He only looked upon the sun,
  And drank the morning air.

He did not wring his hands nor weep,
  Nor did he peek or pine,
But he drank the air as though it held
  Some healthful anodyne;
With open mouth he drank the sun,
  As though it had been wine!

And I and all the souls in pain,
  Who tramped the other ring,
Forgot if we ourselves had done
  A great or little thing,
And watched with gaze of dull amaze
  The man who had to swing.

And strange it was to see him pass
  With a step so light and gay,
And strange it was to see him look
  So wistfully at the day,
And strange it was to think that he
  Had such a debt to pay.

. . . . . .

For oak and elm have pleasant leaves
  That in the spring-time shoot:
But grim to see is the gallows-tree,
  With its adder-bitten root,
And, green or dry, a man must die
  Before it bears its fruit!

The loftiest place is that seat of grace
  For which all worldlings try:
But who would stand in hempen band
  Upon a scaffold high,
And through a murderer's collar take
  His last look at the sky?

It is sweet to dance to violins
  When Love and Life are fair:
To dance to flutes, to dance to lutes
  Is delicate and rare:
But it is not sweet with nimble feet
  To dance upon the air!

So with curious eyes and sick surmise
  We watched him day by day,
And wondered if each one of us
  Would end the self-same way,
For none can tell to what red Hell
  His sightless soul may stray.

At last the dead man walked no more
  Amongst the Trial Men,
And I knew that he was standing up
  In the black dock's dreadful pen,
And that never would I see his face
  In God's sweet world again.

Like two doomed ships that pass in storm
  We had crossed each other's way:
But we made no sign, we said no word,
  We had no word to say;
For we did not meet in the holy night,
  But in the shameful day.

A prison wall was round us both,
  Two outcast men we were:
The world had thrust us from its heart,
  And God from out His care:
And the iron gin that waits for Sin
  Had caught us in its snare.

III

In Debtors' Yard the stones are hard,
  And the dripping wall is high,
So it was there he took the air
  Beneath the leaden sky,
And by each side a Warder walked,
  For fear the man might die.

Or else he sat with those who watched
  His anguish night and day;
Who watched him when he rose to weep,
  And when he crouched to pray;
Who watched him lest himself should rob
  Their scaffold of its prey.

The Governor was strong upon
  The Regulations Act:
The Doctor said that Death was but
  A scientific fact:
And twice a day the Chaplain called,
  And left a little tract.

And twice a day he smoked his pipe,
  And drank his quart of beer:
His soul was resolute, and held
  No hiding-place for fear;
He often said that he was glad
  The hangman's hands were near.

But why he said so strange a thing
  No Warder dared to ask:
For he to whom a watcher's doom
  Is given as his task,
Must set a lock upon his lips,
  And make his face a mask.

Or else he might be moved, and try
  To comfort or console:
And what should Human Pity do
  Pent up in Murderers' Hole?
What word of grace in such a place
  Could help a brother's soul?

. . . . . .

With slouch and swing around the ring
  We trod the Fools' Parade!
We did not care: we knew we were
  The Devil's Own Brigade:
And shaven head and feet of lead
  Make a merry masquerade.

We tore the tarry rope to shreds
  With blunt and bleeding nails;
We rubbed the doors, and scrubbed the floors,
  And cleaned the shining rails:
And, rank by rank, we soaped the plank,
  And clattered with the pails.

We sewed the sacks, we broke the stones,
  We turned the dusty drill:
We banged the tins, and bawled the hymns,
  And sweated on the mill:
But in the heart of every man
  Terror was lying still.

So still it lay that every day
  Crawled like a weed-clogged wave:
And we forgot the bitter lot
  That waits for fool and knave,
Till once, as we tramped in from work,
  We passed an open grave.

With yawning mouth the yellow hole
  Gaped for a living thing;
The very mud cried out for blood
  To the thirsty asphalte ring:
And we knew that ere one dawn grew fair
  Some prisoner had to swing.

Right in we went, with soul intent
  On Death and Dread and Doom:
The hangman, with his little bag,
  Went shuffling through the gloom:
And each man trembled as he crept
  Into his numbered tomb.

. . . . . .

That night the empty corridors
  Were full of forms of Fear,
And up and down the iron town
  Stole feet we could not hear,
And through the bars that hide the stars
  White faces seemed to peer.

He lay as one who lies and dreams
  In a pleasant meadow-land,
The watchers watched him as he slept,
  And could not understand
How one could sleep so sweet a sleep
  With a hangman close at hand.

But there is no sleep when men must weep
  Who never yet have wept:
So we — the fool, the fraud, the knave —
  That endless vigil kept,
And through each brain on hands of pain
  Another's terror crept.

Alas! it is a fearful thing
  To feel another's guilt!
For, right within, the sword of Sin
  Pierced to its poisoned hilt,
And as molten lead were the tears we shed
  For the blood we had not spilt.

The Warders with their shoes of felt
  Crept by each padlocked door,
And peeped and saw, with eyes of awe,
  Grey figures on the floor,
And wondered why men knelt to pray
  Who never prayed before.

All through the night we knelt and prayed,
  Mad mourners of a corse!
The troubled plumes of midnight were
  The plumes upon a hearse:
And bitter wine upon a sponge
  Was the savour of Remorse.

. . . . . .

The grey cock crew, the red cock crew,
  But never came the day:
And crookèd shapes of Terror crouched,
  In the corners where we lay:
And each evil sprite that walks by night
  Before us seemed to play.

They glided past, they glided fast,
  Like travelers through a mist:
They mocked the moon in a rigadoon
  Of delicate turn and twist,

And with formal pace and loathsome grace
The phantoms keep their tryst.

With mop and mow, we saw them go,
Slim shadows hand in hand:
About, about, in ghostly rout
They trod a saraband:
And the damned grotesques made arabesques,
Like the wind upon the sand!

With the pirouettes of marionettes,
They tripped on pointed tread:
But with flutes of Fear they filled the ear,
As their grisly masque they led,
And loud they sang, and long they sang,
For they sang to wake the dead.

'*Oho!*' they cried, '*The World is wide,*
But fettered limbs go lame!
And once, or twice, to throw the dice
Is a gentlemanly game,
But he does not win who plays with Sin
In the Secret House of Shame.'

No things of air these antics were,
That frolicked with such glee:
To men whose lives were held in gyves,
And whose feet might not go free,
Ah! wounds of Christ! they were living things,
Most terrible to see.

Around, around, they waltzed and wound;
Some wheeled in smirking pairs;
With the mincing step of a demirep
Some sidled up the stairs:
And with subtle sneer, and fawning leer,
Each helped us at our prayers.

The morning wind began to moan,
But still the night went on:
Through its giant loom the web of gloom
Crept till each thread was spun:
And, as we prayed, we grew afraid
Of the Justice of the Sun.

The moaning wind went wandering round
The weeping prison-wall:
Till like a wheel of turning steel
We felt the minutes crawl:
O moaning wind! what had we done
To have such a seneschal?

At last I saw the shadowed bars,
Like a lattice wrought in lead,
Move right across the whitewashed wall
That faced my three-plank bed,
And I knew that somewhere in the world
God's dreadful dawn was red.

At six o'clock we cleaned our cells,
At seven all was still,
But the sough and swing of a mighty wing
The prison seemed to fill,
For the Lord of Death with icy breath
Had entered in to kill.

He did not pass in purple pomp,
Nor ride a moon-white steed.
Three yards of cord and a sliding board
Are all the gallows' need:
So with rope of shame the Herald came
To do the secret deed.

We were as men who through a fen
Of filthy darkness grope:
We did not dare to breathe a prayer,
Or to give our anguish scope:
Something was dead in each of us,
And what was dead was Hope.

For Man's grim Justice goes its way,
And will not swerve aside:
It slays the weak, it slays the strong,
It has a deadly stride:
With iron heel it slays the strong,
The monstrous parricide!

We waited for the stroke of eight:
Each tongue was thick with thirst:
For the stroke of eight is the stroke of Fate
That makes a man accursed,
And Fate will use a running noose
For the best man and the worst.

We had no other thing to do,
Save to wait for the sign to come:
So, like things of stone in a valley lone,
Quiet we sat and dumb:
But each man's heart beat thick and quick,
Like a madman on a drum!

With sudden shock the prison-clock
Smote on the shivering air,
And from all the gaol rose up a wail
Of impotent despair,
Like the sound that frightened marshes hear
From some leper in his lair.

And as one sees most fearful things
In the crystal of a dream,
We saw the greasy hempen rope
Hooked to the blackened beam,
And heard the prayer the hangman's snare
Strangled into a scream.

And all the woe that moved him so
That he gave that bitter cry,
And the wild regrets, and the bloody sweats,
None knew so well as I:

For he who lives more lives than one
  More deaths than one must die.

IV

There is no chapel on the day
  On which they hang a man:
The Chaplain's heart is far too sick,
  Or his face is far too wan,
Or there is that written in his eyes
  Which none should look upon.

So they kept us close till nigh on noon,
  And then they rang the bell,
And the Warders with their jingling keys
  Opened each listening cell,
And down the iron stair we tramped,
  Each from his separate Hell.

Out into God's sweet air he went,
  But not in wonted way,
For this man's face was white with fear,
  And that man's face was grey,
And I never saw sad men who looked
  So wistfully at the day.

I never saw sad men who looked
  With such a wistful eye
Upon that little tent of blue
  We prisoners called the sky,
And at every careless cloud that passed
  In happy freedom by.

But there were those amongst us all
  Who walked with downcast head,
And knew that, had each got his due,
  They should have died instead:
He had but killed a thing that lived,
  Whilst they had killed the dead.

For he who sins a second time
  Wakes a dead soul to pain,
And draws it from its spotted shroud,
  And makes it bleed again,
And makes it bleed great gouts of blood,
  And makes it bleed in vain!

. . . .

Like ape or clown, in monstrous garb
  With crookèd arrows starred,
Silently we went round and round
  The slippery asphalte yard;
Silently we went round and round
  And no man spoke a word.

Silently we went round and round,
  And through each hollow mind
The Memory of dreadful things
  Rushed like a dreadful wind,
And Horror stalked before each man,
  And Terror crept behind.

. . . .

The Warders strutted up and down,
  And kept their herd of brutes,
Their uniforms were spick and span,
  And they wore their Sunday suits,
But we knew the work they had been at,
  By the quicklime on their boots.

For where a grave had opened wide,
  There was no grave at all:
Only a stretch of mud and sand
  By the hideous prison-wall,
And a little heap of burning lime,
  That the man should have his pall.

For he has a pall, this wretched man,
  Such as few men can claim:
Deep down below a prison-yard,
  Naked for greater shame,
He lies, with fetters on each foot,
  Wrapt in a sheet of flame!

And all the while the burning lime
  Eats flesh and bone away,
It eats the brittle bone by night,
  And the soft flesh by day,
It eats the flesh and bone by turns,
  But it eats the heart alway.

. . . .

For three long years they will not sow
  Or root or seeding there:
For three long years the unblessed spot
  Will sterile be and bare,
And look upon the wondering sky
  With unreproachful stare.

They think a murderer's heart would taint
  Each simple seed they sow.
It is not true! God's kindly earth
  Is kindlier than men know,
And the red rose would but blow more red,
  The white rose whiter blow.

Out of his mouth a red, red rose!
  Out of his heart a white!
For who can say by what strange way,
  Christ brings His will to light,
Since the barren staff the pilgrim bore
  Bloomed in the great Pope's sight?

But neither milk-white rose nor red
  May bloom in prison air;
The shard, the pebble, and the flint,
  Are what they give us there:
For flowers have been known to heal
  A common man's despair.

So never will wine-red rose or white,
  Petal by petal, fall
On that stretch of mud and sand that lies

By the hideous prison-wall,
To tell the men who tramp the yard
That God's Son died for all.

. . . .

Yet though the hideous prison-wall
Still hems him round and round,
And a spirit may not walk by night
That is with fetters bound,
And a spirit may but weep that lies
In such unholy ground,

He is at peace — this wretched man —
At peace, or will be soon:
There is no thing to make him mad,
Nor does Terror walk at noon,
For the lampless Earth in which he lies
Has neither Sun nor Moon.

They hanged him as a beast is hanged:
They did not even toll
A requiem that might have brought
Rest to his startled soul,
But hurriedly they took him out,
And hid him in a hole.

They stripped him of his canvas clothes,
And gave him to the flies:
They mocked the purple swollen throat,
And the stark and staring eyes:
And with laughter loud they heaped the shroud
In which their convict lies.

The Chaplain would not kneel to pray
By his dishonoured grave:
Nor mark it with that blessèd Cross
That Christ for sinners gave,
Because the man was one of those
Whom Christ came down to save.

Yet all is well; he has but passed
To life's appointed bourne:
And alien tears will fill for him
Pity's long-broken urn,
For his mourners will be outcast men,
And outcasts always mourn.

V

I know not whether Laws be right,
Or whether Laws be wrong;
All that we know who lie in gaol
Is that the wall is strong;
And that each day is like a year,
A year whose days are long.

But this I know, that every Law
That men have made for Man,
Since first Man took his brother's life,
And the sad world began,
But straws the wheat and saves the chaff
With a most evil fan.

This too I know — and wise it were
If each could know the same —
That every prison that men build
Is built with bricks of shame,
And bound with bars lest Christ should see
How men their brothers maim.

With bars they blur the gracious moon,
And blind the goodly sun:
And they do well to hide their Hell,
For in it things are done
That Son of God nor Son of Man
Ever should look upon!

. . . .

The vilest deeds like poison weeds,
Bloom well in prison-air;
It is only what is good in Man
That wastes and withers there:
Pale Anguish keeps the heavy gate,
And the Warder is Despair.

For they starve the little frightened child
Till it weeps both night and day:
And they scourge the weak, and flog the fool,
And gibe the old and grey,
And some grow mad, and all grow bad,
And none a word may say.

Each narrow cell in which we dwell
Is a foul and dark latrine,
And the fetid breath of living Death
Chokes up each grated screen,
And all, but Lust, is turned to dust
In Humanity's machine.

The brackish water that we drink
Creeps with a loathsome slime,
And the bitter bread they weigh in scales
Is full of chalk and lime,
And Sleep will not lie down, but walks
Wild-eyed, and cries to Time.

. . . .

But though lean Hunger and green Thirst
Like asp with adder fight,
We have little care of prison fare,
For what chills and kills outright
Is that every stone one lifts by day
Becomes one's heart by night.

With midnight always in one's heart,
And twilight in one's cell,
We turn the crank, or tear the rope,
Each in his separate Hell,
And the silence is more awful far
Than the sound of a brazen bell.

And never a human voice comes near
  To speak a gentle word:
And the eye that watches through the door
  Is pitiless and hard:
And by all forgot, we rot and rot,
  With soul and body marred.

And thus we rust Life's iron chain
  Degraded and alone:
And some men curse, and some men weep,
  And some men make no moan:
But God's eternal Laws are kind
  And break the heart of stone.

. . . . . .

And every human heart that breaks,
  In prison-cell or yard,
Is as that broken box that gave
  Its treasure to the Lord,
And filled the unclean leper's house
  With the scent of costliest nard.

Ah! happy they whose hearts can break
  And peace of pardon win!
How else may man make straight his plan
  And cleanse his soul from Sin?
How else but through a broken heart
  May Lord Christ enter in?

. . . . . .

And he of the swollen purple throat,
  And the stark and staring eyes,
Waits for the holy hands that took
  The Thief to Paradise;
And a broken and a contrite heart
  The Lord will not despise.

The man in red who reads the Law
  Gave him three weeks of life,
Three little weeks in which to heal
  His soul of his soul's strife,
And cleanse from every blot of blood
  The hand that held the knife.

And with tears of blood he cleansed the hand,
  The hand that held the steel:
For only blood can wipe out blood,
  And only tears can heal:
And the crimson stain that was of Cain
  Became Christ's snow-white seal.

VI

In Reading gaol by Reading town
  There is a pit of shame,
And in it lies a wretched man
  Eaten by teeth of flame,
In a burning winding-sheet he lies,
  And his grave has got no name.

And there, till Christ call forth the dead,
  In silence let him lie:
No need to waste the foolish tear,
  Or heave the windy sigh:
The man had killed the thing he loved,
  And so he had to die.

And all men kill the thing they love,
  By all let this be heard,
Some do it with a bitter look,
  Some with a flattering word,
The coward does it with a kiss,
  The brave man with a sword!

1898

John Davidson * (1857–1909)

A BALLAD OF HEAVEN

He wrought at one great work for years;
  The world passed by with lofty look:
Sometimes his eyes were dashed with tears;
  Sometimes his lips with laughter shook.

His wife and child went clothed in rags,
  And in a windy garret starved:
He trod his measures on the flags,
  And high on heaven his music carved.

Wistful he grew but never feared;
  For always on the midnight skies
His rich orchestral score appeared
  In stars and zones and galaxies.

He thought to copy down his score:
  The moonlight was his lamp: he said,
'Listen, my love'; but on the floor
  His wife and child were lying dead.

Her hollow eyes were open wide;
  He deemed she heard with special zest:
Her death's-head infant coldly eyed
  The desert of her shrunken breast.

'Listen, my love: my work is done;
  I tremble as I touch the page
To sign the sentence of the sun
  And crown the great eternal age.

'The slow adagio begins;
  The winding-sheets are ravelled out
That swathe the minds of men, the sins
  That wrap their rotting souls about.

'The dead are heralded along;
  With silver trumps and golden drums,
And flutes and oboes, keen and strong,
  My brave andante singing comes.

* By permission of Dodd, Mead and Company, Inc.

'Then like a python's sumptuous dress
The frame of things is cast away,
And out of Time's obscure distress,
The thundering scherzo crashes Day.

'For three great orchestras I hope
My mighty music shall be scored:
On three high hills they shall have scope
With heaven's vault for a sounding-board.

'Sleep well, love; let your eyelids fall;
Cover the child; goodnight, and if . . .
What? Speak . . . the traitorous end of all!
Both . . . cold and hungry . . . cold and stiff!

'But no, God means us well, I trust:
Dear ones, be happy, hope is nigh:
We are too young to fall to dust,
And too unsatisfied to die.'

He lifted up against his breast
The woman's body stark and wan;
And to her withered bosom pressed
The little skin-clad skeleton.

'You see you are alive,' he cried.
He rocked them gently to and fro.
'No, no, my love, you have not died;
Nor you, my little fellow; no.'

Long in his arms he strained his dead
And crooned an antique lullaby;
Then laid them on the lowly bed,
And broke down with a doleful cry.

'The love, the hope, the blood, the brain,
Of her and me, the budding life,
And my great music — all in vain!
My unscored work, my child, my wife!

'We drop into oblivion,
And nourish some suburban sod:
My work, this woman, this my son,
Are now no more: there is no God.

'The world's a dustbin; we are due,
And death's cart waits: be life accurst!'
He stumbled down beside the two,
And clasping them, his great heart burst.

Straightway he stood at heaven's gate,
Abashed and trembling for his sin:
I trow he had not long to wait,
For God came out and led him in.

And then there ran a radiant pair,
Ruddy with haste and eager-eyed
To meet him first upon the stair —
His wife and child beatified.

They clad him in a robe of light,
And gave him heavenly food to eat;
Great seraphs praised him to the height,
Archangels sat about his feet.

God, smiling, took him by the hand,
And led him to the brink of heaven:
He saw where systems whirling stand,
Where galaxies like snow are driven.

Dead silence reigned; a shudder ran
Through space; Time furled his wearied wings;
A slow adagio then began
Sweetly resolving troubled things.

The dead were heralded along:
As if with drums and trumps of flame,
And flutes and oboes keen and strong,
A brave andante singing came.

Then like a python's sumptuous dress
The frame of things was cast away,
And out of Time's obscure distress
The conquering scherzo thundered Day.

He doubted; but God said 'Even so;
Nothing is lost that's wrought with tears:
The music that you made below
Is now the music of the spheres.'

1894

A BALLAD OF HELL

'A LETTER from my love to-day!
Oh, unexpected, dear appeal!'
She struck a happy tear away,
And broke the crimson seal.

'My love, there is no help on earth,
No help in heaven; the dead-man's bell
Must toll our wedding; our first hearth
Must be the well-paved floor of hell.'

The colour died from out her face,
Her eyes like ghostly candles shone;
She cast dread looks about the place,
Then clenched her teeth and read right on.

'I may not pass the prison door;
Here must I rot from day to day,
Unless I wed whom I abhor,
My cousin, Blanche of Valencay.

'At midnight with my dagger keen
I'll take my life; it must be so.
Meet me in hell to-night, my queen,
For weal and woe.'

She laughed although her face was wan,
  She girded on her golden belt,
She took her jewelled ivory fan,
  And at her glowing missal knelt.

Then rose, 'And am I mad?' she said;
  She broke her fan, her belt untied;
With leather girt herself instead,
  And stuck a dagger at her side.

She waited, shuddering in her room,
  Till sleep had fallen on all the house.
She never flinched; she faced her doom:
  They two must sin to keep their vows.

Then out into the night she went,
  And stooping crept by hedge and tree;
Her rose-bush flung a snare of scent,
  And caught a happy memory.

She fell, and lay a minute's space;
  She tore the sward in her distress;
The dewy grass refreshed her face;
  She rose and ran with lifted dress.

She started like a morn-caught ghost
  Once when the moon came out and stood
To watch; the naked road she crossed,
  And dived into the murmuring wood.

The branches snatched her streaming cloak;
  A live thing shrieked; she made no stay!
She hurried to the trysting-oak —
  Right well she knew the way.

Without a pause she bared her breast,
  And drove her dagger home and fell,
And lay like one that takes her rest,
  And died and wakened up in hell.

She bathed her spirit in the flame,
  And near the centre took her post;
From all sides to her ears there came,
  The dreary anguish of the lost.

The devil started at her side,
  Comely, and tall, and black as jet.
'I am young Malespina's bride;
  Has he come hither yet?'

'My poppet, welcome to your bed.'
  'Is Malespina here?'
'Not he! To-morrow he must wed
  His cousin Blanche, my dear!'

'You lie, he died with me to-night.'
  'Not he! it was a plot.' 'You lie.'
'My dear, I never lie outright.'
  'We died at midnight he and I.'

The devil went. Without a groan
  She, gathered up in one fierce prayer,
Took root in hell's midst all alone,
  And waited for him there.

She dared to make herself at home
  Amidst the wail, the uneasy stir.
The blood-stained flame that filled the dome,
  Scentless and silent, shrouded her.

How long she stayed I cannot tell;
  But when she felt his perfidy,
She marched across the floor of hell;
  And all the damned stood up to see.

The devil stopped her at the brink:
  She shook him off; she cried, 'Away!'
'My dear, you have gone mad, I think.'
  'I was betrayed: I will not stay.'

Across the weltering deep she ran;
  A stranger thing was never seen:
The damned stood silent to a man;
  They saw the great gulf set between.

To her it seemed a meadow fair;
  And flowers sprang up about her feet.
She entered heaven; she climbed the stair
  And knelt down at the mercy-seat.

Seraphs and saints with one great voice
  Welcomed that soul that knew not fear;
Amazed to find it could rejoice,
  Hell raised a hoarse half-human cheer.

1894

Francis Thompson* (1859–1907)

TO OLIVIA

I FEAR to love thee, Sweet, because
Love's the ambassador of loss;
White flake of childhood, clinging so
To my soiled raiment, thy shy snow
At tenderest touch will shrink and go.
Love me not, delightful child.
My heart, by many snares beguiled,
Has grown timorous and wild.
It would fear thee not at all,
Wert thou not so harmless-small.
Because thy arrows, not yet dire,
Are still unbarbed with destined fire,
I fear thee more than hadst thou stood
Full-panoplied in womanhood.

1893

* *Complete Poems*, The Modern Library, Inc. By permission of the Publishers.

THE HOUND OF HEAVEN

I FLED Him, down the nights and down the days;
I fled Him, down the arches of the years;
I fled Him, down the labyrinthine ways
Of my own mind; and in the mist of tears
I hid from Him, and under running laughter.
Up vistaed hopes I sped;
And shot, precipitated,
Adown Titanic glooms of chasmèd fears,
From those strong Feet that followed, followed after.
But with unhurrying chase,
And unperturbèd pace,
Deliberate speed, majestic instancy,
They beat — and a Voice beat
More instant than the Feet —
'All things betray thee, who betrayest Me.'

I pleaded, outlaw-wise,
By many a hearted casement, curtained red,
Trellised with intertwining charities;
(For, though I knew His love Who followèd,
Yet was I sore adread
Least, having Him, I must have naught beside)
But, if one little casement parted wide,
The gust of His approach would clash it to.
Fear wist not to evade, as Love wist to pursue.
Across the margent of the world I fled,
And troubled the gold gateways of the stars,
Smiting for shelter on their clangèd bars;
Fretted to dulcet jars
And silvern chatter the pale ports o' the moon.
I said to dawn: Be sudden — to eve: Be soon;
With thy young skiey blossoms heap me over
From this tremendous Lover!
Float thy vague veil about me, lest He see!
I tempted all His servitors, but to find
My own betrayal in their constancy,
In faith to Him their fickleness to me,
Their traitorous trueness, and their loyal deceit.
To all swift things for swiftness did I sue;
Clung to the whistling mane of every wind.
But whether they swept, smoothly fleet,
The long savannahs of the blue;
Or whether, Thunder-driven,
They clanged his chariot 'thwart a heaven,
Plashy with flying lightnings round the spurn o' their feet: —
Fear wist not to evade as Love wist to pursue.
Still with unhurrying chase,
And unperturbèd pace,
Deliberate speed, majestic instancy,
Came on the following Feet,
And a Voice above their beat —
'Naught shelters thee, who wilt not shelter Me.'

I sought no more that, after which I strayed,
In face of man or maid;
But still within the little children's eyes
Seems something, something that replies,
They at least are for me, surely for me!
I turned me to them very wistfully;
But, just as their young eyes grew sudden fair
With dawning answers there,
Their angel plucked them from me by the hair.
'Come then, ye other children, Nature's — share
With me' (said I) 'your delicate fellowship;
Let me greet you lip to lip,
Let me twine with you caresses,
Wantoning
With our Lady-Mother's vagrant tresses,
Banqueting
With her in her wind-walled palace,
Underneath her azured daïs,
Quaffing, as your taintless way is,
From a chalice
Lucent-weeping out of the dayspring.'
So it was done:
I in their delicate fellowship was one —
Drew the bolt of Nature's secrecies.
I knew all the swift importings
On the wilful face of skies;
I knew how the clouds arise
Spumèd of the wild sea-snortings;
All that's born or dies
Rose and drooped with — made them shapers
Of mine own moods, or wailful or divine —
With them joyed and was bereaven.
I was heavy with the even,
When she lit her glimmering tapers
Round the day's dead sanctities.
I laughed in the morning's eyes.
I triumphed and I saddened with all weather,
Heaven and I wept together,
And its sweet tears were salt with mortal mine;
Against the red throb of its sunset-heart

I laid my own to beat,
And share commingling heat;
But not by that, by that, was eased my human smart.
In vain my tears were wet on Heaven's grey cheek.
For ah! we know not what each other says,
These things and I; in sound *I* speak —
Their sound is but their stir, they speak by silences.
Nature, poor stepdame, cannot slake my drouth;
Let her, if she would owe me,
Drop yon blue bosom-veil of sky, and show me
The breasts o' her tenderness:
Never did any milk of hers once bless
My thirsting mouth.
Nigh and nigh draws the chase,
With unperturbèd pace,
Deliberate speed, majestic instancy;
And past those noisèd Feet
A voice comes yet more fleet —
'Lo! naught contents thee, who content'st not Me.'

Naked I wait Thy love's uplifted stroke!
My harness piece by piece Thou hast hewn from me,
And smitten me to my knee;
I am defenceless utterly, .
I slept, methinks, and woke,
And, slowly gazing, find me stripped in sleep.
In the rash lustihead of my young powers,
I shook the pillaring hours
And pulled my life upon me; grimed with smears,
I stand amid the dust o' the mounded years —
My mangled youth lies dead beneath the heap.
My days have crackled and gone up in smoke,
Have puffed and burst as sun-starts on a stream.
Yea, faileth now even dream
The dreamer, and the lute the lutanist;
Even the linked fantasies, in whose blossomy twist
I swung the earth a trinket at my wrist,
Are yielding; cords of all too weak account
For earth with heavy griefs so overplussed.
Ah! is Thy love indeed
A weed, albeit an amaranthine weed,
Suffering no flowers except its own to mount?
Ah! must —
Designer infinite! —
Ah! must Thou char the wood ere Thou canst limn with it?
My freshness spent its wavering shower i' the dust;
And now my heart is as a broken fount,
Wherein tear-drippings stagnate, spilt down ever
From the dank thoughts that shiver
Upon the sighful branches of my mind.
Such is; what is to be?
The pulp so bitter, how shall taste the rind?
I dimly guess what Time in mists confounds;
Yet ever and anon a trumpet sounds
From the hid battlements of Eternity,
Those shaken mists a space unsettle, then
Round the half-glimpsèd turrets slowly wash again;
But not ere him who summoneth
I first have seen, enwound
With glooming robes purpureal, cypress-crowned;
His name I know, and what his trumpet saith.
Whether man's heart or life it be which yields
Thee harvest, must Thy harvest fields
Be dunged with rotten death?
Now of that long pursuit
Comes on at hand the bruit;
That Voice is round me like a bursting sea:
'And is thy earth so marred,
Shattered in shard on shard?
Lo, all things fly thee, for thou fliest Me!

'Strange, piteous, futile thing!
Wherefore should any set thee love apart?
Seeing none but I makes much of naught' (He said),
'And human love needs human meriting:
How hast thou merited —
Of all man's clotted clay the dingiest clot?
Alack, thou knowest not
How little worthy of any love thou art!
Whom wilt thou find to love ignoble thee,
Save Me, save only Me?
All which I took from thee I did but take,
Not for thy harms,
But just that thou might'st seek it in My arms.
All which thy child's mistake
Fancies as lost, I have stored for thee at home:
Rise, clasp My hand, and come!'

Halts by me that footfall:
Is my gloom, after all,
Shade of His hand, outstretched caressingly?

'Ah, fondest, blindest, weakest,
I am He Whom thou seekest!
Thou dravest love from thee, who dravest Me.'

1895

ENVOY

Go, songs, for ended is our brief, sweet play;
Go, children of swift joy and tardy sorrow:
And some are sung, and that was yesterday,
And some unsung, and that may be to-morrow.

Go forth; and if it be o'er stony way,
Old joy can lend what newer grief must borrow:
And it was sweet, and that was yesterday,
And sweet is sweet, though purchasèd with sorrow.

Go, songs, and come not back from your far way:
And if men ask you why ye smile and sorrow,
Tell them ye grieve, for your hearts know To-day,
Tell them ye smile, for your eyes know To-morrow.

1897

Robert Bridges * (1844–)

ELEGY

ON A LADY WHOM GRIEF FOR THE DEATH OF HER BETROTHED KILLED

ASSEMBLE, all ye maidens, at the door,
And all ye loves, assemble; far and wide
Proclaim the bridal, that proclaimed before
Has been deferred to this late eventide:
For on this night the bride,
The days of her betrothal over,
Leaves the parental hearth for evermore;
To-night the bride goes forth to meet her lover.

Reach down the wedding vesture, that has lain
Yet all unvisited, the silken gown:
Bring out the bracelets, and the golden chain
Her dearer friends provided; sere and brown
Bring out the festal crown,
And set it on her forehead lightly:
Though it be withered, twine no wreath again;
This only is the crown she can wear rightly.

Cloke her in ermine, for the night is cold,
And wrap her warmly, for the night is long,
In pious hands the flaming torches hold,
While her attendants, chosen from among
Her faithful virgin throng,
May lay her in her cedar litter,
Decking her coverlet with sprigs of gold,
Roses, and lilies white that best befit her.

Sound flute and tabor, that the bridal be
Not without music, nor with these alone;
But let the viol lead the melody,
With lesser intervals, and plaintive moan
Of sinking semitone;
And, all in choir, the virgin voices
Rest not from singing in skilled harmony
The song that aye the bridegroom's ear rejoices.

Let the priests go before, arrayed in white,
And let the dark-stoled minstrels follow slow,
Next they that bear her, honoured on this night,
And then the maidens, in a double row,
Each singing soft and low,
And each on high a torch upstaying:
Unto her lover lead her forth with light,
With music, and with singing, and with praying.

'T was at this sheltering hour he nightly came,
And found her trusty window open wide,
And knew the signal of the timorous flame,
That long the restless curtain would not hide
Her form that stood beside;
As scarce she dared to be delighted,
Listening to that sweet tale, that is no shame
To faithful lovers, that their hearts have plighted.

But now for many days the dewy grass
Has shown no markings of his feet at morn:
And watching she has seen no shadow pass
The moonlit walk, and heard no music borne
Upon her ear forlorn.
In vain has she looked out to greet him;
He has not come, he will not come, alas!
So let us bear her out where she must meet him.

Now to the river bank the priests are come:
The bark is ready to receive its freight:
Let some prepare her place therein, and some
Embark the litter with its slender weight:

* By permission of John Murray, Publisher.

The rest stand by in state,
And sing her a safe passage over;
While she is oared across to her new home,
Into the arms of her expectant lover.

And thou, O lover, that art on the watch,
Where, on the banks of the forgetful streams,
The pale indifferent ghosts wander, and snatch
The sweeter moments of their broken dreams, —
Thou, when the torchlight gleams,
When thou shalt see the slow procession,
And when thine ears the fitful music catch,
Rejoice, for thou art near to thy possession.

1890

I LOVE ALL BEAUTEOUS THINGS

I love all beauteous things,
I seek and adore them;
God hath no better praise,
And man in his hasty days
Is honoured for them.

I too will something make
And joy in the making;
Although tomorrow it seem
Like the empty words of a dream
Remembered on waking.

1890

THE IDLE LIFE I LEAD

The idle life I lead
Is like a pleasant sleep,
Wherein I rest and heed
The dreams that by me sweep.

And still of all my dreams
In turn so swiftly past,
Each in its fancy seems
A nobler than the last.

And every eve I say,
Noting my step in bliss,
That I have known no day
In all my life like this.

1890

NIGHTINGALES

Beautiful must be the mountains whence ye come,
And bright in the fruitful valleys the streams, wherefrom
Ye learn your song:
Where are those starry woods? O might I wander there,
Among the flowers, which in that heavenly air
Bloom the year long!

Nay, barren are those mountains and spent the streams:
Our song is the voice of desire, that haunts our dreams,
A throe of the heart,
Whose pining visions dim, forbidden hopes profound,
No dying cadence nor long sigh can sound,
For all our art.

Alone, aloud in the raptured ear of men
We pour our dark nocturnal secret; and then,
As night is withdrawn
From these sweet-springing meads and bursting boughs of May,
Dream, while the innumerable choir of day
Welcome the dawn.

1894

William Watson * (1858–)

WORDSWORTH'S GRAVE

I

The old rude church, with bare, bald tower, is here;
Beneath its shadow high-born Rotha flows;
Rotha, remembering well who slumbers near,
And with cool murmur lulling his repose.

Rotha, remembering well who slumbers near.
His hills, his lakes, his streams are with him yet.
Surely the heart that read her own heart clear
Nature forgets not soon: 't is we forget.

We that with vagrant soul his fixity
Have slighted; faithless, done his deep faith wrong;
Left him for poorer loves, and bowed the knee
To misbegotten strange new gods of song.

Yet, led by hollow ghost or beckoning elf
Far from her homestead to the desert bourn,
The vagrant soul returning to herself
Wearily wise, must needs to him return.

* By arrangement with the Author.

To him and to the powers that with him dwell: —
Inflowings that divulged not whence they came;
And that secluded spirit unknowable,
The mystery we make darker with a name;

The Somewhat which we name but cannot know,
Ev'n as we name a star and only see
His quenchless flashings forth, which ever show
And ever hide him, and which are not he.

II

Poet who sleepest by this wandering wave!
When thou wast born, what birth-gift hadst thou then?
To thee what wealth was that the Immortals gave,
The wealth thou gavest in thy turn to men?

Not Milton's keen, translunar music thine;
Not Shakespeare's cloudless, boundless human view;
Not Shelley's flush of rose on peaks divine;
Nor yet the wizard twilight Coleridge knew.

What hadst thou that could make so large amends
For all thou hadst not and thy peers possessed,
Motion and fire, swift means to radiant ends? —
Thou hadst, for weary feet, the gift of rest.

From Shelley's dazzling glow or thunderous haze,
From Byron's tempest-anger, tempest-mirth,
Men turned to thee and found — not blast and blaze,
Tumult of tottering heavens, but peace on earth.

Nor peace that grows by Lethe, scentless flower,
There in white languors to decline and cease;
But peace whose names are also rapture, power,
Clear sight, and love: for these are parts of peace.

III

I hear it vouched the Muse is with us still; —
If less divinely frenzied than of yore,
In lieu of feelings she has wondrous skill
To simulate emotion felt no more.

Not such the authentic Presence pure, that made
This valley vocal in the great days gone! —
In *his* great days, while yet the springtime played
About him, and the mighty morning shone.

No word-mosaic artificer, he sang
A lofty song of lowly weal and dole.
Right from the heart, right to the heart it sprang,
Or from the soul leapt instant to the soul.

He felt the charm of childhood, grace of youth,
Grandeur of age, insisting to be sung.
The impassioned argument was simple truth
Half-wondering at its own melodious tongue.

Impassioned? ay, to the song's ecstatic core!
But far removed were clangour, storm and feud;
For plenteous health was his, exceeding store
Of joy, and an impassioned quietude.

IV

A hundred years ere he to manhood came,
Song from celestial heights had wandered down,
Put off her robe of sunlight, dew and flame,
And donned a modish dress to charm the Town.

Thenceforth she but festooned the porch of things;
Apt at life's lore, incurious what life meant.
Dextrous of hand, she struck her lute's few strings;
Ignobly perfect, barrenly content.

Unflushed with ardour and unblanched with awe,
Her lips in profitless derision curled,
She saw with dull emotion — if she saw —
The vision of the glory of the world.

The human masque she watched, with dreamless eyes
In whose clear shallows lurked no trembling shade:

The stars, unkenned by her, might set and rise,
Unmarked by her, the daisies bloom and fade.

The age grew sated with her sterile wit.
Herself waxed weary on her loveless throne.
Men felt life's tide, the sweep and surge of it,
And craved a living voice, a natural tone.

For none the less, though song was but half true,
The world lay common, one abounding theme.
Man joyed and wept, and fate was ever new,
And love was sweet, life real, death no dream.

In sad, stern verse the rugged scholar-sage
Bemoaned his toil unvalued, youth uncheered.
His numbers wore the vesture of the age,
But, 'neath it beating, the great heart was heard.

From dewy pastures, uplands sweet with thyme,
A virgin breeze freshened the jaded day.
It wafted Collins' lonely vesper-chime,
It breathed abroad the frugal note of Gray.

It fluttered here and there, nor swept in vain
The dusty haunts where futile echoes dwell, —
Then, in a cadence soft as summer rain,
And sad from Auburn voiceless, drooped and fell.

It drooped and fell, and one 'neath northern skies,
With southern heart, who tilled his father's field,
Found Poesy a-dying, bade her rise
And touch quick Nature's hem and go forth healed.

On life's broad plain the ploughman's conquering share
Upturned the fallow lands of truth anew,
And o'er the formal garden's trim parterre
The peasant's team a ruthless furrow drew.

Bright was his going forth, but clouds ere long
Whelmed him; in gloom his radiance set, and those
Twin morning stars of the new century's song,
Those morning stars that sang together, rose.

In elvish speech the *Dreamer* told his tale
Of marvellous oceans swept by fateful wings. —
The *Seer* strayed not from earth's human pale,
But the mysterious face of common things

He mirrored as the moon in Rydal Mere
Is mirrored, when the breathless night hangs blue:
Strangely remote she seems and wondrous near,
And by some nameless difference born anew.

V

Peace — peace — and rest! Ah, how the lyre is loth,
Or powerless now, to give what all men seek!
Either it deadens with ignoble sloth
Or deafens with shrill tumult, loudly weak.

Where is the singer whose large notes and clear
Can heal, and arm, and plenish, and sustain?
Lo, one with empty music floods the ear,
And one, the heart refreshing, tires the brain.

And idly tuneful, the loquacious throng
Flutter and twitter, prodigal of time,
And little masters make a toy of song
Till grave men weary of the sound of rhyme.

And some go prankt in faded antique dress,
Abhorring to be hale and glad and free;
And some parade a conscious naturalness,
The scholar's not the child's simplicity.

Enough; — and wisest who from words forbear.
The kindly river rails not as it glides;
And suave and charitable, the winning air
Chides not at all, or only him who chides.

VI

Nature! we storm thine ear with choric notes.
Thou answerest through the calm great nights and days,
'Laud me who will: not tuneless are your throats;
Yet if ye paused I should not miss the praise.'

We falter, half-rebuked, and sing again.
We chant thy desertness and haggard gloom,
Or with thy splendid wrath inflate the strain,
Or touch it with thy colour and perfume.

One, his melodious blood aflame for thee,
Wooed with fierce lust, his hot heart world-defiled.
One, with the upward eye of infancy,
Looked in thy face, and felt himself thy child.

Thee he approached without distrust or dread —
Beheld thee throned, an awful queen, above —
Climbed to thy lap and merely laid his head
Against thy warm wild heart of mother-love.

He heard that vast heart beating — thou didst press
Thy child so close, and lov'dst him unaware.
Thy beauty gladdened him; yet he scarce less
Had loved thee, had he never found thee fair!

For thou wast not as legendary lands
To which with curious eyes and ears we roam.
Nor wast thou as a fane 'mid solemn sands,
Where palmers halt at evening. Thou wast home.

And here, at home, still bides he; but he sleeps;
Not to be wakened even at thy word;
Though we, vague dreamers, dream he somewhere keeps
An ear still open to thy voice still heard, —

Thy voice, as heretofore, about him blown,
For ever blown about his silence now;
Thy voice, though deeper, yet so like his own
That almost, when he sang, we deemed 't was thou!

VII

Behind Helm Crag and Silver Howe the sheen
Of the retreating day is less and less.
Soon will the lordlier summits, here unseen,
Gather the night about their nakedness.

The half-heard bleat of sheep comes from the hill.
Faint sounds of childish play are in the air.
The river murmurs past. All else is still.
The very graves seem stiller than they were.

Afar though nation be on nation hurled,
And life with toil and ancient pain depressed,
Here one may scarce believe the whole wide world
Is not at peace, and all man's heart at rest.

Rest! 't was the gift *he* gave; and peace! the shade
He spread, for spirits fevered with the sun.
To him his bounties are come back — here laid
In rest, in peace, his labour nobly done.

1890

WHEN BIRDS WERE SONGLESS

WHEN birds were songless on the bough,
I heard thee sing.
The world was full of winter, thou
Wert full of spring.

To-day the world's heart feels anew
The vernal thrill,
And thine beneath the rueful yew
Is wintry chill.

1890

ENGLAND MY MOTHER

I

ENGLAND my mother,
Wardress of waters,
Builder of peoples,
Maker of men, —

Hast thou yet leisure
Left for the muses?
Heed'st thou the songsmith
Forging the rhyme?

Deafened with tumults,
How canst thou hearken?
Strident is faction,
Demos is loud.

Lazarus, hungry,
Menaces Dives;
Labour the giant
Chafes in his hold.

Yet do the songsmiths
Quit not their forges;

Still on life's anvil
 Forge they the rhyme.

Still the rapt faces
Glow from the furnace:
Breath of the smithy
 Scorches their brows.

Yea, and thou hear'st them?
So shall the hammers
Fashion not vainly
 Verses of gold.

II

Lo, with the ancient
Roots of man's nature,
Twines the eternal
 Passion of song.

Ever Love fans it,
Ever Life feeds it;
Time cannot age it,
 Death cannot slay.

Deep in the world-heart
Stand its foundations,
Tangled with all things,
 Twin-made with all.

Nay, what is Nature's
Self, but an endless
Strife toward music,
 Euphony, rhyme?

Trees in their blooming,
Tides in their flowing,
Stars in their circling,
 Tremble with song.

God on His throne is
Eldest of poets:
Unto His measures
 Moveth the Whole.

III

Therefore deride not
Speech of the muses,
England my mother,
 Maker of men.

Nations are mortal,
Fragile is greatness;
Fortune may fly thee,
 Song shall not fly.

Song the all-girdling,
Song cannot perish:
Men shall make music,
 Man shall give ear.

Not while the choric
Chant of creation
Floweth from all things,
 Poured without pause,

Cease we to echo
Faintly the descant
Whereto for ever
 Dances the world.

IV

So let the songsmith
Proffer his rhyme-gift,
England my mother,
 Maker of men.

Grey grows thy count'nance,
Full of the ages;
Time on thy forehead
 Sits like a dream:

Song is the potion
All things renewing,
Youth's one elixir,
 Fountain of morn.

Thou, at the world-loom
Weaving thy future,
Fitly may'st temper
 Toil with delight.

Deemest thou, labour
Only is earnest?
Grave is all beauty,
 Solemn is joy.

Song is no bauble —
Slight not the songsmith,
England my mother,
 Maker of men.

1892

THE WORLD IN ARMOUR

I

UNDER this shade of crimson wings abhorred
That never wholly leaves the sky serene,
While Vengeance sleeps a sleep so light, between
Dominions that acclaim Thee overlord,—
Sadly the blast of Thy tremendous word,
Whate'er its mystic purport may have been,
Echoes across the ages, Nazarene:
Not to bring peace Mine errand, but a sword.
For lo, Thy world uprises and lies down
In armour, and its Peace is War, in all
Save the great death that weaves War's dreadful crown;
War unennobled by heroic pain,
War where none triumph, none sublimely fall,
War that sits smiling, with the eyes of Cain.

II

When London's Plague, that day by day enrolled
His thousands dead, nor deigned his rage to abate
Till grass was green in silent Bishopsgate,
Had come and passed like thunder, — still, 't is told,
The monster, driven to earth, in hovels old
And haunts obscure, though dormant, lingered late,
Till the dread Fire, one roaring wave of fate,
Rose, and swept clean his last retreat and hold.
In Europe live the dregs of Plague today,
Dregs of full many an ancient Plague and dire, —
Old wrongs, old lies of ages blind and cruel.
What if alone the world-war's world-wide fire
Can purge the ambushed pestilence away?
Yet woe to him that idly lights the fuel!

III

A moment's fantasy, the vision came
Of Europe dipped in fiery death, and so
Mounting re-born, with vestal limbs aglow,
Splendid and fragrant from her bath of flame.
It fleeted; and a phantom without name,
Sightless, dismembered, terrible, said: 'Lo,
I am that ravished Europe men shall know
After the morn of blood and night of shame.'
The spectre passed, and I beheld alone
The Europe of the present, as she stands,
Powerless from terror of her own vast power,
'Neath novel stars, beside a brink unknown;
And round her the sad Kings, with sleepless hands,
Piling the fagots, hour by doomful hour.

1893

THE SAINT AND THE SATYR

SAINT ANTHONY the eremite
He wandered in the wold,
And there he saw a hoofèd wight
That blew his hands for cold.

'What dost thou here in misery,
That better far wert dead?'
The eremite Saint Anthony
Unto the Satyr said.

'Lorn in the wold,' the thing replied,
'I sit and make my moan,
For all the gods I loved have died,
And I am left alone.

'Silent, in Paphos, Venus sleeps,
And Jove, on Ida, mute;
And every living creature weeps
Pan and his perished flute.

'The Faun, his laughing heart is broke;
The nymph, her fountain fails;
And driven from out the hollow oak
The Hamadryad wails.

'A God more beautiful than mine
Hath conquered mine, they say. —
Ah, to that fair young God of thine,
For me I pray thee pray!'

1893

I DO NOT ASK

I DO not ask to have my fill
Of wine, or love, or fame.
I do not, for a little ill,
Against the gods exclaim.

One boon of Fortune I implore,
With one petition kneel:
At least caress me not, before
Thou break me on thy wheel.

1895

SONG

APRIL, April,
Laugh thy girlish laughter;
Then, the moment after,
Weep thy girlish tears!
April, that mine ears
Like a lover greetest,
If I tell thee, sweetest,
All my hopes and fears,
April, April,
Laugh thy golden laughter,
But, the moment after,
Weep thy golden tears!

1897

Rudyard Kipling* (1865–)

THE BALLAD OF FISHER'S BOARDING-HOUSE

THAT night, when through the mooring-chains
The wide-eyed corpse rolled free,

* *Verse*, Inclusive Edition, Doubleday, Page & Co. Copyright, 1891–1919. By permission of Author and Publishers.

To blunder down by Garden Reach
  And rot at Kedgeree,
The tale the Hughli told the shoal
  The lean shoal told to me.

'T was Fultah Fisher's boarding-house,
  Where sailor-men reside,
And there were men of all the ports
  From Mississip to Clyde,
And regally they spat and smoked,
  And fearsomely they lied.

They lied about the purple Sea
  That gave them scanty bread,
They lied about the Earth beneath,
  The Heavens overhead,
For they had looked too often on
  Black rum when that was red.

They told their tales of wreck and wrong,
  Of shame and lust and fraud,
They backed their toughest statements with
  The Brimstone of the Lord,
And crackling oaths went to and fro
  Across the fist-banged board.

And there was Hans the blue-eyed Dane,
  Bull-throated, bare of arm,
Who carried on his hairy chest
  The maid Ultruda's charm —
The little silver crucifix
  That keeps a man from harm.

And there was Jake Without-the-Ears,
  And Pamba the Malay,
And Carboy Gin the Guinea cook,
  And Luz from Vigo Bay,
And Honest Jack who sold them slops
  And harvested their pay.

And there was Salem Hardieker,
  A lean Bostonian he —
Russ, German, English, Halfbreed, Finn,
  Yank, Dane, and Portugee,
At Fultah Fisher's boarding-house
  They rested from the sea.

Now Anne of Austria shared their drinks,
  Collinga knew her fame,
From Tarnau in Galicia
  To Jaun Bazaar she came,
To eat the bread of infamy
  And take the wage of shame.

She held a dozen men to heel —
  Rich spoil of war was hers,
In hose and gown and ring and chain,
  From twenty mariners,
And, by Port Law, that week, men called
  Her Salem Hardieker's.

But seamen learnt — what landsmen know —
  That neither gifts nor gain
Can hold a winking Light o' Love
  Or Fancy's flight restrain,
When Anne of Austria rolled her eyes
  On Hans the blue-eyed Dane.

Since Life is strife, and strife means knife,
  From Howrah to the Bay,
And he may die before the dawn
  Who liquored out the day,
In Fultah Fisher's boarding-house
  We woo while yet we may.

But cold was Hans the blue-eyed Dane,
  Bull-throated, bare of arm,
And laughter shook the chest beneath
  The maid Ultruda's Charm —
The little silver crucifix
  That keeps a man from harm.

'You speak to Salem Hardieker;
  You was his girl, I know.
I ship mineselfs to-morrow, see,
  Und round the Skaw we go,
South, down the Cattegat, by Hjelm,
  To Besser in Saro.'

When love rejected turns to hate,
  All ill betide the man.
'You speak to Salem Hardieker' —
  She spoke as woman can.
A scream — a sob — 'He called me — names!'
  And then the fray began.

An oath from Salem Hardieker,
  A shriek upon the stairs,
A dance of shadows on the wall,
  A knife-thrust unawares —
And Hans came down, as cattle drop,
  Across the broken chairs.

. . . .

In Anne of Austria's trembling hands,
  The weary head fell low: —
'I ship mineselfs to-morrow, straight
  For Besser in Saro;
Und there Ultruda comes to me
  At Easter, und I go

'South, down the Cattegat — What's here?
  There — are — no — lights — to — guide!'
The mutter ceased, the spirit passed,
  And Anne of Austria cried
In Fultah Fisher's boarding-house
  When Hans the mighty died.

Thus slew they Hans the blue-eyed Dane,
  Bull-throated, bare of arm,
But Anne of Austria looted first
  The maid Ultruda's charm —
The little silver crucifix
  That keeps a man from harm.

1886

GUNGA DIN

You may talk o' gin and beer
When you 're quartered safe out 'ere,
An' you 're sent to penny-fights an' Aldershot it;
But when it comes to slaughter
You will do your work on water,
An' you 'll lick the bloomin' boots of 'im that 's got it.
Now in Injia's sunny clime,
Where I used to spend my time
A-servin' of 'Er Majesty the Queen,
Of all them black-faced crew
The finest man I knew
Was our regimental bhisti, Gunga Din.
    He was 'Din! Din! Din!
  You limpin' lump o' brick-dust, Gunga Din!
    Hi! Slippery *hitherao!*
    Water, get it! *Panee lao!*
  You squidgy-nosed old idol, Gunga Din!'

The uniform 'e wore
Was nothin' much before,
An' rather less than 'arf o' that be'ind,
For a piece o' twisty rag
An' a goatskin water-bag
Was all the field-equipment 'e could find.
When the sweatin' troop-train lay
In a sidin' through the day,
Where the 'eat would make your bloomin' eyebrows crawl,
We shouted 'Harry By!'
Till our throats were bricky-dry,
Then we wopped 'im cause 'e couldn't serve us all.
    It was 'Din! Din! Din!
  You 'eathen, where the mischief 'ave you been?
    You put some *juldee* in it
    Or I 'll *marrow* you this minute
  If you don't fill up my helmet, Gunga Din!'

'E would dot an' carry one
Till the longest day was done;
An' 'e didn't seem to know the use o' fear.
If we charged or broke or cut,
You could bet your bloomin' nut,
'E 'd be waitin' fifty paces right flank rear.
With 'is mussick on 'is back,
'E would skip with our attack,
An' watch us till the bugles made 'Retire,'
An' for all 'is dirty 'ide
'E was white, clear white, inside
When 'e went to tend the wounded under fire!
    It was 'Din! Din! Din!'
  With the bullets kickin' dust-spots on the green.
    When the cartridges ran out,
    You could 'ear the front-ranks shout,
  'Hi! ammunition-mules an' Gunga Din!'

I sha'n't forgit the night
When I dropped be'ind the fight
With a bullet where my belt-plate should 'a' been.
I was chokin' mad with thirst,
An' the man that spied me first
Was our good old grinnin', gruntin' Gunga Din.
'E lifted up my 'ead,
An' 'e plugged me where I bled,
An' 'e guv me 'arf-a-pint o' water green.
It was crawlin' and it stunk,
But of all the drinks I 've drunk,
I 'm gratefullest to one from Gunga Din.
    It was 'Din! Din! Din!
  'Ere 's a beggar with a bullet through 'is spleen;
    'E 's chawin' up the ground,
    An' 'e 's kickin' all around:
  For Gawd's sake, git the water, Gunga Din!'

'E carried me away
To where a dooli lay,
An' a bullet come an' drilled the beggar clean.
'E put me safe inside,
An' just before 'e died,
'I 'ope you liked your drink,' sez Gunga Din.
So I'll meet 'im later on
In the place where 'e is gone —
Where it 's always double drill and no canteen.
'E 'll be squattin' on the coals
Givin' drink to pore damned souls,
An' I 'll get a swig in hell from Gunga Din!
    Yes, Din! Din! Din!
  You Lazarushian-leather Gunga Din!
    Though I 've belted you an' flayed you,
    By the livin' God that made you,
  You 're a better man than I am, Gunga Din!

1892

L'ENVOI

WHEN Earth's last picture is painted and the tubes are twisted and dried,
When the oldest colours have faded, and the youngest critic has died,
We shall rest, and, faith, we shall need it — lie down for an æon or two,
Till the Master of All Good Workmen shall put us to work anew.

And those that were good shall be happy: they shall sit in a golden chair;
They shall splash at a ten-league canvas with brushes of comets' hair.
They shall find real saints to draw from — Magdalene, Peter, and Paul;
They shall work for an age at a sitting and never be tired at all!

And only the Master shall praise us, and only the Master shall blame;
And no one shall work for money, and no one shall work for fame,
But each for the joy of the working, and each, in his separate star,
Shall draw the Thing as he sees It for the God of Things as They are!

1896

THE VAMPIRE

A FOOL there was and he made his prayer
(Even as you and I!)
To a rag and a bone and a hank of hair
(We called her the woman who did not care)
But the fool he called her his lady fair —
(Even as you and I!)

Oh, the years we waste and the tears we waste
And the work of our head and hand
Belong to the woman who did not know
(*And now we know that she never could know*)
And did not understand!

A fool there was and his goods he spent
(Even as you and I!)
Honour and faith and a sure intent
(And it wasn't the least what the lady meant)
But a fool must follow his natural bent
(Even as you and I!)

Oh, the toil we lost and the spoil we lost
And the excellent things we planned
Belong to the woman who didn't know why
(*And now we know she never knew why*)
And did not understand!

The fool was stripped to his foolish hide
(Even as you and I!)
Which she might have seen when she threw him aside —
(But it isn't on record the lady tried)
So some of him lived but the most of him died —
(Even as you and I!)

'And it isn't the shame and it isn't the blame
That stings like a white hot brand —
It's coming to know that she never knew why
(*Seeing, at last, she could never know why*)
And never could understand!'

1897

RECESSIONAL

GOD of our fathers, known of old,
Lord of our far-flung battle-line,
Beneath whose awful Hand we hold
Dominion over palm and pine —
Lord God of Hosts, be with us yet,
Lest we forget — lest we forget!

The tumult and the shouting dies;
The Captains and the Kings depart:
Still stands Thine ancient sacrifice,
An humble and a contrite heart.
Lord God of Hosts, be with us yet,
Lest we forget — lest we forget!

Far-called our navies melt away;
On dune and headland sinks the fire:
Lo, all our pomp of yesterday
Is one with Nineveh and Tyre!
Judge of the Nations, spare us yet,
Lest we forget — lest we forget!

If, drunk with sight of power, we loose
Wild tongues that have not Thee in awe,
Such boastings as the Gentiles use,
Or lesser breeds without the Law —
Lord God of Hosts, be with us yet,
Lest we forget — lest we forget!

For heathen heart that puts her trust
In reeking tube and iron shard,
All valiant dust that builds on dust,
And, guarding, calls not Thee to guard,
For frantic boast and foolish word —
Thy mercy on Thy People, Lord!

1897

William Butler Yeats * (1865–)

THE DEATH OF CUCHULAIN

A MAN came slowly from the setting sun,
To Forgail's daughter, Emer, in her dun,
And found her dyeing cloth with subtle care,
And said, casting aside his draggled hair:
'I am Aleel, the swineherd, whom you bid
Go dwell upon the sea cliffs, vapour hid;
But now my years of watching are no more.'

Then Emer cast the web upon the floor,
And stretching out her arms, red with the dye,
Parted her lips with a loud sudden cry.

Looking on her, Aleel, the swineherd, said:
'Not any god alive, nor mortal dead,
Has slain so mighty armies, so great kings,
Nor won the gold that now Cuchulain brings.'

'Why do you tremble thus from feet to crown?'

Aleel, the swineherd, wept and cast him down
Upon the web-heaped floor, and thus his word:
'With him is one sweet-throated like a bird,
And lovelier than the moon upon the sea;
He made for her an army cease to be.'

'Who bade you tell these things?' and then she cried
To those about, 'Beat him with thongs of hide
And drive him from the door.' And thus it was;
And where her son, Finmole, on the smooth grass
Was driving cattle, came she with swift feet,
And called out to him, 'Son, it is not meet
That you stay idling here with flocks and herds.'

'I have waited, mother, for those words;
But wherefore now?'

'There is a man to die;
You have the heaviest arm under the sky.'

'My father dwells among the sea-worn bands,
And breaks the ridge of battle with his hands.'

'Nay, you are taller than Cuchulain, son.'

'He is the mightiest man in ship or dun.'

'Nay, he is old and sad with many wars,
And weary of the crash of battle cars.'

'I only ask what way my journey lies,
For God, who made you bitter, made you wise.'

'The Red Branch kings a tireless banquet keep,
Where the sun falls into the Western deep.
Go there, and dwell on the green forest rim
But tell alone your name and house to him
Whose blade compels, and bid them send you one
Who has a like vow from their triple dun.'

Between the lavish shelter of a wood
And the gray tide, the Red Branch multitude
Feasted, and with them old Cuchulain dwelt,
And his young dear one close beside him knelt,
And gazed upon the wisdom of his eyes,
More mournful than the depth of starry skies,
And pondered on the wonder of his days;
And all around the harp-string told his praise,
And Conchubar, the Red Branch king of kings,
With his own fingers touched the brazen strings.

At last Cuchulain spake, 'A young man strays
Driving the deer along the woody ways.
I often hear him singing to and fro,
I often hear the sweet sound of his bow,
Seek out what man he is.'

One went and came.
'He bade me let all know he gives his name
At the sword point, and bade me bring him one
Who had a like vow from our triple dun.'

'I only of the Red Branch hosted now,'
Cuchulain cried, 'have made and keep that vow.'

After short fighting in the leafy shade,
He spake to the young man, 'Is there no maid
Who loves you, no white arms to wrap you round,
Or do you long for the dim sleepy ground,
That you come here to meet this ancient sword?'

* *Poetical Works*, The Macmillan Company, 1911. By permission of the Publishers.

'The dooms of men are in God's hidden hoard.'
'Your head a while seemed like a woman's head
That I loved once.'
Again the fighting sped,
But now the war rage in Cuchulain woke,
And through the other's shield his long blade broke,
And pierced him.
'Speak before your breath is done.'

'I am Finmole, mighty Cuchulain's son.'

'I put you from your pain. I can no more.'

While day its burden on to evening bore,
With head bowed on his knees Cuchulain stayed;
Then Conchubar sent that sweet-throated maid,
And she, to win him, his gray hair caressed;
In vain her arms, in vain her soft white breast.
Then Conchubar, the subtlest of all men,
Ranking his Druids round him ten by ten,
Spake thus, 'Cuchulain will dwell there and brood,
For three days more in dreadful quietude,
And then arise, and raving slay us all.
Go, cast on him delusions magical,
That he might fight the waves of the loud sea.'
And ten by ten under a quicken tree,
The Druids chaunted, swaying in their hands
Tall wands of alder and white quicken wands.

In three days' time, Cuchulain with a moan
Stood up, and came to the long sands alone:
For four days warred he with the bitter tide;
And the waves flowed above him, and he died.

1892

THE WHITE BIRDS

I WOULD that we were, my belovèd, white birds on the foam of the sea!
We tire of the flame of the meteor, before it can fade and flee;
And the flame of the blue star of twilight, hung low on the rim of the sky,
Has awaked in our hearts, my belovèd, a sadness that may not die.
A weariness comes from those dreamers, dew dabbled, the lily and rose;
Ah, dream not of them, my belovèd, the flame of the meteor that goes,
Or the flame of the blue star that lingers hung low in the fall of the dew:
For I would we were changed to white birds on the wandering foam: I and you!
I am haunted by numberless islands, and many a Danaän shore,
Where Time would surely forget us, and Sorrow come near us no more;
Soon far from the rose and the lily, and fret of the flames would we be,
Were we only white birds, my belovèd, buoyed out on the foam of the sea!

1892

Stephen Phillips * (1868–1915)

FACES AT A FIRE

DAZZLED with watching how the swift fire fled
Along the dribbling roof, I turned my head;
When lo, upraised beneath the lighted cloud
The illumed unconscious faces of the crowd!
An old grey face in lovely bloom upturned,
The ancient rapture and the dream returned!
A crafty face wondering simply up!
That dying face near the communion cup!
The experienced face, now venturous and rash,
The scheming eyes hither and thither flash!
That common trivial face made up of needs,
Now pale and recent from triumphal deeds!
The hungry tramp with indolent gloating stare,
The beggar in glory and released from care,
A mother slowly burning with bare breast,
Yet her consuming child close to her prest!
That prosperous citizen in anguish dire,
Beseeching heaven from purgatorial fire!
Wonderful souls by sudden flame betrayed,
I saw; then through the darkness went afraid.

1898

THE APPARITION

MY dead Love came to me, and said:
'God gives me one hour's rest,
To spend upon the earth with thee:
How shall we spend it best?'

* By permission of Dodd, Mead and Company, Inc.

'Why as of old,' I said, and so
We quarrelled as of old.
But when I turned to make my peace,
That one short hour was told.

Nine nights she did not come to me:
The heaven was filled with rain;
And as it fell, and fell, I said,
'She will not come again.'

Last night she came, not as before,
But in a strange attire;
Weary she seemed, and very faint,
As though she came from fire.

She is not happy! It was noon;
The sun fell on my head:
And it was not an hour in which
We think upon the dead.

She is not happy! I should know
Her voice, much more her cry;
And close beside me a great rose
Had just begun to die.

She is not happy! As I walked,
Of her I was aware:
She cried out, like a creature hurt,
Close by me in the air.

Under the trembling summer stars,
I turned from side to side;
When she came in and sat with me,
As though she had not died.

And she was kind to me and sweet,
She had her ancient way;
Remembered how I liked her hand
Amid my hair to stray.

She had forgotten nothing, yet
Older she seemed, and still:
All quietly she took my kiss,
Even as a mother will.

She rose, and in the streak of dawn
She turned as if to go:
But then again came back to me;
My eyes implored her so!

She pushed the hair from off my brow,
And looked into my eyes.
'I live in calm,' she said, 'and there
Am learning to be wise.'

'Why grievest thou? I pity thee
Still turning on this bed.'
'And art thou happy?' I exclaimed.
'Alas!' she sighed, and fled.

I woke: she had been standing by,
With wonder on her face.
She came toward me, very bright,
As from a blessèd place.

She touched me not, but smiling spoke,
And softly as before.
'They gave me drink from some slow stream;
I love thee now no more.'

The other night she hurried in,
Her face was wild with fear:
'Old friend,' she said, 'I am pursued,
May I take refuge here?'

1898

I IN THE GREYNESS ROSE

I IN the greyness rose;
I could not sleep for thinking of one dead.
Then to the chest I went,
Where lie the things of my belovèd spread.

Quietly these I took;
A little glove, a sheet of music torn,
Paintings, ill-done perhaps;
Then lifted up a dress that she had worn.

And now I came to where
Her letters are; they lie beneath the rest;
And read them in the haze;
She spoke of many things, was sore opprest.

But these things moved me not;
Not when she spoke of being parted quite,
Or being misunderstood,
Or growing weary of the world's great fight.

Not even when she wrote
Of our dead child, and the hand-writing swerved;
Not even then I shook:
Not even by such words was I unnerved.

I thought, she is at peace;
Whither the child is gone, she too has passed.
And a much needed rest
Is fallen upon her, she is still at last.

But when at length I took
From under all those letters one small sheet,
Folded and writ in haste;
Why did my heart with sudden sharpness beat?

Alas, it was not sad!
Her saddest words I had read calmly o'er.
Alas, it had no pain!
Her painful words, all these I knew before.

A hurried happy line!
A little jest, too slight for one so dead:
This did I not endure:
Then with a shuddering heart no more I read.

1898

John Masefield * (1875–)

SEA-FEVER

I MUST go down to the seas again, to the lonely sea and the sky,
And all I ask is a tall ship and a star to steer her by,
And the wheel's kick and the wind's song and the white sail's shaking,
And a gray mist on the sea's face and a gray dawn breaking.

I must go down to the seas again, for the call of the running tide
Is a wild call and a clear call that may not be denied;
And all I ask is a windy day with the white clouds flying,
And the flung spray and the blown spume, and the sea-gulls crying.

I must go down to the seas again to the vagrant gipsy life,
To the gull's way and the whale's way where the wind 's like a whetted knife;
And all I ask is a merry yarn from a laughing fellow-rover,
And quiet sleep and a sweet dream when the long trick 's over.

1902

A WANDERER'S SONG

A WIND 's in the heart of me, a fire 's in my heels,
I am tired of brick and stone and rumbling wagon-wheels;
I hunger for the sea's edge, the limits of the land,
Where the wild old Atlantic is shouting on the sand.

Oh I'll be going, leaving the noises of the street,
To where a lifting foresail-foot is yanking at the sheet;
To a windy, tossing anchorage where yawls and ketches ride,
Oh I'll be going, going, until I meet the tide.

And first I'll hear the sea-wind, the mewing of the gulls,
The clucking, sucking of the sea about the rusty hulls,
The songs at the capstan in the hooker warping out,
And then the heart of me 'll know I'm there or thereabout.

Oh I am tired of brick and stone, the heart of me is sick,
For windy green, unquiet sea, the realm of Moby Dick;
And I 'll be going, going, from the roaring of the wheels,
For a wind 's in the heart of me, a fire 's in my heels.

1902

Alfred Noyes † (1880–)

RALEIGH

BEN was our only guest that day. His tribe
Had flown to their new shrine — the Apollo Room,
To which, though they enscrolled his golden verse
Above their doors like some great-fruited vine,
Ben still preferred our *Mermaid*, and to smoke
Alone in his old nook; perhaps to hear
The voices of the dead,
The voices of his old companions,
Hovering near him, — Will and Kit and Rob.
'Our Ocean-shepherd from the Main-deep sea,
Raleigh,' he muttered, as I brimmed his cup,
'Last of the men that broke the fleets of Spain,
'T was not enough to cage him, sixteen years,
Rotting his heart out in the Bloody Tower,
But they must fling him forth in his old age
To hunt for El Dorado. Then, mine host,
Because his poor old ship *The Destiny*
Smashes the Spaniard, but comes tottering home
Without the Spanish gold, our gracious king,
To please a catamite,
Sends the old lion back to the Tower again.
The friends of Spain will send him to the block

* *Poems*, The Macmillan Company, 1922. By permission of the Publishers.
† *Tales of the Mermaid Tavern*, Frederick A. Stokes Company, 1913. By permission of the Publishers.

This time. That male Salome, Buckingham,
Is dancing for his head. Raleigh is doomed.'
A shadow stood in the doorway. We looked up;
And there, but O, how changed, how worn and grey,
Sir Walter Raleigh, like a hunted thing,
Stared at us.
'Ben,' he said, and glanced behind him.
Ben took a step towards him.
'O, my God,
Ben,' whispered the old man in a husky voice,
Half timorous and half cunning, so unlike
His old heroic self that one might weep
To hear it, 'Ben, I have given them all the slip!
I may be followed. Can you hide me here
Till it grows dark?'
Ben drew him quickly in, and motioned me
To lock the door. 'Till it grows dark,' he cried,
'My God, that you should ask it!'
'Do not think,
Do not believe that I am quite disgraced,'
The old man faltered, 'for they 'll say it, Ben;
And when my boy grows up, they 'll tell him, too,
His father was a coward. I do cling
To life for many reasons, not from fear
Of death. No, Ben, I can disdain that still;
But — there 's my boy!'
Then all his face went blind.
He dropt upon Ben's shoulder and sobbed outright,
'They are trying to break my pride, to break my pride!'
The window darkened, and I saw a face
Blurring the panes. Ben gripped the old man's arm,
And led him gently to a room within,
Out of the way of guests.
'Your pride,' he said,
'That is the pride of England!'
At that name —
England! —
As at a signal-gun, heard in the night
Far out at sea, the weather and world-worn man,
That once was Raleigh, lifted up his head.
Old age and weakness, weariness and fear
Fell from him like a cloak. He stood erect.
His eager eyes, full of great sea-washed dawns,
Burned for a moment with immortal youth,
While tears blurred mine to see him.
'You do think
That England will remember? You do think it?'
He asked with a great light upon his face.
Ben bowed his head in silence.

. . . . .

'I have wronged
My cause by this,' said Raleigh. 'Well they know it
Who left this way for me. I have flung myself
Like a blind moth into this deadly light
Of freedom. Now, at the eleventh hour,
Is it too late? I might return and —'
'No!
Not now!' Ben interrupted. 'I'd have said
Laugh at the headsman sixteen years ago,
When England was awake. She will awake
Again. But now, while our most gracious king,
Who hates tobacco, dedicates his prayers
To Buckingham —
This is no land for men that, under God,
Shattered the Fleet Invincible.'
A knock
Startled us, at the outer door. 'My friend
Stukeley,' said Raleigh, 'if I know his hand.
He has a ketch will carry me to France,
Waiting at Tilbury.'
I let him in, —
A lean and stealthy fellow, Sir Lewis Stukeley, —
I liked him little. He thought much of his health,
More of his money bags, and most of all
On how to run with all men all at once
For his own profit. At the *Mermaid Inn*
Men disagreed in friendship and in truth;
But he agreed with all men, and his life
Was one soft quag of falsehood. Fugitives
Must use false keys, I thought; and there was hope
For Raleigh if such a man would walk one mile
To serve him now. Yet my throat moved to see him
Usurping, with one hand on Raleigh's arm,
A kind of ownership. '*Lend me ten pounds*,'
Were the first words he breathed in the old man's ear,
And Raleigh slipped his purse into his hand.

. . . . . .

Just over Bread Street hung the bruised white moon
When they crept out. Sir Lewis Stukeley's watch-dog,

A derelict bo'sun, with a mulberry face,
Met them outside. 'The coast quite clear, eh, Hart?'
Said Stukeley. 'Ah, that 's good. Lead on, then, quick.'
And there, framed in the cruddle of moonlit clouds
That ended the steep street, dark on its light,
And standing on those glistening cobble-stones
Just where they turned to silver, Raleigh looked back
Before he turned the corner. He stood there,
A figure like foot-feathered Mercury,
Tall, straight and splendid, waving his plumed hat
To Ben, and taking his last look, I felt,
Upon our *Mermaid Tavern*. As he paused,
His long fantastic shadow swayed and swept
Against our feet. Then, like a shadow, he passed.

'It is not right,' said Ben, 'it is not right.
Why did they give the old man so much grace?
Witness and evidence are what they lack.
Would you trust Stukeley — not to draw him out?
Raleigh was always rash. A phrase or two
Will turn their murderous axe into a sword
Of righteousness —
Why, come to think of it,
Blackfriar's Wharf, last night, I landed there,
And — no, by God! — Raleigh is not himself,
The tide will never serve beyond Gravesend.
It is a trap! Come on! We 'll follow them!
Quick! To the river side!' —
We reached the wharf
Only to see their wherry, a small black cloud
Dwindling far down that running silver road.
Ben touched my arm.
'Look there,' he said, pointing up stream.
The moon
Glanced on a cluster of pikes, like silver thorns,
Three hundred yards away, a little troop
Of weaponed men, embarking hurriedly.
Their great black wherry clumsily swung about,
When, with twelve oars for legs, came striding down,
An armoured beetle on the glittering trail
Of some small victim.
Just below our wharf
A little dinghy waddled.
Ben cut the painter, and without one word
Drew her up crackling through the lapping water,
Motioned me to the tiller, thrust her off,
And, pulling with one oar, backing with the other,
Swirled her round and down, hard on the track
Of Raleigh. Ben was an old man now but tough,
O tough as a buccaneer. We distanced them.
His oar blades drove the silver boiling back.
By Broken Wharf the beetle was a speck.
It dwindled by Queen Hythe and the Three Cranes.
By Bellyn's Gate we had left it, out of sight
By Custom House and Galley Keye we shot
Through silver all the way, without one glimpse
Of Raleigh. Then a dreadful shadow fell
And over us the Tower of London rose
Like ebony; and, on the glittering reach
Beyond it, I could see the small black cloud
That carried the great old seamen slowly down
Between the dark shores whence in happier years
The throng had cheered his golden galleons out,
And watched his proud sails filling for Cathay.
There, as through lead, we dragged by Traitor's Gate,
There, in the darkness, under the Bloody Tower,
There, on the very verge of victory,
Ben gasped and dropped his oars.
'Take one and row,' he said, 'my arms are numbed.
We 'll overtake him yet!' I clambered past him,
And took the bow oar.
Once, as the pace flagged,
Over his shoulder he turned his great scarred face
And snarled, with a trickle of blood on his coarse lips,
'Hard!' —
And blood and fire ran through my veins again,
For half a minute more.
Yet we fell back.
Our course was crookèd now. And suddenly
A grim black speck began to grow behind us,
Grow like the threat of death upon old age.

Then, thickening, blackening, sharpening, foaming, swept
Up the bright line of bubbles in our wake,
That armoured wherry, with its long twelve oars
All well together now.
'Too late,' gasped Ben,
His ash-grey face uplifted to the moon,
One quivering hand upon the thwart behind him,
A moment. Then he bowed over his knees
Coughing. 'But we 'll delay them, we 'll be drunk,
And hold the catch-polls up!'
We drifted down
Before them, broadside on. They sheered aside.
Then, feigning a clumsy stroke, Ben drove our craft
As they drew level, right in among their blades.
There was a shout, an oath. They thrust us off;
And then we swung our nose against their bows
And pulled them round with every well-meant stroke.
A full half minute, ere they won quite free,
Cursing us for a pair of drunken fools.
We drifted down behind them.
'There 's no doubt,'
Said Ben, 'the headsman waits behind all this
For Raleigh. This is a play to cheat the soul
Of England, teach the people to applaud
The red fifth act.'
Without another word we drifted down
For centuries it seemed, until we came
To Greenwich.
Then up the long white burnished reach there crept
Like little sooty clouds the two black boats
To meet us.
'He is in the trap,' said Ben,
'And does not know it yet. See, where he sits
By Stukeley as by a friend.'
Long after this,
We heard how Raleigh, simply as a child,
Seeing the tide would never serve him now,
And they must turn, had taken from his neck
Some trinkets that he wore. 'Keep them,' he said
To Stukeley, 'in remembrance of this night.'
He had no doubts of Stukeley when he saw
The wherry close beside them. He but wrapped
His cloak a little closer round his face.
Our boat rocked in their wash when Stukeley dropped
The mask. We saw him give the sign, and heard
His high-pitched quavering voice — 'IN THE KING'S NAME!'
Raleigh rose to his feet. 'I am under arrest?'
He said, like a dazed man.
And Stukeley laughed.
Then, as he bore himself to the grim end,
All doubt being over, the old sea-king stood
Among those glittering points, a king indeed.
The black boats rocked. We heard his level voice,
'*Sir Lewis, these actions never will turn out*
To your good credit.' Across the moonlit Thames
It rang contemptuously, cold as cold steel,
And passionless as the judgment that ends all.

. . . . .

Some three months later, Raleigh's widow came
To lodge a se'nnight at the Mermaid Inn.
His house in Bread Street was no more her own,
But in the hands of Stukeley, who had reaped
A pretty harvest . . .
She kept close to her room, and that same night,
Being ill and with some fever, sent her maid
To fetch the apothecary from Friday Street,
Old 'Galen' as the Mermaid christened him.
At that same moment, as the maid went out,
Stukeley came in. He met her at the door;
And, chucking her under the chin, gave her a letter.
'Take this up to your mistress. It concerns
Her property,' he said. 'Say that I wait,
And would be glad to speak with her.'
The wench
Looked pertly in his face, and tripped upstairs.
I scarce could trust my hands.
'Sir Lewis,' I said,
'This is no time to trouble her. She is ill.'
'Let her decide,' he answered, with a sneer.
Before I found another word to say
The maid tripped down again. I scarce believed
My senses, when she beckoned him up the stair.
Shaking from head to foot, I blocked the way.
'Property!' Could the crux of mine and thine

Bring widow and murderer into one small room?
'Sir Lewis,' I said, 'she is ill. It is not right!
She never would consent.'
He sneered again,
'You are her doctor? Out of the way, old fool!
She has decided!'
'Go,' I said to the maid,
'Fetch the apothecary. Let it rest
With him!'
She tossed her head. Her quick eyes glanced,
Showing the white, like the eyes of a vicious mare.
She laughed at Stukeley, loitered, then obeyed.

And so we waited, till the wench returned,
With Galen at her heels. His wholesome face,
Russet and wrinkled like an apple, peered
Shrewdly at Stukeley, twinkled once at me,
And passed in silence, leaving a whiff of herbs
Behind him on the stair.
Five minutes later,
To my amazement, that same wholesome face
Leaned from the lighted door above, and called
'Sir Lewis Stukeley!'
Sir Judas hastened up.
The apothecary followed him within.
The door shut. I was left there in the dark
Bewildered; for my heart was hot with thoughts
Of those last months. Our Summer's Nightingale,
Our Ocean-Shepherd from the Main-deep Sea,
The Founder of our Mermaid Fellowship,
Was this his guerdon — at the Mermaid Inn?
Was this that maid-of-honour whose romance
With Raleigh, once, had been a kingdom's talk?
Could Bess Throckmorton slight his memory thus?
'It is not right,' I said, 'it is not right.
She wrongs him deeply.'
I leaned against the porch
Staring into the night. A ghostly ray
Above me, from her window, bridged the street,
And rested on the goldsmith's painted sign
Opposite.
I could hear the muffled voice
Of Stukeley overhead, persuasive, bland;
And then, her own, cooing, soft as a dove
Calling her mate from Eden cedar-boughs,
Flowed on and on; and then — all my flesh crept
At something worse than either, a long space
Of silence that stretched threatening and cold,
Cold as a dagger-point pricking the skin
Over my heart.
Then came a stifled cry,
A crashing door, a footstep on the stair
Blundering like a drunkard's, heavily down:
And with his gasping face one tragic mask
Of horror, — may God help me to forget
Some day the frozen awful eyes of one
Who, fearing neither hell nor heaven, has met
That ultimate weapon of the gods, the face
And serpent-tresses that turn flesh to stone —
Stukeley stumbled, groping his way out,
Blindly, past me, into the sheltering night.

. . . .

It was the last night of another year
Before I understood what punishment
Had overtaken Stukeley. Ben, and Brome —
Ben's ancient servant, but turned poet now —
Sat by the fire with the old apothecary
To see the New Year in.
The starry night
Had drawn me to the door. Could it be true
That our poor earth no longer was the hub
Of those white wheeling orbs? I scarce believed
The strange new dreams; but I had seen the veils
Rent from vast oceans and huge continents,
Till what was once our comfortable fire,
Our cozy tavern, and our earthly home
With heaven beyond the next turn in the road,
All the resplendent fabric of our world
Shrank to a glow-worm, lighting up one leaf
In one small forest, in one little land,
Among those wild infinitudes of God.
A tattered wastrel wandered down the street,
Clad in a seaman's jersey, staring hard
At every sign. Beneath our own, the light

Fell on his red carbuncled face. I knew him —
The bo'sun, Hart.
He pointed to our sign
And leered at me. 'That 's her,' he said, 'no doubt,
The sea-witch with the shiny mackerel tail
Swishing in wine. That 's what Sir Lewis meant.
He called it blood. Blood is his craze, you see.
This is the Mermaid Tavern, sir, no doubt?'
I nodded. 'Ah, I thought as much,' he said.
'Well—happen this is worth a cup of ale.'
He thrust his hand under his jersey and lugged
A greasy letter out. It was inscribed
THE APOTHECARY AT THE MERMAID TAVERN.
I led him in. 'I knew it, sir,' he said.
While Galen broke the seal. 'Soon as I saw
That sweet young naked wench curling her tail
In those red waves. — The old man called it blood.
Blood is his craze, you see. — But you can tell
'T is wine, sir, by the foam. Malmsey, no doubt.
And that sweet wench to make you smack your lips
Like oysters, with her slippery tail and all!
Why, sir, no doubt, this was the Mermaid Inn.'

'But this,' said Galen, lifting his grave face
To Ben, 'this letter is from all that 's left
Of Stukeley. The good host, there, thinks I wronged
Your Ocean-shepherd's memory. From this letter,
I think I helped to avenge him. Do not wrong
His widow, even in thought. She loved him dearly.
You know she keeps his poor grey severed head
Embalmed; and so will keep it till she dies;
Weeps over it alone. I have heard such things
In wild Italian tales. But *this* was true.
Had I refused to let her speak with Stukeley
I feared she would go mad. This letter proves
That I — and she perhaps — were instruments
Of some more terrible chirurgery
Than either knew.'
'Ah, when I saw your sign,'
The bo'sun interjected, 'I 'd no doubt
That letter was well worth a cup of ale.'
'Go — paint your bows with hell-fire somewhere else,
Not at this inn,' said Ben, tossing the rogue
A good French crown. 'Pickle yourself in hell.'
And Hart lurched out into the night again,
Muttering 'Thank you, sirs. 'T was worth all that.
No doubt at all.'
'There are some men,' said Galen,
Spreading the letter out on his plump knees,
'Will heap up wrong on wrong; and, at the last,
Wonder because the world will not forget
Just when it suits them, cancel all they owe,
And, like a mother, hold its arms out wide
At their first cry. And, sirs, I do believe
That Stukeley, on that night, had some such wish
To reconcile himself. What else had passed
Between the widow and himself I know not;
But she had lured him on until he thought
That words and smiles, perhaps a tear or two,
Might make the widow take the murderer's hand
In friendship, since it might advantage both.
Indeed, he came prepared for even more.
Villains are always fools. A wicked act,
What is it but a false move in the game,
A blind man's blunder, a deaf man's reply,
The wrong drug taken in the dead of night?
I always pity villains.
I mistook
The avenger for the victim. There she lay
Panting, that night, her eyes like summer stars,
Her pale gold hair upon the pillows tossed
Dishevelled, while the fever in her face
Brought back the last wild roses of her youth
For half an hour. Against a breast as pure
And smooth as any maid's, her soft arms pressed
A bundle wrapped in a white embroidered cloth.
She crooned over it as a mother croons
Over her suckling child. I stood beside her.
— That was her wish, and mine, while Stukeley stayed. —
And, over against me, on the other side,
Stood Stukeley, gnawing his nether lip to find
She could not, or she would not, speak one word
In answer to his letter.

'Lady Raleigh,
You wrong me, and you wrong yourself,' he cried,
'To play like a green girl when great affairs
Are laid before you. Let me speak with you
Alone.'
'But I am all alone,' she said,
'Far more alone than I have ever been
In all my life before. This is my doctor.
He must not leave me.'
Then she lured him on,
Played on his brain as a musician plays
Upon the lute.
'Forgive me, dear Sir Lewis,
If I am grown too gay for widowhood.
But I have pondered for a long, long time
On all these matters. I know the world was right;
And Spain was right, Sir Lewis. Yes, and you,
You too, were right; and my poor husband wrong.
You see I knew his mind so very well.
I knew his every gesture, every smile.
I lived with him. I think I died with him.
It is a strange thing, marriage. For my soul
(As if myself were present in this flesh)
Beside him, slept in his grey prison-cell
On that last dreadful dawn. I heard the throng
Murmuring round the scaffold far away;
And, with the smell of saw-dust in my nostrils,
I woke, bewildered as himself, to see
That tall black-cassocked figure by his bed.
I heard the words that made him understand:
The Body of our Lord — take and eat this!
I rolled the small sour flakes beneath my tongue
With him. I caught, with him, the gleam of tears,
Far off, on some strange face of sickly dread.
The Blood — and the cold cup was in my hand,
Cold as an axe-heft washed with waterish red.
I heard his last poor cry to wife and child. —
Could any that heard forget it? — *My true God,*
Hold you both in His arms, both in His arms.
And then — that last poor wish, a thing to raise
A smile in some. I have smiled at it myself
A thousand times.
'Give me my pipe,' he said,
'*My old Winchester clay, with the long stem,*
And half an hour alone. The crowd can wait,
They have not waited half so long as I.'
And then, O then, I know what soft blue clouds,
What wavering rings, fragrant ascending wreaths
Melted his prison walls to a summer haze,
Through which I think he saw the little port
Of Budleigh Salterton, like a sea-bird's nest
Among the Devon cliffs — the tarry quay
Whence in his boyhood he had flung a line
For bass or whiting-pollock. I remembered
(Had he not told me, on some summer night,
His arm about my neck, kissing my hair)
He used to sit there, gazing out to sea;
Fish, and for what? Not all for what he caught
And handled; but for rainbow-coloured things,
The water-drops that jewelled his thin line,
Flotsam and jetsam of the sunset-clouds;
While the green water, gurgling through the piles,
Heaving and sinking, helped him to believe
The fast-bound quay a galleon plunging out
Superbly for Cathay. There would he sit
Listening, a radiant boy, child of the sea,
Listening to some old seaman's glowing tales,
His grey eyes rich with pictures —
Then he saw,
And I with him, that gathering in the West,
To break the Fleet Invincible. O, I heard
The trumpets and the neighings and the drums.
I watched the beacons on a hundred hills.
I drank that wine of battle from *his* cup,
And gloried in it, lying against his heart.
I sailed with him and saw the unknown worlds!
The slender ivory towers of old Cathay
Rose for us over lilac-coloured seas
That crumbled a sky-blue foam on long shores
Of shining sand, shores of so clear a glass
They drew the sunset-clouds into their bosom
And hung that City of Vision in mid-air
Girdling it round, as with a moat of sky,
Hopelessly beautiful. O, yet I heard,
Heard from his blazoned poops the trumpeters
Blowing proud calls, while overhead the flag
Of England floated from white towers of sail —
And yet, and yet, I knew that he was wrong,

And soon he knew it, too.
I saw the cloud
Of doubt assail him, in the Bloody Tower,
When, being withheld from sailing the high seas
For sixteen years, he spread a prouder sail,
Took up his pen, and, walled about with stone,
Began to write — his *History of the World.*
And emperors came like Lazarus from the grave
To wear his purple. And the night disgorged
Its empires, till, O, like the swirl of dust
Around their marching legions, that dim cloud
Of doubt closed round him. Was there any man
So sure of heart and brain as to record
The simple truth of things himself had seen?
Then who could plumb that night? The work broke off!
He knew that he was wrong. I knew it, too!
Once more that stately structure of his dreams
Melted like mist. His eagles perished like clouds.
Death wound a thin horn through the centuries.
The grave resumed his forlorn emperors.
His empires crumbled back to a little ash
Knocked from his pipe. —
He dropped his pen in homage to the truth.
The truth? *O, eloquent, just and mighty Death!*

Then, when he forged, out of one golden thought,
A key to open his prison; when the King,
Released him for a tale of faerie gold
Under the tropic palms; when those grey walls
Melted before his passion; do you think
The gold that lured the King was quite the same
As that which Raleigh saw? You know the song:

'Say to the King,' quoth Raleigh,
'I have a tale to tell him;
Wealth beyond derision,
Veils to lift from the sky,

Seas to sail for England,
And a little dream to sell him,
Gold, the gold of a vision
That angels cannot buy.'

Ah, no! For all the beauty and the pride,
Raleigh was wrong; but not so wrong, I think,
As those for whom his kingdoms oversea
Meant only glittering dust. The fight he waged
Was not with them. They never worsted him.
It was *The Destiny* that brought him home
Without the Spanish gold. — O, he was wrong,
But such a wrong, in Gloriana's day,
Was more than right, was immortality.
He had just half an hour to put all this
Into his pipe and smoke it. —
The red fire,
The red heroic fire that filled his veins
When the proud flag of England floated out
Its challenge to the world — all gone to ash?
What! Was the great red wine that Drake quaffed
Vinegar? He must fawn, haul down his flag,
And count all nations nobler than his own,
Tear out the lions from the painted shields
That hung his poop, for fear that he offend
The pride of Spain? Treason to sack the ships
Of Spain? The wounds of slaughtered Englishmen
Cried out — *there is no law beyond the line!*
Treason to sweep the seas with Francis Drake?
Treason to fight for England?
If it were so,
The times had changed and quickly. He had been
A school-boy in the morning of the world
Playing with wooden swords and winning crowns
Of tinsel; but his comrades had outgrown
Their morning-game, and gathered round to mock
His battles in the sunset. Yet he knew
That all his life had passed in that brief day;
And he was old, too old to understand
The smile upon the face of Buckingham,
The smile on Cobham's face, at that great word
England!
He knew the solid earth was changed
To something less than dust among the stars —
And, O, be sure he knew that he was wrong,
That gleams would come,
Gleams of a happier world for younger men,
That Commonwealth, far off. This was a time

Of sadder things, destruction of the old
Before the new was born. At least he knew
It was his own way that had brought the world
Thus far, England thus far! How could he change,
Who had loved England as a man might love
His mistress, change from year to fickle year?
For the new years would change, even as the old.
No — he was wedded to that old first love,
Crude flesh and blood, and coarse as meat and drink,
The woman—England; no fine angel-isle,
Ruled by that male Salome — Buckingham!
Better the axe than to live on and wage
These new and silent and more deadly wars
That play at friendship with our enemies.
Such times are evil. Not of their own desire
They lead to good, blind agents of that Hand
Which now had hewed him down, down to his knees,
But in a prouder battle than men knew.

His pipe was out, the guard was at the door.
Raleigh was not a god. But, when he climbed
The scaffold, I believe he looked a man.
And when the axe fell, I believe that God
Set on his shoulders that immortal head
Which he desired on earth.
O, he was wrong!
But when that axe fell, not one shout was raised.
That mighty throng around that crimson block
Stood silent — like the hushed black cloud that holds
The thunder. You might hear the headsman's breath.
Stillness like that is dangerous, being charged,
Sometimes, with thought, Sir Lewis! England sleeps!
What if, one day, the Stewart should be called
To know that England wakes? What if a shout
Should thunder-strike Whitehall, and the dogs lift
Their heads along the fringes of the crowd
To catch a certain savour that I know,
The smell of blood and saw-dust? —
Ah, Sir Lewis,
'T is hard to find one little seed of right
Among so many wrongs. Raleigh was wrong,
And yet — it was because he loved his country
Next to himself, Sir Lewis, by your leave,
His country butchered him. You did not know
That I was only third in his affections?
The night I told him — we were parting then —
I had begged the last disposal of his body,
Did he not say, with O, so gentle a smile,
"*Thou hadst not always the disposal of it*
In life, dear Bess. 'T is well it should be thine
In death!"'
'The jest was bitter at such an hour,
And somewhat coarse in grain,' Stukeley replied.
'Indeed I thought him kinder.'
'Kinder,' she said,
Laughing bitterly.
Stukeley looked at her.
She whispered something, and his lewd old eyes
Fastened upon her own. He knelt by her.
'Perhaps,' he said, 'your woman's wit has found
A better way to solve this bitter business.'
Her head moved on the pillow with little tossings.
He touched her hand. It leapt quickly away.
She hugged that strange white bundle to her breast,
And writhed back, smiling at him, across the bed.
'Ah, Bess,' he whispered huskily, pressing his lips
To that warm hollow where her head had lain,
'There is one way to close the long dispute,
Keep the estates unbroken in your hands
And stop all slanderous tongues, one happy way.
We have some years to live; and why alone?'
'Alone?' she sighed. 'My husband thought of that.
He wrote a letter to me, long ago,
When he was first condemned. He said — he said —
Now let me think — what was it that he said? —
I had it all by heart. "*Beseech you, Bess,*
Hide not yourself for many days," he said.'
'True wisdom that,' quoth Stukeley, 'for the love
That seeks to chain the living to the dead
Is but self-love at best!'

'And yet,' she said,
'How his poor heart was torn between two cares,
Love of himself and care for me, as thus:
"*Love God! Begin to repose yourself on Him!*
Therein you shall find true and lasting riches;
But all the rest is nothing. When you have tired
Your thoughts on earthly things, when you have travelled
Through all the glittering pomps of this proud world
You shall sit down by Sorrow in the end.
Begin betimes, and teach your little son
To serve and fear God also.
Then God will be a husband unto you,
And unto him a father; nor can Death
Bereave you any more. When I am gone,
No doubt you shall be sought unto by many
For the world thinks that I was very rich.
No greater misery can befall you, Bess,
Than to become a prey, and, afterwards,
To be despised."'
'Human enough,' said Stukeley,
'And yet — self-love, self-love!'
'Ah no,' quoth she,
'You have not heard the end: "*God knows, I speak it*
Not to dissuade you" — not to dissuade you, mark —
"*From marriage. That will be the best for you,*
Both in respect of God and of the world."
Was *that* self-love, Sir Lewis? Ah, not all.
And thus he ended: "*For his father's sake*
That chose and loved you in his happiest times,
Remember your poor child! The Everlasting,
Infinite, powerful, and inscrutable God,
Keep you and yours, have mercy upon me,
And teach me to forgive my false accusers" —
Wrong, even in death, you see. Then — "*My true wife,*
Farewell!
Bless my poor boy! Pray for me! My true God,
Hold you both in His arms, both in His arms!"
I know that he was wrong. You did not know,
Sir Lewis, that he had left me a little child.
Come closer. You shall see its orphaned face,
The sad, sad relict of a man that loved
His country — all that 's left to me. Come, look!'
She beckoned Stukeley nearer. He bent down
Curiously. Her feverish fingers drew
The white wrap from the bundle in her arms,
And, with a smile that would make angels weep,
She showed him, pressed against her naked breast,
Terrible as Medusa, the grey flesh
And shrivelled face, embalmed, the thing that dropped
Into the headsman's basket, months agone, —
The head of Raleigh.
Half her body lay
Bare, while she held that grey babe to her heart;
But Judas hid his face. . . .
'Living,' she said, 'he was not always mine;
But — dead — I shall not wean him' —
Then, I too
Covered my face — I cannot tell you more.
There was a dreadful silence in that room,
Silence that, as I know, shattered the brain
Of Stukeley. — When I dared to raise my head
Beneath that silent thunder of our God,
The man had gone —
This is his letter, sirs,
Written from Lundy Island: "*For God's love,*
Tell them it is a cruel thing to say
That I drink blood. I have no secret sin,
A thousand pound is not so great a sum;
And that is all they paid me, every penny.
Salt water, that is all the drink I taste
On this rough island. Somebody has taught
The sea-gulls how to wail around my hut
All night, like lost souls. And there is a face,
A dead man's face that laughs in every storm,
And sleeps in every pool along the coast.
I thought it was my own, once. But I know
These actions never, never, on God's earth,
Will turn out to their credit, who believe
That I drink blood."
He crumpled up the letter
And tossed it into the fire.
'Galen,' said Ben,
'I think you are right — that one should pity villains.'

. . . .

The clock struck twelve. The bells began to peal.
We drank a cup of sack to the New Year.
'New songs, new voices, all as fresh as may,'
Said Ben to Brome, 'but I shall never live
To hear them.'
All was not so well, indeed,
With Ben, as hitherto. Age had come upon him.
He dragged one foot as in paralysis.

The critics bayed against the old lion, now,
And called him arrogant. 'My brain,' he said,
'Is yet unhurt although, set round with pain,
It cannot long hold out.' He never stopped,
Never once pandered to that brainless hour.
His coat was thread-bare. Weeks had passed of late
Without his voice resounding in our inn.
'The statues are defiled, the gods dethroned,
The Ionian movement reigns, not the free soul.
And, as for me, I have lived too long,' he said.
'Well — I can weave the old threnodies anew.'
And, filling his cup, he murmured, soft and low,
A new song, breaking on an ancient shore:

I

Marlowe is dead, and Greene is in his grave,
  And sweet Will Shakespeare long ago is gone!
Our Ocean-shepherd sleeps beneath the wave;
Robin is dead, and Marlowe in his grave.
Why should I stay to chant an idle stave,
  And in my Mermaid Tavern drink alone?
For Kit is dead and Greene is in his grave,
  And sweet Will Shakespeare long ago is gone.

II

Where is the singer of the Faerie Queen?
  Where are the lyric lips of Astrophel?
Long, long ago, their quiet graves were green;
Ay, and the grave, too, of their Faerie Queen!
And yet their faces, hovering here unseen,
  Call me to taste their new-found œnomel;
To sup with him who sang the Faerie Queen;
  To drink with him whose name was Astrophel.

III

I drink to that great Inn beyond the grave!
  — If there be none, the gods have done us wrong. —
Ere long I hope to chant a better stave,
In some great Mermaid Inn beyond the grave;
And quaff the best of earth that heaven can save,
  Red wine like blood, deep love of friends and song.
I drink to that great Inn beyond the grave;
  And hope to greet my golden lads ere long.

He raised his cup and drank in silence. Brome
Drank with him, too. The bells had ceased to peal.
Galen shook hands, and bade us all good night.
Then Brome, a little wistfully, I thought,
Looked at his old-time master, and prepared
To follow.
  'Good night — Ben,' he said, a pause
Before he spoke the name. 'Good night! Good night!
My dear old Brome,' said Ben.
  And, at the door,
Brome whispered to me, 'He is lonely now.
There are not many left of his old friends.
We all go out — like this — into the night.
But what a fleet of stars!' he said, and shook
My hand, and smiled, and pointed to the sky.
And, when I looked into the room again,
The lights were very dim, and I believed
That Ben had fallen asleep. His great grey head
Was bowed across the table, on his arms.
Then, all at once, I knew that he was weeping;
And like a shadow I crept back again,
And stole into the night.
  There as I stood
Under the painted sign, I could have vowed
That I, too, heard the voices of the dead,
The voices of his old companions,
Gathering round him in that lonely room,
Till all the timbers of the Mermaid Inn
Trembled above me with their ghostly song:

I

Say to the King, quoth Raleigh,
  I have a tale to tell him,
    Wealth beyond derision,
      Veils to lift from the sky,
Seas to sail for England
  And a little dream to sell him, —
    Gold, the gold of a vision,
      That angels cannot buy.

II

Fair through the walls of his dungeon,
  — What were the stones but a shadow? —
    Streamed the light of the rapture,
      The lure that he followed of old,
The dream of his old companions,

The vision of El Dorado,
  The fleet that they never could capture,
  The City of Sunset-gold.

III

Yet did they sail the seas
  And, dazed with exceeding wonder,
  Straight through the sunset-glory
  Plunge into the dawn:
Leaving their home behind them,
  By a road of splendour and thunder,
  They came to their home in amazement
  Simply by sailing on.

1913

Rupert Brooke* (1887–1915)

PINE-TREES AND THE SKY: EVENING

I'D watched the sorrow of the evening sky,
And smelt the sea, and earth, and the warm clover,
And heard the waves, and the seagull's mocking cry.

And in them all was only the old cry,
That song they always sing — 'The best is over!
You may remember now, and think, and sigh,
O silly lover!'
And I was tired and sick that all was over,
And because I,
For all my thinking, never could recover
One moment of the good hours that were over.
And I was sorry and sick, and wished to die.

Then from the sad west turning wearily,
I saw the pines against the white north sky,
Very beautiful, and still, and bending over
Their sharp black heads against a quiet sky.
And there was peace in them; and I
Was happy, and forgot to play the lover,
And laughed, and did no longer wish to die;
Being glad of you, O pine-trees and the sky!

1911

FAILURE

BECAUSE God put His adamantine fate
  Between my sullen heart and its desire,
I swore that I would burst the Iron Gate,
  Rise up, and curse Him on His throne of fire.
Earth shuddered at my crown of blasphemy,
  But Love was as a flame about my feet;
Proud up the Golden Stair I strode; and beat
Thrice on the Gate, and entered with a cry —

All the great courts were quiet in the sun,
  And full of vacant echoes: moss had grown
Over the glassy pavement, and begun
  To creep within the dusty council-halls.
An idle wind blew round an empty throne
  And stirred the heavy curtains on the walls.

1911

THE GREAT LOVER

I HAVE been so great a lover: filled my days
So proudly with the splendour of Love's praise,
The pain, the calm, and the astonishment,
Desire illimitable, and still content,
And all dear names men use, to cheat despair,
For the perplexed and viewless streams that bear
Our hearts at random down the dark of life.
Now, ere the unthinking silence on that strife
Steals down, I would cheat drowsy Death so far,
My night shall be remembered for a star
That outshone all the suns of all men's days.
Shall I not crown them with immortal praise
Whom I have loved, who have given me, dared with me
High secrets, and in darkness knelt to see
The inenarrable godhead of delight?
Love is a flame: — we have beaconed the world's night.
A city: — and we have built it, these and I.
An emperor: — we have taught the world to die.
So, for their sakes I loved, ere I go hence,
And the high cause of Love's magnificence,
And to keep loyalties young, I'll write those names
Golden for ever, eagles, crying flames,
And set them as a banner, that men may know,
To dare the generations, burn, and blow

* By permission of Dodd, Mead & Company, Inc.

Out on the wind of Time, shining and streaming. . . .
These I have loved:
White plates and cups, clean-gleaming,
Ringed with blue lines; and feathery, faery dust;
Wet roofs, beneath the lamp-light; the strong crust
Of friendly bread; and many-tasting food;
Rainbows; and the blue bitter smoke of wood;
And radiant raindrops couching in cool flowers;
And flowers themselves, that sway through sunny hours,
Dreaming of moths that drink them under the moon;
Then, the cool kindliness of sheets, that soon
Smooth away trouble; and the rough male kiss
Of blankets; grainy wood; live hair that is
Shining and free; blue-massing clouds; the keen
Unpassioned beauty of a great machine;
The benison of hot water; furs to touch;
The good smell of old clothes; and other such —
The comfortable smell of friendly fingers,
Hair's fragrance, and the musty reek that lingers
About dead leaves and last year's ferns. . . .
Dear names,
And thousand others throng to me! Royal flames;
Sweet water's dimpling laugh from tap or spring;
Holes in the ground; and voices that do sing;
Voices in laughter, too; and body's pain,
Soon turned to peace; and the deep-panting train;
Firm sands; the little dulling edge of foam
That browns and dwindles as the wave goes home;
And washen stones, gay for an hour; the cold
Graveness of iron; moist black earthen mould;
Sleep; and high places; footprints in the dew;
And oaks; and brown horse-chestnuts, glossy-new;
And new-peeled sticks; and shining pools on grass; —
All these have been my loves. And these shall pass,
Whatever passes not, in the great hour,
Nor all my passion, all my prayers, have power
To hold them with me through the gate of Death.
They'll play deserter, turn with the traitor breath,
Break the high bond we made, and sell Love's trust
And sacramented covenant to the dust.
— Oh, never a doubt but, somewhere, I shall wake,
And give what's left of love again, and make
New friends, now strangers. . . .
But the best I've known
Stays here, and changes, breaks, grows old, is blown
About the winds of the world, and fades from brains
Of living men, and dies.
Nothing remains.

O dear my loves, O faithless, once again
This one last gift I give: that after men
Shall know, and later lovers, far-removed,
Praise you, 'All these were lovely'; say, 'He loved.'

1915

HAUNTINGS

In the grey tumult of these after years
Oft silence falls; the incessant wranglers part;
And less-than-echoes of remembered tears
Hush all the loud confusion of the heart;
And a shade, through the tossed ranks of mirth and crying,
Hungers, and pains, and each dull passionate mood, —
Quite lost, and all but all forgot, undying,
Comes back the ecstasy of your quietude.

So a poor ghost, beside his misty streams,
Is haunted by strange doubts, evasive dreams,
Hints of a pre-Lethean life, of men,
Stars, rocks, and flesh, things unintelligible,
And light on waving grass, he knows not when,
And feet that ran, but where, he cannot tell.

1915

PROSE

Edmund Gosse (1849–)

THE WHOLE DUTY OF WOMAN *

It is universally conceded that our great-grandmothers were women of the most precise life and austere manners. The girls nowadays display a shocking freedom; but they were partly led into it by the relative laxity of their mothers, who, in their turn, gave great anxiety to a still earlier generation. To hear all the 'Ahs' and the 'Well, I nevers' of the middle-aged, one would fancy that propriety of conduct was a thing of the past, and that never had there been a 'gaggle of girls' (the phrase belongs to Dame Juliana Berners) so wanton and rebellious as the race of 1895. Still, there must be a fallacy somewhere. If each generation is decidedly wilder, more independent, more revolting, and more insolent than the one before, how exceedingly good people must have been four or five generations ago! Outside the pages of the people so sweetly advertised as 'sexual female fictionists,' the girls of to-day do not strike one as extremely bad. Some of them are quite nice; the average is not very low. How lofty, then, must have been the standard one hundred years ago, to make room for such a steady decline ever since! Poor J. K. S. wrote: —

'If all the harm that 's been done by men
Were doubled and doubled and doubled again,
And melted and fused into vapour, and then
Were squared and raised to the power of ten,
There wouldn't be nearly enough, not near,
To keep a small girl for a tenth of a year.'

This is the view of a cynic. To the ordinary observer, the 'revolting daughters,' of whom we hear so much, do not revolt nearly enough to differentiate them duly from their virtuous great-grandmothers.

We fear that there was still a good deal of human nature in girls a hundred, or even two hundred, years ago. That eloquent and animated writer, the author of *The Whole Duty of Man*, published in the reign of Charles II, a volume which, if he had had the courage of his opinions, he would have named *The Whole Duty of Woman*. Under the tamer title of *The Ladies' Calling* it achieved a great success. In the frontispiece to this work a doleful dame, seated on what seems to be a bare altar in an open landscape, is raising one hand to grasp a crown dangled out of her reach in the clouds, and in the other, with an air of great affectation is lifting her skirt between finger and thumb. A purse, a coronet, a fan, a mirror, rings, dice, coins, and other useful articles lie strewn at her naked feet; she spurns them, and lifts her streaming eyes to heaven. This is the sort of picture which does its best to prevent the reader from opening the book; but *The Ladies' Calling*, nevertheless, is well worth reading. It excites in us a curious wish to know more exactly what manner of women it was addressed to. How did the great-grandmothers of our great-grandmothers behave? When we come to think of it, how little we know about them!

The customary source of information is the play-book of the time. There, indeed, we come across some choice indications of ancient woman's behaviour. Nor did the women spare one another. The woman dramatists outdid the men in attacking the manners of their sex, and what is perhaps the most cynical comedy in all literature was written by a woman. It will be some time before the Corinnas of *The Yellow Book* contrive to surpass *The Town Fop* in outrageous frankness. Our ideas of the fashions of the seventeenth century are, however, taken too exclusively, if they are taken from these plays alone. We conceive every fine lady to be like Lady Brute, in *The Provoked Wife*, who wakes about two o'clock in the afternoon, is 'trailed' to her great chair for tea, leaves her bedroom only to descend to dinner, spends the night with a box and dice, and does not go to bed until the dawn. Comedy

* By permission of the Author.

has always forced the note, and is a very unsafe (though picturesque) guide to historic manners. Perhaps we obtain a juster notion from the gallant pamphlets of the age, such as *The Lover's Watch* and *The Lady's Looking-Glass;* yet these were purely intended for people whom we should nowadays call 'smart,' readers who hung about the outskirts of the Court.

For materials, then, out of which to construct a portrait of the ordinary women of the world in the reign of Charles II, we are glad to come back to our anonymous divine. His is the best-kept secret in English literature. In spite of the immense success of *The Whole Duty of Man*, no one has done more than conjecture, more or less vaguely, who he may have been. He wrote at least five works besides his most famous treatise, and in preparing each of these for the press he took more pains than Junius did a century later to conceal his identity. The publisher of *The Ladies' Calling*, for example, assures us that he knows no more than we do. The MS. came to him from an unknown source and in a strange handwriting, 'as from the Clouds dropped into my hands.' The anonymous author made no attempt to see proofs of it, nor claimed his foundling in any way whatever. In his *English Prose Selections*, the recent third volume of which covers the ground we are dealing with, Mr. Craik, although finding room for such wretched writers as Bishop Cumberland and William Sherlock, makes no mention of the author of *The Whole Duty*. That is a curious oversight. There was no divine of the age who wielded a more graceful pen. Only the exigencies of our space restrain us from quoting the noble praise of the Woman-Confessor in the preface to *The Ladies' Calling*. It begins 'Queens and Empresses knew then no title so glorious'; and the reader who is curious in such matters will refer to it for himself.

The women of this time troubled our author by their loudness of speech. There seems some reason to believe that with the Restoration, and in opposition to the affected whispering of the Puritans, a truculent and noisy manner became the fashion among Englishwomen. This was, perhaps, the 'barbarous dissonance' that Milton deprecated: it is, at all events, so distasteful to the writer of *The Ladies' Calling* that he gives it an early prominence in his exhortation. 'A woman's tongue,' he says, 'should be like the imaginary music of the spheres, sweet and charming, but not to be heard at distance.' Modesty, indeed, he inculcates as the first ornament of womanhood, and he intimates that there was much neglect of it in his day. We might fancy it to be Mrs. Lynn Linton speaking when, with uplifted hands, he cries, 'Would God that they would take, in exchange for that virile Boldness, which is now too common among many even of the best Rank,' such a solidity and firmness of mind as will permit them to succeed in keeping a secret! Odd to hear a grave and polite divine urging the ladies of his congregation not to 'adorn' their conversation with oaths and imprecations, of which he says, with not less truth than gallantry, that 'out of a woman's mouth there is on this side Hell no noise that can be more amazingly odious.' The revolting daughters of to-day do not curse and swear; at all events, they do not swear in print, where only we have met the shrews. On the other hand, they smoke, a contingency which does not seem to have occurred to the author of *The Ladies' Calling*, who nowhere warns the sisterhood against tobacco. The gravity of his indictment of excess in wine, not less than the evidence of such observers as Pepys, proves to us that drunkenness was by no means rare even among women of quality.

There never, we suppose, from the beginning of the world was a man-preacher who did not warn the women of his congregation against the vanity of fair raiment. The author of *The Ladies' Calling* is no exception; but he does his spiriting in a gentlemanlike way. The ladies came to listen to him bedizened with jewels, with all the objects which lie strewn at the feet of his penitent in the frontispiece. He does not scream to them to rend them off. He only remonstrates at their costliness. In that perfectly charming record of a child's mind, the Memoir of Marjorie Fleming, the delicious little wiseacre records the fact that her father and mother have given a guinea for a pineapple, remarking that that money would have sustained a poor family during the entire winter. We are reminded of that when our divine tells his auditors that 'any one of the baubles, the loosest appendage of the dress, a fan, a busk, perhaps a black patch, bears a price that would warm the empty bowels of a poor starving wretch.' This was long before the days of very elaborate and expensive patches, which were still so new in Pepys' days that he remarked on those of Mr. Penn's pretty sister when he saw her in the new coach, 'patched and very fine.' Our preacher is no ranter, nor does he shut the door of mercy on entertainments; all he deprecates is their excess. His penitents are not forbidden to spend an afternoon at the theatre, or an evening in dancing or at cards; but they are desired to remember that, delightful as these occupations are, devotion is more delightful still.

The attitude of the author to gaming is curious. 'I question not the lawfulness of this recreation,' he says distinctly; but he desires his ladies not to make cards the business of their life, and especially not to play on Sundays. It appears that some great ladies, in the emptiness of their heads and hearts, took advantage of the high pews then always found in churches to play ombre or quadrille under the very nose of the preacher. This conduct must have been rare; the legends of the age prove that it was not unknown. The game might be concealed from every one if it was desisted from at the moment of the sermon, and in many cases the clergyman was a pitiful, obsequious wretch who knew better than to find fault with the gentlefolks 'up at the house.' It was not often that a convenient flash of lightning came in the middle of service to kill the impious gamester in his pew, as happened, to the immense scandal and solemnization of everybody, at Withycombe, in Devonshire.

On the whole, it is amusing to find that the same faults and the same dangers which occupy our satirists to-day were pronounced imminent for women two hundred years ago. The ladies of Charles II's reign were a little coarser, a little primmer, a good deal more ignorant than those of our age. Their manners were on great occasions much better, and on small occasions much worse, than those of their descendants of 1895; but the same human nature prevailed. The author of *The Ladies' Calling* considered that the greatest danger of his congregation lay in the fact that 'the female Sex is eminent for its pungency in the sensible passion of love'; and, although we take other modes of saying it, that is true now.

1895

George Bernard Shaw (1856–)

THE CASE FOR THE CRITIC-DRAMATIST *

A discussion has arisen recently as to whether a dramatic critic can also be a dramatic author without injury to his integrity and impartiality. The feebleness with which the point has been debated may be guessed from the fact that the favorite opinion seems to be that a critic is either an honest man or he is not. If honest, then dramatic authorship can make no difference to him. If not, he will be dishonest whether he writes plays or not. This childish evasion cannot, for the honor of the craft, be allowed to stand. If I wanted to ascertain the melting-point of a certain metal, and how far it would be altered by an alloy of some other metal, and an expert were to tell me that a metal is either fusible or it is not — that if not, no temperature will melt it; and if so, it will melt anyhow — I am afraid I should ask that expert whether he was a fool himself or took me for one. Absolute honesty is as absurd an abstraction as absolute temperature or absolute value. A dramatic critic who would die rather than read an American pirated edition of a copyright English book might be considered an absolutely honest man for all practical purposes on that one particular subject — I say on that one, because very few men have more than one point of honor; but as far as I am aware, no such dramatic critic exists. If he did, I should regard him as a highly dangerous monomaniac. That honesty varies inversely with temptation is proved by the fact that every additional penny on the income-tax yields a less return than the penny before it, showing that men state their incomes less

* *Dramatic Opinions and Essays*, Brentano's, 1906. By permission of the Publishers.

honestly for the purposes of taxation at sevenpence in the pound than sixpence. The matter may be tested by a simple experiment. Go to one of the gentlemen whose theory is that a man is either honest or he is not, and obtain from him the loan of half-a-crown on some plausible pretext of a lost purse or some such petty emergency. He will not ask you for a written acknowledgment of the debt. Return next day and ask for a loan of £500 without a promissory note, on the ground that you are either honest or not honest, and that a man who will pay back half a crown without compulsion will also pay back £500. You will find that the theory of absolute honesty will collapse at once.

Are we then to believe that the critic-dramatist who stands to make anything from five hundred to ten thousand pounds by persuading a manager to produce his plays, will be prevented by his honesty from writing about that manager otherwise than he would if he had never written a play and were quite certain that he never should write one? I can only say that people who believe such a thing would believe anything. I am myself a particularly flagrant example of the critic-dramatist. It is not with me a mere case of an adaptation or two raked up against me as incidents in my past. I have written half-a-dozen 'original' plays, four of which have never been performed; and I shall presently write half-a-dozen more. The production of one of them, even if it attained the merest success of esteem, would be more remunerative to me than a couple of years of criticism. Clearly, since I am no honester than other people, I should be the most corrupt flatterer in London if there were nothing but honesty to restrain me. How is it, then, that the most severe criticisms of managers come from me and from my fellow critic-dramatists, and that the most servile puffery comes from writers whose every sentence proves that they have nothing to hope or fear from any manager? There are a good many answers to this question, one of the most obvious being that as the respect inspired by a good criticism is permanent, whilst the irritation it causes is temporary, and as, on the other hand, the pleasure given by a venal criticism is temporary, and the contempt it inspires permanent, no man really secures his advancement as a dramatist by making himself despised as a critic. The thing has been tried extensively during the last twenty years; and it has failed. For example, the late Frank Marshall, a dramatist and an extravagantly enthusiastic admirer of Sir Henry Irving's genius, followed a fashion which at one time made the Lyceum Theatre a sort of court formed by a retinue of literary gentlemen. I need not question either their sincerity or the superiority of Canute to their idolatry; for Canute never produced their plays: 'Robert Emmet' and the rest of their masterpieces remain unacted to this day. It may be said that this brings us back to honesty as the best policy; but honesty has nothing to do with it: plenty of the men who know that they can get along faster fighting than crawling, are no more honest than the first Napoleon was. No virtue, least of all courage, implies any other virtue. The cardinal guarantee for a critic's integrity is simply the force of the critical instinct itself. To try to prevent me from criticizing by pointing out to me the superior pecuniary advantages of puffing is like trying to keep a young Irving from going on the stage by pointing out the superior pecuniary advantages of stockbroking. If my own father were an actor-manager, and his life depended on his getting favorable notices of his performance, I should orphan myself without an instant's hesitation if he acted badly. I am by no means the willing victim of this instinct. I am keenly susceptible to contrary influences — to flattery, which I swallow greedily if the quality is sufficiently good; to the need of money, to private friendship or even acquaintanceship, to the pleasure of giving pleasure and the pain of giving pain, to consideration for people's circumstances and prospects, to personal likes and dislikes, to sentimentality, pity, chivalry, pugnacity and mischief, laziness and cowardice, and a dozen other human conditions which make the critic vulnerable; but the critical instinct gets the better of them all. I spare no effort to mitigate its inhumanity, trying to detect and strike out of my articles anything that would give pain without doing any good. Those who think the things I say severe, or even malicious, should just see the things I do *not* say. I do my best to be partial, to hit out at remediable abuses rather than at accidental shortcomings, and at strong and responsible people rather than weak and helpless ones. And yet all my efforts do not alter the result very much. So stubborn is the critic within me, that with every disposition to be as good-natured and as popular an authority as the worst enemy of art could desire, I am to all intents and purposes incorruptible. And that is how the dramatist-critic, if only he is critic enough, 'slates' the actor-manager in defiance of the interest he has in conciliating him. He cannot help himself, any more than the ancient mariner could help telling his story. And the actor-manager can no more help listening than the wedding guest could. In short, the better formula would have been, that a man is either a critic or not a critic; that to the extent to which he is one he will criticize the managers in spite of heaven and earth; and that to the extent to which he is not, he will flatter them anyhow, to save himself trouble.

The advantage of having a play criticized by a critic who is also a playwright is as obvious as the advantage of having a ship criticized by a critic who is also a master shipwright. Pray observe that I do not speak of the criticism of dramas and ships by dramatists and shipwrights who are not also critics; for that would be no more convincing than the criticism of acting by actors. Dramatic authorship no more constitutes a man a critic than actorship constitutes him a dramatic author; but a dramatic critic learns as much from having been a dramatic author as Shakespeare or Mr. Pinero from having been actors. The average London critic, for want of practical experience, has no real confidence in himself: he is always searching for an imaginary 'right' opinion, with which he never dares to identify his own. Consequently every public man finds that as far as the press is concerned his career divides itself into two parts: the first, during which the critics are afraid to praise him; and the second, during which they are afraid to do anything else. In the first, the critic is uncomfortably trying to find faults enough to make out a case for his timid coldness: in the second, he is eagerly picking out excellencies to justify his eulogies. And of course he blunders equally in both phases. The faults he finds are either inessential or are positive reforms, or he blames the wrong people for them: the triumphs of acting which he announces are stage tricks that any old hand could play. In criticizing actresses he is an open and shameless voluptuary. If a woman is pretty, well dressed, and self-satisfied enough to be at her ease on the stage, he is delighted; and if she is a walking monument of handsome incompetence, so much the better, as your voluptuary rarely likes a woman to be cleverer than himself, or to force him to feel deeply or think energetically when he only wants to wallow in her good looks. Confront him with an actress who will not condescend to attack him on this side — who takes her work with thorough seriousness and self-respect — and his resentment, his humiliation, his sense of being snubbed, break out ludicrously in his writing, even when he dare not write otherwise than favorably. A great deal of this nonsense would be taken out of him if he could only write a play and have it produced. No dramatist begins by writing plays merely as excuses for the exhibition of pretty women on the stage. He comes to that ultimately perhaps; but at first he does his best to create real characters and make them pass through three acts of real experiences. Bring a critic who has done this face to face with the practical question of selecting an actress for his heroine, and he suddenly realizes for the first time that there is not such a galaxy of talent on the London stage as he thought, and that the handsome walking ladies whom he always thought good enough for other people's plays are not good enough for his own. That is already an immense step in his education. There are other steps, too, which he will have taken before the curtain falls on the first public representation of his play; but they may be summed up in the fact that the author of a play is the only person who really wants to have it well done in every respect, and who therefore has every drawback brought fully home to him. The man who has had that awakening about one play will thenceforth have his eyes open at all other plays; and there you have at once the first moral with the first technical qualification of the critic — the determination to have every play as well done as possible, and the knowledge of what is standing in the way of that consummation. Those of our critics who, either as original dramatists or adapters and translators, have superintended the production of plays with paternal anxiety, are never guilty of the wittily disguised indifference of clever critics who have never seen a drama through from its first beginnings behind the scenes. Compare the genuine excitement of Mr. Clement Scott, or the almost Calvinistic seriousness of Mr. Wm. Archer, with the gaily easy what-does-it-matterness of Mr. Walkley, and you see at once how the two critic-dramatists influence the drama, whilst the critic-playgoer only makes it a pretext for entertaining his readers. On the whole there is only as much validity in the theory that a critic should not be a dramatist, as in the theory that a judge should not be a lawyer nor a general a soldier. You can not have qualifications without experience; and you can not have experience without personal interest and bias. That may not be an ideal arrangement; but it is the way the world is built; and we must make the best of it.

1895

Gilbert Keith Chesterton (1874–)

A DEFENCE OF NONSENSE *

There are two equal and eternal ways of looking at this twilight world of ours: we may see it as the twilight of evening or the twilight of morning; we may think of anything, down to a fallen acorn, as a descendant or as an ancestor. There are times when we are almost crushed, not so much with the load of the evil as with the load of the goodness of humanity, when we feel that we are nothing but the inheritors of a humiliating splendour. But there are other times when everything seems primitive, when the ancient stars are only sparks blown from a boy's bonfire, when the whole earth seems so young and experimental that even the white hair of the aged, in the fine biblical phrase, is like almond-trees that blossom, like the white hawthorn grown in May. That it is good for a man to realize that he is 'the heir of all the ages' is pretty commonly admitted; it is a less popular but equally important point that it is good for him sometimes to realize that he is not only an ancestor, but an ancestor of primal antiquity; it is good for him to wonder whether he is not a hero, and to experience ennobling doubts as to whether he is not a solar myth.

The matters which most thoroughly evoke this sense of the abiding childhood of the world are those which are really fresh, abrupt and inventive in any age; and if we were asked what was the best proof of this adventurous youth in the nineteenth century we should say, with all respect to its portentous sciences and philosophies, that it was to be found in the rhymes of Mr. Edward Lear and in the literature of nonsense. 'The Dong with the Luminous Nose,' at least, is original, as the first ship and the first plough were original.

It is true in a certain sense that some of the greatest writers the world has seen — Aristophanes, Rabelais and Sterne — have written nonsense; but unless we are mistaken, it is in a widely different sense. The nonsense of these men was satiric — that is to say, symbolic; it was a kind of exuberant capering round a discovered truth. There is all the difference in the world between the instinct of satire, which, seeing in the Kaiser's moustaches something typical of him, draws them continually larger and larger; and the instinct of nonsense which, for no reason whatever, imagines what those moustaches would look like on the present Archbishop of Canterbury if he grew them in a fit of absence of mind. We incline to think that no age except our own could have understood that the Quangle-Wangle meant absolutely nothing, and the Lands of the Jumblies were absolutely nowhere. We fancy that if the account of the knave's trial in 'Alice in Wonderland' had been published in the seventeenth century it would have been bracketed with Bunyan's 'Trial of Faithful' as a parody on the State prosecutions of the time. We fancy that if 'The Dong with the Luminous Nose' had appeared in the same period every one would have called it a dull satire on Oliver Cromwell.

* *The Defendant*, 1901. By permission of the Author.

It is altogether advisedly that we quote chiefly from Mr. Lear's 'Nonsense Rhymes.' To our mind he is both chronologically and essentially the father of nonsense; we think him superior to Lewis Carroll. In one sense, indeed, Lewis Carroll has a great advantage. We know what Lewis Carroll was in daily life: he was a singularly serious and conventional don, universally respected, but very much of a pedant and something of a Philistine. Thus his strange double life in earth and in dreamland emphasizes the idea that lies at the back of nonsense — the idea of *escape,* of escape into a world where things are not fixed horribly in an eternal appropriateness, where apples grow on pear-trees, and any odd man you meet may have three legs. Lewis Carroll, living one life in which he would have thundered morally against any one who walked on the wrong plot of grass, and another life in which he would cheerfully call the sun green and the moon blue, was, by his very divided nature, his one foot on both worlds, a perfect type of the position of modern nonsense. His Wonderland is a country populated by insane mathematicians. We feel the whole is an escape into a world of masquerade; we feel that if we could pierce their disguises, we might discover that Humpty Dumpty and the March Hare were Professors and Doctors of Divinity enjoying a mental holiday. This sense of escape is certainly less emphatic in Edward Lear, because of the completeness of his citizenship in the world of unreason. We do not know his prosaic biography as we know Lewis Carroll's. We accept him as a purely fabulous figure, on his own description of himself:

'His body is perfectly spherical,
He weareth a runcible hat.'

While Lewis Carroll's Wonderland is purely intellectual, Lear introduces quite another element — the element of the poetical and even emotional. Carroll works by the pure reason, but this is not so strong a contrast; for, after all, mankind in the main has always regarded reason as a bit of a joke. Lear introduces his unmeaning words and his amorphous creatures not with the pomp of reason, but with the romantic prelude of rich hues and haunting rhythms.

'Far and few, far and few,
Are the lands where the Jumblies live,'

is an entirely different type of poetry to that exhibited in 'Jabberwocky.' Carroll, with a sense of mathematical neatness, makes his whole poem a mosaic of new and mysterious words. But Edward Lear with more subtle and placid effrontery, is always introducing scraps of his own elvish dialect into the middle of simple and rational statements, until we are almost stunned into admitting that we know what they mean. There is a genial ring of common sense about such lines as,

'For his aunt Jobiska said "Every one knows
That a Pobble is better without his toes,"'

which is beyond the reach of Carroll. The poet seems so easy on the matter that we are almost driven to pretend that we see his meaning, that we know the peculiar difficulties of a Pobble, that we are as old travellers in the 'Gromboolian Plain' as he is.

Our claim that nonsense is a new literature (we might almost say a new sense) would be quite indefensible if nonsense were nothing more than a mere æsthetic fancy. Nothing sublimely artistic has ever arisen out of mere art, any more than anything essentially reasonable has ever arisen out of the pure reason. There must always be a rich moral soil for any great æsthetic growth. The principle of *art for art's sake* is a very good principle if it means that there is a vital distinction between the earth and the tree that has its roots in the earth; but it is a very bad principle if it means that the tree could grow just as well with its roots in the air. Every great literature has always been allegorical — allegorical of some view of the whole universe. The 'Iliad' is only great because all life is a battle, the 'Odyssey' because all life is a journey, the Book of Job because all life is a riddle. There is one attitude in which we think that all existence is summed up in the word 'ghosts'; another, and somewhat better one, in which we think it is summed up in the words 'A Midsummer Night's Dream.' Even the vulgarest melodrama or detective story can be good if it expresses something of the delight in sinister possibilities — the healthy lust for darkness and terror which may come on us any night in walking down a dark lane. If, therefore, nonsense is really to be the literature of the future, it must have its own version of the Cosmos to offer; the world must not only be the tragic, romantic, and religious, it must be nonsensical also. And here we fancy that nonsense will, in a very unexpected way, come to the aid of the spiritual view of things. Religion has for centuries been trying to make men exult in the 'wonders' of creation, but it has forgotten that a thing cannot be completely wonderful so long as it remains sensible. So long as we regard a tree as an obvious thing, naturally and reasonably created for a giraffe to eat, we cannot properly wonder at it. It is when we consider it as a prodigious wave of the living soil sprawling up to the skies for no reason in particular that we take off our hats, to the astonishment of the park-keeper. Everything has in fact another side to it, like the moon, the patroness of nonsense. Viewed from that other side, a bird is a blossom broken loose from its chain of stalk, a man a quadruped begging on its hind legs, a house a gigantesque hat to cover a man from the sun, a chair an apparatus of four wooden legs for a cripple with only two.

This is the side of things which tends most truly to spiritual wonder. It is significant that in the greatest religious poem existent, the Book of Job, the argument which convinces the infidel is not (as has been represented by the merely rational religionism of the eighteenth century) a picture of the ordered beneficence of the Creation; but, on the contrary, a picture of the huge and undecipherable unreason of it. 'Hast Thou sent the rain upon the desert where no man is?' This simple sense of wonder at the shapes of things, and at their exuberant independence of our intellectual standards and our trivial definitions, is the basis of spirituality as it is the basis of nonsense. Nonsense and faith (strange as the conjunction may seem) are the two supreme symbolic assertions of the truth that to draw out the soul of things with a syllogism is as impossible as to draw out Leviathan with a hook. The well-meaning person who, by merely studying the logical side of things, has decided that 'faith is nonsense,' does not know how truly he speaks; later it may come back to him in the form that nonsense is faith.

1901

Herbert George Wells (1866–)

MY FIRST FLIGHT *

Hitherto my only flights have been flights of imagination, but this morning I flew. I spent about ten or fifteen minutes in the air; we went out to sea, soared up, came back over the land, circled higher, planed steeply down to the water, and I landed with the conviction that I had had only the foretaste of a great store of hitherto unsuspected pleasures. At the first chance I will go up again, and I will go higher and further.

This experience has restored all the keenness of my ancient interest in flying, which had become a little fagged and flat by too much hearing and reading about the thing and not enough participation. Fifteen years ago, in the days of Langley and Lilienthal, I was one of the few journalists who believed and wrote that flying was possible — it affected my reputation unfavorably, and produced in the few discouraged pioneers of those days a quite touching gratitude. Over my mantel as I write hangs a very blurred and bad but interesting photograph that Professor Langley sent me thirteen years ago. It shows the flight of the first piece of human machinery heavier than air that ever kept itself up for any length of time. It was a model, a little affair that would not have lifted a cat; it went up in a spiral and came down unsmashed, bringing back, like Noah's dove, the promise of tremendous things.

That was only thirteen years ago, and it is amusing to recall how cautiously even we out-and-out believers did our prophesying. I was quite a desperate fellow; I said outright that in my lifetime we should see men flying. But I qualified that by repeating that for many years to come it would be an enterprise only for quite fantastic daring and skill. We conjured up stupendous difficulties and risks. I was deeply impressed and greatly discouraged by a paper a distin-

* *American Magazine*, December, 1912. By permission of the Author.

guished Cambridge mathematician produced to show that a flying-machine was bound to pitch fearfully, that as it flew on its pitching *must* increase, until up went its nose, down went its tail, and it fell like a knife. We exaggerated every possibility of instability. We imagined that when the airplane wasn't 'kicking up ahind and afore' it would be heeling over to the lightest side wind. A sneeze might upset it. We contrasted our poor human equipment with the instinctive balance of a bird, which has had ten million years of evolution by way of a start. . . .

(The waterplane in which I soared over Eastbourne this morning with Mr. Grahame White was as steady as a motor-car running on asphalt.)

Then we went on from those anticipations of swaying insecurity to speculations about the psychological and physiological effects of flying. Most people who look down from the top of a cliff or high tower feel some slight qualms of dread, many feel a quite sickening dread. Even if men struggled high into the air, we asked, wouldn't they be smitten up there by such a lonely and reeling dismay as to lose all self-control? And, above all, wouldn't the pitching and tossing make them quite horribly seasick?

I have always been a little haunted by that last dread. It gave a little undertow of funk to the mood of lively curiosity with which I got aboard the waterplane this morning — that sort of faint, thin funk that so readily invades one on the verge of any new experience; when one tries one's first dive, for example, or pushes off for the first time down an ice-run. I thought I should very probably be seasick — or, to be more precise, airsick; I thought also that I might be very giddy, and that I might get thoroughly cold and uncomfortable. None of those things happened.

I am still in a state of amazement at the smooth steadfastness of the motion. There is nothing on earth to compare with that, unless — and that I can't judge — it is an ice-yacht traveling on perfect ice. The finest motor-car in the world on the best road would be a joggling, quivering thing beside it.

To begin with, we went out to sea before the wind, and the plane would not readily rise. We went with an undulating movement, leaping with a light splashing pat upon the water, from wave to wave. Then we came about into the wind, and rose; and looking over I saw that there were no longer those periodic flashes of white foam. I was flying. And it was as still and steady as dreaming.

I watched the widening distance between our floats and the waves. It wasn't by any means a windless day — there was a brisk fluctuating breeze blowing out of the north over the downs. It seemed hardly to affect our flight at all.

And as for the giddiness of looking down, one does not feel it at all. It is difficult to explain why this should be so, but it is so. I suppose in such matters I am neither exceptionally steady-headed, nor is my head exceptionally given to swimming. I can stand on the edge of cliffs of a thousand feet or so and look down, but I can never bring myself right up to the edge, nor crane over to look to the very bottom. I should want to lie down to do that. And the other day I was on that Belvedere place at the top of the Rotterdam skyscraper, a rather high wind was blowing, and one looks down through the chinks between the boards one stands on upon the heads of the people in the streets below; I didn't like it. But I looked directly down on a little fleet of fishing-boats over which we passed, and on the crowds assembling on the beach, and on the bathers who stared up at us from the breaking surf with an entirely agreeable exaltation. And Eastbourne in the early morning sunshine had all the brightly detailed littleness of a town viewed from high up on the side of a great mountain.

When Mr. Grahame White told me we were going to plane down, I will confess I tightened my hold on the sides of the car, and prepared for something like the downgoing sensation of a switchback railway on a larger scale. Just for a moment there was that familiar feeling of something pressing one's heart up towards one's shoulders and one's lower jaw up into its socket, and of grinding one's lower teeth against the upper, and then it passed. The nose of the car and all the machine was slanting downward, we were gliding quickly down, and yet there was no feeling that one rushed, not even as one rushes in coasting a hill on a bicycle. It wasn't a tithe of the thrill of those three descents one gets on the great mountain railway in the White City. There one gets a disagreeable quiver up one's backbone from the wheels, and a real sense of falling.

It is quite peculiar to flying that one is incredulous of any collision. Some time ago I was in a motor-car that ran over and killed a small dog, and this wretched little incident has left an open wound upon my nerves. I am never quite happy in a car now; I can't help keeping an apprehensive eye ahead. But you fly with an exhilarating assurance that you cannot possibly run over anything or run into anything — except the land or the sea, and even those large essentials seem a beautifully safe distance away.

I had heard a great deal of talk about the deafening uproar of the engine. I counted a headache among my chances. There again reason reinforced conjecture. When in the early morning Mr. Travers came from Brighton in this Farman in which I flew, I could hear the hum of the great insect when it still seemed abreast of Beachey Head, and a good two miles away. If one can hear a thing at two miles, how much the more will one not hear it at a distance of two yards. But at the risk of seeming too contented for anything I will assert I heard that noise no more than one hears the drone of an electric ventilator upon one's table. It was only when I came to speak to Mr. Grahame White, or he to me, that I discovered that our voices had become almost infinitesimally small.

And so it was that I went up into the air at Eastbourne with the impression that flying was still an uncomfortable, experimental, and slightly heroic thing to do, and came down to the cheerful gathering crowd upon the sands again with the knowledge that it is a thing achieved for everyone. It will get much cheaper no doubt, and much swifter, and be improved in a dozen ways, — we *must* get self-starting engines, for example, for both our aëroplanes and motor-cars, — but it is available to-day for any one who can reach it. An invalid lady of seventy could have enjoyed all that I did if only one could have got her into the passenger's seat. Getting there was a little difficult, it is true; the waterplane was out in the surf, and I was carried to it on a boatman's back, and then had to clamber carefully through the wires, but that is a matter of detail.

This flying is indeed so certain to become a general experience that I am sure that this description will in a few years seem almost as quaint as if I had set myself to record the fears and sensations of my First Ride in a Wheeled Vehicle. And I suspect that learning to control a Farman waterplane now is probably not much more difficult than, let us say, twice the difficulty in learning the control and management of a motor bicycle. I cannot understand the sort of young man who won't learn how to do it if he gets half a chance.

The development of these waterplanes is an important step towards the huge and swarming popularization of flying which is now certainly imminent. We ancient survivors of those who believed in and wrote about flying before there was any flying, used to make a great fuss about the dangers and difficulties of landing and getting up. We wrote with vast gravity about 'starting rails' and 'landing stages,' and it is still true that landing an aëroplane, except upon a well-known and quite level expanse, is a risky and uncomfortable business. But getting up and landing upon fairly smooth water is easier than getting into bed. This alone is likely to determine the aëroplane routes along the line of the world's coast-lines and lake groups and water-ways.

The airmen will go to and fro over water as the midges do. Wherever there is a square mile of water the waterplanes will come and go like hornets at the mouth of their nest. But there are much stronger reasons than this convenience for keeping over water. Over water the air, it seems, lies in great level expanses; even when there are gales it moves in great uniform masses, like the swift still rush of a deep river. The airman, in Mr. Grahame White's phrase, can go to sleep on it.

But over the land, and for thousands of feet up into the sky, the air is more irregular than a torrent among rocks; it is — if only we could see it — a waving, whirling, eddying, flamboyant confusion. A slight hill, a plowed field, the streets of a town, create riotous, rolling, invisible streams and cataracts of air, that catch the aviator unawares, make him drop disconcertingly, try his nerve. With a powerful enough engine he climbs at once again, but these sudden downfalls are the least pleasant and most dangerous experience in aviation. They exact a tiring vigilance. Over lake or sea, in sunshine, within sight of land — this is the perfect way of the flying tourist. Gladly would I have set out for France this morning instead of returning to Eastbourne. And then coasted round to Spain and into the Mediterranean. And so by leisurely stages to India. And the East Indies. . . .

I find my study unattractive to-day.

1912

John Galsworthy (1867-)

CASTLES IN SPAIN *

We of the modern world, what do we dream of? What are our castles in Spain?

The thought came to me in Seville Cathedral, the stone fabric of man's greatest dream in those ages to which we have been accustomed to apply the word 'dark.' They who, traveling in Spain, consult their guide-books, may read these words: 'On the eighth day of July in the year 1401 the Dean and Chapter of Seville assembled in the court of the elms and solemnly resolved: "Let us build a church so great that those who come after us may think us mad to have attempted it!" . . . The church took one hundred and fifty years to build.'

Men dreamed in those 'dark' days, and carried out their dreams. In that silent building, incredibly beautiful, in that grove of sixty great trees of stone, whose vast trunks are jeweled by sunlight filtering through the high stained glass, in that stupendous and perfected work of art, raised by five succeeding generations to the glory of themselves and their God, one stood wondering wherein lay the superiority of ourselves, Children of Light, over those Sons of Darkness.

We, too, dream. I have seen some of the results — the Great Dam at Assuan, the Roosevelt Dam in Arizona, the Woolworth Building, the Forth Bridge, the Power Works at Niagara — not yet the greatest of them all, the Panama Canal (which actually took one-tenth of the time it took the Sons of Darkness to achieve Seville Cathedral). But all these were dreamed and fabricked out for immediate material benefit.

The builders of the giant mosques, the Temples of the Sun, the marvelous old churches, builded for no physical advantage in this life. They carved and wrought and slowly lifted stone on stone, to remote, and, as they thought, spiritual ends.

We moderns mine and forge, and mason up our monuments, to the immediate profit of our bodies. Have we raised anything really great in stone or brick *for a mere idea*, since Christopher Wren built St. Paul's Cathedral?

Now, the Sons of Darkness and the Children of Light, both, I think, have worshipped a half-truth. In the streets of Spain, in the Indian or Egyptian village, to this day you may see the shadow of these ancient great buildings fall as if with dark weight on a miserably poor humanity. The ancients builded for to-morrow in another world; they forgot that all of us have a to-day in this. They spent riches and labor to save the souls of their hierarchy, but they kept their laborers so poor that they had no souls to save. They left astounding testimony to human genius and tenacity, majestic creations which can uplift the spirit of anyone who has eyes to see; but with all their dreams in stone to the glory of their gods, they kept simple man a beast of burden. And it never seems to have ruffled their consciousness that they purchased much of that ideal beauty with slavery, misery, and blood.

We moderns have gone another way to work, worshipping our half-truth. In place of those ideals for which the ancients worked — art, and the future life of their princes, politicians, and prelates — we moderns pursue what we call 'progress.' All our stupendous achievements have this progressive notion at their back. We worship industry and trade. We think that if we make the wheels go round fast enough, mankind is bound to rise on the wings of wealth. Look

* *Yale Review*, October, 1921. By permission of Author and Publishers.

after the body, we say, and the spirit will look after itself. Whether we save a greater proportion of our bodies than the ancients did of souls, is more than doubtful. But no such trifling doubts shake our belief in 'progress.'

Our modern castle in Spain is, in a word, 'production,' and we have no other. It terrifies us, it paralyzes us, it is like a snake in front of a rabbit. It is like that Chinese general at whose name a million trembled. And what was his name? 'Wu.'

It is machinery, of course, which has divided us from the ancients, given us a new culture and ideal.

Machinery has quietly and gradually shifted the central point of man's philosophy. Before the industrial era set in, men used to make things by hand; they were in some sort artists, with the artist's — or at least the craftsman's — pride in their work. Now they press buttons, they turn wheels; they don't make completed articles, they work with monotony at the section of an article; so many hours of machine-driving per day, the total result of which is never a man's individual achievement. 'Intelligent specialism,' says an English writer, 'is one thing. It consists in one man learning how to do one thing specially well. But the sort of specializing which consists in setting thousands of human beings during their whole working lives to such a soul-destroying job as fixing the bristles into a hair-brush, pasting labels on jam-pots, or nearly any one of the varieties of machine minding, is quite another thing. It is an utter negation of human nature.'

A man's real interest in life is now not in his working day, but outside of it. The old artificers drew in their culture, such as it was, from their work; in these days, culture, such as it is, is grafted on to the workman in his leisure, as a sort of antidote to wheel driving. I don't want to exaggerate — hewers, delvers, drawers of water could never have taken much pride in their work, and, on the other hand, we still have many among us to whom their work is of absorbing interest. The modern architect and engineer, for example, have a great deal of the artist in them — they have a passion for the perfection of their job, which they communicate to many of those working under them. But though they may raise in Brooklyn Bridge, or the Woolworth Building, a marvel of efficiency, which in certain lights is also a thing of beauty, Society did not commission them to erect these wonders primarily for the sake of their beauty, or in order that Presidents Wilson and Harding might go to heaven. And, on the whole, I think there has been a great change; pride of quality has given way to pride of quantity. Men used to make things as well as they could for the pride they took in making them (and because they sometimes used the thing themselves). Now it is to their interest to turn out the cheapest, most quickly made, and lowest form of article that the public will take; and we have to rely for quality, not on the maker's pride of work, but on a grafted culture which keeps the public up to demanding a better sort of article. In old days the good thing was naturally supplied, nowadays it is artificially demanded.

Of course there is much truth in the vague modern notion that if you take care of the body the spirit will take care of itself. Only, you must really take care of the body, and not just pretend to. And the trouble about this progress of ours — which is supposed to take care of our bodies, and of which machinery is the mistress — is that it doesn't progress. We used to have the manor-house, with half a dozen hovels in its support. Now we have, say, twenty miles of handsome residences, with a hundred and twenty miles of ugly back streets, reeking with smoke and redolent of dulness, dirt, and discontent. Proportions are unchanged. The purple patches of our great towns are too often as rouge on the cheeks and salve on the lips of a corpse. Real progress would level up and gradually extinguish the disproportion between manor and hovel, residence and back street.

Let us be fantastic for a moment and conceive the civic authorities of London on the eighth day of July in the year 1922, solemnly resolving: 'We will remake of London a city so beautiful and sweet to dwell in that those who come after us shall think us mad to have attempted it.' It might well take five generations, but it would be real progress. Alas! Our civic authorities have not been brought up to care a button for anything so unpractical as a castle in Spain. And say what you will in favor of democracy, there is always the trouble of getting any far-sighted and unbroken policy pursued. If anyone can furnish an antidote to the wasting tendency of short immediate policies, inherent in the system of government by bodies elected for short terms, he will be the greatest benefactor of the age. The life of a civic body is, I believe, about four years; we should want a procession of civic bodies who steadily loved castles in Spain, to make of London a stainless city of Portland stone, full of baths and flowers and singing birds — not in cages.

But, seriously, we are very unfortunate in letting our civic life be run in the main by those who were born seeing two inches before their noses, and whose education, instead of increasing, has reduced those inches to one. It seems ungrateful to criticize the practical business man whose faculties and powers, stamina and energy, make the more imaginative person gasp. One owes him, in fact, so much, that one would like to owe him more. But does his vision as a rule extend beyond keeping pace with the present? And without vision the people perish! Why, the age is so practical that the word 'visionary' has actually a slighting significance. And yet the really great practical administrators have all had vision — men like Cæsar, Chatham, Lincoln. And great men apart, there are really many naturally both practical and visionary. But in an age of specialism our method of education ever tends to develop one side of our natures at the expense of the other.

If we can't incorporate beauty in our scheme of life to-day, and foster the love of beauty in our children, the life of to-morrow and the children thereof must necessarily be as far from beauty as we are now. Surely it is strange to set men to direct the education, housing, and amusements of their fellow citizens, if they haven't a love of beauty, and some considerable knowledge of art! And is it really going too far to say that the present generation of business men — with, of course, many notable exceptions — have a sort of indulgent contempt for art and beauty? Would they admit that art has been the greatest of all factors in raising mankind from its old savage state? And yet it is the contemplation of beautiful visions, emotions, thoughts, and dreams, expressed beautifully in stone, metal, paint, words, and music, which has slowly, generation by generation, lifted man to his present stature, such as it is, and mollified his savage nature. If it hasn't been that, ask yourselves what it has been! Religion? The uplifting part of religion is the beautiful expression of exalted feeling. The rest of religion is but superstition. Think of the thousand wars fought in the name of superstition; of the cannibal feasts, the human sacrifices; the tortures of the Inquisition; the persecutions, intolerances, and narrow cruelties perpetrated even to this day. The stories and teachings of Buddha, of Christ, of St. Francis d'Assisi, were the beautiful expressions of exalted feeling, simple, and touching the hearts of men, as all true beauty does; and so they have done their ennobling work. They belong to the cult of beauty.

Has trade, perhaps, been the mollifying influence and elevator of mankind? I think, only so far as it has widened the reach of beauty, brought beauty within the range of multitudes, by opening up the lines of communication. In that sense, no doubt, trade has helped. But trade as trade has no real elevating influence — rather the contrary.

No! Only beauty, in the largest sense of the word, the yearning for it, the contemplation of it, has civilized mankind. And yet we don't really take beauty seriously. Immediate profit rules the roost of us all in this age of ours. I leave it to the conscience of the age to decide whether that is good. For every age has a conscience, but it never comes to life till the age is on its death-bed.

The fault of all ages has been this: beauty — the knowledge and the love of it — has been kept as a preserve of the few, as the possession of a caste or clique. No great proportion of us are capable of creating or expressing beauty; but an immensely greater proportion of us are capable of appreciating it than ever have been given a real chance of so doing.

It should be our castle in Spain to clear our age of that defect, and put beauty within the reach of all. Machinery has come to stay, so that we must perforce rely on grafted culture — in other words, on education. We must teach the young now to feel and see the beauties of nature and art. The modern age is not easy to teach. But we have exceptional facilities in these days for teaching what helps to keep life dignified, besides those simple accomplishments, cooking and keeping clean; we could bring an inkling at least of the fine arts, the architecture, literature, and music of the past to children even in the humblest schools. And why should not the children of labor have as much chance to be familiar with beauty as the children of the rich? All economic revolution or evolution is hollow unless it means more demand for beauty — greater dignity of human life. Without that it must be simply retrograde, destroying what beauty and love of it we have, with all to begin over again. What use in B's despoiling A, if B is going to use his spoils no better, probably worse, than A? A mere lap of luxury would only make B fat.

This is all platitude; and a great fuss about beauty, which cannot feed or clothe or warm the body, whatever it may do to that sentimental appanage, the spirit.

I read in a journal not long ago: 'One always suspects Mr. Galsworthy of a certain deep-seated sentimentalism.' I think the writer must have sold his castles in Spain at a loss. The fact is, one must be sentimental in this life to do anything except make money, and it is really better to have a castle in Spain than a villa at Newport or Cannes.

The precise definitions of beauty are without number or — value, to speak of. I just use the word to mean everything which promotes the real dignity of human life. To illustrate the width of the word beauty as I am using it, I mention what we all understand: good sportsmanship. To be a good 'sportsman,' a man shuns that which lowers his dignity, that which dims his idea of his own quality; and — his conception of quality derives obscurely from his sense of beauty. The dignity of human life demands in fact not only such desirable embroideries as pleasant sound, fine form, and lovely color, but health, strength, cleanliness, balance, joy in living, just conduct and kind conduct, for there is no beauty in the sight of tortured things. A man who truly loves beauty hates to think that he enjoys it at the expense of starved and stunted human beings or suffering animals. A cruel or pettifogging æstheticism has sometimes smeared the word beauty and given it a bad odor. But that is not the beauty which gleams on the heights in the sunrise. That is not our castle in Spain.

But to put aside for a moment the sentimental, and come to business. Beauty, and the love of it, is surely the best investment modern man can make; for nothing else — most certainly not trade — will keep him from destroying the human species.

Consider what science has become in the hands of engineers and chemists; its destructive powers increase a hundred-fold with each decade; and the reproductive powers and inclinations of the human being do not vary. Recollect that nothing in the world but the love of beauty in its broad sense stands between man and the full and reckless exercise of his competitive greed; and remember the great war — a little war compared to that which, through the development of scientific destruction, we shall be able to wage next time! Remembering all this, we get an inkling of the sheer necessity there is for us to invest in beauty and the love thereof. No other investment will give us interest on our money and our money back. Unbalanced trade, science, industry, will give us a high momentary rate of interest, but only till the crash comes again, and the world goes even more bankrupt than it is at present.

The professor who has invented a rocket which will go to the moon and find out all about it (though whether it is to be boomerang enough to come back with the story, we are not told), that professor would, I venture to think, have done more real good if he had taught a school full of children to see the beauty of — moonshine.

The next war will be fought from the air with explosives and gas, and may very likely be over before war is declared. The war after that will be fought with the germs of disease, distributed by wireless or something choice of that character. The final war necessary for the complete extirpation of mankind will be fought with radium or atomic energy; and we shall have no need to examine the moon, for the earth will be as lifeless.

So much for business! To go back to sentiment, which is really what makes the wheels go round. Not even 'big business' rules our instincts, and our passions. Imperialists, chemists, engineers, merchants, militarists — we are all deep-seated sentimentalists. The only question for us is: What shall we be sentimental about? Which is the fairer castle in Spain — quantity or quality?

Consider for a moment the ideals which have been offered us instead of the pursuit of beauty, or quality, if that be a preferable word.

Take, for instance, the ideal of happiness in a future life. If there be a future life for the individual, we obviously cannot reach happiness therein without having longed for and served quality in this, without having had that kind and free and generous philosophy which belongs to the cult of beauty and alone gives peace of mind. The pursuit of beauty includes, then, whatever may be true in the ideal — happiness in a future life.

Take the ideal of material comfort in this life. But the cult of beauty, of quality, includes all that is good in this ideal, for it surely demands physical health and well-being; sane minds in sane bodies, which depend of course on a sufficiency of material comfort. All the rest of the ideal of wealth is mere fat, sagging beyond the point of balance. As a fact, modern civilization is offering us a compound between happiness in a future life, and material comfort in this, lip-serving the first, and stomach-serving the second. We get the keys of heaven from our banks, and we don't get them if we haven't a good balance. Modern civilization is, on the whole, camouflaged commercialism, wherein to do things well, *for the joy of doing them well,* is rarer than we think. We have even commercialized salvation — for so much virtue, so much salvation. Always — always — *quid pro quo.*

But let us give the devil its due. Let us admit at once that in spite of everything this is still the best age on the whole that man has lived in. It is in its own way very thorough — our modern civilization. It has made advertisement into a fine art, equipped bedrooms with telephones; it diagnoses maladies with extreme punctilio. A doctor examined a young lady the other day, and among his notes were these: 'Not afraid of small rooms, ghosts, or thunderstorms; not made drunk by hearing Wagner; brown hair, artistic hands; had a craving for chocolate in 1918.' The age is thorough in its way. But there 's a kind of deadly practicality about its production: all for to-day, none for to-morrow! The future will never think us mad for attempting what we do attempt; we build no Seville cathedrals. We don't get ahead of time.

We have just let slip, in England, the chance to get our country life going thoroughly once more. At demobilization we might have put hundreds of thousands on the land, which needs them so badly for a dozen reasons. How many have we put? Not so many as the war took away from the land. Admitted that life on the land means hard work, burnt faces, and maybe bowed backs; it also means hearty stock for the next generation. A nation concerned only with its present is like the man who was fishing, and, feeling sleepy, propped his rod up on the bank, with the line in the water. A wag spied him sleeping, took the rod, waded across the river, propped up the rod on the opposite bank, and lay down behind a hedge to watch for the awakening. Such is the awakening in store for nations which enjoy their present and forget there is a future.

The pursuit of beauty as a national ideal, the building of that castle in Spain, is no picnic. Idlers need not apply. Consider the rank growth which must be cut down, the stumps and roots to be burned out and cleared, the swamps to be drained, before even the foundations can be laid. And — after — what long and patient labor and steadfastness of ideal before we begin to see rise a fair edifice of human life upon this earth.

Members of a practical race will say: 'Well, what do you want us to do? Cut the flower and come to the fruit?' Alas! All literary men can tell people what they oughtn't to be; that 's — literature. But to tell them what they ought to do is — politics, of which no literary man is guilty; for politics and literature afford the only instance known — in virtuous countries — of divorce by mutual consent. The contempt of politicians for literary men is only equalled by the contempt of literary men for politicians. It would be impertinent, then, for a literary man to suggest anything practical. Let me, however, make a few affirmations. I do believe that, on the whole, modern man is a little further from being a mere animal than the men of the Dark Ages, however great the castles in Spain those men built and left for us to look upon; but I am sure we are in far greater danger than ever they were, of a swift decline. From that decline I am convinced that only the love and cult of beauty will save us!

By the love and cult of beauty I mean a great deal — *higher and wider conception of the dignity of human life;* the teaching of what beauty is, to all, not merely to the few; the cultivation of good will so that we wish and work and dream that not only ourselves but everybody may be healthy and happy; and, above all, the fostering of the habit of doing things and making things well for the joy of the work and the pleasure of achievement, rather than for the gain they will bring us. With these as the rules, the wheels of an insensate industrialism, whose one idea is to make money and get ahead of other people — careless of direction towards hell or heaven — might conceivably be spoked.

As it seemed to me, the great lack of our age is an ideal, expressed with sufficient concreteness to be like a vision, beckoning. To me there is no other ideal worthy of us, or indeed possible to us in these unsuperstitious days, save beauty — or call it, if you will, the dignity of human life. One or two writers of late have urged the need of more *spiritual* beauty in our lives. They mean what I mean, but it is unfortunate to talk of *spiritual* beauty. We must be able to smell, and see, hear, feel, and taste our ideal as well. We must know by plain evidence that it is lifting human life, that it is the heritage of all, not merely of the refined and leisured among us. The body and soul are one for the purpose of all real evolution, and I regret any term which suggests a divorce between them. But nobody, I think, can mistake what is meant by quality, or the dignity of human life. Anything which crosses and offends against that ideal is our Satan. And the only way in which each one can say '*Retro Satana*' is to leave his or her tiny corner of the universe a little more dignified, a little more lovely and lovable than he or she found it.

It may seem absurd to be writing like this in a world whose general mood at the moment is utter disillusionment and gloomy spite. The world is cross-eyed just now; when it weeps out of one eye, the tear runs down the other cheek. And it is difficult to be in love with a lady like that. I, for one, find it extremely hard not to be a cynic. Latest opinion assigns eight or ten thousand years as the outside length of time during which what we know as civilization has been at work. Still — ten thousand years is a considerable period of mollification. One had rashly hoped that mankind was not to be so speedily stampeded; that traditions of gentleness, fair play, chivalry, had a little more strength among Western peoples than they have been proved to have had since 1914; that mob feeling might be less, instead of, as it seems, more potent than it used to be. Only very constant self-reminding that the fault was in one's self, that one was a facile observer, a dreamer who did not look deeply enough beneath the surface; a rider before the hounds; only that, and a constant self-reminding of the individual patience, good humor, endurance, and heroism which goes so queerly hand in hand with stupidity, savagery, greed, and mob violence, can save a man from turning his back on the world with the words: 'Cats and monkeys, monkeys and cats, all life is there!'

Fear is at the back of nearly all the savagery in the world; and if there be not present in the individual that potent antidote — the sense of human dignity, which is but a love of and a belief in beauty, he must infallibly succumb to fear. There are tremendous difficulties in the way of coherent progress, of all fair and far ideals under the régime of short-lived elective bodies, a régime essentially exposed to stampede through popular opinion and the emotions of the moment. Seeing the violence of which military autocracy is capable, one is liable to become too blind a devotee of democracy. But democracy has no greater enemies than her unthinking friends. Short sight is her danger, short sight verging on blindness. What will happen if democracy really goes blind? She must have an ideal, a star on which to fix her eyes — something distant and magnetic to draw her on, something to strive towards, beyond the troubled and shifting needs, passions, and prejudices of the moment. Lovers of beauty, those who wish to raise the dignity of human life, should try to give her that ideal, to equip her with the only vision which can save the world from spite and the crazy competition which leads thereto.

We of this still young century may yet leave to those who come after us at least the foundations of a castle in Spain such as the world has not yet seen; leave our successors in mood and heart to continue our work; so that one hundred and fifty years perhaps from now, human life may really be dignified and beautiful, not just a breathless, grudging, visionless scramble from birth to death, of a night with no stars out.

Dreamer — deep-seated sentimentalist — the immortal Don riding his Rosinante on the bare brown uplands of Spain never saw so crazy a vision, so fickle-shining a mirage! Who knows? The world is changing. It *must* change, or perish; the forces of destruction, the inherent futilities of the present order, are too great. And there is in human nature, after all, the instinct of self-preservation, a great saving common-sense.

The past six years have been the result of the past six hundred years. The war was no spasmodic visitation; it was the culmination of age-long competitions. The past six years have devoured many millions of grown men, more millions of little children — prevented their birth, killed them, or withered them for life. If we begin again these crazy competitions, without regard for beauty or the dignity of human life, we shall live to see ten millions perish for every million perished in this war. We shall live to curse the day — this day when, at the end of so great a lesson, we were too sane to take it to heart; too sensible and practical and business-like and unemotional to see visions and dream dreams, and build our castle in Spain.

1921

NOTES

OLD ENGLISH PERIOD

References in poetry are to lines; in prose are to pages, columns (a and b), and lines.

References to pages and columns are printed in bold-face type.

2a BEOWULF

Beowulf is the most ancient epic of the Germanic peoples and the only Old English poem that attempts a picture of life among the primitive Teutons on a large scale. Of the author we know nothing except what can be inferred from the text: he was a man of genius who knew how to write in the high epic style and liked to throw a veil of Christian morality over the pagan life of the long-gone past. The poem was composed probably during the seventh or early eighth century after Christ. Though there is reason to believe that Beowulf, the hero, was a real person (cf. note to l. 1202), his exploits as here described belong largely to the realm of folk-lore and mythology. He is the Christianized ideal of the ancient warrior and gentleman, and much of the poem is devoted to "noble sentiments and counsels of modesty and wisdom." In spite of its sustained dignity and high moral tone, *Beowulf* contains grave faults of structure and makes an impression of cold and sombre sadness in a world where the sun never shines and even the finest of life is but vanity. It lacks the cheery note that so strikingly marks later English literature. *Beowulf* consists of four separate stories: (1) the hero's fight with Grendel, (2) the fight with Grendel's mother, (3) the triumphant return of the hero to his home, (4) the fight with the dragon. The poem opens with a brief survey of the ancestors of Hrothgar, King of the Danes, whose palace of Heorot is wasted by the nightly attacks of Grendel, a giant ogre of the race of Cain, the first murderer. Beowulf, with some brave Geats, crosses the sea (a day's journey) to Hrothgar's assistance, and in a terrible encounter, tears off the arm of Grendel, who flees mortally wounded to his lair beneath a lake. Grendel's mother comes to avenge her son. Beowulf follows her to her home in a cave under the water, where he finds Grendel dead and by means of a magic sword overcomes the mother. He returns to Heorot in triumph, bearing Grendel's head. Beowulf becomes king of the Geats and reigns over them until, after fifty years, he is mortally wounded in a conflict with a dragon that guards a treasure.

As the translation follows the original line for line and attempts to reproduce some of the peculiar metrical and stylistic effects, the following remarks should be carefully noted. (1) In the original every complete line is made up of two halves, each consisting of two accents and a varying number of unaccented syllables. The two parts are separated by a cæsura (pause) and are united by alliteration. Alliteration is the rhyming of the initial sounds of words or of syllables. In Anglo-Saxon poetry alliteration and accent, though not always found together, combine to emphasize the most important words or syllables of the line. In the following example the alliterating letters are printed in bold-face type:

With **w**arlike **w**eapons and **w**eeds of battle.

(2) The style is more abrupt and there are more separate, disconnected words in apposition than in modern English.
(3) Compound words are abundant; *e.g.*, "land-prince" for "prince of the land"; "war-speed" for "success in war."
(4) An object is frequently designated by a roundabout compound without ever being directly spoken of; *e.g.*, "whale-road" for "the sea"; "earl's raiment" for "armor." Such poetic metaphors are called "kennings."
(5) The pronoun often anticipates its antecedent, the subject of the sentence is changed without warning, and the style is frequently inverted in a fashion somewhat puzzling until one gets the hang of it; *e.g.*, "He thought that he would, ere day came, divide, the terrible monster, of every one, the life from the body," for "The terrible monster thought that ere day came, he would divide the life of every one from the body."

The following genealogical tables will be of assistance in understanding the relationship of the characters:

GENEALOGICAL TABLES

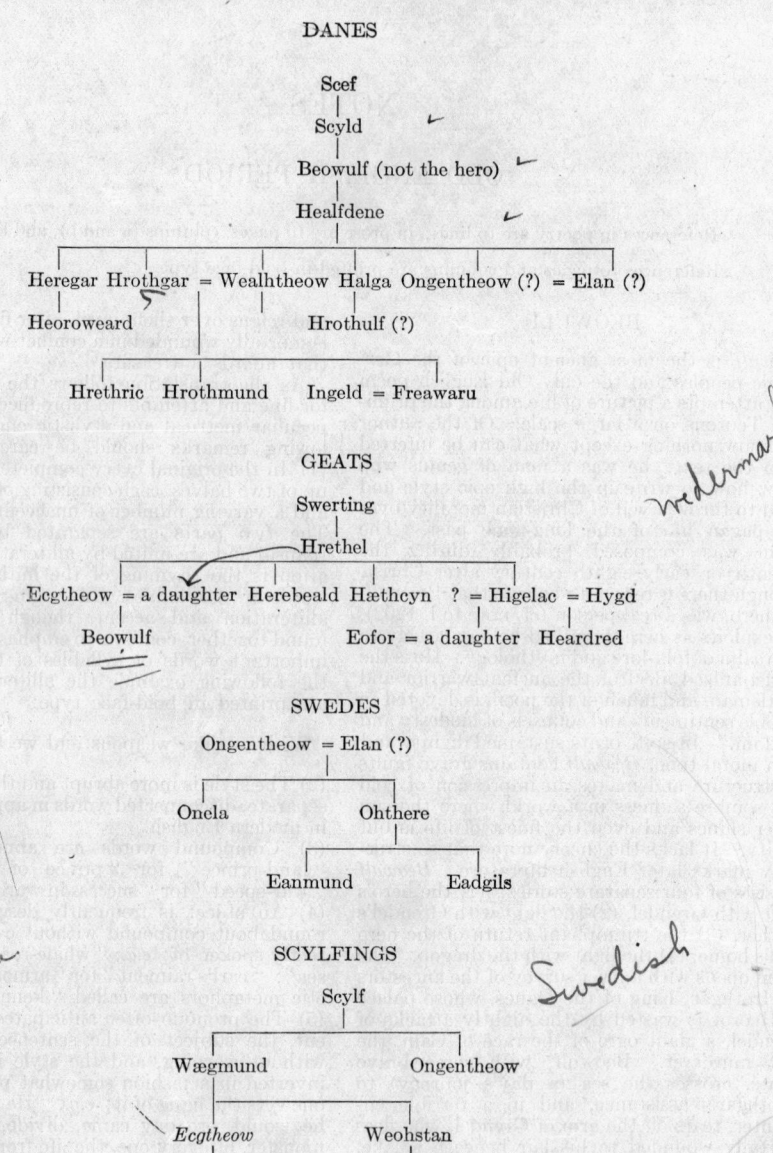

DANES

Scef

Scyld

Beowulf (not the hero)

Healfdene

Heregar Hrothgar = Wealhtheow Halga Ongentheow (?) = Elan (?)

Heoroweard Hrothulf (?)

Hrethric Hrothmund Ingeld = Freawaru

GEATS

Swerting

Hrethel

Ecgtheow = a daughter Herebeald Hæthcyn ? = Higelac = Hygd

Beowulf Eofor = a daughter Heardred

SWEDES

Ongentheow = Elan (?)

Onela Ohthere

Eanmund Eadgils

SCYLFINGS

Scylf

Wægmund Ongentheow

Ecgtheow Weohstan

Beowulf Wiglaf

6. **earl.** The word here conveys the general idea of nobility rather than of specific rank.
7. **Found thus forlorn.** According to tradition Scyld, the founder of the Scylding dynasty, was washed ashore as a child in a boat, in which he was pillowed upon a sheaf of grain; hence his name "son of Scef (Sheaf)." Cf. l. 45.
18. **Beowulf,** a Danish king, not the hero of the poem. The name, so confusing here to the beginner, seems to have been inserted at this point by some copyist in place of the word "Beaw," which stood in the original. Beaw was probably a god of the ancient Scandinavians.
19. **Scedelands,** Denmark.
30. **Scyldings,** the Danes. See genealogical tables.
35. **Giver of rings.** Royal favor was shown by gifts of rings used as armlets, necklaces, etc.
35. **On the deck.** The passage refers to the ancient Teutonic custom of ship-burial. The body of the dead king was placed on shipboard along with armor and treasures, and allowed to drift away to sea. See further ll. 3014 ff.
40. **Bills and burnies,** swords and coats of mail.
43. **Not at all with less gifts.** A fine example of litotes or understatement, a favorite figure in Anglo-Saxon poetry. (Cf. l. 1304.) The poet here means that the treasure far exceeded what had come in the boat that brought the king, when a helpless child, to shore.
50. **Men,** etc. Compare this passage with the close of Tennyson's *The Passing of Arthur* (p. 908).
63. **Scylfing's.** The Scylfings were perhaps a Swedish people.
78. **Heorot.** The name "Heort (Heorot)," which means "hart," seems to have been given to the hall because, with its decorated gables, it bore a fancied resemblance to a stag's head with antlers. The building was probably rectangular, with opposite doors and a hearth in the middle of the large hall.
83. **hateful fire.** Presumably a reference to the fact that Heorot, like other mediæval houses of wood, was destined ultimately to be destroyed by fire. The burning is not referred to elsewhere.
86. **fell spirit,** the giant ogre Grendel, not referred to by name until l. 102.
91. **creation.** The creation of the world was a favorite theme with Old English poets. Compare Cædmon's "Hymn" (p. 39). Though the Danes are heathens, the minstrel is represented as reciting a story told in the Bible!
103. **mark-stepper,** one who dwells on the borders.
107. **Cain's kin.** It was a common tradition during the Middle Ages that Cain, because of his wickedness and of God's curse (Genesis iv, 8), was the ancestor of many uncanny creatures. Cf. l. 1261 and note.
112. **Eotens,** giants.
123. **thanes,** nobles attending upon the king in his court. After the Norman Conquest the title was replaced by that of *baron*.
151. **Sadly in songs.** Poets, who acted as journalists and purveyors of news during the Dark Ages, spread abroad Grendel's fame in sorrowful songs.
156. **nor with money compound.** Grendel did not even offer monetary compensation for his crimes, as was permitted by Germanic law. Cf. l. 470.
168. **Yet must he,** etc. The passage is difficult. It may mean either that (a), as rendered here, Grendel could not approach the throne because of his evil deeds, or that (b) Hrothgar could not approach his throne because of the will of God.
177. **destroyer of spirits,** a name given by the Christian poet to the god of the heathen Danes.
194. **Higelac's thane,** Beowulf, the hero of the poem. Higelac (Hygelac) was king of the Geats (Goths), a people settled in southern Sweden or Jutland.
199. **war-king,** Hrothgar.
200. **swan-road,** a kenning for the "sea."
202. **cunning churls,** retainers skilled in arms and council. The word "churl" is used here without any low connotation.
212. **stied,** mounted. Cf. Modern English "stirrup"; *i.e.*, a "sty-rope," a rope to mount by.
223. **nesses,** headlands.
225. **Weders' people,** Geats.
226. **battle-sarks,** shirts of mail.
236. **wood,** spear.
259. **word-hoard unlocked,** spoke. A characteristic epic formula. Cf. l. 2791 f.
268. **Healfdene's son,** Hrothgar. See genealogical tables.
270. **mickle,** great, important.
298. **Wedermark,** the land of the Geats, Beowulf's home.
303. **boar's likeness,** the figure of a boar worn as an ornament on top of the helmet. The boar was sacred to Freyr, a favorite god of the ancient Scandinavians.
307. **the well-built hall,** Heorot.
372. **I knew him of old.** That Hrothgar knows Beowulf and his lineage is evidence of the latter's noble origin.
374. **Hrethel.** See genealogical tables.
408. **many exploits.** The youthful exploits (*enfances*) of a hero are a favorite theme of epic and romance. Of Beowulf's youthful deeds the poet gives us nothing except the swimming match with Breca, introduced incidentally (l. 506 ff.). See also l. 2426 ff.

422. **nickers,** sea-monsters.
445. **Hrethmen,** Danes.
454. **Hrædla's,** Hrethel's. See l. 374. The armor, bequeathed to Beowulf by his grandfather, is here said to have been made by Weland, a famous smith, the Vulcan of Germanic mythology.
455. **Weird,** Fate. The pagan idea of the unalterable character of Destiny, is frequently mentioned by Anglo-Saxon Christian writers. At times Weird is apparently identified with Divine Providence.
467. **Heregar.** See genealogical tables.
493. **bold-minded,** Beowulf and his companions.
499. **Hunferth,** the official orator or spokesman of Hrothgar's court. Cf. l. 1165. His discourtesy, Beowulf implies (l. 531), is due to drunkenness. The word-battle between him and Beowulf is called a *fliting.*
521. **Brondings,** Breca's people. The episode of Beowulf's swimming-match with Breca is famous.
524. **Son of Beanstan,** Breca.
541. **Not at all,** etc. "He could not outswim me; I would not outswim him."
569. **let,** hinder.
570. **Bright beacon,** a common kenning for the sun.
580. **Finns' land,** land of the Laplanders.
607. **giver of treasure,** Hrothgar.
612. **Wealhtheow.** The part here played by the queenly Wealhtheow speaks well for the status of women in early Germanic society.
620. **Helmings'.** The Helmings were the tribe to which Wealhtheow belonged.
634. **I throughout,** etc. "I would fulfill the desire of your people completely."
637. **end-day mine,** my last day.
675. **spoke . . . boastful words.** In early Germanic society the warrior was privileged to boast, provided he made good his words. After the coming of chivalry, with its more sophisticated standards, the ideal gentleman is praised for modesty, and boastfulness is frowned upon. Compare Gawain's words (p. 100b, 30 f.) and what is said of Chaucer's Knight (p. 140, l. 43 ff.).
688. **Warlike.** Supply "Beowulf."
743. **Soon.** Used in the older sense of "immediately."
747. **Warrior,** Beowulf.
761. **Outwards.** Supply "go."
788. **He,** Beowulf.
798. **They knew not.** When they attacked Grendel, they were unaware that the monster could not be injured by mortal weapons.
825. **ere,** formerly.
875. **Sigemund,** son of Wæls (*i.e.*, Wælsing), the father of Fitela (l. 879) by his own sister, Signy. The story told here belongs to a large body of epic tradition which includes the legends of the Volsunga Saga and the Nibelungenlied, made familiar to modern readers by Wagner's operas and William Morris's *Sigurd the Volsung.* In these better known versions of the story it is Sigemund's son, Sigurd or Sigfried, who slays the dragon (cf. l. 886).
891. **Worm,** dragon.
901. **Heremod.** Mentioned here and again (l. 1709 ff.) as a stock example of a bad king. Sigemund is compared with Beowulf, the slayer of monsters and the friend of men; Heremod serves for contrast.
913. **He,** Beowulf.
915. **him,** Heremod.
917. **they,** those coming to see Grendel's hand. The poet, having completed his account of the singer's lay, returns somewhat abruptly to the main thread of his narrative.
924. **mead-path,** path from the women's apartment to the great hall, or mead-house.
928. **thanks.** Note that Christian sentiments are here put into the mouth of a heathen. Cf. note to l. 91. See also l. 1397 ff.
977. **bale,** sorrow.
980. **son of Ecglaf,** Hunferth, who had made little of Beowulf's exploits. See l. 499 ff.
995. **webs,** brocaded tapestries.
1008. **Shall sleep after feast.** Every one must die. Truisms emphasizing the shortness of life and the certainty of death are common in the literature composed under the influence of early English Christianity. Cf. ll. 1386 f., 2590 f. The Anglo-Saxons were fond of aphorisms. Cf. l. 1059.
1017. **Hrothulf,** the nephew of Hrothgar. See genealogical tables. He lives at Hrothgar's court. Nephew and uncle are here at peace (l. 1164); it appears that later they fell out. See note to l. 1181.
1030. **'Round the crown,** etc. The passage seems to mean that the crown of the helmet was crossed by a ridge of wires to prevent its being cut by swords hardened with files.
1035. **earl's defence,** Hrothgar.
1036. **to lead,** etc. During the Middle Ages halls were frequently of such a construction that horses could be led into the building.
1044. **Ingwins,** Danes.
1068. **Finn's sons.** The Lay of Finn, covering lines 1068 to 1159, presents numerous difficulties. It belongs to a larger body of epic material of which part is preserved in a fragment known as the *Fight at Finnsburgh.* It appears that Finn, a Frisian chieftain, abducted Hildeburh, daughter of Hoc, King of Danemark. The father pursued the fugitives, but was slain in

the ensuing fight. Later Hoc's sons, Hnæf and Hengest, invade Finn's country to revenge their father's death, but are both slain — Hengest, by the son of Hunlaf. Two of their retainers, Guthlaf and Oslaf, escape to Danemark and, returning with fresh troops, slay Finn and carry off Hildeburh.

1181. **Hrothulf.** Wealhtheow appeals to Hrothulf (who is none too trustworthy) as the natural guardian of her two sons, Hrethric and Hrothmund (l. 1189).

1190. **The youth.** On formal occasions a special place in the hall was assigned to the "youth" or younger members of the band, who were called *geogoth*, as opposed to the *duguth*, or seasoned warriors of the chieftain's retinue (*comitatus*).

1199. **Brosings' collar.** According to Scandinavian mythology, the Brosings' (really Brisings') necklace belonged originally to the goddess Freyja and was stolen from her by the god Loki. It was later carried off by Hama (Heime) when he fled from Earmenric (the Hermanric of history), king of the Ostrogoths (l. 1201). Another echo of an ancient epic.

1202. **Higelac.** The poet tells us that the collar given to Beowulf passed into the hands of Beowulf's lord Hygelac, who lost it during the encounter which cost him his life. Hygelac is a historical personage who was slain about A.D. 512 while on a raid into Frisian territory (cf. ll. 1207, 2914 ff.). Beowulf, who is said to have escaped by swimming (l. 2360), may also be historical.

1214. **The hall resounded.** That is, resounded with applause when the gifts were given to Beowulf. Having completed the history of the necklace, the poet returns to the scene in Heorot.

1239. **Emptied,** etc. They set aside the movable benches and covered the floor with beds and bolsters for sleeping.

1240. **A certain beer-servant.** Æschere, one of Hrothgar's retinue. He is referred to in l. 1294, but his name is not given till l. 1323.

1243. **boards.** The shields were made of boards.

1248. **in each one.** That is, both at home and on military expeditions.

1261. **Cain.** Cf. l. 107 ff. A modern narrator would hardly indulge in this repetition.

1270. **he,** Beowulf.

1306. **old king,** Hrothgar.

1312. **one of earls,** Beowulf.

1345. **I,** etc. "I have heard my people say that," etc.

1357. Note the passage describing nature (ll. 1357–1375). Such extensive descriptions of nature are rare in Anglo-Saxon poetry. For the underground water, cf. "the sacred river" in Coleridge's *Kubla Khan* (p. 714).

1392. **he.** The reference is of course to Grendel's mother, though Beowulf uses the masculine pronoun.

1412. **He,** probably Hrothgar.

1435. **holm,** sea.

1438. **hooked swords.** The reference is to the boar spears, which were hooked and barbed.

1456. **Hrothgar's orator,** Hunferth. See l. 499 and note.

1457. **Hrunting,** the "Thruster." Ancient Germanic swords frequently had names. This weapon, because of a spell, failed Beowulf at need (l. 1522). Later he returns it to Hunferth (l. 1807).

1485. **Hrethel's son,** Hygelac. See genealogical tables.

1489. **The wonderful sword,** Beowulf's own sword or the one given him by Hrothgar.

1502. **Not sooner,** etc. That is, she did not injure.

1513. **sea-hall.** Beowulf is overcome by Grendel's mother and dragged to her lair, a great hall situated under but free from the water.

1537. **Seized,** etc. Beowulf seized Grendel's mother and threw her on the floor.

1546. **brown-edged,** burnished, bright.

1581. **Slew,** etc. Grendel had seized and eaten fifteen of Hrothgar's men while they slept.

1584. **he,** Beowulf.

1600. **The ninth hour.** Probably the close of the day.

1601. **he,** Hrothgar.

1602. **the strangers,** Beowulf's companions.

1605. **The sword.** The story returns abruptly to Beowulf in the hall under water. Because of the heat of the monster's blood the sword melted in bloodstained drops. Cf. l. 1667.

1686. **Sceden-ig,** the Danish kingdom.

1700. **that he may say,** etc. "Whoever remembers as far back as I do may well say, as I say, that," etc.

1734. **For his lack of wisdom.** So great is his empire that he, because of his folly, expects his kingdom to last forever.

1747. **that cursed spirit,** the devil.

1749. **for boasting,** because of pride.

1801. **joy of heaven,** a kenning for the sun.

1804. **æthelings,** men of noble birth.

1873. **hope of both.** The translation is doubtful. The passage seems to mean that the old king had in mind two alternatives — he might not or he might live to see Beowulf again; he hoped for the latter.

1926. **Hygd,** Hygelac's queen.

1931. **Modthrytho,** etc. Probably a better rendering of this and the following line would be: "Not Thryth's pride showed she (Hygd), folk-queen famed, or that fell deceit." In any case, Thryth, the proud and cruel wife of the Anglian king Offa and the mother of Eomer, is here introduced in striking contrast to the gentle Hygd.

1942. **peace-weaver,** a kenning for a wife.
1945. **kinsman of Heming,** her husband, whom she slew.
1946. **less did inflict.** She inflicted none at all. See note to l. 43.
1948. **given to the young warrior.** Perhaps Thryth belonged to that class of heroines who, like Katherina in Shakespeare's *Taming of the Shrew*, lose their ill nature after they are tamed by the right man.
1963. **the brave,** Beowulf.
1968. **Ongentheow,** king of the Swedes, slain by Hygelac. See genealogical tables. For the strife between the Swedes and the Geats, see ll. 2472 ff., 2922 ff.
1978. **Kinsman.** Hygelac is Beowulf's uncle.
2025. **Froda's . . . son,** Ingeld, son of Froda and king of the Heathobards (l. 1032). The Heathobards are perhaps the Langobards (Lombards), near neighbors of the Angles and Saxons on the Continent.
2036. **bequest of the aged.** Froda, it appears, was slain by a Danish warrior, who leaves the weapon to his son. This son accompanies the young princess Freawaru to Ingeld's court. When the sword is recognized and the circumstances recalled by an old warrior, the feud is reopened. The Dane is killed, but the murderer (" the other," l. 2061) escapes.
2085. **glove.** Or rather a sort of bag into which he intended to stuff his prey.
2158. **Hiorogar,** Heregar. See genealogical tables.
2187. **slothful.** The story of the sluggish, stupid boy who later becomes a hero of renown is a favorite in epic and romance, especially in the literature of Scandinavia.
2190. **earl's defence,** Hygelac.
2199. **better.** The passage seems to mean not that Hygelac was morally " better " than Beowulf but that, being king, he occupied a higher position.
2201. **Hygelac died.** See note to l. 1202.
2202. **Heardred.** See genealogical tables. Heardred was slain by Onela. See also l. 2385 ff.
2205. **Battle-Scylfings.** See note to l. 63.
2206. **nephew of Hereric,** Heardred.
2207. **After Beowulf,** etc. After the death of Hygelac, Beowulf acted as guardian of Heardred. (See l. 2370 ff. and notes.) After Heardred was slain, Beowulf succeeded to the throne and ruled long and well.
2212. **a treasure protected.** The story of a treasure protected by a dragon is a common theme both in Classical and in mediæval tradition. Compare Jason's winning of the Golden Fleece and the story of the Nibelungs referred to above (note to l. 875).
2213. **steep stony mountain.** Great stone mounds, or barrows, are prominent landmarks in certain parts of England. See, for example, Mr. Thomas Hardy's Egdon Heath. Some barrows have been found with a secret entrance somewhat like that described in this passage.
2215. **Some one of men.** The same person as " the innocent warrior (man) " referred to below (ll. 2221 and 2227). The finder of the treasure was banished, though innocent. The stolen vessel he carried as a " peace offering " to his lord (l. 2283).
2233. **Some one of men.** Not the finder of the treasure but some ancient warrior, the last of a noble race, who had concealed the treasure in the barrow and then "banning words spoke." (l. 2246); *i.e.*, laid a curse upon it that it might never be touched. There is a mass of folk-lore about the dangers of meddling with buried treasure. As to the curse, see further l. 3052.
2239. **that,** death.
2275. **He . . . earth.** The translation is a guess. Perhaps better: " He shall seek treasure in the earth."
2300. **That,** the fact that the treasure had been robbed.
2307. **At the will of,** as wished.
2333. **fire-drake,** dragon.
2358. **died.** See note to l. 1202.
2363. **Hetwaras,** one of the tribes against whom Hygelac was fighting when he was slain.
2370. **The child,** Heardred.
2373. **Not sooner.** Beowulf refused the crown but consented to act as guardian of the young king.
2380. **Ohthere's sons.** See genealogical tables.
2384. **A mighty prince,** Onela, who pursued his nephew to the Geats' court and slew Heardred.
2439. **Missed he the mark.** Hæthcyn killed his brother Herebeald by accident.
2441. **fee-less fight.** Under the circumstances the father could claim no wergild or monetary recompense from one brother for killing the other.
2445. **his son hang.** The poet does not mean that Hrethel actually hanged Hæthcyn; he is merely supposing.
2460. **he,** the father.
2487. **the aged Scylfing,** Ongentheow, slain by Eofor.
2488. **sword-pale,** pale in death.
2494. **Gifths,** a name for the Gepidæ, a tribe living near the Baltic Sea.
2502. **Hugs'.** The Hugs were perhaps the Franks, among whom Hygelac met his death. See note to l. 1202.
2546. **burn's,** stream's.
2577. **relic,** sword.
2602. **Weohstan's.** Weohstan, Wiglaf's father, was a kinsman of Hygelac and Beowulf (see above, l. 2151). While in the service of the Swedish king Onela (l. 2616), he had killed Eanmund (l. 2611) and won his arms.

2680. **Nægling,** the name of Beowulf's sword.

2684 ff. **that hand . . . better.** No sword Beowulf tried could stand his strength. Epic heroes, especially those who, like Beowulf, were slothful in youth, are apt to be represented as possessing superhuman strength.

2695. **The earl,** Wiglaf.

2738 f. **nor . . . swore many oaths falsely.** That is, "I swore no false oaths."

2756. **The seat.** That is, the seat where Beowulf was.

2772. **took.** That is, "had taken."

2785. **the high-minded,** Beowulf.

2791 f. **word's point . . . breast-hoard.** A dignified poetic phrase for "spoke."

2805. **Whale's ness.** Other epic poets represent their heroes as buried beside the sea. In the *Odyssey* (xxiv, 103), for example, Achilles' bones are buried under a mound overlooking the Hellespont.

2814. **Wægmundingas,** the family to which Beowulf and Wiglaf belong. See genealogical tables.

2829. **leavings of hammers,** a kenning for swords.

2836 ff. **to few of men throve,** etc. Few (*i.e.*, none) succeeded in meeting the dragon's breath.

2846. **cowardly ones,** the rest of Beowulf's companions.

2860 f. **from the youth . . . valor.** Any one who had yielded to fear, easily got an answer from Wiglaf. Wiglaf did not hesitate to express his opinion of the cowards.

2880. **He . . . worse,** his strength constantly waned.

2881. **stronger.** Read "less strongly."

2892. **hedge,** enclosure, fortification.

2895 ff. **in expectance . . . man.** They were in doubt whether Beowulf would meet his "final day" (*i.e.*, death) or would return alive.

2899–3025. These lines, giving the speech of the herald or messenger, may be omitted at the first reading.

2977. **Thane of Hygelac,** Eofor, who avenged the blow dealt his brother Wulf (l. 2993).

3015 ff. **No earl shall wear,** etc. The herald foresees misfortune as a result of Beowulf's death.

3041. **scorched with flames,** burned by his own fire.

3050. **A thousand winters.** Poetical exaggeration. The phrase merely signifies a long time.

3119. **barb,** point of the arrow.

3147. **house of bone,** a kenning for human body.

3150. **the spouse.** That this is the only reference in the poem to Beowulf's queen is not surprising. Generally speaking, women play only a minor part in popular heroic poetry. Perhaps Beowulf had married Hygd. So far as we know, however, he had no immediate family ties and hence, by his lonely position, was better fitted for the single-minded deeds of unselfishness and heroism that mark the ideal epic hero.

CÆDMON

38b HYMN

Because of its antiquity the so-called Hymn is here given in the original as well as in translation. The Anglo-Saxon version represents the Old English language as written in the northern monasteries during the eighth century after Christ. Cædmon is often referred to as "the father of English poetry" and several metrical paraphrases of biblical stories were attributed to him as early as the seventeenth century, but these are now known to be the work of several authors and the Hymn is the only composition that can with any degree of probability be assigned to the heaven-inspired poet whose legend is so beautifully told by Bede in one of our selections (pp. 45 f.).

7. **middle-yard.** A common expression for "the earth," derived from pagan Germanic mythology. It implies an abode above and another below the earth.

38b JUDITH

The author of *Judith* is unknown. The poem is based on the book of Judith, one of the books of the Bible which, though excluded from the Canon (and hence called apocryphal), was extremely popular during the Middle Ages. Although a part of the beginning of the poem is lacking, the portion preserved gives the impression of an artistic whole, and probably not much is lost. The Hebrew city of Bethulia is menaced by an Assyrian army under the command of the redoubtable Holofernes. Judith, a Hebrew maiden, cuts off Holofernes' head while the heathen lies in a drunken stupor, and, accompanied by her maidservant, carries back the trophy to Bethulia. The Assyrians are now routed by the Hebrews. The author of our poem thinks of the characters and the action in terms of Germanic rather than Hebrew conditions. The warriors might well have stepped out of *Beowulf*, and Judith, no longer a Hebrew, has become an orthodox Christian with a high and holy mission. The poem dates probably from the ninth century. The translation is by Henry Morley.

20. **his woe,** his benighted, hence woeful, condition.

21 ff. **There were,** etc. The description of

the drinking scene is famous. It is based on a bare suggestion in the original.

85 ff. **Son of the Almighty,** etc. Judith, though a Hebrew, includes the Christian Savior in her petition.

106. **Scather-foe,** enemy who works harm.

198 ff. **lank wolf . . . raven.** The wolf and the raven (or eagle) are constantly represented in Old English epic poetry as hovering around the battle field and feeding on the corpses. See also l. 275.

228. **thanes.** The leaders of the Assyrian army are transformed into Anglo-Saxon thanes. See also " earls " in l. 308 and note.

PROSE

42a ADAMNAN

Adamnan was born about A.D. 625 in Donegal, Ireland. He entered the monastery of Iona, where he rose to the dignity of abbot in 679. He was noted for his piety and learning. He died in 709. He was a kinsman of St. Columba and wrote in Latin his biography within a century after the great missionary's death. Adamnan's *Life of Columba* is one of the most complete biographies written during the Middle Ages and as such gives us a valuable picture of early Christian culture in the north of Britain.

LIFE OF COLUMBA

Columba (521–597) was the great Irish missionary who introduced Christianity into the north of Britain as Augustine did into the south. He was of royal blood and was prominent both as a statesman and as an ecclesiastic. He became famous for his activity in copying manuscripts, in founding churches, and in spreading the Gospel among the Celts of Ireland and Scotland. In 563 he emigrated to Scotland, where he founded the monastery of Iona on a small island off the coast of the larger island of Mull. From Iona Christian culture spread throughout a large part of Scotland and as far south as Northumbria.

43a 3. **oratory,** a small chapel set apart for private prayer.

19. **So far the Saint.** The words mark the close of the quotation.

44a 11. **Scotic . . . Dalriadic.** During the early Middle Ages the term " Scotic " was applied to the Irish Celts. During the fifth or sixth century after Christ a band of Irish crossed from Antrim to the opposite coast of Scotland and founded the Dalriadic kingdom in what is now Argyleshire. The prophecy foretells that the Celts of Ireland and Scotland alike shall honor Iona.

26. **Baithene.** Said to have been Columba's nephew.

44b BEDE

Bede, usually called the Venerable, was the most learned theologian and the most accurate Church historian of early England. He was brought up in Wearmouth Abbey, and spent most of his life in the neighboring monastery of Jarrow, where he imbibed the simple, ardent faith and mysticism of the Irish monks settled in Northumbria. (Read his account of himself, p. 47.) He was a man of varied interests and broad knowledge. Besides his *Ecclesiastical History of the English People* (written in Latin), from which our selections are taken, he composed treatises on metrics and natural history and lives of saints and martyrs. His style is simple and clear, and conveys, even when viewed through the medium of the present English translation, a vivid impression of the glowing enthusiasm and childlike faith which breathes through the life of early Christian England. The translation is that of J. A. Giles, 1843.

ECCLESIASTICAL HISTORY OF THE ENGLISH NATION

44b 27. **man of God,** Paulinus. The Roman missionary Augustine landed in England in 595. Paulinus, one of his followers, accompanied the Kentish princess Æthelburh when she went north to become the wife of Eadwine (Edwin), the powerful king of Northumbria (617–633). The conversion of Edwin took place in 627.

29. **that sign,** the laying of his hand on the king's head. The sign was intended to remind Edwin of his promise made to a heavenly visitor before he became king.

45a 28 ff. **The present life of man,** etc. The following passage has been often quoted as an admirable example of an extended simile.

45b 52 ff. **The Poet Cædmon.** For directness, simplicity, and genuine artistry the story of Cædmon has rarely been surpassed. It is probably not altogether the product of Bede's imagination, for there are other mediæval tales of men inspired to compose in dreams, and Coleridge wrote his famous *Kubla Khan* (p. 714) under similar circumstances.

46a 6. **English, which was his native language.** The word "English" was first used of the tongue of the Angles, among whom Cædmon lived. Later the name was applied to the speech of the Anglo-Saxons in general.

46a 45 ff. **How,** etc. This is Bede's Latin prose version of Cædmon's Hymn. The Anglo-Saxon text is given on p. 38.

47a 19. **The Eucharist,** Holy Communion, the Lord's Supper.

33. **viaticum,** provision for a journey. Here applied to the last communion administered before death.

THE ANGLO-SAXON CHRONICLE

The Anglo-Saxon Chronicle began as a series of records kept by various Saxon monasteries, the monks of each monastery inscribing in their chronicle brief disconnected notes of events which seemed important to them. Toward the close of the ninth century the chronicle kept at Winchester was gone over and filled out until it became a sort of national history. The work of revision is attributed to King Alfred the Great. After Alfred's death (901) the chronicle at Peterborough was continued till nearly a century after the Norman Conquest. It ceases at the year 1154. Though rude and condensed, the Anglo-Saxon Chronicle is often vigorous in style and is the most important existing source for the history of early England.

47b 45. **A.D. 435.** Alaric, king of the Goths, captured Rome A.D. 410. The consequent withdrawal of the Roman legions from Britain, which they had held since the invasions of Julius Cæsar (the Gaius Julius referred to in l. 51), left the country at the mercy of the Germanic invaders. This event made a profound impression upon the minds of the people. This and the following entry (A.D. 449) are of course not contemporary with the events.

52. **A.D. 449.** This date is incorrect. Marcian and Valentinian III became joint rulers of the Roman Empire A.D. 450. The Germanic invasion here described took place probably about A.D. 428.

48a 7. **Picts,** a people occupying a portion of the north of Scotland. They are often referred to as joining with the Scots (Irish) against the Britons or the Anglo-Saxons.

30. **Woden,** the highest of the ancient Germanic gods. Mediæval genealogists were fond of tracing noble families back to divine ancestors.

48b 15. **alderman,** chief officer of a shire or county.

49a 8. **A.D. 897.** The correct date is A.D. 896. The passage describes the last great campaign of Alfred against the Vikings.

25. **horse-thane,** a marshal, an officer of the royal household who had charge of the horses.

31. **esks.** The esk (*æsc*) was a kind of Danish ship.

49b 15. **Frieslander.** Alfred's men were not very good sailors, so the king made some use of the Frisians because of their experience in nautical matters.

17. **neat-herd,** keeper of cattle.

34. **A.D. 1137.** The remainder of the selection is a translation of one of the last entries in the version of the Chronicle written at Peterborough Abbey, in Northampton. Besides representing the Middle English language as written less than a century after the Norman Conquest, it is extremely valuable as a source for the history of the troubled period of Stephen and Matilda. It is against such a historical background as this that Scott presents the action of *Ivanhoe,* though the events are placed somewhat later.

38. **his treasure.** The treasure is said to have amounted to £100,000.

43. **council at Oxford.** The council was held in June, 1139.

53 ff. **every rich man . . . him.** Every rich (*i.e.,* powerful) man built himself castles and held them against Stephen.

50a 21. **crucet-house.** Literally, "torture-house."

27. **Rachenteges.** Literally, "chain fetters."

40. **tenserie,** a kind of irregular taxation. This and other French words found in the original furnish valuable evidence that the importation of French into the English vocabulary had already begun.

49. **for a while.** More probably to be translated "formerly."

50b 13. **To till . . . the sea.** To plough the ground was as futile as to attempt to cultivate the sea.

14. **corn,** grain, not maize, or Indian corn.

16. **Christ . . . saints.** Christ and the saints no longer cared for the welfare of men.

50b KING ALFRED

Alfred ranks as one of the noblest sovereigns who ever ruled in England. When, after a bitter struggle, he succeeded in saving his native Wessex from the Danish yoke, he set himself wholeheartedly and disinterestedly to re-establish the Christian culture which had existed before the Danes began their destructive invasions (A.D. 787). From the close of the seventh through most of the eighth century learning had so flourished in England, especially in the monasteries of the north, that students came even from abroad to study in English institutions. The low state to which learning had fallen by 871 Alfred describes in the passage translated here. In order to remedy the evil, Alfred, like Charlemagne nearly a century before, gathered scholars about him and encouraged learning. He translated into the vernacular several highly esteemed Latin works, among them Pope Gregory's famous treatise on the duties of the clergy, and to him has been attributed an important part in compiling the Anglo-Saxon Chronicle. The translation is that of the Jubilee edition of Alfred's Works, 1858.

PREFACE TO THE *CURA PASTORALIS*

50b 22. The *Cura Pastoralis* is the work of Pope Gregory the Great (*ca.* 540–604). It deals with the duties of the office of bishop and was long held in high esteem as an authority — facts which explain Alfred's having copies of his translation placed "in each bishop's see" in the kingdom (see p. 51b l. 41).

50b 26. **Wærferth,** Bishop of Worcester.

30. **formerly,** that is, before the Danish invasion. Lindisfarne, Whitby (the home of Cædmon), Jarrow (that of Bede), and other Northumbrian monasteries first came into prominence as centres of culture early in the eighth century. A century or so later, after the coming of the Danes, the chief centres of culture were in Alfred's own kingdom. The best period of Anglo-Saxon learning was that of Alcuin (730?–804), who was educated in Northumbria and who, after the Scandinavians had begun their work of destruction, was called (790) by Charlemagne to help restore the culture of France.

49. **the Humber.** The river Humber marked the southern boundary of Northumbria.

50. **service,** religious service.

51a 2. **Thames.** The river Thames marked roughly the northern boundary of Alfred's dominions.

3. **When I . . . kingdom.** Alfred came to the throne A.D. 871.

5. **Stall,** pulpit.

18. **them,** the churches.

19. **laid waste,** etc. The Danes, being heathen, showed no respect for the Christian churches, but plundered and burned them without scruple.

42. **reckless,** ill advised.

47. **the Law,** the divine law as given in the Old Testament. Alfred here argues for translating into the vernacular.

51b 10 ff. **so bring it about . . . that,** etc. Alfred here urges the importance of elementary popular education.

11. **rest,** peace, quietude.

31. **Pastoralis . . . Hind's book.** "Hind's book," *i.e.,* "shepherd's book." The Latin word *pastor,* from which the adjective *pastoralis* is derived, means "shepherd"; the bishop is the pastor or shepherd of his people.

42. **æstel,** a book-mark or clasp.

43. **mancuses,** coins of the value of 30 pence each.

46. **minster,** monastery. The word is preserved in the name "Westminster." It has no connection with "minister" or the Latin *ministerium.*

47. **so learned bishops.** Conditions had improved greatly during Alfred's time.

51. **write others,** that is, make manuscript copies. It should be remembered that in the centuries before the invention of printing, books were multiplied only by copying out with the hand. The mediæval monks were, however, industrious transcribers and manuscripts were not so rare as one might imagine.

52a ÆLFRIC

Ælfric was educated under Bishop Æthelwold, who flourished about the middle of the tenth century and was active in carrying on the work of disseminating culture begun by Alfred. Ælfric is chiefly memorable for his educational and religious writings. Besides compiling a work for teaching Latin by the conversational method and a glossary which is the first Latin-English dictionary, he composed some eighty homilies, or sermons, on the lives of the saints venerated by the Anglo-Saxon church. Ælfric's homilies were designed to be spoken, not read as Alfred's prose was. The order of the words is so rhythmical as to suggest verse almost as much as prose, and the general effect is that of clearness and finish. Ælfric's style shows a distinct advance over that of Alfred. The translation is that of Benjamin Thorpe, *Homilies of the Anglo-Saxon Church* (Ælfric Society), 1844.

THE SECOND SUNDAY AFTER PENTECOST

52a 2. **Pentecost,** also called Whitsunday.

4. **Homo quidam,** etc. This is the text for the sermon that follows. In the King James translation it runs: "There was a certain rich man, which was clothed in purple and fine linen and fared sumptuously every day" (Luke XVI, 19). It forms the beginning of Jesus' famous story of the Rich Man and Lazarus. Ælfric, following the custom of the Catholic Church, quotes his text from

the Latin Vulgate. In Ælfric's day only a small part of the Bible had been translated into English.

14. **pope Gregory.** See note, p. 50b, 22.

34. **in another place,** Matthew xi, 7–15.

52b 53. **vapour.** A translation of the Latin word *chaos* (vs. 26), which in the King James version is rendered "gulf."

53a 9. **fordone,** undone, ruined.

42. **dark likeness,** in the older sense of body or background.

53b 10 ff. **Gain,** etc. Christ's actual words as given in the King James version are: "Make to yourselves friends of the mammon of unrighteousness; that when ye fail, they may receive you into everlasting habitations" (Luke xvi, 9).

22 ff. **I was hungry,** etc. Matthew xxv, 35–36.

27. **Lycaonia,** a district of Asia Minor.

48 **Martyrius.** There are several mediæval saints named Martyrius. According to tradition the one referred to here lived in Lycaonia and, after his death, his relics were deposited in the diocese of Toulouse in France. One of the breviaries of the Roman Church gives his feast day as August 26. The story suggests the legend of St. Christopher, who carried Christ disguised as a little child over a river.

54a 5 ff. **That which ye do,** etc. Compare Matthew xxv, 40: "Inasmuch as ye have done it unto one of the least of these my brethren, ye have done it unto me."

ANSELM

Though an Italian by birth, Anselm spent nearly half his life in Normandy and was for more than a decade (1093–1109) Archbishop of Canterbury. He has been well called the second Augustine (not the person of that name who brought Christianity to England but the great author of *The City of God*). Skilled in the niceties of mediæval logic and fired with a burning enthusiasm for spiritual truth, he wrote voluminously — discussions of various theological questions, prayers, sermons, and letters.

The *Proslogium* (from which our selection is translated) and the *Monologium* are Latin treatises on God, His existence and attributes. Throughout his writings Anselm takes his stand on a high plane: the seeker after religious truth can understand only if he believes first. Unbelievers, he says, fail to understand because they do not believe; we strive to understand because we do believe. In religion faith plays the same part that experience does in worldly things. In clarity of style and in spiritual fervor Anselm's works furnish an admirable example of the type of religious writings which was to influence English religious and didactic literature for the next three centuries.

33. **thy Word, that is, thy Son.** Compare John i, 1: "In the beginning was the Word, and the Word was with God, and the Word was God," and John i, 14: "The Word was made flesh, and dwelt among us."

55a 7. **Wisdom v. 15.** The reference is to the Wisdom of Solomon, one of the apocryphal books of the Bible and hence not to be found in the version used by the Protestant Church. The verse reads: "But the righteous live for evermore; their reward also is with the Lord, and the care of them is with the Most High."

56b 6 ff. **thou dost command . . . ask.** The reference is to one of Christ's oft-quoted sayings in the famous Sermon on the Mount: "Ask, and it shall be given you; seek, and ye shall find; knock, and it shall be opened unto you" (Matthew vii, 7).

MIDDLE ENGLISH PERIOD

IRISH

59a THE FEAST OF BRICRIU

THE CHAMPION'S BARGAIN

The Feast of Bricriu (pronounced Bríc-riu) is one of the finest of the older sagas of Ireland. "The Champion's Bargain," which forms the closing episode of the story in its present form, was originally an independent tale and as such may be considered as a separate literary entity. It should be known to all students of English literature, not only because it is an early example of good story-telling in the literature of the British Isles but also because it represents the Celtic source of the most distinguished piece of Middle English narrative poetry outside the works of Chaucer. An Irish story of a beheading game similar to that described in "The Champion's Bargain" furnished the inspiration for the picture of the Green

Knight, and for Gawain's exploit at the beginning and the return blow at the end of the fourteenth-century English romance of *Gawain and the Green Knight.* See especially pp. 98 ff. and 117 ff.

The *Feast of Bricriu* belongs to the Ulster or Red Branch cycle of early Irish literature (which includes also the Ossianic cycle [see note to p. 62b] and the so-called Mythological cycle). The stories of the Ulster cycle centre around the court of King Connor (Conchobar), who, according to tradition, ruled ancient Ulster about the beginning of the Christian era. Many of the Red Branch tales, such as the *Feast of Bricriu*, recount the exploits of the youthful Cuchulainn (pronounced: Cu-hoolin), beloved hero of early Irish epic and romance. In its present form the *Feast of Bricriu* consists of a series of loosely connected episodes in which Cuchulainn, Conall, and Leary (Loegaire) — the three most renowned champions of Ulster — contend by feats of bravery for the choicest tidbits ("the hero's portion") of a feast given by Bricriu. The final and deciding contest is described in our selection. "The Champion's Bargain" is based on a widespread folk-tale of a supernatural being whose head comes off and on with ease and who proposes to mortals a game which only the chosen hero can win. Sometimes, as in the story of the Sphynx in Greek mythology, the uncanny creature asks a riddle; in other versions, as in the Irish story, he proposes a beheading game. In certain Slavic countries there is a terrible supernatural woman who asks difficult questions of mortals that happen to come under her influence and slays them if they cannot answer.

The author of the *Feast of Bricriu* is unknown.

5. **Emain,** pronounced: Ǻvin. Emain, or Emain Macha, as it is usually called, was the capital of ancient Ulster. To-day nothing of it remains except an extensive artificial earthwork, the ruins of the mound on which the ancient palace (doubtless thought of as much like Hrothgar's hall in *Beowulf*, l. 78 and note) and its outbuildings are said to have stood. As the Ulster sagas go back to a period before the establishment of a centralized government in Ireland, Tara, the capital of Ireland immortalized by Tom Moore in "The Harp that once through Tara's Halls" (p. 805), had not yet become a centre of romantic tradition. Emain, now called "Navan fort," is situated near the little town of Navan in county Louth not far from the hill of Tara.

6. **Conchobar,** king of Ulster. His character is more typical of the popular epic than are the characters of Hrothgar and Hygelac in *Beowulf*. He is not always portrayed in a favorable light; he is often deceitful, and, although elderly, is uxorious. The Irish pagan epics have in general been less christianized than those of the Anglo-Saxons and hence are more valuable as pictures of pre-Christian culture. Read the introductory note to *Beowulf*, p. 1.

6. **Fergus mac Roig.** Fergus mac Roig (pronounced: Rő-igh) is the chief noble of Connor's court.

10. **Cuchulainn,** the chief hero of the Ulster cycle. According to tradition, his name, originally Setanta, was changed to Cu-Chulainn (Hound of Culann) because, when a little boy, he slew a terrible watch-dog belonging to the Ulster smith Culann, and, to make amends, took the animal's place. Irish saga writers never tired of recounting his exploits. He has been called the Achilles of ancient Irish epic literature. He is the son of King Connor's sister (or daughter) by a supernatural father. Like other popular heroes, he is precocious. He begins his heroic deeds at the age of seven. One of the finest epic passages preserved from the literature of the Middle Ages describes his death, which took place when he was twenty-seven years old. His stronghold is placed by tradition at Dun Delgan (modern Dundalk). Though boastful, vindictive, and cruel, he is not without feelings of modesty, friendship, and honor, and is doubtless intended to exemplify the ideals of pagan Celtic chivalry. Contrast the character of Beowulf.

10. f. **Conall . . . Laegaire.** See introductory note to the *Feast of Bricriu.*

38. **Duach of the Chafer Tongue,** so called because of his rough, biting, satirical speech. Duach (pronounced: Dōō-ach) is the doublet of Bricriu, called "Poison-Tongue" because of the bitterness of his language. Both are usually represented as fomenting strife and discord. They are stock epic figures corresponding to Thersites in the Homeric epic, and to Sir Kay in Arthurian romance.

59b 1. **Erin,** Ireland.

2. **Alba,** Britain.

3. **Scythia,** an ancient name for the remoter northern regions of Europe and Asia.

4. **Pillars of Hercules,** the two great promontories that guard the straits of Gibraltar.

5. **Brigantium,** in Spain.

5. **Gades,** Cadiz. This and the other names of places are doubtless introduced merely to indicate vaguely a vast extent of territory.

22. **Sencha mac Ailill,** pronounced: Shĕn-cha mac Ăl-ill. Sencha is the type of the old, wise counselor — a stock epic figure.

31. **I may cut off his head.** The giant, with grim humor, at first proposes the beheading game in reverse order. The real bargain, which seems so "strange" to the mortals, is that the first blow shall be given by the Ulsterman, the return blow on the next night by the giant.

35. **Munremar, son of Gercenn,** literally, "Fat-Neck son of Short-Head," next to Cuchulainn one of the most redoubtable heroes of Ulster. His nickname is said to have been derived from the fact that a Connaught warrior cast a spear at him and struck him in the neck, which swelled and became thick in consequence.

40. **centaurs,** mythical creatures, half men and half horses, who figure in Greek mythology as especially savage and strong. They fought against Hercules.

47. f. **By my people's god.** Just what gods the pagan Irish worshipped is doubtful. They probably adored the sun and other natural objects such as fountains and trees.

60a 36. ff. **Loegaire . . . . Conall.** Clearly Loegaire and Conall agreed to the bargain and beheaded the giant, but failed to keep the promise to abide the return blow.

38. **Champion's Portion,** the choicest part of the feast prepared by Bricriu and described at the beginning of the saga. It consisted of a hogshead of wine, a whole boar, a bull, and a hundred gigantic cakes cooked in honey. The strain of burlesque which runs through the *Feast of Bricriu* and other Irish sagas has been compared with the work of the great French humorist Rabelais.

60b 25. f. **I would rather have death with honor.** This is a fine epic sentiment. Cuchulainn's delicate sense of personal honor is emphasized elsewhere in Irish literature.

34. **stretched out his neck,** etc. Cuchulainn is noted for his contortions, some even more fantastic than this.

61a CONNLA OF THE GOLDEN HAIR, AND THE FAIRY MAIDEN

The story of Connla is an admirable example of the type of ancient Celtic tale that stimulated the imagination of continental and English poets during the Middle Ages and produced an abundant crop of romances and lays telling of love affairs between seductive fairy women and their mortal lovers. Such stories have furnished a storehouse for English poets from Chaucer till the nineteenth century. Read the introductory note to *Guingamor* (p. 70). Connla's departure to fairy land should be compared with the Passing of Arthur as described by Layamon (p. 97), Malory (p. 134b, 14 ff.), and Tennyson (p. 913, l. 361 ff.). The author is unknown.

26. **Conn the Hundred-fighter,** according to tradition, high-king of Ireland from A.D. 123 to 158.

27. **Hill of Usna,** one of the royal residences, situated in the district now known as Westmeath.

32. **Land of the Living,** also called "Land of the Young" (*Tír na n-Óg*, pronounced: Tēēr na nōag) and the "Pleasant Plain" (Moy Mell): see l. 45, below. It is the earthly paradise or Elysium of the pagan Irish. It is localized in various places, frequently, as here, on an island in the Atlantic Ocean. To this land of perpetual pleasure and eternal summer chosen mortals were sometimes transported, there to enjoy youth and love for ever, or to return only to find, like Guingamor (p. 74a), that what had seemed an absence of three days had really been three hundred years.

61b 7. **druid.** Little is known of the specific functions of the Irish druids. Like the medicine-men of the American Indians, they practiced magic and acted as intermediaries between mortals and the powers of the unseen world. Here the druid by his "medicine" counteracts the charm of the fairy woman.

9. **fairy woman,** a rendering of the Irish *bean-sidhe* (pronounced: bånshee), literally "woman of the *shee*, or fairy hill." The fairy woman of early Irish literature, like the fée of Arthurian romance, is young, beautiful, dignified, imperious. The modern Irish banshee is generally thought of as a lugubrious old hag whose appearance foretells death or other misfortune. Modern Irish fairies still carry off mortals to the other world.

20. **apple.** In folk-lore the apple is the symbol of love. Apple-trees figure prominently in the earthly paradise of the Celts. The *Avalun* to which Arthur departs in Layamon's *Brut* (p. 97, l. 325) is popularly supposed to be one of the names for the Celtic other world and to be connected with the Welsh word *avall* (apple). Tennyson makes his Arthur refer to it as "Avilion . . . with orchard lawns" (p. 913, l. 427 ff.).

47. **A just one.** The reference is to St. Patrick, who, according to tradition, overcame the druids.

62a 14. **canoe.** The Irish writer had in mind a *curragh* (cf. p. 62b, l. 26), or framework covered with skins — a type of boat used by the ancient Irish.

62b OSSIAN

Most students of English literature are aware that the rhythmical prose poems published between 1760 and 1763 by James Macpherson (see p. 588 ff.) and by him attributed to a mythical third-century Caledonian bard named Ossian are spurious, but few students are acquainted with the large body of authentic Gaelic poetry composed during the Middle Ages and attributed to the mythical Irish poet Ossian. The poems here translated are printed in order to illustrate the kind of literature that furnished the background for Macpherson's greatly admired imitations. Like Macpherson's work, it is tinged with melancholy, but it is simple and direct, whereas Macpherson's *Ossian* is grandiose and vague. The Ossian of authentic tradition was an Irishman, the son of the famous Finn mac Cumhail (Co͞o-ul), who figures in mediæval Irish legend as the leader of the Fiana, a distinguished band of hunters and warriors whose exploits took place, according to the Irish annals, in the third century after Christ. In the earliest Irish Ossianic literature Ossian is not the only poet who sings the exploits of Finn's band; gradually he became the bard *par excellence* of the Fiana. As seen through the eyes of eighteenth-century sentimentalists, he was a great natural genius — the Homer of the ancient Celts. The earliest Ossianic poetry is not melancholy in tone, but as the centuries progress, the poems attributed to Ossian embody more and more Ireland's longing for her departed glories. The name "Ossian" (spelled in Irish "Osin," "Oisin") is pronounced Ŭsh-een in Munster, Ŏsh-in in Ulster and in Scotland.

WELSH

63a THE MABINOGION

The literary men of ancient Wales practiced a highly technical art and were required to undergo a very careful training. Speaking strictly, the *Mabinogion* (pronounced: Măb-i-nō-gion) includes a group of four mediæval Welsh tales (called the "Four Branches of the Mabinogi") which formed a sort of textbook for the young *mabinog*, or aspirant to the title of bard. More generally, the term "Mabinogion" is applied to a collection of some dozen stories (including the four just referred to) which illustrate the cultural and literary background of mediæval Wales. Although written in Welsh, they should be known to all students of English literature for more than one reason. First, they are told in delightful style and are packed with motifs drawn from the superstition and fancies of the folk. Even more important is the fact that they help us to visualize the cultural background against which some of the most fascinating of the legends of the Round Table should be viewed. The Four Branches (from one of which our selection is taken) do not mention Arthur and hence may go back to ancient pagan Welsh mythology before Arthur became a popular hero. Others of the *Mabinogion* contain Arthurian figures, but represent them as highly grotesque and markedly different from the courtly knights of Anglo-Norman romance. See the note to Geoffrey of Monmouth's *History*, p. 75a.

PWYLL PRINCE OF DYVED

Pwyll, pronounced: Po͞o-ill, the *ll* sounded somewhat like the *lli* in "million." Pwyll was an ancient, probably mythical, Welsh prince, said to have been a contemporary of King Arthur. **Dyved,** pronounced: Dŭv-eth. "Dyved" is an ancient name for the western part of South Wales. The *mabinogi* of *Pwyll* combines a number of folk-lore themes often used both in mediæval and in modern popular fiction. Especially noteworthy is the story of Rhiannon, who, like Connla's mistress (p. 61) and the fairy heroines of numerous Arthurian romances and Breton lays, visits mortal soil in search of her lover.

16. **Gorsedd Arberth,** the mound (or seat) of Arberth (or Narberth, l. 10 above). Such mounds are often associated in Celtic tradition with supernatural appearances or with buried treasure, and hence are dangerous. See the notes to *Beowulf*, ll. 2213 and 2223.

64a 52 f. **My chief quest . . . thee.** So in Arthurian romance fairy ladies are not slow in betraying the purpose of their visits.

64b 4. **Rhiannon** (pronounced: Rēēan-on), one of the most charming and unfortunate of the heroines of mediæval romance. She belongs to a long line of ladies in folk-lore and romance who, in the face of the greatest misfortunes, carry to incredible lengths the virtue of patience under adversity. Perhaps the most famous example is Griselda, another heroine of mediæval romance. The mediævals were fond of depicting virtues and vices carried to extremes.

5. **Heveydd Hên** (pronounced: Hĕv-a-ith Hane), Heveydd "the Old," another probably mythical Welsh king.

52. **Nay.** The stranger who arrives just in time for dinner and enforces a request by refusing to accept hospitality till his boon be granted is a common figure in mediæval romance.

65a 3 ff. **'What boon . . . have.'** Custom required that King Arthur and other worthies of mediæval romance should grant whatever boon was asked on a high festival. When once the king's promise was given, it must be kept at any cost (see l. 23 below).

20. **Gwawl,** pronounced: Goo-owl.

66a 50. **sureties.** That is, sureties that he will keep his promise.

67b 51. **Teirnyon Twryv Vliant,** pronounced: Têir-nion Too-riv Vlee-ant.

52. **Gwent Is Coed,** an ancient name for the eastern division of South Wales. Compare the position of Dyved (note to *Pwyll*, p. 63a, above).

68a 24. **struck off the arm.** Compare the scene in *Beowulf* (p. 11, l. 815 ff.), where the hero tears off Grendel's arm. Both *Beowulf* and *Pwyll* illustrate the ancient and oft-repeated theme of the haunted house — a building beset by a demon or other supernatural creature. In a folk-tale from the South the hero cuts off the claw of a demon cat and so rids a dwelling of the monster's visits.

68b 6. **Gwri Wallt Euryn,** Gwri (pronounced: Goor-ee) "of the golden hair."

69b 9. **Pendaran,** pronounced: Pen-dăran. According to tradition, Pendaran was a powerful Welsh chieftain and possessed an immense herd of swine.

10. **Pryderi,** pronounced: Prid-ĕri. The name is suggested by the fact that Rhiannon has just used the word *pryderi*, which means "trouble."

70a 7. **Cantrevs.** The *cantrev*, literally "a hundred villages," was a measure of land used anciently both in Britain and in Ireland.

11. **Ystrad Tywi,** part of Carmarthenshire.

ANGLO-NORMAN FRENCH

THE LAY OF GUINGAMOR

Guingamor (pronounced: Gwin-ga-more) belongs to a group of short narrative poems written mostly in French during the twelfth and thirteenth centuries and known as "Breton" lays because of their supposed origin in the Celtic folk-lore of Brittany or Britain (*Bretagne*). Some of them were translated into Middle English. Chaucer's *Franklin's Tale* claims to be a Breton lay. They are generally love stories and include such folk-lore themes as human beings transformed into wolves (were-wolves), self-effacing wives (see note to p. 64b 4), boats that sail by magic, and mortals enamored of fairy women. *Guingamor*, one of the most fascinating of the Breton lays, is based on a theme that was widely popular both on the continent and in England — the story of a mortal beloved by a fairy woman (compare *Connla*, p. 61 ff. and *Pwyll*, p. 63 ff.) and by her lured through the agency of a fairy hunt to her happy other world. In no less than three Breton lays (one in Middle English) the hero is tempted by a queen, refuses her love, wins a fairy mistress, and departs to dwell in her land. In *Guingamor*, as in numerous Celtic and other folk-tales, the hero returns to mortal soil only to find that he has been absent for three hundred years. Compare the story of Herla, p. 82b.

Of the writers of Breton lays, Marie of France is deservedly the most famous. Little is known of her life. She was certainly well educated and was probably a lady of rank. Though born in France, she lived and wrote in England, perhaps at the court of Henry II (1154–1189), and although she wrote in French, her work deserves to be recognized as part of the literary heritage of the English people. Taking as the subject of her poems stories told in the Norman castles by minstrels who were acquainted with Celtic tradition, she wrote in clear and simple style and with admirable narrative art.

14. **Brittany.** The translation is uncertain; the rendering should perhaps be Britain.

23 ff. **he knew how to promise . . . courtesy.** Guingamor, like Chaucer's knight (p. 140b, l. 45 ff.), was a perfect gentleman according to the standards of Chivalry. Our ideals in this respect have improved little since the Middle Ages.

30. **bled.** Until comparatively recent years "bleeding" was practiced not only as a remedy but also as a preventive against disease.

35. **seneschal,** a sort of steward of the royal household, who had charge of feasts and other domestic ceremonies.

70b 24. **The queen.** The behavior of the queen and of Guingamor on this occasion should be compared with the story of Potiphar's wife and Joseph in the Bible (Genesis xxxix).

72a 31. **burghers,** citizens.

72b 50 ff. **the adventurous land . . . the perilous river . . . the meadow-land.** These are all stock features of descriptions of journeys to fairyland.

73b 8. **taking her robes.** The explanation of this unknightly act, so contrary to Guingamor's general character, is to be found in the nature of the story on which the lay is based. The girl here introduced is a supernatural being somewhat like a swan-maiden — a type of creature who lays aside her swan garment or skin at times and can be captured only by the one who gets possession of her covering. Fairies, swan-maidens, and witches easily become confused in the popular mind. Compare the capture of the fairy woman in Walter Map's story (p. 83a).

48 ff. **He looked upon her gently,** etc. Compare the love at first sight in *Connla* (p. 61a), *Pwyll* (p. 64a), and *Courtiers' Trifles* (p. 83b).

74a 14. **Each knight . . . lady.** Lovers accompanied by perpetual fairy mistresses are a common feature in the fairy world of Celtic folklore and mediæval courtly romance.

74b 10. **neither eat nor drink.** Mortals who, like Guingamor, have spent a long period of time in the fairy world are in grave danger if they again eat mortal food or even set foot on mortal soil. See Walter Map's story, p. 82b, ll. 21 ff. In fact, consorting with the fairy folk in any fashion is likely to render mortals abnormal. Compare the behavior of the knight in Keats' *La Belle Dame sans Merci*, p. 790a.

75a 8. **nones,** originally about 3 P.M., the ninth hour of the day reckoning from six in the morning. Later "nones" was shifted so as to mean "midday," our noon.

LATIN

GEOFFREY OF MONMOUTH

Geoffrey of Monmouth was a monk and at one time was archdeacon of Monmouth in Wales. He may have been a Welshman. His *History of the Kings of Britain*, written in Latin, *ca.* 1136, claims to be a translation of an ancient British book. Since no such book has been discovered, literary historians have been accustomed to speak of Geoffrey as one of the greatest liars in history. However much Geoffrey may have derived from Celtic tradition, to him is due the credit of establishing Arthur as a great emperor, the conqueror of many lands, whose court is a centre of culture to which all resort who wish to learn the proper rules of courtly etiquette and chivalry. To Geoffrey may safely be ascribed the establishment of Arthur's court and his Round Table as chivalric institutions. Whatever be the Celtic background of Arthurian romance, the chief characters are essentially mediæval ladies and gentlemen. He also introduced into polite literature the story of King Lear and other stories used later by playwrights and poets. The passages here translated give us an excellent picture of a coronation and other doings of high society during the early twelfth century at an Anglo-Norman court such as that of Henry I (1100–1135). Geoffrey's *History* was popular throughout the Middle Ages.

HISTORY OF THE KINGS OF BRITAIN, BK. IX

40. **Whitsuntide,** the week of Whitsunday, the seventh Sunday after Easter. Cf. note to p. 53a, 2.

75b 23. **City of Legions,** Caerleon, situated upon the Usk river near the Severn in Wales.

76a 5. **busking,** preparing.

76b 4. **Trojans.** According to a favorite tradition, perpetuated by Geoffrey's *History*, Britain was first settled by the descendants of refugees from Troy.

14. **vair,** perhaps a kind of fur of mixed grey and white.

19. **brave,** fine.

34 ff. **And the dames . . . for their love.** This passage is especially important as illustrating the intimate connection which Chivalry established between knightly prowess and love.

JOCELIN OF BRAKELOND

77a CHRONICLE OF ST. EDMUNDSBURY

The chronicle from which the selections in the text are taken was written in Latin during the latter part of the twelfth century by one Jocelin, a monk of the monastery of St. Edmundsbury, or Bury St. Edmonds, in Suffolk. Jocelin's work is of especial importance to the student of English literature for two reasons. First, it gives us an exceedingly realistic picture of monasticism, which played so important a part in the life of the Middle Ages. Second, it inspired a large portion of Thomas Carlyle's *Past and Present* (1843).

A monastery was an abode of men or women who, in order to escape from temptation and save their own souls, lived together in common, ate at the same table, slept in the same dormitory, worshipped in the same church, and were buried in the same graveyard. The numbers of inmates sometimes ran into hundreds, the activities were numerous and far-reaching, and the influence upon life both secular and religious enormous. The essential buildings of a monastery were the church, the cloister, the dormitory, the refectory, and the chapter-house. An abbey was a monastery that owed no allegiance to some larger establishment.

The Abbot Samson, referred to in the first line, became abbot in 1182 and ruled over the monastery for thirty years. His abbacy covers wholly or in part the reigns of three English Kings: Henry II, Richard I, and John. He was a man of marked personality with a keen sense of duty, strong common sense, and great self-reliance. He is the hero of Jocelin's narrative. Of Jocelin we know little. He reminds us of James Boswell, who six centuries later recorded in such detail the sayings and doings of Dr. Samuel Johnson (see p. 627 ff.).

77a 14. **the lord abbot,** Samson.

15. **The night before.** Samson became abbot on March 21, 1182.

27. **Benedictus Dominus,** "Blessed is the Lord." Compare Luke i, 68. This and the following Latin phrases are taken from the service of the mediæval Catholic church.

29. **Martiri adhuc,** "The martyrs up to the present."

30. **St. Edmund or Edmund,** a ninth-century king of East Anglia (including Norfolk and Suffolk), was taken prisoner by the Danes, bound to a tree, and, like St. Sebastian, shot to death with arrows. The monastery was founded in his honor.

34 f. **Omnipotens . . . huic,** "All-powerful eternal God, have mercy upon this person," part of the Roman liturgy.

38. **precentor,** leader of the choir.

41. **Te Deum laudamus,** "We praise Thee, O God."

43. **prior,** the officer next below the abbot in dignity, a sort of prime minister or chief executive to the abbot.

46. **chapter.** See note to p. 79a, l. 5, below.

48. **Benedicite,** "Bless ye"; "Bless ye the Lord."

77b 6. **Wimer,** sheriff of the counties of Norfolk and Suffolk.

34. **mitred effigy,** a figure or likeness of himself wearing a mitre to indicate his high dignity.

78a 16. **Ranulf de Glanville.** Ranulf (Randolph) Glanville was justiciar or chief justice of England from 1180 to 1189 under Henry II. He was a distinguished lawyer and wrote the first treatise on English law. He died A.D. 1190.

28. **demanded an aid . . . knights.** Monasteries were great landowners. Knights occupying monastery lands owed military service in payment for their lands, or "fees." In place of rendering this service they might pay a sum of money — *scutage*, literally "shield money" (see l. 34 below). Under these circumstances the abbot became extremely powerful and occupied a position on a level with the higher feudal nobles.

43. **villeins,** villagers, peasants, somewhat above the serfs, or slaves.

78b 6. **cultivation.** The monks did excellent work in clearing land and improving methods of agriculture.

23. **hundreds.** The "hundred" was a measure of land next below a "shire" in size.

33 f. **leets and suits,** districts marked off for purposes of legal enforcement.

34. **hidages.** Hidage was the income due from a "hide," theoretically the amount of land required to support one family.

79a 5. **chapter,** a meeting of the monks for the transaction of business.

20. **subsacristan,** assistant to the sacristan, or sexton, who had charge of the utensils and movables of the abbey church.

36. **this,** the sternness of the abbot's manner.

42. **Melun,** the school of mediæval logic founded by Peter Abelard, the great twelfth-century theologian, best known for his love affair with the beautiful Héloïse.

79b 31. **Almoner,** the officer who distributed the charity, or alms, of the abbey.

80a 10. **the fall of Jerusalem.** Jerusalem was taken from the Crusaders by the great Mohammedan leader Saladin on October 2, 1187. The event shocked the Christian world profoundly.

80b 21. **On his manors;** *i.e.*, absent from the monastery on some one of his estates.

81a 2. **offices,** outhouses such as kitchens, stables, etc.

10. **I . .. guests.** Jocelin had obviously long wished for a new guest-house and now he was to have one.

35. **alienated,** transferred or disposed of to raise money.

36. **Mildenhall,** a manor which had belonged originally to the abbey but had passed into the hands of the king at the time of the Conquest. Abbot Samson bought it back from Richard I for one thousand marks.

36 f. **the ransom of King Richard.** Returning from his crusade, Richard I fell into the hands of his enemy, Henry VI of Germany, and was held for ransom. All the English monasteries were obliged to hand over their gold and silver to the government in order to help make up the sum demanded — 100,000 marks, an enormous ransom for that time. Richard was released in 1194.

WALTER MAP

Genial, urbane, friendly, sympathetic, mildly satirical, Walter Map (or Mapes) reminds us more of Chaucer than does any other man of his time. He was born of gentle parentage on the border of Wales (perhaps in Herefordshire), studied at the great university of Paris, became a member of the brilliant court of Henry II of England, served the crown in various capacities, notably as ambassador to Rome in 1179, and became Archdeacon of Oxford in 1197. He was popular at court and was acquainted with John of Salisbury, Thomas à Becket, Geraldus Cambrensis (Gerald of Wales), and other distinguished men of his day. His arrogance, his superstition, and his prejudice, which appear everywhere in his pages, were but faults of the courtiers of his day. Clergyman, courtier, gentleman, aristocrat, cosmopolitan, man of letters, he stands out as one of the most interesting personalities in an age when interesting personalities were not uncommon at the English court. Anyone who sets out to understand the English temper of the twelfth century and neglects Walter Map, is guilty of a serious omission.

81b COURTIERS' TRIFLES

Map has been called "The first English essayist." Instead of expending his learning on tiresome discussions of mediæval theology, he has given us in his *Courtiers' Trifles* (written in Latin) something far more valuable — court gossip, good stories, and vivid reminiscences of interesting people of twelfth-century England, and scraps gleaned from his reading in many books. *Courtiers' Trifles* is not a systematic treatise; it is a series of disconnected notes and memoranda, made over a series of a dozen years, but it is all the more valuable on that account. It gives us a glimpse of the daily talk and mental furniture of a gentleman at the English court during the latter part of the twelfth century. Though Map's Latin is often cluttered up with classical and biblical learning, the author is a born story-teller, a master of brief narrative. He lived in an age when superstition was well-nigh universal, and he has succeeded in imparting to the stories of King Herla and of Edric Wilde an eerie fascination which eight hundred years have not wholly destroyed. He calls his work "Trifles," but to us the trifles of that far-off age are as significant as its serious annals. For mediæval superstitions accepted as scientific fact, see p. 89 ff.

To Map have been attributed certain versions of the legend of the Holy Grail and numerous convivial, amorous, or satirical Latin lyrics known as Goliardic (see note to "The Glutton's Confession," p. 85b), but the evidence of his authorship is unreliable.

81b **The Story of King Herla.** With this Welsh version of the "Journey to the Other World," the student should compare the Irish *Connla* (p. 61a ff.) and the Anglo-Norman *Guingamor* (p. 70a ff.). See also the notes to p. 61a, l. 32 and 74b, l. 10.

83a **The Story of Wild Edric.** The story of the capture of a supernatural wife by a mortal and her subsequent disappearance when her commands are broken is found in the folk-lore of many peoples. Map's version appears to come from Welsh tradition and represents a phase of popular literature which was reflected in the romances and lays of England and the continent.

83a 9 f. **Edric Wilde.** Edric the Wild (*Silvaticus*) figures in history as a powerful lord of the Welsh frontier who resisted William the Conqueror and for years maintained his independence.

14 f. **North Ledbury,** in Hereford on the border of Wales.

40. **plagues.** Map playfully refers to all women as plagues.

44. **Dictinna,** the Greek goddess Diana. Actæon spied upon Diana while she was bathing and was punished by being changed into a stag and eaten by his own dogs. As Map observed, it is dangerous to pry into the affairs of supernatural beings.

45. **Dryads,** minor female divinities of Greek mythology. They are associated with fountains, caves, trees, etc.

45. **Spectral squadrons.** Creatures of the world of ghosts, demons, and witches are often confused with fairies. Compare the character of Geraldine in Coleridge's *Christabel* (p. 708 ff.).

83b 12. **seized her.** Here, as in *Guingamor* (see note to p. 73b, l. 8), the woman is won by force. Some authorities tell us that the true Celtic fée, uncontaminated by swan-maidens and other weak creatures, is never captured. They point to the fairy woman of *Connla* (p. 61a ff.) as more truly typical.

29 ff. **until thou shalt cast, etc.** Fairies, like other supernatural beings, shrink from publicity. In stories of the type represented here the fairy woman usually forbids her husband to reproach her with her origin or to mention her name in public. As here, failure to observe the prohibition or *tabu,* brings disaster.

33. **anent,** concerning.

42. **William,** the Conqueror (reigned 1066–1087).

84a **Three Hermits and Their Wonderful Penance.** This is one of many stories told of the penances imposed upon themselves by mediæval religious devotees who believed that Heaven could be attained only by excessive mortification of the flesh. In some instances the penances were far more severe than that described here.

84b **Advice of Valerius to Ruffinus Not to Marry.** Many attacks upon women were composed during the Middle Ages. Map's tract, originally independent of *Courtiers' Trifles,* was widely known and greatly admired. It was, however, long supposed to be the work of the Roman writer, Valerius Maximus, the mistake being due to the accidental identity of names. The Valerius of Map's work is Map himself, and the treatise is addressed to a friend (whom Map calls Ruffinus) about to marry. We need not take Map's bitterness against women too seriously. Contrast the mediæval idea of a good wife (p. 86 f.) and the more liberal views of the seventeenth-century poet, Pomfret (p. 446b).

84b 20. **The first wife of the first man.** According to the Bible (Genesis ii, 17; iii, 3, 6) Eve ate of the fruit of "the tree of knowledge of good and evil" in disobedience to God's command and so caused the fall of man.

84b 32. **I have found a man,** etc. 1 Samuel xiii, 14; Acts xiii, 22.

35. **from adultery to homicide.** The story of King David's unlawful love for Bathsheba and the death of her husband Uriah the Hittite through the treachery of the king is first recorded in the Bible (2 Samuel xi, 3–17). It has often been retold in literature and depicted in art.

45. **Delilah,** the mistress of the famous biblical strong man Samson. Through her wiles Samson was led to reveal the secret of his strength and so fell into the hands of his enemies (Judges xvi, 4–20).

51. **Solomon,** famed not only as the richest of the ancient kings of Israel but as the wisest of men. According to 1 Kings xi, 4, his wives caused him to turn away from God and worship heathen idols.

85a 4. **Baal,** the chief male divinity of certain heathen neighbors of the ancient Israelites.

7. **Phœbus,** Apollo (or Helios), the Sun-god, one of the most important divinities of the ancient Greeks. He allowed his son Phaeton (or Phaethon) to drive his chariot, but Phaeton, being too weak to hold the horses, allowed them to come so near the earth as almost to set it on fire. As a punishment Phaeton was dashed down by a flash of lightning and Apollo was forced to serve a mortal for one year. He accordingly became the shepherd of Admetus, a mythical king of the Pheræ in ancient Thessaly.

15. **the phœnix.** See note to *A Praise of his Lady*, p. 203, l. 18.

25. **Lucretia,** a lady of ancient Rome famous for her chastity. Her rape by Sextus Tarquinius led to the dethronement of Tarquinius Superbus and the establishment of the republic. **Penelope,** the wife of Ulysses. Throughout her husband's long absence during and after the Trojan war, she maintained her chastity in spite of the importunities of many suitors. The story is told in Homer's *Odyssey;* see especially Books xiv, xxi, and xxii.

26. **Sabine women,** the women of a tribe near ancient Rome, raped, according to tradition, by the followers of Romulus, who lacked wives.

85a **The Decadence of Society.** It was a common opinion in early times that man was not so tall of stature, so long of life, or so pure of morals as he had been immediately after the creation. According to a Jewish tradition, man was created so tall that his head reached the heavens. We are informed in Genesis v, 5 that Adam lived 930 years. The depressing idea that, as the result of Adam's original sin (Genesis iii, 1–23), the human race was gradually degenerating in morals and in physique is in strong contrast with the more optimistic philosophy which became popular in Europe during the Romantic period (see pp. 404, 646). The Latins and Greeks also believed in the degeneration of the human race from a state of happiness and perfection in the Golden Age.

47. **eighty years.** Compare Psalm xc, 10.

ANONYMOUS LYRICS

85b THE GLUTTON'S CONFESSION

This and the following song are given in order to illustrate one of the lighter aspects of mediæval life, of which we are too apt to lose sight if we read only the literature of religion or instruction. *The Glutton's Confession* is one, perhaps the most famous, of a large body of poems composed in Latin during the Middle Ages by wandering students who migrated from university to university and who sang in jocund or irreverent vein of the clergy or of wine, women, and song. These poems are known as Goliardic and are attributed to one Golias, the imaginary head of a fraternity of vagrant and lawless students. *The Glutton's Confession* was known in England and has been attributed, though incorrectly, to Walter Map (see notes to p. 81b). In general the Goliardic poems attributed to Map express the protest of a considerable part of the English people against the abuses of the twelfth and thirteenth centuries. **ichor,** in Classical mythology "an ethereal fluid that supplied the place of blood in the veins of the gods"; here merely the inspiration resulting from wine.

GAUDEAMUS IGITUR

The title, which means "Let us rejoice therefore," forms the first line of the original. *Gaudeamus Igitur* is another student song, the Latin form of which was well known during the Middle Ages and has retained its popularity down to our own day.

BARTHOLOMEW

86b A MEDIÆVAL ENCYCLOPEDIA

The passages quoted are taken from the fourteenth-century English translation of the *De Proprietatibus Rerum* (Concerning the Properties of Things), a Latin encyclopedia of general information compiled by Bartholomew (Bartholomæus Anglicus), an English friar who wrote about 1250. Bartholomew's work was designed for men of little learning and was probably the most popular of the numerous compilations of universal knowledge composed during the thirteenth century — the great century of mediæval encyclopedias. It gives an excellent idea of the notions of the ordinary mediæval man regarding astronomy, physiology, physics, chemistry, geography, and natural history, as well as many matters of social etiquette. In addition to its purely historical value, the English translation possesses unusual interest because of its quaint phraseology and genuine literary quality.

21. **might and strength.** The writer apparently imagines that *vir* is derived from *virtus*, "strength."

27 f. **Maritus . . . Matrem.** The etymological connection between *maritus* (married man, husband) and *matrem* (mother) is fanciful. Mediæval etymologies are frequently based upon fancied or accidental similarity rather than upon fact.

32. **behoveth and obligeth.** *Spondere* signifies "to pledge one's self solemnly," "to place one's self under obligation."

87a 7. **cheer,** look, appearance. This is the older meaning.

29. **passing and ayencoming,** going and returning.

87b 7. **of grace than of kind,** endowed rather with heavenly grace than with earthly qualities.

22. **entaileth,** bestoweth as a heritage.

45. **forms,** benches. In the older schools each class was known as a "form" because the students were supposed to sit on the same bench.

88a 3. **messes.** Properly a "mess" was a service of food for four persons. To have only two people at a mess, as in the opening scene of *Gawain and the Green Knight*, was extremely sumptuous.

11. **wash . . . their hands.** The guests ate with their fingers. Forks for table use were not introduced into England until after the Middle Ages.

MEDICINE

Note the crudeness of the diagnosis and method of treatment.

43. **nice,** foolish.

GEOGRAPHY

88b 9. **most,** largest.

25. **Brute.** According to a fanciful mediæval etymology Britain derived its name from one Brutus (Brute), a descendant of refugees from Troy. See p. 97 and note to p. 76b, l. 4. Numerous mediæval chronicles giving the traditional history of Britain were called *Brutes*. Compare Layamon's *Brut* (p. 94).

40. **Anglia.** The etymologies of the name *Anglia* given here are of course fanciful. The word is derived from the fact that the district was settled by Angles, representatives of one of the Germanic tribes that invaded England in the fifth century. On the basis of *Angle* are formed the words "England" and "English." The story of Gregory and the English children was first told by Bede and has often been repeated.

NATURAL HISTORY

89a Lore such as that presented in this section not only served for popular Natural History during the Middle Ages but furnished material for literary allusion long after it had become antiquated as science.

49. **Hexameron,** a work more properly attributed to Basil the Great, *ca.* 330–379.

89b 33. **kept away beasts,** etc. Compare the ballad of "The Three Ravens" (p. 163).

37 f. **Garamantus.** An excellent illustration of how stories sometimes start. This king and the report concerning him probably owe their existence to a mistranslation of a passage in Pliny's *Natural History*, a popular source-book during the Middle Ages. Pliny says that two hundred dogs brought back *Garamantum regem* (the king of the Garamantes) out of exile and fought against those who resisted. The translator mistook *Garamantum* (genitive plural) for an accusative singular, and so manufactured a new king whom he represents as bringing, not being brought by, the dogs. The Garamantes were an African people described by some classical authorities as weak and unwarlike.

44. **Saint Anthony.** St. Anthony of Egypt, called "the Great" (A.D. 251–356?), the reputed founder of Christian monasticism. He is said to have sold his property, given the proceeds to the poor,

and retired to the desert, where he was often tempted by the devil and encountered many strange creatures. The Temptation of St. Anthony is a theme famous in literature and art.

89b 50. **Cynocephali,** a Greek word meaning *Dogs' Heads.*

51 f. **by the working,** by their actions.

90a 2. **Cyclops.** The *cyclopes,* giants with round or circular eyes, belong to Greek mythology. They are described differently by different writers. According to Homer, each of them had only one eye in the center of his forehead.

15. **Scythia,** an ancient name for the remoter parts of northern Europe and Asia.

18. **Ethiopia,** a name for ancient Abyssinia.

25. **Cynopodes,** dog-footed creatures.

29. **Lybia,** an ancient name for Africa.

34. **sirens,** in classical mythology sea maidens who had the power of charming all who heard their song. They sat on the shore and lured sailors to destruction. Later tradition represented them as having wings.

37. **some-deal,** partly.

46. **Physiologus,** a widely known and often quoted mediæval work in which fabulous qualities of various animals are used for moral instruction. The Middle English version of the *Physiologus,* dating from the early thirteenth century, is called the *Bestiary.*

90b 9 f. **the great Alexander's story.** Alexander the Great, 356–323 B.C., was one of the most popular figures in mediæval romantic literature. Before the beginning of the Christian era the Alexander legend had been set down in a Greek work called the *Pseudo-Callisthenes,* which furnished directly or indirectly many strange tales. In England stories concerning Alexander "had a continuous history from the close of the Anglo-Saxon period to the accession of Elizabeth."

RICHARD DE BURY

PHILOBIBLON, OR LOVE OF BOOKS

Richard Aungerville, or, as he is more generally known, Richard de Bury (*i.e.,* Bury St. Edmonds) is one of the most interesting figures in the life of mediæval England. Born of a distinguished line, he early became the tutor of the young prince (afterward Edward III), and later achieved high distinction in church and state. He was a great patron of learning and an insatiable collector of books. He is said to have possessed a larger library than all the other English bishops of his time. He was, moreover, a genuine lover of books; his Latin *Philobiblon,* completed just before his death, is not only one of the best books in praise of books ever written but also one of the clearest evidences of literary culture in England during the thirteenth century.

34. **treasure.** Cf. Proverbs xxi, 20.

34 ff. **The desirable treasure,** etc. One of the best indexes of culture is the regard in which books are held. Even to-day it would be difficult to find a more enthusiastic appreciation of the treasures of wisdom to be found in books than this one from the thirteenth century.

36 f. **infinitely surpasses . . . world.** Suggested by a passage in the apocryphal book of the Wisdom of Solomon vii, 8–9.

40. **at whose splendour . . . to look upon.** Cf. Wisdom of Solomon vii, 29.

43. **are bitter.** Cf. Wisdom of Solomon viii, 16.

44. **that fadeth not.** Cf. Wisdom of Solomon vi, 12.

48. **the Father of lights.** Cf. James i, 17.

91a 1 f. **those who eat . . . thirst.** Suggested by a passage in the apocryphal book of Ecclesiasticus, or the Wisdom of Jesus the Son of Sirach xxiv, 21.

7. **By thee kings reign.** Cf. Proverbs viii, 15.

13 ff. **would have melted . . . ploughshares.** That is, would have adopted an inglorious mode of life. The reference is to Isaiah ii, 4, where the prophet foretells that at the coming of Christ's kingdom universal peace shall prevail; "they (men) shall beat their swords into plough-shares, and their spears into pruning-hooks." Cf. Joel iii, 10.

16. **the prodigal.** The reference is to the story of the Prodigal Son, one of the most beautiful of Christ's parables. See Luke xv, 11–32.

23 ff. **everyone who asks . . . opened.** Cf. Matthew vii, 8.

26. **cherubim,** an order of angels especially noted for their wisdom. See also Exodus xxv, 20. The word *cherubim* is the Hebrew plural of *cherub,* which now has a very different suggestion.

33 f. **celestial, terrestrial, and infernal.** Cf. Philippians ii, 10.

38. **the ideas of Plato.** Plato, 429?–347 B.C., was a distinguished philosopher of ancient Greece and one of the most influential moral teachers in history. He taught that wisdom is the attribute of God and that moral abstractions, such as wisdom, truth, and love, correspond to actual ideas in the mind of God. Plato's philosophy grew out of that of his teacher Socrates; and he himself was the instructor of the great philosopher and rhetorician, Aristotle, who in turn was tutor to Alexander the Great. See also note to p. 91b, 19 ff.

39. **the chair of Crato.** Obscure. Perhaps *Crato* is a mistake for *Cato.* The Roman philosopher Cato, 95–46 B.C., was famed

for his stern moral virtue (cf. l. 53 below). He has been repeatedly introduced into literature, notably in Addison's once famous drama which bears his name.

53. **Fabricius.** A story famous in Roman annals tells how the Roman statesman Fabricius (third century before Christ) refused the bribes of Pyrrhus, king of Epirus, and remained faithful to his country. He is noted for his simplicity of life and integrity of character.

91b 11 f. **Ptolemy . . . Almagest.** Claudius Ptolomæus, or Ptolemy (second century before Christ), celebrated during the Middle Ages as a mathematician, astronomer, and geographer, wrote numerous influential treatises, of which the *Almagest* deals with astronomy. Ptolemy's system of astronomy, which made the earth the center of the universe, was accepted throughout the Middle Ages and was used in literature (*e.g.*, in Milton's *Paradise Lost*) even after it had been largely discarded by scientists. Ptolemy also wrote a geography which was a standard authority during the Middle Ages.

17. **things new and old.** Cf. Matthew xiii, 52.

19 ff. **which . . . friendship.** The idea comes ultimately from Aristotle, whose doctrines, reinterpreted by mediæval scholars, were extremely influential during our period. See also note to p. 91a, 38.

22. **holy Boethius.** Boëthius (A.D. 470?–524) was a Roman statesman and philosopher. His *Consolation of Philosophy*, written while the author was in prison, consists of a dialogue between Boëthius and Philosophy, who comforts him in his misfortunes and proves to him that the only true happiness lies in the soul and that wisdom and virtue are the only things that matter. The sentiments of the book are noble and exalted, and, although Boëthius does not mention Christianity, he was famed throughout the Middle Ages as one of the greatest Christian philosophers. The *Consolation of Philosophy* was known to practically all cultured people during the Middle Ages. It was translated by Alfred the Great, Chaucer, and Queen Elizabeth. In the history of human thought Boëthius stands out as one of the most important intermediaries between Platonic philosophy (see note to p. 91a, 38) and Christianity.

26 f. **the meaning of the voice . . . sound.** Cf. 1 Corinthians xiv, 11.

27 f. **wisdom that is hid.** Cf. Ecclesiasticus xx, 30.

92a 17. **given us by inspiration of God.** Cf. 2 Timothy iii, 16.

28. **golden pots.** Cf. Hebrews ix, 4.

29. **rocks flowing . . . honey.** Cf. Deuteronomy xxxii, 13.

31. **garners ever full.** Cf. Psalms cxliv, 13.

31 f. **the tree of life.** Cf. Genesis ii, 9; Revelation xxii, 2.

32. **the fourfold river of Paradise.** Cf. Genesis ii, 10.

35. **the ark of Noah.** Cf. Genesis vi, 14–16.

35 f. **the ladder of Jacob.** See Genesis xxviii, 12.

36 f. **the troughs, etc.** Cf. Genesis xxx, 38.

38. **the stones of testimony.** Cf. Joshua iv, 7.

39. **Gideon.** Cf. Judges vii, 16.

40 f. **David . . . Goliath.** Cf. 1 Samuel xvii.

42 f. **the arms of the soldiers of the church.** Cf. 2 Corinthians x, 4.

44. **darts of the wicked.** Cf. Ephesians vi, 16.

45. **vines of Engadi.** Engedi (Engadi), a place in Palestine celebrated for its vineyards (Song of Solomon i, 14).

46. **burning lamps.** Cf. Luke xii, 35.

92b 15. **the Lord's body,** the holy sacrament.

51. **halm,** straw, stalk of grain.

93a 7. **wallet,** the bag in which clerical students received the alms which they got by begging from door to door.

24. **quatrefoil,** a leaf with four leaflets, as sometimes that of clover.

44. **the Latinist and sophister.** Students in mediæval universities were required to use Latin in ordinary conversation; hence they might be called "Latinists." In the third year of his residence at the university the student was allowed to become a "sophister," and to take part in logical discussions.

93b 4. **anathema,** curse. Here used jocosely.

8 f. **no grease-stained finger.** Read note to p. 88a, 11.

17. **clerk,** scholar, learned man. Cf. Chaucer's Clerk (*Prologue*, l. 285 ff).

32 ff. **Moses . . . Take, he says, etc.** Cf. Exodus xxv, 16.

43 f. **S. Luke.** The reference is to Luke iv, 20.

LAYAMON

Layamon (Lagamon), or Lawman, seems to have been a Saxon priest and to have resided on the Severn river in northern Worcestershire near the border of Wales. He writes more like a Saxon *scop* (cf. p. 1) than a Norman courtly poet. In spite of his probable Germanic ancestry, his sympathies as expressed in the *Brut* are all with the Britons and against the Saxons — a fact which shows how completely the two races, so long enemies, had become one people by the close of the twelfth century. Layamon's work is pervaded by a spirit of simple earnestness and genuine emotionalism. He was a true poet and a sincere patriot. Of the mediæval poets who treated the Arthurian story, he is the first to make King Arthur the hero of the English people.

94a **BRUT**

Layamon's *Brut* is a rhymed chronicle giving the legendary history of Britain from the fall of Troy (see notes to p. 76b, 4, and p. 88b, 25) to the late seventh century; that is, a hundred years or so after the traditional date of Arthur's death. It exists in two versions: the earlier dating from about 1205, the later a revision made some fifty years afterward to suit the rapidly changing English language. It is written in one form of the Southern dialect. In style, in language, and in subject matter it is a work of great significance for students of English literary history. In style (observe particularly the alliteration) it resembles the Anglo-Saxon epic (see introductory note to *Beowulf*, p. 1).[1] In language it represents the transition from Anglo-Saxon to Middle English. The story of King Arthur and the legendary history of Britain, which had been given in Latin prose by Geoffrey of Monmouth about 1135 (see note to Geoffrey, p. 75a) and in courtly French verse by the Norman poet Wace about 1155, appears here for the first time as the adopted heritage of the English people. On the name *Brut*, see note to p. 88b, 25.

THE PASSING OF ARTHUR

Through ostensibly a translation of Wace's *Brut*, Layamon's poem is about twice as long as its original and contains much material barely suggested or not even referred to by Wace. Layamon's additions are particularly important in the parts of the poem that deal with King Arthur. Layamon, for example, gives us for the first time a full account of the founding of the Round Table and the Passing of Arthur. The latter, perhaps drawn from Welsh popular tradition, was afterward to make its literary fortune at the hands of Malory (p. 134) and Tennyson (p. 913, l. 361 ff.).

1. **Modred,** Arthur's sister's son, the villain of the story. For the further development of his character, see note to p. 130b, 14. Malory spells his name *Mordred*. At the point where our selection begins Modred has seized the kingdom and married Queen Guenevere during Arthur's absence on the continent.

17. **Whitsond,** Wissant, on the French coast near Calais.

30. **Romerel,** probably Romney in Kent.

94b 43. **Walwain,** Gawain, Arthur's nephew and, according to the older tradition, Modred's brother. Gawain is one of the most famous knights of the Round Table. He is the hero of several independent romances. (See *Gawain and the Green Knight*, p. 97 ff.) In the older romances Gawain is the "father of courtesy" (see p. 106a, 19), the beau ideal of the mediæval gentleman; in Malory he is an interesting mixture of attractive and unattractive qualities; in Tennyson he is almost entirely bad. See the account of his character on p. 103b.

47. **Childriches.** Elsewhere in the poem we learn that Childerich was a powerful emperor in Alemaine (Germany). He had come to Britain and had been vanquished by Arthur.

53. **an eorle Sexisne,** a Saxon earl.

61. **mine swevene.** Earlier in the poem Arthur had a dream (*sweven*) which seemed to portend the death of Gawain and the calamities that follow.

63. **Angel,** a king of Scotland whom Arthur had helped. The name *Angel* may have developed out of the Scotch *Angus*.

69. **Æfne than worde,** accordingly with speed. Literally, "even with the word." Cf. l. 337.

95a 88. **Lundene,** London.

94. **Winchestre.** Winchester is situated in Hampshire (see Literary Map). It was the seat of Alfred's kingdom and, according to one tradition, of Arthur's. It has been identified with the Camelot of Arthurian romance. But see note to l. 247 ff.

107. **Tha a there,** then on that.

113 ff. **He bihehte . . . neoden,** He promised the citizens ever more free laws provided they would help him at high (great) need.

95b 139. **lette him to cleopien,** had called to him.

144. **the feond hine aye,** may the devil take him.

145 f. **that folc gode . . . for-wurthe,** left all that good people there perished (gone wrong).

152. **Hamtone,** Southampton, in Hampshire not far from Winchester. See note to l. 94.

155 ff. **nom . . . neode,** took all the ships that were good there, and forced all the pilots to the ships.

159. **Cornwalen,** Cornwall. See Literary Map. The extremity of Cornwall and the submerged territory off Land's End have been identified with the Lyonesse of Arthurian romance.

160. **forcuthest . . . dayen,** most cowardly of kings in those days.

172. **while,** formerly.

175. **Merlin,** the magician and prophet of Arthur's court. A considerable body of romance recounts his sayings and doings.

177. **Eouwerwic,** Evorwic, an older form of *York*. See Literary Map.

179. **Wenhaver,** Guenevere (Guinevere), Arthur's famous queen.

[1] For convenience the two halves of each line are here printed separately.

96a 186. **on life,** alive.
189. **Karliun,** Caërleon. For location, see note to p. 75b, 23.
193 ff. **me . . . wife,** one (they) covered her head with a holy veil, and she was there a nun, most sorrowful of women.
197 ff. **Tha nusten . . . watere.** Then men knew not concerning the queen what had become of her, nor for many years afterward was it known truly whether she were dead [and how she went hence] or whether she had drowned herself. The bracketed half-line, added from another manuscript, breaks the continuity of the sense.
208. **a-neoste,** the correlative of *a-neouste* in l. 210. Translate the two: "first," "next."
209. **Sex-londe,** land of the Saxons.
220. **tha neode cuman weneth,** when he believes need is coming. The reading is a guess.
227 f. **sonde yeond,** messengers throughout.
231. **tha . . . weoren,** that to fight were brave.
96b 247 ff. **Tambre . . . Camelford.** The writers of Arthurian chronicles and romances do not agree as to the place of Arthur's last battle, usually referred to as the battle of Camlan. The Tambre may be the river Tamar, which forms the northern boundary of Cornwall. There is a Camelford in northern Cornwall, but it is some twenty miles from the river Tamar. Malory (p. 132a, 39) places the battle "by the seaside" near Salisbury (in Wiltshire). The fact that after the battle Arthur is transported to a neighboring shore and departs across the water seems to favor northern Cornwall as the scene of the battle. The present Camelford, it should be noted, is near Tintagel Castle, a noble ruin on the Cornish coast closely associated with Arthurian romance (see, for example, note to l. 324). Camelford has been identified with Camelot, the capital of Arthur's dominions in the romances, but here again another tradition identifies Camelot with Cadbury in Somersetshire. In the *Lady of Shalott* (p. 877 f.) Tennyson, following an Italian source, places Camelot near the sea. For another identification, see note to l. 94. Everything considered, it seems best to think of the dream city of Camelot as located near Tintagel and not far from the wild rocky coast of northern Cornwall. The Welsh annals treat Arthur's last battle as historical and date it A.D. 537.
263. **luken . . . longe,** long swords interlock.
287. **Bruttes,** Britons.
97a 295. **i thare lasten;** *i.e.*, into the smallest of Arthur's wounds.
298. **i . . . lave,** in that fight as a remnant.
304. **wunder ane swithe,** wonderfully much, very sorely.
320. **thines lifes ende,** Translate "to thy life's end."
324. **Utheres,** Uther's. Uther Pendragon was the father of Arthur by Igerna, wife of Gorlois, Duke of Cornwall, who had his stronghold at Tintagel Castle. See note to l. 247 ff.
97b 325. **Avalun.** Avalon (Avalun) is the name given in Arthurian romance to the Happy Other World or Earthly Paradise corresponding to the Land of Youth of Irish tradition. Read the note to p. 61a, 32 and compare the Irish story of *Connla of the Golden Hair* (p. 61 f.). Geoffrey of Monmouth merely refers to the place as an island. Avalon was early identified with Glastonbury in Somerset, where, according to one tradition, Arthur was buried. Mediæval etymologists connected *Avalon* with the French word *val*, "valley," and with the Welsh word *aval*, "apple," and hence spoke of the place sometimes as a valley, sometimes as the "Isle of Apples." Tennyson had both ideas in mind when, in the *Passing of Arthur*, he describes Avalon (which he calls "the island-valley of Avilion") as "fair with orchard lawns" (p. 913, l. 430).
327. **Argante.** This lady's name is a puzzle, but her character is perfectly clear. She is mentioned neither by Geoffrey of Monmouth nor by Wace, Layamon's immediate source. Her name is perhaps connected with that of Morgan le Fay, a fairy queen of Arthurian romance who, in Malory's account, is one of the ladies who carry the wounded king away in the magic boat (see p. 135b, 3). As regards her character, she belongs to the same class of Celtic supernatural beings as the fairy woman who transports Connla to the Land of the Young (see note to p. 61a, 32). In l. 354, Arthur refers to her as "fairest of all elves."
333. **seothe ich cumen wulle,** etc., afterward I will come, etc. The disappearance of a popular hero and the belief that he will ultimately return is found in the folklore of many peoples, but seems to have appealed particularly to the imagination of the Celts. See, further, note to p. 135b, 31 f.
338 ff. **ther com of se,** etc. This, the first appearance in English literature of the romantic tradition of Arthur's passing, should be carefully compared with the more elaborate account given by Malory (p. 134b, 14 ff.) and the highly mystical and richly ornate description by Tennyson (p. 913, l. 361 ff.).

97a SIR GAWAIN AND THE GREEN KNIGHT

Of the author of *Gawain and the Green Knight* we know only what can be derived from his work. He seems to have been well educated and was obviously acquainted with the best society of his time. He was intimately versed in the practice of chivalry and may have belonged to the knightly class. At the same time, he shows deep religious feeling and has been credited with the authorship of a religious poem called *Pearl* and other works of a moral character. Whoever he was, he was a conscious and highly trained literary artist. *Gawain and the Green Knight* is one of a number of Middle English verse romances based on French originals, but it far surpasses the rest in narrative excellence. Aside from the work of Chaucer, it is easily the best piece of narrative verse that has come down to us from English literature of the fourteenth century. It is a stirring account, full of the best traditions of honor and purity. It belongs to a small group of Middle English poems written in exceedingly difficult alliterative verse and in a dialect known as North-West Midland. The impetus that gave rise to these writings is generally spoken of as the Alliterative Revival, the supposition being that in them alliteration, which is so striking a feature of Anglo-Saxon verse (see introductory note to *Beowulf*, p. 1), was "revived." It is, however, more probable that Old English alliterative verse, though not used for literary purposes from the Norman Conquest till the fourteenth century, maintained a continuous existence during that period.

Although most critics are agreed that Arthurian romance owes much to the imaginative literature of the Celts, *Gawain and the Green Knight* is one of the few romances of the Round Table whose debt to Celtic is universally acknowledged. The beheading episode near the beginning and the account of the return blow at the end of the English romance go back, probably through a French intermediary (see note to p. 98b, l. 19) to a Celtic story resembling part of the early Irish saga of the *Feast of Bricriu* (p. 59 ff.). The Irish tale should be compared carefully with the English romance.

97a 1. **Troy.** On the tradition that Britain was settled by descendants of Trojan refugees, see notes to p. 76b, l. 4 and p. 88b, l. 25.

97b 5. **Felix Brutus.** Brutus, according to tradition, was the great grandson of Æneas. See note to p. 88b, l. 25. The source of the name "Felix" is unknown.

10. **Western Isles,** the countries west of Troy, including Britain.

98a 9. **Camelot.** On the location of Camelot, see note to Layamon's *Brut*, p. 96b, 247 ff.

16. **carols.** The carol was a kind of round dance accompanied by singing. See also p. 107a, 18. Contrast the meaning as used on p. 181.

42. **daïs,** a platform on which sat the more distinguished members of the household.

44. **Tars,** a place often referred to during the Middle Ages as famous for silks and tapestries.

98b 19. **à la dure main,** French for "of the hard hand." Our romance is based on a French original, now lost. See the reference to "the book," p. 103b, 53. Agravain was one of Gawain's brothers.

21. **Bawdewyn,** Baldwin.

22. **Ywain,** Yvain, known as the "Knight of the Lion," the hero of a fine romance by Chrétien de Troyes. On Chrétien, see Chronological Outline.

34. **to each two, etc.**; that is, there were only two instead of four (the usual number) at a mess. This was unusually sumptuous. See note to p. 88a, l. 3.

99a 49. **ell-yard,** an old measure of length. The English ell was forty-five inches.

100a 16. **jest.** *Gomen*, the word in the original, means "game."

100b 17. **Gawain.** See note to p. 94b, l. 43.

30 f. **the weakest . . . the feeblest of wit.** Notice Gawain's humility, and contrast Beowulf's boasting (note to p. 9, l. 675).

102a 5. **dossal,** a frame hung with tapestry above the daïs.

30 ff. **each season, etc.** Such long and sympathetic descriptions of the various seasons are exceedingly rare in mediæval literature. If you read the romance through with your eye out for nature descriptions, you will find an unusually large number.

32. **Lent,** a period of forty days beginning with Ash Wednesday and continuing until Easter, observed by most Christian churches in memory of Christ's fast in the wilderness (Matthew iv, 1–11; Luke iv, 1–13; Mark i, 12–13). Called "crabbed" because those who observe Lent are supposed to deny themselves certain worldly pleasures during that period.

102b 8. **Michaelmas,** autumn. In the church calendar Michaelmas is September 29, the feast of the archangel Michael.

11. **All Hallows Day,** All Saints Day, November 1.

103a 2. **byrny.** See note on *burnies* (*Beowulf*, l. 40).

10. **bawdrick,** sash.

13. **hearkened Mass**; that is, heard Mass, as a good Catholic should. Mass is a service of the Catholic Church that includes the consecration and offering of the Sacred Host, the body of the Lord.

19. **Gringalet,** Gawain's famous horse.

32. **vintail,** or ventail, part of the visor, or movable front portion of the helmet, intended to admit air (French *vent*).

42. **pentangle,** a five-pointed figure used here as Gawain's heraldic device. The elaborate interpretation that follows is an interesting evidence of the mediæval fondness for allegory.

103b 8 ff. **the five wounds . . . the five joys.** The five wounds of Christ and the five joys of the Virgin Mary are often referred to in mediæval literature.

104a 2. **Logres,** often used in mediæval romance as a name for England or Britain.

8. **Anglesey,** an island off the northwest coast of Wales. Just outside Anglesey lies the smaller island of Holyhead (l 10).

9 f. **foreland,** headland.

11. **wilderness of Wirral,** on the northwest side of Cheshire near the Welsh border. Gawain has traveled northward through Wales and then turned east.

104b 19. **matins,** the morning devotional service in the Catholic and certain other Christian churches.

20 f. **Paternoster,** "Our Father," the Lord's prayer. *Ave,* the first word of the *Ave Maria,* "Hail, Mary," — the words of the angel who announced to Mary that she was to become the mother of Christ (Luke ii, 29). *Credo,* "I believe," the Creed (from Latin *credo*). All appear in the service of the Catholic Church.

30. **castle.** The author appears to have in mind a real castle. The Green Knight's dwelling apparently was somewhere in Cheshire or Derbyshire.

37. **Saint Julian,** the patron saint of travelers, noted for providing his votaries with good lodging.

40. **hostel,** lodging.

51. **corbels,** carved stone brackets supporting the battlements.

105a 21. **by Saint Peter.** The porter very properly swears by St. Peter, who bears the keys of Heaven.

44. **the lord.** Really the Green Knight, though Gawain does not recognize him.

105b 47. **sodden,** boiled.

106b 5. **gorget,** a sort of ruff worn around the neck.

5. **wimple,** a covering for the neck worn by men and elderly ladies.

34. **fool it with the best,** etc., compete with the best in acting the fool, so as not to lose his hood.

38. **light the tapers,** *i.e.*, as a signal to go to bed.

107a 14. **Saint John's Day,** December 27.

34. **behest,** command.

46. **wend,** go.

107b 28. **solace,** pleasure.

38. **waked,** kept awake, stayed up late.

108a 21. **mails,** bags, trunks.

27. **sop,** slight repast, snack.

109a 2. **rede,** advise.

4. **my knight whom I have captured.** The episode should be compared with that in *Guingamor,* p. 70b, 24 ff. The essential difference consists in the fact that here the lady, unlike the queen in *Guingamor,* is not really in love with the knight. She is merely testing him. See p. 118b, l. 29 ff.

109b 45. **holt and heath,** grove and open country. Cf. Chaucer, *Prologue,* l. 6.

110a 4. **tale,** count, sum.

23. **gramercy,** thanks.

112b 7. **prime,** about 9 A.M.

38. **spinney,** small thicket.

113b 33. **marks.** The mark was a coin formerly used in England and worth a little over thirteen shillings.

114a 43. **assoiled,** absolved.

114b 47. **mine is behind.** Apparently, "my gift is behind yours in value."

53. **Rood,** the Cross on which Christ was crucified.

115a 17. **deal the doom of my weird,** take the judgment of my fate.

115b 18. **did on,** put on. The past tense of *do on,* "don."

21. **cognizance,** device or sign used in heraldry to identify a knight when he wore armor and hence would otherwise be unrecognizable.

116b 31. **let,** hinder.

45. **greet,** weep.

117a 7. **mound.** Compare the association of mounds with uncanny happenings in *Beowulf* (see notes to ll. 2213, 2223) and the Welsh *Pwyll* (note to p. 63a, 16).

22. **oratory.** See note to p. 43a, 3.

25 f. **in five wits,** in my five wits.

117b 1. **dight,** made ready.

10. **brent.** Read *bent,* hillside. Cf. *Squyr of Lowe Degre,* l. 65.

118b 45. **covetousness,** one of the seven deadly or most heinous sins, according to mediæval belief.

51. **largess,** liberality, freedom in giving — a virtue highly prized during the Middle Ages.

119a 34 ff. **Adam . . . Solomon . . . Samson . . . David,** famous examples often cited during the Middle Ages of men who were brought to sorrow through their relations with women. Read again the notes to Walter Map's "Advice of Valerius to Ruffinus" (p. 84b).

44. **samite,** a rich silk fabric woven or embroidered with gold. Tennyson uses the word in a famous line in the *Passing of Arthur* (p. 911, l. 199, and p. 912, l. 327). The word *samite* is derived from the Greek.

49. **pride,** the first of the seven deadly sins. See note to p. 118b, 45.

119b 5. **Morgain le Fay,** a famous supernatural woman of Arthurian romance. See note to Layamon's *Brut,* p. 97b, 327. Here she is at enmity with Guenevere (l. 16), probably because Arthur has rejected her love and married her rival.

29 f. **Prince of Paradise,** Christ.

120a 27. **Brutus.** See note to p. 88b, 25.

THE SQUYR OF LOWE DEGRE

Composed within a century after *Gawain and the Green Knight* (p. 97 ff.), the *Squyr of Lowe Degre* is one of the best of the small number of Middle English romances for which no single French source is known or suspected. It is made up almost entirely of stock themes, of which two — (1) the youth who, in spite of many obstacles, rises from comparative obscurity to wealth and power, (2) a pair of young lovers who, though separated for a time, are finally united — have an eternal and irresistible appeal, especially to the young. The *Squyr* marks a step in the gradual evolution of the modern novel of manners; it is valuable for the light it throws not only on the mental furniture of the fiction writer of the fifteenth century but also on the courtly life of the time. The unknown author shows considerable skill in weaving together his various materials and unusual freshness and delicacy in his general treatment. "Though often neglected in the ordinary histories of English literature as being a mere type of a class, the *Squyr*, in its brilliancy of description and in its passages of genuine poetry, rises far above the level of the average fifteenth-century romance." It was widely popular in its day and maintained its vogue till well on into the age of Elizabeth.

1. **squyer.** Compare the description of Chaucer's squire, *Prologue*, l. 79 ff.

1. **of lowe degre,** of low estate or station, not menial. In l. 20 he is called a "gentill" (well-born) man.

2. **the kings doughter of Hungre,** daughter of the king of Hungary. Hungary is here merely a distant country, fit setting for a romantic story.

7. **seven yere,** the conventional number of years for such service.

8. **set the lords.** It was his duty as marshal to arrange them in order of rank.

11. **styll mornyng,** "always mourning" because of ill success in love.

120b 15. **Christente,** Christendom, the whole Christian world.

28. **arber,** here "a garden of fruit trees."

31 ff. **The tre it was,** etc. Such lists of trees were popular in mediæval literature and were introduced by imitators of romance such as Chaucer (in *Sir Thopas*) and Spenser (in the *Faerie Queene*, p. 217, l. 69 ff.).

32. **Jesu chese.** The cypress, according to mediæval tradition, was one of the trees that furnished wood for Christ's cross; hence Christ may be said to have "chosen" it.

52. **mery,** sweet, pleasant, agreeable, without reference to mirth (Campbell). Cf. the phrase "Merry England."

65. **bente.** See note to p. 117b, 10.

67. **lened his backe to a thorne.** By leaning his back against a thorn he places himself in a state of bodily discomfort in harmony with his unhappy state of mind. To the mediævals the plaintive note of the nightingale, the bird of love, suggested that it was leaning against a thorn. See l. 801.

121a 78. **Syr Lybius,** Sir Libeaus Desconus (The Fair Unknown), hero of a famous Middle English romance. The poet gives a brief summary of the romance later (l. 615 ff.).

80. **Syr Guy,** Sir Guy of Warwick, the hero of a popular mediæval romance.

82. **Syr Colbrande,** a giant Danish champion slain by Guy of Warwick. See note to l. 80.

90. **sowned,** swooned. The heroes and heroines of mediæval romance were given to fainting under emotional stress. In the sentimental fiction of the eighteenth century swooning again became popular.

93. **oryall,** an oriel or bay window.

95. **Fulfylled . . . with ymagery,** filled with painted figures.

96. **by and by,** one after another.

98. **Sperde,** fastened.

116. **it,** the mourning.

121b 140. **Lynen cloth . . . were;** *i.e.*, I will forego soft raiment and wear rough clothing.

148. **his love that harowed hell.** According to a tradition which was widespread and exceedingly influential during the Middle Ages, Christ, after his crucifixion, descended into hell, where he rebuked Satan and comforted the damned souls. There are versions of the story in Old and in Middle English, and it is the theme of the oldest English mystery play, *The Harrowing of Hell.*

162. **and,** if.

163. **woyng,** wooing.

168. **drawe,** the past participle of *drawe*, which means "to extract the bowels from." Compare the phrase "hang, draw, and quarter," used of criminals.

172. **chyvalry.** Cf. note to p. 76b, l. 34 ff.

174 **wynne your shone,** or, as we should say, "win your spurs." Cf. l. 248.

122a 184. **by and by,** one (night) after another.

198. **the Rodes,** Rhodes, an island in the eastern Mediterranean which knights errant, as well as palmers and pilgrims bound for the holy sepulcher in Jerusalem, would naturally visit on their journeys.

199 f. **I hold . . . But,** I do not count you worthy of praise unless, etc.

204. **sable,** a dark, almost black, color used in heraldry. Compare the description of the Squire's armor with that of Gawain in *Gawain and the Green Knight* (p. 102b, l. 50 ff.).

210. **true loves,** true lovers' knots.
214. **A reason . . . me,** a motto. The motto, given in the next two lines, is *Amor,* Love. Compare the motto of Chaucer's Prioress, *Prologue,* l. 162.
229. **cote armoure,** a coat worn over the armor, upon which the wearer's coat of arms was usually embroidered.
232. **yemen.** Cf. Chaucer's yeoman, *Prologue,* l. 101 ff.
122b 236. **Jerusalem.** After the completion of his fighting, the Squire must, like many other mediæval knights, make a pilgrimage to the sepulcher of Christ in Jerusalem.
244. **on lyve,** alive.
251. **to,** for.
258. **whele of vyctory,** the wheel of victory; *i.e.,* "may the wheel of victory (like the wheel of fortune) turn to your advantage." Or perhaps *whele* simply means *wele,* "welfare," "success." See also l. 592.
288. **bewraye,** betray.
123a 304. **gente,** graceful, pretty.
305 ff. **he araied him,** etc. Cf. the gay dress of Chaucer's squire, *Prologue,* l. 89 f.
308. **barres,** stripes or bands on the belt.
317 ff. **deynty meates,** etc. Cf. the description of a meal in Bartholomew's *Encyclopedia* (p. 87b, l. 42 ff.) and in Chaucer's *Prologue,* l. 341 ff. The mediævals were hearty eaters and were fond of elaborate and highly seasoned dishes.
123b 352. **can he fle,** did he flee.
364. **to longe,** to long for, to desire.
380. **purchase,** the acquisition of an estate by any method other than descent (herytage).
386. **For,** on account of.
392. **fame,** defame.
399. **And,** if.
400. **dede,** death.
124a 430. **Or,** before.
437. **But yf,** unless.
124b 461. **panter . . . butler.** Originally the pantler had charge of the bread (French *pain*), the butler (botler) of the bottles.
464. **bordes.** The tables consisted of boards, which were brought in and laid on trestles and were removed after the meal. Hence "voyding the borde" (cf. l. 468) was a more serious matter than it is now.
486. **can gone,** did go.
125a 517. **yet,** even then.
524. **by his owne,** by himself.
526. **tyll,** to. Still used in Scotland.
534. **'Your dore undo!'** etc. This scene became so popular that the phrase "Undo your door" was sometimes used as a title for the whole poem.
543. **but,** unless.
125b 578. **make slee,** cause you to be slain.
583. **at,** at the hands of.
588. **Otherwyse . . . to,** you shall win me in some other way.
597. **worshyp,** honor.
611. **symple kynne.** A yeoman might be referred to as of "simple kin" in contrast to the gentry (nobles).
615 ff. **When the dwarfe and mayde Ely,** etc. The following passage gives a summary of the romance of *Sir Libeaus Desconus* (see note to l. 78), where, however, the lady's name is Elene.
617. **kyng.** The correct word is knight. It was Sir Libeaus, not Arthur, who won the lady of Synadowne.
623. **semeth,** befits.
126a 626. **distaunce,** dissension (?).
627. **They . . . victory.** Apparently: when they (the maiden and the dwarf) saw that Sir Libeaus had won the victory for them.
637. **in-fere,** together.
638 ff. **Theyr enemyes approched,** etc. The following scene needs a word of explanation. Although the attack upon the Squire was contrary to the king's orders, we must understand that it was the king who sent the armed men and who after the fight agrees with the Squire to test the lovers' affection for seven years. There is some confusion in the account of the fight — who ordered the Steward's body to be disfigured, disguised, and laid at the Lady's door, is not clear.
663. **wemme,** injury.
667. **cast thee,** planned, resolved.
675. **weale away!** wo alas wo, welaway.
126b 699. **closed hym,** etc. The story of a lady who kept her dead lover's head in her chamber was told by Boccaccio and furnished the inspiration for Keats' *Isabella.*
692. **gynnes,** devices, contrivances.
704. **offre to them.** Offerings for the dead were common during the Middle Ages and even in more recent times.
713. **ruddy read,** complexion red.
714. **browes bent,** arched eyebrows, regarded as a sign of beauty during the Middle Ages.
720. **oryent,** bright.
127a 737. **every deale,** every part, bit. Cf. Modern English "great deal."
750. **Trapped,** supplied with trappings.
753 ff. **rumney,** etc. Lines 753–762 contain a list of various sorts of wine.
772. **his rechase.** Perhaps, the recall of the hounds after the deer had been brought down.
776. **egle horne,** a kind of hawk.
127b 790. **countre note and dyscant,** counterpoint and descant, musical terms.
816. **or,** before.
128a 841. **fustyane.** See footnote to Chaucer's *Prologue,* p. 141a, l. 75.
858. **thore,** there.
878. **The whyles,** the times.
885 ff. **Tuskayne,** etc. Cf. p. 140, l. 51 ff.
894. **the sepulture,** the Holy Sepulcher. Cf. l. 243 ff.

128b 911. **Let none . . . meyne,** let none of my household know.

923. **Nor . . . she knew,** For she knew not.

940. **Fy,** Fie. In the older language *fie* was a much stronger word than it is to-day.

129a 957. **for,** in respect to any relations with.

129b 1026. **dyd of,** took off.

130a 1070 ff. **harpe,** etc. Lines 1070–1077 include a list of musical instruments.

1088. **thee,** succeed.

1112. **comunalte,** the common people.

SIR THOMAS MALORY

Sir Thomas Malory came of an ancient and distinguished family. He seems to have been born about 1400 (the year of Chaucer's death) in Warwickshire, the county of Shakespeare. He was brought up according to the best ideas of what a fourteenth-century gentleman should be. As a youth he served in the retinue of the Earl of Warwick, who was known as "the father of courtesy" and who made a point of keeping up the customs of chivalry, which had gradually become antiquated during the three centuries since their establishment in England (see Introduction to Middle English Period, p. 58). It was in this environment that young Malory doubtless imbibed the romantic admiration for knighthood and knightly exploits that inspired the *Morte Darthur*. In 1445 Malory was a knight and sat in Parliament for Warwickshire. During his late years he seems to have devoted himself to the extensive reading that must have preceded the writing of his great romance. He died in 1471.

130b LE MORTE DARTHUR

Malory's *Morte Darthur* (usually written thus rather than according to modern spelling, *Morte d'Arthur*) is one of several mediæval romances bearing the same name. It is the most famous Arthurian romance of the Middle Ages and probably the only romance of mediæval England that is widely read to-day. The name *Morte Darthur* means the "Death of Arthur," but the book is far more than an account of Arthur's passing. It is a great treasury of Arthurian romance based largely upon French sources (cf. p. 131b, 16) and so arranged by Malory as to give a complete history of the knights of the Round Table from Arthur's birth till his last battle. Though not the first to undertake such a task, Malory was the first to make Arthur the central figure of his narrative, and he shows a certain amount of originality in the choice and arrangement of his materials, though he omits some good stories, such as *Gawain and the Green Knight* (p. 97 ff.). He is not altogether just to Gawain (see note to p. 94b, l. 43), and in recounting the death of Tristram (Tristan) he uses a far less poetic tradition than that preserved in Wagner's opera. At times Malory's characters are portrayed as fifteenth-century ladies and gentlemen, but in general they lack the flesh-and-blood reality to be found in the epic and in realistic fiction. Taken altogether, however, his book embodies the finest ideals of chivalry and the best traditions of "old romance." The *Morte Darthur* is the chief source of Tennyson's *Idylls of the King* (see note to *The Lady of Shalott*, p. 877a).

1. **Sir Mordred.** See note to p. 94a, 1. Malory, following an older though probably not original tradition, makes Mordred the son of Arthur (p. 131a, 17) by his half-sister, the daughter of Igerna by her first husband, Duke Gorlois (see note to p. 97a, 324). Hence Arthur's downfall comes as a retribution for his youthful sin.

14. **his uncle's wife and his father's wife.** According to Malory, Arthur is both Mordred's uncle and his father. See note to l. 1.

131a 6. **shot great guns.** From age to age the Arthurian stories have been more or less made over to suit contemporary conditions. The mediævals were especially lacking in historical perspective. The original Arthurian romances, of course, knew nothing of cannon fired with gunpowder, which did not come into use in England until the fourteenth century.

16 f. **to let . . . to land.** See footnote to p. 126, l. 668. Contrast the meaning of *let*, "to cause to," in l. 30, below.

27. **maugre,** in spite of.

131b 15. **he was shriven,** he had made his last confession.

19 f. **King Lot's son of Orkney,** son of King Lot of Orkney. A common form of expression in Middle English. See note to p. 120a, l. 2.

23. **The old wound.** The battle in which this wound was received is described by Malory in Bk. XX, Chap. xxi.

44. **straitly bestead with,** hard beset by.

132a 12. **his Saviour,** the last Sacrament.

39. **by the seaside . . . Salisbury.** On this and other traditional locations of Arthur's last battle, see note to p. 96b, l. 247 ff.

52. **by,** during.

132b 5. **condescended,** agreed.

133a 24 ff. **your night's dream,** etc. During the preceding night Arthur had two dreams in one of which the ghost of Sir Gawain appeared and warned him against doing battle the next day.

35. **avail,** advantage.

133b 11 f. **do me to wit,** cause me to know.

21. **harness,** armor.
31. **works,** turns.

134a 7 f. **Excalibur.** Arthur's famous sword Excalibur came originally from the fairy world (cf. p. 912, l. 272 ff.). Tennyson (p. 911, l. 197 ff.), following a passage in Malory not given here, tells how Arthur received the sword from a mysterious hand that rose out of a lake. Malory's account of the disposal of the sword by Sir Bedivere should be compared carefully with the corresponding passage in Tennyson's *Passing of Arthur* (p. 911, l. 204 ff.).

29. **lief,** beloved.

134b 15 ff. **hoved a little barge.** Compare the earlier account of Arthur's passing by Layamon (p. 97, l. 337 ff.) and the later version by Tennyson (p. 913, l. 361 ff.). The mourning of the ladies is probably due to a confusion between two traditions: (1) Arthur was wounded, but departed alive to fairy land, (2) Arthur died and was buried in mortal soil (cf. p. 135a, l. 11 ff., p. 135b, l. 30 ff.), and hence was to be lamented.

21. **softly,** carefully.
36. **Avilion,** Malory's spelling for Avalon, on which see especially note to p. 97b, 325.
42. **took the forest,** took to the woods.

135a 6. **deeming,** inference.

135b 3. **Morgan le Fay.** See notes to p. 119b, 5, and p. 97, l. 327.

6. **Nimue,** a fairy personage sometimes identified, as here, with the Lady of the Lake, Arthur's supernatural helper and the giver of Excalibur. Under the variant form of Vivien she is the beloved of Merlin.

31 f. **Hic jacet . . . futurus,** Here lies Arthur, king formerly and destined to be king again.

WILLIAM LANGLAND

An old tradition attributes *Piers the Plowman* to one William Langland (or Langley), and an imaginary life has been made up for the poet; but it is now believed that the poem in its various forms is the combined work of several different authors of varying degrees of technical skill and originality. The authors all agree in satirizing contemporary society and in urging a return to the customs of the past. Chaucer and many other mediæval writers give the point of view of the aristocracy; *Piers the Plowman* is noteworthy because its authors give a picture of the times as viewed by the masses.

136a PIERS THE PLOWMAN

Piers the Plowman exists in three forms or versions: Version *A*, about 1362; Version *B* (the one printed here), about 1377; Version *C*, about 1397. The poem was exceedingly popular during the fourteenth and fifteenth centuries and still remains one of the most important pieces of social criticism in the English language. It is satire in that it points out abuses, but the authors are not reformers in the sense that they have new ideas to propose nor are they opposed to the Church or Society as a whole. Piers the Plowman is the type of the hard-working, honest, conservative laborer. The poem is an allegory in that many parts have a double meaning — one literal, the other figurative. For example, the "faire felde ful of folke" near the beginning of the poem not only gives a satirical picture of actual fourteenth-century English society but also represents allegorically the world with its labors, amusements, and other interests. Piers is the typical representative of the lower classes; he is also a sort of humble Christ. And so on. An even more elaborate allegory is found in the *Faerie Queene* (see introductory note to p. 216a). *Piers the Plowman* also belongs to what is known as "vision literature," of which Dante's *Divine Comedy* is the best mediæval representative. The seer falls asleep and has a vision — in this case a vision of the great panorama of fourteenth-century society.

The poem is written in Old English alliterative verse and was composed under the same impetus that gave rise to the so-called "alliterative revival" of the fourteenth century (see introductory note to *Gawain and the Green Knight*, p. 97).

136a 2 f. **shepe . . . heremite.** The dress of a shepherd is said to have resembled that of a hermit.

5. **Malverne hulles,** a range of hills separating Worcester from Hereford. The real scene of the poem is, however, London with its varied occupations and types of humanity. See also note on the "faire felde," l. 17.

17. **A faire felde ful of folke.** The "fair field" is the world (Matthew xiii, 38). The whole vision surveys the world, heaven, and hell. Visions, especially visions of heaven and hell, were popular during certain periods of the Middle Ages. The part of our poem beginning with l. 17 is often referred to as the "vision of the field full of folk."

136b 22. **wonnen . . . destruyeth,** won that which wasteful men spend in gluttony.

23. **putten hem to pruyde,** take to pride, behave proudly.
26. **ful streyte,** very strictly.
27. **hevene-riche blisse,** the bliss of the kingdom of heaven.
33. **murthes,** mirths.

36 ff. **Feynen,** etc. This passage may be ren-

dered thus: "Feign fancies for themselves, and make fools of themselves, and (yet) have their wit at their will, (able) to work if they were obliged. As for such fellows, that which Saint Paul (2 Thessalonians iii, 10) preaches about them, I will not adduce it here; (else I might be blameworthy myself, since) he who speaks slander is Lucifer's (Satan's) servant" (Skeat). The passage which the author refuses to quote for fear of speaking slander, reads: "*Si quis non vult operari, non manducet,*" — "If any one will not work, neither shall he eat." The lines in *Piers the Plowman* are interesting for the light they throw on the minstrels and wandering entertainers of the fourteenth century.

40. **Bidders,** beggars.

41. **her bagges,** the bags carried by beggars to receive whatever was given them.

42. **atte ale,** at the alehouse.

137a 43. **hii,** they.

45. **evre,** ever, always.

47. **Seynt James,** the famous shrine of St. James of Campostella, in Galicia, Spain.

47. **seyntes in Rome.** There were many shrines in Rome.

51. **To eche a tale,** in regard to each tale.

54. **Walsyngham,** the shrine of Our Lady of Walsingham, in Norfolk. It was a popular resort of pilgrims. The followers of John Wyclif were opposed to pilgrimages thither.

57. **shopen hem,** arrayed themselves as.

58. **the foure ordres,** the four great orders of friars: Carmelites (white friars), Augustines (Austin friars), Dominicans (black friars), and Minorites (gray friars). During the Middle Ages the friars fulfilled much the same functions as the Salvation Army does to-day. Originally they labored among the poor and owned no property. They should be carefully distinguished from the monks, who separated themselves from the world and were property owners. See especially note to p. 78a, l. 28.

60. **Glosed . . . lyked,** interpreted the gospel as it pleased them well.

62. **this maistres freris,** these master friars.

62. **at lykyng,** as they like.

64. **sith . . . lordes,** since love (charity), the special function of the friars, has turned peddler, selling absolution instead of giving it, and since the friars have devoted themselves chiefly to shriving lords.

65. **ferlis,** strange things.

66. **But . . . togideres.** The regular clergy and the friars quarreled as to which had the right to hear confession. Sometimes (see l. 81) they agreed to share the profits. Here the poet says, "Unless they hold together better, the greatest mischief in the world will result."

68. **Pardoner,** an officer of the mediæval church commissioned to travel through the country and dispense absolution.

69. **bulle,** a bull, a letter or edict of the pope.

70 f. **assoilen hem alle Of falshed of fastyng,** absolve them all from the sin of breaking their vows of fasting.

137b 74. **blered here eyes,** deceived them.

78. **Were the bischop yblissed,** if the bishop were really a holy man, as he should be.

79. **sent to deceyve;** *i.e.,* sent to the pardoner to be used by him in deceiving.

80. **by,** against.

81. **parten,** divide.

82. **yif thei nere,** if it were not for them.

83. **Persones,** parsons.

83. **pleyned hem,** complained.

84. **sith the pestilence tyme.** The reference is perhaps to the Black Death, which appeared in England in 1348.

85. **To have,** etc.; that is, they petitioned the bishop that they might have, etc. Chaucer praises his Parson because he did not rent his country living and hurry up to London to get a more lucrative position (*Prologue,* l. 507 ff.).

87. **bachelers,** novices in the church.

88. **cure,** a cure, or care, of souls; a position as priest or curate.

91. **an elles,** and at other times.

93. **chalengen his dettes,** claim the debts due the king. The exchequer decided all cases dealing with revenue due the king from the various wards of the city and also claimed for him all waifs and strays — *i.e.,* property without owner.

97. **oures,** prayers recited at stated hours of the day.

99. **consistorie.** The last great court held by Christ at the day of judgment is likened to a consistory or council of the mediæval Church.

101. **as the boke telleth.** The reference is to the famous words of Christ to Peter (Matthew xvi, 19): "I will give unto thee the keys of the kingdom of heaven: and whatsoever thou shalt bind on earth, shall be bound in heaven: and whatsoever thou shalt loose on earth, shall be loosed in heaven."

138a 102 ff. **he it left,** etc.; *i.e.,* Peter left the power of the keys, delegated to him by Christ, to the four cardinal virtues — Prudence, Temperance, Fortitude, and Justice. The poet refers to these as "closyng gatis" because the adjective "cardinal," applied to them, is connected with the Latin word *cardo,* "a hinge."

111. **I can and can naughte,** I *can* speak more, but I must not, out of respect for the holy power which the cardinals possess of electing the pope.

113. **Might of the comunes . . . regne,** the power of the commons caused the king to reign. Note the democratic idea that the king derives his power from the people.

114. **kynde wytte,** common sense.
114. **clerkes,** learned men. Cf. the picture of Chaucer's Clerk, *Prologue,* l. 285 ff.
117. **Casten,** planned.
117. **hem-self fynde,** provide for themselves.
118. **kynde witte craftes,** handicrafts that could be practiced by means of ordinary intelligence.
120. **travaile,** labor.
122. **Shope,** disposed, ordered.
123. **a lunatik.** Perhaps the reference is to the poet himself because his doctrine seemed like that of a madman to his contemporaries.
129 ff. **for lewed men ne coude,** etc. The poet ironically says that ignorant men ought not to be told how to justify themselves.
138b 132 ff. **Sum Rex,** etc., "(You may say) 'I am a king, I am a prince,' (but if you are not careful,) you will be neither ere long. O thou who dost administer the special laws of Christ the king, as thou art just, be also merciful, in order that thou mayst do this better! Justice, naked, desires to be clothed by thee with mercy; such crops as thou desirest to reap, these sow. If justice is stripped bare (by thee), let bare justice be measured out to thee; if mercy is sown (by thee), mayst thou reap mercy." The angel speaks Latin, the language of the Church and of official communications.
139. **a Goliardeys.** Originally the goliard was a reciter of irreverent stories and rhymes (see note to "Anonymous Lyrics," p. 85b); here the goliard is a "glutton of words," a user of many words.
141 f. **Dum rex,** etc., "While the king may be said to have his name (*rex*) from *regere* (to rule), he has the name without the thing itself unless he is zealous to keep the laws." The goliard's words involve a sort of pun.
145. **Precepta Regis,** etc., "The King's precepts are for us the bonds of the law." Note that the common people know only the Latin that the rulers would have them know.
146 ff. **a route of ratones,** etc. The following is one of the best versions of the old fable of the rats and mice holding a parliament to determine who shall hang a bell on their enemy the cat. Here the story is a political allegory, and would be appropriate in 1377, when the old king Edward III was lying ill and the heir apparent was Richard, then eight years old (see note to l. 190). The "old cat" may, however, be John of Gaunt. If so, the poem comes somewhat later in time. The "rats" are the more influential men among the commons; the "mice" the people of less importance.
155. **us lotheth,** we loathe.
155. **or,** before.
157. **aloft,** beyond his reach.
159. **for a sovereygne help to hymselve,** so far as he was concerned.
139a 165. **beighe,** collar.
180. **helden hem unhardy,** thought themselves not daring enough.
183. **Stroke forth . . . alle,** brushed quickly past the rest and stood before them all.
189. **is sevene yere ypassed,** seven years ago.
139b 190. **kitoun,** Richard, son of Edward the Black Prince, who, while still a boy, ascended the throne of England in 1377 as Richard II.
192. **Ve terre,** etc. Woe to the land where the king is a child. The words are a paraphrase of Ecclesiastes x, 16.
193. **may no renke,** etc. The mouse suggests that the rats themselves (the more powerful of the commons) need to be kept in order and that the real trouble is that the true cat (the king) is a child.
195 f. **better is a litel losse,** etc. The meaning is, "The confusion in which we are (a litel losse) is better than having a depraved ruler (a shrewe)."
197 ff. **many mannes malt,** etc. We mice would destroy many a man's malt (for making ale and beer) and you rats would tear men's clothes, were it not for that court cat, which can catch you.
201. **I se so mykel after,** I foresee so much that will come afterward.
203. **costed me nevre,** would have cost me nothing (for I would have given nothing toward its purchase).
204 ff. **though it had coste me catel,** etc. The general sense is, "Though I had contributed to the purchase of the bell, I would not acknowledge it, but would let him do what he likes; both the cat and the kitten, coupled together or uncoupled, may catch what they can."
207. **uche a wise wighte,** every wise man.
207. **wite,** guard.
208. **bemeneth,** means, signifies.
209. **Devine ye, for I ne dar,** Guess ye the meaning, for I dare not.
211. **Serjauntz,** lawyers, who wore coifs as a sign of their profession.
213. **unlese,** unclose.
215. **but,** unless.
216. **bonde-men,** peasants.
216. **als,** also.
140a 222. **Of . . . somme,** of laborers of every kind there leaped forth some.
223. **dykers,** ditchers.
224. **dryven forth . . . Emme!** pass the livelong day singing, "God save you, dame Emme!" (evidently the refrain of some popular song). The meaning is that the laborers wasted their time.
225. **knaves,** servants.
225. **Hote pies,** etc. It was the custom for cooks, shopkeepers, etc., to advertise their goods by such cries as these.
229. **the roste to defye,** to digest the roast.

CHAUCER

Geoffrey Chaucer was a fourteenth-century English man of affairs who, in the leisure hours snatched from a busy life, wrote poetry. His business brought him in contact with all classes of society; and although his training was aristocratic, he was a sympathetic observer of the lower orders. Few poets have ever been more gifted and none more thoroughly human than Chaucer.

He was the son of a substantial London wholesale merchant and exporter. He early entered the service of the court, where he occupied in turn the positions of page, squire, diplomat, and public official. For many years he seems to have been regarded with special favor by John of Gaunt, Duke of Lancaster. In 1359, while still a youth, he went to the continent as a soldier, fought against the French in the Hundred Years' War, was taken prisoner, and was ransomed by the King. In the late sixties or early seventies he married Philippa, a lady in waiting to the Queen. From 1366 till the end of his life he received various pensions, special evidences of royal favor. In 1370 he went to the continent on the first of several diplomatic missions. In 1372 he visited Italy for the first time. In 1374 he was appointed controller of customs on wools and hides for the port of London, and in 1382 controller of petty customs. In 1386 he was a knight and a member of Parliament for Kent. In 1389 he was appointed Clerk of the King's Works, in which capacity he had the oversight of the buildings and repairs of Westminster Palace, the Tower of London, and various royal manors. In 1391 he was appointed a subforester of one of the estates of the Earl of March. In 1394 he received from Richard II a pension, which was increased considerably by Henry IV (cf. notes to *The Compleint of Chaucer to His Empty Purse*, p. 159a). He died about 1400 and was buried in Westminster Abbey.

Chaucer was a great reader, but, like many other poets, he was not learned, nor was he a scholar, even when judged by the standards of his own day. He was an urbane, genial, kindly, mildly satirical man of the world whose genius for portraying humanity elevated him to a place among the immortals.

His genius seems to have developed late. As the court in which he grew up was largely French and as the most influential literature read and discussed there was of French origin, he naturally began his poetical career by imitating French models. Among his early works imitative of French are a translation of part of the great French allegorical love-poem the *Roman de la Rose* ("Romance of the Rose") and a poem commemorating the death of Blanche, the wife of John of Gaunt. In what is usually called his "second period" (beginning about 1379) Chaucer showed clearly that he had felt the spirit of the Renaissance, which had already begun in Italy. In 1372 and again in 1378 he went to Italy on diplomatic missions, and these visits influenced profoundly the development of his genius. He became acquainted with the works of Dante, Petrarch, and Boccaccio (see Chronological Outline), and from them derived not only new poetic material but a new conception of literary art. In the second period belong the *House of Fame* and the *Legend of Good Women*, both considerably indebted to Italian models, and *Troilus and Criseyde*, which is based largely on a work by Boccaccio. As Chaucer developed further in intellect and creative power, he depended less and less upon foreign models. His third, or "English," period includes the *Canterbury Tales*, the plan of which seems to have been conceived by the poet about 1385. The work as a whole is essentially national and English.

140a THE *CANTERBURY TALES*

THE PROLOGUE

The *Canterbury Tales* are the fruit of Chaucer's ripest genius. They are the most readable of the numerous collections of stories made during the Middle Ages. Most of the tales had been told many times before Chaucer took them up, but in Chaucer's hands they generally acquired added picturesqueness and charm. Like the stories in Boccaccio's *Decameron*, Gower's *Confessio Amantis* (see introductory note, p. 159a), and other mediæval and modern collections, Chaucer's tales are fitted into a "frame," or plot, but Chaucer's frame owes little to its predecessors. Moreover, the tales are so skillfully adapted to the character and profession of the narrators that they make no impression of being lugged in as do the tales in many frame-stories. Though the tales are not all told with equal zest and success, the best, among which are the two given here, are supreme examples of the art of narration.

Prefixed to the *Canterbury Tales* is a prologue, which explains how the characters came to be in company and introduces them to the reader. One day in May (the sixteenth, to be precise) Chaucer, so he tells us, found assembled at the Tabard Inn in Southwark some thirty persons, all bound on a pilgrimage to the famous shrine of Saint Thomas à Becket at Canterbury, about fifty-six miles distant. Chaucer, who is also going to Canterbury, soon makes the acquaintance of the other pilgrims, and, being a good mixer, is admitted to their "fellowship." Harry Bailey, the genial host of the inn, proposes that they pass the time on the road by telling stories. Each pilgrim is to tell four tales — two going and two on the return journey (cf. note to *Prologue*, l. 794). The host even offers to accompany them and act as master of ceremonies and as judge of the relative merit of their stories, the teller of the best tale to have a supper at the expense of the rest on their return. The proposal is accepted, and on the next morning the company ride forth. When they have gone about two miles and have stopped to water their horses, lots are drawn, and the "cut" by good luck falls to the Knight, the most distinguished person present, who forthwith begins his tale of chivalry. Chaucer never completed the ambitious program he thus laid out. He wrote only twenty-four of the more than one hundred tales called for; he never got his pilgrims to Canterbury, much less back to Southwark; and the "frame" contains numerous gaps.

The Canterbury pilgrims represent almost every class of fourteenth-century English society. Each is thoroughly typical of his class or profession, but the pilgrims are far more than mere types. They are rendered much more interesting by the discovery that, in some cases at least, they reveal characteristics borrowed from actual individuals with whom Chaucer's varied activities had brought him in contact. (See especially Professor J. M. Manly, *Some New Light on Chaucer*, 1926.) In reading the *Canterbury Tales*, we should remember that the stories are told not to us but to a holiday group of individuals who represent various more or less antagonistic classes or professions, who are trying to obliterate for the time being all social distinctions, but who constantly reveal their personal peculiarities and their class prejudices, even in their tales.

Chaucer and the English Language. — Before the Norman Conquest the Germanic inhabitants of England spoke various dialects, of which those most frequently adopted for literary purposes were (1) Northumbrian, used in the northern monasteries (cf. introductory note to Cædmon's *Hymn*, p. 38a), and (2) West Saxon, the language of Alfred the Great (see introductory note to "Alfred the Great," p. 50b, and note to p. 50b, 30). During the Middle-English period, extending roughly from the early twelfth to the late fifteenth century, the confusion and variety of language became less marked as some one dialect gained the day over the others in the various parts of England. As a result the Middle-English language came to embrace three important dialects: Southern (the language of the south of England and of the region west of the Thames), Northern (the language of ancient Northumbria enriched by contributions from Scandinavian and spoken over a territory considerably larger than its old domain), and Midland (the language spoken in the territory between Northern and Southern). London, it will be remembered, is situated in the Midland district. Its importance as the capital of the country caused the form of English spoken by Londoners (called the "King's English") to become gradually the most important of the Middle English dialects. Thus Midland English, with a considerable admixture of Northern forms, became the basis of the standard modern language. By boldly adopting his native London English as a vehicle for literature, Chaucer not only gave it a dignity it had never possessed before but he made it the beautiful and flexible medium of poetic expression that it still remains.

The Pronunciation of Chaucer's English. — Though the beginner need not learn to pronounce Middle English in order to derive either pleasure or profit from his reading, it is important for him to remember that great changes have taken place in the pronunciation of the English language since the Middle Ages and that the English of Chaucer was in general fuller and rounder in tone and hence more musical than modern English (note especially the long open vowels). Consequently some of the best effects are lost if the text of Chaucer is not read with some approximation to the original pronunciation. The following list includes some of the Middle-English vowels and consonants the sounds of which should be noted especially by the modern reader.

long *a* is pronounced like the *a* in *art:* ga-men, grace.

short *a* like the *a* in *artistic:* fat, carl.

long "open" *e* like the *e* in *there:* ded (dead), heed, hede (head).

long "close" *e* like the *ey* in *they:* feld, scheld.

short *e* like the *e* in *men*: fell, slep-te.

long *i* (or *y*) like the *i* in *machine:* lif (lyf), prime.

short *i* like the *i* in *pin:* wiht, simp-le.

long "open" *o* like the *o* in *lord:* cold, rose.

long "close" *o* like the *o* in *note:* god (good), cok (cook).

short *o* like the *o* in *not:* of, long. In some cases,

as in Modern English, the sound is represented by an *o* but is pronounced like the *u* in *put:* sonne, som.

long *u* somewhat like the *u* in *juice*, or, more correctly, like French *u* and German *ü:* just, nature.

short *u* like the *u* in *full:* drunken, us.

ai (*ay*), *ei* (*ey*) like the *ey* in *they:* dai (day), streit.

au (*aw*) like the *ow* in *how:* felawe, cause.

eu (*ew*) like the *ew* in *few:* knew, hewe.

oi (*oy*) like the *oy* in *joy:* clois-ter, joint.

ou usually like the *oo* in *boot:* now, flour.

ch like the *ch* in *rich:* chirche, speche.

gg usually like *j:* jugg-en (judge), hegge (hedge). But sometimes like *g* in *get* where the hard *g*-sound occurs in modern English: dogge, pig-ges.

gh after a vowel like *ch* in the German word *ach:* knight, dogh-ter.

f between vowels like *v:* wyfes, lyfes.

final *s* like the *s* in *this:* was, wys.

s between vowels like *z:* ese, les-en (lose).

In pronouncing *kn* both letters are sounded: knowe, knave.

r is trilled.

In Chaucer's day many words were written with an *e* at the end, this *e* being the last remaining sign of some termination in the older language. In poetry "final *e*," as this letter is called, might be pronounced or not according to the requirements of the meter. As most of Chaucer's lines in the *Canterbury Tales* are of the five-accent, ten-syllable type familiar in Shakespeare's plays and in Tennyson's *Idylls of the King*, the beginner will have little trouble with the final *e*'s if he will remember that they are pronounced as a separate syllable, much like the *er* in such words as *better*, *bother*, etc., whenever a syllable is required to produce the rhythmic alternation of accented and unaccented syllables, and sometimes when a line contains eleven syllables. In the following lines the pronounced final *e*'s are printed in bold face type:

And sma'|le fo'w|les ma'|ken me'|lody'e
The te'n | dre crop | pes, a'nd | the yo'n | ge so'nne
Ne we'tte | hir fi'ng | res i'n | hir sa'u | ce de'pe.

140a 1 ff. **Whan that Aprille,** etc., "When April with his sweet showers hath pierced the drought of March to the root, and bathed every vein in that sap by whose power (*vertu*) the flower is engendered, and when Zephyr (the West Wind) also with his sweet breath hath inspired the tender shoots in every grove and space of open country, and the young sun hath run half his course in the constellation of the Ram." The Ram (Aries), one of the signs of the Zodiac, covers the period from March 21 till April 11. According to one form of the calendar used during the Middle Ages, the year began on March 25; hence the sun might be called "young" in April. Chaucer was fond of astronomy and is here telling us in roundabout, astronomical language that April had come in and that the sun had run through the part of the Ram that lies in that month; in other words, it was after April 11.

13. **palmers,** pilgrims who went to the Holy Land and brought back palm branches as a token; hence their name "palmers."

17. **The holy blisful martir,** Thomas à Becket, whose tomb at Canterbury was the most famous shrine in mediæval England. Thomas was a distinguished churchman under Henry II, but quarreled with the King and was murdered at Canterbury by four of the King's knights. Henry was blamed for the act, and Thomas was worshiped as a saint.

140b 18. **holpen,** the past participle of *helpen*.

19. **Bifel,** it happened.

20. **Southwerk,** Southwark, across the Thames from London on the south.

20. **Tabard.** Chaucer represents his pilgrims as putting up at an inn that had as its sign a tabard, or jacket without sleeves.

22. **corage,** heart.

24. **Wel,** quite.

25 f. **y-falle In felawshipe,** fallen into association.

46. **fredom,** generosity.

48. **therto,** besides.

49. **hethenesse,** heathen lands, as opposed to Christendom.

51 ff. **Alisaundre,** etc. Mediæval knights frequently fought in foreign countries that happened to be at war (cf. *Squyr of Lowe Degre*, p. 122, l. 190 ff. and p. 128, l. 885 ff.). Chaucer gives a list of the countries and places where the Knight had traveled or fought: Alexandria (Alisaundre), Prussia (Pruce), Lithuania (Lettow), Russia (Ruce), Granada (Gernade), Algezir (in Spain), Belmarye (a Moorish kingdom in Africa), Lyeys (in Armenia), Satalye, Tramissene, Palatye (all three in Asia Minor). He had also been at many a noble landing of troops in the Grete (Mediterranean) Sea.

52 f. **ofte tyme,** etc., "often in Prussia he had been honored by being placed at the head of the table above all other nations."

62 f. **foughten,** etc. Three times had he fought for our faith in the lists (where tournaments were held) in the Moorish kingdom of Tramissene.

65. **Sometyme,** at one time, formerly.

141a 67. **sovereyn prys,** exceedingly great renown.

71. **no maner wight,** no kind of person.

74. **His hors were gode . . . gay,** "His horses were good, but he himself was not

gaudily dressed." *Hors* is an old neuter plural (cf. l. 598).

77 f. **For he was,** etc. Without changing his clothes, he went to perform his pilgrimage, which he had vowed in gratitude for his safe return.

79. **Squyer,** esquire. He attended on the knight and bore his lance and shield.

80. **lovyere,** one skilled in the niceties of courtly love (an elaborate code governing the relationship between the sexes).

80. **bacheler,** a young aspirant to knighthood.

86. **Flaundres,** etc., Flanders, Artois, and Picardy — ancient provinces of northern France. The Squire, though young, had already seen service.

87. **space,** length of time.

88. **stonden . . . grace,** stand well in his lady's favor. *Lady* is an old genitive.

92. **fresh.** The word has none of the modern suggestion of fresh in the sense of "impudent." Note the contrast between the simplicity of the father's dress and the gay attire of the son.

94. **faire,** gracefully.

98. **sleep,** slept, an old past tense.

100. **carf,** carved, an old past tense. The Squire was well brought up according to the ideas of the time.

101. **Yeman,** yeoman, a servant of the degree next above a groom. Cf. Locksley in Scott's *Ivanhoe.*

103. **he,** the Yeoman.

104. **A sheef of pecock-arwes,** a sheaf of arrows with peacock's feathers.

109. **not-heed,** head with hair cut short.

141b 115. **Cristofre,** a figure of St. Christopher worn as a good-luck charm.

120. **by sëynt Loy.** As the patron saint of travelers, St. Loy was an appropriate saint for the Prioress to swear by under the circumstances. Swearing was common among ladies in old times. The Prioress's oath is a very mild and ladylike one.

125. **Stratford atte Bowe,** a Benedictine convent near London. The Prioress was head of the convent school, a sort of young ladies' seminary. She spoke, not Parisian French, but the particular kind of Anglo-French used at Stratford atte Bowe. Chaucer is not ridiculing her pronunciation.

137. **of greet disport,** readily amused.

138. **port,** carriage.

139 f. **peynèd hir . . . court,** took great pains to imitate courtly manners.

142a 160. **shene,** bright.

161. **crownèd A.** The *A* stood for *Amor,* Love or Charity.

162. **Amor vincit omnia,** "Love conquers all things." Unless *Amor* stood for "heavenly love," this was hardly an appropriate motto for the Prioress.

164. **three.** This seems to be a mistake; only one priest is mentioned elsewhere (cf. introductory note to *Nonne Preestes Tale,* p. 149b).

165. **a fair for the maistrye,** suitable for the highest place.

166. **out-rydere.** The Monk was appointed to ride out and inspect the manors, farms, etc., belonging to his monastery. He was also in charge of a "cell," one of the branches of the monastery.

173. **seint Maure — seint Beneit.** St. Benedict (Benet) formulated early in the sixth century the oldest of the "rules," or sets of monastic regulations, of the Roman Church. The Benedictine "rule" was introduced into France by St. Benedict's disciple, St. Maur, and into England by St. Augustine (cf. note, l. 187).

176. **He held . . . space.** He governed himself according to the new state of things. When monasteries grew rich, it was of course difficult to enforce the old strict regulations such as those of St. Benedict, which were particularly insistent upon the importance of manual labor.

177. **yaf,** etc. We should say, "He didn't care a rap," or something of the kind.

177. **pullèd hen.** Plucked hens were said not to lay.

184. **What,** why.

187. **Austin.** St. Austin (Augustine) introduced Christianity into England in 597 (see Introduction to the Old English Period). He, like Chaucer's monk, was a Benedictine.

187. **How . . . be servèd?** How shall the business of the world get done?

193. **seigh,** saw.

194. **of a lond,** in the land.

200. **in good point,** in good condition (French *embonpoint*).

202. **stemèd . . . leed,** shone like a furnace under a cauldron.

142b 208. **Frere.** With Chaucer's description of the Friar, compare what is said of friars in general in *Piers the Plowman,* l. 58 ff. Recall also Friar Tuck in Scott's *Ivanhoe.*

208. **wantown,** lively.

209. **limitour,** a friar who begged within a certain "limitation," or assigned district.

210. **ordres foure.** See note to *Piers the Plowman,* l. 58.

210. **Can,** knows.

211. **daliaunce and fair langage,** gossip and flattery.

214. **post,** pillar or support.

217. **worthy,** respected.

219. **curat,** a minister in charge of a parish. See note to *Piers the Plowman,* l. 88. On the disagreement between the friars and the parish clergy as to the right of hearing confession, see note to *Piers the Plowman,* l. 66.

224. **Ther as he wiste to han,** where he expected to receive.

226. **y-shrive,** confessed.
237. **he bar the prys,** he carried away the prize.
239. **There-to,** besides.
243 ff. **For,** etc., for in the case of such a respected man as he it was not becoming, considering his natural gifts, to deal with such poor people. Contrast the proper work of the friars as indicated in the note to *Piers the Plowman*, l. 58.
250. **lowly of servyse,** humble in offering his services.
251. **vertuous,** capable.
253. **sho,** shoe.

143a 254. **'In principio,'** "In the beginning." Friars in going from house to house were accustomed to repeat in Latin the first verse of the first chapter of the gospel according to St. John, "In the beginning was the word," etc.
258. **love-dayes,** days fixed for settling differences out of court by arbitration. The umpire was frequently a friar.
263. **That rounded . . . presse.** His semicope (short cape), which was round as a bell, had just been pressed.
264. **for his wantownesse,** out of affectation.
270. **forked berd.** Forked beards were fashionable in Chaucer's day.
272. **Flaundrish . . . hat.** Flaundrish (Flemish) hats were popular in England.
273. **faire and fetisly,** gracefully and neatly.
276. **kept for any thing,** kept (safe from piracy) at any cost.
277. **Middelburgh and Orewelle.** Middleburgh, a port of the island of Walcheren, off the Netherlands; Harwich, formerly Orewelle, on the English coast directly opposite.
285. **Clerk.** The term "clerk" might be applied to any learned man. Here, of course, the Clerk is a university student preparing for the ministry.
286. **logik.** The Clerk had long since taken up the study of the philosophy of Aristotle; *i.e.*, he had entered the higher realms of mediæval education. See l. 295 and the notes to p. 91a, 38, and p. 91b, 19 ff.
288. **undertake,** affirm.
291 f. **he had geten,** etc., "he had not yet obtained a position as a priest nor was he worldly enough to get a secular office." One of the easiest ways for a young scholar to rise in the world was to enter administrative work or the service of some rich nobleman (cf. note to l. 507 ff.).

143b 297 f. **al be that,** etc. A philosopher might be at the same time an alchemist and so be chiefly interested in searching for the philosopher's stone, which would turn the baser metals into gold. Chaucer, with delicate humor, observes that although the Clerk was a philosopher, he was not an alchemist, for he had but little gold (money).
307. **souninge,** tending to.
310. **parvys,** the portico of St. Paul's Church, in London, where lawyers commonly met for consultation. See also note to *Piers the Plowman*, l. 211. The title "sergeant" was given only to lawyers of the highest rank.
319. **Al was . . . effect.** The Sergeant was clever enough to avoid any legal encumbrance and so pass the property on to the heirs free from all limitations or conditions. He was a specialist in settling estates.
323. **In termes,** at his command.
327. **coude,** knew.
331. **Frankeleyn,** a substantial though not a noble landholder and a man of importance in his community. In the fourteenth century the franklin occupied approximately the same position as a modern English country gentleman. Chaucer's Franklin was sheriff and a knight of the shire (l. 355 f.).
336. **Epicurus owne sone.** Epicurus was a Greek philosopher (342–270 B.C.). He taught that pleasure of a high and ethical character is the chief end to be aimed at in life; later he was said to have emphasized sensual pleasure. Chaucer, following the popular notion, observes that the Franklin, who was a good liver, was a true son or disciple of Epicurus.
340. **Seynt Iulian,** the patron saint of hospitality. Cf. note to p. 104b, 37.
340. **contree,** countryside.
341. **after oon,** of the same quality.

144a 345. **snewèd.** So abundant a provider was the Franklin that it fairly snowed meat and drink in his house.
351. **but-if,** unless.
353. **His table dormant.** Cf. note to p. 124b, l. 464. The fact that the Franklin's table was always set was a sign of his hospitality.
363. **clothed in o liveree.** Each was clad in the distinctive dress of the guild (fraternitee) or union of the trade that he followed.
372. **alderman,** head of a guild (cf. note to l. 363).
377. **vigilyës,** meetings of the parishioners in the church or churchyard on the eve of a festival. On such occasions it was a fine thing to have precedence over the wives of other tradesmen.
379. **for the nones,** for the occasion. Literally, "for the once."
385. **it thoughte me,** it seemed to me.

144b 389. **Dertemouthe,** Dartmouth on the south coast of Devonshire.
390. **as he couthe,** as well as he was able. Being a sailor, he was little accustomed to riding horses. This is one of the fine touches of realism that characterize Chaucer's descriptions. Chaucer must have known shipmen intimately through his connection with the customs.

396 ff. **Ful many a draughte,** etc. Full many a draught of wine had he drawn (stolen) from Bordeaux on the coast of France while the merchant to whom the wine belonged was asleep, for he cared nothing for delicate conscientious scruples. If he had a fight at sea and got the better of his enemies, he made them walk the plank (sent them home by water). The Shipman, like most sailors of his day, was a thief and somewhat of a pirate.

404. **Cartage,** Carthage in Spain.

406. **With . . . shake.** This is a highly poetical and justly famous line.

410. **Maudelayne.** There was a real vessel called the *Maudelayne* belonging to Dartmouth during the latter part of the fourteenth century. This is another instance of Chaucer's use of details borrowed from real life.

415 f. **kept . . . magic naturel.** According to mediæval astrology, human events were largely determined by the position of the planets with regard to each other and to the horizon at important moments such as that of birth or of beginning some undertaking. The Physician, by means of "natural magic" (*i.e.*, magic produced by natural means), was able to bring it about that the patient was treated at just the moment when the "ascendant" (the relation of the planets to the horizon) was favorable. The "natural magic" used consisted in treating a little image (l. 418) made to resemble the patient. Such images might be used either for good purposes as the physician used them, or for evil, as in Rossetti's *Sister Helen*. Witches have long been accustomed to torture little images of clay or wax in order to injure their enemies.

420. **hoot or cold, or moiste, or drye.** According to mediæval science, the world is composed of four elements — earth, air, fire, and water — which represent four qualities — hot, cold, dry, and moist. These qualities or "humors" (l. 421) are the causes of the four "complexions" or characteristic temperaments of men — the melancholy (cold and dry) temperament, in which black bile predominates; the choleric (hot and dry) temperament, in which choler predominates; the phlegmatic (cold and moist) temperament, in which phlegm predominates; and the sanguine (hot and moist) temperament, in which warm blood predominates. Our modern adjectives "melancholy," "choleric," "phlegmatic," and "sanguine" derive their meanings ultimately from mediæval medical science.

429 ff. **Esculapius,** etc. Chaucer here gives a list of the chief authorities on medicine during the Middle Ages. Esculapius was the god of Medicine among the Ancients; Dioscorides, Rufus, Hippocrates, and Galen were Greek physicians; Haly, Rhasis, Damascenus, Serapion, and Avicenna were Arabians; Averroës was a Moorish scholar; Constantyn was a monk of Monte Cassino in Italy; "Gilbertyn" is perhaps the celebrated English medical authority, Gilbertus Anglicus; Bernard was a professor of medicine at Montpellier; and John of Gatisden was a noted physician of Oxford. The two last named were contemporaries of Chaucer.

145a 438. **His studie,** etc. Doctors were commonly regarded as skeptics. Cf. Sir Thomas Browne's words at the beginning of his *Religio Medici*.

442. **wan in pestilence,** acquired during the pestilence. See note to *Piers the Plowman*, l. 84. Besides the great plague of 1348–1349, there were lesser plagues in England in 1362, 1369, and 1376.

443 f. **gold . . . cordial.** Powdered gold in oil was regarded as a remedy for certain diseases. Chaucer jokingly observes that the Physician, knowing the value of gold (money), loved it especially. The Doctor charged high for his services.

445. **A good Wyf . . . of bisyde Bathe.** Chaucer's picture of the Wife of Bath is one of the best in the *Prologue*. It seems that the poet had in mind a real woman who lived in a small village near Bath in Somerset.

447. **clooth-making.** In Chaucer's day and long afterward Bath and the surrounding district were famous for cloth making.

448. **Ypres and Gaunt,** Ypres and Ghent, towns in Flanders famous for manufacturing clothing.

449 f. **ne was ther noon.** No woman in the parish could go ahead of her when the congregation went forward to kiss the relics and make an offering.

453. **coverchiefs,** coverings for the head.

453. **ground,** texture.

454. **ten pound.** Mediæval headdresses were often heavy with gold and silver network.

457. **moiste,** soft.

460. **chirche-dore.** Marriages were celebrated at the church door.

461. **Withouten other companye,** besides other lovers.

465. **Boloigne.** There was an image of the Virgin at Boulogne in France.

466. **Galice.** See note to *Piers the Plowman*, l. 47.

466. **Coloigne.** At Cologne were said to be preserved the bones of the three kings (or wise men) who came from the East to worship the new-born Christ.

468. **gat-tothèd . . . seye,** to tell the truth, her teeth were set wide apart. An old saying has it that, if your teeth are wide

apart, you will travel. The Wife of Bath was a great traveler.

475. **remedyes of love.** The reference is to Ovid's *Remedia Amoris* ("Remedies of Love"), a well-known book during the Middle Ages.

476. **the olde daunce,** the old game of the art of administering love remedies.

478. **Persoun.** The Parson, a representative of the parish clergy, is described with the greatest sympathy, a fact which shows that Chaucer recognized and approved the spirit of true religion when he found it. With Chaucer's portrait should be compared that by Goldsmith in the *Deserted Village* (p. 572b, l. 141 ff.).

145b 486. **Ful looth were him,** etc. He disliked extremely to excommunicate those who refused to pay tithes, monetary obligations to the church.

494. **muche and lyte,** high and low.

503. **take keep,** take care.

507 ff. **He sette nat,** etc. He did not leave his parishioners in the care of a strange priest while he sought at St. Paul's in London the easy and lucrative position of a chantry or joined a brotherhood in order to save living expenses. Chantries were establishments founded by men who wished to employ priests to pray for their souls.

525. **wayted after,** looked for, expected.

529. **Plowman.** Compare Chaucer's Plowman with Piers the Plowman — the type of unspoiled humanity and true religion (see introductory note to *Piers the Plowman*).

146a 534. **him gamed or smerte,** it was pleasant or unpleasant to him.

541. **mere.** Had the Plowman been a man of quality, he would have scorned to ride a mare.

542. **Reve.** The Reeve was a sort of steward or overseer in charge of an estate.

543. **Somnour.** The business of a sommoner was to act as bailiff to summon offenders against ecclesiastical law before the ecclesiastical courts. It should be remembered that in Chaucer's day the Church had its own system of courts for the trial of offenses against church law.

543. **Pardoner,** see note to *Piers the Plowman*, l. 68, and *Prologue*, l. 687.

545. **for the nones.** Here probably means "extremely." For another meaning, see l. 379.

548. **ram,** the usual prize at wrestling matches.

560. **goliardeys.** See introductory notes to Anonymous Lyrics, p. 85b, and to *Piers the Plowman*, l. 139.

562. **tollen thryes,** take toll, or payment, three times for grinding the grain.

563. **a thombe of gold.** A miller tested the output of his mill with his thumb, and his profits depended upon his skill in testing. "An honest miller," runs an old saying, "has a thumb of gold." The meaning is that, since no miller actually has a thumb of gold, no miller is honest. Chaucer's Miller was not honest, but he had a thumb of gold, nevertheless, for he paid himself well for his labor.

567. **A gentle Maunciple . . . of a temple.** A manciple's business was to purchase supplies for a monastery, a college, or, as here, a "temple," one of the inns of court or community houses occupied by a legal society.

571. **achat,** buying.

572. **ay biforn,** always ahead.

573 ff. **Now,** etc. Now is it not a goodly gift of God that an unlearned man like the Manciple can hoodwink ("set the cap of," l. 586) a whole household of men trained in the law? See note to l. 567.

146b 581. **propre,** own.

582. **but he were wood,** unless he were mad.

587. **colerik.** Cf. note to l. 420.

594. **auditour,** an auditor, a person appointed to check the Reeve's accounts.

604. **he,** the Reeve.

605. **the deeth,** the plague.

619. **Northfolk.** The spelling indicates the etymology of the word *Norfolk*.

622. **route,** company.

147a 624. **cherubinnes face.** Cherubs were usually depicted as having red faces.

642 f. **a jay,** etc. A jay can pronounce the name "Wat" (Walter) as well as any *man*, even the pope. The English jay can be trained to talk.

646. **'Questio quid iuris',** "The question is, what is the law (bearing on the case)?" This is one of the scraps of Latin picked up by the Summoner while attending the law courts.

650. **good felawe,** disreputable person. This was a slang usage in Chaucer's day.

652. **a finch . . . coude he pulle,** he knew how to trick an ignorant person.

654 ff. **He wolde techen,** etc. He would teach the offender not to fear excommunication if he possessed money, for by paying a certain sum he could escape punishment, except that, of course, entailed by the loss of his money. The archdeacon was the officer who presided over the lowest ecclesiastical court.

660. **him drede,** be afraid.

662. **war him of,** let him beware of.

662. **significavit,** the writ issued by the secular authorities for the apprehension of an excommunicated person.

665. **was al hir reed,** was entirely their adviser.

666 f. **gerland . . . ale-stake.** Extending from the front of alehouses was commonly a pole, or "ale-stake," to which was attached a "bush," made of ivy leaves, and a "garland," made of three hoops set at right angles to each other and covered with ribbon.

147b 670. **Rouncival,** perhaps the London branch or "cell" (cf. note, l. 166) of the Priory of Roncevaux in Navarre, France.
673. **bar . . . burdoun.** The Summoner sang deep bass. The song seems to be lost.
682. **the newe jet,** the new fashion, the one described in the preceding lines.
692. **fro Berwick into Ware,** *i.e.*, from one end of England to the other.
702. **up-on lond,** in the country.
148a 726. **n'arette it . . . vileinye,** do not ascribe it to my ill breeding. Chaucer skillfully shifts to the shoulders of his characters the responsibility for some of the shady stories he tells.
734. **large,** coarsely.
740. **vileinye,** vulgarity.
741. **Plato.** This saying of Plato comes from Boethius' *Consolation of Philosophy,* on which cf. note, p. 91b, 22.
752. **marshal.** See *Squyr of Lowe Degre,* l. 7 and l. 311 ff.
753. **stepe,** large.
754. **Chepe,** Cheapside in London.
765. **herberwe,** inn.
148b 770. **The blisful martir . . . mede,** May the blessed martyr reward you.
785. **Us thoughte . . . wys,** it seemed to us not worth while to make it a matter of deliberation.
788. **Lordinges,** Gentlemen.
794. **othere two.** This would make each pilgrim tell four tales. As a matter of fact, Chaucer never completed one tale for each. There are actually only twenty-four Canterbury Tales.
795. **whylom,** formerly.
798. **sentence,** meaning.
799. **our aller cost,** at our joint expense.
149a 817. **In heigh and lowe,** in all respects.
826. **watering of seint Thomas,** a place for watering horses at a brook two miles out from London on the road to St. Thomas' shrine at Canterbury.
829. **forward,** agreement.
838. **draweth cut,** draw lots, draw straws.
848. **composicioun,** agreement.

149b THE NONNE PREESTES TALE

The story that Chaucer puts into the mouth of the nun's priest (see note to *Prologue,* l. 164) is one of the most charming and characteristic of The Canterbury Tales. A convincing evidence of Chaucer's skill is the fact that though he attributes to Chanticleer and Pertelote (Partlet) the language and behavior of fourteenth-century courtly gentlemen and ladies, he never overdoes it; they are still interesting as barnyard fowls. The following points should be remembered in connection with the tale. (1) It is not a fable, like those of Æsop; *i.e.*, a story in which the animal characters are merely used to point a moral. The *Nonne Preestes Tale* bears no heavy burden of moral instruction, and hence is all the more delightful. (2) It belongs to a vast body of literature known as the "beast epic," in which animals play the part of human beings. It is, however, different from simple folk tales with animal heroes, such, for example, as the Br'er Rabbit stories of our own country; nor is it a biting and at times vulgar satire on society like the great animal epic of *Renard the Fox,* which flourished during the Middle Ages. Chaucer is a perfectly conscious artist, individual in his treatment, and, although he uses the high epic style, he does so only in gentle mockery (cf. notes to l. 359 ff. and l. 407 f.). (3) In its frequent digressions, which introduce *exempla* (illustrative stories designed to hammer in the moral: ll. 165 ff., 247 ff., 406 ff., 505 ff.), it is much like a mediæval sermon and hence is appropriate to the priest.
12. **bour.** In mediæval castles the *bour* (bower) consisted of the private apartments set aside especially for the use of the ladies of the family; the hall was the public living and dining room. The humor of Chaucer's line may consist in Chaucer's having visualized the widow's cottage as containing but one room which was without fireplace or chimney — hence sooty with smoke — and which served as a roosting place for the chickens (l. 64) and as "hall" and "bower" for the widow and her daughters.
29. **Chauntecleer,** the name for the cock in the beast epic of *Renard the Fox* (see introductory note). The word means the "Clear Singer."
31. **orgon.** In Chaucer's day the word "orgon" (organ) was treated as plural, doubtless because the instrument has a number of pipes.
35 ff. **knew he,** etc. The meaning is that the cock by instinct knew how to estimate the time required for the sun to move one degree in the latitude in which he lived; whenever it had ascended 15°, *i.e.*, one hour, he crew. Chaucer was interested in astronomy and wrote a treatise on the subject. See also note to *Prologue,* l. 415 ff.
150a 54. **in hold,** in possession.
59. **'my lief is faren in londe',** my beloved has gone away. The title of a popular song of the time.
71. **verray,** true, sound.
74. **me mette,** I dreamed. Cf. the phrase "me thought."
81. **wolde han had me deed,** would have killed me.
94. **free,** generous.
150b 96. **tool,** weapon.
105. **humours.** See note to *Prologue,* l. 420.
106. **met,** dreamed. Cf. note to l. 74.
108. **rede colera,** sometimes called "red hu-

mor," the result of too much bile and blood. It was said to cause one to dream of red things just as melancholy caused dreams of black things. See note to *Prologue*, l. 420.

112. **lyte,** little.

120. **Catoun,** Dionysius Cato, a writer of unknown date, to whom is attributed a collection of moral precepts called "Distichs," from which Dame Partlet quotes. The book was much read during the Middle Ages.

121. **do no fors of,** take no notice of.

122. **flee fro the bemes;** *i.e.*, fly down from the rafters on which they roosted.

124. **Up,** upon.

132. **kynde,** nature.

135. **colerik.** See note to *Prologue*, l. 420.

139. **fevere terciane,** tertian fever, an intermittent fever recurring every other day.

151a 146. **yve,** ivy.

146. **mery,** pleasant. The herbs prescribed by Dame Partlet are really unpleasant to the taste, but she conceals this fact from her husband.

148. **fader,** father's. An old genitive.

150. **graunt mercy,** great thanks.

155. **many a man,** etc. Dreams and their significance were discussed seriously in old times.

164. **Oon of the gretteste auctours.** The reference is to Cicero's treatise *De Divinatione* ("On Divination"). The story told by the cock is a typical *exemplum* (see introductory note to the *Nonne Preestes Tale*).

170. **o,** one, a single.

151b 190. **took of this no keep,** paid no attention to the matter.

222. **gapinge upright,** lying flat on the back with the mouth open.

223. **crye out on,** call upon.

224. **kepe,** guard.

225. **Harrow,** a cry of distress.

227. **out-sterte,** hastened out.

152a 243. **to drede,** to be feared.

256. **that oo,** one of the two.

258. **agayn,** toward.

264. **lette,** leave off, abandon.

269. **my thinges,** my business affairs.

280. **what mischaunce it eyled,** what mischance was responsible for it.

152b 281. **casuelly,** by chance.

290. **Kenelm.** According to tradition Kenelm, the seven-year old son of Kenulph, king of Mercia in the early ninth century, had a vision portending his death and was later murdered by order of his aunt. He was afterward made a saint.

303. **Macrobeus.** The *Somnium Scipionis* ("Scipio's Dream"), a work composed by the fifth-century Roman grammarian Macrobius on the basis of a passage in Cicero's *De Republica* ("Republic"), was widely read during the Middle Ages. Though primarily philosophic in purpose, the book contains much dream lore.

308. **Daniel.** Read the whole of the second chapter of the book of Daniel.

310. **Joseph.** Read Genesis xl, 5–23.

318. **Cresus,** Crœsus, king of Lydia from 560 to 546 B.C. He is most famous for his power and wealth.

321. **Andromacha.** This story is not found in Homer. It occurs in an apocryphal history of the Trojan War, written probably during the sixth century after Christ and attributed to one Dares Phrygius, an alleged eyewitness. Dares' work was widely read during the Middle Ages.

334. **I ne telle . . . store,** I consider laxatives of no value.

153a 343 f. **In principio . . . confusio.** See note to *Prologue*, l. 254. The cock says, "As surely as *In principio* (or, as we should say, 'as sure as gospel'), woman is man's undoing." But notice that he says it in Latin, knowing that Dame Partlet, being a lady, does not understand the language. The translation that he palms off on her is given in l. 346.

359 ff. **He loketh,** etc. The mock-heroic strain that runs throughout the tale is here obvious. Chaucer describes Chanticleer as if he were an epic hero. Note also the comparison of the fox to famous traitors of antiquity (l. 407 f.). See also note to l. 535 ff.

367 f. **The month,** etc. Mediæval theologians taught that the world was created in March. Compare the old method of beginning the year in March (*Prologue*, note to l. 1 ff.).

368. **That highte March,** that is called March. Chaucer means that March had passed and thirty-two days more; in other words, that it was the third of May. Instead of "thirty dayes and two," Chaucer should have said that two months and two days had passed since March began. Chaucer is not always exact when he tries to turn astronomical computations into verse.

374. **Taurus,** the Bull, one of the twelve signs of the Zodiac. Compare note to *Prologue*, l. 1 ff.

377. **pryme,** 9 A.M.

153b 384. **fil a sorweful cas,** befell a sorrowful event.

389. **sovereyn notabilitee,** a thing supremely worthy of note.

391 f. **al-so — as,** as — as.

392. **Launcelot de Lake,** one of the most famous Arthurian romances, especially popular with women because it tells the love story of Lancelot and Guenevere. It is full of incredible tales.

394. **sentence,** subject, main thread of my story.

395. **col-fox,** a sly fox; a fox with more black fur than ordinary; also a deceitful fox.

397. **forn-cast,** foreordained.
407 f. **Scariot,** etc., Judas Iscariot, who betrayed Christ; **Genilon,** who, according to the *Chanson de Roland,* betrayed and caused the death of Roland; **Sinon,** who induced the Trojans to bring the wooden horse inside the walls of Troy and so caused the fall of the city.
420 f. **I ne can not,** etc. During the Middle Ages, as during other periods in the history of the Christian church, disputes regarding predestination, free will, and salvation by merit or by free grace, were common. Of the questions involved Chaucer says, "I cannot sift the matter out." **Augustyn,** Saint Augustine (A.D. 354–430), the most illustrious of the Latin Church Fathers and the great advocate of predestination. **Boëce,** Boethius (see note to p. 91b, l. 22). **Bradwardyn,** professor and chancellor of the university of Oxford and Archbishop of Canterbury, another distinguished opponent of free will. He flourished about the middle of the fourteenth century.
425. **simple necessitee,** absolute predestination, as contrasted with "necessitee condicionel" (l. 430), limited freedom of the will.
154a 436. **colde,** baneful. The line is an old proverb.
438. **made Adam fro paradys to go.** See note to p. 84b, l. 20.
440. **But for I noot,** but because I don't know.
445 f. **Thise been,** etc. A delightful touch.
450. **mermayde.** See p. 90a, l. 34 ff.
451. **Phisiologus.** See p. 90a, l. 46, and note.
456. **No-thing ne liste,** not at all did it please.
467. **If I,** etc., if I should do you any harm or act of rudeness.
471. **stevene,** voice.
474. **Boëce,** Boethius (see note to p. 91b, l. 22) was an authority on music and wrote a treatise on the subject.
480. **So mote . . . tweye,** as I hope to enjoy the use of my two eyes.
154b 492 ff. **daun Burnel the Asse.** This is an allusion to a twelfth-century poem written by Nigellus Wireker and entitled *Burnellus seu Speculum Stultorum* ("Burnel, or the Mirror of Fools"). It is here that Chaucer found the story of the cock who, to revenge himself on the priest who had struck him on the leg, when he was young and nice (foolish), failed to waken his enemy on the morning of his ordination and so caused him to lose his benefice.
509. **Ecclesiaste,** the apocryphal book of Ecclesiasticus, or the Wisdom of Jesus the Son of Sirach, xii, 10–12 and 16. For other references to this popular work, see notes to p. 91a, l. 1 ff.
513. **for the nones.** See note to *Prologue,* l. 379.
521 f. **Friday — Venus.** Friday is Venus' day, and Venus, being the goddess of Love, should have been specially favorable to the cock.
527 ff. **Gaufred.** Geoffrey de Vinsauf about 1200 wrote a treatise on poetry into which he introduced a lament for the death of Richard I. Chaucer is here making fun of Geoffrey's bombastic tirade against Friday, the day on which Richard was slain.
155a 535 ff. **swich cry,** etc. Again the mock-heroic.
539. **Eneydos,** Virgil's *Æneid.*
543. **Hasdrubales wyf.** Hasdrubal, king of Carthage, killed himself when the Romans sacked Carthage (146 B.C.), and his wife burned herself. He should not be confused with Hasdrubal, the brother of Hannibal, who was slain in battle and whose head was thrown into Hannibal's camp.
155b 573. **benedicite.** Literally "bless ye (the Lord)"; here a mere expletive about equivalent to "bless my soul!" "goodness me!" or some similar expression.
574. **Jakke Straw.** Jack Straw's rebellion (1381) resulted in the death of many Flemish merchants.
588. **as wis God helpe me,** so may God truly help me.
156a 621. **seint Paul seith.** Cf. 2 Timothy iii, 16.
625. **my lord,** the Archbishop of Canterbury, head of the Church in England. William Courtnay occupied this position at the time Chaucer wrote these words.

THE PARDONERS TALE

The Pardoner (see *Prologue,* l. 669 ff., and note to *Piers the Plowman,* l. 68), when asked for a moral tale, preaches a sermon which, along with extensive digressions, contains the tale given here. The story is extremely old and, because of its highly dramatic character and its obvious moral, was often told during the Middle Ages. Chaucer's version, with its background of fourteenth-century England, where death stalked abroad in the form of the plague (see note to *Prologue,* l. 442), makes an irresistible impression of tragic fatality.
1. **Flaundres.** See note to *Prologue,* l. 86.
2. **haunteden,** followed after.
11. **grisly,** terrible.
12. **to-tere.** According to the teachings of the mediæval Church, swearing by any part of Christ's body wounded him in that member. In l. 44 one of the characters swears by God's (*i.e.,* Christ's) arms.
16. **belle clinke.** At funerals during the Middle Ages a bell was carried by the sexton before the corpse.
18. **knave,** servant.
24. **felawe,** companion.
31. **this pestilence,** during this plague. See note to *Prologue,* l. 442.

36. **dame,** mother.
156b 47. **avow,** vow.
69. **carl,** churl, country fellow.
74. **Inde,** India.
83. **leve moder,** dear mother. The earth is his mother (as she is of us all).
86 ff. **cheste.** He would gladly exchange for a shroud (l. 88) the chest that holds all his earthly possessions. The furniture of a mediæval bedroom usually included a chest for holding clothing and valuables.
157a 92. **vileinye,** discourtesy.
95 f. **Agayns,** etc. Cf. Leviticus xix, 32. *Agayns* means " before," " in the presence of."
96. **reed,** advice.
103. **hasardour,** gambler.
117. **ook,** oak.
118. **boghte agayn,** redeemed.
157b 142. **doon us honge,** cause (men) to hang us, cause us to be hanged.
144. **slyly,** secretly, carefully.
145. **rede,** advise.
145. **cut,** lots.
168. **noot,** a shortened form of *ne wot,* "know not."
180. **ryve,** rive, pierce.
158a 185. **lustes,** desires.
194 f. **the trone Of god,** heaven.
215. **corn,** grain.
218. **a paas,** in walking.
226. **swinke,** toil.
158b 237. **par cas,** by chance.

TRUTH

BALADE DE BON CONSEYL

2. **Suffyce . . . smal,** Be content with thy property, though it be small.
3. **climbing,** ambition.
6. **that,** thou who.
7. **trouthe shal delivere.** " The Truth shall make you free " (John viii, 32).
8. **Tempest thee noght,** etc., Do not distress yourself by trying to reform the world.
9. **hir that . . . bal,** Fortune. The figure of fickle Fortune with her wheel revolving like a ball and determining arbitrarily the fates of men was constantly present to the mediæval mind.
10. **Gret reste stant,** etc., Much repose consists in abstinence from fussiness (Skeat).
11. **be war to sporne,** be wary of kicking. Cf. " It is hard for thee to kick against the pricks (*i.e.*, an awl) " (Acts ix, 5).
12. **Stryve noght,** etc., strive not. A reference to Æsop's fable about the sad fate of the earthenware pot that struck against one of brass. An earthen pot would fare even worse if it strove against a wall.
13. **Daunte thy-self,** etc., Thou that subduest the deeds of another, subdue thyself.
19. **look up,** look up to thy country, which is Heaven. There is an old saying that beasts look down, man up.
19. **Of al,** for all things.
159a 21. **Envoy.** An envoy is an explanatory postscript.
22. **thou vache.** This address, so long a puzzle, may involve a pun. The French word *vache* not only has the obvious meaning of " cow " (cf. *beste* in l. 18), but it also forms part of the name of Sir Philip la Vache or de la Vache, who married Elizabeth, daughter of Chaucer's friend, Sir Lewis Clifford. The poem may therefore be addressed to Sir Philip.

THE COMPLEINT OF CHAUCER TO HIS EMPTY PURSE

In this charming poem Chaucer applies the language of courtly love to his purse. The envoy is addressed to Henry IV, who, after having ousted Richard II, was acknowledged King by Parliament on September 30, 1399. We need not take Chaucer's complaint of dire poverty too seriously; but if he was in want, it is pleasant to know that he received an additional pension from the crown on October 13 of the same year. If Chaucer died in 1400, which is not absolutely certain, this poem is one of his latest compositions.

10. **colour,** a reference to the color of gold coins.
19. **I am shave,** etc., I am shaved as clean of money as a friar's tonsure, or shaven crown, is of hair.
22. **conquerour of Brutes Albioun,** Henry IV, who defeated Richard II (see Daniel's *Civil Wars,* p. 234 ff. and notes) and claimed the throne by right of descent and of conquest. On Brute, see note to p. 88b, l. 25. It will be recalled that Henry IV was John of Gaunt's son, a fact that may account for Chaucer's addressing a petition to him and for the king's gracious response in the form of a pension.

JOHN GOWER

John Gower owned extensive estates both in Kent and in other counties. Though he was widely read and was acquainted with court life, he lacked the delicacy of taste, sense of humor, and the joy of living that characterize Chaucer's work. He tried literature in the lighter vein, but he was not successful at it. His French poems mark him as the last of the Anglo-Norman poets. In general he seems to have been a typical conservative aristocrat.

Gower's chief works are three long poems — the *Miroir de l'Omme* ("Mirror of

Man"), a sermon written in French and dealing with the virtues and vices, the life of man, and the way of salvation; the *Vox Clamantis* ("Voice of One Crying in the Wilderness"), written in Latin and attributing the evils of the day, especially the peasant revolt under Wat Tyler and Jack Straw, to the baseness of human society; and the *Confessio Amantis* ("Lover's Confession"), an immense compilation written in English and consisting of a discussion of various sins with some hundred illustrative stories awkwardly inserted. Venus, who has little love for the poet, advises him to confess to her priest, Genius. Genius, on being consulted, discusses the seven deadly sins and various minor offences, pointing the moral of each by means of a story. When the confession is ended, Venus makes fun of the poet, who is too old to love. Gower was not a great poet, but some of his stories are excellent examples of the art of narration. His practice of writing in three different languages is illustrative of the uncertainty that prevailed in fourteenth-century England regarding the proper language for literary composition (see note on the Language of Chaucer).

PHYLLIS AND DEMOPHON

Demophon (or Demophoön) was one of the heroes who accompanied the Greeks against Troy. On his return he gained the love of Phyllis, daughter of Sithon, king of Thrace, and promised to marry her. He departed to arrange for the wedding, but as he remained away longer than Phyllis expected, she committed suicide. She was later transformed into a tree.

159b 4. **Rhodopeie,** Rhodopeia, a country near the mountain range of Rhodope in Thrace. Gower calls it a city (l. 10). Phyllis's father was king of Thrace.

5. **Æolus,** the god of the winds.

36. **as innocent,** like one who was innocent.

46. **monthe day,** a month.

160a 103. **all hir owne,** all alone.

160b 111. **ever in one,** continually.

123. **spille,** destroy.

130. **dede,** placed, tied.

135. **ayein the slowe,** against slow people. The story is told as a sort of *exemplum* of slowness or forgetfulness in love.

139. **Philliberd.** Phyllis was transformed into a filbert tree.

CEIX AND ALCEONE

Alcyone (or Halcyone), the daughter of Æolus, was the wife of Ceyx. The pair were so happy that when Ceyx perished in a shipwreck and Alcyone in grief threw herself into the sea, the gods transformed husband and wife into birds. "It was fabled that during the seven days before, and as many after, the shortest day of the year, while the bird *alcyone* was breeding, there always prevailed calms at sea." According to tradition the alcyone was the kingfisher, the ceyx a kind of sea gull. One form of the story is told by Ovid, from whom Chaucer derived most of the version which he incorporates in his *Book of the Duchess.*

7. **Dedalion,** Dædalion, who out of grief for the death of his daughter threw himself from Parnassus, but was changed into a falcon (*goshauk*, l. 9).

161a 12. **pelrinage,** pilgrimage.

19 f. **reformèd, Of that,** etc., formed over again from the shape into which he had been transformed.

51. **high estage,** the lofty dwelling of the gods.

61. **Chimerie.** See note to Milton's *l'Allegro*, l. 10.

65 ff. **Under a hille,** etc. Cf. Spenser's description of the dwelling of the god of Sleep, p. 221, l. 345 ff.

161b 85. **Lethes,** Lethe, the personification of Oblivion; also a river in the lower world whose waters caused those who drank to forget the past.

91. **Hebenus,** ebenus, the ebon tree, the juice of which was supposed to cause drowsiness.

100. **So.** *Read* She.

113. **Morpheus,** the god of dreams.

113. **the whose,** whose.

162a 128 f. **other while . . . jape,** sometimes is true evidence, sometimes only a trick.

139. **sih hym dien,** saw him die.

144. **Whiche,** etc., who feared for their lady.

146 ff. **she . . . Hir swevene hath told,** etc. On the importance attached to dreams during the Middle Ages, see Chaucer's *Nonne Preestes Tale*, l. 155 ff. and notes.

BALLADS

A ballad may be defined as a song that tells a story. A popular ballad differs from other narrative poems in the following important respects. (1) It reflects the mind of simple, unlettered folk with common interests. (2) It is traditional; *i.e.*, it is handed down from one generation to another by word of mouth. (3) It is impersonal in tone; *i.e.*, the emotions expressed are as much those of the community as they are those of the author. It may deal with almost any matter that stirs the homogeneous group — the story of an unfaithful lover or mistress, a returned ghost, the deeds of a bold outlaw who spoils the rich but befriends the poor — or it may grow out of a common occupation, as is the case with weaving songs, cowboy songs, and songs of the cotton fields. In all cases it is simple in plot, in technique, and in metrical structure, and the emotions portrayed are elementary — love, hate, fear, jealousy, etc. The great sometimes figure in the ballads, but the kings and queens of popular literature are portrayed with the naïve technique of folk and fairy tales. (See note to *Sir Patrick Spens*, p. 164b.) Whether the popular ballads originated with individual authors or were composed by various members of a group acting under a common impulse, they were written for the folk, they are the property of the folk, and in substance and spirit they reveal nothing of that personal, individual reaction which is so important in lyric poetry. They pass from mouth to mouth and in so doing undergo various alterations, additions, and subtractions. In England the great flourishing period of the popular ballad included the fourteenth and fifteenth centuries, but popular ballads have been composed since the Middle Ages whenever the common interest and stimulus and the proper degree of remoteness from sophisticated and bookish influences have been present. Many popular ballads reveal high poetic genius; many more ballads that pass for popular are vitiated by vulgarity or commonplaceness of style or content.

When eighteenth-century England began to seek new sources of inspiration in the past and in simple life (see Introduction to Restoration and Eighteenth Century), many ballads were recorded and published and many imitations were composed. Among the most important collections were Bishop Percy's *Reliques of Ancient English Poetry*, 1765, and Sir Walter Scott's *Minstrelsy of the Scottish Border*, 1802. Several eighteenth-century imitations and forgeries are printed on pages 532 ff. of this volume. They vary all the way from Lady Wardlaw's *Hardyknute*, which smacks little of the popular, to the clever imitations by Scott, who was soaked in the lore of popular tradition, but they always betray somehow their literary origin. The eighteenth-century enthusiasm for popular ballads was part of a general romantic interest in folk literature, which has increased until to-day any song or tale that shows popular characteristics is seized upon with avidity by the reading public.

163a EDWARD

Edward has been called "one of the noblest and most sterling specimens of the popular ballad." It illustrates admirably the repetition of phrases and ideas which is so characteristic of genuine folk poetry. It is still sung in parts of the southern United States.

163b THE THREE RAVENS

"True love at its best, stronger than death" (Gummere).

164a THOMAS RYMER

Thomas Rymer and the romance of *Thomas of Erceldoune* deal with the same theme.

164b SIR PATRICK SPENS

Sir Patrick Spens, like many other ballad heroes, is not mentioned in history, but there are at least two historical or semi-historical accounts of thirteenth-century princesses and their suites lost at sea while going to or from Britain.

LORD THOMAS AND FAIR ANNET

The fickle or perfidious lover or mistress is a favorite personage in ballad literature. In this ballad the tragic interest is heightened by a double murder and a suicide.

166b SWEET WILLIAM'S GHOST

The whole tribe of the ghost world, especially the dead lover or maiden who returns to ask back an unfulfilled promise of marriage, have an eerie fascination for the imagination of the folk. Here the lover returns, not, as the present version says, from "afar beyond the sea," but from the neighboring churchyard. Cf. *William and Margaret*, p. 538 f., a tinkered eighteenth-century "improvement" on a genuine old ballad.

167a THE WIFE OF USHER'S WELL

From a version taken down some years ago in North Carolina it appears that the children's motive for returning was to warn their mother against the danger of obstinate grief, but no such motivation is needed to heighten the effect.

168a ROBIN HOOD AND GUY OF GISBORNE

History says nothing of Robin Hood. The Robin Hood of the ballads is probably an idealized composite of numerous individuals who aroused the patriotic enthusiasm of the English common people by resisting the tyranny of the Norman conquerors and by taking the part of the peasants against the encroachments of church and state. Because perhaps of the gap between lines

8 and 9 of our ballad, the story is rather difficult to trace on the first reading. Robin Hood has apparently just had a dream in which he was beaten and bound by two men. Having faith in dreams, he sets out to find them. They turn out to be his enemies, Guy of Gisborne and the Sheriff of Nottingham.

171b THE HUNTING OF THE CHEVIOT

The best introduction to this stirring heroic ballad is Sir Philip Sidney's comment in his *Defense of Poesy* (p. 293a, 1 ff.). Both *The Hunting of the Cheviot* and another ballad, *The Battle of Otterburn,* are founded upon the historical battle of Otterburn, fought between the English and the Scots in August, 1388; but here, as always when the popular imagination begins to work upon historical material, the facts are distorted. In this case the changes are to the advantage of the English.

175a JOHNIE ARMSTRONG

The historical John Armstrong was a daring freebooter who made raids both on the English and the Scottish side of the border during the first half of the sixteenth century. He was taken prisoner in 1530 by King James V of Scotland and executed. His capture, it seems, was effected by means dishonorable to the crown, and his execution apparently was not the result of a fair trial. The brave outlaw is always an appealing figure, especially when he appears to be the victim of injustice.

LYRICS

176a Besides the stream of mediæval poetry illustrated by the Latin lyrics translated on p. 85 f., there were composed in English a large number of lyrics which prove that during the Middle Ages England was fully awake to the charms of springtime and love and to the emotional appeal of religion. In material and form the secular lyrics given below show the influence of French poetry, but in their sincerity and in their fresh, unconventional treatment of nature and love, they are genuinely English. The *Hymn to the Virgin* owes most to the mediæval hymns of the Latin Church, of which a great many are preserved. For later Middle English lyrics, see page 181 ff.

176a CUCKOO SONG

For this song we have not only the words but the music. It is the oldest English nonreligious composition in four parts that has come down to us.

SPRINGTIME

8. **Away is huere wynter wo.** The mediæval poet is seldom enthusiastic over winter. We must wait until the eighteenth century for anything like the modern appreciation of the cold season (see Thomson's *Winter*, p. 542 f.).

176b A HYMN TO THE VIRGIN

2. **Velut maris stella,** like a star of the sea.
4. **Parens et puella,** a parent and yet a mere girl.
7. **Tam pia,** so kind, good.
11. **Eva peccatrice,** because Eve sinned.
13. **De te genetrice,** with thee for a mother.
16. **Salutis,** of Salvation.
18. **Virtutis,** of efficacy, of virtue.
20. **Rosa sine spina,** rose without a thorn.
22. **Gratia divina,** divine grace.
25. **Electa,** chosen.
26 f. **es Effecta,** thou art become.

177a 29. **Felix fecundata,** blessed one made fruitful.
31. **Mater honorata,** honored mother.
34. **In cruce,** on the cross.
36. **In luce,** in light.
38. **Ventre quem portasti,** whom thou borest in thy womb.
40. **Parvum quem lactasti,** whom thou didst nurse when he was small.
43. **Superni,** of Heaven.
45. **Inferni,** of hell.

GEOFFREY CHAUCER

178b BALADE

This *balade* is introduced in Chaucer's *Legend of Good Women*, a poem celebrating a number of famous heroines who were true in love, "Cupid's saints."

1. **Absolon,** Absalom, the handsome but undutiful son of King David. Cf. 2 Samuel xiv, 26.
3. **Jonathas,** Jonathan, noted for his friendliness toward David. Cf. 1 Samuel xix, 2 ff.

4 ff. **Penalopee,** etc. Penelope, the faithful wife of Ulysses (see note to p. 85a, 25); Marcia Cato, who showed her complaisance in consenting to be lent to her husband's friend; Isoude (Isolt), the unfortunate mistress of Sir Tristan (Tristram); Eleyne, Helen of Troy, also unlucky in love; Lavyne (Lavinia), the heroine of the latter part of Virgil's *Æneid;* Lucresse (see note to p. 85a, 25); Polixene (Polyxena), daughter of Priam, who was loved by Achilles but was sacrificed on his tomb; Cleopatra, famed for her passionate loves and her suicide; Tisbe (Thisbe), the beloved of Pyramus — she slew herself on the body of her dead lover; Herro (Hero), who

drowned herself when she discovered the dead body of her lover, Leander; Dido, the mistress of Æneas in the *Æneid* — she committed suicide when her lover deserted her; Laudomia (Laodamia), the wife of Protesilaus — she died rather than survive her husband; Phyllis (see Gower's "Phillis and Demophon" and notes); Canace, daughter of Æolus and beloved by Macareus; Ysiphile (Hypsipyle), the mistress of Jason of the Argonauts; Ypermistre (Hypermnestra), who saved her husband's life although her forty-nine sisters, by common agreement, slew theirs; Ariadne, who fell in love with Theseus and assisted him in his effort to slay the Minotaur but found her lover false at last.

ROBERT HENRYSON

The fifteenth century is the glorious period of Scotland's older native poetry. Scottish poetry of this epoch offers a pleasant contrast to the general aridness of contemporary literature in England. Though allegory and the imitation of Chaucer were the vogue, the poetry written was artistic in form and vital in spirit. Aside from the royal poet, King James I of Scotland (1394–1436), one of the most significant Chaucerian imitators was Robert Henryson, who, according to tradition, was a schoolmaster in Dunfermline but of whose life otherwise nothing is known. His *Robin and Makyne*, the gem of his productions, is based on the pastoral tradition of Dresden-china shepherds and shepherdesses and their amorous disputes (see note to *The Nutbrowne Maide*, p. 181a), but it is pervaded by a fresh country atmosphere and a general unconventionality that make it one of the most charming poems dealing with the pastoral theme. Of all the Scottish poets of the time Henryson combines most rustic realism with true poetry.

WILLIAM DUNBAR

Of the Scottish poets of the fifteenth century William Dunbar is regarded as the greatest. He began his career as a Franciscan friar, became at one time a wandering preacher, rose to positions of minor importance at court, went on embassies to London and Paris, and received a considerable pension. He became a sort of uncrowned poet laureate of Scotland. His poems, of which he wrote more than a hundred on various subjects and in various meters, show him to be a true artist. Though he generally uses old themes, his treatment is new and his poetry is full of dazzling color and real music. If we are to judge by what has come down to us, the Scottish poets of the fifteenth century achieved a success denied to their English neighbors.

181a THE NUTBROWNE MAIDE

The unknown author of this poem was clearly a person of genius. Some authorities have thought that *The Nutbrowne Maide* was written by a woman, but the interpretation of woman's character is rather that of a man. The poem takes the form of a *debat*, or friendly altercation, and was doubtless intended to be recited as a dialogue. Coming as it probably does just at the end of the Middle Ages, it proves that, however little intrinsically meritorious literature has come down to us from the fifteenth century, English poetic genius was not dead.

ELIZABETHAN AND PURITAN PERIODS

SIR THOMAS WYATT

The first of the great line of "courtly makers" or courtier poets of the Renaissance in England was Sir Thomas Wyatt, son of Sir Henry Wyatt, privy councillor and favorite at the courts of both Henry VII and Henry VIII. The place of his birth was his father's residence, Allington Castle in Surrey, and the year was probably 1503. At the age of twelve he entered St. John's College, Cambridge, and proceeded B.A. in 1518 and M.A. in 1520. In the latter year, when no more than seventeen, he was married to the Lady Elizabeth, daughter of Lord Cobham. He was attached to the court early and made rapid advancement. One of several diplomatic missions took him in 1526–1527 to Italy, where he came into intimate contact with Italian life and literature. He was knighted in the spring of 1536–1537, served on several diplomatic missions to the continent, was brought to the Tower by intriguing enemies on the downfall of the minister, Cromwell, but was pardoned, and continued in royal favor until his death at Sherborne, Dorsetshire, while on a mission of state, in 1542. In boyhood he became acquainted with Anne Boleyn, and long after his own marriage he was regarded as her lover. In the general suspicion which attended her fall he was himself in grave danger, but wholly without cause. Those of his poems which appear to be most personal seem to echo this attachment. He introduced the sonnet into English from Italy and with Surrey helped to give it vogue. He translated his model, Petrarch, freely but simplified the meter and form of the great Italian. (See note to l. 1 of "That Petrarch Cannot, etc.," p. 204.) His poetry lacks smoothness and grace, and in sentiment and style it is often strained, but it possesses a rugged strength of content which is seldom found in the more polished measures of his contemporary, the Earl of Surrey. His poems were first published in Tottel's *Songs and Sonnets* ("Miscellany") in 1557.

187a THE LOVER FOR SHAMEFASTNESS, etc.

5. **learns,** teaches.
6. **lust,** pleasure, joy.
7. **reined,** ruled.
8. **hardiness,** bravery, persistency.

THE LOVER UNHAPPY, etc.

6 f. **Mishaps unhappy,** etc. Evidently Wyatt believed May to be his unlucky month. His commitment to the Tower in connection with the trial of the queen, Anne Boleyn, occurred in May.
9. **Stephan,** probably an astrologer.

THE LOVER COMPARETH, etc.

This sonnet is a translation of Petrarch, Sonnet 156.

187b THE LOVER LAMENTS, etc.

4. **still,** always.
5. **hap,** chance, fortune.
11. **careful,** full of care.

A RENOUNCING OF LOVE

3. **Senec,** Seneca, a Roman philosopher and tragic poet of the first century after Christ.
3. **Plato.** See note to p. 91a, l. 38.
8. **lever,** dearer.
14. **Me list,** it pleases me.

188a THE LOVER DESPAIRING, etc.

2. **may,** can, be able.
13. **'Noli me tangere.'** "Do not touch me." The lady of this sonnet is understood to be Anne Boleyn after her espousal to Henry VIII.

THE DESERTED LOVER, etc.

1. **Divers doth use,** various ones are accustomed.
3. **lynn,** cease.
13. **kind,** nature.

THE LOVER TAUGHT, etc.

2. **doubt,** fear.
7. **For dread to fall.** Probably in reference to his precarious position, as former lover to Queen Anne, during her brief reign.

188b 17. **ure,** use.

189a THE LOVER COMPLAINETH, etc.

1. **My lute, awake.** Skill in music was a regular part of the equipment of the complete gentlemen of the time.
24. **Unquit,** unrequited.
24. **playn,** complain, lament.

189b THE LOVER'S LUTE, etc.

20. **quit,** acquit, reply.
40. **silly,** empty.

THE LOVER BESEECHETH, etc.

190a 17. **thine own approved,** thy accepted lover.
18. **which.** Used properly as a relative for persons until a much later date.

OF HIS LOVE CALLED ANNA

Anna of this poem is generally taken to be Anne Boleyn, but the date is uncertain.

3. **wot,** knows.
5. **meedeth,** rewards.
7. **eke,** also.

HENRY HOWARD, EARL OF SURREY

The Earl of Surrey was probably born at his grandfather's residence, Kenninghall, in Norfolk. There and at his father's residence, Stoke Hall, in Suffolk, and at Hunsdon in Hertfordshire, another of his grandfather's places, he spent his early youth. He was carefully educated, was well read in classical and modern literature, and began to write verse early. In 1531–1532 he was married to the daughter of the Earl of Oxford, but on account of his extreme youth he lived apart from his wife until 1535. He spent some time in France for the cultivating influences of travel, and later won distinction abroad in military service. Naturally of a proud and imperious disposition, in his zeal to advance his father's interests toward the regency on the anticipated death of Henry VIII, he very imprudently, though with entire right by royal grant, quartered the arms of Edward the Confessor with his own.

The act was construed by his enemies as treason, and he was brought to trial, condemned, and beheaded on Tower Hill in January, 1547. He read and imitated the Italian poets, but there is no evidence that he ever was in Italy. He was a student of Wyatt's literary work, but differing widely in politics and religion, the two, despite the prevailing notion, were never very intimate friends. Apart from his help in establishing the sonnet in English, with Wyatt he introduced "ottava rima" (an English adaptation of an Italian eight-line stanza with an especial rhyme scheme) into English poetry. But his greatest claim as an innovator is in his use, for the first time in English, of blank verse in five-stress iambic measure in his translation of a part of Virgil's *Æneid.* In his poetry he was a disciple of Wyatt, but he is superior to his master at every point except perhaps in native strength. His poems, like Wyatt's, were published for the first time in Tottel's *Miscellany.*

DESCRIPTION OF THE RESTLESS STATE, etc.

190b 4. **And new again begins.** The time is early autumn.
14. **reduceth,** leads back, brings about.
24. **use,** practice, custom.
33. **cheer,** countenance.
36. **lace,** net.
44. **agazed,** at gaze, aghast.
191a 51. **teen,** sorrow.
54. **rue on,** have pity on.

PRISONED IN WINDSOR, etc.

For suspected sympathy with a Yorkshire rebellion, Surrey was placed in confinement at Windsor in 1537. While there he spent his time in writing poetry.

3. **With a king's son.** Surrey was for a while companion to the King's natural son, Henry Fitzroy, and spent the years 1530–1532 with him at Windsor.
4. **Priam's sons of Troy.** Priam, king of Troy at the time of its destruction, had fifty sons.
6. **to hove,** to hover.
13. **palm-play,** tennis court.
16. **bait,** tempt.
17. **gravel,** ground, place of tournament.
17. **with sleeves tied on the helm.** Referring to the custom of the knight's wearing his lady's favor as he went into the field.
21. **With silver drops, etc.** Dewsprent lawns where wrestling and other sports were held.

191b 29. **holts,** woods, copses.
42. **berain,** bedew, as with rain.
44. **Upsupped,** supped up, drank.
46. **accompt,** account.
46. **fere,** companion, fellow.
48. **lief,** dear.

COMPLAINT OF THE ABSENCE, etc.

Rarely in the conventional love poetry of the time is expression attempted of the lady-love's "sorrows," as in this poem. The reference is probably to the poet's own domestic life, which was happily regular.

192a 8. **freight,** fraught, laden.
14. **avail,** profit, advantage.
33. **drencheth,** drowns.

THE LOVER EXCUSETH, etc.

3. **passèd,** failed.
3. **spot,** stain.
4. **honesty,** honor.
5. **fancy,** love.
6. **wite,** censure, or be censured.
11. **a pease,** a pea.

192b 24. **far-forth,** far.
30. **the gander's foe,** the fox.
43. **lese,** lose.
46. **Want,** lack.

THE MEANS TO ATTAIN HAPPY LIFE

Translated from Martial, a Roman epigrammatic poet of the first century after Christ.

5. **egall,** equal.
9. **mean,** moderate.
16. **Ne . . . ne,** neither . . . nor.

193b OF THE DEATH OF SIR T[HOMAS] W[YATT]

1. **quick,** alive.
2. **encreasèd by disdain.** It was an additional grace in him not to be proud of his gifts.
7. **stithe,** forge, or anvil.
21. **none affect,** no affection, no personal interest.
29. **corse,** body, physique.

HOW NO AGE IS CONTENT, etc.

193b 7. **that feels his bones with pains oppress,** that is, from work, not from sickness or infirmity.
10. **more,** greater.
12. **chop,** shift, change.
16. **chews,** cheeks, jaws.
22. **two ages past, the third now coming in,** youth and manhood, and age.
23. **wanton,** sportive, playful.
26. **Truss up thy pack, and trudge.** Pack up thy wares, as a peddler, and go.

194a DESCRIPTION OF SPRING, etc.

1. **soote**, sweet.
4. **turtle**, dove.
4. **make**, mate.
6. **hung his old head**, shed his antlers.
9. **The adder all her slough away she slings.** The snake throws off her skin.
11. **mings**, mixes, mingles, prepares.

DESCRIPTION AND PRAISE, etc.

Geraldine of this poem was the lady Elizabeth, daughter of the Earl of Kildare. At the time of the poet's imprisonment at Windsor, she was only nine years of age. Attempts to make her out as the lady of his other songs and sonnets are without substantiation.

1. **Tuscan**, Tuscany.
2. **her**, their.
3. **The Western isle**, Ireland.
4. **Camber's cliffs**, the cliffs of Wales.
4. **did give her lively heat**, afforded her birth.
9. **Hunsdon**, a town in Hertfordshire, where the poet first saw Geraldine.
10. **hight**, is called.
11. **Hampton**, Hampton Court, a royal palace on the Thames a few miles above London.
12. **Windsor**, Windsor Castle, a royal residence on the Thames above London.

194b VIRGIL'S *ÆNEID*

2. **gan**, did.
9. **Argive**, Greek.
11. **fray**, make afraid, frighten.
15. **me thought**, it seemed to me.
19. **shene**, bright, shining.
28. **sith**, since.
32. **Ceres**, Earth Mother, the goddess of Agriculture in classical mythology.
37. **woode**, mad, insane.

195a 39. **Ascanius**, Iulus, his son.
40. **Anchises**, his aged father.
50. **ugsome**, ugly.
51. **aghast my sprite**, made my spirit afraid.

195a 59. **Juno's sanctuair**, the temple of Juno.
60. **Phenix, Ulysses**, Grecian heroes. The latter, celebrated for his wisdom, is hero of the *Odyssey*.
69. **clepes**, calls.
71. **sithes**, times.
75. **woxe**, grew, became.
76. **stack**, stuck.

195b 85. **Hesperian**, western.
86. **Lidian Tiber**, the river Tiber, on which Rome is situated.
92. **Myrmidons**, Greeks of Thessaly.
92. **Dolopes**, other Greeks of Thessaly.
94. **son of Venus.** Æneas was the son of Aphrodite or Venus.
96. **the God's great mother**, Cybele, the wife of Saturn and the mother of the gods. Creusa probably means that she will pass into the half-deified state of an attendant upon Cybele.
102. **raught**, reached.
109. **each-where**, everywhere.
112. **Lucifer**, the morning star.
113. **Ide**, Mt. Ida near Troy.

THOMAS SACKVILLE, LORD BUCKHURST

Thomas Sackville, an only son, was born of upper-class parentage at Buckhurst in Sussex. He became a student of the Inner Temple, of which his father, Sir Richard, was governor, and was called to the bar. In early life he devoted himself mainly to literature. By 1557 he became interested in a work fashioned on Lydgate's *Fall of Princes*, to which he contributed his *Induction* as a poetical preface, and wrote one tale, the *Complaint of the Duke of Buckingham*, for the plan. These compositions give to the collection, the *Mirror for Magistrates*, its only claim to literary merit. But of even greater interest in literary history is the part he took in the first tragedy of the language in blank verse, *Gorboduc*, which was presented at the Inner Temple in 1560–1561. He was interested in music and freemasonry as well, but politics became the real business of his life. Wealthy, traveled, cultivated, favored at court, he rose rapidly from parliamentary and diplomatic positions to the Privy Council and ultimately to the Lord Treasurership of the realm. He was knighted in 1567, and on the same day was raised to the peerage as Lord Buckhurst. In 1591 he was made chancellor of Oxford University. Other honors and emoluments continued to come to him throughout the rest of his long life. But for his occupancy with public affairs he doubtless would have attained an even greater place in literature. As it is, his is the most illustrious name in English poetry between Chaucer and Spenser.

THE INDUCTION

2. **treen**, trees.
3. **Saturnus**, Saturn, the planet of evil influence.

196a 7. **tapets**, tapestries, foliage.
8. **erst**, first, once, erstwhile.
11. **Boreas**, the North Wind.
24. **Hermes**, messenger of the gods.
25. **Mars**, god of War.
27. **Virgo**, the Virgin, a constellation due south of the handle of the Dipper.
28. **Thetis**, goddess of the Sea.
29. **Scorpio . . . Sagittarius**, southern constellations, eighth and ninth signs of the zodiac.

32. **The Bear,** a constellation.
36. **Phaeton,** the sun god Helios, or, according to other traditions, the son of Helios.
40. **stent,** stopping-place, end.
42. **Titan,** the Sun.
43. **Cynthea,** the Moon.
45. **noonstead,** point of noon, the zenith.

196b 48. **chare,** car, chariot.
57. **leams,** flames, rays.
60. **Phœbus,** the sun god.
68. **peers,** noblemen of high rank, lords.
69. **descrive,** describe, write about.
74. **wight,** creature, person.
74. **forewaste,** wasted away.
75. **brast,** burst.
78. **forewithered and forespent,** all withered and worn.
80. **welkèd,** withered.
80. **besprent,** besprinkled.

197a 90. **doom,** judgment, opinion.
93. **distrained,** distraught, pained.
97. **dewle,** lamentation, dole.
102. **dure,** endure.
102. **attaint,** touched, afflicted.
103. **all forefaint,** very faint.
107. **aslake,** abate.
109. **the Furies,** three merciless sisters with snaky locks, daughters of Night, whose duty it was to punish guilty souls after death.
110. **Pluto,** brother of Jupiter and Neptune and ruler of the Underworld.
111. **Lethe,** the river of Oblivion, situated in the lower world.

197b 120. **out brayed,** gasped out.
122. **shright,** shrieked.
123. **to-dashed,** dashed to pieces.
125. **eft,** again, anew.
128. **appale,** make pale, appall.
131. **avale,** fall or sink down.
132. **foredone,** undone.
135. **drear,** dreariness, gloom.
141. **stike,** stich, a stanza or verse.
143. **Æölus,** god of the Winds.
145. **bedrent,** drenched.
152. **ruing,** sorrowing, repenting.
156. **whilere,** erewhile, formerly.

198a 161. **won,** dwelling.
164. **glass,** mirror.
174. **godhead,** godhood.
179. **swing,** sway.
191. **unmeet,** unmeasured.

198b 202. **Astoined,** astounded.
208. **anon,** at once.
210. **Avern,** Avernus, a lake near Naples, supposed to be the entrance to Hades.
212. **swelth,** overflow.

199a 236. **staring,** standing on end.
243. **farforth,** far, to such a degree.
250. **fet,** fetched.
253. **somedeal,** somewhat.
258. **scrip,** wallet.
271. **breres,** briars.
273. **tawèd,** hardened.

199b 284. **keep,** heed, care.
294. **Crœsus,** king of Lydia about 550 B.C., fabulously wealthy.
294. **Irus,** a Homeric beggar of gigantic size, who kept watch over the suitors of Penelope and by them was employed as messenger.
299. **Sisters,** the Fates — Clotho, Lachesis, and Atropos, who severally spun, twisted, and severed the thread of life.
309. **But and,** although.
313. **eld,** old age.
314. **all were it,** although it were.

200a 318. **reckless,** heedless.
331 **Went on three feet,** walked with the support of a staff.
333. **pilled,** bare.
333. **forlore,** utterly lost.
342. **recure,** recovery.

200b 361. **maw,** stomach.
371. **Enthrilling,** piercing in.
372. **by and by,** at once.
381. **eftsoons,** very soon, forthwith.
382. **affrayèd,** frightened.
383. **dight,** clad, provided.
383. **pardé,** pardy, Fr. *par Dieu.* Here means little more than "in truth."

201a 398. **forehewed,** cut to pieces.
400. **depainted,** depicted.
405. **Darius,** king of Persia, 521–486 B.C., who with an innumerable host failed at Marathon in 490 to conquer Greece. It was Darius III, however, whom Alexander overthrew.
407. **Macedo,** Alexander the Great, 356–323 B.C.
410. **Duke,** leader.
410. **Hannibal,** 247–183 B.C., greatest of the Carthaginian generals who fought against Rome. He defeated the Romans disastrously at the Trebia River in 218, at Lake Trasimene in 217, and at Cannæ in 216, where the consul Paulus fell. He was overcome by Scipio Africanus at Zama in Africa in 202.
422. **Cæsar weeping over Pompey's head.** Pompey was treacherously murdered in Egypt shortly after his defeat by Cæsar at Pharsalia in 48 B.C. At sight of his severed head Cæsar is said to have wept.
423. **Sulla and Marius.** The civil war between Marius and Sulla began in 88 B.C. and resulted ultimately in the triumph of the latter and his elevation to the dictatorship in 82.
425. **Cyrus,** "the Younger," slain on the battlefield of Cunaxa, 401 B.C., in his attempt to overthrow his brother Artaxerxes with the aid of the Ten Thousand Greeks celebrated in the *Anabasis* of Xenophon.
426. **the queen,** etc., Parysatis, the mother of Cyrus. She is reported to have inflicted atrocious punishments on those of his enemies whom she overcame after his death.

428. **Xerxes,** *ca.* 519–464 B.C., king of Persia, defeated at Salamis in 480 in his attempted conquest of Greece.
432. **Thebes,** an ancient city of Bœotia in Greece, destroyed by Alexander the Great.
433. **Tyrus,** the most important city of ancient Phœnicia, much reduced though not utterly destroyed by Alexander.
201b 441. **lin,** cease, restrain myself.
443. **force,** perforce, of necessity.
445. **quail,** fall, perish.
449. **Hector,** son of Priam and greatest of the defenders of Troy. His death at the hands of Achilles, as recorded in the twenty-second book of the *Iliad,* is one of the tragic events of world literature.
451. **boot,** reward.
463. **Cassandra,** a prophetess, daughter of Priam, condemned by Apollo not to have her prophecies believed, though true.
464. **Pallas' house,** the temple of Pallas Athena.
467. **Pyrrhus,** one of the heroes concealed in the wooden horse, and slayer of Priam; in legend the son of Achilles, later married to Andromache, wife of Hector.
468. **baign,** bath.
474. **can,** know.
475. **gledes,** coals.
476. **Neptunus,** god of the Sea.
202a 480. **Acheron,** a river of the Underworld.
482. **Charon,** aged ferryman who transported souls across the rivers of the lower world.
491. **fraughted,** freighted, laden.
494. **hoise,** hoist, raise.
497. **A three-sound bark.** Cerberus, the monstrous dog on guard at the entrance of Hades, had three heads.
501. **Foredinning,** making a deafening noise or din.
504. **peased,** was appeased, became silent.
202b 512. **puled,** whimpered, whined.
517. **yfear,** together.
521. **stillèd,** distilled.
532. **kesar,** Cæsar (cf. kaiser, czar), ruler, emperor.
533. **Henry, Duke of Buckingham.** Henry Stafford, second duke of Buckingham, foremost supporter of Richard III in his usurpation of the throne of England, was betrayed in a conspiracy and beheaded. He is the subject of Sackville's tale in the *Mirror for Magistrates* (see introductory note on Sackville).
534. **forworn,** worn out.
537. **lorn,** lost.
542. **molt,** melted.

THOMAS, LORD VAUX

The second Lord Vaux was born and chiefly resided at Harrowden in Northamptonshire. He succeeded to the barony at the age of thirteen, and apparently was educated at Cambridge. Almost his only claim to prominence in his day, apart from the reputation he enjoyed as a poet, was his attainment of the order of the Bath and the captaincy of the Isle of Jersey. He belonged to the cultured group which distinguished the courts of Henry VIII and Edward VI. His known works are lyrics, in inditing which he manifestly had before him as models the works of Wyatt and Surrey. He shows metrical skill and a reflective vein, which caught the popular fancy in his time and have preserved his name in English literature.

203a OF A CONTENTED MIND

Compare Dyer's better-known poem of similar import on page 250. The attitude of philosophic calm here portrayed was hardly typical of the English state of mind in the sixteenth century.

6. **deem,** judge, think.
12. **casual,** subject to by accident.

ANONYMOUS

A PRAISE OF HIS LADY

203b 10. **a naked boy,** the image or reflection of Cupid.
18. **the Phenix kind,** a mythical bird said to have come from Arabia. Rarity was the essence of its nature. It appeared only once every five hundred years, and then singly.
21. **Diana,** goddess of Hunting and Chastity.
31. **redier,** ruddier.
33. **Bacchus,** god of Wine and Revelry.
36. **stray,** a straying person or animal.
38. **shamefastness,** steadfastness in virtue. The modern form of the word is misspelled and misinterpreted.
47. **gilli-flower,** clove-pink or carnation.
204a 49. **graff,** bud or scion.

THAT PETRARCH CANNOT, etc.

1. **Petrarch.** The Italian writer Petrarch, 1304–1374, was the great model and storehouse of the English courtly makers in the sixteenth century. They imitated, adapted, and translated him freely, and in their own experiences relived, or imagined themselves to relive, his unfortunate love for Laura. See note to Ralegh's *A Vision,* p. 253.
3. **file,** foil.
5. **mean,** medium.
7. **sleight,** cunning, skill.
12. **lay my life to wed,** pledge my life in a wager.
13. **Momus,** a divinity personifying Censure and Mockery.

THE PROMISE OF A CONSTANT LOVER

4. **fret,** break; literally, to chafe.

204b THAT EACH THING IS HURT OF ITSELF

8. **to-fret,** eaten to pieces.
11. **envy,** hatred, animosity.

AN OLD LOVER TO A YOUNG GENTLEWOMAN

5. **trill the ball,** as a toy before a child, to attract its attention; to tantalize.
14. **pound,** a place for confining animals caught astray.
18. **lime,** birdlime, snare.
19. **feared,** afraid.
26. **at price for every ware,** know the cost of every commodity before buying.
27. **good cheap,** at a bargain.
29. **on head,** ahead.

205a ALE SONG

One of the most celebrated drinking songs in the language. It belongs earlier, but cannot be definitely placed before the period here represented.

4. **him that wears a hood,** that is, any man.
14. **crab,** crab apple.
15. **do me stead,** be sufficient for me.
17. **trow,** trust, believe.
25. **trowl,** pledge with a gesture or flourish.
29. **wink,** sleep.

RICHARD EDWARDES

A native of Somersetshire, Edwardes became a student and fellow of Oxford; but after being created M.A. in 1547, he interested himself in playmaking and poetry in London. Only one of his plays, of indifferent quality at best, has come down to us, but a number of his poems have been preserved, chiefly in the celebrated *Paradyse of Daynty Devises* of 1576, to which he was principal contributor. He was greatly admired as a poet by his contemporaries, whose judgment has been approved by his retention, in a moderate way, to fame down to the present time. His chief characteristics are grace and tenderness, and a thoughtful outlook on life.

AMANTIUM IRA, etc.

A translation of the title may be found in the closing line of each stanza.

206a 35. **some beck, some check,** some nod approval, some hold in or refuse.

37. **at cap and knee,** the posture of a courtly bow or formal salutation.

GEORGE GASCOIGNE

In his day Gascoigne's reputation as a poet suffered from his excesses as a man. Coming from a better-class Bedfordshire family, he spent some time at Cambridge without taking a degree, and then, ostensibly in the study of law, he lived somewhat the life of a rakehell in London as an inn-of-court man. Charges of gambling, debt, atheism, and even of manslaughter are recorded against him. Among worse things, he is denominated "a common rymer and a deviser of slanderous pasquils against divers persones of great calling." He is important as a literary pioneer. His *Supposes* is the first English comedy in prose, his *Steele Glas* is the first regular verse satire in the language, and his *Certain Notes of Instruction concerning the Making of Verse* must be placed as the first critical essay in English. In his poetry he is certainly facile, but evidently he used his muse too much for his own personal advancement. He is best in his short poems, in which he attained an ease and a smoothness that are rarely discoverable in English Renaissance poetry before his day.

THE LULLABY OF A LOVER

206b 42. **ware,** need, caution.

A STRANGE PASSION OF A LOVER

16. **grutch,** complaint, ill temper.
25. **Philomene,** Philomel, the nightingale.
28. **wray,** bewray, beguile.
31. **wench,** girl, without the ill suggestion which the word later carries.

EDWARD DE VERE, EARL OF OXFORD

Edward de Vere, seventeenth earl of Oxford, is a good example, even in the unfavorable light in which Ascham has depicted the type, of the Italianate Englishman at the English court in the period of the Renaissance. Despite many rich inheritances, he was constantly in jeopardy and was frequently brought to the verge of ruin by his reckless temper and profligate manner of living. He was a dissolute fop. In his artistic tastes he turned to music and poetry, and in the latter art he ranks high among the courtly group of his day. The charm of his verse is evident in the more than twenty of his poems which have come down to us from the anthologies of the period.

207a IF WOMEN COULD BE FAIR

1. **fond,** foolish.
8. **Phœbus,** Apollo, the personification of manly beauty and excellence.
8. **Pan,** the god of flocks and shepherds. His favorite residence was in Arcadia.
9. **haggards,** wild or ill-trained falcons.

207b 17. **their fancy try,** put their love to the test.

WILLIAM CAXTON

The first English printer, William Caxton, was born in the Weald of Kent of parents whose names and condition are not known. After some routine of education, he was apprenticed to a mercer or merchant in London, on whose death he removed to Bruges in Holland for the completion of his apprenticeship, and there gradually rose to the position of governor of the English Merchants' Association. About 1469 he gave up his business career and became a translator and printer under the patronage of the Duchess of Burgundy, an English princess. In 1476 he returned to England with his new art and the following year issued from his press in Westminster his *Dictes and Sayings of the Philosophers*, which was the first book to be printed in England. From that time until his death in 1491 he displayed marvellous industry and energy as a printer and translator. Within fourteen years he published about eighty separate books, some in more than one edition, a total of eighty thousand pages in print, and translated by his own hand more than twenty works. He was versatile in French and knew Latin, was esteemed at court, and enjoyed some court patronage. As a translator he had much to do with fixing the literary usage of the language in the sixteenth century.

207a PREFACE TO *LE MORTE D'ARTHUR*

11. **demanded,** asked.
12. **do made,** caused to be made.

13 f. **Saint Greal,** Holy Grail, the cup from which Christ drank on the night of the Last Supper or, according to another tradition, the vessel used to catch the blood from Christ's wounds as he hung on the cross. It is intimately associated with English romantic material from the tradition that Joseph of Arimathea transported the cup to England and deposited it in the monastery of Glastonbury, whence it vanished in the early Dark Ages and was known to reappear in vision here and there to any one who was virtuous enough to see it. It early became identified with the Arthurian material. Compare Tennyson's idyl, *The Holy Grail.*

22. **Paynims,** pagans.
33. **behest,** promise.

207b 1 f. **Judas Maccabæus,** the defender and preserver of Jewish religious and political liberty in the first half of the second century before Christ.

5. **stalled,** installed.
14. **Godfrey of Boloine,** a leader in the first crusade, latter half of the eleventh century. Caxton's book, *The History of Godfrey of Boulogne,* was printed in 1481.

208a 5. **aretted,** imputed, adjudged.

9. **Glastonbury.** In southwest England, now Somersetshire. See notes to Thomas Warton's *Grave of King Arthur*, p. 597a, ll. 86 and 116.

9 f. **Policronicon,** an historical work in Latin by Ralph Higden, fourteenth century.

14. **Bochas,** Boccaccio, 1313–1375, Italian poet and novelist, author of the *Decameron.* His *De Casu Principum* ("On the Fall of Princes") belongs to the same literary type as the *Mirror for Magistrates.* See introductory note to Sackville, p. 195.

16 f. **Galfridus in his British book,** Geoffrey of Monmouth, *History of the Kings of Britain, ca.* 1136. See p. 75 ff.

21. **St. Edward,** Edward the Confessor, *ca.* 1004–1066.
27. **Winchester,** in Hampshire; according to one tradition, Camelot, the seat of Arthur's kingdom.
41. **Camelot,** Arthur's capital city, by Caxton here located in Wales. See also especially note to p. 96b, l. 247 ff.

46 f. **the Word of God.** See Matthew xiii, 57.

208b 10. **conning,** knowledge, skill.

12. **enprised,** undertaken.
15. **Sir Thomas Malorye,** author of *Le Morte Darthur*, at one time a knight in the retinue of Richard Beauchamp, Earl of Warwick. See introductory note to Malory, p. 130.
29. **honest,** honorable.
35. **hardiness,** bravery.
38. **renommee,** renown.

209a PREFACE TO THE *ÆNEID*

8. **clerk,** scholar.
13. **Eneas departed,** etc. See the Earl of Surrey's translation above, p. 194 ff.
33. **delibered,** deliberated.

49 f. **evidences,** legal documents.

209b 14. **Forland,** the extreme northeast point of land in Kent at the mouth of the Thames.

41. **uplondished man,** countryman.
50. **entermete,** meddle with.

210a 1. **lightly,** quickly, easily.

10. **Master John Skelton,** a noted English

humanist and poet, *ca.* 1460–1529, protégé of Henry VII and tutor of the future Henry VIII. He was made poet laureate of Oxford in 1489.

13. **address and expown,** straighten out and explain.
18. **Epistles of Tully,** Marcus Tullius Cicero's letters.
18 f. **Diodorus Siculus,** Diodorus of Sicily, a Greek historian, second half of the first century before Christ.
21. **craftily,** skillfully.
26 f. **appropred,** appropriated.
28. **Helicon's well,** Hippocrene, a fountain on Mt. Helicon in Bœotia, sacred to the Muses.
35 f. **to-coming,** future.
36. **Arthur.** This prince died and his brother succeeded to the throne as Henry VIII on the death of Henry VII in 1509. Arthur's widow was the Catherine of Aragon so celebrated in Henry VIII's matrimonial history.

ROGER ASCHAM

Roger Ascham was born at Kirby Wiske of a native Yorkshire family. He received his earliest education from his father, who was both a wise and a good man. While still a child, he was adopted into the home of Sir Anthony Wingfield and there brought up in learning. Under his patron he made rapid progress in English and classical studies, and developed a liking for archery, which remained with him through life. At fifteen he entered St. John's College, Cambridge, won recognition soon for his proficiency in Latin and Greek, and became an accomplished musician and penman. He attained both degrees in the Arts and was made a fellow of his college. As Greek reader he was popular, but university dissensions annoyed him so much that he sought employment elsewhere. In 1545 appeared his *Toxophilus* with a dedication to the King, who was so pleased with the work that he settled a pension of £10 on the author. The book is celebrated for the vigor, purity, and flexibility of its style, and for the plea it makes in the prefatory address for the literary use of the English tongue as opposed to Greek and Latin. In 1546 Ascham was made public orator of the University, a position which entailed heavy correspondence for several years afterwards. For two years, 1548–1550, he was tutor to Elizabeth, then residing at Cheshunt. On the accession of Mary he became her Latin Secretary, at a salary of £20, and acquitted himself well in the office. He continued in royal favor in Elizabeth's reign but was continually harassed by ill health and insufficient means for his family responsibilities. His last years were devoted to his second great work, the *Scolemaster,* which appeared two years after his death, in 1570. Ascham was one of the great humanists (see p. 186), but his chief merit lies in his simple, direct, and easy-flowing use of the English language, "for the good of all Englishmen."

210b TOXOPHILUS

The title means lover of the bow.

7. **Bias the wise man,** one of the Seven Sages of Greece, famous for his apothegms.
12 f. **news but these.** The word *news* was used frequently in the plural sense until after Shakespeare's day.

211a 30. **in such a mean,** in such a moderate way.

211b 11. **Aristotle,** a Greek philosopher, 384–322 B.C., the fountainhead of western criticism. See also notes to p. 91a, 38, and p. 91b, 19 ff.
38 f. **books of feigned chivalry,** romances.

212a 4. **outshoot,** overshoot.
9. **plucketh down a side,** shoots aside into the ground (?).
25. **a-good,** in earnest.
43. **stark nought,** absolutely nothing.
53. **fletchers,** arrow makers.

212b 1. **bowyers,** makers of bows.
46. **artillery,** the science of shooting.

JOHN FOXE

John Foxe, the greatest of martyrologists, was a native of Boston in Lincolnshire. His father died early, but he luckily succeeded to a good stepfather. He early displayed a zeal for study. By the help of friends he was enabled to enter Oxford at sixteen. He became a fellow of Magdalen in 1539 and proceeded M.A. in 1543; but because of his advanced religious views, he resigned his fellowship in 1545. For five years, 1548–1553, he was tutor to the orphan children of the Earl of Surrey, but fled the country at the beginning of Mary's persecutions. He returned on the accession of Elizabeth and in 1563 issued his *Acts and Monuments,* which became known at once as the "Book of Martyrs." The work was long the chief authority for Protestant church history, a storehouse of arguments against the Catholics, and a treasury of stories and sermon material for Protestant clergymen. But, despite the deep earnestness which gives the work its vigorous style, the author was too violent a partisan to be accurate or just. Nevertheless, in its large amount of first-hand material the work is valuable, and it reflects the social habits and religious tone of Protestant thought during the Reformation.

213a DEATH OF CRANMER

7. **Cranmer.** Cranmer became Archbishop of Canterbury in 1533, was committed to the Tower for treason on the accession of Mary, and was subsequently tried for heresy, condemned, and burned at the stake on March 31, 1556.
8. **Bocardo,** the old north gate at Oxford, used as a prison.
9. **the university,** Oxford.
17. **Nunc dimittis,** the first words of the vulgate Latin version of Luke ii, 29, which in the King James translation reads: "Lord, now lettest thou thy servant depart in peace, according to thy word."
23. **Cole,** Henry Cole, D. D., *ca.* 1500–1580, provost of Eton. He was privately requested by Mary to prepare a special sermon for Cranmer's execution.
40. **presently,** immediately.

213b 17. . . . A resumé of Cole's sermon here follows.

18. **the standers-by,** etc. Contrary to the general expectation, and to the complete chagrin of his persecutors, Cranmer at the conclusion of the sermon resolutely renounced his former recantation of the Protestant faith.

214a 22 f. **Hugh Latimer and Nicholas Ridley.** The two were burned at the stake on October 16, 1555.

214b 3. **Brazennose,** one of the colleges of Oxford.

11. **he put his right hand,** etc. He had formerly signed his recantation and written in defense of it, hence his open and declared purpose to let the offending hand suffer first. A famous passage.
24. **the words of Stephen.** See Acts vii, 60. Stephen, stoned for his boldness in preaching the Gospel, has been called the first Christian martyr.

CICELY ORMES OF NORWICH

30. **About the 23rd day,** etc. In 1557.
31. **the other above mentioned,** John Noyes, burnt at the stake at Laxfield, near Norwich, September 22, 1557.
32. **Norwich,** the chief city of Norfolk.

215a 30. **East Dereham,** a town a few miles west of Norwich.

DEATH OF MARY

215b 41. **Mary's reign.** Mary "the Bloody," so called from the many persecutions of her reign, was queen of England from 1553 to 1558.

216a 10. **the year above said,** 1558.

12. **her sister.** Both Mary and Elizabeth were daughters of Henry VIII but by different mothers, the former by Catherine of Aragon and the latter by Anne Boleyn.
14. **tympany,** tympanites.
21. **the king's majesty her husband,** etc., Philip II of Spain, whose dislike of England and neglect of Mary are well known.

216b 8. **department,** departure.

10. **'Calais lying in my heart.'** The loss of Calais to the French in the last year of Mary's reign was a source of bitter grief to the queen.
18. **king Lucius,** a legendary hero, called the first Christian king in Britain, supposed to have lived in the second century.

EDMUND SPENSER

A Londoner by birth, Spenser came, as he says, of "an house of ancient fame," which, while it doubtless was old, belonged at best only to the humbler order of gentry. He attended the Merchant Taylors' School in London, which had just opened its doors. He entered Cambridge as a sizar in 1569, and, despite poverty and ill health, distinguished himself for his wide reading and his thorough knowledge of Greek, Latin, French, and Italian. Chief among his notable associates there was Gabriel Harvey, the scholar, who remained his firm friend for life. On the attainment of the M. A. degree in 1576, he left the university and went up to London as a secretary in Leicester's household in the Strand. There with Sir Philip Sidney, for whom he developed a deep and lasting friendship, and others was perhaps formed the celebrated literary club called the Areopagus. Probably amid these surroundings he began his *Faerie Queene.* Certainly, out of his experimentations with verse there, he developed the celebrated measure employed in his great poem, which since has borne his name. His *Shepheards Calender* appeared in 1579 (or, rather, early in 1580), and met with favor at once. In 1580 he went to Ireland as secretary to the Lord Deputy. For seven years he was an official and a popular figure in and about Dublin, but the country suited his nature and undertakings best; so in 1586 in a "plantation" scheme in Munster he secured a grant of three thousand acres of land, including the old castle of Kilcolman in Cork, and settled there in 1588. To Sir Walter Ralegh, his neighbor, he showed in 1589 the first three books complete of the *Faerie Queene.* Delighted with the discovery, Ralegh hurried with him across the Channel to communicate his find to his sovereign and reinstate himself, if possible, in favor. Spenser's reading from his cantos before the Court is one of the most dramatic events in literary history. Elizabeth was captivated. Spenser felt assured of preferment, but after some delay received a formal grant only of £50 per annum. In disappointment he returned to his estate in Ireland. There in 1594 he married Elizabeth Boyle, whom he had addressed in his sonnets, *Amoretti*. He returned to England in 1596 and published the second three books of the *Faerie Queene*, without reward. In a peasants' uprising in 1598 his castle was burned to the ground, and he fled the country with his family. He reached London shattered in spirit and health, and died there a month after his arrival, "for want of bread," according to Ben Jonson. He was buried in Westminster Abbey only a few yards from Chaucer. Spenser's literary gifts were as rich as they were manifold. His lyrical power was of the very highest order; he displayed the rarest talent for epical narrative, in a medium of his own masterful contrivance; he expressed the English Renaissance best in several of its larger aspects, its aspiration, its fondness for allegory, and its luxury of color; only Milton and Gray among the English poets have surpassed him in learning; and in sheer imaginative splendor he excels all others who have written in English.

217a FAERIE QUEENE

The *Faerie Queene* is an epic poem in which Spenser, using as a plot many themes from mediæval romance, sets forth an elaborate allegory designed, as he tells us, "to fashion a gentleman or noble person in virtuous or gentle discipline." Prince Arthur is in love with the Faerie Queene, from whose court the Red Cross Knight and the heroes of the remaining books set forth on their various quests. The allegory is threefold — moral, religious, and political. Arthur, for example, represents Magnificence, which, according to Aristotle (see notes to p. 91a, l. 38 and p. 91b, l. 19 ff.) is the perfection of the moral virtues. He also represents divine grace. The Red Cross Knight represents Holiness and the Church of England. As a figure in the political allegory, Arthur suggests Leicester, the favorite of Queen Elizabeth, who is represented by the Faerie Queene. Duessa represents Mary Queen of Scots. And so on. The allegory is complicated and at times obscure and confused. The *Faerie Queene* is written in a nine-line stanza invented by Spenser and named in his honor. It consists of eight ten-syllable lines followed by a twelve-syllable line called an "alexandrine." The rhyme scheme is *ababbcbcc*.

The *Faerie Queene* is a noble poem. For us its interest consists not in the allegory or the moral lesson, but in the music and dignity of the verse and the unsurpassed variety and beauty of the descriptions that crowd its pages.

1. **A gentle knight,** the hero of the first book, exemplifying Holiness.
1. **pricking,** spurring.
5. **Yet arms,** etc. The Red Cross Knight, like the hero of the romance of *Sir Libeaus Desconus*, has just been knighted and is wearing second-hand armor.
9. **giusts,** jousts.
17. **cheere,** countenance.
20. **Gloriana,** Queen Elizabeth.
21. **Faery Lond,** England.
27. **a dragon,** the Devil. See Revelation xii, 9.
28. **A lovely ladie,** Una, or Truth.

217b 43. **that infernall feend,** the Dragon.
44. **Forwasted,** laid waste.
46. **a dwarfe,** Prudence, Common Sense.
52. **lemans,** lovers.
53. **everie wight to shrowd it,** etc., it compelled every creature to seek cover.
54. **eke,** also.
60. **perceable,** pierceable, penetrable.

218a 68. **can,** did.
69. **The sayling pine,** so called from its use in making sailing vessels. For the catalogue of trees, compare note to p. 120b, l. 31 ff.
71. **The builder oake,** the oak used in building.
74. **still,** always.
76. **eugh,** yew.
77. **sallow,** a species of willow.
78. **The mirrhe sweete,** etc., the Arabian myrtle, which exudes a bitter but fragrant gum. Myrrha was the mother of Adonis. Wounded by her father, she fled to Arabia and was there changed into the myrtle.
79. **The warlike beech,** so called from its use in making spears, etc.
79. **the ash for nothing ill.** Ashwood was used for many purposes.
80. **platane,** plane tree.
81. **The carver holme.** The evergreen oak was used in carving.
84. **weening,** thinking.
88. **doubt,** fear.
94. **about,** out of.
98. **Eftsoones,** very soon, quickly.

218b 110. **wot,** know.
113. **retrate,** retreat.
114. **the wandring wood,** the wood in which men wander or go astray.
116. **read,** advice.
118. **hardiment,** bravery, daring.
129. **boughtes,** folds.
134. **uncouth,** unknown, strange.
136. **effraide,** frightened.

139. **entraile,** coil.
219a 145. **Elfe,** the Knight, as belonging to Fairyland.
147. **trenchand,** cutting, sharp.
149. **bray,** cry out harshly.
152. **enhaunst,** uplifted.
156. **attonce,** at once.
158. **Tho,** then.
168. **His gall did grate,** etc., his ire was aroused from pain and disgust.
170. **gorge,** throat.
174. **gobbets,** lumps.
177. **bookes and papers,** that is, the literature on which Error is nourished.
178. **frogs and toades,** very venomous animals, according to the mediæval notion.
180. **parbreake,** vomit.
181. **Nilus,** the river Nile.
219b 185. **avale,** subside.
189. **reed,** perceive.
194. **sinke,** hoard.
200. **welke,** grow pale, wane.
206. **clownish,** rustic.
212. **lin,** cease.
220a 227. **unkindly,** unnatural.
254. **An agèd sire,** Archimago, an enchanter, exemplifying Hypocrisy.
254. **weedes,** garments.
262. **louting,** bowing.
263. **quited,** requited, returned.
267. **Silly,** simple.
268. **Bidding his beades,** counting his beads, praying.
270. **mell,** meddle.
277. **weare,** spend.
280. **wastfull,** barren.
285. **forwearied,** wearied out.
288. **baite,** refresh.
295. **take up your in,** have lodging.
302. **edifyde,** built.
221a 313. **file,** make smooth.
315. **Ave-Mary.** See note to p. 104b, l. 20 f.
318. **Morpheus,** god of Sleep.
320. **riddes,** conducts.
328. **Plutoes griesly dame,** Proserpine, queen of the Underworld.
332. **Great Gorgon,** Demogorgon.
333. **Cocytus . . . Styx,** rivers of wailing and hate in the Underworld.
338. **fray,** frighten.
343. **spersèd,** dispersed.
221b 348. **Tethys,** Ocean. Tethys was a Titan and wife of Oceanus, god of the Ocean-Stream, which, according to classical mythology, flowed around the world.
349. **Cynthia,** the Moon.
360. **keepe,** heed.
372. **mought,** might.
381. **Hecate,** a malignant deity of the Underworld, presiding over witchcraft and enchantment.
222a 391. **careful carke,** sorrow full of care.
392. **starke,** stiff.
411. **borne without her dew,** born unnaturally.
422. **playned,** complained.
422. **false wingèd boy,** Cupid.
222b 430. **the Graces,** the three daughters of Jupiter and Eurynome — Aglaia, Euphrosyne, and Thalia, attendants of Venus. See l. 14 ff. of Milton's *L'Allegro*.
431. **Hymen Iö Hymen.** From a Roman marriage song addressed to Hymen, god of Marriage.
447. **To prove,** etc., to try his senses and put her to the test to see if she were genuine.
454. **the blind god,** Cupid.
454. **amate,** subdue.
223a 473. **redoubted,** doughty.
476. **shend,** shame.
488. **light,** fickle.
494. **he,** the dream-spright.
1. **northerne wagoner,** constellation of Boötes, containing the bright star Arcturus.
2. **sevenfold teme,** the seven stars making up the Great Bear, or Dipper.
2. **stedfast starre,** pole star.
6. **Chaunticlere,** the cock.
223b 16. **Proserpines wrath.** See note to Canto I, l. 328.
22. **lustyhed,** pleasure.
34. **wex,** grows.
40. **ment,** mixed, mingled.
43. **yblent,** blinded.
224a 50. **Yrkesome,** tired, weary.
51. **Hesperus,** the evening star.
55. **the rosy fingred Morning,** etc. The goddess Aurora loved the Trojan Prince Tithonus and won for him, by consent of the gods, immortality, but neglected to ask for eternal youth. He wasted away until nothing was left of him but his weak, rasping voice, and then the goddess in pity changed him into a grasshopper. Cf. Tennyson's *Tithonus*.
58. **Titan,** the Sun.
60. **baser,** too mean or lowly.
63. **stowre,** distress, misfortune.
83. **science,** knowledge, skill.
85. **Proteus,** the son of Poseidon. He was gifted with prophecy but was averse to using his powers. When seized and importuned, he would change his shape many times in order to escape, but at last would yield the benefits of his gifts.
224b 96. **discolourd,** many-colored.
99. **Saint George,** the patron saint of England.
105. **Sarazin,** Saracen, pagan.
107. **Sans foy,** literally, Without Faith.
109. **a faire companion,** Duessa, or Falsehood.
111. **Purfled,** bordered.
111. **assay,** quality.
113. **owches,** jewels.
117. **bosses,** studs.
118. **disport,** play, sport.

118. **courting,** courtly.
128. **dispiteous,** without pity, cruel.
225a 134. **Astonied,** astonished.
135. **rebutte,** recoil.
144. **broken reliques,** splintered lances.
147. **quyteth,** requites, repays.
148. **envies,** hates.
155. **bitter fitt,** agony of death.
157. **forwarnèd,** prevented.
171. **Whether,** whither, whereto.
225b 186. **emmove,** move, excite to pity.
198. **Tiberis,** the river Tiber.
200. **haire,** heir.
206. **fone,** foes.
212. **assaid,** assailed, tried.
226a 224. **Sansjoy,** Without Joy.
225. **Sansloy,** Without Law.
239. **chear,** countenance.
243. **so dainty, they say, maketh derth.** Rarity, they say, makes very valuable.
226b 258. **mote,** might.
261. **tide,** while, time.
268. **girlond,** wreath, garland.
269. **rifte,** fissure.
273. **embard,** barred in, imprisoned.
278. **Astond,** astounded.
278. **up his heare did hove,** his hair stood on end.
284. **Limbo lake.** Limbo is a region bordering on Hell.
227a 291. **Fradubio,** Brother Doubtful.
295. **Boreas,** the North Wind.
316. **take in hand,** maintain.
322. **dye of warre,** fortune of war.
323. **prise martiall,** prize of war.
227b 332. **Fraelissa,** True-Faith-in-Doubt.
339. **her,** Fraelissa's.
342. **she,** Duessa.
342. **when none,** etc., 'when in reality no one in the place was fair.'
351. **treen mould,** form of a tree.
353. **unweeting,** not knowing.
354. **wist,** knew.
355. **everie prime,** every springtime.
358. **origane,** a species of mint, sweet marjoram.
228a 376. **pight,** placed.
382. **living well,** flowing well, spring or fountain.
385. **well,** well-being.
386. **kynd,** nature.
388. **hight,** called.
391. **dreriment,** sorrow.
228b 4. **freakes,** tricks.
14. **touch,** touchstone, by which gold was tested.
21. **preace,** press.
229a 32. **fillet,** band of cloth for the hair.
32. **undight,** unloosed.
33. **stole,** a long robe or garment.
38. **A ramping lyon,** a bounding lion. Here exemplifying Reason(?).
39. **salvage,** savage.
48. **weet,** know, recognize.
229b 87. **hore,** hoar, old.
90. **sad,** firm.
102. **whereas,** where.
106. **affray,** terror.
110. **wicket,** gate, door.
230a 116. **Pater nosters.** The Pater Noster (Our Father) is the Lord's Prayer in Latin form.
117. **Aves.** See note to p. 104b, l. 20 f.
121. **bitt,** bit of food.
125. **hardly doen,** done with difficulty.
136. **Aldeboran,** a bright star in the group Hyades of the constellation Taurus.
137. **Cassiopeias chaire,** a constellation opposite the Great Bear on the other side of the pole star.
143. **stelths,** thefts.
144. **purchas criminall,** robbery.
147. **poore mens boxes of their due reliefe,** alms-boxes of their contents.
230b 150. **carelesse,** free from care.
157. **Abessa,** Superstition.
157. **Corceca,** Blind Devotion.
172. **Him booteth,** it profits him.
231a 185. **that long wandring Greeke,** Ulysses, the hero of the *Odyssey,* who refused Calypso's offer of immortality that he might return to Penelope.
192. **Kirkrapine,** Robber of Kirks (churches).
196. **amazèd deare,** frightened deer.
204. **her rayling,** she, the elder, Corceca, of course; the other was dumb.
211. **embost,** arrayed.
214. **traynes,** wiles, guile.
231b 248. **meere,** absolute, out and out.
250. **kindly,** natural.
252. **liefe,** dear.
232a 257. **deface,** disfigure, harm.
271. **beaten,** storm-beaten.
276. **fierce Orions hound,** Sirius, the Dog Star.
279. **Nereus,** after Poseidon, the most important of the sea deities of classical mythology, kindly and benevolent, presiding over the Ægean Sea in particular.
232b 294. **chauffed,** chafed, irritated.
307. **Paynim,** pagan, infidel.
321. **Lethe lake,** the river of Oblivion in Hades.
233a 323. **Furies.** See note to Sackville's *Induction,* p. 197a, l. 109.
323. **doen aslake,** cause to abate.
345. **hether,** hither.
233b 376. **thrilling,** piercing.
377. **launcht,** split in twain.
382. **spill,** destroy.

SAMUEL DANIEL

Daniel was the son of a music master in the neighborhood of Taunton in Somerset. He entered Oxford as a commoner in 1579 but left in three years without a degree. After traveling for some time on the Continent, he became tutor in 1590 or soon after to William Herbert, later Earl of Pembroke, and thus became a member of the celebrated Mary Sidney's circle, residing at Wilton, the family estate in Wiltshire. Without his knowledge and greatly to his embarrassment, twenty-seven of his sonnets were published with Sidney's *Astrophel and Stella* in 1591. His corrected edition, *To Delia,* appeared the following year, and was well received. In 1595 he issued the first four books of his historical poem, *The Civil Wars,* which, next to the *Faerie Queene,* is one of the longest poems of the period. The work was inspired in part by the enthusiastic patriotism, following the triumph over Spain, which sought to glorify English achievements, and in part by his own notion that men are influenced more by epical narrative than by any other writings. About 1599 he became tutor to the young daughter of Margaret, Countess of Cumberland (see p. 241a), at Skipton in Yorkshire. His associations in his new position were congenial, but he found the duties of tuition irksome. Early in the reign of James he was a figure at Court, but his popular favor was waning. He retired to Wiltshire in his later years, continued his literary work there, and died at Beckington in 1619. In his literary work he is reflective rather than passionate. He is at his best in his *Delia* sonnets, which possess a sweetness of rhythm, a delicacy of imagery and sentiment, and a beauty and purity of language which place them among the best of the sonnet series of the time. In his longer poems his pure, clear, stately, modern diction justifies the epithet given him by his contemporaries of "well-languaged" Daniel.

234a THE CIVIL WARS

The portion given is from stanza 19 to the end of the Third Book. Compare Shakespeare's *Richard II* for a treatment of the same subject.

1. **The parliament, which now is held.** Richard was deposed by act of Parliament, September 30, 1399.

2. **the king,** Henry Bolingbroke, now King Henry IV.

11. **Close prisoner.** After his deposition Richard was confined in Pontefract Castle in Yorkshire until his assassination.

17. **Carlile,** the Bishop of Carlisle.

26. **Aventine-retire,** post of refuge or safety. The Aventine was farthest south of the seven hills of Rome.

234b 46. **assecure,** make sure or certain.

57. **accident,** incident, event.

66. **th' abbot's skill of Westminster.** The plot to kill King Henry and restore Richard to the throne was laid at the house of the Abbot of Westminster.

235a 89. **Bewray,** betray, disclose.

106. **Surrey,** Thomas, Duke of Surrey.

235b 120. **dash,** destroy.

120. **fact,** deed.

145. **Blount,** Sir Thomas Blount.

151. **warier carriage in the thing,** a more cautious conduct in the business.

236a 184. **cast the worst of ill,** forecast the worst that may befall.

236b 215. **raise another head,** organize another power or army.

237a 245. **Aumarle,** Edward, Duke of Aumerle, son to the Duke of York.

237b 289. **foregoes,** goes before, anticipates.

290. **eminent,** imminent, near at hand.

290. **woful king,** Richard.

293. **rose,** rose in revolt.

299. **he,** Henry IV.

238a 311. **a knight,** Sir Pierce of Exton.

341. **Pomfret,** Pontefract Castle in the West Riding of Yorkshire. See note to l. 11.

342. **laid in hold,** committed to prison.

346. **near genius,** presiding spirit or "good angel."

238b 351. **prophetising,** prophetical.

359. **unquick,** lacking life or luster.

368. **Conferring,** comparing.

382. **restraint,** confinement.

239a 393. **Diocletian,** a Roman emperor who, after a troubled reign of twenty-one years, longed for repose and abdicated A.D. 305. He spent the remainder of his life among his gardens in Illyria.

418. **Whenas,** when, whereupon.

419. **Enforced them strain who,** compelled them to make a nice point as to who.

239b 437. **Marius' soldier at Minternum.** In the civil war with Sulla in 88 B.C., Marius took refuge at Minturnæ in the lowlands of Latium. The soldier sent to kill him quailed at a look from the old general and fled, exclaiming, "I cannot kill Caius Marius!"

446. **presently,** immediately.

466. **being laid to sore,** being hard pressed.

240a 473. **proditorious,** treacherous.

487. **So th' wolf,** etc., referring to the well-known fable of Æsop.

488. **Betraying,** deceiving.

503. **check,** rebuke.

506. **th' oblation,** sacrifice, offering.

240b 548. **Of mild access,** easy to approach.

241a 556. **being the simple usager,** etc., he being simply the agent or user only for the state.

561. **concussèd,** violently shaken, agitated.

565. **revocate,** revoke.

569. **Syndick,** organized body of control or management.

573. **president,** precedent, principle of procedure.

573. **of pestilent import,** of pernicious character.

581. **calls up many's hopes,** etc., excites hope in many, but brings gratification to few.

583. **their.** The antecedent is "kings," l. 579.

TO THE LADY MARGARET, COUNTESS OF CUMBERLAND

241b 7. **seat,** site, situation.
18. **stately,** of or pertaining to the state.
20. **ill-succeeding,** turning out ill.
22. **Great pirate Pompey,** etc. In little more than a month in 67 B.C., Pompey the Great drove the Mediterranean pirates from the sea. Because of his unscrupulous and almost successful effort to dominate the Roman world, Pompey might be spoken of as a pirate.
35. **sits,** in judgment as a magistrate.
48. **not strange, but as foredone,** as not being unnatural, because foreordained.
242a 57. **madam.** See the title.
67. **kind,** womankind, nature.
68. **head,** armed force, power.
69 f. **hue The world can cast,** color or shade the world can contrive by way of illusion.
82. **use to do,** are accustomed to do.
242b 101 f. **dispense With,** grant dispensation to.
106. **cast the sum,** reckoned the total.
114. **set,** set up, as in music.
117. **union,** unison.
119. **accord,** concord, harmony.

MICHAEL DRAYTON

Drayton was born in the northern part of Shakespeare's county of Warwickshire, preceded him by a year in birth, and is said by Aubrey to have had a butcher to his father, a trade that is also associated with Shakespeare's name. Drayton himself says he was "nobly bred," which probably means he was brought up in the household of Sir Henry Goodere of Powlesworth. There is no evidence that he was ever at either university. He published in 1591 some portions of Scripture metrically rendered. A volume of eclogues followed in 1593. The next year appeared his *Idea* sonnets, which fill a worthy place among the numerous cycles of the time. Then for a decade or more he was in part a playwright, usually in collaboration with others, but mainly, like Samuel Daniel, a poet of the heroical in English history. His *Heroical Epistles* appeared in 1597 and his *Barons' Wars* in 1603. Parts of his *Poly-olbion*, a versified geography of England, appeared in 1613. It is his *magnum opus*, representing many years of industrious labor and containing amid much solid matter passages of great sweetness and light, but it fell unnoticed from the press because the wave of patriotic fervor which prevailed in England at the time of its inception had subsided. His dainty and inimitable fairy poem *Nymphidia* appeared in 1627. The tone and metrical form are derived from Chaucer's *Sir Thopas*, but in general *Nymphidia* owes little to its predecessors. Nothing better of its kind has ever been done. Drayton died in 1631 and received interment in Westminster Abbey. He was a man of life upright and a poet of unusual talent and marvellous industry. Many plaudits came to him in his day, which have not yet ceased to echo the fame of his poetry.

NYMPHIDIA

An interesting comparison, for the treatment of the fairy element in literature, may be made with Shakespeare's *A Midsummer Night's Dream*, which, strange to say, Drayton forgets to mention.

243a 1. **Topas.** Sir Thopas, the hero of Chaucer's burlesque romance of the same name, set out to seek an elf queen.
2. **Rabelais.** François Rabelais, *ca.* 1490–1553, a French humorist, was the author of the celebrated "novel" *Pantagruel*, which contains much learned fooling and is based on the romances of chivalry.
3. **Dowsabel,** a favorite name for a rustic sweetheart in pastoral poetry. It came from the French *douce et belle*, "sweet and pretty."
18. **Or of the later, or the old,** either in recent times or in the past.
25. **Nymphidia.** The poet's muse and informant is one of the spirits in attendance upon Queen Mab.
243b 49. **Obe,** Oberon, King of Fairyland.
54. **upright,** face upwards.
55. **the mare that hight.** The nightmare was supposed to be an incubus or evil spirit that oppressed people in sleep.
63. **dancing hays,** dancing in a ring.
65. **sluttery,** slatternliness, slovenliness.
79. **oaf,** an elf's child, in reference to the popular belief in the changeling.
102. **emmet's eyes,** eyes of the ant.
244a 118. **may,** the hawthorn flower.
132. **letting,** prevention, hindrance.
244b 160. **diswitted,** deprived of wit or sense.
182. **as mad as any hare,** "as mad as a March hare," in reference to the wild actions of the hare in the breeding season.
190. **About his head he lets it walk.** He swings it about his head as a club.
193 f. **The Tuscan poet.** Ariosto, 1474–1533, in his *Orlando Furioso*, "Roland in Madness," recounts the semimythical exploits of Roland, one of the "paladins," or distinguished followers of Charlemagne.
196. **Alcides,** Hercules, a celebrated Greek hero, driven mad by Juno.
197. **Ajax Telamon,** a Grecian hero in the Trojan War, called Ajax the Greater. After being defeated by Ulysses, he went mad.
199. **Bedlam,** mad. The word is a corruption of Bethlehem, an institution in London

for the care of returned crusaders who had become insane.

245a 240. **moilèd,** bedaubed, defiled.

259. **chop,** come or go suddenly or violently.

245b 274. **Don Quixote,** the Knight of La Mancha, hero of Cervantes' celebrated burlesque romance by the same name. Sancho Panza is his famous squire.

280. **gravel,** perplex, run aground.

282. **Puck,** an English popular sprite, known by several names but with one character. See Shakespeare's *A Midsummer Night's Dream* for the greatest of all delineations of him.

291. **bush,** thicket.

246a 326. **hautboy,** ancestor of the present oboe.

246b 371. **her over-match,** more than a match for her.

383. **out of hand,** forthwith, instantly.

385. **fern-seed doth bestow.** According to the popular notion, fernseed had the power to render the possessor invisible.

386. **kernel of the mistletoe.** Mistletoe was consecrated to religious purposes by the ancient Celts. The present custom of kissing under the mistletoe at Christmas time is a relic of an old superstition.

389. **night-shade,** henbane.

390. **vervain,** a species of verbena, used as a cooling remedy.

390. **dill,** a member of the carrot family, with aromatic seeds, used in pickling.

396. **lunary,** moonwort.

397. **molewarp,** the mole.

398. **pismire,** the ant.

247a 417. **mandrake's dreadful groans.** Mandragora, so named from the rough resemblance of its forked root to a man. When torn from the soil, it was reputed to utter a shriek, which drove any hearer insane. It was supposed to have strong medicinal properties.

418. **lubrican,** the leprechaun, in Irish superstition a pygmy sprite given to serving human beings when treated well.

422. **fire-drake,** a fire-breathing monster or dragon. See *Beowulf*, l. 2200 ff.

426. **stound,** stroke.

428. **fear us,** cause us to fear.

430. **night-raven,** the night-heron.

436. **she doth only mind him,** she is apprehensive of, or gives attention to, him only.

455. **case,** skin.

247b 476. **madding,** acting madly.

490. **cockle-shell,** shell of a species of mollusk.

493. **a bent,** a rush stalk.

495. **pile,** point or head.

248a 546. **quoint,** quaint, pretty.

249a 648. **poke,** bag or sack.

651. **pother,** a smothering cloud of smoke, dust, etc.

662. **eschew his blame,** avoid his punishment.

249b 701. **mickle,** much, great.

THOMAS HOWELL

Thomas Howell, of whom very little is known, was probably a native of Dunster in Somerset. At the time of his *Arbor of Amitie*, "by Thomas Howell, Gentleman," 1568, he appears to have been employed in the household of the Earl of Shrewsbury. His last work, so far as known, was his *Devises,* "for his own exercise and his Friends pleasure," in 1581, when he was in service to the Countess of Pembroke, at Wilton. Here, while in temporary retirement from court, Sidney wrote for his incomparable sister his *Arcadia*, which Howell almost certainly saw in manuscript and celebrated in his best known poem. He belongs to the school of Wyatt and Surrey and wrote on the approved themes. In his metrical variety he points the way to the lyrical riches of form which were soon to follow.

249a WRITTEN TO A MOST EXCELLENT BOOK, etc.

The book was most probably the *Arcadia*, by Sir Philip Sidney, which was not published until 1590.

1. **Pallas,** Pallas Athena, goddess of Wisdom.

3. **Pan,** a popular rural divinity, god of Flocks and Herds.

3. **Zoylus,** a Greek rhetorician of the fourth century before Christ, called the "Scourge of Homer" because of his severe criticism of the great bard.

4. **lower at thy laud,** frown upon thy praise.

249b 9. **dight,** prepare, indite.

11. **filèd,** polished.

13 f. **How much they err,** etc. The book in its conclusion shows how wrong people are who try to set aside fate.

250a 25. **Minerva's mirrour.** Minerva's shield was polished like a mirror. By its reflection Perseus slew the Gorgon.

26. **y-fret,** adorned.

33. **The worthy Countess,** Mary Sidney, Countess of Pembroke, Sir Philip's sister and a patroness of letters, for whom the *Arcadia* was written.

A DREAM

250b 11. **hire,** reward.

12. **When hope with hap,** etc., when hope in realization may enjoy its object.

SIR EDWARD DYER

Dyer was born at Sharpham Park in Somerset, the birthplace later of the novelist, Henry Fielding. He attended Oxford but took no degree. After some travel he rose to a high place at Court, winning for himself the honor of a comparison with Sir Philip Sidney in his sovereign's esteem. He was patronized by Leicester, and like Sidney, with whom he was intimate, was a master spirit of the Areopagus Club. Little is known of his last years. He enjoyed considerable fame as a poet, specifically in elegy, during the last quarter of the century, receiving mention by the contemporary critic of the *Arte of English Poesie* for his "sweet solemn and high conceit." But his poems were not collected at the time, and from those that remain it is hard to judge either of his general merits as a poet or of his works by classes or kinds. His poem on the contentment of a quiet mind is a household possession.

MY MIND TO ME A KINGDOM IS

5. **want,** lack.
10. **No shape to feed a loving eye,** no bodily form to attract love by good looks.
19. **stay,** reliance, comfort.

EDMUND SPENSER

251a PROTHALAMION

The word *prothalamion* means "a song in celebration of a marriage." Spenser's poem was written in celebration of the double marriage of the ladies Elizabeth and Katherine Somerset, daughters of the Earl of Worcester, to Henry Guilford and William Peter in 1596 while Spenser was sojourning in London.

2. **Zephyrus,** the West Wind.
6. **my long fruitlesse stay,** etc. Spenser had long waited expectantly, though in vain, for preferment from Elizabeth because of the delight she had expressed at the early books of his *Faerie Queene.*
12. **rutty,** rooty.

251b 27. **feateously,** neatly.
33. **vermeil,** vermilion.
37. **two swannes of goodly hewe,** representing the brides to be.
40. **Pindus,** a range of mountains separating Thessaly and Epirus in ancient Greece.
43. **Leda,** the mother of Clytæmnestra, Helen, and Castor and Pollux. She was wooed by Zeus in the form of a milk-white swan.

252a 63. **Venus silver teeme.** Venus is often represented as being drawn through the air in a pearl shell by a team of white doves or pigeons, sometimes sparrows.
67. **Somers-heat,** a play on the word "Somerset," the family name of the brides.
78. **Peneus,** a river in Thessaly running through the Vale of Tempe.
97. **heart-quelling sonne,** Cupid.

252b 100. **assoile,** absolve.
110. **undersong,** burden, refrain.
121. **shend,** put to shame.
128. **my most kyndly nurse,** etc. Spenser was born in London.
130. **from another place,** etc. Spenser's family, it is thought by some, long resided in Lincolnshire.
132. **those bricky towres.** The Temple, formerly the property of the Knights Templar until the suppression of the order by Edward II, was occupied by students of law.
137. **a stately place,** Leicester House. After Leicester's death in 1588 the place became the property of the Earl of Essex and was known as Essex House.

253a 145. **a noble peer,** the Earl of Essex.
147. **through all Spaine did thunder.** Essex commanded the land forces in the expedition against Cadiz in 1596, which resulted in its capture.
148. **Hercules two pillors,** the rocks on each side of the Strait of Gibraltar.
157. **Elisaes,** Queen Elizabeth's.
164. **Hesper,** the evening star.
169. **Two gentle knights,** the bridegrooms.
173. **the twins of Jove,** Castor and Pollux, the constellation Gemini.

SIR WALTER RALEGH

Sir Walter Ralegh (or Raleigh) was the most restless and many-sided spirit of Elizabeth's reign. Like Sidney he satisfied well the ideal of the complete gentleman, but unlike Sidney he was not a universal favorite, because of his overweening hauteur and pride. He came of seaman stock of Devonshire, the son of a country gentleman by a third wife. He was at Oxford for a while, and in 1576 was a member of the Middle Temple, more as a passing lodger, however, than as a serious student of the law. He saw service at sea against the Spaniards and in Ireland against the native rebels. Rising rapidly at court, he was knighted in 1584, and represented his native shire in Parliament. In 1586 he obtained the grant of a vast estate (40,000 acres) in Ireland and became a neighbor of Spenser while temporarily out of favor at court. Meanwhile he had interested himself in explorations and discoveries in America, which resulted in the addition of Virginia to the Queen's dominions. He was denied the privilege of accompanying the expedition to the Azores in 1591, but his responsibility in the enterprise gave us his celebrated account of the glorious fight of the *Revenge* (p. 295 ff.). At the beginning of James's reign the partisans of the late Earl of Essex, Ralegh's arch enemy, succeeded in bringing him to trial on charges of the highest treasonable offense against the country and the crown. He was convicted and sentenced to execution on December 11, 1603; but he was reprieved the day before he was to suffer, his property was confiscated, and he was committed to the Tower. He languished in prison for many years, engaging in scientific experiments, writing his *History of the World*, and solacing himself with the friendship of the gallant Henry, Prince of Wales. At last in a desperate venture to regain his freedom, he went on an expedition to the Orinoco, engaging to return with a shipload of gold as the price of his liberty, or forfeit his life. After a year of fruitless voyaging under the worst of circumstances, he returned to England to meet his fate. His execution took place on October 29, 1618. In gratification of his lifelong passion for literature, he cultivated, during his leisure in London, the friendship of scholars and men of letters. His prose, which is ever stately and lucid, becomes nobly eloquent when he is aroused. When it is narrative in character, as it frequently is, it is the best of its kind at the time. Poetry was an occupation with him all his life, but only a slender remnant of his verse has been preserved. That remnant, mirroring as it does the aristocratic personality of the author, is aptly described by a contemporary as "most lofty, insolent, and passionate."

253b A VISION UPON THIS CONCEIT, etc.

This sonnet was prefixed to the first book of the *Faerie Queene*.

1. **Laura.** The lady to whom Petrarch addressed some three hundred sonnets during an acquaintanceship of fifteen or twenty years has been identified as Laure de Noves, later Madame de Sale, a French woman of Avignon, 1308–1348.
6. **the Fairy Queen,** Queen Elizabeth.

REPLY TO MARLOWE'S PASSIONATE SHEPHERD

See Marlowe's poem, p. 259.

12. **fancy,** love.

254a THE LIE

Some doubt remains whether this poem is by Ralegh's hand.

2. **arrant,** errand.

254b 44. **tickle points of niceness,** questions of trivial but fastidious import.

49. **physic,** medical skill.

255a 70. **virtue least preferreth,** merit is advanced least.

HIS PILGRIMAGE

The tone and imagery of this poem are explained by its probable composition in 1603, after Ralegh's condemnation and before his reprieve.

1. **scallop-shell,** shell of a species of mollusk, worn by pilgrims.
3. **scrip,** wallet.
9. **palmer,** pilgrim in general; specifically one returning from Jerusalem bearing a palm-branch.
25. **suckets,** delicacies, sweetmeats.

255b 41. **without degrees,** without regard to rank.

42. **angels,** a play on the word in the sense of a coin.
48. **Unblotted,** untainted.

THE CONCLUSION

This poem is said to have been written the night before Ralegh's execution. It was found afterwards in his Bible.

JOHN LYLY

John Lyly was a native of the Weald of Kent. He was registered at Oxford as "*plebeii filius*," proved an indifferent student but attained both degrees, and later was incorporated M.A. of Cambridge. His *Euphues* appeared in 1579 and brought him at once into fame but not into fortune. He became a playwright for children's companies and aspired to the Mastership of the Revels. But the boys' companies suffered legal restrictions, after a few years he was superseded by better dramatists, and, disappointed at court, he died in obscurity in 1606. He attained the high-water mark of artificiality of style in his *Euphues*, a work that was enormously imitated in his day, affecting even the speech of the time, and since has provided the language with a new critical term, *Euphuism*. His plays are pleasant reading, but ultimately they cloy. While showing some skill in comedy, he is not a great acting dramatist. His finest work is in his lyrics.

APELLES' SONG

1. **Campaspe,** a Theban captive, Alexander's favorite, with whom the painter Apelles fell in love. The song appears in Lyly's play of *Campaspe*.
4. **team of sparrows.** See note to *Prothalamion*, p. 252a, l. 63.

256a TRICO'S SONG

Trico is an Athenian youth in Lyly's play of *Campaspe*.

2. **the ravished nightingale.** Philomela, daughter of King Pandion, was violated by her brother-in-law, Tereus, and deprived of her tongue that she might not divulge her shame. Divine pity transformed her into the nightingale, whence she is represented as singing on a thorn tree with a prickle at her breast in token of her wrong.
3. **tereu,** representing the name of her ravisher, Tereus.
5. **Brave,** fine.
5. **prick-song,** a song with the harmony written or pricked down.

ROBERT GREENE

The most facile writer and probably the best writer of fiction during the Elizabethan age was Robert Greene, the son of poor but honest parents of Norwich. He attended Cambridge as a sizar and in due time won both the Arts degrees. After a period of travel he returned to his native city, and was married and resided there in the mid-eighties, but deserted wife and child and settled permanently in London to try his fortune as a " university wit." He was essentially a religious being at heart, but, innately weak in character, in conduct he fell hopelessly short of the bounties of grace and virtue with which his pen is so fluent. His associations with the London underworld he often turned to his own profit in his penitential pamphlets, when his nobler impulses were dominant. Improvidence was his bane, and he died in squalor in London when not much more than half the number of his days were fulfilled. He was both a prolific and a popular writer in his day. His works comprise pamphlets, plays, and romances. His greatest service was in prose fiction. His plays are more important in the history of English drama than they are intrinsically significant. His poems, found chiefly in his romances, are justly famous. Noble in sentiment, tender in sympathy, refined and elegant in phrase, they are among the treasures of English lyrical poetry.

SEPHESTIA'S SONG TO HER CHILD

Sephestia is the banished daughter of King Damocles in Greene's *Menaphon*.

256b THE SHEPHERD'S WIFE'S SONG

This song is found in the *Mourning Garment*, a tract which adopted for its theme the Biblical story of the Prodigal Son.

35. **More sounder.** Double comparatives are common in Elizabethan usage.

257a 36. **spill,** lose, destroy.
42. **tide or sithe,** time or occasion.

SONG

This song occurs in one of the author's numerous penitential tracts, the *Farewell to Folly*. Compare Dyer's poem on the same theme, p. 250.

9. **The mean,** suggestive of " the golden mean "; in music, the middle part of a three-part harmony.

GEORGE PEELE

Peele was the son of a London citizen of Devonshire stock. He was brought up in Christ's Hospital School, where his father for many years was clerk and a teacher of commercial subjects. He went up to Oxford in 1571 and continued through to his M.A. degree in 1579. He enjoyed some reputation as a poet during his university career. Later he acquired a reputation for being extremely wild. With his eclectic genius he pursued the calling of playwright and actor until his life came to a miserable end while he was still under forty years of age. " He is a less witty and more poetic Lyly." His lyrics were popular in literary circles and have continued the best preservers of his fame down to the present time.

CUPID'S CURSE

In *The Arraignment of Paris*.

257b 10. **bin,** are.
11. **roundelay,** a song in which a simple strain is oft repeated, suitable for singing to a dance in a circle.

THOMAS LODGE

Thomas Lodge was the second son of the Lord Mayor of London, though not certainly born in the city. He attended the Merchant Taylors' School and Oxford University, and became a member of Lincoln's Inn. But he soon gave up law for literature, thus adding one more name to the brilliant group of " university wits " who were adorning literature in London at the close of the century. He tried his hand at play making for a while, mainly in collaboration with Greene, without great success. Then he turned adventurer and voyaged as far as South America. From his travel came his Euphuistic romance of *Rosalynde*, the best of the time, from which Shakespeare drew his plot for *As You Like It*. In 1596 he abandoned literature for medicine, and for the remainder of his rather long life he was a fashionable practitioner in London. His prose is ornate, though languid, and modern readers find it tedious. He best deserves remembrance for his lyrical poems, where, though fervor is often lacking, he charms with his unique artistry.

ROSALIND'S MADRIGAL

In *Rosalynde.* Among the many representations of love in the poetry of the time, this one is unique in that love is compared to a bee.

ROSALIND'S DESCRIPTION

1. **highest sphere,** the empyrean or sphere of pure fire, according to the Ptolemaic system of astronomy.

258a 43. **for her fair,** as for her beauty.

NICHOLAS BRETON

Breton came of an ancient family, originally settled in Essex, but his father removed to London, amassed a fortune there in trade, and died in 1558, when the son was some twelve years of age. Ten years later his mother was married to George Gascoigne, the poet. He may have attended Oxford. By 1577, the year of his stepfather's death, he was settled in London and lodging in Holborn. He was married in 1592, and from the records of the births and deaths of his children he resided in Cripplegate. He was referred to as a gentleman, but no record remains of his death. Voluminous works in prose and verse appeared from his pen regularly from 1577 to 1626. He was patronized early by Mary Sidney, Countess of Pembroke. He wrote with great facility and wrote too often and too much. Versatility and refinement are his characteristics. He is best in his pastoral lyrics, where he is always sincere, often gay without being gross, and quite regularly melodious and fresh without being notable for originality of thought or weight of content.

A SWEET LULLABY

Compare Greene's *Sephestia's Song to Her Child,* p. 256.

258b 39. **rascal,** an inferior deer or other animal, unfit for the chase.

PHYLLIDA AND CORYDON

259a 6. **Phyllida and Corydon,** conventional names of pastoral lovers.

ROBERT SOUTHWELL

The Catholic poet Robert Southwell was born near Norwich in Norfolk. His maternal grandmother was a Shelley, from which line descended the great lyric poet of the nineteenth century. He received his early schooling at Douay and Paris under Jesuit instruction. He prepared for orders in the Jesuit Society and studied at Rome, becoming in due time prefect of studies in the English College there. He was ordained priest in 1584, and by his own wish was nominated for the English mission, where from the rigor of the penal laws priests were in the utmost peril. On his arrival in England he became at once active and, very soon, influential. His headquarters were in London. In time he was arrested and tortured to extort confession, but in vain. Finally, after an extremely hazardous life of nearly ten years, he was tried, sentenced, and met the fate he had long invited, by hanging at Tyburn in February, 1595. He left much writing ready for the press, including his chief volume of verse, *St. Peter's Complaint, with Other Poems,* which was published soon after his death. Piratical reprints and other volumes of his poetry attest his popularity. He was acquainted with the poetry of his contemporaries, but his constant effort, he declared, was to show that virtue and piety are as worthy topics for a poet's pen as the worldly subjects usually treated. To this end he uses the artificial and "conceited" manner introduced from Italy as a vehicle for his ardent religious fervor.

CHRISTOPHER MARLOWE

Christopher Marlowe, the second greatest personage in English drama, was the son of a Canterbury shoemaker. He was educated at the king's School of his native town. In 1580 he proceeded to Cambridge as a pensioner. The following year he was admitted to a six-years' scholarship and continued for the B.A. and M.A. degrees, the latter of which he received in 1587. He probably went up to London at once and began playwriting. He was early attached to the Lord Admiral's Company, the company of the great Edward Alleyn, which produced most of his plays. His *Tamburlaine,* in two parts, of which the first appeared in 1587 and opened a new vein for English tragedy, is written in a flexible blank verse form, which has since been called "Marlowe's mighty line." His *Dr. Faustus* followed, probably the next year, and his *Jew of Malta* a year or two later. This brilliant succession showed clearly the possibilities of the great tragic passions in English drama. *Edward II,* an historical play, about 1592, is generally acknowledged to be the best of its kind in the language. His other dramatic pieces are inferior. A short while before his death he attracted attention by his radical religious views, and was under close surveillance when he was stabbed to death in a drunken brawl in Deptford. Marlowe was Shakespeare's senior by only a few weeks, and at his death he was a greater dramatist. His early decease by violence may well be deplored.

259b THE PASSIONATE SHEPHERD

See Ralegh's *Reply*, p. 253.

THOMAS NASHE

"The Young Juvenal," as Thomas Nashe was called in recognition of his undoubted satirical talent, was baptized at Lowestoft in Norfolk near the end of the year 1567. He was in Cambridge for seven years, lacking one quarter, by which he narrowly missed the M.A. degree, and, according to his own statement, "might have been a fellow if I had would." He was settled in London by 1588, seeking a livelihood with his pen. He tried for a patron and courted assiduously the favor of the Earl of Southampton, but to the end of his life he suffered the direst poverty. He displayed a talent for satire early. By him, probably more than by any other, the Martinists were discomfited in the Mar-Prelate Controversy between Episcopalians and Puritans. His inveterate enemy, the Puritan Gabriel Harvey (the friend of Spenser), engaged him in a duel of words but was hopelessly worsted. Harvey had angered Nashe by speaking ill of his friend Greene (p. 256a) after that poet's death. In 1594 appeared his *Unfortunate Traveler, or Jack Wilton*, a picaresque or rogue romance which is generally recognized as a landmark in the history of realistic fiction. He tried playwriting for a while without conspicuous success, and was dead by 1601. Nashe opposed the euphuistic practices so current in his day, cultivated pretentious words in his own vocabulary to offset the effects, as he regarded it, of the too abundant "small change" in the language, and wrote a few poems which amply maintain the high lyrical quality of the age.

DEATH'S SUMMONS

This poem was written during a visitation of the plague. The refrain, "Lord, have mercy on us," accompanied by a cross, was often officially placed on the doors of infected houses.

260a 19. **Helen,** Helen of Troy.
25. **her gate,** the grave.
31. **Hell's executioner,** the plague.
33. **vain art,** medical skill.
36. **each degree,** persons of every rank.

WILLIAM SHAKESPEARE

The known facts of Shakespeare's life are not numerous. The family name, a compound, deriving from the Conquest, was prevalent in England in the sixteenth century. John Shakespeare, the poet's father, was a general merchant in Stratford, a small town on the Avon River in Warwickshire, which has been called "the heart of England." In 1557 John Shakespeare, then a prosperous burgess, was married to Mary Arden, the daughter of a house which had belonged to the landed gentry of the shire since before the Conquest. On April 26, 1564, the first son of the union, William, was baptized in the parish church. Other children followed, and the family continued prosperous, the father at one time being chief magistrate of the town. At the usual age, it is reasonably assumed, the poet entered the Free Grammar School and remained until about 1578, when the family fortunes were so low as probably to necessitate his withdrawal from school. There is no evidence that he afterwards continued his education anywhere. In 1582 he was married to Anne Hathaway, eight years his senior, of the neighboring village of Shottery. In the following year a daughter Susanna was born, and in 1585 came the twins Hamnet and Judith. By 1590 he was in London, beginning his career as actor and playwright. He was mentioned enviously by the dying Greene in 1592, and in 1598 was cited by Francis Meres as "most excellent" for both comedy and tragedy. (For another contemporary estimate, see p. 267b.) The following year he became a shareholder in the newly erected Globe Theatre, occupied by the Lord Chamberlain's Company. Before 1600 the majority of his plays were histories and comedies. From 1600 to 1607 he was engaged mainly on his great tragedies. From the latter year until the end of his career as playwright he wrote the anomalous group called the romances. At some time between 1610 and 1613 he gave up his professional life and retired to his native Stratford, where probably his family had remained all the while, and there in some affluence spent his few remaining years. He died in 1616, on April 23, which, according to tradition, was the anniversary of his birth. His lyrics and sonnets fully attest the supreme quality of his genius.

ON A DAY, ALACK THE DAY!

In *Love's Labour's Lost.*

260b 19. **for Jove,** that he was Jove.

SPRING

The closing song in *Love's Labour's Lost.*

2. **lady-smocks,** a variety of meadow flower.
3. **cuckoo-buds,** probably buttercups.
6. **Mocks married men,** etc. The note of the cuckoo was vulgarly supposed to prognosticate cuckoldry.
12. **turtles,** turtledoves.

WINTER

20. **blows his nail,** that is, to warm his hands.
27. **keel,** cool, stir.
29. **saw,** old saying, proverb.
32. **crabs,** crab apples.

WHO IS SILVIA

In *The Two Gentlemen of Verona.*

261a TELL ME WHERE IS FANCY BRED

In *The Merchant of Venice.*

1. **fancy,** romantic love.

UNDER THE GREENWOOD TREE

In *As You Like It.*

3. **turn,** suit, adapt.

BLOW, BLOW, THOU WINTER WIND

In *As You Like It.*

261b 14. **warp,** congeal, freeze.

IT WAS A LOVER AND HIS LASS

In *As You Like It.*

4. **ring time,** time for exchanging rings in troth plight.
17. **crownèd with the prime,** crowned with the best of everything, is at its best.

O MISTRESS MINE

In *Twelfth Night.*

262a COME AWAY, COME AWAY, DEATH

In *Twelfth Night.*

1. **Come away,** come hither.
2. **cypres,** crape for the dead.

FEAR NO MORE THE HEAT O' TH' SUN

The justly famous dirge in *Cymbeline.*

14. **thunder-stone,** thunderbolt.
19. **exorciser,** one who controls spirits, a conjurer.
21. **unlaid,** unappeased.

COME UNTO THESE YELLOW SANDS

In *The Tempest.*

262b 5. **featly,** neatly, gracefully.

FULL FATHOM FIVE THY FATHER LIES

In *The Tempest.*

WHERE THE BEE SUCKS

Ariel's song in *The Tempest.*

CRABBED AGE AND YOUTH

This poem appeared in *The Passionate Pilgrim* of 1599, a piratical publication by W. Jaggard, and its attribution to Shakespeare has therefore been doubted.

THOMAS CAMPION

Of the early life and associations of Thomas Campion little is known. He was educated at Cambridge and may have obtained an M.D. degree in some foreign university, although he did not practice medicine until late in life. He entered Gray's Inn in 1586 but withdrew from the society in 1595. In the same year he published his first volume of verse. By 1601 he was recognized as an authority on music, at which time appeared his first *Book of Airs*, containing both music and lyrics of a high order. Other song books followed at intervals until his death in 1620. He intentionally used English airs in preference to those from France and Italy, which were popular in his day. His songs are of various kinds — pious and passionate, polished and rustic. His work illustrates the fondness for songs which characterized all classes of English society during the Elizabethan age. Physician, scholar, accomplished musician, he cannot have regarded poetry as anything more than an avocation, but the results give him a high rank among the very best song writers of the time.

263a TO LESBIA

Translated from Catullus.

3. **heaven's great lamps,** the sun and moon.

THE MAN OF LIFE UPRIGHT

11. **vaults to fly**, vaults to which to fly.

263b JACK AND JOAN THEY THINK NO ILL

7. **Lash out**, risk, venture.
7. **feast**, fair.
9. **nappy**, strong, heady.
19. **tutties**, posies.
24. **ever thinks**, etc. In speech he is ever forethoughtful.

THERE IS A GARDEN IN HER FACE

4. **flow**, flourish.
6. **'Cherry ripe,'** the cry of the fruit vender on the street.

MICHAEL DRAYTON

264a AGINCOURT

Addressed to the Cambro-Britons, or Welsh, for their valiant service in the English monarch's invasion of France in 1415 to make good his claim to the French throne.

8. **King Harry**, King Henry V. See the treatment of the battle in Shakespeare's *Henry V*, Act III, scenes v–vii, and the whole of Act IV.
11. **Agincourt**, in the northern neck of France, south of Calais.

264b 15. **the French general**, Constable d'Albret.
27. **to one be ten.** The French forces outnumbered the English about four to one.
41. **Poitiers and Cressy**, scenes of celebrated English victories in the Hundred Years' War, the latter in 1346 and the former in 1356.
45. **our Grandsire great**, John of Gaunt, 1340–1399, fourth son of Edward III.
48. **the French lilies**, the national emblem of France.
49. **Duke of York**, Edward, second Duke of York, slain in the battle.
53. **Exeter**, Duke of Exeter, uncle of Henry V.
66. **Erpingham**, Sir Thomas Erpingham, of the King's household, who gave the signal to the English forces in ambush to advance.

265a 73. **Spanish yew**, a favorite wood for the making of bows.
74. **Arrows a cloth-yard long**, the longest arrows used in European archery, slightly longer than the ordinary unit of long measure.
82. **bilboes**, swords, from Bilboa, in Spain, famous for its weapons.
91. **ding**, strike.
97 ff. **Gloucester . . . Clarence**, brothers of the King.
105 ff. **Warwick . . . Oxford . . . Suffolk . . . Beaumont . . . Willoughby . . . Ferrers . . . Fanhope**, English noblemen who fought at Agincourt.
113. **St. Crispin's Day**, October 25.
118. **fill a pen**, inspire poetry.

SIR JOHN DAVIES

Sir John Davies was born at Tisbury in Wiltshire. His father, a gentleman, apparently died early and the mother bred the son to learning. He was educated at Winchester and Oxford, receiving his B.A. degree in 1590, when already a member of the Middle Temple. In 1596 appeared his *Orchestra*, an exceedingly ingenious and fanciful poem on dancing, nearly a thousand lines long, but said to have been composed in fifteen days. For a personal attack on a fellow Templer he was expelled from the society and debarred the practice of law. In retirement at Oxford he wrote his *Nosce Teipsum* (1599), a poem on the soul, which is remarkable for its clear and technical exposition of a vague and abstract subject. In the same year appeared his *Hymns of Astrea*, thirty-six cleverly designed and beautiful acrostics addressed to the Queen. The *Nosce Teipsum* recommended its author highly to James on his accession. In the same year Davies was made Solicitor-General of Ireland, and from this time on he resided in that country. In 1606 he became Attorney-General of Ireland, was knighted the following year, and in 1626 was appointed Lord Chief Justice, but died of apoplexy before assuming office. Davies lacks the color and emotionality of his time, and hence has little popular appeal, but his fancy and classic intellectuality have won for him a class of readers whose delight is sufficient warrant for his fame.

265b HYMNS OF ASTREA

These Hymns, addressed to the Queen (*Astrea*, star), are written in acrostic form, the initial letters of each poem spelling "Elizabeth Queen" in the Latin form, ELISABETHA REGINA.

TO SPRING

11. **this nymph of ours**, the Queen.

TO THE LARK

2. **clark**, clerk.
9. **set to some sweet sphere**, a reference to the fabled music of the spheres.

TO ENVY

266a 16. she, *i.e.*, my Muse.

THOMAS DEKKER

Thomas Dekker was born in London. He was probably a "gentleman" residing with his family in Cripplegate and Bishopsgate. The first definite mention of him is in an entry for January, 1597, in the diary of the well-known theatrical manager, Philip Henslowe, by whose assistance he was soon afterwards released from prison. He was a principal in the celebrated Stage Quarrel just at the close of the century. Henslowe records eight plays written by him single-handed between 1598 and 1602. Thereafter he did much in collaboration. His plays were recklessly done, and they show many inartistic touches, yet they are regularly mentioned among the great masterpieces of English drama. His lyrics are characterized by tenderness, optimism, lightness of touch, and genuine poetic charm. He is best as a pamphleteer. His *Guls Hornbook*, 1609, a sort of mock guide for the man about town, presents in sterling English the best of all pictures of the profligates, dupes, and swindlers of the time.

O SWEET CONTENT

In *The Patient Grissell.*

RICHARD BARNFIELD

The poet Barnfield was the eldest son of Richard Barnfield, gentleman, of Norbury in Shropshire. His mother died when he was six, leaving him to the care of an aunt. He was given a career at Oxford, whence he was graduated B.A. in 1592. His first volume of verse, *The Affectionate Shepherd*, 1594, was dedicated to the Stella of Sidney's sonnets, then Lady Rich. Three other volumes followed in rapid succession, after which he disappears from sight, apparently settling down as a country gentleman of considerable property in Staffordshire. He died at Dorlaston in 1627. Too often his poems, as being dedicated to sentiments of friendship, are unrestrained and extravagant, even for his time, cloying the reader before they convince or charm. On the other hand, the high quality of two or three of his poems is evidenced by the fact that they were long regarded as Shakespeare's.

AS IT FELL UPON A DAY

For the legend of the nightingale, see the notes to Lyly's *Trico's Song*, p. 256 and to p. 120b, l. 67.

BEN JONSON

Ben Jonson was born a posthumous child in Westminster. It is said he inherited border blood, which may account for his combative disposition. His stepfather was a bricklayer, and the boy was poorly brought up. He attended Westminster School but probably did not receive university training, being set instead to his stepfather's trade. To escape this he fled to Flanders and took service with the English against the Spaniards, slew an adversary in a personal encounter, and returned to London under unknown circumstances about 1592. He was married, but apparently was not happy in his wife and children. In 1597 he was both a player and a playwright for the Lord Admiral's men, an important theatrical company of the time. The following year he was mentioned by Meres as one of the chief contemporary writers of tragedy. In several comedies he represented one side, to wit, his own, in the celebrated Stage Quarrel at the turn of the century. Early in the reign of James he began the series of masques which have since distinguished his name above all others in the type. He stood high at court and occupied a position of unique authority over the younger writers of the time. Under Charles he declined in favor and suffered in health until death relieved him in 1637. As a playwright he was great, as a scholar and critic supreme for his time, and as a lyrical poet known and appreciated then and since for his vigorous and refined thought, his classical poise, and his neatly wrought expression.

266b

HYMN TO DIANA

In *Cynthia's Revels.*

3. **Seated in thy silver chair.** Diana is here addressed as the Moon goddess.

EPITAPH ON S[ALATHIEL] P[AVY]

The subject was one of the children connected with Queen Elizabeth's Chapel, who is reported to have acted in one or two of Jonson's plays.

11. **three filled zodiacs,** three years, three dramatic seasons.

267a 15. **Parcæ,** the Fates.

TO CELIA

In *The Forest.*

SONG: TO CELIA

In *Volpone.* Translated from Catullus.

267b *SIMPLEX MUNDITIIS*

In *Epicœne.* The title is from one of the odes of Horace and means "of simple elegance," or, as Milton translated it, "plain in thy neatness."

EPITAPH ON ELIZABETH, L. H.

The full name of this unfortunate subject has not been discovered. The form of the initials would suggest some gentlewoman. Cf. also l. 10.

TO THE MEMORY, etc.

See introductory note to William Shakespeare, p. 260a.

2. **thy book,** the First Folio edition of Shakespeare's works, 1623, to which this poem was prefixed.

268a 19. **I will not lodge thee by, etc.** See William Basse's *Elegy on Shakespeare,* p. 273.

26. **disproportioned,** inferior to his own.

27. **of years,** limited in time. Cf. l. 43.

28. **peers,** contemporaries.

30. **Marlowe's mighty line.** Marlowe was the first to employ really powerful blank verse in English tragedy and to demonstrate its possibilities. See introductory note to Marlowe, p. 259b.

33 f. **Æschylus, Euripides, and Sophocles,** the three great Greek tragic dramatists, fifth century before Christ.

35. **Pacuvius, Accius,** Latin tragic writers of the second century before Christ.

35. **him of Cordova dead,** Seneca.

36. **buskin,** thick-soled footwear of the actors of classical tragedy.

37. **socks,** thin-soled wear employed by actors in comedy.

51. **Aristophanes,** greatest of the Greek comic writers, late fifth and early fourth centuries before Christ.

52. **Terence — Plautus,** famous Latin comic dramatists of the early part of the second century before Christ. Their works were widely known and imitated during the age of Shakespeare.

268b 69. **shake a lance,** a pun on Shakespeare's name. Punning was a habit, almost a disease, with the Elizabethans.

71. **Sweet Swan of Avon,** a reference to Shakespeare's birthplace, Stratford-on-Avon in Warwickshire.

74. **Eliza, and our James,** Queen Elizabeth and her successor King James I.

DR. JOHN DONNE

John Donne was born in London of a family of Welsh extraction, and was left an orphan by the death of his father, a prosperous citizen and ironmonger, when he was only two or three years old. He entered Oxford at the age of eleven but left after three years and went abroad for three more. In 1592 he was admitted to Lincoln's Inn. He soon became intimate with the remarkable band of poets and wits who were the leaders of their day. He accompanied Essex on the expedition to Cadiz in 1596, and on his return was made secretary to Sir Thomas Egerton, Lord Keeper of the Seal. His position brought him into intimate contact with the Lord Keeper's niece, the pair fell inconsiderately in love, and were secretly married in 1600. The rash act ruined his fortunes. He was dismissed from his position without a chance of reinstatement. For a number of years the couple lived amid extremely embarrassing circumstances. Gradually he regained favor at court but received no appointment. He was told by James he must rise by the Church if at all. At last in 1615 he took orders and straightway was made chaplain to James. He soon came to be recognized as the greatest divine of his age. He was made dean of St. Paul's in 1621 and died ten years later. The best period of his poetry coincides with the time of his secular fortunes. Although it was not published at the time, it was popular in manuscript. It is love poetry in the exaggerated vein of the age. Vague, subtle, clever, far-fetched in imagery, and fantastic in expression, it is the source of much of the so-called "metaphysical" usage which prevailed so widely among the seventeenth-century lyricists. His religious poetry is inferior to his secular compositions. It is too much given to speculation and is too often lacking in feeling and deep spiritual experience to make it memorable in the general body of sacred poetry of the language.

SONG

Donne here, and in some of his poems which follow, derides the extravagant sentiments of the "sonneteers." His example had much to do with discouraging the vogue of the sonnet early in the seventeenth century.

2. **a mandrake root.** See note to Drayton's *Nymphidia,* p. 247a, l. 417.

269a THE INDIFFERENT

1. **fair and brown.** Only the fair or blondes satisfied the conventional ideal of beauty in Elizabethan times. By including brunettes, Donne makes himself a heretic to the Venus cult of his day.

15. **Let me,** allow me, take me for an example.

A VALEDICTION FORBIDDING MOURNING

269b 16. **elemented it,** gave it its elements, created it.

19. **Inter-assurèd of the mind,** mutually, or by common agreement of mind.

26. **As stiff twin compasses,** etc. Here follows a good example of the "conceit," which was so prevalent in the lyrical poetry of the seventeenth century.

LOVE'S DEITY

9. **godhead,** godhood.

270a 15. **modern,** commonplace.

18. **purlieu,** domain occupied or possessed through usurpation.

22. **Rebel and atheist,** that is, to the prevailing creed of love.

SIR HENRY WOTTON

Wotton was born at Boughton Hall in Kent. He attended Winchester School and went up to Oxford as a commoner, where he began a friendship with Donne which was ended only by the latter's death. He was abroad on the continent and in Italy for seven years after his university career. In 1595 he was back in London and was admitted to Lincoln's Inn. He became an agent and secretary to Essex. On the great earl's fall, Wotton left England for Italy and remained away until the Queen's death. He was knighted under James and received the post of ambassador to Venice, which he occupied, though not continuously, for nearly twenty years. While in England in 1611 he courted the favor of Prince Henry and the Princess Elizabeth, the latter with her charms inspiring in him an enthusiastic esteem, which he celebrated in beautiful verse. From 1625 to his death in 1639 he was provost of Eton, where he died and was buried. His poetry, though small in amount, is of surpassingly high quality.

270b THE CHARACTER OF A HAPPY LIFE

8. **breath,** talk.

ON HIS MISTRESS, THE QUEEN OF BOHEMIA

Elizabeth, eldest daughter of James, married the elector palatine and titular king of Bohemia.

FRANCIS BEAUMONT

Francis Beaumont, third son of a judge of the common pleas in London, was born at Grace-Dieu in Leicestershire, the family seat. His Oxford career was interrupted suddenly in his second year by the death of his father. He was entered in the Inner Temple in 1600, but was more probably a frequenter of the celebrated Mermaid Tavern than a serious student of the law. His name is inextricably associated with the name of Fletcher, who was several years his senior. The two lodged together and apparently had all things in common on the Bankside in Southwark. Their joint literary work arose as a natural consequence, and not from any sordid managerial arrangement of collaboration. Beaumont died in mid career in 1616 and was interred in Westminster Abbey. He is above all a dramatist, but the occasional high quality of his few short poems explains Coleridge's wish that he had been a lyric poet.

271a LINES ON THE TOMBS IN WESTMINSTER

5. **they lie, had,** etc., they lie who had, etc.

JOHN FLETCHER

John Fletcher was born at Rye in Sussex, prior to the elevation of his father, Dr. Richard Fletcher, to the bishopric of London. He probably was the John Fletcher of London registered in 1591 in one of the Cambridge colleges, of which his father had been master. He was on intimate terms with Beaumont in 1607, from which year it is customary to date their long and successful work of collaboration as dramatists. In their joint work he excelled in brilliant dialogue and sprightly repartee. He attempted to give greater elasticity to blank verse and in so doing marks the beginning of the end of the great poetical drama which so signalized the age. He collaborated with other playwrights as well, notably Massinger, and there is good evidence that he had a hand in *The Two Noble Kinsmen* and *Henry VIII* of Shakespeare. He wrote a number of plays without assistance, and continued actively as a dramatist to the end of his life. He died of the plague in 1625 and was buried, it is said, in the same grave with Massinger in Southwark. He did his best work in comedy. His comedies reveal lively wit and fancy, freshness, and variety, qualities that are recognizable also in his lyrics.

271b ASPATIA'S SONG

Aspatia is the unfortunate heroine of *The Maid's Tragedy*.

WHAT IS LOVE?

In *The Captain.*

CARE-CHARMING SLEEP

In *Valentinian.*

JOHN WEBSTER

John Webster was the son of a London tailor. He was apprenticed to his father's trade, and for a while at least practiced it, but he early identified himself with a life of letters. He soon made literary friends and began writing for the stage in collaboration with others, but after a year or two he quit the practice of collaborating and for the most part wrote alone. His dark genius matured best when free of the restraints imposed by association with inferior talents. He was a disciple of Shakespeare, and in tragic power, among all the brilliant dramatists of the time, approached him nearest. In the treatment of unrelieved tragic horror he is unequaled. In two plays, *The White Devil* and *The Duchess of Malfi,* he attained tragic heights that are rare in any drama. His occasional songs, dirgelike and somber, are *par excellence* the best of their kind.

272a

DIRGE

In *The White Devil.*

DIRGE

In *The Duchess of Malfi.*

2. **the whistler shrill,** the plover.

WILLIAM DRUMMOND

William Drummond was associated with Hawthornden near Edinburgh. His father was first laird of Hawthornden, on whose death, in 1610, he succeeded to the title and estate. He attended the Edinburgh High School and proceeded to the University, whence he received the M.A. degree in 1605. On coming into his inheritance, he repaired to his estate, collected a good library there, and read widely. His first publication was in 1613, an elegy on the death of Prince Henry. His betrothed died in 1615, and the following year he issued a book of poems memorializing her. At the end of 1618 he was visited for two or three weeks by Ben Jonson and took careful notes on their conversations. These notes have since been important in Jonsonian biography. Drummond refrained as far as possible from participation in the civil war troubles, but the execution of Charles is said to have hastened his death, which took place at the end of the year 1649. He is a learned poet, and excels in his sonnets.

EPITAPH

2. **The paragon of princes,** Henry, Prince of Wales, who died in his nineteenth year, on November 6, 1612.
6. **the Destinies,** the Parcæ or Fates.
9. **immortal amaranthus,** an imaginary poetical flower supposed never to fade.
10. **that sweet flower,** the hyacinth. See note to Milton's *Lycidas,* l. 106.

272b 13. **Gades,** the remotest colony of the Phœnicians in the west; modern Cadiz in Spain.

WILLIAM BROWNE

Next to Spenser, the most distinguished among the Elizabethan writers of pastoral poetry was William Browne. Little is known of him except his works. He was born at Tavistock in Devonshire, went to Oxford but did not remain for a degree, and became a member of the Inner Temple in London. When he was no more than twenty-five, he retired to the country, where, as a man of some means, he devoted his time to literary pursuits. Like some of his contemporaries, he ventured into print first with an elegy on Prince Henry in 1613. In the same year appeared the first book of his *Britannia's Pastorals.* The second came in 1616, but the third and last was not published until long after his death. He wrote in imitation of Spenser and employed regularly the machinery and sentiments of conventional pastoral poetry; but by his genuine love of rural scenes, he breathed through the whole the spirit of the Devonshire life of his time. His best vein is in his pastoral descriptions. He has always been a favorite with the poets, and in this way shares further a likeness to Spenser.

ON THE COUNTESS DOWAGER OF PEMBROKE

Mary Sidney, 1577–1621, Countess of Pembroke, a poet herself, was one of the greatest patrons of letters of her time.

3. **Pembroke,** William Herbert, Earl of Pembroke, according to some authorities the Fair Friend of Shakespeare's sonnets.
7. **Marble piles,** etc. This stanza is suspected by some to have been written by another hand.
10. **Niobe,** the proud mother of fourteen children, who, having lost all her offspring through the anger of Apollo and

Diana, was transformed into a marble statue but still continued to weep for her losses.

AN EPITAPH ON MRS. EL: Y.

Compare Ben Jonson's *Epitaph*, p. 267, of which this, though quite as noble, seems in part an echo.

WILLIAM BASSE

Not much more dependable evidence than mere speculation identifies William Basse with Oxfordshire. Apparently his first verse was published in 1602, and in 1613 he ventured an elegy on Prince Henry. No other volume of his poems was issued in his lifetime. But two other manuscript collections prepared for the press are still extant. He probably lived to a ripe age, as fifty-one years elapsed between his first and last publications. He is best known for his occasional verse, especially for his epitaph on Shakespeare, of which several versions remain in manuscript. His poetry is distinguished by pleasant homeliness and an enthusiastic love of country life.

273a ELEGY ON SHAKESPEARE

1 f. **Spenser . . . Chaucer . . . Beaumont.** These are all interred close together in the Poets' Corner in Westminster Abbey.

9. **If your precedency,** etc. The choice of place of interment allowed in the poem seems to indicate composition immediately after Shakespeare's death, before his burial place was decided upon.

16. **by thee.** Shakespeare was buried in Stratford in a grave seventeen feet deep under an inscription which forbids with a curse any molestation of his bones.

GEORGE WITHER

George Wither lived a few years into the Restoration period, and his writings represent the changing character of the literature of the time; but as a lyrical poet he well may be regarded as the last of the great Elizabethans. He was born at Brentworth in Hampshire, where the family, originally from Lancashire, had lived for five generations. He spent two years at Oxford and in 1610 settled in London to study law. From the first, however, he devoted his best energies to literature. Some satirical performances of his gave offence, and he was several times cast into the Marshalsea prison, where he penned some excellent verse. His early poetry is his best. With the changing time, he, like Milton, became a staunch Puritan, and thereafter devoted his pen to the causes of conscience and liberty. He took an active part in the strife and became the panegyrist of the new order of government after the fall of the monarchy. He was arrested and imprisoned at the Restoration, but was released. He died at his house in the vicinity of the Savoy palace after a residence in London of nearly sixty years. His religious poetry is nowhere equal to his secular lyrics, all of which were written early. His perennial high spirits, his joy in living, his buoyancy, his occasional felicities of expression, and withal his colloquial ease, make him one of the most wholesome spirits of his time.

SHALL I, WASTING IN DESPAIR

273b 14. **Turtle-dove or pelican.** Traditionally, the turtledove mates but once, and the pelican sheds its blood to nourish its young.

SIR PHILIP SIDNEY

Probably no other Englishman ever attained so nearly an universal admiration at home and abroad as did Sir Philip Sidney. He combined the virtues of the mediæval knight with the polish of the Renaissance courtier. In him the lofty ideal of the age, "the complete gentleman," seemed to be realized in full measure. He was born at Penshurst in Kent. His father was Sir Henry Sidney, Lord President of Wales, later Lord Deputy of Ireland. He entered Shrewsbury School in 1564, on the same day with Fulke Greville, later Lord Brooke, and formed with him a friendship which lasted till death. He went up to Oxford in 1568 but left three years later, while the plague was raging, without taking a degree. The next year he went abroad, was in Paris at the massacre of St. Bartholomew, passed thence into the German states, where he met the great scholar, Languet, and was accompanied by him into Italy. On his return he went to Poland, where he is said to have rejected the suggestion that he become a candidate for the crown. He rose rapidly at Court. As an attendant courtier at the Earl of Essex' seat, Chartley Castle, he probably met the Stella of his sonnets, Penelope Devereux, the Earl's daughter, then twelve years of age. It was the Earl's dying request that the pair should be married, but her sudden union with Lord Rich in 1581, under compulsion by her guardians, it is said, prevented this consummation, probably with tragic consequences to each. Literature was uppermost in Sidney's interests in London. Because of his vehement protest in 1580 against the Queen's marriage to the Duke of Anjou, he was banished the court. He retired to his sister's estate at Wilton and there wrote his (or her) *Arcadia.* In 1583 he was married to Frances Walsingham, the daughter of the great secretary. He interested himself in affairs in America and is reported at one time to have been on the point of migrating to the new country when he was suddenly restrained by the Queen. In the latter part of 1585 he left England for the Low Countries to take up the Protestant cause against the encroachments of the Spaniards. He was wounded in the attack on Zutphen and a few weeks later died from the effects. He was brought back to England, given a great public funeral, and buried in St. Paul's Cathedral. He published nothing in his lifetime; but his works, circulating in manuscript, were widely known, and no man, conjointly in his life and works, ever influenced the literature of his time more than he. He made three notable contributions to English literature. His pastoral romance *Arcadia* stemmed the tide of euphuism and started English prose on its way back to sanity and naturalness. His *Astrophel and Stella* was the first real sonnet cycle in the language, and his great example gave the type vogue. His *Defense of Poesy* (see p. 290), the first regular bit of formal criticism in English, treats practically all the important critical problems of the day.

273a ASTROPHEL AND STELLA

The title means "Star-lover and Star." The former is Sidney, and the latter is Penelope Devereux. Their ill-starred love is one of the most celebrated events in literature. The sentiments expressed in the sonnets are generally regarded as sincere.

The sonnet is a poetic form introduced into England from Italian sources, chiefly Petrarch, by Wyatt and Surrey (see introductory notes to pp. 187 and 190). Though varying in form, the English sonnet may be defined in general as a poem of fourteen ten-syllable iambic (×´) lines divided into an octave (the first eight lines) and a sextet (the last six), each part having a separate and rather complicated rhyme-scheme. The age of Elizabeth was characterized by an extraordinary outburst of sonnet writing, and the decade from 1590 to 1600 witnessed the appearance of more than a dozen sonnet cycles or sequences, including Sidney's *Astrophel and Stella,* Daniel's *To Delia* (p. 276b), Spenser's *Amoretti* (p. 278b), and most if not all of Shakespeare's collection (p. 281a). Of later sonnet writers, we should remember at least Milton (p. 345a) and Wordsworth (p. 699b), and of sonnet sequences Elizabeth Barrett Browning's *Sonnets from the Portuguese* (p. 960a) and Rossetti's *House of Life* (p. 992a). See also Wordsworth's *Scorn Not the Sonnet* (p. 700b) and Eugene Lee-Hamilton's *What the Sonnet Is* (p. 1098a).

I

The student will note the free employment of the six-stress line in some of Sidney's sonnets.

4. **might pity win.** The sonnet lover ever sues for pity, because, "Pity is akin to love."

273b 9. stay, support.

11. **feet,** poetical feet, measures.

III

274a 1. **cry on the Sisters nine,** urge the Muses, as hunters encourage their hounds.

3. **Pindar's apes,** imitators of Pindar.

8. **Of herbs or beasts,** a reference to the habit of forcing comparisons from natural history, inherited from mediæval and classical writers. See note to p. 90a, l. 46.

VI

5. **Jove's strange tales.** To avoid the suspicions of his justly jealous wife, Juno, Jove often assumed the form of some animal when in pursuit of an amour. As a bull he wooed Europa and, as a swan, Leda.

XV

2. **Parnassus,** a mountain, mainly in Phocis in ancient Greece, celebrated as the home of the Muses.

274b 7. **Petrarch.** See notes to the anonymous *That Petrarch,* etc., p. 204, and Ralegh's *A Vision,* etc., p. 253.

9. **far-fet,** far-fetched.

10. **a want of inward touch,** a lack of sincerity and originality.

XXI

2. **windlass,** wring, constrain.

9. **mad Mars,** etc. Not the least of Sidney's many accomplishments was skill in arms. Cf. Sonnet XLI.

XXXI

4. **That busy archer,** Cupid.

8. **my state descries,** describes or reveals my condition.

275a XXXIII

1. **I might,** etc. This sonnet appears to have been written upon Penelope Devereux' sudden marriage with Lord Rich. (See introductory note to Sir Philip Sidney.) Presumably Sidney had been too sure of her affection.

6. **No lovely Paris,** etc. Paris won Helen while he was a guest in her household during the absence of her husband, King Menelaus, and eloped with her before his return.

XXXIX

2. **The baiting-place,** the feeding place.
9. **Tak thou of me,** receive thou at my hands, as an offering for the grace of sleep.
11. **A rosy garland,** a garland of roses.

XLI

1. **Having this day.** This sonnet has all the appearance of celebrating an actual event in the author's life, a tournament in which he came off victorious.
4. **that sweet enemy France.** France was the traditional enemy of England but here called "sweet" because of the English admiration for French culture during the Renaissance.

5 f. **advance,** commend, praise.

275b 7. **sleight,** skill.

LXX

5. **Sonnets be not bound prentice to annoy.** Sonnets need not necessarily celebrate only the sorrows of love. Conventionally they rarely did else.
6. **Trebles,** sopranos.
7. **the boy,** Cupid.

LXXIV

1. **Aganippe well,** a fountain near Mt. Helicon in Bœotia, ancient Greece, sacred to the Muses.
2. **Tempe,** a deep vale, celebrated for its beauty, between Olympus and Ossa in ancient Thessaly.

276a 3. **Muses scorn with vulgar brains to dwell,** a reference to the belief in the courtly quality of poetical talent. Cf. the term "courtly makers." Recognition of poetic genius in a person has ever tended, from King David and Cædmon to Burns and John Clare, to raise the possessor's fortunes socially.

7. **blackest brook of hell,** Lethe.

LXXXIV

1. **Highway.** This sonnet seems to indicate that Sidney often composed his poetry while traveling on horseback about the country in his manifold interests.
7. **of duty,** in duty, in acknowledgment of obligation.
11. **for blood,** for shedding of blood by highwaymen.

XC

6. **A nest,** etc., in hope of a reputation as a poet. The laurel was sacred to Apollo, the god of poetry.

276b CIII

9. **Æol's youth,** sons of Æolus, the winds.

CIV

12. **moral notes,** moralizing inferences.
13. **puffing,** enlarging.

SAMUEL DANIEL

TO DELIA

Little is known of the Delia of Daniel's addresses, if indeed she ever existed, except perhaps that she dwelt on the Avon River, probably the Avon in Wiltshire. See Sonnet LVIII.

II

2. **Minerva-like.** Minerva or Athena, goddess of Wisdom, sprang full-grown from the brow of Zeus.

277a VI

11. **had she pity.** See note to l. 4 of Sonnet I in *Astrophel and Stella.*

XVII

5. **to make her live forever.** The sonneteer freely promised immortality to his subject by his verse, rather for her worth than for any inherent quality of his rhymes.
13. **Favours, I think.** Cf. l. 5 and note to Sonnet LXX in *Astrophel and Stella.*

277b XIX

2. **Cytherea's son,** Cupid. Cytherea is another name for Venus.
2. **those arcs of love,** Delia's eyebrows.
6. **breathing sweet,** her pleasant conversation.
8. **Thetis,** goddess of the Sea, famed for her beautiful ankles.
12. **Hyrcan tigers,** tigers of Hyrcania, a district to the south and southeast of the Caspian Sea. They were reputed to be excessively fierce. The idea probably derives from Pliny's *Natural History* (see note to p. 89b, l. 37) or Virgil's *Æneid,* iv, 367.

XXXIII

6. **aspects,** astrological predominance.

278a XLII

9 ff. **This may remain,** etc. See note to Sonnet XVII, l. 5.

10. **happily,** haply, perchance.

278b LIV

Cf. Fletcher's *Care-Charming Sleep,* p. 271. Both treatments represent classical conceptions.

6. **The shipwreck,** etc., because of his unrequited love for Delia, not that his youth was wayward.
8. **the night's untruth,** night's unrealities or high imaginings.
13. **embracing clouds in vain,** oblivious, and therefore happy, though in vain.

LVIII

9. **respects,** appertains to.
9. **nor theatres.** Daniel was not a playwright.
11. **Avon,** probably the Avon of Wiltshire.

EDMUND SPENSER

AMORETTI

The word is an Italian plural form of *amoretto*, a diminutive from the Latin *amor*, and means *love sonnets*, or *persons enamored*. These sonnets celebrate Spenser's love for Elizabeth Boyle, whom he married in 1594.

I

6. **lamping,** shining.

279a 9 f. **the sacred brooke Of Helicon,** the fountain Hippocrene on Mt. Helicon, haunt of the Muses.

10. **whence she derivèd is.** As the inspiration of his poems she is therefore a Muse.

XV

3. **both the Indias,** the East and the West Indies.

279b XXIV

8. **Pandora.** According to classical mythology, Pandora was the first woman, through whom evil came into the world. She was created by Zeus as a source of punishment to man for accepting the gift of fire stolen from heaven by Prometheus.

XXXIII

2. **that most sacred empresse,** Queen Elizabeth.
3. **Queene of Faëry.** The first three books of the *Faerie Queene* were complete by 1589. The second three did not appear until 1596. In the meantime Spenser had other interests.
4. **dead,** when she is dead.
5. **Lodwick,** Lodowick Bryskett, one of Spenser's friends. He held an official position in Ireland.
5. **aread,** explain, tell.
8. **All were it,** although it were.

280a XXXIV

10. **Helice,** constellation of the Great Bear.

L

3. **leach,** physician.
5. **priefe,** experience.
9. **cordialls,** heart remedies.

LXIII

This sonnet, as the reader will note, marks the turn of the poet's fortune in love.

9. **atchyve,** achieve.

280b LXXIV

The poet's mother, Queen, and wife were all named Elizabeth.

LXXV

11. **My verse,** etc. See note to l. 5, Sonnet XVII, of Daniel's *To Delia*, p. 277.

WILLIAM SHAKESPEARE

SONNETS

Shakespeare's sonnets comprise two general groups or cycles: (a) those (1–126) addressed to a Male Friend, a practice quite unusual in the sonnet fashions of the time; and (b) those (127–154), constituting the remainder, which have to do with a Dark Woman. All are unified in a sort of triangular friendship and rivalry of Friend, Poet, and Woman. Along with a good deal of conventional material and machinery, there is enough of unconventional usage, and of what appears to have a specific and particular reference in both relationships, to suggest a strong likelihood that both attachments were real.

281a I — THE FAIR FRIEND

The Friend has been variously identified as the Earl of Southampton, the Earl of Pembroke, and other contemporaries of Shakespeare, but no entirely satisfactory identification has yet been made. In the first four sonnets, the Friend is urged to get married that his fine parts may be "eternized" in his offspring.

I

5. **contracted to thine own bright eyes,** etc. The Friend is guilty of a strong self-love.
12. **niggarding,** acting as a niggard.

II

3. **Thy youth's proud livery,** etc. The Friend is young, very handsome, and much admired.
11. **sum my count,** complete my account.
11. **make my old excuse,** make excuse or compensate for my age.

XII

281b 8. **Borne on the bier,** *i.e.*, carted away at harvest time.

XVIII

If the Friend will not marry, then his perfections must be immortalized in the poet's verse.

10. **ow'st,** ownest.
12. **When in eternal lines,** etc. See note to l. 5, Sonnet XVII, of Daniel's *To Delia*, p. 277.

XX

Though of manly form and constancy, the Friend has the facial features and the gentle heart of a woman.

282a 12. **to my purpose nothing,** of no use to me.

XXIX

1. **When in disgrace,** etc. These lines are often taken as indicating Shakespeare's keen sense of the social ban he was under from his connection with the theater, rather as actor than as playwright.

282b XXXII

5. **the bettering of the time.** English poetry has been consistently progressive to the poet's own day. He has a right to expect succeeding poets to surpass him, but his poetry may be cherished for his love.

XXXIII

9. **Even so my sun,** etc. The Friend has committed against the poet some wrong which stains their perfect amity.
12. **The region cloud,** a cloud of the surrounding air.

XLI

The wrong is a lascivious one, involving some one dear to the poet, probably the Dark Woman.

283a LV

For the theme of this and the three following sonnets, see note to l. 5, Sonnet XVII of Daniel's *To Delia*, p. 277.

283b LXVI, LXXI, LXXIII

From world-weariness and advancing years the poet meditates on death. Sonnet writers were fond of speaking of themselves as growing old.

284a LXXVIII

Rival pens, even those of the learned, are aping the poet in paying addresses to the Friend.

284b XCVII

The poet is absent for a season or two.
7. **prime,** spring.

CIV

Three years have elapsed since the poet first saw the Friend.

CVI

Former poets who have celebrated beauty have but prefigured the poet's Friend.

285a CXVI

Love defined — it may be platonic love.

CXXVI

Time, which hitherto has but indulged the Friend, will finally undo him.
12. **her quietus is to render thee.** Nature will receive her acquittance in her account with Time only when she yields up thee. This, the *envoy* of the cycle to the Friend, is in couplets and lacks two lines.

II — THE DARK WOMAN

CXXVII

The poet is or pretends to be enamored of some beautiful but dark-hued woman, and the attachment is not entirely honorable to him.
1. **black,** of dark complexion.

285b 10. **so suited,** black, too.

CXXX

The Dark Woman is negatively described.

CXXXVIII

The poet is not deceived, though gratified, by the Dark Woman's flatteries.

CXLIV

The Poet suspects the Dark Woman of infidelity to him with the Fair Friend, possibly the lascivious wrong committed against him earlier. See Sonnet XLI.
2. **like two spirits,** referring to the long prevalent idea of two rival spirits contending for control over a man's life and fate.

286a CXLVI

The poet will regard his body less and his soul more.

286b CLIV

At a watering place, probably Bath, for cure, the Poet cannot forget his love.

RALPH HOLINSHED

Holinshed, it seems, was a native of Cheshire. He appears to have been a Cambridge man. Early in the reign of Elizabeth he was a translator in a London printing office. Ten years before the accession of Elizabeth the printer Wolfe had projected a kind of universal history. Holinshed assisted him in the enterprise, and much was done on England, Scotland, and Ireland; but at the end of twenty-five years, when Wolfe died, no part of the work was ready for publication. Three well-known publishers engaged to continue the project but to limit it to England, Scotland, and Ireland. The work was issued in two folio volumes in 1577, and was immediately successful, but the chronicler himself did not long survive. His will a year later describes him as of Bramcote in Warwickshire, where he is said to have died in 1580. The work was carried on by his successors. It is one of the results of the patriotic interest in the past that characterized the age of Elizabeth. The style is clear but not elevated. The author's claim that he kept "an especial eye on the truth of things" is justifiable. The work was a great storehouse for Elizabethan dramatists, including Shakespeare, who not only adopted the material but at times used the phraseology of the original.

286a CHRONICLES OF ENGLAND, SCOTLAND, AND IRELAND

MACBETH AND THE WEIRD SISTERS

Compare this passage with Shakespeare's *Macbeth*, especially Act I, scenes ii and iii.

11. **Fores,** on the Moray Firth in northern Scotland.
15 f. **in the midst of a land,** the blasted heath of Shakespeare.
18. **elder world,** older, other world.
287a 1 f. **long order of continual descent.** Traditionally, but almost certainly erroneously, Banquo was regarded as the ancestor of the Stuart line of monarchs in Scotland and England.
11. **the weird sisters,** etc. Literally, Sisters of Fate. Shakespeare gives them a threefold character derived from (a) the Classical Fates, (b) the Scandinavian Norns, (c) the vulgar broomstick witches of his own day.
14. **necromantical science,** skill in the black art.
37 f. **Prince of Cumberland,** the title of the successor to the throne, whenever he was designated in the lifetime of the sovereign.
46. **next of blood.** Macbeth was first cousin to King Duncan, and from his position as generalissimo of Scotland, he had some right to expect the rule by fair means.
49. **quarrel,** cause.
287b 11. **Envernes,** Inverness, at the head of Moray Firth in northern Scotland.
16. **Scone,** in Perthshire on the river Tay, where from early times the Scottish monarchs were crowned.
20. **Elgin,** in northern Scotland on the Moray Firth.
22. **Colmkill,** now Iona, a small island on the west coast of Scotland — "the church of Columba," the great Irish missionary to Scotland. See Adamnan, p. 44 and note.

SIR THOMAS NORTH

By reason of such men as Sir Thomas North, the Elizabethan age was great in translations as it was in nearly every other branch of literature. He was the second son of the first Baron North. It is believed that he attended Cambridge. In 1557 he entered Lincoln's Inn, but soon turned his attention to literature. Provision was made for him by his father and by his generous brother, the second baron, but apparently he was always in need. He attended his brother on an embassy to France in 1574; he was a captain in command of three hundred men of Ely in the days of the Armada; he was knighted about 1591; and for a number of years he maintained some position in Cambridgeshire, being a commissioner of the peace there in 1592. In 1601, when nearly seventy years of age, he was granted a pension of £40 a year by the Queen. There is no record of his death. His literary work was almost wholly in translation, but it exerted a powerful influence on the writers of the time. His translation of Plutarch's *Lives*, by which he is best remembered, appeared in 1579, rendered from the French of Amyot. It was dedicated to Elizabeth and proved one of the most popular books of her reign. Appearing simultaneously with Lyly's *Euphues*, it stands in striking contrast in the elements of style. Its nervous idiomatic English and noble simplicity of expression resemble the language of the English Bible. Shakespeare used it as "a storehouse of classical learning," not only employing its material for his plays but taking over many of its speeches bodily and adapting them in his dialogue.

TRANSLATION OF PLUTARCH'S LIVES

ASSASSINATION OF CÆSAR

In the *Life of Brutus*. Compare this passage with Shakespeare's *Julius Cæsar*, especially Act III.

41. **Pompey's image,** the statue of Pompey, surnamed "the Great," a famous Roman statesman and general, 106–48 B.C.
43. **Antonius,** Mark Anthony, a Roman triumvir and general, *ca.* 83–30 B.C.
288a 50. **Consul with Cæsar.** Anthony took sides with Cæsar in the civil war with Pompey, commanded a wing of his army at Pharsalia, and was made consul in 44 B.C., the year of Cæsar's assassination.
289a 4. **Tellus,** goddess of Earth.
289b 5. **seventy-five drachmas,** worth about twelve dollars in American money. The purchasing power of money was, of course, far greater than at present.
28. **Clodius,** Publius Clodius or Claudius, a Roman politician, *ca.* 93–52 B.C.
290a 12. **Antium,** a city of Latium about thirty miles south of Rome.

SIR PHILIP SIDNEY

290a DEFENSE OF POESY

Of English literature in general Sidney has a low opinion, but of poetry he has the highest possible conception, regarding the poet as superior to the lawgiver, the historian, and the philosopher.

ITS SUPREMACY

7. **conceits,** conceptions.
16. **margent,** margin. To a few lines of text the schoolmen often added a long and learned commentary.
32. **take their physic at their ears,** have their ears boxed.

290b 11. **as Aristotle saith.** See *Poetics*, iv. See also note to p. 211b, l. 11.
15. **Amadis de Gaule,** a Spanish prose romance of the early fourteenth century. A French version of about 1548 was popular in Sidney's day.
20 f. **Æneas carrying old Anchises on his back.** See Surrey's translation, p. 194.
23. **Turnus,** King of the Rutulians in Italy, when Æneas arrived.
26 f. **Fugientem,** etc. "Shall this land behold (Turnus) in flight? Is it so very base a thing to die?"
29. **Where the philosophers,** etc. The reference is to the Stoics and some of their stock questions for discussion.

291a 1. **Boethius.** See note to p. 91b, l. 22.
5 f. **indulgere genio,** to indulge their genius or tastes.
18. **The one of Menenius Agrippa,** patrician ambassador to the revolted plebeians at the Sacred Mount about 494 B.C.
44. **Nathan the Prophet.** 2 Samuel xii, 1 ff.

291b 3 f. **that heavenly Psalm of mercy.** Psalm li.
29. **Sanazzar,** an Italian poet, 1458–1530, author of *Arcadia,* a pastoral romance of mixed prose and verse.
42. **poor pipe,** pipe or flute of the shepherds.
43. **Melibeus,** a shepherd in Virgil's first eclogue.
45. **Titirus,** a character in Virgil's first eclogue.

292a 4 f. **Hæc memini,** etc. "These (things) I remember and conquered Thyrsis striving in vain; from that time we have had Corydon, only Corydon."
11. **Heraclitus,** a Greek philosopher, late sixth century before Christ, called "the weeping philosopher" because he wept over the follies of mankind.
17. **Iambic.** In Greek literature satirical works were often written in iambic (×́) measure.
21. **Omne vafer,** etc., "Cunningly touching every vice, he moves his friend to laughter."
27. **Circum præcordia ludit,** "He plays about the heart."
31. **Est Ulubris animus,** etc. "We are for Ulubræ, if equanimity fails us not." Ulubræ, a town of Latium, was notable for its desolation.
43. **oblique,** oblique angle or triangle.
52. **Demea,** the "heavy father" in the *Adelphi* of Terence.
52. **Danus,** a conventional name for a slave in Latin comedy, as in the *Phormio* of Terence.
53. **Gnatho,** a parasite and flatterer in the *Eunuchus* of Terence.
53. **Thraso,** a braggart in the *Eunuchus* of Terence.

292b 9. **Pistrinum,** a "mill" or place of punishment for slaves.
27. **Qui sceptra sævus,** etc. "The tyrant with his scepter, who rules with an iron sway, is afraid of those who fear him; fear recoils against the inventor."
32. **Alexander Pherœus,** a tyrant of Pheræ in Thessaly, fourth century before Christ, cited in the *Life of Pelopidas*.
51. **natural Problems,** points in natural history.

293a 2 f. **the old song of Percy and Douglas.** See *The Hunting of the Cheviot,* p. 171 and note.
5 f. **Crowder,** a fiddler.
10. **Pindar,** the chief lyrical poet of Greece, fifth century before Christ.
15. **Lacedemonians,** ancient inhabitants of the most southerly of the peninsulas of Greece.
29. **Philip of Macedon,** Philip II of Macedonia, father of Alexander the Great.
30. **Olympus,** *i.e.,* the Olympic games.
41. **Tideus,** a Greek hero, king of Argos, who fell in the expedition against Thebes.
41. **Rinaldo,** a distinguished warrior, who appears in Tasso's *Gerusalemme Liberata,* Ariosto's *Orlando Furioso,* and other heroic poems.
41 f. **who doth not only teach,** etc. The common Renaissance interpretation was that the great heroical or epical poems of the past were intended to teach lessons, their heroes to shadow forth ideal princes or rulers.
47. **Tully,** Marcus Tullius Cicero, a Roman orator and statesman, 106–43 B.C.

293b 14. **Dido,** queen of Carthage, loved and deserted by Æneas as described in Virgil's *Æneid.*
28. **Melius Chrisippo et Crantore.** "Better than Chrysippus and Crantor," philosophers of the third and late fourth centuries before Christ.
44 f. **gave divine names unto it,** etc. In Greek ποιητής signifies "maker"; in Latin one word for poet is *vates,* "seer" or "prophet."

294a 12. **the flowers of it,** its imagery, illustrative fictions, and the like.

BEN JONSON

TIMBER

Timber, or Discoveries upon Men and Matter, is, as the title suggests, a succession of brief discussions of various subjects.

25. **Non nimium,** etc., "Trust not too much to the ancients."
39. **Non domini,** etc., "They are not our masters, but our leaders."
40. **several,** individual property.
40 ff. **Patet omnibus,** etc., "Truth abides for all; not yet has it been mastered. Much of it remains for the future as well."
44. **De Shakespeare nostrat. — Augustus in Hat.** "About our fellow-countryman Shakespeare — Augustus (said) of Haterius."

294b 8. **Sufflaminandus erat.** "He should have been clogged."
9. **Haterius,** a senator and rhetorician under Augustus and Tiberius.
15. **'Cæsar did never wrong,'** etc. See Shakespeare's *Julius Cæsar,* III, i, 47.
21. **Dominus Verulamius,** Lord Verulam, *i.e.,* Francis Bacon.
23 f. **ever grew up to his author,** ever equaled his model.
30. **pressly,** closely, concisely.
37. **at his devotion,** at his pleasure.
41 ff. **Consuetudo,** etc. These words are explained in the context which follows.

295a 16. **aquai and pictai,** older forms for *aquæ* and *pictæ.*
16. **Lucretius,** a Roman philosophical poet, *ca.* 96–55 B.C.
16. **scabrous,** rough.

295b 1. **Paronomasies,** plays upon words, puns.
2 f. **Quæ per salebras,** etc., which through rough ways and lofty rocks fall.
15. **veer out,** spread out, as a sailing vessel under a favorable wind.
17. **argument,** subject.

RICHARD HAKLUYT

Hakluyt's ancestors, originally from Holland perhaps, had been settled for several centuries in Herefordshire. He was educated at Westminster School and at Oxford, where he received both the B.A. and M.A. degrees. At Westminster he first gave attention to geography and the history of discovery. At Oxford he became enthusiastic over these subjects lecturing in them for a while after becoming Master of Arts. He seems to have taken orders at the usual age. He was chaplain to the ambassador to France in 1583. In France he continued his researches in voyages to America, through French and Spanish sources. In 1589, a year after his return to England, he issued his *Principal Navigations.* It proved to be his life work. Repairing to Wetheringsett in Suffolk, he continued his work of collection and compilation and reissued it in three volumes ten years later. Upon his death in 1616 he left a body of manuscript sufficient for a fourth volume, which fell to his disciple and heir, Samuel Purchas. Froude calls his work "the prose epic of the modern English nation."

295a RALEGH'S LAST FIGHT OF THE REVENGE

This pamphlet is one of several accounts of the battle which appeared between 1591 and 1600. Though it is a piece of war propaganda inspired largely by imperialistic pride and unreasoning religious animosity, it is important as reflecting the English state of mind immediately after the destruction of the Spanish Armada and as furnishing the background for an intelligent appreciation of Tennyson's spirited poem, *The Revenge.*

8. **this late encounter.** The engagement took place off the Azores "the last of August, 1591." Rumor had been busy with slanders against Ralegh, who was second in command in the expedition but was required at the last minute by the Queen to give up his office and remain behind.

295b 4. **Sir Richard Grenville,** Ralegh's cousin, vice admiral of the expedition and real hero of the battle.
10. **advisos,** dispatches.
14. **1588,** the year in which the Great Armada attempted to conquer England.

296a 7. **Caracks,** large vessels, galleons.
14. **Lizard in Cornwall,** southernmost point in England.
15. **Portland,** a peninsula in Dorset, southern England.
20. **squibs,** rocketlike explosive missiles.
29. **coupled in halters,** with ropes about their necks in pairs.
47 ff. **Sir Francis Drake,** a great English seaman, *ca.* 1540–1596. His successful operations in "their Indies" were made in 1585–1586.

296b 2 f. **Earl of Essex,** Robert Devereux, second Earl of Essex.
24. **consumption of two billets,** burning of two pieces of wood.
51. **all pestered and rummaging,** *i.e.,* disarranged and everything out of order.

297a 30. **very hardly,** with great difficulty.
45. **sprang their luff,** gave up sailing close against the wind.

297b 4. **carged,** carved or built (?).
6. **laid the Revenge aboard,** lay aboard the *Revenge,* attacked her at close quarters.
12. **three tier of ordnance,** three ranks or lines of guns.
14. **chase,** bows.
23. **crossbar shot,** projectiles fastened in pairs for destroying rigging or for general execution.

298a 1. **hulks,** transports.
14. **withal his surgeon,** notwithstanding the skill of his surgeon.

32 f. **composition,** terms of peace.
50. **hold,** the hold or interior of the ship.
299a 26. **free from galley,** free from service as galley slaves.
300a 44. **keep the weather gage,** keep to windward.
300b 39. **empery,** dominion, control.
53. **better sort,** higher rank.
301a 46. **holds,** strongholds, positions.
301b 2. **drawn, and quartered,** disemboweled and cut in four pieces. See note to p. 121a, l. 168.
14. **be reformed,** have become Protestant.
23. **Jesuits,** the Society of Jesus, founded by Loyola in 1534.
35. **the Turk.** For centuries after the crusades the word "Turk" was synonymous with tyranny and enmity toward Christianity.
38. **the low countries,** the Netherlands.
51 f. **Agnus Dei,** a prayer beginning with the words *Agnus Dei,* "Lamb of God." It is found in the liturgy of the Roman and Protestant churches.
302a 6. **Hispaniola,** Haiti.
15. **Bartholomew de las Casas,** a Spanish missionary known as the "Protector of the Indians," 1474–1566.

ROBERT GREENE

A GROATSWORTH OF WIT

This tract, though doubtless not actually written by Greene, is valuable as a contemporary Puritan estimate of him and some of his associates. It was published by Henry Chettle almost immediately after his death.

302b 2. **gracer of tragedians,** Christopher Marlowe, notorious at the time for his "blasphemies" or atheistical opinions.
11. **Machiavellian policy.** Niccolo Machiavelli, 1469–1527, Italian statesman whose book on the cold-blooded methods of statesmen brought the author into abhorrence because of his supposed advocacy of the policy set forth.
303a 4. **Sic volo, sic jubeo,** As I wish, so I command.
5. **Fas et nefas,** right and wrong.
11. **brocher,** broacher or founder, probably Francis Kitt, A.M. of Cambridge, burnt at Norwich, Greene's native town, 1589, for his obnoxious opinions.
15. **Quam inscrutabilia,** etc. How inscrutable are the judgments of God!
20. **Julian,** a Roman emperor, 361–363, called "the Apostate" because of his abandonment of Christianity. His death in battle by an arrow became a classic example of the fate of atheists.
30. **young Juvenal,** Thomas Nashe. See introductory note to p. 259.
41. **blame not scholars.** In his *Pierce Penniless,* licensed for printing a month before Greene's death, Nashe attacked the Harveys, two Cambridge scholars.
44. **thou no less deserving,** George Peele. See introductory note to p. 257.
303b 1. **puppets,** players.
8. **an upstart Crow,** etc. This passage is generally acknowledged to refer to Shakespeare. As such, it is the first definite mention of him after his arrival in London and one of the few references to him by his contemporaries.
10. ***Tigers heart,*** etc. A parody on Shakespeare's "O tiger's heart, wrapt in a woman's hide" (*3 Henry VI,* I, iv, 137), referring to his pretensions as an actor as well as a playwright.
13. **Johannes fac totum,** Johnny-do-all, Jack-of-all-trades.
26. **two more,** probably Thomas Lodge and another.

THOMAS DEKKER

304a THE GULL'S HORN-BOOK

Dekker's well-known take-off is understood by its lifelike pictures and speech to have detracted from its own popularity and effectiveness. See also introductory note to Dekker, p. 266. The selection in the text comprises Chapter VI.

Gull, a greenhorn.
Horn-Book, primer or ABC book for the young pupil, so named from its cover of horn to prevent abuse.
32. **the great beast,** the public.
34. **factors,** helpers.
39. **chapmen,** merchants, tradesmen.
42. **groundling,** occupant of the pit at the theater.
42. **gallery-commoner,** a commoner who could afford a seat in the gallery.
43. **haggler,** huckster.
45. **Sithence,** since.
46. **a stool,** a portable seat at the theater for any who could afford the price for it.
47. **templer,** a member of the Temple.
304b 1. **Momus.** See note to p. 204a, l. 13.
9. **throne of the stage.** The gallants often occupied seats on the stage itself.
10. **lord's room,** corresponding to the first-floor boxes of to-day.
14. **sharers,** shareholders, stockholders.
18. **rushes.** Rushes strewn on the floor served the place of carpets.
19. **Cambises,** the king of rant in stage parlance of the time.
20. **estridge,** ostrich.
24. **cast up a reckoning,** make an account.
34 f. **girder,** one who gibes, a satirist.
49. **Fleet street gentleman,** a resident or frequenter of Fleet street, where all kinds of shows were offered.
52. **'we three,'** a representation similar to the modern postcard with two asses de-

picted and an inscription such as, "When shall we three meet again?" the third person being the reader.

305a 12. **the boys,** the ushers or helpers.

14. **infants.** Women's parts were taken by boys in their early teens.

19. **dawcock,** the male daw; an empty, chattering fellow.

29 f. **'Away with the fool,'** the cry of the spectators when tired of the extemporizings of the jester. Dekker deftly turns the joke on the gallant.

37 f. **the quaking Prologue.** For the new play the Prologue or introductory speech was, of course, important, as creating the first impression of the production.

39 f. **the trumpets their cue.** The opening of a play was heralded by trumpet blasts from the roof.

45. **teston,** originally a French coin, later the shilling of Henry VIII.

53. **the Counter,** a prison in London in the Poultry. Another by the same name was located in Southwark, and a third in Wood Street.

305b 1. **bastome,** a cudgel or club.

8 f. **inn-o'-court man,** a member of one of the inns of court, where the young gallants, ostensibly studying law, were acquiring fashion and awaiting court preferment.

9. **zany,** a subordinate fool or clown who aped the tricks of his principal.

11. **beagle,** a small hunting dog.

14. **morris,** a country dance.

14 f. **Pelion upon Ossa.** In the war against the gods in Grecian mythology the Titans piled the mountains Pelion and Ossa one upon the other in an attempt to scale heaven.

21. **watch.** The time of night was indicated by the periods of watching. Thieves seized convenient times between watches, or while the guards were being changed, to commit assaults. Some of the gallants of the time were thieves at night, and had associates among the thugs. Cf. Falstaff and the Eastcheap group in Shakespeare's *1 Henry IV*.

23. **pass,** escape.

39. **shoulder-clapping,** elbowing through the crowds.

40. **cockatrice,** mistress.

43. **sculler,** a waterman who drove a scull or light boat for public hire.

306a 1. **upon ticket,** upon credit.

5. **draw,** draw your purse to pay cash.

14. **upon the third sound,** the last sound of the trumpet announcing the beginning of the play.

27. **bastinado,** a cudgeling.

306b 2. **mimics,** actors.

5. **frets,** a play on the word in the sense of annoyance; in stringed instruments, a bar or stop across the fingerboard. Shakespeare uses the same pun in *Hamlet*, III, ii, 388.

17. **felt and feather,** hat.

18. **punk,** a bawd.

23 f. **play-scraps,** fragments of speeches from the play.

29. **shittlecock,** a game or sport.

JOHN FLORIO

John Florio was the son of an Italian Protestant refugee who came to England shortly before the reign of Edward VI to escape persecution. For the same reason the family probably retired during the reign of Mary to the continent, where the son began his education. Later he attended Oxford. By 1600 he was a teacher of languages in London and on intimate terms with the men of letters and literary patrons of the time. In 1603 his translation of Montaigne's *Essays* was published. In the same year he became reader in Italian to Queen Anne. Late in life he retired to Fulham and died there in 1625. He is not an accurate translator but he is a genuine interpreter. Many of the riches of his great original he has transferred to English as no one without his genius and not of his time could have done.

Michel Eyquem de Montaigne, 1533–1592, was a French courtier and later mayor of Bordeaux. He is celebrated for his *Essais*, first published in 1580. In them he discusses with an amused and subtly skeptical tolerance various aspects of human life, usually in relation to some general truths regarding history or society. They are familiar in style and are full of pleasant digressions. His philosophy is: Do not expect *too* much, accept life with cheerful resignation, don't take yourself too seriously. Though he cannot be said to have invented the essay, he was the first to give it a thoroughly literary flavor. His essays were read with delight by Bacon (p. 314b) and Shakespeare, and they exercised a considerable influence upon Addison, Steele, and other essayists of the eighteenth century.

TRANSLATION OF MONTAIGNE'S ESSAYS

306a OF IDLENESS

307a 4. **Sicut aquæ,** etc. A free verse translation follows, as in other quotations throughout the work.

47. **cariere,** career, roadway.

49. **Chimeræs,** monsters. The classical Chimera was a fire-breathing monster, part lion, part goat, and part dragon, that laid waste ancient Lycia. It was slain by Bellerophon mounted on Pegasus.

307b OF THE CANNIBALS

This essay is significant, not only because we know that it was read and used by Shakespeare (see note to p. 309b, 48) but because its general theme — the superiority of primitive over civilized and sophisticated man — was later to become the cardinal principle for a considerable body of radical romanticists during the eighteenth century. Montaigne's picture of the American Indians lays the foundation for Cooper's later idealization.

5. **King Pyrrhus,** *ca.* 318–272 B.C., king of Epirus and one of the greatest generals of antiquity. His operations against Rome took place 280–275, when he was defeated at Beneventum.

13. **Flaminius,** *ca.* 230–*ca.* 174 B.C., a Roman general. He defeated Philip V of Macedon in 197 and proclaimed the freedom of Greece at Corinth in 196. See note to l. 14.

14. **Philip,** king of Macedonia, 220–178 B.C. (not to be confused with Philip of Macedonia, the father of Alexander the Great).

16 f. **Publius Sulpitius Galba,** a Roman consul who held Macedonia during part of Philip's reign.

25. **Villegaignon,** a French soldier in charge of an expedition to Brazil. He planted a colony, which later was destroyed, in the Bay of Rio in 1555.

39. **the general Deluge.** Most of the ancient nations bear testimony to a general inundation which destroyed the race at some period in its history. The Greek account strongly resembles the Biblical.

308a 42. **febricitant,** affected with fever or convulsions.

44. **Dordoigne,** a river of France emptying into the Garonne a few miles below Bordeaux.

308b 6. **Medoc,** a district of Gironde in France.

309a 4. **hyperbolize,** exaggerate.

28. **scantling,** bit, modicum.

309b 36 f. **Lycurgus,** a Spartan lawgiver, probably of the ninth century before Christ.

45. **genuity,** race or condition.

48. **It is a nation,** etc. The next six lines include the famous passage used by Shakespeare in the *Tempest,* II, i, 139 ff.

310a 26 f. **champain,** plain, level.

53. **Suidas,** author of a famous encyclopædic Greek lexicon, probably second half of the tenth century after Christ.

310b 12. **Corianders,** belonging to the parsley family, the seeds of which were used in flavoring.

14. **wallowish,** flat, nauseous.

311a 19. **Scythians,** in ancient times the inhabitants of the more remote parts of north and northeast Europe and Asia.

26 f. **coni-catch,** dupe, cheat.

37. **broaches,** any one of several pointed instruments.

311b 34. **mammocks,** fragments.

40. **Chrysippus and Zeno,** Greek philosophers of the third century before Christ, the latter the founder and the former the most eminent disciple of the Stoic sect.

46. **city of Alexia,** Alesia, the capital of the Mandubii, a tribe of central Gaul, famous for its defense by Vercingetorix and capture by Cæsar in 52 B.C.

312a 18. **uberty,** abundance.

312b 35 f. **porterly-rascal,** a low, mean, porterlike fellow.

313a 9. **Salamis,** scene of the victory over the Persians by the Greek fleet under Themistocles in 480 B.C.

9. **Platæa,** scene of the final repulse of the Persians by the Greeks in 479 B.C.

9. **Mycale,** a mountain in Lydia, Asia Minor, near which on the same day as the battle of Platæa the Greeks overcame the Persian naval forces.

10. **Sicilia,** probably the unsuccessful attempt of the Carthaginians to make a conquest of Sicily in the same year as the battle of Salamis above.

12. **King Leonidas,** king of Sparta, slain in his defense of Thermopylæ in 480 B.C.

313b 47. **Lea, Rachel,** etc. See Genesis xvi and xxx.

49. **Livia,** Livia Drusilla, *ca.* 56 B.C.–A.D. 29, wife of Augustus Cæsar. She was charged with various crimes in her attempts to secure the succession for her son Tiberius by her former husband.

314a 14 f. **canzonet,** a short song or vocal piece. This fragment was several times rendered into English verse and served during the Romantic period as a standard illustration of poetry composed by means of simple native genius and without the application of rules. See Introduction to Restoration and Eighteenth Century, p. 404 f.

25. **Anacreontic.** Anacreon, *ca.* 563–478 B.C., was a distinguished Greek lyric poet who sang the praises of love and wine.

52. **Switzers,** Swiss guards.

The student will not miss the delicious humor in the great essayist's irrelevant conclusion.

FRANCIS BACON

Francis Bacon, a younger son of Sir Nicholas Bacon, Lord Keeper of the Great Seal, was born at York House in the Strand. His mother, the daughter of Sir Anthony Cooke, tutor to Edward VI, was a woman of scholarly inclinations and literary talent. Not much is known of his early life and education, except that he was delicate in health and of grave demeanor. In 1573 he entered Trinity College, Cambridge, and interested himself in science and philosophy. All previous investigations in both these branches he came to regard as generally wrong, and with this idea in mind, after three years, he quitted the University. In 1576 he was admitted to Gray's Inn, and the same year went to Paris in the suite of the English ambassador. He was recalled to England in 1579 by the death of his father. Embarrassed by a limited provision from the estate, he set himself to the study of law and sought advancement at court. He entered Parliament in 1584. He seems to have been acquainted with the Earl of Essex by 1588; by 1591 he was a diligent adviser to him; and in 1595 the Earl bestowed on him an estate of land. Meanwhile he was in ill favor with the Queen. In the reign of James his fortunes improved. He became Solicitor-General in 1607, Attorney-General in 1613, Privy Councillor in 1616, and Lord Chancellor in 1618, with the title of Baron Verulam. In January, 1621, he was created Viscount St. Alban, and in March of that year he was impeached for corruption in office. Admitting the charges, he was fined £40,000, sentenced to imprisonment at the King's pleasure, and debarred forever afterward from holding office in the state. His remaining five years he lived in seclusion, devoting his time to philosophical and literary pursuits. He died at Highgate in April, 1626. The first edition of his *Essays* appeared in 1597. He reissued them, with several additions, in 1612, and in 1625 they were published in their final form, fifty-eight in number. Their remarkable terseness of expression and compactness of thought and style make them the most memorable examples of their kind in the language. As a philosopher and scientist Bacon was one of the first to perceive the essential unity and the practical end of all knowledge, and he is popularly regarded as the first to apply the experimental method, now universally employed by scientific men. His method and his classification of science are set forth in the *Novum Organum*, published in 1621.

314b OF TRUTH

47. **jesting Pilate.** See John xviii, 38.

315a 9. **One of the later school,** etc., probably the "New Academy," a sect of Greek philosophers who came to the conclusion that mankind has no criterion by which to judge of truth.

13. **as with poets.** The common ascription of lying to poets is only in the sense of "feigning," that is, of fabricating or creating from the imagination.

31 f. **One of the fathers,** Jerome or Augustine.

33. **vinum dæmonum,** the wine of devils.

46. **sovereign good,** the *summum bonum,* "the highest good," which has been sought by the philosophers of all ages.

315b 1 f. **The poet,** etc., Lucretius, in his great philosophical poem, *De Natura Rerum.*

2. **the sect,** the Epicureans, who held that pleasure is the highest good. See note to Chaucer's *Prologue*, l. 336.

32. **Montaigne saith,** etc. Second book of Essays, Chapter 18.

44. **it being foretold.** See Luke xviii, 8.

OF ADVERSITY

316a 17 f. **Prometheus,** a Titan. He stole fire from heaven and bestowed it on man against the express prohibition of Zeus, who in anger caused him to be fixed to a rock on Mount Caucasus and tormented daily by a vulture eating at his vitals. After many centuries Hercules released him.

23. **in a mean,** in a general way.

OF MARRIAGE AND SINGLE LIFE

316b 24 f. **humorous,** given to humors, or having peculiar temperaments. See note to Chaucer's *Prologue*, l. 420.

38. **hortatives,** exhortations.

52. **Ulysses,** hero of the Odyssey. He was offered immortality by Calypso, but he preferred his old wife to immortality.

317a 8 f. **he was reputed,** etc., the Greek philosopher Thales, *ca.* 640–*ca.* 546 B.C.

OF LOVE

28. **syren.** The Sirens were three sea nymphs who sang so entrancingly that sailors were lured to destruction on the rocks where they lived. See also note p. 90a, 34.

29. **fury.** See note to Sackville's *Induction*, l. 109.

38. **Appius Claudius,** a Roman judge who fell criminally in love with Virginia, 449 B.C. See Chaucer's *Physician's Tale*, Macaulay's *Lays of Ancient Rome*, Sheridan Knowles' *Appius and Virginia*, etc.

46 f. **Satis magnum,** etc. We are a sufficiently ample spectacle one to another.

317b 6. **it hath been well said,** etc., by Plutarch.

12. **it was well said,** etc., by Publius Syrus.

22. **the poet's relation,** Ovid in his *Epistles.*

23 f. **he that preferred Helana,** Paris. Juno offered him Asia, and Athena renown in war, but he awarded the prize to

Venus for the return gift of Helen. See Tennyson's *Œnone.*

318a OF GREAT PLACE

10 f. **The rising unto place,** etc. This passage is a sad but apt commentary on Bacon's own rise and fall.

16 f. **Cum non sis,** etc. Since you are no longer what you were, there is no reason why you should wish to live.

38 f. **Illi mors gravit,** etc. Death weighs heavily on him who, too well known to all, dies unknown to himself.

42. **not to can,** not to be able.

53 f. **Et conversus Deus,** etc. And God turned to behold the works which his hands had made, and saw they were very good. A paraphrase of the Latin version of Genesis i, 31.

318b 28. **de facto,** as a fact.

319a 3. **inward,** intimate, confidential.

13. **Salomon saith.** Cf. Proverbs xxviii, 21.

18 f. **omnium consensu,** etc. By consent of all he was fit for rule — if he had never ruled.

20 f. **solus imperantium,** etc. Of the emperors Vespasian alone changed for the better.

OF YOUTH AND AGE

319b 7. **Septimius Severus,** a Roman emperor, A.D. 198–211.

8 f. **Juventutem egit,** etc. He spent a youth full of errors, even of madness.

13. **Cosmos,** Cosimo de Medici, 1519–1574, called "the Great." He became Duke of Florence in 1537.

13. **Gaston de Fois,** a French general of the early sixteenth century.

51. **A certain Rabbin,** Isaac Abrabanel, fifteenth century.

52. **Your young men,** etc. Joel ii, 28, and Acts ii, 17.

320a 11. **Hermogenes,** a Greek rhetorician of the second century after Christ.

19. **Hortensius,** 114–50 B.C., an eminent Roman orator, Cicero's great rival.

19 f. **idem manebat,** etc. He remained the same when it was no longer becoming.

23. **Scipio Africanus,** *ca.* 234–183 B.C., a Roman general who defeated Hannibal at Zama, 202 B.C., and thus ended the second Punic War.

24 f. **ultima primis cedebant.** His end was not equal to his beginning.

OF STUDIES

320b 29. **Abeunt studia in mores.** One's studies become at length a part of one's nature. This famous sentence comes from Ovid.

30. **stond,** drawback, hindrance.

31. **wit,** understanding.

34. **stone and reins,** bladder and kidneys.

42. **cymini sectores,** hairsplitters. *Cymini sector* means, literally, "splitter of a cumin seed (a very small seed)."

JOSEPH HALL

Joseph Hall received his early education at his birthplace, Ashby-de-la-Zouch in Leicestershire. He went up to Cambridge in 1589 and in course of time received the B.A., M.A., B.D., and D.D. degrees, "with great applause." He wrote verses early and enjoyed some reputation as a satirist. He took orders at the end of the century and occupied rural appointments for several years. At the beginning of his residence at Waltham he published his *Characters of Vices and Virtues,* 1608. His *Contemplations,* which contain much of his best work, appeared in eight volumes between 1612 and 1626. In 1627 he was made Bishop of Exeter, whence he was transferred to Norwich in 1641, only to be ousted soon after by the fortunes of civil war. He spent his last years at Higham, a village near Norwich, and died there in 1656. He wrote with great fluency and energy and perhaps with fewer digressions from the broad course of eloquence than any other of the clerical writers of his time. His satirical sketches give us interesting glimpses of contemporary manners and are instructive experiments in the portrayal of character. See, further, observations on the "character" in the introductory sketch to Sir Thomas Overbury, p. 322b.

321a THE HONEST MAN

33. **overseen,** overlooked or omitted.

45. **providence,** sense or instinct for providing.

321b THE HYPOCRITE

24. **player,** actor.

322a 2. **tables,** notebook.

18. **every occurrent,** everything that happens.

30. **all gnats,** etc. See Matthew xxiii, 24.

43 f. **so fast a closure,** so quickly coming to terms or understanding.

SIR THOMAS OVERBURY

A native of Warwickshire, Sir Thomas Overbury attended Oxford as a gentleman commoner, took the B.A. degree in 1598, and set up in London as a member of the Middle Temple. He was knighted at Greenwich in 1608 and attained prominence as a courtier, partly by his own merit and partly by his friendship for the favorite, Rochester, whom he had met as Robert Carr in Edinburgh several years before. When Rochester's intrigue with the abandoned Countess of Essex began to show promise of culminating in marriage, Overbury protested vehemently. The vindictive Countess procured his imprisonment in the Tower, suborned the attendants, and accomplished his death by slow poisoning a few months later. Within two years the secret came out, the accomplices were executed, and the principals, now Earl and Countess of Somerset, were committed to the Tower for a time and disgraced. Overbury was a singularly gifted and cultivated man. As a courtier he did more than any other of his time to foster and encourage literature and art. To the second edition of his popular poem, *The Wife*, 1614, there was appended a set of "characters," or sketches of typical representatives of various classes of society. The English "character" has important continental models, but the "characters" of Overbury and his contemporaries are important as early examples of a form that was to reach its highest perfection in the Sir Roger de Coverley Papers of Addison and Steele (p. 521 ff. and p. 524 ff.).

322b AN AMORIST

The amorist or lover here delineated unfavorably is the conventional lover portrayed in the sonnets.

18 f. **Is,** etc., A lover (amorist) is a man blighted and, as it were, driven mad by the influences of the planets.
19. **the dog that leads,** etc. He is to the little blind god Cupid merely like a dog that leads a blind beggar.
22. **musk comfits,** scented sweetmeats.
43 f. **not at home,** his mind wanders.
44. **scotcheth,** wounds, passes.

A FAIR AND HAPPY MILK-MAID

323a 12. **tissue,** fabrics.
16. **conditions,** disposition.
39. **bravery,** finery.
51 f. **a Friday's dream.** Of all the days of the week Friday is most regarded with superstition.

JOHN EARLE

John Earle was born at York of parents who were in easy circumstances. He went to Oxford, received the B.A. and M.A. degrees, and was incorporated M.A. of Cambridge. In 1628 his *Microcosmographie, or Essays and Characters* appeared. An edition the following year contained twenty-three new pieces, after which it is doubtful if he ever gave the work further concern. He became tutor to Prince Charles about 1641, was abroad with him during the Commonwealth, and remained closely attached to and highly esteemed by him afterwards. He was in favor at the Restoration, and wisely used his power and influence for tolerance and moderation. He became Bishop of Worcester in 1662 and later was transferred to Salisbury. He died at Oxford in attendance at the court while it was temporarily exiled from London on account of the plague. His book of "characters" ran through several editions within a few years after its first appearance, thus evincing its great popularity. The sketches themselves are inimitably drawn, exhibit the spirit of a philosopher, humorist, and artist, and throw much light on the social conditions of the time. On the "character," see introductory note to Sir Thomas Overbury, p. 322b.

323b A CHILD

28. **tice,** entice.

324a A PLAIN COUNTRY FELLOW

7. **the punishment of Nebuchadnezzar.** See Daniel iv, 29 ff.
15. **gee and ree,** expressions used in directing a team.
31. **copyhold,** tenure of land.

324b 4. **hobnail,** homely, rustic, from the peasant's shoe with large nails in it.
5. **clout,** patch or mend.

A CRITIC

This "character" is more of the Renaissance schoolman or pedant than of the critic as we know him to-day.

28 f. **desunt multa's,** many things lacking.
35. **sophicate,** sophisticated, adulterated.
36. **bastard,** a sweet Spanish wine; here the meaning is, apparently, impure.
38. **Varro,** Marcus Terentius Varro, 116–*ca.* 27 B.C., scholar and author, "the most learned of the Romans."
39. **Plautus,** a Roman comic dramatist. He lived nearly two centuries before the Golden Age of Latin literature. His work was known and imitated during the Renaissance in England.
39 f. **omneis . . . quicquid,** antiquated forms employed by the pedantic critic.

325a BIBLE

The Authorized Version of the Bible was largely the result of the stimulus given the enterprise by James I, hence the popular name, "King James's Bible." The plan was proposed at the Hampton Court Conference, at which the King presided. In the months which followed he directed the project and superintended the selection of the fifty-four translators who were to perform the work. By 1606 forty-seven scholars were definitely set to the task. They worked deliberately and systematically, under a definite code of instructions, in six general companies, two meeting at Oxford, two at Cambridge, and two at Westminster. Smaller groups worked separately from each other, making frequent comparison of their labors, and submitting their joint achievements to the larger units for incorporation or rejection. The final revision represented the combined efforts and consensus of views of the whole learned body. They brought under contribution not only the Greek and Hebrew originals but also all previous versions from Wyclif down. In this way the work was an evolution, the final results representing the best talent and scholarship, not only of England but of the continent, for many generations. The book was issued by Robert Barker, the King's printer, in 1611. Apart from its spiritual significance, no other work of the language has exercised so profound and far-reaching an influence upon the thought, speech, and literature of the nation.

MARRIAGE OF SAMSON

Samson was the strong man of the Hebrew race, more nearly its epic hero than any other. The episodical character of the love story here indicates epical treatment.

4. **Timnath,** a town in northern central Judæa.
6. **Philistines,** a race of people probably of Semitic origin, inhabiting southern Palestine and owing allegiance to Egypt, hereditary enemies of the Hebrews.
23. **Israel,** people of Israel, descendants of Jacob. See Genesis xxxii, 28.

325b 43. **Ashkelon,** one of the chief cities of the Philistines, on the coast of Judæa.

326a THE WOMAN AT THE WELL

The author was John, the beloved disciple. He was the son of Zebedee and by trade was a fisherman. He enjoyed the closest intimacy with Christ, and at the crucifixion was charged with the care of Christ's mother. He is believed to be the author of the three epistles that bear his name and of Revelation. After an exile on the Isle of Patmos in the Ægean, he is thought to have returned to Ephesus and to have died there at a very advanced age.

7. **Pharisees,** a very strict or puritanical order of the Jews.
8. **John,** John the Baptist, *ca.* 5 B.C.–*ca.* A.D. 30, last of the Hebrew prophets and forerunner of Christ.
13. **Samaria,** a district lying between Judæa and Galilee.
15. **Sychar,** in southern central Samaria. Jacob's well and Joseph's tomb are near.
16. **Jacob gave to his son Joseph.** See Joshua xxiv, 32.
29. **Samaritans.** The Samaritans were of foreign origin, having come from Babylonia and some of the Assyrian provinces.

327a CHARITY

The writer was Paul, "apostle to the Gentiles." He was born in Tarsus, learned the trade of tent making, studied at Jerusalem, persecuted the Christians, was miraculously converted on the way to Damascus, and became the greatest Christian preacher of all time. He made missionary tours into various countries and suffered martyrdom in Rome about 67.

31. **charity.** A better English word for the Greek original ἀγάπη is *love,* which is given in the Revised Version.

JOHN MILTON

John Milton, the greatest of the sacred poets of England and one of the greatest epic writers of all time, was born December 9, 1608, in Bread Street, Cheapside, London, where his family resided for the first sixteen years of the poet's life. His father, a native of Oxfordshire and a scrivener by trade, was an accomplished man, particularly in music, and from all accounts was an entirely adequate father for so gifted a son. His mother, Sarah Jeffrey, was an excellent woman. His first schooling was at St. Paul's School close by his native street. He entered Christ's College, Cambridge, as a "lesser pensioner," at sixteen years and two months, and remained there nearly seven and a half years. He was not generally popular because of his independent demeanor, which got him into trouble with his tutor. The sobriquet of "the Lady of Christ's" was given him partly in compliment to his elegance and refinement and partly in scorn of his fastidious tastes. Before leaving the university, he wrote some excellent poems, including his ode on the Nativity, the epitaph on Shakespeare, and his sonnet on reaching the age of twenty-three. Meanwhile the family had retired to Horton in Buckinghamshire, a few miles west of London. The next six years, spent in studious self-improvement there, were productive of some of his best poetry — *L'Allegro*, *Il Penseroso*, *Comus*, and *Lycidas*. After the death of his mother in 1637, he went abroad but was induced to return in little more than a year by increasing rumors of disquieting conditions in England. For a while he employed his powers in controversial writings; he was married to Mary Powell (who very soon left him) in 1643; and for a few years he was engaged in teaching. For his *The Tenure of Kings and Magistrates*, issued within two weeks after the death of Charles I, he was made Latin Secretary under Cromwell. The duties of the office were heavy, his devotion to the cause was great, his sight began to fail, and by 1653 he became totally blind. For the remainder of the Protectorate his life was of an even tenor. At the Restoration he went down in the general obloquy which attended the Puritan fall, and for a time he retired into concealment to save his life. How he escaped execution is yet, to some extent, a mystery. By 1665 *Paradise Lost*, which he had begun in 1658 and completed under the severest trials, was ready for publication. It appeared two years later, and considering the author's circumstances and the temper of the time was well received, bringing him again into the public eye. He continued productive until his death, which occurred at his house in Bunhill, November 8, 1674, of "gout struck in." He was buried in the church of St. Giles in Cripplegate. In the possession of solid learning, high intellectuality, and rare imaginative force and splendor, Milton probably excels all other poets who have written in English. His style and characteristic treatment best represent what has so often been inaptly called in others "the grand manner." Other poets often attain sublimity, but with Milton it is well-nigh a constant state. His deficiencies, as often pointed out, are a lack of human warmth and an almost complete dearth of humor, both of which were denied him more by his inherent nature than by the conditions of his life and time. His environment, however, affected his writings greatly, even determining largely the scope and character of his great epic. If he could have remained free to treat the great body of genuine epic material of the English nation, the matter of Arthur, as he long contemplated doing, we cannot but wonder what might have been the result.

327a ON SHAKESPEARE

This poem appeared first among some commendatory verses in the Second Folio edition of Shakespeare's works, 1632.

11. **unvalued,** invaluable.
12. **Delphic,** inspired, oracular. Delphi, on the southern slope of Mt. Parnassus, was the seat of the famous oracle of Apollo.

L'ALLEGRO

L'Allegro ("The Cheerful Man") and *Il Penseroso* ("The Thoughtful Man") are experiments in describing two contrasting attitudes toward life. They belong to the literature of "character" writing (see p. 321 ff. and notes).

2. **Cerberus,** the three-headed dog that guarded the entrance to the Underworld.
5. **uncouth,** strange, unknown.
7. **night-raven,** probably the owl or night heron.
10. **Cimmerian desert,** land of mist and darkness beyond the Ocean Stream.
11. **ycleped,** called.

328b 12. **Euphrosyne,** one of the three Graces, who, as the name implies, presided over the kindly and pleasing offices or charities of life.

15. **two sister Graces,** Aglaia (the bright) and Thalia (the blooming).
19. **Zephyr with Aurora,** the West Wind and Dawn.
27. **Quips,** short, sharp, witty sayings.
27. **Cranks,** turns of wit.
29. **Hebe's,** goddess of youth, Jove's cup-bearer until superseded, because of an awkward fall, by Ganymede.
40. **unreprovèd,** that cannot be reproved.

329a 62. **dight,** decked, clad.

67. **tells his tale,** counts his flock.
70. **landskip,** landscape.
80. **Cynosure,** constellation of the pole star; here the center of attraction.
83 ff. **Corydon, Thyrsis, Phillis, Thestylis,** conventional names in pastoral literature. Milton, who sees English country life through bookish spectacles, gives English peasants classical names.
94. **rebecks,** fiddles.
102. **fairy Mab the junkets eat.** Mab, queen of the fairy world, ate whatever dainties the peasants set out.
102. **junkets,** a general name for country delicacies.
104. **Friar's lanthorn,** will-o'-the-wisp, jack-o'-lantern, *ignis fatuus*.
105. **drudging Goblin,** Puck, Robin Goodfellow. See Drayton's *Nymphidia*, page 243, and Shakespeare's *Midsummer Night's Dream*.

329b 132. **Jonson's learnèd sock.** See note to Jonson's *To the Memory of My Beloved Master William Shakespeare*, l. 37.

133. **Fancy's.** The word "fancy" was more general in Milton's time than now. Was Shakespeare really an artless genius who merely "warbled" like a bird?

136. **Lydian airs,** according to the Greeks, the softest, mellowest kind of music.

139. **bout,** fold, twist.

145. **Orpheus,** son of Apollo and Calliope, celebrated for his musical powers; patron of music.

149. **Pluto,** god of the Infernal Regions.

150. **Eurydice,** wife of Orpheus, who won her back from Hades by the power of his music but lost her by a forbidden look before they had regained the upper air.

IL PENSEROSO

6. **fond,** foolish.

330a 18. **Prince Memnon,** an Ethiopian hero noted for his comeliness, slain by Achilles in the Trojan War. His sister Hemera (day) was by implication most beautiful among women.

19. **that starred Ethiop queen,** Cassiopeia, wife of Cepheus, king of Ethiopia, who incurred the anger of the sea nymphs by her boast of her superior beauty. She was transformed into the constellation Cassiopœia.

23. **Vesta,** goddess of the Hearth. To her father, Saturn or Cronos, is attributed the origin of civilization. Milton's melancholy is therefore born of Retirement and Culture.

24. **Saturn,** supreme deity until dethroned by his son Zeus or Jupiter.

29. **woody Ida,** Mt. Ida, near Troy, a favorite resort of the gods, or Mt. Ida in Crete.

33. **darkest grain,** violet.

35. **stole,** veil or hood.

36. **decent,** comely, beautiful.

56. **Philomel,** the nightingale. See note to Lyly's *Trico's Song*, l. 2.

330b 83. **the Bellman's drowsy charm.** The night watchman was often given to singing pious songs or reciting charms while on duty.

87. **Bear,** constellation of the Great Bear, which in northern countries never sets.

88. **thrice great Hermes,** Hermes Trismegistus, a legendary learned Egyptian philosopher, often confused with the god Hermes.

93. **Dæmons,** spirits, genii. The Greek imagination peopled well-nigh everything with presiding divinities.

98. **pall,** outer garment, often richly embroidered.

99. **Thebes,** chief city of ancient Bœotia; according to legend, the scene of martial exploits that are surpassed only by those of Troy.

99. **Pelops,** the good son of the cruel Tantalus, king of Lydia. Defeated in a war with Troy, he was favored by Neptune in winning the beautiful Hippodamia in a chariot race, and became the prosperous ruler of Southern Greece for many years, hence the name Peloponnesus. Æschylus wrote three plays on the murder of Agamemnon, a descendant of Pelops.

100. **tale of Troy divine.** The reference is not to Homer but to Æschylus, Sophocles, and Euripides, the great classical dramatists who composed tragedies dealing with the stories of Thebes, Pelops' line, and Troy.

102. **the buskined stage.** See note to Jonson's *To the Memory of My Beloved Master William Shakespeare*, l. 36.

104. **Musæus,** a mythical Greek poet.

108. **made Hell grant,** etc. See note to *L'Allegro*, l. 150.

109. **him that left half-told,** etc. Chaucer in his unfinished *Squire's Tale*.

116. **great Bards beside.** Spenser, for example, in his *Faerie Queene*.

122. **civil-suited,** clad in conventional attire.

123. **tricked and frounced,** adorned and with curled hair.

124. **Attic boy,** Cephalus, loved by Aurora.

127. **still,** gentle.

134. **Sylvan.** Sylvanus, a Roman divinity, was god of the Woods.

331a 156. **pale,** enclosure.

158. **antick,** antique.

159. **storied,** furnished with stories or scenes from Scripture.

161. **the pealing organ,** the pipe organ. Milton was skilled in music. It is common to speak of the organlike qualities of his great poetry.

170. **spell,** interpret.

COMUS

A masque in honor of the Earl of Bridgewater as Lord President of Wales, presented at Ludlow Castle upon his entrance upon the duties of his office in the autumn of 1634.

7. **pinfold,** enclosure for stray cattle.

331b 20. **high and nether Jove,** Jupiter or Zeus and Pluto.

27. **this Isle,** England.

29. **quarters,** divides in four, referring to the four divisions of government in the island — London, Edinburgh, the North, and Wales.

29. **blue-haired,** cerulian- or skyey-haired, a common representation of the sea gods on the stage.

31. **A noble Peer,** John Egerton, Earl of Bridgewater.

34. **his fair offspring.** The earl's children — Lord Brackley, Thomas, and Lady Alice —, the main figures of the masque, were children of about ten to fourteen years of age.

48. **the Tuscan mariners,** etc., Etruscan or Tyrrhenian pirates who attempted to sell Bacchus into slavery and were transformed into dolphins for their pains.

50. **Circe's island,** Ææa, off the coast of Italy. See *Odyssey*, Bk. X.

332a 58. **Comus.** The wicked enchanter of the masque is not a well-defined figure in classical mythology. His birth and character are largely Milton's own.

60. **Celtic and Iberian fields,** France and Spain.

79. **adventurous,** full of adventures.

83. **Iris,** the Rainbow.

92. **viewless,** invisible.

93. **The star,** Hesperus, or the evening star.

93. **Fold,** gather his sheep into the fold.

332b 97. **steep,** deep.

105. **rosy twine,** wreaths of roses.

116. **morrice,** a Moorish dance imported from Spain into England by John of Gaunt in the fourteenth century; a popular country dance.

121. **wakes,** watches.

129. **Cotytto,** a Thracian goddess of low revelry and debauchery.

135. **Hecat',** Thracian goddess of Witchcraft.

139. **nice,** fastidious.

333a 147. **shrouds,** hiding places.

151. **wily trains,** train of wiles, dupery.

155. **blear,** dimming.

161. **glozing,** deceitful.

167. **gear,** business.

168. **fairly,** softly.

176. **Pan,** god of Flocks and Herds, chief of the rural divinities.

189. **Votarist,** one who has vowed a pilgrimage.

190. **wain,** wagon, chariot, or car.

333b 204. **single darkness,** darkness alone.

230. **Echo,** a mountain nymph enamored of Narcissus. Her love was unrequited, and she repined until nothing was left but her voice. As a punishment Narcissus fell in love with his own image and wasted away, until at last he was changed into the flower which bears his name.

232. **Meander,** a winding river in Phrygia not far from Troy.

334a 241. **Parley,** conversation, debate. The speech of Echo is ever a reply.

253. **Sirens three.** See note to p. 317b, l. 28.

254. **Naiades,** nymphs of fresh-water springs and lakes.

257. **Scylla,** at first a beautiful maiden but transformed by Poseidon's jealous wife, the sea nymph Amphitrite, into a monster with twelve feet, six heads, and the voice of a dog. She infested a rocky cave on the Italian side of the Straits of Messina.

259. **Charybdis,** a dangerous whirlpool opposite the rock of Scylla.

334b 293. **swinked hedger,** tired common laborer.

313. **bosky bourn,** brook or stream, bordered with bushes or trees.

335a 341. **star of Arcady.** Callisto, daughter of Lycaon, king of Arcadia in the upland portion of the Peloponnesus, was changed by the jealous Hera into a bear; and, when slain unintentionally by her protectress, Artemis, was made the constellation of the Great Bear by her former lover, Zeus.

342. **Tyrian Cynosure,** a constellation of the pole star, or Lesser Bear, by which the Tyrian seamen steered their course.

344. **wattled cotes,** enclosures made by intertwining boughs of trees or young saplings while green.

345. **pastoral reed with oaten stops,** the shepherd's pipe made of oaten straws.

358. **savage hunger,** hungry beast.

358. **savage heat,** bestial passion or appetite.

335b 380. **to-ruffled,** much ruffled.

382. **i' th' centre,** the center of the earth, which, according to the Ptolemaic system, was the center of the universe.

393. **Hesperian tree,** etc. The Hesperides, three daughters of Atlas, dwelt on an island in the west and guarded a tree bearing golden apples, Gæa's gift to Hera on her marriage with Zeus. They were deprived of their office for tasting the forbidden fruit, and their place was taken by the dragon Ladon.

404. **it recks me not,** I care not.

336a 434. **unlaid,** unexorcised.

447. **snaky-headed Gorgon shield.** Perseus presented the Gorgon's head to his divine patroness Pallas Athena, the Roman Minerva, who placed it in the center of her shield. See note to *Paradise Lost*, II, l. 611.

336b 468. **Imbodies and imbrutes,** grows fleshly and brutish.

478. **Apollo's lute.** The most beautiful and glorious of all the sons of Zeus, Phœbus Apollo, is fabled to have cried to his foster nurse Themis, upon springing full-grown to young manhood, "The golden lyre shall be my friend," whence he became the special patron of music.

337a 517. **Chimeras.** See note to p. 307a, l. 49. Montaigne's essay, *Of Idleness*.

539. **unweeting,** unknowing, unawares.

337b 580. **furder,** further.

338a 604. **Acheron,** the river of Sorrow in Hades.

605. **Harpies,** three female supernatural creatures with the faces of maidens but the bodies of vultures. They were afflicted with insatiable hunger.

605. **Hydras.** The Hydra of classical lore was a water monster or serpent with nine heads, one of which was immortal. The task of destroying her was one of the labors of Hercules.

635. **clouted shoon,** patched shoes.

636. **Moly,** a fabulous herb of magic power.

637. **Hermes once,** etc. Cf. *Odyssey* X, 281–306.

338b 638. **Hæmony,** an ancient name for Thessaly, the land of magic; hence Milton's probable coinage of the word.

641. **Furies' apparition.** See note to Sackville's *Induction*, l. 109.

646. **lime-twigs of his spells,** the precincts of his enchantment, referring to the practice of ensnaring birds by spreading birdlime on the boughs and twigs of trees.

649. **necromancer's,** sorcerer, dealer in the black art.

655. **sons of Vulcan.** Vulcan had his great forge in Mt. Ætna. He was for a while the husband of Venus and later married one of the Graces. His children were mostly monsters, such as Cacus, Periphetes, and Cercyon.

661. **as Daphne was,** etc. Daphne, daughter of the river god Peneus, was sought by Apollo. In her flight she prayed for aid and was changed into a laurel tree, which since has been Apollo's symbol.

675. **Nepenthes,** a drink which had the power of dispelling sorrow.

675. **the wife of Thone,** Polydamna, whom Homer no further characterizes than as an Egyptian woman and the wife of Thone.

676. **Jove-born Helena.** Helen of Troy was the daughter of Zeus and Leda.

339a 689. **wanted,** lacked.

695. **oughly,** ugly.

700. **lickerish,** tempting to any of the appetites.

707. **budge doctors of the Stoic fur,** the pedantic disciples of the ancient Stoics, a school of philosophers who held the chief aim in life was to school oneself into indifference to all strokes of fortune.

708. **Cynic tub.** Diogenes, the greatest of the Cynic philosophers, lived in a tub in scorn of the conventions and common comforts of life.

719. **hutched,** stored up.

721. **pulse,** peas, beans, etc.

722. **frieze,** a coarse woolen cloth, originally from Friesland.

750. **grain,** color.

751. **sampler,** a pattern in embroidery and other needlework.

751. **tease,** comb.

751. **huswife,** housewife.

339b 760. **bolt,** to sift or refine as in milling.

340a 791. **fence,** art of defense.

804. **Erebus,** the Netherworld of darkness.

805. **Saturn's crew.** The Titans who supported Saturn after his overthrow were, like the fallen hosts from heaven, cast down into utter darkness or the Underworld.

340b 822. **Melibœus,** a conventional name in pastoral poetry.

823. **soothest,** truest.

825. **Severn stream,** the Severn River.

826. **Sabrina,** the goddess of the Severn River, not far from Ludlow Castle. The story of Sabrina was told by Geoffrey of Monmouth and afterwards used by various English poets, including Spenser and Drayton.

828. **Brute.** See notes to p. 88b, 25, and 76b, 4.

830. **Guendolen,** first wife of Locrine, whom he divorced for the fair Estrildis, mother of Sabrina.

835. **Nereus,** an important and beneficent sea deity, father of the Nereides, fifty in number.

838. **lavers,** baths.

838. **asphodil,** daffodil or narcissus. Originally the asphodel was a plant growing in the Greek Elysium.

845. **urchin blasts,** mildew or other blight sent on grain or cattle by an elf that took the form of an urchin, or hedgehog.

341a 846. **the shrewd meddling Elf,** Robin Goodfellow or one of his kind.

868. **Oceanus,** god of the great Ocean Stream, which flowed around the earth.

869. **Neptune's mace,** the trident.

870. **Tethys,** wife of Oceanus.

872. **Carpathian wizard,** Proteus, a soothsayer who inhabited an island in the Carpathian Sea. He was able to change his shape at pleasure.

873. **Triton,** son of Poseidon and Amphitrite, and "herald of the Sea."

874. **Glaucus,** a Bœotian fisherman who was transformed into a sea beast from eating enchanted grass. He was endowed with the gift of prophecy.

875. **Leucothea,** the daughter of Cadmus, who plunged into the sea with her son to escape her demented husband, and was changed into a sea goddess. "Lovely hands" is by analogy with her "fair ankles."

879. **Parthenope,** a sea nymph whose body was washed ashore at Naples. A shrine was erected to her there.

880. **Ligea,** one of the Sirens.

891. **osier,** a species of willow. **Dank,** damp.

341b 921. **Amphitrite's,** a sea nymph espoused by Poseidon.

923. **Anchises',** aged father of Æneas.

342a 963. **Mercury,** a Roman divinity, identified with Hermes, the wing-footed messenger of the gods.

964. **Dryades,** wood nymphs.

981 f. **Gardens fair of Hesperus.** See note to l. 393.

986. **Hours.** The Horæ or Seasons, three beautiful maidens, daughters of Zeus and Themis, who presided over the smaller divisions of time as well. Only three seasons were recognized, spring, summer, and autumn, nature being regarded as dead or asleep in winter, hence the joyous, beneficent character of these divinities.

342b 1002. **Assyrian queen,** Astoreth or Astarte, the Phœnician Venus. The Phœnician Adonis is to be equated with Thammuz, also slain by a wild boar.

1005. **Psyche,** a beautiful princess espoused by Cupid, the god of Love, but under strict prohibition not to look upon him. Urged on by her sisters she beheld him asleep by the light of a taper but aroused him, whereupon he left her. She wandered disconsolate through the world suffering great hardships, including a journey to Hades, but at last was reunited with him in heaven, to the glad acclaim of all the gods.

1017. **corners,** horns.

1021. **sphery chime,** music of the spheres.

LYCIDAS

Lycidas is one of four famous laments in English, the other three being Shelley's *Adonais*, Tennyson's *In Memoriam*, and Arnold's *Thyrsis*.

Edward King, contemporary of the poet at Cambridge, was drowned off the Welsh coast on August 10, 1637, at the age of twenty-five.

8. **Lycidas.** The name is from the seventh idyll of Theocritus, the father of pastoral poetry. It occurs frequently in pastoral literature.

10 f. **he knew Himself to sing,** etc., he himself knew how to sing, etc. Some Latin verses by King have been preserved.

15. **Sisters of the sacred well,** the nine Muses, either of Aganippe well on Mount Helicon in Bœotia or of the Pierian spring at the foot of Mount Olympus.

21. **he,** some poet, referred to as the Muse in l. 19.

23. **the self-same hill,** Cambridge.

343a 29. **Battening,** fattening.

34. **Satyrs,** rough, wild woodland spirits.

34. **Fauns,** a class of sportive deities of the Romans, somewhat like the satyrs of the Greeks.

36. **Damœtas,** a conventional pastoral name. Possibly Milton's tutor Chappell at Christ Church is referred to.

45. **canker,** cankerworm.

52. **the steep,** probably Kerig y Druidion in Denbighshire, a reputed burial ground of the druids.

53. **Druids,** priests of the primitive Celtic religion or worship. They were poets as well.

54. **Mona,** the island of Anglesey off the Welsh coast.

55. **Deva,** the River Dee. Chester, the port from which King sailed, is on this stream.

58. **the Muse herself.** Calliope, chief of the nine, was the mother of Orpheus by Apollo.

62. **His gory visage.** Orpheus was slain by some Thracian women, in resentment at his indifference to them, and his head was thrown into the River Hebrus.

343b 68 f. **Amaryllis . . . Neæra,** conventional names of women in pastoral writings.

75. **the blind Fury,** etc., Atropos, one of the Fates, who cut the thread of life. **Blind,** undiscriminating.

85. **fountain Arethuse.** Arethusa was a nymph of Elis loved by the river god Alpheus. In her flight from him she was changed by Diana into a fountain and led under the sea to reappear again near Syracuse in Sicily.

86. **Mincius,** a river emptying into the Po near Mantua, Virgil's birthplace.

89. **Herald of the Sea,** Triton. See note to *Comus*, l. 873.

90. **plea,** defense.

96. **Hippotades,** Æolus, god of the Winds.

99. **Panopê,** a Nereid. The Nereides, fifty in number, were Mediterranean nymphs, the daughters of Nereus and Doris.

103. **Camus,** the spirit or divinity of the river Cam, on which Cambridge University is situated.

344a 106. **that sanguine flower,** the hyacinth, whose petals the Greeks imagined were marked with the word meaning *alas!* from Apollo's sorrow at the accidental death, of which he was the innocent cause, of his friend Hyacinthus.

109. **Pilot of the Galilean Lake,** St. Peter (see Matthew xiv, 25 ff.). The passage following is an attack on the corrupted clergy of the time. King was preparing for orders.

110. **Two massy keys.** Cf. Matthew xvi, 19.

112. **mitered.** The miter was the official papal headdress.

114. **Anow,** enough.

115. **the fold,** the Church.

122. **What recks it them?** What do they care?

124. **scrannel,** screechy.

128. **the grim Wolf,** the Roman Catholic Church.

130. **two-handed engine.** (Specific meaning unknown.)

132. **Alphëus,** a river in southern Greece. See note to l. 85.

133. **Sicilian Muse,** Theocritus.

138. **the swart star,** the dog star.

344b 142. **rathe,** early.

149. **amaranthus,** emblematic of immortality.

151. **laureate,** adorned with laurel.

156. **Hebrides,** a group of islands northwest of Scotland.

158. **monstrous world,** world of monsters.

160. **Bellerus.** The name was coined by Milton from *Bellerium*, a name for St. Michael's Mount, off the coast of Cornwall near Land's End. According to Milton, Bellerus was a legendary Cornish giant.

161. **Vision of the guarded mount,** St. Michael's

Mount in Cornwall, where the angel Michael is said to have been seen.

162. **Namancos and Bayona's hold,** points on the Spanish coast, the one probably a tower and the other a castle.

173. **Him that walked the waves.** Cf. Matthew xiv, 22 ff.

345a 186. **uncouth Swain,** the unknown rustic, the poet Milton.

188. **Doric lay,** a simple song; here a simple elegy in the pastoral style.

ON HIS BEING ARRIVED, etc.

Written at Cambridge soon after Milton had taken his M.A. degree.

4. **my late spring.** Milton's literary powers appeared relatively late in life. He was first designed for the Church.

5. **Perhaps my semblance.** See the biographical sketch for Milton's reputation at the university.

TO THE LORD GENERAL CROMWELL, etc.

Fourteen members of the Rump Parliament made up a committee on church affairs. To this body proposals were made that preachers should receive public maintenance.

7. **Darwen stream.** Preston in Lancashire, on the Darwen, was the scene of Cromwell's victory over the Scots, August 17, 1648.

8. **Dunbar field,** in Haddingtonshire, Scotland, the scene of another defeat of the Scots, September 3, 1650.

9. **Worcester,** the scene of Cornwell's decisive victory over Charles II and his Scottish allies, September 3, 1651.

345b ON THE LATE MASSACRE IN PIEDMONT

In 1655 the Protestants of northwest Italy were subjected to a bloody persecution by the court of Turin because they refused to accept Catholicism. The English government took cognizance in a solemn protest to the Duke of Savoy, under whose rule the territory lay.

4. **When all our fathers,** etc. Before the Reformation when England was a Catholic country.

12. **The triple Tyrant,** the Pope, from his triple crown, signifying his threefold power in heaven, earth, and hell.

14. **Babylonian woe.** The Puritan identified Rome with the Babylon of Scriptural imprecation. See Revelation xviii.

ON HIS BLINDNESS

Milton was totally blind by 1653.

3. **that one Talent.** Cf. Matthew xxv, 14 ff.

346a TO CYRIACK SKINNER

10. **conscience,** consciousness.

10. **lost them over-plied.** Milton at least hastened his blindness by his severe application to his duties as Latin Secretary.

ON HIS DECEASED WIFE

The poet's second wife, Catherine Woodcock, died in childbirth in 1658 — a little more than a year after their marriage.

2. **Alcestis,** the beautiful wife of Admetus, king of Pheræ in Thessaly. By the favor of Apollo immortality was granted to the king on condition that some member of his family should take his place when death summoned. His parents failing him at this crisis, Alcestis secretly gave herself to the sacrifice and expired in his arms. As she was being committed to the tomb, Hercules appeared and compelled death to release her.

6. **the Old Law.** Cf. Leviticus xii.

10. **Her face was veiled.** Milton probably never had had sight of her.

PARADISE LOST

I

346b 1. **Man's first disobedience,** etc. Cf. Genesis iii.

4. **one greater Man,** the Messiah.

6. **Heavenly Muse,** the Spirit, Jehovah.

7. **Oreb, or of Sinai,** the mountain range of Horeb with Mt. Sinai where the law was given to Moses. See Exodus xix–xxxiv.

8. **That Shepherd,** Moses.

8. **the chosen seed,** the Israelites.

10. **Sion hill,** one of the hills on which Jerusalem was built.

11. **Siloa's brook,** the pool of Siloam at the foot of the hill on which the temple in Jerusalem stood.

15. **Aonian mount,** Mt. Helicon. See note to *Lycidas*, l. 15.

21. **Dove-like.** Cf. Luke iii, 22.

29. **grand Parents,** Adam and Eve.

29. **that happy state,** in Eden, generally believed to have been in Mesopotamia.

32. **For one restraint.** Cf. Genesis ii, 12.

347a 34. **The infernal Serpent,** Satan in the form of a serpent.

36. **what time his pride,** etc. Cf. Revelation xii, 7 ff.

59. **ken,** know, have powers of sight.

70. **Such place,** etc. In his conception of the universe, Milton reverts to the Ptolemaic system with Christian adaptations

74. **from the center thrice to the utmost pole.** Three times the distance from the center of the earth to the *Primum Mobile* or tenth circle.

FIG. 1

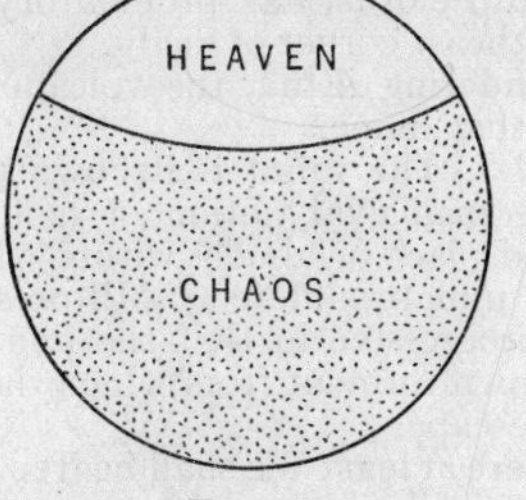

FIG. 2

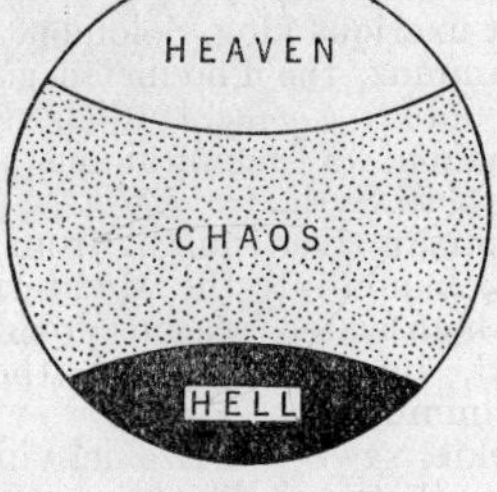

FIG. 3

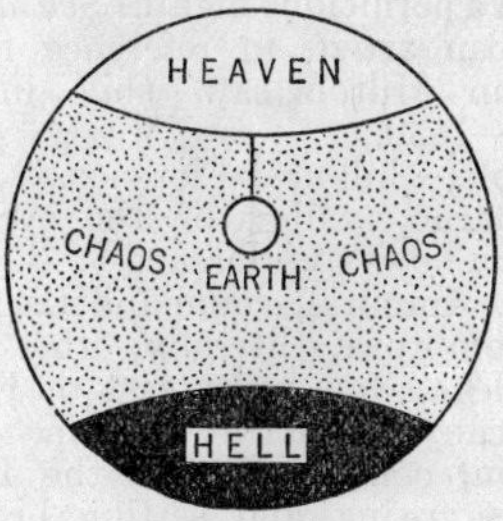

FIG. 4

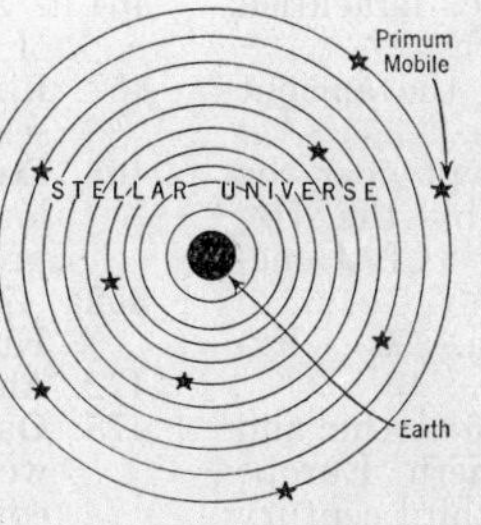

FIG. 5

347b 81. **Beelzebub,** sun god of the Philistines.

82. **thence in Heaven called Satan.** Satan before his fall was an archangel; his name was blotted out from the Book of Life after his fall and the new name given for his new state. Cf. l. 361 ff.

93. **He with his thunder,** Jehovah. The poet mixes freely pagan and Christian conceptions. Thunder was the special weapon of punishment of Zeus or Jupiter.

348b 197 ff. **whom the fables name,** etc. From the union of Uranus and Gæa (Earth) sprang two races of earth-born beings: three Giants, each with fifty heads and a hundred hands, possessing powerful brute strength, and able to shake the universe; and twelve Titans, who had great intellectual as well as physical powers. Both at one time or another rebelled against the gods. Titanian is a general name for the Titans. Briareus was a Giant. Typhon was the youngest born of Tartarus and Gæa He had a hundred heads and eyes that could strike terror to the beholder. He threatened gods and men, but was overcome by Zeus. The gods fled him and assumed animal shapes in Egypt. Accounts of the whole are mixed.

200. **ancient Tarsus,** capital of Cilicia in Asia Minor.

201. **Leviathan,** a sea monster of the Bible, identified with the whale.

349a 232. **Pelorus,** a promontory at the northeast corner of Sicily.

233. **thundering Ætna,** the volcano in Sicily by that name.

349b 254 f. **The mind is its own place,** etc. The mediæval notion of hell was of a fixed place or abode, within which alone the inmate suffered. Milton's theology is progressive in that the mind is made its own torment from which there can be no escape.

258 f. **Here at least We shall be free.** Liberty, specifically of conscience, was the great end sought by the Puritans in their struggle.

282. **such a pernicious highth!** See note to l. 74.

288. **Tuscan artist,** in reference to Galileo, whom Milton saw while in Italy in 1638–1639.

289. **Fesolè,** a hill near Florence.

290. **Valdarno,** valley of the Arno River, which flows by Florence.

350a 294. **Ammiral,** commander's flagship.

303. **Vallombrosa,** literally, the valley of shades, a few miles east of Florence in Tuscany or ancient Etruria.

305. **Orion,** constellation of the Huntsman, whose rising and setting brought bad weather.

307. **Busiris,** an early king of Egypt, here made the pharaoh of the Israelitish exodus (cf. Exodus xiv, 5 ff.).

307. **Memphian.** Memphis was the ancient capital of Egypt.

309. **Goshen,** the portion of Egypt near the eastern frontier occupied by the Hebrews before their exodus. Cf. Genesis xlvii, 27 f.

350b 339. **Amram's son,** Aaron. Cf. Exodus vi, 20.

351. **the populous North,** etc., the Gothic and Vandal invasions of southern Europe and northern Africa in the third century and later.

353. **Rhene or the Danaw,** the Rhine or Danube.

351a 392. **Moloch,** the Canaanitish sun god in his fiercer aspects. His worship included human sacrifice.

397. **Rabba,** the capital city of the Ammonites, who dwelt on the eastern border of Palestine.

398. **Argob . . . Basan,** districts east of Palestine.

399. **Arnon,** a river flowing westward into the Dead Sea.

402. **His temple.** Solomon in his later idolatrous days built a temple to Moloch next to the Mount of Olives, hence "opprobrious hill."

404. **Hinnom,** a valley lying west and south of Jerusalem.

404. **Tophet,** etc. Tophet and Gehenna are Old Testament names for hell.

406. **Chemos,** the chief deity of the Moabites, who occupied the district east of the Dead Sea and south of the Arnon. His worship was licentious.

407 ff. **From Aroar,** etc. These places mark pretty definitely the limits of Moab.

411. **Asphaltick Pool,** the Dead Sea.

413. **Israel in Sittim,** etc. See Numbers xxv.

418. **good Josiah.** See 2 Kings xxiii.

420. **brook that parts,** the River Besor.

422. **Baalim and Ashtaroth.** Both words are plural, including in general the Phœnician "heavenly host," who were represented in licentious forms of worship.

351b 438. **Astoreth,** the Phœnician Venus.

441. **Sidonian.** Sidon was the oldest city of Phœnicia, a seaport.

444. **that uxorious king,** Solomon.

446. **Thammuz,** the Phœnician god of Love. See note to *Comus*, l. 1002.

447. **Lebanon,** a mountainous district in southern Syria.

450. **Adonis,** a river running from the heights of Lebanon into the Mediterranean Sea, in high-water seasons reddened with mud, by interpretation the blood of Thammuz.

455. **Ezekiel saw.** Cf. Ezekiel viii, 14.

460. **grunsel,** threshold.

462. **Dagon,** a sea god, national deity of the Philistines along the seacoast.

464 ff. **Azotus . . . Gaza,** the five chief cities of the Philistines.

467. **Rimmon,** a gluttonous divinity whose seat of worship was Damascus.

468. **Damascus,** an historical city of Syria, long celebrated for its beauty and prosperity.

352a 471. **A leper once,** Naaman. Cf. 2 Kings v.

472. **Ahaz.** Cf. 2 Kings xvi.

478. **Osiris, Isis, Orus,** Egyptian deities worshiped in the forms of the bull, the cow, and the sun, respectively.

484. **The calf in Oreb.** Cf. Exodus xxxii.

484. **the rebel king,** Jeroboam, who set up a golden calf each at Bethel and at Dan. Cf. 1 Kings xii, 28 f.

487. **in one night,** etc. Cf. Exodus xii, 29.

490. **Belial,** the spirit of evil personified.

495. **Eli's sons.** Cf. 1 Samuel ii, 12 ff.

503. **Sodom.** Cf. Genesis xix.

504. **In Gibeah.** Cf. Judges xix.

508. **Ionian,** Greek.

508. **Javan,** the grandson of Noah by Japhet.

510. **Titan,** perhaps to be equated with Uranus, father of the Titans. Uranus was dethroned by his youngest son Cronos, or Saturn, and Saturn in turn was deposed by Zeus, or Jove.

514. **in Crete.** Mt. Ida in Crete was the birthplace of Zeus.

352b 517. **Delphian cliff,** the oracle of Apollo on Mt. Parnassus.

518. **Dodona,** the oracle of Zeus in Epirus.

519. **Doric**, Greek.
520. **Adria**, Adriatic Sea.
520. **Hesperian fields**, Italy.
521. **Celtic**, Celtic lands, *i.e.*, France and Spain.
521. **utmost Isles**, British Isles.
534. **Azazel.** Cf. Leviticus xvi, 8.
543. **Chaos and old Night.** Chaos, according to Greek mythology, was not so much a spirit or being as a condition, amorphousness or confusion, although even that, with the active imagination of the Greek, was conceived of as vitalized by an essence, hence the vague divinity Chaos. Nyx or Night was his daughter, and in turn was the mother of mysteries, such as Death, Sleep, etc. She was clad in black, wore a veil, rode in a chariot drawn by black horses attended by the stars, and abode in the lower or outer world, but was withal a beautiful woman.
550. **Dorian mood**, martial music, grave and stern.
551. **recorders**, wind instruments somewhat like the flute.

353a 575. **that small infantry**, the battle of the pygmies and the cranes, mentioned in the *Iliad*, Bk. III.
577. **Phlegra**, a headland on the peninsula of Chalcidice in the Ægean Sea, the scene of the defeat of the Giants by the gods.
580. **Uther's son**, King Arthur.
581. **Armoric**, Briton.
583. **Aspramont**, etc., battle scenes in chivalric history and romance.
587. **Fontarabbia.** In the oldest of the French *chansons de gestes*, the *Song of Roland*, Charles and his twelve peers are defeated by an overwhelming host of Saracens at Roncesvalles near Fontarabia in Spain.

353b 609. **amerced**, punished.

354a 651. **a fame**, a story.
678. **Mammon**, the personification of riches. Cf. Matthew vi, 24.

354b 694. **Babel.** Cf. Genesis xi, 1 ff.
694. **works of Memphian kings**, the Pyramids.
703. **founded**, melted, as in a foundry.
718. **Alcairo**, Memphis in Egypt.
720. **Belus**, Bel or Baal, an Assyrian god.
720. **Serapis**, an Egyptian deity, lord of the Underworld.

355a 739. **Ausonian land**, Italy.
740. **Mulciber**, the Greek Hephæstus, who was hurled from Olympus for siding with Juno in a dispute with Jove.
756. **Pandæmonium**, " hall of all the demons," the capitol of Hell.
764. **Soldan's**, sultan.
765. **Panim**, pagan, specifically Mohammedan.

355b 769. **Taurus**, the Bull, one of the signs of the Zodiac.
780. **pygmean race.** See note to l. 575.
781. **the Indian mount**, Mt. Ophir.

II

2. **Ormus**, an island city at the entrance to the Persian Gulf, a rich emporium in the sixteenth and seventeenth centuries.

356b 69. **Tartarean**, Tartarus was a vast and gloomy region far below Hades.
74. **forgetful lake**, the lake of fire into which they had first fallen.
77. **To us is adverse**, etc. As the moral, so the physical forces of the universe were reversed to them.

357a 113. **Dropt manna.** Cf. Exodus xvi, 31.
133. **realm of Night.** See note to Bk. I, l. 543.

359a 294. **Michaël**, the Archangel.
306. **Atlantean.** Atlas was a Titan who was condemned by Zeus to stand at the western verge of the world and support the heavens. At sight of the Gorgon's head borne in the hands of Perseus, he was changed into the mountains which bear his name.

360b 405 ff. **dark, unbottomed, infinite Abyss . . . palpable obscure . . . vast Abrupt,** etc., the region of Chaos between hell and the earth. See Figure 4 above.
410. **happy Isle**, the earth.
430. **Empyreal.** The Empyrean was the highest heaven, composed of a substance like sublimated fire.
439. **unessential**, without essence or substance.

361b 513. **horrent**, bristling.

362a 528. **sublime**, sublimated, rarefied.
530. **Olympian games**, celebrated games or contests held every four years at Olympia in Elis, the national seat of the worship of Zeus.
530. **Pythian fields.** The chief seat of the worship of Apollo was at Delphi. Here the Pythian games were held every four years in honor of his victory over the Python at that place.
539. **Typhœan.** See note to Bk. I, l. 197.
542. **Alcides**, Hercules. Œchalia was the capital of Eubœa, which Hercules had just reduced and from which he was returning with the beautiful Iole. In his preparations for an offering, his wife Deianeira supplied him with a sacrificial robe sprinkled with the Centaur's blood, thinking thereby to prevent the loss of her husband's affection. The great hero died in the severest agony from the poisoned garment.
545. **Lichas**, the messenger who bore the poisoned robe to Hercules. He was changed into an island.
545. **Œta**, a mountain in the southern part of Thessaly, the scene of Hercules' death.

362b 577 ff. **Styx**, etc. The four rivers here named are borrowed from the *Odyssey*, Bk. X, 513 f.
592. **Serbonian bog**, a lake and quicksand in

Egypt between the city of Damietta and the sand mound called Mount Casius.

596. **Furies.** See note to Sackville's *Induction*, l. 105.

363a 611. **Medusa,** the most celebrated of the three sister Gorgons. She was originally a beautiful maiden, priestess of Athena, but forgetting her vows of celibacy she was married to Poseidon and as a punishment was changed by the goddess into the most frightful of monsters, whose gaze could change to stone. She was relieved at last by death at the hands of Perseus.

614. **Tantalus,** a great king of Lydia, who was especially favored by the gods, but for his presumptions he was placed in Tartarus, and afflicted with a burning thirst, in water that receded before him, and with an insatiable hunger, in the presence of fruit that forever eluded his grasp.

638. **Bengala,** according to the older notion, a prosperous country of the Indies.

639. **Ternate and Tidore,** two of the Molucca islands in the East Indies.

641. **Ethiopian,** the Indian Ocean.

641. **Cape,** the Cape of Good Hope.

363b 655. **Cerberean.** See note to Sackville's *Induction*, l. 497, and *L'Allegro*, l. 2.

660. **Scylla.** See note to *Comus*, l. 257.

661. **Calabria,** a district in southern Italy.

661. **Trinacrian,** Sicily, so called from its triangular shape.

662. **the night-hag,** Hecate, archsorceress of the ancients.

665. **Lapland,** the traditional home and favorite resort of witches.

364a 692. **the third part of Heaven's Sons.** See Revelation xii, 4, 9.

709. **Ophiuchus,** Serpentarius or Serpent-bearer, a northern constellation over against Scorpio.

721. **but once more.** See Revelation xx.

366b 904. **Barca or Cyrene,** cities of northern Africa.

919. **frith,** an arm of the sea.

367a 922. **Bellona,** the Roman goddess of War.

939. **Syrtis,** treacherous quicksands in the region of Tripoli in northern Africa.

945. **Arimaspian,** a mythical Scythian race who fought with the griphons for gold in the mines of which these monstrous half-eagle, half-lion creatures were guardians.

367b 964. **Orcus and Ades,** divinities of the realm of death. The former brought spirits under the power of death and the latter ruled over them there.

965. **Demogorgon,** a mysterious, terrible, and evil divinity who had in subjection the inhabitants of Hades.

1002 f. **first Hell.** See Figure 3 of Book I above.

368a 1004. **Earth, another world.** See Figure 4 of Book I above.

1017. **Argo,** the ship which carried Jason and his fifty heroes on their quest of the Golden Fleece.

1018. **justling rocks,** the Symplegades at the entrance of the Euxine from the Bosporus, two great rocky islands which floated about and constantly crashed together and then parted. After the passage of the Argo they became permanently joined and fixed to the bottom of sea.

368b 1029. **utmost Orb,** the tenth or outer circle of the stellar universe. See Figure 5 of Book I above.

GEORGE HERBERT

The most devotional of the numerous sacred poets of England, George Herbert, was born in 1593 at Montgomery Castle in Wales. His father, Sir Richard Herbert, died early, and the education of the several sons, the oldest of whom became the celebrated Lord Herbert of Cherbury, was left to the mother. She was a woman of singular piety and great personal charm, at one time a patroness of the poet Donne, and strongly impressed her character on her son George. George attended Westminster School and Cambridge University, and became a good classical scholar. He received the M.A. degree in 1616 and continued in his college as a fellow. In 1619 he was made university orator and thus was brought into contact with the life of the court. Encouraged by his mother, he had contemplated divinity early, but with the chance of a political career, he hesitated over his life work for some years. The King's death, however, in 1625, spoiled his prospects at court. This fact and his own failing health determined him for the church. He was granted the living at Leighton Bromswold in Huntingdonshire, and on his ordination in 1630 was presented with the vicarage of Bemerton near Salisbury. It was here mainly that he won the fame which has since caused him to be known as "saintly George Herbert." Within three years he died of consumption and was buried under the altar of his church. None of his English poems were published in his lifetime. He left a body of manuscript, however, to his friend Nicholas Ferrar of Little Gidding, who issued it as *The Temple* soon after his death. Its popularity is shown by the several editions which followed within a few years. He was a disciple of Donne in his over-elaboration and fastidious literary artistry. His shortcomings are discernible in his limited range of subject matter and his obvious artificiality. His greatest service was in the wholesome restraint which he exercised, by his sincere piety and devotional fervor, on the too licentious tendency of much of the amatory poetry of the time.

368a JORDAN

8. **sped,** prospered.

368b 17. **There is in love,** etc. Compare l. 14, Sonnet I, of Sidney's *Astrophel and Stella*, p. 273.

369a THE ALTAR

1. **A broken Altar,** etc. Cf. Psalms li, 17.

EASTER WINGS

19. **imp,** graft, repair.

VIRTUE

5. **angry and brave,** very red and defiant.

369b 11. **My music.** Herbert was an excellent musician.

11. **closes,** stops, end.

14. **gives,** gives way, warps.

THE QUIP

2. **train-bands.** A trainband was a force of citizen soldiery in London.

23. **at large,** generally or vaguely.

THE COLLAR

1. **the board,** the table.

5. **store,** abundance.

6. **in suit,** in supplication for a favor.

8. **let me blood,** cause me to shed blood.

9. **cordial,** in the derivative sense of appertaining to the heart (Latin *cor, cordis*).

370a 26. **wink,** close the eyes, sleep.

29. **thy death's head,** a *memento mori*.

THOMAS CAREW

Thomas Carew was a genuine Caroline in both his manner of living and in his poetry. He was a younger son of Sir Matthew Carew and seems to have formed bad habits early. He was at Oxford but did not remain for a degree. When his father's family was in straitened circumstances by 1613, he was an indifferent student of the law at the Middle Temple. Soon afterward he became attached in some secretarial capacity to the embassy of Sir Dudley Carleton to Italy, but gave up his post in a huff on his return in 1616. For some years he idled his time away in some ill repute and in want of preferment. After a visit with his friend, Lord Herbert of Cherbury, to France in 1619, he became attached to the English court, and received from the King the royal domain of Sunninghill in Windsor Forest. He made a maudlin kind of deathbed repentance for his irregular life, and died in 1638. He was acquainted with most of the literary men of his day, and was especially intimate with the young dramatist Davenant and with Sir John Suckling. He wrote the elaborate masque, *Cœlum Britannicum*, but is remembered for his lyrics, which were composed, it is said, with great difficulty, but which possess melody, cultivated ease, and a certain feeling of classical decorum, which gave them a high rank in literature.

370b A CRUEL MISTRESS

9. **Vesta,** the goddess of Fire and the Family Hearth.

13. **The Assyrian king,** Nebuchadnezzar. Cf. Daniel iii.

371a ASK ME NO MORE, etc.

11. **dividing,** producing music.

18. **the phœnix.** See p. 89a, l. 29 ff., and note to p. 203b, l. 18.

FRANCIS QUARLES

Francis Quarles, another of the religious poets of the time, was born at his father's manor house at Romford in Essex. He was educated in a country school and at Cambridge University, where he was awarded the B.A. degree in 1608. From the study of law in Lincoln's Inn he rose to the position of cupbearer to the Princess Elizabeth, and on her marriage to the Elector Palatine in 1613 attended her to Germany. For his scriptural paraphrases and religious tracts he was made secretary to Archbishop Ussher of Armagh in 1629, and lived in Dublin for a few years. By 1633 he seems to have been in retirement at Roxwell in his native Essex, where he prepared his chief volume of poetry, *Emblems*, published in 1635. Four years later he was made chronologer to the city of London. At the outbreak of the Civil War he cast in his lot with the Royalist cause, suffered the loss of his property and was publicly traduced for his active adherence, and died, it is said, from a sense of his wrongs in 1644. The wretchedness of man's estate is the general theme of his writings. His poetry abounds in conceits, but contains flashes of genuine poetic fire. The qualities which made him popular in his day, such as liveliness, good sense, and rough humor, continue to preserve his fame.

A GOOD NIGHT

3. **he that keeps,** etc. Cf. Psalms cxxi, 3 f.

SWEET PHOSPHOR, BRING THE DAY

3. **Phosphor,** the morning star.

371b 15. **fray,** frighten away.

31. **Vulcan's forge.** See note to p. 338b, l. 655.
38. **Heaven's loitering lamp,** the moon.
43. **our greater taper,** the sun.
44. **the lesser,** the moon.

ROBERT HERRICK

Robert Herrick was one of the greatest of the seventeenth-century lyrical poets. He was the fourth son of Nicholas Herrick, a goldsmith of Cheapside in London, derived from an ancient family of Leicestershire. The father did not survive the son's infancy. In 1607 the boy was apprenticed to his uncle for ten years but did not serve his time. By 1613 he was a fellow commoner at Cambridge, and after the attainment of the M.A. degree in 1620 he returned to London, where he remained for nearly a decade. In 1629 he was made vicar of Dean Prior Church in Devonshire. Much of his poetry obviously was written before, but by his own confession the best was written after this significant change in his life. Probably poor as a preacher, but evidently high in esteem with the gentry for his conversation, he remained at Dean Prior until he was ousted by the Puritan government in 1647. While in London the following year he published his only book, *Hesperides*, together with his *Noble Numbers*, in one volume. In the one he is frankly pagan and in the other sincerely Christian. Two years after the recall of King Charles II to the throne, Herrick's parish was restored to him. He died there in 1674. He left nearly thirteen hundred lyrics. Jonson is his master in English, and Horace, Catullus, and Martial in Latin; but when he borrows most, his spirit is always freshly original, and however foreign his material, he never fails to make his productions entirely English. He shows great metrical variety, and is always a consummate artist. In general, his poems are characterized by a great natural charm.

372a THE ARGUMENT OF HIS BOOK

3. **hock-carts,** harvest-home carts.
3. **wakes,** watches.
6. **cleanly wantonness.** This may be taken as a keynote to all Herrick's secular poetry. His revelry is but the riot of imagination.

CHERRY RIPE

1. **Cherry ripe,** See note to l. 6 of Campion's *There Is A Garden*, etc., p. 263.

372b DELIGHT IN DISORDER

Cf. Jonson's *Simplex Munditiis*, p. 267.

6. **stomacher,** front piece for the pit of the stomach and breast, often richly embroidered and ornamented with jewels.

CORINNA'S GOING A MAYING

2. **the god unshorn,** Apollo, the Sun.
17. **Flora,** the goddess of Flowers. She was the wife of Zephyrus and the fairest of the lesser gods. Her festival was generally celebrated in May.
25. **Titan,** the Sun.

373a 51. **green-gown,** a grass-stained dress.

373b HIS POETRY HIS PILLAR

24. **Pyramides,** pyramids.

374a TO BACCHUS A CANTICLE

1. **whorry,** hurry.

374b THE NIGHT PIECE, TO JULIA

7. **slow-worm,** a species of lizard.

375a AN ODE FOR BEN JONSON

5. **The Sun,** etc. Names of taverns in London. The Dog was a favorite resort of the "Tribe of Ben," disciples of Ben Jonson.

HIS PRAYER FOR ABSOLUTION

This and the selections following are from his religious verse or *Noble Numbers*, published with the *Hesperides* but with a separate title page.

6. **my book,** the *Hesperides* proper.

375b HIS LITANY TO THE HOLY SPIRIT

13. **artless,** without art or skill.
15. **runs on the lees,** runs low, fails.
21. **passing-bell,** death bell.
27. **more than true,** greater than are true.

376a A THANKSGIVING, etc.

22. **unflead,** unflayed, uncut.
31. **worts,** potherbs, vegetables.

376b ANOTHER GRACE FOR A CHILD

3. **paddocks,** toads.

SIR JOHN SUCKLING

Sir John Suckling excelled in the courtly graces of excellent wit, a handsome presence, the habit of gaming, and a happy but careless gallantry, generosity, and a turn for poetry. His birthplace was Whitton in Middlesex. His father, of an ancient Norfolk family, was a prominent official and man of affairs, rising ultimately to a Secretaryship of State and the Privy Council. The poet went to Cambridge and left without a degree, but his attainments were respectable. He was a man of polite rather than profound learning. Coming into some rich estates on his father's death in 1627, he was able to make himself conspicuous at court, soon becoming known as the greatest gallant of his time. He was knighted by the King at Theobald's in 1630. Attached to the Royalist cause from the first, he led a troop of horse against the Scots, and tried by a sudden attack to secure the command of the army for the King, but his plot was discovered and he fled the country. He died probably by self-poisoning in Paris in 1642. His *Fragmenta Aurea*, published four years after his death, contains his best work. His dramas are dreary, their chief merit consisting in an occasional good lyric, such as "Why so pale," etc., in *Aglaura*. Gaiety and ease are his best traits, often atoning for his irresponsible air and the general frivolity of his subject matter.

377a THE CONSTANT LOVER

5. **moult away,** shed.

BALLAD UPON A WEDDING

The occasion was the marriage of Roger Boyle, later Earl of Orrery, to Lady Margaret Howard, daughter of the Earl of Suffolk, at Northumberland House in London in 1640.

1. **Dick,** the poet, Richard Lovelace.

377b 7. **Charing-Cross,** near Haymarket Square in London.

32. **Whitsun-ale,** a Whitsuntide festival, usually celebrated by feasting, drinking, and playing games, in the vicinity of a church.

34. **kindly,** naturally.

378a 77. **trained band.** Cf. Herbert's *The Quip*, p. 369b, l. 2 and note.

JAMES SHIRLEY

Shirley is usually recognized as the last of the great Elizabethan line of English dramatists. He was born in London and attended the Merchant Taylors' School. He entered Oxford but migrated to Cambridge and received the B.A. degree about 1618. He became a priest in the Church of England, but on becoming a Roman Catholic abandoned a clerical and scholastic career and "set up for a play-maker" in London. His plays followed each other in rapid succession from 1626 to 1642, when the closing of the theaters put an end to his career as playwright. He published plays during the Commonwealth and engaged in teaching in London. He died in 1666 from his miseries and losses occasioned, it is said, by the great fire. He wrote few lyrics, but a poet who could pen "No Armour against Fate," found in his masque of *The Contention*, possessed no mean lyrical ability.

RICHARD CRASHAW

Richard Crashaw was the only son of the poet and Puritan divine, William Crashaw of London. He attended the Charterhouse School, was admitted to Cambridge in 1631, became noted for his proficiency in languages, received his B.A. degree in 1684 and his M.A. as a fellow of Peterhouse four years later. In 1643 he lost his position by the exigencies of war, and by 1646 had become a Catholic and was living in Paris. He went to Italy in 1649, was an attendant upon Cardinal Palotta at Rome, but falling out with his household was made a subcanon for his own protection in the church of Our Lady at Loretto, and died there in 1649. A volume of his poems, both sacred and secular, *Steps to the Temple, and Delights of the Muses*, was published in 1646, and a mass of manuscript survived him at his death, only part of which has been preserved. His devotional poems are noted for their passionate fervor and richness of imagery. As a class, they are usually reckoned his best, but the lover of poetry in its less spiritual essence often finds greater pleasure in the sweetness and delicate artistry of an occasional secular piece, such as his *Wishes to His (Supposed) Mistress*.

378b WISHES TO HIS (SUPPOSED) MISTRESS

6. **shady leaves of destiny,** the Book of Fate.

14. **her to,** to her.

18. **tire,** attire.

18. **shoe-tie,** an ornamental shoe lace, sometimes very elaborate.

379a 20. **tissue,** a cloth interwoven with gold or silver.

33. **ru'th,** falls in love with.

64. **bin,** are.

379b 82. **Sidneian,** etc., an allusion to Sir Philip Sidney's conversation, or the dialogue of his *Arcadia*.

94. **Her flattery,** etc. Let her know only the flattery of painting and poetry.

380a 120. **her Story,** her true story, true of her.

EDMUND WALLER

The poet Waller, the eldest son of Sir Robert Waller, was born at Coleshill in what is now Buckinghamshire. He was at Eton and attended Cambridge without taking a degree. He became a member of Lincoln's Inn and is said to have entered Parliament at the age of sixteen. His sensational marriage in 1631 to Anne, daughter of John Banks, made him, with his own ample fortune, the richest poet, except Samuel Rogers, in English literature. After his marriage he retired to Beaconsfield, with which his name is intimately associated, and after the death of his wife devoted himself more closely to letters. He had no deep political convictions but sided with the King against Parliament as the easiest way to peace. He was not the originator but became a principal in "Waller's Plot" to secure the city of London for the King. The design failed on the eve of its execution, and he turned informant to save himself. He was fined £10,000 and banished the realm, but was pardoned in 1651 and returned to England. After the Restoration he again entered Parliament and remained until his death in 1687. His poems circulated freely in manuscript, but no edition was published before 1645. His social prominence, his eloquence, and his great personal charm were mainly responsible for his popularity in his own time. To-day he is remembered for his use of the couplet and for a few graceful lyrics that express the courtly ideals of the age.

ON A GIRDLE

6. **pale,** enclosure.

RICHARD LOVELACE

The Cavalier poet Richard Lovelace was born at Woolwich in 1618, the scion of an old Kentish family. He was educated at the Charterhouse and at Oxford, where he was advanced to the M.A. degree, after only two years attendance, at the request of a great lady in her admiration for his handsome appearance and fine parts. Thereafter he employed his time at court or in the field. On the attainment of his majority he took possession of large holdings in Kent and was selected to present the Kentish petition to Parliament in the King's behalf. For the offense he was committed to prison for a few weeks, within which time he wrote his celebrated *To Althea from Prison*. He aided the king by personal service and by the use of his ample fortune. He was abroad for a while after the fall of the monarchy, but returned to London and lived in poverty and wretchedness until his death in 1658. He was a follower of Donne, probably his closest disciple, and a fastidious writer of "conceits." A few of his lyrics have achieved great popularity.

380b TO LUCASTA, ON GOING TO THE WARS

4. **To war and arms,** Lovelace served against the Scots in 1639 and took the Cavalier side in the Civil War in 1642.

TO ALTHEA, FROM PRISON

10. **no allaying Thames,** undiluted.

ANDREW MARVELL

Andrew Marvell was born at Winestead in Yorkshire. He attended the Hull Grammar School under his father's tuition and entered Cambridge as a sizar in 1633. After 1638, when he was awarded the B.A. degree, little is known of him for a dozen years. He came into intimate contact with the new government first in 1651 as tutor in the family of Lord Fairfax in Yorkshire. In 1657 he was made Milton's colleague in the Latin secretaryship. Meanwhile he became preëminently the poet of Cromwell and the Commonwealth, but as only one of his poems in defense of the new order was published, his associations were not in his way at the Restoration. He entered Parliament in 1660 and continued actively in public life, particularly by the use of his pen as a satirist though rarely publishing his productions of this kind, until his sudden death in 1678. His literary work is varied. He was known in his day as a pamphleteer, and by the succeeding age as a political satirist. Both these reputations are past, and he now stands out in some vividness of outline as a poet of the pre-Restoration period. His amatory addresses and the verses that reveal his delight in natural charms represent him in his best vein.

381a TO HIS COY MISTRESS

Compare Donne's *The Computation*, p. 270, for similar imagery.

7. **Humber.** The poet was born near the mouth of the Humber river in Yorkshire.
11. **vegetable love,** etc., *i.e.*, growing or increasing like a plant.
40. **slow-chapt,** slowly consuming.
45 f. **our sun stand still.** Cf. Joshua x, 12 ff.

THE GARDEN

381b 29. **Apollo hunted Daphne.** See note to *Comus*, l. 661.
31. **Pan did after Syrinx speed.** The beautiful nymph Syrinx fled the embraces of the rustic Pan. On the bank of the river Ladon she prayed for succor and was changed into a reed. The sound of the wind-swayed reeds charmed her pursuer and he tried to reproduce it. Getting seven reeds of unequal length he partially succeeded and thus fashioned the pipe or Syrinx which has been associated with his name.
57. **that happy garden-state,** the Garden of Eden.

HENRY VAUGHAN

Henry Vaughan, the "Silurist" by his own designation, was born of an ancient and honorable Welsh family in southern Wales. He entered Oxford but left without a degree. He then studied law for a while in London, but changed to medicine, and lived a practicing physician in high repute in his native Brecknockshire until his death. After passing through a crucial spiritual experience about 1647–1648 he produced his *Silex Scintillans* in 1650. The second part followed five years later. The two contain his best poetry. He lived nearly through the Restoration, dying in 1595, but was as much out of place in it as he had formerly been in the early Puritan régime. He remained unknown throughout most of the eighteenth century but has since been given a high and unique place in English poetry. He was much indebted to Herbert, but possessed a better wit. His mystic rapture is his main source of appeal.

382a THE RETREAT

1. **Happy those early days,** etc. The poet imagined himself to have lived in an innocent happy state before his birth into the world. Compare Wordsworth's *Ode on Intimations of Immortality*, which derives in part from this poem.

THE WORLD

382b 12. **knots,** love-knots.
38. **epicure.** See Chaucer's *Prologue*, l. 336 and note.
45. **sat counting by,** sat by enumerating or estimating.

383b DEPARTED FRIENDS

35. **Resume,** take back.
38. **perspective,** glass, telescope.

SIR THOMAS BROWNE

English prose has no more remarkable instance of a highly ornate yet pleasing style than that of Sir Thomas Browne. He was born in London of a good Cheshire family, and was educated at Winchester and Oxford. He was made B.A. in 1626 and M.A. three years later. He studied medicine at Leyden, where he received a degree. Upon his return he settled at Shipley Hall in Yorkshire for a few years and there wrote his most celebrated work, *Religio Medici*. In 1637 he was made M.D. of Oxford and removed to Norwich. His sympathies were with the Royalists in the Civil War, but he seems to have been as little affected by the strife as any considerable figure of the time. He prospered in his profession, grew renowned for his encyclopædic knowledge and his interest in science, was knighted by the King in 1671, and died in Norwich on the anniversary of his birth in 1682. The range of his interests is indicated by his best known works — the doctor's religion, *i.e.*, his own, in *Religio Medici*, popular errors or superstitions in *Pseudodoxia Epidemica*, and ancient burial customs in *Hydriotaphia or Urn-Burial*. His remarkable style echoes his curious-mindedness, his unusual learning, his tinge of melancholy, and his whimsical humor.

RELIGIO MEDICI

384a 8. **toad,** a venomous animal, according to the older notion.
18. **constellated,** astrologically fitted.
30. **composition,** agreement.
38. **Hydra.** See note to *Comus*, l. 605.
40 f. **set down by Solomon.** Cf. Proverbs viii, 4 ff.

384b 1. **Doradoes,** a general and popular name for a fish of the dolphin or porpoise family.
21 f. **this noble virtue,** charity.
25. **graffs,** grafts.

385a 17. **bushes,** wreaths of ivy hung by wine dealers at the doors of their shops.
25. **Adam assigned,** etc. See Genesis ii, 19 f.
29. **à la volée,** at random.
36. **Chiromancy,** palmistry.
40 f. **vagabond and counterfeit Egyptians,** gypsies, popularly thought to be Egyptians by race.

386a 38. Βατραχομυομαχία, "The Battle of the Frogs and Mice," a poem ascribed to Homer.

39. **S. and T. in Lucian.** Lucian was a celebrated Greek satirist, A.D. 120–200. In his *Judicium Vocalium* Sigma complains of Tau's interference with other consonants.

43. **Si foret in terris,** etc. "If it should be among mortals, Democritus would laugh." Democritus, *ca.* 460–*ca.* 357 B.C., was called "the laughing philosopher" because he laughed at the follies of mankind.

50 f. **Actius his razor.** Accius, according to Livy, cut a whetstone through with a razor.

53. **basilisco,** a piece of ordnance.

386b 26 ff. **Le mutin Anglois,** etc. "The obstinate English, and the swaggering Scotch, and the foolish French, and the cowardly Roman, and the rogue of Gascony, the proud Spaniard, and the drunken German."

30. **St. Paul,** etc. See Titus, Bk. I, 12 f.

40. **Heraclitus,** a celebrated Greek philosopher, *ca.* 535–*ca.* 475 B.C., called "the weeping philosopher."

387a 5. **Satyr,** a satire.

33. **quadrate,** agree.

46. **Non occides.** "Thou shalt not kill," the sixth commandment. Cf. Exodus xx, 13.

49. **Atropos,** the third Fate, who with her shears cut the thread of life.

387b 17. **the greatest affliction of Job,** the commiseration of his friends. See the Book of Job.

42. **Damon and Pythias,** Syracusans of the first half of the fourth century before Christ. Damon substituted for Pythias, under sentence of death, while the latter "set his house in order." On his return the offender was pardoned because of the fidelity of the two friends.

43. **Achilles and Patroclus.** Patroclus was the fast friend of Achilles, the hero of the *Iliad*. It was only by his death that Achilles was aroused from his sulks to proceed to the destruction of Troy.

46. **lay down his life,** etc. See John xiv, 13.

388a 18. **two natures in one person,** Christ, who was both human and divine.

19. **three persons in one nature,** the Trinity.

19 f. **one soul in two bodies,** the ideal of true love.

388b 26. **the story of the Italian.** He deluded his enemy into a renunciation of his faith to save his life and then slew him to prevent repentance and insure eternal death.

389a 3. **battle of Lepanto,** a naval victory of the Italians and Spaniards over the Turks, October 7, 1571.

11. **peccadillo,** a slight offense.

29 f. **that lecher,** etc. Pygmalion, a sculptor and king of Cyprus. He fashioned an image of the nymph Galatea and fell in love with it. At his earnest importunities Aphrodite gave it life, and the new being became his wife.

31. **Spintrian,** from *spintry,* a male prostitute.

389b 30. **confusion of Babel.** Cf. Genesis xi, 1 ff.

51. **simpled,** gathered or studied herbs, botanized.

51. **Cheapside,** a well-known section of old London near the Thames.

390a 5. **Homer pined away,** etc. See Plutarch's Life of Homer.

11. **Euripus,** the channel between Eubœa and the mainland, remarkable for its changes of current.

17 f. **Peripatetics,** Stoics, or Academics, schools of Grecian philosophers.

20. **Janus,** an important Roman divinity, usually represented with two faces, one turned to the past and the other to the future.

390b 49 f. **Tacitus,** in the very first line. See *Annales* i.

51 ff. **Cicero . . . a perfect hexameter.** See *Pro Archia.*

391a 4. **ephemerides,** a calendar.

24 f. **those three noble professions,** medicine, law, and divinity.

391b 9 f. **Magnæ virtutes,** etc., "Neither great virtues, nor less vices."

14. **Antiperistasis,** the antagonism of natural qualities.

31 f. **the man without a navel,** Adam.

39. **Numquam minus,** etc. "Never less alone than when alone." — Publius Scipio.

392a 42 f. **Ruat cœlum,** etc. "Though the skies should fall, let Thy will be done."

392b 23. **Scorpius,** a southern constellation, eighth sign of the Zodiac.

24. **planetary hour of Saturn,** under the influence of Saturn.

41. **Galen,** a celebrated Greek physician of the second century after Christ.

393a 13. **Themistocles,** a famous Greek statesman and commander (d. *ca.* 460 B.C.), chiefly responsible for saving Greece from destruction by the Persians.

17. **Lucan and Seneca.** They were allowed by Nero to choose the manner of their deaths.

394a 7. **Peru,** synonymous with great wealth.

31. **Statists,** statesmen.

35. **the prophecy of Christ.** Cf. John xii, 8.

394b 23. **Copernicus,** 1473–1543, the founder of modern astronomy.

24. **Crambe,** tiresome repetition.

30. **summum bonum,** literally, the highest good, the end sought by all sects of philosophy.

38. **Pliny,** A.D. 23–79, a famous Roman naturalist.

39. **Boccaccio,** 1313–1373, Italian poet and

novelist, whose *Decameron* is one of the most celebrated collections of tales made during the Middle Ages.

JOHN MILTON

395a LETTER ON EDUCATION

5. **Master Hartlib,** 1600?–1670? a prominent Prussian philanthropist, who settled in London as a merchant about 1628.

395b 15. **Januas and Didactics,** abbreviated titles of educational works of Comenius, 1592–1671, a Czechic educational reformer.

25. **The end then of learning,** etc. One of the most celebrated definitions of education in any language.

396a 29. **praxis,** use, practice.

397a 22. **Lily,** William Lily, 1468?–1522, author of a celebrated Latin grammar.

23. **commencing,** finishing for a degree.

37. **grammar,** *i.e.*, Latin grammar.

397b 2. **Cebes,** a Greek philosopher and disciple of Socrates of the fifth century, B.C.

5. **Quintilian,** a teacher of oratory in Rome. The first two books of his *Institutio Oratoria* give his plan for the education of youth.

36. **Cato, Varro, and Columella,** Latin writers, authors of three important treatises dealing with agriculture, and all entitled *De Re Rustica*.

44. **one of Hercules' praises,** *i.e.*, the reclamation of land made waste by the ravages of some monster, as the Nemean lion or the wild boar of Erymanthus, both of which Hercules slew.

398a 6. **Theophrastus,** 372–287 B.C., a botanical writer, pupil of Aristotle.

8 f. **Vitruvius,** a contemporary of Augustus, author of *De Architectura*.

9. **Seneca's natural questions,** *Naturales Quæstiones*, chiefly on meteorology and astronomy.

10. **Mela, Celsus, Pliny, or Selinus,** Latin writers of the early Christian era on geography, medicine, and natural history.

16. **enginery,** engineering.

25. **a crudity,** indigestion.

47 f. **Orpheus, Hesiod,** etc. Greek and Roman poets from the earliest or mythical times to the fourth century after Christ.

398b 1. **Proairesis,** choice between right and wrong.

9 f. **the moral works of Plato,** etc., the moralizing or philosophical works of these celebrated Greek and Roman writers.

11. **Locrian remnants,** Timæus of Locris, fourth century before Christ, was one of the masters of Plato. A work "On the Soul of the World and Nature" has been ascribed to him.

25. **Trachiniæ, Alcestis,** plays, respectively, of Sophocles and Euripides, both of which deal with the suffering and sacrifice of a faithful wife.

36. **Moses.** Cf. Exodus xxiv, 12 ff., etc.

39. **Lycurgus, Solon,** etc., lawgivers of Sparta, Athens, and southwestern Italy and Sicily.

41. **Justinian,** called "the Great," 483–565, emperor of Rome and codifier of the Roman law.

399a 1. **Attic tragedies,** the plays of the Athenian tragic dramatists, Æschylus, Euripides, and Sophocles.

20 f. **Plato, Aristotle,** etc., Plato's *Phædrus*, for its discussion of rhetoric, Aristotle's *Rhetoric*, Phalerius' *Elocution* (?), Cicero's *Rhetorica*, Hermogenes' fine works on rhetoric, and Longinus' *On the Sublime*.

29. **Horace,** his *Ars Poetica*.

30 f. **Castlevetro, Tasso, Mazzoni,** Castlevetro's translation and exposition of Aristotle's *Poetics*, Tasso's *Discourses on Epic Poetry*, and Mazzoni's *Defense of Dante's Divine Comedy*.

399b 19. **Pythagoras, Plato,** etc. Pythagoras taught philosophy to a group of his disciples at Crotona in Italy; Plato founded the Academy; Isocrates had a school of rhetoric in Athens; Aristotle founded the peripatetic school of philosophy.

24. **Cyrene and Alexandria.** The former was celebrated for its school of medicine and its general intellectuality; the latter was the home of literature and science.

26 f. **a defect . . . of Sparta,** that both the legal and educational systems tended to encourage war.

30. **the gown,** the garment of peace.

401a 17 f. **Homer gave Ulysses.** See *Odyssey*, Bk. XXI.

THOMAS FULLER

Thomas Fuller was born at Aldwinkle in Northamptonshire, later the birthplace of Dryden. At thirteen he entered Cambridge and proceeded B.A. and M.A. He entered the church and enjoyed some appointments in the west but probably remained in the University until he obtained the B.D. degree in 1635. In politics he was a moderate, but leaned to the Royalist side. At the beginning of hostilities he surrendered his interests in the west and came up to London. During the conflict and the new order of government he lectured and preached and wrote, working mainly at his *Worthies of England*. At the Restoration he recovered his appointments, became D.D. by king's letters, and was made chaplain extraordinary to the King. He died of a fever in the summer of 1661.

His exuberant wit, his playfulness, kindliness, and simplicity, and his shrewd English sense endeared him to his time, and secured for him an enduring fame among the great masters of English prose. He was one of the earliest English writers to live by his pen unaided by the patronage of the great.

WORTHIES OF ENGLAND

JOHN TIPTOFT

40. **in this,** Bedfordshire. Fuller lists his worthies by counties.
49. **Civil Wars,** the Wars of the Roses.
401b 23. **de facto . . . de jure,** in fact . . . by right.

THOMAS CORIAT

41. **this county,** Somerset.
49 f. **ad duo . . . ad decem,** to the second degree . . . to the tenth.
52. **counters,** round pieces of metal used in making up accounts.
402a 5. **Prince Henry.** See note to Drummond's *Epitaph*, p. 272a, l. 2.

WILLIAM SHAKESPEARE

38. **this country,** Warwickshire, "the heart of England."
402b 21. **Poeta non fit,** etc. "The poet is not made, but born."
39. **anno Domini 16 —.** Fuller's ignorance of Shakespeare's death year indicates how little was known of the great poet in the seventeenth century.

RESTORATION AND EIGHTEENTH CENTURY

SAMUEL BUTLER

Samuel Butler was the son of a small farmer of Worcestershire. His formal education probably ended with his career in the Worcester Grammar School. As early as 1628 he seems to have been in attendance upon the Countess of Kent at Wrest in Bedfordshire, where he attained to some proficiency in painting. For a number of years he appears to have been clerk to a succession of country gentlemen, one of whom was Sir Samuel Luke of Cople Hoo near Bedford, a stiff Presbyterian and an officer in Cromwell's army, the original of Hudibras, though the satire is general rather than personal. He published nothing until he was nearly fifty years old, when an anonymous tract brought him an appointment with the Lord President of Wales and the stewardship of Ludlow Castle in 1660. A few months after his marriage in the same year he gave up his position, apparently in expectation of a competency from his wife's dower, which was never realized. The first part of *Hudibras*, published in 1663, brought him fame almost over night and strongly recommended him to the King. He was, however, allowed to live on in poverty and obscurity — probably he was not by nature easy to help — until his death by consumption in London in 1680. His satire, a mock-heroic romance like *Don Quixote*, was the most popular book of the Restoration because it expressed so well the scorn of the age for its antithetical predecessor, the Puritan régime. Its genuine wit and cleverness and its unusual verse, doggerellike in effect, have perpetuated the author's fame.

406a HUDIBRAS

1. **civil fury,** the Civil War in England, which culminated in the Commonwealth.
6. **punk,** bawdry.
13. **Sir Knight.** See the foregoing biography.
19 f. **Nor put up blow,** etc., nor endured blow except the one from his monarch which made him knight.
22. **chartel,** a letter of defiance, a challenge.
24. **swaddle,** bind up, swathe.
26. **styled of War,** etc. Sir Samuel Luke was a colonel in the Puritan army, as well as a justice of the peace.
406b 38. **As Montaigne,** etc. "When my cat and I entertain each other with mutual apish tricks . . . who knows but she laughs at, and censures my folly, for making her sport, and pities me for understanding her no better?" — *Essays*, Bk. II, xii.
40. **Sir Hudibras.** Butler probably took the name from Spenser's *Faerie Queene*, II, ii, 17.
407a 74. **Comittee-men and Trustees.** The former were committees appointed by Parliament, in certain counties, to fine and imprison.
91. **Babylonish,** Babel-like, confused.
100. **Babel.** Cf. Genesis xi, 1 ff.
113. **the orator,** Demosthenes.
118. **Tycho Brahe,** a celebrated Dutch astronomer, 1546–1601.
118. **Erra Pater,** probably a nickname for the

English astrologer, William Lilly, 1602–1681.

407b 143. **Entity and Quiddity,** abstract terms in scholastic philosophy.

150. **Irrefragable,** Alexander of Hales, a noted English theologian (d. 1245), surnamed "Doctor Irrefragabilis," *i.e.,* the "Invincible Doctor."

151. **Thomas,** Thomas Aquinas, an Italian theologian and scholastic philosopher, *ca.* 1225–1274, called the "Father of Moral Philosophy."

152. **Duns,** Duns Scotus, a famous Scotch scholastic philosopher, *ca.* 1265–*ca.* 1308.

175. **What Adam dreamt of,** etc. Cf. Genesis ii, 21 ff.

408a 228. **Like Mahomet's,** etc. Mahomet dreamed the angel Gabriel sent him a milk-white beast resembling an ass, to carry him into the presence of God. *Widgeon,* or silly fellow, is substituted for *pigeon,* which Mahomet trained to eat out of his ear, to give the impression that he received inspired messages from it.

232. **advowson,** right of appointment.

408b 249. **Samson's heart-breakers.** See Judges xiv-xvi.

256. **Cordeliere,** a strict Franciscan order in France, so named from the knotted cord worn about the waist by the adherent.

277. **Taliacotius,** an Italian physician and surgeon of the sixteenth century, who taught the transfer of sensations by grafting flesh for flesh.

281. **Nock,** buttocks, rump.

295. **white-pot,** a dish resembling rice- or bread-pudding, baked in a pot or bowl.

306. **siege of Bullen,** the siege of Boulogne in 1544 by Henry VIII.

409a 334. **farthingal,** a hoop skirt.

342. **nuncheons,** a light meal, or luncheon.

355. **Toledo,** a city in Spain celebrated for the manufacture of swords.

409b 368. **Serjeant Bum,** etc. See l. 287 f.

375. **dudgeon,** a short sword or dagger.

420. **With mouth of meal and eyes of wall,** mealy-mouthed and wall-eyed.

410a 453. **A Squire . . . Ralph.** Several persons have been suggested as the original of the squire. He represents the Anabaptists or Independents, religious sects of the time.

463. **The mighty Tyrian Queen,** Dido. See *Æneid,* I, 360 ff.

472. **Trojan Knight,** Æneas. See *Æneid,* VI.

410b 531. **Terra Incognita,** literally, unknown land, a term used in philosophical speculations.

535. **Sir Agrippa,** 1486–1535, a German philosopher and student of alchemy and magic. His *De Occulta Philosophia* was noted for its extravagance.

537. **Anthroposophus,** a nickname for Thomas Vaughan of Bedfordshire, author of *Anthroposophia Theomagica,* which Swift characterized as "the most unintelligible fustian that perhaps was ever published in any language."

537. **Floud,** Robert Floud of Kent, a physician and dealer in occult philosophy.

538. **Jacob Behmen,** a celebrated German mystic, 1575–1624.

411a 541. **Rosicrucian.** The Rosicrucians, a sect of self-styled philosophers during the seventeenth and early eighteenth centuries, claimed to be able to prolong life and to discover many secrets by means of magic formulæ.

562. **fair of Barthol'mew,** a fair formerly held at Smithfield in London, notorious for its licentious amusements.

579. **Knights o' th' Post,** infamous persons who attended the courts of law to swear for hire to things they knew nothing of.

594. **nimmed,** took, stole.

411b 599. **Like him that took,** etc. A story is told, by Henry Stephen (in his apology for Herodotus), of a rustic who bolted down the doctor's prescription and was cured.

636. **familiar,** a familiar spirit or attendant demon, often referred to in the literature of witchcraft. Witchcraft was much discussed during the late seventeenth century.

642. **Withers, Pryn, and Vickars,** Presbyterian poetasters and pamphleteers.

653. **th' forked hill,** Parnassus.

412a 678. **Isthmian and Nemean games,** national festivals of the ancient Greeks, the former being held on the Isthmus of Corinth in honor of Neptune, and the latter in the forest of Nemea in celebration of Hercules' triumph over the lion.

412b 714. **Pharos,** the lighthouse of Pharos, one of the seven wonders of the world.

722. **coincidere,** happen.

723. **Quantum in nobis,** a number of us.

732. **Cov'nant,** the solemn agreement drawn up by the Scotch in 1638 to uphold the Presbyterian doctrine and governmental ideas as the religion of the country. The adherents were fond of calling their party "the Cause."

738. **Though ev'ry *nare olfact* it not,** though every nose does not smell it.

743. **plus satis,** more than enough.

744. **cane et angue pejus,** worse than dog and serpent.

748. **cynarctomachy,** bear baiting with a dog. The word is a humorous invention of Butler.

754. **averruncate,** avert or ward off.

413a 773. **Indians,** Hindoos.

776. **mordicus,** valiant.

782. **boute-feus,** incendiaries.

812. **worshipping of Dagon.** See note to *Paradise Lost,* I, l. 462.

816. **ad amussim,** according to rule.

818. **Jure divino,** by divine right.
820. **Totidem verbis,** in just as many words.
827. **Provincial, or Parochial Classis,** a local governing body or tribunal.

413b 838. **Mira de lente,** marvelous things out of an insignificant matter.

847. **ejusdem generis,** of the same kind.

414a 892. **Mamaluke,** a member of a celebrated corps of cavalry which had great political power in Egypt down to the nineteenth century.

906. **the Phrygian Knight,** Laöcoön. See *Æneid*, II, 40 ff.

JOHN WILMOT, EARL OF ROCHESTER

The Earl of Rochester doubtless expended his best energies in living the life of a libertine, but his undoubted talent has left something worth while in English poetry. Born at Ditchley in Oxfordshire, he succeeded to the earldom, though without great possessions, at the age of ten. He attended school at Burford and entered Oxford as a fellow commoner, and was created M.A. when fourteen years old. He traveled in France and Italy, and saw naval service, but meanwhile was identified with the most dissolute of the courtier set. Though often out of favor, he enjoyed the closest intimacy with the King. His epigram on Charles is famous — he "never said a foolish thing, and never did a wise one." As the result of excesses his health failed in 1679. He repaired to his residence at Woodstock Park, a royal gift, made a death-bed confession, which has become famous, and died in 1680. His best talent is in satire, and his best strain is in his reactions from satiety. He is a free borrower, his *Satire against Mankind* being imitated from Boileau. His lyrical gift is sprightly, but his amorous verse, where he best employs it, is too often marked by obscenity and by artificiality of sentiment.

A SATIRE AGAINST MANKIND

15. **Errour's fenny bogs.** In his allegorical abstractions Rochester echoes Spenser, whom he read and admired.

415a 69. **Ingelo,** Nathaniel Ingelo, *ca.* 1621–1683, author of a religious romance called *Bentivolio and Urania.*

70. **Patrick's Pilgrim,** Simon Patrick, 1626–1707, an English divine, author of *The Parable of the Pilgrim*, etc.

70. **Sibb's Soliloquies,** Richard Sibbes, a prolific English devotional writer, 1577–1635.

86. **a whimsical philosopher,** Diogenes, a Greek Cynic philosopher *ca.* 412–323 B.C. See note to *Comus*, l. 708.

JOHN DRYDEN

Dryden was born of landed gentry at Aldwinkle in Northamptonshire. He attended Westminster School and entered Cambridge in 1650. After receiving his B.A. degree in 1654, he probably remained in the university three years longer. In 1657 or a year later he settled in London. By the family leanings he inclined to the Puritan side, hence his self-introduction to the world of letters in 1658 with an adulatory poem on the death of the Protector. But he was equally facile two years later when, in his courtly panegyric *Astræa Redux,* he welcomed Charles back to the English throne. His attainments were soon recognized in London by his election to the Royal Society in 1662. He was married the following year, in 1668 was created M.A. of Cambridge by king's request, and in 1670 was made poet laureate and city chronologer. The first fifteen years of his career were given mainly to play writing. Within this time he developed the heroic play, with its idealizations of character, its standards of classical drama borrowed from the French, and its refinements upon the old couplet measure. In the political and religious strife that began with the Popish Plot in 1678 and agitated rights of succession to the throne several times within the next ten years, he found opportunity for the exercise of his best talent — satire. In 1681 he contributed his brilliant political satire, *Absalom and Achitophel,* to the Tory cause, in the interests of the Catholic James. The next year came *The Medal,* directed against the Whigs, and *Mac Flecknoe,* a masterpiece of personal invective. James ascended the throne in 1685, and the same year Dryden became a Catholic. In defense of his new faith he produced two years later his last great satire, *The Hind and the Panther.* The revolution of 1688 brought ruin upon him, but he accepted his fate with dignity. With all his offices and awards gone, he turned to play making and translation for a living. But he is best seen in those years of misfortune as a sympathetic master and instructor of younger poets, as Jonson had been before him. He died in London in 1700. He was the first great English critic, the chief dramatist of a great dramatic period, and as a satirist has not been surpassed in the language. He was also a master of the classical ode in its adaptation in English. If one disregards the few who have written by the sheer magic of inspiration, he is one of the greatest figures in English literature.

416b ABSALOM AND ACHITOPHEL

The Earl of Shaftesbury, deposed minister of Charles II, had been active in behalf of Charles's illegitimate son, the Duke of Monmouth, as heir to the English throne, against the rightful heir, James, Duke of York, a Catholic. The poem was published late in 1681, when Shaftesbury was in the Tower awaiting trial for high treason. Despite its manifest design to influence the public and the jury, Shaftesbury was acquitted. He is represented in the poem as Achitophel and Absalom is the unfortunate Monmouth. The scriptural parallel was in the air before Dryden adopted it. For the original, see 2 Samuel xv ff.

7. **Israel's monarch,** King David, representing Charles II. Israel is England.

11. **Michal,** the daughter of Saul who was given in marriage to David (cf. 1 Samuel xviii, 20 ff.), representing Charles II's queen, Catherine of Portugal.

13. **Several mothers bore.** See 2 Samuel iii, 2 ff.

18. **Absalom,** the third son of David. James Scott, Duke of Monmouth and Buccleuch, was the son of Charles II by Lucy Walters, a beautiful young woman of good Welsh family.

417a 30. **the charming Annabel,** Anne Scott, Countess of Buccleuch, to whom the Duke of Monmouth was married by the King's interference.

35. **Amnon's murder.** Cf. 2 Samuel xiii, 28 ff. Probably a reference to a brutal assault by some of Monmouth's troopers upon Sir John Coventry, a member of Parliament and a critic of the King's amours.

38. **Sion,** London.

41. **The Jews,** the English people.

53. **Saul,** Oliver Cromwell.

54. **Ishbosheth,** Richard Cromwell. Cf. 2 Samuel iii f.

55. **Hebron,** Scotland, where Charles had been crowned ten years before his coronation in England.

417b 78. **The Good Old Cause,** the cause of the Commonwealth.

81. **Jerusalem,** London.

82. **Jebusites,** Roman Catholics.

84. **the chosen people,** the Protestants.

104. **that Plot,** the Popish Plot.

418a 114. **Egyptian,** French.

418b 171. **the triple bond,** the Triple Alliance — England, Holland, and Sweden, against France (1668).

184. **Abbethdin,** an officer of the high court of justice of the Jews, who represents Shaftesbury as Lord Chancellor of England.

193. **one immortal song,** probably Psalms iii (cf. 2 Samuel xviii, 33), as Achitophel, according to the satirical interpretation, would then not have prevailed upon Absalom to rebel.

419a 209. **the king himself a Jebusite.** Charles died a Catholic and was probably sympathetic with the Catholic interests throughout his reign.

419b 260. **Gath,** Brussels, where Charles while in exile long resided.

266. **Jordan's sand,** Dover.

277. **Pharaoh,** Louis XIV, in alliance with Charles.

420b 349. **His brother,** James Duke of York, later James II.

421a 386. **Sanhedrin,** the supreme council of the Jews; Parliament.

422a 509. **Solymæan rout,** the London rabble.

422b 513. **Ethnic plot,** the Popish Plot.

515. **Hot Levites,** etc., Presbyterian clergymen, forced out of the Church of England in 1662 by the Act of Uniformity.

516. **the Judges' days,** the Commonwealth.

521. **Aaron's race,** the priesthood.

537. **Hydra.** See note to l. 605 of Milton's *Comus.*

540. **Zimri.** The brilliant and unscrupulous genius, George Villiers, Duke of Buckingham, had satirized Dryden in *The Rehearsal.* The portrait is one of the best in satirical literature.

546. **chymist,** chemist.

423a 555. **In squand'ring wealth.** By the accident of the Restoration he came into an estate of £20,000 a year, which he was at liberty to squander in any way his wild brain directed.

570. **Balaam,** the Earl of Huntingdon.

570. **Caleb,** Lord Grey.

571. **canting Nadab,** Lord Howard of Escrick, a debauchee now and then turned pious.

577. **bull-faced Jonas,** Sir William Jones, the attorney general who directed the prosecution against offenders in the Popish Plot.

580. **Heav'n's anointed,** David. Cf. 2 Samuel xvi, 5 ff.

581. **Shimei,** Slingsby Bethel, one of the two Whig sheriffs of London, a writer against both the Commonwealth and royalty.

591. **vare,** a wand or staff of authority.

594. **The sons of Belial,** the Whigs.

423b 613. **Rechabite.** Cf. Jeremiah xxxv, 14.

628. **Corah,** Titus Oates, contriver of the Popish Plot. Cf. Numbers xvi.

630. **the serpent,** etc. Cf. Numbers xxi, 8 ff.

639. **Stephen.** Cf. Acts vi, 11 ff.

424a 672. **Agag's murther.** Cf. 1 Samuel xv, 8 ff. Sir Edward Berry Godfrey, the magistrate before whom Oates made his deposition, was mysteriously murdered soon afterward.

424b 693. **Hybla-drops.** Hybla in Sicily was celebrated for its honey.

701. **Tyrus,** Holland.

706. **Bathsheba,** the Duchess of Portsmouth.

425a 734. **Issachar,** Thomas Thynne of Wiltshire, who extended hospitality to

Monmouth in his progress through the kingdom in 1680.

746. **a brother and a wife.** Oates tried to involve both the Duke of York and Queen Catherine in his plot.

425b 813. **Barzillai.** Cf. 2 Samuel xix, 31 ff. The aged Duke of Ormond was a companion in exile, and later a loyal servant, to Charles.

816. **In regions waste,** etc. As Lord Lieutenant of Ireland, Ormond had served the Royalist cause across the Irish Channel.

426a 827. **His eldest hope.** The Earl of Ossory, a distinguished seaman and warrior, died of a fever in 1680.

860. **Zadoc the priest,** the Archbishop of Canterbury.

426b 862. **the Sagan of Jerusalem,** the Bishop of London, Henry Compton, son of the Earl of Northampton.

864. **Him of the western dome,** John Dolben, dean of Westminster.

866. **The prophet's sons,** the boys of Westminster School.

873. **Adriel,** the Earl of Mulgrave, John Sheffield, patron to Dryden, himself a gifted poet.

878. **Jothan,** the Marquis of Halifax, George Savile, a poet and political peacemaker.

884. **Hushai,** Viscount Hyde. Cf. 2 Samuel xv ff.

895. **Amiel,** Edward Seymour, Speaker of the House of Commons from 1673 to 1679.

906. **th' unequal ruler of the day,** Phæton, son of Apollo, who came to disaster while trying to guide the sun chariot across the heavens.

427a 940. **Th' offenders,** etc. The Whigs had questioned the King's pardoning power over offenders against the state.

427b 951. **my young Samson,** etc. Cf. Judges xvi, 25 ff.

978. **Esau's hands,** etc. Cf. Genesis xxvii, 22.

MAC FLECKNOE

The poet Richard Flecknoe (d. 1678) was a Catholic priest of Irish descent. Dryden selected him apparently for no other reason except that for years he had had the reputation of being a bad poet.

T. S. is Thomas Shadwell, Dryden's rival and enemy. Shadwell had scurrilously abused Dryden in an answer to *The Medal.*

428b 29. **Heywood and Shirley,** Thomas Heywood and James Shirley, late Elizabethan dramatists, in no sense contemptible, as Dryden, perhaps through ignorance of their writings, here makes them.

33. **Norwich drugget,** a coarse woolen fabric, apparently associated with the poorer class of poets.

36. **King John of Portugal.** Flecknoe visited Portugal and boasted of the king as his patron.

42. **Epsom blankets,** a reference to a scene in which a person is tossed in a blanket in Shadwell's *Virtuoso* and to his play of *Epsom Wells.*

43. **the new Arion.** Arion was a Greek musician of about 700 B.C. Shadwell boasted of his skill in music.

429a 51. **St. André,** a popular French dancing master of the time.

52. ***Psyche,*** a bad operatic piece by Shadwell.

55. **Singleton,** a musician and opera singer of the time.

57. **Villerius,** a leading character in Davenant's *Siege of Rhodes.*

62. **Augusta,** a Roman name for London. At the time London was in constant fear of popish plots.

70. **a Nursery,** a theater erected under royal patent in 1664 to train young actors for the stage.

74. **Maximins.** Maximin is a ranting hero in Dryden's own early play of *Tyrannic Love.*

75. **Great Fletcher,** John Fletcher. See p. 271 and notes.

76. **greater Jonson,** Ben Jonson. See p. 266 and notes.

77. **Simkin,** a stage clown of the time.

80. **Panton,** a celebrated punster, according to some references.

83. **Dekker,** Thomas Dekker. See p. 266 and notes.

89. **Raymond families . . . tribes of Bruce.** Raymond and Bruce are characters respectively in Shadwell's *Humorists* and *Virtuoso.*

429b 93. **Bunhill . . . Watling Street,** near each other in the older part of London.

98. **Ogleby,** John Ogleby, 1600–1676, a Scotch translator and bad poet.

101. **Herringman,** Dryden's London publisher for a number of years.

104. **Ascanius,** Shadwell — an adaptation from Virgil.

108 f. **As Hannibal,** etc. According to Livy, Hannibal, at nine years of age, was required by his father to swear eternal hatred against Rome.

118. ***Love's Kingdom,*** a play by Flecknoe, the only one ever acted.

430a 147 f. **gentle George,** etc. Sir George Etheredge, a leading comic dramatist of the time. Dorimant, Loviet, etc., are characters in his plays.

159. **Sedley,** Sir Charles Sedley, a brilliant wit and minor poet of the time, suspected of aiding Shadwell in his *Epsom Wells.*

164. **Sir Formal,** a character in *The Virtuoso,* called by the author "the orator, a florid coxcomb."

168. **Jonson's hostile name.** Shadwell praised

Ben Jonson as a comic dramatist so lavishly as to intimate kinship with him.

175. **Prince Nicander,** a character in Shadwell's *Psyche.*

430b 201. **wings display and altars raise,** referring to fanciful verse forms of the metaphysical poets. See George Herbert's *Easter Wings* and *The Altar,* p. 368 f.

206. **Bruce and Longville,** characters in the *Virtuoso,* who dispose of Sir Formal by a trap.

DANIEL DEFOE

Defoe is generally acknowledged the greatest journalist in English literature. The son of James Foe, a London butcher and Nonconformist, he attended a Dissenters' school for three or four years, but did not proceed to the university. Except for a brief experience as a soldier, his interests for some score of years were mainly commercial. His arrival in English literature came in 1701 with his *True-born Englishman,* which brought him wide popularity and royal favor. It was followed the next year with equal effectiveness but with loss of favor by his prose satire, *The Shortest Way with the Dissenters.* In his *Review,* 1704, he anticipated in several vital particulars Addison and Steele in the *Tatler* and *Spectator* papers. When he was nearly sixty, he began with *Robinson Crusoe,* 1719, that remarkable series of prose fictions which constitute his greatest work and which proclaim him our first regular novelist. He died in London in 1731. His tireless energy, his variety, his remarkably simple, straightforward style, his journalistic sense for "news value," his gift for making fiction read like fact, and his marvelous productiveness in the domain of realistic narrative are the chief reasons for his fame.

THE TRUE-BORN ENGLISHMAN

The poem was a reply to the general objection to King William, 1689–1702, as a foreigner, and to the specific attack by the satirist Tutchin upon him as a Dutchman. It immediately turned the tide of public favor toward the King. It ran through many editions and was widely read.

431b 60. **Luther, Calvin, or by Rome,** *i.e.,* the Church of England, the dissenting branches, or, the Roman Catholic Church, in the satirist's own country and time.

432b 160. **the Norman Bastard,** William the Conqueror, the natural son of Robert, Duke of Normandy, and Helena, daughter of a tanner of Falaise.

433a 196. **fifth Henry's time,** Henry V, king of England, 1413–1422.

204. **Walloons,** the people of southern Belgium chiefly, descended from the ancient Belgæ, with a mixture of Germanic or Roman elements.

205. **Vaudois,** Waldensians, a reforming body of Christians, under Peter Waldo of Lyons, from about 1170.

205. **Valtolins,** inhabitants of Valtellina, a small district in northern Italy.

213. **David at Hackelah.** Cf. 1 Samuel xxiii, 19 ff.

218. **The royal branch,** etc. James VI of Scotland became James I of England.

222. **Tay,** the longest river in Scotland.

224. **the locusts,** etc. Cf. Exodus x, 4 ff.

433b 243. **Lindsey,** etc., representatives of English noble houses on the Royalist side in the Civil War.

249. **Italian Castlemain.** Lady Castlemaine and Duchess of Cleveland was the mistress of Charles II, by whom she became the mother of the Dukes of Cleveland, Grafton, and Northumberland.

250. **Portsmouth,** the Duchess of Portsmouth, mother of the Duke of Richmond by Charles II.

250. **Tabby Scott,** doubtless Lucy Walters (see note to *Absalom and Achitophel,* l. 18).

250. **Cambrian,** Welsh. Nell Gwyn is said (doubtfully) to have been the daughter of Captain Thomas Gwyn, "of an ancient family in Wales." The name appears to be of Welsh origin. She was the mother of the Duke of St. Albans by Charles.

256. **Schomberg.** Friedrich von Schomberg, a Prussian general, accompanied William of Orange to England and was made Duke of Schomberg.

256. **Portland.** William Bentinck of Holland, personal attendant and diplomatic agent of William of Orange, went with him to England, and was made first Earl of Portland.

434a 304. **Wales strove to separate,** etc. Wales was not subjugated by the Romans, the Germanic tribes, or the Normans, and acknowledged but a half-fealty to England until conquered by Edward I in 1277.

434b 361. **Blue-coat Hospitals, and Bridewell,** Charity schools such as Christ's Hospital. The Bridewell, originally a school of the same kind, later became a reformatory.

ABRAHAM COWLEY

Abraham Cowley was born a posthumous child in a family of seven in London. At fifteen, while he was in Westminster School, he produced his first volume of poetry. He continued his writing in Cambridge and seems to have become a major fellow there. Ejected in 1643, he repaired to Oxford and there became intimate with the Royalist leaders. For ten years after 1646 he was a member of the royal household in France. He was back in England seeking retirement in 1656, when the most important edition of his poems was published. It included in addition to the poems of the *Mistress*, which had been for ten years the favorite love poems of the age, his Pindaric odes and his ponderous unfinished epic *Davideis*. At the Restoration he retired to private life at Barn Elms and Chertsey, and died in 1667. His reputation was highest in his own time when he was regarded as a model of the cultivated poet. He survives to-day in the few examples of his poetry where he condescends to be unaffected, and in his simple, graceful, charming essays, among the first of their kind in the language.

435a ODE VI, etc.

15. **the horse,** pack horse.
24. **Nestor,** King of Pylus, the oldest counsellor of the Greeks against Troy.

THE RESURRECTION

435b 14. **quire,** choir.
436a 54. **Pindaric,** Pindar, *ca.* 522–478 B.C., the greatest of the Greek lyric poets and father of the ode in western literatures, whom Cowley is imitating.

JOHN DRYDEN

MRS. ANNE KILLIGREW

Anne Killigrew, niece to the dramatists Thomas and William Killigrew, died in 1685 at the age of twenty-five. An edition of her poems was issued the same year. Dryden's ode was published in the volume. In Dryden's day the title "Mrs." was used for both married and unmarried women.

436b 26. **Thy father,** Henry Killigrew, a divine, who wrote a tragedy, *The Conspiracy*, which was published in 1638.
33. **Sappho,** a Greek lyric poetess who flourished about 600 B.C., known as "the Tenth Muse." Of her nine books of lyrics all are lost except a single ode to Aphrodite and a few fragments.
43. **trine,** the favorable aspect of two stars 120° apart.
437a 68. **Arethusian stream.** See note to l. 85 of *Lycidas*.
82. **Epictetus,** a Stoic philosopher of the first century after Christ. Dryden probably confused him with Diogenes.
437b 103. **demains,** demesnes, domains.
103. **the Dumb Sister,** the muse of Painting.
128. **Our martial king,** James II.
438a 134. **Our Phœnix queen.** Mary of Este, queen of England, was "as eminent for beauty as rank." See note to l. 18 of *A Praise of His Lady*, p. 203.
162. **Orinda,** Mrs. Katherine Philips, 1631–1664, "The Matchless Orinda." Both she and Anne Killigrew died of smallpox.
165. **her warlike brother,** Henry Killigrew, a naval officer, who rose ultimately to the rank of admiral.
438b 175. **Pleiads,** the seven stars, part of the constellation Taurus.
180 f. **Valley of Jehosophat.** Cf. Joel iii, 2, 12.

A SONG FOR ST. CECILIA'S DAY

St. Cecilia was a Christian martyr of the third century and by tradition the patron saint of music. From about 1683 a musical society in London had been celebrating November 22 annually as St. Cecilia's Day.

439a 17. **Jubal.** See Genesis iv, 21.
44. **The sacred Organ.** Cecilia is represented by the poet, perhaps without authority, as being the inventress of the organ.

439b ALEXANDER'S FEAST

The poem celebrated the Feast of St. Cecilia in London in 1697. The historical time is after the battle of Arbela in 351 B.C.

1. **for Persia won,** celebrating the conquest of Persia.
2. **Philip's warlike son,** Alexander the Great.
9. **Thais,** an Athenian courtesan, mistress of Alexander, reputed to have incited him to fire the Persian palace at Persepolis.
20. **Timotheus,** musician to Alexander, not to be confused with the celebrated Athenian poet who lived also, though a little earlier, in the fourth century before Christ.
28. **A dragon's fiery form,** etc. The poet represents Jove as wooing Olympia(s), Alexander's mother, in the form of a dragon and begetting, or inspiring the conception of, her all-conquering son.
29. **spires,** coils.
440a 75. **Darius,** Darius III, the last king of Persia.
440b 97. **Lydian,** sweet, melting.
441a 132. **Furies,** etc. See note to l. 109 of Sackville's *Induction*.

WILLIAM CONGREVE

William Congreve was preëminently a dramatist. He was born at Bardsey near Leeds, and on the removal of the family to Ireland was educated, a contemporary and friend of Swift, in the famous Kilkenny School and at the University of Dublin. From the university he entered the Middle Temple but soon gave up law for literature. He began his dramatic career in 1692 and was highly successful until the end of the century, when, finding the public taste changing, under the attacks of Collier, toward a reformed drama, he gave up the profession of playwright and in several public appointments lived a life of ease and literary sovereignty until his death in 1729. He was a writer of poems, as well as plays, but these have not generally added to his fame.

441b ODE

At a time when ode writing was popular, this ode was written to correct the mistaken notion that the English ode of the time, following the examples of Cowley, was a true imitation of Pindar, and to some extent to show by example what a genuine Pindaric should be.

2. **Calliope,** the muse of Heroic Poetry. The Muses were the daughters of Zeus and Mnemosyne (Memory).
3. **Anna,** Anne, daughter of James II, queen of England, 1702–1714.
7. **Castalian spring,** a fountain on the slope of Parnassus, sacred to Apollo and the Muses.
14. **Pierian heights,** the legendary birthplace of Orpheus and the Muses in northern Thessaly.
16. **Alcides,** Hercules.
19. **Cyllene's shady Hill,** the mountain on which Hermes or Mercury was born, in Arcadia.
23. **Latona's son,** Apollo.

442a 35. **Mantuan.** Mantua was the early home and probably the birthplace of Virgil.

35. **Mæonian,** Homeric. According to one account, Homer was a native of Mæonia in Asia Minor.
41. **Boyn,** a river in Ireland, beside which William III defeated the army of James II in 1690.
43. **Augusta,** London.
45. **Tithon,** Tithonus. See note to p. 224a, l. 56.
56. **Halcyon.** See note to Gower's *Ceix and Alceone*, p. 160b.
61. **a world of wars,** the war of the Spanish Succession.

442b 75. **Zembla,** Nova Zembla, in the Arctic Ocean, north of Russia.

82. **Astræa,** the goddess of Justice.
84. **Marlbro',** John Churchill, first duke of Marlborough, the greatest military genius produced by the war of the Spanish Succession.
90. **Ister,** Latin name of the Danube River.
95. **When bold Bavaria,** etc. The celebrated Battle of Blenheim (a Bavarian village on the Danube) was fought on August 13, 1704. Marlborough was its hero. See Addison's *The Campaign*, p. 471.

443a 117. **Belgia,** Belgium.

117. **Brabant,** the Netherlands.
118. **Ramilia's day.** The triumph at Ramillies in Belgium, May 23, 1706, was one of Marlborough's great achievements, as it meant the expulsion of the French from the Low Countries.
119. **Cannæ . . . Pharsalia.** See note to ll. 410, 422 of Sackville's *Induction*.

JOHN WILMOT, EARL OF ROCHESTER

43b UPON DRINKING IN A BOWL

Paraphrased from a song ascribed to the ancient Greek poet Anacreon.

11. **Maestrick,** a city in the Netherlands captured by the French in 1673. The English were allies of the French.

444a 15. **Sir Sidrophel,** an astrologer in Butler's *Hudibras*.

JOHN OLDHAM

The poet John Oldham, born at Shipton-Moyne in Gloucestershire, was the son of a Nonconformist divine who was "silenced" when the poet was only ten years old, and the lad consequently was brought up in straitened circumstances. He had a career at Oxford, however, but quit on receiving the B.A. degree in 1670, although his attainments were recognized. He became usher in a school at Croydon, where Rochester and other courtiers sought his acquaintance from an interest in his wit. As a tutor in various places in or about London, he came to know the literary celebrities and won favor by his satires. He died of smallpox near Nottingham in his thirtieth year. In his satires he displayed original power and was capable of strong invective, but he is perhaps best in the care-free small way of the libertine, suggestive of Rochester.

THE CARELESS GOOD FELLOW

1. **this fooling and plotting of late,** in reference to the Popish Plot of 1678 and subsequent events deriving from it.
9. **Tyburn,** a place of execution near Hyde Park in London.

444b 15. **damn us to woollen,** condemn us to woolen garments instead of silken as becomes gentlemen.

20. **right and succession.** England was much agitated over the matter of Charles II's successor, whether it should

be the Protestant Duke of Monmouth or the Catholic Duke of York. See Dryden's *Absalom and Achitophel* and notes.

25. **leagues with the Hollander.** The chief business of Sir William Temple's life from about 1665 till 1680 was arranging treaties in some way involving Holland. He succeeded in a general pacification only about 1680.

26. **Sidney and Monsieur D'Avaux.** Algernon Sidney, 1622–1683, an English statesman, commissioned to intrigue with the French monarch, was implicated in the Rye House Plot and beheaded. Count D'Avoux, 1640–1709, a French diplomat, helped to negotiate the treaty of Nymwegen in 1678.

27. **Cassel,** a town in France, taken by the French from the Prince of Orange in 1677.

31. **The bully of France,** Louis XIV.

39. **Smithfield,** a place in the older part of London where in Queen Mary's day heretics were burnt.

40. **Mr. Fox,** John Foxe, author of the *Book of Martyrs*. See p. 213.

JOHN POMFRET

John Pomfret was born at Luton in Bedfordshire, the son of the vicar of the place. He was educated at the Bedford Grammar School and at Cambridge, where he received both the B.A. and M.A. degrees. Taking orders, he became rector of Maulden in his native shire in 1695. He had already begun to dabble in verse. In 1700 appeared his *The Choice,* which for the general reader is almost his only claim to remembrance. It was vaguely fashioned on Sir William Temple, and in neatly turned verse represents the "empty epicureanism of a cultivated man." Johnson said of it, "Perhaps no poem of our language has been so often perused." Pomfret died at Maulden in 1702.

446a THE CHOICE

94. **friends to Cæsar,** loyal to their sovereign.

446b 157. **I'd have no wife.** This declaration stood in the way of Pomfret's preferment with the Bishop of London. Pomfret had been married at Luton eight years before.

ABRAHAM COWLEY

447a OF OBSCURITY

24. **Mr. Broom,** Alexander Broom or Brome, 1620–1666, whose songs are said to have greatly aided the Restoration.

35. **Quintilian,** a Roman rhetorician, A.D. 35–95.

447b 17. **Achates,** the faithful attendant of Æneas in Virgil's *Æneid.*

24 f. **Demosthenes' confession.** The story is told by Cicero in his *Tusculan Disputations,* v, 103.

37. **Epicurus.** See note to Chaucer's *Prologue,* l. 336.

448a 28. **Bucephalus,** the favorite horse of Alexander the Great.

29. **Incitatus,** the horse of the Roman emperor Domitian, A.D. 51–96.

40. **that of St. Peter.** See Acts v, 15.

43. **Cato and Aristides,** Cato "the Censor," a Roman statesman, 234–149 B.C.; Aristides, an Athenian statesman and general of the fifth century before Christ, surnamed "the Just."

448b 13. **Augustus,** Octavius Cæsar, 63 B.C.–A.D. 14, the first Roman emperor.

OF MYSELF

32 f. **these precedent discourses.** Cowley's essays were first published as *Several Discourses,* etc., in 1668, the year after his death.

449a 30. **Horace might envy,** etc. The country villa of the Roman poet Horace, 65–27 B.C., given him by his friend Mæcenas, was situated in the Sabine Hills. It is celebrated in his poetry.

449b 16. **that violent public storm,** the Civil War, which ended with the establishment of the Commonwealth.

48 f. **business of great and honorable trust.** During part of the exile of the King and Queen Cowley was intrusted with their correspondence in cipher.

450b 38. **Take thy ease.** Cf. Luke xii, 16 ff.

44. **Non ego perfidum,** etc. I took no oath upon it.

SIR WILLIAM TEMPLE

The events of Sir William Temple's life belong to statecraft rather than to letters. He was born in London, spent his early years at Penshurst in Kent in the absence of his father as master of the rolls in Ireland, attended Cambridge without taking a degree, and spent many years at home and abroad as a diplomat. He retired to private life in 1680. After 1686 he lived at Moor Park in Surrey, where he had as secretary the rising young genius Jonathan Swift, and interested himself in gardening and literature until his death. In all his writing he gives the impression of "the gentleman at his ease." In his essays, or *Miscellanea,* he touches on a variety of subjects, and, without treating anything deeply, treats all with an ease and grace that mark him as a writer of unusual taste. He shares with Dryden the honor of writing the first English prose that can properly be called modern. His style was greatly admired and often imitated during the eighteenth century.

451a OF HEROIC VIRTUE

9. **Canaries and Maderas,** islands off the northwest coast of Africa.

20. **Tercera islands,** the Azores.

22. **Columbo,** Christopher Columbus.

30 f. **a certain Prince of Wales,** Madoc, who is said to have founded a colony in a land across the sea to the southwest of Ireland.

32. **The Ancient Carthaginians.** Most of the older nations have had claims advanced at some time or other of discovering America prior to Columbus.

451b 20. **Montezuma,** Montezuma II, 1477?–1520, Aztec war chieftain or "emperor" of Mexico at the time of the Spanish conquest.

49. **Atahualpa,** 1495?–1533, a sovereign of Peru, captured, mistreated, and at length executed by the Spaniards during their conquest of the country.

452a 21. **Mango Copac,** Manco Capac, the traditional founder of the Inca monarchy in Peru.

24. **a mighty lake,** Lake Titicaca, between Peru and Bolivia.

452b 50. **Cozco,** the present Cuzco, in southern Peru.

454a 7. **Acosta.** José de Acosta, 1540–1600, a Jesuit historian and archæologist, was in Peru and Mexico for several years between 1570 and 1590.

10. **Lycurgus,** a Spartan lawgiver, probably of the ninth century before Christ.

10. **Numa,** Numa Pompilius, the second king of Rome, 715–672 B.C., according to legend the author of many Roman institutions.

455b 42. **Pachacamac,** the supreme deity of the ancient Peruvians. A coastal town by this name, a few miles south of Lima, contains extensive ruins of a very old temple.

JOHN DRYDEN

OF HEROIC PLAYS

The "heroic plays" dealt with highly idealized persons placed in impossible situations and in remote settings. They treated of love and honor and employed exaggerated language, according to the approved method of heroic romance, as established in particular by Ariosto. Dryden's play, *The Conquest of Granada*, to which was prefixed his "*Essay*" in 1672, was the play *par excellence* of the type.

456a 5. **heroic verse,** a form of verse adapted to the treatment of lofty themes, in English iambic pentameter (five-accent) measure rhyming in couplets.

456b 23 f. **Sir William D'Avenant,** 1606–1668, an important figure in English drama bridging the gap from 1642 to 1660, and chief among the early Restoration dramatists.

457a 6 f. ***Siege of Rhodes,*** first brought out in 1656 as a kind of opera.

36. **Ariosto,** a great Italian poet, 1474–1533, author of the heroic poem, *Orlando Furioso.*

39 f. **Le donne, i cavalier,** etc. I sing of ladies, knights, arms, loves, courtesy, and bold enterprises.

457b 44. **Petronius Arbiter,** a Roman satirical "novelist" of the first century after Christ.

50 ff. **Non enim res gestæ,** etc. For a poem should not deal with actual events, which historians do far better: but the poet should by suggestions and interventions of the gods give vent to a free inspiration that there may rather appear the prophecy of the inspired intelligence than the testimony of a scrupulously exact statement.

458a 5. **Lucan,** a Roman poet and prose writer, author of *Pharsalia,* an epic poem in ten books on the civil war between Cæsar and Pompey.

22. **Erictho,** a Thessalian witch consulted by Pompey in Lucan's *Pharsalia.*

27. **Statius,** a Roman poet, A.D. *ca.* 45–*ca.* 96, author of the epic *Thebais.*

27. **Tasso,** Torquato Tasso, 1544–1595, a celebrated Italian poet, author of the *Gerusalemme Liberata* ("Jerusalem Delivered").

458b 6. **Mr. Hobbs,** Thomas Hobbes, 1588–1679, a celebrated English philosopher.

27 f. **Mr. Cowley's verses before Gondibert.** See *To Sir William Davenant, upon His Two First Books of Gondibert,* etc.

33. **Davideis,** an epic poem, 1656, by Cowley on David, king of the Hebrews.

34. **Godfrey.** Tasso's poem was first issued under this title, from Godfrey of Bouillon, a leader in the First Crusade and hero of Tasso's *Jerusalem Delivered* (see p. 458a, l. 27).

48 ff. **Segnius irritant,** etc. Things sent through the ears stir the mind more tardily than those subjected to the faithful eyes.

459a 34. **Almanzor,** the hero of *The Conquest of Granada.*

43. **Rinaldo,** a famous warrior in Tasso's *Jerusalem Delivered.*

45. **Calprenède,** La Calprenède, 1610–1663, a French "novelist" and dramatist. Artaban is a character in his *Cléopâtre.*

459b 7 f. **Οἰνοβορὲς,** etc. Sot, having the eye of a dog and the head of a deer.

9. **Δημοβόρος,** etc. Tyrant King.

14. **Ἕλκετο,** etc. And drew his great sword from the sheath.

23 ff. **'Αλλ' ὅδ ἀνὴρ,** etc. But this man wishes

to be above all others, wishes to get possession of all, and to rule over all.

29 ff. **Honoratum si fortè,** etc. If perchance you restore Achilles, let him be active, wrathful, obstinate, sharp, let him deny native rights, and let him appropriate to himself everything by arms.

41 ff. **Venga egli,** etc. Let him (Godfrey) come or send, I will stand firm; arms and destiny will be arbiters between us. Whoever presents himself, there will ensue a tragedy to delight the foe. — *Ger. Lib.*, V, xliii, 5 ff. (Strunk).

460a 4. **Cyrus,** a figure in Madame Scudéry's *Artamène ou Le Grand Cyrus.*

5. **Oroondates,** a prominent character in Calprenède's romance, *Cassandra.*

10 f. **Almahide, of Ozmyn, and Benzayda,** characters in *The Conquest of Granada.*

24. **Cethegus,** Caius Cethegus, a character in Ben Jonson's *Catiline.*

460b 3. **juego de toros,** bullfight.

6. **Abdalla,** a brother of the King in *The Conquest of Granada.*

24. **Duke of Guise,** Henry Lorraine, fifth Duke of Guise, 1614–1664.

37. **Ast opere in tanto,** etc. But in so great a work it is lawful to be surprised by sleep.

JOHN EVELYN

The diarist Evelyn was a man of great probity of character as well as of singular polish of manner. He was born at Wotton in Surrey, which became celebrated as his home in his last years. He spent some time at Oxford, at twenty was left a considerable fortune by his father, and had a brief experience as a soldier in the Royalist cause. Hopeless of a return of the former régime, in 1652 he settled down at Sayes Court, Deptford, to the life for which he has since been remembered, gardening and literature. A decade or more before his death he returned to Wotton and died there in 1706. He is known almost exclusively by his Diary, which gives an admirable account of the life of a cultured English gentleman of the seventeenth century. It is remarkable for its unaffected simplicity and for its well-nigh perfect perspicuity of style and expression.

DIARY

461a

5. **Deptford,** a suburb of London.

462a 2. **the return of the Jews,** *i.e.*, from the Babylonian captivity.

17 f. **the Three Cranes,** the name of a tavern on Upper Thames Street.

462b 32. **non enim,** etc. Cf. Hebrews xiii, 14.

33 f. **London was,** etc. The great fire destroyed the London of the older times almost completely.

42. **When King James,** etc. James II fled England December 22, 1688.

463a 21 f. **Lord teach me,** etc. See Psalms xc, 12.

SAMUEL PEPYS

Pepys' name is a synonym for the best in private literature. The reason for his preëminence over all others in the field must be sought in the fact that, with his engaging personality and gift of expression, he least of all diarists expected his work to come to light. In this way he committed to record the most intimate suggestions of his active brain and fertile imagination. His *Diary* is therefore the acme of confessional writing. He was the son of a London tailor. He went to Cambridge for a while, was married early, obtained a clerkship in the navy office at the Restoration, and gradually rose to the Secretaryship of the Admiralty. He died at his favorite residence, Clapham, in 1703.

DIARY

51 f. **The King and the two dukes,** Charles II and the Dukes of York and Gloucester.

463b 22. **General Monk.** After the death of Richard Cromwell, General Monk as head of the army reorganized Parliament and became head of the new Council, which voted the restoration of the monarchy on May 1, 1660.

464a 3. **C. R.,** *Carolus Rex,* "Charles the King."

10. **'Beggar's Bush,'** a comedy by Fletcher and others.

18 f. **the Spanish Curate,** a comedy by Fletcher and Massinger.

465b 44. **a pair of Virginall's,** a popular musical instrument of the time, ancestor of the modern piano.

467a 28 f. **French,** etc. England was continually harassed in the reign of Charles II by the aggressions of Louis XIV of France in Alliance with other powers.

37. **'The Mayd's Tragedy,'** a tragic romantic drama by Beaumont and Fletcher.

38 f. **Sir Charles Sedley,** 1639?–1701, one of the most celebrated of the court poets and wits of the time.

JONATHAN SWIFT

Jonathan Swift, the greatest prose satirist in English, was born a posthumous child of English parents in Dublin in 1667. By the aid of his uncles he went through the Kilkenny School and the University of Dublin, finishing B.A. by special grace in 1686. After the revolution of 1688 he entered the household of Sir William Temple at Moor Park, where he became acquainted with Esther Johnson ("Stella") and wrote two of his greatest works, *A Tale of a Tub* and *The Battle of the Books*. Having taken orders, he returned to Ireland after the death of Temple in 1699, and was granted the living of Laracor near Dublin and other benefices. Stella joined him there in 1701, superintended his household, but with Mrs. Dingley occupied a separate establishment. From 1710 to 1713, the years of the celebrated *Journal*, he was a man of the highest consequence in London. In the same years his acquaintanceship with Esther Van Homerigh (" Vanessa ") ripened into a friendship which became a tragedy for her a few years later. After his appointment to the deanship of St. Patrick's he interested himself more in the affairs of Ireland. His principal works done then were the *Drapier Letters* in 1724 and *Gulliver's Travels* in 1726. Vanessa died in 1723 and Stella in 1728. Mental decay set in soon after, and finally Swift relapsed into complete insanity. He died peacefully in 1745. His epitaph, written by himself,

Ubi sæva indignatio
Cor ulterius lacerare nequit,

best explains the character of his work. He was a partisan writer, with an innate grudge against humanity, in everything he did, and he expressed his partisanship, in his savage animosity against his race, with all the vigor and fervor of his big inconsiderate genius.

467b JOURNAL TO STELLA

Stella was Esther Johnson, ward to Sir William Temple of Moor Park, where Swift met the young lady and became her tutor. There is a well-grounded belief that he was married to her about 1716. The *Journal* is addressed to both Stella and her companion, Mrs. Dingley, in his "little language," under a solemn pledge that it was to be shown to no one. *M. D.*, " my dears," stands for Stella and Dingley, though sometimes only for the former; *D.* is for Dingley; and *D. D.* is for Dingley and Stella, though at times only for the latter. *PDFR* and *Presto* represent Swift himself.

468a 9. **all the ministry.** Swift was an ardent Tory and a potent influence in the last ministry of Queen Anne. The reasons for his presence in London at the time were political. Owing to the personal dislike of the Queen he was rewarded for his services only with the deanery of St. Patrick's in Dublin.

32 f. **My head,** etc. Swift long suffered from fits of giddiness, which he attributed to indigestion from a surfeit of golden pippins in 1689.

48. **Vanhomrigh's,** *i.e.*, Vanessa and her mother.

468b 1. **Parvisol,** Swift's agent at Laracor, a Frenchman.

22. **Mr. Secretary,** Henry St. John, 1678–1751. He became Secretary of State in 1710 and was made Viscount Bolingbroke in 1714.

42. **Lord Keeper,** Sir Simon Harcourt.

42. **Mr. Harley,** Robert Harley, 1661–1724. He became premier and Earl of Oxford in 1711.

469b 29. **against a peace.** The War of the Spanish Succession had been waging since 1701. It was brought to a close by the Treaty of Utrecht in 1713.

36. **Parnell's poem,** *An Essay on the different styles of Poetry*, in verse.

53. **famous moving picture.** There were several exhibitions of the kind at the time. See the *Tatler*, No. 113.

470a 10. **Windsor or St. Patrick's,** *i.e.*, the bishopric of Windsor or the deanery of St. Patrick's in Dublin, as a reward for his services to the ministry.

13. **Lady Masham,** an intimate friend and keeper of the privy purse to Queen Anne.

JOSEPH ADDISON

Addison in his writings represents the acme of good taste and urbanity. His elegance, however, is not that of the courtier, certainly not the courtier of his time, but of an inherently well-regulated life, of a superb classical culture, and of a nature that was instinctively artistic. He was born at Milston in Wiltshire, the son of a prominent clergyman, attended the Charterhouse School, where he met Steele, and had an enviable career at Oxford. Winning some recognition by his writings in the last years of the century, when men of literary talent were in demand in political life, he made an extended sojourn abroad to prepare himself for a diplomatic career. He had just returned and was living in retirement in London at the time of the battle of Blenheim, when he was sought out by the Whig ministry to celebrate the victory in appropriate verse. His poem, fittingly called a "gazette in rhyme," was well received, and his preferment began, leading ultimately to the Secretaryship of State a year before his death in 1718. His play *Cato*, undramatic at best, was popular at the time for its accepted political significance. As a writer, however, he really found himself only in his association with Steele in the *Tatler* and *Spectator* papers, 1709–1712. Neither writer, strictly speaking, was the originator of the short familiar essay, but Addison soon proved himself the finished master of the type. His grace, his ease, his evident good breeding, and his prevailing genteel humor remain unexcelled in English literature.

471a THE CAMPAIGN

4. **Anna,** Queen Anne.
5. **great leader,** John Churchill, *ca.* 1650–1722, created Duke of Marlborough in 1702, a great English general in the War of the Spanish Succession, and hero of the poem.
13. **The haughty Gaul,** Louis XIV.
15. **Pirene's lofty barriers,** the Pyrenees Mountains. When Charles II of Spain died, bequeathing his crown to Philip of Anjou, the French King cried, "The Pyrenees no longer exist," *i.e.*, as a political barrier between France and Spain.
17. **Ausonia's states,** the Italian peninsula.
24. **Germania,** the countries of central Europe.
25. **Great Leopold,** Leopold I, 1640–1705, emperor of the Holy Roman Empire and one of the claimants to the Spanish throne.

471b 51. **Moselle,** a river in France which joins the Rhine at Coblenz.

472a 68. **Maese,** the river Meuse in France and Belgium.

75. **the burning Scorpion.** See note to l. 29, Sackville's *Induction.*
87. **the Neckar,** a river in Würtemberg and Baden joining the Rhine at Mannheim.
98. **great Bourbon,** Louis XIV.
100. **Eugenio,** Prince Eugene, 1663–1736, a celebrated Austrian general and co-victor at Blenheim.

472b 128. **Schellenberg,** a hill near Donauwerth, Bavaria, where the French and Bavarians were defeated July 2, 1704.

473b 185. **Belgian mounds,** the dikes of Belgium.

197. **Donawert,** Donauwerth, a small town on the Danube in Bavaria, north of Augsburg.
204. **Landau,** a town in Rhenish Bavaria west of the Rhine.
207. **Deluded prince,** Philip of Anjou, 1683–1746, whose accession to the Spanish throne on the death of Charles II caused the war of the Spanish Succession. He was the grandson of the French king.

474b 287. **So when an angel,** etc. This celebrated figure, more than anything else, made Addison famous and prepared the way for his rapid rise in politics.

289. **Such as of late,** etc., in reference to a devastating storm which passed over England in 1703.

475a 309. **Dormer,** Philip Dormer, an officer in the 1st foot guards, killed at Blenheim.

321 ff. **Soane . . . Rhone . . . Seine . . . Loire,** rivers of France.

326. **Scythian seas,** the Black Sea.

335. **Tallard,** Duc de Tallard, 1652–1728, marshal of France, and commander at Blenheim.

475b 361. **Memminghen,** a town in Neuburg, southwestern Bavaria.

361. **Augsburg,** chief city of the district of Swabia and Neuburg in Bavaria.

365. **Ulm,** a town and imperial fortress on the Danube in eastern Würtemberg.

476a 402. **Hochstet's fatal plain.** "Hochstädt" is the German name for Blenheim.

407. **Austria's young monarch,** Joseph I, 1678–1711, son of Leopold I, of the Hapsburg line.

420. **Nireus,** the handsomest Greek in the Trojan War.

421 ff. **great father of almighty Rome,** Æneas, son of the goddess Aphrodite. She was sometimes called Cytherea from the island Cythera or from Cythera in Crete.

476b 437. **Treves,** a town in Rhenish Prussia.

438. **Traerbach,** a town in the vicinity of Coblenz.

455. **Ister's states.** "Ister" is a Latin name for the Danube.

ALEXANDER POPE

Pope is usually spoken of as the most distinguished representative of English classicism. Apart from his literary career, his life was uneventful. He was born in London of Catholic parents, and, inheriting a sickly body, received little systematic schooling. By the aid of his friends, however, and his own inquisitive nature he managed to gain considerable learning of a desultory kind. His claim to have "lisped in numbers" was well-nigh literally true, for he began writing verse early. His first work of real worth, however, was his *Essay on Criticism*, written by the time he was twenty-one and published two years later. In 1712 came his *Rape of the Lock*, which is the daintiest bit of mock-heroic poetry in English. For the next decade he was occupied primarily with his translations of the *Iliad* and the *Odyssey*, both of which continue to be the best-known English versions of the great originals. His satirical powers produced their best effects in maturity, in proportion as his literary squabbles multiplied. Preëminent among his satirical works are *The Dunciad* and the *Epistle to Dr. Arbuthnot*, representing his endeavors from 1728 to the end of his life. He died of dropsy and asthma in 1744 at his celebrated villa of Twickenham on the Thames, which has since become one of the most famous literary shrines in England. His ideal in poetry was correctness. He was content to dispense with strict originality and to say what had been thought and said before, but to say it surpassingly well. His works therefore contain more stock quotations than any others of similar scope in the language. He perfected the old five-accent couplet and employed it with biting effectiveness in his satirical writings.

477b AN ESSAY ON CRITICISM

34. **Mævius,** an inferior Latin poet of the first century before Christ, who shared with Bavius, his contemporary, friend, and equal, a dislike for Horace and Virgil.

478a 84. **the Muse's steed,** Pegasus.

478b 129. **the Mantuan Muse,** Virgil.

130. **Maro,** the family name of Virgil.

138. **the Stagyrite,** Aristotle, from his birthplace, Stagira. The poetical doctrines of the English classicists were based largely upon the supposed doctrines of Aristotle.

479a 180. **Homer nods.** Cf. Horace's *Ars Poetica*, l. 359.

480a 267. **La Mancha's knight,** the hero of Cervantes' celebrated work, *Don Quixote.*

480b 270. **Dennis,** John Dennis, 1657–1734, an English critic. The reference is to his commentary on Aristotle.

481a 328. **Fungoso in the play,** a character in Jonson's *Everyman out of His Humour.*

481b 356. **Alexandrine,** a six-stress iambic line, as represented in the next line following in the text. See introductory note to Spenser's *Faerie Queene.*

361. **Denham,** Sir John Denham, 1615–1669, a minor English poet.

361. **Waller.** Cf. p. 380 and notes.

370. **Ajax,** etc. Cf. *Iliad*, Bk. VII, l. 265 ff. In l. 370 f. and l. 372 f. Pope skillfully illustrates in his own composition the slow and the swift movements he is discussing.

372. **Camilla.** Cf. *Æneid*, Bk. VII, l. 803 ff.

374 ff. **Timotheus' varied lays,** etc. The reference is to Dryden's *Alexander's Feast*, p. 439.

376. **the son of Lybian Jove,** Alexander the Great. See note to l. 28 ff. of Dryden's *Alexander's Feast.*

482b 444. **Scotists and Thomists,** followers of the thirteenth-century scholastic philosophers Duns Scotus and Thomas Aquinas.

445. **Duck Lane,** a place in London where second-hand books were sold, near Smithfield.

463. **Blackmores.** Sir Richard Blackmore, 1652–1729, an indefatigable producer of commonplace epic poems.

463. **Milbourns.** The Reverend Luke Milbourn was a critic of Dryden's *Virgil.*

465. **Zoilus.** See note to l. 3 of Howell's *Written to a Most Excellent Book*, etc., p. 249.

483b 545. **Socinus,** Lælius Socinus, 1525–1562, and Faustus Socinus, 1539–1604, Italian theologians, founders of Socinianism.

484a 585. **Appius,** in reference to the play *Appius and Virginia*, by John Dennis, who became insanely critical of Pope for this and other references. See note to l. 270.

484b 617. **Durfey,** Thomas D'Urfey, *ca.* 1650–1753, a mediocre English playwright and humorous poet.

619. **Garth,** Sir Samuel Garth, 1661–1719, a physician and author of the mock-heroic poem, *The Dispensary.*

485a 648. **Mæonian star,** Homer, who, according to one account, was a native of Mæonia, an ancient name for Lydia, in Asia Minor.

665. **Dionysius,** of Halicarnassus, first century after Christ, a Greek rhetorician and historian.

667. **Petronius.** See note to p. 457b, l. 44.

485b 675. **Longinus,** *ca.* A.D. 210–273, the most celebrated of the Greek critics after Aristotle.

693. **Erasmus,** *ca.* 1465–1536, the greatest of the humanistic scholars and theologians.

696. **those holy vandals,** the indolent, ignorant priesthood.

697. **Leo's golden days.** Pope Leo X, 1475–1521, under whose pontificate the Reformation began, was a liberal patron of art and literature.

704. **Raphael,** 1483–1520, a great Italian painter.

704. **Vida,** *ca.* 1480–1566, an Italian Latin poet.

707. **Cremona,** Vida's birthplace.

714. **Boileau,** 1636–1711, a famous French poet and critic of the classical school.

486a 725. **Roscommon,** Wentworth Dillon, *ca.* 1633–1685, Earl of Roscommon, a minor English poet of the Restoration who wrote an essay on the art of versified translation.

729. **Walsh,** William Walsh, 1663–1708, an English writer who inspired Pope to be a "correct" poet.

THE RAPE OF THE LOCK

The poem celebrates the incident of Lord Petre's purloining a lock of hair from the head of Arabella Fermor, a fashionable belle of the time. Pope wrote the poem, in mock-heroic vein, at the request of his friend John Caryll, to allay the ill feeling which arose in consequence between the two families. All, including the poet and the friend, belonged to a small Catholic circle living near Windsor.

4. **Belinda,** the offended beauty, Miss Fermor.

486b 23. **a Birthnight Beau,** a fine gentleman such as might attend a royal birthday fête.

44. **the Box,** at the theater.
44. **the Ring,** a circular promenade or driveway in Hyde Park.

487a 56. **Ombre,** a fashionable game of cards borrowed from Spain, usually played by three persons, the eights, nines, and tens being omitted from the hands.

60. **Salamander's name.** According to an old notion, the salamander could live in fire.

488a 148. **Betty,** the waiting maid.

489b 133. **Ixion,** king of the Lapithæ and murderer of his father-in-law. He was condemned by Jupiter, for making love to Juno, to perpetual punishment by being bound on a revolving wheel of fire in Tartarus.

3. **a structure of majestic frame,** Hampton Court, a royal palace.
7. **great Anna,** Queen Anne.

490a 33. **a Matadore,** one of the three high cards in omber.

49. **Spadillio,** the ace of spades.
51. **Manillio,** the deuce of clubs of a black trump, or the seven of a red.
53. **Basto,** the ace of clubs.

490b 61. **Pam,** the knave of clubs, high card in the game of loo, a game which has some features similar to poker.

92. **Codille,** the condition of a double loss to a player who fails to get as many tricks as one of his opponents.

491a 122. **Scylla,** the daughter of King Nisus of Megara, who gave to the Cretan leader Minos, at war against her father, the purple lock of the latter's hair on which depended the safety of the state, and was punished by being changed into a bird.

491b 165. **Atalantis,** *The New Atlantis,* a work by Mrs. Manley popular at the time.

492a 8. **Cynthia when her,** etc. Diana or Cynthia, the ancient goddess of Chastity; in general any maiden so modest as to be upset at having her mantle pinned awry.

492b 51. **Homer's Tripod.** Cf. *Iliad,* Bk. XVIII, l. 372 ff.

82. **Ulysses held the winds.** Cf. *Odyssey,* Bk. X, l. 19 ff.

493a 89. **Thalestris,** Mrs. Morley, sister of Sir George Brown.

118. **sound of Bow.** Grub Street and other Bohemian haunts, where wits would scorn to live, lay within earshot of the Bow bells.
121. **Sir Plume,** Sir George Brown. He took offense at the representation.

493b 156. **Bohea,** a kind of tea.

494a 5 f. **the Trojan,** etc. Æneas was resolute to leave Carthage despite the passionate grief of Dido and the solicitations of her sister Anna. See *Æneid,* Bk. IV.

7. **Clarissa.** This character does not appear in the first edition of the poem.

495a 62. **Dapperwit.** Cf. Wycherley's *Love in a Wood.*

63. **Sir Fopling.** Cf. Etherege's *The Man of Mode.*
65. **Mæander,** a winding river in Asia Minor.

495b 125. **Rome's great founder,** Romulus.

126. **Proculus,** a Roman senator to whom Romulus is said to have expressed a wish for deification as Quirinus.
129. **Berenice's locks.** Berenice was an Egyptian queen who dedicated her beautiful hair to Venus for the safe return of her husband from war. On the fulfillment of the pledge the goddess transformed the hair into a comet.
136. **Rosamonda's lake,** a miniature lake in St. James's Park.
137. **Partridge,** John Partridge, an astrologer and almanac maker, ridiculed by Swift.
138. **Galileo's eyes,** the telescope.

496a 140. **Louis,** Louis XIV of France.

EPISTLE TO DR. ARBUTHNOT

Dr. John Arbuthnot, a popular physician, classical scholar, and writer, was an ardent friend of most of the literary wits of the time. To him Pope drew up and addressed in his celebrated *Epistle,* "a sort of bill of complaint" against his age.

1. **good John,** John Searl, a servant to Pope for a long while.
4. **Bedlam.** See note to l. 199 of Drayton's *Nymphidia.*
12. **Sabbath day,** *i.e.,* a day of rest.
13. **the Mint,** a place in Southwark where insolvent debtors were not liable to arrest.
21. **Twit'nam,** Pope's villa, Twickenham.
23. **Arthur,** Arthur Moore, a politician.
25. **Cornus,** Sir Robert Walpole, 1676–1745, the famous prime minister.

496b 40. **"Keep your piece nine years."** See Horace, *Ars Poetica,* l. 388.

43. **Term,** the London "season."
49. **Pitholeon,** the name of a foolish poet of Rhodes.
53. **Curll,** Edmund Curll, a piratical bookseller.
62. **Lintot,** Bernard Lintot, Pope's publisher after 1712.

497a 69. **Midas.** King Midas of Lydia was rewarded with a pair of ass's ears for unjustly giving the prize in a musical contest to his own favorite flute player instead of to Apollo.

85. **Codrus,** a poetaster in Juvenal.
99. **Bavius.** See note to l. 34 of *An Essay on Criticism.*
100. **one Bishop,** etc., Bishop Bolter, patron of Ambrose Philips, Pope's rival in pastoral poetry.
101. **Sappho,** Lady Mary Wortley Montague, one of the most brilliant women of her time.

497b 117. **Ammon's great son,** Alexander the Great, who claimed descent from Jove Ammon.

135. **Granville,** George Granville, Lord Lansdowne, 1667–1735, at whose suggestion Pope published his *Windsor Forest* in 1713.

139. **Talbot, Somers, Sheffield,** noblemen and statesmen who encouraged Pope's early literary endeavors.

140. **mitred Rochester,** Francis Atterbury, Bishop of Rochester.

141. **St. John's self,** Henry St. John, Viscount Bolingbroke, 1678–1751, orator and statesman, whose shallow philosophy influenced many of the writers of the time.

146. **Burnets, Oldmixons, Cookes,** writers of secret and disreputable histories, according to Pope.

149. **gentle Fanny,** Lord Hervey.

498a 151. **Gildon,** Charles Gildon, an abusive critic of Pope.

164. **Bentleys,** Richard Bentley, 1662–1742, one of the great classical scholars and critics of the time.

164. **Tibbalds,** Lewis Theobald, 1688–1744, a notable Shakespearean editor, the hero of the *Dunciad*.

190. **Tate,** Nahum Tate, at one time poet laureate.

498b 193. **were there one.** The characterization of Addison which follows is one of the best in satirical literature. Atticus was a Roman scholar and bookseller of the first century before Christ.

222. **great George,** George II, king of England.

230. **Bufo,** probably Charles Montague, Earl of Halifax, statesman, poet, and patron of letters.

230. **Castalian state,** realm of poetry.

499a 256. **Gay.** See p. 503 and notes.

260. **Queensb'ry.** The Duke and Duchess of Queensbury, in whose house Gay died, gave him a monument in Westminster Abbey.

276. **Balbus,** the Earl of Kinnoul.

499b 280. **Sir Will,** Sir William Yonge.

280. **Bubo,** George Bubb Dodington, a politician and patron of letters.

299. **Dean and Silver Bell,** the unknown person who represented to the Duke of Chandos that Pope in the *Essay on Taste* had ridiculed the furnishings of that nobleman's residence, the Canons.

305. **Sporus,** Lord Hervey. Sporus was an effeminate favorite of Nero.

500a 363. **Japhet in a jail,** Japhet Crook, who was put in jail for a forgery conveying an estate to himself.

500b 373. **Cibber,** Colley Cibber, 1671–1757, actor, playwright, and small poet, who superseded Theobald as hero of the *Dunciad*.

373. **Moore,** James Moore-Smythe, author of much verse and a play.

375. **Welsted,** Leonard Welsted, a Whig pamphleteer.

378. **Budgell,** Eustace Budgell, friend and kinsman of Addison, charged with forging a will to his own profit.

391. **Bestia,** probably the Duke of Marlborough. Bestia was a Roman proconsul who accepted bribes from Jugurtha for a dishonorable peace.

MATTHEW PRIOR

A few years after the birth of the poet Prior at Wimborne in Dorsetshire, of working-class Presbyterian parents, the family removed to London, where the boy, apparently an apprentice in a tavern, was discovered by the Earl of Dorset through his facility in verse and sent to Westminster. He proceeded to Cambridge for a full career and was made a fellow of his college at the time of the Revolution of 1688. Under the changed régime he became a diplomat and political figure, rising in 1699 to the position of Undersecretary of State, and continued in public life until his death of a fever at Wimpole in 1621. His satires, epistles, and epigrams were well received in his day, but he was best known for his lyrics of a familiar tenor and cast, an estimate which posterity has approved.

501b A SIMILE

14. **Pindus,** a mountain range in Greece.

AN ODE

4. **Cloe,** Mrs. Elizabeth Coxe, the wife of a London coachman. Because the couple were his friends, the poet is thought to have set the pair up in business.

THOMAS PARNELL

Thomas Parnell came of a long-established Cheshire family which had migrated to Ireland at the Restoration. He was born in Dublin and received his education at Trinity College in that city, where he took his M.A. degree in 1700. Entering the Church, he became archdeacon of Clogher in 1706 and after the death of his wife five years later was brought by Swift to London and introduced to the literary and political leaders. By 1713 he had become intimate with Pope, under whose influence he remained until his premature death at Chester, by his own intemperate habits, in 1718. He had the usual stylistic refinements of the poets of the time, and, like many of them, tried to be merry, but he is best in a grave or even elegiac vein, in which he definitely anticipates Gray.

JOHN GAY

In the actualities of life Gay was a poet who needed and usually found protection in the households of persons of quality. He was born into an impoverished family at Barnstaple in Devonshire, and losing both parents by the time he was ten, served an apprenticeship to a London silk merchant. Giving up the trade and devoting himself to literature, he managed by his pen and various private sinecures to live a life of ease and to amass a considerable amount of money. His most conspicuous literary achievement was *The Beggar's Opera* in 1728, which has been called "the first popular success of the modern English stage." He is best in the lighter lyric, in which he resembles Prior. His love of nature associates him with the romantic writers who were then beginning to express a new spirit in English poetry.

A BALLAD

In *The What D' Ye Call It.*

504a SWEET WILLIAM'S FAREWELL, etc.

1. **Downs,** a roadstead for shipping off the coast of Kent.

JOHN HUGHES

John Hughes was placed by both his great contemporaries, Swift and Pope, "among the mediocribus in prose as well as verse," but each acknowledged his gravity as beyond them. He was born at Marlborough in Wiltshire and attended a dissenting academy where he had as contemporary the hymn writer Isaac Watts. In 1715 he published the works of Spenser with glossarial helps, — the first attempt at a critical edition of that poet and consequently to be reckoned a part of the great Spenserian revival which became prominent later in the century (see introductory note to Thomas Warton). He was a constant invalid and in narrow circumstances during the greater part of his life, but in 1717 he was appointed to a secretaryship which afforded him independence until his death. He died of consumption in London on the opening night of his one successful play, *The Siege of Damascus*, February 17, 1720.

504b THE PICTURE

3. **Apelles,** a famous Greek painter of the time of Philip and Alexander. His greatest picture, perhaps the greatest of antiquity, was the Aphrodite (Venus) of the temple of Æsculapius in Cos.
16. **parrot-pride,** herb-lily.
25. **Juno's bird,** the peacock.
26. **Iris' bow,** the rainbow. See note to l. 46 of Gower's *Ceix and Alceone*, p. 161.

HENRY CAREY

Next to nothing is known of the life of Henry Carey. According to report, he was an illegitimate child of George Savile, Marquis of Halifax, whose family supplied him with a pension for life. He became known in London as the author of many lively poems in manuscript, of several successful farces and burlesques, and of a number of songs, the music of which he often composed himself. It is said that he died by his own hand with quite as much gayety of spirit as he had lived. He survives in English literature for the critical term, "Namby-Pamby," applied by him in ridicule to the mediocre verse of Ambrose Philips, and for his inimitable song-poem with music, *Sally in Our Alley*.

MARK AKENSIDE

Akenside, like several other significant English writers, was a physician. He was born at Newcastle-on-Tyne the son of a butcher. He was educated at a free school of his native town and in a private academy. His poetical talent developed early. At sixteen he produced in his *Virtuoso* a remarkable imitation of Spenser. At seventeen he began the poem by which he is best remembered, *Pleasures of the Imagination*. He studied medicine in Edinburgh and abroad, and before he was twenty-five was a practicing physician and had a reputation as a poet. His creative powers subsided early. He became merely a fashionable physician in London and developed a reputation for cruelty and arrogance. He died before he was fifty, in the bed, it is said, in which Milton expired. His own phrase from one of his odes, "Reason clad in strains of harmony," best explains his poetry.

506b FOR A GROTTO

2. **Actæa,** a Nereid, adopted by the poet as a local divinity.
5. **Glycon,** a conventional classical name for a shepherd.
6. **lychnis,** a kind of rose.

DANIEL DEFOE

507a THE SHORTEST WAY WITH THE DISSENTERS

The Dissenters or Nonconformists were treated with consideration by William and Mary; but with the accession of Anne, a Stuart, and the appointment of a Tory ministry in 1702, all dissenting elements were threatened with severe measures by Parliament. In the face of the dangers Defoe wrote his pamphlet to show the High Church Party the absurdity of its position, but his satire was so clever and covert that it was at first mistaken by both sides. When its real import was discovered, Defoe was arrested, fined, pilloried, and imprisoned, and his tract was burned by the common hangman.

1. **Sir Roger L'Estrange,** 1616–1704, an English journalist and pamphleteer.

27 f. **the purest and most flourishing church,** etc., the Church of England, since the Revolution of 1688.

507b 12. **Act of Toleration,** by which, 1689, the Nonconformists were relieved of the penalties for not attending services of the Church of England.

40 ff. **one King . . . another . . . a third . . . the fourth,** Charles I . . . James II . . . William III . . . Queen Anne.

508a 3 f. **Dutch monarch.** Before his accession William III was Prince of Orange.

29. **The first execution,** etc., dating from the Hampton Court Conference in 1604.

52. **a sordid impostor,** Oliver Cromwell.

509a 4. **preferred,** gave preferment to.

11. **the Rye House Plot,** a conspiracy in 1683, it was thought, to murder Charles II and his brother James.

509b 2 f. **the Observator,** an extremely partisan Whig organ begun April 1, 1702, by John Tutchin.

510a 8. **Protestants in France.** By the revocation of the Edict of Nantes in 1685, the Huguenots were driven from the country in great numbers.

37. **a time of war.** The War of the Spanish Succession began in 1701.

510b 33. **Monmouths and Shaftesburys.** See Dryden's *Absalom and Achitophel* and notes.

34. **Argyles,** the Earl of Argyll, beheaded in Scotland in 1685 for complicity in Monmouth's Rebellion.

43. **post est occasio calva,** Opportunity is bald behind.

511a 50. **de heretico comburendo,** for burning heretics.

511b 19. **Delenda est Carthago,** Carthage must be destroyed.

42. **Amalekite race.** Cf. I Samuel xv.

512a 7. **Moses,** etc. Cf. Exodus xxxii, 25 ff.

22. **the counter.** See note to p. 305a, l. 53.

512b 43. **Thirty-nine Articles.** The religious belief of the English Church, formulated under Edward VI, was reduced and codified in the Thirty-nine Articles in the fifth year of the reign of Elizabeth.

JONATHAN SWIFT

514a A MEDITATION UPON A BROOMSTICK

This essay is a humorous imitation, "according to the style and manner," of the philosophical musings of Robert Boyle, 1627–1691.

514b 35. **besom,** the broom.

A MODEST PROPOSAL

49. **this great town,** Dublin.

515a 8. **the pretender in Spain.** James Stuart, son of James II, intrigued with the Spaniards in an attempt to recover the crown of England.

9. **Barbadoes,** an island in the British West Indies.

515b 37. **county of Cavan,** in northern central Ireland.

517a 13. **Psalmanaazar,** author of a fictitious *Description of Formosa,* 1705, which was widely believed to be authentic.

518b 11. **Topinamboo,** a district in Brazil.

519b 16 f. **I have no children,** etc. See introductory note to the *Journal to Stella,* p. 467, for Swift's possible marital relations.

SIR RICHARD STEELE

Like Goldsmith and to some extent like Gay, Richard Steele by his very irresponsibility in practical matters, has endeared himself to English readers as few writers have done. He was born in Dublin, attended the Charterhouse School in London with Addison and proceeded with him to Oxford, but left without a degree for a career in the army. His first authorship of any consequence was in drama, where, by a succession of comedies at the beginning of Queen Anne's reign, he led the return to decency on the stage, and, with the *Conscious Lovers* nearly twenty years later, proved himself a leader in the sentimental drama of his century. After two years' experience as Gazetteer he undertook the publication of the *Tatler*, but soon found it needful to call Addison to his aid, and the two in the *Tatler* and *Spectator* established the short familiar essay in English. For his fearless championship of the Hanoverian line he was knighted in 1715. He continued prominent in the literary and political life of the time and enjoyed several lucrative appointments, but was recklessly prodigal in all matters appertaining to money. Finally, embarrassed by his financial difficulties, he retired to Wales in 1724 and died there five years later. His good nature, constantly reflected in his writings, often got him into trouble. In his literary character he is known and loved for his ready sympathies, for his childlike innocence and unaffected simplicity, and for his unfailing humor in all relations of life.

519a RECOLLECTIONS OF CHILDHOOD

17. **manes,** spirits of the dead.

520a 27. **battledore,** a bat.

SIR ROGER IN LOVE

522a 8. **a murrain to,** an oath, from *murrain*, a pestilence affecting cattle.

523a 13. **by posing her,** *i.e.*, by answering her riddles, and thus overcoming her.

51 f. **dum tacet hanc loquitur.** While he is silent he talks of her.

JOSEPH ADDISON

523b WESTMINSTER ABBEY

33. Γλαῦκόν τε, etc., Glaucus and Medon and Thersilochus, warriors on the Trojan side.

524a 20. **the poetical quarter,** Poet's Corner.

23. **the present war,** War of the Spanish Succession, 1701–1714.

40. **Sir Cloudesly Shovel's,** 1650–1707, an English admiral, commander of the fleet the last three years of his life.

524b 9. **rostral crowns,** crowns conferred on naval commanders.

526b SIR ROGER AT THE ASSIZES

36. **cast,** bring in a verdict against, defeat at law.

39. **business of the willow-tree,** *i.e.*, a lawsuit of long standing about a willow tree.

THE DEATH OF SIR ROGER

531a 14. **the quorum,** justices of the peace whose presence was necessary to constitute a bench.

LADY WINCHILSEA

Lady Winchilsea was the daughter of Sir William Kingsmill of Sidmonton. She was a personal attendant upon the Duchess of York, but before the accession of the Duke of York to the throne as James II, she was married to Colonel Finch, later Earl of Winchilsea, and withdrawing from court settled at Eastwell in Kent, known for its beauty. In her London days she was acknowledged as a wit and thought of as having a talent for rhyming somewhat after the approved fashion. But in her verses composed amid her new surroundings she displayed her native love for country things and expressed her appreciation in terms and images that were unusual in poetry at the time. In this way she is a genuine forerunner in the back-to-nature movement in English poetry.

532a A NOCTURNAL REVERIE

19. **Salisbury,** Lady Salisbury, whose mother was an intimate friend of the author.

LADY GRIZEL BAILLIE

Lady Grizel Baillie was the eldest daughter of Sir Patrick Hume or Home, later Earl of Marchmont, and was born at Redbraes Castle in Berwickshire. She developed a thoroughly capable and responsible character early. While her father, a political refugee, lay in hiding in the family vault at Polwarth, she as a mere child supplied him, sometimes only by the utmost shifts, with daily food. During their exile in Holland, she was the mainstay of the family. On the accession of William their misfortunes were relieved, she was married to her childhood lover, and lived an incomparable married life for nearly half a century. The only one of her songs that has been preserved entire indicates the appealing quality of her verse.

532b WERNA MY HEART LICHT, etc.

1. **may,** maiden.
2. **biggit,** built.
3. **Dool,** dole, ill luck.
7. **hecht,** promised.
7. **braw,** fine.
9. **titty,** sister.
14. **dwam,** sudden illness.
22. **dribbles,** drops.
22. **draff,** lees, dregs.
23. **pickles,** small quantities.
23. **mill-e'e,** eye or outlet of the mill.
28. **een,** eyes.
28. **trow,** trust, believe.
32. **dowie,** sad, dreary.
32. **corn-bing,** heap of corn.
33. **daund'ring,** sauntering.
33. **dykes,** ditches.
34. **dow,** be able.
34. **hund,** set on, urge.
34. **tykes,** dogs.
35. **steeks,** closes.

LADY ELIZABETH WARDLAW

Lady Elizabeth Wardlaw was the daughter of Sir Charles Halket of Pitfirrane, Scotland. She became Lady Wardlaw by her marriage with Sir Henry Wardlaw of Pitrevie. Her one recovered poem belongs to the literature of forgery. She professed to have discovered it, a relic of an age long past, written upon shreds of paper, but was later induced to own its authorship. Though its first line is one of the few derived from genuine ballad tradition, the poem is an ingenious imitation. It deceived Gray and fascinated Scott. It was first printed by Allan Ramsay (p. 536a). See also introductory note to Popular Ballads, p. 163.

533a **HARDYKNUTE**

The historical event represented in the poem was the invasion of Scotland by Haco, King of Norway, in the reign of Alexander III, 1263.

1. **wa'**, wall.
10. **a-hight**, on high.
14. **deimt**, deemed.
15. **marrow**, mate, match.
20. **bot**, without.
27. **jimp**, slender.
35. **the isle.** After seizing the islands of Bute and Arran, Haco landed at Largs in Ayrshire.
38. **dyne**, dinner.

533b 48. **seyed**, tried.
82. **leal**, loyal, true.
93. **harnisine**, harness, armor.

534a 107. **twirtle twist**, intertwined cord.
108. **plet**, plaited.
109. **dyce**, an ornamental pattern of cubes or squares.
113. **muir**, moor.
130. **lowan's**, flaming.
131. **menzie**, followers, army.
145. **hyne**, hence.
145. **attour**, over, across.

534b 157. **feirs**, comrades.
158. **reevers**, robbers.
173. **stoupe of weir**, prop of war.
180. **dart**, hurt.
185. **sindle**, seldom.
185. **bruiked**, enjoyed.
188. **sen**, since.
194. **mense the faught**, open the battle.
196. **unsonsie**, unlucky.

535a 207. **quat**, let go, quit.
208. **eard**, earth.
213. **ettled**, aimed.
216. **meid**, appearance, bearing.
217. **jupe**, mantle, coat.
236. **height**, promised.
240. **garred**, made, caused.
248. **lout**, bow.
251. **darred**, hurt.
253. **ferliet**, wondered.

535b 268. **leugh**, laughed.
268. **jeir**, jeer.
276. **fey**, fated to die.
286. **meise**, soften.
289. **wailowit**, faded.
303. **thole**, suffer, endure.

536a 317. **bleise**, blaze.
330. **ceist**, ceased.

ALLAN RAMSAY

A good deal of credit for the return of naturalness, in both materials and language, into English poetry is due to Allan Ramsay, as well for his own gifts as for the interest he fostered by his publications. He was born at Leadhills in Lanarkshire and received a common-school education at Crawford. Losing both parents early he was apprenticed at fifteen to a wigmaker in Edinburgh, in due time set up a shop of his own, and became a substantial citizen. About 1715 he began the regular exercise of his rhyming gifts, turned bookseller a year or two later, and gave up wig-making. After 1730 he practically ceased to write verses but lived on in comfort and in some renown for nearly thirty years. His pastoral drama, *The Gentle Shepherd*, is the crowning achievement of his own work as a poet, but he performed a greater service for literature with his celebrated *Tea-Table Miscellany*, which was enormously popular and helped to lay the foundation for the later appreciation of Burns.

MY PEGGY IS A YOUNG THING

8. **wauking**, watching.
8. **fauld**, fold, sheepfold.
14. **lave**, rest, others.
15. **gars**, makes, causes.

536b 31. **wale**, choice.

THE LASS WITH A LUMP OF LAND

11. **gear**, property.
12. **dowf**, dull, hollow.
14. **poortith**, poverty.
18. **siller and gowd**, silver and gold.
20. **tint**, lost.
22. **riggs**, measures of land.
24. **well-tochered**, well dowered.

WILLIAM HAMILTON OF BANGOUR

William Hamilton, the son of an advocate, was born at Bangour. He inherited a frail constitution and developed a turn for poetry early. He espoused the cause of the Stuarts, was in hiding for a while after their reverses, and finally escaped to France. By the aid of friends he was allowed to return, but his health was undermined and he again sought the continent. He died of consumption at Lyons in 1754. He is remembered almost solely by his exquisite *Braes of Yarrow*.

THE BRAES OF YARROW

The poem is a trialogue, the speakers being the bridegroom, a bystander, and the bride. The Yarrow is a river in Selkirkshire, Scotland.

1. **Busk,** adorn.
537a 4. **braes,** banks, hills.
8. **birks,** birch trees.
17. **maun,** must.
25. **reid,** red.
537b 50. **gowan,** daisy.
53. **Tweed,** a boundary river between England and Scotland.
538a 79. **to-fall,** etc., evening, nightfall.

DAVID MALLET

David Mallet or Malloch was born apparently of a well-to-do farmer class of Perthshire. He attended school at his native Crieff and went up to the University of Edinburgh, where he became a friend of James Thomson, author of the *Seasons*. In 1723 he entered the household of the Duke of Montrose as tutor. Attaining to some eminence in politics, he lived principally in London until his death in 1765. A persistent tradition attributes to him the authorship of *William and Margaret*, but it is now known that Mallet's *William and Margaret* is really a genuine traditional ballad touched up by so-called "improvements." Its tremendous popularity during the eighteenth century is another evidence of increased interest in the older literature of England. See further, introductory note to Popular Ballads, p. 163. *Rule, Britannia* has been assigned both to him and to Thomson.

WILLIAM AND MARGARET

Compare *Sweet William's Ghost*, p. 166.

JOHN DYER

John Dyer was the son of a solicitor of Abberglasney in Wales. He was educated at Westminster and placed in his father's office, but upon the latter's death he turned artist and spent some time in rambling over south Wales and the adjoining English counties, thus anticipating, in his experience and appreciations, the great nature poets, Wordsworth and Coleridge, three-quarters of a century later. His *Gronger Hill* in 1727 brought him an enviable reputation. He studied painting in Italy, but failing of success as an artist, he entered the church and occupied appointments in Lincolnshire until his death in 1758. His love of natural scenery at a time when such love was not common in English poetry has given him a unique place in literature.

539b GRONGAR HILL

Grongar Hill was an elevation near the poet's birthplace.

1. **Silent nymph,** the muse of Painting.
23. **Towy's flood,** the river Towy in Wales.
540a 61. **taper grows,** diminishes, grows smaller and smaller.

JAMES THOMSON

It was reserved for James Thomson, among a group of minor bards, really to lead the way "back to nature" in English poetry. His genius was great enough and his works sufficiently striking, in his early productive years, to give him a prestige that could be claimed by no other poet between Pope and Gray. He came of genteel parentage and was born at Ednam on the Scottish border. He grew up amid romantic surroundings in Roxburghshire and was educated for the church in the Scottish capital. He wrote *Winter*, the first of his celebrated *Seasons*, in 1725 under straitened circumstances in London, where he had repaired to make his fortune. Its success was complete. The other parts followed, and the poem was published entire in 1730. It proved to be his masterpiece. He altered it, revised it, and added to it at pleasure for the rest of his life. About 1738 he began the best of the eighteenth-century Spenserian imitations in his *Castle of Indolence*, but thereafter his poetical vein ran thin. His dramas, done in his mature years, add nothing to his fame. He died of a neglected cold in the summer of 1748, amid the general lament of his contemporaries. The reader who has been schooled in Wordsworth will miss some warmth in Thomson's treatment of nature, but to the readers of his day it was as genuine and reassuring as its want was manifest in the other writings of the time.

540b SUMMER

The passage in the text comprises ll. 352–432 of the final version of the poem.

541b 77. **her dreadful thunder,** etc. These

lines are not in the original edition. They were added later, when England and France were at war.

AUTUMN

Ll. 950–1036 of the final version.

542b WINTER

Ll. 223–321 of the final version.

1 ff. **fuming dun . . . Thick clouds ascend,** thick clouds composed of dark confused vapors ascend.

544a THE CASTLE OF INDOLENCE

Canto I, stanzas ii–vii and xxiii–xliii.

12. **kest,** cast.

544b 22. **vacant,** idle.

26. **coil,** noise.

545a 59. **The pride of Turkey,** etc. The "halls" were furnished out as with the riches of oriental luxury, Turkish hangings, Persian carpets, and the like.

74. **ancient maiden's gall,** an old maid's rancor.

75. **saintly spleen,** puritanical criticism.

85. **Arcadian or Sicilian vale.** Arcadia was a remote district of Greece noted for the simplicity of its inhabitants. Sicily was the home of Theocritus, the traditional father of pastoral poetry.

92. **Depeinten,** depicted.

93. **Dan Abraham,** etc. See Genesis xi, 31 ff. *Dan* is an archaic title of honor equivalent to "Master."

545b 107 f. **Lorraine . . . Rosa . . . Poussin,** French and Italian landscape painters of the seventeenth century.

126. **The Harp of Æolus,** "an instrument, called Æolus's harp, which, when placed against a little rushing or current of air, produces the effect here described." — Author's note.

546a 137 ff. **Of Caliphs old,** etc. "The Arabian Caliphs had poets among the officers of their court whose office it was to do what is here mentioned." — Author's note.

149. **mell,** mix, mingle.

WILLIAM SHENSTONE

Shenstone was born at Halesowen in Worcestershire, where his father was a churchwarden. His first teacher was an old dame, Sarah Lloyd, whom he celebrated, with better memory than most poets, in his *The Schoolmistress.* He attended school at his native place and was a contemporary of Dr. Johnson in Pembroke College, Oxford, but left without a degree. From 1745 he gave himself up to a life of ease and landscape gardening at Leasowes, until his death in 1763. Though most of his verse is artificial and unreal, the burlesque of Spenser's style in *The Schoolmistress* is noteworthy for its excellence, and the character of the schoolmistress herself is portrayed with rare skill.

THE SCHOOLMISTRESS

546b 18. **unconned,** unstudied, inelegant.

18. **shent,** put to shame, blamed.

547a 41. **perdie,** a very mild oath.

51. **Tway,** two.

56 f. **Eol's train,** etc., Æolus and the attendant winds.

547b 76. **additions,** titles.

79. **eld,** age.

548a 119. **Sternhold,** Thomas, *ca.* 1500–1549, one of the authors of a metrical version of the Psalms.

123 ff. **How Israel's sons,** etc. See Psalms cxxxvii.

130 ff. **when truth,** etc. That is, she was well read in Foxe's *Book of Martyrs.* See p. 213 and notes.

133. **nould,** would not.

136. **that of Scottish stem,** the coronation chair at Westminster, which contains the famous stone of Scone, once part of the coronation chair of the Scottish kings.

139. **liefest,** dearest, most beloved.

548b 157. **pellucid horn,** etc. See note to Dekker's *The Gull's Horn-Book,* p. 304.

160. **St. George's high achievements,** St. George's fight with the dragon.

165. **the bard,** etc. Spenser. Kilcolman Castle, Spenser's home in Ireland, was situated near the Mulla River.

169. **brogues,** breeches.

549b 211. **form,** a long seat or bench. See note to p. 87b, l. 45.

242. **Vernon's patriot soul,** Edward Vernon, 1684–1757, a distinguished English admiral and hero of many stirring engagements against the Spaniards.

550a 255. **Dennis,** John Dennis the critic.

550b 279. **kesar,** emperor, ruler (cf. *Cæsar*).

287. **Thilk,** this or that same.

306. **Salopia.** Salop was an older name for Shropshire in England, through which the Severn River runs.

EDWARD YOUNG

Edward Young is a remarkable example of the late maturity of the poetic powers. He published nothing until he was past thirty. At sixty he collected his verse in two volumes. Afterward he produced the work which, in some respects, places him first among the group who constitute the School of Melancholy or "Graveyard School" in English poetry. He was born at Upham in Hampshire, attended school at Winchester and Oxford, sought political advancement for a number of years without success, and when nearly fifty decided to enter the church. He chafed long under the humiliation of withheld preferment, but becoming well off by marriage lived a life of dignity at Welwyn until his death in 1765. His *Complaint, or Night Thoughts*, particularly in its celebrated first book, is significant for its nervous force, the elevation and harmony of its numbers, the sustained beauty of its phrase, and its quiet undertone of romantic despair.

551b THE COMPLAINT, etc.

555a 321. **Lorenzo,** "an infidel lay-figure," against whom the poet is constantly vindicating orthodoxy.

555b 344. **Mine died with thee.** Young began the poem soon after the death of his wife, and not long after the loss of other members of his family.

557a 449. **Mæonides,** a surname of Homer.

ROBERT BLAIR

Robert Blair aligns himself with his contemporary, Edward Young, as a poet of melancholy. He was born in Edinburgh and was educated in the university there. He was, it seems, licensed to preach at an early age but lived on for several years in his native city without an appointment. In 1731 he was given the living at Athelstaneford in East Lothian and there leisurely completed his poem, *The Grave,* which he had begun in Edinburgh. It was an instant and signal success, but he could never again be tempted away from solitude or the ease of retirement into the world of letters. He died in 1748. *The Grave* remains one of the most prominent poems of a gloomy cast in a century in which poems of the kind were plentiful.

THE GRAVE

Compare William Cullen Bryant's *Thanatopsis*, which Bryant wrote soon after reading *The Grave.*

1. **affect,** choose.

14 f. **Dark as was chaos,** etc. Compare Milton's conception of the universe as shown in the notes and figures to l. 70 of *Paradise Lost*, Bk. I.

557b 34. **night's foul bird.** See l. 43.

558b 99. **yonker,** a young man, a simpleton.

100. **clubs,** contributes to the club, or common stock [of stories].

101. **catch,** a song.

SAMUEL JOHNSON

Dr. Samuel Johnson was the high priest of English classicism in the period of its decline. He was a man of strong prejudices, which made him in some respects one of the most partisan of writers, but at the same time he possessed a rugged honesty and a sturdy common sense which compelled him to acknowledge many good qualities in the new literature and to condemn much that was false in the old. He was the son of a bookseller in Lichfield, where he received the rudiments of his fine classical learning. He entered Oxford when past the age of most college youths of his time, but left without a degree. After some experience in teaching he married a woman nearly twice his age, and with her money set up a school near Lichfield. Failing in the enterprise, he set out for London in 1737, accompanied by his former pupil, David Garrick, to try his fortune as a writer. His poem *London*, published the following year, brought him some recognition. A decade later appeared his rhetorical and gloomy *Vanity of Human Wishes*, which has aptly been called the most Roman poem in the language. The celebrated *Dictionary*, projected in 1747, was issued in two volumes in 1755. Its preface, intensely personal though it is, remains an important document in the history of English linguistics. It emphasizes the importance of freeing the language from foreign influences by utilizing the treasures of Elizabethan English. While engaged on the *Dictionary*, Johnson, following the traditions of the *Spectator*, conducted the *Rambler* through a brief career. He continued his periodical writing with the *Idler*, but his essays published in these periodicals, while relieved more than his other writings by a gentle humor, show too clearly the faults of his "sesquipedalian" style, from which his writings are never free. His allegorized oriental tale of *Rasselas*, suggesting the pessimism of Voltaire's *Candide*, was the work of the evenings of a single week, to pay the expenses of his aged mother's funeral. By a pension granted him in 1762 he at last became free of the financial want that had distressed him since childhood. Two years later was founded the famous Club, which has given us, in the pages of Boswell, our most familiar glimpses of the great man. In 1765 his edition of Shakespeare, famous for its interpretative notes, made its appearance. The succession of fifty-two *Lives of the English Poets*, 1777–1781, constituting a rough biographical account of English poetry from the Restoration, entitles him to rank as a distinguished critic; but here, more than anywhere else, the great critic displayed his invincible suspicion of anything that savored of innovation in his country's literature. His last two or three years were clouded with gloom and melancholy. Attended by a few intimate friends, he died at his house in Bolt Court in 1784. He was interred in Westminster Abbey. As Carlyle observed, he is as nearly an heroical figure as is possible in a life wholly devoted to letters.

561a THE VANITY OF HUMAN WISHES

This poem is an imitation of the tenth satire of Juvenal. It consists of a series of pictures of disappointed ambitions.

561b 49. **Democritus.** See note to Sir Thomas Browne's *Religio Medici*, p. 386b, l. 38.

562a 84. **palladium,** an image of Pallas Athena at Troy, on the preservation of which the safety of the city depended. Here a picture of some ancestor, once honored but now taken down and removed to the kitchen or auction room to make way for the likeness of an upstart.

99. **Wolsey,** Cardinal Wolsey, the great prime minister of Henry VIII. See Shakespeare's *Henry VIII*.

562b 124. **Trent,** a river in central England. Lichfield is situated not far from its banks.

129. **great Villiers,** George Villiers, first Duke of Buckingham, an English courtier assassinated by John Felton in 1628.

130. **Harley.** See note to Swift's *Journal to Stella*, p. 468b, l. 42.

131. **murdered Wentworth,** Thomas Wentworth, 1593–1641, Earl of Strafford, a famous English statesman, condemned for treason by the Long Parliament and executed.

131. **exiled Hyde,** Edward Hyde, Earl of Clarendon, an English statesman and historian, banished from England in 1667.

139. **Bodley's dome,** a library of Oxford University, named for Sir Thomas Bodley, who rebuilt it in 1597–1602.

140. **Bacon's mansion,** etc., an allusion to the tradition that the study of Roger Bacon, an English scientist of the thirteenth century who lived at Oxford, would fall when a greater man than he passed it.

563a 164. **Lydiat's life.** Lydiat was a man of various learning but troubled life, including sufferings for the Royalist cause. He died in indigence in 1642.

164. **Galileo's end.** He died of a slow fever.

168. **Laud,** Archbishop Laud, 1573–1645, impeached by the Long Parliament and beheaded on Tower Hill.

181 f. **the Briton's shine,** etc. Cf. Addison's *Campaign*, p. 471 and notes.

563b 192. **Swedish Charles,** Charles XII, 1682–1718, king of Sweden. He defeated the Russians in 1700. See note to l. 210.

210. **Pultowa's day.** Charles XII was defeated by Peter the Great of Russia at Pultowa on July 8, 1709. He escaped to Turkey, where he was hospitably entertained. After various political intrigues he was mysteriously shot at Fredericks-hall in Norway.

224. **Persia's tyrant.** See l. 227.

224. **Bavaria's lord,** Charles Albert, Elector of Bavaria, who became emperor of the Holy Roman Empire in 1742 under the title of Charles VII. See l. 241. He became involved in the troubles centering around Maria Theresa (see note to l. 245) during the War of the Austrian Succession and came to grief. The events were fresh in the public mind when Johnson wrote his poem.

227. **Xerxes.** See note to p. 201a, l. 428.

564a 245. **fair Austria,** Maria Theresa, 1717–1780, Archduchess of Austria and queen of Hungary and Bohemia, daughter of the emperor Charles VI.

249. **Croatian.** Croatia was a titular kingdom in Austria-Hungary.

249. **Hussar,** the light cavalry of Poland and Hungary.

564b 313. **Lydia's monarch,** Crœsus (see note to p. 199b, l. 294), who in his prosperity regarded himself as the happiest of mortals but was assured by Solon that no man could be sure of happiness in his lifetime. On his funeral pyre, when misfortune had overtaken him, he was overheard to murmur "Solon! Solon! Solon!"

565a 317. **Marlborough's eyes,** etc. Marlborough was afflicted with paralysis in his last years.

318. **Swift expires,** etc. See p. 467 and notes. Swift died in 1745, four years before Johnson's poem was written.

321. **Vane,** Lady Vane, the mistress of Lord Berkeley and others.

322. **Sedley cursed,** etc. Sedley's daughter, Catherine, became the favorite mistress of James II and by him was made Countess of Dorchester.

OLIVER GOLDSMITH

The unusual affection in which Goldsmith is held is due, on the one hand, to his utter irresponsibility in practical matters, for which the reader has a sympathetic regard, and, on the other, to the easy grace and charming assurance of his writings. He was born in Ireland, the son of a clergyman, whose portrait is preserved in the village preacher and the humble vicar, Dr. Primrose. Goldsmith attended a local school and managed to get through the University of Dublin. He was rejected when examined for the ministry; he gave up a tutorship that had been secured for him; he set out for America, but squandered his passage money before sailing; and he at last studied medicine in Edinburgh and obtained an obscure medical degree on the Continent. On his return he failed in the practice of his profession and turned writer. Dr. Johnson discovered his talent and took him under his protection, where he remained with many vicissitudes of fortune until his death in London in 1774. So far as is known, *The Traveller* is his first poem, belonging in part, at least, to his period of vagrancy in Europe. *The Deserted Village* in 1770, representing his mature muse, is a household possession. In his poetry Goldsmith is conventional in form and diction, but he uses the couplet with an ease and grace that neither Dryden nor Pope possessed, and in spirit and sentiment he is often richly romantic. His one novel, *The Vicar of Wakefield*, 1766, hardly contains a plot, and yet it is the best example of prose fiction in the century. In 1768 he turned playwright, and with *The Goodnatured Man* and *She Stoops to Conquer* directed the way to a liberation of English drama from the sentimental spirit which had enslaved it since Steele. Finally, in his essays, found in the periodicals of the time and in his loosely connected *Citizen of the World*, he displayed a talent worthy of Addison and Steele. In nearly all his writings he employs his own experiences. He is the Traveller in the poem by that name; he revives many childish memories in *The Deserted Village;* he moves through the pages of the *Vicar* in the character of George; and in his best play he recounts his own "mistakes of a night." The best criticism of him is contained in Johnson's famous epitaph:

Nullum fere scribendi genus non tetigit,
Nullum quod tetigit non ornavit.

"There is almost no form of writing that he did not touch,
And he touched none that he did not adorn."

565b THE TRAVELLER

The *Traveller* belongs to a class of philosophical poems popular in Goldsmith's day and admired by his friend Johnson. Cf. Johnson's *Vanity of Human Wishes*, p. 561 ff.

3. **Carinthian,** of the district of Carinthia in Austria-Hungary.
5. **Campania's plain,** a fertile plain on the west coast of ancient Italy.
9. **my brother,** his elder brother Henry, to whom the poem is dedicated.

566a 69. **the line,** the equator.

566b 84. **Idra,** a town in Austria-Hungary, northeast of Trieste, celebrated for its quicksilver mines.

84. **Arno,** a river in Tuscany, Italy.

569a 313. **Belgic sires,** the Belgæ of northern Gaul, among the most formidable of the ancient tribes encountered by Cæsar.

320. **Hydaspis,** a celebrated river in India.

569b 334. **learns to venerate himself.** The development of self-consciousness among the lower classes is a marked characteristic of the movement toward democracy during the eighteenth century.

570a 401 f. **Opulence — Depopulation.** The possible effects of luxury and emigration upon society were subjects of serious discussion during a considerable part of the eighteenth century. See *The Deserted Village,* ll. 51 ff. and 339 ff. and note to p. 571b, l. 63.

570b 411. **Oswego,** a river in New York flowing into Lake Ontario.

436. **Luke's iron crown.** Luke and George Dosa were engaged in a peasants' war in Hungary in 1514, in which George, not Luke, suffered torture by a red-hot iron crown, a means of punishment inflicted on regicides and rebels.

436. **Damiens' bed of steel.** Damiens was put to death by torture for his attempt on the life of Louis XV in 1757.

THE DESERTED VILLAGE

1. **Auburn.** The village is rather an idealized English village than one of any definite recollection of the poet.

571b 63. **Trade's unfeeling train.** In Goldsmith's opinion as set forth in this poem, three dangers threatened the civilization of England: luxury, emigration, commerce. See especially ll. 385, 399, and 427. See also note to *The Traveller*, p. 570a, l. 401 f.

572b 141 ff. **A man he was,** etc. Cf. the description of Chaucer's Parson, *Prologue*, p. 145a, l. 477 ff.

573b 232. **The twelve good rules,** rules of conduct ascribed to Charles I, as follows: 1. Urge no healths. 2. Profane no divine ordinances. 3. Touch no state matters. 4. Reveal no secrets. 5. Pick no quarrels. 6. Make no comparisons. 7. Maintain no ill opinions. 8. Keep no bad company. 9. Encourage no vices. 10. Make no long meals. 11. Repeat no grievances. 12. Lay no wagers.

232. **the royal game of goose,** the game of fox and geese.

575a 344. **Altama,** the Altamaha River in the state of Georgia.

576a 418. **Torno's cliffs,** the heights of Lake Torno in northern Sweden.

418. **Pambamarca,** a mountain in Ecuador.

RETALIATION

This poem was written only a few weeks before the author's death. It grew out of a playful contest in writing epitaphs on those present at a dinner held at St. James Coffee-house early in 1774.

1. **Scarron,** Paul Scarron, a French burlesque poet and dramatist of the seventeenth century.

5. **Our Dean,** Thomas Barnard, dean of Derry in Ireland.

6. **Burke,** Edmund Burke, the statesman.

7. **Will,** William Burke, a cousin of the statesman.

576b 8. **Dick,** Richard Burke, brother of the statesman.

9. **Cumberland,** Richard Cumberland, popular sentimental dramatist.

10. **Douglas,** John Douglas, canon of Windsor.

11. **Garrick,** David Garrick, the great actor.

14. **Ridge,** John Ridge, an Irish barrister.

14. **Reynolds,** Sir Joshua Reynolds, the portrait painter.

15. **Hickey,** Tom Hickey, an Irish attorney.

34. **Tommy Townshend,** a Whig member of Parliament, later Lord Sydney.

577b 86. **Dodds,** William Dodd, a clergyman and author, executed three years after the appearance of the *Retaliation* for forging a note for £4,200.

86. **Kenricks,** William Kenrick, a reviewer and playwright, unfriendly to the poet.

87. **Macpherson,** James Macpherson, author of the so-called poems of Ossian. See introductory sketch to Macpherson, p. 588.

89. **Lauders,** William Lauder, a Scottish literary impostor.

89. **Bowers,** Archibald Bower, a Scotch Jesuit and historian, who in 1740 was in ill repute in England for taking part in a questionable financial enterprise.

578a 115. **Kellys,** Hugh Kelly, a sentimental dramatist.

115. **Woodfalls,** William Woodfall, publisher of the *Morning Chronicle*.

118. **be-Rosciused,** in allusion to Churchill's *Rosciad*, a satirical criticism of English actors. Roscius, first century before Christ, was the greatest of the Roman comic actors.

124. **Beaumonts and Bens,** the Elizabethan dramatists Francis Beaumont and Ben Jonson.

578b 145. **Correggios,** Antonio Correggio, a famous Italian painter contemporary with Raphael.

146. **trumpet,** ear trumpet. Sir Joshua Reynolds was deaf.

WILLIAM COLLINS

William Collins was the son of a hatter in Chichester, Sussex. He entered Winchester College, where he was a student with Joseph Warton (see introductory note to Thomas Warton), and later went to Oxford. He showed himself precocious by composing while still at the university his *Persian Eclogues* in 1742 — the very year, it should be noted, that Gray began his *Elegy* (see introductory note to Thomas Gray). At about the same time he began to show signs of the mental disorder that was later destined to overwhelm him in madness. Without deciding upon any profession, he thought vaguely of literature as a career, went up to London, and in 1746 published a thin volume of *Odes*, containing *To Evening* and *The Passions*. In 1749 he composed his ode on the death of the poet Thomson and *On the Popular Superstitions of the Highlands of Scotland* (published 1788), but the ill success of his published volume discouraged him, and he wrote little after 1746. In 1749 a modest legacy rendered him financially independent, and he retired to the place of his birth, where he became the prey of periodical melancholia and finally died insane.

The work of Collins marks a decided step in the romantic progress that can be traced onward through Gray, Chatterton, Warton, and Bowles to Coleridge. He was an admirer of Spenser, Shakespeare, and Milton and helped to increase their influence. Though he uses too many personified abstractions and too often admits into his verses the false prettinesses and artificialities of the outworn classical diction, he shows in his verse the perfect finish of Greek form, and his sentiments are elevated far above the commonplace by genuine sincerity and a true lyric gift. He shares with Gray and the other poets of the "Graveyard School" an elegiac strain and a fondness for solitude and night, but he rises above them in his ability to idealize his emotions and to transmit them, morbid though they sometimes are. His *Ode on the Popular Superstitions of the Highlands* is significant for its early use of folklore as literary material as well as for its thoroughly romantic tone.

DIRGE IN CYMBELINE

See Shakespeare's *Cymbeline* IV, ii, 258 ff.

578a 1. **Fidele's grassy tomb.** The dirge is sung by Guiderus (Shakespeare's Guiderius) and Arviragus over the body of Imogen (whose assumed name is Fidele, *Cymbeline* III, vi, 60).

578b ODE TO SIMPLICITY

The poem illustrates the romantic reaction against artificiality and emphasizes the importance of unadorned simplicity as indispensable to true poetry.

579a 5 ff. **Fancy,** etc. According to the poet,

Simplicity or Pleasure is the parent of Fancy (Creative Imagination).

10. **decent,** decorous, unpretentious.

11. **Attic robe,** a robe marked by the simplicity that characterized ancient Athenian art and life.

14. **Hybla's thymy shore.** Hybla was an ancient city on the east coast of Sicily, celebrated for the honey produced in the vicinity.

18. **sad Electra's poet's ear.** The Greek dramatist Sophocles represents his character Electra, in the drama that bears her name, as being soothed in sorrow by the song of the nightingale.

19. **Cephisus,** a river in Attica, flowing by the city of Athens.

21. **thy green retreat,** Athens.

23. **When holy Freedom died.** Compare Gray, *Progress of Poesy*, p. 586a, l. 77 ff. Collins thinks of Simplicity as having abandoned Greece after the conquest of that country by Alexander the Great (335 B.C.) and as having found "no equal haunt" to allure her "future feet." Gray, on the other hand, represents the true muse of Poetry as having abandoned conquered Greece for Rome and as having departed thence to England. It is well to note the constant emphasis laid by eighteenth-century romantic theorists upon freedom as necessary for the production of true poetry.

32 ff. **virtue's patriot theme.** As long as Rome esteemed above all other poetry that inspired by patriotic virtue (heroic manhood), Simplicity loved her hills and inspired her "laureate band" (poets), but when Freedom (the Republic) had departed and the Empire had been established, Simplicity remained long enough to sing during one distinguished reign (that of Augustus), and then "fled [the] altered land."

579b ODE TO EVENING

Note the fact that the poem is composed in unrhymed stanzas.

1. **If.** The conclusion of this if-clause begins with l. 15.

7. **With brede ethereal wove,** woven with braid (or embroidery) made of the more subtle (ethereal) elements of the atmosphere.

21. **folding star,** "the star that bids the shepherd fold" (Milton's *Comus*, l. 93).

580a 23. **Hours.** See note to Milton's *Comus*, l. 986.

41. **wont,** is wont, (accustomed) to do.

46 ff. **Winter . . . Affrights,** etc. A poetical way of saying that winter shortens evening and makes it give place quickly to night.

49 f. **So long,** etc. Collins seems to imply that Evening under proper circumstances favors imagination, friendship, etc.

THE PASSIONS

When Music on one occasion happened to lay aside her instruments, the Passions (emotions) seized them and proceeded to express themselves. At the close of the poem, ll. 95–118, Collins calls on Music to resume her former position of preëminence.

580b 11. **myrtles.** In classical mythology and literary tradition the myrtle is associated with Apollo and the Muses.

35. **She called on Echo still.** The meaning seems to be that Hope depends on some encouragement from the Future, even though the call be but an echo.

43. **denouncing,** announcing, proclaiming.

52. **ball of sight,** eyeball.

581a 75. **oak-crowned sisters, and their chaste-eyed queen,** wood nymphs and their queen, the chaste Diana.

581b 91. **zone,** girdle.

92. **he,** Love, Cupid.

101. **mimic,** skilled in imitation.

108. **thy recording sister's page,** history. Clio was the muse of History.

114. **Cecilia's . . . world of sound.** On St. Cecilia, see notes to Dryden's *Song for St. Cecilia's Day*, p. 438, and *Alexander's Feast*, p. 439.

ODE ON THE DEATH OF MR. THOMSON

While a young man, Collins was befriended by the older nature poet, Thomson, p. 540, whose death in 1748 he lamented in the present "ode," or elegy.

1. **druid.** To the eighteenth-century poetic mind the bards (poets) of ancient Britain were closely associated with the druids (magicians). As a modern representative of the magic art of poetry, Thomson might be referred to in the conventional phraseology of the time as a druid.

THOMAS GRAY

Thomas Gray was born in London in 1716. His father, a ne'er-do-well scrivener, and his mother, an industrious milliner in Cornhill, had twelve children, of whom Thomas alone survived. He entered Eton College (see his *Ode on a Distant Prospect of Eton College*), where his mother's brothers were assistant masters. Here he became the friend of Richard West (son of the Lord Chancellor of Ireland) and Horace Walpole (son of the Prime Minister), who was afterward to play so prominent a part in the literary world, (see introductory note to Walpole, p. 639). At school Gray had few associates, took no part in athletics, and was regarded as somewhat effeminate. In fact, as Walpole said of him, he " was never a boy." In 1734 he and Walpole entered Cambridge University, where Gray became a pensioner at Peterhouse and his friend a member of King's College. At Cambridge he was a diligent student of the Latin and Greek classics and the modern languages, but he found the regular curriculum a bore, and in 1738 left the university without a degree. In 1739 he went abroad with Horace Walpole and remained for two years, making the " grand tour " of Europe. The year 1742 is noteworthy in his career. He spent the summer at Stoke Poges, where his now widowed mother had taken up her residence and whither he often returned in later years. In the same year he composed his *Ode on a Distant Prospect of Eton College* and his sonnet *On the Death of Richard West*, and commenced his *Elegy Written in a Country Church-Yard* — the latter not completed, and none of them published till years afterward. In the winter of 1742 he returned to Cambridge, where he spent most of the remainder of his life in seclusion. In 1744 he graduated as LL.B., but he never practiced law. In 1757 he was offered the position of poet laureate, but declined the honor. In 1768 he was appointed professor of modern history, but delivered no lectures. He collected many notes for a history of English poetry, but upon learning that Thomas Warton had undertaken a similar task, he gave up the project, (see introductory note to Thomas Warton, p. 596). Though he was always of a sensitive and retiring nature and lived for the most part in the world of books, he was, as his writings show, interested in the social and political life of his day. He was a voluminous reader and was regarded, probably not without justice, as the most learned man in contemporary Europe.

Gray was an academic poet. His verse is small in volume, and is rarely spontaneous; but it is in general highly artistic and is especially significant as showing more obviously than is often the case the development of a literary genius under new influences. In his poetic work can be traced the history of English Romanticism. His *Ode on a Distant Prospect of Eton College*, composed in 1742 soon after the death of his friend West, is sincere in its gloomy pessimism, but its language is tinged with the " poetic diction " of the school of Pope (see notes to p. 582b, l. 25 ff.). The *Elegy*, begun the same year and completed nearly a decade later, is classical in little but form; in its delicate feeling for nature, its pensive enjoyment of evening and melancholy, and its emphasis on the nobility of simple folk, it is romantic. In 1754 he composed *The Progress of Poesy*, a Pindaric ode on the conventional theme of "progress" (see Shakespeare's Sonnet XXXII and note), but smacking of romanticism in its enthusiasm over older English poetry and its emphasis on original genius. In the same year he wrote *The Fatal Sisters* and *The Descent of Odin*, both based on mediæval Scandinavian tradition and both thoroughly romantic both in form and in spirit, and *The Bard*, a poem completely inspired by romantic enthusiasm over the character and genius of the ancient British poet. Contrast Johnson's opinion of Gray, p. 622 ff.

ODE ON A DISTANT PROSPECT OF ETON COLLEGE

Eton College, one of the most famous English public schools, is situated in the valley of the Thames River twenty-two miles west of London and just below the eminence on which stands the town and royal castle of Windsor. It was founded in 1440 by Henry VI, 1422–1461. Gray attended Eton (see introductory note).

582a 2. **watery glade,** the valley of the Thames.

12. **beloved in vain.** Gray had recently been estranged from one of his Eton friends (Walpole) and had lost by death another (West); hence he might in temporary bitterness of soul speak of his early loves as having been in vain.

582b 25 f. **to cleave . . . glassy wave.** The poets of the classical school believed that poetry should have a special, or " poetical," vocabulary. This doctrine resulted in artificiality. The reaction culminated with Wordsworth's doctrine of simplicity in poetic diction (see Preface to *Lyrical Ballads*, p. 815, and note). The phrase quoted here is simply the pseudo-classicist's way of saying: " to swim in thy clear water."

29. **To chase,** etc., to play at rolling the hoop. Another classical artificiality — a refusal to call things by their simple names.

30. **urge the flying ball,** play cricket (see notes to ll. 25 f. and 29.

583a

SONNET

ON THE DEATH OF RICHARD WEST

Gray and, later, Warton (see p. 597) helped to restore to popularity the sonnet which had fallen into disuse since the time of Milton. The revival of the sonnet is one of the marks of the revolt against the regularity of eighteenth-century classical verse. See introductory note to Sir Philip Sidney's *Astrophel and Stella*, p. 273a. To get an idea of the development of the romantic theory of poetic diction during the eighteenth century, see note to p. 582b, l. 25 f., and then Wordsworth's criticism of Gray's sonnet, p. 818b, l. 14 ff. See, further, introductory note to William Lisle Bowles, p. 599. West (see introductory note to Thomas Gray) died in 1742.

3. **descant.** Gray applies to the songs of the birds a technical term used in music. A descant is a tune with various modulations.

ELEGY WRITTEN IN A COUNTRY CHURCH-YARD

This celebrated poem was begun in 1742, but was not finished until 1750. In 1751 Gray got Walpole to have it published to prevent it from being pirated.

The term "elegy" may be applied to any serious poem pervaded by a tone of actual grief or reflective melancholy. Gray's *Elegy* carries on the tradition of reflective verse exemplified by Milton's *Il Penseroso* and represents the high-water mark of the contemporary poetry of night and melancholy. Its tremendous popularity is due to its striking and melodious phraseology, its democratic sentiments, and its universality of appeal.

The "church-yard" in which the poem is represented as written is that of Stoke Poges, a village situated in Buckinghamshire twenty-three miles from London and not far from Eton. It is the resort of thousands of literary pilgrims yearly. For Gray's association with the place, see introductory sketch.

583b 35. **Awaits.** This seems to be bad grammar, but it is the reading that Gray obviously preferred. The meaning appears to be: "The inevitable hour of death is waiting for all — the great, the beautiful, and the rich."

39. **fretted vault,** a vault crossed by moldings intersecting in such a fashion as to form diamonds or other geometrical figures.

584a 57. **some village Hampden,** some one who will oppose unjust local taxes as the famous English statesman, John Hampden, 1594–1643, resisted the unjust taxation of Charles I.

59. **Milton.** In their enthusiasm over the importance of untutored genius as opposed to technical training and polish as an essential to great poetry, eighteenth-century theorists believed that the highest genius might ere long be discovered among unlettered rustics. When Burns finally appeared, they triumphantly asserted that their claims were justified.

60. **Cromwell guiltless of his country's blood,** a man with Cromwell's greatness but without his guilt.

73. **Far from the madding crowd's ignoble strife.** We might expect "maddening," but Gray's use of "madding" has merely helped to establish the participial form of the verb "to mad," which already existed. The line suggested the title to one of Mr. Thomas Hardy's best-known novels.

584b 81. **spelt by the unlettered Muse.** Some of the inscriptions in Stoke Poges church-yard are misspelt.

85 ff. **For who,** etc. The meaning seems to be: "Who ever resigned this pleasing, though anxious, life to be a prey to forgetfulness, and left no memorial behind?"

585a 125 ff. **No farther,** etc. The "dread abode" is not, as would appear from the construction, the "bosom of his Father and his God."

THE PROGRESS OF POESY

The ode was originally a form of lyric poem expressive of exalted or enthusiastic emotion, written in a somewhat complicated though regular metrical form, and intended for singing. Abraham Cowley (see p. 435) adopted an irregular type of ode, which became extremely popular during the late seventeenth and early eighteenth centuries. Gray, familiar as he was with the original Pindaric form, divides his ode into three stanzas with forty-one lines each. The individual stanzas are divided into three parts — strophe, antistrophe, and epode, corresponding to the "turn," the "counterturn," and the "stand," of the Greek chorus. Aside from its other excellences, the poem is an admirable example of symmetrical structure. It is full of Miltonic echoes. See, further, note to Congreve's *Ode*, p. 441.

1. **Æolian lyre,** an invocation to Pindar (*ca.* 522 B.C. to 443 B.C.), the greatest of the Greek lyric poets and a member of the Æolian division of the Greeks.

3 f. **Helicon's harmonious springs,** etc., the fountain of the Muses on Mount Helicon, from which flow the streams of the world's poetry.

9. **Ceres' golden reign,** fields of grain, presided over by Ceres (Demeter), the divinity of crops.

13. **Sovereign of the willing soul,** music and poetry — the lyre, here called a "shell" because the first lyre was said to have been made out of a tortoise shell.

17 f. **On Thracia's hills the Lord of War,** etc. The inhabitants of Thrace (the entire northern region of ancient Greece) were particularly noted for their fierceness; hence the special association of their country with Mars, the god of War.

21. **the feathered king,** Jove's eagle.

585b 27. **Idalia's velvet-green.** Idalium, a town on the coast of Cyprus, contained a temple sacred to Venus (Cytherea, l. 29), who was sometimes called Idalia.

53. **Hyperion's march,** the rising of the sun.

54 ff. **In climes,** etc. Lines 54 to 65 are especially significant as indicating (1) some of the new sources of inspiration which were being opened to English poets during the eighteenth century and (2) Gray's conviction, which he shared with some of his contemporaries, that poetic genius is not confined to civilized peoples. In a note on this passage he writes, "Extensive influence of poetic genius over the remotest and most uncivilized nations: its connection with liberty, and the virtues that naturally attend on it." He then refers to several collections of supposedly primitive poetry which had been printed before the note was written.

56. **The Muse has broke the twilight gloom.** Gray is probably referring to certain Lapland songs that were known to the English public of his day.

59 ff. **Chili's boundless forests,** etc. Gray is here probably thinking of the Indian love song given by Montaigne in his essay *Of the Cannibals*, p. 314a.

586a 68. **Ilissus,** a small river that flows through Athens.

69. **Mæander's amber waves,** a small, winding river in western Asia Minor famous in Greek heroic tradition. Cf. Milton's *Comus*, l. 232.

77 ff. **Till the sad Nine,** the Nine Muses. Ancient Greece, Gray tells us, was full of poetry, but when she lost her freedom the Muses departed and took up their abode in Italy ("the Latian plains," l. 78); when Rome fell, they emigrated to Britain ("Albion," l. 82).

83. **Far from the sun,** etc., far from sunny Italy — in England, where the climate is less genial.

84. **Nature's darling,** Shakespeare.

92 f. **This can unlock the gates of Joy, Of horror that,** etc.; *i.e.*, Shakespeare by reason of his genius was master of comedy, of tragedy, and in general of the means of moving the human emotions.

95. **second he, that rose sublime,** Milton. The references in the following lines are of course to *Paradise Lost* and to the poet's blindness.

586b 105. **Two coursers,** the two lines of the heroic couplet, Dryden's favorite verse form.

108. **Fancy,** Imagination.

112 ff. **what daring spirit Wakes thee now?** etc. The remaining lines imply that Gray himself is the "daring spirit" who disregards convention and soars on the wings of inspiration.

115. **Theban Eagle,** Pindar.

121. **keep his distant way,** a reference to Gray's retiring disposition.

THE BARD

The Bard was begun in 1754, but was not finished until 1757. It is based on a meager and unhistorical tradition that Edward I, upon the English conquest of Wales in 1276–1284, ordered all the bards that came in his way to be put to death. Most of the poem is thus the work of Gray's imagination. The events of the poem are probably thought of as having occurred in 1282, when Gilbert de Clare (see note to l. 13), after having conducted a campaign in south Wales, joined with King Edward on his expedition into the northwest.

Ruin seize thee, etc. The original plan of the poem is given thus by the author: "The army of Edward I., as they march through a deep valley, and approach Mount Snowdon, are suddenly stopped by the appearance of a venerable figure seated on the summit of an inaccessible rock, who, with a voice more than human, reproaches the king with all the desolation and misery which he had brought on his country; foretells the misfortunes of the Norman race, and with prophetic spirit declares that all his cruelty shall never extinguish the noble ardour of poetic genius in this island; and that men shall never be wanting to celebrate true virtue and valour in immortal strains, to expose vice and infamous pleasure, and boldly censure tyranny and oppression. His song ended, he precipitates himself from the mountain, and is swallowed up in the river that rolls at its foot."

4. **idle state,** useless ostentation.

8. **Cambria's.** Cambria is Wales.

11. **Snowdon's shaggy side,** the wooded side of Mount Snowdon, a range of high peaks in Carnarvonshire and Merionethshire, north Wales.

13. **Glo'ster,** "Gilbert de Clare, surnamed the Red, Earl of Gloucester and Hertford, son-in-law to King Edward" (Gray).

14. **Mortimer,** "Edmond de Mortimer, Lord of Wigmore" (Gray). He and Gloucester were among those especially commissioned by the king to guard the Welsh frontier.

16. **Conway's . . . flood.** The Conway is a small river in north Wales emptying into Beaumaris Bay.

587a 18. **the Poet.** The image of the Bard, Gray informs us, is taken from a famous painting by Raphael, representing God in the vision of Ezekiel. In accordance with eighteenth-century notions about original genius, the bard is thought of as composing spontaneously and under the influence of strong emotion. He resembles contemporary pictures of Homer as an untutored but great composer of rhapsodies.

27 f. **Cambria's fatal day,** etc. Since the conquest of Wales the bards have been silent. Hoel was a prince as well as a bard. Llewellyn (ap Gruffydd), who became prince of Wales in 1246, was slain in 1282 by one of Mortimer's knights; his death was lamented by several bards.

28. **Soft Llewellyn's lay,** the lay celebrating the mild, or tender-hearted Llewellyn.

29 ff. **Cadwallo's tongue . . . Urien . . . Modred.** Gray here introduces Cadwallo, Urien, and Modred as ancient Welsh bards. No bard named Modred is known.

34. **Plinlimmon,** a famous mountain on the border of Cardigan and Montgomery in Wales.

35. **Arvon's shore,** "the shores of Caernarvonshire opposite to the isle of Anglesey" (Gray).

54 ff. **Severn . . . Berkley's roofs . . . shrieks of an agonizing King . . . She-wolf of France.** King Edward II, son of Edward I, was brutally murdered (1327) in Berkeley Castle (near the Severn River) partly through the machinations of his faithless wife, Isabella of France.

587b 60 ff. **The scourge of Heaven,** etc. Edward III, son of Edward II, after a troubled though successful reign marked by devastating wars, especially in France, survived his distinguished son, the Black Prince ("the Sable Warrior," l. 67), and died lonely and deserted.

71 ff. **Fair laughs the morn,** etc. Gray in a note tells us that the following lines refer to the magnificence of the reign of Richard II, son of Edward the Black Prince.

81. **Fell Thirst and Famine scowl.** According to the authorities followed by Gray, Richard II was starved to death. Cf. Daniel's *Civil Wars*, p. 234a ff. The source used by Shakespeare in his *Richard II* attributes the King's death to Sir Pierce of Exton; this story, Gray asserts, "is of much later date." As one writer observes, "the tongues of rumour are always busy when the great ones of the earth die suddenly."

83 ff. **Heard ye the din,** etc. The following lines, according to Gray, refer to the "ruinous civil wars of York and Lancaster," the Wars of the Roses.

87 ff. **Ye towers of Julius,** etc. "Henry the Sixth, George Duke of Clarence, Edward the Fifth, Richard Duke of York, etc., believed to be murthered secretly in the Tower of London. The oldest part of that structure is vulgarly attributed to Julius Cæsar" (Gray).

89 f. **Revere his consort's faith,** etc. Margaret of Anjou, "a woman of heroic spirit, who struggled hard to save her Husband (Henry VI) and her crown" (Gray). His father was Henry V.

588a 90. **the meek usurper's holy head.** "Henry the Sixth came very near being canonized. The line of Lancaster had no right of inheritance to the Crown" (Gray).

91 f. **the rose of snow . . . her blushing foe,** "the white and red roses, devices of York and Lancaster" (Gray).

93 f. **The bristled Boar in infant gore,** etc. Richard III, whose badge was a silver boar, caused the death of the two young sons of Edward IV in the Tower of London and waded through blood to the throne.

99. **Half of thy heart,** etc. Edward I was deeply attached to his queen, Eleanor of Castile, who died in 1290.

104. **They,** the slaughtered bards referred to in l. 47 ff.

109. **Arthur.** On the Welsh national faith that King Arthur would return, see note to p. 97b, l. 333.

110. **ye genuine kings.** "Both Merlin and Taliessin (an ancient Welsh bard, l. 121) had prophesied that the Welsh should regain their sovereignty over this island; which seemed to be accomplished in the House of Tudor (Henry VII, Henry VIII, Edward VI, Mary, and Elizabeth)" (Gray).

588b 127. **Truth severe, by fairy Fiction drest.** The reference is to Spenser's *Faerie Queene*, with its allegory cloaked by "fairy fiction." See introductory note to Edmund Spenser, p. 217.

128 ff. **In buskined measures move.** A reference to Shakespeare's tragedies.

131 ff. **A Voice,** etc., Milton.

133 f. **distant warblings,** etc., "the succession of poets after Milton's time" (Gray).

141. **Be thine Despair.** Edward had a troubled reign and died a worn-out old man.

JAMES MACPHERSON

James Macpherson was born in the Highlands of Scotland. After studying at the Universities of Aberdeen and Edinburgh, he began life as a schoolmaster. While acting as private tutor to a young nobleman, he met the dramatist John Home, to whom he showed a number of short pieces which he claimed were translations of poems composed by a third-century Caledonian bard named Ossian. Under the patronage of the distinguished Edinburgh critic, Hugh Blair, Macpherson's *Fragments of Ancient [Gaelic] Poetry* appeared in 1760. This volume was followed in 1761 and 1763 by *Fingal* and *Temora,* two longer compositions which Macpherson called "epics" and also attributed to Ossian. Later Macpherson wrote numerous political pamphlets dealing with the struggle between Great Britain and the American colonies. He spent some time in Pensacola, Florida. His last years were divided between London and his native Highlands, where he died in 1796.

The eighteenth-century enthusiasm over mediæval poetry which encouraged imitations and forgeries of English and Scottish ballads (see notes to pp. 163, 533, and 538) helped to insure the success of Macpherson's alleged translations of ancient Celtic epic verse. Ossian, especially the *Fragments,* achieved immediate popularity throughout Europe and exercised a profound influence, particularly upon romantic poets in their younger and more sentimental compositions. By many critics Ossian was hailed as triumphant evidence that Original Genius, unhampered by classical rules and operating among a simple and untutored folk such as the ancient Caledonians were believed to have been, could produce epic poetry comparable to that of Homer (see note to p. 607b, l. 37 f.). From the beginning, however, doubt existed as to whether Macpherson's prose poems were the genuine remains of an ancient Celtic Homer or entirely modern compositions. The result was a long literary controversy which was not finally settled till comparatively recent years. Noteworthy among the contemporary skeptics was Dr. Johnson (p. 628b, l. 33), who, when Macpherson threatened him, replied in a famous letter (p. 638).

Macpherson, it appears, knew little Gaelic, the language from which he claimed to have translated his Ossian. Aside from a few proper names, a few wisps of Gaelic story, and perhaps a touch of sentimentalism and melancholy, Ossian contains nothing that is likely to have been derived, even indirectly, from Celtic sources. The author's genius consists in the skill with which he combined his scanty Celtic materials with the parallelism and cadenced style of the Psalms, the language of Pope's Homer and of eighteenth-century classical poetry, the melancholy of the "Graveyard School," and contemporary ideas regarding the excessive delicacy and sentimentalism of primitive man, to form a whole which illustrated even better than Homer contemporary theories of what a primitive epic should be. In thus reconstructing the "lost epic" of the Scottish people, Macpherson was only following the tendencies of his age. Just how far he intended to deceive we do not know. In any case, his Ossian possesses a grandiose and vague beauty which shows the author to have been a man of real poetic genius. For a sample of genuine Ossianic poetry and the facts concerning the Irish Ossian, see p. 62b and note.

THE DEATH OF CUTHULLIN

In this prose poem, as in most of Macpherson's Ossianic works, the thread of the narrative is obscure without some preliminary explanation. According to the author, the story on which it is based runs as follows: Cuthullin, the guardian of the young king Cormac of Ireland, is attacked by the rebel Torlath, who advances upon Tara (Temora) to dethrone Cormac. "Cuthullin marched against him, came up with him at the Lake of Lego, and totally defeated his forces. Torlath fell in battle by Cuthullin's hand; but as he [Cuthullin] too eagerly pressed on the enemy, he was mortally wounded."

Macpherson's account, it should be observed, has no justification in authentic Irish tradition. According to the ancient Irish epic, Cuchulainn, forced by an inexorable fate, encountered a number of his enemies and fell heroically, overpowered by numbers. For another version, the product of a nineteenth-century poetic imagination, see Yeats's poem, p. 1123 f.

1. **Fingal,** the name used by Macpherson and the older English poets generally for the Irish Finn. See note to Ossian, p. 62.

5. **Bragela . . . Sorglan.** These, like others of Macpherson's proper names, are apparently imaginary.

7. **Cuthullin's sails.** *Cuthullin* is Macpherson's spelling for Cuchullin or Cuchulainn, who is the chief hero of the Ulster or Red Branch cycle of early Gaelic literature, and, according to Irish tradition, flourished nearly three centuries before Finn. See especially the introductory note to *The Feast of Bricriu,* p. 59a, and the note to p. 59a, l. 10.

11. **Semo.** According to Macpherson, Cuchulainn was the son of Semo, another imaginary personage. In authentic tradition he is the son of Sualtam or Sualtach.

13. **Togorma,** one of the Hebrides (Macpherson).

589a 7. **Dunscai's walls,** the walls of the *dun* (fortress) of Skye (?). Skye, the largest and most northerly of the Inner Hebrides Islands, is associated in tradition with the name of Cuchulainn.

13 f. **The feast of shells.** Contrary to all justification in ancient Celtic tradition, Macpherson makes his heroes drink out of shells.

14 f. **Carril strikes the harp.** In connection with the romantic interest in early poets and poetry, note throughout the poem the prominence given to the bards and their songs.

20. **Connal.** See note to p. 59a, l. 10.

22. **Cormac.** According to the Irish annals, Cormac, who figures in Irish Ossianic literature as a contemporary of Finn, was high king of Ireland, A.D. 218–254. Macpherson represents Cormac as a young king under the guardianship of Cuthullin (Cuchulainn), whom tradition fixes several centuries earlier.

36 f. **Temora's echoing halls.** *Temora* is one of Macpherson's spellings for Temair, Temrach, the Tara of Irish tradition. See note to p. 59a, l. 5.

589b 18. **Slimora,** apparently manufactured by Macpherson from the Gaelic *sliabh mór*, great mountain.

45. **Caithbat.** This figure is probably borrowed from Cathbad, who appears as a powerful druid in the Ulster cycle of ancient Irish literature. See note to *The Feast of Bricriu*, p. 59.

590a 7 ff. **'Who,'** etc. "Alcletha speaks" (Macpherson).

19 ff. **"But it is covered,** etc. "Alcletha speaks" (Macpherson).

38. **The ghost of Calmar.** The feeble, insubstantial spirits with which Macpherson's Ossian teems are quite different from the forthright, virile ghosts of genuine folk tradition.

590b 39. **Lochlin's seas.** Lochlann is the Gaelic name for Scandinavia.

591a 21. **Tura's,** apparently another of Macpherson's spellings for Temora (Tara). See note to p. 589a, l. 36 f.

37. **Selma — Morven's woody land,** Macpherson's names respectively for the capital and domain of Fingal.

THOMAS CHATTERTON

Thomas Chatterton was the posthumous son of a poor schoolmaster in Bristol and was brought up under the shadow of the noble mediæval minster of St. Mary Redcliffe, which Queen Elizabeth had called "the fairest, the goodliest, and most famous parish-church in England." Lonely, introspective, precocious, Chatterton while still a child pored over books of antiquarian lore and early formed a plan to deceive his fellow townsmen, especially a certain gullible antiquarian named George Catcott, with forged documents bearing on the history of Bristol. By the help of some ancient vellum manuscripts preserved in the muniment room of the church, where his uncle was sexton, he manufactured documents containing spurious historical information. He also made up from his reading a crude vocabulary of archaic words which, without much attention to grammar or syntax, he used in composing a series of poems attributed by him to a mythical fifteenth-century monk whom he called Thomas Rowley. In 1769 he sent some of his writings to Horace Walpole (see introductory note to Walpole, p. 639), who was deceived at first (see his letter, p. 640), but later dropped the matter, much to Chatterton's chagrin. In 1770 he went up to London, where, after an unsuccessful attempt at a literary career, he became desperate and at last when on the verge of starvation tore his latest prose and verse to bits and poisoned himself with arsenic in a Holborn attic before he was eighteen years old. In spite of the fact that Chatterton's writings were recognized during his life time as spurious, in the eyes of the later romantic poets he became a great original genius and the boy martyr of romanticism.

In composing his Rowley poems Chatterton, inspired by Ossian (see introductory note to Macpherson, p. 588) and the common eighteenth-century desire to unearth further remains of mediæval genius, was far more than a naughty boy playing tricks on his elders. Though his ungrammatical and laborious archaisms deceived many in an age when little was known of the Middle English language, the facts have long since been discovered; to-day the problem is not linguistic but psychological. He died too young for his work to furnish more than promise of future accomplishments, but even on the basis of what he left he may be called in certain respects the most romantic poet of his time. Lonely, sensitive, gifted, he brooded in the gloomy shadows of St. Mary's till his soul was flooded by a longing for the past, and his creative genius responded by catching at times the true spirit of mediæval poetry. Chatterton's work is the work of a child, but a child of exalted, though irregular, genius.

591b BRISTOWE TRAGEDIE

The source of Chatterton's poem was probably some account of the execution at Bristol of Sir Baldwin Fulford, by act of attainder, after the accession of Edward IV, in 1461. Fulford had opposed Edward's claims to the throne. Bristowe is Bristol.

Chatterton's poems are easier to read if one recalls that, in addition to introducing old spellings, he frequently doubles letters without any justification.

5. **Kynge Edwarde,** Edward IV.

17. **Sir Canterlone,** an adaptation of the name Cantlow or Cantelow.

592a 45. **Maister Canynge,** William Canynge, a merchant and mayor of Bristol in the reigns of Henry VI and Edward IV.

593a 141. **goddelyke Henrie.** King Henry VI lived in captivity for a number of years after his dethronement. On the applicability of "goddelyke," see note to p. 588a, l. 90.

593b 183. **Richard's sonnes,** Edward IV and Richard, Duke of Gloucester, later Richard III.

594b 276. **bataunt,** a stringed instrument, which apparently was the product of Chatterton's imagination.

595b MYNSTRELLES SONG

In *Ælla*

8. **cryne,** hair.
9. **rode,** skin.
17. **codgelle,** cudgel.
17. **stote,** stout.

596a 25. **heie,** they.

38. **Nee,** not.
39. **celness,** coldness.
43. **dente,** fix, arrange.
44. **gre,** grow.
45. **Ouphante,** elfin.
53. **nete,** night.
57. **reytes,** water flags.
58. **leathalle,** deadly.

THOMAS WARTON

Thomas Warton, Jr., the brother of Joseph Warton, the distinguished eighteenth-century critic of Pope, was born at Basingstoke, Hampshire, some forty miles southwest of London, where his father, also named Thomas, was vicar and master of the grammar school. After studying the classics and reading widely under his father's supervision, young Warton entered Oxford in his sixteenth year. In spite of his rather easy-going and convivial habits, he was soon elected one of the twelve scholars of Trinity College. After taking the A.B. and A.M. degrees, he was appointed to a fellowship, and he remained a tutor and fellow of Trinity for the rest of his life. He became poet laureate in 1785 and also at one time occupied the poetry professorship of the university, a position formerly held by his father. Immediately after his first degree, 1747, he became a clergyman, but his only charges were small village churches near Oxford. Though he was not distinguished as a preacher and was generally lacking in ambition, he was a learned and indefatigable antiquarian and had a wide circle of correspondents among the literary men of his day. He composed verse both in Latin and in English, but in the estimation of most literary historians his importance rests upon his *Observations on the Faerie Queene* of Spenser, 1754, which was the first successful attempt to rescue that poet from the neglect into which he had fallen, and his *History of English Poetry*, 1774–1789, a work of great erudition, which not only brought to light many samples of early English poetic genius but is actually the first history of English literature to apply the modern historical method of criticism.

Thomas Warton's father, though a friend of Pope, was to some extent influenced by the new romantic spirit. His small body of verse, published by his son Joseph after his death, proves that he was interested in Spenser and in the literature of primitive peoples and of the Middle Ages, and it is probably from him that Joseph and Thomas, Jr. derived the fondness for the past and the highly developed historical sense that enabled the elder brother to estimate more sanely than his contemporaries the accomplishments of the great idol of the classicists, Pope, and the younger to perceive the genius of a much neglected poet of an earlier period. It was from his father too, as well as from his environment, that Thomas acquired his first stimulus toward antiquarian research, which resulted ultimately in a small body of verse including the ode on *The Grave of King Arthur* and the sonnets on Dugdale's *Monasticon* and on Stonehenge. These three poems are genuinely romantic in their enthusiastic idealization of ancient times. In spirit at least, if not in form, they were surpassed by none of Warton's successors in the Romantic Movement. Warton also contributed somewhat toward the development of the romantic feeling for nature.

THE GRAVE OF KING ARTHUR

As pointed out in the note to p. 134b, l. 15 ff., there were two mediæval traditions regarding the fate of Arthur after his last battle. What may be called the "romantic" tradition is the one that has most frequently been treated by English poets (see the versions of Layamon, Malory, and Tennyson, referred to in the note just cited). The other, or "realistic," account is the one emphasized by Warton in *The Grave of King*

Arthur. According to the chroniclers and other sober "historians" of the Middle Ages, Arthur was actually slain in the battle of Camlan and was afterward buried in the "vale of Avalon," which was identified with Glastonbury abbey in Somerset (see note to p. 97b, l. 325). The claim was even made that Henry II of England had caused the grave to be opened and the body disclosed, thus destroying forever the hopes of the Welsh people that Arthur would ultimately return to liberate his country.

6. **Henry,** Henry II of England, who ruled 1154–1189.

7 f. **Prepared to stain,** etc. Warton represents the events of the poem as taking place just before Henry's invasion of Ireland in 1171. The Shannon lakes are situated in the south of Ireland, where Henry was chiefly active.

12. **metheglin,** mead, once a favorite drink among the Welsh.

596b 20 **Mona,** the island of Anglesea, famous in ancient times as a seat of the druids and bards.

21 f. **Teivi,** a small river in southwestern Wales; **Elvy's vale,** valley of the river Elwy, in northwestern Wales; **Cader's crown,** Cader Idris is a prominent mountain in northwestern Wales. The poet simply means that bards had come from all over Wales.

24. **Ierne's hoarse abyss,** the Irish Sea.

26 **Radnor's.** Radnor is a mountainous county in the heart of Wales.

33. **Tintagell's topmost tower.** On Tintagel, see note to p. 96b, l. 247 ff.

40. **Camlan's crimsoned banks.** The Welsh annals treat Arthur's death as historical and date the battle of Camlan A.D. 537.

54. **Arabia,** here simply a far-off land of enchantment.

597a 76. **a bard.** Compare the description of a similar figure in Gray's *Bard*, p. 586b, l. 15 ff.

85. **read,** advice, story.

100. **Locrine,** son of the mythical Brutus (see note to p. 88b, l. 25), one of the traditional kings of Britain.

104. **Clyder's head,** a mountain in Carnarvonshire.

116 f. **Joseph's towered fane,** etc. According to a tradition preserved in mediæval romance, Glastonbury was founded by Joseph of Arimathea, who came to Britain after the crucifixion of Christ bringing with him the Holy Grail. On the identification of Glastonbury with Avalon, see note to p. 97b, l. 325.

127. **the ruthless Dane.** On the destruction of church property by the Danes, see note to p. 51a, l. 19.

597b 134. **Yon recreant isle,** Ireland.

142. **gigantic stature.** Arthur, like other heroes of romance, was early endowed with supernatural strength and size.

154. **Harald's bay,** the bay of Dublin, named for the Norwegian king Harald Fairhair, the reputed founder of the city.

158. **Roderick's heart.** Roderick O'Connor, king of Connaught and, before the English invasion, high king of Ireland, long resisted the invaders and did not render submission until 1175.

171. **Pictish kings.** Among the enemies of the ancient Britons were the Picts, a people from the north of Britain; hence Arthur may be thought of as having fought against them.

SONNETS

WRITTEN IN A BLANK LEAF OF DUGDALE'S *MONASTICON*

Sir William Dugdale, 1605–1686, was a distinguished antiquary and the better known of the two authors of the *Monasticon Anglicanum*, 1655–1673, a famous history of the monastic orders of England. Warton made great use of the book as a source for his *History of English Poetry*.

598a 5. **Henry's fiercer rage.** At the time that Henry VIII disestablished the monasteries of England, 1536–1540, there was wholesale destruction of church property.

13 f. **Not rough . . . flowers.** These lines express admirably the romantic attitude toward antiquarian research.

WRITTEN AT STONEHENGE

Stonehenge is a celebrated prehistoric group of standing stones on Salisbury Plain, Wiltshire. The question of its origin fascinated and baffled antiquarians of the eighteenth century as it has archæologists and other scholars of a later date. It appears to have been built as a sun temple, and was associated with the dead, but by whom it was constructed nobody knows. Warton here summarizes some of the theories current in his day.

2. **Scythia's shore.** See note to p. 59b, l. 3.

3. **Amber's fatal plain.** The name *Amber Isles* was applied by the Greek to Britain and other lands thought of vaguely as lying in the North Sea. Camden calls the site of Stonehenge *Amber's plains* (Mant.).

5. **Hengist's guile.** Hengist, according to tradition, was one of the leaders of the Saxon invaders of Britain. He is here represented as in conflict with Uther Pendragon, the father of King Arthur. Some modern scholars believe that Stonehenge was erected as a sepulchral monument. See also l. 10 f.

11. **Brutus' genuine line.** See note to p. 88b, l. 25.

TO THE RIVER LODON

The Lodon is a small river near Basingstoke, where Warton's early years were spent (see introductory note to Thomas Warton). The poem is therefore to some extent autobiographic. In its reminiscent idealization of early life seen through the haze of memory it is genuinely romantic.

ROBERT FERGUSSON

Born in Edinburgh, Robert Fergusson, the son of a bank clerk, was educated in the high school of the city and at the University of St. Andrew's, but before finishing his career he was recalled from the latter institution by the death of his father and found employment as a copying clerk in a lawyer's office. Soon afterward he began contributing sprightly songs to Ruddiman's *Weekly Magazine;* and possessing a vivacious wit and some skill in music, he was much sought after in the easier social circles of the Scottish capital. Under this stimulus he fell into intemperate habits and impaired his naturally frail constitution, his mind gave way, and he was committed to a madhouse and died there at the early age of twenty-three. Though he is known chiefly as a precursor and inspirer of Burns, his undoubted talent, coupled with the circumstances of his tragic life and early death, rendered him an even more potent force in English literature. Burns, in his passionate admiration, erected a stone at his own cost to Fergusson's memory as " an elder brother in misfortune."

598b THE DAFT DAYS

The daft days are certain days of the Christmas season which were usually celebrated with wild festivities.

2. **rigs,** ridges, stretches of corn land.
10. **Borean cave,** the cave of the North Wind.
11. **dwyning,** failing, pining.
18. **weir,** war, struggle.
19. **Auld Reikie,** Edinburgh, so called because of its smoke (reik).
19. **canty,** merry, cheerful.
20. **bield,** shelter.
20. **caldrife,** cool, spiritless.
22. **couth,** comfortable.
23. **bicker,** bowl.
26. **scantlins,** scarcely.
28. **gusty,** savory.
29. **kickshaws,** delicacies.
30. **fairn-year,** last year.
31. **browster,** brewer.
31. **bra,** fine.
33. **tither,** the other.
35. **the Well of Spa.** Spa is a watering place in Belgium, celebrated for its medicinal springs.

599a 44. **roset,** rosin.
45. **Italian tricks,** Italian songs and turns of playing.
48. **'Tullochgorum,'** a famous old Scotch tune and song.
63. **capernoity,** ill-humored.

WILLIAM LISLE BOWLES

The Rev. William Lisle Bowles, descended from a clerical family, was born at King's Sutton, Northamptonshire. He attended school at Winchester, where Joseph Warton was head master, went up to Oxford as a scholar of Trinity College, and won the Chancellor's prize for Latin verse in 1783. Meeting with a disappointment in love, he spent some time in wandering over northern England, Scotland, and the Continent, and wrote the sonnets (published in 1789) which constitute his chief claim to remembrance. During the new century he published often, engaged in a heated controversy with Byron on the poetry of Pope, rose to a canonry in Salisbury Cathedral, 1828, lived to hear other harps sound " far more sublime chords," and died in the same year as Wordsworth at the age of eighty-eight. He followed Gray and Warton in the revival of the sonnet in English poetry (see note to Gray's sonnet *On the Death of Richard West,* p. 583a), and by his own examples, with their true feeling for nature, their mellow sentiment, their gentle harmony, and their genuine simplicity, influenced nearly all the great romantic poets. He is the immediate predecessor of the Lake School. To Coleridge in particular his sonnets were an inspiration.

599a BAMBOROUGH CASTLE

1. **Ye holy Towers.** Bamborough Castle, on the coast of Northumberland, was built about 547.

599b DOVER CLIFFS

1. **On these white cliffs.** From the time of Shakespeare's famous description in *King Lear,* IV, vi, Dover, with its imposing chalk cliffs and its protected harbor, has been a source of inspiration to English poets. With Bowles's sonnet compare Matthew Arnold's *Dover Beach,* p. 980.

600a RETROSPECTION

1. **these leaves,** the sonnets already written.

HYMNS

English hymn writing began with translations and imitations of the Latin hymns of the mediæval church. Since the Middle Ages there has been an increasing stream of poetical talent striving to express in the vernacular the religious faith and experience of the English race in the form of sacred songs. During the eighteenth century, under the stimulus of the reëlevation of natural feeling to a place of dignity and the renewed emphasis on individual responsibility, the impulse became more widely spread and more concerted, and during the progress of romanticism developed well nigh into the proportions of a movement. The hymns thus composed survive in great abundance in modern hymnals, and, though often altered without being improved and frequently set to new music, they still continue to be the consolation and joy of the race in its religious strivings and aspirations.

ISAAC WATTS

Isaac Watts was born at Southampton, the son of a clothier who dabbled in verse. He is said to have begun Latin at five, and at seven or eight to have composed some devotional pieces to gratify his mother. He attended a Nonconformist academy at Stoke Newington but was debarred by his religious views from the universities. He became the pastor of an independent congregation in London, but gave more time to hymn writing and theological works than to preaching. His collections of sacred hymns, specifically *Horæ Lyricæ*, 1706, and *Divine and Moral Songs for Children*, 1720, contain many excellent hymns. He employs a pure though somewhat artificial English, breathes a simple and unaffected fervor, and realizes a manly sweetness attained by few other writers. He composed as many hymns approaching a high standard of excellence and at the same time suited for congregational use as any other writer in the modern Christian world.

A CRADLE HYMN

19. **brutal,** brutish.

CHARLES WESLEY

Charles Wesley, the brother of John Wesley, the great founder of the Methodists, was the eighteenth child of the rector of Epworth in Lincolnshire, who was himself a writer of religious verse. He attended Winchester School and Oxford University. After his ordination he went to Georgia as secretary to the governor of the colony, but returned within a year, and became the poet of the evangelical revival. He lived chiefly in Bristol and London. He died in London in 1788.

Charles Wesley is generally regarded as the greatest English hymn writer. He composed nearly seven thousand hymns. The expression of his fervor in poetry was almost a second sense to him. His hymns are usually supplicatory and reveal a consciousness of the mystical bond between the human and the divine. He often loses force by repetition, but he has great truth, depth, and variety of feeling, and employs a manly, passionate diction.

601a IN TIME OF PRAYER AND TEMPTATION

1. **lover.** "From an early date this tender expression was felt by many to be beneath the solemn dignity of the Divine Being" (Julian). As a result the reading *Savior* or *Refuge* is often adopted. The second line is also often found altered to meet the same objection.

AUGUSTUS M. TOPLADY

Augustus Toplady was born at Farnham in Surrey. He was educated at Westminster and at Trinity College, Dublin. He became a minister and occupied appointments in Devonshire, but the last two or three years of his life he resided in London, where he died when under forty years of age in 1778. Few writers of hymns have possessed higher gifts. Adhering closely to Calvinistic principles, he was often in controversy with John Wesley; but his very intemperateness as a theologian lent warmth, richness, and spiritual fervor to his hymns. His *Rock of Ages*, with its pure lyricism scarcely touched by dogma, is usually regarded as the greatest hymn in the language.

601b ROCK OF AGES

In a few passages emendations (introduced in 1815) have been substituted for the original readings.

5. **the double cure.** The water and the blood (l. 3) that flowed from Christ's side when it was pierced by a Roman soldier (John xix, 34) cleanse from sin and insure salvation. The double emphasis has good scriptural precedent (1 John v, 6, 8).

602a 14. **My eyes shall close,** originally, "My eyestrings break."

JOHN NEWTON

John Newton was born in London. His mother, a pious woman, taught him the Scriptures assiduously but died when he was eleven. He then went with his father to sea, where he had many thrilling adventures and lived a godless and abandoned seafaring life until he was twenty-one. Becoming converted, he embraced a somewhat stern and Calvinistic type of religious faith. After a period of study he was ordained in 1764 and became curate of Olney in Buckinghamshire. Here about 1767 he formed a warm friendship with the poet Cowper and collaborated with him in the celebrated *Olney Hymns*. In spite of much that is bald and tame, Newton's hymns show a manliness, a natural cast of imagination, a genuine repentance for sin, and a conviction of ultimate pardon which mark them as among the best called forth by the emotional and mystical revival of the eighteenth century.

WILLIAM COWPER

(For a fuller account of Cowper see p. 647 and notes.)

At Olney in Buckinghamshire, about the year 1767, Cowper came into contact with the zealous minister and hymn writer John Newton (see note above). He had already written hymns, the outpourings of his deeply religious nature, and readily came under the sway of the austere divine. Newton, recognizing his talent and ardent spirituality, engaged him in an enterprise of hymn writing which resulted ultimately in the *Olney Hymns*, the joint work of the two authors (see Cowper's letters to Newton, p. 641 ff.). The collection, published in 1779, is the best single body of sacred hymns in English. Cowper's contributions reflect the author's profound and at times anguished spiritual experiences; and being the products of his gifted muse, they are among the prized possessions of their kind in the language.

602b PRAISE FOR THE FOUNTAIN OPENED

7 f. **And there have I . . . washed,** etc. In some modern hymnals intended for revival services these lines have been altered to read: " And there may I . . . wash," etc. This reading completely spoils the beautiful confidence and fine lyric rapture of Cowper's lines.

SAMUEL JOHNSON

603b THE GARRET

3. **professors of literature,** followers of the literary profession, that is, writers.

22. **Pythagoras,** a famous Greek philosopher and mathematician of the sixth century before Christ.

30. **Tibullus,** a Roman elegiac poet of the first century before Christ.

42. **Lucretius,** a Roman philosophical poet of the first century before Christ.

604b 19 f. **Hippocrates,** a famous Greek physician, " the Father of Medicine," *ca.* 460–*ca.* 377 B.C.

605a 51. **Aretæus,** a Greek physician of the first century after Christ. He gives the interesting case of a joiner who was sane when employed but became mad when away from the seat of his employment.

605b 8. **Solomon's house,** " The College of the Six Days Work," described by Bacon in *The New Atlantis*.

OLIVER GOLDSMITH

JUSTICE AND GENEROSITY

42. **Lysippus.** The historical Lysippus was a Greek sculptor of the fourth century before Christ, a favorite of Alexander the Great and author of most of his portraits in sculpture. The personage here is fictitious.

607b ADVERSITIES OF POETS

26. **Pope Urban the Eighth,** Maffeo Barberini, a Florentine, who became Pope in 1623.

37 f. **he was blind and sang his ballads about the streets.** The notion that Homer was a poor itinerant ballad composer found great favor among eighteenth-century critics. See introductory note to James Macpherson, p. 588, and note to p. 587a, l. 18.

45. **Boëthius.** See note to p. 91b, l. 22.

608a 4. **Bentivoglio,** Ercole Bentivoglio, a sixteenth-century Italian satirist and comic dramatist of noble birth.

12. **Cervantes,** the greatest writer in Spanish literature, author of *Don Quixote.* He lived the greater part of his life in want and died in comparative poverty, according to tradition, on the same day as Shakespeare, April 23, 1616. The report that he starved to death appears to be unfounded.

14. **Camoëns,** a celebrated Portuguese poet, *ca.* 1524–1580.

18. **Vaugelas,** Claude Favre, 1585–1650, Baron Vaugelas. He spent thirty years in translating Quintus Curtius.

36. **Cassander.** François Cassandre, a gifted seventeenth-century courtier and man of letters, fell into poverty, became misanthropic, refused the help of Boileau, and died miserably.

608b 10 f. **Spenser . . . Butler . . . Dryden.** See introductory notes to Spenser, p. 216 Butler, p. 406, and Dryden, p. 416.

11. **Otway,** Thomas Otway, a distinguished dramatic poet of the Restoration. He spent his last days in a sponging house and died in a baker's shop.

19. **a good and a generous master.** It is interesting to note that this essay was written before Goldsmith had made any conspicuous success as a writer.

SAMUEL JOHNSON

PREFACE TO THE ENGLISH DICTIONARY

See Johnson's letter to Lord Chesterfield, p. 637 and note.

610a 22 f. **Quid te exempta,** etc. What does it help you to have one thorn removed out of many?

610b 43. **Hammond,** Henry Hammond, 1605–1660, English clergyman and author. Dr. Johnson liked his works and often gave them as presents to young men about to be ordained as ministers.

611a 13. **Hooker,** Richard Hooker, *ca.* 1553–1600, one of the great English prose masters, author of the *Laws of Ecclesiastical Polity*.

612a 4. **Junius,** Franciscus Junius (1589–1677), a distinguished continental scholar who lived most of his life in England. He was an authority on early English, collected Anglo-Saxon manuscripts, and edited several works in the older language, including the poems attributed to Cædmon. His *Etymologicum Anglicanum* was first edited in 1743.

4. **Skinner,** Stephen Skinner, 1623–1667, an English lexicographer. His *Etymologicon Linguæ Anglicanæ* was published in 1671.

613b 41. **Bailey,** Nathan Bailey, d. 1642, whose English dictionary was the standard before Johnson's. Johnson and his helpers worked on an interleaved copy of Bailey.

41. **Ainsworth,** Robert Ainsworth, 1660–1743, author of a Latin-English dictionary published in 1736.

41. **Philips,** Edward Phillips, 1630–1696, author of *A New World of Words, or A General Dictionary.*

614b 39 f. **the twelve tables,** the tables on which were engraved (451 and 450 B.C.) the principal rules of Roman law.

616b 44. **Sidney,** Sir Philip Sidney.

619a 1. **academicians della Crusca.** The *Accademia della Crusca* was founded at Florence in 1582 by the poet Grazzini to purify the Italian language and literature.

619b 41. **Amelot,** Abraham Nicholas Amelot de la Houssaye, 1634–1706, a French historian, translator of Fra Paolo Sarpi's *History of the Council of Trent.*

42. **Le Courayer,** Pierre François, 1681–1776, a later translator of Fra Paolo Sarpi's *History of the Council of Trent.* The translation is dedicated to the queen of England and is accompanied by a long preface.

46. **Caro,** Annibale Caro, a sixteenth-century Italian poet.

620b 19. **Swift . . . petty treatise,** etc., *A Proposal for Correcting the English Language,* 1712.

621b 15. **Scaliger,** Joseph Scaliger, 1540–1609, "the greatest scholar of modern times" — *Britannica.*

52. **embodied criticks of France,** etc. In 1639 the French Academy undertook to construct a dictionary of the French language. The work did not appear until 1694.

622a 7. **those whom I wished to please,** etc. Mrs. Johnson had died three years before.

GRAY

See p. 582 ff. and notes, and p. 629.

36. **Mr. Horace Walpole.** See p. 639 and notes.

622b 24. **Mr. Mason.** William Mason, author of the *Life and Letters of Gray,* 1775.

623a 47. **Warburton,** William Warburton, 1698–1779, an English prelate, controversialist, and critic.

623b 6. **Mr. Whitehead,** William Whitehead, who became poet laureate in 1751.

30. **Dr. Beattie,** James Beattie, 1735–1803, poet and professor in Mareschal College, Aberdeen.

624a 11. **Mr. Boswell.** See p. 627 and notes.

624b 30. **Shaftesbury,** Anthony Ashley Cooper, 1671–1713, third Earl of Shaftesbury, a celebrated English moralist and philosopher.

625b 8 f. **O Diva, gratum quæ regis Antium,** "O goddess, who rulest pleasant Antium," the first line of one of the odes of Horace.

626a 36. **Algarotti, 1712–1764, an Italian nobleman and litterateur.**

37. **the prophecy of Nereus.** See Horace, *Car.* I, xv.

48. **Incredulus odi,** Incredulous as I am, I hate it.

626b 14 f. **the ballad of Johnny Armstrong.** See p. 175.

JAMES BOSWELL

James Boswell was the son of a Scottish judge and was reared at the family seat of Auchinleck in Ayrshire. He received his education in Edinburgh and Glasgow and adopted the legal profession. In 1760 he migrated to London for the better opportunity of indulging his tastes for good fellowship and there began the exercise of his talent for making the acquaintance of celebrities. In 1763 he had the good fortune to meet Johnson (see his own account, p. 627). It was the greatest event of his life. By his ingratiating genius he was soon successful in cultivating an intimate friendship, and for the next twenty years he was an integral part, as his pages reflect, of the great man's presence. In 1773 he became a member of the famous literary Club, and in the same year made a journey with his great patron to the Hebrides, an account of which he later published. He continued his attachment unabated until within a few months of Johnson's death, when he took leave in what each seemed to feel was a final farewell. With Johnson's death, apparently, the last tie was severed which bound him in any way to a life of rectitude. He relapsed into loose living, sustained only by application to his great biography, and died prematurely in London in 1795. In his memorable *Life* he adopted the theory, employed by Mason in his *Life and Letters of Gray*, of letting the subject tell his own story. In execution he was eminently successful. He never intrudes himself upon the attention of the reader but busies himself only with his subject and maintains without interruption the impression of complete dominance by it The result is one of the greatest biographies ever written.

627b 44 f. **' Look, my lord,'** etc. *Hamlet* I, iv, 38.

628a 2 f. **Sir Joshua Reynolds,** 1723–1792. The famous literary club was established at his suggestion. The portrait referred to is the one usually seen of Johnson.

35 f. **an order . . . for Miss Williams,** *i.e.*, for a complimentary seat. Some years before, at Johnson's request, Garrick had given a benefit night " to this very person, by which she had got two hundred pounds."

628b 17 f. **Thornton, Wilkes, Churchill, and Lloyd,** literary wits and publicists of the time.

23. **Dr. Blair,** Hugh Blair, 1718–1800, a distinguished critic, professor at the University of Edinburgh. See introductory note to James Macpherson, p. 588.

33. **James Macpherson.** See introductory note to p. 588.

629a 28. **Gray.** See p. 582 and notes, and p. 622.

629b 28. **Dr. Oliver Goldsmith.** See p. 565 and notes. Boswell's portrait, as is well known, is not just to Goldsmith. There was no good will lost between the two, probably because of the envy each felt of the other for Johnson's favor.

35 f. **Mr. Malone,** Edmond Malone, 1741–1812, the Shakespearean scholar, who carefully revised Boswell's *Life of Johnson*.

630a 34. **un étourdi,** a blunderer.

630b 32. **Mrs. Piozzi,** formerly Mrs. Thrale, an intimate friend of Johnson for twenty years. She greatly offended him a few months before his death by her marriage to the Italian musician Piozzi (see p. 639). Her *Anecdotes* of his life appeared in 1785.

32. **Sir John Hawkins,** 1719–1789, author of a life of Johnson and editor of his works in 1787.

631a 13. **Νυξ γαρ ερχεται.** For the night cometh. Cf. John ix, 4.

25. **Mr. Steevens,** George Steevens, 1736–1800, a Shakespearean scholar. He assisted Johnson in his edition of Shakespeare.

631b 38. **Mr. Thrale's.** The Thrales kept a room in their home in Southwark for Johnson's accommodation.

49. **Hermippus redivivus,** Hermippus revived. Hermippus was a Greek poet of the old comedy, an early contemporary of Aristophanes.

632a 16 f. **the Bishop of Killaloe,** Dr. Barnard, a member of the celebrated Club.

18. **Hannah More,** 1745–1833, an English Bluestocking popular in the literary London of Johnson's day.

632b 24. **Dr. Taylor,** John Taylor, Prebend of Westminster.

PHILIP DORMER STANHOPE, EARL OF CHESTERFIELD

Chesterfield was the son of an earl and grandson of a marquis. He was educated at Cambridge and abroad. On coming of age he was made a gentleman of the bedchamber and entered Parliament. Like Sir Philip Sidney, whom he resembles in outward manners, he became a fashionable figure in foreign courts. In 1726 he was seated in the House of Lords. The Walpole ministry was inimical to his advancement in politics, but under the Pelhams he became in 1745 Lord Lieutenant of Ireland, and the year following was made a secretary of state. In 1748 he withdrew from public affairs, and lived in dignified ease and retirement, though remaining influential, until his death in 1773. His inimitable *Letters*, written to his natural son and godson between 1737 and 1770, constitute his only claim to literary fame. In philosophy they are shallow and in morals indifferent, but in the elements of fine manners, set forth with a nervous elegance and grace that have not been surpassed, they are the best things the language possesses.

THOMAS GRAY

635b TO HORACE WALPOLE

See p. 639 ff. and notes.

TO THE REV. WILLIAM MASON

See note to Johnson's *Gray*, p. 622b, l. 24.

636a 20. **Rowe,** Nicholas Rowe, dramatist and poet, who became poet laureate in 1714.

22. **Settle.** Elkanah Settle, a second-rate Restoration dramatist, was official poet of the city of London.

23. **Eusden,** Lawrence Eusden, d. 1730, a clergyman and mediocre poet.

48. **Strawberry Hill,** Walpole's famous villa a few miles above London on the Thames.

636b TO HORACE WALPOLE

8 f. **the two specimens of Erse poetry,** two of the alleged translations of Gaelic poetry which Macpherson had given to Home (see p. 588 and notes).

20. **'Hardicanute.'** See p. 533 and notes.

TO THE REV. NORTON NICHOLLS

Norton Nicholls was a Cambridge undergraduate when Gray first became attached to him, about 1760. He later became a country clergyman in Suffolk.

637a 4. **thirteen years ago.** Gray's mother died March 11, 1753, aged sixty-seven.

34. **the New Bath Guide,** a succession of satirical epistles in verse by Christopher Anstey, 1724–1805.

47. **Mr. Brown,** the Rev. James Brown, fellow and later master of Pembroke, an intimate friend of Gray.

SAMUEL JOHNSON

TO THE RIGHT HONORABLE, THE EARL OF CHESTERFIELD

See p. 633 and notes.

Johnson addressed the plan of his dictionary in 1747 to Chesterfield, but was neglected by the earl until his work was nearing completion. The would-be patron then inserted some papers adulatory of Johnson in *The World*, hoping thereby to make sure of the dedication. These papers furnished the occasion for Johnson's celebrated letter.

637b 28. **Le vainqueur,** etc. The conqueror of the conqueror of the world.

49 f. **The shepherd in Virgil,** etc. See *Eclogue* viii, 42 ff.

638a 7 f. **till I am solitary,** etc. See note to the Preface to the Dictionary, p. 622a, l. 7.

TO BENNET LANGTON

Bennet Langton, 1737–1801, an English classical scholar, was an intimate friend of Johnson. After Johnson's death he became professor of ancient literature at the Royal Academy.

48. **Streatham,** a village just south of London, where the Thrales had a home.

53. *Κύριε ἐλέησον.* Lord, have mercy.

638b 7 ff. *Τὸν τάφον εἰσοράας,* etc. You, Stranger, who look upon the tomb of Oliver, tread not with careless feet his honored dust. But in him — in whom nature, the gift of numbers, and the things of old delighted — lament the poet, the historian, and the natural philosopher.

TO JAMES MACPHERSON

See p. 588 and notes.

Johnson's letter was a reply to Macpherson's letter threatening Johnson with violence for his attack on the Ossianic poems as impostures.

36. **your Homer,** Macpherson's translation of the *Iliad*, published in 1773.

TO MRS. PIOZZI (THRALE)

See note to Boswell's *Life of Johnson*, p. 630b, l. 32.

HORACE WALPOLE

Horatio Walpole was the youngest son of the great statesman, Sir Robert Walpole, and was born in London. Despite his delicate health, he entered Eton at ten, and there became acquainted with the poet Gray (see p. 582 and notes). His career at Cambridge was interrupted by the death of his mother in 1737, after which he set out on his tour of the continent with his friend Gray. At Florence he met Sir Horace Mann, with whom he maintained a correspondence for nearly fifty years. On his return he entered Parliament and retained his seat until 1768. The various sinecures which he enjoyed through the offices of his father supplied him with an income of nearly £4,000 a year, with which he could indulge his pampered tastes much as he liked. He became a virtuoso and antiquary. To satisfy his dilettantism he built near Twickenham a mansion, redolent of the Middle Ages with its Gothic form and atmosphere of mystery, called Strawberry Hill, and spent amid its luxuries a large part of his life. He died in London in 1797. In literature he was little more than a gossip. By his social prominence, his interest in and acquaintance with letters, and his undeniable talent, he influenced others in writing more than he performed himself. In his *Castle of Otranto*, 1764, he must be accorded the credit of a pioneer: it is the first of the Gothic romances, which led directly to Scott. But he is interesting mainly for the remarkable *corpus* of his correspondence. Though it fills many volumes, none of it is positively bad. His letters lack the warm spontaneity of Cowper and the scholarly yet natural mastery of Gray, but as the products of a gentle and cultivated gift of writing they are supreme.

TO GEORGE MONTAGU

George Montagu was a contemporary of Walpole and Gray at Eton. He later occupied several secretarial positions in England and Ireland.

639b 5 f. **Mr. Hume's England,** *A History of England,* 1754–1761, by David Hume, Scottish philosopher and historian.

15. **Fingal,** one of Macpherson's Ossianic epics (see introductory note to p. 588).

640a 7. **Garrick * * *** The remainder of the letter is lost.

TO THOMAS CHATTERTON

See p. 591 and notes.
Chatterton sent to Walpole, as the author of *Anecdotes of Painting,* a fictitious manuscript, among others, called *The Ryse of Peynctynge yn Englande,* ascribing the work to a mythical fifteenth-century writer, Thomas Rowley. Walpole's letter was an acknowledgment. A few months later, having his suspicions aroused, he returned the manuscripts without comment, an injury the youthful poet never forgave.

39. **The Abbot John's verses.** Abbot John, a priest of St. John's Church in Bristol, was the creation of Chatterton's imagination.

640b TO THE REV. WILLIAM COLE

William Cole, 1714–1782, was an English clergyman and antiquary.

30. **Herculaneum,** an ancient city of Italy, situated at the foot of Mount Vesuvius. It was overwhelmed by an eruption A.D. 79.

35. **Waller and Prior.** See pp. 380 and 501 respectively, and notes.

36. **Lord Surrey.** See p. 190 and notes.

TO THE COUNTESS OF [OSSORY]

Lady Ossory was the daughter of Henry Liddell, Baron Ravensworth. She became Lady Ossory by her runaway marriage with John Fitzpatrick, Earl of Upper Ossory, in 1768. She was one of Walpole's most frequent correspondents.

641a 25. **Methusalem.** See Genesis v, 21 ff.

39. **twelfth-cakes,** cakes prepared for the celebration of Twelfth Night, or the festival of Epiphany, twelve days after Christmas.

643a WILLIAM COWPER

TO THE REV. JOHN NEWTON

See p. 602 and notes.

51 f. **my last volume,** *The Task,* published with the *Tirocinium* in 1785.

643b 13. **Henderson,** John Henderson, 1747–1785, an English actor, second only to Garrick in the public esteem.

644b 12 ff. **Seasons return,** etc. The passage is a paraphrase of *Paradise Lost,* III, 41 ff.

NINETEENTH CENTURY

WILLIAM COWPER

Outwardly the life of William Cowper was uneventful; inwardly it was made up of experiences that were rarely without tragic consequence to his supersensitive nature. He was born of gentle blood in the rectory of Great Berkhampstead in Hertfordshire, where his father was incumbent. The death of his mother when he was only six and the cruelty of a bully in his first school made a profound impression on his affectionate and retiring nature. He spent seven years at Winchester School, where he was taught the classics and learned to love Homer. After a three years' apprenticeship and some study of law in the Temple he was admitted to the bar at the age of twenty-three. Meanwhile he was exercising his talent in verse, enjoying renewed associations with his old Winchester friends, and taking part in the friendly gayety of the Nonsense Club. The death of his father in 1756 and separation from his cousin Theodora, whom he wished to marry, aggravated his innate despondency and prepared him for the crash which came in 1763. He was appointed to the clerkship of the journals in the House of Lords, but the appointment was contested, and he was required to appear before the house for examination. The prospect so oppressed him that he tried to escape the ordeal by suicide. His mind gave way, and he was placed in an asylum at St. Albans for a year and a half. On his recovery he removed to Huntingdon and there lived a simple life during his remaining years. The Reverend Morley Unwin and his young wife Mary, the zealot Newton, the vivacious Lady Austen, and Cowper's kinswoman Lady Hesketh all sympathized with him in his mental distresses, encouraged him to write poetry, and contributed as much happiness as possible to his perturbed life. *The Task*, his greatest poem, begun at the suggestion of Lady Austen, was published in 1785. By its employment of blank verse, its treatment of simple scenes of nature, and its depiction of lowly country life, it carries on the traditions of Thomson, but it shows a warmth of appreciation and a prevailing geniality that were unknown to the author of *The Seasons*. *John Gilpin*, his most humorous work, written also at the request of Lady Austen, appeared the same year. The two poems brought him fame. His last years, filled with gloom from his settled conviction that salvation was denied him, are reflected in his terrible *Castaway*, 1799. He died peacefully at East Dereham in 1800. He is one of the great heralds of the romantic triumph in English poetry at the close of the eighteenth century.

647a JOHN GILPIN

3. **trainband,** a force of citizen soldiery in London.

23. **calender,** a calendrer or operator in one of the finishing processes of cloth or paper making, *i.e.*, of pressing the fabric to make it smooth and even.

649b THE TASK

650a 49. **placemen,** incumbents of appointive government positions.

650b 86. **Katterfelto,** a quack doctor and conjurer whose advertisements filled the London papers about 1782.

651b 189. **'Oh evenings worthy of the gods!'** Cf. Horace, *Satires*, II, vi, 65.

652b 269 f. **he of Gath,** etc. Cf. 1 Samuel xvii, 23 ff.

655a 473. **Indian fume,** tobacco smoke.

507. **Midas,** a king of Phrygia who, through a gift of Dionysus, turned to gold everything he touched.

655b 515 f. **Arcadian scenes,** etc. Virgil in his *Eclogues*, and Sir Philip Sidney in his *Arcadia*.

656b 627. **balloted,** conscripted for service.

657b 707. **Tityrus,** the name of the shepherd in the first *Eclogue* of Virgil.

723. **ingenious Cowley.** See p. 435 ff. and notes.

728. **Chertsey,** a village in Surrey where Cowley spent his last years.

658a 765. **The Frenchman's darling,** Mignonette.

658b ON THE RECEIPT OF MY MOTHER'S PICTURE

The picture was a gift to the poet from his cousin, Ann Bodham, in 1790, more than fifty years after his mother's death.

659b 97. **'Where tempests,'** etc. This line is inexactly quoted from *The Dispensary* of Samuel Garth, 1660–1718.

108 f. **I deduce my birth,** etc. Cowper was descended from Henry III.

660a THE LOSS OF THE ROYAL GEORGE

The poem celebrates the loss of Rear Admiral Kempenfelt's flagship while being repaired at Spithead, off the southern coast of England, on August 29, 1782. It was written at the request of Lady Austen, "who wanted words to the march in Scipio."

660b THE CASTAWAY

This, the last of Cowper's original poems, was founded on an incident in Anson's *Voyage around the World*, 1748. The personal application in the poet's case is evident.

7. **No braver chief.** Lord George Anson, 1692–1762, was an heroic English admiral in the days of exploration and colonization in the Americas.

GEORGE CRABBE

The life experiences of no other English poet have more definitely determined the bent of his genius than did those of George Crabbe. He was born in the unattractive little fishing village of Aldburgh on the "frowning coast" of Suffolk, where his father was a collector of the salt tax. An apprenticeship to a surgeon and the practice of medicine for a brief period brought him that intimacy with the struggles of the poor and the sterner side of nature for which his work is distinguished. Failing as a doctor, he went to London to try his hand at literature, and after much discouragement attracted the attention of Burke, whose patronage enabled him to publish *The Library*, 1781, and *The Village*, 1783. By his patron's advice he took orders and devoted himself to parish work for the rest of his life. Among his later works, *The Parish Register*, 1807, and *The Borough*, 1810, draw largely upon his personal contacts during this period. Although he used the poetic forms and methods of the eighteenth century, he was a realist in the current sense of the word, and the background of his work was the sordid life he knew almost too well. He died at Trowbridge in 1832.

661a THE VILLAGE

The village described is Aldburgh, the poet's native place.

661b 12. **Corydons,** shepherds.

15. **Mincio's banks.** The Mincio is a river flowing into the Po below Mantua, the home of Virgil.

16. **Tityrus.** See note to l. 707 of *The Task.*

27. **Duck.** The reference may be to Stephen Duck, a poor thresher mentioned by Johnson in his *Life of Savage.* Some of Duck's contemporaries imagined for a time that he was a great original genius.

662b 97. **Ajax,** Ajax Telamon, one of the greater Greek heroes in the Trojan War.

663a 144. **Dog-star,** the star Sirius in the constellation *Canis Major*, the brightest of the fixed stars.

665a 284. **drowsy Bench,** the lax laws governing the practice of medicine.

303. **He, 'passing rich,'** etc., an allusion to the parson in Goldsmith's *Deserted Village*, p. 572b, l. 137 ff.

665b 341. **the moping owl.** Cf. l. 10 of Gray's *Elegy.*

ROBERT BURNS

Robert Burns was born in Ayrshire beside the "bonnie Doon." He was the eldest of seven children, and the struggle of the family for existence on the small unproductive farm was unrelenting. He endured long hours of laborious toil, and had few books and little schooling, but developed a love of nature, generous emotions, and acute powers of observation which later were to inspire him with spontaneous song. When twenty-three he tried flax-dressing at Irvine; but acquiring only the bad habits and practices of the seaport town, he returned to farming, in partnership with his brother at Mossgiel. Soon afterward he met Jean Armour, who was to become his wife in 1788. During these years most of his finest work was done. By 1786 his wayward life had led him into difficulties, and he resolved to leave Scotland forever. He decided to go to Jamaica, but money was needed for the passage. He wrote to a friend, "You have heard that I am going to commence poet in print — it is just the last foolish action I intend to do; and then turn a wise man as fast as possible." In this way the famous Kilmarnock edition of his poems, 1786, came into existence. Its success was instantaneous, and as a result he was invited to the Scottish capital to meet the social and literary élite. At the end of the second winter, however, he realized the uncongeniality of city life both to his social tastes and to his muse, and returned to his native district. With the proceeds of a second edition of his poems he stocked a few acres at Ellisland in Dumfriesshire and with Jean Armour settled down to a short period of contentment if not of prosperity. To add to his earnings he obtained a post in the excise at Dumfries, but again he was tempted into habits of intemperance, to the detriment of both health and reputation. He died in Dumfries, broken and embittered, at the age of thirty-seven. He had written of the life he knew, the tenderness and passion of simple folk, the tears and mirth that are essentially human, with a sincerity and power that made his poetry a vitalizing element for the new age.

665b THE COTTER'S SATURDAY NIGHT

Burns dedicated this poem to his friend and patron, Robert Aiken, 1739–1807, an Ayrshire solicitor. He got the suggestion for the poem from Fergusson's *Farmer's Ingle.*

10. **sugh,** wail.

666a 21. **stacher,** totter.

22. **flichterin',** fluttering.

23. **ingle,** fireplace.

26. **kiaugh,** worry.

28. **Belyve,** soon.

29. **tentie rin,** heedful run.

31. **cannie,** careful.

31. **neebor town,** a neighboring farm, including its buildings.

38. **spiers,** asks.

40. **uncos,** strange things.

44. **Gars,** makes.

44. **claes,** clothes.

48. **eydent,** busy, diligent.

49. **jauk,** trifle.

666b 62. **hafflins,** partly.

67. **kye,** cows.

69. **blate and laithfu',** shy and bashful.

72. **lave,** rest, others.

92. **parrich,** porridge.

93. **soupe,** milk.

93. **hawkie,** cow.

667a 94. **hallan,** partition.

96. **weel-hained kebbuck, fell,** well-saved ripe cheese.

99. **towmond,** etc., twelve months old since flax was in the flower.

105. **lyart haffets,** gray side locks.

111 ff. **Dundee . . . Martyrs . . . Elgin,** names of well-known sacred melodies.

113. **beets,** kindles.

122. **the royal Bard,** King David.

667b 133. **he, who lone,** etc., St. John on the Isle of Patmos.

138. **'springs exulting,'** etc., an inexact quotation from Pope's *Windsor Forest*, l. 112.

150. **sacerdotal stole,** priestly robe.
166. **'An honest man,'** etc. Pope, *Essay on Man,* Epistle IV, l. 248.
668a 182. **Wallace,** William Wallace, 1274?–1305, a Scotch patriot and national hero. Cf. *Scots, Wha Hae,* p. 675a and note.

TO A MOUSE

4. **bickering brattle,** hurrying scamper.
15. **A daimen icker,** etc., an occasional ear in a sheaf or shock.
21. **big,** build.
668b 22. **foggage,** coarse grass.
24. **snell,** bitter.
29. **coulter,** plough.
34. **hald,** abode.
35. **thole,** endure.
36. **cranreuch,** hoarfrost.
37. **no thy lane,** not alone.
40. **gang aft agley,** go often awry.

TO A MOUNTAIN DAISY

4. **stoure,** dust.
21. **bield,** shelter.
669a 23. **histie,** barren.
39. **card,** compass, chart.

EPISTLE TO JOHN LAPRAIK

John Lapraik, 1727–1807, was an Ayrshire poet.

2. **paitricks,** partridges.
3. **poussie whiddin,** the hare scudding.
7. **Fasten-e'en,** evening before Lent.
7. **rockin,** social meeting.
8. **crack,** tale, chat.
11. **yokin,** a set-to.
13. **ae sang,** Lapraik's *When I upon the Bosom Lean.*
14. **Aboon,** above.
669b 22. **Beattie.** See note to Johnson's *Gray,* p. 623b, 30.
23. **chiel,** young fellow.
25. **fidgin-fain,** tingling wild.
26. **spier't,** asked.
28. **ingine,** genius.
32. **douce,** sober.
35. **Inverness an' Teviotdale.** The former is in northern Scotland on the Moray Firth, the latter in Roxburghshire on the English border.
38. **graith,** implements, gear.
39. **cadger pownie,** a peddler's pony.
40. **dyke-back,** back of a turf fence or wall.
45. **crambo-jingle.** In the game of crambo one player supplies a rhyme to a word given by another.
49 ff. **I am nae poet,** etc. The five stanzas here following may be called Burns's confession of faith, or poetical creed, as opposed to the classical notion of the origin and essence of poetry.
64. **sairs,** serves.
66. **knappin-hammers,** hammers used for breaking stones.
670a 69. **stirks,** young steers.
79. **spunk,** spark.
79. **Allan.** See p. 536 and notes.
80. **Fergusson.** See p. 598 and notes.
80. **slee,** clever, sly.
83. **lear,** learning.
87. **fow,** full.
94. **roose,** praise.
99. **plack,** a Scotch coin of small denomination.
103. **Mauchline,** a town near Burns's farm of Mossgiel, where he married Jean Armour.
109. **chap,** drinking cup.
110. **kirsen,** christen.
111. **whitter,** a hearty draught.
115. **warly,** worldly.
116. **havins,** manners, conduct.
118. **Catch-the-Plack,** the hunt for coin.
670b 129. **fissle,** tingle.

OF A' THE AIRTS

1. **airts,** points of the compass, directions.
14. **shaw,** a wood or grove.

671a JOHN ANDERSON, MY JO

1. **jo,** sweetheart.
4. **brent,** smooth.
5. **beld,** bald.
7. **pow,** head.
11. **cantie,** jolly, cheerful.

AULD LANG SYNE

9. **pint-stowp,** a drinking vessel.
14. **gowans,** daisies.
15. **fit,** foot, step.
17. **burn,** brook.
671b 21. **fiere,** comrade.
23. **waught,** a copious draught.

TAM O' SHANTER

When Burns wrote *Tam O' Shanter,* Alloway Kirk, but a short distance from the poet's birthplace, had been long in ruins, and many legends had gathered about it, among them that of Douglas Graham, who was noted for his convivial habits, and whose experience probably gave Burns the suggestion for this poem.

1. **chapman billies,** peddler fellows.
5. **nappy,** ale.
7. **Scots miles.** The Scottish mile was longer by an eighth or thereabout than the English mile.
8. **slaps,** breaches or gates in the fences.
19. **skellum,** a good-for-nothing.
20. **blethering,** talking nonsense.
20. **blellum,** a babbler.
23. **ilka melder,** every meal grinding.
25. **ca'd,** driven.
31. **warlocks,** male witches.
33. **greet,** weep.
39. **bleezing,** blazing.

40. **reaming swats,** foaming new ale.
41. **Souter,** shoemaker.
672a 69. **That hour . . . the keystane,** midnight.
81. **skelpit,** scurried, cantered.
81. **dub,** puddle.
84. **sonnet,** song.
86. **bogles,** bogies, hobgoblins.
88. **houlets,** owls.
90. **smoored,** smothered.
91. **birks,** birches.
93. **whins,** furze.
93. **cairn,** a pile of stones.
103. **bore,** chink.
672b 107. **tippenny,** small beer.
108. **usquebae,** whisky (Gaelic *uisque beathad,* water of life).
110. **deils a boddle,** devils a bit.
117. **strathspeys,** lively Scotch dances.
119. **winnock-bunker,** a window seat.
121. **A tousie tyke,** a shaggy dog.
123. **skirl,** squeal.
124. **dirl,** ring, tingle.
127. **cantraip,** magic.
132. **span-lang,** only a span long.
132. **unchristened,** unbaptized, and therefore gone to perdition.
134. **gab,** mouth.
147. **cleekit,** took hold.
148. **carlin,** an old woman, a hag.
149. **duddies,** clothes.
149. **to the wark,** for the work (orgie).
150. **linkit,** danced with the utmost activity.
151. **queans,** young women.
153. **creeshie flannen,** greasy flannel.
154. **seventeen-hunder linen,** fine linen with seventeen hundred threads to a width.
155. **Thir,** these.
155. **breeks,** breeches.
157. **hurdies,** hips.
160. **Rigwoodie,** ancient or lean.
160. **spean,** wean (by disgust).
673a 161. **crummock,** a crooked staff.
163. **brawlie,** perfectly.
164. **wawlie,** choice, handsome.
166. **Carrick,** the southern district of Ayrshire.
169. **bear,** barley.
171. **cutty sark,** a short skirt.
171. **Paisley harn,** coarse linen made in Paisley, a town in Renfrewshire.
176. **coft,** bought.
185. **fidged,** fidgeted.
186. **hotched,** jerked (with his arm, as a bagpiper).
193. **fyke,** fret, fuss.
194. **herds,** herders.
194. **byke,** hive.
195. **pussie,** a hare.
200. **eldritch,** unearthly.
201. **fairin,** reward.
213. **ettle,** aim, intent.

674a HIGHLAND MARY

The Mary of this poem was Mary Campbell, whose sudden death in the fall of 1786 brought real sorrow to the poet.

2. **castle o' Montgomery,** Coilsfield House, near Tarbolton.
4. **drumlie,** muddy.

675a SCOTS, WHA HAE

This poem celebrates the victory of the Scots under Bruce over the English under Edward II at Bannockburn in Sterlingshire, June 24, 1314.

2. **Bruce,** Robert Bruce, 1274–1329, a national hero. He became king of Scotland in 1306.

A MAN'S A MAN FOR A' THAT

8. **gowd,** gold.
10. **hoddin grey,** coarse grey woolen cloth.
17. **birkie,** fellow.
20. **cuif,** a dolt, ninny.
675b 28. **fa',** lay claim to.
36. **gree,** prize.

WILLIAM BLAKE

William Blake's poetry and pictorial art are closely linked together as the expression of a visionary and dreamer. He was born in London in the household of a clothier. His systematic education was meager, but his father apparently recognized his artistic temper and gave him the training that was most congenial to his talent. For four years he attended a drawing school and for seven more was an apprentice to a prominent engraver by the name of Besire. On completing his apprenticeship he began to engrave for the trade but continued his studies in art at the Royal Academy. He was married to Catherine Boucher in 1782, and with her sympathetic interest and help literally made his own books in every detail. He engraved his poems with a decorative design on copper plates and afterward added coloring by hand, by a process revealed to him, he affirmed, in a dream. His *Poetical Sketches* appeared in 1783, *Songs of Innocence* in 1789, and *Songs of Experience* in 1794. Although little known at the time, these have been recognized since as component parts of the Romantic Movement in its lyrical exuberance and mystical longing. As he grew older his artistry improved but his poetry became more vague and incoherent. Some of his *Prophetic Books,* as he called them, are unintelligible. He continued in poverty to the end of his long life, and died in London in 1827. In his mystical view of Nature he suggests Wordsworth, and in his lyrical intensity and employment of materials of the spirit world he forecasts Shelley.

WILLIAM WORDSWORTH

William Wordsworth was the second of five children born to John Wordsworth, an attorney in the little town of Cockermouth, situated on the river Derwent in a picturesque district of northern England diversified by mountains and lakes and known as the "Lake District." As a boy he was physically vigorous and active but of a moody disposition and a violent temper. His mother dying when he was eight years old (1778), he was sent to the grammar school at Hawkshead, near Esthwaite Lake, where he remained for six years. Here he acquired the rudiments of an education and wandered among the neighboring lakes and forests, in which he rejoiced with a boyish enthusiasm already somewhat spiritualized by the mystical insight that was afterward to play so large a part in his poetical theory and practice. In 1787 he entered Cambridge University, where he took his B.A. in 1791. During his college career he usually spent his vacations in excursions through the beautiful scenery of Derbyshire, Yorkshire, Westmoreland, and Cumberland in company with his sister Dorothy and her friend, Mary Hutchinson. In 1790 he made a walking tour in France, where his radical social tendencies were intensified by the French revolutionary movement, then in its early stages. In 1791 and again in 1792 he was back in France, and, urged by sympathy for the revolutionary ideals, even thought of joining the Girondists (moderate republicans), but was forced to return home by lack of money. Spiritual perturbation over an affair with a French girl whom he believed he could not marry, the apparent failure of the high ideas of French republicanism after the Reign of Terror (1793–1794), and the declaration of war between France and England plunged Wordsworth into black despair. As a result his outlook on moral and social questions became for the time being utterly confused, but his mental vision was gradually clarified by communion with Nature and by the tender ministrations of his beloved sister Dorothy (cf. *Tintern Abbey*, l. 115 ff.). He now no longer believed in the theories of the French Revolution, but he had, through his struggle, acquired a greater respect for Man, a deeper sympathy with human joys and sorrows, and a keener feeling for the spiritual values that lay for him within the heart of Nature. He had begun writing verse in boyhood, and in 1793 he published *Descriptive Sketches*, his first collection of poetry. Uncertain how to make a living, he thought of taking up journalism, but a fortunate legacy of £900, bequeathed him in 1795, enabled him to abandon the plan and devote himself to literature. He and his sister took up their abode in a farmhouse at Racedown, Dorsetshire, where he continued his literary exercises and wrote a tragedy, *The Borderers* (published in 1842). Here, probably in 1796, he met Coleridge (cf. introductory note to p. 701), who became his intimate friend and was of great assistance in focusing his poetic gifts. Late in the same year Coleridge took a cottage at Nether Stowey not far from the Quantock Hills and near Bristol Channel. Here and at the neighboring estate of Alfoxden, where William and Dorothy soon settled, took place the collaboration between the two poets which resulted in the celebrated *Lyrical Ballads*, 1798 (cf. introductory note to *Preface*, p. 815). After a winter in Germany, whither they had gone with Coleridge, the Wordsworths settled (1799) in Dove Cottage at Town-end, Grasmere in the Lake District. Here Wordsworth resided for the next seven or eight years. In 1800 appeared a new edition of the *Lyrical Ballads*, with an added second volume and an important introduction (p. 815 ff.). In 1802 Wordsworth married Mary Hutchinson, the friend of his earlier years. In 1803 the Wordsworths, accompanied part of the way by Coleridge, crossed the border into Scotland on an excursion which inspired some of Wordsworth's most spiritual productions. During this tour he met Sir Walter Scott. In 1805 he finished *The Prelude* (published in 1850), a long poem of the greatest importance not only for its fine poetry but for its record of the growth of the poet's mind. As years passed and children were born, Dove Cottage became too small for Wordsworth's family, and in the winter of 1806–1807 the poet removed to a farmhouse at Coleorton in Leicestershire. Here his friendship with Coleridge, now suffering from melancholy, was renewed, and here in 1807 he published in two volumes his *Poems*, containing a series of sonnets, the poems of the Scottish tour, *Resolution and Independence*, and his Ode on the *Intimations of Immortality*. The reviews were unfavorable, but Wordsworth was not discouraged. In 1808 he returned to Grasmere but not to Dove Cottage. He had in his house as guests Coleridge and, for a time, De Quincey (see introductory note to p. 855). In 1813 the death of a beloved little daughter caused Wordsworth to move again, this time to Rydal Mount, two miles from Grasmere. In 1814 appeared Wordsworth's second long poem, *The Excursion.* About this time his poetic disrepute was at its height, and *The Excursion* was not well received. In 1815 he published the first collected edition of his poems. In spite of his early loss of faith in the French Revolution, Wordsworth had retained his interest in politics, and his enthusiasm over the defeat of Napoleon at Waterloo (1815) found expression in a number of poems, published in 1816. The remainder of his life was occupied with the quiet routine of Rydal Mount and excursions to various parts of the British Isles and the continent. As he grew older, his poetical powers gradually waned and he became more conservative in his social and political opinions. In 1843 he was appointed poet laureate. Saddened by the loss of friends and dear ones, he died in 1850 and was buried in Grasmere churchyard.

The various faculties of Wordsworth's genius were unusually well balanced and unified; yet he was far from being the mild and gentle soul so often portrayed in the textbooks. He was a man of strong passions, but passions controlled by a powerful conviction of the moral significance of human life. His fondness for simple things and his faith in the essential nobility of common men, which grew out of his French Revolutionary experiences and the whole body of English thought that lay behind him in the eighteenth century (see p. 646) never left him. It found expression not only in his political creed but also in his poetry, notably in the *Lyrical Ballads.* For Wordsworth the center of art is in the uncontaminated human soul, and he found his inspiration in Nature and in the idealized spiritual life of childhood and of humble and lowly humanity. As pointed out above (p. 405), a few of the earlier romanticists had recognized the poetry of common life; Wordsworth elevated it to a dignity with which it had never before been invested. To the romantic treatment of Nature, he also added a new element. More clearly than Blake, with whom he has much in common, he saw with the eye of the Christian Platonist (cf. note to p. 91a, l. 38) a mystical reality behind external phenomena. He regarded the external world not only as a veil through which we at times catch glimpses of the Divine but as a humanizing influence which cements the bond of brotherhood between man and man (cf. especially *Tintern Abbey*, l. 22 ff.). But Wordsworth was not merely a sentimental, dreamy mystic. He had a definite theory of art. He distinguished between Fancy (an inferior faculty of collecting artistic materials) and Imagination, the superior faculty by which the poet illumines the external facts with the light of inner reality. With him Imagination was not, as it is in the minds of most people, divorced from reality. He was lyrical only in the sense that his poetry is a personal interpretation. He believed that real truth is arrived at by the constructive imagination operating upon mental pictures in quiet retirement — "emotion recollected in tranquillity" (cf. note to p. 679b, l. 23 f.). His language is simple, at times childishly prosaic, and his descriptions are often striking in their realism; yet he was thoroughly romantic in spirit. He sought "to give the charm of novelty to things of every day, and to excite a feeling analogous to the supernatural, by awakening the mind's attention to the lethargy of custom, and directing it to the loveliness and the wonders of the world before us." He was not learned, and he lacked a sense of humor; but as a poet who took his high calling seriously, who linked his art intimately with Nature and humanity, and who discreetly and inoffensively turned it to the edification of his readers, he has never been surpassed. He was a great philosopher and a great poet. In attempting to appreciate his work, we should compare it, not with the present, but with the relatively meager accomplishments of his eighteenth-century predecessors.

678a WE ARE SEVEN

We are Seven was composed in 1798 and appeared the same year in Wordsworth and Coleridge's famous collection of poems entitled *Lyrical Ballads* (cf. introductory note to the *Preface* to the *Lyrical Ballads*, p. 815). Wordsworth's contribution consisted of poems in which he attempted to shed an ideal light over reality. This poem, like others written by Wordsworth, is an analysis of the mental reaction of the simple and lowly — here the inability of a child to conceive of death. In order to understand this aspect of the poem, the student should compare it with the *Ode on Intimations of Immortality from Recollections of Early Childhood* (p. 695), which suggests a solution of the great question of immortality by "the heaven-taught wisdom of the child." Aside from the prosaic character of the language the poem suffers from a lack of "the spontaneous overflow of powerful feelings," which, Wordsworth tells us, is characteristic of all true poetry. The stanza form resembles that of the popular ballads in its simplicity.

1. **A simple child.** The child was a little

cottage girl whom Wordsworth met at Goodrich Castle on an excursion through the valley of the Wye River in 1793. The poem was not written till five years later. Until 1815 the first line read, " A simple child, dear brother Jim," — a rather prosaic line, even for Wordsworth.

678b 65 ff. **'But they are dead,'** etc. The last stanza, Wordsworth tells us, was written first.

679a LINES WRITTEN IN EARLY SPRING

5 ff. **To her fair works,** etc. Note the emphasis upon Nature as a harmonizing influence.

11 f. **'tis my faith,** etc. To Wordsworth Nature was really alive.

EXPOSTULATION AND REPLY

This and the following poem are companion pieces — the first put into the mouth of William Taylor (the " Matthew" of l. 15), Wordsworth's old teacher at Hawkshead; the second, the poet's reply. In both, Wordsworth's point of view predominates. Though the poem was written at Alfoxden, Somerset, in 1798, the scene is laid at Hawkshead, Lancashire, where Wordsworth attended school as a boy.

679b 23 f. **we can feed,** etc. By calm meditation, " a wise passiveness," we can transmute into truth the thoughts and emotions of our busier hours. Cf. *Tintern Abbey*, l. 64 f.

THE TABLES TURNED

9 ff. **Books! 'tis a dull and endless strife,** etc. Wordsworth is not opposed to books; he is here simply emphasizing the importance of the vision of truth that comes only from " a wise passiveness." He distrusted science only "when it chained the spirit of man to merely material things."

680a LINES COMPOSED A FEW MILES ABOVE TINTERN ABBEY

Tintern Abbey, one of the most romantic ruins in England, is situated in the valley of the Wye River not far from the Severn. Regarding the present poem Wordsworth wrote, " No poem of mine was composed under circumstances more pleasant for me to remember." The actual work of composition was done during a five-day tramp with his sister Dorothy in 1798. The poem is important for an understanding of Wordsworth's philosophy of nature.

1. **Five years have passed.** Wordsworth had visited the place in 1793.

680b 65 ff. **And so I dare to hope,** etc. The poet's previous experiences, as here outlined, may be divided into three periods: (1) that in which the animal enjoyment of Nature, mingled with an uncomprehended deeper pleasure, predominated; (2) that in which the love of man was uppermost; (3) that in which a spiritual presence was revealed by a deeper sympathy with man and with Nature.

681a 115 ff. **my dearest Friend,** etc. This tribute to Dorothy should be noted particularly. She was Wordsworth's constant inspiration and has left us in her *Journal* the completest extant record of his life. As Professor Saintsbury observes in one of his rare flashes of inspiration, she was " a woman in a million."

681b LUCY POEMS

Whether the Lucy of these five poems was a real person or the creature of Wordsworth's imagination, we do not know. If she was imaginary, we have in the " Lucy Poems " an illustration of a truth too often forgotten by readers of poetry: namely, that a great poet can so completely identify himself with the characters he creates that for the time being he is one with them. Certainly love, with its " anxious foreboding, profound sorrow, and calm despair," has never been more simply or poignantly portrayed.

682a SHE DWELT AMONG THE UNTRODDEN WAYS

2. **Dove,** a river forming part of the boundary between Derby and Stafford.

682b A SLUMBER DID MY SPIRIT SEAL

5 ff. **No motion,** etc. This is one of the finest expressions in literature of tragic grief all the more terrible because of its repression.

LUCY GRAY

This poem, suggested by the story of a little Yorkshire girl lost in a snowstorm, is intended, according to Wordsworth, " to exhibit poetically entire solitude." The theme is admirably suited to the simple language and the simple ballad stanza.

683a 20. **the moon,** " the day-moon, which no town or village girl would ever notice" (Robinson).

683b MICHAEL

Of the composition of this poem Wordsworth says, " The character and circumstances of Luke were taken from a family to whom had belonged, many years before, the house we lived in at Town-end." The sheepfold, then in ruin, was connected with this property. The style of *Michael* is noteworthy for its simplicity and directness. It is remarkably free from artificial poetic diction. In it the author attempts to portray the conflict in an honest and humble soul of two powerful forces — parental affection and love of ancestral property.

2. **Green-head Ghyll,** a valley near Dove Cottage. *Ghyll,* according to Wordsworth, is the local name for a steep, narrow valley with a stream running through it.

685a 134. **Easedale,** near Grasmere.

134. **Dunmail-Raise,** a pass about three miles from Grasmere.

689a MY HEART LEAPS UP

This poem has been called the keynote to Wordsworth's poetry.

9. **piety,** used in the Latin sense of "filial reverence." The child is father of the man, and the poet desires that his early childish delight in Nature may be retained and cherished during the years of manhood.

689b RESOLUTION AND INDEPENDENCE

690a 43. **Chatterton.** See introductory note to Chatterton, p. 591.

45 f. **Him who walked,** etc. The reference is to Robert Burns. See introductory note to Burns, p. 665.

691a TO H. C.

These sympathetic lines (written in 1802) were addressed to Hartley, the eldest son of Samuel Taylor Coleridge. See introductory note to Hartley Coleridge, p. 810.

1. **O thou! whose fancies,** etc. Compare *Intimations of Immortality,* p. 695 ff.

691b AT THE GRAVE OF BURNS

This poem grew out of Wordsworth's visit to the tomb of Burns in 1803.

19 f. **the flower, whose modest worth He sang.** The reference is to Burns's *To a Mountain Daisy,* p. 668.

33. **Whose light,** etc. The first (Kilmarnock) edition of Burns's poems appeared in 1786, when Wordsworth was sixteen.

39. **Criffel's hoary top.** Crowfell (Criffel) is a hill near Dumfries in the county of Kirkcudbright.

692a 40. **Skiddaw,** a mountain about three thousand feet high near Keswick in the Lake District.

78. **For which it prayed.** Cf. Burns's *To Ruin.*

TO A HIGHLAND GIRL

Wordsworth and his companions saw the girl here described on the border of Loch Lomond during a drenching rain and amid considerable discomfort, but the idealized picture omits all that is unpleasant and spiritualizes the girl and her surroundings. The unskilled critic may regard the stark simplicity of Wordsworth's style as somewhat prosaic.

693a THE SOLITARY REAPER

This poem is based partly on Wordsworth's own observations during his Highland tour of 1803, partly on a sentence found by him in an account of the Highlands written by some one else. Both in temper and in technique it is one of Wordsworth's most exquisite poems. The romance of the Highland girl singing in Gaelic alone on the hillside is conveyed in language carefully chosen for its musical effects.

17. **Will no one tell me what she sings?** She is singing in Gaelic, hence the observer's failure to understand her song.

693b TO THE CUCKOO

Wordsworth writes of the cuckoo in several poems. This one he often revised in an effort to convey in words "the imaginative influence" of the bird's voice.

SHE WAS A PHANTOM OF DELIGHT

This poem (written in 1804) was inspired by Mary Hutchinson, whom the poet had married in 1802. The first four lines were originally intended as part of another poem, *To a Highland Girl,* p. 692 f.

694a 22. **machine.** Perhaps the word "machine" (so often criticized for its prosaic suggestion) is intended to apply, not to the poet's wife, but to the whole household machine of which she is the center.

I WANDERED LONELY AS A CLOUD

Of the circumstances by which this poem was inspired, Dorothy Wordsworth wrote: "When we were in the woods beyond Gowbarrow Park (on the lake of Ullswater) we saw a few daffodils close by the water-side . . . as we went along there were more, and yet more; and at last under the boughs of the trees we saw that there was a long belt of them along the shore . . . I never saw daffodils so beautiful . . . They . . . tossed and reeled and danced and seemed as if they verily laughed with the wind that blew directly over the lake to them."

1. **I wandered lonely.** In reality the poet was not alone and only a few daffodils were seen at first. Again a simplification and idealization of experience.

19 ff. **For oft,** etc. Poetry, according to Wordsworth, is "emotion recollected in tranquillity." See also note to *Expostulation and Reply*, p. 679b, l. 23 f.

ODE TO DUTY

"I would rather a child of mine should know and feel the high, imaginative teachings of Wordsworth's *Ode to Duty* than any piece of uninspired prose morality in the language" (Reed).

694b 28. **Too blindly have imposed my trust.** The dangers of being led by impulse alone became more obvious to Wordsworth as he grew older.

695a ELEGIAC STANZAS

SUGGESTED BY A PICTURE OF PEELE CASTLE, ETC.

The Peele Castle portrayed in the picture is in Lancashire. Near it Wordsworth spent several weeks during one of his college vacations.

695b 39. **The feeling of my loss,** etc. Wordsworth's brother, Captain John Wordsworth, was drowned at sea in 1805, the year the poem was written.

ODE

INTIMATIONS OF IMMORTALITY FROM RECOLLECTIONS OF EARLY CHILDHOOD

This poem is one of the finest creations of English poetic genius. Contrary to the common opinion, it is not an argument either for a prenatal existence or for immortality; it is merely a poetic treatment of the themes in question. Wordsworth was, however, greatly impressed by the possibilities of the subject. He begins his poem by saying that, though the poet can no longer feel the beauty of Nature as he once did, he can at least refrain from useless sorrow. He tries to share the common joy of the beasts, the little child, the flower at his feet — but in vain. The new-born baby brings with it from its heavenly abode a glory which enshrouds the things of earth but which gradually disappears and fades into "the light of common day" as the child grows to manhood and becomes more and more the slave of earth. Though the radiance that was so bright in childhood is now forever taken from the poet's sight, the early impressions cannot be completely destroyed. The passing years have brought a deeper love of Nature inspired by a philosophic mind, a more profound human sympathy, and the hope of immortality. It is because of sympathy with Man that even the "meanest flower" can affect the poet too deeply for tears. With this poem compare Wordsworth's lines *Composed upon an Evening of Extraordinary Splendour and Beauty*, p. 698. Wordsworth's hypothesis regarding immortality is derived ultimately, though probably not directly, from one of Plato's doctrines (see note to p. 91a, l. 38).

696b 58 ff. **Our birth is but a sleep,** etc. Cf. Vaughan's exquisite lines in *The Retreat*, p. 382, and the note to l. 1.

102. **The little Actor,** etc. Wordsworth is thinking of Jaques's speech on the world as a stage (Shakespeare's *As You Like It* II, vii, 139 ff.). The "humorous stage" is the part in life taken by a man as the result of his disposition or "humor" (see note to Chaucer's *Prologue*, l. 420).

697b 166. **see the Children sport upon the shore.** The Man or Boy, though he has traveled some distance into the great continent of life, still has glimpses of the ocean on which he sailed thither from the Other World and can still see the newly arrived children playing on the shore.

698a COMPOSED UPON AN EVENING OF EXTRAORDINARY SPLENDOUR AND BEAUTY

698b 61 ff. **Such hues,** etc. Wordsworth directs the reader to compare this stanza with the opening of his *Intimations of Immortality*, p. 695.

TO A SKYLARK

8. **A privacy of glorious light.** Compare Shelley's *To a Skylark*, p. 769, l. 36 f.: "Like a Poet hidden In the light of thought."

699a 10. **with instinct more divine.** Compare James Hogg's *The Skylark*, p. 795, l. 12: "Thy lay is in heaven, thy love is on earth."

EXTEMPORE EFFUSION UPON THE DEATH OF JAMES HOGG

James Hogg, a Scottish shepherd and poet, was known as the "Ettrick Shepherd" from the fact that he lived in the Ettrick Forest, Selkirkshire. Wordsworth tells us that he wrote the poem immediately after reading of Hogg's death in a newspaper.

1 f. **When first . . . I saw,** etc. The reference is to Wordsworth's tour in Scotland in 1814.

2. **Yarrow,** a small river in Selkirkshire.

8. **Border-minstrel,** Scott, who died in 1832. The poem was written in 1835.

12. **the Shepherd-poet's eyes.** The reference is to Hogg.

15. **Coleridge,** died in 1834.

19. **Lamb,** died in 1834.

25 f. **lids . . . earlier raised.** All except Crabbe were younger than Wordsworth.

31. **Crabbe,** died in 1832. Wordsworth had frequently met Crabbe on the elder poet's annual visits to London.

32. **Hampstead,** Hampstead Heath, just outside London.

39 f. **Her who . . . Has sunk,** etc., Mrs. Felicia Hemans, a sentimental poet of considerable ability who lived near the Wordsworths on Windermere. She died in 1835.

699b 1 ff. **old romantic sorrows,** etc. The reference is to Hogg's ballads.

COMPOSED UPON WESTMINSTER BRIDGE, SEPTEMBER 3, 1802

Perhaps the best known and certainly one of the noblest of Wordsworth's sonnets. It was not composed in September, but a month or two earlier. On the sonnet in English literature, see introductory note to Sidney's *Astrophel and Stella*, p. 273.

LONDON, 1802

1. **Milton.** Milton, were he alive with his free, bold spirit, might call England back from artificiality and corruption to her ancient heritage of simple, inward happiness.

700a THE WORLD IS TOO MUCH WITH US

In our lust for worldly pleasure and possessions, we have lost sight of that in Nature which is ours — beauty. Rather than be thus out of tune Wordsworth would even be a pagan, for if he were, Imagination would enable him to see the poetry in Nature represented by the ancient classical divinities.

TO SLEEP

Compare Daniel's Sonnet LIV, p. 278. See further Shakespeare's *Macbeth*, II, ii, 35 ff.; *Midsummer Night's Dream*, III, ii, 431 f.; *2 Henry IV*, III, i, 5 ff.

700b NUNS FRET NOT

3. **pensive citadels,** strongholds or refuges where they can think at leisure.

6. **Furness-fells,** the downs or uplands of Furness, on the coast of Lancashire.

SCORN NOT THE SONNET

1. **Scorn not the Sonnet.** During the early part of the eighteenth century the sonnet was out of favor. Through the work of Gray, Warton, and Bowles it gradually returned to popularity as a literary form (see pp. 583, 597 f., 599 ff., and notes).

3. **Shakspeare unlocked his heart.** We do not now believe as fully as Wordsworth did in the autobiographical character of Shakespeare's sonnets.

AFTER-THOUGHT

This is the last of a series of thirty-four sonnets composed during a long period of years and entitled *The River Duddon.* The river Duddon rises at the point where Westmoreland, Cumberland, and Lancashire meet.

SAMUEL TAYLOR COLERIDGE

Coleridge was born two years later than Wordsworth. His education began at his birthplace, Ottery St. Mary, in Devonshire, where his father, an amiable and unworldly parson, was vicar of the parish and master of the local grammar school. As a child Coleridge was precocious and moody. Upon the father's death in 1781 the family was forced to leave the vicarage, and Coleridge was sent to Christ's Hospital, an ancient and famous charity school in London. Here he made many friends, among them Charles Lamb, astonished his fellow pupils by talking neo-Platonic philosophy and reciting Greek poetry on the playground, fell in love, took the highest honors the school afforded, and, in general, became known as "the inspired charity boy." His poetical faculty, already evident, was stimulated when in 1789 he read Bowles's sonnets (see introductory note to Bowles, p. 599), which had just appeared. In 1791 he entered Cambridge University as a "sizar" or poor student. At Cambridge he became somewhat of a radical in politics and religion, but had made a respectable record in his studies when suddenly in 1793 he left the university, probably because of bad debts and disappointed love, and enlisted in the army under the name of Silas Tomkyn Comberbach. Finding himself quite unfitted for the life of a dragoon, he succeeded in procuring a discharge and returned to the university, but he took no degree. On a visit to Oxford in 1794 he met Southey (see introductory note to Southey, p. 799), and the two conceived a wild plan called Pantisocracy, the purpose of which was to gather a select company of twelve ladies and twelve gentlemen, emigrate to America, and found an ideal community on the banks of the Susquehanna, which was chosen because of "its excessive beauty and its security from Indians and bisons!" With Pantisocracy in mind Southey and Coleridge engaged themselves to two young ladies named Fricker, whom they soon afterward married. In order to gather money for their enterprise the two youthful enthusiasts tried lecturing; but Coleridge earned little, his love for Sara Fricker wavered, he quarreled with Southey, and Pantisocracy came to nothing. In October, 1795, he married Miss Fricker in the church of St. Mary Redcliffe, Bristol, and the two settled in a small and ill-furnished establishment on Coleridge's meager and uncertain income. After numerous unsuccessful efforts to earn a competency, Coleridge became greatly depressed, contracted neuralgia, and began the use of opium, a habit which held him in subjection and weakened his powers throughout most of his remaining life. In 1796 he published his first volume of poems. In the same year his first child, Hartley (see introductory note to Hartley Coleridge, p. 810), was born (see his *To a Friend*, etc., p. 701, and Wordsworth's *To H. C.*, p. 691). In 1796 also he first met William and Dorothy Wordsworth (see introductory note to Wordsworth, p. 678), whose influence steadied his determination and during 1796 and the two following years stimulated his finest poetic work. At the close of the year 1796 he removed to a small cottage at Nether Stowey not far from Alfoxden, in Somerset, whither the Wordsworths migrated soon afterward. In 1797 Wordsworth and Coleridge conceived the plan that resulted a year later in that epoch-making volume, the *Lyrical Ballads* (see Coleridge's *Biographia Literaria*, p. 826 ff., and the Preface to the *Lyrical Ballads*, p. 815 ff.). Coleridge's chief contribution was *The Ancient Mariner* (p. 701 ff.). To this period also belong *Kubla Khan* and the first part of *Christabel*. In the fall of 1798 he went to Germany with the Wordsworths, but left them in order to study German literature and metaphysics at Göttingen University. After his return to England he settled at Greta Hall in Keswick, some twelve miles away from the Wordsworths' cottage at Grasmere. He now became reconciled with Southey and renewed his associations with the Wordsworths, whom he assisted in issuing the famous second edition of the *Lyrical Ballads*, 1800. About this time he became estranged from his wife, resumed the use of opium, and went through a period of vacillation marked by fits of despondency which were only temporarily relieved by advances of money from friends or publishers and which are reflected in his *Dejection: an Ode* (p. 717), written in 1802. After a sojourn on the continent he returned little improved in health and continued to waste his own time and his friends' money in fruitless comings and goings and in unremunerative undertakings, including a short-lived publication called *The Friend*. During the next fifteen years he did various sorts of political writing and literary hack work and gave several courses of lectures, which contain some excellent literary criticism. In 1817 appeared the *Biographia Literaria*, which throws valuable light on the author's life, philosophic opinions, and literary theories. After making many literary false starts, trying various places of abode, and attempting without success to abandon the use of stimulants and narcotics, Coleridge placed himself under the care of a Dr. Gillman, who resided at Highgate, a London suburb. Here he spent the last sixteen years of his life, sunk for the most part, as Carlyle says, in "putrescent indolence," but adored by a wide circle of admirers, especially among the younger generation, for his lovable nature and his high and fascinating discourse.

In striking contrast with the harmoniously balanced faculties of his friend Wordsworth, Coleridge's personality lacked stability. Like Wordsworth, he passed through a stage of political and religious radicalism, but unlike Wordsworth he was never able to apply successfully in his own life the more conservative doctrines that he afterward preached. He shrank from pain and hence took to opium. He avoided duty, and his morale weakened progressively. He lacked the power of concentrated, continuous effort, and his work became fragmentary and his knowledge scattering. He possessed an unusually warm and lovable disposition, but his relations with his wife were seldom harmonious. In spite, however, of his grievous personal shortcomings, he ranks in criticism as one of the greatest interpreters of English literature and in poetry as an almost unique combination of high intellectuality, delicate feeling for style, and exalted lyric genius. In reading Coleridge's poetry we receive the same impression of finality as from Shakespeare's most inspired lines. For his theories of literary art, see his *Biographia Literaria*, p. 826 ff.

701a DOMESTIC PEACE

From the historical drama, *The Fall of Robespierre*, 1794. It was also printed separately.

3. **Halcyon,** calm, tranquil. The adjective derives its significance from an ancient tradition that fair weather always prevails during the period that the *halcyon* (kingfisher) is breeding. See note to Gower's *Ceix and Alceone*, p. 160b.

TO A FRIEND, etc.

Chiefly notable for the beauty of the last two lines.

1. **Charles.** The poem is probably addressed to Charles Lamb or to another of Coleridge's friends, Charles Lloyd. The child is Hartley, born in 1796.

701b THE RIME OF THE ANCIENT MARINER

This famous poem was first printed in the *Lyrical Ballads*, 1798. For the literary theories that underlie its composition, see Coleridge's *Biographia Literaria*, p. 826 ff., and the introductory note to the *Preface to the Lyrical Ballads*, p. 815. *The Ancient Mariner* is an imitation ballad (see pp. 532 ff. and the introductory note to Ballads, p. 163). The horrible and the supernatural elements were introduced partly under the influence of the popular ballads, partly under the inspiration of the so-called Gothic School, or School of Terror, whose gruesome productions were popular during the late eighteenth century. The poem was "founded upon a dream of one of Coleridge's friends" and was begun by Coleridge and Wordsworth jointly during a walk near Alfoxden in the autumn of 1797. Before they had got far, however, they perceived that their methods did not harmonize, and Coleridge completed the poem alone, Wordsworth composing other poems in accordance with the division of labor described by Coleridge in the *Biographia Literaria*. Among the few contributions made by Wordsworth to *The Ancient Mariner*, perhaps the most important was the killing of the albatross. This, as he explained, was to serve as a crime the commission of which, coupled with the long wandering, should bring the spectral persecution upon the Ancient Mariner. Coleridge afterward said that he regarded the theme of moral responsibility as inappropriate in a work of imagination. In spite of this possible defect, the poem stands as the high-water mark of English poetry dealing with the supernatural.

701b 8. **May'st,** thou may'st.

12. **Eftsoons,** immediately. This and other obsolete words introduced throughout the poem are intended to help reproduce the atmosphere of the old ballads.

25. ff. **The Sun came up,** etc. The ship is thought of as sailing south in the Atlantic Ocean. The student should trace the course of the vessel.

30. **over the mast at noon.** The ship is near the equator.

32. **bassoon,** a musical wind instrument. Coleridge had probably been impressed with the sound of a bassoon which had been recently added to the resources of the village choir at Stowey.

702a 46. **who,** one who. What is the comparison suggested in this and the following lines?

55. **clifts,** cliffs.

57. **ken,** see, descry.

62. **swound,** swoon.

64. **Thorough,** an old form of *through*.

75. **shroud.** The shrouds are ropes attached to the sides of the ship and used to support the masts.

76. **vespers,** used in the Latin sense of "evenings."

81. **cross-bow.** In arming the Ancient Mariner thus, Coleridge was doubtless attempting to suggest that the action took place before the use of firearms became common.

83. **The Sun now rose,** etc. The ship has doubled Cape Horn and turned north into the Pacific. Before writing the poem, Coleridge had been reading numerous accounts of voyages in the South Seas.

702b 92. **'em,** for them.

98. **uprist,** modern uprose. Cf. the form *riz*, used by many unlettered persons as the past of "rise."

128. **death-fires,** St. Elmo's fires or dead men's candles, electrical discharges which sometimes appear on the rigging of ships and are believed by sailors to foretell disaster.

703a 168. **weal,** happiness, good.

170. **steadies,** comes steadily along.

184. **gossameres,** gossamers, wisps of cobweb floating in the air.

703b 197. **'The game is done!'** etc. Life-in-Death and Death are playing at dice to decide the Mariner's punishment.

199 f. **The Sun's rim dips,** etc., a splendid description of a tropical sunset.

209. **clomb,** the old past tense of *climb*.

210 f. **The hornèd Moon,** etc. No star can be seen through any part of the moon. Coleridge is inaccurately but poetically using the nautical superstition that when

a star "dogs" (follows closely) the moon, misfortune will result.

226 f. **And thou art long,** etc. These two lines were supplied by Wordsworth.

232 ff. **Alone, alone,** etc. This stanza is one of the most perfect expressions in literature of the terror of utter loneliness.

704a 267 f. **Her beams,** etc. To the Mariner the moon seemed to be mocking the hot sea by making the surface look as though covered with frost.

282 ff. **O happy living things!** etc. "Coleridge's strange creatures of the sea are not the hideous worms which a vulgar dealer in the supernatural might have invented. Seen in a great calm by the light of the moon, these creatures of God are beautiful in the joy of their life" (Dowden).

704b 290 f. **The Albatross fell off,** etc. This is the dramatic center of the story.

297. **silly,** empty, useless.

314. **fire-flags,** perhaps the phenomenon known in the northern hemisphere as the Aurora Borealis, or northern lights.

314. **sheen,** beautiful.

705a 333. **had been,** would have been.

362. **jargoning,** used in the older (French) sense of chirping, chattering.

705b 394. **have not,** have not the ability.

706b 472 ff. **The harbour-bay,** etc. "How pleasantly, how reassuringly, the whole night-mare story is made to end among the clear, fresh sounds and lights of the bay where it began" (Walter Pater).

512. **shrieve my soul,** cleanse my soul by receiving my confession.

707a 535. **ivy-tod,** clump of ivy.

707b 575. **crossed his brow,** made the sign of the Cross on his brow to avert evil.

708a 623. **of sense forlorn,** deprived of his senses.

CHRISTABEL

The first part of *Christabel* was written in 1797 and 1798, the remainder in 1800. Coleridge made various efforts to complete the poem but never succeeded. Like *The Ancient Mariner*, it derives its charm largely from its skillful use of the supernatural. According to Coleridge, it was partly founded on the notion that "the virtuous of this world save the wicked." It represents the struggle of the heroine against the forces of evil as embodied in Geraldine. The title and something of the general theme are derived from the old ballad-romance of *Sir Cauline*, and the poem is full of suggestions borrowed from other mediæval romantic literature. The character and appearance of Geraldine owe much to a mediæval belief that witches and other demonic creatures can assume partially beautiful forms. The ghostly surroundings, the mediæval setting, the whole atmosphere of terror suggest the work of the Gothic School (see introductory note to *The Ancient Mariner*). The spirit of mediæval superstition and of the popular ballads is here "refined and made subtle by delicate modern reflection." The richness and detail of the scenes in the castle remind us of Keats's *Eve of St. Agnes* (p. 781 ff.) and the work of the pre-Raphaelites (see introductory note to John Keats, p. 779, and also p. 981 ff.).

The verse form is novel. Each line has four accented and a varying number of unaccented syllables. The lines do not rhyme with perfect regularity, and the stanzas are of varying length. Each variation is designed to produce some particular musical or imaginative effect.

708b 49 ff. **The one red leaf,** etc. Note the change in the movement of the lines to correspond to the dancing of the leaf.

709a 129 f. **The lady sank,** etc. The fact that Geraldine cannot cross the threshold (which has probably been blessed by the church as the thresholds of all Christian homes should be) shows that she is a witch or a demon.

142. **I cannot speak.** Like other witches, Geraldine cannot pray.

709b 149. **what can ail,** etc. Animals have a specially keen sense of the presence of supernatural creatures.

159. **A tongue of light,** etc. The flame leaps up to greet a creature so closely associated with the fiery regions of hell.

710a 205. **Off, wandering mother!** etc. The demonic Geraldine has power to drive away the beneficent spirit of Christabel's mother.

252. **Behold! her bosom and half her side.** A key to Geraldine's character is furnished by one manuscript of *Christabel*, in which this line is followed by the words "Are lean and old and foul of hue."

711a 344. ff. **Bratha Head,** etc. The places referred to in this and the following lines are all in the Lake District, but the real scene of *Christabel* is in the world of "old, unhappy, far-off things" and fairy enchantment.

712a 408 ff. **Alas! they had been friends,** etc. Coleridge called lines 408–426 "the best and sweetest" he ever wrote.

714a 656 ff. **A little child,** etc. This so-called conclusion seems to have so little connection with the rest of the poem that one is tempted to believe that it was not originally intended as a part of *Christabel*.

714b

KUBLA KHAN

Kubla Khan has been called "a splendid curiosity," and such indeed it is. Sometime during the summer of 1798, Coleridge's most fruitful poetic year, the author, according to his own account, became slightly indisposed and retired to a lonely farmhouse about twenty miles from Nether Stowey. While there, he had recourse to an "anodyne" (? laudanum), from the effects of which he fell asleep while reading in Purchas's *Pilgrimage* (a famous seventeenth-century book of travel) a brief account of how Kubla Khan, the great mediæval founder of the Mogul dynasty in China, built a sumptuous palace of pleasure surrounded by a beautiful garden, the whole enclosed by a wall ten miles in circumference. "The Author," Coleridge goes on, "continued for about three hours in a profound sleep, at least of the external senses, during which time he has the most vivid confidence, that he could not have composed less than from two to three hundred lines; if that indeed can be called composition in which all the images rose up before him as *things*, with a parallel production of the correspondent expressions, without any sensation or consciousness of effort. On awaking he appeared to himself to have a distinct recollection of the whole, and taking his pen, ink, and paper, instantly and eagerly wrote down the lines that are here preserved. At this moment he was unfortunately called out by a person on business from Porlock (a neighboring village), and detained by him above an hour, and on his return to his room, found, to his no small surprise and mortification, that though he still retained some vague and dim recollection of the general purport of the vision, yet, with the exception of some eight or ten scattered lines and images, all the rest had passed away like the images on the surface of a stream into which a stone has been cast, but, alas! without the after restoration of the latter." Coleridge was doubtless sincere in his belief that he recovered only a small part of what he had composed in his sleep, but none the less *Kubla Khan* is perfectly unified in the effect produced by its assemblage of images. From the "stately pleasure-dome" in far-off Xanadu to the end of the poem, we are confronted with words and pictures gathered by Coleridge in his waking hours, treasured because of their romantic associations, and here fused by the power of his genius into one of the most perfect pieces of purely romantic description in literature. On the general subject of poems composed in dreams, see the note on the poet Cædmon, p. 45b, l. 52 ff.

1. **Xanadu.** Purchas gives "Xaindu" as the name of the place where Cublai Can (Kubla Khan) had his palace erected.

39 ff. **Abyssinian maid . . . Mount Abora.** *Abyssinian* and *Mount Abora* are merely words suggesting remoteness and romance.

715a 53 f. **For he on honey-dew,** etc. These two lines have often been applied to Coleridge himself.

FROST AT MIDNIGHT

This poem reveals Coleridge's genuinely lovable and loving humanity. It was composed during one of his long midnight meditations at Nether Stowey in February, 1798.

7. **My cradled infant,** Hartley.

26. **stranger.** According to an old superstition, a film of soot sticking to the grate foretells the coming of a stranger.

715b 37. **stern preceptor's face.** The reference is to Boyer, Coleridge's stern, though in the main just, master at Christ's Hospital.

42. **sister more beloved,** Coleridge's elder sister Ann, who died in 1791.

50 ff. **thou shalt learn far other lore,** etc. This was prophetic. Coleridge was soon to move to Greta Hall, but he did not know this fact when he wrote these lines.

716a FRANCE: AN ODE

Coleridge, like Wordsworth, began by sympathizing with the French Revolution as a great movement toward liberty and democracy. The present composition is a magnificent poetical expression of the author's reaction against the excesses that followed the triumph of the revolutionists (see introductory note to Wordsworth, p. 678). Its immediate occasion was the invasion of Switzerland (Helvetia, l. 66) by France in 1798.

30 f. **The Monarchs marched,** etc. France declared war against Austria and Prussia in April, 1792; against England, Holland, and Spain in February, 1793.

716b 43. **Blasphemy's loud scream.** During the Reign of Terror, 1793–1794, women dressed to represent the Goddess of Reason were enthroned in some of the Christian churches of Paris.

717b DEJECTION: AN ODE

This, probably the saddest of Coleridge's poems, was composed in its original form in April, 1802, not long before Wordsworth and Mary Hutchinson were happily married and after Coleridge's disagreement with his wife had become chronic. It was originally addressed to Wordsworth, but after Coleridge's estrangement from his friend it was altered (see notes). Out of the depth of his own misery Coleridge sings of the pure human love of another.

2. **Sir Patrick Spence.** See p. 164.

25. **O Lady!** In the earlier version the word *William* took the place of *Lady* here and elsewhere in the poem.

718a 40. **these,** the beauties of Nature.

718b 99 ff. **Thou Wind,** etc. Cf. Shelley's *Ode to the West Wind*, p. 767.

104. **Lutanist,** one who plays on a lute.

719a 120. **Otway's,** originally *William's.*

HYMN BEFORE SUN-RISE, etc.

Coleridge "had never been at Chamouni (one of the highest mountain valleys in the Savoy Alps), but he expanded a German poem by Frederica Brun addressed to Klopstock. The sights and sounds with which this solemn and beautiful psalm begins gradually become so intimately associated with the thoughts which they awaken, that his soul is swept onward and upward until it creates the spiritual vision of it all as an emanation from God" (George).

3. **Blanc,** Mont Blanc, which rises above the Vale of Chamouni.

4. **Arve and Aveiron,** rivers.

720a THE PAINS OF SLEEP

In 1803 Coleridge started with the Wordsworths on a walking tour through the Highlands (see introductory note to Wordsworth, p. 678), but separated from them at Inversnaid, ostensibly because of weariness, partly no doubt in order that he might have more unrestrained liberty to indulge in narcotics. The dreams which he had during his journey alone, "with all their mockery of guilt, rage, unworthy desires, remorse, shame, and terror, formed at that time the subject of some verses" (Coleridge). De Quincey, in his *Confessions of an English Opium Eater*, describes a similar experience.

720b YOUTH AND AGE

This poem, composed in 1823, is one of the last evidences of Coleridge's poetic genius at anything like its best.

721a WORK WITHOUT HOPE

Composed in February, 1827.

722b EPITAPH

The childlike faith and love that breathe through this poem should be compared with the somewhat contemptuous tone of Walter Savage Landor's lines composed under somewhat similar conditions (p. 814). The *Epitaph* stands on Coleridge's grave in Highgate churchyard.

WALTER SCOTT

Walter Scott was the son of a writer to the Signet and was born in Edinburgh. He was descended from border ancestry, in which he took great pride, and spent his rather delicate childhood in the beautiful country about Kelso, acquainting himself with scenes that later were to figure in his poems, and storing his memory with native tradition and history. He was a precocious child and early developed a habit of omnivorous reading, which remained with him for life. At neither the high school nor the University of Edinburgh was he distinguished for scholarship. He studied for the bar with greater industry than pleasure and being admitted in 1792 entered upon his profession as a hard worker but a heartier player. The tastes and instincts of the country gentleman in him led him after his marriage in 1797 to make his home for part of the year at Lasswade on the Esk. In 1789 he was appointed sheriff of Selkirkshire, and later removed to Ashestiel on the Tweed. Finally, when his various revenues, as he thought, gave him warrant, he built on the same river Abbotsford, an extensive and costly residence which was to be his home for the rest of his life. In his "raids" among the hospitable dalesmen, while performing the duties of his office, he gathered much of the material for his first publication of importance, the *Minstrelsy of the Scottish Border*, 1802–1803. This collection of popular poetry is second only to Percy's *Reliques* in the romantic revival of the mediæval ballads. *The Lay of the Last Minstrel*, 1805, with its brilliant descriptive coloring, its rapid movement, and its new verse form, adapted from the yet unpublished *Christabel* (see introductory note to *Christabel*, p. 708), established the author's fame, which *Marmion*, 1808, and *The Lady of the Lake*, 1810, confirmed, at the same time contributing substantially to his growing fortune. In 1812 Byron "awoke one morning and found" himself famous in working a poetical vein which had made Scott's reputation. Sensing the change of popular favor from himself to the younger and more spectacular genius, Scott generously gave up poetry and turned to the novel, a type in which he was to gain high distinction. *Waverley* appeared anonymously in 1814. It was the first of the great series which ended with *Castle Dangerous* only a year before the author's death. In 1820 he was created a baronet. In 1825 came the failure of his publishers, the Ballantynes, and with it vanished his dreams of founding a great house, that of Scott of Abbotsford. A touch of heroism was added to these years when he assumed the responsibility of paying his share of the debt, amounting to considerably more than £100,000, by the sheer efforts of his pen. The obligation was discharged in full by royalties accruing from his writings not long after. He died at Abbotsford in 1832 and was buried at Dryburgh Abbey nearby. In his verse Scott did more than any other writer to popularize romantic poetry, especially that dealing with British history. His best work is in his novels, in which he proved himself a master of romantic narrative.

LOCHINVAR

Lady Heron in the fifth canto of *Marmion* sings this song. In a slight degree it is founded on the ballad of "Katharine Janfarie" in *Minstrelsy of the Scottish Border*.

722a 20. **the Solway.** The Solway Firth, between England and Scotland on the west, has very swift tides.

32. **galliard,** a lively dance for two persons.

722b MARMION

In 1512–1513 Henry VIII was involved in a struggle with France. During his absence James IV of Scotland, yielding to the entreaties of the French king, led an army across the Border into Northumberland, but was met by the English under the Earl of Surrey and defeated at Flodden Field on September 9, 1513. James himself was slain. The battle in the poem, according to the author, is the culmination of "the private adventures of a fictitious character." By his splendid descriptive account Scott displays his powers of recreating the historic past and overlaying it with the glamour of romance.

8. **Terouenne,** a town of Artois southwest of Calais, under siege by Henry VIII.

13. **the good Countess,** the Countess of Angus, wife of Douglas, whose two sons perished at Flodden.

25. **Tantallon,** Tantallon Castle on the Scotch coast in Haddingtonshire.

34. **The Bloody Heart,** a symbol in the Douglas coat of arms commemorating the commission of Robert Bruce to Sir James Douglas to bear his heart to the Holy Land. Sir James lost his life in the performance of the task.

723a 67. **Whitby's fane.** Clare was a "novice unprofessed" (*i.e.*, she had not taken vows as a nun) at Whitby Abbey on the coast of Yorkshire, the place of Cædmon's fame. The reference is inaccurate, as there were no nuns at Whitby in Henry VIII's time. Hilda was the first abbess of Whitby.

723b 128. **Red de Clare,** Gilbert de Clare, who married a daughter of Edward I.

138. **Wilton,** Ralph de Wilton, Marmion's rival in love and arms.

724b 271. **fight on Otterburne.** See the *Hunting of the Cheviot*, p. 171b, and note.

275. **Angus,** Archibald Douglas, fifth Earl of Angus, called "Bell-the-Cat."

725a 280. **Twisel glen,** at the junction of the Till and Tweed, where James encamped before going to Flodden.

327. **A bishop . . . stood.** Gawain Douglas, *ca.* 1474–1522, a Scotch poet, son of the fifth Earl of Angus (see note to l. 275). He translated the *Æneid* into Scottish verse. He became Bishop of Dunkeld in 1515.

726a 435. **Saint Bride,** Saint Bridget.

726b 456. **Saint Jude,** St. Judas, one of the Apostles, not Iscariot.

460. **Saint Bothan,** a kinsman of Columba and his successor at the monastery of Iona. See *Life of Columba*, p. 42 f.

481. **spell the trick,** explain the mystery.

499. **Sheriff Sholto,** probably one of Douglas's sons.

500. **the Master,** Douglas's oldest son.

727a 507. **Henry,** Henry VIII.

512. **Cotswold.** De Wilton was vanquished by Marmion in the lists at Cotswold, Gloucestershire.

531. **Constance,** Constance de Beverley, carried away from a convent by Marmion and later left by him to a tragic fate imposed by the Church, while he pursued the Lady Clare.

540. **Lennel's convent,** a Cistercian convent near Flodden.

545. **A reverend pilgrim,** Scott's literary friend, Patrick Brydone.

727b 609 f. **Douglas . . . Randolph,** famous lieutenants of Bruce.

728a 616. **Bannockbourne.** See Burns's *Scots, Wha Hae*, p. 675, and note.

652. **the falcon's claw.** Marmion's crest was a falcon.

657. **Leat,** a small tributary of the Tweed.

730b 920. **A little fountain cell.** The well and Sibyl Grey are not historic.

731a 1000. **Fontarabian.** See note to p. 353a, l. 587.

732a 1071 ff. **View not,** etc., an allusion to the idle rumor that Home murdered the King at Home Castle.

1090. **Lichfield's lofty pile,** Lichfield Cathedral, in Staffordshire.

1095. **fanatic Brook,** a Puritan leader in the attack on Lichfield under garrison by the Royalists in 1643.

1097. **Saint Chad,** Ceadda, a bishop of Lichfield in the latter part of the seventh century. Brook was slain on St. Chad's Day.

1108. **Ettrick Woods,** Ettrick Forest in southeastern Scotland.

732b 1155. **Holinshed or Hall.** See introductory note to Ralph Holinshed, p. 286a.

1167. **Wolsey,** the Cardinal, prime minister to Henry VIII.

733a 1168. **More, Sands, and Denny,** Sir Thomas More (later Lord Chancellor), Lord Sands, and Anthony Denny, courtiers at the court of Henry VIII.

1170. **Catherine's hand,** etc. Catherine of Aragon was the first wife of Henry VIII. It was customary after the wedding to throw a stocking after the bride or groom.

SOLDIER, REST!

In *The Lady of the Lake*, I.

15. **pibroch,** a martial strain performed on the bagpipe, sometimes used of the bagpipe itself.

CORONACH

In *The Lady of the Lake*, III.

" The *coronach* of the Highlanders, like the *ululatus* of the Romans, and the *ululoo* of the Irish, was a wild expression of lamentation, poured forth by the mourners over the body of a departed friend " (Scott).

733b 17. **correi,** a hillside or cove.

18. **cumber,** trouble.

BRIGNAL BANKS

In *Rokeby*, III.

Brignal was an estate " on the banks of the Greta, below Rutherford Bridge " in Yorkshire.

PROUD MAISIE

In *The Heart of Midlothian*.

734a 7. **braw,** handsome.

GEORGE GORDON (LORD) BYRON

English romanticism culminated in the life and writings of Lord Byron. His noble but wayward blood, his Apollolike physical appearance, the mystery of his lonely but eventful life, his tumultuous passions, his spontaneous genius, and his lordly disdain of the ordinary conventions of life, all are of the very essence of romanticism in the popular conception. He was born in London, the son of a graceless father, Captain John Byron, and a " mad Gordon," descended from James I. Deserted by his scapegrace father, he spent his early years with his mother amid wild surroundings in Aberdeenshire, Scotland. At the age of ten he became heir to the barony and was brought by his mother to the ancestral home of the Byrons, Newstead Abbey, in Nottinghamshire. After some desultory schooling under tutors, he went to Dulwich, passed to Harrow, and in 1805 entered Cambridge. Three years later he received the M.A. degree by the special privilege of a peer. A scathing review, in the *Edinburgh Magazine*, of his juvenile verses in *Hours of Idleness*, 1807, elicited his spirited satire, *English Bards and Scotch Reviewers*, 1809. Soon afterward he left for a two years' sojourn in southern Europe and the near East. On his return he published the first cantos of his *Childe Harold's Pilgrimage* and acquired instant fame. With his succession of oriental and romantic tales, such as *The Giaour*, *The Bride of Abydos*, *The Corsair*, and *Lara*, written, as he characteristically said, *stans pede in uno* (standing on one foot) while undressing after balls, and echoing, it was supposed, his own life, he realized a popularity that has never been equaled by any other English poet. His separation from Lady Byron early in 1816 (for causes that have never been definitely known and after only a year of married life) reversed his fortunes, and a few months later he left England never to return. The *Prisoner of Chillon*, *Mazeppa*, and the last two cantos of *Childe Harold* followed during his trip across the continent and during the early part of his residence in Italy. In Italy he learned the language well, identified himself with the social and political interests of the country, domesticated himself with a countess, and came to know Italian life as few English writers have done. His dramas contributed little to his fame, but a long poem, *Don Juan*, 1819–1824, in some respects his masterpiece, proved him to be the greatest satirist in verse of modern times. A few months before his death he left Italy for Greece, to take part in the struggle for independence, but died of a fever at Missolonghi in the spring of 1824. His lyrics add only a few individual great pieces to English poetry. His plays, by which he tried to reform English drama, are good reading but are unsuited for the stage. His romantic narratives, carrying on the traditions of Scott, his descriptions of Nature in its big picturesqueness, and his masterful use of satire give him a major place in English literature.

THE PRAYER OF NATURE

Nature in Byron is not as in Wordsworth a being in itself permeated by a divine sentiency in sympathy with man, but an inscrutable and elemental force exercising control over man and presenting only in its more awful and sublime aspects a means of soothing him into quiet or awaking him to noble aspiration and expression. In this poem Nature means the natural man with all his baser impulses, as fully exemplified in the poet himself.

734b 7. **the sparrow's fall.** Cf. Matthew x, 29.

14. **the pile,** the sacred edifice.

735a WHEN WE TWO PARTED

This poem doubtless refers to his boyhood sweetheart, Mary Chaworth, for whom he cherished, or imagined he cherished, a real affection. She was married to a Mr. Musters and later suffered the ill fame of a separation.

MAID OF ATHENS, ERE WE PART

The Maid of Athens is usually taken to be Theresa Macri, in whose house Byron lodged during his first stay in Athens. The Greek subtitle means, "My life, I love you."

735b 21. **Istambol,** Constantinople.

SHE WALKS IN BEAUTY

The lady celebrated in this poem was Anne Horton of Catton Hall, Derbyshire.

736a THE DESTRUCTION OF SENNACHERIB

For the Biblical account, cf. 2 Kings xviii f.

21. **Ashur,** Assyria.

736b STANZAS FOR MUSIC

This poem and *Stanzas*, etc., p. 737, represent the usual romantic glorification of youth and inconsolable regret at its passing. Cf. Coleridge's *Youth and Age*, p. 720, and Browning's *Abt Vogler*, p. 941.

FARE THEE WELL

These stanzas, as one of the poems of the Separation, refer to Lady Byron. They were published in April, 1816.

737b TO THOMAS MOORE

The Irish poet, Thomas Moore (see p. 805 and introductory note), was a boon companion and friend of Byron for many years. He was Byron's authorized biographer.

738a CHILDE HAROLD'S PILGRIMAGE

Childe Harold has fittingly been called a glorified guidebook. In following the adventures of one person it is epical; in its pictorial elements it is descriptive; and in its emotional outbursts it is lyrical. It gives the poet's reactions, in the character of the thinly disguised Harold, to the scenes of his travel in southern Europe in 1809–1811 and of his trip across the continent to, and residence in, Italy in 1816–1818. In its most sustained parts it is a commemoration of "the glory that was Greece and the grandeur that was Rome."

1. **my fair child.** Byron never saw his daughter after she was a few weeks old.

738b 20. **The wandering outlaw,** Childe Harold, in cantos I and II of the poem.

739b 118. **the Chaldean.** The ancient Chaldeans were celebrated astronomers.

740a 155. **the deadly Waterloo.** The battle of Waterloo took place on June 18, 1815, only a year before these stanzas were written.

158. **'pride of place,'** a term in falconry. See *Macbeth* II, iv, 12.

165. **One,** Napoleon.

740b 180. **Harmodius drew,** etc. Harmodius and Aristogeiton, with swords concealed in myrtle during a religious procession, slew the Athenian tyrant Hipparchus, 514 B.C.

181 ff. **a sound of revelry by night,** etc. The scene described is that of the Countess of Richmond's ball in Brussels on the eve of the Battle of Quatrebras and three days before the Battle of Waterloo.

200. **Brunswick's fated chieftain,** Frederick William, Duke of Brunswick, slain early in the Battle of Quatrebras. His father was killed at Auerstadt in 1806.

741a 226. **'Cameron's gathering,'** the rallying cry of the Scotch Highland clan of the Camerons. Donald Cameron of Lochiel was the chieftain of the clan who fought at Culloden in 1745 (see Campbell's *Lochiel's Warning*, p. 802). Sir Evan Cameron was his ancestor.

227. **Albyn,** the Gaelic name for Scotland, more specifically the Highlands.

235. **Ardennes,** "The wood of Soignies . . . a remnant of the forest of Ardennes" (Byron).

741b 254 ff. **one . . . gallant Howard,** Byron's kinsman, the Hon. Frederick Howard, son of the Earl of Carlisle. He fell in a final charge at Waterloo.

256. **I did his sire some wrong.** Byron satirized his guardian, the Earl of Carlisle, in *English Bards and Scotch Reviewers.*

742a 303 f. **apples on,** etc. According to Tacitus (*Hist.* V, 7), the apples on the ancient lake Asphaltites, or Dead Sea, were fair without but ashes within.

307. **The Psalmist numbered,** etc. Cf. Psalms xc, 10.

316 ff. **the greatest,** etc., Napoleon.

743a 366. **Philip's son,** Alexander the Great.

368. **Diogenes,** a Greek cynic philosopher.

744b 476. **one fond breast,** Byron's half sister, Augusta.

496. **Drachenfels.** The castle of Drachenfels crowns a summit on the right bank of the Rhine above Bonn.

745a 541. **Marceau,** a French general who captured Coblenz in 1794 and was slain at Altenkirchen two years later.

745b 554. **Ehrenbreitstein,** a fortress on the Rhine opposite Coblenz, captured by the French in 1799.

746a 601. **Morat,** a small town in Switzerland where the Swiss won a decisive victory over Charles the Bold, Duke of Burgundy, in 1476.

608. **Cannæ.** See note to Sackville's *Induction,* p. 201a, l. 411.

609. **Marathon.** See note to Sackville's *Induction,* p. 201a, l. 405.

616. **Draconic.** The Athenian code of laws, formulated by Draco in the seventh century before Christ, provided so freely for the death penalty that they were said to have been written in blood.

625. **Aventicum,** the ancient capital of Helvetia, now Avenches, in Switzerland.

627. **Julia,** according to a Latin inscription (discovered to be a fabrication since Byron's day), Julia Alpinula, a young Aventian priestess, who vainly tried to save her father from death on a charge of treason and who died soon after.

746b 644. **Lake Leman,** Lake Geneva in Switzerland.

747b 725. **Rousseau,** Jean Jacques Rousseau, 1712–1778, who spent his youth at Geneva, his birthplace.

743. **Julie,** the heroine of Rousseau's novel, *La Nouvelle Héloïse.*

745 ff. **This hallowed,** etc. Byron's note to this passage cites the account in Rousseau's *Confessions* of Rousseau's passion for the Comtesse d'Houdetot and of his daily walk for the single conventional kiss common among French acquaintances.

748a 762. **Pythian's mystic cave,** the oracle of Apollo at Delphi. Its prophetess was called Pythia.

748b 809. **Jura,** a mountain range in western and northern Switzerland.

749a 848. **Cytherea's zone,** the girdle of the Cytherean Aphrodite, which was fabled to bring love to its wearer.

750a 923. **Clarens,** a village on Lake Geneva, celebrated in Rousseau's *Le Nouvelle Héloïse.*

750b 972. **Love his Psyche's zone,** etc. See note to *Comus,* l. 1005.

751a 977. **Lausanne! and Ferney!** residences respectively of Gibbon and Voltaire.

986. **The one,** Voltaire.

991. **Proteus.** See note to the *Faerie Queene,* canto ii, l. 85.

995. **The other,** Gibbon.

751b 1024. **the fierce Carthaginian,** Hannibal. See note to Sackville's *Induction,* p. 201a, l. 410.

752b THE PRISONER OF CHILLON

The Castle of Chillon is situated at the eastern end of Lake Geneva. After a visit to the place in company with the Shelleys in June, 1816, Byron wrote his poem in two days' time from a very inadequate knowledge of the historical personage whose afflictions he has celebrated. François de Bonnivard, 1493–1570, was a Swiss patriot and religious reformer. For his opposition to the House of Savoy he was imprisoned at Chillon from 1530 until its capture by his own party in 1536. Byron's Prisoner is a romantic idealization of the facts. The brothers are imaginary.

THE ISLES OF GREECE

This "hymn," as Byron called it, is in *Don Juan,* III.

756a 4. **Delos,** a small island of the Cyclades in the Ægean, the fabled birthplace of Apollo. It is said to have risen from the sea.

7. **the Scian and the Teian muse,** Homer who, according to one tradition, was born at Scio; and Anacreon, whose birthplace was Teos in Asia Minor. Homer's poetry is heroic and Anacreon's amatory.

12. **'Islands of the Blest,'** ἁι τῶν μακάρων νῆσοι, or Islands of the Blest, situated, according to Greek fable, in the far Atlantic; the abode of the blest after death. Cf. notes to p. 61a, l. 32, and p. 886b, l. 63.

19 f. **A king,** etc. See note to Sackville's *Induction,* p. 201a, l. 428.

756b 42. **Thermopylæ,** the scene of the heroic action of King Leonidas and his three hundred Spartans in an attempt to defend Greece against the Persian hordes in 480 B.C.

55. **Pyrrhic dance,** an ancient Grecian war dance, in quick and light measure, named for Pyrrhichos, the inventor.

56. **Pyrrhic phalanx,** *i.e.,* the ancient Greek mode of war and valor in arms, as exemplified in King Pyrrhus of Epirus, *ca.* 318–272 B.C., one of the greatest generals of ancient times. See note to p. 307b, l. 5.

59. **Cadmus,** the legendary founder of Thebes. He is said to have brought

from Phœnicia the letters which make the Greek alphabet.

61. **Samian,** etc. While a refugee from his native land, Anacreon was hospitably entertained at Samos by the tyrant Polycrates, a patron of art and literature.

67. **The tyrant,** etc. Miltiades, the hero of Marathon, for several years previous to the battle was "tyrant" of the Chersonesus.

74. **Suli's rock,** a fortress on a height overlooking the river Suli in Albania.

74. **Parga,** a seaport in Albania.

78. **Heracleidan.** The Heraclidæ, or descendants of Hercules, are fabled to have conquered the Peloponnesus before the Trojan War.

757a 91. **Sunium,** the promontory at the southeastern extremity of Attica, now Cape Colonna.

DON JUAN

Don Juan represents the reactions of the world-weary Byron to contemporary conditions in his later years. His purpose was, as he declared, to be "a little quietly facetious about everything" — society, politics, and literature. He took as his hero the traditional Spanish libertine, Don Juan, and in a loosely constructed narrative conducts him from an intrigue in his native land to the islands of the East, through Turkey and Russia, and into England, where he leaves him at the end of the sixteenth canto. The narrative is interrupted freely by the author's commentary, grave, gay, or flippant, as the mood prevails. The tone was borrowed from the Italian of Pulci and had been lately employed in England by John Hookham Frere. The poem was begun in 1818 and was left unfinished at the time of Byron's departure for Greece in the late summer of 1823. Byron regarded the poem as "the comic epic of the human race." The public at the time, mistaking it for "an eulogy of vice," was shocked by its license. Critical opinion since has regarded it as the greatest verse satire in English.

21. **'falls into the yellow Leaf.'** Cf. *Macbeth* V, iii, 23.

757b 43. **Pulci,** an Italian poet of the fifteenth century, author of the burlesque epic, *Il Morgante Maggiore.*

44. **Quixotic.** Cervantes ridicules the decadent romances of chivalry in his great satirical burlesque *Don Quixote.*

762b 411. **Cassandra.** See note to Sackville's *Induction,* p. 201b, l. 463.

418. **Phlegethontic rill,** Phlegethon, a river of fire in Hades.

431. **Fez,** a sultanate in the northern part of Morocco.

763a 455. **Numidian.** Numidia was a country of northern Africa.

763b 485. **Laocoön,** a famous antique group in sculpture, showing the Trojan priest of Apollo and his two sons ensnared and bitten to death by pythons.

486. **ever-dying Gladiator,** the Dying Gaul, a famous statue, showing a half-reclining gladiator reluctantly yielding to death.

764b 576. **Cyclades,** a group of islands southeast of Greece in the Ægean Sea.

ON THIS DAY, etc.

This poem was written in Greece, January 22, 1824. Byron died April 19, following.

PERCY BYSSHE SHELLEY

Percy Bysshe Shelley, the greatest of English lyrical poets, stands in striking contrast to Keats, whom he admired and elegized, in his idealization of intellectual rather than sensuous beauty and in the employment of the great body of his poetry for his philosophy of reform. He was the son of a bluff Tory squire and was born and spent his early youth at Field Place, the family estate in Sussex. As an oldest son he was heir to the baronetcy which came into the family in 1806. At the age of ten he was sent to Sion House Academy, near London, and two years later went to Eton, where he showed himself a rebel to school tradition and published a romance called *Zastrozzi.* He entered Oxford in 1810 and began at once to gratify his intellectual avidity by reading widely in philosophy, specifically Hume, Locke, and Godwin, and when the year was no more than half over issued his first formal protest against "tyranny," *The Necessity of Atheism.* His expulsion in consequence brought on a family rupture. Taking up lodgings in London, he met a pink-and-white school-girl beauty of sixteen, Harriet Westbrook, who readily adopted his revolutionary doctrines. Sympathizing with her rebellious attitude toward parental and school authority, he eloped with her to Edinburgh. The next two or three years, spent in migrations from place to place in the British Isles, are significant mainly for the publication of his *Queen Mab,* 1813, and for his sojourn in Ireland to aid the cause of political and religious liberty by tracts and addresses. By the spring of 1814 he was intimate with the Godwins in London. Mary Godwin attracted him by her delicate beauty and intellectuality, Harriet was neglectful and spent much time away from him, and after apprising Harriet of his purpose to separate from her he eloped with Mary to the continent. Harriet drowned herself in the Serpentine two and a half years afterward, having had in the meanwhile other attachments. Shelley and Mary were again in England after a brief stay abroad. They spent the summer of 1816 with Byron in Switzerland, returned to England for another year and a half, and in the spring of 1818 left the country for good. These years are notable mainly for *Alastor*, 1816, and the long *Revolt of Islam*, 1817, both of which show the effects on his poetry of his speculations on reform. In Italy, where he spent his remaining years, he found his realm; the climate suited him, a few friends were congenial, and he was far from the scenes of his early agitations. Here from 1819 to 1821 he produced in rapid succession the great works which have given him an enduring fame: *Prometheus Unbound*, *The Cenci*, *Adonais*, *Epipsychidion*, and his unrivaled lyrics. In the spring of 1822 he went to Lerici, on the bay of Spezzia, to spend the summer. On July 8, while he was returning from a meeting with Byron and Leigh Hunt in Pisa, his little sailing craft *Ariel* was foundered in a storm. His body, discovered on the shore a few days later with that of his friend Williams, was burned, and his ashes were placed in the Protestant cemetery at Rome near the grave of Keats. For the greater part of his career he imagined himself a reformer and used his poetry as a means of freeing the race from its social, political, and religious shackles, but in his last years he became reconciled to the calling of a poet and wrote more as an inspired representative of pure art. Though he idealizes intellectual beauty, he is far from being unsympathetic or cold. He is a neo-Platonist, and the prototype of his intellectual idealism is Love (see note to p. 91a, l. 38). In his combination of noble aspiration, profound emotion, and exquisite technique, he is the supreme lyric genius of the language.

765a HYMN TO INTELLECTUAL BEAUTY

In this poem Shelley announces his ideal of life, the pursuit of intellectual beauty. His conception is essentially Platonic. The beauties of earth are but partial and imperfect reflections of a higher essence of pure beauty. It is man's duty and privilege to aspire to an understanding and realization of this higher archetype, which when attained will transform his whole being and suffuse it with brotherly love.

765b 49 ff. **While yet a boy,** etc. The romantic picture here presented of the poet's boyhood is made up of real memories.

766a OZYMANDIAS

The statue of Ozymandias, according to Diodorus Siculus, was reputed to be the largest in Egypt.

766b 8. **The hand that mocked them,** etc. The hand of the sculptor drew in imitation in marble those passions which the heart of the king nourished.

STANZAS WRITTEN IN DEJECTION NEAR NAPLES

30 ff. **I could lie down,** etc. In this stanza the poet appears to have had a premonition of his own death by drowning.

767a ODE TO THE WEST WIND

This ode is one of Shelley's greatest lyrical achievements. It was "conceived and chiefly written in a wood that skirts the Arno, near Florence, and on a day when that tempestuous wind" was actually blowing. In its treatment of Nature the poem illustrates his unique myth-making faculty and his power of gradual mergence into the object he describes until he becomes one with it and sings as the inspired object itself. The stanzaic form of the poem is unusual in English, being an adaptation of the popular Italian *terza rima*.

9. **Thine azure sister,** etc., the south wind laden with blue haze.

767b 21. **Maenad,** a priestess of Bacchus.

32. **Baiae's bay,** near Naples, a favorite resort of the ancient Romans.

769a TO A SKYLARK

Compare Wordsworth's *To A Skylark*, p. 698, and James Hogg's *The Skylark*, p. 795. According to Mrs. Shelley, the poem was inspired by "the caroling of the skylark" one "beautiful summer evening."

6 ff. **Higher still,** etc. This stanza has often been taken as characterizing fittingly Shelley himself as a lyrical poet.

770a TIME LONG PAST

Many of Shelley's late poems reveal a chastened air of retrospection and a seeming prescience of death, not only an evident wish for it as a relief but an unmistakable anticipation of its actual imminence.

772a ADONAIS

Adonais, one of the great elegies, is Shelley's spontaneous tribute to the memory of Keats. After Keats's death the erroneous notion prevailed that he had been hurried to his grave by the savage criticism of his *Endymion* in the *Quarterly Review*. Shelley knew Keats, though not intimately, and greatly admired him. When he heard of this last act of tyranny, he "dipped his pen in consuming fire for Keats's destroyers." The elegy therefore had a double motive in its inception — sympathy for the young genius as the victim of oppression and righteous indignation against unjust and indiscriminate reviewers. In execution, however, the former motive prevailed, and the poem became one of the most beautiful threnodies in any language. The name "Adonais" is the poet's own formation from Adonis, the beautiful youth loved by Aphrodite and killed by a wild boar.

772b 12. **Urania,** Uranian Aphrodite, with some elements of the Muse Urania.

30. **the Sire,** etc., Milton. Shelley's poem is reminiscent of *Lycidas* as well as of Bion's *Lament for Adonis* and Moschus' *Elegy on Bion*.

36. **the third,** the other two being Homer and Shakespeare, or, among epic poets, Homer and Dante.

41. **Others more sublime,** perhaps such as Chatterton and Burns.

44. **some yet live,** such as Byron and Wordsworth.

773a 55. **that high Capital,** Rome.

774a 127. **Lost Echo.** See note to *Comus*, p. 333b, l. 230.

140. **Hyacinth.** See note to *Lycidas*, p. 344a, l. 106.

152 f. **his head who,** etc., the reviewer in the *Quarterly*, J. W. Croker. Shelley supposed the author was H. H. Milman, an English clergyman.

775b 238. **the unpastured dragon,** the critical world.

244 ff. **The herded wolves . . . ravens . . . vultures,** etc., the critics who served party ends.

250 f. **The Pythian of the age,** etc., Byron, in allusion to *English Bards and Scotch Reviewers*.

264 ff. **The Pilgrim of Eternity,** etc., Byron, in allusion to *Childe Harold's Pilgrimage*.

268 ff. **Ierne,** Ireland. Thomas Moore, the Irish poet (see p. 805 f.), in several poems sang the tragic fate of the patriot, Robert Emmet.

776a 271. **one frail Form,** Shelley himself.

276. **Actaeon,** a young hunter who saw Diana bathing with her nymphs. He was changed into a stag by the goddess and destroyed by his own hounds.

284 ff. **a dying lamp,** etc. See note to *Time Long Past*, p. 770a.

307 ff. **What softer voice,** etc., Leigh Hunt.

776b 317 ff. **What deaf and viperous murderer,** etc. See note to l. 152 f.

777b 399. **Chatterton.** See p. 591a and notes.

401. **Sidney.** See p. 273 and notes.

404. **Lucan.** See note to p. 458a, l. 5.

778a 439 ff. **a slope of green access,** the Protestant cemetery, where Keats was buried and where a few months later Shelley's ashes were interred.

444 ff. **one keen pyramid,** etc., the tomb of Cajus Cestius.

451 ff. **Here pause,** etc. For the vein of personal reference from this point on, see note to *Time Long Past*, p 770.

779a WITH A GUITAR, TO JANE

1. **Ariel to Miranda.** See Shakespeare's *The Tempest*. The Miranda of the poem was Mrs. Jane Williams, whose husband, Edward Williams, was drowned with Shelley. They were intimate friends of the Shelleys. Mrs. Williams used often to delight Shelley with music. The guitar which accompanied the poem is preserved in the Bodleian Library at Oxford.

10. **Prince Ferdinand,** Edward Williams, the lady's husband.

JOHN KEATS

John Keats died when he was little more than twenty-five years old. He was not unusually precocious. His active literary career extended over scarcely half a dozen years; yet unlike any other English writer of so brief a career, he is reckoned one of the major poets of the language. He was born in Moorfields, London, the son of a stableman who had married his proprietor's daughter. He attended school at Enfield, near London, and there came into contact with Charles Cowden Clarke, who more than any other influenced him in his literary development. At fifteen he was removed from school and apprenticed to a surgeon; but surgery was uncongenial to his tastes and temperament, and in the winter of 1816–1817 he definitely decided to devote himself to poetry. In 1817 appeared his first volume, containing along with other good juvenile pieces his celebrated sonnet on Chapman's Homer. His *Endymion*, written in fulfillment of a pact with Shelley, was published the following year. The poem contains passages of exquisite beauty, but its obscurity and his association with Leigh Hunt (see introductory note to Leigh Hunt, p. 807) and the so-called Cockney School called down on him the wrath of the Tory reviewers. Meanwhile his health showed signs of decline; and the breaking up of the little family group, by the departure of one brother for America, the death of another to whom he was devotedly attached, and isolation from his sister Fanny by an unsympathetic guardian, affected him greatly. About the same time he became engaged to Fanny Brawne, his violent passion for whom proved a real affliction. In 1820 appeared the volume on which his fame chiefly rests. It contained along with other notable poems *Isabella*, *The Eve of St. Agnes*, the great odes, and the fragmentary *Hyperion*. Meanwhile the condition of his health made it necessary for him to spend the cold season in a warmer climate. Accordingly in the autumn of 1820 he set out for Italy in company with the painter Severn, whose devoted friendship in those last months is one of the beautiful things in literary biography. But hereditary consumption, as it was called at the time, had progressed too far. The friends spent the winter in anguish at Rome, and just before its close the poet died. He was buried in the Protestant cemetery near the mound of Caius Cestius, where the following year the ashes of Shelley were laid. He is noteworthy in English poetry for his idealization of sensuous beauty; in his own words, "a thing of beauty is a joy forever." He even goes so far as to regard Beauty as supreme Truth—truth discovered by imaginative power rather than by scientific analysis (see the closing lines of the *Ode on a Grecian Urn*, p. 787). He is frequently regarded as one of the chief English exponents of the principle of "art for art's sake." The little group of artist poets led by Rossetti (see introductory notes to Dante Gabriel Rossetti, p. 981; William Morris, p. 996; and Algernon Charles Swinburne, p. 1006) and called "pre-Raphaelites" because of their advocacy in painting and poetry of the artistic principles that prevailed before Raphael, found a kinship in his works which caused them to regard him as their great predecessor and exemplar. Some of his sonnets are among the best in the language; he is the greatest ode writer in English; and in his fragment of *Hyperion*, Matthew Arnold in *Sohrab and Rustum* alone perhaps excepted, he has written the best epic poetry since Milton.

779b KEEN FITFUL GUSTS

780a 10. **a little cottage**, Leigh Hunt's residence in the Vale of Health at Hampstead, on the occasion of Keats's first visit to the place.

11 f. **Milton's eloquent distress**, etc. See *Lycidas*, p. 342, and notes.

13. **Laura.** See note to p. 253b, l. 1. One picture describes Laura as dressed in green.

14. **Petrarch.** See note to p. 204a, l. 1. Petrarch was crowned poet laureate at Rome in 1341.

ON FIRST LOOKING INTO CHAPMAN'S HOMER

Chapman's Homer, 1598–1616, is one of the classical translations of the great Greek epics, *Iliad* and *Odyssey*. Keats's appreciation was written after a night's reading in Homer, lasting until daybreak, with Charles Cowden Clarke.

11. **Cortez.** Substitute Balboa. The mistake is the poet's.

780b ON LEAVING SOME FRIENDS AT AN EARLY HOUR

The friends were the congenial group at Hunt's cottage in Hampstead.

ADDRESSED TO [HAYDON]

The historical painter, Benjamin Robert Haydon, 1786–1846, was one of Keats's close friends and doubtless did much to awaken the poet's interest in Greek sculpture and antiquities.

2 ff. **He of the cloud**, etc., Wordsworth.

3. **Helvellyn's summit**, a mountain peak in Cumberland.

5. **He of the rose**, etc., Leigh Hunt.

7. **And lo! — whose**, etc., Haydon.

781a BRIGHT STAR

4. **Eremite**, hermit.

THE EVE OF ST. AGNES

St. Agnes, a Roman virgin and martyr, was beheaded in the reign of Diocletian. The poem is founded on the superstition that if a maiden, after certain rites, retired fasting on the night before St. Agnes's Day (January 21), her future husband would appear and feast with her in her dreams. The story is of Keats's own creation. It is feudal in setting and spirit, and by its richness of color and imagery it suggests the pre-Raphaelitism which found chief expression in the poetry of Rossetti, Morris, and Swinburne later in the century.

782a 70. **amort**, deadened, dazed.

71. **her lambs unshorn.** On account of her name (cf. Latin *agnus*, lamb) and innocence, St. Agnes's symbol was a lamb. Her proper sacrifice was two unshorn lambs.

782b 115 ff. **by the holy loom,** etc. The wool of the sacrificial lambs was dressed, spun, and woven into cloth by the nuns.

783a 171. **Merlin paid his Demon,** etc. Merlin, the son of a demon, disappeared in a violent storm in the forest of Broceliande by the magic of an enchantress, to whom he had confided the secret of the spell which overcame him. To the poet his "monstrous debt" was his existence, which he owed to the Devil for the gift of his magic.

784a 241. **a missal,** etc., a Christian prayer-book with pictures of converted heathen at prayer.

784b 269. **Fez,** a district in northern Morocco. The city of Fez is an important commercial center.

270. **silken Samarcand,** a city in Turkestan, Asiatic Russia, celebrated for its manufacture of cotton goods, silks, etc.

270. **cedared Lebanon,** a mountain range in southern Syria, noted from time immemorial for its cedars.

292. **'La belle dame sans mercy,'** the title of a poem by Alain Chartier, an early fifteenth-century French poet. See Keats's own poem by the same title, p. 790.

785b ODE TO A NIGHTINGALE

During his general depression in the spring of 1819, following the death of his brother Tom, Keats was at times delighted by the song of a nightingale which had built its nest near Wentworth Palace, where he was residing. He composed his ode one morning while seated under a plum tree, listening to the bird's ravishing strains.

786a 15. **O for a beaker,** etc. Keats was very fond of claret wine.

32. **pards,** leopards. Bacchus is often represented as riding in a car drawn by leopards or other wild beasts.

786b 66. **the sad heart of Ruth.** See Ruth ii.

ODE ON A GRECIAN URN

The particular urn which is generally understood to have inspired this ode is still preserved, though in a weather-beaten condition, at Holland House in London.

787b 41. **brede,** braid, ornament.

ODE TO PSYCHE

1. **Goddess.** See note to Milton's *Comus*, p. 342b, l. 1005.

14. **Tyrian,** of a purple color.

26. **Phœbe's . . . star,** the moon.

27. **Vesper,** the evening star, the planet Venus when east of the sun and appearing after sunset.

788a 67. **the warm love,** Cupid.

789a BARDS OF PASSION AND OF MIRTH

This poem was written on the blank page before Beaumont and Fletcher's tragicomedy, *The Fair Maid of the Inn*, and must therefore be understood to be addressed to these poets rather than to poets in general.

789b LINES ON THE MERMAID TAVERN

The Mermaid Tavern was "the club-house of Shakespeare, Ben Jonson, and other choice spirits" of the late Elizabethan age. It is said to have been founded by Sir Walter Ralegh.

790a LA BELLE DAME SANS MERCI

This poem is of Keats's own romantic creation and has nothing to do with the "ancient ditty" referred to in l. 291 f. of *The Eve of St. Agnes* (see note to p. 784b, l. 292).

790b HYPERION

Keats completed only two books and a part of a third of *Hyperion.* He left the poem unfinished partly because of his declining health, partly because of the unfavorable reception of *Endymion*, and because it contained "too many Miltonic inversions." If he had completed it, it would have treated, so says a friend, the dethronement of Hyperion (the god of physical light) by Apollo, of Saturn by Jupiter, of Oceanus by Neptune, and the like, and the war of the Titans for Saturn's restoration. The mythology represented is but darkly suggested in the Greek and Roman poets. The incidents would have been, as in the parts achieved, the poet's own imaginative creation. In the general character of its subject and treatment and in its masterful blank verse, the poem ably suggests Milton.

23. **there came one,** Thea, a Titan, the sister of Saturn and Hyperion.

30. **Ixion's wheel.** See note to the *Rape of the Lock*, i, p. 489b, l. 133.

792a 147. **The rebel three,** Zeus or Jupiter, Neptune, and Pluto.

793a 246. **Tellus,** the goddess of Earth.

794a 307. **Cœlus,** god of the Sky.

JAMES HOGG

James Hogg, known as the "Ettrick Shepherd," came of ancestors who had been shepherds for centuries. He had almost no schooling and grew up well-nigh ignorant of books. At the age of twenty, after several years of herding for various masters, he was employed by a Mr. Laidlaw of Blackhouse, through whose kindness he found access to a good library. He read and taught himself while he was attending his flocks. In 1801 he produced his *Scottish Pastorals*. On Scott's recommendation, in return for some assistance in the *Border Minstrelsy*, his *Mountain Bard* was published by Constable in 1807. He tried farming in Dumfriesshire for three years without success; and failing of employment as a shepherd in his native district, he set out for Edinburgh in 1810 to try his fortune as a literary venturer. His *Queen's Wake* in 1813 made his reputation. At the request of the Duchess of Buccleuch, to whom he had dedicated his *Forest Minstrel*, 1810, he was given a lease for life of the farm of Eltrive in Yarrow, and there he remained, without relaxing his literary endeavors, for the rest of his life. During his later years he wrote considerable prose, and was kept continually before the public by his connection with *Blackwood's Magazine*. Fame came to him in both England and Scotland only a few years before his death in 1835 (see Wordsworth's *Extempore Effusion*, etc., p. 699). He is known in English literature mainly as a great peasant poet. Some of his lyrics are exquisite, and occasionally, as in his romantic ballad of *Kilmeny*, he shows an absorption in the ideal and supernatural that has rarely been excelled in any poetry.

794b WHEN THE KYE COMES HAME

11. **mirk,** dark.
17. **birk,** birch tree.
22. **bigs,** builds.
31. **blewart,** blue wort, a small blue flower.
34. **fauldit,** closed.
35. **laverock,** lark.

795a 40. **pawkie,** sly, wily.
44. **downa,** cannot.

THE SKYLARK

Compare Wordsworth's *To a Skylark*, p. 698, and Shelley's *To a Skylark*, p. 769.

13. **fell,** moor, down.

795b KILMENY

This story in ballad form is one of a collection of original poems, called *The Queen's Wake*, purporting to be recited by the Scotch minstrels at Holyrood, before Mary Queen of Scots at Christmas, on the occasion of her return to her native country. The theme of a journey to fairyland is a common one. particularly among the Celts (see notes to *Connla of the Golden Hair*, p. 61a f.).

5. **yorlin,** the yellow bunting, yellow-hammer.
7. **hypp,** the dog rose or wild brier.
10. **minny,** mother.
11. **shaw,** grove, thicket.
13. **greet,** weep.
22. **its lane,** alone.
23. **lowed,** blazed.
23. **leme,** gleam.
26. **dean,** a sandy tract or low hill.
29. **joup,** mantle.
30. **snood,** a fillet worn around the hair.
36. **emerant,** emerald.

796a 48. **swa'd,** swelled.
52. **waik,** a trail.
53. **wene,** a path.
54. **maike,** a mate (matchless one).
67. **speer,** ask.
70. **fere,** comrade, companion.
72. **Eident,** busy, attentive.
74. **feminitye,** womanhood.

796b 89. **littand,** giving color.
115. **kythes,** appears.
127. **blow,** full bloom.

797a 139. **gleid,** spark.
141. **gouden,** golden.
150. **wained,** conveyed.

797b 206. **leifu',** loyal.
211. **hundit,** hounded, set on.
220. **girned,** grinned, made grimaces.
222. **weir,** war.

798a 226. **gowled,** howled.
228. **gecked,** derided.
229. **arles,** a pledge (of possession).
239. **herkèd,** hearkened.
244. **lened,** granted.
246. **swinked,** struggled.
247. **brainzelled,** rushed headlong.
250. **mooted,** moulted.
270. **unmeled,** uncontaminated.

798b 286. **seymar,** a loose upper garment, a scarf.
290. **raike,** range.
305. **boughts,** enclosures.
306. **goved,** stared idly or vacantly.
311. **corby,** crow, raven.
311. **houf,** haunt.
315. **leveret,** a hare in its first year.
316. **attour,** above.
317. **forhooyed,** forsook.

ROBERT SOUTHEY

Robert Southey was the son of an unsuccessful linen draper of Bristol. Most of his childhood was spent at Bath under the care of a maternal aunt. At fourteen he entered Westminster School, and four years later was expelled for an article against the discipline of the institution. At Oxford he lived a life apart and left without a degree. In 1794 he met

Coleridge, who inspired him with Pantisocracy (see introductory note to Coleridge, p. 701), the only practical result of which was to make the men brothers-in-law. He began his residence at Greta Hall in 1803, and there spent the remainder of his life, with the added responsibility of Coleridge's family after 1809. His admiration for Coleridge was tempered somewhat by close acquaintance with his failings; Wordsworth he admired greatly, but the two were never at any time intimate. He became a writer for the *Quarterly Review* but had nothing to do with its policy of harsh criticism. In 1813 he was made poet laureate after Scott's refusal of the office. His mature years are remembered chiefly for his quarrel with Byron. His last years were clouded by family losses and afflictions, and after 1839 he was almost entirely incapable from the decline of his own powers. He died in 1843. The amount of his work is enormous; and because of its general inferiority, it will probably never all be collected. His poetry is always disappointing, largely because it contains too much prosaic commonplace. His ponderous epics, such as *Thalaba*, 1801, and the *Curse of Kehama*, 1810, when not "wildly impossible" are "incurably dull." His prose, written with ease and grace, is his best work. His *Life of Nelson* is a model of the short biography.

799a THE BATTLE OF BLENHEIM

See Addison's *The Campaign*, p. 471 and notes.

799b MY DAYS AMONG THE DEAD ARE PAST

Southey possessed a library of about fourteen thousand well-selected volumes and spent much of his time in it. He was a great reader, and even after his powers of comprehension were gone he found pleasure in walking about his shelves and mechanically examining his beloved books.

800a THE CATARACT OF LODORE

The cascade of Lodore is on the Derwent River in Cumberland. As suggested in the poem, Southey wrote the piece for his children. It is one of the best examples in the language of sustained onomatopœia.

22. **I was Laureate.** Southey was made poet laureate in 1813.

THOMAS CAMPBELL

Thomas Campbell, born in Glasgow and educated in the schools and the university there, is another of the poets popular in their own day upon whom later critics have passed a more discriminating judgment. In view of what has been found enduring in his verse, the two most significant episodes of his life were a long vacation spent in the western Island of Mull in 1795, where he enriched his imagination with images of the savage beauty of nature and lonely men, and a trip to the continent in 1800, when his earlier enthusiasm for the French Revolution, the struggles of Poland, and his own native history, gloried anew in the outward pageantry of battle. He became inspired by the terrible sublimity of war, from watching the battle of Ratisbon and from hearing the distant guns of Hohenlinden. It was after these experiences that his great war-songs were written. In 1802 he settled in London and made literature his profession. He wrote for the magazines and even tried a verse romance, *Gertrude of Wyoming*, 1809. He was instrumental in founding the University of London, and became lord rector of Glasgow University. He died at Boulogne.

801a YE MARINERS OF ENGLAND

The patriotic ardor of this poem is explained partly by its composition abroad and partly by the recent naval victories over the French, particularly those of Cape St. Vincent, 1797, and the Nile, 1798.

15. **Blake,** Robert Blake, a famous English admiral of the Commonwealth. He died at sea, near Plymouth, in 1757.

15. **mighty Nelson.** Horatio Nelson, the greatest of English admirals, "fell" sorely wounded at the battle of Copenhagen, April 2, 1801. He was slain at Trafalgar four years after the date of the poem.

801b THE EXILE OF ERIN

The Exile was Anthony McCann, who had been implicated in the rebellion of 1798. Campbell met him in Hamburg during the winter of 1800 and felt a deep sympathy for him as well as for several of his countrymen who were in the same plight.

8. **'Erin go bragh!'** Ireland forever!

802a 40. **"Erin mavournin,"** Ireland, my darling.

HOHENLINDEN

The village of Hohenlinden is in Upper Bavaria not far from Munich. It was the scene of a decisive victory of the French over the Austrians on December 3, 1800.

802b LOCHIEL'S WARNING

On Donald Cameron of Lochiel (see note to *Childe Harold's Pilgrimage*, l. 226), chief of the Camerons, rested the responsibility of deciding whether his clan should cast its lot with the Young Pretender in 1745. The chieftain met the prince and tried to dissuade him from attempting to establish his claim, but was unsuccessful. To the taunt that he should hear of his prince's victories from the newspapers, his reply was, "I will share the fate of my Prince and so shall every man over whom nature or fortune hath given me any power." He was wounded at the Battle of Culloden, near Inverness, April 16, 1746.

7. **Proud Cumberland,** William Augustus, a younger son of George II and Duke of Cumberland, commanded the English forces at Culloden.

15. **Albin,** a Gaelic name for Scotland, particularly the Highlands.

804a THE BATTLE OF THE BALTIC

The Battle of the Baltic, or Copenhagen, between the English fleet and the Danish land and naval forces, was fought on April 2, 1801. The English admiral, Sir Hyde Parker, remaining in reserve, sent Nelson in to the attack. When it appeared that the English were in distress, he gave the signal to discontinue the action, but Nelson applying his blind eye to the telescope declared he could not see the signal and ordered his fleet to close in. He offered generous terms of surrender, and on landing was given a hearty ovation by the people for his brotherly treatment of the Danish wounded.

804b 63. **Elsinore,** a seaport near Copenhagen, famous as the scene of *Hamlet*.

67. **the gallant good Riou,** Captain Edward Riou, in command of the smaller craft. He was killed in the action.

LORD ULLIN'S DAUGHTER

The scene of the poem is the Island of Mull on the west coast of Scotland, where the poet spent several months as a private tutor in 1795. Ulva is a small island near Mull on the southwest.

THOMAS MOORE

The Irish poet, Thomas Moore, was born in Dublin. He was the son of a prosperous grocer and wine merchant, and was well educated. At Trinity College, Dublin, he formed a friendship with the patriot Robert Emmet, whose tragic fate he commemorated in several of his best lyrics. In 1799 he entered the Middle Temple to study law, but by the exercise of his lyrical gift and his talents as a musician and singer he soon became the most fashionable poet in England. For a harsh review of some of his amatory poems, 1806, in the *Edinburgh Magazine* he challenged the editor and writer, Francis Jeffrey, to a duel. A meeting took place, but officers of the law interfered; his antagonist's pistol was found without charge; and the ludicrous affair resulted in a warm friendship between the two men. Throughout life he was sensitive in matters of personal honor, but affectionate, generous, and high-minded. He was successful in satire, but his best work was in his *Irish Melodies*, begun in 1807 and continued until 1834. These poems show a command over the harmony of numbers and an elevation of the simpler emotions which suggest a kinship with the nobler strains of Burns and Wordsworth. They constitute an imposing body of Anglo-Irish verse; and in spite of a certain amount of false sentiment, their combination of fancy, melody, and pathos with a genuinely national quality established for the author the reputation (which he still holds) of being the lyric poet of Ireland. His long poem, *Lalla Rookh*, 1817, which cloaks "Irish patriotic aspirations under the garb of oriental romance" and which in its day was one of the most admired poems in the English language, still maintains a measure of popularity. His last significant work, the *Life and Letters*, 1830, of his friend Byron, gave the world just the sort of biography that the age required and is in its way a classic. In his mature years he saw his popularity wane before that of the greater Romantic poets, and was harassed by debt. His last child died in 1845, and from that time until his death in 1852 he was a total wreck. He is remembered as a charming lyricist and as the author of *Lalla Rookh*. As a poet he ranks high for his troubadour-like combination of poetry with music.

805a THE LAKE OF THE DISMAL SWAMP

Moore came to Bermuda as registrar of the Admiralty Court in 1803. Disliking the place, he left his office to a deputy and after a few months' visit to the United States returned to England. While in Norfolk, Virginia, he heard the legend of a crazed lover whose sweetheart had disappeared, it was supposed, in the Dismal Swamp and was never heard of afterward. The poem is built on the legend.

805b THE HARP THAT ONCE THROUGH TARA'S HALLS

1. **Tara,** in county Meath northwest of Dublin, a royal residence in the early history of Ireland. See note to p. 59a, l. 5.

806a SHE IS FAR FROM THE LAND

The person celebrated in this poem was Sarah Curran, the fiancée of the Irish patriot, Robert Emmet. Emmet was captured on his return from hiding in the Wicklow Mountains to bid her good-by, and was tried for high treason and executed in 1803.

CHARLES WOLFE

No English poet has greater fame for the composition of one short poem than has Charles Wolfe for his *Burial of Sir John Moore at Corunna.* It is one of the most stirring and affecting war poems in the language. No other work of the author is worthy of record. He was born in County Kildare, Ireland. He was educated in English schools and at Trinity College, Dublin, where he enjoyed some reputation as a poet while still an undergraduate. He entered the ministry in 1817 and occupied curacies in County Tyrone. He died at Cork when he was only thirty-one years of age.

806b THE BURIAL OF SIR JOHN MOORE AT CORUNNA

Sir John Moore, 1761–1809, was an English general in command of the operations against France in Spain in 1808. He was slain at Corunna, and according to his wishes was buried in the citadel during the night of January 16–17, 1809. The poem accurately describes the event as it was reported in the *Edinburgh Annual Register.*

THOMAS LOVE PEACOCK

Thomas Love Peacock was born at Weymouth on the coast of Dorsetshire. He was the only son of a well-to-do London glass merchant, who died when the boy was three. He early gave evidence of the marked individualism that characterized his adult years. When about sixteen he left school and continued his education by wide though desultory reading in the British Museum. His earliest works consisted of poems, published between 1810 and 1815, but it is upon his novels, which appeared at intervals during the next fifty years, that his fame chiefly rests. As a young man he seems to have been somewhat of a dreamer. He was fond of wandering through romantic country districts, especially through Wales, where he met Jane Gryffydh (Griffith), who afterward became his wife, and where he gathered the inspiration for some of his best work. For more than a quarter of a century he filled with distinction a position in the office of the East India Company in London until his retirement in 1856, when he settled down in the country and devoted the remaining ten years of his life to his grandchildren, his library, and his garden.

Peacock is a puzzling figure. Though he was a close friend of Shelley, he had much of the common-sense satirical attitude of the eighteenth-century realists, and he made fun of "that egregious confraternity of Rhymsters," as he called Coleridge and his fellow adherents of poetical simplicity. Like the romanticists he shrank from the modern world and loved the past, but he looked at the past with no tender, Ossianic retrospect. To him the Middle Ages were only a vantage ground from which to ridicule the follies of his own time. Unlike the typical dreamy romantic social reformer, he was an unusually practical and successful man of affairs who proposed no theories and recommended no cure-alls. He hated the extremes of affectation and conventionality. His novels are still read for their humorous satire on contemporary writers and literary fads, but his memory is best preserved from oblivion by the admirable ballads and songs that are scattered through their pages.

807a THE FRIAR'S SONG

This song occurs in *Maid Marian.* The friar who sings it resembles Friar Tuck in his drinking propensities.

807b THE WAR-SONG OF DINAS VAWR

In the *Misfortunes of Elphin,* a satirical novel based on the early Welsh romance of *The History of Taliessin.* The meter is an interesting example of the three-accent iambic (× ´) line with double rhyme (*sweeter: meeter*, etc.) and an unaccented syllable at the end. The second line also has an extra syllable at the beginning. Dinas Vawr is represented as a petty Welsh king of King Arthur's time, whose castle was surprised by King Melvas from beyond the Severn.

9. **Dyfed.** See introductory note to *Pwyll, Prince of Dyved*, p. 63.

LEIGH HUNT

Leigh Hunt was a thoroughgoing man of letters. He was an editor, a prolific reviewer and critic, a familiar essayist, an exponent of dramatic reform, a patron of younger writers, and a poet of no mean ability. He was the son of a clergyman and was born at Southgate, near London. At Christ's Hospital School he indulged his fancy in some crude attempts at verse. Here too he met Lamb. Leaving a clerkship in the War Office, he became editor, together with his brother, of the *Examiner* in 1808, and soon won for the publication a high reputation. For what was adjudged a personal libel on the Prince Regent in 1812 he was fined heavily and imprisoned for two years. In 1816 he published his *Story of Rimini*, a notable achievement in poetical narrative and an important influence on English metrical art. In the pages of his *Indicator*, started in 1818, he generously befriended both Shelley and Keats during their reverses. For years he struggled against poverty and adverse fortune, but an annuity by Mrs. Shelley in 1844 and a crown pension three years later relieved him, and he spent his last years in easier circumstances. He died at Putney in 1859. His taste was not sure or elevated, and he wrote too much to be uniformly good. As an essayist he is surpassed by Lamb in range and variety, but in other respects he is often Lamb's equal. His poetry in general is bright, animated, and harmonious. In personality he was cheerful, courageous, lovable, forgiving. "He is perhaps the best teacher in our literature of the contentment which flows from a recognition of everyday joys and blessings" (Ireland).

ABOU BEN ADHEM

Line 14, which contains the central idea of this charming little fable, has been applied to Hunt himself and stands inscribed over his grave. The name "Abou Ben Adhem" (which means "Father of the Son of Adam" if it means anything) is the product of Hunt's fancy.

RONDEAU

808a This poem celebrates, it is said, Mrs. Carlyle's delight at Hunt's announcement that a publisher had accepted her husband's *Frederick the Great.*

GEORGE DARLEY

George Darley undoubtedly possessed genius; but though he was accepted by his contemporaries for his occasional literary gems, he has since been forgotten by a public that is unwilling to extract his beauties from the rubbish in which they are set. He was born of an Irish family of good standing and independent means residing in Dublin. In the absence of his parents in America during his early years he was left to the care of his grandfather at Springfield near Dublin. Many of his lyrics were inspired by his happy recollections of the place. He entered Trinity College in 1815 and was graduated in 1820, but he was hampered in his career by an incurable stammer, which, as he says, made him a "solitudinarian" for life. Adopting literature as a profession, he settled in London, issued his first volume of verse in 1822, and became a regular contributor to the *London Magazine*, then in its heydey. The connection brought him in contact with many of the leading writers of the day, and won for him in particular the esteem of Lamb. He was abroad for a time, and on his return became a dramatic reviewer for the *Athenæum;* but his criticism displayed such truculency and personal bias, even against the best writers, that it is worth little. His poetical dramas — *Sylvia*, 1827; *Thomas à Becket*, 1840; and *Athelstane*, 1841 — though showing evidence of splendid talent, were not written for the stage. He was a good mathematician and wrote some treatises and texts on mathematical subjects. He continued his connection with the *Athenæum* until his death, which occurred in London in the autumn of 1846. His poetry is not sustained, it often lacks taste and finish, and it not infrequently fails in definiteness of meaning for the general reader, but he has occasional outbursts and entire lyrics that deserve to be remembered. His unfinished *Nepenthe*, 1835, contains his best poetry.

THE FALLEN STAR

808b 5. **the orb of fire.** See note to *Rosalind's Description*, p. 257b, l. 1.

26. **Uriel,** one of the seven archangels.

THOMAS HOOD

Thomas Hood was the son of a London bookseller. After the death of his father, when the boy was twelve, his mother removed to Islington, where he passed through a brief but agreeable period of schooling. While still a boy he entered the countinghouse of a family friend; but the work proved detrimental to his health, and he was sent to his father's relatives in Dundee. Returning to London in 1818, he studied engraving sufficiently to enable him later to set off his humorous writings with effective drawings and illustrations. In 1821 he was made subeditor of the *London Magazine* and thus came into contact with some of the best writers of the day — Lamb, De Quincey, Hartley Coleridge, and others. His first volume, *Odes and Epistles*, appeared in 1825; and two years later he produced his *Plea of the Midsummer Fairies*, a body of serious poetry which proved him a not unworthy follower of Keats. The public, however, neglected his serious verse and looked to him for humorous productions — an attitude which largely determined the nature of his work for the remainder of his life. In the *Comic Annual* from 1830 to 1838, and in contributions to other periodicals, he produced the mimicry, word-jugglery, caricature, and buffoonery, for which he was famed. At the same time he did here and there the serious pieces which have given him a permanent place in English poetry. In his later years he conducted two magazines of his own. Through a long period of ill health he endured very straitened circumstances, but was relieved to some extent by a pension in the last year or two of his life, and died at Hampstead in 1845. In a few poems, which deal with the tragic sufferings of the unfortunate and oppressed, he displays a command of pathos that is rare in English poetry.

HARTLEY COLERIDGE

Hartley Coleridge, the oldest son of Samuel Taylor Coleridge, was born at Clevedon, near Bristol. His early years were spent under Southey's care at Keswick in the Lake District and in school at Ambleside a few miles away. He entered Oxford as a scholar in 1815 and won an Oriel fellowship but lost it soon afterward by his intemperate habits. Some amends for the loss, however, were made him by the award of a stipend of three hundred pounds. He spent two years in London and contributed some short poems to the *London Magazine*. He next became a biographer of Yorkshire and Lancashire celebrities for a Leeds publisher, a venture which resulted in his largest work, *Biographia Borealis*. A volume of his poems appeared in 1833. The remainder of his life, except for brief intervals, he spent quietly at Grasmere and Rydal, loved by the country people and as familiar a figure as Wordsworth. His "woeful impotence of weak resolve," which he inherited from his father, increased with maturity, and for the last ten years possessed him entirely. He died in 1849 and was buried, at Wordsworth's request, in Grasmere churchyard. He is remembered to-day as a gifted sonneteer.

THOMAS BABINGTON MACAULAY

Thomas Babington Macaulay was born at Rothley Temple in Leicestershire. His precocity was extraordinary, and he developed a memory that is scarcely equaled elsewhere in English history. Among the remarkable achievements of his very early youth, he wrote, before he was eight, a *Compendium of Universal History* from creation to 1800 and a romance of three cantos in the manner of Scott, called *The Battle of the Cheviot*. He had a distinguished career as a fellow of Trinity College, Cambridge, and became a barrister in 1826. His *Essay on Milton*, contributed to the *Edinburgh Magazine* in 1825, made his literary reputation; and being a brilliant talker as well as an able critic, he was soon a popular idol in London society. He entered Parliament in 1830 and ere long rose to such prominence in statecraft that he had little time for literary work. From 1834 to 1838 he was in India as a member of the Supreme Council and there acquired the material for his best historical essays, *Lord Clive* and *Warren Hastings*. On his return he reëntered Parliament and soon rose to the position of a cabinet minister. In 1842 appeared the volume on which his fame as a poet chiefly rests, the *Lays of Ancient Rome*. By party reverses in 1847 he lost his seat in Parliament and retired to private life with genuine relief. At the close of the following year the first two volumes of his *History of England* appeared. The work presented a new point of view in historical writing — that history is not so much the biography of great men as it is a record of the familiar and intimate events of the life of a people. The early volumes were deservedly popular and were followed by others in 1855. Meanwhile the author was suffering from ill health. He was raised to the peerage in 1857, died two years later, and was buried in the Poets' Corner in Westminster Abbey. He is one of the great English prose masters. With his writings, present-day prose may be said to have begun. His straightforward, clear-cut, short sentences, his freedom from structural involutions, his well-ordered paragraphs, his pure diction, his unimpassioned tone — all represent the ideals of English prose during the late nineteenth and early twentieth centuries. His poetry cannot be called great, but, being usually martial in subject, it has the romantic charm of old heroic exploits and possesses an eloquence of tone which makes it good reading.

811b IVRY

This poem, also called *A Song of the Huguenots,* commemorates the victory on March 14, 1590, of the Huguenots or French Protestants, under Henry of Navarre (Henry IV of France), over the Catholic League led by the Dukes of Mayenne and Aumale. Henry was fighting also for the rightful possession of his throne against Philip II of Spain. The League employed many hired troops from the Low Countries and from Austria and Switzerland, which are alluded to in the poem. Ivry is a village in the department of Eure, France, west of Paris.

5. **Rochelle,** a stronghold of the Protestants during the religious wars. It is situated on the coast of France.

14. **Appenzel,** a canton in German Switzerland.

14. **Egmont,** a famous Flemish general and popular hero, executed in 1568. The allusions are to the mercenary troops employed against the Protestants in the battle.

15. **false Lorraine.** The great ducal family of Guise in Lorraine were the Catholic claimants of the French throne.

18. **Coligni's hoary hair,** Admiral Coligni, a famous Huguenot leader and victim of the massacre of St. Bartholomew.

812a 34. **Guelders,** a province of the Netherlands.

34. **Almayne,** a general term for Germany.

46. **'Remember Saint Bartholomew.'** The Massacre of St. Bartholomew, having as its object the extinction of the Huguenots in Paris and the provinces, began on August 24, 1572.

54. **the good Lord of Rosny.** Maximilian, Baron de Rosny, was a friend and adviser of Henry.

812b 66. **St. Genevieve,** the patron saint of Paris, reputed to have saved Paris from Attila, by her prayers, in 451.

THOMAS LOVELL BEDDOES

Thomas Lovell Beddoes, the son of a physician, was born at Clifton, near Bristol. From the Bath Grammar School he passed to the Charterhouse in London. During his school days he was distinguished for his daring deeds of mischief and his love of Elizabethan literature. He also wrote a good deal of verse. He entered Oxford in 1820 and while in residence composed some dramatic pieces after the manner of the Elizabethans, particularly Webster and Tourneur. He was among the first to recognize Shelley's genius and imitated him in some of his lyrics. After his graduation in 1825, he went to Germany to study, and in 1832 won his doctorate in medicine. Meanwhile he had developed revolutionary views which made the continent more congenial to his tastes than England. He settled at Zurich, though not permanently, and rarely returned to England for the remainder of his life. In his later years he seems not to have been entirely sane. He died at Basel in Switzerland of complications arising from an attempt at suicide. His plays suggest the drama of the late sixteenth and early seventeenth centuries. Many of his short poems echo his masters, but his best lyrics are the products of his own somber poetical fancy and as such they are among the gems of nineteenth-century poetry.

DIRGE

This dirge is chanted over the bier of the knight Wolfram in the church at Ancona, in *Death's Jest-Book.*

813a SONG

A song by attendants at the couch of Veronica in the unfinished drama of *Torrismond.*

WALTER SAVAGE LANDOR

Walter Savage Landor was born at Warwick of a family of good standing and considerable means. He was educated at Rugby and Oxford, and receiving an allowance from his father, adopted no profession. At the age of twenty he issued a volume containing some fine juvenile poems. In 1798 he published his *Gebir,* which might have been as important as the celebrated *Lyrical Ballads* of Wordsworth and Coleridge the same year, had the author been less immature. Really it is an incoherent failure. On his father's death in 1805 he came into possession of an independent fortune.

His noble tragedy of *Count Julian,* 1812, was the result of his operations in Spain during the Napoleonic Wars with a troop which he had fitted out at his own expense. After his impulsive marriage in 1811, he resided for a short while in Wales and then went to Italy and settled in Florence. In 1824 he began his *Imaginary Conversations,* on which his fame since has chiefly rested. After 1835 he again lived in England, but returned to Florence for the last six years of his life and died there amid domestic distractions in 1864. His poems are numerous and his prose works fill volumes. The former were done at various intervals in his long career, but the latter were the products mainly of his last forty years. In both media his style is classically pure and reserved. In poetry he is the most considerable figure after Byron and before Tennyson.

813b ROSE AYLMER

Rose Aylmer was the daughter of Henry (Baron) Aylmer. She was Landor's friend and companion during the years 1795–1798, when he was in Wales. His elegy was written after hearing of her death in India in 1800.

YES; I WRITE VERSES

814a 31. **Essex.** Robert Devereux, second Earl of Essex, was a favorite of Queen Elizabeth.

TO ROBERT BROWNING

This tribute was written just after the marriage of Robert Browning to Elizabeth Barrett (see pp. 917 and 950 and introductory notes).

13. **Sorrento and Amalfi,** seaports in Italy a few miles south of Naples.

TO YOUTH

Compare the treatment of age in this and the following poems of Landor with that of Coleridge in *Youth and Age,* p. 720, and of Browning in *Rabbi Ben Ezra,* p. 943.

814b ON HIS SEVENTY-FIFTH BIRTHDAY

1. **I strove with none,** etc. It will be remembered that Landor had no profession.

WILLIAM WORDSWORTH

PREFACE TO THE 'LYRICAL BALLADS'

This Preface was prefixed to the first volume of the two-volume second edition of the *Lyrical Ballads,* 1800, and was later enlarged. It represents (1) a reaction against the whole poetical theory and practice of the classical school of the eighteenth century, and (2) a crystallization of ideas about poetry that had been more or less in solution for more than a century. In these respects it is a kind of "Declaration of Independence" of the Romantic School. The peculiar traits which, according to Wordsworth, characterize the poems contributed by him to the *Lyrical Ballads* are: (1) they deal with incidents and situations from common life; (2) they are written, not in an artificial poetical vocabulary, but in words selected from the language really spoken by men; the events and persons involved are so treated (3) that there is thrown over them "a certain colouring of imagination, whereby ordinary things [are] presented to the mind in an unusual way," and (4) that they reveal, "truly though not ostentatiously, the primary laws of our nature." Wordsworth adds that low and rustic life was generally chosen as his theme because poor and simple country folk speak a (1) plainer and (2) more emphatic language, and lead a life in which their feelings (3) are more elementary and simple and less under restraint, and (4) are "incorporated with the beautiful and permanent forms of nature." Wordsworth's theory of simplicity in theme and treatment is also illustrated in the stanza forms of his and Coleridge's poems in the *Lyrical Ballads,* which are often written in balladlike meters, and in the very title of the work, which suggests a connection between the contents and the poetry of the folk, long admired by the earlier romanticists. In connection with Wordsworth's revolutionary theory of poetry the student should read Coleridge's criticism in his *Biographia Literaria,* p. 826 ff.

In accordance with the original plan of the *Lyrical Ballads* (described by Coleridge in the *Biographia Literaria*) Wordsworth, in his contributions, attempted "to give the charm of novelty to things of every day," while Coleridge dealt with "persons and characters supernatural, or at least romantic; yet so as to transfer from our inward nature a human interest and a semblance of truth sufficient to procure for these shadows of imagination that willing suspension of disbelief for the moment, which constitutes poetic faith."

815b 32 ff. **age of Catullus . . . that of Statius,** etc., the classical period . . . the silver period, of Latin literature.

818b 23 ff. **'In vain to me,'** etc., *Sonnet on the Death of Richard West* (see p. 583).

823b 49. **' Clarissa Harlowe,'** a novel, 1748, by Samuel Richardson.

49 f. **the ' Gamester,'** a tragedy, 1753, by Edward Moore.

825b 4 ff. **' I put my hat,'** etc., a famous parody on *The Hermit of Warkworth*, 1771, a ballad by Bishop Percy.

10. **' Babes in the Wood,'** an English ballad of unknown authorship.

SAMUEL TAYLOR COLERIDGE

BIOGRAPHIA LITERARIA

The author has described this work as the history of his opinions and literary life, a treatise on the true nature of poetic diction. Though it is without sequence and often confused, it is perhaps the most revealing commentary we have of Coleridge's mental world, his habits of thought, his theories and judgments. In connection with the *Biographia Literaria* the student should read Wordsworth's Preface to the *Lyrical Ballads* and the introductory note thereto.

827b 3. **The Dark Ladie,** i.e., *The Ballad of the Dark Lady*, a mere fragment. Neither it nor *Christabel* appeared in the *Lyrical Ballads*.

828a 31. **his recent collection,** the *Poems* of 1815, in which the original preface is transferred to the end.

829a 1. **Bathyllus,** a beautiful youth beloved and often referred to by the Greek erotic poet and voluptuary, Anacreon. Cf. especially Anacreon, Ode XXIX.

2. **Alexis,** a character in Virgil's second eclogue.

829b 20 f. **Præcipitandus est,** etc., "the free spirit ought to be urged forward by its own choice." From the *Satiricon* of Petronius Arbiter. See note to p. 457b, l. 44.

28. **Jeremy Taylor,** 1613–1667, an English bishop and theological writer, called the "prose Shakespeare."

29. **Burnet's Theory of the Earth,** *Telluris Theoria Sacra* ("Sacred Theory of the Earth,"), 1681, by Thomas Burnet, 1635–1715, a Cambridge scholar.

830a 25. **laxis effertur habenis,** is borne along with loose reins.

46 ff. **' Doubtless this,'** etc. *Nosce Teipsum*, iv. See p. 265 and notes.

WILLIAM HAZLITT

William Hazlitt was the son of a Unitarian minister. In his home surroundings in Ireland, in America, and at Wem in Shropshire, before he was twenty, he imbibed the spirit of radicalism which tinges much of his work. At fifteen he was sent to a Nonconformist seminary at Hackney, but soon decided that he could not preach. After some desultory studies in painting he met Coleridge, and was inspired to write. From that time until his death in 1830 he was a busy and energetic writer, a quarrelsome friend, and a gifted talker and lecturer. With Coleridge he assisted the English public to its first real appreciative understanding of Shakespeare, and with Lamb he performed the same service for other Elizabethans. In his *Spirit of the Age*, 1825, he fearlessly interpreted his contemporaries, with rare taste and good judgment. Whatever he wrote, he wrote with enthusiasm, if at times with pardonable partiality. He is one of the last masters of English prose before its modernization by such writers as Macaulay and Matthew Arnold.

830b ON FAMILIAR STYLE

831b 11. **cum grano salis,** with a grain of salt.

832a 18. **Mr. Cobbett,** William Cobbett, 1762–1835, an English political writer.

832b 17. **old English authors,** etc. The writers named belong mainly to the first half of the seventeenth century.

28. **' Mrs. Battle's Opinions on Whist,'** *London Magazine*, February, 1821.

31. **' A well of native English undefiled,'** *Faerie Queene*, IV, ii, 32.

36 f. **Erasmus's Colloquies,** *Colloquia*, 1519, of Desiderius Erasmus, 1466–1536, a great continental scholar and theologian.

45 f. **' What do you read? '** etc. *Hamlet* II, ii, 195 ff.

833a 2. **florilegium . . . tulipomania,** literally, a culling of flowers, an anthology . . . a craze for tulips.

18 f. **Sermo humi,** etc., speech which creeps on the ground.

37. **Ancient Pistol,** a braggart in Shakespeare's *2 Henry IV* and *Henry V*.

42. **fantoccini beings,** puppets.

43. **' That strut and fret,'** etc. *Macbeth* V, v, 25.

50. **' And on their pens,'** etc., an adaptation from *Paradise Lost*, IV, 988 f.

834a 17 f. **Cowper's description,** etc. *The Task*, V, 173 ff.

MR. WORDSWORTH

834b 9 f. **' Nihil humani,'** etc., I think nothing human is alien to me. — Terence, *Heautontimoroumenos*, I, i, 25.

835a 5 f. **de novo . . . tabula rasa,** anew . . . blank page.

19. **Alcaeus,** *ca.* 611–580 B.C., a famous Greek lyric poet.

39. **' To the bare trees,'** etc. See Wordsworth's poem, *To My Sister*, l. 7 f.

50. **' Beneath the hills,'** etc. See *The Excursion*, VI, 531.

836a 8. **' To him,'** etc. See Wordsworth's

ode, *Intimations of Immortality*, p. 698b, l. 202 f.

836b 24. **Cole-Orton,** the home of Sir George Howland Beaumont to whom Wordsworth dedicated the 1815 edition of his poems.

33. **' Calm contemplation,'** etc. Cf. *Laodamia*, l. 72.

837a 11. **' Fall blunted,'** etc. Cf. Goldsmith's *The Traveller*, p. 568, l. 232.

52. **toujours perdrix,** always partridges. The allusion is to a story told of Henry IV of France, who, to prove the importance of variety, ordered his confessor to be fed for a time on nothing but his favorite dish, which was partridge.

837b 3. **Holbein's heads,** the portraits of Hans Holbein, *ca.* 1497–1543, a German painter and wood engraver.

50 f. **' Flushed with,'** etc. See Dryden's *Alexander's Feast*, p. 440, l. 51 f.

838a 6. **Titian,** 1477–1576, a famous Venetian painter, called " the Divine."

32 ff. **' Action is momentary,'** etc., quoted inaccurately from *The Borderers*, Act III, l. 405 ff.

50 f. **' Let observation,'** etc. See p. 561.

838b 9 f. **Drawcansir,** a character in the Duke of Buckingham's *The Rehearsal*, 1671.

18. **Walton's Angler,** Izaak Walton's *Compleat Angler*, 1653.

18. **Paley,** William Paley, 1743–1805, a popular theological and philosophical writer.

22. **Bewick,** Thomas Bewick, 1753–1828, an English wood engraver.

23. **Waterloo,** Antoine Waterloo, a seventeenth-century French painter, engraver, and etcher.

27. **Nicolas Poussin,** 1594–1665, a noted French landscape painter.

37. **Rembrandt,** 1607–1669, a great Dutch painter.

49. **' he hates conchology,'** etc. Hazlitt quotes from his own *Lecture on the Living Poets*.

839a 1 f. **' Where one,'** etc. *Hudibras*, II, i, 29–30.

CHARLES LAMB

Charles Lamb was born in London and, except for brief intervals, spent his life there. Unlike most of his great romantic contemporaries, he loved the city and affected to despise the country. His works, therefore, reflect an aspect of romanticism that is unique — an interest in urban subjects, usually old or replete with infinite suggestiveness, over which he casts the characteristic halo of the genuine romanticist. At Christ's Hospital, where he was educated, he began a friendship with Coleridge which lasted for life. When he was fifteen he found employment as a clerk in the South Sea Office. Three years later he removed to a desk in the East India House and there remained till his superannuation more than thirty years later. The strain of insanity to which the family was subject at times affected with peculiar violence his sister Mary. During a sudden attack in 1796 she stabbed their mother to death. Thereafter Lamb gave himself to caring for her during the remainder of his life. Except for brief intervals, when her malady returned, she proved a sympathetic and helpful companion. She collaborated with him in his first important work, *Tales from Shakespeare*, 1807. With his *Specimens* of the Elizabethan dramatists the following year, Lamb proved himself one of the great pioneer critics of the older literature. To the *London Magazine* from 1820 to 1826 he contributed the *Essays of Elia,* his best work. He lived nearly a decade after his retirement without doing anything to add to his fame, and died at Edmonton in 1834. The range, variety, quaint humor, perennial good spirits, and gentleness that characterize his work have made him one of the most popular prose writers of the language.

840a DREAM CHILDREN: A REVERIE

In the *Essays of Elia* Lamb is James Elia (El-ya) and Mary is Bridget.

11 f. **great-grandmother Field . . . in Norfolk.** Lamb's grandmother, Mary Field, lived at Blakesware in Hertfordshire, where for more than fifty years she was housekeeper for the Plumers, a Hertfordshire family. Lamb himself was never married.

18. **Children in the Wood.** See note to p. 825b, l. 10. In the ballad the redbreasts cover the dead children with leaves.

841a 39. **John L —.** John Lamb, brother of Charles, died in 1821. His death appears to have inspired the tender vein of reminiscence and regret in the essay.

841b 36 f. **Alice W—n.** Alice Winterton (Lamb's fictitious name for the young lady) was probably Ann Simmons, a Hertfordshire girl who married Mr. Bartram, a pawnbroker in London.

842a A DISSERTATION UPON ROAST PIG

Lamb borrowed his idea of the discovery of roast pig from his friend, Thomas Manning, who had traveled in China. The details, except the historical figure of Confucius, are all fictitious.

843b 53 f. **mundus edibilis,** world of eatables.

844a 2. **princeps obsoniorum,** the chief of dainties.

7 f. **amor immunditiæ,** love of filth.

11 f. **præludium,** prelude.

52 f. **' Ere sin,'** etc. See Coleridge's *Epitaph on a Young Infant*, l. 1 f.

845b 11. **St. Omer's,** a Jesuit college in France. Lamb, of course, never attended it.

POOR RELATIONS

49. **Agathocles,** a tyrant of Syracuse, son of a potter.

49 f. **Mordecai.** Cf. Esther ii, 5 ff.

50. **Lazarus.** Cf. Luke, xvi, 19 ff.

847a 9. **Richard Amiet, Esq.,** a character in *The Confederacy*, a play by Sir John Vanbrugh.

27. **Poor W—.** Lamb tells us elsewhere that W— was his friend Favell, who "left Cambridge because he was ashamed of his father, who was a house-painter there."

847b 1 f. **Nessian venom,** *i.e.*, the blood of the centaur Nessus. See note to *Paradise Lost*, II, l. 542.

3 f. **Latimer . . . Hooker.** Both these famous men were servitors, the former at Christ's College, Cambridge, the latter at Corpus Christi College, Oxford.

20 f. **N—, near Oxford.** The place is Cambridge. See note to l. 27 above.

848a 18 f. **St. Sebastian.** St. Sebastian in Spain was besieged and taken by Wellington in 1813.

848b 21. **Grotiuses.** Hugo Grotius, 1583–1645, a Dutch jurist, etc., "founder of the science of international law."

849a THE SUPERANNUATED MAN

29 f. **Sera tamen,** etc., Freedom though late has taken thought of me.

31 f. **A Clerk I was,** etc. Probably not quoted from John O'Keefe, but from a farce by George Colman, *Inkle and Yarico*, first produced in 1787.

45. **six-and-thirty years,** *i.e.*, three years in the South Sea Office and thirty-three in the East India House.

849b 38. **my native . . . Hertfordshire.** Lamb was born in London, but passed part of his early life with his grandmother in Hertfordshire. See note to p. 840a, l. 11 f.

850b 27 f. **Boldero . . . Lacy.** These are fictitious names which Lamb gives of the officials of the company.

30. **Esto perpetua!** Be thou perpetual!

37. **Old Bastile,** a state prison in Paris, destroyed at the beginning of the Revolution in 1789.

851a 21 f. **—' that's born,'** etc. Quoted from Middleton's *The Mayor of Queenborough*.

851b 1 f. **a tragedy,** etc., *The Vestal Virgin, or the Roman Ladies.*

42 ff. **Ch — . . . Pl —,** John Chambers, Henry Dodwell, W. D. Plumley.

46. **Gresham,** Sir Thomas Gresham, 1519?–1579, founder of the Royal Exchange.

47. **Whittington.** Sir Richard Whittington, *ca.* 1356–1423, who rose from poverty to the lord mayorship of London, celebrated in nursery rhyme with his equally celebrated cat.

852a 2. **my ' works!',** *i.e.*, his ledgers, with perhaps a little pathetic suggestion of what he might otherwise have done in literature.

5. **Aquinas.** See note to *Hudibras*, l. 151.

17. **Carthusian,** a strict monastic order founded by St. Bruno about 1084.

39. **the Elgin marbles,** relics of the ancient Parthenon in Athens brought to the British Museum by Lord Elgin.

852b 19. **Lucretian pleasure.** Lucretius' *De Rerum Natura*, Bk. II, opens thus: "It is sweet, when on the great sea the winds trouble its waters, to behold from land another's deep distress."

35. **' As low,'** etc. *Hamlet* II, ii, 527.

43. **cum dignitate,** adapted from the phrase, *otium cum dignitate*, ease with dignity.

48. **opus operatum est.** The labor has been performed.

LEIGH HUNT

853a GETTING UP ON COLD MORNINGS

1. **Giulio Cordara,** Giulio Cesare Cordara, 1704–1785, an Italian poet and historiographer of the Jesuits.

853b 14 ff. **They are ' haled,'** etc. See *Paradise Lost*, II, 596 ff.

854a 12 f. **the degenerate King,** probably Francis I, 1494–1547, who is reputed to have been the first French monarch to shave his beard.

15. **Emperor Julian,** Julian "the Apostate," 331–363.

17 f. **Cardinal Bembo,** Pietro Bembo, 1470–1547, an Italian cardinal and man of letters.

18. **Titian.** See note to p. 838a, l. 6.

24. **Haroun Al Raschid,** 763–809, the most magnificent of the caliphs of Bagdad, renowned in the *Arabian Nights*.

24 f. **Bed-ridden Hassan,** probably Hassan ben Sabbah, the "Old Man of the Mountains," founder of the Moslem Order of the Assassins about 1090.

25. **Wortley Montague,** Edward Wortley Montagu, 1713–1776, author and traveler, son of Lady Mary Wortley Montagu, one of the most versatile and talented women in English literary history.

36 f. **'Sweetly recommends itself,'** etc. *Macbeth* I, vi, 2 f.

44 f. **Thomson.** See p. 540 ff.

855a 13. **vis inertiæ,** power of inertia.

THOMAS DE QUINCEY

Thomas De Quincey, the son of a well-to-do merchant of good descent, was born in the manufacturing city of Manchester. His early life was subject to several touching bereavements, including the death of his father when he was seven. His schooling was intermittent, and his life became irregular. At seventeen he ran away from the Manchester Grammar School, wandered through Wales, and passed a year in vagabondage in London. He was in residence at Oxford for several years but left without a degree in 1808. The following year he decided upon a literary life and settled at Grasmere, near Wordsworth. His real career, however, began in 1820 when he removed to London to write for the *London Magazine*, by which time he had become a complete slave to opium. The next year appeared his best and most characteristic work, the *Confessions of an English Opium Eater*, the addict, of course, being De Quincey himself. For the last thirty years of his life he maintained relations with the Edinburgh magazines, chiefly *Blackwood's*, and resided in the Scotch capital and at Lasswade near by. His marvelous faculty for dreams, enhanced as it was by the use of opium, produced during his mature years the finest products of his genius — the *Suspiria de Profundis* ("Sighs from the Depths"), 1845, and the *Dream-Fugue* in the *English Mail-Coach*, 1849. He died in Edinburgh in 1859. He is one of the great English essayists. His works, largely biographical as they are, belong to journalism, but they are among its very finest flowers. His style is his own — variegated, daring, gorgeous, and devoid of artifice. It gives the impression of consummate ease and naturalness.

LEVANA AND OUR LADIES OF SORROW

856a 10. **Euclid,** a famous Greek geometer of the third or fourth century before Christ, associated with Alexandria.

38. **Parcæ,** the Fates.

857a 3 f. **Rama,** etc. Cf. Jeremiah xxi, 15 and Matthew ii, 16 ff.

858a 8 f. **the tents of Shem.** Cf. Genesis ix, 26 f.

21. **Cybele,** the mother of the gods, usually represented with a mural crown.

858b DREAM FUGUE

50. **tumultuosissimamente,** in a most tumultuous manner.

861a 33 f. **Campo Santo,** a "cemetery at Pisa composed of earth brought from Jerusalem from a bed of sanctity" (De Quincey).

862b 5. **sanctus,** a chant with the word "holy" as a refrain.

THOMAS CARLYLE

Thomas Carlyle chose to interest himself mainly in history and philosophy, but he enveloped whatever he wrote with a moral grandeur that is unequaled elsewhere in his century, and in all his writings he proved himself a maker of literature. He came of the peasant class and was the son of a stone mason of Ecclefechan in Dumfriesshire. After the sparsest of educational beginnings in his native village, he entered the grammar school of Annan at ten, and four years later matriculated at the University of Edinburgh. He was essentially unacademic. His whole school career was devoid of unusual events and even of promise of any future renown. Leaving the university in 1814 without a degree, he thought vaguely of the ministry, but gave up the idea and became a teacher of mathematics at Annan and Kirkcaldy. Tiring of this occupation, he turned to law; but meeting with Madame de Staël's *De l'Allemagne* in 1817, he immersed himself in German philosophy and literature. The first result was his *Life of Schiller*, which appeared in the *London Magazine* in 1823–1824. Meanwhile he had met Jane Welsh of Haddington, a woman of remarkable gifts, who became his wife in 1826. The next six or seven years, spent meanly enough amid the dreary moors of Craigenputtock, are celebrated only for his first great work, *Sartor Resartus*. In 1834, with little means at their command, the Carlyles decided to risk their fortunes in London and removing there settled in Cheyne Row, Chelsea, where they resided for the rest of their lives. Meanwhile, in spite of adverse criticism of his *Sartor*, Carlyle labored unremittingly at his next great work, *The French Revolution*. The manuscript of the first volume was accidentally burned, but he doggedly rewrote it, and its appearance in 1837 brought him fame. In the meantime, he had become a lecturer and in 1840 produced the series *Heroes and Hero Worship*, which set forth his famous theory that history is the biography of great men. Within two months in 1843 he wrote his most spontaneous work, *Past and Present*, which, though written in prose, reveals a highly poetic imagination. His *Oliver Cromwell*, over which he long agonized, appeared in 1845 and amply maintained his fame both as a historian and as an artist. His last great work was *Frederick the Great*, 1858–1865. In 1865 he became lord rector of Edinburgh University. During his absence the following spring for the purpose of delivering his inaugural address in Edinburgh, Mrs. Carlyle died suddenly in London. He lived on for fifteen years and died in 1881. He was buried in his native Ecclefechan.

Carlyle is a romanticist in his reaction against his age; but unlike certain other romanticists, he wishes, after destroying, to rebuild on a solid foundation. For a generation he preached to England and America, thundering with white-hot moral indignation against whatever he considered as weak, false, artificial, or mechanical, and calling men back to sincerity in ideals, honesty in labor, and in general to what he regarded as true democracy — "government by the best not by the worst." The complexity and contortion of his style and his romantic mysticism have been made his reproach, but the marvelous abundance, yet compression, of his thought, his fiery vehemence and sincerity, and his rich but thoroughly assimilated store of knowledge, have been sufficient to make him a commanding figure in English literature.

863a DEATH OF GOETHE

26. **Elijah-translation.** Cf. 2 Kings ii, 1 ff.
864b 9. **Vates.** Cf. note to p. 293b, l. 44 f.
865a 21. **David Hume,** 1711–1776, an eminent Scottish historian and philosopher.
867a 12. **Mignon,** a character in *Wilhelm Meisters Lehrjahre.*
13. **Mephistopheles,** the devil in *Faust.*
46. **Carl August,** Duke Charles Augustus, a patron of literature, by whose invitation Goethe settled at Weimar.

THOMAS BABINGTON MACAULAY

867b OLIVER GOLDSMITH

See p. 565 ff. and notes.
868a 39 f. **Rapparee chiefs,** etc. The word *rapparee* means first "wild fellow," then "bandit." Hugh Baldearg O'Donnell (d. 1704) was one of the most noted of these bandits.
41 f. **Peterborough and Stanhope,** etc. Charles Mordaunt, 1658–1735, Earl of Peterborough, and James, Lord Stanhope, 1673–1721, were commanders who acquired fame in the War of the Spanish Succession, especially in the battles mentioned in the text.
50. **Carolan,** Turlogh Carolan, 1670–1738, an Irish wandering minstrel.
868b 9 f. **the Glorious and Immortal Memory,** *i.e.*, of William III. The phrase was often used by the Whigs in toasting this King.
21. **Knowle,** Lord Sackville's country seat in Kent. Goldsmith's portrait is by Sir Joshua Reynolds.
869a 3 f. **the woolsack . . . the episcopal bench,** *i.e.*, a judgeship or a bishopric.
869b 31. **Fontenelle,** Bernard le Bovier de Fontenelle, 1657–1757, a noted French writer.
870a 39. **Beau Nash,** Richard Nash, 1674–1761, a celebrated leader of fashion and predecessor of Beau Brummel.
871a 26. **'The Traveller.'** See p. 565 ff.
871b 48 f. **'False Delicacy,'** by Hugh Kelly, 1739–1777.
872a 9. **'The Deserted Village.'** See p. 570 ff.
15. **'The Rehearsal,'** a play by the Duke of Buckingham satirizing Dryden under the name of Bayes.
872a 26. **finest poem in the Latin language,** the Epicurean poem *De Rerum Natura* of Lucretius.
872b 32. **Cumberland.** See note to p. 576b, l. 9.
873a 3. **Naseby,** in Northamptonshire, the scene in 1845 of a victory by Cromwell over the Royalists.
8. **Montezuma.** See note to p. 451b, l. 20.
22. **Maupertuis,** Pierre Louis Moreau de Maupertuis, 1698–1759, a noted French mathematician and astronomer.
873b 5 f. **Beauclerk,** Topham Beauclerk, 1739–1780, an English gentleman of distinguished talent and wit.
18. **Horace Walpole.** See p. 639 ff. and notes.
20. **Chamier,** Frederick Chamier, 1796–1870, an English novelist.
24. **Boswell.** See p. 627 ff. and notes.
874a 35 f. **George Steevens.** See note to p. 631a, l. 25.
874b 15. **Lord Clive,** Robert, Lord Clive, 1725–1774, founder of the British Empire in India.
16. **Sir Lawrence Dundas,** a contractor for the British army in Germany from 1748 to 1759. He made a large fortune and was knighted in 1762.
875a 21 f. **a little poem,** the *Retaliation.* See p. 576 f.
875b 8. **Nollekens,** Joseph Nollekens, 1737–1832, an English sculptor.
24. **Lyttelton,** George, Lord Lyttelton, 1709–1773, a writer of mediocre prose and verse.
31. **Mr. Prior,** Mr. (afterward Sir) James Prior, 1790?–1869, a biographer and surgeon.
31. **Washington Irving,** 1783–1859, a noted American author and humorist.
32. **Mr. Forster,** John Forster, 1812–1876, an English historian and biographer.

ALFRED (LORD) TENNYSON

Alfred Tennyson was the fourth child of a family of twelve, two others of whom became poets. He spent his early years in the cultured atmosphere of an English clergyman's family, his father being rector of Somersby, a village in north Lincolnshire. When not yet eighteen he published, with his brother Charles, a small collection of verses imitative of Ossian, Byron, Moore, and other poets popular at the time. In 1828 he entered Trinity College, Cambridge, where he became one of the "twelve apostles," a remarkable group of young men of whom one, Arthur Hallam, became his dearest friend. In 1831 he returned home on account of the ill health of his father, who died soon afterward. In 1830 he published his first independent volume of verse, which, though largely imitative and experimental, shows remarkable metrical skill and some depth of spiritual feeling. In 1832 he published another volume, containing, along with other poems, *The Lady of Shalott* and *The Palace of Art;* but the reviews were harsh, and Tennyson, though continuing to write, published nothing more for nearly a decade. In the meantime he read widely in many literatures, practiced writing verse, and became what he remained for the rest of his life, essentially a family man. In 1833 he was plunged in profound grief by the death of his friend Hallam, at the time engaged to his sister Emily, and he began a series of fragmentary verses some of which seventeen years later formed sections of *In Memoriam.* In 1842 he published two volumes entitled *Poems,* which established him at once as the greatest living English poet. Partially relieved from financial burdens by a government pension of £200 a year and encouraged by the success of *In Memoriam,* 1850, he married in 1850 Emily Sellwood, to whom he had been engaged for sixteen years. In the same year, upon the death of Wordsworth, Tennyson was made poet laureate, and from this time till his death more than forty years later, he remained the official poetic voice of the English nation. In order to escape intrusion he purchased in 1853 a house on the Isle of Wight known as Farringford, which remained his chosen abode during the remainder of his life except during the summer, when he moved to Aldworth, another house built by him in Surrey in 1868. In 1855 he was awarded the degree of D.C.L. by Oxford University. In the same year appeared his series of dramatic monologues and lyrics entitled *Maud.* In 1859 he published *The Idylls of the King,* a collection of four poems on the story of the Round Table — a theme which had fascinated him since boyhood and which was to hold his interest to the end of his life. The *Idylls* were received with universal praise, and the other Arthurian poems, published in 1870, 1872, and 1885, only added to his fame. In 1862 he was presented to Queen Victoria, who remained his friend ever afterward. In 1864 he published the volume entitled *Enoch Arden,* which contained, besides the title poem, the first of Tennyson's humorous poems in dialect. In 1875 he wrote *Queen Mary,* the first of a series of dramas which, though carefully modeled on Shakespearean lines, showed that Tennyson lacked the highest dramatic sense. After much hesitation he accepted, in 1884, a peerage, which he had already declined once. He spent his later years as unostentatiously as his fame would permit, traveling for his health, revising old poems, and composing new. He worked almost to the very end, which came in the early morning of October 6, 1892. He was buried in Westminster Abbey next to Robert Browning.

Both in versatility and in poetic genius Tennyson is one of the greatest writers England has ever produced. He wrote songs, idylls, ballads, laments, dramatic monologues, and epics, as well as several other kinds of poetry; and in all he showed a range of intellect, a power of imagination, a perfection of technique, and an exquisiteness of melody that have seldom, if ever, been surpassed. Moreover, living as he did in an age when the romantic spirit of revolt was yielding to the conservatism of the Victorian era, he reconciled more of the conflicting elements than any other writer. His most striking characteristic was admiration for law and order, and both in his life and his writings he constantly protested against the reckless individualism and the unrestrained passion of the typical romanticist. Though he never relaxed his high standards of art in order to cater to a cheap public taste, he was, in the best sense of the word, the most popular poet of the nineteenth century. His emphasis upon personal morality and his extreme delicacy in treating sexual matters result not, as some critics suppose, from hypocrisy or ignorance, but from an exalted conception of the poet's art and mission.

CLARIBEL

This and the following poem, first published in Tennyson's earliest volume, are instructive as experiments in fanciful description and melodious phrasing.

876a 15. **lintwhite,** linnet.
16. **mavis,** thrush.
19. **crispeth,** a word used by Tennyson in describing little waves.

MARIANA

The suggestion for this poem was found by Tennyson in Shakespeare's words: "There, at the moated grange, resides this dejected Mariana" (*Measure for Measure* III, i).

8. **moated grange,** a large old country house surrounded by a moat, or ditch.

876b 18. **trance,** cast a spell over.
20. **glooming flats,** low grounds becoming dusky (with night).
40. **marish-mosses,** "the little marsh-moss lumps that float on the surface of the water" (Tennyson). In accuracy and detail of observation Tennyson far surpasses most other poets of nature.

877a THE LADY OF SHALOTT

In this, Tennyson's first published poem on an Arthurian subject, he used as his source, not Malory's *Morte Darthur* (see p. 130 and introductory note), which was his favorite version, but an Italian romance, *Donna di Scalotta* ("Lady of Scalott"). "Shalott," the author explained in a footnote, was substituted for "Scalott" because it had a softer sound. It is originally the same word as "Astolat," the name of the heroine's home in another version of the story, which is found in Malory and which furnished the source of Tennyson's idyll of *Lancelot and Elaine*. Besides its superficial meaning, *The Lady of Shalott* has a secondary or symbolical significance, the key to which, according to Tennyson, is found in the closing lines to Part II: "The new-born love for something, for some one in the wide world from which she has been so long excluded, takes her out of the region of shadows into that of realities." On its first appearance the poem was severely criticized. In its wealth of sensuous beauty it suggests both Keats and the Pre-Raphaelites.

5. **Camelot.** See note to p. 96b, l. 247 ff.
11. **dusk and shiver.** The words suggest admirably the effect of little puffs of wind upon the surface of a smooth stream.

877b 56. **pad,** an easy-paced horse.

878a 76. **greaves,** armor covering the legs.
84. **Galaxy,** the Milky Way.
87. **baldric.** See note to p. 103a, l. 10.

879a THE PALACE OF ART

The poem is an allegory designed, as the author explained, to show that intellectuality, imaginative power, and cultured pride, when attended by selfishness and contemptuous isolation, cause us to lose sight of our proper relation to man and to God.

Tennyson was accustomed to think of his descriptions in terms of pictures and to describe them as such. It is therefore important that those who wish to get the best out of his poetry read it slowly and carefully so as to miss none of the pictorial suggestions in his carefully chosen words. In richness and color of description this and the following poem resemble the work of the Pre-Raphaelites.

15 f. **Saturn whirls . . . ring.** As seen through a telescope the shadow of the planet Saturn, thrown on the luminous ring surrounding it, appears to be motionless. Tennyson was greatly interested in astronomy as well as in other branches of science and constantly introduced into his poems what he regarded as the latest scientific discoveries.
23. **gorge,** throat.
30. **lent broad verge,** gave a broad horizon.
41. **she,** my soul.

879b 49. **traced,** ornamented with traced decorations.
61. **arras,** tapestry.
79 f. **prodigal in oil . . . wind.** The uplands were clothed with olive trees. "The under side of the olive leaf is white" (Tennyson).

880a 93 ff. **Or the maid-mother,** etc. The picture was probably suggested by certain images of the Virgin seen in Paris shops.
99. **St. Cecily.** See notes to *St. Cecilia's Day*, p. 438.
102. **Houris,** beautiful women who people the heaven of the Mohammedans, of whom Tennyson's Islamite was one.
105. **Uther's . . . son,** King Arthur. See Tennyson's *Passing of Arthur*, p. 913b, l. 432, and note to p. 134b, l. 15 ff.
107. **Avalon.** See note to p. 97b, l. 325.
109. **his.** The reference is to the King.
11. **Ausonian king,** Numa Pompilius, the second king of Rome, who is said to have received his laws from the wood-nymph Egeria. Ausonia is a poetic name for southern Italy.
113. **engrailed,** indented, a term in heraldry.
115. **Cama,** the Cupid, or god of Love, of Hindu (Brahmanic) mythology; also called Camdeo, etc.
117. **Europa,** a maiden carried off to Crete by Zeus in the form of a bull. The abduction is represented in a famous painting by the Italian artist Titian.
121. **Ganymede,** a beautiful boy whom Zeus in the form of an eagle carried off to Olympus, where he became cupbearer to the gods.
126. **Caucasian,** applied to the white race.

880b 135. **world-worn.** Dante's face as represented in art wears a look of profound melancholy.

135. **grasped his song.** In Giotto's famous portrait of Dante, the poet is holding a book.

137. **Ionian father,** Homer.

149 ff. **The people here,** etc., the people of France before and during the Revolution.

159. **Oriels.** See note to p. 121a, l. 93.

163. **Verulam,** Francis Bacon. See introductory note to p. 314.

881a 171. **Memnon,** a colossal statue near Thebes, believed to represent the Greek sun god and hence said to give forth music at sunrise.

186. **anadems,** crowns.

188. **hollowed moons of gems,** gems hollowed out for lamps.

204. **drives them,** etc. Cf. Matthew viii, 32 ff.

881b 219. **Like Herod,** etc. Cf. Acts xii, 21 ff.

227. **' Mene, mene,'** part of the tragic phrase written mysteriously on the wall at Belshazzar's feast (Daniel v, 25 ff).

242. **fretted,** worm-eaten.

882a 255. **Circumstance,** the surrounding sphere of the universe. According to the Ptolemaic system of astronomy, the earth was scooped out of chaos.

275. **dully,** dull.

882b A DREAM OF FAIR WOMEN

This poem is particularly rich in colorful images and in reminiscences of Tennyson's wide reading in ancient, mediæval, and renaissance literature. Though suggested by Chaucer's *Legend of Good Women* (see introductory note to Chaucer, p. 140), it owes much — *e.g.*, the cold, damp forest where the vision takes place — to other sources, and the ornate style is quite different from Chaucer's easy simplicity. The only one of Chaucer's ladies whom Tennyson takes is Cleopatra.

1. **before my eyelids dropped their shade,** an artificial way of saying, " before I went to sleep."

5. **Dan,** a title of respect derived from the Latin *dominus*, " master." Cf. note to p. 545a, l. 93.

5 ff. **the first warbler . . . sounds that echo still.** Tennyson means that Chaucer's work was a sort of prelude to the tremendous outburst of literary activity during the Elizabethan period, the influence of which is felt even in the nineteenth century. Unlike certain writers of to-day, Tennyson believed that the poet should not disregard his predecessors.

27. **tortoise,** (1) a movable shed used in ancient warfare for protecting soldiers brought close to a wall, or (2) a body of such troops with their shields interlocked above their heads for protection and hence resembling a tortoise's back. As the poet falls asleep, he has a confused vision of ancient wars about which he has read.

36. **seraglios,** harems.

883a 54. **an old wood.** Tennyson tells us that the wood is to be allegorically interpreted as " the Past," but no such secondary significance is necessary to a clear understanding of the poem.

883b 87. **daughter of the gods,** Helen of Troy, the daughter of Zeus and Leda, or, according to another tradition, of Zeus and Nemesis.

95. **Many drew swords,** etc., *i.e.*, in the Trojan War.

100. **one that stood beside,** Iphigenia, who was doomed to be sacrificed to Diana (Artemis) because her father, Agamemnon, had slain a stag sacred to the goddess. The events are said to have taken place at Aulis (l. 106), where the goddess detained the Greek fleet on its way to Troy until her wrath should be appeased (cf. l. 104). Tennyson represents Iphigenia as actually slain; according to another tradition, Diana relented at the last moment and left a hind to be substituted in her place. The legend of Iphigenia was often treated in Greek dramas, some of which were read by Tennyson.

101. **averse,** turned away.

884a 127. **A queen,** Cleopatra. The description was suggested largely by Shakespeare's *Antony and Cleopatra.*

127. **swarthy,** sunburnt. The historical Cleopatra was a Greek and hence probably fair and blue-eyed, but the Cleopatra of Shakespeare and Tennyson is an artistic creation, not an historical personage.

139. **Cæsar,** Octavius Cæsar, whom she could not captivate.

140 ff. **Mark Antony,** etc. See Shakespeare's play.

146. **Canopus,** one of the brightest stars in the heavens.

150. **Hercules.** Antony is said to have claimed descent from Hercules and to have imitated the traditional dress of that hero.

884b 155. **with a worm,** etc. After Antony's death Cleopatra committed suicide by the bite of a snake (worm) rather than be carried captive to Rome by Octavius.

174. **they drew . . . two burning rings.** The figure is inappropriate.

177. **undazzled,** recovered from the dazzling effect.

178. **some one,** Jephthah's daughter. Cf. Judges xi.

179. **the crested bird,** the lark.

181 ff. **' The torrent brooks,'** etc. This is the Hebrew maiden's song.

885a 196. **To save her father's vow.** Jephthah had vowed that in exchange for victory over his enemies he would sacrifice to God the first thing that came out of his house to meet him on his return. He was met by his daughter.

214. **maiden blame,** blame for not having given birth to a male child.

885b 243. **Thridding the sombre boskage,** threading the dark thickets.

251. **Rosamond,** "Fair Rosamond," Rosamond Clifford, the mistress of Henry II, said to have been slain or forced to drink poison by Henry's jealous queen, Eleanor (l. 255), at Woodstock in 1177.

259. **Fulvia's waist.** Cleopatra, thinking of her own tragedy, puts the name of Antony's wife for that of Eleanor, wife of Rosamond's paramour.

263. **The captain of my dreams,** Venus, the morning star.

266 f. **her, who clasped,** etc., Margaret Roper, daughter of Sir Thomas More, who, fourteen days after her father's execution, claimed his severed head as a precious relic. She was buried with it in her arms.

886a 269 ff. **her who knew,** etc. "Eleanor, wife of Edward I., went with him to the Holy Land (1269), where he was stabbed at Acre with a poisoned dagger. She sucked the poison from the wound" (Tennyson).

ULYSSES

Homer's *Odyssey*, after telling how Ulysses arrived safely at his home, Ithaca, from his long wanderings after the fall of Troy, leaves him there; but this, though the most famous, is not the only ending to the story. Earlier in the *Odyssey* (xi, 100 ff.) Tiresias foretells that, after returning to Ithaca, Ulysses shall set forth on a mysterious voyage; and Dante, in a famous passage in the *Divine Comedy* (*Inferno*, xxvi, 90 ff.), represents Ulysses as telling Dante how he had set out, not from home, but from Circe's island and, urged by "an ardor to gain experience of the world," had sailed with his companions through the straits of Gibraltar and had finally been swallowed up by a whirlpool. Tennyson's chief source is Dante. As to the meaning of the poem, the author tells us that, written as it was in the sad period following the death of Hallam, it expressed the poet's feeling of the need of going forward and braving the struggle of life in the face of all obstacles and discouragements. In beauty of phrasing, in elevation of conception, and in dramatic appropriateness this is one of Tennyson's finest accomplishments in the monologue form. On the dramatic monologue, see note to Browning's *My Last Duchess*, p. 919a.

886a 3. **agêd wife,** Penelope.

10. **Hyades,** a group of stars in the constellation Taurus. They are associated with wet weather.

886b 49. **you,** Ulysses' companions. The attitude of Tennyson's Ulysses toward his old shipmates is distinctly modern.

63. **Happy Isles,** an imaginary archipelago located in the Atlantic Ocean by early geographers. They were identified with the Elysian Fields as the abode of the blessed dead and in general with the transatlantic Other World. Cf. notes to pp. 61a, l. 32, and 97b, l. 325.

LOCKSLEY HALL

Though this poem does not show the high imagination and brilliant phrasing that characterize some of Tennyson's other works, it is one of his most complete and original monologues. The speaker, though not a mere type without individuality, might, as the late Professor Alden pointed out, represent young America of to-day as well as it represented the young England of Tennyson's time. The speaker is portrayed as a young man who, having been disappointed in love, becomes embittered against what he regards as the materialism of the age, but recalls that the eternal law of progress must be fulfilled though the individual suffer disaster. Recovering from his somewhat morbid, though not unnatural, state of mind, he concludes that the fundamental law of the universe is progress and he foresees some of the great changes to be wrought in future ages. The poem has always been especially popular with young people.

Note that Tennyson in this poem uses the rather unusual trochaic (´x) instead of the common iambic (x´) meter; *i.e.*, the accent falls on the first instead of the second syllable of each foot.

887 1. **Comrades.** The hero, having returned to Locksley Hall, his boyhood home, on a hunting trip, stops to muse while his companions go on.

8. **Orion,** one of the most conspicuous constellations in the heavens.

9. **Pleiads.** See note to p. 438b, l. 175.

888 68. **crow,** rook.

75. **comfort scorned of devils,** in *Paradise Lost*, Bks. I and II.

75 f. **the poet,** etc., Dante, *Inferno*, v, 121 ff: "There is no greater sorrow than to remember happy times when one is in misery."

79. **he,** Amy's husband, a coarse, fox-hunting squire — at least so the discarded lover represents him.

889 121 ff. **Saw the heavens,** etc. This passage has often been regarded as a prophetic glimpse of modern aviation and the World War.

128. **Federation of the world.** Cf. the modern idea of the League of Nations.

138. **process of the suns,** passing of the years.

890 155. **in wild Mahratta-battle,** etc. Tennyson represents his hero as having been born in India, the son of a British soldier who fell in battle against the Mahrattas, a people inhabiting central India.

180. **Joshua's moon in Ajalon.** Joshua commanded the sun to stand still, and by the power of Jehovah it did so (Joshua x, 12 f.).

182. **the ringing grooves of change.** When Tennyson first traveled on a railroad train, he thought the wheels ran in a groove. He here applies the notion to the movement of the world as it spins down the centuries.

184. **a cycle of Cathay,** an indefinitely long period, an age, spent in China.

891 190. **for me,** so far as I am concerned.

SIR GALAHAD

Of the various mediæval traditions regarding the quest for the Holy Grail (see notes to pp. 207a, l. 13 f. and 597a, l. 116 f.), probably the latest in development and certainly the most popular in modern times, is that which represents the holy vessel as having been finally discovered by Galahad, the virgin knight, son of Lancelot and the daughter of the Grail-King Pelles. Tennyson gives various accounts of the quest in his idyll of *The Holy Grail.* Tennyson's Galahad, in his combination of military prowess with monastic celibacy and ecstatic mysticism, is a sort of nineteenth-century idealization of a mediæval religious warrior.

891b 68 ff. **odours haunt my dreams.** As Tennyson probably knew, the things heard, seen, and smelt by Galahad have at times been actual psychological experiences of real mystics.

892a BREAK, BREAK, BREAK

This is one of the poems that grew out of Tennyson's sorrow for the death of Arthur Hallam.

11. **a vanished hand,** Hallam's.

SONGS FROM THE PRINCESS

Into the 1850 version of *The Princess,* the primary purpose of which is to present certain aspects of the problem of woman's rights, Tennyson introduced several justly admired lyrics, three of which are given here.

THE SPLENDOUR FALLS

Suggested by the echoes from a bugle heard by the poet at Killarney, Ireland, in 1848.

10. **Elfland.** In Ireland the fairy world is especially close to the world of mortals.

TEARS, IDLE TEARS

"This song came to me on the yellowing autumn-tide at Tintern Abbey (see note to Wordsworth's *Tintern Abbey,* p. 680a), full for me of its bygone memories. It is the sense of the abiding in the transient" (Tennyson).

892b IN MEMORIAM A. H. H.

Tennyson's dearest friend, Arthur Henry Hallam, the lovable and gifted son of the historian Henry Hallam, died suddenly at Vienna in September, 1833. *In Memoriam,* composed in his memory, is one of the noblest elegies or laments (see introductory note to Milton's *Lycidas,* p. 342b) in the English language. It consists of a series of one hundred and thirty-one lyrics composed over a period of seventeen years and reflecting various degrees of sorrow and various attitudes toward life, death, and immortality. In general the temper of the lyrics moves from blank despair to increasing faith until, in the prologue (ll. 1–44), which was composed last, the poet triumphantly states his conviction that faith alone can fathom the eternal purpose of God and solve the problem of immortality. The "In Memoriam stanza," with its unusual rhyme scheme *abba,* was, Tennyson at first believed, his own invention, but he later discovered that it had been used during the Elizabethan period.

893a 25. **Let knowledge grow,** etc. See note to l. 169 ff.

45. **him,** Goethe.

893b 73 ff. **from the Italian shore,** etc. Hallam's body was brought home and buried at Clevedon, on the Severn River.

82. **Phosphor,** Lucifer, the morning star.

894b 169 ff. **Are God and Nature then at strife,** etc. Here and in other passages in the poem Tennyson attempts to reconcile the apparent conflict between science and orthodoxy which was beginning to agitate the public even before the appearance of Darwin's supposedly new ideas in *The Origin of Species,* 1859.

895a 185. **You,** probably Tennyson's sister Emily, who had been engaged to Hallam.

189. **one,** Hallam.

209 ff. **Ring out,** etc. This famous lyric marks the third New Year after Hallam's death. In it the poet, disregarding his personal

sorrow, thinks only of the universal message of love and peace to all mankind — "the Christ that is to be."

895b 241 ff. **Thy voice is on the rolling air,** etc. Hallam, by a kind of new Platonism, becomes identified with the spirit of the universe.

257. **O living will,** "Free-will in man" (Tennyson).

896a ODE ON THE DEATH OF THE DUKE OF WELLINGTON

Arthur Wellesley, first Duke of Wellington, 1769–1852, was at the time of his death field marshal of the British Army and held an almost unparalleled record of military victories. Tennyson's poem, written on the day of the duke's funeral, is one of the most artistic of all the poet's official compositions as poet laureate and one of the finest funeral odes in literature. It belongs to the type of ode known as "irregular." Cf. notes to Gray's *Progress of Poesy*, p. 585a, and Congreve's Ode, p. 441b. See also Cowley's odes, p. 435a ff. The movement of the verse, a notable early example of "free rhythm," follows the action. "The opening strophe suggests the irregular movement of the crowds in the streets . . . In the second our attention is turned toward St. Paul's Cathedral, and in the third the procession begins to move. Later we approach the cathedral, and hear the sound of tolling bell mingle with that of the music within. The movement of the remaining strophes is one of thought rather than action, but at the close we find ourselves inside the cathedral, hearing the dead march, the 'Dust to dust' of the burial service, and the final prayer" (Alden).

42. **World-victor's victor,** the conqueror of Napoleon, the world-victor.

896b 49. **cross of gold,** on St. Paul's Cathedral, where the duke was buried.

56. **Bright let it be,** etc. The names of Wellington's victories were inscribed on the funeral car.

80 ff. **Who is he,** etc. "These lines are spoken by the 'mighty seaman' Nelson, who lies in St. Paul's" (Tennyson). Horatio, Viscount Nelson, 1758–1805, vice-admiral of the British navy, the idol of the sailors, and the hero of many sea battles, was slain at Trafalgar in 1805.

99. **Assaye,** a small town in Hindostan, where Wellington (then General Wellesley) won his first great victory, in 1803. He defeated an army of thirty thousand with a force of less than five thousand.

897a 101. **underneath another sun,** in Spain.

123. **that loud sabbath,** the day of the battle of Waterloo, Sunday, June 18, 1815.

137. **the Baltic and the Nile,** battles fought by Lord Nelson. For the former, see Campbell's *Battle of the Baltic*, p. 804, and notes.

897b 170. **wink,** shut the eyes.

196. **all her stars.** Wellington was a knight of twenty-six orders, as well as viscount, earl, marquis, and duke.

898b THE CHARGE OF THE LIGHT BRIGADE

The famous charge took place on October 25, 1854, at Balaclava, in the Crimean War, fought against Russia. Though Tennyson composed his poem without Drayton's *Agincourt* (p. 264) in mind, *The Charge of the Light Brigade* is written in the same meter as Drayton's poem and should be compared with it as one of the noblest war poems in literature. Other notable examples of martial verse are Campbell's *Hohenlinden* (p. 802) and *The Battle of the Baltic* (p. 804) and Tennyson's *Last Fight of the Revenge* (see introductory note to p. 295).

6. **he.** A certain Captain Nolan delivered the order. It is not known who was responsible for the original command that sacrificed so many lives uselessly (cf. l. 12).

899a 38. **Not the six hundred.** Only one hundred and ninty-five returned.

MAUD; A MONODRAMA

A monodrama is "a series of monologues . . . spoken by the same person, and passing from one scene to another somewhat in the dramatic manner — as if the story of Hamlet should be told by his soliloquies alone" (Alden). In a series of twenty-eight such monologues Tennyson traces several chapters in the history of a soul — a morbid, sentimental young man with a touch of hereditary insanity has a tragic love affair with Maud, a girl with whose family he is at enmity. After achieving a somewhat less jaundiced view of life as the result of his love for Maud, he loses his sweetheart by death and goes insane, but finally recovers, and decides that he is ready to take up again the burden of life with courage and hope. Though the individual monologues in *Maud* are not of uniform excellence, some of those that are more specifically lyric in tone are among the best of Tennyson's poems.

900b SONG OF THE BROOK

This charming lyric, broken into several sections, is inserted in a longer narrative poem with the same title. Its extraordinary popularity is probably due to the simple, childlike attitude toward nature which it reflects.

GUINEVERE

Guinevere is the eleventh of a series of twelve poems by Tennyson called *Idylls of the King* and dealing with the story of King Arthur — the chief heroic legend in English literary history. Aside from *The Marriage of Geraint* and *Geraint and Enid* (originally one idyll), which are based on the Welsh *Mabinogion* (see introductory note to p. 63a), Tennyson's chief and almost only source was Malory's *Morte Darthur* (see introductory note to p. 130b).

Beginning perhaps as a body of heroic legend current among the British Celts and dealing with the exploits of a chieftain who defended his country against the invading Saxons, the Arthurian story developed into a vast body of romance including not only the love affair between Guinevere and Lancelot but also a large number of knightly exploits and quests, especially that of the Holy Grail — the whole suffused with the ideals of chivalry and courtly love. From the large collection of legends furnished by Malory Tennyson chose as his central theme the age-old story of marital inconstancy as illustrated in Lancelot and Guinevere, and around it built his *Idylls*, which he composed at various times over a period of nearly half a century. Though following in the main the outlines of the old narratives, he introduces elements of characterization and symbolism not found in the original: (1) Guinevere becomes a modern wife, whose husband, engrossed in big business, neglects her and so forces her into the arms of a handsome lover. The failure of Arthur's high endeavor is due not, as in certain of the older versions, to his youthful slip (see note to p. 130b, l. 1), but to the subtle poison of Guinevere's infidelity. (2) As in Spenser's *Faerie Queene*, the poem has a secondary or allegorical as well as a primary meaning: the tragedy of Arthur's failure to build up an ideal kingdom in the face of Guinevere's guilty love represents the eternal war between the Soul (Arthur) and Sense (Guinevere); Merlin represents Intellect; etc. (3) The progress of the twelve idylls follows the course of the months, from the coming of Guinevere in spring through the Tournament of Dead Innocence in autumn to Arthur's last battle late in December. As the *Idylls* were composed at various times over a long period of years and as the final order is not in every case the order of composition, the allegory is not consistently carried out.

Though characters, plot, and allegory give the *Idylls* a certain unity, Tennyson thought of his Arthurian poems as individual pictures; he calls them "idylls," *i.e.*, works descriptive of simple scenes in which the pictorial element predominates. In artistic finish, in nobility of sentiment, and in exaltation of theme the *Idylls* rank as the greatest treatment of the Arthurian legend.

2. **Almesbury,** in Wiltshire, about seven miles from Salisbury. The nunnery, to which Guinevere has fled after her parting with Lancelot, is the scene of her final repentance and her last interview with her injured husband.

901a 10. **Modred.** See note to p. 94a, l. 1.

15. **Lords of the White Horse,** Hengist and Horsa, the traditional leaders of the earliest Saxon invaders of Britain (see Anglo-Saxon Chronicle at the year 449, p. 47b and note). Both *Hengist* and *Horsa* mean "horse," and Hengist's standard was said to have been a figure of a white horse.

901b 87. **thine own land,** France.

902b 166. **'Late, late,'** etc. Cf. Matthew xxv, 1 ff.

903b 221. **Camelot.** See note to p. 96b, l. 247 ff.

903b 234. **Lyonesse,** a district often referred to in Arthurian romance. According to an ancient tradition, it sank beneath the waves, its position being marked in historic times only by the Scilly Isles off Land's End, the extreme point of Cornwall.

904a 286. **false son of Gorloïs.** See note to p. 97a, l. 324.

289. **Bude and Bos,** places on the coast of Cornwall.

292. **Tintagil.** See note to p. 96b, l. 247 ff.

905a 395. **Dragon,** the standard of Uther Pendragon, Arthur's father.

905b 419 f. **one I honoured.** Guinevere's father was Leodogran, king of Cameliard.

906a 453. **when the Roman left us.** See Anglo-Saxon Chronicle at the year 435, p. 47a, l. 53 ff., and note.

485. **Tristram and Isolt.** Had Tennyson been able to foresee the tremendous popularity which the love story of Tristan (Tristram) and Isolt was destined to enjoy later, he would perhaps have treated this famous pair of star-crossed lovers more sympathetically.

906b 500. **Usk.** See note to p. 75b, l. 23.

907a 535. **the flaming death,** burning at the stake as an adulteress.

908b THE PASSING OF ARTHUR

Except for the first one hundred and sixty-nine and the last thirty lines, this poem stands as it appeared, under the title *Morte d'Arthur*, in the 1842 volume. For epic sweep and dignity the *Morte d'Arthur* is surpassed by none of Tennyson's other Arthurian poems.

909a 27. **My God, thou hast forgotten me,** etc. Cf. Christ's dying words, Matthew xxvii, 46.

909b 56. **Light was Gawain,** etc. See note to p. 94b, l. 43.

77. **one lying in the dust at Almesbury.** See *Guinevere*, l. 524 ff.

90 f. **the great light . . . lowest,** "the winter solstice (December 21)" (Tennyson).

94. **last, dim, weird battle,** "A Vision of Death" (Tennyson).

910b 168. **Excalibur.** See note to p. 134a, l. 7 f.

912a 278. **his own conceit,** his own conception regarding the matter.

307. **streamer of the northern morn,** the Aurora Borealis.

308. **moving isles of winter,** icebergs.

913a 361 ff. **there hove a dusky barge,** etc. Cf. the earlier accounts of Arthur's passing: pp. 97b, l. 338 ff, and 134b, l. 14 ff.

383. **cuisses,** plate armor for the front of the thighs.

913b 400 f. **the light that led,** etc., the Star of Bethlehem. Cf. Matthew ii, 9 ff.

427. **Avilion.** See note to p. 97b, l. 325.

914a FLOWER IN THE CRANNIED WALL

Tennyson was tremendously interested in science and was constantly using the results of scientific research in his poetry. The flower which he has just plucked from a cranny in a wall suggests the whole problem of human science.

914b RIZPAH

This, the most pathetic of Tennyson's dramatic monologues, was suggested by a magazine account of an old woman of Brighton who, after her son had been hanged for highway robbery, visited the gallows on dark and stormy nights, gathered up the bones as they fell from the disintegrating corpse, and buried them in the hallowed soil of the churchyard. When the poem opens, the old mother is talking to a visiting lady in a hospital where she is dying. The title was of course suggested by the biblical account of Rizpah's watch over the dead bodies of her sons, hanged by order of David (2 Samuel xxi, 10).

916a 'FRATER AVE ATQUE VALE'

Tennyson was steeped in the classics, and his poems are full of reminiscences of his reading. This poem, written upon his visit to Italy in 1880, is a splendid tribute to one of his favorite Latin poets. The title, which means "Brother, Hail and Farewell," is taken from Catullus' lament for his brother.

1. **Desenzano,** a town on Lake Garda a little west of Sirmione, where Catullus' villa was situated.

2. **'O venusta Sirmio!'** "O beautiful Sirmio!" quoted from Catullus.

8. **Lydian.** The Etruscans, settled near Lake Garda, were supposed to be of Lydian origin.

MERLIN AND THE GLEAM

This poem gives an allegorical account of Tennyson's poetical career. The Gleam, he explained, means "the higher poetic imagination."

14. **learned,** taught, once good usage but now obsolete.

917a CROSSING THE BAR

A few days before his death Tennyson directed that this poem should be placed at the end of all editions of his works.

ROBERT BROWNING

Robert Browning came of good though mixed middle-class stock and was born and bred in a suburb of London. His father, a clerk in the Bank of England, was scholarly, artistic in temperament, a linguist, and versatile in general affairs. The poet was hardly less fortunate in his mother, who was a woman of good musical talent and a lover of art. His formal education was slight — some tutoring, a little private schooling, and a term or two in the University of London. By the aid of his father, however, and by his own resources he acquired a mass of knowledge which, though unsystematic and ill-organized, has been equaled by few. Relieved by family circumstances from the necessity of making a living, he decided early upon a literary career and became a devotee of Shelley. His first poem, *Pauline*, 1833, attracted little attention, but his dramatic piece, *Paracelsus*, 1835, brought a request from the actor-manager Macready for a play. For several years afterward, Browning wrote dramas, but did not realize any great success on the stage. In 1840 he produced his long and obscure poem *Sordello*, which for years did his reputation positive harm. In consequence his next works were issued in cheap editions at his own expense. Two of these, *Dramatic Lyrics*, 1843, and *Dramatic Romances*, 1845, contain many of his best poems. In 1845 he became acquainted with the gifted Elizabeth Barrett, whose reputation as a poet was already better than his own. After a brief unconventional courtship and marriage in 1846, the pair left England for Italy, where they lived a life of almost ideal happiness and congeniality until her death in 1861. His *Men and Women*, 1855, and *Dramatis Personæ*, 1864, conclude the better known collections of his shorter poems. After Mrs. Browning's death he set to work on his masterpiece, *The Ring and the Book*, 1868–1869, a long psychological study from various angles of an old Roman murder trial. He continued to write until the end of his long life, but his later work is injured by his tendency to philosophical speculation and by indulgence in grotesqueness of rhyme, expression, and even of thought. His genius was recognized, however; he became a familiar figure about London, where he resided most of the time; he was honored with degrees by both Oxford and Cambridge; and with his naturally buoyant nature was reasonably happy. He died in Venice just after the appearance of his last volume of verse, *Asolando*, and was brought back to England for interment in Westminster Abbey. As in the case of Carlyle, his extremely individual style has been made an objection against him. His peculiar turns of expression to characterize his exuberance of thought, the inverted and artificial order of his sentence structure, and his penchant for odd rhymes often detract from what would otherwise be a permanent level of high seriousness in his poetry. The same faults, too, are largely responsible for the charge, made against him, of obscurity. But his oddity of style and obscurity of meaning are mainly the faults of his inferior works. The great body of his best poetry is quite free from such defects, and in its good qualities — its intense revelations of character, its wholesome tone and hopeful outlook, its superabundant fullness of ideas, its artistic imagery and phrase, and its genuine music — justifies the place that has been assigned to Browning, in the forefront of the great English poets.

917b SONG FROM *PIPPA PASSES*

This song is sung by the little silk weaver of Asolo in the dramatic poem which bears her name. It is a brief compendium of Browning's philosophy of life.

CAVALIER TUNES

The first of these "tunes" is evidently imagined as originating in 1642, when civil war in England was beginning, and Pym, Hampden, and Hazelrig (Hazlerigg) were members of Parliament in opposition to King Charles I. The second and third speak of a somewhat later period, when Pym and Hampden are dead and Cromwell (Noll) is the head of the army.

I. MARCHING ALONG

2. **crop-headed.** Cropped hair was worn by the Puritan, long curls by the Cavalier aristocrat. Hence the Puritans were called "Roundheads."

7. **Pym,** John Pym, 1584–1643, an able statesman and orator, one of the leaders of the popular party against Charles. He was not an extreme Puritan.

918a 13 f. **Hampden,** etc., John Hampden, a patriot and statesman, coleader with Pym of the popular party; Sir Arthur Hazelrig, a leader in the Long Parliament; John Fiennes, a prominent cavalry officer; Sir Henry Vane the younger, a prominent member of the Long Parliament.

15. **Rupert,** Prince Rupert, a nephew of Charles and a picturesque cavalry leader on the Royalist side.

22. **Nottingham,** a town in central England where Charles raised his standard at the beginning of the civil war in 1642.

918b INCIDENT OF THE FRENCH CAMP

Ratisbon in Bavaria was taken by Napoleon in April, 1809. The incident described is said to have happened, but the hero was a man, not a boy.

11. **Lannes,** a famous marshal of France.

29. **flag-bird.** Napoleon's standard bore an eagle on the central stripe.

919a MY LAST DUCHESS

In this excellent dramatic monologue a Duke of Este is imagined as negotiating a marriage settlement with the ambassador of "the Count" and entertaining him, probably by design, with the story of his former wife's shortcomings. The capital of the magnificent House of Este during the Renaissance was Ferrara in northern Italy, not far from Venice.

A dramatic monologue is a poem, essentially short, in which (1) a speaker divulges aloud (2) some crucial experience through which he at the time is passing to (3) a listener (or listeners) who silently influences to some extent what he says. The type, as Browning fashioned and perfected it, proved a marvelous vehicle for the revelation of character in brief flashes, as was peculiarly suited to his dramatic genius. His dramatic monologues are his best poems.

3. **Frà Pandolf,** Brother Pandolf, an imaginary character, represented as a monk. Many of the Renaissance painters were monks.

919b 56. **Claus of Innsbruck.** Claus is an imaginary person. Innsbruck, the capital of Tyrol in Austria, is celebrated for its work in bronze representing the figure, ancestry, and achievements of Maximilian I.

THE LABORATORY

This poem is mediæval in spirit and setting. The story and characters are imaginary.

920b THE LOST LEADER

Wordsworth's change to Toryism gave Browning his idea for his *Lost Leader*. But the Seer of the Lakes was only " a sort of painter's model " for the portrait of a popular leader who basely deserts a great cause for a paltry consideration of money and honors.

921a HOW THEY BROUGHT THE GOOD NEWS, etc.

In writing this poem Browning doubtless had vaguely in mind the Pacification of Ghent in 1576, although there is no specific historical foundation for the story. Ghent is in Flanders, some ninety miles from Aix-la-Chapelle in West Prussia. The other places named lie almost directly between.

922b HOME-THOUGHTS FROM THE SEA

This poem was inspired by Nelson's victories at Cape St. Vincent in 1797 and at Trafalgar in 1805.

THE BISHOP ORDERS HIS TOMB, etc.

Praxedis was an early Christian saint. Her church is in Rome. The materials and characters of the poem are imaginary.

923a 46. **Frascati,** a town near Rome, anciently a villa.

923b 77. **Tully,** Marcus Tullius Cicero.

79. **Ulpian,** Ulpianus Domitius, *ca.* 170–228, a Roman jurist.

99. **elucescebat,** an example of Ulpian's bad Latin, a wrong formation from *elucere*. In an epitaph it means " was noted " or " was notable."

924a 108. **Term,** a bust on a square base, like the statues of Terminus, the god of boundaries.

924b EVELYN HOPE

This poem, probably the most popular of the author's lyrics, is fictitious throughout. It denies the evanescence of human love, a favorite theme with Browning.

925a LOVE AMONG THE RUINS

This poem was probably suggested by the ruins of the Campagna in Rome, where it was written in the winter of 1853–1854. By its line arrangement and rhyme effect it is intended to represent echo, which has its haunt among ruins.

926a A TOCCATA OF GALUPPI'S

A toccata (Ital. *toccare*, to touch) is a composition for the organ or the harpsichord, in a free and brilliant style. Baldassare Galuppi, 1706–1785, was a popular musical composer in his day. During his last years he was organist in St. Mark's Cathedral in Venice.

926b 6. **wed the sea with rings.** Pope Alexander III in 1174 instituted the ceremony of " wedding the Adriatic." He gave the doge a ring in token of the victory of the Venetians over Frederick Barbarossa and desired the doge to throw a similar ring into the sea annually, to commemorate the event.

8. **Shylock's bridge,** the Rialto. Cf. *The Merchant of Venice*.

19 ff. **lesser thirds,** etc. The technical musical terms used here will be found explained in a good dictionary. The general meaning is sufficiently clear from the context.

927a 'DE GUSTIBUS'

The full phrase is *de gustibus non est disputandum,* " there is no accounting for tastes."

927b 36. **liver-wing,** right arm. The king was the cruel and despotic Ferdinand II, 1810–1859.

40. **Queen Mary's saying.** See the *Death of Mary,* p. 215b f.

MY STAR

The " Star " of this poem is usually understood to be Mrs. Browning.

4. **angled spar,** a mineral crystalline formation which gives off colored lights.

929a A GRAMMARIAN'S FUNERAL

This poem depicts well nigh perfectly the Renaissance love of learning. As indicated in the title, the deceased subject is simply *a* grammarian or scholar, without any definite historical antecedent. The speaker is the leader of the procession, a former student of the dead master.

929b 86. **Calculus,** the stone, a disease.

88. **Tussis,** a cough.

930a 129. **Hoti,** the Greek particle ὅτι, "that," etc.

130. **Oun,** the Greek particle, οὖν, "then," "now then," etc.

131. **De,** the enclitic δε, "toward," not the contrastive δε, "but."

930b CHILDE ROLAND, etc.

The suggestion for this poem was Edgar's song in *King Lear* III, iv. Such objects as a tower in the Carrara Mountains, a painting in Paris, and the figure of a horse in the tapestry of the Browning drawing-room, contributed slightly to its make-up; otherwise the entire composition is a fiction, and it is best to interpret it, as doubtless Browning intended, without a moral meaning. It is a realistic study in the forbidding and grotesque, and as such is one of the most powerful poems in the language.

932b 143. **Tophet.** See note to *Paradise Lost*, I, l. 404.

160. **Apollyon.** See Revelation ix, 11.

933a FRA LIPPO LIPPI

Fra Lippo Lippi, 1406–1469, was a noted Florentine painter. Browning interprets his life and art from the account of him in Vasari's *Lives*.

933b 7. **Carmine,** a Carmelite monastery in Florence.

17. **Cosimo,** etc., Cosimo de Medici, surnamed "the Elder," 1389–1464, a banker, statesman, and patron of art, and practically ruler of the Florentine Republic.

934a 67. **Saint Laurence,** the church of San Lorenzo.

73. **Jerome,** St. Jerome, *ca.* 340–420, author of a Latin version of the Bible known as the Vulgate.

88. **Old Aunt Lapaccia,** Lippi's paternal aunt, Mona Lapaccia.

935a 139. **Camaldolese,** monks of the convent of Camaldoli, near Florence.

140. **Preaching Friars,** Dominican friars.

935b 189. **Giotto,** Giotto di Bondone, 1276–1337, a Florentine painter, architect, and sculptor.

196. **Herodias.** Cf. Matthew xiv.

936a 235. **Brother Angelico,** Giovanni da Fiesole, 1387–1455, a painter who followed the ideals of the earlier ascetic school.

236. **Brother Lorenzo,** Lorenzo Monaca, a monk of Camaldoli, who showed the same tendencies in painting as Brother Angelico.

936b 276. **Guidi,** Tommaso Guidi Masaccio, 1401–1443, a famous Italian painter, founder of the modern naturalistic school of painting.

937a 323. **Saint Laurence.** St. Laurence suffered martyrdom by broiling on a gridiron in 258.

324. **Prato,** a town near Florence.

937b 339. **Chianti,** a region south of Florence, celebrated for its wines.

346. **Sant' Ambrogio's,** the convent of St. Ambrose in Florence.

347 ff. **I shall paint,** etc. The picture described is the *Coronation of the Virgin* in the Academy of Fine Arts at Florence.

354. **Saint John,** John the Baptist, the patron saint of Florence.

938a 377. **Iste perfecit opus,** that one did the work.

387. **Saint Lucy.** According to tradition, a Christian martyr about 303.

ANDREA DEL SARTO

Andrea del Sarto, called "the Faultless Painter," was born about 1486 and died in 1531. According to Vasari, his love for Lucrezia del Fede, who became his wife in 1512, caused him to neglect work, parents, and even honor. He used funds, entrusted to him by Francis I of France for the purchase of pictures, to build a house for her in Florence. Recent historians have given her a better character. The poem has often been called Browning's best dramatic monologue, and as such it is the best in English poetry.

15. **Fiesole,** a village on a ridge above Florence, visible from Andrea's house.

938b 25. **a model.** Lucrezia, wholly or in reminiscence, is discernible in almost all of the women of Del Sarto's pictures.

939a 93. **Morello,** a mountain near Florence.

105. **The Urbinate,** Raphael, from Urbino, the place of his birth.

940a 150. **Fontainebleau,** a royal palace near Paris.

941a 263. **Leonard,** Leonardo da Vinci, 1452–1519, one of the greatest of Italian painters.

941b PROSPICE

This poem is Browning's *Crossing the Bar*. It was written in the autumn after Mrs. Browning's death and contains in its conclusion a glowing tribute to her. The title means, "Look forward."

ABT VOGLER

George Joseph Vogler of Bavaria, 1749–1814, was a Catholic priest and a popular musical composer, though reviled by some as a charlatan. About 1786 he invented the "orchestrion," on which he is represented as extemporizing in the poem.

3 f. **Solomon willed,** etc. According to a Moslem tradition, Solomon, by the power of a ring containing the name of God, could command " armies of angels " and demons to his service.

942a 23. **Rome's dome,** St. Peter's Cathedral, illuminated for Easter.

943b ✓ RABBI BEN EZRA

Ibn Ezra, 1092–1167, born in the intellectual center of Toledo, was a great Jewish scholar, philosopher, and poet. His writings contain some of the ideas expressed in the poem, but Browning makes of the whole one of the best expositions of his own philosophy of life. Contrast in the poem his view of old age with that of the romantic poets and of Fitzgerald in the *Rubaiyat.*

945a 151. **that Potter's wheel.** The figure of the potter's wheel is characteristically oriental. See various passages in the Old Testament and the *Rubaiyat,* l. 327 ff., etc.

945b ✓ CALIBAN UPON SETEBOS

See *The Tempest* for the figure of Caliban. The poem is a study of " Natural Theology in the Island." Caliban, a rudimentary thinking being, is represented as having just emerged into a consciousness of an overruling divinity, whose character he interprets in terms of himself and the life he knows.

946a 20. **Prosper and Miranda.** See *The Tempest.*

24. **Setebos,** Caliban's divinity; a god, or devil, " worshipped by the Patagonians " in South America.

947b 170. **His dam.** Caliban's mother was the witch Sycorax.

949b APPARENT FAILURE

Browning wrote this poem, as he says, to save the " Doric little Morgue " in Paris, which, according to a newspaper report, was to be destroyed. Seven years before, while in Paris to witness the baptism of Louis Napoleon, he had visited the little building, where lay three suicides by drowning, one from disappointed ambition, one from the failure of his socialistic ideals, and one from love. At that time the Congress of the European Powers was in session in the city, attended by Prince Gortschakoff, the Russian minister; Cavour, the Italian statesman; and Count Buol, the Austrian foreign minister. The poem avows Browning's belief in an ultimate opportunity for such " apparent " failures as the suicides.

12. **Petrarch's Vaucluse,** a valley near Avignon, where Petrarch spent four years in study and writing. The Sorgue is a river flowing through the valley.

39. **the Tuileries,** a royal palace and grounds in Paris.

950a ✓ EPILOGUE

This poem, appended to Browning's last volume of verse, *Asolando,* 1889, is celebrated for the poet's almost perfect characterization of himself.

ELIZABETH BARRETT BROWNING

Elizabeth Barrett was born at Coxhoe Hall in Durham, in 1806. Her poetry amply reflects the associations of her childhood in the country, chiefly at Hope End, near the Malvern Hills. When she was twelve her indulgent father printed her *Battle of Marathon,* an epic poem in eleven or twelve books. Her didactic poem, *An Essay on Mind,* written in imitation of Pope when she was seventeen or eighteen, she " long repented of." She was an ardent student of Greek; and when in her constant ill health she feared the prohibition of her studies by her physician, she had her beloved Greek authors bound as novels that she might continue to have access to them. In 1832 the family removed to Sidmouth in Devonshire, where she translated the *Prometheus Unbound* of Æschylus, revised later into one of the great popular Greek poems in English. In London, which became her home in 1835 and continued to be so until the family was broken up, she cultivated literary friends, contributed poems to magazines, and issued one or two volumes of verse. She had suffered a spinal affection since girlhood; her lungs became weak from the unwholesome London climate; she ruptured a blood vessel and became an invalid, confining herself almost wholly indoors. The loss of her beloved brother, while she was at Torquay in the interest of her health, distressed her sorely. In 1844 her poems appeared in two volumes and brought her an acquaintance with Browning. Their remarkable courtship, which followed speedily, has given us the best known body of love letters in English literature. Because of unreasonable objections by her father, they were married clandestinely in the fall of 1846, and thereafter made their home in Italy. Her *Sonnets from the Portuguese* appeared in 1847 and *Casa Guidi Windows* in 1851. Her long personal epic, *Aurora Leigh,* was completed and published in 1856 and won instant success. She continued to write till the end of her life, dying in Florence in 1861. She was talented, intellectual, and by nature subjective. She wrote usually from the fervor of a glowing heart, but not always from inspiration. Her masterpiece, as she regarded it, *Aurora Leigh,* has hardly maintained its fame. Her gifts are essentially lyrical. Some of her short poems, such as *The Cry of the Children,* have had a wide appeal. By her *Sonnets from the Portuguese,* voicing her perfect love for Browning, she raised herself to a position among the few great sonneteers of the language.

950b LADY GERALDINE'S COURTSHIP

This poem is in the form of a rhymed epistle from the lover Bertram to a "friend and fellow student." By its expressed admiration of Browning (see l. 163 f.) it served to bring the two poets together, and resulted ultimately in their union.

951a 36. **spectrum of the salt.** In mediæval England the salt was placed on the table at the dividing line between gentry and commonalty.

952b 115. **Lough,** John Graham Lough, *ca.* 1804–1876, an English sculptor.

953a 152. **Tuscan,** *i.e.*, a composition like the Tuscan Petrarch's love poetry.

953b 162. **Howitt,** William Howitt, 1792–1879, an English poet and miscellaneous writer.

163. **some 'Pomgranate,'** an allusion to Browning's *Bells and Pomgranates,* 1841–1846.

954b 227. **Camoëns.** See note to p. 608a, l. 14.

955a 268. **Pythian height,** *i.e.*, of inspiration or intoxication like the priestess of Apollo at Delphi.

956a 311. **Parias,** members of the lowest social caste in India.

957a 367. **Phemius,** Polyphemus, a one-eyed giant blinded by Ulysses. See *Odyssey,* IX, 371 ff.

378. **Parian.** Paros, an island of the Cyclades, was famed in ancient times for its white marble.

958a THE CRY OF THE CHILDREN

This poem had its inception in an official report on child labor in the English mines and factories, and is therefore a product of the humanitarian movement near the middle of the century, which inspired such novelists as Dickens and Kingsley in some of their works.

960a SONNETS FROM THE PORTUGUESE

These sonnets are Mrs. Browning's artistic expression of the motive which inspired her life, her love for her poet husband, Robert Browning. The phrase "from the Portuguese" was merely a veil to disguise from the public the personal import of the poems.

1. **Theocritus,** a Greek idyllic poet of the third century before Christ. Cf. *Idyl,* xv, 104 f.

MATTHEW ARNOLD

Matthew Arnold was born and reared in an academic atmosphere. At the time of his birth his father, the later famous Dr. Thomas Arnold, was a teacher at Laleham, near Staines. In 1828 Arnold removed with the family to Rugby upon his father's becoming head master of the public school there. After attending Rugby and Winchester, he entered Balliol College, Oxford, where he held a classical scholarship. In 1845 he was elected to a fellowship in Oriel College. He soon left Oxford to become private secretary to the Marquis of Lansdowne, through whose influence he was appointed inspector of schools in 1851, and from this time until his retirement on a pension in 1883 he devoted his energies conscientiously and unremittingly to the drudgery of his position. To the inspectorship was added, 1857, the relatively light duties of professor of poetry at Oxford, an appointment which he held for ten years. He made lecture tours in the United States in 1884 and 1886, when such tours were not as common as they are to-day.

Arnold's literary talents developed late. His early prose is crude, and his verse was of little value before the appearance in 1849 of *The Strayed Reveller and Other Poems* (published under a penname), which is too unequal in quality and too slight in bulk to afford a basis for sound generalization. In 1852 appeared his *Empedocles on Etna,* which contained, besides the title poem and a collection of lyrics, a version of the mediæval legend of Tristram and Iseult and which showed the author to be a poet of mature if irregular genius. In 1853 he published a volume containing, along with other poems, his noble epic, *Sohrab and Rustum.* He later published other collections of poetry, notably the volumes containing *Thyrsis,* 1861, and *Rugby Chapel,* 1869; but in general his poetic vein, never very abundant, grew thinner as the years passed. He turned his attention more and more to prose criticism, and during the last twenty years of his life he came to be recognized as a leader, if not a dictator, in this field. Some of his more important utterances are to be found in *On Translating Homer*, 1861; *On the Study of Celtic Literature*, 1867; *Culture and Anarchy*, 1869; *Literature and Dogma*, 1873; *The Study of Literature*, 1880; and *Discourses in America*, 1885.

In his published prose and in his public lectures Arnold, like Carlyle, was an apostle of the higher life. For more than twenty years he strove to impress his ideals of culture and criticism upon the generally unresponsive but always respectful public of England and America. He would help us to save ourselves from "Philistinism" — narrow-mindedness, self-satisfaction, and vulgarity. He would have us strive after "culture," which he defines as "a pursuit of our total perfection by means of getting to know, on matters which must concern us, the best which has been thought and said in the world." In literary criticism his standards are ethical rather than æsthetic, an assertion which will perhaps be clearer when it is remembered that he regards poetry as "a criticism of life" rather than a "thing of beauty." His test of "high seriousness" as a criterion of the greatest literature is indeed a searching one, but it applies rather to the spiritual than to the æsthetic content.

Personally Arnold is said to have been entirely lacking in the attitude of condescension which characterizes his criticism. His prose is usually light and vivacious in tone, whereas his poetry is pervaded by a profound hopelessness regarding this life and the world to come. This pessimistic philosophy, which is said to reflect Arnold's real attitude, is usually attributed to the fact that he lived in a period of transition when the old foundations of human faith appeared to be weakening under the influence of apparently revolutionary theories in science and religion that have since become commonplaces.

961b TO A FRIEND

Arnold here expresses that extreme reverence for classical literature and philosophy which is revealed throughout his work.

2. **the old man,** Homer, who, according to tradition, was blind.

3. **The Wide Prospect, and the Asian Fen,** names for Europe and Asia respectively. "The name Europe (Εὐρώπη, *the wide prospect*) probably describes the European coast to the Greeks on the coast of Asia Minor opposite. The name Asia, again, comes, it has been thought, from the muddy fens of the rivers of Asia Minor" (Arnold). Matthew Arnold's etymologies, it may be observed, are more valuable as poetry than as linguistics.

4. **Tmolus,** a mountain in Asia Minor. Homer, according to one tradition, lived in Asia Minor.

4. **Smyrna,** situated on the west coast of Asia Minor, one of the many towns claimed as the birthplace of Homer.

6. **That halting slave,** the distinguished Stoic philosopher, Epictetus, *ca.* A.D. 60–120. Banished from Rome by the Emperor Domitian, son of Vespasian, he went to Nicopolis, where he had as a pupil the historian and philosopher Arrian, to whom we owe most of our information regarding the master.

8 ff. **his . . . whose even-balanced soul,** etc., Sophocles, 497–406 B.C., a celebrated Greek dramatist. His works are marked by freedom from the intrusion of contemporary disturbing elements.

14. **Colonus.** Sophocles was born at Colonus near Athens.

SHAKESPEARE

1. **Others abide our question. Thou art free.** This may mean one of two things: (1) Others answer our questions, whereas thou tellest us nothing of thyself or of thy philosophy of life; or (2) thou art supreme in the world's judgment, whereas others still await humanity's final verdict.

11. **unguessed at.** Arnold means that, if Shakespeare's contemporaries had realized fully his ultimate place in the world's opinion, they would have preserved more biographical facts about him. We really know very little of Shakespeare's life.

A PICTURE AT NEWSTEAD

Newstead Abbey in Nottinghamshire was the ancestral home of the Bryon family.

962a THE FORSAKEN MERMAN

This deservedly famous monologue is based on a theme widespread in folklore — the story of a union between a mortal and a being from another, in this case a watery, world. Arnold's merman, an ocean king, has married a mortal woman. At the moment of the poem she has returned to her kinfolk on land at Easter and has decided not to go back to her subaqueous family for fear she may lose her soul. *The Forsaken Merman* is perhaps the best known of Arnold's lyrics. The variations in meter are unusually effective in indicating changes in the rapidity of the action.

962b 69. **sea-stocks**, sea gillyflowers.

963a 81. **sealed**, fastened.

82. **shut stands the door.** According to popular belief, fairies and certain other supernatural beings are excluded from Heaven and from all other benefits of Christianity.

963b SOHRAB AND RUSTUM

Sohrab and Rustum is based on a summary of an episode in the great mediæval Persian epic, *Shah Namah*, "Book of Kings" (tenth century). The chief figure in the original is Rustum, the most illustrious of Persian heroes, who, according to tradition, lived about 600 B.C. His combat with his unknown son belongs to the realm of folk tradition. Arnold's poem is a magnificent example of epic dignity and restraint. It is one of the most thoroughly Greek productions of Arnold's pen. The frequent epic similes (see note to l. 111 ff.) are especially reminiscent of Homer and Milton.

2. **Oxus**, the largest river in central Asia.

3. **Tartar.** Sohrab, though a Persian by birth, is represented as serving under Afrasiab, the Tartar king. The Tartars were a group of wandering savage tribes in central Asia and southern Russia.

11. **Peran-Wisa**, leader of Afrasiab's army, which is composed of various Tartar tribes.

15. **Pamere**, a lofty plateau in central Asia.

25. **thick-piled**, having a thick pile, or nap.

964a 40. **Samarcand**, a city in Turkestan, once the capital of Tartary.

42. **Ader-baijan**, the northwest province of Persia, the home of Sohrab's mother, Tahminah (see l. 590).

60. **common**, general.

964b 82. **Seïstan**, a district on the borders of Persia and Afghanistan.

101. **Kara-Kul**, a district in south-central Asia. Cf. the name "caracul" now used of a kind of fur.

107. **Haman**, second in command to Peran-Wisa (l. 11).

111 ff. **As when**, etc. This is an example of an "epic" simile; *i.e.*, an extended simile, common in epic literature, in which the things compared do not correspond in all the details enumerated. Thus in the present case much that is said about the cranes is not intended to throw light on the behavior of the Tartar horsemen. See *Paradise Lost*, I, ll. 200 ff., 351 ff., etc.

115. **frore**, frozen.

965a 119. **Bokhara**, an extensive district in central Asia.

120. **Khiva**, a district in the valley of the lower Oxus.

121. **Toorkmuns**, Turkomans, a branch of the Turks living in central Asia.

123. **Attruck**, a river in northern Persia.

128. **Ferghana**, a district in Turkestan to the east of Samarcand.

129. **Jaxartes**, a former name of the Sir-Daria River, which flows through Turkestan.

131. **Kipchak**, a district in central Asia.

132. **Kalmuks . . . Kuzzaks.** Kalmucks, wandering Mongolian tribes living in central Asia and western Siberia; Kuzzaks, or Cossacks, a warlike people of southern Russia and southwestern Asia.

133. **Kirghizzes**, a nomadic people of northern Turkestan.

138. **Khorassan**, the northeastern province of Persia. "*Ilyats* means tribes" (St. Quintin).

965b 160. **Cabool**, Kabul, an important commercial city of northern Afghanistan.

161. **Indian Caucasus**, the mountain range between Turkestan and Afghanistan.

966a 217. **Iran**, now the official name for Persia, formerly applied to a larger area.

223. **Kai-Khosroo.** He has been identified with Cyrus the Great, sixth century before Christ, the founder of the Persian Empire.

967a 293. **swathe**, a line of mown grain or grass.

968b 412. **Hyphasis . . . Hydaspes**, rivers in northern India.

969a 452. **autumn Star**, Sirius, the Dog Star, whose coming was associated among certain ancient peoples with hot, dry weather and with fevers.

971a 570. **glass**, reflect.

592. **Koords**, Curds, a warlike people of northwestern Persia.

973a 736. **big warm tears.** Cf. p. 44b f.

751 f. **Helmund . . . Zirrah**, in Seïstan, Afghanistan.

973b 763 ff. **Moorghab . . . Tejend, Kohik . . . Sir**, rivers in Afghanistan.

974b 861. **Jemshid**, or Jamshid, a semimythical king of Persia; his capitol was Persepolis. Cf. note to p. 1020b, l. 18.

878. **Chorasmian waste**, the modern Khiva (see note to p. 965a, l. 120).

880. **Orgunjè**, a village on the Oxus not far from where it enters the Aral Sea.

975a 890. **home of waters**, the Aral Sea.

REQUIESCAT

The title means "Let her rest." It often occurs in Latin inscriptions on tombstones. Like some others of Arnold's lyrics, this poem is marked by clarity rather than intensity of feeling.

12. **laps**, enfolds.

13. **cabined**, etc., her spirit which, though longing to expand, was confined (as in a cabin) by the limitations of human life.

RUGBY CHAPEL

This poem commemorates the poet's father, Dr. Thomas Arnold, 1795–1842, who during the fifteen years that he was head master of Rugby did much to regenerate public education in England by impressing upon his students the importance of knowledge and the sacredness of duty. He is the "Doctor" of *Tom Brown's School Days*, 1857. Arnold's poem is marked by perfection of form and, unlike some of his other lyrics, by genuine feeling. The short unrhymed lines, with their unusual combination of accents (mingled iambic and anapæstic feet), are peculiarly suited to the pathetic tone of the poem.

975b 29. **unforeseen.** Dr. Arnold died suddenly, of angina pectoris.

976b 162. **Servants of God.** See note to l. 190. Cf. John xv, 15.

190. **Ye,** the "Servants of God" referred to in l. 162.

977a THYRSIS

This poem was written in commemoration of Arnold's friend, the poet Arthur Hugh Clough (see introductory note to p. 1014). Clough was possessed of "remarkable gifts, strength of character, and personal charm." The diction of the poem, Arnold tells us, was modeled on that of Theocritus, the celebrated Greek pastoral poet, and was intended to be "so artless as to be almost heedless." It ranks with Milton's *Lycidas* and Shelley's *Adonais* as among the noblest of the English pastoral laments. It combines classical clarity and restraint with true feeling. It is written in the same meter as *The Scholar Gipsy* and serves as a complement to that poem. It is full of reminiscences of the days spent with Clough in Oxford and its environs.

On the name "Thyrsis," see notes to Milton's *L'Allegro*, l. 83 ff.

2. **the two Hinkseys,** villages near Oxford. Numerous other places in or near Oxford are mentioned in the poem. The poet represents himself as standing on one of the hills overlooking the city and the Thames valley.

15. **the youthful Thames.** The Thames is about fifty yards wide at Oxford.

19. **that sweet City,** Oxford.

977b 29. **the Scholar-Gipsy,** a reference to Arnold's poem, in which a young scholar, driven by poverty, leaves the University of Oxford and becomes a member of a gipsy band. According to Arnold's source, the Scholar-Gipsy lived in the seventeenth century.

36 f. **this many a year,** etc. Arnold is saying, in the language of pastoral poetry, that he has not written any poetry for a long time.

40. **Thyrsis of his own will went away.** Clough resigned his fellowship in Oriel College, Oxford, in 1848. He appears to have done so voluntarily on account of his religious beliefs.

45. **silly,** simple.

49. **storms that rage.** Much of Clough's poetry reveals the poet's spiritual struggles.

978a 80. **Corydon.** See notes to Milton's *L'Allegro*, l. 83 ff.

82. **when Sicilian shepherds lost a mate,** an apparent reference to the lament for Bion attributed to the Sicilian pastoral poet Moschus.

86 ff. **relax Pluto's brow,** etc. Cf. notes to Milton's *L'Allegro*, l. 145 ff.

92. **Dorian,** Sicilian.

978b 95. **Enna,** the place in Sicily from which Proserpine was carried off by Pluto.

107. **fritillaries,** flowers somewhat like lilies.

979a 135. **sprent,** sprinkled.

137. **pausefully,** so as to make it pause.

979b 167. **Arno.** Clough died in Italy and was buried in Florence by the River Arno.

175. **boon,** benign, bounteous.

177. **the great Mother's train.** Arnold imagines that Clough's spirit has gone to be an attendant upon Cybele, the mother of the gods.

180. **Apennine.** The Apennines are a celebrated mountain range forming the backbone of Italy.

185. **Daphnis.** There are numerous classical stores about Daphnis, the reputed founder of pastoral poetry. According to one, he was blinded by a nymph whose love he had slighted, consoled himself by playing on the pipes, and was later raised to heaven. According to another, he had a reaping contest with Lityerses, king of Phrygia, but was enabled to win by the help of Hercules, and was thus saved from the death which Lityerses inflicted upon all contestants whom he overcame.

980b DOVER BEACH

In contrast with the light, occasionally even playful, tone of Arnold's prose, his poetry is suffused with a pessimism so uniformly gloomy and despairing that one is at times tempted to doubt its complete sincerity. In spite of its mood of disillusionment, *Dover Beach* ranks, both in technical excellence and in imaginative power, as one of the most perfect reflective lyrics in the English language.

With *Dover Beach* compare note to Bowles's sonnet *Dover Cliffs*, p. 599b, l. 1.

15. **Sophocles.** Cf. note to p. 961b, l. 8 ff.

The specific reference is apparently to Sophocles' *Antigone*, l. 583 ff.

DANTE GABRIEL ROSSETTI

Dante Gabriel Rossetti was both a poet and a painter. He early felt himself to be a painter and fashioned his life accordingly, but as an innovator in art he wrote to disseminate his ideas, applied his principles in verse, and achieved a renown as a poet that is even greater than his fame as a painter. He was born in London, the son of an English-Italian mother and a refugee Italian father who was himself a poet. He began his education at a private school in London but after one year was transferred to King's College School, where he remained from 1836 to 1843. On leaving school he was placed in Cary's Art Academy, passed thence about 1846 to the Royal Academy Antique School, and for a while received technical instruction from the artist Brown. In the autumn of 1848, in conjunction with half a dozen others, including the painter Millais and the sculptor Woolner, he formed an organization which had for its aim a recovery of the neglected opportunities of the mediæval past and a reinterpretation rather than a strict revival of the principles of the Italian painters before Raphael. Impelled as it was by the enthusiasm of its sponsor, the new order was aggressive, and at once became known as the Pre-Raphaelite Brotherhood. For the next fifteen years Rossetti was a productive painter, striving to realize the lost world of romance, wonder, and spiritual beauty which was known to the old masters but which eluded them because of their slavery to clerical tradition. He had written some of his best poetry by his twentieth year; but his first published pieces appeared in the *Germ*, the official organ of the Brotherhood, in 1850–1851. Slowly he accumulated a body of verse, which, as it circulated freely in manuscript, vitally influenced the poetry of the time long before his poems appeared in print. To his poetry he transferred the principles of his art, and by his practice won for himself the leadership of the "renascence of wonder" both in poetry and in painting. In 1860 he married a beautiful young woman of artistic talent to whom he was passionately attached. His wife died in 1862, and in his grief he buried his manuscript poems in the grave with her. In 1869–1870 they were recovered and published. They provoked an attack by Robert Buchanan, who charged Rossetti with fostering a "fleshly school" of poetry, a charge which the critic later retracted but not before the poet had suffered great depression from its manifest injustice. For several years he had been a sufferer from insomnia and an addict to the use of narcotics. Notwithstanding his naturally genial disposition, he became morose and despondent, shrank from society, and found ease only in the presence of his immediate family or with a few intimate friends, such as William Morris. In 1881 appeared his second and last volume of original poetry, *Ballads and Sonnets*. Meanwhile his health had given way. He repaired to Birchington-on-Sea, but derived no benefit from the change and died there in the spring of 1882. In both his poetry and painting he represents the culmination of the renascence of wonder. To go beyond him in either art would be to vanish into mysticism. With Blake, Coleridge, Shelley, and Keats he manifests a close kinship in the elements of vision, mystery, and a longing to recreate the romance-world of the past. The prevailing characteristic of his work, which he shares with other Pre-Raphaelites, is the realism with which he visualizes the unseen world. His style is marked by an unusual though fearless nicety of expression, a colorful loveliness of language, a luxuriant wealth of suggestive imagery, and a musical richness that is perennially haunting. His lyrics are exquisite, his romantic ballads have rarely been surpassed, and his sonnets are among the best in the language.

981a THE BLESSED DAMOZEL

Rossetti's intimate knowledge of Dante served him as a background for his conception in this poem, the figure of a deceased loved one in heaven bereft of her earthly lover. His immediate inspiration, however, was Poe's *Raven*, published in 1845, in which the poet presents the earthly lover yearning hopelessly for an ultimate reunion with his lost love. Rossetti declared it but remained for him to depict the longing of the beatified one for her mortal lover. In all her lineaments and impulses his damozel is earthly still. The poem was composed as early as 1847 or 1848, but was revised for the 1870 edition of his works, and included touches that are suggestive of his own bereavement.

981b 54. **The stars sang in their spheres,** an allusion to the fabled music of the spheres, by which order arose out of chaos.

87. **the Dove,** symbolizing the third member of the Trinity, the Holy Spirit.

982a 107 f. **Cecily, Gertrude,** etc., mediæval Christian saints.

MY SISTER'S SLEEP

Apparently this poem is without personal foundation in the poet's own life, but it has the highest poetical likeness of truth and contains all the pathos of actuality. It employs the stanza of *In Memoriam* with a genuine dirgelike effect.

983a SUDDEN LIGHT

That is, the light of recognition of some one loved in a former existence. On the general theme, cf. Vaughan's *The Retreat*, p. 382 and notes, and Wordsworth's *Ode on Intimations of Immortality*, p. 695 and notes.

THE WOODSPURGE

Woodspurge is a species of widely distributed weed or plant which exudes a viscid or milky fluid. The title is only incidental. The poem expresses the romantic conception of the receptiveness of the human mind to strange bits of knowledge, even in its abandonment to "perfect grief."

THE KING'S TRAGEDY

James I, king of Scotland, was slain at Perth on February 20, 1437, by Robert Graham (Græme) and his followers, in the manner described with striking fidelity in the poem. The events of the story are historical, as are also the personages represented, including the prophetess, the unfaithful Stewart, the "King of Love," and, of course, the heroine, Catherine Douglas (Kate Barlass). The details of the setting and the circumstances of the retribution are also actual. The poem is a great example of the historical ballad. The heroine tells the story in her old age to a group of "modern" lasses, among them, it may be, her own descendants.

8. **the palm-play ball**, a game like the modern tennis, in which the ball was struck by the hand instead of a racquet.

983b 11. **a true lord's head.** According to Rossetti, Kate was married to Alexander Lovell of Bolunnie.

16. **King Robert**, Robert III, who before his accession in 1390 was John, Earl of Carrick.

19. **James was pent.** Upon the death of his elder brother David, at the instigation of his uncle, the Duke of Albany, James was despatched to France for safety about 1405, but his vessel was intercepted by the English. He was taken into custody, and detained as a prisoner in various places in England for nearly twenty years.

22 ff. **the elder Prince**, etc. See note above.

26. **the Bass Rock fort**, a small island at the entrance to the Firth of Forth, where James embarked for France.

28. **Henry the subtle**, etc., Henry IV.

35 ff. **For once**, etc. James tells his own romance in the *King's Quair*. Like Palamon and Arcite in Chaucer's *Knight's Tale*, he fell in love with his "lady of royal blood" on sight from his prison window at Windsor. She was Joan Beaufort, the young daughter of the Earl of Somerset. The couple were married in Southwark in February, 1424, and were crowned at Scone in May of the same year.

41. **a sweeter song**, the *King's Quair*.

984a 68 ff. **England's wrong renewed**, *i.e.*, depredations by the English on the Scottish border and attempts to kidnap James's daughter while on her way to France. For these outrages James attacked Roxburgh in October, 1436, but withdrew his forces after a fifteen-day siege.

74 ff. **a tale of dread**, etc., the mutiny of a group of the barons.

984b 105. **Three Estates**, the nobility, the clergy, and the commonalty, according to the mediæval grades of society.

128. **country of the Wild Scots**, the Highlands, in northern Scotland.

141. **Perth**, on the river Tay in Perthshire, a partial seat of government at the time.

985a 176. **the Duchray and the Dhu**, a small stream west of Loch Lomond and a lake in Aberdeenshire.

179. **Inchkeith Isle**, a small island in the Firth of Forth.

183. **Links of Forth**, the land bordering on the River Forth near Stirling, Scotland.

986b 316 ff. **'Worship, ye lovers,'** etc. This and the later stanzas in the poem printed in italics are, as the poet tells us, adapted from the *King's Quair*.

987b 388. **pearl-tired**, pearl-attired, adorned with pearls.

414. **Voidee-cup**, a spiced wine served before retiring.

424. **brast**, broken, burst.

988a 462. **bitter dule to dree**, to suffer bitter sorrow.

469. **Aberdour**, a town on the north shore of the Firth of Forth, across from Edinburgh.

989a 566. **stanchion-hold**, a staple or socket for securing the bar which fastened the door.

992a THE HOUSE OF LIFE

These sonnets were composed during a period of thirty-three years, 1848–1881. It is impossible to determine the order of their succession or to make out their associations in the poet's own life. Undoubtedly many of them represent his most intimate experiences. They have all the appearance of reality characteristic of Shakespeare's sonnets and on attempted analysis prove quite as elusive. In their poetical qualities — their gorgeous word painting, their infinite suggestiveness of thought and imagery, and their seductive melody — they are most like his among all the great sonnet sequences of the language.

XVIII. GENIUS IN BEAUTY

993a 3. **Michael's hand,** etc., Michael Angelo, an allusion to his figures of Night, Day, Evening, Twilight, etc.

993b XLIX–LII. WILLOWWOOD

The term "Willowwood" is poetical for the Woodland of Weeping, suggestive of the "soul-struck widowhood" of Sonnet 3, l. 3.

994a 4

2. **wellaway,** sighing, lamentation.

995a LXI. SONG–THROE

The title means the poetical *urge* or *passion.* The sonnet is interesting as giving Rossetti's idea of the source and nature of poetry.

9. **The Song-god . . . the Sun-god,** Apollo.

996a CHIMES

This poem should be read for the sound effect of chimes, which it attempts to reproduce. Notable in it, to this end, is the alliteration, the selection and combination of vowels, the use and arrangement of heavy and light syllables, and the variations in tone from high to low and vice versa. It represents only a succession of poetical sensations; hence no consistent general meaning need be sought.

WILLIAM MORRIS

William Morris, born at Walthamstow, was the son of a discount broker. As a child he was delicate, but he very early showed a disposition to reading and study. By the time he was four he was familiar with the Waverley novels. By the time he was nine the outdoor life around Woodford, the family residence, and in Epping Forest near by brought him health and vigor. At nine he was placed in school at Walthamstow and four years later was transferred to Marlborough, where he developed a taste for architecture. His Oxford career, 1852–1855, was important chiefly for his association with a group of intellectual young men called "the Brotherhood," who held exalted views of the aims of life and who directed their own studies accordingly. At Oxford too he had his initiation into poetry. The story is told that three of his friends one evening listened in his room to a reading of one of his compositions, a "perfectly original" and "truly striking and beautiful" poem, *The Willow and the Red Cliff.* To their expressions of favor he replied, "If this is poetry, it is very easy to write." Thereafter poetry was a source of pleasure to him, although it never became a preoccupation. He thought of entering the ministry, but abandoned the idea for social work and decided to become an architect. In 1858 his *Defence of Guenevere* appeared but attracted little attention. Meanwhile through a magazine venture he had become acquainted with Rossetti. By 1860 his "house beautiful" at Upton in Kent was ready for occupancy by him and his young wife, but the location proved unhealthful, and a few years later he removed to town. His next venture was the formation of a company, with Rossetti, Burne-Jones, and others as "craftsmen," for the manufacture of house furnishings and interior decorations. The company prospered under his management, and he was forced to give much of his attention to business, but he still found time for literature. His *Life and Death of Jason* appeared in 1867 and was followed in 1868–1870 by his master work, *The Earthly Paradise.* By this time he was recognized as one of the foremost English poets of the age, a reputation which was amply maintained by *Sigurd the Volsung* in 1876. In his later years he was much interested in social work, but continued to write. One of his last great ventures was the establishment in Hammersmith of the Kelmscott Press for beautifying and improving the art of printing, the crowning achievement of which was the Kelmscott edition of Chaucer, issued only a few months before his death. He wrote much prose fiction, but he was preëminently a narrative poet. Chaucer was his model, and he always wrote of remote times and places. His works lack the wider human reaches, but the spirit of beauty breathes through all his productions in literature and art. He composed with ease and despite his manifold activities produced extensively, but, notwithstanding his facility, he wrote sufficiently well to give him a high place among the poets of the century.

997a AN APOLOGY

This apology is prefixed to the cycle of stories called *The Earthly Paradise.* "Certain gentlemen and mariners of Norway" set sail to find the Earthly Paradise. After many years they reach a "Western land" inhabited by descendants of the ancient Greeks, who entertain them with semimonthly feasts for a year. At each feast a tale is told, alternately between the inhabitants and the wanderers. The stories of the former are from Greek mythology and those of the latter are of Norse or Romance origin. *Atalanta's Race*, a rendition of the well-known myth, is the first of the twenty-four stories making up the cycle.

997b 25. **the ivory gate,** *i.e.*, of the dwelling of Morpheus, through which issued dreams that were not true.

ATALANTA'S RACE

998b 63. **the Fleet-foot One,** Mercury, or Hermes, the messenger of the gods.

1000a 184. **the sea-born one,** Venus.

1000b 208. **Adonis' bane,** the wild boar. Adonis was slain by an enraged wild boar which he had wounded.

211. **Argive cities,** cities of Argolis in southern Greece.

1001a 275. **the threeformed goddess,** Diana, or Artemis.

1002a 340. **sleepy garland,** a wreath of poppies.

352. **Argos,** a town in Argolis.

1004b 534. **Diana's raiment,** the symbol of virginity.

535. **Saturn's clime,** a fabled age of innocence and plenty, which prevailed in Saturn's reign.

ALGERNON CHARLES SWINBURNE

The last of the great Victorian poets, Algernon Charles Swinburne, came of distinguished ancestry on both sides of his family. His father was an English admiral, and his mother was the daughter of the Earl of Ashburnham. He was born in London, but his infancy and childhood were spent partly on his grandfather's estate in Northumberland and partly on that of his father in the Isle of Wight. His associations with the latter place are doubtless responsible for the atmosphere of the sea that pervades his poetry. After some private tutoring he went to Eton for five years and passed to Oxford for three more, but left without a degree. At the university he developed a passionate love for Greek literature. The year of his leaving, 1860, he published his remarkable youthful dramas, *The Queen Mother* and *Rosamond.* During a brief stay in Italy he met the aged poet Walter Savage Landor, who was already a potent influence in his work. In 1865 his drama, *Atalanta in Calydon*, replete with Hellenism, appeared; and the following year he published his *Poems and Ballads*, by which, though severely criticized for their revolt against moral conventions, he established himself as one of the foremost poets of the age and the leader of a younger group, to whom he was both master and prophet. By the removal of the family to Holmwood in the Thames valley he was brought into contact with the literary life of London, and became a vital part of the Pre-Raphaelite movement then in full career. With his *Songs before Sunrise*, 1871, echoing Victor Hugo but displaying his own independent manner and spirit, he became a poet of revolt against political and ecclesiastical conditions. The next decade is celebrated for his second series of *Poems and Ballads,* 1878, which contains some of his best poems; for the completion of his Mary Stuart trilogy of plays; and for the production of some of his most remarkable critical studies. After 1880 his life was uneventful. He continued to write poetry, which maintained but added little to his fame, and he was prolific in criticism. The collected edition of his *Poems and Dramas* begun in 1904, an important event in itself, seems to close the great period of creative Victorian poetry. He died in London in the spring of 1909. He is a master of phrase in prose and verse. In poetry he is one of the great metrical geniuses. Probably more than any other English poet, he was able to maintain a high and exuberant poetic level by sheer richness of melody and imaginative suggestiveness without much wealth of thought content. His long poems, like classical music, are recognized and admired but will never be popular. He is perhaps best in a few great lyrics. In his criticism he is creative and impressionistic. He rarely touches a subject without illuminating it; but he is often inaccurate, his taste falters at times, and he is usually too subject to personal likes and dislikes for sane judgment and sustained good sense.

1006b A SONG IN TIME OF ORDER

Louis Napoleon became emperor of France in 1852. The poem voices the sentiments of three "red" liberalists against his régime as representing political tyranny and oppression. It echoes also the failure during the period of some popular movements in central Europe.

34. **The old red,** the flag of the revolution which resulted in the French republic in 1848.

1007a 38. **Pope.** Pope Pius IX was driven from Rome by the Italian statesman Garibaldi, but was restored by the aid of the French army in 1849.

50. **Cayenne,** the capital of French Guiana, a place of banishment for political prisoners.

50. **the Austrian whips,** an allusion to Austrian oppression in Italy.

BEFORE THE BEGINNING OF YEARS

A chorus in *Atalanta in Calydon.* In the religious views expressed in his poetry Swinburne is often frankly pagan.

1008b ROCOCO

The title implies a rich and expensive style of ornamentation in art, popular in the seventeenth and eighteenth centuries, but the term is usually used contemptuously of the style as a meaningless system of conglomerate symbols in works of art.

1009b THE GARDEN OF PROSERPINE

According to the Greek conception, the groves of Proserpine formed a realm of shades near the entrance to the underworld. The poet uses the idea to express "that brief total pause of passion and of thought, when the spirit . . . thirsts only after the perfect sleep."

1010a HERTHA

Hertha was the ancient Teutonic divinity of the Earth, but Swinburne's conception is much vaster — an all-enveloping, all-producing, all-evolving Whole. He said of the poem, "Of all I have done I rate 'Hertha' highest as a single piece."

1012b A FORSAKEN GARDEN

The scene of this poem is East Dene on the Isle of Wight, where the poet spent much of his youth.

ARTHUR HUGH CLOUGH

Arthur Hugh Clough was born in Liverpool, of good Welsh and Yorkshire stock. His father was a cotton merchant. His childhood was spent mostly in Charleston, South Carolina, but his education was English. In 1829 he came under the influence of the great Dr. Arnold at Rugby, and in 1837 he entered Oxford as a scholar, where he was a contemporary and friend of Matthew Arnold. He was influenced greatly by the High Church Movement, then in full sway under the leadership of Newman. He remained in the university as a fellow of Oriel College until 1848, when, under the conviction that further tenure was inconsistent with his growing unorthodoxy, he resigned his position. He tried his fortune at tutoring and writing in Cambridge, Massachusetts, for a short while, but returned to England. In 1853 he was appointed to a position in the Education Office and led an official life for his remaining years. In 1860 his health failed. He tried a change of climate, but died at Florence late in the following year. His pastoral poem, the *Bothie of Toper-na-Vuolick,* appeared in 1848. A year later he was joint author, with Thomas Burbidge, of *Ambervalia,* a collection of shorter poems of various dates. Some idyls, lyrics, and elegiac pieces make up the best of his remaining poetry. He wrote no great amount, and he never led a wholly detached literary life. He has melody and strength of thought but possesses little originality, and to-day his moral tone seems rather severely conventional. It is no aspersion of his character or talent to say that his best service to English poetry was his friendship with Matthew Arnold, which, after his death, inspired *Thyrsis,* one of the great elegies.

1014a QUA CURSUM VENTUS

The title in paraphrase means, "As the wind blows, so the vessel takes its course." The Latin words form part of a line in Virgil's *Æneid,* Bk. III, l. 269. The poem reflects Clough's break with William George Ward, 1812–1882, a religious controversialist who became a Catholic in 1845.

CHARLES KINGSLEY

Charles Kingsley was born at Holne in Devonshire. His early life was spent in the Fen country and in north Devonshire. He was greatly impressed by the scenery of both districts, bits of which he vividly described in his writings later. He was educated at private schools, at King's College in London, and at Cambridge. In 1842 he became curate and soon afterward rector of Eversley in Hampshire, where he continued to reside for the remaining thirty-three years of his life. His professorship of modern history at Cambridge from 1860 to 1869 is celebrated mainly for his controversy with J. H. Newman, in which Kingsley was completely discomfited. He became chaplain to Queen Victoria and canon of Chester and Westminster, and died at Eversley in 1875. He was not a scholar, but he had wide and varied knowledge, and by his books and personality he exercised a great influence upon the thought of his time. He is mainly a novelist. *Alton Locke* and *Yeast* are great novels of purpose, and *Hypatia* and *Westward Ho!* rank as highly in historical fiction. He wrote little poetry, but some of his lyrics are memorable, and in his longer *Andromeda* he perhaps succeeded best among English poets in the attempt to naturalize the classical hexameter in English.

1014b THE SANDS OF DEE

The River Dee flows through northern Wales and Cheshire into the Irish Sea.

1015a WHEN ALL THE WORLD IS YOUNG

In *Water Babies*, one of the great classics for children.

SYDNEY DOBELL

Sydney Dobell was born the son of a wine merchant at Cranbrook, Kent. His mother was a woman of much strength and force of character. He was educated privately and became an ardent liberal. In a number of his early poems he displayed a passionate zeal for political reform. In 1855 he produced a succession of sonnets on the Crimean War, followed a year later by a volume on the same theme entitled *England in War Time.* Ill health made it necessary for him to spend his winters abroad, and in 1869 he met with an accident in a fall from a horse, which made him an invalid for the rest of his life. His death occurred at Barton End, Gloucestershire, in 1874. He was prominent in what has been called the "spasmodic school" of poetry, which was distinguished by a dissatisfaction with the conditions of existence, a sense of the futility of human effort and of the inequitable distribution of rewards for struggle, a skepticism regarding accepted religion, and a restless striving after the impossible. In style the writers of the spasmodic school are characterized by an excessive use of metaphor and a general extravagance of language, but they often show freshness and originality. In his own poetry Dobell is very uneven, but at times he attains an excellence that is not often surpassed.

AMERICA

At the time of the Crimean War, 1853–1856, which inspired much of Dobell's poetry, it was thought that opinion in the United States was hostile to England.

1015b 14. **Helena and Hermia.** Shakespeare's *Midsummer Night's Dream.*

1016a HOME WOUNDED

Experiences in the recent World War give the subject and sentiments of this poem a renewed interest at the present time.

EDWARD FITZGERALD

Edward Fitzgerald was born at Bredfield in Suffolk. While he was a boy the family lived abroad for a few years. On their return in 1821 he was placed in school at Bury St. Edmunds. Five years later he went to Cambridge. He adopted no profession and lived a secluded life in various places in his native section until his death. He was devoted to flowers, music, and literature, but allowed his friends Tennyson and Thackeray to outstrip him far in creative work. His first book, *Euphranor,* 1851, in platonic dialogue, echoes his Cambridge life. After some studies and translations in Spanish poetry he turned to Persian, from which he translated his *Rubaiyat*, 1859. It appeared anonymously in pamphlet form and at first attracted no attention. The following year Rossetti discovered it, as did Swinburne and Lord Houghton soon afterward. In 1868 Fitzgerald was induced to print a revised edition. His greatly enlarged final revision appeared in 1879. After 1861 his greatest interest was in the sea. Aboard his own vessel or among his books and flowers he grew old and died asleep at Merton in Norfolk in 1883. The melody, profundity of thought, and wealth of imagery of his great philosophical song have made it one of the immortal poems of the language.

1020b THE RUBAIYAT OF OMAR KHAYYAM

Omar Khayyam (Omar the Tentmaker) was a Persian poet and astronomer of the late eleventh and early twelfth centuries. Fitzgerald says: "The original Rubáiyát are independent Stanzas, consisting each of four Lines of equal, though varied, Prosody; sometimes all rhyming, but oftener (as here imitated) the third line a blank. Somewhat as in the Greek Alcaic, where the penultimate line seems to lift and suspend the Wave that falls

meter next to last

over in the last. As usual with such kind of Oriental Verse, the Rubáiyát follow one another according to Alphabetic Rhyme — a strange succession of Grave and Gay. Those here selected are strung into something of an Eclogue, with perhaps a less than equal proportion of the 'Drink and make-merry,' which (genuine or not) occurs over frequently in the Original. Either way, the Result is sad enough: saddest perhaps when most ostentatiously merry: more apt to move Sorrow than Anger toward the old Tentmaker, who, after vainly endeavoring to unshackle his Steps from Destiny, and to catch some authentic Glimpse of TOMORROW, fell back upon TODAY (which has outlasted so many Tomorrows!) as the only Ground he had got to stand upon, however momentarily slipping from under his Feet." Fitzgerald's translation, in no sense literal, is one of liberal interpretation and free paraphrase.

5. **False morning,** a transient light on the horizon about an hour before the true dawn; a well-known phenomenon in the East (Fitzgerald).

13. **the New Year.** The Persian new year began with the vernal equinox.

15 f. **the White Hand of Moses,** etc. Cf. Exodus iv, 6. According to a Persian version, Moses' hand was not *leprous*, but "*white* as our May-blossom in spring." The Persians believed also that Jesus' healing power resided in his breath.

17. **Iram,** a garden planted by King Shaddad, now obliterated somewhere in the sands of Arabia.

18. **Jamshyd,** a legendary Persian king. His seven-ringed divining cup typified the seven heavens, seven planets, seven seas, etc.

1021a 21. **David,** etc. Pehlevi was the old heroic language long since obsolete. David's tongue is forgotten, but the nightingale still cries in ancient Pehlevi, "Wine!" etc.

29. **Naishápúr,** a village in Persia, formerly one of the four great cities of Khorassan; Omar's native place.

36. **Kaikobád,** founder of the Kaianian dynasty, the most celebrated of all the dynasties of ancient Persia. According to legend, he was placed on the throne by the help of Rustum (see note to p. 963b).

38. **Kaikhosrú,** etc. See note to p. 966a, l. 223.

39. **Zál and Rustum.** The latter was the Hercules of Persia; the former was his father. See Matthew Arnold's *Sohrab and Rustum*, p. 963 ff.

40. **Hátim,** a well-known type of Oriental Generosity (Fitzgerald).

44. **Mahmúd,** the sultan, a title. Mahmud the Great, *ca.* 971–1030, was one of the great Mohammedan conquerors.

1021b 70. **The Courts,** etc. Jamshyd's capital was Persepolis.

71. **Bahrám,** a Sassanian sovereign who sank in a swamp while pursuing a wild ass.

75. **Hyacinth.** See note to *Lycidas*, l. 344.

1022a 122. **Saturn,** the lord of the seventh heaven.

1022b 153 ff. **a drop . . . we throw,** etc., an allusion to the custom of throwing a little wine on the ground before drinking. To Omar it signified: "The liquor is not lost, but sinks into the ground to refresh the dust of some poor Wine-worshiper foregone."

169. **the Angel of the darker Drink,** Death, or Azräel, who, according to one tradition, performs his mission "by holding to the nostril an apple from the Tree of Life."

1023a 179. **Ferrásh,** a servant, camp follower.

183. **Sáki,** wine bearer.

198. **Alif,** the first letter of certain ancient alphabets.

203. **from Máh to Máhi,** *i.e.*, from fish to moon.

1023b 225. **my Computations.** Omar was one of eight learned men employed to reform the calendar under the sultanate of Malik Shah.

234. **Two and Seventy,** etc., the number of religions which were "supposed to divide the world."

237 ff. **Mahmúd,** etc., an allusion to Sultan Mahmud, conqueror of "India and its people."

277 ff. **The Ball,** etc., the game of polo, of ancient Persian origin.

1024b 299. **Parwin and Mushtarí,** the Pleiades and Jupiter. See note next above.

302. **Dervish,** an Islamitish devotee.

1025a 326. **Ramazán,** the fasting month of the Moslems.

346. **a Súfi,** an adherent of a pantheistic religious sect in Persia.

358. **The little Moon,** etc., the new moon announcing the end of the month of fasting.

360. **the Porter's shoulder-knot,** etc., *i.e.*, from bearing in wine.

CHRISTINA ROSSETTI

Christina Rossetti, the sister of Dante Gabriel, was born in London. Her father was an Italian poet and a liberal in politics, and she grew up in the mixed society of Italian exiles and English eccentrics who frequented his house. When she was seventeen, a volume of her *Verse* was privately printed, and at twenty she contributed some of her finest lyrics to the Pre-Raphaelite organ, the *Germ*. After her father's death in 1854 she suffered from poverty and ill health, and developed a deeply religious nature, which was only intensified by affliction and disease in her later life. *The Goblin Market* appeared in 1862 and was received with enthusiasm. In 1866 she published *The Prince's Progress.* A third volume, showing a loss of power, appeared in 1881, from which time on she produced little except religious prose. Her last years were spent in retirement and broken health in Bloomsbury, where she died in 1894. Her gifts were lyrical. Her poetry shows the narrow range of her sympathies and experiences, but it often possesses genuine music, and sometimes it rises to pure splendor. It is pervaded by a tone of austerity and sanctity, and a spirit of melancholy reverie envelops the whole.

JAMES THOMSON

James Thomson, the second of the name in English poetry (see p. 540 ff.), was born at Port Glasgow in Scotland. His father was a sailor who suffered from ill health. On the death of his mother, a deeply religious woman, when he was seven, he was placed in an orphan asylum. In 1850 he entered the model school of the Military Asylum in Chelsea, from which he emerged an assistant army schoolmaster. At a garrison near Cork in Ireland he fell ardently in love with a beautiful and cultivated girl, who returned his passion, but whose sudden death two years later "prostrated him in mind and body." Thenceforth his life was one of gloom and poverty rarely relieved by sunlight or better fortune. In 1862 he was dismissed from the army for a trival act of insubordination and became successively an attorney's clerk, a secretary to a mining company, a war correspondent in Spain, and a free lance in journalism. He maintained connections with several magazines, chiefly the *National Reformer*, to which he contributed his masterpiece, *The City of Dreadful Night*, in 1874. From 1866 to the end of his life he lived alone in London. His intemperate habits and his inveterate tendency to moral gloom and pessimism denied him a successful career. The publication of his *City of Dreadful Night and Other Poems* in 1880 commanded some attention. He died in London in 1882. The nature of his writing shows a sympathetic kinship with De Quincey. His lyrical gift was genuine, and his lighter pieces are often gay and sunny, as one side of his life was genial. His most characteristic poetry, however, touches the limits of an absolute despair. Its merits lie in its imaginative power, in its awe-inspiring splendor, and in its haunting music.

1027a THE CITY OF DREADFUL NIGHT

The City of Dreadful Night is of course imaginary, the City of Despair, total and absolute. The mood portrayed, common to humanity, though in less intensified form, was greatly emphasized in Thomson's own character; the subject was congenial to his tastes; and on the basis of its ordinary human association, he built, with his great imaginative powers, his structure, forbidding as it is, just as other poets have reared other structures to typify in exaggerated vein other moods and passions. The poem is a mere phantasy of only a possibly conceivable mental state, and is to be read without thought of any moral purport or ethical significance whatever. It is one of the great imaginative creations of the language.

1028b 136. **God's-acre,** a cemetery.

1031a 317. **Pandora's box.** See note to p. 279b, l. 8.

1037b 838. **the pure sad artist,** Albrecht Dürer, 1471–1528, a famous German painter and engraver. His "Melancholia" is one of his most celebrated engravings.

THOMAS EDWARD BROWN

Thomas Edward Brown, the sixth of ten children in the home of a clergyman, was born at Douglas on the Isle of Man. When he was two, the family removed to Kirk Braddan near by, where his youth was spent amid pleasant surroundings. After some local schooling and private instruction, chiefly by the elder Brown, he went to King William's College and in 1849 entered Oxford. In 1854 he attained the highest honor of an Oxford career, a fellowship at Oriel, and was ordained deacon; but not taking kindly "to the life of an Oxford Fellow" he returned to his native island as vice-principal of King William's. During his three years' tenure of a head mastership at Gloucester he met and influenced deeply the young poet W. E. Henley (see p. 1043). In 1864 he joined the teaching staff of Clifton College and for twenty-eight years led there a kind of twofold existence, publicly living the life of a really great teacher and schoolman, and privately following his literary inclinations and writing his poetry. In 1892 his health gave way, and he retired to the Isle of Man. His recovery was rapid, and the remaining five years were all his own, to follow happily at will the literary vocation which he had long felt belonged to him by nature. He died suddenly while delivering an address to the boys of his old school. His works include *Fo'c's'le Yarns*, 1881; *The Doctor*, etc., 1887;

The Manx Witch, etc., 1889; *Old John*, etc., 1893; and his *Collected Poems*, 1900, 1901. He was a mystic, like Vaughan and Blake, though in a far less pronounced degree than the latter. His poetry is not always clear, and his expression often overbalances his thought. He shows a command of both humor and pathos, and with his range and variety in form and method, as well, he is never monotonous. His dialect pieces suffer from being written in a language that is in itself unbeautiful. His lyrics are the best known of his works, but one or two of his stories should have a very high rank in English narrative poetry.

1039a IBANT OBSCURÆ

The title means, "They passed in darkness."

12. **Andromeda,** the daughter of Cepheus and Cassiope. On account of her mother's pride she was bound to a rock to be devoured by a sea monster, but was freed and married by Perseus. She was made a constellation by Athena.

1039b OPIFEX

The artificer or maker represented in the title is Brown himself. The poem is therefore interesting as his estimate of his own talent.

THE VOICES OF NATURE

1040a 6. **Damnonian Briton,** a Briton from ancient Cornwall.

17. **bourdon,** a bass stop in an organ or harmonium.

27. **dulse,** a kind of seaweed.

JUVENTA PERENNIS

The title means, "Perennial Youth."

ARTHUR O'SHAUGHNESSY

Arthur O'Shaughnessy was born in London and spent his life there. At seventeen he became a transcriber in the library of the British Museum. Two years later he was transferred and made an assistant in the department of natural history. His constitution was never vigorous, and he succumbed to the effects of a chill at the age of thirty-seven. Despite his work and associations, his inclinations were all literary. His *Epic of Women* appeared in 1870 and *Music and Moonlight* in 1874. During his last seven years he published no volume of poetry, but *Songs of a Worker* was issued posthumously in 1881, the year of his death. His themes are never important, and he rarely has real dignity of thought; but with his genuine song-gift he produced some melodies that are unforgettable.

1040b ODE

19. **Nineveh.** Cf. Genesis x, 11 f., and the book of Jonah.

20. **Babel.** Cf. Genesis xi, 1 ff.

ROBERT LOUIS STEVENSON

Robert Louis Stevenson was the only child of the civil engineer Thomas Stevenson, and was born in Edinburgh. His health was frail from infancy. He was educated mainly in Edinburgh and prepared to follow the family profession. The outdoor life suited him, but it overtaxed his physical endurance; hence in 1871 he gave up the career of engineer and went to Edinburgh to study law. He was called to the bar in 1875, but never practiced. Meanwhile he was working assiduously at a better style of writing and began publishing some original essays in magazines. His *Inland Voyage*, 1878, and *Travels with a Donkey*, 1879, were the results of a wandering existence in France, Germany, and Scotland, three or four years before in search of health. In August, 1879, he came to California to renew his suit to, and the following year to marry, a Mrs. Osborne whom he had met in France several years before. The next few years are a record of migration from place to place in England, Scotland, and southern Europe, to improve his health. His first popular work, *Treasure Island*, was published in 1883. In 1885 appeared his *Child's Garden of Verses* and in 1887 his volume of lyrical poems called *Underwoods*. In the latter year he left England on a long voyage in search of health, never to return. In the mountains of New York State he wrote most of his *Master of Ballantrae* and many of his best essays. In the summer of 1888 he crossed the continent to San Francisco and set out on a voyage in the Pacific. After several months of cruising he settled in Samoa, one of the Gilbert Islands, and spent there the last four years of his life, amid picturesque surroundings and in better health than he had ever known. He lived as an island chieftain but continued his writing to the end. He died suddenly at the close of the year 1894 and was buried on a peak overlooking the ocean. His adventurous life and engaging personality to some extent have increased his literary reputation. By his talent and remarkable influence he is, however, one of the important figures in Victorian literature. He resembles Steele and Goldsmith in the variety of his work, and he equals them in the general excellence of the whole. He revived the romantic novel; he is a great essayist, a master of the short story, and a popular poet. He is a past master of style and a romanticist in everything he wrote.

1041b REQUIEM

This is Stevenson's own fitting epitaph of himself. It is carved on his tomb in Samoa.

1042a HEATHER ALE

This poem, the author tells us, is based on a Galloway legend.

23. **Brewsters,** brewers.

WILLIAM ERNEST HENLEY

William Ernest Henley was a native of Gloucester. In the Crypt Grammar School of that city he had the singular good fortune to come under the influence of the poet T. E. Brown (see p. 1039 and introductory note), whose kindness to him, at a time when he needed it most, he repaid with a life-long admiration and in later years with the stanch support of his pen. He was afflicted with a physical infirmity and at twenty-five was lodged in a hospital in Edinburgh. While confined there he contributed to the *Cornhill Magazine* his poems on his hospital experiences. A visit from Stevenson at the time resulted in a warm friendship between the two men. In 1877 he went to London and became an editor. In 1888 his *Book of Verse* appeared, followed in 1892 by his *Song of the Sword*, or *London Voluntaries*, as it was called in the second edition the year after. He published collections of verse in 1898 and again in 1901. Meanwhile he had written much prose and engaged in dramatic authorship with Stevenson. He died at Woking in Surrey in the summer of 1903. His prose represents a high order of journalism. His poetry is celebrated for its reflection of the author's indomitable courage under the severest trials.

1043b OUT OF THE NIGHT, etc.

This, the most popular of Henley's poems, is also known by the title, *Invictus*, " Unconquered."

JOHN HENRY NEWMAN

John Henry Newman was the son of a banker and was born in London. At the age of seven he entered a private school at Ealing, where he was distinguished by his studious habits and good conduct rather than by the usual boyish interest in sports. An important event in his life was his conversion under Calvinistic influences at fifteen, his last year at school. In 1817 he entered Oxford and in 1822 won the enviable honor of an Oriel fellowship. He was ordained in 1824, presented to a curacy at Oxford, and began to write. While on a trip to southern Europe and Italy in 1832–1833, he was profoundly impressed by his visit to Rome. During these years he wrote most of the short poems appearing in the *Lyra Apostolica* as well as his beautiful hymn, *Lead Kindly Light*. In July, 1833, he heard at Oxford Keble's sermon on " National Apostasy," which he regarded as the definite beginning of the Oxford Movement. Later in the same month an organization was effected by a group of high churchmen, not including Newman, to fight for " the apostolic succession and the integrity of the Prayer-Book." A few weeks later Newman, apparently on his own account, began his *Tracts of the Times*, whence the movement came to be called " Tractarian." The aim was to secure a definite basis of doctrine and discipline for the Church of England, in its threatened disruption and desertion by the high church party. Newman became editor of the *British Critic* and through its columns and in lectures defended the Anglican Church as a *via media* " between Romanism and popular Protestantism." With his *Tract 90* in 1841 he ended his celebrated series, by which time he had come to doubt the Anglican position. In 1843 he published a retraction of his strictures against the Catholic Church, and two years later he was formally received into its fold. In 1846 he went to Rome, where he was ordained priest and awarded the D.D. degree by the Pope. On his return to England he settled at Edgbaston near Birmingham, where, except for his official years in Ireland, he lived in comparative seclusion the rest of his life. In 1854 he became rector of the new Catholic University at Dublin, but lacking a practical talent for organization he retired after a tenure of four years. The experience, however, resulted in his volume of lectures called the *Idea of a University*, containing probably his best work. His controversy with Kingsley (see p. 1014 and introductory note), in which he came off triumphant, gave him the needed opportunity for his *Apologia pro Vita Sua*, published serially, in which he justified his change to Catholicism. In 1879 he was made cardinal from simple priest — a procedure that was in itself unusual, — and the act was applauded by Catholics and Protestants throughout Christendom. He died at the Oratory in Edgbaston in 1890. As a preacher and controversialist, he exercised a powerful influence. He had genuine poetical gifts, but his most congenial medium was prose, in which he is recognized as one of the great modern masters. His style is clear, direct, straightforward, full of thought and varied with the finest distinctions, acutely logical, grand in simplicity, and always inspired by a genuine sincerity.

1044a WHAT IS A UNIVERSITY

40. **litera scripta**, written letters.

1044b 17. **The Sibyl**, the Cumean Sibyl, an ancient prophetess who wrote her predictions on the leaves of trees. See note to p. 1099b, l. 64.

24 f. **sermons in stones, etc.** *As You Like It* II, i, 16.

1046a 26. **beau monde**, the world of fashion.

31. **au courant**, up-to-date.

1047b 45. **St. Irenæus**, an early Christian saint, Bishop of Lyons, probably martyred in the reign of Septimius Severus.

52. **St. Anthony.** See note to p. 89b, l. 44, and p. 1119a, l. 1 ff.

1048a 2. **Didymus**, 309?–394?, surnamed "the Blind," an ecclesiastical writer and teacher of Alexandria.

1048b 20. **Patrick**, *ca.* 389–*ca.* 461, the patron saint of Ireland.

JOHN RUSKIN

John Ruskin was the only child of two Scottish cousins and was born in London. His father was a wine merchant, a man of great ability and probity, who provided a cultured home in which to rear his gifted son. The boy's early years were passed under faithful nursing and care. Throughout his adolescence he was favored with the means and opportunity of travel about England and Scotland and on the continent, in search of everything that was beautiful in nature and art. No other writer in English literature ever had better æsthetic training. His literary education, mainly private, was irregular and on the whole unsuccessful. He early became a bookworm and at a tender age showed an inclination to write. His Oxford career was marked by one signal triumph, and one only, the Newdigate prize for poetry. He was graduated in 1842. Meanwhile his real study had been, and continued to be, nature, art, and literature. Long previously he had begun his career as a writer with some nature studies and art criticism. His first great work, however, was *Modern Painters*, the first volume of which appeared in 1843 and produced a sensation. By parental arrangement in 1848 he was married to a brilliant social beauty, but the union was dissolved after her departure from his home in 1854. In his *Modern Painters* he presented the thesis that truth is the standard of excellence in art and that nature is the source of truth and of inspiration. He expanded his ideas to include other arts in *The Seven Lamps of Architecture*, 1849, and *The Stones of Venice*, 1851–1853. With the last volume of *Modern Painters* in 1860 his work on art subjects strictly as such came to an end. The last forty years of his life were given up to enlarging his doctrines in a long series of lectures, letters, serial articles, essays, and the like, on social, industrial, educational, moral, and religious topics. Better known among his works of this kind are *Unto this Last*, 1861; *Sesame and Lilies*, 1865; *The Crown of Wild Olive*, 1866; and the expansive *Fors Clavigera*, 1871–1884. In 1869 he was elected Slade professor of art at Oxford and filled the position with distinction for many years. In 1871 he purchased the property of Brantwood on Coniston Water in the Lake District and resided there for the rest of his life. His last years were loaded with honors from all sources. He died from influenza at Brantwood in 1900. His literary work, with its evident culture, its high ethical tone, its rich phrase and rosy imagery, and its varied and suggestive thought content, is an important part of the great prose heritage of the language.

TRAFFIC

This essay was first delivered as a lecture in the town hall in Bradford, Yorkshire, and afterward published in *The Crown of Wild Olive*.

1049b 50 f. **Teniers**, etc., David Teniers, 1610–1690, a famous Flemish realistic painter. Cf. his "Peasants Playing Dice," 1646.

1050a 8. **Turner.** Joseph Mallord William Turner, 1775–1851, a great English landscape painter. He inspired Ruskin's *Modern Painters*.

38 f. **Newgate Calendar**, a publication named from Newgate prison in London. It gives accounts of sensational crimes.

1050b 32 ff. **'They carved,'** etc. Scott's *Lay of the Last Minstrel*, I, 31 ff.

1051a 39. **Armstrongs**, big guns, from the name of the manufacturers, Armstrong, in England.

44. **black eagles**, symbols of the Austrian arms.

1051b 19. **Inigo Jones**, 1578–1652, a distinguished English architect, designer of Whitehall Palace in London.

20. **Sir Christopher Wren,** 1632–1723, a great English architect, designer of St. Paul's Cathedral in London.

1052a 2 ff. **Hawes . . . Brough . . . Wharnside.** These places lie along the Penine hills between Bradford in West Yorkshire, where the lecture was delivered, and Carlisle, the chief city of Cumberland.

10 ff. **a dream,** etc. Cf. Genesis xxviii, 10 ff.

45 ff. **' Thou, when thou prayest,'** etc. Cf. Matthew vi, 5 f.

1053b 26 ff. **to the Jews,** etc. Cf. 1 Corinthians i, 23.

37 ff. **Athenaic symbols,** etc. The representation here is of the Athena *Parthenos* by Phidias.

42. **Gorgon, on her shield.** See note to *Comus*, l. 447.

1054b 2. **Tetzel,** Johann Tetzel, the seller of papal indulgences who provoked the ire of Martin Luther.

5 f. **bals masqués,** masked balls.

13. **Revivalist,** *i.e.*, of classical architecture, as represented in the palace of Versailles and the Vatican.

1055a 28 f. **strong evidence,** etc. Matthew xxi, 12 f.

1055b 49 f. **Perdix fovit,** etc., the partridge has fostered what she brought not forth. (The Vulgate, Jeremiah, xvii, 11.)

1056a 1. **Gennesaret.** The reference may be to Matthew viii, 28–34, particularly the last verse. Gennesaret is a beautiful and fertile district west of the Sea of Galilee.

21. **Agora,** market place.

50 ff. **an Olympus,** etc. See note to p. 305b, l. 14 f. Cf. *Hamlet* V, i, 305.

1056b 13. **Plutus,** the god of riches.

1057b 8 ff. **Solomon made gold,** etc. Cf. 1 Kings x, 14 ff.

37. **Bolton priory,** a beautiful old abbey in the West Riding of Yorkshire.

41 f. **' men may come,'** etc. See Tennyson's *The Brook*, p. 900.

1058b 32 f. **plain of Dura,** in the province of Babylon, where Nebuchadnezzar set up "an image of gold." Cf. Daniel iii, 1.

ROBERT LOUIS STEVENSON

1059a ÆS TRIPLEX

The title of this essay is taken from Horace (*Odes*, I, iii). It means, literally, "threefold brass."

36. **dule trees,** trees used as gallows.

1060a 4 f. **blue peter,** a blue flag with a white square in the center, used to indicate immediate sailing. The truck is a cap at the top of the mast or flagstaff.

37. **Balaclava.** See Tennyson's *Charge of the Light Brigrade*, p. 898 and notes.

41 f. **Curtius,** etc. According to a Roman legend, a gulf opened in the Forum in 362 B.C., and the soothsayers declared it could be stopped only by the sacrifice of the city's most valuable possession, whereupon, Marcus Curtius, a patriotic youth, fully armed and mounted, plunged into the abyss, which immediately closed.

52. **the Derby,** *i.e.*, the Derby races.

1060b 1. **the deified Caligula,** Gaius Cæsar Caligula, A.D. 12–41, one of the cruelest of the Roman emperors. He claimed divine honors and instituted a priesthood to attend to his worship. The Prætorian guards were a special body of picked soldiers in his service.

3. **Baiæ bay.** See note to p. 767b, l. 32.

1061b 4. **the Commander's statue.** In the story of Don Juan, the famous rake accepts an invitation from a statue to supper.

25. **bag's end,** etc., a *cul-de-sac*.

41. **our respected lexicographer,** Dr. Samuel Johnson.

1062b 1 f. **' A peerage,'** etc. Before the battle of the Nile, Nelson is said to have exclaimed to his officers, "Before this time to-morrow, I shall have gained a peerage or Westminster Abbey."

1063a PULVIS ET UMBRA

The title means, "Dust and Shadow."

1065a 14. **Assiniboia,** a small town in Saskatchewan, Canada.

MATTHEW ARNOLD

THE STUDY OF POETRY

This essay formed the introduction to *The English Poets*, edited by T. H. Ward in 1880. For an estimate of the value of Arnold's test of "high seriousness" as a criterion of poetic excellence, see introductory note to p. 961b. *The Study of Poetry* should be read by all persons who desire to read poetry intelligently.

1066a 36. **these words,** quoted, with slight differences, from Arnold's Introduction to *The Hundred Greatest Men*, 1879.

1066b 30 ff. **' the impassioned expression,'** etc., quoted from the Preface to the *Lyrical Ballads*, p. 821b, l. 16 ff.

34 f. **' the breath,'** etc., quoted from the same passage as the words in the preceding note.

1067a 7. **Sainte-Beuve,** 1804–1869, the most distinguished French critic of the nineteenth century. Arnold's familiar, at times almost chatty, style of essay-writing owes much to Sainte-Beuve.

1068a 14. **Pellisson,** Paul Pellisson, a seventeenth-century French man of letters.

16. **politesse stérile et rampante,** barren and cringing civility.

21. **d'Héricault,** a nineteenth-century French novelist and scholar.

22. **Marot,** 1497?–1544, a French poet of the Renaissance.

1068b 32. **Methuselah.** According to Genesis v, 27, he lived nine hundred and sixty-nine years.

1069a 27. **Imitation,** the *Imitation of Christ*, written originally in Latin — a famous work of pious instruction which has probably been translated into more languages than any other book except the Bible. It is attributed to Thomas à Kempis, *ca.* 1380–1471.

29 f. **Cum multa,** etc. When you have read and come to know many things, it behooves you always to return to the beginning (*Imitation* III, xliii, 2).

43. **Cædmon.** See introductory note to Cædmon, p. 38, and Bede's account of Cædmon, p. 45.

47. **Vitet,** Ludovic, 1802–1873, a French dramatist and politician.

49. **Chanson de Roland.** See Chronological Outline.

50 f. **joculator or jongleur,** best translated by the English word "minstrel."

1069b 3. **Roncevaux,** or Roncevalles, a mountain pass on the Spanish frontier of France, the traditional scene of the events described in the central episode of the *Chanson de Roland*.

4 f. **Turoldus.** It is not certain whether Turoldus, who is referred to at the end of the Oxford manuscript of the *Roland*, is the author who wrote the poem, the minstrel who recited it, or the scribe who copied it.

31 ff. **'De plusurs choses,'** etc. "Then he began to call many things to remembrance, — all the lands which his valour conquered, and pleasant France, and the men of his lineage, and Charlemagne his liege lord who nourished him" (Arnold).

39 f. Ὣς φάτο, etc.

"So said she; they long since in Earth's soft arms were reposing,
There, in their own dear land, their fatherland, Lacedæmon
— *Iliad*, iii, 243, 244 [translated by Dr. Hawtrey]" (Arnold.)

1070a 17 ff. Ἀ δειλώ, etc. "Ah, unhappy pair, why gave we you to King Peleus, to a mortal? but ye are without old age, and immortal. Was it that with men born to misery ye might have sorrow? — *Iliad*, xvii, 443–445" (Arnold).

24. Καὶ σέ, etc. "Nay, and thou too, old man, in former days wast, as we hear, happy. — *Iliad*, xxiv, 543" (Arnold).

28 f. **Ugolino's . . . words.** Ugolino was an Italian political leader who was seized by the inhabitants of Pisa in 1288 and thrown into prison along with his two sons and two grandsons, where all died of starvation in a few days. The case was famous in Dante's time.

30 f. **'Io no piangeva,'** etc. "I (Ugolino) wailed not, so of stone I grew within; — *they* (the children) wailed" (Arnold). The passage occurs in the *Inferno*, xxxiii, 49 f.

34 ff. **'Io son fatta,'** etc. "Of such sort hath God, thanked be his mercy, made me, that your misery toucheth me not, neither doth the flame of this fire strike me. — *Inferno*, ii. 91–93" (Arnold).

39. **'In la sua volontade,'** etc. "In His will is our peace. — *Paradiso*, iii. 85" (Arnold).

42 ff. **'Wilt thou,'** etc. *2 Henry IV*, III, i, 18 ff.

1070b 1 ff. **'Darkened so,'** etc. See p. 353b, l. 599 ff.

7 f. **'And courage,'** etc. See p. 347b, l. 108 f.

12 f. **'. . . which cost,'** etc. See *Paradise Lost*, iv, 271 f.

1071a 9 f. φιλοσοφώτερον, etc., more philosophic and serious.

1071b 42 ff. **Brunetto Latini . . . Treasure . . . la parleure en,** etc. Brunetto Latini, *ca.*1210–*ca.* 1294, was a distinguished Italian philosopher and scholar and was a friend of Dante. While in exile in France, he wrote in French his prose *Trésor* ("Treasure"), a great encyclopedia of human knowledge, and in Italian his *Tesoretto* ("Little Treasure"), which is an abridgment of the *Trésor*. Of the French language he said that "its manner of expression is more pleasant and more common to all people."

48. **Christian of Troyes,** Chrétien de Troyes. See Chronological Outline. The passage quoted is found in one of Chrétien's early Arthurian romances, *Cligès*, l. 30 ff.

1072a 24 ff. **nourished on this poetry,** etc. Arnold overemphasizes the Italian element in Chaucer's poetry. See introductory note to Chaucer, p. 140.

33 f. **Wolfram of Eschenbach,** an early thirteenth-century German courtly poet, the author of *Parzival*, one of the best-known versions of the legend of Perceval.

1072b 10 f. **Dryden's,** in the Preface to the *Fables*.

25. **Johnson,** in his *Lives of the Poets*.

28. **Gower.** See p. 159 ff.

53. **'O martyr,'** etc. Cf. *The Prioresses Tale*, l. 127. Chaucer's line has "to" instead of "in."

1073a 10 f. **The Prioress's Tale,** l. 197 ff.

19. **O Alma,** the first words of a Latin hymn of the mediæval church, beginning: *Alma Redemptoris mater*, "O gracious mother of the Redeemer."

1073b 42. **Villon.** François Villon, a fifteenth-century French assassin, thief, crook, and underworld character, has left us some of the most beautiful poems in literature, especially lyrics picturing the physical decay of youth and loveliness.

44. **La Belle Heaulmière.** The name *heaulmière* (cf. Modern French *heaume*, helm) is said to be derived from the special headdress worn as a sign by courtesans. In the last stanza of the poem the old courtesan is represented as saying: "Thus amongst ourselves we regret the good time, poor silly old things, low-seated on our heels, all in a heap like so many balls; by a little fire of hemp-stalks, soon lighted, soon spent. And once we were such darlings! So fares it with many and many a one" (Arnold).

1074a 31 ff. **'that the sweetness,'** etc. From *An Essay of Dramatic Poesy.*

38 ff. **'there is,'** etc. From the Preface to the *Fables.*

1074b 24. **Chapman.** See note to Keats's *On First Looking*, etc., p. 780a.

34. **Milton.** In his *Apology for Smectymnuus*, one of his prose tracts.

42. **Dryden.** In the Postscript to the Reader affixed to his translation of Virgil's *Æneid.*

42. **Dryden.** In the preface to his translation of Virgil's *Æneid.*

52. **after the Restoration.** See p. 404.

1075a 42 f. **'A milk-white Hind,'** etc., *The Hind and the Panther*, l. 1 f.

49 f. **'To Hounslow Heath,'** etc., *Second Satire*, l. 143 f.

1075b 30 f. **the position of Gray is singular.** See introductory note to p. 582a.

50. **Burns.** See introductory note to p. 665b.

1076a 8 ff. **'Mark ruffian Violence,'** etc. From *On the Death of Robert Dundas, Esq.*

17. **Clarinda's love poet, Sylvander.** The reference is to the correspondence which Burns (under the poetical name of Sylvander) carried on with Mrs. Maclehose (whom he addresses as Clarinda).

19 ff. **'These English songs,'** etc., Burns to Mr. Thomson, October 19, 1794.

1076b 11 ff. **'Leeze me on drink!'** etc. From *The Holy Fair.*

33 ff. **'A prince can mak,'** etc. From *A Man's a Man for A' That*, p. 675b, l. 25 ff.

45 ff. **'The sacred lowe,'** etc. From the *Epistle to a Young Friend.*

1077a 1 ff. **'Who made,'** etc. From *Address to the Unco Guid.*

11 ff. **'To make a happy,'** etc. From *To Dr. Blacklock.*

50. **Burns . . . Chaucer.** The inadequacy of Arnold's test is obvious from the fact that it excludes Chaucer and Burns from the ranks of the greatest poets.

1077b 7 ff. **'Had we never,'** etc. From *Ae Fond Kiss*, p. 674a, l. 13 ff.

22 ff. **'Thou Power Supreme,'** etc. From *Winter.*

1078a 1 f. **Auerbach's Cellar.** A famous scene of revelry near the beginning of Goethe's *Faust* is represented as taking place in Auerbach's Cellar, a wine cellar in Leipzig. Carlyle has an essay on Goethe, p. 863 ff.

4. **Aristophanes,** *ca.* 450–*ca.* 380 B.C., the greatest of the ancient Greek comic dramatists.

11 f. **the address to the Mouse.** See p. 668a.

28 ff. **'We twa hae paidl't,'** etc. From *Auld Lang Syne*, p. 671a, l. 17 ff.

41. **'Pinnacled,'** etc. From Shelley's *Prometheus Unbound*, III, iv, last line.

46 ff. **'On the brink,'** etc. From *Prometheus Unbound*, II, v, opening lines.

WALTER PATER

Walter Horatio Pater was born at Shadwell in east London. His father, a physician, died in the son's infancy, and the family removed to Enfield, where Pater spent his youth. At King's School in Canterbury he showed an interest in art but none in literature. His undergraduate career at Oxford was uneventful. He considered entering the ministry, but after his graduation he settled down (1864) as a fellow of Brasenose, where he remained the rest of his life. At Brasenose he began to interest himself in literature and to write criticisms for various magazines. His articles, with some additions, were collected and published as *Studies in the History of the Renaissance* in 1878. By this time, despite his native reserve, he was a man of influence at Oxford and had a considerable following. His masterpiece, *Marius the Epicurean*, in which he set forth his ideals of beauty and the æsthetic life, was published in 1885. His essays in philosophic fiction, *Imaginary Portraits*, appeared in 1887, and two years later he issued his *Appreciations, with an Essay on Style*. Other significant works were published both before and after his death. He died at Oxford in the prime of his powers in 1894. By nature he was contemplative and reflective. His style, with its careful attention to structure and phrase and its conscious cadence, without appearing florid or affected, has a magnificence that has rarely been equaled in English. Dominant in the deep and earnest philosophy of life which he presents is a strain of alert idealism, and through all his writings runs the strong though chastened desire to live in keeping with the highest conceptions of life and its promised fulfillments.

1079a STYLE

35. **Michelet,** Jules Michelet, 1798–1874, a French historian and man of letters.

1080a 13. **Pascal,** Blaise Pascal, 1623–1662

an eminent French mathematician, philosopher, and man of letters.

50. **Tacitus,** Cornelius Tacitus, *ca.* 55–*ca.* 120, a well-known Roman historian and orator.

1081b 47. **le cuistre,** the downright pedant.

1082b 34. **Montaigne.** See introductory note to John Florio, p. 306.

45. **ascêsis,** a Greek word meaning exercise, training, art.

1083a 9. **Esmond,** *Henry Esmond,* a novel by William Makepeace Thackeray.

24. **Schiller,** Johann Christoph Friedrich von Schiller, 1759–1805, a famous German dramatist and critic.

44 f. **Flaubert's Madame Bovary,** a novel by the French writer, Gustave Flaubert, 1821–1880.

45 f. **Stendhal's Le Rouge,** etc., a novel by the French author, Henri Beyle, 1783–1842, whose pen name was Stendhal.

1084a 28. **Dean Mansel.** Henry Longueville Mansel, 1820–1871, an English metaphysical writer, dean of St. Paul's.

1085b 14 f. **Swedenborg,** Emanuel Swedenborg, 1688–1772, a Swedish scientist, philosopher, and mystic.

15. **Tracts of the Times.** See introductory note to John Henry Newman, p. 1044.

1086a 4 ff. **Gustave Flaubert.** See note to p. 1083a, l. 44. Flaubert's letters to Madame X (Madame Colet), written in 1846, often disparage human love in favor of the love of art.

1086b 29 ff. **a sympathetic commentator,** etc., Guy de Maupassant, in his Introduction to the *Lettres de Gustave Flaubert à George Sand.*

1088a 10. **Buffon,** Georges Louis Leclerc, 1707–1788, Comte de Buffon, a French naturalist, author of a *discours sur le style.*

1089b 7. **Bach,** Johann Sebastian Bach, 1685–1750, a famous German musician.

ALGERNON CHARLES SWINBURNE

1090a KING LEAR

17. **Æschylus,** 525–468 B.C., one of the great Greek dramatists.

47 f. **the trilogy of the Oresteia,** the *Agamemnon, Choephoroi,* and *Eumenides* of Æschylus.

51. **Agamemnon . . . Prometheus,** plays by Æschylus.

1090b 9 f. **Clytæmnestra,** the criminal queen of Agamemnon.

20. **Antigone,** the gentle daughter of Œdipus, who accompanied him in his blind exile. She is the heroine of Sophocles' play *Antigone.*

39. **the house of Atreus,** the descendants of Atreus, specifically Agamemnon and his immediate household. Atreus, the father of Agamemnon and Menelaus, was the ancient king of Mycenæ.

1091a 22. **Gadarean sow.** Cf. Mark v, 1 ff.

27 ff. **'Where's thy drum,'** etc. *King Lear* IV, ii, 55 ff.

38. **François-Victor Hugo,** 1828–1873, translator of Shakespeare's works into French, 1850–1867.

1091b 9 ff. **'I pant,'** etc. *King Lear* V, iii, 243 ff.

1092b 38. **Tolstoi,** Count Leo Tolstoi, 1828–1910, a great Russian novelist and social reformer. In his late years he became a very hostile critic of Shakespeare.

38. **Suderman,** Herman Sudermann, 1857–, a German dramatist.

1093a 50. **Choephoræ,** a tragedy by Æschylus.

51. **Ugolino.** See note to p. 1070a, l. 28 f., and Dante's *Inferno,* xxxiii, 49 f.

CHRISTOPHER MARLOWE

1094a 30. **Hallam,** Henry Hallam, 1777–1859, an English historian.

1094b 6. **the son of Victor Hugo.** See note to p. 1091a, l. 38.

34. **vision of Helen,** scene xiv.

49. **monologue,** scene xvi.

1095a 23. **the king's deposition,** Act V, scene i.

26 f. **the corresponding scene,** etc., Act IV, scene i.

1095b 4. **Mr. Collier,** John Payne Collier, 1789–1883, a Shakespearean critic.

22. **Nathanial Lee,** *ca.* 1653–1692, an English dramatist. He wrote *The Massacre of Paris* and collaborated with Dryden in *The Duke of Guise,* a play on the same theme.

28. **loss,** Marlowe's death, in 1593.

29. **Thomas Nash.** See p. 259 and notes.

39. **Greene.** See pp. 256 and 302 f. and notes.

1096a 43 f. **the soliloquy,** etc., scene xix.

1096b 13. **Jack Cade,** an Irishman by birth, leader of the rebellion in 1450 which bears his name.

22. **the author of,** etc., Swinburne himself, *A Study of Shakespeare,* 1880.

25. **Mr. Dyce,** the Rev. Alexander Dyce, 1798–1869, an English editor and critic. He issued an edition of Marlowe in 1850 and one of Shakespeare in 1857.

47. **Peele.** See p. 257 and notes.

1097a 36. **Passionate Shepherd.** See p. 259.

EDMUND GOSSE

Edmund Gosse, the son of a distinguished naturalist, was born in London. He was educated privately in Devonshire, and at eighteen became an assistant in the library of the British Museum. In 1875 he was made translator to the Board of Trade. From 1884 to 1890 he was a lecturer in English literature at Cambridge, and in 1894 he became librarian to the House of Lords. He has received honorary degrees from both Oxford and

Cambridge, as well as from several other institutions, in recognition of his eminence in letters. During the first part of his career he was a graceful poet and published numerous volumes of verse. Since about 1900 he has written on a variety of subjects, chiefly in literary history and criticism, and has proved himself a master of an easy and fluent style and an exponent of a broad and sympathetic culture. His greatest service perhaps is in acquainting English readers with foreign literature, chiefly that of Holland and Scandinavia. He was knighted in 1925. He resides in London.

1098a IMPRESSION

In this poem the writer aptly characterizes contemporary English poetry of the close of the Victorian era.

EUGENE LEE-HAMILTON

Born in an atmosphere of relative affluence, Eugene Lee-Hamilton was educated with the greatest care. He attended Oxford University, where he won a scholarship during his first term. After leaving the university, he became an attaché to the British legation in Paris and later secretary of the Alabama Claims Commission in Geneva. In 1873 he fell a victim to spinal meningitis and for twenty years was confined to bed, at times with excruciating pain. During this period he composed his *Sonnets of the Wingless Hours*, 1894, and supervised the studies of his gifted half-sister Violet Paget, who later became well known as a critic under the pen-name of Vernon Lee. By 1894 Lee-Hamilton had largely recovered his health. He later married Annie F. Holdsworth, the Scottish novelist. The death of their infant daughter is lamented in the poet's *Mimma Bella*, which includes some of the best sonnets in recent English literature. He died in 1907. His earliest volume of poems, which appeared in 1878, gave little promise of his later achievements. He is chiefly memorable for his work in the sonnet, a difficult metrical form in which he attained great skill. His sonnets are often tender and elevated in tone, and they leave an impression of spontaneity rarely accomplished in this form of stanza. On the sonnet, see introductory note to Sidney's *Astrophel and Stella*, p. 273a.

WHAT THE SONNET IS

1098b 7. **Faustus,** the chief figure in an ancient legend of a man who sold his soul to the devil in return for worldly gifts and finally had to pay the price. The theme has been used frequently in literature, notably by Marlowe and Goethe.

ALFRED AUSTIN

Alfred Austin was born at Headingly near Leeds, where his father was a merchant. He received his early schooling at Stonyhurst and Oscott, and afterward attended the University of London, where he was graduated in 1853. Four years later he was called to the bar from the Inner Temple but soon abandoned law for literature and travel. In 1896 he was appointed to the poet laureateship, which had been vacant since Tennyson's death. In England he lived in the country, finding recreation in riding, gardening, and fishing, and died at Swinford Old Manor near Ashford in Kent. In his early poetry, which was satirical, he attacked some of his great contemporaries but proved himself extremely uncritical. He wrote several plays without attaining any success on the stage. His poetry reveals a thoroughly English patriotism and a deep and intimate love of nature. His lyrics often lack the fervor and glow of a compelling spontaneity, but they possess a freshness and an orderly charm that make them delightful reading.

1099a AT SHELLEY'S HOUSE AT LERICI

The Shelleys removed from Pisa to Lerici on the bay of Spezzia in April, 1822. In July following Shelley was drowned while on the way home from a trip to Pisa.

1099b 64. **thrice-spurned Sibyl.** The Cumean Sibyl offered one of the Tarquins nine books for three hundred pieces of gold. On his refusal she burned three of the books and offered him the rest at the same price. Again the king refused, and she burned three more, asking for the remaining ones the original price of all. Struck by the strangeness of the case, he bought the three and found them to contain important prophesies concerning Rome. Cf. note to p. 1044b, l. 17.

86 f. **Pentecostal Peace,** etc. Cf. Acts ii, 1 ff.

88. **this bay,** the bay of Spezzia.

92. **Manfredonia,** a town and district in Apulia, southeast Italy.

93. **satraps,** subordinate rulers, colonial governors.

95. **mammoth-monsters.** Austria from time immemorial has been the proverbial enemy of Italy.

98. **Porto Venere,** "the port of Venus," a small town on a point of land enclosing the bay of Spezzia on the west.

OSCAR WILDE

Oscar Wilde, the son of the Irish surgeon and antiquary Sir William Robert Wilde, was born in Dublin. He was educated at the royal school in Enniskillen, at the University of Dublin, and at Oxford. His career at Oxford was remarkable. He stood high in scholastic attainments, won the Newdigate prize for poetry, founded a movement on the doctrine of Art for Art's sake, and led a brilliant but hectic existence by trying to live up to the " blue china " of his new cult. After a lecture tour in America and a quiet life in London for five or six years, he began in 1888 a career of almost unprecedented literary activity. He wrote with ease prose fiction of various kinds, but in such plays as *Lady Windermere's Fan*, 1892; *Salomé*, written in French, 1893; and *The Importance of Being Earnest*, 1895, he excelled all other Victorian dramatists in brilliancy of dialogue, literary finish, and dramatic effectiveness. In 1895, while engaged in a lawsuit for libel against the Marquis of Queensberry, he was found to be criminally liable himself. He was arrested, tried, and sentenced to two years' imprisonment with hard labor. This was the end of his literary career, except for an apologetic account of his life written in prison and his powerful rhetorical *Ballad of Reading Gaol*, 1898. After his release from jail he went abroad and died of cerebral meningitis in Paris in 1900. His reputation as a writer has suffered from his life as a man. His best work is to be found in his plays, but his poetry possesses a fascinating but sinister beauty, the beauty of decay.

1101b REQUIESCAT

See Matthew Arnold's poem by the same title, p. 975. This poem is said to memorialize the author's little sister Isola, who, according to the attending physician, was a " most gifted and lovable child." She died on February 23, 1867, and was buried at the home of Maria Edgeworth, the novelist.

5. **golden hair.** According to a legend, golden hair does not tarnish in the tomb.

1102a THE BALLAD OF READING GAOL

Reading is an important town in Berkshire west of London. Wilde spent part of his imprisonment, 1895–1897, in Reading jail and later was removed to Wandsworth prison in London.

1103a 96. **the kiss of Caiaphas,** the kiss of Judas bought with the pay received from Caiaphas the high priest for the betrayal of Christ. Cf. Matthew iii.

1103b 158. **Trial Men,** men sentenced by a " court of the first instance," or preliminary court, the verdict of which might be appealed.

1106b 485 f. **the barren staff,** etc. Rods and staffs that bloom spontaneously are a part of the machinery of mediæval saints' lives.

1107b 572. **latrine,** a privy.

1108a 621 f. **the holy hands,** etc. Cf. Luke xxiii, 39 ff.

623 f. **a broken,** etc. Cf. Psalms li, 17.

JOHN DAVIDSON

John Davidson was born a minister's son in a small town near Glasgow. He spent his youth in school and at work in Greenock, and in 1876–1877 attended the University of Edinburgh. For a dozen years thereafter he taught in various places in Scotland and attempted playwriting under the impression that he was a born dramatist. In 1890 he removed to London to devote himself entirely to literature. His first poetry in the metropolis was received coldly, but his *Fleet Street Eclogues*, 1893, brought him recognition. Several subsequent volumes and a successful play or two increased his reputation but failed to provide him with a competent income. He lived in hard circumstances in Penzance during his last years and in 1909 disappeared under suspicion of suicide by drowning. His poetry is fresh and full of thought, vigorous and bold in expression and imagery, and replete with a passionate but unembittered reproachfulness of life as he had known it. Such intense ballads as his *Heaven* and *Hell* deserve to be remembered.

1108b A BALLAD OF HEAVEN

25. **adagio,** a piece of music, or a movement in music, in adagio (*i.e.*, slow and graceful) time.

32. **andante,** a musical piece or movement in moderate time.

1109a 36. **scherzo,** in music a movement of lively character.

FRANCIS THOMPSON

Francis Thompson was born at Preston in Lancashire. He was bred a Catholic and educated in that faith at Upshaw College near Durham. Preparatory to following his father's profession, he studied medicine at Owens College near Manchester but was interested only in literature. Failing in practical life, he became friendless and solitary. After several obscure years in which he suffered ill health and great destitution he was discovered in London and rescued from starvation if not from self-destruction by a Mr. and Mrs. Meynell, adherents of his own faith, who had been attracted to him by his offer of a poem for the *Merrie England* magazine. They gave him a home and procured a publisher for his first volume, *Poems*, 1893. The book met with critical favor, and the opinion was confirmed by his *Sister Songs*, 1895, and *New Poems*, 1897. During his last years he was a victim of tuberculosis and lived a shadowy existence partly at a Capuchin monastery in north Wales and partly at Storrington in Sussex, until his death in London in 1907. Some of his poetry is marred by eccentricity in both speech and manner, but his genuine inspiration and a certain high distinction of thought and utterance justify the unique place he occupies in English poetry.

1110b TO OLIVIA

This poem is characteristic of Thompson's poetry about children in its attitude of intimate reverence for childhood.

1111a THE HOUND OF HEAVEN

The Hound of this poem is the poet's daring representation of God. The poem reflects its author's deeply religious nature and the profound spiritual experience through which he passed.

ROBERT BRIDGES

Robert Bridges, now poet laureate, though for years a practicing physician in London, has long been identified with the cultured literary and academic life of England. He was educated at Eton and Oxford and studied medicine in London, but retired from practice while he was yet under forty. His early poetry was printed privately and had a limited but admiring circle of readers. He published numerous volumes but did not reach his full maturity as a poet until his *Shorter Poems* in 1890. He has continued productive to the present time, although he is now past eighty. Within the new century he was won wide recognition as a scholar, as attested by the many honorary degrees he has received from various institutions. He became poet laureate on the death of Alfred Austin in 1913, and resides at Oxford. His poetry illustrates his own poetic theory, which emphasizes stress rather than uniformity in the number of syllables, but at the same time it carries on the older traditions of restraint, purity, and precision, and is not lacking in strength.

1113a ELEGY, etc.

This elegy, though written in a somewhat difficult stanza, fully sustains the quality of other great elegies, and is inferior, if in aught, only in its brevity.

WILLIAM WATSON

William Watson was born at Burley-in-Wharfedale, Yorkshire, and was reared in Liverpool, whither the family had removed in the interest of his father's business. His early poems, which appeared in the eighties, passed unnoticed, but his volume containing *Wordsworth's Grave*, 1890, won recognition. From this time until his important *New Poems* in 1909 he produced numerous works in verse of a critical, philosophical, and political character. His political poetry is usually understood to have interfered with his appointment as poet laureate in 1913. Since the beginning of the World War he has continued to issue volumes of poetry at regular intervals without doing anything to surpass the quality of his previous work. His lyrics are often good, but he is best in a contemplative vein, which comports only moderately well with the lyrical spirit. His poetry is compact with thought expressed in a refined and stately diction, often with striking epigrammatic effect, and at times glows with a sincere and sustained eloquence. It displays a classical turn in its regularity, fastidiousness of taste, and chastened and restrained general tone.

1114b WORDSWORTH'S GRAVE

Wordsworth was buried at Grasmere. In addition to its excellent criticism of Wordsworth, this poem is noteworthy for the writer's wide knowledge of English poetry during the eighteenth and nineteenth centuries. His characterization of the classical régime in section iv is excellent.

2. **Rotha,** a small river flowing through Grasmere churchyard.

1116a 89. **rugged scholar-sage,** Dr. Samuel Johnson.

95. **Collins' lonely vesper-chime.** See his *Ode to Evening*, p. 579.

96. **frugal note of Gray.** Gray's published verse is unusually small in volume.

100. **Auburn,** Goldsmith's Deserted Village.

101 ff. **one 'neath northern skies,** etc., Robert Burns.

111 ff. **Twin morning stars,** etc., Wordsworth and Coleridge. The former is the *Seer* and the latter the *Dreamer*.

1116b 121 ff. **Ah, how the lyre,** etc. Compare Mr. Gosse's *Impression*, p. 1098, for a like contemporary estimate of the poetry of the Nineties.

127 f. **one . . . one, one . . . another,** without definite reference.

1117a 149 ff. **One,** etc., Wordsworth.

173. **Helm Crag and Silver Howe,** elevations just north and south of Grasmere.

1117b ENGLAND MY MOTHER

This poem is an excellent example of the unrhymed lyric which has been popular in English poetry since about the middle of the nineteenth century. Cf. Tennyson's *Tears, Idle Tears*, p. 892.

12. **Demos,** personification for the crowd, populace.

13 f. **Lazarus,** etc. Cf. Luke xvi, 19 ff.

1118b THE WORLD IN ARMOUR

It may be noted that the second (l. 9 ff.) and third sonnets of this group contain a striking prophecy of the World War twenty years before its beginning in 1914.

1119a 1 ff. **London's Plague . . . dread Fire.** The plague, or black death, which had visited England, at times with devastating effects, since the fourteenth century, was particularly virulent in 1664–1666; hence it was known as the Great Plague. It disappeared finally from the country after the Great Fire of 1666.

14. **him that idly,** etc., literally, the person or persons who shot to death at Serajevo on June 28, 1914, Archduke Francis Ferdinand of Austria, an act which precipitated the World War.

THE SAINT AND THE SATYR

1. **the eremite,** the hermit. See note to p. 89b, l. 44.

1119b 13. **Paphos,** a town in Cyprus, one of the favorite resorts of Venus.

14. **Ida,** a mountain in Crete where Zeus was concealed to escape being devoured by his father Saturn.

RUDYARD KIPLING

Rudyard Kipling, the son of an English colonial official, was born in Bombay, India. He was educated at a college in north Devonshire and at seventeen returned to India to become an editor. At twenty-one he published his *Departmental Ditties*, and within the next three years produced a succession of prose fictions that brought him fame. In 1892 he issued his second volume of verse, *Barrack Room Ballads*. These and other poems of the nineties opened up a new literary field — the life of the common soldier and sailor beyond England's natural borders. They were written in a racy if low language that all classes could understand, and they made Kipling a genuinely popular poet. In 1894–1895 he produced in the *Jungle Books* the work that will probably live longest of all his writings. He traveled in the Orient and South America, lived a few years in America, settled in England, in 1907 won the Nobel prize for distinction in literature, and has continued to the present time a fluent and prolific writer. In both his prose and his poetry he has described from the ranks the life of the British service, not so much as it was but as it came to be under the influence of his writings. He is one of the supreme masters of the modern short story. His home is at Burwash in Sussex.

THE BALLAD OF FISHER'S BOARDING HOUSE

The place-names in this poem are unimportant for an interpretation of it as a ballad. They illustrate well the author's mastery of proper names for poetical uses. They serve to suggest remoteness, strangeness, and the like.

1121a GUNGA DIN

3. **Aldershot,** a district in Hampshire where a permanent military camp is located.

12. **bhisti,** a water carrier.

16. **Panee lao,** bring water in a hurry.

27. **'Harry By,'** O brother.

32. **juldee,** speed.

1121b 41. **mussick,** mussuk, a leather water bag.

70. **dooli,** a kind of litter or army ambulance.

1122a THE VAMPIRE

A vampire is thought of as a preternatural creature of malignant nature which secures its nourishment by sucking the blood of a sleeping person. The poem was written to elucidate a picture by Kipling's cousin, Philip Burne-Jones, representing a man in the last agonies of death, by whose side is seated a woman with a cold hard look on her face.

1122b RECESSIONAL

This poem was written to celebrate the diamond jubilee (sixtieth anniversary) of Queen Victoria's reign, in 1897. In ecclesiastical usage the recessional is the hymn of retirement sung at the close of the service.

WILLIAM BUTLER YEATS

William Butler Yeats, son of the distinguished Irish artist J. B. Yeats, was born in Dublin. After attending schools in London and Dublin, he took up the study of art but soon abandoned it for literature. Encouraged by Oscar Wilde, he went to London in 1888, and in 1889 published his first volume of verse, *The Wanderings of Oisin,* containing a narrative poem based on one of the most charming and characteristic episodes in the Irish Ossianic legend (see introductory note to Ossian, p. 62b). This was followed by other volumes, notably *The Celtic Twilight*, 1893, and *The Wind among the Reeds*, 1899, which, together with his collected *Poems*, 1895, established his position as a poet of ability. He has also written numerous dramas on ancient or modern Irish themes, some of them involving allegories of Ireland's national aspirations. Especially significant among his plays are *Kathleen ni Houlihan* and *The Land of Heart's Desire*. He is a literary critic of distinction, has edited several collections of Irish folk tales, and was one of the editors of the works of the English poet and mystic William Blake. Of late years he has become interested in Japanese literature and has written several plays under Japanese influence.

Mr. Yeats's first volume is said to have inaugurated the so-called modern Celtic renaissance, or Anglo-Irish literary movement, and throughout his career the author has striven to create for Ireland a national literature written in English but independent of foreign influences. Stimulated more or less by oriental philosophy, William Blake, the Pre-Raphaelites, and modern occultism, he has attempted to convey in his poetry that lively faith in an other world of fairy folk and magic which is so striking a characteristic of the native Irish mind. In his treatment both of ancient Celtic themes, such as *The Death of Cuchulain,* and of modern Irish superstitions, as in *The Land of Heart's Desire*, he has sought to catch the feeling for nature and the wistful charm of ancient Celtic romance. His style is almost proselike in its simplicity and naturalness. He has always had a leaning toward mysticism, but before he became obsessed with modern spiritualism and necromancy and with things Japanese, he held practically undisputed his position as the most representative writer of the new spirit in the literature of Ireland. He resides in London.

1123a THE DEATH OF CUCHULAIN

The chief source of this poem is an ancient Irish version of the theme of the father-and-son combat, best known perhaps through Arnold's *Sohrab and Rustum* (p. 963b ff.): Cuchulainn, while learning feats of arms abroad, becomes the father of a son whom he later meets and unknowingly slays. Cuchulainn's famous wife Emer does not figure in the older story, nor is Cuchulainn an old man when he slays his son (Conlach). Yeats's version should be compared with Macpherson's (see p. 588 f. and introductory note).

1123b 39. **Red Branch.** See note to *The Feast of Bricriu*, p. 59a.

1124a 90. **quicken,** the mountain ash, or rowan tree, associated with magic and hence with druidism.

THE WHITE BIRDS

1. **I would . . . white birds.** This fanciful poetic idea may have been suggested by the common appearance in early Irish tradition of fairies or transformed mortals in the form of white birds.

1124b 9. **Danaän.** In ancient Irish tradition the Tuatha Dé Danaan are represented as one of the ancient races of Ireland. They are possessed of magical powers and inhabit a fairy world beneath the earth or water, or even in the many-isled elysium beyond the ocean (see *Connla of the Golden Hair*, p. 61a, and note to p. 61a, l. 32). They are often identified with the *sidhe*, or fairy folk (see note to p. 61b, l. 9).

STEPHEN PHILLIPS

Stephen Phillips was born at Somertown near Oxford. He was educated at Stratford and later at Peterborough, where his father was precentor in the cathedral. For six years he was a minor actor in a theatrical company. He attracted attention as a poet first by his *Christ in Hades*, 1896, and with his *Poems* the following year he was recognized as a genius of unusual magnitude. His reputation brought a request from a theatrical manager for a play, whereupon he turned to drama and produced a succession of poetical plays which gratified the popular taste but which have since been neglected. His last volume, *Lyrics and Dramas*, 1913, representing his maturer thought and style, came after his vogue had declined. He died at Deal in 1915. He drew his inspiration from the past. His plays are based on old stories and are modeled upon Greek drama. In his poetry he is Victorian in both manner and style. His fame is preserved best by his shorter poems.

JOHN MASEFIELD

John Masefield was born in Hertfordshire. Urged by the love of adventure which has marked a large part of his life and which shines constantly through his work, he ran away to sea and for some years underwent the hard experiences which furnished him with abundant materials for literary treatment. The character of his first volume of poems, published in 1902, is indicated by the title, *Salt-Water Ballads;* and much of his later verse, notably *The Everlasting Mercy*, 1911, deals with the vicissitudes of the sailor or the wanderer. He has written several novels, the first, *Captain Margaret*, appearing in 1908, and a number of plays, of which *The Tragedy of Nan*, 1909, shows unusual dramatic intensity. In his forthright, uncompromising view of life Mr. Masefield is distinctly a modern, but in imaginative power and clear-eyed idealism he rises above most of the contemporary realists.

1126a A WANDERER'S SONG

7. **ketches,** two-masted vessels of one to two hundred tons burden.

1126b 11. **hooker,** a one-masted fishing smack.

14. **Moby Dick,** a whale in the famous sea romance of the same name, by the American novelist Herman Melville, 1819–1891.

ALFRED NOYES

Alfred Noyes was born in Staffordshire and was educated at Oxford. His first volume of poetry was published in 1902. His collected poems appeared in 1910. From 1914–1923 he was professor of modern English literature at Princeton University. He published several volumes during the period of the World War. In meter, vocabulary, and theme Mr. Noyes carries on the tradition of the Victorians and of the older literature. He is steeped in the poetry and heroic traditions of the Elizabethan age and revives them with a fine enthusiasm. His verse is significant for its melody, which has rarely been surpassed, rather than for any profound philosophy or theory of life.

RALEIGH

In its main outlines this poem is historical; hence to understand and appreciate it in full the student should read an account of Ralegh's life and acquaint himself with the conditions of the time. The personages represented familiarly as Ben, Will, Kit, and Rob, are, of course, the great dramatists Jonson, Shakespeare, Marlowe, and Greene. The *Mermaid* was the celebrated tavern which they frequented. The story is dramatically told long afterward by mine host to an imagined listener or listeners.

1. **His tribe.** The younger poets who owned their discipleship to Jonson delighted to call themselves the Sons of Ben.

12. **'Last of the men,'** etc. See p. 253 and notes, and p. 295 ff.

16. **El Dorado,** the "Land of Gold," believed by the Spaniards and by Sir Walter Ralegh to exist in the upper course of the Amazon River in South America.

20. **catamite,** a male pervert.

1127a 23. **Salome.** Salome was the daughter of the beautiful and unscrupulous Herodias, whose marriage to Herod Antipas, 4 B.C.–A.D. 39, after her divorce from Herod's half-brother Philip, caused the wrath of John the Baptist. Cf. Mark vi, 17 ff.

1127b 73 f. **king . . . hates tobacco.** Ralegh is reputed to have introduced the use of tobacco into England. James was its avowed enemy. By his *Counterblast to Tobacco*, 1604, he imagined himself to have said the last word on the subject.

80. **ketch.** See note to p. 1126a, l. 7.

81. **Tilbury,** a town near the mouth of the Thames.

1128a 122. **Gravesend,** a town a few miles below London on the Thames.

125. **wherry,** a light rowboat.

136. **dinghy,** a small light skiff.

1128b 157. **Cathay.** See note to p. 890, l. 184.

1129a 197. **Greenwich.** At this time Greenwich was, of course, an independent village outside London.

1130b 296 f. **the face,** etc. See note to *Paradise Lost*, II, 611.

307 ff. **our poor earth,** etc. The Copernican theory was announced three-quarters of a century before Ralegh's death.

318. **wastrel,** a good-for-nothing.

1131a 324 f. **The sea-witch,** etc., the figure of the mermaid represented on the tavern signboard. See note to Keats's *Lines*, etc., p. 789b.

351. **wild Italian tales.** See Boccaccio, *Decameron*, Day iv, Nov. 5, and Keats's *Isabella*.

1132a 423. **black-cassocked figure,** the priest who administered the sacrament and heard the prisoner's confession before the execution.

1132b 444. **Budleigh Salterton,** a small town on the southern coast of Devonshire, where Ralegh was born.

1133a 487. **like Lazarus,** etc. Cf. John xi.

503. **O, eloquent,** etc. With this passage Ralegh closed his *History of the World.*

1134a 589 ff. **the Stewart,** etc., a forecast of the civil war which dethroned and executed the Stuart Charles I and resulted in the Commonwealth.

591. **Whitehall,** a royal palace in London.

1135b 677. **Medusa,** the Gorgon. See note to *Paradise Lost,* II, 611.

691. **Lundy Island,** situated at the entrance to the Bristol Channel.

1136a 723. **Ionian movement.** Ionia was a small district of Asia Minor bordering on the Ægean, settled, it was supposed, by native Greeks, whose descendants in time came to dominate Greek commerce and art.

737. **Astrophel,** Sir Philip Sidney.

741. **œnomel,** a mixture of wine and honey, used as a drink by the ancient Greeks.

RUPERT BROOKE

Rupert Brooke was born at Rugby, where his father was an assistant master. At school he was a successful athlete and won a prize for a poem. He attended Cambridge University, where he was known as one of the leading young intellectuals, though he was regarded as somewhat of a "socialist" and a "crank." After leaving Cambridge, he studied in Germany. On his return to England he settled near Cambridge and gave himself up to voluminous reading and outdoor exercise. In 1913 he passed through the United States and Canada on his way to the South Seas. When the World War broke out, he obtained a commission, but while on the way to the Dardanelles, he died of blood poisoning on board a hospital ship in the harbor of Scyros. He was strikingly handsome and possessed great personal charm. As a poet he showed unusual versatility. After the beginning of the war the fanciful social theories of his earlier years gave way to unreserved patriotism, and his later writings reflect the fearless, heroic spirit of England's youth in the presence of the national calamity. His verse occupies a high place in recent English poetry.

1137b THE GREAT LOVER

15. **inenarrable,** indescribable; literally, untellable.

EDMUND GOSSE

THE WHOLE DUTY OF WOMAN

1139a 16 f. **Juliana Berners,** Juliana Barnes or Berners, prioress of Sopewell, near St. Albans, late in the fifteenth century.

31. **J. K. S.,** James Kenneth Stephen, 1859–1892, an English barrister and small poet. The quotation occurs in his *A Thought.*

46 f. **The Whole Duty of Man,** once attributed to Richard Sterne, now ascribed to the Royalist divine Richard Allestree, 1619–1681, and revised by Allestree's literary executor, John Fell.

1139b 27. **play-book,** a book of plays or dramatic pieces.

33 f. **most cynical comedy,** etc., *The Town Fop* by Mrs. Aphra Behn, 1640–1689.

35. **Corinnas,** etc., *i.e.,* characters in contemporary light fiction. Corinna was a Greek poetess who triumphed over Pindar in certain public contests.

41. **The Provoked Wife,** a play by Sir John Vanbrugh, 1664–1726.

1140a 21. **Junius,** the pen-name under which appeared a succession of brilliant political letters contributed to the *London Advertiser,* 1769–1772. It appears that "Junius" was Sir Francis Philip, 1740–1818.

32. **Mr. Craik,** Sir Henry Craik, 1846 ——, a Scottish educator and author, editor of *English Prose Selections,* 1892–1896.

34. **Bishop Cumberland,** Richard Cumberland, 1732–1811, Bishop of Peterborough.

34 f. **William Sherlock,** 1641?–1707, dean of St. Paul's.

1140b 10 f. **Mrs. Lynn Linton,** 1822–1898, an English novelist and miscellaneous writer.

49. **Marjorie Fleming,** Margaret Fleming, 1803–1811, a remarkably gifted child, the friend of Sir Walter Scott.

1141a 28. **ombre.** See note to Pope's *Rape of the Lock,* l. 56.

28. **quadrille,** a game of cards played by four persons, the eights, nines, and tens being omitted from the pack.

GEORGE BERNARD SHAW

George Bernard Shaw was born in Dublin of English Protestant stock. He attended school in his native city, but his formal education ceased at the age of fifteen, when he began to earn his own living. In 1876 he removed with his family to London. He spent several years as a clerk in the offices of a land agent and of the Edison Telephone Company. He early undertook to write novels, but found little sale for his literary work. He adopted socialistic views, which he defended both as a pamphleteer and as a street orator. About 1885 he began journalism, and has since published many essays of literary or social criticism. Beginning with *Widowers' Houses,* written partly in 1885, he has composed more than two dozen plays, mainly satirical, the nature of which is to some extent indicated by the title *Plays Pleasant and Unpleasant*, given to a collection of his dramas published in two volumes in 1898. In their published form his plays are often supplied with extensive stage directions and character sketches designed to help the reader visualize the action, and with elaborate prefaces explaining the author's literary and social theories. His *Common Sense and the War*, published soon after the outbreak of the European conflict, caused widespread comment.

If we are to judge by his writings, Mr. Shaw believes that many things in the world need reforming, but he goes about the reformation in his own way. He is a socialist, but he believes that socialism will accomplish its ends best by using Fabian (waiting) tactics. Both in his essays and in his dramas he attacks conventionality and sham — or what he regards as conventionality and sham —, but he does so by the indirect method of reducing to absurdity the institution condemned. His criticisms are often valuable not so much because they are just as because they stimulate thought. He has helped to raise the prose drama again to the level of literature, and he has succeeded in popularizing his plays in printed form with a public accustomed to the explicitness of the novel.

1142b THE CASE OF THE CRITIC DRAMATIST

6. **Frank Marshall,** 1840–1889, editor of the "Henry Irving" edition of Shakespeare.

7 f. **Sir Henry Irving,** 1838–1905, a great English actor.

12. **Canute,** a Danish king of England, 1017–1035.

14. **'Robert Emmet,'** a play by Francis (Frank) Marshall.

1143a 18. **wedding guest.** See Coleridge's *Ancient Mariner*.

38. **Mr. Pinero,** Sir Arthur Wing Pinero, 1855 ——, a prominent English dramatist and fiction writer.

1144a 11. **Clement Scott,** 1841–1904, an English journalist and dramatic critic.

13. **Wm. Archer,** 1856 ——, an English dramatic critic.

14. **Mr. Walkley,** Arthur Bingham Walkley, 1855–1926, a dramatic critic.

GILBERT KEITH CHESTERTON

Gilbert Keith Chesterton is descended from a family of realty dealers in London, where he was born. He was educated at St. Paul's School, but at seventeen abandoned his studies for a career in art. His inclination to write, however, soon triumphed. He wrote some art criticism for *The Bookman,* published a volume of verse (*The Wild Gallant*), and about 1900 began, with signed articles for various Liberal papers, the regular career of a journalist. His decided personality, pugnacious disposition, and dogmatic assertiveness soon made him a reputation which he has maintained unabated until the present time. His works have been frequently republished, and he has constantly added new productions on all sorts of subjects and of various types. His medleylike range and versatility and his remarkable ingenuity and dexterity have made him one of the most prominent of modern writers. His style is marked by pungency and incisiveness, freely interspersed with paradox, often provoking in its militancy, but relieved by a racy humor that rarely weakens or fails. He resides at Beaconsfield.

A DEFENCE OF NONSENSE

1144b 18. **Edward Lear,** 1812–1888, an English artist and humorous poet. For the 'Dong,' the 'Quangle-Wangle,' the 'Jumblies,' and the like, see his poetry.

25. **Rabelais.** See note to p. 243a, l. 2.

25. **Sterne,** Lawrence Sterne, 1713–1768, an English humorous novelist.

37 f. **the present Archbishop,** etc., Frederick Temple, D.D., 1821–1902.

47. **'Trial of Faithful.'** See *Pilgrim's Progress*.

1145a 5. **Lewis Carroll,** the Reverend Charles Lutwidge Dodgson, 1832–1898, an English mathematician, who wrote stories for children under the pen name of Lewis Carroll.

10 f. **Philistine,** a person lacking in liberal culture and enlightenment.

40 f. **'His body,'** etc., prefatory poem to *Nonsense Songs*.

1145b 1 f. **'Far and few,'** etc., a refrain in *The Jumblies*.

16 f. **'For his aunt,'** etc., misquoted from *The Pobble Who Has No Toes*.

1146a 38 ff. **'Hast Thou,'** etc. Cf. Job xxxviii, 26.

49. **Leviathan,** a fabulous sea monster of Scripture, sometimes identified with the behemoth. Cf. Job xli.

HERBERT GEORGE WELLS

Herbert George Wells, the son of a professional cricket player, was born at Bromley in Kent. He was educated in a private school of his native town, in the grammar school of Midhurst, and in the Royal College of Science. After his graduation at the University of London in 1888 he engaged in private teaching. In 1893 he became dramatic critic of the

Pall Mall Gazette and began contributing articles to other magazines. His first success came with his stories and romances, beginning with *The Time Machine* in 1895. In these he employed the newest scientific knowledge and set forth his views on politics and sociology. He also wrote some expository treatises further elucidating his sociological doctrines. Meanwhile he had begun his career as novelist, which he pursued with eminent success through the World War. In recent years the great fame of his novels has been eclipsed by his mammoth *Outline of History*, 1919–1920, in which he disparaged the conventional historic method and as a modern scientific theorizer attempted to give the story of the race devoid of the usual national prejudices and distinctions. In his writings he is not without marked originality. In his thought processes he is speculative rather than scientific. In all his expressions of opinion he is vigorous and decided. A strong personal element and a pervasive optimistic tone make whatever he writes good reading.

MY FIRST FLIGHT

1146b 26. **Langley,** Samuel Pierpont Langley, 1834–1906, an American physicist, early designer and constructor of airplanes.

26. **Lilienthal,** Otto Lilienthal, 1848–1896, a German aëronautical engineer.

1147a 15. **Eastbourne,** a town on the coast of Sussex.

15 f. **Grahame White,** 1880 ——, a noted English publicist.

1148a 4. **the White City,** an amusement park at Shepherd's Bush in London.

24. **Brighton,** a coastal town a few miles west of Eastbourne.

JOHN GALSWORTHY

John Galsworthy was born at Coombe in Surrey. He was educated at Harrow and Oxford, and was called to the bar in 1890, but devoted himself mainly to literature. His earliest novel appeared in 1898. From the first recognition of his ability as revealed in *The Island Pharisees* in 1904 and *The Man of Property* in 1906, the intelligent public has welcomed with ever increasing interest the series of literary works that have come from his pen. Besides novels, he has written essays, short stories, and plays, the latter marked by realistic treatment and strong emotional appeal. If we judge by Mr. Galsworthy's novels alone, with their emphasis on sex relationships and the futility of human endeavor in the face of convention and scandal, we may conclude that his philosophy is one of pessimistic realism. If, however, we consider his whole literary output, including his essays, he appears not only as a surpassingly subtle literary artist but as a kindly and even hopeful spectator of human society.

1149a CASTLES IN SPAIN

26 f. **Seville Cathedral.** Except St. Peter's in Rome and the Mezquita in Cordova, the great cathedral of Santa Maria de la Sede in Seville, Spain, is the largest church structure in the world — 414 feet long, 271 feet wide, and 100 feet high at the nave. It was begun in 1402 and completed in 1519.

52. **Assuan,** a town in upper Egypt on the Nile.

1149b 2. **Forth Bridge,** the great cantilever bridge over the Firth of Forth above Edinburgh.

19 f. **Christopher Wren,** etc. See note to p. 1051b, l. 20.

1151b 19. **St. Francis d'Assisi,** 1182?–1226, the Italian founder of the Franciscan order of friars, famous for his Christlike life and teachings.

1153a 47. **quid pro quo,** an adequate return; literally, "something for something."

1154b 3. **'Retro Satana.'** Get thee behind me, Satan. Cf. Mark viii, 23 (Vulgate).

1155a 25 f. **Dreamer . . . Don,** etc. See note to p. 245b, l. 274.

INDEX OF AUTHORS

INDEX OF TITLES

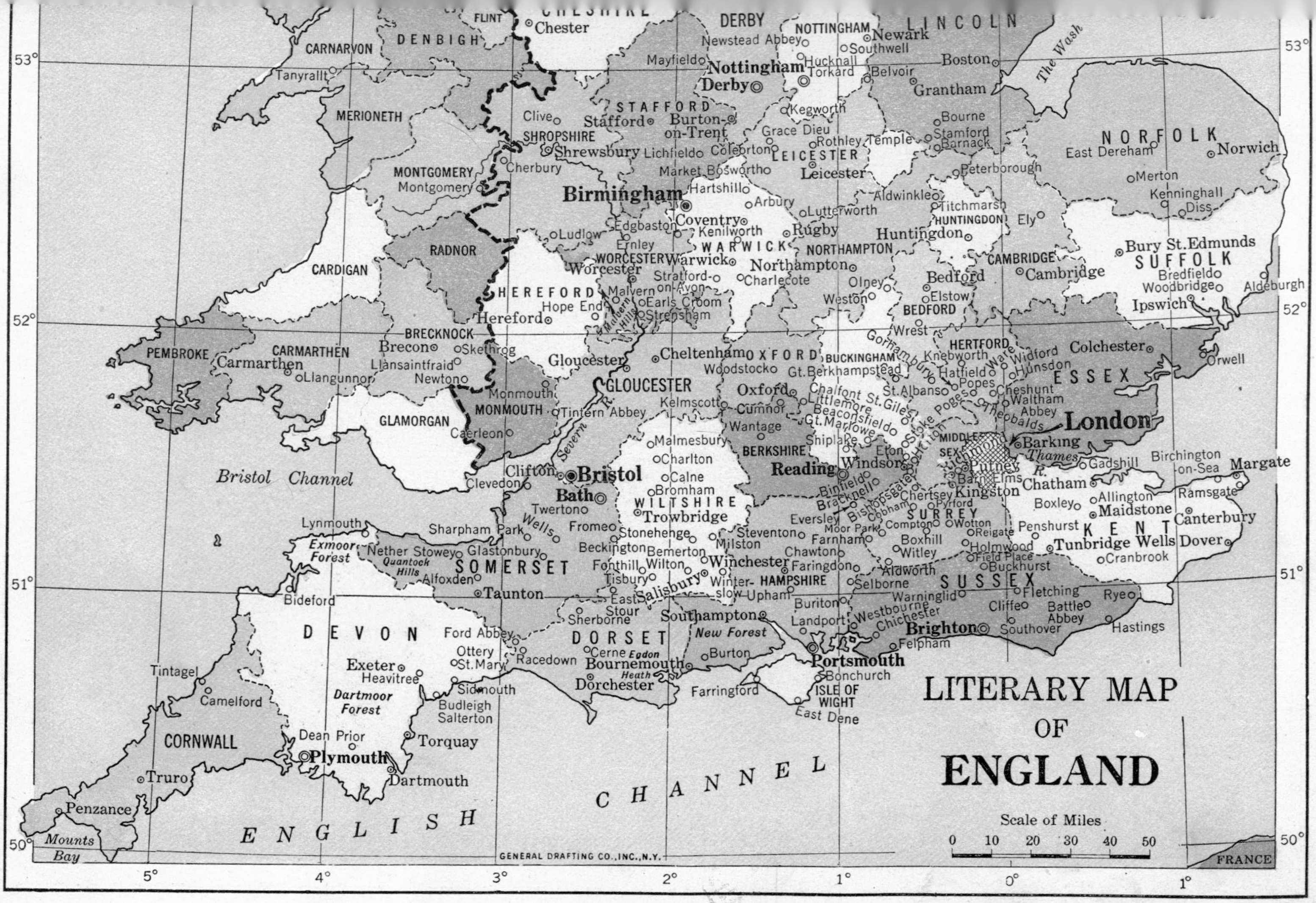
LITERARY MAP OF ENGLAND
Scale of Miles
0 10 20 30 40 50
GENERAL DRAFTING CO., INC., N.Y.
ENGLISH CHANNEL
Bristol Channel
The Wash
Mounts Bay
FRANCE
CORNWALL
DEVON
SOMERSET
DORSET
WILTSHIRE
HAMPSHIRE
SUSSEX
KENT
SURREY
MIDDLESEX
ESSEX
BERKSHIRE
OXFORD
BUCKINGHAM
HERTFORD
BEDFORD
CAMBRIDGE
HUNTINGDON
NORTHAMPTON
SUFFOLK
NORFOLK
LINCOLN
NOTTINGHAM
DERBY
LEICESTER
WARWICK
STAFFORD
SHROPSHIRE
WORCESTER
HEREFORD
GLOUCESTER
MONMOUTH
GLAMORGAN
BRECKNOCK
CARMARTHEN
PEMBROKE
CARDIGAN
RADNOR
MONTGOMERY
MERIONETH
CARNARVON
DENBIGH
FLINT
ISLE OF WIGHT
Exmoor Forest
Dartmoor Forest
Quantock Hills
New Forest
Egdon Heath
Malvern Hills
Severn R.
Thames R.
London
Birmingham
Bristol
Bath
Nottingham
Derby
Plymouth
Portsmouth
Brighton
Reading
Oxford
Cambridge
Colchester
Norwich
Bury St. Edmunds
Ipswich
Canterbury
Dover
Margate
Tunbridge Wells
Maidstone
Chatham
Winchester
Salisbury
Southampton
Bournemouth
Dorchester
Exeter
Taunton
Penzance
Truro
Tintagel
Camelford
Dartmouth
Torquay
Chester
Shrewsbury
Coventry
Stratford-on-Avon
Leicester
Northampton
Huntingdon
Bedford
Hereford
Worcester
Gloucester
Cheltenham
Carmarthen
Brecon
Windsor
Kingston
Putney
Barking
Boston
Grantham
Newark

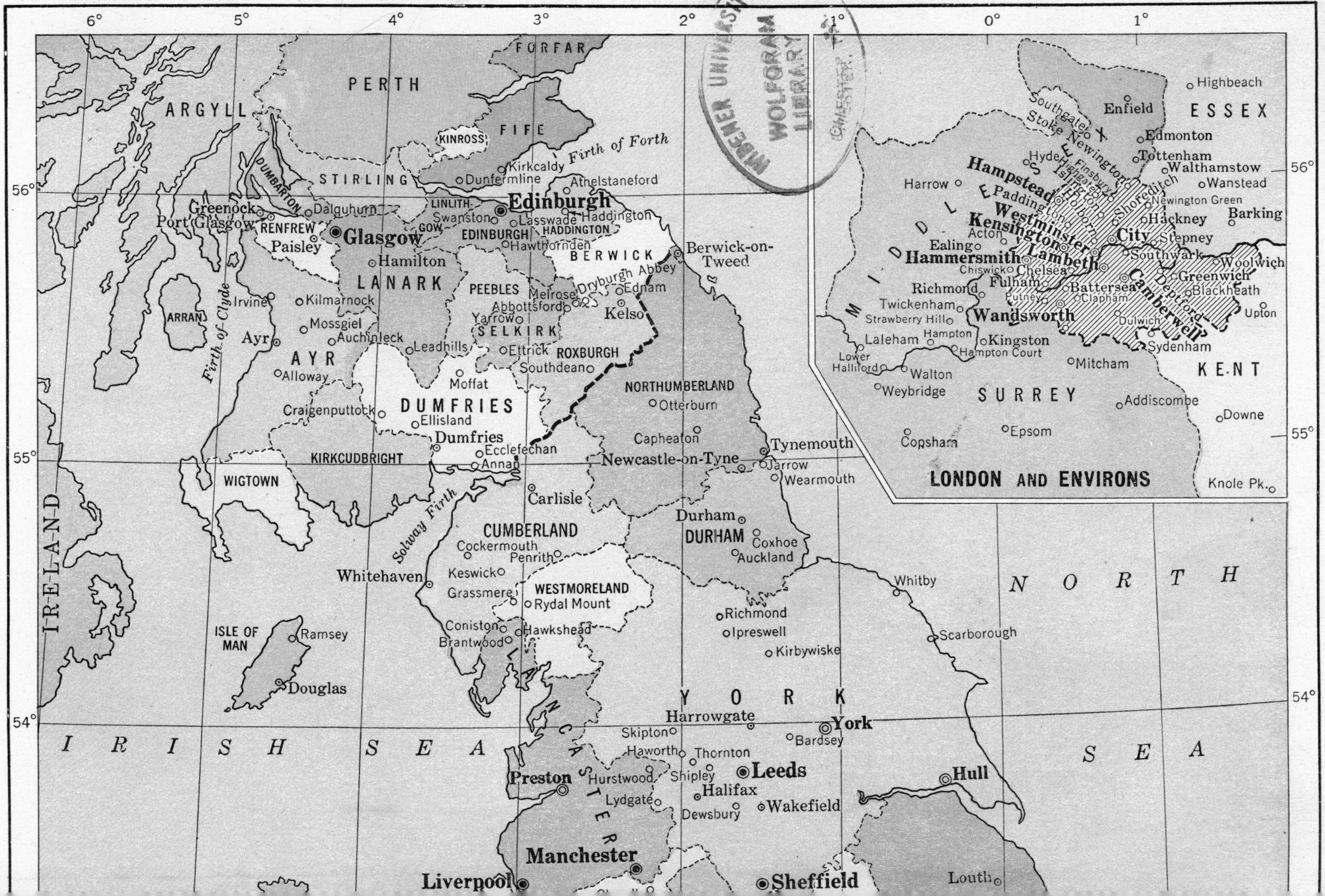
IRELAND
ARGYLL
PERTH
FORFAR
FIFE
KINROSS
STIRLING
DUMBARTON
LINLITH-GOW
EDINBURGH
HADDINGTON
BERWICK
RENFREW
LANARK
PEEBLES
SELKIRK
ROXBURGH
AYR
ARRAN
DUMFRIES
KIRKCUDBRIGHT
WIGTOWN
NORTHUMBERLAND
CUMBERLAND
WESTMORELAND
DURHAM
ISLE OF MAN
LANCASTER
YORK
Firth of Forth
Firth of Clyde
Solway Firth
IRISH SEA
NORTH SEA
Greenock
Port Glasgow
Paisley
Glasgow
Dalguhurn
Hamilton
Kilmarnock
Irvine
Mossgiel
Auchinleck
Ayr
Alloway
Leadhills
Craigenputtock
Moffat
Ellisland
Dumfries
Ecclefechan
Annan
Swanston
Edinburgh
Lasswade
Haddington
Hawthornden
Athelstaneford
Kirkcaldy
Dunfermline
Melrose
Abbottsford
Yarrow
Ettrick
Southdean
Dryburgh Abbey
Ednam
Kelso
Berwick-on-Tweed
Otterburn
Capheaton
Newcastle-on-Tyne
Tynemouth
Jarrow
Wearmouth
Carlisle
Durham
Coxhoe
Auckland
Cockermouth
Penrith
Keswick
Whitehaven
Grassmere
Rydal Mount
Coniston
Hawkshead
Brantwood
Ramsey
Douglas
Whitby
Richmond
Ipreswell
Kirbywiske
Scarborough
Harrowgate
Skipton
York
Bardsey
Haworth
Thornton
Shipley
Leeds
Halifax
Wakefield
Dewsbury
Preston
Hurstwood
Lydgate
Hull
Manchester
Liverpool
Sheffield
Louth
6°
5°
4°
3°
2°
1°
0°
56°
55°
54°
LONDON AND ENVIRONS
MIDDLESEX
ESSEX
KENT
SURREY
Highbeach
Enfield
Edmonton
Tottenham
Walthamstow
Wanstead
Southgate
Stoke Newington
Harrow
Hampstead
Hyde
Highgate
Finsbury
Islington
Paddington
Holborn
Shoreditch
Newington Green
Hackney
Barking
Westminster
Kensington
Acton
City
Stepney
Ealing
Hammersmith
Lambeth
Southwark
Chiswick
Chelsea
Woolwich
Greenwich
Deptford
Blackheath
Richmond
Fulham
Battersea
Putney
Clapham
Twickenham
Strawberry Hill
Wandsworth
Dulwich
Camberwell
Upton
Laleham
Hampton
Kingston
Hampton Court
Sydenham
Lower Halliford
Walton
Mitcham
Weybridge
Addiscombe
Downe
Epsom
Copsham
Knole Pk.